2023 DIR National Minority and Women-Owned Business Directory
Fifty-Fourth Edition

HISTORY
Diversity Information Resources was founded in Minneapolis in 1968 by H. Peter Meyerhoff, a Honeywell aeronautics engineer, who sought to advance race relations by improving economic conditions for Blacks after the assassination of Dr. Martin Luther King, Jr. Meyerhoff and his wife were European Jews who managed to escape Hitler at the outset of World War II. Themselves victims of discrimination, they were motivated by Dr. King's death to launch the "Buy Black" directory, a 10-page directory of black-owned businesses.

In 2001 DIR partnered with an IT firm and developed an online Supplier Diversity Database Management Portal. The dynamic portal allows corporations online access to certified minority and women-owned businesses, veteran, service-disabled veteran, LGBT and HUBZone businesses, supplier registration, certification validation, and data cleansing. Please contact Diversity Information Resources at (612) 781-6819 or www.diversityinforesources.com for more information. A Board of Directors, representative of major U.S. corporations set policy and direction for Diversity Information Resources.

MISSION
To develop, maintain, and provide information resources that enhance supplier diversity initiatives and support the development and economic growth of diverse businesses.

INCLUSION CRITERIA AND LISTING PROCESS
In identifying minority-owned businesses, fifty-one percent of the business must be owned, operated and controlled by minority group members who are U.S. citizens, capable of national and/or regional sales and physically located in the United States or its trust territories. In identifying woman-owned businesses, at least fifty-one percent or more is owned by a woman (or women), who is a U.S. citizen, and who controls the firm by exercising the power to make policy decisions and operates the business by being actively involved in day-to-day management. It must be profit seeking and capable of national and/or regional sales.

CERTIFICATION
Information on certification(s) held is also validated and reported. Buyers are advised to contact firms directly if clarification on certification is needed. The following certifications are validated:

- State — State Agencies
- City — City Agencies
- WBENC — Women's Business Enterprise National Council
- NWBOC — National Women Business Owners Corporation
- NMSDC — National Minority Supplier Development Council
- CPUC — California Public Utilities Commission (M/WBE Clearinghouse)
- SDB — Small Business Administration's Small Disadvantaged Business
- 8(a) — SBA's 8(a) Business Development Program

OWNERSHIP CLASSIFICATION
The following code indicates ownership type:

- AA — African American
- Hisp — Hispanic American
- Nat Ame — Native American
- As-Pac — Asian Pacific American
- As-Ind — Asian Indian American

LIABILITY DISCLAIMER
Although the information listed herein has been compiled with the utmost care and is believed by the publisher to be reliable, its accuracy or completeness cannot be guaranteed. The publishers and sponsors assume no responsibility for transactions resulting from the use of information herein and do not guarantee the quality or reliability of products or services listed. The content of the advertising copy contained in this Directory is the sole responsibility of those firms, which submitted it. Diversity Information Resources assumes no responsibility for its accuracy.

USING THE DIRECTORY

Directory Format:

- The Table of Classifications on the next page gives the section numbers for each category and the range of numbers in that category. The Table of NAIC codes list the two-digit NAIC code for each category.
- Firms are listed by state, in alphabetical order, in each category.
- An alphabetical listing of companies (page ii-1) appears at the back of the directory.
- See codes to identify certification and ownership type on the back of the first printed page: "2023 DIR National Minority and Women-Owned Business Directory Fifty-Fourth Edition."

An Example:

If you are looking for a supplier to print a company brochure, first you look up "brochure" in the Keyword Index. You will see that the Keyword Index refers you to the "Printing and Engraving" category.

Turning to the "Printing and Engraving" section, you will find suppliers listed alphabetically, according to the state in which they reside. A typical entry might appear as follows:

7600   ABC Printing Company
       1234 XYZ Avenue NE New York, NY 10001
       (212) 555-1234   R. Smith, pres.
       Fax: (212) 555 5678
       Email: Rsmith@www.net
       Web Site: www.print.com
       4-5 color offset presses. In-house 4-color, bindery, die cutting,
       mounting & finishing. (AA, est. 1965, empl 45, sales $4,000,000, cert: State, NMSDC, SDB)

OTHER PRODUCTS AND SERVICES PROVIDED BY DIVERSITY INFORMATION RESOURCES

"The Business of Supplier Diversity: A Handbook of Essential Contacts and Information for Navigating the Industry"

This ninth edition combines the best of DIR's previously published "Purchasing People in Major Corporations" and the "Supplier Diversity Information Resource Guide". This book provides a road map for diverse-owned suppliers and supplier diversity professionals by combining who-to-call with where-to-look. DIR, the leader in supplier diversity data management, combines a detailed contact list of over 1500 supplier diversity and procurement contacts from major corporations, government agencies, large nonprofit organizations, and educational institutions. It also details information on certification, legislation, regional and national networking opportunities, diverse business resources and much more.

Corporate Supplier Diversity Seminars

Now in their 37th year, these seminars teach methods to establish or enhance Supplier Diversity Programs. Diversity Information Resources offers "Building Strategic Phases of a Supplier Diversity Process" seminar and the "Best Practices in Supplier Diversity Strategies and Initiatives" seminar.

For further information on any of the above resources, please contact DIR at (612) 781-6819 or visit www.diversityinforesources.com

TABLE OF CLASSIFICATIONS

TABLE OF NAICS

Arkansas

1000   Creative Merchandise Displays Inc.
1839 W 1st Ave
Mesa, AZ 85202
Contact: Debra Mendoza COO
Tel: 480-668-7225
Email: deb@cmdracks.com
Website: www.cmdracks.com
Mfr point-of-purchase display racks, point-of-purchase display design, engineering, manufacturing, finishing, assembly & packaging. (Woman, estab 2008, empl 12, sales $686,921, cert: City, WBENC, SDB)

Arizona

1001   Double T. Signs Inc.
1835 S Alvernon Ste 214
Tucson, AZ 85711
Contact: David Torres President
Tel: 520-750-0189
Email: dave@doubletsigns.com
Website: www.doubletsigns.com
Mfr & install signs: billboards, displays, electrical, neon, signboards, display lettering services, sign lettering, window dressing, ad displays, identification plates & tags. (Hisp, estab 1993, empl 6, sales $601,161, cert: State, City)

1002   Language Concepts Consulting LLC
8502 E Princess Dr, Ste 230
Scottsdale, AZ 85255
Contact: Katherine Paredes Managing Dir
Tel: 480-626-2926
Email: kathy.paredes@languageconceptsllc.com
Website: www.languageconceptsllc.com
Translation services: English, Spanish, Chinese, Portuguese, Korean, German & Vietnamese. Document Translation, Linguistic Validation, Linguist Testing and Bug Reporting (sites), Multilingual graphic design, Localization, Transcription. (Minority, Woman, estab 2009, empl 1, sales $112,000, cert: NMSDC)

California

1003   1-Stop Translation
3700 Wilshire Blvd, Ste 630
Los Angeles, CA 90010
Contact: Diana Chi Mktg Mgr
Tel: 213-480-0011
Email: diana@1stoptr.com
Website: www.1stoptr.com
Translation and interpretation services with a specialty in Asian languages, including typesetting, desktop publishing, web localization, software testing, budding & subtitling services. (As-Pac, estab 2001, empl 8, sales , cert: CPUC)

1004   3V Signs & Graphics, LLC
434 Pacific Coast Hwy
Hermosa Beach, CA 90254
Contact: Pat Dacy Sec/Treas
Tel: 310-372-0888
Email: pat@3vsigns.com
Website: www.3Vsigns.com
Sign & graphic consultation & design, production, delivery & installation services: architectural signs, window, wall, ground or vehicle graphics, point-of-purchase posters or a building identification signs. (Minority, Woman, estab 2010, empl 5, sales $186,000, cert: City)

1005   Aahs Entertainment, Inc.
10707 Camarillo St, Ste 312
Toluca Lake, CA 91602
Contact: Gwenn Smith President
Tel: 818-279-2416
Email: gwenn@aahsentertainment.com
Website: www.aahsentertainment.com
Video Production Services, Media Production, Media Services, Advertising, Marketing, Content Creation, Branded Content, Brand Marketing, DVD Extras, DVD Special Features, Marketing, Advertising, EPKs. (Woman/AA, estab 2011, empl 1, sales , cert: WBENC)

1006   Artisan Creative Inc.
1830 Stoner Ave Ste 6
Los Angeles, CA 90025
Contact: Katty Douraghy President
Tel: 310-312-2062
Email: kattyd@artisancreative.com
Website: www.artisancreative.com
Design & development solutions: marketing, advertising, communications & production teams in the digital, broadcast, mobile & print space. (Woman, estab 1996, empl 15, sales $3,000,000, cert: WBENC)

1007   Canela Media
2715 Palomino Circle
La Jolla, CA 92037
Contact: Annette Salinas Dir
Tel: 858-699-6640
Email: annette@canelamedia.com
Website: www.canelamedia.com
Create multimedia programs for brand and/or co-opt efforts. (Hisp, estab 2019, empl 12, sales $1,000,000, cert: NMSDC)

1008   Carmazzi of Florida, Inc.
8926 Beckington Dr
Elk Grove, CA 95624
Contact: Angela Carmazzi President
Tel: 888-452-6543
Email: sales@carmazzi.com
Website: www.carmazzi.com/
Translations, interpretations & transcriptions. (Minority, Woman, estab 1998, empl 8, sales $1,900,000, cert: CPUC)

1009 Coast sign inc
      1500 W Embassy St.
      Anaheim, CA 92802
      Contact: Charlie President
      Tel: 714-999-1900
      Email: charlie.alemi@coastsign.com
      Website: www.coastsign.com
Mfr electrical signage, ATM surrounds & kiosks, project
management, design, engineering, lighting, installation,
service & maintenance. (Woman, estab 1964, empl 220,
sales $80,535,032, cert: WBENC)

1010 Competitive Edge Media Management
      3261 S Higuera St Ste 110
      San Luis Obispo, CA 93401
      Contact: Suzy da Silva President
      Tel: 805-788-0966
      Email: suzy@cemm.com
      Website: www.cemm.com
Media buying, brand promotion plans, product launch,
direct-to-consumer sales strategy, hybrid campaigns.
(Woman, estab 2007, empl 8, sales $6,874,176, cert:
WBENC)

1011 CR&A Custom, Inc.
      312 W Pico Blvd
      Los Angeles, CA 90015
      Contact: Carmen Rad Acct Exec
      Tel: 213-749-4440
      Email: carmen@cracustom.com
      Website: www.cracustom.com
Large format digital printing, embroidery, promotional
products, custom designs, carwraps, banners, billboards,
tents, POP displays. (Minority, Woman, estab 1993, empl
31, sales $5,900,000, cert: NMSDC, CPUC, 8(a))

1012 Direct Results Radio, Inc.
      815 Hamton Dr, Ste 2
      Venice, CA 90291
      Contact: Sheri White Business Dev Dir
      Tel: 310-441-9100
      Email: sheriwhite@directresults.com
      Website: www.directresults.com
Advertising agency, audio & radio. (Woman, estab 2007,
empl 20, sales , cert: NWBOC)

1013 Everfield Consulting, LLC
      2075 W 235th Pl
      Torrance, CA 90501
      Contact: Delbara Dorsey Partner
      Tel: 310-251-7165
      Email: deldorsey@everfieldconsulting.com
      Website: www.everfieldconsulting.com
Marketing Consulting Services, Administrative & Manage-
ment, Display Advertising, Advertising, Public Relations,
Media Buying, Direct Mail Advertising, Advertising
Material Distribution Services. (Woman/AA, As- Pac, estab
2011, empl 2, sales , cert: State, City, CPUC)

1014 Exponential Interactive, Inc.
      5858 Horton St, Ste 300
      Emeryville, CA 94608
      Contact: Catherine Avenido Sr Mgr, Intl Ops
      Tel: 510-250-5500
      Email: mbe@exponential.com
      Website: www.exponential.com/
Advertising intelligence & digital media solutions. (As-Ind,
estab 2000, empl 690, sales $219,740,000, cert: NMSDC,
CPUC)

1015 Fraser/White, Inc.
      1631 Pontius Ave
      Los Angeles, CA 90025
      Contact: Renee Fraser CEO
      Tel: 310-319-3737
      Email: rfraser@frasercommunications.com
      Website: www.frasercommunications.com
Advertising, marketing, market research, display
advertising, media planning, media buying, qualitative
research, quantitative research, strategic planning,
outdoor advertising. (Woman, estab 1998, empl 25,
sales $40,000,000, cert: WBENC)

1016 Frisson, Inc.
      12 Geary St, Ste 607
      San Francisco, CA 94108
      Contact: Deboran N Loeb President
      Tel: 415-922-1482
      Email: purchasing@brainchildcreative.com
      Website: www.brainchildcreative.com
Advertising agency; marketing-branding vonsulting
services; commercial production services. (Woman,
estab 2001, empl 7, sales $16,700,000, cert: CPUC,
WBENC)

1017 Global Language Solutions
      19800 MacArthur Blvd Ste 750
      Irvine, CA 92612
      Contact: Inna Kassatkina President
      Tel: 949-798-1400
      Email: info@globallanguages.com
      Website: www.globallanguages.com
Translation svcs: document & web site translations,
conference interpretation, multimedia production &
graphic design services. (Woman, estab 1994, empl 50,
sales $16,300,000,000, cert: WBENC)

1018 I. Studio, Inc.
      51 E Colorado Blvd
      Pasadena, CA 91105
      Contact: Gabriel Avalos Principal
      Tel: 626-683-3101
      Email: g.avalos@interiorstudioinc.com
      Website: www.interiorstudioinc.com
I, Studio, Inc, is a full service Interior Planning & Design
Firm. Our services included programming, schematic
design, design development, contract documents,
construction administration. (Hisp, estab 2006, empl 3,
sales , cert: State, NMSDC)

1019 IW Group, Inc.
      6300 Wilshire Blvd. Ste 2150
      Los Angeles, CA 90048
      Contact: Nita Song President
      Tel: 310-289-5500
      Email: nita.song@iwgroupinc.com
      Website: www.iwgroupinc.com/
Advertising & PR, creative development, research, media
planning, media buying, production, events, cultural
training. (As-Pac, estab 1990, empl 50, sales
$10,506,000, cert: NMSDC, CPUC)

1020 Kramer Translation
      893 Massasso St
      Merced, CA 95341
      Contact: Keith Ensminger Principal
      Tel: 209-385-0425
      Email: keith@kramertranslations.com
      Website: www.kramertranslations.com
Translation svcs: personal, business & government documents. (Minority, Woman, estab 1995, empl 3, sales $701,672, cert: State, NMSDC, CPUC)

1021 Limelight Media LLC, Inc.
      15619 Gaymont Dr
      La Mirada, CA 90638
      Contact: Christina Roach President
      Tel: 818-501-4043
      Email: christina@limelightmedia.net
      Website: www.limelightmedia.net
Advertising and PR campaigns. (Woman, estab 2004, empl 1, sales $2,000,000, cert: WBENC)

1022 Local Concept
      1510 Front St, Ste 200
      San Diego, CA 92101
      Contact: Localization Solutions Specialist
      Tel: 619-295-2682
      Email: info@localconcept.com
      Website: www.localconcept.com
Localization, translation, foreign language typesetting & multimedia for all languages. (Hisp, estab 1985, empl 25, sales $1,435,306, cert: NMSDC)

1023 Motivate, Inc.
      4141 Jutland Dr Ste 300
      San Diego, CA 92117
      Contact: SVP Finance
      Tel: 866-664-4432
      Email: hello@motivateroi.com
      Website: www.MotivateROI.com
Media representation, consumer event marketing services. (Woman, estab 1977, empl 25, sales $40,690,000, cert: WBENC)

1024 Muse Communications, Inc.
      5358 Melrose Ave West Bldg, Ground Fl
      Hollywood, CA 90038
      Contact: Norma Keffer
      Tel: 323-960-4080
      Email: norma@museusa.com
      Website: www.musecordero.com
Advertising, marketing, promotions & public relations programs. (AA, estab 1985, empl 35, sales $5,975,000, cert: CPUC)

1025 Nonpareil Ventures LLC
      710 C St, Ste 206
      San Rafael, CA 94901
      Contact: Nicolas Campos Mgr
      Tel: 415-404-7409
      Email: drcampos2002@yahoo.com
      Website: www.instalogistics.biz
Advertising services, sign manufacturing, repair & maintenance. (As-Ind, estab 2011, empl 5, sales $250,000, cert: State)

1026 Paragon Language Services, Inc.
      5055 Wilshire Blvd Ste 835
      Los Angeles, CA 90036
      Contact: Marina Mintz President
      Tel: 323-966-4655
      Email: marina@paragonls.com
      Website: www.paragonls.com
Foreign language translation, adaptation, interpreting, typesetting/desktop publishing, internationalization, globalization, localization, cultural and linguistic consulting, dialog/dialect coaching, captioning, subtitling, narrations. (Woman, estab 1991, empl 10, sales $2,600,000, cert: City, CPUC, WBENC)

1027 Quigley-Simpson & Heppelwhite, Inc.
      11601 Wilshire Blvd 7th Fl
      Los Angeles, CA 90025
      Contact: Gerald Bagg Co-Chairman
      Tel: 310-996-5820
      Email: geraldb@quigleysimpson.com
      Website: www.quigleysimpson.com
Direct response advertising agency. (Woman, estab 2002, empl 180, sales , cert: WBENC)

1028 RBG Marketing, Inc. dba Crescendo
      5000 Executive Pkwy Ste 350
      San Ramon, CA 94583
      Contact: A.K. AHUJA Managing Dir
      Tel: 925-939-1800
      Email: aka@crescendoagency.com
      Website: www.crescendoagency.com
Marketing & advertising, creative, media planning & media buying in-house. (As-Ind, estab 2003, empl 30, sales $9,000,000, cert: State, NMSDC, CPUC)

1029 RP & Associates, Inc.
      2205 Pacific Coast Hwy
      Hermosa Beach, CA 90254
      Contact: Lisa Pola CEO
      Tel: 310-372-9709
      Email: lpola@mac.com
      Website: www.rpandassociates.com
Marketing solutions, branded products & programs, custom packaging, premiums & promotional items. (Minority, Woman, estab 1988, empl 34, sales $2,306,595,900, cert: NMSDC)

1030 Sensis Inc.
      1651 South Central Ave, Ste A
      Glendale, CA 91204
      Contact: Dreux Dougall
      Tel: 213-341-0171
      Email: ddougall@sensisagency.com
      Website: www.sensisagency.com
Advertising, digital marketing & communications services, online media & marketing, web design & development, online creative strategy, analytics & planning. (Hisp, estab 1998, empl 90, sales $24,000,000, cert: NMSDC)

1031 Simply Displays
      12200 Los Nietos Rd
      Santa Fe Springs, CA 90670
      Contact: Mila Thompson President
      Tel: 888-767-0676
      Email: mthompson@simplydisplays.com
      Website: www.simplydisplays.com
Mfr Point of Purchase Displays & Store Fixtures, Sign Holders, Hospitality & Retail Signage (Woman, estab 2002, empl 16, sales $36,000,000, cert: WBENC)

1032 Think Ink
      927 Mariner St
      Brea, CA 92821
      Contact: Mary Sanchez Dir of Sales
      Tel: 714-672-0017
      Email: info@thinkinkinfo.com
      Website: www.thinkinkinfo.com
Creative marketing, graphic design, print & promotions.
(Hisp, estab 2002, empl 5, sales $1,105,519, cert: NMSDC,
CPUC)

1033 Tylie Jones & Associates, Inc.
      58 E Santa Anita Ave
      Burbank, CA 91502
      Contact: Sheri Lawrence President
      Tel: 818-955-7600
      Email: slawrence@tylie.com
      Website: www.tylie.com
Broadcast advertising services: SD & HD audio & video
spot duplication & digital distribution; post production,
closed captioning, tagging, versioninig, encoding; production element vaulting/storage. (Woman, estab 1971, empl
35, sales , cert: WBENC)

1034 Unique Image, Inc.
      19365 Business Center Dr. Bldg. 1
      Northridge, CA 91324
      Contact: Wafa Kanan President
      Tel: 818-727-7785
      Email: kelly@uniqueimageinc.com
      Website: www.uniqueimageinc.com
Printing & marketing svcs: strategic campaigns, print
media, design & direct mail. (Woman, estab 1992, empl
10, sales $1,200,000, cert: CPUC, WBENC)

1035 Weldon Works, Inc.
      1650 Mabury Rd
      San Jose, CA 95133
      Contact: Jennifer Easom CEO
      Tel: 408-251-1161
      Email: jenn@weldonworks.com
      Website: www.weldonworks.com
Plastic Fabrication & Signage, Interior & Exterior Signs,
ADA Signage, Lobby Signs, Window Graphics & Lettering,
Menu Boards, Isle Signage, Banner, Stencils, Reflective
Road Work/ Parking Signs, Full Color Digital Printing.
(Woman, estab 1982, empl 3, sales $100,000, cert: State)

1036 Zeesman Communications, Inc.
      6255 Sunset Blvd. Ste 1040
      Los Angeles, CA 90028
      Contact: Bonnie Nijst President
      Tel: 323-658-8000
      Email: bonnie@zeesman.com
      Website: www.zeesman.com
Marketing, advertising & design: branding programs,
logos, corporate identity, collateral, direct mail, print
advertising & web design. (Minority, Woman, estab 1990,
empl 4, sales $570,000, cert: NMSDC, CPUC, WBENC)

Connecticut

1037 Andrew Associates, Inc.
      6 Pearson Way
      Enfield, CT 06082
      Contact: Dir Marketing & Business Dev
      Tel: 860-918-5041
      Email:
      Website: www.andrewdm.com
Data management, digital printing, bulk mailing services,
labeling, inserting, stamping, sorting & literature fulfillment services. (Woman, estab 1985, empl 60, sales
$7,600,000, cert: WBENC)

1038 Crew Design Inc.
      PO Box 400
      Kent, CT 06757
      Contact: Gil Aviles CEO
      Tel: 860-927-5001
      Email: gil@crewdesign.com
      Website: www.crewdesign.com
Custom in store display & merchandising equipment:
signage, merchandising fixtures, point of purchase
displays. (Hisp, estab 1998, empl 25, sales $11,000,000,
cert: NMSDC)

1039 Desai Communication
      34 Oakwood Ave Ste 102
      Norwalk, CT 06850
      Contact: Amanda Desai Acct Exec
      Tel: 203-324-6000
      Email: amanda@desaicomm.com
      Website: www.desaicomm.com
Web design & hosting, promotions, premiums, fulfillment, graphic design, computer graphics, digital
retouching, power point pesentations, pint avertising &
promotional material, trade show displays, B/W & color
printing. (Minority, Woman, estab 1979, empl 11, sales
$1,500,000, cert: State, NMSDC)

1040 Point View Displays, LLC
      200 Morgan Ave
      East Haven, CT 06512
      Contact: Cynthia Sedlmeyer Owner
      Tel: 203-468-0887
      Email: cindy@pointviewdisplays.com
      Website: www.pointviewdisplays.com
Press conference backdrops, displays, indoor/outdoor
banner stands & graphics. (Woman, estab 2001, empl 4,
sales $400,000, cert: WBENC)

1041 Tanen Directed Advertising
      12 South Main St
      South Norwalk, CT 06854
      Contact: President
      Tel: 203-855-5855
      Email: ilene@tanendirected.com
      Website: www.tanendirected.com
Advertising, direct marketing, integrated marketing,
online marketing, direct mail, email, print ads, collateral,
sales presentations, human resources communications,
benefits communications materials, employee communications. (Woman, estab 1985, empl 10, sales
$1,865,652, cert: WBENC)

District of Columbia

1042 APCO Worldwide LLC
      1299 Pennsylvania ave NW
      Washington, DC 20005
      Contact: Jim Moorhead
      Tel: 202-778-1000
      Email: jmoorhead@apcoworldwide.com
      Website: www.wwwapcoworldwide.com
Global communication consulting: advertising, antitrust
& competition, branding, broadcast film, video &
multimedia production, business diplomacy, coalition
building, corporate restructuring communication.
(Woman, estab 1984, empl 638, sales $172,200,000,
cert: WBENC)

1043 SRB Communications, LLC
      1020 16th St, NW Ste 400
      Washington, DC 20036
      Contact: Sheila Brooks CEO
      Tel: 202-775-7721
      Email: sbrooks@srbcommunications.com
      Website: www.srbcommunications.com
Media & communications: video production, advertising,
lay-out & design, copywriting services, media placement &
webcasting. (Woman/AA, estab 1990, empl 7, sales , cert:
State, City, NMSDC)

Delaware

1044 Keen Branding
      17601 Coastal Hwy., Ste. 11-416
      Nassau, DE 19969
      Contact: Alicia Stack Principal
      Tel: 302-644-6885
      Email: astack@keenbranding.com
      Website: www.keenbranding.com
Identity creation & design: logos, packaging, look & feel
programs, identity mgmt. (Woman, estab 2000, empl 14,
sales , cert: WBENC)

1045 Meetings by Design, Inc.
      312 Nonantum Dr
      Newark, DE 19711
      Contact: Jan White President
      Tel: 302-738-8318
      Email: info@MeetingsbyDesign.net
      Website: www.meetingsbydesign.net
Business meetings & special events production. (Woman,
estab , empl , sales $200,000, cert: State, WBENC)

Florida

1046 Adventures in Advertising dba Resource Marketing
      2520 Illinois St
      Orlando, FL 32803
      Contact: Christyl Seymour President
      Tel: 407-228-0881
      Email: cseymour@advinadv.com
      Website: www.resourcemarketinginc.net
Graphic design/art services, product research support,
custom design, online store solution, fulfillment svcs,
direct import, promotional svcs, website searchable
database, promotion design & implementation. (Woman,
estab 2002, empl 1, sales $3,175,125, cert: WBENC)

1047 Avanza Advertising
      5465 NW 36 St Ste 100
      Miami Springs, FL 33166
      Contact: Alejandro Perez-Eguren CEO
      Tel: 786-565-7601
      Email: alejandro@avanzaad.com
      Website: www.avanzaad.com
Advertising, design, digital media & video. (Hisp, estab
2013, empl 6, sales $500,000, cert: NMSDC, CPUC, 8(a))

1048 Baron Sign Manufacturing
      900 W 13th St
      Riviera Beach, FL 33404
      Contact: Jerry Foland CEO
      Tel: 800-531-9558
      Email: jerry@baronsign.com
      Website: www.baronsign.com
Interior & exterior signage, awards, plaques. (Woman,
estab , empl , sales , cert: State, City)

1049 Black Dog Inc.
      4803 George Rd Ste 370
      Tampa, FL 33634
      Contact: Dorothy Johnson President
      Tel: 813-249-6398
      Email: djohnson@nextdaysignstampa.com
      Website: www.nextdaysignstampa.com
Vinyl signs, banners, digital printing, vehicle & boat
graphics & lettering, directional signs, promotional
signs, trade show & conventions, sandblasted, electrical,
coroplast, point of purchase, magnets, screen printing,
real estate, constrcution. (Woman, estab 2003, empl 3,
sales $429,460, cert: State)

1050 BroadBased Communications, Inc.
      1301 Riverplace Blvd, Ste 1830
      Jacksonville, FL 32207
      Contact: Jan Hirabayashi CEO
      Tel: 904-398-7279
      Email: jan@bbased.com
      Website: www.bbased.com
Marketing plans, branding, direct mail, publication
design, exhibit design, annual reports, web sites, fleet
graphics, copywriting, art direction. (Woman, estab
1996, empl 7, sales $1,381,791, cert: WBENC)

1051 Certified Translations LLC
      11663 Vicolo Loop
      Windermere, FL 34786
      Contact: Mara Cawthorn Managing Dir
      Tel: 407-205-9494
      Email: certifiedtranslationsllc@gmail.com
      Website: www.certifiedtranslationsllc.com
Language Translation & Interpreting Services: Legal,
Technical, Mechanical, Medical, & Business / Finance.
Spanish, Portuguese, Creole, Mandarin, Cantonese,
French, Italian, German, etc. (Minority, Woman, estab
2013, empl 2, sales , cert: NMSDC)

1052 Doubletake Studios, Inc.
      105 S Fielding Ave, Ste A & B
      Tampa, FL 33606
      Contact: Terri Hall President
      Tel: 813-251-6308
      Email: Info@doubletakeFL.com
      Website: www.doubletakestudios.com
Advertising agency & creative marketing, creative
coaching, branding, web site design & development &
print advertising. (Woman, estab 1999, empl 7, sales
$725,000, cert: WBENC)

1053 Eco Graphics Media
      7034 NW 50th St
      Miami, FL 33166
      Contact: Jose Contreras Project Mgr
      Tel: 305-640-9600
      Email: info@ecogm.com
      Website: www.ecogm.com/index.html
Corporate Image and Concept, Product and Trade Mark
Campaigns • Billboards • Trade shows and displays•
Banners - Posters • Gran Format prints • Signs and
Graphics • vehicle wraps • Trade Shows • Custom
Displays • Store Fixtures. (Hisp, estab 2005, empl 11,
sales $820,000, cert: NMSDC)

1054 Kreative Kontent Co.
3019 Ravenswood Road Ste 110
Fort Lauderdale, FL 33312
Contact: Debbie Margolis-Horwitz Exec Producer
Tel: 954-312-3660
Email: debbie@kreativekontent.com
Website: www.kreativekontent.com
Production specializing in content creation, broadcast, web based, theatrical & marketing fulfillment programs, broadcast commercials, corporate video communications, product placement, branded content, promotional products. (Woman, estab 2010, empl 4, sales $2,000,000, cert: State, WBENC)

1055 KVJINC Consulting
7016 San Ramon Pl Ste. 202
Tampa, FL 33617
Contact: Kimberly Jackson Owner
Tel: 813-987-9083
Email: kvjinc@yahoo.com
Website: www.kvjincpr.com
Public, media relations, strategic, crisis communications, press conferences, kits, event planning, image consulting, sponsorship procurement & market research. (Woman/AA, estab 1999, empl 3, sales $100,000, cert: State, City)

1056 LanguageSpeak, Inc.
5975 Sunset Dr Ste 803
Miami, FL 33143
Contact: Annette Taddeo CEO
Tel: 305-668-9797
Email: acct@languagespeak.com
Website: www.languagespeak.com
Language svcs: document translation, language instruction, conference interpretation, software localization, website translation, cross cultural training. (Minority, Woman, estab 1995, empl 5, sales , cert: NMSDC, WBENC)

1057 MarkMaster, Inc.
11111 N 46th St
Tampa, FL 33617
Contact: Deborah Jordan Sales Rep
Tel: 813-988-6000
Email: sales@markmasterinc.com
Website: www.markmasterinc.com
Mfr rubber stamps, engraved & screened signage & badges; industrial marking equip. (Hisp, estab 1933, empl 65, sales $8,700,993, cert: NMSDC)

1058 Multi Image Group, Inc.
1701 Clint Moore Rd
Boca Raton, FL 33487
Contact: Jim Ballentine President
Tel: 917-319-8127
Email: ballentine@mig.cc
Website: www.mig.cc
Meeting production & staging, video & audio production, graphic design, signage printing, set construction, web & teleconferencing services, trade show exhibits, lighting rentals. (Woman, estab 1979, empl 106, sales $28,400,000, cert: NWBOC)

1059 Retail Solution Center
475 N Cleary Road
West Palm Beach, FL 33413
Contact: Deborah Leo CEO
Tel: 561-567-9000
Email: debleo@rsc-ny.com
Website: www.rsc-ny.com
Point of purchase displays, merchandising systems, mfr & design. (Woman, estab 2003, empl 49, sales $8,110,000, cert: WBENC)

1060 Sunlure, Inc.
3700 NW 124 Ave Unit 140
Coral Springs, FL 33065
Contact: Craig Sage Mgr
Tel: 754-484-7929
Email: craig.sage@sunlure.com
Website: www.sunlure.com
Promotional Products, Apparel Products, Custom imprinted apparel, Writing Products, Candy, Food and Water, Customized Drinkware Products, Bags for Marketing Campaigns, Toys and Novelties, Office products, Outdoor and Leisure, Health and Personal Care. (Minority, Woman, estab 2003, empl 7, sales $900,000, cert: State, NMSDC)

1061 T Wynne Art & Design Inc.
1401 Manatee Ave W, Ste 1005
Bradenton, FL 34205
Contact: Tanya Wynne Williams President
Tel: 941-906-7124
Email: tanya@twynne.com
Website: www.twynne.com
Package graphic design & and point of sale (POS) design. (Woman, estab 1991, empl 8, sales $2,430,822, cert: WBENC)

1062 Thomas Sign and Awning Company, Inc.
4590 118th Ave N 33762
Clearwater, FL 33762
Contact: Aimee Pavlovich Marketing Mgr
Tel: 727-573-7757
Email: aimee.pavlovich@thomassign.com
Website: www.thomassign.com
Design, mfr, install & service illuminated electrical signs. LED, neon, vinyl graphics, permit acquisition, variance applications, turnkey project mgmt. (Woman, estab 1969, empl 156, sales $21,000,000, cert: WBENC)

Georgia

1063 AEE Productions
1650 Westfork Dr, Ste 110
Lithia Springs, GA 30122
Contact: Yergan Jones President
Tel: 404-352-2201
Email: yerganjones@aeeproductions.com
Website: www.aeeproductions.com
Audio visual services. (AA, estab 1990, empl 6, sales $975,000, cert: NMSDC)

1064 American Systems, Inc. dba Simon Sign Systems
2158 Sylvan Rd
Atlanta, GA 30344
Contact: Simon Robinson President
Tel: 404-766-5208
Email: gen-info@simonsignsystems.com
Website: www.simonsignsystems.com
Mfr signs: interior & exterior, banners, digital & screen printing, posters, corporate apparel & promotional items. (AA, estab 1989, empl 5, sales $300,670, cert: NMSDC)

1065   Basiqa, LLC
       1555 Oakbrook Dr Ste 135
       Norcross, GA 30093
       Contact: Winston Dzose VP Digital Marketing
       Tel: 678-824-6460
       Email: winston@basiqa.com
       Website: www.basiqa.com
Direct mail, advertising, material preparation services for
mailing or other direct distribution, digital printing. (AA,
estab 2009, empl 16, sales $3,000,000, cert: NMSDC)

1066   CK&M Direct Mail Advertising, Inc.
       1250 Northmeadow Pkwy Ste 116
       Roswell, GA 30076
       Contact: Gary Kern General Mgr
       Tel: 770-442-2166
       Email: gkern@ckmdirect.com
       Website: www.ckmdirectmail.com
Lettershop services, fulfillment, distribution, warehousing,
list broker. (Hisp, estab 1992, empl 7, sales $1,992,000,
cert: NMSDC)

1067   Cloud Track, LLC
       36111 Indigo Creek Trail NW
       Kennesaw, GA 30144
       Contact: Samir Mullick CEO
       Tel: 404-934-7408
       Email: Samir.Mullick@cloudtrackusa.com
       Website: www.cloudtrackusa.com
Digital Branding, Lead Generation. (As-Ind, estab 2014,
empl 2, sales , cert: NMSDC)

1068   Display America
       195 Andrew Dr
       Stockbridge, GA 30281
       Contact: Carlos Quinones CEO
       Tel: 770-416-7047
       Email: carlos@displayamerica.com
       Website: www.displayamerica.com
Dist exhibit marketing products & turnkey services: image
& identity, rent exhibits, high impact graphics, trade
shows, conventions, expositions, hospitality & retail
environments. (Hisp, estab 2003, empl 15, sales
$1,400,000, cert: NMSDC)

1069   Dove Direct
       5601 Fulton Industrial Blvd SW
       Atlanta, GA 30336
       Contact: Travis L Benjamin Business Dev Exec
       Tel: 404-629-0122
       Email: tbenjamin@dovedirect.com
       Website: www.dovedirect.com
First class barcoding, third class mail, lettershop svcs,
personalization, list, data mgmt, fulfillment svcs, design
analysis, etc. (Woman/AA, estab 1987, empl 59, sales
$24,000,000, cert: NMSDC)

1070   Exhibits South
       1000 Satellite Blvd Ste 120
       Suwanee, GA 30024
       Contact: Nichole Holliday VP
       Tel: 678-225-5200
       Email: nholliday@exhibitssouth.com
       Website: www.exhibitssouth.com
Dist & rent portable, modular & custom displays, graphic
production & design department, tradeshow services,
logistics & exhibit storage. (Woman, estab 1983, empl 35,
sales $10,750,000, cert: WBENC)

1071   Jones Worley Design, Inc.
       723 Piedmont Ave
       Atlanta, GA 30308
       Contact: Cynthia Jones Parks President
       Tel: 404-876-9272
       Email: cjonesparks@jonesworley.com
       Website: www.jonesworley.com
Graphic design svcs: print graphics & signage, design,
planning & implementation. (Woman/AA, estab 1990,
empl 15, sales $939,838, cert: WBENC)

1072   Mail Centers Plus LLC
       17 Executive Park Dr Ste 230
       Atlanta, GA 30329
       Contact: John Smithson Business Devel Analyst
       Tel: 404-321-1010
       Email: jsmithson@mailcentersplus.com
       Website: www.mailcentersplus.com
Document distribution & mail center solutions. (AA,
estab 2000, empl 140, sales $5,500,000, cert: NMSDC)

1073   PM Publicidad
       1776 Peachtree St
       Atlanta, GA 30309
       Contact: Philip Polk EVP General Mgr
       Tel: 404-844-5757
       Email: info@pm3.agency
       Website: www.pm3.agency
Multicultural advertising solutions in the Hispanic
market segment, account services, broadcast production, media planning & buying, sports marketing, market
research, strategic account planning, experiential &
event marketing. (Hisp, estab 2004, empl 35, sales
$23,307,370, cert: NMSDC)

1074   Profitmaster Displays Inc.
       6190 Powers Ferry Rd Ste 510
       Atlanta, GA 30339
       Contact: President
       Tel: 800-633-5454
       Email: sales@ProfitmasterDisplays.com
       Website: www.profitmasterdisplays.com
Point of purchase displays & racks: wire, sheet metal,
wood, plastic & corrugated paperboard. (Woman, estab
1984, empl 18, sales $20,000,000, cert: WBENC)

1075   Shared Vision LLC
       225 Ottley Dr NE Ste 140
       Atlanta, GA 30324
       Contact: Doug Jackson Principal
       Tel: 678-694-1965
       Email: djackson@shared-vision.net
       Website: www.shared-vision.net
Marketing & advertising, strategic & creative services.
(Woman/AA, estab 2006, empl 20, sales $1,700,000,
cert: NMSDC)

1076   TDEFERIAMEDIA, Inc.
       9795 Talisman Dr
       Johns Creek, GA 30022
       Contact: Antenor Tony President
       Tel: 404-630-0639
       Email: contact@tdeferiamedia.com
       Website: www.tdeferiamedia.com
Marketing, branding consulting & creative production,
ethnic market study & plans, media buying, translation
& interpretation in Spanish, digital & social media
expertise. (Hisp, estab 2007, empl 1, sales $140,000,
cert: NMSDC)

1077 The Symmetry Group, LLC
      600 W Peachtree St Ste 510
      Atlanta, GA 30308
      Contact: Scott Robinson President
      Tel: 404-237-2378
      Email: scott@tsgatl.com
      Website: www.tsgatl.com
Graphic design, radio/TV production, print/outdoor
advertising production, event development, management
& production, promotion development & execution. (AA,
estab 2001, empl 6, sales $1,200,000, cert: NMSDC)

1078 Viswam Bala Enterprises
      440 Barrett Pkwy, Ste 33
      Kennesaw, GA 30144
      Contact: Giridhar Iyer President
      Tel: 770-421-8110
      Email: giri.iyer@fastsigns.com
      Website: www.fastsigns.com/201
Marketing strategy creation, brand /product identity
creation, graphic design services, production/printing &
installation services, static signs, banners, posters, decals,
vehicle art/wraps, cutting-edge digital signs & visual
magnetic solutions. (As-Ind, estab 1994, empl 6, sales
$1,047,000, cert: City, NMSDC)

1079 Yellobee Studio
      750 Hammond Dr Ste 350 Bldg 15
      Atlanta, GA 30328
      Contact: Alison Scheel Creative Dir
      Tel: 404-249-6407
      Email: ascheel@yellobee.com
      Website: www.yellobee.com
Bilingual design & marketing, promotional communications, brand identity & packaging, direct mail design,
brochures, newsletters, web design, banner & poster art,
tradeshow displays, court graphics, typography,
illustration,photography. (Woman, estab 1998, empl 4,
sales $850,000, cert: WBENC)

Iowa

1080 Hawthorne Direct LLC
      2280 W Tyler Ave, Ste 200
      Fairfield, IA 52556
      Contact: Karla Crawford Kerr VP Marketing
      Tel: 310-844-0606
      Email: diversity@hawthornedirect.com
      Website: www.hawthornedirect.com/
Advertising, strategic planning, creative development,
production, media planning, buying, analytics & campaign
management. (Woman, estab 1986, empl 61, sales
$11,500,000, cert: WBENC)

Illinois

1081 1st Metropolitan Translation Services, Inc.
      875 North Michigan Ave Ste 3100
      Chicago, IL 60611
      Contact: Shannon Ewasiuk President
      Tel: 312-621-1500
      Email: firstmetro@sbcglobal.net
      Website: www.1stmetropolitan.info
Foreign language interpreters & translations. (Woman,
estab 2000, empl 1, sales $222,810, cert: State, WBENC)

1082 2.718 Marketing
      54 W Hubbard St, Ste LLE
      Chicago, IL 60654
      Contact: Liz Brohan President
      Tel: 312-661-1050
      Email: lbrohan@2718marketing.com
      Website: www.2718marketing.com
B2B & B2C advertising, marketing, creative development
& design, internet & email marketing & consulting.
(Woman, estab 1988, empl 20, sales $2,500,000, cert:
WBENC)

1083 Angel Flight Marketing Services, Inc.
      1006 S. Michigan Ave Ste 606
      Chicago, IL 60605
      Contact: Gabriel Mitchell President
      Tel: 312-933-1878
      Email: gmitchell@angelfly.com
      Website: www.angelfly.com
Direct mail, graphic design, call center, market research.
(AA, estab 1992, empl 10, sales $1,220,000, cert: City,
NMSDC)

1084 Bluedog Design, LLC
      403 N Carpenter
      Chicago, IL 60642
      Contact: Michelle Hayward President
      Tel: 312-243-1101
      Email: michelle@bluedogdesign.com
      Website: www.bluedogdesign.com
Brand strategy & package design: brand positioning,
identity development & revitalization, innovation,
nomenclature, consumer research &bstrategic graphic
design. (Woman, estab 1999, empl , sales $4,334,286,
cert: WBENC)

1085 commonground
      600 W Fluton Fl 4
      Chicago, IL 60661
      Contact: Sherman Wright Managing Partner
      Tel: 312-384-1906
      Email: alicepollard@discovercg.com
      Website: www.discovercg.com
Marketing, advertising, cultural consulting, brand
strategy, promotions. (AA, estab 2003, empl 75, sales
$24,367,000, cert: NMSDC)

1086 Cor Creative, Inc.
      1412 W Jarvis
      Chicago, IL 60626
      Contact: Linda Tuke-Larkin President
      Tel: 773-381-3811
      Email: linda@corcreate.com
      Website: www.corcreate.com
Design, advertising, production, web site design &
programming, strategy, branding, social media, marketing, creative, media placement. (Woman, estab 2006,
empl 1, sales $100,000, cert: City)

1087 J.C. Schultz Enterprises, Inc./FlagSource
      951 Swanson Dr
      Batavia, IL 60510
      Contact: Joseph Smurawski Controller
      Tel: 800-323-9127
      Email: jsmurawski@flagsource.com
      Website: www.flagsource.com
Mfr flags & banners: screen printing, appique, dye sub, 4
color process, table banners, vinyl & polyethylene POP
banners, flag poles. (Woman/As-Ind, estab 1920, empl
65, sales $8,500,000, cert: WBENC)

1088 Jayne Agency, LLC
      1231 Eastwood Ave
      Highland Park, IL 60035
      Contact: Brooke Foley CEO
      Tel: 312-464-8100
      Email: brooke@jayneagency.com
      Website: www.jayneagency.com
Creative, Strategy, Media, Digital Strategy & Technology.
(Woman, estab 2009, empl 4, sales $484,000, cert:
WBENC)

1089 Linguanational Translations, Inc.
      401 N Michigan Ave Ste 1200
      Chicago, IL 60611
      Contact: Janie Markos President
      Tel: 312-833-1399
      Email: jmarkos@linguanational.com
      Website: www.linguanational.com
Translation services: interpretation, typesetting, transcription & desktop publishing. (Woman, estab 2009, empl 3,
sales , cert: WBENC)

1090 Mail Everything, Inc.
      325 N Fourth St
      Libertyville, IL 60048
      Contact: Mary Trifunovich President
      Tel: 847-573-9999
      Email: mary@maileverything.com
      Website: www.maileverything.com
Direct mail & fulfillment services: addressing, inserting,
tabbing, folding, mailing lists, printing, warehousing, dist
literature, product & promotional items, kitting & assembly. (Woman, estab 2002, empl 16, sales $3,000,000, cert:
WBENC)

1091 Medius & Associates, Inc.
      13175 Cold Springs Dr
      Huntley, IL 60142
      Contact: Karen Holmes President
      Tel: 847-609-8165
      Email: kholmes@mediusinc.com
      Website: www.mediusinc.com
Graphic design, illustration, photography & printing:
brochures, catalogs, ads, point of purchase, tradeshow
graphics & web design. (Woman, estab 1993, empl 2, sales
, cert: WBENC)

1092 NorthStar Strategies, Inc.
      448 Greenwood Ave
      Glencoe, IL 60022
      Contact: Dinny Cosyns Sr Partner
      Tel: 847-242-9107
      Email: dinny@northstarstrategies.biz
      Website: www.northstarstrategies.biz
Marketing & advertising agency. (Woman, estab 2004,
empl 3, sales $240,000, cert: State, WBENC)

1093 Suncraft Technologies, Inc.
      1301 Frontenac Road
      Naperville, IL 60563
      Contact: Holly Winters Diversity Lead
      Tel: 630-369-7900
      Email: hwinters@suncraft-tech.com
      Website: www.suncraft-tech.com
Inline and conventional direct mail with variable data.
digital storefront, signage, inventory management,
creative format design, graphic design, fulfillment, kitting
and mailing services. (Woman, estab 1993, empl 100, sales
$30,000,000, cert: WBENC)

Indiana

1094 Deborah Wood Associates, Inc.
      630 W Carmel Dr Ste 200
      Carmel, IN 46032
      Contact: Dana Walker Strategic Acct Dir
      Tel: 317-208-3600
      Email: dana_walker@avanthcm.com
      Website: www.dwahcg.com
Comprehensive launch & mature-product strategy,
promotional programming strategy design
& implementation, scientific content development,
thought leader & emerging leader identification,
advisory board identification, recruitment. (Woman,
estab 1994, empl 150, sales $23,000,000, cert: WBENC)

1095 L & D Mail Masters Inc.
      110 Security Pkwy
      New Albany, IN 47150
      Contact: Jill Peden Business Devel Mgr
      Tel: 812-981-7161
      Email: jpeden@ldmailmasters.com
      Website: www.ldmailmasters.com
Direct mail processing. (Woman, estab 1986, empl 110,
sales $25,000,000, cert: WBENC)

1096 RLR Associates, Inc.
      1302 N Illinois St
      Indianapolis, IN 46202
      Contact: Ryan Scott President
      Tel: 317-632-1300
      Email: ryan@rlr.biz
      Website: www.rlr.biz
Professional design services: corporate identity &
branding, signage, wayfinding programs, interiors &
interpretive spaces. (AA, estab 1994, empl 6, sales
$710,000, cert: State, City)

Kansas

1097 Callahan Creek, Inc.
      805 New Hampshire
      Lawrence, KS 66044
      Contact: Sarah Etzel VP Mktg Svcs
      Tel: 785-838-4774
      Email: cmaude@callahancreek.com
      Website: www.callahancreek.com
Advertising & marketing, graphic design, qualitative,
quantitative & competitive intelligence research,
interactive, brand development, media planning &
placement. (Woman, estab 1982, empl 35, sales
$6,000,000, cert: WBENC)

Kentucky

1098 John F. Ruggles, Inc.
      93 Industry Dr
      Versailles, KY 40383
      Contact: Tim Cambron President
      Tel: 859-879-1199
      Email: tim@rugglessign.com
      Website: www.rugglessign.com
Mfr & install signage. (Woman, estab 1946, empl 95,
sales $16,000,000, cert: WBENC)

1099   Life's Eyes Media, LLC
     1717 Dixie Hwy, Ste 150
     Fort Wright, KY 41011
     Contact: Kristan Getsy CEO
     Tel: 859-363-3916
     Email: kgetsy@lifeseyesmedia.com
     Website: www.lifeseyesmedia.com
Corporate Video, Commercial Video Production, Motion Graphics, After Effects, DSLR Production, DSLR, Creative, Creative Agency, Agency, Non-Profit Video, Scriptwriting, Scripting, Web Video, Social Media Video. (Woman, estab 2005, empl 3, sales $263,704, cert: WBENC)

1100   Madison Design Group
     515 Madison Ave, Ste 201
     Covington, KY 41011
     Contact: Julie Courtney Partner
     Tel: 859-655-9900
     Email:
     Website: www.madison-design.com
Design services: editorial layout, collateral, point-of-sale, fundraising mailings, newsletter design & layout, annual reports, website design, brand identity creation. (Woman, estab 1998, empl 7, sales $159,498,680, cert: WBENC)

1101   New West LLC
     9630 Ormsby Station Rd
     Louisville, KY 40223
     Contact: Melvin Graham Managing Dir
     Tel: 888-867-7811
     Email: mgraham@newwestagency.com
     Website: www.newwestagency.com
Advertising, Public Relations, Brand Strategy, Website & Mobile App Development, Social Media, Multicultural Marketing, SEO/SEM/PPC, Event Planning & Video Production. (AA, estab 2002, empl 28, sales $5,500,000, cert: NMSDC)

1102   Vest Marketing Design, LLC
     3007 Sprowl Rd
     Louisville, KY 40299
     Contact: Keith Searles Healthcare Marketing Dir
     Tel: 502-267-5335
     Email: bizdev@urbangis.com
     Website: www.vestadvertising.com
Digital, video, print & comprehensive media strategy & implementation. (Woman, estab 1991, empl 40, sales $8,500,000, cert: WBENC)

Massachusetts

1103   Buyer Advertising & Talent Solutions
     189 Wells Ave Ste 201A
     Newton, MA 02459
     Contact: Charles Buyer President
     Tel: 617-404-0860
     Email: cbuyer@buyerads.com
     Website: www.buyerads.com
Website Design & Development, Search Engine Optimization (SEO), Search Engine Marketing, Mobile marketing, Social Networking, Facebook Advertising, Facebook Applications, Employer Brand Development, market Research & Analysis. (Woman, estab 1966, empl 32, sales $15,877,337, cert: State)

1104   Carroll Communications Group
     PO Box 401
     Milton, MA 02186
     Contact: Marc Carroll Principal
     Tel: 781-248-2125
     Email: mcarroll@carrollcommunications.net
     Website: www.carrollcommunications.net
Advertising agency: web design, graphic design, branding strategies, social media strategies, on-line marketing, media planning & media buying. (AA, estab 2008, empl 3, sales $100,000, cert: State)

1105   Color Media Group, LLC
     4 Copley Pl, Ste 120
     Boston, MA 02116
     Contact: Josefina Bonilla President
     Tel: 617-266-6961
     Email: josefina@colorboston.com
     Website: www.colormagazineusa.com
Web advertising, signature events, event management, strategic marketing initiatives, new markets, media buying services, public relations. (Minority, Woman, estab 2007, empl 3, sales $289,000, cert: State)

1106   National Electric Corporation
     57 Providence Hwy
     Norwood, MA 02062
     Contact: Rhonda Rothberg Sr Acct Mgr
     Tel: 888-344-4632
     Email: rrothberg@natlelec.com
     Website: www.natlelec.com
Provide electrical and sign services for retail stores nationwide plus Canada and Puerto Rico. (Woman, estab 1999, empl 10, sales $1,500,000, cert: WBENC)

1107   Rapport International, LLC
     93 Moore Rd
     Sudbury, MA 01776
     Contact: Owner, Exec Dir
     Tel: 978-443-2540
     Email: rapport@rapportintl.com
     Website: www.rapporttranslations.com
Translation & interpretation services in over 100 languages. (Woman, estab 1987, empl 5, sales $1,200,000, cert: WBENC)

1108   Spectrum Broadcasting Corporation
     114 Wrentham St
     Boston, MA 02124
     Contact: Tessil Collins CEO
     Tel: 617-287-8770
     Email: thewiz@spectrumbroadcasting.com
     Website: www.spectrumbroadcasting.com
Media streaming & production, advertising creative services, training & management, internet, television, radio, graphic & web design, product & artist management, training, facilitation & consultation services. (AA, estab 1998, empl 5, sales , cert: State, City)

1109   TSM Design, Inc.
     293 Bridge St
     Springfield, MA 01103
     Contact: Nancy Urbschat Principal
     Tel: 413-731-7600
     Email: nancy@tsmdesign.com
     Website: www.tsmdesign.com
Integrated branding, multi-channel marketing & standout graphic design services. (Woman, estab 2005, empl 7, sales $900,000, cert: State)

Maryland

1110 21st Century Expo Group, Inc.
3321 75th Ave, Ste P
Landover, MD 20785
Contact: Leslie McFarland President
Tel: 301-386-9771
Email: lmcfarland@21stceg.com
Website: www.21stceg.com
Exhibit mgmt, marketing, dist displays & decorating svcs.
(Woman/AA, estab 1991, empl 9, sales , cert: NMSDC,
WBENC)

1111 A. Bright Idea
210 Archer St
Bel Air, MD 21014
Contact: CEO
Tel: 410-836-7180
Email:
Website: www.abrightideaonline.com
Advertising, public relations & graphic design support.
(Woman, estab 1996, empl 35, sales $2,100,000, cert:
WBENC)

1112 American International Mailing, Inc.
3916 Vero Rd Ste K
Baltimore, MD 21227
Contact: Tom Parry VP
Tel: 410-247-4900
Email: tomp@aimmailing.com
Website: www.aimmailing.com
International mailing & distribution svcs: letter mail, direct
mail, catalogs, publications, parcels & freight. (Woman,
estab 2004, empl 25, sales $8,000,000, cert: WBENC)

1113 ArachnidWorks, Inc.
5104 Pegasus Court Ste B
Frederick, MD 21704
Contact: Monica Kolbay CEO
Tel: 240-285-9844
Email: monica@arachnidworks.com
Website: www.arachnidworks.com
Advertising, internet marketing, logo design, print media,
ad creation & copywriting, web design & development.
(Woman, estab 2008, empl 3, sales $158,335, cert: State)

1114 Barb Clapp Advertising and Marketing, LLC
6115 Falls Rd
Baltimore, MD 21209
Contact: Barb Clapp President
Tel: 410-561-8886
Email: lisa@barbclapp.com
Website: www.clappcommunications.com
Advertising, marketing & public relations. (Woman, estab
2000, empl 6, sales $354,737, cert: State)

1115 Catalpha Advertising & Design
6801 Loch Raven Blvd
Towson, MD 21286
Contact: Karen Kerski Principal
Tel: 410-337-0066
Email:
Website: www.catalpha.com
Design & produce product & event promotional signs &
materials: banners, fact tags, headers, danglers, hang tags,
counter cards. (Woman, estab 1986, empl 6, sales
$720,000, cert: State)

1116 Harvey & Daughters, Inc.
952 Ridgebrook Rd, Ste 1000
Sparks, MD 21152
Contact: Jade Reider Office Mgr
Tel: 410-771-5566
Email: jreider@harveyagency.com
Website: www.harveyagency.com
Brand activation, purchasing strategy, package design,
logo development & graphic design. (Woman, estab
1986, empl 35, sales $6,000,000, cert: WBENC)

1117 Herrmann Advertising|Branding|Technology
30 West St
Annapolis, MD 21401
Contact: Jane Farrell Sr Acct. Exec.
Tel: 410-267-6522
Email: jane@herrmann.com
Website: www.herrmann.com
Advertising agency: market research, creative design,
media management, print management, photography,
copy writing & technology. (Woman, estab 1979, empl
14, sales $3,663,968, cert: State, City, WBENC)

1118 Media Works, Ltd.
1425 Clarkview Rd Ste 500
Baltimore, MD 21209
Contact: Michele Selby President
Tel: 443-470-4400
Email: mselby@medialtd.com
Website: www.medialtd.com
Advertising agency, research, plan & place media.
(Woman, estab 1989, empl 34, sales $887,604, cert:
City)

1119 Pure Advertising, LLC
137 National Plaza Ste 300
Oxon Hill, MD 20745
Contact: Rick Tyner Managing Partner
Tel: 301-646-4392
Email: rick.tyner@prosum.com
Website: www.pureadsww.com
Outdoor advertising & graphic design, taxi advertising,
transit, airport advertising & billboards. (AA, estab 2010,
empl 2, sales $200,000, cert: State, NMSDC)

Michigan

1120 BlueWater Technologies Group Inc.
24050 Northwestern Hwy
Southfield, MI 48075
Contact: Suzanne Schoeneberger President
Tel: 248-356-4399
Email: sue@bluewatertech.com
Website: www.bluewatertech.com
Retail POP and POS displays, complete turn key mer-
chandising solutions, Literature displays, Audio Visual
Systems. (Woman, estab 1985, empl 187, sales
$148,000,000, cert: WBENC)

1121 Graphicolor Systems, Inc.
12788 Currie Court
Livonia, MI 48150
Contact: Anita Mitzel President
Tel: 248-347-0271
Email: anita@graphicolor.com
Website: www.graphicolor.com
Design trade show displays & corporate signage.
(Woman, estab 1984, empl 8, sales $1,002,000, cert:
WBENC)

1122   Immersion Graphics Inc.
1020 Metro Dr
Commerce, MI 48390
Contact: Pat Hernandez President
Tel: 248-624-6520
Email: pat@immersion-graphics.com
Website: www.immersion-graphics.com
Engineering & audio visual systems solutions. (Hisp, estab 1998, empl 10, sales $3,439,000, cert: NMSDC)

1123   LA Exhibits, Inc.
1091 Centre Rd Ste 130
Auburn Hills, MI 48326
Contact: Della Dotson President
Tel: 248-340-1144
Email: della@laexhibits.com
Website: www.laexhibits.com
Design, build & support tradeshow displays & events, portable, modular & custom displays, design & production, warehousing. (Woman, estab 1991, empl 3, sales , cert: WBENC)

1124   Languages International Inc.
4665 - 44th St SE Ste A1101
Grand Rapids, MI 49512
Contact: Beverly Wall Owner
Tel: 616-285-0005
Email: beverly@lang-int.com
Website: www.lang-int.com
Foreign language translation & interpreting services. (Woman, estab 1988, empl 7, sales $400,000, cert: WBENC)

1125   Marketing Displays, Inc.
38271 W Twelve Mile Rd
Farmington, MI 48331
Contact: Lisa Sarkisian President
Tel: 248-553-1900
Email: lisa.sarkisian@mdiworldwide.com
Website: www.mdiworldwide.com
Custom & stock retail display products & Traffic Control Products for temporary traffic control devices. (Woman, estab , empl , sales $30,639,000, cert: WBENC)

1126   PALS International
900 Wilshire Dr, Ste 105
Troy, MI 48084
Contact: David Schroeder VP Business Dev
Tel: 248-362-2060
Email: dschroeder@palsintl.com
Website: www.palsintl.com
Translations & interpretations; language instruction; cross-cultural programs; accent reduction; global relocation; videovoice-overs. (Minority, Woman, estab 1983, empl 80, sales $1,509,900, cert: NMSDC, WBENC)

1127   Pro-Motion Technology Group
29755 Beck Rd
Wixom, MI 48393
Contact: Brian Flewelling Acct Mgr
Tel: 248-668-3100
Email: hello@promotion.tech
Website: www.promotion.tech
Audiovisual technology solutions. (Woman, estab 2002, empl 45, sales $25,000,000, cert: WBENC)

1128   Stage 3 Productions
1532 N. Opdyke Rd Ste 700
Auburn Hills, MI 48326
Contact: Andre LaRoche President
Tel: 248-955-1250
Email: andre@stage3.com
Website: www.stage3.com
Commercial, advertising photography, digital imaging, illustration, graphic design, stage rental. (AA, estab 1984, empl 8, sales , cert: NMSDC)

1129   STS Marketing Services, LLC
22840 Woodward Ave
Ferndale, MI 48220
Contact: Theresa Bland Business Mgr
Tel: 248-548-1011
Email: tbland@stsmktg.com
Website: www.stsmktg.com
Editorial boutique editing, internal/external corporate communications packages, production services. (AA, estab 1994, empl 1, sales , cert: NMSDC)

1130   The Ajamu Group, LLC.
29155 Northwestern Hwy, Ste 687
Southfield, MI 48034
Contact: Cheryl D Parks Ajamu CEO
Tel: 248-223-0904
Email: cheryl.ajamu@ajamugroup.com
Website: www.ajamugroup.com
The Ajamu Group, LLC. secures print, digital and mobile advertising for national media companies, and also provides Event Management services for local and national companies. (Woman/AA, estab 2004, empl 1, sales , cert: NMSDC, WBENC)

1131   Tiger Studio Co.
418 E 8th St
Holland, MI 49423
Contact: Luciano Hernandez Owner
Tel: 616-748-7532
Email: luciano@tigerstudiodesign.com
Website: www.tigerstudiodesign.com
Product, Interaction, Brand, and Strategy. (Hisp, estab 2000, empl 4, sales , cert: NMSDC)

1132   Trent Design LLC
114 E Second St
Rochester, MI 48307
Contact: Marilyn Trent Principal
Tel: 248-652-8307
Email: marilyn@trentcreative.com
Website: www.trentcreative.com
Graphic design, digital media, web design & development, advertising, social media marketing. (Woman, estab 1991, empl 5, sales $600,000, cert: WBENC)

1133   Wensco of Michigan Corporation
5760 Safety Dr NE
Belmont, MI 49306
Contact: Yolanda Cain Inside Sales Support
Tel: 800-253-1569
Email: ycain@wensco.com
Website: www.wensco.com
Dist signs: digital inkjet media & laminates, cut vinyls, banners, neon, l.e.d.'s, ballasts, plywood, metal & plastic substrates, aluminum, polycarbonate, acrylic, plexiglass, aluminum composite panels. (Woman, estab 1937, empl 50, sales , cert: WBENC)

Minnesota

1134 Bella Creative LLC
16860 Judicial Rd
Lakeville, MN 55044
Contact: Stacy A Parizek Owner
Tel: 952-232-6411
Email: stacy@bella-creative.net
Website: www.bellaexhibts.com
Mfr trade show exhibits, off-the-shelf displays to custom booths. (Woman, estab 2008, empl 1, sales $108,353, cert: WBENC)

1135 Betmar Languages, Inc.
6260 Hwy 65 NE, Ste 308
Minneapolis, MN 55432
Contact: President
Tel: 763-572-9711
Email:
Website: www.betmar.com
Translation svcs: on site interpreters; voice-over services for audio, video & interactive projects; typesetting; document translation; cultural diversity training. (Woman, estab 1985, empl 4, sales $949,266, cert: WBENC)

1136 cmnd+m LLC
867 Pierce Butler Route
St. Paul, MN 55104
Contact: Krista O'Malley
Tel: 612-867-6273
Email: accounting@cmndm.com
Website: www.cmndm.com
Design, production, engineering, retail, advertising, project management, construction, and training. (Minority, Woman, estab 2011, empl 11, sales $700,000, cert: NMSDC, WBENC)

1137 Deep Well, Inc.
123 N 3rd St Ste 700
Minneapolis, MN 55401
Contact: Phil Nelson
Tel: 612-338-7947
Email: phil@crash-sues.com
Website: www.crash-sues.com
Advertising, marketing, production, video editing, animation, 3D, traditional animation, stop motion, graphics, effects, color, media, web apps, strategy, creative, branding, brand development, ideation, web development, post-production. (Woman, estab 2008, empl 12, sales $1,600,000, cert: WBENC)

1138 Designer Sign Systems
9975 Flanders Ct NE
Blaine, MN 55449
Contact: Karen Fisher CEO
Tel: 763-784-5858
Email: customerservice@designersign.com
Website: www.designersign.com
Mfr & design architectural interior & exterior signage. (Woman, estab 1984, empl 30, sales $5,246,000, cert: WBENC)

1139 Dudak Production, Inc.
582 Bavaria Lane
Chaska, MN 55318
Contact: Shirley Dudak President
Tel: 952-443-0097
Email: shirley.dudak@dudakproductioninc.com
Website: www.dudakproductioninc.com
Advertising, Graphic Design Services, Marketing Consulting Services, Commercial Gravure Printing, Commercial Screen Printing, Print Advertising, Direct Marketing Fulfillment, Printing, Brand Marketing. (Woman, estab 1996, empl 3, sales $1,675,000, cert: WBENC)

1140 IN Food Mktg & Design, Inc.
600 N Washington Ave Ste C101
Minneapolis, MN 55401
Contact: Anita M Nelson President
Tel: 612-353-3410
Email: anita@infoodmktg.com
Website: www.infoodmktg.com
Marketing & communications: brand building & product promotions. (Woman, estab 1995, empl 12, sales $1,215,000, cert: WBENC)

1141 Intercross Design, Inc.
2238 Edgewood Ave S
Minneapolis, MN 55426
Contact: Lori Fuller VP
Tel: 952-935-2080
Email: lori.fuller@intercross.com
Website: www.intercross.com
Advertising agency: branding, videos, websites, collateral & advertising. (Woman, estab 1997, empl 17, sales $3,876,000, cert: WBENC)

1142 JPG & Associates, Inc.
8991 33rd St N
Lake Elmo, MN 55042
Contact: Jerry Grohovsky President
Tel: 651-779-1072
Email: jerry@jpgassoc.com
Website: www.jpgassoc.com
Graphic design, desktop publishing, web site development, web-based help development. (Woman, estab 1993, empl 30, sales $2,000,000, cert: WBENC)

1143 KJ International Resources, LTD
800 Washington Ave N Ste 905
Minneapolis, MN 55401
Contact: Kristem Giovanis
Tel: 612-288-9494
Email: kgiovanis@kjinternational.com
Website: www.kjinternational.com
Language translation & validation, desktop publishing, web translation & localization, voice-overs, etc. (Woman, estab 1994, empl 30, sales $6,400,000, cert: WBENC)

1144 KNOCK, inc.
1307 Glenwood Ave
Minneapolis, MN 55405
Contact: Tom Newton VP Business Dev
Tel: 612-333-6511
Email: tom.newton@KNOCKinc.com
Website: www.KNOCKinc.com
Graphic design, branding, marketing, advertising, packaging, illustration, photo art direction. (Minority, Woman, estab 2001, empl 102, sales $24,145,000, cert: NMSDC, WBENC)

1145   Latitude Prime LLC
      80 S 8th St Ste 900
      Minneapolis, MN 55402
      Contact: Nat LeBrun
      Tel: 888-341-9080
      Email: email@latitudeprime.com
      Website: www.latitudeprime.com
Multilingual translation services, media & document translation, interpretation, localization, transcription, proofreading/editing & DTP services. (Minority, Woman, estab 2009, empl 15, sales , cert: State, City, NMSDC, WBENC, 8(a))

1146   Media Bridge, Inc.
      212 3rd Ave N
      Minneapolis, MN 55401
      Contact: Shannon Knoepke SVP Marketing
      Tel: 612-353-6077
      Email: Procurement@mediabridgeadvertising.com
      Website: www.mediabridgeadvertising.com
Ad agency. Media buying, strategy, branding, creative services, social media and video production. (Woman, estab 2010, empl 26, sales $24,420,385, cert: WBENC)

1147   Northcott Banners, Inc.
      2645 - 26th Ave S, Ste 400
      Minneapolis, MN 55406
      Contact: Millie Northcott Owner
      Tel: 612-722-1733
      Email: millie@northcottbanner.com
      Website: www.northcottbanner.com
Mfr banners: fabric, vinyl, interior & exterior applications. (Woman, estab 1984, empl 9, sales $712,698, cert: WBENC)

1148   Oceandrum LLC dba Zydeco Design
      231 2nd St
      Excelsior, MN 55331
      Contact: Nathalie Wilson President
      Tel: 612-202-7421
      Email: nathaliew@zydecodesign.com
      Website: www.zydecodesign.com
Brand & design, branding strategy, brand experience strategy, brand architecture, naming, identity, image system, packaging, annual reports, corporate social responsibility & sustainable development. (Woman, estab 2009, empl 2, sales $300,000, cert: State, WBENC)

1149   Peggy Lauritsen Design Group, Inc.
      125 SE Main St Ste 340
      Minneapolis, MN 55414
      Contact: Linda Gosslin Sr Acct Dir
      Tel: 612-623-4200
      Email: lgosslin@pldg.com
      Website: www.pldg.com
Corporate & brand identity, graphic & communications sesign, marketing communications, website design, event communications, print or electronic media. (Woman, estab 1979, empl 9, sales , cert: WBENC)

1150   Portage Marketing
      2401 Sheridan Ave S
      Minneapolis, MN 55405
      Contact: Laureen Carlson President
      Tel: 612-381-0621
      Email: lcarlson@portagemarketing.com
      Website: www.portagemarketing.com
Advertising agency & media placement. (Woman, estab 2000, empl 1, sales $5,000,000, cert: WBENC)

1151   Tembua Inc (fka Precision Language Services)
      17595 Kenwood Trail Ste 120
      Lakeville, MN 55044
      Contact: Paula Town Exec Admin Assist
      Tel: 952-435-8178
      Email: office@tembua.com
      Website: www.tembua.com
Document translation: bilingual, bicultural translations. (Woman, estab 1993, empl 36, sales $700,000, cert: WBENC)

1152   Wrap City Graphics
      62 6th Ave S
      Hopkins, MN 55343
      Contact: President
      Tel: 952-920-4664
      Email: sales@wrapcitygraphics.com
      Website: www.WrapCityGraphics.com
Commercial signage & digitally printed wide-format adhesive backed vinyl graphics for vehicle graphics/wraps, window/wall graphics, dimensional letters/logos & architectural products. (Woman, estab 2005, empl 7, sales $745,000, cert: WBENC)

Missouri

1153   Brighton Agency, Inc.
      7711 Bonhomme Ave Ste 100
      Saint Louis, MO 63105
      Contact: Tina VonderHaar CEO
      Tel: 314-726-0700
      Email: accounting@brightonagency.com
      Website: www.brightonagency.com
Strategic planning, brand development, digital marketing & production, marketing consulting, public relations, advertising, promotions, media planning, audio & video production, event marketing, online, mobile & app development. (Woman, estab 1989, empl 71, sales $9,030,143, cert: State, WBENC)

1154   Language Solutions Inc.
      230 South Bemiston Ave. Ste 610
      St. Louis, MO 63105
      Contact: Melissa Wurst President
      Tel: 314-725-3711
      Email: melissa@langsolinc.com
      Website: www.langsolinc.com
Written translation & multilingual typesetting: over 40 languages. (Woman, estab 1998, empl 2, sales $677,610, cert: WBENC)

1155   Schisla Design, LLC dba Enrich
      12 N Sarah St
      St. Louis, MO 63108
      Contact: Suzanne Duvald'Adrian Marketing & Social Media
      Tel: 314-553-9500
      Email: suzanne@enrichcreative.com
      Website: www.enrichcreative.com
Branding programs: audits & research, Strategy and Development, Naming, Logo Design, Strategic Messaging, Positioning, Brand Guides & Product, Service and Event Branding. (Woman, estab 2002, empl 4, sales $438,502, cert: WBENC)

North Carolina

1156 Crutchfield & Associates Inc.
515 College Rd, Ste 14
Greensboro, NC 27410
Contact: Bernadette Trinidad President
Tel: 336-297-1222
Email: bernadette@ca-ideas.com
Website: www.ca-ideas.com
Advertising agency, integrated, strategic & innovative marketing & communications solutions. (Minority, Woman, estab 1985, empl 3, sales $121,707, cert: NMSDC)

1157 Fly My Photo, LLC
560 Davidson Gateway Dr Ste 101
Davidson, NC 28036
Contact: Susan Boaz President
Tel: 855-347-4922
Email: susan@flagology.com
Website: www.flagology.com
Mfr decorative flags, printed & appliqued, photo flags, monogram flags, signage, flag poles & brackets, door mats, monograms & personalized flags. (Woman, estab 2013, empl 1, sales , cert: WBENC)

1158 Jervay Agency, LLC
338 S Sharon Amity, Ste 302
Charlotte, NC 28211
Contact: Adria Jervay Media Acct Rep
Tel: 704-780-7004
Email: adria@thejervayagency.com
Website: www.TheJervayAgency.com
Advertising & marketing materials. (Woman/AA, estab 2012, empl 3, sales , cert: City)

1159 Language Resource Center Inc.
PO Box 18066
Charlotte, NC 28218
Contact: Abdullahi Sheikh CEO
Tel: 704-464-0016
Email: abdullah.sheikh@languagerc.com
Website: www.languagerc.com
Interpretation & translation service providers. (Woman/AA, estab , empl , sales $1,428,268, cert: State, City)

1160 Main Street Mobile Billboards
2610 Tuckaseegee Rd
Charlotte, NC 28208
Contact: Brendon Henderson CEO
Tel: 888-788-7492
Email: brendon@mainstreetmobilebillboards.com
Website: www.mainstreetmobilebillboards.com
Mobile truck billboard & walking billboards advertising. (AA, estab 2013, empl 2, sales , cert: State, City, NMSDC)

1161 Moving Ideas, Inc.
7519 Royal Bliss Ct, Ste 205
Denver, NC 28037
Contact: Jennifer Moates President
Tel: 704-655-2870
Email: jmoates@movingideasinc.com
Website: www.movingideasinc.com
Advertising, Branding & Identity, Copywriting & Content, Creative Campaigns, Direct Mail, Infographics, Email Marketing, Graphic Design, Strategic Marketing Plans, Naming, Social Media, Tradeshow, Video, Websites. (Woman, estab 2005, empl 5, sales $500,000, cert: WBENC)

New Hampshire

1162 Kelley Solution, Inc.
210 West Rd Unit 3
Portsmouth, NH 03801
Contact: Lisa Finneral President
Tel: 603-431-3881
Email: lfinneral@kelleysolutions.com
Website: www.kelleysolutions.com
E-business solutions & svcs: online fulfillment, graphic design, strategic sourcing, warehousing, distribution, integrated marketing campaigns & direct mail management. (Woman, estab 1972, empl 6, sales $2,200,000, cert: WBENC)

1163 Polaris Direct
300 Technology Dr
Hooksett, NH 03106
Contact: Judith Maloy Dir & CEO
Tel: 603-626-5800
Email: diversity@polarisdirect.net
Website: www.polarisdirect.net
Direct mail, data processing, ink jet & laser personalization, mailing services, bindery & print management. (Woman, estab 2003, empl 78, sales $25,546,966, cert: WBENC)

New Jersey

1164 Clark Media Corp.
655 Jersey Ave
Jersey City, NJ 07302
Contact: Ken Clark COO
Tel: 800-872-6752
Email: kclark@resptrans.com
Website: www.responsivetranslation.com
Translation & interpretation services: machine translation, translation memory, content management systems & multi-platform publishing in 157 languages. (Minority, Woman, estab 1990, empl 2, sales $1,628,455, cert: WBENC)

1165 CQ fluency, Inc.
2 University Plaza, STE 406
Hackensack, NJ 07601
Contact: Elisabete Miranda President
Tel: 201-487-8007
Email: info@cqfluency.com
Website: www.cqfluency.com
Translation services: 180 languages, web localization, cultural consulting, desktop publishing, phone interpretation, multimedia production, tape transcription. (Minority, Woman, estab 2000, empl 82, sales $3,844,722, cert: State, NMSDC, WBENC)

1166 Digital Outdoor Advertising
788 Shrewsbury Ave
Tinton Falls, NJ 07724
Contact: Christine Lanziano President
Tel: 732-491-8726
Email: christine@digitaloutdooradvertising.com
Website: www.digitaloutdooradvertising.com
Digital & static outdoor billboards, mall kiosks & bus advertising. (Woman, estab 2012, empl 7, sales $6,000,000, cert: WBENC)

1167 Eclipse Marketing Services Inc.
      490 Headquarters Plaza North Tower, 10th Fl
      Morristown, NJ 07960
      Contact: Margaret Boller President
      Tel: 800-837-4648
      Email: mboller@eclipse2.com
      Website: www.eclipsemarketingservices.com
Advertising Services: campaigns; Hispanic Marketing
Consulting; Website design; Promotional printing;
Magazine advertising and publishing; Coop Marketing &
promotion; Digital & social media. (Woman, estab 1992,
empl 39, sales $10,980,994, cert: WBENC)

1168 Encore Events, ltd. dba ENCORE DESIGN
      31 Industrial Ave., Ste 7
      Mahwah, NJ 07430
      Contact: Kathleen Orbe Principal
      Tel: 973-890-0088
      Email: encoredesign@mac.com
      Website: www.encoredesign.com
Design services: strategic identity & branding. (Woman,
estab 1994, empl 5, sales $425,000, cert: WBENC)

1169 Expect Advertising, Inc.
      1033 Route 46
      Clifton, NJ 07013
      Contact: Ravi Sachdev President
      Tel: 973-777-8886
      Email: ravi.sachdev@expectad.com
      Website: www.expectad.com
Medical marketing & communications: advertising,
promotion, branding, web design, web marketing, sales
incentive programs, premiums, trade shows, public
relations, media planning, market research. (As-Ind,
estab 1996, empl 16, sales $2,000,000, cert: NMSDC)

1170 Graphic Matter, Inc.
      601 Route 206, Ste 26-405
      Hillsborough, NJ 08844
      Contact: Beverly Thomas President
      Tel: 908-359-8760
      Email: wbe@graphicmatter.com
      Website: www.graphicmatter.com
Creative services: print & web. (Woman, estab 2002,
empl 6, sales $297,570, cert: State, WBENC)

1171 Iris Communications LLC
      11 Belaire Dr
      Roseland, NJ 07068
      Contact: Barbara Bochese Managing Dir
      Tel: 973-902-7027
      Email: bbochese@iriscommunications.org
      Website: www.iriscommunications.org
Marketing services, corporate communications &
branding, presentations-internal/corporate, brand
deliverables, educational/training, video production &
animation, website design & development, media
planning & buying. (Woman, estab 2011, empl 12, sales ,
cert: State, NWBOC)

1172 Jouard Wozniak LLC dba JWDesign
      165 Passaic Ave Ste 410
      Fairfield, NJ 07004
      Contact: Faith Wozniak President
      Tel: 973-244-9191
      Email: faith@jwadv.com
      Website: www.jwadv.com
Advertising & design, creative, design & marketing
services, web & print, trade show graphics, promotional
events, video & audio production, photography &
retouching. (Woman, estab 1989, empl 4, sales
$178,000, cert: WBENC)

1173 Newtype, Inc.
      447 Route 10 East
      Randolph, NJ 07869
      Contact: Jo Ann Porto CEO
      Tel: 973-361-6000
      Email: accounting@newtypeinc.com
      Website: www.newtypeinc.com
Translations & desktop publishing svcs in over 130
languages. (Woman, estab 1966, empl 12, sales , cert:
WBENC)

1174 Para-Plus Translations, Inc.
      2 Coleman Ave
      Cherry Hill, NJ 08034
      Contact: Carlos Santiago VP
      Tel: 856-547-3695
      Email: csantiago@para-plus.com
      Website: www.para-plus.com
Translation & interpretation svcs: technical reports,
medical reports, legal documents, oral & written
depositions, audio tapes, video tapes, patents, manuscripts, manuals, product literature, web sites. (Minority,
Woman, estab 1980, empl 15, sales $3,028,000, cert:
State)

1175 Personal Mail International, Inc.
      5 Cold Hill Rd S, Ste 28
      Mendham, NJ 07945
      Contact: Debra Seyler President
      Tel: 973-543-6001
      Email: dseyler@pmipmi.com
      Website: www.pmipmi.com
International & domestic mail & package forwarding
services. (Woman, estab 1987, empl 11, sales $950,000,
cert: WBENC)

1176 Seliger-Braun Inc. dba Keylingo Translations
      116 Village Blvd, Ste 200
      Princeton, NJ 08540
      Contact: Managing Dir
      Tel: 609-423-1077
      Email:
      Website: www.keylingo.com/
Translations services: localization, transcreation,
interpretation & tele-interpretation. (Woman, estab
2011, empl 2, sales $106,775, cert: State, WBENC)

1177 Sign Up Inc.
      255 Route 3 E
      Secaucus, NJ 07094
      Contact: President
      Tel: 201-902-8640
      Email: 153@fastsigns.com
      Website: www.fastsigns.com/153
Signs: vinyl, wood, windows, walls or vehicles, channel
letters, window graphics, trade show booths, exhibits
and displays, flags and banners, cut-outs, dimensional
letters, banner stands, vehicle graphics, vinyl lettering,
posters, murals. (Woman, estab 1992, empl 8, sales
$87,542,162, cert: State)

1178 Sunset Printing and Engraving Corp
      10 Kice Ave
      Wharton, NJ 07885
      Contact: Deron Wainer
      Tel: 732-335-2165
      Email: dwainer@sunsetcorpid.com
      Website: www.sunsetcorpid.com
Corporate identity campaigns: printing, engraving,
embossing & foil stamping. (Hisp, estab 1945, empl 28,
sales $3,820,000, cert: NMSDC)

1179 The S3 Agency
      716 Main St
      Boonton, NJ 07005
      Contact: Denise Blasevick CEO
      Tel: 973-257-5533
      Email: dblasevick@thes3agency.com
      Website: www.theS3agency.com
Advertising & marketing: print, tv, radio, outdoor, online,
public relations, collateral, direct mail & direct marketing,
e-marketing, websites, product launches, POP, business-to-
business & consumer marketing, internal communications.
(Woman, estab 2001, empl 25, sales $3,800,000, cert:
WBENC)

1180 TriStar Fulfillment Services, Inc.
      520 Pedricktown Rd
      Bridgeport, NJ 08014
      Contact: Susan Harker Owner
      Tel: 972-355-6256
      Email: sharker@tristarfulfillment.com
      Website: www.tristarfulfillment.com
Rebates, gift cards, merchandise, sweepstake offers, online order entry, reporting, tracking, billing, data entry,
data processing, telemarketing, ondemand printing,
sampling, direct mail, warehousing & distribution.
(Woman, estab 1976, empl 135, sales $30,000,000, cert:
WBENC)

Nevada

1181 El Mundo, Ltd.
      760 N Eastern Ave, Ste 110
      Las Vegas, NV 89101
      Contact: Hilda Escobedo CEO
      Tel: 702-649-8553
      Email: hescobedo@elmundo.net
      Website: www.elmundo.net
Advertising, display advertising, graphic design, Spanish
publication, Spanish readers, advertising in Spanish,
display ads in Spanish, Spanish, newspaper, (Minority,
Woman, estab 1980, empl 9, sales $1,347,788, cert: State)

1182 The Design Factory, LLC
      4318 W Cheyenne Ave
      North Las Vegas, NV 89032
      Contact: Mgr
      Tel: 702-656-0555
      Email:
      Website: www.dflv.com
Exhibit design & sales, exhibit rental, graphic design,
graphic printing, vinyl production, event services, furniture
rental, floral rental, carpet rental, custom exhibit production, convention labor, sales of signs & banners. (Woman,
estab 1999, empl 12, sales $2,081,369, cert: WBENC)

New York

1183 ADDO, LLC
      155 W 118th St, Ste 1
      New York, NY 10026
      Contact: S Courtney Booker, CEO
      Tel: 212-933-0670
      Email: courtney@theaddo.com
      Website: www.theaddo.com
Brand marketing. (AA, estab 2006, empl 1, sales , cert: City,
NMSDC)

1184 Adventium Marketing & Design
      320 E 35th St, Ste 5B
      New York, NY 10016
      Contact: Penny Chuang President
      Tel: 212-481-9576
      Email: penny@adventium.net
      Website: www.adventium.net
Marketing collateral, graphic design, brochures, advertising, direct mail, corporate communications, newsletters,
catalogs, videos, invitations, logo design, media kits,
posters, signage, trade show exhibits, web design &
architecture, web banners. (Minority, Woman, estab
1992, empl 3, sales $370,000, cert: State, City)

1185 Baseline Design, Inc
      236 W. 30th St 5th Fl
      New York, NY 10001
      Contact: Flanders Founder & Chief Brand Strate-
      gist
      Tel: 212-925-1656
      Email: darcy@baselinedesign.com
      Website: www.baselinegroupny.com/
Design solutions, printing, logo design & corporate
identity programs, fund rollouts, conference support
materials, brochures, catalogs, newsletters, direct mail
pieces, advertising
& annual reports. (Woman, estab 1997, empl 8, sales ,
cert: State, WBENC)

1186 Big Apple Visual Group Inc.
      3 Oval Dr
      Islandia, NY 11749
      Contact: Mobin Shroff Sr Sales Exec
      Tel: 631-342-0303
      Email: mobin@bigapplegroup.com
      Website: www.bigapplegroup.com
Design & mfr interior & exterior architectural signs:
subsurface graphics, cut out letters & logos, directional
& informational signs, fabricated letters, POP displays,
engraved signs, etc. (As-Pac, estab 1979, empl 82, sales
$19,000,000, cert: NMSDC)

1187 Brand Cool Marketing, Inc.
      2300 East Ave
      Rochester, NY 14610
      Contact: Sue Kochan CEO
      Tel: 585-381-3350
      Email: doorsopen@brandcoolmarketing.com
      Website: www.brandcool.com
Advertising services. (Woman, estab 1997, empl 20,
sales $4,360,000, cert: WBENC)

1188 Butler/Till Media Services, Inc.
      260 E Broad St
      Rochester, NY 14604
      Contact: Andria DiFelice Group Acct Dir
      Tel: 585-274-5108
      Email: adifelice@butlertill.com
      Website: www.butlertill.com
Advertising agency: research analysis, media planning &
placement, post-buy analysis & reconciliation, results
measurement & analysis, & independent media audit
services. (Woman, estab , empl , sales , cert: WBENC)

1189　Crown Sign Systems
　　　7 Odell Plaza
　　　Yonkers, NY 10701
　　　Contact: Michelle Strum President
　　　Tel:　914-375-2118
　　　Email: mstrum@crownsigns.com
　　　Website: www.crownsigns.com
Mfr interior & exterior architectural signage. (Woman,
estab 1994, empl 14, sales $22,000,000, cert: State)

1190　DePirro/GarroneLLC
　　　25 W 13th St Ste 6NN
　　　New York, NY 10011
　　　Contact: Lisa Garrone CEO
　　　Tel:　212-206-6967
　　　Email: lgarrone@depirrogarrone.com
　　　Website: www.depirrogarrone.com
Creative advertising, size or media channel, traditional or
digital, online or offline. Flexible & scalable. (Woman,
estab 2008, empl 8, sales $1,000,000, cert: City, WBENC)

1191　Eriksen Translations Inc.
　　　360 Court St, #37
　　　Brooklyn, NY 11231
　　　Contact: Vigdis Eriksen President
　　　Tel:　718-802-9010
　　　Email: vigdis.eriksen@eriksen.com
　　　Website: www.eriksen.com
Multilingual services, translation, interpreting, typesetting,
project management, web localization & cultural consult-
ing in over 75 languages. (Woman, estab 1986, empl 35,
sales $8,040,294, cert: State, City, WBENC)

1192　Fusia Communications, Inc.
　　　45 Main St, Ste 212
　　　Brooklyn, NY 11201
　　　Contact: Elizabeth Kay President
　　　Tel:　718-643-0311
　　　Email: ekay@fusia.net
　　　Website: www.fusia.net
Marketing, strategic consulting, media planning & buying,
media tracking, design/production, copywriting, transla-
tions. (Minority, Woman, estab 2002, empl 4, sales
$514,627, cert: City, WBENC)

1193　Harquin Graphics, Inc.
　　　80 Surrey Dr
　　　New Rochelle, NY 10804
　　　Contact: Sherry Bruck President
　　　Tel:　914-738-9620
　　　Email: sbruck@harquin.com
　　　Website: www.harquin.com
Graphic design, printing & web design. (Woman, estab
1992, empl 9, sales $450,000, cert: State, City)

1194　JUICE Pharma Worldwide
　　　322 8th Ave, 10th Fl
　　　New York, NY 10001
　　　Contact: Howard Nagelberg CFO
　　　Tel:　212-647-1595
　　　Email: hnagelberg@juicepharma.com
　　　Website: www.juicepharma.com
Professional, patient, and consumer promotion and
advertising. (Woman, estab 2002, empl 169, sales
$45,000,000, cert: WBENC)

1195　Keeper of the Brand
　　　894 Otsego Rd
　　　West Hempstead, NY 11552
　　　Contact: Donyshia Boston-Hill CEO
　　　Tel:　917-697-1699
　　　Email: db@keeperofthebrand.com
　　　Website: www.keeperofthebrand.com/
Marketing Plans & Strategies, Media Buying, TV, Radio,
Print & Digital Solutions, Broadcast Media Distribution,
Brand Development, Consumer Insight, Copyright,
Transactional Engagement, Programming & Campaign
Mgmt, Graphic Design, Creative Services. (Woman/AA,
estab 2013, empl 6, sales , cert: State, NMSDC, WBENC)

1196　MAD Studio LLC
　　　1123 Broadway, Ste 707
　　　New York, NY 10010
　　　Contact: FirstName LastName Principal
　　　Tel:　212-982-4613
　　　Email: smatiz@mad-nyc.com
　　　Website: www.mad-nyc.com
Brand marketing & design: positioning, logo develop-
ment, stationery, brochures, email campaigns, websites,
exhibits, packaging, promotional items, advertising.
(Woman, estab 2011, empl 3, sales , cert: City, WBENC)

1197　Millennium Signs & Display, Inc.
　　　90 W Graham Ave
　　　Hempstead, NY 11550
　　　Contact: Saj Khalfan President
　　　Tel:　516-292-8000
　　　Email: saj@msdny.com
　　　Website: www.msdny.com
Signs and Graphics; Point of Purchase Displays; Large
Format Digital Printing; Wayfinding Signage; 3-Dimen-
sional Letters and Logos; Lenticular Graphics; Laser &
Waterjet Cutting; Architectural Signage. (Minority, estab
2008, empl 28, sales $5,255,000, cert: City, NMSDC)

1198　Mix On Digital, LLC
　　　1867 Amsterdam Ave Ste 3F
　　　New York, NY 10034
　　　Contact: Christina Mixon Managing Dir
　　　Tel:　917-383-8121
　　　Email: christina@mixondigital.com
　　　Website: www.mixondigital.com
Digital media design & consulting, social, mobile &
digital platforms. (Woman/AA, As- Pac, estab 2012, empl
2, sales $385,000, cert: City)

1199　Signs & Decal Corp.
　　　410 Morgan Ave
　　　Brooklyn, NY 11211
　　　Contact: Hasnain Khalfan VP Sales & Marketing
　　　Tel:　718-486-6400
　　　Email: salesadmin@signsanddecal.com
　　　Website: www.signsanddecal.com
Mfr & install signage, signs. (Minority, estab 1972, empl
30, sales $7,204,781, cert: City)

1200　SpikeDDB, LLC
　　　437 Madison Ave 20 FL
　　　New York, NY 11201
　　　Contact: Sterling Green
　　　Tel:　718-596-5400
　　　Email: joel@spikeddb.com
　　　Website: www.spikeddb.com
Advertising agency. (AA, estab 1997, empl 30, sales
$6,000,000, cert: NMSDC)

1201 Squeaky
55 Broadway 3th Fl
New York, NY 10006
Contact: Mailet Lopez Managing Dir
Tel: 212-994-5270
Email: mailet@squeaky.com
Website: www.squeaky.com
Design interface, web design, flash animation, e-commerce, database. (Hisp, estab 2001, empl 30, sales $1,754,683, cert: State, NMSDC)

1202 The Language Shop
114-26 146th St
Jamaica, NY 11436
Contact: Deborah Lockhart Dir of Operations
Tel: 646-245-4129
Email: deborah.lockhart@thelanguageshop.org
Website: www.languageshop.org
Translation & interpreting legal, medical, financial, corporate, commercial, marketing, online games, website translation & localization. (Minority, Woman, estab 2007, empl 1, sales $122,000, cert: City)

1203 TITANIUM Worldwide LLC
350 7th Ave Ste 1403
New York, NY 10001
Contact: Streisand Chief Financial Operations Officer
Tel: 646-952-8440
Email: accounting@titaniumww.com
Website: www.titaniumww.com
Media, marketing, communications & consulting: Branding/Creative/Strategy, Content/Messaging, Digital/Social/Mobile, Film/Video Production, Event Marketing, Business Intelligence, Data Warehousing, Development/Deployment. (Woman, estab 2014, empl 4, sales , cert: WBENC)

1204 Uniworld Group Inc.
One Metro Tech Center North 11th Fl
Brooklyn, NY 11201
Contact: Ronald Hughes Group Acct Dir
Tel: 212-219-1600
Email: ronald.hughes@uwgatl.com
Website: www.uwginc.com
Multicultural advertising agency. (AA, estab 1969, empl 138, sales $18,717,000, cert: NMSDC)

1205 Visual Citi Inc.
110-30 Dunkirk St
St. Albans, NY 11412
Contact: Mirza Kermani Acct Exec
Tel: 718-479-5500
Email: mirza@visualciti.com
Website: www.visualciti.com
Digitally Printed Signs & Graphics, Banners, POP Displays, Window Signs & Graphics, Cutout logos & letters, Silk Screen printing, ADA Signs, Etched Signs & Custom Fabrication. (As-Ind, estab 2004, empl 25, sales , cert: City, NMSDC)

1206 Weinrib & Connor Associates, Inc.
297 Knollwood Rd
White Plains, NY 10607
Contact: President
Tel: 914-686-3900
Email:
Website: www.weinconn.com
Advertising agency. (Woman, estab 1993, empl 7, sales $1,300,000, cert: WBENC)

1207 Womenkind, LLC
114 E 25th St, Ste 710
New York, NY 10010
Contact: Sandy Sabean Partner/Chief Creative Officer
Tel: 212-660-0400
Email: sandy@womenkind.net
Website: www.womenkind.net
Advertising & marketing communications. (Woman, estab 2007, empl 2, sales $1,800,000, cert: WBENC)

Ohio

1208 Baker Creative Ltd.
386 Main St
Groveport, OH 43125
Contact: Michele Cuthbert Principal
Tel: 614-836-3845
Email: mbaker@baker-creative.com
Website: www.baker-creative.com
Graphic Design, Marketing Consulting, Advertising, Public Relations, Display Advertising. (Minority, Woman, estab 2003, empl 10, sales , cert: State, WBENC, SDB)

1209 Blink Marketing LLC dba Blink Signs; BlinkSwag
1925 St. Clair Ave NE
Cleveland, OH 44114
Contact: Todd Davis Natl Sales
Tel: 216-503-2568
Email: t.davis@blinksigns.com
Website: www.blinksigns.com
Manufacture all types of illuminated or non-illuminated interior signage (including ADA) and exterior signage including awnings, sign service and maintenance. (Minority, Woman, estab 2007, empl 65, sales $9,069,699, cert: State, City)

1210 Bright Future Partners, Inc. dba RED212
5509 Fair Lane
Cincinnati, OH 45227
Contact: Donna Zaring Dir Business Devel
Tel: 513-772-1020
Email: donnazaring@red212.com
Website: www.red212.com
Marketing communications, production & post production services. (Woman, estab 2001, empl 18, sales $3,971,726, cert: WBENC)

1211 Commercial Cutting & Graphics, LLC
208 Central Ave
Mansfield, OH 44905
Contact: Natl Sales Exec
Tel: 714-493-4714
Email: custservice@commercialcutting.com
Website: www.commercialcutting.com
Design & mfr temporary point of purchase displays. (Woman, estab 1986, empl 42, sales $6,800,001, cert: WBENC)

1212 Dayton Mailing Services, Inc.
888 Dayton St
Yellow Springs, OH 45387
Contact: Barbara Deer Sales Exec
Tel: 937-222-5056
Email: barbara.deer@dmsink.us
Website: www.daytonmailing.com
Digital printing, variable printing, direct mail, inserting, inkjetting, product fulfillment, collation, labeling, tipping, folding/glue. (Minority, Woman, estab , empl , sales $8,625,000, cert: State, WBENC)

1213 INNERSOURCE Inc.
      755 Wick Ave
      Youngstown, OH 44505
      Contact: Gloria Byce Principal
      Tel: 330-799-7619
      Email: gbyce@innersourceinc.com
      Website: www.innersourceinc.com
Interior Signage, Exterior Signage, ADA Signage, Room
Identification Signage, Way Finding, Directories, Tempo-
rary Signage, Modular Systems, Custom Signage, Donor
Plaques, Dimensional Letters, Corporate Identity, Digital
Printing, Banners. (Woman, estab 1996, empl 7, sales ,
cert: WBENC)

1214 Modern Technique, LLC
      1050 Lear Industrial Pkwy
      Avon, OH 44011
      Contact: Kristi Blosser President
      Tel: 440-497-8547
      Email: kristi@whatsyourtechnique.com
      Website: www.whatsyourtechnique.com
Advertising, digital & mobile media development, website
design, SEO & email marketing, broadcast & social media
planning & devel, mobile app devel & mobile marketing.
(Woman, estab 2012, empl 4, sales $250,000, cert:
WBENC)

1215 MRA Advertising/Production Support Services, Inc.
      3979 Erie Ave
      Cincinnati, OH 45208
      Contact: Stacey St. John Dir Business Dev
      Tel: 513-561-5610
      Email: diversity@mraservices.com
      Website: www.mraservices.com
Advertising production management & cost control.
(Minority, Woman, estab 1980, empl 25, sales $4,900,000,
cert: WBENC)

1216 Skyline Exhibits of Central Ohio, LLC
      2801 Charter St
      Columbus, OH 43228
      Contact: Mark Armbrust President
      Tel: 614-684-2050
      Email: mark@skylineohio.com
      Website: www.skylineohio.com
Exhibits, displays, kiosks, graphics, accessories & services
for trade shows & events, pop ups, banner stands, portable displays, custom modular exhibits, hanging signs &
structures. (Woman, estab 2001, empl 12, sales
$3,108,655, cert: WBENC)

1217 Swath Design, LLC
      30 Garfield Place Ste 1020
      Cincinnati, OH 45202
      Contact: CEO
      Tel: 513-421-1773
      Email: people@swathdesign.com
      Website: www.swathdesign.com
Environmental graphic design, wayfinding, signage,
interior design, architectural design, branding, marketing
& print communications & interactive media. (Woman,
estab 1991, empl 6, sales , cert: State, WBENC, SDB)

1218 Vocalink, Inc.
      405 W First St
      Dayton, OH 45402
      Contact: Jill A. Mead Compliance Counsel
      Tel: 877-492-7754
      Email: rfp@vocalinkglobal.com
      Website: www.vocalinkglobal.com/
Translation & web localization services: documentation
& online content, multimedia
Linguistic asset mgmt, terminology mgmt, web content
& e-commerce sites, server side scripting. (Minority,
Woman, estab 1995, empl 450, sales , cert: State,
NMSDC, WBENC)

1219 Xela Group, LLC dba Grupo Xela
      1775 Mentor Ave, Ste 404
      Cincinnati, OH 45212
      Contact: Jose D. Cuesta Managing Partner
      Tel: 513-351-2200
      Email: info@grupoxela.com
      Website: www.grupoxela.com
Hispanic marketing research: questionnaire dev, focus
groups, bilingual moderators, surveys, data collection &
tabulation, interpreting, corporate identity, collateral
design, media buying, web dev, translation svcs. (Hisp,
estab 2002, empl 10, sales , cert: State)

Oregon

1220 Hanlon Brown Design
      2130 NW 29th Ave
      Portland, OR 97210
      Contact: Noma Hanlon Sr Acct Exec
      Tel: 503-944-1000
      Email: matthew@hbdesign.com
      Website: www.hbdesign.com
Design services: print, web, interactive & catalog,
graphic design, programming, software engineering,
quality assurance & project management. (Woman,
estab 1978, empl 25, sales $5,500,000, cert: State,
WBENC)

Pennsylvania

1221 Anderson Advertising dba The Anderson Group
      879 Fritztown Rd
      Sinking Spring, PA 19608
      Contact: Julie LaSalle
      Tel: 610-678-1506
      Email: jlasalle@theandersongrp.com
      Website: www.theandersongrp.com
Brand development & continuity programs: strategic
planning, corporate identity, advertising & creative
services, interactive services, media placement & public
relations. (Woman, estab 1987, empl 18, sales
$2,961,323, cert: State, WBENC)

1222 Communications Media, Inc.
      2200 Renaissance Blvd Ste 160
      King of Prussia, PA 19406
      Contact: Theresa Heintz Exec Dir
      Tel: 484-322-0880
      Email: theintz@cmicompas.com
      Website: www.cmimedia.com
Media planning specializing in Healthcare media.
(Minority, estab 1989, empl 40, sales $6,000,000, cert:
NMSDC)

1223 ConnectedSign, LLC
120A W Airport Rd
Lititz, PA 17543
Contact: Loren Bucklin President
Tel: 866-833-2723
Email: lbucklin@connectedsign.com
Website: www.connectedsign.com
Digital Signage Software, Navori Tycoon Software, Digital Signage Hardware, Digital Signage Content, Website Development and Content, Kiosks Software, Kiosks Hardware, Kiosks Content. (Woman, estab 2003, empl 12, sales $1,000,000, cert: WBENC)

1224 DMC Design
120 Ave A
Pittsburgh, PA 15221
Contact: Dorothy Clark Owner
Tel: 412-824-7844
Email: dmcdesign@verizon.net
Website: www.dmcdesign.com
Design tradeshow exhibits, graphic design, print, promotional items, embroidered or silkscreened apparel. (Woman, estab 1991, empl 1, sales , cert: WBENC)

1225 Domus Inc.
Two Bala Plaza, Ste 300
Bala Cynwyd, PA 19004
Contact: Lisa Samara President
Tel: 215-772-2800
Email: lsamara@domusinc.com
Website: www.domusinc.com/
Traditional advertising, public relations, soical media, online advertising, internal/corporate communications. (Woman, estab 1993, empl 13, sales $6,659,848, cert: WBENC)

1226 Harmelin Media
525 Righters Ferry Rd
Bala Cynwyd, PA 19004
Contact: Mary Meder President
Tel: 610-668-7900
Email: mmeder@harmelin.com
Website: www.harmelin.com
Media planning & buying company. (Woman, estab 1982, empl 204, sales $25,000,000, cert: WBENC)

1227 Hoffmann Murtaugh Advertising, Inc.
355 Chestnut St
Sewickley, PA 15143
Contact: Adele Lawhead Controller
Tel: 412-741-8618
Email: shea@hoffmannmurtaugh.com
Website: www.hoffmannmurtaugh.com
Media Immersion & Discovery, Discovery Worksheets, Custom Exercises, Data Mining, Competitive/Challenge Identification, Goal Setting, Brainstorming/ideation, Media Research & Insights, 1st Party Data Analysis, Nielsen Ratings, MRI. (Woman, estab 2004, empl 17, sales $2,145,000, cert: WBENC)

1228 Ideamart Inc.
232 Conestoga Rd
Wayne, PA 19087
Contact: Tom King Owner
Tel: 610-971-2000
Email: tom@23k.com
Website: www.23k.com
Advertising, direct marketing, interactive, social media, branding/identity, packaging & retail POS. (As-Pac, estab 1991, empl 15, sales $2,185,947, cert: NMSDC)

1229 Language Services Associates
455 Business Center Dr Ste 100
Horsham, PA 19044
Contact: Jerry Lotierzo Strategic Sales Mgr
Tel: 215-259-7000
Email: jlotierzo@lsaweb.com
Website: www.lsaweb.com
Foreign language translation & interpretation: 175 languages, sign language. (Minority, Woman, estab 1991, empl 200, sales $45,000,000, cert: NMSDC, WBENC)

1230 Media Advantage, Inc.
78 Second St Pike
Southampton, PA 18966
Contact: Adraiane Thomson President
Tel: 800-985-5596
Email: athomson@mediaadvantage.com
Website: www.mediaadvantage.com
Sign and graphic design. (Woman, estab 2009, empl 8, sales $675,000, cert: State)

1231 Mendoza Group Inc.
3813 West Chester Pike
Newtown Square, PA 19073
Contact: Mia Mendoza CEO
Tel: 484-445-4017
Email: mmendoza@mendozagroup.com
Website: www.mendozagroup.com
Translation, marketing & advertising agency. (Minority, Woman, estab 1995, empl 7, sales $1,984,611, cert: State, NMSDC, WBENC)

1232 MTM LinguaSoft
705 S 50th St, 2nd Fl
Philadelphia, PA 19143
Contact: Myriam Siftar President
Tel: 215-729-6765
Email: siftar@mtmlinguasoft.com
Website: www.mtmlinguasoft.com
Translation & localization services: websites, software & online applications, e-learning modules, document translation & multilingual desktop publishing services. (Woman, estab 2003, empl 5, sales $496,685, cert: WBENC)

1233 Munroe Creative Partners
121 S. Broad St. Ste 1900
Philadelphia, PA 19107
Contact:
Tel: 215-563-8080
Email:
Website: www.munroe.com
Corporate identity launches, brochures, print and online advertising, direct mail campaigns, and web site creation. (Woman, estab 1989, empl 20, sales $2,019,757, cert: State, WBENC)

1234 NetPlus Marketing, Inc.
625 Ridge Pike, Blg E, Ste 300
Conshohocken, PA 19428
Contact: Robin Neifield CEO
Tel: 610-897-2380
Email: rn@netplusmarketing.com
Website: www.netplusmarketing.com
Online advertising: branding & direct response objectives, sponsorships, email marketing & search engine marketing. (Woman, estab 1996, empl 18, sales , cert: WBENC)

1235 PMG, Inc.
      583 Skippack Pike, Ste 200
      Blue Bell, PA 19422
      Contact: Peg Fitzpatrick
      Tel: 215-628-4737
      Email: p.fitzpatrick@pmginc.net
      Website: www.pmginc.net
Marketing & creative development, print mgmt, web development. (Woman, estab 1990, empl 8, sales $1,500,000, cert: WBENC)

1236 SSKJ Enterprises Inc. dba Vital Signs
      2812 Idlewood Rd
      Carnegie, PA 15106
      Contact: Sandy Burkett President
      Tel: 412-494-3308
      Email: sandy@vitalsignspgh.com
      Website: www.VitalSignsLLC.net
Mfr interior & exterior signage, large digital format printing, promotional items, ADA signage, architectural, banners, bar code labels, business graphics, buttons, channel letters, commercial awnings, corporate identification, custom displays. (Minority, Woman, estab 2005, empl 4, sales $342,350, cert: NMSDC)

Puerto Rico

1237 Arteaga & Arteaga Advertising
      PO Box 70336
      San Juan, PR 00926
      Contact: Juan Arteaga VP Strategy & New Business
      Tel: 787-620-1600
      Email: jat@arteaga.com
      Website: www.arteaga.com
Advertising, marketing, public relations, media, creative, interactive, packaging design, event planning, strategic planning, youth marketing. (Hisp, estab 1984, empl 40, sales $21,000,000, cert: NMSDC)

Tennessee

1238 FlagCenter.com, LLC
      4550 Summer Ave
      Memphis, TN 38122
      Contact: Maureen Criscuolo Owner
      Tel: 901-762-0044
      Email: maureen@flagcenter.com
      Website: www.flagcenter.com
Mfr custom nylon & vinyl signs, street banners, banners, flags, table covers & banners. (Woman, estab 2006, empl 6, sales $550,000, cert: State, City)

1239 nomADic genius, LLC
      5049 Trousdale Dr
      Nashville, TN 37220
      Contact: Regis Dir of Operations
      Tel: 615-336-6678
      Email: regis@nomadicgenius.com
      Website: www.nomadicgenius.com
Non traditional advertising company specializing in mobile billboards and street teams. (Woman, estab 2009, empl 4, sales $400,000, cert: State, WBENC)

1240 Three Point Graphics, Inc.
      750 Eaton St
      Memphis, TN 38120
      Contact: Sabrina Owner
      Tel: 901-537-0537
      Email: sabrina@threepointgraphics.com
      Website: www.3ptgraphics.com
Mission critical & complex graphic & signage products. (Woman, estab 2004, empl 1, sales $100,000,000, cert: State, City)

Texas

1241 Asher Media, Inc.
      15303 Dallas Pkwy Ste 1300
      Addison, TX 75001
      Contact: Kalyn Asher President
      Tel: 972-732-6464
      Email: kalyn@ashermedia.com
      Website: www.ashermedia.com
Strategic planning & buying solutions. (Woman, estab 1999, empl 27, sales , cert: State, WBENC)

1242 B2B Enterprises Inc. dba Prism Sign Group
      3645 Dallas Pkwy, Ste 535
      Plano, TX 75093
      Contact: Bill Brooks CEO
      Tel: 972-403-7770
      Email: bbrooks@prismsigngroup.com
      Website: www.prismsigngroup.com
Mfr signs: banners, vehicle wraps, advertising specialties, business cards, awards/recognition. (AA, estab 2007, empl 4, sales , cert: State, NMSDC)

1243 Blue Sun LLC
      4650 Lockheed Lane, Unit 104
      Denton, TX 76207
      Contact: Gulnara Balic Owner
      Tel: 800-238-6064
      Email: gulnara@dallasdigitalsigns.com
      Website: www.dallasdigitalsigns.com
Mfr, install & repair Interior & exterior electrical signs, graphic design. (Minority, Woman, estab 2012, empl 6, sales $360,000, cert: State)

1244 Brown Graphics Inc.
      11404 Chairman Dr
      Dallas, TX 75243
      Contact: Melanie Brown President
      Tel: 214-553-9988
      Email: melanie@browngraphics.com
      Website: www.browngraphics.com
Designs & mfr architectural signs: monuments, wayfinding, suite signs, cubicle, reception area, garage, directories, crown & building signage. (Woman, estab 1989, empl 8, sales $765,816, cert: State)

1245 Cartel Creativo, Inc.
      5835 Callaghan Rd Ste 600
      San Antonio, TX 78228
      Contact: Sean Salas CEO
      Tel: 210-602-8880
      Email: ssalas@thecartel.com
      Website: www.thecartel.com
Advertising agency: research & planning, creative development, production & in-house audio. (Hisp, estab 1994, empl 10, sales $4,400,000, cert: NMSDC)

1246 Castle Business Solutions, LLC
      2777 North Stemmons Frwy Ste 1242
      Dallas, TX 75207
      Contact: Sharon King CEO
      Tel: 214-599-2880
      Email: sharon@castlebusinesssolutions.net
      Website: www.castlebusinesssolutions.com/
Directory & mailing list publishing, direct mail advertising,
packaging & labeling services, warehousing & storage,
custom computer programming services, data processing,
hosting & related services. (Woman/AA, estab 2010, empl
3, sales $615,880, cert: State, NMSDC)

1247 Desert Star Enterprises, Inc
      8409 Sterling St Ste B
      Irving, TX 75063
      Contact: Myra Brown President
      Tel: 972-915-6970
      Email: myra@highvaluesigns.com
      Website: www.highvaluesigns.com
Create & install signs: wayfinding signs, banners, car wraps
& monument signs. (Woman, estab 2014, empl 3, sales
$300,000, cert: State, WBENC)

1248 Digital Thrive, LLC
      1910 Anita Dr
      Austin, TX 78704
      Contact: Kevin Co-Founder, CMO
      Tel: 512-900-7699
      Email: kevin@digthrive.com
      Website: www.digthrive.com
Graphic design & media: website design, mobile application design & development, animation & video production, print collateral & promotional materials. (Woman,
estab 2010, empl 10, sales , cert: State, WBENC)

1249 DMN3
      2190 North Loop W, Ste 200
      Houston, TX 77018
      Contact: Pamela Lockard President
      Tel: 713-868-3000
      Email: accounting@dmn3.com
      Website: www.dmn3.com
Direct mail & print advertising, e-marketing, multicultural
marketing, event promotions, internal communication,
radio & TV placement, data processing & mgt, interactive
& promotional mktg, outdoor media, sponsorships, print
colateral. (Woman, estab 1985, empl 9, sales $4,267,600,
cert: State, City, WBENC)

1250 Duncan/Day Advertising, LP
      6513 Preston Rd Ste 200
      Plano, TX 75024
      Contact: Leslie Duncan COO
      Tel: 469-429-1974
      Email: duncan@duncanday.com
      Website: www.duncanday.com
Advertising, brand development, copywriting, credit card
marketing, corporate identity, corporate communications,
design, direct marketing, email marketing, event planning,
interactive marketing, logo design & devel. (Woman, estab
1986, empl 7, sales $1,470,755, cert: WBENC)

1251 Enigma, LLC
      100 Crescent Ct. Ste 700
      Dallas, TX 75201
      Contact: Sherilyn K Smith-Rudolph President
      Tel: 214-459-8208
      Email: sherilyn@enigmallc.com
      Website: www.enigmallc.com
Advertising & marketing agency. (Woman/AA, estab
2003, empl 4, sales , cert: NMSDC, 8(a))

1252 Excalibur Exhibits
      7120 Brittmoore Rd, Ste 430
      Houston, TX 77041
      Contact: Peggy Swords President
      Tel: 713-856-8853
      Email: pswords@excaliburexhibits.com
      Website: www.excaliburexhibits.com
Design & build custom, portable, modular & system
solutions. (Woman, estab 1997, empl 26, sales
$5,628,500, cert: WBENC)

1253 Gilbreath Communications, Inc.
      15995 N Barkers Landing, Ste 100 Ste 100
      Houston, TX 77079
      Contact: Debra Johnson VP
      Tel: 281-649-9595
      Email: debra@gilbcomm.com
      Website: www.gilbcomm.com
Advertising: ad campaigns, promotional materials,
media relations, public relations, press relations,
community relations, employee communications, press
conferences, press releases, press kits, speeches &
scripts, graphic design, etc. (Woman/AA, estab 1990,
empl 11, sales , cert: State, City, WBENC)

1254 J.O. Agency
      440 S Main St
      Fort Worth, TX 76104
      Contact: Business Dev Mgr
      Tel: 817-335-0100
      Email:
      Website: www.joagency.com
Full service marketing, public relations and advertising:
branding, public relations, graphic design, market
research, marketing campaigns, digital marketing, etc.
(Woman, estab 1998, empl 10, sales $950,825, cert:
WBENC)

1255 Latinworks
      410 Baylor St
      Austin, TX 78703
      Contact: Marly Ramstad CEO
      Tel: 512-479-6200
      Email: m.ramstad@latinworks.com
      Website: www.latinworks.com
Advertising agency. (Hisp, estab 1998, empl 174, sales ,
cert: State, NMSDC)

1256 Limb Design LLC
      1702 Houston Ave
      Houston, TX 77007
      Contact: Partner
      Tel: 713-529-1117
      Email:
      Website: www.limbdesign.com
Marketing, graphic design & web site design.
 (Woman, estab 1983, empl 14, sales $1,600,000, cert:
WBENC)

1257 Lopez Marketing Group, Inc.
      11169 La Quinta Pl
      El Paso, TX 79936
      Contact: Jose Luis Lopez President
      Tel: 915-772-8018
      Email: jllopez1@lopezgroup.com
      Website: www.lopezgroup.com
Advertising, Hispanic marketing, public relations. (Hisp, estab 1989, empl 16, sales $4,500,000, cert: State, NMSDC)

1258 Lopez Negrete Communications, Inc.
      3336 Richmond Ave Ste 200
      Houston, TX 77098
      Contact: Alex Lopez Negrete President
      Tel: 713-877-8777
      Email: alex@lopeznegrete.com
      Website: www.lopeznegrete.com
Brand Leadership, Media Planning & Buying, Creative, Production, Social Media, Public Relations. (Hisp, estab 1985, empl 100, sales $14,265,000, cert: State, NMSDC, CPUC)

1259 MasterWord Services, Inc.
      303 Stafford St
      Houston, TX 77079
      Contact: Ludmila Golovine President
      Tel: 281-589-0810
      Email: hr@masterword.com
      Website: www.masterword.com
Translation, interpretation, language training & assessments, cultural intelligence training & language compliance consulting. (Woman, estab 1993, empl 96, sales $14,620,522, cert: WBENC)

1260 Metromarketing Services Inc
      8707 Katy Freeway, Ste 100
      Houston, TX 77024
      Contact: Becky Dunn Grider
      Tel: 713-973-7900
      Email: becky.dunn@metromkt.com
      Website: www.metromkt.com
Graphic design, promotional products & fine printing, catalogs & e-store programs. (Woman, estab 1975, empl 13, sales , cert: WBENC)

1261 One Pytchblack, LLC DBA PytchBlack
      1612 Summit Ave Ste 415
      Fort Worth, TX 76102
      Contact: Andre Yanez Owner/Managing Partner
      Tel: 817-570-0915
      Email: aryanez@pytchblack.com
      Website: www.pytchblack.com
Advertising agency, website design, trademark and identity design, product design, media buying & graphic design. (Hisp, estab 2013, empl 2, sales $115,000, cert: State, NMSDC)

1262 Preferred Translations, Inc.
      PO Box 42065
      Houston, TX 77242
      Contact: Gina Guerrero Managing Dir
      Tel: 281-882-3080
      Email: projects@preferredtranslationsinc.com
      Website: www.preferredTranslationsInc.com
Language Translation, Interpretation, Multilingual Desktop Publishing, Transcription, Voiceover, and subtitling. (Minority, Woman, estab 2012, empl 1, sales , cert: State)

1263 Reach Media Inc.
      13760 Noel Rd Ste 750
      Dallas, TX 75240
      Contact: Reggie Denson VP Sales
      Tel: 972-789-1058
      Email: reggie.denson@reachmediainc.com
      Website: www.reachmediainc.com
African-American advertising for the Tom Joyner Morning Show. (AA, estab 2001, empl 92, sales $53,000,000, cert: State, NMSDC)

1264 St. Julien Communications Group, LLC
      PO Box 3724
      Houston, TX 77253
      Contact: Jaa St. Julien CEO
      Tel: 713-965-7084
      Email: jaa@stjuliencg.com
      Website: www.stjuliencg.com
Advertising, public relations, marketing, media placement, strategy development, graphic & web design, web development, mobile app development, photography, videography consulting, community outreach. (Minority, estab 2007, empl 1, sales $196,000, cert: State, NMSDC)

1265 SuperLatina Inc.
      4200 South Frwy Ste 2370
      Fort Worth, TX 76115
      Contact: Andres Suarez CEO
      Tel: 214-431-5783
      Email: andres@aganarmedia.com
      Website: www.aganarmedia.com
Multicultural marketing services, video & interactive campaigns for television & digital (Minority, Woman, estab 2007, empl 8, sales $787,000, cert: NMSDC)

1266 Techstyle Group LLC
      PO Box 692347
      Houston, TX 77269
      Contact: Laurel Prokop CEO
      Tel: 281-251-2436
      Email: lp.info@techstyle.com
      Website: www.techstylegroup.com
Document, presentation & written-content production. (Woman, estab 1986, empl 5, sales , cert: City)

1267 Universal Display & Fixtures
      726 E Hwy 121
      Lewisville, TX 75057
      Contact: Michele Skene Dir Marketing
      Tel: 972-829-2402
      Email: barbara.stoddard@udfc.com
      Website: www.udfc.com
Design & mfr displays & fixtures, components, project management, EDI, fulfillment & installation coordination. (Nat Ame, estab 1961, empl 200, sales $56,000,000, cert: State, NMSDC)

1268 Web-Hed Technologies, Inc. dba Webhead
      1710 N Main Ave
      San Antonio, TX 78212
      Contact: Juanita I . Gonzalez CEO
      Tel: 210-354-1661
      Email: contracts@webheadtech.com
      Website: www.webheadtech.com
Hispanic interactive marketing svcs: media & animated graphics, online & interactive games & sweepstakes. (Minority, Woman, estab 1995, empl 15, sales , cert: State)

1269 What's the Big Idea?
      5603 Kingston Court
      Richardson, TX 75082
      Contact: Tracy Cink President
      Tel: 972-509-0081
      Email: tracy_cink@wtbi.com
      Website: www.wtbi.com
Advertising & graphic design. (Woman, estab 0, empl ,
sales , cert: WBENC)

Utah

1270 Infinite Scale Design Group
      16 Exchange Place
      Salt Lake City, UT 84111
      Contact: Molly Mazzolini Managing Member
      Tel: 801-363-1881
      Email: molly@infinitescale.com
      Website: www.infinitescale.com
Brand strategy, logo design, creative briefs, identity
systems, collateral, website design, environmental graphics, master plan, interpretive design, wayfinding signage,
recognition & donor, signage, uniform systems, vehicle
graphics. (Woman, estab , empl , sales , cert: State)

1271 U.S. Translation Company
      320 W 200 S
      Salt Lake City, UT 84101
      Contact: Kathy Sprouse Dir of Operations
      Tel: 801-393-5300
      Email: kathy@ustranslation.com
      Website: www.ustranslation.com
Language services, document formatting, interpreting
services. (Hisp, estab 1995, empl 15, sales $2,987,864,
cert: NMSDC)

Virginia

1272 AB Design, Inc.
      10005 Stonemill Rd
      Richmond, VA 23233
      Contact: Gladys Brenner President
      Tel: 804-346-4771
      Email: gbrenner@abdesignonline.com
      Website: www.abdesignonline.com
Environmental graphic design: interior & exterior signage,
dev wayfinding systems & architectural graphics, site
analysis/evaluation, master planning & comprehensive
wayfinding systems. (Minority, Woman, estab 1991, empl
3, sales $182,000, cert: State)

1273 Advanta Pacific International
      9336 Braymore Circle
      Fairfax Station, VA 22039
      Contact: Adam Tran Managing Dir
      Tel: 703-226-1605
      Email: contact@vernacularlanguage.com
      Website: www.vernacularlanguage.com
Translation & interpretation services in over 200 languages
and dialects, including sign language. (Minority, Woman,
estab 2009, empl 4, sales $150,000, cert: State)

1274 Capital Exhibits
      8245-B Backlick Rd
      Lorton, VA 22079
      Contact: Jennifer Warren Sales
      Tel: 540-219-9372
      Email: jennifer@capitalexhibits.com
      Website: www.capitalexhibits.com
Indoor & outdoor signage, tradeshow displays, banners,
channel lettering, wayfinding & directional signage, hard
or thick signage, custom flirting titles, fabric & vinyl signs.
(As-Ind, estab 1994, empl 6, sales , cert: State)

1275 Eighth Day Design
      7653 Leesburg Pike
      Falls Church, VA 22043
      Contact: Carol Muszynski President
      Tel: 703-562-3636
      Email: info@eighthday.com
      Website: www.eighthday.com
Productivity & image solutions, architecture & design,
programming, space planning, design dev, sustainable
design, exhibit design, construction documents, construction administration, move coordination & facilities
maintenance support. (Woman, estab 1989, empl 25,
sales $3,800,000, cert: WBENC)

1276 Hybrid Studios LLC
      1940 Duke St Ste 200
      Alexandria, VA 22314
      Contact: Susan Yates Mgr
      Tel: 703-671-6975
      Email: susan@hybrid-studios.com
      Website: www.hybriddc.com
Communications solutions: print, interactive development, advertising, corporate identity, direct marketing &
social media marketing services. (Woman, estab 2002,
empl 2, sales $532,000, cert: State)

1277 Mail Call Direct LLC
      5616 Eastport Blvd
      Henrico, VA 23231
      Contact: Lisa Jacoby Co-Owner
      Tel: 804-222-0608
      Email: lisa@mailcalldirect.com
      Website: www.MailCallDirect.com
Direct mail services, digital lasering, inkjet & insert, data
processing, mailing lists, barcode printing, variable data,
stamping, metering, permits, hand fulfillment, parcel
fulfillment, folding bindery services, glue dotting, poly
bagging. (Woman, estab 2014, empl 8, sales , cert: State)

1278 Nvision Media Group, LLC
      114 W Hicks St
      Lawrenceville, VA 23868
      Contact: David Fant Owner
      Tel: 866-848-8822
      Email: david.fant@nvisn.net
      Website: www.nvisn.net
Indoor advertising. (Woman/AA, estab 2006, empl 6,
sales $100,000, cert: State)

1279 Tandem By Design LLC
      306 N 26th St, Ste 227
      Richmond, VA 23223
      Contact: Bev Gray President
      Tel: 804-239-2539
      Email: bev@tandembydesign.com
      Website: www.tandembydesign.com
Marketing & advertising solutions,one-to-one marketing, B2B sales collateral, B2C POP/POS, packaging
design, corporate communications, corporate & brand
videos, grassroots campaigns, social media. (Woman,
estab 2012, empl 1, sales , cert: State)

1280 Trusted Translations, Inc.
      108 N Virginia Ave
      Falls Church, VA 22046
      Contact: Diversity Manager Acct Mgr
      Tel: 877-255-0717
      Email: mbe@trustedtranslations.com
      Website: www.trustedtranslations.com
English to Spanish translation agency. (Hisp, estab 2003,
empl 10, sales $2,400,000, cert: City)

1281 West Cary Group
      5 W Cary St
      Richmond, VA 23220
      Contact: Moses Foster CEO
      Tel: 804-343-2029
      Email: mfoster@westcarygroup.com
      Website: www.westcarygroup.com
Marketing communications & advertising. (AA, estab 2007, empl 20, sales $2,586,876, cert: State, NMSDC)

Washington

1282 Dynamic Language
      15215 52nd Ave S, Ste 100
      Seattle, WA 98188
      Contact: Rick Antezana Partner
      Tel: 206-244-6709
      Email: rick@dynamiclanguage.com
      Website: www.dynamiclanguage.com
Foreign language translation, desktop publishing services, narration, language & ASL interpreting services. (Minority, Woman, estab 1985, empl 50, sales $10,155,200, cert: NMSDC)

1283 TDW+Co
      92 Lenora St #888
      Seattle, WA 98121
      Contact: Tim Wang Principal
      Tel: 206-623-6888
      Email: biz@tdwandco.com
      Website: www.tdwandco.com
Marketing communications & advertising agency. (As-Pac, estab 2004, empl 25, sales $10,015,295, cert: State, NMSDC, CPUC)

1284 The Garrigan Lyman Group
      1524 Fifth Ave
      Seattle, WA 98101
      Contact: Jean Zartman Mgr Business Devel
      Tel: 206-223-5548
      Email: jean.zartman@glg.com
      Website: www.glg.com
Brand & interactive strategic insight, creative vision & technology-forward solutions. (Woman, estab 1993, empl 65, sales , cert: WBENC)

1285 Thinking Cap Communications & Design
      9 S Washington Ste 201
      Spokane, WA 99201
      Contact: Marvin Reguindin President
      Tel: 509-747-4930
      Email: marvo@tcapdesign.com
      Website: www.tcapdesign.com
Advertising & graphic design, creative & account services, websites, radio & TV/video spots. (As-Pac, estab 1995, empl 3, sales $124,753, cert: State, NMSDC)

1286 Translation Solutions Corp.
      1201 Pacific Ave Corp Ste 600
      Tacoma, WA 98402
      Contact: Rosa Capdevielle Project Management
      Tel: 808-404-1270
      Email: rosa@translationsolutions.org
      Website: www.translationsolutions.org
Translations & interpretation services. (Minority, Woman, estab 1994, empl 5, sales , cert: State, NMSDC)

1287 Trio Northwest Business Solutions, Inc.
      239 SW 41st St
      Renton, WA 98057
      Contact: Jeffrey Quint EVP Sales & Mktg
      Tel: 206-728-8181
      Email: info@triogroupnw.com
      Website: www.triogroupnw.com/
Brand management, advertising, marketing, strategy, campaign development, project management, marcom strategy, web development, mobile app development, media buying, social media strategy & deployment. (Nat Ame, estab 2000, empl 6, sales $1,300,000, cert: NMSDC)

1288 Worktank Enterprises, LLC
      400 E Pine St, Ste 301
      Seattle, WA 98122
      Contact: Leslie Rugaber CEO
      Tel: 206-658-2555
      Email: leslie@worktankseattle.com
      Website: www.worktankseattle.com
Media strategy & production: integrated media & marketing campaigns, video & film production, CD, DVD & web content production, software & product demos, webcast management & production staffing services. (Woman, estab 2001, empl 10, sales , cert: WBENC)

Wisconsin

1289 Everbrite, LLC
      4949 S 110th St
      Greenfield, WI 53228
      Contact: Nicki LaFrance Sales Admin
      Tel: 414-529-3500
      Email: supplierdiversity@everbrite.com
      Website: www.everbrite.com
Outdoor illuminated identification signage. (Woman, estab 1927, empl 850, sales , cert: WBENC)

1290 Revelation, LLC
      222 N Midvale Blvd Ste 18
      Madison, WI 53705
      Contact: Brian Lee President
      Tel: 608-622-7767
      Email: brian@experiencerevelation.com
      Website: www.experiencerevelation.com
Public relations, media buying, ad buying, advertising, social media consulting, internet marketing, web marketing & speaking engagements. (As-Pac, estab 2010, empl 3, sales $170,000, cert: NMSDC)

1291 The Geo Group
      6 Odana Court
      Madison, WI 53719
      Contact: Georgia Roeming President
      Tel: 608-230-1000
      Email: georgia.roeming@thegeogroup.com
      Website: www.thegeogroup.com
Translation of radio, TV, website & print advertising. (Woman, estab 1991, empl 20, sales , cert: WBENC)

ADVERTISING SPECIALTIES
Supply advertising specialties, premium and promotional products, or travel incentives. Includes frims which do silkscreening and embroidery on various products. NAICS Code 42

Alabama

1292 Concepts & Associates
      105 19th St S
      Birmingham, AL 35210
      Contact: Tim Hennessy President
      Tel: 205-870-1111
      Email: tim@conceptsusa.com
      Website: www.conceptsusa.com
Corporate gifts & promotional products, embroidery & fulfillment center. (Woman, estab 1983, empl 15, sales , cert: State, WBENC)

1293 LogoBranders Inc.
      1161 Lagoon Business Loop
      Montgomery, AL 36117
      Contact: Dean Flynn Branding Specialist
      Tel: 334-277-1144
      Email: dean@logobranders.com
      Website: www.logobranders.biz/
Promotional items, executive gifts, embroidery, screen print, hardline, health and safety, computer and electronic products, wearables, bags, writing instruments, drinkwear, desk/office business accessories, calenders, person products, etc. (Woman, estab 1993, empl 34, sales $6,000,000, cert: WBENC)

Arizona

1294 Everyone Loves Buttons Inc.
      24825 N 16th Ave Ste 100
      Phoenix, AZ 85085
      Contact: Maura Statman President
      Tel: 623-445-9975
      Email: maura@elbusa.com
      Website: www.custombuttons.com
Promotional products, buttons. (Woman, estab 1997, empl 12, sales $1,350,000, cert: WBENC)

California

1295 Apropos Promotions
      1401 N Broadway Ste 280
      Walnut Creek, CA 94596
      Contact: Ann Auelmann President
      Tel: 925-274-5700
      Email: ann@apropospromotions.com
      Website: www.apropospromotions.com
Promotional merchandise: tradeshow giveaways, staff appreciation, gifts, special events, etc. (Woman, estab 2002, empl 4, sales , cert: WBENC)

1296 Avid Promotions
      499 Nibus St Unit C
      Brea, CA 92821
      Contact: Dena Gibbs CEO
      Tel: 949-387-9890
      Email: dena@avidpromotions.com
      Website: www.AvidPromotions.com
Promotional products, marketing materials, and apparel/corporate uniforms. (Hisp, estab 2009, empl 4, sales $540,000, cert: NMSDC, CPUC)

1297 Beyond Zebra Inc.
      1443 E Washington Blvd, Ste 641
      Pasadena, CA 91104
      Contact: CFO
      Tel: 818-435-8202
      Email: info@beyondzebra.net
      Website: www.beyondzebra.net
Promotional products: bags, desk accessories, apparel, hats, memo pads, housewares, sales incentive & corporate gift programs. (Minority, Woman, estab 2000, empl 4, sales $1,043,151, cert: WBENC)

1298 Caden Concepts
      13412 Ventura Blvd #300
      Sherman Oaks, CA 91423
      Contact: Katie Llanos Acct Dir
      Tel: 707-486-6017
      Email: annie@cadenconcepts.com
      Website: www.cadenconcepts.com
Dist advertising specialties: logoed corporate wearables, giveaways, incentives, employee awards & tradeshow projects, embroidery silk screen & pad printing. (Woman, estab 1998, empl 9, sales , cert: CPUC, WBENC)

1299 Elementi Designs
      1655 22nd Ave
      San Francisco, CA 94122
      Contact: Ken Lou President
      Tel: 415-887-3889
      Email: elementidesigns@gmail.com
      Website: www.elementidesigns.com
Corporate promotional items, apparel & printing, fashion jewelry & accessories, wedding party supplies, gift items, home decor products & car assortments. (Minority, Woman, estab 2004, empl 5, sales $194,902, cert: CPUC)

1300 Ellen's Silkscreening, Inc.
      1500 Mission St
      South Pasadena, CA 91030
      Contact: Ellen Daigle President
      Tel: 626-441-4415
      Email: info@ellenssilkscreening.com
      Website: www.ellenssilkscreening.com
Screen printed & embroidered goods & promotional products. (Woman, estab 1978, empl 15, sales $2,087,125, cert: WBENC)

1301 Gorilla Marketing
      4100 Flat Rock Dr, Ste A
      Riverside, CA 92505
      Contact: Chris Arranga CEO
      Tel: 951-353-8133
      Email: chris@gorillamarketing.net
      Website: www.gorillamarketing.net
Imprinted promotional products, advertising specialties. (Hisp, estab 1985, empl 10, sales $1,700,000, cert: NMSDC)

1302 Infocus Specialties, Inc.
      1655 Hauser Circle
      Thousand Oaks, CA 91362
      Contact: Steve Leo Co-Owner
      Tel: 805-379-9192
      Email: steve@infocusspecialties.com
      Website: www.infocusspecialties.com
Promotional and advertising impressions. (Woman, estab 2013, empl 2, sales $720,000, cert: WBENC)

1303 Intention Advertising
      2995 Bonnie Lane
      Pleasant Hill, CA 94523
      Contact: Mara Villa Owner
      Tel: 925-274-1774
      Email: mara@intentionadvertising.com
      Website: www.intentionadvertising.com
Promotional products, t-shirts to pens, etc. (Woman, estab
2011, empl 1, sales $400,000, cert: State)

1304 Janco & Winnex Inc
      3018 Durfee Ave, Ste E
      El Monte, CA 91732
      Contact: Jennifer Renshaw President
      Tel: 626-454-4882
      Email: jenniferjan@yahoo.com
      Website: www.jancoline.com
Dist folding chairs, promotional stationery & bags. (Minority, Woman, estab 1996, empl 9, sales , cert: State, 8(a))

1305 JLT Promotions Inc.
      24238 Hawthorne Blvd
      Torrance, CA 90505
      Contact: John Tulchin CFO
      Tel: 310-791-7006
      Email: jtulchin@thepromotionsdept.com
      Website: www.instadiumpromotions.com
Sports & team promotional items & stadium giveaways.
(Woman, estab 1990, empl 10, sales $5,700,000, cert:
State, CPUC)

1306 KV & Associates, LLC
      5694 Mission Center Rd, Ste 357
      San Diego, CA 92108
      Contact: Kathy Valadez President
      Tel: 858-277-7036
      Email: info@kvapromotions.com
      Website: www.KVAPromotions.com
Promotional & merchandise, graphic design, corporate
apparel, women, men, infant, jackets, polo's, long sleeve,
short sleeve, caps, visors, T-shirts, embroidery, silk screen,
writing pens, pencils, markers, cups. (Minority, Woman,
estab 2000, empl 1, sales $640,500, cert: NMSDC, WBENC,
SDB)

1307 Laughing Willow, Inc.
      1110 Quintana Rd
      Morro Bay, CA 93442
      Contact: Elizabeth Espy CEO
      Tel: 805-772-4770
      Email: liz@doghousepromotions.com
      Website: www.doghousepromotions.com
Advertising specialty, apparel, awards, bags, banners,
brand names, conventions, corporate gifts, custom
merchandise, drink ware, eco-friendly, embroidery, gift
baskets, headwear, hospitality, incentive programs.
(Woman, estab 1998, empl 4, sales $2,029,491, cert:
WBENC)

1308 Lexicon Promo
      1281 Ninth Ave, Unit 2004
      San Diego, CA 92101
      Contact: Brandon Christopher CEO
      Tel: 760-681-8248
      Email: jbsc@trylexicon.com
      Website: www.trylexicon.com
Carbon neutral, full-service print and promo (swag) agency
with capabilities of fulfilling orders of any size from 100
quantity to 100,000 quantity. (AA, estab 2019, empl 1,
sales $315,000, cert: NMSDC)

1309 Macro Industries, Inc
      5595 Daniels St Ste F
      Chino, CA 91710
      Contact: Cynthia Phillips Marketing Mgr
      Tel: 909-364-8100
      Email: sales106@goldensundirect.com
      Website: www.3cfactory.com
Dist safety vests, safety t-shirts, safety jackets, ANSI/ISEA
107-2004 Class 2, Class 3, gloves, caps, hats, uniforms,
bags, backpacks, tote bags, custom-made orders,
imprint, embroidery. (As-Pac, estab 2001, empl 7, sales
$1,020,000, cert: CPUC)

1310 Matel Manufacturing Inc.
      13205 Estrella Ave Unit A
      Gardena, CA 90248
      Contact: Nagendra Bolla President
      Tel: 310-217-9111
      Email: bobbolla@matelinc.com
      Website: www.matelinc.com
Leather & Metal desk accessories, letter trays, form
holders, business cards, desk pads, pen sets, bill holders,
book ends, memo boxes, coasters & conference pads.
(As-Ind, estab 1985, empl 7, sales $720,000, cert: CPUC)

1311 O2 Marketing & Design, Inc.
      367 Civic Dr Ste 15
      Pleasant Hill, CA 94523
      Contact: Sabina Rica Treasurer
      Tel: 510-553-0202
      Email: sabina@o2marketing.com
      Website: www.O2MARKETING.COM
promotional products: tradeshow giveaways, corporate
branding, employee incentive programs, awards.
(Woman/As-Ind, estab 2000, empl 8, sales , cert: CPUC,
WBENC)

1312 PMP Products Inc.
      1210 W Jon St, Ste B
      Torrance, CA 90502
      Contact: Peter Newhouse President
      Tel: 310-547-8064
      Email: petern@american-casuals.com
      Website: www.american-casuals.com
Promotional products, apparel (soft goods) headwear,
hard goods. (Minority, Woman, estab 2003, empl 10,
sales , cert: NMSDC, WBENC)

1313 Premium Resource
      5460B Lincoln Way
      Felton, CA 09018
      Contact: Andrea Casella CEO
      Tel: 408-777-0711
      Email: andrea@premiumresource.com
      Website: www.premiumresource.com
Full-service advertising specialties & promotional items.
(Minority, Woman, estab 2001, empl 2, sales , cert:
CPUC)

1314 Red Cloud LLC
      1600 Sawtelle Blvd, Ste 108
      Los Angeles, CA 90025
      Contact: Denise Lyons Controller
      Tel: 310-444-5583
      Email: denise@redcloudllc.com
      Website: www.redcloudpromotions.com
Promotional products, advertising specialties. (Woman,
estab 2005, empl 10, sales , cert: WBENC)

1315 Seba International
1210 W Jon St
Torrance, CA 90502
Contact: Mariah M. Qian CEO
Tel: 310-549-5122
Email: seba@globalxlr.com
Website: www.sebaintl.com
Promotional items: sports Jerseys, shirts, jackets, sweatshirts, caps & hats. (Minority, Woman, estab 2013, empl 8, sales $5,171,671, cert: NMSDC)

1316 Sun Coast Merchandise Corporation
6315 Bandini Blvd
Los Angeles, CA 90040
Contact: Dilip Bhavnani President
Tel: 800-432-4274
Email: dilip@sunscopeusa.com
Website: www.sunscopeusa.com
Promotional products. (As-Pac, estab 1943, empl 48, sales $108,000,000, cert: NMSDC)

1317 The Corporate Gift Service, Inc.
4120 W Burbank Blvd
Burbank, CA 91505
Contact: Lydia Eltringham Accounting Dept
Tel: 818-845-9500
Email: accounting@corpgiftservice.com
Website: www.thecorporategiftservice.com
Handmade Custom Gift Baskets, Embroidered Corporate Apparel, High End Corporate Gifts, Branded Promotional Products & Advertising Specialties. (Woman, estab 1990, empl 7, sales $1,600,000, cert: WBENC)

1318 TSG Direct LLC
20992 Avenida Amapola
Lake Forest, CA 92630
Contact: Gregg Moschides Dir of Sales
Tel: 650-224-9146
Email: gmoschides@tsgdirectllc.com
Website: www.tsgdirectllc.com
Print, direct mail & fulfillment services, promotional products, branded apparel, uniforms & office supplies. (Woman, estab 2014, empl 5, sales , cert: State, CPUC)

1319 Wearable Imaging, Inc.
26741 Portola Pkwy Ste 1E, 608
Foothill Ranch, CA 92610
Contact: Robin Richter President
Tel: 949-888-7837
Email: robin@wearableimaging.com
Website: www.wearableimaging.com
Screenprinting & embroidered apparel: t-shirts, polo's, hats & caps, pens, travel mugs, etc. (Minority, Woman, estab 1992, empl 5, sales $941,828, cert: CPUC, WBENC)

Colorado

1320 AC Flag & Banner, Inc.
11616 Shaffer Pl Unit S-103
Littleton, CO 80127
Contact: Wendy Willson President
Tel.: 303-948-9774
Email: wendy@acflag.com
Website: www.acflagandbanner.com
Custom logo flags & banners. (Woman, estab 2004, empl 4, sales $225,000, cert: WBENC)

1321 Artistic Promotions
2168 S Birch St
Denver, CO 80222
Contact: Radhika Hess Sales Assoc
Tel: 303-759-5559
Email: sharon@artisticpromo.com
Website: www.artisticpromo.com
Advertising specialties: marketing programs, special events, promotional products, logo apparel, incentive & safety programs, events items, trade shows, convention gifts, corporate awards, etc. (Woman, estab 1991, empl 4, sales , cert: WBENC)

Connecticut

1322 Church Hill Classics
594 Pepper St
Monroe, CT 06468
Contact: Sales & Marketing Rep
Tel: 800-477-9005
Email: info@diplomaframe.com
Website: www.diplomaframe.com
Corporate frames & gifts: custom designed insignias awards, recognition certificates & events. (Woman, estab 1991, empl 73, sales , cert: WBENC)

1323 GBG The Corporate Gift Source, Inc.
204 Spring Hill Rd
Trumbull, CT 06611
Contact: Charlotte O'Banion President
Tel: 203-459-4424
Email: charlotte@gbginc.com
Website: www.gbginc.com
Promotional products, logoed apparel, warehousing & catalog programs, fulfillment services, employee award redemption programs, premiums & sales incentives. (Minority, Woman, estab 1987, empl 6, sales $3,700,000, cert: NMSDC)

1324 John Michael Associates, Inc.
94 Holmes Rd
Newington, CT 06111
Contact: Paul Sposito Exec VP
Tel: 860-666-1414
Email: paul@jmalogos.com
Website: www.jmalogos.com
Logo apparel & merchandise, corporate online stores, awards, recognition & loyalty programs, fulfillment, event, incentive & sales marketing, importing, trade shows & fundraisers, kitting, collating & custom packaging, creative services. (Woman, estab 1980, empl 27, sales $12,000,000, cert: State, WBENC)

1325 Preferred Promotions, LLC
1801 Berlin Turnpike
Berlin, CT 06037
Contact: Dottie Nelson Owner
Tel: 860-829-1317
Email: dnelson@preferredpromo.com
Website: www.preferredpromos.com
Promotional products: imprinted wearables, engraved awards.. (Minority, Woman, estab 2003, empl 5, sales $725,000, cert: State)

1326 Stay Visible, LLC
1 Pinewood Dr
New Fairfield, CT 06812
Contact: Theresa Gonzalez President
Tel: 203-746-2111
Email: theresa@stayvisible.com
Website: www.stayvisible.com
Promotional products, Direct mail and fulfillment services; Design and print services; Custom packaging. (Woman, estab 2000, empl 1, sales , cert: State, WBENC)

District of Columbia

1327 The Hamilton Group
      4406 Gault Place NE
      Washington, DC 20019
      Contact: Kaari Hamilton President
      Tel: 202-689-4304
      Email: kayhhpbp@verizon.net
      Website: www.thehamiltongroupllc.net
Dist office supplies, advertisement & promotional products, office equipment & clothing wearables. (Woman/AA, estab 2007, empl 1, sales $731,000, cert: City, NMSDC, WBENC)

Delaware

1328 Promo Victory, Inc.
      4142 Ogletown-Stanton Rd, Ste 238
      Newark, DE 19713
      Contact: Vicki Lam President
      Tel: 800-385-7573
      Email: vlam@promovictory.com
      Website: www.promovictory.com
Promotional products. (Minority, Woman, estab 2008, empl 1, sales , cert: State, WBENC)

Florida

1329 Ad Specs of Delaware,LLC d/b/a Levy Recognition
      2415 N Albany Ave, Unit 1
      Tampa, FL 33607
      Contact: Michele Adams President
      Tel: 813-868-3923
      Email: michele.adams@levyrecognition.com
      Website: www.levyrecognition.com
Mfr medals, medallions & emblematic jewelry, custom design awards, promotional products, branded apparell & business gifts. (Woman, estab 1960, empl 38, sales $4,000,000, cert: WBENC)

1330 Ad Specs of FL, LLC dba Proforma Global Sourcing
      2415 N Albany Ave Unit 1
      Tampa, FL 33607
      Contact: Michele Adams President
      Tel: 716-553-1655
      Email: michele.adams@proforma.com
      Website: www.proformaglobalsourcing.com
Print & promotional products. (Woman, estab 2005, empl 5, sales $1,230,000, cert: WBENC)

1331 American Traders Enterprises, Inc.
      2900 Glades Circle, Ste 1250
      Weston, FL 33327
      Contact: Josie Musch President
      Tel: 954-888-9206
      Email: josie@americantraders.com
      Website: www.americantraders.com
Promotional products. (Minority, Woman, estab 1996, empl 6, sales , cert: NMSDC)

1332 American Trading International Co, LLC
      13866 SW 256 Terr
      Homestead, FL 33032
      Contact: Juan Penso Owner
      Tel: 813-810-1610
      Email: sales@atipromotions.com
      Website: www.atipromotions.com
Promotional products, gifts, awards, souvenirs, business cards, advertising specialties. (Hisp, estab 2007, empl 1, sales , cert: State, NMSDC)

1333 Bilmor with Advertising Specialties Inc.
      16155 SW 117th Ave, Unit B-19
      Miami, FL 33177
      Contact: Andrew Headley Dir
      Tel: 305-232-3323
      Email: support@bilmoradv.com
      Website: www.bilmoradv.com
Dist promotional items: custom embroidery, heat transfers, pad printing, hot stamping, awards & recognition gifts. (AA, estab 1985, empl 4, sales $614,000, cert: State)

1334 CottonImages.com, Inc.
      10481 NW 28th St
      Miami, FL 33172
      Contact: Scott Hertzbach CEO
      Tel: 305-251-2560
      Email: scott@cottonimages.com
      Website: www.cottonimages.com
Embroidered garments, imprinted mugs, umbrellas & promotional products. (Woman, estab 1989, empl 85, sales $6,700,000, cert: WBENC)

1335 Design & Promotions Corp.
      12333 SW 132nd Ct
      Miami, FL 33186
      Contact: Vicente Buraglia President
      Tel: 305-232-8119
      Email: service@design-promotions.com
      Website: www.design-promotions.com
Custom promotional products, custom packaging, custom displays, P.O.P. material, graphic design. (Hisp, estab 1990, empl 4, sales , cert: NMSDC)

1336 Entertainment Retail Enterprises, LLC
      2437 E LandSt Rd
      Orlando, FL 32824
      Contact: Melinda Wenderlein Dir of Finance
      Tel: 407-649-6552
      Email: melinda@ere-sri.com
      Website: www.ere-sri.com
CAT workwear, menswear, thermos, lunch bags, mugs (Woman, estab 2008, empl 102, sales $45,000,000, cert: WBENC)

1337 I Love Promos, Inc.
      6627 NW 25th Way Ste 100
      Boca Raton, FL 33496
      Contact: Mary Turel SVP
      Tel: 866-546-7001
      Email: mary@ilovepromos.com
      Website: www.ilovepromos.com
Promotional products, apparel, writing instruments, eco-friendly items. (Minority, Woman, estab 2013, empl 2, sales $3,200,000, cert: WBENC)

1338 Ingage, LLC
      1395 Black Willow Trail
      Altamonte, FL 32714
      Contact: Lisa Marcheskie CEO
      Tel: 407-521-7777
      Email: info@ingageincentives.com
      Website: www.ingageincentives.com
Recognition Incentives and Promotional Products. (Woman, estab 2012, empl 25, sales $15,000,000, cert: State, WBENC)

1339 Jamapchi LLC
      13885 SW 151ST Ln
      Miami, FL 33186
      Contact: Pamela Chin Managing Dir
      Tel: 786-708-9623
      Email: pam@jamapchi.com
      Website: www.her-mine.com
Corporate gifting items for retirement, appreciation, on-boarding and women self-care gift boxes for personal care and well being. We also supply school items and toys for children ages 4 through 12. (AA, estab 2015, empl 5, sales $193,000, cert: State, City)

1340 JT Promotions
      4378 LB Mcleod Rd
      orlando, FL 32811
      Contact: James Stillwell Owner
      Tel: 407-730-7990
      Email: info@aclipsemarketing.net
      Website: www.aclipsemarketing.net
Embroidery, silk screening, promotional & novelty items, event planning & execution. (AA, estab 2003, empl 4, sales $250,000, cert: NMSDC)

1341 Merchandise Partners
      11111 N 46th St
      Tampa, FL 33617
      Contact: Wendy Knapp
      Tel: 404-460-7190
      Email: wendy@merchandisepartners.com
      Website: www.merchandisepartners.com
Corporate promotions, merchandising solutions, retail programs, sponsorship promotions, sales promotions, dealer networks, web stores. (Hisp, estab 2006, empl 6, sales $35,000,000, cert: NMSDC)

1342 MH Specialties LLC
      9896 White Sands Place
      Bonita Springs, FL 34135
      Contact: Tondalaya (Mike) Herbert CEO
      Tel: 313-268-5907
      Email: mike@mhspecialties.com
      Website: www.mhspecialties.com
Rewards & Recognition, wall/desk custom designed plaques, recognition jewelry, awards rings & promotional jewelry, premium incentives gifts for Safety Programs & Training, employees recognition awards, corporate awards/gifts. (Woman, estab 2002, empl 1, sales $300,000, cert: WBENC)

1343 Rimco Marketing Products, Inc.
      6344 All American Blvd
      Orlando, FL 32810
      Contact: Connie Jones President
      Tel: 407-290-0883
      Email: connie@rimcoinc.com
      Website: www.rimcoinc.com
Custom packaging: binders, tabs, boxes, folding cartons, bags, totes, mailers, portfolios & bound books, briefcases, menus, guest service directories, gifts, incentives & promotional products, fulfillment, warehousing & shipping. (Woman, estab 1984, empl 8, sales $4,600,000, cert: WBENC)

1344 SpringboardPC
      4517 W. Dale Ave
      Tampa, FL 33609
      Contact: Wendy Pepe President
      Tel: 813-918-0371
      Email: wendy@springboardpc.com
      Website: www.springboardpc.com
Advertising specialty, promotional products. (Woman, estab 1992, empl 5, sales $2,400,000, cert: State, City, WBENC)

1345 Tampa T-Shirts
      5112 N 22nd St
      Tampa, FL 33610
      Contact: Juan Davis Mgr
      Tel: 813-879-3298
      Email: juan@fastlaneclothing.com
      Website: www.fastlaneclothing.com
Apparel, logo shirts, lab coats, promotional items. (Minority, Woman, estab 1985, empl 19, sales $1,480,000, cert: State, City)

1346 Think Tank Studio
      626 Lakeview Rd, Ste A
      Clearwater, FL 33756
      Contact: Marlies Schoenau President
      Tel: 727-441-4488
      Email: mus@thinktankstudio.com
      Website: www.thinktankstudio.com
Promotional marketing services, logo apparel, hats, drink ware, office items, pens, bags, awards, signage, trade-show hand-outs. (Woman, estab 1998, empl 7, sales $1,487,596, cert: WBENC)

1347 Underground Graphics Inc.
      13355 Belcher Rd S Unit H
      Largo, FL 33773
      Contact: Grace Newcomer President
      Tel: 727-535-9582
      Email: grace@undergroundgraphics.us
      Website: www.undergroundgraphics.us
Promotional products: pens, mugs, keychains etc. (Woman, estab 1993, empl 4, sales $165,000, cert: State)

1348 Wendt Productions Inc.
      17301 Solie Rd
      Odessa, FL 33556
      Contact: Susan Wendt President
      Tel: 813-920-5000
      Email: swendt@wendtpro.com
      Website: www.wendtpro.com
Advertising, marketing & promotional products. (Woman, estab 1986, empl 9, sales $1,450,000, cert: State, City)

1349 Y-Not Design & Mfg. Inc.
      1041 E 24th St
      Hialeah, FL 33013
      Contact: Angelina Garcia CEO
      Tel: 855-843-1422
      Email: contactus@y-not.com
      Website: www.y-not.com/
Promotional & gifts products. (Minority, Woman, estab 2005, empl 61, sales $86,000,000, cert: NMSDC, WBENC)

Georgia

1350 Atlanta Brand Central LLC
      880 Glenwood Ave se unit 1317
      Atlanta, GA 30316
      Contact: Darryl Armstrong Owner
      Tel: 404-312-8777
      Email: darryl@abcatl.com
      Website: www.abcatl.com
Promotional products & sourcing. (AA, estab 2008, empl 4, sales $170,000, cert: NMSDC)

1351 Atlanta Promotional Products
      911 High Green Court
      Marietta, GA 30068
      Contact: Glynis Holihan Managing Partner
      Tel: 770-310-9860
      Email: glynis@atlpromo.com
      Website: www.atlpromo.com
Advertising specialty, logoed merchandise, corporate gifts
& apparel. (Woman, estab 2004, empl 3, sales $1,196,294,
cert: CPUC)

1352 Barazzo, LLC
      2221 Peachtree Rd NE Ste D357
      Atlanta, GA 30309
      Contact: Quiana Lloyd Member
      Tel: 888-716-5785
      Email: quiana@barazzo.com
      Website: www.barazzo.com
Custom gift & accessory solutions, corporate brand
identity & marketing solutions. (Woman/AA, estab 2009,
empl , sales , cert: State, NMSDC, SDB)

1353 Blue Rose Promotions, LLC
      2660 Holcomb Bridge Road Ste 200
      Alpharetta, GA 30022
      Contact: Jennifer Pines VP Sales
      Tel: 770-695-7673
      Email: jennifer@bluerosepromotions.com
      Website: www.bluerosepromotions.com
Promotional marketing with access to over 700,000
products. (Woman, estab 2013, empl 4, sales $4,165,561,
cert: WBENC)

1354 Brand Spirit Inc.
      245 N Highland Ave NE Ste 230-272
      Atlanta, GA 30307
      Contact: Jenna Banks President
      Tel: 877-804-7906
      Email: jenna@gobrandspirit.com
      Website: www.gobrandspirit.com
Branded gifts, promotional items, printed materials,
business forms, logo apparel, badges & credentials,
awards, uniforms, lanyards, brochures & business cards.
(Woman, estab 2012, empl 1, sales $430,400, cert:
NWBOC)

1355 Capital Ideas, Inc.
      990 Hammond Dr Ste 620
      Atlanta, GA 30328
      Contact: Gina Sealey Acct Mgr
      Tel: 678-320-1630
      Email: gsealey@capitalideas.net
      Website: www.capitalideas.net
Promotional products. (Woman, estab 1987, empl 8, sales
$4,162,000, cert: WBENC)

1356 Choice Premiums
      560 Arlington Pl
      Macon, GA 31201
      Contact: President
      Tel: 478-741-8888
      Email: request@choicepremiums.com
      Website: www.choicepremiums.com
Promotional products & marketing. (Woman, estab 1996,
empl 4, sales $402,067, cert: WBENC)

1357 CKSports and Associates LLC
      3655 Altama Ave
      Brunswick, GA 31520
      Contact: Charles Loving CEO
      Tel: 912-547-7504
      Email: charles@cksportsandassociates.com
      Website: www.cksportsandassociates.com
Football Helmet Shaped Cooler-Carrier on Wheels,
Baseball Cap and Player Head Cooler-Carrier on Wheels,
Football Helmet Grill, Baseball Helmet Grill, Racecar
Grill. (AA, estab 2016, empl 6, sales , cert: NMSDC)

1358 Creative Corporate Ideas Inc
      1010 Huntcliff Ste.1350
      Atlanta, GA 30350
      Contact: Creative Corporate Ideas Inc Owner
      Tel: 404-252-2588
      Email: cwalina@bellsouth.net
      Website: www.creativecorporateideas.com
Promotional items, logo merch & wearables. (Woman,
estab 1993, empl 2, sales $500,000, cert: WBENC)

1359 Creative Innovators, Inc.
      1797 Spring Rd, Ste 6
      Smyrna, GA 30080
      Contact: Omar Horton Mgr
      Tel: 770-435-7552
      Email: sales@creativeinnovators.net
      Website: www.creativeinnovators.net
Embroidery, screen printing, signs, banners, advertising
specialty & promotional items. (AA, estab 1999, empl 3,
sales $150,000, cert: State, City)

1360 FireSign Inc. Promotional Products & Print
      4480-H S Cobb Dr, Ste 540
      Smyrna, GA 30080
      Contact: Jen Lyles Lead Ignitor
      Tel: 678-574-2461
      Email: jlyles@firesigninc.com
      Website: www.firesigninc.com
Promotional product & print services, (Woman/AA,
estab 2003, empl 5, sales $1,295,000, cert: NMSDC)

1361 Henry-Aaron Inc.
      754 Woodson St
      Atlanta, GA 30315
      Contact: Aaron Turpeau President
      Tel: 404-622-4308
      Email: info@aarongroup.us
      Website: www.henry-aaroninc.logomall.com/
Premium & promotional items. (AA, estab 1991, empl 3,
sales $2,189,931, cert: State, NMSDC)

1362 Jansen Advertising
      5565 Glenrich Court
      Atlanta, GA 30338
      Contact: Paige Jansen-Nichols VP Sales
      Tel: 770-452-0252
      Email: paige@jansenadvertising.com
      Website: www.jansenadvertising.com
Custom promotional, incentive & recognition merchandise. (Woman, estab 1993, empl 9, sales , cert: WBENC)

1363 NorthStar Print, LLC
      6050 Peachtree Pkwy Ste 240359
      Norcross, GA 30092
      Contact: Jacki Suckow President
      Tel: 770-490-6251
      Email: jacki@northstarprint.net
      Website: www.northstarprint.net
Print & promotional products, marketing materials,
traditional business forms, POP items, just-in-time digital
printing, distribution & kitting services. (Woman, estab
1991, empl 8, sales $3,000,000, cert: NWBOC)

1364   The Corporate Shop, Inc.
       11455 Lakefield Dr Ste 200
       Johns Creek, GA 30097
       Contact: Wendy Neubauer CEO
       Tel: 770-242-0090
       Email: wendy@thecorporateshop.com
       Website: www.thecorporateshop.com
Corporate promotional products & logoed apparel.
(Woman, estab , empl , sales $3,000,000, cert: WBENC)

1365   Universal Graphics, Inc.
       2931 Lewis St, Ste 301
       Kennesaw, GA 30144
       Contact: Celia Reed Sales
       Tel: 678-581-1221
       Email: ccmem@aol.com
       Website: www.ugiinc.biz
Silk screening, embroidery, promotional items, corporate
apparel, printing. (AA, estab , empl , sales , cert: NMSDC)

Iowa

1366   World of Colors - Break The Cycle LLC
       1624 7th Ave SE, Ste 7000
       Cedar Rapids, IA 52403
       Contact: Rick Rodriguez Owner
       Tel: 319-447-7282
       Email: rrodri7855@aol.com
       Website: www.worldofcolors.us
Design, print & dist screen printed bags, shirts, hats &
specialty items. (Hisp, estab 2012, empl 5, sales , cert:
NMSDC)

Illinois

1367   Action Bag Company
       1001 Entry Dr.
       Bensenville, IL 60640
       Contact: Martha Quintero
       Tel: 866-349-8853
       Email: mquintero@actionbag.com
       Website: www.actionhealth.com
Printed bags, bags, retail packaging products, printed
promotional products, promotional items, packaging
supplies, labels, tissue paper, gift cards, specialty packaging, custom bags, custom printed items, rush orders, in-
stock products. (Woman, estab , empl , sales , cert: City,
WBENC)

1368   B. Gunther & Company, Inc.
       4742 Main St
       Lisle, IL 60532
       Contact: Jeanne Brommer President
       Tel: 630-969-5595
       Email: jeanne@bgunther.com
       Website: www.bgunther.com
Promotional products, business gifts, imprinted pens to
the leather portfolio or high end wearables. (Woman,
estab 1985, empl 9, sales $1,220,000, cert: WBENC)

1369   Brilliant Gifts LLC
       1605 S Waukegan Rd
       Waukegan, IL 60085
       Contact: Nick Phillips Dir of Business Dev
       Tel: 773-885-3532
       Email: nick@brilliantmade.com
       Website: www.brilliantmade.com
Curate and produce memorable gifts, branded merchandise and custom products, while providing our clients with
a suite of tools to enable distribution, analytics, and ROI
measurement. (Woman, estab 2015, empl 100, sales
$25,000,000, cert: WBENC)

1370   Corporate Identity, Inc.
       223 W Main St
       Barrington, IL 60010
       Contact: Debbie Story Sales Mgr
       Tel: 847-304-8550
       Email: msparks@Corpid.com
       Website: www.corpid.com
Promotional products, awards, logo apparel, trade
show giveaways, corporate gifts, notepads, golf balls,
banners, table throws, business forms, labels, folders,
nameplates, tags. (Woman, estab 1976, empl 9, sales ,
cert: WBENC)

1371   eLead Resources, Inc. DBA eLead Promo
       125 S Clark St 17th Fl
       Chicago, IL 60603
       Contact: Michael Wheeler VP
       Tel: 888-420-1788
       Email: mike@eleadresources.com
       Website: www.eleadresources.com
Promotional marketing products & brand consulting.
(AA, estab , empl , sales $4,328,835, cert: NMSDC)

1372   Essential Creations Chicago, Inc.
       2112 W 95th St
       Chicago, IL 60643
       Contact: Sandtricia Andrews-Strickland'
       President
       Tel: 773-238-1700
       Email: sandtricia@ecreations2000.com
       Website: www.ecreations2000.com
Custom Embroidery, Patches, Screen Printing and
Sublimation. We also do promotional Products. (AA,
estab 2000, empl 3, sales $222,000, cert: State,
WBENC)

1373   Excel Screen Printing & Embroidery, Inc.
       10507 Delta Pkwy
       Schiller Park, IL 60176
       Contact: Leon Johnson President
       Tel: 847-801-5200
       Email: leon@excelscreenprinting.com
       Website: www.excelscreenprinting.com
Screen printed & embroidered apparal, imprinted
glassware, premiums, etc. (AA, estab 2005, empl 63,
sales $4,500,000, cert: State)

1374   Fancy That
       3712 N Broadway, Ste 336
       Chicago, IL 60613
       Contact: Deborah Epstein Owner
       Tel: 888-369-8428
       Email: fancythatpromos@cs.com
       Website: www.fancythatpromos.com
Promotional items, corporate giftware, awards &
trophies. (Woman, estab 1991, empl 1, sales , cert:
WBENC)

1375   Global Sourcing Connection, Ltd.
       2610 Lake Cook Road Ste 190
       Riverwoods, IL 60015
       Contact: Jennifer Arenson CEO
       Tel: 847-317-9000
       Email: jarenson@gloso.com
       Website: www.gloso.com
Mfr & import headwear, apparel & promotional items.
(Woman, estab 2001, empl 24, sales $9,200,000, cert:
WBENC)

1376   Graphic Source Group, Inc.
      1119 W Algonquin Rd Ste B
      Lake in the Hills, IL 60156
      Contact: Sharon Meyer President
      Tel: 847-854-2670
      Email: sharon@graphicsourcegroup.com
      Website: www.graphicsourcegroup.com
Promotional products, screen printing, embroidery.
(Woman, estab 1993, empl 6, sales $2,050,000, cert:
WBENC)

1377   Konik and Company, Inc.
      7535 North Lincoln Ave
      Skokie, IL 60076
      Contact: Amy Lederer Owner
      Tel: 847-933-1805
      Email: amy@konik.com
      Website: www.konik.com
Premium & promotional products: apparel, drinkware,
dental sampling bags, bag, plush toys, technology items,
brand name products, desk accessories, conference items,
awards/recognition gifts, etc. (Woman, estab 1991, empl
18, sales $11,000,000, cert: WBENC)

1378   L and N Promotions, Inc.
      99 Oak Leaf Lane #203
      Vernon Hills, IL 60061
      Contact: Kristi Marquardt President
      Tel: 847-612-9215
      Email: lnpromotionsinc@aol.com
      Website: www.companycasuals.com/lnpromotions
Promotional, incentive & specialty premium items.
(Woman, estab 1996, empl 2, sales $585,000, cert:
WBENC)

1379   LinJen Promotions, Inc.
      15519 Harbor Town Dr
      Orland Park, IL 60462
      Contact: Linda Heyse-Highland President
      Tel: 708-478-8222
      Email: sales@linjen.com
      Website: www.linjen.com
Promotional solutions ideas & products. (Woman, estab
2000, empl 6, sales $1,250,000, cert: WBENC)

1380   M.R. Nyren Company
      600 Academy Dr Ste 110
      Northbrook, IL 60062
      Contact: Kim Nyren Acct Exec
      Tel: 800-323-8066
      Email: kim@nyren-tms.com
      Website: www.companycasuals.com/nyrencompany
Textile & promotional products: apparel, bags, hats,
towels, blanets, golf accessories, etc. (Woman, estab 1963,
empl 7, sales $4,880,454, cert: WBENC)

1381   Overture, LLC
      800 S Northpoint
      Waukegan, IL 60085
      Contact: Brian Lisinski VP Client Services
      Tel: 847-573-6080
      Email: brianl@overturepromo.com
      Website: www.overturepromotions.com
Promotional products, awards, incentive & recognition
programs, giveaways, logo merchandise, ad specialties,
apparel, t-shirts, fulfillment. (Woman, estab 2001, empl
135, sales $47,091,020, cert: WBENC)

1382   Premium Surge Promotions, L.L.C.
      640 N. LaSalle Ste 540
      Chicago, IL 60654
      Contact: Pam Crain EVP Mktg/Client Service
      Tel: 312-951-2303
      Email: pcrain@surge-innovations.com
      Website: www.surge-creates.com/
Marketing, creative & promotional product design and
manufacturing. (Minority, estab 2001, empl 15, sales
$33,000,000, cert: NMSDC)

1383   Pro Biz Products LLC
      350 N Orleans St Ste 9000N
      Chicago, IL 60654
      Contact: Richard Smith President
      Tel: 312-961-4513
      Email: r.smith@probizproducts.com
      Website: www.probizproducts.com
Screen printing or embroidery, office supplies,
furniture, janitorial products & promotional items.
(AA, estab 2014, empl 6, sales $15,000,000, cert:
State, NMSDC)

1384   Silk Screen Express, Inc.
      7611 W 185TH ST
      TINLEY PARK, IL 60477
      Contact: Dawn Coleman President
      Tel: 708-845-5600
      Email: dcoleman@silkscreenx.com
      Website: www.silkscreenx.com
Silk screened & embroidered apparel, promotional
items, uniforms & safety programs. (Woman, estab ,
empl , sales $3,000,000, cert: WBENC)

1385   Stitch Me LLC
      329 W 18th St, Unit 308
      Chicago, IL 60616
      Contact: Brenda Nelson Owner
      Tel: 312-933-2608
      Email: brenda@stitchmeapparel.com
      Website: www.stitchmeapparel.com
Embroidered Sportswear, Hats, Caps, Jackets, T-Shirts,
Fleece, Sweaters, Tote Bags, Cut Goods, Finished
Goods, Polo Shirts, Women's Wear, Promotional
Products Screen Printed Apparel - T-shirts, Jackets,
Hats, Team Uniforms, Sports (Woman/AA, estab 2011,
empl 3, sales , cert: City, NMSDC, WBENC, 8(a))

1386   TBK Promotions, Inc.
      3055 W 111th St 2 South
      Chicago, IL 60655
      Contact: Kevin Flynn Dir of Sales
      Tel: 773-239-2222
      Email: k@tbkpromotions.com
      Website: www.tbkpromotions.com
Promotional products, advertising specialties &
branded wearable items. (Woman, estab 1990, empl
5, sales $502,500, cert: State, WBENC)

1387   The Certif-a-gift Company Inc.
      1625 E Alqonqion Rd
      Arlington Heights, IL 60005
      Contact: Trish Duh President
      Tel: 847-718-0300
      Email: tduh@certif-a-gift.com
      Website: www.certif-a-gift.com
Incentive programs. (Woman, estab 1954, empl 50,
sales $15,600,000, cert: WBENC)

1388 Windy City Silkscreening, Inc.
      2715 S Archer
      Chicago, IL 60608
      Contact: Jessica Trojanowski Cstmr Service
      Tel: 312-842-0030
      Email: jessicat@wcstshirts.com
      Website: www.wcsshirts.com
Custom screen printed apparel: t-shirts, sweats, hats,
jackets, towels, hot-market printing, rally towels, promotional products. (Woman, estab 1978, empl 36, sales
$1,380,000, cert: WBENC)

1389 World Of Promotions
      1310 Louis Ave
      Elk Grove Village, IL 60007
      Contact: Layla Rosenfeld President
      Tel: 847-439-7930
      Email: rosenfeldlayla@yahoo.com
      Website: www.aworldofpromotions.com
Promotional products: pens, mugs, hats, clothing, bags.
(Woman, estab 2003, empl 8, sales $1,120,000, cert: State)

Indiana

1390 Awards Unlimited, Inc.
      3031 Union St
      Lafayette, IN 47904
      Contact: Stacey Shirar President
      Tel: 765-447-9413
      Email: sjs@awardsunlimitedinc.net
      Website: www.awardsunlimitedinc.net
Advertising specialties. (Woman, estab 1978, empl 12,
sales $500,000, cert: WBENC)

1391 Bardach Awards, Inc.
      4222 W 86th St
      Indianapolis, IN 46268
      Contact: Diane Bardach Beck CEO
      Tel: 317-872-7444
      Email: dbardach@bardachawards.com
      Website: www.bardachawards.com
Custom corporate awards: plaques, trophies, crystal,
acrylic, plates, marble, glass, leather items such as portfolios, name badges, medals, ribbons, bronze castings, donor
recognition, signage, jewelry, executive gifts. (Woman,
estab 1969, empl 36, sales $2,960,000, cert: State)

1392 Karm Corporation
      2017 N Bedford Ave
      Evansville, IN 47711
      Contact: Kena Campbell President
      Tel: 812-426-1323
      Email: kcampbell@promarkin.com
      Website: www.promarkin.com
Screen printing, embroidery, labels, stickers, decals,
promotional products, t-shirts, uniforms. (Woman, estab
1976, empl 24, sales $2,900,000, cert: State, WBENC)

1393 Linz and Company
      8231 Hohman Ave Ste 200
      Munster, IN 46321
      Contact: Heather Koetteritz Sales/Import Mgr
      Tel: 708-757-7800
      Email: heather@linzco.com
      Website: www.linzco.com
Promotional products: apparel, housewares, novelties,
personal care items, etc. (Woman, estab 2000, empl 4,
sales $3,007,000, cert: WBENC)

1394 M. Nelson and Associates
      4011 Vincennes Rd
      Indianapolis, IN 46268
      Contact: Carolina Pimental-Nelson President
      Tel: 317-228-1422
      Email: carolina@mnelson.com
      Website: www.mnelson.com
Promotional products, printing services, graphic design
& screen-print/embroidery of apparel. (Minority,
Woman, estab 1991, empl 4, sales , cert: State, 8(a))

1395 Metro Printed Products, Inc.
      1001 Commerce Pkwy South Dr Ste H
      Greenwood, IN 46143
      Contact: Gloria James Marketing
      Tel: 317-885-0077
      Email: gloria.james@proforma.com
      Website: www.metroprintedproducts.com
Advertising specialties and promotional products.
(Woman, estab 1989, empl 6, sales $2,361,600, cert:
WBENC)

1396 OmniSource Marketing Group, Inc.
      8945 N Meridian St Ste 150
      Indianapolis, IN 46260
      Contact: Janet Calderon Goldberg President
      Tel: 317-575-3318
      Email: jgoldberg@omnisourcemarketing.com
      Website: www.omnisourcemarketing.com
Custom promotional products & packaging, embroidery,
fulfillment, graphic services & design, screen printing.
(Woman, estab 1988, empl 30, sales $10,400,000, cert:
WBENC)

1397 PlaqueMakerPlus, Inc.
      5713 Park Plaza Ct
      Indianapolis, IN 46220
      Contact: Edson Pereira President
      Tel: 317-594-5556
      Email: edson@plaquemakerplus.com
      Website: www.plaquemakerplus.com
Mfr awards, plaques, name badges, name plates & signs.
(Woman, estab 1995, empl 6, sales $640,000, cert:
State)

1398 Pro-Am Team Sports
      1650 US Hwy 41 Ste E
      Schererville, IN 46375
      Contact: Mary Dolan Owner
      Tel: 219-515-6900
      Email: mary@pro-amteamsports.com
      Website: www.pro-amteamsports.com
Branded, customized name-brand apparel & equipment.
(Woman, estab 2014, empl 60, sales $4,200,000, cert:
WBENC)

1399 Smiling Cross Inc.
      700 S College Ave, Ste A
      Bloomington, IN 47403
      Contact: Rula Hanania President
      Tel: 812-323-9290
      Email: rhanania@smilepromotions.com
      Website: www.smilepromotions.com
Promotional products. (Minority, Woman, estab 2003,
empl 10, sales $2,400,000, cert: State, NMSDC)

1400   Table Thyme Designs
217 W 10th St Ste 125
Indianapolis, IN 46202
Contact: Laurie Rice Owner
Tel: 317-634-0281
Email: coloredthreads@sbcglobal.net
Website: www.colored-threads.com
Promotional prods, embroidered apparel, screen printing.
(Woman, estab 2002, empl 2, sales , cert: State, City)

1401   Thomas E. Slade, Inc.
6220 Vogel Road
Evansville, IN 47715
Contact: Lisa Slade President
Tel: 812-437-5233
Email: tom@sladeprint.com
Website: www.sladeprint.com
Printing, graphic design, website design, wide format
posters & banners, mailing, promotional products,
letterhead, envelopes, business cards, labels, tags, inserts,
marketing services, augmented reality, QR codes for
tracking, signs. (Woman, estab 1993, empl 17, sales
$2,500,000, cert: State)

1402   Wolf Run Marketing
6020 N Emerson Ave
Indianapolis, IN 46220
Contact: Susan Fryer Owner
Tel: 317-445-5180
Email: susan@wolfrunmarketing.com
Website: www.wolfrunmarketing.com
Promotional products, logoed apparel, service & safety
awards, employee & customer recognition awards,
tradeshow handouts, conference materials, incentives,
safety apparel, graphic design, logo devel. (Woman, estab
2009, empl 2, sales $200,000, cert: City)

Kansas

1403   Grapevine Designs, LLC
8406 Melrose Dr
Lenexa, KS 66214
Contact: Bob Offord VP Business Dev
Tel: 913-307-0225
Email: bob.offord@abrandcompany.com
Website: www.grapevinedesigns.com/
Promotional marketing, promotional products, creative
design, corporate giveaways, tradeshow giveaways,
corporate branding, branded merchandise. (Woman, estab
2000, empl 72, sales $8,000,000, cert: WBENC)

1404   Promo Depot Inc.
2266 N Ridge Rd
Wichita, KS 67205
Contact: Rick McKay President
Tel: 316-722-2500
Email: rick@4mypromo.com
Website: www.4mypromo.com
Promotional products: logo wearables & printed ad
specialty products, embroidery & screeen printing, wards
& recognition products. (Hisp, estab 1997, empl 15, sales
$2,600,000, cert: NMSDC)

Kentucky

1405   Ad-Venture Promotions
2625 Regency Rd
Lexington, KY 40503
Contact: Cathy Stafford Owner
Tel: 859-263-4299
Email: cathy@ad-venturepromotions.com
Website: www.ad-venturepromotions.com
Advertising specialties & promotional products. (Woman,
estab 2004, empl 6, sales , cert: WBENC)

1406   Presence Inc.
2311 Mohican Hill Ct
Louisville, KY 40207
Contact: Gail Iwaniak President
Tel: 502-365-4616
Email: gail@stuffology.com
Website: www.stuffology.com
Promotional marketing & products. (Woman, estab
1989, empl 2, sales $350,000, cert: City)

1407   The Logo Warehouse
1963 Meadowcreek Dr
Louisville, KY 40218
Contact: Leah Scott Owner
Tel: 502-451-5421
Email: lscott@thelogowarehouse.com
Website: www.thelogowarehouse.com
Promotional products & apparel. (Woman/AA, estab
2008, empl 1, sales , cert: City, WBENC)

1408   Walker Flags, Inc.
8134 New LaGrange Rd, Ste 200
Louisville, KY 40222
Contact: Donna Walker Mancini Owner
Tel: 502-394-1474
Email: customercare@walkerflags.com
Website: www.walkerflags.com
Flags, Banners, Flagpoles, Flag & Flagpole Accessories.
(Woman, estab 1960, empl 3, sales , cert: State)

Louisiana

1409   Augie Leopold Advertising Specialties, Inc.
3214 Roman St
Metairie, LA 70001
Contact: Leeanne Leopold CEO
Tel: 504-836-0525
Email: leeanne@augieleopold.com
Website: www.augieleopold.com
Advertising specialties, promotional items, premium
gifts, casino monthly giveaways, safety programs.
(Woman, estab 0, empl , sales , cert: WBENC)

1410   Impress Marketing Studios, LLC
PO Box 38845
Shreveport, LA 71133
Contact: Janelle Marks Owner
Tel: 888-773-0183
Email: jmarks@impressmarketingstudios.com
Website: www.ImpressMarketingStudios.com
Marketing & promotional, premiums, advertising
specialties, apparel & signage. (Woman/AA, estab 2014,
empl 2, sales $127,000, cert: NMSDC)

1411   The Creative Touch, Inc.
7725 Jefferson Hwy
Baton Rouge, LA 70809
Contact: Maureen Kahl President
Tel: 225-925-0022
Email: maureen@creativetouchembroidery.com
Website: www.createyourtouch.com
Embroidery, silk screening, promotional prods, (Woman,
estab 1982, empl 7, sales $489,000, cert: WBENC)

1412   Wilkin Enterprises, Inc.
2323 Bainbridge St, Bldg B, Ste 13
Kenner, LA 70062
Contact: Kathleen Wilkin President
Tel: 504-464-2520
Email: kwilkin@gosafeguard.com
Website: www.safeguardprints.com
Full color printing, promotional items & embroidered
apparel. (Woman, estab 1993, empl 7, sales $1,458,066,
cert: WBENC)

Massachusetts

1413 Ellco Promotions, Inc.
     113 Smoke Hill Ridge Road
     Marshfield, MA 02050
     Contact: Max Cohen VP
     Tel: 508-641-6274
     Email: max@ellcopromotions.com
     Website: www.ellcopromotions.com
Promotional/premium product & apparel agency.
(Woman, estab 2010, empl 2, sales $150,000, cert: State)

1414 GAP Promotions LLC
     1 Washington St
     Gloucester, MA 01930
     Contact: Gayle Piraino President
     Tel: 978-281-0083
     Email: gayle.piraino@gappromo.com
     Website: www.gappromo.com/
Promotional programs and products. (Woman, estab 2006, empl 10, sales $5,602,133, cert: WBENC)

1415 Infinart, Inc.
     44 Mechanic St
     Newton, MA 02464
     Contact: Felicity Green President
     Tel: 617-964-3279
     Email: felicityinfinart@gmail.com
     Website: www.infinart.com
Custom branding, logo embroidery, silk screening, imprinted promotional products, awards, corporate gifts incentives, signage, banners. (Woman, estab 1980, empl 5, sales , cert: State)

1416 Jazzy Sportswear Promotional Co.
     90 Munroe
     Lynn, MA 01903
     Contact: Vincent Williams President
     Tel: 781-593-7197
     Email: jazzypc@jazzysportswear.com
     Website: www.jazzysportswear.com
Screen printing, embroidery, and a wide array of promotional items, banners, awards. (AA, estab 1997, empl 1, sales $189,000, cert: State, NMSDC)

Maryland

1417 APISource, Inc.
     7850 Walker Dr Ste 400
     Greenbelt, MD 20770
     Contact: Jinni Kerns Accounting Specialist
     Tel: 301-731-6100
     Email: accounting@apisource.com
     Website: www.apisource.com
Promotional products: t-shirts, collared shirts, polo shirts, hats, jackets, bags, computer accessories, pens, note pads, mugs, novelties, giveaways, awards, premiums, incentives, fulfillment services. (Woman, estab 1965, empl 150, sales , cert: WBENC)

1418 Debbie Lynn, Inc.
     952 Ridgebrook Rd Ste 1100
     Sparks, MD 21152
     Contact: Stephanie Bloom Operations Mgr
     Tel: 443-595-8178
     Email: stephanie@debbielynn.net
     Website: www.debbielynn.net
Writing instruments, office accessories, Back to School & novelty products. (Woman, estab 1998, empl 5, sales $10,200,000, cert: WBENC)

1419 Lord & Mitchell, Inc.
     9205 Locksley Rd
     Fort Washington, MD 20744
     Contact: Toya Mitchell President
     Tel: 800-491-8026
     Email: toya@lord-mitchell.com
     Website: www.lord-mitchell.com
Promotional products distributors and wholesale trade agents/brokers. (Woman/AA, estab 1991, empl 3, sales $1,475,910, cert: NMSDC, WBENC)

1420 Products 2 Brand, LLC
     8217 Cloverleaf Dr
     Millersville, MD 21108
     Contact: Macgill Antor President
     Tel: 301-787-0077
     Email: macgill@products2brand.com
     Website: www.products2brand.com
Promotional product brand merchandise, tradeshow registration bags, totes, briefcases, luggage, lanyards, name badges. (Woman, estab 2007, empl 22, sales , cert: City)

1421 Williams Solutions Group, LLC
     20140 Scholar Dr, Ste 315
     Hagerstown, MD 21742
     Contact: Peter E. Perini, Sr. VP
     Tel: 301-739-7532
     Email: peter.perini@williamssolutionsgroup.com
     Website: www.WilliamsSolutionsGroup.com
Promotional items, marketing items, tchotchkies, giveaway items, logo branded items. (AA, estab 2009, empl 2, sales $100,000, cert: State)

Michigan

1422 Alfie Logo Gear
     2425 Switch Dr
     Traverse City, MI 49684
     Contact: Bonnie Alfonso President
     Tel: 800-507-0040
     Email: bonnie@goalfie.com
     Website: www.GoAlfie.com
Logowear, embroidery, screen printing & promotional products, uniforms, rewards & incentives, trade show giveaways. (Woman, estab 1990, empl 18, sales $2,863,520, cert: WBENC)

1423 Antina Promotions, LLC
     84 Leslie Lane
     Waterford, MI 48328
     Contact: Christina Concord Managing Partner
     Tel: 248-254-3845
     Email: christina@antinapromo.com
     Website: www.antinapromo.com
Promotional Products, Exhibit Displays, Corporate Gifts, Awards, Signage, Branded Apparel, Company Stores, Custom Packaging, Marketing Materials. (Woman, estab 2010, empl 2, sales , cert: WBENC, SDB)

1424 CE Competitive Edge LLC
     5924 Red Arrow Hwy
     Stevensville, MI 49127
     Contact: Mary Tomasini CEO
     Tel: 269-429-0404
     Email: mjtomasini@competitive-edge.net
     Website: www.competitive-edge.net
Incentive & promotional products, ideas & services. (Woman, estab 1993, empl 15, sales , cert: WBENC)

1425 CompleteSource Inc.
      4455 44th St SE
      Grand Rapids, MI 49512
      Contact: VP Sales
      Tel: 800-868-7018
      Email: customerservice@completesource.com
      Website: www.completesource.com
Commercial printing, promotional products, awards &
incentives, embroidery & silk screened apparel & uni-
forms, saftey awards & incentives, banners & signs.
(Woman, estab 1989, empl 11, sales $2,000,000, cert:
WBENC)

1426 Graphix 2 Go
      7200 Tower Rd
      Battle Creek, MI 49014
      Contact: Amy Howard Sales Mgr
      Tel: 269-969-7321
      Email: amy@graphix2goinc.com
      Website: www.graphix2goinc.com
Promotional products. (Woman, estab 1997, empl 8, sales
$2,500,000, cert: WBENC)

1427 InmartGroup, Ltd.
      37570 Hills Tech Dr
      Farmington Hills, MI 48331
      Contact: Stephanie Master Acct Exec
      Tel: 248-489-0344
      Email: stephanie@inmartgroup.com
      Website: www.inmartgroup.com
Custom imprinted promotional & premium items, branded
merchandise, warehouse, distribution & on-line payment.
(Woman, estab 1989, empl 6, sales , cert: WBENC)

1428 Krystal Marketing, Inc.
      1120 E Long Lake Rd, Ste 200
      Troy, MI 48085
      Contact: Carolyn Boccia Mktg Mgr
      Tel: 248-619-9000
      Email: carolyn@krystalmarketing.com
      Website: www.krystalmarketing.com
Promotional products, awards & incentives. (Woman,
estab 1987, empl 10, sales , cert: WBENC)

1429 Mendoza Enterprises LLC
      1847 N Main St
      Royal Oak, MI 48073
      Contact: Sue Johnson President
      Tel: 248-588-0335
      Email: sue@mendozaenterprises.us
      Website: www.mendozaenterprises.us
Printing and promotional products. (Hisp, estab 0, empl ,
sales , cert: NMSDC)

1430 Mercury P&F
      35610 Mound Rd
      Sterling Heights, MI 48310
      Contact: Betsy Canova Business Dev Mgr
      Tel: 586-825-9300
      Email: canovab@mercuryfs.com
      Website: www.mercuryfs.com
Branded merchandise & premiums. (Woman/AA, estab
1996, empl 70, sales $25,000,000, cert: NMSDC, WBENC)

1431 Mixed Promotions, LLC
      3759 S Baldwin Rd, Ste 222
      Lake Orion, MI 48359
      Contact: Lona Carson CEO
      Tel: 248-783-4099
      Email: lcarson@mixedpromotions.com
      Website: www.mixedpromotions.com
Promotional products. (Minority, Woman, estab 2000,
empl 1, sales $462,000, cert: NMSDC, WBENC)

1432 Promotion Concepts Inc.
      414 S Burdick St
      Kalamazoo, MI 49007
      Contact: Lauren A. Powers President
      Tel: 269-488-2987
      Email: laurene.powers@promotionconcepts.com
      Website: www.promotionconcepts.com
Incentive marketing svcs, sales promotion, promotional
products, premium incentives programs, awards,
recognition, brand-building. (Woman, estab 1982, empl
18, sales , cert: WBENC)

1433 Promotional Solutions LLC
      48530 Van Dyke Ave
      Shelby Township, MI 48317
      Contact: Kathy Ferguson Member
      Tel: 586-739-1132
      Email: promotionalsolutions@onemain.com
      Website: www.promotionalsolutionsonline.com
Advertising specialty goods & services. Logowear
embroidered or screen print,
wwards & trophys, special event gifts, employee
appreciation items. (Woman, estab 2001, empl 8, sales
$622,000, cert: WBENC)

1434 The Bradley Company, Inc.
      26777 Central Park Blvd Ste 180
      Southfield, MI 48076
      Contact: Marci Taran CEO
      Tel: 248-538-1909
      Email: marcit@thebradco.com
      Website: www.thebradco.com
Advertising specialties, Assembly, Awards, Branded
merchandise, Branding, Commemorative items, Corporate apparel, Corporate gifts, Corporate identity,
Corporate webstores, Custom packaging, etc. (Woman,
estab 2004, empl 11, sales $5,000,000, cert: WBENC)

1435 Tier One Marketing
      3160 Belle Terre
      Commerce Township, MI 48382
      Contact: Jeanne Snyder President
      Tel: 313-274-1179
      Email: jeannesnyder@sbcglobal.net
      Website: www.tierone.biz
Ad specialties: coffee cups, pens, portfolios, golf items,
technology driven give-a-ways, coolers, tote bags,
flashlights, key chains, awards, custom pieces,
collectables. (Woman, estab 2003, empl 2, sales
$250,000, cert: WBENC)

1436 Unique Expressions, LLC
      22050 Woodward Ave
      Ferndale, MI 48220
      Contact: Beverly Bantom CEO
      Tel: 248-547-9300
      Email: info@uniquex.net
      Website: www.UniqueX.net
Dist promotional products. (AA, estab 1999, empl 6,
sales $1,000,000, cert: NMSDC)

Minnesota

1437 2020 Brand Solutions
      135 Grand Ave East
      South St. Paul, MN 55075
      Contact: Dan Livengood VP Sales & Mktg
      Tel: 651-451-3850
      Email: dan.livengood@2020brands.com
      Website: www.2020collection.com
Corporate Apparel & Uniform Programs, Branded
Merchandise, Incentives & Recognition, Print Management & Specialty Fulfillment. (Nat Ame, estab 2014,
empl 62, sales $20,000,000, cert: NMSDC)

1438   A.K. Rose Inc.
       3701 Shoreline Dr Ste 200B
       Wayzata, MN 55391
       Contact: Barb DeRonde Cstmr Service
       Tel: 952-474-3050
       Email: barb@akrose.com
       Website: www.akrose.com
Promotional merchandise. (Woman, estab 1985, empl 4,
sales $1,200,000, cert: WBENC)

1439   Corporate Advertising & Incentives
       6289 Niagara Lane N
       Maple Grove, MN 55311
       Contact: Loni Spence Promotional Consultant
       Tel: 763-559-8388
       Email: lspence@corpadvertising.net
       Website: www.corpadvertising.net
Promorional products. (Woman, estab 2003, empl 3, sales
$150,000, cert: WBENC)

1440   Creality Promo+Retail, inc.
       3201 West County Rd. 42 Ste 105
       Burnsville, MN 55306
       Contact: Tony Pesante President
       Tel: 952-854-9202
       Email: tonyp@crealitypromo.com
       Website: www.crealitypromo.com
Promotional products, logo merchandise, custom apparel,
gift store merchandise, give-away items, premiums,
awards. (Minority, Woman, estab 1999, empl 19, sales
$6,850,000, cert: NMSDC)

1441   Creative Resources Agency
       1208 5th St South
       Minneapolis, MN 55343
       Contact: Caren Schweitzer CEO
       Tel: 952-988-9407
       Email: caren@acreativeresource.com
       Website: www.acreativeresource.com
Promotional products, direct mail, trade show give-aways,
corporate holiday gifts, lead generators & client thank-you
gifts. (Woman, estab 1995, empl 24, sales $5,700,000,
cert: WBENC, 8(a))

1442   High Five, LLC
       750 2nd St NE Ste 122
       Hopkins, MN 55343
       Contact: Co-President
       Tel: 952-746-0355
       Email: info@highfiveonline.com
       Website: www.highfiveonline.com
Promotional products & advertising specialties. (Woman,
estab 2003, empl 4, sales $455,000, cert: WBENC)

1443   Ithaca Promotions
       PO Box 220
       Wahkon, MN 56386
       Contact: Katrina Chang President
       Tel: 612-669-7833
       Email: katrina@ithacapromotions.com
       Website: www.ithacapromotions.com
Promotional, incentive, corporate gifts, gift certificates,
gift checks, American Express Gift Cheques, banners, etc.
(Minority, Woman, estab 1991, empl 1, sales $631,227,
cert: State, NMSDC)

1444   J Michael Industries
       1086 W 7th St
       St. Paul, MN 55102
       Contact: Jamie Flynn Owner
       Tel: 651-698-3333
       Email: jamiemm@extendedexposure.com
       Website: www.extendedexposure.com
Design, create & source give-away mementos, memorable keepsakes & corporate gifts. (Woman, estab 1999,
empl 7, sales $1,200,000, cert: WBENC)

1445   M Plus Embroidery & Promotions
       5 Viking Dr W
       Little Canada, MN 55117
       Contact: Beth Mulcahy Owner
       Tel: 651-777-3624
       Email: beth@mplus-embroidery.com
       Website: www.mplus-embroidery.com
Embroidery, silk screening, direct to garment, polo's, t-
shirts, sweatshirts/pants, caps, hats, bags, etc. (Woman,
estab 1984, empl 7, sales $324,800, cert: WBENC)

1446   Rutabaga Rags, Inc.
       8700 West 36th St Ste 3E
       St. Louis Park, MN 55426
       Contact: Julie Miller Owner
       Tel: 952-938-4841
       Email: julie@rutabagarags.com
       Website: www.rutabagaragsshop.com
Promotional products & stadium giveaways: baseball
caps, jerseys, bats, gloves, toys, banks, bracelets, lip
balm, magnets, pens, schedules, memo pads, padfolios,
portfolios, duffles, bags, backpacks, cinch sacks, mugs,
coffee tumblers, stuffed animals. (Woman, estab 1993,
empl 3, sales $600,000, cert: WBENC)

1447   Spartan Promotional Group, Inc.
       711 Hale Ave N
       Oakdale, MN 55128
       Contact: Dan Perdue Sales Assoc
       Tel: 309-827-2215
       Email: phyllisohenwald@spartanpromo.com
       Website: www.spartanpromo.com/index.html
Advertising specialties: keychains, magnets, pens,
distribution services, promotional marketing programs.
(Woman, estab 1966, empl 80, sales , cert: WBENC)

Missouri

1448   Accent Group Solutions
       1154 Reco Ave
       St. Louis, MO 63126
       Contact: Erica Hughes CEO
       Tel: 314-965-5388
       Email: ehughes@accentgroupsolutions.com
       Website: www.AccentGroupSolutions.com
Warehousing, Distribution Services, Pick Pack & Ship,
Custom Fulfillment, Publisher Services, Logo Apparel &
Promotional Products, Printing, Converting Printed
Materials, Literature Fulfillment, Container Manage-
ment. (Woman, estab 2003, empl 26, sales $6,621,042,
cert: WBENC)

1449   Blue Sky Apparel & Promotions, LLC
       12732 Pennridge Dr
       Bridgeton, MO 63044
       Contact: Kathy Gralike Owner
       Tel: 314-739-4531
       Email: kgralike@aol.com
       Website: www.blueskypromotion.com/
Promotional products: pens, coffee mugs, apparel &
caps. (Woman, estab 2002, empl 5, sales $1,369,654,
cert: State)

Mississippi

1450   Zebra Marketing Corporation
       289 Commerce Park Dr, Ste E
       Ridgeland, MS 39157
       Contact: Sharon Thompson Sales Exec
       Tel: 251-438-2422
       Email: sharon.thompson@zebrapromos.com
       Website: www.zebrapromos.com
Advertising specialties, service awards, clothing-jackets, t-shirts, sport shirts, trade show give aways. (Woman, estab 2000, empl 14, sales $7,000,000, cert: WBENC)

North Carolina

1451   Adsource Media, Inc.
       8313-101 Six Forks Rd
       Raleigh, NC 27615
       Contact: Darlene Brand Acct Exec
       Tel: 919-871-9990
       Email: darlene@am3adsource.com
       Website: www.am3adsource.com
Branded merchandise, decorated apparel, medical educational material, dimensional packaging, imported product, trade show supplies, direct mailing, signage, training board games. (Woman, estab 1999, empl 4, sales $675,000, cert: WBENC)

1452   Austin Business Forms Inc.
       PO Box 1905
       Matthews, NC 28016
       Contact: Acct Exec
       Tel: 704-821-6165
       Email: sales@printwithaustin.com
       Website: www.printwithaustin.com
Printing, graphic design, screen printing & embroidery, promotional products. (Woman, estab 1991, empl 6, sales $1,514,990, cert: WBENC)

1453   Blue Dove Promotions
       1471 Brookwood Dr
       Winston-Salem, NC 27106
       Contact: Joyce Williams Owner
       Tel: 336-624-5223
       Email: jwilliams@bluedovepromotions.com
       Website: www.bluedovepromotions.com
Promotional products. (Woman, estab 2012, empl 1, sales , cert: State, NMSDC)

1454   Bob Williams Specialty Co.
       5539 Monroe Rd
       Charlotte, NC 28212
       Contact: Janet VP Sales
       Tel: 704-568-3411
       Email: janet@bobwilliamsspecialty.com
       Website: www.bobwilliamsspecialty.com
Imprinted promotional products. (Woman, estab 1961, empl 5, sales $800,000, cert: City)

1455   BrandRPM, LLC
       4910 Starcrest Dr
       Monroe, NC 28110
       Contact: Keith Brent VP Strategic Sales
       Tel: 704-225-1800
       Email: keithb@brandrpm.com
       Website: www.brandrpm.com
Corporate apparel & branded merchandise. (Minority, Woman, estab 2008, empl , sales $5,000,000, cert: State, NMSDC)

1456   Crown Trophy Winston-Salem
       2871 Reynolda Rd
       Winston-Salem, NC 27106
       Contact: Michael Robinson President
       Tel: 336-723-7400
       Email: crowntrophy419@bellsouth.net
       Website: www.crowntrophy.com
Awards & recogniton: badges, signage, corporate awards, plaques, trophies, ribbons, medallians, promotional items, cast bronze, etc. (Woman/AA, estab , empl , sales , cert: State, City)

1457   Daybreak Marketing Services, LLC
       14460 Falls of Neuse Rd Ste 149-326
       Raleigh, NC 27614
       Contact: Dawn Nakash COO
       Tel: 919-926-1452
       Email: dawn@daybreakmarketing.com
       Website: www.DaybreakMarketing.com
Promotional Products, Advertising Specialties, Silk Screening, Embroidery, Debossing, Embossing Imprinted, Pens, mugs, t-shirts, magnets, pins, buttons, uniforms, awards, bags, desk and auto accessories, flash drives, power banks. (Woman, estab 1998, empl 1, sales $150,000, cert: State)

1458   G. ALAN Inc.
       5317 Highgate Dr Ste 212
       Durham, NC 27713
       Contact: Gregory Harris
       Tel: 919-544-0055
       Email: gregory@imwithg.com
       Website: www.imwithg.com
Embroidery, screenprinting & promotional products. (AA, estab 1994, empl 2, sales $422,500, cert: State, NMSDC)

1459   PIA International LLC
       PO Box 481232
       Charlotte, NC 28269
       Contact: Donna Daniels Owner
       Tel: 704-593-1256
       Email: donna@piapromo.com
       Website: www.piapromo.com
Promotional products, ad specialties, t-shirts, sports uniforms & equipment, safety wear, etc. (Woman/AA, estab 2003, empl 1, sales , cert: State, NMSDC)

1460   PROMOQUEST Inc.
       1308 Ballyclare Ct
       Raleigh, NC 27614
       Contact: Pam Williams President
       Tel: 919-845-3448
       Email: pam@promoquest.com
       Website: www.promoquest.com
Imprinted promotional products: screenprinting, embroidery, lithography, digital printing, emboss, deboss, laser, t-shirts, jackets, fleece, athletic apparel, pants, bumper stickers, signs, buttons, pens note pads. (Woman/AA, estab 1994, empl 1, sales , cert: State)

New Jersey

1461   3D Promoplastic, Inc.
       31 Summer Rd
       Flemington, NJ 08822
       Contact: Sibel Toy Owner
       Tel: 469-955-6282
       Email: mail@3dpromoplastic.com
       Website: www.3d-promo.com
Promotional products, plastic promotional products, custom mold clip pens, promotional give aways, ballpoint pens, pen holders & eco friendly products. (Woman, estab 2002, empl 50, sales , cert: State)

1462   Aberson Narotzky & White
       945 Lincoln Ave E
       Cranford, NJ 07016
       Contact: Shelly Aberson President
       Tel: 908-789-2700
       Email: shelly@anwinc.com
       Website: www.anwinc.com
Advertising specialties, promotional products. (Woman, estab 1989, empl 7, sales $3,100,000, cert: WBENC)

1463   Action Calendar & Specialty Co., Inc.
       5 Underwood Ct
       Delran, NJ 08075
       Contact: Lora Dunnigan President
       Tel: 856-764-4000
       Email: lora.dunnigan@renpromo.com
       Website: www.wellnesseducationkits.com
Dist promotional products, on-site distribution center, graphic arts, web dev, customer care call center, on-line company stores. (Woman, estab 1975, empl 10, sales $6,121,000, cert: WBENC)

1464   Balady Promotions, Inc.
       1719 Route 10 Ste 103
       Parsippany, NJ 07054
       Contact: Balady CEO
       Tel: 973-682-8440
       Email: jbalady@balady.com
       Website: www.balady.com
Promotional product & decorated apparel programs, trade show exhibits, signage & giveaways, business gifts/ premiums & award programs for employee achievement, sales rewards & years of service. (Woman, estab 1989, empl 7, sales $2,951,425, cert: WBENC)

1465   Blank2Branded powered by Axis
       160 Main Rd
       Montville, NJ 07045
       Contact: Marcia Tarnoff President
       Tel: 973-917-3100
       Email: marcia@blank2branded.com
       Website: www.blank2branded.com
Promotional solutions. (Woman, estab 2013, empl 5, sales $1,900,000, cert: WBENC)

1466   Compas, Inc.
       4300 Haddonfield Rd Ste 200
       Pennsauken, NJ 08109
       Contact: Robert Kadar SVP
       Tel: 856-667-8577
       Email: rkadar@cmicompas.com
       Website: www.compasonline.com
Media & promotional svcs. (AA, estab , empl , sales $250,000,000, cert: NMSDC)

1467   Cotapaxi Custom Design & Manufacturing, LLC
       338 Hackensack St
       Carlstadt, NJ 07072
       Contact: Vincent Sposito Sr Vice President
       Tel: 201-507-5111
       Email: vsposito@cotapaxi.com
       Website: www.cotapaxi.com
Create, develop, and deliver effective, high value, low cost exclusive promotional products. (Minority, Woman, estab , empl , sales $87,000,000, cert: NMSDC)

1468   Focus Merchandising
       127 E Ridgewood Ave
       Ridgewood, NJ 07450
       Contact: Allison Rao President
       Tel: 201-445-5858
       Email: allisonr@focusmc.com
       Website: www.focusmerchandising.com
Promotional marketing & premium items. (Woman, estab 2003, empl 8, sales $8,000,000, cert: WBENC)

1469   Glazer Design, LLC
       330 Franklin Turnpike
       Mahwah, NJ 07430
       Contact: TRISH GLAZER Office Mgr
       Tel: 201-684-1132
       Email: trish@glazerpromos.com
       Website: www.glazerpromos.com
Promotional products. (Woman, estab 2002, empl 7, sales $669,828, cert: City, WBENC)

1470   Graphics Solutions
       473 Chapel Heights Rd
       Sewell, NJ 08080
       Contact: Steven Riggs Owner
       Tel: 877-931-1636
       Email: support@graphics-solution.com
       Website: www.graphics-solution.com
Marketing communications products, print products, promotional products, customized apparel, signage, graphic design, web design, marketing consulting, audio/video production. (AA, estab 2008, empl 5, sales $423,000, cert: NMSDC)

1471   Ideas to Impress, LLC
       35 Longman St
       Toms River, NJ 08753
       Contact: Debbie Dennerlein President
       Tel: 201-750-0222
       Email: debbie@ideastoimpress.com
       Website: www.ideastoimpress.com
Dist promotional products, company brand / logo, customized printed, embroidered & laser etched products: t-shirts, polo shirts, sweatshirts & uniforms, pens, desk accessories, to signs, and table covers, executive gift & give-aways. (Woman, estab 2006, empl 1, sales $103,211, cert: WBENC)

1472   Impact Dimensions, LLC and Affiliate
       725 Hylton Rd
       Pennsauken, NJ 08110
       Contact: Norbert McGettigan COO
       Tel: 856-382-4501
       Email: norbertm@impactdimensions.com
       Website: www.impactdimensions.com
Embroidery & apparel, advertising specialties, and corporate gifts. (Hisp, estab 2002, empl , sales $12,368,000, cert: NMSDC, SDB)

1473   Imprint Source LLC
       15 Charles St
       Westwood, NJ 07675
       Contact: Karen Adler Acct Exec
       Tel: 201-358-1010
       Email: karen@theimprintsource.com
       Website: www.TheImprintSource.com
Imprinted promotional products. (Woman, estab 1994, empl 6, sales , cert: WBENC)

1474 LeRoe Corporate Gifts, Inc.
      43 Haytown Rd
      Lebanon, NJ 08833
      Contact: Rochelle Moneta Owner
      Tel: 908-236-8754
      Email: rmoneta@leroe.com
      Website: www.LeRoe.com
Promotional, incentive & business gifts, employee recognition & gifts. (Woman, estab 1999, empl 2, sales $250,000, cert: WBENC)

1475 Marissa L. Promotions
      1020 Campus Dr W
      Morganville, NJ 07751
      Contact: Marissa Harkavay Partner
      Tel: 732-689-2299
      Email: hello@creativesolutions.net
      Website: www.creativesolutions.net
Promotional & advertising specialties: trade show giveaways, corporate gifts, screen printing, graphic design. (Woman, estab 1990, empl 20, sales , cert: WBENC)

1476 Nygala Corp.
      115 Moonachie Ave
      Moonachie, NJ 07074
      Contact: Giancarlo Carrillo Key Accounts Mgr
      Tel: 201-288-6400
      Email: Giancarlo@flomousa.com
      Website: www.flomoglobal.com
Dist school supplies, gift bags & accessories. (Minority, Woman, estab 1992, empl 18, sales , cert: NMSDC, WBENC)

1477 Progressive Promotions Inc.
      145 Cedar Lane
      Englewood, NJ 07631
      Contact: Julie Levi President
      Tel: 201-945-0500
      Email: julie@progressivepromotions.com
      Website: www.progressivepromotions.com
Promotional products: corporate apparel, gifts, awards, uniforms, web stores, fulfillment, packaging & assembly. (Woman, estab 1987, empl 30, sales , cert: WBENC)

1478 Sabella Gabino Inc. dba Bella Marketing Inc.
      5 Deer Path
      Holmdel, NJ 07733
      Contact: Isabella Petruzzelli Founder/CEO
      Tel: 917-951-3025
      Email: isabella@bellamarketinginc.com
      Website: www.bellamarketinginc.com
Custom designed, promotional branded products specializing in the medical & pharmaceutical industry. (Minority, Woman, estab 2001, empl 1, sales , cert: NMSDC, WBENC)

1479 Significant Printz
      663-665 Elizabeth Ave
      Newark, NJ 07112
      Contact: TIffany Ryan Owner
      Tel: 862-755-8658
      Email: significantprintz@gmail.com
      Website: www.significantprintz.com
In-house graphic tshirt, hoodies and other apparel printing & production capabilities. (AA, estab 2020, empl 1, sales , cert: State)

1480 Stackable Sensations
      2200 Rt. 10 West, Ste 206
      Parsippany, NJ 07054
      Contact: Shari Verrone President
      Tel: 973-442-2831
      Email: Shariv@stackablesensations.com
      Website: www.stackablesensations.com/
Promotional marketing solution, online stores, fulfillment, global unique promotional items. (Woman, estab 2003, empl 14, sales $2,802,447, cert: WBENC)

1481 Thomas Direct Sales, Inc.
      30 Plymouth St
      Fairfield, NJ 07004
      Contact: Guy DAndrea COO
      Tel: 973-614-2307
      Email: mmarinzulich@thomasdirect.com
      Website: www.thomasdirect.com
Promotional products, premium & incentive programs, importing, on-site design & illustration, graphic arts, technology & website development. (Woman, estab 1986, empl 12, sales $1,000,000, cert: WBENC)

1482 Wisco Promo Uniform, INC.
      160 US Hwy 46
      Saddle Brook, NJ 07663
      Contact: Linda Briscoe President
      Tel: 973-767-2022
      Email: briscoe_linda@yahoo.com
      Website: www.wiscopnu.com
Mfr apparel, uniforms & aprons, silk screen & embroidery, promotional products, corporate identity & promotion. (Minority, Woman, estab 1999, empl 10, sales , cert: NMSDC)

Nevada

1483 Eagle Promotions
      4575 W Post Rd Ste 100
      Las Vegas, NV 89118
      Contact: Mario Stadtlander President
      Tel: 702-388-7100
      Email: mario@eaglepromotions.com
      Website: www.eaglepromotions.com
Advertising specialties: apparel, awards, catalog, company store fulfillment programs. (As-Pac, estab 2001, empl 203, sales $36,400,000, cert: NMSDC)

New York

1484 AIA New Dimensions in Marketing, Inc.
      124 S Central Ave
      Elmsford, NY 10523
      Contact: Maria Perex President
      Tel: 914-348-4872
      Email: perez@effectivepromos.com
      Website: www.effectivepromos.com
Promotional & specialty advertising items. (Minority, Woman, estab 1999, empl 3, sales $355,000, cert: State, WBENC)

1485 Dakota Print and Premiums LLC
      150 Barton Road
      White Plains, NY 10605
      Contact: Stuart Standard President
      Tel: 914-831-9101
      Email: stuart@fuseprinting.com
      Website: www.fuseprinting.com
Promotional products, commercial printing, wide format & transit advertising, vehicle wraps, directories, transit & marketing tools provider, screen printing, banners, posters, postcards, journals, award items, etc. (Woman/AA, estab 2004, empl 3, sales $606,000, cert: State, City, NMSDC)

1486 Don Jagoda Associates, Inc
      100 Marcus Dr
      Melville, NY 11747
      Contact: Rich Fascianella Acct Dir
      Tel: 631-454-1800
      Email: rfascianella@dja.com
      Website: www.dja.com
Full-service promotion marketing, sweepstakes, contests, instant win games, and consumer incentive, reward, and loyalty programs. (Woman, estab 1962, empl 55, sales $11,107,000, cert: WBENC)

1487 Freestyle Marketing, LLC
      362 Fifth Ave Ste 1003
      New York, NY 10001
      Contact: Caryn Stoll President
      Tel: 212-599-5995
      Email: info@freestylemktg.com
      Website: www.freestylemktg.com
Promotional marketing materials & premiums. (Woman, estab 2001, empl 40, sales $7,000,000, cert: WBENC)

1488 Innovative Premiums Inc.
      3571 Hargale Rd
      Oceanside, NY 11572
      Contact: VP
      Tel: 516-766-3800
      Email: contactus@innovativepremiums.com
      Website: www.innovativepremiums.com
Custom & standard promotional merchandise. (Woman, estab 1980, empl 14, sales $9,000,000, cert: WBENC)

1489 inQueue Designs LLC
      25 Central Park W
      New York, NY 10023
      Contact: Alison Schneiderman Co-Owner
      Tel: 917-699-8259
      Email: alison@inqueuedesigns.com
      Website: www.inQueuedesigns.com
Custom branded, designed products, stationery goods, seasonal promotions, corporate gifts, journal books, log books, die-cut folders & boxes, ipad book case, (Woman, estab 2010, empl 2, sales , cert: WBENC)

1490 KarSun Enterprises, Inc.
      1133 Broadway, Ste 1311
      New York, NY 10010
      Contact: Sung Park President
      Tel: 212-420-6688
      Email: sung@customdirectpromo.com
      Website: www.karsunenterprises.com
Promotional & merchandise bags, backpacks & duffels. (Minority, Woman, estab 1996, empl 10, sales $3,500,000, cert: NMSDC)

1491 Multi Media Promotions
      33 Southwick Court S
      Plainview, NY 11803
      Contact: FirstName LastName Managing Partner
      Tel: 516-935-0553
      Email: beth@mmpromos.com
      Website: www.mmpromos.com
Promotional advertising & premium incentives, logos, graphic design, printing, imprinting, embroidery, embossing & engraving. (Woman, estab 2004, empl 3, sales $1,200,000, cert: State, City, WBENC)

1492 National Gifts Ltd.
      6 Poole St
      Oceanside, NY 11572
      Contact: Elaine Goodman CEO
      Tel: 516-763-9000
      Email: elaine@nationalgifts.com
      Website: www.nationalgifts.com
Advertising specialities, premiums, gifts, awards, trophies, wearables, promotional items, etc. (Woman, estab 1983, empl 6, sales $12,250,000, cert: WBENC)

1493 Print & Mail Partners, Inc.
      2152 Ralph Ave Ste 317
      Brooklyn, NY 11234
      Contact: Rose Mazzone President
      Tel: 646-771-4245
      Email: rose.mazzone@theperfectpromo.com
      Website: www.theperfectpromo.com
Custom imprinted T-shirts, advertising specialties, promotional items, buttons, badges, premiums, corporate merchandise & giveaways. (Woman, estab 1997, empl 3, sales , cert: State, City)

1494 Sauerbach Associates
      1745 Merrick Ave Ste 27
      Merrick, NY 11566
      Contact: Janet Silver President
      Tel: 516-868-9650
      Email: customerservice@sauerbach.com
      Website: www.sauerbach.com
Sales incentive programs, promotional products programs, company stores, trade show marketing, new product launches, road shows, sales training meetings. (Woman, estab 1954, empl 6, sales $1,600,000, cert: WBENC)

1495 Sentec Promotions, Inc
      4367 Harlem Rd
      Amherst, NY 14226
      Contact: Susan Cataudella President
      Tel: 716-839-2294
      Email: susiespec@aol.com
      Website: www.susiespecialties.com
Promotional products.
 (Woman, estab 1994, empl 3, sales $1,090,404, cert: WBENC)

1496 United Print Group, Inc.
      36-36 33rd St
      Long Island City, NY 11106
      Contact: Bob Sanchez President
      Tel: 718-392-4242
      Email: rsanchez@unitedpg.com
      Website: www.unitedpg.com
Promotional products, commerical printing, signage & table skirts. (Hisp, estab , empl , sales $6,000,000, cert: NMSDC)

1497 Von Pok & Chang
      60 E 42 St, Ste 666
      New York, NY 10165
      Contact: Peter Sebastian Sales
      Tel: 212-599-0556
      Email: peter.sebastian@vonpok.com
      Website: www.vonpok.com
Contract mfr & import promotional products. (As-Pac, estab 1981, empl 8, sales , cert: NMSDC)

Ohio

1498 Airmate Company
16280 County Rd D
Bryan, OH 43506
Contact: Carol Czech President
Tel: 419-636-3184
Email: carol@airmatecompany.com
Website: www.airmatecompany.com
Safety signs, promotional products, custom fabrication, custom printing. (Woman, estab 1946, empl 35, sales $4,200,000, cert: WBENC)

1499 Arrasmith Promotions LLC
6115 Wiehe Rd
Cincinnati, OH 45237
Contact: Jerry Arrasmith Jr. President
Tel: 513-681-9400
Email: sales@arrasmithpromotions.com
Website: www.arrasmithpromotions.com
Advertising specialties & promotional items. (Woman, estab 2003, empl 6, sales $2,100,000, cert: WBENC)

1500 Bouzounis LLC dba Artina Promotional Products
50 S Liberty St Ste 250
Powell, OH 43065
Contact: Lesley Jennings Sr Acct Exec
Tel: 614-635-8865
Email: ljennings@artina.com
Website: www.artina.com
Promotional products. (Woman, estab 1967, empl 22, sales $4,353,500, cert: WBENC)

1501 Eat It Read It Placemats
45 W Main St
McConnelsville, OH 43756
Contact: Heather Hill CEO
Tel: 740-962-6899
Email: hbhill@ergraphics.com
Website: www.ergraphics.com
Advertising specialties, apparel, uniforms, signs, website design, printing. (Woman/AA, estab 2001, empl 3, sales $175,000, cert: State)

1502 EB ART EB ADS LLC
9045 Spooky Ridge Ln
Cincinnati, OH 45242
Contact: Eileen Bloustein CEO
Tel: 513-405-6469
Email: sales@ebartebads.com
Website: www.ebartebads.com
Dist promotional products: corporate awards, portraits, limited editions giclee, digital art & sculpture. (Woman, estab 1999, empl 1, sales , cert: WBENC)

1503 Global Promotions & Incentives, LLC
3375 Gilchrist Rd
Mogadore, OH 44260
Contact: Jonathan Thornton Reg Dir, Key Accts
Tel: 330-798-5175
Email: jdthornton@aswglobal.com
Website: www.shopglobalpai.com/
Promotional & incentive products, programs & event planning. (AA, estab 2002, empl 31, sales $5,500,000, cert: NMSDC)

1504 Ketterer Company
12110 Ellington Ct
Cincinnati, OH 45249
Contact: Kimberly W. Ketterer CEO
Tel: 513-247-0100
Email: kim_ketterer@kettererco.com
Website: www.getLOGOstuff.com
Promotional advertising: logo design, graphic art, warehousing, distribution & fulfillment services, company stores & online rewards programs. (Woman, estab 1955, empl 6, sales $3,609,077, cert: WBENC)

1505 Leader Promotions, Inc.
790 E Johnstown Rd
Columbus, OH 43230
Contact: Stephanie Leader CEO
Tel: 614-416-6565
Email: supplierdiversity@leaderpromos.com
Website: www.leaderpromos.com
Fulfillment programs, corporate apparel, promotional products & uniforms. (Woman, estab 1995, empl 105, sales $50,000,000, cert: WBENC)

1506 LIZard Apparel & Promotions
775 Congress Park Dr
Dayton, OH 45459
Contact: Kelly Davis VP Sales
Tel: 937-848-7100
Email: kelly@lizardap.com
Website: www.lizardap.com
Promotional, recognition & rewards programs, uniform fittings, Shoe programs, Uniform accessories, name badges, stethoscopes, scissors, arm sleeves. (Woman, estab 2013, empl 10, sales $1,231,824, cert: WBENC)

1507 Outreach Promotional Solutions
111 Liberty St Ste 101
Columbus, OH 43215
Contact: Nevin Bansal President
Tel: 216-452-5319
Email: bansal@outreachpromos.com
Website: www.outreachpromos.com
Provides creative promotional product solutions. (As-Ind, estab 2012, empl 12, sales $1,000,000, cert: State)

1508 Palmer Promotions
5245 Indian Run
Cincinnati, OH 45243
Contact: Steven Palmer Owner
Tel: 800-697-0053
Email: steve@palmerpromotions.com
Website: www.palmerpromotions.com
Promotional products, awards, business gifts & decorated apparel. (As-Pac, estab 1983, empl 2, sales $578,066, cert: NMSDC)

1509 Park Place Services
8800 E Pleasant Valley Rd
Cleveland, OH 44131
Contact: Bill Byrne President
Tel: 216-520-8400
Email: bbyrne@proforma.com
Website: www.proforma.com/parkplace
Printing, Promotional products, Corporate Apparel, Marketing literature, Packaging, Trade Show Supplies & giveaways, Business Forms, labels, envelopes. (Woman, estab 1996, empl 700, sales $500,000,000, cert: NWBOC)

1510   Proforma Albrecht & Co.
       1040 Technecenter Dr
       Milford, OH 45150
       Contact: Suzette Albrecht
       Tel: 202-237-2828
       Email: suzette@albrechtco.com
       Website: www.albrechtco.com
Promotional products, tees & clothing, custom logos &
designs, decorated corporate gifts. (Woman, estab 1999,
empl 150, sales $2,200,000, cert: WBENC)

1511   Proforma Joe Thomas Group
       13500 Pearl Rd, Ste 139-107
       Cleveland, OH 44136
       Contact: Joe Thomas President
       Tel: 440-268-0881
       Email: joe@proformajoethomasgroup.com
       Website: www.proformajoethomasgroup.com
Advertising specialties. (As-Ind, estab 1999, empl 2, sales
$1,123,000, cert: NMSDC)

1512   PromoHits! Ltd.
       141B N Main St
       Bluffton, OH 45817
       Contact: Melinda Bowden Owner
       Tel: 419-358-0700
       Email: mbowden@wcoil.com
       Website: www.promohitsltd.com
Promotional items: gift & specialty baskets, jackets,
shirts, sweatshirts, pants, hats, windshirts, mousepads,
pencil holders, pens, paperclips, USB drives, flash drives/
memory drives. (Woman, estab 2000, empl 4, sales
$382,780, cert: WBENC)

1513   Promotions Etc., LLC
       5000 Acme Dr. Unit A
       Fairfield, OH 45014
       Contact: Julie Holderbach CEO
       Tel: 513-795-7021
       Email: julie@mypromotionsetc.com
       Website: www.mypromotionsetc.com
Promotional products: apparel & uniforms, corporate
gifts, give-a-ways, awards, engraved items, decals, labels,
trade show give-a-ways, booth display & signage.
(Woman, estab 2012, empl 2, sales $125,000, cert: State)

1514   Race Ahead
       7100 Euclid Ave Ste 175
       Cleveland, OH 44103
       Contact: Beth Eaton President
       Tel: 440-554-7018
       Email: beth@raceaheadcle.com
       Website: www.raceaheadcle.com
Customized apparel & branded accessories. (Woman,
estab 2016, empl 1, sales $260,000, cert: City)

1515   RJ Manray - Promotional Products
       9500 Springfield Rd, Unit 5
       Poland, OH 44514
       Contact: Rowena Henderson CEO
       Tel: 234-201-0160
       Email: rrlimos18@gmail.com
       Website: www.rjmanray.com/
Dist personalized and custom logo tote bags. (Woman,
estab 1986, empl 11, sales $640,000, cert: WBENC)

1516   Schaffer Partners, Inc.
       6545 Carnegie Ave
       Cleveland, OH 44103
       Contact: Susan Mayrant VP Business Dev
       Tel: 863-299-6392
       Email: susan.mayrant@spihq.com
       Website: www.pfi-awards.com
Incentive merchandise fulfillment & program administration resources, design & manage online & paper
based solutions, brand name merchandise awards,
travel rewards & event tickets. (Woman, estab 1968,
empl 40, sales $10,017,858, cert: WBENC)

1517   Ten 10 Design LLC
       119 Main St
       Chardon, OH 44024
       Contact: Casey Zulandt Owner
       Tel: 440-286-4367
       Email: casey@ten10design.com
       Website: www.ten10design.com
Printing (offset and digital), promotional items, ad
specialties, mailing services, labels & decals,
graphic design, web design. (Woman/AA, estab 2009,
empl 5, sales $3,093,663, cert: State, NMSDC, WBENC)

1518   The AG Group, Inc. dba AG PrintPromo Solutions
       960 Graham Rd, Ste 1
       Cuyahoga Falls, OH 44221
       Contact: Anup Gupta President
       Tel: 330-315-9600
       Email: agupta@theaggroup.com
       Website: www.theaggroup.com
Dist promotional products, gifts, corporate apparel,
embroidered & screen printed. (Minority, Woman, estab
1996, empl 5, sales $3,300,000, cert: State)

1519   The Callard Company
       811 Green Crest Dr Ste 300
       Westerville, OH 43081
       Contact: Robin Welch Acct Exec
       Tel: 614-933-0303
       Email: rwelch@callard.com
       Website: www.callard.com
Promotional products & creative marketing: awards,
trade show giveaways, team rewards, client gifts,
recruitment incentives & golf outing supplies. (Woman,
estab 1987, empl 24, sales , cert: WBENC)

1520   The John K. Howe Company, Inc.
       7188 Main St
       Cincinnati, OH 45244
       Contact: CEO
       Tel: 513-651-1888
       Email: salesinfo@ehowe.com
       Website: www.ehowe.com
Branded apparel, promotional products & business
recognition. (Woman, estab 1972, empl 10, sales
$2,232,110, cert: WBENC)

1521   Vorce & Associates
       1335 Dublin Rd Ste 216C
       Columbus, OH 43215
       Contact: Donna Vorce Owner
       Tel: 614-488-5450
       Email: donna@firstimpressionsohio.com
       Website: www.firstimpressionsohio.com
Promotional & imprinted apparel. (Woman, estab 1983,
empl 2, sales $810,000, cert: State)

Oregon

1522 Enthusias Media Group
      1631 NE Broadway, Ste 614
      Portland, OR 97232
      Contact: Marcy Hall Reg acct Mgr
      Tel: 503-376-6839
      Email: info@enthusiastmediagroup.com
      Website: www.enthusiastmediagroup.com
Promotional & print items. (Woman, estab 2005, empl 7,
sales $2,000,000, cert: State)

Pennsylvania

1523 As You Wish Promotions
      3801 Germantown Pike Ste 202
      Collegeville, PA 19426
      Contact: Alyssa Heininger Client Relationship Coord
      Tel: 484-973-6565
      Email: aheininger@wishpromo.com
      Website: www.wishpromo.com
Promotional products, graphic arts capabilities, marketing,
service, client support & customer relations, trade show
give-aways, corporate gifts, promotional apparel &
employee awards. (Woman, estab 1992, empl 5, sales
$1,913,640, cert: WBENC)

1524 BDJ Ventures, LLC
      3024 Bainbridge Dr
      Lansdale, PA 19446
      Contact: Bernard Wright Principal
      Tel: 215-266-2062
      Email: bwright@bdjventuresllc.com
      Website: www.bdjventuresllc.com
Premiums & promotional products. (AA, estab 2009, empl
3, sales , cert: State, NMSDC)

1525 Bry-Lex Promotional LLC
      19 Nelson Dr
      Southampton, PA 18966
      Contact: Bev Kaytes CEO
      Tel: 800-251-9101
      Email: bev@brylex.com
      Website: www.bry-lex.com
Promotional items, imprinted logos, blank logos, embroi-
dery/silkscreen. (Woman, estab 1996, empl 11, sales
$550,000, cert: State, WBENC)

1526 Carol Philp Inc
      336 1st St
      Pittsburgh, PA 15215
      Contact: Carol Philp President
      Tel: 412-782-2675
      Email: info@cpicreative.com
      Website: www.cpicreative.com
Design & fulfil custom programs: service awards, safety,
sales incentives, fundraising, trade shows, education,
product introduction, ad specialties & innovative products.
(Woman, estab 1994, empl 5, sales $3,370,160, cert:
WBENC)

1527 Diversified Business Consultants, Inc.
      1009 Sage Rd
      West Chester, PA 19382
      Contact: President
      Tel: 610-692-3600
      Email: jerry@DiversifiedCorp.com
      Website: www.diversifiedcorp.com
Promotional products & printing services. (Woman/As-Ind,
estab 2000, empl 4, sales , cert: WBENC)

1528 Signature Promotions
      715 Twining Road Ste 107
      Dresher, PA 19025
      Contact: Maureen Coffey Owner
      Tel: 215-641-1168
      Email: sigpro@comcast.net
      Website: www.sigpromo.com
Promotional advertising products, grahic design, product
development & fulfillment capabilities. (Woman, estab
1992, empl 1, sales , cert: WBENC)

1529 The Jay Group
      700 Indian Springs Dr
      Lancaster, PA 17601
      Contact: Nicole Sensenig Administrative Asst
      Tel: 717-285-6200
      Email: nicole.sensenig@jaygroup.com
      Website: www.jaygroup.com
Product, literature & catalog fulfillment services,
inbound call center, customer service support, co-
packing, promotional processing, information technology, sampling services, promotional products, e-business
solutions. (Woman, estab 1965, empl 300, sales
$25,887,011, cert: WBENC)

Rhode Island

1530 Ahlers Designs, Inc.
      999 Main St, Unit 707
      Pawtucket, RI 02860
      Contact: Gail Ahlers CEO
      Tel: 401-365-1010
      Email: operations@ahlersdesigns.com
      Website: www.ahlersdesigns.com
Designs & mfr custom corporate gifts & awards, engraving, custom cards or packaging. (Woman, estab 1989,
empl 3, sales $132,751, cert: State, WBENC)

South Carolina

1531 2 Oceans Promotions, LLC
      6175 Caravelle Court
      Awendaw, SC 29429
      Contact: Michele Johnson Owner
      Tel: 843-971-8499
      Email: michele@2oceanspromotions.com
      Website: www.2oceanspromotions.com
Promotional marketing & products. (Woman, estab
2001, empl 6, sales , cert: WBENC)

1532 Promotions Unlimited, LLC
      327 Miller Rd, Ste E
      Mauldin, SC 29662
      Contact: Jo Dir of Sales
      Tel: 864-527-1193
      Email: jo@promoultd.com
      Website: www.promoultd.com
Promotional Items, Uniform Programs (Woman, estab
2005, empl 9, sales $2,254,086, cert: State, WBENC)

1533 Pueri Elemental LLC dba Bonk Fit
      412 Hwy 90 E
      Little River, SC 29566
      Contact: Donna Brin Managing Member
      Tel: 866-639-1430
      Email: donna@bfive40.com
      Website: www.bfive40.com
Digital printer and full-service sew and embroidery
operation, offering sustainable solutions for apparel,
uniforms and printed signage, especially designed to
minimize environmental impact, with a mission of net
zero waste. (Woman, estab 2014, empl 14, sales
$1,250,000, cert: WBENC)

1534   Red Iron Brand Solutions, LLC
       104 Saluda Run Dr
       Piedmont, SC 29673
       Contact: Vishnu Jampala Owner
       Tel: 800-325-3824
       Email: vishnujam@rwts.net
       Website: www.redironbrand.com
Mfr & import event display items: Tablecovers & runners
in stretch fabric, polyester, polyvalue, plastic (cut table
covers and imprinted banquet rolls), and 400 denier.
(Woman, estab 2016, empl 10, sales , cert: State, WBENC)

Tennessee

1535   Imagination Specialties, Inc.
       623 Old Hickory Blvd.
       Old Hickory, TN 37138
       Contact: Lori Armes Controller
       Tel: 615-255-5688
       Email: loria@imaginationbranding.com
       Website: www.imaginationbranding.com
Ad specialty & promotional products, corporate gifts,
baskets, event planning, event room drops, custom
printing, invitations, mail outs, online company stores,
warehousing, distribution & fulfillment services. (Woman,
estab 1989, empl 39, sales $11,275,000, cert: WBENC)

1536   Signet, Inc.
       1801 N Shelby Oaks Dr, Ste 12
       Memphis, TN 38134
       Contact: Elizabeth Tate CEO
       Tel: 901-387-5555
       Email: etate@gosignet.com
       Website: www.gosignet.com
Promotional products, branding, kitting, warehousing,
event management. (Woman, estab 0, empl , sales
$11,000,000, cert: WBENC)

1537   The Barr Group, Inc.
       230 Great Circle Road, Ste 234
       Nashville, TN 37228
       Contact: Jim Barr Dir of Sales
       Tel: 615-612-0444
       Email: jim@barrgroupinc.com
       Website: www.barrgroupinc.com
Promotional products, printing, indoor & outdoor signage,
corrugated packagin, MRO items, transportation brokerage
& hauling. (Minority, Woman, estab 1999, empl 6, sales
$2,505,000, cert: WBENC)

Texas

1538   Ad-Image Creative Promotions Co.
       851 Lakeview Dr
       Coppell, TX 75019
       Contact: Terri Finazzo President
       Tel: 972-462-0919
       Email: adimagedallas@aol.com
       Website: www.adimagedallas.com
Advertising specialties & promotional products. (Woman,
estab 1999, empl 2, sales , cert: State, WBENC)

1539   Austin Ad Group
       5960 W Parker Rd, Ste 278
       Plano, TX 75093
       Contact: Rhonda Aicklen President
       Tel: 972-307-7100
       Email: orders@austinadgroup.com
       Website: www.AustinAdGroup.com
Promotional logo/branded items: apparel, pens, bags,
hats, cups, trinkets, coolers, armbands, badges, etc.
(Woman, estab 1993, empl 7, sales , cert: State)

1540   Aztec Promotional Group, LP
       2815 Manor Rd
       Austin, TX 78722
       Contact: Patti Winstanley President
       Tel: 512-744-0195
       Email: patti@aztecworld.com
       Website: www.aztecworld.com
Sscreen printed & embroidered textiles, advertising
specialty items & design. (Woman/AA, estab 1995,
empl 25, sales $1,350,000, cert: State, WBENC)

1541   Beehive Specialty Co.
       8701 Wall St, Ste 900
       Austin, TX 78754
       Contact: Kelli Dillon Mgr/new business dept
       Tel: 512-912-7940
       Email: kelli@specialbee.com
       Website: www.beehivespecialty.com
Promotional products, custom product fabrication, online programs, high impact mail, packaging, fulfillment
& integrated project management. (Woman, estab
1998, empl 12, sales $8,000,000, cert: WBENC)

1542   Cadena Specialty Advertising
       PO Box 150655
       Arlington, TX 76015
       Contact: Olga Quiroz Owner
       Tel: 817-459-4474
       Email: olga_cadenaspecialty@yahoo.com
       Website: www.cadenausa.com
Dist promotional marketing products: pens, cups, key
tags, calendars, silkscreened & embroidered caps &
apparel, employee recognition & safety awards & gifts.
(Woman/Hisp estab 1993, empl 1, sales $155,000, cert:
State, City)

1543   CFJ Manufacturing
       701 Eight Twenty Blvd. Ste 145
       Fort Worth, TX 76106
       Contact: Sharon Evans CEO
       Tel: 817-625-9559
       Email: marketing@cfjmfg.com
       Website: www.cfjmfg.com
Promotional marketing & employee recognition
solutions. (Woman, estab 1983, empl 201, sales
$50,000,000, cert: WBENC)

1544   Creative Menus & Folders, LLC dba Texas Covers
       409 Old Hwy 80
       Olden, TX 76466
       Contact: Renee Forguson Asst Production Mgr
       Tel: 254-653-2775
       Email: reneeforguson@texascovers.com
       Website: www.texascovers.com
Presentation/Executive Binders, folders, business cards,
printing (screen, digital, offset, foil stamp, deboss,
specialty color cast printing, plastic ID badge holders, ID
badges, name tags, souvenir printing, banners, signage,
laminating, caps. (As-Pac, estab 2015, empl 19, sales ,
cert: NMSDC)

1545   Davis & Stanton, Inc.
       4002 W Miller Rd, Ste 140
       Garland, TX 75041
       Contact: Charlee Castillo Owner
       Tel: 214-340-1321
       Email: charlee@davstan.com
       Website: www.davstan.com
Advertising specialties, promotional products, plaques
& awards & police commendation bars. (Minority,
Woman, estab 1949, empl 26, sales $5,000,000, cert:
State, WBENC)

1546 DBS Marketing & Promotions LLC
      24466 Pipestem Dr
      Magnolia, TX 77355
      Contact: Sue Becknell President
      Tel: 281-356-2386
      Email: sue@dbspromo.com
      Website: www.dbspromo.com
Logo branded promotional products, corporate apparel,
awards, pens, notepads, shirts, caps, jackets, screen
printing, laser engraving, embroidery, pad folios, backpacks, duffel bags, flyers, etc. (Woman, estab 2005, empl
3, sales $1,230,000, cert: WBENC)

1547 Distinctive Marketing Ideas
      3415 Custer Rd, Ste 133
      Plano, TX 75023
      Contact: Bonnie Shackelford Owner
      Tel: 972-612-0050
      Email: bonnie.shack@dmipromotions.com
      Website: www.dmipromotions.com
Promotional productss/premiums, warehouse & fulfill-
ment. (Woman, estab 1992, empl 4, sales $1,750,000, cert:
State, WBENC)

1548 Fuel7 Inc.
      11910 Greenville Ave, Ste 275
      Dallas, TX 75243
      Contact: Steven Pratt
      Tel: 888-669-4009
      Email: steven@fuel7.com
      Website: www.fuel7.com
Fuel7 provides embedded development services, both
hardware and software, specializing in new embedded
Linux projects. From design and architecture through
development and board bringup (Hisp, estab 2004, empl
12, sales $2,200,000, cert: NMSDC)

1549 Graves Group Promotions
      3851 Camp Bowie Blvd Ste 300
      Fort Worth, TX 76107
      Contact: President
      Tel: 817-738-8446
      Email: info@gravesgroup.com
      Website: www.gravesgroup.com
Custom promotional products: apparel, awards, novelty,
golf, computer, sports & leisure items. (Woman, estab
1997, empl 4, sales , cert: WBENC)

1550 Henya Direct LLC
      5555 W University Blvd
      Dallas, TX 75209
      Contact: Terence Johnson Natl Accts Mgr
      Tel: 214-701-0671
      Email: tjohnson@henyadirect.com
      Website: www.henyadirect.com
Promotional merchandise: uniforms, hats, cups, stress
balls, pens, bags, watches, etc. (Woman, estab 2007, empl
3, sales $1,500,000, cert: WBENC)

1551 Holden Custom Products
      7920 Beltline Rd Ste 960
      Dallas, TX 75254
      Contact: Marnie Holden Dir Major Accounts
      Tel: 214-543-1133
      Email: holdenll@flash.net
      Website: www.holdenbrand.com
Corporate packaging, promotional products, imports &
wearables. (Woman, estab 1978, empl 16, sales
$9,500,000, cert: State)

1552 I Chispa, LLC
      129 Thunderbird
      El Paso, TX 79912
      Contact: Horacio Arras VP Sales & Mktg
      Tel: 915-239-7430
      Email: horacio@ichispa.us
      Website: www.ichispa.us
Promotional & sports items. (Minority, Woman, estab
2010, empl 5, sales , cert: State, NMSDC)

1553 IncentiveAmerica, Inc.
      18208 Preston Rd Ste D924
      Dallas, TX 75252
      Contact: Elizabeth Montgomery President
      Tel: 972-380-9990
      Email: elizabethm@incentiveamerica.com
      Website: www.incentiveamerica.com
Pre-paid MasterCard gift cards & dining gift cards,
personalized, premium note card & gold-embossed
greeting card. (Woman/AA, estab , empl , sales
$968,290, cert: State, NMSDC, 8(a))

1554 Insignia Marketing
      32731 Egypt Lane Ste 301
      Magnolia, TX 77354
      Contact: Christine McAtee President
      Tel: 281-465-0040
      Email: orders@visicare.com
      Website: www.VisiCare.com
Promotional advertising: corporate brand identity,
creativity, pens, coffee mugs, t-shirts & awards.
(Woman, estab 2002, empl 3, sales $2,000,000, cert:
State, WBENC)

1555 Malkoff Promotions
      4904 Stony Ford Dr
      Dallas, TX 75287
      Contact: Lynne Malkoff President
      Tel: 972-248-4354
      Email: lynne@lmpspecialties.com
      Website: www.lmpspecialties.com
Marketing & promotional solutions. (Woman, estab
1989, empl 5, sales , cert: State, WBENC)

1556 Network Embroidery Inc.
      10600 Shadow Wood Dr Ste 201
      Houston, TX 77043
      Contact: Lily Clark President
      Tel: 713-865-8032
      Email: micael.shea@networkinterstateco.com
      Website: www.networkinterstateco.com
Mfr & dist promotional products, catalog programs,
awards, trophies, graphics, warehousing & fulfillment.
(Woman, estab 0, empl , sales , cert: WBENC)

1557 Potenza Promotions, LLC
      810 Genoa
      Argyle, TX 76226
      Contact: Laura Hulke President
      Tel: 940-595-9555
      Email: lhulke@potenzapromotions.com
      Website: www.potenzapromotions.com
Promotional products: mugs, pens, stress balls, awards,
office items, USB pens, etc. (Woman, estab 2006, empl
6, sales $147,000, cert: State)

1558 Power Of Two Productions, LLC
9901 Brodie Ln, Ste 160-279
Austin, TX 78748
Contact: LeeAnn Wick CEO
Tel: 512-872-5000
Email: leeann@ptwopromo.com
Website: www.PTwoPromo.com
Promotional products, business gifts, trade show give-aways, wellness programs, incentives, awards, safety, screen printing, embroidery, apparel, employee retention, sustainable, eco friendly, tote bags, promotions. (Minority, Woman, estab 2007, empl 3, sales $419,000, cert: State, NMSDC, WBENC)

1559 Radia Enterprises Inc.
3800 Juniper St
Houston, TX 77087
Contact: Rupendra Radia CEO
Tel: 713-645-6383
Email: rradia56@gmail.com
Website: www.spectrumuniforms.com
Uniforms and promotional products. (As-Ind, estab 1992, empl 20, sales $3,500,000, cert: NMSDC)

1560 RG Apparel Co.
2912 N MacArthur, Ste 103
Irving, TX 75062
Contact: Joe Temple COO
Tel: 972-793-0583
Email: jt@rgapparel.com
Website: www.rgapparel.com
Mfr textiles: uniforms, work shirts, polos, tees, woven button up shirts & headwear, promotional marketing items & gifts. (AA, estab 2006, empl 6, sales $3,200,000, cert: State, NMSDC)

1561 The Donna Bender Company
6860 North Dallas Pkwy Ste 200
Plano, TX 75024
Contact: Donna Bender President
Tel: 214-520-8577
Email: donna@donnaco.com
Website: www.donnaco.com
Promotional products; specialty advertising; business gifts; service, achievement & recognition awards; incentive & awareness programs. (Woman, estab 2007, empl 3, sales , cert: State, WBENC)

1562 TLC Adcentives LLC
21101 Kingsland Blvd. Ste. 1113
Katy, TX 77450
Contact: Terri Hornsby President
Tel: 281-828-2270
Email: terri@tlcadcentives.com
Website: www.tlcadcentives.com
Promotional incentives, awards & trophies, cups & mugs, apparel & headgear, desk accessories, writing instruments, portfolios, briefcases. (Woman/AA, estab 1995, empl 4, sales $175,000, cert: State, NMSDC, WBENC)

1563 Trademarks Promotional Products
11333 Todd St
Houston, TX 77055
Contact: Kelli Cochran Acct Mgr
Tel: 713-680-3000
Email: tpp@tmarks.com
Website: www.trademarkspromos.com
Promotional products, screenprinting, embroidery, direct digital garment printing, graphic design, award engraving, ad specialty items. (Woman, estab 1979, empl 60, sales $7,100,001, cert: State, WBENC)

1564 Trinity Enterprise Group LLC
400 S Zang Blvd, Ste 240
Dallas, TX 75208
Contact: Casey Gonzales COO
Tel: 214-785-6741
Email: casey@tegroup.biz
Website: www.tegroup.biz
Advertising items, Apparel, Uniforms, Hats, Gifts, Trophies, Awards, Nameplates, PPE, Sports Bags, Pens, Business Supplies, Technology items, Signage, and Custom ordered goods. (Hisp, estab 2020, empl 5, sales , cert: NMSDC)

1565 W. M. Martin Advertising
PO Box 795818
Dallas, TX 75379
Contact: Wendy Fahle Owner
Tel: 972-732-8040
Email: cs@wmmadv.com
Website: www.wmmadv.com
Advertising specialties: pens, shirts, caps, calendars, golf items. (Woman, estab 1983, empl 4, sales $850,000, cert: State, WBENC)

Virginia

1566 E&R Sales Inc.
4800 Market Square Lane
Midlothian, VA 23112
Contact: Elissa Mast President
Tel: 804-744-8000
Email: headcoach@ersales.com
Website: www.ersales.com
Balloons, pens and novelty trend items. (Minority, Woman, estab , empl , sales , cert: WBENC)

1567 Fishnet, LLC
PO Box 7311
Charlottesville, VA 22906
Contact: David Goloversic Sr Acct Exec
Tel: 434-409-6177
Email: contactus@fishnetllc.com
Website: www.fishnetllc.com
Printing & promotional products: writing instruments, office accessories, food and drink ware, doormats, banners, flags, tents, table covers, displays, retractors, bags, health and safety items, coloring books, business cards. (Minority, Woman, estab 2006, empl 2, sales , cert: State)

1568 Global Partner's of Virginia, LLC
3005 E Boundary Terr, Ste G
Midlothian, VA 23112
Contact: Norm Falkner VP
Tel: 804-744-8112
Email: logos@globalpromosonline.com
Website: www.globalpromosonline.com
Logo wear, embroidery, silk screen, screen printing, direct to garment ink jet printing, heat transfer. Corporate apparel, mens, ladies, kids, uniforms. Promotional Products, pens, magnets, calendars, Bags, towels, luggage, sportwear, team uniforms. (Woman, estab 2001, empl 4, sales $350,000, cert: State)

1569 It's A Breeze Specialties, LLC
8221 Little Florida Rd
Mechanicsville, VA 23111
Contact: Shirley Husz President
Tel: 804-779-0183
Email: shirley@itsabreez.com
Website: www.itsabreez.com
Promotional products, corporate apparel, screen printed &
embroidered, awards, incentives & award programs.
(Woman, estab 2002, empl 2, sales $140,000, cert: State)

1570 Rivanna Natural Designs, Inc.
3009 Lincoln Ave
Richmond, VA 23228
Contact: Crystal Mario President
Tel: 434-244-3447
Email: cmario@rivannadesigns.com
Website: www.rivannadesigns.com
Environmentally responsible gifts, plaques & awards.
(Woman, estab , empl , sales , cert: State)

1571 The Advertising Specialist, L.C.
PO Box 5325
Midlothian, VA 23112
Contact: Jeanette Mayo President
Tel: 804-744-0044
Email: advertisingspecialist@verizon.net
Website: www.advertisingspecialist.com
Promotional products, banners, sport uniforms, T-Shirts,
Website Design, Screen Printing & Embroidery. (Woman/
AA, estab 1997, empl 3, sales , cert: State)

Washington

1572 Brand|Pride
6523 California Ave SW, Ste 329
Seattle, WA 98136
Contact: Elise Lindborg CEO
Tel: 206-938-8828
Email: glittertheunicorn@brand-pride.com
Website: www.brand-pride.com
Promotional products. (Woman, estab 2000, empl 3, sales
$1,100,000, cert: CPUC, WBENC)

1573 Bravo! Promotional Products
569 Occidental Ave S
Seattle, WA 98104
Contact: Peggie Dickens President
Tel: 206-682-3953
Email: peggie@bravobranding.com
Website: www.bravobranding.com
Offshore sourcing, fulfillment services, creative art
services, event fulfillment. (Woman, estab 1995, empl 12,
sales $5,969,545, cert: WBENC)

1574 Gifts by Design, Inc.
66 S Hanford St Ste 100
Seattle, WA 98134
Contact: Andy Sroufe Acct Exec
Tel: 206-286-6688
Email: andy@giftsbydesign.net
Website: www.giftsbydesign.net
Dist art objects, wearables, logo items, awards, baskets,
etc. (Woman, estab 1988, empl 11, sales $2,950,000, cert:
WBENC)

1575 Unique Experience Custom Embroidery & Screen-
Print
234 First St
Bremerton, WA 98337
Contact: Ronald Flemister Mgr
Tel: 360-373-2076
Email: un234@silverlink.net
Website: www.companycasuals.com/
uniqueexperience
Custom embroidery, screen printing & promotional
products. (Woman/AA, estab 1990, empl 3, sales
$250,000, cert: State)

Wisconsin

1576 A Branovan Company, LLC.
6505 W Calumet Rd
Milwaukee, WI 53223
Contact: Marie Branovan CEO
Tel: 414-352-5000
Email: marie@abcgifts.com
Website: www.abcgifts.com
Advertising specilties: custom embroidery & screen
printing apparel. (Woman, estab 1996, empl 12, sales
$3,712,200, cert: WBENC)

1577 Actualink Designs LLC
N65W12525 Sycamore Ln
Menomonee Falls, WI 53051
Contact: Anthony Martin Owner
Tel: 414-349-4367
Email: info@actualinkdesigns.com
Website: www.actualinkdesigns.com
Embroidery, screen printing & digital printing, polo
shirts, caps, graphic design studio. (AA, estab 2012, empl
3, sales , cert: NMSDC)

1578 Madison Avenue Worldwide, LLC
5515 Catfish Court
Westport, WI 53597
Contact: Donna Smith Business Mgr
Tel: 608-850-9663
Email:
donna.smith@madisonavenueworldwide.com
Website: www.madisonavenueworldwide.com
Promotional & marketing agency. (Woman, estab 2008,
empl 8, sales $2,100,000, cert: WBENC)

1579 on3 Promotional Partners, LLC
1543 Sheridan Rd
Kenosha, WI 53140
Contact: Lora Lehmann Owner
Tel: 262-551-8715
Email: llehmann@on3promopartners.com
Website: www.on3promopartners.com
Promotional products, incentive & loyalty programs,
fulfillment, packaging & collateral print needs. (Woman,
estab 2005, empl 6, sales $1,850,000, cert: State,
WBENC)

1580 Promolux Inc.
      6027 W Vliet St
      Milwaukee, WI 53213
      Contact: CEO
      Tel: 414-771-1831
      Email: sales@epromolux.com
      Website: www.epromolux.com
Dist promotional products: screen printed & embroidered
apparel, employee uniforms, trade show giveaways,
customer loyalty programs, custom souvenirs & gifts, sales
incentives, corporate identity programs, marketing
premiums, etc. (Woman, estab 2003, empl 6, sales , cert:
WBENC)

1581 Royal Recognition, Inc.
      S83 W19105 Saturn Dr
      Muskego, WI 53150
      Contact: Joseph Cull VP
      Tel: 262-679-6050
      Email: jcull@royalrec.com
      Website: www.royalrec.com
Employee service awads, corporate apparel, recognition/
sales awards & promotional items. (Woman, estab 1983,
empl 52, sales , cert: State)

ALARM SYSTEMS
Manufacturers or wholesalers of fire, security, intercom, CCTV, or other alarm components or systems. NAICS Code 33

Arizona

1582 American Fire Equipment
      3107 W Virginia Ave
      Phoenix, AZ 85009
      Contact: Rose Koppy Admin
      Tel: 602-433-2484
      Email: info@americanfire.com
      Website: www.americanfire.com
Sells, designs, installs, services & repairs all types of fire protection systems, special hazards fire protection, building fire alarm, mass notification, fire sprinkler, kitchen fire suppression. (Woman, estab 1992, empl 125, sales $12,331,853, cert: WBENC)

California

1583 Aponi Products and Services
      3805 Florin Rd Ste 1228
      Sacramento, CA 95823
      Contact: Lisa M Davis lacy Owner
      Tel: 916-392-6571
      Email: lisad@aponitelecommunication.com
      Website: www.aponitelecom.com
Telecommunication Equipment, Installation, Voice, Data, Cabling, Maintenance, Repair, Security System, DVR, Security Cameras. (Minority, Woman, estab 2007, empl 7, sales $360,000, cert: State, 8(a))

1584 EARL Security, Inc.
      745 E Valley Blvd, Ste 518
      San Gabriel, CA 91776
      Contact: Lynn Chen CEO
      Tel: 626-285-9178
      Email: lynn.chen@earl-security.com
      Website: www.earl-security.com
Install & maintain burglar/intrusion alarms, fire alarms, intercoms, access control closed circuit TV surveillance, metal detectors, electrical. (Minority, Woman, estab 1988, empl 6, sales $596,987, cert: CPUC)

District of Columbia

1585 MJS Communications LLC
      1343 First St NW
      Washington, DC 20001
      Contact: Marlon Boykin President
      Tel: 888-829-1658
      Email: mboykin@mjscommunications.biz
      Website: www.mjscommunications.biz
Information technology, telecommunications services, structure cabling system, voice/data cabling, CCTV cabling, POS & wireless, CCTV, digital video recorders, Interior/exterior cameras, monitors, perimeter security. (AA, estab 2009, empl 2, sales $110,000, cert: State, City)

Florida

1586 Aegis Fire and Integrated Services, LLC
      156 Industrial Loop S
      Orange Park, FL 32073
      Contact: Shelli Schmid Reg Sales
      Tel: 904-215-9669
      Email: sschmid@afps.com
      Website: www.aegisfis.com
Fire sprinkler, extinguishers & alarm systems. (As-Pac, estab 2004, empl 42, sales , cert: State, NMSDC)

1587 Audio Video Systems, Inc.
      1860 Old Okeechobee Rd, Ste 104
      West Palm Beach, FL 33409
      Contact: Angela Barnard President
      Tel: 561-686-4473
      Email: angela@cctvrepair.com
      Website: www.cctvrepair.com
Commercial audio, video & electronic security projects, sales, service, installation & integration: burglar alarm, access control, CCTV/video surveillance, commercial audio, commercial video, business class projectors & displays. (Woman, estab 1981, empl 6, sales $800,000, cert: State, City)

1588 AVI Integrators Inc. dba Security 101
      1520 N Powerline Rd
      Pompano Beach, FL 33069
      Contact: Stacy Bjork Controller
      Tel: 954-984-4282
      Email: sbjork@security101.com
      Website: www.Security101.com
Card access, Badging, CCTV, Intercom, Alarms, IP video, Wireless mesh systems. (Hisp, estab 2005, empl 37, sales $7,296,000, cert: State)

1589 Blue Wave Communications, Inc.
      8399 NW 30th Terrace
      Doral, FL 33122
      Contact: Michelle Fernandez Sales Coord
      Tel: 305-436-8886
      Email: mfernandez@bluewavemiami.com
      Website: www.bluewavemiami.com
Low Voltage Cabling, Audio Visual, CCTV/ IP Surveillance Systems, Access Control, Sound Masking/ White Noise, Wireless Installations, Nurse Call Systems (Hisp, estab , empl , sales , cert: State)

1590 Carter Brothers Security Services LLC
      1 Portofino Dr
      Pensacola Beach, FL 32561
      Contact: John F. Carter CEO
      Tel: 770-954-7010
      Email: cbregistrations@carterbrothers.com
      Website: www.carterbrothers.com
Project & program management, fire safety & security systems. (AA, estab 2019, empl 4, sales $350,000, cert: State, NMSDC)

1591 Mainstream IP Solutions, Inc.
      6905 El Dorado Dr
      Tampa, FL 33615
      Contact: Arnie Solomon Acct Mgr
      Tel: 813-549-7768
      Email: asolomon@mcsoftampa.com
      Website: www.mainstreamipsolutions.com
Electrical, structured cabling, audio-visual, security & fire
alarm systems. (AA, estab 2010, empl 5, sales $250,000,
cert: State, NMSDC, 8(a), SDB)

Georgia

1592 AAA Fire Protection Resources, Inc.
      PO Box 1122
      Lawrenceville, GA 30046
      Contact: President
      Tel: 770-963-0887
      Email:
      Website: www.aaafirepro.com
Fire Extinguisher Sales & Service, Recharging & Inspections, Emergency Exit Lighting. (Woman, estab 1982, empl
4, sales $977,756, cert: WBENC)

1593 Alliance Fire Protection Services, Inc.
      PO Box 1798
      Loganville, GA 30052
      Contact: Angie Jordan Office Mgr
      Tel: 770-554-5004
      Email: acjordan@alliancefire.com
      Website: www.alliancefire.com
Life Safety Inspections & Service, Fire Alarm, Fire Sprinkler,
Extinguishers, Hydrants, Backflows & Fire Pumps. (Woman,
estab 1999, empl 75, sales $7,768,000, cert: City, WBENC)

1594 DH Security Solutions
      303 Perimeter Center N Ste 300
      Atlanta, GA 30346
      Contact: Tina Dungy President
      Tel: 678-341-9451
      Email: tdungy@dhsecuritysolutions.com
      Website: www.dhsecuritysolutions.com
Locksmith, access control, card readers, door hardware,
door closers, electronic gates, safes, vaults, CCTV, door
repair, high security solutions. (Woman/AA, estab 2011,
empl 12, sales $510,000, cert: NWBOC)

1595 Strickland Security & Safety Solutions
      541 Tenth St NW, Ste 135
      Atlanta, GA 30318
      Contact: Robert Strickland Owner
      Tel: 800-422-9075
      Email: rob@stricklandsecurity.com
      Website: www.stricklandsecurity.com
Service & equipment replacement: CCTV & alarm systems
components. (AA, estab 2007, empl 12, sales $2,150,000,
cert: NMSDC)

Illinois

1596 Applied Controls & Contracting Services, Inc.
      537 W Taft Dr
      South Holland, IL 60473
      Contact: George Kinnison President
      Tel: 708-596-7400
      Email: gkinnison@accshome.com
      Website: www.accshome.com
Engineering design, project management & estimations,
technical analysis, emergency dispatch services installation, design security ad alarm systems, fire detection
systems, closed circuit tv system & card access. (AA,
estab 1990, empl 11, sales $1,090,522, cert: State,
NMSDC)

Indiana

1597 Geyer Fire Protection, LLC
      700 N High School Rd
      Indianapolis, IN 46214
      Contact: Rosemily Geyer
      Tel: 317-490-9357
      Email: rosemily@geyerfire.com
      Website: www.geyerfire.com
Design, install, serve & maintain fire sprinkler systems,
fire extinguishers & alarms. (Minority, Woman, estab
2011, empl 12, sales $686,733, cert: State, City, NMSDC)

Louisiana

1598 Fire Boss of Louisiana, Inc.
      7905 Hwy 90 W
      New Iberia, LA 70560
      Contact: Debra Denais Romero President
      Tel: 337-365-6729
      Email: debbie@fireboss.com
      Website: www.fireboss.com
Fire & safety protection services, DBI/SALA authorized
distributor/repair center, fire & gas detection/suppres-
sion system design, engineering & installation, commercial inspection of portable fire extinguishing systems,
foam & water systems. (Woman, estab 1975, empl ,
sales , cert: WBENC)

1599 Fire Tech Systems, Inc.
      721 N Ashley Ridge Loop
      Shreveport, LA 71106
      Contact: Linda Biernacki President
      Tel: 318-688-8800
      Email: lbiernacki@firetechsystems.com
      Website: www.firetechsystems.com
Design, install & service fire sprinkler systems, fire
suppression systems, fire extinguishers. (Woman, estab
1990, empl 85, sales , cert: WBENC)

Maryland

1600 Digital Video Solutions, Inc.
      7526 Connelley Dr Ste A
      Hanover, MD 21076
      Contact: John Webster President
      Tel: 240-547-0143
      Email: jwebster@remoteeyes.com
      Website: www.digitalvideosolutions.biz
Designs & integrate physical security systems: CCTV,
access control, alarm, public address & intercom
systems. (AA, estab 2008, empl 3, sales $302,000, cert:
State, NMSDC)

Michigan

1601   Edgewood Electrical, LLC
       3633 Michigan Ave Ste 100
       Detroit, MI 48216
       Contact: Robert Bell Sr Project Mgr
       Tel: 313-263-0440
       Email: robertb@edgewoodelectric.com
       Website: www.edgewoodelectric.com
Electrical Installations, Design/Build, Design/Assist, Fire
Alarm & Low Voltage Systems. (AA, estab 2008, empl 45,
sales $12,000,000, cert: NMSDC)

Minnesota

1602   Castle Cop Inc.
       17003 E Lake Netta Dr
       Ham Lake, MN 55304
       Contact: Barb Underdahl CEO
       Tel: 763-438-2761
       Email: castlecopinc@earthlink.net
       Website: www.castlecop.com
Dist stainless steel doorjamb reinforcing device. (Woman,
estab 2003, empl 1, sales , cert: State)

1603   Lloyd Security Incorporated
       5051 Hwy 7 Ste 270
       Minneapolis, MN 55416
       Contact: Me'Lea Connelly GM
       Tel: 612-874-9295
       Email: info@lloydsecurity.com
       Website: www.lloydsecurity.com
Installation, repair, service & monitoring of security
systems, access control, surveillance and video, perimeter
detection, safe rooms, CCTV & ballistic solutions. (Woman,
estab 2001, empl 14, sales , cert: State, City)

Missouri

1604   Mark One
       909 Troost
       Kansas City, MO 64106
       Contact: Rosana Privitera Biondo President
       Tel: 816-842-7023
       Email: rosana.priviterabiondo@markone.com
       Website: www.markone.com
General Electrical Construction, Fire Alarm, Security, CCTV,
Utilities, Lighting, Electrical Engineering, Specialty Electri-
cal Construction. (Woman, estab 1974, empl 250, sales
$40,000,000, cert: State, WBENC)

Mississippi

1605   HC Services Fire Protection
       1455 West Dr
       Laurel, MS 39440
       Contact: Sue Bridges President
       Tel: 601-399-4800
       Email: sue@hcservicesinc.com
       Website: www.hcservicesinc.com
Dist, service & install fire protection products: extinguish-
ers, fire systems, detection, fire alarms, access control,
sprinklers, Fm-200, inergen, halon & speciality hazards.
(Woman, estab 1991, empl 13, sales $13,000,000, cert:
State, City, WBENC)

North Carolina

1606   SAF Technologies, Inc.
       2032 Independence Commerce Dr Ste B
       Matthews, NC 28105
       Contact: Alan Weeks President
       Tel: 704-844-0955
       Email: alan.weeks@saftechnologies.com
       Website: www.saftechnologies.com
Install, program & maintain security Systems, fire alarm,
CCTV, surveillance & access control. (Woman, estab
2004, empl 40, sales , cert: WBENC)

1607   Video & Security Specialists
       2313 Wedgewood Dr
       Matthews, NC 28104
       Contact: Erika Gordon Partner
       Tel: 704-821-9396
       Email: egordon@carolina.rr.com
       Website: www.videoandsecurityspecialists.com
Dist electrical & security products: alarm/security
systems, fire alarm systems, structured wiring, access
control, security cameras, networking, phone system,
intercom & gates. (Woman, estab 1975, empl 7, sales
$220,866, cert: State)

New Jersey

1608   DGX, LLC
       840 Bergen Ave
       Jersey City, NJ 07306
       Contact: Sal Austin Sr VP
       Tel: 201-370-4761
       Email: Sal@dgxsecurity.com
       Website: www.dgxsecurity.com
Electronic security: dist, install & miantain video surveillance camera systems, alarm systems, access control
systems, card access readers & intercom systems. (AA,
estab 2003, empl 20, sales $15,030,000, cert: State)

Nw York

1609   ASM Security Inc.
       8003 Myrtle Ave
       Glendale, NY 11385
       Contact: Simon Ruderman President
       Tel: 718-839-6000
       Email: sruderman@asmintegrators.com
       Website: www.asmintegrators.com
Design, engineering, filing & expediting fire alarm &
security systems. (Minority, Woman, estab 2006, empl
28, sales $2,000,000, cert: State, City)

1610   Care Security Systems Inc
       9 Hemion Road
       Montebello, NY 10952
       Contact: Eli Ribowsky Acct Mgr
       Tel: 845-282-1245
       Email: eribowsky@care-inc.com
       Website: www.caresecuritysystems.com
Design, assembly, testing, installation, maintenance, and
management of high-level integrated security systems.
(Woman, estab 1987, empl 30, sales , cert: City, WBENC)

Ohio

1611 ABEL Building Systems
1185 Prairie
Cincinnati, OH 45215
Contact: Mgr
Tel: 513-772-0401
Email:
Website: www.abelbuildingsystems.com
Test, maintain, service & install fire alarm, security systems, surveillance cameras, card readers, intercom systems. (Woman/AA, estab 2000, empl 20, sales $2,000,000, cert: WBENC)

1612 Advance Federated Protection
2000 lee road #202
Cleveland Heights, OH 44118
Contact: Alan Lewis Managing General Partner
Tel: 216-321-1369
Email: afp044@aol.com
Website: www.afpsecurity.net
Low Votage Technolgy Burglar Alarm system, Surveillance Cameras-CCTV Fire System, Access Control Medal Detectors (Walk Thru), Guards/ Consulting. (AA, estab 1984, empl 9, sales $184,622, cert: State, City)

1613 Gene Ptacek & Son Fire Equipment Co, Inc.
7310 Associate Ave
Brooklyn, OH 44144
Contact: Gene Ptacek VP
Tel: 216-651-8300
Email: gene@gpsfire.com
Website: www.gpsfire.com
Fire extinguishers, fire suppression systems, Fire alarm & fire sprinkler systems, Inspections, fire extinguisher training, dist fire hose, brass adapters & nozzles. (Woman, estab 1975, empl 52, sales , cert: City)

1614 Rika Group Corporation
13701 Enterprise Ave
Cleveland, OH 44135
Contact: Ryan Temple Dir of Operations
Tel: 216-325-1006
Email: ryan@pcsurveillance.net
Website: www.pcsurveillance.net
Design, dist & install surveillance equipment & systems. (Woman, estab 2001, empl 20, sales $1,600,000, cert: City)

1615 TaiParker Consulting LLC
4020 Sara Dr
Uniontown, OH 44685
Contact: Tai Parker Owner
Tel: 330-472-2115
Email: tai@taiparkerconsulting.com
Website: www.taiparkerconsulting.com
Video Systems Installation / Monitoring / Service, Real Time Remote Video Monitoring, Remote Video Storage, Cellular Only Video Camera Solutions, WiFi / IP Video Camera Solutions, Alarm Systems Installation / Monitoring / Service. (AA, estab 2010, empl 1, sales , cert: State, NMSDC)

Pennsylvania

1616 Arora Systems Group, LLC
61 Wilmington-West Chester Pike Ste 100
Chadds Ford, PA 19317
Contact: Adam Oliver GM
Tel: 610-500-0714
Email: aoliver@arorasystemsgroup.com
Website: www.arorasystemsgroup.com
Facility Maintenance, testing, management, and code consulting, Fire Alarm testing, maintenance & repair, Fire Suppression, sprinkler system testing maintenance & repair, Hydrant, Standpipe & Fire extinguisher testing. (As-Ind, estab 2004, empl 17, sales $2,885,827, cert: City, NMSDC)

1617 Fire Fighter Sales & Service Company
791 Commonwealth Dr
Warrendale, PA 15086
Contact: Richard Malady VP
Tel: 724-720-6000
Email: rmalady@all-lines-tech.com
Website: www.firefighter-pgh.com
Alarms, sprinkler systems & fire protection. (Woman, estab 1946, empl 125, sales $12,500,000, cert: WBENC)

1618 Gabba LLC
630 W Germantown Pike Ste 120
Plymouth Meeting, PA 19462
Contact: Finance & Office Ops
Tel: 877-933-2288
Email: support@isgprotect.com
Website: www.invisionsecuritygroup.com
Security system installation. (Woman, estab 2010, empl 15, sales $3,500,000, cert: State, WBENC)

Puerto Rico

1619 Guardmax Corporation
N 20, Ste B, Fagot Ave
Ponce, PR 00716
Contact: Manuel Santana CEO
Tel: 787-806-5525
Email: manuelsantana@guardmaxpr.com
Website: www.guardmaxpr.com
Security services, security technology integration, service & maintenance, access control, asset conservation, automatic door repair & service, burglar alarms, CCTV, analog & Matrix Systems, IP Systems, Wireless IP. (Hisp, estab 2014, empl 16, sales , cert: NMSDC)

1620 One Corps, Inc
PO Box 79767
Carolina, PR 00984
Contact: Sonia Fuentes
Tel: 787-776-0062
Email: sfuentes@one-corps.com
Website: www.one-corps.com
Armed & Unarmed Security Guards, IP Monitoring Station with Patrol Response Service, Sales, Installation & Maintenance of Cameras, Access Control, Fire Watch. (Hisp, estab 2007, empl 134, sales $2,641,716, cert: NMSDC)

1621　Puerto Rico Alarm Systems, Inc.
　　　PO Box 488
　　　Dorado, PR 00646
　　　Contact: Jose Sanchez President
　　　Tel:　787-883-4587
　　　Email: jsanchez@pralarms.com
　　　Website: www.pralarms.com
Dist, install & service commercial fire, access control,
burglar, page, close circuit tv, nurse call, interlock & infant
protection systems, security alarm monitoring service &
conduits. (Hisp, estab 1997, empl 20, sales $1,823,161,
cert: NMSDC)

1622　The Security Group Corp.
　　　Urb. Villa Blanca 42 Aquamarina
　　　Caguas, PR 00725
　　　Contact: Luis Benet President
　　　Tel:　787-743-3299
　　　Email: info@securitygroupcorp.com
　　　Website: www.securitygroupcorp.com
Electronic security & automation: design, sale, installation,
programming, service & maintenance of electronic
security & automation systems. (Hisp, estab 1988, empl
18, sales $901,822, cert: NMSDC)

South Carolina

1623　Quintech Security Consultants, Inc.
　　　102 Sangaree Park Court Ste 4
　　　Summerville, SC 29483
　　　Contact: Harold Gillens President
　　　Tel:　843-695-0170
　　　Email: hgillens@quintechengineering.com
　　　Website: www.quintechengineering.com
Security risk assessments, emergency response planning,
security site surveys, surveillance system design, alarm
system design, access control systems, AV/intercom
systems. (AA, estab 1997, empl 11, sales $5,227,488, cert:
NMSDC)

Texas

1624　Action Fire Alarm and Action Automatic Sprinkler
　　　200 Sharron Dr
　　　Woodway, TX 76712
　　　Contact: Patricia Green Sales Coord
　　　Tel:　254-235-8300
　　　Email: pbreen@actionfirepros.com
　　　Website: www.actionfirepros.com
Inspect, service & install fire extinguishers, fire alarms, fire
sprinkler & backflows. (Woman, estab 1993, empl 73, sales
$9,005,218, cert: State, WBENC)

1625　Asez Inc.
　　　1716 S San Marcos, Ste 120
　　　San Antonio, TX 78207
　　　Contact: Robert Lozano CEO
　　　Tel:　210-736-6200
　　　Email: corporate@asezinc.com
　　　Website: www.asezinc.com
Armed & unarmed security officers, security systems
services, security alarm systems, fire alarm systems, access
control, closed circuit television, alarm monitoring,
intergraded system. (Hisp, estab 2000, empl 75, sales
$2,575,000, cert: State, 8(a))

1626　Champion Life Safety Solutions
　　　2701 W. Plano Pkwy Ste 500
　　　Plano, TX 75075
　　　Contact: Chuck Henderson President
　　　Tel:　972-663-5000
　　　Email:
　　　charles.henderson@championfiresecurity.com
　　　Website: www.championfiresecurity.com
Design, install, inspect & monitor fire sprinkler & other
suppression systems, fire alarm systems & security
systems for new construction, retrofit to existing
facilities. (AA, estab 2001, empl 112, sales $14,200,000,
cert: State, NMSDC)

1627　CLS Technology, Inc.
　　　5206 E 3rd St
　　　Katy, TX 77493
　　　Contact: Amber Wolfe Accounting Clerk
　　　Tel:　281-347-7973
　　　Email: monitoring@clstechnology.net
　　　Website: www.clstechnology.net
Fire alarm and sound systems, annual inspections,
installations, sound, shooter detection, temperature
taking devices, access control systems and install.
(Woman, estab 2006, empl 50, sales $8,000,000, cert:
WBENC)

1628　Laredo Technical Services, Inc.
　　　22011 Roan Bluff
　　　San Antonio, TX 78259
　　　Contact: Joseph Lukowski President
　　　Tel:　210-705-2904
　　　Email: joseph@laredotechnical.com
　　　Website: www.laredotechnical.com/
Dist SpiderTech Security perimeter detection systems.
(Hisp, estab 2007, empl 23, sales $6,210,000, cert: State,
NMSDC, 8(a))

1629　Nationwide Investigations & Security, Inc.
　　　2425 West Loop South, Ste 200
　　　Houston, TX 77027
　　　Contact: Allen G Hollimon CEO
　　　Tel:　713-297-8830
　　　Email: ahollimon@ntwinvestigations.com
　　　Website: www.ntwinvestigations.com
Security guard services, investigations, dignitary protec-
tion, communications cabling, CCTV/CATV, alarms,
automated controls, networking, home theaters. (AA,
estab 1999, empl 123, sales , cert: State, NMSDC)

1630　TotalCom Management Inc
　　　PO Box 460230
　　　San Antonio, TX 78246
　　　Contact: Moe Oroian President
　　　Tel:　210-366-1116
　　　Email: moe@totalcom-inc.com
　　　Website: www.totalcom-inc.com
Dist, install & service voice & data cabling, fire systems,
security systems, access control systems, CCTV/CATV,
cameras & DVR recording systems, alarm monitoring,
telephone systems, blown fiber. (As-Ind, estab 1994,
empl 19, sales $1,755,237, cert: State)

Virginia

1631   Quality CCTV Systems, Inc.
       3513 Gregory Pond Rd
       Richmond, VA 23236
       Contact: Dianne Rust President
       Tel: 804-276-7300
       Email: dianne@qualitycctv.net
       Website: www.qualitycctv.net
Install & maintain security systems to include: video
surveillance, CCTV, access control systems, burglar & fire
systems, etc. (Woman, estab 1989, empl 14, sales
$1,240,000, cert: State)

Wisconsin

1632   Hurt Electric Inc.
       N57 W14502 Shawn Circle
       Menomonee Falls, WI 53051
       Contact: Henry Hurt President
       Tel: 262-252-0500
       Email: hurtelectric@hotmail.com
       Website: www.hurtelectric.com
Fire alarm systems, lighting systems & controls, motor
control. (AA, estab 1996, empl 27, sales $4,500,000, cert:
State)

APPAREL

Manufacturers or wholesalers of men's and women's clothing, accessories and notions. Many firms listed are contract sewing houses. NAICS Code 54

Alabama

1633   At Work Sales Corporation
PO Box 40
Orange Beach, AL 36561
Contact: CEO
Tel: 251-981-6701
Email: online@atworkuniforms.com
Website: www.atworkuniforms.com
Mfr & dist uniform & career apparel, embroidery & screen-printing. (Woman, estab 1991, empl 58, sales 10,000,000, cert: WBENC)

California

1634   Abell Marketing Group, Inc.
15057 Avenida De Las Flores
Chino Hills, CA 91709
Contact: James Lohan Project Mgr
Tel: 909-456-8905
Email: james@abellmarketinggroup.com
Website: www.abellmarketinggroup.com
Protective clothing & medical/industrial nitrile, vinyl & latex gloves. (Woman, estab 1998, empl 2, sales 375,000, cert: WBENC)

1635   Alpha Athletics Sports LLC
220 11th St
Redlands, CA 92374
Contact: Juan Ramirez Owner
Tel: 909-747-7707
Email: Owner@AgloveAbove.com
Website: www.alphaathletics.net
Design, mfr & dist AAA high performanace sport gloves & apparel for men, women and youth. (Hisp, estab 2019, empl 1, sales , cert: State)

1636   Blubandoo Inc.
27128-B Paseo Espada Ste 602
San Juan Capistrano, CA 92675
Contact: Cindy Benedict President
Tel: 949-240-2617
Email: cindy@blubandoo.com
Website: www.blubandoo.com
Cooling headwear: caps/hats, fashionable visors, neckbands, cool ties, headbands & doorags. (Woman, estab 1993, empl 2, sales 5,500,000, cert: CPUC)

1637   Clipper Corporation
21124 Figueroa St
Carson, CA 90745
Contact: Deena Conner VP Business Units
Tel: 310-533-8585
Email: deena.conner@clippercorp.com
Website: www.clippercorp.com
Mfr & dist uniforms & smallwares. (Minority, Woman, estab , empl 45, sales 30,000,000, cert: NMSDC, WBENC)

1638   ECO Trend Cases, LLC
14242 Ventura Blvd Ste 203
Sherman Oaks, CA 91423
Contact: Sandy Rouse CEO
Tel: 310-770-6422
Email: srouse@ecostylecases.com
Website: www.ecostylecases.com
Mfr laptop, netbook & iPad cases: topload shoulder case, backpack, messenger case, rolling case & sleeves. (Woman, estab 2009, empl 4, sales 150,000, cert: WBENC)

1639   Kool Breeze Solar Hats, Inc.
827 E Princeton
Fresno, CA 93704
Contact: Tommie Nellon Owner
Tel: 559-456-8510
Email: tnellon@koolbreezesolarhat.com
Website: www.koolbreezesolarhat.com
Mfr solar cooling hats, Kool Breeze Solar Hats. (Woman/AA, estab 2012, empl 11, sales , cert: City)

1640   L.A. Rag Maker, LLC
8939 S Sepulveda, Ste 102
Los Angeles, CA 90045
Contact: George Arrington Owner
Tel: 213-407-4508
Email: g@laragmaker.com
Website: www.barbecuewhizz.com
Mfr & dist grilling aprons. (AA, estab 2021, empl 1, sales , cert: NMSDC)

1641   The Green Garmento, LLC
20109 Nordhoff St
Chatsworth, CA 91311
Contact: Jennie Nigrosh CEO
Tel: 323-512-2600
Email: jennie@thegreengarmento.com
Website: www.thegreengarmeno.com
A reusable dry-cleaning bag, eco-friendly all-in-one laundry, reusable hanging garment bag, carrying & duffel bag, hanger hamper, "green" drycleaning bag. (Woman, estab 2008, empl 6, sales 0, cert: WBENC)

Connecticut

1642   PrintabiliTees, LLC
180 Turn Of River Rd Ste 13D
Stamford, CT 06905
Contact: Jere Eaton President
Tel: 203-322-3390
Email: jere@printabilitees.com
Website: www.printabilitees.com
Custom apparel: screen printing, embroidery, document printing & promotional products. (Woman/AA, estab 2004, empl 1, sales 180000, cert: State, NMSDC)

Florida

1643   Global Trading, Inc.
7500 NW 25 St, Unit 12
Miami, FL 33122
Contact: Viraj Wikramanayake President
Tel: 305-471-4455
Email: accounting@gtim.com
Website: www.gtim.com
Provide safety footwear. (As-Ind, estab 1991, empl 20, sales , cert: State)

1644 Supreme Discount Uniforms, LLC
7410 SW 15th St
Plantation, FL 33317
Contact: Victor Albo Dir Sales/Marketing
Tel: 877-535-2540
Email: victor@supremediscountuniforms.com
Website: www.discountuniformsonline.com
Uniforms, embroidered lab coats, maintenance uniforms, housekeeping uniforms & embroidered polo t-shirts. (Hisp, estab 2009, empl 2, sales 168,000, cert: State)

1645 Tampa T-Shirts
5112 N 22nd St
Tampa, FL 33610
Contact: Juan Davis Mgr
Tel: 813-879-3298
Email: juan@fastlaneclothing.com
Website: www.fastlaneclothing.com
Apparel, logo shirts, lab coats, promotional items. (Minority, Woman, estab 1985, empl 19, sales 1,480,000, cert: State, City)

1646 Tavarez Sporting Goods
1840 22nd St
Miami, FL 33145
Contact: Manuel Tavarez Managing Partner
Tel: 347-441-9690
Email: tavarezsports@gmail.com
Website: www.tavarezsports.com
Sporting goods & fitness apparel, baseballs, softballs, baseball bats, gloves, batting gloves, catcher's equipment, helmets, volleyballs, soccer balls, basketballs, boxing equipment, martial arts equipment, sports bags to sports apparel. (Hisp, estab 2014, empl 5, sales , cert: NMSDC)

Georgia

1647 ERB Industries, Inc.
1 Safety Way
Woodstock, GA 30188
Contact: Jackie Barker EVP
Tel: 770-926-7944
Email: jbarker@e-erb.com
Website: www.e-erb.com
Mfr & dist personal protective equipment & uniform apparel: head, eye, face, body & hand protection, hard hats, safety glasses, high visibility apparel, aprons, smocks, lab coats. (Woman, estab 1956, empl 100, sales 0, cert: WBENC)

1648 O.G.I.H. Enterprises, Inc.
201 17th St NW, Ste 30303
Atlanta, GA 30363
Contact: Benny Nesbitt, Jr. CEO
Tel: 404-478-7852
Email: b.nesbitt@ogih-enterprises.com
Website: www.invisibleigloves.com
Dist work safety gloves, protective clothing. (AA, estab 2012, empl 4, sales , cert: State)

1649 Staffwear 2
155 Westridge Pkwy, Ste 307
McDonough, GA 30253
Contact: Towanda Scott President
Tel: 800-727-9289
Email: t.scott@staffwear2.com
Website: www.staffwear2.com
Corporate branded apparel & national uniform programs. (Woman/AA, estab 2008, empl 10, sales 502,438, cert: NMSDC)

Hawaii

1650 Coradorables,LLC
1707 Mahani Loop
Honolulu, HI 96819
Contact: Cora Spearman CEO
Tel: 808-782-4267
Email: coraspearman@hotmail.com
Website: www.coradorables.com
Men , women, children's hats and clothing, specializing in men's button down s/s shirts, boys button down s/s shirts, girls dresses. (Woman, estab 2010, empl 20, sales , cert: WBENC)

Illinois

1651 JERO Medical Equipment & Supplies, Inc.
4108 W Division St
Chicago, IL 60651
Contact: President
Tel: 312-829-5376
Email:
Website: www.jeromedical.com
Mfr disposbable wearing apparels, kit assembler, 1st aid, disaster, admission. (AA, estab 1987, empl 24, sales 4,000,000, cert: City)

1652 McKlein Company, LLC
4447 W. Cortland St
Chicago, IL 60639
Contact: Parinda Saetia CEO
Tel: 773-235-0600
Email: psaetia@mckleincompany.com
Website: www.mckleincompany.com
Mfr briefcases, computer cases, luggage, travel bags. (Minority, Woman, estab 1997, empl 7, sales 7,507,695, cert: WBENC)

Indiana

1653 RiverCity Workwear LLC
4020 Earnings Way
New Albany, IN 47150
Contact: Tina Dotson
Tel: 812-948-9020
Email: tina@rivercityworkwear.com
Website: www.rivercityworkwear.com
Dist safety glasses, hard hats, safety vest, shirts, rainwear, steel & non steel toe boots, tshirts, polos, jackets. (Woman, estab 2004, empl 3, sales , cert: State)

Louisiana

1654 Abform, Inc.
167 Industrial Pkwy
Lafayette, LA 70508
Contact: Kim Leblanc Comptroller
Tel: 337-837-9675
Email: kim@abform.com
Website: www.abform.com
Dist uniforms & work wear. (Woman, estab 1981, empl 20, sales 0, cert: WBENC)

1655 Company Apparel Safety Items, Inc.
     802 N Range Ave
     Denham Springs, LA 70726
     Contact: Nancy David President
     Tel: 225-664-2713
     Email: nancyestilldavid@gmail.com
     Website: www.companyapparelsafetyitems.com
Mfr disposable garments: medical scrubs, lab jackets, lab coats & multi-purpose coveralls. (Woman, estab 1994, empl 22, sales , cert: WBENC)

1656 Denison Consulting Group LLC
     6221 S Claiborne Ave Ste 450
     New Orleans, LA 70125
     Contact: Dianne Denison CEO
     Tel: 504-982-6110
     Email: sales@denisonconsultinggroup.com
     Website: www.denisonconsultinggroup.com/
Dist corporate work wear, uniforms, apparel, protective work wear, industrial clothing, flame retardant (FR) clothing, FR shirts, FR pants, FR coveralls, FR coats, FR jackets, FR jeans, rainwear, raingear. (Woman, estab 2015, empl 6, sales , cert: WBENC)

Maryland

1657 janlitlfeather
     3813 Terka Circle
     Randallstown, MD 21133
     Contact: Stephanie Gladden CEO
     Tel: 410-830-9244
     Email: janlitlfeather@aol.com
     Website: www.janlitlfeather.com
Signature feathered ponytail holder, key chains, car mirror hangs, bow ties, earrings, neck ties, hat clips & hair accessories. (Woman/AA, estab 2010, empl 1, sales , cert: NMSDC)

1658 Unitec Distribution Systems
     289 E Green St
     Westminster, MD 21157
     Contact: Elise Elfman CEO
     Tel: 410-876-6227
     Email: eelfman@unitec-corp.com
     Website: www.unitec-corp.com
Provide uniforms & Total Uniform Management Solution (TUMS). (Woman, estab 1927, empl 22, sales 5,000,000, cert: State, WBENC)

Michigan

1659 BluCase
     6026 Kalamazoo Ave. Ste. 237
     Grand Rapids, MI 49508
     Contact: Bill McCurdy CEO
     Tel: 708-263-9522
     Email: bmccurdy@blucase.com
     Website: www.blucase.com
Mfr innovative cellphone accessory products. (AA, estab 2014, empl 5, sales 12,000,000, cert: NMSDC)

1660 POSHnFIT
     17910 Van Dyke
     Detroit, MI 48234
     Contact: Tyanieka Jackson Owner
     Tel: 313-282-6008
     Email: admin@poshnfit.com
     Website: www.poshnfit.com
Creates fitness accessories for women. (Woman/AA, estab 2017, empl 1, sales , cert: NMSDC, WBENC)

1661 Stars Clothing Manufacturing Company
     300 River Place, Ste 5350
     Detroit, MI 48226
     Contact: Darrell Washington President
     Tel: 734-476-6709
     Email: dw@starsactivewear.com
     Website: www.starsactivewear.com
Mfr men and women apparel. (AA, estab 2017, empl 3, sales , cert: NMSDC)

1662 StarSource Management Services, Inc.
     39080 Webb Dr
     Westland, MI 48185
     Contact: Melvin Brown CEO
     Tel: 734-721-8540
     Email: sales@starsourceinc.com
     Website: www.starsourceinc.com
Dist uniforms, protective clothing, cutting tools, fasteners, janitorial chemical supplies, cleaning equipment, paper towels, plastic liners, welding supplies, automotive cleaning supplies, cooling tower chemicals, laundry services. (AA, estab , empl , sales 6,000,000, cert: NMSDC)

Minnesota

1663 Amaril Uniform Company
     8020 University Ave NE
     Fridley, MN 55432
     Contact: CEO
     Tel: 763-717-2037
     Email: cartsales@amaril.com
     Website: www.amaril.com
Dist uniforms, fire resistant clothing, actionwear, tailoring,e mbroidering, logos, stocking caps, neckwarmers, hardhat linner, rain gear. (Woman, estab 2000, empl 10, sales 1,257,080, cert: WBENC)

Missouri

1664 Cherry
     1712 Main St, Ste 232
     Kansas City, MO 64108
     Contact: Thalia Cherry President
     Tel: 816-377-1832
     Email: info@cherrysportsgear.com
     Website: www.cherrysportsgear.com
Sporting goods, corporate apparel, tee shirts, athletic equipment & uniforms. (AA, estab 2011, empl 3, sales , cert: NMSDC)

North Carolina

1665 Century Hosiery, Inc.
     PO Box 1410
     Denton, NC 27239
     Contact: Kathy Martin President
     Tel: 336-859-3806
     Email: kmartin@centuryhosiery.com
     Website: www.centuryhosiery.com
Mfr hosiery products. (Woman, estab 1989, empl 120, sales 6,000,000, cert: State, WBENC)

1666 Darlyng & Co.
1585 Yanceyville St
Greensboro, NC 27405
Contact: Tara Darnley Co-Founder
Tel: 929-376-8584
Email: info@darlyngandco.com
Website: www.darlyngandco.com
Fun and innovative line of baby products and apparel. (AA, estab 2014, empl 4, sales 350,000, cert: City)

1667 Transportation Safety Apparel
11 Conrad Industrial Dr
Weaverville, NC 28787
Contact: Rob DeLoach Natl Sales Dir
Tel: 828-767-9632
Email: rob.deloach@tsasafety.com
Website: www.tsasafety.com
Dist OCEA approved ANSI safety apparel, safety vests, tshirts, sweat shirts raingear, hardhats, gloves, uniforms, custom workshirts. (Woman, estab 2003, empl 15, sales 5,100,000, cert: WBENC)

New Jersey

1668 Design Alternatives NY LLC
169 Boyd Ave
Jersey City, NJ 07304
Contact: Cenia Peredes President
Tel: 973-583-9553
Email: cenia@ceniany.com
Website: www.goo.gl/3f8E3Q
Women's Apparel (Minority, estab , empl 2, sales 0, cert: NMSDC)

1669 Shani International Corporation
8 Conifer Dr
Warren, NJ 07059
Contact: Arti Mohin VP
Tel: 908-484-7070
Email: arti@shaniintl.com
Website: www.shaniintl.com
Mfr & import uniforms (knit & woven tops & bottoms), lab & chef coats, aprons, non-woven bags & basic fashion items. (Woman/As-Ind, estab 2005, empl 4, sales , cert: NMSDC)

1670 Tronex International Inc
300 International Dr
Mount Olive, NJ 07828
Contact: Edmund Tai VP Healthcare Division
Tel: 973-355-2888
Email: etai@tronexcompany.com
Website: www.tronexcompany.com
Dist disposable gloves & apparel products. (As-Pac, estab 1989, empl 75, sales , cert: NMSDC)

1671 Wisco Promo Uniform, INC.
160 US Hwy 46
Saddle Brook, NJ 07663
Contact: Linda Briscoe President
Tel: 973-767-2022
Email: briscoe_linda@yahoo.com
Website: www.wiscopnu.com
Mfr apparel, uniforms & aprons, silk screen & embroidery, promotional products, corporate identity & promotion. (Minority, Woman, estab 1999, empl 10, sales , cert: NMSDC)

Nevada

1672 Dellrone Services LLC
8550 W Charleston Blvd, Ste 228
Las Vegas, NV 89117
Contact: Willie Endsley President
Tel: 702-457-7855
Email: admin@dellroneservices.com
Website: www.dellroneservices.com
Dist safety clothing & equipment: fire safety jacket & pants, helmets, construction safety clothing: helmets, jackets, parkas, rain coats, safety vest, goggles & shoes. (Woman/AA, estab 2010, empl 4, sales , cert: NMSDC)

New York

1673 American Fashion Network, LLC
5852 Heritage Landing Dr
East Syracuse, NY 13057
Contact: Jacob Lewis Corporate Acct Exec
Tel: 315-560-3652
Email: jlewis@americanfashionnetwork.com
Website: www.americanfashionnetwork.com
Knit and woven apparel and a supplier of knit and woven apparel to American and Multi-National Corporations. Our apparel categories include corporate, event, swag, uniforms, workwear, lab coats, masks, and PPE. (Woman, estab 2005, empl 35, sales 26,665,000, cert: CPUC, WBENC)

1674 Hamburger Woolen Company
23 Denton Ave
New Hyde Park, NY 11040
Contact: Ilene Rosen President
Tel: 516-352-7400
Email: irosen@hwcny.com
Website: www.hwcny.com
Dist uniform fabrics, law enforcement & public safety equipment: duty belts, flashlights, raincoats, reflective vests, protective eyewear & earwear. (Woman, estab 1940, empl 12, sales 6,105,831, cert: State, City)

1675 PKP Industries, Inc.
1407 Broadway Ste 3412
New York, NY 10018
Contact: Puneet Pasricha
Tel: 646-586-3044
Email: puneet@pkpindustries.com
Website: www.pkpindustries.com
Wholesale apparel, clothing, women's tops, bottoms, skirts, dresses, pants. (Woman/As-Ind, estab 2014, empl 1, sales , cert: NMSDC)

1676 S & H Uniform Corp.
1 Aqueduct Rd
White Plains, NY 10606
Contact: ROSA GRECO VP
Tel: 914-937-6800
Email: info@sandhuniforms.com
Website: www.sandhuniforms.com
Workwear & footwear, outerwear/jackets, coveralls, hats, shirts, polos, t-shirts, pants, shorts, vests, flame resistant wear, Hi visibility, boots & shoes, medical uniforms, aprons, chef's apparel. (Woman, estab 1969, empl 40, sales 8,500,000, cert: City)

1677   Salsa-The Designer Solution LLC.
1441 Broadway 3 Fl, Ste 3021
New York, NY 10018
Contact: Gigi De Jesus-Frerichs President
Tel: 212-575-6565
Email: gigi@gicleeapparel.com
Website: www.SalsaProfessionalApparel.com
Mfr uniforms, sports apparel, collegiate apparel, varsity-wear, tees, tanks, polo shirts, sweatshirts, shorts, pants, lounge-wear & pajamas. (Minority, Woman, estab 2000, empl 6, sales 10,000,000, cert: State, City, NMSDC, WBENC)

Ohio

1678   Liniform Service
1050 Northview Ave
Barberton, OH 44203
Contact: Jennifer Peroli VP
Tel: 330-825-6911
Email: jenniferperoli@liniform.com
Website: www.liniform.com
Uniforms: lab coats, scrubs, jackets, warm-up jackets, maintenance uniforms, chef coats & cook apparel. Linens: patient gowns, mammo capes, sheets, pillowcases, blankets, towels & washcloths, tablecloths, skirting, napkins. (Woman, estab 1924, empl 60, sales 4,700,000, cert: WBENC)

1679   MASCOT Workwear
320 Springfield Dr, Ste 150
Fairlawn, OH 44333
Contact: Michael Allio Sales
Tel: 330-618-3997
Email: michael@maworkwear.com
Website: www.mascotworkwear.com
Dist MASCOT Workwear in North America. (Woman, estab 2013, empl 7, sales 1,000,000, cert: WBENC)

1680   RJ Manray - Promotional Products
9500 Springfield Rd, Unit 5
Poland, OH 44514
Contact: Rowena Henderson CEO
Tel: 234-201-0160
Email: rrlimos18@gmail.com
Website: www.rjmanray.com/
Dist personalized and custom logo tote bags. (Woman, estab 1986, empl 11, sales 640,000, cert: WBENC)

1681   VDP Safety & Uniforms Ltd.
11811 Shaker Blvd Ste 416
Cleveland, OH 44120
Contact: Phoebe Lee President
Tel: 216-352-1026
Email: info@vdpsafety.com
Website: www.vdpsafety.com
Uniform apparel & safety supplies/equipment: high visibility shirts, safety vests, hard hats, traffic cones, jackets, hospital uniforms. (Woman/AA, estab 2013, empl 1, sales , cert: State)

Pennsylvania

1682   Tyndale Company
5050 Applebutter Rd
Pipersville, PA 18947
Contact: Barbara Fitzgeorge Marketing Specialist
Tel: 215-766-5660
Email: Marketing@TyndaleUSA.com
Website: www.tyndaleusa.com
Mfr & dist flame resistant clothing. (Woman, estab 1982, empl 120, sales 40,000,000, cert: WBENC)

South Carolina

1683   MVP Textiles and Apparel, Inc.
1031 Le Grand Blvd
Charleston, SC 29492
Contact: Mary Propes CEO
Tel: 843-216-8380
Email: marypropes@mvpgroupint.com
Website: www.mvptextiles.com
Mfr textiles. (Woman, estab 2005, empl 15, sales 16,800,000, cert: WBENC)

Texas

1684   Career Uniforms
3800 Juniper
Houston, TX 77087
Contact: President
Tel: 713-645-3600
Email: sales@careeruniforms.com
Website: www.careeruniforms.com
Mfr uniforms: medical, governmental & restaurant. (As-Ind, estab 1980, empl 25, sales , cert: NMSDC)

1685   Fresh Comfort, Inc.
3200 Rifle Gap Rd, Ste 1470
Frisco, TX 75034
Contact: Maria E. Valencia President
Tel: 214-705-0408
Email: maria.valencia@freshcomfortinc.com
Website: www.freshcomfortinc.com
Adaptive intimate apparel (bras, panties, boxers), front Velcro & zipper closure bras for easy dressing & undressing, seamless bra & underwear. (Minority, Woman, estab 2012, empl 1, sales , cert: State)

1686   Radia Enterprises Inc.
3800 Juniper St
Houston, TX 77087
Contact: Rupendra Radia CEO
Tel: 713-645-6383
Email: rradia56@gmail.com
Website: www.spectrumuniforms.com
Uniforms and promotional products. (As-Ind, estab 1992, empl 20, sales 3,500,000, cert: NMSDC)

1687   RG Apparel Co.
2912 N MacArthur, Ste 103
Irving, TX 75062
Contact: Joe Temple COO
Tel: 972-793-0583
Email: jt@rgapparel.com
Website: www.rgapparel.com
Mfr textiles: uniforms, work shirts, polos, tees, woven button up shirts & headwear, promotional marketing items & gifts. (AA, estab 2006, empl 6, sales 3,200,000, cert: State, NMSDC)

1688 Santex
      4211 W Illinois, Ste 100
      Dallas, TX 75211
      Contact: Jose Lopez Owner
      Tel: 214-256-2169
      Email: karla.leal@santexallsports.com
      Website: www.santexallsports.com
Manufacturing business uniforms. (Hisp, estab 2013, empl
4, sales 160000, cert: State)

1689 Wholesale T-shirts Depot, Inc.
      11311 Harry Hines Blvd, Ste 201
      Dallas, TX 75229
      Contact: Joe Turner Exec VP
      Tel: 972-243-4785
      Email: info@wtdapparel.com
      Website: www.wtdapparel.com
Licensed military branded apparel & accessories. (As-Pac,
estab 2006, empl 18, sales 2,500,000, cert: NMSDC)

Virginia

1690 First Due Gear
      2111 Apperson Dr
      Salem, VA 24153
      Contact: Sarah Fuhrman Owner
      Tel: 540-725-8850
      Email: firstduegear@yahoo.com
      Website: www.firstduegear.com
Dist Fire, EMS, swiftwater & technical rescue gear, apparel
& equipment. (Woman, estab 2006, empl 1, sales , cert:
State)

1691 Global Partner's of Virginia, LLC
      3005 E Boundary Terr, Ste G
      Midlothian, VA 23112
      Contact: Norm Falkner VP
      Tel: 804-744-8112
      Email: logos@globalpromosonline.com
      Website: www.globalpromosonline.com
Logo wear, embroidery, silk screen, screen printing, direct
to garment ink jet printing, heat transfer. Corporate
apparel, mens, ladies, kids, uniforms. Promotional Products, pens, magnets, calendars, Bags, towels, luggage,
sportwear, team uniforms. (Woman, estab 2001, empl 4,
sales 350,000, cert: State)

1692 Sayre Enterprises Inc.
      45 Natural Bridge School Rd
      Natural Bridge Station, VA 24579
      Contact: Danielle Ayres Commericial Rep
      Tel: 800-552-6064
      Email: dayres@sayreinc.com
      Website: www.sayreinc.com
Reflective products: vests, belts, headbands, wrist & arm
bands. (Woman, estab 1987, empl 104, sales 9,092,000,
cert: State)

1693 The Uniform Store, LLC
      10 Weems Lane
      Winchester, VA 22601
      Contact: Lisa B Beggs President
      Tel: 540-678-8711
      Email: lisa@uniformstoreonline.com
      Website: www.uniformstoreonline.com
Dist ChefWorks, Edwards Garments & Uncommon Threads
for men & women in chef coats (executive chef & basic),
kitchen shirts, pants, aprons, headwear, neckwear, front of
the house (shirts, blouses, pants, vests, ties). (Woman,
estab 2009, empl 5, sales 455,781, cert: State, WBENC)

Washington

1694 Bootie Shoe Cover Inc
      5616 NE 55 Circle
      Vancouver, WA 98661
      Contact: Marla Gillette President
      Tel: 360-903-0992
      Email: info@bootieshoecover.com
      Website: www.bootieshoecover.com
Dist reusable shoe covers. (Woman, estab 2009, empl 3,
sales , cert: WBENC)

Wisconsin

1695 Straight-Up, Inc.
      1190 Richards Rd
      Hartland, WI 53029
      Contact: Craig Zirbel Mktg Exec
      Tel: 608-335-3676
      Email: zirbs@straightupinc.com
      Website: www.straightupinc.com
Embroidery svcs: up to 14 color screen print presses.
(Woman, estab 1994, empl 84, sales 22,200,000, cert:
WBENC)

ARCHITECTS

Most firms have agreements with other state architects permitting them to work anywhere in the nation. Nearly all are members of the American Institute of Architects (AIA). (See ENGINEERING & SURVEYING SERVICES for civil, structural, electrical and mechanical engineers).   NAICS Code 54

Arizona

1696   Fore Dimensions LLC
3337 E. Sells Dr
Phoenix, AZ 85018
Contact: Lisa Foreman Principal
Tel: 602-748-4664
Email: lisa@foredimensions.com
Website: www.foredimensions.com
Architectural consulting, remodel, tenant improvements & new construction for transportation facilities, wet & dry labs, clean rooms, testing buildings, office & training centers. (Woman, estab 2001, empl 2, sales $500,000, cert: State, City, WBENC)

California

1697   Aetypic, Inc.
7 Freelon St
San Francisco, CA 94107
Contact: Dennis Wong
Tel: 415-762-8388
Email: dennis.wong@aetypic.com
Website: www.aetypic.com
Architecture & engineering services: structural engineering, civil engineering, construction engineering & inspection, technology integration, & sustainable design. (As-Pac, estab 2011, empl 25, sales , cert: State, NMSDC)

1698   Blackbird Associates, Inc.
2320 J St
Sacramento, CA 95816
Contact: Franc Blackbird President
Tel: 916-446-6227
Email: franc@blackbirdassoc.com
Website: www.blackbirdassoc.com
Architecture and Project Management. (Minority, Woman, estab 1994, empl 7, sales $1,311,000, cert: NMSDC, WBENC)

1699   CDS Architects, Inc.
12220 El Camino Real Ste 200
San Diego, CA 92130
Contact: Dir Business Dev
Tel: 858-793-4777
Email: info@sca-sd.com
Website: www.sca-sd.com
Architectural & drafting services, interior space planning, project mgmtt & consulting services, LEED AP. (Woman, estab 1988, empl 18, sales $5,898,423, cert: WBENC)

1700   Development One, Inc.
2020 E. 1st St, Ste 525
Santa Ana, CA 92705
Contact: Geoff Chapluk Dir Marketing & Operations
Tel: 714-689-0298
Email: gchapluk@developmentone.net
Website: www.developmentone.net
Architecture/engineering, CADD, environmental. (Hisp, estab 1987, empl 25, sales , cert: State, NMSDC)

1701   H. Hendy Associates
4770 Campus Dr Ste 100
Newport Beach, CA 92660
Contact: Heidi Hendy Principal
Tel: 949-851-3080
Email: hhendy@hhendy.com
Website: www.hhendy.com
Interior architecture firm. (Woman, estab 1979, empl 30, sales $4,800,000, cert: CPUC, WBENC)

1702   Line2Line Architectural Design Group, LLP
2413 Webb Ave Ste D
Alameda, CA 94501
Contact: Angelus Cheng Principal
Tel: 510-995-8278
Email: info@line2lineadg.com
Website: www.line2lineadg.com
Architectural & design, Feasibility Studies, ADA Consultation, Sustainability, Programming, Urban/Site Planning, Entitlement, Due Diligence, Project Mgmt, Site & Building Evaluations, Interior Design, Design presentations. (Minority, Woman, estab 2012, empl 4, sales $354,156, cert: NMSDC)

1703   M+M Design Construction Project Management (MPJI)
1503 Bainum Dr
Topanga, CA 90290
Contact: Mohan Joshi President
Tel: 310-455-0064
Email: mjoshi@mpji.net
Website: www.mpji.net
Architecture, interior design, planning & advisory services. (As-Ind, estab 2002, empl 1, sales , cert: NMSDC, 8(a))

1704   Quezada Architecture, Inc.
639 Front St 1st Fl
San Francisco, CA 94111
Contact: Kate Albee Marketing Dir
Tel: 415-331-5133
Email: kate@qa-us.com
Website: www.qa-us.com
Architectural svcs: architecture, planning, interior architecture, design. (Minority, Woman, estab 1994, empl 10, sales , cert: NMSDC, WBENC)

1705   Source West
1631 Aspen Grove Lane
Diamond Bar, CA 91765
Contact: Roberto Manzini Dir Business Dev
Tel: 909-872-0010
Email: r.manzini@greencubicles.com
Website: www.greencubicles.com
Commercial architecture & interior design. (Woman, estab 1988, empl 25, sales $2,500,000, cert: State)

1706   Torres Architects, Inc.
400 Crenshaw Blvd Ste 200
Torrance, CA 90503
Contact: Denise Torres Managing Principal
Tel: 310-320-6285
Email: denise@tarci.com
Website: www.tarci.com
Architect, Interior Design, Computer Aided Drafting, Design, Mechanical Engineering, Electrical Engineering, Plumbing Engineering. (Hisp, estab 1991, empl 5, sales $1,127,237, cert: NMSDC)

1707 TSAO Design Group
      160 Pine St, Ste 650
      San Francisco, CA 94111
      Contact: Jonathan Tsao Principal
      Tel: 415-398-5500
      Email: jtsao@tsaodesign.com
      Website: www.tsaodesign.com
Architectural & interior design. (As-Pac, estab 1981, empl 12, sales $1,750,000, cert: CPUC)

Colorado

1708 Coover-Clark & Associates, Inc.
      1936 Market St
      Denver, CO 80202
      Contact: Carol Coover-Clark President
      Tel: 303-783-0040
      Email: marketing@cooverclark.com
      Website: www.cooverclark.com
Architectural planning & design services, commercial & military aviation facilities. (Woman, estab 1987, empl 22, sales $2,800,000, cert: WBENC)

Connecticut

1709 Bavier Design, LLC
      277 Rowayton Ave
      Rowayton, CT 06853
      Contact: Anne Bavier Principal
      Tel: 203-388-1818
      Email: abavier@bavierdesign.com
      Website: www.bavierdesign.com
Architectural & interior design. (Woman, estab 2004, empl 8, sales $1,255,000, cert: WBENC)

District of Columbia

1710 Systems Design, Inc.
      1420 9th St NW
      Washington, DC 20001
      Contact: Darlene Mathis CEO
      Tel: 202-232-5631
      Email: meka_mathis@msn.com
      Website: www.systemsdesignbuild.com
Interior design, space planning, architectural design svcs, also dist lamps, tables, tile, window treatments & systems furniture. (Woman/AA, estab 2002, empl 6, sales $700,000, cert: 8(a))

Florida

1711 Architechnical, Inc.
      2908 Clubhouse Dr
      Plant City, FL 33566
      Contact: Erick Gulke President
      Tel: 813-312-2455
      Email: egulke@architechnical.biz
      Website: www.architechnical.biz
Architectural design solutions & environments. (Hisp, estab 2008, empl 3, sales , cert: City)

1712 Architectural Design Collaborative
      235 Alcazar Ave
      Coral Gables, FL 33134
      Contact: Raymundo Feito President
      Tel: 305-442-1188
      Email: rfeito@adcinternational.net
      Website: www.adcinternational.net
Architectural, planning & interior design. (Hisp, estab 1984, empl 25, sales $7,600,000, cert: NMSDC)

1713 MGE Architects, Inc.
      3081 Salzedo St, 3rd Fl
      Coral Gables, FL 33134
      Contact: Jose Estevez President
      Tel: 305-444-0413
      Email: jestevez@mgearchitects.com
      Website: www.mgearchitects.com
Architectural services: private health systems, major government hospitals, teaching facilities & small community hospitals. (Hisp, estab 1982, empl 23, sales $7,937,182, cert: State)

1714 Rhodes+Brito Architects
      605 E Robinson St, Ste 750
      Orlando, FL 32801
      Contact: Ruffin Rhodes Principal
      Tel: 407-648-7288
      Email: info@rbarchitects.com
      Website: www.rbarchitects.com
Architectural Services. (AA, estab 1996, empl 19, sales $3,024,653, cert: State, City, 8(a))

Georgia

1715 Arseal Technologies, LLC
      5900 Windward Pkwy, Ste 475
      Alpharetta, GA 30005
      Contact: Edith Lakip CEO
      Tel: 678-387-1200
      Email: edith.lakip@arseal.com
      Website: www.arseal.com
Architectural & engineering design-build, electrical, mechanical & civil, CADD design services, project management & procurement. (Minority, Woman, estab 1999, empl 18, sales $1,500,000, cert: State, NMSDC)

1716 GSB Architects & Interiors, Inc.
      3500 Lenox Rd. Ste 1500
      Atlanta, GA 30326
      Contact: Jennifer Mercier Interior Designer
      Tel: 404-233-6450
      Email: jennifer@gsbarchitects.com
      Website: www.gsbarchitects.com
Architectural services, interior design, construction mgmt, project mgmt, space planning, move mgmt. (Minority, Woman, estab 1998, empl 5, sales $1,414,000, cert: NMSDC, WBENC)

1717 SpaceCraft International
      195 14th St, NE Ste 2908
      Atlanta, GA 30309
      Contact: Managing Dir
      Tel: 404-348-4732
      Email: info@spacecraftintl.com
      Website: www.spacecraftintl.com
Architectural & interior design svcs. (Woman, estab 2003, empl 10, sales , cert: WBENC)

1718 Utilicon Services, Inc.
      13275 Hwy 231
      Davisboro, GA 31018
      Contact: Tom Glover COO
      Tel: 478-348-3233
      Email: tom.glover@utilicon.net
      Website: www.utilicon.net
Architecture Services. (Woman/Nat Ame, estab 1998, empl 140, sales $12,800,000, cert: WBENC)

Illinois

1719   Bailey Edward Design, Inc.
35 E Wacker Dr Ste 2800
Chicago, IL 60601
Contact: Ellen B. Dickson President
Tel: 312-440-2300
Email: edickson@baileyedward.com
Website: www.baileyedward.com
Architectural services, Interior design services, Drafting services, Building inspection services
Engineering Services, Historical Preservation, Cost Estimating (Woman, estab 1991, empl 39, sales $2,973,760, cert: State, City, WBENC, NWBOC)

1720   Bauer Latoza Studio, Ltd.
2241 S Wabash
Chicago, IL 60616
Contact: Edward Torrez President
Tel: 312-567-1000
Email: etorrez@bauerlatozastudio.com
Website: www.bauerlatozastudio.com
Architectural design, evaluation & renovation services. (Hisp, estab 1990, empl 12, sales $2,195,986, cert: State)

1721   Brook Architecture
2325 S Michigan Ave Ste 300
Chicago, IL 60616
Contact: Jeanne Franks Dir of Marketing
Tel: 312-528-0890
Email: jfranks@brookarchitecture.com
Website: www.brookarchitecture.com
Design, urban planning, consulting, project management & services, new construction & renovation of institutional, residential, office & retail spaces. (Woman/AA, estab 1995, empl 6, sales $1,495,915, cert: State, City, NMSDC, 8(a))

1722   EC Purdy & Associates
53 W Jackson Blvd Ste 1631
Chicago, IL 60604
Contact: Elizabeth Purdy Architect
Tel: 312-408-1631
Email: ecpurdy@ecpurdy.com
Website: www.ecpurdy.com
Architectural, interior design planning services. (Minority, Woman, estab 1994, empl 1, sales $563,878, cert: State)

1723   Muller & Muller Ltd.
700 N Sangamon
Chicago, IL 60642
Contact: Mark Stromberg Principal
Tel: 312-432-4180
Email: mstromberg@muller2.com
Website: www.muller2.com
Architectural services: Feasibility Studies; Building Analysis; Schematic Design; Design Development; Construction Documents; LEED; ADA Review; Presentations; Renderings; 3D Animations; Specifications; Cost Estimating. (Woman, estab 1984, empl 20, sales $2,000,000, cert: State, City)

1724   Studio AH LLC dba HPZS
213 West Institute Place Ste 502
Chicago, IL 60610
Contact: April Hughes Owner
Tel: 312-944-9600
Email: ahughes@hpzs.com
Website: www.hpzs.com
Architectural design, Interior Design, Historic Preservation, Facade Maintenance & Sustainable Design, green renovation & design services. (Woman, estab 2015, empl 4, sales $133,310, cert: State, WBENC)

1725   Sumac Inc.
3701 N Ravenswood Ave Ste 202
Chicago, IL 60613
Contact: Liliana Gonzalez VP
Tel: 773-857-7906
Email: lgonzalez@sumacinc.com
Website: www.sumacinc.com
Architecture & construction management: architectural design, sustainable design, project scheduling, cost estimating, construction procurement, construction management services & general contracting. (Hisp, estab 2008, empl 10, sales $2,000,000, cert: NMSDC)

1726   Tigerman McCurry Architects
444 N Wells St Ste 206
Chicago, IL 60654
Contact: Margaret McCurry President
Tel: 312-644-5880
Email: tma@tigerman-mccurry.com
Website: www.Tigerman-McCurry.com
Architectural & interior design services. (Woman, estab 1967, empl 10, sales $1,200,000, cert: City)

Indiana

1727   Brenner Design Incorporated
620 N Delaware St
Indianapolis, IN 46204
Contact: Diana Brenner President
Tel: 317-262-1220
Email: dbrenner@brennerdesign.com
Website: www.brennerdesign.com
Architecture; Interior Architecture; Historic Preservation; Interior Design; Furniture Management Services; Owner's Representative Services; Space Planning; Project Management. (Woman, estab 1992, empl 10, sales , cert: State, City, WBENC)

1728   Jung Design, Inc.
8910 Purdue Rd Ste 680
Indianapolis, IN 46268
Contact: Connie Jung President
Tel: 317-471-1221
Email: cjung@jungdes.com
Website: www.jungdes.com
Architectural & interior design services, master planning, signage, programming, space planning. (Woman, estab 2004, empl 3, sales $200,000, cert: State)

1729   Rowland Design, Inc.
702 N Capitol Ave
Indianapolis, IN 46204
Contact: Sarah Schwartzkopf CEO
Tel: 317-636-3980
Email: smschwartzkopf@rowlanddesign.com
Website: www.rowlanddesign.com
Architecture, interior design & graphic design. (Woman, estab 1968, empl 32, sales $4,050,000, cert: State)

1730 Studio 3 Design, Inc.
8604 Allisonville Rd Ste 330
Indianapolis, IN 46250
Contact: Heather Leslie President
Tel: 317-595-1000
Email: hleslie@studio3design.net
Website: www.studio3design.net
Architectural & interior design services. (Woman, estab 2002, empl 7, sales , cert: State)

1731 WDi Architecture, Inc.
15 W 28th St
Indianapolis, IN 46208
Contact: Williams-Dotson Daryl CEO
Tel: 317-251-6172
Email: daryl_wd@wdiarchitecture.com
Website: www.wdiarchitecture.com
Architectural design, space planning & programming, feasibility studies, facilities evaluation, project managment & existing conditions documentation. (Woman/AA, estab 1995, empl 5, sales $400,000, cert: State, City, WBENC)

Kentucky

1732 First World Architects Studio, PSC
15 E 9th St
Covington, KY 41011
Contact: B. Charles Alexander President
Tel: 859-431-1999
Email: alexcama@fuse.net
Website: www.1stworldarchitectsstudio.com
Architectural & engineering services: master planning & project mgmt, construction mgmt, design/build, facility assessments. (AA, estab 1982, empl 6, sales $415,000, cert: State, 8(a))

Louisiana

1733 Marrero Couvillon & Associates, LLC
4354 S Sherwood Forest Blvd, Ste D200
Baton Rouge, LA 70816
Contact: Stacey Vincent Production Mgr
Tel: 225-408-8249
Email: svincent@mca-llc.com
Website: www.mca-llc.com
Mechanical, Electrical, Plumbing, Fire Protection Engineering Services, Architectural Services and Construction Management (Hisp, estab 1968, empl 17, sales $2,800,000, cert: State, NMSDC, 8(a), SDB)

Maryland

1734 K. Dixon Architecture, PLLC
137 National Plaza, Ste 300
National Harbor, MD 20745
Contact: K. Dixon Principal
Tel: 301-364-5053
Email:
Website: www.kdixonarchitecture.com
Architectural design & planning services: commercial, education, government, residential, and institutional. (Woman/AA, estab 2003, empl 1, sales $100,000, cert: State, City, WBENC)

1735 Mimar Architects & Engineers, Inc.
7004 Security Blvd Ste 210
Baltimore, MD 21244
Contact: Maria Khalid Marketing Coord
Tel: 410-944-4900
Email: mkhalid@mimarch.net
Website: www.mimarch.net
Architectural-engineering, architectural/planning, interior/graphic design, engineering & construction management services. (Minority, estab 1995, empl 25, sales $3,991,379, cert: State)

1736 NFD, Inc.
124 Lakefront Dr
Hunt Valley, MD 21030
Contact: Laura Schlicht Business Dev Dir
Tel: 410-785-7795
Email: lschlicht@nfd.com
Website: www.nfd.com
Commercial interior design & planning: programming & budgeting; schematic design; furniture/equipment inventorying; space planning; 3D modeling; furniture & finish specs; project coordination. (Woman, estab 1978, empl 9, sales $973,000, cert: State, City, WBENC)

1737 Sugar Associates, LLC
2909 Old Court Rd
Baltimore, MD 21208
Contact: Karen Sugar President
Tel: 410-602-2909
Email: karen@sugarassociates.com
Website: www.sugarassociates.com
Interior design & planning, space programming, 24-hour-turn-around space planning & facility planning services. (Woman, estab , empl , sales $212,000, cert: State, City)

Michigan

1738 Gala & Associates Inc.
31455 Southfield Rd
Beverly Hills, MI 48025
Contact: Chuni Gala President
Tel: 248-642-8610
Email: cgala@galaandassociates.com
Website: www.galaandassociates.com
Electrical, mechanical, structural, civil & architectural engineering svcs, CAD services. (As-Ind, estab 1987, empl 50, sales $6,000,000, cert: NMSDC)

Minnesota

1739 Studio Hive Inc.
901 N Third St, Ste 228
Minneapolis, MN 55401
Contact: Shari Bjork Principal
Tel: 612-279-0430
Email: sbjork@studiohive.com
Website: www.studiohive.com
Architectural & interior design. (Woman, estab 2003, empl 8, sales $1,098,036, cert: State)

Missouri

1740 Arcturis, Inc.
720 Olive St Ste 200
St. Louis, MO 63101
Contact: Julie Keil Principal
Tel: 314-206-7100
Email: jkeil@arcturis.com
Website: www.arcturis.com
Architecture, interior design, landscape architecture, urban planning, graphic design, workplace optimization, master planning, site planning & building evaluation services. (Woman, estab 1977, empl 50, sales $8,500,000, cert: State, WBENC)

1741 Bozoian Group Architects, LLC
2201 S Brentwood Blvd Ste 105
St. Louis, MO 63144
Contact: Katherine Bozoian President
Tel: 314-962-4100
Email: information@bozoiangroup.com
Website: www.bozoiangroup.com
Architectural svcs: master planning, facility & needs assessment, new building design, renovation, interior design, adaptive re-use, re-purpose, sustainable design, owners representation, construction administration. (Woman, estab 1996, empl 6, sales $958,000, cert: State, WBENC)

1742 CORE10 Architecture
4501 Lindell Blvd Ste 1a
St. Louis, MO 63108
Contact: Michael Byrd
Tel: 314-726-4858
Email: mbyrd@core10architecture.com
Website: www.core10architecture.com
Architecture, Interior Design, Master Planning, Sustainable Design, LEED, Residential, Mixed Use, Multi-Family, Commercial, Office, Industrial. (Minority, estab 2007, empl 6, sales $881,934, cert: State, City)

1743 Gray Design Group, Inc.
Nine Sunnen Dr, Ste 110
Saint Louis, MO 63143
Contact: Lorrie Kramer
Tel: 314-646-0400
Email: lkramer@graydesigngroup.com
Website: www.graydesigngroup.com
Commercial architecture & interior design. (Woman, estab , empl , sales $2,397,779, cert: State, City)

1744 Kennedy Associates/Architects, Inc.
2060 Craigshire Rd
St. Louis, MO 63146
Contact: Michael B. Kennedy, Jr. President
Tel: 314-241-8188
Email: kaibuild@kai-db.com
Website: www.kai-db.com
Architecture, planning & interior design, mechanical engineering, electrical, plumbing. (AA, estab 1980, empl 110, sales $26,000,000, cert: State, City, NMSDC)

1745 Oculus Inc.
1 S Memorial Dr, Ste 1500
St. Louis, MO 63102
Contact: Shevaun McNaughton Marketing Dir
Tel: 314-367-6100
Email: shevaunm@oculusinc.com
Website: www.oculusinc.com
Architecture, strategic planning, interior design & move management. (Woman, estab 1994, empl , sales $6,338,825, cert: State, WBENC)

1746 Pendulum Studio LLC
1512 Holmes St
Kansas City, MO 64108
Contact: Jonathan Cole Owner
Tel: 816-399-5251
Email: jonathan@pendulumkc.com
Website: www.pendulumkc.com
Architectural svcs: master planning, new facility design, green building strategy, accessibility consulting, existing facility renovation, strategic expansion planning, facility assessment. (AA, estab 2007, empl 9, sales $1,120,578, cert: State, City, NMSDC)

North Carolina

1747 Arcons Design Studio Professional Corporation
10550 Independence Point Pkwy Ste 300
Matthews, NC 28105
Contact: Rajeev Bhave President
Tel: 704-542-5252
Email: rbhave@arconsds.com
Website: www.arconsds.com
Architectural services, retail, commercial, institutional and mixed use projects. (As-Ind, estab 2004, empl 7, sales $1,400,000, cert: State)

1748 CSBO Architecture P.C.
1589 Skeet Club Rd Ste 102-172
High Point, NC 27265
Contact: Carlos Sanchez President
Tel: 336-617-3079
Email: carlos.sanchez@csboinc.com
Website: www.csboinc.com
Architectural design services. (Hisp, estab 2002, empl 2, sales , cert: State)

1749 Espinosa Architecture + Consulting, PC
937 Bryansplace Rd
Winston-Salem, NC 27104
Contact: Carlos V Espinosa President
Tel: 336-407-8419
Email: arlos@espinosaarchitecture.com
Website: www.espinosaarchitecture.com
Architecture services, architectural design, space planning, needs evaluation & programming, evaluation of existing structures, cost analysis, interior design. (Hisp, estab 2014, empl 3, sales , cert: State)

1750 McCulloch England Associates Architects, Inc.
100 Queens Rd, Ste 200
Charlotte, NC 28204
Contact: Grace Murray COO
Tel: 704-372-2740
Email: gmurray@mceaa.com
Website: www.mccullochengland.com
Architecture & design services, healthcare architecture, interior design, planning, programming, schematic design, design development, construction documents, bidding documents, construction administration. (Hisp, estab 1971, empl 24, sales , cert: State, NMSDC)

1751 Neighboring Concepts, PLLC
      1230 W Morehead St Ste 204
      Charlotte, NC 28208
      Contact: Robin Holloway Dir of Mktg/Business Dev
      Tel: 704-374-0916
      Email: robin@neighboringconcepts.com
      Website: www.neighboringconcepts.com
Architectural design: concept, construction, post-construction services, urban planning, development & revitalization. (Minority, estab 1996, empl 17, sales $1,903,763,
cert: State)

New Jersey

1752 Gramieri Design Services
      353 Georges Rd, Ste C
      Dayton, NJ 08810
      Contact: Frank Gramieri President
      Tel: 732-274-9540
      Email: fgramieri@gdsinc.net
      Website: www.gdsinc.net
Interior architectural & engineering services: site analysis,
design development, project budgeting & programming,
space planning, schematics design, 3D rendering &
modeling, architectural & engineering contract documents. (Minority, estab 1992, empl 7, sales $638,903, cert:
City, NMSDC)

1753 Kamlesh Shah Designs Inc.
      18 Lovell Dr
      Plainsboro, NJ 08536
      Contact: Kamlesh Shah Principal
      Tel: 609-655-9908
      Email: kshah@ksdarchitects.com
      Website: www.ksdarchitects.com
Architectural, Interior Space Planning, Programing, Lab
Design, Process Manufacuring Design, Mechanical,
Electrical, Plumbing, Engineering Services. (As-Pac, estab
1998, empl 6, sales $2,115,234, cert: State)

1754 O&S Associates, Inc.
      145 Main St
      Hackensack, NJ 07601
      Contact: Kelly O'Leary Dir Business Devel
      Tel: 201-488-7144
      Email: kaoleary@oandsassociates.com
      Website: www.oandsassociates.com
Planning, Design and Restoration of full building envelope,
inclusive of roof, windows, facade. Specializing in parking
planning, design & restoration. Engineers and Architects.
(Minority, estab 1996, empl 40, sales $6,500,000, cert:
NMSDC)

Nevada

1755 KME Architects LLC
      231 W Charleston Blvd
      Las Vegas, NV 89102
      Contact: Melvin Green Principal
      Tel: 702-888-2088
      Email: melvin@kmearchitects.com
      Website: www.kmearchitects.com/
Architectural services, interior design, landscape design,
sustainable design, Historic preservation, tenant improvements, fire code violations, master planning, laser scanning. (AA, Hisp, estab 2009, empl 9, sales , cert: NMSDC)

New York

1756 Avinash K. Malhotra Architects (AKM)
      148 W 24th St
      New York, NY 10706
      Contact: Richard Saunderson Associate
      Tel: 212-808-0000
      Email: rsaunderson@akmarch.com
      Website: www.akmarch.com
Architectural solutions: high-rise buildings, large scale
conversions, historical preservation & landmarks re-use,
renovations & architectural interiors. (As-Ind, estab
1982, empl 10, sales $1,900,000, cert: State, City,
NMSDC)

1757 AWA Lighting Designers Inc.
      61 Greenpoint Ave
      Brooklyn, NY 11222
      Contact: Abhay Wadhwa CEO
      Tel: 212-473-9797
      Email: abhay@awalightingdesigners.com
      Website: www.awalightingdesigners.com
Architectural lighting design, design & implement
lighting solutions for commercial, civic, cultural &
residential projects. (As-Ind, estab 2011, empl 27, sales ,
cert: State)

1758 Foit-Albert Associates, Architecture, Engineering
      and Surveying, P.C.
      215 W 94th St, Ste 517
      New York, NY 10025
      Contact: Gregory Carballada President
      Tel: 716-856-3933
      Email: cstoebe@foit-albert.com
      Website: www.foit-albert.com
Architecture, Engineering, Environmental & Land
Surveying Consulting. (Hisp, estab 1977, empl 70, sales
$10,000,000, cert: State, City)

1759 Kahn Architecture & Design, PC
      2 West 45th St Ste 501
      New York, NY 10036
      Contact: Heidi Kahn President
      Tel: 646-253-9864
      Email: hwiley@kahnarchitecture.com
      Website: www.kahnarchitecture.com
Architecture, interior design & planning solution services
to commercial and retail clients. (Woman, estab 2005,
empl 17, sales $2,200,000, cert: State, City, WBENC)

1760 Kenne Shepherd Interior Design Architecture PLLC
      54 W 21st St, Ste 1208
      New York, NY 10010
      Contact: Kenne Shepherd Principal
      Tel: 212-206-6336
      Email: kshepherd@kenneshepherd.com
      Website: www.kenneshepherd.com
Multi-disciplinary interior architectural, workspace, retail
store or residence, strategic planning, site evaluation,
code/zoning analysis, lease/workletter review, architectural design, sustainable design, construction documents, construction observation (Woman, estab 1993,
empl 3, sales , cert: WBENC)

1761 Lewandowska Architect PLLC
      14 Wall St, 20th Floor
      New York, NY 10005
      Contact: Barbara Lewandowska Principal
      Tel: 212-787-4558
      Email: barbara@lewandowskaarchitect.com
      Website: www.LewandowskaArchitect.com
Architectural, interior design & space planning services.
(Woman, estab 2002, empl 3, sales $200,000, cert: State,
City)

1762 SWITZER Architecture, P.C.
      255 W 36th St Ste 1101
      New York, NY 10018
      Contact: Gregory T Switzer Principal
      Tel: 212-391-1519
      Email: gswitzer@switzerarchitecture.com
      Website: www.switzerpc.com
Architectural design & holistic management. (AA, estab
2003, empl 6, sales $750,000, cert: NMSDC)

1763 The Switzer Group
      3 E 54th St
      New York, NY 10022
      Contact: Wendy Hall Principal, Client Devel
      Tel: 212-922-1313
      Email: whall@theswitzergroup.com
      Website: www.theswitzergroup.com
Interior design. (AA, estab 1975, empl 70, sales
$13,500,000, cert: City, NMSDC)

1764 ZELJKA ONE Management LLC dba: Green Way
      Pavement
      PO Box 2927
      Binghamton, NY 13902
      Contact: Robert V Gerard Co-Owner
      Tel: 607-724-2438
      Email: robertgerard@me.com
      Website: www.greenwaypavements.com
LEED architects & construction services. (Woman, estab
2011, empl 2, sales $11,000,000, cert: State)

Ohio

1765 Brockman Designs LLC
      27600 Chagrin Blvd Ste 260
      Cleveland, OH 44122
      Contact: Sharon Brockman Principal
      Tel: 216-504-4040
      Email: sbrockman@brockmandesigns.com
      Website: www.brockmandesigns.com
Interior design, healthcare spaces & facilities, higher
education & corporate offices, interior space planning,
interior finish selections & specifications, furniture
planning & specifications, project coordination. (Woman,
estab 2001, empl 2, sales , cert: State, City)

1766 DNK Architects, Inc.
      2616 Central Pkwy
      Cincinnati, OH 45214
      Contact: Guinette Kirk VP
      Tel: 513-948-4146
      Email: gkirk@dnkarchitects.com
      Website: www.dnkarchitects.com
Interior design & space planning services, Cadd drafting.
(AA, estab 1986, empl 20, sales $2,000,000, cert: State,
NMSDC)

1767 Quinn Engineering & Employment Network LLC
      125 W Market St, Ste 221
      Warren, OH 44481
      Contact: Candys Mayo Owner
      Tel: 330-423-1923
      Email: info@queen-ohio.com
      Website: www.queen-ohio.com
Computer Aided Drafting and Engineering/Architecture
support, Naval Architecture and Aerospace. (AA, estab
2015, empl 2, sales , cert: State)

1768 Robert P Madison International, Inc
      1215 Superior Ave E Ste 110
      Cleveland, OH 44114
      Contact: R. Kevin Madison, AIA President
      Tel: 216-861-8195
      Email: rklann@rpmadison.com
      Website: www.rpmadison.com
Architectural svcs; civil, structural, electrical & mechanical engineering. (Woman/AA, estab 1954, empl 13, sales
$1,692,000, cert: State, City)

1769 Ubiquitous Design, Ltd.
      3443 Lee Rd
      Shaker Heights, OH 44120
      Contact: W. Daniel Bickerstaff, II Founder &
      Principal Architect
      Tel: 216-752-4444
      Email: arcatek@udltd.com
      Website: www.udltd.com
Architectural design services, conceptual design/
feasibility analysis, construction administration. (AA,
estab 2001, empl 2, sales $200,000, cert: City)

1770 WA, Inc. (dba WA Architects, Inc.)
      807 Broadway St 2nd Fl
      Cincinnati, OH 45202
      Contact: Wade Price Principal
      Tel: 513-641-0111
      Email: wprice@wa-inc.biz
      Website: www.wa-architectsinc.com
Healthcare Design & Planning. (AA, estab 1971, empl 16,
sales $1,750,000, cert: State, NMSDC)

1771 Wanix Architects, LLC
      4208 Prospect Ave
      Cleveland, OH 44103
      Contact: Xin Wan Owner
      Tel: 440-570-9829
      Email: xinwan@wanixarchitects.com
      Website: www.wanixarchitects.com
Architectural design, site planning, interior space
planning & 3D. (Minority, Woman, estab 2008, empl 2,
sales , cert: City)

Pennsylvania

1772 Alexander Perry Inc.
      2929 Arch St, Ste 1700
      Philadelphia, PA 19104
      Contact: Patricia Sanford CEO
      Tel: 215-948-8148
      Email: psanford@alexanderperryinc.com
      Website: www.alexanderperryinc.com
Interior design, project management, construction
management, flooring & window treatments, furniture,
signage. (Woman/AA, estab 1992, empl 13, sales , cert:
State, City, NMSDC, WBENC)

1773 DJDC Inc.
      12300 Perry Hwy, Ste 204
      Wexford, PA 15090
      Contact: Marcia Guth Principal
      Tel: 412-996-6771
      Email: mguth@djdc.com
      Website: www.djdc.com
Interior architecture design, space planning & facilities
planning svcs. (Woman, estab 1972, empl 6, sales
$243,000, cert: WBENC)

1774 Genesis Architects Inc.
      1850 N Gravers Rd
      Plymouth Meeting, PA 19462
      Contact: Meryl Towarnicki President
      Tel: 610-592-0280
      Email: mtowarnicki@geiarc.com
      Website: www.geiarc.com
Architecture, Engineering, Commissioning & Construction
Management. (Woman, estab 2017, empl 50, sales
$60,480,129, cert: WBENC)

1775 MKSD. LLC
      1209 Hausman Rd, Ste A
      Allentown, PA 18104
      Contact: President
      Tel: 610-366-2081
      Email:
      Website: www.mksdarchitects.com
Architecture, planning, design & construction for new
buildings, additions & renovations. (Woman, estab 2005,
empl 16, sales $3,103,884, cert: State, WBENC)

1776 SMC Consulting, LLC d/b/a/ Studio SMC
      379 Insurance St
      Beaver, PA 15009
      Contact: Sam McWilliams Managing Partner
      Tel: 724-728-8625
      Email: sam@studio-smc.com
      Website: www.studio-smc.com
Interior Design, Space Planning, Furniture Planning,
Furniture Specification, Move Management, Project
Management, Construction Administration. (Woman,
estab 1999, empl 5, sales $213,544, cert: State)

1777 Styer & Associates, Inc.
      412 Dekalb St
      Norristown, PA 19401
      Contact: Amy Styer Tahtabrounian Principal
      Tel: 610-275-6000
      Email: amy@styergroup.com
      Website: www.styergroup.com
Architecture, engineering, interior design, construction,
project management, purchase management. (Woman,
estab 1985, empl 9, sales $190,000,000, cert: WBENC)

Puerto Rico

1778 CMA Architects & Engineers LLC
      1509 Ave FD Roosevelt
      Guaynabo, PR 00968
      Contact: Jorge A. Tirado, PE Managing Member
      Tel: 787-792-1509
      Email: jtirado@cmapr.com
      Website: www.cmapr.com
Architectural design services, preparation of construction
documents, field & construction management, environmental & permitting, electrical, mechanical, structural,
transportation & infrastructure engineering. (Hisp, estab
1959, empl 90, sales $8,300,000, cert: NMSDC, SDB)

1779 UNIPRO Architects Engineers LLP
      PO Box 10914
      San Juan, PR 00922
      Contact: Jose R. Gonzalez Dir planning/Projects
      Tel: 787-793-3950
      Email: jgonzalez@uniproaep.net
      Website: www.uniproaep.com
Architecture, civil engineering, structural engineering,
mechanical engineering, electrical engineering, environmental engineering, construction management. (Hisp,
estab 1980, empl 30, sales $3,200,000, cert: NMSDC)

Texas

1780 Architect for Life - A Professional Corporation
      2450 Louisiana St, Ste 400-233
      Houston, TX 77006
      Contact: Lolalisa King
      Tel: 888-986-7771
      Email: lking@architectforlife.com
      Website: www.architectforlife.com
Green consulting professional services, develop &
manage energy efficient strategies, programs, &
projects, retrofit strategies, benchmarking building
energy performance, long-term energy management &
water saving goals assessment. (Woman/AA, estab
1995, empl 12, sales , cert: City)

1781 BSA Design Group Inc.
      8750 N Central Expressway, Ste 1725
      Dallas, TX 75231
      Contact: Vanessa Witliff President
      Tel: 214-818-0563
      Email: vwittliff@bsa-designgroup.com
      Website: www.bsa-designgroup.com
Architectural, interior design, design build, project
management, programming and scheduling, studies and
analyses, specifications, furnishing procurement.
(Woman, estab 1989, empl 13, sales $5,000,000, cert:
WBENC)

1782 Interprise/Southwest Interior & Space Planning
      5080 Spectrum Dr Ste 115E
      Addison, TX 75001
      Contact: Lesley Leahy VP Business Dev
      Tel: 972-385-3991
      Email: lleahy@interprisedesign.com
      Website: www.interprisedesign.com
Commerical interior design & space planning. (Woman,
estab 1981, empl 36, sales $4,500,000, cert: WBENC)

1783 R & T Architects, Inc.
      3300 S Gessner, Ste 119
      Houston, TX 77063
      Contact: Spencer Tsui Principal
      Tel: 713-974-2008
      Email: rtarch@swbell.net
      Website: www.rtarch.net
Architectural services: design & built. (As-Pac, estab
1982, empl 4, sales $110,000, cert: State, City)

1784 STOA International Architects, Inc.
6001 Savoy Dr, Ste 100
Houston, TX 77036
Contact: Alice Hu
Tel: 713-995-8784
Email: stoaintl@globalxlr.com
Website: www.stoaintl.com
Architectural design, interior design, planning, construction management, architectural rendering. (As-Pac, estab 1995, empl 10, sales $750,000, cert: State, City, NMSDC)

1785 VAI Architects Inc.
16000 N Dallas Pkwy, Ste 200
Dallas, TX 75248
Contact: William Vidaud Principal
Tel: 972-934-8888
Email: wvidaud@vaiarchitects.com
Website: www.vaiarchitects.com
Architecture, master planning, feasibility analysis, interior planning & design, building condition assessments, CADD, renovation, alteration & expansion, demolition specifications, roofing assessments/corrective design. (Hisp, estab 1985, empl 28, sales $4,945,000, cert: State)

Virginia

1786 nbj Architecture
11537-B Nuckols Rd
Glen Allen, VA 23059
Contact: Neil Bhatt President
Tel: 804-273-9811
Email: nbhatt@nbjarch.com
Website: www.nbjarch.com
Architectural, space planning, interior design, construction administration, feasibility studies & value engineering. (Minority, estab 2000, empl 12, sales $2,000,000, cert: State)

1787 SandHurst-AEC
1069 W Broad St, Ste 777
Falls church, VA 22046
Contact: Kwafo Djan Principal
Tel: 703-533-1413
Email: kdjan@sandhurstaec.com
Website: www.sandhurstaec.com
Architecture & Urban Planning, Program Management, Site Analysis, Feasibility Studies, Architectural Design, Construction, Documentation, Interior Design Services, Space Planning, Project Management. (AA, estab 2013, empl 3, sales , cert: State, 8(a))

Washington

1788 Ato Apiafi Architects PLLC
10940 NE 33rd Place Ste 208
Bellevue, WA 98004
Contact: Jeff Thompson
Tel: 425-202-7760
Email: jeff.t@atoapiafi.com
Website: www.atoapiafi.com
Full service architectural firm. (AA, estab 2004, empl 2, sales , cert: State, NMSDC)

1789 Magellan Architects
8383 158th Ave NE, Ste 280
Redmond, WA 98052
Contact: Principal
Tel: 425-885-4300
Email: office@magellanarchitects.com
Website: www.magellanarchitects.com
Architectural design services & construction administration. (Hisp, estab 2000, empl 30, sales $1,928,209, cert: NMSDC)

Wisconsin

1790 Continuum Architects + Planners, S.C.
228 S First
Milwaukee, WI 53204
Contact: Ursula Twombly Principal
Tel: 414-220-9649
Email: ursula.twombly@continuumarchitects.com
Website: www.continuumarchitects.com
Master planning site selection site planning, pre-design studies. (Woman, estab 1996, empl 13, sales $1,700,000, cert: City)

AUTOMOBILES
New and used car dealerships. Distributors of single cars, trucks and fleet sales. Provide rental and leasing services. NAICS Code 44

California

1791   Premiere Solutions, LLC
11501 Dublin Blvd Ste 200
Dublin, CA 94568
Contact: Holly Michael
Tel: 925-467-1000
Email: holly@premieresolutionsllc.com
Website: www.premieresolutionsllc.com
Fleet management services: vehicle acquisition (lease, purchase or rental), vehicle disposal, fuel card, preventative maintenance, accident management, roadside assistance, transportation, licensing & registration. (AA, estab 2005, empl 7, sales $15,807,000, cert: NMSDC, CPUC)

1792   Rotolo Chevrolet, Inc.
16666 S Highland Ave
Fontana, CA 92336
Contact: Jamie Harshman Dir Fleet Sales
Tel: 909-822-1111
Email: jamie@rotolo.com
Website: www.rotolochevy.com
Sell & service Chevrolet light duty cars & trucks. (Woman, estab 1971, empl 104, sales $81,651,283, cert: CPUC)

Colorado

1793   Burt Fleet Services, Inc.
5210 S Broadway
Englewood, CO 80113
Contact: Lloyd Chavez CEO
Tel: 303-789-6701
Email: lgchavezjr@burt.com
Website: www.burt.com
National fleet vehicle sales & leasing. (Minority, Woman, estab 2009, empl 6, sales $600,001, cert: NMSDC)

Florida

1794   NM1, LLC
16725 NW 57th Ave
Miami Gardens, FL 33055
Contact: Rogelio (Roger) Tovar President
Tel: 888-423-7756
Email: rogeliotovar@gmail.com
Website: www.palmetto57nissan.com
Sell new & used cars, parts & service. (Hisp, estab 2012, empl 110, sales $74,101,851, cert: NMSDC)

1795   Sun State International Trucks, LLC
6020 Adamo Dr
Tampa, FL 33619
Contact: Dave Metcalf VP, Dir of Sales
Tel: 813-769-2541
Email: dave.metcalf@sunstateintl.com
Website: www.sunstateintl.com
Medium & heavy duty commercial truck dealership. (AA, estab 1982, empl 163, sales $115,000,000, cert: NMSDC)

Illinois

1796   Advantage Chevrolet
9510 W. Joliet Rd
Hodgkins, IL 60525
Contact: Rick Zureick GM
Tel: 847-561-5281
Email: rzureick@advantagechev.com
Website: www.advantagechev.com
Automotive & commercial truck sales. (AA, estab 2000, empl 122, sales $91,265,959, cert: NMSDC)

1797   Sutton Ford, Inc.
21315 Central
Matteson, IL 60443
Contact: Michael Miller Fleet Mgr
Tel: 708-720-8034
Email: mmiller@suttonford.com
Website: www.suttonford.com
Ford cars, trucks, sales, service & parts. (AA, estab 1989, empl 80, sales , cert: State, NMSDC, CPUC)

Indiana

1798   Truck City of Gary, Inc.
PO Box 64800
Gary, IN 46401
Contact: Gerri Davis-Parker CEO
Tel: 219-949-8595
Email: wbe@mytruckcity.com
Website: www.mytruckcity.com
Heavy Duty Trucks: Agricultural, Landscaping, Bucket, Vacuum, Fuel, Aerial, Welding, Digger Derrick, Pole, Straight, Box, Flat-bed, Bucket, Service, Platform, Dump, Runway Snow Plow, Railway, Refuse, Logging, Mounted Cranes, etc. (Woman, estab 1946, empl 58, sales $45,799,499, cert: State, WBENC)

Massachusetts

1799   Minuteman Trucks, Inc.
2181 Providence Hwy
Walpole, MA 02081
Contact: William L Witcher COO
Tel: 508-668-3112
Email: bwitcher@minutemantrucks.com
Website: www.minutemantrucks.com
Medium & Heavy Duty Truck Support Center. (Minority, estab 1990, empl 87, sales $47,359,662, cert: State, NMSDC)

Maryland

1800   K. Neal International Trucks, Inc.
5000 Tuxedo Rd
Hyattsville, MD 20781
Contact: Sharon Calomese CEO
Tel: 301-772-5100
Email: scalomese@knealinternational.com
Website: www.knealinternational.com
Commercial truck dealership: International, Hino, Mitsubishi Fuso trucks & IC Bus. Sales, service, parts & body shop services, leasing & rental services. (AA, estab 1982, empl 90, sales $110,000,000, cert: State, City, NMSDC)

Michigan

1801   Hall Whitener Investments, Inc.
       13475 Portage Rd
       Vicksburg, MI 49097
       Contact: Laura Awe Customer Relations Dir
       Tel: 269-649-2000
       Email: laura.awe@vicksburgchrysler.com
       Website: www.vicksburgchryslerdodgejeepram.com
Sale & service Chrysler, Dodge, Jeep , Ram vehicles. (AA,
estab 2013, empl 32, sales , cert: NMSDC)

1802   Vicksburg Chrysler Dodge Jeep
       13475 Portage Rd
       Vicksburg, MI 49097
       Contact: Monti Long President
       Tel: 269-649-2000
       Email: mlong007@comcast.net
       Website: www.VicksburgChryslerDodge.com
New & used cars, lease & fleet services. (AA, estab 1989,
empl 46, sales $22,521,322, cert: NMSDC)

Minnesota

1803   Holt Motors, Inc
       245 Cokato St W
       Cokato, MN 55321
       Contact: Kate Keith GM
       Tel: 320-286-2176
       Email:
       Website: www.holtmotors.com
Ford Vehicles, Commercial Ford Fleet Program. (Woman,
estab 1951, empl 48, sales , cert: WBENC)

Nevada

1804   SVI. Inc.
       440 Mark Leany Dr
       Henderson, NV 89011
       Contact: Nancy Munoz Sales Mgr
       Tel: 702-567-5256
       Email: nancy.munoz@specialtyvehicles.com
       Website: www.specialtyvehicles.com
Sales & distributer of people mover products, ie Buses,
Trams, Trolleys, Golf Carts, Ground Maintence Vehicles and
vehicle parts. (Minority, Woman, estab 2003, empl 13,
sales $14,036,900, cert: State, WBENC)

New York

1805   Fleet Maintenance, Inc.
       67 Ransier Dr
       West Seneca, NY 14224
       Contact: Deborah Gawron President
       Tel: 716-675-9220
       Email: debg@fmibuffalo.com
       Website: www.fmifreightliner.com
Truck dealership, Daimler Truck North America franchise
agreements. (Woman, estab 1979, empl 40, sales
$70,000,000, cert: State, WBENC)

1806   TransPerfect Global, Inc.
       3 Park Ave, 40th Fl
       New York, NY 10016
       Contact: Andrew Majalya Acct Exec
       Tel: 561-687-3331
       Email: amajalya@translations.com
       Website: www.transperfect.com
Multilingual Brand Management Cultural Consulting
(Woman, estab , empl , sales $472,000,000, cert: WBENC)

Ohio

1807   Auld Technologies, LLC
       2030 Dividend Dr
       Columbus, OH 43228
       Contact: Project Coord
       Tel: 614-755-2853
       Email: info@auldtech.com
       Website: www.auldtech.com
Dist decorative emblems, trim, labels, overlays & coating
solutions. (Woman, estab 2009, empl 26, sales
$3,500,000, cert: WBENC)

1808   Bob Ross Auto Group
       85 Loop Rd
       Centerville, OH 45459
       Contact: Fleet FSP Mgr
       Tel: 937-433-0990
       Email: fleet@bobrossauto.com
       Website: www.bobrossauto.com
New Vehicle Dealer, automobiles & light/medium duty
trucks: Buick, GMC Light Duty Trucks, Vans and SUVs;
Fiat Automobiles; Alfa Romeo Automobiles, Fleet &
Commercial Vehicles. (Woman/AA, estab 1974, empl 92,
sales $66,226,386, cert: State, WBENC)

Pennsylvania

1809   Buick GMC of Moosic Inc.
       4230 Birney Ave
       Moosic, PA 18507
       Contact: Lori Guitson President
       Tel: 570-414-1000
       Email: lori@sunbpg.com
       Website: www.sunbuickgmc.com
New Buick GMC's, economical cars to vehicles for
executives. (Woman, estab 2004, empl 18, sales
$14,000,000, cert: WBENC)

Texas

1810   Ancira
       10807 W IH 10
       San Antonio, TX 78230
       Contact: Betty Ferguson Mgr
       Tel: 210-558-1500
       Email: ljust@ancira.com
       Website: www.ancira.com
Automobile dealership. (Hisp, estab 1985, empl 25, sales
, cert: State)

1811   Kahlig Enterprises, Inc
       351 IH 35 South
       New Braunfels, TX 78130
       Contact: Larry Brown Exec Dir Fleet Sales
       Tel: 210-426-3295
       Email: lbrown@kahligauto.com
       Website: www.kahligauto.com
New Ford, Lincoln & Jeep automobiles, light trucks &
SUVs. (Hisp, estab 1984, empl 212, sales $343,000,000,
cert: NMSDC)

1812   Rio Motor
       4350 E Hwy 83
       Rio Grande City, TX 78582
       Contact: O.C. Canales President
       Tel: 956-487-2596
       Email: riomotorco@aol.com
       Website: www.riomotors.com
Sell Chevrolet cars, trucks, van parts & servicing. (Hisp,
estab 1953, empl 29, sales , cert: State)

AUTOMOTIVE PARTS & ACCESSORIES
Manufacturers of batteries, cables, recapping of tires, remanufacturing of auto parts, etc. Also lists wholesale distributors of automotive supplies & equipment. NAICS Code 42

California

1813   Concours Direct, Inc.
3212 El Camino Real
Atascadero, CA 93422
Contact: William M Vega
Tel: 805-466-4040
Email: wvega@concoursdirect.com
Website: www.concoursdirect.com
Dist Automotive & Truck Performance Parts, Ford Performance Racing Parts, Edelbrock, MSD, Airaid, Readylift, MBRP, Moroso, Diablosport, Bullydog, Performance Automatic, Centerforce, Tremec, Powermaster, Holly, etc. (Hisp, estab 2005, empl 2, sales $2,412,993, cert: NMSDC, CPUC)

1814   VIAIR Corporation
15 Edelman
Irvine, CA 92618
Contact: Alan Basham Dir of Operations
Tel: 949-585-0011
Email: alanb@viaircorp.com
Website: www.viaircorp.com
Dist Air Compressor, Air Tank, LED Light, Air accessories for automotive industry. (As-Pac, estab 1998, empl 32, sales $22,000,000, cert: NMSDC)

Florida

1815   Astra/CFX Holdings, LLC
11971 NW37th St
Coral Springs, FL 33065
Contact: Sharon McTurk President
Tel: 954-494-3948
Email: smcturk@astraservices.com
Website: www.astraservices.com
3PL Tire and Wheel Assembly, heavy Sub Assembly for all major vehicle modules. (Minority, Woman, estab 1989, empl 217, sales $8,950,000, cert: NMSDC, WBENC)

1816   Indus Solutions LLC
4260 NW 1st Ave
Boca Raton, FL 33433
Contact: Sandeep Vijay
Tel: 248-875-8010
Email: sv@indus-sol.com
Website: www.indus-sol.com
Mfr automotive parts & components, sub assemblies & assemblies of door, hood & tailgate systems, exhaust, steering & suspension, gaskets, rubber mounts, engine, electrical & electronics parts, wire harness & integrated products & prototyping. (As-Ind, estab 2015, empl 15, sales , cert: NMSDC)

1817   NM1, LLC
16725 NW 57th Ave
Miami Gardens, FL 33055
Contact: Rogelio (Roger) Tovar President
Tel: 888-423-7756
Email: rogeliotovar@gmail.com
Website: www.palmetto57nissan.com
Sell new & used cars, parts & service. (Hisp, estab 2012, empl 110, sales $74,101,851, cert: NMSDC)

1818   Vehicle Maintenance Program, Inc.
3595 N Dixie Hwy, Bay 7
Boca Raton, FL 33431
Contact: Penny Brooks CEO
Tel: 561-362-6080
Email: accounting@vmpparts.com
Website: www.vmpparts.com
Dist vehicle repair parts: filters, wiper blades, lenses, lamps, bulbs, mirrors, batteries, seals, bearings, brake drums. (Woman, estab 1988, empl 15, sales $23,443,700, cert: State, WBENC)

Georgia

1819   Battle and Battle Distributors, Inc
2410 Park Central Blvd.
Decatur, GA 30035
Contact: Sylvia Battle VP
Tel: 770-987-8147
Email: sylvia@battleandbattle.net
Website: www.battleandbattle.net
Dist industrial batteries, automotive, batteries & battery equip. (AA, estab , empl , sales , cert: NMSDC)

Illinois

1820   Bearings & Industrial Supply
431 Imen Ave
Addison, IL 60101
Contact: Sejal Khandwala Acct Exec
Tel: 630-628-1966
Email: Sejal@BearingsNow.Com
Website: www.bearingsnow.com
Dist bearings & power transmission products; pump & pump repair parts, HVAC & electrical parts. (As-Pac, estab , empl , sales , cert: NMSDC)

1821   Chicago Parts & Sound, LLC
1150 Lively Blvd
Elk Grove Village, IL 60007
Contact: Dennis Hoffberg Sales Mgr
Tel: 630-350-1500
Email: sales@clickoncps.com
Website: www.clickoncps.com/
Dist automotive parts, commodity lines such as Anco wiper blades. (Minority, Woman, estab 1978, empl 80, sales , cert: City)

1822   J&J's Creative Colors, Inc.
19015 S Jodi Rd - Ste E Ste E
Mokena, IL 60448
Contact: Terri Sniegolski
Tel: 708-478-1437
Email: terri@creativecolorsintl.com
Website: www.WeCanFixThat.com
On-site repair for leather, vinyl, fabric and plastics to the auto industry. (Woman, estab 1980, empl 21, sales $18,384,759, cert: WBENC)

1823 Reliance Distributing
3609 Pebble Beach Rd
Northbrook, IL 60062
Contact: Anne Chessick CEO
Tel: 847-372-6125
Email: annieparts@aol.com
Website: www.reliancedistributing.com
Automotive & truck lighting, flashers, wiper blades, fuses, hose clamps, halogen headlight sockets, permatex products (Woman, estab 2012, empl 1, sales , cert: WBENC)

Indiana

1824 Wingard Wheel Works, LLC
1521 Kepner Dr
Lafayette, IN 47905
Contact: David Oliver GM
Tel: 765-449-3509
Email: doliver@wingard.biz
Website: www.wingardllc.com
Wingard Wheel Works specializes in Tire and Wheel Assembly as well as offering services in logistics management and procurement of material. (AA, estab 2007, empl 20, sales $51,432,000, cert: NMSDC)

Kentucky

1825 HJI Supply Chain Solutions
13200 Complete Court
Louisville, KY 40223
Contact: Lynn Moore VP Finance & Admin
Tel: 502-638-8064
Email: lmoore@hjisolutions.com
Website: www.hjisolutions.com
Automotive parts: door panel/trim, switch bezels, running boards, driveshafts, shocks, corner pillars, floor mats & hub caps. (Woman, estab 0, empl , sales , cert: NMSDC)

1826 LB Manufacturing
360 Industry Dr
Springfield, KY 40069
Contact: Keith Hamilton CEO
Tel: 859-336-0090
Email: hamiltonk@leanbmfg.com
Website: www.leanbmfg.com
Automotive stamping, welding & mfg assemblies, mig & resistance, robotic, window glass & exhaust system assemblies. (AA, estab 1998, empl 40, sales $17,000,000, cert: NMSDC)

Michigan

1827 Advanced Assembly Products, Inc.
1300 East Nine Mile Road
Hazel Park, MI 48030
Contact: Ron Waring IT Systems Mgr
Tel: 248-543-2427
Email: rwaring@aapincorp.com
Website: www.aapincorp.com
Body hardware, door hinges, door checks, strikers, hood hinges, deck lid hinges, stampings, welded assemblies, mechanical assemblies. (As-Ind, estab 1993, empl 140, sales $18,000,000, cert: NMSDC)

1828 BBW Holdings Inc.
318 John R Rd
Troy, MI 48083
Contact: Barry Williams President
Tel: 248-935-6161
Email: barry@bbwholdings.com
Website: www.bbwholdings.com
Vehicle manage solutions, vehicle inspection, processing tracking storage. (AA, estab 2009, empl 37, sales , cert: NMSDC)

1829 CAMACO, LLC
40000 Grand River Ste 110
Novi, MI 48375
Contact: Pamela Cooper Admin Coord
Tel: 248-442-6800
Email: pcooper@camacollc.com
Website: www.camacollc.com
Mfr auto components & assemblies. (As-Ind, estab 1987, empl 68, sales , cert: NMSDC)

1830 Capsonic Automotive & Aersopace
3121 University Dr, Ste 120
Auburn Hills, MI 48326
Contact: George E. Albrecht CQA
Tel: 248-754-1100
Email: georgea@capsonic.com
Website: www.capsonic.com
Automotive assemblies. (AA, estab 1996, empl 449, sales $18,000,000, cert: NMSDC)

1831 Concept Industries, Inc.
4950 Kraft Ave SE
Grand Rapids, MI 49512
Contact: David Foote, Troy Caswell CFO
Tel: 616-554-9000
Email: dfoote@conceptind.com,
troyc@conceptind.com
Website: www.conceptind.com
Thermoforming, interior acoustical applications, engine side noise absorbers, dash insulators, package trays, load floors, undercarpet absorbers, headliners, trunk liners, needle punch, laminating, plastic vacuum forming, die cut. (Minority, Woman, estab 1984, empl 150, sales $20,000,000, cert: NMSDC)

1832 Dawson Mfg Co. - Benton Harbor Division
1042 N Crystal Ave
Benton Harbor, MI 49022
Contact: Neil Trivedi VP
Tel: 269-925-0100
Email: neil.trivedi@vibracoustic.com.com
Website: www.dawsonmfg.com
Mfr body mounts, engine mounts, strut mounts, link assemblies & bushings, dist anti-vibration components, rubber injection molding. (As-Pac, estab 1988, empl 90, sales $36,000,000, cert: NMSDC)

1833 Detroit Chassis LLC
6501 Lynch Rd
Detroit, MI 48234
Contact: Darin Burns VP Business Dev
Tel: 313-571-2100
Email: dburns@detroitchassis.com
Website: www.detroitchassis.com
Niche vehicle, motor home chassis & commercial truck assembly; complex sub-assemblies & sub-assemblies. (AA, estab 1998, empl 150, sales $7,615,052, cert: NMSDC)

1834 Diversitech, Inc.
16620 Industrial St
Roseville, MI 48066
Contact: Roger Olle President
Tel: 586-445-7600
Email: rho@div-techusa.com
Website: www.div-techusa.com
Design & build automation assembly machines, leak test, special machines for powertrain & body & assembly, parts feeding & handling systems. (As-Ind, estab 2009, empl 4, sales $1,500,000, cert: NMSDC)

1835 Firstronic LLC
1655 Michigan St NE
Grand Rapids, MI 49503
Contact: Tony Bellitto Quality Dir
Tel: 616-808-3878
Email: tbellitto@firstronic.com
Website: www.firstronic.com
Dist automotive components: lighting controls, various sensors & control modules. (Woman, estab 1995, empl 50, sales $20,000,000, cert: WBENC)

1836 Global Enterprises
26909 Woodward Ave
Huntington Woods, MI 48070
Contact: Pat Vizcarra Business Dev
Tel: 248-542-2000
Email: pvizcarra@globalent.org
Website: www.globalent.org
Extrusion, die-cutting, compression molding, laminating & glueing interior trim components & assemblies. (Minority, Woman, estab 1998, empl 280, sales , cert: WBENC)

1837 H.R. Technologies, Inc.
32500 N. Avis Dr
Madison Heights, MI 48071
Contact: Tushar Patel President
Tel: 248-284-1170
Email: tpatel@hrtechinc.com
Website: www.hrtechinc.com
Laminate fabrics & vinyl, carpet, die cutting, headliner glass fiber reinforcements, headliner glass polypropylene substrate materials. (As-Ind, estab 1996, empl 48, sales $11,000,000, cert: NMSDC)

1838 Integrated Manufacturing and Assembly, LLC
5200 Auto Club Dr
Dearborn, MI 48126
Contact: Leslie Thumm Financial Anyalyst
Tel: 313-593-9246
Email: lthumm@lear.com
Website: www.comerholdings.com/about.htm
Interior Systems; seat assemblies, foam & trim assemblies & injection molded & painted interior components - Exterior Systems; Exterior mirror assemblies, inection molded & painted interiors. (AA, estab 1996, empl 700, sales , cert: NMSDC)

1839 Intex Technologies LLC
3133 Highland Dr
Hudsonville, MI 49426
Contact: Randi Sniegowski Sales
Tel: 616-662-0276
Email: randi.sniegowski@intextech.net
Website: www.intextech.net
Mfr integral skin flexible foam automotive interior parts: arm rests, center console, console door, sun visor, steering wheel, soft-touch points on door handles, cup holders, seals, jounce bumpers & insulation components. (Hisp, estab 2008, empl 50, sales $14,800,000, cert: NMSDC)

1840 La Solucion Corp.
19930 Conner
Detroit, MI 48234
Contact: Patricia Leon CEO
Tel: 313-893-9760
Email: patleon@la-solucion.com
Website: www.la-solucion.com
Mfr & dist liquid & air filtration systems. (Minority, Woman, estab 1999, empl 4, sales , cert: NMSDC, WBENC)

1841 Marimba Auto, LLC
41133 Van Born Rd Ste 200
Belleville, MI 48111
Contact: Venkat Chigulla VP Admin
Tel: 734-398-9000
Email: vchigulla@marimbaauto.com
Website: www.marimbaauto.com
Import tubing, tube processing, global supply mgmt, in-house engineering, warehousing. (As-Pac, estab 2003, empl 35, sales $17,000,000, cert: NMSDC)

1842 McKechnie Vehicle Components
27087 Gratiot Ave, 2 Fl
Roseville, MI 48066
Contact: Linda Torakis President
Tel: 586-491-2622
Email: ltorakis@mvcusa.com
Website: www.mvcusa.com
Mfr decorative trim products: nickel chrome plating on plastic and stainless surfaces, plastic injection molding, metal stamping, base and clear coat painting and assembly. (Woman, estab 0, empl , sales , cert: WBENC)

1843 Need a Part Now, LLC
1157 Manufacturers Dr
Westland, MI 48186
Contact: Erin Brazill VP
Tel: 888-201-9061
Email: erina@needapartnow.com
Website: www.needapartnow.com
Mfr parts from AutoCad, blueprints, drawings, sketches, or reverse engineer. (Woman, estab 2006, empl 20, sales , cert: WBENC)

1844 NYX Inc.
30111 Schoolcraft Rd
Livonia, MI 48150
Contact: Dan DePalma VP Sales
Tel: 734-462-2385
Email: sales@nyxinc.com
Website: www.nyxinc.com
Automotive interior solutions: Door Panels, Center
Consoles, Overhead Consoles, Glove Box Systems, Knee
Bolster Assemblies, Interior Garnish, Seating Components,
Rear Shelf package Trays, Design and Engineering. (As-Pac,
estab 1985, empl 2100, sales , cert: NMSDC)

1845 Piston Automotive
12723 Telegraph Rd
Redford, MI 48239
Contact: James Edwards Sales Mgr
Tel: 313-541-8674
Email: jedwards@pistongroup.com
Website: www.pistongroup.com
Manufacturing, module assembly & sequencing, & logistics
management. (AA, estab 1995, empl 750, sales , cert:
NMSDC)

1846 Sigma International
36800 Plymouth Rd
Livonia, MI 48150
Contact: Alessandra Konopczyk Operations Mgr
Tel: 248-230-9681
Email: akonopczyk@sigmaintl.com
Website: www.sigmaintl.com
Mfr labels, decals, badges, chrome abs parts, wheel center
caps, dimensional graphics, stone chip protection film. (AA,
estab 2003, empl 10, sales , cert: NMSDC)

1847 Sino Brite (USA), Inc.
30600 Telegraph Rd, Ste 1131
Bingham Farms, MI 48025
Contact: Julinda Kong President
Tel: 659-819-7871
Email: sales@sinobrite-sg.com
Website: www.sinobrite-sg.com
Motor Vehicle Supplies & New Parts Merchant Wholesal-
ers. (As-Pac, estab 2003, empl 5, sales , cert: NMSDC)

1848 Ventura Manufacturing
471 E Roosevelt
Zeeland, MI 49464
Contact: Ana Figueroa Finance
Tel: 616-772-7405
Email: ana.figueroa@venturamfg.com
Website: www.venturamfg.com
Mfr automotive dimming rearview mirror components,
wire processing components, overhead grabhandles.
(Minority, Woman, estab 1997, empl 140, sales
$26,000,000, cert: NMSDC)

Minnesota

1849 DV Roland Enterprises, Inc.
15171 Freeland Ave N
Hugo, MN 55038
Contact: Kenny Scamp General Mgr
Tel: 651-429-9012
Email: ken@jtservicesinc.com
Website: www.jtservicesinc.com
Dist & service industrial diesel engines & diesel engine
parts. Supporting diesel engines for aerial lifts, air
compressors, backhoes, dozers, excavators, forklifts,
generators, light towers, rollers, skid steer loaders,
tractors, welders. (AA, estab 2004, empl 6, sales
$1,433,333, cert: City, NMSDC)

Missouri

1850 JCM Machine, Inc.
5655 Old Hwy 21
House Springs, MO 63051
Contact: Laura Borrini Owner
Tel: 636-942-4567
Email: lborrini@jcmmachineandcoatings.com
Website: www.jcmmachineandcoatings.com
Automotive machine shop, cylinder head & engine
rebuilding, certified ceramic coatings applicators & dry
film lubricants. (Woman, estab 1976, empl 4, sales
$223,000, cert: State)

New Jersey

1851 Suburban Auto Seat Co., Inc.
35 Industrial Rd
Lodi, NJ 07644
Contact: Amy Winfield President
Tel: 973-778-9227
Email: amyw@suburbanseats.com
Website: www.suburbanseats.com
Dist aftermarket truck seats, delivery truck seats, truck
parts, material handling equipment seats, truck & cab
accessories, safety equipment. (Woman, estab 1947,
empl 10, sales $7,002,253, cert: WBENC)

1852 Wexco Industries
3 Barnet Rd
Pine Brook, NJ 07058
Contact: Paula Lombard President
Tel: 973-244-5777
Email: plombard@wexcoind.com
Website: www.wexcoind.com
Dist complete windshield wiper systems. (Woman, estab
1991, empl 30, sales $18,367,600, cert: WBENC)

Tennessee

1853 Wingard Quality Supply, LLC
5901 Shallowford Rd Ste 20
Chattanooga, TN 37421
Contact: James Wingard President
Tel: 423-521-4600
Email: james@wingard.biz
Website: www.wingardll.com
Automotive assembly: tire & wheel. (AA, estab 2002,
empl 25, sales $60,000,000, cert: NMSDC)

CHEMICALS

Manufacturers and distributors of organic and inorganic chemicals, fertilizers, blasting materials, radioactive, cosmetic & industrial chemicals, paints, glues, drilling mud, oil derivatives, pharmaceutical preservatives, blowing agents, coatings, lubricants and solvents. Also chemical and custom packaging. NAICS Code 42

Alabama

1854 Stutton Corporation
1256 McCaig Rd
Lincoln, AL 35096
Contact: Lorraine Studin President
Tel: 205-763-2000
Email: info@stuttoncorp.com
Website: www.stuttoncorp.com
Mfr & dist chemicals: lubricants, greases, degreasers, cleaners, sealers, epoxy strippers, paint strippers, citrus solvents, deodorizers, corrosion barriers, rust penetrants, spray insulation, sealers, adhesives. (Woman, estab 1977, empl 12, sales $1,900,000, cert: State)

Arizona

1855 Chemical Distribution Solutions, LLC
1125 Oak St Ste 303
Conway, AR 72032
Contact: Anthony Wilmington President
Tel: 501-978-1111
Email: admin@chemicalds.com
Website: www.chemicalds.com
Custom Blending, Valued Products, Chemical Distribution (AA, estab 2011, empl 4, sales $7,198,033, cert: NMSDC)

Arkansas

1856 Welsco, Inc.
9006 Crystal Hill Rd
North Little Rock, AR 72113
Contact: Chris Layton President
Tel: 501-771-1204
Email: chris.layton@welsco.com
Website: www.Welsco.com
Welding gases and Supplies, industrial supplies and Spec gases. (Woman, estab 1941, empl 127, sales $40,000,000, cert: NWBOC)

California

1857 Anahau Energy, LLC
2041 Rosecrans Ave, Ste 322
El Segundo, CA 90245
Contact: Suyen Pell CEO
Tel: 310-414-2300
Email: proposals@anahauenergy.com
Website: www.anahauenergy.com
Electric power, natural gas, and renewable products. (As-Pac, estab 2005, empl 10, sales , cert: NMSDC)

1858 Apac Chemical Corp.
150 N. Santa Anita Ave, Ste 850
Arcadia, CA 91006
Contact: Tom Kusaka
Tel: 626-203-0066
Email: sales@apacchemical.com
Website: www.apacchemical.com
Mfr Sorbic acid & Potassium sorbate. (As-Pac, estab 1999, empl 7, sales $19,000,000, cert: NMSDC)

1859 Cervantes Distribution Companies, Inc.
471 W Lambert Rd, Ste 100
Brea, CA 92821
Contact: Rick Gross President
Tel: 714-990-3940
Email: rsg@cervantes-delgado.com
Website: www.cervantesdistribution.com
Marketing and distributing dry urea and urea solutions for SCR and SNCR NOx systems. (Hisp, estab 2001, empl 3, sales , cert: CPUC)

1860 Ensunet Consulting Corporation
10679 Westview Pkwy, 2nd Fl
San Diego, CA 92126
Contact: Paul Robinson President
Tel: 858-348-4690
Email: paul.robinson@ensucorp.com
Website: www.ensunet.com
Dist lubricants, fuel additives & safety fluids. (AA, estab 2008, empl 8, sales , cert: NMSDC)

1861 Ferco Color
2315 Baker Ave
Ontario, CA 91761
Contact: Jennifer Thaw President
Tel: 909-930-0773
Email: info@fercocolor.com
Website: www.fercocolor.com/
Mfr color & additives for plastics, bottles, closures. (Woman, estab 1994, empl 48, sales $16,000,000, cert: WBENC)

1862 Genard, inc. dba Lennova
1717 Boyd St
Santa Ana, CA 92705
Contact: Tony Genova VP Sales & Mktg
Tel: 562-860-3213
Email: tony@lennova.net
Website: www.lennova.net
Install epoxy & urethane protective floor & wall coatings. (Hisp, estab 2000, empl 15, sales $2,387,000, cert: CPUC)

1863 Impact Absorbents, Inc.
5255 Traffic Way
Atascadero, CA 93422
Contact: Tammy Rayner Dir of Corporate Sales
Tel: 800-339-7672
Email: trayner@spillhero.com
Website: www.spillhero.com
Mfr & dist granular absorbents, sorbent pads, sorbents socks, spill clean up programs and products, non-hazardous, earth friendly, cost effective. XSORB, FiberDuck, FiberLink, Spill Station, Spill Caddy, Spill Rack, Biohazard Kit. (Woman, estab 1992, empl 30, sales $5,300,000, cert: State)

1864   LMC Enterprises, dba Chemco Products Company
      6401 Alondra Blvd
      Paramount, CA 90723
      Contact: Erica Utz Wochna VP Human Resources
      Tel: 866-243-6261
      Email: erica@chemcoprod.com
      Website: www.chemcoprod.com
Chemical commodities: sodium hydroxide, potassium hydroxide, sulfuric acid, phosphoric acid, citric acid, sodium hypochlorite. (Woman, estab 1976, empl 125, sales $43,324,790, cert: WBENC)

1865   Merrimac Energy Group
      1240 E Wardlow Rd
      Long Beach, CA 90807
      Contact: Mary Hazelrigg President
      Tel: 562-427-6565
      Email: mhazelrigg@merrimacenergy.net
      Website: www.merrimacenergy.net
Transportation and generator fuels. (Woman, estab 1988, empl 5, sales $30,000,000, cert: CPUC)

1866   Pinnacle Petroleum, Inc.
      16651 Gemini Lane
      Huntington Beach, CA 92647
      Contact: Liz McKinley President
      Tel: 714-841-8877
      Email: lmckinley@pinnaclepetroleum.com
      Website: www.pinnaclepetroleum.com
Dist petroleum & lubricants, fuel management services. (Woman, estab 1995, empl 25, sales $176,000,000, cert: WBENC)

1867   Pynergy, LLC
      4495 S Santa Fe Dr
      Englewood, CA 80110
      Contact: Darrell Jackson President
      Tel: 303-292-5005
      Email: djackson@pynergy.com
      Website: www.pynergy.com
Dist Diesel, On-Site Refueling, Gasoline, Wet Hose Refueling, High Octane Fuels, Diesel Generator Fuel Delivery, Ethanol, Diesel Fuel Treatment Program, Biodiesel Kerosene, Lubricant/Fuel Management, Aviation Fuel & Lubricants. (Woman/AA, estab 1999, empl 44, sales $31,103,590, cert: City)

1868   Ramos Oil Company, Inc.
      1515 S River Rd
      West Sacramento, CA 95691
      Contact: Sarah Russell
      Tel: 916-371-2570
      Email: sarahr@ramosoil.com
      Website: www.ramosoil.com
Dist fuel & oils. (Hisp, estab 1951, empl 185, sales , cert: CPUC)

1869   RCI Technologies, Inc.
      462 Borrego Ct, Ste D
      San Dimas, CA 91773
      Contact: Gabriel Gutierrez President
      Tel: 909-305-1241
      Email: gabeg@rcitechnologies.com
      Website: www.rcitechnologies.com
Dist diesel fuel purification products, universal fuel purifiers, portable tank cleaning units & automatic fuel recirculating systems. (Minority, Woman, estab 1994, empl 5, sales $2,042,449, cert: WBENC)

1870   STARDUST Spill Products, LLC
      45 Mirador
      Irvine, CA 92612
      Contact: Timothy McDuffie CEO
      Tel: 714-550-4999
      Email: tim@stardustspillproducts.com
      Website: www.stardustspillproducts.com
Mfr STARDUST Super Absorbent™: absorbs animal, vegetable, mineral, petroleum & chemical liquids. (AA, estab 2018, empl 4, sales $1,017,723, cert: NMSDC)

1871   Western States Distributing
      1790 S 10 St
      San Jose, CA 95112
      Contact: Louis Burford Admin
      Tel: 482-292-1041
      Email: slopes@lubeoil.com
      Website: www.lubeoil.com
Dist petroleum. (Hisp, estab 1956, empl 44, sales , cert: CPUC)

Colorado

1872   Birko Corporation
      9152 Yosemite St
      Henderson, CO 80640
      Contact: Kelly Green President
      Tel: 303-289-1090
      Email: kgreen@birkocorp.com
      Website: www.birkocorp.com
Mfr & dist chemicals, industrial hygiene, hand soaps & sanitizers, surface sanitizers & cleaners, specialty white-oil based lubricants, chemical dispensing equipment, chemical allocation tracking equipment, steam/water temperature control valves. (Woman, estab 1952, empl 59, sales , cert: WBENC)

Connecticut

1873   Hartford Technologies, Inc.
      1022 Elm St, Ste 201
      Rocky Hill, CT 06067
      Contact: Vickie Brown Dir Natl Sales
      Tel: 860-571-3602
      Email: vbrown@hartfordtechnologies.com
      Website: www.hartfordtechnologies.com
Dist adhesives & coatings. (Woman, estab 1930, empl 129, sales , cert: WBENC)

1874   Prochimie International, Inc.
      2 Waterside Crossing
      Windsor, CT 06095
      Contact: Anna Malz VP
      Tel: - -
      Email: amalz@prochimieinternational.com
      Website: www.prochimieinternational.com
Chemical products: Automotive/Tire, Agrochemical, Oil field, Water Treatment, Pharmaceutical, Photographic and Specialty chemicals. (Woman, estab 1975, empl 10, sales $6,000,000, cert: WBENC)

1875   U.S. Chemicals, LLC
      22 Thorndal Circle
      Darien, CT 06820
      Contact: Carol Piccaro President
      Tel: 203-202-2808
      Email: cpiccaro@uschemicals-wob.com
      Website: www.uschemicals-wob.com
Dist chemicals. (Woman, estab 0, empl 15, sales $90,000,000, cert: WBENC)

Delaware

1876   KRETETEK Industries, LLC
       1000 N West St
       Wilmington, DE 19801
       Contact: Joshua Moore Owner
       Tel: 855-573-8383
       Email: support@kretetek.com
       Website: www.ghostshield.com
Mfr concrete sealing products designed to provide long-lasting protection for their concrete projects. (Hisp, estab 2013, empl 10, sales , cert: NMSDC)

Florida

1877   Algon Corporation
       12000 SW 132 Court
       Miami, FL 33186
       Contact: Eduardo Suarez-Troconis Dir
       Tel: 305-253-6901
       Email: edal@algon.com
       Website: www.algon.com
Chemical raw materials, laboratory supplies & machine parts. (Minority, Woman, estab 1989, empl 24, sales $20,570,883, cert: NMSDC)

1878   Bell Performance
       1340 Bennett Dr
       Longwood, FL 32750
       Contact: Deb Moon Dir of Sales
       Tel: 407-831-5021
       Email: dmoon@bellperformance.net
       Website: www.bellperformance.com
Mfr commercial grade treatments for diesel, ethanol, gasoline, fuel oil & power plant fuels. (Woman, estab , empl 16, sales $1,543,035, cert: WBENC)

1879   Burck Oil Co., Inc.
       1401 53rd St
       West Palm Beach, FL 33407
       Contact: Jefffrey Burck President
       Tel: 561-842-3600
       Email: jeffburck@burckoil.com
       Website: www.burckoil.com
Dist oil, grease & lubricants; food grade lubricants. (Woman, estab 1996, empl 4, sales $3,600,000, cert: State)

1880   Chemical Systems
       PO Box 810
       Zellwood, FL 32798
       Contact: Corky Thein President
       Tel: 407-886-2329
       Email: corky.thein@chemicalsystems.com
       Website: www.chemicalsystems.com
Mfr sanitation & specialty chemicals. (Hisp, estab 1979, empl 23, sales $20,000,000, cert: State, NMSDC)

1881   Graham Trading Company, LLC
       3001 N. Rocky Point Dr. East, Ste 200
       Tampa, FL 33607
       Contact: Darrell Graham CEO
       Tel: 855-256-8237
       Email: info@gratraco.com
       Website: www.gratraco.com
Dist diesel, gasoline, jet fuel & lubricants. (AA, estab 2014, empl 2, sales $250,000, cert: State, NMSDC)

1882   Osceola Supply, Inc.
       915 Commerce Blvd
       Midway, FL 32343
       Contact: Doro Hittinger President
       Tel: 850-580-9800
       Email: dhittinger@osceolasupply.com
       Website: www.osceolasupply.com
Dist chemicals. (Woman, estab 1991, empl 46, sales $13,000,000, cert: State)

1883   Petruj Chemical Corporation
       8055 NW 98th St
       Hialeah Gardens, FL 33016
       Contact: Adrian Garcia Sales Dir
       Tel: 305-556-1271
       Email: adrian@formula88.com
       Website: www.formula88.com
Dist chemicals. (Minority, Woman, estab 1976, empl 12, sales $2,552,032, cert: NMSDC)

Georgia

1884   DES Wholesale, LLC
       601 West Crossville Road
       Roswell, GA 30075
       Contact: Allison Sheffield de Aguero President
       Tel: 404-671-9593
       Email: info@diversified.energy
       Website: www.diversifiedenergy.com/
Dist natural gas, electric power & fleet fuel. (Woman/Hisp, estab 2011, empl 20, sales $149,224,828, cert: CPUC, WBENC)

1885   DJG Chemical, Inc.
       4761 Hugh Howell Rd D
       Tucker, GA 30084
       Contact: Carla Doleman CEO
       Tel: 404-244-4606
       Email: cdoleman@djgchem.com
       Website: www.djgchemical.com
Mfr & dist chemical products: adhesives, janitorial, lubricants, raw materials, water treatment chemicals, foam soaps, herbicides, cosmetic chemicals, etc. (AA, estab 2003, empl 8, sales , cert: NMSDC)

1886   PS Energy Group, Inc.
       4480 North Shallowford Rd Ste 100
       Dunwoody, GA 30338
       Contact: Allison Laudano Sales & Marketing Assistant
       Tel: 800-334-7548
       Email: allison.laudano@psenergy.com
       Website: www.psenergy.com
Dist natural gas, vehicle fleet fuel mgmt, diesel fuel, gasoline, jet fuel, propane, etc. (Minority, Woman, estab , empl , sales $165,000,000, cert: NMSDC, WBENC)

1887   Simcol Group, LLC
       3455 Peachtree Rd NE, 5th Fl
       Atlanta, GA 30326
       Contact: Simon Guobadia CEO
       Tel: 404-995-7037
       Email: simon@simcolgroup.com
       Website: www.simcolgroup.com
Fuel, gasoline, jet fuel, aviation fuel, diesel fuel, lubricants, wax. (AA, estab 2009, empl 10, sales , cert: NMSDC)

1888 Supreme Resources, Inc.
      285 E Smoketree Terr
      Alpharetta, GA 30005
      Contact: Victor Tan Business Dir
      Tel: 770-475-4638
      Email: victortan@supremeresources.com
      Website: www.supremeresources.com
Dist chemicals, resins, adhesives & raw materials. (As-Pac, estab 1988, empl 10, sales , cert: NMSDC)

1889 TDMC Enterprises Inc.
      370 Great Southwest Pkwy
      Atlanta, GA 30336
      Contact: Chuck Smith President
      Tel: 404-699-5404
      Email: cesmith@chemstationatlanta.com
      Website: www.chemstation.com
Mfr industrial chemicals: cleaners, degreasers, vehicle & airplane cleaners, food processing, odor control, parts washing, scrubber soaps, asphalt release products, strippers, etc. (AA, estab 1991, empl 14, sales $870,000, cert: NMSDC)

Iowa

1890 Searle Petroleum Co.
      PO Box A
      Council Bluffs, IA 51502
      Contact: David Bills VP
      Tel: 712-323-2441
      Email: davidb@redgiantoil.com
      Website: www.redgiantoil.com
Dist engine oils, hydraulic, compressor, journal, grease. (Woman, estab , empl 88, sales $53,500,000, cert: WBENC)

Illinois

1891 Blackdog Corporation
      2305 Enterprise Dr
      Westchester, IL 60154
      Contact: Marc Whitaker Chief Marketing Officer
      Tel: 877-617-4104
      Email: marc@blackdogcorp.com
      Website: www.blackdogcorp.com
Dist fuel, oil & lubricants. (As-Pac, estab 2006, empl 46, sales $23,500,000, cert: City, NMSDC)

1892 Budnick Converting Inc.
      200 Admiral Weinel Blvd
      Columbia, IL 62236
      Contact: Lori Baltz Acct Mgr
      Tel: 800-282-0090
      Email: samwi@budnickconverting.com
      Website: www.budnickconverting.com
Convert & dist adhesive tapes & foams, cutting, slitting, laminating, printing & spooling. (Woman, estab 1952, empl 85, sales $20,000,000, cert: WBENC)

1893 Cedar Concepts Corporation
      4342 S Wolcott Ave
      Chicago, IL 60609
      Contact: Roxanne Hubbard Marketing Mgr
      Tel: 773-890-5790
      Email: roxanne@cedarconcepts.net
      Website: www.cedarconcepts.net
Mfr surfactants & chemical intermediates. (Woman/AA, estab 1991, empl 41, sales $15,000,000, cert: WBENC)

1894 Celta Chemical, Inc.
      1301 W First St, Ste 1A
      Granite City, IL 62040
      Contact: Patrick Riordan VP
      Tel: 314-440-6194
      Email: pat@celtachem.com
      Website: www.celtachem.com
Chemical & food ingredient toll manufacturer and supplier. (Woman, estab 2014, empl 8, sales $15,000,000, cert: WBENC)

1895 Essential Water Technologies LLC
      6625 N. Avondale Ave
      Chicago, IL 60631
      Contact: Lori Hilson Cioromski President
      Tel: 630-344-6770
      Email: lori@essentialwatertech.com
      Website: www.essentialwatertech.com
Water treatment chemicals & services. (Woman, estab 2011, empl 8, sales $902,221, cert: WBENC)

1896 Petrochem, Inc.
      6N999 Whispering Trail Rd
      St. Charles, IL 60175
      Contact: Jill Dohner VP
      Tel: 630-513-6350
      Email: jdohner@petrochem1.com
      Website: www.petrochem1.com
Dist synthetic lubricants: proofer chains, food grade lubricants for cooler chains, gears & hydraulics. (Woman, estab 1998, empl 2, sales $1,000,000, cert: WBENC)

1897 Quimex, Inc.
      14702 S Hamlin
      Midlothian, IL 60445
      Contact: Felipe Estrada Acct Mgr
      Tel: 708-597-6201
      Email: quimex@quimexinc.com
      Website: www.quimexinc.com
Dist industrial chemicals, oils, lubricants, solvents & coatings. (Hisp, estab 1975, empl 14, sales $6,309,695, cert: City)

1898 West Fuels Inc.
      82 S La Grange Road Ste 201
      La Grange, IL 60525
      Contact: Deborah Stange President
      Tel: 708-588-1900
      Email: dstange@westfuels.com
      Website: www.westfuels.com
Dist petroleum products. (Woman, estab 1991, empl 9, sales $10,600,000, cert: State, City, WBENC)

Indiana

1899 Advance Energy LLC
      3580 N Hobart Rd, Ste C
      Hobart, IN 46342
      Contact: Vance Kenney Managing Partner
      Tel: 219-794-1277
      Email: vance.kenney@advanceegy.com
      Website: www.advanceegy.com
Petroleum related products & services: gas, diesel & oil related products. (AA, estab 2012, empl 10, sales , cert: NMSDC)

1900 Harris and Ford, LLC
      9307 E 56th St
      Indianapolis, IN 46216
      Contact: Tim Harris II Business Devel
      Tel: 317-591-0000
      Email: tth@harrisandford.com
      Website: www.harrisandford.com
Dist chemicals & ingredients. (AA, estab 1994, empl 50, sales $220,000,000, cert: NMSDC)

1901 J2 Systems and Supply, LLC
      803 E 38th St
      Indianapolis, IN 46205
      Contact: James Leonard Owner
      Tel: 317-602-3940
      Email: jleonard@j2ssllc.com
      Website: www.j2systemsandsupply.com
Dist chemicals: water treatment, waste-water treatment, metal surface cleaning & coating, food ingredients & additives, industrial floor & general purpose cleaners. (AA, estab 2007, empl 5, sales $245,949, cert: State, NMSDC)

1902 Lemak, LLC dba Lemak Lubricants
      PO Box 1381
      Noblesville, IN 46061
      Contact: Elizabeth Reynolds President
      Tel: 260-906-6433
      Email: beth@lemakllc.com
      Website: www.lemakllc.com/
Dist petroleum & chemicals: Industrial & Automotive Lubricants, Propane, Fuels, Coolants and Cutting Fluids, Antifreeze, Specialty & Commodity Chemicals. (Woman, estab 2008, empl 2, sales $3,289,096, cert: State, WBENC)

1903 Mays Chemical Company
      5611 E 71st St
      Indianapolis, IN 46220
      Contact: Julie Brown Inventory Planning Admin
      Tel: 317-558-2045
      Email: julieb@mayschem.com
      Website: www.mayschem.com
Dist process chemicals: bags, drums & totes, technical, reagent & USP/FCC grades. Electronic grade chemicals, antifreeze, caustic soda, etc. (Hisp, estab 1980, empl 70, sales $95,000,000, cert: NMSDC)

1904 Supreme Oil Company
      1319 Vincennes St
      New Albany, IN 47150
      Contact: Matt Sexton VP
      Tel: 812-945-5266
      Email: msexton@heritageoil.com
      Website: www.supremelubricants.com
Mobil & Chevron oils, lubricants & greases, hydraulic oil, motor oil, gear oil, synthetic oil, biodegradeable oil, antifreeze, coolants & cleaners. (Woman, estab 1937, empl 7, sales $15,359,000, cert: NWBOC)

1905 VTI Contracting, Inc.
      831 Elston Dr
      Shelbyville, IN 46176
      Contact: Judy Montgomery President
      Tel: 317-398-7911
      Email: jm@vtitotalsolutions.com
      Website: www.vtitotalsolutions.com
Concrete coatings, sealants, epoxy and resinous coatings, polishing, repair, staining, traffic coatings, striping, caulking, expansion joints, joint filler, fire proof caulking, air barriers, waterproofing. (Woman, estab 1985, empl 30, sales $3,000,010,000, cert: State, City)

Kentucky

1906 Hexagon Technologies, Inc.
      PO Box 23163
      Louisville, KY 40223
      Contact: Mr. Kiran Shah President
      Tel: 502-429-8990
      Email: hexafloc@bellsouth.net
      Website: www.hexagontech.net
Water & wastewater treatment chemicals & services. (As-Ind, estab 1982, empl 6, sales , cert: NMSDC)

Louisiana

1907 Golden Leaf Energy, Inc.
      PO Box 3605
      Harvey, LA 70059
      Contact: Troy Clark CEO
      Tel: 504-252-4838
      Email: troyclark@goldenleafenergy.com
      Website: www.goldenleafenergy.com
Mfr biodiesel, bio-based lubricants & other products. (AA, estab 2011, empl 9, sales , cert: State)

1908 Rig-Chem Inc.
      132 Thompson Rd
      Houma, LA 70363
      Contact: Lori Davis President
      Tel: 985-873-7208
      Email: ldavis@rigchem.com
      Website: www.rigchem.com
Mfr & dist specialty chemicals. (Woman, estab 1980, empl 11, sales , cert: WBENC)

Massachusetts

1909 Grimes Oil Co., Inc.
      PO Box 276
      West Tisbury, MA 02575
      Contact: Calvin Grimes, Jr. President
      Tel: 617-825-1200
      Email: sales@grimesoil.com
      Website: www.grimesoil.com
Dist distillate & risidual heating oils, diesel fuels & gasoline. (AA, estab 1940, empl 4, sales $3,925,000, cert: State, City, NMSDC)

Maryland

1910 HIC Energy, LLC
      5937 Belair Rd
      Baltimore, MD 21206
      Contact: Troy Holland Mgr
      Tel: 410-914-7161
      Email: th@hicenergy.com
      Website: www.hicenergy.com
Dist natural gas. (AA, estab 2015, empl 5, sales , cert: NMSDC)

1911 Maryland Chemical Company, Inc.
      1551 Russell St
      Baltimore, MD 21230
      Contact: Sandra Dove inside Sales
      Tel: 410-752-1800
      Email: sandradove@mdchem.com
      Website: www.marylandchemical.com
Dist chemicals: alums, ammonia, hydrogen peroxide, ice-melt products, ketones, mineral spirits, potassium, sodium silicates, soil amendments, solvating agents. (Woman, estab 1955, empl 18, sales , cert: WBENC)

Michigan

1912   2V Industries, Inc.
       48553 West Rd
       Wixom, MI 48393
       Contact: Sharron Craig
       Tel: 248-624-7943
       Email: scraig@2vindustries.com
       Website: www.2vindustries.com
Dist metalworking compounds, coolants, RPS, cleaners, etc. (As-Ind, estab 1968, empl 20, sales , cert: NMSDC)

1913   Adhesive Systems, Inc.
       14410 Woodrow Wilson
       Detroit, MI 48238
       Contact: Randall Jaymes Tech Sales Acct Mgr
       Tel: 313-530-6654
       Email: randallj@dchem.com
       Website: www.dchem.com
Mfr hot melt, water base & pressure sensitive adhesives. (AA, estab 1985, empl 28, sales $60,000,000, cert: NMSDC)

1914   Adhezion, Inc.
       7730 Childsdale Ave
       Rockford, MI 49341
       Contact: Chris Telman Reg Acct Mgr
       Tel: 616-726-1775
       Email: ctelman@adhezioninc.com
       Website: www.adhezioninc.com
Adhesives & coatings. (Woman, estab 2010, empl 7, sales , cert: WBENC)

1915   Americhem Sales Corporation
       340 North St
       Mason, MI 48854
       Contact: Matthew Bueche Govt Business Devel
       Tel: 517-676-7718
       Email: buechem@americhemsales.com
       Website: www.americhemsales.com
Dist solvents, chemicals & lubricants, custom oil blends. (Minority, estab 1997, empl 25, sales $22,300,000, cert: NMSDC)

1916   C.J. Chemicals, LLC
       47635 Old US 23
       Brighton, MI 48114
       Contact: Eric Earl Reg Mgr
       Tel: 269-788-2317
       Email: eric@cjchemicals.net
       Website: www.cjchemicals.net
Dist Chemicals, Solvents & Oils used for water & wastewater treatment, cleaning, painting, metal finishing & other industrial & commercial applications. (Woman, estab 2011, empl 10, sales , cert: WBENC)

1917   Chemico Systems, Inc.
       50725 Richard W. Blvd.
       Chesterfield, MI 48051
       Contact: Paul Duff Natl Accts mgr
       Tel: 248-723-3263
       Email: pduff@chemicosystems.com
       Website: www.chemicosystems.com
Mfr & dist chemicals: building maintenance, janitorial, paint shop & process cleaners; coating removal svcs, chemical mgmt svcs. (AA, estab 1989, empl 90, sales $20,000,000, cert: NMSDC)

1918   ChemicoMays, LLC
       25200 Telegraph Rd
       Southfield, MI 48034
       Contact: Dave Macleod VP Bus Dev
       Tel: 248-723-3263
       Email: dmacleod@chemicomays.com
       Website: www.chemicomays.com
Chemical management, purchasing, distribution & logistics. (AA, estab 2005, empl 250, sales $86,000,000, cert: NMSDC)

1919   Chrysan Industries, Inc.
       14707 Keel St
       Plymouth, MI 48170
       Contact: Suk-Kyu Koh CEO
       Tel: 734-451-5411
       Email: skoh@chrysanindustries.com
       Website: www.chrysanindustries.com
Mfr industrial lubricants, cleaners, rust-preventatives, cutting fluids, stamping compounds, specialty chemicals, chemical mgmt. (As-Pac, estab 1977, empl 21, sales $10,300,000, cert: NMSDC)

1920   Diversified Chemical Technologies, Inc.
       15477 Woodrow Wilson
       Detroit, MI 48238
       Contact: Michael Joseff Dir of Sales
       Tel: 313-530-6630
       Email: mjoseff@dchem.com
       Website: www.dchem.com
Dist chemicals. (AA, estab 1971, empl 185, sales $80,000,000, cert: NMSDC)

1921   Infiniti Energy & Environmental, Inc.
       24755 W Five Mile Rd Ste 100
       Redford, MI 48239
       Contact: Sherman Larkins President
       Tel: 313-538-0172
       Email: sl@infinitigroup.us
       Website: www.infinitigroup.us
Dist natural gas, oil, lubricant & petroleum products, waste recycling, consulting & industrial cleaning, waste hauling. (AA, estab 1997, empl 5, sales $2,300,000, cert: NMSDC)

1922   Infiniti Energy & Environmental, Inc. dba Infiniti
       15930 19 Mile Rd, Ste 150
       Clinton Township, MI 48038
       Contact: Mark Coaster Marketing Mgr
       Tel: 616-583-9292
       Email: coaster@lakeshoreenergy.com
       Website: www.lakeshoreenergy.com
Natural gas brokering & supply management. (AA, estab 1997, empl 8, sales $3,000,000, cert: NMSDC)

1923   Ipax Cleanogel, Inc.
       8301 Lyndon
       Detroit, MI 48238
       Contact: Veronika Maltsev CEO
       Tel: 313-933-4211
       Email: vmaltsev@ipax.com
       Website: www.ipax.com
Mfr & dist quality cleaning & maintenance products. (Woman, estab 1988, empl 12, sales $1,680,000, cert: WBENC)

1924 LCF - Farmer Group
       4581 S. Lapeer Road Ste G
       Lake Orion, MI 48359
       Contact: Forest Farmer President
       Tel: 248-322-7079
       Email: rfarmer@mti-farmergrp.com
       Website: www.thefarmergroup.com
Paints, cleaners, wipes, rags, paint-booth related products, cleaning supplies, oil, lubricants, janitorial and floor care. (AA, estab 1994, empl 7, sales $2,822,500, cert: NMSDC)

1925 MCEM LLC
       31153 Plymouth Rd
       Livonia, MI 48150
       Contact: BK Masti President
       Tel: 517-881-1226
       Email: bkm@mcem.co
       Website: www.mcem.co
Lubricants, valves, conduit fittings. (As-Pac, estab 2011, empl 5, sales , cert: NMSDC)

1926 Parson Adhesives Inc.
       3345 Auburn Rd, Ste 107
       Rochester Hills, MI 48309
       Contact: Hammie Dogan NA Acct Mgr
       Tel: 248-299-5585
       Email: hammie@parsonadhesives.com
       Website: www.parsonadhesives.com
Industrial adhesives in small and large packing sizes, (As-Pac, estab 2002, empl 45, sales , cert: NMSDC)

1927 RKA Petroleum Company, Inc.
       28340 Wick Rd
       Romulus, MI 48174
       Contact: Timothy Dluzynski Natl Acct Exec
       Tel: 734-946-2202
       Email: tdluzynski@rkapetroleum.com
       Website: www.rkapetroleum.com
Dist refined & renewable fuel products and fuel management solutions. (Woman, estab 1969, empl 49, sales $675,365,826, cert: WBENC)

1928 Roy Smith Company
       14650 Dequindre
       Detroit, MI 48212
       Contact: Peter Wong Owner
       Tel: 313-883-6969
       Email: angela.summers@rscmain.com
       Website: www.rscmain.com
Industrial gases & welding, dist industrial bulk gas systems, packaged & cylinder specialty gases, welding equipment & consumables. (As-Pac, estab 1924, empl 20, sales $24,000,000, cert: NMSDC)

Minnesota

1929 LKT Laboratories, Inc.
       545 Phalen Blvd
       Saint Paul, MN 55130
       Contact: Luke Lam President
       Tel: 651-644-8424
       Email: llam@lktlabs.com
       Website: www.lktlabs.com/
Mfr biochemicals for life science research, inhibitors, activators, modulators, and many other high purity small molecules, phytochemical isolation and analysis. (As-Pac, estab 1990, empl 11, sales $1,300,000, cert: NMSDC)

Missouri

1930 The Kiesel Company
       4801 Fyler Ave
       St. Louis, MO 63166
       Contact: Larry Gooden VP
       Tel: 314-351-5500
       Email: larry.gooden@kieselco.com
       Website: www.thekieselcompany.com
Dist fuels & lubricants, emergency response services to chemical & petroleum product releases, railroad tank car cleaning, barge cleaning, non-hazardous & hazardous waste disposal, demolition & petroleum-contaminated waste water treatment & disposal. (Woman, estab , empl 48, sales $75,010,000, cert: City)

1931 TransChemical, Inc.
       419 East Desoto Ave
       Saint Louis, MO 63147
       Contact: Marilyn Stovall FitzGerald President
       Tel: 314-231-6905
       Email: marilyn.stovall@transchemical.com
       Website: www.transchemical.com
Dist chemicals. (Woman, estab 1973, empl 25, sales $26,000,000, cert: WBENC)

1932 Wallis Oil Company
       106 E Washington St
       Cuba, MO 65453
       Contact: Dave Anthes Managing Dir
       Tel: 573-885-2277
       Email: dave.anthes@wallisco.com
       Website: www.wallisco.com
Dist petroleum. (Woman, estab 1968, empl 550, sales $266,169,874, cert: State)

North Carolina

1933 Continental Chemicals, LLC
       4525 Park Rd Ste B-202
       Charlotte, NC 28209
       Contact: Brandon Lowery Natl Acct Exec
       Tel: 704-535-1215
       Email: blowery@continentalchemicals.com
       Website: www.continentalchemicals.com
Dist chemicals & raw materials. (Nat Ame, estab 1975, empl 5, sales $30,100,000, cert: NMSDC)

1934 NDR Energy Group, LLC
       4822 Albemarle Rd Ste 209
       Charlotte, NC 28205
       Contact: Solomon RC Ali CEO
       Tel: 888-756-0555
       Email: solomon.ali@ndrenergy.us
       Website: www.ndrenergy.us
Dist natural gas, propane, refined products, fuels & energy efficient lighting, asset management services. (AA, estab 2005, empl 7, sales $65,000,000, cert: NMSDC)

1935 PHT International Inc.
       8133 Ardrey Kell Road Ste 204
       Charlotte, NC 28277
       Contact: Ansley Proctor Cockerham Acct Rep
       Tel: 704-246-3480
       Email: acockerham@phtchemical.com
       Website: www.phtchemical.com
Mfr & source fine chemicals, organic intermediates & API's. (Minority, Woman, estab 1993, empl 112, sales $88,900,000, cert: NMSDC, WBENC)

1936   PolySi Technologies, Inc.
5108 Rex McLeod Dr
Sanford, NC 27330
Contact: Lynn Richardson Operations Mgr
Tel: 919-775-4989
Email: lynn@polysi.com
Website: www.polysi.com
Mfr silicone, synthetic greases & silicone fluids, industrial packaging, retail packaging, contract filling & custom packaging. (Woman, estab 1995, empl 25, sales $7,000,000, cert: WBENC)

1937   Red Star Oil Company
802 Purser Dr
Raleigh, NC 27603
Contact: Paula Milliron Acct Mgr
Tel: 919-772-1944
Email: paula@redstaroil.com
Website: www.redstaroil.com
Deliver gasolines, diesel, non highway fuel, bio fuel,kerosene. Sell motor oils, provide fuel polishing. (Minority, estab 1969, empl 30, sales $38,489,046, cert: State)

1938   Texican Natural Gas Company
7301 Carmel Executive Park Dr Ste 316
Charlotte, NC 28226
Contact: Aubrey Hilliard President
Tel: 704-544-7121
Email: ahilliard@texican.com
Website: www.Texican.com
Dist Natural gas, fuel oil, propane, Natural gas consulting. (Hisp, estab 1985, empl 38, sales $500,000,000, cert: NMSDC)

New Jersey

1939   Ash Ingredients, Inc.
65 Harristown Rd, Ste 307
Glen Rock, NJ 07452
Contact: Phetmany Falconi Acct Mgr
Tel: 201-689-1322
Email: phet@ashingredients.com
Website: www.ashingredients.com
Mfr over 81 complex Intermediates for customers with CDA's in place. (Minority, Woman, estab 1999, empl 4, sales , cert: State, City)

1940   Assaycell Technologies LLC
36 Chestnut St
Avenel, NJ 07001
Contact: Dir
Tel: 732-429-0199
Email: info@assaycell.com
Website: www.assaycell.com
Dist biochemical reagents, bacterial & mammalian cell culture media, reagents, assaykits, molecular biology reagents, plastic ware glassware, laboratory supplies, technical consultation. (Minority, Woman, estab 2017, empl 2, sales $120,000, cert: State, SDB)

1941   Bel-Ray Co.
PO Box 526
Wall, NJ 07719
Contact: Bob Shrewsbury Acct Mgr
Tel: 270-585-9005
Email: rshrewsbury@belray.com
Website: www.belray.com
Mfr & dist high performance lubricants made for the Mining, Industrial & Powersports markets world wide. (Woman, estab 1946, empl 150, sales , cert: State)

1942   BKM Resources, Inc. Global Chemicals
PO Box 327
Eatontown, NJ 07724
Contact: Nancy Engkilterr President
Tel: 732-264-2300
Email: nengkilterra@bkmresources.com
Website: www.bkmresources.com
Dist commodity & specialty chemicals. (Woman/AA, estab 1986, empl 10, sales $7,000,000, cert: NMSDC)

1943   Elan Chemical Co., Inc.
268 Doremus Ave
Newark, NJ 07105
Contact: Isabel Couto VP
Tel: 973-344-8014
Email: icouto@elan-chemical.com
Website: www.elan-chemical.com
Natural benzaldehyde, flavors, natural ingredients, synthetic ingredients, vanilla, extracts, acetaldehyde, ethyl benzoate, iso amyl alcohol, aldehydes, natural esters, ethyl caproate, acetic acid, natural aromatic chemicals, ethyl-2-methyl. (Woman, estab 1985, empl 50, sales , cert: State, WBENC)

1944   Foodtopia, Inc.
11 Harrisotwn Rd, Ste 101
Glen Rock, NJ 07452
Contact: Tae Kim GM
Tel: 201-444-8810
Email: tkim@foodtopiausa.com
Website: www.foodtopiausa.com
Food Additives, Nutritional Raw Materials, Amino Acids, Sweeteners, Food Chemicals (As-Pac, estab 1997, empl 7, sales $4,000,000, cert: State)

1945   GJ Chemical
40 Veronica Ave
Somerset, NJ 08873
Contact: Fiore Masci Sr Acct Mgr
Tel: 973-589-4176
Email: customerservice@gjchemical.com
Website: www.gjchemical.com
Mfr & dist raw chemical. (Woman, estab 1974, empl 75, sales $30,000,000, cert: WBENC)

1946   Global Essence Inc.
8 Marlen Dr
Hamilton, NJ 08691
Contact: Jeanna Johnson VP Sales
Tel: 732-677-1100
Email: jjohnson@globalessence.com
Website: www.globalessence.com
Dist flavor & fragrance raw materials: essential oils, organic essential oils, oleoresins, concretes, absolutes an& d synthetic aroma chemicals. (Woman, estab 1993, empl 34, sales $54,700,000, cert: State, WBENC)

1947   INDOFINE Chemical Company
121 Stryker Ln Bldg 30, Ste 1
Hillsborough, NJ 08844
Contact: Sujata Moton VP
Tel: 908-359-6778
Email: indofine@indofinechemical.com
Website: www.indofinechemical.com
Provide custom synthesis, contract research & process development. (Woman/As-Ind, estab 1981, empl 8, sales $1,000,000, cert: NMSDC, WBENC)

1948 Kingchem
      5 Pearl Ct
      Allendale, NJ 07401
      Contact: Daniel Kukovski Diversity Supplier Mgr
      Tel: 201-825-9988
      Email: d.kukovski@kingchem.com
      Website: www.kingchem.com
Mfr fluoro-organic compounds. (As-Pac, estab 1994, empl
13, sales $69,780,000, cert: NMSDC)

1949 Su International Group, Inc.
      1430 Rte 206, Ste 210
      Bedminster, NJ 07921
      Contact: Dan Downs Project Mgr
      Tel: 908-901-0102
      Email: ddowns@suintl.com
      Website: www.suintl.com
Mfr chemicals: synthetic vitamins, food chemical, &
artificial sweeteners. (Minority, Woman, estab 1996, empl
6, sales $18,946,253, cert: NMSDC, NWBOC)

1950 Vitusa Products Inc.
      343 Snyder Ave
      Berkeley Heights, NJ 07922
      Contact: Angela Grande CEO
      Tel: 908-665-2900
      Email: agrande@vitusaproducts.com
      Website: www.vitusaproducts.com
Provide food grade products: Glycerine, Sodium Bicarbon-
ate, Ammonium Bicarbonate, Triacetin, Food Grade
Phosphates & Acids. (Woman, estab , empl , sales
$95,000,000, cert: WBENC)

New York

1951 Ampak Co., Inc.
      1890 Palmer Ave, Ste 203
      Larchmont, NY 10538
      Contact: Cindy Sturm Business Devel
      Tel: 914-833-7070
      Email: csturm@ampakcompany.com
      Website: www.ampakcompany.com
Dist amino acids, antioxidants, preservatives, cellulosics,
hight intensity sweetners, humectants, hydrocolloids,
phosphates, colors, vitamins & minerals. (As-Ind, estab
1978, empl 22, sales $85,041,406, cert: NMSDC)

1952 Crescent Chemical Co., Inc.
      2 Oval Dr
      Islandia, NY 11749
      Contact: President
      Tel: 631-348-0333
      Email: creschem@aol.com
      Website: www.crescentchemical.com
Dist pesticides & herbicides. (Woman, estab 1947, empl 8,
sales $3,000,000, cert: City, WBENC)

1953 Infinite Energy Corp dba Definite Energy Group
      410 Park Ave, 15th Fl
      New York, NY 10022
      Contact: Deborah Pinto President
      Tel: 212-759-7426
      Email: dpinto@definiteenergy.com
      Website: www.definiteenergy.com
Dist petroleum products. (Woman, estab 1994, empl 2,
sales $16,814,844, cert: State, City, WBENC)

1954 M&R Energy Resources Corporation
      259 Main St
      Cornwall, NY 12518
      Contact: Melissa Massimi CEO
      Tel: 845-534-5462
      Email: mmassimi@mandrenergy.com
      Website: www.mandrenergy.com
Dist natural gas: residential, commercial, retail, hospitals
& municipalities. (Woman, estab 2002, empl 10, sales
$15,000,000, cert: City, WBENC)

1955 Tra-Lin Corp.
      248 Buell Road
      Rochester, NY 14624
      Contact: Linda Fedele President
      Tel: 585-254-6010
      Email: lindafedele@rochester.rr.com
      Website: www.samsonfuel.com
Dist fuel & additives. (Woman, estab 1984, empl 10,
sales $663,110, cert: State)

Ohio

1956 Accurate Lubricants & Metalworking Fluids Inc.
      PO Box 3807
      Dayton, OH 45401
      Contact: Marilyn Kinne President
      Tel: 937-461-9906
      Email: mgkinne@acculube.com
      Website: www.acculube.com
Sales & technical support of industrial lubricants,
metalworking fluids, water treatment chemicals &
ancillary sales & services. (Woman, estab 0, empl , sales ,
cert: WBENC)

1957 Calvary Industries, Inc.
      9233 Seward Rd
      Fairfield, OH 45014
      Contact: Austin Morelock New Business Dev Mgr
      Tel: 513-874-1113
      Email: acmorelock@calvaryindustries.com
      Website: www.calvaryindustries.com
Mfr industrial & inorganic chemicals. (Nat Ame, estab
1983, empl 120, sales $78,000,000, cert: NMSDC)

1958 Coolant Control, Inc.
      5353 Spring Grove Ave
      Cincinnati, OH 45217
      Contact: Jorge Costa Owner
      Tel: 513-471-8770
      Email: jcosta@coolantcontrol.com
      Website: www.coolantcontrol.com
Site chemical management services, mfr emulsifiers,
corrosion inhibitors, cleaners, washers, coolants, coolant
additives & odor control. (Hisp, estab 1975, empl 29,
sales , cert: NMSDC)

1959 Creekwood Energy Partners, LLC
      312 Walnut St Ste 3540
      Cincinnati, OH 45202
      Contact: Ron DeLyons CEO
      Tel: 513-762-7808
      Email: ron.delyons@creekwoodadvisors.com
      Website: www.creekwoodenergy.com
Fuel procurement & supply chain mgmt: diesel, biodiesel
& biodiesel blended fuels. (AA, estab 2004, empl 1, sales
, cert: State, City, NMSDC)

1960 Global Environmental Products
4624 Interstate Dr
Cincinnati, OH 45406
Contact: Mike Mamaligas President
Tel: 513-984-5444
Email: info@gepltd.com
Website: www.gepltd.com
Dist absorbents, oil & chemical spill cleanup products. (AA, estab 2002, empl 5, sales $1,200,000, cert: NMSDC)

1961 Hightowers Petroleum Company
3577 Commerce Dr
Middletown, OH 45005
Contact: Stephen L. Hightower President
Tel: 513-423-4272
Email: steve@hightowerspetroleum.com
Website: www.hightowerspetroleum.com
Dist & transport fuel & petroleum products: gasoline, diesel fuel, lubricants, oils, greases, speciality chemicals. (AA, estab 1985, empl 37, sales $219,922,573, cert: NMSDC)

1962 Lianda Corporation
8285 Darrow Rd Ste 200
Twinsburg, OH 44087
Contact: Lifang Mao President
Tel: 330-653-8341
Email: lmao@liandacorp.com
Website: www.liandacorp.com
Import & dist synthetic rubber & related chemicals. (Minority, Woman, estab 1995, empl 11, sales , cert: NMSDC)

1963 Next Generation Fuel, LLC
3589 Commerce Dr
Middletown, OH 45005
Contact: Bernita MCCann Hightower President
Tel: 888-410-6448
Email: bmccann@nxtgenfuel.com
Website: www.nxtgenfuel.com
Dist unleaded gasoline, high & low sulfur diesel fuels, bio-diesel, ethanol & fuel additives. (Woman/AA, estab 2013, empl 5, sales $8,494,467, cert: NMSDC, CPUC, WBENC)

1964 Orchem Corporation
4927 Beech St
Cincinnati, OH 45212
Contact: Denise Ramey COO
Tel: 513-874-9700
Email: denise.ramey@orchemcorp.com
Website: www.orchemcorp.com
Mfr cleaning & sanitation chemicals. (Woman/AA, estab 1996, empl 28, sales $4,200,000, cert: NMSDC)

1965 Phymet
75 N Pioneer Blvd
Springboro, OH 45066
Contact: Amy Minck President
Tel: 937-743-8061
Email: alachman@micropoly.com
Website: www.micropoly.com
Mfr MicroPoly, a solid lubricant system made of plastics & oil used in bearing lubrication and conveyor chain lubrication. (Woman, estab 1986, empl 18, sales $3,000,000, cert: WBENC)

1966 Stand Energy Corporation
1077 Celestial St. Ste 110
Cincinnati, OH 45202
Contact: Kate Bedinghaus
Tel: 513-621-1113
Email: kbedinghaus@standenergy.com
Website: www.standenergy.com
Manage & supply natural gas to thousands of manufacturers, hospitals, hotels, universities, government facilities and smaller businesses. (Woman, estab 1984, empl 28, sales $95,195,066, cert: WBENC)

1967 Stevenson Oil & Chemical Corp.
30130 Lakeland Blvd
Wickliffe, OH 44092
Contact: Suzanne Harkey
Tel: 440-943-3337
Email: info@stevensonoil.com
Website: www.stevensonoil.com
Dist industrial lubricants: engine oil, hydraulic oil, gear oil, cutting oil, metalworking fluid, turbine oil, general purpose lubricants, transmission oil, quenching oil, bio-friendly lubricants, grease & solvents. (Woman, estab 1969, empl 3, sales $1,904,092, cert: WBENC)

1968 Tedia Company, Inc.
1000 Tedia Way
Fairfield, OH 45014
Contact: Jennifer Herber Key Accounts Mgr
Tel: 513-889-6468
Email: jherber@tedia.com
Website: www.tedia.com
Mfr & dist high purity solvents & reagents: research, industrial & analytical applications. (Minority, Woman, estab 1975, empl 120, sales , cert: NMSDC)

1969 Zephyr Solutions, LLC.
1050 Lear Industrial Pkwy
Avon, OH 44011
Contact: Matt Knotts Natl Acct Mgr
Tel: 440-420-9907
Email: mknotts@zephyrsolutions.com
Website: www.zephyrsolutions.com
Aluminum helium tank, air inflators, regulators, helium tank safety equipment, balloon corrals, LED balloons. (Woman, estab 2008, empl 17, sales $30,000,000, cert: WBENC)

Oklahoma

1970 Advance Research Chemicals
1110 W Keystone Ave
Tulsa, OK 74015
Contact: Mat Cleveland Sales Mgr
Tel: 918-266-6789
Email: mathercleveland@fluoridearc.com
Website: www.fluoridearc.com
Inorganic fluorides (As-Ind, estab 1987, empl 125, sales $50,000,000, cert: NMSDC)

1971 Sage Energy Trading, LLC
8023 E 63rd Pl, Ste 350
Tulsa, OK 74133
Contact: Cindy Hughes President
Tel: 918-362-2310
Email: chughes@sageenergytrading.com
Website: www.sageenergytrading.com
Dist natural gas. (Woman, estab 2004, empl 2, sales $9,359,750, cert: WBENC)

1972 Tiger Natural Gas, Inc.
      1422 E 71st St, Ste J
      Tulsa, OK 74136
      Contact: Johnathan Burris VP Marketing
      Tel: 918-491-6998
      Email: diversity@tigernaturalgas.com
      Website: www.tigernaturalgas.com
Dist natural gas. (Minority, Woman, estab 1991, empl 46, sales , cert: NMSDC, WBENC)

Oregon

1973 YOLO Colorhouse LLC
      519 NE Hancock St, Ste B
      Portland, OR 97212
      Contact: Rick Barnard VP Operations
      Tel: 503-493-8275
      Email: rick@colorhousepaint.com
      Website: www.colorhousepaint.com
Premium paints: no-VOC, low-odor & earth friendly. (Woman, estab 2006, empl 11, sales $780,000, cert: WBENC)

Pennsylvania

1974 American Energy Supply Corporation
      1704 Chichester Ave
      Upper Chichester, PA 19061
      Contact: Kristen Baiocco President
      Tel: 610-494-4874
      Email: kb@fueloilnow.com
      Website: www.fueloilnow.com
Diesel Fuel Delivery and Fuel Tanks for rent or sale. (Woman, estab 2009, empl 9, sales $2,454,000, cert: WBENC)

1975 Biopeptek Pharmaceuticals LLC
      5 Great Valley Pkwy Ste 100
      Malvern, PA 19355
      Contact: John Zhang CEO
      Tel: 610-643-4881
      Email: johnzhang@biopeptek.com
      Website: www.biopeptek.com
Mfr custom peptides services. (As-Pac, estab , empl , sales $5,000,000, cert: NMSDC)

1976 Crystal Inc. PMC
      601 W Eighth St
      Lansdale, PA 19446
      Contact: Karen Roorda Exec Asst
      Tel: 215-368-1661
      Email: kroorda@pmc-group.com
      Website: www.crystalinc-pmc.com
Specialty & performance chemicals, sodium & potassium stearates, wax emulsions, specialty antifoams, rubber & plastics additives, process chemicals & cable filling jellies. (As-Pac, estab 1929, empl 80, sales , cert: NMSDC)

1977 Crystal, Inc.
      601 W 8th St
      Lansdale, PA 19446
      Contact: Lynne Currie Exec/Mktg Asst
      Tel: 215-368-1661
      Email: epalincrystal@pmc-group.com
      Website: www.pmc-group.com
Dist specialty & performance chemicals, sodium & potassium stearates, wax emulsions, specialty antifoams, rubber & plastics additives, process chemicals & cable filling jellies. (Minority, estab 1929, empl 80, sales , cert: NMSDC)

1978 EMSCO Scientific Enterprises, Inc.
      5070 Parkside Ave
      Philadelphia, PA 19131
      Contact: Roderick Clifford Assistant VP
      Tel: 215-477-5601
      Email: rpclifford2@emscoscientific.com
      Website: www.emscoscientific.com
Dist production & laboratory chemicals. (AA, estab 1980, empl 9, sales $19,800,000, cert: City, NMSDC)

1979 GRP Services
      PO Box 41
      Pittsburgh, PA 15221
      Contact: Ernest Groover President
      Tel: 412-271-5231
      Email: egroover@grpservices.net
      Website: www.grpservices.net
Natural gas brokerage, utility cost recovery, telecommunications svcs. (AA, estab 2002, empl 3, sales $100,000, cert: NMSDC)

1980 Muscle Products Corp.
      752 Kilgore Rd
      Jackson Center, PA 16133
      Contact: Sharon Murphy-Dittrich President
      Tel: 814-786-0166
      Email: sharon@mpclubricants.com
      Website: www.mpclubricants.com
Manufacture Lubricants & Greases, for General Industry & Automotive Use. (Woman, estab 1986, empl , sales , cert: WBENC)

1981 Naughton Energy Corp.
      Rte 940
      Pocono Pines, PA 18350
      Contact: Sean Naughton VP
      Tel: 570-646-0422
      Email: sean@naughtonenergy.com
      Website: www.naughtonenergy.com
Energy products, energy services & lubricants: gasoline, heating oil, diesel, marine, kerosene,jet, residual & re-refined oil, Anthracite, Bituminous & Synfuel, natural gas. (Minority, Woman, estab 1976, empl 8, sales $14,000,000, cert: State, City, NMSDC)

Puerto Rico

1982 Lanco Manufacturing Corp.
      Urb. Aponte 5
      San Lorenzo, PR 00954
      Contact: Nelson Soto Category Mgr
      Tel: 787-736-4221
      Email: nsoto@lancopaints.com
      Website: www.lancopaints.com
Paints (Water and Oil Based), Enamels, Caulking, Spackling, Wood Stains, Wood Fillers, Adhesive, Roof Sealers, Concrete Bonding Agents and Solvents(Paint removers, Lacquer Thinners, Mineral Spirits). (Hisp, estab 1978, empl 250, sales $69,320,794, cert: NMSDC)

1983   Sachs Chemical Inc.
PO Box 191670 KM 0 02 LOT, 18 RR 175
San Juan, PR 00725
Contact: Laura Conde Accountant
Tel: 787-745-2520
Email: laura@sachschem.com
Website: www.sachschem.com
Dist chemicals. (Hisp, estab 1986, empl 33, sales $32,000,000, cert: NMSDC)

South Carolina

1984   AmberTech Technologies LLC
2037 Summerton Hwy
Summerton, SC 29148
Contact: Tom Massey Dir
Tel: 803-696-1152
Email: tmassey001@sc.rr.com
Website: www.ambertech-global.com
A USDA certified 99% bio-based metal conditioner used in all lubrication applications to reduce friction and heat. (Woman, estab 2011, empl 7, sales $1,600,000, cert: NWBOC)

1985   Sims Petroleum Company, LLC
1201 Main St, Ste 1840
Columbia, SC 29201
Contact: Wayne Sims CEO
Tel: 803-600-7941
Email: wsims@simspetroleum.com
Website: www.simspetroleum.com
Dist Bulk Fuel Products; Gasoline, Diesel, Biodiesel, Ethanol and Jet Fuel. (AA, estab 2017, empl 1, sales $414,539, cert: State, NMSDC)

Tennessee

1986   CGS, Inc.
14225 Hickory Creek Rd
Lenoir City, TN 37771
Contact: Joy McCabe President
Tel: 865-988-9080
Email: joym@cgs-inc.com
Website: www.cgs-inc.com
Sales agency and distributor of natural gas distribution products, (Woman, estab 1986, empl 5, sales , cert: WBENC)

1987   Quality Adhesives LLC
3791 Air Park
Memphis, TN 38118
Contact: curtis hunt President
Tel: 901-375-3991
Email: curtish@qualityadhesivesinc.com
Website: www.qualityadhesivesinc.com
Mfr & dist hot melt & liquid adhesives. (AA, estab 1999, empl 8, sales $8,000,000, cert: NMSDC)

Texas

1988   American Chemie, Inc.
13706 Research Blvd Summit Exec Ctr, Ste 302
Austin, TX 78750
Contact: Mike Kamdar President
Tel: 512-219-7400
Email: mike@americanchemie.com
Website: www.americanchemie.com
Dist Emulsifiers, Emollients, Esters, Fatty alcohols, Eco-Cert Natural Refined Shea Butter and other body Butters, Preservatives & Surfactants. (Woman/As-Ind, estab 1991, empl 9, sales $10,086,762, cert: State, NMSDC, WBENC)

1989   AmPac Chemical Company Inc.
PO Box 272848
Houston, TX 77277
Contact: Sonia Fujimoto President
Tel: 713-660-9383
Email: sonia@ampacchemical.com
Website: www.ampacchemical.com
Dist chemicals. (Minority, Woman, estab 1996, empl 1, sales $2,217,678, cert: City, NMSDC)

1990   Arrow Magnolia International, Inc.
2646 Rodney Ln
Dallas, TX 75229
Contact: Tanya Shaw Chairwoman
Tel: 972-247-7111
Email: tshaw@arrowmagnolia.com
Website: www.arrowmagnolia.com
Dist safety & first aid, floor care products, disinfectants, deodorants, solid waste chemicals, kitchen & restroom sanitation, machine & automotive products, insecticides, repellents, weed killers, grease & lubricants, boiler & water products. (Minority, Woman, estab , empl , sales , cert: NMSDC, WBENC)

1991   Atlantic Petroleum & Mineral Resources Inc.
723 Main St, Ste 207
Houston, TX 77002
Contact: Donald Sheffield
Tel: 713-223-2767
Email: drsheffield@atlantic-petro.com
Website: www.atlanticpetro.com
Dist branded & unbranded petroleum products. (AA, estab 2005, empl 8, sales $476,200, cert: State, City, NMSDC)

1992   Avalon Chemicals, Inc.
10101 Southwest Frwy Ste 400
Houston, TX 77074
Contact: Vinay Deshmane President
Tel: 713-219-1457
Email: info@avalonchemicals.com
Website: www.avalonchemicals.com
Phenolic antioxidants (BHT, TBHQ, BHA), antioxidants (DODPA). (As-Ind, estab 2002, empl 2, sales $1,260,000, cert: State, NMSDC)

1993   BHP Engineering & Construction, LP
715 Oak Park Ave
Corpus Christi, TX 78408
Contact: Mary Pham Treasurer
Tel: 361-693-6283
Email: viki.pham@bhpeng.com
Website: www.bhpeng.com
Engineering consulting design services for refinery & petrochemical industries. (Minority, estab 1983, empl 60, sales , cert: CPUC)

1994   Champion Fuel Solutions
PO Box 210191
Bedford, TX 76095
Contact: Patti Russell President
Tel: 877-909-9191
Email: prussell@championfs.com
Website: www.championfs.com
Dist gasoline & diesel fuel, biodiesel, kerosene, oils & lubricants. (Woman, estab 2010, empl 2, sales , cert: State, WBENC)

1995 Cole Chemical & Distributing, Inc.
      1500 S Dairy Ashford Ste 450
      Houston, TX 77077
      Contact: Rebecca Cooper President
      Tel: 713-465-2653
      Email: weborders@colechem.com
      Website: www.colechem.com
Mfr & dist thermoformed products. (Minority, Woman,
estab 0, empl 0, sales $47,000,000, cert: State, City,
NMSDC, WBENC)

1996 Dien, Inc.
      3510 Pipestone Rd
      Dallas, TX 75212
      Contact: Dian Davis President
      Tel: 214-905-1528
      Email: dian@dieninc.com
      Website: www.dieninc.com
Dist chemicals: industrial, food, solvents, greases &
lubricants, pharmaceutical & personal care. (Minority,
Woman, estab , empl , sales $46,627,700, cert: State,
NMSDC)

1997 Diversified Chemical and Supply, Inc.
      PO Box 1297
      Humble, TX 77347
      Contact: Donna Rosenstein President
      Tel: 713-461-9610
      Email: dcsupply@sbcglobal.net
      Website: www.diversifiedchem.com
Dist janitorial & industrial chemicals & supplies.
(Woman, estab 1990, empl 3, sales $2,508,119, cert:
State, WBENC)

1998 Elevation Energy Group LLC
      PO Box 6036
      Austin, TX 78762
      Contact: Gwen Kyle President
      Tel: 317-333-7281
      Email: tri@elevationeg.com
      Website: www.elevationeg.com
Natural gas supply and associated services. (As-Pac,
estab 2014, empl 15, sales , cert: NMSDC)

1999 Energy Utility Group, LLC
      1402 Clearview Loop
      Round Rock, TX 78664
      Contact: Melinda Zito O'Brien CEO
      Tel: 512-805-8321
      Email: melinda@energyutilitygroup.com
      Website: www.energyutilitygroup.com
Energy consulting & electricity & natural gas brokering
company. (Woman, estab , empl , sales , cert: State, City,
CPUC, WBENC)

2000 FSTI Inc.
      6300 Bridge Point Pkwy, Ste 1-200
      Austin, TX 78730
      Contact: Coulter Gibson Dir of Packaged Products
      Tel: 512-278-8800
      Email: cgibson@fstichem.com
      Website: www.fstichem.com
Dist chemicals. (Woman, estab 1998, empl 50, sales
$19,100,000, cert: State, WBENC)

2001 Gasochem International LLC
      9509 Pemberton Crescent Dr
      Houston, TX 77025
      Contact: Charu Jain President
      Tel: 713-837-6116
      Email: charu@gasochem.com
      Website: www.gasochem.com
Dist chemicals: oilfield, water treatment, industrial,
agricultural & pharmaceutical. (Minority, Woman, estab
2012, empl 2, sales $167,000, cert: State, WBENC)

2002 Genoa International
      2245 Texas Dr, Ste 300
      Sugar Land, TX 77479
      Contact: Pamela Kahn Principal
      Tel: 281-313-0120
      Email: pkahn@genoaint.com
      Website: www.genoaint.com
Specialty chemicals, surfactants, drilling fluids, solvents,
lubricants & commodities. (Woman, estab 0, empl , sales
$4,000,000, cert: State, WBENC)

2003 Global Amchem Inc.
      407 E Methvin, Ste 200
      Longview, TX 75606
      Contact: Debbie Scott Office Admin
      Tel: 903-236-0138
      Email: debbie@amcheminc.com
      Website: www.amcheminc.com
Dist solvents & chemicals. (Hisp, estab 1993, empl 6,
sales $430,505, cert: State, NMSDC)

2004 GND Consulting & Supply LLC
      1836 Snake River Rd, Ste A
      Katy, TX 77449
      Contact: Jose Camacho Sales Mgr
      Tel: 832-415-4100
      Email: camachojo@gndsc.com
      Website: www.gndsc.com
Dist non-toxic, environmentally-safe cleaners,
degreasers, solvents, lubricants & specialty chemical
products. (Minority, Woman, estab 2011, empl 8, sales
$603,242, cert: State, NMSDC, WBENC)

2005 New K-Stone Management, Inc.
      10718 Sentinel St
      San Antonio, TX 78217
      Contact: Dana Stone President
      Tel: 210-494-0507
      Email: dstone@kstoneinc.com
      Website: www.kstonesupply.com
Industrial chemicals for automotive, animal shelters,
food processing plants, physical plant supplies &
chemicals for lab animal research. (Woman, estab 1997,
empl 15, sales $1,147,125, cert: State)

2006 One Nation Energy Solutions, LLC
      4404 Blossom St
      Houston, TX 77007
      Contact: Terry Pierce President
      Tel: 713-861-0600
      Email: tpierce@onenationenergy.com
      Website: www.onenationenergy.com
Dist & market gas & power. (Woman, estab 2003, empl
1, sales $68,601,802, cert: City, CPUC, WBENC)

2007 Oxyde Chemicals, Inc.
      225 Pennbright Dr Ste 101
      Houston, TX 77090
      Contact: Elva Rojas Sales agent
      Tel: 281-874-9100
      Email: rojase@oxydeusa.com
      Website: www.oxydeusa.com
Dist petrochemicals & plastics. (Hisp, estab 1950, empl 60, sales $650,000,000, cert: State, NMSDC)

2008 Premier Polymers LLC
      16800 Imperial Valley, Ste 200
      Houston, TX 77060
      Contact: Melwani Kwan Supply Chain Mgr
      Tel: 281-902-0909
      Email: mkwan@premierpolymers.com
      Website: www.premierpolymers.com
Dist Plastic Resin. (As-Pac, estab 2009, empl 22, sales , cert: State, NMSDC)

2009 Ricochet Fuel Distributors, Inc.
      1201 Royal Pkwy
      Euless, TX 76040
      Contact: Jason Cox Mktg Coord
      Tel: 800-284-2540
      Email: sales@ricochetfuel.com
      Website: www.ricochetfuel.com
Dist diesel, gasoline, oil, antifreeze & kerosene, fuel mgmt & monitoring programs. (Woman, estab 1988, empl 27, sales $63,847,000, cert: WBENC)

2010 SolvChem, Inc.
      1904 Mykawa
      Pearland, TX 77546
      Contact: Stacey Barrett Acct Mgr
      Tel: 832-300-4067
      Email: stacey_barrett@solvchem.com
      Website: www.solvchem.com
Dist aircraft chemicals, chemicals blends, calibrating fluids, purging fluids. (Hisp, estab 1980, empl 40, sales $2,707,198, cert: State, NMSDC)

2011 Sun Coast Resources, Inc.
      6405 Cavalcade, Building 1
      Houston, TX 77026
      Contact: Susan Tyler President
      Tel: 713-844-9600
      Email: styler@suncoastresources.com
      Website: www.suncoastresources.com
Dist petroleum products (gasoline, diesel, etc.). (Woman, estab 1985, empl 1270, sales $860,000,000, cert: WBENC)

2012 The Green Chemical Store, Inc.
      11837 Judd Ct, Ste 104
      Dallas, TX 75243
      Contact: The Green Chemical Store President
      Tel: 972-429-1719
      Email: operations@thegreenchemicalstore.com
      Website: www.thegreenchemicalstore.com
Dist chemicals for building maintenance trades. (Woman, estab 2009, empl 5, sales $150,000, cert: WBENC)

2013 Tri-Chem Specialty Chemicals, LLC
      PO Box 2056
      Cresson, TX 76035
      Contact: CEO
      Tel: 972-745-6875
      Email: contact@tri-chem.net
      Website: www.tri-chem.net
Custom liquid & dry chemical blending, chemical & additive distribution. (Minority, Woman, estab 1989, empl 14, sales $4,777,000, cert: WBENC)

2014 XD Ventures, LLC
      2555 South Shore Blvd. Ste C
      League City, TX 77573
      Contact: Xan Difede President
      Tel: 832-557-6622
      Email: xan@fidelityfuels.com
      Website: www.fidelityfuels.com
Dist aliphatic solvents, mineral spirits & mineral seal oils. (Woman, estab 2014, empl 1, sales , cert: State, WBENC)

Utah

2015 CP Industries, LLC
      560 North 500 West
      Salt Lake City, UT 84116
      Contact: Erica Sellers President
      Tel: 801-521-0313
      Email: info@cpindustries.net
      Website: www.cpindustries.net
Mfr ice melting compounds, customer chemical blending, liquid & powder detergents. (Woman, estab 1949, empl 19, sales $5,510,415, cert: WBENC)

2016 FYVE STAR, Inc.
      1972 E Dan Dr
      Layton, UT 84040
      Contact: Celeste Gleave CEO
      Tel: 801-552-9100
      Email: celeste@fyvestar.com
      Website: www.fyvestar.com
Mfr & dist deicers. Calcium Chloride, Blends, Solar Salt, Water Conditioning Salts, primary supplier to the US Military on Liquid Runway & Aircraft Deicers. (Woman, estab 1993, empl 2, sales $400,000, cert: State)

2017 The Horrocks Company LLC dba Volu-Sol
      5095 West 2100 South
      Salt Lake City, UT 84120
      Contact: Celeste Horrocks Owner
      Tel: 801-974-9474
      Email: celeste.horrocks@volusol.com
      Website: www.volusol.com
Mfr chemicals, alcohols, reagents, diagnostic stains & counterstains. (Woman, estab 2013, empl 10, sales $470,000, cert: WBENC)

Virginia

2018 Coyanosa Gas Services Corporation
      1765 Greensboro Station Place Ste 900
      McLean, VA 22102
      Contact: Jerry Curry President
      Tel: 703-938-7984
      Email: jerry@coyanosagasservices.com
      Website: www.coyanosagasservices.com
Dist natural gas & energy utilization consulting. (AA, estab 1995, empl 3, sales $20,000,000, cert: NMSDC, CPUC, SDB)

2019   Creative Maintenance Solutions, LLC
       1171 Polk Rd
       Edinburg, VA 22824
       Contact: Nancy Barnett
       Tel: 540-984-8172
       Email: nancy@cmsolutionsus.com
       Website: www.cmsolutionsus.com
Dist polymer/epoxy & coatings. (Woman, estab , empl ,
sales , cert: State)

2020   Enspire Energy, LLC
       134 N Battlefield Blvd
       Chesapeake, VA 23320
       Contact: julie hashagen Dir of Operations
       Tel: 757-963-9123
       Email: jhashagen@enspireenergy.com
       Website: www.enspireenergy.com
Natural gas marketing & transportation. (Woman, estab
2005, empl , sales $979,376, cert: WBENC)

2021   James River Solutions
       10487 Lakeridge Pkwy
       Ashland, VA 23005
       Contact: Elizabeth Austin Commercial Project Mgr
       Tel: 804-358-9000
       Email: eaustin@jrpetro.com
       Website: www.JamesRiverPetroleum.com
Bulk Deliveries, Gasoline, Diesel, Dyed Diesel, Heating Oil,
DEF, Mobile Fueling, Fleet Fueling Cards. (Woman, estab
2005, empl 61, sales $251,000,000, cert: State)

2022   Quad Chemical Corporation
       1008 Old Virginia Beach Rd, Ste 500
       Virginia Beach, VA 23451
       Contact: Karin Harrigan Natl Acct Mgr
       Tel: 757-422-2486
       Email: kharrigan@quadchemical.com
       Website: www.quadchemical.com
Dist bulk process manufacturing chemicals. (Woman, estab
1991, empl 6, sales , cert: WBENC)

Washington

2023   Allied Fuel LLC
       2400 Harbor Ave SW, Ste 100
       Seattle, WA 98126
       Contact: James E Hasty President
       Tel: 206-582-2020
       Email: james@alliedfuel.net
       Website: www.alliedfuel.net
Dist fuel. (AA, estab 2009, empl 5, sales $51,350,000, cert:
NMSDC)

2024   PetroCard, Inc.
       PO Box 40
       Kent, WA 98035
       Contact: Tamara Torklep Dir Corporate Marketing
       Tel: 253-867-3218
       Email: ttorklep@petrocard.com
       Website: www.petrocard.com
Cardlock, Mobile Fueling, Lubricants, Retail Gas Stations
and Bulk Fuels. (Nat Ame, estab 1985, empl 187, sales
$744,000,000, cert: NMSDC)

2025   Walla Walla Environmental
       4 W Rees Ave
       Walla Walla, WA 99362
       Contact: Cassie Rothstrom CEO
       Tel: 509-522-0490
       Email: cassie@wwenvironmental.com
       Website: www.wwenvironmental.com
Dist mildewcide, insecticide & flame retardant paint
additives. (Woman, estab 1990, empl 16, sales , cert:
WBENC)

Wisconsin

2026   ChemCeed LLC
       1720 Prosperity Court
       Chippewa Falls, WI 54729
       Contact: Myra Detienne Sales Rep
       Tel: 715-726-2300
       Email: customerservice@chemceed.com
       Website: www.chemceed.com
Dist chemicals in bulk tankwagons, drums, totes, or
custom packaging, ethanols, alcohols, reagents, & other
solvents. (Minority, Woman, estab 2009, empl 10, sales ,
cert: NMSDC, WBENC)

2027   Power Lube Industrial LLC
       4930 S 2nd St, Ste 300
       Milwaukee, WI 53207
       Contact: Sarah Herr Exec VP Sales
       Tel: 800-635-8170
       Email: sarah@powerlubeind.com
       Website: www.powerlubind.com
Automatic lubrication equipment and supplies,
Memolub, Greaseomatic, and ATS Electrolub single point
and multi- point product lines. (Woman, estab 1998,
empl 10, sales $2,200,000, cert: WBENC)

CLEANING PRODUCTS, SUPPLIES & SERVICES
Manufacturers and distributors of maintenance supplies: all purpose cleaners, deodorizers, floor waxes, wax removers, oven cleaners, dishwashing & laundry detergents, soaps, hand cleaners, furniture & metal polishes, rug & upholstery shampoos, ammonia, janitorial services, etc. Janitorial services. NAICS Code 32

Arizona

2028   Maintenance Mart
       4648 N 7th Ave
       Phoenix, AZ 85013
       Contact: Shelley Krauss President
       Tel: 602-252-9402
       Email: shelley@maintenancemart.com
       Website: www.maintenancemart.com
Dist commercial janitorial supplies, tools, motorized equipment, paper, trash liners, walk-off mats, indoor & outdoor receptacles & ash urns. (Minority, Woman, estab 2000, empl 20, sales $7,200,000, cert: City)

California

2029   Avery Group Inc.
       8941 Dalton Ave
       Los Angeles, CA 90047
       Contact: Leatora Morse President
       Tel: 310-217-1070
       Email: leatora@averygroup-inc.com
       Website: www.averygroup-inc.com
Mfr restroom hygiene products. (Woman/AA, estab 2003, empl 2, sales $100,000, cert: State, NMSDC)

2030   Ayota, LLC
       122 15th St, Ste 681
       San Diego, CA 92014
       Contact: Toya McWilliams Acct Mgr
       Tel: 914-548-6193
       Email: tm@ayotainternational.com
       Website: www.ayotainternational.com
Dist janitorial supplies. (Woman/AA, estab 2012, empl 3, sales , cert: State)

2031   BriteWorks, Inc.
       620 Commerical Ave.
       Covina, CA 91723
       Contact: Anita Ron President
       Tel: 626-337-0099
       Email: anitaron@briteworks.com
       Website: www.briteworks.com
Commercial & industrial janitorial services. General cleaning, construction cleaning, floor care & carpet care, window cleaning. (Minority, Woman, estab 1997, empl 130, sales $6,866,357, cert: NMSDC, CPUC, WBENC)

2032   Continental Building Maintenance
       13316 Mapledale St
       Norwalk, CA 90650
       Contact: Sanggwon Kim President
       Tel: 562-926-7474
       Email: sgkim@continentalbm.com
       Website: www.continentalbm.com
Janitorial Services & Supplies. (As-Pac, estab 2003, empl 120, sales $2,950,000, cert: CPUC)

2033   Corporate Image Maintenance
       2700 S Main St, Ste D
       Santa Ana, CA 92707
       Contact: Gil Gamboa President
       Tel: 714-966-5325
       Email: corpimage@sbcglobal.net
       Website: www.cimservices.com
Janitorial services: office, industrial & warehouse, carpet cleaning, pressure washing & window cleaning. (Hisp, estab 1995, empl 70, sales $1,176,190, cert: State)

2034   Diamond Wipes International
       4651 Schaefer Ave
       Chino, CA 91710
       Contact: Rebecca Liu Natl Sales
       Tel: 909-230-9888
       Email: rliu@diamondwipes.com
       Website: www.diamondwipes.com
Mfr wiper based cleansing products: white board, furniture polishing wipes, antibacterial wipes, shoe shine, grease & graffiti remover wipes. (Minority, Woman, estab 1994, empl 88, sales , cert: WBENC)

2035   Eurow & O'Reilly Corp.
       51 Moreland Rd
       Simi Valley, CA 93065
       Contact: Martin Mair Dir Inside Sales
       Tel: 805-421-4310
       Email: mmair@eurow.com
       Website: www.eurow.com
Dist janitorial cleaning products. (Woman, estab 1983, empl 26, sales $40,000,000, cert: WBENC)

2036   Global Building Services, Inc.
       25570 Rye Canyon Rd Ste F
       Valencia, CA 91355
       Contact: Charles Herrera Sr Dir operations
       Tel: 800-675-6643
       Email:
       charlesherrera@globalbuildingservices.com
       Website: www.globalbuildingservices.com
Complete janitorial services, building & grounds maintenance, window washing, complete floor care, pressure washing, parking lot maintenance, high dusting, green cleaning. (Hisp, estab 1986, empl 1200, sales $33,339,000, cert: NMSDC)

2037   Mar-Len Supply Inc.
       23159 Kidder St
       Hayward, CA 94545
       Contact: Shirley Winter Owner
       Tel: 510-782-3555
       Email: marlensupply@aol.com
       Website: www.marlensupply.com
Dist & service industrial cleaning equipment & cleaning agents. (Woman, estab 1956, empl 4, sales $1,000,000, cert: CPUC)

2038   NMS Management Inc.
       155 W 35th St Ste A
       National City, CA 91950
       Contact: Dir Business Devel
       Tel: 619-425-0440
       Email: cynthia@nmsmanagment.com
       Website: www.nms-management.com
Custodial services for military establishments, healthcare facilities, institutions of higher education, public housing agencies, public transportation authorities & federal, state & municipal agencies. (Hisp, estab 1985, empl 168, sales $3,822,801, cert: CPUC)

2039 Right Tek Enterprises
      1775 N Lee St
      Simi Valley, CA 93065
      Contact: Sandy Cohen Owner
      Tel: 877-208-3717
      Email: righttek@pacbell.net
      Website: www.righttekenterprises
Dist preventative maintenance cleaning products:
magentic card readers, bill validators, thermal printers,
point of sale (pos) machines and key lock systems.
(Woman, estab 2001, empl 1, sales $272,000, cert:
WBENC)

2040 SBM Management Services
      5241 Arnold Ave
      McClellan, CA 95652
      Contact: Dan Berardelli Dir Strategic Solutions
      Tel: - -
      Email: dberardelli@sbmcorp.com
      Website: www.sbmmanagement.com
Facilities support, janitorial, clean-room & laboratory
sanitizing, general building maintenance, recycling &
environmental awareness programs, move-add-change
support services, vendor management. (Minority, estab
1982, empl 10000, sales $430,000,000, cert: NMSDC)

2041 SDI Systems Division, Inc.
      21 Morgan
      Irvine, CA 92618
      Contact: Jon Korbonski President
      Tel: 949-583-1001
      Email: sdi@sdinetwork.com
      Website: www.sdinetwork.com
Manufacture and distribute cleaning equipment &
supplies. (Hisp, estab 2008, empl 20, sales $3,700,000,
cert: NMSDC)

2042 SeaYu Enterprises Inc.
      236 West Portal
      San Francisco, CA 94127
      Contact: Quincy Yu CEO
      Tel: 415-566-9677
      Email: qyu@sea-yu.com
      Website: www.becleanandgreen.com
Natural cleaners, stain removers and odor eliminators that
are effective, easy to use, biodegradable and safe for
people, pets and the planet. (Minority, Woman, estab
2001, empl 2, sales , cert: NMSDC)

2043 Signature Building Maintenance, Inc.
      PO Box 110340
      Campbell, CA 95011
      Contact: Anna Murphy President
      Tel: 408-377-8066
      Email: anna@signaturefacilities.com
      Website: www.signaturefacilities.com
Facilities services, commercial janitorial services & general
contractor interior improvements. (Woman, estab , empl ,
sales $8,125,433, cert: WBENC)

2044 Supply Solutions
      17625 Fabrica Way
      Cerritos, CA 92691
      Contact: Jeffrey Lerma CEO
      Tel: 888-901-5011
      Email: jlerma@casupplysolutions.com
      Website: www.casupplysolutions.com
Dist janitorial products, paper supplies, can liners, chemicals, and equipment. (Hisp, estab 2006, empl 27, sales
$12,500,000, cert: NMSDC)

2045 Ultimate Maintenance Services, Inc.
      4237 Redondo Beach Blvd
      Lawndale, CA 90260
      Contact: Sherly Cstmr Service
      Tel: 310-542-1474
      Email: sherly@umscorporation.com
      Website: www.umscorporation.com
Janitorial services & construction clean up services.
(Minority, Woman, estab 1990, empl 50, sales , cert:
State)

2046 UNISERVE Facilities Services
      2363 S Atlantic Blvd
      Commerce, CA 90040
      Contact: Eugene Hwang Dir of Mktg
      Tel: 213-533-1000
      Email: ehwang@uniservecorp.com
      Website: www.uniservecorp.com
Janitorial services. (As-Pac, estab 1966, empl 750, sales
$25,000,000, cert: NMSDC)

2047 US Metro Group, Inc.
      135 S State College Blvd, Ste 200
      Brea, CA 92821
      Contact: Phil Gregg Contracts Compliance
      Tel: 213-382-6435
      Email: phil.g@usmetrogroup.com
      Website: www.usmetrogroup.com/
Janitorial maintenance services. (As-Pac, estab 1975,
empl 1000, sales $15,908,576, cert: NMSDC, CPUC)

Colorado

2048 AFL Maintenance Group, Inc.
      1075 S. Yukon St, Ste 300
      Lakewood, CO 80226
      Contact: Bonnie Nash Business Devel
      Tel: 303-984-7400
      Email: b.nash@afsg-us.com
      Website: www.afsg-us.com
Facility maintenance, management & real estate
services. (Minority, Woman, estab 1989, empl 500, sales
$19,500,000, cert: NMSDC)

Connecticut

2049 C & C Janitorial Supplies, Inc.
      665 New Britain Ave
      Newington, CT 06111
      Contact: Grace Cafe President
      Tel: 860-594-4200
      Email: gracec@ccsupplies.com
      Website: www.ccsupplies.com
Dist janitorial products, paper products & equip.
(Minority, Woman, estab , empl , sales , cert: NMSDC,
WBENC)

2050 Citra Solv, LLC
      188 Shadow Lake Rd
      Ridgefield, CT 06877
      Contact: Steve Zeitler Co-Founder
      Tel: 203-778-0881
      Email: szeitler@citrasolv.com
      Website: www.citrasolv.com
Plant-based ingredients, environmentally friendly
cleaners and air fresheners. (Woman, estab 1996, empl
7, sales $15,000,000, cert: State)

2051   Horizon Services Company
     250 Governor St
     East Hartford, CT 06108
     Contact: Thomas Baerlein Sr Acct Exec
     Tel: 860-291-9111
     Email: tbaerlein@horizonsvcs.com
     Website: www.horizonsvcs.com
Custodial services, supply & management, window cleaning, clean room environmental svcs, hazardous material site labor, exterior cleaning & landscaping, post construction cleaning. (As-Pac, estab 1991, empl 412, sales $7,400,000, cert: State, NMSDC)

2052   KeeClean Management Inc.
     494 Bridgeport Ave Ste 180
     Shelton, CT 06484
     Contact: Keith Jang President
     Tel: 203-397-2532
     Email: keithjang@keeclean.com
     Website: www.keeclean.com
Commercial cleaning, custodial & janitorial services: floor care service, carpet cleaning, window washing services. (As-Pac, estab 2007, empl 5, sales $3,444,178, cert: State, City, NMSDC)

Delaware

2053   Star Building Services, Inc.
     106 Quigley Blvd
     New Castle, DE 19720
     Contact: Ernie Martin VP Sales & Mktg
     Tel: 302-983-0275
     Email: emartin@sbsclean.com
     Website: www.sbsclean.com
Janitorial Services, Medical Device Cleaning Services. (Woman, estab 1953, empl 300, sales , cert: WBENC)

Florida

2054   ABCO Products, Inc.
     6800 NW 36th Ave
     Miami, FL 33147
     Contact: Luis Janania Sales Mgr
     Tel: 786-223-0944
     Email: luisj@abcoproducts.com
     Website: www.abcoproducts.com
Dist cleaning supplies. (Hisp, estab 1979, empl 54, sales , cert: State, NMSDC)

2055   All Pro Janitorial Service Inc.
     3843 N Tanner Rd
     Orlando, FL 32826
     Contact: Glenda Lee President
     Tel: 407-649-8878
     Email: glenda@allprojan.com
     Website: www.procarpetcleanerorlando.com
Commercial janitorial cleaning, carpet cleaning, upholstery cleaning, ceramic tile & grout cleaning, floor stripping, waxing, buffing & water restoration. (Woman/AA, estab 2000, empl 15, sales , cert: State, City, NMSDC)

2056   Clean Clean, Inc.
     3580 NW 56th St, Ste 106C
     Fort Lauderdale, FL 33309
     Contact: Gary Plancher Sales Mgr
     Tel: 954-777-9555
     Email: gplancher@cleancleaninc.com
     Website: www.cleancleaninc.com
Mfr personal wipes. (Woman/AA, estab 2004, empl 6, sales , cert: NMSDC)

2057   Cube Care Company
     6043 NW 167th St Ste A-23
     Miami Lakes, FL 33015
     Contact: Susana Robledo Founder & CEO
     Tel: 305-556-8700
     Email: susana@cubecare.com
     Website: www.cubecare.com
Janiorial Supplies, Window Treatments & Curtains, (Minority, Woman, estab 1999, empl 70, sales $6,685,526, cert: NMSDC, WBENC)

2058   D&A Building Services, Inc.
     321 Georgia Ave
     Longwood, FL 32750
     Contact: Albert Sarabasa CEO
     Tel: 407-831-5388
     Email: al@dabuildingservices.com
     Website: www.dabuildingservices.com
Janitorial, window washing, pressure cleaning, caulking, carpet, cleaning, construction cleaning, seal buildings, light painting. (Hisp, estab 1985, empl 550, sales $8,200,000, cert: State, City)

2059   GEM Janitorial LLC
     9031 Pembroke Rd
     Pembroke Pines, FL 33025
     Contact: Richard Addison President
     Tel: 954-682-3594
     Email: homeownersservicesfla@gmail.com
     Website: www.gemjanitorialcorp.com
Cleaning, Commercial Remodeling and Repair, Painting, Pressure Cleaning, Carpentry, Doors & Windows Installation, Drywall Repairs and Installation, Flooring Installation. (Woman/AA, estab 2006, empl 6, sales $320,000, cert: NMSDC)

2060   Grosvenor Building Services Iinc.
     3398 Pkwy Center Ct
     Orlando, FL 32808
     Contact: Lee McDaniel Business Devel Mgr
     Tel: 407-292-3383
     Email: lmcdaniel@grosvenorservices.com
     Website: www.grosvenorservicescom
Janitorial Services. (Woman, estab 1984, empl 400, sales $6,000,000, cert: WBENC)

2061   Harvard Services Group, Inc.
     201 S Biscayne Blvd FL 24
     Miami, FL 33131
     Contact: Nathalie Doobin CEO
     Tel: 305-351-7300
     Email: ndoobin@harvardservices.com
     Website: www.harvardsg.com
Janitorial services & maintenance services. (Woman, estab 1986, empl 1500, sales , cert: WBENC)

2062   Jimco Maintenance Inc.
     710 Commerce Dr, Ste 107
     Venice, FL 34292
     Contact: Lynn Moseley President
     Tel: 800-392-8678
     Email: lynn@jimcos.com
     Website: www.jimcos.com
Janitorial services. (Woman, estab 1983, empl 90, sales $12,180,000, cert: WBENC)

2063 Merton Partners LLC
      692 Solana Court
      Marco Island, FL 34145
      Contact: Nanette Rivera President
      Tel: 609-773-0145
      Email: wordehoff@mertonpartners.com
      Website: www.mertonpartners.com
Operations Management Consultants: SPC; facilities; maintenance; engineering; construction; validation; manufacturing; yield; optimization (Minority, Woman, estab 2007, empl 50, sales $1,200,000, cert: NMSDC)

2064 RagsWarehouse & Cleaning Supplies
      7221 NW 35th Ave
      Miami, FL 33147
      Contact: Luther Pierre Sales Mgr
      Tel: 202-531-9225
      Email: luther.pierre@ragswarehouse.com
      Website: www.ragswarehouse.com
Dist wiping materials ideal for painters or cleaners. (Woman/AA, estab 2015, empl 2, sales , cert: State)

2065 Siboney Contracting Co.
      1000 Southern Blvd, Ste 300
      West Palm Beach, FL 33405
      Contact: Dante Sevi VP
      Tel: 561-832-3110
      Email: dsevi@siboneycc.com
      Website: www.siboneycc.com
Hauling fill and aggregates, hauling hurricane debris (Hisp, estab 1972, empl 8, sales $23,789,190, cert: City)

2066 The American Cleaning Services Inc
      8270 Woodland Center Blvd.
      Tampa, FL 33614
      Contact: Marty Hales GM
      Tel: 813-961-6970
      Email: callus1st@americancleaningservice.com
      Website: www.americancleaningservice.com
Complete janitorial services, commercial & construction. (Minority, Woman, estab 1989, empl 1, sales $367,000, cert: State)

2067 The Green Glider Company LLC
      830 Harbor Cir
      Palm Harbor, FL 34683
      Contact: Tanya Lewis President
      Tel: 727-504-9441
      Email: info@gogreenglider.com
      Website: www.gogreenglider.com
Green Glider Mop Pad, Reusable, Washable, Durable & Adjustable mop pad that fits onto virtually all of the Swiffer style/type mopping systems. (Woman, estab 2010, empl 1, sales $225,000, cert: WBENC)

2068 Treasure Enterprise, Inc.
      11026 Oak Ridge Dr N
      Jacksonville, FL 32225
      Contact: Fidelis Odeh President
      Tel: 904-683-8114
      Email: info@treasureenterprise.com
      Website: www.treasureenterprise.com
Janitorial maintenance, carpet cleaning, lawn services, roadside litter removal services, and the numerous services that we offer. (AA, estab 1998, empl 56, sales $1,250,000, cert: City)

Georgia

2069 5 Star Enterprise, Inc.
      4705-G Bakers Ferry Rd SW
      Atlanta, GA 30336
      Contact: Tracey Felder President
      Tel: 404-924-4290
      Email: tfelder@5starchemicals.com
      Website: www.5starchemicals.com
Mfr Green cleaning, soaps & detergent products, green certified chemicals. (Woman/AA, estab 2006, empl 10, sales $2,450,000, cert: WBENC)

2070 Frederick Hart Co. Inc.
      4963 S Royal Atlanta Dr
      Tucker, GA 30084
      Contact: Dean-Paul Hart President
      Tel: 404-373-4030
      Email: deanpaul@compacind.com
      Website: www.compacind.com
Mfr cleaning products: garbage disposal cleaner & deodorizer, scented sink strainer, bathroom, kitchen, auto, cleaners, closet & air fresheners. (AA, estab 1979, empl 15, sales $3,500,000, cert: NMSDC)

2071 General Building Maintenance, Inc.
      3835 Presidential Pkwy Ste 200
      Atlanta, GA 30340
      Contact: Joe Woodson Sr VP
      Tel: 770-457-5678
      Email: marketing@gbmweb.com
      Website: www.gbmweb.com
Janitorial svcs: carpets, stripping & waxing floors, marble & stone care, clean room cleaning & recycling. (As-Pac, estab 1983, empl 271, sales , cert: NMSDC)

2072 GMI Group, Inc.
      130 Stone Mountain St
      Lawrenceville, GA 30046
      Contact: Kayla Dang CEO
      Tel: 678-482-5288
      Email: kayla.dang@gmigroupinc.com
      Website: www.thegmigroup.com
Commercial janitorial cleaning, marble maintenance & restoration, ReKRETE waterless concrete cleaning, pressure washing, graffiti removal, construction clean up. (Minority, Woman, estab 2005, empl 72, sales $4,867,904, cert: NMSDC, WBENC)

2073 ShockTheory Interactive, Inc.
      12705 Century Dr Ste C
      Alpharetta, GA 30004
      Contact: Sonja Williams VP
      Tel: 877-747-4625
      Email: sonja.williams@shocktheory.com
      Website: www.shocktheory.com
Web design and development, Interactive marketing, User Interface design, and social networking, collaboration and integration, ROI measurement and SEO strategies. (Woman/AA, estab 2003, empl 9, sales , cert: NMSDC)

2074 The Burks Companies, Inc.
      2780 Bert Adams Road Ste 225
      Atlanta, GA 30339
      Contact: James Weisbrodt President & COO
      Tel: 678-686-3203
      Email: jweis@theburkscompanies.com
      Website: www.theburkscompanies.com
Janitorial services. (AA, estab 1991, empl 181, sales $7,980,000, cert: NMSDC)

Hawaii

2075   Building Maintenance Services, LLC
       1541 S Beretania St, Ste 204
       Honolulu, HI 96826
       Contact: Barbara Beckmeier Owner
       Tel: 808-983-1269
       Email: barbara@bmsnationwide.com
       Website: www.bmsnationwide.com
Janitorial services. (Woman, estab 2000, empl 45, sales ,
cert: WBENC)

Iowa

2076   Midwest Janitorial Service
       1395 N Center Pt. Rd
       Hiawatha, IA 52233
       Contact: Aaron Schulze VP
       Tel: 319-393-6162
       Email: customerservice@mjsia.com
       Website: www.midwestjanitorial.com
Commercial janitorial cleaning company, offering specialty
services, carpet cleaning, floor care and window cleaning.
(Woman, estab 1958, empl 650, sales $10,150,000, cert:
NWBOC)

Illinois

2077   A&R Janitorial Service, Inc.
       10127 w. Roosevelt Rd.
       Westchester, IL 60154
       Contact: Deborah Pintor Sr Exec VP
       Tel: 708-656-8300
       Email: dpintor@arjanitorial.com
       Website: www.arjanitorial.com
Janitorial services, commercial cleaning, carpet care, floor
care, power washing, snow removal, after construction
cleanup & emergency response cleaning. (Minority,
Woman, estab 1967, empl , sales $19,752,715, cert: City,
NMSDC, WBENC)

2078   B & B Maintenance, Inc.
       537 Capital Dr
       Lake Zurich, IL 60047
       Contact: Pamela Seiser VP Sales
       Tel: 847-550-6060
       Email: pseiser@bandbmaint.com
       Website: www.bandbmaint.com
Building maintenance: janitorial, window cleaning, &
painting, carpet care, power washing, hard surfaced floor
care, tile restoration, fire safety programs, porter service &
support personnel. (Woman/Hisp, estab 1979, empl 550,
sales , cert: City, NMSDC, WBENC)

2079   Clean Impressions Corp.
       127 N Northwest Hwy
       Palatine, IL 60067
       Contact: Teresa Garvin President
       Tel: 847-776-0706
       Email: cic@cleanimpressionscorp.com
       Website: www.cleanimpressionscorp.com
Janitorial service, building maintenance, floor care,
stripping & refinishing floor tile, carpet cleaning, stone
care, crystalizing & acoustical tile cleaning. (Woman, estab
1998, empl 40, sales , cert: WBENC)

2080   EBM, Inc. (Executive Building Maintenance)
       2238 Landmeier Rd
       Elk Grove Village, IL 60007
       Contact: Vtio M. D'Ambrosio Dir Sales
       Tel: 224-203-4090
       Email: vdambrosio@ebmclean.com
       Website: www.ebmcleaning.com
Janitorial services. (Woman, estab 1963, empl 450, sales
$14,000,000, cert: State, City, WBENC, NWBOC)

2081   ELB Enterprises, Inc.
       4709 Bond Ave
       Alorton, IL 62207
       Contact: Rhonda Jones
       Tel: 618-394-1912
       Email: rjones@elb1inc.com
       Website: www.elbenterprisesinc.com
Dist janitorial supplies. (AA, estab 1993, empl 12, sales ,
cert: State, NMSDC)

2082   Emeric Facility Services
       918 S Green Bay Rd
       Waukegan, IL 60085
       Contact: Michael Ramirez Acct Exec
       Tel: 847-623-6912
       Email: mramirez@emericservices.com
       Website: www.emericservices.com
Janitorial services & carpet cleaning. (Minority, Woman,
estab 2011, empl 46, sales $932,000, cert: City, WBENC)

2083   IDSC, Inc.
       PO Box 1055
       Woodstock, IL 60098
       Contact: Milissa Dooley President
       Tel: 815-337-8066
       Email: milissa_ids@att.net
       Website: www.idscinc.com
Dist sanitation supplies & equipment, PPE, paper goods,
maintenance supplies & equipment, hoses. (Woman,
estab 1990, empl 7, sales $480,000, cert: WBENC)

2084   Jelmar LLC
       5550 W Touhy Ste 200
       Skokie, IL 60007
       Contact: Glenn Poticha VP Sales
       Tel: 800-323-5497
       Email: glenn@jelmar.com
       Website: www.jelmar.com
Dist cleaning products. (Woman, estab , empl , sales
$36,745,934, cert: WBENC)

2085   LACOSTA Facility Support Services, Inc.
       440 W Bonner Rd
       Wauconda, IL 60084
       Contact: Jeffrey Johnson Natl Dir Business Dev
       Tel: 847-487-3103
       Email: sales@cms4.com
       Website: www.lacostaservices.com
Janitorial services, painting services, facility
maintanance services. (Minority, Woman, estab 1988,
empl 1700, sales $64,000,000, cert: NMSDC)

2086   United Building Maintenance, Inc.
       165 Easy St
       Carol Stream, IL 60188
       Contact: Amy Cabrera-Goddard Dir Sales & Mktg
       Tel: 630-653-4848
       Email: agoddard@ubm-usa.com
       Website: www.ubm-usa.com
Janitorial, painting, pressure washing, snow removal,
parking lot maintenance & landscape design. (Hisp,
estab 1979, empl 1500, sales $63,800,000, cert: NMSDC)

2087 White Glove Janitorial Services & Supply, Inc.
      356 E Irving Park Rd
      Wood Dale, IL 60191
      Contact: Joyce Dickens Owner
      Tel: 630-766-7466
      Email: whtglove@msn.com
      Website: www.whiteglovejanitorialservices.com
Janitorial svcs: carpet cleaning, landscaping, power
washing, food plant sanitation, floor scrubbing. (Woman,
estab 1975, empl 105, sales $2,476,000, cert: City)

Indiana

2088 Suzy Q Cleaning Services
      2401 N Tibbs Ave
      Indianapolis, IN 46222
      Contact: Suzett Moffitt Owner
      Tel: 317-755-7664
      Email: suzettsuzett@gmail.com
      Website: www.suzyqcleaning.net
Janitorial, ground & bldg maintenance, Commercial,
Renovation, Construction, Bridge, Road, Side Walk Repair.
(Woman/AA, estab 2009, empl 10, sales , cert: State, City)

2089 Titan Associates, Inc. dba A.G. Maas Company
      8402 E 33rd St
      Indianapolis, IN 46226
      Contact: Cindy Schum President
      Tel: 317-632-8315
      Email: cindy@agmaas.com
      Website: www.agmaas.com
Dist Janitorial Supplies, Safety Supplies, Bathroom Parti-
tions & Accessories, site Furnishings, Indoor/Outdoor
Mats, Rock Salt, Ice Melt & Water Softener Salt,
Breakroom Supplies, Office Supplies. (Woman, estab 1969,
empl 4, sales $2,200,000, cert: City, WBENC)

Kentucky

2090 Facility Maintenance & Services Group
      147 E Loudon Ave
      Lexington, KY 40505
      Contact: Frank HAll CEO
      Tel: 859-554-6584
      Email: info@facilitymsg.com
      Website: www.facilitymsg.com
Janitorial, Facility Maintenance, Painting, Lawn Care,
Pressure washing, High Dusting. (AA, estab 2015, empl 42,
sales $1,000,019, cert: NMSDC)

2091 Superior Maintenance Co.
      141 Howell Dr
      Elizabethtown, KY 42701
      Contact: Sid Shurn VP
      Tel: 270-769-2553
      Email: sid@smc.cc
      Website: www.smc.cc
Janitorial & grounds maintenance, window cleaning, pest
control, facility maintenance, HVAC, plumbing, chemicals,
janitorial supplies & equip. (AA, estab 1988, empl 1200,
sales , cert: NMSDC)

Louisiana

2092 Economical Janitorial & Paper Supplies
      1420F Sams Ave, Ste F
      Harahan, LA 70123
      Contact: Suzie Migliore President
      Tel: 504-464-7166
      Email: suzie@economicaljanitorial.com
      Website: www.econoomicaljanitorial.com
Dist janitorial supplies, paper supplies, janitorial equipment, food service supplies. (Woman, estab 1983, empl
85, sales $31,015,000, cert: WBENC)

Massachusetts

2093 Dependable Facility Cleaning Services, LLC
      1074 Hyde Park Ave, Ste 4
      Hyde Park, MA 02136
      Contact: Chuck Ojoko Managing Dir
      Tel: 857-261-4582
      Email: charles@dependablefacilitycleaning.com
      Website: www.dependablefacilitycleaning.com
Commercial cleaning & janitorial services. (AA, estab
2015, empl 6, sales , cert: NMSDC)

2094 Milhench Supply Company
      121 Duchaine Blvd
      New Bedford, MA 02745
      Contact: Angie Prevost Inside Sales
      Tel: 508-995-8331
      Email: angie@milhench.com
      Website: www.milhench.com
Dist janitorial, paper, packaging & facility maintenance
supplies. (Woman, estab 1932, empl 32, sales
$16,315,760, cert: State, City)

2095 Moura's Cleaning Service, Inc.
      349 Lunenburg St
      Fitchburg, MA 01420
      Contact: Andre Thibodeau Sales Mgr
      Tel: 978-562-1839
      Email: andre@mourascleaningservice.com
      Website: www.mourascleaningservice.com
Janitorial services: office cleaning, floor strip & wax,
restroom service, odor control service, concrete cleaning, maintenance & sealing, carpet & upholstery steam
cleaning, window cleaning, power wash bldgs. (Hisp,
estab 1988, empl 150, sales $2,100,000, cert: State)

2096 Savin Products Co., Inc.
      214 High St
      Randolph, MA 02368
      Contact: Dona D'Ambrosia President
      Tel: 781-961-2743
      Email: donamarie@savinproducts.com
      Website: www.savinproducts.com
Mfr cleaning products. (Woman, estab 1968, empl 10,
sales , cert: State)

2097 Unic Pro Inc.
      415 Boston Tpk Ste 211B
      Shrewsbury, MA 01545
      Contact: Lilian Radke CEO
      Tel: 877-881-8642
      Email:
      Website: www.unicpro.com
Commercial Cleaning Services, Carpet Cleaning, Floor
Washing & Waxing, Green Cleaning Services, Industrial
Cleaning, Nightly Office Cleaning, Post-Construction
Cleaning. (Minority, Woman, estab 2007, empl 54, sales
$2,450,000, cert: State, WBENC)

Maryland

2098 Associated Building Maintenance Co., Inc.
      2140 Priest Bridge Court Ste 3
      Crofton, MD 21114
      Contact: Kurt Bender VP Sales
      Tel: 410-721-1818
      Email: kbender@abmcoinc.com
      Website: www.abmcoinc.com/
Commercial general contract cleaning, window cleaning,
carpet cleaning, snow removal, floor stripping & other
building related services. (Woman, estab 1987, empl
1000, sales $25,599,000, cert: State)

2099   Bolana Enterprises, Inc.
10739 Tucker St Ste 270
Beltsville, MD 20705
Contact: Valarie Dock President
Tel: 301-595-2577
Email: vdock@bolanainc.com
Website: www.bolanainc.com
Green & sustainable janitorial services, carpet cleaning, floor care, and garage cleaning. (Woman/AA, estab 2004, empl 355, sales $11,000,000, cert: NMSDC, WBENC)

2100   C.J. Maintenance, Inc.
9254 Bendix Rd
Columbia, MD 21045
Contact: Tyler Yoon Acct Exec
Tel: 410-720-5157
Email: cjmaintenance@hotmail.com
Website: www.cjmaint.com
Janitorial, custodial & housekeeping svcs: carpet cleaning, hard wood floors, marble floor restoration. (As-Pac, estab 1985, empl 700, sales $14,499,999, cert: State, NMSDC)

2101   Red Coats, Inc.
4520 East-West Hwy
Bethesda, MD 20814
Contact: Page Pollock Dir of Reg Sales & Marketing
Tel: 301-280-4414
Email: ppollock@redcoats.com
Website: www.redcoats.com
LEED compliant cleaning services. (Woman, estab 1960, empl 7000, sales $203,366,500, cert: WBENC)

2102   Viking Chemicals, Inc.
2325 Banger St
Baltimore, MD 21230
Contact: Shannon Hodges VP
Tel: 410-525-2100
Email: shodges@vikingchem.com
Website: www.vikingjanitorsupplies.com
Dist janatorial supplies: paper, floor care equipement, sweepers, vacuums, matting, brooms, brushes, trash cans & trash can liners. (Woman, estab 1974, empl 6, sales $2,206,148, cert: State, City)

Michigan

2103   Caravan Facilities Management, LLC
1400 Weiss St
Saginaw, MI 48602
Contact: Victor Gomez Business Devel Mgr
Tel: 989-798-0977
Email: vg10@caravanfm.com
Website: www.caravanfm.com
Facilities mgmt: janintorial, landscaping, snow removal, HVAC, fleet mgmt & building services. (Hisp, estab 1997, empl 2344, sales $139,000,000, cert: NMSDC)

2104   Caravan Technologies, Inc.
3033 Bourke
Detroit, MI 48238
Contact: Robert Charleston CEO
Tel: 313-341-2551
Email: cti3033@aol.com
Website: www.caravantech.com
Mfr industrial & commercial cleaning solutions, disinfecting agents & parts washer detergents. (AA, estab 1979, empl 10, sales $495,961, cert: NMSDC)

2105   Choctaw-Kaul Distribution Company
3540 Vinewood
Detroit, MI 48208
Contact: Caitlin Johnson Customer Dev Mgr
Tel: 313-895-3165
Email: cjohnson@choctawkaul.com
Website: www.choctawkaul.com
Mfr gloves & safety products, mgmt svcs, janitorial svcs, industrial specialty cleaning, paint booth cleaning, chemical mgmt, recycling, filter maintenance, truck repair, construction mgmt, parking lot maintenance, temp manpower, etc. (Minority, estab 1998, empl 350, sales $107,000,000, cert: NMSDC)

2106   CMS Sourcing Solutions
29700 Harper Ave, Ste 2
St. Clair Shores, MI 48082
Contact: Cheryl A King Exec VP Sales
Tel: 586-879-0669
Email: cheryl.king@cmsgroup.us
Website: www.cmsgroup.us
Janitorial services, management, labor, supplies, equipment & systems. (Woman, estab 2009, empl 150, sales $5,500,110, cert: NMSDC)

2107   Contract Direct, LLC
24300 Southfield Rd, Ste 210
Southfield, MI 48075
Contact: Bill Dreyer Sr Corp Sales Exec
Tel: 248-395-1199
Email: elizabeth@contractdirect.net
Website: www.contractdirect.net
Contract Cleaning Janitorial Services, Custodial Services, Food Plant Sanitation, Silo Cleaning. (Woman, estab 2002, empl 450, sales $15,000,000, cert: WBENC)

2108   DFM Solutions (Devon Facility Management LLC)
777 Woodward Ave Ste 500A
Detroit, MI 48226
Contact: Chad Starnes Dir Business Devel
Tel: 313-221-1510
Email: cstarnes@dfm.solutions
Website: www.dfm.solutions
Facility management, janitorial & building maintenance & industrial cleaning services. (Woman, estab 2007, empl 298, sales $45,000,000, cert: WBENC)

2109   Ipax Cleanogel, Inc.
8301 Lyndon
Detroit, MI 48238
Contact: Veronika Maltsev CEO
Tel: 313-933-4211
Email: vmaltsev@ipax.com
Website: www.ipax.com
Mfr & dist quality cleaning & maintenance products. (Woman, estab 1988, empl 12, sales $1,680,000, cert: WBENC)

2110   LCF - Farmer Group
4581 S. Lapeer Road Ste G
Lake Orion, MI 48359
Contact: Forest Farmer President
Tel: 248-322-7079
Email: rfarmer@mti-farmergrp.com
Website: www.thefarmergroup.com
Paints, cleaners, wipes, rags, paint-booth related products, cleaning supplies, oil, lubricants, janitorial and floor care. (AA, estab 1994, empl 7, sales $2,822,500, cert: NMSDC)

2111 Macomb Wholesale Supply Corp.
17730 E 14 Mile Rd
Fraser, MI 48026
Contact: Catherine David President
Tel: 586-415-7400
Email: online@macombwholesale.com
Website: www.macombwholesale.com
Dist Packaging, Safety, Janitorial & Facility Maintenance
Supplies, corrugated, poly bags, tape, paper, chemical,
packaging, gloves, safety & facility cleaning supplies.
(Woman, estab 1988, empl 10, sales $2,500,000, cert:
WBENC)

2112 Midwest Maintenance Services, Inc.
3704 Trade Center Dr
Ann Arbor, MI 48108
Contact: Linda Johnson President
Tel: 734-222-5902
Email: linda@midwestms.com
Website: www.midwestms.com
Janitorial services & building maintenance. (Woman, estab
1989, empl 35, sales , cert: WBENC)

2113 Perfection Commercial Services, Inc.
905 N Church St
Tekonsha, MI 49092
Contact: Lori Smith Controller
Tel: 888-933-3103
Email: lori@pcsmichigan.com
Website:
www.perfectioncommercialservicesinc.com
Janitorial services and supplies, which includes window
and floor care. (Woman, estab 1991, empl 212, sales
$5,785,000, cert: WBENC, NWBOC)

2114 Polstar Commercial Cleaning Services
5124 Pontiac Trail
Ann Arbor, MI 48105
Contact: Kamil Krainski Sales Mgr
Tel: 800-557-9120
Email: kamil@polstar.us
Website: www.polstar.us
Contract janitorial & commercial cleaning services, floor
stripping & waxing, disinfection service, antimicrobial
coatings, carpet cleaning. (Woman, estab 2000, empl 25,
sales $903,146, cert: WBENC)

2115 Sparkle Janitorial Service
4100 Woodward Ave, Ste 9
Detroit, MI 48201
Contact: Loretta Watson President
Tel: 313-831-1535
Email: watsonlorettam@sparklejani.com
Website: www.saniglaze535.com
Complete janitorial service, window cleaning, carpet
cleaning, construction clean-up, tile & grout restoration.
(AA, estab 1989, empl 25, sales , cert: NMSDC)

2116 StarSource Management Services, Inc.
39080 Webb Dr
Westland, MI 48185
Contact: Melvin Brown CEO
Tel: 734-721-8540
Email: sales@starsourceinc.com
Website: www.starsourceinc.com
Dist janitorial chemical supplies, cleaning equipment,
paper towels, plastic liners, welding supplies, automotive
cleaning supplies, cooling tower chemicals, laundry
services. (AA, estab , empl , sales $6,000,000, cert:
NMSDC)

2117 Tri County Cleaning Supply, Inc.
7109 Dan McGuire Dr
Brigton, MI 48116
Contact: Geri Gee President
Tel: 810-229-6500
Email: g.gee@tcclean.com
Website: www.tcclean.com
Dist cleaning supplies. (Woman, estab 0, empl , sales ,
cert: WBENC)

Minnesota

2118 Allied National Services
6066 Shingle Creek Pkwy #1105
Minneapolis, MN 55430
Contact: President
Tel: 763-503-0707
Email: sales@alliedns.com
Website: www.alliedns.com
Contract cleaning services. Floor care Restroom sanita-
tion. (AA, estab 2002, empl 541, sales $17,610,000, cert:
City, NMSDC, 8(a))

2119 Diverse Maintenance Solutions Inc.
1523 94th Lane NE
Blaine, MN 55449
Contact: Rita Dumra President
Tel: 763-230-7488
Email: rita.dumra@dmsimn.com
Website: www.dmsimn.com
Dist maintenance supplies, janitorial supplies,
rubbermaid products, paper products, equipment, office
supplies & tools. (Woman/As-Ind, estab 1988, empl 7,
sales $966,055, cert: NMSDC, WBENC)

2120 Innovative Chemical Corporation
7769 95th St South
Cottage Grove, MN 55016
Contact: Shelly Meyers Sales Marketing Dir
Tel: 651-649-1762
Email: smeyers@iccmn.com
Website: www.iccmn.com
Mfr eco friendly cleaning & maintenance products,
green cleaning products. (As-Ind, estab 1994, empl 13,
sales $2,000,000, cert: NMSDC)

2121 SDQ, Ltd.
4737 County Rd 101, Ste 250
Minnetonka, MN 55345
Contact: Scott Bak VP
Tel: 952-929-5263
Email: scott@sdqltd.com
Website: www.sdqltd.com
Janitorial svcs: cleaning, clean room cleaning, carpet
cleaning, hard floor surface cleaning. (Woman, estab
1983, empl 250, sales $10,800,000, cert: WBENC)

Missouri

2122 HI-Gene
1836 Linn St
North Kansas City, MO 64116
Contact: Barrie Evans Acct Mgr
Tel: 816-472-4118
Email: barrie@higenesjanitorial.com
Website: www.higenesjanitorial.com
Janitorial services. (Woman, estab 1969, empl 275, sales
$6,151,289, cert: NWBOC)

2123   J&B Franchise Venture, Inc.
       11684 Lilburn Park Rd
       St. Louis, MO 63146
       Contact: Janet Mann President
       Tel: 314-989-9997
       Email: janet.mann@jan-prousa.com
       Website: www.stlouis.jan-pro.com
Janitorial services, commercial cleaning, carpet cleaning,
floor cleaning services. (Woman, estab 2004, empl 8, sales
$2,000,000, cert: State)

2124   Peistrup Paper Products, Inc.
       1185 Research Blvd
       St. Louis, MO 63132
       Contact: Dennis Burjoski Acct Exec
       Tel: 314-993-0970
       Email: dburjoski@peistruppaper.com
       Website: www.peistrup.com
Dist janitorial, paper & safety supplies. (Woman, estab
1960, empl 9, sales , cert: State, WBENC)

2125   Rockwell Labs Ltd.
       1257 Bedford Rd
       North Kansas City, MO 64116
       Contact: Cisse Spragins CEO
       Tel: 816-283-3167
       Email: cspragins@rockwelllabs.com
       Website: www.rockwelllabs.com
Mfr & dist pest management & biological cleaning products: baits for roaches, ants bed bugs & other crawling
insects. (Woman, estab 1998, empl 11, sales , cert:
NWBOC)

2126   Tier One Property Services
       8601 E 63rd St
       Kansas City, MO 64133
       Contact: Joel Sanders Business Devel
       Tel: 816-285-7439
       Email: jsanders@tier1usa.com
       Website: www.tier1usa.com
Janitorial services. (AA, estab 2011, empl 750, sales
$27,200,000, cert: NMSDC)

2127   Wexford Labs, Inc.
       325 Leffingwell Ave
       Kirkwood, MO 63122
       Contact: Mary Anne Auer CEO
       Tel: 800-506-1146
       Email: maryanne.auer@wexfordlabs.com
       Website: www.wexfordlabs.com
Mfr hard surface, EPA registered disinfectants, floor care
products, general purpose cleaners, hand soaps, alcohol
hand sanitizers. (Woman, estab , empl , sales $2,966,970,
cert: State)

Mississippi

2128   Jefferson Cleaning Services, LLC
       06 Ray C. Nicks Rd
       Jayess, MS 39641
       Contact: Jan Jefferson President
       Tel: 601-803-1601
       Email: Jefferson.jan@gmail.com
       Website:
       www.jeffersoncleaningservices.weebly.com
Commercial janitorial services, corporate buildings, post
construction clean up, office space, hospitals, schools,
daycares, retail centers, etc. (Woman/AA, estab 2014, empl
1, sales , cert: City, WBENC)

North Carolina

2129   Century Products LLC
       404 Edwardia Dr
       Greensboro, NC 27409
       Contact: Evette Darden AVP Gov Accts
       Tel: 336-292-8090
       Email: edb@centuryproductsllc.com
       Website: www.centuryproductsllc.com
Dist janitorial cleaning tools: mops, brooms, brushes for
institutions & food industry. (AA, estab 1987, empl 21,
sales , cert: NMSDC)

2130   Coverall Health Based Cleaning System
       2401 Whitehall Park
       Charlotte, NC 28273
       Contact: Shannon Krieser Sr Lead Generation
       Sales Associate
       Tel: 704-209-7113
       Email: shannon.krieser@coverall.com
       Website: www.coverall.com
Janitorial services. (Minority, estab 1985, empl 300, sales
, cert: NMSDC)

2131   Green's Commercial Cleaning
       4421 Stuart Andrew Blvd Ste 604
       Charlotte, NC 28217
       Contact: Kimberly Grace Dir of Sales
       Tel: 704-201-6209
       Email: kimberly@greenscommercialcleaning.com
       Website: www.greenscommercialcleaning.com
Janitorial services, medical curtain cleaning, floor &
carpet care, pressure washing & building maintenance.
(AA, estab 2003, empl 165, sales $2,300,000, cert: City,
8(a))

2132   JAC Janitorial Services
       1101 Tyvola Rd, Ste 205
       Charlotte, NC 28217
       Contact: Jose Jaramillo Sales Mgr
       Tel: 980-201-9099
       Email: jjaramillo@jacjanitorialservice.com
       Website: www.jacjanitorialservice.com
Cleaning services, hospitals, schools, business parks,
government buildings, and more. (Hisp, estab 2006,
empl 15, sales , cert: State, City)

2133   Solid Surface Care, Inc.
       3820 Rose Lake Dr
       Charlotte, NC 28217
       Contact: Vanesah Noechel Business Devel
       Tel: 202-281-7742
       Email: vnoechel@solidcare.com
       Website: www.solidcare.com
Stone, Terrazzo, Metal & Wood Maintenance & Restora-
tion, Carpet & Upholstery Cleaning, Tile & Grout
Maintenance & Restoration, High Performance Coatings
& Concrete Refinishing. (Minority, estab 1996, empl 130,
sales $16,604,415, cert: State, CPUC)

2134   Yu Ken Cut It Inc.
       3121 Sweeten Creek Rd
       Asheville, NC 28803
       Contact: Jonathan Bae Marketing Mgr
       Tel: 828-651-9770
       Email: jonathanbae@yukencutit.com
       Website: www.yukencutit.com
Janitorial services. (Minority, Woman, estab 1995, empl
300, sales $5,365,000, cert: NMSDC)

Nebraska

2135 Meylan Enterprises, Inc.
6225 S. 60th St
Omaha, NE 68117
Contact: Tori Peitz President
Tel: 402-339-4880
Email: tpeitz@meylan.net
Website: www.meylan.net
Industrial cleaning services to include; 10,000-40,000 psi high pressure waterblasting, vacuum services, blast wave services (explosives) and specialty projects. (Woman, estab , empl 160, sales , cert: WBENC)

New Jersey

2136 BRAVO! Building Services, Inc.
29 King George Road
Green Brook, NJ 08812
Contact: Frank S. Wardzinski COO
Tel: 732-465-0707
Email: fwardzinski@bravobuildingservices.com
Website: www.bravogroupservices.com
Janitorial svcs, day porters & matrons, HVAC, mail room services. (Minority, Woman, estab 1997, empl , sales $95,000,000, cert: NMSDC)

2137 Capstone Facilities Group LLC
609 Park Ave
Brielle, NJ 08730
Contact: Jrhosaboy President
Tel: 877-765-2242
Email: jrhosaboyj@gmail.com
Website: www.capstonefacilities.com
Dist foodservice, healthcare & janitorial disposables & equipment: paper towels, toilet paper, handsoap, cleaning chemicals, flatware, napkins. (AA, estab 2012, empl 3, sales , cert: NMSDC)

2138 CSS Building Services Inc
846 Livingston Ave
North Brunswick, NJ 08902
Contact: Liz Coury VP Internal Operations
Tel: 609-655-5000
Email: lcoury@cssbuildingservices.com
Website: www.cssbuildingservices.com
Janitorial, builiding maintenance. (Woman, estab 1976, empl 450, sales $40,000,000, cert: WBENC)

2139 Janel Inc.
7 Mountain Ave
Bound Brook, NJ 08805
Contact: Colleen McAteer President
Tel: 732-271-4700
Email: colleenm@janelinc.com
Website: www.janelonline.com
Dist cleaning products, assemble, test & repair electronic equipment. (Woman, estab 1960, empl 8, sales $2,897,219, cert: State, WBENC)

2140 Shore Manufacturing LLC
1709 Hwy 34 Unit 5
Wall, NJ 07727
Contact: William Vogel President
Tel: 732-894-9810
Email: williamjvogel@aol.com
Website: www.shoremfgllc.com
Mfr non woven disposable food service wipers. (Woman, estab 2013, empl 8, sales , cert: State, WBENC)

New Mexico

2141 Specialized Services, LLC
3150 Carlisle NE Ste, 6
Albuquerque, NM 87110
Contact: Faith St. Clair
Tel: 505-881-5237
Email: faith.specializedservices@gmail.com
Website: www.specializedservicesnm.com
Commercial maintenance, floor maintenance, strip & waxing, cleaning & disinfecting tile & grout. (Hisp, estab 2009, empl 26, sales $125,165,468, cert: NMSDC)

Nevada

2142 Kamco Industries LLC
6969 Speedway Blvd, Ste 107
Las Vegas, NV 89115
Contact: Delicia Liu President
Tel: 702-518-1253
Email: delicia@kamco-online.com
Website: www.kamco-online.com
Mfr & distribute nontoxic, plant-based industrial cleaner, EPA-registered disinfectant and foaming hand sanitizer. We also offer professional consultation for janitorial issues for hotels, (As-Pac, estab 2010, empl 1, sales $130,000, cert: State, NWBOC)

2143 Smalls Senibaldi Services LLC
4127 Falcons Flight Ave
North Las Vegas, NV 89084
Contact: Iris Senibaldi CEO
Tel: 702-636-1316
Email: iris@smaseni.com
Website: www.smaseni.com
Commercial & residential cleaning, janitorial services. (Woman/AA, estab 2013, empl 20, sales , cert: NMSDC)

2144 Smart Cleaning Solutions LLC
57 Spectrum Blvd
Las Vegas, NV 89101
Contact: Salvador Canales Mgr
Tel: 702-685-7055
Email: scanales@mysmartcleaningsolutions.com
Website: www.smartcleaningsolutionsllc.vom
Escalator Step Cleaning & Refurbishment, Powder Coating, Demarcations Lines, Commercial Cleaning, Industrial Cleaning, Final Cleaning, Power Wash, Custodial & Janitorial Services. (Minority, Woman, estab 2011, empl 38, sales $950,000, cert: State)

New York

2145 A&A Maintenance Enterprise, Inc.
965 Midland Ave
Yonkers, NY 10704
Contact: Armando Rodriguez Jr. CEO
Tel: 914-969-0009
Email: arodriguez@aamaintenance.com
Website: www.aamaintenance.com
Janitorial services. (Hisp, estab 1983, empl 2600, sales $23,000,000, cert: City, NMSDC)

2146 Alliance Supply, Inc.
1743-48 St
Brooklyn, NY 11204
Contact: FirstName LastName President
Tel: 347-564-0022
Email: sylviasadv@yahoo.com
Website: www.alliancesupply.net
Dist janitorial supplies & food service disposables. (Woman, estab 2005, empl 4, sales $850,000, cert: City)

2147 American Maintenance Janitorial Services &
Supplies Co. Corp.
1074 Home St
Bronx, NY 10459
Contact: Jessica Ortiz-Gonzalez Acct Mgr
Tel: 718-409-0021
Email: americanmaintenance3jss@gmail.com
Website: www.americanmaint1807.com
Commercial janitorial services; custodial services
floor & carpet care; construction cleanup; window
cleaning; building maintenance. (Hisp, estab 2004, empl
25, sales $800,000, cert: State, City, NMSDC)

2148 Anthony's Janitorial/Maintenance Service Ltd.
24-20 Jackson Ave
Long Island City, NY 11101
Contact: Anthony Fisher President
Tel: 718-737-5806
Email: anthonyjanitorialmaintenance@gmail.com
Website: www.anthonysjanitorialmaintenance.com
Janitorial Supplies & Services. (AA, estab 2010, empl 100,
sales , cert: City)

2149 Gilbert International Inc.
1001 Ave of the Americas 12th Fl
New York, NY 10018
Contact: Kevin Gilbert President
Tel: 212-628-5305
Email: kevin@gilbertinternational.com
Website: www.gilbertinternational.com
Integrated facilities services, janitorial & facilities support.
(Minority, Woman, estab 1992, empl 266, sales
$22,760,946, cert: State, City, NMSDC, WBENC)

2150 Global Traders, Inc.
496 Powell St
Brooklyn, NY 11212
Contact: Charles Ossa President
Tel: 347-240-9900
Email: cossa@globaltradersusa.us
Website: www.globaltradersusa.us
Cavicide surface disinfectant & decontaminant cleaner.
(Woman/AA, estab 1999, empl 4, sales $400,000, cert:
State, City)

2151 H. Weiss LLC
12 Labriola Court
Armonk, NY 10504
Contact: Elizabeth Weiss Managing Member
Tel: 914-273-4400
Email: eweiss@hweiss.net
Website: www.hweiss.net
Dist disposables, janitorial wares & supply items for the
kitchen. (Minority, Woman, estab 2003, empl 46, sales
$958,779,300, cert: WBENC)

2152 Premier Supplies
460 W 34th St
New York, NY 10001
Contact: Brad Singer Dir Jan/San Div
Tel: 732-240-6900
Email: bsinger@premiersupplies.com
Website: www.premiersupplies.com
Dist cleaning products & equipment. (Woman, estab 1962,
empl 7, sales $1,250,000, cert: State)

2153 Quality Building Services
801 Second Ave 8th Fl
New York, NY 10017
Contact: ANDREA BARRAGAN Research & Dev
Tel: 212-883-0009
Email: andrea.b@qbs.co
Website: www.qualitybuildingservices.com
Janitorial services: offices, conference rooms, kitchens,
bathrooms, lobbies and other common spaces. (Woman,
estab 2000, empl 600, sales $50,050,000, cert: City,
WBENC)

2154 Snappy Solutions
106 Sycamore Dr
East Hampton, NY 11937
Contact: Fairlie President
Tel: 212-748-9030
Email: maureen@snappysolutions.com
Website: www.snappysolutions.com
Dist janitorial, material maintenance products & safety
products. (Woman, estab 2003, empl 2, sales $430,000,
cert: WBENC)

Ohio

2155 Cummins Facility Services, LLC
1798 Marion Cardington Rd E
Marion, OH 43302
Contact: Christa Cloud Business Devel Mgr
Tel: 740-726-9800
Email: sales@cumminsfs.com
Website: www.cumminsfs.com
Janitorial services, vendor management, building
management, snow removal, ice melt, landscaping,
security, floor work and carpet care (Woman, estab
1972, empl 500, sales $15,000,000, cert: WBENC)

2156 Ecoprocleaningsolutions Inc.
9001 Portage Pointe Dr, Ste R103
Streetsboro, OH 44241
Contact: Kevin White President
Tel: 330-689-8196
Email: kwhite@ecoprocleaningsolutions.com
Website: www.ecoprocleaningsolutions.com
Full service janitorial service, carpet cleaning; floor
stripping; sanding; waxing; burnishing & window
cleaning. (Minority, estab 2012, empl 1, sales , cert:
NMSDC)

2157 J.T. Dillard, LLC dba ZayMat Distributors
25906 Emery Rd
Cleveland, OH 44128
Contact: Terrell Dillard President
Tel: 440-605-9000
Email: terrell.dillard@zaymat.com
Website: www.zaymat.com
Full-service commercial cleaning services. (AA, estab
2003, empl 6, sales $2,600,000, cert: State, NMSDC)

2158 Janitorial Services Inc.
5795 Canal Rd
Valley View, OH 44125
Contact: Ronald Martinez Jr. VP
Tel: 216-341-8601
Email: rmartinez@jsijanitorial.com
Website: www.jsijanitorial.com
Commercial Cleaning Services, Construction Cleaning,
Window Washing, Wall Washing, Carpet Cleaning, Hard
Surface Floor Care. (Hisp, estab 1972, empl 400, sales ,
cert: NMSDC)

2159　Ohio Services-CLE, LLC dba Jani-King of Cleveland
9075 Town Centre Dr, Ste 200
Broadview Heights, OH 44147
Contact: Joe Carollo President
Tel:　440-546-0000
Email: jcarollo@janikingcleveland.com
Website: www.janiking.com/cleveland
Janitorial services: general commercial cleaning, carpet cleaning, floor care, trash disposal, window cleaning, wall cleaning, etc. (Woman, estab 1991, empl 1000, sales $14,860,813, cert: WBENC)

Pennsylvania

2160　CSI International, Inc.
105 Terry Dr Ste 116
Newtown, PA 18940
Contact: Jamie Moore COO
Tel:　800-258-3330
Email: jmoore@csiinternational.com
Website: www.csiinternational.com
Janitorial Services, Integrated Facility Services, Building Operations & Maintenance Services. (Minority, Woman, estab 1994, empl 1915, sales $61,000,000, cert: WBENC)

2161　Homeland Industrial Supp
3045 McCann Farm Dr, Unit 102
Garnet Valley, PA 19060
Contact: Donna King CEO
Tel:　844-350-1550
Email: support@homelandindustrialsupply.com
Website: www.homelandindustrialsupply.com
Dist specialty maintenance products & janitorial supplies. (Woman, estab 2014, empl 11, sales $1,500,000, cert: State, City)

2162　T. Frank McCall's, Inc.
601 Madison St
Chester, PA 19013
Contact: Lisa Witomski President
Tel:　610-876-9245
Email: lisa@tfrankmccalls.com
Website: www.tfrankmccalls.com
Janitorial, maintenance & dist paper. (Woman, estab , empl 23, sales , cert: WBENC)

2163　Team Clean, Inc.
104 N 63rd St
Philadelphia, PA 19139
Contact: Donna Allie President
Tel:　267-514-8326
Email: dallie@team-clean.com
Website: www.team-clean.com
Janitorial cleaning, nightly office & commercial cleaning, hot water pressure washing, sanitizing garbage holding areas, window washing, carpet shampooing & full kitchen cleaning. (Woman/AA, estab 1989, empl 366, sales $17,271,812, cert: NMSDC, WBENC)

Rhode Island

2164　Universal Cleaning Concept LLC
77 Burgess Ave
East Providence, RI 02914
Contact: Evanisio Oliveira Owner
Tel:　401-952-2844
Email: universalcc14@gmail.com
Website: www.universalcleaning.org
Commercial office cleaning services. (AA, estab 2007, empl 14, sales , cert: State, 8(a), SDB)

South Carolina

2165　Clean Advantage, Inc.
5 N Watson Rd
Taylors, SC 29687
Contact: Linda Black President
Tel:　800-322-6641
Email: linda@cleanadvantage.com
Website: www.cleanadvantage.com
Mfr & package specialty cleaning products, private label packaging. (Woman, estab 1993, empl 25, sales , cert: WBENC)

2166　Quality Touch Janitorial Service, Inc.
7252 Investment Dr
North Charleston, SC 29418
Contact: John Brown President
Tel:　843-552-7303
Email: jbrown@qualitytouchjanitorial.com
Website: www.wwwqualitytouchjanitorial.com
Janitorial services, general cleaning, construction cleanup & floor maintenance. (Woman/AA, estab , empl , sales $1,650,000, cert: State, City, SDB)

Tennessee

2167　Action Chemical, Inc.
275 Cumberland St
Memphis, TN 38112
Contact: Charles E. Barnes President
Tel:　901-522-8783
Email: charles@actionjps.com
Website: www.actionchemical.com
Dist janitorial supplies & equipment, maintenance supplies & equipment, industrial supplies, paper products, safety products, cleaning chemicals, odor control products, skin care, personal hygiene products, mops, brooms, brushes. (AA, estab 1994, empl 16, sales $5,481,460, cert: State, City, NMSDC)

2168　Fayette Janitorial Service LLC
PO Box 866
Sommerville, TN 38068
Contact: Michael Kellon General Sales Mgr
Tel:　901-465-1529
Email: mburns@fayettejanitorialservice.com
Website: www.fayettejanitorialservice.com
Janitorial services. (Woman, estab 1995, empl 15, sales $24,481,341, cert: CPUC, WBENC)

2169　Ladd Safety, LLC
3901 Lighthouse Lane
Lakeland, TN 38002
Contact: Jessica Ladd Owner
Tel:　901-268-2098
Email: admin@laddsafety.com
Website: www.laddsafety.com
Dist Safety PPE & Janitorial supplies. (Woman, estab 2016, empl 3, sales , cert: WBENC)

2170　Mason's Professional Cleaning Service, LLC
1422 Menager Rd
Memphis, TN 38106
Contact: Dorothy Mason President
Tel:　901-775-7778
Email: dotm20032003@yahoo.com
Website: masonprofessionalcleaningservicellc.com
Commercial janitorial cleaning services, carpet cleaning, hard surface flooring cleaning, pressure washing, groundskeeping/landscaping service. (Woman/AA, estab 2000, empl 21, sales $550,000, cert: State, City, NMSDC)

2171　Premiere Building Maintenance Corporation
1416 McCalla Ave
Knoxville, TN 37915
Contact: Tom Poovey Dir of Business Dev
Tel:　865-773-9524
Email: tpoovey@premierebuilding.com
Website: www.premierebuilding.com
Janitorial Service, Maintenance & Facility Mgmt (AA, estab 1996, empl 500, sales $13,900,000, cert: State, NMSDC)

2172　Universal Sanitizers and Supplies, Inc.
P.O.Box 50305
Knoxville, TN 37853
Contact: Emilia Rico-Munoz CEO
Tel:　865-573-7296
Email: emirico@msn.com
Website: www.universalsanitizers.com
Sanitation cleaners & sanitizers, conveyor lubricants, janitorial products, sanitation consulting, training & audits, contract cleaning, fogging, sanitation equipment, water treatment, environmental testing. (Minority, Woman, estab 1994, empl 15, sales $3,000,000, cert: WBENC)

Texas

2173　AHI Facility Services, Inc.
625 Yuma Ct
Dallas, TX 75208
Contact: Bethany Lorentzen Marketing Coord
Tel:　800-472-5749
Email: bethanylorentzen@ahifs.com
Website: www.ahifs.com
Janitorial svcs, carpet & floor care, landscaping, groundskeeping, parking lot sweeping & striping, garage maintenance, window washing, power washing, document shredding, recycle programs. (Woman, estab 1968, empl 1500, sales $39,000,000, cert: WBENC)

2174　Aztec Facility Management, LP
11000 S Wilcrest, Ste 125
Houston, TX 77099
Contact: Andrea Bradshaw Proposal & Mktg Mgr
Tel:　281-668-9000
Email: andrea@aztec1.com
Website: www.aztecfacility.com
Facility management & support services: janitorial, grounds & preventive maintenance, pest control, parking lot maintenance, construction clean-up, property warehousing, environmental services. (Woman/AA, estab 1981, empl 900, sales $23,500,000, cert: State, NMSDC)

2175　Bell Janitorial Supplies & Services, Inc.
2828 Reward Ln
Dallas, TX 75220
Contact: Susan Morrissey President
Tel:　214-352-7775
Email: susan@belljanitorial.com
Website: www.belljanitorial.com
Dist janitorial supplies & services. (Woman, estab , empl , sales , cert: WBENC)

2176　CalGar Enterprises, LLC
3712 Arapaho Rd
Addison, TX 75001
Contact: Rick Calabrese
Tel:　972-437-6555
Email: rbraucht@calgar-ent.com
Website: www.calgar-ent.com
Maintenance & Detailed Cleaning of Cleanrooms, Data Center, Sub-Flooring Cleaning, Terminal Cleaning, Construction Clean Services, Site Preparation Contractors, Janitorial, Custodial, Green Cleaning, LEED. (Hisp, estab 2005, empl 30, sales $1,200,000, cert: State)

2177　Competitive Choice, Inc.
PO Box 35743
Houston, TX 77235
Contact: Aundrea Williams President
Tel:　832-724-5300
Email: aundrea@competitivechoice.net
Website: www.competitivechoice.net
Dist industrial maintenance & cleaning chemicals: lubricants, solvents, degreasers, hand cleaners & wipes, disinfectants, deodorizers, greases & oils, coil cleaners & pan tabs, drain & sewer maintainers, insecticdes & safety supplies. (Woman/AA, estab , empl , sales $700,000, cert: WBENC)

2178　Contractors Corner, LLC
9515 Maverick Point
San Antonio, TX 78240
Contact: Eduardo Garcia Owner
Tel:　210-462-3110
Email: agarcia@concorusa.com
Website: www.concorusa.com
Commercial janitorial services, floor care, strip & wax, buffing, polishing concrete floors & building maintenance services. (Hisp, estab 2009, empl 72, sales $1,000,000, cert: State)

2179　Entrust One Facility Services, Inc.
11142 Shady Trail
Dallas, TX 75229
Contact: Lupe Fernandez Marketing Coord
Tel:　972-669-8485
Email: lupe@entrust1.com
Website: www.entrust1.com
Janitorial Services, hard floor maintenance, carpet cleaning, marble restoration,powerwashing, window cleaning. (Minority, Woman, estab 1983, empl 600, sales , cert: State, NMSDC)

2180　Evelyn's Professional Janitorial Services, Inc.
1617 N Central Exprwy
Dallas, TX 75075
Contact: Tammy Pearce Business Devel Dir
Tel:　972-516-9550
Email: customerservice@alljanitorial.net
Website: www.alljanitorial.net
Janitorial service; window cleaning; power washing; floor maintenance; janitorial supplies; window cleaning equipment; window cleaning supplies; floor scrubbers; floor buffers; cleaning chemicals; floor sweepers; carpet vacuum. (Minority, Woman, estab 1992, empl 110, sales $1,258,040, cert: State, NMSDC, WBENC)

2181   Industrial Solution Company
       2514 Oak Hill Dr
       Arlington, TX 76006
       Contact: Barbara Oldums Owner
       Tel: 214-200-6535
       Email: industrialsolutions513@yahoo.com
       Website: www.indsolbo.com
Mfr Disposable Towel TUF Towels, Dist Cloth Towels,
Gloves, Safety Supplies, Packaging Supplies & Janitorial
Supplies. (Woman/AA, estab 2011, empl 2, sales , cert:
State, City)

2182   La Med Facility Maintenance
       10815 Gulfdale
       San Antonio, TX 78216
       Contact: Eduardo Tijerina CEO
       Tel: 210-464-0107
       Email: edwardtij@hotmail.com
       Website: www.lamedfm.com
Facility maintenance, commercial cleaning, transportation.
(Minority, Woman, estab 2011, empl 32, sales $1,250,987,
cert: State)

2183   Lim Service Industries Inc.
       5829 W Sam Houston Pkwy N, Ste 907
       Houston, TX 77041
       Contact: Frank Gortot Jr. VP Business Dev
       Tel: 954-899-2257
       Email: f.gortot.exit@gmail.com
       Website: www.limsii.com
Janitorial nation wide. (As-Pac, estab 2013, empl 32, sales
$6,000,000, cert: City, 8(a))

2184   M.A.N.S. Distributors, Inc.
       6719 Levelland Dr Ste 200
       Dallas, TX 75252
       Contact: Project Mgr
       Tel: 972-380-2062
       Email: sales@mans.us
       Website: www.mans.us
Dist industrial janitorial & maintenance supplies. (Minority,
Woman, estab 1980, empl 5, sales $3,500,000, cert: State)

2185   MarFran Cleaning, LLC
       15502 Old Galveston Rd, Ste 718
       Webster, TX 77598
       Contact: Naomi Scales Managing Member
       Tel: 832-885-6692
       Email: naomi@marfrancleaning.com
       Website: www.marfrancleaning.com
Custodial/Janitorial Services, Landscaping Services, Car-
pet & Upholstery Cleaning, Facilities Maintenance Support,
Painting & Flooring, Minor Construction, Remodeling &
Renovations. (Woman/AA, estab 2006, empl 15, sales
$543,650, cert: State, City, 8(a))

2186   Prestige Maintenance USA Ltd.
       1808 10th St
       Plano, TX 75074
       Contact: Rachel Sanchez CEO
       Tel: 972-578-9801
       Email: rsanchez@prestigeusa.net
       Website: www.prestigeusa.net
Contract cleaning: retail, office, industrial & warehouse
facilities. (Woman, estab 1976, empl 777, sales , cert:
WBENC)

2187   Redlee/SCS, Inc.
       10425 Olympic Dr, Ste A
       Dallas, TX 75220
       Contact: John Gendreau CEO
       Tel: 214-357-4753
       Email: jgendreau@redleescs.com
       Website: www.redleescs.com
Commerical janitorial services, carpet cleaning, & hard
surface flooring maintenance & restoration. (Nat Ame,
estab 1982, empl 225, sales $30,353,905, cert: State,
NMSDC)

2188   San Benito Textile Inc.
       201 N Travis St
       San Benito, TX 78586
       Contact: Carlos Sanchez Mgr
       Tel: 956-361-0282
       Email: jenny@sanbenitotextiles.com
       Website: www.sanbenitotextiles.com
Dist recycled wiping rags that clean grease, oil, petroleum, gasoline, chemicals & paint as well as buffing,
polishing, & waxing. (Hisp, estab 1990, empl 15, sales ,
cert: NMSDC)

2189   SOYAC Industrial
       12514 Willow Breeze Dr
       Tomball, TX 77377
       Contact: Roberto Schnakofsky President
       Tel: 877-243-0445
       Email: roberto@soyacindustrial.com
       Website: www.soyacindustrial.com
Environmentally & Regulatory Friendly Solvents,
Degreasers, Cleaners, Penetrating Lubricants. (Hisp,
estab 2004, empl 3, sales $273,532, cert: State, City)

2190   Supply Sanitation Systems
       1450 Preston Forest Sq, Ste 209
       Dallas, TX 75230
       Contact: Sally Seegers Sales
       Tel: 972-458-2555
       Email: sallys@supplysystemsusa.com
       Website: www.supplysystemsusa.com
Mfr & dist cleaning chemicals. (Woman, estab 1992,
empl 6, sales , cert: State)

2191   Texas Microfiber Incorporated
       2515 Tarpley Rd, Ste 118
       Carrollton, TX 75006
       Contact: President
       Tel: 800-742-2913
       Email: Sales@texasmicrofiber.com
       Website: www.texasmicrofiber.com
Mfr microfiber mop pads, mops, cloths, towels, telescopic microfiber high dusters & duster socks, aluminum
mop handles & heads, cotton hand towels, bar towels,
logo cotton towels, logo microfiber towels. (Woman,
estab 2010, empl 4, sales $725,000, cert: State, WBENC)

2192   The Entermedia Group, LLC
       900 RR620 S Ste C101-153
       Austin, TX 78734
       Contact: Lorraine Jordan CEO
       Tel: 512-553-8341
       Email: lorraine.jordan@tegteam.com
       Website: www.tegteam.com
Procurement opportunities to minority, women and
disabled veteran-owned business (Woman/AA, estab
2010, empl 10, sales , cert: State, NMSDC, WBENC)

2193 Total Building Maintenance, Inc.
      PO Box 35669
      Dallas, TX 75235
      Contact: Erica Vasquez Office Mgr
      Tel: 214-350-8293
      Email: evasquez@totalbuildingmaintenance.com
      Website: www.totalbuildingmaintenance.com
Commerical janitorial services. (Minority, Woman, estab 2005, empl 32, sales $2,500,000, cert: WBENC)

2194 XD Ventures, LLC
      2555 South Shore Blvd. Ste C
      League City, TX 77573
      Contact: Xan Difede President
      Tel: 832-557-6622
      Email: xan@fidelityfuels.com
      Website: www.fidelityfuels.com
Dist aliphatic solvents, mineral spirits & mineral seal oils. (Woman, estab 2014, empl 1, sales , cert: State, WBENC)

Virginia

2195 A&L Service Industries, Inc
      10366A Democracy Lane
      Fairfax, VA 22030
      Contact: Andrea Sax President
      Tel: 703-359-0555
      Email: diversity@alsi.us.com
      Website: www.alsi.us.com
Janitorial services, commercial & residential buildings, new construction cleanup, parking lot/garage cleaning, day porter service, carpet cleaning, window cleaning, floor restoration. (Woman, estab 1978, empl 62, sales $3,244,673, cert: State)

2196 Hutchins & Hutchins, Inc.
      39 Hutchwood Lane
      Waynessboro, VA 22980
      Contact: Kristyn H Marketing Mgr
      Tel: 540-949-6663
      Email: marketing@yourcleanroomsupplier.com
      Website: www.yourcleanroomsupplier.com/
Dist clean room supplies & safety apparel. (Woman, estab 1984, empl 17, sales $4,503,300, cert: State)

2197 ROCK SOLID Janitorial, Inc.
      2705 W Mercury Ave
      Hampton, VA 23666
      Contact: Arvella Gardner President
      Tel: 757-766-7223
      Email: calltherock@aol.com
      Website: www.rocksolidjanitorial.com
Certified green janitorial services: Complete Floor Care Services (hard surface and carpet), Day & Evening Custodial Support, Construction Cleanup. (AA, estab 1997, empl 226, sales $4,025,000, cert: State)

Washington

2198 AMEX Investments, LLC
      730 West A St
      Pasco, WA 99301
      Contact: Deborah Bermudez Owner
      Tel: 509-545-3903
      Email: deb@acompletejanitorial.com
      Website: www.acompletejanitorial.com
Cleaning supplies, chemicals, equipment & parts. (Minority, Woman, estab 2012, empl 6, sales $500,000, cert: State)

2199 Nexo Services LLC
      12819 SE 38th St
      Bellevue, WA 98006
      Contact: Fatima Sotelo Principal
      Tel: 206-518-3235
      Email: patty@nexoservices.net
      Website: www.nexoservices.net
Janitorial, Maintenance, Office, Industrial, Foodservice Supplies. (Minority, Woman, estab 2014, empl 1, sales , cert: State)

Wisconsin

2200 Lavelle Industries, Inc.
      665 McHenry St
      Burlington, WI 53105
      Contact: Megan Schmidt Natl Acct Mgr
      Tel: 262-757-2213
      Email: mschmidt@lavelle.com
      Website: www.lavelle.com
Mfr Korky brand toilet repair products: toilet flappers, toilet fill valves & flush valves. (Woman, estab , empl 450, sales , cert: WBENC)

2201 Modern Maintenance Building Services, Inc.
      2125 S 162nd St
      New Berlin, WI 53151
      Contact: Steve Ogden VP Business Devel
      Tel: 262-785-1962
      Email: steven.o@mmbuildingservices.com
      Website: www.mmbuildingservices.com
Complete janitorial services, General Cleaning, Carpet & Upholstery Cleaning, Hard Floor Care, Construction Cleaning, Parking Lot Cleaning. (Minority, Woman, estab 1984, empl 225, sales , cert: State, NMSDC)

2202 Performance Clean LLC
      One Brewers Way
      Milwaukee, WI 53214
      Contact: Steven O'Connell General Mgr
      Tel: 414-902-4439
      Email: info@performanceclean.com
      Website: www.performanceclean.com
Janitorial & building maintenance. (AA, estab 2001, empl 350, sales $4,381,330, cert: NMSDC)

2203 Rebel Green LLC
      1009 Glen Oaks Lane
      Mequon, WI 53092
      Contact: Ali Florsheim Owner
      Tel: 262-240-9992
      Email: kristina@rebelgreen.com
      Website: www.rebelgreen.com
Mfr & dist eco-friendly cleaning products that do not contain harsh chemicals. (Woman, estab 2009, empl 8, sales $7,000,000, cert: WBENC)

Alaska

2204 Teya Technologies, LLC
      101 E 9th Ave, Ste 9B
      Anchorage, AK 99501
      Contact: Ronald Perry CEO
      Tel: 907-339-4901
      Email: ron.perry@teyatech.com
      Website: www.teyatech.com
Construction, demolition, project management, custodial and janitorial services, administrative services, product manufacturing, housing maintenance, and conference and event planning/management. (Nat Ame, estab 2005, empl 46, sales $14,422,189, cert: NMSDC)

Alabama

2205 Dine Modular Construction, LLC
      2515 11th Ave
      Haleyville, AL 35565
      Contact: Pam Morton Sr Project Mgr
      Tel: 205-485-1267
      Email: pparrish@dineconstruction.com
      Website: www.dineconstruction.com
General construction: design/build construction, pre-engineered steel & modular buildings. (Minority, Woman, estab 2003, empl 6, sales $1,000,002, cert: WBENC)

Arizona

2206 Caliente Construction, Inc.
      485 W Vaughn St
      Tempe, AZ 85283
      Contact: Lorraine Bergman CEO
      Tel: 480-894-5500
      Email: lbergman@calienteconstruction.com
      Website: www.calienteconstruction.com
Licensed commercial, residential and general engineering General Contractor. (Woman, estab 1991, empl 90, sales $69,838,941, cert: CPUC, WBENC)

2207 DAP Construction Management, LLC
      516 W Vermont Ave
      Phoenix, AZ 85013
      Contact: Alicia Hernandez
      Tel: 602-541-0229
      Email: ahernandez@dapconstructionmgt.com
      Website: www.dapconstructionmgt.com
General construction: self performing, rough framing, landscaping, roofing, painting, flooring & material supplies. (Minority, Woman, estab 2009, empl 2, sales $102,000, cert: State, City, WBENC)

2208 Eagle EGC dba Miura Contracting
      4001 S Contractors Way, Ste 121
      Tucson, AZ 85716
      Contact: Liz Joye Office Mgr
      Tel: 520-292-3939
      Email: ljoye@miuracontracting.com
      Website: www.miuracontracting.com/
General Contracting, horizontal construction projects (highway, road, utilities, and site development) & vertical construction projects (commercial building and building improvements). (Hisp, estab 2008, empl 13, sales $1,400,000, cert: City, 8(a), SDB)

2209 RJC Contracting, Inc.
      2824 N Power Rd, Ste 113
      Mesa, AZ 85215
      Contact: Kristi Carpenter President
      Tel: 480-357-0868
      Email: kristi@rjccontracting.com
      Website: www.rjccontracting.com
Civil construction, commercial building, professional engineering, concrete construction, inspecting, formwork & falsework design. (Woman, estab 1996, empl 6, sales , cert: City)

2210 Sentinel Fence and Contracting LLC
      6908 East Thomas Road
      Scottsdale, AZ 85251
      Contact: Sharon Hamilton President
      Tel: 602-828-4866
      Email: sharonh@sentinelfence.com
      Website: www.sentinelfence.com
General contracting, commercial renovations, high security fencing, gates, bollards, barriers & barricades. (Minority, Woman, estab 2002, empl 15, sales $3,219,351, cert: City, WBENC)

2211 Troon Inc.
      16441 N 90th St
      Scottsdale, AZ 85260
      Contact: Ray Garcia President
      Tel: 480-626-4300
      Email: ray@trooninc.com
      Website: www.trooninc.com
General contracting. (Hisp, estab 2002, empl 11, sales $11,000,000, cert: State)

California

2212 Ahtna Government Services Corporation
      3100 Beacon Blvd.
      West Sacramento, CA 95691
      Contact: Craig O'Rourke President
      Tel: 916-372-2000
      Email: info@ahtnagov.com
      Website: www.ahtnagov.com
Comprehensive general construction; construction management; engineering; environmental engineering and remediation; professional and staffing services; and program management services. (Nat Ame, estab 1999, empl 120, sales $60,100,000, cert: CPUC)

2213　Anderson Burton Construction
121 Nevada St
Arroyo Grande, CA 93420
Contact: Joni Anderson President
Tel:　805-481-5096
Email: joni@andersonburton.com
Website: www.andersonburton.com/
General Engineering, Procurement, General Contracting,
Energy (Minority, Woman, estab 1999, empl 155, sales
$30,198,963, cert: CPUC)

2214　Aqual Corp.
7951 North Ave
Lemon Grove, CA 91945
Contact: Lanette McAfee Business Operations
Tel:　619-741-9028
Email: lanette@aqualcorp.com
Website: www.aqualcorp.com
Construction Management Cost Plus, GMP Design Build &
Lump Sum, Multi Family Commercial & Industrial Tenant
Improvements, Concrete, horizontal/vertical, drywall &
taping, painting, framing, carpentry, tile, doors, plumbing.
(AA, As-Pac, estab 2008, empl 4, sales $1,049,692, cert:
NMSDC)

2215　Bjork Construction Co. Inc.
4420 Enterprise Place
Fremont, CA 94538
Contact: Jean Bjork President
Tel:　510-656-4688
Email: jbjork@bjorkconstruction.com
Website: www.bjorkconstruction.com
General contracting: self preforms, construction manage-
ment, carpentry rough & finish, metal stud framing,
sheetrock systems & painting. (Woman, estab 1988, empl
115, sales $22,000,000, cert: CPUC, WBENC)

2216　Cabral Roofing & Waterproofing Corp.
675 W. Terrace Dr
San Dimas, CA 91773
Contact: Desi Cabral PR/Sales
Tel:　323-832-9100
Email: desi@cabralroofing.com
Website: www.cabralroofing.com
General contracting: roofing & waterproofing (Hisp, estab
1997, empl 70, sales , cert: CPUC)

2217　Casco Contractors, Inc.
9850 Irvine Center Dr.
Irvine, CA 92618
Contact: Cheryl Osborn President
Tel:　949-679-6880
Email: cheryl@cascocontractors.com
Website: www.cascocontractors.com
General contracting, TI construction, construction manage-
ment. (Woman, estab 2001, empl 44, sales $32,000,000,
cert: CPUC, WBENC)

2218　Christian Brothers Mechanical Services, Inc.
11140 Thurston Lane
Mira Loma, CA 91752
Contact: Steve Knisley VP Service
Tel:　951-361-2247
Email: steve@cbhvac.com
Website: www.cbhvac.com
Commercial HVAC. (Nat Ame, estab 1985, empl 100, sales
$18,500,000, cert: State)

2219　Commercial Site Improvements, Inc.
192 Poker Flat Rd
Copperopolis, CA 95228
Contact: Kim Batch Owner
Tel:　209-785-1920
Email: mainoffice@comimprovementsinc.com
Website: www.comsiteimprovementsinc.com
Construction maintenance & remodeling. (Woman,
estab 2012, empl 50, sales $130,000,000, cert: CPUC)

2220　Excel Construction Services, Inc.
1950 Raymer Ave
Fullerton, CA 92833
Contact: Karen Ratzlaff CEO
Tel:　714-680-9200
Email: karen@excelconstruction.biz
Website: www.excelconstruction.biz
Commercial maintenance and construction services.
(Woman, estab 2004, empl 125, sales $22,316,621, cert:
WBENC)

2221　Fasone Construction inc
9124 Norwalk Blvd
Santa Fe Springs, CA 90670
Contact: Andrea N Garrido
Tel:　562-322-0828
Email: andrea@fasonegbc.com
Website: www.fasonegbc.com
Design & general construction contracting. (Minority,
Woman, estab 1995, empl 21, sales $3,800,500, cert:
City, CPUC, WBENC, 8(a))

2222　FS3, Inc.
1201 Puerta del Sol, #314
San Clemente, CA 92673
Contact: Garrett Terlaak Principal
Tel:　949-445-3734
Email: garrett@fs3h.com
Website: www.fs3h.com
Project Management, Construction Management, CPM
Scheduling, Cost Estimating, Inspection, Constructibility
Analysis, Risk Management (Hisp, estab 2011, empl 10,
sales $1,200,000, cert: State)

2223　Health Education Services
1000 Varian St, Ste A
San Carlos, CA 94070
Contact: Jenny Fernando
Tel:　650-321-6500
Email: jfernando@healtheducationservices.net
Website: www.healtheducationservices.net
Health Education Services provides turnkey AED pro-
gram implementation and management - sales, compli-
ance, maintenance, database tracking, training.
(Woman, estab 1979, empl 18, sales $900,000, cert:
CPUC, WBENC)

2224　Hollister Construction Company
4065 E La Palma Ave Ste C
Anaheim, CA 92807
Contact: Holli Evelyn Carpenter President
Tel:　714-632-1800
Email: holli@hollico.net
Website: www.hollico.net
General contracting, turn-key design & constuction
services. (Woman, estab 1992, empl 12, sales
$2,150,000, cert: CPUC, WBENC)

2225 Interior Plus, Inc.
      8620 Sorenson Ave, Ste 2
      Santa Fe Springs, CA 90670
      Contact: Stephen Muñoz President
      Tel: 562-464-6950
      Email:
      Website: www.interiorplusinc.us
General contracting, commercial & industrial interior
construction & improvements, tenant improvements.
(Hisp, estab 1992, empl 11, sales $2,261,918, cert: CPUC,
8(a))

2226 KW Construction
      841 F St
      West Sacramento, CA 95605
      Contact: Dennis Horton Projects Est
      Tel: 916-372-8600
      Email: dhorton@kwc-usa.com
      Website: www.kwconstruction.us
General contracting: electric, plumbing, HVAC, painting,
grading & paving, finish & rough carpentry. (Woman, estab
1989, empl 15, sales $4,072,182, cert: State)

2227 Menco Pacific, Inc.
      15110 Keswick St.
      Van Nuys, CA 91405
      Contact: Jenna Lockstedt procurement Mgr
      Tel: 760-747-4405
      Email: jlockstedt@menco-pacific.com
      Website: www.menco-pacific.com
Construction services. (Hisp, estab 2007, empl 100, sales
$20,500,000, cert: State, CPUC)

2228 MSH Construction Co., Inc.
      15301 Connector Lane
      Huntington Beach, CA 92649
      Contact: Lisa Moss President
      Tel: 714-899-9509
      Email: lmoss@mshconstruction.com
      Website: www.mshconstruction.com
General contractoring: tenant improvement & civil
construction, concrete, demolition, grading & general
maintanence labor. (Woman, estab 2003, empl 12, sales
$6,679,909, cert: CPUC, WBENC)

2229 OST Trucks and Cranes, Inc.
      2951 N Ventura Ave
      Ventura, CA 93002
      Contact: L. Dennis Zermeno President
      Tel: 805-643-9963
      Email: ostcranes@aol.com
      Website: www.ostcranes.com
General & hazardous substance removal & remedial
action, hydraulic cranes 5 to 140. (Hisp, estab 1947, empl
69, sales , cert: State, NMSDC, CPUC)

2230 Paradigm General Contractors
      1017 Macdonald Ave
      Richmond, CA 94801
      Contact: CEO
      Tel: 510-478-1121
      Email: KARLA@PARADIGMGC.COM
      Website: www.paradigmgc.com
General construction, construction mgmt svcs, tenant
improvement & rennovation. (Woman, estab 1990, empl
17, sales , cert: WBENC)

2231 Petrochem Insulation, Inc.
      2300 Clayton Road, Ste 1050
      Concord, CA 94590
      Contact: Ian Broste Business Devel Mgr
      Tel: 707-644-7455
      Email: ian.broste@petrocheminc.com
      Website: www.petrocheminc.com
Insulation, Siding, Scaffolding, Fireproofing, Coatings &
Linings, Removable Blankets, Tracing, and Lead &
Asbestos Abatement. (Woman/Nat Ame, estab 1974,
empl 900, sales $102,247,202, cert: NMSDC)

2232 ProWest Engineering, Inc.
      1442 E Lincoln St Ste 360
      Orange, CA 92865
      Contact: Sherri Barrera Sales/Mktg Dir
      Tel: 866-278-0572
      Email: sherri@prowest-engineering.com
      Website: www.prowest-engineering.com
General contracting, asphalt paving removal or
maintainance, concrete repairs, seal/slurry coat,
stenciling & re-striping & ADA compliant (Minority,
Woman, estab 2005, empl 8, sales $1,500,000, cert:
CPUC)

2233 Pub Construction, Inc.
      23441 Golden Springs Dr, Ste 104
      Diamond Bar, CA 91765
      Contact: Chris Yi President
      Tel: 909-455-0187
      Email: pubconstruction@yahoo.com
      Website: www.pubconstruction.com
General contracting services, building, carpet, flooring,
tile, painting. (As-Pac, estab 2000, empl 13, sales
$15,000,000, cert: NMSDC)

2234 Shames Construction Company, Ltd
      5826 Brisa St, Ste E
      Livermore, CA 94550
      Contact: Carolyn Shames President
      Tel: 925-606-3000
      Email: cshames@shames.com
      Website: www.shames.com
Commercial construction. (Woman, estab 1987, empl
48, sales $70,847,336, cert: CPUC)

2235 South City Construction Inc.
      1111 Rancho Conejo Blvd Ste 205
      Newbury Park, CA 91320
      Contact: Andrew Solimine President
      Tel: 805-376-2000
      Email: a.solimine@southcityconstruction.com
      Website: www.southcityconstruction.com
General contracting, construction management, program management, value engineering, scheduling, cost
estimating. (Woman, estab 2011, empl 8, sales
$100,000, cert: CPUC)

2236 The G Crew
      225 E Broadway Ste 202
      Glendale, CA 91205
      Contact: Ella Daya VP
      Tel: 818-240-4157
      Email: info@thegcrew.com
      Website: www.thegcrew.com
Inspection, Construction Management, & Project
Support services (Minority, Woman, estab 2001, empl 9,
sales , cert: CPUC)

2237 True Champions
5234 Cushman Pl, Ste 200
San Deigo, CA 92110
Contact: Kristi Vega Admin Mgr
Tel: 619-276-6999
Email: kristi@truechampions.net
Website: www.truechampions.net
General contracting, design build, concrete restoration/ protective coatings, waterproofing & commercial flooring. (Hisp, estab 1995, empl 23, sales , cert: State, CPUC)

2238 Vanir Construction Management, Inc.
4540 Duckhorn Dr, Ste 300
Sacramento, CA 95834
Contact: Dorene Dominguez Business Dev Dir
Tel: 916-575-8888
Email: melinda.guzman@vanir.com
Website: www.vanir.com
Construction management services. (Minority, Woman, estab 1980, empl 334, sales $129,308,942, cert: NMSDC, CPUC)

2239 WMB Financial Solutions
1999 Harrison St Ste 1800
Oakland, CA 94612
Contact: Franck Waota President
Tel: 510-210-8052
Email: fwaota@wmbgc.com
Website: www.wwww.wmbgc.com
General construction, tenant improvement & remodeling, design build, operation & maintenance of real estate properties (Residential & commercial). (Woman/AA, estab 2004, empl 25, sales $3,700,000, cert: State, 8(a))

Colorado

2240 Alvarado Construction, Inc.
924 W Colfax Ave Ste 301
Denver, CO 80204
Contact: Jennifer Coons VP
Tel: 303-629-0783
Email: jcoons@alvaradoconstruction.com
Website: www.alvaradoconstruction.com
Commercial General Contracting, Construction Manager, Development, Design/Build & Property Management. (Minority, Woman, estab 1976, empl 50, sales , cert: NMSDC, WBENC)

2241 B&M Construction, Inc.
3134 Beacon St
Colorado Springs, CO 80907
Contact: Barbara Myrick
Tel: 719-577-4550
Email: bmyrick@bmc-i.com
Website: www.bmc-i.com
Project Management, Design-Build Services, Furniture Acquisition & Procurement, Electrical Design & Installation, Construction/Infrastructure, Tenant Finish/Renovation Services, Satellite Communications Repair & Overhaul. (Woman/AA, estab 2005, empl 33, sales $13,000,000, cert: State, NMSDC, WBENC)

2242 Rhinotrax Construction, Inc.
1035 Coffman St
Longmont, CO 80501
Contact: Michele Noel President
Tel: 303-682-9906
Email: michelenoel@rhinotrax.com
Website: www.rhinotraxconstruction.com
General contracting: demolition, rough concrete, masonry, drywall & framing, doors & hardware, etc. (Woman, estab 2004, empl 12, sales $4,500,000, cert: City)

2243 Torix General Contractors a Tepa Company
5045 List Dr
Colorado Springs, CO 80919
Contact: Marvin Maples GM
Tel: 719-596-8114
Email: marvin.maples@tepa.com
Website: www.tepa.com
New construction & rennovations: design-build, general contracting & construction management. (Nat Ame, estab 1988, empl 180, sales $105,000,000, cert: NMSDC)

Connecticut

2244 Diggs Construction, LLC
1010 Wethersfield Ave Ste 201
Hartford, CT 06114
Contact: Derrick Diggs VP
Tel: 860-296-1664
Email: ddiggs@diggsconstruction.com
Website: www.diggsconstruction.com
Program Management, Construction Management, Contract Administration & General Contracting solutions. (AA, estab 1999, empl 35, sales $11,000,000, cert: State, NMSDC)

2245 TRI-CON Construction Managers, LLC
59 Amity Rd, Ste 11
New Haven, CT 06515
Contact: Larry Stewart Exec Project Mgr
Tel: 203-772-4229
Email: lmstewart@tri-con.org
Website: www.tri-con.org
Construction management, general contracting, project management, value engineering, contract administration, estimating,owners representation services. (AA, estab 2002, empl 11, sales , cert: State, NMSDC)

2246 West Reach Construction Company, Inc.
PO Box 1328
Manchester, CT 06045
Contact: Kerry Hainsey Owner
Tel: 860-649-7607
Email: westreachcon@wrconstruction.net
Website: www.westreachconstruction.com
General contracting, commercial, industrial construction. (Woman, estab 1987, empl 15, sales , cert: State, WBENC)

District of Columbia

2247 Columbia Enterprises
      1018 7th St SE
      Washington, DC 20003
      Contact: President
      Tel: 202-547-7979
      Email:
      Website: www.columbiadb.com
Construction management & general contracting services.
(AA, estab 1993, empl 15, sales $5,200,000, cert: State,
NMSDC)

2248 Drake Incorporated
      4315 Sheriff Rd NE
      Washington, DC 20019
      Contact: Stephanie Y Drake CEO
      Tel: 202-291-3174
      Email: sdrake@drake-inc.com
      Website: www.drake-inc.com
Construction, design / build & project management.
(Woman/AA, estab 2002, empl 24, sales $7,088,479, cert:
State)

2249 Motir Services, Inc.
      1508 E Capitol St, NE
      Washington, DC 20003
      Contact: Emmanuel Irono President
      Tel: 202-371-9393
      Email: eirono@motirservices.com
      Website: www.motirservices.com
Industrial Building Construction, Commercial & Institu-
tional Building Construction, Office Moving/Relocation,
Management Consulting, Information Technology, Data
Processing, Facilities Management, Janitorial Services.
(Minority, estab 1994, empl 193, sales $17,635,639, cert:
State, NMSDC, SDB)

2250 The ELOCEN Group
      1341 H St, NE Ste 301
      Washington, DC 20002
      Contact: Taryn Lewis Dir of Operations
      Tel: 202-644-8500
      Email: tarynl@elocengroup.com
      Website: www.elocengroup.com
Program & Project Management, Construction Manage-
ment, Interior Design, Information Technology, Facilities/
Logistics, and Healthcare Facilities/Logistics/Management.
(Woman/AA, estab 2007, empl 62, sales $20,089,894, cert:
State, City, WBENC, 8(a))

Delaware

2251 M. Davis & Sons, Inc.
      19 Germay Dr
      Wilmington, DE 19804
      Contact: Christina MacMillan VP Strategic Dev
      Tel: 952-742-4096
      Email: mdsregistrations@mdavisinc.com
      Website: www.mdavisinc.com
Industrial construction company. (Woman, estab , empl
450, sales $82,717,195, cert: WBENC)

Florida

2252 Albu & Associates, Inc.
      2711 W Fairbanks Ave
      Winter Park, FL 32789
      Contact: Jason Albu President
      Tel: 407-788-1450
      Email: jasonalbu@albu.biz
      Website: www.albu.biz
General contracting, design build, construction
management & consulting. (Hisp, estab 1994, empl 20,
sales $20,000,000, cert: City, NMSDC)

2253 Arkren Inc.
      6278 N Federal Hwy Ste 430
      Fort Lauderdale, FL 33308
      Contact: Mark Barati Sr VP
      Tel: 954-210-8886
      Email: mark@arkren.com
      Website: www.arkren.com
Telecommunications, general construction(commercial
and residential), design, Procurement, logistics, warehousing, transportation, temporary housing/life support, professional/craft labor, O&G/LNG. (Woman, estab
2013, empl 15, sales $960,000, cert: WBENC)

2254 Certified Constructors' Services Inc.
      5330 Fairfield Dr
      Crestview, FL 32536
      Contact: Tommy Henderson Sr VP
      Tel: 850-682-8953
      Email: ccsithenderson@aol.com
      Website: www.ccsipower.com
Provide onsite mechanical construction services for the
Power Generating and General Industry. (Woman, estab
2004, empl 250, sales $42,000,000, cert: WBENC)

2255 Cortes Construction Services, LLC
      720 Anclote Rd
      Tarpon, FL 34689
      Contact: Michael Corral VP
      Tel: 727-937-4700
      Email: mcorral@cortesconstruction.com
      Website: www.cortesconstruction.com
Commercial construction company specializing in hotel
renovations. (Hisp, estab 2004, empl 30, sales
$5,178,771, cert: State)

2256 Dominion Builders, LLC
      4942 S LeJeune Rd Ste 203
      Coral Gables, FL 33146
      Contact: Mark Gemignani President
      Tel: 305-661-2700
      Email: mgemignani@dominionbuild.com
      Website: www.dominionbuild.com
General contracting services. (Nat Ame, estab 2008,
empl 7, sales $5,000,000, cert: State, 8(a))

2257 Fine Line Construction contractors, Inc.
      6500 Georgia Ave
      Florida, FL 33405
      Contact: Bob Waskiwicz VP
      Tel: 561-582-7880
      Email: bobw@finelinecontractors.com
      Website: www.finelinecontractors.com
General contracting, commercial construction,
commecial buildout & renovations, interior remodel,
building expansion, full buildout, interior improvements,
warehouse expansion, warehouse renovations. (Woman,
estab 2010, empl 15, sales $5,867,874, cert: WBENC)

2258 Hatcher Construction & Development, Inc.
      3300 S Congress Ave Ste 15
      Boynton Beach, FL 33426
      Contact: William Hatcher
      Tel: 561-752-4100
      Email: hatchergc@bellsouth.net
      Website: www.hatcher-construction.com
Commercial Institutional Bldg, General Contractor, Asphalt
roofing, Asphalt Coating & Sealing, Concrete, Painting,
spraying, or coating, Facilities Support Mgmt, Electrical,
Residential Construction, multifamily, Landscaping. (AA,
estab 1999, empl 7, sales $1,350,000, cert: State, 8(a))

2259 IBC, Inc. - International Builders & Consultants
      5135 Starfish Ave
      Naples, FL 34103
      Contact: Brandy McCombs President
      Tel: 816-220-0812
      Email: brandy@ibcinc.biz
      Website: www.IBCinc.biz
General contracting, install/repair drywall, cabinets,
counter tops, doors, frames, hardware, paint and
specailties. (Woman, estab 2008, empl 70, sales
$12,500,000, cert: State, City)

2260 J & K Mechanical
      2176 NW 82nd Ave
      Miami, FL 33122
      Contact: Jaime Monserrat VP
      Tel: 305-278-7171
      Email: jmonserrat@tropicac.com
      Website: www.tropicmechanical.com
HVAC mechanical contractor, Engineering and design, New
construction installation, Controls design, installation and
programming. (Hisp, estab 2004, empl 56, sales
$19,000,000, cert: State)

2261 LEGO Construction Co.
      1011 Sunnybrook Rd Ste 905
      Miami, FL 33136
      Contact: Luis Garcia President
      Tel: 305-381-8421
      Email: lgarcia@legocc.com
      Website: www.legocc.com
General Contractor. (Hisp, estab 2006, empl 40, sales
$40,000,000, cert: State, SDB)

2262 Lemartec Corporation
      11740 SW 80th St, 3rd Fl
      Miami, FL 33183
      Contact: Maira Suarez Mgr Strategic Partnerships
      Tel: 305-273-8676
      Email: cjaramillo@lemartec.com
      Website: www.lemartec.com
EPC/EPCM, Design-Build, and Construction Management
Firm. (Hisp, estab 1979, empl 88, sales $60,000,000, cert:
NMSDC)

2263 Nakitare Builders LLC
      11806 Foxglove Dr
      Clermont, FL 34711
      Contact: Robert Mack GM
      Tel: 352-857-0000
      Email: buld2006@aol.com
      Website: www.sustainable-roofs.com
Construction services, inspections. (AA, estab 2006, empl
5, sales $390,000, cert: NMSDC)

2264 R L Burns Inc.
      1203 W Gore St
      Orlando, FL 32805
      Contact: Elizabeth Duncan
      Tel: 407-839-1131
      Email: eduncan@rlburnsinc.com
      Website: www.rlburnsinc.com
Construction management svcs: project management,
consulting, cost estimating, pre-construction planning &
design, schedule / CPM management, general construction, design/build, new construction, renovation. (AA,
estab 1994, empl 9, sales $3,000,000, cert: City)

2265 T&G Corporation
      8623 Commodity Circle
      Orlando, FL 32819
      Contact: Mark Knott Dir Business Devel
      Tel: 407-352-4443
      Email: officedepot@t-and-g.com
      Website: www.t-and-g.com
General contracting: facility operation/maintenance
support services, commercial building, construction
management & design-build services. (Hisp, estab 1987,
empl 85, sales $23,214,524, cert: State, NMSDC)

2266 Thomco Enterprises Inc.
      745 Hollywood Blvd NW
      Fort Walton Beach, FL 32548
      Contact: Darryl Embrey President
      Tel: 850-244-0811
      Email: darryle@thomcoent.com
      Website: www.thomcoent.com
Construction, construction management, facility
maintenance, renovations, upgrades, vertical construction, bank facility construction, commercial & government construction, development, project management.
(AA, estab 1993, empl 35, sales $11,245,342, cert: State)

2267 Thornton Construction Company, Inc.
      13290 NW 42nd Ave
      Miami, FL 33054
      Contact: Nataly Guevara Business Devel Mgr
      Tel: 305-649-1995
      Email: nguevara@thornton-inc.com
      Website: www.thornton-inc.com
Contracting and construction management firm. (Hisp,
estab 1998, empl 55, sales $55,978,278, cert: State)

2268 Validus Construction Services LLC
      7130 S Orange Blossom Trail Ste 111
      Orlando, FL 32809
      Contact: Nicole Wickens Owner
      Tel: 407-413-5022
      Email: validuscs@gmail.com
      Website: www.validuscs.net
New construction, remodel, remediation, design-build,
renovation, office renovations, warehouse renovations,
landscaping, parking lot, sidewalks, windows, doors,
flooring, interiors, exteriors, HVAC, plumbing, electrical.
(Woman, estab 2012, empl 9, sales $5,337,114, cert:
WBENC)

2269 Veatic dba of Proxy Management Group
2450 Smith St, Ste P
Kissimmee, FL 34744
Contact: Jon Andreasson Project Dev
Tel: 888-474-2999
Email: jandreasson@veatic.com
Website: www.veatic.com
General Contractor, Site Development, Excavation,
Retention, Disaster Response, Grading, Foundations,
Underground Utilities, Demolition, Site Restoration, New
Building Construction. (Hisp, estab 2008, empl 32, sales
$3,801,885, cert: State, City, NMSDC)

Georgia

2270 Bryson Constructors, Inc.
2847 Main St, Ste 200
East Point, GA 30344
Contact: Steve Barnes CEO
Tel: 404-762-1000
Email: sbarnes@brysonconstructors.com
Website: www.brysonconstructors.com
Design/build commercial construction. (AA, estab , empl ,
sales $7,351,431, cert: NMSDC)

2271 Colliers Facility Solutions, LLC
1230 Peachtree St Ste 800
Atlanta, GA 30309
Contact: Holly Hughes CEO
Tel: 404-574-1014
Email: holly.hughes@colliers.com
Website: www.colliers.com/atlanta
Facility management, project management, construction
management, interior, exterior & maintenance, energy
efficiency, systems optimization, risk mitigation & cost
savings. (Woman, estab 2014, empl 160, sales
$19,500,000, cert: WBENC)

2272 Pinnacle Services Group, Inc.
10270 Oxford Mill Circle
Alpharetta, GA 30022
Contact: Jerry Peljovich President
Tel: 770-355-7156
Email: jerryp@psginc-ga.com
Website: www.PSGinc-ga.com
General contracting. (Hisp, estab 2004, empl 5, sales
$3,207,000, cert: State, City, NMSDC)

2273 Pioneer Construction, Inc.
31 Park of Commerce Way Ste 100
Savannah, GA 31405
Contact: Whitney Butler Dir Mktg
Tel: 912-650-1850
Email: wbutler@pioneersavannah.com
Website: www.pioneersavannah.com
General Contractors specializing in commercial construc-
tion. (Minority, Woman, estab 1994, empl 20, sales
$10,000,000, cert: State)

2274 Quantum Installation Group
889 Franklin Gateway, Ste 100
Marietta, GA 30067
Contact: Bob Turner VP Business Dev
Tel: 706-506-2262
Email: bob.turner@quantuminstall.com
Website: www.quantuminstall.com
General construction contractor, millwork, fixture & decor
installation contractor. (Woman/As-Pac, estab 2012, empl
150, sales , cert: NMSDC, WBENC)

2275 Synergy Development Partners, LLC
83 Walton St, NW Ste 400
Atlanta, GA 30303
Contact: Brittany Montgomery Operations Mgr
Tel: 404-254-4755
Email: bmontgomery@synergydp.com
Website: www.synergydp.com
General contracting, construction management, drywall,
framing, renovation, restoration, roof repair, carpentry,
flooring, paint, trim, tentant build-out & new construc-
tion. (Woman/AA, estab 2003, empl 15, sales
$3,568,712, cert: City, NMSDC)

2276 The Chester Group, Inc.
231 Peters St SW
Atlanta, GA 30313
Contact: Wallace Chester President
Tel: 786-586-3941
Email: wchester@thechestergroup.com
Website: www.thechestergroup.com
General contracting & construction mgmt: renovation;
design/build; maintenance; roofing; concrete place-
ment; debris removal; fencing; asphalt resurfacing;
masonry; interior build-out; windows; doors; painting;
flooring; electrical. (AA, estab 2002, empl 1, sales
$100,000, cert: State)

2277 Time Out Systems, Inc.
308 Indian Creek Circle
Adel, GA 31620
Contact: Tim LeBlanc CFO
Tel: 229-896-6190
Email: admin@timeoutsystems.com
Website: www.timeoutsystems.com
General Construction, Remolding, Roofing, Painting,
Security, Surround Sound, Televisions, Home Automa-
tion, Yard Maintenance, Door and Window Replace-
ment, Blind Installation, Deck Construction, Bathroom
Remolding. (Woman, estab 1991, empl 150, sales
$13,000,000, cert: WBENC)

Hawaii

2278 Arita-Poulson General Contracting, LLC
PO Box 1035
Puunene, HI 96784
Contact: John Evarts Sr Project Engineer
Tel: 808-871-4787
Email: jevarts@aritapoulson.com
Website: www.aritapoulson.com
General Contracting. (As-Pac, estab 1986, empl 62, sales
$50,000,000, cert: NMSDC)

Iowa

2279 Gethmann Construction Company, Inc.
PO Box 160
Marshalltown, IA 50158
Contact: Jill Craft President
Tel: 641-753-3555
Email: jill@gethmann.com
Website: www.gethmannconstruction.com
Concrete work, excavation, backfill, foundations, slabs,
pads, elevated slabs, concrete demo, structural steel fab,
crane rental & operators. (Woman, estab 1937, empl 67,
sales $22,000,000, cert: WBENC)

Illinois

2280 Continental Painting and Decorating
2255 S Wabash Ave
Chicago, IL 60616
Contact: Constance Williams President
Tel: 312-225-6100
Email: cwilliams@continentalpainting.com
Website: www.continentalpainting.com
Painting, wallcovering, wood refinishing, drywall taping. (AA, estab 1994, empl 68, sales $11,700,000, cert: State, City, NMSDC)

2281 Cotter Consulting, Inc.
100 S Wacker Dr Ste 920
Chicago, IL 60606
Contact: Anne Edwards-Cotter President
Tel: 131-269-6120
Email: a.cotter@cotterconsulting.com
Website: www.cotterconsulting.com
Construction program & project management services. (Woman, estab 1990, empl 100, sales $18,650,000, cert: State, WBENC)

2282 CREA Construction
161 N Clark, Ste 4700
Chicago, IL 60601
Contact: Rea Johnson President
Tel: 312-371-3827
Email: rea1_23@yahoo.com
Website: www.creagc.com
Construction management, general contracting, estimating & engineering services. (Woman/AA, estab 2007, empl 10, sales $1,000,000, cert: State, NMSDC)

2283 GACC Video Electronics Inc.
700 Nicholas Blvd Ste 103
Elk Grove Village, IL 60007
Contact: Jennifer Chang Secretary
Tel: 312-733-5774
Email: jennifer@gaccvideo.com
Website: www.gaccvideo.com
Audio and Video Service and repair. Audio and Video Sales of microphones, cameras, decks, monitors in such brands as Sony, Lectrosonics, Sound Devices, Josephson, Sanken, Panasonic, JVC, Canon, Fujinon. Audio Video Rental in (Minority, Woman, estab 2000, empl 3, sales $450,000, cert: City)

2284 Integrated Construction Technology Corp.
126 S Villa Ave
Villa Park, IL 60181
Contact: Les Shy President
Tel: 630-993-1800
Email: lshy@integratedusa.com
Website: www.integratedusa.com
Design & build construction, general contracting, property managment, supplies & services. (AA, As-Pac, estab 1994, empl 30, sales $18,000,000, cert: City)

2285 LiveWire Electrical Systems, Inc.
12900 S. Throop St
Calumet Park, IL 60827
Contact: Angela Drexel VP
Tel: 708-535-6001
Email: adrexel@livewire-systems.com
Website: www.livewire-systems.com
New Construction & renovations, phase electrical systems, Switchgear, Back up generators, Power systems for process/production. (AA, estab 2006, empl 65, sales $23,046,514, cert: State, NMSDC)

2286 Maman Corp.
346 W Colfax
Palatine, IL 60067
Contact: Rodney Pace Dir of Operations
Tel: 847-358-2688
Email: megan@maman-corp.com
Website: www.maman-corp.com
General contractors, commercial construction, project management. (Woman, estab 1997, empl 18, sales , cert: WBENC)

2287 Otis Construction Company
111 W Jackson Blvd Ste 1105
Chicago, IL 60604
Contact: Glenn Otis, Jr. President
Tel: 312-786-9877
Email: gotis@otiscc.com
Website: www.otiscc.com
Construction svcs: interior building alterations, commercial & industrial facilities, green construction & maintenance, specialty projects, facilities maintenance, emergency repairs. (AA, estab 1999, empl 4, sales $1,500,000, cert: NMSDC)

2288 Sumac Inc.
3701 N Ravenswood Ave Ste 202
Chicago, IL 60613
Contact: Liliana Gonzalez VP
Tel: 773-857-7906
Email: lgonzalez@sumacinc.com
Website: www.sumacinc.com
Architecture & construction management: architectural design, sustainable design, project scheduling, cost estimating, construction procurement, construction management services & general contracting. (Hisp, estab 2008, empl 10, sales $2,000,000, cert: NMSDC)

2289 The Landmark Group Companies LLC
6735 Vistagreen Way Ste 100
Rockford, IL 61107
Contact: Bob Sanches CEO
Tel: 815-639-0034
Email: bsanches@lmcos.com
Website: www.lmcos.com
Construction management of new & existing facilities. (Hisp, estab 2006, empl 8, sales $30,000,000, cert: NMSDC)

2290 Total Response Technology, LLC
1921 Richfield Ave
Highland Park, IL 60035
Contact: Sandra Bast President
Tel: 312-513-0478
Email: sandra@trt-llc.com
Website: www.totalresponsetechnology.com
Total Response Technology (Minority, Woman, estab 2009, empl 20, sales $1,400,000, cert: City, WBENC)

2291 Trinidad Construction, LLC
9850 190th St Ste N
Mokena, IL 60448
Contact: Brian Ortiz President
Tel: 773-429-4600
Email: bortiz@trinidadllc.com
Website: www.trinidadllc.com
General contracting, construction management. (Hisp, estab 2010, empl 75, sales $25,000,000, cert: NMSDC)

2292 Vistara Construction Services, Inc.
728 W Jackson Blvd, Ste 402
Chicago, IL 60661
Contact: Bina Nair President
Tel: 312-986-8660
Email: info@vistara.com
Website: www.vistara.com
General construction. (Woman/As-Ind, estab 1994, empl 10, sales , cert: City)

Indiana

2293 Custom Mechanical Systems, Corp.
691 Industrial Blvd
Bargersville, IN 46106
Contact: William Beach VP Business Dev
Tel: 617-803-0714
Email: wbeach@cms-corporation.com
Website: www.cms-corporation.com
New construction, renovations, energy & sustainability, building operations maintenance & repairs. (Hisp, estab 1996, empl 110, sales $42,753,323, cert: State, NMSDC)

2294 Finch Constructors, Inc.
5528 W 84th St
Indianapolis, IN 46268
Contact: Tammy Brooks Operations Mgr
Tel: 317-916-6770
Email: tbrooks@finchconstructors.com
Website: www.finchconstructors.com
Industrial, commercial & municipal construction & management services: mechanical piping, equipment erection, HVAC & electrical services. (AA, estab 2004, empl 42, sales $20,000,000, cert: NMSDC)

2295 Harmon Construction, Inc.
621 S State St
North Vernon, IN 47265
Contact: Ardell Mitchell Sr Project Mgr/Estimator
Tel: 812-346-2048
Email: ardell.mitchell@harmonconstruction.com
Website: www.harmonconstruction.com
Contracting, design-build capabilities. (AA, estab 1955, empl 81, sales $8,478,000, cert: State, NMSDC)

2296 K&S Construction Group, Inc.
9148 Louisiana St, Unit F
Merrillville, IN 46410
Contact: Vance R. Kenney CEO
Tel: 219-794-9550
Email: vkenney@k-sconstruction.com
Website: www.k-sconstruction.com
Heavy construction, construction mgmt, demolition, design build, excavation, reinforced concrete, concrete forming, sidewalk, curb, crushed granite, levees, revetments, carpentry, railroad construction, fencing, environmental. (AA, estab 1992, empl 25, sales $3,200,000, cert: State, NMSDC)

2297 Powers & Sons Construction Co, Inc.
2636 W 15th Ave
Gary, IN 46404
Contact: Kelly Powers Baria Dir Business Dev
Tel: 219-949-3100
Email: kbaria@powersandsons.com
Website: www.powersandsons.com
Construction services. (AA, estab 1967, empl , sales $30,390,330, cert: State, NMSDC)

2298 Shawnee Construction and Engineering
7701 Opportunity Dr
Fort Wayne, IN 46825
Contact: Matt Schenkel President
Tel: 260-489-1234
Email: matt@shawneeconstruction.com
Website: www.ShawneeConstruction.com
General contracting, new construction & remodeling, commercial & industrial. (Hisp, estab 1968, empl 42, sales $17,300,000, cert: State, City)

Kentucky

2299 AAECON General Contractors, LLC.
1147 Logan St
Louisville, KY 40204
Contact: Troy Ansert VP
Tel: 502-291-3976
Email: tansert@aacongc.com
Website: www.aacongc.com
Design/build, construction management & general construction. (AA, estab 2005, empl 33, sales , cert: NMSDC, 8(a))

Louisiana

2300 Lafayette Steel Erector
313 Westgate Rd
Lafayette, LA 70506
Contact: John Prudhomme President
Tel: - -
Email: janice@l-s-e.com
Website: www.LSEcrane.com
Crane, steel erection, precast erectors, equipment installation. (Nat Ame, estab 1957, empl 115, sales , cert: NMSDC)

Massachusetts

2301 Chicopee Industrial Contractors
107 N Chicopee St
Chicopee, MA 01020
Contact: Carol Campbell President
Tel: 413-538-7279
Email:
Website: www.chicopeeindustrial.com
Rigging, millwrighting, heavy equipment hauling, plant relocation, concrete, foundations, pre-fab building erection, demolition, welding, fabrication. (Woman, estab 1992, empl 20, sales $1,725,000, cert: WBENC)

2302 Essex Newbury North Contracting Corporation
65 Parker St, Unit 5
Newburyport, MA 01950
Contact: Delano Brooks President
Tel: 978-463-5414
Email: delano_br@yahoo.com
Website: www.essexnewburynorth.com
General Contracting, construction management, commercial & industrial construction, lead abatement & asbestos remediation, finish carpentry, commercial & institutional bldg construction, painting & wall coverings, site preparation. (AA, estab 1997, empl 400, sales $31,000,000, cert: State, City, NMSDC)

2303 General Air Conditioning and Heating Inc.
7 Gaston St
Dorchester, MA 02121
Contact: Felicia Pinckney Dir Business Dev
Tel: 617-427-7370
Email: felicia@genairheat.net
Website: www.genairheat.net
Mechanical Contractors, Heating, Air Conditioning, Plumbing, Refrigeration and Energy. (AA, estab 1985, empl 50, sales $29,000,000, cert: City)

2304 J&J Contractors, Inc.
101 Billerica Ave Bldg 5 Ste 2
North Billerica, MA 01862
Contact: Kamlesh Patel CEO
Tel: 978-452-9898
Email: kamp@jjcontractor.com
Website: www.jjcontractor.com
Construction management, general contracting & design/build. (As-Ind, estab 1997, empl 50, sales , cert: State)

Maryland

2305 Buch Construction Inc.
11292 Buch Way
Laurel, MD 20723
Contact: Denise Buch Controller
Tel: 301-369-3500
Email: dbuch@buch.us.com
Website: www.buchconstruction.com
General contracting, interior construction, carpentry, drywall, electric, painting, new construction, doors & hardware, structural steel. (Woman, estab 1984, empl 65, sales $6,210,000, cert: WBENC)

2306 Capital Brand Group, LLC
12501 Prosperity Dr, Ste 400
Silver Spring, MD 20904
Contact: Max Brand President
Tel: 301-358-1377
Email: mbrand@capitalbrandgroup.com
Website: www.capitalbrandgroup.com
Construction, Construction Management, A/E Services, Facility Management, Janitorial, Energy and Sustainability, landscaping, HVAC and Construction Services. (Hisp, estab 2013, empl 30, sales $3,512,178, cert: State, 8(a))

2307 Estime Enterprises, Inc.
4640 Forbes Blvd Ste 100
Lanham, MD 20706
Contact: Lunique Estime President
Tel: 301-731-8316
Email: lestime@estimeinc.com
Website: www.estimeinc.com
Construction management, renovation, environmental consulting services, green sustainable solutions (wind power generation, solar harvesting, triban antimicrobial systems, and photovoltaic roofing solutions). (AA, estab 1996, empl 35, sales $4,296,512, cert: State, NMSDC)

Michigan

2308 3.L.K. Construction, LLC
18401 S Weaver
Detroit, MI 48228
Contact: Lorenzo Walker President
Tel: 313-493-9101
Email: lesa@3lkconstruction.com
Website: www.3lkconstruction.com
General Contractor, Construction Manager (AA, estab 1998, empl 20, sales , cert: NMSDC)

2309 Associated Design & Services, Inc.
1177 Wadhams Rd, Bldg E
Smiths Creek, MI 48074
Contact: Mary Insley President
Tel: 810-650-2809
Email: minsley1@advnet.net
Website: www.ads800callus.com/
Commercial Industrial & Structural Maintenance and Repairs, Millwrighting, Rotating Equipment and Mechanical Services. (Woman, estab 2003, empl 7, sales $831,602, cert: WBENC)

2310 Blaze Contracting, Inc.
5640 St. Jean
Detroit, MI 48213
Contact: Gayl Turk Dir Business Dev
Tel: 313-361-1000
Email: gturk@blazecontracting.net
Website: www.blazecontracting.com
Site Preparation Contractor; Excavation, Grading, Storm Sewer, Sanitary Sewer, Watermain, Water Detention Systems; (AA, estab 2000, empl 120, sales $19,000,000, cert: NMSDC)

2311 Commercial Construction Inc.
7428 Kensington Rd
Brighton, MI 48116
Contact: Robert Garcia President
Tel: 248-685-3263
Email: pgarcia@cci-rigging.com
Website: www.cci-rigging.com
Millwright & migging contractor, install machinery, conveyors, robots, automation for automotive industry, industrial process. (Hisp, estab 1991, empl 40, sales $3,100,000, cert: NMSDC)

2312 Hale Contracting, Inc.
18407 Weaver St
Detroit, MI 48228
Contact: Lawrence Hale President
Tel: 313-272-9400
Email: lawrence.hale@halecontracting.com
Website: www.Halecontracting.com
General contracting. (AA, estab 0, empl , sales , cert: NMSDC)

2313 Hamilton Contracting
30375 Northwestern Hwy Ste 102
Farmington Hills, MI 48334
Contact: Melissa Grundy Business Devel Exec
Tel: 734-895-3547
Email: mgrundy@hamilton-contracting.com
Website: www.hamilton-contracting.com
General contracting: demolition, machinery installation & relocation, conveyor installation, structural installation, platform installation, preventative maintenance & machine precision alignments. (Woman, estab 2011, empl 45, sales $5,400,000, cert: WBENC)

2314 Harris Design & Construction Services
2512 W Grand Blvd, Ste 100
Detroit, MI 48208
Contact: Karl Harris CEO
Tel: 313-444-3307
Email: kharris@harrisdesignconstruction.com
Website: www.harrisdesignconstruction.com
Architectural design and construction services. (AA, estab 2014, empl 1, sales $100,000, cert: NMSDC)

2315 Ideal Contracting, LLC
2525 Clark St
Detroit, MI 48209
Contact: Kevin Foucher VP
Tel: 313-843-8000
Email: kfoucher@idealcontracting.com
Website: www.idealcontracting.com
General contracting, construction management & design/build services. (Hisp, estab 1998, empl 325, sales $191,613,602, cert: NMSDC)

2316 Jenkins Construction, Inc.
985 E Jefferson, Ste 300
Detroit, MI 48207
Contact: Darwyn Parks Project Exec
Tel: 313-625-7200
Email: dparks@jenkinsconstruction.com
Website: www.jenkinsconstruction.com
Design/build, construction management, general contractor & excavation. (AA, estab 1989, empl 50, sales $65,000,000, cert: NMSDC)

2317 Optimum Contracting Solutions
2211 Devonshire Rd
Bloomfield Hills, MI 48302
Contact: Anamaria Tet Owner
Tel: 248-346-3069
Email: anamaria.optimum@att.net
Website: www.optimum1.net
General Contracting, Project Management, Residential Building & Remodeling Services , Commercial Remodeling Services, Roofing, Siding, Additions, Drywall, Rough and Finish Carpentry ,Painting, Electrical, HVAC, Doors & window installation. (Woman, estab 2010, empl 10, sales $400,000, cert: WBENC)

2318 PAT USA, Inc.
2927 Waterview Dr
Rochester Hills, MI 48309
Contact: Fenar Mayes Sr Project Mgr
Tel: 248-299-2410
Email: fenar@pat-engineering.com
Website: www.pat-engineering.com
General contracting services, engineering & construction services. (Woman, estab 2011, empl 10, sales , cert: WBENC)

2319 Powerlink Electrical
217 Fisher Building
Detroit, MI 48202
Contact: Sherwood Merrill Chairman
Tel: 313-309-2020
Email: smerrill@powerlinkonline.com
Website: www.powerlinkonline.com
Facilities management, maintenance services, & construction. (AA, estab 2002, empl 350, sales $15,900,000, cert: NMSDC)

2320 R.B. Construction Company
6489 Metro Pkwy
Sterling Heights, MI 48312
Contact: Russell Beaver President
Tel: 586-264-9478
Email: rbeaver@rb-construction.com
Website: www.rb-construction.com
Construction, renovation, building, pre-engineered building, remodel. (Nat Ame, estab 1984, empl 7, sales $3,318,000, cert: NMSDC, 8(a))

2321 Rickman Enterprise Group, LLC
15533 Woodrow Wilson
Detroit, MI 48238
Contact: Lawrence Bost CEO
Tel: 313-454-4000
Email: lawrence@rickmanenterprise.com
Website: www.rickmanenterprise.com
Industrial Painting/Environmental, Flooring, Demo. (AA, estab 2007, empl 131, sales $10,000,000, cert: NMSDC)

2322 Sieler Construction
11119 E US 223
Blissfield, MI 49228
Contact: Jeff Sieler VP
Tel: 517-486-3050
Email: lue@sielerconstruction.com
Website: www.sielerconstruction.com
General Contracting, excavation, concrete, steel trades, steel fabrication, holding tanks, shut-down / machinery relocation, water & fire main repairs, water lines. (Woman, estab 2000, empl 12, sales , cert: WBENC)

2323 Stenco Construction Company, LLC
12741 Farmington Rd
Livonia, MI 48150
Contact: Nick Schallmo General Mgr
Tel: 734-427-8843
Email: nschallmo@stencoconstruction.com
Website: www.stencoconstruction.com
General contruction: interior finish, earthwork, concrete, steel & rigging projects. (As-Pac, estab 1998, empl 75, sales $33,650,000, cert: NMSDC)

2324 The Ideal Group
2525 Clark St
Detroit, MI 48209
Contact: Linzie Venegas Sales
Tel: 313-842-7290
Email: linzie@idealshield.com
Website: www.weareideal.com
Architectural & engineering svcs; general contracting & construction mgmt, rigging. Mfr, dist, fabricate & erect structural & misc steel. Patent for "Ideal Shield" Protective Guard Rail System. (Hisp, estab 1979, empl 120, sales , cert: NMSDC)

2325 Tooles Contracting Group LLC
500 Griswold St, Ste 1620
Detroit, MI 48226
Contact: Laura Ottman Mgr Business Devel
Tel: 313-221-8500
Email: laura.ottman@toolesgroup.com
Website: www.toolesgroup.com
Commercial & industrial construction, general contracting, construction & pogram management, equipment installation, self perform services & design build. (AA, estab 2002, empl 38, sales $119,996,211, cert: NMSDC)

2326 W-3 Construction Company
7601 Second Ave
Detroit, MI 48202
Contact: Walter E. Watson, Jr. CEO
Tel: 313-875-8000
Email: w3@w3group.net
Website: www.w3group.net
General contracting, project managers, self perform concrete, drywall & accoustical. (AA, estab 1987, empl 49, sales $19,901,023, cert: NMSDC)

2327 Zebing Solutions LLC
15617 Marksman Rd
Lanse, MI 49946
Contact: Arlan Friisvall President
Tel: 877-585-8171
Email: info@zebingsolutions.com
Website: www.zebingsolutions.com
Construction, electrical, mechanical & engineering services. (Nat Ame, estab 2011, empl 20, sales $500,000, cert: NMSDC)

Minnesota

2328 Loeffler Construction and Consulting, LLC
20520 Keokuk Ave, Ste 100
Lakeville, MN 55044
Contact: Doug Loeffler President
Tel: 952-955-9119
Email: dloeffler@loefflerconstruction.com
Website: www.loefflerconstruction.com
Construction and consulting services, new construction & remodeling projects. (Minority, Woman, estab 2010, empl 6, sales $21,922,187, cert: NMSDC)

2329 Meyer Contracting Inc.
11000 93rd Ave N
Minneapolis, MN 55369
Contact: Scott Kerzman CEO
Tel: 763-391-5959
Email: skerzman@meyercontractinginc.com
Website: www.meyercontractinginc.com
Water & sewer line construction, highway, street & bridge construction, site preparation, commercial & institutional building. (Minority, Woman, estab 1987, empl 41, sales $69,786,884, cert: NMSDC)

2330 Moltron Builders Inc.
2900 North 2nd St
Minneapolis, MN 55411
Contact: Patrick Buckner President
Tel: 612-354-2730
Email: patrick.buckner@moltronbuilders.com
Website: www.moltronbuilders.com
General Construction, Construction Management & Design Build. (AA, estab 2007, empl 5, sales , cert: State, City)

2331 Shaw-Lundquist Associates, Inc.
2757 W Service Rd
St. Paul, MN 55121
Contact: Hoyt Hsiao CEO
Tel: 651-454-0670
Email: hhsiao@shawlundquist.com
Website: www.shawlundquist.com
General construction & mgmt: commercial, industrial & institutional, multi-unit residential, tenant improvements, contract service work, etc. (As-Pac, estab 1974, empl 98, sales $185,879,100, cert: NMSDC)

2332 Shingobee Builders, Inc.
669 N Medina St
Loretto, MN 55357
Contact: Mike Melton President
Tel: 763-479-1300
Email: mmelton@shingobee.com
Website: www.shingobee.com
General construction. (Minority, Woman, estab 1980, empl 55, sales $49,882,025, cert: WBENC)

2333 Total Construction and Equipment, Inc.
10195 Inver Grove Trail
Inver Grove Heights, MN 55076
Contact: William Krech VP
Tel: 651-451-1384
Email: info@total-const.com
Website: www.total-const.com
General and electrical contracting, large facility maintenance. (Woman, estab 1972, empl 350, sales $53,000,000, cert: WBENC)

2334 Welsh Construction, LLC
4350 Baker Rd Ste 400
Minnetonka, MN 55343
Contact: Linda Solberg Corporate Services Dir
Tel: 952-897-7854
Email: lsolberg@welshco.com
Website: www.welshconstruct.com
General contracting, commercial new construction, office & industrial, expansions & renovations of existing office & industrial space. (Woman, estab 1977, empl 43, sales $73,308,502, cert: WBENC)

Missouri

2335 Amodu Engineering Solutions, LLC
1201 Garden Village Dr
Florissant, MO 63031
Contact: Anthony Osuma President
Tel: 314-249-8623
Email: aosuma@amodu-engineering.com
Website: www.amodu-engineering.com
Mechanical design & consulting services, electrical plumbing & fire protection systems, construction admin services. (AA, estab 2007, empl 5, sales $100,000, cert: State, City, NMSDC)

2336 Legacy Building Group
3242 S. KingsHwy
Saint Louis, MO 63139
Contact: Todd Weaver President
Tel: 314-361-3535
Email: weavert@legacybg.com
Website: www.legacybg.com
Doors & frames installation & concrete footings & foundations. (AA, estab 2003, empl 20, sales $7,123,000, cert: State, City, NMSDC)

2337 Pro Circuit, Inc.
4925 Deramus Ave
Kansas City, MO 64120
Contact: Monica Bury President
Tel: 816-474-9292
Email: monicabury@procircuitinc.com
Website: www.procircuitinc.com
Electrical, low voltage, Construction, design build, Service, industial, commercial, cabling, wiring, Motor control, panels, IR Scan, Power quality, Arc flash, data cabling, fiber, fire alarm, security, paging, water, wastewater, PLC, Controls. (Woman, estab 1993, empl 100, sales $17,706,683, cert: State, City, WBENC)

2338 Schweiger Construction Company
      8300 Troost Ave
      Kansas City, MO 64131
      Contact: Denise Holt VP
      Tel: 816-523-5875
      Email: dholt@schweigercc.com
      Website: www.schweigercc.com
General building construction & construction mgmt:
critical facilities, office structures, food service facilities,
new build, expansion, renovation. (Woman, estab , empl
50, sales $19,000,000, cert: WBENC)

2339 Tarlton Corporation
      5500 W Park Ave
      St. Louis, MO 63110
      Contact: Ted Guhr Dir Business Devel
      Tel: 314-633-3354
      Email: taguhr@tarltoncorp.com
      Website: www.tarltoncorp.com
General contracting & construction management.
(Woman, estab 1945, empl , sales $207,000,000, cert:
State, WBENC)

North Carolina

2340 Golden Sands General Contractors
      10924 Granite St, Ste 700
      Charlotte, NC 28273
      Contact: Jody Pinkston Project Coord
      Tel: 704-727-6000
      Email: jody.pinkston@goldensandsgc.com
      Website: www.goldensandsgc.com
Design/Build, New Construction, Tenant Improvements,
Major & Minor Renovations, Dedicated Facilities
Maintenance Department, Dedicated Disaster Recovery
Department. (Woman, estab 1988, empl 167, sales
$62,000,000, cert: WBENC)

2341 Holt Brothers Construction LLC
      421 Fayetteville St Stes 1300
      Raleigh, NC 27601
      Contact: Terrence Holt President
      Tel: 919-787-1981
      Email: terrence@holtbrothersinc.com
      Website: www.holtbrothersconstruction.com
Construction management, design-build & general
contracting services. (AA, estab 2007, empl 22, sales
$32,500,000, cert: State)

2342 Lakeside Project Solutions
      405 North Pilot Knob Rd
      Denver, NC 28037
      Contact: Ronnie Massingale Business Devel
      Tel: 704-483-3739
      Email: workorders@lakesideps.com
      Website: www.lakesideps.com
General Contracting, Drywall, Painting, Doors and
Hardware, Carpentry, Ashpalt, Concrete. (Woman, estab
2009, empl 55, sales $42,000,000, cert: WBENC)

2343 Marand Builders, Inc.
      4534 Old Pineville Rd Ste A
      Charlotte, NC 28217
      Contact: Francisco Alvarado CEO
      Tel: 704-525-1824
      Email: falvarado@marandbuilders.com
      Website: www.marandbuilders.com
Commercial & industrial general contracting: demolition, new construction & renovations. (Hisp, estab 1999,
empl 15, sales $75,822,000, cert: NMSDC)

2344 Metcon Inc.
      763 Comtech Dr
      Pembroke, NC 28372
      Contact: Aaron Thomas CEO
      Tel: 910-521-8013
      Email: athomas@metconus.com
      Website: www.metconus.com
General contracting, panelized metal studs & truss. (Nat
Ame, estab 1999, empl 75, sales $24,180,330, cert:
NMSDC)

2345 Miles McClellan Construction Co., Inc.
      2201-E Crownpoint Executive Dr
      Charlotte, NC 28227
      Contact: Melia Mauldin Sales & Marketing Coord
      Tel: 704-900-1170
      Email: melia.mauldin@mmbuildings.com
      Website: www.mmbuildings.com
Design & build, construction mgmt, general contracting,
masonry. (AA, estab 1978, empl 75, sales $50,889,458,
cert: State, NMSDC)

2346 Modern Construction Services, LLC
      5900 Harris Technology Ste D
      Charlotte, NC 28031
      Contact: Tracy Snowdy President
      Tel: 704-765-9937
      Email: tsnowdy@modernconstructionsvc.com
      Website: www.modernconstructionsvc.com
General Contractor & Facility Repairs, Interior demolition & up-fits, exterior refreshes, parking lot repairs/
resurfacing, doors, windows, drywall, painting, rough &
finish carpentry, ADA upgrades. (Woman, estab , empl
20, sales $5,300,000, cert: State, City, WBENC)

2347 Vega Construction Company, Inc.
      147 Clover Ln
      Mount Airy, NC 27030
      Contact: Marlene Lopez Finance Officer
      Tel: 336-756-3477
      Email: mlopez@vega-constructionco.com
      Website: www.vega-constructionco.com
Construction services. (Hisp, estab 2018, empl 48, sales
$5,290,564, cert: State)

New Jersey

2348 A&A Industrial Piping
      6 Gardner Rd
      Fairfiled, NJ 07004
      Contact: Jennifer Simmons Exec Asst
      Tel: 973-882-2622
      Email: jenn@a-agroup.com
      Website: www.a-agroup.com
Install & services HVAC, Plumbing, Process Piping
systems. (Woman, estab 1990, empl 45, sales
$26,106,745, cert: WBENC)

2349 BTII Institute
      414 Eagle Rock Ave Ste 100 D
      West Orange, NJ 07052
      Contact: Sharon Bussey Managing Partner
      Tel: 973-325-9001
      Email: Sharon.Bussey.SD@BTIIInstitute.com
      Website: www.btiiglobal.com
Project Management, Professional Development and
Microsoft. BTII's Portfolio/Program/Project Management
services better enable organizations to achieve strategic
objectives and a sustaina (Woman/AA, estab 2009, empl
5, sales $300,000, cert: NMSDC)

2350   Ferreira Construction Co Inc.
31 Tannery Rd
Branchburg, NJ 08876
Contact: Megan Carton Dir of Mktg
Tel: 908-534-8655
Email: mcarton@ferreiraconstruction.com
Website: www.ferreiraconstruction.com
Utility Construction: Gas, Transmission and Distribution,
Foundations, Water, Sewer, Fiber Optic. Heavy Civil
Construction: Bridges, Highways, Airports, Excavation,
Sitework
Marine Construction: Dredging, Seawalls, Docks/Piers
(Hisp, estab 1988, empl 1000, sales $410,000,000, cert:
State, CPUC)

2351   HC Constructors, Inc.
PO Box 855
Whitehouse Station, NJ 08889
Contact: Lisa Chowansky President
Tel: 908-534-3833
Email: lchowansky@hcconstructors.com
Website: www.hcconstructors.com
General contracting: Underground Excavation for Electri-
cal & Telecommunication, Masonry, Bridgework, Sound
Walls, Concrete - Wall, foundations & floors. (Woman,
estab 1989, empl 15, sales $15,000,000, cert: WBENC)

2352   Hydro-Marine Construction Company, Inc.
1345 Route 38 West
Hainesport, NJ 08036
Contact: Castle President
Tel: 609-261-6353
Email: hmc@wjcastlegroup.com
Website: www.wjcastlegroup.com
Marine structures construction services: repair, replace-
ment & maintenance of bulkhead & pier construction &
rehabilitation, cable inspection & location, bridge under-
mining repairs, pile repair, underwater concreting, steel
sheeting cofferdams. (Woman, estab 1997, empl 13, sales
$2,000,000, cert: WBENC)

2353   Maysonet LLC
4 Orchard Terrace
Clark, NJ 07066
Contact: Mark Maysonet Managing Member
Tel: 732-396-0873
Email: info@maysonetllc.com
Website: www.maysonetllc.com
Commercial & residential construction: carpentry, drywall,
framing, general contracting. (Hisp, estab 2005, empl 18,
sales $751,588, cert: State)

2354   NC & Sons The Nicholson Corporation
201 Chambersbrook Rd
Branchburg, NJ 08876
Contact: Brandon Nicholson President
Tel: 908-575-0055
Email: accounting@nicholsoncorp.com
Website: www.nicholsoncorp.com
General contracting &construction management. (Minor-
ity, Woman, estab 1997, empl 225, sales $70,336,810,
cert: State, NMSDC, WBENC)

2355   Wu & Associates, Inc.
100 Gaither Dr, Ste C
Mount Laurel, NJ 08054
Contact: Kirby Wu President
Tel: 856-857-1639
Email: info@wuassociates.com
Website: www.wuassociates.com
General contracting: govt, commercial, institutional &
industrial, renovations, new construction, environ
cleanups. (As-Pac, estab 1990, empl 25, sales
$14,474,000, cert: State, NMSDC)

Nevada

2356   KMG Solutions, Inc.
7800 Via Costada St
Las Vegas, NV 89123
Contact: Kat Welniak CEO
Tel: 503-754-7592
Email: Kat@KMGSolutionsInc.com
Website: www.KMGSolutionsInc.com
General Contracting & Construction Management,
Carpentry, Painting & Flooring. (Woman, estab 2002,
empl 5, sales , cert: WBENC)

New York

2357   ACC Construction Corporation
519 Eighth Ave 7th Floor
New York, NY 10018
Contact: Michele Medaglia President
Tel: 212-686-9331
Email: mmedaglia@acc-construction.com
Website: www.acc-construction.com
General contracting & construction mgmt, phased,
interior renovations. (Woman, estab 1984, empl 55,
sales $28,748,041, cert: State, City, WBENC)

2358   Al-Pros Construction Inc.
109-20 121 St
South Ozone Park, NY 11420
Contact: Imran Ali Office Mgr
Tel: 718-848-3666
Email: iali@alprosconstruction.com
Website: www.alprosconstruction.com
General contracting & maintenance services. (As-Pac,
estab 1995, empl 30, sales $500,000, cert: City)

2359   Brinco Mechanical Services, Inc.
111 Plainfield Ave
Floral Park, NY 11001
Contact: Renee Prager
Tel: 516-354-8707
Email: renee@brinco.com
Website: www.brinco.com
National Maintenance & service, HVAC & refrigeration
work. (Woman, estab 1997, empl 40, sales $20,000,000,
cert: WBENC)

2360   C.W. Brown Inc.
1 Labriola Court
Armonk, NY 10504
Contact: Erin Griffin Business Devel Mgr
Tel: 914-219-8323
Email: info@cwbrown.com
Website: www.cwbrown.com
General contracting/construction management.
(Woman, estab 1984, empl 72, sales $48,000,000, cert:
City, WBENC)

2361 Con Rac Construction Group LLC
1895 Walt Whitman Rd Ste 2
Melville, NY 11747
Contact: John Coleman EVO
Tel: 631-756-0101
Email: jcoleman@conracgroup.com
Website: www.conracgroup.com
General contracting & construction management.
(Woman, estab 2010, empl 4, sales $13,009,136, cert:
State, City)

2362 Construction and Service Solutions Corp.
216 Main Rd
Akron, NY 14001
Contact: Suzanne Witnauer President
Tel: 716-570-1352
Email: suzanne@csscbuilds.com
Website: www.csscbuilds.com
General contractor: drywall, doors & hardware, acoustic
ceilings, siding, windows, cabinetry, countertops,
framing, trim & finish carpentry installations. (Woman,
estab 2002, empl 15, sales , cert: State, City, WBENC)

2363 Genesus One Enterprise, Inc.
43-24 54th Rd Ste 203
Maspeth, NY 11378
Contact: David Turner CEO
Tel: 718-361-7516
Email: office@genesusconstruction.com
Website: www.genesusconstruction.com
General contracting, construction management, interiors
construction, site work, pavement, concrete, masonry,
metal work & other trades. (AA, estab 1999, empl 16,
sales $3,500,000, cert: State)

2364 Henegan Construction Co., Inc.
250 W 30th St
New York, NY 10001
Contact: MAUREEN HENEGAN CEO
Tel: 212-947-6441
Email: mahenegan@henegan.com
Website: www.henegan.com
Construction management & general contracting:
interior building alterations, renovations & infrastructure
upgrades. (Woman, estab 1959, empl 150, sales
$238,724,000, cert: City, WBENC)

2365 Ideal Interiors Group, LLC
450 7th Ave, 21st Fl
New York, NY 10123
Contact: Ricardo Rivera President
Tel: - -
Email: kkolley@ideal-interiors.com
Website: www.ideal-interiors.com
Construction management, general contracting, and
design/build services. (Hisp, estab 2008, empl 25, sales ,
cert: State, City, NMSDC)

2366 K-Pak Consulting, Inc.
29 Elves Ln
Levittown, NY 11756
Contact: Khurram Bajwa President
Tel: 718-813-7755
Email: bajwa@kpakconsulting.com
Website: www.kpakconsulting.com
General contracting: remodeling, renovations, carpentry,
drywall, cement, flooring, masonry, demolition, painting,
doors & windows. (As-Ind, estab 2012, empl 4, sales
$169,960, cert: State)

2367 Mamais Contracting Corp.
256 West 124th St
New York, NY 10027
Contact: Mamais-Lorino President
Tel: 212-865-1666
Email: voula@mamais.com
Website: www.mamais.com
General contracting, high-end alterations & renovations,
rapid repair services. (Woman, estab 1968, empl 142,
sales $17,367,537, cert: City, WBENC)

2368 Milestone Construction Partners
100 Tech Park Dr, Ste C
Rochester, NY 14623
Contact: President
Tel: 585-247-5179
Email: info@milestoneconstructionpartners.com
Website: milestoneconstructionpartners.com
General contracting: commercial & multi-family projects.
(Woman, estab 2001, empl 14, sales , cert: WBENC)

2369 Professional Retail Services
3249 Route 112 Ste 2 Bldg 4
Medford, NY 75028
Contact: Robbye Chasteen Natl sales/mktg
Tel: 888-834-2411
Email: rchasteen@profretail.com
Website: www.profretail.com
Commercial facility maintenance, construction & project
services. (Woman, estab 2001, empl 51, sales
$13,000,000, cert: WBENC)

2370 Theodore Williams Construction Company, LLC
641 Lexington Ave
New York, NY 10022
Contact: Shelby Johnson President
Tel: 212-593-9700
Email: sjohnson@twcc-llc.com
Website: www.twcc-llc.com
General contracting & construction management:
interior buildouts, alterations, restorations & base
building construction. (Woman, estab 1972, empl 24,
sales $21,727,000, cert: WBENC)

2371 VRD Contracting, Inc.
25 Andrea Rd
Holbrook, NY 11741
Contact: Sapienza Exec VP
Tel: 631-956-7000
Email: joe@vrdcontracting.com
Website: www.vrdcontracting.com
General contracting & construction management
services. (Woman, estab 1993, empl 60, sales
$22,000,000, cert: State)

Ohio

2372 Bambeck & Vest Associates, Inc.
49 E Fourth St, Ste 1020
Cincinnati, OH 45202
Contact: Ed Roark President
Tel: 513-621-5654
Email: ed@bambeckandvest.com
Website: www.bambeckandvest.com
General contracting, office renovations, new buildings,
general repair work. (Woman, estab 1964, empl 35, sales
$10,000,000, cert: WBENC)

2373 Better Built Construction Services, Inc.
PO Box 467
Middletown, OH 45042
Contact: Karen S. Tipton President
Tel: 513-727-8637
Email: ksh@betterbuiltcs.com
Website: www.betterbuiltcs.com
Pre-engineered steel building, steel erection. (Minority, Woman, estab 1995, empl 5, sales $1,245,340, cert: State)

2374 C&B Construction Company Ltd.
3713 Lee Rd
Cleveland, OH 44120
Contact: Barbara Coker President
Tel: 216-905-2617
Email: candbcont@sbcglobal.net
Website: www.candbconstoh.com
General construction, rehab, new construction, residential & commercial properties. (Woman/AA, estab 2007, empl 4, sales $990,000, cert: State)

2375 Construction Support Solutions, LLC
PO Box 48
Avon Lake, OH 44012
Contact: Anna Klee President
Tel: 440-541-6642
Email:
anna.klee@constructionsupportsolutions.com
Website: www.constructionsupportsolutions.com
Construction mgmtt: scheduling, estimating, constructability review, contract admin, project controls, on site inspections & close out services. (Woman, estab 2008, empl 3, sales $250,000, cert: State, WBENC)

2376 Cook Paving & Construction Co., Inc.
4545 Spring Road
Brooklyn Heights, OH 44131
Contact: Linda Fletcher President
Tel: 216-267-7705
Email: linda.fletcher@cookpaving.com
Website: www.cookpaving.com
Construction management, underground utilities installation & maintenance telecommunication & electrical ductbank systems, directional boring, site development, commercial & heavy hwy hotmix asphalt & concrete paving, excavation & trenching. (Woman/AA, estab 1950, empl 100, sales , cert: State, City, NMSDC)

2377 D.A.G. Construction Company, Inc.
4924 Winton Rd
Cincinnati, OH 45232
Contact: Lindsay Wilhelm Mktg Dir
Tel: 513-542-8597
Email: lwilhelm@dag-cons.com
Website: www.dag-cons.com
General construction, construction management, design/build & renovations. (AA, As-Pac, estab 1990, empl 35, sales $21,000,000, cert: NMSDC)

2378 Dawn Incorporated
106 E Market St Ste 505
Warren, OH 44481
Contact: Dawn Ochman President
Tel: 330-652-7711
Email: dawn@dawnincorporated.com
Website: www.dawnincorporated.com
General contracting, pre-construction planning, quality control & customer service. (Woman, estab 1993, empl 15, sales $1,014,000, cert: State)

2379 Dynamix Engineering Ltd.
855 Grandview Ave, 3rd Fl
Columbus, OH 43215
Contact: Eugene Griffin President
Tel: 614-443-1178
Email: ggriffin@dynamix-ltd.com
Website: www.dynamix-ltd.com
Electrical, mechanical, plumbing, technology systems design; assessements & standard operating & maintenance procedures. (AA, estab 1997, empl 40, sales $11,700,000, cert: State, NMSDC)

2380 G. Stephens, Inc
133 N Summit St
Akron, OH 44304
Contact: Glen Stephens President
Tel: 330-762-1386
Email: compliance@gstephensinc.com
Website: www.gstephensinc.com
Project & construction management, engineering services, real estate procurement, general contracting, managing consulting, contract compliance, specializing government, public, private sectors. (AA, estab 1992, empl 62, sales , cert: State, City)

2381 JWT&A LLC
3615 Superior Ave, Bldg 31-1J
Cleveland, OH 44114
Contact: John Todd President
Tel: 216-426-1580
Email: jwtassoc@sbcglobal.net
Website: www.jwta-construction.com
Construction management, general contractor, acoustical ceilings, drywall, drywall insulation, framing, gypsum board, metal studs & taping. (AA, estab 2005, empl 7, sales $969,473, cert: City)

2382 Kerricook Construction, Inc.
20355 Vermont St
Litchfield, OH 44253
Contact: Ann Smith Owner
Tel: 440-647-4200
Email: ann@kerricook.com
Website: www.kerricook.com
Ground-up construction, design build construction, tenant build-out construction, open store remodels, facilities maintenance. (Woman, estab 2003, empl 20, sales $5,393,450, cert: WBENC)

2383 MBJ Consultants, Inc.
30 W 3rd St, Ste 4M
Cincinnati, OH 45202
Contact: Monroe Barnes President
Tel: 513-631-9600
Email: mbarnes@mbjconsultants.com
Website: www.mbjconsultnats.com
General contracting & construction management. (AA, estab 1992, empl 30, sales $1,300,000, cert: NMSDC)

2384 McTech Corp.
8100 Grand Ave
Cleveland, OH 44104
Contact: Mark F. Perkins President
Tel: 216-391-7700
Email: mctechadmin@mctech360.com
Website: www.mctech360.com
General contracting, construction mgmt, design build, building renovation, restoration, roadway construction, waterline, sewerline. (AA, estab 1997, empl 45, sales , cert: NMSDC)

2385 Mel Lanzer Co.
2266 N Scott St
Napoleon, OH 43545
Contact: Lyndsey Lucas President
Tel: 419-592-2801
Email: llucas@mellanzer.com
Website: www.mellanzer.com
General contracting: renovations, additions, or new construction. (Woman, estab 1950, empl 30, sales $17,000,000, cert: WBENC)

2386 Ozanne Construction Co., Inc.
1625 E 25th St
Cleveland, OH 44114
Contact: Dominic L. Ozanne CEO
Tel: 216-696-2876
Email: dozanne1@ozanne.com
Website: www.ozanne.com
Multi-Diciplenary Construction Management; Construction Management Agency, Construction Management at Risk, Design-Build, Design-Bid-Build/General Contracting, Owner's Representative, Program Management, Task Order Contracting. (AA, estab 1956, empl 37, sales $50,000,000, cert: State, City, NMSDC)

2387 Precision Engineering & Contracting, Inc.
31340 Solon Rd, Stes 25 & 26
Solon, OH 44139
Contact: Sekhar Narendrula President
Tel: 440-349-1204
Email: kmoomaw@precisioneng.us
Website: www.precisioneng.us
Site work, demolition & construction. (As-Ind, estab 2001, empl 37, sales , cert: State)

2388 ProjDel Corporation
One North Commerce Park Dr, Level G
Cincinnati, OH 45215
Contact: Eric Browne Principal
Tel: 513-931-0900
Email: brownee@projdel.com
Website: www.projdel.com
Construction management, project management & construction technologies. (AA, estab 1995, empl 13, sales $1,500,000, cert: NMSDC)

2389 R L Hill Management, Inc.
31875 Aurora Road
Solon, OH 44139
Contact: Ralphael Hill President
Tel: 440-439-0490
Email: pam@rlhillmgmt.com
Website: www.rlhillmgmt.com
General contracting, construction management, architectural millwork, drywall, etc. (AA, estab 1998, empl 12, sales $1,744,631, cert: State, City)

2390 R.J. Runge Company, Inc.
3539 NE Catawba Rd
Port Clinton, OH 43452
Contact: Amy Runge President
Tel: 419-740-5781
Email: arunge@rjrunge.com
Website: www.rjrunge.com
Construction Management, CM at Risk, General Contracting, Scheduling, Cost Management, Pre Construction Services, Electrical Contractor, Carpentry, Concrete, Site Work, Rough Carpentry, Interior Finishes. (Woman, estab 2004, empl 30, sales $5,571,511, cert: State, City)

2391 Regency Construction Services Inc.
14600 Detroit Ave, Ste 1495
Lakewood, OH 44107
Contact: Tari Rivera President
Tel: 216-529-1188
Email: riverat@regencycsi.com
Website: www.regencycsi.com
General contracting & construction. (Woman, estab 1994, empl 70, sales $10,302,000, cert: City, WBENC)

2392 The Coniglio Co.
4400 Commerce Ave.
Cleveland, OH 44103
Contact: Gwenay Reaze-Coniglio President
Tel: 216-391-1800
Email: coniglioco@aol.com
Website: www.theconigliocompany.com
General contracting services, general trades, carpentry, custom cabinetry, pre-fabricated office structures. (Woman/AA, estab 1994, empl 20, sales $1,091,271, cert: City, NMSDC)

2393 Welling Inc.
7781 Cooper Rd
Cincinnati, OH 45242
Contact: Amy Smith Acctg Mgr
Tel: 513-793-6900
Email: amy@wellinginc.com
Website: www.wellinginc.com
Commercial Construction; install trash & linen chutes, security screens, interior window shading systems. (Woman, estab 1987, empl 6, sales $900,000, cert: WBENC)

2394 Wise Construction Management, Inc.
1705 Guenther Rd
Dayton, OH 45427
Contact: David Abney President
Tel: 937-854-0281
Email: dfa@wiseconstructionco.com
Website: www.wiseconstructionco.com
Construction management, design/build. (AA, estab 2001, empl 7, sales $804,000, cert: NMSDC)

Oklahoma

2395 DBG Construction, LLC
PO Box 674
Oklahoma City, OK 73101
Contact: Deemah Ramadan Managing Partner
Tel: 405-601-2700
Email: info@dbgconstruction.com
Website: www.dbgconstruction.com
Commercial Construction, Pre-Construction, Design/Build, General Contracting & Construction Management. (Woman, estab 2007, empl 15, sales $7,000,000, cert: WBENC)

2396 Red Stone Construction Services, LLC
2738 E 51st St, Ste 140
Tulsa, OK 74105
Contact: Andrea L Gibson Natl Acct Exec
Tel: 918-747-7410
Email: andrea.gibson@redstonecs.com
Website: www.redstonecs.com
Construction technology: BIM, 3D-based conceptual estimate, laser scanning existing building conditions & field validation, 3D visualization. (Nat Ame, estab 2009, empl 40, sales , cert: State, NMSDC)

2397 The Ross Group Construction Corporation
510 E 2nd St
Tulsa, OK 74120
Contact: Tammy Pameticky Mgr Contracts Admin
Tel: 918-234-7675
Email: tammy.pameticky@withrossgroup.com
Website: www.withrossgroup.com
General contracting, construction management & facilities maintenance services. (Nat Ame, estab 1979, empl 125, sales $88,398,046, cert: NMSDC)

Oregon

2398 Art Cortez Construction, Inc.
15783 NW Dairy Creek Rd
North Plains, OR 97133
Contact: Art Cortez President
Tel: 503-841-5732
Email: art@artcortezconstruction.com
Website: www.artcortezconstruction.com
Commercial construction, general contracting, steel frame construction & interior systems, MEP services. (Hisp, estab 2007, empl 25, sales $3,185,945, cert: State)

Pennsylvania

2399 84 Lumber Company
1019 Route 519
Eighty Four, PA 15330
Contact: Amy Criss Govt Sales
Tel: 724-228-8820
Email: amy.criss@84lumber.biz
Website: www.84lumber.com
General Construction Contracting Services. (Woman, estab 1954, empl 5000, sales $3,800,000,000, cert: WBENC)

2400 AHJ Construction, LLC
1208 Main St
Darby, PA 19023
Contact: Henry Robinson President
Tel: 215-900-3508
Email: hrobinson@ahjconstructionco.com
Website: www.ahjconstructionco.com
Commercial & industrial construction projects. (AA, estab 2010, empl 8, sales $360,235, cert: State)

2401 Berner Construction, Inc.
1101 Quarry Rd
Gap, PA 17527
Contact: Andrea Irey President
Tel: 717-442-3110
Email: andrea.irey@bernerconstruction.com
Website: www.bernerconstruction.com
Construction, environmental remediation, renovation, utility installation. (Woman, estab 2002, empl 25, sales $5,317,916, cert: WBENC)

2402 CD & Associates, Inc.
725 Skippack Pike, Ste 140
Blue Bell, PA 19422
Contact: Lisa Casiello President
Tel: 215-793-9069
Email: LCasiello@CDandAssociatesInc.com
Website: www.CDandAssociatesInc.com
Design & construction. (Woman, estab 1989, empl 24, sales $67,671,317, cert: WBENC)

2403 Crawford Consulting Services, Inc.
239 Highland Ave
East Pittsburgh, PA 15112
Contact: Crawford
Tel: 412-823-0400
Email: lschroeder@crawfordconsultingservices.com
Website: www.crawfordcs.com
Construction consulting services: cost estimating, value engineering, inspections, project (CPM) scheduling, project mgmt, construction mgmt, owner's representation & general construction. (Woman, estab 1993, empl 23, sales $1,050,000, cert: State, WBENC)

2404 DK Cleaning Contractors, LLC
6418 Woodland Ave Ste 1FF
Philadelphia, PA 19142
Contact: Chidozie Dike President
Tel: 610-883-3133
Email: cdike@dkconstructionservicesllc.com
Website: www.dkconstructionservicesllc.com
Project & Construction Management, Repair & Renovation, Drywall & Insulation, Painting & Wall Covering, Framing, Masonry, & Siding Contractors, Plumbing, HVAC, Electrical, Mechanical, Carpentry, Demolition, Site work. (AA, estab 2010, empl 5, sales $300,000, cert: City, 8(a))

2405 ecoservices, LLC
407 W Lincoln Hwy, Ste 500
Exton, PA 19341
Contact: Denenno President
Tel: 484-872-8884
Email: ldenenno@eco-pa.com
Website: www.eco-pa.com
Construction management / project management, industrial site rehabilitation, demolition, asbestos abatement, roof removal, lead & mold abatement & remediation. (Woman, estab 2009, empl 30, sales $5,293,485, cert: State, City)

2406 Northeast Construction Contractors, Inc.
4827 Wingate St
Philadelphia, PA 19136
Contact: April Slobodrian President
Tel: 215-624-3667
Email: info@northeastconstructioninc.com
Website: www.northeastconstructioninc.com
General construction management, construction related property maintenance, snow removal & general carpentry work, walls, wall coverings, FRP, ACT, ceilings, doors, windows, hardware, accessories, drywall, painting, electrical, interior. (Woman, estab 2004, empl 12, sales $1,520,000, cert: State)

2407 Perryman Building and Construction Services, Inc.
4548 Market St
Philadelphia, PA 19139
Contact: Angelo Perryman President
Tel: 215-243-4109
Email: admin@perrymanbc.com
Website: www.perrymanbc.com
Genenral construction: commercial interiors, building & project management services. (AA, estab 1998, empl 26, sales , cert: NMSDC, 8(a))

2408 Robert Ganter Contractors, Inc.
595 E Pumping Station Rd
Quakertown, PA 18951
Contact: Donna Ganter President
Tel: 215-538-3540
Email: dganter@gantercontractors.com
Website: www.gantercontractors.com
Architectural roofing & sheet metal servicing, commercial, industrial builders & architects. (Woman, estab 2000, empl 25, sales $37,735,416, cert: WBENC)

2409 Tracy Becker Construction, Inc.
7280 Dragonfly Lane
Macungie, PA 18062
Contact: Tracy Becker President
Tel: 610-421-8590
Email: tb@tbcinstalls.com
Website: www.tbcinstalls.com
General contracting & construction. (Woman, estab 1997, empl 15, sales $3,748,957, cert: WBENC)

2410 U.S Construction Group Inc.
6100 Henry Ave Ste 2N
Philadelphia, PA 19128
Contact: Yaw Danso President
Tel: 215-756-1364
Email: ydanso@usconstructgroup.com
Website: www.usconstructgroup.com
General Construction, Sitework, Utilities, Demolition, waste disposal, Hazardous waste disposal, Paving. (AA, estab 2008, empl 5, sales $517,000, cert: State, City, NMSDC)

2411 U.S. Facilities, Inc. PRWT Services Company
30 N 41st St Ste 400
Philadelphia, PA 19104
Contact: David Groomes Sr VP
Tel: 215-564-1448
Email: david.groomes@usfacilities.com
Website: www.usfacilities.com
Facilities support svcs, building operations & maintenance, subcontract mgmt svcs, project mgmt. (AA, estab 2000, empl 462, sales , cert: City, NMSDC)

Puerto Rico

2412 Aireko Construction, LLC
PO Box 2128
San Juan, PR 00922
Contact: Alejandro Nazario Business Dev Dir
Tel: 787-653-6300
Email: anazario@aireko.com
Website: www.aireko.com
Integrated construction & building maintenance services, planning, financing, building and servicing leading industrial, commercial & institutional facilities. (Hisp, estab 1963, empl 450, sales , cert: NMSDC)

2413 BNS Engineering Inc.
Rafael Cordero, Ste 140 HC 02 Box 14212
Gurabo, PR 00778
Contact: Bienvenido Negron
Tel: 787-745-4848
Email: b.negron@bns-eng.com
Website: www.bns-eng.com
Construction design/build, project management, equipment, maintenance, turnarounds, program/project management, procurement & safety. (Hisp, estab 2001, empl 25, sales $1,599,871, cert: NMSDC)

2414 CIC Construction Group, SE
PO Box 29726
San Juan, PR 00929
Contact: Jose Torrens VP
Tel: 787-287-3540
Email: jtorrens@cic-pr.com
Website: www.cicconstruction.com/
General contractors doing construction at pharmaceuticals, hotels, hospitals etc. (Hisp, estab 1983, empl 480, sales $70,743,703, cert: NMSDC)

2415 CPM PR, LLC
44 Road 20 Ste 201
Guaynabo, PR 00966
Contact: Francisco Martínez Business Dev Mgr
Tel: 787-999-4000
Email: fmartinez@cpmintl.com
Website: www.cpmintl.com
Program, project & construction management & consulting services. (Hisp, estab 1991, empl 125, sales $9,849,191, cert: NMSDC)

2416 CSCG Inc.
PO Box 991
Aguada, PR 00602
Contact: Victor Jose Garcia Ruiz VP
Tel: 787-868-4030
Email: vgarciaruiz@cscginc.com
Website: www.cscginc.com
Pre construction: Conceptual Estimating, Budget Development, Project Phasing, General Contractor, Cost Monitoring & Control, Subcontractor Management, Safety Assurance, Quality Control, Civil and Structural Works. (Hisp, estab 2000, empl 60, sales $13,107,533, cert: NMSDC)

2417 Ideal Engineering Solutions, PSC
RR 3 Box 7266
Cidra, PR 00739
Contact: Ismael Robles President
Tel: 787-378-2948
Email: irobles.ies@gmail.com
Website: www.idealengineeringsolutions.com
General Construction, Electrical and Mechanical Installations, Instrumentation and Control Systems, Gypsum Board works. (Hisp, estab 2007, empl 5, sales $300,000, cert: NMSDC, 8(a))

2418 JCD Engineering, Inc.
PO Box 192372
San Juan, PR 00919
Contact: Juan C. del Pino President
Tel: 787-787-7211
Email: jcdelpino@jcdengineering.com
Website: www.jcdengineering.com
Civil, electrical & mechanical engineering: concrete & steel small buildings, interiors work, hung ceilings, floors, gypsum board, electrical power & controls, fiber optics, local area networks (LAN), process and AHU control systems. (Hisp, estab 1996, empl 11, sales $1,327,000, cert: NMSDC)

South Carolina

2419 Built Right Construction, LLC
 1524 Ashley River Rd
 Charleston, SC 29407
 Contact: Chris Pelletier Owner
 Tel: 843-882-7632
 Email: chris@brcsc.com
 Website: www.brcsc.com
Construction management, equipment rental, development, HVAC & plumbing & facility operations & maintenance. (Nat Ame, estab 2007, empl 10, sales $1,000,000, cert: State, City)

2420 CCCS International, LLC
 2414 Clements Ferry Rd
 Charleston, SC 29492
 Contact: Calvin Whitfield CEO
 Tel: 843-856-4874
 Email: cwhitfield@cccsinternational.com
 Website: www.cccsinternational.com
On-site construction management, project operations, site security, site clearing, site utilities, deep foundations, waterproofing & sealants, pre-treatment for mold & termites, concrete slab on grade, miscellaneous concrete, masonry. (Woman/AA, estab , empl , sales $2,500,000, cert: State, City, NMSDC, SDB)

2421 Greenwood, Inc.
 160 Milestone Way
 Greenville, SC 29615
 Contact: Sherry Harris Dir Sales/Marketing
 Tel: 540-298-2628
 Email: sharris@gwood.com
 Website: www.GreenWoodInc.com
Construction, maintenance & workforce solutions. (Woman, estab 1990, empl 680, sales $60,000,000, cert: WBENC)

2422 Landmark Construction Company, Inc.
 3255 Industry Dr
 North Charleston, SC 29418
 Contact: Sam Hayes Business Devel Dir
 Tel: 843-552-6186
 Email: shayes@landmark-sc.com
 Website: www.landmark-sc.com
Construction services: grading, drainage, utilities, paving (concrete and asphalt), foundations, steel erection, and vertical wall construction. (Woman, estab 1965, empl 135, sales $11,000,000, cert: City)

2423 Lipscomb Plant Services, Inc.
 160 Milestone Way Ste B
 Greenville, SC 29376
 Contact: Eric Burnette Business Devel
 Tel: 864-244-9669
 Email: eburnette@gwood.com
 Website: www.LIPSCOMBINC.COM
Industrial maintenance, construction, construction management & workforce solutions. (Woman, estab 2009, empl 4, sales $2,635,406, cert: WBENC)

Tennessee

2424 Gipson Mechanical Contractors Inc.
 6863 E Raleigh LaGrange Rd
 Memphis, TN 38134
 Contact: Winston Gipson President
 Tel: 901-388-6149
 Email: info@gipsonmech.com
 Website: www.gipsonmech.com
Commercial and industrial mechanical, HVAC & Plumbing, installation, renovation & repair. (AA, estab 1983, empl 71, sales $20,000,000, cert: State, NMSDC)

2425 MC Builders, LLC
 2115 Chapman Rd Ste 131
 Chattanooga, TN 37421
 Contact: Linda Stooksbury Dir of Sales
 Tel: 423-355-8118
 Email: linda@mc-buildersllc.com
 Website: www.mcbuildersllc.construction
Retail, Restaurant, Multi-Family Housing, Property Management, Hospitals, Universities, Commercial and Industrial Building maintenance. (Woman, estab 2012, empl 36, sales $4,000,000, cert: WBENC)

2426 SRS, Inc.
 131 Saundersville Rd, Ste 210
 Hendersonville, TN 37075
 Contact: Charles Pickett CEO
 Tel: 615-230-2966
 Email:
 Website: www.srsincorp.com
Construction Management and Disaster Recovery Services (AA, estab 2001, empl 55, sales $16,974,636, cert: NMSDC)

Texas

2427 3i Construction, LLC
 400 N Saint Paul St Ste 700
 Dallas, TX 75201
 Contact: Micheal Williams VP Business Dev
 Tel: 214-231-0675
 Email: mwilliams@3iconstruction.com
 Website: www.3iconstruction.com
General commercial construction. (AA, estab 2001, empl 27, sales $22,146,587, cert: State, NMSDC)

2428 American Renewable Energy
 3890 North Frwy, Unit F
 Houston, TX 77022
 Contact: JC Avila Mgr
 Tel: 713-690-1116
 Email: jca@arebuildingco.com
 Website: www.arebuildingco.com
General contracting & design construction. (Minority, Woman, estab 2010, empl 20, sales $5,000,000, cert: WBENC, 8(a))

2429 Argent Associates, Inc.
 2800 E Plano Pkwy Ste 400
 Plano, TX 75074
 Contact: Betty Manetta VP Supply Chain
 Tel: 732-512-9009
 Email: bmanetta@argentassociates.com
 Website: www.argentassociates.com
Inventory mgmt, warehousing, dist, logistics, packaging, installation & commercial construction. (Minority, Woman, estab 1998, empl 65, sales $181,676,013, cert: NMSDC, CPUC, WBENC)

2430 Beach Construction, Inc.
      1271 Record Crossing
      Dallas, TX 75235
      Contact: Denice VanBuren
      Tel: 214-920-9100
      Email: denice@beachconstructiontx.com
      Website: www.beachconstructiontx.com
Commerical general contracting. (Minority, Woman, estab 2002, empl 10, sales $2,740,000, cert: State)

2431 Bird Electric Enterprises, LLC
      8787 IH 20
      Eastland, TX 76448
      Contact: Jeffrey Walter VP
      Tel: 254-653-2950
      Email: jwalter@birdelectricinc.com
      Website: www.birdelectricinc.com
Distribution Line Construction, Maintenance and Repair. (AA, estab 2012, empl 275, sales $115,673,000, cert: NMSDC)

2432 Davitz Group
      6220 Pine Ridge Blvd
      McKinney, TX 75070
      Contact: Earl Davis President
      Tel: 972-746-6045
      Email: tarad@davitzgroup.com
      Website: www.davitzgroup.com
Construction, design / build, LEED project design & construction, building information modeling (BIM), large projects & small task orders, procurement services. (AA, estab 2006, empl 3, sales $2,000,000, cert: State, 8(a))

2433 Diversity Resources Group
      101 E Park Blvd Ste 600
      Plano, TX 75074
      Contact: Wayne Lawrence President
      Tel: 214-352-2284
      Email: wlawrence@diversityroofing.com
      Website: www.diversityroofing.com/
Construction management, commercial roofing services. (AA, Hisp, estab 2015, empl 80, sales , cert: State, NMSDC)

2434 DMG Commercial Construction Services, Inc.
      3939 Beltline Rd Ste 540
      Addison, TX 75001
      Contact: Stephanie Hilburn President
      Tel: 972-630-6900
      Email: stephanie@dmginc.net
      Website: www.dmginc.net
General contracting: renovations, finish out, additions & new build construction. (Woman, estab 2006, empl 17, sales $3,600,000, cert: State, WBENC)

2435 Falkenberg Construction Company, Inc.
      2435 109th St
      Grand Prairie, TX 75050
      Contact: Trish Gomez Business Devel Mgr
      Tel: 214-324-4779
      Email: pag@falkenbertconstruction.com
      Website: www.falkenbergconstruction.com
Commercial general contracting. (Hisp, estab , empl , sales $6,000,000, cert: State)

2436 High Plains Contactors and Management Group
      414 S. Dumas Ave.
      Dumas, TX 79029
      Contact: Michael Ramirez President
      Tel: 806-935-5858
      Email: michael.ramirez@highplainsmanagement.com
      Website: www.highplainsmanagement.com
General construction, project management, plumbing, dry ice blasting & powder coating services. (Hisp, estab 2009, empl 12, sales $8,500,000, cert: State, 8(a))

2437 HJD Capital Electric, Inc.
      5424 W Hwy 90
      San Antonio, TX 78227
      Contact: Heather Washburn Proposal Admin
      Tel: 210-681-0954
      Email: marketing@hjdcapital.com
      Website: www.hjdcapital.com
Design Build, General construction, electrical, Plumbing, Sitework, SWPPP, Erosion control, Underground electrical, Overhead electrical, Datacomm, Telecommunications, Pole lighting bases, Electrical meters, Gas meters, Outside plant copper fiber. (Hisp, estab 1994, empl 150, sales $17,354,379, cert: State, City)

2438 Kings Aire, Inc.
      1035 Kessler Dr
      El Paso, TX 79907
      Contact: Beama Hernandez Dispatcher
      Tel: 915-592-2997
      Email: service@kingsaire.com
      Website: www.kingsaire.com
HVAC, Commercial & Residential, Installs, Maintainance & Repair Low Temp, Commercial Electrical, Duct Fab. (Hisp, estab 1980, empl 196, sales $15,921,442, cert: State)

2439 Largin Construction Services LLC
      1959 Saratoga Blvd, Bldg. 10
      Corpus Christi, TX 78417
      Contact: Billy Largin VP
      Tel: 361-723-1573
      Email: billy@larginconstruction.com
      Website: www.larginconstruction.com
General contracting: construction, new buildings, remodel & maintenance, new custom housing, remodel & repair, site work, concrete, masonry, metals, carpentry, environmental, doors & windows, finishes, specialties, equipment. (Woman, estab 2006, empl 25, sales $3,500,000, cert: State)

2440 Marvin Groves Electric Company, Inc.
      PO Box 2305
      Wichita Falls, TX 76307
      Contact: Marvin Groves President
      Tel: 940-767-2711
      Email: m.groves@marvingroveselectric.com
      Website: www.marvingroveselectric.com
Install electrical wiring for new and exist bldg. (Nat Ame, estab 1972, empl 13, sales , cert: State)

2441 Midwest Steel Company, Inc.
      9825 Moers Rd
      Houston, TX 77075
      Contact: Christopher Given VP
      Tel: 713-991-7843
      Email: chrisgiven@midwest-steel.com
      Website: www.midwest-steel.com
Dismantling & demolition contracting. (Woman, estab 1968, empl 89, sales $10,755,892, cert: State, WBENC)

2442 Minority Print Media, LLC
2646 South Loop West Ste 600
Houston, TX 77054
Contact: Barry Simmons Advertising Dir
Tel: 713-748-6300
Email: advertising@stylemagazine.com
Website: www.stylemagazine.com
educated Urban view inside the worlds of
celebrity, business, fashion, beauty, health, travel, transportation, culinary, real estate,
arts, cultural and entertainment. (AA, estab 1989, empl 15,
sales $539,868, cert: State, City, NMSDC)

2443 North American Commercial Construction, LP
11577 Goodnight Lane
Dallas, TX 75229
Contact: Lynn Dunlap Managing Partner
Tel: 972-620-9975
Email: lynn@naccolp.com
Website: www.naccolp.com
General Contractor. (Woman, estab 2004, empl 10, sales
$12,000,000, cert: WBENC)

2444 Office Design Concepts, LLC
6750 Brittmoore Rd
Houston, TX 77041
Contact: Joseph Sylvan President
Tel: 713-849-3611
Email: admin@odc-llc.com
Website: www.odc-llc.com
Office furniture, carpet & flooring, moving services,
furniture installation, and painting (AA, estab 1999, empl
5, sales , cert: State, NMSDC)

2445 Pecos Construction
8111 LBJ Freeway Ste 625
Dallas, TX 75251
Contact: Mitzi Green Business Devel Mgr
Tel: 214-299-4900
Email: mdgreen@pecosconstruction.com
Website: www.pecosconstruction.com
Pre-construction, construction management, general
contracting, design-build projects, large projects & self-
perform services. (AA, estab 2003, empl 20, sales
$16,616,224, cert: State)

2446 Prim Construction LLC
252 Roberts Cut Off Rd
Fort Worth, TX 76114
Contact: Trent Prim COO
Tel: 817-885-7851
Email: tprim@primconstruction.com
Website: www.primconstruction.com
Commercial general contracting, end user/tenant improve-
ment/retail, mission critical, corporate campuses, health
care & institutional service providers. (Woman, estab
2007, empl 10, sales $10,000,000, cert: State, WBENC)

2447 Samaripa Oilfield Services, LLC
2855 N Mechanic St
El Campo, TX 77437
Contact: Amy Samaripa President
Tel: 979-257-9385
Email: amy@samaripaofs.com
Website: www.samaripaofs.com
Pressure washing services, oil & chemical spill clean up,
disaster cleanup & disposal, construction site clean up &
reclamation, general construction, general labor hands &
transport of equip & supplies. (Minority, Woman, estab
2011, empl 15, sales $850,000, cert: NMSDC, WBENC)

2448 Sun Builders Co.
15012 FM 529 Rd
Houston, TX 77095
Contact: Mary Miller Sec/Treas
Tel: 281-815-1020
Email: mmiller@sunbuildersco.com
Website: www.sunbuildersco.com
General Contractor. (Woman, estab 1979, empl 25, sales
$16,919,787, cert: WBENC)

2449 Synergy Project Consultants, Inc.
1801 Wyoming, Ste 204
El Paso, TX 79902
Contact: Mark Young COO
Tel: 915-613-1442
Email: mcyoung@spc-pm.com
Website: www.spc-pm.com
General contracting, construction renovation & repairs,
design-build construction, architectural, engineering
design management, construction project management,
commissioning. (Hisp, estab 2007, empl 29, sales
$2,100,000, cert: State)

2450 Tejas Premier Building Contractor, Inc.
9200 Broadway, Ste 120
San Antonio, TX 78217
Contact: Julissa Carielo President
Tel: 210-821-5858
Email: julissa@tejaspremierbc.com
Website: www.tejaspremierbc.com
Commercial general contracting. (Minority, Woman,
estab 2006, empl 15, sales $2,280,000, cert: WBENC)

2451 The Trevino Group, Inc.
11410 Brittmoore Park
Houston, TX 77041
Contact: Erin Trevino Sec/Treas
Tel: 713-863-8333
Email: etrevino@trevinogroup.com
Website: www.trevinogroup.com
General contracting, construction management, design/
build. (Hisp, estab 1976, empl 65, sales $32,000,000,
cert: State, NMSDC)

2452 UCS Group LLC
5910 N. Central Expy Ste 900
Dallas, TX 75206
Contact: Henry Rodriguez Dir of Marketing
Business Dev
Tel: 214-349-1600
Email: henryr@universaltx.com
Website: www.universaltx.com
General contracting, tenant improvements, renovations,
design & build, construction management, ground up,
office space remodeling, restaurant build out. (Hisp,
estab , empl , sales $5,000,000, cert: State, NMSDC)

2453 Vanguard Electrical Services, LLC
12002 Forestgate Dr
Dallas, TX 75243
Contact: Dustin Sample Business Devel
Tel: 214-534-0627
Email: dsample@vesdfw.com
Website: www.vesdfw.com
Commercial & Industrial Electrical Contractor, Design
Build/Assist & Engineering. (Hisp, estab 2009, empl 115,
sales $16,000,000, cert: State)

Virginia

2454   Alkat Electrical Contractors, Inc.
PO Box 6903
Richmond, VA 23230
Contact: Katherine Mickens
Tel: 804-354-0944
Email: katherinemickens@alkatelectric.com
Website: www.alkatelectric.com
Integrated building systems, conduits, raceways, fittings, etc. (AA, estab 1983, empl 45, sales $4,780,000, cert: State, NMSDC)

2455   Bay Electric Co., Inc.
627 36th St
Newport News, VA 23607
Contact: John F. Biagas President
Tel: 757-595-2300
Email: johnfbiagas@bayelectricco.com
Website: www.bayelectricco.com
General contracting, design/build, electrical, security, technology & power quality solutions & services. (AA, estab 1962, empl 95, sales $62,173,000, cert: NMSDC)

2456   BFE Construction, Inc.
7620 Whitepine Rd
Richmond, VA 23237
Contact: Travis Bowers President
Tel: 804-714-2540
Email: tbowers@bfe-llc.com
Website: www.bfe-llc.com
General contracting: bonded, commercial. (AA, estab 1998, empl 19, sales , cert: State, NMSDC)

2457   Davis & Green, Inc.
PO Box 35418
Richmond, VA 23235
Contact: Teddi Bartlett Project Mgr
Tel: 804-231-9684
Email: teddi@dgelectrical.com
Website: www.dgelectrical.com
Electrical Contractor, service and supplies. (Woman, estab 1985, empl 95, sales $11,400,000, cert: State, WBENC)

2458   Diamonds Management Group, Inc.
10117 Residency Rd
Manassas, VA 20110
Contact: Glenn Bertrand President
Tel: 703-257-0017
Email: dmgincservices@outlook.com
Website: www.diamondsmanagement.com/
General contracting. (AA, estab 1994, empl 4, sales $300,000, cert: State)

2459   J. R. Caskey, Inc.
PO Box 305
Oilville, VA 23129
Contact: Ginger Caskey President
Tel: 804-784-8001
Email: gec@jrcaskey.com
Website: www.jrcaskey.com
Engineering, Layout & Surveying, Clearing & Demolition, Earthwork, Grading & Excavation, Erosion & Sediment Control, Traditional Stormwater Management Systems, Low-Impact Development Systems, Underground Water & Sanitary Sewer Utilities. (Woman, estab 1985, empl 42, sales $6,630,000, cert: State)

2460   Prestige Construction Group, Inc.
219 Turner Rd
Richmond, VA 23225
Contact: John Scott President
Tel: 804-745-0000
Email: johns@prestigeconstruction.com
Website: www.prestigeconstruction.com
General contracting, construction management. (AA, estab 1991, empl 25, sales $10,919,532, cert: State)

2461   ProTech Restoration, LLC
3730 Glenmore Rd
Scottsville, VA 24590
Contact: Frank Trimble President
Tel: 434-960-4456
Email: protechrestorationva@gmail.com
Website: www.protechva.com
Disaster restoration & construction services. (Woman, estab 2015, empl 1, sales , cert: State)

2462   RMT Construction & Development Group, Inc.
571 Southlake Blvd
Richmond, VA 23236
Contact: Warren Thomas VP Construction
Tel: 804-464-2673
Email: wthomas@rmt-construction.com
Website: www.rmt.construction.com
Commercial & industrial construction. (Woman/AA, estab 2007, empl 10, sales $2,000,000, cert: State)

2463   T. K. Davis Construction, Inc.
711 Dawn St
Richmond, VA 23222
Contact: Thomas Davis
Tel: 804-321-7822
Email: smosby@tkdavis.com
Website: www.tkdavis.com
General contracting: commercial, light industrial, retail, medical, office, storage facilities, athletic facilities, multi-family, design build, construction mgmt. (AA, estab 2001, empl 9, sales $21,819,325, cert: State, NMSDC)

2464   United Unlimited Construction, Inc.
213 East Clay St, Ste A
Richmond, VA 23219
Contact: Merlin Hargrove President
Tel: 804-343-7266
Email: mharuuc@cavtel.net
Website: www.uucirichmondva.com
General contracting: painting, concrete, demolition, renovations & retrofit, masonry, carpentry, miscellaneous & structural steel. (AA, estab 1983, empl 32, sales $1,946,879, cert: State)

2465   Wunna Contracting Corporation
43695 John Mosby Hwy
Chantilly, VA 20152
Contact: Darnell Ingram Business Devel Dir
Tel: 703-957-4266
Email: dingram@wunnacontracting.com
Website: www.wunnacontracting.com
Concrete installation, rehabilitation & repair, building entrances; foundations, driveways; walkways; stairs; colums, walls, patios; landscape; retaining walls. (Minority, estab 2007, empl 30, sales $3,000,000, cert: State)

2466   **A&D Quality Construction Company, LLC**
220 SW Sunset Blvd Ste E202
Renton, WA 98057
Contact: Annette Demps Owner
Tel: 425-271-7751
Email: annette@adqualityco.com
Website: www.In-Work
General contractoring: commercial & residential construction, demolition, excavation, site clearing, grading, dirt removal, utilities, footing, foundation & concrete. (Woman/AA, estab 1991, empl 2, sales $270,000, cert: State)

2467   **Apollo Mechanical Contractors**
1133 W. Columbia Dr
Kennewick, WA 99336
Contact: Janelle LaFlamme Business Devel
Tel: 509-586-1104
Email: janelle.laflamme@apollomech.com
Website: www.apollomech.com
General contracting services. (Nat Ame, estab 1981, empl 1800, sales $625,000,000, cert: NMSDC)

2468   **JTS Manage Services**
526 Yale Ave North, Ste A
Seattle, WA 98109
Contact: Douglas Hamilton Marketing Coord
Tel: 206-861-8000
Email: douglas@jtsmanageservices.com
Website: www.jts-seattle.com/
Construction management & project controls. (Woman/AA, estab 1993, empl 10, sales $650,000, cert: State)

2469   **Laboratory Design & Construction, Inc.**
6659 Kimball Dr Ste D404
Gig Harbor, WA 98335
Contact: Elia Grogan Sales Mgr
Tel: 253-858-7835
Email: elia@laboratorydesign.net
Website: www.laboratorydesign.net
Build laboratory facilities. (Woman, estab 1996, empl 2, sales , cert: State)

2470   **MACNAK Construction LLC**
2624 112th St S, Ste A1
Lakewood, WA 98499
Contact: Santiago Mateo Project Mgr
Tel: 253-212-2378
Email: smateo@macnak.com
Website: www.macnak.com
General Construction Design-Build & Design-Bid-Build projects, site work, concrete, rough carpentry, finish carpentry, plumbing, mechanical, electrical, painting & roofing, fire alarm system & access control systems. (Minority, estab 2007, empl 35, sales $84,000,000, cert: State)

2471   **RHD Enterprises, Inc.**
817 78th Ave SW
Tumwater, WA 98501
Contact: Rozanne Garman President
Tel: 360-705-9459
Email: rozanne@rhdenterprises.com
Website: www.rhdenterprises.com
General contracting: marine/subsea construction, remodels, design/build services, new construcion, pre-engineered metal buildings, modular facilities, laboratory modernizations. (Minority, Woman, estab 2005, empl 25, sales $13,199,569, cert: NMSDC, WBENC, 8(a))

2472   **Sybis LLC**
9925 NE 134th Ct Ste 100
Kirkland, WA 98034
Contact: Jonathan Djajadi Partner
Tel: 206-686-8463
Email: jon@sybissolution.com
Website: www.sybissolution.com
CyberLock is an innovative electronic lock system that easily converts existing mechanical locks into an access control system, helping organization increase key control and accountability. With electronic lock cylinders, programmable keys (As-Pac, estab 2012, empl 3, sales $198,621, cert: State, NMSDC)

2473   **Arteaga Construction, Inc.**
4000 S Pine Ave
Milwaukee, WI 53207
Contact: Anthony Arteaga President
Tel: 414-744-7944
Email: anthony@arteagaconstruction.com
Website: www.arteagaconstruction.com
General contracting: masonry, carpentry, concrete, demolition & HVAC. (Hisp, estab 1986, empl 75, sales $25,000,000, cert: State, NMSDC)

2474   **Sirrah Construction & Co, LLC**
3430 N 53rd St
Milwaukee, WI 53216
Contact: James Harris Managing Member
Tel: 414-442-7477
Email: james@sirrahconstruction.net
Website: www.sirrahconstruction.net
General contracting: flatwork concrete & asphalt paving, demolition services. (AA, estab 2005, empl 6, sales $1,250,000, cert: State, City)

DIR Products and Services

Diversity Information Resources, Inc. (DIR) helps corporations build the best possible supplier diversity programs through verified and validated data, data management and other managed services, educational seminars and trusted print resources. Our exceptional products and services support both corporations and suppliers, facilitating the advancement of corporate diversity as a whole.

DIR's Supplier Diversity Resource Services include:
- Data Scrubbing, Validation and Reporting
- Sourcing Diverse Suppliers: Online database
- Sourcing Requests: DIR conducts specific supplier searches for upcoming opportunities, RFI's, etc.
- National Minority & Women Owned Business Directory
- The Business of Supplier Diversity: A Handbook of Essential Contacts and Information for Navigating the Industry
- Corporate Supplier Diversity Seminars: Building Strategic Phases of a Supplier Diversity Process and Best Practices in Supplier Diversity Strategies & Initiatives

Data Scrubbing and Validation
DIR's data scrubbing/validation service allows you to classify your current suppliers that fall into diverse categories and accurately analyze and report spend. Categories include: Small, Minority, Women, Veteran, Service-disabled Veteran, LGBT, HUBZone, 8a and Disability-Owned Business Enterprises. Diverse certifications are also classified. Certifications include: National Minority Supplier Development Council (NMSDC); Women Business Enterprise National Council (WBENC); Small Business Administration SDB, 8(a) and HUBZone; National LGBT Chamber of Commerce (NGLCC); State and City Agencies (DOT, Dept. of Commerce, Economic Development, etc.) DIR offers competitive pricing and quick turn-around.

Sourcing Diverse Suppliers
Access to a high-quality database of certified and personally validated diverse suppliers: Small, Minority, Women, Veteran, Service-disabled Veteran, LGBT, HUBZone, 8a and Disability-Owned Business Enterprises certified by NMSDC, WBENC, NWBOC, CPUC, 8(a), NGLCC, USBLN, WEConnect, CAMSC, State and City, MSDUK and more. Monthly or annual subscriptions available. DIR can also conduct specific supplier searches for upcoming opportunities, RFI's, etc.

Corporate Supplier Diversity Seminars
DIR's sought-after educational seminars are designed to give supplier diversity professionals valuable insight they can then leverage to improve the performance of their own programs. Presented by experienced supplier diversity practitioners with world-class programs, these seminars share best practices, current trends and issues impacting supplier diversity programs today. In person or virtual.

For more information and pricing please call DIR at (612) 781-6819 or email <u>*info@diversityinforesources.com*</u>

> **COSMETICS**
> Formulate, manufacture & distribute face and eye products, hair care products, perfumes, hand and body lotions, wig cleaners and sprays, and cosmetics for men. NAICS Code 32

California

2475 Garcoa, Inc.
      26135 Mureau Rd Ste 100
      Calabasas, CA 91302
      Contact: Deborah Reidy
      Tel: 818-225-0375
      Email: debbie@garcoa.com
      Website: www.Garcoa.com
Mfr branded, private label, control label & branded external liquid fill health & beauty products. (Woman, estab 1983, empl 48, sales 126000000, cert: WBENC)

2476 Plantlife Natural Body Care
      961 Calle Negocio
      San Clemente, CA 92673
      Contact: Nancy Baldini Sales Mgr
      Tel: 888-708-7873
      Email: nbaldini@plantlife.net
      Website: www.plantlife.net
Mfr All Natural Organic Aromatherapy products: Soaps, Lotions, Essential Oils, Body/Massage Oils, Bath Salts, Natural Homeopathic Pain Relief, Natural Pest repellent. (Woman, estab 1994, empl 20, sales 3000000, cert: WBENC)

Colorado

2477 Crossing Cultures LLC
      1821 Lefthand Cir, Ste D
      Longmont, CO 80501
      Contact: Dennis O'Toole Natl Sales Mgr
      Tel: 303-651-3678
      Email: dennis@goddessgarden.com
      Website: www.goddessgarden.com
Organic skincare products. (Woman, estab 2009, empl 12, sales 1429113, cert: WBENC)

District of Columbia

2478 Shea Yeleen Health and Beauty, LLC
      417 H St NE Ste 2
      Washington, DC 20002
      Contact: Rahama Wright CEO
      Tel: 202-285-3435
      Email: rwright@sheayeleen.com
      Website: www.sheayeleen.com
Premium natural & organic shea butter bodycare products. (Woman/AA, estab 2012, empl 1, sales , cert: NMSDC)

Florida

2479 High End Beauty Inc.
      1120 Holland Dr, Ste 2
      Boca Raton, FL 33487
      Contact: CEO
      Tel: 561-665-1968
      Email: CustomerService@Highendbeauty.com
      Website: www.highendbeauty.com
Dist hair, skin, cosmetics & nail products. (Woman, estab 2011, empl 6, sales , cert: WBENC)

2480 NAIWBE Natural As I Wanna Be
      421 W Church St Ste 601
      Jacksonville, FL 32202
      Contact: President
      Tel: 904-634-7607
      Email: info@naiwbellc.net
      Website: www.naiwbellc.net
Organic Skin Care Products. (Woman/AA, estab 2011, empl 3, sales 100000, cert: State, City)

Indiana

2481 Elwood Staffing Services, Inc.
      4111 Central Ave
      Columbus, IN 47202
      Contact: Kimberly Randall Dir Business Dev
      Tel: 812-372-6200
      Email: hope.lane@elwoodstaffing.com
      Website: www.elwoodstaffing.com
Organic skincare products. (AA, estab 1980, empl 260, sales 95010000, cert: NMSDC)

Michigan

2482 Universal Products
      854 Edgemont Park
      Grosse Pointe Park, MI 48230
      Contact: Jose Reyes CEO
      Tel: 313-804-0042
      Email: jose.reyes@universalproductsmarketing.com
      Website: www.universalproductsmarketing.com
Health & beauty care, hair growth treatments and vitamin supplements. (Hisp, estab 1988, empl 6, sales 4000000, cert: NMSDC)

North Carolina

2483 TWT Distributing Inc.
      11107-C S Commerce Blvd
      Charlotte, NC 28273
      Contact: Daniel Owens Business Devel Mgr
      Tel: 704-588-1746
      Email: dowens@twtdist.com
      Website: www.twtdistributing.com
Dist African American & Hispanic health and beauty care products. (AA, estab 1993, empl 14, sales 0, cert: NMSDC)

New Jersey

2484 Custom Essence
      53 Veronica Ave
      Somerset, NJ 08873
      Contact: Colin O'Such President
      Tel: 732-249-6405
      Email: cosuch@customessence.com
      Website: www.CustomEssence.com
Manufacture Fragrance & Cosmetic Products. (As-Ind, estab 1985, empl 43, sales , cert: NMSDC)

2485 G&D Coffee Mud LLC
      5 Mathews Ave
      Riverdale, NJ 07457
      Contact: Giovanna Cicillini Owner
      Tel: 973-709-0090
      Email: giovannaskincare@gmail.com
      Website: www.gdnaturalskincare.com
Manufacture skin care moisturizers. (Woman, estab 2008, empl 2, sales , cert: State)

2486   Health and Natural Beauty Corp LLC (SprinJene is a
       trade name)
       140 Ethel Rd, Ste W
       Piscataway, NJ 08854
       Contact: Alexandra DePierro Sales & Marketing Mgr
       Tel: 732-640-1832
       Email: a.depierro@sprinjene.com
       Website: www.sprinjene.com
Mfr oral care products. SprinJene is our line of superior
toothpastes combining the power of black seed oil, zinc,
and xylitol. (AA, estab 2012, empl 11, sales , cert: State)

2487   US Organic Group Corp.
       90 Dayton Ave. STE 132 Bldg 18, Unit 1P
       Passaic, NJ 07055
       Contact: Leonard Moon President
       Tel: 201-252-4269
       Email: mij3461@us-organic.com
       Website: www.us-organic.com
Mfr USDA certified organic topical & personal care
products. (As-Pac, estab 2011, empl 7, sales 590303, cert:
NMSDC)

2488   Xenna Corporation
       33 Witherspoon St Ste 200
       Princeton, NJ 08542
       Contact: Carol Buck CEO
       Tel: 609-921-1101
       Email: cbuck@xenna.com
       Website: www.xenna.com
Dist personal care products for foot care & hair care.
(Woman, estab 1996, empl 5, sales 3355705, cert: WBENC)

Ohio

2489   Shema Global, LLC
       825 N Houk Rd
       Delaware, OH 43015
       Contact: mark butler Managing Dir
       Tel: 740-953-0292
       Email: contact@shemaglobal.com
       Website: www.shemaglobal.com
Mfr & dist all natural hair & body care products. (Woman/
AA, estab 2009, empl 2, sales , cert: State)

Tennessee

2490   Keystone Laboratories, Inc.
       1103 Kansas St
       Memphis, TN 38106
       Contact: Melinda Menke Owner
       Tel: 901-774-8860
       Email: mmburns@earthlink.net
       Website: www.keystone-labs.com
Personal care products, ethnic hair care, skin care, toilet-
ries. (Woman, estab 1934, empl 21, sales 3793002, cert:
WBENC)

Texas

2491   826 & Co. LLC
       4301 Greatview Dr
       Round Rock, TX 78665
       Contact: Jaime Masters CEO
       Tel: 913-284-5536
       Email: jaime@826andco.com
       Website: www.826andCo.com
A full service botanical-based aromatherapy, skin and hair
care company. (AA, estab 2010, empl 1, sales , cert: State)

2492   Clavél
       4150 E Overland Trail
       Abilene, TX 79601
       Contact: Dason Williams EVP Sales & Marketing
       Tel: 325-676-9655
       Email: dason@clavel.com
       Website: www.clavel.com
Private label, over the counter skin creams, pain creams,
and scar creams. (Woman, estab 1988, empl 11, sales
2854152, cert: WBENC)

2493   Naterra International
       13525 Denton Dr
       Dallas, TX 75234
       Contact: Dan Zarazan VP Sales & Mktg
       Tel: 972-241-9665
       Email: dan@naterra.com
       Website: www.naterra.com
Mfr beauty products. (As-Pac, estab 1994, empl 51, sales
0, cert: NMSDC)

2494   NTE Legacy, LLC
       2919 Commerce St, Ste 480
       Dallas, TX 75226
       Contact: Nathan Townsie CEO
       Tel: 469-708-7546
       Email: ntownsie@naturelovesyouskincare.com
       Website: www.naturelovesyouskincare.com
Hand & Surface Sanitizer (Vegan), Citrus, Lavender, Rose,
Japanese Blossom, Lemongrass, Cucumber Melon, 4-in-1
Shave Oil (Organic), Moisturizing Rejuvenation Serum
(Organic). (AA, estab 2016, empl 1, sales , cert: NMSDC)

2495   Synergy Bodycare LLC.
       5653 Winding Woods Trail
       Dallas, TX 75227
       Contact: Rosie Hill CEO
       Tel: 214-460-1500
       Email: rosielh@synergibody.com
       Website: www.synergibody.com
Performance Skin & Hair Care**Cal** for women & men of
all skin types, tones & hair. (Woman/AA, estab 2009,
empl 1, sales , cert: State, NMSDC)

Virginia

2496   Tree Naturals Inc.
       4204 Riding Place Rd
       Richmond, VA 23223
       Contact: LaTresha Sayles CEO
       Tel: 804-514-4423
       Email: customerservice@treenaturals.com
       Website: www.treenaturals.com
Natural hair and body line created to add moisturize to
dry hair & skin. (Woman/AA, estab 2011, empl 1, sales ,
cert: State)

> **DETECTIVE & SECURITY AGENCIES**
> Provide civil, criminal and private investigations; security consulting services and security guard services. NAICS Code 54

Alaska

2497 NMS Security Services, LLC
     800 E Domind Blvd, Ste 3-450
     Anchorage, AK 99515
     Contact: Patrick Hayes Exec Dir, Sales US
     Tel: 952-233-4014
     Email: patrick.hayes@nmsusa.com
     Website: www.nmsusa.com
Security and investigative services. (Nat Ame, estab 1978, empl 2850, sales $187,737,520, cert: NMSDC)

Alabama

2498 Dothan Security Inc. dba DSI Security Services
     600 W Adams St
     Dothan, AL 36303
     Contact: Boyd Clark Dir Sales/Marketing
     Tel: 334-793-5720
     Email: bclark@dsisecurity.com
     Website: www.dsisecurity.com
Uniformed security officers. (Woman, estab 1969, empl 4000, sales $52,000,000, cert: WBENC)

2499 Employment Screening Services
     2500 Southlake Park
     Birmingham, AL 35244
     Contact: Jared Balint Enterprise Sales Mgr
     Tel: 314-282-0154
     Email: jbalint@es2.com
     Website: www.es2.com
Criminal checks, credit checks, drug testing, motor vehicle checks, electronic fingerprinting, education, employment & reference verifications. (Woman, estab 1994, empl 85, sales $12,500,000, cert: WBENC)

2500 Workable Solutions Investigative & Protective Services, LLC
     5925 Carmichael Rd Ste D
     Montgomery, AL 36117
     Contact: Tyron Works CEO
     Tel: 334-262-0432
     Email: info@wsips.net
     Website: www.workable-solutions.org/
Security Guards & Patrol Services, Investigation Services, Special Events Security, Background Investigations, CCTV Monitoring, Loss Prevention, Home Watch, Protection/ Bodyguard Services, Security Training. (AA, estab 2009, empl 25, sales , cert: State)

Arizona

2501 Anderson Security Agency, Ltd.
     PO Box 42690
     Phoenix, AZ 85080
     Contact: Kimberly Matich CEO
     Tel: 602-331-7000
     Email: kmatich@andersonsecurity.com
     Website: www.andersonsecurity.com
Armed & unarmed uniformed security officers, executive protection service, patrol service, investigations & background checks. (Woman, estab 1994, empl 388, sales , cert: WBENC)

2502 Hope Capital LLC
     PO Box 74554
     Phoenix, AZ 85087
     Contact: Sarah Hope CEO
     Tel: 602-899-1606
     Email: sarah@verticalidentity.com
     Website: www.verticalidentity.com
Develop, implement & provide screening programs, background investigations, Employment Verification, Criminal Background Checks, Motor Vehicle Record Check, Government Watch Lists, Fingerprinting. (Minority, Woman, estab 2014, empl 6, sales , cert: WBENC)

2503 Law Enforcement Specialists, Inc.
     PO Box 11656
     Glendale, AZ 85318
     Contact: Bonnie Lucas CEO
     Tel: 623-825-6700
     Email: bonnie@lesaz.com
     Website: www.offdutypoliceofficers.com
Law Enforcement Officers off-duty armed, uniformed & plain clothes. (Woman, estab 1994, empl 8, sales $5,610,458, cert: WBENC)

California

2504 Accurate Background
     7515 Irvine Center Dr
     Irvine, CA 92618
     Contact: Matthew Schneider Enterprise Acct Exec
     Tel: 949-609-2277
     Email: mschneider@accuratebackground.com
     Website: www.accurate.com
Background screening: criminal background checks, drug screening, fingerprinting, verifications, & compliance services. (Hisp, estab 1997, empl 1700, sales $350,000,000, cert: NMSDC)

2505 AccuSource, Inc.
     30650 Rancho California Road Ste D406-215
     Temecula, CA 92591
     Contact: Cynthia Woods VP Sales & Mktg
     Tel: 888-649-6272
     Email: diversity@accusource-online.com
     Website: www.accusource-online.com
Screening services: criminal backgrounds checks, social security traces, DMV records, drug testing, international criminal & reference, employment verfications, domestic employment verification, license verification, I-9 compliance. (Woman, estab 1999, empl 30, sales $4,603,876, cert: WBENC)

2506 A-Check Global
     1501 Research Park Dr
     Riverside, CA 92507
     Contact: Mike Primbsch Dir of Marketing
     Tel: 951-750-1501
     Email: diversity@acheckglobal.com
     Website: www.acheckglobal.com
Screening services: background & drug-screening. (Woman/AA, estab 1998, empl 209, sales $24,200,000, cert: NMSDC, CPUC, WBENC)

2507 American Eagle Protective Services Inc.
425 West Kelso St
Inglewood, CA 90301
Contact: Maria Moreno Business Devel
Tel: 213-427-0715
Email: officeadmi@aeprotectiveservices.com
Website: www.aeprotectiveservices.com
Security guard services & patrol services. (Woman/AA, estab 2012, empl 102, sales , cert: NMSDC, CPUC)

2508 American Executive Private Security Inc.
2930 W Imperial Hwy, Ste 518
Inglewood, CA 90303
Contact: Eric Hall President
Tel: 323-920-6463
Email: aeps.security@gmail.com
Website: www.aepsecurityservices.com
Security and patrol services. (AA, estab 2014, empl 36, sales $1,548,909, cert: NMSDC)

2509 Apex Investigative Services Inc.
11171 Sun Center Dr Ste 120
Rancho Cordova, CA 95670
Contact: JR Robles CEO
Tel: 916-858-2999
Email: jr@apexpi.com
Website: www.apexpi.com
Investigation svcs: surveillance, workers compensation fraud, liability, disability mgmt, sexual harassment, due diligence, SIU fraud, employee terminations, background investigation, discrimination, witness interviews, etc. (Hisp, estab 1997, empl 55, sales $1,555,730, cert: NMSDC)

2510 Diversified Risk Management
8137 3rd ST. 2nd Fl
Downey, CA 90241
Contact: Patricia Kotze-Ramos President
Tel: 800-810-9508
Email: bids@drminc.us
Website: www.diversifiedriskmanagement.com
Licensed investigation firm that assists the federal government, corporations, non-profit organizations, high-net-worth individuals and law firms in identifying, responding, and mitigating risk through a comprehensive and integrated suite of professional (Woman, estab 2002, empl 10, sales $1,300,000, cert: State, CPUC, WBENC)

2511 Global Unit 1
15603 Firmona Ave
Lawndale, CA 90260
Contact: Ferdinand Ndedi COO
Tel: 310-760-1957
Email: ferdinandd@globalunit1.com
Website: www.globalunit1.com
Security guards, patrol services, access control, perimeter patrol, vehicle & bike patrol, special events & parties, control room surveillance, gate house & reception services. (Woman/AA, estab 2010, empl 500, sales , cert: State, City)

2512 Infortal Associates, Inc. dba Infortal Worldwide
1590 The Alameda Ste 100
San Jose, CA 95126
Contact: Candice Tal CEO
Tel: 408-298-9700
Email: ctal@infortal.com
Website: www.infortal.com
Global security & risk mitigation, risk management & investigation services, business due diligence, reputation due diligence, M&A, board advisory, international executive travel, competitive intelligence, FCPA due diligence. (Woman, estab 1985, empl 12, sales $1,159,505, cert: WBENC)

2513 Inter-Con Security Systems, Inc.
210 S De Lacey Ave
Pasadena, CA 91105
Contact: Matthew Reeser VP
Tel: 626-535-2639
Email: solutionsdesign@icsecurity.com
Website: www.icsecurity.com
Security services. (Hisp, estab 1973, empl 35000, sales $378,022,000, cert: State, NMSDC)

2514 JLR Invesitgations
9375 Archibald Ave, Ste 103
Rancho Cucamonga, CA 91730
Contact: Ruth Riddle CEO
Tel: 909-888-8880
Email: ruth@jlrinvestigations.com
Website: www.jlrinvestigations.com
Investigative services, Surveillance & Sub Rosa, Background Investigations, AOE/COE Statements & Field Interviews, Activity Checks, Database Searches, Mortgage fraud Investigations. (Woman/AA, estab 2004, empl 34, sales , cert: NMSDC)

2515 Locked on Referrals Protection Inc.
4202 Atlantic Ave, Ste 212
Long Beach, CA 90807
Contact: Kris Potter CEO
Tel: 562-552-7972
Email: lorprotection@gmail.com
Website: www.lorprotection.com
Security guard services. (Woman/AA, estab 2013, empl 30, sales , cert: NMSDC, CPUC)

2516 National Eagle Security, Inc.
3200 Wilshire Blvd, Ste 1208
Los Angeles, CA 90010
Contact: Maria Castillo Business Devel
Tel: 213-637-0200
Email: nesbestone@yahoo.com
Website: www.nationaleaglesecurity.com
Security Officers, Public Relations Officers, Vehicle Patrol. (AA, estab 2014, empl 45, sales $768,194, cert: NMSDC, CPUC)

2517 Pacific Protection Services, Inc.
22144 Clarendon St, Ste 110
Woodland Hills, CA 91367
Contact: Bob Pina CEO
Tel: 818-313-9369
Email: bob.pina@pacific-protection.com
Website: www.pacific-protection.com
Uniform unarmed, armed security guard services & Law Enforcement Experience Agents (ODO). (AA, estab 1984, empl 400, sales $5,123,267, cert: NMSDC, CPUC)

2518   Private Eyes, Inc
2700 Ygnacio Valley Rd, Ste 100
Walnut Creek, CA 94598
Contact: Sandra James CEO
Tel: 925-927-3333
Email: sandra@pebackgroundchecks.com
Website: www.privateeyesbackgroundchecks.com
Pre-employment screening, employment background
investigations. (Woman, estab 1999, empl 45, sales
$6,500,000, cert: WBENC)

2519   RCI Associates
5030 Business Center Dr Ste 280
Fairfield, CA 94534
Contact: Mitchell Brooks
Tel: 866-668-4732
Email: mbrooks@rciassociatesinc.com
Website: www.rciassociatesinc.com
Corporate & Insurance Investigations, Security Consulting,
Global Threat Management, Special Events & Specialized
Unarmed & Armed Uniform Services. (Nat Ame, estab
2012, empl 5, sales $1,495,000, cert: NMSDC, 8(a))

2520   Rene Garza and Associates, Inc.
2660 W. Shaw Lane, Ste 110
Fresno, CA 93711
Contact: Audra da Rosa President
Tel: 559-399-3113
Email: audra@rga-pi.com
Website: www.rga-pi.com
Investigative Services: Workers Compensation, Criminal
Defense, Pre-Employment Background & Reference
Checks. (Hisp, estab 2009, empl 5, sales $284,000, cert:
NMSDC)

2521   RMI International
8125 Somerset Blvd
Paramount, CA 90723
Contact: Roxanne Rodriguez President
Tel: 562-806-9098
Email: roxanner@rmiintl.com
Website: www.rodbat.com
Security svcs: armed & unarmed security, off-duty law
enforcement protection, background screening, investiga-
tions, security system design & engineering, training,
worldwide executive protection & consulting services.
(Minority, Woman, estab 1996, empl 60, sales , cert:
NMSDC)

2522   Servexo Protective Services
1515 W 190th St, Ste 170
Gardena, CA 90248
Contact: Nick Chaires Dir of Corporate Accts
Tel: 323-527-9994
Email: nchaires@servexousa.com
Website: www.servexo.com
Security Services, Security solutions. (AA, estab 2013, empl
300, sales $5,000,000, cert: NMSDC, CPUC)

2523   Spearhead Protection Inc.
PO Box 605
Antioch, CA 94509
Contact: Cherokee Martin Admin Asst
Tel: 925-308-7778
Email: cherokee.spearheadpro@hotmail.com
Website: www.spearheadpros.com
Security services. (AA, estab 2006, empl 22, sales
$400,000, cert: State)

Colorado

2524   IBC
PO Box 1052
Arvada, CO 80001
Contact: Bob Linderman Dir Business Dev
Tel: 303-403-0807
Email: blinderman@industrialbuyers.com
Website: www.intelligentbackground.com
Employment background screening, workers comp
credit identity, investigations. (Hisp, estab 1991, empl
35, sales , cert: NMSDC)

Florida

2525   American Guard Services, Inc.
7011 N Atlantic Ave, Ste 200
Cape Canaveral, FL 32920
Contact: John Boyle Dir Business Dev
Tel: 321-784-1893
Email: jboyle@americanguardservices.com
Website: www.americanguardservices.com
Security personnel for the maritime environment,
government facilities, campus safety, commercial
security, industrial security. (Woman/As-Ind, estab 1997,
empl 2500, sales $20,300,000, cert: State)

2526   Darwin Securities, LLC
16350 Bruce B Downs, Ste 47178
Tampa, FL 33646
Contact: Michael Dastolfo Owner
Tel: 813-468-3504
Email: michael@darwinsecurities.com
Website: www.darwinsecurities.com
Private Investigation, Executive Protection &
Process Service Agency. (As-Pac, estab 2005, empl 2,
sales , cert: State)

2527   Drakonx, Inc.
127 Grand Ave
Coral Gables, FL 33133
Contact: Fernando Alvarez President
Tel: 866-224-1245
Email: info@drakonx.com
Website: www.drakonx.com
Private Investigations, Surveillance, Background Checks,
Due Diligence, Skip Tracing, Executive Protection, Risk
Assessments, Insurance Fraud, Employee Misconduct
Investigations. (Hisp, estab 2003, empl 2, sales , cert:
NMSDC)

2528   First Choice Background Screening
4611 S. University Dr Box 314
Davie, FL 33328
Contact: Nicole Morales
Tel: 888-222-9688
Email: sales@firstchoicebackground.com
Website: www.firstchoicebackground.com
Pre-employment background screening & drug testing,
criminal history, motor vehicle records, social security
verification, credit report. (Minority, Woman, estab
1996, empl 48, sales $4,600,000, cert: NMSDC, WBENC)

2529 Westmoreland Protection Agency, Inc.
10194 NW 47th St
Sunrise, FL 33351
Contact: Paul Spence President
Tel: 954-318-0532
Email: pspence@wpafla.com
Website: www.wpafla.com
Security svcs: armed & unarmed security officers. (AA, estab 2002, empl 101, sales $2,901,382, cert: NMSDC)

Georgia

2530 ALL(n)1 Security Services, Inc.
3915 Cascade Rd, Ste 340
Atlanta, GA 30331
Contact: Mary Parker CEO
Tel: 404-691-4915
Email: rrobinson@alln1security.com
Website: www.allin1security.com
Security officers, off-duty police, background checks, motor vehicle reports, drug screening, security surveys, risk assessment analysis, consulting, seminars & workshops & security system designs, CCTV monitors. (Woman/AA, estab , empl , sales $20,000,000, cert: State, NMSDC, WBENC)

2531 Confidential Security Agency, Inc.
PO Box 55188
Atlanta, GA 30308
Contact: Patrice Adams VP
Tel: 404-888-0801
Email: padams@confidentialsecurityagency.net
Website: www.confidentialsecurityagency.net
Security guard protective services. (AA, estab 1972, empl 267, sales $6,000,000, cert: State, NMSDC)

2532 Ekeholm and Associates, LLC
550 Parkbrook Trace
Alpharetta, GA 30004
Contact: Kirsti Ekeholm Member
Tel: 877-219-0732
Email: info@screensafecheck.com
Website: www.ScreenSafeCheck.com
Background screening, nationwide pre-employment background checks, criminal records checks, credit history, motor vehicle driving records, identity trace, credential verification & healthcare sanction history searches. (Woman, estab 1998, empl 25, sales , cert: WBENC)

2533 ESA Investigations & Security, LLC
70 Whitaker Way
Midway, GA 31320
Contact: Gerard Easley President
Tel: 912-312-9510
Email: gerard.easley@gmail.com
Website: www.esainvestigations.com
Investigative and security solutions. (AA, estab 2020, empl 15, sales , cert: NMSDC)

2534 Global Bureau of Security & Investigations
240 Auburn Ave
Atlanta, GA 30303
Contact: Robert Conley President
Tel: 404-876-7273
Email: chez@gbsillc.com
Website: www.gbsillc.com
Full service private investigation & security firm. (AA, estab 2012, empl 8, sales , cert: NMSDC)

2535 Global Investigations Inc.
PO Box 473
Fayetteville, GA 30214
Contact: Tracey Brown
Tel: 770-477-9879
Email: tbrown@globalpi.us
Website: www.globalpi.us
Surveillance, background checks & liability cliams. (Woman/AA, estab 2003, empl 10, sales , cert: NMSDC)

2536 Hawque Protection Services, LLC.
3017 Bolling Way
Atlanta, GA 30305
Contact: Chris Rich President
Tel: 502-767-7479
Email: chris@hawque.com
Website: www.hpg.global
Veteran Security Personnel – Military and LEO, GPS tracked movement – monitored and recorded, Licensed, Armed and Trained in multiple weapons platforms (Pistol, Shotgun and Patrol Rifle) based on threat and client needs. (AA, estab 2019, empl 25, sales $400,000, cert: NMSDC)

2537 InfoMart
1582 Terrell Mill Rd
Marietta, GA 30067
Contact: Michelle Summers Supplier Diversity Admin
Tel: 770-984-2727
Email: infomartwbe@backgroundscreening.com
Website: www.backgroundscreening.com
Background checks, criminal history searches, reference checks, education verification, professional license certification, drug screening, business reports, credit/driving history. (Woman, estab 1989, empl 140, sales $19,376,578, cert: WBENC, NWBOC)

2538 IPROVEIT.COM
6340 Sugarloaf Pkwy Ste 200
Duluth, GA 30097
Contact: Vaughn Harvey President
Tel: 770-239-1707
Email: vharvey@iproveit.com
Website: www.iproveit.com
Background screening, investigations, fingerprint services, fingerprint equipment. (AA, estab 2005, empl 3, sales $315,000, cert: NMSDC)

2539 Safeguard Security Solutions LLC
1781 Hwy 42 N
McDonough, GA 30253
Contact: Rahul Anand CEO
Tel: 404-545-3023
Email: mrandall@safeguardsecurityllc.com
Website: www.safeguardsecurityllc.com
Security guards, staffing & janitorial services. (AA, estab 2010, empl 5, sales $348,000, cert: NMSDC, 8(a))

2540 The Cedalius Group LLC
2900 Delk Rd, Ste 700
Marietta, GA 30067
Contact: Melissa Foiles CEO
Tel: 404-963-9772
Email: mfoiles@thecedaliusgroup.com
Website: www.thecedaliusgroup.com
Background screening, criminal, credit reports an& d drug screening, talent selection research support, vendor/franchisee vetting & international searches. (Hisp, estab 2012, empl 5, sales , cert: NMSDC)

2541　The Guardian Protective Services, LLC
2839 Church St
Atlanta, GA 30344
Contact: Jennifer Rocke VP Acctg/Business Dev
Tel:　404-766-2611
Email: jenniferr@theguardiansecurity.com
Website: www.theguardiansecurity.com
Security guard service, armed & unarmed, security consultation & analysis, loss prevention, security concierge services, patrol services. (Woman/AA, estab 1998, empl 200, sales , cert: State)

Iowa

2542　3rd Degree Screening Inc.
100 E. Broadway Ste 201
Council Bluffs, IA 51503
Contact: Jeanie Waters President
Tel:　712-256-1701
Email: jeanie.waters@3rddegreescreening.com
Website: www.3rddegreescreening.com
International comprehensive background screening, verifications services & drug testing services. (Woman, estab 2012, empl 8, sales $646,000, cert: WBENC)

Illinois

2543　AGB Investigative Services, Inc.
2033 W 95th St
Chicago, IL 60643
Contact: John Griffin Jr. President
Tel:　773-445-4300
Email: john,griffin@agbinvestigative.com
Website: www.AGBinvestigativeservices.com
Asset protection, risk mitigation, computer forensics & network security, fraud management, assurance services, private security services. (AA, estab 1999, empl 100, sales $2,600,000, cert: State, City, 8(a))

2544　Allpoints Security & Detective, Inc.
2112 E 71st St
Chicago, IL 60649
Contact: Rhone Llevelyn CCO
Tel:　773-955-6700
Email: lrhone@allpointssecurityinc.com
Website: www.allpointssecurityinc.com
Armed/unarmed security guard & mobile patrol services. (Woman/AA, estab 2000, empl 210, sales $4,940,000, cert: State, City)

2545　Fact Finders Group, Inc.
4747 Lincoln Mall Dr, Ste 300
Matteson, IL 60443
Contact: Kenneth Webb Sr. CEO
Tel:　708-283-4200
Email: kenwebb@factfindersgroup.com
Website: www.factfindersgroup.com
Investigative & security consulting agency. (AA, estab 1996, empl 16, sales $1,000,000, cert: State, City, NMSDC, 8(a))

2546　Lincoln Security Services, LLC
6735 W Archer Ave
Chicago, IL 60638
Contact: Gregory Ramirez Exec VP
Tel:　773-796-7900
Email: gramirez@lincolnsecurityllc.com
Website: www.lincolnsecurityllc.com
Unarmed Security Guards, Security Guards in Vehicle Patrol and Off Duty Law Enforcement Officers. (Hisp, estab 2011, empl 451, sales $2,350,791, cert: City)

2547　Page Security Inc.
9453 S Ashland Ave
Chicago, IL 60620
Contact: Henry Page COO
Tel:　773-239-5256
Email: pagesecurity@msn.com
Website: www.pagesecurityagency.net
Armed & unarmed security guards, live scan fingerprinting & background. (AA, estab 2001, empl 100, sales $1,500,000, cert: State)

2548　Securatex Ltd.
651 W Washington Blvd Ste 105
Chicago, IL 60661
Contact: Patricia J. DuCanto
Tel:　708-536-3771
Email: pducanto@securatex.com
Website: www.securatex.com
Armed & unarmed physical security/guards, patrol services, background investigations, pre-employment screenings. (Woman, estab 1986, empl 838, sales $12,518,000, cert: State, City)

2549　Security Professionals of Illinois, Inc.
7120 Windsor Lake Pkwy Ste 102
Loves Park, IL 61111
Contact: Angela Larson Dir of Dev
Tel:　815-637-6950
Email: alarson@getspi.com
Website: www.getspi.com
Security risk management services & solutions. (Hisp, estab 2003, empl 50, sales , cert: State, City, 8(a))

Louisiana

2550　L&R Security Services, Inc.
3930 Old Gentilly Rd
New Orleans, LA 70126
Contact: Edward Robinson President
Tel:　504-943-3191
Email: ejrobinson@lrsecurity.com
Website: www.lrsecurity.com
Security guard & special events services. (AA, estab 1979, empl 250, sales , cert: NMSDC)

2551　Pinnacle Security & Investigation Inc.
332 N Jefferson Davis Pkwy
New Orleans, LA 70119
Contact:　VP Dir of Business Dev
Tel:　504-934-1411
Email: info@securitybypinnacle.com
Website: www.securitybypinnacle.com
Security Guard Services, armed security, unarmed security, security patrols, CCTV monitoring, and security consulting. (Hisp, estab 2011, empl 175, sales $3,200,000, cert: NMSDC)

2552   Tracepoint, LLC
PO Box 24059
New Orleans, LA 70184
Contact: Kristi Barranco Owner
Tel: 504-284-2285
Email: kristi@tracepointllc.com
Website: www.tracepointllc.com
Background & drug screening. (Woman, estab 2012, empl 3, sales , cert: WBENC)

Maryland

2553   AU & Associates Inc.
3100 Ritchie Rd, Ste F
District Heights, MD 20747
Contact: Ade Uiyoshioria President
Tel: 301-909-0076
Email: adeu@auanda.com
Website: www.auanda.com
Personality Fitting & Proficiency Testing, In-Depth Background Research, Drug Screening & Urinalysis Testing, Prior Work History Inspections, Information Technology Solutions. (Woman/AA, estab 2003, empl 5, sales $1,094,799, cert: State)

2554   Bradley Technologies Inc.
8701 Georgia Ave Ste 804
Silver Spring, MD 20910
Contact: Angela Bradley President
Tel: 301-562-9201
Email: angelabradley@btisecurity.com
Website: www.btisecurity.com
Unarmed & armed guard security guard services, access control & monitoring services. (Woman/AA, estab 2000, empl 157, sales $9,116,610, cert: State, NMSDC, WBENC, 8(a))

2555   National Background Investigations, Inc.
PO Box 966
Stevensville, MD 21666
Contact: Lori Holmes Grail VP
Tel: 410-604-6200
Email: lori@nationalbackground.com
Website: www.nationalbackground.com
Pre & post employment screening, felony & misdemeanor court record searches, motor vehicle reports, credit profiles, sex offender registry, SSN tracing, employment verification, civil record searches. (Woman, estab 1996, empl 9, sales , cert: WBENC)

2556   PChange LLC
4400 Stamp Rd Ste 302
Temple Hills, MD 20748
Contact: Rosa Griffin
Tel: 240-619-3507
Email: r.griffin@pchangellc.com
Website: www.pchangellc.com
Guard services & patrol. (Woman/AA, Hisp, estab 2003, empl 165, sales $5,388,000, cert: State, City)

2557   Security 1 Solutions LLC
845 Quince Orchard Blvd Ste Q
Gaithersburg, MD 20878
Contact: Bruce Alexander President
Tel: 301-926-4957
Email: balexander@security1solutions.com
Website: www.security1solutions.com
Security solutions, Security staffing, Emergency response services, Special event security, Safety auditing & awareness, Security training, Conceptual security systems design. (AA, estab 2012, empl 80, sales $2,400,000, cert: State)

Michigan

2558   Del Ray Security
34215 Jefferson
Harrison Township, MI 48045
Contact: Rudy Garcia President
Tel: 586-415-4518
Email: delraypd@aol.com
Website: www.delraysecurity.com
Armed/unarmed security guard services. (Hisp, estab 1998, empl 25, sales $400,000, cert: NMSDC)

2559   Lagarda Security
2123 S Center Rd
Burton, MI 48519
Contact: Elena Rathburn Accounting specialist
Tel: 877-944-8400
Email: elenarathburn@lagardasecurity.com
Website: www.lagardasecurity.com
Security officers. (Woman, estab , empl , sales , cert: WBENC)

2560   Pyratech Security Systems, Inc.
20150 Livernois
Detroit, MI 48221
Contact: Larry Teamer Sales
Tel: 313-345-2000
Email: larry@pyratechsecurity.com
Website: www.pyratechsecurity.com
Security service: homeland security, alarm system design, uniformed security guards, private investigations, security & fire detection systems. (AA, estab 1993, empl 45, sales , cert: NMSDC)

2561   Tricon Security Group, LLC
3011 W Grand Blvd, Ste 407
Detroit, MI 48202
Contact: Michael Whittaker CEO
Tel: 877-641-2600
Email: mwhittaker@rsigsecurity.com
Website: www.triconsecurity.com
Uniformed security officers, loss prevention education, personal protection training, executive protective, event security. (AA, As-Pac, estab 2004, empl 1100, sales $10,000,000, cert: NMSDC)

Minnesota

2562   Guardem Security Group Inc.
601 Carlson Pkwy, Ste 1050
Minnetonka, MN 55305
Contact: Daniel Claybrook CEO
Tel: 888-314-0613
Email: info@guardemsecuritygroup.com
Website: www.guardemsecuritygroup.com
Security services, armed & unarmed, cybersecurity, private protection & construction security . (AA, estab 2018, empl 18, sales , cert: NMSDC)

2563 Twin City Security, Inc.
519 Coon Rapids Blvd
Coon Rapids, MN 55433
Contact: Jeff Flattum Reg Accounts/ Sales Mgr
Tel: 763-784-4160
Email: j.flattum@twincitysecurity.com
Website: www.twincitysecurity.com
Armed & unarmed security guard services. (Woman, estab 1974, empl 650, sales , cert: State)

Missouri

2564 Discreet Check, LLC
655 NE Swann Circle
Lees Summit, MO 64086
Contact: Owner
Tel: 816-600-6200
Email: info@DiscreetCheck.com
Website: www.discreetcheck.com
Global Criminal Background Checks, National Criminal Background Checks, National Background Screenings, National Drug Testing. (Woman, estab 2012, empl 1, sales , cert: CPUC, WBENC)

North Carolina

2565 J.P. Investigative Group, Inc.
9716-B Rea Rd, Ste 211
Charlotte, NC 28277
Contact: Joe Paonessa Co-Owner
Tel: 704-243-1137
Email: info@jpinvestigations.com
Website: www.jpinvestigations.com
Video surveillance & special investigations for potentially fraudulent workers' compensation, property/casualty & general liability claims. (Woman, estab 2000, empl 15, sales $499,636, cert: State, WBENC)

2566 Mind Your Business Inc.
500 Beverly Hanks Ctr
Hendersonville, NC 28792
Contact: Christina Beckworth Contract Specialist
Tel: 828-698-9900
Email: mail@mybinc.com
Website: www.mybinc.com
Pre-employment screening: background investigation, civil, federal & state criminal checks, motor vehicle records, credit history, social security traces, employment/education verifications, workers compensation, drug testing, professional licenses checks (Woman, estab 1996, empl 15, sales $1,600,000, cert: WBENC)

2567 Professional Police Services Inc
9731 Southern Pine Blvd Ste A
Charlotte, NC 28273
Contact: Candace Ratliff COO
Tel: 704-442-9499
Email: clratliff@pssprotection.com
Website: www.pssprotection.com
Security guard and patrol services, law enforcements services, alarm response, crowd control, surveillance, escorts, personal protection. (Woman/AA, estab 2000, empl 95, sales , cert: State)

2568 Safe & Secure Worldwide Protection Group
4925 W Market St Ste 1142
Greensboro, NC 27409
Contact: Lance Jones President
Tel: 888-476-6388
Email: chiefjones@safesecureworldwide.com
Website: www.safesecureworldwide.com
Security guards, armed guards, loss prevention agents, executive protection agents. (Woman/AA, estab 2009, empl 157, sales , cert: NMSDC)

2569 Sunstates Security, LLC
801 Corporate Center Dr Ste 300
Raleigh, NC 27607
Contact: Carol Drumheller Sales & Marketing Coordinator
Tel: 919-987-1409
Email: radams@sunstatessecurity.com
Website: www.sunstatessecurity.com
Security services. (Woman, estab 1998, empl 2302, sales $58,957,564, cert: WBENC)

2570 TriMetro Security Services LLC
224 E Holding Ave, Unit 935
Wake Forest, NC 27588
Contact: Terry Walser CEO
Tel: 919-623-4354
Email: terrywalser@trimetrosecurity.com
Website: www.TriMetroSecurity.com
Guard staffing & patrol services. (AA, estab 2009, empl 9, sales , cert: State)

New Hampshire

2571 STANDA, Inc.
41 Micah Terr
Milton, NH 03851
Contact: David G Duchesneau GM
Tel: 603-652-7225
Email: info@standa.com
Website: www.standa.com
Security & Investigations consultant. (Woman, estab 1991, empl 8, sales $150,000, cert: State)

New Jersey

2572 Data Access Inc.
999 McBride Ave Ste C205
Woodland Park, NJ 07424
Contact: Karen Jacobsen President
Tel: 973-774-0030
Email: karen@datascreening.com
Website: www.datascreening.com
Background screening for pre-employment & tenant screening. (Woman, estab 1996, empl 5, sales $300,000, cert: State, City, WBENC)

2573 Motivated Security Services, Inc.
34 W Main St Ste 204
Somerville, NJ 08876
Contact: Sheref Shahid VP Sales
Tel: 908-526-1140
Email: sshahid@motivatedsecurity.com
Website: www.motivatedsecurity.com
Armed & unarmed uniform security officers. (Woman, estab 1969, empl 650, sales $16,300,000, cert: WBENC)

2574 We See You limited liability
116 N 2nd St Ste 208
Camden, NJ 08102
Contact: Raymond Jones President
Tel: 609-914-5775
Email: weseeyoullc@gmail.com
Website: www.we-see-you.net
Unarmed security & safety, uniformed & plain clothes, foot
& vehicle patrols. (AA, estab 2010, empl 75, sales , cert:
NMSDC, 8(a), SDB)

New York

2575 A.C. Roman & Associates, Inc.
1350 RXR Plaza West Tower
Uniondale, NY 11556
Contact: Kamil Podlinski VP of Operations
Tel: 516-596-3300
Email: info@romansearch.com
Website: www.romansearch.com
Insurance, corporate, fraud, surveillance & criminal
investigation services. (Hisp, estab 1998, empl 70, sales
$4,000,000, cert: City)

2576 AWICS Security & Investigations, Inc.
962 East 31 St
Brooklyn, NY 11210
Contact: Barrington Pinto President
Tel: 718-338-0882
Email: awicslisa@gmail.com
Website: www.iawics.com
Security, training, investigative & emergency management
operations, armed & unarmed Peace Enforcement Offic-
ers, private investigators. (AA, estab 2000, empl 12, sales ,
cert: State)

2577 Bay Ridge Security Service, Inc.
110 Bay Ridge Ave
Brooklyn, NY 11220
Contact: Anthony La Bella
Tel: 718-238-2974
Email: alabella@bayridgesecurity.com
Website: www.bayridgesecurity.com
Uniformed & plainclothes security guard services, armed
& unarmed, executive protection, vehicle patrol & armed
transportation. (Woman, estab 1973, empl 175, sales
$3,159,632, cert: State, City)

2578 BBG Consulting, LLC
8 Rosa Dr
White Plains, NY 10607
Contact: New Supplier Managing Dir
Tel: 917-727-1173
Email: cnbell@thebellbuskeygroup.com
Website: www.thebellbuskeygroup.com
Business Registry Checks, Fraud and Financial Investiga-
tions, BSA Investigations, Civil and Criminal, Due Diligence
Investigations, Litigation Checks, Asset Forfeiture Checks,
Court Ordered Monitoring,Background Investigations, Law
Enforcement, Security D (AA, estab 2012, empl 2, sales
$100,000, cert: State, NMSDC)

2579 Care Security Systems Inc
9 Hemion Road
Montebello, NY 10952
Contact: Eli Ribowsky Acct Mgr
Tel: 845-282-1245
Email: eribowsky@care-inc.com
Website: www.caresecuritysystems.com
Design, assembly, testing, installation, maintenance, and
management of high-level integrated security systems.
(Woman, estab 1987, empl 30, sales , cert: City, WBENC)

2580 ISS Action, Inc.
158-12 Rockaway Blvd
Queens, NY 11434
Contact: Pamela Newman CEO
Tel: 718-978-3000
Email: cdcohen@issaction.com
Website: www.issaction.com
Armed & unarmed uniformed security guard services.
Aviation security, ramp security, mobile security.
Security planning FCL Clearance Federal security
contractor. (Woman, estab 1991, empl 200, sales
$11,340,577, cert: State, City, 8(a))

2581 Johnson Security Bureau, Inc.
609 Walton Ave
Bronx, NY 10451
Contact: Jessica A. Johnson President
Tel: 718-402-3600
Email: info@johnsonsecuritybureau.com
Website: www.johnsonsecuritybureau.com
Watch, guard & patrol agency: armed & unarmed guard
services. (Woman/AA, estab 1962, empl 120, sales
$5,635,000, cert: City, NMSDC, WBENC)

2582 Lemire LLC
44 Wall St, Fl 12
New York, NY 10005
Contact: Christine O'Sullivan Analyst
Tel: 212-461-2158
Email: cosullivan@lemirellc.com
Website: www.lemirellc.com
Investigative due diligence, complex investigations,
monitorships, background screening, sexual misconduct
investigations, construction integrity monitoring & cyber
forensics. (Woman, estab 2013, empl 10, sales , cert:
State, City, WBENC)

2583 Miracle Security Inc.
193-49 Williamson Ave, Ste B
Queens, NY 11413
Contact: James Obayagbona President
Tel: 718-525-8030
Email: jambona193@aol.com
Website: www.miracle4security.com
Security guard services. (AA, estab 2005, empl 150, sales
$200,000,000, cert: State)

2584 Outsource Consultants, Inc.
237 W 35th St, Fl 12A
New York, NY 10001
Contact: Diego Caballero President
Tel: 212-732-6933
Email: dcaballero@outsourceconsultants.com
Website: www.outsourceconsultants.com
building code and zoning consultation, offering a broad
scope of services that includes approvals, permit
expediting, and sign offs. (Minority, estab 1993, empl 50,
sales $5,500,000, cert: NMSDC)

Ohio

2585 Amerisearch Background Alliance
2529 S Ridge Rd E
Ashtabula, OH 44004
Contact: Kelley Groff Sales & Marketing
Tel: 800-569-6133
Email: kelleygroff@hotmail.com
Website: www.amerisearchbga.com
Background screening, electronic I-9s solutions, drug
screening, behavioral assessments & information services.
(Woman, estab 2006, empl 11, sales $750,000, cert:
WBENC)

2586 Crimcheck
150 Pearl Rd
Brunswick, OH 44212
Contact: Michelle Ackley EA to CEO
Tel: 877-992-4325
Email: mackley@crimcheck.com
Website: www.crimcheck.net
Pre-employment screening & background checks. (As-Pac,
estab 1991, empl 77, sales $15,759,628, cert: NMSDC)

2587 National Alliance Security Agency, Inc.
7918 N Main St
Dayton, OH 45415
Contact: President
Tel: 937-387-6517
Email: administrative@nationalalliancesecurity.com
Website: www.nationalalliancesecurity.com
Uniformed armed & unarmed security guard services.
(Woman, estab 2005, empl 92, sales $1,091,995, cert:
State, WBENC)

2588 Safe Choice LLC
11811 Shaker Blvd, Ste 415
Cleveland, OH 44120
Contact: Anthony Spencer VP
Tel: 216-231-7233
Email: safechoice1@att.net
Website: www.Safechoicellc.com
Armed & Unarmed Security Guards & Police Officers,
Security for Public & Private Events, Traffic Control,
Employee Investigations, Theft, Drug & Alcohol Testing,
Professional & Secure, employee Removal Assistance, Body
Guard Services. (Woman/AA, estab 2010, empl 382, sales
$3,115,948, cert: State, SDB)

Oklahoma

2589 Superior Security
4419 N. Bryan Ave.
Shawnee, OK 74804
Contact: Louis Maltos CEO
Tel: 405-275-9072
Email: lmaltos@superiorsecurityusa.com
Website: www.superiorsecurityusa.com
Security svcs: physical security, executive & personal
protection, access control, CCTV cameras, life safety, on
call emergency response, pre-employment screening,
terrorism watch list searches, security guard analysis, crisis
mgmt. (Hisp, estab 1994, empl 140, sales $8,000,000, cert:
NMSDC)

Pennsylvania

2590 Century Security Services, Inc.
6 Rose Lane
Wilkes Barre, PA 18702
Contact: President
Tel: 800-927-0524
Email: info@centurysecurityservices.com
Website: www.centurysecurityservices.com
Armed & unarmed security officers, ambulance stand-
by, medical transports. risk assessment, general security
consultation, private investigation, alarm & surveillance
equipment. (Woman, estab 1984, empl 70, sales , cert:
State)

2591 Gentile and Associates, Inc.
3645 Brodhead Rd
Monaca, PA 15061
Contact: Christine Selden Principal
Tel: 724-775-3511
Email: cselden@gentilesecurity.com
Website: www.gentilesecurity.com
Pre-employment background screening, risk manage-
ment, workplace investigations, vulnerability analysis,
executive protection, surveillance, security guards.
(Woman, estab 2009, empl 314, sales $15,000,000, cert:
WBENC)

2592 Peak Security Inc.
103 Yost Blvd, Ste 100
Pittsburgh, PA 15221
Contact: Sales Consultant
Tel: 412-349-0850
Email: info@peaksecurityinc.com
Website: www.peaksecurityinc.com
Armed & unarmed guard services, emergency opera-
tions planning & design, ID badging, security system
services. (Woman, estab 1997, empl 150, sales , cert:
State)

2593 Tactical Response Security Consulting Inc.
3565 Sepviva St
Philadelphia, PA 19134
Contact: Luis Torres President
Tel: 888-755-9111
Email: tacresp@msn.com
Website: www.tacticalresponsesecurity.com
Security & detective services, armed & unarmed security
& investigative services. (Hisp, estab 2008, empl 50,
sales $1,800,000, cert: NMSDC)

Puerto Rico

2594 One Corps, Inc
PO Box 79767
Carolina, PR 00984
Contact: Sonia Fuentes
Tel: 787-776-0062
Email: sfuentes@one-corps.com
Website: www.one-corps.com
Armed & Unarmed Security Guards, IP Monitoring
Station with Patrol Response Service, Sales, Installation
& Maintenance of Cameras, Access Control, Fire Watch.
(Hisp, estab 2007, empl 134, sales $2,641,716, cert:
NMSDC)

South Carolina

2595 G&I Security Company, LLC.
9444 Two Notch Rd Ste B-1
Columbia, SC 29223
Contact: Melvin Dewitt CEO
Tel: 803-661-9221
Email: info@gisecuritycompany.com
Website: www.gisecuritycompany.com
Security services. (AA, estab 2011, empl 30, sales , cert: State)

Tennessee

2596 Metropolitan Security Inc. dba Walden Security
100 E Tenth St Ste 400
Chattanooga, TN 37402
Contact: Lauren Tudor EVP Marketing & Sales
Tel: 423-702-8200
Email: marketinginfo@waldensecurity.com
Website: www.waldensecurity.com
Security services. (Woman, estab 1990, empl 4550, sales $232,247,039, cert: WBENC)

2597 Phelps Security Inc.
4932 Park Ave
Memphis, TN 38117
Contact: Andrew Phelps Business Mgr
Tel: 901-365-9728
Email: andy@phelpssecurity.com
Website: www.phelpssecurity.com
Armed/unarmed security officers, commercial/residential patrols, commercial alarm/emergency response, investigations. (Woman, estab 1953, empl 375, sales $8,000,000, cert: WBENC)

2598 Security Walls LLC
130 N Martinwood Rd
Knoxville, TN 37923
Contact: Juanita Walls Chief Mgr
Tel: 865-546-2597
Email: jwalls@securitywalls.net
Website: www.securitywalls.net
Security & Protective Services: security guard services, armed & unarmed, visitor/access control, SCIF security, international visitor escort/control, post & roving patrols, electronic security monitoring, CCTV systems, emergency plans & procedures. (Woman/AA, estab 2003, empl 376, sales $15,000,000, cert: State, City)

Texas

2599 Ameritex Guard Services
100 N Central Expwy, Ste 350
Richardson, TX 75080
Contact: Christopher ONeal Sr Acct Exec
Tel: 972-231-6395
Email: isf972@earthlink.net
Website: www.ameritexguardsaervices.com
Uniformed security guards. (Minority, Woman, estab 1994, empl 256, sales $7,400,000, cert: State, NMSDC)

2600 Asez Inc.
1716 S San Marcos, Ste 120
San Antonio, TX 78207
Contact: Robert Lozano CEO
Tel: 210-736-6200
Email: corporate@asezinc.com
Website: www.asezinc.com
Armed & unarmed security officers, security systems services, security alarm systems, fire alarm systems, access control, closed circuit television, alarm monitoring, intergraded system. (Hisp, estab 2000, empl 75, sales $2,575,000, cert: State, 8(a))

2601 Boutchantharaj Corporation
5705 Airport Freeway
Fort Worth, TX 76117
Contact: Kit Boutchantharaj President
Tel: 817-831-2000
Email: kit@dfwsecurityprotectiveforce.com
Website: www.dfwsecurityprotectiveforce.com
Provide unarmed & armed on-site security guard services. (As-Pac, estab 2000, empl 250, sales $7,000,000, cert: State, 8(a))

2602 Nationwide Investigations & Security, Inc.
2425 West Loop South, Ste 200
Houston, TX 77027
Contact: Allen G Hollimon CEO
Tel: 713-297-8830
Email: ahollimon@ntwinvestigations.com
Website: www.ntwinvestigations.com
Security guard services, investigations, dignitary protection, communications cabling, CCTV/CATV, alarms, automated controls, networking, home theaters. (AA, estab 1999, empl 123, sales , cert: State, NMSDC)

2603 Night Eyes Protective Services Inc.
2407 E Yandell, Ste C
El Paso, TX 79903
Contact: Barbara Rodriguez VP
Tel: 915-549-0501
Email: nebarb01@night-eyes.com
Website: www.night-eyes.com
Security officers/guards, patrol officers & armored courier services. (Hisp, estab 1999, empl 200, sales $3,400,000, cert: State, NMSDC)

2604 RGG Services Inc.
5959 Westheimer Rd, Ste 107
Houston, TX 77057
Contact: G. Gallardo President
Tel: 713-972-1719
Email: marketing@rggservices.org
Website: www.rggservices.org
Bilingual (English/Spanish) security guards, body guards, private investigators, civil process svcs. (Minority, Woman, estab 1978, empl 50, sales , cert: City)

2605 Ruiz Protective Service, Inc.
2646 Andjon Dr
Dallas, TX 75220
Contact: Sales Mgr
Tel: 214-357-0820
Email: info@myliedetect.com
Website: www.ruizservices.com
Security guard & patrol services: armed & unarmed guard services. (Hisp, estab 1998, empl 550, sales $6,000,000, cert: State)

2606 Thomas Protective Service, Inc.
      PO Box 883
      Kaufman, TX 75142
      Contact: Larry Thomas Security Sales
      Tel: 972-962-3686
      Email: larry@thomasprotective.com
      Website: www.securityguardservices.com
Armed & Unarmed Security Officers, Private Investigations,
Alarm Systems & CCTV Systems. (Woman, estab 1981,
empl 485, sales $15,000,000, cert: WBENC)

2607 Z-MAS International
      2626 South Loop West, Ste 250
      Houston, TX 77054
      Contact: Janie Pinkney Managing Dir
      Tel: 832-489-0960
      Email: securitieszmas@outlook.com
      Website: www.zmassecurity.wixsite.com/
      zmassecurity
Certified, licensed, insured & bonded security officers,
armed guards, unarmed guards, investigations. (AA, estab
2017, empl 5, sales , cert: State)

Virginia

2608 AIVI Global Inc.
      6412 Brandon Ave, Ste 712
      Springfield, VA 22150
      Contact: Raphaela O'Brien President
      Tel: 703-851-4521
      Email: ella.obrien@aiviglobal.com
      Website: www.aiviglobal.com
Security integration and engineering consulting, Physical
Access Control installation and management, Video
installation and management, IP infrastructure and
Security Investigations. (Minority, estab 2019, empl 4,
sales , cert: State)

2609 Top Guard, Inc.
      PO Box 55030
      Norfolk, VA 23505
      Contact: Chris Stuart VP
      Tel: 757-722-3961
      Email: cstuart@topguardinc.com
      Website: www.topguardinc.com
Guard services, uniformed private security officers.
(Woman, estab 1996, empl 575, sales $15,250,000, cert:
State)

2610 Goldbelt Specialty Services LLC
      200 W Thomas, Ste 420
      Seattle, WA 98119
      Contact: Gino DCafango Business Dev Mgr
      Tel: 206-234-8759
      Email: g.dcafango@gbss.us
      Website: www.gbss.us
Security services: aromored transpot, vehicle, foot patrol
& stationary security officers. (Nat Ame, estab 2005, empl
18, sales $996,994, cert: NMSDC)

2611 Nexus Pest Solutions, Inc.
      3900 W Brown Deer Rd
      Brown Deer, WI 53223
      Contact: Will White President
      Tel: 414-355-3732
      Email: wwhite@nexuspestsolutions.com
      Website: www.nexuspestsolutions.com
We Provide pest control services for
commercial,industrial,institutional,manufacturing, and
hospitality facilities. (AA, estab 2007, empl 4, sales
$126,000, cert: State, City, NMSDC)

> **EDUCATIONAL MATERIALS**
> Manufacturers and wholesale distributors of text books, films, tapes, posters, magazines and teaching guides. NAICS Code 42

California

2612 El Mundo Communications
7444 E Chapman Ave Ste B
Orange, CA 92869
Contact: Martha Montoya Publisher
Tel: 714-366-3225
Email: martha@elmundous.com
Website: www.elmundous.com
Spanish language newspaper. (Hisp, estab 1988, empl 7, sales $700,000, cert: NMSDC)

Indiana

2613 Briljent, LLC
7999 Knue Road, Ste. 200
Indianapolis, IN 46250
Contact: Jennifer Duszynski Mgr Client Services
Tel: 317-220-1563
Email: jduszynski@briljent.com
Website: www.briljent.com
Develop customized technical writing, education manuals, systems documentation, training & adult learner educational programs. (Woman, estab 1998, empl 120, sales $35,250,000, cert: State)

2614 HPC International, Inc.
5261 Fountain Dr, Ste A
Crown Point, IN 46307
Contact: Lynn Bell CEO
Tel: 219-922-4868
Email: lbell@hpcinterantionalinc.com
Website: www.hpcinternationalinc.com
Trade publishing: books, pamphlets, brochures, booklets, journals, newsletters, to comic books, e-zines, interactive DVD's, e-learning & web-based content. (AA, estab 1996, empl 20, sales , cert: NMSDC)

2615 MPM Marketing, Inc
8918 Squire Ct
Indianapolis, IN 46250
Contact: Mary Pat McKee President
Tel: 317-440-9376
Email: marypat@mpmmarketinginc.com
Website: www.indyboomer.com
Publish an annual visitor guides for several hospitals in Indiana, sell advertising & work with large marketing departments. (Woman, estab 2005, empl 1, sales , cert: State)

Massachusetts

2616 Victory Productions, Inc.
55 Linden St
Worcester, MA 01609
Contact: President
Tel: 508-798-6218
Email:
Website: www.victoryprd.com
Develop educational products: print & electronic products in English and Spanish, concept development, design, editorial, translation, technology, & production. (Minority, Woman, estab 1996, empl 35, sales $5,500,000, cert: NMSDC, WBENC)

Minnesota

2617 Free Spirit Publishing Inc.
6325 Sandburg Road, Ste 100
Golden Valley, MN 55427
Contact: April Neske Asst to President
Tel: 612-338-2068
Email: neske@freespirit.com
Website: www.freespirit.com
Publish learning materials that support social & emotional development, counseling & educational needs, professional development, special needs, gifted & talented, counseling, bullying & conflict resolution, character education & service learning. (Woman, estab 1983, empl 31, sales $5,600,000, cert: WBENC)

New Jersey

2618 American Overseas Book Company, Inc.
550 Walnut St
Norwood, NJ 07648
Contact: Peter Lieb Dir of Operations
Tel: 201-767-7600
Email: plieb@aobc.com
Website: www.aobc.com
Dist books, CDs, DVDs & journal subscriptions. (Woman, estab 1969, empl 7, sales $4,500,000, cert: State)

2619 Horizon Group USA
45 Technology Dr
Warren, NJ 07059
Contact: Penn Wilder VP Sales
Tel: 908-810-1111
Email: pwilder@hgusa.com
Website: www.horizongroupusa.com/
broad array of activity kits, kids crafts, finished decor, fashion accessories and educational products. (As-Pac, estab , empl 340, sales $257,000,000, cert: NMSDC)

2620 Infopro Learning Inc
103 Morgan Ln, Ste 102
Plainsboro, NJ 08536
Contact: Ashhish Handa Regional VP Sales
Tel: 609-606-9012
Email: ash.handa@infoprolearning.com
Website: www.infoprolearning.com
Instructor Led/ Web Based/ Blended Training: Therapeutic Training, Sales Training, Product Training, Physician Training. (As-Ind, estab 2006, empl 1100, sales $262,418,117, cert: NMSDC)

New York

2621 Black Enterprise
130 Fifth Ave, 10 Fl
New York, NY 10011
Contact: Shareen Maison Staff Acct
Tel: 212-242-8000
Email: careers@blackenterprise.com
Website: www.blackenterprise.com
Publishing services. (AA, estab 1970, empl 100, sales $23,555,540, cert: State)

2622 Hudson Valley Press LLC
PO Box 2160
Newburgh, NY 12550
Contact: Chuck Stewart Editor
Tel: 845-562-1313
Email: sales@hvpress.net
Website: www.HudsonValleyPress.com
Minority newspaper that gives coverage to Orange, Dutchess, Westchester, Rockland, and Ulster Counties in the Hudson Valley of New York State. (AA, estab 1983, empl 3, sales $135,000, cert: State)

Texas

2623 Minority Business News
13111 N Central Expressway, Ste 400
Dallas, TX 75044
Contact: Mia Smith Project Mgr
Tel: 214-369-3200
Email: mbnusa@globalxlr.com
Website: www.mbnusa.biz
Magazine/internet supplier diversity publishing. (AA, estab 1988, empl 10, sales $1,300,000, cert: NMSDC)

2624 Minority Opportunity News, Inc.
PO Box 763866
Dallas, TX 75376
Contact: Thurman Jones Publisher
Tel: 972-516-4191
Email: businessoffice@northdallasgazette.com
Website: www.northdallasgazette.com
Newspaper: advertising & media, paper & internet. (AA, estab 1991, empl 5, sales , cert: State)

2625 Southern Chinese Daily News LLC
11122 Bellaire Blvd
Houston, TX 77072
Contact: Mia Smith Project Mgr
Tel: 281-498-4310
Email: scdn@globalxlr.com
Website: www.scdaily.com/
Publishing, advertising. (As-Pac, estab 1978, empl 19, sales $2,327,224, cert: City, NMSDC)

Wisconsin

2626 Best Ed, LLC
10936 N Port Washington Rd, Ste 269 Ste 269
Mequon, WI 53092
Contact: June Perry-Stevens Co-Owner
Tel: 414-313-9762
Email: contact@bestedbusiness.com
Website: www.bestedbusiness.com
Dist school supplies, games, materials. (Woman/AA, estab 2004, empl 2, sales $525,000, cert: State, City, NMSDC)

```
┌─────────────────────────────────────┐
│          ELECTRONIC ASSEMBLY         │
│  Electro-mechanical job shops. Man-  │
│  ufacturers of electro-mechanical    │
│  devices: PC boards, wire har-       │
│  nesses, cables, circuit components, │
│  housing, power supplies, etc. (See  │
│  also ELECTRONIC & ELECTRICAL        │
│  DIST. and ELECTRONIC & ELECTRICAL   │
│  MFG.) NAICS Code 33                 │
└─────────────────────────────────────┘
```

Alabama

2627　Mtronics.com, Inc.
　　　325 Electronics Blvd SW Ste C
　　　Huntsville, AL 35824
　　　Contact: Mary Fields Mgr, Quality Admin
　　　Tel:　256-461-8883
　　　Email: mary@mtronics.com
　　　Website: www.mtronics.com
Mfr automotive electronic assemblies. (As-Ind, estab 1987, empl 61, sales 53431545, cert: NMSDC)

Arizona

2628　EDS Manufacturing Inc.
　　　765 N Target Range Rd
　　　Nogales, AZ 85621
　　　Contact: Tony Milo VP Sales & Marketing
　　　Tel:　520-287-9711
　　　Email: tmilo@edsmanufacturing.com
　　　Website: www.edsmanufacturing.com
Molding, wire harness assembly, automatic cut, strip & crimp. (Hisp, estab 1990, empl 1800, sales 45687820, cert: NMSDC)

California

2629　Aeroflite Enterprises
　　　261 Gemini
　　　Brea, CA 92821
　　　Contact: Pamela DePape Sales Mgr
　　　Tel:　714-773-4251
　　　Email: pdepape@aeroflite.com
　　　Website: www.aeroflite.com
Dist aerospace electronics, custom cable assemblies & electrical connectors assemblies. (Woman, estab 1977, empl 65, sales 20000000, cert: NWBOC)

2630　Black Diamond Manufacturing Company
　　　755 Bliss Ave
　　　Pittsburg, CA 94565
　　　Contact: Barbara Williams Supplier Diversity Admin
　　　Tel:　925-439-9160
　　　Email: bwilliams@bwc.com
　　　Website: www.blackdiamondmfg.com
Mechanical sub-assemblies, manufacture specialty parts, in-house manufacturing experiences & capabilities, single source solution for custom sub-assemblies. (Woman, estab 2008, empl 3, sales , cert: WBENC)

2631　Cal-Am Switch & Relay Co., Inc.
　　　8837 Lankershim Blvd
　　　Sun Valley, CA 91352
　　　Contact: Max Beno COO
　　　Tel:　818-252-0507
　　　Email: lg@welcoelectronics.com
　　　Website: www.welcoelectronics.com
Avionic components, batteries, bearings, bushings, cables assemblies, cable ties, capacitors, connectors, expando sleeve, fuses, circuit breakers, lacing cords, relays, resistors, semiconductors, switches, wire, cable, tubing. (Minority, Woman, estab 1971, empl 7, sales 1250000, cert: NMSDC)

2632　Calpak USA, Inc.
　　　13750 Prairie Ave
　　　Hawthorne, CA 90250
　　　Contact: Danish Qureshi VP
　　　Tel:　310-937-7335
　　　Email: danish@calpak-usa.com
　　　Website: www.calpak-usa.com
Electronic Design, Electronics Engineering, Contract Manufacturing Services (CMS), Electronic Manufacturing Services (EMS), PCB Layout, PCB Design, PCB Assembly. (As-Pac, estab 1978, empl 15, sales 2400000, cert: State, NMSDC, SDB)

2633　LeeMAH Electronics Inc.
　　　1088 Sansome St
　　　San Francisco, CA 94111
　　　Contact: Brent Liebel Business Devel
　　　Tel:　972-570-7170
　　　Email: bliebel@leemah.com
　　　Website: www.leemah.com
Cable harness, printed circuit board stuffing; SMT assembly. Machine-programmed auto. printed circuit board testing, coil winding, transformer production, radio frequency cables. Mfr for special communications systems. Custom injection molding. (As-Ind, estab 1971, empl 650, sales 46000000, cert: NMSDC)

2634　Micro Analog Inc.
　　　1861 Puddingstone Dr
　　　La Verne, CA 91750
　　　Contact: Kim Bickmeier Dir of Sales
　　　Tel:　909-392-8277
　　　Email: kimbickmeier@micro-analog.com
　　　Website: www.micro-analog.com
Mfr electronics: printed circuit board assembly PCBA, custom cable & wire harness assembly, box/system build. (Minority, Woman, estab 1991, empl 155, sales 15698000, cert: NMSDC)

2635　Sierra Proto Express, Inc.
　　　1108 W Evelyn Ave
　　　Sunnyvale, CA 94086
　　　Contact: Greg Lawson Acct Rep
　　　Tel:　　408-735-7137
　　　Email: gregl@protoexpress.com
　　　Website: www.protoexpress.com
Mfr & assemble Printed Circuit Boards manufacturer, quick turn PCBs & medium production. (Minority, Woman, estab 1986, empl 353, sales , cert: NMSDC)

2636　Surface Art Engineering Inc
　　　81 Bonaventura Dr
　　　San Jose, CA 95134
　　　Contact: Jennifer Lee CEO
　　　Tel:　　-　-
　　　Email: sandy@surfaceart.com
　　　Website: www.surfaceart.com
PCB assembly, system mfg, design analysis, test solutions. (As-Pac, estab 1996, empl 40, sales , cert: NMSDC)

Colorado

2637　Premier Manufactuirng and Supply Chain Services
　　　7755 Miller Dr
　　　Frederick, CO 80504
　　　Contact: Edmond Johnson President
　　　Tel:　　303-776-4145
　　　Email: ejohnson@pmscs.com
　　　Website: www.pmscs.com
Contract mfr of printed circuit board assemblies for prototypes, production, sub assemblies, cable harness & test. (AA, estab 2000, empl 55, sales 12000000, cert: NMSDC)

Connecticut

2638　Accutron Inc.
　　　149 Addison Rd
　　　Windsor, CT 06095
　　　Contact: Jim Foss Outside Sales Mgr
　　　Tel:　　860-683-8300
　　　Email: jfoss@accutroninc.com
　　　Website: www.accutroninc.com
Printed circuit board assembly, surface mount assembly, thru-hole assembly, box build assembly, ICT, functioanl testing, flying probe testing. (As-Pac, estab 1989, empl 130, sales 25000000, cert: NMSDC)

2639　ICDI Inc.
　　　407 Brookside Rd
　　　Waterbury, CT 06708
　　　Contact: Steve Villodas President
　　　Tel:　　203-753-8551
　　　Email: svillodas@icdi-inc.com
　　　Website: www.icdi-inc.com
Contract mfr electronic high tech equip & systems, turnkey program mgmt, eng design, microprocessor systems, PC layout, PC board & automated surface-mount assembly, wave soldering, vapor degreasing, custom cables, ATE testing. (Hisp, estab 1975, empl 22, sales 3019307, cert: NMSDC)

Florida

2640　Circuitronix, LLC
　　　3131 SW 42nd St
　　　Fort Lauderdale, FL 33312
　　　Contact: ken peterson VP Sales
　　　Tel:　　231-459-4670
　　　Email: kenp@circuitronix.com
　　　Website: www.circuitronix.com
Supplier of rigid, flexible and rigid-flexible printed circuit boards in small, medium and high volumes. (As-Pac, estab 2000, empl 20, sales 0, cert: NMSDC)

2641　Hyper IC Florida Inc.
　　　5015 49th Ave N
　　　Saint Petersburg, FL 33703
　　　Contact: Nathalie Ouellet President
　　　Tel:　　727-822-7129
　　　Email: nathalie@hypericflorida.com
　　　Website: www.hypericflorida.com
Integrated Circuit. (Woman, estab 2008, empl 3, sales 0, cert: WBENC)

Georgia

2642　Roytec Industries LLC
　　　306 Bell Park Dr
　　　Woodstock, GA 30188
　　　Contact: Amanda Chapman CEO
　　　Tel:　　770-926-5470
　　　Email: mchapman@roytecind.com
　　　Website: www.roytecind.com
Mfr electrical wire harnesses & electrical wire assemblies. (Woman, estab 1984, empl 500, sales 36734238, cert: WBENC)

Illinois

2643 Alpha Circuit Corporation
      730 N Oaklawn Ave
      Elmhurst, IL 60126
      Contact: Steven Ryan Business Dev
      Tel: 630-617-5555
      Email: stever@alphacircuit.com
      Website: www.alphacircuit.com
Mfr single sided, double sided & multilayer printed circuit boards. (As-Ind, estab 1981, empl 42, sales 3200000, cert: NMSDC)

2644 American Standard Circuits
      475 Industrial Dr
      West Chicago, IL 60185
      Contact: Anaya Vardya CEO
      Tel: 630-639-5444
      Email: anaya@asc-i.com
      Website: www.asc-i.com
Mfr quality rigid, metal-backed, flex & rigid-flex printed circuit boards, RF/microwave printed circuit boards. (As-Ind, estab 1988, empl 135, sales 31000000, cert: NMSDC)

2645 Casco Manufacturing, Inc
      600 Territorial Dr Unit C
      Bolingbrook, IL 60440
      Contact: David Cohen Sales Rep
      Tel: 630-771-9555
      Email: dc@cascomanufacturing.com
      Website: www.cascomanufacturing.com
Mfr custom cable assemblies, wiring harnesses, fiber-optic cables, patch cords, capabilities to solder, tin, and/or crimp our terminals. (Woman, estab 1997, empl 25, sales 3100000, cert: State)

2646 Circom, Inc.
      505 W Main St
      Bensenville, IL 60106
      Contact: Victor Bossov Business Devel Mgr
      Tel: 630-595-4460
      Email: vbossov@circominc.com
      Website: www.circominc.com
Printed circuit board assembly & electronic control design services, wire & cable harness assemblies, enclosures & panels. (Woman, estab 1968, empl 25, sales 5200000, cert: WBENC)

2647 Circuitronics LLC
      201 N Gables Blvd
      Wheaton, IL 60510
      Contact: Shelley Lara VP Sales
      Tel: 630-668-5407
      Email: shelleylara@yahoo.com
      Website: www.circuitronicsllc.com
Mfr high tech printed circuit boards, exotic materials and alternate finishes (As-Ind, estab 1993, empl 55, sales 18000000, cert: NMSDC)

2648 General Circuit Corporation
      1370 Lively Blvd
      Elk Grove Village, IL 60007
      Contact: JANICE ROSARIO Sales/Mktg
      Tel: 847-758-8000
      Email: janice@deltapcb.com
      Website: www.Deltapcb.com
Mfr printed circuit boards: single, double & multi-layers in small, medium & high volumes. (As-Ind, estab 1996, empl 25, sales 4600000, cert: NMSDC)

2649 KLI Inc.
      304 Roma Jean Pkwy
      Streamwood, IL 60107
      Contact: Lisa Carso President
      Tel: 630-213-1283
      Email: support@kli-inc.com
      Website: www.kli-inc.com
Mfr electronic components; electronic assembly; main harness & cable to mil specs. (Minority, Woman, estab 1987, empl 15, sales 0, cert: State, NMSDC)

2650 Midwest Molding, Inc.
      1560 Hecht Dr
      Bartlett, IL 60103
      Contact: Sanjay Patel Dir of Purchasing
      Tel: 224-208-1110
      Email: sanjay.patel@mwmolding.com
      Website: www.mwmolding.com
Injection molding, insert molding, two shot molding, IMD molding, wire harness assembly & multi-component assembly. (As-Pac, estab 1996, empl 70, sales 0, cert: NMSDC)

Indiana

2651 Precision Wire Assemblies, Inc.
      551 E Main St
      Hagerstown, IN 47346
      Contact: Penny Wickes President
      Tel: 765-489-6302
      Email: penny@pwawire.com
      Website: www.pwawire.com
Mfr wire harnesses & assemblies, cable assemblies. (Woman, estab 1987, empl 75, sales 6130594, cert: State)

Kansas

2652 S and Y Industries, Inc.
      606 Industrial Rd
      Winfield, KS 67156
      Contact: Dir Sales/Marketing
      Tel: 620-221-4001
      Email: info@sandyindustries.com
      Website: www.sandyindustries.com
Printed circuit boards, wire harnesses, cable assemblies, connectors, surface mount. (Woman, estab 1984, empl 80, sales 7660639, cert: WBENC)

Massachusetts

2653   Cable Harness Resources, Inc.
One Robert Bonazzoli Ave
Hudson, MA 01749
Contact: Kim Nguyen
Tel: 978-562-4352
Email: knguyen@cableharnessresources.com
Website: www.cableharnessresources.com
Electrical wire harness& cable asembly, Mil-Spec source, cut, strip, tin, twist, splice, crimp, solder, coil, end-prep, connector/component installation. (Minority, Woman, estab 2008, empl 10, sales 800000, cert: NMSDC)

Michigan

2654   Advanced-Cable, LLC
1179 Chicago Rd
Troy, MI 48083
Contact: Deanna Zwiesele Owner
Tel: 248-268-3167
Email: deanna@advanced-cable.com
Website: www.advanced-cable.com
Mfr custom cable assemblies (molded and non molded) & wire harnesses, dist bulk wire, cable & various electronic components. (Woman, estab 2012, empl 15, sales 2000000, cert: WBENC)

2655   American Hydrostatics Distribution Co.
6626 Sims Dr
Sterling Heights, MI 48313
Contact: Drew Parikh Business Devel
Tel: 248-649-2587
Email: dp@americanhydrostatics.com
Website: www.americanhydrostatics.com
Build small automation & assembly equipment, rebuild machines & general assembly services. (As-Pac, estab 1982, empl 25, sales 42000000, cert: NMSDC)

2656   Detroit Manufacturing Systems
12701 Southfield Rd Bldg A
Detroit, MI 48223
Contact: Sung Moon Business Devel Mgr
Tel: - -
Email: casey.smith@dmsna.com
Website: www.dmsna.com
Provide assembly and sub-assembly services. (Woman/AA, estab 2012, empl 1400, sales 900000000, cert: NMSDC)

2657   Embedded Logix Inc.
50644 Sabrina Dr
Shelby, MI 48315
Contact: Deborah McLeod President
Tel: 586-709-2025
Email: dmcleod@emlogix.net
Website: www.emlogix.net
Product design for automotive, commercial & medical, test equipment design, test consulting, service, connector build, harness build, assembly test equipment. Embedded design, embedded programming, labview programming. (Woman, estab 0, empl , sales 0, cert: WBENC)

2658   GM&T Engineering, Inc.
775 Davis St Ste 4
Plymouth, MI 48170
Contact: Carlos Gutierrez President
Tel: 734-679-8340
Email: cgutierrez@gmt-engineering.com
Website: www.gmt-engineering.com
Testing of Electrical Distribution Systems (Wire Harnesses, batteries), Engineering of EDS, Process and Product quality audits, Staffing and recruiting Wire Harnesses and prototypes, Testing tooling and equipment. (Hisp, estab 2005, empl 16, sales , cert: NMSDC)

2659   Newtech 3, Inc.
28373 Beck Rd Ste H7
Wixom, MI 48393
Contact: Gail Gyenese Dir of Sales
Tel: 248-912-1062
Email: ggyenese@newtech3inc.com
Website: www.newtech3.com
Mfr lower to mid volume wire harness & circuit board assemblies. (AA, estab 2009, empl 32, sales 3965000, cert: NMSDC)

2660   Orri Corporation
5385 Perry Dr
waterford, MI 48329
Contact: Angelo Doa Sales
Tel: 248-618-1104
Email: Sales@orricorp.com
Website: www.orricorp.com
Wire harnesses, cable assemblies, electrical test fixtures, robotic vision guidance software. (Woman, estab 2001, empl 12, sales 0, cert: WBENC)

2661   Saturn Electronics Corporation
28450 Northline Rd
Romulus, MI 48174
Contact: Parthiv Trivedi Dir Business Dev
Tel: 734-941-8100
Email: parthiv@saturnelectronics.com
Website: www.saturnelectronics.com
Printed circuit boards: prototype & production; 1 to 20 layers. (As-Ind, estab 1985, empl 190, sales 40025000, cert: NMSDC)

2662 Wolverine Assemblies, LLC
      30260 Oak Creek Dr
      Wixom, MI 48393
      Contact: Adam Claytor Sr Lead Analyst
      Tel: 248-822-8056
      Email: aclaytor@taghold.com
      Website: www.wolverine-llc.com/
Modular assembly, warehousing, sequencing, import &
export, fabrication, machining, kitting, supply chain
management, pre delivery inspection, repack and test,
containment & sorting. (AA, estab 2010, empl 6, sales
12000000, cert: NMSDC)

2663 Wotko LLC
      229 South St
      Rochester, MI 48307
      Contact: Dustin Coon President
      Tel: 248-266-6016
      Email: dcoon@wotkollc.com
      Website: www.wotkollc.com
Custom cable & harness specialty products, prototype,
fiber cables. (Nat Ame, estab 2013, empl 2, sales , cert:
State)

Minnesota

2664 Aero Assemblies, Inc.
      12012 - 12th Ave S
      Burnsville, MN 55337
      Contact: Anthony Winick President
      Tel: 952-894-5552
      Email: tonyw@aeroassemblies.com
      Website: www.aeroassemblies.com
Contract manufacturing, wire rope assembly, electronic
cable assembly, print finishing, bindery, eyeletting (As-Pac,
estab 1972, empl 16, sales 3000000, cert: NMSDC)

2665 Quantronic Corporation
      8300 89th Ave N
      Brooklyn Park, MN 55445
      Contact: Gabriela Faouen Acct Mgr
      Tel: 763-425-2602
      Email: gfaouen@quantronic.net
      Website: www.quantronic.net
Surface Mount & Thru Hole Assemblies, Incircuit &
Functional testing, Prototype & Product development,
Circuit Board Rework & modifications, Complete Product &
and sub assemblies, Packaging Solutions, Conformal
Coating. (Hisp, estab 1995, empl 65, sales 15000000, cert:
NMSDC)

New Jersey

2666 Delaire USA, Inc.
      1913 Atlantic Ave
      Manasquan, NJ 08736
      Contact: President
      Tel: 732-528-4520
      Email: sales@delaireusa.com
      Website: www.delaireusa.com
Mfr custom RF & fiber optic cables & assemblies, box
level assemblies, precision soldering & testing. (Woman,
estab 1994, empl 19, sales 0, cert: State, WBENC)

2667 Precision Graphics, Inc.
      21 County Line Rd
      Somerville, NJ 08876
      Contact: Alec Weissman VP
      Tel: 908-707-8880
      Email: aweissman@precisiongraphics.us
      Website: www.precisiongraphics.us
Mfr printed circuit board assemblies, surface mount,
through hole, or RoHs processing. (Woman, estab 1971,
empl 55, sales 13000000, cert: NWBOC)

Nevada

2668 Power Assemblies LLC
      7061 W Arby Rd Ste 120
      Las Vegas, NV 89113
      Contact: Patricia Knowles Owner
      Tel: 541-610-6494
      Email: gknowles@powerassemblies.com
      Website: www.powerassemblies.com
Assemble portable power & industrial products, flexible
power cable assemblies, connectors, generator docking
stations, enclosed variable speed drives & cam lock
panels, custom portable power products ranging from
20A to 4000A. (Woman, estab 2006, empl 9, sales
350000, cert: State, WBENC)

New York

2669 Hazlow Electronics
      49 St. Bridgets Dr
      Rochester, NY 14605
      Contact: Crain CEO
      Tel: 585-263-7852
      Email: rdwiz@aol.com
      Website: www.hazlow.com
Wire harnesses, printed circuit boards, cable assemblies,
sub assembly. (Minority, Woman, estab 1971, empl 40,
sales 3500000, cert: State, WBENC)

Pennsylvania

2670   Contine Corporation
1820 Nagle Rd
Erie, PA 16510
Contact: Constance Ellrich President
Tel: 814-899-0006
Email: cellrich@continedbe.com
Website: www.continedbe.com
Mfr mechanical & electro mechanical assemblies.
(Woman, estab 1981, empl 43, sales 9175996, cert: CPUC, WBENC)

2671   John A. Romeo & Associates, Inc.
890 Pittsburgh Rd, Ste 7
Butler, PA 16002
Contact: Pamela Romeo CEO
Tel: 724-586-6961
Email: sales@jara-mfg.com
Website: www.jara-mfg.com
Mfr Custom Cables, Wiring Harnesses & Electromechanical Assemblies. (Woman, estab 1990, empl 15, sales 1506698, cert: WBENC)

South Carolina

2672   North American Assemblies, LLC
2222 Cale Yarborough Hwy
Timmonsville, SC 29161
Contact: William Rucker
Tel: 248-342-6500
Email: warucker@naa-llc.com
Website: www.naa-llc.com
Mfg & assembly services. (AA, estab 2004, empl 17, sales 3000000, cert: NMSDC)

Texas

2673   Accurate Connections Inc.
13801 Hutton Dr, Ste 100
Farmers Branch, TX 75234
Contact: President
Tel: 972-484-8500
Email: info@accurateconnections.com
Website: www.accurateconnections.com
Cable assemblies, fiber optic & copper. (Woman, estab 2003, empl 26, sales 3246807, cert: State, WBENC)

2674   Arise Solutions Inc.
5862 Cromo Ste 149
El Paso, TX 79912
Contact: Daniel Laing President
Tel: 915-345-9134
Email: sales@arisesolutions.biz
Website: www.arisesolutions.biz
Custom designed wire harness, cable assembly, bulk wire, signal cable, specialty bolts, screws, Nut Rivets, Inserts, Fasteners, Spacers, Connectors & Fittings for automotive industry. (As-Pac, estab 2012, empl 5, sales 1000000, cert: State, NMSDC)

2675   Electro Plate Circuitry, Inc.
1430 Century Dr
Carrollton, TX 75006
Contact: Nicolas Garcia President
Tel: 972-466-0818
Email: nickg@eplate.com
Website: www.eplate.com
Mfr printed circuit boards: GF,GI, RF, insulators, heatsinks, blind buried vias, controlled impedance. (Hisp, estab 1981, empl 80, sales 9000000, cert: NMSDC)

2676   Electronic Assembly Services, Inc.
4501 S Pinemont, Ste 108
Houston, TX 77041
Contact: Evelyn Fletcher CEO
Tel: 713-686-4390
Email: efletcher@easinchou.com
Website: www.eashouston.com/
Custom electric & electronic assemblies & sub-assemblies: control panels, cable wire harnesses, electro-mechanical assemblies, printed circuit board assemblies, rack-mount assemblies. (Minority, Woman, estab 1987, empl 13, sales 1500000, cert: State, NMSDC)

2677   Galaxy Electronics Company
201 E Arapaho Rd
Richardson, TX 75081
Contact: Will Moore Sales Mgr
Tel: 972-234-0065
Email: wmoore@galaxyee.com
Website: www.galaxyee.com
Fiber optic & copper cable assembly. (As-Pac, estab 1988, empl 31, sales 0, cert: State, NMSDC)

2678   JVB Electronics dba Multilayer Technology
3835 Conflans Rd
Irving, TX 75061
Contact: Johnnie Feathers Dir of Sales
Tel: 972-790-0062
Email: johnnie@multilayer.com
Website: www.multilayer.com
Mfr printed circuit boards. (As-Ind, estab 1986, empl 45, sales , cert: State, NMSDC)

2679 Optical Interconnect
       2621 Summit Ave Ste 100
       Plano, TX 75074
       Contact: Steve Wade Acct Exec
       Tel: 214-239-3988
       Email: swade@opticalinterconnect.com
       Website: www.opticalinterconnect.com
Dist fiber optic cable assemblies, copper cable assemblies,
rack/wall mount metal enclosures. (Woman, estab 2004,
empl 15, sales , cert: State, WBENC)

2680 THT Electronics Company, Inc.
       6645 Fairway Dr
       Westworth Village, TX 76114
       Contact: Scott Sewell CEO
       Tel: 972-505-6769
       Email: scott.sewell@thtelec.com
       Website: www.thtpromo.com
Electronic components, cable assemblies. (Nat Ame, estab
1996, empl 6, sales 126000, cert: State, NMSDC)

2681 Trendsetter Electronics
       2500 NE Inner Loop Bldg 1 Ste 105
       Georgetown, TX 78626
       Contact: Carol Williams President
       Tel: 512-310-8858
       Email: stacyb@trendsetter.com
       Website: www.trendsetter.com
Stocking programs & stocking replinishment, kitting, cable
& harness assemblies, lead forming & modifying, part
sleeving & custom transformers. (Woman, estab 1995,
empl 12, sales 5536114, cert: WBENC)

2682 Trilogy Circuits, Inc.
       1717 Firman Dr Ste 200
       Richardson, TX 75081
       Contact: Mark T McCrocklin
       Tel: 972-907-2727
       Email: mark@trilogycircuits.com
       Website: www.trilogycircuits.com
Printed circuit board design/layout. (As-Pac, estab 2001,
empl 27, sales 5000000, cert: State, NMSDC)

Wisconsin

2683 A1 Cable Solutions, Inc.
       665 Commercial Ave
       Waterloo, WI 53594
       Contact: Laurie Hoffmann President
       Tel: 608-444-3072
       Email: ljhoffmann@usa1cable.com
       Website: www.usa1cable.com
Battery Cables, Ground Straps, Wire Harnesses, Electromechanical Assemblies, Panel Assembly & Wiring, Prototypes,
Testing & Reporting. (Woman, estab 2001, empl 2, sales ,
cert: WBENC)

ELECTRONICS & ELECTRICAL DIST.
Distribute a wide range of electrical or electronic products: battery chargers, communications equipment, video equipment, radios, measuring instruments, etc. (See also ELECTRONIC ASSEMBLY and ELECTRONICS & ELECTRICAL MFG.) NAICS Code 42

Arizona

2684   Aegis Electronic Group, Inc.
1465 North Fiesta Blvd. Ste 101
Gilbert, AZ 85233
Contact: Michelle Witt Technical Sales Rep
Tel: 480-635-8400
Email: michelle@aegiselect.com
Website: www.aegis-elec.com/
Dist industrial imaging equipment: cameras, lenses, monitors, cables, connectors, power supplies, frame grabbers, software, etc. (Woman, estab 1989, empl 17, sales $9,000,000, cert: WBENC)

2685   Spirit Distribution and Logistics, Inc.
23910 N 19th Ave Ste 26
Phoenix, AZ 85085
Contact: Vickie Wessel President
Tel: 480-998-1533
Email: v.wessel@spiritelectronics.com
Website: www.spiritelectronics.com
Dist passive components, memory products, obsolete & hard-to-find semiconductors & electromechanical devices. (Minority, Woman, estab 1979, empl 15, sales $29,307,000, cert: NMSDC, WBENC)

California

2686   AAA Electrical Supply, Inc.
1014 S Montebello Blvd
Montebello, CA 90640
Contact: Alfred J. Alvarez President
Tel: 323-721-2700
Email: zirma@aaaelectricalsupply.com
Website: www.aaaelectricalsupply.com
Dist electrical supplies: conduit fittings, wire, cable, steelboxes, weatherproof boxes, lighting, ballasts, hand tools, circuit breakers, panelboards, switchgear, transformers, wiring devices, lamps, incandescent, fluorescent, HID & LED lighting. (Hisp, estab 1988, empl 7, sales $3,426,300, cert: State, City, CPUC)

2687   Aeroflite Enterprises
261 Gemini
Brea, CA 92821
Contact: Pamela DePape Sales Mgr
Tel: 714-773-4251
Email: pdepape@aeroflite.com
Website: www.aeroflite.com
Dist aerospace electronics, custom cable assemblies & electrical connectors assemblies. (Woman, estab 1977, empl 65, sales $20,000,000, cert: NWBOC)

2688   American Industrial Control, Inc.
170 N Maple St Ste 104
Corona, CA 92880
Contact: Monica Pratt President
Tel: 951-520-0613
Email: monica@aicesupply.com
Website: www.aicesupply.com
Dist electrical supplies, mfr industrial control panels. (Minority, Woman, estab 2000, empl 4, sales $1,010,254, cert: NMSDC, CPUC, WBENC)

2689   AREA51-ESG
51 Post
Irvine, CA 92618
Contact: Khanh Hoang OEM Sales
Tel: 949-387-0054
Email: khanh.hoang@area51esg.com
Website: www.area51esg.com
Dist electronic components, cables, hardware, mil spec hardware, rotables, expandables, etc. (As-Pac, estab 2000, empl 53, sales $24,900,000, cert: NMSDC)

2690   AutoCell Electronics
7311 Greenhaven Dr
Sacramento, CA 95831
Contact: Mark Hardwick Acct Mgr
Tel: 888-393-6668
Email: mark@autocell.net
Website: www.autocell.net
CFLs (compact fluorescent lights), linear fluorescent lights, LED (Light Emitting Diode) lights, indoor & outdoor hardwired light fixtures (luminaires), LED Desk Lamps. (As-Pac, estab 2000, empl 5, sales $2,000,000, cert: CPUC)

2691   Bright Light LED Inc.
7751 Alabama Ave, Warehouse 7-8
Canoga Park, CA 91304
Contact: Rami Vardi CEO
Tel: 310-987-6670
Email: rvardi@brightlightled.net
Website: www.brightlightled.net
Residential & commercial LED bulbs & fixtures. (Woman, estab 2008, empl 200, sales $2,050,000, cert: NMSDC)

2692   C Plus Electronics, Inc.
17842 Irvine Blvd. Ste B144
Tustin, CA 92780
Contact: Carrie Fill Purchasing
Tel: 714-783-7141
Email: carrie.fill@cpluselectronics.com
Website: www.cpluselectronics.com
Dist electronic components: ICs, passives; interconnect products, memory modules & other computer related products. (Minority, Woman, estab 2003, empl 15, sales $5,000,000, cert: NMSDC, SDB)

2693   Callor Sales, Inc
3850 Cedar Ave
Long Beach, CA 90807
Contact: Lori Nelson Owner
Tel: 562-426-6209
Email: lori.nelson@callorsales.com
Website: www.callorsales.com
Dist electrical, electronic & telecommunications materials & equipment. (Woman, estab 2005, empl 1, sales , cert: State)

2694 CE Supply
1111 W Victoria St
Compton, CA 90220
Contact: MobileVision Sales/Mktg
Tel: 310-735-2078
Email: customerservice@cesupply.com
Website: www.mobilevisionus.com/
Dist wireless & electronics accessories. (Minority, Woman, estab 1990, empl 3, sales $2,879,544, cert: CPUC, WBENC)

2695 DWY Inc.
911 S Primrose Ave, Ste I
Monrovia, CA 91016
Contact: Daniel Yohannes
Tel: 626-357-0500
Email: honeylyn@ecads-na.com
Website: www.ecads-na.com
Dist LED & solar products, energy saving LED bulbs & solar panels. (AA, estab 2001, empl 4, sales , cert: NMSDC)

2696 Forza Electronics
1110 S El Camino Real Ste C
San Clemente, CA 92672
Contact: James Cassano President
Tel: 949-276-8686
Email: james@forzaelectronics.com
Website: www.forzaelectronics.com
Dist electronics components, semiconductors, capacitors, resistors, switches, relays, connectors, diodes, computer peripherals, computer hardware & electromechanical devices. (Woman, estab 2006, empl 5, sales $794,000, cert: WBENC)

2697 FTS Lighting Services, Inc.
160 S. Cypress St
Orange, CA 92866
Contact: Michele Davidson President
Tel: 714-289-1957
Email: michele@ftslighting.com
Website: www.ftslighting.com
Energy Saving Lights & Analysis, LEDs, Induction, tubes, ballast, fixtures, aircraft, xenon, HID, Metal halide. (Minority, Woman, estab 2010, empl 1, sales $350,000, cert: State, CPUC, WBENC)

2698 Integra Electronics, Inc.
1363 Lewis St
Anaheim, CA 92805
Contact: Victor Montez President
Tel: 714-282-4990
Email: vicm@integrasmp.com
Website: www.integrasmp.com
Dist electronic components: Lampholders, Panel Mount indicator lights, incandescent & neon indicator lights, LED Panel lenses & Cable assemblies, Electro-Mechanial products. (Hisp, estab 1997, empl 11, sales $3,960,000, cert: State, NMSDC)

2699 MCV Technologies Inc.
6640 Lusk Blvd, Ste A102
San Diego, CA 92121
Contact: Edward Liang VP
Tel: 858-450-0468
Email: eliang@mcv-microwave.com
Website: www.mcv-microwave.com
Mfr & dist RF/Microwave Filter, Antenna, Dielectric Resonator and Microelectronic Circuit. Bandpass Filter, Notch Filter, Lowpass Filter, Highpass Filter, Duplexer, Triplexer, Multiplexer. (Minority, Woman, estab 1995, empl 25, sales $2,000,000, cert: CPUC)

2700 Meritke Electronics Corp.
5160 Rivergrade Rd.
Baldwin Park, CA 91706
Contact: Oliver Su President
Tel: 626-373-1728
Email: sales@meritekusa.com
Website: www.meritekusa.com
Dist electronics. (As-Pac, estab 1983, empl 36, sales $20,000,000, cert: NMSDC)

2701 Onesource Distributors, Inc.
3951 Oceanic Dr
Oceanside, CA 92056
Contact: Jeremy Schmidt Dir Diversity Devel
Tel: 760-966-4500
Email: jschmidt@1sourcesupplysolutions.com
Website: www.1sourcedist.com
Dist electrical related materials. (Hisp, estab 1983, empl 310, sales $250,000,000, cert: NMSDC)

2702 Perfect Parts Corporation
7545 Irvine Center Dr, Ste 200
Irvine, CA 92618
Contact: Lulu Jaff Owner
Tel: 949-209-1655
Email: lulu@perfectelectronicparts.com
Website: www.perfectelectronicparts.com
Dist electronic components. (Woman, estab 2013, empl 5, sales , cert: WBENC)

2703 RAK Technologies LLC
23122 Mountain Pine
Mission Viejo, CA 92692
Contact: Mark Meeks President
Tel: 949-633-9845
Email: mark@rak-techca.com
Website: www.raktechca.com
Dist electronic components: semiconductors, connectors, power, sensors, relays etc. (Nat Ame, estab 2007, empl 4, sales , cert: NMSDC)

2704 SilenX Corporation
10606 Shoemaker Ave Ste A
Santa Fe Springs, CA 90670
Contact: PK Karunphan Sales Mgr
Tel: 562-941-4200
Email: pkarun@silenx.com
Website: www.silenx.com
Replace & install energy-efficient LED light tubes. (As-Pac, estab 2004, empl 6, sales $2,077,409, cert: NMSDC)

2705 Steven Engineering, Inc.
230 Ryan Way
South San Francisco, CA 94080
Contact: Bonnie A. Walter VP Mktg
Tel: 800-258-9200
Email: bonnie_walter@steveneng.com
Website: www.stevenengineering.com
Dist electronic pneumatic products, electronic components, electrical parts, industrial automation & controls. (Woman, estab 1975, empl 123, sales $46,500,000, cert: CPUC, WBENC)

2706   telCade.Com
2914-24th Ave
San Francisco, CA 94132
Contact: Jerry Chan VP Sales
Tel: 408-955-9268
Email: jerry@telcade.com
Website: www.catalog.telcade.com/
Custom cable & wire harness, coaxial connector & cables, xDSL/ VDSL filter/splitter, connectors, optical cables & connectors, power cord, power supply adapter/chargers. (Minority, Woman, estab 1993, empl 168, sales $6,100,000, cert: CPUC)

2707   THISAI LLC
1834 Blazewood St
Simi Valley, CA 93063
Contact: Ramalingam Subramaniam Owner
Tel: 747-206-3886
Email: ram@thisaillc.com
Website: www.thisaillc.com
Electrical products, cables, switches, wire, lighting fixtures, metal products, aluminum, sheet metal, laser cut, bent & fabricated. (Minority, estab 2015, empl 2, sales , cert: State)

2708   Unical Aviation Inc.
4775 Irwindale Ave
Irwindale, CA 91706
Contact: Ray Daljeet Mgr
Tel: 626-813-1901
Email: rdaljeet@unical.com
Website: www.unical.com
Kitts, connector, wire, hardware, flight component, Avionic, engine component, MROs. (As-Pac, estab 1990, empl 160, sales $2,000,000, cert: NMSDC)

2709   Waisun Corporation
13321 Alondra Blvd, Ste D
Santa Fe Springs, CA 90670
Contact: Albert Hui President
Tel: 562-394-6922
Email: optolight@msn.com
Website: www.optolight.com
Dist LED products, LED light bulbs, recess downlight, etc. (As-Pac, estab 1988, empl 8, sales , cert: CPUC)

Colorado

2710   Innov8 Solutions USA,LLC
1500 W 47th Ave
Denver, CO 80211
Contact: Dan Montoya Dir of Sales operations
Tel: 303-328-8888
Email: dmontoya@innov8supplies.com
Website: www.innov8solutions.com
Dist electrical & telecommunications supplies, warehouse services of cable stubbing, custom cutting, order fulfillment & kitting operations. (Hisp, estab 2001, empl 20, sales , cert: NMSDC)

District of Columbia

2711   Ideal Electrical Supply Corporation
3515 V St NE
Washington, DC 20018
Contact: Cora Williams President
Tel: 202-526-7500
Email: cwilliams@idealelectric.com
Website: www.idealelectric.com
Dist electrical, industrial, data & telecommunications, networking products, lighting tools & safety equipment. (Woman/AA, estab 1991, empl 17, sales $59,000,000, cert: NMSDC, WBENC)

Florida

2712   Aero Supply USA
21941 US Hwy 19 N
Clearwater, FL 33765
Contact: Robert Ramirez Business Devel Mgr
Tel: 727-754-4915
Email: rramirez@aerosupplyusa.com
Website: www.aerosupplyusa.com
Dist aerospace parts & electronic components. (Minority, Woman, estab 2012, empl 12, sales $0, cert: NMSDC, SDB)

2713   Chase Components LLC
647 Arnau Dr
New Smyrna Beach, FL 32168
Contact: Cristal Dongilli CEO
Tel: 386-426-1367
Email: cristal@chasecomponents.com
Website: www.chasecomponents.com
Dist board level electronic components. (Woman, estab 2003, empl 10, sales $2,907,439, cert: WBENC)

2714   Efficient Lighting Technologies
12555 Orange Dr Ste 4002
Fort Lauderdale, FL 33330
Contact: Jose Trevino Dir of Operations
Tel: 954-623-7102
Email: jtrevino@elt-us.com
Website: www.elt-us.com
Dist LED light bulbs & linear fluorescent lamps. (Hisp, estab 2005, empl 22, sales $10,123,250, cert: NMSDC)

2715   LedZed International Inc.
2240 Palm Beach Lakes Blvd
West Palm Beach, FL 33409
Contact: Helena Lahtinen CEO
Tel: 954-629-0768
Email: helena@ledzed.com
Website: www.ledzed.com
Mfr & dist energy efficiency led lights. (Woman, estab 2011, empl 1, sales , cert: City)

2716   LXI Components Inc.
2802 Leslie Road
Tampa, FL 33619
Contact: Wolmar Busche President
Tel: 813-663-9682
Email: wolmar.busche@lxicomponents.com
Website: www.lxicomponents.com
Dist passive & interconnect electronic components. (AA, estab 1994, empl 10, sales $2,926,437, cert: NMSDC)

2717 The Bernd Group Inc.
1251 Pinehurst Rd
Dunedin, FL 34698
Contact: Pilar Bernd President
Tel: 727-733-0122
Email: businessdevelopment@berndgroup.com
Website: www.berndgroup.com
Material handling equip, safety products, hand & power tools, pumps & compressors, motors, generators, electrical hardware, batteries, lighting fixtures, lockers, bins, shelving, lab equip. (Minority, Woman, estab 1992, empl 66, sales $0, cert: NMSDC)

Georgia

2718 AC & DC Power Technologies
125 Cavalier Ct
Fayetteville, GA 30215
Contact: Charles McCartha Office Mgr
Tel: 404-361-3788
Email: charles@acdcpowertechnologies.com
Website: www.acdcpowertechnologies.com
Integrate, dist & engineer electrical systems: transformers, switchgear, batteries, generators, capacitor banks, resistors, ground fault protection. (Minority, Woman, estab 1997, empl 14, sales $3,800,000, cert: State, NMSDC, WBENC)

2719 B & S Electric Supply Co., Inc
4505 Mills Place
S.W. Atlanta, GA 30336
Contact: Clarence Robie
Tel: 404-696-8284
Email: c.robie@b-s-electric.com
Website: www.bandselect.com
Dist electrical supplies. (AA, estab , empl , sales $0, cert: NMSDC)

2720 GC Electrical Solutions, LLC
120 Cecil Court
Fayetteville, GA 30214
Contact: George Lottier President
Tel: 770-716-5400
Email: glottier@gcelectrical.com
Website: www.gc-es.com
Dist electrical components: lamps, wire, conduit, panel boards, transformers, fixtures, wiring devices. (AA, estab 2003, empl 5, sales $0, cert: NMSDC)

2721 NAECO, LLC
100 NAECO Way
Peachtree City, GA 30269
Contact: Steven Jones Dir Sales & Marketing
Tel: 770-487-6006
Email: stevej@naeco.net
Website: www.naeco.net
Dist Electrical Contacts, Contact Assemblies, Tungsten based Heavy Metal Products & Machined Parts. (Minority, estab 1999, empl 25, sales $11,111,301, cert: NMSDC)

2722 Quality Standby Services, LLC
1649 Sands Place SE Ste C
Marietta, GA 30067
Contact: Paul Whitaker General Mgr
Tel: 770-916-1747
Email: paul@qualitystandbyservices.com
Website: www.qualitystandbyservices.com
Dist, install, maintain & test standby power systems: batteries, battery racks, chargers & spill containment. (Woman, estab 2006, empl 19, sales $8,558,834, cert: WBENC)

Illinois

2723 Bearings & Industrial Supply
431 Imen Ave
Addison, IL 60101
Contact: Sejal Khandwala Acct Exec
Tel: 630-628-1966
Email: Sejal@BearingsNow.Com
Website: www.bearingsnow.com
Dist bearings & power transmission products; pump & pump repair parts, HVAC & electrical parts. (As-Pac, estab , empl , sales $0, cert: NMSDC)

2724 Electric Motor Corporation
3865 N Milwaukee Ave
Chicago, IL 60641
Contact: Isabell Siegel President
Tel: 773-725-1050
Email: isabell@electricmotorcorp.us
Website: www.electricmotorcorp.us
Electric motor repair. (Woman, estab 1960, empl 25, sales $2,488,000, cert: WBENC)

2725 Electro-Kinetics Inc.
859 N Sivert Dr
Wood Dale, IL 60191
Contact: Aileen Sonderman President
Tel: 630-595-6700
Email: aileens@e-kinetics.com
Website: www.e-kinetics.com
Dist electric & electronic components: sensors, relays, contactors, controls, fuses, fuse blocks, circuit breakers, solenoids, timers, transducers, boots/seals, cable cordsets, cable ties, connectors, cord grips, current operated switches. (Minority, Woman, estab 1957, empl 8, sales $2,400,000, cert: NMSDC, WBENC)

2726 Electro-Wire Inc.
933 E Remington
Schaumburg, IL 60173
Contact: Mike Schmidt VP
Tel: 847-944-1500
Email: mschmidt@electrowire.com
Website: www.electrowire.com
Dist wire & cable, cable assemblies, mechanical cable, harness assemblies & electromechanical sub-assemblies. (As-Pac, estab 1978, empl 100, sales $80,000,000, cert: NMSDC)

2727 Global Test Equipment Inc.
1424 Centre Cir
Downers Grove, IL 60515
Contact: Jay Perry Acct Mgr
Tel: 630-678-0400
Email: jay@4gte.com
Website: www.4gte.com
Dist, rent & lease electronic test equipment. (Woman, estab 2003, empl 4, sales $0, cert: WBENC)

2728 Go Green LED-Alternatives, LLC
6621 State Route 71
Yorkville, IL 60560
Contact: Sandra Goeken CEO
Tel: 630-802-4213
Email: s.miles@gogreenled.com
Website: www.gogreenled.com
LED, light, lighting, security, value added reseller, control systems, street lighti (Woman, estab 2008, empl 2, sales $2,937,513, cert: CPUC, WBENC)

2729 Gordon Electric Supply Co.
1290 N Hobbie
Kankakee, IL 60901
Contact: Randy Molthan CFO
Tel: 800-892-1866
Email: rmolthan@gordonelec.com
Website: www.gordonelectricsupply.com
Dist elelctrical supplies. (Woman, estab 0, empl 20, sales $8,500,000, cert: State, WBENC)

2730 Halogen Lighting Products Corp.
PO Box 229
Kaneville, IL 60144
Contact: Gloria Stewart President
Tel: 800-621-0001
Email: info@halogen-lighting.com
Website: www.halogen-lighting.com
LED & fluorescent industrial machine lights with with a wide range of wattages, lumens capable of operating in environments of 90 - 260 volts & some are compatible with 24VDC. (Woman, estab 1993, empl 5, sales , cert: City, NWBOC)

2731 Hinsdale Lighting
777 N York Rd Ste 19
Hinsdale, IL 60521
Contact: David Laughter Warehouse Mgr
Tel: 630-734-0662
Email: hlighting@hinsdalelighting.com
Website: www.hinsdalelighting.com
Lighting design, light fixture & light bulb distributor. (Woman, estab 2008, empl 6, sales $1,100,000, cert: WBENC)

2732 JP Simons & Co.
1426 Brook Dr
Downers Grove, IL 60641
Contact: Jean Bradfield President
Tel: - -
Email: roger@jpsimons.net
Website: www.jpsimons.com
Dist wiring devices & switches, electrical tapes, fittings, wire, cable & cords, transformers, electrical boxes, tools & testers, terminals & lugs, circuit breakers, fuses & terminal strips, cables ties, etc. (Woman, estab , empl 7, sales $10,000,000, cert: State)

2733 Midco Electric Supply
7237 W 90th Pl
Bridgeview, IL 60455
Contact: Tony Niedospial Sales
Tel: 888-446-4326
Email: tony@midcoelectric.com
Website: www.midcoelectric.com
Dist motor controls, fuses, wire & wiring devices, circuit breakers, switches, transformers, tie wraps, conduit & accessories, liquid tight & fittings, signal towers, PLC's, HMI's, relays, enclosures, timers, light fixtures, ballasts, batteries, tape, etc (Woman, estab 1979, empl 11, sales $13,500,000, cert: State, City, WBENC)

2734 Ottsie, LLC
1412 Sioux Dr
Ottawa, IL 61350
Contact: Sally Rutledge Ott President
Tel: 815-378-7841
Email: ottsiesupply@gmail.com
Website: www.ottsiesupply.com
Dist electrical & plumbing supplies, generators. (Woman, estab 2014, empl 1, sales $437,000, cert: State)

Indiana

2735 Diesel Electrical Equipment, Inc.
139 N Griffith Blvd
Griffith, IN 46319
Contact: Susan Pappas President
Tel: 219-922-1848
Email: susan@dieselelectricalequipment.com
Website: www.dieselelectricalequipment.com
Dist & service diesel electric locomotive components. (Woman, estab 0, empl , sales $0, cert: WBENC)

2736 First Electric Supply
2225 N College Ave
Indianapolis, IN 46205
Contact: Tony Frost VP
Tel: 317-931-3675
Email: michaelb@firstelectricsupply.com
Website: www.firstelectricsupply.com
Dist electrical components: ballats, batteries, cable, fuses, generators. (Woman/AA, estab 2004, empl 35, sales $60,000,000, cert: State, City, NMSDC)

2737 UV Solutions, LLC
9118 Pinecreek Court
Indianapolis, IN 46256
Contact: Calvin Stewart CEO
Tel: 317-345-9899
Email: calvin@uvsolutions-indy.com
Website: www.uvsolutions-indy.com
UV germicidal equipment & LED lighting. (AA, estab 2007, empl 3, sales $350,000, cert: State)

Kansas

2738 AJ Smith Enterprise Inc
9320 Johnson Dr
Merriam, KS 66203
Contact: Leon Delmez
Tel: 913-677-3008
Email: leon.delmez@wattsuplighting.com
Website: www.wattsuplighting.com
Dist lighting supplies: light bulbs, ballasts, sockets, fixtures, capacitors, starters, lenses, emergency batteries & emergency ballasts, lighting fixtures, LED bulbs & LED tape. (Hisp, estab 1985, empl 7, sales $3,000,000, cert: NMSDC)

Kentucky

2739 Asia-Link, Inc.
12540 Westport Rd
Louisville, KY 40245
Contact: Andrew Lorenz Admin Mgr
Tel: 502-394-3900
Email: andrew.lorenz@asialnk.com
Website: www.asialnk.com
Data & communication, coaxial cables & connectors, communication connectors & kits, data/LAN cables, telephone cords, voice & data connectors, wire terminals, insulation displacement connectors, shrink tubing. (Woman, estab 1986, empl 18, sales $16,000,000, cert: WBENC)

2740 BFW Inc.
445 Baxter Ave, Ste 175
Louisville, KY 40204
Contact: Lynn Cooper President
Tel: 502-899-1808
Email: lynn@bfwinc.com
Website: www.bfwinc.com
High intensity LED portable and tethered headlights and light sources. (Woman, estab 1994, empl 5, sales $4,200,000, cert: WBENC)

Massachusetts

2741 C & D Electronics
28 Appleton St
Holyoke, MA 01040
Contact: Shelly Kubereit Acct Mgr
Tel: 413-493-1217
Email: skubereit@cdindustries.com
Website: www.cdindustries.com
Dist electronic parts & equipment. (Woman/AA, estab 1982, empl 18, sales $11,000,000, cert: NMSDC)

2742 Eastern States Components, LLC dba ES Components
108 Pratts Junction Rd
Sterling, MA 01564
Contact: Michelle Aubrey President
Tel: 978-422-7641
Email: maubrey@escomponents.com
Website: www.escomponents.com
Dist electronic components. (Woman, estab 1981, empl 20, sales , cert: WBENC)

2743 Integrated Control Solutions Inc.
28 Bridge Ave
Scituate, MA 02066
Contact: Tara Miller President
Tel: 781-545-5100
Email: icstara@comcast.net
Website: www.icsonline.net
Japanese, Korean, and Chinese MRO parts.
Omron, Fuji Electric, Mitsubishi, Idec Relays, motors, gear reducer, sensors, solenoids, breakers, switches, timers,counters (Woman, estab 1990, empl 3, sales $1,400,000, cert: WBENC)

2744 Port Electronics Corporation
60 Island St
Lawrence, MA 01840
Contact: Louise Elliott Exec VP
Tel: 603-894-6000
Email: LElliott@PortNH.com
Website: www.PortNH.com
Premier distributor and supply chain solutions supporting the Aerospace and Defense industries. (Minority, Woman, estab 1988, empl 10, sales $90,021,883, cert: NMSDC)

Maryland

2745 GreenerVolts
801 N East St Ste 9A
Frederick, MD 21701
Contact: Business Devel
Tel: 888-495-3629
Email:
Website: www.greenervolts.com
LED lighting, lighting controls, warehousing & fulfillment. (Hisp, estab 2010, empl 5, sales $1,800,000, cert: NMSDC)

2746 IVS Solutions, LLC
1040 West St
Laurel, MD 20707
Contact: Brian Smith President
Tel: 240-487-0295
Email: brian.smith@ivssolutions.net
Website: www.ivssolutions.net
IVS Solutions is a supplier diversity data management company that provides customized information technology solutions to manage and enrich supplier diversity data for corporations. Formed in 2011 to address industry needs of (AA, estab 2011, empl 2, sales , cert: NMSDC)

2747 MX4 Electronics, Inc.
2203 Greenspring Dr
Timonium, MD 21093
Contact: Susan Grill Owner
Tel: 410-252-1192
Email: susan@mx4elect.com
Website: www.mx4elect.com
Dist electronic components & accessories. (Woman, estab 1976, empl 3, sales $2,821,076, cert: State)

Michigan

2748 Arrow Motor & Pump Inc.
692 Central Ave
Wyandotte, MI 48192
Contact: Gloria Marquess Inside Sales
Tel: 734-285-5700
Email: sales@arrowmotor.net
Website: www.arrowmotor.net
Sales & repair electric motors, pumps & power transmission products, reducers, gearmotors, etc. (Woman, estab 1988, empl 14, sales $2,128,352, cert: WBENC)

2749 Bluecolt Lighting LLC
4403 Concourse Dr STE B
Ann Arbor, MI 48108
Contact: Jaspreet Sawhney
Tel: 734-864-5533
Email: service@falconinnovations.com
Website: www.bluecoltlighting.com
L.E.D. (Light Emitting Diode) lighting. (As-Ind, estab 2003, empl 9, sales $3,000,000, cert: NMSDC)

2750 Ebinger Manufacturing Company
7869 Kensington Ct
Brighton, MI 48116
Contact: Janny Lu President
Tel: 248-486-8880
Email: emc@ebinger-mfg.com
Website: www.ebinger-mfg.com
Dist electrical, plumbing, work gloves, HVAC & safety products. (Minority, Woman, estab 1974, empl 1, sales $0, cert: NMSDC)

2751 Empire Electric
3575 Vinewood
Detroit, MI 48208
Contact: Bob Pauline vp
Tel: 313-895-1920
Email: bob@empireec.com
Website: www.empirewc.com
Dist electrical, industrial & networking products & supplies. Also mfr wire harnesses & cable assemblies. (AA, estab 2003, empl 10, sales $1,005,000,000, cert: NMSDC)

2752   Industrial Control Service, Inc.
      9267 Riley St
      Zeeland, MI 49464
      Contact: Dale Venema VP
      Tel: 800-087-8672
      Email: dale@industrialcontrol.com
      Website: www.industrialcontrol.com
Dist controls: Cognex, DVT, Banner, Turck, Sunx, X-Rite, Spectrum Illumination,Nerlite, RFID, Microscan, Eaton Cutler-Hammer, Parker, Danaher, IAI, Panasonic, Hyde Park, Giddings & Lewis, Nachi, Encoder Products, GE Industrial. (Nat Ame, estab 1975, empl 10, sales $5,157,803, cert: NMSDC)

2753   Manufacturing & Automation Cost Solutions, LLC
      28795 Goddard Rd, Bldg 6, Ste 201
      Romulus, MI 48174
      Contact: Kenneth M President
      Tel: 248-321-2433
      Email: kgutierrez@macostsolutions.com
      Website: www.macostsolutions.com
Dist non-production maintenance spare parts in the Electrical and Mechanical sector to support machines, robots, automation and clean rooms. (Hisp, estab 2016, empl 2, sales $500,000, cert: NMSDC)

2754   Sawyer Services Inc.
      56851 Gratiot Ave
      Chesterfield, MI 48051
      Contact: Kim Sawyer Office Mgr
      Tel: 586-646-5181
      Email: electrical@sawyerservices.net
      Website: www.sawyer-services.com
Design, installation, management & maintenance of facility lighting, electrical & sign systems to achieve significant energy cost savings and more efficient facility operations. (Minority, Woman, estab 2009, empl 20, sales $3,000,000, cert: NMSDC, WBENC)

2755   Strike Group LLC
      18800 Fairway Dr, Ste 10
      Detroit, MI 48221
      Contact: Lane coleman President
      Tel: 313-586-0003
      Email: lanec@strikegroup.org
      Website: www.strikegroup.org
Dist electrical products. (AA, estab 1998, empl 3, sales $3,200,000, cert: NMSDC)

2756   York Electric Motors, Inc.
      611 Andre St
      Bay City, MI 48706
      Contact: Thomas Hunter Acct Mgr
      Tel: 989-684-7460
      Email: tomh@yorkelectric.com
      Website: www.yorkelectric.com
Dist & svc electric motors, generators, transformers, inverters, pumps, etc. (Nat Ame, estab 1971, empl 37, sales $0, cert: NMSDC)

Minnesota

2757   Carlo Lachmansingh Sales, Inc.
      4801 4th Ave S
      Minneapolis, MN 55419
      Contact: Carl Lachmansingh VP
      Tel: 612-827-2211
      Email: carlo@carloelectrical.com
      Website: www.carloelectrical.com
Dist electrical supplies. (As-Ind, estab 1990, empl 2, sales $2,800,000, cert: State, 8(a))

2758   JCB Enterprises, Inc. dba Reluminate
      1408 Northland Dr, Ste 105
      Mendota Heights, MN 55120
      Contact: Brigid Brady CEO
      Tel: 612-378-1677
      Email: brigid@reluminate.com
      Website: www.reluminate.com
Commercial lighting service, interior & exterior lighting. (Woman, estab 2014, empl 10, sales $1,450,000, cert: WBENC)

2759   Recycle Technologies, Inc.
      4000 Winnetka Ave North, Ste 210
      Minneapolis, MN 55427
      Contact: Lynn Petros CEO
      Tel: 763-559-5130
      Email: lynn@recycletechnologies.com
      Website: www.recycletechnologies.com
Recycle fluorescent bulbs, ballasts, batteries, electronics, computers, mercury containing devices, & special industrial waste. (Woman, estab 1993, empl 18, sales $2,010,000, cert: WBENC)

Missouri

2760   Butler Supply, Inc.
      965 Horan Dr
      Fenton, MO 63026
      Contact: Warren Baker Diversity Program Mgr
      Tel: 314-952-7564
      Email: wbaker@butlersupply.com
      Website: www.butlersupply.com
Dist electrical, plumbing and telecommunications products and services. (Woman, estab , empl , sales $105,000,000, cert: State, WBENC)

2761   Communications & Electrical Supplies, Inc.
      13288 Newt Dr
      Neosho, MO 64850
      Contact: Amanda Murphy Accounting Mgr
      Tel: 417-451-1789
      Email: amanda@ceslive.com
      Website: www.ceslive.com
Dist tools & electrical equipment. (Woman, estab 1990, empl 8, sales $3,000,000, cert: WBENC)

2762   Cooling Components Inc.
      69 N Gore Ave
      Saint Louis, MO 63119
      Contact: morgan brewster Dir of Sales
      Tel: 314-772-8311
      Email: morgan@coolingcomponents.com
      Website: www.ccicoolingtowerparts.com
Dist, service, repair & erect cooling towers & related equipment. (Woman, estab 2000, empl 10, sales $0, cert: WBENC)

2763   Electronic Supply Co, Inc.
      4100 Main St
      Kansas City, MO 64111
      Contact: Bob Niekamp Mgr
      Tel: 816-931-0250
      Email: bobn@eskc.com
      Website: www.eskc.com
Dist electronic parts, wire/cable, tools, test equipment, security cameras & systems, access control systems, computer networking equipment. (Woman, estab 1952, empl 33, sales $17,300,000, cert: City)

2764 US Electronics Inc.
      1590 Page Industrial Blvd
      Saint Louis, MO 63132
      Contact: Anil Arekapudi President
      Tel: 314-423-7550
      Email: anil@us-electronics.com
      Website: www.us-electronics.com
Dist electrical & electronic components. Mfr electrical
bulbs, Halogen, energy saving & LED bulbs. (As-Ind, estab
1995, empl 15, sales $2,200,000, cert: NMSDC)

North Carolina

2765 Tiger Controls Inc.
      7615 Business Park Dr
      Greensboro, NC 27409
      Contact: Neeta Singh President
      Tel: 336-889-6265
      Email: neeta@tigercontrols.com
      Website: www.tigercontrols.com
Dist electronic, electrical & industrial supplies. (Minority,
Woman, estab , empl , sales $9,005,000, cert: NMSDC)

2766 Video & Security Specialists
      2313 Wedgewood Dr
      Matthews, NC 28104
      Contact: Erika Gordon Partner
      Tel: 704-821-9396
      Email: egordon@carolina.rr.com
      Website: www.videoandsecurityspecialists.com
Dist electrical & security products: alarm/security systems,
fire alarm systems, structured wiring, access control,
security cameras, networking, phone system, etc.
(Woman, estab 1975, empl 7, sales $220,866, cert: State)

New Jersey

2767 Samson Electrical Supply Co Inc
      1764 New Durham Road
      South Plainfield, NJ 07080
      Contact: Joan Cohen President
      Tel: 732-393-7070
      Email: yourdiversesupplier@samsonelectrical.com
      Website: www.samsonelectrical.com
Dist electrical supplies. (Woman, estab 1949, empl 51,
sales $40,200,000, cert: State, City, WBENC)

2768 Weissco Power Limited Liability Company
      516 Route 513
      Califon, NJ 07830
      Contact: Stacy Weiss President
      Tel: 908-832-2173
      Email: sweiss@weisscopower.com
      Website: www.weisscopower.com
DIst uninterruptible power supply products & services,
preventative maintenance, emergency services, load
testing, battery installation & removal, equipment removal
& battery maintenance. (Woman, estab 1999, empl 10,
sales $2,700,000, cert: State, WBENC)

Nevada

2769 Codale Energy Services & Supply, LLC
      3920 W Sunset Rd, Ste A
      Las Vegas, NV 89118
      Contact: Oscar Aliaga President
      Tel: 702-384-8500
      Email: oscara@codaleess.com
      Website: www.codaleess.com
Dist electrical supplies: commercial construction, hospitality MRO, solar, comm data, Outside plant, & Utility. (Hisp,
estab 2010, empl 21, sales $21,500,000, cert: NMSDC)

New York

2770 Aurora Electric Inc.
      141 Federal Circle
      Jamaica, NY 11430
      Contact: Veronica Rose President
      Tel: 718-371-0385
      Email: vrose@auroraelectric.org
      Website: www.auroraelectric.org
Data communication & electrical installation & maintenance. (Woman, estab 1993, empl 17, sales $795,628,
cert: State, City)

2771 Deep Roof Lighting
      27 Hall St
      Brooklyn, NY 11205
      Contact: Jay Chen Exec
      Tel: 718-243-9388
      Email: deeproof@aol.com
      Website: www.deerooflighting.com
Software controlled patent daylight harvest dimming
control system. Dimmanble LED, Dimmable and Non-dim
Fluorescent, HID, Halogen Recess housings, Track
lighting, Pendant lights, Flush mount ceiling. (As-Pac,
estab 1997, empl 7, sales $2,000,000, cert: City)

2772 East Coast Metallic Tubing & Hardware Supply
      Corp
      1951 Ocean Ave, Unit 4
      Ronkonkoma, NY 11779
      Contact: Ehmann CEO
      Tel: 631-676-5570
      Email: eastcoastmthsc@aol.com
      Website: www.eastcoastmetallic.com/
Dist metallic & conduit hardware. (Woman, estab 2001,
empl 2, sales , cert: State)

2773 Edge Electronics Inc.
      75 Orville Dr.
      Bohemia, NY 11716
      Contact: Mitchel Auerbach VP Operations
      Tel: 631-471-3343
      Email: mauerbach@edgeelectronics.com
      Website: www.edgeelectronics.com
Dist electronics. (Woman, estab 1990, empl 34, sales
$33,009,000, cert: City, WBENC)

2774 Linrose Electronics Inc.
      29 Cain Dr
      Plainview, NY 11803
      Contact: Debra Freedman President
      Tel: 516-293-2520
      Email: debra@linrose.com
      Website: www.linrose.com
Dist CML - Led indicators. (Woman, estab 1964, empl 5,
sales $510,000, cert: WBENC)

2775 North Shore Components Inc.
      9 Sawgrass Dr
      Bellport, NY 11713
      Contact: David Hochhauser Acct Mgr
      Tel: 631-504-6038
      Email: davidh@nscomponents.com
      Website: www.nscomponents.com
Dist IC's, semiconductors, capacitors, connectors,
resistors, diodes, etc. (Woman, estab 2001, empl 22,
sales $0, cert: WBENC)

2776　Serendipity Electronics, Inc.
　　　152 E Main St
　　　Huntington, NY 11743
　　　Contact: Yovanna Camargo Acct Mgr
　　　Tel:　631-424-2244
　　　Email: yovannac@serendipityelectronics.com
　　　Website: www.serendipityelectronics.com
Dist electronic components; capacitors, resistors, diodes,
computer peripherals, active & passive components.
(Woman, estab 1992, empl 9, sales $19,000,000, cert:
WBENC)

2777　Southtown Electronics Inc.
　　　75 Lake St
　　　Hamburg, NY 14075
　　　Contact: Heather Sidorowicz Owner
　　　Tel:　716-648-6565
　　　Email: heather@southtownav.com
　　　Website: www.southtownav.com
Dist & install commercial Audio Video Technology Solu-
tions: Audio Video Systems, Digital Signage, Electronics
Sales (TVs, Speakers, Racking Equipment), Music Systems,
interactive Rooms & Conference rooms. (Woman, estab
1984, empl 6, sales , cert: State)

2778　Venus Power-Com Supply, LLC
　　　54-07 46th St
　　　Maspeth, NY 11378
　　　Contact: King President
　　　Tel:　646-248-7050
　　　Email: sheena@venussupply.com
　　　Website: www.venussupply.com/
Dist electrical, data & power products. (Woman, estab
2014, empl 5, sales , cert: City, WBENC)

Ohio

2779　Daycoa, Incorporated
　　　50 Walnut Rd
　　　Medway, OH 45341
　　　Contact: Tamela Chenault Sales Consultant
　　　Tel:　937-849-1315
　　　Email: tami@daycoa.com
　　　Website: www.daycoa.com
Dist lighting products. (Woman, estab 1957, empl 14, sales
$33,866,096, cert: WBENC)

2780　E-Z Electric Motor Service, Inc.
　　　8510 Bessemer Ave
　　　Cleveland, OH 44127
　　　Contact: Demetrius Ledgyard VP Sales
　　　Tel:　216-581-8820
　　　Email: demetrius@ezelectricmotor.com
　　　Website: www.ezelectricmotor.com
Dist & repair electric motors: complete rewinds, rebuild,
machine shop services, repair pumps, & gearboxes, dynamic
balancing. (AA, estab 1965, empl 16, sales , cert: State,
NMSDC)

2781　Mars Electric
　　　6655 Beta Dr, Ste 200
　　　Mayfield Village, OH 44143
　　　Contact: Michael Doris Exec VP
　　　Tel:　440-946-2250
　　　Email: mldoris@mars-electric.com
　　　Website: www.mars-electric.com
Electrical dist: lighting (fixtures and lamps), distribution
equipment, switches, conduit, wire, etc. (Woman, estab
1952, empl 160, sales $84,000,000, cert: City)

2782　Mirg Corporation
　　　6270 Este Ave
　　　Cincinnati, OH 45232
　　　Contact: Michael Griffie President
　　　Tel:　513-679-2020
　　　Email: mgriffie@mirgcorp.com
　　　Website: www.mirgcorp.com
Dist electrical supplies, electrical contracting. (AA, estab
1989, empl 9, sales $0, cert: State, NMSDC)

2783　Peak Electric, Inc.
　　　320 N Byrne Rd
　　　Toledo, OH 43607
　　　Contact: Milton McIntyre President
　　　Tel:　419-726-4848
　　　Email: mmcintyre@peakelectrictoledo.com
　　　Website: www.peakelectrictoledo.com
Dist lighting, LED indoor & outdoor, fixtures, lamps,
ballast & components, switchgear, transformers,
panelboards & disconnects, fuses, wire, conduits, fittings
& boxes, telecommunication equip, high voltage equip.
(Woman/AA, estab 2000, empl 3, sales $7,000,000, cert:
State, City, NMSDC)

2784　US Communications and Electric
　　　4933 Neo Pkwy
　　　Garfield Heights, OH 44128
　　　Contact: Jim Connole COO
　　　Tel:　216-478-0810
　　　Email: jconnole@uscande.com
　　　Website: www.uscande.com
Technology-based communications cabling systems,
design & install outdoor copper systems, horizontal
copper cabling solutions. (Woman, estab , empl , sales
$17,000,000, cert: State, City, WBENC)

2785　Wheatley Electric Service Co.
　　　2046 Ross Ave
　　　Cincinnati, OH 45212
　　　Contact: Dorothy Elsbrock President
　　　Tel:　513-531-4951
　　　Email: motor@fuse.net
　　　Website: www.wheatleyelectric.com
Dist & repair electric motors & pumps, recondition,
rebuild & re-design motors. (Woman, estab 1934, empl
9, sales $0, cert: WBENC)

Oklahoma

2786　Electro Enterprises, Inc.
　　　3601 N I-35 Service Road
　　　Oklahoma City, OK 73111
　　　Contact: Nathan Little Dir Global Sales
　　　Tel:　405-427-6591
　　　Email: nathan.little@electroenterprises.com
　　　Website: www.electroenterprises.com/
Dist interconnect, electro-mechanical, wire/cable and
harness management systems, connector assembly,
fiber optic cable assembly, kitting, marking, built to
print, military packaging and labeling. (Minority,
Woman, estab 1970, empl 227, sales $109,000,000, cert:
State)

Oregon

2787 Super Stores Service
11170 SW 5th St
Beaverton, OR 97005
Contact: Mary Kroger Acct Mgr
Tel: 800-462-2370
Email: maryk@superstoresservice.com
Website: www.superstoresservice.com
Dist replacement parts for manual & electric pallet jacks used to handle palletized goods. (Woman, estab 1986, empl 20, sales $4,200,000, cert: WBENC)

Pennsylvania

2788 Decision Distribution America, Inc.
4548 Market St, Ste 215
Philadelphia, PA 19139
Contact: Bernie Hopewell President
Tel: 215-493-4400
Email: bernie@ddistribution.com
Website: www.ddistribution.com
Dist electrical, hvac, mechanical, plumbing, supplies & equipment. (AA, As-Pac, estab 2004, empl 7, sales $14,000,000, cert: State, NMSDC)

2789 DEW Electric, Inc.
189 Enterprise Ln
Connellsville, PA 15425
Contact: Wendy Wiltrout CEO
Tel: 724-628-9711
Email: wendy@dewelectric.com
Website: www.dewelectric.com
Dust & repair motors, electronic drives, gearboxes, generators, control panel fabrication. (Woman, estab 1993, empl 4, sales $935,000, cert: WBENC)

2790 Electrical Systems & Construction Supplies
5131-37 N 2nd St, Bldg 12
Philadelphia, PA 19120
Contact: Bernard Hopewell CEO
Tel: 215-324-3291
Email: bhopewell@escsinc.net
Website: www.escsinc.net
Dist electrical equipment, construction supplies, wire & cable & lighting. (AA, estab 2003, empl 3, sales $1,440,000, cert: State, City)

2791 Habsco Inc.
12th St Bldg 240
New Kensington, PA 15068
Contact: George Hubbard CEO
Tel: 724-337-9498
Email: george@habscoinc.com
Website: www.habscoinc.com
Dist Westinghouse Reactor Coolant Pump (RCP) & motor replacement components. (AA, estab , empl , sales $1,000,000, cert: NMSDC)

2792 Manna Supply, Inc.
3015 Blackswift Rd
East Norriton, PA 19403
Contact: Elaine Prince President
Tel: 610-222-4775
Email: eprince@mannasupply.com
Website: www.mannasupply.com
Dist electrical & electronic equipment & supplies: data & communications, network integration, telecom & conferencing, mechanical & general construction. (Minority, Woman, estab 1993, empl 6, sales $9,000,548, cert: WBENC)

2793 R. Scheinert & Sons, Inc.
10092 Sandmeyer Ln
Philadelphia, PA 19116
Contact: Sheree Miller President
Tel: 215-673-9800
Email: sheree@scheinert.com
Website: www.scheinert.com
Repair, rewind & dist AC & DC electric motors, pump repair & refurbish, new cooling tower technology, eliminating gearboxes, warranty center. (Woman, estab , empl 24, sales $6,000,000, cert: City, WBENC)

2794 Valenko Incorporated
4124 Clendenning Rd
Gibsonia, PA 15044
Contact: Jim Perko VP
Tel: 888-908-6322
Email: info@valenko.com
Website: www.valenko.com
Dist electrical products: custom transformers, panels, wire, cable, power distribution equipment, hand tools, conduit, couplings, cable assemblies, cable management, UPS, data center. (Woman, estab 2007, empl 5, sales $4,013,000, cert: State)

Puerto Rico

2795 Wholesale Electric Caribe Inc.
PO Box 2057
Barceloneta, PR 00617
Contact: Miguel Barrios President
Tel: 787-846-5755
Email: sales@wecipr.com
Website: www.wecipr.com
Dist electronic products: automation & control products. (Hisp, estab 1999, empl 43, sales $7,331,560, cert: NMSDC)

South Carolina

2796 Carolina Product Solutions, LLC
PO Box 12901
Florence, SC 29504
Contact: Sean Tanner President
Tel: 843-409-6922
Email: stanner@cpsled.com
Website: www.cpsled.com
LED Lighting. (Nat Ame, estab 2008, empl 4, sales $2,800,000, cert: NMSDC)

2797 Electritex
321 Alliance Pkwy
Williamston, SC 29697
Contact: Tracie Craft President
Tel: 864-226-4438
Email: andersonoffice@electritex.com
Website: www.electritex.com
Dist & service electric motors. (Woman, estab 1980, empl 20, sales , cert: WBENC)

Tennessee

2798 Brighter Days & Nites, Inc.
2165 Troyer Aven
Memphis, TN 38114
Contact: Dorothy Sinclair CEO
Tel: - -
Email: csallie@bdnincorp.com
Website: www.bdnincorp.com
Dist electrical materials. (Woman/AA, estab 2003, empl 5, sales $13,000,000, cert: NMSDC, WBENC)

2799 Diversified Supply, Inc.
210 N Highland Park Ave
Chattanooga, TN 37404
Contact: Janice Brown Sales Marketing Mgr
Tel: 423-544-8964
Email: jbrown@diversifiedsupply.com
Website: www.diversifiedsupply.com
DIst electrical & instrument materials. (AA, estab 1987, empl 58, sales $0, cert: NMSDC)

2800 Edwards Supply Company
315 Oak Ridge Turnpike
Oak Ridge, TN 37830
Contact: Tracie Miller CEO
Tel: 865-483-1766
Email: tracie@edwardssupply.com
Website: www.edwardssupply.com
Dist electrical supplies: ballast, batteries, conduit, electric, electrical, janitorial, lamps, lighting, motors, tools, wire. (Minority, Woman, estab 1993, empl 23, sales $24,472,449, cert: NMSDC, WBENC)

Texas

2801 Advanced Equipment Co. dba Prime Distributing Co.
PO Box 946
Allen, TX 75013
Contact: Carole Booth Inside Sales
Tel: 972-562-0170
Email: caroleb@primedistributing.com
Website: www.primedistributing.com
Dist electronic components. (Woman, estab 1972, empl 8, sales $1,135,426, cert: WBENC)

2802 Arbor Electronics Inc.
4257 Arbor Creek Dr
Carrollton, TX 75010
Contact: Janice President
Tel: 972-939-7092
Email: janice@goarbor.com
Website: www.goarbor.com
Dist electronics. (Woman, estab 1999, empl 2, sales $850,000, cert: WBENC)

2803 BG Technologies of Austin, LLC
2301 Denton Dr, Ste A
Austin, TX 78758
Contact: Linda Gibson President
Tel: 512-336-2299
Email: linda@bg-technologies.com
Website: www.bg-technologies.com
Dist electronic components. (Woman, estab 2001, empl 6, sales $16,400,000, cert: State)

2804 Demand Lighting USA Inc
1321 Rutherford Lane Ste 150,
Austin, TX 78753
Contact: Gary Morrissey COO
Tel: 512-822-1100
Email: garymorrissey@demandlighting.com
Website: www.demandlighting.com
Dist DLC, Energy Star LED lighting solutions. (Woman, estab 2013, empl 15, sales $1,000,000, cert: State, WBENC, SDB)

2805 IDM Products
10500 Metric Dr, Ste 119
Dallas, TX 75243
Contact: Gerald Grimes President
Tel: 888-908-4580
Email: gerald@idmproducts.com
Website: www.idmproducts.com
Dist LED Lighting, Building Maintenance & Office Products, Industrial Products, Food Service Disposables and Healthcare Products. (AA, estab 2018, empl 4, sales $1,000,000, cert: NMSDC)

2806 Mavich LLC
525 Commerce St.
Southlake, TX 76092
Contact: Vincent Manfredini Operations
Tel: 682-503-4484
Email: vincent.manfredini@mavich.com
Website: www.mavich.com
Dist MRO & industrial supplies: electronic components, connectors, passives, resistors, etc. (Minority, Woman, estab 2010, empl 10, sales $3,000,000, cert: State)

2807 NOVA Electronic Materials LLC
1189 Porter Rd
Flower Mound, TX 75022
Contact: Lauri Boudreaux President
Tel: 972-478-7002
Email:
Website: www.novawafers.com
Dist silicon wafers & cleanroom consumables. (Woman, estab 1989, empl 5, sales $4,216,523, cert: State)

2808 Portable Power Systems Inc.
2890 Market Loop
Southlake, TX 76092
Contact: Jordan Hamill VP Sales
Tel: 303-460-8261
Email: sales@portablepower.com
Website: www.portablepower.com
Dist OEM battery and power products. (Woman/AA, Hisp, estab 1992, empl 13, sales $4,000,000, cert: State)

2809 Specialty Optical Systems, Inc.
10210 Forest Ln
Dallas, TX 75243
Contact: Terry Nelson
Tel: 214-340-8574
Email: sales@sossupply.com
Website: www.soslightbulbs.com
Dist lightbulbs: lamps & bulbs, ballasts & fixtures. (Woman, estab 1981, empl , sales $5,015,000, cert: WBENC)

2810 Supa Tech Inc.
17304 Preston Rd Ste 800
Dallas, TX 75252
Contact: Sue Glover President
Tel: 972-238-8958
Email: sglover@supatech.net
Website: www.supatech.net
Information technology products & printed circuit boards. (Woman, estab 1980, empl 3, sales $285,000, cert: State)

2811 Telecom Electric Supply Company
1304 Capital Ave
Plano, TX 75074
Contact: Christy Moses Sales Exec
Tel: 972-422-0012
Email: cmoses@tes85.com
Website: www.tes85.com
Dist electric, utility, construction & telecommunication supplies. (AA, estab , empl , sales $33,858,031, cert: State, NMSDC)

2812 Wholesale Electric Supply of Houston
4040 Gulf Fwy
Houston, TX 77004
Contact: Pam McKellop President
Tel: 713-749-8461
Email: khighland@wholesaleelectric.com
Website: www.wholesaleelectric.com
Dist electrical & data communications material. (Woman, estab 1949, empl 284, sales $0, cert: WBENC)

Virginia

2813 Bright Regards LLC
5837 Governors Hill Dr
Alexandria, VA 22310
Contact: Yvonne Herrera President
Tel: 703-349-1709
Email: yvonne@brightregards.com
Website: www.brightregards.com
Commercial LED, induction & solar lighting solutions. (Minority, Woman, estab 2014, empl 1, sales , cert: State)

2814 Delta Automation, Inc.
2704 Charles City Rd
Richmond, VA 23231
Contact: Margarete Culley CEO
Tel: 804-236-2800
Email: plc@deltaautomation.com
Website: www.deltaautomation.com
Industrial electronic control equipment, PLCs & drives. (Woman, estab 1996, empl 19, sales $0, cert: State)

2815 Jo Kell, Inc.
1716 Lambert Ct
Chesapeake, VA 23320
Contact: Patricia Galiney Sales
Tel: 904-260-8420
Email: customerservice@jokell.com
Website: WWW.JOKELL.COM
Dist electrical apparatus & equipment, wiring supplies & related equipment. (Woman, estab 1977, empl 50, sales $30,383,075, cert: WBENC)

2816 Old Dominion Electrical Supply Co Inc
2509 N Lombardy St
Richmond, VA 23220
Contact: Harold Parker President
Tel: 804-344-5440
Email: odessales@gmail.com
Website: www.olddominionelectricalsupply.com
Dist electrical supplies: batteries, light bulbs, specialty lighting, circuit breakers, panel boxes, ballast, fuses, light fixtures, etc. (AA, estab 1983, empl 5, sales $4,457,015, cert: State, City)

2817 Reynolds Lighting Supply Co.
606 Research Rd
Richmond, VA 23236
Contact: Valerie Reynolds President
Tel: 804-897-2300
Email: valarie@reynoldslighting.com
Website: www.reynoldslighting.com
Dist replacement light bulbs, ballasts, fixtures, electrical & electronic items. (Woman, estab 1987, empl 7, sales $2,250,000, cert: State)

Vermont

2818 Granite City Electric Supply
14 Morse Rd
Bennington, VT 05201
Contact: Phyllis Papani Godwin Chairman of the Board
Tel: 617-472-6500
Email: phyllisg@granitecityelectric.com
Website: www.granitecityelectric.com
Dist electrical products. (Woman/As-Ind, estab 1923, empl 70, sales $90,000,000, cert: State)

Washington

2819 1 Industrial Source
17627 E Lake Desire Dr SE
Renton, WA 98058
Contact: Tammie Cook Owner
Tel: 206-354-4295
Email: tammiecook@1industrialsource.com
Website: www.1industrialsource.com
Supplier of LED lighting, hand dryers and other products used in electrical upgrades. (Woman, estab 2009, empl 1, sales , cert: State)

2820 Mobile Electrical Distributors, Inc.
14050 Lake City Way NE
Seattle, WA 98125
Contact: Sales
Tel: 206-363-2400
Email:
Website: www.mobileelec.com
Dist electrical supplies: ballasts, boxes, conduit & fittings, lighting, service gear, tools, testers, wire, wiring devices, motor controls, fuses, etc. (Woman, estab 1956, empl 11, sales $925,000, cert: State, WBENC)

Wisconsin

2821 First American Engineered Solutions, LLC
136 Jackson St, Ste C
Oshkosh, WI 54901
Contact: Gerald Morris President
Tel: 920-231-8501
Email: gmorris@firstamericanllc.com
Website: www.firstamericanllc.com
Dist electronics, electrical equipment, industrial equipment & supplies, office equipment & supplies & ordnance. (Nat Ame, estab 1997, empl 12, sales $4,500,000, cert: NMSDC, 8(a))

ELECTRONICS & ELECTRICAL MFG.

Firms design, develop and make (turnkey) electro-mechanical devices on contract or market their own products such as power supplies, test equipment, guidance systems, robotics, radar, CMOS-IC, connectors, modems, military trainers, motors, etc. NAICS Code 33

Alabama

2822 Amphenol Tecvox, LLC.
4900 Bradford Dr Ste 1
Huntsville, AL 35805
Contact: Ryan Brown Financial Analyst
Tel: 256-417-4338
Email: ryan.brown@tecvox.com
Website: www.tecvox.com
Mfr finish electronic components, single, dual & multi channel headphones & remote contols, plastic & rubber products, metal stamping & cable assemblies. (Minority, estab 2002, empl 50, sales $3,300,000, cert: NMSDC)

2823 Global Manufacturing, Inc.
248 N Main St
Arab, AL 35016
Contact: Kathy Bennefield Mgr
Tel: 256-789-0948
Email: kathy@globalmanufacturing.us
Website: www.globalmanufacturing.us
Custom fabricated wire harnesses & cables, Data cables, MIL-SPEC, Coaxial, Power assemblies. (Hisp, estab 2014, empl 17, sales $1,824,260, cert: NMSDC)

Arizona

2824 Transtek Magnetics Inc.
1900 W Grant Rd
Tucson, AZ 85745
Contact: Mary Yanez Office Mgr
Tel: 520-792-4415
Email: mary@ttkm.co
Website: www.transtekmagnetics.com
Mfr & dist electronic components, custom magnetic coils, TableTop PowerStation, A/C, USB & wireless charging power to laptops, cell phones. (As-Pac, estab 1999, empl 1400, sales $30,000,000, cert: NMSDC)

California

2825 American Industrial Control, Inc.
170 N Maple St Ste 104
Corona, CA 92880
Contact: Monica Pratt President
Tel: 951-520-0613
Email: monica@aicesupply.com
Website: www.aicesupply.com
Dist electrical supplies, mfr industrial control panels. (Minority, Woman, estab 2000, empl 4, sales $1,010,254, cert: NMSDC, CPUC, WBENC)

2826 Berkeley Integration Group dba Fiber.com
2200 Powell St, Ste 1200
Emeryville, CA 94608
Contact: Sophia Mendoza-Hirano Account/Sales Mgr
Tel: 510-227-5583
Email: sophia@fiber.com
Website: www.fiber.com
Fiber optic cables, connectors and accessories, fiber jumpers, patch cords, pigtails, multi-strand, armored, aerial, indoor/outdoor, plenum, LSZH. (As-Pac, estab 1989, empl 4, sales , cert: NMSDC)

2827 Calpak USA, Inc.
13750 Prairie Ave
Hawthorne, CA 90250
Contact: Danish Qureshi VP
Tel: 310-937-7335
Email: danish@calpak-usa.com
Website: www.calpak-usa.com
Electronic Design, Electronics Engineering, Contract Manufacturing Services (CMS), Electronic Manufacturing Services (EMS), PCB Layout, PCB Design, PCB Assembly. (As-Pac, estab 1978, empl 15, sales $2,400,000, cert: State, NMSDC, SDB)

2828 Century Wire & Cable
7400 E Slauson Ave
Commerce, CA 90040
Contact: Bob Arthur Acct Exec
Tel: 800-999-5566
Email: arthur@centurywire.com
Website: www.centurywire.com
Mfr electrical wire & cable products. (Hisp, estab 1965, empl 110, sales $40,000,000, cert: City)

2829 Doc Stephens Scientific
5851 S Garth Ave
Los Angeles, CA 90056
Contact: David Stephens CEO
Tel: 310-568-9082
Email: david.stephens@dsscientific.com
Website: www.dsscientific.com
Equipment & electronic manufacturing services related to infrared, visual cameras & imaging systems, RF & high speed fiber optic telecommunication circuits, sensor designs, silicon III-V semiconductor processing. (AA, estab 2014, empl 2, sales , cert: NMSDC)

2830 Evolve Manufacturing Technologies Inc
47300 Bayside Pkwy
Fremont, CA 94538
Contact: Acct Analyst
Tel: 510-690-8959
Email: services@evolvemfg.com
Website: www.evolvemfg.com
Contract manufacturer: assembly, precision & electro-mechanical products, component sourcing, turnkey supply chain management, prototyping, production, testing, product configuration. (Woman, estab 1998, empl 70, sales $20,000,000, cert: WBENC)

2831 Frontier Electronics
667 E Cochran St
Simi Valley, CA 93065
Contact: Jeannie Gu President
Tel: 805-522-9998
Email: jeannie@frontierusa.com
Website: www.frontierusa.com
Mfr electric coil, transformers & inductors. (Minority, Woman, estab 1985, empl 25, sales $5,400,000, cert: WBENC)

2832 Johnson-Peltier Electric
12021 S Shoemaker Ave
Santa Fe Springs, CA 90670
Contact: Greg Kelley Business Devel
Tel: 562-944-3408
Email: gkelley@johnson-peltier.com
Website: www.johnson-peltier.com
Industrial electrical contracting, including power distribution, medium & high voltage line work, control systems, instrumentation, and communication integration. (Nat Ame, estab 1957, empl 85, sales , cert: NMSDC, CPUC)

2833 KR Wolfe, Inc.
10015 Maine Ave
Lakeside, CA 92040
Contact: Kasey Pitchford Dir of Client Relations
Tel: 619-368-1544
Email: kasey.pitchford@krwolfe.com
Website: www.krwolfe.com
Low voltage systems installation & integration, design, layout & installation/integration of A/V & control systems. (Woman, estab 2007, empl 34, sales $5,500,000, cert: WBENC)

2834 Ledtronics, Inc.
23105 Kashiwa Court
Torrance, CA 90505
Contact: Janelle Mika-Palmer Manufacturer Rep
Tel: 630-243-0412
Email: janemika@mikasales.com
Website: www.ledtronics.com
Design & mfr light emitting diodes (LEDs). (Minority, estab 1983, empl 125, sales $12,470,700, cert: NMSDC, CPUC)

2835 Magnuson Products LLC
1990 Knoll Dr Bldg A
Ventura, CA 93003
Contact: Nader Rayes Brand Mgr
Tel: 805-765-5562
Email: nader.rayes@magnusonproducts.com
Website: www.magnusonsuperchargers.com
Design, fabrication & mfr superchargers. (Woman, estab 2010, empl 60, sales $14,649,000, cert: WBENC)

2836 Micro Analog Inc.
1861 Puddingstone Dr
La Verne, CA 91750
Contact: Kim Bickmeier Dir of Sales
Tel: 909-392-8277
Email: kimbickmeier@micro-analog.com
Website: www.micro-analog.com
Mfr electronics: printed circuit board assembly PCBA, custom cable & wire harness assembly, box/system build. (Minority, Woman, estab 1991, empl 155, sales $15,698,000, cert: NMSDC)

2837 Myers Power Products, Inc.
2950 E Philadelphia St
Ontario, CA 91761
Contact: Diana Grootonk CEO
Tel: 909-923-1800
Email: diana.grootonk@myerspower.com
Website: www.myerspower.com
Mfr low voltage & med voltage electrical distribution equipment, 5,15,27 & 38kv switchgear, LV switchgear, switchboards, panel boards, inverters, converters & electrical products & circuit breakers. (Woman, estab 2001, empl 500, sales $263,101,084, cert: CPUC, WBENC)

2838 NexEco Energy Conservation, Inc.
9370 Studio Court, Ste 168
Elk Grove, CA 95758
Contact: Nick Potter Acct Mgr
Tel: 855-711-6868
Email: nick@nexeco.net
Website: www.nexeco.net
Mfr energy efficient LED lighting products, LED Bulbs, LED Fixtures, LED Hardwired Interior Ceiling Fixture, LED Hardwired Exterior Porch lanterns, LED Hardwired Vanity Fixture. (Minority, Woman, estab 2016, empl 5, sales $800,000, cert: State)

2839 One-E-Way, Inc.
3016 E Colorado Blvd Ste 70848
Pasadena, CA 91107
Contact: Cedric Woolfork CFO/VP
Tel: 310-743-4081
Email: cedric@one-e-way.com
Website: www.wayvz.com/
Design & mgr electronic products. (AA, estab 2004, empl 5, sales , cert: NMSDC)

2840 Philatron Wire and Cable
15315 Cornet Ave
Santa Fe Springs, CA 90670
Contact: Phillip Ramos III GM
Tel: 562-802-2570
Email: p3@philatron.com
Website: www.philatron.com
Design & mfr electrical, electronic, instrumentation, control & communication wire & cable. (Hisp, estab 1974, empl 85, sales $24,000,000, cert: NMSDC)

2841 Pro-Lite
3505 Cadillac Ave, Bldg D
Costa Mesa, CA 92626
Contact: Andy Kaoh President
Tel: 714-668-9988
Email: ak@pro-lite.com
Website: www.pro-lite.com
Mfr LED signs & LED displays. (As-Pac, estab 1981, empl 400, sales , cert: CPUC)

2842 Solartech Power, Inc.
901 E Cedar St
Ontario, CA 91761
Contact: Sherry Fu Owner
Tel: 714-630-8880
Email: sherry.fu@solartechpower.com
Website: www.solartechpower.com
Mfr solar photovoltaic panels & equipment. (Minority, Woman, estab 2001, empl 10, sales $3,000,000, cert: CPUC)

2843 Steren Electronics International, LLC
      6260 Sequence Dr Ste 110
      San Diego, CA 92121
      Contact: E'Lisa Jones Dir Business Devel
      Tel: 800-266-3333
      Email: elisa@steren.com
      Website: www.sterenusa.com
Mfr voice, video & data connectivity solutions. (Hisp, estab
1978, empl 100, sales $56,000,000, cert: CPUC)

2844 Unicorp, Inc.
      5780 Smithway St
      Commerce, CA 90040
      Contact: VP Business Dev
      Tel: 323-890-9246
      Email: customerservice@uninex.com
      Website: www.uninex.com
LED lighting technology, Indoor & Outdoor Electric Lighting
Fixtures, Residential Electrical Lighting Fixture, Commer-
cial, Industrial, Institutional Electrical Lighting Fixture,
Other Lighting Equipment. (As-Pac, estab 1989, empl 14,
sales , cert: State, CPUC)

Colorado

2845 Colorado Lighting, Inc.
      1831 E 73rd Ave
      Denver, CO 80229
      Contact: Christy Kidwell Cont/Sales Support Admin
      Tel: 303-288-3152
      Email: quotes@cli-services.com
      Website: www.coloradolighting.com
Electrical, Lighting, Sign Work, Fire Alarms, Energy Analysis, and Emergency Lighting service for commercial and
retail facilities. (Woman, estab 1977, empl 70, sales
$17,950,000, cert: WBENC)

2846 Premier Manufactuirng and Supply Chain Services
      7755 Miller Dr
      Frederick, CO 80504
      Contact: Edmond Johnson President
      Tel: 303-776-4145
      Email: ejohnson@pmscs.com
      Website: www.pmscs.com
Contract mfr of printed circuit board assemblies for
prototypes, production, sub assemblies, cable harness &
test. (AA, estab 2000, empl 55, sales $12,000,000, cert:
NMSDC)

2847 Quality Concepts Manufacturing Inc.
      1635 S Murray Blvd
      Colorado Springs, CO 80911
      Contact: Robert Millemon Program Mgr
      Tel: 719-574-1013
      Email: robert@qcmi.com
      Website: www.qcmi.com
Electronic Manufacturing Services, Quick-turn prototyping,
pre-production & full production support services,
mechanical assembly. (Woman, estab 1988, empl 30, sales
, cert: City)

Connecticut

2848 ICDI Inc.
      407 Brookside Rd
      Waterbury, CT 06708
      Contact: Steve Villodas President
      Tel: 203-753-8551
      Email: svillodas@icdi-inc.com
      Website: www.icdi-inc.com
Contract mfr electronic high tech equip & systems,
turnkey program mgmt, eng design, microprocessor
systems, PC layout, PC board & automated surface-
mount assembly, wave soldering, vapor degreasing,
custom cables, ATE testing. (Hisp, estab 1975, empl 22,
sales $3,019,307, cert: NMSDC)

Florida

2849 123GermFree, LLC dba TrackedMobility
      4537 Prime Terr
      North Port, FL 34286
      Contact: Cordell Jeter President
      Tel: 888-976-2525
      Email: cjeter@trackedmobility.us
      Website: www.compositemotors.com
Design & mfr electrical motors & controllers. (AA, estab
2010, empl 1, sales , cert: State, NMSDC)

2850 CableNetwork Associates Inc.
      4800 N Federal Hwy, Ste E300
      Boca Raton, FL 33431
      Contact: Marcela Gutierrez
      Tel: 954-312-1200
      Email: mgutierrez@cablenetwork.net
      Website: www.cablenetwork.net
Mfr coax cable, drop & trunk cable. (Hisp, estab 1997,
empl 300, sales $2,284,358,226, cert: NMSDC)

2851 ElectraLED, Inc.
      12722 62nd St N Ste 200
      Largo, FL 33773
      Contact: Ryan Begin Marketing Mgr
      Tel: 727-561-7610
      Email: ryan.begin@electraled.com
      Website: www.electraled.com
Mfr & dist LED light fixtures. (Woman, estab 2002, empl
18, sales , cert: WBENC)

2852 LedZed International Inc.
      2240 Palm Beach Lakes Blvd
      West Palm Beach, FL 33409
      Contact: Helena Lahtinen CEO
      Tel: 954-629-0768
      Email: helena@ledzed.com
      Website: www.ledzed.com
Mfr & dist energy efficiency led lights. (Woman, estab
2011, empl 1, sales , cert: City)

2853 Mainstream IP Solutions, Inc.
      6905 El Dorado Dr
      Tampa, FL 33615
      Contact: Arnie Solomon Acct Mgr
      Tel: 813-549-7768
      Email: asolomon@mcsoftampa.com
      Website: www.mainstreamipsolutions.com
Electrical, structured cabling, audio-visual, security &
fire alarm systems. (AA, estab 2010, empl 5, sales
$250,000, cert: State, NMSDC, 8(a), SDB)

2854 PowerLogics, Inc.
1115 Marbella Plaza Dr
Tampa, FL 33619
Contact: Barbara Smith Sales Assoc
Tel: 813-645-2971
Email: barbarasmith@powerlogics.com
Website: www.powerlogics.com
Transient voltage surge suppression, uninterruptible power systems, power conditioning equip, battery replacements, generators, automatic transfer switches, AC & DC invertors. (Woman, estab 1981, empl 6, sales $4,000,000, cert: State)

Georgia

2855 Georgia Green Energy Services
335 Wilma Ct SW
Atlanta, GA 30331
Contact: Gavin Ireland CEO
Tel: 404-334-3323
Email: gireland@gagreenenergysvc.com
Website: www.gagreenenergysvc.com
Light retrofitting, LED lighting, occupancy sensors, solar power systems, alternative & renewable energy systems, Energy auditing & reduction reports, energy audits. (AA, estab 2007, empl 1, sales $1,099,000, cert: NMSDC, 8(a))

2856 Roytec Industries LLC
306 Bell Park Dr
Woodstock, GA 30188
Contact: Amanda Chapman CEO
Tel: 770-926-5470
Email: mchapman@roytecind.com
Website: www.roytecind.com
Mfr electrical wire harnesses & electrical wire assemblies. (Woman, estab 1984, empl 500, sales $36,734,238, cert: WBENC)

2857 Southern States, LLC
30 Georgia Ave
Hampton, GA 30228
Contact: Amit Modi Sr Reg Mgr
Tel: 770-946-4562
Email: a.modi@southernstatesllc.com
Website: www.southernstatesllc.com
Mfr high voltage electrical airbreak switchgear, power fuses, circuit switchers & capacitor bank switching devices. (As-Ind, estab , empl 300, sales , cert: NMSDC)

Illinois

2858 AC Gentrol, Inc.
100 S Fourth St
Chillicothe, IL 61523
Contact: Allan Capati President
Tel: 309-274-5486
Email: acapati@acgentrol.com
Website: www.acgentrol.com
Mfr specialized electrical controls systems. (Minority, Woman, estab , empl , sales $1,100,000, cert: State)

2859 Capsonic Group, LLC
460 S Second St Slot B-8
Elgin, IL 60123
Contact: George Albrecht Reg Sales Mgr
Tel: 847-888-7242
Email: georgea@capsonic.com
Website: www.capsonicgroup.com
Insert & composite molding: product design, prototype, automation. (AA, estab 1968, empl 225, sales , cert: NMSDC)

2860 CEC Industries Ltd.
599 Bond St
Lincolnshire, IL 60069
Contact: Michelle Draper
Tel: 847-599-6132
Email: michelle@cecindustries.com
Website: www.ceclighting.com
Mfr miniature halogen lamps, LED lamps, electronic turn signal flashers. (Minority, estab 1979, empl 66, sales , cert: NMSDC)

2861 KLI Inc.
304 Roma Jean Pkwy
Streamwood, IL 60107
Contact: Lisa Carso President
Tel: 630-213-1283
Email: support@kli-inc.com
Website: www.kli-inc.com
Mfr electronic components; electronic assembly; main harness & cable to mil specs. (Minority, Woman, estab 1987, empl 15, sales , cert: State, NMSDC)

2862 PowerVolt Inc. (DBA Ensign Corporation)
300 W Factory Rd
Addison, IL 60101
Contact: Ajay Sharma VP Sales & Mktg
Tel: 630-628-9999
Email: ajays@powervolt.com
Website: www.ensigncorp.com
Mfr power transformers & DC power supplies. (As-Ind, estab 1986, empl 39, sales $3,330,000, cert: NMSDC)

2863 Tempco Electric Heater Corp.
607 N Central Ave
Wood Dale, IL 60191
Contact: William Kilberry CFO
Tel: 630-350-2252
Email: williamkilberry@tempco.com
Website: www.tempco.com
Mfr thermal component products: electric heating elements, temperature controls, temperature sensors & turnkey process heating systems. (Hisp, estab 1972, empl 330, sales $28,500,000, cert: NMSDC)

2864 WarmlyYours.com Inc.
590 Telser Rd, Ste B
Lake Zurich, IL 60047
Contact: Julia BIllen President
Tel: 800-875-5285
Email: jbillen@warmlyyours.com
Website: www.WarmlyYours.com
Manufacturer Electric Radiant Floor Heating Systems. (Woman, estab 1999, empl 28, sales $14,441,282, cert: WBENC)

Indiana

2865 ATEC Electrical Contractors
419 Ransdell Rd
Lebanon, IN 46052
Contact: C. Shane Conner President
Tel: 765-482-8926
Email: s.conner@atec-electric.com
Website: www.atec-electric.com
Electrical and telecommunications sales, service and support, engineering, project management and sustainable energy consulting and installation. (Hisp, estab 2005, empl 25, sales $5,547,137, cert: NMSDC)

2866   Carson Manufacturing Company, Inc.
5451 N Rural St
Indianapolis, IN 46220
Contact: Barbara Ferguson President
Tel: 317-257-3191
Email: receptionist@carson-mfg.com
Website: www.carson-mfg.com
Contract mfg electromechanical assemblies & equipment, mfr emergency vehicle sirens, rotary switches & voting machines. Prototyping, testing, quick turns, stocking programs & turn-key capabilities. (Woman, estab 1946, empl 20, sales $2,500,000, cert: State, City)

2867   Continental Manufacturing, LLC
1524 Jackson St
Anderson, IN 46016
Contact: Chris Petty Natl Sales Mgr
Tel: 765-298-8030
Email: cpetty@solasray.com
Website: www.solasray.com
Mfr, design, engineer & test LED technology lighting solutions for commercial, industrial & educational applications. (Woman, estab 2007, empl 10, sales $900,000, cert: State, WBENC)

2868   Electric Motors and Specialties, Inc.
701 W King St
Garrett, IN 46738
Contact: Rick Moore President
Tel: 847-559-6132
Email: rmoore@emsmotors.com
Website: www.emsmotors.com
Design, mfg & application of shaded pole, PSC & electronically commutated unit bearing motors. (Woman, estab 1946, empl 200, sales , cert: WBENC)

Kansas

2869   Global Control Systems, Inc.
11605 S Alden St
Olathe, KS 66062
Contact: Manual David President
Tel: 913-681-9261
Email: sales@gcsks.com
Website: www.webcontrolsystems.com
Systems integration, configuration & programming SCADA system & industrial networks, intelligent batch mgmt systems, process equipment, packaging systems, robotics systems, vision systems, material handling controls. (Hisp, estab 2000, empl 8, sales $1,027,400, cert: City, NMSDC)

Kentucky

2870   Dollar Aisle, LLC
165 Woods Dr
Brandenburg, KY 40108
Contact: rahul anand President
Tel: 502-303-4518
Email: dollaraisle@gmail.com
Website: www.wenlighting.com
Mfr led tube lights, wall packs, hig bays, led light bulbs etc. (As-Pac, estab 2011, empl 3, sales $650,000, cert: NMSDC)

Massachusetts

2871   Adcotron EMS
12 Channel St
Boston, MA 02210
Contact: Don MacNeil Business Devel Sales Rep
Tel: 617-598-3000
Email: donimac@comcast.net
Website: www.adcotron.com
Electronic mfg service, printed circuit board assembly, system integration, system assembly. (Minority, Woman, estab 1977, empl 100, sales $30,200,000, cert: State)

2872   International Coil, Inc.
15 Jonathan Dr Unit 1
Brockton, MA 02301
Contact: George Machadinho President
Tel: 508-580-8515
Email: gmachadinho@internationalcoil.com
Website: www.internationalcoil.com
Mfr Transformers (wire wound products) & Power Supplies. (AA, estab 1995, empl 12, sales $1,000,000, cert: State)

Maryland

2873   Armacost Lighting LLC
140 Baltic Ave
Baltimore, MD 21225
Contact: Terry Armacost President
Tel: 410-354-6000
Email: tarmacost@armacostlighting.com
Website: www.armacostlighting.com
Architectural quality LED lighting fixtures, LED tape lighting is ultra-thin, flexible, fully dimmable, can be cut to size or multiple strips. (Woman, estab 2009, empl 10, sales $3,700,000, cert: WBENC, NWBOC)

2874   JEM Engineering, LLC
8683 Cherry Ln
Laurel, MD 20707
Contact: Nancy Lilly CEO
Tel: 301-317-1070
Email: nlilly@jemengineering.com
Website: www.jemengineering.com
Design & prototype military & commercial antennas: HF to millimeter-wave, microstrip patch antennas & arrays, wire, aperture, broadband, active & low-observable antennas. (Minority, Woman, estab 2001, empl 30, sales , cert: State)

Michigan

2875   AG Manufacturing Inc.
319 Industrial Pkwy
Harbor Beach, MI 48441
Contact: Marlo Klaus Customer Service
Tel: 989-479-9590
Email: mklaus@agmanufacturing.com
Website: www.agmanufacturing.com
Mfr wire harnesses. (AA, estab 2004, empl 101, sales , cert: NMSDC)

2876 Amtech Electrocircuits, Inc.
701 Minnesota Dr
Troy, MI 48083
Contact: Jay Patel President
Tel: 248-583-1801
Email: jrp@amelectro.com
Website: www.amelectro.com
Electronic manufacturing services, contract manufacturer, printed circuit boards, wire harnesses & electronic assemblies. (As-Ind, estab 1997, empl 10, sales $800,000, cert: NMSDC)

2877 Eisen Electric Corporation
3340 Pinetree Rd
Lansing, MI 48911
Contact: Lokesh Kumar GM
Tel: 517-393-5850
Email: lkumar@eisennet.com
Website: www.eisennet.com
Mfr terminal screws, electrical fasteners & springs. (As-Ind, estab 1994, empl 72, sales $4,200,000, cert: NMSDC)

2878 Empire Electric
3575 Vinewood
Detroit, MI 48208
Contact: Bob Pauline vp
Tel: 313-895-1920
Email: bob@empireec.com
Website: www.empirewc.com
Dist electrical, industrial & networking products & supplies. Also mfr wire harnesses & cable assemblies. (AA, estab 2003, empl 10, sales $1,005,000,000, cert: NMSDC)

2879 Excel Electrocircuit Inc.
50 Northpointe Dr
Orion, MI 48359
Contact: Nipur Shah President
Tel: 248-373-0700
Email: sales@excelcircuits.com
Website: www.excelelectro.com
Mfr printed circuit boards. (As-Ind, estab 1970, empl 25, sales , cert: NMSDC)

2880 Hart Precision Products, Inc.
12700 Marion
Redford, MI 48239
Contact: Darlene Hart President
Tel: 313-537-0490
Email: d.hart@hart-precision.com
Website: www.Hart-Precision.com
Mfr precision components & assemblies for the Transportation Industry. (Woman, estab 1953, empl 48, sales $5,100,000, cert: WBENC)

2881 Hybrid Design Services
2479 Elliott Dr
Troy, MI 48083
Contact: James Pinon President
Tel: 248-298-3400
Email: jpinon@hybriddesignservices.com
Website: www.hybriddesignservices.com
Engineering, design, prototyping, testing services specializing in hybrid vehicles & systems, electric vehicles & systems, HEV systems, EV systems, hybrid and electric vehicle R&D, high voltage systems, energy storage. (Hisp, estab 2007, empl 20, sales $2,000,000, cert: NMSDC)

2882 Industrial Control Repair - ICR Services
28601 Lorna Ave
Warren, MI 48092
Contact: Marlies Davis Business Devel
Tel: 586-582-1500
Email: mdavis@icrservices.com
Website: www.icrservices.com
Dist & repair industrial electronics: robots, PLCs drives, welders, encoders, temperature controls, displays, monitors, power sources, etc. (Hisp, estab 1992, empl 155, sales $80,000,000, cert: NMSDC)

2883 JA Quality Assurance Group, LLC
537 Bradford
pontiac, MI 48341
Contact: Julio Rodriguez CEO
Tel: 248-506-3316
Email: jrodriguez@jaqualityassurance.com
Website: www.jaqualityassurance.com
Mfr prototype harnesses. (Hisp, estab 2002, empl 469, sales $7,850,000, cert: NMSDC)

2884 JMC Electrical Contractor, LLC dba JMC Technologies
33651 Giftos
Clinton Township, MI 48035
Contact: Bob Locklear VP Technologies
Tel: 586-773-8026
Email: blocklear@jmcelectricllc.com
Website: www.jmcelectricllc.com
Electrical service, installation, Structured Cable, Fiber Optic Cable, Voice, Data, Security, CCTV, Intrusion Detection, Access Control, Audio/Visual, CATV, Wireless, Wi-Fi, DAS & Building Automation Systems installation. (Woman, estab 2010, empl 45, sales $6,000,000, cert: WBENC)

2885 Johnico LLC
400 Monroe St Ste 480
Detroit, MI 48226
Contact: john economy Managing Partner
Tel: 248-895-7820
Email: johneconomy@yahoo.com
Website: www.americasgreenline.com
Commercial & industrial LED manufacturer. (Woman, estab 2011, empl 10, sales $3,500,000, cert: WBENC)

2886 Lotus International Company
6880 Commerce Blvd
Canton, MI 48187
Contact: Darren Ivey Dir Sales/Marketing
Tel: 734-245-0140
Email: divey@licus.com
Website: www.licus.com
Electrical & electro-mechanical contract mfg, wire harness, navigation CRT & LCD displays, aluminum & zinc die cast, electronics repair. (As-Ind, estab 1991, empl 200, sales $50,000,000, cert: NMSDC)

2887 Myron Zucker, Inc.
36825 Metro Ct
Sterling Heights, MI 48312
Contact: Mary Anderson Buyer
Tel: 586-979-9955
Email: dzobel@myronzucker.com
Website: www.myronzucker.com
Engineer & mfr low-voltage power products: power factor correction capacitors, harmonic filters & surge suppressors. (Woman, estab 1967, empl 10, sales $1,050,000, cert: WBENC)

2888   Newtech 3, Inc.
28373 Beck Rd Ste H7
Wixom, MI 48393
Contact: Gail Gyenese Dir of Sales
Tel: 248-912-1062
Email: ggyenese@newtech3inc.com
Website: www.newtech3.com
Mfr lower to mid volume wire harness & circuit board assemblies. (AA, estab 2009, empl 32, sales $3,965,000, cert: NMSDC)

2889   Orri Corporation
5385 Perry Dr
waterford, MI 48329
Contact: Angelo Doa Sales
Tel: 248-618-1104
Email: Sales@orricorp.com
Website: www.orricorp.com
Wire harnesses, cable assemblies, electrical test fixtures, robotic vision guidance software. (Woman, estab 2001, empl 12, sales , cert: WBENC)

Minnesota

2890   Electro Mechanical Industries (EMI)
13300 6th Ave N
Plymouth, MN 23606
Contact: Holly Hicks Sales/Mktg
Tel: 763-546-5998
Email: hhicks@e-m-i.com
Website: www.e-m-i.com
Low voltage switchgear, metal clad & metal enclosed medium voltage switchgear, paralleling switchgear, control panels, special wire ways, wall & floor ducts, pull boxes & sound-attenuated generator enclosures. (Woman, estab 1981, empl 36, sales $8,522,000, cert: WBENC)

2891   Telamco, Inc.
636 Industrial Dr SE
Lonsdale, MN 55046
Contact: Tracy Humann President
Tel: 507-744-5504
Email: tracy@telamcoinc.com
Website: www.telamcoinc.com
Mfr custom heat sealed membrane switches & quality assemblies. (Woman, estab 1968, empl 11, sales $1,500,000, cert: NWBOC)

Missouri

2892   Staco Electric Construction Co
11030 Hickman Mills Dr
Kansas City, MO 64134
Contact: Kristen Bilyeu Admin Asst
Tel: 1515-707-3513
Email: kbilyeu@stacoelectric.com
Website: www.stacoelectric.com
Commercial Electrical Contracting, Data centers, Manufacturing, Maintenance, Voice/Data services, Design/Build. (Woman, estab 1971, empl 120, sales $27,532,139, cert: NWBOC)

North Carolina

2893   Adams Electric Company
PO Box 958
Reidsville, NC 27323
Contact: Joy Jones Business Devel
Tel: 800-349-6283
Email: joyjones@adams-electric.com
Website: www.adams-electric.com
Electrical design-build, clean rooms, critical power, pharmaceuticals, health care, industrial & large commercial. (Woman, estab 1928, empl 300, sales $35,000,000, cert: State)

2894   Freedom Industries, Inc.
PO Box 7099
Rocky Mount, NC 27804
Contact: Jeff Groover VP Operations
Tel: 252-984-0007
Email: jgroover@freedomind.us
Website: www.freedomind.us
Electrical, Mechanical, HVAC, Plumbing & Fabrication. (Woman, estab 2004, empl 105, sales $28,140,000, cert: State)

2895   TEC Electric, LLC
6612G East WT Harris Blvd
Charlotte, NC 28215
Contact: Donald James President
Tel: 704-394-5097
Email: donald.james@harriselec.com
Website: www.harriselec.com
Electical contracting, engineering, controls & conveyor installation. (AA, estab 2006, empl 15, sales $3,000,000, cert: NMSDC)

2896   Thermal Control Products
6324 Performance Dr
Concord, NC 28027
Contact: Geoff Nilsen Commercial Sales Exec
Tel: 704-454-7605
Email: gnilsen@thermalcontrolproducts.com
Website: www.thermalcontrolproducts.com
Mfr thermal & protective components, Protective shielding / robotics, Weld splatter shielding, Weld head covers, Gun Bags, Computer monitor protectors, Weld screens, Transport bags. (Woman, estab 1993, empl 40, sales , cert: State)

Nevada

2897   VaOpto, LLC
5178 W Patrick Lane
Las Vegas, NV 89118
Contact: Charles Li Acct Mgr
Tel: 702-517-5789
Email: charles.li@vaopto.com
Website: www.vaopto.com
Mfr LED lightings & LED fixtures. (As-Pac, estab 2010, empl 5, sales $6,000,000, cert: NMSDC)

New York

2898 Integrated Control Corporation
748 Park Ave
Huntington, NY 11743
Contact: CEO
Tel: 631-673-5100
Email: sales@goicc.com
Website: www.goicc.com
Mfr electronic control & communication devices, system integrated design. (Woman, estab 1986, empl 21, sales $6,100,000, cert: WBENC, NWBOC)

Ohio

2899 S & V Industries, Inc.
3535 S Smith Rd
Fairlawn, OH 44333
Contact: Denise Uher Acct Exec
Tel: 330-408-3078
Email: denise.uher@svindustries.com
Website: www.svindustries.com
Mfr gears, spur, helical, double helical, worm straight bevel, spiral bevel, herringbone, gear boxes, worm gear boxes, helical gear boxes, bevel helical gear boxes, custom or special gear boxes, geared motors. (As-Pac, estab 1993, empl 30, sales $40,000,000, cert: NMSDC)

2900 Watkins Lighting & Sign Mtc, Inc.
300 Karl St
Berea, OH 44017
Contact: Tonia Watkins Owner
Tel: 440-243-3444
Email: tonia@watkinslighting.com
Website: www.watkinslighting.com
Lighting maintenance, LED lighting, Light poles service & installation, Interior and Exterior lighting. Sign Installation, Sign service, sign change. (Woman/Hisp, estab 2003, empl 6, sales $103,837,787, cert: State, City)

Oregon

2901 Powin Energy Corporation
20550 SW 115th Ave
Tualatin, OR 97062
Contact: Victor Liu Sales
Tel: 503-598-6659
Email: victorl@powinenergy.com
Website: www.powinenergy.com
Design & develop advanced battery management technology & manufactures battery energy storage solutions. (As-Pac, estab 2011, empl 43, sales , cert: NMSDC)

Pennsylvania

2902 American Cable Co., Inc.
231 E Luzerne St
Philadelphia, PA 19124
Contact: Rolando Sanchez Business Devel
Tel: 215-456-0700
Email: rsanchez@americancableco.com
Website: www.americancableco.com
Mfr battery cable assemblies, wire harnesses, and ground straps. (Hisp, estab 1976, empl 150, sales $15,000,000, cert: NMSDC)

2903 Butler Technologies, Inc.
231 W Wayne St
Butler, PA 16001
Contact: Marilyn Suchy Sales Admin
Tel: 724-283-6656
Email: msuchy@butlertechnologies.com
Website: www.butlertechnologies.com
Mfr graphic overlays, membrane switches, labels, decals & printed electronics. (Woman, estab 1990, empl 61, sales $6,974,188, cert: WBENC)

2904 John A. Romeo & Associates, Inc.
890 Pittsburgh Rd, Ste 7
Butler, PA 16002
Contact: Pamela Romeo CEO
Tel: 724-586-6961
Email: sales@jara-mfg.com
Website: www.jara-mfg.com
Mfr Custom Cables, Wiring Harnesses & Electromechanical Assemblies. (Woman, estab 1990, empl 15, sales $1,506,698, cert: WBENC)

Puerto Rico

2905 Advanced Control Services, Inc.
425 Rd. 693, PMB 205, Ste 1
Dorado, PR 00646
Contact: Victor M. Taveras Operations Mgr
Tel: 787-502-8752
Email: victor@advcontrolservices.com
Website: www.advcontrolservices.com
Engineering & validation services, systems integration svcs, control panels, VFDs, electrical services, SCADA, HMI, instrumentation services. (Hisp, estab 1999, empl 7, sales $621,123, cert: NMSDC)

2906 AG Group Inc.
Centro Industrial Minellas, Carr. 174TH KM 3.0
Bayamon, PR 00959
Contact: Elliott Gonzalez Sales Mgr
Tel: 787-707-0022
Email: info@aggpr.com
Website: www.aggroupinc.com
Engineering, System Integration, Installations, Calibrations, Validations. (Hisp, estab 1997, empl 105, sales $7,892,343, cert: State, NMSDC)

2907 Hi-Tech Products Inc.
PO Box 4956
Carolina, PR 00984
Contact: Daisy Maldonado Admin Officer
Tel: 787-257-1707
Email: admin@hi-techproducts.com
Website: www.hi-techproducts.com
Mfr reps for industrial control products, electronics, electrical & pneumatics. (Hisp, estab 1991, empl 30, sales , cert: NMSDC)

2908 Invision Engineering Corp.
PO Box 6567
Mayaguez, PR 00681
Contact: Jose Vazquez President
Tel: 787-831-0070
Email: jvazquez@invisioneng.com
Website: www.invisioneng.com
Automation, Control System Design, System Integrations, Instrumentation, Calibrations and Installations, Electrical Installations, Computer System Validations, Software Validations, Software design. (Hisp, estab 2002, empl 35, sales $3,137,957, cert: NMSDC)

2909   Lord Electric company of PR, Inc.
8 Simon Madera Ave. Rio Piedras, Parcelas Falu
San Juan, PR 00924
Contact: Manuel Rosabal CEO
Tel: 787-758-4040
Email: mrosabal@lordelectric.com
Website: www.lordcg.com
Electrical, mechanical & piping contractors. (Hisp, estab 1959, empl 300, sales $26,200,000, cert: NMSDC)

South Carolina

2910   Amec, LLC
4601 E White Horse Rd
Greenville, SC 29611
Contact: Kevin Lindsey Project Mgr
Tel: 864-269-0222
Email: kevin@amecllc.net
Website: www.amecsc.net
Industrial & commercial electrical applications, industrial electrical maintenance, thermal imaging, de-energized maintenance, studies for lighting improvements, breaker testing, power analysis, installation of service entrance equipment. (Woman, estab 2009, empl 11, sales $838,385, cert: State)

2911   Arva, LLC
3705 Centre Circle
Fort Mill, SC 29715
Contact: Shahil Amin Dir
Tel: 803-336-2235
Email: shahilamin@arva.us
Website: www.hyliteledlighting.com/
Mfr energy-efficient, indoor & outdoor LED & Induction Lighting & Retrofit Kits. (Woman/As-Ind, estab 2010, empl 7, sales $1,200,000, cert: NMSDC)

Tennessee

2912   TLC Investments, LLC
1244 Gallatin Pike S
Madison, TN 37115
Contact: Jami Hall CEO
Tel: 615-885-0019
Email: jhall@stonesriverelectric.com
Website: www.stonesriverelectric.com
Provides electrical and lighting management and installation services on a national basis. (Woman, estab , empl , sales $44,750,424, cert: State, WBENC)

Texas

2913   Blackhawk Management
1322 Space Park Dr Ste A220
Houston, TX 77058
Contact: Gabrielle Busby Admin
Tel: 832-536-3703
Email: busbyg@blackhawkmgmt.com
Website: www.blackhawkmgmt.com
Electrical & mechanical engineering design services, prototyping, short production runs, printed circuit board design, 3D machining, digital, analog design, power electronics. (Minority, Woman, estab 1992, empl 24, sales $10,000,000, cert: WBENC, SDB)

2914   Electro Plate Circuitry, Inc.
1430 Century Dr
Carrollton, TX 75006
Contact: Nicolas Garcia President
Tel: 972-466-0818
Email: nickg@eplate.com
Website: www.eplate.com
Mfr printed circuit boards: GF,GI, RF, insulators, heatsinks, blind buried vias, controlled impedance. (Hisp, estab 1981, empl 80, sales $9,000,000, cert: NMSDC)

2915   FASIC Design LLC
4105 Front Range Lane
Austin, TX 78732
Contact: Scott Buchanan Managing Member
Tel: 214-298-7810
Email: scott.buchanan@fasicdesigns.com
Website: www.fasicdesigns.com
Design large to small semiconductor designs at low to large process nodes(350 nm to 4nm).
. (AA, estab 2008, empl 1, sales $151,366, cert: NMSDC)

2916   GCI Technologies
1301 Precision Dr
Plano, TX 75074
Contact: Hinkki Chen CEO
Tel: 972-423-8411
Email: mike.beauchamp@gcitechnologies.com
Website: www.gcitechnologies.com
Mfr magnetics: engineering, telecom, audio, power transformers, external power supplies, chokes, ferrite beads, cores. (As-Pac, estab 1982, empl 420, sales $25,000,000, cert: NMSDC)

2917   Krypton Solutions
3060 Summit Ave 75074
Plano, TX 75074
Contact: Carol Primdahl Dir of Sales
Tel: 214-882-2363
Email: carol@krypton-solutions.com
Website: www.krypton-solutions.com
Electronic contract manufacturer. (As-Pac, estab 2005, empl 51, sales $5,100,000, cert: State)

2918   PanAmerica Supply, Inc.
21414 Provincial Blvd
Katy, TX 77450
Contact: Shaun Choi President
Tel: 281-646-8472
Email: sychoi@pasihouston.com
Website: www.pasihouston.com
Mfr power cables (HV, Med XLPE), transformer (up to 230kV). (As-Pac, estab 2005, empl 3, sales $8,000,000, cert: City)

2919   Perau Power Technology, Inc.
PO Box 540067
Houston, TX 77254
Contact: President
Tel: 713-522-5808
Email: information@peraupower.com
Website: www.peraupower.com
Backup power supplies: telecommunications, computers, emergency equip, engineering, install, maintenance. (Woman, estab 2001, empl 1, sales , cert: WBENC)

2920 Roman Industries, Inc.
10945 Estate Ln, Ste E115
Dallas, TX 75238
Contact: Shawn Quiroga Owner
Tel: 214-503-3100
Email: shawn@romanindustriesinc.com
Website: www.romanindustriesinc.com
Mfr custom cable, dist power lugs & RF connectors.
(Woman, estab 2008, empl 3, sales , cert: State)

2921 Southwest Synergistic Solutions, LLC
215 N Center, Ste 701
San Antonio, TX 78202
Contact: Juan Cienfuegos Managing Member
Tel: 956-645-5265
Email: jc@everythingtactical.com
Website: www.everythingtactical.com
Mfr & dist lighting solutions. (Hisp, estab 2010, empl 1,
sales , cert: State)

2922 Telco Intercontinental Corporation
9812 Whithorn Dr
Houston, TX 77095
Contact: Paolo Longo Dir of Sales
Tel: 281-855-2218
Email: plongo@telcointercon.com
Website: www.telcointercon.com
Mfr electric motors, Permanent Magnet DC motor, PMDC,
coreless, core-less DC, gearmotor, high speed, high torque,
miniature, stepper, Brushless DC motor, BLDC, green
energy efficient ECM motor, fan, blower. (As-Pac, estab
1985, empl 22, sales $19,000,000, cert: NMSDC)

2923 Texas Mgt Associates, Inc
7001 Fairgrounds Pkwy
San Antonio, TX 78238
Contact: Dora Mendoza Business Devel
Tel: 210-673-8422
Email: dmendoza@t-m-a.com
Website: www.t-m-a.com
Electrical engineering & mfg: cable harnesses, electrical
components, test station fixtures, circuit boards, restraint
test stations, electrical housings, both complex & simple.
(Hisp, estab 1991, empl 20, sales $4,368,852, cert: State,
NMSDC)

Virginia

2924 Atomized Products Group of Chesapeake, Inc.
808 Curtis Saunders Ct
Chesapeake, VA 23321
Contact: Lee Puckett Exec VP/Chief Operating
Officer
Tel: 757-793-2922
Email: lee.puckett@atomizedproductsgroup.com
Website: www.atomizedproductsgroup.com
Mfr & dist negative plate expander for lead-acid battery
applications. (Woman, estab 2013, empl 13, sales , cert:
WBENC)

Washington

2925 CETS LLC
1441 N Northlake Way, Ste 211
Seattle, WA 98103
Contact: Tim Tracey Purchasing
Tel: 206-588-1239
Email: info@cetsinc.com
Website: www.cetsinc.com
Develop & build new electrical systems; constructing
additions, alterations & repairs,
UL508 LISTED Open & Closed Industrial Panel, marine
electrical construction services, electrical power
distribution design & repair. (AA, estab 2013, empl 12,
sales $1,500,000, cert: City, NMSDC)

2926 Charter Controls, Inc.
1705 NE 64th Ave Ste B
Vancouver, WA 98661
Contact: Randy Ayala VP Industrial Sales
Tel: 360-695-2161
Email: randy@chartercontrols.us
Website: www.chartercontrols.us
Design, engineer & mfr industrial control systems.
(Woman, estab 2004, empl 15, sales $3,000,000, cert:
State)

2927 Cherry City Electric
8100 NE St. Johns Rd
Vancouver, WA 98665
Contact: Ray Ellis President
Tel: 503-566-5600
Email: rellis@cherrycityelectric.com
Website: www.cherrycityelectric.com
Provide electrical construction, electrical remodels and
electrical repair. Provide voice/data installations.
(Woman, estab 1968, empl 275, sales $49,800,000, cert:
WBENC)

2928 Eworld Solutions, Inc.
19550 7th Ave NE
Shoreline, WA 98155
Contact: Nasir Junejo CEO
Tel: 206-659-1988
Email: nasir@eworldsolutions.com
Website: www.eworldsolutions.com
Contractor placement for design and verification.
Specializing in SystemVerilog, UVM and Mixed Signal
verification. Consulting Service to audit verification and
design environments, Consulting Service to create re-
usable template (As-Ind, estab 2010, empl 3, sales , cert:
NMSDC)

2929 Reliable Investments LLC
801 2nd Ave Ste 800
Seattle, WA 98104
Contact: Anthony Obiako President
Tel: 800-918-4380
Email: anthony@reliableinvestmentsllc.com
Website: www.reliableinvestmentsllc.com
Procurement & supply chain management, field
engineering, installation, repair, calibration and rental
services. (AA, estab 2010, empl 3, sales $2,000,000,
cert: State)

Wisconsin

2930 Arnev Products, Inc.
      N1530 Spring Glen Rd
      Keshena, WI 54135
      Contact: Patricia Evensen President
      Tel: 715-799-5944
      Email: arnev@frontiernet.net
      Website: www.arnev.com
Mfr decorative electrical hardware. (Woman, estab 1990, empl 2, sales $550,000, cert: State)

2931 Convenience Electronics, Inc.
      4405 Triangle St
      McFarland, WI 53558
      Contact: J. Harry Lum President
      Tel: 608-838-4300
      Email: hlum@convenienceelectronics.com
      Website: www.convenienceelectronics.com
Mfr custom computer cables & harnesses, fiber optic cables, molded cables, etc. (As-Pac, estab 1989, empl 45, sales $4,000,000, cert: NMSDC)

2932 Dairyland Electric Co, Inc.
      12770 W. Custer Ave
      Butler, WI 53007
      Contact: Chris Martinez President
      Tel: 262-783-1550
      Email: cmartinez@dairylandelectric.com
      Website: www.dairylandenergy.com/
Electrical construction, data & communication, cabling, testing & certifying, electrical, telecom, fiber, alarms & video installation. (Hisp, estab 1998, empl 11, sales , cert: State, NMSDC)

2933 Electrical Testing Solutions
      2909 Green Hill Ct, Ste I
      Oshkosh, WI 54904
      Contact: Scott Banaski Business Devel Mgr
      Tel: 920-420-2986
      Email: sbanaski@electricaltestingsolutions.com
      Website: www.electricaltestingsolutions.com
Power system components for low, medium voltage & parallel switchgear troubleshooting, commissioning, design, analysis, repair & testing. (Hisp, estab 2005, empl 25, sales $4,300,000, cert: State, NMSDC)

2934 Professional Power Engineering Company, LLC
      W266 N7220 Kettle Ridge Ct
      Sussex, WI 53089
      Contact: Glenn Wilder President
      Tel: 262-372-4220
      Email: gwilder@ppecompany.com
      Website: www.ppecompany.com
Uninterruptible power supply systems, generator sets, automatic transfer switches, batteries, battery racks & cabinets & preventive maintenance services. (AA, estab 2006, empl 3, sales $105,000, cert: NMSDC)

DIR

DIVERSITY INFORMATION RESOURCES

DIVERSITY411 excerpts from DIR's Blog: www.diversityinforesources.blogspot.com

Top 10 Ways to Effectively (and Memorably) Reach Out to Supplier Diversity Professionals

DIR works directly with diverse-owned suppliers, and helps to bring them to the procurement discussion table. Using this book is a fantastic first step. Keep in mind that these contacts and information are best used:
- to establish business relationships
- reinforce business matchmaking

After years of discussions with people on both sides of the procurement "fence," we offer our Top 10 Ways to make the most out of this resource:

#10: Don't send information blindly: Let the buyer ask you for samples, line cards and other company specific information.

#9: Let corporate contacts know what you've done and ask about the best next steps ("I've registered," "I've researched your products/services." etc.). Use references within their industry.

#8: Keep track of conversations: What was said. With whom. What to do next. Schedule follow-ups.

#7: Ask about a corporation's "prime suppliers". You may not be able to work directly with a global conglomerate, but you most likely are able to work with one of their prime suppliers ... ask about them!

#6: Take advantage of any "personal" time you can get. Utilize business events to their fullest potential, reconnecting face-to-face with contacts you meet locally or at national business fairs.

#5: Do your homework about regional outreach groups: Chambers of Commerce, Economic Development Agencies, state or regional divisions of national organizations. Check them all out and be tenacious about following up with their matchmaking opportunities.

#4: Practice your introductions, and have more than one 'ready'. Know what you're going to say to someone experienced or inexperienced in your industry. Educate efficiently!

#3: Do your due diligence in researching what a Supplier Diversity contact needs to bring your information forward to their procurement department. You'll often find their preferences and needs listed on their Web site's supplier diversity page.

#2: Develop targeted marketing lists, and be specific when following up ("Good to meet you at NMSDC on Monday," etc.). Recall a piece of information that distinguishes you from everyone else ("Thank you for commenting on the effectiveness of my capabilities brochure.").

#1: Use names and titles and use them correctly in all your correspondence. If you send an email that says "Dear Ray" to a Ramona, it'll be deleted at first glance.

ENGINEERING SERVICES
Most of these firms are engaged in civil, structural and sanitation engineering services. May also do land surveying, environmental impact studies, testing and sampling, R&D, systems engineering, manufacturing, etc. Included are plant noise studies, digital design, radio active waste disposal, nuclear power. (See also ENVIRONMENTAL SERVICES). NAICS Code 54

Alabama

2935 Building & Earth Sciences, Inc.
5545 Derby Dr
Birmingham, AL 35210
Contact: Matt Adams Dir Corp Client Dev
Tel: 205-836-6300
Email: madams@buildingandearth.com
Website: www.buildingandearth.com
Consulting Engineering, geotechnical, environmental & construction materials testing & special inspection services. (Minority, Woman, estab 1998, empl 215, sales $28,000,000, cert: City, WBENC)

2936 GASmith Enterprises, Inc.
464 Cahaba Park Cir
Birmingham, AL 35242
Contact: George A. Smith President
Tel: 205-981-5391
Email: info@signarama-bham.com
Website: www.signarama-bham.com
SIGN-A-RAMA is your full service sign center. We use the latest technology and highest quality products to produce custom signs for your business. We can make the perfect signs to advertise your products or to inform your (AA, estab 2010, empl 6, sales $3,000,000, cert: State, NMSDC)

2937 Manufacturing Technical Solutions, Inc.
7047 Old Madison Pike Ste 302
Huntsville, AL 35806
Contact: Emily Tanksley Contract Admin
Tel: 256-890-9090
Email: emily.tanksley@mts-usa.com
Website: www.mts-usa.com
Engineering and science, logistics, program management, business management, and information technology. (Woman, estab 2001, empl 135, sales $17,326,179, cert: WBENC)

2938 Mesa Associates Inc.
480 Production Ave
Madison, AL 35758
Contact: Darrell Christman Exec VP
Tel: 865-671-5401
Email: dchristman@mesainc.com
Website: www.mesainc.com
Civil, electrical, mechanical, structural engineering services: integration, surveying, transmission, substation, controls, panel build, telecommunication, fiber optic engineering, robotic vehicle payloads & devices. (Minority, Woman, estab 1988, empl 356, sales $36,000,000, cert: NMSDC, WBENC)

Arizona

2939 G.D. Barri & Associates, Inc.
6860 W Peoria Ave
Peoria, AZ 85345
Contact: CEO
Tel: 623-773-0410
Email: gdbarri@gdbarri.com
Website: www.gdbarri.com
Engineering, management & technical support: environmental assessment, analysis, design, systems, baseline engineering, training, procedure development, quality assurance & quality control. (Woman/AA, estab 1989, empl 331, sales $54,435,707, cert: CPUC, WBENC)

California

2940 Aetypic, Inc.
7 Freelon St
San Francisco, CA 94107
Contact: Dennis Wong
Tel: 415-762-8388
Email: dennis.wong@aetypic.com
Website: www.aetypic.com
Architecture & engineering services: structural engineering, civil engineering, construction engineering & inspection, technology integration, & sustainable design. (As-Pac, estab 2011, empl 25, sales , cert: State, NMSDC)

2941 Blackstone Consulting, Inc.
11726 San Vicente Blvd Ste 550
Los Angeles, CA 90049
Contact: Leila Arrants Admin Services Mgr
Tel: 310-826-4389
Email: Leila@blackstone-consulting.com
Website: www.blackstone-consulting.com
Facilities Maintenance. (AA, estab 1991, empl 6000, sales $350,000,000, cert: NMSDC)

2942 Blair, Church & Flynn
451 Clovis Ave, Ste 200
Clovis, CA 93612
Contact: David Mowry Principal
Tel: 559-326-1400
Email: dmowry@bcf-engr.com
Website: www.bcf-engr.com
Engineering, land surveying, planning, civil engineering, landscape architecture & construction management. (Nat Ame, estab 1958, empl 49, sales $5,200,000, cert: CPUC)

2943 Calvada Surveying, Inc.
411 Jenks Cir Ste 205
Corona, CA 92880
Contact: Armando Dupont President
Tel: 951-280-9960
Email: armando@calvada.com
Website: www.calvada.com
Environmental site surveying & mapping, design topographic surveying & mapping, boundary surveys, construction staking, encumbrance mapping. (Hisp, estab 1989, empl 35, sales $4,200,000, cert: NMSDC, CPUC)

2944 Engineering/Remediation Resources Group, Inc.
4585 Pacheco Blvd Ste 200
Martinez, CA 94553
Contact: Tyson Appel Sr Project Mgr
Tel: 925-969-0750
Email: tyson.appel@errg.com
Website: www.errg.com
Engineering & remediation services, environmental, civil &
geotechnical engineers, geologists, soil physicists, scien-
tists, construction mgrs, construction superintendents,
equipment operators, certified hazardous waste techni-
cians. (Minority, Woman, estab 1997, empl 175, sales
$81,494,792, cert: CPUC)

2945 Faith Com, Inc.
3850 E Gilman St
Long Beach, CA 90815
Contact: PATRICIA WATTS CEO
Tel: 562-719-9300
Email: patwatts@fcimgt.com
Website: www.fcimgt.com
Consulting, strategic energy solutions for corp, residential,
commercial & industrial clients; govt & municipal agencies.
(Woman/AA, estab 1998, empl 50, sales $16,100,000, cert:
State, City, NMSDC, CPUC, WBENC)

2946 GDSTA, LLC
2000 Wyatt Dr, Ste 10
Santa Clara, CA 95054
Contact: Daphne Liu President
Tel: 408-980-8399
Email: daphneliu@gdsta.net
Website: www.gdsta.net
Light emitting diode (LED) lighting & smart lighting
devices, reduce carbon dioxide emission, energy usage,
energy cost, lighting pollution, waste & ROI. (Minority,
Woman, estab 2009, empl 8, sales , cert: NMSDC)

2947 Integrated Circuit Development, Inc.
405 E Santa Clara St
Arcadia, CA 91006
Contact: George Johnson Dir Operations
Tel: 626-599-8566
Email: gjj@heateflex.com
Website: www.heateflex.com
Deionized Water Heaters, In-Line Acid Heaters, Gas
Heaters, Immersion Heaters, DI Water Heating Systems.
(Hisp, estab 1974, empl 37, sales , cert: CPUC)

2948 Mercado Associates
25583 Ave Stanford
Valencia, CA 91355
Contact: Lizandro Mercado Principal
Tel: 661-753-9295
Email: monicaf@mercadoassociates.com
Website: www.mercadoassociates.com
Structural consulting engineering services. (Hisp, estab
1998, empl 5, sales $480,000, cert: State, NMSDC)

2949 National Relocation Services, Inc. dba NRS, Inc.
2671 Pomona Blvd
Pomona, CA 91768
Contact: Irene Ito CEO
Tel: 909-869-5748
Email: icito@nrsca.com
Website: www.nrsca.com
Asset mgmt, online inventory, project & move mgmt,
space planning, warehousing, inventory & bar coding,
furniture installation, workstation, cubicle reconfiguration,
furniture planning, CAD & CAFM. (Minority, Woman, estab
1994, empl 48, sales $4,373,000, cert: State, CPUC)

2950 Pari & Gershon Inc.
2053 Lincoln Ave Ste A
San Jose, CA 95125
Contact: Romena Jonas President
Tel: 408-966-7184
Email: rjonas@pgiinc.net
Website: www.pgicompany.com
Environmental Consulting, Engineering Design &
Construction. (Woman, estab 2009, empl 5, sales
$100,000, cert: State, WBENC)

2951 Pivox Corporation
3240 El Camino Real Ste 230
Irvine, CA 92602
Contact: Sean Shahin VP
Tel: 949-727-1400
Email: sean@pivox.com
Website: www.pivox.com
Remediation of soil & groundwater, demolition, project
& construction management, permitting, design,
feasibility study, treatment system installation (civil,
mechanical, electril, and instrumentation). (Woman,
estab 2004, empl 20, sales $8,000,000, cert: CPUC)

2952 Quest Project Controls, Inc.
114 W Colorado Blvd
Monrovia, CA 91016
Contact: Robyn Coates CEO
Tel: 626-639-2613
Email: robyn@thecmsolution.com
Website: www.thecmsolution.com
Project controls services & staff augmentation, project
scheduling & planning, cost engineering, estimating &
management of change. (Woman, estab 2002, empl 23,
sales $1,959,183, cert: State, City, CPUC, WBENC)

2953 R.J. Roberts, Inc.
145 John Glenn Dr
Concord, CA 94520
Contact: Terri Van De Veire Acct Mgr
Tel: 925-689-8080
Email: van_t@robertscompanies.net
Website: www.robertscompanies.net
Consulting engineering services: civil, structural,
electrical & mechanical. (Woman, estab 1978, empl 80,
sales $9,712,761, cert: WBENC)

2954 RFE Engineering, Inc.
8680 Greenback Ln, Ste 107
Orangevale, CA 95662
Contact: Bob Eynck President
Tel: 916-989-3285
Email: reynck@rfeengineering.com
Website: www.RFEengineering.com
Surveying, boundary & topographic surveys, aerial
control, ALTA/ACSM, parcel/subdivision maps, construc-
tion staking planning, military facility master planning,
development feasibility analysis, zoning & use permits,
master planning. (Hisp, estab 2003, empl 8, sales
$640,000, cert: State, CPUC, 8(a))

2955 Solartech Power, Inc.
901 E Cedar St
Ontario, CA 91761
Contact: Sherry Fu Owner
Tel: 714-630-8880
Email: sherry.fu@solartechpower.com
Website: www.solartechpower.com
Mfr solar photovoltaic panels/equip. (Minority, Woman,
estab 2001, empl 10, sales $3,000,000, cert: CPUC)

2956 SW Safety Solutions Inc.
33278 Central Ave, Ste 102
Union City, CA 94587
Contact: Mike Kimberley Business Devel & Diversity
Solutions Leader
Tel: 510-429-8692
Email: mkimberley@swsafety.com
Website: www.swsafety.com/
Manufacturing, R&D and hand health technologies to
provide premium hand protection products that enhance
worker performance. (Minority, Woman, estab 1984, empl
28, sales $102,000,000, cert: NMSDC, WBENC)

2957 TEC, Inc.
510 S. La Brea Ave.
Inglewood, CA 90301
Contact: Steven Youschak Sales
Tel: 949-450-8200
Email: syouschak@teccm.com
Website: www.teccm.com
Engineering & construction mgmt svcs: CPM scheduling,
cost control, constructability review, claims analysis,
design mgmt & contract administration. (AA, estab 1988,
empl 32, sales , cert: NMSDC, CPUC)

2958 The CAD-Scan Connection
1111 Riveside Ave Ste 405
Paso Robles, CA 93446
Contact: Linda Martini Posner CEO
Tel: 805-237-9347
Email: lindap@cadscanconnection.com
Website: www.cadscanconnection.com
Engineering/architectural technical support services,
Conversion to CAD architectural, engineering drawings to
AutoCAD. Revit, Map 3D, ArcView,GIS, Large format
Description scanning. (Woman, estab 1998, empl 3, sales ,
cert: CPUC)

2959 The R.E.M. Engineering Co., Inc.
1575 N Lake Ave, Ste 204
Pasadena, CA 91104
Contact: Robert Milton, Jr. General Mgr
Tel: 626-296-7200
Email: remeng@remengr.com
Website: www.remengr.com
Engineering services: civil, structural, electrical & mechani-
cal, design & design-build, scheduling, project status
reporting, construction management. (AA, estab 1979,
empl 7, sales $265,826, cert: State, CPUC)

2960 Vistam, Inc.
2375 Walnut Ave
Signal Hill, CA 90755
Contact: Arley Tamayo Sales
Tel: 562-912-7779
Email: art.tamayo@vistam.com
Website: www.vistam.com
Electrical engineering & testing services, substation
maintenance & commissioning projects, scheduled
maintenance programs. (As-Pac, estab 1992, empl 18,
sales $1,752,000, cert: State)

2961 WRW Engineering
2104 Martin Way
Pittsburg, CA 94565
Contact: Barbara Williams SD Admin
Tel: 925-439-8272
Email: bwilliams@wrweng.com
Website: www.wrweng.com
Mechanical, electrical & software engineering, auto-
mated flexible testing stations, smart products &
autonomous machines. (Woman, estab 2012, empl 2,
sales , cert: WBENC)

2962 Zelos Consulting, LLC
2400 Wyandotte St Ste A
Mountain View, CA 94043
Contact: Sabrina Sirwet Business Devel Mgr
Tel: 650-462-1696
Email: sabrina.sirwet@zelos.com
Website: www.zelos.com
Turnkey & customized engineering: staffing services,
payroll services, engineering project design services.
(Minority, Woman, estab 1996, empl 40, sales
$3,000,000, cert: CPUC, WBENC)

Colorado

2963 F&D International, LLC
5723 Arapahoe Ave Ste 1B
Boulder, CO 80303
Contact: Teri Ficken President
Tel: 303-652-3200
Email: teri@fdi-one.com
Website: www.fdi-one.com
F&Engineering, architecture & construction manage-
ment, engineering consulting (civil & structural), facility
condition assessments, site plans, construction consult-
ing, architectural design & CAD drawings. (Woman,
estab 2001, empl 10, sales $1,400,000, cert: WBENC)

2964 KIRA, Inc.
2595 Canyon Blvd Ste 240
Boulder, CO 80302
Contact: Constance O''Brien Sr Accountant
Tel: 303-402-1526
Email: cobrien@kira.com
Website: www.kira.com
Facilities maintenance and base operations support
services contractor. (Nat Ame, estab 1987, empl 500,
sales $49,524,857, cert: NMSDC)

2965 Samuel Engineering, Inc.
8450 E Crescent Pkwy, Ste 200
Greenwood Village, CO 80111
Contact: DJ Alemayehu CEO
Tel: 303-714-4840
Email: dj@samuelengineering.com
Website: www.samuelengineering.com
Engineering & architectural svcs: electrical, instrumenta-
tion, controls, civil, structural, process, chemical,
mechanical, piping, HVAC. (Woman/AA, estab , empl
200, sales $2,934,704, cert: NMSDC)

Connecticut

2966 Butler America, LLC
2 Trap Falls Rd
Shelton, CT 06484
Contact: Cynthia Lashley Acct Exec
Tel: 765-464-5551
Email: clashley@butler.com
Website: www.butler.com
Engineering Solutions, Extensive recruiting network, rapid deployment, Turnkey Design Center development, Cost reduction. (Woman, estab 2009, empl 2500, sales $101,387,490, cert: WBENC)

Delaware

2967 Bethrant Industries LLC
7 Midfield Rd
New Castle, DE 19720
Contact: Ashly Bethrant President
Tel: 302-322-0521
Email: ashly17@comcast.net
Website: www.bethrantdesign.com
Design, engineering, CAD, graphics, illustration, rendering, prototype models & fixture fabrication, point of purchase displays, shelving design, exhibit booth & bathom furniture design. (Woman/AA, Hisp, estab 2016, empl 4, sales , cert: NMSDC)

2968 Mechanical Design Solutions, Inc.
5577 S DuPont Pkwy
Smyrna, DE 19977
Contact: Dianne Bingham President
Tel: 302-659-0233
Email: dbingham@mds13.com
Website: www.mds13.com
Mechanical, electrical & instrument system design & engineering, P&ID walkdown, verification, fabrication orthography, isometrics, bill of material & scopes of work, stress analysis (Rebis and AutoPIPE), PSV survey & modeling, Installation. (Minority, Woman, estab 1998, empl 6, sales $875,000, cert: State)

2969 Mountain Consulting, Inc.
103 S Bradford St
Dover, DE 19904
Contact: Kim Adams President
Tel: 302-744-9875
Email: kadams@mountainconsultinginc.com
Website: www.mountainconsultinginc.net
Engineering, land survey & technical services: Military Housing Privatization, Resident Construction Management, Contract Program Management, Title II Services, and Project Oversight. (Woman/AA, estab 2003, empl 5, sales , cert: State, NWBOC, 8(a))

Florida

2970 Brindley Pieters & Associates, Inc.
2600 Maitland Center Pkwy Ste 180
Maitland, FL 32751
Contact: Brindley Pieters President
Tel: 407-830-8700
Email: bpieters@bpa-engineers.com
Website: www.bpa-engineers.com
Civil & structural engineering svcs & construction management & inspection. (AA, estab 1991, empl 35, sales $6,234,839, cert: City)

2971 Diversified Technology Consultants
650 Central Ave Unit 3
Sarasota, FL 34236
Contact: Robert Hammersley Program Mgr
Tel: - -
Email: robert.hammersley@teamdtc.com
Website: www.teamdtc.com
Civil, environmental, transportation, structures, water pollution control, solid/hazardous waste mgmt, survey, electrical, mechanical, construction inspection & admin, CADD svcs, landscape architecture. (As-Pac, estab 1979, empl 55, sales $6,724,276, cert: State)

2972 EAC Consulting, Inc.
815 NW 57th Ave, Ste 402
Miami, FL 33126
Contact: Enrique Crooks President
Tel: 305-264-2557
Email: eac@eacconsult.com
Website: www.eacconsult.com
Civil structural, bridge & highway design, construction engineering & inspection svcs. (AA, estab 1994, empl 34, sales , cert: State)

2973 EDF Company
8390 Currency Dr, Ste 4
Riviera Beach, FL 33404
Contact: Karla Watkins Dir
Tel: 561-863-6770
Email: karla@edfinc.com
Website: www.edfinc.com
Complex design & engineering support services to the Aerospace industry. Test Facilities & Test Equipment Design/Build for multiple Engine Test Programs, F100/F14, F119/F22, Joint Strike Fighter (JSF). (Woman, estab 1978, empl 25, sales $3,355,920, cert: WBENC)

2974 Engineered Design Services LLC
1035 S State Rd 7 Ste 315
Wellington, FL 33411
Contact: Craig McKenzie President
Tel: 561-600-1776
Email: craigmckenzie@edsengineers.com
Website: www.edsengineers.com
Mechanical & Electrical Engineering, Process Design, Pumping Systems, 3D Modeling, Food Grade Piping Design, Structural/Concrete
Vessel Design, Dry Material Handling, Material Conveying & Dust Collection. (AA, estab 2013, empl 4, sales $119,829, cert: State)

2975 Frazier Engineering, Inc.
6767 N. Wickham Road, Ste 304
Melbourne, FL 32940
Contact: Michelle Shoultz President
Tel: 321-253-8131
Email: mshoultz@fraziereng.com
Website: www.fraziereng.com
Civil, structural, environmental engineering & surveying: design, permitting & construction administration of site plans, utility improvements, water, sewer, reuse, drainage, roadway improvements, bridges. (Minority, Woman, estab 1992, empl 20, sales $17,700,000, cert: State, NMSDC)

2976   Holland Engineering Inspection Services dba HEIS
       3900 Hollywood Blvd Ste 303
       Hollywood, FL 33021
       Contact: Catherine MacAskill CEO
       Tel: 954-626-0550
       Email: catherine@heisflorida.com
       Website: www.heisflorida.com/
Civil engineering inspections & certifications, 5-Year
Surface Water Management Renewals, Stormwater
Certifications, Stormwater Drainage Cleaning & Repairs,
SSES. (Woman, estab 2016, empl 2, sales $400,000, cert:
State)

2977   ITG Global, LLC
       11235 St. Johns Industrial Pkwy N Ste 2A
       Jacksonville, FL 32246
       Contact: Joseph Lukowski CEO
       Tel: 904-425-4760
       Email: almaferrante@itgtec.com
       Website: www.itgtec.com
Automation Design, PLC Programming, Software Development, Technologies Consulting, Motion Design, Robot
programming, MES, OEE, Data Analytics, Condition
Monitoring, Control System Design, UL 508A Panel Shop,
Control Panel. (Minority, Woman, estab 2003, empl 27,
sales $3,000,000, cert: NMSDC)

2978   RLJ Enterprises Inc. dba Genesis VII, Inc.
       1605 White Dr
       Titusville, FL 32780
       Contact: Robert Jordan CEO
       Tel: 321-383-4813
       Email: robert.jordan@genesisvii.com
       Website: www.genesisvii.com
Engineering, Logistics & Constructions Services, Design
Engineering, 3D CAD, Reverse Engineering, Procurement
(Wholesale Procurement), Facilities Management, Con-
struction Management. (AA, estab 1989, empl 9, sales
$3,900,000, cert: NMSDC, SDB)

2979   Southern Energy Solution Group, LLC
       2336 S East Ocean Blvd, Ste 204
       Stuart, FL 34996
       Contact: Oswald Hoffler Managing Member
       Tel: 772-919-2844
       Email: ohoffler@soenergy-grp.com
       Website: www.soenergy-grp.com
Renewable Energy Generation and RECs (AA, estab 2010,
empl 5, sales $250,000, cert: CPUC)

Georgia

2980   BREED Enterprises, Inc.
       4501 Circle 75 Pkwy Ste A-1160
       Atlanta, GA 30339
       Contact: Bobby Reed CEO
       Tel: 678-324-0105
       Email: breed@breedenterprisesinc.com
       Website: www.breedenterprisesinc.com
LEED programs, LED lighting products. (AA, estab 2005,
empl 45, sales $2,500,000, cert: State, NMSDC)

2981   Greenspeed Energy Solutions, LLC
       2148 Hills Ave NW Ste H
       Atlanta, GA 30318
       Contact: Thomas McNeill Business Devel Mgr
       Tel: 404-924-7400
       Email: tmcneill@greenspeedenergy.com
       Website: www.greenspeedenergy.com
Design/build energy services, audit & design, implemen-
tation (installation) of energy efficiency measures.
(Minority, estab 2006, empl 20, sales $4,000,000, cert:
State, NMSDC)

2982   Murzan Inc.
       2909 Langford Rd Ste 1-700
       Norcross, GA 30071
       Contact: Alberto Bazan VP
       Tel: 770-448-0583
       Email: albertobazan@murzan.com
       Website: www.murzan.com
Diaphragm Pumps, Transfer Pumps, Unloading Systems,
Paw Pumps, Gizzard Pumps, Chicken Breast Pumps, CIP
Systems, PLC Programming, Liver Pumps, Engineering
Services. (Hisp, estab 1984, empl 50, sales $10,400,000,
cert: NMSDC)

2983   Present Energi LLC
       411 S Greenwood St Ste B
       LaGrange, GA 30240
       Contact: Renee Warrick Managing Partner
       Tel: 706-883-7336
       Email: renee@presentenergi.com
       Website: www.presentenergi.com
Solar Photovoltaic & Solar Thermal systems for residential, commercial, industrial & utility scale customers;
engineering, project management & construction for
large scale systems. (Woman, estab 2009, empl 2, sales ,
cert: WBENC)

2984   Prime Power Services
       8225 Troon Circle
       Austell, GA 30168
       Contact: Addie Mathes President
       Tel: 770-739-2300
       Email: gmaddox@primepower.com
       Website: www.primepower.com
Power generation svcs: maintenance & emergency
response, testing, inspection, calibration & repair,
rentals, installations, retrofit, commissioning, ngineering
studies & analysis, support, investigation & consulting,
training. (Woman, estab 1992, empl 50, sales
$11,600,000, cert: WBENC)

2985   R2T, Inc.
       580 W Crossville Road Stes 101-102
       Roswell, GA 30075
       Contact: Kimberly Ajy President
       Tel: 770-569-7038
       Email: kim.ajy@r2tinc.com
       Website: www.r2tinc.com
Civil & environmental engineering & construction
services: watershed/stormwater mgmt, conceptual
planning, water & wastewater system design, design/
build construction. (Woman/AA, estab 2005, empl 57,
sales $6,810,190, cert: City, NMSDC, WBENC)

2986 The Black Book, Inc.
       3500 Lenox Ste 1500
       Atlanta, GA 30326
       Contact: Rochelle Brown Owner
       Tel: 888-808-9542
       Email: rochelle@theblackbookvip.com
       Website: www.theblackbookvip.com
The BLACK BOOK is a premiere luxury concierge service
and lifestyle management agency. We serve a plethora of
individuals from athletes and sports organizations ,
entertainers and production companies to high-net-
individuals (Woman/AA, estab 2013, empl 5, sales , cert:
NMSDC)

Iowa

2987 ACT Safe, LLC
       4121 Gordon Dr
       Sioux City, IA 51106
       Contact: Lorna Puntillo Managing Member
       Tel: 712-204-9274
       Email: lorna@actsafellc.com
       Website: www.actsafellc.com
Occupational Safety & Health (OSHA), Environmental (EPA)
– Due Diligence & Remediation, Engineering (A&E),
Construction services. (Woman, estab 2011, empl 12, sales
$750,000, cert: City, 8(a))

Illinois

2988 Advanced Cad/Cam Service dba EngineeringPeople
       801 W Main St
       Peoria, IL 61606
       Contact: Jim Montelongo CEO
       Tel: 309-621-5792
       Email: jim@engineeringpeople.com
       Website: www.engineeringpeople.com
Engineering service support, mechanical, electrical,
hydraulic, structural, engineering staffing. (Hisp, estab
1991, empl 60, sales $5,700,000, cert: NMSDC)

2989 DeAmertek
       300 Windsor Dr
       Oak Brook, IL 60523
       Contact: Dan Anderson Sales
       Tel: 630-667-4687
       Email: anderson@deamertek.com
       Website: www.deamertek.com
Electrical Power Steering; AFS: Adaptive Front-lighting
System and Fuel Delivery Modules (FDM). (As-Pac, estab
1997, empl 25, sales , cert: NMSDC)

2990 Environmental Systems Design, Inc.
       233 south wacker Dr Ste 5300
       Chicago, IL 60606
       Contact: Tony Kempa Chief Marketing Officer
       Tel: 312-580-0534
       Email: akempa@esdglobal.com
       Website: www.esdglobal.com
Consulting-engineering services. We deliver value by
making building occupants more healthy and productive
and your facility more cost effective, flexible, reliable, and
sustainable. Utilizing an integrative design process, (As-
Pac, estab 1967, empl 250, sales $53,537,753, cert:
NMSDC)

2991 KAE Consultants, Inc.
       1750 E Golf Rd Ste 490
       Schaumburg, IL 60173
       Contact: Karen Eng President
       Tel: 847-605-0080
       Email: keng@csmius.com
       Website: www.csmius.com
Engineering & design services: project management,
electrical, mechanical, packaging, automation engineering & CAD services. (Minority, Woman, estab 1983, empl
11, sales $5,309,251, cert: State, WBENC)

2992 Mat Holdings Inc
       6700 Wildlife Way
       Long Grove, IL 60047
       Contact: Tatiana Sokolov Sr Tax Analyst
       Tel: 847-821-9630
       Email: tatiana.sokolov@matholdingsinc.com
       Website: www.matholdingsinc.com
Global manufacturing, marketing and distribution
company (As-Pac, estab 1984, empl 11000, sales , cert:
NMSDC)

2993 Milhouse Engineering and Construction, Inc.
       333 S. Wabash Ave. Ste 1501
       Chicago, IL 60604
       Contact: William Whitaker Sr Business Mgr
       Tel: 312-987-0061
       Email: milhousebd@milhouseinc.com
       Website: www.milhouseinc.com
Engineering design services, site civil, transportation,
mechanical, electrical, plumbing, fire protection, water/
waste water, preconstruction, quality assurance &
control, post construction & construction. (AA, estab
2001, empl 200, sales $32,000,000, cert: NMSDC)

2994 Nest Builders
       303 W Erie St Ste 510
       Chicago, IL 60654
       Contact: Victor Avila Principal
       Tel: 312-915-0557
       Email: vavila@dbhms.com
       Website: www.dbhms.com
Engineering services: mechanical, electrical, plumbing &
fire protection design. (Hisp, estab 2002, empl 60, sales ,
cert: City)

2995 PMA Consultants of Illinois LLC
       333 W Wacker Dr, Ste 880
       Chicago, IL 60606
       Contact: Gui Ponce de Leon Managing Principal
       Tel: 312-920-0404
       Email: kflood@pmaconsultants.com
       Website: www.pmaconsultants.com
Engineering consulting services: CPM scheduling, claims
mitigation, change order management, contract document review, cost estimating, value engineering, training
& expert analysis and testimony. (Hisp, estab 1971, empl
190, sales , cert: State, NMSDC)

2996   Prairie Engineers
107 N Main St, Ste 3C
Columbia, IL 62236
Contact: Michelle Chambliss Business Devel
Tel: 217-605-0403
Email: mchambliss@prairieengineers.com
Website: www.prairieengineers.com
Engineering services: planning, project management, civil
engineering, water resources engineering, land surveying,
land acquisition, environmental science & natural re-
sources management & construction management.
(Woman, estab 2010, empl 20, sales $2,000,000, cert: City,
WBENC, 8(a))

2997   Primera Engineers
100 S Wacker Dr Ste 700
Chicago, IL 60606
Contact: Al Perla
Tel: 312-606-0910
Email: aperla@primeraeng.com
Website: www.primeraeng.com
Engineering design: mechanical, electrical, plumbing, fire
protection, architecture, commissioning, structural, civil,
telecommunications, utility distribution & substation
engineering. (Hisp, estab 1987, empl 170, sales
$21,910,784, cert: State, City, NMSDC)

2998   Quality Tools & Abrasives
605 Bonnie Lane
Elk Grove Village, IL 60007
Contact: Matthew Lombardo Sales Devel
Tel: 800-640-2110
Email: mattl@qualitytools.com
Website: www.qualitytools.com
Industrial distributor, supply chain integrator, fluid man-
agement, Six Sigma consulting, vending machines, engi-
neering/process improvements. (Minority, estab 1974,
empl 39, sales $24,000,000, cert: NMSDC)

2999   Solved Engineering
55 E Monroe, Ste 3800
Chicago, IL 60603
Contact: Edward William Prinicpal Engineer
Tel: 800-975-9723
Email: ewilliam@solvedeng.com
Website: www.solvedeng,com
Electrical Engineer & and Consulting, Engineering Design,
Subject Matter Testimony & Engineering Calculation /
Studies Service. (AA, estab 2015, empl 5, sales , cert: City,
NMSDC, CPUC)

3000   Sterling Engineering, Inc.
Two Westbrook Corporate Center Ste 300
Westchester, IL 60154
Contact: Rama Kavaliauskas President
Tel: 630-993-3433
Email: rama@sterling-engineering.com
Website: www.sterling-engineering.com
Engineering & technical staff augmentation solutions.
(Woman, estab 1969, empl 75, sales $2,691,294, cert:
WBENC)

3001   Structure Designs, Inc.
309 W Washington St Ste 325
Chicago, IL 60606
Contact: Olufemi Oladeinde President
Tel: 312-551-9780
Email: oao@structuredesignsinc.com
Website: www.sdiengr.com
Civil Engineering, Structural Engineering, Architectural
Engineering, Land Surveying, Construction management.
(AA, estab 1994, empl 30, sales $12,500,000, cert:
NMSDC, 8(a))

3002   Valdes Architecture and Engineering
100 W 22nd St
Lombard, IL 60148
Contact: Max Mather Business Devel Mgr
Tel: 630-792-1886
Email: mmather@valdeseng.com
Website: www.valdeseng.com/
Engineering svcs to process facilities, chemical, food,
pharmaceutical, power & steel mfg plants in piping
design, mechanical, civil & structural engineering,
architecture & process engineering. (Hisp, estab 1992,
empl 200, sales , cert: NMSDC)

Indiana

3003   Americas Engineers, Inc.
1449 Kimber Ln, Ste 101
Evansville, IN 47715
Contact: KC Jain President
Tel: 812-473-1905
Email: kcjain@americasengineers.com
Website: www.americasengineers.com
Civil engineering: surveying, site plans, drainage sys-
tems, grading & approach roads, access roads & storm
water management. (As-Ind, estab 2004, empl 7, sales
$1,200,000, cert: NMSDC)

3004   Consulting Management Inspection Design, Inc.
1402 N Capitol Ave Ste 250
Indianapolis, IN 46202
Contact: Stacey L. Harrell Exec Admin Assist
Tel: 317-917-4244
Email: sharrell@cmidinc.com
Website: www.cmidinc.com
Architectural, structural, mechanical, electrical, environ-
mental, civil, commissioning & construction manage-
ment & inspection services. (AA, estab 1996, empl 24,
sales $3,500,000, cert: State, City)

3005   Continental, Inc.
1524 Jackson St
Anderson, IN 46016
Contact: Paul Wysong CEO
Tel: 765-778-9999
Email: paul@continentalinc.com
Website: www.continentalinc.com
Engineering Services, Drafting Services, Human Re-
sources & Executive Search, Consulting Services
(Woman, estab 1985, empl 147, sales $11,350,000, cert:
WBENC)

3006 Falcon Manufacturing LLC
164 S Park Blvd
Greenwood, IN 46143
Contact: Larry Waskom Exec VP
Tel: 317-884-3600
Email: lwaskom@falcon-manufacturing.com
Website: www.falcon-manufacturing.com
Containment/Inspection, Repack/Kitting Operations, Global Sourcing & Procurement, Packaging and Parts Washing, Vendor-Managed Inventory (VMI), EDI Management, Customer Service. (As-Pac, estab 1991, empl 225, sales $120,000,000, cert: State, NMSDC)

3007 K & S Engineers, Inc.
9715 Kennedy Ave
Highland, IN 46322
Contact: Debbie Pilawski President
Tel: 219-924-5231
Email: dpilawski@kandsengineers.com
Website: www.kandsengineers.com
Geotechnical engineering & consulting, drilling soil borings & caissons, rock coring, lab & field testing of soil, concrete, asphalt & steel, environmental consulting & forensic investigation of construction materials. (As-Ind, estab 1984, empl 36, sales $4,515,115, cert: State, NMSDC)

Kansas

3008 Choson Resource LLC
1999 N Amidon, Ste 100B
Wichita, KS 67203
Contact: Kim Silcott President
Tel: 316-729-0312
Email: kim@chosonresource.com
Website: www.Chosonresource.com
Aerospace engineering & staffing services for the air, defense & space industries. (Minority, Woman, estab 2010, empl 4, sales $4,254,100, cert: NMSDC)

Kentucky

3009 Foam Design Inc.
444 Transport Ct
Lexington, KY 40511
Contact: Chris Harrod Sales Engineer
Tel: 502-682-8562
Email: charrod@foamdesign.com
Website: www.foamdesign.com
Commercial and industrial foam conversion capabilities and design, intricate parts cut to precise tolerances. (Woman, estab 1974, empl 102, sales $18,500,000, cert: WBENC)

3010 LECGI Inc.
13113 Eastpoint Park Blvd Ste D
Louisville, KY 40223
Contact: Don Liu President
Tel: 502-425-1647
Email: dliu@lecgi.us
Website: www.lecgi.us
Engineering design & structural steel detailing, structural steel connection design & structural analysis of steel structures, handrails, and stairs for steel fabricators. (As-Pac, estab 2004, empl 10, sales $633,000, cert: State, 8(a))

3011 Pioneer Logistics Group, Inc.
2208 Sieger Villa Ct
Louisville, KY 40218
Contact: Phillip Shoulders President
Tel: 502-479-3546
Email: pioneergroupse@msn.com
Website: www.pioneergroupse.com
Logistics, inventory control management, warehouse services, facilities management, (AA, estab 2010, empl 25, sales $2,000,000, cert: NMSDC)

Louisiana

3012 Gulf South Engineering & Testing, Inc.
2201 Aberdeen St Ste B
Kenner, LA 70062
Contact: Chad Poche VP
Tel: 504-305-4401
Email: cpoche@gulfsoutheng.com
Website: www.gulfsoutheng.com
Geotechnical engineering, foundation engineering, soil borings, facility permitting, laboratory testing, construction materials testing & inspection, concrete testing, pile testing & inspection. (AA, estab 2010, empl 8, sales $550,000, cert: City)

3013 Omega Natchiq, Inc.
4418 Pesson Rd
New Iberia, LA 70560
Contact: Scott McKay GM Business Devel
Tel: 337-365-6028
Email: info@asrcenergy.com
Website: www.asrcenergy.com/
Turnkey Fabrication, Operations and Maintenance Services, Subsea Components, Construction Crews, and ASME Pressure Vessel Design and Fabrication. (Nat Ame, estab 1988, empl 450, sales $71,009,754, cert: NMSDC)

Massachusetts

3014 Corporate Environmental Advisors, Inc.
127 Hartwell St
West Boylston, MA 01583
Contact: Scott Soucy Health, Safety & Compliance
Tel: 800-358-7960
Email: contactus@cea-inc.com
Website: www.cea-inc.com/
Environmental engineering, consulting & contracting firm. (Woman, estab 1985, empl 20, sales $3,878,000, cert: State)

3015 Green International Affiliates, Inc.
100 Ames Pond Dr, Ste 200
Tewksbury, MA 01876
Contact: Adel Shahin Sr VP
Tel: 978-923-0400
Email: ashahin@greenintl.com
Website: www.greenintl.com
Consulting civil, environmental & structural engineers. (Minority, estab 1954, empl 28, sales , cert: State)

3016 RRMAE Engineering LLC
      46 Loring Ave
      Boxborough, MA 01719
      Contact: Anton Edmund Owner
      Tel: 508-517-4913
      Email: anton.edmund@rrmaeengineering.com
      Website: www.rrmaeengineering.com
Process Design, Process Improvement, Risk assessment,
Process Validation, Validation, Commissioning & Qualification, Quality Engineering, Data analysis, Lean management, Process Automation. (As-Ind, estab 2013, empl 2,
sales $267,000, cert: State)

Maryland

3017 Robotic Research, LLC
      555 Quince Orchard Road, Ste 300
      Gaithersburg, MD 20878
      Contact: Alberto Lacaze President
      Tel: 240-631-0008
      Email: lacaze@roboticresearch.com
      Website: www.roboticresearch.com
Robotics, intelligent control, sensor processing & specialized computer programming. (Hisp, estab 2002, empl 15,
sales $3,000,000, cert: State)

3018 Site Resources, Inc.
      14315 Jarrettsville Pike
      Phoenix, MD 21131
      Contact: Sharon Elliott Marketing Mgr
      Tel: 410-683-3388
      Email: selliott@siteresourcesinc.com
      Website: www.siteresourcesinc.com
Civil engineering, landscape architecture & land planning
services. (Woman, estab 1994, empl 28, sales $4,126,649,
cert: State, City)

Michigan

3019 4D Systems
      4130 Market Place
      Flint Twp, MI 48507
      Contact: Jean-Pierre Rasaiah President
      Tel: 248-535-0758
      Email: jp.rasaiah@4dsysco.com
      Website: www.4dsysco.com
Robotic Systems Build (Specializing in glass handling),
Robot Programming (All applications), Robotic Simulation,
Siemens software reseller, NX Design, Robcad Simulation,
Process Simulate Simulation, Controls Design, Panel build.
(As-Pac, estab 2010, empl 65, sales $8,000,000, cert:
NMSDC)

3020 ABE Associates, Inc.
      440 Burroughs St, Ste. 605
      Detroit, MI 48221
      Contact: Andre Brooks President
      Tel: 313-961-5170
      Email: andreb@abe-engineers.com
      Website: www.abe-engineers.com
Architectural design, civil, environmental, fire protection,
mechanical & structural engineering, project management,
program management, drafting, surveying, construction
inspection, land acquisition services. (AA, estab 1997, empl
3, sales $250,000, cert: State, NMSDC)

3021 AMBE Engineering, LLC
      15424 Prestwick Circle
      Northville, MI 48168
      Contact: Rashmi Zaveri VP
      Tel: 734-667-3167
      Email: rashmis@ambeeng.com
      Website: www.ambeeng.com
Engineering: corrective actions implementations, design
optimization, CAD/CAE design support, quality containment support. (Woman/As-Ind, estab 2001, empl 120,
sales $8,000,000, cert: NMSDC, WBENC)

3022 Array of Engineers, LLC
      2350 Oak Industrial Dr NE Ste 1
      Grand Rapids, MI 49505
      Contact: Stacy Paul CEO
      Tel: 989-858-1855
      Email: Stacy.paul@arrayofengineers.com
      Website: www.arrayofengineers.com/
Lifecycle and certification process related to DO-178,
MIL-STD-882E and similar standards. We specialize in all
aspects of hardware and software design from concep-
tion through product realization. (Woman, estab 2018,
empl 19, sales $1,200,000, cert: WBENC)

3023 Automotive Quality & Logistics, Inc.
      14744 Jib St
      Plymouth, MI 48170
      Contact: Joe Nosek VP
      Tel: 734-459-1670
      Email: jnosek@aql-inc.com
      Website: www.aql-inc.com
Sorting, inspection, containment, rework, engineering
support, supplier development, technical staffing,
warehousing. (Woman/As-Ind, estab 1994, empl 820,
sales $22,000,000, cert: NMSDC, WBENC)

3024 Bigelow Family Holdings LLC
      3223 15 Mile Rd
      Sterling Heights, MI 48310
      Contact: President
      Tel: 586-306-8962
      Email: info@mettleops.com
      Website: www.mettleops.com
Program management, engineering, and business
development. (Woman, estab 2013, empl 10, sales ,
cert: WBENC, 8(a))

3025 Byce & Associates, Inc.
      487 Portage St
      Kalamazoo, MI 49007
      Contact: Brenda Longman VP
      Tel: 269-381-6170
      Email: Accounting@byce.com
      Website: www.byce.com
Structural, mechanical & electrical engineering design
services. (Hisp, estab 1959, empl 34, sales , cert:
NMSDC)

3026 CAD Engineering Resources, Inc.
      6100 Auburn Rd
      Shelby Township, MI 48317
      Contact: Samantha Rutherford Mgr
      Tel: - -
      Email: dmurphy@cergroupna.com
      Website: www.cergroupna.com
Dimmensional support, CMM inpsection, 3rd party
quality containment & rework, quality residency
engineering, assembly and warehouseing. (Nat Ame,
estab 2003, empl 600, sales $20,000,000, cert: NMSDC)

3027 Capitol Reproductions, Inc.
215 E 12 Mile Rd
Madison Heights, MI 48071
Contact: Laura Muresan GM
Tel: 313-564-4820
Email: lauram@capitolgroup.net
Website: www.capitolgroup.net
Engineering, CAD design & technical Illustration services. (Woman, estab 1946, empl 48, sales $6,750,000, cert: WBENC)

3028 CTI and Associates, Inc.
34705 W 12 MILE RD Ste. 230
Farmington Hills, MI 48331
Contact: Jennifer Armstrong Admin
Tel: 248-486-5100
Email: jarmstrong@cticompanies.com
Website: www.cticompanies.com
Engineering consulting & construction management. (As-Ind, estab 1976, empl 150, sales $21,000,000, cert: NMSDC)

3029 Dakkota Integrated Systems, LLC
1875 Holloway Dr
Holt, MI 48842
Contact: Jessica Haughton Engineering Change Coordinator
Tel: 517-803-0755
Email: jessica.haughton@dakkotasystems.com
Website: www.dakkotasystems.com
Full-Service Interior Integration Management, Supplier Management, Assembly & Sequencing, JIT Product Delivery.
 (Woman/Nat Ame, estab 2001, empl 1114, sales $625,000,000, cert: NMSDC, WBENC)

3030 Detroit Engineered Products (DEP).
850 E Long Lake Rd
Troy, MI 48085
Contact: John Gelmisi Dir Business Devel
Tel: 248-219-9838
Email: john_gelmisi@depusa.com
Website: www.depusa.com
Reverse Engineering, Benchmarking, Scanning, Prototyping, Project Outsourcing, Offshore/Domestic Design support, and Technical Services. (As-Ind, estab 1998, empl 380, sales $18,000,000, cert: NMSDC)

3031 Doshi Associates, Inc.
5755 New King St Ste 210
Troy, MI 48098
Contact: Shailesh Doshi CEO
Tel: 248-247-3030
Email: shailesh.doshi@doshigroup.net
Website: www.doshigroup.net
Architecturel, civil, structural, mechanical & electrical engineering. (As-Pac, estab 1991, empl 30, sales $2,550,000, cert: NMSDC)

3032 Embedded Logix Inc.
50644 Sabrina Dr
Shelby, MI 48315
Contact: Deborah McLeod President
Tel: 586-709-2025
Email: dmcleod@emlogix.net
Website: www.emlogix.net
Product design for automotive, commercial & medical, test equipment design, test consulting, service, connector build, harness build, assembly test equipment. Embedded design, embedded programming, labview programming. (Woman, estab 0, empl , sales , cert: WBENC)

3033 Engineering Design Solutions PLC
5220 Lovers Lane, Ste LL-120
Portage, MI 49002
Contact: Irfan Ahmed, MSCE, PE President
Tel: 269-903-2652
Email: irfan.ahmed@enggdesigns.com
Website: www.enggdesigns.com
Manufacturing & industrial building design & CAD designing automobile facilities. (As-Ind, estab 2004, empl 8, sales $600,000, cert: NMSDC)

3034 ETCS Inc.
275 Executive Dr
Troy, MI 48083
Contact: Ravi Kapur Dir of Sales
Tel: 248-763-9467
Email: ravi@etcsinc.com
Website: www.etcsinc.com
Engineering, reverse engineering, tool design, staffing, offshore component sourcing. (Minority, estab 2003, empl 52, sales $4,826,000, cert: NMSDC)

3035 Feamold, Inc.
1441 W Long Lake Rd, Ste 240
Troy, MI 48098
Contact: Shrikant Oak President
Tel: 248-680-4628
Email: oak@feamold.com
Website: www.feamold.com
Engineering Consulting. (Minority, estab 1994, empl 5, sales , cert: NMSDC)

3036 Future Technologies, Inc.
2490 E Midland Rd
Bay City, MI 48706
Contact: Brent Waldie Applications Engineer
Tel: 989-686-6200
Email: brentw@futuretechnologies.com
Website: www.futuretechnologies.com
Custom leak testing systems, function testing equipment, welding & assembly automation & calibrated standard leaks. (Hisp, estab 1989, empl 33, sales , cert: NMSDC)

3037 Gala & Associates Inc.
31455 Southfield Rd
Beverly Hills, MI 48025
Contact: Chuni Gala President
Tel: 248-642-8610
Email: cgala@galaandassociates.com
Website: www.galaandassociates.com
Electrical, mechanical, structural, civil & architectural engineering svcs, CAD services. (As-Ind, estab 1987, empl 50, sales $6,000,000, cert: NMSDC)

3038   Generalety, LLC
5820 N Canton Center Rd Ste 140
Canton, MI 48187
Contact: Sheng-Dong Liu CEO
Tel: 734-522-1488
Email: sliu@generalety.com
Website: www.generalety.com
Computer aided design (CAD) & computer aided engineering (CAE) services in the automotive industry. (As-Pac, estab 2003, empl 60, sales $1,250,000, cert: NMSDC)

3039   Global Supply Innovative Engineering LLC
200 E Big Beaver
Troy, MI 48083
Contact: Dayle Farrimond VP
Tel: - -
Email: dfarrimond@gsiengineering.com
Website: www.gsiengineering.com
Injection Mold Building, Program Mgmt, Engineering, Sample Facility, Production Mfg Facility. (Woman, estab 2005, empl 7, sales $2,800,000, cert: WBENC)

3040   Gonzalez Aerospace
29401 Stephenson Hwy
Madison Heights, MI 48071
Contact: Pablo Calzada NBD Dir
Tel: 248-867-8212
Email: pcalzada@gonzalezaerospace.com
Website: www.gonzalezaerospace.com
Production Systems; Manufacturing Engineering, Program Management, Automated Assembly System Integration, Contingent Workforce Services. (Hisp, estab 1975, empl 130, sales $64,000,000, cert: NMSDC)

3041   Hybrid Design Services
2479 Elliott Dr
Troy, MI 48083
Contact: James Pinon President
Tel: 248-298-3400
Email: jpinon@hybriddesignservices.com
Website: www.hybriddesignservices.com
Engineering, design, prototyping, testing services specializing in hybrid vehicles & systems, electric vehicles & systems, HEV systems, EV systems, hybrid and electric vehicle R&D, high voltage systems, energy storage. (Hisp, estab 2007, empl 20, sales $2,000,000, cert: NMSDC)

3042   I*LOGIC, Inc.
999 Tech Row
Madison Heights, MI 48071
Contact: Sharon Weatherspoon President
Tel: 248-616-4506
Email: sweatherspoon@goilogic.com
Website: www.goilogic.com
Program management, containerization mgmt, industrial engineering, material flow engineering, procurement services, design services & IT services. (Minority, Woman, estab 1995, empl 32, sales , cert: NMSDC, WBENC)

3043   Magnys Innovative Solutions LLC
42500 W Eleven Mile Rd Ste B
Novi, MI 48375
Contact: Mary Willy Office Mgr
Tel: 248-449-2600
Email: mwilly@magnys.com
Website: www.magnys.com
Design, oversee process, project engineering services, manufacturing engineering, 3-D simulation & PLC emulation software modeling. (AA, estab 1999, empl 210, sales $25,000,000, cert: NMSDC)

3044   MPS Group, Inc.
38755 Hills Tech Dr
Farmington Hills, MI 48331
Contact: Bryon Lawrence Dir Sales/Marketing
Tel: 313-841-7588
Email: blawrence@mpsgrp.com
Website: www.mpsgrp.com
Environmental Consulting & Engineering. (AA, estab 1995, empl 495, sales $46,200,000, cert: NMSDC)

3045   Optimal Computer Aided Engineering, Inc.
47802 W Anchor Court
Plymouth, MI 48170
Contact: Song Young CEO
Tel: 734-414-7933
Email: ksrinivas@optimalinc.com
Website: www.optimalinc.com
CAD/CAM/CAE/PDM services, contract engineering services & metrology product sales & support. (As-Pac, estab 1986, empl 100, sales $10,000,000, cert: NMSDC)

3046   PAT USA, Inc.
2927 Waterview Dr
Rochester Hills, MI 48309
Contact: Fenar Mayes Sr Project Mgr
Tel: 248-299-2410
Email: fenar@pat-engineering.com
Website: www.pat-engineering.com
General contracting services, engineering & construction services. (Woman, estab 2011, empl 10, sales , cert: WBENC)

3047   Process Control & Engineering Inc.
1091 Centre Rd, Ste 290
Auburn Hills, MI 48326
Contact: Theresa Dies Treasurer
Tel: 248-340-1888
Email: tdies@pcemonarch.com
Website: www.pcemonarch.com
Monitoring & Control System for process air & fluid parameters, VOC emissions, air and fluid handling equipment. Monitoring and Control system for: Process parameters: air velocities, humidity, temperature, fluid flows, viscosity, chemical parameters. (Minority, estab 1994, empl 15, sales $9,000,000, cert: NMSDC)

3048   Renaissance S & S Inc.
26637 Golfview
Dearborn Heights, MI 48127
Contact: Smith Sylvester CEO
Tel: 313-561-3897
Email: rssgroup@sbcglobal.net
Website: www.renaissancessgroup.com
Engineering consulting services. (AA, estab 1996, empl 4, sales , cert: NMSDC)

3049   Sigma Associates, Inc.
1900 St. Antoine St
Detroit, MI 48226
Contact: Kathy Cotton Administrative Asst
Tel: 313-963-9700
Email: kcotton@sigmaassociates.com
Website: www.sigmaassociates.com
Multi-disciplinary engineering, architectural, program management, construction contract admin, construction management, design-build capabilities & information technology services. (Woman, estab 1978, empl 51, sales , cert: State, WBENC, SDB)

3050 SoundTech Inc.
      3880 SoundTech Ct
      Grand Rapids, MI 49512
      Contact: Amy Sparks President
      Tel: 616-575-0866
      Email: asparks@soundtechinc.com
      Website: www.soundtechinc.com
Engineer acoustic & thermal insulation solutions. (Woman, estab 1987, empl 90, sales $29,011,176, cert: WBENC)

3051 Universal Tool Equipment & Controls, Inc.
      6525 Center Dr
      Sterlng Heights, MI 48312
      Contact: Bill Bartolotta VP
      Tel: 586-268-4380
      Email: bbartolotta@universaltecinc.com
      Website: www.universaltecinc.com
Automation & welding systems, robotics, weld guns, vision systems, sealant systems, drawn arc welders, projection welders, material handling end effectors & welding fixtures. (Woman/AA, estab 2009, empl 29, sales $10,000,000, cert: WBENC)

3052 WFQ, Inc.
      5751 S. Sheldon Rd
      Canton, MI 48188
      Contact: Jennifer McGuire Sales Acct Mgr
      Tel: 734-512-6284
      Email: jmcguire@wfqinc.com
      Website: www.wfqinc.com
GP12/Launch support, Resident Liaison / Customer representation Quality Engineering services (placement or hire) Containment, Inspection & Re-work Solutions Sequence / Kitting solutions Warehouse capabilities Proprietary Web-based Reporting System. (Woman, estab 2013, empl 150, sales $5,780,000, cert: WBENC)

3053 Willie Horton Inc.
      7784 Ronda Dr
      Canton, MI 48187
      Contact: Deryl Horton President
      Tel: 248-855-2215
      Email: dhorton@horton-inc.com
      Website: www.horton-inc.com
Heat-treating, hardening, surface engineering, tool steel, mechcanical & electrical engineering. (AA, estab 2003, empl 20, sales , cert: NMSDC)

Minnesota

3054 EVS, Inc.
      10025 Valley View Rd Ste 140
      Eden Prairie, MN 55344
      Contact: Andy Kim President
      Tel: 952-646-0236
      Email: akim@evs-eng.com
      Website: www.evs-eng.com
Civil engineering, site development, surveying & environmental, permits, assessments & NEPA documentation. (As-Pac, estab 1979, empl 61, sales $7,432,378, cert: NMSDC)

3055 Fourth Factor Engineering, LLC
      10636 Maryland Ave S
      Bloomington, MN 55438
      Contact: Elizabeth Becker President
      Tel: 612-708-2562
      Email: liz.becker@fourth-factor-engineering.com
      Website: www.fourth-factor-engineering.com
Engineering analysis: system safety, software safety, human factors, reliability, maintainability, testability & logistics analysis. (Woman, estab 2010, empl 6, sales $1,049,233, cert: State, WBENC)

3056 Hansen Thorp Pellinen Olson, Inc.
      7510 Market Place Dr
      Eden Prairie, MN 55344
      Contact: Tim Johnson Business Devel Dir
      Tel: 952-829-0700
      Email: tjohnson@htpo.com
      Website: www.htpo.com
Engineering svcs: land surveying, civil engineering, landscape architecture design & construction. (Woman, estab 1980, empl 23, sales $2,876,105, cert: City)

3057 L.W. Survey Engineering & Design Company
      1 E First St
      Duluth, MN 55802
      Contact: Richard Grogan Dir Business Dev
      Tel: 218-722-8211
      Email: r.grogan@lwsurvey.com
      Website: www.lwsurvey.com
Engineering, drafting (AutoCAD), surveying, inspection, right of way, project management. (Nat Ame, estab 1998, empl 35, sales , cert: NMSDC)

3058 Questions & Solutions Engineering
      1079 Falls Curve
      Chaska, MN 55318
      Contact: Rebecca Ellis
      Tel: 612-309-0503
      Email: rebecca.ellis@qseng.com
      Website: www.QSEng.com
Commissioning program development, training & project execution, existing building troubleshooting, retro-commissioning, re-commissioning, HVAC system planning & implementing capital projects. (Woman, estab 2005, empl 4, sales $181,000, cert: City, WBENC)

3059 Sambatek
      14800 28th Ave N, Ste 140
      Plymouth, MN 55447
      Contact: Erik Miller Sales
      Tel: 763-476-6010
      Email: emiller@sambatek.com
      Website: www.sambatek.com
Civil engineering, land planning & surveying, water & waste water treatment process engineering, enviornmental assesments. (As-Pac, estab 1966, empl 46, sales $5,269,743, cert: State)

3060 SM Engineering Co.
      9 Ninth Ave N
      Hopkins, MN 55343
      Contact: Wayne Peterson COO
      Tel: 952-938-7407
      Email: wayne@smeng.com
      Website: www.smeng.com
Utility management: electricity, natural gas, water & sewer. (As-Ind, estab 1982, empl 13, sales $2,921,000, cert: NMSDC)

Missouri

3061   Ameri-Pac, Inc.
751 S 4TH ST
Joseph, MO 65501
Contact: Robert Colescott President
Tel: 816-233-4530
Email: bobc@ameri-pac.com
Website: www.ameri-pac.com
Mfr animal nutrition specialty products. (Woman, estab 1985, empl 45, sales , cert: WBENC)

3062   Civil Design Inc.
5220 Oakland Ave
St. Louis, MO 63110
Contact: Lori Daiber Business Devel Mgr
Tel: 314-916-1178
Email: ldaiber@civildesigninc.com
Website: www.civildesigninc.com
Civil & Site Engineering, Land Surveying, Transportation, Water Resources, Infrastructure & Analytics. (Woman, estab 1996, empl 52, sales $5,800,000, cert: State, WBENC, NWBOC)

3063   David Mason & Associates, Inc.
800 S Vandeventer Ave
St. Louis, MO 63110
Contact: Taylor Mason Business Devel
Tel: 314-534-1030
Email: tmason@davidmason.com
Website: www.davidmason.com
Professional survey, civil & structural engineering services. (AA, estab 1989, empl 50, sales $48,327,574, cert: NMSDC)

3064   EFK Moen, LLC
13523 Barrett Pkwy Dr Ste 250
St. Louis, MO 63021
Contact: Darrell Eilers VP
Tel: 314-729-4104
Email: dleilers@efkmoen.com
Website: www.EFKMoen.com
Civil engineering & land surveying, roadway/highway engineering, bridge/structural design, site/development engineering, water/wastewater, traffic/transportation engineering. (Woman, estab 1998, empl 35, sales $2,700,000, cert: State)

3065   Peoria Contract Services, LLC
6428 Lipizzaner Dr
Imperial, MO 63052
Contact: Kyle Pogue CEO
Tel: 314-761-5470
Email: kyle@peoriacontractservices.com
Website: www.pcs-energy.com
Engineering, Electrical, Mechanical, Chemical, Process, Civil, Structural, Patented Modular Extrusion Process; ASME/API Storage Vessels; Bulk Material Handling/ Storage; Automation; Piping Design & Pipe Supply; Hydraulic & Pneumatic. (Nat Ame, estab 2012, empl 5, sales , cert: State, NMSDC)

3066   Webb Engineering Services, Inc.
4670 Lansdowne Ave, Ste 111
St. Louis, MO 63116
Contact: Stanley Webb President
Tel: 314-351-0440
Email: webbs@webb-engineering.com
Website: www.webb-engineering.com
Mechanical, electrical, fire protection, plumbing, & civil design services. (AA, estab 1999, empl 8, sales $1,000,000, cert: City, 8(a))

North Carolina

3067   ENPULSE Energy Conservation, Inc.
100 N Elm St, Ste 138
Greensboro, NC 27401
Contact: Derrick Giles President
Tel: 336-370-1088
Email: info@enpulse.com
Website: www.enpulse.com
Engineering services, energy management, utility bill audits, engineering studies, measurement & verification, building commissioning (AA, estab 2002, empl 3, sales , cert: State, City)

3068   ImmunoReagents Inc.
6003 Chapel Hill Road Ste. 153
Raleigh, NC 27607
Contact: Ann Black CEO
Tel: 919-831-2240
Email: sales@immunoreagents.com
Website: www.immunoreagents.com
Mfr highly purified polyclonal antibodies used in the life sciences & immunodiagnostic industries. (Woman, estab 2005, empl 14, sales $1,636,402, cert: WBENC)

3069   John Davenport Engineering, Inc.
305 W Fourth St Ste 2A
Winston-Salem, NC 27101
Contact: Shari Mauk Chief Admin Officer
Tel: 336-744-1636
Email: smauk@davenportworld.com
Website: www.davenportworld.com
Roadway design, traffic signal design, transportation engineering, civil engineering, transportation planning, construction support, construction engineering & inspection, traffic data collection, turning movement counts. (AA, estab 2002, empl 21, sales $1,629,947, cert: State, City, 8(a))

3070   RDAF Energy Solutions
6201 Fairview Rd Ste 200
Charlotte, NC 28210
Contact: Rickey Hart Chairman
Tel: 980-205-1220
Email: rickey.hart@rdafenergy.net
Website: www.rdafenergy.net
Energy consulting & management, market & sell power, natural gas, renewable & sustainable energy & services. (AA, estab 2016, empl 5, sales $16,096,148, cert: NMSDC, CPUC)

3071   Sud Associates PA
1813 Chapel Hill Rd
Durham, NC 27707
Contact: Ish Sud President
Tel: 919-493-5277
Email: sudmain@sudassociates.com
Website: www.sudassociates.com
Energy svcs & studies: recycling process produced heat, energy conserving HVAC, electrical, plumbing. (Minority, estab 1980, empl 23, sales $2,000,000, cert: State, City)

New Jersey

3072 3A Engineering & Validation LLC
122 Lexington Ave
Maplewood, NJ 07040
Contact: Adebayo Boboye Principal Engineer
Tel: 973-715-0541
Email: adebayo.boboye@3a-engineering.com
Website: www.3a-engineering.com
Engineering services, qualification, commissioning & validation of manufacturing processes & products. (AA, estab 2007, empl 1, sales $120,000, cert: NMSDC)

3073 Consolidated Energy Design, Inc.
1933 Hwy 35 Ste 105
Wall, NJ 07719
Contact: Rey Montalvo President
Tel: 732-681-8800
Email: reym@cedinternational.com
Website: www.fadrs.com
Smart Grid and Smart Micro Grid technology. (Hisp, estab 1987, empl 2, sales $101,432, cert: NMSDC)

3074 Economic Project Solutions, Inc.
2 King Arthur Ct, Ste E
North Brunswick, NJ 08902
Contact: Sabrina Staats Mgr of Corporate Compliance
Tel: 732-248-1110
Email: sstaats@economicprojects.com
Website: www.economicprojects.com
Construction consulting, facilities mgmt, move mgmt, OSHA fire & safety, property mgmt & technical design services. (Woman, estab 1997, empl 72, sales $21,172,800, cert: WBENC)

3075 IFSI General Contractor, Co.
1245 Main St Apt 232
Rahway, NJ 07065
Contact: Rita (Joanie) George CEO
Tel: 908-339-2842
Email: sales@ifsgc.com
Website: www.industrialfiberglassservices.com
Civil, Mechanical, FRP Repair & Installation. (Woman, estab 2000, empl 7, sales $3,000,000, cert: WBENC)

3076 inRange Solutions II, LLC
695 Route 46 W, Ste 103
Fairfield, NJ 07004
Contact: Edwin Gomez President
Tel: - -
Email: ss@inrange-llc.com
Website: www.inrangesolutions.com
DAS, Wireless and Telecom Design and Engineering, Site Acquisition, Real Estate Negotiation, Zoning and Permitting, Project Management, Architectural Engineering and Design, Electrical Engineering and Design, Mechanical Engineering and Design. (As-Pac, estab 2011, empl 24, sales $6,000,000, cert: State, City, NMSDC)

3077 KS Engineers, P.C.
2 Riverfront Plaza 3rd Fl
Newark, NJ 07102
Contact: KAMAL SHAHID President
Tel: 973-623-2999
Email: info@kseng.com
Website: www.kseng.com
Engineering, surveying & construction management. (As-Ind, estab 1991, empl 275, sales $25,000,000, cert: State, City, NMSDC)

3078 Matrix New World Engineering, Land Surveying and Landscape Architectur
26 Columbia Trnpke 2nd Fl
Florham Park, NJ 07932
Contact: Jayne Warne, PE President
Tel: 973-240-1800
Email: jwarne@mnwe.com
Website: www.matrixneworld.com
Environmental, geotechnical, civil engineering, survey & building facility consulting & engineering firm. (Woman, estab 1990, empl 200, sales $28,899,396, cert: State, City, WBENC)

3079 MFS Consulting Engineers & Surveyor, DPC
2780 Hamilton Blvd
South Plainfield, NJ 07080
Contact: Jeffrey Clark Sr Project Admin
Tel: 908-922-4622
Email: jac@mfsengineers.com
Website: www.MFSengineers.com
Site/civil, structural, geotechnical & foundation, environmental engineering, construction layout, sustainable design & construction management services. (Minority, estab 2009, empl 32, sales $4,403,207, cert: State, City, 8(a))

3080 Sovereign
111 A North Gold Dr
Robbinsville, NJ 08691
Contact: Michael Hanlon Mgr
Tel: 609-259-8200
Email: mhanlon@sovcon.com
Website: www.sovcon.com
Environmental consulting & remediation services, environmental, civil & geotechnical engineering; remediation system evaluation, optimization, design & construction/installation; environmental, land use & natural resources permitting. (As-Pac, estab 1999, empl 165, sales $35,466,433, cert: NMSDC)

New York

3081 Airosmith Development
32 Clinton St
Saratoga Springs, NY 12866
Contact: Ann DAlessandro Dir Business Devel
Tel: 518-350-4060
Email: adalessandro@airosmithdevelopment.com
Website: www.airosmithdevelopment.com
Provide Make ready survey & design engineering, outside plant engineering, 3rd party application processing, easements and permitting, GIS mapping, asset management, project management & site acquisition. (Woman, estab 2004, empl 75, sales $17,917,031, cert: WBENC)

3082 Associated Renewable
1370 Broadway 5th Fl
New York, NY 10018
Contact: Manoj Patel CEO
Tel: 212-444-8214
Email: mbe@associatedrenewable.com
Website: www.associatedrenewable.com/
Energy management, cut energy costs, reduce energy wastage, meet regulatory requirements, building energy audits, install new energy-efficient equipment, supply electricity, natural gas & renewable energy. (As-Pac, estab 2010, empl 8, sales $420,000, cert: NMSDC)

3083 DESMAN, Inc. dba DESMAN Associates
     3 W 35th ST 3rd Fl
     New York, NY 10001
     Contact: ANUP CHHABRA CFO
     Tel: 212-686-5360
     Email: achhabra@desman.com
     Website: www.desman.com
Parking consulting, design, planning and restoration. (As-Ind, estab 1984, empl 100, sales $18,000,000, cert: NMSDC)

3084 Dose Engineering, PLLC
     15 W 38TH ST Fl. 4, Ste 736
     New York, NY 10018
     Contact: Anostere Jean Principal
     Tel: 646-715-2096
     Email: ajean@dose-engineering.com
     Website: www.dose-engineering.com
Engineering design, engineering design drawings, due diligence reports Mechanical: HVAC Electrical: Lighting and Power Plumbing Fire Alarm Fire Protection LEED: Leadership in Energy and Environmental (AA, estab 2009, empl 5, sales $300,000, cert: State, City, NMSDC)

3085 Environmental Design & Research, DPC
     217 Montgomery St Ste 1000
     Syracuse, NY 13202
     Contact: Joanne Stewart Associate
     Tel: 315-471-0688
     Email: jstewart@edrdpc.com
     Website: www.edrdpc.com
Landscape architecture, civil engineering, community planning, visualization, environmental regulatory, ecological, geographic information systems mapping & analysis, historic preservation, cultural resources, archeology. (Woman, estab 1979, empl 38, sales $4,500,000, cert: State)

3086 Foit-Albert Associates, Architecture, Engineering
     and Surveying, P.C.
     215 W 94th St, Ste 517
     New York, NY 10025
     Contact: Gregory Carballada President
     Tel: 716-856-3933
     Email: cstoebe@foit-albert.com
     Website: www.foit-albert.com
Architecture, Engineering, Environmental & Land Surveying Consulting. (Hisp, estab 1977, empl 70, sales $10,000,000, cert: State, City)

3087 Karp Strategies, LLC
     26 Broadway
     New York, NY 10004
     Contact: Rebecca Karp CEO
     Tel: 718-530-1728
     Email: rebecca@karpstrategies.com
     Website: www.karpstrategies.com
Urban strategy consultancy, community-economic development planning, community and stakeholder engagement, and real estate and urban planning. (As-Pac, estab 2015, empl 16, sales , cert: State, City)

3088 KLD Engineering PC
     1601 Veterans Memorial Hwy Ste 340
     Islandia, NY 11749
     Contact: Kacie Larson HR & Contract Mgr
     Tel: 631-524-5940
     Email: klarsen@kldcompanies.com
     Website: www.kldcompanies.com
Transportation Engineering Consultant. Professional Engineering services concentrated in three primary areas: (1) Traffic Engineering & ITS; (2) Evacuation & Emergency planning; (3) GIS & other support services to "1" & "2" (As-Ind, estab 1997, empl 25, sales , cert: State, City, CPUC)

3089 Sabir, Richardson & Weisberg Engineers PLLC
     37 W 39th St, Ste 1005
     NYC, NY 10018
     Contact: Yvette Richardson Principal
     Tel: 646-863-6160
     Email: info@srw-eng.com
     Website: www.srw-eng.com
Engineering svcs: architectural, mechanical, electrical, fire protection & plumbing consulting. (Woman/AA, Hisp, estab 2004, empl 1, sales $2,018,954, cert: State, City)

3090 SoundSense, LLC
     46 Newtown Lane Ste 1
     East Hampton, NY 11937
     Contact: Maryann Buquicchio Sr admin asst
     Tel: 631-324-2266
     Email: maryann@soundsense.com
     Website: www.soundsense.com
Acoustic consulting & design services, efficacy & compliance testing, site inspection services & innovative acoustical products. (Woman, estab 1981, empl 9, sales $2,623,444, cert: City, WBENC)

3091 Toll International LLC
     303 Fifth Ave Ste 211
     New York, NY 10016
     Contact: Nure M Aiza Bezares President
     Tel: 212-710-2633
     Email: nure.aiza@tollintl.com
     Website: www.tollintl.com
Construction experts, schedulers, construction managers, estimators, business consultants and information technology experts. (Hisp, estab 2005, empl 11, sales $2,410,000, cert: State, City, NMSDC)

3092 W. Allen Engineering PLLC
     400 Strawtown Rd
     West Nyack, NY 10994
     Contact: Wayne Allen Principal
     Tel: 646-398-7870
     Email: info@wallenengineering.com
     Website: www.wallenengineering.com
Civil & mechanical engineering, construction inspection/management services, contract admin, owner representation, cost estimating, lead based paint abatement, drafting, HVAC design. (AA, estab 1997, empl 12, sales $1,200,000, cert: State, City)

3093 Watts Engineering & Architecture, P.C.
95 Perry St Ste 300
Buffalo, NY 14203
Contact: Edward Watts President
Tel: 716-836-1540
Email: ewatts@wattsengineers.com
Website: www.wattsengineers.com
Civil, environmental, mechancial & electrical engineering
& architecture consulting. (AA, estab 1986, empl 73, sales
$6,800,000, cert: City, NMSDC)

3094 WM Group Services, LLC
Two Penn Plaza Ste 552
New York, NY 10121
Contact: Hemant Mehta Controller
Tel: 646-827-6400
Email: hmehta@wmgroupeng.com
Website: www.wmgroupeng.com
Study, Design, optimization of Central Utilities Systems:
cooling, heating & power. (As-Pac, estab , empl , sales
$2,697,396, cert: NMSDC)

Ohio

3095 Advanced Engineering Consultants, Ltd.
1405 Dublin Road
Columbus, OH 43215
Contact: Sam Reed Principal
Tel: 614-486-4778
Email: samr@aecmep.com
Website: www.aecmep.com
Mechanical, Electrical, Plumbing, Fire Protection, Technol-
ogy engineering design & construction administration
services. (Minority, Woman, estab 1998, empl 70, sales
$13,925,055, cert: State, City)

3096 Airecon Manufacturing Corporation
5271 Brotherton Court
Cincinnati, OH 45227
Contact: Josh Jacobs President
Tel: 513-561-5522
Email: josh@airecon.com
Website: www.airecon.com
Design, fabricate & install industrial dust, mist & fume
control equipment & systems, fume exhaust pneumatic
conveying, supply & exhasut ventilation, clean air rooms &
other industrial air handling systems. (Hisp, estab 1979,
empl 40, sales $9,000,000, cert: NMSDC)

3097 AMG, Inc.
1497 Shoup Mill Rd
Dayton, OH 45414
Contact: LeAnn Thompson VP Engineering
Tel: 937-274-0736
Email: jbaddour@amg-eng.com
Website: www.amg-eng.com
Feasibility studies, conceptual design, capital cost
esimtates, detailed design engineering, project manage-
ment through construction management, commissioning.
(Hisp, estab 1980, empl 40, sales $16,921,031, cert:
NMSDC)

3098 Atmos360, Inc
64 Circle Freeway Dr
Cincinnati, OH 45246
Contact: Icy Williams President
Tel: 513-330-6688
Email: iwilliams@atmos360.com
Website: www.atmos360.com
Engineering & design of air system &
custom/specialty fabricated products, Dust/Aerosol
Control, Process Air, Central
Vacuum Cleaning, HVAC and Heated air Make-up
Systems. (Woman/AA, estab 1989, empl 40, sales
$17,000,000, cert: State, NMSDC, WBENC)

3099 Balance Product Development, Inc.
3615 Superior Ave. Ste 4402B
Cleveland, OH 44114
Contact: Rene Polin President
Tel: 440-247-4711
Email: rene@balanceinc.com
Website: www.balanceinc.com
Industrial Design, product design, CAD development,
prototype development, concept ideation, packaging
design, graphic design, innovation, engineering, product
research, ergonomic research, user interface design.
(Hisp, estab 2004, empl 10, sales , cert: NMSDC)

3100 CAD Concepts, Inc.
2323 West 5th Ave Ste 120
Columbus, OH 43204
Contact: Joyce K Johnson
Tel: 614-485-0670
Email: certifications@ccitechs.com
Website: www.ccitechs.com
Engineering support services: CAD, GIS, field work &
administrative services. (Woman, estab 1984, empl 26,
sales , cert: State, WBENC)

3101 CTL Engineering, Inc.
2860 Fisher Rd
Columbus, OH 43204
Contact: C.K. Satyapriya President
Tel: 614-276-8123
Email: ctl@ctleng.com
Website: www.ctleng.com
Geotechnical, construction inspection, environmental,
mining engineering, analytical chemistry, forensic
science, metallurgy, product testing, research & development, roof engineering, existing structure evaluation,
asbestos inspection. (Minority, estab 1928, empl 187,
sales , cert: NMSDC)

3102 DHDC Engineering Consulting Services, Inc.
2390 Advanced Business Center Dr
Columbus, OH 43228
Contact: Savvas Sophocleous President
Tel: 614-527-7656
Email: sophocleous@dhdcinc.com
Website: www.dhdcinc.com
Laboratory testing services, geotechnical (engineering,
drilling, and laboratory) & subsurface utility engineering
(SUE). (As-Pac, estab 2012, empl 15, sales $500,000,
cert: State)

3103   DLZ Industrial, LLC
6121 Huntley Rd
Columbus, OH 43229
Contact: Kurt Schmiegel CEO
Tel: 614-888-0040
Email: mbe@dlz.com
Website: www.dlz.com
Industrial surveying, close tolerance machinery surveying, setting & realignment, construction, topographical, hydrographic & property surveying. (Minority, estab 1989, empl 568, sales , cert: NMSDC)

3104   Moody Engineering, LLC
300 Spruce St Ste 200
Columbus, OH 43215
Contact: President
Tel: 614-280-8999
Email:
Website: www.moody-eng.com
Stormwater management, Site design, Sediment and erosion control, Roadway, Permits - NPDES, PTI, zoning, Vehicular access, Grading, Pedestrian traffic, Drainage, Parking lots, Wet and dry ponds, Utility design, Domestic water, Underground infrastructure. (AA, estab 2015, empl 10, sales $1,924,000, cert: State, City)

3105   Noble Technologies Corp. (DBA NobleTek)
1909 Old Mansfield Road
Wooster, OH 44691
Contact: Nathan Kramar Business Devel
Tel: 360-391-0055
Email: nathan.kramar@nobletek.com
Website: www.nobletek.com
3D CAD & Drafting. (As-Pac, estab 2009, empl 42, sales , cert: NMSDC)

3106   On Line Design, Inc.
12059 Sheraton Ln
Cincinnati, OH 45246
Contact: Kimberly Persiani Client Advisor
Tel: 513-476-3113
Email: Persiani.K@o-l-design.com
Website: www.o-l-design.com
Engineering & technical personnel: plant & capital projects, design/build equipment. (Woman, estab 1989, empl 50, sales $2,200,000, cert: WBENC)

3107   R Engineering Team, LLC
3100 E 45th St, Ste 306
Cleveland, OH 44127
Contact: Tom Roberts President
Tel: 216-361-2500
Email: rengineeringteam@gmail.com
Website: www.rengineeringteam.com
Consulting engineering in the disciplines of electrical engineering, mechanical engineering, construction administration, and computer CAD drafting. (AA, estab 2008, empl 7, sales $687,194, cert: State, City, NMSDC)

3108   Resource International
1740 St. Clair Ave
Cleveland, OH 44114
Contact: Brian Winslett Dir of Operations
Tel: 216-781-2820
Email: brianw@resourceinternational.com
Website: www.resourceintl.com
Civil engineering & engineering support services: environmental assessments, geotechnical engineering, surveying & construction material testing. (Minority, Woman, estab 1974, empl 100, sales $10,000,000, cert: WBENC)

3109   THORS, LLC
5054 Paramount Blvd.
Medina, OH 44256
Contact: Senthil Kumar Founder
Tel: 330-576-4448
Email: sales@thors.com
Website: www.thors.com
Mfg process training for procurement, design engineers & quality teams in commodities such as - castings, machining, gears, steel manufacturing, forgings, polymers with a tools center that includes a supplier manager, tooling manager & parts manager. (Minority, Woman, estab 2010, empl 11, sales , cert: NMSDC)

3110   Williams Engineering LLC
1836 Dana Ave
Cincinnati, OH 45207
Contact: Kennard Williams President
Tel: 513-731-6400
Email: keino.williams@williamsenginedesign.com
Website: www.williamsenginedesign.com
Engineering & mfg services, 3D CAD modeling & product development of machine tools, aerospace, medical and automotive aftermarket parts. (AA, estab 2005, empl 1, sales , cert: State)

Oklahoma

3111   Cameron Glass
3550 W Tacoma St
Broken Arrow, OK 74012
Contact: Angie Mann Customer Service Mgr
Tel: 918-307-4720
Email: angiem@camglass.com
Website: www.camglass.com
Glass fabrication, Glass bending, Tempering, Saftey glass, Screen printing. (Nat Ame, estab 1978, empl 120, sales $18,000,000, cert: NMSDC)

3112   Excellence Engineering, LLC
8670 S Peoria Ave
Tulsa, OK 74132
Contact: Deyona Hays CEO
Tel: 918-298-5500
Email: dee.hays@eeinco.com
Website: www.eeinco.com
Engineering, civil, structural, process, piping, mechanical, electrical, instrument, controls, startup & commissioning. (Woman, estab 2001, empl 40, sales , cert: WBENC)

Oregon

3113   Elcon Associates, Inc.
12670 NW Barnes Rd
Portland, OR 97229
Contact: Donna Freeman Marketing Mgr
Tel: 503-644-2490
Email: dfreeman@elcon.com
Website: www.elcon.com
Electrical energy: high voltage, project management, studies, cost estimating, and construction management, utility power systems, power distribution, PLC based control systems, energy management/SCADA. (As-Ind, estab 1975, empl 47, sales $5,600,000, cert: NMSDC)

Pennsylvania

3114 Advantus Engineers
300 Bilmar Dr Ste 150
Pittsburgh, PA 15205
Contact: Alicia Avick President
Tel: 412-489-9090
Email: aavick@advantusengineers.com
Website: www.advantusengineers.com
Facilities design engineering, commissioning, project management & construction management services for the commercial, institutional & light industrial markets. (Minority, Woman, estab 2004, empl 10, sales $550,000, cert: State, WBENC)

3115 Aquatech International Corporation
1 Four Coins Dr
Canaonsburg, PA 15317
Contact: Francis D'sa Reg Sales Mgr
Tel: 724-746-5300
Email: aic@aquatech.com
Website: www.aquatech.com
Mfr water & waste water treatment equip & systems. ASME tank & piping fabricators. (Minority, Woman, estab 1981, empl 450, sales $80,000,000, cert: NMSDC)

3116 Biopharm Project Solutions
119 Jaffrey Rd
Malvern, PA 19355
Contact: Surjit Sengha President
Tel: 484-614-0869
Email: surjs@biopharmprojects.com
Website: www.biopharmprojects.com
Process engineering, equipment, utilities & equipment cleaning/sterilization systems, automation engineering, project management & engineering staffing, equipment design engineering, factory testing, start-up. (As-Ind, estab 1987, empl 10, sales $2,500,000, cert: NMSDC)

3117 C & R Communications Group
2814 Guilford St
Philadelphia, PA 19152
Contact: Marc Carroll President
Tel: 215-480-0130
Email:
marc.carroll@candrcommunicationsgroup.com
Website: www.candrcommunicationsgroup.com
Engineering, Procurement, Installation, and Certification of Communication Infrastructure Solutions. (Hisp, estab 2009, empl 15, sales , cert: NMSDC)

3118 Chester Engineers, Inc.
1555 Coraopolis Heights Rd
Moon Township, PA 15108
Contact: Elaine Talak Exec Asst
Tel: 412-809-6576
Email: etalak@chesterengineers.com
Website: www.chesterengineers.com
Engineering consulting services, construct. mgmt., water resource mgmt., scientific research & environmental mgmt. (AA, estab 1987, empl 200, sales $14,500,000, cert: NMSDC)

3119 Dawood Engineering, Inc.
2020 Good Hope Rd
Enola, PA 17025
Contact: Kristal Martinez
Tel: 717-732-8576
Email: kmartinez@dawood.cc
Website: www.dawood.cc
Civil Site Design, Survey & Mapping, Environmental Consulting, Mechanical & Electrical Engineering, Geotechnical Engineering Structural Engineering. (Minority, estab 1992, empl 161, sales $20,100,000, cert: NMSDC)

3120 Diversified Global Systems, LLC.
721 Arbor Way Ste 100
Blue Bell, PA 19422
Contact: Dale Hobbie Managing Dir
Tel: 703-963-4942
Email: dale.hobbie@diversifiedglobalsystems.com
Website: www.diversifiedglobalsystems.com
Finance, Site Development, Design, Engineering, Procurement Management, Construction Management (Pre-Construction and Construction), Project Management, Program Management & Operations & Maintenance services. (Nat Ame, estab 2016, empl 5, sales $265,000, cert: NMSDC)

3121 First Capital Engineering
48 S Richland Ave
York, PA 17404
Contact: Ann Luciani CEO
Tel: 717-845-3227
Email: annl@fcap.com
Website: www.fcap.com
Civil engineering, land surveying, landscape architecture, environmental & construction inspection services. (Woman, estab 1995, empl 17, sales $1,949,255, cert: State, WBENC)

3122 GAI Construction Monitoring Services, Inc. dba CMT Services Group
24 Portland Rd
Conshohocken, PA 19428
Contact: Valerie Moody President
Tel: 610-731-0430
Email: v.moody@cmtservicesgroup.com
Website: www.cmtservicesgroup.com
Geotechnical engineering, environmental consulting, construction materials testing, special inspections, engineering materials forensic investigations. (Woman, estab 1986, empl 23, sales $2,200,000, cert: WBENC)

3123 IES Engineers
1720 Walton Rd
Blue Bell, PA 19422
Contact: Lisa Wallis Mgr, Accounting & Administrative Services
Tel: 610-828-3078
Email: lwallis@iesengineers.com
Website: www.iesengineers.com
Engineering & environmental, health & safety consulting, regulatory compliance. (As-Ind, estab 1991, empl 30, sales $8,223,000, cert: NMSDC)

3124   RNDT, Inc.
       228 Maple Ave
       Johnstown, PA 15901
       Contact: VP Technical Dir
       Tel: 814-535-5448
       Email: info@rndt.net
       Website: www.rndt.net
Nondestructive testing services, radiographic, magnetic
particle, liquid penetrant, ultrasonic and visual testing
services. Also offer Positive Material Identification (PMI),
remote video, certified welding inspector services (CWI).
(Woman, estab 2002, empl 35, sales $5,800,000, cert:
WBENC)

3125   Rodriguez Consulting LLC
       1301 N 2nd St
       Philadelphia, PA 19122
       Contact: Yarelis Franco Marketing Coord
       Tel: 215-839-8087
       Email: yfranco@rodriguezconsulting.biz
       Website: www.rodriguezconsulting.biz
Civil engineering, site design, environmental engineering,
land surveying, traffic data collection and engineering,
construction inspection & geographic information systems
(GIS) services. (Hisp, estab 2007, empl 22, sales $909,000,
cert: City, 8(a))

3126   TesTex, Inc.
       535 Old Frankstown Rd, Ste A
       Pittsburgh, PA 15239
       Contact: Robert Gormley President
       Tel: 412-798-8990
       Email: r.gormley@testex-ndt.com
       Website: www.testex-ndt.com
Electromagnetic NDT systems & services: inspect ferrous
& non-ferrous components. (Minority, estab 1987, empl
50, sales $14,700,000, cert: NMSDC)

3127   TREC Group, Inc.
       900 Old Marple Rd.
       Springfield, PA 19064
       Contact: Dir Business Devel
       Tel: 610-328-6465
       Email: info@trecgroup.com
       Website: www.trecgroup.com
Mechanical, electrical & civil engineering, project management, construction management, drafting & AUTOCAD
capabilities. (Woman, estab 2001, empl 11, sales , cert:
State, WBENC)

3128   ValSource, Inc.
       918A Horseshoe Pike
       Downingtown, PA 19335
       Contact: Deborah Stanton President
       Tel: 610-269-2808
       Email: dstanton@valsource.com
       Website: www.valsource.com
Commissioning, Qualification and Validation Services
(Woman, estab 1996, empl 220, sales $34,000,000, cert:
WBENC)

Puerto Rico

3129   Aireko Construction Management Services, LLC
       PO Box 2128
       San Juan, PR 00922
       Contact: Alejandro Nazario Business Dev Dir
       Tel: 787-653-4700
       Email: emarrero@amscm.com
       Website: www.amscm.com
Pre-construction management & financial Viability
Planning, Project Development Services, Engineer,
Procure & Construct, Capital Structuring & Performance
Guarantees. (Hisp, estab 1999, empl 10, sales , cert:
NMSDC)

3130   CRB Caribe, LLP
       BBVA Center Mail Box 21, 1738 Amarillo St #314
       San Juan, PR 00926
       Contact: Tom Forester GM
       Tel: 787-622-2720
       Email: shirley.nieves@crbusa.com
       Website: www.crbusa.com
Engineering & Architectural Consulting & Design
Services, Construction and Use Permitting, Inspections
and Construction Support (Hisp, estab 2004, empl 60,
sales $8,729,275, cert: NMSDC)

3131   JCD Engineering, Inc.
       PO Box 192372
       San Juan, PR 00919
       Contact: Juan C. del Pino President
       Tel: 787-787-7211
       Email: jcdelpino@jcdengineering.com
       Website: www.jcdengineering.com
Civil, electrical & mechanical engineering: concrete &
steel small buildings, interiors work, hung ceilings,
floors, gypsum board, electrical power & controls, fiber
optics, local area networks (LAN), process and AHU
control systems. (Hisp, estab 1996, empl 11, sales
$1,327,000, cert: NMSDC)

3132   LabChemS
       PO Box 1022
       Boqueron, PR 00622
       Contact: Efrain Rivera Torres CEO
       Tel: 787-920-4657
       Email: efrain.rivera@labchemspr.com
       Website: www.labchemscorp.com/
Engineering Consulting, Manufacturing & Packaging
Equipments, Facilities & Manufacturing Process Validation, Quality Engineering & Six Sigma tools. (Hisp, estab
2009, empl 10, sales $1,200,000, cert: NMSDC)

3133   NOVO Consulting Group LLC
       PMB 9 6400
       Cayey, PR 00737
       Contact: Claritza Millan President
       Tel: 787-413-7379
       Email: cmillan@novo-pr.com
       Website: www.novo-pr.com
Design Qualification, Engineering Studies, Installation
Qualification, Operational Qualification, Performance
Qualification, Process Verification/Validation, Project
Management, Process Improvement/Optimization,
Quality Assurance, CAPA, NCRs. (Minority, Woman, estab
2015, empl 2, sales , cert: NMSDC)

3134 SQS, Inc. (Successful Quality Systems)
Palmas Industrial Park Road 869 KM. 2.0 Street 4
Catano, PR 00962
Contact: WILDA AGUIRRE President
Tel: 787-275-2424
Email: wildaaguirre@sqswarehouse.com
Website: www.sqswarehouse.com
Specialized Storage and Inventory Management Services of materials and products for the pharmaceutical, medical devices, biotech and consumer industries as well as to the safe-guarding of documents (Minority, Woman, estab 2003, empl 8, sales $2,500,000, cert: NMSDC)

3135 UNIPRO Architects Engineers LLP
PO Box 10914
San Juan, PR 00922
Contact: Jose R. Gonzalez Dir planning/Projects
Tel: 787-793-3950
Email: jgonzalez@uniproaep.net
Website: www.uniproaep.com
Architecture, civil engineering, structural engineering, mechanical engineering, electrical engineering, environmental engineering, construction management. (Hisp, estab 1980, empl 30, sales $3,200,000, cert: NMSDC)

3136 Visional Technology LLC
400 Calle Calaf, Ste 49
San Juan, PR 00918
Contact: Joyce Rotger President
Tel: 787-717-0881
Email: joycemar@visionaltechnology.com
Website: www.visionaltechnology.com
Engineering services, dimensional metrology solutions, vision systems, coordinate measurement machines (CMM), laser measurements, 3D scanning, reverse engineering & computer aided inspections. (Minority, Woman, estab 2013, empl 5, sales , cert: NMSDC)

South Carolina

3137 Amee Bay LLC
915 Commerce Cir
Hanahan, SC 29410
Contact: William Messing Sr Program Mgr
Tel: 843-725-6800
Email: bmessing@ameebay.com
Website: www.ameebay.com
General/mechanical contracting, power & pressure process piping installation, repair mechanical systems on commercial and industrial pressure vessels, conveyors & auxiliary systems. (Nat Ame, estab 2006, empl 184, sales $26,000,000, cert: State)

3138 Atlantic South Consulting Services
3030 Ashley Town Center Dr Ste 101A
Charleston, SC 29414
Contact: Adrian Williams
Tel: 843-266-3998
Email: awilliams@atlanticsouthconsulting.com
Website: www.atlanticsouthconsulting.com
Engineering, surveying, and right-of-way acquisition services, transportation & utility designs, site development & land planning, construction inspection & management services, easement. (AA, estab 2004, empl 6, sales $668,000, cert: State)

3139 Diverse Industries, Inc.
260 Morley Court, Ste A
Duncan, SC 29334
Contact: Laura Charles Office Mgr
Tel: 864-400-9741
Email: laurac@diverseii.com
Website: www.diverseii.com
We experience implementing solutions & fixes for many customers in a variety of industries. Contract Robot Programming, Panel View & Thin Client HMI's, Training, Robot & PLC, Vision, Robot Guidance, Inspection & Code Reading. (Woman, estab 2007, empl 40, sales $5,114,985, cert: State)

3140 US&S, Inc.
50 Grand Ave
Greenville, SC 29607
Contact: Shontel Babb Regional Sales Mgr
Tel: 864-233-8035
Email: sbabb@usands.com
Website: www.usands.com
Facilities maintenance and support services. (AA, estab 2003, empl 137, sales $31,000,000, cert: State, NMSDC)

Tennessee

3141 GQSI
3777 Winchester Rd Ste 1
Memphis, TN 38118
Contact: Williette Graham President
Tel: 901-365-9566
Email: willgraham@gqsi.net
Website: www.gqsi.net
Engineering & technical services, medical devices, process & special processes equipment & validation, laser marking, CMM inspection services, product inspection, engineering support, supplier support services. (Woman/AA, estab 2005, empl 6, sales , cert: NMSDC)

Texas

3142 Aguirre Roden Inc.
10670 N Central Expressway 6th Fl
Dallas, TX 75231
Contact: Peter Aguirre, CFM SVP Program Devel
Tel: 972-789-2662
Email: paaguirre@aguirre.com
Website: www.aguirreroden.com
Architecture, mechanical, electrical & structural engineering, general contracting. (Hisp, estab 1960, empl 65, sales , cert: State, NMSDC)

3143 ALTECOR Engineering
3617 Flamingo Ave
McAllen, TX 78504
Contact: T. G. Altecor Sr Staff Engineer
Tel: 956-687-7389
Email: info@altecoreng.com
Website: www.altecoreng.com
Structural dynamics & control systems engineering, equipment-machinery installations, optimizations, maintenance, reliability. (Woman, estab 2007, empl 7, sales $100,000, cert: State)

3144 Arias & Associates, Inc.
142 Chula Vista
San Antonio, TX 78232
Contact: Jeremy Arias VP
Tel: 210-308-5884
Email: purchaseorders@ariasinc.com
Website: www.ariasinc.com
Geotechnical engineering svcs, construction materials testing & observation, environmental svcs. (Hisp, estab 1996, empl 96, sales , cert: State, City, SDB)

3145 Balance Vibration Technologies, Inc.
2426 Lacy Ln
Carrollton, TX 75006
Contact: Savanna Cole President
Tel: 214-733-8771
Email: mferrante@balancevibration.com
Website: www.balancevibration.com
Vibration analysis, condition monitoring, motor current analysis, laser alignment, dynamic balancing service, spectrographic oil analysis, infrared thermography, ultrasound, electrical repair service, switchgear relay, ground fault testing. (Woman, estab 2005, empl 11, sales $2,983,487, cert: WBENC)

3146 Basal Solutions LLC
1301 Texas Ave Ste 122
Houston, TX 77002
Contact: Branden Morris
Tel: 713-393-8767
Email: branden@basalsolutionsllc.com
Website: www.basalsolutionsllc.com
Engineering & business management consulting, project management, develop, test & integrate 0-D/1-D dynamic mathematical models, create FMEA & DFMEA for various vehicle platforms, test script design & implementation. (AA, estab 2014, empl 10, sales , cert: State, NMSDC)

3147 Bastion Technologies, Inc.
17625 El Camino Real
Houston, TX 77058
Contact: Jorge Hernandez President
Tel: 281-283-9330
Email: jhernandez@bastiontechnologies.com
Website: www.bastiontechnologies.com
Engineering design, analysis, systems engineering, information technology applications, engineering research, mechanical engineering, structural engineering, safety & reliability engineering, systems safety, hazard analysis. (Hisp, estab 1998, empl 400, sales $42,711,000, cert: State, NMSDC)

3148 BEPC, Inc.
3240 Executive Dr
San Angelo, TX 76904
Contact: Liza Dennis Dir of New Business
Tel: 325-944-0169
Email: liza.dennis@bepcinc.com
Website: www.bepcinc.com
Engineering services: validations of equipment, processes, audit & qualification of external suppliers, quality systems & validations, R&D product design & testing. (Hisp, estab 2005, empl 460, sales $20,038,327, cert: State, NMSDC)

3149 Charles Gojer & Associates, Inc.
11615 Forest Central Dr, Ste 303
Dallas, TX 75243
Contact: Charles Gojer President
Tel: 214-340-1199
Email: cgojer@cgojer.com
Website: www.cgojer.com
Civil & structural engineering. (Hisp, estab 1973, empl 10, sales , cert: State, NMSDC)

3150 Elements of Architecture, Inc.
1201 6th Ave Ste 100
Fort Worth, TX 76104
Contact: Debbie Fulwiler President
Tel: 817-333-2880
Email: info@elementsofarc.com
Website: www.elementsofarc.com
Architectural & engineering svcs: environmental, structure & facility, electrical, mechanical, fire protection, alarming. (Woman, estab 1996, empl 7, sales , cert: State, WBENC)

3151 Elevan LLC dba Elevate Systems
1919 NW Loop 410, Ste 200
San Antonio, TX 78213
Contact: Scott Gray CEO
Tel: 210-807-9981
Email: scott.gray@elevatesystems.com
Website: www.elevatesystems.com
Engineering and logistics services for Department of Defense Aging Weapon Systems, Subsystems, Components, Parts and Pieces. (Minority, Woman, estab 2012, empl 4, sales $1,100,000, cert: State, SDB)

3152 First Assured Quality Systems, LLC
PO Box 535812
Grand Prairie, TX 75053
Contact: Brittany Stovall President
Tel: 817-538-9240
Email: bstovall@assuredqualitysystems.com
Website: www.assuredqualitysystems.com
Quality Control Services- Containment, Sorting, Rework, Inspection, Liaison Support, Engineering Support & Launch Support. (Woman/AA, Hisp, estab 2013, empl 35, sales $2,872,632, cert: NMSDC, WBENC)

3153 Gap Engineering
21703 Kingsland Blvd, Ste 103
Katy, TX 77450
Contact: Mike Homma
Tel: 281-578-0500
Email: mhomma@gap-eng.com
Website: www.gap-eng.com
Engineering, design & drafting services, develop instrument Specs, Detail Design, Distributive Control Systems (DCS), Fieldbus, Programmable Logic Controllers (PLC), Safety Instrumented Systems (SIS), Fiber Optic Comm Networks. (As-Pac, estab 2004, empl 25, sales $2,800,000, cert: NMSDC, 8(a))

3154 GMR Protection Resources, Inc.
1629 Smirl Dr, Ste 200
Heath, TX 75032
Contact: Scott Crawford Sr Dir of Business Dev
Tel: 469-267-9144
Email: smcrawford@gmr1.com
Website: www.gmr1.com
ADA compliance inspections and risk/security assessments, security incident response assessments, security compliance reviews & crime report data development. (Woman, estab 1991, empl 105, sales $16,000,000, cert: WBENC)

3155 JAT Energy Services LLC
111 Soledad St, Ste 1900
San Antonio, TX 78205
Contact: Keith Allen President
Tel: 916-429-9096
Email: keith@jatenergies.com
Website: www.JATEnergies.com
Energy solutions, engineering & management firm, custom engineered solutions to reduce energy consumption in commercial & industrial spaces. (AA, estab 2012, empl 8, sales $500,000, cert: State, NMSDC)

3156 Johnson & Pace Inc.
1201 NW Loop 281, Ste 100
Longview, TX 75604
Contact: Linda Bennett President
Tel: 903-753-0663
Email: LindaB@johnsonpace.com
Website: www.johnsonpace.com
Engineering services: civil, mechanical, electrical, structural, architectural services, land surveying. (Woman, estab 1995, empl 45, sales $7,930,735, cert: State, WBENC)

3157 JQ Infrastructure, LLC
100 Glass St Ste 201
Dallas, TX 75207
Contact: Stephen Lucy Principal
Tel: 972-392-7340
Email: slucy@jqeng.com
Website: www.jqieng.com/
Surveying services, building, structures & components consulting, engineering consulting, civil engineering, concrete engineering, drainage engineering, foundation engineering, inspection, general/engineering. (As-Pac, estab 2003, empl 105, sales $6,471,893, cert: State, NMSDC)

3158 M.E.P. Consulting Engineers, Inc.
2928 Story Rd W
Irving, TX 75038
Contact: Camilla Beavers Admin Asst
Tel: 972-870-9060
Email: mail@mepce.com
Website: www.mepce.com
Mechanical, electrical, plumbing, fire protection & information technology design engineering & commissioning for aviation facilities, municipalities, educational facilities, government, health care & commercial facilities. (Woman, estab 1998, empl 14, sales $4,000,000, cert: State, WBENC)

3159 Maslowski Controls, LLC
1751 Hurd Dr, Ste 111
Irving, TX 75038
Contact: Jacqueline Sikorski President
Tel: 817-999-1662
Email: jsikorski@maslowskicontrols.com
Website: www.maslowskicontrols.com
Control System Engineering, PLC Programming, Historian, SCADA, HMI
Control Systems signal/instrumentation, troubleshooting, testing, simulation, staff training. (Woman, estab 2017, empl 3, sales , cert: WBENC)

3160 MULTATECH
2821 W 7th St Ste 400
Fort Worth, TX 76107
Contact: Hong P. Chen President
Tel: 817-877-5571
Email: hchen@multatech.com
Website: www.multatech.com
mechanical, electrical, plumbing & civil consulting engineering services, architectural design services. (Hisp, estab 1986, empl 74, sales $11,048,061, cert: State, NMSDC)

3161 NSM Inc.
1535 Industrial Dr
Missouri City, TX 77489
Contact: Vini Gupta CEO
Tel: 281-880-8188
Email: sales@cornerstonevalve.com
Website: www.cornerstonevalve.vom
Custom Engineered Design and Manufacturing Solutions, Wide array of metallurgies, Temperature range -350F to 1500F, Metal seated bubble tight leakage, High cycling up to 1.5 million cycles per year. (As-Ind, estab 2019, empl 17, sales $4,500,000, cert: NMSDC)

3162 Oil Field Development Engineering
12121 Wickchester Lane, Ste 700
Houston, TX 77079
Contact: Jay Chen President
Tel: 281-679-9060
Email: jay.chen@ofdeng.com
Website: www.ofdeng.com
Project management, engineering and design for offshore and onshore oil and gas production and transportation facilities. (As-Pac, estab 2002, empl 64, sales , cert: State)

3163 SeaMax Corporation
3720 W Alabama St Ste 3108
Houston, TX 77027
Contact: BRENDAN ISIDIENU Structural Engineer
Tel: 713-584-3643
Email: ibrendan@seamax.org
Website: www.seamax.org
Engineering consulting, structural engineering & and design of offshore & onshore soil & gas structures. (AA, estab 2015, empl 10, sales , cert: NMSDC)

3164 Standard Industrial Products Company
12610 Galveston Rd
Webster, TX 77059
Contact: Walter Gomez Dir Operation & Mktg
Tel: 281-480-8711
Email: wgomez@sipco-mls.com
Website: www.sipco-mls.com
Engineering, Electro - Mechanical Design, Validation & System Integration, CNC Milling, CNC Turning, Sawing, Mechanical System assembly & integration, Gearing - Design, Sourcing, Assembly & System Integration. (Hisp, estab 1984, empl 15, sales $2,099,000, cert: NMSDC)

3165 Sunland Group
10400 Westoffice Dr, Ste 116
Houston, TX 77042
Contact: Sales/Marketing
Tel: 713-467-8484
Email: info@sunlandgrp.com
Website: www.sunlandgrp.com
Design build: civil, structural, environmental engineering, architecture, design & construction surveying, value engineering. (Hisp, estab 1985, empl 85, sales $8,200,000, cert: State)

3166 Systems Integration, Inc.
7316 Business Pl
Arlington, TX 76001
Contact: Rhonda Smith Acct Mgr
Tel: 817-468-1494
Email: rsmith@sitexas.com
Website: www.sitexas.com
Engineering & Design, Reverse Engineering, Fabrication, Installation, Structural & Civil, Manufacturing, Machinery, Mechanical, CNC Machining, Electrical & Controls, Test Structures, Tooling. (Hisp, estab 1992, empl 20, sales $4,000,000, cert: State)

3167 Taylor & Hill, Inc.
9941 Rowlett
Houston, TX 77075
Contact: Natalie Langford Business Devel Mgr
Tel: 713-941-2671
Email: mwhittington@taylorandhill.com
Website: www.taylorandhill.com
Contract/direct hire personnel & in-house engineering services, computerized electronic measurement (AEMS) & high definition laser scanning for plant design purposes. (Hisp, estab 1974, empl 100, sales $16,300,000, cert: State, NMSDC)

3168 United Geo Technologies LLC
7715 Mainland Dr, Ste 110
San Antonio, TX 78250
Contact: Patricia Ingram President
Tel: 210-684-2147
Email: pingram@unitedgeotech.com
Website: www.unitedgeotech.com
Softcopy photogrammetric mapping, digital orthophotography, GIS services, geospatial database architecture, raster/vector data layer production, CAD to GIS data integration, remotely updating of GIS layers & solution development. (Woman, estab 2011, empl 6, sales , cert: State)

Virginia

3169 Ashe Consultants, PLLC
950 Herndon Pkwy Ste 320
Herndon, VA 20170
Contact: Sharon M. Gorick, PE President
Tel: 703-230-2500
Email: sgorick@asheconsultants.com
Website: www.asheconsultants.com
Mechanical, electrical & plumbing engineering design services for buildings. (Woman, estab 2008, empl 5, sales $130,660, cert: State, WBENC)

3170 INTERSPEC, LLC
464 S Independence Blvd Ste C-104
Virginia Beach, VA 23452
Contact: Sean Murphy Business Devel Dir
Tel: 757-622-6299
Email: murphys@interspecllc.net
Website: www.interspecllc.net
Tank, piping & pressure vessel inspections, STI storage tank inspections, Non-Destructive Examination/Testing steel structures, Spill Prevention Control & Countermeasure (SPCC) plans, Oil Discharge Control Plans (ODCP. (Nat Ame, estab 2001, empl 22, sales $1,200,000, cert: State, 8(a))

3171 Lu Smith Engineers
4604 Sadler Grove Way
Glen Allen, VA 23060
Contact: Dawen Lu President
Tel: 804-519-9306
Email: dlu6838@gmail.com
Website: www.lsengineers.net
Building system commissioning services, energy modeling/audit services, geothermal system study & design, sustainable design/LEED consultation & administration, mechanical, electrical, plumbing & fire protection system design. (As-Pac, estab 2012, empl 12, sales $1,400,000, cert: State)

3172 MKAssociates, Inc.
6593 Commerce Ct, Ste 100
Warrenton, VA 20187
Contact: Michelle Kilby-Miranda Principal
Tel: 540-428-3550
Email: info@mkassociates.com
Website: www.mkassociates.com
Land surveying coordination. (Woman, estab 1998, empl 12, sales $350,000,000, cert: WBENC)

3173 Raul V. Bravo + Associates, Inc.
1889 Preston White Dr Ste 202
Reston, VA 20191
Contact: Claudio Bravo VP
Tel: 703-326-9092
Email: procurement@rvba.com
Website: www.RVBA.com
Rail Car Design, Mechanical, CADD, Electrical schematics, Telecommunication Design, Security Design, Electrical Diagrams Wiring, Smoke Detector Layout, CCTV & MATV Design, Power Supplies. (Hisp, estab 1979, empl 63, sales , cert: State)

3174 T3 Design Corporation
10340 Democracy Ln, Ste 305
Fairfax, VA 22030
Contact: Tandrumn Reid WBENC Liaison
Tel: 770-813-0882
Email: treid@t3design.us
Website: www.streetsmarts.us
Transportation engineering, civil/site engineering, transportation planning, intelligent transportation systems, traffic engineering, survey services, subsurface utility engineering, data collection, geographic information systems & public involvement. (Woman, estab , empl , sales $9,500,000, cert: State)

3175 Unified Industries Inc.
6551 Loisdale Ct Ste 400
Springfield, VA 22150
Contact: Tom Callahan
Tel: 703-922-9800
Email: callahan@uii.com
Website: www.uii.com
Metrology & calibration services, life cycle logistics planning, supply chain support, ship outfitting, distance support, obsolescence analysis. (AA, estab 1970, empl 200, sales $16,045,000, cert: State)

Washington

3176 CS3W Associates, Inc.
2821 167th Ave NE
Bellevue, WA 98008
Contact: Christopher Sims President
Tel: 425-922-5900
Email: csims@cs3w.com
Website: www.cs3w.com
Engineering & management services, electrical & structural/seismic engineering services, project management & analysis support. (AA, estab 1999, empl 8, sales $671,000, cert: State)

3177 Garry Struthers Associates, Inc.
3150 Richards Rd
Bellevue, WA 98005
Contact: Garry Struthers President
Tel: 425-519-0300
Email: garrys@gsassoc-inc.com
Website: www.gsassoc-inc.com
Engineering, construction, environmental science, facilities maintenance. (AA, estab 1988, empl 106, sales $21,000,000, cert: NMSDC)

3178 GeoTest Services, Inc.
741 Marine View Dr
Bellingham, WA 98225
Contact: Jeremy Wolf VP
Tel: 360-733-7318
Email: jeremyw@geotest-inc.com
Website: www.geotest-inc.com
Geotechnical engineering, environmental services, special inspection & materials testing, facilities, structures, roads, bridges & all types of infrastructure. (Woman, estab 1993, empl 33, sales $6,000,000, cert: State)

3179 Land Development Consultants, Inc.
14201 NE 200th St Ste 100
Woodinville, WA 98072
Contact: Frank Lemos President
Tel: 425-806-1869
Email: flemos@ldccorp.com
Website: www.ldccorp.com
Civil Engineering, Land Survey, Land Use Planning/Permitting, A/E Design, Commercial Site Design, Roadway Design, Drainage Design and Reporting, GIS ESRI Mapping, Water Systems. (Hisp, estab 2003, empl 40, sales $5,354,378, cert: State, NMSDC)

3180 Professional CAD Services, Inc. dba PCSI Design
18916 N Creek Pkwy Ste 103
Bothell, WA 98011
Contact: Carlos Veliz CEO
Tel: 425-485-3420
Email: carlos@pcsidesign.com
Website: www.pcsidesign.com
Product design & engineering services focused on assisting companies to translate conceptual design into market-ready production products. Our product & solution offerings extend to many industries. (Hisp, estab 1997, empl 5, sales $1,116,889, cert: NMSDC)

3181 WHPacific, Inc.
12100 NE 195th St Ste 300
Bothell, WA 98011
Contact: Carl Romig Dir ICS
Tel: 425-951-4000
Email: cromig@whpacific.com
Website: www.WHPacific.com
Accessibility/Universal Access, Aviation Planning & Design, Bridge Design and Rehabilitation, Civil Engineering, Commissioning, Community & Urban Design, Construction Inspection, Construction Management, Construction Management. (Nat Ame, estab 1981, empl 351, sales $55,249,100, cert: NMSDC)

Wisconsin

3182 Barrientos Design & Consulting, Inc.
205 W Highland Ave Ste 303
Milwaukee, WI 53203
Contact: President
Tel: 414-271-1812
Email: admin@barrientosdesign.com
Website: www.barrientosdesign.com
Architecture, structural engineering, civil & site engineering: industrial, office, training, warehousing, maintenance facilities, field operations, substations & power plant enclosures, space needs analysis, building programming, site selection. (Hisp, estab 1998, empl , sales $1,010,000, cert: NMSDC)

3183 Datasyst Engineering & Testing
S14 W33511 Hwy 18
Delafield, WI 53018
Contact: Rose Hoisington CFO
Tel: 800-969-4050
Email: mhoisington@datasysttest.com
Website: www.datasysttest.com
Mechanical & electrical equipment testing & engineering: medical, telecommunications, construction, mining & process, industrial, automotive. (Minority, Woman, estab 1990, empl 11, sales , cert: NMSDC)

3184 Fusion Integrated Solutions LLC
416 Security Blvd
Green Bay, WI 54313
Contact: Seaphes Miller CEO
Tel: 920-593-4200
Email: solutions@fusion-etc.com
Website: www.fusion-etc.com
Mechanical, civil & structural, electrical & process engineering & design svcs, project management, materials procurement, construction field supervision, electrical panel construction & custom machine design & manufacture. (AA, estab 2004, empl 60, sales $9,113,000, cert: State, NMSDC)

3185 K. Singh & Associates, Inc.
3636 N 124th St
Wauwatosa, WI 53222
Contact: Pratap Singh CEO
Tel: 262-821-1171
Email: gmiller@ksaconsultants.com
Website: www.ksaconsultants.com
Environmental engineering & management services, transportation, structural, environmental & civil engineering, land surveying & construction management. (As-Ind, estab 1987, empl 33, sales $3,000,000, cert: State)

3186 PSJ Engineering, Inc.
7665 N Port Washington Rd
Milwaukee, WI 53217
Contact: Parmjit Jaspal CEO
Tel: 414-352-2211
Email: jesse@psjengineering.com
Website: www.psjengineering.com
Consulting engineering svcs: heating, ventilation, air conditioning, plumbing & fire protection. (As-Pac, estab 1986, empl 13, sales $1,186,006, cert: State, City)

ENVIRONMENTAL SERVICES
Firms are engaged in underground and above ground storage tank removal and installation, assessment and remediation, lead and asbestos abatement, hazardous waste management, pollution, etc. NAICS Code 54

Alabama

3187 One Stop Environmental, LLC
      4800 Division Ave
      Birmingham, AL 35222
      Contact: Elizabeth Hinson Marketing Dir
      Tel: 205-595-8188
      Email: ehinson@onestopenv.com
      Website: www.onestopenv.com
Hazardous waste transport & disposal, confined space entry, industry cleaning, emergency response, remediation, oil/water separator, lead/asbestos abatement, environmental consulting. (Woman, estab 1999, empl 42, sales $4,000,000, cert: WBENC)

3188 Orrs Environmental, LLC
      515 Sparkman Dr
      Huntsville, AL 35756
      Contact: Debra Sanders Mgr
      Tel: 256-556-1220
      Email: orrsenvironmental@gmail.com
      Website: www.orrsenvironmental.com
Rail, air, water, trucking multimodal service, general & climate control warehousing, waste management assessments, spill response supplies & PPE, safety training, haz mat disposal & recycling services. (Woman/AA, estab 2004, empl 12, sales , cert: State)

3189 Slade Land Use, Environmental & Transportation Planning LLC
      1500 1st Ave N, Unit 54
      Birmingham, AL 35203
      Contact: L'Tryce Slade Owner
      Tel: 205-413-4685
      Email: lslade@sladellc.com
      Website: www.sladellc.com
General Contracting, Environmental Consulting, Geotechnical Services, Construction Material Testing, Urban Planning. (Woman/AA, estab 2006, empl 6, sales $644,986, cert: NMSDC, WBENC, 8(a))

3190 Vulcan Industrial Contractors Co., LLC
      4625-A Valleydale Rd
      Birmingham, AL 35242
      Contact: Kristi Lawler CEO
      Tel: 205-313-4766
      Email: KLawler@vindco.com
      Website: www.vindco.com
Asbestos & lead removal. (Woman, estab 1949, empl 727, sales $68,000,000, cert: WBENC)

Arizona

3191 Archaeological Consulting Services, Ltd.
      424 W Broadway Rd
      Tempe, AZ 85282
      Contact: Margerie Green President
      Tel: 480-894-5477
      Email: mgreen@acstempe.com
      Website: www.acstempe.com
Cultural resource services, class I to class III studies, testing, & data recovery, environmental services, biological assessments/evaluations, environmental project management, paleo environmental analysis, GIS mapping. (Woman, estab 1977, empl 34, sales $1,945,942, cert: State, City, CPUC)

3192 Beck Environmental and Remediation, Ltd.
      772 S Holmes Rd
      Apache Junction, AZ 85119
      Contact: Julie Beck President
      Tel: 480-671-1365
      Email: julie.beck@earthlink.net
      Website: www.beckenvironmental.com
Environmental assessments, site characterizations, remediation, air monitoring, hazardous materials management, environmental impact statements, health & safety, environmental engineering, mitigation modeling. (Woman, estab 1998, empl 5, sales $292,915, cert: WBENC, 8(a))

3193 Darling Geomatics
      9040 S Rita Rd, Ste 2350
      Tucson, AZ 85747
      Contact: Mary Darling CEO
      Tel: 520-298-2725
      Email: marydarling@darlingltd.com
      Website: www.darlingltd.com
Environmental consulting. (Woman, estab 1997, empl 15, sales $2,000,000, cert: City, CPUC, WBENC)

3194 Gutierrez-Palmenberg, Inc.
      2922 W Clarendon Ave
      Phoenix, AZ 85017
      Contact: Jason Weed Engineer
      Tel: 602-234-0696
      Email: jason.w@gpimail.com
      Website: www.gpieng.com
Environmental consulting & engineering support services, site characterizations, design, identifying potential environmental impacts of planned operations, remediation, monitoring and protecting valued resources. (Hisp, estab 1980, empl 25, sales $2,250,273, cert: NMSDC)

3195 The Green Way Environmental Group, LLC.
      PO Box 5705
      Scottsdale, AZ 85261
      Contact: Chris McNally Business Dev Mgr
      Tel: 480-639-0389
      Email: chris@gweg-az.com
      Website: www.greenway-environmental.com
Environmental, construction & restoration, sampling & clearance sampling of asbestos, lead based paint & microbial, environmental compliance, consulting, industrial hygiene & occupational safety. (Woman, estab 2010, empl 5, sales $616,000, cert: WBENC)

California

3196 CAL Inc.
2040 Peabody Rd
Vacaville, CA 95687
Contact: David Esparza President
Tel: 707-446-7996
Email: desparza@cal-inc.com
Website: www.cal-inc.com
General contracting: Asbestos & Lead Abatement, Demolition, Remediation Services & Environmental & Safety Training. (Hisp, estab 1979, empl 40, sales $4,786,000, cert: CPUC)

3197 California Hazardous Services Inc
1431 E St Andrew PL
Santa Ana, CA 92705
Contact: Tammy Taylor Sales Mgr
Tel: 714-434-9995
Email: bids@calhaz.com
Website: www.calhaz.com
Fuel tank service, cleaning, waste disposal, water intrusion pump-outs, environmental compliance tank testing, tank removals, tank installations, tank upgrades. (Woman, estab 1988, empl 24, sales $4,960,000, cert: CPUC, WBENC)

3198 EFR Environmental Services Inc.
PO Box 2669
Alpine, CA 91903
Contact: Laura L Harris President
Tel: 619-722-6781
Email: accounting@efrenviro.com
Website: www.efrenviro.com
Transport hazardous waste and non-hazardous waste, Drum, Rolloff Services, Bulk Services, Vacuum Services, Site Cleanups and Waste Categorization and Profiling. (Woman, estab 1999, empl 17, sales $2,506,684, cert: State, CPUC)

3199 Engineering/Remediation Resources Group, Inc.
4585 Pacheco Blvd Ste 200
Martinez, CA 94553
Contact: Tyson Appel Sr Project Mgr
Tel: 925-969-0750
Email: tyson.appel@errg.com
Website: www.errg.com
Engineering & remediation services, environmental, civil & geotechnical engineers, geologists, soil physicists, scientists, construction managers, construction superintendents, equipment operators, certified hazardous waste technicians. (Minority, Woman, estab 1997, empl 175, sales $81,494,792, cert: CPUC)

3200 FRS Environmental
1414 E Sixth St
Corona, CA 92879
Contact: President
Tel: 951-898-1888
Email: info@frsenvironmental.com
Website: www.frsenvironmental.com
Emergency response, containment & recommendation, hazardous waste mgmt & disposal, facility decontamination & remediation, analytical & testing svcs, lab pack svcs, vacuum pumping. (Woman, estab 1995, empl 10, sales $2,000,000, cert: WBENC)

3201 Future Power Corporation
66 Franklin St Ste 300
Oakland, CA 94607
Contact: Dahlia Moodie President
Tel: 510-647-8450
Email: dahlia@ecoptions.biz
Website: www.ecoptions.biz
Facility energy audits, energy savings solution recommendation & technology solution implementation. (Woman/AA, Hisp, estab 2008, empl 7, sales $1,175,198, cert: CPUC)

3202 GGG Demolition Inc.
1130 W Trenton Ave
Orange, CA 92867
Contact: President
Tel: 714-699-9350
Email:
Website: www.gggdemo.com
Structural Demolition, Asbestos/Lead Abatement, Mold Remediation, Soil Remediation. Selective Demolition. (Woman, estab 2013, empl 150, sales $12,000,000, cert: CPUC, WBENC)

3203 Greenway Solid Waste & Recycling, Inc.
PO Box 1453
Claremont, CA 91711
Contact: Charles Elias VP
Tel: 909-518-7943
Email: celias@greenwayrecyclinginc.com
Website: www.greenwayrecyclinginc.com
Electronic waste recycling, nonhazardous waste treatment & disposal. (Minority, Woman, estab 2006, empl 3, sales $321,000, cert: State, 8(a))

3204 H2O Engineering, Inc.
189 Granada Dr
San Luis Obispo, CA 93401
Contact: Jeff Cedillos Sales Coord
Tel: 866-987-0303
Email: marketing@h2oengineering.com
Website: www.h2oengineering.com
Create tailored water treatment solutions for industrial process water, ultra-pure water, water reuse, and groundwater remediation. (Hisp, estab 2000, empl 16, sales $4,200,000, cert: NMSDC)

3205 Impact Absorbents, Inc.
5255 Traffic Way
Atascadero, CA 93422
Contact: Tammy Rayner Dir of Corporate Sales
Tel: 800-339-7672
Email: trayner@spillhero.com
Website: www.spillhero.com
Mfr & dist granular absorbents, sorbent pads, sorbents socks, spill clean up programs and products, non-hazardous, earth friendly, cost effective. XSORB, FiberDuck, FiberLink, Spill Station, Spill Caddy, Spill Rack, Biohazard Kit. (Woman, estab 1992, empl 30, sales $5,300,000, cert: State)

3206 Integrated Science Solutions (ISSI)
1777 N California Blvd Ste 305
Walnut Creek, CA 94596
Contact: Cecelia Mccloy President
Tel: 925-979-1535
Email: info@issi-net.com
Website: www.issi-net.com
Earth & environmental science, engineering, regulatory compliance, occupational safety & health, homeland security, emergency response, & energy, water & natural resource development. (Woman, estab 1999, empl 40, sales $5,035,703, cert: CPUC, WBENC)

3207 Ninyo & Moore
      5710 Ruffin Rd.
      San Diego, CA 92123
      Contact: Elizabeth Brooks Corp Business Dev Mgr
      Tel: 858-576-1000
      Email: ebrooks@ninyoandmoore.com
      Website: www.ninyoandmoore.com
Geotechnical & environmental sciences consulting:
geotechnical engineering, engineering geology, engineering geophysics, hydrogeology, soil & materials testing &
environmental sciences. (Hisp, estab 1986, empl 492, sales
$92,662,074, cert: City, NMSDC, CPUC)

3208 Northstar Environmental Remediation
      26225 Enterprise Ct
      Lake Forest, CA 92630
      Contact: Katherine Tweidt President
      Tel: 949-580-2800
      Email: ktweidt@cox.net
      Website: www.northstarremediation.com
Environmental consulting & remediation of soil & groundwater, equipment fab, installation, & operation, permitting, consulting, soil & groundwater characterization, well
installation, reporting, compliance activities. (Woman,
estab 2002, empl 6, sales $1,250,000, cert: CPUC)

3209 OST Trucks and Cranes, Inc.
      2951 N Ventura Ave
      Ventura, CA 93002
      Contact: L. Dennis Zermeno President
      Tel: 805-643-9963
      Email: ostcranes@aol.com
      Website: www.ostcranes.com
General & hazardous substance removal & remedial
action, hydraulic cranes 5 to 140. (Hisp, estab 1947, empl
69, sales $0, cert: State, NMSDC, CPUC)

3210 Pari & Gershon Inc.
      2053 Lincoln Ave Ste A
      San Jose, CA 95125
      Contact: Romena Jonas President
      Tel: 408-966-7184
      Email: rjonas@pgiinc.net
      Website: www.pgicompany.com
Environmental Consulting, Engineering Design & Construc-
tion. (Woman, estab 2009, empl 5, sales $100,000, cert:
State, WBENC)

3211 Piper Environmental Group, Inc.
      11600 California St
      Castroville, CA 95012
      Contact: Jane Piper CEO
      Tel: 831-632-2700
      Email: jpiper@peg-inc.com
      Website: www.peg-inc.com
Design ozone solutions, turn-key ozone trailer systems,
ozone sparging systems. (Woman, estab 1992, empl 3,
sales $1,483,616, cert: CPUC, WBENC)

3212 Pivox Corporation
      3240 El Camino Real Ste 230
      Irvine, CA 92602
      Contact: Sean Shahin VP
      Tel: 949-727-1400
      Email: sean@pivox.com
      Website: www.pivox.com
Remediation of soil & groundwater, demolition, project &
construction management, permitting, design, feasibility
study, treatment system installation (civil, mechanical,
electril, and instrumentation). (Woman, estab 2004, empl
20, sales $8,000,000, cert: CPUC)

3213 RORE, Inc.
      5151 Shoreham Place
      San Diego, CA 92122
      Contact: Gita Murthy
      Tel: 858-404-7393
      Email: rore, inc.
      Website: www.roreinc.com
General & hazardous waste contracting, environmental
investigation & remediation. (Woman/As-Ind, estab
2003, empl 70, sales $15,000,000, cert: State)

3214 SCA Environmental, Inc.
      320 Justin Dr
      San Francisco, CA 94112
      Contact: Christina Codemo President
      Tel: 415-882-1675
      Email: ccodemo@sca-enviro.com
      Website: www.sca-enviro.com
Environmental consulting services, O & M plans.
(Woman, estab 1992, empl 11, sales $0, cert: WBENC)

3215 Spring Rivers Ecological Sciences LLC
      PO Box 153
      Cassel, CA 96016
      Contact: Maria Ellis Aquatic Ecologist
      Tel: 530-335-5446
      Email: maria@springrivers.com
      Website: www.springrivers.com
Aquatic ecology & resources consulting. (Woman, estab
1994, empl 15, sales $0, cert: CPUC)

3216 TERRA Solutions & Services, LLC
      3478 Buskirk Ave Ste 100
      Pleasant Hill, CA 94523
      Contact: Bruce Borup Owner
      Tel: 925-651-6388
      Email: bborup@sircorporation.com
      Website: www.terras2.com
Environmental engineering, Phase I & Phase II property
assessment & site investigation,
underground storage tank assessment, removal, & site
restoration services, environmental construction &
remediation system installation. (Nat Ame, estab 2011,
empl 11, sales $664,000, cert: CPUC)

3217 Thomas Land Clearing Company
      2170 W Esther St
      Long Beach, CA 90813
      Contact: Bernice Antimo President
      Tel: 562-436-6025
      Email: tlc.demo@verizon.net
      Website: www.jesdbes.com
Demolition, asbestos abatement, lead based paint
removal & general land clearing. (AA, estab 1985, empl
5, sales $1,700,000, cert: State, CPUC)

3218 Three Squares International Inc.
      1507 7th St, Ste 05
      Santa Monica, CA 90401
      Contact: Jaime Nack President
      Tel: 310-403-6225
      Email: jnack@threesquaresinc.com
      Website: www.threesquaresinc.com
Environmental consulting, strategy, planning & implementation of sustainability initiatives. (Woman, estab
2008, empl 4, sales $500,000, cert: State, City, CPUC)

3219   Tycho Services, Inc.
      3906 W. Burbank Blvd.
      Burbank, CA 91505
      Contact: Raj Chhina President
      Tel: 818-840-9404
      Email: raj@tychoservices.com
      Website: www.tychoservices.com
Pre & post event clean-up & biohazard waste removal and clean-up. (As-Ind, estab 2009, empl 81, sales $1,600,000, cert: NMSDC, CPUC)

3220   UltraViolet Devices, Inc.
      26145 Technology Dr
      Valencia, CA 91355
      Contact: Kathi Million Inside Sales Mgr
      Tel: 661-295-8140
      Email: marys@uvdi.com
      Website: www.uvdi.com
Mfr & dist ultraviolet sanitation devices that purify surfaces, air and water. UV-C Disinfection. (Hisp, estab , empl , sales $0, cert: State, NMSDC)

3221   Veridian Environmental, Inc.
      425 Merchant St, Ste 101
      Vacaville, CA 95688
      Contact: Charlotte R. Symms President
      Tel: 707-449-4400
      Email: csymms@veridianenv.com
      Website: www.veridianenv.com
Quality assurance environmental chemistry consulting services: human health & ecological risk assessment, lab audits, lab data validation, environmental data mgmt, technical liaison services, QA/QC programs & documents, litigation. (Woman, estab 2001, empl 5, sales $210,000, cert: State, CPUC)

3222   West Coast Environmental Solutions
      2650 Lime Ave
      Signal Hill, CA 90755
      Contact: Beatriz Esparza Business Devel Mgr
      Tel: 562-448-9510
      Email: beaesparza@westcoastes.com
      Website: www.westcoastes.com
24-hour hazardous & non-hazardous emergency response spill cleanup; pipeline, facility, marine, rail, highway, container spills, river, stream, harbor, shoreline, drug lab, containment & protective booming, product skimming/ recovery & storage. (Woman, estab 2010, empl 35, sales $5,768,900, cert: CPUC)

3223   Wildscape Restoration, Inc.
      2500 Channel Dr Ste A-1
      Ventura, CA 93003
      Contact: Noreen Cabanting Principal
      Tel: 805-644-6852
      Email: noreen@wildscaperestoration.com
      Website: www.wildscaperestoration.com
Environmental consulting & contracting: habitat restoration, non-native invasive species removal, biological surveys & monitoring, permitting & environmental planning. (Minority, Woman, estab 2006, empl 8, sales $415,369, cert: State)

3224   Zero Waste Solutions Inc.
      PO Box 1485
      Newark, CA 94560
      Contact: Shavila Singh CEO
      Tel: 510-461-1433
      Email: marketing@zerowastesolutions.com
      Website: www.zerowastesolutions.com
Recycling services, waste management, janitorial services, waste reduction programs, construction recycling, construction debris, trash, hauling services. (Minority, Woman, estab 2002, empl 110, sales $17,500,000, cert: WBENC)

Colorado

3225   Colorado's Advanced Restoration Experts, LLC
      PO Box 1592
      Lyons, CO 80540
      Contact: Theodore Pangilinan President
      Tel: 303-588-6796
      Email: theo@restorationwithcare.com
      Website: www.restorationwithcare.com
Water damage mitigation, mold remediation, carpet cleaning, fire & smoke restoration, odor control & upholstery cleaning. (As-Pac, estab 2015, empl 12, sales $350,000, cert: State)

3226   Diamond T Services Inc.
      112 N Rubey Dr Ste 101
      Golden, CO 80403
      Contact: Vanessa Ingalls CEO
      Tel: 303-459-5499
      Email: vanessa.ingalls@dtservices.com
      Website: www.diamondtservices.com
Soil stabilization & welding solutions, access & environmental matting, primary & secondary containment, surface rentals, certified welding services for pipeline & well sites, fabrication, roustabout, heavy equipment, trucking & environmental services. (Woman, estab 2009, empl 30, sales $7,434,245, cert: WBENC)

3227   Impact Mitigation Consultants LLC.
      9851 Castleridge Cir
      Highlands Ranch, CO 80129
      Contact: James Balman Owner
      Tel: 720-285-9918
      Email: james@imcnow.com
      Website: www.imcnow.com
Environmental testing. Air quality, asbestos, mold, lead. Mitigation consulting Construction services not exceeding 2MMPlastic mold injection & design, IT development. (Nat Ame, estab 2016, empl 5, sales , cert: State)

3228   Property Doctors Inc.
      14700 W 66th Place Unit 7
      Arvada, CO 80004
      Contact: Nancy Rees President
      Tel: 888-456-0911
      Email: information@property-drs.com
      Website: www.property-drs.com
Asbestos abatement & removal, asbestos testing, asbestos consulting, carpet cleaning. (Woman, estab 2005, empl 12, sales $17,000,000, cert: City, WBENC)

3229 RDS Environmental, Inc.
      11603 Teller St
      Broomfield, CO 80020
      Contact: Tammy Linton President
      Tel: 303-444-5253
      Email: tammy@rdsenvironmental.com
      Website: www.rdsenvironmental.com
Environmental consulting, asbestos testing, mold testing,
mold remediation/removal, radon testing, radon mitigation installation. (Woman, estab 1978, empl 6, sales
$1,032,000, cert: WBENC)

3230 RMC Consultants, Inc.
      12345 W Alameda Pkwy Ste 205
      Lakewood, CO 80228
      Contact: Richard Valdez President
      Tel: 303-980-4101
      Email: rvaldez@rmc-consultants.com
      Website: www.rmc-consultants.net
Environmental services consulting: science & engineering,
project mgmt, planning & documentation, compliance,
mine reclamation, heavy equipment operation, waste
mgmt, remediation services. (Hisp, estab 1990, empl 56,
sales $3,980,000, cert: State, City)

3231 TerraNext
      155 S Madison, Ste 311
      Denver, CO 80209
      Contact: Martin President
      Tel: 303-399-6145
      Email: kmartin@terranext.net
      Website: www.terranext.net
Environmental consulting & engineering: regulatory &
historical reviews & compliance projects, phase I ESAs,
NEPA, Section 106 reviews & remedial activity. (Woman,
estab 1997, empl 45, sales $5,000,000, cert: WBENC)

Connecticut

3232 Material Management
      363 New Britain Rd
      Kensington, CT 06037
      Contact: Karen Gamer Owner
      Tel: 860-829-2000
      Email: kg@materialmanagement.us
      Website: www.materialmanagement.us
Recycling services: paper, plastics & metal. (Woman, estab
2002, empl 4, sales $16,000,000, cert: WBENC)

District of Columbia

3233 Windjammer Environmental
      1001 G St NW Ste 800
      Washington, DC 20001
      Contact: Damien Hammond President
      Tel: 888-270-8387
      Email: hammond@wjenviro.com
      Website: www.wjenviro.com
Industrial Hygiene Services: Indoor air Quality Surveys,
Mold & Moisture Investigation, General Air & Waterborne
Contaminate Sampling, Asbestos Management Services &
Lead Management Services, Environmental Health &
Occupational Safety Services. (AA, estab 2012, empl 5,
sales $350,000, cert: State, City, 8(a))

Delaware

3234 BrightFields, Inc.
      801 Industrial St
      Wilmington, DE 19801
      Contact: Donald Short CFO
      Tel: 302-656-9600
      Email: dshort@brightfieldsinc.com
      Website: www.brightfieldsinc.com
Environmental consulting svcs: phase I & II investigations, multi-media sampling, above & underground
storage tanks, soil & groundwater remediation,
brownfield redevelopment, asbestos & lead svcs.
(Woman, estab 2003, empl 45, sales $5,907,000, cert:
WBENC)

Florida

3235 Advantage Environmental Services, Inc.
      2325 5th Ave N
      St. Petersburg, FL 33713
      Contact: Project Dir
      Tel: 727-323-1902
      Email:
      Website: www.aesenv.com
Remediation, waste management & construction
services. (Woman/AA, estab 1994, empl 3, sales
$1,351,000, cert: State, City)

3236 AirQuest Environmental, Inc.
      6851 SW 45th St
      Fort Lauderdale, FL 33314
      Contact: Boyle President
      Tel: 954-792-4549
      Email: traci@airquestinc.com
      Website: www.airquestinc.com
Environmental consulting: due diligence investigations,
Phase I & II site assessments, mold & asbestos surveys,
abatement mgmt, indoor air quality surveys, soil &
groundwater assessment & remediation, etc. (Woman,
estab 2002, empl 28, sales $6,575,064, cert: State,
WBENC)

3237 Ambient Technologies, Inc.
      4610 Central Ave
      St. Petersburg, FL 33711
      Contact: Carlos Lemos President
      Tel: 727-328-0268
      Email: ambtec@aol.com
      Website: www.ambienttech.com
Environmental & geotechnical drilling, geophysics &
utility designating services. (Hisp, estab 1992, empl 30,
sales $3,000,000, cert: State, NMSDC)

3238 Clark Environmental, Inc.
      755 Prairie Industrial Pkwy
      Mulberry, FL 33860
      Contact: Beth Clark President
      Tel: 863-425-4884
      Email: bclark@clarkenvironmental.com
      Website: www.ThermalTreatment.com
Thermal treatment facility: dispose petroleum contaminated soil, waste processing, hazardous & non-hazardous waste disposal & transportation services. (Woman,
estab 1991, empl 23, sales $0, cert: State)

3239   J. J. Sosa & Associates, Inc.
      6911 Pistol Range Rd, Ste 101A
      Tampa, FL 33635
      Contact: Josh Taxon President
      Tel: 813-888-6525
      Email: jjsosa@jjsosa.com
      Website: www.jjsosa.com
General contracting, industrial hygiene, asbestos abatement, environmental remediation. (Hisp, estab 1992, empl 45, sales , cert: State)

3240   Meryman Environmental, Inc.
      10408 Bloomingdale Ave
      Riverview, FL 33578
      Contact: Charles CEO
      Tel: 813-626-9551
      Email: meryman@merymanenvironmental.com
      Website: www.merymanenvironmental.com
Environmental consulting services: scientists, geologists, ecologists, forestry experts, & laboratory scientists. (Nat Ame, estab 1974, empl 9, sales $928,261, cert: State)

3241   OHC Environmental Engineering
      101 S. Hoover Blvd Unit 101
      Tampa, FL 33609
      Contact: James Rizk President
      Tel: 813-376-2005
      Email: ohcadmin@ohcnet.com
      Website: www.ohcnet.com
Environmental consulting: asbestos & lead surveys, indoor air quality investigations, phase I & II assessments, subsurface investigations, asbestos, lead & mold remediation & hazardous material management. (AA, estab 1983, empl 15, sales $2,000,000, cert: State)

3242   Pinnacle Environmental Management Support, Inc.
      2001 W Sample Rd, Ste 101
      Pompano Beach, FL 33064
      Contact: Cynthia Williams CEO
      Tel: - -
      Email: nhaddy@pinnacleems.com
      Website: www.pinnacleems.com
Environmental claims management and cost-control services for petroleum-impacted sites. (Woman, estab 1995, empl 65, sales , cert: WBENC)

3243   Progressive Engineering & Construction, Inc.
      12402 N. 56th St
      Tampa, FL 33617
      Contact: Jill Doyle Office Admin
      Tel: 813-930-0669
      Email: jdoyle@progressiveec.com
      Website: www.progressiveec.com
Environmental engineering, construction management services, environmental feasibility/technology evaluations, remedial/closure strategy development, remedy construction & enhancement. (Woman, estab 1999, empl 9, sales $2,811,000, cert: WBENC)

3244   Pure Air Control Services, Inc.
      4911 Creekside Dr, Ste C
      Clearwater, FL 33760
      Contact: Alan Wozniak President
      Tel: 800-422-7873
      Email: awozniak@pureaircontrols.com
      Website: www.pureaircontrols.com
Indoor environmental svcs: IEQ training, building & home diagnostics, mold identification, industrial hygiene svcs, forensic IEQ testimony, environmental lab svcs, environmental project mgmt, IAQ-screen test kits, HVAC cleaning. (Hisp, estab 1982, empl 35, sales $2,500,000, cert: State, NMSDC)

3245   Spaulding Decon, LLC
      9420 Lazy Lane, E-9
      Tampa, FL 33614
      Contact: Laura Spaulding Owner
      Tel: 813-298-7122
      Email: spaulding911@yahoo.com
      Website: www.spauldingdecon.com
Bio-hazard clean up svcs: blood, vomit, feces, urine removal, odor abatement, dead animal removal. (Woman, estab 2005, empl 7, sales $1,500,000, cert: City, WBENC)

3246   Stone Environmental Services
      6151 Lake Osprey Dr
      Sarasota, FL 33946
      Contact: Anna Milantoni Owner
      Tel: 941-628-5693
      Email:
      amilantoni@stoneenvironmentalservices.com
      Website: www.stoneenvironmentalservices.com
Dist metal/plastic cleaning chemistry, refrigerants, disposal of non-hazardous & hazardous waste disposal, cleaning equipment. (Woman, estab 2001, empl 1, sales $446,000, cert: WBENC)

3247   Urban E Consulting, Inc.
      5630 E Powhatan Ave
      Tampa, FL 33610
      Contact: Dellinda Rabinowitz President
      Tel: 813-512-6998
      Email: dell@urbanerecycling.com
      Website: www.urbanerecycling.com
Provide, pick up, data destruction, recycling, and certification. (Woman, estab 2012, empl 24, sales $2,556,300, cert: WBENC)

Georgia

3248   Accura Analytical Laboratory, Inc.
      6017 Financial Dr
      Norcross, GA 30071
      Contact: Besa Trenova Business Dev
      Tel: 770-449-8800
      Email: besa@accura.com
      Website: www.accura.com
Environmental analytical lab svcs; inorganic, organic, geotechnical & radiochemical testing. (As-Ind, estab 1988, empl 35, sales $0, cert: State, City)

3249   Basha Services, LLC
      2336 Wisteria Dr Ste 510
      Snellville, GA 30078
      Contact: Neville Anderson President
      Tel: 678-344-1161
      Email: nanderson@bashaservices.com
      Website: www.bashaservices.com/
Environmental services: remediation, emergency & spill response, soil remediation, excavation & restoration, groundwater remediation, UST/AST closure, cleaning, inspection & installation. (AA, estab 2007, empl 11, sales , cert: State, NMSDC)

3250 Cape Environmental Management Inc.
500 Pinnacle Court, Ste 100
Norcross, GA 30071
Contact: MICHAEL HEALY Business Devel Mgr
Tel: 610-470-1189
Email: mhealy@cape-inc.com
Website: www.cape-inc.com
Environ remediation & consulting: base closures, USTS, ASTS, assessments, lead based paint, radon, asbestos, environ communication programs, hazardous wastes, soil & groundwater. (Hisp, estab 1985, empl 455, sales $128,148,143, cert: NMSDC)

3251 Corporate Environmental Risk Management
1990 Lakeside Pkwy Ste 300
Tucker, GA 30084
Contact: Al Edwards Managing Dir
Tel: 678-999-0173
Email: certification@cerm.com
Website: www.cerm.com
Environmental mgmt & remediation, civil engineering & site dev, water resources mgmt, program & construction mgmt. (AA, estab 1995, empl 112, sales $2,960,000, cert: State)

3252 Environmental International Corporation
161 Kimball Bridge Rd Ste 100
Alpharetta, GA 30009
Contact: Phil Perley Tech Svcs Mgr
Tel: 770-772-7100
Email: pperley@eicusa.com
Website: www.eicusa.com
Environ compliance, site assessment, remedial investigation, feasibility study, soil & ground remediation, risk & hazard evaluation, litigation support, hazardous waste mgmt, etc. (Minority, Woman, estab 1994, empl 15, sales $1,000,000, cert: WBENC)

3253 Kemron Environmental Services, Inc.
1359-A Ellsworth Industrial Blvd
Atlanta, GA 30318
Contact: John Dwyer Exec VP
Tel: 404-636-0928
Email: mbe@kemron.com
Website: www.kemron.com
Environ svcs: consulting, site remediation, environ assessment, investigation & engineering, analytical svcs, geotechnical testing, treatability studies & technology evaluation. (Hisp, estab 1975, empl 165, sales $47,127,478, cert: NMSDC)

Illinois

3254 A3 Environmental, LLC.
3030 Warrenville Rd, Ste 418
Lisle, IL 60532
Contact: Tim Allen Business Devel
Tel: 630-507-9002
Email: Tim@A3E.com
Website: www.A3E.com
Environmental Due Diligence, Phase I Environmental Site Assessments, Phase II Environmental Site Assessments, Record Search w/ Risk Assessment (RSRA), Environmental Screens, Transaction Screen Assessments (TSA) Preliminary Environmental Site Assessments. (Woman, estab 2015, empl 18, sales $2,600,000, cert: WBENC)

3255 All Service Contracting Corp.
2024 E Damon Ave
Decatur, IL 62526
Contact: CEO
Tel: 217-233-3018
Email: info@allservice.com
Website: www.allservice.com
Dist, remove & install filter media, water & waste water plants, industial & municipal. (Woman, estab 1996, empl 12, sales $0, cert: WBENC)

3256 Anderson & Egan, Co.
124 N Water St Ste 206
Rockford, IL 61107
Contact: Jennifer Anderson President
Tel: 815-962-9000
Email: janderson@andersonenveng.com
Website: www.andersonenveng.com
Air monitoring, asbestos abatements, environmental consulting & engineering, permitting assistance, underground storage tank removals, environmental site assessments. (Woman, estab 2003, empl 5, sales $469,000, cert: State, City)

3257 Endure, Inc.
360 Beinoris Dr
Wood Dale, IL 60191
Contact: Angelia Hopson Enviro Safety/Training
Tel: 630-616-9700
Email: ahopson@endure-inc.com
Website: www.endureinc.com
Safety, health & environmental consulting, training for regulatory compliance to OSHA, EPA & DOT requirements. (Woman/AA, estab 2010, empl 17, sales $1,845,500, cert: City, NMSDC)

3258 NES Incorporated
19015 Jodi Rd Unit B
Mokena, IL 60448
Contact: Kyla Lawson Secretary
Tel: 708-478-5497
Email: klawson@nesincorp.com
Website: www.nesincorp.com
Asbestos abatement, operations & maintenance, inspections & sampling, lead removal, mitigation, sampling & testing, mold remediation, inspections & sampling, hazardous materials clean-up & infrared investigations. (Hisp, estab 2000, empl 10, sales $1,800,000, cert: State, NMSDC)

Indiana

3259 Gurman Container & Supply Co.
800 N 3rd St
Terre Haute, IN 47807
Contact: Michael Roberts Sales Mgr
Tel: 800-448-7626
Email: mike@gurmancontainer.com
Website: www.gurmancontainer.com
Removal of used or damaged drums for reconditioning or disposal. (Woman, estab 1922, empl 13, sales $1,654,920, cert: State, WBENC)

3260　Hoosier Equipment Service, Inc.
　　　8149 Network Dr
　　　Plainfield, IN 46168
　　　Contact: Anne DaVega VP Business Dev
　　　Tel:　317-838-8988
　　　Email: adavega@hoosierequipment.com
　　　Website: www.hoosierequipment.com
Environmental services, underground & aboveground storage tank work (removals, installs, repairs), oil/water separator cleanouts, & environmental remediation work, excavate contaminated soil. (Woman, estab 1978, empl 13, sales $3,169,000, cert: WBENC)

3261　Keramida Environmental, Inc.
　　　401 N College Ave
　　　Indianapolis, IN 46202
　　　Contact: Tim Higgins VP
　　　Tel:　317-414-9862
　　　Email: thiggins@keramida.com
　　　Website: www.keramida.com
Environmental, health & safety engineering & consulting, remediation, site assessments, permitting. (Woman, estab 1988, empl 123, sales $21,043,881, cert: WBENC)

Kansas

3262　EMR, Inc.
　　　2110 Delaware, Ste B
　　　Lawrence, KS 66046
　　　Contact: Connie Cook VP Marketing & Busines Devel
　　　Tel:　785-842-9013
　　　Email: ccook@emr-inc.com
　　　Website: www.emr-inc.com
Environmental consulting: compliance, industrial hygiene, mold, asbestos, lead paint, UST/AST investigation, hazardous waste mgmt, recycling, soil & groundwater remediation. (Minority, Woman, estab 1988, empl 250, sales $44,000,000, cert: WBENC)

Kentucky

3263　Evergreen Environmental
　　　7416 Hwy 329
　　　Crestwood, KY 40014
　　　Contact: Hollis Flora Project Mgr
　　　Tel:　502-241-4171
　　　Email: hflora@evgusa.com
　　　Website: www.evgusa.com
Compliance plan dev, environmental process & RCRA audits, property audits, UST mgmt, hazard risk analysis, OSHA training & consulting, soil & groundwater remediation, permitting & closure plans, industrial cleaning, hazardous & waste mgmt, etc. (Woman, estab 1986, empl 26, sales $4,300,000, cert: WBENC)

3264　Specific Waste Industries
　　　3600 Chamberlain Lane, Ste 104
　　　Louisville, KY 40241
　　　Contact: Victor Anderson President
　　　Tel:　502-425-2770
　　　Email: vanderson@a-solutionsinc.com
　　　Website: www.specificwaste.com
Regulated Medical Waste Removal & Treatment, Pharmaceutical Waste (Haz and Non-Haz), Sharps Waste (Reusable Sharps Program). (AA, estab , empl , sales $500,000, cert: NMSDC)

Louisiana

3265　Quaternary Resource Investigations, LLC
　　　13588 Florida Blvd
　　　Baton Rouge, LA 70819
　　　Contact: Mary Ruiz VP Sales
　　　Tel:　225-292-1400
　　　Email: info@qri.com
　　　Website: www.qri.com
Litigation & strategy support; environmental sampling & lab data mgmt; groundwater geophysical svcs; remediation implementation; regulatory compliance; coastal & wetlands svcs. (Woman, estab 1986, empl 18, sales $31,000,000, cert: WBENC)

Massachusetts

3266　Capaccio Environmental Engineering Inc.
　　　293 Boston Post Road West
　　　Marlborough, MA 01752
　　　Contact: Lisa Wilk President
　　　Tel:　508-970-0033
　　　Email: lwilk@capaccio.com
　　　Website: www.capaccio.com
Environmental engineering & consulting services, environmental compliance & permitting, occupational safety & health consulting services, environmental, health & safety management systems. (Woman, estab , empl , sales $3,139,945, cert: State, WBENC)

3267　Corporate Environmental Advisors, Inc.
　　　127 Hartwell St
　　　West Boylston, MA 01583
　　　Contact: Scott Soucy Health, Safety & Compliance
　　　Tel:　800-358-7960
　　　Email: contactus@cea-inc.com
　　　Website: www.cea-inc.com/
Environmental engineering, consulting & contracting firm. (Woman, estab 1985, empl 20, sales $3,878,000, cert: State)

3268　CR Environmental Inc
　　　639 Boxberry Hill Road
　　　East Falmouth, MA 02536
　　　Contact: Charlotte Cogswell President
　　　Tel:　508-563-7970
　　　Email: charlotte@crenvironmental.com
　　　Website: www.crenvironmental.com
Ecological risk assessments & characterizations of terrestrial, wetland & aquatic habitats. (Woman, estab 1994, empl 7, sales $1,314,475, cert: State, City)

3269　Essex Newbury North Contracting Corporation
　　　65 Parker St, Unit 5
　　　Newburyport, MA 01950
　　　Contact: Delano Brooks President
　　　Tel:　978-463-5414
　　　Email: delano_br@yahoo.com
　　　Website: www.essexnewburynorth.com
General Contracting, construction management, commercial & industrial construction, lead abatement & asbestos remediation, finish carpentry, commercial & institutional bldg construction, painting & wall coverings, site preparation. (AA, estab 1997, empl 400, sales $31,000,000, cert: State, City, NMSDC)

3270 Strategic Environmental
      362 Putnam Hill Rd
      Sutton, MA 01590
      Contact: Ross Hartman Exec VP
      Tel: 508-757-7782
      Email: info@strategic-es.com
      Website: www.strategic-es.com
Transportation & disposal management svcs: environmental testing & on-site field svcs, site clean-up & remediation, groundwater mgmt. (Woman, estab 2001, empl 48, sales $26,000,000, cert: WBENC)

Maryland

3271 Environmental Health and Safety Solutions, LLC
      13 Pheasant View Place
      Parkton, MD 21120
      Contact: Frank Damato Dir of Safety/Training
      Tel: 904-556-6422
      Email: fdamato@ehssgroup.com
      Website: www.EHSSGroup.com
Environmental services, industrial hygiene monitoring services, air & noise monitoring surveys. (Woman, estab 2011, empl 5, sales $760,000, cert: State)

3272 SodexoMagic (Magic Food Provision, LLC)
      9801 Washingtonian Blvd
      Gaithersburg, MD 20878
      Contact: Ken Holdman Dir Strategic Sales
      Tel: 918-430-6514
      Email: ken.holdman@sodexomagic.com
      Website: www.sodexomagic.com
Food and catering services groundkeeping facilities and plant operations and maintenance, environmental & engineering services & laundry & linens. (AA, estab 2006, empl 4900, sales $283,400,000, cert: NMSDC)

3273 Turtle Wings Inc.
      1771 Olive St
      Capitol Heights, MD 20743
      Contact: Elizabeth Wilmot President
      Tel: 301-583-8399
      Email: info@datakillers.com
      Website: www.datakillers.com
Environmental services. (Woman, estab 2005, empl 13, sales $1,200,000, cert: State, WBENC)

Michigan

3274 Advanced Environmental Management Group, LLC
      44339 Plymouth Oaks Blvd
      Plymouth, MI 48170
      Contact: Linda Leonard Office Admin
      Tel: 734-354-9070
      Email: admin@aemgroup.biz
      Website: www.aemgroup.biz
Environmental permitting, compliance assessments, dispersion modeling, stack & ambient air testing, due diligence & remediation svcs, ISO 14001 EMS svcs, facility closure & decommissioning services, spill & contingency plans. (As-Ind, estab 1998, empl 11, sales $0, cert: NMSDC)

3275 A-Global Solution, LLC DBA Environmental Services of North America, In
      10455 Ford Rd
      Dearborn, MI 48126
      Contact: Joe Coelho Owner
      Tel: 313-945-7400
      Email: jcoelho@esnainc.com
      Website: www.esnainc.com
Facility svcs: waste disposal & recycling, snow removal, parking lot sweeping, power washing, janitorial services & supplies, landscaping, onsite & offsite document shredding, asbestos, lead based paint & mold, waste containers. (AA, estab , empl , sales $0, cert: NMSDC)

3276 Atier
      24074 Gibson Dr
      Warren, MI 48089
      Contact: Patricia Schrenk Acct Mgr
      Tel: 586-759-4240
      Email: patti.schrenk@atierpro.com
      Website: www.atierpro.com
Total Quality Management & Engineering Consulting, Quality & Industrial Engineering, Containment, Supplier Representation, ISO & TS Implementation Audits, Quality Inspection, Launch support, Scrap Reduction, Project Management. (AA, estab 2012, empl 100, sales $4,700,000, cert: NMSDC)

3277 Cadena, LLC.
      1099 Highland Dr, Ste A
      Ann Arbor, MI 48108
      Contact: Armando Ojeda CEO
      Tel: 734-418-1977
      Email: aojeda@cadenaco.com
      Website: www.cadenaco.com
Environmental services, lab data, Level II & Level IV validations, environmental laboratory audits, archiving environmental data. (Hisp, estab 2013, empl 2, sales $384,654, cert: NMSDC, CPUC)

3278 EKS Services Incorporated
      7451 Third St
      Detroit, MI 48202
      Contact: Clarence E. Carpenter III CEO
      Tel: 313-963-1433
      Email: clarencecarpenter@eksservices.com
      Website: www.eksservices.com
Environmental consulting & construction mgmt. (AA, estab 2000, empl 20, sales $1,500,000, cert: NMSDC)

3279 Environmental Compliance Office Inc.
      3011 W Grand Blvd, Ste 420
      Detroit, MI 48202
      Contact: Vimala Anishetty, Ph.D. President
      Tel: 313-285-8401
      Email: vanishet@ecomain.com
      Website: www.ecomain.com
Environmental engineering & consulting svcs: air, water, waste, auditing, reporting & training. (Minority, Woman, estab 2007, empl 4, sales $310,000, cert: WBENC)

3280 Environmental Testing and Consulting Inc.
      38900 W Huron River Dr
      Romulus, MI 48174
      Contact: Patricia Stephen Business Devel Mgr
      Tel: 734-955-6600
      Email: sales@2etc.com
      Website: www.2etc.com
Environmental consulting firm, asbestos, lead based paint,
mold surveys, risk assessments, clearances, O&M plans,
project management and training, indoor air quality
assessments. (Woman, estab 1989, empl 75, sales
$3,270,519, cert: WBENC)

3281 Infiniti Group International, LLC
      241 Keelson Dr
      Detroit, MI 48215
      Contact: Melvin Gilmer Member
      Tel: 586-995-5331
      Email: mg@infinitigroup.us
      Website: www.infinitigroupinternational.org
Environmental Products and Services. (AA, estab 2014,
empl 2, sales , cert: NMSDC)

3282 Integrated Recycling Industries
      PO Box 581
      Wyandotte, MI 48192
      Contact: Richard Pacheco President
      Tel: 734-818-9835
      Email: rpacheco.iri@gmail.com
      Website: www.integratedrecyclingindustries.com
Recycle Ferrous and Non-Ferrous scrap metals, Cardboard
and Plastics. (Hisp, estab 2015, empl 2, sales $100,000,
cert: NMSDC)

3283 Merit Laboratories, Inc.
      2680 E Lansing Dr
      East Lansing, MI 48823
      Contact: Maya Murshak President
      Tel: 517-332-0167
      Email: mayamurshak@meritlabs.com
      Website: www.meritlabs.com
Environmental testing laboratory, RCRA remediation
analytical, testing for soil, water & waste. We work with
large and small industries, engineering firms, municipalities (Woman, estab 1987, empl , sales $0, cert: WBENC)

3284 MPS Group, Inc.
      38755 Hills Tech Dr
      Farmington Hills, MI 48331
      Contact: Bryon Lawrence Dir Sales/Marketing
      Tel: 313-841-7588
      Email: blawrence@mpsgrp.com
      Website: www.mpsgrp.com
Environmental Consulting & Engineering. (AA, estab 1995,
empl 495, sales $46,200,000, cert: NMSDC)

3285 Unlimited Recycling, Inc.
      PO Box 363
      Richmond, MI 48062
      Contact: Maria Marin-McInturf President
      Tel: 586-784-4980
      Email: maria@unlimitedrecyclinginc.com
      Website: www.unlimitedrecyclinginc.com
Recycling svcs: spent electric lamps, batteries, electronic
equipment, mercury containing devices. In addition,
hazardous & non-hazardous waste, oil, solvents, paint,
antinfreeze. (Woman/Hisp, estab 1999, empl 7, sales ,
cert: NMSDC, WBENC)

3286 VMX International, LLC
      3011 W Grand Blvd Ste 2401
      Detroit, MI 48202
      Contact: Vickie Lewis CEO
      Tel: 313-875-9450
      Email: vlewis@vmxi.com
      Website: www.vmxi.com
International waste management & recycling services.
(Woman/AA, estab 2001, empl 54, sales $3,140,800,
cert: NMSDC, WBENC)

Minnesota

3287 EnviroBate, Inc.
      3301 E 26th Sttreet
      Minneapolis, MN 55406
      Contact: Dana Krakowski VP Sales & Marketing
      Tel: 612-437-5797
      Email: dkrakowski@envirobate.com
      Website: www.envirobate.com
Environmental remediation, asbestos & lead abatement,
mold remediation & Indoor Air Quality (Duct Cleaning),
hazardous waste disposal to include mercury, lead &
PCB's. (Woman, estab 1991, empl 80, sales $14,000,000,
cert: City, WBENC)

Missouri

3288 Ahrens Contracting, Inc.
      140 Lafayette Ave
      St. Louis, MO 63104
      Contact: Patricia Ahrens President
      Tel: 314-631-7799
      Email: pahrens@ahrenscontracting.com
      Website: www.ahrenscontracting.com
Hauling Dirt, Rubbish, Trash, Special Waste, Hazardous
Waste, Clean Fill, etc. (Woman, estab , empl , sales $0,
cert: WBENC)

3289 Cardinal Environmental Operations Corp.
      4518 Woodson Rd
      Saint Louis, MO 63134
      Contact: Paula Milligan President
      Tel: 314-890-2088
      Email: pmilligan@callcardinal.com
      Website: www.callcardinal.com
Asbestos abatement, lead abatement, environmental
remediation, mold remediation, soil/water remediation,
UST/AST removal & installation, duct cleaning services,
consulting services, site assessments, demolition.
(Woman, estab 1993, empl 25, sales $2,000,000, cert:
State, City)

3290 CCI Environmental, Inc.
      6913 Noble Dr
      Hazelwood, MO 63024
      Contact: Mark Briguglio President
      Tel: 314-974-3893
      Email: marksbriguglio@gmail.com
      Website: www.ccienv.info
Asbestos abatement, inspections, testing, project
management & estimating to air monitoring & project
consulting. (Nat Ame, estab 1994, empl 7, sales
$930,000, cert: State)

3291 Global Environmental, Inc.
6439 Plymouth Ave Ste 119
Wellston, MO 63133
Contact: John Dingus Project Mgr
Tel: 314-875-9501
Email: john@globalabatement.com
Website: www.globalabatement.com
Environmental remediation & consulting. (Minority,
Woman, estab 1991, empl 10, sales $10,500,000, cert:
State, 8(a))

3292 Haz-Waste, Inc.
12951 Gravois Rd Ste 110
St. Louis, MO 63127
Contact: Kimberly Medlock VP
Tel: 800-429-9783
Email: kmedlock@haz-waste.com
Website: www.haz-waste.com
Air pollution permitting, asbestos, abatement, byproduct
mgmt, environmental audits, field service, industrial
compliance, OSHA compliance, Phase I & II site work,
plant closures, pollution prevention. (Woman, estab 1993,
empl 34, sales $6,200,000, cert: WBENC)

3293 The Kiesel Company
4801 Fyler Ave
St. Louis, MO 63166
Contact: Larry Gooden VP
Tel: 314-351-5500
Email: larry.gooden@kieselco.com
Website: www.thekieselcompany.com
Dist fuels & lubricants, emergency response services to
chemical & petroleum product releases, railroad tank car
cleaning, barge cleaning, non-hazardous & hazardous
waste disposal, demolition & petroleum-contaminated
waste water treatment & disposal. (Woman, estab , empl
48, sales $75,010,000, cert: City)

Mississippi

3294 Advanced Environmental Consultants, Inc.
5430 Executive Place, Ste 2A
Jackson, MS 39206
Contact: DeJonnette Grantham-King CEO
Tel: 601-362-1788
Email: dgking@advancedenviroconsultants.com
Website: www.advancedenviroconsultants.com
Asbestos inspections, abatement & disposal, lead inspec-
tions, abatement & disposal, mold inspections, air
monitoring, phase I site assessments. (Woman/AA, estab
1996, empl 10, sales $410,000, cert: WBENC)

North Carolina

3295 AB & Law, Inc. dba A-1 Supply Company
638 Person St
Fayetteville, NC 28301
Contact: Owner
Tel: 910-323-3871
Email: sales@a1supplycorp.com
Website: www.a1supplycorp.com
Microfiber, Secondary Containment Units, Mold and Algae
Cleaners, Remendiation Products, Absorbents, Absobent
pads, Loose Absorbents, Sorb-sox and Booms, Spill kits, Air
Care, Floor Care, Skin Care, Insecticides and Herbicides.
(Woman, estab 1990, empl 4, sales $1,000,000, cert:
State)

3296 Environmental Process Solutions, PLLC
7000 Stinson Hartis Rd Ste F
Indian Trail, NC 28079
Contact: CEO
Tel: 980-202-2377
Email: info@epscharlotte.com
Website: www.EPSCharlotte.com
Environmental Consulting, Industrial wastewater
treatment, engineering services. (Woman, estab 2010,
empl 5, sales , cert: WBENC)

3297 Environmental Service Systems, LLC
5550 77 Center Dr. Ste 160
Charlotte, NC 28217
Contact: Ciara Lilly VP Diversity & Inclusion
Tel: 704-527-4099
Email: clilly@environmentalss.com
Website: www.environmentalss.com
Facility maintenance & janitorial services. (AA, estab
1998, empl 10000, sales $250,000,000, cert: NMSDC)

3298 FireWater CleanUp Crew Corp.
PO Box 78145
Greensboro, NC 27427
Contact: Jamal Mention President
Tel: 336-666-1913
Email: jamalmention@firewatercleanupcrew.com
Website: www.firewatercleanupcrew.com
Remediation/restoration services for smoke, fire & water
damage. Trauma scene cleanup. (AA, estab 2016, empl
3, sales , cert: State)

3299 Porter Scientific Inc.
PO Box 1359
Pembroke, NC 28372
Contact: Freda Porter President
Tel: 910-521-0549
Email: fporter@porterscientific.com
Website: www.porterscientific.com
Environmental consulting, assessments, remediation &
cleanup, pollution prevention, regulatory compliance,
water, sewer & solid waste project management.
(Minority, Woman, estab 1997, empl 18, sales
$3,458,000, cert: City)

3300 Reliable Solutions Construction, LLC dba Reliable
Restorations
12220 Nations Ford Rd Ste A
Pineville, NC 28134
Contact: Johanna Suarez Operations Mgr
Tel: 704-909-7616
Email: johanna@reliablerestorations.net
Website: www.reliablerestorations.net
Disaster emergency response services, board ups, water
extraction, fire & water damage restoration, odor &
mold remediation, contents clean up & pack-outs, Non-
Destructive Mold Remediation, Smoke & odor deodor-
ization, Removal. (Minority, Woman, estab 2009, empl
15, sales $1,426,000, cert: State)

New Hampshire

3301 Absolute Resource Associates, LLC
124 Heritage Ave Unit 16
Portsmouth, NH 03801
Contact: Susan Sylvester President
Tel: 603-436-2001
Email: sues@absoluteresourceassociates.com
Website: www.absoluteresourceassociates.com
Environmental laboratory testing & indoor air quality
assessments. (Woman, estab 1994, empl 25, sales $0,
cert: WBENC)

New Jersey

3302　BGI Resources International Corporation
205 Barclay Pavilion W
Cherry Hill, NJ 08034
Contact: Bassey Akpan CEO
Tel:　856-888-2396
Email: info@bgiresourcesintl.com
Website: www.BGIResourcesIntl.com
Air, Water Soil Sampling, Phase I, II, III Projects, GIS Mapping, Preliminary Assessments. (AA, estab 2010, empl 3, sales , cert: State)

3303　Brinkerhoff Environmental Services, Inc.
1805 Atlantic Ave
Manasquan, NJ 08736
Contact: Laura Brinkerhoff CEO
Tel:　732-223-2225
Email: lbrinkerhoff@brinkenv.com
Website: www.brinkenv.com
Environmental services, Environmental Engineering, Environmental Site assessments, NEPA Evaluation Reports, Environmental Planning & Permitting, Wetland Services, Brownfield Redevelopment, Underground Storage Tank management, Geologic and Hydro-geologic. (Woman, estab 1989, empl 40, sales $7,505,209, cert: State, WBENC)

3304　Cornerstone EHS, LLC
PO Box 1102
Mullica Hill, NJ 08062
Contact: Marianne Payne President
Tel:　856-776-0455
Email: mpayne@cornerstoneehs.com
Website: www.cornerstoneehs.com
Environmental, health, safety consulting & services, EHS program development & management; comprehensive EHS compliance & management system auditing; EHS related training, management systems development & implementation. (Woman, estab 2011, empl 1, sales $332,065, cert: WBENC)

3305　Environmental Industrial Services Corp. of NJ
288 Oak Grove Rd
Swedesboro, NJ 08085
Contact: Robert Feller Business Devel
Tel:　856-467-5001
Email: rfeller@eisco4service.com
Website: www.eisco4action.com
Environmental remediation services, soil remediation, capping, stabilization, UST & AST cleaning & closure, subsurface exploratory/test pits, groundwater remediation, install systems, pump & treat, vapor extraction, vacuum enhanced recovery. (Woman, estab 1990, empl 55, sales $3,211,964, cert: State)

3306　Fortune Metal Group
900 Leesville Ave
Rahway, NJ 07065
Contact: Tina Chen Buyer
Tel:　732-388-0709
Email: tinac@fortunegroup.net
Website: www.fortunemetalrecycling.com
Full-service metal recycling facility. (As-Pac, estab 2006, empl 500, sales , cert: State)

3307　Fortune Metal Inc. of RI
900 Leesville Ave
Rahway, NJ 07065
Contact: Rick Gosselin Natl Sales Dir
Tel:　401-725-9100
Email: rickgosselin@fortunegroup.net
Website: www.fortunegroup.net
Buy & recycle scrap metals & plastics. (As-Pac, estab 1998, empl 128, sales $110,856,318, cert: NMSDC)

3308　Matrix New World Engineering, Land Surveying and Landscape Architectur
26 Columbia Trnpke 2nd Fl
Florham Park, NJ 07932
Contact: Jayne Warne, PE President
Tel:　973-240-1800
Email: jwarne@mnwe.com
Website: www.matrixneworld.com
Environmental, geotechnical, civil engineering, survey & building facility consulting & engineering firm. (Woman, estab 1990, empl 200, sales $28,899,396, cert: State, City, WBENC)

3309　Prestige Environmental, Inc.
220 Davidson Ave Ste 307
Somerset, NJ 08873
Contact: Girish Mehta President
Tel:　908-757-9700
Email: girish.mehta@prestige-environmental.com
Website: www.prestige-environmental.com
Environmental consulting & contracting svcs: site assessments & feasibility studies; removal & installation of petroleum tanks; soil & groundwater investigations; site remediation; design, installation & operation of remediation systems. (As-Ind, estab 1993, empl 6, sales $1,092,700, cert: State)

3310　Sovereign
111 A North Gold Dr
Robbinsville, NJ 08691
Contact: Michael Hanlon Mgr
Tel:　609-259-8200
Email: mhanlon@sovcon.com
Website: www.sovcon.com
Environmental consulting & remediation services, environmental, civil & geotechnical engineering; remediation system evaluation, optimization, design & construction/installation; environmental, land use & natural resources permitting. (As-Pac, estab 1999, empl 165, sales $35,466,433, cert: NMSDC)

Nevada

3311　The Westmark Group
2430 N Decatur Blvd Ste 140
Las Vegas, NV 89108
Contact: Leslie Mujica Dir of BD & gov affairs
Tel:　702-839-2960
Email: marketing@westmarkgroup.net
Website: www.westmarkgroup.net
Consulting & project management, environmental consulting, occupational safety & health services & waste management services. (Hisp, estab 1999, empl 25, sales $5,000,000, cert: State)

New York

3312 Abtron Associates Corp.
60A Corbin Ave
Bay Shore, NY 11706
Contact: Robert Green President
Tel: 631-392-1330
Email: rgreen@abtronassociatescorp.com
Website: www.abtronassociatescorp.com
Environmental hazards/non-hazards services. (AA, estab 1997, empl 30, sales $1,055,000, cert: NMSDC)

3313 American Environmental Assessment & Solutions, Inc
679 Lafayette Ave, 3rd Fl
Brooklyn, NY 11216
Contact: Antoinette Ollivierre Principal
Tel: 718-209-0653
Email: aollivierre@aeasinc.com
Website: www.aeasinc.com
Environmental services: Phase I, II and III Environmental Site Assessments (ESA), soil & groundwater investigation, remediation of contaminated sites, NYC E-designation investigation and compliance. (Woman/AA, estab 2006, empl 9, sales , cert: State, City)

3314 Atlantic Testing Laboratories, Limited
6431 US Hwy 11
Canton, NY 13617
Contact: Eric M. Van Alstyne Business Devel Mgr
Tel: 315-386-4578
Email: evanalstyne@atlantictesting.com
Website: www.atlantictesting.com
Subsurface investigations, water-based investigations, geotechnical engineering, construction materials engineering & testing, special inspection services, pavement engineering, nondestructive testing & environmental services. (Woman, estab 1967, empl 260, sales $16,190,692, cert: State, City)

3315 Chenango Contracting, Inc.
29 Arbutus Rd
Johnson City, NY 13790
Contact: Carl Burdick Project Mgr
Tel: 607-729-8500
Email: cburdick@chenangocontracting.com
Website: www.chenangocontracting.com
Supply & Install Environmental Geosynthetics. (Nat Ame, estab 1992, empl 45, sales , cert: State)

3316 CSA Central, Inc.
55 Broadway, 14th Fl
New York, NY 10006
Contact: Frederik Riefkohl Sr VP
Tel: 305-461-5484
Email: friefkohl@csagroup.com
Website: www.csagroup.com
Program & project mgmt, environmental services, architecture & engineering, Construction Management, Operation & Maintenance. (Hisp, estab 1995, empl 55, sales $4,963,359, cert: NMSDC)

3317 Environmental Design & Research, DPC
217 Montgomery St Ste 1000
Syracuse, NY 13202
Contact: Joanne Stewart Associate
Tel: 315-471-0688
Email: jstewart@edrdpc.com
Website: www.edrdpc.com
Landscape architecture, civil engineering, community planning, visualization, environmental regulatory, ecological, geographic information systems mapping & analysis, historic preservation, cultural resources, archeology. (Woman, estab 1979, empl 38, sales $4,500,000, cert: State)

3318 Foit-Albert Associates, Architecture, Engineering and Surveying, P.C.
215 W 94th St, Ste 517
New York, NY 10025
Contact: Gregory Carballada President
Tel: 716-856-3933
Email: cstoebe@foit-albert.com
Website: www.foit-albert.com
Architecture, Engineering, Environmental & Land Surveying Consulting. (Hisp, estab 1977, empl 70, sales $10,000,000, cert: State, City)

3319 Gianco Environmental Services Inc.
37 North Grand Boulevard
Brentwood, NY 11717
Contact: Michael Gianchetta VP
Tel: 631-952-9900
Email: michaelg@gianco.com
Website: www.gianco.com
Facilities management, hazard & non-hazard waste removal & recycling. (Woman, estab 2001, empl 4, sales $1,024,193, cert: WBENC)

3320 Innovative Recycling Technologies, Inc.
690 N Queens Ave
Lindenhurst, NY 11757
Contact: John Ewen Sales
Tel: 631-225-3044
Email: jewen@irtwaste.com
Website: www.irtwaste.com
Coordinating & implementing cost-effective, ihazardous & non-hazardous waste, waste classification, labelling, storage, transportation, and disposal solutions. (Woman, estab , empl , sales $0, cert: State, City)

3321 International Asbestos Removal, Inc.
68-08 Woodside Ave
Woodside, NY 11377
Contact: Karen Grando President
Tel: 718-335-0304
Email: kgrando@aol.com
Website: www.iaronline.com
Asbestos & lead removal, insulation, heat, cold, sound, firestopping, etc. (Woman, estab 1987, empl 25, sales $0, cert: WBENC)

3322 LEADCARE, Inc.
10-25 44th Ave
Long Island City, NY 11101
Contact: Sarah Attias-Dunn President
Tel: 718-706-8383
Email: dunn@leadcare.com
Website: www.leadcare.com
Environmental testing, consultating & remediation project management, asbestos, lead, mold & indoor air quality investigations. (Woman, estab 1992, empl 10, sales $1,100,000, cert: State, City)

3323　Mechanical Testing, Inc.
　　　70 Lake Ave.
　　　Saratoga Springs, NY 12866
　　　Contact: Eileen Venn CEO
　　　Tel:　　518-450-7292
　　　Email: eileenv@mechtest.com
　　　Website: www.mechtest.com
Testing, Adjusting & Balancing of HVAC Systems, Indoor Air Quality Testing, Performance Tests for HVAC Equipment, Sound Testing, In Room/Space Pressure Relationship Testing, Duct Pressurization, SMACNA. (Woman, estab 1967, empl 27, sales $3,800,000, cert: State, WBENC)

3324　Miller Environmental Group, Inc.
　　　538 Edwards Ave
　　　Calverton, NY 11933
　　　Contact: Carl Fiore VP Business Dev
　　　Tel:　　631-369-4900
　　　Email: cfiore@millerenv.com
　　　Website: www.millerenv.com
Environmental and Industrial Services Equipment, Emergency Response and Industrial Cleaning services. (Minority, estab 1971, empl 160, sales $30,000,000, cert: NMSDC)

3325　NPTS, Inc.
　　　2060 Sheridan Dr
　　　Buffalo, NY 14223
　　　Contact: Hormoz Mansouri President
　　　Tel:　　716-876-8066
　　　Email: rbroman@eiteam.com
　　　Website: www.npts.net
Engineering consulting: nuclear, fossil, petrochem, risk assessment, thermohydraulic, design, outage mgmt, technical support svcs, etc. (As-Ind, estab 1983, empl 15, sales $1,521,462, cert: NMSDC)

3326　Sienna Environmental Technologies, LLC
　　　350 Elmwood Ave
　　　Bufalo, NY 14222
　　　Contact: Susanne Kelley President
　　　Tel:　　716-332-3134
　　　Email: skelley@siennaet.com
　　　Website: www.siennaet.com
Asbestos inspections & contamination assessments, lead-based paint inspection & risk assessment, indoor air quality, microbial & radon testing & investigative services, air, soil, dust, water & solid waste sampling. (Minority, Woman, estab 2000, empl 17, sales $2,000,000, cert: State, City)

3327　Universal Environmental Consulting, Inc.
　　　900 Merchants Concourse Ste 214
　　　Westbury, NY 11590
　　　Contact: Lisa Giaquinto President
　　　Tel:　　800-552-0309
　　　Email:
　　　Website: www.uecny.com
Collection management of solid waste & recyclables. (Woman, estab 1995, empl 20, sales $33,785,084, cert: WBENC)

Ohio

3328　Ace Healthy Products LLC
　　　907 W Fifth St
　　　Dayton, OH 45402
　　　Contact: Anthony Watson CEO
　　　Tel:　　866-891-5338
　　　Email: acehealthyproducts11@gmail.com
　　　Website: www.eaglewatchproducts.com/
Mfr unique and patented environmentally friendly products globally. (AA, estab 2015, empl 8, sales , cert: City)

3329　CAP-STONE & Associates, Inc.
　　　748 Green Crest Dr
　　　Westerville, OH 43081
　　　Contact: Mary Sharrett President
　　　Tel:　　614-865-1874
　　　Email: marysharrett@stoneenvironmental.com
　　　Website: www.StoneEnvironmental.com
Assessment, Permitting, Design & Compliance, air, water, soil, waste streams, hazardous materials, storm water, natural resources, site civil, utilities, and structures. (Woman, estab 1989, empl , sales $1,400,000, cert: State, City, WBENC)

3330　CTL Engineering, Inc.
　　　2860 Fisher Rd
　　　Columbus, OH 43204
　　　Contact: C.K. Satyapriya President
　　　Tel:　　614-276-8123
　　　Email: ctl@ctleng.com
　　　Website: www.ctleng.com
Geotechnical, construction inspection, environmental, mining engineering, analytical chemistry, forensic science, metallurgy, product testing, research & development, roof engineering, existing structure evaluation, asbestos inspection. (Minority, estab 1928, empl 187, sales $0, cert: NMSDC)

3331　Environmental and Safety Solutions, Inc.
　　　544 Tohatchi Dr
　　　Cincinnati, OH 45215
　　　Contact: Cindy Tomaszewski President
　　　Tel:　　513-383-7703
　　　Email: ctomaszewski@theessinc.com
　　　Website: www.essinc.info
Enviromental, health & safety services. (AA, estab 2002, empl 9, sales $3,034,000, cert: State, NMSDC)

3332　Iron Eagle Enterprises, LLC
　　　4991 Belmont Ave
　　　Youngstown, OH 44505
　　　Contact: M. McKenzie Business Devel
　　　Tel:　　330-759-2760
　　　Email: mmckenzie@ironeagleent.com
　　　Website: www.IronEagleEnt.com
Custom frac & storage tank rentals, Vacuum truck service—wet & dry materials, Professional cleaning—disposal wells, drains, holding tanks, frac tanks, Solid waste disposal & hauling—rentals of vac boxes & sealed top boxes. (Woman, estab 2010, empl 14, sales $4,500,000, cert: WBENC)

3333 MCFS Enterprises, Inc.
      PO Box 30207
      Middleburg Heights, OH 44130
      Contact: Carrie Scaravelli Owner
      Tel: 440-888-0497
      Email: cscaravelli@cox.net
      Website: www.rainbowintl.com/cleveland
Water & fire restoration, smoke & odor remediation, mold,
lead & asbestos testing & abatement, hazardous waste
specialist. (Woman, estab 2007, empl 5, sales $798,000,
cert: State, City)

3334 Superior Environmental Corp.
      1132 Luschek Dr
      Cincinnati, OH 45241
      Contact: Michael Weinstein Sr Project Mgr
      Tel: 513-923-9000
      Email: m.weinstein@superiorenvironmental.com
      Website: www.superiorenvironmental.com
Environmental consulting: remedial design & implementation, property transfers. (Woman, estab 1989, empl 83,
sales $12,200,000, cert: WBENC)

Oregon

3335 Paul Carlson Associates, Inc.
      5775 Jean Rd. Ste 101
      Lake Oswego, OR 97035
      Contact: Joel McCarthy Industrial Hygienist
      Tel: 503-652-6040
      Email: joelm@pcasafety.com
      Website: www.pcasafety.com
HAZsolutions designed to manage hazardous materials and
waste in retail. (Woman, estab 1988, empl 12, sales , cert:
State)

Pennsylvania

3336 Environmental Data Validation, Inc.
      1326 Orangewood Ave
      Pittsburgh, PA 15216
      Contact: Maxine Wright-Walters President
      Tel: 412-341-5281
      Email: mwalters@edv-inc.com
      Website: www.edv-inc.com
Chemical & radiochemical data validation, environmental
health & safety training, occupational health & safety
consulting, industrial hygienist services, building inspections, environmental site assessments, risk assessment,
hazard assessment. (Woman/AA, estab 1990, empl 8, sales
$350,000, cert: State)

3337 Environmental Equipment + Supply, LLC
      491-L Blue Eagle Ave, Ste L
      Harrisburg, PA 17112
      Contact: Lisa Reeves President
      Tel: 717-901-8891
      Email: reevesl@envisupply.com
      Website: www.envisupply.com
Environmental equipment rental and sales. (Woman, estab
2018, empl 9, sales $1,260,211, cert: WBENC)

3338 Environmental Strategy Consultants, Inc.
      1528 Walnut St Ste 1812-1818
      Philadelphia, PA 19102
      Contact: Lorna Velardi President
      Tel: 215-731-4200
      Email: lmv@envirostrat.com
      Website: www.envirostrat.com
Environmental & safety management: air permitting &
outsourcing, waste, emergency planning & safety &
health services. (Woman, estab 1986, empl 5, sales
$546,532, cert: WBENC)

3339 JD2 Environmental, Inc.
      800 E Washington St
      West Chester, PA 19380
      Contact: Donna Hymes VP
      Tel: 610-430-8151
      Email: dhymes@jd2env.com
      Website: www.jd2env.com
Environmental consulting: storage tank mgmt &
remediation, phase I/II environmental site assessments
& expert witness services. (Woman/AA, estab 2001,
empl 15, sales $0, cert: WBENC)

3340 Keating Environmental Management, Inc.
      835 Springdale Dr
      Exton, PA 19341
      Contact: Keith Choper President
      Tel: 484-876-2200
      Email: kchoper@kempartners.com
      Website: www.kempartners.com
Engineering, environmental engineering and consulting,
brownfields redevelopment, groundwater studies,
subsurface evaluations, geology, remediation management, asbestos, site assessments and environmental
auditing. (Woman, estab 1988, empl 13, sales
$2,250,000, cert: State, City, WBENC)

3341 Niche Waste Reduction and Recycling Systems, Inc
      PO Box 245246
      Philadelphia, PA 19119
      Contact: Maurice Sampson II CEO
      Tel: 267-269-6912
      Email: msampson@nicherecycling.com
      Website: www.nicherecycling.com
Waste Management & recycling planning & consultation
svcs: site survey/waste assessments, Waste Audits,
Architectural Design Consultation for Waste Management, In-house container, brochure, poster training &
orientation. (AA, estab 1995, empl 1, sales , cert: State)

3342 Novel Geo-Environmental, LLC
      171 Montour Run Rd
      Moon Township, PA 15108
      Contact: Grace Aiken Office Mgr
      Tel: 412-722-1970
      Email: gaiken@ngeconsulting.com
      Website: www.ngeconsulting.com
Environmental & geotechnical engineering consulting,
Multi- Media Compliance Auditing, Permitting, Report-
ing & Plan Development, Environmental Management
Systems Design & Implementation. (Woman, estab 2002,
empl 34, sales $5,579,823, cert: State)

3343 Polaris Engineering, Inc.
5015 Preakness Pl
Bethlehem, PA 18020
Contact: Fidel Gonzalez President
Tel: 610-698-7185
Email: fidel@polarisengineeringinc.com
Website: www.polarisengineeringinc.com
Civil engineering: feasibility studies, roadways, storm
water management facilities, water line design, sanitary
sewer design, site layout & site grading. (Hisp, estab 2007,
empl 2, sales , cert: State)

3344 SLM Waste & Recycling Services Inc.
80-90 N Main St
Sellersville, PA 18960
Contact: Susan V. Daywitt President
Tel: 888-847-4449
Email: sdaywitt@slmwaste.com
Website: www.slmwaste.com
Waste & recycling svcs: cardboard, plastics, aluminum,
monitors & computer recycling. (Woman, estab 1998,
empl 37, sales $12,939,507, cert: WBENC)

3345 W. K. Merriman, Inc.
7038 Front River Rd
Pittsburgh, PA 15225
Contact: Mary Ann Merriman CEO
Tel: 412-262-7024
Email: m.merriman@wkmerriman.com
Website: www.wkmerriman.com
Dist commodity chemicals & environmental technology,
neutralize wastewater, reduce sluge & cost saving alterna-
tives. (Woman, estab 1986, empl 6, sales $6,377,400, cert:
WBENC)

Rhode Island

3346 Full Circle Recycling
23 Green Hill Rd
Johnston, RI 02919
Contact: Maria Vinagro President
Tel: 401-464-5996
Email: maria@fullcircleri.com
Website: www.fullcirclerecyclingri.com
Full service recycling facility for metal, plastic, paper, fiber,
and electronic post-industrial and post-consumer scrap
materials and components. (Woman/AA, estab 2007, empl
30, sales , cert: WBENC)

South Carolina

3347 Air Hub, LLC
PO Box 2535
Mount Pleasant, SC 29465
Contact: Terri Sciarro Owner/Member
Tel: 843-343-3618
Email: tls@airhubllc.com
Website: www.airhubllc.com
Air permitting, air modeling, noise modeling & studies,
stormwater pollution prevention plans (SWPPP), spill
prevention control & countermeasure (SPCC), environmen-
tal consulting. (Woman, estab 2011, empl 1, sales , cert:
State)

Tennessee

3348 Bionomics, Inc.
PO Box 817
Kingston, TN 37763
Contact: Karen McCormick President
Tel: 865-220-8501
Email: karenbionomics@comcast.net
Website: www.bionomics-inc.com
Transportation & disposal of hazardous, radioactive &
mixed waste. (Woman, estab 1988, empl 7, sales
$4,000,000, cert: WBENC)

3349 EGSE Holdings, LLC. dba Emergency Response
Team
195 Omohundro Pl, Unit H
Nashville, TN 37210
Contact: Kevin Seats Sales Assoc
Tel: 615-525-9075
Email: kseats@ertnashville.com
Website: www.fireandfloodexperts.com
Water Restoration, Fire & Smoke Mitigation, Mold
Remediation. (AA, estab 2004, empl 5, sales $470,000,
cert: State, NMSDC)

3350 iSustain Inc.
12249 Wildlife Place
Soddy Daisy, TN 37379
Contact: President
Tel: 423-668-0111
Email: huberda@me.com
Website: www.isustain.expert
Recycling & Waste Management. (Woman, estab 2014,
empl 4, sales $2,653,697, cert: WBENC)

3351 Microbial Insights, Inc.
10515 Research Dr
Knoxville, TN 37932
Contact: Anita Biernacki VP Operations
Tel: 865-573-8188
Email: info@microbe.com
Website: www.microbe.com
Environmental biotechnology, bioremediation of
chlorinated hydrocarbons, biofilm formation in drinking
water systems. (Woman, estab 1992, empl 15, sales
$2,951,477, cert: WBENC)

3352 Tioga Environmental Consultants, Inc.
357 North Main St
Memphis, TN 38112
Contact: Larkin Myers VP
Tel: 901-791-2432
Email: lmyers@tiogaenv.com
Website: www.tiogaenv.com
Lead based paint inspections, mold sampling, IAQ
investigations, asbestos inspections, environmental
sampling, soil & groundwater sampling, environmental
compliance, SWPPP, SPCC Plans, waste water studies,
erosion control. (Woman, estab 2009, empl 7, sales
$730,000, cert: State, City)

Texas

3353 Architect for Life - A Professional Corporation
2450 Louisiana St, Ste 400-233
Houston, TX 77006
Contact: Lolalisa King
Tel: 888-986-7771
Email: lking@architectforlife.com
Website: www.architectforlife.com
Green consulting professional services, develop & manage energy efficient strategies, programs, & projects, retrofit strategies, benchmarking building energy performance, long-term energy management & water saving goals assessment. (Woman/AA, estab 1995, empl 12, sales , cert: City)

3354 Bocci Engineering, LLC
12709 Pine Dr
Cypress, TX 77429
Contact: Lianne Lami Principal
Tel: 713-575-2400
Email: LBLami@bocciengineering.com
Website: www.bocciengineering.com
Efficiency & Optimization, Renewable Resources, Combined Heat & Power, Distributed Generation, Central Plant Projects, Emissions Reduction, Waste Recovery, & Sustainability. Expect Engineering Excellence. (Woman, estab 2007, empl 13, sales , cert: CPUC, WBENC, SDB)

3355 Dougherty Sprague Environmental, Inc.
3902 Industrial St Ste A
Rowlett, TX 75088
Contact: John Dougherty VP Marketing
Tel: 972-412-8666
Email: jdougherty@dsei.com
Website: www.dsei.com
Environmental consulting, phase I & II site assessments, groundwater modeling, industrial compliance, UST removal & site clean-up, litigation support & expert witness testimony. (Woman, estab 1998, empl 25, sales $2,000,000, cert: State, WBENC)

3356 Lynx Ltd
PO Box 591540
Houston, TX 77259
Contact: Darlene Sanchez VP
Tel: 281-797-2546
Email: darlene.sanchez@lynxltd.com
Website: www.lynxltd.com
Environmental compliance & mechanical svcs: hazardous waste mgmt, hazardous waste permit compliance, environmental training, NPDES compliance, air quality compliance, spill response, NEPA review & compliance, asbestos & lead. (Hisp, estab 1998, empl 2, sales $119,640, cert: State, City)

3357 Nation Waste Inc.
12006 Proctor St
Houston, TX 77038
Contact: Brendan Goodnough Cheif Marketing Officer
Tel: 713-649-7776
Email: bgood@nationwaste.us
Website: www.nationwaste.us
Commercial waste disposal: Construction, Demolition, Commercial & Industrial Non-Hazardous Waste Removal, Portable Toilets & Recycling services. (Minority, Woman, estab 1997, empl 24, sales $3,200,000, cert: State, City)

3358 RNDI Companies, Inc.
2255 Ridge Rd, Ste 216
Rockwall, TX 75087
Contact: Diana Cross President
Tel: 214-771-3977
Email: diana@rndicompanies.com
Website: www.rndicompanies.com
Environmental services: asbestos, lead, mold remediation & abatement, demolition. (Minority, Woman, estab 2005, empl 20, sales $2,000,000, cert: State)

3359 Separation Systems Consultants, Inc.
17041 El Camino Real, Ste 200
Houston, TX 77058
Contact: Helen Hodges President
Tel: 281-486-1943
Email: ssci@sscienvironmental.com
Website: www.sscienvironmental.com
Risk-based corrective action, remediation & closure, engineering & consulting, waste mgmt, petroleum storage tank, environmental site assessments, health, safety & environmental compliance audits, plans, permits & training. (Woman, estab 1986, empl 23, sales $4,000,000, cert: State, WBENC)

3360 SIA Solutions, LLC
17171 Park Row Ste 370
Houston, TX 77084
Contact: Mark Knight Program Mgr
Tel: 866-768-4625
Email: mjknight@siasolutions.com
Website: www.siasolutions.com
Environmental Consulting & Engineering • Asset Management and Energy Consulting • Environmental Remediation • Radiological Services • Hazardous, Toxic & Radioactive Waste (HTRW) Management. (As-Ind, estab 2012, empl 49, sales $2,100,000, cert: City, 8(a))

3361 Southern Global Safety Services, Inc.
2986 County Rd 180
Alvin, TX 77511
Contact: Julie Wernecke President
Tel: 281-331-3667
Email: possumloo@hotmail.com
Website: www.southernglobalsafetyservices.com
Environmental consulting: surveys identification & assesement, project design, specifications, indoor air quality testing, radon testing & mitigation, norm testing & hearing conservation. (Woman, estab 2001, empl 21, sales $3,127,872, cert: WBENC)

3362 TGE Resources, Inc.
8048 Northcourt Rd
Houston, TX 77040
Contact: Robin Franks President
Tel: 713-744-5800
Email: melanie.rivas@tgeresources.com
Website: www.tgeresources.com
Full Service Environmental and Consulting & Managment Services (Woman, estab 1994, empl 20, sales $2,360,000, cert: State, City, WBENC)

Virginia

3363 Aegis Environmental, Inc.
11511 Allecingie Pkwy
Richmond, VA 23235
Contact: Matthew Markee President
Tel: 804-378-6015
Email: mmarkee@aegisenv.com
Website: www.aegisenv.com
Air permitting & compliance, air dispersion modeling analyses, pollution control technology analyses, emissions estimates, environmental training & compliance, contingency planning, environmental mgmt systems dev & auditing. (Woman, estab 1996, empl 20, sales $3,000,000, cert: State)

3364 CMMD Enterprises, Inc.
7001 Loisdale Rd Ste C
Springfield, VA 22150
Contact: Carolyn Marina CEO
Tel: 703-646-2900
Email: carolyn.m@cmmdinc.com
Website: www.cmmdinc.com
Critical maintenance management & distribution, rotating process plant systems, wastewater treatment systems, potable water systems, chemical processes. (Woman/AA, estab 2001, empl 5, sales $483,000, cert: State, NMSDC)

3365 Environmental Waste Specialists, Inc.
4451 Brookfield Corporate Dr Ste 206
Chantilly, VA 20151
Contact: Dawn Walker Recycling Mgr
Tel: 703-502-0100
Email: dawn@ewsihazmat.com
Website: www.ewsihazmat.com
Package, transport, dispose & recycle hazardous & non-hazardous materials. (Woman/AA, estab 1994, empl 4, sales $1,700,000, cert: State)

3366 Froehling & Robertson, Inc.
3015 Dumbarton Rd
Richmond, VA 23228
Contact: Jackie Clingenpeel Exec Asst
Tel: 804-264-2701
Email: jclingenpeel@fandr.com
Website: www.fandr.com
Environmental services: phase I & II ESAs, EIRs, EIS, wetland & stream delineations, hazardous materials assessments, industrial hygiene svcs, asbestos & lead testing, environmental planning, property condition assessments. (Minority, Woman, estab , empl 400, sales $0, cert: State)

3367 INTERSPEC, LLC
464 S Independence Blvd Ste C-104
Virginia Beach, VA 23452
Contact: Sean Murphy Business Devel Dir
Tel: 757-622-6299
Email: murphys@interspecllc.net
Website: www.interspecllc.net
Tank, piping & pressure vessel inspections, STI storage tank inspections, Non-Destructive Examination/Testing steel structures, Spill Prevention Control & Countermeasure (SPCC) plans, Oil Discharge Control Plans (ODCP. (Nat Ame, estab 2001, empl 22, sales $1,200,000, cert: State, 8(a))

3368 J. R. Caskey, Inc.
PO Box 305
Oilville, VA 23129
Contact: Ginger Caskey President
Tel: 804-784-8001
Email: gec@jrcaskey.com
Website: www.jrcaskey.com
Engineering, Layout & Surveying, Clearing & Demolition, Earthwork, Grading & Excavation, Erosion & Sediment Control, Traditional Stormwater Management Systems, Low-Impact Development Systems, Underground Water & Sanitary Sewer Utilities. (Woman, estab 1985, empl 42, sales $6,630,000, cert: State)

3369 Mac-Par Services, LLC
20 B Research Dr
Hampton, VA 23666
Contact: David Parham President
Tel: 866-622-7271
Email: dparham@macparservices.com
Website: www.macparservices.com
Interior demolition, material & debris hauling, lead paint & asbestos abatements, mold remediation & HVAC duct cleaning. (AA, estab 1999, empl 3, sales $370,000, cert: State)

3370 Sea Consulting Group
325 Mason Ave
Cape Charles, VA 23310
Contact: Ann Hayward Walker President
Tel: 757-331-1787
Email: ahwalker@seaconsulting.com
Website: www.seaconsulting.com
Environmental consulting. (Minority, Woman, estab 1983, empl 10, sales $0, cert: WBENC)

Washington

3371 EHS-International, Inc.
1011 SW Klickitat Way, Ste 104
Seattle, WA 98134
Contact: Nancy Yee Marketing
Tel: 425-455-2959
Email: nancyy@ehsintl.com
Website: www.ehsintl.com
Environmental engineering & industrial hygiene svcs: workplace & environmental health & safety, hazards identification & removal, assessments & remediation, employee training & abatement management. (Hisp, estab 1996, empl 21, sales $1,489,983, cert: State)

3372 Environmental Assessment Services, LLC
350 Hills St Ste 112
Richland, WA 99354
Contact: Brett Tiller
Tel: 509-375-4212
Email: brett.tiller@easbio.com
Website: www.easbio.com
Environmental characterization, Spill Response & Natural Resource Damage Assessments, Hazardous Waste Site Remedial Investigations, Risk Assessments, & Environmental Surveillance, Ecological Characterization & Restoration. (Nat Ame, estab 2005, empl 44, sales $2,700,000, cert: NMSDC)

3373 GeoTest Services, Inc.
741 Marine View Dr
Bellingham, WA 98225
Contact: Jeremy Wolf VP
Tel: 360-733-7318
Email: jeremyw@geotest-inc.com
Website: www.geotest-inc.com
Geotechnical engineering, environmental services, special inspection & materials testing, facilities, structures, roads, bridges & all types of infrastructure. (Woman, estab 1993, empl 33, sales $6,000,000, cert: State)

Wisconsin

3374 K. Singh & Associates, Inc.
3636 N 124th St
Wauwatosa, WI 53222
Contact: Pratap Singh CEO
Tel: 262-821-1171
Email: gmiller@ksaconsultants.com
Website: www.ksaconsultants.com
Environmental engineering & management services, transportation, structural, environmental & civil engineering, land surveying & construction management. (As-Ind, estab 1987, empl 33, sales $3,000,000, cert: State)

3375 OGC Construction, LLC
W171 n10330 Wildrose Ln
Germantown, WI 53022
Contact: Michael Owens President
Tel: 414-383-4205
Email: mowens@ogcconstruction.com
Website: www.ogcconstruction.com
Hazardous waste removal remediation, construction lead asbestos abatement. (AA, estab 2005, empl 18, sales , cert: NMSDC)

3376 White Glove Environmental
8326 N Stevens Rd
Milwaukee, WI 53223
Contact: London Thomas President
Tel: 414-760-1733
Email: london@wgginc.net
Website: www.wgginc.net
Environmental services, safe abatement & removal. (AA, estab 2005, empl 11, sales , cert: NMSDC)

3377 White Glove Group, Inc.
8326 N Stevens Rd
Milwaukee, WI 53223
Contact: Joseph Njuguna Sales Dir
Tel: 414-760-1733
Email: joe@wgginc.net
Website: www.wgenvironmental.com
Environmental services, facility maintenance, demolition, construction & demolition waste recycling program mgmt, green construction final cleaning, LEED consulting, sustainable product procurement for new construction & existing buildings. (AA, estab 2003, empl 25, sales $700,000, cert: State)

FOOD PRODUCTS AND SERVICES
Products include coffees, teas, bottled water, water filtration units, milk and milk products, juices, soft drinks, candies, cookies, jellies, pastries, snacks, dressings, flavorings, sauces, spices, syrups, ethnic foods, fish, seafood & prepared meats, fruits & vegetables. NAICS Code 31

Alabama

3378   The Widget Development & Trading Company, LLC
10 S Perry St
Montgomery, AL 36104
Contact: David Martin President
Tel: 404-695-0141
Email: davidmartin@widgetdtc.com
Website: www.widgetdtc.com
Dist nuts, meats, sauces, baked goods. (Woman/AA, estab 2011, empl 2, sales , cert: NMSDC)

Arkansas

3379   My Brother's Salsa LLC
PO Box 922
Bentonville, AR 72712
Contact: Helen Lampkin Founder
Tel: 479-271-9404
Email: helen@mybrotherssalsa.com
Website: www.mybrotherssalsa.com
Produce 9 salsa varieties some available in multiple heat levels. Salsas range from smooth to textured consistencies with flavor profiles the span from earthy to smoky to sweet and savory. (Woman, estab 2003, empl 5, sales , cert: WBENC)

Arizona

3380   Sir Aubrey's Tea Company, Ltd
15941 N 77th St Ste 3
Scottsdale, AZ 85260
Contact: Kathryn Petty President
Tel: 480-607-5300
Email: kpetty@whiteliontea.com
Website: www.whiteliontea.com
White Lion Tea offers a collection of rare & beautiful teas from the world's finest gardens. (Woman, estab 1998, empl 8, sales $998,470, cert: WBENC)

California

3381   AG Commodties, Inc.
12815 Stevens Dr
Tustin, CA 92782
Contact: Theresa Bailey VP Business Dev
Tel: 612-839-3385
Email: ach112350@gmail.com
Website: www.agcommoditiesinc.com
Natural sweeteners & natural maltodextrins, rice maltodextrin, tapioca maltodextrin, rice syrups: brown & clarified, medium invert sugar cane syrup, clear tapioca syrups, organic sugar cane, organic glycerin, organic acacia powder, etc. (As-Ind, estab 2006, empl 10, sales $3,500,000, cert: NMSDC)

3382   Andytown LLC
3655 Lawton St
San Francisco, CA 94122
Contact: Lauren Crabbe Owner
Tel: 619-823-4359
Email: lauren@andytownsf.com
Website: www.andytownsf.com/
Coffee beans and ground coffee to companies large and small. (Woman, estab 2014, empl 55, sales $3,900,000, cert: WBENC)

3383   Asiana Cusine Enterprises (ACE Sushi)
22771 S. Western Ave
Torrance, CA 90501
Contact: Gary Chin CFO
Tel: 310-327-2223
Email: gary.chin@acesushi.com
Website: www.acesushi.com
Dist Sushi. (As-Pac, estab 1998, empl 35, sales , cert: City)

3384   Cacique, Inc.
14940 Proctor Ave
City of Industry, CA 91746
Contact: Bob Cashen Dir of Sales
Tel: 626-961-3399
Email: rcashen@caciqueinc.com
Website: www.caciqueinc.com
Mfr & dist food (dairy) products. (Hisp, estab 1973, empl 350, sales , cert: NMSDC)

3385   Carlos Steffens, Inc.
3061 Independence Dr, Ste E
Livermore, CA 94550
Contact: Carlos Steffens President
Tel: 925-838-2336
Email: carlos@steffenscorp.com
Website: www.steffenscorp.com
Industrial ingredient brokers, concentrated fruit juice products. (Hisp, estab 2000, empl 6, sales , cert: NMSDC)

3386   Creative Research Management
PO Box 7843
Stockton, CA 95267
Contact: Cheryl R. Mitchell President
Tel: 209-598-7565
Email: cheryl@crmcorp.net
Website: www.crmcorp.net
Produce Sucramask™, RiceLife® Brown Rice-Milk syrups, TherMoPectin and our line of GrainLife™ products including RiceLife® and CornLife™. (Woman, estab 2000, empl 3, sales $5,000,000, cert: NWBOC)

3387   C-Shore International Inc.
1010 N Central Ave
Glendale, CA 91202
Contact: Jacques Isaac CEO
Tel: 818-909-4684
Email: mirline@aol.com
Website: www.beantrader.com
Peas, beans, lentils, pre cooked flour, bread flour, wheat flour, dried malt extract roasted barley. (AA, estab 1988, empl 3, sales $0, cert: NMSDC)

3388   Encore Fruit Marketing, Inc.
       120 W Bonita Ave, Ste 204
       San Dimas, CA 91773
       Contact: Kandi Ashcraft VP Finance
       Tel: 909-394-5640
       Email: kashcraft@encorefruit.com
       Website: www.encorefruit.com
Acai, Acerola, Agave, Apple, Apricot, Aronia, Banana,
Bilberry, Blackberry, Black Currant, Blueberry, Boysenberry,
Cherry, Cranberry, Date (domestic), Dragon Fruit, Elder-
berry, Fig, Gac Fruit, Goji Berry, Grape, etc. (Woman, estab
1989, empl 15, sales $16,050,000, cert: WBENC)

3389   F. Gavina & Sons, Inc.
       2700 Fruitland Ave
       Vernon, CA 90058
       Contact: Angela Day Natl Sales Mgr
       Tel: 323-351-5616
       Email: Angela.Day@gavina.com
       Website: www.gavina.com
Coffee roasting, new blend development or matching of
your current blend, brand & marketing support, brewing &
espresso service & training. (Hisp, estab 1967, empl 265,
sales $127,485,828, cert: NMSDC)

3390   Frieda's Inc.
       4465 Corporate Center Dr
       Los Alamitos, CA 90720
       Contact: Karen Caplan CEO
       Tel: 714-826-6100
       Email: karen.caplan@friedas.com
       Website: www.friedas.com
Specialty Fruits (including Fresh Tropicals and Dried Fruits),
Specialty Vegetables (including cooking vegetables and
leafy greens), Hispanic Fruits & Vegetables (including fresh
& dried chile peppers), Asian Fruits & Vegetables.
(Woman, estab 1962, empl 75, sales $46,000,000, cert:
WBENC)

3391   Fusion Ranch, Inc. dba Fusion Jerky
       405 S Airport Blvd
       South San Francisco, CA 94080
       Contact: Kaiyen Mai CEO
       Tel: 650-589-8899
       Email: kaiyen@fusionranch.com
       Website: www.fusionjerky.com
Jerky, Sausage, Ham, Shredded Pork. (Minority, Woman,
estab 2014, empl 46, sales , cert: NMSDC, WBENC)

3392   Got Broccoli, Inc.
       6201 Progressive Ave Ste 400
       San Diego, CA 92154
       Contact: Art Sanchez Dir
       Tel: 619-661-0909
       Email: art@gotbroccoli.com
       Website: www.frugo.com.mx
IQF Vegetables, Asparagus, Broccoli, Cauliflower, Celery,
Cucumber, Jalapeno, Spinach, Kale. (Hisp, estab 2010,
empl 2, sales $10,000,000, cert: NMSDC)

3393   Kruger Foods Inc.
       18362 E Hwy 4
       Stockton, CA 95215
       Contact: Kara Kruger CEO
       Tel: 209-941-8518
       Email: k.kruger@krugerfoods.com
       Website: www.krugerfoods.com
Pickles, Sweet Pickle Relish, Dill Pickle Relish, Hot Pepper
Relish, Jalapeno Peppers (sliced, diced, whole), Banana
Wax Peppers, Peppers, Giardinera. (Woman, estab 1930,
empl 158, sales $65,400,000, cert: WBENC)

3394   Laxmi's Delights
       98 Brevensville Dr
       San Ramon, CA 94583
       Contact: Laxmi Hiremath Owner
       Tel: 925-833-0115
       Email: laxmihiremath@gmail.com
       Website: www.laxmisdelights.com
Organic flaxseed spreads. (Woman/As-Ind, estab 2000,
empl 1, sales $100,000, cert: WBENC)

3395   National Raisin Company
       PO Box 219
       Fowler, CA 93625
       Contact: Joe Leon VP Business Dev
       Tel: 559-834-5981
       Email: jleon@nationalraisin.com
       Website: www.nationalraisin.com
High industrial specifications for confection, cereal &
baking, using the California grown Natural Seedless
Select and Small raisins, sugar coated raisins, glycerin
infused raisins, juice concentrates, pastes and purees.
(Woman, estab 1969, empl 450, sales , cert: WBENC,
NWBOC)

3396   NC Moving & Storage Solutions
       3146 Corporate Pl
       Hayward, CA 94545
       Contact: Johanna Lobation Business Devel Mgr
       Tel: 510-385-4441
       Email: jlobaton@ncmss.com
       Website: www.ncmss.com
NC Moving & Storage Solutions is a full service household goods provider for both domestic and international
moving services. We are an agent for North American
Van Lines. (Minority, Woman, estab 2006, empl 19, sales
$1,165,000, cert: NMSDC, CPUC, WBENC)

3397   NiuSource Inc.
       14266 Euclid Ave
       Chino, CA 91710
       Contact: Linda Lin General Mgr
       Tel: 909-631-2895
       Email: Linda.lin@niusource.com
       Website: www.NiuSource.com
Sweeteners business, like Aspartame, Sucralose, AceK,
Stevia, Monk Fruit, Etc. (Woman/As-Pac, estab 2014,
empl 15, sales $32,000,000, cert: NMSDC, WBENC)

3398   P.S. Let's Eat Inc.
       3943 Irvine Blvd, Ste 610
       Irvine, CA 92602
       Contact: Preya Patel Bhakta President
       Tel: 855-998-3554
       Email: preya@elliquark.com
       Website: www.elliquark.com
Produce German style Quark products. (Minority,
Woman, estab 2011, empl 2, sales , cert: WBENC)

3399   Peas of Mind LLC
2339 3rd St Unit 53-3R
San Francisco, CA 94107
Contact: Jill Litwin CEO
Tel: 415-504-2556
Email: jill@peasofmind.com
Website: www.peasofmind.com
Mfr healthy eating options. (Woman, estab 2005, empl 4, sales $2,800,000, cert: WBENC)

3400   Planet Popcorn, Inc.
1616 E Wilshire Ave
Santa Ana, CA 92705
Contact: Sharla Gandy-Caldaronello CEO
Tel: 949-278-1312
Email: sharla@planetpopcorn.com
Website: www.planetpopcorn.com
Hand-crafted gourmet popcorn. (Woman, estab 2005, empl 23, sales $2,009,000, cert: WBENC)

3401   Somax Inc.
339 S Notre Dame Ave
Orange, CA 92869
Contact: Grace Knight Owner
Tel: 714-633-6614
Email: graceknight@sanluissausage.com
Website: www.sanluissausage.com
Healthy, preservative free pork & chicken gourmet sausages. (Woman, estab 1991, empl 2, sales $2,200,286, cert: WBENC, NWBOC)

3402   Valley Lahvosh Baking Co.
502 M St
Fresno, CA 93721
Contact: Lori Miller President
Tel: 559-485-2700
Email: customerservice@valleylahvosh.com
Website: www.valleylahvosh.com
Mfr valley lahvosh crackerbreads & pita breads. (Woman, estab , empl , sales $8,578,874, cert: WBENC)

3403   Zego LLC
912 Cole St, Ste 294
San Francisco, CA 94117
Contact: CEO
Tel: 415-622-8115
Email: customerservice@zegofoods.com
Website: www.zegofoods.com
Mfr & dist Oats, Muesli, Sacha Inchi Protein Powder, Nutrition Bars, and Mix-Ins Trail Mix all free of the top 12 most common allergens and gluten. (Woman, estab 2013, empl 3, sales $410,000, cert: WBENC)

Colorado

3404   All American Seasonings, Inc.
10600 E 54th Ave, Unit B & C
Denver, CO 80239
Contact: Andy Rodriguez President
Tel: 303-623-2320
Email: andyr@allamericanseasonings.com
Website: www.allamericanseasonings.com
Custom blenders of food ingredients. (Hisp, estab 1968, empl 40, sales $18,000,000, cert: NMSDC)

3405   Mona's Granola and Cookies, Inc.
651 Eldorado
Broomfield, CO 80021
Contact: Mona Gale CEO
Tel: 727-420-0707
Email: mona@monasinc.com
Website: www.monasinc.com
All natural no white sugar nutrient rich granola cereal & ice cream toppings. (Woman, estab 1981, empl 27, sales $600,000, cert: WBENC)

3406   Toddy, LLC
3706 Aldrin Dr
Loveland, CO 80538
Contact: Mike Skillins Key Acct Cstmr Advocacy
Tel: 970-493-0788
Email: diversity@toddycafe.com
Website: www.toddycafe.com
Developed cold brewing solutions for food service, home users and also as consumer packaged goods. (Woman, estab 1964, empl 50, sales $14,324,000, cert: WBENC)

Connecticut

3407   Aurora Product Inc.
205 Edison Road
Orange, CT 06477
Contact: Stephanie Blackwell Business Devel
Tel: 203-375-9956
Email: sblackwell@auroraproduct.com
Website: www.auroranatural.com
Natural & organic snacks: almonds, cashews, mixed nuts & peanuts, salted, unsalted & raw, dried fruits. (Woman, estab 1998, empl 225, sales $60,000,000, cert: WBENC)

3408   Carla's Pasta, Inc.
50 Talbot Lane
South Windsor, CT 06074
Contact: Sandro Squatrito VP Business Dev
Tel: 860-436-4042
Email: abiel@carlaspasta.com
Website: www.carlaspasta.com
Produce pasta & pesto products, Cheeseburger Ravioli, Buffalo Chicken Ravioli & Stromboli Ravioli. (Woman, estab 1978, empl 182, sales , cert: NWBOC)

3409   Gelato Giuliana, LLC
240 Sargent Dr
New Haven, CT 06511
Contact: Deborah Cairo Mktg Mgr
Tel: 203-772-0607
Email: dcbottega@sbcglobal.net
Website: www.gelatogiuliana.com
Mfr & dist gelato under our label Gelato Giuliana. (Woman, estab 2006, empl 10, sales $882,662, cert: State)

3410   Heidi's Real Food LLC
47 Hillside Rd
Greenwich, CT 06830
Contact: Heidi Matonis Owner
Tel: 203-219-4202
Email: heidi@heidisrealfood.com
Website: www.heidisrealfood.com
Heidi's Meatless "Meat"balls also available in bulk for food service and prepared foods. (Woman, estab 2013, empl 1, sales , cert: WBENC)

3411 The Bites Company
PO Box 122
Westport, CT 06881
Contact: Dina Upton Owner
Tel: 203-296-2482
Email: sales@thebitescompany.com
Website: www.thebitescompany.com
All natural, round, bite size pieces of Biscotti in 5 flavors; almond, orange, lemon, cocoa & coffee. (Woman, estab 2011, empl 1, sales , cert: State)

District of Columbia

3412 Tribes-A-Dozen, LLC
PO Box 42063
Washington, DC 20015
Contact: Leah Hadad President
Tel: 202-684-8256
Email: leah@tribesadozen.com
Website: www.tribesadozen.com
Mfr three all-natural & kosher (OU) Voil! Hallah Egg Bread Mixes: Traditional, Wholey Wheat & Simply Spelt. (Woman, estab 2012, empl 1, sales , cert: WBENC)

3413 Village Tea Company Distribution Inc.
1342 Florida Ave., NW Ste 225-B
Washington, DC 20009
Contact: Janon Costley CEO
Tel: 888-406-1138
Email: janon@villageteaco.com
Website: www.villageteaco.com
100% organic & natural tea in biodegradable packaging, foodservice tea, bulk tea, tea dispensers, tea machines, packaged tea, tea in bags, loose leaf tea, loose tea, organic tea, natural tea. (AA, estab 2008, empl 12, sales , cert: NMSDC)

Florida

3414 ARA Food Corporation
8001 NW 60th St
Miami, FL 33166
Contact: Oscar Tanaka President
Tel: 305-592-5558
Email: marta@arafood.com
Website: www.arafood.com
Mfr plantain & cassava chips. (Hisp, estab 1975, empl 30, sales , cert: NMSDC)

3415 Brisk/RCR Coffee Company
507 N. 22nd St
Tampa, FL 33605
Contact: Richard Perez CEO
Tel: 813-248-6264
Email: customer@briskcoffee.com
Website: www.briskcoffee.com
Coffee importing, roasting, grinding, packaging & shipping. (Hisp, estab 1968, empl 30, sales , cert: State)

3416 COEX Coffee International Inc.
525 NW 27th Ave
Miami, FL 33125
Contact: Robert Menos Sr Trader
Tel: 305-459-5180
Email: lmones@coexgroup.com
Website: www.coexgroup.com
Coffee trading, importing green coffee from all major global coffee producing countries. (Hisp, estab 1980, empl 45, sales $415,000,000, cert: NMSDC)

3417 Delina Inc.
1068 Pine Branch Dr
Weston, FL 33326
Contact: President
Tel: 954-306-0628
Email: sales@delinainc.com
Website: www.delinainc.com
Dist asparagus spears, green pickled asparagus spears, cornichons, roasted red peppers, artichoke hearts, hearts of palm & organic coffee. (Minority, Woman, estab 1998, empl 2, sales , cert: City)

3418 GFIS
2525 Ponce de Leon Blvd Ste 300
Coral Gables, FL 33134
Contact: Andrea Cordova Mgr
Tel: 305-521-9094
Email: acordova@foodingredientsolution.com
Website: www.foodingredientsolution.com
Frozen, Aseptic, No pasteurized, Unpasteurized, IQF, Fruitm Vegetables, Puree, Juice, Concentrate, NFC, Single Straight, Organic, Conventional, Acai, Acerola, Apple, Blackberry, Blueberry, Cherry, Grapefruit, Guava, Kiwi, Lemon, Lime, Mango, and more. (Minority, Woman, estab 2016, empl 4, sales $1,500,000, cert: State)

3419 Henry Roberts BBQ Sauce
2001 Art Museum Dr
Jacksonville, FL 32207
Contact: Anthony Ammons VP
Tel: 904-591-8102
Email: anthony.ammons@gmail.com
Website: www.HenryRoberts.com
Bottle & distribute barbecue sauce & chow chow. (Woman/AA, estab 1985, empl 4, sales $160,000, cert: City)

3420 M&G Expresso, Inc
13311 SW 132 Ave, Unit 3
Miami, FL 33186
Contact: Gabriel Cortina VP
Tel: 786-200-9802
Email: mgexpressinc@gmail.com
Website: www.ladybeehoney.net
Dist Lady Bee Honey. (Minority, Woman, estab 2009, empl 3, sales $1,996,000, cert: NMSDC)

3421 MH Food Group LLC
1800 Sunset Harbour Dr, Ste P
Miami Beach, FL 33139
Contact: Calvin Harris President
Tel: 954-501-6215
Email: charris@mhfoodgroup.com
Website: www.mhfoodgroup.com
Pack & dist frozen fruit & industrial food ingredients. (Minority, Woman, estab 2014, empl 4, sales $1,000,000, cert: NMSDC)

3422 Quirch Foods Co.
2701 S. LeJeune Rd. 12th Fl
Miami, FL 33134
Contact: Elijah Davis Natl Acct Sales Mgr
Tel: 305-691-3535
Email: elijah.davis@quirchfoods.com
Website: www.quirchfoods.com
Dist & export meat & seafood. (Hisp, estab 1967, empl 500, sales $747,373,931, cert: NMSDC)

3423   Sweet Additions, Inc.
     4440 PGA Blvd, Ste 600
     Palm Beach Gardens, FL 33410
     Contact: Ken Valdivia President
     Tel: 561-472-0178
     Email: kvaldivia@sweetadditions.com
     Website: www.sweetadditions.com
Mfr & dist cane & grain based sweeteners. (Hisp, estab 2004, empl 3, sales $5,000,000, cert: NMSDC)

3424   The Best Direct Marketing Group LLC
     250 N Orange Ave Ste 990
     Orlando, FL 32801
     Contact: Latif Qadri
     Tel: 407-730-6569
     Email: latif@bestdirectgroup.com
     Website: www.bestdirectgroup.com
Direct mail & staffed event company that can fulfill all print needs ad creative design. (As-Ind, estab 2012, empl 4, sales $112,000, cert: NMSDC)

Georgia

3425   82's, LLC
     1475 Buford Dr Ste 403-227
     Lawrenceville, GA 30043
     Contact: Reginald Kelly Owner
     Tel: 770-402-2226
     Email: contact@kyvan82.com
     Website: www.kyvan82.com
All Natural Honey Apple Salsa (Hot & Mild), Sesame Garlic BBQ Sauce, Sweet BBQ Sauce, Hot Sauce. (AA, estab 2008, empl 7, sales $100,000, cert: NMSDC)

3426   Brooksmade Gourmet Foods
     8000Avalon Blvd, Ste 100
     Alpharetta, GA 30009
     Contact: Antoinette Brooks Exec Asst
     Tel: 770-231-2601
     Email:
     antoinette.brooks@brooksmadegourmetfoods.com
     Website: www.brooksmadegourmetfoods.com
Ketchups and seasonings. (AA, estab 2004, empl 10, sales $500,000, cert: NMSDC)

3427   Diaz Foods
     5501 Fulton Industrial Blvd SW
     Atlanta, GA 30336
     Contact: Jorge Antona EVP
     Tel: 404-344-5421
     Email: jorge.antona@diazfoods.com
     Website: www.diazfoods.com
Hispanic grocery distributor, grocery, frozen, dairy, meats & produce. (Hisp, estab 1980, empl 323, sales $168,000,000, cert: NMSDC)

3428   Fire & Flavor Grilling Co.
     1160 S Milledge Ave, Ste 230
     Athens, GA 30605
     Contact: Davis Knox CEO
     Tel: 706-369-9466
     Email: davis@fireandflavor.com
     Website: www.fireandflavor.com
Dist spices, seasonings, sauces, brines, grilling planks, wood chips, charcoal & fire starters. (Woman, estab 2003, empl 6, sales $5,000,000, cert: WBENC)

3429   H. Walker Enterprises, LLC
     22 E Montgomery Crossroads
     Savannah, GA 31406
     Contact: Herschel Walker CEO
     Tel: 912-961-0002
     Email: hwrmi34@aol.com
     Website: www.34promotions.com
Mfr & dist poultry, beef & pork food products. (AA, estab 2002, empl 4, sales $0, cert: NMSDC)

3430   JCPG LLC DBA Popbar
     4573 Bogan Meadows Ct
     Buford, GA 30519
     Contact: Charel Palmer Owner
     Tel: 678-783-9688
     Email: alpharetta@pop-bar.com
     Website: www.pop-bar.com
Hand crafted, all natural and preservative free gelato, yogurt, vegan gelato and sorbet in a new way, on a stick! With 5 chocolate dippings. (AA, estab 2017, empl 15, sales , cert: City, NMSDC)

3431   Seeds of Nature, LLC
     1456 Lechemin Dr
     Snellville, GA 30078
     Contact: Patricia Nowell Managing Member
     Tel: 877-277-9260
     Email: pnowell@prodigy.net
     Website: www.seedsofnature.com
Premium Cocoa Beans sourced from Ivory Coast, Nigeria & Ghana. (Woman/AA, estab 2009, empl 3, sales $300,000, cert: NMSDC)

Iowa

3432   Young G's Barbecue Sauce, LLC
     8211 Brookview Dr.
     Urbandale, IA 50322
     Contact: Gerald Young President
     Tel: 515-331-8001
     Email: youngsbbq@gmail.com
     Website: www.ygsbbq.com
Young G's is a gluten free low sodium content with no high fructose corn syrup. (AA, estab 2010, empl 1, sales , cert: NMSDC)

Illinois

3433   Baldwin Richardson Foods Co.
     One Tower Lane Ste 2390
     Oakbrook Terrace, IL 60181
     Contact: Cara Hughes Dir Sales/Marketing
     Tel: 630-607-1780
     Email: chughes@brfoods.com
     Website: www.brfoods.com
Mfr custom sauces, condiments, syrups, toppings & fillings. (AA, estab 1997, empl 287, sales $0, cert: NMSDC)

3434   Bell Marketing, Inc.
     10135 S Roberts Rd
     Palos Hills, IL 60465
     Contact: Mary Ann Bell President
     Tel: 708-598-8873
     Email: maryann@bellmarketing.com
     Website: www.bellmarketing.com
Fruit concentrates, purees, puree concentrates IQF frozen fruit, all natural colors from fruit & vegetable juice concentrates, extracts, ice cream inclusions. (Woman, estab 1986, empl 5, sales $10,000,000, cert: WBENC)

3435   CBC Sales, Inc.
       5117 S Normandy Ave
       Chicago, IL 60638
       Contact: Desiree Alonzo President
       Tel: 773-218-9563
       Email: desiree@cbcsalesinc.com
       Website: www.cicerobloodymary.com
Gourmet beverages, Craft Sodas & Bloody Mary Mixes,
Salted Caramel Root beer, Bacon Bloody Mary Mix.
(Woman, estab 2008, empl 1, sales $400,000, cert:
WBENC)

3436   Chapin LLC
       1350 N Wells St Ste F109
       Chicago, IL 60610
       Contact: Jennifer Alexander Monzón
       Tel: 312-493-6976
       Email: jennifer@chapincoffee.com
       Website: www.ChapinCoffee.com
Specialty coffee, whole bean, ground & single serve (k-
cup). (Hisp, estab 2013, empl 2, sales , cert: NMSDC)

3437   Compact Industries
       3945 Ohio Ave
       St. Charles, IL 60174
       Contact: Dan Matyus VP Business Dev
       Tel: 630-513-9600
       Email: matyus@compactind.com
       Website: www.compactind.com
Contract manufacturer of dry food products. (Woman,
estab 1963, empl 120, sales $98,000,000, cert: WBENC)

3438   Cornfields, Inc.
       3898 Sunset Ave
       Waukegan, IL 60087
       Contact: JB Weiler VP Sales
       Tel: 847-263-7000
       Email: info@cornfieldsinc.com
       Website: www.cornfieldsinc.com
Mfr natural & organic snacks. (Woman, estab 1991, empl
60, sales $12,000,000, cert: WBENC)

3439   Cristina Foods, Inc.
       4555 S Racine Ave
       Chicago, IL 60609
       Contact: Cesar Dovalina President
       Tel: 312-829-0360
       Email: cdovalina@cristinafoods.com
       Website: www.cristinafoods.com
Dist fresh produce, frozen foods, spices, grocery & canned
goods, meats, dairy, poultry, seafood, disposable paper &
plastics. (Hisp, estab 1989, empl 42, sales $21,750,000,
cert: NMSDC)

3440   DAMRON Corporation
       4433 W Ohio St
       Chicago, IL 60624
       Contact: Amariah Bradford Marketing Media
       Specialist
       Tel: 773-826-6000
       Email: amariahbradford@damroncorp.com
       Website: www.damroncorp.com
Healing Tea Leaves of the World brand of Specialty Tea - 25
ct. teabag cartons (25% more than National Brands),
quality fully equal to or better than National Brands. (AA,
estab 1985, empl 50, sales $5,800,000, cert: City, NMSDC)

3441   Frey Produce
       RR 1 Box 89
       Keenes, IL 62851
       Contact: Renee Mattingly VP Sales & Mktg
       Tel: 618-835-2536
       Email: reneemattingly@freyproduce.com
       Website: www.freyproduce.com
Grow, pack & dist fresh fruits & vegetables: watermel-
ons, cantaloupe, green bell peppers, sweet corn,
pumpkins, squash, soybeans, wheat. (Woman, estab
1996, empl 20, sales $50,000,000, cert: WBENC)

3442   Harris Ice Company
       3927 W 5th Ave
       Chicago, IL 60624
       Contact: Walker Harris President
       Tel: 773-826-3110
       Email: harrisice1@sbcglobal.net
       Website: www.harrisicechicago.com
Harris Ice Company manufactures and delivers ice
throughtout the City of Chicago and surrounding
suburbs. (AA, estab 1970, empl 15, sales $1,423,175,
cert: City, NMSDC)

3443   Mullins Food Products, Inc.
       2200 S 25th Ave
       Broadview, IL 60155
       Contact: Andy Camp Dir of Sales
       Tel: 708-344-3224
       Email: acamp@mullinsfood.com
       Website: www.mullinsfood.com
Custom mfr & package liquid condiments: sauces, salad
dressings, ketchup, mayonnaise, picante sauce, salsa
sauce, pizza sauce, asian style sauces, flavored syrups,
icing. (Woman, estab 1934, empl 350, sales , cert:
WBENC)

3444   Navisource Holdings LLC dba Golden Hill Foods
       LLC
       851 W Grand Ave 2nd Fl
       Chicago, IL 60642
       Contact: Demetrio Garcia VP Business Dev
       Tel: 312-226-5900
       Email: dgarcia@goldenhillfoods.com
       Website: www.goldenhillfoods.com
Import & dist dehydrated vegetables & spices. (Hisp,
estab 2005, empl 6, sales $2,500,000, cert: NMSDC)

3445   Reggios' Pizza, Inc.
       340 W 83rd St
       Chicago, IL 60620
       Contact: Darryl Humphrey Sales & Marketing Dir
       Tel: 773-488-1411
       Email: dhumphrey@reggiospizzainc.com
       Website: www.reggios.com
Chicago Style Famous Buttercrust Pizza. (AA, estab 1972,
empl 42, sales , cert: City)

3446   Stern Ingredients, Inc.
       1030 N State St #10BC
       Chicago, IL 60610
       Contact: Joni Stern President
       Tel: 773-472-0301
       Email: joni@sterningredients.com
       Website: www.sterningredients.com
Dist ingredients: confectionery, bakery, nutritional &
snack food products. (Woman, estab 1990, empl 2, sales
$434,255, cert: WBENC)

3447   Subco Foods
1150 Commerce Dr
West Chicago, IL 60185
Contact: Nadia Attia Dir of Sales
Tel: 630-231-0003
Email: nattia@subcofoods.com
Website: www.subcofoods.com
Dist dry food products: randed, private label & contract packaging, drink mixes, gelatin & puddings, coffee creamer, hot chocolate, cappuccino, cake mixes, gravy mixes, seasonings, pancake mixes, soup bases, rice products, nutraceuticals. (As-Pac, estab 1994, empl 90, sales $16,560,000, cert: NMSDC)

3448   Sulpice Better Bites
PO Box 70
Barrington, IL 60011
Contact: Anne Shaeffer Founder
Tel: 630-301-2345
Email: anne@sulpicechocolat.com
Website: www.sulpicechocolat.com
Milk chocolate with salt and almonds; dark chocolate with cinnamon and cayenne pepper; dark chocolate with ginger and lemon; 70% dark chocolate with sea salt; white chocolate with cake batter. (Woman, estab 2009, empl 2, sales $300,000, cert: WBENC)

3449   Suzy's Swirl
703 Rockland Rd
Lake Bluff, IL 60044
Contact: Founder
Tel: 224-544-5189
Email: laine@suzysswirl.com
Website: www.suzysswirl.com
Frozen desserts, liquor-infused frozen yogurts and sorbets. (Woman, estab 2012, empl 8, sales $350,000, cert: WBENC)

3450   The Edlong Corporation
225 Scott St
Elk Grove Village, IL 60007
Contact: Gail Scott Exec Asst
Tel: 847-631-6775
Email: diversity@edlong.com
Website: www.edlong.com
Dairy: cheese, butter, milk & cream, cultured, sweet & functional dairy. (Woman, estab , empl 100, sales , cert: WBENC)

3451   Thomas Imports LLC
1327 W. Washington BLVD Ste 3D
Chicago, IL 60607
Contact: Chris Cottrell Sales
Tel: 312-929-2699
Email: ccottrell@isiahinternational.com
Website: www.isiahimports.com
Corn tortillas, flour tortillas, flavored tortilla flour wraps; jalapeno wrap, tomato basil wrap, chipotle wrap, roasted garlic wrap, cheese, wraps corn chips, spices, chile peppers, canned sauces, frozen foods. (AA, estab 2016, empl 8, sales $0, cert: NMSDC)

3452   V&V Supremo Foods Inc.
2141 S Throop St
Chicago, IL 60608
Contact: John Brandley Natl Sales Mgr
Tel: 312-421-1020
Email: johnb@vvsupremo.com
Website: www.vvsupremo.com
Produce Hispanic cheese, creams & Chorizo. (Hisp, estab 1964, empl 184, sales $67,142,000, cert: NMSDC)

Indiana

3453   Williams, West & Witt's Product Co.
3501 W Dunes Hwy
Michigan City, IN 46360
Contact: Joanne Tica Steiger Natl Dir Bus Dev
Tel: 219-879-8236
Email: jtsteiger@integrativeflavors.com
Website: www.cooksdelight.com
Mfr healthy soup bases & innovative food flavor additives for the institutional, food service, corporate and government user channels. (Woman, estab 1938, empl 19, sales $2,500,000, cert: State, WBENC)

Louisiana

3454   Bridge Foods, Inc.
PO Box 58698
New Orleans, LA 70158
Contact: Henry Chigbu President
Tel: 504-254-9770
Email: hchigbu@bridgefoods.com
Website: www.ashantifoods.com
Condiments: hot sauce, wing sauce, steak sauce, worcestershire sauce, etc. (AA, estab 1993, empl 5, sales $15,000,000, cert: NMSDC)

Massachusetts

3455   600 lb Gorillas, Inc.
558 Washington St
Duxbury, MA 02332
Contact: Paula White CEO
Tel: 781-452-7273
Email: paula@600lbgorillas.com
Website: www.600lbgorillas.com
Dist premium frozen cookie dough. (Woman, estab 2000, empl 2, sales $3,000,000, cert: WBENC)

3456   Adonai Spring Water Inc.
31 West St, Ste 4
Randolph, MA 02368
Contact: Gloria Olatunji President
Tel: 844-273-7672
Email: gloolat@aol.com
Website: www.adonaisprings.com
Bottled water 5 Gallons, Bottled Water Coolers, Point of Use Coolers, Drinking Water Fountains
Biodegradable & Compostable hot and cold cups, lids, straws, trays, napkins, plates, trays clamshells, Table top & Dinnerware. (Woman/AA, estab 2014, empl 2, sales , cert: State, WBENC)

3457 Boston Baking, Inc.
      101 Sprague St
      Boston, MA 02136
      Contact: Julee Robey-Boschetto President
      Tel: 617-364-6900
      Email: julee@bostonbaking.com
      Website: www.bostonbaking.com
Wholesale manufacturer of baked goods. (Woman, estab
2004, empl 54, sales $4,900,000, cert: City)

3458 Cape Cod Select LLC
      73 Tremont St
      Carver, MA 02330
      Contact: Cindy Rhodes Owner
      Tel: 508-866-1149
      Email: crhodes@capecodselect.com
      Website: www.capecodselect.com
Harvest, pack & dist cranberries. (Woman, estab 2009,
empl 3, sales $0, cert: WBENC)

3459 Harbar LLC
      320 Turnpike St
      Canton, MA 02021
      Contact: Keith Brennan Retail Sales Mgr
      Tel: 800-881-7040
      Email: kbrennan@harbar.com
      Website: www.harbar.com
Mfr corn & flour tortillas. (Minority, Woman, estab 1986,
empl 140, sales , cert: NMSDC)

3460 HimalaSalt - Sustainable Sourcing, LLC
      1375 Boardman St
      Sheffield, MA 01257
      Contact: melissa kushi CEO
      Tel: 413-446-8927
      Email: melissa@himalasalt.com
      Website: www.himalasalt.com
Dist pink Himalayan sea salt produced in our owned facility
that is certified organic, Non-GMO, Gluten-Free, Kosher for
Passover & powered by 156 solar panels. (Woman, estab
2006, empl 12, sales $2,500,000, cert: State)

3461 Jensay Co.
      61 Maple St
      Acton, MA 01720
      Contact: Stephen Chen President
      Tel: 978-929-9797
      Email: stephenchen@joycechenfoods.com
      Website: www.joycechenfoods.com
Asian, Chinese cooking sauces, oils, comdiments, spices &
Asian frozen prepared food products. (As-Pac, estab 2006,
empl 1, sales $950,000, cert: State)

3462 Monsoon Kitchens, Inc.
      165 Memorial Dr Unit F
      Shrewsbury, MA 01545
      Contact: Lineman, Janice President
      Tel: 508-842-0070
      Email: jan@monsoonkitchens.co
      Website: www.monsoonkitchens.com
Mfr Indian style frozen chicken entrees, vegetarian entress
& appetizers. (As-Ind, estab 2003, empl 6, sales
$5,000,000, cert: NMSDC)

3463 Nella Pasta LLC
      859 Willard St Ste 400
      Quincy, MA 02169
      Contact: Leigh Foster Member
      Tel: 860-888-9686
      Email: nellapasta@gmail.com
      Website: www.nellapasta.com
Pasta manufacturing. (Woman, estab 2009, empl 1, sales
$145,879, cert: WBENC)

3464 R Square Desserts LLC
      PO Box 990031
      Boston, MA 02199
      Contact: Susie Parish Co-Owner
      Tel: 857-263-8833
      Email: susie@batchicecream.com
      Website: www.batchicecream.com
Ice cream made from real ingredients & without additives. (Woman, estab 2009, empl 5, sales , cert: WBENC)

3465 Signature Breads, Inc.
      100 Justin Dr
      Chelsea, MA 02150
      Contact: Heidi Keathley VP Sales & Mktg
      Tel: 617-819-3105
      Email: heidi.keathley@signaturebreads.com
      Website: www.signaturebreads.com
Mfr par-baked breads: dinner rolls, sandwich rolls,
baguettes, ciabattas, breadsticks, pieggas & artisan
breads, individual & bulk packaging, frozen or par-baked.
(Hisp, estab 2006, empl 280, sales $48,000,000, cert:
NMSDC)

3466 SJB Bagel Makers of Boston
      77 Rowe St
      Newton, MA 02466
      Contact: Jeff Malich Dir of Sales
      Tel: 617-213-8400
      Email: jeff@finagleonline.com
      Website: www.finagleabagel.com/
Artisan all natural bagel baker. We product 2 oz - 5 oz
premium bagels. (Woman, estab 1992, empl 130, sales
$12,000,000, cert: State, WBENC)

3467 VSR Enterprise, LLC
      1675 Dorchester Ave
      Boston, MA 02121
      Contact: Vernon Barsatee CEO
      Tel: 617-514-4711
      Email: vernon@vsrenterprise.com
      Website: www.vsrenterprise.com
Food Brokerage, Import & Export of consumer sized
packaged (CPG), frozen foods, spices, dairy products,
meats, health & beauty aids. (As-Pac, estab 2012, empl
2, sales , cert: NMSDC)

Maryland

3468 Better and Best Corporation
      1601 Knecht Ave
      Halethorpe, MD 21227
      Contact: Patricia Lobel President
      Tel: 410-902-5701
      Email: patricia.lobel@avenuegourmet.com
      Website: www.avenuegourmet.com
Dist natural/organic products: sauces, marinades, fruit
butters & spreads, cookies, crackers, cooking oils,
vinegars, snacks, condiments & beverages. (Woman,
estab 2000, empl 20, sales $0, cert: State)

3469 Caribbean Blue Organic Foods, LLC
      6701 Democracy Blvd Ste 300
      Bethesda, MD 20817
      Contact: Lenore Travers President
      Tel: 301-564-4322
      Email: sales@caribbeanbluewater.com
      Website: www.CaribbeanBlueWater.com
Caribbean Blue Natural Spring Water. (AA, estab 2011,
empl 1, sales $185,000, cert: State)

3470 CharmedBar, LLC
      120 Canfield Hill Dr
      Gaithersburg, MD 20878
      Contact: Debbi Ascher President
      Tel: 202-430-5637
      Email: debbi@charmedbar.com
      Website: www.charmedbar.com
CharmedBars are kosher, baked fruit & nut bars (nutrition/
energy bars) that are certified gluten free and free of
grains, dairy, soy, egg, refined sugars, GMOs, preservatives
& artificial ingredients. (Woman, estab 2013, empl 2, sales
$188,000, cert: WBENC)

3471 Collaborative Food & Beverage, LLC (DBA Mayorga
      Coffee)
      15151 Southlawn Ln
      Rockville, MD 20850
      Contact: Martin Mayorga President
      Tel: 301-315-8093
      Email: martin@mayorgacoffee.com
      Website: www.mayorgacoffee.com
Roasted whole bean specialty coffees, ground "portion
packed" specialty coffees, custom blends, private labeling.
(Minority, Woman, estab 1997, empl 87, sales
$17,500,000, cert: State)

3472 Demeter's Pantry (dba): GreenFood Associates LLC
      419 Greenbrier Dr
      Silver Spring, MD 20910
      Contact: Maria Kardamaki Robertson Managing
      Partner
      Tel: 301-587-0048
      Email: maria@demeterspantry.com
      Website: www.thegreektable.net
Dist ethnic foods, Mediterranean (Greek prepared foods,
entrées, side dishes & bean salad dishes. (Woman, estab
2003, empl 2, sales $490,058, cert: State)

3473 MAS Foods International, LLC
      PO Box 2886
      Montgomery Village, MD 20886
      Contact: Michael Short Chief Managing Officer
      Tel: 301-591-9728
      Email: mshort@masfi.com
      Website: www.masfi.com
Gourmet chicken sausage & personal chicken pizza made
from halal products. (AA, estab 2004, empl 2, sales , cert:
NMSDC)

3474 SodexoMagic (Magic Food Provision, LLC)
      9801 Washingtonian Blvd
      Gaithersburg, MD 20878
      Contact: Ken Holdman Dir Strategic Sales
      Tel: 918-430-6514
      Email: ken.holdman@sodexomagic.com
      Website: www.sodexomagic.com
Food and catering services groundkeeping facilities and
plant operations and maintenance, environmental &
engineering services & laundry & linens. (AA, estab
2006, empl 4900, sales $283,400,000, cert: NMSDC)

3475 SoFine Food
      4825 Cordell Ave, Ste 200
      Bethesda, MD 20814
      Contact: Sophia Maroon CEO
      Tel: 301-979-9555
      Email: sophia@sofinefood.com
      Website: www.dressitupdressing.com
Produce all-natural, shelf-stable vinaigrettes, called
Dress It Up Dressing, gluten-free, sugar-free & vegan.
(Woman, estab 2012, empl 2, sales , cert: WBENC)

3476 Soft Stuff Distributors, Inc.
      8200 Preston Court Ste L
      Jessup, MD 20794
      Contact: Lois Gamerman President
      Tel: 301-604-3300
      Email: loisg@gosoftstuff.com
      Website: www.gosoftstuff.com
Dist breads, bagels, cakes, cheesecakes, muffin batters &
baked muffins, frozen doughs, preproofed danish &
croisants, cookies-frozen doughs & prebaked, pizzas,
soups fresh & frozen, catering dessert items. (Woman,
estab 1989, empl 35, sales $10,500,000, cert: State,
WBENC)

Maine

3477 Bixby & Co., LLC
      248 Norport Ave Ste C
      Belfast, ME 04915
      Contact: Kate McAleer Owner
      Tel: 845-346-6591
      Email: kate@bixbyco.com
      Website: www.bixbyco.com
Mfr healthy gluten free candy bars. Produces three
vegan flavors. Kosher certified. (Woman, estab 2011,
empl 1, sales , cert: WBENC)

3478 Blue Sky Produce
      243 Tory Hill Rd
      Phillips, ME 04966
      Contact: Lynn Thurston Owner
      Tel: 207-684-2172
      Email: hope@tdstelme.net
      Website: www.blueskyproduce.com
Pesticide Free & Conventionally grown Frozen Wild
Blueberries packed in 14 oz containers. (Woman, estab
1987, empl 6, sales , cert: WBENC)

Michigan

3479 Dual Sales & Associates, Inc.
PO Box 725
Grand Blanc, MI 48480
Contact: Donna Bromm Owner
Tel: 248-505-7128
Email: donna@dualsales.com
Website: www.dualsales.com
Dist shelled walnuts & pecans, specialty dried fruits.
(Woman, estab 1993, empl 1, sales , cert: WBENC)

3480 Ebonex
18400 Rialto
Melvindale, MI 48122
Contact: Shelly Toenniges Principal
Tel: 313-388-0063
Email: stoenniges@ebonex.com
Website: www.keystoneuniversal.com
Dist baking ammonium carbonate: lump, chip or powder.
(Woman, estab , empl 12, sales $0, cert: WBENC)

3481 Flamm Pickle & Packing Co., Inc.
4502 Hipps Hollow Rd
Eau Claire, MI 49111
Contact: Dorothy Munao President
Tel: 269-461-6916
Email: dorothymunao@flammpickle.com
Website: www.flammpickle.com
Mfr dill pickles & sweet pickle relishes. (Woman, estab ,
empl 16, sales $1,885,000, cert: WBENC)

3482 Jogue, Inc.
14731 Helm Ct
Plymouth, MI 48170
Contact: Andrew Huber CFO
Tel: 734-207-0100
Email: andrew@jogue.com
Website: www.jogue.com
Mfr dry flavors and beverage bases. (As-Ind, estab 1984,
empl 48, sales $17,933,000, cert: NMSDC)

Minnesota

3483 Aarthun Enterprises, LLC dba Taste of Scandinavia
111 E County Rd F
Vadnais Heights, MN 55127
Contact: CFO
Tel: 651-483-9242
Email: office@tasteofscandinavia.com
Website: www.tasteofscandinavia.com
Hand crafted Cakes & Tortes, Cupcakes & Cookies both
traditional & custom request. (Woman, estab 2004, empl
118, sales $7,062,388, cert: WBENC)

3484 Catallia Mexican Foods, LLC
2965 Lone Oak Circle
Eagan, MN 55121
Contact: Cathy Cruz Gooch President
Tel: 651-647-6808
Email: cathy@catallia.com
Website: www.catallia.com
Mfr premium flour tortillas. (Woman/Hisp, estab 2005,
empl 150, sales $0, cert: NMSDC)

3485 Healthy America, LLC
13570 Grove Dr#372
Maple Grove, MN 55311
Contact: Sunil Kumar President
Tel: 651-666-0375
Email: sunil.kumar@theamazingchickpea.com
Website: www.theamazingchickpea.com
Produce Chickpea Spread that tastes like peanut butter
but does not contain any Nuts, Gluten Free and Dairy
Free. "The Amazing Chickpea - Creamy", "The Amazing
Chickpea - Crunchy","The Amazing Chickpea - Tradi-
tional". (As-Pac, estab 2016, empl 5, sales $200,000,
cert: NMSDC)

3486 Sweet Harvest Foods Management Company
15100 Business Pkwy
Rosemount, MN 55068
Contact: Joel Rengel Sales Dir
Tel: 507-263-8599
Email: jrengel@sweetharvestfoods.com
Website: www.sweetharvestfoods.com
Mfr honey, ingredient honey, pancake syrup (table
syrup), corn syrup & branded peanut butter. (Woman,
estab 1923, empl 50, sales , cert: WBENC)

North Carolina

3487 Calvine's Coffee LLC
PO Box 3005
Matthews, NC 28106
Contact: John Williamson President
Tel: 800-545-8553
Email: john@cadprinting.biz
Website: www.calvinescoffee.com
Gourmet specialty roast blend of coffee beans from
many origins around the world, including small farms
and farmers. Our beans are roasted in small batches in a
San Franciscan Artisan Roaster. (Woman/AA, estab 2015,
empl 1, sales , cert: State)

3488 Dover Foods, Inc.
353 Banner Farm RD
Mills River, NC 28759
Contact: Kathy Milner Natl Acct Mgr
Tel: 828-890-8344
Email: kathy@americanqualityfoods.com
Website: www.aqf.com
Mfr & dist sugar free & gluten free dessert mixes:
cookies, cream pie fillings, cheesecakes, gelatin, mousse
mixes, drink mixes, cake mixes, frosting & pie shells.
(Woman, estab 1994, empl 35, sales $5,000,000, cert:
WBENC)

3489 FDY, Inc.
2459 Wilkinson Blvd Ste 300
Charlotte, NC 28208
Contact: Keith Haywood VP Sales & Mktg
Tel: 704-523-6605
Email: khaywood@fdyinc.com
Website: www.fdyinc.com
Food service mgmt: cafeteria, dining services, vending,
catering, design. (Woman/AA, estab 1983, empl 275,
sales $10,870,702, cert: City)

3490   High Country Springs LLC
PO Box 238
Pilot Mountain, NC 27041
Contact: Linda Tucker Partner
Tel: 336-374-7474
Email: ltucker@highcountrysprings.com
Website: www.highcountrysprings.com
Provide 5-gallon, 3-gallon & 1-gallon Spring, Distilled, RO (Reverse Osmosis), Deionized, and Fluoride Water, water dispensers & coffee service. (Woman, estab 1992, empl 10, sales $605,431, cert: State)

3491   MyThreeSons Gourmet, LLC
2309 Lafayette Ave
Greensboro, NC 27408
Contact: Cheryl Barnett President
Tel: 336-324-5638
Email: mtsgourmet@gmail.com
Website: www.mtsgourmet.com
Mfr natural gourmet pimento cheese spread. (Woman, estab 2010, empl 10, sales $3,800,000, cert: WBENC)

3492   Nirav Dye & Chemicals Inc.
6420 Rea Rd Ste A1-357
Charlotte, NC 28277
Contact: Shaili Doshi Dir
Tel: 704-509-1677
Email: shaili@niravgroup.com
Website: www.niravingredients.com
Dist food grade products, emulsifiers, functional ingredients, natural extracts and other ingredients. (As-Ind, estab 1994, empl 3, sales $25,000,000, cert: NMSDC)

3493   The Busha Group LLC
302 Lord Court
Cramerton, NC 28032
Contact: Julie Busha CEO
Tel: 704-879-4411
Email: jbusha@slawsa.com
Website: www.slawsa.com
Mfr Slawsa, slaw-salsa hybrid condiment, all natural, fat-free, cholesterol-free, gluten-free, low in sodium & kosher. (Woman, estab 2013, empl 1, sales $363,320, cert: WBENC)

3494   Tropical Nut & Fruit Co
1100 Continental Blvd
Charlotte, NC 28273
Contact: Angela Bauer Owner
Tel: 704-588-0400
Email: abauer@tropicalfoods.com
Website: www.tropicalfoods.com
Mfr & dist nuts, seeds, dried fruit, snack mixes, candy & specialty foods. (Woman, estab 1977, empl , sales $88,000,000, cert: WBENC)

New Hampshire

3495   Healthy Solutions Spice Blends, LLC
PO Box 1094
Hampton, NH 03843
Contact: Shelly Wolcott Mgr
Tel: 603-622-8744
Email: shelly@spiceblends.com
Website: www.spiceblends.com
Produce all natural, high quality, recipe ready spice blends. (Woman, estab 2013, empl , sales , cert: WBENC)

3496   Homefree, LLC
PO Box 491
Windham, NH 03087
Contact: Jill Robbins President
Tel: 603-898-0172
Email: info@homefreetreats.com
Website: www.homefreetreats.com
Mfr all natural or organic, ready-to-eat whole grain baked goods free of gluten & common food allergens. (Woman, estab 2009, empl 18, sales $624,408, cert: WBENC)

New Jersey

3497   Advanced Food Systems
21 Roosevelt Ave
Somerset, NJ 08863
Contact: Al Rose Midwest Sales Mgr
Tel: 732-873-6776
Email: ajrose@charter.net
Website: www.afsnj.com
Food ingredients: gums, starches, proteins, spices, flavors, lab services. (As-Pac, estab 1980, empl 40, sales $50,000,000, cert: NMSDC)

3498   Crispy Green Inc.
10 Madison Rd
Fairfield, NJ 07004
Contact: Angela Liu President
Tel: 973-679-4515
Email: angela@crispygreen.com
Website: www.crispygreen.com
Crispy Green Fruit product line is created using a sophisticated freeze-drying process where water is removed from the fresh fruit in a cold (freezing) vacuum condition, leaving behind the true essence of the fruit in a light and crispy texture. (Minority, Woman, estab 2004, empl 10, sales , cert: State)

3499   Harris Freeman & Co LP
344 New Albany Rd
Moorestown, NJ 08057
Contact: Steve Sernka Natl Sales Mgr
Tel: 856-793-0290
Email: steve.sernka@harrisfreeman.com
Website: www.HarrisTea.com
Manufacturer tea. (As-Ind, estab 1997, empl 129, sales , cert: NMSDC)

3500   JK Enterprise Solutions LLC
1000 Delsea Dr Building I Unit 1
Westville, NJ 08093
Contact: Abdul Ahad Butt Owner
Tel: 856-228-5934
Email: ahad@jkens.com
Website: www.jkens.com
Dist snack food products: Bud's Best Cookies, Uncle AL's Cremes, Lil Dutch maid wirecut cookies, Mayfair Candy Carnival, Select Sweets Candy, Daddy Rays fruit bars, Marco Polo Preserves, Caribbean Ice pops, Kisko Freezies. (As-Ind, estab 2014, empl 1, sales $187,000, cert: NMSDC)

3501 JVM Sales Corp.
3401a Tremley Point Rd
Linden, NJ 07036
Contact: Justin Tomasino Owner
Tel: 908-862-4866
Email: justintomasino@aol.com
Website: www.jvmsales.com
Provide Grated, Shredded & Shaved Cheeses, Hard Italian Cheese, Custom blended cheeses. (Woman, estab 1983, empl 200, sales $50,000,000, cert: WBENC)

3502 Soul Sisters Foods, Inc.
41 Prince St, Ste B11
Paterson, NJ 07505
Contact: Betty Dixon President
Tel: 973-742-8255
Email: betty.dixon@unilever.com
Website: www.soulroll.com
Retail frozen food, Soul Rolls: collard greens, marinated meats, cheddar cheese, onions, green peppers, and tomatoes, seasoned to perfection in a crispy flour tortilla. (Woman/AA, estab 2006, empl 2, sales , cert: WBENC)

3503 Suzanne's Specialties, Inc.
421 Jersey Ave, Ste B
New Brunswick, NJ 08901
Contact: Susan Morano President
Tel: 732-828-8500
Email: suzspec@earthlink.net
Website: www.suzannes-specialties.com
Mfr natural sweeteners: rice syrups, malt extracts, molasses, honey, agave syrup, invert, co-extracts, rice sweetener jellies, rice syrup based aerated toppings. (Woman, estab 1984, empl 25, sales $15,000,000, cert: WBENC)

3504 The Dessert Ladies
266 Main Ave
Stirling, NJ 07980
Contact: Lindsay Smith Owner
Tel: 908-340-7321
Email: lindsay.smith@bienscc.com
Website: www.dessertladies.com/
Custom edible gifts, hand-decorated, branded chocolate products and baked goods. (Woman, estab 2010, empl 10, sales $3,000,000, cert: WBENC)

Nevada

3505 Tortillas Inc.
2912 N Commerce St
North Las Vegas, NV 89030
Contact: Gustavo Gutierrez President
Tel: 702-399-3300
Email: gus@tortillasinc.com
Website: www.tortillasinc.com
Corn tortillas, flour tortillas, flavored tortilla flour wraps; jalapeno wrap, tomato basil wrap, chipotle wrap, roasted garlic wrap, cheese, wraps corn chips, spices, chile peppers, canned sauces, frozen foods. (Hisp, estab 1979, empl 76, sales $8,000,000, cert: NMSDC)

New York

3506 Chocolate Promises, Inc.
PO Box 694
Merrick, NY 11566
Contact: Zakalik Cindy President
Tel: 516-299-6400
Email: cindy@chocolatepromises.com
Website: www.chocolatepromises.com
Personalized chocolate with edible images. We'll custom print your full color logo, picture, design and/or special message directly on delicious chocolate coins, lollipops, Belgian truffles and more. (Woman, estab 2012, empl 2, sales , cert: State, City, WBENC)

3507 Golden Glow Cookie Co. Inc.
1844 Givan Ave
Bronx, NY 10469
Contact: Joan Florio Mgr
Tel: 718-379-6223
Email: ggcookies@aol.com
Website: www.thecookiefactory.com
Wholesale bakery, cookies & other related bakery items in bulk , plastic clamshells & individually wrapped. (Woman, estab 1954, empl 15, sales , cert: City)

3508 IMK Products, Inc.
244 Fifth Ave Ste D146
New York, NY 10001
Contact: Ilona Kovacs President
Tel: 914-500-8127
Email: imkproductsinc@gmail.com
Website: www.truetastebar.com
Dist nutritional bars, organic/non gmo, no added sugar, vegan, gluten free, soy free, dairy free. (Woman, estab 2011, empl 2, sales , cert: WBENC)

3509 Lugo Nutrition Inc.
51 N Broadway, Ste 2B
Nyack, NY 10960
Contact: Nick Lugo VP
Tel: 302-573-2301
Email: nlugo@lugonutrition.com
Website: www.lugonutrition.com
Gelatin, beta carotene. Bitterness masking, sweetness enhancing, natural preservative/flavoring. (Hisp, estab 2010, empl 5, sales $4,500,000, cert: NMSDC)

3510 SFR&R Inc.
9 Soundview Lane
Sands Point, NY 11050
Contact: Giovannina Bellino Owner
Tel: 516-767-7286
Email: goddess6x8@aol.com
Website: www.flavorbombs.net
Mfr frozen cooking bases & foods. Low Sodium, Gluten Free, All Natural products. (Woman, estab 2008, empl 1, sales , cert: WBENC)

3511 Thunder Island Coffee Roasters, L.L.C.
PO Box 1275
Southampton, NY 11969
Contact: Benjamin Haile CEO
Tel: 631-204-1110
Email: info@thunderislandcoffee.com
Website: www.thunderislandcoffee.com
Coffee roasting and packaging. (Nat Ame, estab 2005, empl 4, sales , cert: State)

Ohio

3512   ABC Cookie Co., Inc.
3 Nationwide Plaza
Columbus, OH 43215
Contact: Dee Tolber CEO
Tel: 614-221-4442
Email: dee@ablessedcookie.com
Website: www.ablessedcookie.com
Fresh baked cookies, muffins, coffee cake, custom shaped, logo design cookies & custom gift items. (Woman/AA, estab 1990, empl 4, sales $185,000, cert: NMSDC)

3513   Super Bakery
1667 E 40th St, Ste 1D3
Cleveland, OH 44103
Contact: Karen Cahill Corporate Admin
Tel: 216-426-8989
Email: karen.cahill@superbakery.com
Website: www.superbakery.com
Baked goods. (AA, estab 1989, empl 27, sales , cert: NMSDC)

3514   Urban Food Concepts LLC
852 E Highland Rd
Macedonia, OH 44056
Contact: Claude Booker President
Tel: 330-908-0493
Email: claude@simplysouthernsides.com
Website: www.simplysouthernsides.com
Fully cooked & seasoned vegetables & side dishes. (Woman/AA, estab 2007, empl 3, sales $4,000,000, cert: State, NMSDC, WBENC)

3515   Whitehall, Inc.
4760 Paddock Rd
Cincinnati, OH 45229
Contact: Shawn Higgins Dir of Natl Sales
Tel: 513-242-1004
Email: shiggins@klostermanbakery.com
Website: www.klostermanbakery.com
Restaurant quality bread, buns & rolls in a unique, handy and more compact retail package. (Woman, estab , empl 560, sales $295,400,000, cert: WBENC)

Oregon

3516   Hood River Juice Company
550 Riverside Dr
Hood River, OR 97031
Contact: David Ryan President
Tel: 541-386-3003
Email: davidr@hrjco.com
Website: www.ryansjuice.com
Natural & organic apple juice, single strength, not from concentrate. (Hisp, estab 1982, empl 113, sales $35,000,000, cert: NMSDC)

3517   Lucky Foods, LLC
7774 SW Nimbus Ave, Bldg 10
Beaverton, OR 97008
Contact: Tammy Jo President
Tel: 503-641-6602
Email: tammyjo@luckyfood.com
Website: www.luckyfood.com
Asian foods. (Minority, Woman, estab 1985, empl 16, sales $1,547,000, cert: State)

Pennsylvania

3518   A.S.K. Foods Inc.
71 Hetrick Ave
Palmyra, PA 17078
Contact: Liz Burkholder Reg Sales Mgr
Tel: 717-838-6356
Email: ldurr@askfoods.com
Website: www.askfoods.com
Mfr prepared deli salads, entrees, side dishes, soups with no preservatives added. (Woman, estab 1947, empl 175, sales $42,200,000, cert: WBENC)

3519   Casalingo LLC
6321 S Highlings Circle
Harrisburg, PA 17111
Contact: Monette Roberto Member
Tel: 717-805-5088
Email: monetteroberto@yahoo.com
Website: www.casalingofoods.com
Four Generation homemade local pasta sauce. (Woman, estab 2013, empl 2, sales , cert: WBENC)

3520   Dutch Gold Honey, Inc.
2220 Dutch Gold Dr
Lancaster, PA 17601
Contact: Jill Clark
Tel: 717-393-1716
Email: jclark@dutchgoldhoney.com
Website: www.dutchgoldhoney.com
Honey & maple syrup processing & packaging. (Woman, estab 1946, empl 75, sales , cert: WBENC)

3521   Enchanted Acres Farm, Inc.
200 N 8th St Ste 500
Reading, PA 19601
Contact: Kelley Huff President
Tel: 877-707-3833
Email: quality@enchantedacresfarm.net
Website: www.enchantedacresfarm.net
Mfr beverages: tea, coffee, cocoa. (Woman, estab 2002, empl 15, sales $700,000, cert: State)

3522   Fallon Trading Co., Inc.
3897 Adler Pl, Ste C150
Bethlehem, PA 18017
Contact: Michele Rossi Office Mgr
Tel: 610-867-5527
Email: michele@fallontrading.com
Website: www.fallontrading.com
Dist conventional and organic fruit and vegetable juice concentrates, purees, NFC, IQF, essences, powders, oils, flavors, colors, and extracts. (Woman, estab 1998, empl 4, sales , cert: WBENC)

3523   Gourmail Inc.
300 Elmwood Ave
Sharon Hill, PA 19079
Contact: Business Mgr
Tel: 610-522-2650
Email: info@jyotifoods.com
Website: www.jyotifoods.com
Ready to serve vegetarian entrees, soups and sauces for at-home cooking, packed in cans. Indian Dals (Legumes), in pouches. (Minority, Woman, estab 1979, empl 25, sales $30,000,000, cert: NMSDC)

3524 Sweet Street Desserts
722 Hiesters Lane
Reading, PA 19605
Contact: Anthony DiGirolamo CFO
Tel: 610-921-8113
Email: cathy.bitler@sweetstreet.com
Website: www.sweetstreet.com
Mfr frozen goumet desserts: cakes, pies, cheesecakes, dessert bars, bundt cakes, loaf cakes, cookies, scones, cupcakes & mousses. (Woman, estab , empl , sales , cert: WBENC)

3525 Zana Cakes, Inc.
12 W Willow Grove Ave, Ste 153
Philadelphia, PA 19118
Contact: Zana Billue President
Tel: 215-248-1575
Email: info@zanacakes.com
Website: www.zanacakes.com
Cakes & pies. (Woman/AA, estab 1988, empl 1, sales , cert: NMSDC)

South Carolina

3526 Charleston Gourmet Burger Company
4206 Sawgrass Dr
North Charleston, SC 29420
Contact: chevalo wilsondebriano Owner
Tel: 843-847-8369
Email: chevalo@charlestongourmetburger.com
Website: www.charlestongourmetburger.com
Charleston Gourmet Burger Marinade -blend of nine herbs & spices. (Woman/AA, Hisp, estab 2012, empl 2, sales $1,000,000, cert: NMSDC)

3527 Chef Belinda LLC dba Chef Belinda Spices
6 Mooney Court
Trenton, SC 29847
Contact: Belinda Smith-Sullivan President
Tel: 803-552-6450
Email: belinda@chefbelinda.com
Website: www.chefbelindaspices.com
Produce all-natural artisan spice blends. (Woman/AA, estab 2009, empl 3, sales , cert: NMSDC)

3528 Pino Gelato, LLC
1000 William Hilton Pkwy, Ste G-1
Hilton Head Island, SC 29928
Contact: Jessica Scott CEO
Tel: 843-842-2822
Email: marketing@pinogelato.com
Website: www.pinogelato.com
Premium gelato & sorbetto. (Woman, estab 2004, empl 6, sales $1,748,000, cert: WBENC)

3529 Spartanburg Meat Processing Co., Inc.
3003 N Blackstock Rd
Spartanburg, SC 29301
Contact: JoAnne LaBounty Business Devel
Tel: 864-621-1520
Email: eatbbqribsjl@aol.com
Website: www.eatbbqribs.com
Meat processing plant, pork, beef & chicken. Baby Back Ribs w/Sauce, Back Ribs, Pulled Pork w/Sauce, Pulled Chicken w/Sauce, Custom Proteins & Sauces. (Woman, estab 1999, empl 51, sales $17,128,586, cert: State, WBENC)

3530 Sweet Bottom Cookies
PO Box 355
Mt. Pleasant, SC 29466
Contact: Michele Lewis President
Tel: 843-693-7366
Email: mlewis@sweetbottomcookies.com
Website: www.SweetBottomCookies.Com
Privately brands & wholesales jumbo (3.5oz), soft, individually wrapped, fudge covered bottom cookies. (Woman, estab 2010, empl 4, sales , cert: WBENC)

3531 The Muffin Mam, Inc.
3129 N Industrial Dr
Simpsonville, SC 29681
Contact: Greg Marshall VP Sales & Mktg
Tel: 800-948-4268
Email: gmarshall@muffinmam.com
Website: www.muffinmam.com
Mfr custom baked CrÃ¨me Cakes, Pound Cakes, Coffee Cakes, Gourmet Muffins, & Brownies. Use recycled & recycle able packaging. (Woman, estab 1990, empl 70, sales $24,500,000, cert: WBENC)

South Dalota

3532 Native American Natural Foods LLC
287 Water Tower Rd
Kyle, SD 57752
Contact: Mark Tilsen President
Tel: 605-455-2187
Email: mtilsen@tankabar.com
Website: www.tankabar.com
Gluten free, nitrate free, MSG free & hormone free Tanka Bar, Tanka Bites, and Tanka Sticks. (Minority, Woman, estab 2007, empl 12, sales $1,525,000, cert: NMSDC)

Texas

3533 Artesia Springs LLC
8130 Interchange Pkwy
San Antonio, TX 78218
Contact: Rudy Ramon President
Tel: 210-637-5554
Email: rudy@artesiasprings.com
Website: www.artesiasprings.com
Bottled water in all sizes from 16.9 liters, 3 and 4 gallon disposable and 5 gallon recycable, Private label options, water coolers, water filtration options. (Minority, Woman, estab 2004, empl 19, sales $1,400,000, cert: State, NMSDC)

3534 Behrnes Pepper Salts
5313 E Side Ave
Dallas, TX 75214
Contact: Jan Olavarri Owner
Tel: 214-724-0581
Email: jan@behrnes.com
Website: www.behrnes.com
Mfr pepper salts blends using Chipotle, Cayenne & Green Jalapeno. (Woman, estab 2012, empl 1, sales , cert: WBENC)

3535 Cadeco Industries, Inc.
       5610 Clinton Dr
       Houston, TX 77020
       Contact: Carlos deAldecoa President
       Tel: 713-670-0700
       Email: carlos@cadeco.cc
       Website: www.cadeco.cc
Bulk coffee processing, storage & distribution services.
(Hisp, estab 1995, empl 45, sales $40,000,000, cert: State,
NMSDC)

3536 Clint's Picante Inc.
       12 Thornhurst
       San Antonio, TX 78218
       Contact: Keri Poulter CFO
       Tel: 210-274-5916
       Email: keripoulter@yahoo.com
       Website: www.clintspicante.com
Mfr Salsa & BBQ sauce. (Woman, estab 1996, empl 2, sales
$29,990,000, cert: State, City)

3537 Cookies by Design
       1865 Summit Ave Ste 607
       Plano, TX 75074
       Contact: Darylyn Phillips Natl Sales Coord
       Tel: 800-347-3110
       Email: dphillips@cookiesbydesign.com
       Website: www.cookiesbydesign.com
Customized, hand-decorated cookie baskets, cookie
bouquets, cookie cakes, individual logo cookies, gourmet
cookies, cupcakes, gluten free & sugar free. (Woman, estab
1983, empl 54, sales $28,000,000, cert: State, WBENC)

3538 Ezbake Technologies
       PO Box 270527
       Flowermound, TX 75027
       Contact: Rita Tolvanen CEO
       Tel: 888-287-8447
       Email: rita@ezbake.net
       Website: www.ezbaketechnologies.com
Dist baking ingredients, enzyme based dough conditioners,
shelf life extenders & specialty conditioners for cookies,
cakes, donuts, English muffins & low moisture products.
(Woman, estab 1993, empl 4, sales $1,000,000, cert:
WBENC)

3539 Global Coffee Company
       6161 Savoy Dr, Ste 821
       Houston, TX 77236
       Contact: Shaheed Momin President
       Tel: 713-222-2291
       Email: shaheed@globalcoffeecompany.com
       Website: www.javatogo.com
Coffee, cappuccino, slushy, iced tea, juices, soda, water,
paper goods, etc. (As-Ind, estab 2007, empl 4, sales
$1,596,400, cert: State, City, NMSDC)

3540 Sociologie Wines Vintage LLC
       3901 Arlington Highlands Blvd Ste 200
       Arlington, TX 76018
       Contact: Mark Hansen Owner
       Tel: 832-871-7917
       Email: mark@sociologiewine.com
       Website: www.sociologiewine.com
Refreshing blends of delicious fruits & natural ingredients,
Red Berry & Blushing Rose wine. (Woman/AA, estab 2012,
empl 3, sales , cert: NMSDC)

3541 Twang Partners, Ltd.
       6255 WT Montgomery Rd
       San Antonio, TX 78252
       Contact: Patrick Trevino VP Business Dev
       Tel: 603-498-7078
       Email: ptrevino@twang.com
       Website: www.twang.com
Mfr premium-flavored salts, sugars & seasonings. (Hisp,
estab 1986, empl 65, sales $0, cert: State, NMSDC)

Utah

3542 Amboseli Foods, LLC
       320 W 1550 N Ste L
       Layton, UT 84041
       Contact: Sylvia Kapsandoy CEO
       Tel: 801-471-4250
       Email: sylvia@amboselifoods.com
       Website: www.usimplyseason.com
Custom seasoning manufacturing services. (AA, estab
2013, empl 4, sales $250,000, cert: NMSDC)

Virginia

3543 A M King LLC
       13241 Otto Rd
       Woodbridge, VA 22193
       Contact: Adima Aniteye CEO
       Tel: 703-855-9822
       Email: amkingllc@gmail.com
       Website: www.queenvictoriaspunch.com
Mfr & dist fruit punches: The Queen-Grapefruit, Pine-
apple, Apple, Orange, The Duchess— Lemon, Pineapple,
Apple, Orange, The Baroness—Pomegranate, Pineapple,
Lemon, Lime, Agave. (Woman/AA, estab 2012, empl 2,
sales , cert: State)

3544 Grandmas Garden
       7044 Sauvage Ln
       Gainesville, VA 20155
       Contact: Amy Weaver President
       Tel: 571-244-1443
       Email: amyweaver@grandmasgarden.us
       Website: www.grandmasgarden.us
All natural "Sweet" & "Spicy Sweet" gourmet relish:
cabbage, peppers, tomatoes, onions & spices. (Woman,
estab 2011, empl 2, sales , cert: State)

3545 Savaspice LLC
       6247 Glen Wood Loop
       Manassas, VA 20112
       Contact: Lova Mitchell Owner
       Tel: 703-895-4800
       Email: savaspice@gmail.com
       Website: www.savaspice.com
Madagascar vanilla & spices. (Woman/As-Ind, estab
2015, empl 1, sales , cert: State)

3546 Thompson Hospitality Services, LLC
       1741 Business Center Dr Ste 200
       Reston, VA 20190
       Contact: Genevieve Stona VP Joint Ventures
       Tel: 703-964-5500
       Email: gstona@thompsonhospitality.com
       Website: www.thompsonhospitality.com
Contract foodservice management, vending & facilities
maintenance. (AA, estab , empl , sales $73,000,000, cert:
NMSDC)

3547 Kylie B's Pastry Case LLC
       4114 B Place NW, Ste 100
       Auburn, WA 98001
       Contact: Sabrina Bacungan Chief Marketing Officer
       Tel: 253-217-6131
       Email: sabrina@kyliebbakery.com
       Website: www.kyliebbakery.com
Hand-made traditional shortbread. (Minority, Woman,
estab 2016, empl 4, sales , cert: WBENC)

3548 Lanier's Fine Candies
       5710 S Bangor St
       Seattle, WA 98178
       Contact: Herman Lanier CEO
       Tel: 206-723-6465
       Email: herman@laniersfinecandies.com
       Website: www.laniersfinecandies.com
Brittle candies: almond, cashew, peanut, pecan & macad-
amia, hand dipped in dark & milk chocolate. (AA, estab
2013, empl 2, sales , cert: NMSDC)

3549 Lynnae's Gourmet Pickles LLC
       3024 S Mullen #F
       Tacoma, WA 98466
       Contact: Lynnae Schneller President
       Tel: 253-226-2370
       Email: lynnae@lynnaesgourmetpickles.com
       Website: www.lynnaesgourmetpickles.com
Mfr all natural, high quality pickles with unique flavor
combinations. (Woman, estab 2011, empl 3, sales
$285,000, cert: State)

3550 Fair Oaks Farms, LLC
       7600 95th St
       Pleasant Prairie, WI 53158
       Contact: Michael Thompson Natl Acct Sales Mgr
       Tel: 262-947-0320
       Email: mthompson@osigroup.com
       Website: www.fairoaksfarms.com
Dist meats. (AA, estab 1985, empl 260, sales $0, cert:
NMSDC)

3551 Jeneil Biotech, Inc.
       400 N Dekora Woods Blvd
       Saukville, WI 53080
       Contact: Stephen Beaver Sales
       Tel: 262-268-6815
       Email: s.beaver@jeneilbiotech.com
       Website: www.jeneilbiotech.com
Mfr natural dairy flavors in pastes & powders, natural
flavor aroma chemicals, soymilk powder, soy-cream
cheese, fermentation, enzymolysis & distillation. (As-Ind,
estab 1998, empl 43, sales $17,000,000, cert: NMSDC)

3552 Nanland LLC
       5959 N Shore Acres Rd
       New Franken, WI 54229
       Contact: Nan Bush President
       Tel: 920-562-9822
       Email: nan@nanlandllc.com
       Website: www.nanlandllc.com
Provides premium, single origin, organic coffee, 100%
Arabica coffees from Peru, Nicaragua, Sumatra and
Colombia packaged in 12 or 42 single serve cup boxes.
(Woman, estab 2016, empl 2, sales , cert: WBENC)

DIR

DIVERSITYINFORMATION**RESOURCES**

Publications from Diversity Information Resources

2023 National Minority and Women-Owned Business Directory - 54th Edition

A unique resource listing over 10,000 nationally certified Minority and Women-Owned Businesses. Data is organized by Category and State; helpful keyword index included. Identifies: Company Name, Address, Contact, Capabilities, Website, Email, Ownership Type, Certifications, Revenue, Number of Employees, etc.

$215.00

A ROAD MAP TO THE SUPPLIER DIVERSITY INDUSTRY
The Business of Supplier Diversity: A Handbook of Essential Contacts and Information for Navigating the Industry - 9th Edition

This comprehensive easy-to-use resource is written for both corporate supplier diversity/ procurement professionals and diverse-owned suppliers (Minority, Women, Veteran, Service-disabled Veteran, 8a, LGBT and HUBZone).

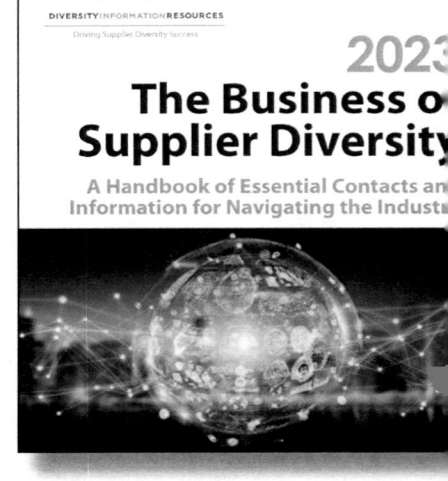

The Business of Supplier Diversity, available in print and as an e-book, combines "who-to-call" with "where-to-look". It combines a detailed contact list of over 1,500 supplier diversity and procurement contacts working at major corporations, government agencies, large non-profit organizations and educational institutions with essential supplier diversity industry information regarding certification, legislation, SBA programs, national councils, international trends and more.

A vital resource for any professional doing business that involves the supplier diversity industry.

$175.00

FURNISHINGS

Manufacturers, distributors or importers of furniture for office and home. Also floor and window coverings, light fixtures, household and kitchen accessories such as wastebaskets, planters, dishes, vases, brooms, dustpans, etc. (See also GIFTWARE, ARTS & CRAFTS and OFFICE SUPPLIES categories. NAICS Code 42

Alabama

3553 E.S. Robbins Corp.
      2802 E Avalon Ave
      Muscle Shoals, AL 35661
      Contact: Bonnie Donato Channel Marketing Mgr
      Tel: 256-248-2494
      Email: badonato@esrobbins.com
      Website: www.esrchairmats.com
Dist office products & furnishings. Mfr polymer products. (Woman, estab 1967, empl 187, sales , cert: WBENC)

Arkansas

3554 Burris Inc.
      113 S Arkansas Ave
      Russellville, AR 72801
      Contact: President
      Tel: 479-968-4888
      Email:
      Website: www.burrisinc.com
Office supplies & office furniture, panel systems, custom millwork, office layout & design. (Woman, estab 1953, empl 15, sales $3,374,600, cert: WBENC)

Arizona

3555 Corporate Interior System
      3311 E Broadway Rd, Ste A
      Phoenix, AZ 85040
      Contact: Lisa K Johnson President
      Tel: 602-304-0100
      Email: ljohnson@cisinphx.com
      Website: www.cisinphx.com
Office Furniture Dealership, modular and system furniture and accessories, and installation of office furniture and accessories. (Woman, estab , empl , sales , cert: WBENC)

3556 Dave Scott & Associates, Inc.
      PO Box 22115
      Phoenix, AZ 85028
      Contact: David R Scott Owner
      Tel: 602-971-1600
      Email: dave.scott@davescottassociates.com
      Website: www.davescottassociates.com
Office Furniture: Systems, Case Goods, Seating, Specialty; Health Care Furniture; Benches, receptacles, bike racks, ash urns; Millwork; Cell phone Charging Station Kiosks, Playgrounds, Design/space planning, Installation. (AA, estab 1999, empl 6, sales $1,360,539, cert: State, City, NMSDC)

3557 Elontec
      5502 W Buckeye Rd, Ste 100
      Phoenix, AZ 85043
      Contact: Jessica Chappell Inside Sales Mgr
      Tel: 602-759-5500
      Email: jchappell@elontec.com
      Website: www.elontec.com
Office furniture: cubicles, case goods, private offices, ect. Planning, design, procurement & installation. (Woman, estab 1997, empl 65, sales $5,200,000, cert: State, WBENC)

California

3558 Alternative Office Solutions
      140 San Pedro Ave, Ste 110
      Morgan Hill, CA 95037
      Contact: Kevin Collier Sales Dir
      Tel: 408-776-2036
      Email: kevin@alt-office.com
      Website: www.alt-office.com
Office space planning & installation of remanufactured Herman Miller AO1 and AO2 cubicles. (Woman, estab 1998, empl 19, sales $2,091,446, cert: CPUC)

3559 American Dawn Inc.
      401 W Artesia Blvd
      Compton, CA 90220
      Contact: Mike Maloney Corp Secretary
      Tel: 310-609-3222
      Email: mmaloney@americandawn.com
      Website: www.americandawn.com
Mfr & dist industrial & hospitality items: linens, towels, etc. (Minority, estab 1975, empl 200, sales , cert: NMSDC)

3560 Compact International
      16161 Ventura Blvd, Ste 382
      Encino, CA 91436
      Contact: Robert Paul Mktg/Sales
      Tel: 818-585-1374
      Email: robert.paul@compactintl.com
      Website: www.compactintl.com
Design, mfr & dist commercial furniture, folding chairs & tables. (AA, estab 1998, empl 4, sales $2,050,000, cert: State)

3561 Decor Interior Design
      2937 E 4th St
      Los Angeles, CA 90033
      Contact: Principal
      Tel: 310-289-2186
      Email: info@designsbydecor.com
      Website: www.designsbydecor.com
Interior Design, Custom Furniture, Window Treatments, Project Management, Interior Landscaping. (Woman/AA, estab 1997, empl 28, sales $552,000, cert: State, NMSDC, CPUC, WBENC)

3562 Environments Plus, Inc.
      1700 1st St
      San Fernando, CA 91340
      Contact: Regina Cordell Owner
      Tel: 866-865-8120
      Email: rcordell@epi-usa.com
      Website: www.Environmentsplus.com
Office Furniture Installation, Office Reconfiguration, Office Moves, Office Furniture Liquidation, Furniture Storage, Project Manager, Design Services, Furniture Lifting. (Woman, estab 1992, empl 45, sales $6,500,000,000, cert: CPUC, WBENC)

3563 HSE USA, Inc.
      5709 E 61st St
      Commerce, CA 90040
      Contact: Nelson Yip President
      Tel: 323-278-0888
      Email: nelson.yip@hseusa.com
      Website: www.hseusa.com
We carry a large selection of candles for the food-service and hospitality industries. (As-Pac, estab 2008, empl 10, sales $4,100,000, cert: NMSDC)

3564 Metro Contract Group
      1111 Broadway Ste 1650
      Oakland, CA 94607
      Contact: Dwight Jackson President
      Tel: 510-254-4281
      Email: dwight@metrocontractgroup.com
      Website: www.metrocontractgroup.com
Contract furniture dealer & design firm. (AA, estab 1993, empl 30, sales $3,010,000, cert: State, NMSDC, CPUC)

3565 MikaPak Inc.
      PO Box 4276
      Walnut Creek, CA 94596
      Contact: Helen Ma President
      Tel: 800-579-0880
      Email: helen@mikapak.com
      Website: www.mikapak.com
Sustainable, compostable products from plate wares, utensils, drink cups, food containers to packaging labels using renewable plant base raw materials. (Minority, Woman, estab 1995, empl 1, sales $279,000, cert: NMSDC)

3566 Southwest Country
      17940 Ventura Blvd
      Encino, CA 91316
      Contact: Fred Fuchs Mgr
      Tel: 818-345-3900
      Email: webmaster@swcountry.com
      Website: www.cowboyindian.com
Mfr & dist southwest, western & country furniture, art & accessories. (Minority, Woman, estab 1989, empl 5, sales , cert: State, City)

3567 Systems Source Inc.
      4685 MacArthur Blvd. Ste 100
      Newport Beach, CA 92660
      Contact: Rosemarie Smith CEO
      Tel: 949-852-0920
      Email: bvente@systemsource.com
      Website: www.systemsource.com
Office furniture, modular furniture systems, demountable walls, design, installation, refinishing, reupholstery & service. (Woman, estab 1982, empl 215, sales $164,000,000, cert: CPUC, WBENC)

3568 Uniworld Omniport
      690 Garcia Ave Ste A
      Pittsburg, CA 94565
      Contact: Chris Smead Dir of Operations
      Tel: 925-439-3070
      Email: chris@bbopokertables.com
      Website: www.BBOPokerTables.com
Mfr & dist folding leg & furniture/dining/conference solid wood poker tables. (As-Pac, estab 2006, empl 5, sales $1,302,000, cert: NMSDC)

Colrado

3569 Premier Commercial Interiors, Inc.
      6830 N Broadway, Unit H
      Denver, CO 80221
      Contact: Brenda Jones President
      Tel: 303-466-8575
      Email: brendaj@pciwindowcoverings.com
      Website: www.pciwindowcoverings.com
Furnish & install window treatments (blinds, roller shades etc.) and projection screens. Clean & repair existing window treatments. (Woman, estab 2004, empl 9, sales , cert: WBENC)

3570 Workplace Elements LLC
      2501 Blake St
      Denver, CO 80205
      Contact: Cameron Gilbreath Controller
      Tel: 303-471-4334
      Email: cgilbreath@workplaceelements.com
      Website: www.workplaceelements.com
Office furniture, furniture storage, flooring, carpet, demountable walls, private office furniture. (Woman, estab 2008, empl 60, sales $38,000,000, cert: WBENC)

Connecticut

3571 De Clercq Office Group
      85 Willow St
      New Haven, CT 06511
      Contact: Deborah Hopewell Declercq President
      Tel: 203-230-9380
      Email: deb@dog-office.com
      Website: www.dog-office.com
Furniture related consulting services, pre-owned furniture & furniture rescue. (Woman, estab 2001, empl 6, sales $11,311,190, cert: WBENC)

3572 People Places and Spaces, LLC
      225 Asylum St
      Hartford, CT 06103
      Contact: Mark Nisbett CEO
      Tel: 860-386-8600
      Email: markn@pps-ct.com
      Website: www.pps-ct.com
Commercial office furniture, adaptable workspaces, and architectural interiors. (AA, estab 2018, empl 3, sales $8,280,210, cert: State, NMSDC)

3573 Workspace Consulting Group, LLC
      2777 Summer St, 2nd Fl
      Stamford, CT 06902
      Contact: Paulina Ribadeneyra Owner
      Tel: 203-548-0305
      Email: paulina@workspacecg.com
      Website: www.workspacecg.com
Office furniture and related consulting services. (Minority, Woman, estab 2010, empl 4, sales $1,591,348, cert: NMSDC)

Delaware

3574   Corporate Interiors, Inc.
       223 Lisa Dr
       New Castle, DE 19720
       Contact: Janice Leone President
       Tel: 302-345-7342
       Email: jleone@corporate-interiors.com
       Website: www.corporate-interiors.com
Sell and install office products. Manufacture & refabricate
office furniture. Installation, reconfiguration & move
services. (Woman, estab 1985, empl 189, sales
$66,461,274, cert: WBENC)

Florida

3575   Above the Sill
       745 C Shamrock Blvd
       Venice, FL 34293
       Contact: Phillip Barone VP Sales & Mktg
       Tel: 941-492-3101
       Email: phil@abovethesill.net
       Website: www.abovethesill.net
Cubicle Curtains and track fabrication and installation,
vertical blinds, roller shades, solar shades, mini blinds, faux
wood blinds, solar panels, shutters, venetian blinds, etc.
(Woman, estab 2004, empl 4, sales , cert: State)

3576   Berwin, Inc.
       3501 Commerce Pkwy
       Miramar, FL 33025
       Contact: Nancy Wolfe A/R Specialist
       Tel: 954-499-6677
       Email: nancy.wolfe@jcwhite.com
       Website: www.jcwhite.com
Design, dist, install & service office furniture, walls &
floors. (Woman, estab 1978, empl 103, sales $43,000,000,
cert: State, WBENC)

3577   Cadence Keen Innovations d/b/a CKI Solutions
       1645 Palm Beach Lakes Blvd #210
       West Palm Beach, FL 33401
       Contact: Gregg Saxton
       Tel: 561-249-2219
       Email: gregg.s@ckisolutions.us
       Website: www.ckisolutions.us
Bed doubling systems, mattress & pillow protectors,
mattress protection systems, disposable luggage protection systems. (Woman, estab 1996, empl 6, sales
$2,211,409, cert: NWBOC)

3578   Furniture Installation Solution Inc
       4740 NW 15th Ave Ste D
       Fort Lauderdale, FL 33309
       Contact: Donovan Williams Operations Mgr
       Tel: 954-638-2432
       Email: info@myfis.biz
       Website: www.myfis.biz
Install, reconfigure & relocate panel (cubicle) system &
case good furniture. (AA, estab 2008, empl 10, sales
$2,400,000, cert: NMSDC)

3579   HNM Enterprises, LLC
       1902 Cypress Lake Dr
       Orlando, FL 32837
       Contact: Juan Barney Business Devel Mgr
       Tel: 407-472-7575
       Email: jbarney@gohnm.com
       Website: www.gohnm.com
Dist & install furniture supplies, furniture, fixtures &
equipment. (AA, estab 2004, empl 27, sales $16,900,000,
cert: NMSDC)

Georgia

3580   Corporate Environments of GA, Inc.
       1636 Northeast Expressway
       Atlanta, GA 30329
       Contact: Sr Acct Mgr
       Tel: 404-679-8999
       Email: rstandard@ceofga.com
       Website: www.corporateenvironments.com
Dist office furniture. (Woman, estab 1973, empl 37, sales
$47,200,000, cert: WBENC)

3581   Nance Carpet & Rug Inc.
       201 Nance Road
       Calhoun, GA 30701
       Contact: Trenna Smith Natl Accounts Specialist
       Tel: 706-629-7731
       Email: trenna.smith@nancecarpet.com
       Website: www.nancefloors.com
Dist area rugs, carpet remnants, carpet by the roll,
carpet tiles & carpet base. (Woman, estab 1972, empl
300, sales $19,000,000, cert: WBENC)

3582   Table Decor International Inc.
       2748 S Cobb Industrial Blvd
       Smyrna, GA 30082
       Contact: Lynn Wells President
       Tel: 770-432-1156
       Email: tdi@tabledecor.com
       Website: www.tabledecor.com
Design & mfr specialty table lighting & unique center-
pieces & table accessory items. (Woman, estab 1984,
empl 5, sales $750,000, cert: WBENC)

3583   Zig Zag Inc.
       4300 Westpark Dr, SW
       Atlanta, GA 30336
       Contact: Gokul Nair CEO
       Tel: 347-558-6767
       Email: gokul@zzincorporation.com
       Website: www.zzincorporation.com
Mfr patio cushions, rugs, door mats & general safety
items. (As-Ind, estab 2008, empl 10, sales $16,000,000,
cert: NMSDC)

Illinois

3584   Corporate Concepts, Inc.
       500 Waters Edge, Ste 200
       Lombard, IL 60148
       Contact: Janet Szyszko Project Mgr
       Tel: 630-691-8800
       Email: jszyszko@corpconc.com
       Website: www.corpconc.com
Design services, space planning, and specifications, chair
re-upholstery, furniture standards programs and
financing consultation. (Woman, estab 1983, empl 55,
sales $54,000,000, cert: WBENC)

3585   Phoenix Woodworking Corporation
       PO Box 459
       Woodstock, IL 60098
       Contact: Sandra Pierce President
       Tel: 815-338-9338
       Email: spierce@phoenixwoodworking.com
       Website: www.phoenixwoodworking.com
Custom & commercial cabinetry & casework, reception
centers, filing cabinets, wooden lockers & millwork,
custom desks & wooden store fixtures. (Woman, estab
1996, empl 10, sales , cert: State, WBENC)

3586   Resource One
321 E Adams
Springfield, IL 62701
Contact: Cynthia Davis President
Tel: 217-753-5742
Email: cdavis@resourceoneoffice.com
Website: www.resourceoneoffice.com
Dist office furniture, carpet, wallcovering, window treatments, refurbishment services, furniture, space-planning & interior design, furniture installation. (Woman, estab 1987, empl 22, sales $8,000,000, cert: State, WBENC)

Indiana

3587   Commercial Office Environments Inc.
7301 Zionsville Road
Indianapolis, IN 46268
Contact: James Bednarski Acct Exec
Tel: 317-876-9200
Email: james@coeindy.com
Website: www.coeindy.com
Furniture & storage equipment, design, install furniture & storage solutions. (Woman, estab 1989, empl 29, sales $13,000,000, cert: State)

3588   Lapsley Inc.
1002 E Rudisill Blvd
Fort Wayne, IN 46806
Contact: Donita Mudd President
Tel: 260-745-3265
Email: dmudd@lapsleyinc.com
Website: www.lapsleyinc.com
Furnish & install window treatments: blinds, shades, draperies, manual or motorized, projection screens, cubicle curtains & cubicle tracks. (Woman/AA, estab 2003, empl 4, sales $140,000, cert: State, 8(a))

3589   Office and Business Resources LLC
244 McConnell Dr
New Albany, IN 47150
Contact: Kahy Brown President
Tel: 502-333-8907
Email: kbrown@officeandbusinessresources.com
Website: www.officeandbusinessresources.com
Office furniture assembly & installation, furniture systems (cubicles), office relocations & interoffice relocations, space planning & design. (Woman, estab 2012, empl 4, sales , cert: NWBOC)

3590   TLS by Design, LLC
10737 Sand Key Circle
Indianapolis, IN 46256
Contact: Jeff Day Dir
Tel: 765-683-1971
Email: sales@tlsbydesign.com
Website: www.tlsbydesign.com
Mfr custom furniture. (Woman, estab 2002, empl 12, sales $780,000, cert: State, WBENC)

Kentucky

3591   Munson Business Interiors
2307 River Rd
Louisville, KY 40206
Contact: Susan Lewis Acct Rep
Tel: 502-588-7368
Email: susan@mbifurniture.com
Website: www.mbifurniture.com
Office furnishings, space planning, design, delivery, installation, project management, warehousing & inventory reports, repair & refinishing, reupholstery panels, chairs & custom furniture. (Woman, estab 1986, empl 21, sales $6,376,824, cert: NWBOC)

Louisiana

3592   Contract Furniture Group, LLC
201 James Dr E
Saint Rose, LA 70087
Contact: Julio Rodriguez President
Tel: 504-412-0080
Email: julio@contractfurnituregroup.com
Website: www.contractfurnituregroup.com
Design & install furniture systems modular furniture, freestanding casegoods, conference room furniture, break rooms, training rooms, healthcare furniture & high density filing systems. (Hisp, estab 2000, empl 20, sales , cert: NMSDC)

Massachusetts

3593   McElroy Scenic Services LLC
PO Box 145
Ashley Falls, MA 01222
Contact: President
Tel: 413-229-9920
Email: info@mcelroyscenic.com
Website: www.mcelroyscenic.com
Decor fabrication, set design & fabrication, custom displays, architectural models, exterior & interior signage, custom corporate furniture & staging, museum exhibits. (Woman, estab 1999, empl 7, sales $1,200,000, cert: State, WBENC)

3594   Wholesale Distribution
PO Box 1497
Cotuit, MA 02635
Contact: Linda Sharp President
Tel: 800-345-4027
Email: linda@facilitiesfurniture.com
Website: www.facilitiesfurniture.com
Dist folding, stack, office & classroom chairs, training & computer, cafeteria & classroom tables & desks, restroom fixtures & components, lockers, flags, communication boards. (Woman, estab 2001, empl 3, sales , cert: State, WBENC)

Maryland

3595   Contemporary Business Interiors, LLC
1369 D Brass Mill Rd
Belcamp, MD 21017
Contact: Christi Member
Tel: 410-272-5559
Email: info@cbillc.com
Website: www.cbillc.com
Dist business furniture: office, hospitality, bar & restaurant, medical, school, space planning & design, project mgmt, installation. (Woman, estab 2006, empl 3, sales $1,300,000, cert: State)

3596 Washington Office Interiors
12354 Carroll Ave
Rockville, MD 20852
Contact: Barbara Barry Prinicpal
Tel: 301-770-4327
Email: bbarry@washingtonoffice.com
Website: www.washingtonoffice.com
Full service contract furniture dealership. (Woman, estab 2005, empl 12, sales $11,300,000, cert: State)

Michigan

3597 Airea
3000 Town Center Ste 80
Southfield, MI 48075
Contact: Yulanda Trout Exec Asst
Tel: 248-226-3971
Email: ytrout@pistongroup.com
Website: www.aireainc.com
Modular walls & ceiling systems, raised-access flooring, floor covering, furniture & lighting. (AA, estab 1995, empl 28, sales $12,000,000, cert: NMSDC)

3598 Designer Installation Services, Inc.
9685 Harrison St, Ste 200
Romulus, MI 48174
Contact: Robert Corona President
Tel: 313-582-9310
danielle.smith@designerinstallationservicesin.com
Website: www.designerinstallationservicesin.com
Dist commercial office furniture, flooring & ancillary items, installation, warehousing, asset management, delivery. (Hisp, estab 1979, empl 25, sales $4,000,000, cert: NMSDC)

3599 Hercules & Hercules, Inc.
19055 W Davison
Detroit, MI 48223
Contact: Belinda Jefferson President
Tel: 313-933-6669
Email: bjefferson@herculesandherculesinc.com
Website: www.herculesandherculesinc.com
Dist maintenance supplies & equip, office supplies & equip, office furniture. (AA, estab , empl , sales $7,000,000, cert: NMSDC)

3600 ISCG
612 N Main St
Royal Oak, MI 48067
Contact: Stephanie Chyz President
Tel: 248-399-1600
Email: schyz@iscginc.com
Website: www.iscginc.com
Contract furnishings (Haworth Preferred Dealer) & Floorcoverings, Facility Asset Management, Project & Move Management, Union & Non. (Woman, estab 1976, empl 21, sales $14,000,000, cert: WBENC)

3601 Remco Storage Systems, Inc.
2328 Livernois Road Ste 1070
Troy, MI 48083
Contact: Donna Tamburo-Wilson President
Tel: 248-362-0500
Email: donna@remcoequipment.com
Website: www.remcoequipment.com
Storage & retrieval systems: vertical lifts & carousels, electric lateral filing systems, movable shelving, rotary files, cabinets, records mgmt systems, color coded labels, custom filing systems, folders & indexes. (Woman, estab 1976, empl 7, sales $2,000,000, cert: WBENC)

Minnesota

3602 AIM Global Trading, LLC
11209 Commerce Dr N
Champlin, MN 55316
Contact: Mahtab Khan CEO
Tel: - -
Email: linenbay3@gmail.com
Website: www.aimglobaltrading.com
Mfr & dist 100% cotton terry towel & Polyester/Cotton Blended Bath Towels, Hand Towels, Wash Cloths, Bath Mats, Pool Towels, & Bar Mops. (As-Pac, estab 2014, empl 3, sales , cert: NMSDC)

3603 Ideal Commercial Interiors LLC
740 Portland Ave. Ste 1418
Minneapolis, MN 55414
Contact: Rick Harris CEO
Tel: 612-759-0955
Email: rick@icinteriors.net
Website: www.icinteriors.net
Office furniture, flooring, fixtures, design, space planning, installation, delivery & project management. (AA, estab 2012, empl 3, sales , cert: NMSDC)

3604 Kelly Computer Supply
2042 Wooddale Dr Ste 250
Woodbury, MN 55125
Contact: Bob Kelly President
Tel: 651-773-1109
Email: bobkelly@kellyrest.com
Website: www.kellyrest.com
Ergonomic equip; mfr "KellyRest" computer products: wrist & foot rests, adjustable copy holders, keyboard drawers & articulating keyboard trays; workstations. (Nat Ame, estab 1983, empl 10, sales , cert: State, NMSDC, CPUC)

3605 R and L Woodcraft, Inc
823 Industrial Park Dr SE
Lonsdale, MN 55046
Contact: Randall Rivers Business Devel
Tel: 507-744-2318
Email: randall@randlwoodcraft.com
Website: www.randlwoodcraft.com
Mfr commercial millwork & casework: cabinets, countertops, workstations, service counters, point of service counters, tables, booths, upholstered seating, running trim, trash recepticles, lockers & toilet partitions. (Woman, estab 1986, empl 22, sales $3,600,000, cert: WBENC)

Mississippi

3606 Commercial Interiors, Inc.
4277 Espy Ave
Long Beach, MS 39560
Contact: President
Tel: 228-452-9540
Email: donna@cidesigns.net
Website: www.cidesigns.net
Commercial FF&E contractor. (Woman, estab 1990, empl 3, sales $555,647, cert: State)

3607 Durfold Corporation
102 Upton Dr
Jackson, MS 11111
Contact: Dawn Warren
Tel: 601-922-4144
Email: dwarren@durfold.com
Website: www.durfold.com
Mfr upholstered healthcare furniture: sleeper chairs &
sofas, trendelenberg recliners, incliners, rocking chairs,
gliders, bariatric seating, patient & guest seating, lounge
seating, lobby furniture & ganged & tandem seating.
(Woman, estab , empl , sales $3,200,000, cert: WBENC)

North Carolina

3608 DARRAN Furniture Industries, Inc.
2402 Shore St
High Point, NC 27263
Contact: Jennifer Hollingsworth President
Tel: 800-334-7891
Email: jlhollingsworth@darran.com
Website: www.darran.com
Mfr high quality, mid-market wood desk collections,
conferencing solutions, reception stations & seating.
(Woman, estab 1977, empl 195, sales $25,559,279, cert:
WBENC)

3609 Excell Home Fashions Inc.
8511 Chatsworth Lane
Waxhaw, NC 28173
Contact: Acct Mgr
Tel: 704-564-2722
Email: bsinger@croscill-living.com
Website: www.croscill-living.com
Mfr Shower Liners, Shower Hooks, Shower Rods & Tub
Mats. (Woman, estab 1932, empl 211, sales $200,000,000,
cert: WBENC, NWBOC)

3610 Forms & Supply, Inc.
PO Box 563953
Charlotte, NC 28256
Contact: Amy Pyles Sr Sales Administrator
Tel: 704-598-8971
Email: amy.pyles@formsandsupply.com
Website: www.fsioffice.com
Furniture, office supplies. (Woman, estab 1962, empl 260,
sales $80,000,000, cert: State, WBENC)

3611 Stuart Page Company, Inc.
1801 Stallings Rd
Matthews, NC 28104
Contact: Kimberly Page President
Tel: 704-545-0695
Email: kim@stuartpagecompany.com
Website: www.stuartpagecompany.com
Furnish and install commercial doors, toilet partitions,
toilet accessories, lockers, wall protection, shelving, flags,
flagpoles, etc. (Woman, estab 1991, empl 24, sales
$37,000,000, cert: State, City)

New Jersey

3612 Business Environments
2001 Route 46 Ste 510
Parsippany, NJ 07054
Contact: John Gardner President
Tel: 973-335-7700
Email: jgardner@be-furniture.com
Website: www.befurniture.com
Office furniture dealer: Cad, project management,
installation & refinishing. (Woman/AA, estab 2005, empl
18, sales $10,000,000, cert: State, WBENC)

3613 Concepts Office Furnishings, Inc.
280 N Midland Ave, Bldg J Unit 204
Saddle Brook, NJ 07663
Contact: Aida DeSoto President
Tel: 201-727-9110
Email: adesoto@conceptsoffice.com
Website: www.conceptsoffice.com
Contract office furniture & equipment, project manage-
ment, furniture installations & re-configurations,
refinishing & reupholstery. (Minority, Woman, estab
1973, empl 15, sales $3,200,000, cert: City)

3614 Contemporary Motives, Inc
445 US-202
Flemington, NJ 08822
Contact: Debbie Hill Dir of Business Dev
Tel: 908-806-4461
Email: dhill@interiormotives.net
Website: www.interiormotives.net
Commercial Interior Design Services, Planning, Design
and installation
Furniture, Fixtures, Decorative Drapery, Decorative
Lighting,
Office Furniture, Office Dividers, Office Desks, Chairs,
Conference Room, Break Room, Carpet, Flooring, Tile,
Cabinets. (Woman, estab 2005, empl 11, sales
$7,200,000, cert: WBENC)

3615 Global Installation Resources LLC
18 Robert St
Clifton, NJ 07014
Contact: Krista Korinis President
Tel: 973-494-9680
Email: kkorinis@gi-resources.com
Website: www.gi-resources.com
Installation services: office furniture, demountable walls,
signage & laboratory case work installations & project
management services. (Woman, estab 2002, empl 10,
sales $1,345,540, cert: State, WBENC)

3616 Image Office Environments, LLC
1122 Route 22 W
Mountainside, NJ 07092
Contact: Tricia Patricco President
Tel: 908-301-0074
Email: tpatricco@image-office.com
Website: www.image-office.com
Interior constructions, raised flooring, moveable walls &
furniture. (Woman, estab 2005, empl 6, sales
$9,000,000, cert: State, WBENC)

3617 JC Office Consultants, LLC
      242 Union Ave
      Somerville, NJ 08876
      Contact: Jackie Orlando CEO
      Tel: 908-842-2150
      Email: jackie@jcofficeconsultants.com
      Website: www.jcofficeconsultants.com
Dist office furniture, installation & reconfiguration
services. Space planning & CAD design. (Minority, Woman,
estab 2009, empl 5, sales $1,900,000, cert: WBENC)

3618 Vaswani Inc
      75 Carter Dr
      Edison, NJ 08817
      Contact: Eric Clark Business Devel
      Tel: 877-376-4425
      Email: eric@vaswaniinc.com
      Website: www.vaswaniinc.com
Provide custom fixtures and furniture. (As-Ind, estab 1993,
empl 120, sales $36,000,000, cert: NMSDC)

New York

3619 A.F.C. Industries, Inc.
      1316 133rd Pl, Ste 2
      Colege Point, NY 11356
      Contact: Donna Tannacore Govt Sales Acct Exec
      Tel: 718-747-0237
      Email: dtannacore@afcindustries.com
      Website: www.afcindustries.com
Ergonomic technical furniture & workstations: mission-
critical control centers, data centers, medical, labs,
military, etc. CPU rack systems & display mount hardware.
(Woman, estab 1994, empl 95, sales $1,010,000, cert:
State)

3620 Alianza Services LLC
      74 N Broadway 2nd Fl S
      Nyack, NY 10960
      Contact: Dawn Cannon VP
      Tel: 845-675-7337
      Email: dcannon@alianzacorp.com
      Website: www.alianzacorp.com
Dist furniture, budgeting, refurbishing, storage & asset
management, rental solutions, service & repair. (Hisp,
estab 2006, empl 6, sales $5,100,000, cert: NMSDC)

3621 Architectural Flooring Resources, Inc.
      135 W 27th St
      New York, NY 10001
      Contact: Mercedes Montano Project Coord
      Tel: 212-290-0200
      Email: mercedes@afrny.com
      Website: www.afrny.com
Carpet, carpet tile, vinyl, composition tile, wood (varies by
species), cork, linoleum & specialty flooring. (Minority,
Woman, estab 1993, empl 19, sales $7,896,224, cert: City,
NMSDC, WBENC)

3622 County Draperies, Inc.
      64 Genung St
      Middletown, NY 10940
      Contact: President
      Tel: 845-342-9009
      Email: info@drape.com
      Website: www.drape.com
Mfr window & bedding products, hardware measuring &
installtion. (Woman, estab 1987, empl 50, sales
$4,520,000, cert: WBENC)

3623 Davies Office Refurbishing, Inc.
      40 Loudonville Rd
      Albany, NY 12204
      Contact: Evelyn Davies Owner
      Tel: 518-449-2040
      Email: evelyndavies@daviesoffice.com
      Website: www.daviesoffice.com
Remanufacture office furniture & office furniture asset
mgmt. (Woman, estab 1975, empl 165, sales , cert:
WBENC)

3624 Kittredge Equipment Company
      17 Pearce Ave
      Tonawanda, NY 14405
      Contact: Jeffrey Mackey COO
      Tel: 800-423-7082
      Email: jmackey@kittredgeequipment.com
      Website: www.kittredgeequipment.com
Dist kitchen equipment, smallwares, tabletop supplies,
warewashing furniture. (Woman, estab , empl 93, sales
$54,500,000, cert: City, WBENC)

3625 Meadows Office Supply Co., Inc.
      885 3rd Ave, 29th Fl
      New York, NY 10022
      Contact: Dina Radoncic Exec VP
      Tel: 212-741-0333
      Email: mofwbe@meadowsoffice.com
      Website: www.meadowsofficeinteriors.com
Dist Haworth furniture products. (Woman, estab 1967,
empl 76, sales $81,500,000, cert: City, WBENC)

3626 Waldner's Business Environments, Inc.
      125 Route 110
      Farmingdale, NY 11735
      Contact: Meredith Stern President
      Tel: 631-844-9342
      Email: mstern@waldners.com
      Website: www.waldners.com
Dist & install office furniture. (Woman, estab 1939, empl
107, sales $92,800,000, cert: City, WBENC)

Ohio

3627 APG Office Furnishings
      PO Box 631850
      Cincinnati, OH 45263
      Contact: Connie L. Goins President
      Tel: 513-239-6814
      Email: cgoins@apgde.com
      Website: www.apgof.com
Dist office furniture, space planning, design, project
management services & product solutions. (Woman,
estab 1969, empl 1, sales $50,000,000, cert: State,
WBENC)

3628 Budget Office Interiors LLC
      1771 E. 30th St
      Cleveland, OH 44114
      Contact: President
      Tel: 216-566-1540
      Email:
      Website: www.budgetofficeinteriorsllc.com
New furniture, used furniture & refinished furniture:
cubicles, workstations, space planning, desks, seating,
conference rooms, training rooms, break rooms, home
offices, telemarketing areas, reception areas, lateral &
vertical filing. (Woman, estab 2005, empl 4, sales
$292,229, cert: City)

3629   Clara I. Brown Interiors, Inc. (CIBI)
5305 Courtney Pl
Columbus, OH 43235
Contact: Clara I. Brown President
Tel: 614-224-9180
Email: jim@cibiinc.com
Website: www.cibiinc.com
Office Furniture, Carpet & Hard Flooring, Carpet Cleaning, Re-upholstery, Mill Work, De-mountable Walls, Wall Coverings, Window Treatments, Interior Design/Space Planning, Furniture Moves, Warehousing. (Minority, Woman, estab 1993, empl 12, sales $3,828,904, cert: NMSDC)

3630   Interior Services Incorporated dba Enriching Spaces
1360 Kemper Meadow Dr
Cincinnati, OH 45240
Contact: Dawn Schwartzman President
Tel: 513-851-0933
Email: dawn@enrichingspaces.com
Website: www.enrichingspaces.com
Office Furniture, Healthcare Furniture, School & University Furniture, Art & Accessories, Carpet Tile, Signage, Interior Design, Branding, Ergonomic Accessories, Ergonomic Chairs, Desks, Workstations, Conference Room. (Woman, estab 1982, empl , sales , cert: WBENC)

3631   King Business Interiors
1400 Goodale Blvd, Ste 102
Columbus, OH 43212
Contact: Darla King Owner
Tel: 614-430-0020
Email: darlaking@kbiinc.com
Website: www.kbiinc.com
Office furniture dealer. (Woman, estab 1998, empl , sales , cert: WBENC)

3632   Master Manufacturing Co, Inc.
9200 Inman Ave
Cleveland, OH 44105
Contact: Bob Ptacek VP Sales
Tel: 800-323-5513
Email: bptacek@mastermfgco.com
Website: www.mastermfgco.com
Mfr furniture casters & self-stick wheels; felt pads, surface protectors, wobble stoppers; furniture movers; door stops; ergonomic support cushions & wire mgmt channels & grommets. (Woman, estab 1951, empl , sales , cert: CPUC, WBENC)

3633   River City Furniture, LLC
6454 Centre Park Dr
West Chester, OH 45069
Contact: Carl Satterwhite President
Tel: 513-612-7303
Email: amy.andrews@thercfgroup.com
Website: www.thercfgroup.com
Design office layout, new furniture, installation, move management & asset management. (AA, estab 2003, empl 100, sales $43,900,000, cert: City, NMSDC)

3634   Vocon Partners, LLC
3142 Prospect Ave
Cleveland, OH 44115
Contact: Deb Donley President
Tel: 216-588-0800
Email: deb.donley@vocon.com
Website: www.vocon.com
Furniture coordination, graphic design. (Woman, estab 1987, empl 180, sales $30,000,000, cert: WBENC)

3635   Williams Interior Designs, Inc
4449 Easton Way, 2nd Floor
Columbus, OH 43219
Contact: Carolyn Williams Francis CEO
Tel: 614-418-7250
Email: carolyn@williamsinteriordesigns.com
Website: www.williamsinteriordesigns.com
Interior design, office furniture, office supplies & window treatments. (Woman/AA, estab 1985, empl 4, sales $2,000,000, cert: NMSDC)

Oregon

3636   Carriage Works, Inc.
1877 Mallard Ln
Klamath Falls, OR 97601
Contact: Barbara Evensizer President
Tel: 541-882-0700
Email: info@carriageworks.com
Website: www.carriageworks.com
Mfr carts: food, espresso, kiosks, beverage, bar, vending & display items. (Minority, Woman, estab 1971, empl 30, sales $4,000,000, cert: State)

Pennsylvania

3637   A. Pomerantz & Co. / Pomerantz Acquisition Corp.
123 S Broad St Ste 1260
Philadelphia, PA 19109
Contact: Elisa V. Feola VP Marketing
Tel: 215-408-2173
Email: feola@pomerantz.com
Website: www.pomerantz.com
Develop productive and efficient workplace environments. (AA, estab , empl 40, sales $37,700,000, cert: NMSDC)

3638   Alpha Office Supplies, Inc.
4950 Parkside Ave Ste 500
Philadelphia, PA 19131
Contact: Chester Riddick CEO
Tel: 215-226-2690
Email: chet.riddick@alphaos.com
Website: www.alphaos.com
Dist office furniture & supplies, paper, computers & accessories; desktop delivery, installation, space planning & project mgmt. (AA, estab 1985, empl 29, sales $26,000,000, cert: NMSDC)

3639   Corporate Facilities of New Jersey, LLC
2129 Chestnut St
Philadelphia, PA 19103
Contact: Amanda Chevalier Principal
Tel: 215-279-9999
Email: achevalier@cfinj-knoll.com
Website: www.cfi-knoll.com
Office furniture. (Minority, Woman, estab 2004, empl 26, sales , cert: NMSDC, WBENC)

3640   Peerless Wall and Window Coverings, Inc.
3490 William Penn Hwy
Pittsburgh, PA 15235
Contact: Bob Cherry Mgr
Tel: 412-823-7660
Email: sales@peerlesswallpaperandblinds.com
Website: www.peerlesswallpaperandblinds.com
Dist & install wallcoverings, window coverings, blinds, shades, shutters & draperies. (Woman, estab 1993, empl 6, sales $761,857, cert: State)

3641 Telrose Corporation
       3801 Ridge Ave
       Philadelphia, PA 19132
       Contact: CEO
       Tel: 215-229-0500
       Email: support@telrosecorp.com
       Website: www.telrosecorp.com
Dist office supplies, equipment & furniture. (AA, estab 1995, empl 19, sales $8,000,000, cert: City, NMSDC)

Puerto Rico

3642 Integrated Design Solutions
       90 Carr 165, Ste 405
       Guaynabo, PR 00968
       Contact: Marlen Diaz VP
       Tel: 787-706-0201
       Email: mdiaz@ids-pr.com
       Website: www.ids-pr.com
Office furniture dealer. (Hisp, estab 1999, empl 17, sales $5,800,000, cert: NMSDC)

South Carolina

3643 Skutchi Designs Inc.
       171 Gardner Lacy Rd
       Myrtle Beach, SC 29579
       Contact: Jeff Little Ecommerce
       Tel: 843-410-0605
       Email: jeff@skutchi.com
       Website: www.skutchi.com
Mfr Office Furniture, Panels Systems, Wall Systems, Conference Tables, Acrylic Screens, Acoustical products, and Desks. We space plan, design and install nationwide. (Woman, estab 2005, empl 30, sales $5,000,000, cert: WBENC)

Texas

3644 B&H Total Office Solutions
       120 Sam Bass Ridge Rd
       Southlake, TX 76092
       Contact: Jeannie Norris President
       Tel: 817-430-8345
       Email: jeannie@bhofficesolutions.com
       Website: www.bhofficesolutions.com
New & used Furniture, refurbished cubicles, Space Planning, Furniture Moves. (Woman, estab 2006, empl 6, sales $650,000, cert: State)

3645 Business Interiors
       1111 Valley View
       Irving, TX 75061
       Contact: Sally Smith President
       Tel: 817-858-2000
       Email: ssmith@businessinteriors.com
       Website: www.businessinteriors.com
Office furniture sales & services: rental, used sales, installation, reconnfiguration, repair, touch up, carpet sales & installation, relocations, storage, design & space planning. (Woman, estab 1970, empl 140, sales $51,517,000, cert: WBENC)

3646 Facilities Connection, Inc.
       240 E Sunset Rd
       El Paso, TX 79922
       Contact: Patty Holland Branch CEO
       Tel: 915-833-8303
       Email: phbranch@facilitiesconnection.com
       Website: www.facilitiesconnection.com
Interior design, furniture layout, space planning, project management, office furniture installation, reconfiguration, relocation, interiors, assets maintenance. (Minority, Woman, estab 1987, empl 25, sales $27,000,000, cert: State)

3647 Facility Interiors Inc.
       PO Box 201828
       Dallas, TX 75320
       Contact: Charles Griggsby President
       Tel: 713-963-0678
       Email: charlesg@fiinc.com
       Website: www.facilityinteriors.com
Furniture installation, design, project management, move services, reconfigurations services. (Woman/AA, estab , empl , sales $80,000,000, cert: State, NMSDC, WBENC)

3648 Intelligent Interiors, Inc.
       16837 Addison Rd Ste 500
       Addison, TX 75001
       Contact: Mindy Casas President
       Tel: 214-239-9886
       Email: mcasas@intelligentinteriors.net
       Website: www.intelligentinteriors.net
Contract office furniture, design, installation, repair refurbishing, carpet, window covering. (Minority, Woman, estab 1996, empl 12, sales $800,000, cert: State, NMSDC)

3649 Modular Installation Services, Inc.
       8606 Wall St Ste 150
       Austin, TX 78754
       Contact: Monica Gould VP
       Tel: 512-835-7706
       Email: mpgould@modularinstall.com
       Website: www.modularinstall.com
Commercial office furniture installation & reconfiguration services. (Hisp, estab 1996, empl 30, sales $1,300,000, cert: State)

3650 Neutral Posture, Inc.
       3904 N. Texas Ave
       Bryan, TX 77803
       Contact: Rebecca Boenigk CEO
       Tel: 979-778-0502
       Email: rboenigk@np-us.com
       Website: www.neutralposture.com
Mfr ergonomic, multipurpose, industrial seating & accessories. (Woman, estab 1989, empl 65, sales , cert: WBENC, 8(a), SDB)

3651 Quiltcraft Industries
       1230 E Ledbetter Dr
       Dallas, TX 75216
       Contact: Janet Pearson President
       Tel: 214-376-1841
       Email: jpearson@quiltcraft.com
       Website: www.quiltcraft.com
Mfr bedspreads, draperies, cubicle curtains, cubicle track, shower curtains, sheets, mattress pads, pillows, hardware, etc. (Minority, Woman, estab , empl , sales , cert: WBENC)

Virginia

3652 Alpha Stone Solutions
2251 Dabney Rd, Ste H
Richmond, VA 23230
Contact: Shion Fenty Acct Exec
Tel: 804-622-2068
Email: shion@alphastone.us
Website: www.alphastone.us
Dist granite products, furniture, fixtures & equipment for hotel industry. (Minority, Woman, estab 2000, empl 20, sales $2,800,000, cert: State)

3653 Finial Showcase, Inc.
720 Third St
Vinton, VA 24179
Contact: Whitney Snyder Corp Acct Mgr
Tel: 540-982-3593
Email: sales@finialshowcase.com
Website: www.finialshowcase.com
Dist accent tables, plant stands, quilt racks, coat racks, dvd/cd cabinets, stacking tables, umbrella stands, waste baskets, desks for home office, magazine racks, luggage racks, mirrors and wall decor, vases, decorative accessories, table lamps. (Woman, estab 1982, empl 5, sales $650,000, cert: WBENC)

3654 Votum Enterprises, LLC
3530 Post Office Rd Ste 5104
Midlothian, VA 23112
Contact: Mark Walton Dir Business Dev
Tel: 804-317-9660
Email: mark@votument.com
Website: www.votument.com
Provides cubicle, modular & systems furniture & related services, installations, reconfigurations, disassembly, moving & storage. (AA, estab 2009, empl 3, sales $257,000, cert: State, NMSDC)

Washington

3655 Apex Facility Resources, Inc.
20219 87th Ave S
Kent, WA 98031
Contact: John Williams Dir of Sales
Tel: 206-686-3357
Email: john@apexfacility.com
Website: www.apexfacility.com
Dist new & used office furnitures: liquidation, installation, project coordination, signage. (Woman, estab 1994, empl 35, sales , cert: WBENC)

3656 Home and Travel Solutions, LLC dba BedVoyage
18915 142nd Ave NE, Ste 230
Woodinville, WA 98072
Contact: CEO
Tel: 425-949-8216
Email: info@bedvoyage.com
Website: www.bedvoyage.com
Mfr eco-luxury bamboo bed linens, towels & blankets. (Woman, estab 2008, empl 7, sales $1,200,000, cert: NWBOC)

Wisconsin

3657 Laacke & Joys LLC
3205 N 124th St
Brookfield, WI 53005
Contact: Joel Vento VP Sales & Mktg
Tel: 800-892-5563
Email: jsvento@conceptseating.com
Website: www.conceptseating.com
Mfr 24/7 intensive use ergonomic office chairs used for dispatch, security, control rooms, surveillance. (Woman, estab , empl 100, sales $9,000,000, cert: WBENC)

GIFTWARES, ARTS & CRAFTS
Manufacture, distribute and import merchandise as well as cooperatives which produce jewelry, carvings, baskets, greeting cards, etc. NAICS Code 42

California

3658 The Corporate Gift Service, Inc.
4120 W Burbank Blvd
Burbank, CA 91505
Contact: Lydia Eltringham Accounting Dept
Tel: 818-845-9500
Email: accounting@corpgiftservice.com
Website: www.thecorporategiftservice.com
Custom Gift Baskets, Embroidered Corporate Apparel, Corp Gifts, Promotional Prods/Advertising Specialties. (Woman, estab 1990, empl 7, sales $1,600,000, cert: WBENC)

Florida

3659 Floral Group, Inc.
2291 NW 82 Ave
Miami, FL 33122
Contact: Dornett Mullings President
Tel: 305-477-5008
Email: dornett@floralgroup.net
Website: www.floralgroup.net
Fresh floral products, foam arrangements, vase arrangements, hand-tied bouquets, rose bouquets. (Woman/AA, estab 2003, empl 12, sales $990,000, cert: NMSDC)

Georgia

3660 Barazzo, LLC
2221 Peachtree Rd NE Ste D357
Atlanta, GA 30309
Contact: Quiana Lloyd Member
Tel: 888-716-5785
Email: quiana@barazzo.com
Website: www.barazzo.com
Custom gift & accessory solutions, corporate brand identity & marketing solutions. (Woman/AA, estab 2009, empl , sales , cert: State, NMSDC, SDB)

3661 Gratitude Goodies, LLC
433 Canton Rd Ste 315
Cumming, GA 30040
Contact: Diane Campbell Owner
Tel: 770-886-9598
Email: diane@gratitudegoodies.com
Website: www.GratitudeGoodies.com
Gift basket with chocolate, savory & gift items. (Woman, estab 2009, empl 4, sales , cert: WBENC, NWBOC)

Illinois

3662 Brilliant Gifts LLC
1605 S Waukegan Rd
Waukegan, IL 60085
Contact: Nick Phillips Dir of Business Dev
Tel: 773-885-3532
Email: nick@brilliantmade.com
Website: www.brilliantmade.com
Gifts, branded merchandise and custom products. (Woman, estab 2015, empl 100, sales $25,000,000, cert: WBENC)

3663 Corporate Artworks, Ltd.
1300 Remington Rd, Ste H
Schaumburg, IL 60173
Contact: Denise Rippinger President
Tel: 847-843-3636
Email: corporateartwork@aol.com
Website: www.corporateartworks.com
Artwork sales & consulting. (Woman, estab 1988, empl 12, sales , cert: WBENC)

3664 Packed with Purpose
2000 W Addison St, Ste 127
Chicago, IL 60618
Contact: Kim Wasney VP Sales & Business Dev
Tel: 844-797-4438
Email: gifts@packedwithpurpose.gifts
Website: www.packedwithpurpose.gifts/
Corporate gifts. (Woman, estab 2016, empl 17, sales $8,697,260, cert: WBENC)

3665 Pearl's Girl Sweet Treats
15222 S LaGrange
Orland Park, IL 60463
Contact: Jacqueline Jackson Owner
Tel: 708-460-3960
Email: gojackiejackson@aol.com
Website: www.kilwins.com
Corporate gift baskets: gourmet caramel apples, handmade fudge, carmel corn, brittles, fine chocolates, dipped strawberries & confectins & 32 flavors of koshers icecream. (Woman/AA, estab 2007, empl 16, sales , cert: NMSDC)

3666 Planet Canit, LLC
843 Kimball Rd
Highland Park, IL 60035
Contact: Virginia Price
Tel: 847-433-1619
Email: vprice@planetcanit.com
Website: www.planetcanit.com
Custom decorative tin-ware packaging. (Woman, estab 2000, empl 1, sales , cert: WBENC)

3667 Vosges, Ltd.
2211 N Elston St Ste 203
Chicago, IL 60614
Contact: Lesley Nosal Dir Corp Sales
Tel: 773-388-5560
Email: vosges@vosgeschocolate.com
Website: www.vosgeschocolate.com
Corporate gifting & events, unique chocolate creations are infused with exotic spices, herbs, roots, flowers, fruits & nuts. (Woman, estab 1997, empl 85, sales $14,000,000, cert: City, WBENC)

Indiana

3668 Trans-Plants Inc.
1260 S Senate Ave
Indianapolis, IN 46225
Contact: Christine Ernst President
Tel: 317-972-6760
Email: admin@trans-plantsindy.com
Website: www.transplants-indy.com
Interior plants & maintenance, design & installation. Floral arrangements, gift baskets, corporate & individual gifts. (Woman, estab 1986, empl 10, sales $360,786, cert: City)

Kentucky

3669 Wall Street Greetings, LLC
3265 Pincakrd Pike
Versailles, KY 40383
Contact: Susan Rice Natl Accounts Specialist
Tel: 859-873-0877
Email: april@wallstreetgreetings.com
Website: www.wallstreetgreetings.com
Corporate greeting cards. (Woman, estab 1992, empl 33, sales $2,628,121, cert: WBENC)

Massachusetts

3670 Madison Floral, Inc.
63B Innerbelt Rd
Somerville, MA 02143
Contact: Edison Chae President
Tel: 781-648-2000
Email: edison@madisonfloral.com
Website: www.madisonfloral.com
Floral design services. (As-Pac, estab 2000, empl 5, sales $180,000, cert: State)

Maryland

3671 Copiosity, LLC
8230 Georgia Ave, 2nd Fl
Silver Spring, MD 20910
Contact: Dianne Harrison Principal
Tel: 301-608-9102
Email: dcharrison@copiosityllc.com
Website: www.copiositygreetings.com
Greeting products: holiday gift wrapping paper; holiday greeting cards; graphic & decorative wall decals; etc. (Woman/AA, estab 2010, empl 2, sales , cert: NMSDC)

Michigan

3672 Mahogani Collections LLC
35323 Plymouth Rd
Livonia, MI 48150
Contact: Phyllis Mitchell Co-Owner
Tel: 313-627-3513
Email: mahoganicollections@aol.com
Website: www.mahoganicollections.com
Mahogani Collections merchandise consists of necklaces, rings, earrings and bracelets for women and men. (AA, estab 2016, empl 2, sales , cert: WBENC)

Minnesota

3673 Schaaf Floral
6554 University Ave NE
Minneapolis, MN 55432
Contact: Marcia Schaaf Owner
Tel: 763-571-4600
Email: flowers@schaaffloral.com
Website: www.schaaffloral.com
Floral arrangement, gifts, etc. (Woman, estab 1970, empl 13, sales $806,748, cert: WBENC)

New Jersey

3674 The Dessert Ladies
266 Main Ave
Stirling, NJ 07980
Contact: Lindsay Smith Owner
Tel: 908-340-7321
Email: lindsay.smith@bienscc.com
Website: www.dessertladies.com/
Custom edible gifts, hand-decorated, branded chocolate products and baked goods. (Woman, estab 2010, empl 10, sales $3,000,000, cert: WBENC)

New York

3675 Chocolate Promises, Inc.
PO Box 694
Merrick, NY 11566
Contact: Zakalik Cindy President
Tel: 516-299-6400
Email: cindy@chocolatepromises.com
Website: www.chocolatepromises.com
Personalized chocolate with edible images. Print full color logo, picture, design and/or special message directly on delicious chocolate coins, lollipops, Belgian truffles , etc. (Woman, estab 2012, empl 2, sales , cert: State, City, WBENC)

Ohio

3676 Independence Flowers & Gifts
6495 Brecksville Rd
Independence, OH 44131
Contact: Laura Gmitro Owner
Tel: 216-524-2800
Email: indyflowers@yahoo.com
Website: www.independenceflorist.com
Florist & gift shop, fruit baskets, gourmet baskets, custom baskets, floral arrangements & gifts. (Woman, estab 2009, empl 4, sales $280,000, cert: City)

3677 K&M International, Inc.
1955 Midway Dr
Twinsburg, OH 44087
Contact: Prathap Shankar Sales
Tel: 800-800-9678
Email: ksprathap@kmtoys.com
Website: www.wildrepublic.com
Mfr & dist Plush, Toys, Corporate Gifts and other distinctive gift products. (Woman/As-Ind, estab 1979, empl 130, sales , cert: NMSDC)

3678 Uniquely Lisa Designs dba Our Favorite Things Boutique
12730 Larchmere Blvd
Shaker Heights, OH 44120
Contact: Lisa McGuthry CEO
Tel: 216-536-7928
Email: info@ourfavoritethingscle.com
Website: www.ourfavoritethingscle.com
Fine gift items and body products. (AA, estab 2019, empl 5, sales $139,000, cert: NMSDC)

Texas

3679 Dessert Gallery Bakery & Cafe
PO Box 981034
Houston, TX 77098
Contact: Sara Brook Founder/CEO
Tel: 713-960-4400
Email: sara@dessertgallery.com
Website: www.dessertgallery.com
Custom photo & logo cookies & cakes, catering- box lunches, office birthday cakes, corporate gifts. (Woman, estab 1995, empl 35, sales , cert: WBENC)

Washington

3680 Gifts by Design, Inc.
66 S Hanford St Ste 100
Seattle, WA 98134
Contact: Andy Sroufe Acct Exec
Tel: 206-286-6688
Email: andy@giftsbydesign.net
Website: www.giftsbydesign.net
Dist, wearables, logo items, awards, baskets. (Woman, estab 1988, empl 11, sales $2,950,000, cert: WBENC)

HARDWARE & TOOLS DIST.
Distribute hardware: screw machine products, plumbing supplies, safety apparel, ladders, etc. (See also HYDRAULIC & COMPRESSED AIR EQUIPMENT and INDUSTRIAL EQUIPMENT & SUPPLIES). NAICS Code 42

Alabama

3681 Ram Tool & Supply Co., Inc.
4500 5th Ave South Bldg A
Birmingham, AL 35222
Contact: Ashley Cato Accounts Receivable Rep
Tel: 205-599-7085
Email: ashley.cato@ramtool.com
Website: www.ram-tool.com
Dist construction material, supplies & tools. (Woman, estab 1985, empl 804, sales , cert: WBENC)

Arizona

3682 Machine Works, LLC
3832 E Illini St
Phoenix, AZ 85040
Contact: carter Trisha Sales/Office Mgr
Tel: 602-426-1035
Email: trisha.c@mworkllc.com
Website: www.machineworksllc.com
Dist aerospace components & assemblies. (As-Pac, estab 1997, empl 12, sales $900,000, cert: NMSDC)

California

3683 ACF Components & Fasteners, Inc.
31012 Huntwood Ave
Hayward, CA 94544
Contact: Bob Henriquez Exec VP
Tel: 510-487-2100
Email: bobh@acfcom.com
Website: www.acfcom.com
Dist industrial fasteners, electronic component hardware, wire, industrial supplies, vmi, kitting, kits, fastener plating, fastener patching, fuses, screws, bolts, terminals. (As-Pac, estab 1976, empl 50, sales $13,000,000, cert: CPUC)

3684 B&B Socket Products, Inc.
1919 Nancita Cir
Placenta, CA 92870
Contact: Robert Huke GM
Tel: 714-985-4360
Email: rchuke@bbsocket.com
Website: www.bbsocket.com
Dist fasteners, hardware & electronic components. (Woman, estab 1976, empl 17, sales , cert: WBENC)

3685 Cordova Bolt, Inc.
5601 Dolly Ave
Buena Park, CA 90621
Contact: Moses E. Cordova President
Tel: 714-739-7500
Email: info@cordovabolt.com
Website: www.cordovabolt.com
Dist nuts, bolts, screws, washers, anchors, A325, A490, GR 2-5-8-L9, etc. (Hisp, estab 1975, empl 34, sales , cert: NMSDC, CPUC)

3686 Mackenzie Aircraft Parts, Inc.
1400 Decision St
Vista, CA 92081
Contact: Toni Mackenzie President
Tel: 760-727-3775
Email: toni@macairparts.com
Website: www.macairparts.com
Dist hardware, screws, nuts, bolts, rivets, washers, bearings & electrical parts. (Woman, estab 1979, empl 11, sales $2,500,000, cert: NWBOC)

3687 Satori Seal, Inc.
8455 Utica Ave
Rancho Cucamonga, CA 91730
Contact: Anne Houlihan President
Tel: 909-987-8234
Email: anne@satoriseal.com
Website: www.satoriseal.com
Dist o-rings, seals, custom molded seals, rotary shaft seals, PTFE seal tape, worm drive hose clamps, gaskets, washers, die cut gaskets, lathe cut gaskets. (Woman, estab 1971, empl 8, sales $2,749,793, cert: WBENC)

3688 STX, Inc. DBA Alta Industries
418 Aviation Blvd, Ste E
Santa Rosa, CA 95403
Contact:
Tel: 800-788-0302
Email: info@altaindustries.com
Website: www.altaindustries.com
Mfr & dist protective knee pads & elbow pads, tool belts for industrial, construction, safety, military & tactical markets. (Woman, estab , empl , sales $3,800,000, cert: NWBOC)

3689 Vampire Tools, Inc.
47 Peters Canyon Rd
Irvine, CA 92606
Contact: Farooqui Ali Admin
Tel: 949-449-5724
Email: ali@vampiretools.com
Website: www.vampiretools.com
Unique pliers for rusted, damaged, stripped screws/nuts/bolts extraction. (Minority, Woman, estab 2010, empl 7, sales $400,000, cert: NMSDC, CPUC)

3690 Widespread Industrial Supplies, Inc.
1220 S Boyle Ave
Los Angeles, CA 90023
Contact: Josh Dorfman President
Tel: 310-793-7315
Email: josh.dorfman@widespreadind.com
Website: www.widespreadind.com
Dist industrial supplies: fasteners, cutting tools, electrical, welding, chemical & safety related supplies, hand & power tools. (Woman, estab 2002, empl 4, sales $820,341, cert: State, City)

Florida

3691 Arrowhead Global, LLC
22033 US 19 N
Clearwater, FL 33765
Contact: Anthony Terranova Sales Mgr
Tel: 727-497-7340
Email: tony@arrowheadglobal.com
Website: www.arrowheadglobal.com
Dist aerospace, military & commercial fasteners, hardware, connectors, electronic components, aircraft parts, adhesives & information technology products & services. (Nat Ame, estab 2013, empl 10, sales $3,100,000, cert: NMSDC, 8(a))

3692 Consolidated Cordage Corp Inc.
      1707 Avenida Del Sol
      Boca Raton, FL 33432
      Contact: Mike Perry Sales Mgr
      Tel: 561-347-7247
      Email: info@consolidatedcordage.com
      Website: www.consolidatedcordage.com
Dist rope, cord, pull cord, twine, elastic shockcord, fall
protection safety equip, multe tape, riggings, hoistings,
etc. (Woman, estab 1993, empl 8, sales , cert: State,
WBENC, NWBOC)

3693 Limitless Investigative Solutions, L.L.C.
      11160 Lost Creek Terrace Ste 205
      Bradenton, FL 34211
      Contact: Miguel Caraballo President
      Tel: 678-458-8538
      Email: miguel@limitlessinv.com
      Website: www.limitlessinv.com
Solid carbide end mills, drills, reamers, burrs, inserts &
specials, in house research & development, custom tool
design for various applications, ools simulation software.
(Hisp, estab 2017, empl 1, sales , cert: State)

3694 The Bernd Group Inc.
      1251 Pinehurst Rd
      Dunedin, FL 34698
      Contact: Pilar Bernd President
      Tel: 727-733-0122
      Email: businessdevelopment@berndgroup.com
      Website: www.berndgroup.com
Material handling equip, safety products, hand & power
tools, pumps & compressors, motors, generators, electrical
hardware, batteries, lighting fixtures, lockers, bins,
shelving, lab equip. (Minority, Woman, estab 1992, empl
66, sales , cert: NMSDC)

3695 Tropic Fasteners LLC
      255 Semoran Comerce Pl
      Apopka, FL 32703
      Contact: Judy Watson President
      Tel: 407-703-1582
      Email: judy@tropicfast.com
      Website: www.tropicfast.com
Dist fastener products. (Woman, estab 1995, empl 50,
sales , cert: WBENC)

Georgia

3696 Stallings Industries Inc.
      869 Pioneer Rd
      Jasper, GA 30143
      Contact: Trevor Wells Minority OppAdmin/Area Mgr
      Tel: 706-253-0440
      Email: trevor@stallingsindustries.com
      Website: www.stallingsindustries.com
Dist Garlock gaskets, packings, expansion joints & oil seals,
PPC mechanical seals & Teadit, aerosol fillers, "O" rings.
(Woman, estab 1988, empl 6, sales , cert: WBENC)

Illinois

3697 Alin Machining Co, Inc. dba Power Plant Services
      3131 W Soffel Ave
      Melrose Park, IL 60160
      Contact: Sonia Gandhi Sales Team Lead
      Tel: 708-345-8600
      Email: sonia@ppsvcs.com
      Website: www.ppsvcs.com
Dist fasteners, studs, nuts, washers, bolts & pins, turbine
valve parts, stems, discs & bushings, turbine blade mfg,
turbine seals & packing, erosion shields. (As-Ind, estab
1998, empl 142, sales $42,000,000, cert: NMSDC)

3698 Hacha Products Corporation
      801 North Main St 60187
      Wheaton, IL 60187
      Contact: Kimberly Meek CEO
      Tel: 630-347-6093
      Email: kmeek@hachaproducts.com
      Website: www.hachaproducts.com
Wire management devices: cable ties, wire nuts, clamps,
nuts, bolts, fasteners, shrink tubing. (Minority, Woman,
estab 2015, empl 2, sales $750,000, cert: NMSDC,
WBENC)

Indiana

3699 Impex International Inc.
      7114 Innovation Blvd
      Fort Wayne, IN 46818
      Contact: Nagin Shah President
      Tel: 260-489-3030
      Email: nshah@impexint.com
      Website: www.impexint.com
Dist fasteners. (As-Ind, estab 1985, empl 6, sales , cert:
NMSDC)

3700 Powell Tool Supply Co., Inc.
      1338 Mishawaka Ave
      South Bend, IN 46615
      Contact: Cari Eaton CEO
      Tel: 574-289-4811
      Email: ceaton@powelltool.com
      Website: www.powelltool.com
Dist industrial supplies: cutting tools, abrasives, chemi-
cals, MRO supplies, material handling, janitorial, etc.
(Woman, estab 1948, empl 20, sales $5,500,000, cert:
WBENC)

3701 Quest Safety Products, Inc.
      5720 W Minnesota St
      Indianapolis, IN 46241
      Contact: Sudhansu (Sam) Yadav President
      Tel: 317-594-4500
      Email: ar@questsafety.com
      Website: www.QuestSafety.com
Dist safety products. (As-Pac, estab 1997, empl 34, sales
$13,600,000, cert: NMSDC)

3702 Thompson Distribution Company
      2225 N College Ave
      Indianapolis, IN 46205
      Contact: John Thompson President
      Tel: 317-923-2581
      Email: johnt@thomdist.com
      Website: www.thomdist.com
Dist pipes, valves, pumps, fittings; plumbing, electrical &
industrial supplies; fasteners, stainless steel. (AA, estab
2001, empl 14, sales , cert: State, NMSDC)

Kentucky

3703 Com Serv LLC
10201 Bunsen Way
Louisville, KY 40299
Contact: Shiva Dhanapal President
Tel: 502-553-1770
Email: sdhanapal@component-supply.com
Website: www.component-supply.com
Specialty screws & customs hardware, engineering special fasteners, tubing, plastic parts, plastic injection molds, packaging supply, jigs for paint line applications, jigs & fixtures, returnable containers/totes, stamping. (As-Ind, estab 2000, empl 7, sales $5,435,800, cert: NMSDC)

3704 Sandy Valley Fasteners, LLC
528 Broadway St
Paintsville, KY 41240
Contact: Christy Henry-Gregory CEO
Tel: 606-788-0222
Email: christy@sandyvalleyfasteners.com
Website: www.sandyvalleyfasteners.com
Dist commercial & aerospace fasteners & supplies: AN, MS, NAS washers, nuts, bolts, screws, rivets, nutplates, electrical connectors & backshells, tools, raw materials, fittings, tubing, bushings, etc. (Woman, estab 1999, empl 13, sales , cert: WBENC)

Louisiana

3705 Best Bolt & Nut Corp.
2726 Lexington Ave
Kenner, LA 70062
Contact: Jason Mangiaracina GM
Tel: 504-469-3585
Email: jason@bestboltandnut.com
Website: www.bestboltandnut.com
Dist hardware. (Hisp, estab 1988, empl 20, sales , cert: NMSDC)

3706 Lightning Bolt and Supply
10626 S Choctaw Dr
Baton Rouge, LA 70815
Contact: Wesley Valverde VP Business Dev
Tel: 225-272-6200
Email: sharon@lightningboltandsupply.com
Website: www.lightningboltandsupply.com
Dist fasteners, nuts, bolts, hex bolts, lock nuts, lock washers, flat washers, fender washers, clips, retaining rings, hex head bolts, socket head cap screws, buttons, lug nuts, studs, double end studs, latches. (Woman, estab 1994, empl 15, sales , cert: WBENC)

Maryland

3707 Absolute Supply and Services, LLC
427 Council Bluffs Ct
Lusby, MD 20657
Contact: Paula Tilghman President
Tel: 301-440-6056
Email: ptilghman@absolutesupplyandservices.com
Website: www.absolutesupplyandservices.com
Dist HVAC, plumbing equipment & replacement parts. (Woman/AA, estab 2007, empl 1, sales $161,000, cert: WBENC)

3708 American General Contractor Inc.
1 Research Ct, Ste 450
Rockville, MD 20850
Contact: Linward Hope VP
Tel: 301-202-4511
Email: americangeneralmd@yahoo.com
Website: www.americangeneralmd.com
Dist construction materials, thermostats, tools, cement, sheet rock, led lights, hardware nails, screws, toilets, tile, all flooring, hand towels, paper towels. (Minority, Woman, estab 2012, empl 2, sales $107,000, cert: State)

3709 Atlantic Hardware Supply
8389 Ardwick Ardmore Rd
Hyattsville, MD 20785
Contact: Jon Gray VP
Tel: 240-249-6047
Email: jgray@atlantic-supply.com
Website: www.atlantic-supply.com
Dist hardware. (Woman, estab 2009, empl 6, sales , cert: State)

3710 B & B Lighting Supply, Inc.
PO Box 68084
Baltimore, MD 21215
Contact: Sharon Bradford CEO
Tel: 410-523-7300
Email: sbradford@bnblightingsupply.com
Website: www.bnblightingsupply.com
Dist lamps, relamping & energy mgmt, const mgmt & svcs, provision & professional. (Woman/AA, estab 1994, empl 2, sales $525,000, cert: State)

Michigan

3711 Ewie Co., Inc.
1099 Highland Dr
Ann Arbor, MI 48108
Contact: Shoki Mullick Dir of diversity
Tel: 734-971-6265
Email: shoki.mullick@ewie.com
Website: www.ewie.com
Dist cutting tools, abrasives, special tools, chemical/lubricants. (Minority, estab 1981, empl 253, sales $122,000,000, cert: NMSDC)

3712 Extreme Tooling LLC
48750 Structural Dr
Chesterfield, MI 48051
Contact: Kurt Schill President
Tel: 586-232-3618
Email: kschill@extremetooling.com
Website: www.extremetooling.com
Dist metal removal & industrial supplies, milling, drilling & industrial products. (Woman, estab 2003, empl 5, sales $3,683,821, cert: WBENC)

3713 Marshall Sales Inc.
14359 Meyers Rd
Detroit, MI 48227
Contact: Brian Tupiak Acct Mgr
Tel: 313-491-1700
Email: btupiak@marshallsales.com
Website: www.marshallsales.com
Fasteners & fastener installation, tooling. (Woman, estab 1958, empl 9, sales $7,000,000, cert: State, WBENC)

3714 Materials Management Services Inc.
      13691 Girardin St
      Detroit, MI 48212
      Contact: Jack Long President
      Tel: 313-365-1290
      Email: jlong@mms-inc.com
      Website: www.mms-inc.com
Mfr & dist industrial work gloves of fabric & leather in a
variety of styles. Also dist tools, tape, coolant, etc. (AA,
estab 1994, empl 11, sales , cert: NMSDC)

3715 Mer Wil Industries, Inc.
      328 S Saginaw St, Ste 902
      Flint, MI 48502
      Contact: Deborah Love Sales Rep
      Tel: 810-239-0600
      Email: mwilliams@merwil.com
      Website: www.merwil.com
Dist hardware & building supplies. (AA, estab 1983, empl
2, sales , cert: State)

3716 National Industrial Supply Co.
      1201 Rochester Rd
      Troy, MI 48083
      Contact: Kathryn Harper President
      Tel: 248-588-1828
      Email: kathybrett@nischain.com
      Website: www.nischain.com
Dist chain, wire rope, nylons, hardware supplies, etc.
(Minority, Woman, estab 1981, empl 20, sales $2,000,000,
cert: NMSDC, WBENC)

3717 New Eagle, LLC
      3588 Plymouth Rd, Ste 271
      Ann Arbor, MI 48105
      Contact: Mickey Swortzel CEO
      Tel: 734-929-4557
      Email: mswortzel@neweagle.net
      Website: www.neweagle.net
Controls system solutions, tools, products & services.
(Woman, estab 2008, empl 25, sales $3,874,600, cert:
WBENC)

3718 Northern Industrial Products Corp.
      20380 Cornillie Dr
      Roseville, MI 48066
      Contact: Andrew Wilson General Mgr
      Tel: 586-293-9544
      Email: awilson@nipcorp.com
      Website: www.nipcorp.com
Dist industrial fasteners, tools, rack & shelving, etc. (AA,
estab 1976, empl 17, sales $5,000,000, cert: NMSDC)

3719 Production Services Management, Inc.
      1255 Beach Court
      Saline, MI 48176
      Contact: Michael Henry Dir - Global Diversity and
      Sustainability
      Tel: 917-690-0179
      Email: mhenry@psmicorp.com
      Website: www.psmicorp.com
Tool Commodity Management, Wholesaler, Integrator, etc.
(As-Ind, estab 2004, empl 400, sales $184,000,000, cert:
NMSDC)

3720 Reggie Mckenzie Industrial Materials, Inc.
      34401 Schoolcraft Rd Ste 200
      Livonia, MI 48150
      Contact: Dan Kapp Office Mgr
      Tel: 734-261-0844
      Email: dkapp@rmimi.com
      Website: www.reggiemckenzieindustrial.com
Dist MRO, Cutting Tools, Abrasives, Industrial Supplies,
Industrial Materials. (AA, estab 2000, empl 3, sales
$6,000,000, cert: NMSDC)

3721 Suburban Bolt and Supply Co.
      27670 Groesbeck
      Roseville, MI 48066
      Contact: Frank Woch Sales
      Tel: 586-775-8900
      Email: defense@suburbanbolt.com
      Website: www.suburbanbolt.com
Fasteners - Socket Products, Bolts, Screws, Pins, NAAMS,
Nuts, Washers, Anchors, Cutting Tools - Drills, Taps,
Counter Bores, Countersinks, Dies, Reamers, End Mills,
Saw Blades, Abrasives- Coated Abrasives, Cut off Wheels,
Flap Wheels and Discs. (Minority, estab 1971, empl 77,
sales $14,004,169, cert: NMSDC)

Minnesota

3722 Bredemus Hardware Co Inc.
      1285 Sylvan St
      St. Paul, MN 55117
      Contact: Betty Bredemus CEO
      Tel: 651-489-6250
      Email: betty@bredemus.com
      Website: www.bredemus.com
Dist hardware, hollow metal doors, frames & wood
doors. (Minority, Woman, estab 1955, empl 29, sales
$5,000,000, cert: State, City)

3723 Wells Technology, Inc.
      4885 Windsor Ct NW
      Bemidji, MN 56601
      Contact: Wendy Knudson VP Contracts/Certs
      Tel: 218-751-1412
      Email: wendy@wellstech.com
      Website: www.wellstech.com
Dist fasteners, brasives, power handtools, hardwares,
paint, varnish & general line industrial supplies. (Nat
Ame, estab 1989, empl 43, sales $132,890,629, cert:
NMSDC, SDB)

Missouri

3724 AMC Industries, LLC
      4251 N Kentucky Ave
      Kansas City, MO 64117
      Contact: Adam French Dir of Sales
      Tel: 816-833-4249
      Email: adam@amc-industries.net
      Website: www.amc-industries.net
Dist pipes, valves, fittings, plumbing fixtures, HVAC
equipment, HVAC accessories, toilet partitions &
washroom accessories. (AA, estab 2001, empl 5, sales
$4,400,000, cert: State, City, NMSDC)

North Carolina

3725 ARTU-USA, Inc.
330 Fields Dr.
Aberdeen, NC 28315
Contact: Beverly Tate-Cooper President
Tel: 910-944-1883
Email: beverly@artu.com
Website: www.artu.com/
Cutting tools, Multi-Purpose Drill Bits, PORC+ Drill Bits, Cobalt Drill Bits, Tungsten Carbide Grit Hole Saws & Saw Blades, SDS Drill Bits, Precision Multi-Purpose Drill Bits & Spline Shanks. (Woman, estab 1989, empl 6, sales $1,636,453, cert: State, CPUC, NWBOC)

3726 C & D Industrial Tools & Supplies Inc.
2415 Penny Road Ste 101
High Point, NC 27265
Contact: Jerry Camp President
Tel: 336-885-6675
Email: jerry@cdi-tools.com
Website: www.cdi-tools.com
Dist cutting tools: drills, end mills, reamers, taps & dies, precision tools, etc. (AA, estab 1988, empl 4, sales $2,500,000, cert: NMSDC)

New Jersey

3727 Edwards & West, Inc. dba Divspec
605 Springfield Rd
Kenilworth, NJ 07033
Contact: Doug Burke NC Sales Mgr
Tel: - -
Email: dougb@divspec.com
Website: www.divspec.com
Dist threaded rod, strut, strut fittings, and fasteners. (Woman, estab 1980, empl 12, sales $5,913,389, cert: WBENC)

3728 Fastenation, Inc.
120 Bright Rd Unit 2
Clifton, NJ 07012
Contact: Stephanie Cherepinsky Sales Rep
Tel: 973-591-1277
Email: stephanie@fastenation.com
Website: www.fastenation.com
Distributor & Converter of VELCRO(R) Brand Fasteners (Die-Cutting, Packaging, Printing, etc.) (Woman, estab 1997, empl , sales $9,000,000, cert: WBENC)

3729 MF Supply Corp.
164 Garibaldi Ave
Lodi, NJ 07644
Contact: Robin Lieberman President
Tel: 973-777-5411
Email: robin@mfsupply.com
Website: www.mfsupply.com
Dist fasteners, Stainless Steel, Inserts & Keenserts, Socket products, Standoffs & Spacers & Mil-Spec fasteners. (Woman, estab 1974, empl 5, sales $823,000, cert: State)

New York

3730 Global Connection Co. of America, Inc.
150-123 Powells Cove Blvd
Whitestone, NY 11357
Contact: Grace King President
Tel: 718-767-5168
Email: gk@madeinchina.net
Website: www.glocoamerica.com
Dist hardware & tools. (Minority, Woman, estab 1992, empl 3, sales $2,107,046, cert: State, NMSDC)

3731 Henssgen Hardware Corporation
PO Box 2078
Queensbury, NY 12804
Contact: Rachel Novak President
Tel: 518-793-3593
Email: rachel@henssgenhardware.com
Website: www.henssgenhardware.com
Sources rigging hardware, Snap Hooks, Pulleys (both Fixed Eye and Swivel with Single Sheave and Double Sheave), Quick Links, Shackles, Wire Rope Clips, Drop Forged Clevis Grab & Clevis Slip Hooks. (Woman, estab 2000, empl 3, sales $548,000, cert: WBENC)

3732 NY Plumbing Wholesale & Supply, Inc.
933 Columbus Ave
New York, NY 10025
Contact: Derek Price President
Tel: 212-678-4900
Email: derek@nyps1.com
Website: www.nyps1.com
Dist plumbing fittings, fixtures, pipe, tools & accessories. (AA, estab 2009, empl 23, sales , cert: City)

3733 South Atlantic Marine Services
342 Cold Spring Rd
Syosset, NY 11791
Contact: Linda Allen President
Tel: 516-449-9000
Email: southatlantic15@yahoo.com
Website: www.southatlantic-services.com
Dist lubricants, greases, additives, hardware, bolts fasteners, tools, fittings, safety products, ropes, chains, hoses, twine, clamps rivet, cables, pumps, valves, bearings, tubing, welding supplies, cutting tools. (Woman, estab 2000, empl 2, sales $889,255, cert: State, City)

Ohio

3734 Bain Enterprises, LLC
4650 Allen Road Ste B
Stow, OH 44244
Contact: Owner
Tel: 513-378-4411
Email:
Website: www.bainenterprises.com
Dist Stanley handheld hydraulic & battery operated tools & accessories. (Woman, estab 2006, empl 2, sales $1,700,000, cert: WBENC)

3735   CJ Industrial Supply Inc.
15326 Waterloo Rd
Cleveland, OH 44110
Contact: Tom Frohwerk VP Sales
Tel: 216-481-4448
Email: tom@cjindustrial.com
Website: www.cjindustrial.com
Industrial hardware, Valves Pumps Steel Fabrication, OSHA Products, Plumbing, Electrical, Cutting Tools, Machine Shop Services, Abrasives, Hand Tools, Power Tools, VOC Compliant Chemicals & Paints, Steel. (Woman, estab 1995, empl 8, sales $2,000,000, cert: State, City)

3736   CryoPlus, Inc.
2429 N Millborne Rd
Wooster, OH 44691
Contact: Kathi Bond President
Tel: 330-683-3375
Email: kathicryo@aol.com
Website: www.cryoplus.com
Cutting tools, blades, knives, dies & punches. (Woman, estab 1994, empl 3, sales , cert: NWBOC)

3737   General Factory/ WD Supply
4811 Winton Rd
Cincinnati, OH 45232
Contact: Pat Priko Sales
Tel: 513-681-6300
Email: patp@gfwdsupply.com
Website: www.gfwdsupply.com
Dist MRO, welding, cutting tools, hand tools & safety. (Woman, estab 2007, empl 32, sales $12,500,000, cert: WBENC)

3738   Power Tool & Supply Co., Inc.
3699 Leharps Rd
Youngstown, OH 44515
Contact: Linda Richardson Dir Business Dev
Tel: 330-792-1487
Email: linda@powertoolandsupply.com
Website: www.powertoolandsupply.com
Dist power tools & supplies. (Woman, estab 1961, empl 18, sales , cert: State, WBENC)

3739   Queensgate Hardware & Security, Inc.
1025 Dalton Ave
Cincinnati, OH 45203
Contact: Sarah Back President
Tel: 513-929-0062
Email: sarah@queensgatehardware.com
Website: www.queensgatehardware.com
Dist commercial grade hardware, wood doors & frames, hollow metal doors & frames, access control systems, toilet partitions & accessories. (Woman, estab 2010, empl 3, sales $768,000, cert: WBENC)

3740   River City Building Solutions, LLC
19885 Detroit Rd, Ste 173
Cleveland, OH 44116
Contact: Peggy Powers President
Tel: 216-333-1491
Email: peggy@rivercitybuildingsolutions.com
Website: www.rivercitybuildingsolutions.com
Dist building materials, sustainable materials, paintings & coatings, roofing materials, flooring, HVAC, plumbing materials, electrical / telecommunications wiring. (Woman, estab 2011, empl 2, sales , cert: State, City)

Puerto Rico

3741   Industrial Fittings & Valves
PO Box 2329
Toa Baja, PR 00951
Contact: Jose Merino President
Tel: 787-251-0840
Email: jmerino@infiva.com
Website: www.infiva.com
Dist industrial valves & fittings. (Hisp, estab 1985, empl 30, sales $6,093,000, cert: NMSDC)

South Carolina

3742   GT Industrial LLC Co.
846 Royle Rd
Ladson, SC 29456
Contact: Teresa Gore President
Tel: 843-873-0290
Email: teresag@gtindustrial.net
Website: www.gtindustrial.com/
Dist tools, cert kits, tape, adhesives, dust masks, respirators, marking crayons, flashlights, batteries, light bulbs. (Nat Ame, estab 1998, empl 6, sales $5,111,180, cert: NMSDC)

3743   Janeice Products Co. Inc
1084 Williston Road
Aiken, SC 29803
Contact: Vernal Sanders Mktg Mgr
Tel: 803-652-3025
Email: sales@janeiceproducts.com
Website: www.janeiceproducts.com
Dist MRO products: abrasives, cutting tools, fans, hand tools, hardware, ladders, lawn & garden, material handling equip & safety prods. (AA, estab 1995, empl 7, sales , cert: NMSDC)

Tennessee

3744   D & J Tool Supply, LLC
PO Box 9601
Knoxville, TN 37940
Contact: Deanna Maurer Owner
Tel: 865-546-0744
Email: deanna@djtoolsupply.com
Website: www.djtoolsupply.com
Dist metalworking & fabricating machinery, machine tool accessories, cutting tools, hand & power tools, metalworking fluids, abrasives, safety supplies, welding consumables. (Woman, estab 1999, empl 2, sales $386,641, cert: State)

Texas

3745   Power Tool Service Co., Inc.
3718 Polk St
Houston, TX 77003
Contact: JB Robertson VP
Tel: 713-228-0100
Email: sales@powertoolservice.com
Website: www.powertoolservice.com
Dist, rent & repair tool & equipment, calibration. (Minority, Woman, estab 1969, empl 18, sales , cert: State)

3746 PowerOne and Associates, LLC
      12320 Barker Cypress Rd Ste 600-300
      Cypress, TX 77429
      Contact: Gus Guerrero BDM
      Tel: 713-955-7888
      Email: gus@power-one-usa.com
      Website: www.powerone-usa.com
Dist High Temperature Pipe, Hose & Cable Wraps (Safety),
MRO products, Hand Tools, Personal Safety Equipment
(PSE), Power transmission equipment (Safety Couplings,
Metal Bellows Coupling, Locking assemblies). (Hisp, estab
2008, empl 10, sales , cert: NMSDC)

3747 Powr-Guardian, Inc.
      1607 Falcon Dr, Ste 101
      DeSoto, TX 75115
      Contact: Von Miller President
      Tel: 972-228-9029
      Email: info@powrguardian.com
      Website: www.powrguardian.com
Dist & service batteries. (AA, estab 1988, empl 11, sales
$1,375,000, cert: State)

Virginia

3748 Apollo Energy Components Inc. t/a Apollo Supply
      2711 Lowesville Rd
      Arrington, VA 22922
      Contact: Christine Manley President
      Tel: 434-277-5556
      Email: apollonrg2711@aol.com
      Website: www.apolloenergycomponents.com
Dist fasteners, pipe fittings, valves, high pressure tube
fittings, abrasives, grinding wheels, cutting tools, saw
blades, aerosols. (Woman, estab 2009, empl 3, sales
$122,080, cert: State)

3749 Machine Tools of Virginia, Inc.
      8147 Shady Grove Rd
      Mechanicsville, VA 23111
      Contact: Cindy Waddell President
      Tel: 804-569-6147
      Email: machinetoolsofva@hotmail.com
      Website: www.machinetoolsofvirginia.com
Dist machine tools: lathes & mills, CNC & standard, lathe &
mill accessories, carbide cutting tools, compressors,
grinders, drills, saws & fabrication equipment. (Woman,
estab 2001, empl 4, sales , cert: State)

Washington

3750 The Part Works Inc.
      2900 4th Ave S
      Seattle, WA 98134
      Contact: Oly Welke Sales & Marketing Mgr
      Tel: 206-305-0448
      Email: oly@thepartworks.com
      Website: www.thepartworks.com
Dist plumbing supplies. (Woman, estab 1980, empl 25,
sales $5,500,000, cert: City, WBENC)

HARDWARE & TOOLS MFG.
Manufacture fasteners and other screw machine products. Many manufacture tools and hand tools (See also HYDRAULIC & COMPRESSED AIR EQUIPMENT and INDUSTRIAL EQUIPMENT & SUPPLIES). NAICS Code 42

Arizona

3751   B&T Tool & Engineering Inc.
2618 E Washington St
Phoenix, AZ 85034
Contact: William Meras President
Tel: 602-267-1481
Email: bnttool@aol.com
Website: www.bnttool.us
Mfr & dist precision cutting tools. (Hisp, estab 1992, empl 21, sales $3,701,273, cert: NMSDC)

3752   Special Carbide Tools
3153 E 36th St
Tucson, AZ 85713
Contact: Jerry Gamboa CEO
Tel: 520-624-0007
Email: jerry@specialcarbide.com
Website: www.specialcarbide.com
Mfr special custom carbide cutting tools: standard drills, endmills & reamers. (Hisp, estab 1999, empl 18, sales $2,000,000, cert: NMSDC)

California

3753   Blue Sky Industries
595 Monterey Pass Rd
Monterey Park, CA 91754
Contact: Denis Gagnier Outside Sales Mgr
Tel: 213-620-9950
Email: dgagnier@blueskyindustries.com
Website: www.blueskyindustries.com
Cherry & Monogram blind rivets & blind bolts, Shear Pins & Collars Hi-locks, Standard Aerospace Bolts, Screws, Nuts & Washers, Single & Double Oversize fasteners, Bushings, Bearings, Spacers, & Shims. (As-Pac, estab 1995, empl 52, sales $15,000,000, cert: NMSDC)

3754   D Unique Tools Inc
5744 International
Oakland, CA 94621
Contact: Nanette Hunter President
Tel: 510-569-9961
Email: nanette@universalsquare.com
Website: www.universalsquare.com
Mfr & dist tools. (Woman/AA, estab 1991, empl 4, sales $125,536, cert: NMSDC)

Connecticut

3755   Chapman Manufacturing Company
471 New Haven Rd
Durham, CT 06422
Contact: Jason Camassar VP
Tel: 860-349-9228
Email: jason@chapmanmfg.com
Website: www.chapmanmfg.com
Mfr screwdriver kits. (Woman, estab 1936, empl 13, sales $683,000, cert: CPUC)

Florida

3756   AAW Products Inc.
825 Brickell Bay Dr Ste 246
Miami, FL 33131
Contact: Andre Woolery CEO
Tel: 305-330-6863
Email: andre@magnogrip.com
Website: www.magnogrip.com
Mfr magnetic work gear "MagnoGrip." MagnoGrip: wristbands, hammer holders, tool pouches & tool belts. (AA, estab 2005, empl 3, sales $4,500,000, cert: NMSDC)

3757   Limitless Investigative Solutions, L.L.C.
11160 Lost Creek Terrace Ste 205
Bradenton, FL 34211
Contact: Miguel Caraballo President
Tel: 678-458-8538
Email: miguel@limitlessinv.com
Website: www.limitlessinv.com
Solid carbide end mills, drills, reamers, burrs, inserts & specials, in house research & development, custom tool design for various applications, ools simulation software. (Hisp, estab 2017, empl 1, sales , cert: State)

3758   Raisman Corporation
5543 NW 72nd Ave
Miami, FL 33166
Contact: Sales
Tel: 786-581-3820
Email: sales@raisman.com
Website: www.raisman.com
Mfr trimmer heads, spindles, primer bulbs, fuel filters, oil pumps, spark plugs, shock absorbers, mufflers, carburetors, carburetor kits, etc. (Hisp, estab 1998, empl 120, sales $15,000,000, cert: State)

Illinois

3759   Foreman Tool & Mold Company
3850 Swenson Ave
St. Charles, IL 60174
Contact: Jeff Gardner Sales Mgr
Tel: 630-377-6389
Email: jgardner@foremantool.com
Website: www.foremantool.com
Complete 3D part design, Pro-E mold design & layout. (Hisp, estab 1984, empl 80, sales $0, cert: NMSDC)

3760   Pioneer Service Inc. - Addison, IL
542 W Factory Rd
Addison, IL 60101
Contact: Beth Swanson VP Sales & Mktg
Tel: 630-628-0249
Email: bswanson@pioneerserviceinc.com
Website: www.pioneerserviceinc.com/
Contract mfr screw machine products & centerless grinding services: shafts, axles, bolts, bushings, dowels, pins, rods, spacers, valve stems, deburring, drilling, flatting, grinding, knurling, slotting, tapping, threading, heat treating. (Woman, estab 1990, empl 40, sales $5,000,000, cert: CPUC, WBENC)

3761　Tag Tool Services, Inc.
　　　3303 N Main St
　　　East Peoria, IL 61611
　　　Contact: Vonda Jones President
　　　Tel:　　309-694-2400
　　　Email: vonda@countyline-tool.com
　　　Website: www.countyline-tool.com
Cutting tool manufacturing & tool refurbishment, regrind Hobs, Shaper Cutters, Broach Bars, Drills, Rota Broaches, Port Tools, Gun Drills, End Mills, Taps, Reamers, Chamfer Tools, Special Form Tools. (Woman, estab 1984, empl 14, sales $1,200,000, cert: WBENC)

Massachusetts

3762　Electrical Safety Products LLC
　　　375 Main St
　　　Woburn, MA 01801
　　　Contact: Tom Wilkie Dir of Sales
　　　Tel:　　781-249-5007
　　　Email: tom.wilkie@electricalsafety-usa.com
　　　Website: www.electricalsafety-usa.com
Mfr ASTM F-1505 certified insulated tools. (Woman, estab 2009, empl 4, sales , cert: WBENC)

Michigan

3763　2K Tool LLC
　　　3025 Madison Ave SE
　　　Wyoming, MI 49548
　　　Contact: Kevin Smith Engineering Mgr
　　　Tel:　　616-452-4927
　　　Email: kevin@2ktool.com
　　　Website: www.2ktool.com
Moldmaker, machining, tooling, plastic injection molds, compression tooling, composite machining, casting machining part Injection molding. (Woman, estab 2004, empl 19, sales $2,269,151, cert: WBENC)

3764　Anderson Express, Inc.
　　　580 W Sherman Blvd
　　　Muskegon Heights, MI 49444
　　　Contact: Angel Ball HR Mgr
　　　Tel:　　231-733-6001
　　　Email: aball@andersonexpressinc.com
　　　Website: www.andersonexpressinc.com
Rapid tooling & tooling prototypes for small & medium projects. (Woman, estab 2011, empl 17, sales $0, cert: WBENC)

3765　Ideal Machine Tool Technologies, LLC
　　　675 E Big Beaver Rd, Ste 105
　　　Troy, MI 48083
　　　Contact: Vincent H. Hylton Owner
　　　Tel:　　248-792-9061
　　　Email: v.hylton@e-imtt.com
　　　Website: www.e-imtt.com
Commodity management services, program management, engineering services, field services in the machine tool industry. (AA, estab 2010, empl 2, sales $0, cert: NMSDC)

3766　Micro Fixtures, Inc.
　　　20448 Lorne
　　　Taylor, MI 48180
　　　Contact: Sue Rade Office Mgr
　　　Tel:　　313-382-9781
　　　Email: microfixtures@msn.com
　　　Website: www.MicroFixtures.com
Design & mfr tools, fixtures, gauges, prototype products. (Nat Ame, estab 1993, empl 4, sales $514,590, cert: NMSDC)

3767　Universal Tool Equipment & Controls, Inc.
　　　6525 Center Dr
　　　Sterlng Heights, MI 48312
　　　Contact: Bill Bartolotta VP
　　　Tel:　　586-268-4380
　　　Email: bbartolotta@universaltecinc.com
　　　Website: www.universaltecinc.com
Automation & welding systems, robotics, weld guns, vision systems, sealant systems, drawn arc welders, projection welders, material handling end effectors & welding fixtures. (Woman/AA, estab 2009, empl 29, sales $10,000,000, cert: WBENC)

Minnesota

3768　Carbide Tool Services, Inc.
　　　1020 Lund Blvd
　　　Anoka, MN 55303
　　　Contact: Julie Reiling President
　　　Tel:　　763-421-2210
　　　Email: julie@carbidetool.com
　　　Website: www.carbidetool.com
Mfr & repair indexable cutting tools, live tooling. (Minority, Woman, estab 1988, empl 40, sales $3,493,686, cert: WBENC)

North Dakota

3769　Posi Lock Puller, Inc.
　　　805 Sunflower Ave
　　　Cooperstown, ND 58425
　　　Contact: Tamara Somerville VP
　　　Tel:　　701-797-2600
　　　Email: t.somerville@posilock.com
　　　Website: www.posilock.com
Mfr gear & bearing pullers. (Woman, estab 1977, empl 45, sales $3,900,000, cert: City)

New Jersey

3770　JDV Products, Inc.
　　　22-01 Raphael St.
　　　Fair Lawn, NJ 07410
　　　Contact: Ron Vradenburg Sales Mgr
　　　Tel:　　201-796-1720
　　　Email: ron@jdvproducts.com
　　　Website: www.jdvproducts.com
Mfr & dist telecom tools: wire wrap & unwrap tools, semi-automatic wire wrap machines, wire strippers, hand & pneumatic power tools, industrial power bits, hand screwdrivers, tool balancer, torque wrenches & accessories, wire & plastics cutting tools. (Woman, estab 1995, empl 19, sales , cert: WBENC)

3771   SMG Services, LLC
       462 W Lookout Ave
       Hackensack, NJ 07601
       Contact: FirstName LastName CEO
       Tel: 201-937-5378
       Email: sweintraub@svcmgmt.com
       Website: www.smgdiamondtools.com
Mfr Diamond Drill Bits, Diamond Plated drill Bits, Diamond
Grinding Tools, Cutting Blades, Impregnated Inserts,
Brazed Diamond Products, Diamond Core Drills, Diamond
Solid Tools, Cstmr specs. (Woman/AA, estab 2009, empl 1,
sales $765,000, cert: State)

3772   SYSMIND LLC
       38 Washington Rd
       Princeton Junction, NJ 08550
       Contact: Business Devel Specialist
       Tel: 609-897-9670
       Email: info@sysmind.com
       Website: www.sysmind.com
Fabricate plastic components & fasteners for computer,
aerospace, electronic, instrumentation, etc. applications.
Prototype to production. Also stock molded nylon fasteners. (Woman/As-Ind, estab 1999, empl 456, sales
$45,000,000, cert: NMSDC, WBENC)

New York

3773   American Pride Fasteners, LLC
       195 S Fehr Way
       Bay Shore, NY 11706
       Contact: Lynda Zacpal President
       Tel: 631-940-8292
       Email: lynda@americanpridefasteners.com
       Website: www.americanpridefasteners.com
Engineering & mfr miniature screws & miniature fasteners.
(Minority, Woman, estab 2004, empl 24, sales $4,200,000,
cert: City)

3774   Burnett Process, Inc.
       545 Colfax St
       Rochester, NY 14606
       Contact: Melissa Shea-Brooks Marketing Dev Mgr
       Tel: 585-254-8080
       Email: burnettprocesscsr@cannonind.com
       Website: www.burnettprocessinc.com
Mfr & dist ozone, pleated, particulate & HEPA filters. (AA,
estab 1957, empl 39, sales $6,000,000, cert: NMSDC)

Ohio

3775   AKKO Fastener, Inc.
       6855 Cornell Rd
       Cincinnati, OH 45242
       Contact: Art Huge Sales Mgr
       Tel: 513-489-8300
       Email: arthuge@comcast.net
       Website: www.akkofastener.com
Mfr fastening products: machine screws, tapping screws,
plascrews, thread cutting screws, & cold formed metal
products. (Minority, Woman, estab 1967, empl 40, sales
$7,000,000, cert: NMSDC)

3776   Cold Headed Fasteners & Assemblies, Inc.
       1875 Harsh Ave SE
       Massillon, OH 44646
       Contact: Oscar Lee President
       Tel: 330-833-0800
       Email: o.lee@coldheaded.us
       Website: www.coldheaded.us
Mfr fasteners & assemblies, sorting & packaging (As-Pac,
estab 2002, empl 15, sales $0, cert: State)

3777   Custom Millcraft Corp.
       9092 Le Saint Dr
       Fairfield, OH 45014
       Contact: Jody Corbett President
       Tel: 513-874-7080
       Email: jcorbett@custommillcraft.com
       Website: www.custommillcraft.com
Mfr wood & plastic laminate store fixtures. (Woman,
estab 1983, empl 45, sales $4,000,000, cert: WBENC)

3778   M.O.M. Tools, LLC
       3659 Green Road Ste 304
       Cleveland, OH 44122
       Contact: Anthony Lockhart
       Tel: 216-464-2992
       Email: axlockhart@toolsbymom.com
       Website: www.toolsbymom.com/
Mfr dual-head piercing tools & dies. (AA, estab 2003,
empl 2, sales $0, cert: NMSDC)

3779   Master Manufacturing Co, Inc.
       9200 Inman Ave
       Cleveland, OH 44105
       Contact: Bob Ptacek VP Sales
       Tel: 800-323-5513
       Email: bptacek@mastermfgco.com
       Website: www.mastermfgco.com
Mfr furniture casters & self-stick wheels; felt pads,
surface protectors, wobble stoppers; furniture movers;
door stops; ergonomic support cushions & wire mgmt
channels & grommets. (Woman, estab 1951, empl , sales
, cert: CPUC, WBENC)

3780   Midwest Ohio Tool Company, Inc.
       215 Tarhe Trail
       Upper Sandusky, OH 43351
       Contact: Stephanie Kettels President
       Tel: 419-294-1987
       Email: skettels@midwestohio.com
       Website: www.midwestohio.com
Mfr custom cutting tools, metal cutting tools, milling
cutters, specialized cutting tools, boring bars, tool
holders, industrial tools. (Woman, estab 1954, empl 9,
sales $500,000, cert: WBENC)

3781   RB Tool & Mfg Co.
       2680 Civic Center Dr
       Cincinnati, OH 45231
       Contact: Scott Schaeper Sales/Marketing Mgr
       Tel: 513-521-8292
       Email: scott@rbtoolandmfg.com
       Website: www.rbtoolandmfg.com
Mfr mills-horizontal and vertical, lathes-CNC and
manuals, EDM-wire and sinker, welding, painting.
(Woman, estab 1957, empl 40, sales $6,000,000, cert:
WBENC)

3782 Steam Turbine Alternative Resources
116 Latourette St
Marion, OH 43302
Contact: Ken Kubinski Sales Mgr
Tel: 740-387-5535
Email: ken@starturbine.com
Website: www.starturbines.com
Mfr steam seals, packing, spill strips hardware, oil seals & deflectors, on-site field installation & machining sevices. (Woman, estab 1986, empl 40, sales $5,610,000, cert: WBENC)

3783 Stelfast Inc.
22979 Stelfast Pkwy
Strongsville, OH 44149
Contact: Todd McRoberts Sales
Tel: 877-619-8231
Email: toddm@stelfast.com
Website: www.stelfast.com
Import & manufacture fasteners. (As-Pac, estab 1973, empl 80, sales $31,500,000, cert: NMSDC)

3784 Talent Tool & Die, Inc.
777 Berea Industrial Pkwy
Berea, OH 44017
Contact: Mylynh Vu President
Tel: 440-239-8777
Email: mylynh@talent-tool.com
Website: www.talent-tool.com
Mfr dies, tools & fixtures; metal stamping & laser cutting. (As-Pac, estab 1989, empl 44, sales $0, cert: NMSDC)

3785 The M.K. Morse Company
1101 11th St SE
Canton, OH 44707
Contact: Ryan Rhodes Customer Service
Tel: 330-453-8187
Email: rhodesr@mkmorse.com
Website: www.mkmorse.com
Mfr saw blades, band saws, reciprocating saws, hole saws, hack saws and frames, wood boring bits, portable band saws, metal cutting circular saws & machines. Made from bimetal, carbon steel, carbide tipped & carbide grit. (Woman, estab 1963, empl 500, sales $84,000,000, cert: WBENC)

Oklahoma

3786 Hover Group, LLC
416 Heritage Green Rd
Edmond, OK 73003
Contact: Nicole Hover CEO
Tel: 405-437-8691
Email: Nicole@hovergroup.net
Website: www.hovergroup.net
Manufacturing and providing composite components, oil and gas downhole tools. (Woman, estab 2016, empl 5, sales $473,000, cert: WBENC)

Texas

3787 Arise Solutions Inc.
5862 Cromo Ste 149
El Paso, TX 79912
Contact: Daniel Laing President
Tel: 915-345-9134
Email: sales@arisesolutions.biz
Website: www.arisesolutions.biz
Custom designed wire harness, cable assembly, bulk wire, signal cable, specialty bolts, screws, Nut Rivets, Inserts, Fasteners, Spacers, Connectors & Fittings for automotive industry. (As-Pac, estab 2012, empl 5, sales $1,000,000, cert: State, NMSDC)

3788 Danrick Industries Inc.
850 Kastrin St
El Paso, TX 79907
Contact: Marco Herrera President
Tel: 915-599-2988
Email: marcoherrera@danrick.net
Website: www.danrick.net
Mfr tooling & precision machining parts, fabrication of parts & components of terminal crimping. (AA, estab 2002, empl 22, sales $0, cert: State, NMSDC)

3789 EZKutter Company
3617 Rabbit Lane
Bryan, TX 77808
Contact: Dora Loria Owner
Tel: 979-778-0825
Email: ezkutter@suddenlink.net
Website: www.ezkutter-usa.com
Mfr hand held cutting tools used for cutting heavy plastic straps, strings & shrink wrapping. (Woman, estab 1992, empl 2, sales , cert: State)

3790 Versatech, LLC
315 N Park Dr
San Antonio, TX 78216
Contact: Diana Grinman Admin
Tel: 210-979-2823
Email: dgrinman@pmtool.com
Website: www.versatech-mfg.com
Advanced tooling, plastic injection molds, tools & dies fields. (Hisp, estab 2006, empl 5, sales , cert: NMSDC)

Virginia

3791 Master Gage & Tool Company
112 Maplewood St
Danville, VA 24543
Contact: Debbye Lyle President
Tel: 434-836-4243
Email: debbyel@mastergt.com
Website: www.mastergt.com
Calibration, specialized tooling & gaging products. (Woman, estab 1986, empl 26, sales $12,010,000, cert: WBENC)

Wisconsin

3792　R.J. Zeman Tool & Mfg. Co., Inc.
　　　W228 N575 Westmound Dr
　　　Waukesha, WI 53186
　　　Contact: Spencer Schreindl President
　　　Tel:　262-549-4400
　　　Email: sschreindl@zemantool.com
　　　Website: www.zemantool.com
Machining, design, mfr & inspect fixtures, special machines, gages, die cast dies, plastic injection molds, permanent molds, core boxes, patterns for sand casting & short and long-run production parts. (Woman, estab 1966, empl 48, sales $9,600,000, cert: WBENC)

3793　Valley Grinding & Mfg, / Mario Cotta America
　　　1717 Hamilton Ct
　　　Little Chute, WI 54140
　　　Contact: TJ Utschig President
　　　Tel:　800-750-7675
　　　Email: tju@valleygrinding.com
　　　Website: www.valleygrinding.com
Manufacturing, sharpening & servicing hard metal, tool steel and carbide cutting tools. (Minority, Woman, estab 1987, empl 84, sales $10,870,000, cert: WBENC)

HYDRAULIC & COMPRESSED AIR EQUIPMENT

Manufacturers and distributors of compressed air equipment, valves, gaskets, fittings, pumps, meters, hoses, special tools, pipe, etc. (See also HARDWARE & TOOLS, INDUSTRIAL EQUIPMENT & SUPPLIES, INDUSTRIAL MACHINES and MATERIAL HANDLING EQUIPMENT). NAICS Code 42

Alabama

3794 Elle Waterworks Supply, LLC
PO Box 205
Leeds, AL 35094
Contact: Courtney Myrick Owner
Tel: 205-352-3240
Email: cmyrick@ellewws.com
Website: www.ellewws.com
Dist process valves, air valves, control valves, ductile iron pipe, steel pipe, pipe supports & hangers, couplings, adapters, pvc pipe & fittings, ductile iron fittings, hydrants, valve boxes, hardware, bolts, nuts, gaskets, safety equipment. (Woman, estab 2011, empl 2, sales $3,800,000, cert: State, WBENC)

Arizona

3795 Stenzel Sealing Solutions, LLC
16809 N 53rd Ave, Ste 5
Glendale, AZ 85306
Contact: Linda Stenzel Owner
Tel: 602-903-1250
Email: linda@azstenzel.com
Website: www.stenzelsealingsolutions.com
Fluid sealing solutions: Gaskets, Seals, Pump/Valve Packing, Duct/Pipe Expansion Joints, Valves, Pipe, Fittings, Flanges & Steam Traps. (Woman, estab 2012, empl 4, sales $1,925,914, cert: CPUC, WBENC)

California

3796 CLEAR Solutions, Inc.
942 Calle Amanecer, Ste D
San Clemente, CA 92673
Contact: Judy McMacking VP
Tel: 949-429-8922
Email: judy@clearsolutionscorp.com
Website: www.clearsolutionscorp.com
Dist filters, filter housings, water purification, filtration, separation, process liquid filtration, HVAC, compressed air & gas filtration, sanitary gaskets, flange gaskets, screen gaskets, hose assemblies, tubing, quick disconnect fittings. (Woman, estab 2010, empl 6, sales , cert: WBENC)

3797 Dexen Industries, Inc.
9220 Norwalk Blvd
Santa Fe Springs, CA 90670
Contact: Yu-Shan Teng President
Tel: 562-699-8490
Email: info@dexen.com
Website: www.dexen.com
Mfr gas valves. (As-Pac, estab 1988, empl 17, sales $11,000,000, cert: CPUC)

3798 VIAIR Corporation
15 Edelman
Irvine, CA 92618
Contact: Alan Basham Dir of Operations
Tel: 949-585-0011
Email: alanb@viaircorp.com
Website: www.viaircorp.com
Dist Air Compressor, Air Tank, LED Light, Air accessories for automotive industry. (As-Pac, estab 1998, empl 32, sales $22,000,000, cert: NMSDC)

Colorado

3799 Die Cut Technologies/Denver Gasket
10943 Leroy Dr
Northglenn, CO 80233
Contact: Evelyn Meyers CEO
Tel: 303-452-4600
Email: evelyn@diecuttech.com
Website: www.diecuttech.com
Mfr gaskets, die cut parts & converted non-metallic materials. Also dist sponge, foam tapes rubber, bridge bearing pads, expansion joints, impact attenuators & adhesives, contract assembly & packaging svcs. (Hisp, estab 1961, empl 20, sales $2,524,000, cert: NMSDC, SDB)

Florida

3800 Amazon Hose and Rubber Company
4105 Seaboard Rd
Orlando, FL 32808
Contact: Jim Donlin President
Tel: 407-843-8190
Email: jimdonlin@amazonhose.com
Website: www.amazonhose.com
Dist industrial & hydraulic hoses & related fittings. (Woman, estab , empl 60, sales $12,698,846, cert: City, WBENC)

3801 Industrial Hose & Hydraulics, Inc.
2450 N Powerline Rd
Pompano Beach, FL 33069
Contact: Joanne R. Heckman Controller
Tel: 954-960-0311
Email: joeyheckman@industrialhose.com
Website: www.industrialhose.com
Dist hoses, fittings, clamps, adapters, fuel hose, hose reels, check valves, lubrication supplies, garden hose & pumps. (Woman, estab , empl , sales , cert: WBENC)

3802 The Bernd Group Inc.
1251 Pinehurst Rd
Dunedin, FL 34698
Contact: Pilar Bernd President
Tel: 727-733-0122
Email: businessdevelopment@berndgroup.com
Website: www.berndgroup.com
Material handling equip, safety products, hand & power tools, pumps & compressors, motors, generators, electrical hardware, batteries, lighting fixtures, lockers, bins, shelving, lab equip. (Minority, Woman, estab 1992, empl 66, sales , cert: NMSDC)

3803   Zabatt Engine Service, Inc.
     4612 Hwy Ave
     Jacksonville, FL 32254
     Contact: Maria Sabatier AP & Credit Mgr
     Tel: 904-421-9848
     Email: maria@zabatt.com
     Website: www.zabatt.com
Generator and Compressor distributor, specializing in sales, service, parts and installation of air compressors and generators. (Hisp, estab 1977, empl 104, sales $31,969,000, cert: State)

Illinois

3804   Bearings & Industrial Supply
     431 Imen Ave
     Addison, IL 60101
     Contact: Sejal Khandwala Acct Exec
     Tel: 630-628-1966
     Email: Sejal@BearingsNow.Com
     Website: www.bearingsnow.com
Dist bearings & power transmission products; pump & pump repair parts, HVAC & electrical parts. (As-Pac, estab , empl , sales , cert: NMSDC)

3805   Chambers Gasket & Manufacturing Co.
     4701 W Rice St
     Chicago, IL 60651
     Contact: Heide Kenny President
     Tel: 773-626-8800
     Email: hkenny@chambersgasket.com
     Website: www.chambersgasket.com
Gaskets; Washers; Strips; Spiral Wound Gaskets; Molded Gaskets; Waterjet cut parts; pressure sensitve adhesive added; kitting; special packaging. (Woman, estab 0, empl , sales , cert: WBENC)

3806   Cylinders Inc.
     580 W 5th Ave
     Naperville, IL 60563
     Contact: Cynthia Crawford President
     Tel: 630-357-5649
     Email: cindy@cylindersinc.com
     Website: www.cylindersinc.com
Repair & recondition hydraulic & pneumatic cylinders. (Woman, estab , empl 7, sales $1,440,992, cert: WBENC)

Indiana

3807   MIDpro Fluid Power and Automation
     444 Johnson Ln
     Brownsburg, IN 46112
     Contact: Cynthia Torrance President
     Tel: 317-852-5920
     Email: ctorrance@midprofluidpower.com
     Website: www.midprofluidpower.com
Pnuematic, hydraulic, electronic & air systems, conveyors, blowers, pumps, dryers, filtration, air tools, cylinders, valves, fittings, power units, PLC controllers, monitors & touch screens. (Woman, estab 1986, empl 11, sales $5,200,000, cert: WBENC)

Kentucky

3808   SealingLife Technology
     1141 Red Mile Rd Ste 201
     Lexington, KY 40504
     Contact: Danette Wilder CEO
     Tel: 859-977-6640
     Email: wilderdj@sealinglife.com
     Website: www.sealinglife.com
Fabricate, mfr & dist sealing, shielding & coating solutions, O-rings, gaskets, molded parts, extrusions, RFI/EMF shielding, vacuum coating & encapsulating. (Woman/AA, estab 2008, empl 9, sales $1,200,000, cert: NMSDC, SDB)

Louisiana

3809   Treco Stainless Solutions, LLC
     366 Technology Lane
     Gray, LA 70359
     Contact: Brenna Treland Owner/Sales
     Tel: 985-858-2880
     Email: brenna@trecostainless.com
     Website: www.trecostainless.com
Stainless Steel Compression fittings, Stainless Steel Instrumentation fittings, Tubing & Piping, Autoclave fittings (up to 60K PSI), Gauges, Hydraulic Hoses, Quick Connects. (Woman, estab 2014, empl 3, sales , cert: WBENC)

Maryland

3810   Phelps Industrial Products
     6300 Washington Blvd
     Elkridge, MD 21075
     Contact: Gina Lehman CEO
     Tel: 410-796-2222
     Email: gmlehman@phelpsgaskets.com
     Website: www.phelpsgaskets.com
Mfr, fabricator & dist Gaskets, Compression Packing, O' Rings, Molded Parts & Sealing Devices. (As-Pac, estab 1945, empl 15, sales , cert: State)

Michigan

3811   Chippewa Systems, Ltd.
     32663 Coach
     Chesterfield, MI 48047
     Contact: Brian Barr VP
     Tel: 586-772-1783
     Email: chippewasystemsltd@gmail.com
     Website: www.chippewasystems.com
Dist vacuum pumps, compressors, blowers, filters, air knives. (Minority, Woman, estab 1986, empl 3, sales $668,000, cert: NMSDC)

3812   Fluid Line Components, Inc.
     638 S Rochester Rd
     Clawson, MI 48017
     Contact: Mary Schmitt CEO
     Tel: 248-583-9070
     Email: mary@fluidlinecomponents.com
     Website: www.fluidlinecomponents.com
Dist air cylinders, air valves, air fittings, air filters, air gauges, air hoist, air hose, air manifolds, air motors, air drills, air presses, air tanks, air-oil tanks, anti-tie down, balancers, ball valves, ball vibrators, blow guns, brass pipe fittings (Woman, estab 1972, empl 4, sales $1,102,252, cert: WBENC)

3813 MCEM LLC
31153 Plymouth Rd
Livonia, MI 48150
Contact: BK Masti President
Tel: 517-881-1226
Email: bkm@mcem.co
Website: www.mcem.co
Lubricants, valves, conduit fittings. (As-Pac, estab 2011, empl 5, sales , cert: NMSDC)

3814 Service Manufacturing & Supply Co.
33380 Groesbeck Hwy
Fraser, MI 48026
Contact: Ryan Maggio General Mgr
Tel: 586-415-0455
Email: sales@servicemanufacturing.com
Website: www.servicemanufacturing.com
Hydraulic & pneumatic components & accessories, brass, steel, stainless steel, malleable & galvanized fittings, JIC 37 degree flare, push-on barbs, adaptors, solid & union barbs, pipe els & extension adaptors, hydraulic tubing. (Woman, estab 1957, empl 7, sales $1,154,683, cert: WBENC)

Minnesota

3815 Chrom Tech, Inc.
5995 W 149th St, Ste 102
Saint Paul, MN 55124
Contact: Jessica Kolsky Technical Sales Rep
Tel: 952-431-6000
Email: jessica@chromtech.com
Website: www.chromtech.com
Dist HPLC & GC instrumentation, supplies & accessories: autosampler vials, columns, filters, fittings, PEEK tubing & fittings, solid phase extraction cartridges, protein crash plates, positive pressure manifolds, evaporators, syringes, tubing. (Woman, estab 1985, empl , sales $10,538,000, cert: WBENC)

3816 Water Technology Resources
9201 E Bloomington Fwy, Ste Z
Bloomington, MN 55420
Contact: Sally Waldor President
Tel: 952-641-9004
Email: sallywaldor@wtrvalves.com
Website: www.wtrvalves.com
Mfr industrial valves. (Woman, estab 2009, empl 5, sales $1,000,000, cert: State)

North Carolina

3817 Raleigh-Durham Rubber & Gasket Co., Inc.
PO Box 90397
Raleigh, NC 27675
Contact: Judy Hooks President
Tel: 919-781-6817
Email: judyh@raleighdurhamrubber.com
Website: www.raleighdurhamrubber.com
Mfr & dist rubber gaskets. (Woman, estab , empl , sales , cert: WBENC)

3818 Smith Seal of NC
8441 Garvey Dr
Raleigh, NC 27616
Contact: Gertraud Smith President
Tel: 919-790-1000
Email: judysmith@smithseal.com
Website: www.smithseal.com
Dist hydraulic seals, gaskets & packings. (Woman, estab 1976, empl 13, sales , cert: WBENC)

New Jersey

3819 Liquid-Solids Separation Corp.
25 Arrow Rd
Ramsey, NJ 07446
Contact: Stacey Painter COO
Tel: 201-236-4833
Email: spainter@nafilter.com
Website: www.leemfiltration.com
Mfr pressure leaf filters and their components for oil seed processing, bio diesel fuel production, chemical processing and water treatment applications. (Woman, estab 1994, empl 42, sales $13,000,000, cert: WBENC)

3820 Sur-Seal, Inc.
12 Edgeboro Rd Unit 6
East Brunswick, NJ 08816
Contact: Donna King Accounting
Tel: 732-651-7070
Email: donnak@sur-sealinc.com
Website: www.sur-sealinc.com
Dist gaskets, gashet sheet, roll material, mechanical packing, compression packing, mechanical seals (new & repairs), pressure gauges & thermometers (new and repairs), hydraulic packings, o-rings, lantern rings, extrusions. (Woman, estab 1979, empl 11, sales $2,263,945, cert: State)

Ohio

3821 Trident Fluid Power, LLC
PO Box 368
Middletown, OH 45042
Contact: Sandy Ewen GM
Tel: 513-217-4999
Email: sewen@tridentfluidpower.com
Website: www.Tridentfluidpower.com
Replace, overhaul, manufacture, fluidpower components (cylinders, pumps, valves, systems), field service, trouble shoot, design, engineer, all coke oven equipment & operations, machine, welding, fabricating. (Woman, estab 2006, empl 17, sales $2,000,000, cert: WBENC)

Oklahoma

3822 PT Coupling Co.
PO Box 3909
Enid, OK 73702
Contact: James Matthew Parrish President
Tel: 580-237-4033
Email: credit03@ptcoupling.com
Website: www.ptcoupling.com
Mfr industrial hose couplings used in the transfer of fluid & dry products at medium to low pressure. (Nat Ame, estab 1951, empl 390, sales $60,000,000, cert: NMSDC)

Puerto Rico

3823 Pharmaceutical Processes Systems, Inc.
PO Box 31411
Manati, PR 00667
Contact: Eduardo Perez Sales Mgr
Tel: 787-854-5477
Email: eduardo.perez@ppspr.com
Website: www.ppspr.com
Dis process instrumentation, pumps, valves & equipment for chemical, food and beverage, pharmaceutical, power generation and water markets (Hisp, estab 1982, empl 10, sales , cert: NMSDC)

South Carolina

3824   Eastern Power Technologies, Inc.
11 Caledon Court
Greenville, SC 29615
Contact: Chet Chea Legal Counsel
Tel: 864-312-3840
Email: chet.chea@easternfirst.com
Website: www.easternpowertech.com
Dist industrial & commercial pipes, valves, fittings & commercial plumbing fixtures. (Woman, estab 2014, empl 15, sales , cert: WBENC)

3825   Filters South, Inc.
656 Wraggs Ferry Rd
Georgetown, SC 29440
Contact: Deborah Powell President
Tel: 843-833-1042
Email: dwillspowell@earthlink.net
Website: www.filterssouth.com
Dist filters: Air, HVAC, Oil, Hydraulic, Dust Collection, Water, Liquid, etc. (Woman, estab 1997, empl 2, sales , cert: State, City)

3826   Greenville Fluid System Technologies
2516 River Rd
Piedmont, SC 29673
Contact: Greg Farley Sales Mgr
Tel: 864-295-6700
Email: greg.farley@swagelok.com
Website: www.swagelok.com/columbiasc
Dist compression & pipe fittings, valves, hoses, tubing, pumps, gauges & regulators, Orbital welding equipment, tube benders, hydraulic swaging units. (Woman, estab 2001, empl 18, sales $3,200,000, cert: WBENC)

Tennessee

3827   Pioneer Air Systems, Inc.
210 Flat Fork Rd
Wartburg, TN 37887
Contact: Sam Basseen CEO
Tel: 423-346-6693
Email: sam@pioneerair.com
Website: www.pioneerair.com
Convert CO to CO2 in compressed air to make it suitable for breathing air purposes, clean & dry Nitrogen, Natural Gas, Hydrogen, Helium, Ethylene, Seal Gas, OxyPurge (with MONEL vessels & Teflon lined piping) etc. (As-Ind, estab 1980, empl 25, sales , cert: NMSDC)

Texas

3828   Asociar, LLC
2800 E Plano Pkwy Ste 400
Plano, TX 75074
Contact: Betty Manetta CEO
Tel: 214-918-1013
Email: bmanetta@asociar1.com
Website: www.asociar1.com
Streamline Supply Chain Management
Total Equipment Rack Integration & Testing
Procure, Rack, Integrate, Deliver, Engineer
Warehousing & Logistics (Minority, Woman, estab 2012, empl 15, sales $185,000,000,000, cert: State, NMSDC, WBENC)

3829   Corley Gasket Company
PO Box 271124
Dallas, TX 75227
Contact: Jody Anderson Office Mgr
Tel: 214-388-7437
Email: janderson@corleygasket.com
Website: www.corleygasket.com
Mfr gaskets. (Woman, estab 1975, empl 19, sales $1,941,386, cert: CPUC)

3830   CVAL Innovations LLC
9701 Raven Ln
Irving, TX 75063
Contact: Jinen Adenwala President
Tel: 214-699-1326
Email: jinen@cvalinnovations.com
Website: www.cvalinnovations.com
Energy Consumption for Industrial and Commercial customers. We conduct Energy Efficiency Audits, recommend and implement the efficiency measures. (Woman/As-Ind, estab 2009, empl 5, sales $1,093,000, cert: State, NMSDC, SDB)

3831   El Paso Industrial Supplies
119 N Cotton
El Paso, TX 79901
Contact: Antonio Herrera Sales Mgr
Tel: 915-533-5080
Email: sales@epis-usa.com
Website: www.epis-usa.com
Dist pneumatic equipment & parts, sensors, sensors for safety, hydraulic equipments & parts, filters, HEPA filters, work mats, signal towers. (Hisp, estab 1988, empl 16, sales $4,000,000, cert: NMSDC)

3832   Indian Industries LP
432 W Fork Dr
Arlington, TX 76012
Contact: Felipe Moncibaiz Sales
Tel: 817-265-6731
Email: info@indian-industries.com
Website: www.indian-industries.com
Mfr custom gaskets & seals. (Nat Ame, estab 1977, empl 13, sales , cert: State, NMSDC)

3833   Industry Junction, Inc.
3427 W. Kingsley Rd., Ste # 6 & 7
Garland, TX 75041
Contact: Rogelio Cabello President
Tel: 972-926-3526
Email: contact@industryjunction.com
Website: www.industryjunction.com/
Dist fluid power valves, industrial Valves, mallable gittings, stainless steel fittings, hydra-sanitary products. (Hisp, estab 2011, empl 4, sales $4,400,000, cert: State, NMSDC)

3834   iSTAFF Solutions, Inc.
PO Box 118440
Carrollton, TX 75011
Contact: Wanda Young Dir
Tel: 972-251-9877
Email: wanda.young@istaffsolutions.org
Website: www.istaffsolutions.org
IT Staffing, Light Warehouse, Admin. (Woman/AA, estab 2010, empl 20, sales , cert: State)

3835   MARS Industries, LLC
PO Box 560
Cedar Creek, TX 78612
Contact: Alvino Rosales President
Tel: 512-303-4413
Email: arosales@marsindustries.us
Website: www.marsindustries.us
Dist pipe, fittings, valves, etc.for the construction of water & wastewater treatment facilities & water & wastewater utilities. (Hisp, estab 2001, empl 1, sales , cert: State, City)

3836   OG Energy Solutions LLC
1836 Snake River Rd Ste A
Katy, TX 77449
Contact: Federico Zamar Reg Sales Rep
Tel: 832-644-0121
Email: fzsales@ogenergys.com
Website: www.ogenergys.com
Pipes, tubes, fitting, flanges; Valves; Automation & Instrumentation (transducers, sensors, transmitters, panels); Heat Exchanger Equipment & Parts; Seals & Gaskets; Non-toxic, environmentally-safe cleaners, degreasers & solvents. (Minority, Woman, estab 2010, empl 8, sales $600,000, cert: WBENC)

3837   OnPoint, LLC
13155 Noel Rd, Ste 900
Dallas, TX 75240
Contact: Amber B D'Amico Partner
Tel: 972-918-5154
Email: amber@onpointlighting.com
Website: www.onpointlighting.com
Energy-efficient LED lighting, surveys, ROI analysis, best-of-breed American-made products, lighting design, installation &
financing. (Hisp, estab 2011, empl 2, sales $750,000, cert: State)

3838   Petroleum Accessories, Inc.
12500 Oxford Park Dr
Houston, TX 77077
Contact: Anna de Chabannes Technical Sales Dir
Tel: 281-589-9337
Email: hydraulics@paihouston.com
Website: www.paihouston.com
Dist hydraulic components: filters, high pressure micro pumps & valves. (Woman, estab 1980, empl 5, sales $2,930,802, cert: WBENC)

3839   Piping Technology and Product Inc.
3701 Holmes Rd
Houston, TX 77051
Contact: Michael Rucker Business Devel Mgr
Tel: 713-731-0013
Email: info@pipingtech.com
Website: www.pipingtech.com
Custom Engineered Hot/Cold Insulated Pipe Shoes and Supports, Fabric Expansion Joints/Metal Bellows, ASME Certified Pressure Vessels, and ASME-U-Stamp rated Hydraulic and Mechanical Snubbers, Custom Engineered (Minority, estab 1978, empl 750, sales $60,000,000, cert: NMSDC)

3840   Professional Choice Fire & Security Systems
1815 N. Hampton Road
DeSoto, TX 75115
Contact: Dwanald Walker President
Tel: 972-298-2303
Email: dwanald@professionalchoicefire.com
Website: www.professionalchoicefire.com
Installation, service and repair for fire sprinkler, fire pump, fire alarm systems in the Dallas-Fort Worth metropolitan areas. * Testing, inspection and maintenance for fire alarm, sprinkler, fire pumps and backflow detetion equipment. * 24 hour central (AA, estab 2004, empl 6, sales $500,000, cert: State, NMSDC)

3841   Texas Seal Supply Co, Inc.
606 N Great Southwest Pkwy
Arlington, TX 76011
Contact: Carol Gallegos Ortega Mgr
Tel: 817-640-1193
Email: carols@texasseal.com
Website: www.texasseal.com
Dist seals: hydraulic, pneumatic, aerospace, oilfield. (Hisp, estab 1971, empl 13, sales , cert: NMSDC)

Virginia

3842   E&R Minority Supplier LLC
21290 Hedgerow Terr
Ashburn, VA 20147
Contact: Esvith Palomino-Quillama President
Tel: 703-932-5045
Email: epalomino@erminoritysupplier.com
Website: www.erminoritysupplier.com
Heavy highway material & industrial hydraulic hoses & fittings. (Hisp, estab 2011, empl 1, sales , cert: State)

Wisconsin

3843   Anderson Seal Inc.
16555 W Lincoln
New Berlin, WI 53151
Contact: Jennifer Hansen President
Tel: 262-821-0344
Email: jennifer@andersonseal.com
Website: www.andersonseal.com
Dist rubber o-rings, custom molded shapes, gaskets, oil seals, kit assemblies, inventory management. (Woman, estab 1990, empl 50, sales $27,000,000, cert: WBENC)

3844   Central Wisconsin Flex
8510 Enterprise Way
Weston, WI 54476
Contact: Carmen Sauer VP
Tel: 715-355-4344
Email: cenflex@cenflex.com
Website: www.cenflex.com
Flexible metal hose, braided metal hose, expansion joints, exhaust tubing and assemblies, laser cutting, plate rolling, fab shop, Teflon hoses, machining. (Minority, Woman, estab 1992, empl 37, sales $8,394,000, cert: NMSDC)

3845   Husco Automotive, LLC
      2239 Pewaukee Rd
      Waukesha, WI 53188
      Contact: Jonathan Hassert Acct Mgr
      Tel: 262-953-6400
      Email: jon.hassert@huscoauto.com
      Website: www.huscoauto.com
Design, develop & mfr electro-hydraulic solenoid valves
& electro-magnetic solenoid actuators. (Hisp, estab
1946, empl 1015, sales $238,000,000, cert: NMSDC)

3846   Roeming Industries, Inc.
      1133 W Liebau Rd
      Mequon, WI 53092
      Contact: Sandy Roeming Schumaker President
      Tel: 262-243-5800
      Email: sschumaker@roeming.com
      Website: www.roeming.com
Contract sewing on vinyl, leather, Kevlar, fiberglass,
plastics and fabric. Distributor of hydraulic packing,
seals, and packing. Gasket cutting. Rubber to metal
bonding. (Woman, estab 1955, empl 13, sales
$1,600,000, cert: WBENC)

DIVERSITY
INFORMATION
RESOURCES

Driving Supplier Diversity Success since 1968.

1960's

1968 The "Buy Black Campaign" is founded by Peter and Rose Meyerhoff as a not-for-profit organization and prints its first directory of black-owned businesses in Minneapolis.

1968 The first Board of Directors is established and an office space is secured on Plymouth Ave. N. in Minneapolis.

1969 DIR publishes the "Buy Black" directory nationally.

1970's

1972 The "Buy Black" directory changes to "TRY US" and includes Black-, Hispanic-, Asian- and Native American-owned businesses.

1975 First edition of "Purchasing People in Major Corporations" directory is published.

1977 DIR's Board of Directors expands to include national corporations.

1980's

1986 DIR holds its first Supplier Diversity Seminars.

1992 First edition of the "Supplier Diversity Information Resources Guide" is published.

1990's

1995 DIR holds its first "Best Practices in Supplier Diversity Strategies and Initiatives"

1998 DIR creates an online, searchable database for its "Purchasing People in Major Corporations" directory.

2000 TRY US becomes Diversity Information Resources, Inc., to reflect the ongoing and ever-changing diverse-supplier categories.

2000's

2001 DIR hires SupplierGATEWAY as a technology partner.

2001 The "Buy Black" directory is now "National Minority and Women-Owned Business Directory" and includes certified women-owned businesses.

2006 DIR's verification and validation expertise expands to include Veteran-, Service-Disabled Veteran, and GLBT-owned businesses.

2011 DIR greatly expands online presence and redesigns identity to better reflect the open horizon for Supplier Diversity development.

2010's

2013 DIR celebrates its 45th Anniversary and looks forward to a thriving future!

2015 DIR responds to corporate and diverse-suppliers request for consolidated information and publishes a new directory and handbook: "The Business of Supplier Diversity".

INDUSTRIAL EQUIPMENT & SUPPLIES

Manufacturers and distributors of food service and restaurant equipment, drive belts, aircraft parts, motors, industrial batteries, underground mining equipment, heaters, bearings, spark plug cleaner, traffic control signs, etc. (See also HARDWARE & TOOLS, HYDRAULIC & COMPRESSED AIR EQUIPMENT, INDUSTRIAL MACHINES and MATERIAL HANDLING EQUIPMENT). NAICS Code 42

Alabama

3847   Alabama Safety Products Inc.
150 Supply Room Rd
Oxford, AL 36203
Contact: Tracy Rouse President
Tel: 256-835-0963
Email: tracyr@alabamasafety.com
Website: www.alabamasafety.com
Dist safety supplies, safety audits, hand protections surveys, respirator fit-testing. (Minority, Woman, estab 1992, empl 8, sales , cert: NMSDC)

3848   Cornerstone Supply, Inc.
340 Production AVe
Madison, AL 35758
Contact: Bonnie Powers President
Tel: 256-461-4147
Email: bonnie@cornerstone-supply.com
Website: www.cornerstone-supply.com
Dist military fasteners, electronic components, MRO equipment & supplies. (Woman, estab 1996, empl 14, sales $6,500,000, cert: WBENC)

3849   Elle Waterworks Supply, LLC
PO Box 205
Leeds, AL 35094
Contact: Courtney Myrick Owner
Tel: 205-352-3240
Email: cmyrick@ellewws.com
Website: www.ellewws.com
Dist process valves, air valves, control valves, ductile iron pipe, steel pipe, pipe supports & hangers, couplings, adapters, pvc pipe & fittings, ductile iron fittings, hydrants, valve boxes, hardware, bolts, nuts, gaskets, safety equipment. (Woman, estab 2011, empl 2, sales $3,800,000, cert: State, WBENC)

3850   Rainbow Technology Corporation
261 Cahaba Valley Pkwy
Pelham, AL 35124
Contact: Larry Steeley VP
Tel: 800-637-6047
Email: lwsteeley@rainbowtech.net
Website: www.rainbowtech.net
Dist industrial equipment & supplies. (Woman, estab 1971, empl 32, sales $13,500,000, cert: State, CPUC)

3851   Vision Global Technology, Inc.
3512-B 6th Ave SE
Decatur, AL 35603
Contact: Frank Roberts Cstmr Devel
Tel: 877-753-3936
Email: frank@vgtcorp.com
Website: www.vgtcorp.com
Dist bulk R134A, 30 lb. cylinders & ISO tank & 12 oz. cans. (Woman/Nat Ame, estab 2003, empl 20, sales $20,000,000, cert: NMSDC)

Arkansas

3852   Welsco, Inc.
9006 Crystal Hill Rd
North Little Rock, AR 72113
Contact: Chris Layton President
Tel: 501-771-1204
Email: chris.layton@welsco.com
Website: www.Welsco.com
Welding gases and Supplies, industrial supplies and Spec gases. (Woman, estab 1941, empl 127, sales $40,000,000, cert: NWBOC)

3853   Air Energy Systems & Services
4202 E Superior Ave, Ste 3
Phoenix, AZ 85040
Contact: Patricia Bewley Owner
Tel: 602-454-0210
Email: pbewley@aesas.com
Website: www.aesas.com
Dist & install commerical, industrial & HVAC air filters, energy products, IAQ products, UVC producst, energy audits. (Minority, Woman, estab 1997, empl 15, sales $2,300,000, cert: NMSDC, WBENC)

3854   Diversified Diamond Products
4634 E Mountain View Ct
Phoenix, AZ 85028
Contact: Mary Dillon CEO
Tel: 480-443-4899
Email: mdillon@diversifieddiamond.com
Website: www.diversifieddiamond.com
Dist safety supplies & equipment, vests, gloves, respirators, test meters, locks, cable protection, prescription safety glasses, fall protection, ear protection, face masks, cutting tools, abrasives, work holding, metal working. (Woman, estab 1989, empl 5, sales $1,295,404, cert: WBENC)

3855   Industrial Specialties Supply, Inc.
3941 E 29th St, Ste 606
Tucson, AZ 85711
Contact: Alan Davila Mgr
Tel: 520-745-5800
Email: indussupply@live.com
Website: www.indussupplyinc.com
Solenoid valves, PLC components, Conveyor belts, Steam traps, High Pressure Valves, Sanitary/Food grade fittings, valves & tubing, industrial concrete coatings, personal safety equipment, Gas detectors. (Hisp, estab 2001, empl 2, sales $1,438,845, cert: State, City)

California

3856   Able Industrial Products, Inc.
2006 S Baker
Ontario, CA 91761
Contact: Courtney Salvidar Sales/Mktg
Tel: 909-930-1585
Email: courtneys@able123.com
Website: www.able123.com
Mfr & convert thermal management materials: gap pads, interface pads & various non-metallic gaskets. (Minority, Woman, estab 1974, empl 40, sales $3,800,000, cert: NMSDC)

3857 Advanced Mechatronics Solutions, Inc.
      10030 Via De La Amistad
      San Diego, CA 92154
      Contact: Arnold Park Project Mgr
      Tel: 619-661-5985
      Email: arnold@ams-fa.com
      Website: www.ams-fa.com
Dist automated factory equipment, design Modular Rack System. (As-Pac, estab 2002, empl 130, sales $4,306,000, cert: NMSDC)

3858 Anita Fire Hose Company Etc.
      7937 North Ave, Ste B
      Lemon Grove, CA 91945
      Contact: Anita Barnes Owner
      Tel: 619-462-3473
      Email: anitafire@sbcglobal.net
      Website: www.anitafirehosecompanyetc.com
Dist fire hoses, fire extinguishers, fire cabinets. (Woman, estab 2003, empl 7, sales , cert: State)

3859 Empire Safety & Supply
      10624 Industrial Ave
      Roseville, CA 95678
      Contact: Monette Crawford CEO
      Tel: 800-995-1341
      Email: monette@empiresafety.com
      Website: www.empiresafety.com
Dist environmental health & safety products. (Woman, estab 1992, empl 14, sales $6,000,000, cert: CPUC)

3860 FTG, Inc.
      12750 Center Court Dr S Ste 280
      Cerritos, CA 90703
      Contact: Pino Pathak President
      Tel: 562-865-9200
      Email: pino@ftginc.com
      Website: www.ftginc.com
Mfr air filters, oil filters, fuel filters, filtration products, custom engineered parts. (As-Pac, estab 1992, empl 20, sales $3,000,000, cert: NMSDC)

3861 Harris Industrial Gases
      8475 Auburn Blvd
      Citrus Heights, CA 95610
      Contact: Tim Lettich GM
      Tel: 916-725-2168
      Email: tlettich@harrisgas.com
      Website: www.harrisgas.com
Dist welding & industrial equipment & industrial gases. (Woman, estab 1936, empl 20, sales $5,000,000, cert: State, CPUC)

3862 Industrial Specialty Products
      7400 Scout Ave, Ste C
      Bell Gardens, CA 90201
      Contact: Paula Mullan President
      Tel: 562-806-2600
      Email: info@gotoisp.com
      Website: www.gotoisp.com
Dist industrial supplies: coatings, paints, chemicals, etc. (Woman, estab 1989, empl 6, sales $0, cert: WBENC)

3863 Liberty Glove, Inc.
      433 Cheryl Lane
      City of Industry, CA 91789
      Contact: Ken Tran Natl Sales Mgr
      Tel: 800-327-8333
      Email: kentran@libertyglove.com
      Website: www.libertyglove.com
Dist safety industrial products. (Minority, Woman, estab 1988, empl 70, sales , cert: NMSDC)

3864 Nathan Kimmel Company, LLC
      1213 S Santa Fe Ave
      Los Angeles, CA 90021
      Contact: Carol Schary President
      Tel: 213-627-8556
      Email: carol@nathankimmel.com
      Website: www.nathankimmel.com
Dist industrial supplies: mfr tarps, construction equipment & parts, motors, mixers, pumps, material handling, janitorial, electrical, pest control equipment, shipping supplies, safety equipment, shovels, tools. (Woman, estab 1996, empl 13, sales $4,740,000, cert: WBENC)

3865 Paramount Safety Supply
      14516 Crenshaw Blvd
      Gardena, CA 90249
      Contact: Joel Pulgarin President
      Tel: 866-200-2975
      Email: info@paramountsafetysupply.com
      Website: www.paramountsafetysupply.com
Personal Protective Equipment, Fall Protection Systems, Gas Monitors/Sniffers, Disaster Preparedness, Emergency Response Supplies, Confined Space Entry/Rescue, Rescue & Descent Systems, Construction Safety. (Hisp, estab 2015, empl 1, sales $500,000, cert: State, CPUC)

3866 R.J. Safety Supply Company Inc.
      7320 Convoy Court
      San Diego, CA 92111
      Contact: Diane Rodriguez VP
      Tel: 858-541-2880
      Email: drodriguez@rjsafety.com
      Website: www.rjsafety.com
Dist safety supplies: PPE products, respiratory, confined space, fall protection, first aid, gloves, boots, rainwear, protective clothing, hazardous material containers, signs, traffic control, safety cabinets, gas detectors. (Woman, estab 1959, empl 17, sales , cert: CPUC)

3867 Safetyvibe
      2530 Corporate Pl, Ste A105
      Monterey Park, CA 91754
      Contact: Lila Don Owner
      Tel: 626-281-8444
      Email: bidops@safetyvibe.com
      Website: www.safetyvibe.com
Dist industrial equipment & supplies. (Minority, Woman, estab 2003, empl 5, sales $1,950,000, cert: State)

3868 Widespread Industrial Supplies, Inc.
      1220 S Boyle Ave
      Los Angeles, CA 90023
      Contact: Josh Dorfman President
      Tel: 310-793-7315
      Email: josh.dorfman@widespreadind.com
      Website: www.widespreadind.com
Dist industrial supplies: fasteners, cutting tools, electrical, welding, chemical & safety related supplies, hand & power tools. (Woman, estab 2002, empl 4, sales $820,341, cert: State, City)

Connecticut

3869　IBC - Industrial Supply Plus
2 Creamery Brook
East Granby, CT 06026
Contact: Ron Nunez CEO
Tel:　860-246-1618
Email: rnunez@industrialbuyers.com
Website: www.industrialbuyers.com
Dist maintenance, repair, operations, production, bearing & power transmission supplies, technical support, inventory control & mgmt, product support & service, consolidated invoicing & sales reporting, minority credits, standardization & rationalization. (Hisp, estab 1999, empl 15, sales $90,000,000, cert: NMSDC)

Florida

3870　Arroyo Process Equipment Inc.
1550 Centennial Blvd
Bartow, FL 33830
Contact: Diane Schleicher President
Tel:　863-533-9700
Email: diane@arroyoprocess.com
Website: www.arroyoprocess.com
Dist pumps, tanks, mixers, meters, filters, water treatment equip. (Woman, estab 1968, empl 32, sales $15,576,805, cert: NMSDC)

3871　O.T. Trans Inc.
201 Babock St
Melbourne, FL 32901
Contact: Dean Danner Business Dev Mgr
Tel:　321-259-9880
Email: ddanner@ottrans.com
Website: www.ottrans.com
Industrial machinery & equip, material handling, hand tools, wiring supplies, industrial supplies safety & rescue equip, tool & hardware boxes, abrasive materials, cabinets, lockers, bins & shelving, winches, hoists, cranes & derricks. (Hisp, estab 1993, empl 15, sales $5,000,000, cert: NMSDC)

3872　Silver Wings Aerospace
25400 SW 140th Ave
Princeton, FL 33032
Contact: Eduardo Montalvo President
Tel:　305-258-5950
Email: eddie@silverwingsaerospace.com
Website: www.silverwingsaerospace.com
Dist & repair aircraft parts. (Hisp, estab 2007, empl 16, sales $12,765,527, cert: NMSDC)

Georgia

3873　Control Specialties, Inc.
2503 Monroe Dr
Gainesville, GA 30507
Contact: Janice Moody CSR
Tel:　770-532-7736
Email: janice@control-specialties.com
Website: www.control-specialties.com
Dist pumps, instrumentation, filtration, controls, valves, energy audits, utility consultations. (Woman, estab 1987, empl 4, sales $1,965,970, cert: WBENC)

3874　H&S Supply Co., Inc.
528 N Main St
Moultrie, GA 31768
Contact: McKenzie Blanchett Sales
Tel:　229-985-4575
Email: mblanchett@hssupplyco.com
Website: www.hssupplyco.com
Dist plumbing & HVAC supplies, drilling supplies. (Nat Ame, estab 1969, empl 10, sales $40,000,000, cert: State)

3875　HeatRep, LLC
400 Galleria Pkwy, Ste 1500
Atlanta, GA 30339
Contact:　Owner
Tel:　404-989-5457
Email: sales@heatrep.com
Website: www.heatrep.com
Industrial equipment supplies, heat exchangers, fired heaters, electric heaters, economizers, condensers, liquid filtration, gas filtration, strainers, automatic strainers, filter separators, knockout tanks, reactors, pulsation bottles, custom fabrication (Woman, estab 2011, empl 1, sales , cert: WBENC)

3876　KACO Supply Company
1950 Lois Pointe Smyrna
Georgia, GA 30080
Contact: Kay Williams President
Tel:　770-435-8902
Email: kay.williams@kacosupplycompany.com
Website: www.kacosupplycompany.com
Dist institutional food, paper & plastic products, janitorial supplies, kitchenwares & equipment. (Woman/AA, estab , empl , sales $1,449,460, cert: City, NMSDC)

3877　Stag Enterprise, Inc.
383 Wilbanks Dr
Ball Ground, GA 30107
Contact: Rachel Niederer VP Operations
Tel:　770-720-8888
Email: racheln@stagenterprise.com
Website: www.stagenterprise.com
Dist industrial supplies, slitting tapes. (Minority, Woman, estab 1993, empl 21, sales $22,000,000, cert: NMSDC, WBENC)

Illinois

3878　AMSYSCO, Inc.
1200 Windham Pkwy
Romeoville, IL 60446
Contact: Neel Khosa VP
Tel:　630-296-8383
Email: nkhosa@amsyscoinc.com
Website: www.amsyscoinc.com
Dist post-tensioning tendons used in concrete reinforcement, barrier cable used in parking garage restraint systems. (As-Pac, estab 1981, empl 30, sales $18,697,191, cert: NMSDC)

3879　Emergent Safety Supply
1055 Kingsland Dr
Batavia, IL 60510
Contact: Jerry Hill VP
Tel:　630-406-9666
Email: jhill@emergentsafety.com
Website: www.Emergentsafety.com
Dist PPE, FR Clothing, Traffic Safety Products, Safety Signage, Spill Containment, Repertory Products. (Woman, estab 1985, empl 28, sales $12,200,000, cert: State, WBENC)

3880 Equity Industrial
2000 S 25th Ave Unit A
Broadview, IL 60155
Contact: Robert Butler President
Tel: 708-450-0000
Email: kevindonnelly@equityind.com
Website: www.equityind.com
Dist industrial supplies. (AA, estab 1996, empl 7, sales $15,000,000, cert: NMSDC)

3881 Freedom Air Filtration Inc.
1712 Arden Place
Joliet, IL 60435
Contact: Linda Freveletti President
Tel: 877-715-8999
Email: linda@freedomairfiltration.com
Website: www.freedomairfiltration.com
HVAC supplies & services. (Woman, estab 2004, empl 5, sales $850,000, cert: WBENC)

3882 Howe Corporation
1650 N Elston Ave
Chicago, IL 60642
Contact: Mary Howe President
Tel: 773-235-0200
Email: howeinfo@howecorp.com
Website: www.howecorp.com
Mfr Flake ice makers, refrigeration & ammonia pump out compressors & refrigeration pressure vessels. (Woman, estab , empl 37, sales $10,000,000, cert: WBENC)

3883 Inter-City Supply Co
8830 S Dobson Ave
Chicago, IL 60619
Contact: Jackie Dyess President
Tel: 773-731-8007
Email: intercity@ameritech.net
Website: www.intercity-supply.com
Dist janitorial, safety & food service. (AA, estab , empl , sales $11,000,000, cert: State, City, NMSDC)

3884 International Filter Manufacturing Corporation
713 W Columbian Blvd
Litchfield, IL 62056
Contact: Cecilia Ewing Hayes President
Tel: 217-324-2303
Email: ifmpres@consolidated.net
Website: www.ifm-corp.com
Mfr air filters for heavy-duty equip: transit vehicles, coal mining. Also dist HVAC, industrial & specailty filters. (Woman/AA, estab 1987, empl 35, sales $0, cert: NMSDC)

3885 ITA, Inc.
150 Pierce Road, Ste 550 60143
Itasca, IL 60143
Contact: Ritu Agrawal Dir of Marketing
Tel: 281-712-7608
Email: ragrawal@itaoffice.com
Website: www.itaoffice.com
Dist Industrial Equipment, Printers, Production Simulation Software, Hazardous & remote sensing robots, Oil filtration equipment, R&D Equipment, Chemiluminesent Oxidation Analyzers, Ferro Magnetic Detector, Automation MRO Products. (As-Pac, estab 1980, empl 10, sales $2,500,000, cert: NMSDC)

3886 Magid Glove & Safety Mfg. Co., LLC
1300 Naperville Dr
Romeoville, IL 60446
Contact: Joe Staron Dir Corp Sales
Tel: 888-380-9282
Email: joestaron@magidglove.com
Website: www.magidglove.com
Manufacturer, Distributor, and Importer of Work Gloves, Protective Clothing and Safety Equipment. (Minority, estab 1946, empl 3000, sales , cert: NMSDC)

3887 One Way Safety, LLC
418 Shawmut Ave
LaGrange, IL 60525
Contact: Anne Callaghan Sales Mgr
Tel: 708-579-0229
Email: anne@onewaysafety.com
Website: www.onewaysafety.com
Dist PPE, gas detection, fall protection, supplied air, respiratory equipment & uniforms, rescue teams, respiratory fit testing, safety training, safety equipment repair & rental, safety supervisors. (Woman, estab 2013, empl 20, sales $2,500,000, cert: WBENC)

3888 Permatron
2020 Touhy Ave
Elk Grove Village, IL 60007
Contact: Leslye Sandberg President
Tel: 847-434-1421
Email: lsandberg@permatron.com
Website: www.permatron.com
Mfr air filters, air intake filters, equipment protection filters. (Woman, estab 1957, empl 40, sales , cert: WBENC)

3889 Production Distribution Companies
9511 S Dorchester ave
Chicago, IL 60628
Contact: Cleo Downs President
Tel: 708-489-0195
Email: cleo@pdcompanies.org
Website: www.pdcompanies.org
Dist electrical, industrial supplies, tools & equipment. (AA, estab 2004, empl 9, sales $5,400,272, cert: City, NMSDC)

3890 Wabash Transformer (PowerVolt and Ensign Corp)
300 W. Factory Rd.
Addison, IL 60101
Contact: Ajay Sharma VP Sales & Mktg
Tel: 630-628-9999
Email: ajays@wabashtransformer.com
Website: www.wabashtransformer.com
Mfr power transformers: medical, dental, HVAC, controls, packaging & automation equipment. (As-Pac, estab 1966, empl 33, sales $3,200,000, cert: NMSDC)

Indiana

3891 Acorn Distributors, Inc.
5820 Fortune Cir W
Indianapolis, IN 46241
Contact: Debbie Schulz Contract Coord
Tel: 317-243-9234
Email: dschulz@acorndistributors.com
Website: www.acorndistributors.com
Dist disposable paper and plastic, janitorial supplies and equipment, chemicals, sanitary maintenance materials and foodservice supply products. (Woman, estab 1976, empl 128, sales $90,000,000, cert: State, City)

3892 Courtney Material Handling, Inc.
PO Box 6925
South Bend, IN 46660
Contact: Beth Courtney President
Tel: 574-231-0094
Email: beth@cmhionline.com
Website: www.cmhionline.com
Dist safety items: hard hats, vests, safety glasses, gloves, tools, fire & detection, bins, cabinets, carts, casters, chairs & stools. (Woman, estab 2003, empl 2, sales $213,673, cert: State)

3893 GM Supply Company, Inc.
6321 E 30th St Ste 205
Indianapolis, IN 46219
Contact: Steven Batts Business Devel
Tel: 317-898-3510
Email: steveb@gmsupplyco.com
Website: www.gmsupplyco.com
Integrated supply services, commodity management services, component assembly services, distribution of cutting tools, abrasives, safety supplies, MRO, packaging, tools, janitorial, electrical, plumbing, power transmission, bearings. (AA, estab 1992, empl 12, sales $22,000,000, cert: NMSDC)

3894 Gripp Inc.
17322 Westfield Park Rd
Westfield, IN 46074
Contact: Judy Gripp President
Tel: 317-896-3700
Email: judyg@grippinc.com
Website: www.grippinc.com
Dist, service, install & calibrate environmental monitoring equipment, open & and closed pipe flow monitoring & wastewater sampling. (Woman, estab 1992, empl 10, sales , cert: State, City)

3895 Powell Tool Supply Co., Inc.
1338 Mishawaka Ave
South Bend, IN 46615
Contact: Cari Eaton CEO
Tel: 574-289-4811
Email: ceaton@powelltool.com
Website: www.powelltool.com
Dist industrial supplies: cutting tools, abrasives, chemicals, MRO supplies, material handling, janitorial, etc. (Woman, estab 1948, empl 20, sales $5,500,000, cert: WBENC)

3896 Rfs Group
PO Box 68506
Indianapolis, IN 46268
Contact: Ramon Morrison Principal
Tel: 317-507-3165
Email: rmorrison@meticulousdb.com
Website: www.meticulousdb.com
Dist maintenance, janitorial & cleaning supplies, equipment & accessories. Also wholesale distributes office, foodservice and safety supplies. (AA, estab 2007, empl 6, sales $0, cert: State, City)

3897 Team Cruiser Supply LLC
PO Box 88255
Indianapolis, IN 46208
Contact: Christopher Barney President
Tel: 317-423-2430
Email: mbarney@teamcruiser.com
Website: www.tcsupplylogistics.com
Dist industrial products. (AA, estab 2013, empl 5, sales $3,345,000, cert: NMSDC)

3898 Worldwide Filters, LLC
3318 Pagosa Court
Indianapolis, IN 46201
Contact: Dawn Codozor Sales Mgr
Tel: 317-808-3719
Email: frank@worldwidefilters.com
Website: www.worldwidefilters.com
Dist filters: commercial, industrial & residential, HEPA filters, air, oil, hydraulic & fuel vehicle filters, water filtration systems. (AA, estab 2004, empl 5, sales $250,000, cert: NMSDC)

Kansas

3899 Sorella Group, Inc.
14844 W 107th St
Lenexa, KS 66215
Contact: Shelia Ohrenberg President
Tel: 913-390-9544
Email: ap@sorellagroup.com
Website: www.sorellagroup.com
Dist specialty products, bathroom partitions & accessories, flagpoles, lockers, fire protection specialties, mailboxes, shelving, mirrors & access flooring. (Woman, estab 2006, empl 30, sales $5,040,322,000, cert: State, City, WBENC, SDB)

3900 Touch Enterprises LLC
117 N Cooper St
Olathe, KS 66061
Contact: Camilo Fernandez Sales Andmin
Tel: 913-440-0770
Email: cfernandez@touchenterprises.com
Website: www.touchenterprises.com/shop
Dist industrial products, safety products, medical supplies, vet supplies, MRO supplies. (As-Pac, estab 2007, empl 15, sales $3,000,000, cert: NMSDC)

Kentucky

3901 Industrial Electronics LLC dba Indel-USA
10312 Bluegrass Pkwy
Louisville, KY 40299
Contact: Vadim Nazarenko Owner
Tel: 888-499-4877
Email: indel@indel-usa.com
Website: www.indel-usa.com
Repair, troubleshooting, retrofitting & design services for industrial electronic equipment. (Woman, estab 2005, empl 4, sales , cert: State)

3902 United American Supply, LLC
100-C Dewey Dr
Nicholasville, KY 40356
Contact: Albert Taylor Managing Partner
Tel: 859-881-1850
Email: al@unitedamericansupply.com
Website: www.unitedamericansupply.com
Dist safety supplies (PPE), machined parts & sanitary maintenance supplies. (AA, estab 2008, empl 8, sales $1,600,000, cert: NMSDC)

Louisiana

3903 Brewster Procurement Group, Inc.
401 West Main St.
Lafayette, LA 70501
Contact: Pat Brewster, C.p.m. Principal
Tel: 337-291-9009
Email: pat@brewsterprocurement.com
Website: www.brewsterprocurement.com
Dist MRO, mill & industrial supplies, electrical, tools, safety products, buyout services. (Minority, Woman, estab 1999, empl 8, sales $113,609,858, cert: NMSDC, WBENC)

3904 Precision Air & Liquid Solutions, LLC
1905 W Thomas St, Ste D271
Hammond, LA 70401
Contact: Cynthia Bourg Chief Exec Mgr
Tel: 504-208-1525
Email: cyndibourg@precisionair-liquid.com
Website: www.precisionair-liquid.com
Dist ventilation fans, fan parts, filtration, replacement filters, cartridges, housings, compressors, turbines & engines, dust, fume & mist control products & flow monitoring equipment. (Woman, estab 2003, empl 2, sales $550,000, cert: State, WBENC)

Massachusetts

3905 New England Die Cutting, Inc.
96 Milk St
Methuen, MA 01844
Contact: Kimberly L Abare President
Tel: 978-374-0789
Email: kabare@nedc.com
Website: www.nedc.com
Mfr gaskets, seals & insulators, die cutting, waterjet cutting & laser etching. (Woman, estab 1982, empl 28, sales $3,900,000, cert: WBENC)

Michigan

3906 Choctaw-Kaul Distribution Company
3540 Vinewood
Detroit, MI 48208
Contact: Caitlin Johnson Customer Dev Mgr
Tel: 313-895-3165
Email: cjohnson@choctawkaul.com
Website: www.choctawkaul.com
Mfr gloves & safety products, mgmt svcs, janitorial svcs, industrial specialty cleaning, paint booth cleaning, chemical mgmt, recycling, filter maintenance, truck repair, construction mgmt, parking lot maintenance, temp manpower, etc. (Minority, estab 1998, empl 350, sales $107,000,000, cert: NMSDC)

3907 Extreme Tooling LLC
48750 Structural Dr
Chesterfield, MI 48051
Contact: Kurt Schill President
Tel: 586-232-3618
Email: kschill@extremetooling.com
Website: www.extremetooling.com
Dist metal removal & industrial supplies, milling, drilling & industrial products. (Woman, estab 2003, empl 5, sales $3,683,821, cert: WBENC)

3908 IMC Products, Inc.
2743 Henry St, Ste 130
Muskegon, MI 49441
Contact: Irmgard Cooper President
Tel: 877-625-8743
Email: irmgard.cooper@imc-products.com
Website: www.imc-products.com
Assembly & kit packaging, contract administration, warehouse & distribution. (AA, estab 1990, empl 12, sales $1,900,000, cert: NMSDC)

3909 JISI Group, LLC
6043 18 Mile Rd
Sterling Heights, MI 48314
Contact: Amber Amato President
Tel: 586-239-9016
Email: a.amato@jisisupply.com
Website: www.jisisupply.com
Concrete construction & repair products. (Woman, estab 2014, empl 2, sales $446,000, cert: WBENC)

3910 Mahar Tool Supply Company, Inc.
7105 Nineteen MIle Rd
Sterling Heights, MI 48314
Contact: Dave Plosky Exec VP Sales
Tel: 586-997-2584
Email: dp@mahartool.com
Website: www.mahartool.com
Dist industrial products & MRO supplies, commodity management, integrated supply, technical staffing, engineering support. (Woman, estab 1947, empl 142, sales $115,200,000, cert: WBENC)

3911 Master Pneumatic Detroit, Inc.
6701 Eighteen Mile Road
Sterling Heights, MI 48314
Contact: Wendy Goscenski Mgr
Tel: 586-254-1000
Email: wgoscenski@aol.com
Website: www.masterpneumatic.com
Mfr filters, regulators & lubrication systems for compressed air systems. (Woman, estab 1950, empl 56, sales $6,500,000, cert: WBENC)

3912 Midwest Safety Products of Michigan
4929 E Paris SE
Grand Rapids, MI 49512
Contact: Vanh Miller CEO
Tel: 616-554-5155
Email: vanhm@midwestsafety.com
Website: www.midwestsafety.com
Dist safety, first aid, janitorial, packaging supplies, Personal Protective Equipment, Gloves, Safety Glasses, Ear Plugs, Disposable Clothing, Respirators, Welding Supplies, Hardhats. (As-Pac, estab 1978, empl 32, sales $10,010,000, cert: NMSDC)

3913 National Integrated Systems
4622 Runway Blvd
Ann Arbor, MI 48108
Contact: Jay Park Sales
Tel: 313-817-0066
Email: jpark@nisusa.com
Website: www.nisusa.com
Dist coated pipe & components, used for modular pipe racking systems. (As-Pac, estab 2003, empl 10, sales $0, cert: NMSDC)

3914 Safety Services, Inc.
5286 Wynn Rd
Kalamazoo, MI 49048
Contact: Kathryn Bowdish CEO
Tel: 269-382-1052
Email: info@safetyservicesinc.com
Website: www.safetyservicesinc.com
Dist industrial safety equipment: personal protective
equipment, gloves, first aid, fall protection, confined space
equipment, handling, storage, instrumentation, spill
control. (Minority, Woman, estab 1948, empl 28, sales $0,
cert: WBENC)

3915 Simon Marketing Group, LLC
4944 Cimarron Dr
Bloomfield Township, MI 48302
Contact: Carol Berg Managing Member
Tel: 248-855-6647
Email: carol@simonmarketinggroup.net
Website: www.parkinglotsafetysolutions.com/
Dist parking lot maintenance safety supplies. (Woman,
estab 2007, empl 4, sales , cert: WBENC)

3916 The Safety Source, LLC
35320 Forton Court
Clinton Township, MI 48035
Contact: Elizabeth VanSickle President
Tel: 866-688-7233
Email: elizabeth@safetysourcellc.com
Website: www.safetysourcellc.com
Dist industrial safety supplies, first aid supplies & miscella-
neous MRO supplies. (Woman, estab 2006, empl 6, sales
$2,200,000, cert: WBENC)

Minnesota

3917 Allied Electrical & Industrial Supply Company Inc.
6112 14th St W
St. Louis Park, MN 55416
Contact: Valerie McKissack President
Tel: 763-544-3600
Email: vmckissack@allied-electrical.com
Website: www.allied-electrical.com
Dist medical, industrial, electrical, safety, janitorial &
construction supplies. (Woman/AA, estab 1994, empl 6,
sales $832,000, cert: NMSDC)

3918 AMKA Global, LLC
6441 Cecilia Circle
Edina, MN 55439
Contact: Bocar Kane CEO
Tel: 952-495-4492
Email: sales@amkasafety.com
Website: www.amkasafety.com
Personal Protective products and work zone safety cones
and equipment. (AA, estab 2006, empl 2, sales $129,000,
cert: City)

3919 Safety Signs
19784 Kenrick Ave
Lakeville, MN 55044
Contact: Sue Blanchard President
Tel: 952-469-6700
Email: sueblanchard@safetysigns-mn.com
Website: www.safetysigns-mn.com
Traffic safety equipment and svcs specializing in traffic
control, permanent signs, pavement striping, pavement
stripe removals & safety apparel. (Woman, estab 1993,
empl 28, sales , cert: State, City)

Missouri

3920 Alliance Industries LLC
2959 N. Martin Ave
Springfield, MO 65803
Contact: Brenda Ryan President
Tel: 417-863-6315
Email: bryan@allianceind.com
Website: www.allianceind.com
Remanufacture OEM torque converters. (Woman/AA,
estab 2002, empl 20, sales $0, cert: NMSDC, WBENC)

3921 King Filtration Technologies, Inc.
1255 Research Blvd
Saint Louis, MO 63132
Contact: Michael Miossi Energy Acct Mgr
Tel: 800-999-8441
Email: michael.miossi@kingfiltration.com
Website: www.kingfiltration.com
Dist filtration products. (Woman, estab 1964, empl 20,
sales $0, cert: WBENC)

3922 Millennium Industrial Equipment, LLC
1475 Legacy Circle
Fenton, MO 63026
Contact: Tony Estopare President
Tel: 314-574-2047
Email: testopare@miequipment.com
Website: www.miequipment.com
Manufacturer's Rep, Bulk Solids (Dry) Material Handling,
Air Handling, and Air Pollution Control Equipment. (As-
Pac, estab 2002, empl 4, sales $630,862, cert: State)

3923 Stainless Integrity
3431 E Bluff Point Dr
Ozark, MO 65721
Contact: Vickie Norton President
Tel: 417-773-6383
Email: vlnorton@stainlessintegrity.com
Website: www.stainlessintegrity.com
Dist stainless steel nickel alloy ASME pressure vessels &
tanks; bioreactor & fermenter skids; field repair; field
modification & field erection, tank cleaning & inspec-
tion, powder hoppers & bins. (Woman, estab 2010, empl
1, sales $0, cert: WBENC)

Mississippi

3924 MS Rubber Company
715 E McDowell Rd
Jackson, MS 39204
Contact: Susan Foster GM
Tel: 601-948-2575
Email: sfoster@msrubber.com
Website: www.msrubber.com
Dist rubber hoses, hydraulic hoses, belting, plastic,
gaskets, safety supplies, o'rings, general hoses, hose
fittings, clamps, rubber tubing, matting, sheet packing,
rainsuit, gloves & boots. (Woman, estab 1963, empl 14,
sales $1,300,000, cert: CPUC, WBENC)

North Carolina

3925 EMI Supply
      5502 Cannon Dr
      Monroe, NC 28110
      Contact: Susan Richardson CEO
      Tel: 704-721-3641
      Email: srichardson@emisupply.com
      Website: www.emisupply.com
Dist electrical & industrial supplies: abrasives, adhesives,
chemicals, cutting tools, safety, tapes. (Woman, estab
1990, empl 7, sales , cert: WBENC)

3926 GP Supply Company
      501 E Washington St
      Greensboro, NC 27401
      Contact: Antonio Wallace CEO
      Tel: 336-274-7615
      Email: awallace@gpsupplycompany.com
      Website: www.gpsupplycompany.com
Dist mechanical supplies, industrial supplies, commercial
plumbing supplies, pipe, valves, fittings, fixtures. (AA,
estab , empl , sales $14,000,000, cert: NMSDC)

New Hampshire

3927 Quintana Associates, Inc.
      8 Puzzle Lane
      Newton, NH 03858
      Contact: Jorge Cruz Sales & Acct Rep
      Tel: 978-689-4411
      Email: jorgec@qaisupply.com
      Website: www.quintanasupply.com
Dist industrial supplies: safety, janitorial, packaging,
material handling equipment, office & clean room supplies. (Hisp, estab 1991, empl 20, sales $8,717,183, cert:
NMSDC)

New Jersey

3928 Automotive and Industrial Equipment LLC
      43 Wilkeshire Blvd
      Randolph, NJ 07869
      Contact: Vijay Srinivasan President
      Tel: 973-343-6432
      Email: autoandindustrialinc@gmail.com
      Website: www.ai-equip.com
Dist materials, tools, equipment & supplies to laboratories,
government facilities & private facilities. (As-Pac, estab
2011, empl 1, sales $375,891, cert: State)

3929 BKC Industries, Inc.
      3288 Delsea Dr Ste B
      Franklinville, NJ 08322
      Contact: Karen Harrison-Carter President
      Tel: 856-694-9400
      Email: bkcindustrial@comcast.net
      Website: www.bkcindustries.com
Dist industrial plant supplies, safety supplies, packaging
materials & construction materials. (Woman/AA, estab
1998, empl 3, sales $1,200,000, cert: State, 8(a))

3930 Centryco Inc.
      300 W Broad St
      Burlington, NJ 08016
      Contact: Mary Gordon President
      Tel: 609-386-6448
      Email: mtg@centryco.com
      Website: www.centryco.com
Mfr point of operation barriers for machinery & equipment: bellows, way covers, telescoping covers, flat
bellows & screens, spring guards/covers. (Woman, estab
1949, empl 35, sales $3,910,958, cert: WBENC)

3931 Forty Nine Corp.
      PO Box 2325
      Paterson, NJ 07509
      Contact: Michael Temkin VP
      Tel: 201-791-0584
      Email: mct@49corp.com
      Website: www.49corp.com
Mfr safety, warning & protective flags, tapes & tarpau-
lins for electric utilities & telephone companies.
(Woman, estab , empl , sales $500,000, cert: State,
WBENC)

3932 Stillwell Hansen, Inc.
      PO Box 7820
      Edison, NJ 08818
      Contact: Carol Stillwell President
      Tel: 732-225-7474
      Email: carol@stillwell-hansen.com
      Website: www.stillwell-hansen.com
Mfrs rep HVAC Equipment, Computer Room Air Conditioning, UPS, Networking Equipment Racks, Fire Protection , Portable Air Conditioning, Service for HVAC,
Computer Room, UPS, Fire Protection. (Woman, estab
1969, empl 70, sales $22,500,000, cert: State)

3933 The Olympic Glove & Safety Co. Inc.
      75 Main Ave
      Elmwood Park, NJ 07407
      Contact: Jerry Lorenc Sales
      Tel: 201-974-9320
      Email: jlorenc@olympicglove.com
      Website: www.olympicglove.com
Safety equipment. Gloves, safety glasses, safety goggles,
disinfecting spray, hand sanitizer, disinfecting wipes, gas
monitors, etc. (Woman, estab , empl 18, sales
$18,000,000, cert: WBENC)

3934 Turtle & Hughes, Inc.
      1900 Lower Rd
      Linden, NJ 07036
      Contact: Scott West President
      Tel: 330-518-0874
      Email: scott.west@turtle.com
      Website: www.turtle.com
Dist MRO, industrial & electrical supplies & equipment.
(Woman, estab 1923, empl 832, sales $760,000,000,
cert: WBENC)

New York

3935 Active Fire Extinguisher Co., Inc.
5-16 47th Ave
Long Island City, NY 11101
Contact: Munich President
Tel:　718-729-0450
Email: m.munich@activefire.com
Website: www.activefire.com
Dist fire extinguishers, pre-engineered automatic kitchen range hood systems, cabinets, fire hoses. (Woman, estab 1942, empl 13, sales $2,600,000, cert: City)

3936 AMKO Trading
129-09 26th Ave Unit D
Flushing, NY 11354
Contact: Tae S Rim Sales Mgr
Tel:　718-505-8401
Email: trim@amkotrading.com
Website: www.amkotrading.com
Dist commercial kitchen equipment. Electric & Gas Rice cookers, Electric rice warmer, Steam pans, PC food pans, Noodle making machines, Stock pots. (Minority, Woman, estab 2001, empl 8, sales $1,000,000, cert: NMSDC)

3937 J.T. Systems, Inc.
8132 Oswego Rd, Rt 57
Liverpool, NY 13090
Contact: Jit Turakhia President
Tel:　315-622-1980
Email: info@jtsystemsinc.com
Website: www.jtsystemsinc.com
Mfr air pollution control equipment: cyclones, scrubbers & baghouses, fans, ventilation, blowers, etc. (As-Pac, estab 1980, empl 5, sales $0, cert: State)

3938 Legacy Construction, LLC
85 Milton Ave
Sag Harbor, NY 11963
Contact: Stephen Watson CFO
Tel:　917-560-5593
Email: swatson@twcurban.com
Website: www.twcurban.com
Dist construction material & supplies. (AA, estab 2004, empl 2, sales , cert: State)

3939 Mechanical Heating Supply, Inc.
476 Timpson Pl
Bronx, NY 10455
Contact: Frank Rivera President
Tel:　718-402-9765
Email: frank@mechheat.com
Website: www.mechheat.com
Dist heating equipment & supplies. (Hisp, estab 1989, empl 11, sales $12,800,000, cert: State)

3940 Nifty Concept
1159 Elton St
Brooklyn, NY 11239
Contact: Cedric Durant VP Project Devel
Tel:　800-830-1665
Email: cedricd@niftyaides.com
Website: www.niftyconcept.com
Janitorial supplies; Medical equipment and supplies; Office supplies and furniture.. (Woman/AA, estab 2014, empl 8, sales $1,850,000,000, cert: State, City)

3941 Strategic Procurement Group
36 Harbor Park Dr
Port Washington, NY 11050
Contact: Donna Kay President
Tel:　516-479-3778
Email: kayd@strategicprocurement.us
Website: www.strategicprocurement.us
Dist MRO supplies. (Minority, Woman, estab 2002, empl 10, sales $13,000,000, cert: NMSDC, WBENC)

3942 Wats International Inc.
200 Manchester Rd
Poughkeepsie, NY 12603
Contact: Josh Anselmo President
Tel:　845-473-2106
Email: josh.anselmo@watsinternational.com
Website: www.watsinternational.com
Dist janitorial, office & MRO supplies. (AA, estab 1980, empl 8, sales $0, cert: State, City, NMSDC)

Ohio

3943 Benchmark Industrial Supply, LLC
1913 Commerce Rd
Springfield, OH 45504
Contact: Ron Tenkman Natl Sales Mgr
Tel:　937-325-1001
Email: rtenkman@benchmarkindustrial.com
Website: www.benchmarkindustrial.com
Dist safety products & industrial supplies. (Woman, estab 2003, empl 18, sales $5,000,000, cert: State, WBENC)

3944 First Star Safety, LLC
310 South Cooper Ave
Cincinnati, OH 45215
Contact:　President
Tel:　513-661-7827
Email: info@firststarsafety.com
Website: www.firststarsafety.com
Dist construction safety quipment: cones, barrels, safety vests, protective eye & ear wear. (Woman, estab 2005, empl 8, sales , cert: WBENC)

3945 Hydro Dyne Inc.
225 Wetmore Ave SE
Massillon, OH 44646
Contact: Kevin Boone Business Devel Mgr
Tel:　330-832-5076
Email: kevin@hydrodyneinc.com
Website: www.hydrodyneinc.com
Design, mfr & repair shell & tube heat exchangers, condensers, evaporators & feedwater heaters. (Woman, estab 1967, empl 30, sales $0, cert: WBENC)

3946 IPS Group LLC
3254 Hill Ave
Toledo, OH 43607
Contact: Michele Bighouse CEO
Tel:　419-241-5955
Email: ipsti@ipstreatment.com
Website: www.ipsgroupllc.com
Derusting, degreasing, washing, deburring, demagnetizing, descaling, pickling, rust inhibiting, surface passivation, chemical paint stripping, bonding removal, assembly, sorting & inspecting, repackaging & shipping. (As-Ind, estab 1994, empl 30, sales $900,000, cert: State, WBENC)

3947   National Access Design, LLC
1924 Losantiville Ave
Cincinnati, OH 45237
Contact: Cheryl White President
Tel: 513-351-3400
Email: cheryl@nationalaccessdesign.com
Website: www.nationalaccessdesign.com
Mfr double acting traffic/impact doors, strip doors, door jambs, blast cell doors, industrial/divider curtains, dock seals & equipment, dist FRP doors, cold storage doors, and air curtains. (Woman, estab 2011, empl 12, sales $0, cert: WBENC)

3948   Niche Consumer Products, LLC
2600 Civic Center Dr
Cincinnati, OH 45231
Contact: Benjamin Moore President
Tel: - -
Email: info@nicheconsumerproducts.com
Website: www.nicheconsumerproducts.com
Licenses, distributes and manufactures non-woven consumer products. (AA, estab 2007, empl 5, sales $330,000, cert: State, NMSDC)

3949   Norfleet Distributors LLC
32493 Jefferson Dr
Solon, OH 44139
Contact: Garrick Norfleet Owner
Tel: 216-832-2038
Email: garrick.norfleet@norfleetdistributors.com
Website: www.norfleetdistributors.com
Construction safety equipment including hard hats, safety vests etc. (AA, estab 2020, empl 2, sales $229,000, cert: NMSDC)

3950   PenCo Industrial Supply, Inc.
300 Industrial Pkwy, Unit D
Chagrin Falls, OH 44022
Contact: Penny Scocos President
Tel: 440-893-9506
Email: penny@pencosupply.com
Website: www.pencosupply.com
Dist MRO, safety & janitorial supplies: fasteners, cutting tools, abrasives, chemicals, eye & ear protection, gloves, respirators, toilet paper, paper towels, cleaning supplies & chemicals. (Woman, estab 2005, empl 5, sales $1,000,000, cert: WBENC)

3951   Quality Building Supplies For Industry, Inc.
17485 Saylor Ln
Grand Rapids, OH 43522
Contact: Edward haynes CEO
Tel: 419-832-2202
Email: qualitybldginc@aol.com
Website: www.qualitybuildingsupplies.com
Dist construction & industrial products: rebar, structural steel, piling, tools & hardware. (AA, estab 1978, empl 5, sales $2,300,000, cert: NMSDC)

3952   Superior Industrial Supply & Services Inc.
1717 Indianwood Circle Ste 200
Maumee, OH 43537
Contact: Stan McCormick President
Tel: 419-697-3700
Email: stan.mccormick@siss.cc
Website: www.superiorindustrialsupply.com
Dist janitorial chemicals & equipment, packaging supplies & equipment, paper supplies, mill & crib. (AA, estab 1972, empl 3, sales $0, cert: NMSDC)

3953   Tradex International Inc.
5300 Tradex Pkwy
Cleveland, OH 44102
Contact: Philip A. Baseil COO
Tel: 216-651-4788
Email: pab@tradexgloves.com
Website: www.tradexgloves.com
Dist gloves, aprons, shoe covers, bouffant caps, toilet seat covers & wipers. (Minority, estab 1988, empl 70, sales $0, cert: NMSDC)

Oklahoma

3954   Omni Packaging Corporation
12322 E 55th St
Tulsa, OK 74146
Contact: Roberta Jones President
Tel: 918-461-1700
Email: ar@omnipackaging.com
Website: www.omnipackaging.com
Dist adhesives/sealants, hose clamps, expansion joints, gaskets, matting, urethane, protective clothing, plastic, etc. (Minority, Woman, estab 1988, empl 65, sales $0, cert: NMSDC)

Pennsylvania

3955   Aquatech International Corporation
1 Four Coins Dr
Canaonsburg, PA 15317
Contact: Francis D'sa Reg Sales Mgr
Tel: 724-746-5300
Email: aic@aquatech.com
Website: www.aquatech.com
Mfr water & waste water treatment equip & systems. ASME tank & piping fabricators. (Minority, Woman, estab 1981, empl 450, sales $80,000,000, cert: NMSDC)

3956   Arbill Industries, Inc.
10450 Drummond Rd
Philadelphia, PA 19154
Contact: Renee Millett Sales Admin
Tel: 215-501-8246
Email: rmillett@arbill.com
Website: www.arbill.com
Mfr & dist industrial safety products. (Woman, estab 1957, empl 76, sales $0, cert: WBENC)

3957   Electrical Systems & Construction Supplies
5131-37 N 2nd St, Bldg 12
Philadelphia, PA 19120
Contact: Bernard Hopewell CEO
Tel: 215-324-3291
Email: bhopewell@escsinc.net
Website: www.escsinc.net
Dist electrical equipment, construction supplies, wire & cable & lighting. (AA, estab 2003, empl 3, sales $1,440,000, cert: State, City)

3958   General Fire Equipment Company, Inc.
220 Broadway Ave
Aston, PA 19014
Contact: Kim McDonnell Exec Asst
Tel: 610-485-8200
Email: kmcdonnell@generalfireequipment.net
Website: www.GeneralFireEquipment.Net
Dist, Service & Inspect Fire Extinguishers, Fire Equipment & Fire Surpession Systems. (Woman, estab 1975, empl 23, sales $0, cert: City)

3959   Industrial Piping Systems, Inc.
1250 Toronita St.
York, PA 17402
Contact: Christine Wardrop President
Tel: 717-846-7473
Email: christine.wardrop@ipspipe.com
Website: www.ipspipe.com
Dist pipes, valves, fittings, pumps, heat exchangers, tube, industrial coatings, lubricants. (Woman, estab 1982, empl 56, sales $17,574,304, cert: WBENC)

3960   Shah Industrial Sales Inc.
5824 Library Rd
Bethel Park, PA 15102
Contact: Barbara Shah President
Tel: 412-831-1224
Email: kara@shahind.com
Website: www.shahind.com
Dist fasteners, seals, o-rings, gaskets. (As-Ind, estab 1988, empl 2, sales $280,000, cert: State, NMSDC)

3961   Supreme Safety Inc.
21 Richard Road
Warminster, PA 18974
Contact: Annette Patchell President
Tel: 215-259-1400
Email: annette@supremesafetyinc.com
Website: www.supremesafetyinc.com
Dist industrial safety supplies & equipment. (Woman, estab 2004, empl 4, sales $1,400,000, cert: State)

Puerto Rico

3962   Interport Trading Corp.
PO Box 51958
Toa Baja, PR 00950
Contact: Antonio Cruz GM
Tel: 787-788-8650
Email: acruz@interportpr.com
Website: www.interportpr.com
Dist & service fire prevention equipment: extinguisher, hose, supresion systems, fire alarms, safety equipment: gloves,coveralls,eye protection, ear protection, showers, boots, caps, etc. (Hisp, estab 1989, empl 10, sales $1,448,600, cert: NMSDC)

3963   Master Products Corp.
Barrio Candelaria
Toa Baja, PR 00949
Contact: Zoila Rivera Sales & Logistics
Tel: 787-740-5254
Email: zrivera@mastergroup-pr.com
Website: www.mastergroup-pr.com
Mfr QUIKRETE Brand cement mixes: Concrete Mixes, Mortars, Flooring Thin-Sets and Grouts, Fast-Setting, Non-Shrink. (Hisp, estab 2005, empl 75, sales $12,758,000, cert: NMSDC)

3964   New York Wiping & Industrial Products, Inc.
698 Calle B
San Juan, PR 00920
Contact: Dr. Mario Julia President
Tel: 787-273-6363
Email: jsantos@nywiping.com
Website: www.nywiping.com
Dist industrial supplies. (Hisp, estab 1989, empl 5, sales , cert: NMSDC)

South Carolina

3965   Atlan-Tec, Inc. (Atlantic Technical Sales & Svc)
3215 Bryson Dr
Florence, SC 29501
Contact: Grace Patterson President
Tel: 843-661-0415
Email: atlreceivables@aol.com
Website: www.atlan-tec.net
Dist industrial equipment. (Woman, estab 1991, empl 6, sales $3,156,683, cert: State)

3966   Bullzeye Equipment & Supply
1383 Old Hwy 52
Moncks Corner, SC 29461
Contact: Kristie Collins Owner
Tel: 843-499-2226
Email: kcollins@bullzeyeequipment.com
Website: www.bullzeyeequipment.com
Dist industrial products, welding supplies, janitorial supplies, safety supplies, packaging supplies, material handling supplies & construction supplies. (Woman, estab 2012, empl 1, sales , cert: State, SDB)

3967   Carolina Industrial Products, Inc.
1872 Old Dunbar Rd
West Columbia, SC 29172
Contact: Dargon Gore President
Tel: - -
Email: dgore@cipbattery.com
Website: www.cipbattery.com
Dist & service industrial batteries, chargers & handling equipment. (Woman, estab 1983, empl 45, sales $13,000,000, cert: WBENC)

3968   Charleston's Rigging and Marine Hardware Inc
PO Box 21255
Charleston, SC 29413
Contact: Jessica Sage President
Tel: 843-723-7145
Email: jsage@charlestonsrigging.com
Website: www.charlestonsrigging.com
Dist rigging & material handling equipment, industrial & safety products, fabricates custom wire rope, chain, & nylon slings. (Woman, estab 1982, empl 47, sales $10,000,000, cert: City)

3969   Indcon Inc.
105 Ben Hamby Dr., Ste E
Greenville, SC 29601
Contact: Collin Atkins Corporate Counsel
Tel: 864-298-8300
Email: collin@indconinc.com
Website: www.indconinc.com
Dist industrial maintenance products, lubrication quality, general equipment maintenance, equipment installation, concrete & industrial repair, maintenance tools & hardware. (Woman, estab 1998, empl 10, sales $6,000,000, cert: WBENC)

3970 Munaco Sealing Solutions, Inc.
      5 Ketron Ct
      Greenville, SC 29607
      Contact: Jeff Adams Business Devel
      Tel: 864-676-2055
      Email: jeff@munaco-online.com
      Website: www.munacosealing.com
Sealing solutions & precision components: gaskets, custom
gaskets, metal seals, piston rings, metal gaskets, fiber
gaskets, spiral-wound gaskets, rubber gaskets, silicone
gaskets, elastomer o-rings, rubber o-rings, FKM, PTFE.
(Woman, estab 1995, empl 13, sales $13,050,000, cert:
WBENC)

3971 The Skinner Company
      1519 Evans Pond Rd
      Greenwood, SC 29649
      Contact: Operations Mgr
      Tel: 864-953-9618
      Email:
      Website: www.skinnerco.com
Dist pipeline clamps: emergency, band, pipe joint, pressed
steel economy clamps. (Woman, estab , empl 7, sales
$1,314,000, cert: WBENC)

Tennessee

3972 Dixon Services, Inc.
      1315 Farmville Rd
      Memphis, TN 38122
      Contact: Charles Dixon President
      Tel: 901-345-6608
      Email: charlesrdixon@dixonservicesinc.com
      Website: www.dixonservicesinc.com
Dist safety & industrial supplies. (Woman/AA, estab 2000,
empl 10, sales , cert: City, NMSDC)

3973 eSpin Technologies, Inc.
      7151 Discovery Dr
      Chattanooga, TN 37416
      Contact: Jay Doshi President
      Tel: 423-267-6266
      Email: jdoshi@exceedfilters.com
      Website: www.eSpintechnologies.com
Mfr & dist low energy consuming, high performance HVAC
air filters. (As-Ind, estab 1999, empl 27, sales $0, cert:
NMSDC, 8(a))

3974 Porter-Walker LLC
      115 Dyer St Ste 3
      Columbia, TN 38401
      Contact: Terrence Bybee Strategic Accounts Mgr
      Tel: 931-560-2428
      Email: tbybee@porter-walker.com
      Website: www.porter-walker.com
Dist safety, industrial & MRO supplies, supply chain mgmt.
(AA, estab , empl 41, sales $35,000,000, cert: State,
NMSDC)

3975 Superior Industrial Supply Co.
      2675 Whitman Ave
      Memphis, TN 38182
      Contact: Rita Montesi CEO
      Tel: 901-327-0450
      Email: info@superiorindsupply.com
      Website: www.superiorindsupply.com
Dist safety, industrial, janitorial, first aid supplies, fire
protection & AED's. (Woman, estab 1981, empl 13, sales
$2,500,000, cert: NWBOC)

3976 T G Inc.
      615 Main St
      Nashville, TN 37206
      Contact: Joseph Towner VP Sales
      Tel: 615-620-5100
      Email: jtowner@t-g-inc.com
      Website: www.t-g-inc.com
Dist industrial & electrical products, construction
supplies, materials & equipment. (Woman/AA, estab
1999, empl 8, sales $2,000,000, cert: NMSDC)

Texas

3977 All-Tex Pipe & Supply, Inc.
      9743 Brockbank
      Dallas, TX 75220
      Contact: Paul Borham Exec Asst
      Tel: 214-389-2201
      Email: paulb@alltexsupply.com
      Website: www.alltexsupply.com
Dist pipe, valves & fittings: acid waste, carbon steel, cast
iron, copper, CPVC, PVC, drainage, stainless steel.
(Woman, estab 1973, empl 120, sales $78,039,000, cert:
State, WBENC)

3978 Battery Consulting
      4020 Christopher Way
      Plano, TX 75024
      Contact: MuMu Moorthi Owner
      Tel: 214-929-6790
      Email: mumu@battery-consulting.com
      Website: www.battery-consulting.com
Dist batteries. (As-Pac, estab 2001, empl 2, sales
$181,000, cert: State)

3979 CASADA Industrial
      PO Box 203161
      Austin, TX 78720
      Contact: Ernest Anguiano Owner
      Tel: 800-828-0934
      Email: ernest@casada-industrial.com
      Website: www.casada-industrial.com
Dist industrial supplies. (Hisp, estab 1993, empl 8, sales
$0, cert: State)

3980 Daxwell
      2825 Wilcrest Dr, Ste 500
      Houston, TX 77042
      Contact: Sam Zhang Advisor
      Tel: 281-669-0622
      Email: samuel.zhang@daxwell.com
      Website: www.daxwell.com
Mfr & dist disposable products: gloves, dinnerware, foil
& paper products. (As-Pac, estab 1996, empl , sales
$69,982,944, cert: State)

3981 Dow-Caide Industrial, Inc.
      1534 Sunset Lane
      Duncanville, TX 75137
      Contact: Michael Downs President
      Tel: 972-421-8662
      Email: dewaye@sbcglobal.net
      Website: www.dowcaidesupply.com
Dist industrial supplies, industrial equipment, safety
supplies, plastic wrap/sheeting, trashbags, corrugated
boxes, lights/ballasts, food products, chemicals, paper
products, tape, labels, packaging supplies & materials
etc. (AA, estab 2011, empl 2, sales $424,660, cert: State,
NMSDC)

3982 Duran Industries Inc.
504 Business Pkwy
Richardson, TX 75081
Contact: Richard Duran President
Tel: 972-238-7122
Email: rduran@duranco.com
Website: www.duranco.com/
Dist industrial, commercial, MRO, safety, scientific & lab products. (Hisp, estab 1995, empl 20, sales $14,050,000, cert: NMSDC)

3983 Evco Partners dba Burgoon Company
PO Box 1168
Galveston, TX 77553
Contact: Donna Hanson President
Tel: 409-766-1900
Email: office@burgooncompany.com
Website: www.burgooncompany.com
Dist industrial supplies & equipment, laboratory & medical supplies, heavy equipment. (Woman, estab 1988, empl 17, sales $20,981,530, cert: State, WBENC)

3984 Guardian Industrial Supply, LLC
10629 Metric Blvd
Austin, TX 78780
Contact: Christina Duncan Managing Member
Tel: 512-973-3500
Email: sales@guardian-industrial.com
Website: www.guardiancatalog.com
Dist industrial supplies: circuit breakers, motor starters, motor control products, transformers, fuses, safety switches, wiring devices, plug, receptacles, softstarters, variable frequency drives, transfer switches, controls, enclosures, contactors, etc. (Woman, estab 2006, empl 10, sales $3,193,459, cert: WBENC)

3985 HLF Distributing, Inc.
1213-B N Post Oak Rd
Houston, TX 77055
Contact: update
Tel: 713-932-9320
Email: info@huskybicycles.com
Website: www.huskybicycles.com
Dist industrial & commercial bicycles & tricycles: wheels, tires, tubes, chains, tools & lubricants. (Woman, estab 1993, empl 7, sales $2,600,000, cert: WBENC)

3986 I AM Safety
4565 FM 466
Seguin, TX 78155
Contact: Lynda President
Tel: 832-715-0375
Email: lynda@iamsafetytx.com
Website: www.iamsafetytx.com
Safety Training (OSHA), Fire, First Aid/CPR/BBP/AED, Safety Products. (Woman, estab 2011, empl 2, sales , cert: State, City)

3987 Industrial Water Services
4500 Turf Rd Cordillera de los Andes 5740-2, El Paso, TX 79938
Contact: Ruben Diaz President
Tel: 915-849-0401
Email: rdiaz@industrialwaterservice.com
Website: www.industrialwaterservice.com
Industrial water equipment parts & service. (Hisp, estab 1997, empl 17, sales $3,800,000, cert: NMSDC)

3988 Mavich LLC
525 Commerce St.
Southlake, TX 76092
Contact: Vincent Manfredini Operations
Tel: 682-503-4484
Email: vincent.manfredini@mavich.com
Website: www.mavich.com
Dist MRO & industrial supplies: electronic components, connectors, passives, resistors, etc. (Minority, Woman, estab 2010, empl 10, sales $3,000,000, cert: State)

3989 Romar Supply
2468 Fabens
Dallas, TX 75229
Contact: Ron Adair VP Operations
Tel: 214-357-2020
Email: rona@romarsupply.com
Website: www.romarsupply.com
Dist pipe, valves, fittings, steam controls, valve actuation, stainless piping products, sanitary stainless piping. (Woman, estab 1983, empl 42, sales $17,000,000, cert: State, WBENC)

3990 Safety Supply, Inc.
12050 Crownpoint, Ste 160
San Antonio, TX 78233
Contact: CRYSTAL TURNER President
Tel: 800-873-9033
Email: CRYSTAL@SAFETYSUPPLYINC.COM
Website: www.safetysupplyinc.com
Dist industrial safety apparel & equipment, fire service & rescue equipment, environmental & health products. (Woman, estab 1983, empl 11, sales $6,400,000, cert: State, WBENC)

3991 Supply Innovations Co, LLC
200 Chihuahua St, Ste 100
San Antonio, TX 78207
Contact: Nancy Flack Mgr
Tel: 210-225-3194
Email: nancy@supplyinnovationsllc.com
Website: www.supplyinnovationsllc.com
Dist industrial supplies: tapes, safety , tools , abrasives, packaging, material handling, hardware, janitorial, adhesive & aircraft supplies. (Woman, estab 2007, empl 4, sales $1,673,122, cert: State, WBENC)

3992 TKC Enterprises Inc. dba Batteries Plus
2703 N Beltline Rd
Irving, TX 75062
Contact: Miguel Yan Owner
Tel: 972-256-2073
Email: miguel@battplus.net
Website: www.batteriesplus.com
Dist batteries. (As-Pac, estab , empl , sales $100,000,000, cert: State, NMSDC)

3993 Track Trading Co./ dba Exaco USA., Exaco Trading
4209 Greystone Dr
Austin, TX 78731
Contact: Kim Cook President
Tel: 512-345-1900
Email: kim@exaco.com
Website: www.exaco.com
Dist metal mixing blades, mixing paint & drywall. (Woman, estab 1987, empl 18, sales $10,000,000, cert: State, WBENC)

3994 V M Graphic Packaging & Safety Products LLC
4413 Fairlake Dr
Garland, TX 75043
Contact: Verna Melton CEO
Tel: 972-303-9102
Email: vmgraph@flash.net
Website:
www.vmgraphicpkgandsafetyproducts.espwebsite.c
Dist style bags & textile bags, industrial supplies, part bags, brooms, trash containers, tilt trucks. (Woman/AA, estab 1988, empl 5, sales $2,015,489, cert: State)

3995 White-Tucker Company
13895 Westfair East Dr
Houston, TX 77041
Contact: Controller
Tel: 281-664-7444
Email:
Website: www.whitetucker.com
Dist industrial equipment & supplies. (Woman, estab , empl 24, sales $8,580,000, cert: WBENC)

Virginia

3996 17 Machinery, LLC
3595 George Washington Mem Hwy
Hayes, VA 23072
Contact: Marie Knapp GM
Tel: 804-642-9400
Email: mknapp@17m2.com
Website: www.17machinery.com
Industrial & marine pumps & parts, valves, filtration, fabricated process systems, dual laminate pipe, fittings & tanks (Woman, estab 2003, empl 2, sales $257,776, cert: WBENC)

3997 Can See Fire Service Co Inc. t/a Fire Solutions
205 Haley Rd
Ashland, VA 23005
Contact: Edward Caldas VP Sales
Tel: 804-752-2366
Email: edward@firesolutionsinc.com
Website: www.firesolutionsinc.com
Install, maintain, service, inspects, relocate & repair fire protection equipment. (Minority, Woman, estab 1987, empl 53, sales $4,901,793, cert: State, NMSDC, WBENC)

3998 Encompass Supply
8000 Towers Crescent Dr Ste 1350
Vienna, VA 22182
Contact: Rudolph Burwell President
Tel: 804-716-0546
Email: info@encompasssuply.net
Website: www.encompasssupply.net
Electrical and industrial supplies, electrical construction & industrial supplies. (AA, estab 2013, empl 3, sales $2,500,000, cert: State)

3999 Parker Battery, Inc.
208 South St
Franklin, VA 23851
Contact: Shaun Parker Sales
Tel: 800-569-6084
Email: shaun@parkerbattery.com
Website: www.parkerbattery.com
Dist batteries, starters & alternators for automotive, commercial & industrial applications. (Woman, estab 1990, empl 9, sales $2,000,000, cert: State)

4000 Weldex Sales Corporation
PO Box 1
Thaxton, VA 24174
Contact: Robin Hartman President
Tel: 540-586-9648
Email: rhartman@weldexsales.com
Website: www.weldexsales.com
Dist industrial electric forklift batteries & chargers. (Woman, estab 1980, empl 29, sales $3,000,000, cert: NWBOC)

Washington

4001 Birch Equipment Rental & Sales
PO Box 30918
Bellingham, WA 98228
Contact: Cara Buckingham Information Dir
Tel: 360-734-5744
Email: planning@birchequipment.com
Website: www.birchequipment.com
Dist & rent equipment & machines: aerators, carpet cleaners, boom ifts, large excavators & forklifts. (Woman, estab 1972, empl 75, sales $15,000,000, cert: WBENC)

4002 Emerald, Inc.
PO Box 14227
Seattle, WA 98168
Contact: President
Tel: 206-767-8909
Email: emeraldinc@msn.com
Website: www.emeraldinc.net
Kitchen Hood Cleaning, Fire Extinguisher Sales/Service, Kitchen Hood Fire System Sales/Service, Safety Equipment Sales. (Hisp, estab 1989, empl 5, sales $300,000, cert: State, City)

4003 Excel Gloves & Safety Supplies, Inc.
6808 26th St E, Ste 102
Fife, WA 98424
Contact: Irene Reyes CEO
Tel: 253-896-1195
Email: glovelady@excelgloves.com
Website: www.excelgloves.com
Import & dist gloves, safety, medical, janitorial & packaging supplies, (Minority, Woman, estab 1993, empl 8, sales $2,000,000, cert: State, NMSDC)

4004 Rohtek Automation LLC
9223 NE 174th Pl
Bothell, WA 98011
Contact: Oscar Rojas President
Tel: 425-318-2179
Email: orojas@rohtek.com
Website: www.rohtekautomation.com
Dist high tech mfg, operating & monitoring solutions. (Hisp, estab 2011, empl 2, sales , cert: State)

Wisconsin

4005 E. R. Abernathy Industrial Inc.
   2000 Pewaukee Rd, Ste 0
   waukesha, WI 53188
   Contact: Edna Abernathy President
   Tel: 262-446-3377
   Email: edna@abernathyco.com
   Website: www.abernathyco.com
Dist safety, construction, electrical & industrial supplies.
(Woman/AA, estab 1991, empl 10, sales $1,354,000, cert:
NMSDC)

4006 First American Engineered Solutions, LLC
   136 Jackson St, Ste C
   Oshkosh, WI 54901
   Contact: Gerald Morris President
   Tel: 920-231-8501
   Email: gmorris@firstamericanllc.com
   Website: www.firstamericanllc.com
Dist electronics, electrical equipment, industrial equip-
ment & supplies, office equipment & supplies & ordnance.
(Nat Ame, estab 1997, empl 12, sales $4,500,000, cert:
NMSDC, 8(a))

INDUSTRIAL MACHINES

Manufacturers and distributors of ovens, vacuum cleaners, air compressors, blasting machines, food processing equipment, paint mixers, tube flaring machines, etc. (See also HARDWARE & TOOLS, HYDRAULIC & COMPRESSED AIR EQUIPMENT, INDUSTRIAL MACHINES and MATERIAL HANDLING EQUIPMENT). NAICS Code 42

Arizona

4007 STRATCO, Inc.
      14821 N 73rd St
      Scottsdale, AZ 85260
      Contact: Diane Graham CEO
      Tel: 480-991-0450
      Email: supplier.diversity@stratcoglobal.com
      Website: www.stratcoglobal.com
Design blending & reaction equipment for grease, lubricants, bio-diesel & petrochemical industries. (Woman, estab 1928, empl 16, sales $5,621,643, cert: WBENC)

California

4008 Combustion Associates, Inc.
      555 Monica Circle Corona
      Corona, CA 92880
      Contact: Preeti Chandan Sales/Mktg
      Tel: 951-272-6999
      Email: pchandan@cai3.com
      Website: www.cai3.com
Food processing systems; integrated skid-mounted process systems; lube oil & gas systems; water heaters & industrial burners; modular aeroderivative power generation systems; packaged. (Woman/As-Ind, estab 1991, empl 45, sales $9,100,000, cert: NMSDC, CPUC)

4009 Lucio Family Enterprises, Inc.
      2150 Prune Ave
      Fremont, CA 94539
      Contact: Sandra Garcia
      Tel: 510-623-2323
      Email: sgarcia@compactormc.com
      Website: www.compactormc.com
Mfr waste & recycling equipment: compactors, containers, balers (all sizes), custom fabrication requests. (Minority, Woman, estab 2006, empl 18, sales $2,500,000, cert: NMSDC)

4010 Turbo Air, Inc.
      1250 Victoria St
      Carson, CA 90746
      Contact: Laura Spears Natl Acct Mgr
      Tel: 310-900-1000
      Email: laura@turboairinc.com
      Website: www.turboairinc.com
Mfr restaurant equipment: refrigerators/freezers, pizza prep tables, sandwich salad units, glass doors, microwave ovens, food warmers, sink tables, sushi cases & air conditioners. (Minority, estab 1997, empl 40, sales , cert: NMSDC)

Florida

4011 New England Machinery, Inc.
      2820 62nd Ave E
      Bradenton, FL 34203
      Contact: Hans Weiden Sales Mgr
      Tel: 941-755-5550
      Email: hweiden@neminc.com
      Website: www.neminc.com
Packaging equipment, Unscramblers, Orienters, Cappers, Retorquers, Pluggers, Pump Placers, Lidding. (Woman, estab 1974, empl 55, sales $15,000,000, cert: WBENC)

4012 Supergreen Inc.
      4051 107th Circle N, Ste 1
      Clearwater, FL 33762
      Contact: Hoang Mai President
      Tel: 727-459-3130
      Email: mike.hoang@supergreenusa.com
      Website: www.supergreenusa.com
Mfr Tankless Water Heaters. (As-Pac, estab 2013, empl 4, sales , cert: NMSDC)

Illinois

4013 AM Manufacturing Company
      14151 Irving Ave
      Dolton, IL 60419
      Contact: Edward Mentz President
      Tel: 708-841-0959
      Email: lserafin@ammfg.com
      Website: www.ammfg.com
Mfr dough processing equipment: dough dividers, dough rounders, pizza / tortilla presses, pizza crust dockers, proofers, cooling conveyors, bagel forming equipment. (Woman, estab 1961, empl 30, sales $7,000,000, cert: City)

4014 Apex Beverage Equipment Distribution Group, LLC.
      450 Tower Blvd, Ste 200
      Carol Stream, IL 60188
      Contact: Christie Tierney President
      Tel: 877-901-2739
      Email: ctierney@totalapex.com
      Website: www.totalapex.com
Dist beverage equipment, replacement parts & installation products. (Woman, estab 2008, empl 11, sales $14,000,000, cert: WBENC)

Indiana

4015 Cici Boiler Rooms Inc.
      7811 Baumgart Rd
      Evansville, IN 47711
      Contact: Penny Duncan Administrative Asst
      Tel: 812-867-0810
      Email: penny@ciciboilers.com
      Website: www.ciciboilers.com
Boilers, HVAC, Deareators, Water Heaters, Air Conditioning, New Equipment, Parts, Service, (Woman, estab 1965, empl 14, sales $4,900,000, cert: State)

4016 Harriman Material Handling
511 N Range Line Rd
Morristown, IN 46161
Contact: Ashley Larochelle President
Tel: 765-763-8985
Email: ashlar@harrimanmaterialhandling.com
Website: www.HarrimanMaterialHandling.com
Overhead Cranes, Hoists, Jib Cranes, Monorails,
Gantry Cranes, Custom Lifting Devices, Slings/Rigging, Fall
Protection Equipment, Crane Components & Parts, Dock
Equipment, Storage Equipment, Drum Handling Equipment
(Woman, estab 2004, empl 5, sales $3,528,300, cert:
WBENC)

Michigan

4017 Amigo Mobility International Inc.
6693 Dixie Hwy
Bridgeport, MI 48722
Contact: Gabriella DeVries Acct Mgr
Tel: 989-921-5073
Email: gdevries@myamigo.com
Website: www.myamigo.com
Provide electric handicap shopping carts to retailers.
(Woman, estab 1968, empl 114, sales $12,400,000, cert:
WBENC)

4018 Manufacturers/Machine Builders Services Co.
13035 Wayne Rd
Livonia, MI 48150
Contact: Glen Neal Managing Partner
Tel: 734-748-3706
Email: mmbswork2@sbcglobal.net
Website: www.mmbscorp
Build & service automated machines: pipe, wire, debug &
install machines. (Minority, Woman, estab 2002, empl 16,
sales $800,000, cert: NMSDC)

4019 Quality Design Services, Inc.
3914 Highwood Pl
Okemos, MI 48864
Contact: Ashish Manek Business Dev Mgr
Tel: 614-946-4749
Email: ashish.manek@qdsautomation.com
Website: www.qdsautomation.com
System Integration: Engine Assembly Lines, Transmission
Assembly Lines, Axle Assembly Lines, Transfer Machines,
Test Systems, Washers, Conveyor Systems, Hydraulic
Systems, Lubrication Systems. (As-Ind, estab 1990, empl
22, sales , cert: NMSDC)

4020 Ultimation Industries LLC
27930 Groesbeck Hwy
Roseville, MI 48066
Contact: Jacqueline Canny CEO
Tel: 586-771-1881
Email: jcanny@ultimationinc.com
Website: www.ultimationinc.com
Design, mfr & install assembly line equipment & services,
automation devices & conveyor systems, tire & wheel
mounting & inflation devices, tire processing lines, TPMS &
soaping machines. (Woman, estab 1989, empl 14, sales
$4,855,120, cert: WBENC)

Minnesota

4021 DV Roland Enterprises, Inc.
15171 Freeland Ave N
Hugo, MN 55038
Contact: Kenny Scamp General Mgr
Tel: 651-429-9012
Email: ken@jtservicesinc.com
Website: www.jtservicesinc.com
Dist & service industrial diesel engines & diesel engine
parts. Supporting diesel engines for aerial lifts, air
compressors, backhoes, dozers, excavators, forklifts,
generators, light towers, rollers, skid steer loaders,
tractors, welders. (AA, estab 2004, empl 6, sales
$1,433,333, cert: City, NMSDC)

Missouri

4022 Erb Equipment Co., Inc.
200 Erb Industrial Dr
Fenton, MO 63026
Contact: Gregg Erb Dir of Sales
Tel: 636-349-0200
Email: greggerb@erbequipment.com
Website: www.erbequipment.com
Construction equipment, rent new & used equipment &
repair parts, repair & maintenance, Backhoe, Wheel
Loaders, Front loaders, excavators, dozers, crawler
loaders, skid steer (bobcat), mini excavators & material
handlers. (Woman, estab 1943, empl 230, sales
$134,737,841, cert: WBENC)

4023 Productive Automoated Systems Corp. (PASCO)
2600 S Hanley Rd, Ste 450
St. Louis, MO 63144
Contact: Nate Mahoney Dir Finance & IT
Tel: - -
Email: nmahoney@pascosystems.com
Website: www.pascosystems.com
Design & Mfr rugged robotic automation systems and
palletizers. (Woman, estab 1976, empl 50, sales
$13,332,000, cert: State)

4024 TSA Sales Associates, LLC
3466 Bridgeland Dr
Bridgeton, MO 63044
Contact: Pamela Sanders Owner
Tel: 314-291-4400
Email: psanders@tsasales.com
Website: www.tsasales.com
Air pollution control equipment, dry bulk solids, han-
dling equipment & storage silos & bins. Design dust,
fume & mist collecion systems. (Woman, estab 2001,
empl 5, sales $374,087, cert: State)

New Jersey

4025 Ana M Fisher dba A & A Glove & Safety Co.
20 Richey Ave
West Collingswood, NJ 08107
Contact: Ashton Goerge Sales
Tel: 800-854-0060
Email: ashton@aaglove.com
Website: www.aasafetyindustrial.com
Safety consulting & sourcing, industrial equipment.
(Minority, Woman, estab 1990, empl 5, sales $400,000,
cert: State, City)

4026 Hop Industries Corp.
1251 Valley Brook Ave
Lyndhurst, NJ 07071
Contact: Melanie Harkin Sales Rep
Tel: 201-438-6200
Email: mharkin@hopindustries.com
Website: www.hopindustries.com
Laminating Supplies & Equipment: laminating rolls, laminating pouches, pouch laminators, roll laminators, Binding Supplies & Equipment: binding combs, twin wire binding, plastic coil binding. (As-Pac, estab 1977, empl 70, sales $43,697,760, cert: NMSDC)

Ohio

4027 ASD - Automation Systems & Design
6222 Webster St
Dayton, OH 45414
Contact: Sunny Kullar CEO
Tel: 937-387-0351
Email: sunny@asddayton.com
Website: www.asddayton.com
Build, design & integrate custom machines. (As-Ind, estab 2000, empl 14, sales $1,500,000, cert: NMSDC)

4028 OCS Process Systems
24142 Detroit Rd
Westlake, OH 44145
Contact: Beth Kloos CEO
Tel: 440-871-6009
Email: bkloos@ocsprocess.com
Website: www.ocsprocess.com
Engineer, design & install food processing systems: liquid & dry powder processing systems, heat transfer, mixing, batching systems, metering systems, distribution systems, COP, CIP, piping, pumps, valves, welding, fabrication & installation. (Woman, estab , empl 40, sales $7,500,000, cert: WBENC)

Pennsylvania

4029 American Kitchen Machinery and Repair Co., Inc.
204 Quarry St
Philadelphia, PA 19106
Contact: Andrea Mahon President
Tel: 215-627-7760
Email: service@akmco.com
Website: www.akmco.com
Parts & service to commercial kitchen equipment: cooking equipment, sanitation & dishwashing equipment, preparation equipment & mixers, refrigeration equipment & ice machines. (Woman, estab 1953, empl 45, sales $7,000,000, cert: WBENC)

4030 D. Gillette Industrial Service, Inc.
46 N Main St
Bangor, PA 18013
Contact: CEO
Tel: 610-588-4939
Email: contact@deegindustries.com
Website: www.dgindustrialservices.com
Mfr & repair commercial equipment: oven rollers, packaging equip, bakery/food equip. (Minority, Woman, estab 2003, empl 12, sales $2,000,000, cert: 8(a))

4031 Gottscho Printing Systems, Inc.
740 Veterans Circle
Warminster, PA 18974
Contact: Aimee Hasson President
Tel: 267-387-3005
Email: sales@gottscho.com
Website: www.gottscho.com
Printing machines, marking machines, bar code printing, ink jet, coding & printing, blister pack printing, hot stamp, thermal printer, T1J printer, C1J printer, flexographic printer, platen printer, UV printer, digital coder, digital printer. (Woman, estab 2009, empl 12, sales , cert: WBENC)

South Carolina

4032 USS Rhino
50 Grand Ave, Ste D
Greenville, SC 29607
Contact: Deeann Holbird Accounting Clerk
Tel: 864-233-8035
Email: accounting@rhinoassembly.com
Website: www.rhinoassembly.com
Dist industrial machinery & equipment merchant. (AA, estab 2015, empl 2, sales , cert: NMSDC)

Texas

4033 Epcon Industrial Systems
PO Box 7060
The Woodlands, TX 77387
Contact: Shan Jamaluddin COO
Tel: 936-273-3300
Email: epcon@epconlp.com
Website: www.epconlp.com
Design, engineer & mfr air pollution control systems, oxidizers, afterburners, deoilers, washlines, spray booths, ovens & furnaces. (As-Pac, estab 1977, empl 99, sales $14,000,000, cert: State, NMSDC)

4034 PLP Enterprises, Inc.
PO Box 578
Blue Ridge, TX 75424
Contact: Phillip Pulliam VP
Tel: 972-752-4837
Email: ppulliam@aps-plp.com
Website: www.aps-plp.com
Build Plastic & Stainless Steel Chemical Delivery Systems, Valve Manifold Boxes, Chemical Process Tanks, Process Hoods, Drain Pans, Chemical Carts, Storage Cabinets. PLC Control Systems, Electrical Panels, Sump Systems. (Woman, estab 2000, empl 6, sales $1,100,000, cert: WBENC)

4035 RECS, Inc.
PO Box 520
Prosper, TX 75078
Contact: Elaine Underwood President
Tel: 972-346-3226
Email: recsmaterials@windstream.net
Website: www.richmondexpress.com
Heavy construction rental equipment: excavators, rock chrushers, bulldozers, motorgraders, dumptrucks, backhoes, wheel loader/w bucket & forks, dredging machines, automobile & pickup rental, truck & trailer rental, generators lightplants. (Minority, Woman, estab 1982, empl 25, sales $5,000,000, cert: State)

Virginia

4036 Crest Foodservice Equipment Company
605 Jack Rabbit Rd
Virginia Beach, VA 23451
Contact: Karen Ricketts Business Devel
Tel: 757-425-8883
Email: karen@cresteq.com
Website: www.crestfoodservice.com
Dist commercial kitchen equipment & ancillary items. (Woman, estab 1984, empl 36, sales $11,531,745, cert: State)

4037 E2C Group, LLC
1418 Jacquelin St
Richmond, VA 23220
Contact: Denise Fields Principal
Tel: 804-358-3334
Email: dif1@aol.com
Website: www.e2cgroup.com
Dist & install commercial foodservice equipment. (AA, estab 2004, empl 6, sales $2,200,000, cert: State)

4038 VMEK Group LLC
2719 Oak Lake Blvd
Midlothian, VA 23112
Contact: Adriana Lovvorn Operations Mgr
Tel: 804-349-9001
Email: adriana@vmek.com
Website: www.vmek.com
Build & support high speed industrial machines powered by advanced vision technology & machine design. (Minority, Woman, estab 2012, empl 9, sales , cert: NMSDC)

Wisconsin

4039 Accuracy Machine
201 Stange St.
Merrill, WI 54452
Contact: Kevin Keiser Project Mgr
Tel: 715-722-0825
Email: kevin.keiser@accuracymachine.com
Website: www.accuracymachine.com
Mfr machines & specialty parts: converting, printing, coating, paper, material handling, packaging, food grade machine, performance automotive, performance marine, aerospace & powertrain industries. (As-Pac, estab 1994, empl 10, sales , cert: State)

4040 Memmert USA, LLC
W355 S9075 Godfrey Ln
Eagle, WI 53119
Contact: Tina M. Binder CEO
Tel: 262-594-3941
Email: tslaboven@memmertusa.com
Website: www.memmertusa.com
Dist ovens, incubators, climate chambers, humidity chamber, vacuum ovens, water baths, oil baths, CO2 incubators, Paraffin Ovens, Climatic test chambers, sterilizers, glassware washers. (Woman, estab 2006, empl 4, sales $2,242,000, cert: WBENC)

4041 Quintec Integration, Inc.
1600 Paramount Dr
Waukesha, WI 53186
Contact: Tony Storniolo President
Tel: 262-754-5900
Email: tstorniolo@quintecconveyor.com
Website: www.quintecconveyor.com
Layout engineering, conveyor hardware, mechanical equipment, electrical controls & programming, mechanical & electrical installation, project management, field training of equipment. (Hisp, estab 1999, empl 7, sales $10,000,000, cert: State)

4042 Trester Hoist Equipment, Inc.
W136 N4863 Campbell Dr, Ste 6
Menomonee Falls, WI 53051
Contact: Robyn Vaupel President
Tel: 262-790-0700
Email: robyn@tresterhoist.com
Website: www.tresterhoist.com
Overhead lifting equipment & service. (Woman, estab 1995, empl 11, sales $5,000,000, cert: WBENC)

West Virginia

4043 Sisterville Tank Works, Inc.
1942 McCoy St
Sisterville, WV 26175
Contact: Jason Morgan Owner
Tel: - -
Email: sales@stwinc.com
Website: www.stwinc.com
Fabricate pressure vessels, heat exchangers, boilers, condensers, cryogenics, evaporators, hoppers, reactors, stills, strippers, tanks, towers, vaporizers, nitrators, columns, autoclaves. (Woman, estab , empl 50, sales , cert: WBENC)

INFORMATION TECHNOLOGY: Services

Includes system engineering/design/research, consulting, programming, information/data management, data entry, microfilming, help desk, mobile applications, etc. (See also INFORMATION TECHNOLOGY: Systems/Machines and ENGINEERING, SPECIAL SERVICES). NAICS Code 54

Alaska

4044 Tuknik Government Services, LLC
3800 Centerpoint Dr Ste 502
Anchorage, AK 99503
Contact: Navid Nekoui
Tel: 301-802-3114
Email: nnekoui@koniag.com
Website: www.tuknikgs.com
Outsourced computer related services, IT support, software installation & security, physical security, program management. (Nat Ame, estab 2014, empl 2, sales , cert: NMSDC)

Alabama

4045 Ariel Information Technology Corporation
1 Chase Corporate Center Ste 400
Birmingham, AL 35244
Contact: Terry Pennington
Tel: 205-705-3100
Email: tpennington@ariel-it.com
Website: www.ariel-it.com
Information technology consulting & services, technology staff augmentation, business analysis, requirements management, software design, system design, software development, quality assurance testing, hardware & software procurement. (AA, estab 2009, empl 1, sales , cert: NMSDC)

4046 CompuCycle, Inc.
8019 Kempwood Dr
Houston, AL 77055
Contact: Kelly Hess CEO
Tel: 713-866-8026
Email: khess@compucycle.com
Website: www.compucycle.com
Local & national environmentally responsible IT asset disposal services & hard drive data destruction as well as data center decommissioning. (Woman, estab 1989, empl 85, sales $15,000,000, cert: State, WBENC)

4047 Daten System Consulting
8225 Old Pascagoula Road 36582
Theodore, AL 36582
Contact: Catina Short
Tel: 866-388-3856
Email: cshort@datensys.com
Website: www.datensystemconsulting.com
Information technology data centric consulting organization. (Woman/AA, estab 2013, empl 5, sales $396,000, cert: State, NMSDC, WBENC)

4048 Horizon Services Corporation
4898 Valleydale Rd Ste B-3
Birmingham, AL 35242
Contact: Frank Davis CEO
Tel: 205-249-8033
Email: contracting@horizonamerica.net
Website: www.horizonamerica.net
Technical products & services. (AA, estab 2001, empl 30, sales $5,200,000, cert: NMSDC)

4049 RedKnot Resource Group, LLC
120 19th St N, Ste 2067
Birmingham, AL 35203
Contact: Carol Pittman CEO
Tel: 205-901-1386
Email: carol@redknotresources.com
Website: www.redknotresources.com
Provide end-to-end outsourced vendor management solution governing external business arrangements for our clients globally. (Woman, estab 2008, empl 8, sales $1,000,000, cert: WBENC)

4050 Safety Research Corporation of America, LLC
133 Research Lane
Dothan, AL 36305
Contact: Susan Crump CEO
Tel: 334-678-7722
Email: scrump@srca.net
Website: www.srca.net
Information technology services: software design & development database applications, websites & graphic design services. (Woman, estab 1993, empl 16, sales $2,517,535, cert: State)

Arkansas

4051 Celerit
2200 N Rodney Parham, Ste 205
Little Rock, AR 72212
Contact: Terry Rothwell President
Tel: 501-312-2900
Email: info@celerit.com
Website: www.celerit.com
IT consulting: full time personnel and custon application development. (Woman, estab 1985, empl 50, sales , cert: WBENC)

Arizona

4052 Inteliblue
15300 Governors Lake Dr
Little Rock, AR 72223
Contact: Priyanka kothakanti Mgr
Tel: 501-251-8918
Email: priya@inteliblue.com
Website: www.inteliblue.com
IT Consulting/Staffing. (Woman, estab 2012, empl 1, sales , cert: State)

4053 Business Partner Solutions Inc.
7362 E Rovey Ave
Scottsdale, AZ 85250
Contact: Katherine Bluma CEO
Tel: 858-337-9020
Email: kat@businesspartnersolutions.com
Website: www.businesspartnersolutions.com
Asset intelligence, encryption, strong authentication & application security & access control. (Woman, estab 2005, empl 7, sales $2,800,000, cert: WBENC, SDB)

4054 Centacor, Inc.
135 Chilton Dr
Chandler, AZ 85225
Contact: Troy Bryan Mgr
Tel: 480-899-9500
Email: info@centacor.com
Website: www.centacor.com
IT products & services. (AA, estab 2009, empl 4, sales ,
cert: NMSDC)

4055 Clutch Solutions LLC
2152 S Vineyard Ave, Building 1, Ste 120
Mesa, AZ 85210
Contact: Michael Burchell Strategic Diversity Partner
Tel: 203-393-5234
Email: mike.burchell@clutchsolutions.com
Website: www.clutchsolutions.com
Information technology: IT Hardware and Software Value
Added Reseller, Solution Architect/engineering, Cyber-
Security, Unified Communications. (Nat Ame, estab 2017,
empl 58, sales $200,000,000, cert: NMSDC)

4056 EDB Warehousing and Logistics, LLC
PO Box 11363
Chandler, AZ 85248
Contact: Eric Bell Owner
Tel: 800-370-8670
Email: eric.bell@edbwarehousing.com
Website: www.edbwarehousing.com
Inventory Management. (AA, estab 2015, empl 2, sales
$100,000, cert: NMSDC)

4057 Electronic Responsible Recyclers, LLC
730 E Southern Ave
Mesa, AZ 85204
Contact: Christopher Ko CEO
Tel: - -
Email: chris@er2.com
Website: www.ER2.com
Provide technology and computer hardware installation,
imaging, disposal, and recycling services. (As-Pac, estab
2010, empl 78, sales $11,300,000, cert: NMSDC)

4058 Executive Technology Inc.
4809 E Thistle Landing Dr Ste 100
Phoenix, AZ 85044
Contact: Linda Perkins Controller
Tel: 480-346-7041
Email: lperkins@exectechdirect.com
Website: www.exectechdirect.com
Information technology products & services. (AA, estab
2001, empl 16, sales , cert: NMSDC)

4059 Identico Print Services (DBA Print.Save.Repeat.com)
4942 S 71st St
Mesa, AZ 85212
Contact: Nathan Carter Business Devel
Tel: 800-587-1173
Email: orders@printsaverepeat.com
Website: www.printsaverepeat.com
Mfr pressure sensitive labels & laser printer toner car-
tridges. (Hisp, estab 1986, empl 51, sales $17,938,582,
cert: NMSDC)

4060 Native Technology Solutions Inc.
7065 W Allison Rd
Chandler, AZ 85226
Contact: Mabel Tsosie
Tel: 480-639-1234
Email: mtsosie@gilarivertel.com
Website: www.native-tech.net
Cabling & computing services, structured cabling,
phone, security systems, video conferencing, & technol-
ogy solutions. (Nat Ame, estab 2007, empl 14, sales
$4,000,000, cert: State)

4061 QCM Technologies, Inc.
9060 E Via Linda Ste 220
Scottsdale, AZ 85258
Contact: Lenny Aupperlee Sales Exec
Tel: 602-412-3539
Email: laupperlee@qcmtech.com
Website: www.qcmtech.com
IT solutions & services, hardware, software & profes-
sional services, design, implement & support enterprise-
wide IT solutions. (Hisp, estab 2001, empl 20, sales
$12,651,000, cert: NMSDC)

4062 TDR Consulting Inc
951 N Forest Ct
Chandler, AZ 85226
Contact: Dean Rosales
Tel: 480-293-4959
Email: deanrosales@tdrconsultinginc.com
Website: www.tdrconsultinginc.com
Engineering consulting, systems engineering, specifica-
tion development, requirements traceability, derived
requirements, schedule development, milestone
tracking, performance tracking & metrics reporting.
(Hisp, estab 2013, empl 1, sales , cert: NMSDC)

4063 Tec Global
9674 E Vantage Point Rd
Scottsdale, AZ 85262
Contact: Richard Stanford President
Tel: 480-575-4333
Email: richard.stanford@tecglobalinc.com
Website: www.tecglobalinc.com
Global Supply Chain optimization Company. (AA, estab
1996, empl 3, sales $150,000, cert: NMSDC)

4064 TIPS Consultants LLC
1412 E Michelle Dr
Phoenix, AZ 85022
Contact: Dr. Charles Fisher CFO
Tel: 713-307-3362
Email: cfisher@tipsconsultants.com
Website: www.tipsconsultants.squarespace.com
Engineering consultant & training services, Enterprise
Project Management (EPM) & Earned Value Manage-
ment (EVM) solutions. (Woman/AA, estab 2015, empl 3,
sales , cert: State)

4065 XL Technology Group, LLC
6895 E Camelback Rd Ste 118
Scottsdale, AZ 85251
Contact: Michael Brown Dir
Tel: 602-324-7474
Email: michael@xltechnologygroup.com
Website: www.xltechnologygroup.com
IT staffing resources for IT implementations & staff
augmentation (contract, contract to hire, & direct hire) .
(AA, As-Pac, estab 2010, empl 20, sales $2,600,000, cert:
NMSDC)

Califorrna

4066   314e Corporation
6701 Koll Center Pkwy #340
Pleasanton, CA 94566
Contact: Alok Sharma COO
Tel: 646-639-1035
Email: alok@314ecorp.com
Website: www.314e.com
IT consulting, staffing & managed services. (As-Ind, estab 2004, empl 350, sales $26,000,000, cert: NMSDC)

4067   360 IT Professionals, Inc.
3031 Tisch Way, 110 Plaza West
San Jose, CA 95128
Contact: Manmeet Manace Business Devel Dir
Tel: 510-254-3300
Email: manmeet@360itpro.com
Website: www.360itpro.com/
Programming Languages, .net, Java, PHP, Android, IOS, Python, Ruby, Enterprise Resource Planning SAP, Oracle, Microsoft AX & GP, Functional IT Positions, Program Managers, Project Managers, Business Analysts & Data. (As-Pac, estab 2013, empl 93, sales $8,948,501, cert: State, NMSDC, SDB)

4068   3K Technologies LLC
161 Mission Falls Ln Ste 201
Fremont, CA 94539
Contact: Krishna Chittabathini CEO
Tel: 408-716-5900
Email: krishna@3ktechnologies.com
Website: www.3ktechnologies.com
Information technology consulting services & staffing. (Woman/As-Ind, estab 2002, empl 65, sales $5,106,000, cert: CPUC)

4069   3S Global Business Solutions
7923 Nita Ave
Canoga Park, CA 91304
Contact: Sam Mookerjee Dir corp affairs
Tel: 818-453-4403
Email: sam.mookerjee@3sgbs.com
Website: www.3sgbs.com
Information technology resources, staff augmentation, project management, IT training, IT development/ maintenance outsourcing. (As-Ind, estab 2007, empl 12, sales $895,000, cert: State, City, CPUC)

4070   4WardTech Inc.
7317 El Cajon Blvd, Ste 111, La Mesa, CA 91942
La Mesa, CA 91942
Contact: Andrew Parker President
Tel: 757-876-1735
Email: andrew@4ward.tech
Website: www.4ward.tech
Information Technology (IT) solutions & services, Cloud Computing, Internet of Things (IoT), Bluetooth Low Energy (BLE) & Beacons, Machine Learning, Chatbots, Blockchain and DevOps. Other Technical Expertise: Mobility Platform. (AA, estab 2016, empl 2, sales $100,000, cert: NMSDC, SDB)

4071   AccountSight
19925 Stevens Creek Blvd Ste 100
Cupertino, CA 95014
Contact: Anita Bist VP Business Dev
Tel: 408-560-3900
Email: abist@accountsight.com
Website: www.accountsight.com
AccountSight time tracking & resource planning software, SaaS solution, eSign Genie esignature software. (Woman/As-Ind, estab 2013, empl 20, sales , cert: NMSDC)

4072   Ace Technologies, Inc.
2880 Zanker Rd, Ste 208
San Jose, CA 95134
Contact: Jessy Jaiswal Mgr
Tel: 408-228-0240
Email: jessy@acetechnologies.com
Website: www.acetechnologies.com
Information technology: software consulting, software recruitment & staffing, SAP project consulting & staffing, application development, software maintenance. (Minority, Woman, estab , empl , sales $15,170,000, cert: WBENC)

4073   Adroit Resources Inc.
39500 Stevenson Place, Ste 202
Fremont, CA 94539
Contact: Prashant Sharma Sr Dir
Tel: 510-573-6102
Email: prashant@adroitresources.com
Website: www.adroitresources.com
Information Technology services. (Minority, Woman, estab 2011, empl 75, sales $7,000,000, cert: NMSDC, CPUC)

4074   Agama Solutions Inc.
39159 Paseo Padre Pkwy Ste 216
Fremont, CA 94538
Contact: Peter Kalra VP
Tel: 510-377-9959
Email: peter@agamasolutions.com
Website: www.agamasolutions.com
IT Consulting services in terms of Project based consulting and Staffing Services of various technical hard to find skills in the area of Information technology. (As-Pac, estab 2006, empl 200, sales $3,000,000, cert: State)

4075   Agile Global Solutions, Inc.
13405 Folsom Blvd, Ste 515
Folsom, CA 95630
Contact: Raja Krishnan President
Tel: 916-353-1780
Email: raja@agileglobal.com
Website: www.agileglobal.com
IT services (staffing) & turnkey solutions. (Woman/As-Ind, estab 2003, empl 62, sales $8,300,000, cert: NMSDC, CPUC)

4076   AgileTalent, Inc.
1900 S Norfolk Ave.
San Mateo, CA 94403
Contact: Jay Singh
Tel: 650-931-2572
Email: jay.singh@agiletalentinc.com
Website: www.agiletalentinc.com
IT contract staffing & recruiting. (As-Ind, estab 2011, empl 48, sales $4,600,000, cert: NMSDC, CPUC)

4077   AgreeYa Solutions, Inc.
605 Coolidge Dr
Folsom, CA 95630
Contact: Ajay Kaul Managing Partner
Tel: 916-294-0075
Email: sales_americas@agreeya.com
Website: www.agreeya.com
IT consulting services, staff or project based. (Minority, Woman, estab 1999, empl 1800, sales $123,300,000, cert: NMSDC, CPUC)

4078   AKRAYA, Inc.
2901 Tasman Dr Ste 106
Santa Clara, CA 95054
Contact: Sonu Ratra President
Tel: 408-907-6400
Email: sonu.ratra@akraya.com
Website: www.akraya.com
IT consulting - Java, Microsoft, databases, Peoplesoft, Oracle, Siebel, SAP, data warehousing. (Woman/As-Ind, estab 2001, empl 390, sales $33,430,000, cert: NMSDC, CPUC, WBENC)

4079   Alicon Group, Inc.
5405 Alton Pkwy, Ste 5A514
Irvine, CA 92604
Contact: Chris Metzger Operations Coord
Tel: 949-294-9634
Email: chris@alicongroup.com
Website: www.alicongroup.com
Oracle applications technology consulting. (Minority, Woman, estab 2001, empl 4, sales $3,980,000, cert: NMSDC, NWBOC)

4080   Allfon LLC
2746 Glendon Ave
Los Angeles, CA 90064
Contact: Roya Hosseinion President
Tel: 310-470-7868
Email: roya@allfon.com
Website: www.allfon.com
Systems integration, offshore development, outsourcing services. (Woman, estab 2000, empl 50, sales $5,390,928, cert: WBENC)

4081   Alpha Omega Solutions, Inc.
3070 Saturn St, Ste 200
Brea, CA 92821
Contact: Benny Wong President
Tel: 714-996-8760
Email: bennywong@aosolutions.com
Website: www.aosolutions.com
Computer software, computer consulting, financial consulting, automotive business consulting. (As-Pac, estab 1993, empl 8, sales $1,000,000, cert: NMSDC)

4082   AMBCO Electronics Corporation
15052 Redhill Ave, Ste D
Tustin, CA 92780
Contact: ADA XIONG
Tel: 714-259-7930
Email: ada@ambco.com
Website: www.ambco.com
Audiometer Manufacturer. 5 year warranty on all Ambco Audiometers from date of purchased. We repair, service, and calibrate all makes of audiometers. (Minority, Woman, estab 1941, empl 4, sales $914,803, cert: State)

4083   Amick Brown LLC
2500 Old Crow Canyon Rd Ste 425
San Ramon, CA 94583
Contact: Karen Gildea Principal
Tel: 925-820-2000
Email: karen.gildea@amickbrown.com
Website: www.amickbrown.com
SAP BI Implementation, SAP HANA, SAP BI, Strategy and Roadmaps, SAP BI Production Support, SAP BI Installations and Upgrade, Reporting, Analytics & Dashboards, SAP BI Training Workshops, SAP BI Security. (Woman/As-Ind, estab 2010, empl 35, sales $7,335,144, cert: State, CPUC, WBENC)

4084   AmmMm Inc.
28364 S Western Ave, Ste 402
Rancho Palos Verdes, CA 90275
Contact: Malee Tansavatdi CEO
Tel: 310-294-1203
Email: malee@ammmminc.com
Website: www.AmmMmInc.com
Web application & design, portals, online branding, database dev, intranet. (Minority, Woman, estab 2007, empl 20, sales , cert: NMSDC)

4085   Apex Computer Systems, Inc.
13875 Cerritos Corporate Dr Unit A
Cerritos, CA 90703
Contact: Ira Klein Dir Partner Alliance
Tel: 562-926-6820
Email: sales@acsi2000.com
Website: www.acsi2000.com
Computer hardware maintenance & support, managed services, project management, accounting/ERP, EDI, data warehousing, (As-Pac, estab 1984, empl 52, sales $17,010,000, cert: State, NMSDC, CPUC, SDB)

4086   APN Software Services Inc.
39899 Balentine Dr, Ste 385
Newark, CA 94560
Contact: Anisha Sodha
Tel: 510-683-9043
Email: anisha@apninc.com
Website: www.apninc.com
IT staffing: contract, contract to hire & direct hire. (As-Ind, estab 1996, empl 300, sales $16,000,000, cert: NMSDC)

4087   Applied Computer Solutions
15461 Springdale St.
Huntington Beach, CA 92649
Contact: Cathy Fancher Operations Mgr
Tel: 714-861-2200
Email: cathy.fancher@acsacs.com
Website: www.acsacs.com
System integration, strategic solutions, enterprise infrastructure, Sun Microsystems, Cisco Systems, HDS, Veritas, Oracle, Network Appliance, Checkpoint, Symantec, StorageTek. (Woman, estab 1989, empl 25, sales $206,523,000, cert: CPUC, WBENC)

4088 Ashunya Inc
642 n. eckhoff St
orange, CA 92868
Contact: Melanie Merchant CEO
Tel: 714-385-1900
Email: melaniem@ashunya.com
Website: www.ashunya.com
Information technology: hardware & software, LAN/WAN wiring, project mgmt, post implementation svcs. (Minority, Woman, estab 1993, empl 8, sales $3,000,000, cert: WBENC)

4089 Automae
7111 Garden Grove Blvd
Garden Grove, CA 92841
Contact: Mbuyi Khuzadi CEO
Tel: 714-816-3000
Email: mbuyi@mail.automae.com
Website: www.automae.com
Technical services: hardware design, systems engineering, software engineering, system safety & health management. (AA, estab 1997, empl 3, sales , cert: City)

4090 Aviana Global Technologies, Inc.
915 W Imperial Hwy Ste 100
Brea, CA 92821
Contact: Donna Sanchez Staffing Consultant
Tel: 714-256-9756
Email: donnas@avianaglobal.com
Website: www.avianaglobal.com
Enterprise planning, reporting, OLAP analysis, dashboards, scorecards, analytics & statutory regulations. (As-Pac, estab 1994, empl 30, sales $53,822,829, cert: CPUC)

4091 Axelliant LLC
21250 Hawthorne Blvd, Ste 500
Torrance, CA 90503
Contact: Mohsin Khan Procurement Mgr
Tel: 310-377-2881
Email: mohsin.khan@axelliant.com
Website: www.axelliant.com
IT Solutions, Cyber Security, Date Center/ Networking, to Mobility, Cloud Life Cycle Management & UC /Collaboration. (Minority, estab 2016, empl 10, sales , cert: NMSDC)

4092 Axiom Global Technologies, Inc.
220 North Wiget Lane
Walnut Creek, CA 94598
Contact: Mohit Arora
Tel: 925-393-5800
Email: mohit.arora@axiomglobal.com
Website: www.axiomglobal.com
Application development, staff augmentation, document management. (Woman/As-Ind, estab 2001, empl 70, sales $6,000,000, cert: NMSDC)

4093 BayInfotech LLC
11501, Dublin Blvd Ste 200
Dublin, CA 94568
Contact: Maulik Shyani Sr Acct Mgr
Tel: 408-480-8501
Email: maulik@bay-infotech.com
Website: www.bay-infotech.com
Contingent Staffing, Beeline, Infrastructure Management: End-to-End Management, Application, Network, Security, Data Center, Service Desk. (Minority, Woman, estab 2011, empl 15, sales $1,101,000, cert: NMSDC, CPUC, WBENC)

4094 BayOne Solutions
4637 Chabot Dr Ste 250
Pleasanton, CA 94588
Contact: Mohammed Ismail Sr Mgr
Tel: 925-399-0595
Email: mismail@bayone.com
Website: www.bayonesolutions.com
IT & Engineering - Development, testing, Mobile Apps, infrastructure, Analytics, Creative/Product & Data Science/Machine Learning. (Minority, estab 2012, empl 187, sales $54,000,000, cert: NMSDC)

4095 Beta Soft Systems Inc.
42808 Christy St Ste 101
Fremont, CA 94538
Contact: Bob Hemnani Sr Sales Mgr
Tel: 510-744-1700
Email: bob@betasoftsystems.com
Website: www.betasoftsystems.com
IT Services & solutions, recruitment, business development, software development & service delivery. (As-Pac, estab 2005, empl 300, sales , cert: State)

4096 BeyondCurious, Inc.
3767 Overland Ave, Ste 115
Los Angeles, CA 90034
Contact: Nikki Barua CEO
Tel: 310-210-1907
Email: nbarua@beyondcurious.com
Website: www.beyondcurious.com
Design & technology, mobile interfaces. (Woman/As-Ind, estab 2011, empl 9, sales $2,289,210, cert: NMSDC)

4097 California Creative Solutions, Inc.
13475 Danielson St, Ste 220
Poway, CA 92064
Contact: Raminder Singh Accountant
Tel: 858-208-4131
Email: mbeprogram@ccsglobaltech.com
Website: www.ccsglobaltech.com
Information & Technology, software engineering, systems analysis, integration, and development. (As-Ind, estab 1997, empl 400, sales $21,600,000, cert: NMSDC)

4098 California Electronic Asset Recovery
3678 LeMay St
Mather, CA 95655
Contact: Stacey Henrikson Corporate Acct Mgr
Tel: 916-952-1711
Email: shenrikson@cearinc.com
Website: www.cearinc.com
Electronic asset recovery & recycling, Total Solution IT Asset Management & Disposition, E-Waste/E-Asset, ITAD, Data Sanitization, Recovery, Destruction/Shred Remarketing, Test, Repair, Reporting. (As-Pac, estab 2000, empl 58, sales $11,000,000, cert: CPUC)

4099 Celer Systems, Inc.
1024 Iron Point Rd, Ste 100
Folsom, CA 95630
Contact: Sree Gaddam VP
Tel: 916-220-2093
Email: sree.gaddam@celersystems.com
Website: www.celersystems.com
IT consulting services, project management, end to end, application development, testing services, database management, data warehouse, staff augmentation. (Minority, Woman, estab 2007, empl 25, sales $3,000,000, cert: NMSDC)

4100   Central Computer Systems Inc.
3777 Stevens Creek Blvd
Santa Clara, CA 95051
Contact: Heidi Co CEO
Tel: 408-248-5888
Email: heidi@centralcomputer.com
Website: www.CentralComputers.com
Custom-build computer systems, repair services, IT services, networking, notebook repair, corporate sales, local government sales, education sales & retail consumer sales. (Minority, Woman, estab 1986, empl 80, sales $25,000,000, cert: NMSDC, WBENC)

4101   Cerna Solutions, LLC
3304 Febo Ct
Carlsbad, CA 92009
Contact: Michelle Yu CEO
Tel: 442-222-0303
Email: michelle@cernasolutions.com
Website: www.cernasolutions.com
IT consulting services. (Minority, Woman, estab 2012, empl 6, sales , cert: NMSDC)

4102   Certified Independent Adjusters, Inc.
25000 Ave Stanford Ste 224
Valencia, CA 91390
Contact: Roosevelt Jackson Owner
Tel: 800-501-6032
Email: rosey@gociai.com
Website: www.gociai.com
Certified Independent Adjusters, Inc. is a nationwide independent adjusting firm. Our adjusters have over 50 years of experience in Insurance industry.

ï¿½Daily Claims
ï¿½Auto Claims
ï¿½Catastrophes
ï¿½Commercial Claims
ï¿½Li (AA, estab 2010, empl 350, sales , cert: NMSDC)

4103   Clovity Inc.
11501 Dublin Blvd, Ste 200
Dublin, CA 94568
Contact: Bhawna Vats Dir Operations
Tel: 925-264-6360
Email: certifications@clovity.com
Website: www.clovity.com/
IoT-as-a-Service platform provider powered by CSensorNet and Digital Transformation professional and managed services provider in IoT Digital, Cloud and Data. (As-Pac, estab 2008, empl 100, sales , cert: NMSDC)

4104   Connexus Hub
14252 Culver Dr, Ste #257
Irvine, CA 92604
Contact: Daniel Jung Managing Partner
Tel: 949-415-4364
Email: dan@connexushub.com
Website: www.connexushub.com
IT solutions products & services that encompass data storage, mobile, cloud technologies, security & networking solutions, IT hardware & software solutions. (Minority, Woman, estab 2014, empl 20, sales $1,700,000, cert: CPUC, 8(a), SDB)

4105   Consult Our Sorce, LLC
2121 26th St, Ste 202
San Francisco, CA 94107
Contact: Bruin Gerber Business Dev Exec
Tel: 937-925-1336
Email: Bruin@consultoursource.com
Website: www.consultoursource.com
ITIL (Information Technology Infrastructure Library), TOGAF (The Open Group Architecture Framework), Project Management (PMP, Agile), Management Consulting Services, Information Security Consulting, Managed Services. (Hisp, estab 2014, empl 5, sales $937,564, cert: NMSDC)

4106   CPAC Inc.
4749 E. Wesley Dr
Anaheim, CA 92807
Contact: Kara Mack Natl Acct Mgr
Tel: 800-778-2722
Email: kmack@cpacinc.com
Website: www.cpacinc.com
Technical support, IT solutions. (Woman, estab 1993, empl 30, sales $20,000,000, cert: CPUC)

4107   Cyber Professionals Inc. DBA Encore Software Servi
2025 Gateway Pl, Ste 385
San Jose, CA 95110
Contact: Radha Krishnan Managing Partner
Tel: 408-573-7337
Email: rkrishnan@encoress.com
Website: www.encoress.com
Mobility, social commerce, Cloud & analytics IT services. (As-Ind, estab 1998, empl 500, sales $10,679,387, cert: NMSDC)

4108   Danta Technologies
561 Rush Dr
San Marcos, CA 92078
Contact: President
Tel: 619-862-3415
Email: office@dantatechnologies.net
Website: www.dantatechnologies.net
IT applications, Infrastructure, IBM WebSphere, Oracle, Sales Force, IOS developer, Network engineer, Big Data, Hadoop, Java, Angular JS, Node JS, etc. (As-Pac, estab 2013, empl 25, sales $864,000, cert: NMSDC)

4109   Delta Computer Consulting, Inc.
25550 Hawthorne Blvd Ste 106-108
Torrance, CA 90505
Contact: Alisa Spiegel VP Sales
Tel: 310-541-9440
Email: A.Spiegel@deltacci.com
Website: www.deltacci.com
Human Capital Recruiting & Deployment, IT Staff Recruiting & Augmentation. (Woman, estab 1987, empl 165, sales $28,000,000, cert: WBENC, NWBOC)

4110   DeltaTRAK Inc.
6140 Stoneridge Mall Rd Ste 180
Pleasanton, CA 94588
Contact: Karen Bustillo
Tel: 925-249-2250
Email: dtsupplierdiversity@deltatrak.com
Website: www.deltatrak.com
Thermal Mapping Analysis. (As-Pac, estab 1989, empl 200, sales $20,415,145, cert: NMSDC)

4111 Dew Software, Inc.
983 Corporate way
Fremont, CA 94539
Contact: Suresh Deopura President
Tel: 510-490-9995
Email: suresh@dewsoftware.com
Website: www.dewsoftware.com
Provide software consultants for short/long term in latest technology as well in legacy systems, develop projects at offsite or offshore. (Minority, estab 1997, empl 25, sales $3,400,000, cert: CPUC)

4112 DFI Technologies, LLC
1065 National Dr Ste 1
Sacramento, CA 95834
Contact: Vieng Phouthachack Technical Sales Engineer
Tel: 916-568-1234
Email: vieng@dfitech.com
Website: www.dfitech.com
High performance computing solutions: Digital Signage, Interactive Kiosk, Gaming, Industrial Automation, Medical Device/Healthcare, Transportation. (As-Pac, estab 1985, empl 70, sales , cert: State)

4113 Digital Mountain
4633 Old Ironsides Dr Ste 401
Santa Clara, CA 95054
Contact: Julie Lewis CEO
Tel: 866-344-3627
Email: supplierdiversity@digitalmountain.com
Website: www.digitalmountain.com
Web-based filtering & review (FileQuest), electronic evidence collection, electronic discovery (including tape restoration), computer forensics, data breach management & expert witness services. (Woman, estab 2003, empl 5, sales $2,006,316, cert: State, CPUC, WBENC)

4114 E-Base Technologies, Inc.
39159 Paseo Padre Pkwy Ste 206
Fremont, CA 94538
Contact: Archana Kaushik President
Tel: 510-790-2547
Email: archana@ebasetek.com
Website: www.ebasetek.com
IT staffing: contract, contract-to-hire & permanent positions. (Woman/As-Ind, estab 2000, empl 69, sales $6,012,054, cert: WBENC)

4115 ECommerce Holdings, Inc.
201 Los Gatos Saratoga Rd, Ste 230
Los Gatos, CA 95030
Contact: Purnims Nandkishore President
Tel: 866-465-3294
Email: purnima@babychangingstations.com
Website: www.babychangingstations.com
Largest stocking Minority owned distributor of Koala baby changing stations and Bathroom Accessories: Fans, Mirrors, Medicine Cabinets, Soap Dishes, Towel Bars and Rings, Plumbing Fixtures and Parts: Water-free Urinals (Woman/As-Ind, estab 2009, empl 2, sales $840,866, cert: NMSDC, CPUC)

4116 eJangar, Inc.
13700 Altin Pkwy, Ste 154
Irvine, CA 92618
Contact: Ayesh Natekal President
Tel: 800-259-9578
Email: ayesha@ejangar.com
Website: www.ejangar.com
IT services: staffing, project mgmt, Cloud architect, SFDC Consultants, Sharrepoint Developers, Salesforce developers, .Net, Java, Offshore Development from India, Onsite Services. (Woman/As-Ind, estab 2009, empl 25, sales , cert: CPUC)

4117 En Pointe IT Solutions, LLC
2121 Rosecrans Ave, Ste 4310 Ste 4310
El Segundo, CA 90245
Contact: Brian Huber Natl Acct Mgr
Tel: 424-220-6700
Email: brian.huber@enpointeits.com
Website: www.enpointeits.com
Provides software, hardware and IT Services. (Minority, estab 2016, empl 25, sales $150,000,000, cert: State, NMSDC, CPUC, WBENC)

4118 En Pointe Technologies Sales, Inc.
18701 S Figueroa St
Gardena, CA 90248
Contact: Michael Rapp VP Sales & Mktg
Tel: 310-337-5200
Email: helpdesk@enpointe.com
Website: www.enpointe.com
IT products & professional services. (Minority, Woman, estab 1993, empl 1200, sales $347,000,000, cert: NMSDC, WBENC)

4119 eTouch Systems
6627 Dumbarton Circle
Freemont, CA 94555
Contact: Amit Shah VP
Tel: 510-795-4800
Email: ashah@etouch.net
Website: www.etouch.net
Information technology services - QA, Automation, Manual, Functional, Performance, Specialized testing, Mobile testing, etc. (As-Ind, estab 1997, empl 700, sales $70,000,000, cert: NMSDC)

4120 EUS IT Solutions, LLC
19327 Broadacres Ave
Carson, CA 90746
Contact: Donald Hale CEO
Tel: 562-731-2244
Email: donhale@eusitsolutions.com
Website: www.eusitsolutions.com
IT consulting, IT Support, pc/laptop/workstation support, Hardware/Software support, smartphone support, tablet support, network support, printer support, cloud support, do projects. (AA, estab 2012, empl 5, sales , cert: NMSDC)

4121　Executive Office Services
　　　PO Box 6621
　　　Oakland, CA 94603
　　　Contact: Detria Mixon HR consultant
　　　Tel:　510-830-9721
　　　Email: dmixon@exeservice.biz
　　　Website: www.exeservice.biz
Executive human resources business consulting services, Sales & Business Development , Finance /Accounting Healthcare / Human & Social Services Engineering & IT Technology (Woman/AA, estab 2008, empl 1, sales , cert: NMSDC, CPUC)

4122　EYP, Inc.
　　　235 E Broadway Ste 800-B
　　　Long Beach, CA 90802
　　　Contact: Troy DuCre CEO
　　　Tel:　310-684-3022
　　　Email: tducre@eypinc.com
　　　Website: www.eypinc.com
Workforce Management - IT and engineering contract services, Software as a Service (SaaS), Talent Management and Learning Management,
Management Consulting - Business Process Improvement. (AA, estab 2011, empl 3, sales $146,000, cert: NMSDC)

4123　Flexon Technologies Inc.
　　　7901 Stoneridge Dr, Ste 390
　　　Pleasanton, CA 94588
　　　Contact: Sandeep Singh VP Sales
　　　Tel:　510-648-8878
　　　Email: ken@flexontechnologies.com
　　　Website: www.flexontechnologies.com
Our offerings are designed to cater to the entire range of clients' technology needs. (As-Ind, estab 2015, empl 52, sales $1,500,000, cert: NMSDC)

4124　Global IT Services
　　　180 Promenade Circle, Ste 300
　　　Sacramento, CA 95834
　　　Contact: Shavinder (Shawn) Phagura President
　　　Tel:　916-414-0311
　　　Email: sphagura@globalitsvcs.com
　　　Website: www.globalitsvcs.com
IT Staffing Services, Cloud & IT Consulting, and Skilled Staffing Solutions. (As-Ind, estab 2014, empl 15, sales $910,000, cert: State, NMSDC, SDB)

4125　Global Software Resources, Inc.
　　　4447 Stoneridge Dr
　　　Pleasanton, CA 94588
　　　Contact: Keith Granucci Dir
　　　Tel:　925-249-2200
　　　Email: keith@gsr-inc.com
　　　Website: www.gsr-inc.com
Engineering services, plant floor operations. (As-Pac, estab 2003, empl 45, sales $4,000,000, cert: CPUC)

4126　GoAhead Solutions LLC.
　　　400 Oyster Point Blvd Ste 407
　　　South San Francisco, CA 94080
　　　Contact: Jaime Mendoza CEO
　　　Tel:　650-873-7255
　　　Email: jaime@goaheadsolutions.com
　　　Website: www.goaheadsolutions.com
IT Staff Augmentation, Consulting Services, Oracle Software Resell & Oracle Audit Representation. (Hisp, estab 2001, empl 46, sales $12,469,516, cert: NMSDC)

4127　Gray Systems, Inc.
　　　3160 Camino del Rio S, Ste 308
　　　San Diego, CA 92108
　　　Contact: Michelle Gray President
　　　Tel:　619-285-5848
　　　Email: mggray@graysys.com
　　　Website: www.graysys.com
Outsource information technology & programming professionals: project managers, helpdesk, programming & development, R&D, LAN administrators. (Woman/AA, estab 1991, empl 30, sales $5,000,000, cert: WBENC)

4128　Grove Technical Resources
　　　9035 Rosewood Ave
　　　West Hollywood, CA 90048
　　　Contact: Debra Polister President
　　　Tel:　786-390-7119
　　　Email: dpolister@grovetr.com
　　　Website: www.grovetr.com
Technical staffing & consulting services. (Woman, estab 2005, empl 2, sales , cert: CPUC, WBENC)

4129　HB Computers, Inc.
　　　17131 Beach Blvd, Ste B
　　　Huntington Beach, CA 92647
　　　Contact: Madiha Rajput CEO
　　　Tel:　714-916-9294
　　　Email: amir@hbcomputerz.com
　　　Website: www.hbcomputerz.com
Test & manage networks cables. (Woman/As-Ind, estab 2005, empl 10, sales , cert: WBENC)

4130　Heritage Global Solutions, Inc.
　　　230 N Maryland Ave Ste 202
　　　Glendale CA, CA 91206
　　　Contact: Jeff Estep President
　　　Tel:　949-501-1038
　　　Email: jeff.estep@heritageglobal.com
　　　Website: www.heritageglobal.com
Information technology solutions, staff augmentation. (Nat Ame, estab 2003, empl 19, sales $2,000,000, cert: State)

4131　Horologiii, Inc.
　　　270 Corte Colina
　　　Novato, CA 94949
　　　Contact: Rod Nash President
　　　Tel:　510-764-8500
　　　Email: rod@horologiii.com
　　　Website: www.horologiii.com
Energy Consulting Services & Information Technology. (AA, estab 2002, empl 1, sales , cert: CPUC)

4132　IGIS Technologies Inc.
　　　10393 San Diego Mission Rd Ste 212
　　　San Diego, CA 92108
　　　Contact: Andres Abeyta CEO
　　　Tel:　619-640-2330
　　　Email: abeyta@igist.com
　　　Website: www.igist.com
GIS consulting, training & application development for the geospatial community. (Hisp, estab 1997, empl 11, sales $1,000,000, cert: CPUC)

4133 IMPEX Technologies, Inc.
880 Apollo St Ste 315
El Segundo, CA 90245
Contact: Rajiv Shah President
Tel: 310-320-0280
Email: rshah@impextechnologies.com
Website: www.impextechnologies.com
Systems integration: computer hardware, software, consulting & project management, enterprise storage systems & mgmt, enterprise backup, regulatory compliance, business continuance & disaster recovery, security solutions & networking. (As-Ind, estab 1992, empl 10, sales $3,000,000, cert: NMSDC)

4134 Infobahn Softworld, Inc.
2010 N 1st St, Ste 470
San Jose, CA 95131
Contact: Nitin Chandra VP Sales
Tel: 408-855-9616
Email: nchandra@infobahnsw.com
Website: www.infobahnsw.com
Technology, professional services and staffing solutions. (Minority, Woman, estab 1996, empl 200, sales $28,100,000, cert: NMSDC, CPUC)

4135 Information Design Consultants, Inc.
222 W 6th St, Ste 400
San Pedro, CA 90731
Contact: President
Tel: 310-707-2532
Email: informationdesign@idcinc.net
Website: www.idcinc.net
Project Management; Systems Integration (Woman/AA, estab 2002, empl 1, sales , cert: CPUC, WBENC)

4136 Infosoft Inc.
7891 Westwood Dr, Ste 113
Gilroy, CA 95020
Contact: Raj Chopra VP
Tel: 408-659-4326
Email: rchopra@infosoft-inc.com
Website: www.infosoft-inc.com
Information technology staffing & consulting. (As-Ind, estab 2000, empl 130, sales $16,330,000, cert: NMSDC)

4137 Infoyogi LLC
2320 #A Walsh Ave
Santa Clara, CA 95051
Contact: Sriram Sundaravaradan Mktg Mgr
Tel: 408-850-1700
Email: info@infoyogi.com
Website: www.infoyogi.com
Information technology, custom computer programming services, systems design services. (As-Ind, estab 1995, empl 15, sales , cert: CPUC)

4138 Integrated Spatial Solutions, Inc.
13879 Penn St
Whittier, CA 90602
Contact: Julie Henry COO
Tel: 562-693-2253
Email: jhenry@issi-gis.com
Website: www.issi-gis.com
Application devel, internet map services, systems integration, strategic planning, needs assessment, data conversion, database design, GIS mapping. (Woman, estab 1999, empl 7, sales $841,279, cert: CPUC)

4139 Intelliswift Software, Inc.
39600 Balentine Dr, Ste 200
Newark, CA 94560
Contact: Payal Kanaiya VP Strategic Initiatives
Tel: 510-370-2619
Email: payal.kanaiya@intelliswift.com
Website: www.intelliswift.com
Systems integration & software services. (As-Pac, estab 2001, empl 1100, sales $80,224,959, cert: NMSDC)

4140 International Word Processing Services, Inc.
PO Box 5053
Downey, CA 90241
Contact: Mary Jones CEO
Tel: 562-900-8359
Email: mary.jones@intlword.com
Website: www.intlword.com
Technical word processing, transcription & employment placement. (Woman/AA, estab 1994, empl 2, sales , cert: State, City, CPUC)

4141 Intrinsyx Technologies
350 N Akron Rd, Bldg.19-102
Moffett Field, CA 94035
Contact: Nabil Afifi Business Coordinator
Tel: 510-266-2721
Email: nabil@intrinsyx.com
Website: www.intrinsyx.com
Information technology solutions. (Woman/As-Ind, estab 2000, empl 50, sales $7,137,776, cert: State, NMSDC)

4142 IP International, Inc.
1510 Fashion Island Blvd, Ste 104
San Mateo, CA 94404
Contact: Margaret Schaninger CEO
Tel: 650-403-7840
Email: info@infoplusintl.com
Website: www.infoplusintl.com
IT consulting services: project mgmt & PMO, ERP, help desk & contact center, cost mgmt savings, bill audit & mgmt, ordering & provisioning, business case development, RFP & RFI creation, vendor mgmt & selection. (Woman, estab 1986, empl 50, sales $15,000,000, cert: CPUC, WBENC)

4143 IsComp Systems Inc.
5777 W Century Blvd, Ste 560
Los Angeles, CA 90045
Contact: Joshlyn Black Sr Acct Exec
Tel: 310-641-3260
Email: jblack@iscompsystems.com
Website: www.iscompsystems.com
Unix system integration, systems engineering, software develop, database mgmt. (AA, estab 1986, empl 20, sales , cert: CPUC)

4144 iTalent Corporation
27 Devine St Ste 20
San Jose, CA 95110
Contact: Silvia Quintanilla Dir
Tel: 408-428-2641
Email: silvia@italentdigital.com
Website: www.italentdigital.com
Global technology consulting services, Software Development Solutions, Innovative & Flexible Consulting Project Resource Solutions, Specialized Practices, Managed Services, Social Knowledge Management, Change Management. (Minority, Woman, estab 2005, empl 150, sales $25,000,000, cert: NMSDC, WBENC)

4145   JAUST Consulting Partners Inc.
3150 Almaden Exprwy Ste 215
San Jose, CA 95118
Contact: Gail D'Silva Founder
Tel: 408-805-0901
Email: gail@jaustpartners.com
Website: www.jaustpartners.com
IT solutions, ERP, CRM, SCM, Analytics & Web services, development & application integration. (Woman/Hisp, estab 2005, empl 8, sales , cert: NMSDC)

4146   JE Components Inc.
8709 Aviation Blvd
Inglewood, CA 90301
Contact: Joni Paulo President
Tel: 310-645-6021
Email: joni@jecom.com
Website: www.jecom.com
Resell PC & network hardware. (Minority, Woman, estab 1995, empl 7, sales , cert: NMSDC, NWBOC)

4147   Kaygen, Inc.
15420 Laguna Canyon Road Ste 270
Irvine, CA 92618
Contact: Rashmi Chaturvedi President
Tel: 949-203-5100
Email: rashmi.chaturvedi@kaygen.com
Website: www.kaygen.com
Oracle Enterprise Resource Planning (ERP). (Minority, Woman, estab 2003, empl 45, sales $13,000,000, cert: State, City, NMSDC, WBENC)

4148   Kutir Corporation
37600 Central Ct, Ste 280
Newark, CA 94560
Contact: Prathiba Kalyan Sr Business Mgr
Tel: 510-870-0227
Email: prathiba@kutirtech.com
Website: www.kutirtech.com
Contract & permanent staffing, custom software development, business & technology consulting, systems integration, technical support, admin, testing & support, data warehousing, business intelligence. (As-Ind, estab 2003, empl 40, sales $3,400,000, cert: NMSDC, CPUC, 8(a))

4149   Laboratory Data Consultants, Inc.
2701 Loker Ave. West Ste 220
Carlsbad, CA 92010
Contact: Laura Soeten Exec Admin
Tel: 760-827-1100
Email: Lsoeten@lab-data.com
Website: www.lab.data.com
Data validation and data management services. (As-Pac, estab 1991, empl 36, sales $3,940,313, cert: CPUC)

4150   LocalBizNetwork
3141 Stevens Creek Blvd, Ste 358
San Jose, CA 95117
Contact: Indu Jayakumar President
Tel: 408-741-8184
Email: info@localbiznetwork.com
Website: www.localbiznetwork.com
Custom software applications: Internet, Internet based online survey forms, computation of survey data, Internet marketing, SEO, Internet publishing, blogging, website development & hosting. (Woman/As-Ind, estab 2002, empl 22, sales , cert: CPUC)

4151   LogixService, Inc.
1383 Calle Avanzado
San Clemente, CA 92673
Contact: Van Boone CEO
Tel: 949-400-6083
Email: vboone@amtek.net
Website: www.amtek.net
Computer Maintenance and Support Services: IBM, HP, DELL, Compaq, Gateway, EMC, NetApp, Cisco, etc. Samsung, Brother Canon, Okidata, etc. (AA, estab 1980, empl 12, sales $2,100,000, cert: State, NMSDC)

4152   Luminous Tec LLC
15481 Red Hill Ave, Ste B
Tustin, CA 92780
Contact: Uma Sharma Dir new business devel
Tel: 949-630-0448
Email: usharma@luminoustec.com
Website: www.luminoustec.com
IT & non IT staffing & consulting services: project managers, business & technical architects, business analysts, applications development resources, systems integration specialists. (Minority, Woman, estab 2006, empl 5, sales $750,000, cert: CPUC)

4153   MalikCo
900 E. Hamilton Ave Ste 100
Campbell, CA 95008
Contact: Stephynie Malik CEO
Tel: 408-879-7447
Email: smalik@malikco.com
Website: www.malikco.com
Information technology svcs, software consulting, architecture, integration & implementation staff consulting. (Minority, Woman, estab 2003, empl 112, sales $461,000,000, cert: WBENC)

4154   Meijun LLC
9888 Carroll Centre Rd Ste#210
San Diego, CA 92126
Contact: Huy Ly
Tel: 619-333-8698
Email: hly@meijun.cc
Website: www.meijun.cc
Web development & marketing agency, custom software solutions, web & mobile development, design & strategy, digital marketing services, SEO, content marketing & marketing automation integration. (As-Pac, estab 2011, empl 5, sales , cert: NMSDC, CPUC)

4155   Metabyte Inc.
39350 Civic Center Dr Ste 200
Fremont, CA 94538
Contact: Unni Krishnan Business Devel Mgr
Tel: 510-494-9700
Email: unnik@metabyte.com
Website: www.metabyte.com
IT Services, High Technology & ISV, Life Sciences & Healthcare, Manufacturing & Logistics, Banking & Financial Services, Speciality Retail, Telecom & Media. (As-Pac, estab 1993, empl 235, sales , cert: NMSDC)

4156 Method360, Inc
      One Post St, Ste 550
      San Francisco, CA 94104
      Contact: Heather Swanson Operations Mgr
      Tel: 415-956-6360
      Email: hswanson@method360.com
      Website: www.method360.com
Business Intelligence & Enterprise Application initiatives.
(Hisp, estab 2001, empl 60, sales , cert: NMSDC, CPUC)

4157 Microland Electronics Corporation
      1883 Ringwood Ave
      San Jose, CA 95131
      Contact: LINY YU Sales Rep
      Tel: 800-632-1688
      Email: linyy@microlandusa.com
      Website: www.microlandusa.com
Computing technology products, services and solutions,
mass storage solutions, controllers, high-end systems,
peripherals and components. (As-Pac, estab 1986, empl
57, sales $67,000,000, cert: NMSDC)

4158 Mission Critical Technologies, Inc.
      2041 Rosecrans Ave Ste 220
      El Segundo, CA 90245
      Contact: Patti Converse
      Tel: 310-246-4455
      Email: patti_converse@mctinc.com
      Website: www.mctinc.com
Technology solutions: relational database, application
design & implementation, custom software dev,
outsourcing, offsite dev projects, graphic design & development. (Woman, estab 1993, empl 50, sales , cert:
WBENC)

4159 Mobilematics, Inc.
      2528 Qume Dr, Ste 2
      San Jose, CA 95131
      Contact: Dominick Borrello Business Devel Mgr
      Tel: 408-609-1220
      Email: dominick@mobilematics.us.com
      Website: www.mobilematics.us.com
IT hardware & software, training, configuration, etc.
(Minority, Woman, estab 2012, empl 5, sales
$100,000,000, cert: State, NMSDC, WBENC)

4160 MSRCOSMOS LLC
      6200 StoneRidge Mall Rd, Ste 300
      Pleasanton, CA 94588
      Contact: Rajkumar Bogam Lead Sales
      Tel: 321-332-6344
      Email: rajj@msrcosmos.com
      Website: www.msrcosmos.com
IT services, mobile application, web applications, cloud
solutions, analytics, infrastructure management & offshore
consulting. (Woman, estab 2008, empl 84, sales
$6,000,000, cert: WBENC)

4161 NexInfo Solutions, Inc.
      1851 E First St Ste 900
      Santa Ana, CA 92705
      Contact: Kate Duffy Client Relations
      Tel: 714-955-6970
      Email: kate.duffy@nexinfo.com
      Website: www.nexinfo.com
ERP solutions, PLM solutions, Supply Chain Planning,
Software implementations, Manged Services, Technical
consulting, Functional consulting, Techno Functional
Consulting, business process design, Global order promis-
ing. (As-Ind, estab 1999, empl 300, sales , cert: NMSDC)

4162 Northbound LLC
      961 E Arques Ave
      Sunnyvale, CA 94085
      Contact: Leena Menon Operations Mgr
      Tel: 408-333-9885
      Email: supplierdiversity@northboundllc.com
      Website: www.northboundllc.com
Information technology contract & full-time placement
services. (Woman/As-Ind, estab 1998, empl 150, sales ,
cert: NMSDC)

4163 Omni2max, Inc.
      1202 Morena Blvd, Ste 100
      San Diego, CA 92110
      Contact: Javonda Franklin Business Devel Mgr
      Tel: 619-269-1663
      Email: javonda.franklin@omni2max.com
      Website: www.omni2max.com
Information Assurance, Information Technology,
Logistics, Engineering, Contract Management, Help Desk
Management & CRM, Systems Engineering, Program
Management & Performance Based Acquisition. (AA,
estab 2009, empl 25, sales $1,500,000, cert: State, 8(a))

4164 Omnikron Systems Inc.
      20920 Warner Center Lane Ste A
      Woodland Hills, CA 91367
      Contact: Robin Borough President
      Tel: 818-223-4115
      Email: robin.borough@omnikron.com
      Website: www.Omnikron.com
Applications development (ERP), database, reporting,
business intelligence, operations, infrastructure, security
& business personnel. (As-Pac, estab 1980, empl 50,
sales $8,000,000, cert: CPUC)

4165 OrangePeople
      300 Spectrum Dr Ste 400
      Irvine, CA 92618
      Contact: Natasha Myers VP
      Tel: 949-667-1762
      Email: natasha.myers@orangepeople.com
      Website: www.orangepeople.com
OrangePeople is one of the fastest growing Technology
Leadership Services company in America. Our team of
consultants bring tremendous hands-on experience in
business strategy, architecture, and program management. (As-Pac, estab 2006, empl 70, sales $1,800,000,
cert: NMSDC)

4166 Partner Engineering and Science, Inc.
      1990 E Grand Ave, Ste 100
      El Segundo, CA 90245
      Contact: Sean Rakhshani Principal
      Tel: 800-419-4923
      Email: srakhshani@partneresi.com
      Website: www.partneresi.com
Software engineering, modeling & simulation, research
& development & consulting services. (Woman, estab
2006, empl 120, sales $22,700,000, cert: WBENC)

4167 Perlinski & Company
   30025 Alicia Pkwy, Ste 107
   Laguna Niguel, CA 92677
   Contact: Isabel Perlinski CEO
   Tel: 949-481-5482
   Email: isabel.perlinski@perlinskico.com
Management consulting (Minority, Woman, estab 1989, empl 2, sales $244,250, cert: NMSDC, WBENC, 8(a))

4168 Pinpoint Resource Group, LLC
   1960 E Grand Ave Ste 1260
   El Segundo, CA 90245
   Contact: Felix Lin President
   Tel: 310-356-8123
   Email: felix@pinpoint.jobs
   Website: www.pinpoint.jobs
Information technology staffing: consultants & direct hire, systems analysts, project managers & management personnel. (As-Pac, estab 2004, empl 15, sales $4,500,000, cert: NMSDC)

4169 PM Business Holdings LLC
   733 Hindry Ave, Ste C205
   Inglewood, CA 90301
   Contact: Derrick Ferguson CEO
   Tel: 310-242-3171
   Email: pmbh14@gmail.com
   Website: www.brilliantmindssolutions.com
Computer Systems Design Services, employment placement & executive search services (AA, estab 2012, empl 1, sales , cert: NMSDC)

4170 Premium Technologies, Inc.
   PO Box 757
   Palm Desert, CA 92261
   Contact: Stanway Wong President
   Tel: 760-340-4603
   Email: stanwong@premium-technologies.com
   Website: www.premium-technologies.com/
Computer software design & development, data integration, physical asset mgmt, computerized maintenance mgmt system (CMMS) & enterprise asset mgmt (EAM) & asset tracking. (As-Pac, estab 1993, empl 1, sales , cert: NMSDC, CPUC)

4171 Progressive Technology Solutions
   500 E Calaveras
   Milpitas, CA 95035
   Contact: Rumi Bordoloi Account/Relationship Mgr
   Tel: 408-507-7106
   Email: hr@ptsol.com
   Website: www.ptsol.com
Business, Functional Technical consultants and permanent staff/workforce, SAP, Oracle, Internet Technology, Data Management and Analysis, ETL and Datawarehousing, Release and Change Management. (Woman/As-Ind, estab 2002, empl 50, sales $6,650,000, cert: NMSDC)

4172 Propane Studio
   1153 Mission St
   San Francisco, CA 94103
   Contact: Neil Chaudhari CXO
   Tel: - -
   Email: neil@propanestudio.com
   Website: www.propanestudio.com
Websites & Applications, Responsive Websites, Tech Arch Consulting, E-Commerce Development, UX Prototyping & Testing, Mobile Applications, Online Applications, Content Strategy & Migration, CMS Consulting, Strategic Digital Consulting. (As-Ind, estab 2003, empl 20, sales $5,000,000, cert: NMSDC)

4173 Prospance Inc
   4221 Business Center Dr. Ste - 1
   Fremont, CA 94538
   Contact: Santhosh Sundaram Dir Client Service
   Tel: 510-240-7085
   Email: santhosh.s@prospanceinc.com
   Website: www.prospanceinc.com
Short and long term IT services in the mainstream and emerging technologies. (Minority, Woman, estab 2009, empl 178, sales $25,000,000, cert: NMSDC, CPUC)

4174 Prosum, Inc.
   2201 Park Place, Ste 102
   El Segundo, CA 90245
   Contact: Ravi Chatwani CEO
   Tel: 310-426-0609
   Email: ravi.chatwani@prosum.com
   Website: www.prosum.com
Technology staffing services, technology consulting services, technology product sales. (Minority, estab 1996, empl 250, sales $38,000,000, cert: NMSDC, CPUC)

4175 Qsolv Inc.
   1735 N First St, Ste 302
   San Jose, CA 95112
   Contact: President
   Tel: 408-429-0918
   Email:
   Website: www.qsolv-inc.com
Cloud Automation Services, Network management and Networking products, virtualization, automation and orchestration solutions. (Minority, Woman, estab 1999, empl 150, sales , cert: NMSDC, WBENC)

4176 QualityWorks Consulting Group, LLC
   6018 S Citrus Ave
   Los Angeles, CA 90043
   Contact: Aurelia Crews VP Sales
   Tel: 310-467-5122
   Email: sales@qualityworkscg.com
   Website: www.qualityworkscg.com
Automated & manual web testing, Automated & manual mobile testing, Integrated automation test frameworks for web & mobile, DevOps/Continuous Integration Support, API/microservices testing, Agile QA coaching & training. (Woman/AA, estab 2010, empl 40, sales $2,287,690, cert: NMSDC, WBENC)

4177 RaviG Inc. dba Salient Global Technologies
      510 Garcia Ave, Ste E
      Pittsburg, CA 94565
      Contact: Ravikanth Ganapavarapu President
      Tel: 925-526-1234
      Email: rganapa@salientglobaltech.com
      Website: www.salientglobaltech.com
End-to-end business applications & IT infrastructure. (As-Pac, estab 1999, empl 45, sales $8,323,350, cert: NMSDC)

4178 Raycom Data Technologies, Inc.
      1320 E Imperial Ave
      El Segundo, CA 90245
      Contact: Ayaz Pandhiani President
      Tel: 310-322-5113
      Email: ayaz@raycomdtech.com
      Website: www.raycomdtech.com
Document archiving software, document management services, document scanning, conversion services, microfiche & microfilm. (As-Pac, estab 1978, empl 10, sales $1,165,000, cert: State)

4179 Related Technologies, Inc.
      81 Blue Ravine Rd Ste 230
      Folsom, CA 95630
      Contact: Cheryl Borgonah Mgr
      Tel: 916-357-5902
      Email: cherylb@relatedtech.com
      Website: www.relatedtech.com/
Technical & Functional SAP consultants & Subject Matter Experts, implementations, upgrades, enhancements & support. (Woman/As-Ind, estab 2002, empl 150, sales , cert: CPUC)

4180 RJT Compuquest
      222 N Sepulveda Blvd. Ste 2250
      El Segundo, CA 90245
      Contact: Vivek Bhatia Sr Accounts Exec
      Tel: 310-421-1297
      Email: vivek@rjtcompuquest.com
      Website: www.rjtcompuquest.com
IT solutions, SAP, Oracle, WB, web development, CRM & archiving solutions, staff augmentation. (As-Pac, estab 1996, empl 300, sales $46,000,000, cert: NMSDC)

4181 RKG Technologies Inc
      11 Antietam
      Irvine, CA 92620
      Contact: Raju Gottimukkala President
      Tel: 949-910-1262
      Email: grkraju@hotmail.com
      Website: www.rkgtech.com
Strategic consulting, staffing and staff augmentation, training, vendor management and outsourcing services. (As-Ind, estab 2004, empl 20, sales $465,000, cert: City, NMSDC, CPUC)

4182 RPM Engineers, Inc.
      102 Discovery
      Irvine, CA 92618
      Contact: RAYMOND PHUA Principal
      Tel: 949-450-1229
      Email: marisolv@rpmpe.com
      Website: www.rpmpe.com
RPM Engineers, Inc. was established 1993 in Irvine, California. An engineering firm under the direction of Mr. Raymond Phua, a registered professional engineer in state of California, providing air conditioning (As-Pac, estab 1993, empl 17, sales $1,727,000, cert: State)

4183 SA Technologies Inc.
      5201 Great America Pkwy, Ste #441 Ste 441
      Santa Clara, CA 95054
      Contact: Priyanka Joshi President
      Tel: 408-986-0152
      Email: priyanka.joshi@satechglobal.com
      Website: www.satechglobal.com
Information technology consulting & staffing. (Woman/As-Ind, estab , empl , sales $10,800,000, cert: NWBOC)

4184 SD Shredding, Inc.
      7263 Engineer Rd Ste C
      San Diego, CA 92111
      Contact: Todd M Hoover CFO
      Tel: 858-492-9600
      Email: todd.hoover@proshred.com
      Website: www.proshred.com
On-site document & computer hard drive shredding. (Woman, estab 2010, empl 3, sales $200,000, cert: WBENC)

4185 Shimento Inc.
      1350 Hayes St, Ste B4
      Benecia, CA 94510
      Contact: Raj Sharma President
      Tel: 877-211-8708
      Email: jake.gaetti@shimento.com
      Website: www.shimento.com
Staff augmentation, SOW (statement of work), IT services and direct hire recruitment. (As-Ind, estab 2009, empl 80, sales $12,000,000, cert: NMSDC)

4186 Sidebench Studios
      10317 Washington Blvd.
      Culver City, CA 90232
      Contact: Nate Schier Dir of Staff & Co-Founder
      Tel: 808-294-5948
      Email: nate@sidebench.com
      Website: www.sidebench.com
App design, development & strategy. (As-Pac, estab 2012, empl 13, sales $1,342,459, cert: NMSDC, CPUC)

4187 Sigmaways, Inc
      39737 Paseo Padre Pkwy
      Fremont, CA 94538
      Contact: Prakash Sadasivam Founder & CEO
      Tel: 510-713-7800
      Email: info@sigmaways.com
      Website: www.sigmaways.com
Software product, technology innovation & staff augmentation. (As-Ind, estab 2006, empl 85, sales $8,300,000, cert: NMSDC)

4188 Sohum Inc
      1055 Minnesota Ave, Ste 6
      San Jose, CA 95125
      Contact: Vandana Patil President
      Tel: 408-265-2391
      Email: marketing@sohum.biz
      Website: www.sohum.biz
Software UX design, web & mobile, Software Design & Development, Cloud based software deployment & monitoring. (Woman/As-Ind, estab 1998, empl 5, sales $300,000, cert: State)

4189 Solugenix Corporation
      7700 Irvine Center Dr Ste 800
      Irvine, CA 92618
      Contact: Dir
      Tel: 949-266-0938
      Email: info@solugenix.com
      Website: www.solugenix.com
Application Lifecycle Management: Project & Requirements Management, Custom Application Development,
Testing & Quality Assurance, Change & Release Management, Level 2 & Level 3 Production Support. (As-Ind, estab
2004, empl 52, sales $27,583,910, cert: NMSDC)

4190 Source Diversified, Inc.
      1206 Vista Cantora
      San Clemente, CA 92672
      Contact: Alfred Ortiz President
      Tel: 949-940-0450
      Email: aortiz@sourced.com
      Website: www.sourced.com
Command & control systems, security alerting systems,
flight test support svcs, aircraft system integration,
software dev, construction automation software, network
installation, mission control room support svcs. (Hisp,
estab 1987, empl 3, sales , cert: State)

4191 SPK and Associates, LLC
      5011 Scotts Valley Dr
      Scotts Valley, CA 95030
      Contact: Michael Roberts VP Sales & Marketing
      Tel: 888-310-4540
      Email: mroberts@spkaa.com
      Website: www.spkaa.com
Information Technology (IT), Infrastructure, IT Services
(implementation, support, training, data migration), IT
Staffing through a MSP, Large Data Storage/Management,
Network Management, Product Development, Software
Programming, Web Administrators (Woman, estab 2003,
empl 17, sales $2,882,705, cert: WBENC)

4192 SRS Consulting Inc.
      39465 Paseo Padre Pkwy, Ste 1100
      Fremont, CA 94538
      Contact: Aswath Panduranga Business Devel Mgr
      Tel: 510-252-0625
      Email: aswath@srsconsultinginc.com
      Website: www.srsconsultinginc.com
IT Development, Custom Software Development, R&D/
Product Development/Re-engineering, Testing and Quality
Assurance, Network Security Services, ERP/EAI consulting
& implementation, CRM, SCP, BPM, CMS, DMS, e-Gover-
nance, Mobile Security. (Woman/As-Ind, estab 2002, empl
250, sales $46,000,000, cert: NMSDC, WBENC)

4193 Stratitude
      6601 Koll Center Pkwy, Ste 132
      Pleasanton, CA 94566
      Contact: Khannan Sankaran CEO
      Tel: 510-461-3981
      Email: khannan@stratitude.com
      Website: www.stratitude.com
IT services, implementation & staffing, software advisory,
design, development & testing services, SAP, Microsoft,
Java, Salesforce.com , Netsuite, Pega BPM, Guidewire
Temenos, Veeva. (As-Ind, estab 2006, empl 36, sales
$3,600,000, cert: NMSDC)

4194 Sun MicroSolutions Inc.
      29 Avanzare St
      Irvine, CA 92606
      Contact: Ruchi Mitra CEO
      Tel: 949-387-9878
      Email: ruchi@sunmicrousa.com
      Website: www.sunmicrousa.com
IT consulting, staffing & training. (Minority, Woman,
estab 2000, empl 5, sales $540,000, cert: City)

4195 Sunny City Enterprises, Inc.
      959 Mount Whitney Ct
      Chula Vista, CA 91913
      Contact: Francisco Esparza President
      Tel: 619-250-5970
      Email: francisco.esparza@sbcitpros.com
      Website: www.sbcitpros.com
IT & Telecom services, Technology Services, Software
Solutions & Applications, Staffing Augmentation. (Hisp,
estab 2007, empl 10, sales $1,500,000, cert: NMSDC,
CPUC)

4196 Sunrise Global Solutions, Inc.
      30 Monroe, Ste 101
      Irvine, CA 92620
      Contact: Neetu Sadhwani President
      Tel: 949-331-3678
      Email: neetu@sunrisegroupinc.com
      Website: www.sunrisegroupinc.com
IT Consulting, Computer related services. (Woman/As-
Pac, estab 2008, empl 2, sales $450,000, cert: CPUC,
WBENC)

4197 SupplierGATEWAY LLC
      20 Corporate Park Ste 118
      Irvine, CA 92606
      Contact: Adenuga Solaru CEO
      Tel: 949-525-9205
      Email: ade.solaru@suppliergateway.com
      Website: www.suppliergateway.com
Information technology solutions & consulting svcs:
developed SupplierGATEWAY an end-to-end collaborative supply chain solution that connects buyers &
suppliers via the Internet. (AA, estab 1997, empl 15,
sales $2,500,000, cert: NMSDC, CPUC)

4198 Svitla Systems, Inc.
      100 Meadowcreek Dr, Ste 102
      Corte Madera, CA 00949
      Contact: Khrystyna Zahorodnichok Dir Enterprise
      Accounts
      Tel: 650-741-1387
      Email: k.zahorodnichok@svitla.com
      Website: www.svitla.com
Support and help desk support. (Woman, estab 2003,
empl 300, sales $12,037,432, cert: WBENC)

4199 Sycomp a Technology Company., Inc.
      950 Tower Lane Ste 1785
      Foster City, CA 94404
      Contact: Stacy Hunter
      Tel: 650-312-8174
      Email: shunter@sycomp.com
      Website: www.sycomp.com
Design, implement & deliver complex, heterogeneous
Infrastructure, Software & Security technology solutions.
(Minority, Woman, estab 1994, empl 80, sales
$120,000,000, cert: NMSDC)

4200 SysIntelli, Inc.
      9466 Black Mountain Road, Ste. 200
      San Diego, CA 92126
      Contact: CEO
      Tel: 858-271-1600
      Email: info@sysintelli.com
      Website: www.sysintelli.com
Software Development Life Cycle, Re-engineering & Legacy
Migration, Database Administration, Quality Assurance
Testing & Validation, E-Commerce, Data Processing,
Software Maintenance & Support. (As-Ind, estab 2005,
empl 55, sales $16,690,351, cert: NMSDC)

4201 Systems Integration Solutions, Inc.
      1255 Treat Blvd. Ste 100
      Walnut Creek, CA 94597
      Contact: Nick Bata Reg acct dir
      Tel: 952-220-7549
      Email: nbata@sisinc.com
      Website: www.sisinc.com
IT consulting & executive search services. (Minority, estab
1990, empl 150, sales $30,000,000, cert: CPUC)

4202 Tap3Solutions
      2279 Eagle Glen Pkwy, Ste 112-444
      Corona, CA 92883
      Contact: Catrina Snell-Rehder President
      Tel: 949-229-1910
      Email: catrina@tap3solutions.com
      Website: www.Tap3Solutions.com
Information technology & human capital solutions.
(Woman/AA, estab 2015, empl 2, sales , cert: State, City)

4203 TechLink Systems, Inc.
      2 Embarcadero Center Ste 2240
      San Francisco, CA 94111
      Contact: Shannon Proverbs Mgr Business Dev
      Tel: 415-732-7580
      Email: sproverbs@techlinksystems.com
      Website: www.techlinksystems.com
Information technology, engineering, scientific & bio-tech,
application development. (Minority, Woman, estab 1998,
empl 141, sales $23,560,181, cert: NMSDC, WBENC)

4204 Technossus LLC
      4000 MacArthur Blvd Ste 100
      Newport Beach, CA 92660
      Contact: Dave LaJeunesse Dir of Sales
      Tel: 949-769-3522
      Email: info@technossus.com
      Website: www.technossus.com
Custom software development, Microsoft technology
stack, application development, desktop, enterprise &
web-based, mobile applications, SharePoint & Dynamics
CRM, proprietary systems development & enhancement.
(As-Ind, estab 2008, empl 25, sales $4,700,000, cert:
NMSDC)

4205 Tellus Solutions, Inc
      3350 Scott Blvd 34A
      Santa Clara, CA 95054
      Contact: HR/Business Dev
      Tel: 408-850-2942
      Email: contact@tellussol.com
      Website: www.tellussol.com
Information technology services. (Minority, Woman, estab
2005, empl 67, sales $5,320,000, cert: NMSDC, WBENC,
8(a))

4206 TESCRA
      2440 Camino Ramon, Ste 263
      San Ramon, CA 94583
      Contact: Pradeep Kumar Marketing Exec
      Tel: 925-415-5290
      Email: pradeepkumar.g@tescra.com
      Website: www.tescra.com
Systems integration & ERP solutions, enterprise solutions. (Minority, Woman, estab 2002, empl 220, sales
$16,000,000, cert: NMSDC)

4207 The LSC Group, Inc.
      200 Spectrum Center Dr 3rd Fl
      Irvine, CA 92618
      Contact: Troy Humphrey CEO
      Tel: 800-572-9280
      Email: troy.humphrey@yourlscgroup.com
      Website: www.yourlscgroup.com
Electronic Discovery, Data Collection, Data Processing,
Data Production, Forensic Date Discovery, Litigation
Support, Records Management, Early Case Assessment,
Webhosting, Project Management, Consulting. (AA,
estab 2007, empl 1, sales $125,000, cert: NMSDC, CPUC)

4208 Thomas Gallaway Corporation
      100 Spectrum Center Dr Ste 700
      Irvine, CA 92618
      Contact: Shari Jones Client Vendor Relations
      Tel: 949-716-9500
      Email: vendorbids@technologent.com
      Website: www.technologent.com
Sun Microsystems hardware & service, multi vendor
support, Finisar, Sharkrak, Storedge Tek, Oracle &
Veritas. (Woman, estab 2002, empl 265, sales
$651,000,000, cert: WBENC)

4209 Thoughtpowers LLC
      1919 Williams St Ste 215
      Simi Valley, CA 93065
      Contact: Surendra Kulkarni President
      Tel: 805-433-4950
      Email: surendra@thoughtpowers.com
      Website: www.thoughtpowers.com
Custom Application IT development & management, IT
consulting services, IT resources, technical resources.
(Minority, estab 2008, empl 1, sales , cert: NMSDC)

4210 Trabus
      3547 Camino Del Rio South
      San Diego, CA 92108
      Contact: Arthur Salindong Principal
      Tel: 619-220-8000
      Email: art@trabus.com
      Website: www.trabus.com
Providing Disruptive Advances in Wireless, Cybersecurity
and Artificial Intelligence (As-Pac, estab 2010, empl 30,
sales , cert: NMSDC)

4211 Trident Consulting
      2410 Camino Ramon, Ste 183
      San Ramon, CA 94583
      Contact: Shabana Siraj CEO
      Tel: 925-683-5166
      Email: Farhaan@Tridentconsultinginc.com
      Website: www.Tridentconsultinginc.com
IT staffing and technology company. (Woman/As-Ind,
estab 2005, empl 80, sales $12,908,447, cert: State,
NMSDC, WBENC)

4212 Trinus Corporation
      225 South Lake Ave, Ste 1080
      Pasadena, CA 91101
      Contact: Harshada Kucheria President
      Tel: 818-246-1143
      Email: harshada_kucheria@trinus.com
      Website: www.trinus.com
IT consulting & implementation services, business consulting, systems integration & outsourcing. (Woman/As-Ind, estab 1995, empl 250, sales , cert: NMSDC, CPUC, WBENC, SDB)

4213 Two Shea Consulting, Inc.
      1009 Oak Hill Rd, Ste 202
      Lafayette, CA 94549
      Contact: Maureen Shea CEO
      Tel: 925-962-7432
      Email: maureen@twoshea.com
      Website: www.twoshea.com
IT consulting & recruiting services. (Woman, estab 2000, empl 25, sales $5,000,000, cert: City, WBENC)

4214 VARITE, Inc.
      111 North Market St, Ste 730
      San Jose, CA 95113
      Contact: Adarsh Katyal CEO
      Tel: 408-977-0700
      Email: katyal@varite.com
      Website: www.varite.com
Technical consulting & staffing, customized onshore, near shore & offshore solutions. (As-Ind, estab 2000, empl 49, sales $9,500,000, cert: NMSDC, CPUC)

4215 Versa Shore Inc.
      1999 S Bascom Ave Ste 700
      Campbell, CA 95008
      Contact: Shawn Rao CEO
      Tel: 408-874-8330
      Email: shawnrao@versashore.com
      Website: www.versashore.com
Consulting, staffing & headhunting, Microsoft APS, Data warehousing, big data, business intelligence, Oracle, Birst, Tableau, Sql Server, Hadoop, MongoDB, Database, Java & IT management skills. (As-Ind, estab 2003, empl 10, sales $3,000,000, cert: NMSDC)

4216 Vertisystem Inc.
      39300 Civic Center Dr, Ste 230
      Fremont, CA 94538
      Contact: Shaloo Jeswani Sr BDM
      Tel: 702-241-5131
      Email: shaloo@vertisystem.com
      Website: www.vertisystem.com
Staff Augmentation, Full-Time Placements, contract to Hire, IT Projects & Consulting. (Minority, Woman, estab 2008, empl 120, sales $20,000,000, cert: City, CPUC)

4217 Vidhwan Inc dba E-Solutions, Inc.
      2 N Market St Ste 400
      San Jose, CA 95113
      Contact: Eric Kumar Acct Mgr
      Tel: 408-239-4647
      Email: eric.kumar@e-solutionsinc.com
      Website: www.e-solutionsinc.com
IT & ITES staffing, recruitment & deployment: permanent, contract, contract to hire & project based staffing. (Woman/As-Ind, estab 2003, empl 450, sales $22,800,000, cert: NMSDC, CPUC)

4218 Visionary Integration Professionals, LLC
      80 Iron Point Cir, Ste 100
      Folsom, CA 95630
      Contact: Stephen Carpenter VP Admin
      Tel: 916-985-9625
      Email: scarpenter@vipincorp.com
      Website: www.trustvip.com
Assists govt agencies use IT to increase productivity & revenue, improve performance, and reduce costs. (Woman/Hisp, estab 1996, empl 410, sales $30,000,000, cert: State, CPUC)

4219 Volante Enterprise Consulting
      3863 Millbrae Terr
      Perris, CA 92571
      Contact: Sheila Volante CEO
      Tel: 310-256-9639
      Email: sheilavolante@volantenc.com
      Website: www.volantenc.com
Scheduling Management, Risk Management, Systems Consulting, Microsoft Project Server, Microsoft Project Professional, Configuration, Office 365 + SharePoint Configuration, Project Management Office Setup & Maintenance. (Woman/AA, estab 2014, empl 2, sales , cert: State)

4220 VXI Global Solutions, LLC
      220 W 1st St 3rd Floor
      Los Angeles, CA 90012
      Contact: Annette Timmins Marketing Solutions & Sales Support
      Tel: 213-637-1300
      Email: annette.timmins@vxi.com
      Website: www.vxi.com
Business process & information technology outsourcing, call center & BPO services, software development, quality assurance testing & infrastructure outsourcing. (As-Pac, estab 1998, empl 30000, sales , cert: NMSDC)

4221 Webbege, Inc.
      7851 Mission Center Ct Ste 108
      San Diego, CA 92108
      Contact: Francis Geraci President
      Tel: 619-786-7075
      Email: frank.geraci@webbege.com
      Website: www.webbege.com
Web Design, Development, and Online Marketing. (Hisp, estab 2011, empl 7, sales $300,000, cert: NMSDC)

4222 WMBE Payrolling, dba TargetCW
      9475 Chesapeake Dr
      San Diego, CA 92123
      Contact: Dave Bakkeby SVP Business Devel
      Tel: 858-810-8038
      Email: dave.bakkeby@targetcw.com
      Website: www.targetcw.com
Payrolling of contingent workers identified by our clients. Employer of record for temporary workers and contractors already sourced across the US and overseas. (Woman, estab 2009, empl 12, sales , cert: State)

4223 Xavient Information Systems, Inc.
2125 Madera Rd, Ste B
Simi Valley, CA 93065
Contact: Melissa Montejano Dir Admin
Tel: 805-955-4140
Email: melissa@xavient.com
Website: www.xavient.com
Application development & integration, testing & quality assurance, IT infrastructure support, application support, core telecom engineering services. (As-Pac, estab 2003, empl 2200, sales $40,000,000, cert: NMSDC)

4224 Xinnovit Inc.
21001 San Ramon Valley Blvd, Ste A4-103
San Ramon, CA 94583
Contact: Client Relations Mgr
Tel: 925-236-2310
Email:
Website: www.xinnovit.com
Information technology services: application development, systems & database management, data warehousing & quality assurance. (Woman/As-Ind, estab 2002, empl 165, sales $12,000,000, cert: NMSDC)

4225 Yadari Enterprises
728 Texas St, Ste 3
Fairfield, CA 94533
Contact: Tara Lynn Gray President
Tel: 707-398-6478
Email: tara@yadari.com
Website: www.yadari.com
Web development, databasese, report writing, business intelligence, visual data displays, management consulting, graphic design, electronic health record, diagnostic imaging systems, laboratory systems, pharmacy systems. (Woman/AA, estab 2004, empl 3, sales $310,000, cert: State, CPUC)

4226 Zebra-net Incorporated
9995 Muirlands Blvd
Irvine, CA 92618
Contact: Jeanie Reese Recruiter
Tel: 949-900-6110
Email: Jeanie.Reese@Zebra-net.com
Website: www.zebra-net.com
Information technology staffing. (Woman, estab 1996, empl 11, sales $5,635,048, cert: WBENC)

Colorado

4227 Aspen Capital Company, Inc.
530 North Jefferson Ave Unit A
Loveland, CO 80537
Contact: Peggy Tomcheck
Tel: 303-716-2898
Email: plapp@aspencapitalcompany.com
Website: www.aspencapitalcompany.com
Custom asset tracking & invoicing solutions, educational laptop program lease structures, unique iPad refresh programs, consignment solutions, electronic invoicing & billing processes, web based equipment stores. (Woman, estab 2001, empl 8, sales $10,385,908, cert: WBENC)

4228 Aureus Tech Systems, LLC
17593 E Euclid Ave
Aurora, CO 80016
Contact: Sujata Bhattarai CEO
Tel: 816-373-1979
Email: sujata@aureustechsystems.com
Website: www.aureustechsystems.com
Customized & needs-based reporting dashboard, Web-based, & and near real-time reporting tools, overall performance optimization reducing lag times & frivolous resource allocation. (Woman/As-Ind, estab 2008, empl 35, sales $2,316,830, cert: WBENC)

4229 BCM Global Technologies Consultants, Inc.
9457 S University Blvd, Ste 329
Highlands Ranch, CO 80126
Contact: President
Tel: 866-761-8880
Email: info@bcmglobaltech.com
Website: www.bcmglobaltech.com
Provide technical resources & solutions. (Woman/AA, estab 2008, empl 20, sales $1,550,000, cert: NMSDC, WBENC, NWBOC, 8(a))

4230 Bross Group LLC
200 Union Blvd, Ste 200
Lakewood, CO 80228
Contact: Cathy Fligger Sr Acct Exec
Tel: 303-945-2700
Email: sales@brossgroup.com
Website: www.brossgroup.com
Information technology consulting & staffing. (Woman, estab 2004, empl 50, sales $3,094,000, cert: WBENC, NWBOC)

4231 Data Destruction LLC
96 Inverness Dr E Ste K
Englewood, CO 80112
Contact: Ginger Patrick President
Tel: 303-388-3282
Email: ginger@data-destruction.com
Website: www.data-destruction.com
Destroy data, hard drives & back-up tapes, mobile hard drive shredding, digital media. (Woman, estab 2014, empl 5, sales , cert: WBENC)

4232 DCM Technology Solutions, Inc.
17011 Moorside Dr
Parker, CO 80134
Contact: Leslie Kleyweg President
Tel: 303-325-5202
Email: info@dcmsolution.com
Website: www.dcmsolution.com
IT services: staffing, low voltage wiring, networking & computer repair/maintenance. (Woman, estab 2002, empl 5, sales $550,000, cert: WBENC)

4233 iBeta, LLC
2675 S Abilene St Ste300
Aurora, CO 80014
Contact: Curt Dusing II Sales & Marketing Exec
Tel: 303-627-1110
Email: cdusing@ibeta.com
Website: www.ibeta.com
Testing services: engineering, automated & manual testing, functionality testing, performance, stress & load testing, hardware & software testing, data conversion testing, usability testing, console certification testing, handheld testing. (Hisp, estab 1999, empl 141, sales $4,500,000, cert: NMSDC)

4234 Istonish
5500 Greenwood Plaza Blvd
Greenwood Village, CO 80108
Contact: Shannon Hickey Business Devel Exec
Tel: 720-529-4550
Email: shickey@istonish.com
Website: www.istonish.com
Technical resources: staff augmentation, perm placement, vendor mgmt svcs, IT solutions, project based svcs, customer call ctr svcs. (Minority, Woman, estab 1990, empl 100, sales $6,883,874, cert: NMSDC, WBENC)

4235 Managed Business Solutions
12325 Oracle Blvd, Ste 200
Colorado Springs, CO 80921
Contact: Jane Kovalik Marketing Mgr
Tel: 719-314-3400
Email: diversity@mbshome.com
Website: www.mbshome.com
IT managed svcs: IT infrastructure support, multi-vendor/platform system admin, storage mgmt & admin, SAN engineering & design, server consolidation, open view service desk support, project mgmt, data center operations & mgmt. (Nat Ame, estab 2009, empl 7, sales $23,513,000, cert: NMSDC)

4236 Maven Companies
1880 Office Club Pointe
Colorado Springs, CO 80920
Contact: Manish Kochhar President
Tel: 719-884-0102
Email: diversity@mavenco.com
Website: www.mavenco.com
IT consulting, Project Management & Business Analysis (PM Coordination, Change and Release Management, Process Analysis), ERP Development & Support (Oracle, PeopleSoft, SAP),Business Intelligence (Business Objects, Cognos, Microstrategy, Crystal Reports). (As-Pac, estab 2003, empl 30, sales $3,000,000, cert: NMSDC)

4237 netRelevance LLC
4865 Hidden Rock Rd
Colorado Springs, CO 80908
Contact: Rick Limas Dir Business Dev
Tel: 719-488-5742
Email: rick.limas@netrelevance.com
Website: www.netrelevance.com
Wireless Network Site Surveys, Design, Installation & Support, Network Equipment Installations and Startup, Computer Room and Data Center Design and Installation, Copper and Fiber Cabling, Performing Network refresh/upgrades, IP Surveillance. (Hisp, estab 2007, empl 9, sales $2,679,948, cert: NMSDC)

4238 Sedulus Group LLC
19511 Good Life View
Calhan, CO 80808
Contact: Julian Candia CEO
Tel: 719-505-8419
Email: julian.candia@cyberlogistix.com
Website: www.cyberlogistix.com
Cybersecurity expertise and operations. (Hisp, estab 2019, empl 3, sales , cert: NMSDC)

4239 The 'Apps' Consultants Inc.
6909 S Holly Circle Ste 350
Centennial, CO 80112
Contact: Kiran Pingali President
Tel: 303-502-5407
Email: kiran@appsconsultants.com
Website: www.appsconsultants.com
IT consulting, ERP/ CRM & Business Intelligence. (Woman/As-Ind, estab 2005, empl 4, sales $546,846, cert: City)

4240 V3Gate, LLC
555 Middle Creek Pkwy, Ste 120
Colorado Springs, CO 80921
Contact: Lindsay Dumanch Business Devel Mgr
Tel: 855-483-4283
Email: lumanch@v3gate.com
Website: www.v3gate.com/
IT solutions provider for the US Public Sector, healthcare, and education. (Hisp, estab 2007, empl 36, sales $314,000,000, cert: NMSDC)

Connecticut

4241 Agilus Global Services, LLC
35 E Main St, Ste 352
Avon, CT 06001
Contact: Dennis Williams CEO
Tel: 860-404-0476
Email: dwilliams@agilusglobal.com
Website: www.agilusglobalservices.com
IT consulting/staffing & recruiting services. (AA, estab 2015, empl 1, sales , cert: NMSDC)

4242 Aquinas Consulting, LLC
154 Herbert St
Milford, CT 06460
Contact: Dir of HR
Tel: 203-876-7822
Email: info@aquinasconsulting.com
Website: www.aquinasconsulting.com
IT & engineering consulting & staffing. (Minority, Woman, estab 2000, empl 27, sales $3,045,910, cert: State)

4243 Aspire Systems
36 Mill Plain Rd
Danbury, CT 06811
Contact: Laura Del Corpo VP Business Dev
Tel: 732-406-4284
Email: laura@aspiresystem.com
Website: www.aspiresystem.com
Information Technology, Staff Augmentation, Technology Deployment & Enterprise support. (As-Pac, estab 2002, empl 45, sales $5,000,000, cert: NMSDC)

4244 Dudas IT Resources & Advisory, Inc.
117 Butternut Lane
Stamford, CT 06903
Contact: Liz Chait CEO
Tel: 203-653-2739
Email: liz@zarit.com
Website: www.zarit.org
Information technology staffing & consulting services. (Woman, estab 2005, empl 8, sales $6,389,623, cert: WBENC)

4245 eRichards Consulting LLC
1381 Burr St Ste 390
Fairfield, CT 06824
Contact: Doreen F. Gebbia President
Tel: 203-944-0816
Email: dgebbia@erichards.com
Website: www.eRichards.com
IT consulting: strategic assessment, internet strategy, application development, project management, IT governance, web development & staff augmentation. (Woman, estab 1996, empl 3, sales , cert: WBENC)

4246 InfoLynx Services, Inc.
325 Danbury Rd
New Milford, CT 06776
Contact: Uelysee Scantling Dir of Sales
Tel: 860-210-1203
Email: contact@infolynx.com
Website: www.infolynx.com
Technical services: project mgmt, technical configuration, system & application engineering, performance tuning, desktop support. (AA, estab 1994, empl 75, sales $6,200,000, cert: State)

4247 iTech Solutions, Inc.
20 Stanford Dr
Farmington, CT 06032
Contact: Salil Sankaran President
Tel: 703-638-1346
Email: salil.sankaran@itechsolutions.com
Website: www.itechsolutions.com
Information technology staffing, consulting & recruting services. (Woman, estab 1995, empl 115, sales $14,092,608, cert: NMSDC, WBENC)

4248 JANUS Software, Inc. (d/b/a JANUS Associates)
2 Omega Dr
Stamford, CT 06907
Contact: Patricia Fisher President
Tel: 203-251-0200
Email: patfisher@janusassociates.com
Website: www.janusassociates.com
Information & telecommunications security solutions; risk analysis & disaster recovery planning; computer forensics & fraud investigations; information mgmt strategies; identity authentication software. (Woman, estab 1988, empl 20, sales , cert: WBENC)

4249 Nadicent Technologies LLC
2389 Main St
Glastonbury, CT 06033
Contact: Frank Gomes Dir
Tel: 860-659-2600
Email: frank.gomes@nadicent.com
Website: www.nadicent.com
Advanced Managed Security, Conferencing, Video, Web & Audio, Cloud Services, Disaster Recovery, Help Desk Services, Microsoft Azure, Office 365 Enterprise Suites, Data Centers, Colocation, Infrastructure. (As-Pac, estab 2003, empl 10, sales $9,000,000, cert: NMSDC)

4250 OutSecure Inc.
Shelton Pointe, 2 Trap Falls Rd Ste 401
Shelton, CT 06484
Contact: Pamela Gupta President
Tel: 203-816-8061
Email: pamela.gupta@outsecure.com
Website: www.outsecure.com
Cyber Security assessment & security programs, risk assessments. (As-Pac, estab 2003, empl 7, sales $300,000, cert: NMSDC)

4251 PCC Technology Group
2 Barnard Lane
Bloomfield, CT 06002
Contact: Jo Gumbs Marketing Coord
Tel: 860-466-7261
Email: jomal.gumbs@pcctg.com
Website: www.pcctg.com
Software development. (AA, As-Pac, estab 1995, empl 50, sales , cert: NMSDC)

4252 PCNet, Inc.
100 Technology Dr
Trumbull, CT 06611
Contact: FirstName LastName VP Finance/ Operations
Tel: 203-452-8559
Email: teric@pcnet-inc.com
Website: www.pcnet-inc.com
Network systems integrator; e-commerce, Internet/ Intranet; resell of personal computer products & svcs. (Hisp, estab 1993, empl 65, sales $26,000,000, cert: NMSDC)

4253 Safety Management Systems, Inc.
5 Eversley Ave, Ste 306
Norwalk, CT 06851
Contact: Business Dev Mgr
Tel: 203-838-8877
Email: info@sms360.com
Website: www.sms360.com
Develop SMS360, an industry-changing, cost effective software tool that enables any organization, large or small, to manage its EHS program on a par with the biggest and the best. (Woman, estab 2004, empl 9, sales $451,000, cert: State, WBENC)

4254 Saisystems International
5 Research Dr
Shelton, CT 06484
Contact: Chirag Modi VP Technology Services
Tel: 203-929-0790
Email: cmodi@saisystems.com
Website: www.saisystems.com
Informatation technology consulting: disaster recovery planning, dataware & database mgmt systems, quality assurance svcs. (Woman/As-Ind, estab 1987, empl 350, sales $12,306,249, cert: State, NMSDC)

4255 Source IT Technologies, LLC
24 East Ave, Ste 244
New Canaan, CT 06840
Contact: Serica King CEO
Tel: 203-252-0439
Email: sking@sourceittech.com
Website: www.sourceittech.com
Technology solutions. (Woman, estab 2012, empl 7, sales $8,696,000, cert: WBENC)

4256 Stratoserve LLC
18 Colonial Ct
Cheshire, CT 06410
Contact: Subroto Roy President
Tel: 203-768-5690
Email: subroto.roy@stratoserve.com
Website: www.stratoserve.com
consulting, research and training for the following NAICS codes:541720,541613,611430 and is committed to provide quick and measurable value to its clients. (As-Pac, estab 2005, empl 1, sales , cert: NMSDC)

4257 Technosteps LLC
3 Hayes Ave Unit B
Norwalk, CT 06855
Contact: Narayan Venugopal President
Tel: 703-864-4848
Email: narayan.venugopal@technosteps.com
Website: www.technosteps.com
IT Staffing. (As-Ind, estab 2012, empl 3, sales $189,000, cert: State)

4258 The Computer Company, Inc.
15 Commerce Dr
Cromwell, CT 06416
Contact: Eileen Hasson President
Tel: 860-635-0500
Email: ehasson@www.computercompany.net
Website: www.computercompany.net
Network engineering, internet connectivity, system firewalls & security, remote system monitoring, IT outsourcing, custom programming & integration. (Minority, Woman, estab 1995, empl 22, sales $3,750,000, cert: State, NMSDC)

4259 The Computer Support People, LLC
16 River St Upper Level
Norwalk, CT 06850
Contact: Cassandre Jean Business Devel
Tel: 203-653-4643
Email: cassandre.jean@tcsp360.com
Website: www.tcsp360.com
Managed Computer Services. Computer Software & Hardware support. (Hisp, estab 2005, empl 8, sales $419,362, cert: State, NMSDC)

4260 The Wellspring Group, Inc.
4 Research Dr, Ste 402
Shelton, CT 06484
Contact: Amy Dain Vincelette President
Tel: 203-261-1616
Email:
Website: www.wellspringgrp.com
Information technology staffing & project management: temps, contract-to-hire, direct-hire. (Woman, estab 2001, empl 59, sales $7,000,000, cert: WBENC)

4261 Transcend Business Solutions, LLC
30 Grassy Plain St, Unit 5A
Bethel, CT 06801
Contact: Linda Rowan President
Tel: 203-790-5222
Email: info@transcendbus.com
Website: www.transcendbus.com
IT consulting firm & employment recruiting. (Woman, estab 2003, empl 10, sales $850,000, cert: WBENC)

4262 Virpie Inc.
1449 Old Waterbury Rd, Ste 208
Southbury, CT 06488
Contact: Shre Thammana President
Tel: 203-264-0999
Email: shre@virpietech.com
Website: www.virpietech.com
Information technology staffing, storage area network design, architecture & administration, disaster recovery, database developers & administrators, senior & project management. (As-Pac, estab 1997, empl 150, sales $4,725,000, cert: NMSDC)

4263 VisionPoint LLC
152 Rockwell Rd
Newington, CT 06111
Contact: Louise Mastroianni Acct Mgr
Tel: 860-436-9673
Email: visionpointct@gmail.com
Website: www.visionpointllc.com
Technology acquisition, integration, design, installation, technical meeting support & service. (Woman, estab 2003, empl 24, sales $7,002,015, cert: WBENC)

District of Columbia

4264 Analytica LLC
1705 DeSales St, NW Ste 400
Washington, DC 20036
Contact: VP Business Dev
Tel: 202-470-4806
Email:
Website: www.analytica.net
Business Intelligence & Analytics, Information Management, Software Development, Financial Management & Analysis, Program Management Support, Cyber Security & Intelligence, GIS Mapping Solutions, IT and Finance Staff Augmentation. (Hisp, estab 2007, empl 19, sales $7,000,000, cert: State)

4265 Centricity Technology Partners, Inc.
621 Quackenbos St NW
Washington, DC 20011
Contact: CEO
Tel: 202-696-5270
Email:
Website: www.centricity-us.com
Cloud, Mobile & SOA Application Development, Enterprise Architecture, Program/Project Management, Architecture & Engineering, Business Process Reengineering, Operations & Maintenance, IT Governance, Independent Validation & Verification. (Woman/AA, estab 2012, empl 4, sales $1,661,362, cert: WBENC, 8(a))

4266 MSys Inc.
1025 Connecticut Ave, NW Ste 1000
Washington, DC 20036
Contact: Raj Thiyagarajan Dir
Tel: 202-629-0353
Email: register@msysinc.com
Website: www.msysinc.com
Software consulting,custom programming & development, web development. (As-Ind, estab 1994, empl 67, sales $5,787,890, cert: NMSDC)

4267 Optimus Technologies, LLC
700 12th St NW Ste 700
Washington, DC 20005
Contact: Donald Jones CEO
Tel: 202-263-7370
Email: djones@optimustech.net
Website: www.optimustech.net
Document scanning, black & white copy, color copy, records mgmt & retention, electronic data processing, computer forensics, foreign language document conversion, web hosting, backup tape restoration, document printing. (AA, estab 2005, empl 20, sales $8,000,000, cert: NMSDC)

4268 Orgro
20 F St NW Ste 700
Washington, DC 20001
Contact: Aditya Dahagam Founder
Tel: 202-505-1431
Email: connect@orgro.team
Website: www.orgro.team
ITSM & ITIL process improvement, Software/Application Development, IT Business Analytics, BPR, Quality Assurance, Systems Engineering, IT & Organizational Strategy. (As-Ind, estab , empl , sales , cert: State, NMSDC, 8(a), SDB)

4269 Peak Technology Solutions, Inc.
1627 K St, NW, Ste 400
Washington, DC 20006
Contact: Mohammad Tariq President
Tel: 202-776-7196
Email: mtariq@peaktsinc.com
Website: www.peaktsinc.com
COTS implementation, system integration, database design & application development services, Geographic Information System (GIS) solutions, and web enabled automation. (Minority, estab 2002, empl 9, sales $645,948, cert: State)

4270 The ELOCEN Group
1341 H St, NE Ste 301
Washington, DC 20002
Contact: Taryn Lewis Dir of Operations
Tel: 202-644-8500
Email: tarynl@elocengroup.com
Website: www.elocengroup.com
Program & Project Management, Construction Management, Interior Design, Information Technology, Facilities/Logistics, and Healthcare Facilities/Logistics/Management. (Woman/AA, estab 2007, empl 62, sales $20,089,894, cert: State, City, WBENC, 8(a))

4271 vTech Solution Inc
1100 H St NW Ste 750
Washington, DC 20005
Contact: Soudeepya Chinni Client Relation Specialist
Tel: 202-919-8964
Email: info@vtechsolution.com
Website: www.vtechsolution.com
IT staffing, permanent & temporary. (As-Ind, estab 2006, empl 49, sales $38,800,000, cert: State, NMSDC, SDB)

Delaware

4272 Alpha Technologies USA, Inc.
704 N King St
Wilmington, DE 19801
Contact: Amrit Gurung COO
Tel: 302-304-8421
Email: amrit@alphait.us
Website: www.alphaIT.us
Information technology staffing & consulting, project mgmt, software devel, systems integration, datacenter mgmt. (Minority, Woman, estab 1997, empl 200, sales $42,000,000, cert: NMSDC)

4273 DecisivEdge LLC
131 Continental Dr Ste 409
Newark, DE 19713
Contact: Michele Frayler
Tel: 302-299-1570
Email: michele.frayler@decisivedge.com
Website: www.decisivedge.com
Business consulting & technology services, business architecture & performance, business analytics, data warehouse strategy, design, development & governance, marketing analytics development. (As-Ind, estab 2007, empl 41, sales $4,739,862, cert: NMSDC)

4274 Frontier Technologies, Inc.
1521 Concord Pike Ste 302
Wilmington, DE 19803
Contact: Reshma Moorthy President
Tel: 302-225-2530
Email:
Website: www.ftiusa.com
Develop & deploy integrated business solutions: front office apps, IT staff augmentation, CRM, supply chain mgmt & computer telephony. (Woman/As-Ind, estab 1989, empl 15, sales $20,000,000, cert: NMSDC, WBENC)

4275 LiivData Inc.
1201 N Orange St Ste 7065
Wilmington, DE 19801
Contact: Dominic Francis Oguejiofo CEO
Tel: 302-235-3040
Email: dom.francis@liivdata.com
Website: www.liivdata.com
Information & systems integration, communications services, Voip technology. (AA, estab 2010, empl 15, sales $3,850,000, cert: State)

Florida

4276 Action 9-A, Inc.
10416 New Berlin Rd
Jacksonville, FL 32226
Contact: William Valentino President
Tel: 904-696-9191
Email: action9a@earthlink.net
Website: www.action9astorage.com
Moving totes/dollies rentals; specialized equipment for modular furniture; breakdown and reconfiguration for modular furniture systems; corporate moving and storage (Hisp, estab 1999, empl 12, sales $800,000, cert: NMSDC)

4277 Advanced IT Concepts, Inc.
1351 Sundial Point
Winter Springs, FL 32708
Contact: Gabriel Ruiz President
Tel: 407-914-2484
Email: eve.maldonado@aitcinc.com
Website: www.aitcinc.com
Telecommunications & Information Technology services. (Hisp, estab 2006, empl 51, sales $24,860,693, cert: City, 8(a))

4278 Almond Consulting Group
5472 Baytowne Place
Oviedo, FL 32765
Contact: Derrick Henry President
Tel: 407-602-8540
Email: derrick.henry@almondconsulting.com
Website: www.almondconsulting.com
Information technology consulting solutions: Project Management, Information Assurance, Certification & Accreditation & Process Improvement. (AA, estab 2001, empl 1, sales , cert: State, City, NMSDC)

4279 Amzur Technologies, Inc.
405 N Reo St Ste 110
Tampa, FL 33609
Contact: Bala Nemani CEO
Tel: 813-600-4060
Email: supplier@amzur.com
Website: www.amzur.com
Information technology, information security, anti-virus, firewalls, operating systems, IT services, Web e-commerce, LAN / WAN, network management, staff augmentation, servers, workflow, imaging, asset management. (Minority, Woman, estab 2004, empl 200, sales $22,173,714, cert: State, NMSDC)

4280 Auritas
4907 International Pkwy, Ste 1001
Sanford, FL 32771
Contact: Anne Cross Dir of Mktg
Tel: 407-834-8324
Email: rfp@auritas.com
Website: www.auritas.com
SAP Consulting Services & Project Management services, Data Lifecycle Management. (Minority, Woman, estab 2003, empl 200, sales $7,400,000, cert: WBENC)

4281 Beacon Systems, Inc.
3928 Coral Ridge Dr
Coral Springs, FL 33065
Contact: Brian Tupiak Contracts Admin
Tel: 954-426-1171
Email: info@beacongov.com
Website: www.beacongov.com
Information technology training & support, security systems, program management, performance consulting, software & program training, systems security, systems & networking engineering support, web design & development. (Minority, Woman, estab 2005, empl 20, sales $500,000, cert: State, NMSDC)

4282 BlueStreak Learning, LLC
PO Box 110435
Naples, FL 34108
Contact: Jennifer De Vries President
Tel: 630-842-1865
Email: info@bluestreaklearning.com
Website: www.bluestreaklearning.com
Technology-based training programs: needs assessments, e-learning strategy, LMS selection, course development svcs, evaluation/ROI analysis. (Woman, estab 2003, empl 3, sales $500,000, cert: WBENC)

4283 Braille Works International, Inc.
941-942 Darby Lake St
Seffner, FL 33584
Contact: Marketing
Tel: 813-654-4050
Email: JEFF@BRAILLEWORKS.COM
Website: www.brailleworks.com
Braille, large print, audio & computerized documents. (Woman, estab 1994, empl 12, sales $1,250,000, cert: WBENC)

4284 Business Information Technology Solutions.Com
100 S. Orange Ave Ste 800
Orlando, FL 32801
Contact: Amy Seaman Acct Exec
Tel: 407-363-0024
Email: amy@abtsolutions.com
Website: www.abtsolutions.com
IT staffing. (Woman, estab 2000, empl 25, sales $4,700,000, cert: State, City)

4285 C&C International Computers and Consultants, Inc.
7777 N Davie Rd Ext Ste 100 A
Hollywood, FL 33024
Contact: Bill James President
Tel: 954-450-0023
Email: bjames@ccintercomputers.com
Website: www.ccintercomputers.com
Value Added Reseller (VAR) Services, Support Services & IT Staffing, Computer Installations, Product Rollouts & Deployments, Consulting Services & Project Management, Onsite & Remote Help Desk Support. (Woman/AA, estab 1995, empl 27, sales , cert: State, City, NMSDC)

4286 Corporate Subscription Management Services, LLC
5763 N Andrews Way
Fort Lauderdale, FL 33309
Contact: Julie Auslander Chief Cultural Officer
Tel: 201-307-9900
Email: jsauslander@couranto.com
Website: www.couranto.com/
Customizable, end-to-end information, contract, and license management solution, publisher negogiations, information asset consulting, custom information hub. (Woman, estab 2003, empl 22, sales $19,985,377, cert: WBENC)

4287 Corpotel, Inc
      2800 Glades Circle Ste. 146
      Weston, FL 33327
      Contact: Elias Benaim Sales
      Tel: 954-364-7045
      Email: ebenaim@corpotel.com
      Website: www.corpotel.com
Telecom expense mgmt, call accounting, multi-store
telecom svcs, call center software dev, bilingual call center
outsourcing. (Hisp, estab 2001, empl 15, sales $1,000,000,
cert: NMSDC)

4288 Craig Technical Consulting, Inc.
      150 N Sykes Creek Pkwy
      Merritt Island, FL 32952
      Contact: Greg Sheppard Dir Business Dev
      Tel: 321-613-5620
      Email: greg.sheppard@craigtechinc.com
      Website: www.craigtechinc.com
Software Design and Development, Systems Engineering
and Integration, Multidisciplinary Engineering, Training
and Courseware Development, Modeling and Simulation,
Information Technology Support and Integrated Logistics
Support. (Minority, Woman, estab 1999, empl 300, sales
$30,000,000, cert: NMSDC, WBENC, SDB)

4289 Curia Document Solutions LLC
      815 North Homestead Blvd. Ste #646
      Homestead, FL 33030
      Contact: Lourdes Cox President
      Tel: 888-516-5193
      Email: sales@curiausa.com
      Website: www.curiausa.com
On-site & Off-site Document Production & Reprographics,
Imaging Services, On-site & Offsite Scanning & Data
Conversion, Document Utilization & Coding, Document
Clustering for Review Prioritization, Auto Coding. (Minor-
ity, Woman, estab 2011, empl 5, sales $100,000, cert:
State)

4290 Damasco Design Inc
      7136 Crescent Creek Way
      Coconut Creek, FL 33073
      Contact: Jorge Castillo President
      Tel: 954-361-6600
      Email: jorge@damascodesign.com
      Website: www.damasco.io
Web Application solutions & Cloud systems integration.
(Hisp, estab 2013, empl 1, sales , cert: State)

4291 DataSavers of Jacksonville, Inc.
      888 Suemac Rd
      Jacksonville, FL 32254
      Contact: Charlene Sullivan CEO
      Tel: 800-884-9538
      Email: charlene.sullivan@datasaversfl.com
      Website: www.datasaversusa.com
Records storage & management, disaster recovery planning & services, media storage & rotations, copying
services, optical imaging. (Woman, estab 1989, empl 22,
sales $3,444,025, cert: WBENC)

4292 Dbsys Inc.
      5224 W State Rd 46, Ste 369
      Sanford, FL 32771
      Contact: Matthew Hudson Field Tech/Mktg
      Tel: 497-322-7832
      Email: matt@dbsys.com
      Website: www.dbsys.com
Hardware Solutions, PCs, Notebooks, Storage & File
Servers Networking Solutions, Certified Novell Engineer
(CNE) on staff Supporting Windows, Sales Solutions.
(Woman, estab 1990, empl 13, sales $2,200,000, cert:
State)

4293 Digital Hands
      400 N Tampa St 17th Fl
      Tampa, FL 33602
      Contact: Karen Krymski Dir strategic initiatives
      Tel: 877-229-8020
      Email: kkrymski@digitalhands.com
      Website: www.digitalhands.com
Outsourced IT managed services: IT security (assurance)
– enterprise data security, data loss prevention, end-
point security, infrastructure security & management.
(Woman, estab 2001, empl 25, sales $2,225,000, cert:
WBENC)

4294 Easy Verification Inc.
      7050 W Palmetto Park Rd Ste 15-256
      Boca Raton, FL 33433
      Contact: Lisa Bruno President
      Tel: 877-904-7770
      Email: lbruno@easyverification.com
      Website: www.easyverification.com
4506-T Fulfillment, IRS Tax Transcript Verification.
Income Verification, SSN & ID Validation. Web-based
verification application. (Woman, estab 2006, empl 3,
sales , cert: State, SDB)

4295 Ebyte Technologies, Inc.
      7855 NW 12th St Ste 214 & 212
      Miami, FL 33126
      Contact: Mgr Business Devel
      Tel: 786-358-9300
      Email: infomiami@ebytetechnologies.com
      Website: www.ebytetechnologies.com
Technology staffing, placing contract, project solutions &
permanent placement opportunities. (Woman/As-Ind,
estab 2009, empl 70, sales $5,400,000, cert: City)

4296 Employer Management Solutions, Inc.
      5550 W Executive Dr Ste 450
      Tampa, FL 33609
      Contact: Jennifer Johnston
      Tel: 813-287-2486
      Email: jjohnston@consultems.com
      Website: www.consultems.com
Info technology svcs: enterprise wide initiatives; vendor
selection, software implementation & project planning
svcs. (Woman, estab 1998, empl 30, sales $4,000,000,
cert: WBENC)

4297 Enterprise Risk Management, Inc.
800 S Douglas Rd, North T s940
Coral Gables, FL 33134
Contact: Suzanne Siberon Sr Business Devel
Tel: 305-447-6750
Email: ssiberon@emrisk.com
Website: www.ermprotect.com
IT Security Design and Implementation
Vulnerability Assessments Penetration Testing Social
Engineering Incident Response Planning Business Continuity Planning Disaster Recovery (Minority, Woman, estab 1998, empl 18, sales $2,543,700, cert: State, City, 8(a))

4298 ExecuSys, Inc.
551 S Apollo Blvd, Ste 104
Melbourne, FL 32901
Contact: Eddie Haralson President
Tel: 321-253-0077
Email: eharalson@execusys.com
Website: www.execusys.com
Software engineering & information technology services, financial management systems support & range operations cost modelling solutions. (AA, estab 1993, empl 20, sales $2,155,571, cert: State)

4299 Freedom Solutions LLC
19046 Bruce B Downs Blvd, Ste 108
Tampa, FL 33647
Contact: Kelli Covel Dir Business Dev
Tel: 404-713-7777
Email: kcovel@freedomsolutionsllc.com
Website: www.freedomsolutionsllc.com
IBM Business partner, dist IBM software & hardware, aintenance, programming services & installation services. (AA, estab 2002, empl 18, sales $12,000,000, cert: NMSDC)

4300 GDKN Corporation
9700 Stirling Road Ste 110
Cooper City, FL 33024
Contact: Gary Dhir VP
Tel: 954-985-6650
Email: gdhir@gdkn.com
Website: www.gdkn.com
Staffing: information technology, engineering, professional, administrative & clerical, IT consulting, custom application development. (As-Ind, estab 1993, empl 400, sales $18,000,000, cert: NMSDC)

4301 Global Information Technology
8905 Regents Park Dr Ste 210
Tampa, FL 33647
Contact: Aruna Ajjarapu VP
Tel: 813-973-1061
Email: araj@git-org.com
Website: www.git-org.com
IT developers, DBA's, project managers & architects. (Minority, Woman, estab 1995, empl 300, sales $36,000,000, cert: State)

4302 ICG Software Corporation
2860 W State Rd 84 Ste 113
Fort Lauderdale, FL 33312
Contact: Tiffany Nutt Office Mgr
Tel: 305-933-9100
Email: info@icgsoftware.us
Website: www.icgsoftware.us
Mfr Point of Sale Software & Hardware for the retail and restaurant industry. (Minority, Woman, estab 2010, empl 5, sales $200,000, cert: State)

4303 ITG Global, LLC
11235 St. Johns Industrial Pkwy N Ste 2A
Jacksonville, FL 32246
Contact: Joseph Lukowski CEO
Tel: 904-425-4760
Email: almaferrante@itgtec.com
Website: www.itgtec.com
Automation Design, PLC Programming, Software Development, Technologies Consulting, Motion Design, Robot programming, MES, OEE, Data Analytics, Condition Monitoring, Control System Design, UL 508A Panel Shop, Control Panel. (Minority, Woman, estab 2003, empl 27, sales $3,000,000, cert: NMSDC)

4304 ITTConnect Inc.
9021 Southern Orchard Rd N
Davie, FL 33328
Contact: Fabio Back CEO
Tel: 954-732-8277
Email: fabio.back@ittconnect.com
Website: www.ittconnect.com
IT Recruiting / Direct Hire / Placement, IT Staffing / Temporary Contractors. (Hisp, estab 2017, empl 2, sales , cert: State, NMSDC)

4305 Kolter Solutions
175 Middle St
Lake Mary, FL 32746
Contact: Kim Carr Partner
Tel: 407-583-9483
Email: kcarr@koltersolutions.com
Website: www.koltersolutions.com
Information Technology Staff Augmentation, Project Teams, Application Design and Development (Java, C/C++, .NET/C#), Business Analysis/Project Management/Program Management, Quality Assurance, Infrastructure/Network/Security. (Woman, estab 2010, empl 28, sales $1,300,000, cert: WBENC)

4306 Lancesoft, Inc.
8804 Fazio Ct Ste 120
Tampa, FL 33647
Contact: Philip J Kalafut VP Healthcare Advisory
Tel: 813-449-1301
Email: phil.kalafut@lancesoft.com
Website: www.lancesoft.com
IT software, staffing & project execution. (Minority, Woman, estab 2000, empl 2000, sales $90,000,000, cert: NMSDC)

4307 LebenTech Innovative Solutions Inc.
PO Box 670832
Coral Springs, FL 33067
Contact: Lennox Bennett President
Tel: 954-796-7107
Email: lennox_bennett@lebentech.com
Website: www.lebentech.com
Technology consultation svcs: CAD designs, product development, RAMS analysis, R&D, FRACAS implementation, product validation, reliability testing. (AA, estab 2004, empl 6, sales , cert: State)

4308 Lodestar Solutions, Inc.
      3212 W Harbor View Ave
      Tampa, FL 33611
      Contact: Heather Cole President
      Tel: 813-415-2910
      Email: hcole@lodestarsolutions.com
      Website: www.lodestarsolutions.com
IBM business analytics/Cognos reseller & IBM support
renewals, IBM Cognos licenses, TM1, Cognos business
intelligence, FSR, SPSS, Varicent & Cognos planning.
(Woman, estab 2004, empl 11, sales $3,949,751, cert:
WBENC)

4309 N2 Services Inc
      13241 Bartram Park Blvd Ste 2301
      Jacksonville, FL 32258
      Contact: Neminathan Ammaiyappan President
      Tel: 904-703-4245
      Email: nemi@n2sglobal.com
      Website: www.n2sglobal.com
Software design, development, analysis a& nd consulting
services, internet application development, E-Commerce
solutions, Web 2.0, n-tier architecture & rapid application
development environments. (As-Pac, estab 2004, empl
140, sales $6,580,000, cert: NMSDC)

4310 Noise Consulting Group, Inc.
      9280 Bay Plaza Blvd Ste 705
      Tampa, FL 33619
      Contact: GINA HANNAH CEO
      Tel: 315-491-0771
      Email: gina.hannah@noisetcd.com
      Website: www.noisetcd.com
IT staffing, consulting & systems integration, technology
solutions & systems integration & implementation services. (Woman/AA, estab 2007, empl 38, sales $1,900,000,
cert: State)

4311 Ospro Systems, LLC
      1327 LaFayette St Ste C
      Cape Coral, FL 33904
      Contact: Prasad Kasireddy BDM-Recruitment
      Tel: 239-309-0319
      Email: prasad@osprosys.com
      Website: www.osprosys.com
Software Implementations, Software Changes, Custom
Software Development, Software validation/Testing,
Maintenance and Support
Project Management, E-commerce, B2B, B2C, Custom Web
Development, Application Web. (Woman/As-Ind, estab
2004, empl 70, sales $2,000,000, cert: State, NMSDC)

4312 Professional Materials Management
      4210 Saltwater Blvd
      Tampa, FL 33615
      Contact: Julie Floen President
      Tel: 813-249-0834
      Email: julie@pm2online.com
      Website: www.pm2online.com
inventory management planning, inventory project
implementation services, database building, (Woman,
estab 0, empl , sales , cert: WBENC)

4313 Professional Translating Services, Inc.
      44 W Flagler St, Ste 1800
      Miami, FL 33130
      Contact: Alexandra Hunt Natl Business Dev
      Tel: 305-371-7887
      Email: ahunt@protranslating.com
      Website: www.protranslating.com
Translate documents, films & websites, interpreting
services & equipment for multilingual meetings. (Minority, Woman, estab 1973, empl 100, sales $8,800,000,
cert: NMSDC)

4314 Qualex Consulting Services, Inc.
      1111 Kane Concourse Ste 320
      Bay Harbor Island, FL 33154
      Contact: Mark Miller Govt Sales
      Tel: 877-887-4727
      Email: mark.miller@qlx.com
      Website: www.qlx.com
Software solutions & consulting services. (Minority,
Woman, estab 1995, empl 26, sales $4,700,000, cert:
State, WBENC)

4315 RADgov Inc.
      6750 N Andrews Ave, Ste 200
      Fort Lauderdale, FL 33309
      Contact: Mark Smith Sr Business Mgr
      Tel: 954-691-4588
      Email: msmith@radgov.com
      Website: www.radgov.com
IT planning services, system planning, development &
implementation, electronic commerce, training &
support, program management. (Minority, Woman,
estab 2005, empl 247, sales $2,900,000, cert: NMSDC,
WBENC)

4316 RIK Data Solutions Inc.
      8875 Hidden River Pkwy Ste 300
      Tampa, FL 33637
      Contact: Chris Kambhampati Principal Architect
      Tel: 941-527-1464
      Email: krk@rds-us.com
      Website: www.rds-us.com
Datacenter Systems Integration, Cloud Brokerage
Services, Software Development,
Graphic Art and Design Services (for Web and Promo-
tional products). (Minority, Woman, estab 2012, empl 6,
sales $1,540,000, cert: NMSDC)

4317 Rudram Engineering, Inc.
      845 Executive Lane Ste 200
      Rockledge, FL 32955
      Contact: Patel Alkesh President
      Tel: 321-735-4159
      Email: alkesh.patel@rudramengineering.com
      Website: www.rudramengineering.com
System design, development, verification & validation,
EMI analysis, Concept analysis, trade studies, emerging
technology research, Software development, embedded
system support, Interface identification, definition,
design and system safety. (As-Ind, estab , empl 20, sales
$1,454,900, cert: State, NMSDC, 8(a), SDB)

4318   SDI International Corp
      2500 N Military Trail,STE. 318
      Boca Raton, FL 33431
      Contact: Carmen Castillo President
      Tel: 561-288-4079
      Email: sdidiversity@sdintl.com
      Website: www.sdintl.com
Staffing & business solutions, staff augmentation, e-vendor mgmt services. (Minority, Woman, estab 1992, empl 1500, sales $600,000,000, cert: NMSDC, WBENC)

4319   Securance LLC
      13904 Monroes Business Park
      Tampa, FL 33635
      Contact: Paul Ashe President
      Tel: 877-578-0215
      Email: supplydiv@securanceconsulting.com
      Website: www.securanceconsulting.com
Independent technology risk consulting & IT auditing services. (AA, estab 2002, empl 12, sales , cert: NMSDC)

4320   SGF US Inc.
      501 Golden Isles Dr, Ste 205
      Hallandale Beach, FL 33009
      Contact: Kevin Cabrera Acct Mgr
      Tel: 954-454-7676
      Email: kcabrera@sgfglobal.com
      Website: www.sgfglobal.com
Technical recruiting & staffing. (Hisp, estab 1997, empl 90, sales $21,929,723, cert: NMSDC)

4321   SGS Technologie
      6817 Southpoint Pkwy, Ste 2104
      Jacksonville, FL 32216
      Contact: Arun Venkatesan CEO
      Tel: 904-332-4534
      Email: bids@sgstechnologies.net
      Website: www.sgstechnologies.net
Custom Software Applications Development, Mobile Apps Development, Website Design, Digital Marketing, SEO, Salesforce Implementation, CRM, SharePoint Development. (As-Pac, estab 2003, empl 150, sales $15,000,000, cert: State, NMSDC)

4322   Simplified Technologies, LLC
      6310 Techster Blvd, Ste 2
      Fort Myers, FL 33966
      Contact: Darius Joseph Owner
      Tel: 239-210-9645
      Email: darius@simplifiedtech.biz
      Website: www.simplifiedtech.biz
Network & systems integration, Windows Servers Business Server, SQL Server, Exchange Server, Windows Desktop, Microsoft Office & Office 365. (AA, estab 2010, empl 10, sales , cert: State)

4323   Sonoi Solutions LLC
      800 6th St N
      St. Petersburg, FL 33701
      Contact: Vienggeun Gertsch President
      Tel: 727-341-5100
      Email: vienggeun.gertsch@sonoisolutions.com
      Website: www.sonoisolutions.com
IT aggregation, logistics & technical services for supply chain diversification. (Minority, Woman, estab 2013, empl 2, sales , cert: NMSDC, WBENC)

4324   Southeastern Aerospace Services, LLC
      1816 SW 7th Ave
      Pompano Beach, FL 33060
      Contact: Julian Tucker Accountability Mgr
      Tel: 305-992-8257
      Email: sales@southeasternaerospace.com
      Website: www.southeasternaerospace.com
Southeastern Aerospace Services, LLC., is a certified FAA Repair Station, FAA 145 Cert 8SIR251C. As an independent MRO facility, we provide repair and overhaul of military and commercial aircraft power generating units, ranging from regional to wide/nar (AA, estab 2016, empl 4, sales , cert: NMSDC)

4325   SpendCheQ, Inc.
      3171 Jasmine Dr
      Delray Beach, FL 33483
      Contact: Mary Ellen Mitchell President
      Tel: 561-870-3171
      Email: mmitchell@spendcheq.com
      Website: www.spendcheq.com
Integrated supply chain & procurement solutions, Catalog Management, Inventory Data Management, Supplier Information Management & Spend Analysis. (Woman, estab 2014, empl 19, sales , cert: State, WBENC)

4326   SurfBigData LLC
      4474 Foxtail Ln
      Weston, FL 33331
      Contact: Andrew Li CEO
      Tel: 954-353-5599
      Email: service@surfbigdata.com
      Website: www.surfbigdata.com
Enterprise Workflow Analysis, Information Technology, Architecture & System Integration, Dev/Ops & Agile Scrum Plan & Management, Web Application Development, Central Information Repository Design, Big Data Platform design. (As-Pac, estab 2015, empl 6, sales $480,000, cert: State)

4327   Synergy Technologies, LLC
      9600 W Sample Rd, Ste 207
      Coral Springs, FL 33065
      Contact: Srikaanth Bollampally Program Mgr
      Tel: 954-775-0064
      Email: sri.b@synergytechs.net
      Website: www.synergyteks.com
Synergy Technologies has excellent domain competencies in verticals such as Banking & Financial Service, Insurance & Healthcare, and Manufacturing. As a diverse end-to-end IT solutions provider, offers a range of expertise aimed at helping customers re-en (Woman/As-Ind, estab 2006, empl 65, sales $5,000,000, cert: NMSDC, WBENC)

4328   System Soft Technologies, Inc
      3000 Bayport Dr Ste 840
      Tampa, FL 33607
      Contact: Sreedhar Veeramachaneni CEO
      Tel: 727-723-0801
      Email: v.sreedhar@sstech.us
      Website: www.sstech.us
Software development & IT services. (As-Pac, estab 2000, empl 800, sales $67,964,203, cert: State, NMSDC)

4329 Tech Army, LLC
      7777 Davie Road Extension Ste 303B
      Hollywood, FL 33024
      Contact: Jay Narang CEO
      Tel: 954-372-2698
      Email: sales@techarmy.com
      Website: www.techarmy.com
IT consulting and staffing augmentation. (As-Ind, estab
2016, empl 18, sales , cert: NMSDC, 8(a))

4330 Techno-Transfers of Florida, Inc.
      4609 NW 26th Ave
      Boca Raton, FL 33434
      Contact: Virginia Mendiola Dir
      Tel: 561-212-2383
      Email: vmendiola@techno-transfers.com
      Website: www.techno-transfers.com
IT personnel for temporary contract, temp-to-perm roles &
full-time positions. (Minority, Woman, estab 1992, empl 6,
sales $350,000, cert: State)

4331 Tec-Link
      16350 BB Downs Blvd, Ste 48942
      Tampa, FL 33646
      Contact: Derek Holmes President
      Tel: 813-929-3222
      Email: derek@tec-link.com
      Website: www.tec-link.com
Information technology professional services & consulting.
(AA, estab 1999, empl 20, sales $2,000,000, cert: NMSDC)

4332 The Ashvins Group, Inc.
      6161 Blue Lagoon Dr Ste 340
      Miami, FL 33126
      Contact: Ivette Boyd Partner, Proj Mgr
      Tel: 305-264-4442
      Email: iboyd@ashvinsgroup.com
      Website: www.ashvinsgroup.com
Consulting, software validation, software quality audits.
(Woman, estab 2000, empl 20, sales $940,000, cert:
WBENC)

4333 The Goal Inc.
      1408 N. Westshore Blvd Ste 705
      Tampa, FL 33607
      Contact: Mary Kate Gowl Managing Dir Business
      Dev
      Tel: 813-319-7015
      Email: mgowl@thegoalinc.com
      Website: www.thegoalinc.com
Technology Consulting, Software Development, Security
Services, and our Government Practice. (Hisp, estab 1998,
empl 250, sales $34,000,000, cert: NMSDC, SDB)

4334 Tropical Surveillance & Investigations, Inc.
      1813 N Tampa St
      Tampa, FL 33602
      Contact: JC Dominguez
      Tel: 813-282-0074
      Email: jc@tsilegal.com
      Website: www.tsilegal.com
Professional services to large and small business law firms
insurance companies and private citizens. (Minority,
Woman, estab 2003, empl 15, sales $1,100,000, cert:
NMSDC)

4335 Vitaver and Associates, Inc.
      401 East Las Olas Boulevard Ste 1400
      Fort Lauderdale, FL 33301
      Contact: Pablo Vitaver CEO
      Tel: 954-382-0075
      Email: pablo@vitaver.com
      Website: www.vitaver.com
IT staff augmentation & software outsourcing. (Hisp,
estab 1993, empl 15, sales $8,309,079, cert: State)

4336 Wayfinder, LLC
      7300 Biscayne Blvd, Ste 200
      Miami, FL 33138
      Contact: Chinmoy Raval CEO
      Tel: 305-496-8663
      Email: letstalk@wayfinder-ux.com
      Website: www.wayfinder-ux.com
Digital application design, website design and product
development. (As-Ind, estab 2004, empl 5, sales
$2,300,000, cert: NMSDC)

Georgia

4337 1Source International, LLC
      925 Woodstock Rd Ste 150
      Roswell, GA 30075
      Contact: Margaret Tinsley VP Operations
      Tel: 770-733-1202
      Email: mtinsley@1source-intl.net
      Website: www.1sourceinternational.com
Audio, video & conferencing solutions. (Woman, estab
2000, empl 11, sales $6,000,000, cert: WBENC)

4338 3i People, Inc.
      5755 N Point Pkwy Ste 234
      Alpharetta, GA 30022
      Contact: Buvi Raj CMO
      Tel: 678-628-4810
      Email: rbuvi@3ipeople.com
      Website: www.3ipeople.com
IT consulting, application dev, project mgmt & contract
staffing. (As-Pac, estab 2002, empl 220, sales
$13,500,000, cert: NMSDC)

4339 Accretive Technologies, Inc.
      330 Research Ct Ste 250
      Norcross, GA 30092
      Contact: Claire Ehrhardt President
      Tel: 678-328-2440
      Email: claire@accretive.com
      Website: www.accretive.com
Information technology consulting & placement services. (Woman, estab 1997, empl 17, sales $1,857,679,
cert: WBENC)

4340 ACS Solutions
      2400 Meadowbrook Pkwy
      Duluth, GA 30096
      Contact: Akshay Reddy Dir Business Dev
      Tel: 630-605-4731
      Email: akshay.reddy@acsicorp.com
      Website: www.acsicorp.com
IT services: staffing, payrolling, vendor management
services, consulting & business solutions. (As-Ind, estab
1998, empl 17000, sales $683,000,000, cert: NMSDC)

4341 Adroix Corp DBA CodeForce 360
3970 Old Milton pkwy, Ste 200 Ste 200
Alpharetta, GA 30005
Contact: Dickson-Lemond VP Sales
Tel: 470-407-4189
Email: amandad@codeforce.com
Website: www.codeforce.com/
IT Staffing & Talent Management. (As-Ind, estab 2010, empl 250, sales $30,000,000, cert: NMSDC)

4342 Allstaff Technical Solutions
1954 Airport Road Ste 220
Atlanta, GA 30341
Contact: Justin Katz VP Business Devel
Tel: 678-281-3063
Email: jkatz@allstafftech.com
Website: www.allstaffsolutions.net/
Infrastructure Support, Cyber Security, Application Development, and Engineering. (Woman, estab 1991, empl 176, sales $14,000,000, cert: WBENC)

4343 Analysts International Corporation (AIC)
2400 Meadowbrook Pkwy
Duluth, GA 55435
Contact: Vicki Bien Sr Dir - Marketing & Sales Enablement
Tel: 800-800-5044
Email: diversitysupplier@aictalent.com
Website: www.analysts.com
Information technology (IT) services. (As-Ind, estab 1966, empl 350, sales $695,000,000, cert: NMSDC)

4344 Applications Technology Group, Inc.
5825 Glenridge Dr, Bldg3, Ste 101
Atlanta, GA 30328
Contact: Trelaine Business Devel Mgr
Tel: 404-552-0191
Email: tnunnally@atgworks.com
Website: www.atgwork.com
Technical & staffing services. (Minority, Woman, estab 2004, empl 105, sales $3,000,000, cert: NMSDC)

4345 Arete Technology Solutions, Inc. dba STATEMENT
3379 Peachtree Road NE Ste 555
Atlanta, GA 30326
Contact: Kendall Flagg Principal
Tel: 800-640-5589
Email: kendall.flagg@statementcorp.com
Website: www.statementcorp.com
Software & IT consulting, Architecture Custom software development Automated Testing Continuous Development and Integration Oracle Database Development noSql Development Services Native tablet/mobile iOS. (AA, estab 2007, empl 12, sales $1,641,519, cert: NMSDC)

4346 Arion Systems, Inc.
2741 Calloway Ct
Duluth, GA 30097
Contact: Michael Brewington II President
Tel: 770-569-3434
Email: michael.brewington@arioncorp.com
Website: www.ArionCorp.com
Implementation & systems integration consulting: business applications & ERP products, PeopleSoft, SAP, Oracle, Siebel, technology solutions, financials, supply chain mgmt, human capital mgmt, enterprise performance mgmt. (Woman/AA, estab 2003, empl 10, sales $2,000,000, cert: NMSDC)

4347 Armedia LLC
200 Galleria Pkwy, Ste 440
Atlanta, GA 30339
Contact: Andre Staten Global Sales Dir
Tel: 678-945-4417
Email: astaten@armedia.com
Website: www.armedia.com
Enterprise content management (ECM): design, implementation, collaboration, web publishing, workflow, digital asset management & compliance. (AA, estab 2002, empl 30, sales $10,000,000, cert: NMSDC)

4348 ASAP Solutions Group, LLC
3885 Holcomb Bridge Rd
Norcross, GA 30092
Contact: Nancy Williams CEO
Tel: 770-246-1718
Email: nancy@myasap.com
Website: www.myasap.com
IT staff augmentation. (Woman, estab 1989, empl 800, sales $60,000,000, cert: CPUC, WBENC)

4349 Bellsoft
PO Box 743622
Atlanta, GA 30374
Contact: Kannan Ramanathan Dir Client Services
Tel: 888-545-7639
Email: kannanr@ameri100.com
Website: www.ameri100.com/
Implement ERP solutions: JD Edwards, SAP & PeopleSoft. (Minority, estab 1996, empl 350, sales $30,000,000, cert: NMSDC)

4350 Blaze Information Systems Inc.
13026 Dartmore Ave
Alpharetta, GA 30005
Contact: Smita Deshpande CEO
Tel: 877-877-5293
Email: smita.deshpande@blazeinfosys.com
Website: www.blazeinfosys.com
Onsite Technical Support, Onsite Temporary Technology Staffing, Remote Temporary Technology Staffing, End-To-End e-Business Solutions. (Minority, Woman, estab 2009, empl 5, sales $116,000, cert: State)

4351 BlueFletch LLC
621 North Ave NE Ste A-150
Atlanta, GA 30308
Contact: Richard Makerson Managing Partner
Tel: 855-529-6349
Email: invoices@bluefletch.com
Website: www.bluefletch.com
Mobile software development, program leadership, business analysis, mobile web application development, legacy integration, MDM management & cloud infrastructure integration. (AA, estab 2008, empl 34, sales $2,906,767, cert: NMSDC)

4352 BMC Solutions, Inc.
3391 Town Point Dr, Ste 300
Kennesaw, GA 30144
Contact: George Hergen Mgr Business Devel
Tel: 770-514-6704
Email: ghergen@bmcsolutions.com
Website: www.BMCSolutions.com
Computer support & services: maintenance, design, implemeny & support networks. (Woman, estab 1990, empl 130, sales $34,645,320, cert: WBENC)

4353   Capricorn Systems, Inc.
       3569 Habersham At Northlake Bldg K
       Tucker, GA 30084
       Contact: Charles Goldman VP Sales
       Tel: 678-514-1080
       Email: cgoldman@capricornsys.com
       Website: www.capricornsys.com
Software consulting: staff augmentation, turnkey custom
application develpment & permanent placements, on site,
offsite & off-shore. (Minority, estab 1991, empl 155, sales
$3,250,000, cert: NMSDC)

4354   Cellworx LLC
       1005 Alderman Ste 110
       Alpharetta, GA 30005
       Contact: Chandrasekhar Anchala
       Tel: 678-254-9094
       Email: csanchala@celworx.com
       Website: www.celworx.com
Wireless & wireline technology design, development,
validation & realization, Software Defined Network, Cloud
& Virtualization. (As-Ind, estab 2008, empl 10, sales
$500,000, cert: NMSDC, CPUC)

4355   Charter Global Inc.
       One Glenlake Pkwy Ste 525
       Altanta, GA 30328
       Contact: Dev Shah Client Engagement Mgr
       Tel: 770-326-9933
       Email: dshah@charterglobal.com
       Website: www.charterglobal.com
Software consulting svcs: client server, web based, e-
commerce. (Minority, estab 1994, empl 1100, sales
$45,000,000, cert: NMSDC)

4356   CI2, Inc.
       200 Galleria Pkwy, Ste 1200
       Atlanta, GA 30339
       Contact: Sharon Mendon VP bus devel
       Tel: 770-425-2267
       Email: info2@ci2.com
       Website: www.ci2.com
Systems integration & engineering, telecommunications
mgmt. (Woman/AA, estab 1993, empl 83, sales
$25,000,000, cert: State, City, NMSDC)

4357   Competent Systems Inc.
       4080 McGinnis Ferry Rd Ste 1504
       Alpharetta, GA 30005
       Contact: Sridhar Konkala Mgr
       Tel: 678-691-7120
       Email: skonkala@competentsystems.com
       Website: www.competentsystems.com
Information Technology Consulting, Development,
Outsourcing & Technology Staffing. (As-Pac, estab 2004,
empl 150, sales $15,000,000, cert: NMSDC)

4358   Concept Software & Services Inc
       11600 Atlantis Place Ste E
       Alpharetta, GA 30022
       Contact: Ravindra Bhave CEO
       Tel: 770-300-9486
       Email: ravi@concept-inc.com
       Website: www.concept-inc.com
Software solutions, IT consulting, application outsourcing
& enterprise consulting services. (As-Ind, estab 1998, empl
57, sales $7,682,520, cert: NMSDC)

4359   Corpnet Consulting LLC
       2300 Lakeview Pkwy, Ste 700
       Alpharetta, GA 30009
       Contact: Faisal Ansari Managing Principal
       Tel: 678-795-1612
       Email: corpnet@corpnetconsulting.com
       Website: www.corpnetconsulting.com
Information security & risk management consultancy
services, IT platform integration services. (Minority,
Woman, estab 2008, empl 15, sales $1,300,000, cert:
WBENC)

4360   Datamatics Consultants Inc.
       3505 Duluth Park Ln Ste 200
       Duluth, GA 30096
       Contact: Frank Kulendran Business Devel Mgr
       Tel: 770-232-9460
       Email: frank@datamatics.us
       Website: www.datamatics.us
Business process management, financial management,
CRP, ERP, consulting & strategy, architecture & integration, custom systems dev, supply chain mgmt, knowledge mgmt, IT strategy, re-engineering & migration
services, maintenance. (As-Ind, estab 1993, empl 95,
sales $10,000,000, cert: NMSDC)

4361   Dataset, Inc.
       145 Noble Ct Ste 100
       Alpharetta, GA 30005
       Contact: Azhar Syed President
       Tel: 678-240-0771
       Email: azhar_syed@dataset-inc.com
       Website: www.datasetcorp.com
Professional consulting services, software & hardware
installation, software training & temporary contractors.
(As-Ind, estab 1994, empl 7, sales $3,009,031, cert:
NMSDC)

4362   Datum Software Inc.
       12000 Findley Road, Ste 350
       Johns Creek, GA 30097
       Contact: Ram Moorthy President
       Tel: 678-740-0265
       Email: ram@datumsoftware.com
       Website: www.datumsoftware.com
Software application devel, system integration & IT
staffing svcs. (Woman/As-Ind, estab 1992, empl 45, sales
$5,702,565, cert: NMSDC, WBENC)

4363   Diversant, LLC
       2400 Meadowbrook Pkwy
       Duluth, GA 30096
       Contact: Spencer Smith Business Dev Mgr
       Tel: 732-222-1250
       Email: ssmith@diversant.com
       Website: www.diversant.com
IT staffing and diversity products, IT staff augmentation,
direct hire, contract. (AA, estab 2010, empl 27000, sales
$1,700,000,000, cert: NMSDC)

4364 Dominus Gray, LLC
1273 Mackintosh Park NW
Atlanta, GA 30318
Contact: Odie Gray CEO
Tel: 404-360-7453
Email: odie.gray@dominusgray.com
Website: www.dominusgray.com
Cybersecurity & IT Diversity Staffing Services as well as the development and administration of cyber security workforce development. (AA, estab 2020, empl 1, sales , cert: NMSDC)

4365 DW Practice, LLC
5901 Peachtree Dunwoody Rd Ste C-160
Atlanta, GA 30328
Contact: Rajani Koneru President
Tel: 678-999-8197
Email: raj.koneru@dwpractice.com
Website: www.dwpractice.com
Software development services, product development services & IT staffing services. (As-Pac, estab 1998, empl 30, sales $4,000,000, cert: NMSDC)

4366 Edge Solutions, LLC
131 Roswell St C-101
Alpharetta, GA 30009
Contact: Julie Ison Haley CEO
Tel: 888-861-8884
Email: jhaley@edge-solutions.com
Website: www.edge-solutions.com
Data center solutions (hardware & software), Application development tools, cloud computing, virtualization, network security, data storage, backup and recovery, archiving, professional & managed services. (Woman, estab 2008, empl 32, sales $71,000,000, cert: WBENC)

4367 Elgia, Inc.
11675 Rainwater Dr
Alpharetta, GA 30009
Contact: Sandra Jackson Marketing Mgr
Tel: 678-242-4000
Email: sjackson@elgia.com
Website: www.elgia.com
Web conferencing applications, WebEx & Live Meeting, software applications. (Woman/AA, estab 2001, empl 20, sales $1,031,000, cert: WBENC)

4368 Enrich Inc
3655 Brookside Pkwy Ste 265
Alpharetta, GA 30022
Contact: Paul Herron VP-Sales & Marketing
Tel: 770-667-0510
Email: info@enrich.com
Website: www.enrich.com
Software deployment lifecycle in Oracle EBS. (Minority, Woman, estab 2004, empl 200, sales $17,624,212, cert: NMSDC)

4369 Entellimetrix LLC
445 Victorian Lane
Johns Creek, GA 30097
Contact: Magha Devan Partner
Tel: 678-779-7673
Email: mdevan@entellimetrix.com
Website: www.entellimetrix.com
Data Management, Business Intelligence and Analytics Services, Teradata, Informatica, DataStage. (Woman/As-Ind, estab 2012, empl 17, sales $2,450,000, cert: State, City, CPUC, 8(a))

4370 Exalt Integrated Technologies LLC
PO Box 888161
Atlanta, GA 30356
Contact: Donald Maycott VP
Tel: 678-920-3019
Email: dmaycott@exaltit.com
Website: www.exaltit.com
Network business consulting, organizational assessment, IT strategic planning, telecommunications services, security assessment, intrusion detection, firewall & DMZ implementation & management. (Woman/AA, estab 2004, empl 15, sales $1,750,000, cert: NMSDC)

4371 Fabulous Sites, Inc.
160 Clairemont Ave, Ste 555
Decatur, GA 30030
Contact: Laron Walker President
Tel: 404-478-2050
Email: walkerla@sciberus.com
Website: www.sciberus.com
Information technology consulting & software development. (AA, estab 2006, empl 5, sales $1,447,158, cert: NMSDC, 8(a))

4372 Firmament Solutions
510 Plaza Dr
College Park, GA 30349
Contact: Adrian Andrews
Tel: 770-742-0385
Email: aandrews@firmamentsolutions.com
Website: www.firmamentsolutions.com
Managed IT Services, Network Services, CAT3 & CAT6 Install, Hosting Software Service, Break FIX, Fiber Patch Panel, Cloud Services, ISP Services, Conduit/Surface Mount, IT Asset Management, Application Support, Voice/Mobile. (AA, estab 2013, empl 10, sales , cert: State, City, NMSDC)

4373 Focused HR-Solutions, LLC
400 Galleria Pkwy, Ste 1500
Atlanta, GA 30309
Contact: Ross Falik President
Tel: 678-385-6120
Email: rfalik@fhr-solutions.com
Website: www.fhr-solutions.com
IT staffing: software development, project management, development, networking. (Woman, estab 2002, empl 71, sales , cert: WBENC)

4374 Global Resource Manangement, Inc.
5400 Laurel Springs Pkwy Ste 902
Suwanee, GA 30024
Contact: Naheed Syed CEO
Tel: 678-456-6992
Email: naheed1@grmi.net
Website: www.grmi.net
IT consulting, telecommunications & staff augmentation. (Minority, Woman, estab 1993, empl 70, sales $2,600,000, cert: NMSDC, WBENC)

4375 Global Technology Services Group, Inc.
2850 Barrett Lakes Blvd NW Ste 500
Kennesaw, GA 30144
Contact: Jacqueline Holland CEO
Tel: 404-551-5189
Email: jacqui@gtservices.net
Website: www.gtservices.net
IT Asset Management, Auditing, Inventory Management, Warehouse & Logistics, Project Management & Deployment, Reverse Logistics & Asset Recovery, NSA Level Data Security, Depot Technology Hardware Repair & Refurbishment. (Woman, estab 2010, empl 44, sales $8,947,059, cert: State, WBENC)

4376 GSquared Group, LLC
3180 Northpoint Pkwy, Ste 301
Alpharetta, GA 30005
Contact: Joan Guillory CEO
Tel: 404-698-1810
Email: contactus@gsquaredgroup.com
Website: www.gsquaredgroup.com
Technology Talent Solutions for contract, contract-to-hire & direct hire positions, Technology Consulting Solutions for short-term, high-touch, high-value engagements. (Woman, estab 2010, empl 25, sales , cert: WBENC)

4377 GTS, Inc.
1325 Satellite Blvd Bldg 1600, Ste 1601
Suwanee, GA 30024
Contact: Dinesh Raturi President
Tel: 770-497-8637
Email: dinesh@gtsamerica.com
Website: www.gtsamerica.com
IT staff augmentation, permanent & contract, software development, requirement analysis & design, outsourcing. (Woman/As-Ind, estab 1998, empl 150, sales $16,500,000, cert: NMSDC, WBENC)

4378 Heagney Logan Group, LLC
2002 Summit Blvd Ste 300
Atlanta, GA 30319
Contact: Jeannette Weigelt Principal
Tel: 404-267-1351
Email: info@heagneylogan.com
Website: www.heagneylogangroup.com
Management Consulting, IT Consultant Staffing, Project Management, ERP Consulting, Remote Development, Contract Technical Staffing. (AA, estab 2009, empl 3, sales $924,954, cert: State, NMSDC)

4379 HireGenics, Inc.
2400 Meadowbrook Pkwy
Duluth, GA 30096
Contact: Nancy Budmayr Program Dir
Tel: 651-470-5240
Email: nancy.budmayr@hiregenics.com
Website: www.hiregenics.com
Technology consulting & solutions: onsite, near-shore, offshore, business intelligence, e-business, database technologies, ERP, CRM. (As-Ind, estab 1998, empl 10000, sales $683,000,000, cert: NMSDC)

4380 IBEX IT Business Experts LLC
3295 River Exchange Dr, Ste 550
Sandy Springs, GA 30092
Contact: Maggie Carter Sales Dir
Tel: 678-752-7542
Email: mcarter@ibexexperts.com
Website: www.ibexexperts.com
IT Service Management, Enterprise Governance, Project Management, IT Security Management. (Woman/AA, estab , empl , sales $7,500,000, cert: NMSDC, WBENC, 8(a))

4381 Impel Professional Consulting, LLC
7058 Wind Run Way
Stone Mountain, GA 30082
Contact: Jerome Potts Business Dev Dir
Tel: 678-410-9245
Email: info@impelprofessional.com
Website: www.impelprofessional.com
Design & develop end-to-end integrated IT Solutions in ERP (SAP, SAP S/4 HANA, PeopleSoft,Oracle, Workday), BI, CRM Assessment for ERP systems and Business process improvements for SAP IT Road Maps and Best Practices. (Woman/AA, estab 2016, empl 2, sales , cert: State, WBENC)

4382 INDU LLC dba intiGrow
2760 Peach tree Ind. Blvd, Ste D
Duluth, GA 30097
Contact: Mike Evans Business Dev Exec
Tel: 678-666-4365
Email: mike@intigrow.com
Website: www.intigrow.com
Managed Security Services, Identity & Access Management, Federated Identity Management, Single Sign On (E-SSO and SSO), Intrusion Detection & Prevention, Vulnerability Assessment & Penetration Testing. (As-Pac, estab 2006, empl 580, sales $13,000,000, cert: NMSDC)

4383 Information Technology Consulting Company
190 Bluegrass Valley Pkwy Ste B7
Alpharetta, GA 30005
Contact: Gary Kallenbach Sr Procurement Advisor
Tel: 614-207-9475
Email: gkallenbach@itc2.net
Website: www.itc2.net
IT resource & infrastrucute consulting. (Hisp, estab 2006, empl 15, sales , cert: NMSDC)

4384 InfoSmart Technologies Inc.
5400 Laurel Springs Pkwy Ste 706
Suwanee, GA 30024
Contact: Karun Kevin Reddy President
Tel: 678-584-5635
Email: kevin@infosmarttech.com
Website: www.infosmarttech.com
Software consulting business, project management, participation & subcontracting, partnership, staff augmentation, software programming, design & area. (As-Ind, estab 1998, empl 75, sales $6,700,000, cert: NMSDC)

4385   Intellectual Concepts LLC
     3300 Buckeye Rd, Ste 601
     Atlanta, GA 30341
     Contact: DeLois Babiker CEO
     Tel: 202-321-4560
     Email: dbabiker@intellectualconcepts.net
     Website: www.intellectualconcepts.net
Information management technology, full life-cycle IT services, communication, content, collaboration & conferencing, contract administration, asset management & IT acquisition services. (Woman/AA, estab 2004, empl 7, sales $817,000, cert: City, NMSDC, WBENC, 8(a))

4386   IT Division, Inc.
     5955 Pkwy North Blvd Unit A
     Cumming, GA 30040
     Contact: Jamie Crosby Dir of Sales
     Tel: 678-649-3022
     Email: jamiec@itdivisioninc.com
     Website: www.itdivisioninc.com
IT staffing & services, application development, application testing & infrastructure services. (Minority, Woman, estab 2006, empl 165, sales $9,332,282, cert: State)

4387   K.L. Scott & Associates LLC
     235 Peachtree St NE Ste 400
     Atlanta, GA 30303
     Contact: Keith Scott CEO
     Tel: 404-692-5552
     Email: keith.scott@klscottassociates.com
     Website: www.klscottassociates.com
Information technology & management consulting, data analytics, analysis, and business growth strategy, Business Process Management (BPM) & (Re)engineering. (AA, estab 2013, empl 10, sales , cert: NMSDC)

4388   Kavi Software Inc.
     250 Gladeside Path
     Suwanee, GA 30024
     Contact: Jegannathan Mehalingam President
     Tel: 678-358-4861
     Email: mjegann@kavisoft.net
     Website: www.kavisoft.net
IT services & temporary staffing: application security implementation. (As-Ind, estab 1999, empl 25, sales $1,500,000, cert: NMSDC)

4389   Lanin Technologies
     730 Stuart Ct
     Alpharetta, GA 30004
     Contact: Mariano Saldana VP Operations
     Tel: 678-620-8210
     Email: msaldana@lanintech.com
     Website: www.lanintech.com
Software development, IT services, custom software development; primarily web, mobile applications & SAP. (Hisp, estab 2015, empl 3, sales , cert: NMSDC)

4390   Management Decisions, Inc. - MDI Group
     35 Technology Pkwy S Ste 150
     Norcross, GA 30092
     Contact: Joel McCreight Client Mgr/Business Devel
     Tel: 770-416-7949
     Email: jmccreight@mdigroup.com
     Website: www.mdigroup.com
IT staffing & contracting, project mgmt, vendor mgmt, direct hire, IT staffing. (Woman, estab , empl , sales $45,800,000, cert: WBENC, NWBOC)

4391   McNeal Professional Services, Inc.
     2593 Kennesaw Due W Rd Ste 200
     Kennesaw, GA 30144
     Contact: Leslie McNeal Dir Business Dev
     Tel: 770-218-2000
     Email: leslie.mcneal@mcnealpro.com
     Website: www.mcnealpro.com
Technical staffing, wireless engineering svcs. (Woman/AA, estab 2001, empl 50, sales $5,600,000, cert: WBENC)

4392   Metasys Technologies
     3460 Summit Ridge Pkwy, #401
     Duluth, GA 30096
     Contact: Romeen Sheth President
     Tel: 678-523-1798
     Email: info@metasysinc.com
     Website: www.metasysinc.com
Information technology svcs: e-business application devel & integration, staff augmentation. (Minority, estab 2000, empl 495, sales $40,900,000, cert: NMSDC)

4393   Milletech Systems Inc.
     11539 Park Woods Cir, Ste 201
     Alpharetta, GA 30005
     Contact: Nasir Mujawar VP
     Tel: 770-619-0095
     Email: nmujawar@milletechinc.com
     Website: www.milletechinc.com
IT services: staffing & consultants, outsourcing, ERP solutions & implementation, application support, upgrades, custom application devel, training, QA & testing, systems integration. (Woman/As-Ind, estab 2000, empl 46, sales $3,900,000, cert: NMSDC)

4394   Next Level Business Services Inc.
     221 Roswell St Ste 150
     Alpharetta, GA 30009
     Contact: Theresa Jackson Dir Strategic Business
     Tel: 678-438-0195
     Email: theresa.jackson@nlbtech.com
     Website: www.nlbservices.com
IT Consultancy and BPO Services. (As-Ind, estab 2007, empl 6000, sales $378,000,000, cert: NMSDC)

4395   Nineteen Eleven Solutions Inc.
     12850 Hwy 9 Ste 600-247
     Alpharetta, GA 30004
     Contact: Daud Haseeb Principal
     Tel: 404-644-3702
     Email: daud@1911solutions.com
     Website: www.nineteenelevensolutions.com/
IT Staffing, ERP (Oracle, PeopleSoft, & SAP), Open Source & Big Data (Hadoop). (AA, estab 2010, empl 9, sales $275,000, cert: NMSDC)

4396   Nutech Systems Inc.
     2675 Paces Ferry Rd Ste 460
     Atlanta, GA 30339
     Contact: Nachu Anbil President
     Tel: 770-434-7063
     Email: nanbil@nutech-inc.com
     Website: www.nutech-inc.com
IT staff augmentation, IT solutions, software development life cycle, support & infrastructure. (As-Ind, estab 1995, empl 120, sales $20,400,000, cert: NMSDC)

4397 Ocher Technology Group
130 Prospect Pl
Alpharetta, GA 30005
Contact: vijay vasudevan CEO
Tel: 678-521-6329
Email: vijay_vasudevan@ochertech.com
Website: www.ochertech.com
IT consulting & staffing. (As-Ind, estab 2007, empl 55, sales $4,945,175, cert: NMSDC)

4398 Olivine LLC
970 Peachtree Industrial Blvd. Ste 100
Suwanee, GA 30024
Contact: Rajeev Maddur Sr Acct Mgr
Tel: 770-596-5155
Email: rajeevm@olivinellc.com
Website: www.olivinellc.com
IT Consulting Services, Contract, Contract to Hire and Direct hire placements. (As-Ind, estab 2006, empl 20, sales , cert: NMSDC)

4399 Open Systems Inc.
6495 Shiloh Rd, Ste 310
Alpharetta, GA 30005
Contact: Karen Ashley Sr Recruiting Mgr
Tel: 770-752-8600
Email: karen.ashley@opensystemsinc.com
Website: www.opensystemsinc.com
IT consulting & custom software development. (Minority, estab 1994, empl 300, sales $15,165,059, cert: NMSDC)

4400 Orpine Inc.
5865 N Point Pkwy, Ste 320
Alpharetta, GA 30022
Contact: Krish Subbiah Partner
Tel: 770-475-1445
Email: krish@orpine.com
Website: www.orpine.com/
Custom application development services, key information, performance, strategies & Operations. (As-Ind, estab 2006, empl 163, sales $18,170,000, cert: NMSDC)

4401 Paramount Software Solutions, Inc
4030 Old Milton Pkwy
Alpharetta, GA 30005
Contact: Srinivas Kumar Business Devel Mgr
Tel: 770-872-7829
Email: srinivas@paramountsoft.net
Website: www.paramountsoft.net/
IT Staffing, IT Consulting, Software outsourcing % development services. (As-Ind, estab 1997, empl 120, sales $178,777,000, cert: NMSDC)

4402 Paramount Software Solutions, Inc.
4030 Old Milton Pkwy
Alpharetta, GA 30005
Contact: Lokesh Shiv Sr Business Exec
Tel: 770-857-8348
Email: lokesh@paramountsoft.net
Website: www.paramountsoft.net
Research and Emerging Technologies. (Minority, estab 1997, empl 200, sales , cert: NMSDC)

4403 PIE Technology Consulting
559 Commons Park Lane
Tucker, GA 30084
Contact: Wesner Charlotin Dir of Operations
Tel: 877-866-2677
Email: wesnerc@pietconsulting.com
Website: www.pietconsulting.com
Planning, design, and implementation services for Microsoft products: Active Directory, Exchange, Lync/Skype for Business, SharePoint, and Office 365. (AA, estab 2014, empl 7, sales $554,276, cert: NMSDC)

4404 Precedent Technologies LLC
3330 Cumberland Blvd SE, Ste 500
Atlanta, GA 30339
Contact: Patrick Carley
Tel: 770-303-0223
Email: pfcarley@precedent-tech.com
Website: www.precedent-tech.com
Strategic IT consulting & project management, voice over IP telephone systems installation & support, web services, network design, installation and support, internet security software/services. (AA, estab 2006, empl 3, sales $196,000, cert: NMSDC)

4405 Primus Software Corporation
3061 Peachtree Industrial Blvd Ste 110
Duluth, GA 30097
Contact: Satish Anand President, Project Sevices
Tel: 678-336-1871
Email: supplier.diversity@primussoft.com
Website: www.primussoft.com
J2EE technology implementation, web services, IBM Websphere, MS .NET Web svcs, data warehousing, Oracle & SYBASE, project management, ERP, CRM and SCM technologies. (Minority, Woman, estab 1996, empl 220, sales $27,000,000, cert: NMSDC, WBENC)

4406 Professional Technology Integration, Inc.
5425 Peachtree Pkwy NW
Peachtree Corners, GA 30092
Contact: Walter Lee Jones, III CEO
Tel: 877-643-6038
Email: walter.jones@professionaltechintegration.com
Website: www.professionaltechintegration.com
Information technology consulting: software, database application development. (AA, estab 2001, empl 1, sales $180,000, cert: NMSDC)

4407 Prosys Information Systems
6025 The Corners Pkwy Ste 120
Norcross, GA 30092
Contact: Becky Brown Acct Exec
Tel: 404-663-1403
Email: becky.brown@prosysis.com
Website: www.prosysis.com
IP telephony & wireless, network integration, outsourcing solutions & technical staff augmentation. (Woman, estab 1997, empl 425, sales $776,000,000, cert: WBENC)

4408   PSR Associates, Inc.
3350 Riverwood Pkwy Ste 1900
Atlanta, GA 30339
Contact: Ernest Ball SVP
Tel: 404-618-0206
Email: eball@psrassociates.com
Website: www.psrassociates.com
Information technology, program management, project management, staff augmentation, web portal, customer relationship management, IT resources, program testing. (As-Pac, estab 2003, empl 43, sales $7,900,000, cert: NMSDC)

4409   Pyramid Consulting, Inc.
3060 Kimball Bridge Rd Ste 200
Alpharetta, GA 30022
Contact: Lara Lundy Exec VP Client Relations
Tel: 678-514-3500
Email: pcistaffing@pyramici.com
Website: www.pyramidci.com
Information technology consulting: staff augmentation, turnkey IT projects. (As-Ind, estab 1996, empl 1150, sales $283,000,000, cert: NMSDC)

4410   Rapid IT, Inc.
4080 McGinnis Ferry Rd, Ste 1206
Atlanta, GA 30005
Contact: Goutham Goli President
Tel: 678-366-3820
Email: contracts@rapiditinc.com
Website: www.rapiditinc.com
Information Technology. (As-Ind, estab 2006, empl 120, sales , cert: NMSDC)

4411   Renovo Data, Inc.
3121 Maple Dr Ste 200
Atlanta, GA 30305
Contact: Charlotta Vinson President
Tel: 404-935-6363
Email: cvinson@renovodata.com
Website: www.renovodata.com
Data backup & disaster recovery solutions: replication services, virtualization, consulting services. (Minority, Woman, estab 2005, empl 9, sales $2,000,000, cert: NMSDC, NWBOC)

4412   ResiliEnt Business Solutions, LLC
11175 Cicero Dr, Ste 100
Alpharetta, GA 30022
Contact: CEO
Tel: 678-242-5242
Email: infoservices@resilientbiz.com
Website: www.resilientbiz.com
SDLC, Business Intelligence, Enterprise Data Management/Reporting, Data Modeling, Governance, warehousing, cleansing, WebFOCUS, WebQuery, ScoreCards, Dashboards Cognos, MicroStrategy, Mobile Development. (Woman, estab 2004, empl 6, sales $1,153,725, cert: WBENC)

4413   RiVi Consulting Group LLC
2475 Northwinds Pkwy, Ste 200
Alpharetta, GA 30009
Contact: Bhushan Mocherla CIO/partner
Tel: 678-643-8133
Email: bmocherla@rivigroup.com
Website: www.rivigroup.com
Technology solutions: SAP, Peoplesoft & Oracle. (Woman/As-Ind, estab 2002, empl 45, sales $6,217,522, cert: NMSDC, WBENC, 8(a))

4414   RTX Technology Partners, LLC
400 Perimeter Center Terr NE Ste 900
Atlanta, GA 30346
Contact: M. Hans Delly Managing Dir
Tel: 404-551-5609
Email: m.hans.delly@rtxpartners.com
Website: www.rtxpartners.com
Global management & technology consulting: business strategy, technology planning & architecture & business process optimization. (AA, estab 2007, empl 25, sales $6,500,000, cert: NMSDC)

4415   Scintel Technologies Inc.
6340 Sugarloaf Pkwy Ste 200
Duluth, GA 30097
Contact: Shailesh Patel Acct Mgr
Tel: 678-775-6874
Email: s.patel@scintel.com
Website: www.scintel.com
Application outsourcing & enterprise consulting solutions. (As-Ind, estab 2003, empl 400, sales $17,500,000, cert: NMSDC)

4416   Scope IT Consulting
3235 Satellite Blvd Bldg 400, Ste 300
Duluth, GA 30096
Contact: Nadir Noorani Principal, Consultant
Tel: 912-580-5929
Email: nadir.noorani@scopeitconsulting.com
Website: www.scopeitconsulting.com
Business Process Management, Project Management, Mobility Solutions, BigData Solutions, Cloud Solutions. (Woman/As-Ind, estab 2015, empl 16, sales , cert: NMSDC, WBENC)

4417   Serenity Infotech, Inc.
950 Scales Rd, Ste 104
Suwanee, GA 30024
Contact: Srini Vangimalla Partner
Tel: 770-242-9966
Email: srini@serenityinfotech.com
Website: www.serenityinfotech.com
Software solutions & consulting services. (As-Pac, estab 1997, empl 120, sales $13,000,000, cert: NMSDC)

4418   Six Consulting, Inc.
5900 Windward Pkwy, Ste 230
Alpharetta, GA 30005
Contact: Sam Yehya VP
Tel: 470-395-0200
Email: sa@sixconsultingcorp.com
Website: www.sixconsultingcorp.com
Custom Application Development & Maintenance, Business Intelligence & Data Warehousing, Enterprise Resource Planning, Business Process Management, Enterprise Content Management. (As-Ind, estab 2007, empl 72, sales $5,472,009, cert: NMSDC)

4419   Smartecute LLC
1266 Wt Paces ferry Rd Ste 196
Atlanta, GA 30327
Contact: Sheldon Mundle CEO
Tel: 404-939-6303
Email: sheldon@smartecute.com
Website: www.smartecute.com
IT Consulting, IT Advisory, IT Network & Wireless Access Points, IT Unified Communications, Voice Communications & Data, PeopleSoft ERP Consulting, Telecommunications, IT Project Management. (AA, estab 2010, empl 2, sales , cert: NMSDC)

4420　Softech Int'l Resources, Inc.
3300 Holcomb Bridge Rd, Ste 216 30092
Norcross, GA 30092
Contact: Balaji HR
Tel:　770-447-8002
Email: supplier@softintl.com
Website: www.softintl.com
IT consulting, project mgmt, analysis, architectural design, object modeling, application devel. (Woman/As-Ind, estab 1995, empl 40, sales $7,415,369, cert: NMSDC)

4421　Softpath System, LLC
3985 Steve Reynolds Blvd Bldg C
Norcross, GA 30093
Contact: Sushumna Roy Jalajam President
Tel:　404-315-1555
Email: supplier@softpath.net
Website: www.softpath.net
IT services: business intelligence & data warehousing. (Minority, Woman, estab 1999, empl 618, sales $53,000,000, cert: City, NMSDC, CPUC, WBENC)

4422　Stellar Consulting Solutions, LLC
2475 NorthWinds Pkwy, Ste 200
Alpharetta, GA 30009
Contact: Varun Jhanjee CEO
Tel:　678-777-7411
Email: varun@stellarconsulting.com
Website: www.stellarconsulting.com
Onsite Technology Staff Augmentation, Contract, Contract to Hire & Permanent Placements, C Level executive search. (As-Ind, estab 2015, empl 11, sales $2,500,500, cert: NMSDC)

4423　STONE Resource, LLC
9755 Dogwood Rd Ste 350
Roswell, GA 30075
Contact: Kelley Gardner Dir Operations
Tel:　678-646-5488
Email: kgardner@stoneresource.net
Website: www.stoneresource.net
Information Technology staffing: Project Management, Business Analysts, Developers, Architects, System Engineers. (AA, estab 2010, empl 85, sales $16,000,000, cert: NMSDC)

4424　Strategic Systems & Technology Corporation
3325 Paddocks Pkwy Ste 250
Suwanee, GA 30024
Contact: Magan McQuiston CEO
Tel:　678-389-7200
Email: magan.mcquiston@sstid.com
Website: www.sstid.com
Computer database, peripherals, printers, application systems, terminals, network interface hardware, terminal remote job entry. (Woman, estab , empl 29, sales $6,200,000, cert: WBENC)

4425　Sun Technologies, Inc.
3700 Mansell Rd
Alpharetta, GA 30022
Contact: Beena George Dir Client Relations
Tel:　770-418-0434
Email: supplierdiversity@suntechnologies.com
Website: www.suntechnologies.com
IT staffing & IT projects. (Minority, Woman, estab 1996, empl 793, sales $40,060,616, cert: NMSDC, WBENC)

4426　Symbioun Technologies, Inc.
4501 Circle 75 Pkwy D4200
Atlanta, GA 30339
Contact: Raj Muppalla Relationship Mgr
Tel:　408-385-1078
Email: srinik@symbiountech.com
Website: www.symbiountech.com
Information technology consulting, staffing services. (As-Ind, estab 1993, empl 140, sales $7,900,000, cert: NMSDC)

4427　Synergy America, Inc.
6340 Sugarloaf Pkwy, Ste 200
Duluth, GA 30097
Contact: Mike Williams CEO
Tel:　770-923-9300
Email: mike@synergyamerica.com
Website: www.synergyamerica.com
IT services: BPO, healthcare, ERP, e-business, & client server environments. (As-Ind, estab 1993, empl 50, sales , cert: NMSDC, 8(a))

4428　TechBios, Inc.
11800 Amberpark Dr, Ste 130
Alpharetta, GA 30004
Contact: Larry Parker President
Tel:　770-569-2721
Email: lparker@techbios.com
Website: www.techbios.com
Information technology contract & permanent staffing; professional, administrative & clerical staffing, help desk & customer svc, software engineering, LAN/WAN installation, maintenance, & support, configuration mgmt & desktop deployment. (AA, estab 2000, empl 18, sales $1,466,970, cert: State, NMSDC)

4429　TechNet Resources
4080 McGinnis Ferry Rd Ste 604
Alpharetta, GA 30005
Contact: Kyle Hardy Sr Acct Mgr
Tel:　678-242-3044
Email: khardy@tnri.net
Website: www.tnri.net
Information technology & information services, contractors & full time. (Woman, estab 1997, empl 147, sales $17,000,000, cert: WBENC)

4430　Technical Communication Concepts Inc.
179 Fulton Ct
Peachtree City, GA 30269
Contact: Yamasia Evans CEO
Tel:　404-234-1468
Email: yamasia@technicalcomm.com
Website: www.technicalcomm.com
A/V production to bring your ideas into fruition with top-of-the-line service. (AA, estab 1998, empl 4, sales $464,769, cert: NMSDC)

4431　The Danby Group, LLP
3060-A Business Park Dr
Norcross, GA 30071
Contact: Genie Ragin Managing Partner
Tel:　770-416-9844
Email: genie@danbygroup.com
Website: www.danbygroup.com
Automatic identification technology (AIT) design & integration, bar code printing stations. (Woman, estab 1982, empl 11, sales $10,000,000, cert: WBENC)

4432 The Ian Thomas Group, LLC
2870 Peachtree Rd, Ste 417
Atlanta, GA 30305
Contact: Kevin Mobley CEO
Tel: 404-993-5698
Email: info@ianthomasgroup.com
Website: www.ianthomasgroup.com
Software performance engineering (SPE) services & solutions: software performance testing, engineering analysis & optimization, database analysis & tuning & operational support. (AA, estab 2007, empl 15, sales $1,451,588, cert: NMSDC, 8(a))

4433 The REIA Corporation
3348 Fieldwood Dr
Smyrna, GA 33080
Contact: Darnell Clarke CEO
Tel: 770-432-6974
Email: darnell@reiacorp.com
Website: www.reiacorp.com
Systems software application development & integration, security mgmt & compliance, custom development, help desk & IT support project & risk management. (Woman/AA, estab 1992, empl 46, sales $5,868,000, cert: State, City, 8(a))

4434 Think Development Systems
6000 Live Oak Pkwy, Ste 102
Norcross, GA 30093
Contact: P I Joy President
Tel: 770-723-7777
Email: joy@thinkdevelopment.com
Website: www.thinkdevelopment.com
Software development & IT consulting, offshore development, wireless application. (Minority, Woman, estab 1998, empl 47, sales $3,085,109, cert: City, NMSDC)

4435 Unicorn Technologies, LLC
4080 McGinnis Ferry Rd Ste 1203
Alpharetta, GA 30005
Contact: Sunil Savili President
Tel: 678-825-8143
Email: sales@unicorntek.com
Website: www.unicorntek.com
IT solutions & staffing services, Fit Gap Analysis, Application Development, Implementation, Upgrades, Quality Assurance, Maintenance & Support, Project Management. (Woman/As-Ind, estab 2012, empl 60, sales $3,700,000, cert: State, WBENC, SDB)

4436 Universal Business Solutions, LLC
4080 McGinnis Ferry Rd Ste 803
Alpharetta, GA 30005
Contact: Jan O'Brien VP Recruitment & Sales
Tel: 770-416-9900
Email: jobrien@ubsolutions.com
Website: www.ubsolutions.com
Information technology svcs & solutions: ERP & CRM systems, application systems, web systems, e-business, security & threat evaluation, telecommunications, telephony consulting, call & contact centers, infrastructure design, project mgmt. (Nat Ame, estab 1995, empl 34, sales , cert: SDB)

4437 VDart Inc.
11180 State Bridge Rd, Ste 302
Alpharetta, GA 30022
Contact: Bruce Hay VP Business Dev
Tel: 309-657-8528
Email: supplier.registration@vdartinc.com
Website: www.vdartinc.com
High growth, global digital solutions, product development and professional services. (Minority, estab 2007, empl , sales $158,580,118, cert: NMSDC)

4438 Virtue Group
5755 N Point Pkwy, Ste 85
Alpharetta, GA 30022
Contact: Lakshmi Manthena President
Tel: 678-578-4554
Email: lmanthena@virtuegroup.com
Website: www.virtuegroup.com
IT professionals: contract, contract-to-hire & direct hire basis. (Woman/As-Ind, estab 2002, empl 250, sales $23,400,000, cert: NMSDC)

4439 VisionSoft International, Inc.
1842 Old Norcross Rd
Lawrenceville, GA 30044
Contact: Jay Kumar Dir-Marketing
Tel: 770-682-2899
Email: jay@vsiiusa.com
Website: www.vsiiusa.com
On-site software consulting, fixed-price dev services, off shore development. (Minority, Woman, estab 1996, empl 150, sales $5,400,000, cert: NMSDC)

4440 Whitty IT Solutions LLC
260 Peachtree St, NW Ste 2200
Atlanta, GA 30303
Contact: Mrs. Charlie Whitfield CEO
Tel: 404-823-6955
Email: charlie@whittyapps.com
Website: www.whittyit.solutions
Software engineering & integration, architecture, design, development & project management, mobile software solutions. (Woman/AA, estab 2011, empl 2, sales , cert: WBENC, 8(a))

4441 XentIT, LLC
5425 Peachtree Pkwy
Norcross, GA 30092
Contact: Tariq Alvi President
Tel: 678-906-4046
Email: talvi@xentit.com
Website: www.xentit.com
Value Added Reseller, System Integrator & Cloud Managed Service provider. (As-Ind, estab 2006, empl 7, sales $2,247,000, cert: NMSDC)

4442 Xtreme Solutions, Inc.
1170 Peachtree St, Ste 1875
Atlanta, GA 30309
Contact: Phyllis Newhouse Project Mgr
Tel: 404-883-2000
Email: pnewhouse@xtremesolutions-inc.com
Website: www.xtremesolutions-inc.com
Engineering & technology services. (Woman/AA, estab 2002, empl 140, sales , cert: NMSDC)

Iowa

4443   Advanced Technology Solutions, Inc.
       416 Creek Side Dr
       Fairfax, IA 52404
       Contact: Debra Kiwala President
       Tel: 319-845-5177
       Email: debra.kiwala@ats-inc.org
       Website: www.ats-inc.org
IT consulting: software devel, system & network engineers, project managers, etc. (Minority, Woman, estab 1997, empl 85, sales $3,233,188, cert: State)

4444   Certintell, Inc.
       317 6th Ave Ste 901
       Des Moines, IA 50309
       Contact: Benjamin Lefever Sales
       Tel: 515-802-1281
       Email: benjamin@certintell.com
       Website: www.certintell.com
Online & on-demand healthcare delivery services, software & remote monitoring that benefit patients, hospitals, employers, payers, physician practice groups & accountable care organizations. (AA, estab 2014, empl 6, sales , cert: NMSDC)

4445   PC Pitstop LLC
       2515 W 22nd St
       Sioux City, IA 51103
       Contact: Scott Palmer Sales Consultant
       Tel: 712-233-4015
       Email: scottp@pcpitstop.com
       Website: www.pcpitstop.com/
Security optimization software, PC Matic. (As-Pac, estab 1999, empl 32, sales $11,913,000, cert: NMSDC)

4446   Qualmar Technology Group, LLC
       10201 University Ave
       Clive, IA 50325
       Contact: Marshall Payne CEO
       Tel: 515-554-8161
       Email: marshall.payne@qualmar.com
       Website: www.qualmar.com
Resell Hardware/Sofware. (AA, estab 2012, empl 1, sales $100,000, cert: NMSDC)

Illinois

4447   3Core Systems, Inc.
       75 Executive Dr, Ste 401I
       Aurora, IL 60504
       Contact: Shyam Reganti Dir PreSales
       Tel: 630-748-8800
       Email: shyam.reganti@3coresystems.com
       Website: www.3coresystems.com
Information Technology services, solutions & consulting, ERP (Enterprise Resource Planning), CRM (Customer Relationship Management), DW/BI (Data Warehousing & Business Intelligence), Application Development & Management. (Minority, estab 2004, empl 45, sales $9,064,920, cert: State)

4448   A1PlusSoft, Inc.
       222 W Merchandise Mart Plaza, Ste 1212
       Chicago, IL 60654
       Contact: Balaji Rengamannar CEO
       Tel: 630-935-6938
       Email: brengamannar@a1plussoft.com
       Website: www.a1plussoft.com
PCI Compliance assessment, Staff Augmentation, Information & Cloud security consulting, Legacy system transformation/modernization, Data & EMV Migration, Testing & Technical Writing. (As-Ind, estab 2002, empl 5, sales $296,000, cert: State, City, NMSDC)

4449   About Xtreme LLC
       401 N Michigan Ave Ste 1200
       Chicago, IL 60611
       Contact: Yasoob Ahmed Dir Business Devel
       Tel: 815-603-5521
       Email: yasoob.ahmed@axtcorp.com
       Website: www.axtcorp.com
Cloud IT Consulting, Microsoft Azure, Amazon AWS, and SalesForce, Office 365, Dynamics 365, SharePoint, SCCM, AI Chatbots, Knowledge Mining, Big Data, and Analytics, Azure and AWS IAAS. (As-Ind, estab 2016, empl 12, sales $1,000,000, cert: NMSDC)

4450   Accede Solutions Inc.
       164 Ela Rd
       Inverness, IL 60067
       Contact: Garvita Sethi Managing Partner
       Tel: 844-522-2333
       Email: garvita@accedesol.com
       Website: www.accedesol.com
IT, Healthcare, Finance & HR staffing & consulting. Enterprise Resource Planning (ERP) Customer relationship management (CRM) Human Resource Management System (HRMS) Software configuration Management (SCM) System. (Minority, Woman, estab 2005, empl 32, sales , cert: City, WBENC)

4451   Advansoft International Inc.
       415 W Golf Rd Ste 55
       Arlington Heights, IL 60005
       Contact: John Ashwin Business Devel Mgr
       Tel: 224-323-1707
       Email: jjashwin@adso.com
       Website: www.adso.com
Supplier to direct clients and major SAP implementation partners. (Woman, estab 1998, empl 261, sales $22,600,000, cert: WBENC)

4452   Ageatia Technology Consultancy Services Inc
       949 N Plum Grove Road
       Schaumburg, IL 60173
       Contact: Chuck Srinivasan President
       Tel: 847-517-8415
       Email: csrinivasan@ageatia.com
       Website: www.ageatia.com
e-gov, systems integration, database admin, software, implementation, software services, Legacy data, conversions, software devel, custom devel, web devel, systems outsourcing & support, technical support, enterprise, Oracle, Microsoft, PeopleSoft, SAP. (Minority, Woman, estab 2005, empl 300, sales $30,000,000, cert: City, NMSDC)

4453 ALC Enterprises, Inc.
      111 E Wacker Dr, Ste 1200
      Chicago, IL 60601
      Contact: President
      Tel: 312-819-8888
      Email: info@teamwerks.com
      Website: www.teamwerks.com
Technology consulting, e-business applications. (Woman/
As-Ind, estab 1997, empl 30, sales $2,000,000, cert:
WBENC)

4454 Aloha Document Services, Inc.
      141 W. Jackson Blvd. S-A100A
      Chicago, IL 60604
      Contact: Virginia Peak President
      Tel: 312-542-1300
      Email: ginger@alohaprintgroup.com
      Website: www.alohaprintgroup.com
Litigation copying, oversize & digital imaging, presentation,
marketing & training materials, multi-media duplication &
electronic archiving. (Woman, estab 2002, empl 16, sales
$2,600,000, cert: City, WBENC)

4455 Ameex Technologies Corp.
      1701 E Woodfield Rd, Ste 710
      Schaumburg, IL 60173
      Contact: Arockia Preethi Marketing Analyst
      Tel: 847-563-3064
      Email: vendor.registration@ameexusa.com
      Website: www.ameexusa.com/
Develop content management solutions, web development,
maintenance & enhanced services. (As-Pac, estab 2007,
empl 180, sales $8,000,000, cert: NMSDC)

4456 AmorServ LLC
      2340 W Touhy Ave Ste B
      Chicago, IL 60645
      Contact: Otse Amorighoye CEO
      Tel: 312-414-0430
      Email: o.amorighoye@amorserv.com
      Website: www.amorserv.com
Turn-key technology service and solutions, white labelled
on-demand / on-site solutions. (AA, estab 2016, empl 10,
sales $593,000, cert: City, NMSDC)

4457 Aonsoft International, Inc
      1600 Golf Rd, Ste 1270
      Rolling Meadows, IL 60008
      Contact: Siddiq Ahmed President
      Tel: 847-999-4060
      Email: siddiq@aonsoft.com
      Website: www.aonsoft.com
IT Consulting Services & Staff Augmentation Services. (As-
Ind, estab 2007, empl 14, sales $661,000, cert: NMSDC)

4458 Aptude, Inc.
      1601 North Bond St, Ste 316
      Naperville, IL 60563
      Contact: Guy De Rosa Principal
      Tel: 630-692-6700
      Email: accounts@aptude.com
      Website: www.aptude.com
Remote data capturing applications, ebusiness solutions,
customer relationship mgmt solutions, data warehousing &
business intelligence, content svcs, CAD/CAM integration,
knowledge mgmt solutions. (As-Ind, estab 2001, empl 100,
sales $15,300,000, cert: State, City)

4459 ARBA Technology, Inc.
      2760 Forgue Dr Ste 104
      Naperville, IL 60564
      Contact: Kathy de la Torre Dir Sales/Marketing
      Tel: 630-620-8566
      Email: kathy@arbapro.com
      Website: www.arbapro.com
Point of Sale (POS), inventory management & cashless
payment solutions. (Minority, Woman, estab 2007, empl
17, sales $881,670, cert: NMSDC)

4460 Ascent Innovations, LLC
      475 N Martingale Rd Ste 820
      Schaumburg, IL 60173
      Contact: Sohena Hafiz President
      Tel: 847-572-8000
      Email: solutions@ascent365.com
      Website: www.ascent365.com
Dynamics AX & Dynamics CRM Consulting, Implementa-
tion, Development, Integration, Support, Upgrades, Data
Migration, SYSPRO ï¿½ Implementation & Integration,
ERP/CRM Integration. (Minority, Woman, estab 2009,
empl 32, sales $780,000, cert: State, WBENC, 8(a))

4461 Aura Innovative Technology
      223 W Jackson Blvd, Ste 1112
      Chicago, IL 60606
      Contact: James Chen President
      Tel: 312-342-4292
      Email: mmrcela@aurachicago.com
      Website: www.aurachicago.com
Microsoft & AWS consulting & custom software/
integration development. (As-Pac, estab 2011, empl 15,
sales , cert: City, NMSDC)

4462 Aurora Solutions, Inc.
      1051 Perimeter Dr, Ste 510
      Schaumburg, IL 60173
      Contact: Sanjeev Srivastava Business Devel
      Tel: 847-274-7777
      Email: sanjeev@auroraworldwide.com
      Website: www.auroraworldwide.com
Data Mining & Business Analytics, ECommerce & Custom
Application Development. (Minority, Woman, estab
1997, empl 30, sales $3,500,000, cert: NMSDC, 8(a))

4463 BitWise Inc.
      1515 Woodfield Rd Ste 930
      Schaumburg, IL 60173
      Contact: Michael Palermo New Business Mgr
      Tel: 847-969-1500
      Email: john.broshar@bitwiseglobal.com
      Website: www.bitwiseglobal.com
Application development, system maintenance &
support, IT consulting. (As-Pac, estab 1996, empl 600,
sales $30,000,000, cert: NMSDC)

4464 Bourntec Solutions, Inc.
      1701 E Woodfield Rd Ste 636
      Schaumburg, IL 60173
      Contact: Srujana Gudur President
      Tel: 224-232-5090
      Email: ssurya@bourntec.com
      Website: www.bourntec.com
Information technology remote Oracle support services,
on-site Oracle implementation & application development services. (Woman/As-Ind, estab 1994, empl 33,
sales $4,500,000, cert: State, NMSDC)

4465 BTR Solutions, LLC
      1300 Thorndale
      Elk Grove Village, IL 60007
      Contact: Business Devel Mgr
      Tel: 630-594-2011
      Email: JOEP@SIPIAR.COM
      Website: www.sipiar.com
IT Asset Disposition, remarket, redeploy, perform DOD
level Data Security. (Woman, estab 1988, empl 300, sales ,
cert: WBENC, NWBOC)

4466 Clerysys Incorporated
      10600 W Higgins Rd, Ste 711
      Rosemont, IL 60018
      Contact: Nicole Lim Business Dev Exec
      Tel: 847-768-0314
      Email: info@clerysys.com
      Website: www.clerysys.com
Application design & devel, ERP, business intelligence,
systems integration, quality assurance, content mgmt &
web-based applications,SAP R/3 implementation svcs, ERP,
CRM, SRM, PLM, BI & data warehousing. (As-Pac, estab
2005, empl 450, sales $10,000,000, cert: NMSDC)

4467 Cogent Data Solutions LLC
      2500 W Higgins Rd Ste 1165
      Hoffman Estates, IL 60169
      Contact: Sumanth Yalavarthy VP IT
      Tel: 866-666-1877
      Email: sumanth@cogentdatasolutions.com
      Website: www.cogentdatasolutions.com
IT services, IT project base & contract staff augmentation,
Information management, Infrastructure Management,
Data Warehousing, Business Intelligence, QA Testing, Web
Development, EHR & EMR. (Woman/As-Ind, estab 2007,
empl 89, sales $5,400,000, cert: State, NMSDC, WBENC)

4468 Com2 Computers and Technologies
      1196C S Main St
      Lombard, IL 60148
      Contact: Saheem Baloch CEO
      Tel: 630-544-1708
      Email: com2@com2computer.com
      Website: www.com2computer.com
IT asset recovery & remarketing, electronic recycling, IT
technical service. (Woman/As-Ind, estab 2002, empl 10,
sales $62,150,000, cert: NMSDC)

4469 Compact Solutions, LLC.
      Two TransAm Plaza Dr Ste 400
      Oakbrook Terrace, IL 60181
      Contact: Pankaj Agrawal President
      Tel: 312-493-9911
      Email: pankaj.agrawal@compactsolutionsllc.com
      Website: www.compactsolutionsllc.com
Enterprise wide data integration, data management &
quality initiatives, data migration/consolidation, data
synchronization, master data management & cross-
enterprise information integration. (As-Ind, estab 2002,
empl 54, sales $5,550,000, cert: NMSDC)

4470 Complex Network Solutions
      7747 W 96th Pl
      Hickory Hills, IL 60457
      Contact: Eduardo Lopez President
      Tel: 708-233-6222
      Email: elopez@complexnetwork.com
      Website: www.complexnetwork.com
IT services, routing switching & wireless, desktop &
server support. (Hisp, estab 2005, empl 7, sales , cert:
NMSDC)

4471 CosaTech, Inc.
      1415 W 22nd St, Tower Fl
      Oak Brook, IL 60523
      Contact: Ann Le VP
      Tel: 630-684-2331
      Email: ann.le@cosatech.com
      Website: www.cosatech.com
Information technology services: systems integration &
applications, development, quality assurance, managed
services, IT staff augmentation, onsite, offsite & offshore
applications dev & maintenance. (Minority, Woman,
estab 1988, empl 350, sales $25,000,000, cert: NMSDC)

4472 CRSGroup, Inc.
      One Pierce Place Ste 325 West
      Itasca, IL 60143
      Contact: YOLANDA GAINES Business Solutions
      Mgr
      Tel: 630-202-5348
      Email: YGAINES@CRSCORP.COM
      Website: www.crscorp.com
Information technology consulting. (AA, estab 1994,
empl 311, sales $17,500,000, cert: State, City, NMSDC)

4473 Cube Hub Inc.
      600 N Commons Dr Ste 109
      Aurora, IL 60504
      Contact: Sunil Bakhshi Business Devel Mgr
      Tel: 630-746-1239
      Email: sunil@cube-hub.com
      Website: www.cube-hub.com
Technology, Training, Staffing & Professional Services,
Staffing/Recruiting services, Software Development, IT,
Engineering, Professional, Marketing, Healthcare,
Clinical, Scientific, Finance/Audit, Telecommunication,
etc. (Minority, Woman, estab 2014, empl 28, sales
$3,580,640, cert: NMSDC)

4474 Cyberbridge Intl. Inc. dba Creospan Inc.
      1515 E Woodfield Rd, Ste 350
      Schaumburg, IL 60173
      Contact: Praj Shah President
      Tel: 847-598-1101
      Email: praj.shah@creospan.com
      Website: www.creospan.com
Software solutions consulting. (Woman/As-Ind, estab
1999, empl 125, sales $12,500,000, cert: NMSDC)

4475 Data Defenders, LLC
      10 W 35th St, Ste 9F5-1
      Chicago, IL 60616
      Contact: Lester McCarroll Business Devel Mgr
      Tel: 312-224-8831
      Email: lester.mccarroll@data-defenders.com
      Website: www.data-defenders.com
Information Security, Managed Technology, Applied
Computer Forensics & Professional Services solutions.
(AA, estab 2005, empl 14, sales $400,000, cert: City)

4476   DivIHN Integration Inc.
2800 W Higgins Rd Ste 240
Hoffman Estates, IL 60169
Contact: Shantanoo A Govilkar VP
Tel: 224-704-1704
Email: sgovilkar@divihn.com
Website: www.divihn.com
Computer software consulting, staff augmentation, custom
software design & development, data management
solutions & services. (As-Ind, estab 2002, empl 55, sales
$11,200,000, cert: NMSDC)

4477   Edgilent Corp.
700 Cooper Ct Ste AF
Schaumburg, IL 60173
Contact: Raj Ponnuswamy President
Tel: 847-839-7388
Email: rponnuswamy@edgilent.com
Website: www.edgilent.com
Information technology svcs: application development,
outsourcing & consulting. (As-Pac, estab 2003, empl 20,
sales $2,500,000, cert: NMSDC)

4478   Edify Technologies, Inc.
1952 Mc Dowell Rd, Ste 112
Naperville, IL 60563
Contact: Acct Exec
Tel: 630-932-9308
Email: info@edifytech.com
Website: www.edifytech.com
Software development & consulting, business process
automation, SharePoint consulting, custom .NET solutions,
testing & quality assurance, project management, staffing,
offshore development. (As-Pac, estab 2002, empl 65, sales
$4,000,000, cert: State, NMSDC)

4479   Electronic Knowledge Interchange, Co.
33 W Monroe St, Ste 1050
Chicago, IL 60603
Contact: Jose Cruz
Tel: 312-762-0129
Email: jcruz@eki-consulting.com
Website: www.eki-consulting.com
Technology solutions: web portals, e-commerce, knowledge
management, employee intranets, workgroup collaboration
& process automation technologies. (AA, estab 1996, empl
91, sales $17,105,910, cert: State, City, NMSDC)

4480   Entelli Consulting LLC
900 N Arlington Hts. Road Ste 170
Itasca, IL 60143
Contact: Suzy Carlson Dir of Sales
Tel: 847-348-7780
Email: scarlson@entelli.com
Website: www.entelli.com/
Contract technical IS consulting. (Minority, Woman, estab
1999, empl 35, sales $1,600,000, cert: WBENC)

4481   Enterprise Solutions Inc
500 E. Diehl Road Ste 130
Naperville, IL 60563
Contact: Ishrat Jan VP
Tel: 408-385-1731
Email: ishratjan@enterprisesolutioninc.com
Website: www.enterprisesolutioninc.com
IT & engineering staffing, direct hire, contract to hire &
contract positions. (As-Ind, estab 2000, empl 350, sales ,
cert: NMSDC, CPUC)

4482   Evanston Technology Partners, Inc.
56 East 47th St
Chicago, IL 60653
Contact: Emmanuel Jackson President
Tel: 312-348-5122
Email: ejackson@evanstontec.com
Website: www.evanstontec.com
Implement & integrate object storage data (partner to
Cleaversafe). Unified & Real Time Communications
platform including Telehealth. (AA, estab , empl , sales
$120,000, cert: NMSDC)

4483   Evolutyz Corp.
1560 Wall St Ste 105
Naperville, IL 60563
Contact: Adriana Perez Dir of Sales
Tel: 312-275-5735
Email: adriana@evolutyz.com
Website: www.evolutyz.com
Application Development, ERP, Mobile Apps, ETL/ BI/
DW, Quality Assurance & Testing, Professional Services,
Staff Augmentation. (Minority, Woman, estab 2011,
empl 25, sales $6,051,748, cert: NMSDC)

4484   Excelsior Consulting Services
PO Box 325
Clarendon Hills, IL 60514
Contact: Dileta Sapokaite Business Mgr
Tel: 973-447-2575
Email: dileta@excelsiorconsulting.net
Website: www.excelsiorconsulting.net
IT staff & contracting resources. (Minority, Woman,
estab 2004, empl 2, sales $790,000, cert: State, WBENC,
8(a))

4485   Frontier Technologies LLC
1601 Bond St, Ste 305
Naperville, IL 60563
Contact: Richard Ewbank Sales Exec
Tel: 630-687-1606
Email: richard@frontiertechllc.com
Website: www.frontiertechllc.com/
IT consulting services. (Minority, Woman, estab 2002,
empl 146, sales , cert: State)

4486   Galmont Consulting, LLC
70 W Madison St, Ste 1400
Chicago, IL 60602
Contact: Jeri Smith President
Tel: 312-214-3261
Email: jerig@galmont.com
Website: www.galmont.com
Software quality assurance, testing & tool automation.
(Woman, estab 2000, empl 50, sales $5,700,000, cert:
WBENC)

4487   Genius Business Solutions, Inc.
1711 5th Ave, Ste 2
Moline, IL 61265
Contact: Sarthak Joshi Founder & CEO
Tel: 309-269-2551
Email: Shivaji@GeniusBSI.com
Website: www.GeniusBSI.com
Information Technology & Engineering Services Consult-
ing, Software licensing, Implementation & Support SAP,
Oracle & Windchill, Custom software development,
Quality assurance & Testing, End User Training, Strategic
Staffing. (As-Ind, estab 2004, empl 70, sales $6,015,657,
cert: NMSDC)

4488 Harrington Technology & Associates, Inc dba HTA
Technology Security
30 S Wacker Dr, 22 Fl
Chicago, IL 60606
Contact: Michelle Chaudry CEO
Tel: 708-862-6348
Email: mchaudry@hta-inc.com
Website: www.hta-inc.com
Technology & information security consulting: risk assessments, protection, independent verification & validation, vulnerability assessments & penetration testing, computer forensics, network & security remediation. (Woman/AA, estab 2001, empl 29, sales $2,778,000, cert: WBENC)

4489 HOBI International, Inc.
1202 Nagel Blvd
Batavia, IL 60510
Contact: Cathy Hill CEO
Tel: 630-761-0500
Email:
Website: www.hobi.com
Recycle electronics, reverse logistics, IT & cellular asset management, resale & re-marketing, data security, data erasure, equipment removal & environmentally safe recycling. (Woman, estab 1992, empl 250, sales $42,000,000, cert: WBENC)

4490 Indusa Technical Corp.
1 TransAm Plaza Dr Ste 350
Oakbrook Terrace, IL 60181
Contact: Hemant Shah Dir Business Dev
Tel: 865-769-0715
Email: hemant.shah@indusa.com
Website: www.indusa.com
Information technology consulting & software solutions. (As-Ind, estab 1989, empl 100, sales , cert: NMSDC)

4491 Innovative Systems Group, Inc.
799 Roosevelt Rd Ste 109
Glen Ellyn, IL 60137
Contact: Jordan Myers Acct Mgr
Tel: 312-861-1745
Email: jordanm@innovativesys.com
Website: www.innovativesys.com/
Information systems consulting, full life cycle systems, application dev & support, project mgmt, business systems analysis, staff augmentation, QA & testing svcs, database architecture & admin, network & systems admin, CRM & enterprise systems. (As-Pac, estab 1991, empl 250, sales $20,000,000, cert: City)

4492 Intellisys Technology, LLC
1000 Jorie Blvd Ste 200
Oak Brook, IL 60523
Contact: Raju Iyer Managing Partner
Tel: 630-928-1111
Email: riyer@intellisystechnology.com
Website: www.intellisystechnology.com
IT consulting: system integration, application development, QA & testing, embedded system technology & staff augmentation. (As-Ind, estab 1998, empl 300, sales $6,000,000, cert: State)

4493 Iyka Enterprises, Inc.
PO Box 3534
St. Charles, IL 60174
Contact: Poonam Gupta-Krishnan President
Tel: 630-372-3900
Email: poonam@iyka.com
Website: www.iyka.com
Custom application software & IT consulting. (Woman/As-Ind, estab 2000, empl 25, sales $500,000, cert: WBENC)

4494 JRE & Associates Inc.
46 E 26th St
Chicago, IL 60616
Contact: Jeffrey Edwards CEO
Tel: 312-326-4327
Email: jedwards@jreitsolutions.com
Website: www.jreitsolutions.com
Logical Identity Controls
Logical Access Control Systems
Telecommunications and Network Security
Computer Operations Security Management
Cryptography & PKI Infrastructure Support (AA, estab 2009, empl 3, sales $150,000, cert: State)

4495 KBS
12549 S Laramie Ave
Alsip, IL 60803
Contact: Anthony R. Kitchens President
Tel: 708-720-5981
Email: tonyk@kbs.us.com
Website: www.kbsgc.com
Technology products & svcs: desktop & notebook support, network admin, voice, video, data & electricity cabling, RFID tagging, WLAN, LAN, wireless cameras, help desk & end-user technical support. (AA, estab 1992, empl 22, sales $16,710,521, cert: NMSDC)

4496 Kristine Fallon Associates, Inc.
11 E Adams St, Ste 1100
Chicago, IL 60603
Contact: Angelica Martinez Marketing Coord
Tel: 312-360-9600
Email: amartinez@kfa-inc.com
Website: www.kfa-inc.com
Information technology consulting services, Building Information Modeling (BIM / COBie), electronic project management & collaboration systems, Facility Management Systems & Transit Asset Management database solutions. (AA, estab 1993, empl 11, sales , cert: City)

4497 LCS Entertainment LLC
4545 S Drexel
Chicago, IL 60653
Contact: Chrishon Lampley CEO
Tel: 773-330-2440
Email: chrishon@lovecorkscrew.com
Website: www.lovecorkscrew.com
LCS Entertainment, LLC offers Love Cork Screw wine to provide consumers a diverse line of
varietals. Regionally produced, and distributed in Illinois, each sleek wine bottle offers a colorful, whimsical and fun experience. (Woman/AA, estab 2014, empl 5, sales , cert: NMSDC, WBENC)

4498   Lead IT Corporation
       1999 Wabash Ste 210
       Springfield, IL 62704
       Contact: Ira Neuman Sales Mgr
       Tel: 217-726-7250
       Email: ira.neuman@leaditgroup.com
       Website: www.leaditgroup.com
IT staffing & HR, executive search, consulting, computer
programming, IT management, technical consulting.
(Minority, Woman, estab 2005, empl 232, sales
$23,712,000, cert: State)

4499   LG Associates Inc. dba Asen Computer Associates
       900 N National Pkwy, Ste 155
       Schaumburg, IL 60173
       Contact: Liza Brigham Acct Mgr
       Tel: 847-995-1300
       Email: lbrigham@asen.com
       Website: www.asen.com/
Information technology & engineering consulting. (Woman,
estab 1975, empl 137, sales $5,985,000, cert: WBENC)

4500   Midwest Solution Providers, Inc.
       21720 W Long Grove Rd, Ste C-227
       Deer Park, IL 60010
       Contact: Raj Andathode Principal Consultant
       Tel: 224-520-1510
       Email: raj@midwest-sp.com
       Website: www.midwest-sp.com
IT Consulting, Database design, database programming,
ETL, solutions using Informatica, Oracle, Teradata, Java,
Web-Services & custom applications. (As-Ind, estab 2004,
empl 1, sales , cert: NMSDC)

4501   Mu Sigma Inc.
       3400 Dundee Rd Ste 160
       Northbrook, IL 60062
       Contact: Shelly Singh Head Sales
       Tel: 847-620-9419
       Email: shelly.singh@mu-sigma.com
       Website: www.mu-sigma.com
Provide data science solutions. (As-Ind, estab , empl , sales
$70,000,000, cert: NMSDC)

4502   MVC Consulting Inc.
       203 N LaSalle St
       Chicago, IL 60601
       Contact: Greg Mummert Recruiting Mgr
       Tel: 312-606-5555
       Email: greg.mummert@mvc-consulting.com
       Website: www.mvc-consulting.com
IT consulting svcs: business intelligence/data warehousing,
compliance, ERP, CRM sales force automation, change
mgmt & project based consulting projects. (Woman, estab
1981, empl 30, sales $2,800,000, cert: WBENC)

4503   MZI Group Inc.
       1937 W Fulton St
       Chicago, IL 60612
       Contact: Nicole Klimenko VP
       Tel: 312-492-8740
       Email: nicole@mzigroup.com
       Website: www.mzigroup.com
Electrical, Mechanical, and Building Services Contractor
(Hisp, estab 1999, empl 110, sales $35,877,000, cert: City,
NMSDC)

4504   National Tek Services, Inc.
       PO Box 6
       Libertyville, IL 60048
       Contact: Terry Sharkey President
       Tel: 847-850-1201
       Email: info@tekservinc.com
       Website: www.tekservinc.com
Information technology solutions. (Woman, estab 2003,
empl 6, sales $1,200,000, cert: WBENC)

4505   Netrion Global Solutions, Inc
       451 Dunham Rd Ste 202
       St. Charles, IL 60174
       Contact: Heather Thompson VP Business Opera-
       tions
       Tel: 630-510-3000
       Email: heather.thompson@netrion.com
       Website: www.netrion.com
IT svcs: ERP implimentation, e-commerce solutions,
database development, project mgmt. (As-Ind, estab
1989, empl 21, sales $1,950,000, cert: NMSDC)

4506   Next Generation, Inc.
       800 West 5th Ave Ste 202
       Naperville, IL 60563
       Contact: Darrell Higueros President
       Tel: 312-739-0520
       Email: dhigueros@nxtgeninc.com
       Website: www.nxtgeninc.com
Customizations, implementation & support Enterprise
Resource Planning software. (Hisp, estab 2001, empl 15,
sales $2,100,000, cert: State)

4507   OnShore Technology Group, Inc.
       505 N Lake Shore Dr Ste 220
       Chicago, IL 60611
       Contact: Valarie King- Bailey CEO
       Tel: 312-321-6400
       Email: vkbailey@onshoretech.com
       Website: www.onshoretech.com
Applied technology products & svcs: engineering, e-govt
support, advanced strategic & tactical mktg svcs, digital
media production, enterprise business intelligence
solutions, digital home networking. (Woman/AA, estab
2004, empl 6, sales $1,534,540, cert: City, NMSDC,
WBENC)

4508   Pace Systems, Inc
       2040 Corporate Ln
       Naperville, IL 60563
       Contact: Nick Taylor
       Tel: 630-395-2191
       Email: ntaylor@pace-systems.com
       Website: www.pace-systems.com
Information technology services & sales. Citrix networking design & consulting. Physical & network security
consulting. (As-Pac, estab 1983, empl 32, sales
$30,000,000, cert: State, City, NMSDC)

4509   Plego Technologies
       5002 Main St Ste 203
       Downers Grove, IL 60515
       Contact: Dir of Business Dev
       Tel: 630-796-2074
       Email:
       Website: www.Plego.com
Web apps development, enterprise web design, systems
integration, mobile app development, business intelligence & staff augmentation. (Minority, estab 2002, empl
20, sales $1,890,332, cert: NMSDC)

4510 Premier Systems, Inc
14489 John Humphrey Ste 202 Ste 202
Orland Park, IL 60462
Contact: Tariq Khan Acct Mgr
Tel: 708-349-9200
Email: tkhan@premiersystemsinc.com
Website: www.premiersystemsinc.com
IT consulting & staffing, project mgmt, systems programming & admin: IBM mainframe midrange, client server, PeopleSoft, SAP & Microsoft based systems; e-commerce devel. (As-Pac, estab 1993, empl 30, sales $2,713,000, cert: City, NMSDC)

4511 PTS Consulting Services LLC
1700 Park St, Ste 212
Naperville, IL 60563
Contact: Reshma Multani Client Servicing Mgr
Tel: 630-635-8328
Email: reshma.multani@ptscservices.com
Website: www.ptscservices.com
IT consulting and Business Consulting Services. (As-Pac, estab 2012, empl 50, sales $7,000,000, cert: NMSDC)

4512 Purple Consulting
2539 Lexington Lane
Naperville, IL 60540
Contact: Purnima Parashar Principal
Tel: 630-303-2706
Email: purnima@consultpurple.com
Website: www.consultpurple.com
Permanent placement of Software Engineers, Network Engineers, Analysts. Positions like Systems Engineers, Project Managers, Trading Engineers, IT Analysts, Business Analysts, Software Engineers, Sales. (Woman/As-Ind, estab 2014, empl 5, sales , cert: City)

4513 Q1 Technologies, Inc.
750 Shoreline Dr
Aurora, IL 60504
Contact: Krishna Bansal Sr Dir
Tel: 630-536-8202
Email: krishna.bansal@q1tech.com
Website: www.q1tech.com
Enterprise software implementation, application integration & tech/functional support, software devel. (As-Pac, estab 2002, empl 50, sales $7,204,257, cert: State, NMSDC)

4514 Quinnox Inc.
400 N. Michigan Ave Ste 1300
Chicago, IL 60611
Contact: Amar Sowani Sr Mgr
Tel: 312-219-6517
Email: amars@quinnox.com
Website: www.quinnox.com
Information technology consulting & staff augmentation. (As-Ind, estab 0, empl , sales $52,000,000, cert: NMSDC)

4515 RK Management Consultants, Inc.
One Tower Lane Ste 2540
Oakbrook Terrace, IL 60181
Contact: Nidhi Kapoor President
Tel: 630-202-3768
Email: nidhi@rkmcinc.com
Website: www.rkmcinc.com
IT solutions & professional consulting, e-commerce & web dev, network infrastructure & support, software mgmt svcs, client server & mainframe computing environments. (Minority, Woman, estab 1988, empl 70, sales $8,200,000, cert: NMSDC, WBENC)

4516 RL Canning Inc.
8700 W. Bryn Mawr Ste 120N
Chicago, IL 60631
Contact: Rachel Canning President
Tel: 773-693-1900
Email: rachel@rlcanning.com
Website: www.rlcanning.com
Information technology consulting & staffing services. (Minority, Woman, estab 1999, empl 48, sales $5,000,000, cert: State, City, WBENC)

4517 S & F Software Solutions Inc.
285 Victor Lane
Lake Zurich, IL 60047
Contact: Asma Farhin
Tel: 847-726-2571
Email: afarhin@sandfbizsolutions.com
Website: www.sandfbizsolutions.com
Project Management, Program/Project Management Office (PMO), Enterprise Risk Management, Business Process Re-engineering (BPR), Strategic Business Analysis, Data Management, Enterprise Quality Management. (Minority, Woman, estab 2011, empl 2, sales , cert: State, NMSDC, WBENC)

4518 Sayers Technology
825 Corporate Woods Pkwy
Vernon Hills, IL 60061
Contact: Adam Shipp Reg Sales Mgr
Tel: 404-695-2707
Email: ashipp@sayers.com
Website: www.sayers.com
IT Solutions, Servers & Storage, Virtualization, Security & Mobility, Networking & Professional Services. Storage, Servers, Cloud, Virtualization, Networking, Data Management, Archiving & Disaster Recovery Security. (AA, estab 1984, empl , sales , cert: NMSDC)

4519 SDA Consulting, Inc.
3011 W 183rd St
Homewood, IL 60430
Contact: Shawn Anderson President
Tel: 708-372-8809
Email: sda@sdaci.com
Website: www.sdaci.com
Technical consulting, staffing, support, development & training, business software, Oracle EBS, PeopleSoft, JDE, Siebel, Hyperion,
Microsoft, SAP, custom software. (Woman/AA, estab 2004, empl 66, sales $9,185,610, cert: State, NMSDC)

4520 SDI Presence LLC
200 East Randolph, Ste 3550
Chicago, IL 60601
Contact: Dawn Pfeiffer Sr Proposal Mgr
Tel: 312-580-7563
Email: dpfeiffer@sdipresence.com
Website: www.sdipresence.com
Traditional or cloud-based systems life-cycle, concept development, systems integration & long-term support. (As-Ind, estab 2015, empl 250, sales , cert: State, NMSDC)

4521　Silveredge Business Systems, Ltd.
　　　4 Westbrook Center, Ste 1020
　　　Westchester, IL 60154
　　　Contact: Sue Boers President
　　　Tel:　708-449-7738
　　　Email: office@silveredgeconsulting.com
　　　Website: www.silveredgeconsulting.com
Computer consulting services, project management, ERP
Implementation, programming, websites, EDI, staff aug-
mentation & outsourcing. (Woman, estab 1987, empl 30,
sales $7,309,357, cert: WBENC)

4522　SNtial Technologies, Inc.
　　　150 N. Michigan Ave Ste 2800
　　　Chicago, IL 60601
　　　Contact: Leon Francisco President
　　　Tel:　630-452-4735
　　　Email: leon.francisco@sntialtech.com
　　　Website: www.sntialtech.com
Information technology services, custom software develop-
ment, systems integration & re-engineering. (As-Pac, estab
2001, empl 8, sales $1,000,000, cert: City, NMSDC)

4523　Swoon Group
　　　300 South Wacker Dr Ste 300
　　　Chicago, IL 60606
　　　Contact: Joseph Matalone EVP
　　　Tel:　312-450-8700
　　　Email: joe.matalone@swoonstaffing.com
　　　Website: www.swoonstaffing.com
Technical staffing. (Woman, estab , empl , sales
$80,000,000, cert: WBENC)

4524　Synchronous Solutions, Inc.
　　　211 W Wacker Dr Ste 300
　　　Chicago, IL 60606
　　　Contact: John Sterling CEO
　　　Tel:　312-252-3700
　　　Email: jsterling@synch-solutions.com
　　　Website: www.synch-solutions.com
Implementations, integrations & upgrades, ERP software
products, Oracle-PeopleSoft & SAP, functional & technical
Consulting, database admin, application integration,
training, project mgmt, strategic IT outsourcing. (AA, estab
1998, empl 75, sales $14,000,000, cert: State, City, NMSDC)

4525　Synectics Inc.
　　　135 S LaSalle St Ste 2050
　　　Chicago, IL 60603
　　　Contact: Melissa Lounds Dir of Global Accounts
　　　Tel:　312-629-1020
　　　Email: m_lounds@synectics.com
　　　Website: www.synectics.com/
Information technology consulting, staff augmentation.
(Woman, estab 1984, empl 300, sales $19,300,000, cert:
CPUC, WBENC)

4526　System Solutions, Inc.
　　　3630 Commercial Ave
　　　Northbrook, IL 60062
　　　Contact: Oliver Patterson Sr Acct Mgr
　　　Tel:　847-272-6160
　　　Email: oliver.patterson@thessi.com
　　　Website: www.THESSI.COM
Information technology: enterprise solution products &
architecture, consulting, staffing, network design &
implementation, hardware & software procurement, onsite
installation services. (As-Pac, estab 1987, empl 20, sales
$24,000,000, cert: State, NMSDC)

4527　TechCircle, Inc.
　　　500 N Michigan Ave Ste 600
　　　Chicago, IL 60611
　　　Contact: Aakash Gajera President
　　　Tel:　312-767-5653
　　　Email: agajera@techcircleinc.com
　　　Website: www.techcircleinc.com
Information technology consulting & staff augmentation
services, project/program management, business system
analysis, quality assurance, verification & validation. (As-
Ind, estab 2015, empl 4, sales $300,000, cert: State,
NMSDC)

4528　Technical Source, Inc.
　　　1447 E Rosita Dr
　　　Palatine, IL 60074
　　　Contact:　President
　　　Tel:　847-705-1730
　　　Email: jgutwein@computerrelocation.com
　　　Website: www.computerrelocation.com
PC Disconnect/Reconnect Corporate Relocation Add,
Moves, Changes. Project Management Information
Technology, IT Management, Help Desk & Support
Disaster Recovery. (Woman, estab 1999, empl 54, sales
$1,025,201, cert: City, WBENC)

4529　Teklink International Inc.
　　　4320 Winfield Rd Ste 215
　　　Warrenville, IL 60563
　　　Contact: Douglas Heck VP
　　　Tel:　630-881-9026
　　　Email: douglas.heck@tli-usa.com
　　　Website: www.tli-usa.com
Data Analytics Services and Business Intelligence
Consulting Services. (As-Pac, estab 1998, empl 78, sales ,
cert: NMSDC)

4530　teksoft ventures, inc.
　　　127 Ridge Lane
　　　Geneva, IL 60134
　　　Contact: Janet Konn President
　　　Tel:　630-232-9630
　　　Email: jan.konn@teksoftventures.com
　　　Website: www.teksoftventures.com
SAP training & education services, live classroom
education & web based remote education. (Woman,
estab 1996, empl 50, sales $5,000,000, cert: WBENC)

4531　The Silicon Blackgroup, LLC
　　　110 W Superior St, Ste 2001
　　　Chicago, IL 60504
　　　Contact: Nikolina Akinula Business Success Mgr
　　　Tel:　312-298-9892
　　　Email: nikolina@thesiliconblackgroup.com
　　　Website: www.thesiliconblackgroup.com
Cybersecurity, Security Compliance, Strategic Advisory
and IT Project Recovery Management. (AA, estab 2020,
empl 10, sales , cert: NMSDC)

4532　TransTech, LLC
　　　248 Spring Lake Dr
　　　Itasca, IL 60143
　　　Contact: Cynthia Conroy Sales Admin
　　　Tel:　630-228-8880
　　　Email: cconroy@transtechit.com
　　　Website: www.transtechit.com
Informational technology staffing solutions. (Woman,
estab 1990, empl 100, sales $34,600,000, cert: WBENC)

4533 Tranzact Technologies, Inc.
360 W Butterfield Rd Ste 400
Elmhurst, IL 60126
Contact: LeAnn DeFalco Sales Asst
Tel: 630-833-0890
Email: diversity@tranzact.com
Website: www.tranzact.com
Sourcing and Spend Management, Constellation TMS,
Supply Chain Edge, Risk Monitoring, Advanced Data mining
& reporting. (Woman, estab 1984, empl 250, sales
$74,228,000, cert: WBENC)

4534 UFC Technology, Inc.
1900 E Golf Rd, Ste 950
Schaumburg, IL 60173
Contact: Lisa Smith-Maxam President
Tel: 908-336-8831
Email: lisa@the-staffroom.com
Website: www.ufctechnology.com/
Contingent Workforce Staffing and IT Consulting services.
(As-Pac, estab 2013, empl 30, sales , cert: CPUC)

4535 VIVA USA Inc.
3601 Algonquin Rd Ste 425
Rolling Meadows, IL 60008
Contact: Vasanthi Ilangovan President
Tel: 847-368-0860
Email: vilangovan@viva-it.com
Website: www.viva-it.com
IT svcs, custom software dev, IT staffing, offsite & offshore
IT project outsourcing. (Woman/As-Ind, estab 1996, empl
380, sales $30,000,000, cert: State, NMSDC, CPUC,
WBENC)

4536 Von Technologies, LLC
1193 Old Creek Ct
Woodridge, IL 60517
Contact: Michelle Vondrasek President
Tel: 630-985-8474
Email: vondrasek.michelle@vontechnologies.com
Website: www.vontechnologies.com
Network solutions: infrastructure design, implementation,
management, refresh, software & hardware configuration,
wireless solutions. (Woman, estab 2006, empl 23, sales ,
cert: State, WBENC)

Indiana

4537 Alliance Group Technologies Company-Calumet, Inc.
911 Broad Ripple Ave, Ste B
Indianapolis, IN 46220
Contact: Michael Weir Dir-Business Dev
Tel: 317-254-8285
Email: mweir@alliancegrouptech.com
Website: www.alliancegrouptech.com
Engineering consulting & technical staffing solutions. (As-
Pac, estab 1975, empl 215, sales , cert: NMSDC)

4538 Anchor Point Technology Resources, Inc
9510 N MERIDIAN ST Ste 200
Indianapolis, IN 46260
Contact: Rachael Schatko President
Tel: 317-225-4141
Email: rachael.schatko@anchorpointtr.com
Website: www.anchorpointtr.com/
Engineering & IT solutions, IT staffing, contract, C2D,
Permanent Placement, Engineering Staffing & Executive
Placement. (Woman, estab 2004, empl 140, sales
$15,500,000, cert: State)

4539 Bottom-Line Performance, Inc.
PO Box 155
New Palestine, IN 46163
Contact: Kirk Boller President
Tel: 317-861-5935
Email: kirk_boller@bottomlineperformance.com
Website: www.bottomlineperformance.com
E-learning, classroom-based training. (Woman, estab ,
empl , sales $1,500,000, cert: WBENC)

4540 CIMCOR Inc.
8252 Virginia St
Merrillville, IN 46410
Contact: Robert Johnson President
Tel: 219-736-4400
Email: johnson.robert@cimcor.com
Website: www.cimcor.com
Protect critical IT infrastructure from malicious expo-
sure. (AA, estab 1997, empl 15, sales $1,359,269, cert:
NMSDC)

4541 Data Integration Consulting, Inc.
7399 N. Shadeland Ave Ste 312
Indianapolis, IN 46250
Contact: Tim Thompson President
Tel: 317-894-2623
Email: tthompson@dataic.com
Website: www.dataic.com
IT consulting, web application development, desktop
application development, computer programming,
network design & administration, database design &
administration. (AA, estab 2003, empl 1, sales , cert:
State)

4542 Esource Resources, LLC
7114 Lakeview Pkwy W Dr
Indianapolis, IN 46268
Contact: Eddie Rivers CEO
Tel: 317-863-0423
Email: erivers@esourceresources.net
Website: www.esourceresources.net
IT staffing, placement, computer and software consult-
ing, virtualization, systems integration, web and graphic
design resources, managed services and software
licensing. (AA, estab 2002, empl 8, sales $15,133,940,
cert: State, NMSDC)

4543 GuideSoft Inc. dba Knowledge Services
5875 Castle Creek Pkwy N Dr Ste 400
Indianapolis, IN 46250
Contact: Cindy Davis Dir
Tel: 317-578-1700
Email: cindyd@knowledgeservices.com
Website: www.knowledgeservices.com
IT staffing; IT training development. project mgmt,
application development, tier I-III help desk & desktop
support. (Woman, estab 1994, empl 130, sales
$13,186,909, cert: State)

4544   Guilford Group LLC
615 W Carmel Dr, Ste 130
Carmel, IN 46032
Contact: Rajan Kapur Dir
Tel: 317-814-1060
Email: rajkapur@guilfordgroup.com
Website: www.guilfordgroup.com
Information technology consulting, IT project management, enterprise application development, mobile development, data management, staffing, cloud storage, systems integrations, web development & graphic design resources. (As-Ind, estab 2003, empl 30, sales $2,922,823, cert: State, NMSDC)

4545   GyanSys Inc.
702 Adams St
Carmel, IN 46032
Contact: Padmaja Una Chairman
Tel: 317-332-3290
Email: padma.una@gyansys.com
Website: www.gyansys.com
Global systems integration: SAP & Microsoft products, mobile platforms. (Woman/As-Ind, estab , empl , sales $17,000,000, cert: State, WBENC)

4546   JumpStart Point of Arrival, LLC
9801 Fall Creek Rd, Ste 410
Indianapolis, IN 46256
Contact: Ek-Leng Chua-Miller CEO
Tel: 317-777-1995
Email: ek-leng@jumpstartpoa.biz
Website: www.jumpstartpoa.biz
Statistical analysis, data analysis, database marketing, data mining, statistical modeling, regression analysis (Minority, Woman, estab 2005, empl 2, sales $442,000, cert: State, NMSDC, WBENC)

4547   LHP Software, LLC
1888 Poshard Dr
Columbus, IN 47203
Contact: Kandace Yamcharern Mgr Payment Process
Tel: 812-418-6331
Email: kandace.y@lhpes.com
Website: www.lhpsoftware.com
Custom software solutions: embedded software, communication software, internet software, testing. (As-Pac, estab 2001, empl 210, sales $26,893,359, cert: NMSDC)

4548   Lucidia IT
6525 E 82nd St, Ste 103
Indianapolis, IN 46250
Contact: Janet Stiller CEO
Tel: 317-953-9800
Email: anikirk@lucidiait.com
Website: www.lucidiait.com/
Data Center Technologies, Cloud Connectivity, Collaboration, End User Technology, Enterprise Networking, Cybersecurity and Project Management. (Woman, estab 2018, empl 11, sales $5,000,000, cert: WBENC)

4549   Morse Communications Inc.
8207 Linden Ave
Munster, IN 46321
Contact: Tim Kerrick Sr Acct Mgr
Tel: 219-314-6029
Email: tkerrick@morsecom.com
Website: www.morsecom.com
Systems integration, communications, networking & electronic safety & security. (Woman, estab 1994, empl 75, sales $17,000,000, cert: State)

4550   Phelco Technologies, Inc.
9801 Fall Creek Rd Ste 131
Indianapolis, IN 46256
Contact: Tasha Phelps CEO
Tel: 317-898-0334
Email: tasha@phelco.com
Website: www.phelco.com
Network infrastructure, disaster recovery, off-site data backup, web development. (Woman/AA, estab 1997, empl 1, sales , cert: State)

4551   Pinnacle Mailing Products, LLC
7701 W Kilgore Ave, Ste 5
Yorktown, IN 47396
Contact: KIMBERLY LAFFOON Owner
Tel: 765-405-1194
Email: kimlaffoon@pinnaclemailing.com
Website: www.pinnaclemailingproducts.net
Address correction & shipping software solutions. (Woman, estab 2009, empl 6, sales $195,000, cert: State)

4552   RCR Technology Corporation
251 N Illinois St Ste 1150, North Tower
Indianapolis, IN 46204
Contact: Robert Reed CEO
Tel: 317-624-9500
Email: rreed@rcrtechnology.com
Website: www.rcrtechnology.com
Information technology consulting, network design, application services & project management. (AA, estab 1997, empl 150, sales $18,000,000, cert: State, City, NMSDC)

4553   Ryan Consulting Group, Inc.
7914 N Shadeland Ave
Indianapolis, IN 46250
Contact: Hubert Goodman COO
Tel: 317-541-9300
Email: sales@consultrcg.com
Website: www.consultrcg.com/
Information technologies, systems integration, design & consulting. (AA, estab 2001, empl 123, sales $25,990,253, cert: NMSDC)

4554   Sondhi Solutions LLC
47 S Pennsylvania St Ste 400
Indianapolis, IN 46204
Contact: Justin Harris Principal
Tel: 3122-222-2222
Email: jmurphy@sondhisolutions.com
Website: www.sondhisolutions.com
Application Development Services, Client-Server Development, Database Development Legacy System & Application Conversions Systems. (As-Ind, estab 2008, empl 95, sales $12,000,000, cert: State, NMSDC)

4555   STLogics
1119 Keystone Way Ste 301
Carmel, IN 46032
Contact: Priya Prasad President
Tel: 800-505-0357
Email: hr@stlogics.com
Website: www.stlogics.com
IT consulting, staff augmentation, managed IT solutions, project management, web & software development, quality assurance, Java applications, sharepoint, SAP, ERP, datawarehouse & network administration. (Woman/As-Ind, estab 2004, empl 120, sales , cert: NMSDC)

Kansas

4556   3 Fuerzas Technology Solutions, LLC
14013 Outlook
Overland Park, KS 66223
Contact: Shawn Hashmi VP Program Management
Tel: 913-744-1163
Email: shashmi@edzsystems.com
Website: www.edzsystems.com
Software Development, IT Consulting Services, Intelligent Resource Management System (Intelligent RMS. (Minority, Woman, estab 2015, empl 5, sales $201,000, cert: NMSDC)

4557   Complete Carpet Care Inc.
324 Fawn Valley Court
Lansing, KS 66043
Contact: Brad Turner President
Tel: 913-351-3550
Email: bradsmegastore@gmail.com
Website: www.notcompletewithoutyou.com
Hi! This is Brad Turner. Thanks very much for your interest in professional carpet cleaning. I am grateful for the opportunity to provide you with information about carpet cleaning and help you choose a carpet cleaning company. (AA, estab 1993, empl 10, sales , cert: NMSDC)

4558   DW Training and Development Incorporated
6019 Hauser Dr
Shawnee, KS 66216
Contact: Jill Evans VP Sales & Mktg
Tel: 913-268-4400
Email: jill@technicallytraining.com
Website: www.technicallytraining.com
Technical writing & database development. (Woman, estab 2001, empl 2, sales $1,970,000, cert: WBENC)

4559   Evolv Solutions, LLC.
7300 West 110th St Ste 700
Overland Park, KS 66210
Contact: Eric Harland VP
Tel: 913-469-8900
Email: eharland@evolvsolutions.com
Website: www.evolvsolutions.com
IT & document mgmt solutions, project mgmt & outsourcing, enterprise solutions, web devel, system integration, tech communication, office assessment, asset mgmt, etc. (AA, estab 2001, empl 8, sales $7,849,351, cert: NMSDC)

4560   Global Control Systems, Inc.
11605 S Alden St
Olathe, KS 66062
Contact: Manual David President
Tel: 913-681-9261
Email: sales@gcsks.com
Website: www.webcontrolsystems.com
Systems integration, configuration & programming SCADA system & industrial networks, intelligent batch mgmt systems, process equipment, packaging systems, robotics systems, vision systems, material handling controls. (Hisp, estab 2000, empl 8, sales $1,027,400, cert: City, NMSDC)

4561   IT Consulting Services, Inc.
901 Kentucky St Ste 105
Lawrence, KS 66044
Contact: Kishor Gohel COO
Tel: 913-972-2321
Email: kgohel@itcscorp.net
Website: www.itcscorp.net
Software Engineering: Application Development (Web, non-Web, Mobile, SharePoint, e-commerce), Legacy systems & data migration, System Integration (SOA based & FOSS Custom Solutions). (Woman/As-Ind, estab 2004, empl 6, sales , cert: State, 8(a))

4562   JMA Chartered
10551 Barkley St Ste 400
Overland Park, KS 66212
Contact: Sanjay Chopra Dir of Western Region
Tel: 913-722-3252
Email: schopra@jmait.com
Website: www.jma-it.com
Infomration technology: systems integration, IT infrastructure planning, IT facilities management, network design & implementation, IT security audits & staff supplementation. (As-Pac, estab 1994, empl 250, sales $13,900,000, cert: NMSDC, CPUC)

4563   Perfect Output, LLC
9200 Indian Creek Pkwy Ste 400
Overland Park, KS 66210
Contact: Angela Pease VP Business Dev
Tel: 913-317-8400
Email: apease@perfectoutput.com
Website: www.perfectoutput.com
Document output devices: printers, fax machines, & digital multi-functional devices, develop & implement document management strategies. (AA, estab 1997, empl 70, sales , cert: State, NMSDC, CPUC)

4564   Technology Group Solutions, LLC
8551 Quivira Road
Lenexa, KS 66215
Contact: Lenora Payne CEO
Tel: 913-451-9900
Email: lpayne@tgs-mtc.com
Website: www.tgs-mtc.com
Information technology soutions. (Woman/AA, estab 2005, empl 79, sales $87,407,949, cert: NMSDC, WBENC)

4565   Veracity Consulting, Inc.
15516 W 81st St, Ste 195
Lenexa, KS 66219
Contact: Angela Hurt CEO
Tel: 913-579-9242
Email: angela.hurt@engageveracity.com
Website: www.veracityconsulting.us
IT contracting services: process improvement, PMO, project Mgt, custom computer programming, systems administration & information security. (Minority, Woman, estab 2006, empl 26, sales , cert: WBENC)

Kentucky

4566 AnITConsultant, LLC
PO Box 22998
Owensboro, KY 42304
Contact: Whaylon Coleman Owner
Tel: 270-883-1450
Email: it@anitconsultant.com
Website: www.anitconsultant.com
IT solutions & consulting services, Game Development (Unity3d), Social Media Consulting (Facebook, LinkedIn, & Twitter), Microsoft Application Development (Sharepoint, Office, Microsoft Dynamics), Mobile & Tablet Apps. (AA, estab 2010, empl 1, sales , cert: State)

4567 Etisbew Technology Group Inc.
7031 Glen Arbor Dr
Florence, KY 41042
Contact: Raj Pakala CEO
Tel: 502-386-4999
Email: bizteam@etisbew.com
Website: www.etisbew.com
E-Business solutions, e-business strategy, architecture & process automation, web based applications development & maintenance. (As-Pac, estab 2000, empl 150, sales $5,321,106, cert: NMSDC)

4568 GlowTouch LLC
9931 Corporate Campus Dr, Ste 1400
Louisville, KY 40223
Contact: Victoria Karrer Exec Admin
Tel: 502-410-1732
Email: victoria@glowtouch.com
Website: www.glowtouch.com
Technology Outsourcing: custom software development, product development, systems integration, mobile applications, QA, testing, and network monitoring. (Woman/As-Ind, estab 2006, empl 2300, sales $27,909,083, cert: NMSDC, WBENC)

4569 V-Soft Consulting Group Inc.
101 Bullitt Lane Ste 205
Louisville, KY 40222
Contact: Vincel Anthony Natl Business Dev Mgr
Tel: 502-425-8425
Email: vanthony@vsoftconsulting.com
Website: www.vsoftconsulting.com
Information technology staffing & consulting services: temporary, contract & permanent placement. (Minority, Woman, estab 1997, empl 230, sales , cert: NMSDC)

Louisiana

4570 A-B Computer Solutions, Inc.
PO Box 1851
Mandeville, LA 70470
Contact: Jason Brady President
Tel: 985-624-3092
Email: jasonb@a-bcomputers.com
Website: www.a-bcomputers.com
Information technology solutions & consulting. (Woman, estab 1997, empl 13, sales $3,060,000, cert: WBENC)

4571 Barrister Global Services Network Inc
42548 Happywoods Road
Hammond, LA 70403
Contact: Melissa Dobson Dir of Service Solutions
Tel: 985-365-0806
Email: mdobson@barrister.com
Website: www.barrister.com
Information technology services. (Woman, estab , empl 147, sales , cert: WBENC)

4572 ComTec Consultants Inc.
2400 Veterans Memorial Blvd Ste 205
Kenner, LA 70062
Contact: Vijay Saradhi VP
Tel: 972-338-3533
Email: vijay@comtecinfo.com
Website: www.comtecinfo.com
Information technology & business process services. (Woman/As-Ind, estab 1996, empl 635, sales $62,550,319, cert: NMSDC)

4573 Morine Networking, Inc.
PO Box 363
Opelousas, LA 70570
Contact: Rodney Morine VP
Tel: 337-942-1790
Email: rodney@morinetrucking.com
Website: www.morinenetworking.com
We are a freight brokering company providing 3rd party property logistics (Woman/AA, estab 2007, empl 2, sales , cert: State, NMSDC)

4574 MSF Global Solutions, LLC
201 St. Charles Ave, Ste 2500
New Orleans, LA 70170
Contact: Marseyas Fernandez CEO
Tel: 504-872-0641
Email: marseyas@msfglobal.net
Website: www.msfglobal.net
Geospatial & location based software & data development, mobile website & app development, staffing & training support services, data & business intelligence services, web & custom software design & development services. (AA, estab 2003, empl 5, sales $400,000, cert: NMSDC)

4575 VINFORMATIX L.L.C.
801 North Boulevard Ste 120
Baton Rouge, LA 70802
Contact: Kelli Cagle Dir Business Devel
Tel: 504-401-0533
Email: kcagle@vinformatix.com
Website: www.vinformatix.com
Custom-built software applications for web & mobile platforms (including OS/Android/Windows mobile apps), software lifecycle services, requirements analysis, design, coding, testing, QA/QC, training & maintenance. (Minority, Woman, estab 2008, empl 27, sales $1,073,605, cert: WBENC)

Massachusetts

4576 Advans IT Services, Inc.
65 Boston Post Rd W Ste 390
Marlborough, MA 01752
Contact: Paul Angelo CRM Mgr
Tel: 508-624-9900
Email: pangelo@advansit.com
Website: www.AdvansIT.com
IT infrastructure, project management & software development & offshore support. (As-Pac, estab 2009, empl 205, sales $21,000,000, cert: State, NMSDC)

4577 Advoqt, LLC
10 Guest St Ste 290
Boston, MA 02135
Contact: Reinier Moquete Founder & CEO
Tel: 617-307-7770
Email: info@advoqt.com
Website: www.advoqt.com
Systems integration & technology advisory firm focused on Hybrid Cloud Computing. (Hisp, estab 2012, empl 10, sales , cert: State)

4578 Aquent LLC
501 Boylston St 3rd Fl
Boston, MA 02116
Contact: Jennifer Cousins Dir Staffing Solutions Dev
Tel: 202-808-0557
Email: jcousins@aquent.com
Website: www.aquent.com
Graphic designers, web designers, production artists, presentation graphics experts, writers & project managers: freelance, permanent & temporary-to-permanent basis. (Minority, Woman, estab 1986, empl 890, sales $500,000,000, cert: NMSDC)

4579 Cambridge Computer Services, Inc.
271 Waverley Oaks Ste 301
Waltham, MA 02452
Contact: Business Operations Customer Advocate
Tel: 781-250-3000
Email: bizops@cambridgecomputer.com
Website: www.cambridgecomputer.com
Data storage & data protection solutions: SAN, NAS, backup, cloud, solid state, archiving solutions, research data management, scientific workflow, metadata, tiered storage, chargebacks, archiving & cloud storage. (Woman, estab , empl , sales , cert: State, WBENC)

4580 Continental Resources Inc.
175 Middlesex Tpke
Bedford, MA 01730
Contact: Louis Novakis DPO
Tel: 781-533-0450
Email: lnovakis@conres.com
Website: www.conres.com
Global IT solutions provider. (Woman, estab 1962, empl 328, sales $410,000,000, cert: WBENC)

4581 CTS Services Inc.
260 Maple St
Bellingham, MA 02019
Contact: Michelle Carlow President
Tel: 508-528-7720
Email: mcarlow@ctsservices.com
Website: www.ctsservices.com
Computer, printer & peripheral repair: touch screen displays, barcode scanning equipment, receipt printer. (Woman, estab 1989, empl 22, sales $2,775,000, cert: State)

4582 Cube Intelligence Corporation
12 Brattle Lane
Arlington, MA 02474
Contact: Hemant Verma President
Tel: 617-275-8254
Email: hsverma@cubeic.com
Website: www.cubeic.com
IT consulting and Staffing augmentationsvcs: data warehousing, data integration, data profiling, data quality, master data management, ODS, Operational Data Stores, Data Mart, Star Schema. (As-Ind, estab 2001, empl 2, sales $178,654, cert: State, NMSDC, 8(a))

4583 Deerwalk, Inc.
430 Bedford St
Lexington, MA 02420
Contact: Jeffrey Gasser President
Tel: 781-325-1775
Email: jgasser@deerwalk.com
Website: www.deerwalk.com
Global data analytics, big data technology & web based data analytics applications, healthcare data analytics, population management & controlling healthcare costs. (As-Ind, estab 2010, empl 400, sales $7,450,000, cert: NMSDC)

4584 Distributed Technology Associates
1740 Massachusetts Ave
Boxborough, MA 01719
Contact: Sanjay Tikku President
Tel: 978-274-0462
Email: office@dtainc.us
Website: www.dtainc.us
Database & systems services, database & systems, Oracle & SQL Server databases, Linux, Solaris & Windows platforms. (As-Ind, estab 1997, empl 7, sales $2,114,602, cert: State, NMSDC)

4585 Dnutch Associates, Inc.
301 Broadway
Methuen, MA 01844
Contact: Stephen Payne CEO
Tel: 978-687-1500
Email: spayne@dnutch.com
Website: www.dnutch.com
Networking & systems integration solutions. (Woman/AA, estab 1993, empl 8, sales $550,000, cert: State, WBENC)

4586 Fenco Global Industries Corp.
       1 Federal St
       Springfield, MA 01105
       Contact: Fenella Sitati President
       Tel: 413-308-8800
       Email: fenella@winningtek.com
       Website: www.winningtek.com
Technology hardware for application security, datacenters
& cloud virtualization, F5 Networks, VMware, Palo Alto,
Cisco Networks, RedHat, Microsoft, NetApp, EMC, HP, IBM,
Dell & ExtraHop. (Woman/AA, estab 2009, empl 5, sales
$450,000, cert: NMSDC)

4587 Hawkins Point Partners LLC
       7 Technology Dr
       North Chelmsford, MA 01863
       Contact: Heather Morris Kyer Sr Principal
       Tel: 781-640-0893
       Email: hmorriskyer@hawkinspointpartners.com
       Website: www.hawkinspointpartners.com
IT consulting, outsourcing reset, application modernization,
information management, mobile solutions & enterprise
architecture & integration. (Woman, estab 2012, empl 5,
sales , cert: State, WBENC)

4588 Inspiration Zone, LLC
       Two Heritage Dr, Ste 302
       Quincy, MA 02171
       Contact: Juliette Mayers CEO
       Tel: 617-328-0953
       Email: info@inspirationzonellc.com
       Website: www.inspirationzonellc.com
Inspiration Zone provides strategic advisory services
primarily for HR/Talent, Diversity, and Inclusion and has
expertise in Multicultural Marketing and Leadership
Development. We offer training and inspirational talks
including workshops and speaking eng (AA, estab 2011,
empl 1, sales $130,000, cert: State, NMSDC)

4589 Integration Technology, Inc.
       167 Washington St Ste 32
       Norwell, MA 02061
       Contact: Sean Stewart Acct mgr
       Tel: 781-569-4949
       Email: sean.stewart@it-inc.us
       Website: www.integration-technology.com
IT, SAP staffing and consulting services (Woman, estab
1998, empl 4, sales $1,300,000, cert: State)

4590 IntePros Incorporated
       750 Marrett Road Ste 301
       Lexington, MA 02421
       Contact: Jeffrey Anderson Branch Mgr
       Tel: 612-916-7387
       Email: janderson@intepros.com
       Website: www.intepros.com
Provide contracted IT consultants, software development
lifecycle, network infrastructure & security. (Woman, estab
1996, empl 350, sales $55,400,000, cert: WBENC)

4591 Interactive Tactical Group
       55 Wallace St
       Somerville, MA 02144
       Contact: Michael Quan President
       Tel: 617-500-7520
       Email: mike@tacticalvr.com
       Website: www.tacticalvr.com
Interactive panoramic imaging for military, security &
industrial organizations. DotProduct3D hand held 3D
scanner, DotProduct3D hand held 3D scanner, DPI-7,
uses Android tablet & Kinect sensor. (As-Pac, estab 2000,
empl 1, sales $150,500, cert: State, NMSDC)

4592 Iterators LLC
       50 Milk St, Fl 16
       Boston, MA 02109
       Contact: Jill Willcox Managing Member
       Tel: 617-909-0564
       Email: jwillcox@iteratorstesting.com
       Website: www.Iteratorstesting.com
Accessibility Testing, Website and Mobile App Testing:
Manual, Accessibility, Automation • Manual Functional
and Regression Testing • Automated Regression Testing.
(Woman, estab 2017, empl 5, sales $264,000, cert:
WBENC)

4593 M & R Consultants Corporation
       700 Technology Park Dr Ste 203
       Billerica, MA 01821
       Contact: Sales Dir
       Tel: 781-273-5050
       Email: info@mrccsolutions.com
       Website: www.mrccsolutions.com
IT consulting: software engineering, client server
technology, internet & intranet, network admin, project
mgmt, product dev. (As-Ind, estab 1996, empl 700, sales
$20,000,000, cert: State)

4594 Martindale Associates, Inc.
       65 Avco Rd, Unit M
       Bradford, MA 01835
       Contact: Laurie Hall President
       Tel: 978-372-2120
       Email: lmh@martindaleassoc.com
       Website: www.martindaleassoc.com
Automated machine & process control systems, data
acquisition systems, barcode data collection, inventory
& asset tracking, RFID, mobile device management,
handheld computers & systems integration.
 (Minority, Woman, estab 1976, empl 7, sales
$1,525,041, cert: State)

4595 On Track Consulting
       317 Eliot St
       Milton, MA 02186
       Contact: Janet McCloskey President
       Tel: 617-653-1409
       Email: jmccloskey@ontrackconsult.com
       Website: www.ontrackconsult.com
Information management services, big data, data
warehousing, business intelligence & data management.
(Woman, estab 1997, empl 1, sales $3,157,077, cert:
State, WBENC)

4596 Online Computer Prodcuts, Inc.
672 Pleasant St
Norwood, MA 02062
Contact: Harry Butters Acct Mgr
Tel: 781-255-9100
Email: hbutters@online-computer.com
Website: www.online-computer.com
Information technology support products, services & solutions. (Woman, estab 1987, empl 24, sales $14,075,000, cert: WBENC)

4597 Onyx Spectrum Technology, Inc. dba Shearwater EM
78 Fisher Ave
Boston, MA 02120
Contact: Adrienne R. Benton President
Tel: 617-407-2826
Email: abenton@onyxspectrum.com
Website: www.onyxspectrum.com
Technical consulting services: data analysis, information security, business process improvement & regulatory concerns. (Woman/AA, estab 2004, empl 5, sales $726,000, cert: State)

4598 ResourceSoft, Inc.
33 Boston Post Rd W Ste 230
Marlborough, MA 01752
Contact: Pyi Phyo VP
Tel: 508-787-0882
Email: pyi@resourcesoft.com
Website: www.resourcesoft.com
Custom computer programming svcs: MS .NET, JAVA/J2EE, quality assurance. (Minority, Woman, estab 1999, empl 55, sales $5,711,183, cert: State, NMSDC)

4599 Roxbury Technology Corp
3368 Washington St
Jamaica Plain, MA 02130
Contact: Elizabeth Williams President
Tel: 617-524-1020
Email: info@roxburytechnology.com
Website: www.roxburytechnology.com
Mfr & dist premium toner cartridges and imaging supplies. (Woman/AA, estab 1994, empl 55, sales $12,000,000, cert: NMSDC)

4600 Scitics Inc.
436 Central St
Acton, MA 01720
Contact: Joan Yu President
Tel: 978-844-1258
Email: jyu@sciticsinc.com
Website: www.sciticsinc.com
Data analytic services, data exploration & discovery, data processing, hosting & related services, custom computer programming services, dashboard & customized business intelligence reports, predictive modeling. (Minority, Woman, estab 2010, empl 3, sales $128,170, cert: State, WBENC)

4601 Shred King Corporation
60 McGrath Hwy
Quincy, MA 02169
Contact: Donald Cornell GM
Tel: 617-221-1600
Email: info@shred-king.com
Website: www.shred-king.com
Document destruction services. (Woman, estab 2006, empl 10, sales , cert: State)

4602 Sigma Systems, Inc.
293 Boston Post Rd W Ste 301 Ste 100
Mar, MA 01752
Contact: Nate Fischer Dir
Tel: 508-925-3233
Email: nfischer@sigmainc.com
Website: www.sigmainc.com
IT consulting, project mgmt, application dev, network mgmt, database mgmt & support, staffing services, custom application dev, data warehousing, business intelligence, CRM, ERP, EAI, quality assurance, systems admin, web dev & custom MIS. (Minority, Woman, estab 1994, empl 97, sales $4,000,000, cert: State, NMSDC)

4603 SJB Enterprises, Inc. dba Sandra Network
25 Goodale St
Peabody, MA 01960
Contact: Sandra Batakis President
Tel: 978-535-0202
Email: wbe@sandranetwork.com
Website: www.sandranetwork.com
IT consulting: PC repair, training & networks. (Woman, estab 1998, empl 5, sales $671,895, cert: State, WBENC)

4604 Softlinx, Inc.
100 Riverpark Dr
North Reading, MA 01864
Contact: Helen Kim Contract Mgr
Tel: 978-881-0575
Email: hkim@softlinx.com
Website: www.softlinx.com
Software, IT development, consulting & training. (Woman/As-Pac, estab 1993, empl 15, sales $1,530,000, cert: NMSDC, WBENC)

4605 Solidus Technical Solutions, LLC
17 Forsythia Rd
Leominster, MA 01453
Contact: Jill Blagsvedt Business Devel Specialist
Tel: 866-765-4387
Email: solidussmallbd@solidus-ts.com
Website: www.solidus-ts.com
Software & systems engineering, life cycle, radar, sensors, fault tolerant, mission planning, intelligence systems, embedded software, networking, integration & test. (Woman, estab 2001, empl 95, sales , cert: WBENC)

4606 Soltrix Technology Solutions Inc.
860 Worcester Road Ste 215
Framingham, MA 01702
Contact: Raghu Nandan President
Tel: 774-293-1293
Email: raghu.nandan@soltrixsolutions.com
Website: www.soltrixsolutions.com
Custom software application design & development services. (Woman/As-Ind, estab 2007, empl 3, sales , cert: State)

4607 Stellar Corporation
594 Marrett Rd
Lexington, MA 02421
Contact: Swapan Roy President
Tel: 781-863-0101
Email: sroy@stlr.net
Website: www.stlr.net
software - custom application development, reengineering, database
engineering - structural engineering (As-Pac, estab 2002, empl 7, sales $614,678, cert: State)

4608 Stemac Inc
      30 Evergreen Dr
      Bridgewater, MA 02324
      Contact: Jane McCarthy President
      Tel: 508-331-1410
      Email: jane@stemacinc.com
      Website: www.stemacinc.com
IT placement, pre screened Supply Chain & SAP Talent,
Customer Service & Consultative. (Woman, estab 2013,
empl 2, sales $400,000, cert: WBENC)

4609 TalentBurst, Inc
      679 Worcester Road
      Natick, MA 01760
      Contact: Jamie Jacobs Dir of Strategic Partnerships
      Tel: 614-382-8840
      Email: jamie.jacobs@talentburst.com
      Website: www.talentburst.com
Information technology staff augmentation, lifesciences,
business & regulatory compliance, accounting, finance & IT
solutions services. (Minority, estab 2002, empl 1405, sales
$84,700,000, cert: NMSDC)

4610 Tanisha Systems Inc.
      75 Federal St Ste 1330
      Boston, MA 02110
      Contact: Gorav Aggarwal VP
      Tel: 617-729-0260
      Email: gaggarwal@tanishasystems.com
      Website: www.tanishasystems.com
Custom application development & end-to-end IT services.
(As-Ind, estab 2002, empl 80, sales $9,700,000, cert: State)

4611 tCognition, Inc.
      70 Kemble St Ste 100
      Boston, MA 02119
      Contact: Manoj Shinde CEO
      Tel: 617-438-4819
      Email: Manoj.Shinde@tCognition.com
      Website: www.tCognition.com
IT/software consulting & outsourcing services. (As-Ind,
estab 2003, empl 65, sales $3,159,484, cert: State, NMSDC)

4612 Vernance, LLC
      745 Atlantic Ave
      Boston, MA 02111
      Contact: Pedro Marcano CEO
      Tel: 936-647-3376
      Email: pmarcano@vernance.com
      Website: www.vernance.com
Cyber & Physical Security Risk Management consulting
services. (Hisp, estab 2014, empl 3, sales $350,000, cert:
State, NMSDC)

Maryland

4613 5 Star Consulting Group, LLC.
      3261 Old Washington Rd Ste 2020
      Waldorf, MD 20602
      Contact: Lethia Dargin President
      Tel: 301-216-3839
      Email: ldargin@5starconsultinggrp.com
      Website: www.5StarConsultingGrp.com
Systems Integration & Design, Computer Integration, SCCM,
Software deployment, Software packaging, Server maintenance, troubleshooting, configuration & build. IT Consulting, software & hardware support. (Woman/AA, estab
2013, empl 5, sales , cert: State, SDB)

4614 Acela Technologies, Inc.
      5115 Pegasus Ct, Ste A
      Frederick, MD 21704
      Contact: Carole Derringer CEO
      Tel: 301-846-9060
      Email: cderringer@acelatechnologies.com
      Website: www.acelatechnologies.com
Wireless solutions engineering & integration, wireless
internet services, VoIP, VoWiFi, wireless video surveillance. (AA, estab 2002, empl 20, sales $3,834,797, cert:
State)

4615 Advanced Engineering Design, Inc.
      6525 Belcrest Road Ste 426
      Hyattsville, MD 20782
      Contact: Reginald Waters CEO
      Tel: 301-683-2112
      Email: rwaters@aedworld.com
      Website: www.aedworld.com
Central office & data center engineering services: site
surveys, computer-aided-design drafting, equipment
inventories & assessments, records development &
space planning. (AA, estab 1991, empl 60, sales
$2,480,000, cert: State, NMSDC)

4616 Alliance Technology Group, LLC
      7010 Hi Tech Dr
      Hanover, MD 21076
      Contact: Lauren Russ Corporate Admin
      Tel: 410-712-0270
      Email: Lauren.Russ@alliance-it.com
      Website: www.alliance-it.com
End-to-end storage technology solutions, computer,
monitor & printer repair, network peripherals, system
upgrades, backup & recovery engineering, data storage
assessments. (Woman, estab 1987, empl 83, sales
$36,903,666, cert: WBENC)

4617 ALTEK Information Technology, Inc.
      241 E Fourth St, Ste 205
      Frederick, MD 21701
      Contact: Anne Lipman CEO
      Tel: 301-695-4440
      Email: cardinalhealth@al-tekinc.com
      Website: www.al-tekinc.com
Information technology staffing & project management:
contract, contract to hire or direct hire. (Woman, estab
2004, empl 150, sales $15,000,000, cert: State, WBENC)

4618 Applications Alternatives, Inc.
      PO Box 4238
      Upper Marlboro, MD 20775
      Contact: David Kiasi-Barnes
      Tel: 301-350-4752
      Email: david.kiasi@appalt.com
      Website: www.appalt.com
Information technology applications consulting in the
area of informational survey processing. (AA, estab
1987, empl 2, sales , cert: State)

4619   Applied Development LLC
       7 S Front St Ste 200
       Baltimore, MD 21202
       Contact: Kimberly Citizen
       Tel: 410-571-4016
       Email: kcitizen@applied-dev.com
       Website: www.applied-dev.com
Process improvement, automation, analytics & cyber
security, project management, business process improvement, strategic communications, cybersecurity & administrative support. (Woman/AA, estab 2011, empl 12, sales
$687,000, cert: State, City, NMSDC, WBENC, 8(a))

4620   Avance IT Solutions LLC
       7 Gondola View Court
       Woodstock, MD 21163
       Contact: Antoinette Gardner CEO
       Tel: 443-955-5107
       Email: partner@avanceits.com
       Website: www.avanceitsolutions.com
IT consulting services, project management, training,
technology assessments, programming, helpdesk, testing
& deployment. (Woman/AA, estab 2007, empl 5, sales ,
cert: State)

4621   BITHGROUP Technologies, Inc.
       113 W Monument St
       Baltimore, MD 21201
       Contact: Robert Wallace President
       Tel: 410-962-1188
       Email: robertwallace@bithgroup.com
       Website: www.bithgroup.com
Information Technology Consulting, Network Engineering,
Application Dev, Wireless Infrastructure Development, e-
learning (AA, estab 1992, empl 60, sales , cert: State)

4622   Business Integra Technology Solutions, Inc.
       6550 Rock Spring Dr Ste 600
       Bethesda, MD 20817
       Contact: Jay Fernandez Sr Dir Business Dev
       Tel: 732-887-5611
       Email: Jay.Fernandez@businessintegra.com
       Website: www.businessintegra.com
Staff augmentation services, information technology
consulting. (Minority, Woman, estab 2001, empl 650, sales
$115,000,000, cert: WBENC)

4623   CAEI Inc.
       9256 Bendix Rd, Ste 102
       Columbia, MD 21045
       Contact: Derrick Burnett Sr Business Devel Exec
       Tel: 443-319-5381
       Email: dburnett@caeiinc.com
       Website: www.caeiinc.com
Help Desk and Customer Service call center
Personnel and management, in addition to our Help Desk
Tier I, Tier II and Tier III experience and past performance.
(AA, estab 2011, empl 125, sales $6,500,000, cert: State,
NMSDC)

4624   Carson Solutions, LLC
       16701 Melford Blvd. Ste. 431
       Bowie, MD 20715
       Contact: Eugene Carson President
       Tel: 800-480-7132
       Email: eugene@carsonsolutionsllc.com
       Website: www.carsonsolutionsllc.com
Information technology solutions & administrative
support. (AA, estab 2000, empl 10, sales $1,850,000, cert:
State)

4625   Cyber Management Systems
       11504 Eastern Red Cedar Ave
       Clinton, MD 20735
       Contact: Cory Coleman CEO
       Tel: 301-613-3717
       Email: corycoleman@cybermss.com
       Website: www.cybermanagementsystems.com
Information Technology consulting, Enterprise IT
Systems Monitoring, Management Consulting & IT
Consulting. (AA, estab 2014, empl 1, sales , cert: State)

4626   Cybern Consulting Group, LLC
       13615 Triadelphia Mill Rd
       Clarksville, MD 21029
       Contact: Serif Mumuney President
       Tel: 410-379-0545
       Email: serif.mumuney@cyberngroup.com
       Website: www.cyberngroup.com
Develop applications using Business Process Management tools running on finely tuned Databases. (AA,
estab 2004, empl 8, sales $400,050, cert: State, 8(a))

4627   Dakota Consulting Inc.
       1110 Bonifant St Ste 310
       Silver Spring, MD 20910
       Contact: Lokesh Sayal VP
       Tel: 240-645-0229
       Email: contracts@dakota-consulting.com
       Website: www.dakotaconsulting.com
Information technology management, telecommunications & networking. (Woman, estab 2015, empl 150,
sales $19,000,000, cert: State)

4628   DB Commercial Group LLC
       8401 Colesville Rd Ste 310
       Silver Spring, MD 20910
       Contact: Kim Harwell CEO
       Tel: 301-363-2790
       Email: kim.harwell@dbcommercialgroup.com
       Website: www.dbcommercialgroup.com
IT Services, Staff Augmentation, Systems Engineering,
Cyber Security, Application Development, Cloud Computing & Multimedia Services. (AA, estab 2014, empl 20,
sales $10,000,000, cert: NMSDC)

4629   Dhaivat Maharaja Enterprises Inc.
       6 Latimore Ct
       Reisterstown, MD 21136
       Contact: Dhaivat Maharaja CEO
       Tel: 443-650-8287
       Email: dhaivat.maharaja@dhaivat.com
       Website: www.dhaivat.com
Enterprise resource planning (ERP), customer relationship management (CRM), Cloud architecture, unified
computing system (UCS), online course development,
service-oriented architecture (SOA). (As-Pac, estab 2006,
empl 3, sales , cert: State)

4630   Diverse Concepts, Inc.
       1131 Benfield Blvd, Ste K
       Millersville, MD 21108
       Contact: CEO
       Tel: 443-698-1052
       Email:
       Website: www.dciits.com
Web Development and Design, System Engineering,
Network Engineering, Information Assurance, Disaster
Recovery, Program Management, (AA, estab 2002, empl
20, sales $1,520,000, cert: State)

4631   DK Consulting, LLC
       8955 Guilford Road Ste 240
       Columbia, MD 21046
       Contact: Dana Kerr CEO
       Tel: 443-552-5851
       Email: contacts@dkconsult.net
       Website: www.dkconsult.net
Management & technological solutions services. (Woman, estab 2003, empl 9, sales $818,570, cert: State, City, WBENC)

4632   Eigennet LLC
       13508 Wisteria Dr
       Germantown, MD 20874
       Contact: Godfrey Pereira President
       Tel: 240-476-5094
       Email: gpereira@eigennet.com
       Website: www.eigennet.com
We are pleased to inform you that Eigennet LLC is now certified Minority Business Enterprise and is participating in all IT supplier diversity programs and staffing models. We request you to include us in any staffing needs that mandate diversity certific (Nat Ame, estab 2016, empl 25, sales , cert: State, NMSDC)

4633   Encore Solutions Inc.
       12300 Twinbrook Pkwy, Ste 330
       Rockville, MD 20852
       Contact: Gary Lewis President
       Tel: 301-998-6191
       Email: glewis@encore-solu.com
       Website: www.encore-solu.com
Technology solutions: systems engineering, acquisition & logistics support, program management & administrative services, records information management. (Woman/AA, estab 2001, empl 3, sales $502,789, cert: State, NMSDC, WBENC)

4634   ERPMatrix LLC
       3620 Turbridge Dr
       Burtonsville, MD 20866
       Contact: Shams Abedin Managing Partner
       Tel: 240-396-4380
       Email: sa@erpmatrix.com
       Website: www.erpmatrix.com
Staffing, enterprise architecture/integration, software devel, database & IT support. (As-Ind, estab 2005, empl 4, sales $178,191, cert: State)

4635   Infinite Computer Solutions Inc.
       15201 Diamondback Dr Ste 125
       Rockville, MD 20850
       Contact: John Stritzl Dir Sales
       Tel: 215-262-8027
       Email: partnership@infinite.com
       Website: www.infinite.com
Applications development, network engineering/operations, help desk support; e-business, client/server & mainframe solutions; network & system migrations; LAN/WAN/MAN svcs. (As-Ind, estab 2001, empl , sales , cert: NMSDC)

4636   Information Protection Solutions
       1997 Annapolis Exchange Pkwy Ste 300
       Annapolis, MD 21401
       Contact: Todd Chamberlain CEO
       Tel: 240-345-4212
       Email: info@ips314.com
       Website: www.ips314.com
Cyber Security • Cloud security • Continuous Monitoring Strategies • Cyber Security Policy Development • System Hardening Implementation • Vulnerability Analysis Information Assurance: • FedRAMP compliance • NIST 800-53 Rev 4 to Rev 5 Prep • Risk Mgmt. (AA, estab 2014, empl 3, sales , cert: State, NMSDC, 8(a))

4637   Information Security Enterprise Consulting, LLC
       6701 Democracy Blvd
       Bethesda, MD 20814
       Contact: Jason Peterson CEO
       Tel: 301-337-2527
       Email: jpeterson@isec-cybersecurity.com
       Website: www.isec-cybersecurity.com
Cyber security, design, develop, deploy, operate & maintain defensive security measures. (AA, estab 2007, empl 20, sales $2,500,200, cert: State, NMSDC)

4638   International Computer Systems, Inc.
       9111 Edmonston Rd, Ste 403
       Greenbelt, MD 20770
       Contact: Tan Aslam President
       Tel: 301-614-3989
       Email: tanaslam@ics-systems.us
       Website: www.ics-systems.us
Systems engineering, satellite ground systems design & dev, raw data processing systems, system specification, interface control documents, system integration & test, independent verification & test, operations & maintenance, system admin. (Woman/As-Ind, estab 1997, empl 2, sales , cert: WBENC)

4639   JuneGem Technologies, Inc.
       3601 Hamilton St Ste 201
       Hyattsville, MD 20782
       Contact: Stephanie Thomas Business Devel Mgr
       Tel: 301-864-2321
       Email: hr@junegemtech.com
       Website: www.junegemtech.com
Information Technology and Enterprise Resource Planning (ERP) solutions, project management, business process engineering, and software & systems development. (Woman/AA, estab 2011, empl 10, sales , cert: State)

4640   Jupiter LLC
       12021 Eaglewood Ct
       Silver Spring, MD 20902
       Contact: E Alex Jupiter President
       Tel: 240-316-2943
       Email: alexj@jupitercybsec.com
       Website: www.jupitercybsec.com
Risk assessment, analysis & management; control vulnerability assessment, data & functional specification; IS/IT security scope management, features, architecture & design; cyber incident response planning; software capability maturity assessment. (AA, estab 2013, empl 3, sales , cert: State, City)

4641   MASAI Technologies Corporation
       201B Broadway St
       Frederick, MD 21701
       Contact: Masai Troutman CEO
       Tel: 301-694-2751
       Email: masai@masai-tech.com
       Website: www.masai-tech.com
Specialized Staffing & Enterprise Resource Planning (ERP)
SAP Software System Integration, implementation &
operational services. (AA, estab 1997, empl 15, sales
$2,000,000, cert: State, NMSDC)

4642   NucoreVision, Inc
       4601 Forbes Blvd, Ste 310
       Lanham, MD 20706
       Contact: Yolanda Murphy
       Tel: 301-577-3999
       Email: ymurphy@nucorevision.com
       Website: www.nucorevision.com
Cybersecurity, Agency IT Operations, IT Program / Project
Management, Management Consulting, IT Services &
Solutions. (AA, estab 1996, empl 25, sales $1,900,000,
cert: NMSDC)

4643   Nu-Pulse Technologies, Inc.
       21 Industrial Park Dr Ste 101
       Waldorf, MD 20602
       Contact: E. Renee Ingram President
       Tel: 301-374-2534
       Email: ringram@nu-pulse.com
       Website: www.nu-pulse.com
Information technology svcs: software design & devel,
LAN/WAN design & implementation, database design &
devel, project mgmt. IT security, fire protection engineer-
ing, voice guidance exit systems, electronic door locks.
(AA, estab 1998, empl 39, sales $3,000,000, cert: State)

4644   Omega Micro Services
       PO Box 1271
       Bowie, MD 20721
       Contact: Paulson Obiniyi CEO
       Tel: 240-602-8624
       Email: info@omicroservices.com
       Website: www.omicroservices.com
Technical Services and Consulting, Enterprise Architecture,
Data & Media Sanitization, Web site Design and develop-
ment, Project and Program Management, Staffing Aug-
mentation, Content Production, Enterprise Content
Management. (AA, estab 2007, empl 2, sales , cert: State)

4645   Pa Na Solutions Inc.
       3504 Waterford Mill Rd
       Bowie, MD 20721
       Contact: Brahim Zahar VP
       Tel: 703-348-6436
       Email: bzahar@panasolutions.com
       Website: www.panasolutionas.com
IT Svcs: Program Management, Finance, Scheduling,
Methodology, Tools, Network Engineering, Strategy &
Planning, Assessment, Architecture & design services,
Integration & deployment, Optimization, & Device Sup-
port, Video Engineering. (AA, estab 2006, empl 28, sales
$4,218,518, cert: State, 8(a))

4646   Peyak Solutions, Inc.
       9250 Bendix Rd N, Ste 150
       Columbia, MD 21045
       Contact: Leah Conover CEO
       Tel: 800-958-2188
       Email: leah.conover@peyaksolutions.com
       Website: www.peyaksolutions.com
IT consulting & support services: network design,
procurement & installation, desktop, internet & database application dev, project & program management,
hardware recycling & confidential data destruction.
(Minority, Woman, estab 2007, empl 2, sales $195,000,
cert: State, City, 8(a))

4647   Planned Systems International, Inc.
       10632 Little Patuxent Pkwy, Ste 200
       Columbia, MD 21044
       Contact: Terry Lin CEO
       Tel: 410-964-8000
       Email: tlin@plan-sys.com
       Website: www.plan-sys.com/
Providing Healthcare IT, management consulting, IT
solutions & services. (As-Pac, estab 1988, empl 350,
sales $105,101,730, cert: State)

4648   Pn Automation
       1521 S Edgewood St
       Baltimore, MD 21227
       Contact: Nitin Baviskar COO
       Tel: 410-409-6730
       Email: nitin@pnautomation.com
       Website: www.pnautomation.com
Software development & IT service. (As-Ind, estab 2004,
empl 25, sales $600,000, cert: State)

4649   Pramac Engineering LLC
       2000 Astilbe Way
       Odenton, MD 21113
       Contact: Kevin Ruffin CEO
       Tel: 410-409-9772
       Email: kfruffin@pramacengineering.com
       Website: www.pramacengineering.com
Java and C/C++ object oriented design and development, web applications Model/View/Controller (MVC)
development, Niagara Files development, Commercial
Off the Shelf (COTS) Integration, Systems Integration and
508 Compliance application implementation. (AA, estab
2017, empl 1, sales $121,000, cert: State)

4650   Realistic Computing, Inc.
       5707 Calverton St
       Baltimore, MD 21228
       Contact: Sequoia Ramsey CEO
       Tel: 410-744-8144
       Email: sramsey@realistic-computing.com
       Website: www.realistic-computing.com
IT support services, network installation, cabling, data &
voice. (Woman/AA, estab 2000, empl 3, sales $200,000,
cert: WBENC)

4651 Reliable Government Solutions Inc.
3002 Gazebo Ct
Silver Spring, MD 20904
Contact: Chieu Le President
Tel: 800-767-0896
Email: chieule@rgsfederal.com
Website: www.rgsfederal.com
Data warehouse, development, architecture & admin, financial applications, IT audits, JCIDS documentation, network admin & security, testing, program & project mgmt, equirements analysis, SME, training, web development. (As-Pac, estab 2001, empl 5, sales $317,842, cert: City)

4652 Rescon Inc.
4526 Cheltenham Dr,
Bethesda, MD 20814
Contact: Prem Singh CEO
Tel: 301-330-5265
Email: resconinc@aol.com
Website: www.resconisit.com
IT technology consulting & staffing, project management, software architects, programmers, systems admin, network engineers, software quality assurance. (As-Ind, estab 1998, empl 14, sales $2,000,000, cert: State)

4653 Resourcesys Inc.
8850 Columbia 100 Pkwy Ste 304
Columbia, MD 21045
Contact: Kolluri VP Sales
Tel: 609-721-4446
Email: anna@resourcesys.com
Website: www.resourcesys.com
IT contract staffing resources: Oracle Java & .NET technologies. (Woman/As-Ind, estab 1999, empl 20, sales $1,800,000, cert: WBENC)

4654 Right Choice Computers & Networks, LLC
PO Box 5324
Capitol Heights, MD 20791
Contact: Pamela Mitchell President
Tel: 301-839-4905
Email: contactus@rchoicecn.com
Website: www.rchoicecn.com
Software & applications, mainframe Legacy Systems, networks topologies, computer hardware & accessories, help desk & support, network installation. (Woman/AA, estab 1994, empl 1, sales , cert: State)

4655 RTH Solutions LLC
10320 Little Patuxent Pkwy, Ste 200
Columbia, MD 21044
Contact: Tanisha Lockett COO
Tel: 240-638-1222
Email: tanisha.lockett@rthsolutions.com
Website: www.rthsolutions.com
Management consulting, staffing & training, business & IT Service Management process consulting, ITIL, Project Management, Cyber Resilia, DevOps, Lean IT, and Scrum. (Woman/AA, estab 2006, empl 2, sales , cert: State, WBENC, NWBOC)

4656 Shakthy Information Systems, Inc.
13910 Falconcrest Rd
Germantown, MD 20874
Contact: Susheela Palaniswamy CEO
Tel: 240-355-6184
Email: hr@shakthy.com
Website: www.shakthy.com
Custom software development services & solutions. (Minority, Woman, estab 2000, empl 5, sales $350,000, cert: State)

4657 Sympora Technologies
5431 Woodland Blvd Ste B
Oxon Hill, MD 20745
Contact: Dean Matthews President
Tel: 800-568-9965
Email: dean.matthews@sympora.com
Website: www.sympora.com
Software development, information technology, web-based training & information security services. (AA, estab 2000, empl 3, sales $158,325, cert: State)

4658 The Aspen Group, Inc.
1100 Wayne Ave Ste 1200
Silver Spring, MD 20910
Contact: Christina Fitts Exec VP
Tel: 410-308-0629
Email: cfitts@theaspengroupinc.com
Website: www.theaspengroupinc.com
Information technology consulting & services. (Woman/AA, estab 1988, empl 400, sales $38,481,357, cert: NMSDC, WBENC)

4659 The net.America Corporation
16201 Trade Zone Ave, Unit 112
Upper Marlboro, MD 20774
Contact: Yasmin Hines Business Devel Analyst
Tel: 301-218-4559
Email: yasmin.hines@netamerica.net
Website: www.discovernetamerica.com
Information technology solutions, contact centers & help desk, information technology, health services, program management, peer review & grants management. (Woman/AA, estab 2000, empl 51, sales $8,226,437, cert: State, WBENC)

4660 The Squires Group
128 Lubrano Dr, Ste 102
Annapolis, MD 21401
Contact: Nancy Squires CEO
Tel: 410-224-7779
Email: nancy@squiresgroup.com
Website: www.squiresgroup.com
ERP staffing & consulting svsc: process reengineering, change mgmt, implementation, upgrades & web-enabled integration. (Woman, estab 1994, empl 75, sales , cert: WBENC)

4661 TMCS, LLC
6910 Wade Ave Ste A
Clinton, MD 20735
Contact: Tynnetta McBeth CEO
Tel: 301-686-8417
Email: tmcbeth@tmcsllc.com
Website: www.tmcsllc.com
Technical & management consulting, design & implementation of LAN/WAN solutions, security, communicatons & mobility, virtual data center solutions, hardware & software resales. (Minority, Woman, estab 2008, empl 3, sales $160,000, cert: State, 8(a))

4662 Unatek, Inc.
1100 Mercantile Lane Ste 115-A
Largo, MD 20774
Contact: Charles Iheagwara Dir
Tel: 301-583-4629
Email: ciheagwara@unatek.com
Website: www.unatek.com
Information technology consulting. (AA, estab 1996, empl 15, sales $1,860,000, cert: State, 8(a))

4663 Vangel Inc.
3020 Nieman Ave
Baltimore, MD 21230
Contact: Valerie Androutsopoulos Principal
Tel: 410-644-2600
Email: valerie@vangelinc.com
Website: www.vangelinc.com
Data destruction & recycling services: on-site & off-site paper shredding, off-site non-paper storage, media shredding. (Woman, estab 1988, empl 15, sales $1,642,150, cert: State)

4664 Victory Global Solutions, Inc.
5950 Symphony Woods Rd, Ste 211
Columbia, MD 21044
Contact: Angela Brown CEO
Tel: 410-884-9310
Email: abrown@victorygs.com
Website: www.victorygs.com
Information technology & networking integration services, systems engineering, consulting. (Woman/AA, estab 2001, empl 30, sales $26,000,000, cert: State, WBENC)

4665 VVL Systems & Consulting, LLC
8840 Stanford Blvd Ste 1550
Columbia, MD 21045
Contact: Vinnie Lima Managing Dir
Tel: 410-864-8659
Email: vlima@vvlsystems.com
Website: www.vvlsystems.com
Information technology & consulting, cloud services, infrastructure & end-user optimization. (Hisp, estab 2008, empl 6, sales $950,000, cert: State, 8(a))

4666 Web Traits, Inc.
9423 Eagleton Lane
Montgomery Village, MD 20886
Contact: Bhaskar Roy President
Tel: 240-731-6120
Email: bhaskar.roy@web-traits.com
Website: www.web-traits.com/
Information systems security & operations (ISSO), cyber security, network operations management, virtualization, certification & accreditation (C&A), independent verification & validation (IV&V). (Minority, estab 2007, empl 7, sales $960,000, cert: State, 8(a))

Maine

4667 CST2000 dba iCST IT Solutions
100 Brickhill Ave Ste C, Lower Level
South Portland, ME 04106
Contact: Sasha Asdourian Finance Mgr
Tel: 207-221-2952
Email: finance@i-cst.com
Website: www.i-cst.com
Software testing & IT solutions: ASP, client server, database, IT staffing, .NET, internet, Java, network admin, mainframe, migration, etc. (As-Pac, estab 1997, empl 70, sales $6,050,000, cert: State)

Michigan

4668 Acro Service Corporation
39209 W. Six Mile Rd.
Livonia, MI 48152
Contact: Todd Kearns Marketing & Proposal Mgr
Tel: 734-591-1100
Email: acrocorp@acrocorp.com
Website: www.acrocorp.com
Staff augmentation: engineering, information technology, light industrial, clerical. Outsourcing; offshore application dev; IT, engineering, project mgmt consulting. (Minority, estab 1982, empl 1, sales $371,000,000, cert: NMSDC)

4669 All About Technology
6450 Michigan Ave
Detroit, MI 48210
Contact: Willie Brake Mgr
Tel: 313-965-5543
Email: isupply@all-about-technology.com
Website: www.all-about-technology.com
Computer Sales, Service, Training & Upgrades. Data Backup & Recovery, Wireless Networking, Microsoft, Adobe, Quicken, Value Added Reseller, Computer Insurance, Website Maintenance & Design. (AA, estab 2001, empl 7, sales $210,000, cert: State, NMSDC, SDB)

4670 Allegiance Technologies Inc.
140 Edgelake Dr
Waterford, MI 48327
Contact: Matthew Montpas President
Tel: 248-425-0252
Email: matt.montpas@allegiance-tech.com
Website: www.allegiance-tech.com
SAP consulting & implementation. (Hisp, estab 1998, empl 10, sales $594,447, cert: NMSDC)

4671 AltaFlux Corporation
3250 W Big Beaver Rd Ste 342
Troy, MI 48084
Contact: John Morrison Natl Sales Mgr
Tel: 248-850-2298
Email: john.morrison@altaflux.com
Website: www.altaflux.com
Business Transformation Consulting, Complete SaaS Solutions, Cloud Computing Solutions, Specialized Technology Staffing, SAP, Oracle, Google Apps, Dell Boomi, OrangeScape (Minority, Woman, estab 2006, empl 48, sales $5,000,000, cert: NMSDC)

4672 Blue Chip Talent
43252 Woodward Ave, Ste 240
Bloomfield Hills, MI 48302
Contact: Steve Gaura Sr Dir of IT Services
Tel: 248-630-7170
Email: steveg@bctalent.com
Website: www.bctalent.com
Information technology project based services, project management, staff augmentation services & security consulting. (Woman, estab 1994, empl 220, sales $26,500,000, cert: WBENC)

4673   Broadgate Inc.
       830 Kirts Blvd, Ste 400
       Troy, MI 48084
       Contact: Kashi Kotha Dir
       Tel: 248-918-0110
       Email: kashi@broadgateinc.com
       Website: www.broadgateinc.com
IT Profetional services, consulting, project services &
software development. (Woman/As-Ind, estab 2006, empl
70, sales $5,000,000, cert: NMSDC)

4674   BSC Solutions, Inc.
       1000 John R. Rd, Ste 203
       Troy, MI 48083
       Contact: Jody Kapale Business Devel Mgr
       Tel: 810-449-3640
       Email: jody@bsc-us.com
       Website: www.BSCSolutionsInc.com
ERP Implementation & support PeopleSoft, Oracle, SAP,
CRM - Siebel & Salesforce, Staff Augmentation/Custom
Application Development, Java, .Net, C#, EDI, Data Ware-
housing, BI, Big Data, Cloud based applications. (As-Ind,
estab 1999, empl 200, sales $11,143,000, cert: NMSDC)

4675   CADworks Solutions, Inc.
       43422 W Oaks Dr, Ste 326
       Novi, MI 48377
       Contact: James Vaughn Jr. President
       Tel: 248-910-9988
       Email: jamesv@cadwrx.com
       Website: www.cadwrx.com
CAD systems integration, lifecycle mgmt consulting. (AA,
estab 1995, empl 5, sales $153,000, cert: NMSDC)

4676   CAEtech International, Inc.
       43000 W 9 Mile Rd, Ste 305
       Novi, MI 48375
       Contact: Vic Havele President
       Tel: 248-342-7661
       Email: havelev@caetech.com
       Website: www.caetech.com
Contract & direct placement staffing svcs, engineering svcs,
IT svcs. (As-Ind, estab 1989, empl 55, sales , cert: NMSDC)

4677   Ciber Global, LLC
       3270 West Big Beaver Road
       Troy, MI 48084
       Contact: Neal King Sr Client Partner
       Tel: 603-661-0146
       Email: nking@ciber.com
       Website: www.ciber.com
Software Eng., Systems Eng., Software and Systems Test,
Configuration Mgmt, Systems Anaylsis, Intelligence, Data
Warehousing, Business Intelligence, Network Security,
Network Engineering, Information Technology (As-Ind,
estab 1974, empl 11000, sales , cert: NMSDC)

4678   CnC Controls
       5745 W Maple #217
       West Bloomfield, MI 48322
       Contact: Abizer Rasheed President
       Tel: 248-681-7722
       Email: arasheed@cnccontrolsusa.com
       Website: www.cnccontrolsusa.com
Information technology: installation, repairs & maintenance
services. (Woman/As-Ind, estab 1983, empl 10, sales
$2,102,000, cert: NMSDC, WBENC)

4679   Cogent Integrated Business Solutions, Inc.
       2855 Coolidge Hwy Ste 112
       Troy, MI 48084
       Contact: Srini Thonta Dir SAP Solutions
       Tel: 248-649-4444
       Email: sthonta@cogentibs.com
       Website: www.cogentIBS.com
IT services & solutions, SAP services. (Minority, Woman,
estab 2005, empl 30, sales $3,795,325, cert: WBENC)

4680   Communications Professionals, Inc.
       2265 Livernois Rd
       Troy, MI 48083
       Contact: Andrew Wallace CEO
       Tel: 248-557-0100
       Email: awallace2@cpgp.com
       Website: www.cpgp.com
Information technology: dev, implementation & application, hardware, software & technological analysis. (AA,
estab 1997, empl 15, sales $15,000,000, cert: NMSDC)

4681   CompuSoft Integrated Solutions, Inc.
       31500 W 13 Mile Rd Ste 200
       Farmington Hills, MI 48334
       Contact: Pratap Koganti CEO
       Tel: 248-538-9494
       Email: pkoganti@compusoft-is.com
       Website: www.compusoft-is.com
Internet & intranet, e-commerce dev, ERP, Oracle, SAP,
PeopleSoft, client/server software. (As-Ind, estab 1997,
empl 80, sales $8,500,000, cert: State, NMSDC)

4682   Computech Corporation
       W 100 Kirby St
       Detroit, MI 48202
       Contact: Sai Kancharla Project Mgr
       Tel: 248-622-1420
       Email: sai.kancharla@computechcorp.com
       Website: www.computechcorp.com
Information technology staffing & project svcs: custom
programming, enterprise resource planning, CRM,
ebusiness, database programming. (Minority, estab
1996, empl 250, sales , cert: NMSDC)

4683   Custom Business Solutions, Inc.
       40480 Grand River Ave, Ste 107
       Novi, MI 48375
       Contact: Jeff Burton President of Sales
       Tel: 248-478-5300
       Email: burtonj@custom-it.com
       Website: www.custom-it.com
IT consulting, project mgmt, system & application
architecture, disaster recovery & business continuity,
business process engineering, software development,
network design & support, internet & web technologies,
ERP systems. (Woman, estab 1995, empl 75, sales
$4,042,000, cert: WBENC)

4684   Dechen Consulting Group, Inc.
       37000 Grand River Ave., Ste. 330
       Farmington Hills, MI 48335
       Contact: Raj Dechen President
       Tel: 248-346-4590
       Email: rdechen@dcg-us.com
       Website: www.dcg-us.com/
IT professional staffing & project-based implementation,
PeopleSoft, SAP & Oracle software application packages,
staff augmentation services, design, develop & implement Business Intelligence. (As-Ind, estab 1998, empl
100, sales $11,000,000, cert: NMSDC)

4685   Emergent Systems Corp.
       3 Parklane Blvd Ste 1120 West
       Dearborn, MI 48126
       Contact: Saleem Qureshi VP- Engineering
       Tel: 313-996-8285
       Email: saleemq@emergentsys.com
       Website: www.EmergentSys.com
Engineering, design, product development & styling, CAD/
CAM/CAE consulting, software development, engineering
design staffing, tooling design, offshore capability, engi-
neering software products, KBE, knowledge management.
(As-Ind, estab 1997, empl 40, sales $7,000,000, cert:
NMSDC)

4686   Epitec
       24800 Denso Dr Ste. 150
       Southfield, MI 48033
       Contact: Kelleen Young
       Tel: 469-454-3649
       Email: businessdevelopment@epitec.com
       Website: www.epitec.com
IT staff augmentation. (AA, estab 1978, empl 1000, sales
$75,000,000, cert: NMSDC)

4687   ESM Group LLC
       43422 W Oaks Dr, Ste 298
       Novi, MI 48377
       Contact: Jayme Rossiter President
       Tel: 248-921-7452
       Email: jrossiter@esmonline.com
       Website: www.esmonline.com
Information technogy services & staffing. (Woman, estab
1992, empl 23, sales $1,800,000, cert: WBENC)

4688   Excel Technical Services, Inc.
       200 Kirts Blvd Ste A
       Troy, MI 48084
       Contact: Pat Kirby Managing Dir
       Tel: 248-310-9413
       Email: patkirby@exceltechnical.com
       Website: www.exceltechnical.com
Technical staffing & document management svcs, supplier
quality & development. (Hisp, estab 1998, empl 30, sales
$2,500,000, cert: NMSDC)

4689   GDI Infotech, Inc.
       3775 Varsity Dr
       Ann Arbor, MI 48108
       Contact: Vishal Chaubal Dir
       Tel: 734-477-6900
       Email: vishal@gdii.com
       Website: www.gdii.com
Enterprise information technology consulting & services.
(As-Ind, estab 1993, empl 125, sales $10,200,000, cert:
NMSDC)

4690   HRU Technical Resources
       3451 Dunckel Road Ste 200
       Lansing, MI 48911
       Contact: Todd Briggs VP Business Dev
       Tel: 517-272-5888
       Email: briggs.todd@hru-tech.com
       Website: www.hru-tech.com
Engineering, IT, design, mfg, technical staffing services:
contract or direct hire. (Woman, estab 1980, empl 215,
sales $20,500,517, cert: WBENC)

4691   HTC Global Services Inc.
       3270 W Big Beaver
       Troy, MI 48084
       Contact: Gary Gozdor Dir
       Tel: 763-245-0746
       Email: kevin.kraft@htcinc.com
       Website: www.htcinc.com
Information technology services and solutions, Business
Process Services. (As-Pac, estab 1990, empl 11000, sales
$450,000,000, cert: NMSDC)

4692   ICONMA, LLC
       850 Stephenson Hwy Ste 612
       Troy, MI 48083
       Contact: Lauren Diener Sales Operations Mgr
       Tel: 888-451-2519
       Email: rfp@iconma.com
       Website: www.iconma.com
IT consultant staffing: contract, contract to hire &
fulltime.
 (Woman, estab 2000, empl 2985, sales $188,000,000,
cert: WBENC)

4693   IGI Detroit dba Villc, LLC
       1020 Metro Dr
       Commerce, MI 48390
       Contact: Pat Hernandez President
       Tel: 248-624-6520
       Email: pat@werigi.com
       Website: www.werigi.com
Large scale, ultra high resolution systems for advanced
visualization applications and commercial AV systems.
Automotive engineering and design, military collaboration and intelligence, oil and gas exploration, command
and control room. (Hisp, estab 2003, empl 1, sales , cert:
NMSDC)

4694   Iknowvate Technologies, Inc.
       17197 N Laurel Park Dr, Ste 307
       Livonia, MI 48152
       Contact: Sriram Rajakumar Sales Dir
       Tel: 734-432-0634
       Email: rkumar@iknowvate.com
       Website: www.iknowvate.com
IT staff augmentation, application dev, maintenance &
support, project mgmt, real time embedded systems, e-
strategize, portals, implement & deploy SCM, CRM, ERP
packaged solutions, business intelligence solutions, etc.
(As-Pac, estab 2001, empl 40, sales $2,000,000, cert:
NMSDC)

4695   Infomatics Inc.
       31313 Northwestern Hwy, Ste 219
       Farmington Hills, MI 48334
       Contact: Ragan Raghunathan Founder
       Tel: 248-865-0300
       Email: rajan@infomatinc.com
       Website: www.infomatinc.com
Information technology staffing, web technologies, Java,
J2EE , ERP/CRM-Oracle, SAP, database administration,
Oracle, DB2 SQL Server, content management. (Minority,
Woman, estab 1998, empl 225, sales $25,000,000, cert:
NMSDC)

4696　Information Systems Resources
　　　1800 Bailey St
　　　Dearborn, MI 48124
　　　Contact: Eric Levy Business Devel Mgr
　　　Tel:　　313-274-6400
　　　Email: elevy@is-resources.com
　　　Website: www.is-resources.com
Computer asset mgmt services, professional services, lifecycle mgmt, dist hardware & software. (AA, estab 1989, empl 48, sales $4,856,426, cert: NMSDC, CPUC)

4697　Internet Operations Center, Inc.
　　　200 Galleria Officentre Ste 109
　　　Southfield, MI 48034
　　　Contact: Rhonda Hall Business Dev Mgr
　　　Tel:　　248-204-8800
　　　Email: thayward@iocenter.net
　　　Website: www.iocenter.net
Managed internet service provider, web development, help center, EDI, TPP appilcation development. (As-Pac, estab 1996, empl 56, sales , cert: NMSDC)

4698　IP Consulting, Inc.
　　　3635 29th St
　　　Kentwood, MI 49512
　　　Contact: Cherri Mosey VP
　　　Tel:　　616-855-9967
　　　Email: cherri.mosey@ipconsultinginc.com
　　　Website: www.ipconsultinginc.com
Information technology solutions, design, implementation & support services. (Hisp, estab 2006, empl 10, sales $1,400,000, cert: NMSDC, 8(a))

4699　IPS Technology Services
　　　363 W Big Beaver Rd Ste 100
　　　Troy, MI 48084
　　　Contact: Pradip Sengupta CEO
　　　Tel:　　248-835-9895
　　　Email: info@ipstechnologyservices.com
　　　Website: www.ipstechnologyservices.com
Information technology services: customer systems development, CAD/CAM/CAE/PDM svcs, systems integration, HR technology implementation, consulting, & ERP implementation. (As-Pac, estab 2000, empl 22, sales $1,200,000, cert: NMSDC)

4700　JRD Systems, Inc.
　　　42450 Hayes Rd Ste 3
　　　Clinton Township, MI 48038
　　　Contact: Melissa Husmillo
　　　Tel:　　586-416-1500
　　　Email: contact@jrdsi.com
　　　Website: www.jrdsi.com
Information technology solutions, services, & staffing. (Minority, estab 2000, empl 80, sales $5,500,000, cert: State, NMSDC)

4701　Logic Solutions, Inc.
　　　2929 Plymouth Rd Ste 207
　　　Ann Arbor, MI 48105
　　　Contact: Grace Lee CFO
　　　Tel:　　734-930-0009
　　　Email: grace@logicsolutions.com
　　　Website: www.logicsolutions.com
Custom web based software development & integration. (As-Pac, estab 1995, empl 104, sales $8,261,867, cert: NMSDC)

4702　Millennium Software Inc.
　　　2000 Town Center Dr Ste, 300
　　　Southfield, MI 48075
　　　Contact: Anu Anand President
　　　Tel:　　248-213-1800
　　　Email: anu@webmsi.com
　　　Website: www.webmsi.com
IT consulting, project developemnt, contract programming, web designing. (Woman/As-Pac, estab 1996, empl 165, sales $23,129,824, cert: NMSDC, WBENC)

4703　Miracle Software Systems
　　　45625 Grand River Ave
　　　Novi, MI 48374
　　　Contact: Pandu Byroj IT SALES LEAD
　　　Tel:　　234-233-1851
　　　Email: pbyroj@miraclesoft.com
　　　Website: www.miraclesoft.com/
IT consulting: SAP, Oracle, PeopleSoft, JDEdwards, Solaris, J2EE. webMethods, MQ, EAI, Cognos, MicroStrategy, VB, ASP,.Net, SQL, Siebel, Informatica, TIBCO, Vitria, etc. (Minority, estab 1994, empl 2750, sales $100,000,000, cert: NMSDC)

4704　Netlink Software Group
　　　999 Tech Row
　　　Madison Heights, MI 48071
　　　Contact: Bob Pniewski Exec Dir NA Sales
　　　Tel:　　248-535-3250
　　　Email: bpniewski@netlink.com
　　　Website: www.netlink.com
IT Business solutions: Automotive, High Tech, Health Care. Education. Solutions experience in Portals, Intranet/Extranet, Software Applications, Exchanges Wireless, eLearning, Program Management (As-Ind, estab 1997, empl 112, sales , cert: NMSDC)

4705　Ocean Inc. dba Omega Systems
　　　5324 Plainfield Ave NE
　　　Grand Rapids, MI 49525
　　　Contact: Nadeem Hamid President
　　　Tel:　　616-361-6677
　　　Email: nadeem.hamid@oceaninc.com
　　　Website: www.oceaninc.com
Computer solutions, components, notebooks, printers, assembly, packing & configuration, web development, web hosting, surveillance camera solutions & installation. (As-Ind, estab 1984, empl 8, sales $600,000, cert: NMSDC)

4706　Ojibway, Inc.
　　　3720 High St
　　　Ecorse, MI 48229
　　　Contact: James Richardson Acct Exec
　　　Tel:　　248-526-0555
　　　Email: jrichardson@theojibwaygroup.com
　　　Website: www.theojibwaygroup.com
Information technology, leasing & financial services, computer equipment & services. (Nat Ame, estab 1988, empl 13, sales $3,500,000, cert: NMSDC)

4707   Open Systems Technologies DE, LLC
       605 Seward NW, Ste 101
       Grand Rapids, MI 49504
       Contact: David Gerrity Exec Dir
       Tel: 616-574-3500
       Email: dgerrity@ostusa.com
       Website: www.ostusa.com
Resell computer hardware & software, business process
solutions, data center solutions, application development,
managed services. (Nat Ame, estab 1997, empl 110, sales
$68,873,026, cert: NMSDC)

4708   OpenLogix Corporation
       28345 Beck Rd Ste 308
       Wixom, MI 48393
       Contact: Rick Pardy Acct Mgr
       Tel: 919-200-4333
       Email: mbe@open-logix.com
       Website: www.open-logix.com
SOA, business integration, portals & business intelligence,
SAP, WebSphere, web svcs, webMethods, Java/J2EE,
Informatica, business objects.. (As-Ind, estab 2006, empl
45, sales $18,000,000, cert: NMSDC)

4709   Paskon, Inc.
       25899 W 12 Mile Rd Ste 380
       Southfield, MI 48034
       Contact: Sharath Konanur CEO
       Tel: 248-440-2334
       Email: sharath@paskon.com
       Website: www.paskon.com
Business & Technology Consulting, SAP Development
Implementations. (Hisp, estab 1999, empl 50, sales
$3,530,000, cert: NMSDC)

4710   Peer Solutions Group, Inc.
       30777 Northwestern Hwy Ste 107
       Farmington Hills, MI 48334
       Contact: Mohamed Irfan Peeran CEO
       Tel: 248-522-7767
       Email: mpeeran@peersolutionsgroup.com
       Website: www.peersolutionsgroup.com
IT Consulting Staffing, Recruiting, Project Management,
Technology Consulting. (As-Ind, estab 2002, empl 60, sales
$5,412,715, cert: NMSDC)

4711   PeoplePlus software Inc.
       3131 South State St. Ste 250
       Ann Arbor, MI 48108
       Contact: Tom Bastian Solutions Consultant
       Tel: 734-531-6620
       Email: tbastian@peopleplussoftware.com
       Website: www.peopleplussoftware.com
Software design & development, SaaS cloud supply chain
software. IT staffing, Mobile app development. (Minority,
Woman, estab 2007, empl 35, sales $1,500,000, cert:
NMSDC)

4712   Preferred Data Systems, LLC
       39100 Country Club Dr Ste 200
       Farmington Hills, MI 48331
       Contact: Chad Muncy
       Tel: 248-522-4442
       Email: cmuncy@pdsnetworking.com
       Website: www.pdsnetworking.com
IT networking infrastructure & consulting services.
(Minority, Woman, estab 1982, empl 12, sales $510,000,
cert: NMSDC)

4713   Prince Technology Solutions, Inc.
       51221 Schoenherr, Ste 106
       Shelby Township, MI 48315
       Contact: Tigi Duraku CEO
       Tel: 810-512-4253
       Email: jessica@princetechnology.com
       Website: www.princetechnology.com
IT consulting services, contract & permanent positions.
(Woman, estab 1998, empl 50, sales $4,500,000, cert:
WBENC)

4714   PROLIM Global Corporation
       30445 Northwestern Hwy Ste 380
       Farmington Hills, MI 48334
       Contact: Prabhu Patil President
       Tel: 248-522-6959
       Email: prabhu.patil@prolim.com
       Website: www.prolim.com
IT & PLM solutions & consulting services. (As-Ind, estab
2005, empl 350, sales , cert: NMSDC)

4715   Pro-Motion Technology Group
       29755 Beck Rd
       Wixom, MI 48393
       Contact: Brian Flewelling Acct Mgr
       Tel: 248-668-3100
       Email: hello@promotion.tech
       Website: www.promotion.tech
Audiovisual technology solutions. (Woman, estab 2002,
empl 45, sales $25,000,000, cert: WBENC)

4716   Ragha Systems, LLC
       8390 Warwick Groves Ct
       Grand Blanc, MI 48439
       Contact: Veera R Thota CEO
       Tel: 810-694-6551
       Email: vthota@raghasys.com
       Website: www.raghasys.com
IT solutions. (Woman/As-Ind, estab 2002, empl 4, sales
$240,000, cert: NMSDC, WBENC)

4717   Ramsoft Systems, Inc..
       29777 Telegraph Rd Ste 2250
       Southfield, MI 48034
       Contact: Rama Gudivada COO
       Tel: 248-354-0100
       Email: rama@ramsoft.net
       Website: www.ramsoft.net
IT solutions, staff augmentation: onsite, offsite,
nearshore, offshore projects. (Minority, Woman, estab
1993, empl 100, sales , cert: NMSDC)

4718   Rapid Global Business Solutions, Inc.
       1200 Stephenson Hwy
       Troy, MI 48083
       Contact: Vivek Thakur Business Dev Mgr
       Tel: 248-589-1135
       Email: vt@rgbsi.com
       Website: www.rgbsi.com
Engineering svcs: staffing, mechanical, electrical &
electronics, mfg, automotive, design & release, embedded systems, systems modeling & simulation, CAD/CAM/
CAE/PIM svcs, software dev, contract & permanent.
(Minority, estab 1997, empl 1800, sales $80,000,000,
cert: NMSDC)

4719   Real World Technologies Inc.
28423 Orchard Lake Rd Ste 203
Farmington Hills, MI 48334
Contact: Vishnu Jampala President
Tel: 248-987-6008
Email: vishnujam@rwts.net
Website: www.rwts.net
Information Technology Solutions & Business Analyst solutions, Application development, Enterprise resource planning, Data-Warehousing, Customer Relationship Management, Business Analysis, Project Management. (As-Pac, estab 2005, empl 40, sales $3,155,012, cert: State, NMSDC, SDB)

4720   Rumba Solutions, LLC
44648 Mound Rd, Ste 190
Sterling Heights, MI 48314
Contact: Jibu Joseph Managing Dir
Tel: 248-978-3674
Email: jibu.joseph@rumbasolutions.com
Website: www.rumbasolutions.com
Application development, staff augmentation & consulting services, Mobile, Web Applications (Cloud and On premise), IoT, Identity & Access Management, Portal Development. (As-Ind, estab 2010, empl 50, sales , cert: NMSDC)

4721   Skansoft Inc.
4681 Amberwood Ct
Rochester, MI 48306
Contact: Srividya Sadasivam President
Tel: 248-276-4770
Email: srividya@skandasoftinc.com
Website: www.skandasoftinc.com
Integrated information technology consulting & placement services, IT professionals. (Woman/As-Ind, estab 2006, empl 11, sales $1,118,340, cert: NMSDC)

4722   SoftCorp International, Inc.
2838 E Long Lake Ste 236
Troy, MI 48085
Contact: Raja Puli President
Tel: 248-918-2224
Email: vinod@softcorpinc.com
Website: www.softcorpinc.com
Staff augmentation, permanent & temporary IT resources. (As-Ind, estab 1997, empl 87, sales $6,100,000, cert: NMSDC)

4723   SoftPath Technologies LLC
16801 Newburgh Rd, Ste 112
Livonia, MI 48154
Contact: Rohith Thumma Reg Sales Mgr
Tel: 248-522-7011
Email: supplier@softpathtech.com
Website: www.softpathtech.com
Global Staffing, Technology, Services & Consulting. (As-Ind, estab 2006, empl 150, sales $6,012,589, cert: NMSDC)

4724   SunSoft Technologies Inc.
21772 Manchester Ct
Farmington Hills, MI 48335
Contact: Rashmi Upadhyaya President
Tel: 248-426-9805
Email: rashmiu@sunsoft.us
Website: www.sunsofttechnologies.com
Engineering & IT staffing. (Minority, Woman, estab 2000, empl 45, sales $3,705,233, cert: NMSDC, WBENC)

4725   Synergy Computer Solutions, Inc,
30700 Telegraph Rd Ste 2615
Bingham Farms, MI 48025
Contact: Ruslan Avshalumov Accountant
Tel: 248-723-7220
Email: ravshalumov@synergycom.com
Website: www.synergycom.com
Information techology & engineering consulting & staffing: implementation & integration, infrastructure support, web solutions, project mgmt, data warehousing, EDI, off shore devel. (As-Pac, estab 1995, empl 250, sales $16,000,000, cert: NMSDC)

4726   Synova Inc.
1000 Town Center Ste 700
Southfield, MI 48075
Contact: Iain McKendrick Dir of Automotive & Mfg
Tel: 248-281-2500
Email: imckendrick@synovainc.com
Website: www.synovainc.com
IT Staffing, Managed Programs, Offshore, Creative Technical Outsourcing, Projects and Solution Service offerings. (As-Pac, estab 1998, empl 1800, sales $117,000,000, cert: NMSDC)

4727   Syntel Inc.
525 E Big Beaver 3rd Fl
Troy, MI 48083
Contact: ShyamSundar Dittakavi Dir- Lifesciences
Tel: 602-391-8868
Email: vendor_registration@syntelinc.com
Website: www.syntelinc.com
IT lifecycle solutions, applications outsourcing, development, enhancements, maintenance, integration & technology transformation & support. (Minority, estab , empl , sales $923,828,000, cert: NMSDC)

4728   Systems Technology Group, Inc. (STG)
3001 W Big Beaver Rd Ste 500e
Troy, MI 48084
Contact: Anup Popat CEO
Tel: 248-712-6702
Email: apopat@stgit.com
Website: www.stgit.com
Application software development outsourcing svcs: onsite & offshore. (Minority, estab 1985, empl 600, sales $102,000,000, cert: NMSDC)

4729   Systems Technology International, Inc.
39555 Orchard Hill Pl, Ste 530
Novi, MI 48375
Contact: Rodney Tesarz Dir of Sales
Tel: 248-735-3900
Email: rodney.tesarz@sti-world.com
Website: www.sti-world.com
Information technology & engineering: contract staffing, off shore services, software development & testing, engineering design & diagnostics. (AA, estab 0, empl , sales $7,500,000, cert: NMSDC)

4730   Technosoft Corporation
1 Towne Square 6th Fl
Southfield, MI 48076
Contact: Radhakrishnan Gurusamy CEO
Tel: 248-603-2666
Email: supplierdiversity@technosoftcorp.com
Website: www.technosoftcorp.com
IT staffing, IT consulting, system integration & business process outsourcing. (Minority, Woman, estab 1996, empl 4000, sales $123,867,758, cert: NMSDC)

4731   Tekshapers Inc.
       2018 Harbor Village Ave
       Keego Harbor, MI 48320
       Contact: Nalini Kolli President
       Tel: 248-470-5733
       Email: nalini@tekshapers.com
       Website: www.tekshapers.com
Software development, consulting services. (Woman,
estab 0, empl , sales , cert: NMSDC)

4732   Touch World, Inc.
       31500 W 13 Mile Rd Ste 101
       Farmington Hills, MI 48334
       Contact: Gordon McKenna President
       Tel: 248-539-3700
       Email: gordon.mckenna@touchworld.com
       Website: www.touchworld.com
Computer software consulting & staff agumentation svcs:
ERP, Client Server, Microsoft, UNIX, workflow, supply chain
mgmt, ILVS, EDI , barcoding, RFID, Gentran, Future 3,
Harbinger, Mercator, Trinary, AS 400, mainframe products.
(As-Pac, estab 1996, empl 17, sales $1,550,000, cert:
NMSDC)

4733   Trillium Teamologies Inc.
       219 S Main St
       Royal Oak, MI 48067
       Contact: Greg Stanalajczo COO
       Tel: 248-584-2080
       Email: stano@trilliumteam.com
       Website: www.trilliumteam.com
IT solutions: 2D & 3D animations, web dev, flash animations, IT consulting, e-commerce, project mgmt, systems
integration & software dev, etc. (Woman, estab 1996,
empl 63, sales , cert: WBENC)

4734   TTi Global
       6001 N. Adams Road Ste 185
       Bloomfield Hills, MI 48304
       Contact: April Bousamra Controller
       Tel: 248-853-5550
       Email: abousamra@tti-global.com
       Website: www.tti-global.com
Training design, development & delivery, outsourcing
services, staffing services. (Woman, estab 1976, empl 780,
sales $38,100,000, cert: WBENC)

4735   Unified Business Technologies Inc.
       315 Indusco Ct
       Troy, MI 48083
       Contact: Allyssia Gutierrez Sales Rep
       Tel: 248-677-9550
       Email: allyssia.gutierrez@ubtus.com
       Website: www.emd.ubtus.com
Software consulting services & staffing. (Minority, Woman,
estab 1997, empl 150, sales , cert: WBENC)

4736   V2Soft Inc.
       300 Enterprise Court
       Bloomfield Hills, MI 48302
       Contact: Varchasvi Shankar President
       Tel: 248-904-1702
       Email: vs@v2soft.com
       Website: www.v2soft.com
Software business solutions, consulting, contract services
& staff augmentation, project outsourcing, offshore
development. (Minority, estab 1998, empl 1200, sales
$37,000,000, cert: NMSDC)

4737   Vigilant Technologies
       1050 Wilshire Dr Ste 307
       Troy, MI 48084
       Contact: Sameera buksh VP
       Tel: 248-396-2665
       Email: sameera@vigilant-inc.com
       Website: www.vigilant-inc.com
Oracle Managed Services, Oracle Professional Services,
Oracle Talent, Staff Augmentation, QA Testing, Oracle
Licensing. (Woman/As-Ind, estab 1999, empl 69, sales
$12,574,008, cert: NMSDC)

4738   Vision Information Technologies, Inc.
       3031 W Grand Blvd, Ste 600
       Detroit, MI 48202
       Contact: Christine Rice President
       Tel: 313-420-2000
       Email: info@visionit.com
       Website: www.visionit.com
IT staffing, e-business consulting & web application dev.
(Hisp, estab 1997, empl 1000, sales $209,000,000, cert:
NMSDC)

4739   Vivek Systems, Inc.
       2163 Avon Industrial Dr
       Rochester Hills, MI 48309
       Contact: Bose Vivek President
       Tel: 248-293-1070
       Email: bvivek@viveksystems.com
       Website: www.viveksystems.com
CAD/engineering solution company. (As-Ind, estab 0,
empl , sales $1,080,000, cert: NMSDC)

4740   WebRunners, Inc. dba W3R Consulting
       1000 Town Center Ste 1150
       Southfield, MI 48044
       Contact: CEO
       Tel: 248-358-1002
       Email: info@w3r.com
       Website: www.w3r.com
Infrastructure planning & design, custom hosting
solutions, directory svcs design, systems admin,
middleware & database support, metrics tools, monitoring & reporting, firewall mgmt & security, VPN architecture, application integration. (AA, estab 1995, empl 400,
sales $36,500,000, cert: NMSDC)

4741   Weldon Enterprise Global IT, LLC
       3031 W Grand Blvd, Ste 695
       Detroit, MI 48202
       Contact: Markeith Weldon CEO
       Tel: 313-687-4990
       Email: mweldon@weglobalit.com
       Website: www.weglobalit.com
IT managed services, technical staffing & non technical
staffing. (AA, estab 2011, empl 10, sales $1,000,000,
cert: NMSDC)

4742   WIT Inc.
       900 Tower Dr Ste 325
       Troy, MI 48098
       Contact: Quaid Saifee President
       Tel: 248-641-5900
       Email: quaid@witinc.com
       Website: www.witinc.com
Web site design & development, internet branding,
graphic design, content management solutions, database design & consulting, web application development,
training, web collaboration. (As-Ind, estab 1996, empl
20, sales $2,500,000, cert: NMSDC)

4743 Youngsoft Inc.
49197 Wixom Tech Dr Ste B
Wixom, MI 48393
Contact: Chris Reaume Dir of Sales Operations
Tel: 248-675-1200
Email: chrisr@youngsoft.com
Website: www.youngsoft.com
Information technology services: staffing support, consulting, solution design & development. (As-Ind, estab 1996, empl 130, sales $11,690,000, cert: NMSDC)

Minnesota

4744 AMI Imaging Systems, Inc.
7815 Telegraph Rd
Bloomington, MN 55438
Contact: Leah Swartzbaugh VP
Tel: 952-828-0080
Email: leahs@ami-imaging.com
Website: www.ami-imaging.com
Content mgmt, document imaging, scanning, imaging systems, workflow, process automation, remittance processing, aperture card scanning, microfilm & microfiche scanning, large format & roll film scanning. (Woman, estab 1982, empl 15, sales , cert: WBENC)

4745 Analytiks International, Inc.
10 S Fifth St Ste 720
Minneapolis, MN 55402
Contact: Mike Regan Marketing & Sales
Tel: 612-305-4312
Email: mregan@aii-3.com
Website: www.aii-3.com
SAS consulting & resource placement services. (As-Ind, estab 2004, empl 6, sales $200,000, cert: NMSDC)

4746 Arrowhead Promotion & Fulfillment Co., Inc.
1105 SE 8th St
Grand Rapids, MN 55744
Contact: Katie Prokop Christmas CEO
Tel: 218-327-1165
Email: katie@apfco.com
Website: www.arrowheadpromotion.com
Software development, customized reporting, fulfillment activities. (Woman, estab 1983, empl 250, sales $13,000,000, cert: WBENC)

4747 Backbone Consultants
50 S 6th St Ste 1360
Minneapolis, MN 55402
Contact: Operations & Acct Mgr
Tel: 612-568-7167
Email: info@backboneconsultants.com
Website: www.backboneconsultants.com
IT Audit Outsource & Co-source, IT Risk Assessment & Advisory, IT Sourcing Risks, Information Security Risk Assessment, Financial Institutions Data Privacy (GLBA) Reviews. (Minority, estab 2008, empl 13, sales $1,897,914, cert: State)

4748 Barnes Business Solutions, Inc.
4857 Island View Dr
Mound, MN 55364
Contact: Maria Barnes President
Tel: 630-715-4452
Email: mbarnes@barnesbusinesssolutions.com
Website: www.BarnesBusinessSolutions.com
Core competency: Custom programming services, Microsoft Access databases, SQL Server databases, Microsoft Excel tools & macros, Microsoft Office integration, Windows-based software solutions. (Woman, estab 2008, empl 1, sales $139,235, cert: WBENC)

4749 BCforward
7701 France Ave S, Ste 325
Edina, MN 55435
Contact: Kortney Cartwright District Branch Mgr
Tel: 954-540-4064
Email: kortney.cartwright@bcforward.com
Website: www.bcforward.com
IT consulting & staffing. (AA, estab , empl , sales $2,500,000, cert: NMSDC)

4750 BPK Inc.
12800 Whitewater Dr, Ste 100
Minnetonka, MN 55439
Contact: Rajeev Bhatia CEO
Tel: 612-293-7585
Email: rajeev@bpktech.com
Website: www.bpktech.com
IT Consulting, Agile, Software Development, IT Services, Financial consulting, Staff augmentation, Staffing solutions, Java, .Net, Project Manager, Sap, SQ, Investment management, Wealth management. (As-Ind, estab 2006, empl 10, sales $4,000,000, cert: NMSDC)

4751 BTM Global Consulting LLC
330 S Second Ave Ste 450
Minneapolis, MN 55401
Contact: Lesli Hines President
Tel: 612-238-8801
Email: lesli.hines@btmgcs.com
Website: www.btmgcs.com
Custom application development, software development, integration, implementation. (As-Pac, estab 2004, empl 85, sales $5,100,000, cert: NMSDC)

4752 Business Technology Solutions, Inc.
7441 Windmill Dr
Chanhassen, MN 55317
Contact: Brian Hugh President
Tel: 612-208-7287
Email: brian.hugh@btsbiz.com
Website: www.btsbiz.com
Information systems integration/development, project management, business/system analysis, large-scale application/infrastructure upgrades, packaged software evaluation/selection & database performance analysis & tuning. (As-Pac, estab 1996, empl 2, sales $290,804, cert: State)

4753   Charter Solutions, Inc.
3033 Campus Dr Ste N160
Plymouth, MN 55441
Contact: Alexander Wittig Sales Exec
Tel: 763-230-6100
Email: alex.wittig@chartersolutions.com
Website: www.chartersolutions.com
Information technology solutions, mgmt consulting,
application dev, system integration & staffing. (Woman,
estab 1997, empl 55, sales $4,000,000, cert: WBENC)

4754   Clarity Tek, Inc.
2859 Aspen Lake Dr NE
Blaine, MN 55449
Contact: Abida Banu President
Tel: 612-567-0835
Email: abida.banu@claritytek.com
Website: www.claritytek.com/
Placement, Recruiting, IT Consulting, IT Services, Staff
augmetation, IT Contractor Services, Software develop-
ment services, Software maintenance services. (Minority,
Woman, estab 2012, empl 4, sales , cert: City)

4755   Crown CyberSystems
160 Birchwood Ave
St. Paul, MN 55110
Contact: Austin Kasper Mgr of Client Partnerships
Tel: 612-207-7423
Email: akasper@crowncybersystems.com
Website: www.crowncybersystems.com/
IT Solutions, managed IT Department Services. (Woman,
estab 2010, empl 10, sales $6,000,000, cert: WBENC)

4756   CS Solutions, Inc.
7525 Mitchell Road Ste 106
Eden Prairie, MN 55344
Contact: Sonia Stephen Staffing Mgr
Tel: 651-271-4477
Email: sonia@cssoln.com
Website: www.cssolutionsinc.com
IT consulting, staff augmentation, project outsourcing,
solution design & develop, data warehousing & admin, e-
commerce security, web develop. (As-Ind, estab 1996,
empl 30, sales $1,200,000, cert: NMSDC)

4757   Denysys Corporation
2400 Blaisdell Ave Ste 202
Minneapolis, MN 55404
Contact: Philip Denny President
Tel: 612-869-7617
Email: philip.denny@denysys.com
Website: www.denysys.com
Information technology, administrative & management
consulting services. (AA, estab 1991, empl 35, sales
$4,100,540, cert: State)

4758   Enclipse Corp.
331 2nd Ave S Ste 703
Minneapolis, MN 55401
Contact: Mohammed Halim Client Relationship Mgr
Tel: 612-360-4713
Email: halimm@enclipse.com
Website: www.enclipse.com
Professional consulting svcs, managed svcs & solutions
design & development: identifying organizational strate-
gies & objectives, design, develop & implement end-to-
end software solutions. (As-Pac, estab 2002, empl 128,
sales $10,000,000, cert: NMSDC)

4759   Genisys Technologies, Inc.
3545 Plymouth Blvd, Ste 115
Plymouth, MN 55447
Contact: Mohan Dhavileswarapu CEO
Tel: 763-205-4883
Email: mohan@genisystechnologies.com
Website: www.genisystechnologies.com
Management, IT staffing & solutions, business informa-
tion, system design, planning, development & imple-
mentation. (As-Ind, estab 2013, empl 15, sales
$2,000,000, cert: NMSDC)

4760   Horizontal Integration, Inc.
1660 Hwy 100 Ste 200
St. Louis Park, MN 55416
Contact: Craig Blake Dir Staffing Operations
Tel: 612-392-7581
Email: finance@horizontalintegration.com
Website: www.horizontalintegration.com
Information technology staff augmentation , software
design & devel, e-commerce, crm apps, enterprise
arcitecture & enterprise app integration, business
performance mgmt app, custom business apps, web app
information architecture & creative design. (As-Pac,
estab 2003, empl 632, sales $101,000,000, cert: NMSDC)

4761   Icon IT Group
3025 Hatbor Ln N, Ste 324
Plymouth, MN 55447
Contact: Shaik Ahmed President
Tel: 612-207-4778
Email: ahmed@iconitgroup.com
Website: www.iconitgroup.com
E-verify Software Development, Web Technologies, ERP
Packages, Data Warehousing, Business Intelligence,
Business Analysis & Quality Assurance. (As-Ind, estab
2013, empl 11, sales $1,200,000, cert: NMSDC)

4762   ILM Professional Services, Inc.
5221 Viking Dr Ste 300
Edina, MN 55435
Contact: Lee Ann Villella Acct Exec
Tel: 952-960-2220
Email: leeann.villella@ilmservice.com
Website: www.ilmservice.com
Integrated, custom web & mobile applications, consult-
ing, project outsourcing on & offsite. (Minority, Woman,
estab 2002, empl 30, sales $4,100,000, cert: NMSDC,
WBENC)

4763   Infinity Systems, Inc.
PO Box 43925
Brooklyn Park, MN 55443
Contact: Michael Perkins Dir of Business Dev
Tel: 612-819-3940
Email: mperknoll@aol.com
Website: www.isimetrics.com
Internet security software. (AA, estab 1993, empl 10,
sales , cert: NMSDC)

4764 Javen Technologies, Inc.
8030 Old Cedar Ave, Ste 225
Bloomington, MN 55425
Contact: Venkat Kota CEO
Tel: 952-698-4454
Email: vkota@javentechnologies.com
Website: www.javentechnologies.com
Oracle, SQL, QA, .Net, Java, Data warehousing, ERP (Peoplesoft, SAP, Oracle Apps) PM, RedPrairie, BA, System admins. (Minority, Woman, estab 2003, empl 80, sales $24,100,000, cert: NMSDC, WBENC)

4765 Jeevtek Inc.
7160 Cahill Rd, Ste 238
Edina, MN 55439
Contact: President
Tel: 612-440-0123
Email: go@jeevtek.com
Website: www.jeevtek.com/
IT staff augmentation & custom software development services, Java, J2EE, web applications, eCommerce, databases, SQL, ERP (Oracle, SAP), .NET, Cloud etc. (Woman/As-Ind, estab 2015, empl 2, sales $230,000, cert: City, WBENC)

4766 JOBMA LLC
13911 Ridgedale Dr, Ste 230
Minnetonka, MN 55305
Contact: Krishna Kant Head of Global Business
Tel: 952-546-3300
Email: krishnak@jobma.com
Website: www.jobma.com/
Cloud based video interview platform, artificial intelligence recruiting, video resumes, and automated recruiting, (Nat Ame, estab 2013, empl 35, sales , cert: NMSDC)

4767 KCS
2395 Ariel St N, Ste A
Saint Paul, MN 55109
Contact: Dorothy C. Richburg CEO
Tel: 651-777-9119
Email: drichburg@keystonecs.com
Website: www.kcscorp.com
IT consulting, technical services, IT training. (Woman/AA, estab 1987, empl 45, sales $9,894,985, cert: State)

4768 Net Anchor, Inc.
202 N 22nd Ave
Minneapolis, MN 55411
Contact: Keni Fegbeboh
Tel: 612-425-2200
Email: kenfegb@netanchor.com
Website: www.netanchor.com
Software & hardware procurement, Help desk support, IT Managed Services, IT Staff Augmentation, Remote monitoring, IT Network Architecture, Network Design & Installation, IT Infrastructure & Data Center, Custom hardware software application development. (AA, estab 2006, empl 1, sales , cert: NMSDC)

4769 New Horizons Computer Learning Center Minnesota
2915 Commers Dr Ste 500
Eagan, MN 55121
Contact: Sammy Peterson Dir of Operations
Tel: 651-900-7203
Email: speterson@newhorizonsmn.com
Website: www.newhorizonsmn.com
IT training. (Woman, estab 2010, empl 18, sales $3,554,749, cert: WBENC)

4770 Performix
7400 Metro blvd Ste 390
Edina, MN 55439
Contact: Sunil Bafna Owner
Tel: 952-893-0143
Email: priya@performixbiz.com
Website: www.performixbiz.com
Software consulting, application integration, database integration, ecommerce application, enterprise application. (Minority, estab 1997, empl 13, sales $1,650,000, cert: State, NMSDC)

4771 Pinnacle Consulting Solutions
17761 Cascade Dr
Eden Prairie, MN 55347
Contact: Ranja Tarafder CEO
Tel: 952-292-4556
Email: ranja@pinnacleconsultingsolutions.com
Website: www.pinnacleconsultingsolutions.com
IT staffing & consulting, Project/Program Management, ITIL Process Management, Application Development, Software Development Life Cycle, Database Design & Development, Business Intelligence, Business Analysis/Data Analysis. (Woman/As-Ind, estab 2014, empl 2, sales $150,000, cert: NMSDC, WBENC)

4772 Pleasant Consulting, LLC
9145 Lyndale Ave S
Bloomington, MN 55420
Contact: Marty Pleasant President
Tel: 952-484-4373
Email: marty@pleasantconsulting.com
Website: www.pleasantconsulting.com
Contract & temporary IT staff, contract to hire staff. (Woman, estab 2012, empl 17, sales $900,000, cert: WBENC)

4773 Procellis Technology Inc.
1330 Lagoon Ave 4th Fl
Minneapolis, MN 55408
Contact: Damian Young CEO
Tel: 612-430-9505
Email: damian.young@procellis.com
Website: www.procellis.com
IT services, servers, storage, virtualization, backup, disaster recovery & cloud services. (AA, estab 2013, empl 19, sales $5,000,000, cert: NMSDC)

4774 SDK Software Inc aka Sudhko Inc.
810 Lilac Dr North Ste #116
Golden Valley, MN 55422
Contact: Hema Arumilli President
Tel: 763-657-7272
Email: sdkhr@sdksoft.com
Website: www.sdksoft.com
Software development svcs, staff augmentation & project mgmt. (Woman/As-Ind, estab 1993, empl 100, sales $13,350,000, cert: City, NMSDC)

4775 Select Source International
13911 Ridgedale Dr, Ste 230
Minnetonka, MN 55305
Contact: Mandeep Sodhi CEO
Tel: 952-546-3300
Email: sales@selectsourceintl.com
Website: www.SelectSourceIntl.com
Temporary Staffing, Information Technology Staffing, Engineering Services, Financial Services, Government Services, Retail Services, Energy & Utility Services, Application Development, Mobile Development. (Nat Ame, estab 2000, empl 771, sales , cert: NMSDC)

4776   TAJ Technologies, Inc.
       7900 International Dr Ste 405
       Bloomington, MN 55425
       Contact: K.C. Sukumar President
       Tel: 651-405-7411
       Email: kcs@tajtech.com
       Website: www.tajtech.com
E-business solutions, e-commerce applications, client/server programming, on-site, off-site & offshore. (As-Ind, estab 1987, empl 208, sales $22,829,532, cert: NMSDC)

4777   Tanson Corp.
       8317 Pillsbury Ave S
       Bloomington, MN 55420
       Contact: Prema Patil President
       Tel: 612-237-5148
       Email: prema@tansoncorp.com
       Website: www.tansoncorp.com
Offer strategic IT staffing, staff augmentation, and direct placement in application development, business intelligence, web solution, quality assurance, & databases. (Woman/As-Ind, estab 2005, empl 20, sales $1,152,872, cert: WBENC)

4778   Tartan Marketing, Inc.
       10467 93rd Ave N
       Maple Grove, MN 55369
       Contact: Margie MacLachlan CEO
       Tel: 763-391-7575
       Email: info@tartanmarketing.com
       Website: www.tartanmarketing.com
We are a full service B2B agency that specializes in helping food, technology and service companies energize their brands and grow their businesses. We employ a completely integrated marketing approach where strategy drives creative execution (Woman, estab 1999, empl 14, sales $2,038,340, cert: WBENC)

4779   Technical Information & Professional Solutions Inc
       15600 35th Ave N Ste 203
       Plymouth, MN 55447
       Contact: Adnan (AJ) Jalil Sales & Marketing Mgr
       Tel: 763-557-7010
       Email: aj@tips2e.com
       Website: www.tips2e.com
Technical staffing: short & long term contract, contract to hire & direct placement staff. (As-Ind, estab 1995, empl 89, sales $9,374,046, cert: NMSDC)

4780   Technology Solutions Group LLC
       60 S 6th St Ste 2800
       Minneapolis, MN 55402
       Contact: Alexandra Farnsworth CEO
       Tel: 888-733-4599
       Email: ali@tsg-mn.com
       Website: www.tsg-mn.com/
BI/Data Mining, IoT & Software Development, Business Intelligence, BI/Data mining, Analytics, Internet of Things, Mobile App Development, Software Development, Web Development, QA/testing. (Woman, estab 2013, empl 1, sales $616,140, cert: WBENC)

4781   The MACRO GROUP, Inc.
       1200 Washington Ave S Ste 350
       Minneapolis, MN 55415
       Contact: Dawn Kuzma Marketing Dir
       Tel: 612-206-3382
       Email: dkuzma@macrogroup.net
       Website: www.macrogroup.net
Project/Program Management, Business Analysis, Process Improvement, Web Application Devel, Application Integration, Electronic Content Management/Electronic Document Management, Technical Analysis & Design, Client/Service Application Devel. (Woman, estab 1987, empl 35, sales $3,700,000, cert: City)

4782   The Sartell Group, Inc.
       800 Hennepin Ave, Ste 400
       Minneapolis, MN 55403
       Contact: Mary Jacobs Dir of Sales
       Tel: 612-548-3101
       Email: mjjacobs@sartellgroup.com
       Website: www.sartellgroup.com
Customized software development. (Woman, estab 1998, empl 16, sales $3,571,250, cert: WBENC)

4783   Titan Data Group Inc.
       6043 Hudson Rd, Ste 399-E
       Woodbury, MN 55125
       Contact: Viswanathan Subramanian President
       Tel: 651-493-0039
       Email: vish@titandata.com
       Website: www.titandata.com
Business strategy, IT consulting, process improvement & technology development. (Woman/As-Ind, estab 2002, empl 20, sales $3,917,883, cert: NMSDC)

4784   Transcomp Inc. DBA: Evolve Systems
       2974 Rice St
       St. Paul, MN 55113
       Contact: Marnie Ochs-Raleigh CEO
       Tel: 651-628-4000
       Email: info@evolve-systems.com
       Website: www.evolve-systems.com
Web development, shopping carts, event management interfaces, Content Management Systems (CMS) & payment forms. (Woman, estab 1993, empl 15, sales $1,128,000, cert: WBENC)

4785   TSG Server and Storage
       10 2nd St NE, Ste 214
       Minneapolis, MN 55413
       Contact: Mike DuBois COO
       Tel: 612-465-0800
       Email: info@tsg-usa.com
       Website: www.tsg-usa.com
Solution Integrator & infrastructure, Hyper-converged infrastructure, cloud and security, networking, storage, server & software, cloud storage, back up & recovery, cybersecurity, IBM Power Systems, IBM Storage. (As-Pac, estab 2001, empl 11, sales , cert: State, City)

4786   Twin Cities Solutions, Inc.
       PO Box 21975
       Eagan, MN 55121
       Contact: Scott Miller CFO
       Tel: 952-583-0367
       Email: smiller@twincs.com
       Website: www.twincs.com
IT consulting: .Net developers, Java developers, business analysts & project managers. (Woman, estab 2000, empl 10, sales $970,000, cert: State)

4787   UpNet Technologies, Inc.
       7825 Washington Ave S Ste 450
       Minneapolis, MN 55439
       Contact: Kevin Amys Controller
       Tel: 952-944-2345
       Email: kevin.amys@upnettec.com
       Website: www.upnettec.com
Information technologies: EDI, XML, CIDX , EDIFACT and
Rosetta net. (Minority, Woman, estab 2000, empl 25, sales
$3,200,000, cert: WBENC)

4788   Virtelligence, Inc
       6216 Baker Road Ste 100
       Eden Prairie, MN 55346
       Contact: Akhtar Chaudhri CEO
       Tel: 952-548-6600
       Email: achaudhri@virtelligence.com
       Website: www.virtelligence.com
Management consulting & technology solutions: project
mgmt, enterprise software dev & integration, business
intelligence & data warehousing, application outsourcing,
staffing. (Minority, estab , empl , sales , cert: NMSDC)

4789   Virtual Matrix Corporation (dba 1 Source, Inc.)
       7200 France Ave S Ste 324
       Edina, MN 55435
       Contact: Bill Hohn Dir
       Tel: 952-835-6400
       Email: hohnb@vmatrixcorp.com
       Website: www.1Source.net
IT staffing/consulting, SAP (HANA certified), ABAP, Java,
PHP, Oracle, Microsoft products (.NETs). (As-Ind, estab
2002, empl 78, sales $3,500,000, cert: State, City, NMSDC)

4790   Visual Consultants, Inc.
       4900 Hwy 169 N, Ste 307
       New Hope, MN 55428
       Contact: Bala Akkina VP
       Tel: 763-533-1000
       Email: bala@visual-consultants.com
       Website: www.visual-consultants.com
IT solutions, enterprise IT applications development & IT
consulting services. (Minority, Woman, estab 2003, empl
42, sales $3,500,000, cert: NMSDC)

4791   Word Tech Secretarial Service Inc.
       6825 York Place N
       Minneapolis, MN 55429
       Contact: Patty Mesenbrink President
       Tel: 612-349-9214
       Email: patty@wordtechtranscription.com
       Website: www.wordtechtranscription.com
Audio Transcription, Digital transcription, Video transcription, transcription, document preparation, audio and video
transcription. (Woman, estab 1986, empl 3, sales , cert:
State, City, SDB)

4792   Xylo Technologies Inc.
       2434 Superior Dr NW Ste 105
       Rochester, MN 55901
       Contact: Dharani Ramamoorthy President
       Tel: 507-289-9956
       Email: dharani@xylotechnologies.com
       Website: www.xylotechnologies.com
IT consulting, web & client/server technolgies, custom
software development & system integration services. (As-
Pac, estab 2000, empl 60, sales $7,043,821, cert: NMSDC)

4793   YFI Technologies
       1422 Thomas Ave
       Saint Paul, MN 55104
       Contact: Reynaldo Lyles President
       Tel: 651-645-4987
       Email: rlyles@yourfutureimage.com
       Website: www.YFItechnologies.com
Mobile & wireless solutions: PDA's, palm devices,
custom software design, mobile database synchronization, IT consulting & staff augmentation. (AA, estab
1994, empl 8, sales , cert: NMSDC)

Missouri

4794   Advanced Resources Group, Inc.
       687 Trade Center Blvd Ste 110
       Chesterfield, MO 63005
       Contact: Sonya Gotto CEO
       Tel: 636-777-4141
       Email: tgeolat@advr.com
       Website: www.advr.com
Contract engineers & IT consultants. (Woman, estab
2002, empl 450, sales $20,000,000, cert: WBENC)

4795   Applications Engineering Group
       12300 Old Tesson Rd, Ste 100-G
       St. Louis, MO 63128
       Contact: Chris Rakel VP Operations
       Tel: 314-842-9110
       Email: chris.rakel@aeg-inc.com
       Website: www.aeg-inc.com
Provide contract, contract to hire & direct hire IT
employment services. (Hisp, estab 1992, empl 35, sales ,
cert: State)

4796   Ares Construction Co, LLC
       4900 Lawn Ave
       Kansas City, MO 64130
       Contact: Quinton Fears CEO
       Tel: 816-285-5933
       Email: qfears@aresconst.com
       Website: www.aresconst.com
Electrical contracting, satellite dishes, computer consulting, network design & installation, web design, data
recovery, customer training, structured cabling & phone
systems. (AA, estab 2002, empl 7, sales , cert: State, City)

4797   Byrne Software Technologies, Inc.
       16091 Swingley Ridge Rd Ste 200
       Chesterfield, MO 63017
       Contact: Tom Allen VP
       Tel: 636-537-2505
       Email: tra@byrnesoftware.com
       Website: www.byrnesoftware.com
IT consulting & software development; custom applications, web sites, Windows applications. (Woman, estab
1985, empl 55, sales $6,538,000, cert: State)

4798   Communitronics Corp.
       970 Bolger Court
       Fenton, MO 63026
       Contact: Rita Leitensdorfer CEO
       Tel: - -
       Email: rital@communitronics.com
       Website: www.communitronics.com
Audio Visual Systems, VTC Systems, Secure/Non-Secure
VTC, Enterprise Collaboration, Video/Media Walls,
Project Engineering, Custom AV Apps, Service Contracts,
FTEs, Information Assurance Compliance (Woman, estab
1969, empl 11, sales $2,000,000, cert: State, NWBOC)

4799 Data Dynamics, Inc.
      500 Oak Leaf Manor Court Ste 1
      St. Louis, MO 63021
      Contact: Thomas Van Cleave Mgr Business Devel
      Tel: 314-607-3758
      Email: thomas.vancleave@datadynamics-inc.com
      Website: www.datadynamics-inc.com
IT consulting, software development, web applications, mobile apps, web sites& custom software development, infrastructure, PCs, server, networks, routers, etc. (Minority, Woman, estab 1996, empl 2, sales $195,836, cert: State)

4800 Digital Partners Incorporated
      8008 Carondelet Ave Ste 103
      Saint Louis, MO 63105
      Contact: Matina Koester President
      Tel: 314-863-8008
      Email: matina@dpipro.com
      Website: www.dpipro.com
System Integration. (Woman, estab 1994, empl 11, sales $8,500,000, cert: WBENC)

4801 Document Imaging Systems of St. Louis
      1463 S Vandeventer Ave
      St. Louis, MO 63110
      Contact: Adrienne Williams President
      Tel: 314-531-0167
      Email: awilliams@disrepro.com
      Website: www.disrepro.com
blueprint document reproduction, project collaboration & document management solutions. (Woman/AA, estab 1995, empl 8, sales $4,095,761, cert: State, City, NMSDC)

4802 ECCO Select Corporation
      1601 Iron St, Ste 200
      North Kansas City, MO 64116
      Contact: Jeanette Prenger President
      Tel: 816-960-3800
      Email: registrations@eccoselect.com
      Website: www.eccoselect.com
Project management, security consulting, network security admin, system security audits. (Minority, Woman, estab , empl , sales $28,172,000, cert: State, NMSDC, WBENC)

4803 Ferguson Consulting Inc.
      1350 Timberlake Manor Pkwy Ste 450
      Chesterfield, MO 63017
      Contact: Paul Woolverton VP Govt Sector
      Tel: 636-728-4408
      Email: pwoolverton@fergcons.com
      Website: www.fci-engr.com
IT solutions. (Woman, estab 1993, empl 110, sales , cert: State)

4804 Geodata IT
      555 Washington Ave, Ste 310
      St. Louis, MO 63101
      Contact: Justin Bennett President
      Tel: 217-390-8085
      Email: justin@geodatait.com
      Website: www.geodatait.com
Agile Software Development, Data Center Consolidation & Cloud Services, Big Data & Data Analytics, Systems Engineering & Integration, Program & Project Management, Enterprise Content Management, Data & Information Engineering. (Hisp, estab 2012, empl 4, sales $120,000, cert: NMSDC, 8(a))

4805 Information Technology Group
      316 Delaware
      Kansas City, MO 64105
      Contact: CEO
      Tel: 816-421-6472
      Email:
      Website: www.itgllc.net
IT staffing svcs, supplier mgmt, fixed price staffing, project outsourcing. (Woman, estab 1999, empl 78, sales $2,000,000, cert: WBENC)

4806 Ingenuity Consulting Partner, Inc.
      410 B SE 3rd St, Ste 102
      Lee's Summit, MO 64081
      Contact: Brenda Riggs CEO
      Tel: 816-272-8145
      Email: briggs@ingenuityconsulting.com
      Website: www.ingenuityconsulting.com
Software development & application integration, web & mobile applications. (Woman, estab 2002, empl 22, sales $1,155,578, cert: State)

4807 Kelly Mitchell Group, Inc.
      8229 Maryland Ave
      Clayton, MO 63105
      Contact: Cassandra Sanford
      Tel: 314-727-1700
      Email: cassandra.sanford@kellymitchell.com
      Website: www.kellymitchell.com
Technology consulting: staff augmentation, project solutions, managed outsourcing & strategic consulting. (Woman, estab 1998, empl 2000, sales $90,000,000, cert: CPUC, WBENC)

4808 NextGen Information Services Inc.
      906 Olive St Ste 600
      Saint Louis, MO 63101
      Contact: Christy Herschbach Admin Asst
      Tel: 314-588-1212
      Email: supplierdiversity@nextgen-is.com
      Website: www.nextgen-is.com
IT consulting services: project mgmt, custom application dev, legacy transition svcs & staff augmentation, staff augmentaion. (Minority, Woman, estab 1997, empl 300, sales , cert: State, City, WBENC)

4809 Pace Solutions, Inc.
      1065 Executive Pkwy Ste 225
      St. Louis, MO 63141
      Contact: Clint Kleinsorge Dir Business Devel
      Tel: 314-560-9641
      Email: clint@pacesi.com
      Website: www.pacesi.com
Information Technology staffing & consulting services. (Minority, Woman, estab 2011, empl 55, sales $5,000,000, cert: NWBOC)

4810 Programmer Resources International Inc.
      221 Clarkson Executive Park
      Ellisville, MO 63011
      Contact: Deanna Wickey Business Devel Mgr
      Tel: 636-256-7172
      Email: deanna@prijbs.com
      Website: www.prijbs.com
IT professionals & innovative technology solutions. (AA, estab 1997, empl 85, sales $16,000,000, cert: NMSDC)

4811　PSRI TecHnologies LLC
113 Eastland Dr
Jefferson City, MO 65101
Contact: Natasha Conley President
Tel:　573-636-9696
Email: cconley@psritech.com
Website: www.psritech.com
Information technology/staff augmentation, project management & call center/help desk operations. (Woman/AA, estab 2001, empl 5, sales $197,053, cert: State)

4812　Quanteq, Inc.
10 Strecker Rd, Ste 1170
Ellisville, MO 63011
Contact: Juan Kuanfung CEO
Tel:　314-329-7799
Email: jkuanfung@quantequsa.com
Website: www.quantequsa.com
Software service solutions: information systems & technology life-cycle, project mgmt, requirement & business studies, package evaluation, system design & dev, system & software integration, database admin, custom programming svcs. (Hisp, estab 1997, empl 1, sales , cert: State, City)

4813　Rose International, Inc.
16305 Swingley Ridge Rd Ste 350
Chesterfield, MO 63017
Contact: Sabina Bhatia CEO
Tel:　636-812-4000
Email: sales@roseint.com
Website: www.roseint.com
Information systems consulting, software devlopment, computer programming & maintenance. (Minority, Woman, estab 1993, empl 7000, sales $424,000,000, cert: State, NMSDC, CPUC, WBENC)

4814　Saigan Technologies Inc.
2300 Main St Ste 900
Kansas City, MO 64108
Contact: Julie Robertson Client Engagement Mgr
Tel:　816-303-1301
Email: diversity@saigantech.com
Website: www.saigantech.com
Information technology IT services & solutions. (Minority, Woman, estab 2004, empl 31, sales $1,701,826, cert: State, NMSDC, WBENC)

4815　ServeKool Technologies LLC
287 Arbor Trails Dr
Ballwin, MO 63021
Contact: Lovelina Bhagat President
Tel:　636-207-8055
Email: info@servekool.com
Website: www.servekool.com
Custom software development, application support outsourcing & staffing services. (Woman/As-Ind, estab 2013, empl 2, sales , cert: NMSDC)

4816　Strategic Staffing Solutions
120 S. Central Ave
St. Louis, MO 63105
Contact: Denice Olson VP
Tel:　630-546-1784
Email: gscharf@strategicstaff.com
Website: www.strategicstaff.com
Information technology consulting. (Woman, estab 1990, empl 2700, sales $642,000,000, cert: WBENC)

4817　Systems Service Enterprises, Inc.
77 Westport Plaza, Ste 500
St. Louis, MO 63146
Contact: Susan Elliott Exec Acct Mgr
Tel:　314-439-4700
Email: susan.elliott@sseinc.com
Website: www.sseinc.com
Information technology svcs: desktop computer solutions, technical support, hardware & software installation. (Woman, estab 1966, empl 115, sales , cert: WBENC)

4818　TechGuard Security LLC
28 Hawk Ridge Blvd, Ste 107
Lake St. Louis, MO 63367
Contact: Carla Stone CEO
Tel:　636-489-2230
Email:
Website: www.techguard.com
IT networking & security services: vulnerability assessments; policy development; secure network infrastructure design; security awareness training; intrusion detection; business continuity/disaster recovery; 24x7 incident response. (Woman, estab 2000, empl 45, sales $7,550,000, cert: State)

4819　TechnoSmarts, Inc.
16090 Swingley Ridge Rd Ste 330
St.Louis, MO 63017
Contact: Rao Vallabhaneni President
Tel:　636-519-0814
Email: rao@technosmarts.com
Website: www.technosmarts.com
IT consulting & staffing services. (As-Ind, estab 1997, empl 30, sales , cert: NMSDC)

4820　TurnGroup Technologies, LLC
2811 Locust St
St. Louis, MO 63103
Contact: Kim St. Onge Business Dev Mgr
Tel:　314-289-8734
Email: kim@turngroup.com
Website: www.turngroup.com
Database development, hardware/software support, internet solutions, LAN/WAN, programming, website development. (AA, estab 2002, empl 9, sales , cert: City)

4821　Unitech Consulting, LLC dba Chameleon
3207 Washington Ave
St. Louis, MO 63103
Contact: Mary Burgess Business Devel Specialist
Tel:　314-773-7200
Email: sales@chameleonis.com
Website: www.chameleonis.com
Program management, software development & integration & infrastructure support services. (Hisp, estab 2003, empl 75, sales $7,742,000, cert: NMSDC)

Mississippi

4822 Omni Sourcing, Inc.
1230 Raymond Road; Box 6
Jackson, MS 39204
Contact: John Perkins President
Tel: 713-628-6929
Email: jperkins@omnisourcing.net
Website: www.omnisourcing.net
Systems integration & quality management, service assurance mgmt & testing, sourcing value creation, business & technology performance improvement, program & project mgmt. (AA, estab 2012, empl 30, sales $3,600,000, cert: NMSDC)

North Carolina

4823 3 Birds Marketing, LLC
505-B W Franklin St
Chapel Hill, NC 27516
Contact: Layton Judd President
Tel: 919-913-2750
Email: layton@3birdsmarketing.com
Website: www.3birdsmarketing.com
Technology, software, integrated marketing platform, marketing, digital marketing, multichannel marketing, email marketing, email newsletters, digital newsletters, social media management, social media marketing. (Woman, estab 2009, empl 60, sales $3,769,500, cert: WBENC, NWBOC)

4824 Active Ergonomics, Inc.
6501 Creedmoor Rd Ste 101
Raleigh, NC 27613
Contact: Shannon A Powell President
Tel: 919-676-8211
Email: spowell@actergo.com
Website: www.actergo.com
Office ergonomic software to help increase worker productivity and reduce repetitive stress injuries. (Minority, Woman, estab 1997, empl 4, sales $934,000, cert: State, NMSDC, WBENC)

4825 Advantco International LLC
8601 Six Forks Road Ste 120
Raleigh, NC 27615
Contact: Kimthanh Le VP
Tel: 919-518-8298
Email: ktdole@advantco.com
Website: www.advantco.com
Pre-built adapters for integrating SAP & Oracle systems with other leading enterprise platforms (As-Pac, estab 2007, empl 10, sales $100,000, cert: State)

4826 Alliance of Professionals & Consultants, Inc.
8200 Brownleigh Dr
Raleigh, NC 27617
Contact: Troy Roberts President
Tel: 919-510-9696
Email: troberts@apcinc.com
Website: www.apcinc.com
Requirements analysis, network architecture definitions & enhancements, information technology, hardware & software upgrades, modifications, installation, operation & maintenance. (Nat Ame, estab 1993, empl , sales $65,872,532, cert: NMSDC)

4827 Banerasoft Inc.
5710 W Gate City Blvd Ste K, 279
Greensboro, NC 27407
Contact: Brenda Zamzow Sales & Customer Relations Mgr
Tel: 864-787-5408
Email: akshata@banerasoft.biz
Website: www.banerasoft.com
Technology Consulting/Outsourcing, Software Development, App Development for all iOS & Android devices, Data Analytics & Business Intelligence, QA & Solutions Integration. (As-Ind, estab 2012, empl 35, sales , cert: NMSDC)

4828 Barrchin, Inc.
326 Morgan Brook Way
Rolesville, NC 27571
Contact: Janet Barrett President
Tel: 919-630-5128
Email: jbarrett@barrchin.com
Website: www.barrchin.com
Information Technology (IT) & Management consulting. (Woman/AA, estab 2013, empl 4, sales , cert: State, City)

4829 Carolina IT Professionals, Inc.
243 W Catawba Ave
Mount Holly, NC 28120
Contact: VP Mktg
Tel: 704-827-8102
Email: gus.brown@citpinc.com
Website: www.citpinc.com
Information technology staff augmentation, solutions & consulting, permanent placements. (Woman, estab 2001, empl 160, sales $19,009,811, cert: WBENC)

4830 Clark-Powell Associates, Inc.
920 Blairhill Rd
Charlotte, NC 28217
Contact: C. Gibson Sales
Tel: 704-525-4223
Email: cgibson@clark-powell.com
Website: www.clark-powell.com
Design, integration & maintenance of AV systems for presentation, videoconferencing, video broadcast & production. (Woman, estab 1983, empl 62, sales $20,000,000, cert: State)

4831 Clinton Gaddy Inc.
717 Green Valley Rd Ste 200
Greensboro, NC 27408
Contact: Gaddy Will CEO
Tel: 336-355-8708
Email: Wmgaddy@gsostaffing.com
Website: www.gsostaffing.com
Contract IT Staffing/Temporary Labor: Systems Analyst, API Development, Data Analyst, Software Developers, DevOps, Lead Architects, IT Audit Managers, Change Management, Incident/Change Management, Technical Lead, IT Directors, Solution Architect. (AA, estab 2017, empl 8, sales $319,000, cert: State)

4832 COMNet Group, Inc.
       301 McCullough Dr, Ste 400
       Charlotte, NC 28262
       Contact: Ana Sai President
       Tel: 704-323-7762
       Email: ana@comnetgroup.com
       Website: www.comnetgroup.com
IT Technology & training services: ERP, offshoring/
outsourcing, agile program management & complex
software development & delivery. (Woman/As-Ind, estab
2005, empl 20, sales $400,000, cert: NMSDC, WBENC)

4833 Data Bridge Consultants LLC
       101 N Tryon St, Ste 1260
       Charlotte, NC 28246
       Contact: Sola Daves Principal Partner
       Tel: 980-319-7635
       Email: sola.daves@databridgeconsultants.com
       Website: www.databridgeconsultants.com
Big data and Artificial Intelligence Consulting, staffing/
BPO. (AA, estab 2013, empl 8, sales $11,300,000, cert:
NMSDC)

4834 DD Consulting and Management
       13016 Eastfield Rd Ste 200-272
       Huntersville, NC 28078
       Contact: Walter Great
       Tel: 704-909-2970
       Email: walter@ddconsultingservice.com
       Website: www.DDConsultingservice.com
IT consulting, data storage, data backup, physical surveillance data, digital evidence & security-sensitive digital
data. (AA, estab 2001, empl 3, sales , cert: NMSDC)

4835 DynPro
       7412 Chapel Hill Rd
       Raleigh, NC 27607
       Contact: Michael Kallam VP-Business Dev
       Tel: 919-747-7114
       Email: mkallam@dynpro.com
       Website: www.dynpro.com
Design & implement internet applications & web-enable,
enterprise solutions, SAP, People Soft & Oracle application
mgmt outsourcing, technical svcs, staff augmentation,
project mgmt, help desk support. (Minority, estab 1996,
empl 90, sales $3,695,000, cert: NMSDC)

4836 Empores LLC
       11020 David Taylor Dr
       Charlotte, NC 28262
       Contact: Satish Prasad Ramamurthy VP Business Dev
       Tel: 703-409-4945
       Email: satish@emporesllc.com
       Website: www.emporesllc.com
Voltage optimization, intelligent PF correction, KVAR
improvements, cloud based energy monitoring & automatic techniques. (Minority, estab 2012, empl 5, sales ,
cert: State, City)

4837 GrimeGuru Janitorial Service
       1531 Westbrook Plaza Dr, Ste A
       Winston-Salem, NC 27103
       Contact: Brigitte Hampton President
       Tel: 336-710-4406
       Email: brigitte@grimeguru.com
       Website: www.grimeguru.com
GrimeGuru Janitorial Services is a Service Disabled
Veteran Owned Small Business (SDVOSB), Woman-
Owned Small Business (WOSB), and minority-owned
green cleaning company located in Winston-Salem,
North Carolina. With a focus on general janitorial
cleaning f (AA, estab , empl , sales , cert: State, WBENC)

4838 IBG Global Consulting
       333 W Trade St
       Charlotte, NC 28202
       Contact: Diondre Lewis President
       Tel: 866-611-3604
       Email: ellie@ibgsoftware.com
       Website: www.ibgsoftware.com
I.T. Resource Procurement / Application Development /
Software Architecture / Project Mangement / I.T Training
& Education / Federal/State government technical
solutions / Block Chain Solutions / Architecting. Engi-
neering/Developing/Middleware Systems. (AA, estab
2008, empl 50, sales $10,850,000, cert: NMSDC)

4839 Infestus Inc.
       PO Box 222
       McLeansville, NC 27301
       Contact: Glasco Taylor CEO
       Tel: 202-794-7280
       Email: glasco.taylor@calibertec.com
       Website: www.calibertec.com/
IT staffing: Cyber Security, Data Center(Virtualization,
Storage, SAN, Networking, Server Hardware, Linux, etc),
Infrastructure Networking. (AA, estab 2014, empl 5, sales
$200,000, cert: NMSDC)

4840 IT People Corporation
       One Copley Pkwy. Ste 216
       Morrisville, NC 27560
       Contact: Sai Nidamarty Business Dev
       Tel: 919-806-3535
       Email: sai@itpeoplecorp.com
       Website: www.itpeoplecorp.com
Information technology staffing, consulting &
outsourcing services. (Minority, Woman, estab 1999,
empl 153, sales $7,459,294, cert: State, NMSDC, WBENC)

4841 Marketing Resource Solutions LLC
       725 W Main St, Ste E
       Jamestown, NC 27282
       Contact: Melita Vick Natl Accts Svc Mgr
       Tel: 336-510-7523
       Email: info@marketingresourcesolutions.com
       Website: www.marketingresourcesolutions.com
Remote Executive Assistance, Database & CRM support,
Basic Internet Research, Data management, Website
content management, Sales & Customer support, Social
Media Optimization Services, Office management.
(Woman, estab 2003, empl 160, sales , cert: NMSDC)

4842   Paula P. White and Associates, Inc dba DataMasters
          PO Box 14548
          Greensboro, NC 27415
          Contact: Dana White Dir Operations
          Tel: 336-373-1461
          Email: dwhite@datamasters.com
          Website: www.datamasters.com
IT staffing, contract, staff augmentation & permanent or
direct hire positions. (Woman, estab 1971, empl 25, sales
$2,500,000, cert: State)

4843   QCentric Consultants, LLC
          624 Tyvola Rd, Ste 103-177
          Charlotte, NC 28217
          Contact: Nuradin Kariye Managing Partner
          Tel: 800-260-5728
          Email: admin@qcentricconsultants.com
          Website: www.qcentricconsultants.com
IT staffing & technology solutions. (AA, estab 2009, empl
45, sales , cert: State)

4844   Refulgent Technologies Inc.
          112 South Tryon St Ste 1270
          Charlotte, NC 28284
          Contact: Horace Worley President
          Tel: 704-405-4238
          Email: horace.worley@refulgent-tech.com
          Website: www.refulgent-tech.com
IT consulting & staffing services, application development
& staffing. (Minority, Woman, estab 2005, empl 22, sales
$1,157,433, cert: NMSDC)

4845   Sajiton LLC
          301 McCullough Dr Ste 400
          Charlotte, NC 28262
          Contact: Nicole Williams Managing Dir
          Tel: 888-828-7991
          Email: nicole.williams@sajiton.com
          Website: www.sajiton.com
Custom Mobile & Web Application Development, Big Data,
Data Analytics, Data Engineering, Data Integration, Master
Data Management. Data Encryption, Data Security in the
Cloud & On Premise - CyberSecurity. (Woman/AA, estab
2014, empl 1, sales , cert: NMSDC, WBENC)

4846   Saponi Industries, Inc.
          3229 Goslen Dr
          Pfafftown, NC 27040
          Contact: Deborah Bare Owner
          Tel: 336-770-5321
          Email: lynn@saponi-industries.com
          Website: www.saponi-industries.com
Saponi Industries is a brokerage company that provides
competitive products by shopping the insurance market
for the customer. Group products include: Universal life,
whole life, term life, accident, critical illness, dental, cancer
and long term care. (Minority, Woman, estab 2010, empl
2, sales , cert: NMSDC)

4847   Spectraforce Technologies, Inc.
          500 W Peace St
          Raleigh, NC 27603
          Contact: Julianne Howard Dir Client Relations
          Tel: 919-280-3064
          Email: supplierdiversity@spectraforce.com
          Website: www.spectraforce.com
IT/Clinical/Scientific/Engineering contingent staffing and IT
Application Development and Maintenance services. (As-
Ind, estab 2004, empl 2500, sales $112,000,000, cert:
NMSDC)

4848   STATProg Inc.
          421 Fayetteville St, Ste 1100
          Raleigh, NC 27601
          Contact: Dany Guerendo Christian President
          Tel: 919-987-2015
          Email: statprogadmin@statproginc.com
          Website: www.statproginc.com
Research and Development, and/or Life Sciences
departments. Statistical Programming and Analysis using
SAS as software. (Woman/AA, estab 2012, empl 2, sales
$162,000, cert: NMSDC, WBENC)

4849   Stonelaurel Consulting, Inc.
          1515 Mockingbird Ln, Ste 800
          Charlotte, NC 28209
          Contact: Ted Shelton Global Accounts Dir
          Tel: 704-333-8878
          Email: bnymellon@stonelaurel.com
          Website: www.stonelaurel.com
Information Technology & Management Consulting. (AA,
estab 1994, empl 100, sales $7,786,344, cert: NMSDC)

4850   Technology Concepts & Design, Inc.
          4510 Weybridge Ln
          Greensboro, NC 27407
          Contact: Lisa Cain CFO
          Tel: 336-232-5800
          Email: l_cain@tcdi.com
          Website: www.tcdi.com
Advanced application & system design services,
eDiscovery, review & production & large-scale case
management products & services to help effectively
manage and reduce costs associated with significant
litigation and investigations. (As-Pac, estab 1988, empl
69, sales , cert: NMSDC)

4851   Third Law Enterprises, LLC
          517 S Front St
          Wilmington, NC 28401
          Contact: Michael Gilbert Managing Partner
          Tel: 910-477-3772
          Email: mgilbert@thirdlawenterprises.com
          Website: www.thirdlawenterprises.com
Data Center Solutions (Computer hardware, software,
implementation services), Servers, Storage, Networking,
Cloud solutions (on premise, off premise) and Hybrid
Cloud Solutions, Personal Computing (PCs, Notebooks,
Backup drives). (Hisp, estab 2004, empl 2, sales
$220,000, cert: State)

4852   United Global Technologies
          338 S. Sharon Amity Road
          Charlotte, NC 28202
          Contact: Manny Rodriguez Market Mgr
          Tel: 980-270-6636
          Email: mrodriguez@ugtechnologies.com
          Website: www.ugtechnologies.com
Systems integration & IT/engineering services. (Woman,
estab 2005, empl 120, sales $21,400,000, cert: State)

4853   VDC Technologies
          513 New Bridge St Ste 600
          Jacksonville, NC 28540
          Contact: Vactronia Russell CEO
          Tel: 910-353-1492
          Email: support@vdctechs.com
          Website: www.vdctechs.com
IT solutions. (Woman/AA, estab , empl , sales , cert:
State)

New Hampshire

4854 Advanced Presentation Systems dba CCS
132 Northeastern Blvd
Nashua, NH 03062
Contact: Chris Gamst VP
Tel: 978-256-2001
Email: cgamst@ccsprojects.com
Website: www.ccsnewengland.com
Audio visual system design, integration, sales, service &
installation for boardrooms, conference rooms, training
rooms & auditoriums. (Woman/As-Ind, estab 1998, empl
23, sales , cert: State)

4855 Apollo Professional Solutions, Inc.
29 Stiles Rd Ste 302
Salem, NH 03079
Contact: Bruce Thomason VP
Tel: 866-277-3343
Email: bthomason@apollopros.com
Website: www.apollopros.com
Recruited & payrolled engineering & information technol-
ogy temporary personnel. (Woman, estab 1983, empl 20,
sales $12,000,000, cert: State, WBENC)

4856 Dataservinc
1 Tara Blvd, Ste 102
Nashua, NH 03062
Contact: Anil Kumar VP Business Dev
Tel: 603-557-0600
Email: contact@dataservinc.com
Website: www.dataservinc.com
IT staffing & IT software development. (Woman/As-Ind,
estab 2005, empl 100, sales $7,000,000, cert: State)

4857 Digital Prospectors Corp.
100 Domain Dr Ste 103
Exeter, NH 03833
Contact: Chris Roos Principal
Tel: 603-772-2700
Email: croos@dpcit.com
Website: www.dpcit.com
Permanent & temporary IT staffing. (Woman, estab 1999,
empl 120, sales $50,201,563, cert: WBENC)

4858 Paramount Technology Solutions LLC
63 Emerald St, Ste 442
Keene, NH 03431
Contact: Beth Wright Dir of Finance & Admin
Tel: 281-617-1400
Email: beth.wright@acuitycloudsolutions.com
Website: www.acuitycloudsolutions.com
Computer software consulting services. (Woman, estab
2008, empl 25, sales , cert: WBENC)

4859 Universal Software Corporation
20 Industrial Park Dr
Nashua, NH 03062
Contact: Sonu Khanna Sr Mgr
Tel: 603-324-4004
Email: sonuk@universal-sw.com
Website: www.universal-sw.com
Information technology: staff augmentation, project
mgmt, project & offshore outsourcing, embedded systems
& hardware design, Oracle/MS SQL, .Net framework, open
source tools, WinNT, Solaris, Unix, Linux. (As-Pac, estab
1992, empl 58, sales , cert: State)

New Jersey

4860 1st Choice Financial Group LLC
1121 Asbury Ave
Asbury Park, NJ 07712
Contact: Kathrina Nease CEO
Tel: 717-599-1907
Email: knease@1stchoicefg.com
Website: www.1stchoicefg.com
Information technology solutions & program/project
management. (Woman, estab 2006, empl 10, sales
$500,000, cert: State)

4861 20/20 Solutions, Inc.
33 Wilson Dr Unit D
Sparta, NJ 07871
Contact: Jody Torre President
Tel: 973-383-8703
Email: j.torre@20-20solutions.com
Website: www.20-20solutions.com
Website dev, website mgmt, search engine optimization,
website design, website hosting, computer program-
ming, computer repair, computer training, computer
equipment, computer maintenance & support. (Woman,
estab 1999, empl 10, sales $450,000, cert: WBENC)

4862 22nd Century Technologies, Inc.
1 Executive Dr Ste 285
Somerset, NJ 08873
Contact: Eva Gaddis-McKnight Contracts Admin
Tel: 732-537-9191
Email: com@tscti.com
Website: www.tscti.com
Computer programming & consulting, IT support. (As-
Pac, estab 1997, empl 4230, sales $284,132,720, cert:
State, NMSDC)

4863 Actuan Global LLC
4 Debra Ct
Scotch Plains, NJ 07076
Contact: Talib Morgan President
Tel: 908-443-1180
Email: talib.morgan@actuanglobal.com
Website: www.actuanglobal.com
Digital innovation & technology consulting, mobile,
personalization, marketing automation, content man-
agement, social media, data & digital systems. (AA, estab
2011, empl 1, sales , cert: NMSDC)

4864 Adaptive Tech Resources Inc.
4400 Route 9 South Ste 1000
Freehold, NJ 07728
Contact: Roland Williams CEO
Tel: 732-683-0800
Email: roland.williams@atrstaffing.com
Website: www.atrstaffing.com
IT consulting/contract & full time staffing services. (AA,
estab 1996, empl 3, sales $862,000, cert: NMSDC)

4865 Agnosco Technologies Inc.
6 Thornhill Dr
Lumberton, NJ 08048
Contact: Kiran Khan Operations Mgr
Tel: 877-933-5439
Email: kiran@agnoscotech.com
Website: www.agnoscotech.com
IT recruitment consultancy services: permanent,
temporary & contract positions, executive search &
outplacement services & solutions. (Minority, Woman,
estab 2013, empl 50, sales , cert: State)

4866 AIT Global Inc.
      228 Route 34
      Matawan, NJ 07747
      Contact: Mittal Shah VP
      Tel: 732-997-9917
      Email: mittals@aitglobalinc.com
      Website: www.aitglobalinc.com
IT Staffing & Solutions, Contract, Contract to Hire or Full-
time Placements. (Woman/As-Ind, estab 2003, empl 135,
sales $14,800,000, cert: NMSDC, WBENC)

4867 AITA Consulting Services Inc.
      6-80 Towne Center Dr
      North Brunswick, NJ 08902
      Contact: Aisha Thomas Business Devel Mgr
      Tel: 732-658-4471
      Email: hello@aishathomas.com
      Website: www.aitacs.com
IT staffing services, Corp To Corp, W2, 1099, contract, full
time, contract to hire, Business Intelligence, Big Data, Web
development, J2EE, Microsoft technologies, Quality
Assurance & Oracle Applications, SAP, Mobile Apps.
(Minority, Woman, estab 2006, empl 182, sales , cert:
NMSDC, WBENC)

4868 Alliance Sourcing Network Inc
      40 Galesi Dr Ste 2
      Wayne, NJ 07470
      Contact: CEO
      Tel: 201-438-2005
      Email: information@asn-corp.com
      Website: www.asn-corp.com
IT consulting services: application design, client server
design, database admin & hardware design & support,
network admin. (Woman, estab 2006, empl 26, sales
$10,893,853, cert: WBENC)

4869 AppliedInfo Partners, Inc.
      28 World's Fair Dr
      Somerset, NJ 08873
      Contact: Betty Lau CEO
      Tel: 732-507-7316
      Email: blau@appliedinfo.com
      Website: www.appliedinfo.com
Software & web dev, computer & IT products & services,
marketing communications. (Minority, Woman, estab
1990, empl 50, sales $10,000,000, cert: NMSDC, WBENC)

4870 APTIVA Corp.
      100 Franklin Square Dr, Ste 210
      Somerset, NJ 08873
      Contact: Paula Philip Sr VP
      Tel: 732-391-1055
      Email: info@applesandorangespr.com
      Website: www.aptivacorp.com
IT Solutions and services. (As-Ind, estab 2007, empl 80,
sales $8,000,000, cert: NMSDC)

4871 Arborsys Group
      3131 Princeton Pike, Bldg 4, Ste 210
      Lawrenceville, NJ 08648
      Contact: Vasu Ranganathan Partner/President
      Tel: 609-843-0225
      Email: vranganathan@arborsys.com
      Website: www.arborsys.com
Business & IT consulting, content lifecycle management,
collaboration, business process management, portal
solutions & electronic records management. (Minority,
Woman, estab 2004, empl 20, sales $5,300,000, cert:
State, NMSDC)

4872 Argo Navis IT
      155 Glen Alpin Rd
      Morristown, NJ 07960
      Contact: CEO
      Tel: 973-285-1202
      Email: bridgens@argonavisit.com
      Website: www.argonavisit.com
Global audio & web conferencing services. Resell HP
hardware. (Woman, estab 2003, empl 1, sales $270,000,
cert: WBENC)

4873 Artech L.L.C.
      360 Mt. Kemble Ave Ste 2000
      Morristown, NJ 07960
      Contact: Ian Olson Managing Dir
      Tel: 206-679-9001
      Email: ian.olson@artech.com
      Website: www.artech.com
Network infrastructure mgmt, web applications dev,
content mgmt, design, internet infrastructure design
devel & maintenance, multitier architecture, client
server, software applications, systems devel & support.
(Minority, Woman, estab 1992, empl 11500, sales
$725,000,000, cert: State, NMSDC, WBENC)

4874 Astir IT Solutions
      50 Cragwood Rd Ste 219
      South Plainfield, NJ 07080
      Contact: Robert Markowitz Exec VP
      Tel: 908-279-8670
      Email: bobm@astirit.com
      Website: www.astirit.com
IT consulting, staffing & outsourced software development. (Minority, Woman, estab 2001, empl 300, sales
$30,700,000, cert: State, NMSDC)

4875 Atlas Data Systems DBA Atlas
      400 Connell Dr Ste 6000
      Berkeley Heights, NJ 07922
      Contact: Lisa Wickey Acct Exec
      Tel: 908-519-8013
      Email: lisa.wickey@chooseatlas.com
      Website: www.chooseatlas.com
Information technology consulting: internet, e-commerce, infrastructure & RDMS consulting. (Woman,
estab 1998, empl 350, sales $31,900,000, cert: State,
WBENC)

4876 Aumtech, Inc.
      710 Old Bridge Turnpike
      East Brunswick, NJ 08816
      Contact: Tom Porter COO
      Tel: 732-254-1875
      Email: tporter@aumtech.com
      Website: www.aumtech.com
IVR & VoIP network solution: speech recognition,
touchtone input, VXML programming tools. (Minority,
estab 1988, empl 38, sales $2,120,000, cert: NMSDC)

4877 Avenues International Inc.
      4 Restrick Court
      Princeton Junction, NJ 08550
      Contact: Anupam Gupta Dir
      Tel: 609-945-1160
      Email: anupam@avenuesinc.com
      Website: www.avenuesinc.com
IT consulting services: Data Analytics, Business Intelligence, Data Warehousing, Big Data Solution & Management Reporting Solutions. (As-Ind, estab 1994, empl 15,
sales $1,870,000, cert: NMSDC)

4878 Axtria Inc.
300 Connell Dr, 5th Floor
Berkeley Heights, NJ 07922
Contact: Maria Poulos Principal
Tel: 1-201-2859
Email: maria.poulos@axtria.com
Website: www.axtria.com
Data analytics, understanding data & training in the latest technologies. (As-Ind, estab , empl , sales $29,600,000, cert: NMSDC)

4879 Blue Planet Solutions Inc.
36 Route 10 W, Ste E
East Hanover, NJ 07936
Contact: Pradeep Darbhe Resource Mgr
Tel: 973-581-1500
Email: pradeep@blueplanetsolutions.com
Website: www.blueplanetsolutions.com
Outsource software development & maintenance, contract programmers, offshore programming. (Woman/As-Ind, estab 1997, empl 20, sales , cert: State)

4880 BNG Consulting, Inc.
12 Sandhill Ct
Jamesburg, NJ 08831
Contact: Biswatosh Guha VP
Tel: 732-631-0003
Email: guha@bngconsulting.com
Website: www.bngconsulting.com
Business intelligence, data warehousing, reporting/ ETL tools, database admin, support, development, maintenanance, enhancements, architecture & design, data modeling. (As-Pac, estab 2003, empl 65, sales $7,000,000, cert: State)

4881 Brillio, LLC
100 Town Square Pl, Ste 308
Jersey City, NJ 07310
Contact: Gautam Arni VP Sales
Tel: 201-744-5759
Email: gautam@brillio.com
Website: www.brillio.com
Business Technology Consulting | PROGRAM MANAGE-MENT | ANALYTICS | Application PORTFOLIO | COST OPTIMIZATION | CHANGE MANAGEMENT | Mobility | VISUALIZATION | ANALYTICS | BIG DATA (As-Ind, estab 2013, empl 2000, sales , cert: NMSDC)

4882 Cardinal Technology Solutions Inc.
1100 Cornwall Rd, Ste 113
Monmouth Junction, NJ 08852
Contact: Dir
Tel: 732-821-7400
Email: nfo@cardinalts.com
Website: www.cardinaltsinc.com
IT and Engineering Staffing and consulting services. (As-Ind, estab 2004, empl 22, sales $8,000,000, cert: NMSDC)

4883 Caresoft Inc.
220 Lincoln Blvd Ste 300
Middlesex, NJ 08846
Contact: Dhaval Desai Business Dev Mgr
Tel: 732-764-9500
Email: ddesai@caresoftinc.com
Website: www.caresoftinc.com
Information technology staff augmentation. (Minority, estab 1994, empl 189, sales $9,000,000, cert: NMSDC)

4884 Cavalier Workforce, Inc
379 Thornall St 6th Fl
Edison, NJ 08837
Contact: Parag Shroff VP- Delivery
Tel: 201-215-2160
Email: parag@cavalierworkforce.com
Website: www.cavalierworkforce.com/
Technology staffing & consulting. (As-Pac, estab 2007, empl , sales $13,000,000, cert: State, NMSDC)

4885 CBS Technologies
191 Main St
Hackensack, NJ 07601
Contact: President
Tel: 201-843-8070
Email: info@cbstechnologies.com
Website: www.cbstechnologies.com
Business analysis, software & hardware architectures, vendor software selection, hosting, application, data-base support, security, business processes, portals, intranets & extranets. (AA, estab 1996, empl 12, sales $800,000, cert: City)

4886 Chenoa Information Services, Inc.
10 Parsonage Rd Ste 312
Edison, NJ 08837
Contact: Michael Fortino EVP Client Solutions
Tel: 732-549-6800
Email: mfortino@chenoainc.com
Website: www.chenoahealth.com
Information technology solutions & staff augmentation. (As-Ind, estab 1998, empl 600, sales $17,000,000, cert: State, NMSDC)

4887 CNC Consulting
50 E Palisades Ave Ste 422
Englewood, NJ 07631
Contact: Fred Seltzer Business Devel Mgr
Tel: 201-541-9122
Email: fseltzer@cncconsult.com
Website: www.cncconsulting.com
IT professionals for consulting contracts. (AA, estab 1996, empl 25, sales $3,000,000, cert: State)

4888 Cognixia Inc.
110 Allen Rd
Basking Ridge, NJ 06584
Contact: Irina Borovitskaya Associate VP
Tel: 973-559-9121
Email: irina.borovitskaya@cognixia.com
Website: www.cognixia.com
IT and business training courses. (Minority, estab 2018, empl 20, sales , cert: NMSDC)

4889 Collabera
110 Allen Road
Basking Ridge, NJ 07920
Contact: Dawn Serpe Sr VP
Tel: 973-889-5200
Email: AR@COLLABERA.COM
Website: www.collabera.com/services/
Information technology & management svcs, customized software solutions, business solutions, implementation, maintenance, support, etc. (Minority, estab 1996, empl 17000, sales $745,000,000, cert: NMSDC)

4890 Combined Computer Resources, Inc.
120 Wood Ave S, Ste 408
Iselin, NJ 08830
Contact: Laura Palamara Controller
Tel: 732-632-2502
Email: laurap@combinedcomputer.com
Website: www.combinedcomputer.com
Information technology consulting: data processing, right-to-hire & full time placement services. (Woman, estab 1994, empl 107, sales $16,500,000, cert: State)

4891 Communication Experts, Inc.
51 Cragwood Rd Ste 304
South Plainfield, NJ 07080
Contact: Shirish R. Nadkarni CEO
Tel: 908-512-9129
Email: srn@comexpinc.com
Website: www.comexpinc.com
I help clients identify and solve problems using analytical abilities I have developed through management education, decades of working with small and large companies and from my own experience of founding and running software product and service companie (As-Ind, estab 2003, empl 8, sales $1,704,000, cert: NMSDC)

4892 Compunnel Software Group, Inc.
103 Morgan Lane Ste 102
Plainsboro, NJ 08536
Contact: Lalitha Reddy AVP Finance & Legal Operations
Tel: 609-606-9010
Email: contracts@compunnel.com
Website: www.compunnel.com
IT Staffing, eLearning, Application Development, Off shore DEvelopment Facility in India. (Minority, estab 1994, empl 1028, sales $262,418,117, cert: NMSDC)

4893 CompuPlus International Inc.
94 Lilac Lane
Paramus, NJ 07652
Contact: David Wei President
Tel: 626-755-0607
Email: davidw@cp-intl.com
Website: www.cp-intl.com
IT staffing & IT consulting, recruitment & service. (As-Pac, estab 1990, empl 7, sales $1,625,219, cert: State)

4894 Compu-Vision Consulting Inc.
2050 Route 27 Ste 202
North Brunswick, NJ 08902
Contact: Rahul Gupta HR Mgr
Tel: 732-422-1500
Email: rahul.gupta@compuvis.com
Website: www.compuvis.com
Information technology consulting, IT staffing & related services. (Minority, Woman, estab 1998, empl 50, sales $7,250,000, cert: NMSDC, WBENC, NWBOC)

4895 Comrise Technology, Inc.
90 Woodbridge Center Dr Ste 360
Woodbridge, NJ 07730
Contact: Michael Ferrara Dir of Operations
Tel: 732-203-6236
Email: mferrara@comrise.com
Website: www.comrise.com
Staff supplementation, IT mgmt consulting, project outsourcing & recruiting svcs. (As-Pac, estab 1984, empl 150, sales $19,000,000, cert: NMSDC)

4896 Connexions Data Inc.
241 Main St, Ste 206
Hackensack, NJ 07601
Contact: Raghu Menon CFA
Tel: 201-210-8938
Email: raghu.menon@cdatainc.com
Website: www.cdatainc.com
Information technology consulting & integration services, SAP, Oracle & Cloud computing. (As-Ind, estab 2004, empl 48, sales , cert: State)

4897 Corporate Training Group, Inc.
120 Wood Ave S Ste 405
Iselin, NJ 08830
Contact: Kathleen Harvey Sr Acct Exec
Tel: 732-635-9033
Email: kharvey@ctgtraining.com
Website: www.ctgtraining.com
Technical & business end user training on Microsoft, Java, J2EE, Linux, Oracle solutions. (Woman, estab 1991, empl 8, sales $2,000,000, cert: State, WBENC)

4898 Cosmic Software Technology, Inc.
14 Benedek Rd
Princeton, NJ 08540
Contact: Ranvir Sinha CEO
Tel: 609-430-8284
Email: ranvir@cosmic-usa.com
Website: www.cosmic-usa.com
System programming, database analysis, design, dev & admin, documentation & content mgmt, software analysis & design, system analysis & architecture, systems integration, interface design & dev, ERP/CRM implementations. (As-Ind, estab 1999, empl 15, sales $950,000, cert: State)

4899 Crave InfoTech LLC
15 Corporate Place S Ste 104
Piscataway, NJ 08854
Contact: President
Tel: 253-310-5371
Email: shrikant@craveinfotech.com
Website: www.craveinfotech.com
Global software and technology services. (Minority, Woman, estab 2007, empl 75, sales $2,439,000, cert: State, NMSDC, CPUC, WBENC)

4900 Crescens Inc.
1200 Route 22 East, Ste 2000-2176
Bridgewater, NJ 08807
Contact: Sophia Samuel President
Tel: 732-305-2858
Email: supplier@crescensinc.com
Website: www.crescensinc.com
IT consulting, application development, maintenance, product engineering services, testing, business intelligence, packaged applications & staffing. (Minority, Woman, estab 2002, empl 25, sales $550,000, cert: State, NMSDC)

4901 Crystal Data LLC
1 Eves Dr Ste 145
Marlton, NJ 08053
Contact: CEO
Tel: 732-766-9292
Email: info@crystaldatasystems.net
Website: www.crystaldatasystems.net
IT Staffing & Services. (Minority, Woman, estab 2008, empl 40, sales $3,009,933, cert: State, City, WBENC)

4902   Cyber Security Consulting Ops
     309 Fellowship Rd, East Gate Center, Ste 200
     Mt. Laurel, NJ 08054
     Contact: Tony Wittock Dir/CTO
     Tel: 888-588-9951
     Email: tonyw@cybersecurityconsultingops.com
     Website: www.cybersecurityconsultingops.com/
Hardware and software security services. (AA, estab 2017, empl 5, sales , cert: NMSDC)

4903   cyberThink, Inc.
     685 Route 202/206 Ste 101
     Bridgewater, NJ 08807
     Contact: Raj Thind Dir
     Tel: 908-429-8008
     Email: rajveer.thind@cyberthink.com
     Website: www.cyberthink.com
IT auditing & assessment, project mgmt, app devel & integration, infrastructure architecture & deployment, database modeling, data warehousing, business intelligence, quality assurance, ebusiness, collaboration & knowledge mgmt, network & sys admin. (Minority, estab 1996, empl 407, sales $42,800,000, cert: State, NMSDC)

4904   Cygnus Professionals Inc.
     3490 US Hwy # 1,
     Princeton, NJ 08540
     Contact: Gurudas Sarkar CEO
     Tel: 732-423-1785
     Email: gurudas@cygnuspro.com
     Website: www.cygnuspro.com
Business-IT transformation solutions and consulting. (As-Pac, estab 2010, empl 250, sales $25,000,000, cert: State)

4905   Databased Solutions Inc.
     1200 Route 22 E Ste 2000
     Bridgewater, NJ 08807
     Contact: Ila Choudhary President
     Tel: 732-309-0872
     Email: ila.choudhary@dbsiservices.com
     Website: www.dbsiservices.com
IT svcs, staffing augmentation, IT products. (As-Ind, estab 1995, empl 50, sales $4,400,000, cert: NMSDC)

4906   DataEdge Consulting, Inc.
     101 Morgan Ln Ste 203B
     Plainsboro, NJ 08536
     Contact: Siva N Kolli VP Operations
     Tel: 609-275-4500
     Email: Shiv@DataEdgeConsulting.com
     Website: www.DataEdgeConsulting.com
Provide broad-based ERP, Web technology and management consulting services. (As-Ind, estab 2007, empl 30, sales $4,000,000, cert: NMSDC)

4907   Datanomics, Inc.
     991 US Hwy 22 West Ste 201
     Bridgewater, NJ 08807
     Contact: Lori Vail CEO
     Tel: 908-707-8200
     Email: vail@datanomics.com
     Website: www.datanomics.com
IT staffing, helpdesk, desktop support, administration, technical writers, validation specialists, business/systems
analysts, programmers, mainframe, client/server, & web. (Woman, estab 1982, empl 100, sales , cert: State)

4908   Decentxposure LLC
     75 Gorge Rd
     Edgewater, NJ 07020
     Contact: Joseph Confreda VP Finance
     Tel: 201-313-1100
     Email: jconfreda@dxagency.com
     Website: www.dxagency.com
Todayï¿½s customer wants more than your product or service, they want a relationship, a 1:1 connection where you keep track of their preferences, the details of past transactions, and anticipate their desires. (Minority, Woman, estab 2004, empl 45, sales $14,896,000, cert: NMSDC, WBENC)

4909   Diverse Lynx LLC
     300 Alexander Park, Ste 200
     Princeton, NJ 08540
     Contact: Hemanth Durvasula Sr Business Dev Mgr
     Tel: 732-452-1006
     Email: hemanth@diverselynx.com
     Website: www.diverselynx.com
Information technology staffing services. (Woman/As-Ind, estab 2002, empl 100, sales $18,000,000, cert: WBENC)

4910   EmployVision, Inc.
     1100 Cornwall Road Ste 115
     Monmouth Junction, NJ 08854
     Contact: Ash Geria Managing Dir
     Tel: 732-422-7100
     Email: ash@emplolyvision.com
     Website: www.employvision.com
Information technology, recruitment, RPO, IT consulting, staffing. (Minority, Woman, estab 2005, empl 10, sales $3,445,280, cert: NMSDC)

4911   Enin Systems, Inc.
     666 Plainsboro Rd
     Plainsboro, NJ 08536
     Contact: Raj Vendra VP
     Tel: 615-710-8582
     Email: su@eninsystems.com
     Website: www.eninsystems.com/
IT Services, Consulting and Business Solutions. (Woman/As-Pac, estab 2019, empl 60, sales , cert: State, NMSDC, WBENC)

4912   eTeam, Inc.
     1001 Durham Ave Ste 201
     South Plainfield, NJ 07080
     Contact: Ann Thakur Dir Strategic Accounts
     Tel: 732-248-1900
     Email: rfp@eteaminc.com
     Website: www.eteaminc.com
IT, Business Consulting, Management Consulting. (Minority, estab 1999, empl 1300, sales $93,586,862, cert: State, NMSDC, CPUC)

4913   Evergreen Technologies, LLC
     2050 Route 27 Ste 202
     North Brunswick, NJ 08902
     Contact: Elan Kling Sr Acct Mgr
     Tel: 732-422-1500
     Email: elank@evergreentechnologies.com
     Website: www.evergreentechnologies.com
Provides top-notch IT talent with a depth of knowledge in the latest cutting-edge technologies. (Minority, Woman, estab 1998, empl 80, sales $3,154,475, cert: State, NMSDC, WBENC)

4914 ExterNetworks Inc.
10 Corporate Place S, Ste 1-05
Piscataway, NJ 08854
Contact: Abdul Moiz Sr Dir
Tel: 908-751-0875
Email: mmoiz@externetworks.com
Website: www.externetworks.com
Staff augumentation, IT professional services, managed services. (Minority, Woman, estab 2001, empl 205, sales $20,000,000, cert: CPUC, WBENC)

4915 Fabergent, Inc.
63 Ramapo Valley Rd, Ste 214
Mahwah, NJ 07430
Contact: Ratna Silpa Gorantla President
Tel: 201-378-0036
Email: ratna@fabergent.com
Website: www.fabergent.com
Contract & full-time positions IT staffing in Java, .Net, SharePoint, SAP, Oracle, BI, Analytics, networking & IT security. (Minority, Woman, estab 2005, empl 125, sales , cert: State)

4916 Fortidm Technologies LLC
103 Carnegie Center Ste 300
Princeton, NJ 08540
Contact: Hariram Hari President
Tel: 609-851-7190
Email: chari@fortidm.com
Website: www.fortidm.com
IT Program management, information security advisory, identity & access management, secured SDLC, vulnerability management services. (Woman/As-Ind, estab 2005, empl 9, sales $900,000, cert: State, City, 8(a), SDB)

4917 Fourth Technologies Inc.
1816 Springdale Road
Cherry Hill, NJ 08003
Contact: Ravi Shankar CEO
Tel: 856-751-4848
Email: ravi@fortek.com
Website: www.fortek.com
IT Solutions & Staffing; Customized, cost-effective, reliable solutions; SEI-CMM assessed & quality conscious; Resource Management Group. (As-Ind, estab 1987, empl 200, sales , cert: NMSDC)

4918 Futran Solutions Inc.
2025 Lincoln Hwy Ste 110
Edison, NJ 08817
Contact: Jyoti Vazirani President
Tel: 908-279-3112
Email: apankaj@futransolutions.com
Website: www.futransolutions.com
IT services, information technology services. (Minority, estab 2010, empl 150, sales $7,000,000, cert: State, NMSDC)

4919 FYI Systems Inc.
3799 Route 46 E
Parsippany, NJ 07054
Contact: Mindy Zaziski
Tel: 973-909-0390
Email: colleen.luzaj@fyisolutions.com
Website: www.fyisolutions.com
IT solutions: corporate performance mgmt, business intelligence, analytics, data warehousing, web dev, systems integration, project mgmt, applications support, testing, etc. (Woman, estab 1984, empl 100, sales $14,500,000, cert: WBENC)

4920 Global IT Solutions, Inc.
200 Centennial Ave Ste 200
Middlesex, NJ 08846
Contact: William Moore President
Tel: 732-667-3578
Email: info@globalitsolutionscorp.com
Website: www.globalitsolutionscorp.com
Software development life cycle. (AA, estab 2008, empl 2, sales , cert: State, NMSDC)

4921 Globalnest LLC
281 State Route 79, Ste 208
Morganville, NJ 07751
Contact: Durga P Mikkilineni Partner
Tel: 732-333-1901
Email: durgam@globalnest.com
Website: www.globalnest.com
IT staffing, software development & design. (Minority, estab 2005, empl 170, sales $12,000,000, cert: NMSDC, CPUC)

4922 Government Systems Technologies, Inc.
3159 Schrader Rd
Dover, NJ 07801
Contact: Prashanth Kalnad Mgr Finance & Contracts
Tel: 973-361-2627
Email: accounting@gstiusa.com
Website: www.gstiusa.com
Consulting services, software products, full service SAP implementations & offshore development and support. (Woman/As-Ind, estab 2002, empl 46, sales $16,367,405, cert: NMSDC)

4923 Hired by Matrix, Inc.
266 Harristwon Rd Ste 202
Rochelle Park, NJ 07452
Contact: Jennifer Catanese Supplier Diversity & Business Devel
Tel: 201-587-0777
Email: jcatanese@hiredbymatrix.com
Website: www.hiredbymatrix.com
IT consulting svcs & permanent placements. (Woman, estab 1986, empl 275, sales $23,000,000, cert: WBENC)

4924 iii Technologies Inc.
100 Horizon Center Blvd, Ste 100
Hamilton, NJ 08691
Contact: Deepak Mandrekar President
Tel: 609-901-8000
Email: drman@iiitech.com
Website: www.iiitech.com
IT & SAP transformation projects, SAP program management, project management, architecture & implementation consulting. (As-Ind, estab 2005, empl 1, sales $150,000, cert: State, NMSDC)

4925 InfoQuest Consulting Group Inc.
68 Culver Road Ste 106
Monmouth Junction, NJ 08852
Contact: Vinita Lobo Business Mgr
Tel: 609-409-5151
Email: vinita@infoquestgroup.com
Website: www.infoquestgroup.com
IT contract staffing: ERP, CRM, business intelligence, infrastructure management, industry verticals. (Minority, Woman, estab 1994, empl 40, sales $4,000,000, cert: NMSDC)

4926 Inforeem
One Quality Pl
Edison, NJ 08820
Contact: Bhal Deshpande CEO
Tel: 732-494-4100
Email: bhal@inforeem.com
Website: www.inforeem.com
IT consulting services. (As-Pac, estab 2004, empl 40, sales $3,000,000, cert: State)

4927 Innospire Systems Corporation
281 State Route 79
Morganville, NJ 07751
Contact: Raj Durai President
Tel: 732-858-1740
Email: vrm@innospire.com
Website: www.innospire.com
IT consulting, custom application development & advanced analytics solutions, Predictive Analytics, Enterprise Performance Management, Mobile & Custom Application development. (As-Ind, estab 1996, empl 5, sales $355,480, cert: NMSDC)

4928 Instaknow.com, Inc.
180 Talmadge Rd, Ste 32
Edison, NJ 08817
Contact: Paul Khandekar CEO
Tel: 908-650-9598
Email: pkhandekar@instaknow.com
Website: www.instaknow.com
Artificial Intelligence software solutions. (As-Ind, estab 1999, empl 3, sales $293,478, cert: NMSDC, CPUC)

4929 Integration International Inc.
1081 Parsippany Blvd, Ste#101
Parsippany, NJ 07054
Contact: Rahul Chitte
Tel: 973-796-2300
Email: rahul.chitte@i3intl.com
Website: www.i3intl.com
IT infrastructure planning & implementation, software dev, ERP design & deployment, offshore software development & network monitoring. (Minority, estab 2000, empl 400, sales $23,000,000, cert: NMSDC)

4930 Intellyk Inc.
15 Corporate Place S Ste 450
Piscataway, NJ 08854
Contact: Vineet Kumar CEO
Tel: 732-399-9510
Email: vineet@intellyk.com
Website: www.intellyk.com/
IT consulting and technology professional services. (As-Pac, estab 2007, empl 200, sales $13,000,000, cert: State, NMSDC)

4931 International Digital Systems
400 Kelby St, 6th Fl
Fort Lee, NJ 07024
Contact: Anthony Han CEO
Tel: 201-983-7700
Email: ahan@idigitalsystems.com
Website: www.idigitalsystems.com
Server, Network management, Helpdesk, Desktop Support. Microsoft .Net C# based system development. Data Cabling, Data Center build up, SAN, NAS, Server & Network Hardware Resell. (As-Pac, estab 2005, empl 20, sales $1,883,584, cert: State)

4932 International Technology Solutions, Inc.
2000 Cornwall Road Ste 220
Monmouth Junction, NJ 08852
Contact: Brian Armstrong Dir Business Dev
Tel: 732-754-7019
Email: brian@itcsolutions.com
Website: www.itcsolutions.com
Information technology consulting & software development services. (Minority, estab 1998, empl 165, sales , cert: NMSDC)

4933 Intuity Technologies, LLC
One Gateway Center Ste 2600
Newark, NJ 07102
Contact: Max Bhavnani VP Operations
Tel: 201-880-0774
Email: mbhavnani@intuitytech.com
Website: www.intuitytech.com
IT Services, Oracle Hyperion tool-set (Essbase, Planning, HFM, DRM/MDM Financial Reporting) & Oracle Business Intelligence (OBIEE, Staff Augmentation, Implementations, Infrastructure, Performance Tuning. (As-Ind, estab 2005, empl 12, sales $1,100,000, cert: State)

4934 iQuanti, Inc.
111 Town Square Place Ste 710
Jersey City, NJ 07310
Contact: Vish Sastry CEO
Tel: 718-223-3403
Email: supplier@iquanti.com
Website: www.iquanti.com/
Web analytics, web development, web design, online marketing, search engine optimization, pay per click. (As-Ind, estab 2008, empl 205, sales $5,867,132, cert: NMSDC)

4935 Iris Software Inc.
200 Metroplex Dr, Ste 300
Edison, NJ 08817
Contact: Jonathan Fabros Dir
Tel: 732-393-0034
Email: jfabros@irissoftinc.com
Website: www.irissoftware.com
Information technology services. (Minority, estab 1994, empl 200, sales $180,000,000, cert: NMSDC)

4936 ISES, Inc
372 Rte 22 West
Whitehouse Station, NJ 08889
Contact: Kathleen Sullivan Dir
Tel: 800-447-4737
Email: ksullivan@isesincorporated.com
Website: www.isesincorporated.com
Information technology consulting: esolutions & ecommerce, B2B, knowledge mgmt, customer relationship mgmt, application dev & support, database dev & admin, data warehousing, telecommunications, systems support & admin. (Woman, estab 1980, empl 142, sales $20,000,000, cert: WBENC)

4937   IT by Design
       120 Wood Ave S Ste 608
       Iselin, NJ 08830
       Contact: Kam Attwal CEO
       Tel: 646-380-0688
       Email: kkaila@itbd.net
       Website: www.itbd.net
Infrastructure management, virtualization/cloud computing, data center hosting, managed backups, implementations/migrations & 24x7x365 Live Help Desk. (Woman/As-Ind, estab 2003, empl 100, sales $3,000,000, cert: WBENC)

4938   IT Staffing, Inc.
       5 Bliss Court Ste 200
       Woodcliff Lake, NJ 07677
       Contact: Jerry G. Myers Dir Business Dev
       Tel: 201-505-0493
       Email: jerry.myers@itstaffinc.com
       Website: www.itstaffinc.com
Strategic contract sourcing, consulting, staff augmentation, managed teams & outsourcing. (Minority, Woman, estab 1998, empl 78, sales $11,500,000, cert: State)

4939   IT Trailblazers
       2050 Route 27, Ste 203
       North Brunswick, NJ 08902
       Contact: Chris Jones Business Head
       Tel: 732-227-1772
       Email: chris@ittblazers.com
       Website: www.ittblazers.com
Information Technology Consulting, onsite and offshore capabilities. (As-Ind, estab 1999, empl 100, sales $37,000,000, cert: State)

4940   ITM Information & Technology Management
       6 Kilmer Rd
       Edison, NJ 08817
       Contact: Jeffrey Snow Business Devel Mgr
       Tel: 732-339-9801
       Email: jeffs@itmsys.com
       Website: www.itmsys.com
Computer consulting, applications development, QA, infrastructure support, SAP implimentation, database administration, maintanance & support, data warehousing, technical support. (Minority, Woman, estab 1989, empl 40, sales $2,750,000, cert: State, NMSDC)

4941   Kavayah Solutions Inc.
       5 Independence Way, Ste 360
       Princeton, NJ 08540
       Contact: Vivek Casula Principal
       Tel: 609-919-9797
       Email: vivek.casula@kavayahsolutions.com
       Website: www.kavayahsolutions.com
Enterprise application management (development and maintenance) & project management services, technology solutions, staff augmentation. (As-Ind, estab 2006, empl 10, sales $1,224,316, cert: State)

4942   LexHarbor, LLC
       1974 State Route 27
       Edison, NJ 08817
       Contact: Akshat Tewary Dir
       Tel: 626-427-2674
       Email: info@lexharbor.com
       Website: www.lexharbor.com
Information technology services. (As-Ind, estab 2007, empl 2, sales $100,000, cert: NMSDC)

4943   Link2consult, Inc.
       1 Bridge Plaza Ste 275
       Fort Lee, NJ 07024
       Contact: Peter McCree President
       Tel: 201-308-9101
       Email: peter.mccree@link2consult.com
       Website: www.link2consult.com
Information technology consulting: PeopleSoft, human resources & finance solutions. (AA, estab 1992, empl 35, sales $5,800,000, cert: State, NMSDC, CPUC)

4944   Logistic Solutions Inc.
       216 Stelton Rd Ste 2
       Piscataway, NJ 08854
       Contact: Al Limaye President
       Tel: 732-743-2300
       Email: al.limaye@logistic-solutions.com
       Website: www.logistic-solutions.com
Information technologies, Mobile (iPhone, Android, Blackberry/RIM) content aggregation services. (As-Pac, estab 1990, empl 715, sales $140,000,000, cert: NMSDC)

4945   Maestro Technologies, Inc.
       510 Thornall St Ste 375
       Edison, NJ 08837
       Contact: Kamal Bathla Managing Dir
       Tel: 908-458-8600
       Email: kamal.s.bathla@maestro.com
       Website: www.maestro.com
Actuarial Sciences, Big Data & Technologies, Data Science, IT Services. (Woman/As-Ind, estab 2003, empl 63, sales $6,800,000, cert: State, City, NMSDC)

4946   Makro Technologies, Inc.
       One Washington Park, Ste 1303
       Newark, NJ 07102
       Contact: Pritesh Dholakia Business Devel
       Tel: 973-481-0100
       Email: pritesh.dholakia@makrocare.com
       Website: www.makrocare.com
Information technology, IT staffing services. (As-Ind, estab 1996, empl 650, sales $45,000,000, cert: State)

4947   Marlabs Inc.
       One Corporate Place S
       Piscataway, NJ 08854
       Contact: Danielle Jennings Assoc Business Dev Mgr
       Tel: 732-694-1000
       Email: danielle.jennings@marlabs.com
       Website: www.marlabs.com
Information technology services & solutions: IT strategy consulting, resources & staff augmentation, application dev, business intelligence solutions, SAP & Oracle, ERP/CRM systems, data warehousing. (As-Pac, estab 1996, empl 2100, sales $92,000,000, cert: NMSDC)

4948   MARVEL INFOTECH Inc.
       45 Knightsbridge Rd Ste 101
       Piscataway, NJ 08854
       Contact: Venkat Sales
       Tel: 732-906-0444
       Email: vbokka@marvelinfotech.com
       Website: www.marvelinfotech.com
Information technology staffing, consulting. (As-Pac, estab 2000, empl 25, sales $1,850,000, cert: NMSDC)

4949 MashPoint, LLC
   100 Wood Ave S Ste 109
   Iselin, NJ 08830
   Contact: KJ Saini President
   Tel: 732-515-7171
   Email: kjsaini@mashpoint.com
   Website: www.mashpoint.com
Staffing services, data management, data quality, data security, business intelligence, web & mobile development & internet marketing services. (As-Ind, estab 2011, empl 55, sales , cert: NMSDC)

4950 Masterex Technologies, Inc.
   379 Princeton-Hightstown Rd, Bldg 2
   Cranbury, NJ 08512
   Contact: Sunny Gupta Business Devel Mgr
   Tel: 302-632-9532
   Email: info@masterexinc.com
   Website: www.Masterexinc.com
IT staffing , application development, project management, framework, on-shore & offshore testing & QA services. (Woman/As-Ind, estab 2002, empl 60, sales $5,000,000, cert: State)

4951 Mercury Systems, Inc.
   5 Independence Way Ste 140
   Princeton, NJ 08540
   Contact: Wing Li Administrative Mgr, VP
   Tel: 609-937-2801
   Email: wli@mercurysystemsinc.com
   Website: www.mercurysystemsinc.com
Consulting, IT Staffing & IT Placement services. (As-Pac, estab 1999, empl 170, sales $10,000,000, cert: State)

4952 microMEDIA Imaging Systems, Inc.
   300-2 Route 17 South, Ste 4
   Lodi, NJ 07644
   Contact: Joseph Wise President
   Tel: 973-685-5164
   Email: jwise@imagingservices.com
   Website: www.imagingservices.com
Document conversion & scanning services, Data Capture, Data Migration, Document Hosting. (Woman, estab 1993, empl 85, sales $3,200,000, cert: State, City)

4953 Millennium Info Tech. Inc.
   101 Morgan Lane Ste 204
   Plainsboro, NJ 08536
   Contact: Ramana Krosuri President
   Tel: 609-750-7120
   Email: ramana@mitiweb.com
   Website: www.mitiweb.com
Application Development, Business Analysis/Project Management, Business Intelligence, Data/Database Management, Document Management, ERP, ETL, Information Security/Compliance, Migration Services. (As-Ind, estab 1999, empl 150, sales $9,500,000, cert: State)

4954 Mindlance, Inc.
   1095 Morris Ave
   Union, NJ 07083
   Contact: Vik Kalra Co-Founder & Managing Dir
   Tel: 201-386-5400
   Email: cws@mindlance.com
   Website: www.mindlance.com
IT contigent staffing, offshore recruitment, IT permanent placement, software, semiconductor, finance & insurance. (As-Ind, estab 1999, empl 5000, sales $300,000,000, cert: NMSDC)

4955 MKI Group, LLC dba IS3 Solutions
   740 Broad St Ste 1
   Shrewsbury, NJ 07702
   Contact: John Marshall President
   Tel: 732-945-0403
   Email: sraffetto@is3sol.com
   Website: www.is3sol.com
Information technology solutions, Services & Staffing programs. (AA, estab 2010, empl 220, sales , cert: NMSDC)

4956 Momento USA LLC
   440 Benigno Blvd Unit A, 2nd Fl
   Bellmawr, NJ 08031
   Contact: Hasheem Himmati Dir
   Tel: 856-432-4774
   Email: info@momentousa.com
   Website: www.momentousa.com
Project Management, Application Development, Business Analysis, Systems Analysis, System Design, ERP, Database Administration, Systems Engineering, Systems Maintenance, Systems Testing, Systems Architecture, Systems Administration. (As-Pac, estab 2009, empl 28, sales $2,128,413, cert: NMSDC)

4957 MSquare Systems Inc.
   35 Journal Sq, Ste 415
   Jersey City, NJ 07306
   Contact: Muthu Natarajan President
   Tel: 201-290-6728
   Email: info@msquaresystems.com
   Website: www.msquaresystems.com
IT consulting services. (As-Pac, estab 2005, empl 5, sales $403,967, cert: NMSDC)

4958 Mutex Systems Inc.
   50 Cragwood Rd Ste 224
   South Plainfield, NJ 07080
   Contact: Bill Scharnikow BDM
   Tel: 908-822-8515
   Email: bill.scharnikow@mutexsystems.com
   Website: www.mutexsystems.com
IT staff augmentation & consulting services. (Minority, Woman, estab 1999, empl 100, sales $10,000,000, cert: State)

4959 NatSoft Corporation
   27 Worlds Fair Dr
   Somerset, NJ 08873
   Contact: Rakesh Kotha Business Devel Mgr
   Tel: 732-939-2969
   Email: rakeshkv@natsoft.us
   Website: www.natsoft.us
Software development, IT consulting, Enterprise application development, ERP implementation & support, Quality assurance services on offshore/Onsite/Nearshore model. (As-Pac, estab 2004, empl 300, sales , cert: State)

4960 NCS Technologies, Inc.
   15 Corporate Place S Ste 200
   Piscataway, NJ 08854
   Contact: Michael Giannotti Sales
   Tel: 732-562-8880
   Email: mgiannotti@ncstech.com
   Website: www.ncstech.com
Data warehousing, business intelligence, enterprise architecture, process engineering & enterprise security. (Hisp, estab 1984, empl 155, sales $29,000,000, cert: NMSDC)

4961 Neo Tech Solutions, Inc.
      1 Cragwood Rd Ste 301
      South Plainfield, NJ 07080
      Contact: CEO
      Tel: 917-385-8717
      Email: info@neotechusa.com
      Website: www.neotechusa.com
IT, telecommunications, program & project management:
(As-Ind, estab 1996, empl 63, sales , cert: NMSDC)

4962 Neotecra, Inc.
      200 Craig Rd Ste 109
      Manalapan, NJ 07726
      Contact: Nirmal Goswamy VP
      Tel: 212-693-3353
      Email: nirmal@neotecra.com
      Website: www.neotecra.com
IT staffing & consulting, data communication, system
programming & administration, client-server application
development. (Minority, Woman, estab 2000, empl 90,
sales $4,020,000, cert: State)

4963 NetTarius Technology Solutions, LLC
      35 College Dr
      East Orange, NJ 07017
      Contact: Derrick Law President
      Tel: 973-788-1955
      Email: sdiversity@nettarius.net
      Website: www.nettarius.com
Business Strategy, Technology Design & Integration, Fiber
Wireless Broadband, Data Network, Video Technology,
Web & Application Development, Cloud Services, Installa-
tion & Support. (AA, estab 2003, empl 5, sales $300,000,
cert: NMSDC)

4964 New Instruction, LLC
      615 Valley Rd
      Upper Montclair, NJ 07043
      Contact: Dir of Training
      Tel: 973-744-3339
      Email: training@newinstruction.com
      Website: www.newinstruction.com/
Instructor-led technology training: systems & software
engineering, project management, programming languages, internet security, telecommunications & networking, management & leadership skills. (Woman, estab 1978,
empl 4, sales $1,000,000, cert: WBENC)

4965 NewAgeSys, Inc.
      4390 US Hwy 1
      Princeton, NJ 08540
      Contact: Gintu Mary Eapen Business Devel Mgr
      Tel: 609-919-9800
      Email: contact@newagesys.com
      Website: www.newagesys.com
Validation & quality mgmt svcs, custom application devel,
SAP upgrade & support svcs, information security, infrastructure services. (Woman/As-Ind, estab 1994, empl 285,
sales $21,000,000, cert: NMSDC, WBENC)

4966 NexAge Technologies USA Inc.
      75 Lincoln Hwy Ste 104
      Iselin, NJ 08830
      Contact: Suresh Kumar CEO
      Tel: 732-494-4944
      Email: minoritymanager@nexageusa.com
      Website: www.nexageusa.com
IT staffing & consulting, software applications. (As-Pac,
estab 2001, empl 65, sales , cert: State, NMSDC)

4967 NIKSUN Inc.
      100 Nassau Park Blvd 3rd Fl
      Princeton, NJ 08540
      Contact: Christopher Dervishian VP Operations
      Tel: 609-936-9999
      Email: cdervish@niksun.com
      Website: www.niksun.com
Develop real time & forensics-based cybersecurity,
network performance management & mobility solutions. (As-Ind, estab 1997, empl 175, sales , cert:
NMSDC)

4968 NPD Global Inc.
      3 Lincoln Hwy Ste 102
      Edison, NJ 07018
      Contact: Nagesh Davuluri President
      Tel: 732-902-6342
      Email: ndavuluri@npdglobal.com
      Website: www.npdglobal.com
IT staffing & recruiting services. (Nat Ame, estab 2006,
empl 30, sales $6,000,000, cert: NMSDC)

4969 Optima Global Solutions, Inc.
      3113 Princeton Pike Bldg. 3, Ste 207
      Lawrenceville, NJ 08648
      Contact: Rajesh Sinha Federal Business Specialist
      Tel: 609-586-8811
      Email: rajesh@optimags.com
      Website: www.optimags.com
IT staffing, BPM, Data Warehousing, Business Intelligence, Microsoft & Enterprise Mobility. (As-Ind, estab
2001, empl 10, sales $3,186,483, cert: NMSDC, 8(a))

4970 PamTen Inc.
      5 Independence Way, Ste # 180
      Princeton, NJ 08540
      Contact: Satish Kommareddy Acct Mgr
      Tel: 609-643-4228
      Email: satish.kommareddy@pamten.com
      Website: www.pamten.com
IT Strategy, Planning, Program/Project Management,
Business Process Management. (Woman/As-Ind, estab
2002, empl 160, sales $13,500,000, cert: State, City,
NMSDC)

4971 Paxton Consultants Limited Liability Company
      50 Brandywine Rise
      Green Brook, NJ 08812
      Contact: Anand Emmanuel CEO
      Tel: 831-210-8850
      Email: anand.emmanuel@paxtonconsultants.com
      Website: www.paxtonconsultants.com
Information Technology (IT) Consulting & Staffing
Solutions. (As-Ind, estab 2007, empl 2, sales , cert: State)

4972 Peri Software Solutions
      570 Broad St
      Newark, NJ 07102
      Contact: Rosemarie Lederer Sr Acct Mgr
      Tel: 973-735-9500
      Email: rlederer@perisoftware.com
      Website: www.perisoftware.com
Open source solutions, IT staff augmentation, offshore
business outsourcing, custom application development.
(Minority, Woman, estab 1999, empl 700, sales
$12,631,398, cert: NMSDC)

4973 Pioneer Data Systems, Inc.
379 Thornall St
Edison, NJ 08837
Contact: Naushad Mulji Dir
Tel: 732-603-0001
Email: nmulji@pioneerdata.com
Website: www.pioneerdata.com
Client-server, e-business, data warehousing, CRM & ERP. (As-Ind, estab 1995, empl 100, sales $5,000,000, cert: NMSDC)

4974 Platys Group
100 Franklin Square Dr
Somerset, NJ 08873
Contact: Darren Cobb VP Business Dev
Tel: 908-888-6007
Email: dcobb@platysgroup.com
Website: www.platygroup.com
IT consulting & software solutions. (Minority, Woman, estab 2008, empl 140, sales $10,000,000, cert: State)

4975 Presafe Technologies, LLC
PO Box 5872
Somerset, NJ 08875
Contact: Robert V Jones CEO
Tel: 732-887-2442
Email: rvjones@presafetech.com
Website: www.presafetech.com
Cybersecurity architecture & design; Secure network planning & design, enterprise system design, network builds, migration upgrades; Data center planning design, consolidation migrations & relocations; network & performance mgmt. (AA, estab 2010, empl 2, sales , cert: State)

4976 Princeton Web Systems Inc.
1901 N Olden Ave Ext, Ste 8A
Ewing, NJ 08618
Contact: Bhavesh Senedhun CEO
Tel: 888-485-9040
Email: bhavesh@princetonwebsystems.com
Website: www.princetonwebsystems.com
Custom software development, software & application development, website design, mobile app development, IT staff augmentation, staffing & networking solutions. (Minority, estab 2014, empl 25, sales $1,000,000, cert: State)

4977 Rang Technologies Inc.
15 Corporate Place S
Piscataway, NJ 08854
Contact: Gary Sacks Sr VP
Tel: 732-947-4119
Email: sales@rangtech.com
Website: www.rangtech.com/
Analytics & Data Science solutions & comprehensive IT staffing services. (As-Ind, estab 2005, empl 474, sales $25,004,426, cert: State, NMSDC)

4978 Rangam Consultants Inc.
270 Davidson Ave Ste 103
Somerset, NJ 08873
Contact: Hetal Parikh President
Tel: 908-704-8843
Email: rci@rangam.com
Website: www.rangam.com
IT staffing & outsourced web application development services. (Minority, Woman, estab 1995, empl 712, sales $42,500,000, cert: State, City, NMSDC, WBENC)

4979 Rapid Response Computer Service Inc.
2313 Route 33
Robbinsville, NJ 08691
Contact: Terry Ikey Owner
Tel: 609-945-2389
Email: tikey@rapidresponsecs.com
Website: www.rapidresponsecs.com
Software development, website design, network installation & support & compuer repair. (Woman, estab 2004, empl 12, sales $750,000, cert: State)

4980 RCI Technologies
1133 Green St
Iselin, NJ 08830
Contact: Gereld Boffa Exec VP
Tel: 732-382-3000
Email: gereld@rci-technologies.com
Website: www.rci-technologies.com
Custom software development & IT staffing, consulting services. (Minority, Woman, estab 1983, empl 63, sales $8,000,000, cert: State, City, WBENC)

4981 Real Soft Inc.
68 Culver Road Ste 100
Monmouth Junction, NJ 08852
Contact: Joel Jerva VP
Tel: 609-409-3636
Email: joel@realsoftinc.com
Website: www.realsoftinc.com
Software development, consulting & staffing, offshore resources, turnkey dev, voice solutions, IVR, VXML. (Minority, estab 1991, empl 450, sales $30,000,000, cert: NMSDC)

4982 RedSalsa Technologies, Inc.
12 Roszel Rd Ste A-204
Princeton, NJ 08540
Contact: Kiran Vallurupalli CEO
Tel: 609-243-9603
Email: k_vallurupalli@redsalsa.com
Website: www.redsalsa.com/
IT consulting services: internet & e-business consulting, system integration, custom application development & application management. (Minority, estab 1993, empl 120, sales , cert: NMSDC)

4983 Reliant Tech., Inc.
2137 Route 35 Ste 365
Holmdel, NJ 07733
Contact: Subhash Kothari President
Tel: 732-583-6244
Email: skothari@relianttech.com
Website: www.relianttech.com
Application development, technical training, Sun Solaris, HP UX certified. (Minority, estab 1985, empl 30, sales $3,000,000, cert: State)

4984 Revision Technologies Inc.
10 Station Place, Ste 3
Metuchen, NJ 08840
Contact: Raja Balan President
Tel: 732-261-9239
Email: raja.balan@revisiontek.com
Website: www.revisiontek.com
Data Center Design, support, maintenance.Networking, IP and SAN products, Project management, Storage Area Networking architect, planning, implementation, system analysis, Big Data, Cloud implementation & support services. (As-Ind, estab 2006, empl 4, sales $17,792,057, cert: NMSDC)

4985   Samiti Technologies, Inc.
      2 Lincoln Hwy Ste 401
      Edison, NJ 08820
      Contact: Akash Kulshrestha Client Relationship
      Specialist
      Tel: 732-516-0066
      Email: rfp@samitimail.com
      Website: www.samititechnology.com
Software development & consulting services. (Minority, Woman, estab 2003, empl 70, sales $11,796,921, cert: State, NMSDC)

4986   Satnam Data Systems, Inc.
      220 Davidson Ave Ste 318
      Somerset, NJ 08873
      Contact: Parita Patel Dir Business Dev
      Tel: 732-961-8383
      Email: parita@satnam.com
      Website: www.satnam.com
Technology Consulting, Professional & Outsourcing services., Staff Augmentation Services, Custom Development Services, Software Integration Services, Custom Solution Services,   Business Applications, Database Development. (Minority, Woman, estab 1994, empl 23, sales $6,500,000, cert: State, NMSDC, CPUC)

4987   Scadea Solutions Inc
      100 Franklin Square Dr Ste 304
      Somerset, NJ 08873
      Contact: Sreekanth Akkapalli CEO
      Tel: 609-937-6699
      Email: sreekanth@scadea.net
      Website: www.scadea.net
ERP, Consulting & Outsourcing Services. (Woman/As-Ind, estab 2011, empl 150, sales $9,000,000, cert: WBENC)

4988   Scalable Systems Inc.
      15 Corporate Place S Ste 222
      Piscataway, NJ 08854
      Contact: Suman Bajaj Acct Mgr
      Tel: 732-333-3191
      Email: sumanb@scalable-systems.com
      Website: www.scalable-systems.com
Software consulting, development & IT outsourcing, offshore & onshore software solutions & integration services. (As-Ind, estab 2005, empl 30, sales $3,000,000, cert: State, NMSDC)

4989   Scalar Solutions, LLC.
      330 Changebridge Rd, Ste 101
      Pinebrook, NJ 07058
      Contact: Mariana C Mgr Sales
      Tel: 973-767-3260
      Email: sales@scalarsol.com
      Website: www.scalarsol.com
IT consulting/staffing, end-to-end IT consulting services, Software Development Services (Java, Dot Net Platform), Database & Data warehouse development (SQL Server, Oracle, MPP Systems, Cloud, Hadoop Big data), Database Administration. (As-Ind, estab 2013, empl 2, sales , cert: State)

4990   SEAL Consulting Inc.
      105 Fieldcrest Ave 4th FL, Raritan Plaza 3
      Edison, NJ 08837
      Contact: John Beaumont VP
      Tel: 732-947-4901
      Email: info@sealconsult.com
      Website: www.sealconsult.com/
Systems integration, implementation services & staffing: ERP, APO, SEM, BW and SRM. (As-Ind, estab 1996, empl 400, sales $50,000,000, cert: NMSDC)

4991   Seven Seven Softwares, Inc.
      217 E Main St
      Rockaway, NJ 07866
      Contact: Adela Sering VP / Global HR Dir
      Tel: 973-586-1817
      Email: dsering@77soft.com
      Website: www.77soft.com
Information technology, business process outsourcing & call center services. (Minority, Woman, estab 1996, empl 335, sales , cert: NMSDC)

4992   Silicon Alley Group, Inc.
      1 Austin Ave. 2nd Fl
      Iselin, NJ 08830
      Contact: Terrance L Sprinkle Business Devel Mgr
      Tel: 732-326-1600
      Email: tsprinkle@sag-inc.com
      Website: www.sag-inc.com
Information technology services & solutions. (Minority, Woman, estab 2003, empl 30, sales $1,901,608, cert: State, 8(a))

4993   Smart Information Management Systems Inc
      103 Morgan Lane
      Plainsboro, NJ 08536
      Contact: Bharath Medisetty Sr Recruitment Exec
      Tel: 609-269-2732
      Email: bharath.medisetty@smartims.com
      Website: www.SmartIMS.com
Information Management Systems, Software Consulting, Recruitment & Staffing, Quality Assurance Testing & Certification, Custom application development services. (Woman/As-Ind, estab 1994, empl 450, sales $23,000,000, cert: State, City, NMSDC)

4994   Smart Source Technologies, Inc.
      622 Georges Rd Ste 203
      North Brunswick, NJ 08902
      Contact: Shaan Kelly Acct Rep
      Tel: 732-729-7700
      Email: subcontract@smartsourcetec.com
      Website: www.smartsourcetec.com
IT staffing, application & web development, database administration & development, data warehousing & systems administration, business analyst & project management. (Minority, Woman, estab 1999, empl 52, sales $6,000,000, cert: State)

4995   Software Professional Solutions, Inc.
      1315 Hwy 34 2nd Fl
      Farmingdale, NJ 07727
      Contact: Suzanne Schlesinger President
      Tel: 732-751-8770
      Email:
      Website: www.spshome.com
Custom software solutions: develop & implementation, system upgrades, software conversions & system integrations. (Woman, estab 1995, empl 40, sales , cert: WBENC)

4996　Software Synergy, Inc.
　　　151 Hwy 33 E Ste 252
　　　Manalapan, NJ 07726
　　　Contact: Rose Oxley CEO
　　　Tel:　732-617-9300
　　　Email: rmo@ssi-corp.com
　　　Website: www.ssi-corp.com
Information technology: automate key business processes, modernize legacy systems, integrate multi system & technology environments, data translations. (Woman, estab 1990, empl 10, sales $1,500,000, cert: WBENC)

4997　Software Technology, Inc.
　　　100 Overlook Center Ste 200
　　　Princeton, NJ 08540
　　　Contact: Scott Mandel VP Sales
　　　Tel:　609-858-0630
　　　Email: scott.mandel@stiorg.com
　　　Website: www.stiorg.com
IT staffing services. (Minority, Woman, estab 2004, empl 45, sales , cert: NMSDC)

4998　Solutions3 LLC
　　　637 Wyckoff Ave
　　　Wyckoff, NJ 07481
　　　Contact: Dianne McKim Exec Business Admin
　　　Tel:　845-365-0675
　　　Email: dianne.mckim@solutions3llc.com
　　　Website: www.solutions3llc.com
Enterprise Network & Systems Management (architecture and implementation), IT Service Management, Service Desk & associated process definitions (Incident & Problem Management, Change & Configuration Management). (Woman, estab 2003, empl 18, sales $2,707,834, cert: State)

4999　Source One Technical Solutions, LLC
　　　1952 Rte 22 East
　　　Bound Brook, NJ 08805
　　　Contact: Linda Ake President
　　　Tel:　732-748-8643
　　　Email: lake@source1tek.com
　　　Website: www.source1tek.com
Information technology staffing services, consulting & permanent placement. (Woman, estab 2003, empl 56, sales $4,036,000, cert: WBENC)

5000　SPHERE Technology Solutions
　　　525 Washington Blvd. Ste 2635
　　　Jersey City, NJ 07310
　　　Contact:　Chelsea White Dir
　　　Tel:　201-659-6204
　　　Email: chelsea.white@sphereco.com
　　　Website: www.sphereco.com
Data Governance, Security & Compliance centering on structured & un-structured data. (Woman, estab 2009, empl 22, sales $6,448,680, cert: State, WBENC)

5001　Spruce Technology, Inc.
　　　1149 Blloomfield Ave, Ste G
　　　Clifton, NJ 07012
　　　Contact: Srini Penumella CEO
　　　Tel:　781-413-5527
　　　Email: spenumella@sprucetech.com
　　　Website: www.sprucetech.net
Information technology consulting svcs: systems deployment, server infrastructure, technology deployment, network infrastructure, executive, management & general support. (As-Ind, estab 2006, empl 69, sales $42,000,000, cert: State, NMSDC)

5002　Sunrise Systems, Inc.
　　　105 Fieldcrest Ave, Ste 504
　　　Edison, NJ 08837
　　　Contact: Sandy Baldino Sr Acct Exec
　　　Tel:　732-395-4446
　　　Email: sandy@sunrisesys.com
　　　Website: www.sunrisesys.com
IT systems integration, systems integration. (As-Ind, estab 1990, empl 500, sales , cert: NMSDC)

5003　Synergem, Inc.
　　　2323 Randolph Ave
　　　Avenel, NJ 07001
　　　Contact: Amy Silverman President
　　　Tel:　732-225-0001
　　　Email: amysilverman@synergem.com
　　　Website: www.synergem.com
Duplicate DVD's, CD's & USBs, custom packaging, custom printing, fulfillment & distribution. (Woman, estab 1985, empl 26, sales $7,344,330, cert: WBENC)

5004　Systemart, LLC
　　　140 Littleton Rd, Ste 303
　　　Parsippany, NJ 07054
　　　Contact: Nitin Shah President
　　　Tel:　973-917-4834
　　　Email: mbe@systemart.com
　　　Website: www.systemart.com
IT related services, custom software dev, business process mgmt svcs. (Woman/As-Ind, estab 1999, empl 75, sales $5,000,000, cert: NMSDC)

5005　SystemGuru,Inc.
　　　900 Rte 9 N Ste 205
　　　Woodbridge, NJ 07095
　　　Contact: Nitin Sohal Business Dev Mgr
　　　Tel:　732-326-3951
　　　Email: nitin.sohal@systemguru.com
　　　Website: www.systemguru.com
Web enabled application development, data modeling & enterprise data architecture, application design & architecture. (As-Pac, estab 2000, empl 100, sales $8,907,001, cert: City)

5006　Technology Concepts Group International, LLC
　　　150 Maple Ave Ste 306
　　　Somerset, NJ 08873
　　　Contact: Elizabeth Shelton Office Mgr
　　　Tel:　732-659-6035
　　　Email: eshelton@technologyconcepts.com
　　　Website: www.technologyconcepts.com
E-business solutions, web design & hosting, systems integration, desktop support. (Woman/AA, estab 2008, empl 7, sales $21,000,000, cert: NMSDC, WBENC)

5007　TechnoSphere, Inc.
　　　21 Addison Rd
　　　Bergenfield, NJ 07621
　　　Contact: Aureo Capiral President
　　　Tel:　201-384-7400
　　　Email: aureo.capiral@technosphere.com
　　　Website: www.technosphere.com
IT staffing, contracting, contract programming svcs. (As-Pac, estab 1994, empl 26, sales $4,171,947, cert: State, NMSDC)

5008   Technovision, Inc.
       10 Stuyvesant Ave
       Lyndhurst, NJ 07071
       Contact: Anju Aggarwal President
       Tel: 732-381-0200
       Email: anju@etechnovision.com
       Website: www.etechnovision.com
IT Consulting. (Woman/As-Ind, estab 1995, empl 35, sales $3,000,000, cert: State, WBENC)

5009   The Sourcium Group
       833 Blanch Ave
       Norwood, NJ 07648
       Contact: Gabriella Lombardi CEO
       Tel: 201-447-1777
       Email: gabriella.lombardi@sourcium.net
       Website: www.sourcium.net
IT procurement, project management, desktop svcs, staff augmentation. (Woman, estab 2002, empl 12, sales , cert: WBENC)

5010   Triveni Group LLP
       71 Union Ave, Ste 208
       Rutherford, NJ 07070
       Contact: Jwalit Shah CEO
       Tel: 307-203-3888
       Email: Pratap.singh@triveniconsulting.com
       Website: www.triveniit.com
Full-service software consulting. (As-Pac, estab 2011, empl 55, sales , cert: NMSDC)

5011   Twintron Data Systems Inc.
       26 Woodbrook Rd
       Voorhees, NJ 08043
       Contact: Dayal Nagasuru President
       Tel: 856-952-8506
       Email: dayal.nagasuru@twintron.com
       Website: www.twintron.com
IT services (Java, C++, SQL, Big Data, .NET, Web Applications). (As-Ind, estab 2004, empl 5, sales $500,000, cert: NMSDC)

5012   Urooj LLC
       301 Route 17N Ste 800
       Rutherford, NJ 07070
       Contact: Salman Mohammed CEO
       Tel: 201-966-7861
       Email: salman@urooj.net
       Website: www.urooj.net
IT solutions, IT staffing, project architecture, design & analysis, project administration & management, web paradigm, e-commerce & web applications, networking & system administration, RF engineering, database admin & management. (As-Ind, estab , empl , sales $2,154,929, cert: City, NMSDC)

5013   US Tech Solutions, Inc.
       10 Exchange Place
       Jersey City, NJ 07302
       Contact: Michelle Vanetti Legal/Compliance Mgr
       Tel: 201-719-9953
       Email: Michelle@ustechsolutions.com
       Website: www.ustechsolutions.com
IT solutions: consulting, outsourcing, software development, engineering, systems integration, ERP, customer relationship management, supply chain mngt, product development, & electronic commerce. (As-Ind, estab 2000, empl 11500, sales $530,000,000, cert: NMSDC)

5014   V Group Inc.
       379 Princeton Hightstown Road Bldg 3, Ste 2A,
       Cranbury, NJ 08512
       Contact: Monika Rohila CEO
       Tel: 609-371-5400
       Email: certifications@vgroupinc.com
       Website: www.vgroupinc.com/
Software development consulting, networking, database admin, systems admin. (Minority, Woman, estab 1999, empl 35, sales $6,256,810, cert: WBENC)

5015   Vedicsoft Solutions Inc.
       100 Wood Ave, Ste 200
       Iselin, NJ 08830
       Contact: Sam Vaghela Strategic Business Alliance Mgr
       Tel: 732-906-3200
       Email: sam@vedicsoft.com
       Website: www.vedicsoft.com
IT technologies: ERP, data warehousing, web & client/server technologies. (As-Ind, estab 1999, empl 300, sales $54,000,000, cert: NMSDC)

5016   Vega Consulting Solutions, Inc.
       3 Romaine Rd
       Mountain Lakes, NJ 07046
       Contact: Carol Jones Dir Business Dev
       Tel: 973-335-7800
       Email: cjones@vegaconsulting.com
       Website: www.vegaconsulting.com
Information technology consulting svcs. (Woman, estab 1994, empl 70, sales , cert: WBENC)

5017   Ventures Unlimited Inc.
       309 Fellowship Rd, Ste 200
       Mount Laurel, NJ 08054
       Contact: Rajesh Varma President
       Tel: 201-377-5954
       Email: rvarma@vui-inc.com
       Website: www.vui-inc.com
IT consulting services: enterprise application services, product life cycle management, business process modeling. (Minority, estab 2004, empl 162, sales $4,500,000, cert: State, NMSDC, 8(a))

5018   Vichara Technologies Inc.
       5 Marine View Plaza Ste 312
       Hoboken, NJ 07030
       Contact: Atul Jain CEO
       Tel: 201-850-1912
       Email: payables@vichara.com
       Website: www.vichara.com
Software development services for financial institutions, banks & asset management firms, hedge funds, private equity firms. (As-Pac, estab 2000, empl 15, sales $7,259,788, cert: NMSDC)

5019   VNB Consulting Services, Inc.
       100 Menlo Park Ste 302B
       Edison, NJ 08837
       Contact: Nirav Shah Dir HR & Finance
       Tel: 732-474-0700
       Email: info@vnbconsulting.com
       Website: www.vnbconsulting.com
IT services, Business Intelligence, Analytics, CRM, Marketing & Application Integration solutions. (As-Ind, estab 2007, empl 25, sales $2,000,000, cert: State)

5020 WisEngineering, LLC
     3159 Schrader Rd
     Dover, NJ 07801
     Contact: Cheryl Hall President
     Tel: 973-783-1000
     Email: chall@wisengineering.com
     Website: www.wisengineering.com
Management information systems, close combat systems, combat ammo systems. (Woman/AA, estab 1998, empl 32, sales $6,338,536, cert: State, NMSDC, WBENC)

5021 XL Impex Inc DBA Atika Technologies
     5 Independence Way Ste 300
     Princeton, NJ 08540
     Contact: Ashish Dua President
     Tel: 732-907-9001
     Email: ash@atikaservices.com
     Website: www.atikatech.com
CRM recruiting, staff augmentation, IT services & Digital Marketing. (As-Pac, estab 2008, empl 22, sales $1,770,777, cert: NMSDC)

5022 Xybion Corporation & Subsidiaries
     105 College Road East
     Princeton, NJ 08540
     Contact: Nagraj Lanka Business Dev Dir
     Tel: 609-512-5790
     Email: nlanka@xybion.com
     Website: www.xybion.com
Compliance/software & services solutions, data migration, data content & compliance management, enterprise asset management, pre-clin/R&D, quality management, validation/software testing & IT consulting services. (As-Ind, estab 1977, empl 33, sales $7,751,400, cert: State, NMSDC)

5023 Z&A Infotek Corporation
     35 Waterview Blvd 2nd Fl
     Parsippany, NJ 07054
     Contact: John Pezzullo EVP
     Tel: 917-751-2299
     Email: johnp@znainc.com
     Website: www.znainc.com
Information technology, consulting & software, ERP & CRM, web enabling applications, RDBMS, project management, network infrastructure tools & management. (As-Ind, estab 2003, empl 90, sales $7,500,000, cert: NMSDC, 8(a))

New Mexico

5024 Westwind Computer Products
     5655 Jefferson St NE, Ste B
     Albuquerque, NM 87109
     Contact: Brigetta Koepke Supplier Diversity AE
     Tel: 505-345-4720
     Email: diversity@wwcpinc.com
     Website: www.wwcpinc.com/
Mobility & End User Computing, Enterprise Storage Solutions, Blade and Rack Server Integration, Large Deployment Rollouts, VDI design and pilots, Cyber Security, Control & Command Solutions, AV Solutions, VOIP / VTC. (Hisp, estab 1992, empl 56, sales $20,000,000, cert: NMSDC)

Nevada

5025 A.R. Acosta, Ltd. dba Alisa Acosta Business Conslt
     18124 Wedge Pkwy
     Reno, NV 89511
     Contact: Alisa Acosta President
     Tel: 702-203-4382
     Email: alisaa@earthlink.net
     Website: www.AlisaAcostaConsulting.com
Business consulting: process reengineering, documentation, process mapping, project management, develop training curriculum & conducting training. (Minority, Woman, estab 1998, empl 1, sales , cert: State, 8(a))

5026 Agilea Solutions, Inc.
     6671 S.Las Vegas Blvd Ste D, Ste 210
     Las Vegas, NV 89119
     Contact: Marce Roth CEO
     Tel: 866-800-1897
     Email: contact@agileasolutions.com
     Website: www.agileasolutions.com
IT consulting firm, systems integration, implement & support enterprise software applications. (Minority, Woman, estab 2005, empl 75, sales $14,110,000, cert: NMSDC, WBENC)

5027 American Project Management LLC
     11700 W Charleston Blvd, Ste 170-315
     Las Vegas, NV 89135
     Contact: Jane Lee Managing Partner
     Tel: 702-220-4562
     Email: jlee@apmlasvegas.com
     Website: www.apmlasvegas.com
Project Scheduling & Cost Control, Earned Value Management System (EVMS) Implementation, Computer Programming & Embedded Software Development Services & Staff Augmentation. (Minority, Woman, estab 2003, empl 2, sales , cert: NMSDC, NWBOC)

5028 Blue Fields Digital LLC
     3172 N Rainbow Blvd, Ste 1120
     Las Vegas, NV 89108
     Contact: Akilah Kamaria Data Security Consultant
     Tel: 949-344-2996
     Email: akilahk@bluefieldsdigital.com
     Website: www.bluefieldsdigital.com
Cybersecurity solutions, security risk assessments, third-party risk management, security engineering & cyber security awareness training. (Woman/AA, estab 2015, empl 2, sales , cert: City)

5029 ECF Data LLC
     6149 S Rainbow Blvd, Ste 400
     Las Vegas, NV 89118
     Contact: Joseph Henderson
     Tel: 702-664-0075
     Email: jhenderson@ecfdata.com
     Website: www.ecfdata.com
Polycom telephones & video equipment, Audio Codes, Dialogic, Acme Packet voice gateways, HP, Dell, Lenovo Server Hardware, Cisco, Juniper, HP network switches and Routers, Contact Center, Voice Response Applications. (AA, estab 2010, empl 4, sales $220,000, cert: NMSDC, 8(a))

5030　Ingenarius, Inc.
　　　29 N 28th St, Ste 14E
　　　Las Vegas, NV 89101
　　　Contact: Ishmael Thomas President
　　　Tel:　　702-763-1419
　　　Email: ishmaellthomas@ingenarius.com
　　　Website: www.solutions.oracle.com/scwar/scr/
　　　Partner/SCP
Software product life cycle (SPLC) services & enterprise
Java software development services, embedded, mobile,
big data & the Internet of Things (IoT), analysis, design,
construction, operation, configuration & maintenance.
(AA, estab 2013, empl 1, sales , cert: State)

5031　Intelligent Image Management Inc.
　　　2850 W Horizon Ridge Pkwy Ste 200
　　　Henderson, NV 89052
　　　Contact: Shuvo Rahman VP Business Dev
　　　Tel:　　801-906-9517
　　　Email: shuvo@iimdirect.com
　　　Website: www.capturedata.com
Business Process Outsourcing (BPO) & document manage-
ment, data entry, indexing, data conversion, data mining,
call center, post scan processing, back office. (As-Ind, estab
1999, empl 3, sales $5,000,000, cert: NMSDC)

5032　Link Tech, LLC
　　　9505 Hillwood Dr Ste 150
　　　Las Vegas, NV 89134
　　　Contact: Banko SBDE
　　　Tel:　　702-233-8703
　　　Email: debbieb@linktechconsulting.com
　　　Website: www.linktechconsulting.com
Information Technology; CAD; Computer Facilities Man-
agement Services; Management Consulting Services
(Woman, estab 2000, empl 82, sales $15,193,470, cert:
WBENC)

5033　OCAA Solutions LLC
　　　170 S Green Valley Pkwy, Ste 300
　　　Henderson, NV 89012
　　　Contact: Foma Odje
　　　Tel:　　702-900-2733
　　　Email: odje@ocaasolutions.com
　　　Website: www.ocaasolutions.com
Identity Management Solutions, Single Sign-On Solutions,
Custom Software Development, Enterprise Architecture
Design, Technical Writing, Remote DBA Services, Business
Analysis, Personal GPS Trackers. (AA, estab 2011, empl 3,
sales $500,446, cert: NMSDC)

5034　XIOSS, Inc.
　　　4730 S. Fort Apache Rd Ste 300
　　　Las Vegas, NV 89147
　　　Contact: Susie Galyardt　CEO
　　　Tel:　　952-941-4000
　　　Email: susie.galyardt@xioss.com
　　　Website: www.xioss.com
IT storage solutions: data & network architecture, data
management, infrastructure management, systems
architecture & disaster recovery. (Woman, estab 2008,
empl 11, sales $1,100,000, cert: WBENC)

New York

5035　A-1 Technology Inc.
　　　115 Broadway, 13th Fl
　　　New York, NY 10006
　　　Contact: Ishwari Singh President
　　　Tel:　　212-397-7481
　　　Email: ishwari.singh@a1technology.biz
　　　Website: www.a1technology.com
Website design, iPhone programming, mobile program-
ming, application development, database , networking,
quality assurance. (As-Ind, estab 2001, empl 45, sales
$4,500,000, cert: City)

5036　Admiral Courier Services Inc.
　　　18 W 30th St 2nd Fl
　　　New York, NY 10001
　　　Contact: Ray Rafeek Owner
　　　Tel:　　212-714-3581
　　　Email: ruqayyah@admiralstaffinginc.com
　　　Website: www.admiralcourier.com
Admiral Courier Services, Inc. is a same day on demand
Courier / Delivery service located in midtown Manhat-
tan, in the heart of the big apple. We are fully computer-
ized, with state-of-the-art-tracking and dispatch systems,
and operate on a (AA, estab 2005, empl 25, sales , cert:
City, NMSDC)

5037　Aimssoft Consultants Inc.
　　　13760 45th Ave Ste- 6 -C
　　　Flushing, NY 11355
　　　Contact: Ambreen Imran President
　　　Tel:　　718-762-2370
　　　Email: imran@aimssoftconsultant.net
　　　Website: www.aimssoftconsultant.net
Aimssoft serves the business clients by locating a
professional candidates, Interviewing and screening
candidates, setting up interviews if necessary Adminis-
tering all hiring paperwork. (As-Pac, estab 2013, empl
45, sales , cert: NMSDC)

5038　Ask IT Consulting Inc
　　　33 Peachtree St., Ste 100
　　　Holtsville, NY 11742
　　　Contact: Gupta President
　　　Tel:　　631-649-1313
　　　Email: manisha.gupta@askitc.com
　　　Website: www.askitc.com
Information technology services. (Woman/As-Ind, estab
2008, empl 10, sales , cert: State, City, SDB)

5039　Avani Technology Solutions Inc.
　　　687 Lee Road Ste 208
　　　Rochester, NY 14606
　　　Contact: Sameer Penakalapati President
　　　Tel:　　585-507-0386
　　　Email: sameer.k@avanitechsolutions.com
　　　Website: www.avanitechsolutions.com
IT Consulting, Software Programming, Application
Management, Application Maintenance Outsourcing, IT
Staff Augmentation. (As-Ind, estab 2008, empl 325, sales
$18,514,969, cert: NMSDC, 8(a))

5040　BruteForce Solutions Inc
545 8th Ave, Ste 540
New York, NY 10018
Contact: Khurshedur Rahman President
Tel:　212-658-0277
Email: info@bruteforcesolution.com
Website: www.bruteforcesolution.com
Staffing & consulting, Information Technology (IT) solutions. (As-Ind, estab 2010, empl 14, sales $1,093,686, cert: State)

5041　Cerami & Associates, Inc.
404 Fifth Ave 8th Fl
New York, NY 10018
Contact: Jennifer Guzman Project Financial Coord
Tel:　212-370-1776
Email: info@ceramiassociates.com
Website: www.ceramiassociates.com
Acoustical, Audiovisual, Information Technology & Security Consulting Services. (Woman, estab , empl , sales $15,400,000, cert: City, WBENC)

5042　Citadel NY Inc.
62 William St 6th Fl
New York, NY 10005
Contact: Imranova Sr Acct Mgr
Tel:　212-931-8830
Email: sevda@citadelny.com
Website: www.citadelny.com
Information Technology Design; Computer Consulting; Information management computer systems integration design services. (Woman, estab 1998, empl 12, sales $10,913,532, cert: State)

5043　Compulink Technologies, Inc.
214 W 29th St Ste 201
New York, NY 10001
Contact: RAFAEL ARBOLEDA CEO
Tel:　212-695-5465
Email: rafael@compu-link.com
Website: www.compu-link.com
Cabling, network consulting, wireless networks, fiber optic cabling, LAN/WAN, computer hardware, software. (Minority, Woman, estab 1989, empl 15, sales $5,000,000, cert: State, City)

5044　Connect Technology Solutions
550 W Old Country Rd, Ste 307
Hicksville, NY 11801
Contact: Donna Chaimanis President
Tel:　516-433-7707
Email: donnac@connectts.com
Website: www.connectts.com
Information technology consulting & staffing services: technical staffing, executive recruiting, project mgmt, process reengineering, networking& system admin, software development & web design. (Woman, estab 1998, empl 30, sales $1,084,139, cert: State)

5045　Controls and Automation Consultants LLC
100 N Main St, Ste L06
Elmira, NY 14901
Contact: Tangela Nixon CEO
Tel:　800-430-4021
Email: tnixon@controls-automation.com
Website: www.controls-automation.com
IT Staffing, Hybrid Technical Staffing TM Project Management & Control, Electrical Engineering, Automation Engineering (AA, estab 2005, empl 4, sales $1,000,000, cert: State, NMSDC)

5046　Corporate Computer Solutions
55 Halstead Ave
Harrison, NY 10528
Contact: Larry Grippo VP Sales
Tel:　914-835-1105
Email: lgrippo@corporatecomputersol.com
Website: www.corporatecomputersol.com
Computer-based business solutions. (Woman, estab 1986, empl 18, sales $12,000,000, cert: State, City, WBENC)

5047　Crossfire Consulting
1940 Commerce St
Yorktown Heights, NY 10598
Contact: Paul Byrne VP Sales
Tel:　914-302-2900
Email: jessica@crossfireconsulting.com
Website: www.crossfireconsulting.com
IT Consulting, Development & Staff Augmentation, consulting, development, program management & onshore outsourcing. (Woman, estab 2000, empl 25, sales , cert: City, CPUC, WBENC, NWBOC)

5048　Datrose
660 Basket Rd
Webster, NY 14580
Contact: Eunice Sonneville Operations Business Partner
Tel:　585-217-0225
Email: esonneville@datrose.com
Website: www.datrose.com
Facilities support mgmt svcs: mailing-repro & steno; computer hardware & software; programming; data processing; systems design. (AA, estab 1976, empl 219, sales $14,765,522, cert: NMSDC)

5049　Deltronix Technologies Inc.
251 New Karner Road
Albany, NY 12205
Contact: Snekalatha Jegadeesan President
Tel:　518-713-5140
Email: hr@deltronixtech.com
Website: www.deltronixtech.com
IT Staff Augmentation: Java, .NET, Siebel, SAP, Peoplesoft, CRM, Database, Kofax, Testing etc. (Minority, Woman, estab 2012, empl 15, sales $888,071, cert: State)

5050　Derive Technologies
40 Wall St
New York, NY 10005
Contact: Bill Eggers Sr VP
Tel:　212-363-1111
Email: beggers@derivetech.com
Website: www.derivetech.com
Hardware fullfillment, computer integration service, iinfrastructure, desktop & printer support. (As-Ind, estab 1986, empl 110, sales $85,000,000, cert: NMSDC)

5051　Doddi Information Technologies
24 Picture Lane
Hicksville, NY 11801
Contact: David Trotman Dir Business Devel
Tel:　646-330-5354
Email: david.trotman@dodditech.com
Website: www.dodditech.com
Professional Services and Software development. (As-Ind, estab 2013, empl 10, sales , cert: State, City, NMSDC)

5052 Donnelly & Moore Corporation
75 Carolina Dr
New City, NY 10956
Contact: TRACY STEIN CEO
Tel: 845-304-8344
Email: tracys@donmor.com
Website: www.donmor.com
IT consulting & full time IT staffing: GUI dev, internet & intranet application dev, quality assurance testing, help desk & desk top support, database dev & administration. (Minority, Woman, estab 1997, empl 50, sales $10,000,000, cert: State, City, NMSDC)

5053 Eclaro International, Inc.
450 7th Ave Ste 1102
New York, NY 10123
Contact: Tom Sheridan Principal
Tel: 212-695-2922
Email: tsheridan@eclaro.com
Website: www.eclaroit.com
Information technology staffing & software development services. (As-Pac, estab , empl , sales $23,100,000, cert: State, City, NMSDC)

5054 eiWorkflow Solutions, LLC
125 Wolf Rd
Albany, NY 12205
Contact: John Andrew CEO
Tel: 518-240-1155
Email: info@eiworkflowsolutions.com
Website: www.eiworkflowsolutions.com
Cloud software consulting, Workflow Management, Customer Service Management, Customer Relationship Management & Human Resource Management. (As-Ind, estab 2006, empl 7, sales $450,000, cert: NMSDC)

5055 Elite Technical Services, Inc.
3281 Veterans Memorial Hwy Ste E17
Ronkonkoma, NY 11779
Contact: Donna Keller President
Tel: 631-256-1399
Email: dkeller@elitetechnical.com
Website: www.elitetechnical.com
Technical consultants & staff augmentation services: information technology, networking & engineering. (Woman, estab 1992, empl 88, sales $14,500,000, cert: State, WBENC)

5056 emedia, LLC
274 Madison Ave Ste 1202
New York, NY 10017
Contact: Shari Lowsky Dir Client Relations
Tel: 212-774-6100
Email: slowsky@emediaweb.com
Website: www.emediaweb.com
Design, build, integrate & maintain custom software applications, Enterprise Resource Planning (ERP) systems, Enterprise Content Management (ECM) systems, Customer Relationship Management (CRM) systems. (Woman, estab 1996, empl 8, sales $1,000,000, cert: State, City, WBENC)

5057 Episerve Corp.
266 Midwood St
Brooklyn, NY 11225
Contact: Sony Titus President
Tel: 917-921-2644
Email: info@episervecorp.com
Website: www.episervecorp.com
Training, consulting, system integration & managed services. (Woman/AA, estab 2003, empl 6, sales $245,000, cert: City)

5058 Espirit Systems, LLC
14 Penn Plaza Ste 2105
New York, NY 10122
Contact: Sales
Tel: 212-631-0188
Email: amcclean@eliteconsulting.com
Website: www.eliteconsulting.com
Application architect & dev, database dev, network admin & architects, systems admin, business analysts, mainframe. (AA, estab 1997, empl 10, sales $5,000,000, cert: State)

5059 Expinfo, Inc.
1621 Central Ave
Albany, NY 12205
Contact: FirstName LastName CEO
Tel: 518-459-4100
Email: nys@expinfo.com
Website: www.expinfo.com
Information technology staffing, HR consulting, custom computer programming, computer systems design, web development & graphic design, custom application development. (Minority, Woman, estab 2005, empl 21, sales $1,800,000, cert: State, City)

5060 Fair Pattern Inc.
1460 Broadway
New York, NY 10036
Contact: Simon Islam Managing Dir
Tel: 800-906-1656
Email: simon@fairpattern.com
Website: www.fairpattern.com
IT staffing, web & mobile application, software engineering & project management. (As-Ind, estab 2015, empl 22, sales $650,000, cert: NMSDC)

5061 Fast Lane Interactive
PO Box 987
New York, NY 11225
Contact: Shalonda Hunter Founder
Tel: 646-389-8495
Email: contactus@flitimes.com
Website: www.flitimes.com
Digital Media & Advertising, Content Development, Web, Mobile, Tablet Device Development & Services, Software Development, Web Security, Information Security, Cloud Services (Email, Web Storage, Telecomm, Data Center Migration). (Woman/AA, estab 2015, empl 5, sales , cert: NMSDC)

5062   Financial Technologies Inc
305 Madison Ave, Ste 4600
New York, NY 10165
Contact: Young Lee CEO
Tel: 212-485-9842
Email: hlee@sciostrategy.com
Website: www.telochain.com/
IT consulting services, web/mobile applications & back end data management & integration solutions. (Minority, Woman, estab 2006, empl 3, sales $527,935, cert: State)

5063   Galica, LLC
620 Park Ave, Ste 216
Rochester, NY 14607
Contact: Carlos Perez Principal
Tel: 585-319-9301
Email: galicaehs@gmail.com
Website: www.galicaehs.com
Galica LLC provides bilingual (Spanish/English) Strategy Support and Lean Facilitation using The Toyota KATA teachings. We specialize in: Rapid Improvement Event Facilitation Lean Program development Training on Strategy development (Hisp, estab 2009, empl 1, sales , cert: State, NMSDC)

5064   GCom Software, Inc.
24 Madison Ave
Albany, NY 12203
Contact: Rebecca Fischer Acct Mgr
Tel: 518-869-1671
Email: PreSales@gcomsoft.com
Website: www.gcomsoft.com
IT Staff Augmentation, fixed cost deliverable, project based services, Web based application development, Data warehousing, Network support, server , security, virtualization, Quality/Testing. (As-Ind, estab 2005, empl 130, sales , cert: State)

5065   GENESYS Consulting Services, Inc.
1 Marcus Blvd, Ste 102
Albany, NY 12205
Contact: Leo Pfohl VP
Tel: 518-459-9500
Email: leo@genesysonline.com
Website: www.genesysonline.com
Information Technology consulting services, design, develop, implement & maintain technology solutions. (Woman, estab 1987, empl 84, sales $12,500,717, cert: State, City)

5066   Globalquest
435 Lawrence Bell Dr, Ste 7
Williamsville, NY 14221
Contact: Lynn Dearmyer Business Devel Mgr
Tel: 716-635-9820
Email: ldearmyer@globalquestinc.com
Website: www.globalqueststaffing.com
IT staffing: contract, contract-to-hire, direct & payroll. (Woman, estab 1994, empl 120, sales $24,000,000, cert: State, City)

5067   Granwood Inc
61-43 186th St
Fresh Meadows, NY 11365
Contact: Glen Greene Managing Dir
Tel: 718-640-2828
Email: ggreene@granwoodinc.com
Website: www.granwoodinc.com
Information technology consulting & staffing. (AA, estab 2005, empl 11, sales $1,200,000, cert: State, City, NMSDC)

5068   ImageWork USA LLC
170 Hamilton Ave, Ste 301
White Plains, NY 10601
Contact: Bikkal President
Tel: 914-681-0700
Email: cbikkal@imagework.com
Website: www.imagework.com
Full life Cycle Recruitment - IT services - Information Technology; Documentation Scanning; Printing; Computing. (Minority, Woman, estab 2009, empl 1, sales , cert: State, City)

5069   Indotronix International Corporation
687 Lee Rd, Ste 250
Rochester, NY 14606
Contact: Venkat S Mantha President
Tel: 845-473-1137
Email: bd@iic.com
Website: www.iic.com
Software applications, e-business initiatives, IT consulting, customer interaction management. (As-Ind, estab 1986, empl 1250, sales $85,000,000, cert: State, NMSDC, CPUC)

5070   InnoSoul, Inc.
24 Fairfield Ave
Albany, NY 12205
Contact: Rashi Shamshabad President
Tel: 518-400-0425
Email: innosoul@gmail.com
Website: www.innosoul.com
Software Product Development & IT Consulting Services, IT Staffing. (Minority, Woman, estab 2003, empl 20, sales $4,000,000, cert: State, City, WBENC)

5071   Integrated Systems Management
303 S Broadway, Ste 101
Tarrytown, NY 10591
Contact: Dave Business Dev Mgr
Tel: 914-332-5590
Email: ndave@ismnet.com
Website: www.omnimd.com
IT solution services & IT staffing: network security, ERP, CRM softwares. (Minority, Woman, estab 1989, empl 35, sales $5,550,000, cert: State)

5072   Jasper Solutions Inc.
21 Melville Rd
Huntington Station, NY 11746
Contact: Anshuman Patel President
Tel: 631-514-8106
Email: contracts@jaspersolutions.com
Website: www.jaspersolutions.com
Enterprise storage, network monitoring, security, private & public Cloud, networking, disaster recovery, application integration, data warehousing, data mining, database implementation, virtualization, hybrid Cloud, Cisco. (As-Ind, estab 2002, empl 3, sales $300,000, cert: State)

5073   Jean Martin Inc.
551 Fifth Ave, Ste 1425
New York, NY 10176
Contact: Shawn Kumar CEO
Tel: 212-883-1000
Email: shawnk@jeanmartin.com
Website: www.jeanmartin.com
Information technology consulting services. (As-Ind, estab 1997, empl 150, sales $16,000,000, cert: City)

5074   JSL Computer Services, Inc.
       447 E Allen St
       Hudson, NY 12534
       Contact: Ed Grossman VP
       Tel: 518-828-7761
       Email: ed@jslinc.com
       Website: www.jslinc.com
E-commerce, web design & dev, JAVA, systems programming, analysis & business requirements, project mgmt, software testing & quality assurance, documentation, database design, data modeling & warehousing, network engineering. (Woman, estab 1978, empl 33, sales $3,610,079, cert: City, WBENC)

5075   KDI Technology Solutions, Inc
       412 Broadway 2nd Fl
       New York, NY 10113
       Contact: John Thomas President
       Tel: 646-724-0875
       Email: jthomas@kditek.com
       Website: www.kditek.com
Database design & development, mobile applications, web development, business & systems analysis. (AA, estab 2007, empl 1, sales $100,000, cert: State, City)

5076   Keystats Inc
       81 Pondfield Rd
       Bronxville, NY 10708
       Contact: Bilal Karriem President
       Tel: 914-337-6883
       Email: bkarriem@keystatsinc.com
       Website: www.keystatsinc.com
Statistically driven analytic solutions (AA, estab 1999, empl 11, sales $100,000, cert: City, NMSDC)

5077   Maureen Data Systems, Inc.
       307 W 38th St Ste 1801
       New York, NY 10018
       Contact: Robert Irvin Dir govt channels
       Tel: 646-744-1000
       Email: rirvin@mdsny.com
       Website: www.mdsny.com
Systems integrator & VAR, UC, Cloud computing, virtualization & storage, networking & security. (Woman, estab 1994, empl 24, sales $8,500,000, cert: State, City, WBENC)

5078   Mola Group Corporation
       450 Park Ave S Fl 3
       New York, NY 10016
       Contact: Emmanuel Ola-Dake Managing Dir
       Tel: 646-217-0727
       Email: contact@molaprise.com
       Website: www.molaprise.com
Cybersecurity Solutions, Threat Detection. (AA, estab 2014, empl 15, sales $5,000,000, cert: State, City, NMSDC)

5079   Motivate Design, LLC
       111 John St, Ste 450
       New York, NY 10038
       Contact: Laura Haykel Client Experience Dir
       Tel: 646-400-5108
       Email: laura@motivatedesign.com
       Website: www.motivatedesign.com
User experience (UX) research, design, and staffing. (Minority, Woman, estab 2009, empl 15, sales $4,000,000, cert: NMSDC, WBENC)

5080   Navatar Consulting Group Inc.
       44 Wall St, 12 Fl
       New York, NY 10005
       Contact: Mgr operations
       Tel: 212-461-2140
       Email: billing@navatargroup.com
       Website: www.navatargroup.com
On-demand CRM, ERP & supply chain. (As-Pac, estab 2002, empl 25, sales $820,000, cert: State)

5081   Netfast Technology Solutions Inc.
       589 8th Ave 22nd Fl
       New York, NY 10018
       Contact: Navid Nawaz Mgr
       Tel: 212-792-5200
       Email: nnawaz@netfast.com
       Website: www.netfast.com
Information security consulting & network integration. (As-Pac, estab 1994, empl 25, sales $13,800,000, cert: City, NMSDC)

5082   New York Technology Partners
       332 Jefferson Rd
       Rochester, NY 14623
       Contact: VP
       Tel: 585-300-4720
       Email:
       Website: www.nytp.com
Software consulting, onsite, offsite, and offshore, IT & Business Consulting, IT Integration, Project Management. (As-Pac, estab 1999, empl 280, sales $4,000,000,000, cert: NMSDC)

5083   Panther Solutions, LLC
       1001 Lee Rd
       Rochester, NY 14606
       Contact: Robert Kleinschmidt Dir Natl Accounts
       Tel: 414-336-8217
       Email:
       robert_kleinschmidt@panthersolutions.com
       Website: www.flowercitygroup
Account management, custom data programming. (AA, estab 2005, empl 45, sales $32,000,000, cert: NMSDC)

5084   Perpetual Solutions LLC
       134 W 29th St, 607
       New York, NY 10001
       Contact: Amish Gandhi CEO
       Tel: 212-904-1497
       Email: b2bsales@perpetualny.com
       Website: www.perpetualny.com
Software User Experience Mobile Development Computer Services, Technology & Engineering Services. (As-Ind, estab 2012, empl 8, sales $1,650,000, cert: NMSDC)

5085   Pride Healthcare, LLC
       420 Lexington Ave 30th Fl
       New York, NY 10170
       Contact: Bhavin Shah Dir
       Tel: 212-235-5309
       Email: bhavin.shah@pride-health.com
       Website: www.pride-health.com
Staff Augmentation, Vendor Management, IT Hardware Procurement Services and Business Processing Outsourcing. (Hisp, estab 2003, empl 350, sales $358,000,000, cert: NMSDC)

5086　Quantilus Inc.
115 Broadway Ste 1202
New York, NY 10006
Contact: Debarshi Chaudhury Dir Business Dev
Tel:　212-768-8900
Email: debarshi.chaudhury@quantilus.com
Website: www.quantilus.com/
IT Strategy, Implementation, Custom Development, Machine Vision, Publishing, Education, Artificial Intelligence, Natural Language Processing3. (As-Ind, estab 2004, empl 22, sales $7,213,447, cert: State, City, NMSDC)

5087　RMK Consulting, Inc.
2 Oregon Hollow Rd
Armonk, NY 10504
Contact: Debra DeWitt Acct Exec
Tel:　914-765-0075
Email: info@rmkconsulting.com
Website: www.rmkconsulting.com
BPO & IT consulting, outsourcing & consulting services for staff augmentation, managed services & project sourcing solutions, on-site, near-site & off-shore staffing/delivery models. (Woman, estab 1998, empl 127, sales $30,000,000, cert: WBENC)

5088　RMS Computer Corp.
1185 Ave of the Americas Fl 32
New York, NY 10036
Contact: Carole Klang
Tel:　212-840-8666
Email: carolee@rmscorp.com
Website: www.rmscorp.com
Contract Information technology professionals: hardware, software, application development, networking, e-commerce, client server & mainframe environments. (Woman, estab 1985, empl 250, sales , cert: WBENC)

5089　Sharp Decisions, Inc.
1040 Ave of the Americas 9th Fl
New York, NY 10018
Contact: Edward McCann Managing Dir
Tel:　212-403-7557
Email: hdteam@sharpdecisions.com
Website: www.sharpdecisions.com
Computer consulting: staff augmentation & contract programming, systems integration, data networks design, development & implementation, business continuity planning, security & firewall design & dev, vendor product evaluation. (Woman, estab 1990, empl 330, sales $60,000,000, cert: NWBOC)

5090　Siwel Consulting, Inc.
213 W 35th St Ste 12 W
New York, NY 10001
Contact: Michael LaPayower Sr Accountant
Tel:　212-691-9326
Email: mlapayower@siwel.com
Website: www.siwel.com
Information technology: contract & fulltime staffing, IBM Premier VAR, ELA & software license, asset management, Linux, VOIP, VMware, server, storage & networking. (Woman, estab 1992, empl 30, sales $52,780,000, cert: WBENC)

5091　Softpath Systems Inc.
75 Maiden Lane, Ste 903
New York, NY 10038
Contact: Shiv Mgr
Tel:　212-405-1894
Email: shiv@softpathsystems.com
Website: www.softpathsystems.com
IT & supply chain staffing. (As-Pac, estab 1997, empl 150, sales , cert: State)

5092　Software Guidance & Assistance, Inc.
200 White Plains Road
Tarrytown, NY 10591
Contact: Craig Rydell Business Devel Mgr
Tel:　914-366-5950
Email: craigr@sgainc.com
Website: www.sgainc.com
IT professionals: programmers, analysts, senior project managers, operating systems, programming, networking, application software & hardware skills & certifications. (Woman, estab 1981, empl 652, sales $78,218,000, cert: City, WBENC)

5093　Software People Inc.
738 Smithtown Bypass, Ste 202
Smithtown, NY 11787
Contact: Sandeep Jain Sr VP
Tel:　631-863-0299
Email: sandeep.jain@softwarepeople.us
Website: www.softwarepeople.us
ERP implementation, systems analysis, system & database admin, web design & application, client/server implementation, relational database design, systems conversion/migration, electronic data interchange. (Woman/As-Ind, estab 1998, empl 5, sales $2,869,583, cert: State)

5094　Source Of Future Technology (SOFT), Inc.
333 Hudson St Ste 202
New York, NY 10013
Contact: Cathy Grubiak President
Tel:　212-633-1515
Email: cgrubiak@soft-inc.com
Website: www.softinc.com
Computer technology solutions: project life cycle. (Woman, estab 1981, empl 75, sales $6,000,000, cert: State, WBENC)

5095　Sphynx Software Solutions LLC
59 Lafayette Ave Ste 2D
Brooklyn, NY 11217
Contact: Yonas Keflemariam CEO
Tel:　917-705-5548
Email: yonas@sphynxsoftware.com
Website: www.sphynxsoftware.com
Technology solutions, enterprise architecture, local & offshore software development resources & technical staff augmentation. (AA, estab 2007, empl 3, sales , cert: City, NMSDC)

5096 Sutherland Global Services
1160 Pittsford-Victor Rd
Pittsford, NY 14534
Contact: Steve Sandt Business Devel Mgr
Tel: 585-586-5757
Email: sandts@sutherlandglobal.com
Website: www.sutherlandglobal.com
Business process outsourcing & call ctr svcs: technical & customer support, systems integration & application development. (As-Ind, estab 1986, empl 33000, sales $500,500,000, cert: NMSDC)

5097 SVAM International Inc.
233 East Shore Rd, Ste 201
Great Neck, NY 11023
Contact: Manav Bhasin Managing Dir
Tel: 516-466-6655
Email: manav@svam.com
Website: www.svam.com
IT staff augmentation, custom software dev, web enabling technologies, workflow automation, content management. (As-Pac, estab 1994, empl 600, sales $100,000,000, cert: State, NMSDC)

5098 Sygma Technology Solutions, Inc.
300 W 135th St, Ste 5J
New York, NY 10030
Contact: Stuart Holland President
Tel: 917-507-1500
Email: stuart.holland@sygmatechnology.com
Website: www.sygmatechnology.com
Custom software development, integrated technology, technology system solutions, application software development,
business information technology, business software development. (AA, estab 2005, empl 20, sales , cert: State, NMSDC, 8(a))

5099 Techolution LLC
3 World Financial Center 24th Fl
New York, NY 10281
Contact: Zachary Kissel Office Mgr
Tel: 201-417-7240
Email: zak@techolution.com
Website: www.techolution.com
Digital transformation: web & mobile, migrating server farms & applications to the cloud (public or private). (As-Pac, estab 2014, empl 50, sales $1,500,000, cert: NMSDC)

5100 Trivision Group Inc.
118-21 Queens Blvd Ste 401
Forest Hills, NY 11375
Contact: Vijay Shenoy CEO
Tel: 212-869-5455
Email: contracts@trivisioninc.com
Website: www.trivisioninc.com
Contract staffing solutions, Project Management and Information Technology Consulting Services, system design, programming, and testing, to post-implementation support and maintenance. (As-Pac, estab 2003, empl 17, sales $1,000,000, cert: State, City)

5101 Ubiqus
601 Bangs Ave
Asbury Park, NY 07712
Contact: TTI of USA CEO
Tel: 646-495-9019
Email: LK@TTIOFUSA.COM
Website: www.ttiofusa.com
IT staff augmentation. (Woman, estab 1996, empl 240, sales $20,182,200, cert: WBENC)

5102 URimagination, Inc.
18 E 41st St Ste 1703
New York, NY 10017
Contact: Alf Baez CEO
Tel: 212-729-9558
Email: info@urimagination.com
Website: www.urimagination.com
Information technology solutions: custom application development, systems integration, maintenance spanning. (Hisp, estab 2007, empl 7, sales $500,000, cert: City, NMSDC)

5103 Vernalis Group Inc
353 Lexington Ave, Ste 1604
New York, NY 10016
Contact: Nanda Rajasek COO
Tel: 647-923-1903
Email: nanda.rajasek@vernal.is
Website: www.vernalisengg.com
Global software & engineering solutions, Microsoft, IBM, JEE, openSource, Mobile, Business Intelligence, Enterprise Application Integration. (As-Ind, estab 2012, empl 300, sales $4,440,000, cert: NMSDC)

5104 VQV Services LLC
204 Forrest Pointe Dr
East Greenbush, NY 12061
Contact: Khuhsbooben Patel President
Tel: 201-920-6170
Email: khush@vqvservices.com
Website: www.vqvservices.com
Quality Engineer, Validation Engineer, Qualification Specialist, Information Technology consultants. (Minority, Woman, estab 2016, empl 2, sales , cert: State)

5105 Xperteks Computer Consultancy, Inc.
132 West 36th St 10th Fl
New York, NY 10018
Contact: Marcial Velez CEO
Tel: 212-206-6262
Email: mvelez@xperteks.com
Website: www.xperteks.com
Apple, PC & network managed services, IT services. (Hisp, estab 2002, empl 17, sales $2,500,000, cert: City, NMSDC)

Ohio

5106 Accelerated Business Results an A Fox Corporation
1530 Sycamore Ridge Dr
Maineville, OH 45039
Contact: Amy Fox Owner
Tel: 513-774-8608
Email: amy.fox@acceleratedbr.com
Website: www.acceleratedbr.com/what-we-do/
Customized content development, design & develop instructor-led training programs, e-Learning solutions & blended learning solutions. (Woman, estab 2002, empl 11, sales $1,678,119, cert: WBENC)

5107   AespaTech, LLC
23800 Commerce Park, Ste A
Beachwood, OH 44122
Contact: President
Tel: 216-928-1919
Email: info@aespatech.com
Website: www.aespatech.com
Information Technology Consulting & Training Services. (Minority, Woman, estab 2014, empl 1, sales $750,000, cert: State, City, WBENC, 8(a))

5108   Alego Health
24651 Center Ridge Rd Ste 400
Westlake, OH 44145
Contact: Jonathan Levoy VP
Tel: 440-617-6516
Email: jlevoy@alegohealth.com
Website: www.alegohealth.com
Healthcare IT, EMR Training, EMR Implementation, EMR Analysts, Hardware Support, Hardware, Software, IT Analysts, IT, Mobile Technology (Woman, estab 2004, empl 127, sales $11,500,000, cert: WBENC)

5109   American Business Solutions, Inc.
8850 Whitney Dr
Lewis Center, OH 43035
Contact: Nitin Sharma Sr Mgr, Business Devel
Tel: 877-781-2274
Email: nitin@absi-usa.com
Website: www.absi-usa.com
Technology Services & Solutions, Business Intelligence & Database Management, Organizational Change Management, Mobile Application Development, Project Management & Support, Quality Assurance & Testing, Cloud Computing Services. (As-Ind, estab 1998, empl 85, sales $19,000,000, cert: State, NMSDC)

5110   Ardent Technologies Inc.
6234 Far Hills Ave
Dayton, OH 45459
Contact: Vas Appalaneni President
Tel: 937-312-1345
Email: ohbids@ardentinc.com
Website: www.ardentinc.com
ITservices & project management, software development & maintenance, systems
analysis, turnkey project implementations, data services (modeling, management and migration),
project outsourcing services. (As-Ind, estab 2000, empl 60, sales $7,300,000, cert: State, SDB)

5111   Ascendum
10290 Alliance Rd
Blue Ash, OH 45242
Contact: Mark Vornwald Dir
Tel: 513-792-5100
Email: mark.vornwald@ascendum.com
Website: www.ascendum.com
IT solutions, technology-inspired solutions to business-driven challenges. (As-Pac, estab 2008, empl 2000, sales $110,000,000, cert: State, NMSDC)

5112   Avantia, Inc.
9655 Sweet Valley Dr, Ste 1
Valley View, OH 44125
Contact: Jeff Ladd Controller
Tel: 216-901-9366
Email: jladd@avantia-inc.com
Website: www.avantia-inc.com
Information technology consulting & systems development. (Woman, estab 2000, empl 35, sales $9,240,331, cert: WBENC)

5113   Barcode Industrial Systems, Inc.
8044 Montgomery road Ste 700
Cincinnati, OH 45236
Contact: Juan Merchan Business Devel Mgr
Tel: 513-772-5252
Email: contracts@bislabels.com
Website: www.BISLabels.com
Mobile data transaction systems, wireless & batch data capture applications: inventory, shipping, receiving & warehouse mgmt via Internet. (AA, Hisp, estab 1990, empl 16, sales $1,010,000, cert: NMSDC)

5114   Cadre Computer Resources Co.
201 E 5th St, Ste 1800
Cincinnati, OH 45202
Contact: Kristen Norris Marketing
Tel: 513-762-7350
Email: kristen.norris@cadre.net
Website: www.cadre.net
Network & information security solutions, design, assessment, installation, training & support of information security systems. (Woman, estab 2001, empl 47, sales $43,383,000, cert: WBENC, NWBOC)

5115   CB Tech
1491 Polaris Pkwy Ste 291
Columbus, OH 43240
Contact: Josh Harris Sr Dir of Business Dev
Tel: 614-339-8550
Email: info@cbtechnow.com
Website: www.cbtechnow.com
IT services & document management solutions. (AA, estab 1990, empl 15, sales $28,300,000, cert: NMSDC)

5116   CGB Tech Solutions Inc
2310 Superior Ave Ste 105
Cleveland, OH 44114
Contact: Jennifer Brunkow Owner
Tel: 216-373-9449
Email: jen@cgbtech.com
Website: www.cgbgtech.com
Network Infrastructure planning, procurement, installation & troubleshooting, server monitoring, evaluation, troubleshooting and repair, User endpoint (desktop/laptop) troubleshooting, remote or in-person
Help Desk services. (Woman, estab 2003, empl 17, sales $1,000,000, cert: City)

5117   Chagrin Consulting Services Inc.
1795 South Belvoir Blvd.
South Euclid, OH 44121
Contact: Ann Allard President
Tel: 216-514-3301
Email: ahallard@chagrinconsulting.com
Website: www.chagrinconsulting.com
Information technology consulting & staffing. (Woman, estab 1993, empl 12, sales $2,451,851, cert: WBENC)

5118 ClemCorp
      714 E Monument Ave
      Dayton, OH 45402
      Contact: Kevin Clemons CEO
      Tel: 937-531-6645
      Email: kevin.clemons@clemcorp.com
      Website: www.ClemCorp.com
IT solution & services: rational capabilities, enterprise
architecture, GCSS, web dev, graphic design, document
mgmt, network design & admin, software dev, project
mgmt, system design, life cycle application support. (AA,
estab 2005, empl 12, sales , cert: State, 8(a))

5119 Corbus, LLC
      1129 Miamisburg Centerville Rd
      West Carrollton, OH 45449
      Contact: Jerry Teuschler Dir Strategic Sales Dev
      Tel: 513-703-2929
      Email: corbusconnects@corbus.com
      Website: www.corbus.com
Software development, offshore IT support, testing &
quality solutions, staff augmentation. (Minority, estab
1994, empl 600, sales , cert: NMSDC)

5120 Cybervation, Inc.
      4150 Tuller Rd, Ste 204
      Dublin, OH 43017
      Contact: Purba Majumder President
      Tel: 614-818-9061
      Email: pmajumder@cybervationinc.com
      Website: www.cybervationinc.com
Technology Services, Website Development, custom
Software Programming, Graphics Design, Animation,
Video, Transcription, Data Entry & Internet Marketing.
(Minority, Woman, estab 1998, empl 32, sales , cert: State,
NMSDC, WBENC)

5121 Cynergies Solutions Group
      26301 Curtiss-Wright Pkwy Ste 400
      Richmond Heights, OH 44143
      Contact: Debbie Holy President
      Tel: 440-565-0168
      Email: debbie_holy@cynergies.net
      Website: www.cynergies.net
Information technology staffing: consulting, contracting,
permanent, executive placement, contract-to-hire,
software devel & training. (Woman, estab 1997, empl 62,
sales , cert: WBENC)

5122 Dedicated Tech Services, Inc.
      545 Metro Pl S Ste 100
      Dublin, OH 43017
      Contact: Patty E Lickliter President
      Tel: 614-695-5990
      Email: sales@dtsdelivers.com
      Website: www.dtsdelivers.com
Application Design & Development, Service Oriented
Architecture (SOA), Database Design & Development,
Client/Server & N-Tier Development, Web & Web Service
Development, Data Warehousing Solutions. (Woman,
estab 2008, empl 41, sales $1,930,000, cert: WBENC,
NWBOC)

5123 Deemsys Inc.
      800A Cross Pointe Rd
      Columbus, OH 43230
      Contact: RT Rajan
      Tel: 614-322-9929
      Email: raj@deemsysinc.com
      Website: www.deemsysinc.com
Application design, development & implementation,
Systems integration/consolidation, Re-engineering,
Implementation, Feasibility & requirement analysis.
(Woman/As-Ind, estab 2004, empl 82, sales $7,550,000,
cert: State, NMSDC)

5124 DevCare Solutions
      131 N High St Ste 640
      Columbus, OH 43215
      Contact: Ron Vogel Dir Business Dev
      Tel: 614-285-2714
      Email: rvogel@devcare.com
      Website: www.devcare.com
On-site/offshore development of software solutions &
Staff Augmentation consultants. (Minority, Woman,
estab 1995, empl 380, sales $22,000,000, cert: State,
NMSDC, WBENC)

5125 Echo Imaging Inc.
      2645 Wooster Rd
      Rocky River, OH 44116
      Contact: Barbara Milloy President
      Tel: 440-356-4720
      Email: barbara@echoimg.com
      Website: www.echoimg.com
Replication svcs: CD-R, CD-ROM, DVD-R, mini CD's,
business card CD's & diskette duplication, full color
custom printed packaging. (Woman, estab 1997, empl 1,
sales $801,642, cert: WBENC)

5126 ERP Analysts, Inc
      425 Metro Place N Ste 510
      Dublin, OH 43017
      Contact: Cory Drescher Dir
      Tel: 727-424-4427
      Email: jvyas@erpagroup.com
      Website: www.erpagroup.com
Project management, ERP Application Implementations
and Major/Minor
Upgrades in PeopleSoft,Oracle, and SAP. Database
Management and Administration, Performance Tuning.
(AA, As-Pac, estab 2003, empl 500, sales $88,000,000,
cert: State, 8(a))

5127 Expeed Software LLC
      659 Lakeview Plaza Blvd, Ste K
      Worthington, OH 43085
      Contact: Rao Chejarla President
      Tel: 614-371-4791
      Email: rao.chejarla@expeedsoftware.com
      Website: www.expeedsoftware.com
Custom Application Development, Mobile Application
Development, Application Integration, Data Warehous-
ing and Business Intelligence, Independent Software,
Verification/Quality Assurance, Project Management.
(As-Pac, estab 2008, empl 35, sales $735,000, cert:
State, NMSDC)

5128　Fiducia TechneGroup LLC
　　　3838 Eileen Dr
　　　Cincinnati, OH 45209
　　　Contact: Alma Bartos CEO
　　　Tel:　　513-418-8217
　　　Email: amartinez@fiduciatg.com
　　　Website: www.fiduciatg.com
Engineering Services, Reliability (Products, Processes and Software), Implement Reliability Life Cycle Management & Benchmarking. (Minority, Woman, estab 2014, empl 2, sales $100,000, cert: NMSDC, WBENC)

5129　Flairsoft, LTD
　　　7720 Rivers Edge Dr Ste 200
　　　Columbus, OH 43235
　　　Contact: Sharon Fraley Sr Business Devel Mgr
　　　Tel:　　614-207-0764
　　　Email: sharon.fraley@flairsoft.net
　　　Website: www.flairsoft.net
Information Technology, e-Business, Professional Services, Systems Integration & Business Process Re-Engineering. (Minority, estab 2001, empl 100, sales $8,000,000, cert: NMSDC)

5130　Global Associates, Inc.
　　　7160 Corporate Way
　　　Dayton, OH 45459
　　　Contact: Kevin Toshok Dir Solutions Sales
　　　Tel:　　937-312-1204
　　　Email: ktoshok@gassociates.com
　　　Website: www.gassociates.com
IT Consulting, Staff Augmentation, Project Outsourcing & Offshore software design & testing. (Minority, Woman, estab 1996, empl 8, sales $15,000,000, cert: NMSDC)

5131　Halcyon Solutions, Inc.
　　　5880 Innovation Dr.
　　　Dublin, OH 43016
　　　Contact: Shaun Frecska VP
　　　Tel:　　614-339-5608
　　　Email: sfrecska@halcyonit.com
　　　Website: www.halcyonit.com
IT consulting and staffing agency. (As-Ind, estab 1992, empl 125, sales , cert: State, NMSDC)

5132　IdentiPhoto Company Ltd.
　　　1810 Joseph Lloyd Pkwy
　　　Willoughby, OH 44094
　　　Contact: Pamela Johnson GM
　　　Tel:　　440-306-9000
　　　Email: pam@identiphoto.com
　　　Website: www.identiphoto.com
Badging, tracking, verification systems, photo ID systems ID badges, ID software ID supplies, ID badge attachments, ID cards, visitor management software/systems, card printers, perimeter management systems, smart cards, proximity. (Woman, estab 1969, empl 15, sales $2,252,840, cert: WBENC)

5133　Integrated Solutions and Services
　　　4055 Executive Park Dr, Ste 450
　　　Cincinnati, OH 45241
　　　Contact: Clarence McGill
　　　Tel:　　513-769-3913
　　　Email: rmcgill@iss-unlimited.com
　　　Website: www.iss-unlimited.com
Information technology hardware integration, network server mgmt, help desk svcs, LAN/WAN, database dev & mgmt, system application support. (AA, estab 1999, empl 5, sales , cert: State)

5134　IT Reserves, LLC
　　　40 Hutchinson Ave, Ste 403
　　　Columbus, OH 43235
　　　Contact: Pierre Ilyamukuru CEO
　　　Tel:　　469-416-8910
　　　Email: pierre.aimable@itreserves.com
　　　Website: www.itreserves.com/
IT and software development, Digital Consulting Services, Experience Design Services, Application Development & Maintenance. (AA, estab 2020, empl 5, sales $300,000, cert: NMSDC)

5135　JASStek, Inc.
　　　555 Metro Place N Ste 100
　　　Dublin, OH 43017
　　　Contact: Praveen Tummalla Business Devel Mgr
　　　Tel:　　614-808-3600
　　　Email: praveen@jasstek.com
　　　Website: www.jasstek.com
Information technology consulting, project staffing, IT staffing, contract programming, contract consultants, technology consultants & contract to hire consultants. (Minority, Woman, estab 2012, empl 9, sales , cert: State, NMSDC, WBENC)

5136　Lightwell Inc.
　　　565 Metro Place S Ste 220
　　　Columbus, OH 43017
　　　Contact: Bryan Scott Acct Exec
　　　Tel:　　614-310-2700
　　　Email: bryan.scott@lightwellinc.com
　　　Website: www.lightwellinc.com
EDI, B2B integration, order management, ecommerce, business management, and supply chain management services. (Woman, estab 1998, empl 225, sales $39,000,000, cert: WBENC)

5137　Logic Soft, Inc.
　　　5900 Sawmill Rd, Ste 200
　　　Dublin, OH 43017
　　　Contact: Louis Viciedo Business Dev Mgr
　　　Tel:　　614-884-5544
　　　Email: louis.viciedo@logicsoftusa.com
　　　Website: www.logicsoftusa.com
IT Managed Services, monitor program activity, detailed program analysis & benchmarking, invoicing, robust supplier management & total workforce solutions. (As-Ind, estab 1997, empl 50, sales $15,000,000, cert: State)

5138　LRSolutions, LLC
　　　5743 Edgepark Dr
　　　Brook Park, OH 44142
　　　Contact: Linda Gutekunst CEO
　　　Tel:　　440-476-9492
　　　Email: linda@lrsolutions.net
　　　Website: www.LRSolutions.net
IT staffing & solutions: permanent placement, staff augmentation & project-based solutions. (Woman, estab 2006, empl 8, sales $500,000, cert: State, NWBOC)

5139   Marinar Technology Co LLC dba VantageOne
        Software
        33801 Curtis Blvd, Ste 112
        Eastlake, OH 44095
        Contact: Erica Martin CEO
        Tel: 440-354-1458
        Email: erica.francis@vantageonesoftware.com
        Website: www.vantageonesoftware.com
IT service engineers & technicians, infrastructure expansion, data migration, system security, disaster planning or basic workstation & server optimization. (Woman, estab 1994, empl 14, sales $975,000, cert: WBENC)

5140   Marketing & Engineering Solutions
        625 Bear Run Lane
        Lewis Center, OH 43035
        Contact: Hiten Shah President
        Tel: 740-201-8112
        Email: hshah@mesinc.net
        Website: www.mesinc.net
Information technology, outsourcing, customer survey processing, database maintenance, OCR & ICR data processing, call center, data processing, data entry, rebate processing. (As-Ind, estab 1999, empl 110, sales $2,700,000, cert: NMSDC)

5141   MAX Technical Training Inc.
        4900 Pkwy Dr
        Cincinnati, OH 45040
        Contact: Patricia Miller CEO
        Tel: 513-322-8888
        Email: patricia@maxtrain.com
        Website: www.maxtrain.com
IT programmers & developers training. (Woman, estab 1998, empl 12, sales $1,950,556, cert: WBENC)

5142   MEDIASCRIPT, LLC
        3982 Powell Rd, Ste 235
        Powell, OH 43065
        Contact: Angela Horne CEO
        Tel: 614-551-3549
        Email: angela@mediascriptllc.com
        Website: www.mediascriptllc.com
Media webinar technology: distance education, online learning & training. (Woman, estab 2009, empl 3, sales $175,000, cert: WBENC)

5143   MurTech Consulting LLC
        4807 Rockside Rd, Ste 250
        Independence, OH 44131
        Contact: Ailish Murphy President
        Tel: 216-328-8580
        Email: amurphy@murtechconsulting.com
        Website: www.murtechconsulting.com
Information technology consulting & placement services. (Woman, estab 2000, empl 25, sales $14,200,000, cert: WBENC)

5144   Myca Multimedia and Training Solutions, LLC
        4555 Lake Forest Dr Ste 650
        Cincinnati, OH 45242
        Contact: Patricia Massey President
        Tel: 513-608-6033
        Email: pmassey@mycagroup.com
        Website: www.mycalearning.com
Interactive & engaging eLearning tools, computer & cloud-based eLearning courseware on harassment prevention, culture & inclusion, bullying. (Woman, estab 1991, empl 15, sales $984,166, cert: WBENC)

5145   N-ovation Technology Group
        10 W. 2nd St Ste 2201
        Dayton, OH 45402
        Contact: Dwayne Coker CEO
        Tel: 937-886-4850
        Email: sales@n-ovationtech.com
        Website: www.n-ovationtech.com
Network Design, Architecture & Integration services, Data Center Solutions, Cyber Security, Wireless DAS deployment, Cloud strategy, Infrastructure Program Management, Process Management & Quality Assurance, Vendor Management. (AA, estab 2015, empl 5, sales $10,000,000, cert: City, NMSDC)

5146   Precise Infotech Inc.
        7315 Royal Portrush Dr
        Solon, OH 44139
        Contact: Kashifa Ahmed President
        Tel: 440-265-0402
        Email: kahmed@preciseinfotech.com
        Website: www.preciseinfotech.com
Software development & consulting. (Minority, Woman, estab 2004, empl 2, sales $274,121, cert: State)

5147   Promark Custom Solutions LLC
        8 Prestige Plaza, Ste 110
        Springboro, OH 45342
        Contact: Lisa Johnson President
        Tel: 937-557-0333
        Email: ljohnson@promarkcs.com
        Website: www.promarkcs.com
Office Productivity, Cyber Security, Security Certifications, IT Certifications, IT Skills, and Business Skills. (Woman, estab 1995, empl 1, sales , cert: WBENC)

5148   R.Dorsey & Company, Inc.
        400 W Wilson Bridge Rd Ste 105
        Worthington, OH 43085
        Contact: Joyce Dorsey CEO
        Tel: 614-486-8900
        Email: jcdorsey@dorseyplus.com
        Website: www.dorseyplus.com
Network Architecture, Application Architecture, Service Oriented Architecture, Data Warehouse, Hosting, Security, Data Backup, Outsourcing (Woman, estab 1996, empl 30, sales , cert: WBENC, 8(a))

5149   Solutions For You Inc.
        470 Olde Worthington Rd Ste 200
        Westerville, OH 43082
        Contact: Robert Johnson
        Tel: 614-410-6648
        Email: robertj@sfyi.com
        Website: www.sfyi.com
Information Technology consulting: Full cycle product development, Business Analysis, Quality Assurance, Project Management, Security (data, network, database), Open Source (language, tools, software), data analysis, Electronic Data Interchange. (Woman/AA, estab 1999, empl 4, sales $423,027, cert: State, City, NMSDC)

5150 StarTech Consulting, Inc.
      6746 Rivercrest Dr, Ste 100
      Cleveland, OH 44141
      Contact: Joe Bains President
      Tel: 440-546-9500
      Email: jbains@startech-consult.com
      Website: www.startech-consult.com
Staff Augmentation, Web applications, Mobile applications, Database development/administrators, Project Managers, Business Analysts, Quality Assurance, etc. (As-Ind, estab 1998, empl 6, sales $2,107,771, cert: State)

5151 Strategic Systems, Inc.
      475 Metro Place South Ste 450
      Dublin, OH 43017
      Contact: Kaushal Vadada Dir of Operations
      Tel: 614-973-7979
      Email: kaushal@strsi.com
      Website: www.strsi.com
Staff Augmentation for Information Technology, Project Management, Hybrid Staff Aumentation, Contract to Hire, and Platform Development/Delivery. (Woman/As-Ind, estab 2004, empl 175, sales $19,000,000, cert: State, NMSDC)

5152 SYSTEMIAN LLC
      555 Metro Place N, Ste 100
      Plain City, OH 43064
      Contact: Wilson Fernando President
      Tel: 614-390-9660
      Email: wilson@systemian.com
      Website: www.systemian.com
IT services, Enterprise Architecture, Intelligent Automation, Cloud Adoption and Migration, Talent Management. (As-Pac, estab 2020, empl 12, sales , cert: NMSDC)

5153 TechSoft Systems, Inc.
      10296 Springfield Pike Ste 400
      Cincinnati, OH 45215
      Contact: Clifford A. Bailey President
      Tel: 513-772-5010
      Email: cabailey@techsoftsystems.com
      Website: www.techsoftsystems.com
IT Consultants/Staffing, On-Site Support (desktop, network, help desk), Remot Support, Manages Services, Hardware & Software purchasing. (AA, estab 1983, empl 10, sales $904,328, cert: City, NMSDC)

5154 Texcel, Inc.
      4415 Euclid Ave
      Cleveland, OH 44103
      Contact: Herman Atkins President
      Tel: 216-514-1818
      Email: batkins@texcelinc.net
      Website: www.texcelinc.net
Digital document rendering. IBM cloud solutions. (AA, estab , empl , sales $6,000,000, cert: State, City, NMSDC)

5155 TMH Solutions LLC
      4176 Menderes Dr
      Powell, OH 43065
      Contact: Theresa Harris President
      Tel: 614-581-4450
      Email: theresa@tmhsolutions.com
      Website: www.tmhsolutions.com
Resell software & services, management & information technology solutions. (Woman/AA, estab 2010, empl 5, sales $5,100,000, cert: State, NMSDC, WBENC)

5156 TPSi, LLC
      11590 Century Blvd
      Cincinnati, OH 45246
      Contact: Matt Bender President
      Tel: 877-682-5300
      Email: mbender@tpsinc.com
      Website: www.tpsinc.com
Technical staffing & engineering services. (Woman, estab 2000, empl 25, sales $2,300,000, cert: WBENC)

5157 UNICON International, Inc.
      241 Outerbelt St
      Columbus, OH 43213
      Contact: Bobby Cameron Dir Client Services
      Tel: 614-861-7070
      Email: bcameron@unicon-intl.com
      Website: www.unicon-intl.com
Information technology solutions. (Minority, Woman, estab 1990, empl 300, sales $31,000,000, cert: City, NMSDC, WBENC)

5158 United Software Group Inc.
      565, Metro Place South, Ste 110
      Dublin, OH 43017
      Contact: Vetri Palaniappan Business Devel Dir
      Tel: 614-588-8530
      Email: vetri.p@usgrpinc.com
      Website: www.usgrpinc.com
Software consulting services. (As-Ind, estab 2002, empl 200, sales $69,000,000, cert: State, NMSDC)

5159 Vertex Computer Systems, Inc
      25700 Science Park Dr Ste 280
      Beachwood, OH 44122
      Contact: Reshmy Kesavadas Office of Supplier Diversity
      Tel: 479-903-6827
      Email: vertex.rfp@vertexcs.com
      Website: www.vertexcs.com
IT development & outsourced services: web, database & middleware. (Woman/As-Ind, estab 1989, empl 200, sales $12,425,234, cert: NMSDC, WBENC)

5160 Warwick Communications, Inc.
      405 Ken Mar Pkwy
      Broadview Heights, OH 44147
      Contact: Heidi Murphy Principal
      Tel: 216-787-0300
      Email: hmurphy@warwickinc.com
      Website: www.warwickinc.com
Information technology managed services, telephone systems, VOIP systems, cloud/hosted systems, wireless systems, data switching equipment, call recording software, support desk services, call accounting systems, call center software. (Woman, estab 1960, empl 40, sales $6,245,000, cert: City)

Oklahoma

5161 Delaware Resource Group of Oklahoma LLC
      3220 Quail Springs Pkwy
      Oklahoma City, OK 73134
      Contact: Meredith Kemp Program Mgmt Assistant
      Tel: 405-721-7776
      Email: meredith.kemp@drgok.com
      Website: www.drgok.com/
Contract instruction services, computer based training, curriculum development & maintenance, computer training materials devel & contract operations maintenance svcs. (Nat Ame, estab 2002, empl 200, sales $21,569,317, cert: NMSDC)

5162 Lynnco Supply Chain Solutions
2448 E 81st St, Ste 2600
Tulsa, OK 74137
Contact: Wendy Buxton President
Tel: 918-664-5540
Email: wendy.buxton@lynnco-scs.com
Website: www.lynnco-scs.com
Supply Chain Analytics, Planning and Execution, Supply Chain Metrics, Continuous Improvement with Lean Methodologies, Supplier Fulfillment & Compliance Programs, Freight Procurement & Optimization. Logistics Management. (Minority, Woman, estab 1991, empl 65, sales $70,000,000, cert: NMSDC, WBENC)

5163 Xyant Technology, Inc.
710 ASP Ave Ste 500
Norman, OK 73069
Contact: Sowmya Sridhar President
Tel: 405-209-7371
Email: sowmyas@xyant.com
Website: www.xyant.com
IT consulting & staff augmentation solutions: application implementation & deployment, maintenance & support, networking svcs, migration upgrades. (As-Pac, estab 1995, empl 50, sales $2,000,000, cert: NMSDC)

Oregon

5164 Cayuse Technologies, LLC
72632 Coyote Rd
Pendleton, OR 97801
Contact: Heather Collins Dir Business Dev
Tel: 541-278-8200
Email: heather.collins@cayusetechnologies.com
Website: www.cayusetechnologies.com
Technology Platforms: Java and .NET-Operating Systems: UNIX and Windows-Programming Languages: Open Source Frameworks; Hibernate, Spring. (Nat Ame, estab 2006, empl 240, sales $15,063,354, cert: State, NMSDC)

5165 Everest Consultants, Inc.
1500 NW Bethany Blvd Ste 235
Beaverton, OR 97006
Contact: Ranya Edupuganti President
Tel: 503-643-3990
Email: ranya@everestinc.com
Website: www.everestinc.com
Software consulting, offshore software dev, systems integration & IS/IT staff augmentation. (Minority, Woman, estab 1993, empl 65, sales $9,500,000, cert: NMSDC)

5166 iBridge LLC
12725 SW Millikan Way, Ste 300
Beaverton, OR 97005
Contact: Desh Urs President
Tel: 503-906-3930
Email: bids@ibridgellc.com
Website: www.ibridgellc.com/
Digitizing, converting, data processing all forms of information, electronic, paper, microfilm, voice or video, e cleanse, format & verify data. (As-Ind, estab 2004, empl 16, sales , cert: State)

5167 Martin's Got You Covered
PO Box 3764
Portland, OR 97208
Contact: Donald Martin President
Tel: 503-289-0278
Email: donald@martinsgotyoucovered.com
Website: www.martinsgotyoucovered.com/
Computer hardware & software, custom-build laptops, notebooks, tablet pcs, monitors, modems, presentation equipment, servers. (AA, estab 2002, empl 1, sales , cert: State)

5168 Mavensoft Technologies
15248 NW Greenbrier Pkwy
Beaverton, OR 97006
Contact: Acct Mgr
Tel: 503-629-4855
Email: sales@mavensoft.com
Website: www.mavensoft.com
IT services, software development, QA, Cloud Engineering, Project Management, Java, .NET, PHP, Angular JS, HP ALM, Selenium, BI Analytics, E-commerce, IBM Websphere, SAP Hybris, Oracle ATG, Magento. (As-Ind, estab 2004, empl 30, sales $2,400,000, cert: NMSDC)

5169 Protech Excellens Inc.
1500 NW Bethany Blvd Ste 200
Beaverton, OR 07006
Contact: Ben Condol CEO
Tel: 866-688-8843
Email: ben@protechexcellens.com
Website: www.protechexcellens.com
Oracle Databases, Oracle Middleware, Oracle applications, Oracle Engineered Systems, Oracle storage, Oracle support. PeoleSoft, Fusion, EBS, CRM. (Minority, Woman, estab 2007, empl 2, sales $170,000, cert: State)

5170 Rapid External Solutions, Inc.
9450 SW Gemini Dr Ste 61944
Beaverton, OR 97008
Contact: Vic Gupta Dir
Tel: 617-616-0986
Email: info@r-e-s.com
Website: www.r-e-s.com
ERP Applications staffing: Oracle, SAP, PeopleSoft, JDE, Siebel, Microsoft. (As-Ind, estab 2009, empl 13, sales $11,000,000, cert: NMSDC)

5171 Triad Technology Group
10300 SW Greenburg Rd, Ste 560
Portland, OR 97223
Contact: Regina Shapiro Acct Mgr
Tel: 503-293-9547
Email: kelley@go2triad.com
Website: www.triadtechnology.com
Information technology staffing & recruiting services. (Hisp, estab 1989, empl 30, sales $3,700,000, cert: State)

Pennsylvania

5172 Abator Information Services, Inc.
615 South Ave
Pittsburgh, PA 15221
Contact: Joanne Peterson CEO
Tel: 412-271-5922
Email: joanne@abator.com
Website: www.abator.com/
Information technology & systems projects. (Woman, estab 1983, empl 9, sales $1,297,485, cert: State, WBENC)

5173   ABOUT-Consulting LLC
       330 Kennett Pike, Ste 205
       Chadds Ford, PA 19317
       Contact: Frances Gatto CEO
       Tel: 610-388-9455
       Email: fgatto@about-consulting.com
       Website: www.about-consulting.com
Project mgmt, internet, intranet & extranet design & dev, business apps & databases, help desk, network systems engineering, architecture & admin, operations & technical svcs. (Woman, estab 2002, empl 20, sales $3,000,000, cert: WBENC)

5174   Advanced Integration Group Inc.
       1 McCormick Rd Ste A
       McKees Rocks, PA 15136
       Contact: Donna Chappel President
       Tel: 412-722-0065
       Email: dchappel@aigcontrols.com
       Website: www.aigcontrols.com
IT & engineering professionals: consultants, contractors & temp to perm personnel. (Woman, estab 1997, empl 35, sales $2,750,000, cert: WBENC)

5175   AptoTek Inc.
       2026 Milta Hill Rd
       Romansville, PA 19320
       Contact: Joe Johnbosco CEO
       Tel: 610-241-2603
       Email: joe.johnbosco@aptotek-inc.com
       Website: www.aptotek-inc.com
Custom Application Development, CRM Solutions, IT staff augmentation, IT outsource Services, Application/software support & maintenance contracts, IT strategy solutions. (As-Ind, estab 2015, empl 1, sales , cert: NMSDC)

5176   Aspect Consulting, Inc.
       20140 Valley Forge Cir
       King of Prussia, PA 19406
       Contact: Nicole Gantzhorn Business Devel Rep
       Tel: 610-783-0600
       Email: ngantzhorn@aspect-consulting.com
       Website: www.aspect-consulting.com
Technical Staffing, Data Mgmt, Business Intelligence, Configuration, Data Warehouse Development, Database Administration, Oracle, SQL Server, Custom Software Development, Application Design & Architecture. (Woman, estab 1994, empl 40, sales $5,300,000, cert: WBENC)

5177   Cognis IT Advisors LLC
       1735 Market St Ste A-485
       Philadelphia, PA 19103
       Contact: Mike Thomas CEO
       Tel: 215-557-4455
       Email: mthomas@cognisit.com
       Website: www.cognisit-advisors.com
Information Technology (IT) Services. (AA, estab 2007, empl 4, sales $489,000, cert: NMSDC)

5178   Computer Enterprises, Inc.
       1000 Omega Dr Ste 1150
       Pittsburgh, PA 15205
       Contact: Joe Esposito Solutions Sales Dir
       Tel: 412-680-4880
       Email: jesposito@ceiamerica.com
       Website: www.ceiamerica.com
Software consulting & system integration services, custom applications & systems software programming services & Internet systems consulting services. (AA, As-Pac, estab , empl 620, sales $71,947,000, cert: NMSDC)

5179   ConnectedSign, LLC
       120A W Airport Rd
       Lititz, PA 17543
       Contact: Loren Bucklin President
       Tel: 866-833-2723
       Email: lbucklin@connectedsign.com
       Website: www.connectedsign.com
Digital Signage Software, Navori Tycoon Software, Digital Signage Hardware, Digital Signage Content, Website Development and Content, Kiosks Software, Kiosks Hardware, Kiosks Content. (Woman, estab 2003, empl 12, sales $1,000,000, cert: WBENC)

5180   CREDO Technology Solutions, Inc.
       110 Sunset Ave Ste 101
       Harrisburg, PA 17112
       Contact: Missy Flexman Dir of Marketing & Communications
       Tel: 717-657-7017
       Email: mflexman@credotsinc.com
       Website: www.credotsinc.com
IT project solutions, ERP software implementations & upgrades. (As-Ind, estab 2010, empl 42, sales $3,130,000, cert: State, NMSDC)

5181   DecisionOne Corporation
       640 Lee Road 3rd Fl
       Wayne, PA 19087
       Contact: Karen Strickler Sr Proposal Specialist
       Tel: 610-296-6183
       Email: karen.strickler@decisionone.com
       Website: www.decisionone.com
Outsourced remote solutions & support desk services, technology centers, hardware & software asset services, forward/reverse logistics & supply chain management services. (As-Ind, estab 1969, empl 800, sales $101,755,000, cert: NMSDC)

5182   Eminent Group, Inc
       2 Walnut Grove Rd Ste 130
       Horsham, PA 19044
       Contact: Katherine Moore CEO
       Tel: 267-387-6487
       Email: kmoore@egiusa.com
       Website: www.egiusa.com
Transportation Management Systems Implementation, Global Trade Management Systems Implementation, Outsourcing:
Transportation Operational Planning, Transportation Optimization. (Woman, estab 2002, empl 38, sales $7,104,089, cert: WBENC)

5183   Futura Services, Inc.
       515 Pennsylvania Ave Ste 100
       Fort Washington, PA 19034
       Contact: Dominic Sambucci COO
       Tel: 215-639-9540
       Email: dsambucci@futuraservices.net
       Website: www.futuraservices.net
Help desk support, spare pool, asset management, staging, kitting, hardware roll-outs & imaging. (Woman, estab 1992, empl 45, sales $9,000,000, cert: WBENC)

5184 Genzeon Corporation
      559 W Uwchlan Ave Ste 120
      Exton, PA 19341
      Contact: Brendan OHayre COO
      Tel: 203-516-1109
      Email: brendan.ohayre@genzeon.com
      Website: www.genzeon.com
Technology solutions, custom application development,
performance engineering & human capital solutions.
(Minority, estab 1999, empl 150, sales $17,500,000, cert:
NMSDC)

5185 Hanabi Networks Systems, LLC
      150 N Radnor Chester Rd, Ste F200
      Radnor, PA 19087
      Contact: Tariq Yusufzai VP Business Dev
      Tel: 484-381-0698
      Email: tyusufzai@ehanabi.com
      Website: www.ehanabi.com
Analyze, design, install, configure, manage & repair global
network infrastructure & application components. (As-Pac,
estab 2016, empl 2, sales $120,000, cert: NMSDC)

5186 iBusiness Solution, LLC
      5000 Lenker St
      Mechanicsburg, PA 17050
      Contact: Narendra Ghuge
      Tel: 717-724-7865
      Email: sales@ibusinesssolution.com
      Website: www.ibusinesssolution.com
IT consulting, technology services, staffing & outsourcing.
(As-Ind, estab 2000, empl 54, sales $9,000,000, cert: State,
NMSDC)

5187 ID Discovery, Inc.
      18 Mainland Rd
      Harleysville, PA 19438
      Contact: Amanda Mortimer Business Dev
      Tel: 215-230-4130
      Email: amanda.mortimer@id-llc.com
      Website: www.id-llc.com
Strategic Project Management, Data Management,
Product Commercialization, eDiscovery, Cyber Security, IT
consulting and Information Governance solutions.
(Woman, estab 2012, empl 30, sales , cert: WBENC)

5188 ImageTech Systsems, Inc.
      3913 Hartzdale Dr
      Camp Hill, PA 17011
      Contact: RJ Oommen Principal
      Tel: 717-761-5900
      Email: rjo@imagetechsys.com
      Website: www.imagetechsys.com
Enterprise Content Management (ECM) & Business Process
automation technologies. (As-Ind, estab 1994, empl 7,
sales $2,000,000, cert: State, NMSDC)

5189 Independent Computer Consulting Group, Inc.
      1 Ivybrook Blvd Ste 177
      Warminster, PA 18974
      Contact: Mihir Shah Sr Business Dev Mgr
      Tel: 215-675-9149
      Email: mshah@iccg.com
      Website: www.iccg.com
Implementations, upgrades & support, Business Intelligence, Qlik, Cognos & Micro Strategy, SAP suite of applications. (Woman/As-Ind, estab 1988, empl 100, sales , cert:
WBENC)

5190 Iron Lady Enterprises Inc.
      1943 Poplar St, 2nd Fl
      Philadelphia, PA 19130
      Contact: Dianna Montague CEO
      Tel: 267-973-8626
      Email:
      dianna.montague@ironladyenterprises.com
      Website: www.ironladyenterprises.com/
We provide ironworking services such as welding and or
repair of bridges and structural units. Our company also
plans to build bridges and building foundations of any
kind using rebar and re-inforcing concrete. (Woman/AA,
estab 2011, empl 2, sales , cert: City, NMSDC)

5191 JCW Computer Consulting, LLC
      7478 Rhoads St, Ste C
      Philadelphia, PA 19151
      Contact: Carl Johnson Sales Assoc
      Tel: 215-879-6701
      Email: carl@jcwcc.com
      Website: www.jcwcc.com
Computer consulting: Microsoft, IBM & Compaq
solutions, workstation & server product lines. (AA, estab
1992, empl 3, sales , cert: City, NMSDC)

5192 KORYAK Consulting, Inc.
      2003 Kinvara Dr
      Pittsburgh, PA 15237
      Contact: Suresh Ramanathan CEO
      Tel: 412-364-6600
      Email: sramanathan@koryak.com
      Website: www.koryak.com
Management & IT consulting: business & IT strategy dev,
supply chain enhancement, E-business integration,
Oracle app implementation & outsourcing, systems dev
& integration. (As-Ind, estab 2000, empl 25, sales
$3,000,000, cert: State, NMSDC)

5193 Lim, Norris & Associates
      12 Fox Hunt Cir
      Plymouth Meeting, PA 19462
      Contact: Yvonne Norris President
      Tel: 610-825-6730
      Email: ynorris@limnorris.com
      Website: www.limnorris.com
Information technology, strategic planning & organization design. (Minority, Woman, estab 1994, empl 3, sales
$953,000, cert: City)

5194 Logix Guru LLC
      3821 Old William Penn Hwy
      Murrysville, PA 15668
      Contact: Singh Ajmani Business Devel Mgr
      Tel: 724-733-4500
      Email: ajmani@logixguru.com
      Website: www.logixguru.com
IT consulting & staff augmentation, engineering,
administrative, information technology. (As-Ind, estab
2000, empl 20, sales $4,200,000, cert: State, NMSDC)

5195 M.A.P. Consulting Services, Inc.
      520 South 3rd St
      Philadelphia, PA 19147
      Contact: CEO
      Tel: 215-315-4175
      Email: info@mapconsult.com
      Website: www.mapconsult.com
IT staffing & consulting, ERP & EDI specialists, project
mgmt expertise, data warehousing. (Woman, estab
1997, empl 2, sales $201,000, cert: WBENC)

5196 Mastech Digital Technologies, Inc.
      1305 Cherrington Pkwy Bldg 210, Ste 400
      Moon Township, PA 15108
      Contact: Michael Kosar Dir of MSP
      Tel: 412-787-9559
      Email: Michael.kosar@mastechdigital.com
      Website: www.mastechdigital.com
IT services: usiness intelligence, data warehousing, architecture & web svcs, enterprise resource planning, custom applications, dev & maintenance, migration, re-engineering, project mgmt, ebusiness solutions. (Minority, estab , empl 750, sales $123,400,000, cert: NMSDC)

5197 Minitab Inc.
      1829 Pine Hall Rd
      State College, PA 16801
      Contact: Justin Callahan Sr Reg Mgr Commercial Sales
      Tel: 814-238-3280
      Email: jcallahan@minitab.com
      Website: www.minitab.com
IT products and services. (Minority, Woman, estab 1983, empl 350, sales , cert: WBENC)

5198 Momentum, Inc.
      2120 Market St Ste 100
      Camp Hill, PA 17011
      Contact: Scott Reilly Exec Dir
      Tel: 717-214-8000
      Email: momentum@m-inc.com
      Website: www.m-inc.com
IT & management consulting, process improvement, project management & implementation support. (Woman, estab 1998, empl 54, sales $9,304,338, cert: State, City)

5199 Ohm Systems, Inc.
      955 Horsham Rd Ste 205
      Horsham, PA 19044
      Contact: Praful Patel President
      Tel: 215-309-6233
      Email: ppatel@ohmsysinc.com
      Website: www.ohmsysinc.com
Software development, support, maintainance, R&D, web, consulting, FAA, telecom, protocols, client/server, java. (Minority, estab 1998, empl 65, sales $6,500,000, cert: NMSDC)

5200 Partner's Consulting, Inc.
      2004 Sproul Road, Ste 206
      Broomall, PA 19008
      Contact: Delivery & Engagement Mgr
      Tel: 215-939-6294
      Email: info@partners-consulting.com
      Website: www.partners-consulting.com
Information technology recruiting for full-time, temp-to-perm & contract positions. (Woman, estab 2006, empl 40, sales $6,000,000, cert: State, WBENC)

5201 Pierson Computing Connection, Inc.
      10 Long Ln
      Mechanicsburg, PA 17050
      Contact: Debra Pierson President
      Tel: 717-796-0493
      Email: deb@pierson.it
      Website: www.pierson.it
Project mgmt, multi-site IT & related installations, printers, cash registers, PC equipment, cabling, networking equipment, etc. (Woman, estab 1993, empl 47, sales $16,900,000, cert: State, WBENC)

5202 Probitas Technology Inc.
      3544 N Progress Ave Ste 104
      Harrisburg, PA 17110
      Contact: Benjamin Williams President
      Tel: 717-773-4208
      Email: sales@probitastek.com
      Website: www.probitastek.com
Computer networking design, installation & maintenance, electronic security. (AA, estab 2004, empl 8, sales $600,000, cert: State, City)

5203 PRWT Services, Inc.
      1835 Market St Ste 800
      Philadelphia, PA 19103
      Contact: Rose Braverman SVP Strategic Planning & Operations
      Tel: 215-569-8810
      Email: rose.braverman@prwt.com
      Website: www.prwt.com
Information & document processing; lockbox processing; call ctr customer care & service; facilities mgmt; web & telephone-based fulfillment; telecommunications construction; help desk functions & toll collections operations. (AA, estab 1988, empl 1000, sales $69,800,000, cert: City, NMSDC)

5204 Raise Tech Solutions, LLC
      606 Liberty Ave, 3rd Fl
      Pittsburgh, PA 15222
      Contact: John R Thomson President
      Tel: 412-267-3069
      Email: contact@raisets.com
      Website: www.RaiseTS.com
IT Services and Consulting. (AA, estab 2017, empl 10, sales , cert: NMSDC)

5205 River Development Corporation
      2005 Garrick Dr
      Pittsburgh, PA 15235
      Contact: Cheryl McAbee
      Tel: 412-243-2005
      Email: crmcabee@riverdevcorp.com
      Website: www.riverdevcorp.com
Records storage: off site, web access inventory, media vault storage & delivery, scan & index, data vaulting, shredding. (Woman, estab 1996, empl 4, sales , cert: State, City, NMSDC)

5206 RST Solutions Inc.
      1005 Azlen Lane Ste 114
      Chalfont, PA 18914
      Contact: Rajan Kaistha VP
      Tel: 610-613-8699
      Email: rajan@rstsolutions.com
      Website: www.rstsolutions.com
ERP services, implementations, upgrade, integrations, JDE Mobile Apps, FRICE/COMLI, etc. (Woman/As-Ind, estab 2003, empl 18, sales $5,000,000, cert: WBENC)

5207 ShazTEK LLP
      500 Office Center Dr, Ste 400
      Fort Washington, PA 19034
      Contact: Zak Khan Dir Sales
      Tel: 267-507-3168
      Email: zkhan@shaztek.com
      Website: www.shaztek.com
Analyze business impact, costs, and regulatory requirements to build a technology roadmap. (As-Ind, estab 2011, empl 27, sales $18,225,000, cert: NMSDC)

5208 Sigma Resources LLC
7950 Saltsburg Rd
Pittsburgh, PA 15239
Contact: Sandy Kaleida VP Consulting
Tel: 412-712-1019
Email: skaleida@sigma-resources.com
Website: www.sigma-resources.com
IT consulting services. (Minority, Woman, estab 1998, empl 24, sales $9,000,000, cert: State, WBENC)

5209 SoftNice Inc.
5050 Tilghman St, Ste 115
Allentown, PA 18104
Contact: Zubin Pardiwala Mgr Business Devel
Tel: 201-603-2635
Email: zubin@softnice.com
Website: www.softnice.com
Global Consulting and IT services. (As-Pac, estab 2001, empl 600, sales $18,007,269, cert: NMSDC)

5210 SoftSages, LLC
17 Mystic Lane, Ste 2A
Malvern, PA 19355
Contact: Jiraj Ruparelia VP
Tel: 484-604-0603
Email: jiraj@softsages.com
Website: www.softsages.com
Software Development Consultants, programming, Database Developments, Networking & mobile development, custom software & security solutions. (Woman/As-Pac, estab 2005, empl 25, sales $8,000,000, cert: State, NMSDC, WBENC)

5211 solutions4networks, Inc.
1501 Reedsdale St Ste 2001
PIttsburgh, PA 15233
Contact: Michele McGough CEO
Tel: 412-638-4341
Email: michele@s4nets.com
Website: www.s4nets.com
Data, voice, wireless & network security consulting: network assessments & design, security assessments, IPv6 planning, MPLS, QoS, project mgmt, product selection, RFP devel. (Woman, estab 2000, empl 25, sales $8,430,000, cert: State, WBENC)

5212 Strother Enterprises Inc.
100 S Broad St Ste 2130
Philadelphia, PA 19110
Contact: Ernest L Strother CEO
Tel: 215-564-5538
Email: elstrother@strotherenterprises.com
Website: www.strotherenterprises.com
Food Service Management; Facilities Management; Commissary Services; Staffing and Training. Knowledge of government contracts, knowledge of compliance and regulatory standards and long-standing (AA, estab 1990, empl 26, sales $3,409,222, cert: State, City, NMSDC)

5213 SwitchLane Inc.
5 Christy Dr Ste 303
Chadds Ford, PA 19317
Contact: Meera Kalyani President
Tel: 267-297-0790
Email: meera@switchlane.com
Website: www.switchlane.com
IT staffing & consulting services. (Woman, estab 2010, empl 10, sales $1,312,407, cert: State, WBENC)

5214 Symphony Enterprises LLC
PO Box 16140
Pittsburgh, PA 15242
Contact: Head Sales & Business Dev
Tel: 412-212-0135
Email: sales@symphonyenterprises.com
Website: www.symphonyenterprises.com
IT staffing & consulting services. (Minority, Woman, estab 2004, empl 4, sales , cert: State)

5215 Synergy EnterPrize, LLC
1150 First Ave, Ste 501
King of Prussia, PA 19406
Contact: Jonathan Ngah Principal
Tel: 610-945-1737
Email: information@synergy-ia.com
Website: www.synergy-ia.com
Audit Support, Information Technology Management & Governance, Business Process Improvement, Project Management, Fraud Risk & Vulnerability Assessment solutions. (AA, estab 2011, empl 10, sales $1,500,000, cert: NMSDC, 8(a))

5216 Systems Staffing Group   Inc.
910 E. Main St Ste 201
Norristown, PA 19401
Contact: Beth Verman CEO
Tel: 610-668-8101
Email: bverman@systemsstaffinggroup.com
Website: www.systemsstaffinggroup.com
Information technology staffing: consultants & permanent employees. (Woman, estab 2000, empl 30, sales $15,000,000, cert: WBENC)

5217 Tan Check Consolidated, Inc.
2 Silver Trail Circle Ste 101
Newtown, PA 18940
Contact: Rebecca Smith Sr Acct Mgr
Tel: 215-860-5031
Email: rsmith@tcci.com
Website: www.tcci.com
IT Staffing, Information Technology Management, Consulting, Permanent Placement, Temp to Perm, Executive Search, Software Development. (Woman, estab 2001, empl 75, sales $6,850,000, cert: State, WBENC)

5218 Techwave Consulting Inc.
1 E Uwchlan Ave
Exton, PA 19341
Contact: Jalpesh Thaker Mgr
Tel: 484-873-4602
Email: infona@techwave.net
Website: www.techwave.net/
Software consulting & staffing services: SAP (BI, BO, BPC, BPM & BW), Oracle (OBIEE), Cognos & BPM products & services. (Woman/As-Ind, estab 2004, empl 150, sales $11,000,000, cert: State)

5219   The Jay Group
       700 Indian Springs Dr
       Lancaster, PA 17601
       Contact: Nicole Sensenig Administrative Asst
       Tel: 717-285-6200
       Email: nicole.sensenig@jaygroup.com
       Website: www.jaygroup.com
Product, literature & catalog fulfillment services, inbound
call center, customer service support, co-packing, promotional processing, information technology, sampling
services, promotional products, e-business solutions.
(Woman, estab 1965, empl 300, sales $25,887,011, cert:
WBENC)

5220   TreCom Systems Group
       99 November Dr
       Camp Hill, PA 17011
       Contact: Phillip Gring COO
       Tel: 717-319-0711
       Email: pgring@trecomsystems.com
       Website: www.trecomsystems.com
Information technology consulting svcs: software dev &
design, enterprise architecture, training, help desk,
programming, networking, documentation, software
testing, staff augmentation, contract programming, Oracle
authorized reseller. (AA, estab 2009, empl 58, sales
$7,000,000, cert: State, NMSDC)

5221   Tri-force Consulting Services Inc.
       650 North Cannon Ave
       Lansdale, PA 19446
       Contact: Manish Gorawala President
       Tel: 215-362-2611
       Email: mgorawala@triforce-inc.com
       Website: www.triforce-inc.com/
Information technology consulting: Java, J2EE, .NET, QA &
open source technologies based business applications
solutions. (Minority, estab 2000, empl 40, sales
$6,285,927, cert: State, City, NMSDC)

5222   TriLogic Corporation
       161 Hillpointe Dr
       Canonsburg, PA 15317
       Contact: Gary Grabowski Operations Mgr
       Tel: 724-745-0200
       Email: ggrabowski@tri-logic.com
       Website: www.tri-logic.com
Design, install & maintain LAN/WANs; wireless networking,
IP telephony, virtual private networks. (AA, estab 1981,
empl 35, sales , cert: NMSDC)

5223   Urban Harvest Partnership, LLC
       6050 Osage Ave
       Philadelphia, PA 19143
       Contact: Jonathan Ford Principal
       Tel: 610-482-4284
       Email: ford@uhpwireless.com
       Website: www.uhpwireless.com/
Technology services: desktop & network services, secure
wireless networking, cabling services, voice, data & audio/
video installations. (AA, estab 2003, empl 7, sales
$960,000, cert: NMSDC)

5224   Velocity Works, LLC
       12330 Perry Hwy, Ste 115
       Wexford, PA 15090
       Contact: Dionisio Lopez CEO
       Tel: 412-398-2679
       Email: al@velocityworks.io
       Website: www.velocityworks.io
Technical staffing and software engineering consulting
to the financial services, healthcare and robotics
industries. (Hisp, estab 2018, empl 30, sales $3,625,433,
cert: NMSDC)

5225   YIKES, Inc.
       204 E Girard Ave
       Philadelphia, PA 19125
       Contact: Mia Levesque Co-Owner
       Tel: 215-238-8801
       Email: info@yikesinc.com
       Website: www.yikesinc.com
Web design & development services, WordPress,
Custom web design, website maintenance, ecommerce,
web/database integration, ColdFusion, custom-built
web-based applications, content management systems.
(Minority, Woman, estab 1996, empl 5, sales $664,693,
cert: City, WBENC)

5226   Zodiac Solutions Inc.
       270 Lancaster Ave Ste h-2
       Malvern, PA 19355
       Contact: VP Operations
       Tel: 484-550-6482
       Email: info@zodiac-solutions.com
       Website: www.zodiac-solutions.com
IT staff augmentation , IT solutions services, managed
services, project management, software development,
knowledge process outsourcing, management consulting. (As-Ind, estab 2011, empl 70, sales $4,751,993, cert:
NMSDC)

Puerto Rico

5227   Beryllium Corporation
       PO Box 5938
       Caguas, PR 00726
       Contact: Jorge Normandia CEO
       Tel: 787-744-5729
       Email: info@berylliumpr.com
       Website: www.berylliumpr.com
Custom Software Design & Development, Pharmaceuti-
cal/Medical Devices Industries, Manufacturing Execution
Systems Integrators. (Hisp, estab 1998, empl 8, sales
$756,288, cert: NMSDC)

5228   Integrated Services for Productivity & Validation
       Acuarela St, Ste 3A Urb Munoz Rivera
       Guaynabo, PR 00969
       Contact: Luis Baez Principal
       Tel: 787-789-4778
       Email: lmbaez@is-pv.com
       Website: www.is-pv.com
Technology, Management, Systems & Productivity
Improvement projects. (Hisp, estab 2007, empl 25, sales
$2,280,441, cert: NMSDC)

5229 Integrated Technology & Compliance Services
PMB 470 Box 4956
Caguas, PR 00726
Contact: Ismael Aviles COO
Tel: 939-579-3846
Email: ismael.aviles@itcspr.com
Website: www.itcspr.com
Information Technology Consulting & cGMP Validation
Consulting & Compliance services. (Hisp, estab 2005, empl
10, sales $977,456, cert: NMSDC)

5230 Jays and Fancy Interiors, Inc.
2A-16 Ave. Carlos Javier Andaluz
Bayamon, PR 00956
Contact: Gavin Davis
Tel: 787-786-9411
Email: gdavis@jaysandfancy.com
Website: www.jaysandfancy.com
GENERAL CONTRACTOR, INTERIOR FINISHES, CONCRETE,
MASONRY, COLD FORMED METAL FRAMING, DRYWALL,
PLASTER, GYPSUM BOARD, TILING, RESILIENT FLOORING,
NORA, INSTALLATION, ACOUSTICAL (Hisp, estab 2001,
empl 25, sales $5,200,000, cert: NMSDC)

5231 JC Automation, Corp.
Calle D #27-C Urb. Los Maestros
Humacao, PR 00791
Contact: Juan Senquiz GM
Tel: 787-719-7315
Email: jsenquiz@jcapr.cmom
Website: www.jcapr.com
IT Management, Compliance & Manufacturing System
Services, Application Design & Development, Systems
Integration. (Hisp, estab 1997, empl 40, sales $4,700,000,
cert: NMSDC)

5232 Mirus Consulting Group Corp
PO Box 851
Humacao, PR 00792
Contact: Giovanni Gomez Dir
Tel: 787-285-0992
Email: ggomez@miruspr.com
Website: www.miruspr.com
Computer system validation & information technology
consulting services. (Hisp, estab 2001, empl 25, sales
$2,900,000, cert: NMSDC)

5233 PharmaBioServ US, Inc. (PBSV)
545 West Germantown Pike 6 Road 696
Dorado, PR 00646
Contact: Armando Morales US Operations Dir
Tel: 787-278-2709
Email: info@pharmabioserv.com
Website: www.pharmabioserv.com
Data Processing, Hosting, and related Services, Internet
Publishing and Broadcasting and Web Search Portals,
Engineering Services. (Hisp, estab 1993, empl 150, sales
$14,000,000, cert: NMSDC)

5234 Real Physics, Inc.
1056 Munoz Riviera Ave Ste 903
San Juan, PR 00927
Contact: Pedro Torres President
Tel: 787-469-1359
Email: ptorres@realphysics.net
Website: www.realphysics.net
Project management, IT consulting, outsourcing, ap-
praisal, validation, aerial photography, scheduling services,
quality & logistics audits. (Hisp, estab 2007, empl 3, sales ,
cert: NMSDC)

5235 Weil Group, Inc.
Urb. Villa Blanca Calle Aquamarina #78 Ste 1
Caguas, PR 00725
Contact: Milagros del R Gonzalez GM
Tel: 787-633-0025
Email: clopez@weilgroup.com
Website: www.weilgroup.com
Temporary employment agency, outsourcing IT &
automation services: management and/or admin, help
desk, servers, WAN, email system, desktop, mainte-
nance, backup & restore. (Hisp, estab 1994, empl 215,
sales $12,000,000, cert: NMSDC)

Rhode Island

5236 Artifex Technology Consulting, Inc.
614 George Washington Hwy
Lincoln, RI 02865
Contact: Jenna Schmidt President
Tel: 401-723-6644
Email: jenna@artifextech.com
Website: www.artifextech.com
Custom software solutions & graphic design. (Woman,
estab 2002, empl 13, sales $2,380,350, cert: WBENC)

5237 CSG LLC
98 Slope Ave
Wakefield, RI 02879
Contact: Meridith Voshell Acct Exec
Tel: 770-377-8955
Email: mvoshell@csg-llc.co
Website: www.csg-llc.co
Information Technology strategies. (Woman, estab 2017,
empl , sales , cert: WBENC)

5238 Granger Warburton Consulting, LLC
79 West St
East Greenwich, RI 02818
Contact: Bethany Warburton Principal Consultant
Tel: 401-965-1288
Email: bethany@grangerwarburton.com
Website: www.grangerwarburton.com
Learning management system design & deployment,
elearning creation, software application development,
project management, business analysis, change manage-
ment, documentation & process design. (Woman, estab
2013, empl 2, sales $127,000, cert: State)

South Carolina

5239 Blue Eye Soft Corp.
44 Pkwy Commons Way
Greer, SC 29650
Contact: Srikanth Kodeboyina Managing Partner
Tel: 864-479-0888
Email: sri@blueyesoft.com
Website: www.blueyesoft.com
IT Consulting Software solutions, BI Analytics, CRM,
Scalable Architecture, Health IT, Program& Project
Management, Human Resource Consulting. (As-Pac,
estab 2017, empl 14, sales $479,000, cert: NMSDC)

5240   Datasoft Technologies Inc.
34 Pkwy Commons Way
Greer, SC 29650
Contact: Manyapu Alka President
Tel: 864-849-9022
Email: amanyapu@datasoft-tech.com
Website: www.datasoft-tech.com
Software devel & consulting: system integration, engineering & architecture, project mgmt, analysis & design. (Minority, estab 1994, empl 41, sales $4,000,000, cert: State, NMSDC)

5241   Globalpundits Technology Consultancy Inc.
4715D Sunset Blvd
Lexington, SC 29072
Contact: Manoj Devulapalli President
Tel: 803-354-9400
Email: manoj@globalpundits.com
Website: www.globalpundits.com
Computer programming services, software design services, project management, business analysts, database administrations, contract engineering, mechanical engineers, stress engineers, electrical engineers, aeronautical engineers, CAD. (Minority, estab 2000, empl 106, sales $13,000,000, cert: State, NMSDC)

5242   Synesis International, Inc.
30 Creekview Ct
Greenville, SC 29615
Contact: Ricardo Studart President
Tel: 864-288-1550
Email: rstudart@synesisintl.com
Website: www.synesisintl.com
Information technology: ERP, MES, business analytics, EDI, bar code & quality control systems. (Hisp, estab 1994, empl 28, sales $3,500,000, cert: NMSDC)

5243   Technology Solutions Inc.
PO Box 212098
Columbia, SC 29221
Contact: Cathy Hill President
Tel: 803-359-6079
Email: cathy@tsisc.com
Website: www.tsisc.com
IT services: contracted programming, analysis, design, development, database analysis & design, technical writing, PC/technical support, systems programming, help desk, LAN/WAN, etc. (Woman, estab 1989, empl 75, sales , cert: WBENC)

Tennessee

5244   Conch Technologies, Inc.
6750 Poplar Ave, Ste 711
Memphis, TN 38138
Contact: Ray Scott VP Natl Sales
Tel: 901-827-5183
Email: contact@conchtech.com
Website: www.conchtech.com
IT consultants & contract programming, pc/client servers, internet/intranet, B2B & e-commerce. (Minority, Woman, estab 2004, empl 55, sales $1,700,000, cert: State)

5245   Stragistics Technology
6263 Poplar Ave, Ste 603
Memphis, TN 38119
Contact: Scott Swanson Business Devel Specialist
Tel: 901-799-0402
Email: sswanson@stragistics.com
Website: www.stragistics.com
Technology solutions, data integration, migration, eCommerce, infrastructure management, proprietary software, SDLC, systems integration. (Woman/AA, estab 1997, empl 8, sales $379,010, cert: State, City, NMSDC, WBENC)

5246   Zycron, Inc.
413 Welshwood Dr
Nashville, TN 37211
Contact: Rochelle Taylor VP Operations
Tel: 615-251-9588
Email: rtaylor@zycron.com
Website: www.zycron.com
System integration,technical consulting, supplemental staffing, configuration mgmt, software analysis, system design & facilities mgmt. (AA, estab 1991, empl 300, sales $29,245,696, cert: State)

Texas

5247   4Consulting, Inc.
1221 Abrams Rd, Ste 326
Richardson, TX 75081
Contact: Vivek Anand President
Tel: 972-333-0041
Email: vivek@4ci-usa.com
Website: www.4ci-usa.com
Consulting services: IT project mgmt, workforce mgmt, custom application dev, process mgmt, .NET technology, J2EE, Legacy, ERP, CRM, business process analyst, SME, data security, infrastructure mgmt. (Minority, Woman, estab 2000, empl 188, sales $15,780,000, cert: WBENC)

5248   A1 Shredding Inc.
PO Box 460085
Houston, TX 77056
Contact: Christopher Passmore President
Tel: 832-545-3949
Email: cpassmore@a1shreddinginc.com
Website: www.a1shreddinginc.com
Document shredding, paper recycling, paper destruction & shredding, IT/computer services. (AA, estab 2007, empl 1, sales , cert: State)

5249   AACANN Mechanical, Inc.
12718 Robert E. Lee
Houston, TX 77044
Contact: Larry Cannon President
Tel: 281-458-2258
Email: aacann@ymail.com
Website: www.aacann.com
Service, repair, installation, maintenance and zone comfort controls/design of HVACR systems designed for industrial and offshore accommodations along with process cooling systems. (AA, estab 1982, empl 4, sales $642,000, cert: NMSDC)

5250 Accolite Inc.
      16479 Dallas North Pkwy, Ste 350
      Addison, TX 75001
      Contact: Matthew McKinley VP Business Dev
      Tel: 469-235-9316
      Email: matthew.mckinley@accolite.com
      Website: www.accolite.com
Contingent staffinng services: contract, contract to hire &
permanent candidates for IT. (As-Pac, estab 2006, empl
280, sales $12,000,000, cert: State, NMSDC)

5251 Ace Delivery
      7308 Gaines Mill Ln
      Austin, TX 78745
      Contact: Tammie Garcia Office Mgr
      Tel: 512-326-3553
      Email: viaace1@gmail.com
      Website: www.acedeliveryatx.com
Ace Delivery we specilize in the medical supply chains. We
help with delivering medical products to all hospitals and
supply chains. We have a 100 mile radius from downtown
Austin. We are vendors to Seton Family of Hospitals, St
Davids (Minority, Woman, estab 1980, empl 7, sales
$947,931, cert: City)

5252 Addison Stuart
      566 Homewood Dr
      Coppell, TX 75019
      Contact: Christina Kolassa Owner
      Tel: 847-707-0429
      Email: ckolassa@addisonstuart.com
      Website: www.addisonstuart.com
Information technology, PPM implementation using CA
Clarity & Oracle PPM tools. (Woman, estab 2012, empl 4,
sales $200,000, cert: WBENC)

5253 Advent Global Solutions, Inc
      12777 Jones Rd, Ste 445
      Houston, TX 77070
      Contact: Chet Mann VP Client Services
      Tel: 281-640-8934
      Email: chet.mann@adventglobal.com
      Website: www.adventglobal.com/
ERP implementation, IT development & systems integration, SAP technology. (As-Ind, estab 1997, empl 1500, sales
$182,000,000, cert: NMSDC)

5254 Alphaworks LLC
      1600 10th St, Ste B
      Plano, TX 75074
      Contact: Don R Joe Operations Mgr
      Tel: 972-509-8837
      Email: rodney.joe@alphaworksnow.com
      Website: www.alphaworksnow.com
IT hardware, software & services: HP, Oracle, SAP, Cisco &
TDi. (As-Pac, estab 2010, empl 16, sales $3,000,000, cert:
NMSDC)

5255 Al-Razaq Computing Services
      6001 Savoy, Ste 505
      Houston, TX 77036
      Contact: Vicki Semander Contract Vehicle Spec
      Tel: 713-839-9613
      Email: vsemander@al-razaqcomputing.com
      Website: www.al-razaqcomputing.com
Database mgmt, systems network integration, computer
hardware & software, educational product dev & training,
financial mgmt, budget dev & execution package, software
dev & computer programming. (AA, estab 1993, empl 48,
sales $3,167,414, cert: State, NMSDC)

5256 American Unit, Inc.
      2901 N Dallas Pkwy Ste 333
      Plano, TX 75093
      Contact: Ramana Mgr
      Tel: 972-398-3335
      Email: ravi@americanunit.com
      Website: www.americanunit.com
Enterprise & e-business implementation, upgrade, &
production support services. (As-Pac, estab 2003, empl
365, sales $30,000,000, cert: NMSDC)

5257 Amtek Consulting LLC
      18170 Dallas Pkwy Ste 104
      Dallas, TX 75287
      Contact: Satya Movva President
      Tel: 214-680-6111
      Email: smovva@amtekconsulting.com
      Website: www.amtekconsulting.com
IT consulting services, system design & implementation,
client-Server solutions, application development,
systems maintenance/operations support. (As-Ind, estab
2004, empl 47, sales , cert: City, NMSDC)

5258 Anblicks
      5055 Keller Springs Rd, Ste 160
      Dallas, TX 75254
      Contact: Srinivas V VP Projects
      Tel: 214-254-4633
      Email: sri@anblicks.com
      Website: www.anblicks.com
Cloud Data Analytics. (As-Pac, estab 2003, empl 300,
sales $13,500,000, cert: NMSDC)

5259 Applied Training Resources Inc.
      6405 Cypresswood Dr, Ste 250
      Spring, TX 77379
      Contact: Rose Bradshaw Controller
      Tel: 281-370-9540
      Email: rbradshaw@atrco.com
      Website: www.atrco.com
Lifecycle management systems: procedure & policy
management, editing, procedure workflow (MOC),
periodic review, incident investigation, action tracking &
integrated learning management. (Woman, estab 1990,
empl 43, sales $6,580,266, cert: WBENC)

5260 ARC Government Solutions, Inc
      9211 Waterford Centre Blvd Ste 202
      Austin, TX 78758
      Contact: Anne Fielding Dir Finance
      Tel: 512-452-0651
      Email: anne.fielding@arc-gs.com
      Website: www.arc-gs.com
IT services, staffing and solutions. (Woman, estab 1984,
empl 43, sales $104,628,999, cert: State)

5261 Argus Talent, LLC
      11739 Willcrest
      Houston, TX 77031
      Contact: Zeyn Patel President
      Tel: 713-465-5985
      Email: info@argustalent.com
      Website: www.argustalent.com
Document Management, Records Management and
Electronic Content Management (ECM) systems,
custom computing services, system design services, and
staff augmentation services. (As-Ind, estab 1989, empl
20, sales $500,000, cert: State, NMSDC)

5262   Armstrong Archives LLC
       1515 Crescent Dr
       Carrollton, TX 75006
       Contact: Sherri Taylor President
       Tel: 972-242-7179
       Email: staylor@aarchives.com
       Website: www.armstrongarchives.com
Secure & Reliable Record Storage, Document Storage, Document Management, Document Scanning, Paper Shredding & Distribution. (Woman, estab 1996, empl 13, sales , cert: WBENC)

5263   Aspiryon, LLC
       711 Nolana, Ste 103-F
       McAllen, TX 78504
       Contact: Neil Crisman GM
       Tel: 919-900-8622
       Email: sales@aspiryon.net
       Website: www.aspiryon.net
Plan & implement information security solutions. (Minority, Woman, estab 2011, empl 12, sales $2,000,000, cert: State)

5264   Assent Solutions LLC
       27311 Bentridge Park Ln
       Katy, TX 77494
       Contact: Venkata Reka VP
       Tel: 713-853-9288
       Email: reka@assentsolutions.com
       Website: www.assentsolutions.com
Information Technology Consulting, Staffing Augmentation, IT Staffing Services, Custom Software Application Development, Web Development. (Woman/As-Ind, estab 2009, empl 10, sales $588,751, cert: City)

5265   Associates Systems LLC
       750 S Mac Arthur Blvd Ste 100
       Coppell, TX 75019
       Contact: Pavan Akula Dir of Sales
       Tel: 972-241-4436
       Email: pavan.akula@associatessystems.com
       Website: www.associatessystems.com
Information technology solutions & services. (Minority, Woman, estab 2002, empl 40, sales , cert: State, NMSDC)

5266   Austin Tele-Services Partners, LP dba Genesis ATS
       4209 S Industrial Dr Ste 300
       Austin, TX 78744
       Contact: Patrick Manning VP Business Dev
       Tel: 512-437-3041
       Email: pmanning@genesis-ats.com
       Website: www.genesis-ats.com
IT, Networking, Telecommunications & Computer related equipment & services. (Hisp, estab 2003, empl 45, sales $25,000,000, cert: State, NMSDC)

5267   AustinCSI LLC
       7950 Legacy Dr Ste 750
       Plano, TX 75024
       Contact: Karen Moree Found & CEO
       Tel: 972-677-6464
       Email: karen.moree@austincsi.com
       Website: www.austincsi.com
Project & Portfolio Delivery (Organizational Change Management, Agile Transformation, DevOps Transformation, Digital Transformation, Big Data, Internet of Things (IoT), Cybersecurity, Process Innovation, Governance, Metrics & Exec Dashboards, Data Center. (Woman, estab 2007, empl 201, sales $31,000,000, cert: WBENC)

5268   Bastion Technologies, Inc.
       17625 El Camino Real
       Houston, TX 77058
       Contact: Jorge Hernandez President
       Tel: 281-283-9330
       Email: jhernandez@bastiontechnologies.com
       Website: www.bastiontechnologies.com
Engineering design, analysis, systems engineering, information technology applications, engineering research, mechanical engineering, structural engineering, safety & reliability engineering, systems safety, hazard analysis. (Hisp, estab 1998, empl 400, sales $42,711,000, cert: State, NMSDC)

5269   Bestica, Inc.
       3463 Magic Dr Ste 303
       San Antonio, TX 78229
       Contact: Harvinder Singh CEO
       Tel: 210-614-4198
       Email: harvinder@bestica.com
       Website: www.bestica.com
IT consulting & staffing firm. (As-Ind, estab 2005, empl 198, sales $7,500,000, cert: NMSDC, 8(a))

5270   Bravo Technical Resources, Inc.
       5301 Alpha Road Ste 80-37
       Dallas, TX 75204
       Contact: Bettina Jones Strategic Acct Mgr
       Tel: 214-422-3620
       Email: bjones@bravotech.com
       Website: www.bravotech.com
IT & engineering staffing: contract, contract to hire, direct hire. (Woman, estab 1996, empl 180, sales $28,500,000, cert: WBENC)

5271   BroadAxis Inc.
       2591 Dallas Pkwy Ste 300
       Frisco, TX 75034
       Contact: Nazish Imran Technical Recruiter
       Tel: 215-280-1992
       Email: nazish@broadaxis.com
       Website: www.broadaxis.com
Technology solutions, infrastructure & security projects, IT projects & staffing. (As-Ind, estab 2014, empl 5, sales , cert: State, NMSDC)

5272   Calpion Inc.
       4835 Lyndon B Johnson Freeway Ste 515
       Dallas, TX 75244
       Contact: Thomas John President
       Tel: 469-242-6056
       Email: thomas@calpion.com
       Website: www.calpion.com
IT consulting & staffing, software development, SAP testing & consulting, Cloud based server & IT resources. (As-Ind, estab 2004, empl 50, sales $2,400,000, cert: State, NMSDC)

5273   Can-Am Wireless LLC dba Can-Am IT Solutions
       1333 Corporate Dr, Ste 110
       Irving, TX 75038
       Contact: Johan Rahardjo Dir of Engineering
       Tel: 866-976-4177
       Email: johan.rahardjo@canamitsolutions.com
       Website: www.canamitsolutions.com
Telecommunications and Information Technology Hardware & Software. (As-Pac, estab 2001, empl 7, sales $1,020,000, cert: NMSDC)

5274 Caravan Consulting, LLC
16947 Old Pond Dr
Dallas, TX 75248
Contact: Richard Bird Mgr
Tel: 469-525-6518
Email: rbird@caravanconsulting.com
Website: www.caravanconsulting.com
Infrastructure Architecture, Data Modeling, Database Management, ETL Architecture & Development, Data Warehouse Architecture & Development. (AA, estab 2009, empl 1, sales $318,000, cert: NMSDC)

5275 Castillo & Associates
6942 FM 1960 E., Ste 290
Humble, TX 77346
Contact: Mike Castillo President
Tel: 281-852-7487
Email: mike.a.castillo@cainfotech.com
Website: www.cainfotech.com
Engineering & technical support services: network infrastructure, telecommunications systems & services, enterprise application support & IT risk analysis. (Hisp, estab 1998, empl 16, sales $3,200,000, cert: State, City)

5276 CBI Consulting Group
9609 Asheboro St
Frisco, TX 75035
Contact: Heriberto Estrada President
Tel: 956-559-0454
Email: heriberto.estrada@cbiconsultinggroup.com
Website: www.cbiconsultinggroup.com
IT professional services, SAP solutions, implementation, system upgrades, education, support, and custom development. (Hisp, estab 2014, empl 5, sales $350,000, cert: State, NMSDC)

5277 CES Network Services, Inc.
PO Box 810256
Dallas, TX 75381
Contact: Enrique Flores President
Tel: 972-241-3683
Email: ehflores@cesnetser.com
Website: www.cesnetser.com
Network engineering services, LAN, WAN & MAN, cell site planning & desig, RFI / EMI analysis, CADD services, satellite design, microwave radio, topographic map studies, digital terrain studies. (Hisp, estab 1988, empl 11, sales $6,200,000, cert: State, City)

5278 CESCO, Inc.
11969 Plano Rd Ste 130
Dallas, TX 75243
Contact: Billie Bryant Schultz CEO
Tel: 214-824-8741
Email: bbryant@cesco-inc.cm
Website: www.cesco-inc.net
Dist & service fax, printers & copiers, pens, paper, furniture, etc. (Woman, estab , empl , sales $4,900,000, cert: State, WBENC)

5279 Cima Solutions Group, Ltd.
118 Lynn Ave Ste 300
Lewisville, TX 75057
Contact: John Alday President
Tel: 972-499-8261
Email: jalday@cimasg.com
Website: www.cimasg.com
IT optization & business continuity. (Hisp, estab 2005, empl 11, sales $2,374,624, cert: State, City, NMSDC)

5280 Cimarron Software Services, Inc.
18050 Saturn Lane, Ste 280
Houston, TX 77058
Contact: Jeannie Crowell CEO
Tel: 281-226-5100
Email: jcrowell@cimarroninc.com
Website: www.cimarroninc.com
Information technology support: computer operations, systems engineering, networking, verification testing, systems analysis & software engineering. (Woman, estab 1981, empl 215, sales $37,477,460, cert: WBENC)

5281 CIS Cenergy International Services
12650 Crossrroads Park Dr
Houston, TX 77065
Contact: June Ressler President
Tel: 713-965-6200
Email: christine.lujan@cenergyintl.com
Website: www.cenergyintl.com
Information technology consulting services: outsourcing, software development, PC repairs & network support, training, project mgmt, GIS consulting, web development, system support, repair & maintenance. (Woman, estab 2006, empl 20, sales , cert: WBENC)

5282 ClearRES LLC
800 E Campbell Rd Ste 170
Richardson, TX 75081
Contact: Dhanya Yalamanchi CEO
Tel: 214-455-7860
Email: dhanya@clearres.com
Website: www.ClearRES.com
IT services & solutions, fixed priced projects, strategic staffing, onshore, offshore developed centers. (Nat Ame, estab 2015, empl 3, sales $100,000, cert: State, NMSDC)

5283 Cognitive Technologies, Inc.
115 Wild Basin Rd S Ste 104
Austin, TX 78746
Contact: Karen McGraw CEO
Tel: 512-380-1204
Email: kmcgraw@cognitive-technologies.com
Website: www.cognitive-technologies.com
Project management, project recovery, business process redesign, implementation planning, change management, testing. (Woman, estab 2001, empl 10, sales $800,000, cert: City)

5284 Compass Technology Group, LLC
14001 N Dallas Pkwy, Ste 1200
Dallas, TX 75240
Contact: Rebecca Zarski Managing Partner
Tel: 214-679-0133
Email: rzarski@compasstgp.com
Website: www.compasstechnologygroup.com
IT staffing & recruiting: contract, contract to hire & direct placement of IT resources. (Woman, estab 2008, empl 10, sales $800,000, cert: WBENC)

5285 CompNova LLC.
300 N Coit Rd Ste 340
Richardson, TX 75080
Contact: Charles Reddy VP
Tel: 214-227-9458
Email: charlesr@compnova.com
Website: www.compnova.com
IT Staff Augmentation, ERP Consulting, Customer Relationship Mgmt (CRM), Evaluation & Implementation, Data Warehouse/DSS/EIS, Dev Data, Architecture Development, (Minority, Woman, estab 1995, empl 1600, sales $85,000,000, cert: State, NMSDC)

5286   CompQsoft, Inc.
505N Sam Houston Pkwy East Ste 682
Houston, TX 77060
Contact: Franklin Benjamin Business Devel Mgr
Tel: 832-932-8732
Email: franklinb@compqsoft.com
Website: www.compqsoft.com
Mobile computing solutions, custom programming,
network support, e-commerce solutions, QA testing svcs,
staffing, on-site training. (As-Ind, estab 1997, empl 170,
sales $12,000,000, cert: NMSDC)

5287   Consultis
8700 Tesoro Dr, Ste 360
San Antonio, TX 78217
Contact: Barbara Fleming CEO
Tel: 210-930-1640
Email: info@consultis.com
Website: www.consultis.com
Information technology staffing, staff augmentation,
outsourcing & direct hires. (Woman, estab 1984, empl 150,
sales $13,000,000, cert: WBENC)

5288   Corporate Records Management Inc.
3141 Hansboro Ave
Dallas, TX 75233
Contact: Denise Chadima Owner
Tel: 214-333-3453
Email: denise@crmfiles.com
Website: www.crmfiles.com
Record storage, archiving, secured shredding, back up tape
rotation. (Woman, estab 1998, empl 12, sales $764,220,
cert: State)

5289   Critical Start LLC
6100 Tennyson Pkwy Ste 250
Plano, TX 75024
Contact: Tera Davis Managing Dir
Tel: 214-810-6760
Email: tera.davis@criticalstart.com
Website: www.criticalstart.com
Network security products & services: risk, compliance,
governance; threat management & incident response.
(Woman, estab 2012, empl 10, sales , cert: State)

5290   Dallas Digital Services, LLC
5316 Bransford Dr
Colleyville, TX 76034
Contact: Howie Evans VP
Tel: 817-577-8794
Email: howie.evans@ddserv.com
Website: www.ddserv.com
IT storage products: Fibre Channel & iSCSI devices, data
center design solutions, Quantum, OverlandStorage, EMC,
SUN, Tek-Tools, Qlogic, Legato, Cisco, NEOScale. (Woman,
estab 1996, empl 14, sales $10,000,000, cert: WBENC)

5291   Decca Consulting LLC
14090 SW Freeway Ste 300
Sugar Land, TX 77478
Contact: Nayeem Amin Managing Partner
Tel: 832-561-0634
Email: amin@deccaconsulting.com
Website: www.deccaconsulting.com
IT staffing & solutions. (Woman/As-Ind, estab 2007, empl
25, sales $1,850,000, cert: State, NMSDC)

5292   Decision Tree Technologies
306 Thunderbird Ln
El Paso, TX 79912
Contact: Bryyan Ritter Client Mgr
Tel: 512-294-0604
Email: ritter@dtreetech.com
Website: www.dtreetech.com
Data center, contact center, IT security, networking &
related IT technologies. (Woman, estab 1989, empl 10,
sales $8,100,000, cert: State)

5293   Defense Support Services, Inc.
3212 Bishop Dr
Arlington, TX 76010
Contact: Deon Moses President
Tel: 817-261-0233
Email: dmoses@dss-inc.net
Website: www.dss-inc.net
Aircraft hardware logistics & distribution, IT design &
services, communications. (AA, estab 1998, empl 15,
sales $3,000,000, cert: NMSDC)

5294   Digital Consulting & Software Services, Inc.
2277 Plaza Dr Ste 275
Sugar Land, TX 77479
Contact: Patricia Patterson CEO
Tel: 713-982-8034
Email: pmpatter@dcss.com
Website: www.dcss.com
Management consulting, professional technical serivces.
(Woman, estab , empl , sales $30,241,907, cert: WBENC)

5295   Direct Line To Compliance, Inc.
9555 W Sam Houston Pkwy S, Ste 333
Houston, TX 77099
Contact: Micha Adeeko Business Devel Mgr
Tel: 713-777-3522
Email: michael.adeeko@dl2c.com
Website: www.dl2c.com
Software & consulting (ColorCodeIT and
ChameleonDocs), form automation, electronic docu-
ment handling & compliance program software.
(Woman/AA, estab 2008, empl 17, sales $1,363,745,
cert: State, NMSDC)

5296   doc2e-file,Inc.
4500 S. Wayside Dr, Ste 102
Houston, TX 77087
Contact: Sherry McManus President
Tel: 713-649-2006
Email: sherrymcmanus@doc2e-file.com
Website: www.doc2e-file.com
Document scanning & indexing, e-records mgmt,
systems & equipment. (Woman, estab , empl , sales ,
cert: State, WBENC)

5297   Doyensys, Inc.
2591 Dallas Pkwy, Ste 300
Frisco, TX 75034
Contact: Chithra Gopalan President
Tel: 972-992-4220
Email: sales@doyensys.com
Website: www.doyensys.com
Information Technology Staffing and Services in tech-
nologies inlcuding but not limited to SAP, Oracle , Siebel,
peoplesoft, Java, Dot net, IBM Mainframe (Minority,
Woman, estab 2006, empl 4, sales $185,000, cert: City)

5298 Dynamic Computing Services
3307 Northland Dr, Ste 250
Austin, TX 78731
Contact: Jenelle Thomas Dir Business Dev
Tel: 800-345-1275
Email: jenelle@dcshq.com
Website: www.dcshq.com
Information technology placements services. (Woman, estab 1990, empl 152, sales $13,926,270, cert: WBENC)

5299 ECOM Consulting, Inc.
2828 W Parker Rd Ste 224
Plano, TX 75075
Contact: Baku Kshatriya President
Tel: 972-578-0191
Email: baku@ecomconsultinginc.com
Website: www.ecomconsultinginc.com
Technical consulting services & staff augmentation. (As-Ind, estab 1995, empl 72, sales , cert: State, NMSDC)

5300 eConsulting Partners Global, Inc
10000 North Central Exprwy Ste 400
Dallas, TX 75231
Contact: Jade Tran Principal
Tel: 214-680-0982
Email: jade.tran@ecpgi.com
Website: www.ecpgi.com
System Integration, Enterprise Application Architecture, Service-Oriented Architecture, and IT Security (Cyber Security, Information Assurance, Computer Forensics). (Minority, Woman, estab 2006, empl 20, sales , cert: State)

5301 eDataWorld LLC
2770 Main St Ste 229
Frisco, TX 75033
Contact: Bhujang Karakavalasa Dir
Tel: 206-504-8739
Email: bhujang.k@edataworld.com
Website: www.edataworld.com
IT consulting, software development & service. (Minority, Woman, estab 2005, empl 100, sales $2,000,000, cert: NMSDC)

5302 ElectroSystems Engineers Inc.
4141 Pinnacle St, Ste 208
El Paso, TX 79902
Contact: Benita R Munoz Dir of Operations
Tel: 915-587-7902
Email: brmunoz@esei.com
Website: www.esei.com
Information technology, integrated solutions, telecommunications engineering, software design, management & consulting, test & evaluation support & intelligence training. (Hisp, estab 1994, empl 20, sales $1,441,208, cert: NMSDC)

5303 Elise Resources, Inc.
950 Echo Lane Ste 200
Houston, TX 77024
Contact: Nadia Clark CEO
Tel: 281-313-4422
Email: nadia@eliseresources.com
Website: www.eliseresources.com
Call center, inbound and outbound customer service and sales related calls. (AA, estab 2015, empl 1, sales , cert: State)

5304 Endata Corporation
3217 Thorne Hill Ct
Richardson, TX 75082
Contact: Ricardo Rossi CTO
Tel: 214-603-4456
Email: ricardo@endata.com
Website: www.endata.com
Information Technology Professional Services, machine learning, sentiment analysis, predictive data analytics, web & app development, artificial intelligence for web, mobile & cloud applications. (Minority, Woman, estab 1997, empl 2, sales $370,808, cert: State, NMSDC)

5305 Enovox Technical Group, LLC
1775 St. James Place, Ste 120
Houston, TX 77584
Contact: Michael Wilson President
Tel: 832-736-5869
Email: mike@enovox.com
Website: www.enovox.com
IT consulting & technology services, telecommunication services, telecommunication/network equipment, program/project management & outsourcing. (AA, estab 2011, empl 2, sales $100,000, cert: State, City)

5306 Enterprise IT Experts LLC dba EITE LLC
4017 Duclair Dr
McKinney, TX 75070
Contact: Ravi Vegesna Managing Partner
Tel: - -
Email: ravi@eitellc.com
Website: www.enterpriseitexperts.com
Information Technology & Computer Software services: Enterprise Architecture, SAP Implementations, Upgrades, Technology Upgrades, Microsoft Technologies - Sharepoint & Office 365, Cloud Architecture, Integration & Custom development. (As-Ind, estab 2011, empl 228, sales $8,700,000, cert: State, NMSDC)

5307 Enterprise Logic, Inc.
7457 Harwin Dr, Ste 208
Houston, TX 77036
Contact: Ajay Thomas CEO
Tel: 832-489-1851
Email: admin@enterprise-logic.com
Website: www.enterprise-logic.com
Staffing company that focuses on staffing all types of IT Skills. (As-Ind, estab 2000, empl 200, sales , cert: City, NMSDC)

5308 ERP Logic
7423 Las Colinas Blvd Ste 103
Irving, TX 75063
Contact: Caldwell Velnambi CEO
Tel: 972-401-3771
Email: caldwell@erplogic.com
Website: www.erplogic.com
SAP-ERP Implementation, Customization, Integration, Business Process, Re-Engineering, Application Development, Management and Staff Augmentation (As-Ind, estab 2009, empl 45, sales $3,000,000, cert: NMSDC)

5309   Expedien Inc.
2925 Richmond Ave Ste 1200
Houston, TX 77098
Contact: Jiten K Agarwal Dir
Tel: 832-607-5335
Email: jkumar@expedien.net
Website: www.expedien.net/
Business Intelligence, Data Warehousing, Data Integration, Data Migration, Data conversion, Master Data Management, SAP, SAP BW, EAI, SAP Netweaver, SAP Portal, Oracle Financials, Application Development, Business Objects. (Woman/As-Ind, estab 2002, empl 72, sales $15,873,000, cert: NMSDC)

5310   Fidelis Companies, LLC
2800 N Dallas Pkwy Ste 250
Plano, TX 75093
Contact: Bryce Shields Business Dev Mgr
Tel: 972-392-9230
Email: bshields@fideliscompanies.com
Website: www.fideliscompanies.com
IT Consulting for Oracle, PeopleSoft, Hyperion, SAP. (Woman, estab 2000, empl 50, sales , cert: State, WBENC)

5311   Fuse Solutions Inc.
4100 Midway Rd Ste 2120
Carrollton, TX 75007
Contact: Jay Jordan COO
Tel: 214-687-7393
Email: jay@fusesolutions.com
Website: www.fusesolutions.com
Strategic consulting, enterprise service delivery, vendor & asset management. (Woman, estab 2014, empl 25, sales , cert: State, WBENC)

5312   Genesis Networks Enterprises, LLC
600 N Loop 1604 E
San Antonio, TX 78232
Contact: Jason McGinnis Dir-Vendor Engagements
Tel: 770-329-6538
Email: jason.mcginnis@genesisnet.com
Website: www.genesisnet.com
Software development, software testing, systems integrator, proto-type development, security, system application mgmt, application mgmt, business process flow, event mgmt, exception mgmt. (Hisp, estab 2001, empl 771, sales $1,100,000,000, cert: State, NMSDC, CPUC)

5313   Gill Digital Services, LLC
4100 Spring Valley Road, Ste 920
Dallas, TX 75244
Contact: Barbara Gill President
Tel: 214-653-8352
Email: bgill@gilldigital.com
Website: www.gilldigital.com
Document Scanning, Database Software, Disaster Recovery Services, Court Reporting (Woman, estab 0, empl , sales , cert: State, WBENC)

5314   Global IT, Inc.
1303 W Walnut Hill Ln Ste 360
Irving, TX 75038
Contact: Sales
Tel: 972-871-9292
Email: info@globalitinc.com
Website: www.globalitinc.com
Information technology: ERP packages, SAP, Oracle Apps & PeopleSoft. (As-Ind, estab 1999, empl 182, sales $13,400,000, cert: State)

5315   GS Infovision LLC   dba Global Systems LLC
1200 Walnut Hill Lane, Ste 2220
Irving, TX 75038
Contact: Shekhar Gupta VP
Tel: 214-717-4344
Email: account@globalsyst.com
Website: www.globalsyst.com
IT Consulting, Staffing, BPO, IT Consulting, temporary, contract, temp to perm & permanent staffing solutions. (Minority, Woman, estab 2005, empl 110, sales $11,000,000, cert: NMSDC)

5316   Hacware, Inc.
1212 E Arapaho Rd Ste 204
Richardson, TX 75081
Contact: Tiffany Ricks CEO
Tel: 214-662-8332
Email: hello@hacware.com
Website: www.hacware.com
Mobile applications and emerging technology solutions. (AA, estab 2017, empl 8, sales , cert: WBENC)

5317   iBizSoft
9300 Wade Blvd Ste 301
Frisco, TX 75035
Contact: Sandeep Kuttiyatur President
Tel: 214-705-3623
Email: vendor@ibizsoftinc.com
Website: www.ibizsoftinc.com
Enterprise application services: system integration & solution development for Oracle ERP, CRM, Endeca & ATG implementation. (As-Ind, estab 2001, empl 100, sales $6,000,000, cert: State)

5318   Independent Professional Management
9525 Katy Freeway, Ste 435
Houston, TX 77024
Contact: Sheila McIlnay CEO
Tel: 713-973-7400
Email: contact@ipm-inc.com
Website: www.ipm-inc.com
IT Staffing, SAP programers, developers & consultants. (Woman, estab 1992, empl 9, sales , cert: State, WBENC)

5319   Infobeam Technologies LLC
1333 Corporate Dr, Ste 262
Irving, TX 75038
Contact: Jay Gajavelli Dir
Tel: 972-365-9928
Email: jay.gajavelli@infobeamtech.com
Website: www.infobeamtech.com
IT consulting. (As-Pac, estab 2009, empl 15, sales , cert: State)

5320   Infolob Solutions, Inc.
909 Lake Carolyn Pkwy Ste 120
Irving, TX 75039
Contact: Vijay Cherukuri CEO
Tel: 972-535-5559
Email: vijay@infolob.com
Website: www.infolob.com
Database services, RAC, Exadata, SOA, Oracle Fusion, Ebusiness, OBIEE, BI, DW, OLTP, networking, J2EE, replication. (Woman/As-Ind, estab 2009, empl 130, sales $50,000,000, cert: State, NMSDC)

5321   InfoVision Consultants, Inc.
       800 E Campbell Road Ste 388
       Richardson, TX 75081
       Contact: John Mendez Practice Head & Dir
       Tel: 972-234-0058
       Email: john.mendez@infovision.com
       Website: www.infovision.com/
Information technology solutions: IT staffing, consulting &
outsourcing. (As-Ind, estab 1995, empl 300, sales
$26,550,000, cert: NMSDC)

5322   Innovation Network Technologies Corporation
       5729 Lebanon Rd, Ste 144
       Frisco, TX 75034
       Contact: Cathy Davis Accounting Mgr
       Tel: 972-624-1222
       Email: cdavis@innetworktech.com
       Website: www.innetworktech.com
Computer Hardware, Computer Software, Licenses,
Subscriptions, A10, A10 Network, F5, Accedian, Cloud
Monitoring, Virtualization, OPTIV, Alert Logic, Algosec,
Firewall Management, Analyzer, Security Policy,
AlienVault, Managed SIEM, Securematics. (Hisp, estab
2009, empl 15, sales $3,922,715, cert: WBENC)

5323   Inoditech LLC, dba Camino Information Services
       14340 Torrey Chase Blvd Ste 210
       Houston, TX 77014
       Contact: Lam Nguyen CEO
       Tel: 281-742-9560
       Email: lam.nguyen@caminois.com
       Website: www.caminois.com
Custom software development & mobile applications.
(Minority, Woman, estab 2012, empl 22, sales $1,273,000,
cert: State, NMSDC)

5324   Instant Data Technologies
       85 NE Loop 410, Ste. 405
       San Antonio, TX 78216
       Contact: Bede Ramcharan CEO
       Tel: 210-344-0012
       Email: bramcharan@indatatech.com
       Website: www.indatatech.com
Physical inventory, RFID technology, asset valuation &
tracking, supplier integration, barcoding, asset procure-
ment, tagging & management, inventory mgmt software.
(AA, As-Pac, estab 2001, empl 31, sales $11,999,837, cert:
State, NMSDC, SDB)

5325   Intras LLC
       101 E Park Ste 769
       Plano, TX 75074
       Contact: Elvan Jones
       Tel: 972-422-1022
       Email: elvanj@intras-it.com
       Website: www.intras-it.com
Global integrator of technology solutions, technology
hardware & applications develop, IT products, IT Services,
IT Consulting & IT Managed services. (AA, estab 2010,
empl 10, sales $3,000,000, cert: State, NMSDC)

5326   IPM Asset Solutions, Inc.
       9525 Katy Freeway Ste 435
       Houston, TX 77024
       Contact: Andy Bishop VP Resource Management
       Tel: 713-973-7400
       Email: andy.bishop@ipm-inc.com
       Website: www.ipmasset.com
Asset management & tracking utilizing bar code & Radio
Frequency Identification (RFID) technology. (Woman,
estab 2006, empl 9, sales , cert: State, WBENC)

5327   JB Software and Consulting, Inc.
       333 E. Bethany Dr Ste J130
       Allen, TX 75002
       Contact: Uzma Shereen CEO
       Tel: 469-878-3639
       Email: info@jbsac.com
       Website: www.jbsac.com
Information technology services & staff augmentation.
(Minority, Woman, estab 2004, empl 38, sales
$6,000,000, cert: NMSDC, CPUC, WBENC)

5328   KEDAR Integration Services, Inc.
       405 State Hwy 121 Bypass Ste A250
       Lewisville, TX 75067
       Contact:
       Tel: 972-317-3577
       Email: charles@kedarit.com
       Website: www.kedarit.com
IT financial management, cost optimization; business
process management; lean transformation; and training.
(AA, estab , empl , sales $586,858, cert: State)

5329   Krasamo Inc.
       1201 W 15th St, Ste 200
       Plano, TX 75075
       Contact: Melissa Amoros President
       Tel: 214-418-3347
       Email: sales_team_00@krasamo.net
       Website: www.krasamo.com
Internet-of-Things and Digital Transformation. (Hisp,
estab 2010, empl 47, sales $3,200,000, cert: WBENC)

5330   Kreative Zeno Systems, Inc.
       12019 Colwick
       San Antonio, TX 78216
       Contact: Thomas Dooley VP
       Tel: 877-768-1574
       Email: tomd@kreativesystemsinc.com
       Website: www.kreativesystemsinc.com
Provide SCSI disk drive assemblies. (Woman, estab 2010,
empl 7, sales , cert: State)

5331   LMG Technology Services, LLC
       134 Vintage Park Blvd, Ste A-791
       Houston, TX 77070
       Contact: Lloyd Gauthier CEO
       Tel: 832-465-4641
       Email: Lloyd@Lmgtechnology.com
       Website: www.lmgtechnology.com
Information technology. (AA, estab 2006, empl 2, sales ,
cert: State, City, NMSDC)

5332 Managed Staffing Inc
15851 Dallas Pkwy | Ste 450, Addison
Dallas, TX 75001
Contact: Mark Miller Sr Mgr
Tel: 469-608-7015
Email: mark@managedstaffing.com
Website: www.managedstaffing.com
IT consulting: contract, contract to hire, or direct placement, outsourcing. (Minority, Woman, estab 2007, empl 300, sales $39,300,000, cert: NMSDC, WBENC)

5333 MB Five Consulting LLC
8013 Blue Hole Ct
McKinney, TX 75070
Contact: Andre Ketter Mgr
Tel: 972-895-2414
Email: aketter@mb5consulting.com
Website: www.mb5consulting.com
IT Services & Industrial Automation services, desktop & server support, Networking & software development. (AA, estab 2014, empl 1, sales $220,000, cert: State, NMSDC)

5334 Milner & Schooley LLC
14000 S Hwy 95
Coupland, TX 78615
Contact: Sheri Milner Mgmt Services
Tel: 512-914-4061
Email: slmilner@milnerschooley.com
Website: www.milnerschooley.com
Information technology svcs: ERP CIS/CRM. (Woman, estab 2005, empl 2, sales $165,000, cert: State)

5335 Mshana Group LLC dba AriesPro
19901 Southwest Frwy
Sugar Land, TX 77479
Contact: Shivani Sangari Dir Business Dev
Tel: 281-410-6930
Email: shivani.sangari@ariespro.com
Website: www.ariespro.com
Information technology consulting: SAP, HANA, BW, ERP, CRM, SCM, Business Objects, FICO, Oracle, Teradata, Big Data, Microsoft, IBM, Java, Microstrategy, Cognos, Hadoop, DB2, DataStage, Informatica, Netezza, Tivoli, Unix, WebSphere. (Woman/As-Ind, estab 2011, empl 5, sales $460,000, cert: City)

5336 MTech Partners, LLC
1464 E. Whitestone Blvd, Ste #1001
Cedar Park, TX 78613
Contact: Tommy Hodinh President
Tel: 512-993-5730
Email: tommy.hodinh@mtechpartners.net
Website: www.mtechpartners.net
Global Digital Transformation services, Legacy Modernization to Distributed Platform, ERP Integration and DevOps Support, SalesForce Cloud Development and Migration, IOT Engineering Design. (AA, estab 2020, empl 1001, sales $23,245,422, cert: NMSDC)

5337 National Systems America, L.P.
6860 Dallas Pkwy Ste 200
Plano, TX 75024
Contact: Mukesh Shah Managing Partner
Tel: 972-212-7434
Email: manager@nsiamerica.com
Website: www.nsiamerica.com
Softwareconsulting: data processing, software development, system integration, client services & quality assurance analysis. (As-Ind, estab 1996, empl 85, sales $9,839,031, cert: NMSDC)

5338 New Renewable Energy Technologies, LLC dba NERETEC
4102 Amhurst Dr
Highland Village, TX 75077
Contact: Phil Fosso Principal
Tel: 217-299-7789
Email: fosso@neretec.com
Website: www.neretec.com
Project Management, Application Development, Technology Migration/Upgrade, Application Maintenance and Support, IT Assessments/Planning, Independent Verification and Validation, Business Intelligence/Data Warehouse, Service Oriented, Architecture (SOA). (AA, estab 2010, empl 2, sales $154,000, cert: State)

5339 NewData Strategies
5339 Alpha Rd Ste 200
Dallas, TX 75240
Contact: Kristen Scott Dir of Sales
Tel: 972-735-0001
Email: tpope@newdata.com
Website: www.newdata.com
Information technology consulting, placement & education. (Woman, estab 1989, empl 70, sales $7,384,599, cert: WBENC)

5340 Next Generation Technology Inc.
6060 N Central Exprwy, Ste 560
Dallas, TX 75206
Contact: Ray Richardson President
Tel: 214-800-2893
Email: rrichardson@nexgentech.us
Website: www.nexgentech.us
Resell Hewlett Packard products, UPS back-up power for Liebert, APC & Powerware, digital video surveillance systems, IT consulting. (AA, estab 2003, empl 5, sales , cert: State, SDB)

5341 Object Information Services, Inc.
1755 North Collins Blvd #220
Richardson, TX 75080
Contact: Mohammad Hafizullah President
Tel: 214-335-6632
Email: mhafiz@objectinformation.com
Website: www.objectinformation.com
Information technology recruiting. (As-Ind, estab 1995, empl 42, sales $3,449,325, cert: NMSDC)

5342 ObjectWin Technology, Inc.
19219 Katy Freeway, Ste 275
Houston, TX 77094
Contact: Pete Adams Sales
Tel: 832-485-1566
Email: mbe@objectwin.com
Website: www.objectwin.com
IT services & staffing, Partners with Microsoft, Oracle SAP. (Minority, estab 1997, empl 220, sales $28,000,000, cert: NMSDC)

5343 Omega Business Systems
      PO Box 8297
      Fort Worth, TX 76124
      Contact: Norman Labrosse President
      Tel: 817-492-4249
      Email: norman@omegabiz.com
      Website: www.omegabiz.com
Network solutions & technical services. (As-Ind, estab
1992, empl 6, sales $2,000,000, cert: State, City, NMSDC,
SDB)

5344 Oveana
      123 W Mills Ave, Ste 400
      El Paso, TX 79901
      Contact: Bill Randag Business Devel
      Tel: 915-533-0549
      Email: bill.randag@oveana.com
      Website: www.oveana.com
Document mgmt, data processing, mail room processing,
scanning, data storage, data entry, data capture & destruction, call center. (Minority, Woman, estab 2013, empl
2200, sales , cert: State)

5345 OverNite Software Inc.
      1212 N Velasco, Ste 110
      Angleton, TX 77515
      Contact: David Stark Mktg Dir
      Tel: 979-849-2002
      Email: david.stark@overnitecbt.com
      Website: www.overnitecbt.com
Computer-based performance systems. (Hisp, estab 1995,
empl 55, sales , cert: State)

5346 Pinnacle Technical Resources, Inc.
      5501 Lyndon B. Johnson Frwy, Ste 600
      Dallas, TX 75240
      Contact: Monica Watkins Managing Dir
      Tel: 214-995-6648
      Email: monica.watkins@pinnacle1.com
      Website: www.pinnacle1.com
Nearshore software development in latin america. (Minority, Woman, estab 1996, empl 3606, sales $306,000,000,
cert: WBENC)

5347 Precision Task Group, Inc.
      9801 Westheimer, Ste 803
      Houston, TX 77042
      Contact: James Morris General Mgr
      Tel: 713-781-7481
      Email: massey@ptg.com
      Website: www.ptg.com
IT staff augmentation. (Hisp, estab 1980, empl 615, sales
$25,000,000, cert: NMSDC)

5348 PriceSenz LLC
      4615 Al Razi St
      Irving, TX 75062
      Contact: Bijith Moopen CEO
      Tel: 469-817-3804
      Email: bijith@pricesenz.com
      Website: www.pricesenz.com
Digital Technology Services, application modernization,
system rationalization, system strategy, Data & staff
augmentation. (As-Ind, estab 2015, empl 38, sales
$1,430,638, cert: NMSDC)

5349 Principle Information Technology
      9301 Southwest Fwy Ste 475
      Houston, TX 77074
      Contact: Nickell Cheruku President
      Tel: 832-434-4016
      Email: reddy@principleinfotech.com
      Website: www.principleinfotech.com
SAP Services, Oracle Service, Big Data, Cloud
Mobility, Luxon. (As-Pac, estab 2009, empl 157, sales ,
cert: State, City, NMSDC, 8(a))

5350 Promacsolution Inc.
      9916 Bundoran Dr
      Austin, TX 78717
      Contact: Srinivas Ande Dir
      Tel: 310-733-3076
      Email: srinivas@promacsolution.com
      Website: www.promacsolution.com
IT consulting, SOA Architecture, Web Services, ERP, Data
warehousing, SAP, Oracle HRMS, .NET,J2EE etc. (Woman/
As-Ind, estab 2004, empl 5, sales $143,086, cert: State)

5351 Prudent Technologies and Consulting Inc.
      1505 LBJ Freeway Ste 327
      Dallas, TX 75234
      Contact: Mario Guerra VP
      Tel: 414-491-9056
      Email: mguerra@prudentconsulting.com
      Website: www.prudentconsulting.com
IT consultants & staffing: Oracle, SAP, PeopleSoft, .Net,
Java, Hyperion, Documentum, Clarity, Crystal Reports,
Testing, Mercury Tools, Compuware Tools, .Net, C#,
Oracle, Oracle ERP, SQL, etc. (As-Ind, estab 1998, empl
70, sales $5,000,000, cert: NMSDC)

5352 Pure Business Solutions, LLC
      219 Gessner Rd
      Houston, TX 77024
      Contact: Andrea Hite CEO
      Tel: 713-750-9500
      Email: ahite@purebizsolns.com
      Website: www.purebizsolns.com
IT Operations Management Software, IT Service Man-
agement, Discovery, Configuration Management
Database, Application & Service Modeling, IT Operations
& Business Analytics, Performance and Availability
Management. (Woman, estab 2015, empl 1, sales , cert:
State, WBENC)

5353 Quality High-Tech Services, Inc.
      11807 Forestgate Dr
      Dallas, TX 75243
      Contact: Mary Rogers President
      Tel: 972-231-6696
      Email: m.rogers@qht.com
      Website: www.QHT.com
IT services and repairs. (Woman, estab 1987, empl 17,
sales $2,492,492, cert: State)

5354 RD Data Solutions
      2340 E Trinity Mills Ste 349
      Carrollton, TX 75006
      Contact: Reuben D'Souza CEO
      Tel: 972-899-2334
      Email: reuben.dsouza@rddatasolutions.com
      Website: www.rddatasolutions.com
Technology staffing: SAP & ERP. (Minority, Woman, estab
2002, empl 26, sales $25,000,000, cert: State, NMSDC)

5355 Reed Global Networks, Inc.
1354 N Loop 1604 E
San Antonio, TX 78232
Contact: Tina Younts Mgr Supplier Diversity Dev
Tel: 210-489-6601
Email: tina.younts@reedglobalnetworks.com
Website: www.reedglobalnetworks.com
End-to-end technology solutions, design, installation, monitoring, and maintenance technology infrastructure. (AA, estab 2021, empl 8, sales $20,000,000, cert: NMSDC)

5356 ReMedi Health Solutions LLC
20333 TX-249, Ste 224
Houston, TX 77070
Contact: Sandeep Hyare CEO
Tel: 832-966-0430
Email: diversity@remedihs.com
Website: www.remedihs.com/
Healthcare IT management and consulting, end-to-end, physician-centric EHR implementation and training, including system selection advisory, system optimization, integration and testing. (As-Ind, estab 2013, empl 12, sales $4,000,000, cert: State, City, NMSDC)

5357 Remedy Technological Services, L.P.
501 N 4th St
Killeen, TX 76541
Contact: Christopher Walton VP & Legal Counsel
Tel: 254-213-4740
Email: cwalton@centextech.com
Website: www.centextech.com
Information Technology, Software Engineering, Project Management, Database Management, ERP Solutions, Data Warehouse & Business Intelligence, Web & App Development, Internet Marketing & Network Administration. (As-Ind, estab 2006, empl 50, sales $1,300,000, cert: State, 8(a))

5358 Research Analysis and Maintenance, Inc.
9440 Viscount Blvd, Ste 200
El Paso, TX 79925
Contact: Richard Jones Contracts Admin
Tel: 915-592-7047
Email: jonesr@ramincorp.com
Website: www.ramincorp.com
IT services, networking & telecommunications, software dev, systems integration & information mgmt. (Woman, estab 1982, empl 650, sales $62,000,000, cert: State)

5359 Resolve Tech Solutions
15851 Dallas Pkwy, Ste 1103
Addison, TX 75001
Contact: Business Devel Mgr
Tel: 703-995-7377
Email: info@resolvetech.com
Website: www.resolvetech.com
Information Technology Staffing, Consulting Services and Implementation. (As-Ind, estab 1996, empl 25, sales $3,000,000, cert: State)

5360 RSI Solutions Inc.
3607 Summer Ranch Dr
Katy, TX 77494
Contact: Principal
Tel: 832-506-0868
Email: contactus@rsisolutions.net
Website: www.rsisolutions.net
Enterprise Resource Planning (ERP) based solutions to both public and private sector entities, SAP BW, HANA. (As-Ind, estab 2011, empl 2, sales $254,000, cert: State, SDB)

5361 Saratoga Software Solutions, Inc.
555 Republic Dr. Ste 200
Plano, TX 75074
Contact: Arlene Carter President
Tel: 469-301-1515
Email: arlene.carter@teamsaratoga.com
Website: www.saratogasoftwaresolutions.com
IT staff augmentation: contract, contract-to-hire & permanent. (Woman, estab , empl , sales $1,400,000, cert: State)

5362 Shirley Hollywood & Associates, Inc.
17585 State Hwy 19 Ste 100
Canton, TX 75103
Contact: Stacie Hollywood-Baber President
Tel: 972-287-8834
Email: stacie@shirleyhollywoodinc.com
Website: www.shirleyhollywoodinc.com
SAP curriculum devel & training delivery resources. (Woman, estab 1996, empl 5, sales $5,000,000, cert: WBENC)

5363 Simplistek, LLC
5050 Quorum Dr, Ste 700
Dallas, TX 75254
Contact: Xavier Hurd VP Talent Acquisition
Tel: 469-675-3594
Email: xhurd@simplistekit.com
Website: www.simplistekit.com
ERP Implementation & support, business process improvement, utilities business consulting & staff augmentation for all areas of Information Technology (IT). (Minority, estab 2014, empl 3, sales $1,200,000, cert: State, NMSDC)

5364 Smart IT Pros Inc.
2305 Ridge Rd Ste 101D
Rockwall, TX 75087
Contact: David Thomas Dir Sales
Tel: 734-238-1553
Email: dave.thomas@smartitpros.com
Website: www.smartitpros.com
IT & Business Services, Application & Business process services. (Minority, Woman, estab 2012, empl 65, sales $3,566,788, cert: NMSDC, WBENC)

5365 Smartbridge
2000 W Sam Houston Pkwy S
Houston, TX 77042
Contact: William Wong Marketing Dir
Tel: 713-360-2500
Email: innovations@smartbridge.com
Website: www.smartbridge.com
Technology consulting services, strategy, implementation, and support to bring each client's digital agenda to reality. (As-Pac, estab 2003, empl 55, sales $14,000,000, cert: State, NMSDC)

5366   SOAL Technologies, LLC
       10900 Research Blvd, Ste. 160C-40
       Austin, TX 78759
       Contact: Ahmed Moledina CEO
       Tel: 512-270-6700
       Email: amoledina@soaltech.com
       Website: www.soaltech.com
Information technology development & consulting. (As-Ind, estab 2009, empl 40, sales $10,600,000, cert: City)

5367   Software Professionals, Inc.
       1029 Long Prairie Road Ste A
       Flower Mound, TX 75022
       Contact: Reena Batra CEO
       Tel: 972-355-0054
       Email: reena@spius.net
       Website: spius.net
Systems integration & computer programming svcs: client/server & mainframe environ; facilities mgmt, help desk support & training; business re-engineering & total quality mgmt. (Minority, Woman, estab 1992, empl 100, sales $15,000,000, cert: NMSDC, WBENC)

5368   Softway Solutions, Inc.
       7324 Southwest Frwy Ste 1600
       Houston, TX 77074
       Contact: Robert Goady VP Client Services
       Tel: 281-914-4381
       Email: robert@softwaysolutions.com
       Website: www.softway.com
Website design & development, Internet marketing services, graphics design & multimedia. (As-Pac, estab 2003, empl 65, sales $5,800,000, cert: NMSDC)

5369   Sontesa Technologies Inc.
       2101 Cedar Springs Rd, Ste 1050
       Dallas, TX 75201
       Contact: Jewel Hale CEO
       Tel: 972-534-2023
       Email: procurement@sontesa.com
       Website: www.sontesa.com
Telecom Network and System Design. (Woman/AA, estab 2007, empl 4, sales , cert: NMSDC, WBENC)

5370   SPAR Information Systems
       7800 Dallas Pkwy, Ste 120
       Plano, TX 75024
       Contact: Abraham Regan VP IT Talent Acquisition
       Tel: 201-528-5324
       Email: abraham.regan@sparinfosys.com
       Website: www.sparinfosys.com
IT Services. (Minority, Woman, estab 2012, empl 380, sales $30,000,000, cert: State)

5371   Storage Assessments LLC
       PO Box 864017
       Plano, TX 75086
       Contact: Carolyn Chambers CEO
       Tel: 972-578-2708
       Email: cc@storageassessments.com
       Website: www.storageassessments.com
Resell, design & support computer storage related products: database, backup & recovers, disaster recovery & file management. (Woman, estab 2003, empl 6, sales $4,774,271, cert: State, WBENC)

5372   Stratium Consulting Group, Inc.
       14785 Preston Rd Ste 550
       Dallas, TX 75013
       Contact: James Gayle Principal
       Tel: 972-789-5566
       Email: opportunities@stratiumconsulting.com
       Website: www.stratiumconsulting.com
Information management services, document management, records management, web portals, digital asset management, business intelligence, data warehouse, enterprise search and integrations with backend systems. (As-Pac, estab 2009, empl 20, sales , cert: State, NMSDC)

5373   Swift Pace Solutions, Inc
       600 E John Carpenter Frwy Ste 175
       Irving, TX 75062
       Contact: Pratima Upadhya Client Partner
       Tel: 972-714-0000
       Email: pratima@spsolinc.com
       Website: www.spsolinc.com
IT Services Consulting, Oracle Gold Partner, SAP Partner, Horton Works Partner Migrate, Integrate & Build Custom Apps. (Woman/As-Ind, estab 2013, empl 12, sales $2,000,000, cert: State, NMSDC)

5374   Systemware Professional Services, Inc.
       15601 Dallas Pkwy, Ste 1000
       Dallas, TX 75001
       Contact: Marisa Hammond VP
       Tel: 972-239-0200
       Email: marisa.hammond@systemware.com
       Website: www.systemware.com
Application system dev, life cycle turnkey solutions, system life cycle development methodology, testing svcs, application support & maintenance. (Woman, estab 1991, empl 100, sales $8,480,000, cert: WBENC)

5375   Talent Logic Inc.
       2313 Timber Shadows Dr Ste 200
       Kingwood, TX 77339
       Contact: Hilda Roper VP
       Tel: 281-358-1858
       Email: hroper@talentlogic.com
       Website: www.talentlogic.com
Computer consulting & programming svcs. (As-Ind, estab 1984, empl 300, sales $17,500,000, cert: NMSDC)

5376   Taylor Smith Consulting, LLC
       16800 Greenspoint Park Dr, STte155N
       Houston, TX 77060
       Contact: Tracy Smith CEO
       Tel: 713-937-3111
       Email: staylor@taylorsmithconsulting.com
       Website: www.taylorsmithconsulting.com
Business Development, Training, Call/Customer Service Center Operations, Staffing, Contracting Services. (Woman/AA, estab 2006, empl 1200, sales $18,001,317, cert: State, City, NMSDC)

5377   Technology Asset LLC
       789 N Grove Rd, Ste 103
       Richardson, TX 75081
       Contact: Tom Earley Reg Sales Mgr
       Tel: 972-318-2600
       Email: tearley@globalassetonline.com
       Website: www.globalassetonline.com
Eco-Friendly IT lifecycle management. (Minority, Woman, estab 2010, empl 40, sales $12,500,000, cert: State)

5378   Technology for Education
658 Alliance Pkwy
Hewitt, TX 76643
Contact: Brandy Mynar-Olson Sales Mgr
Tel: 254-741-2450
Email: sales@tfeconnect.com
Website: www.tfe-wordpress.tfeconnect.com
Structured cabling & networking, Data Center, IP Communications, Audio Visual & Physical Security. (Woman, estab 1998, empl 50, sales $31,709,451, cert: State, WBENC)

5379   TechTrans International, Inc.
2200 Space Park Dr, Ste 410
Houston, TX 77058
Contact: Joel Anderson VP
Tel: 281-335-8000
Email: janderson@tti-corp.com
Website: www.tti-corp.com
International logistics, translation, interpretation, language training, and global support. (Woman, estab 1993, empl 145, sales $13,843,636, cert: NWBOC)

5380   Techway Services
12880 Valley Branch Ln Ste 120
Farmers Branch, TX 75234
Contact: Cathi Coan CEO
Tel: 855-832-4929
Email: cathi@techwayservices.com
Website: www.techwayservices.com
E-data destruction services & used computer asset remarketing. (Woman, estab 2004, empl 52, sales $607,751,300, cert: State, WBENC)

5381   Tek Leaders, Inc
4975 Preston Park Blvd, Ste 500, Plano 75093
Plano, TX 75093
Contact: 774001 VP Enterprise Accounts
Tel: 214-244-3753
Email: hr@tekleaders.com
Website: www.tekleaders.com
IT Services, IT Staffing, Data Analytics and Business Intelligence. (As-Pac, estab 2008, empl 150, sales $20,000,000, cert: NMSDC)

5382   TELA Technologies, Inc.
10310 Harwin Dr. East Wing
Houston, TX 77036
Contact: Jaime Flores President
Tel: 713-863-1411
Email: jflores@telatechnologies.com
Website: www.telatechnologies.com
Document management solutions, electronic document storage & retrieval solutions. (Hisp, estab 2003, empl 15, sales $1,050,000, cert: State, NMSDC)

5383   The Ternio Group LLC
8285 El Rio Ste 120
Houston, TX 77054
Contact: Luis Romero Principal
Tel: 210-519-7933
Email:
Website: www.terniogroup.com
Consulting & project management services: supply chain, logistics, distribution, medical-surgical & pharmacy inventory management, consignment, resource management, data processing, data cleansing, e-commerce, ERP. (Hisp, estab 2012, empl 10, sales $1,960,000, cert: State)

5384   Themesoft Inc.
13601 Preston Rd, Ste W860
Dallas, TX 75240
Contact: Pascal Vinoth Dir
Tel: 972-474-8787
Email: vinoth@themesoft.com
Website: www.themesoft.com
Custom Software Development & Consulting, Java, J2EE, SAP, Networking, Infrastructure, QA, Project Management. (Woman/As-Ind, estab 2004, empl 200, sales $42,845,261, cert: State, NMSDC, WBENC)

5385   Third Term Inc.
6 Meadowridge Pl
The Woodlands, TX 77381
Contact: Carolina Denkler Project Mgr
Tel: 713-357-6666
Email: carolina.denkler@thirdtermlearning.com
Website: www.thirdtermlearning.com
eLearning, computer based training, web based Training, Learning Management Systems, LMS. (Hisp, estab 2013, empl 2, sales $266,000, cert: NMSDC)

5386   Traveling Coaches Inc.
2805 Dallas Pkwy Ste 150
Dallas, TX 75093
Contact: Lyndi Lockhart Acct Mgr
Tel: 214-742-6224
Email: llockhart@travelingcoaches.com
Website: www.travelingcoaches.com
Software, consulting, integration & training. (Woman, estab 1995, empl 35, sales $10,637,000, cert: State, WBENC)

5387   Tunabear, Inc.
13155 Noel Rd Ste 900
Dallas, TX 75240
Contact: James Knowles
Tel: 888-923-8889
Email: james@tunabear.com
Website: www.tunabear.com
Staff Augmentation, Project Management, Upgrades, Implementation, Development, Strategy Development, Infrastructure Planning, Training / Change Management, Technologies, Peoplesoft, Hyperion / Data Warehousing. (As-Pac, estab 2010, empl 6, sales $1,444,000, cert: City)

5388   Valbrea Technologies, Inc.
PO Box 1516
Addison, TX 75001
Contact: President
Tel: 972-661-2268
Email: info@valbrea.com
Website: www.valbrea.com
Custom software development, database solutions, custom applications & programming services. (Woman, estab 1999, empl 14, sales , cert: WBENC)

5389   VCM Technologies, Inc.
25 Highland Park Village, Ste 100-149
Dallas, TX 75205
Contact: CEO
Tel: 817-571-6335
Email: info@beaconsystems.com
Website: www.beaconsystems.com
Information technology staff augmentation, SAP consultants. (Woman, estab 2002, empl 6, sales $14,200,000, cert: WBENC)

5390 Vensiti Inc
300 East Royal Lane Ste 104
Irving, TX 75039
Contact: Vijaya Saradhi Sr Dir Staffing
Tel: 972-887-7995
Email: saradhi.v@vensiti.com
Website: www.vensiti.com
Information tehcnology staffing & consulting services.
(Woman/As-Ind, estab 2004, empl 52, sales $4,340,000,
cert: State)

5391 Verge Information Technologies, Inc.
1305 Cheyenne Trail
Corinth, TX 76210
Contact: Mark McLaughlin Operations Mgr
Tel: 940-279-1390
Email: mark@vergeit.com
Website: www.vergeit.com
Information technology & IS consulting & staff augmenta-
tion. (Nat Ame, estab 2000, empl 25, sales $5,342,852,
cert: State, NMSDC)

5392 ViewTech Group, LLC
1332 Crampton St
Dallas, TX 75207
Contact: Jessica Landestrait CEO
Tel: 817-717-9600
Email: support@viewtechgroup.com
Website: www.viewtechgroup.com
Business Intelligence consulting and comprehensive digital
signage solutions, integrated design, hardware procurement and installation, software implementation and
ongoing maintenance, creative content, and technical
supplies. (Woman, estab 2018, empl 20, sales $2,251,558,
cert: WBENC)

5393 Virtuo Group Corporation
6700 Woodlands Pkwy Ste 230-322
The Woodlands, TX 77382
Contact: Theresa Blackwell CEO
Tel: 281-298-8571
Email: tblackwell@virtuogroup.com
Website: www.virtuogroup.com
PMO, Cyber Security, application modernization, migration
& consolidation technology services. (Woman/AA, estab
2001, empl 35, sales , cert: City, NMSDC)

5394 VKNetworks IT Solutions
638 Quail Run Dr
Murphy, TX 75094
Contact: Dr. Rajan Subramanian President
Tel: 469-323-3345
Email: drrajs@vknetworks.com
Website: www.vknetworks.com
IT/SAP STAFFING & Consulting, SAP Projects, AM, AD.
Big Data, SAP HANA, S/4 HANA, SAP Vistex, EDI, Business
Intelligence and Analytics, BW4HANA, ERP, BPC, HCM, SAP
Fiori, RDS, POC, HEC, BI Reporting (Webi, Crystal Reports,
Dash Boards. (Woman/As-Ind, estab 1999, empl 10, sales ,
cert: State)

5395 Wave Technologies
2340 E Trinity Mills Rd Ste 240
Carrollton, TX 75006
Contact: Phillip Radcliff VP Business Dev
Tel: 972-820-6950
Email: pradcliff@wavehitech.com
Website: www.wavehitech.com
Voice, data, cabling, inside & outside plant design, PC's,
network appliances, servers, printers, routers, switches
& network design, systems integration, network admin
& configuration mgmt, database dev, email & calendar-
ing, systems upgrades & support. (Woman, estab 1990,
empl 12, sales $3,000,000, cert: State)

5396 Wise Men Consultants Inc
1500 S Dairy Ashford Ste 285
Houston, TX 77077
Contact: Rosa Delgado-Batchan Dir of Operations
Tel: 281-953-4511
Email: rosa.batchan@wisemen.com
Website: www.wisemen.com
IT staffing, project mgmt, team leads, onshore &
offshore custom software development. (Minority,
Woman, estab 1997, empl 220, sales , cert: NMSDC,
WBENC)

5397 XBI Tech Corporation
7670 Woodway Dr, Ste 370
Houston, TX 77063
Contact: Trieu Nguyen CEO
Tel: 713-999-1286
Email: trieu.nguyen@xbitech.com
Website: www.xbitech.com
Comprehensive web development & management
services: web design & development, accessibility, web
content management, web training, maintenance &
support, web application/software development &
business intelligence. (As-Pac, estab 2007, empl 5, sales
$1,300,000, cert: State)

5398 Xpediant Solutions
2425 W Loop South
Houston, TX 77027
Contact: Suparna Mahesri Dir
Tel: 713-335-5550
Email: qusai@xpediantsolutions.com
Website: www.xpediantsolutions.com
Digital experience consulting and systems integration,
Cloud installation, configuration and staffing support.
(As-Ind, estab 2001, empl 25, sales $4,800,000, cert:
City)

5399 XTGlobal, Inc.
2701 N Dallas Pkwy, Ste 550
Plano, TX 75093
Contact: Ananth Ramaswamy President
Tel: 972-755-1800
Email: ananth@xtglobal.com
Website: www.xtglobal.com
Professional design, development, integration & support
services: Microsoft. NET, SQL, BizTalk, SharePoint, .NET
Web-based & Desktop Application development. (As-
Ind, estab 1998, empl 170, sales $26,500,000, cert:
State, NMSDC)

5400 YASME Soft Inc.
      1212 Corporate Dr Ste 150
      Irving, TX 75038
      Contact: Sandeep Kilaru President
      Tel: 214-529-3693
      Email: sam@yasmesoft.com
      Website: www.yasmesoft.com
IT consulting solution services: Oracle, SAP, Microsoft & IT
staff augmentation. Application devel, maintenance &
support, enterprise applications, practices, consulting. (As-
Ind, estab 2007, empl 70, sales $6,000,000, cert: State,
NMSDC)

5401 Zepol Productions, Inc. dba KiloTech
      1991 Rawhide Dr
      Round Rock, TX 78681
      Contact: Michael Jones Strategic Acct Exec
      Tel: 512-831-3663
      Email: michael.jones@kilotechusa.com
      Website: www.kilotechusa.com
Information technology sales and services. (Hisp, estab
2011, empl , sales $8,500,000, cert: NMSDC, 8(a))

Virginia

5402 Aarisha Inc.
      11890 Sunrise Valley Dr Ste 201
      Reston, VA 20191
      Contact: Shailesh Akhouri President
      Tel: 703-579-8510
      Email: supplier@aarisha.com
      Website: www.aarisha.net
Software development life cycle, Oracle Fusion Middle
ware Administration, Oracle Fusion Middle ware Development, Oracle Database Administration, Business Intelligence and Data warehousing, Software Development. (As-
Pac, estab 2005, empl 6, sales $1,059,708, cert: NMSDC)

5403 ACI Solutions Inc.
      131 E Broad St
      Falls Church, VA 22046
      Contact: Jovan Silva Business Devel Mgr
      Tel: 703-766-4070
      Email: jsilva@acisolutions.net
      Website: www.acisolutions.net
Information technology, data & voice networking products
& services. (AA, As-Pac, estab 2001, empl 25, sales , cert:
NMSDC)

5404 Advanced Computer Concepts
      7927 Jones Branch Dr Ste 600 N
      Mclean, VA 22102
      Contact: Mark Braxton Sr Acct Exec
      Tel: 571-395-4117
      Email: bill@acconline.com
      Website: www.acconline.com
IT hardware, software sales & network engineering
services, wireless network design & implementation, IT
security, IT storage systems, VOIP design & implementation. (Woman, estab 1982, empl 45, sales $55,000,000,
cert: WBENC)

5405 Affigent, LLC
      13873 Park Center Rd Ste 127
      Herndon, VA 20171
      Contact: Joe Clagett Acct Exec
      Tel: 301-305-9513
      Email: joe.clagett@affigent.com
      Website: www.affigent.com
Dist IT product & systems integration. (Nat Ame, estab
2004, empl 5, sales , cert: NMSDC)

5406 AhaApps LLC
      11608 Timberton Ct
      Glen Allen, VA 23060
      Contact: Satish Reddy CEO
      Tel: 804-366-9979
      Email: satish@ahaapps.com
      Website: www.ahaapps.com
Design & build mobile applications for iOS (iPhone,
iPad), Android phone & tablets, web applications,
ASP.NET, ASP.NET MVC, Ruby on Rails, Java,
Salesforce.com implementation & integration. (As-Pac,
estab 2010, empl 15, sales , cert: State, NMSDC)

5407 Alliant Global Strategies Inc.
      4607 W. Broad St
      Richmond, VA 23230
      Contact: James Wallace
      Tel: 804-283-2203
      Email: jwallace@alliantglobalstrategies.com
      Website: www.alliantglobalstrategies.com
Business process outsourcing (BPO) & technology
training solutions. (AA, estab 2011, empl 5, sales
$137,000, cert: State, NMSDC)

5408 Alltech International, Inc.
      8298-B Old Courthouse Rd
      Vienna, VA 22182
      Contact: Nathan Sanders Client Svcs Mgr
      Tel: 703-506-1222
      Email: alltech-raytheon@alltech.net
      Website: www.alltech.net
Applications Development & Engineering, Systems
Administration & Engineering, Database Development &
Administration, Security & Training. (Woman/Hisp, estab
1993, empl 150, sales $18,000,000, cert: State)

5409 Ampcus Inc.
      14900 Conference Ctr Dr, Ste 500
      Chantilly, VA 20151
      Contact: Donna Howell Sr VP
      Tel: 703-429-0550
      Email: donna.howell@ampcus.com
      Website: www.ampcus.com
Information technology and application development
services that are aligned with our clients business
objectives. (Minority, Woman, estab 2004, empl 1350,
sales $77,550,031, cert: State, NMSDC, CPUC, WBENC)

5410   Apex CoVantage
         198 Van Buren St Ste 200
         Herndon, VA 20170
         Contact: Mike Lohneis Dir Proposal & Contract
         Tel: 703-709-3000
         Email: mlohneis@apexcovantage.com
         Website: www.apexcovantage.com
Process engineering, knowledge & content management,
imaging, document management, forms processing &
digital assets creation, engineering: data conversion,
purification & conflation, work order posting, inspections,
audits. (Minority, estab 1988, empl 2500, sales , cert:
State, NMSDC)

5411   Applied Integrity Consulting, LLC
         40646 Weaver Ct
         Leesburg, VA 20175
         Contact: Loan Clarke CEO
         Tel: 703-868-3886
         Email: lclarke@aic-llc.us
         Website: www.aic-llc.us
Enterprise IT & Software Engineering support and services.
Expertise in Microsoft technologies. (Minority, Woman,
estab 2011, empl 2, sales , cert: State)

5412   Astyra Corporation
         411 East Franklin St, Ste 105
         Richmond, VA 23219
         Contact: Lee Rattigan VP Strategy & Dev
         Tel: 804-433-1117
         Email: lrattigan@astyra.com
         Website: www.astyra.com
IT staff augmentation & IT solutions: Medicaid & HIPAA
application dev & project management. (AA, estab 1997,
empl 150, sales $15,000,000, cert: State, NMSDC, SDB)

5413   Atlantic Resource Group, Inc.
         4880 Cox Rd, Ste 105
         Glen Allen, VA 23060
         Contact: Deborah J. Dowdy President
         Tel: 804-262-4400
         Email: Debbie.Dowdy@AtlanticResource.com
         Website: www.AtlanticResource.com
Information technology, staff augmentation & project
mgmt. (Woman, estab 1990, empl 45, sales , cert: WBENC)

5414   Avineon, Inc.
         1430 Spring Hill Road Ste 300
         McLean, VA 22102
         Contact: Charles Erdrich VP Business Devel
         Tel: 703-671-1900
         Email: cerdrich@avineon.com
         Website: www.avineon.com
Information technology, geospatial, and engineering
support services. (As-Pac, estab 1992, empl 142, sales
$36,021,678, cert: State, CPUC)

5415   Balance Technology Group, Inc.
         8136 Old Keene Mill Rd Ste A207
         Springfield, VA 22152
         Contact: Tracy Betts CEO
         Tel: 703-451-8675
         Email: tracy.betts@balanceinteractive.com
         Website: www.balanceinteractive.com
Web design & development agency. (Woman, estab 1997,
empl 13, sales $1,600,000, cert: WBENC)

5416   Benten Technologies
         13996 Parkeast Circle 105
         Herndon, VA 20171
         Contact: President
         Tel: 703-788-6560
         Email:
         Website: www.bententech.com
IT consulting. (As-Pac, estab 2000, empl 4, sales
$2,050,615, cert: State)

5417   Betis Group. Inc.
         1420 Beverly Rd, Ste 330
         McLean, VA 22205
         Contact: Hernan Cortes CEO
         Tel: 703-532-2008
         Email: hcortes@betis.com
         Website: www.betis.com
Staff augmentation and technology deployments,
systems integration services. (Hisp, estab 1995, empl 36,
sales $22,000,000, cert: State, NMSDC)

5418   Biswas Information Technology Solutions Inc.
         2612 Litchfield Dr
         Herndon, VA 20171
         Contact: Sumita Biswas
         Tel: 202-203-0982
         Email: sbiswas@b-itsinc.com
         Website: www.b-itsinc.com
Database centric applications, dbase mgmt & development. (Minority, Woman, estab 2006, empl 5, sales
$383,733, cert: NMSDC, WBENC, 8(a))

5419   BlueAlly Technology Solutions, LLC
         8609 Westwood Center Dr Ste 100
         Vienna, VA 22182
         Contact: Hope Jepson Proposal & Certification
         Mgr
         Tel: 919-249-1509
         Email: hjepson@blueally.com
         Website: www.blueally.com
Big Data, Business Intelligence, Micro Strategy cognos,
project management office model. (As-Pac, estab , empl
, sales $46,000,000, cert: NMSDC)

5420   Burke Consortium, Incorporated
         5500 Cherokee Ave, Ste 510
         Alexandria, VA 22312
         Contact: Thomas Nodeen COO
         Tel: 703-941-0600
         Email: tnodeen@bcinow.com
         Website: www.bcinow.com
Information technology solutions, software development, cyber security, independent verification &
validation. (Woman, estab 1982, empl 44, sales
$10,500,000, cert: WBENC)

5421   Capital Legal Solutions dba Capital Novus
         10521 Rosehaven St Ste 300
         Fairfax, VA 22030
         Contact: Ramesh Purohit Business Dev Mgr
         Tel: 703-226-1500
         Email: rpurohit@capitalnovus.com
         Website: www.capitalnovus.com
Forensic data collection from project sites around the
world, data preservation, processing, and presentation,
web hosting services & loading (Minority, Woman, estab
2002, empl 250, sales $21,560,000, cert: State, WBENC)

5422 Cetan Corp.
  1001 Scenic Pwy, Ste 203
  Chesapeake, VA 23323
  Contact: Brad Scott President
  Tel: 757-548-6420
  Email: brad.scott@cetancorp.com
  Website: www.cetancorp.com
Enterprise and Business Service Management (BSM) software and services. (Nat Ame, estab 2007, empl 16, sales , cert: State, NMSDC)

5423 Cheshil Consultants, Inc.
  8136 Old Keene Mill Rd, Ste B-201
  Springfield, VA 22152
  Contact: Chet Bhimani President
  Tel: 703-569-8763
  Email: cvbhimani@ccione.com
  Website: www.ccione.com
Information technology consulting. (As-Ind, estab 1991, empl 13, sales $1,226,303, cert: State)

5424 CompuGain LLC
  13241 Woodland Park Rd, Ste 100 Ste 100
  Herndon, VA 20171
  Contact: Manita Hota VP Client Dev
  Tel: 703-956-7005
  Email: srinivasa.chowdary@compugain.com
  Website: www.compugain.com
Application development, business intelligence, data management, systems integration, project management, support & maintenance services. (Minority, estab 2000, empl 500, sales $100,000,000, cert: NMSDC)

5425 Conviso Inc.
  312 E Main St, Ste 200
  Luray, VA 22835
  Contact: Uday Malhan President
  Tel: 703-980-7074
  Email: umalhan@convisoinc.com
  Website: www.convisoinc.com
Application Development & Maintenance lication security & applications portfolio rationalization, .NET, Java, PeopleSoft, Systems Integration. (As-Ind, estab 2010, empl 18, sales $1,590,000, cert: State)

5426 CoreLogix Consulting Incorporation
  1900 Campus Commons Dr Ste 100
  Reston, VA 20191
  Contact: Inderbir Singh President
  Tel: 703-665-0813
  Email: inder@clx-inc.com
  Website: www.clx-inc.com
IT & management consulting services. (As-Ind, estab 2011, empl 25, sales $1,400,000, cert: State)

5427 CurtMont Global Services, Inc.
  9501 Hull St Rd, Ste D
  Richmond, VA 23236
  Contact: Curtiss Stancil President
  Tel: 804-982-9349
  Email: cstancil@curtmont.com
  Website: www.curtmont.com
Contracted foodservices, facility management, and transportation support services through our operating companies (CurtMont Foodservices and TransitServcorp). We are minority owned certified in 20 states in the USA. (AA, estab 2014, empl 105, sales , cert: State)

5428 Cyber Clarity Inc.
  15722 Ryder Court
  Haymarket, VA 20169
  Contact: Ed Kraemer VP
  Tel: 571-982-6710
  Email: ed@cyberclarity.com
  Website: www.cyberclarity.com
Cyber Intelligence, Operational Continuity, Computer network Defense, Incident Response & Compliance. (Woman, estab 2011, empl 12, sales $1,700,000, cert: State, City)

5429 Cynet Systems Inc.
  21000 Atlantic Blvd #700
  Sterling, VA 20166
  Contact: Arpit Paul VP Strategy & Partnerships
  Tel: 571-442-1007
  Email: arpitp@cynetsystems.com
  Website: www.cynetsystems.com
IT & engineering staffing consulting, direct/full time hiring, contract (temp hiring) or contract to hire services. (Minority, estab 2010, empl 1200, sales $65,000,000, cert: NMSDC)

5430 Data Concepts
  4405 Cox Rd Ste 140
  Glen Allen, VA 23060
  Contact: Dennis Woomer Dir Business Dev
  Tel: 804-968-4700
  Email: dennis.woomer@dataconcepts-inc.com
  Website: www.dataconcepts-inc.com/
Application development, Microsoft, Java & Mobile technologies.. (Minority, Woman, estab 1997, empl 20, sales $15,000,000, cert: State)

5431 DayBlink
  1595 Spring Hill Road Ste 300
  Vienna, VA 22182
  Contact: Michael Wong CEO
  Tel: 703-869-1309
  Email: minority.supplier@dayblink.com
  Website: www.dayblink.com
IT, Procurement, Contact Center, Finance, HR, Marketing, and Supply Chain. (As-Pac, estab 2013, empl 63, sales $13,720,845, cert: NMSDC)

5432 Deque Systems, Inc.
  2121 Cooperative Way Ste 210
  Reston, VA 20191
  Contact: Preety Kumar CEO
  Tel: 703-225-0380
  Email: preety.kumar@deque.com
  Website: www.deque.com
IT consulting & services. (Woman/As-Ind, estab 1999, empl 25, sales $1,745,001, cert: State, WBENC)

5433 Desktop Service Center, Inc.
  111 N 17th St
  Richmond, VA 23219
  Contact: Philise Conein CEO
  Tel: 804-249-8720
  Email: info@techead.com
  Website: www.techead.com
IT staff augmentation svcs, web & graphics training, website devel, Linux platform. (Woman, estab 1988, empl 100, sales $7,000,000, cert: State, WBENC)

5434 Digilent Consulting, LLC
2612 Amanda Ct
Vienna, VA 22180
Contact: Vinny Raj Managing Dir
Tel: 412-657-2219
Email: vinnyraj@digilentconsulting.com
Website: www.digilentconsulting.com
SMAC (Social, Mobile, Analytics and Cloud), Cyber Security expertise/capabilities. (Woman/As-Ind, estab 2006, empl 5, sales $450,000, cert: State, NMSDC)

5435 Digital Intelligence Systems, LLC
8270 Greensboro Dr Ste 1000
McLean, VA 22102
Contact: Arthur Levitt VP Strategic Accounts
Tel: 703-752-7900
Email: FHLBNY@disys.com
Website: www.disys.com
Information technology service, staff augmentation & recruitment, hardware & software, wireless & mobile systems design, implementation & mgmt. (As-Ind, estab 1994, empl 9500, sales $888,064,538, cert: NMSDC)

5436 DISYS Solutions, Inc.
4151 Lafayette Center Dr Ste 600
Chantilly, VA 20151
Contact: Vinu Luthra COO
Tel: 703-802-0500
Email: supplier.diversity@disyssolutions.com
Website: www.disyssolutions.com
Information technology products & services. (As-Ind, estab 2010, empl 45, sales $62,000,000, cert: State)

5437 End To End Computing
1800 Diagonal Rd Ste 600
Alexandria, VA 22301
Contact: Esteve Mede Principal
Tel: 833-720-7770
Email: emede@eecomputing.com
Website: www.eecomputing.com
Vendor agnostic solutions, infrastructure solution, network architectureand design, network security architecture, unified communications, data center design, Cloud data center design, information assurance, policy implementation & procedure. (AA, estab 2012, empl 31, sales $3,800,000, cert: State)

5438 Enterprise ITech Corp.
10014 Manor Pl
Fairfax, VA 22032
Contact: Pals Nagaraj
Tel: 703-731-7881
Email: pnagaraj@enterpriseitech.com
Website: www.enterpriseitech.com
Full Software Development Lifecycle, Business Analytics, Business Intelligence, Enterprise Web Development, Enterprise Legacy System Modernization, Mobile application development, Database Design, Data Warehouse ETL. (As-Ind, estab 2000, empl 2, sales $300,000, cert: State, NMSDC)

5439 EsteemLogic
722 E Market St
Leesburg, VA 20176
Contact: K. Francis CEO
Tel: 571-235-9284
Email: kfrancis@esteemlogic.com
Website: www.esteemlogic.com
IT consulting and training firm that implements sustainable, scalable solutions to ensure organizations optimize engagement with its people, customers and the communities they serve. (AA, estab 2017, empl 2, sales , cert: State, WBENC)

5440 eTechSecurityPro, LLC
851 French Moore Jr. Blvd
Abingdon, VA 24210
Contact: Alain Sadeghi CTO
Tel: 202-587-2750
Email: alain@etechsecurity.com
Website: www.etechsecurity.com
Health I/T Patient Registration, History and Secure Access Control Solution Security Auditing Services GLBA /FDICIA /Guidelines NCUA / Guidelines FFIEC/ IT Examination /Sarbanes-Oxley/Homeland Security/Security Management and Social Engineering (Woman, estab 2004, empl 14, sales $1,200,000, cert: State)

5441 ETELIC Inc.
5388 Twin Hickory Rd
Glen Allen, VA 23059
Contact: Mark Murphy President
Tel: 866-240-3395
Email: mark.murphy@etelic.com
Website: www.etelic.com
Computer programming svcs: systems design, facilities management, consulting, database & data warehouse. (As-Pac, estab 2004, empl 20, sales $2,400,000, cert: State, NMSDC)

5442 EvereTech LLC
2705 Main Sail Ct
Henrico, VA 23233
Contact: Andrew Everett Principal
Tel: 804-986-9998
Email: andrew.everett@everetech.com
Website: www.everetech.com
Systems Administration & Engineering , Network Design, Network Administration & Network Engineering, Software Development & Engineering, Project Management, COTS/GOTS Systems Integration & Configuration. (AA, estab 2014, empl 7, sales $300,000, cert: State)

5443 eWaste Tech Systems, LLC
501 E Franklin St Ste 726
Richmond, VA 23219
Contact: Felipe Wright Managing Member
Tel: 804-716-3577
Email: fwright@ewastetech.com
Website: www.ewastetech.com
Green Information technology sustainability & asset mgmt, data destruction & disposition services, electronic waste disposal. (AA, estab 2012, empl 16, sales , cert: State, NMSDC)

5444   Force 1 Global, LLC
       1050 Temple Ave Ste 214
       Colonial Heights, VA 23834
       Contact: DeAlteman Beasley CEO
       Tel: 804-723-1164
       Email: dbeasley@force1global.com
       Website: www.force1global.com
Staffing, outsourcing & technology integration. (AA, estab
2014, empl 1, sales , cert: State, NMSDC)

5445   G2 Global Solutions, LLC
       202 Church St SE Ste 538
       Leesburg, VA 20176
       Contact: Elizabeth Lauren Galati CEO
       Tel: 703-349-7787
       Email: lgalati@g2gs.net
       Website: www.g2gs.net
Cyber Exploitation, Information Technology Services,
Intelligence. (Minority, Woman, estab 2012, empl 86, sales
$8,000,000, cert: State, 8(a), SDB)

5446   G2 Ops Inc.
       205 Business Park Dr
       Virginia Beach, VA 23462
       Contact: Robert Gregorio COO
       Tel: 757-965-8330
       Email: bobg@g2-ops.com
       Website: www.g2-ops.com
Model based systems engineering & cybersecurity,
acquiring data, modeling systems & processes, identifying
cyber vulnerabilities, performing analyses, identifying
capability gaps and/or areas for improvement. (Woman,
estab 2005, empl 15, sales $2,200,000, cert: State,
WBENC)

5447   Geologics Corporation
       5285 Shawnee Rd, Ste 300
       Alexandria, VA 22312
       Contact: John Hildreth Dir Consulting Services
       Tel: 978-524-8152
       Email: jhildreth@geologics.com
       Website: www.geologics.com
Technical services: systems engineering, spacecraft, space
systems, software dev, science applications. (Hisp, estab
1989, empl 500, sales $79,434,480, cert: NMSDC)

5448   Global Geographic Inc.
       11511 Cavalier Landing Ct
       Fairfax, VA 22030
       Contact: Sameer Chandra VP
       Tel: 703-594-5181
       Email: schandra@globalgeographic.com
       Website: www.globalgeographic.com
IT Services, resourcing, customized software devel,
program & project mgmt. (As-Pac, estab 2006, empl 3,
sales , cert: State, NMSDC)

5449   GovSmart, Inc.
       706 Forest St
       Charlottesville, VA 22903
       Contact: JASON GAVIRIA Owner
       Tel: 434-326-5656
       Email: jason@govsmart.com
       Website: www.govsmart.com
Authorized Reseller of IT Technology. (As-Pac, estab 2009,
empl 50, sales $155,000,000, cert: State, 8(a), SDB)

5450   Gupton & Associates, Inc.
       901 N Pitt St Ste 230
       Alexandria, VA 22314
       Contact: Clara Lee Client Engagement Mgr
       Tel: 703-419-3048
       Email: clarablee@guptonassociates.com
       Website: www.guptonassociates.com
Program/Project Management; Application Architecture;
Information Assurance/Cyber Security; Network Ser-
vices; Virtualization & Consolidation; Cloud Computing;
Engineering Services; Data Analysis & Generation.
(Woman, estab 2002, empl 5, sales $19,200,000, cert:
State)

5451   Hanusoft Inc.
       7206 Impala Dr, Ste 214
       Richmond, VA 23228
       Contact: Bala Kamuju President
       Tel: 804-484-2400
       Email: kamuju@hanusoftinc.com
       Website: www.hanusoftinc.com
Computer related services, implementation requirements, computer applications, implementing customize
hardware systems, updating & modifying existing
programs. (As-Ind, estab 2005, empl 46, sales
$4,816,708, cert: State)

5452   HyperGen Inc.
       7810 Carvin St
       Roanoke, VA 24019
       Contact: Sherry Dyer VP Sales
       Tel: 540-992-6500
       Email: sales@hypergeninc.com
       Website: www.hypergeninc.com
PeopleSoft® functional & technical consulting svcs:
implementation, upgrade, system analysis, custom
developed. (Woman, estab 1992, empl 25, sales
$5,000,000, cert: State, WBENC)

5453   Idexcel, Inc.
       459 Herndon Pkwy, Ste 10
       Herndon, VA 20170
       Contact: Prasad Alapati President
       Tel: 703-230-2600
       Email: palapati@idexcel.com
       Website: www.idexcel.com
Staff augmentation, software development, network
design, systems integration & business process improvement. (Minority, estab 1998, empl 615, sales
$44,289,871, cert: NMSDC)

5454   Inficare, Inc.
       22375 Broderick Dr Ste 225
       Dulles, VA 20166
       Contact: Sumar Mathur President
       Tel: 703-945-1800
       Email:
       Website: www.inficaretech.com
IT consulting, staff augmentation. (As-Ind, estab 2001,
empl 465, sales $29,000,000, cert: State)

5455 Infomatics Corporation
23465 Rock Haven Way, Ste 100
Dulles, VA 20166
Contact: Shahil Shariff CEO
Tel: 703-786-4824
Email: jeff@infomaticscorp.com
Website: www.infomaticscorp.com
Digital Transformation, Application Modernization. (Woman/As-Ind, estab 2005, empl 67, sales $15,000,000, cert: State)

5456 Inoventures, LLC/SciMetrika, LLC
7601 Lewinsville Road Ste 101
McLean, VA 22102
Contact: Meena Krishnan CEO
Tel: 703-917-6622
Email: meenak@inoventures.com
Website: www.inoventures.com
Information Technology, Big Data, Software Engineering and Development, Systems Integration, Cloud Migration, and Talent Acquisition. (Minority, estab 2008, empl 53, sales $4,550,315, cert: WBENC)

5457 Integrated Support Systems Inc (ISSi)
PO Box 2402
Arlington, VA 22202
Contact: Frank Duron CEO
Tel: 703-892-6100
Email: fduron@integratedsupport.com
Website: www.integratedsupport.com
Web design, develop & content mgmt, imaging, form conversion, records & docuemnt mgmt, workflow & litigation solutions, systems integration & custom solutions. (Hisp, estab 1984, empl 22, sales $2,334,042, cert: NMSDC)

5458 IntellectFaces, Inc.
23397 Minerva Dr
Ashburn, VA 20148
Contact: Kishore Kochi CEO
Tel: 703-340-6445
Email: kkochi@intellectfaces.com
Website: www.intellectfaces.com
IT and managed services. (Woman/As-Pac, estab 2011, empl 10, sales $854,791, cert: NMSDC, WBENC, 8(a))

5459 iQuasar, LLC
6 Pidgeon Hill Dr Ste 305
Sterling, VA 20165
Contact: Amin Bhat Chief Business Officer
Tel: 703-962-6001
Email: amin.bhat@iquasar.com
Website: www.iquasar.com
Information technology solutions & services, IT consulting, staffing & recruitment services. (As-Pac, estab 2004, empl 15, sales $2,070,152, cert: State, NMSDC)

5460 iWorks Corporation
1889 Preston Shite Dr Ste 100
reston, VA 20191
Contact: Jothi Radhakrishnan Sr VP
Tel: 571-485-2004
Email: jradhakrishnan@iworkscorp.com
Website: www.iworkscorp.com
Information technology consulting & staff augmentation. (As-Ind, estab 2005, empl 9, sales $8,000,000, cert: State)

5461 JPI Technology LLC
9720 Capital Court, Ste 301
Manassas, VA 20155
Contact: Haris Perwaiz VP
Tel: 703-828-5651
Email: harris@jpitechnology.com
Website: www.jpitechnology.net
Information consulting, contracting, application development, e-commerce/ERP, application integration, infrastructure & staff augmentation. (Minority, Woman, estab 2011, empl 9, sales $1,300,000, cert: State)

5462 Key Concepts Knowledgebase LLC
4031 University Dr
Fairfax, VA 22030
Contact: Kim de Peiza President
Tel: 703-966-1364
Email: kdepeiza@keyknowledgebase.com
Website: www.keyknowledgebase.com
Technical and customer centric documentation, SOPsService Desk supportLAN/WAN Infrastructure and Systems Administration supportSoftware Web Development, SOA development, mobile computing, Web 2.0 (AA, estab 2004, empl 10, sales $450,000, cert: NMSDC, 8(a))

5463 Knowledge Connections, Inc.
610 Herndon Pkwy Ste 900A
Herndon, VA 20170
Contact: Marion Bonhomme-Knox President
Tel: 571-203-9120
Email: marion.bk@theknowledgeconnection.com
Website: www.knowledgeconnector.com
Systems engineering & telecommunications. (Woman/AA, estab 1996, empl 150, sales $4,000,000, cert: State)

5464 Knowledge Information Solutions, Inc.
227 South Rosemont Road
Virginia Beach, VA 23452
Contact: Terry Kreamer CFO
Tel: 757-463-0033
Email: terry.kreamer@kisinc.net
Website: www.kisinc.net
Information technology products & services: inside/outside plant cabling & wireless solutions, security systems, telephone systems, computer products & services, web development, data base dev & mgmt, network architecture & engineering. (Minority, Woman, estab 1983, empl 100, sales $30,200,000, cert: State)

5465 Loyola Enterprises Inc.
2984 S Lynnhaven Rd Ste 101
Virginia Beach, VA 23452
Contact: Benito Loyola President
Tel: 757-498-6118
Email: benito@loyola.com
Website: www.Loyola.com
TS/SCI, Modeling & Simulation Information Technology, Web Portal and Multimedia. (Hisp, estab 1991, empl 30, sales $7,325,312, cert: State)

5466 MAI Enterprises, Inc.
PO Box 1194
Annandale, VA 22003
Contact: Bonnie Norem President
Tel: 703-750-2228
Email: bonnie@maienterprises.com
Website: www.maienterprises.com
System engineering, graphic illustration, desktop publishing, proposals, tech editing & writing, computer hardware & software products. (Woman, estab 1986, empl 15, sales $763,400, cert: State)

5467 Meta Dimensions Inc.
7115 Leesburg Pike, Ste 213
Falls Church, VA 22043
Contact: Amit Prakash
Tel: 571-969-4140
Email: amit@metadim.com
Website: www.metadim.com
Analytics service, Big Data Lake, Data Visualization, Enterprise Information Management, Intelligent Enterprise Roadmap, Master Data Management. (Minority, Woman, estab 2007, empl 85, sales $2,064,955, cert: State, NMSDC, WBENC)

5468 MicroAutomation, Inc.
5870 Trinity Pkwy, Ste 600
Centreville, VA 20120
Contact: Suresh Gursahaney CEO
Tel: 703-543-2100
Email: Sgursahaney@microautomation.com
Website: www.microautomation.com
Computer telephony integration, speech recognition, interactive voice response, reporting, workforce mgmt & digital recording. (Minority, estab 1991, empl 34, sales $7,900,000, cert: NMSDC)

5469 MicroTechnologies, LLC
8330 Boone Blvd, Ste 600
Vienna, VA 22182
Contact: Aaron Drabkin SVP Contracts
Tel: 703-891-1073
Email: adrabkin@microtech.net
Website: www.MicroTech.net
Program mngt, database mgmt & admin, change mgmt & process re-engineering, sys eng svcs, info sys sustainment & support, IT svcs & solns, collaboration svcs & info sharing apps, network solns & sys modernization, & IT enterprise transformation. (Hisp, estab 2004, empl 420, sales $780,000,000, cert: State, NMSDC)

5470 Mindseeker, Inc.
20130 Lakeview Center Plaza, Ste 320
Ashburn, VA 20147
Contact: Cassie Kelly VP Client Services & Operations
Tel: 304-549-9281
Email: ckelly@mindseeker.com
Website: www.mindseeker.com
Information Technology, Financial, Clerical and Enterprise Performance Management services and solutions. (Woman, estab , empl 234, sales $2,000,000, cert: State, WBENC)

5471 Mosaic Solutions, Inc.
209 Elden St, Ste 204
Herndon, VA 20170
Contact: Vikash Nangalia program Mgr
Tel: 703-707-1680
Email: vikash@mosaic-us.com
Website: www.mosaic-us.com/
Systems integration, program mgmt, enterprise resource mgmt, customer relationship mgmt, data mgmt, database admin & warehousing, knowledge mgmt, networking, desktop & help desk svcs, business process outsourcing & supply chain mgmt. (As-Ind, estab 1996, empl 17, sales $1,170,660, cert: NMSDC)

5472 NETHOST, Inc.
1750 Tysons Blvd. Ste 1500
McLean, VA 22102
Contact: Ikram Koreshi CEO
Tel: 571-236-0781
Email: ikoreshi@nethostus.com
Website: www.nethostus.com
Network systems & data communication, engineering, business processes, ERP & CRM functional areas & technical consulting. (As-Ind, estab 2002, empl 3, sales $300,000, cert: State)

5473 NetVision Resources
2201 Cooperative Way Ste 600
Herndon, VA 20171
Contact: Sunny Nangia Dir Resource Management
Tel: 703-342-4284
Email: snangia@netvisionresources.com
Website: www.netvisionresources.com
Information technology svcs: staff augmentation, on-site, off-site & off-shore software development. (Minority, estab 1999, empl 100, sales , cert: NMSDC)

5474 NexThreat
7686 Richmond Hwy Ste 116
Alexandria, VA 22306
Contact: Ruben Gavilan CEO
Tel: 202-796-1676
Email: ruben@nexthreat.com
Website: www.Nexthreat.com
Cyber Security. Emerging SIEM Tool Optimization (Splunk, Qradar, Arcsight Partner), Insider Threat Detection, Incident Response, SOC/NOC Support Services, Continuous Data Analytics, IA, IT Security, Vulnerability Assessments. (Hisp, estab 2016, empl 15, sales $1,000,000, cert: State)

5475 Nirvana International Inc.
2108 Gunnell Farms Dr
Vienna, VA 22181
Contact: Pritish Nawlakhe President
Tel: 571-215-0072
Email: pritish@nirvana-international.com
Website: www.nirvana-international.com
Oracle EBS/ERP Solutions, INFOR Solutions, Program & Project Management, Staff Augmentation, PCI Compliant Credit Card Solutions, Business Intelligence & Analytics solutions, Social Media Integration. (Woman/As-Ind, estab 2012, empl 5, sales $158,000, cert: State)

5476 Pan Asia Resources Pte Ltd.
      44031 Pipeline Plaza Ste 305
      Ashburn, VA 20147
      Contact: Aparnaa Vinod President
      Tel: 571-269-2778
      Email: aparnaa@panasiagroup.net
      Website: www.panasiaresources.com
Information Technology, Marketing & Telecommunications.
(Woman/As-Ind, estab 2003, empl 35, sales , cert: State)

5477 Pantheon Inc.
      1801 Robert Fulton Dr Ste 160
      Reston, VA 20191
      Contact: Sarah Johnson Sales Dir
      Tel: 469-387-9775
      Email: sarah.johnson@pantheon-inc.com
      Website: www.odyssey-automation.com
Technology consulting services, Cloud engineering services. SAP services, Salesforce consulting services, Cyber
Security services, Web development services, IT staff
augmentation services, TaaS services, Customer Technology Solutions. (Woman/As-Pac, estab 1997, empl 1200,
sales $247,000,000, cert: NMSDC, NWBOC)

5478 PeopleNTech LLC
      8133 Leesburg Pike, Ste 220
      Vienna, VA 22182
      Contact: Chandra Sharma Dir Business Dev
      Tel: 703-982-7034
      Email: chandra.sharma@email.peoplentech.com
      Website: www.peoplentech.com
IT & Engineering solutions, Development, Outsourcing &
Consulting. (Minority, Woman, estab 2005, empl 57, sales
$9,600,000, cert: State, City, NMSDC)

5479 Pretek Corporation
      800 Corporate Dr Ste 301
      Stafford, VA 22554
      Contact: Exec Dir
      Tel: 703-855-7148
      Email: info@pretek.com
      Website: www.pretek.com
Enterprise architecture, agile application development,
DevOps, enterprise data management, IT infrastructure,
systems engineering, and security. (Woman/As-Ind, estab
2002, empl 25, sales $2,800,000, cert: State, 8(a))

5480 Protege LLC
      12359 Sunrise Valley Dr Ste 260
      Reston, VA 20191
      Contact: Shyam Monaysar Sr Business Devel Mgr
      Tel: 703-953-2535
      Email: shyam@protegellc.com
      Website: www.protegellc.com
Web/Application Dev (.Net, Java, J2EE, JSP, HTML, DHTML,
CSS, Ajax, Flash, C#, C++, C), Web Services(WebLogic,
WebSphere, Apache, TeamSite, Windows Admin),
SharePoint. (Woman/As-Ind, estab 2004, empl 60, sales
$3,500,000, cert: State)

5481 Qassurance Technology Inc.
      5821 Maybrook Court
      Glen Allen, VA 23059
      Contact: Gurushyam Mony CEO
      Tel: 814-441-9634
      Email: support@qassurancetechnology.com
      Website: www.qassurancetechnology.com
Information technology consulting services. (As-Ind, estab
2012, empl 2, sales $145,000, cert: State)

5482 QSACK & Associates, Inc.
      2111 Wilson Blvd, Ste 700
      Arlington, VA 22201
      Contact: C. Anthony Cusack CEO
      Tel: 703-351-5035
      Email: cac@qsack1.com
      Website: www.qsack1.com
Professional, information technology & business support
services, systems integration; information assurance;
systems security services; information technology
services, program & project management. (AA, estab
2001, empl 35, sales $3,879,000, cert: State)

5483 Savi Solutions, Inc.
      8200 Greensboro Dr, Ste 900
      McLean, VA 22102
      Contact: Smita Iyer CEO
      Tel: 571-258-7602
      Email: siyer@savisolutions.biz
      Website: www.savisolutions.biz
Strategic Planning, Program/Project Management,
Merger & Acquisition Support, Systems Implementation
(ERP/CRM/SCM), Cloud Based Implementation Solu-
tions, Business Requirement Analysis, System Design
and Development. (Minority, estab 2010, empl 3, sales
$552,551, cert: WBENC)

5484 Secured Network Solutions, Inc.
      929 Ventures Way Ste 113
      Chesapeake, VA 23320
      Contact: Alphonzo Barney President
      Tel: 757-819-7647
      Email: abarney@teamsns.com
      Website: www.teamsns.com
Telecommunications & information technology: cabling,
design, install, fiber optics single/multi-strand, fiber
fusion & splicing, LAN/WAN/wireless network engineering, drafting & information systems security. (AA, estab
2006, empl 11, sales , cert: State)

5485 Shivan Technologies, Inc.
      12818 Owens Glen Dr
      Fairfax, VA 22030
      Contact: Rekha Bathula President
      Tel: 703-595-6879
      Email: contact@stgxinc.com
      Website: www.stgxinc.com
Information Technology (IT), Network Management,
Computer Facilities Management, Program Management, Consulting, Administrative & Professional Support
Services, Information Assurance, Enterprise Architecture, Cloud. (Minority, Woman, estab 2007, empl 4, sales
, cert: State, 8(a))

5486 SilTek, Inc.
      13454 Sunrise Valley Dr Ste 250
      Herndon, VA 20171
      Contact: Silvia M. Park President
      Tel: 703-620-9130
      Email: info@siltek.com
      Website: www.siltekinc.com
Computer hardware, IT svcs, systems integration,
computer training. (Minority, Woman, estab 1997, empl
1, sales , cert: State)

5487 SMART Resources, Inc.
      10442 Patterson Ave
      Richmond, VA 23238
      Contact: Van Williams Principal
      Tel: 804-864-9150
      Email: vanw@smartva.net
      Website: www.smartva.net
Information Technology and Human Resources Consulting
Services. (Woman, estab 2007, empl 28, sales
$13,800,000, cert: State)

5488 Solvitur Systems LLC
      202 Church St SE Ste 526
      Leesburg, VA 20176
      Contact: Ade Odutola Managing Dir
      Tel: 703-348-3544
      Email: aodutola@solvitursystems.com
      Website: www.solvitursystems.com
Regulatory Compliance & Security Assessments, Privacy
Impact Analysis, Cloud Security Services, CSA, Assessment
& Authorization, independent Verification & Validation.
(AA, estab 2007, empl 5, sales $230,000, cert: State, 8(a))

5489 Spurgetech, LLC
      21580 Atlantic Blvd, Ste 220B
      Sterling, VA 20166
      Contact: Susetha Balabishegan President
      Tel: 703-652-6576
      Email: susetha@spurgetech.com
      Website: www.spurgetech.com
Information Technology Consulting, contract & permanent
staffing solutions, On-site, off-site or remote, ERP Resources, SAP, Oracle & Peoplesoft. (Minority, Woman,
estab 2006, empl 5, sales $900,000, cert: State, WBENC)

5490 Stanton Secure Technologies, LLC
      2054 S Shirlington Rd
      Arlington, VA 22204
      Contact: Lisa Wallace CEO
      Tel: 703-568-0553
      Email: johnson@sst-llc.com
      Website: www.sst-llc.com
Information Assurance services, training & security
management, Cyber Security Program Management,
Assessment & Authorization, Security Engineering,
Remediation Solutions, Security Awareness & Training.
(Woman/AA, estab 2005, empl 2, sales $180,000, cert:
State)

5491 Summit Information Solutions, Inc.
      3957 Westerre Pkwy Ste 120
      Richmond, VA 23233
      Contact: Vickie Quigg Comms & Mktg Mgr
      Tel: 804-201-4356
      Email: vickie.quigg@summitis.com
      Website: www.summitis.com
Enterprise Architecture; Change Management; Informa-
tion Technology; SCORM; Virtual; 3D; Training; Atomic
Layering; ALD; Banking; Finance; Aerospace Engineering;
Big Data; Data Analytics; Resource Management; Portfolio
Management; Cloud; Procurement; AGIL. (Minority,
Woman, estab 2002, empl 37, sales $8,326,000, cert:
NMSDC)

5492 Sygna Technologies Inc
      4000 Legato Rd Ste 1100
      Fairfax, VA 22033
      Contact: Paul Shakya President
      Tel: 571-445-4800
      Email: paul@sygnatechnologies.com
      Website: www.sygnatechnolgies.com
Temporary contract IT Staffing. (Minority, estab 2014,
empl 1, sales , cert: State)

5493 Synapse Business Systems
      11350 Random Hills Rd, Ste 800
      Fairfax, VA 22030
      Contact: Shivani Kaushal Sales Head
      Tel: 703-782-0007
      Email: hr@synapsebsystems.com
      Website: www.synapsebsystems.com
Staff Augmentation, Experienced, dedicated and
qualified core staffs, Network of IT Professional, System-
atic and well-defined process to recruit and hire new
talent. (Minority, Woman, estab 2013, empl 63, sales
$2,911,046, cert: WBENC)

5494 Synaptein Solutions Inc.
      1568 Spring Hill Road Ste 402
      Mclean, VA 22102
      Contact: Sharad Dayma CEO
      Tel: 703-209-2350
      Email: sharad.d@synap-one.com
      Website: www.synapteinsolutions.com
Staff Augmentation & Resource Planning Services, BPM
Solutions, Product Development, Customer Support,
Professional Services, Enterprise Solutions Provider,
Business Intelligence & DSS, Off-& and On-site. (As-Ind,
estab 2011, empl 15, sales $1,196,000, cert: State,
NMSDC, 8(a))

5495 Talteam,Inc
      13800 Coppermine Rd Ste 120
      Herndon, VA 20171
      Contact: Bobby Toe Exec VP
      Tel: 571-315-4958
      Email: bobbyt@talteam.com
      Website: www.talteam.com
IT professional Services, Salesforce & Java technologies.
(Minority, Woman, estab 2011, empl 100, sales
$9,000,000, cert: WBENC)

5496 Team Askin Technologies, Inc
      13135 Lee Jackson Memorial Hwy Ste 340
      fairfax, VA 22033
      Contact: steve askin COO
      Tel: 703-230-0111
      Email: steve.askin@teamaskin.com
      Website: www.teamaskin.com
Software engineering & development, electronic
commerce (Internet and Intranet Web Sites, G2C,G2G),
Java Applets, XML, Graphical User Interface (GUI), Front
Page, Cold Fusion, Dreamweaver. (Minority, Woman,
estab 1992, empl 50, sales $9,000,000, cert: State,
WBENC)

5497 Technalink, Inc.
      8000 Towers Crescent Dr Ste 600
      Vienna, VA 22182
      Contact: Alka Dhillon CEO
      Tel: 703-627-1916
      Email: adhillon@technalink.net
      Website: www.technalink.net
Informaiton technology staffing solutions. (Woman/As-Ind,
estab 2000, empl 20, sales , cert: WBENC)

5498 Technology Assurance Group, Inc.
      2114 Tomlynn St
      Richmond, VA 23230
      Contact: Angela Taylor CEO
      Tel: 804-323-7480
      Email: ahtaylor@tagva.com
      Website: www.tagva.com
Systems integration: LAN/WAN, VP & wireless networks,
bandwidth mgmt tools, file & directory svcs, storage,
messaging, databases, IP telephony, desktop support.
(Woman, estab 2002, empl 10, sales $850,000, cert: State)

5499 Terralogic Integrated Systems Analysts, Inc.
      2001 N Beauregard St Ste 600
      Alexandria, VA 22311
      Contact: Tony Swetich Business Devel Mgr
      Tel: 313-416-1741
      Email: tony.s@terralogic.com
      Website: www.terralogic.com
Computer Systems Services, Project Management, Process
Engineering, Site Planning, Safety Engineering, PC Deploy-
ments, Hardware/Software Upgrades, Deskside Support,
Help desk, Asset Management, Hardware Maintenance.
(As-Ind, estab 1980, empl 1000, sales $11,000,000, cert:
NMSDC)

5500 The Mt. Olivet Group, LLC
      PO Box 56415
      Virginia Beach, VA 23456
      Contact: Jon McGlothian President
      Tel: 757-271-8681
      Email: jon@tmogllc.com
      Website: www.mtolivetgroup.com
The Mt Olivet Group, LLC (TMOG) is set up as a Project
Management Office. As such we provide power, lighting,
security and data products. We provide training and
development services as well as execute (AA, estab 2007,
empl 2, sales , cert: State)

5501 Total System Services US, Inc.
      1900 Campus Commons Dr #100
      Reston, VA 20191
      Contact: Aniths Paalepu
      Tel: 703-732-6063
      Email: anithapaalepu@tsysus.com
      Website: www.tsysus.com
IT consulting solutions, distributed operating & computing
systems, storage, networking, systems knowledge. (Minority, Woman, estab 2012, empl 3, sales , cert: NMSDC)

5502 Unicom Government, Inc.
      2553 Dulles View Dr Ste 100
      Herndon, VA 20171
      Contact: Margaret Dooley Systems Integrator
      Tel: 703-502-2937
      Email: maggie.dooley@unicomgov.com
      Website: www.unicomgov.com
Integration, Logistics, Warehouse Warehousing, Cloud
Computing, IT Products Computers, laptops Desktops
Servers Switches Cables Software, Supply Chain
Outsourcing, procurement, Financial Services Leasing.
(As-Pac, estab 1986, empl 199, sales $193,000,000, cert:
NMSDC)

5503 USM Business Systems, Inc.
      14175 Sullyfield Circle Ste 400
      Chantilly, VA 20151
      Contact: USM Business Systems SVP Business Dev
      Tel: 832-881-7903
      Email: joshuar@usmsystems.com
      Website: www.usmsystems.com
Staffing & implementation solutions, computer software
programming, application dev, web dev, data warehouse
dev & ERP implementations. (As-Ind, estab 1999, empl
400, sales $45,000,000, cert: State)

5504 Weiatech, LLC
      22584 Hammersmith Pl
      Ashburn, VA 20148
      Contact: Akomala Akouete Operation Dir
      Tel: 703-665-9603
      Email: aakouete@weiatech.com
      Website: www.weiatech.com
Information technology equipment, solutions, and
services. (AA, estab 2016, empl 5, sales , cert: State)

5505 Worldgate, LLC
      1760 Reston Pkwy Ste 312
      Reston, VA 20190
      Contact: Katelyn Montgomery Dir Client Services
      Tel: 703-349-0493
      Email: kmontgomery@worldgatellc.com
      Website: www.worldgatellc.com
IT systems integration consulting, technology platforms,
operating systems & infrastructures, data warehouse,
business intelligence, ERP, project managment, call
center/service desk. (Woman, estab 2002, empl 20, sales
$1,200,000, cert: State, WBENC)

5506 Zeva Inc
      10300 Eaton Place Ste 305
      Fairfax, VA 22030
      Contact: Sam I Shihadeh Dir Diversity & Inclusion
      Tel: 301-518-3705
      Email: sshihadeh@zeva.us
      Website: www.zevainc.com
Cloud Services, Public Key Ennoblement (PKE), Identity,
Credentialing and Access Management. (Woman, estab
2005, empl 55, sales $10,000,000, cert: WBENC)

5507 Zillion Technologies, Inc.
20745 Williamsport Pl Ste 150
Ashburn, VA 20147
Contact: Kimberlee Sours Business Devel Mgr
Tel: 703-592-6949
Email: kimberlee@zilliontechnologies.com
Website: www.zilliontechnologies.com
Business consulting & technology solutions, strategic outsourcing & application management. (As-Ind, estab 2002, empl 350, sales $38,000,000, cert: NMSDC, SDB)

5508 Zirtex Systems Corporation
7371 Atlas Walk Way, Ste 152
Gainesville, VA 20155
Contact: Rajeev Jessani President
Tel: 800-536-4982
Email: rjessani@zirtexsystems.com
Website: www.zirtexsystems.com
Management consulting & technology services. (As-Ind, estab 2006, empl 2, sales $328,832, cert: NMSDC)

5509 Zolon Tech Solutions, Inc.
13921 Park Center Rd, Ste 500
Herndon, VA 20171
Contact: Goutham Amarneni President
Tel: 703-636-7370
Email: supplier.diversity@zolon.com
Website: www.zolontech.com
Information technology consulting services: integration, modification, unification, secure & customized, applications & enterprise software solutions. (Minority, estab 1998, empl , sales $66,000,000, cert: NMSDC)

Vermont

5510 iTech US, Inc.
20 Kimball Ave, Ste 303N
South Burlington, VT 05403
Contact: Kishore Khandavalli CEO
Tel: 802-383-1500
Email: kk@itechus.com
Website: www.itechus.com
Software consulting services, application development, business process outsourcing solutions & offshore project development. (As-Pac, estab 2001, empl 1150, sales $53,000,000, cert: NMSDC)

Washington

5511 Amreli Technology Solutions, LLC
17530 NE Union Hill Rd, Ste 290
Redmond, WA 98052
Contact: Atul Hirpara CEO
Tel: 425-881-6971
Email: atul@amrelitech.com
Website: www.amrelitech.com
IT intelligence, dashboards & scorecards, software, integration of disparate systems & applications. (As-Pac, estab 2004, empl 32, sales $3,400,000, cert: State, NMSDC)

5512 Axelerate
13401 Bel Red Rd, Ste B8
Bellevue, WA 98005
Contact: Sr Client Services Mgr
Tel: 425-429-6720
Email: info@axelerate.com
Website: www.axelerate.com
IT consulting & staffing. (Woman, estab 2003, empl 5, sales , cert: WBENC)

5513 BiSoft Consultancy Services
16310 NE 80th St, Ste 104
Redmond, WA 98052
Contact: Balaji Udayshankar CEO
Tel: 401-450-1672
Email: bala@bisoftllc.com
Website: www.bisoftllc.com
Information technology svcs, website design, wed development & maintenance, SEO optimization, application software. (As-Ind, estab 2015, empl 1, sales $2,000,000, cert: NMSDC)

5514 Chameleon Technologies, Inc.
520 Kirkland Way Ste 101
Kirkland, WA 98033
Contact: Principal
Tel: 425-827-1173
Email: sales@chameleontechinc.com
Website: www.chameleontechinc.com
Technical staffing: software testers, software developers, network engineers & admins, database admins & developers, project mgrs, business & systems analysts, technical writers, etc. (Minority, Woman, estab 2000, empl 30, sales $722,000, cert: WBENC)

5515 Eastside Groups LLC
P.O.Box 165
Mercer Island, WA 98040
Contact: Jessie Wang Owner
Tel: 206-466-6649
Email: main@catandena.com
Website: www.catandena.com
Software solutions, financial applications, web sites & web services, from stand-alone scale to enterprise scale. (Minority, Woman, estab 2014, empl 1, sales , cert: State)

5516 ELYON International Inc.
1111 Main St, Ste 405
Vancouver, WA 98660
Contact: Carmen Nazario President
Tel: 360-696-5892
Email: carmen@elyoninternational.com
Website: www.elyoninternational.com
Consulting & technology svcs: software devel, systems integration, offshore solutions delivery, etc. (Minority, Woman, estab 1997, empl 148, sales $23,000,000, cert: State, NMSDC, WBENC)

5517 General Microsystems Inc.
3220 118th Ave SE
Bellevue, WA 98005
Contact: Earl Overstreet President
Tel: 425-644-2233
Email: earl@gmi.com
Website: www.gmi.com
Information technology: systems, storage management solutions. (AA, estab 1983, empl 13, sales $32,330,000, cert: State, NMSDC)

5518 Hansell Tierney, Inc.
2955 80th AVE SE #103
Mercer Island, WA 98040
Contact: Acct Mgr
Tel: 206-232-3080
Email: info@hanselltierney.com
Website: www.hanselltierney.com
IT consulting services & recruiting. (Woman, estab 2001, empl 35, sales $2,800,000, cert: State)

5519 i9 Systems, Inc.
16928 NE 38th Place
Bellevue, WA 98008
Contact: Sukhjot Basi CEO
Tel: 206-412-7918
Email: basi@i9systems.com
Website: www.i9systems.com
Staffig, consulting, software development & testing, program/project management, database & network administrations, business requirements, full software development life cycle. (Woman/As-Ind, estab 1999, empl 16, sales $500,000, cert: State)

5520 Idea Entity Corporation
16625 Redmond Way Ste M 009
Redmond, WA 98052
Contact: John Strathy CFO
Tel: 425-454-2905
Email: john.strathy@ideaentity.com
Website: www.ideaentity.com
Project, staff, development, testing, onsite, offsite, offshore, application developmen, custom application development & packaged solution integration. (As-Ind, estab 2006, empl 45, sales , cert: State, NMSDC)

5521 InConsulting Inc.
12901 181st Ave NE
Redmond, WA 98052
Contact: Aparna Mahadevan CEO
Tel: 425-880-5996
Email: services@inconsultinginc.com
Website: www.inconsultinginc.com
Information staffing & placement, IT services, Consulting, Systems planning, Web Design & development. (Woman/As-Ind, estab 2010, empl 40, sales , cert: State)

5522 Kaasm, LLC
900 1st Ave S, Ste 302
Seattle, WA 98134
Contact: Shawn Sandoval President
Tel: 206-735-3882
Email: shawns@kaasm.com
Website: www.kaasm.com
SCADA software, Industrial computers, networking components, alarm notification software & Enterprise Asset Management. (Hisp, estab 2013, empl 3, sales $150,000, cert: City, NMSDC)

5523 Kathcart Open Systems & Consulting, Inc.
17311 135th Ave NE, Ste B500
Woodinville, WA 98072
Contact: CEO
Tel: 425-402-0258
Email: info@dimension-systems.com
Website: www.dimension-systems.com
Information technology consulting services. (Woman, estab 1993, empl 20, sales $42,000,000, cert: WBENC)

5524 Martirx Infotech LLC
1017 4th Ave E Ste 6
Olympia, WA 98506
Contact: Narasimha Varakantham CEO
Tel: 360-545-4089
Email: reddy@matrixinf.com
Website: www.matrixinf.com
Information technology services, contingent workforce staffing solutions, technology support, consulting & development, software to hardware. (Woman/As-Ind, estab 2014, empl 3, sales $105,253, cert: State)

5525 New Era Contract Sales Inc.
5838 S Adams St
Tacoma, WA 98409
Contact: Brenda Valentine President
Tel: 253-272-3553
Email: brenda@newerasalesteam.com
Website: www.newerasalesteam.com
Customized purchasing software. (Woman, estab 1988, empl 9, sales $15,200,000, cert: WBENC)

5526 Nvelup Consulting
19125 North Creek Pkwy Ste 120
Bothell, WA 98011
Contact: Chris Barrios CEO
Tel: 206-419-2584
Email: chris@nvelupconsulting.com
Website: www.nvelupconsulting.com
Performance Management (Budgeting, Planning & Forecasting) & Business Intelligence (Data Analysis & Reporting) solutions. (Minority, estab 2014, empl 15, sales $936,000, cert: State, NMSDC, SDB)

5527 Online Training Solutions, Inc.
PO Box 951
Bellevue, WA 98009
Contact: Joan Preppernau President
Tel: 888-308-6874
Email: biz@otsi.com
Website: www.otsi.com
Publishing & programming services. (Woman, estab 1987, empl 13, sales $1,120,873, cert: WBENC)

5528 P2 Solutions Group LLC
2296 W Commodore Way, Ste 300
Seattle, WA 98199
Contact: Tonjia Borland
Tel: 206-226-8433
Email: tborland@p2solutionsgroup.com
Website: www.p2solutionsgroup.com
Technical, system administrator, programming, developer, engineering, finance, marketing & project management staff. (Hisp, estab 2002, empl 120, sales $10,600,000, cert: City, NMSDC)

5529 PeopleTech Group
15809 Bear Creek Pkwy Ste 410
Redmond, WA 09082
Contact: Exec VP
Tel: 425-444-6174
Email:
Website: www.peopletech.com
ERP Services, Oracle, PeopleSoft, SAP, Microsoft Dynamics, Implementation, Upgrade, Application Development, Testing & Consulting, Big Data, DWH & BI, OBIEE, BO, Micro Strategy, Microsoft. (Minority, Woman, estab 2006, empl 1200, sales $22,000,000, cert: NMSDC)

5530 Prowess Consulting, LLC
5701 Sixth Ave S Ste 374
Seattle, WA 98108
Contact: Aaron Suzuki CEO
Tel: 206-443-1117
Email: info@prowesscorp.com
Website: www.prowesscorp.com
Content program management, technical content development & editing, training content development, IT & content systems management & digital marketing services. (As-Pac, estab 2003, empl 80, sales $11,800,000, cert: State, NMSDC)

5531   S3Global Consulting Services, LLC
       10532 82nd Ave Court SW
       Lakewood, WA 98498
       Contact: Morris Sterling III, MBA CEO
       Tel: 877-470-1900
       Email: morris.sterling@s3goglobal.com
       Website: www.s3goglobal.com
Information technology & business-based enterprises,
project, program & product management, technical
writing & communications, continuous process improvement, business analysis & intelligence. (Woman/AA, estab
2012, empl 5, sales , cert: State, City)

5532   ScrumPoint
       1110 112th Ave Northeast Ste 350
       Bellevue, WA 98052
       Contact: Michael Mpare President
       Tel: 509-714-4842
       Email: michael@scrumpoint.com
       Website: www.scrumpoint.com
Custom software applications, SSIS & SSRS management,
SharePoint portals, custom web applications, Windows
Azure Cloud Services. (AA, estab 2011, empl 6, sales , cert:
NMSDC)

5533   Tam Partners Consulting, LLC
       18350 204th Ave NE
       Woodinville, WA 98077
       Contact: Lisa Tam Founder
       Tel: 425-998-8401
       Email: lisatam@tpartnerscg.com
       Website: www.tpartnerscg.com
Engineering: Power BI, Excel Power Pivot, ETL, SSIS, SSAS,
T-SQL, Data Marts, Data Warehouse, SQL Server Manage-
ment Studio, Business Intelligence Development StudioBig
Data Analytics: JSon, HiveQL, Microsoft Azure HDInsight |
Cloud Hadoop, Azure Managem (Woman, estab 2016,
empl 1, sales $114,784, cert: WBENC)

5534   TripleNet Technologies, Inc.
       1122 E Pike St, Ste 509
       Seattle, WA 98122
       Contact: Hans Gomez President
       Tel: 206-260-8998
       Email: hansgomez@triplenettech.com
       Website: www.triplenettech.com
IT staffing, network architecture & design, software
development, wireless network design & implementation,
data storage plan, disaster recovery. (Hisp, estab 1997,
empl 18, sales $500,000, cert: State, City, NMSDC)

5535   TSS Redmond
       8461 154th Ave NE, Bldg G
       Redmond, WA 98052
       Contact: Lisa Roeder CEO
       Tel: 425-749-3030
       Email: lroeder@tssredmond.com
       Website: www.tssredmond.com
Software, computer, technical development, soft skills,
project management, business development & leadership
training. (Woman, estab 2000, empl 20, sales $700,000,
cert: State)

5536   Zones, LLC
       1102 15th St SW Ste 102
       Auburn, WA 98001
       Contact: Bruce Heather Field Acct Mgr
       Tel: 253-205-3227
       Email: bruce.heather@zones.com
       Website: www.zones.com
Information technology products & services, resell
computer hardware & software. (As-Ind, estab 1986,
empl 2744, sales $2,900,000,000, cert: State, NMSDC)

Wisconsin

5537   Abaxent LLC
       N28 W23050 Roundy Dr. Ste 200
       Pewaukee, WI 53072
       Contact: Adonica Randall President
       Tel: 414-587-2950
       Email: arandall@abaxent.com
       Website: www.abaxent-global.com
Information technology services, project management,
software development, network engineering & consult-
ing/design. (Woman/AA, estab 2002, empl 10, sales ,
cert: State, NMSDC, WBENC)

5538   Comcentia, LLC
       1025 W Glen Oaks Lane Ste 211
       Mequon, WI 53092
       Contact: Darrell Caldwell President
       Tel: 414-871-1100
       Email: info@comcentia.com
       Website: www.comcentia.com
IT Consulting, Custom Applications & Database Development, Custom web based or windows desktop application development, Application Management of Existing
Systems, Ongoing & and ad hoc changes. (AA, estab
2006, empl 6, sales $612,112, cert: NMSDC, 8(a))

5539   CTL Resources (Caribou Thunder)
       8558 N County Rd K
       Hayward, WI 54843
       Contact: Rita Peterson Owner
       Tel: 719-412-3754
       Email: rita@ctlresources.com
       Website: www.ctlresources.com
Project Management,   Process Re-engineering,
Process Change, Enterprise application integration,
Engineering. (Minority, Woman, estab , empl , sales
$10,000,000, cert: NMSDC)

5540   Excel Global Solutions Inc.
       2727 N Grandview Blvd Ste 117
       Waukesha, WI 53188
       Contact: Jerry Sorci VP
       Tel: 262-347-4911
       Email: jerry.sorci@excelglobalsolution.com
       Website: www.excelglobalsolution.com
IT services, solutions & products, Big Data Predictive
intelligence Product, Automated Application Testing
Product, Vehicle Maintenance Management Product.
(Minority, Woman, estab 2010, empl 250, sales , cert:
State)

5541 Genome International Corporation
8000 Excelsior Dr Ste 202
Madison, WI 53717
Contact: Sue Seshadri HR Mgr
Tel: 608-833-5855
Email: sue@genome.com
Website: www.genome.com
IT staffing, technical consulting, enterprise application developement. (Minority, Woman, estab 1992, empl 120, sales $9,100,000, cert: WBENC)

5542 Malleswari Inc.
11512 N Port Washington Rd, Ste 101-I
Mequon, WI 53092
Contact: Trinadha Pattem
Tel: 262-308-3480
Email: trinadha@malleswari.com
Website: www.malleswari.com
End to End SAP ERP/SRM/BI/Mobile Technology Solutions. (Woman/As-Ind, estab 2004, empl 5, sales $2,350,227, cert: State, City, NMSDC)

5543 Valicom Corp
2923 Marketplace Dr Ste 104
Fitchburg, WI 53719
Contact: Marketing
Tel: 800-467-7226
Email: sales@valicomcorp.com
Website: www.valicomcorp.com
IT & telecom invoice audit & management: RFP facilitation, contract negotiation & management, network design & engineering, help desk, invoice payment & general ledger coding. (Woman, estab 1991, empl 20, sales , cert: State, WBENC)

5544 Vanguard Computers, Inc.
13100 W Lisbon Rd, Ste 100
Brookfield, WI 53005
Contact: Owner
Tel: 262-317-1900
Email: sales@vanguardinc.com
Website: www.vanguardinc.com
Dist, svc & rent computer equipment & peripherals; network configuration, installation & maintenance. (Minority, Woman, estab 1982, empl 39, sales , cert: WBENC)

5545 Wissen Infotech Inc
2325 Parklawn Dr Ste G
Waukesha, WI 53186
Contact: Upendra Rachupaly Operations Mgr
Tel: 262-510-2900
Email: upendra.rachupally@wisseninfotech.com
Website: www.wisseninfotech.com
IT services, onsite, offsite & offshore service, End to end Mobility application, development, Analytics, Cloud Management, Media & Entertainment, Embedded Systems, Big data & Hadoop. Enterprise Resource Planning, Remote Infrastructure Management (As-Ind, estab 2001, empl 800, sales $12,000,000, cert: State)

5546 Fusion Plus Solutions Inc.
17 Cherokee Dr
Moundsville, WV 26041
Contact: Mark Thomas Dir
Tel: 732-250-9048
Email: mark@fusionplusinc.com
Website: www.fusionplusinc.com
IT Staff Augmentation, Information Technology Solutions, Consulting/Staffing Services, System Integration, Software Products. (Minority, Woman, estab 2009, empl 1000, sales , cert: State)

INFORMATION TECHNOLOGY: Supplies
Manufacture or distribute magnetic media supplies such as , disketts, paper, printers, fascimilies, toner cartridges, keyboards, computer peripherials. NAICS Code 42

Arizona

5547   Centacor, Inc.
135 Chilton Dr
Chandler, AZ 85225
Contact: Troy Bryan Mgr
Tel: 480-899-9500
Email: info@centacor.com
Website: www.centacor.com
IT products & services. (AA, estab 2009, empl 4, sales , cert: NMSDC)

5548   Cybergear, Inc.
4711 E Falcon Dr Ste 202
Mesa, AZ 85215
Contact: President
Tel: 480-926-6470
Email: sales@cybergearUSA.com
Website: www.cybergearusa.com
Dist computer hardware, consumer electronics, electronic test & measurement, computer software & software licensing, POS/bar code equipment, wireless voice/data products & services. (Woman, estab 1998, empl 2, sales , cert: City, WBENC)

5549   ESI Ergonomic Solutions, LLC
4030 E Quenton Dr Ste 101
Mesa, AZ 85215
Contact: Carol Keogh CEO
Tel: 480-517-1871
Email: ckeogh@esiergo.com
Website: www.esiergo.com
Mfr & dist articulating arms, keyboard platforms, flat screen monitor arms & ergonomic accessories. (Woman, estab 1988, empl 25, sales $15,000,000, cert: NWBOC)

5550   Herco Technology div. of Hernandez Companies
3734 E Anne St
Phoenix, AZ 85040
Contact: Mike Pena Acct Exec
Tel: 602-438-7825
Email: info@hernandezcompanies.com
Website: www.hernandezcompanies.com/
Dist computer & networking cable & cable accessories: fiber optic cables, coaxial, custom assemblies, racks, shelving, wire mgmt, Cat5E patch cables. (Minority, Woman, estab 1975, empl 75, sales , cert: NMSDC)

5551   Swift Office Solutions
2429 W 12th St Ste#6
Tempe, AZ 85281
Contact: Edward Swift President
Tel: 480-966-2100
Email: eswift@sosnet.com
Website: www.sosnet.com
Dist computers, hardware, software, and office products. (Minority, estab 1981, empl 9, sales $5,000,000, cert: NMSDC)

California

5552   Alliant Event Services
196 University Pkwy
Pomona, CA 91768
Contact: Heather Milianak Sr Sales Mgr
Tel: 909-354-4469
Email: hmilanak@asn-corp.com
Website: www.AlliantEvents.com
Rental technology & event production solutions: laptop & desktop computers, printers, copiers, audio-visual, sound & lighting products. (As-Ind, estab 2003, empl 38, sales $4,150,000, cert: State)

5553   CDCE Inc.
22755-G Savi Ranch Pkwy
Yorba Linda, CA 92887
Contact: Kim Hufford Natl Acct Mgr
Tel: 714-282-8881
Email: khufford@cdce.com
Website: www.cdce.com
Wireless, computer vehicle installations, ruggedized notebooks & tablets. (Woman, estab 1984, empl 25, sales , cert: CPUC, WBENC)

5554   ComputerSuppliers.Com
7377 Convoy Court, Ste A
San Diego, CA 92111
Contact: Jay Satpute Bids Specialist
Tel: 858-268-7370
Email: bids@computersupplies.com
Website: www.computersupplies.com
Dist inks, toners, monitor filters, furniture, pens, printers, ribbons, and storage media such as DVD, CD, LTO, SDX, AIT, 4mm & 8mm cartridges. (Woman/As-Ind, estab 2002, empl 7, sales $6,000,000, cert: City)

5555   Conversions Technology
1740 Emerson Ave
Oxnard, CA 93033
Contact: Kevin Williams VP Sales
Tel: 800-596-2037
Email: kevin@conversionstechnology.com
Website: www.ConversionsTechnology.com
Mfr & dist cable accessory & PC peripheral components. (Minority, Woman, estab 2006, empl 25, sales $1,000,000, cert: CPUC)

5556   GC Micro Corporation
3910 Cypress Dr
Petaluma, CA 94954
Contact: Ashley Kidd Acct Mgr
Tel: 800-426-4276
Email: bg@gcmicro.com
Website: www.gcmicro.com
Dist personal computers, microcomputer hardware, software, peripherals, IBM, HP, AST, Epson authorized dealer. (Minority, Woman, estab 1986, empl 35, sales , cert: State, NMSDC, CPUC, WBENC)

5557   Gear One Enterprise
34450 Calle Sereno
Temecula, CA 92592
Contact: Brad Barnes Sr Acct Mgr
Tel: 949-276-7924
Email: brad@gearonecom.com
Website: www.gearonecom.com
Network peripherals & connectivity products: optical transceivers, network memory, media converters & cable solutions. (Woman, estab 2012, empl 6, sales $1,511,024, cert: WBENC)

5558 Kambrian Corporation
2707 E Valley Blvd
West Covina, CA 91792
Contact: Cathy Hsieh CEO
Tel: 626-374-3933
Email: cathyh@kambrian.com
Website: www.kambrian.com
Resell IT products: software, hardware & services. (Minority, Woman, estab 2009, empl 7, sales $10,469,102, cert: NMSDC, WBENC, 8(a))

5559 MelroseMAC, Inc.
6614 Melrose Ave
Hollywood, CA 90038
Contact: Jonathan Strayhorn CEO
Tel: 323-937-4600
Email: jon@mac330.com
Website: www.melrosemac.com
Resell Apple products. (Woman, estab 2003, empl 80, sales $55,000,000, cert: CPUC, WBENC)

5560 Mobile ID Solutions, Inc.
1574 N Batavia St, Ste 1
Orange, CA 92867
Contact: Rick Fahilga Acct Exec
Tel: 714-922-1134
Email: rfahilga@mobileidsolutions.com
Website: www.mobileidsolutions.com
Mobile Computers, printers. Barcode Printers, Scanners, verifiers. ID Card Printers and supplies. IP Cameras. Cellular Routers, modem, POS Equipment, Satellite phones. (As-Pac, estab 2004, empl 9, sales $4,800,000, cert: NMSDC)

5561 On-Site LaserMedic Corp.
21540 Prairie St, Unit D
Chatsworth, CA 91311
Contact: Gail Solomon CEO
Tel: 818-772-6911
Email: sd@onsitelasermedic.com
Website: www.onsitelasermedic.com
Laser printer, fax & deskjet service & repair, dist toner. (Woman, estab 1992, empl 46, sales $5,318,472, cert: WBENC)

5562 Performance Designed Products
14144 Ventura Blvd Stė 200
Sherman Oaks, CA 91423
Contact: Theresa Harrell Natl Acct Mgr
Tel: 479-445-8612
Email: theresa.harrell@pdp.com
Website: www.pdp.com
Design & mfr video game peripherals & accessories: PS2, PS3, PSP PS Vita, Xbox, Xbox 360, Wii, Wii U, 3DS, DS Lite. (Woman, estab 1990, empl 200, sales , cert: WBENC)

5563 PNH Technology, Inc.
15375 Barranca Pkwy Ste F-108
Irvine, CA 92618
Contact: Thacher Grauer Office Mgr
Tel: 949-614-4102
Email: thacher@pnhtech.com
Website: www.pnhtech.com
Dist servers, rack, tower, blades, memory, hard drives, server accessories, storage (SAN, NAS, DAS), storage accessories. networking switches, routers, firewalls, network accessories, desktops, PCs & laptops. (As-Pac, estab 2008, empl 6, sales $3,000,000, cert: State)

5564 RC & JT Inc. dba Computer Masters
6185 Cornerstone Court Ste 103
San Diego, CA 92121
Contact: Jessie Thorell Acct Mgr
Tel: 858-444-2966
Email: jthorell@computermastersinc.com
Website: www.computermastersinc.com
Dist computer hardware, software, printers, supplies & networking products & services. (Minority, Woman, estab 1990, empl 4, sales , cert: State)

5565 Saitech Inc.
42640 Christy St
Fremont, CA 94538
Contact: Ernesto Juarez Business Devel
Tel: 510-440-0256
Email: ernesto@esaitech.com
Website: www.saitechincorporated.com/
Dist telecom, network & computer components & equipment. (Minority, estab 2002, empl 18, sales $18,721,958, cert: NMSDC, CPUC)

5566 Source Graphics
1530 N. Harmony Circle
Anaheim, CA 92807
Contact: Sy Hussaini Sr Acct Mgr
Tel: 714-701-1500
Email: sy.h@sourcegraphics.com
Website: www.sourcegraphics.com
Dist & svc plotter scanners, printers & digitizers. (As-Pac, estab 1989, empl 10, sales , cert: CPUC)

5567 Southland Technology Inc.
8053 Vickers St
San Diego, CA 92111
Contact: Jack Lowrey Acct Exec
Tel: 858-634-4136
Email: jlowrey@southlandtechnology.com
Website: www.southlandtechnology.com
Computer, computer hardware, software, cables, peripherals, IT, information technology, audio, video, A/V, sound systems, servers, storage, virtualization, fiber cables, workstations, notebooks, voip, projectors, monitors. (Minority, Woman, estab 2001, empl 43, sales $45,000,000, cert: CPUC)

5568 Varitek, Inc.
1100 E. Orangethorpe Ave Ste 195
Anaheim, CA 92801
Contact: Moe Moalemi VP
Tel: 714-224-0361
Email: moalemi@varitekinc.com
Website: www.varitekinc.com
Dist & service network solutions, computers, printers, barcode printers, plotters, point of sale, copiers, faxes, office equipment consumables. (Minority, Woman, estab 1982, empl 12, sales $1,030,000, cert: State)

5569 ViewSonic Corporation
381 Brea Canyon Rd
Walnut, CA 91789
Contact: Julie Yao Legal Assistant
Tel: 909-444-8613
Email: legal@viewsonic.com
Website: www.viewsonic.com
Dist visual display technology products: liquid crystal displays, LCD, monitors, cathode ray tube, CRT, monitors, projectors, LCD TVs, plasma displays, tablet personal computers & PCs, wireless monitors. (As-Pac, estab 1987, empl 700, sales $1,093,000,000, cert: NMSDC)

5570 Vision Specialties, Inc.
10330 Regis Ct
Rancho Cucamonga, CA 91730
Contact: Donn DeMarzio VP
Tel: 800-499-8176
Email: donn.demarzio@visionspecialties.com
Website: www.visionspecialties.com
Mfr & dist Category Cable, HDMI Cable, Audio/Video Cable, Batteries, Injection Molding products & services. (Woman, estab 1995, empl 14, sales $6,000,000, cert: CPUC)

5571 Zetta Pros - Total IT Solutions
2201 E Willow St, Ste D232
Signal Hill, CA 90755
Contact: Sarom Hong CEO
Tel: 562-252-3673
Email: sarom.hong@zettapros.com
Website: www.zettapros.com
Computers, hardware, software, printers, computer peripherals, cables. (Minority, Woman, estab 2005, empl 4, sales $600,000, cert: NMSDC, CPUC, 8(a))

Colorado

5572 Image Projections West, Inc.
14135 E 42nd Ave Ste 40
Denver, CO 80239
Contact: Kedar Morarka CEO
Tel: 888-576-9477
Email: josephf@ipwusa.com
Website: www.ipwusa.com
Mfr advance technology toner cartridges. (Woman/As-Ind, estab 1996, empl 172, sales $31,200,000, cert: NMSDC, WBENC)

5573 SK&T Integration Inc.
10495 S. PROGRESS WAY
Parker, CO 80112
Contact: Kathy Lawson President
Tel: 720-851-9108
Email: info@skandt.com
Website: www.skandt.com
Dist stock & custom labels, ribbons, bar code & specialty printers, asset tracking & inventory management systems, bar coding software, scanners, mobile computers & wireless switches. (Woman, estab , empl , sales $3,200,000, cert: WBENC)

5574 Systec101
1027 Fenwick Dr
Fort Collins, CO 80524
Contact: Murat Yildirim Owner
Tel: 970-646-2706
Email: murat.yildirim@systec101.com
Website: www.systec101.com
Dist networking equipment, manufacture & resell, cat5e, cat6, cat6a cables & accessories. (Minority, estab 2012, empl 3, sales $277,000, cert: State)

Connecticut

5575 Hartford Toner & Cartridge
6 Wapping Rd
Broad Brook, CT 06016
Contact: Timothy Golubeff Sr Sales
Tel: 860-292-1280
Email: tgolubeff@hartfordtoner.com
Website: www.hartfordtoner.con
Hp authorized service center, repair laser printers & supplies. (Woman, estab 1998, empl 9, sales $1,000,100, cert: State)

District of Columbia

5576 Borrowed Time Enterprises, Inc.
4460 Alabama Ave, SE
Washington, DC 20019
Contact: Vanessa Brooks CEO
Tel: 202-581-0406
Email: borrowedte@rcn.com
Website: www.btenterprise.us
Dist computers, parts, software & hardware, office supplies, digital signage & content management software installation & services. (Woman/AA, estab 1999, empl 1, sales $127,000, cert: State, City)

5577 Mall Lobby.com, Inc.
1775 Eye St, NW Ste 1150
Washington, DC 20006
Contact: Lang Maith CEO
Tel: 301-807-2422
Email: lang.maith@malllobby.com
Website: www.malllobby.com
Dist computers, software, network equipment, office products, electronics, cellular phones, pagers, merchant accounts, microfilm/microfiche, CD/DVD production, etc. (AA, estab 1995, empl 15, sales $500,000, cert: State)

Delaware

5578 Laser Tone, Inc.
24 S W Front St
Milford, DE 19963
Contact: Debra Cromer President
Tel: 302-422-2323
Email: emailus@laser-tone.net
Website: www.lasertoneinc.com
Laser printer service, repairs, preventive maintenance & supplies, toner supplies. (Woman, estab 1989, empl 13, sales , cert: State)

Florida

5579 BIT DIRECT
2202 N Westshore Blvd, Ste 200
Tampa, FL 33607
Contact: Duane Turner Sr VP& GM
Tel: 813-343-0879
Email:
Website: www.bitdirect.com
Dist audio & headsets, digital cameras, LCD & plasma TV's & projectors, handheld computers, removable media, optical dives, keyboards & mice, software & licenses, flash drives, cables, hard drives, media tapes, computer furniture. (Woman, estab 2002, empl 11, sales $700,000,000, cert: City, WBENC)

5580   Card Quest, Inc.
6630 Rowan Rd
New Port Richey, FL 34655
Contact: Shannon Capshaw President
Tel: 727-816-8401
Email: sales@cardquest.com
Website: www.cardquest.com
Dist proximity cards, readers, photo ID printers, ribbons, accessories, cards. (Woman, estab 2001, empl 4, sales $750,000, cert: State)

5581   Innovative Software Solution
3762 NW 124th Ave
Coral Springs, FL 33065
Contact: Kareline Duverge Office Mgr
Tel: 954-800-7552
Email: kduverge@isoftwaresolution.com
Website: www.isoftwaresolution.com
Mfr ink & toner cartridges. Authorized distributors of HP, Lexmark & Ricoh products & supplies, general office supplies, toner & ink cartridges. (Woman/AA, estab 2012, empl 15, sales $1,590,000, cert: State, NMSDC)

5582   Keiki Enterprises LLC
200 Crandon Blvd Ste 327
Key Biscayne, FL 33149
Contact: Karina Diaz VP
Tel: 305-361-0623
Email: karina@dsignage.net
Website: www.dsignage.net
We are system integrator specialized in providing reliable digital signage with dynamic and/or interactive solutions for the health care industry by representing the best software and hardware manufacturers in the digital signage (Minority, Woman, estab , empl , sales $441,317, cert: City)

5583   LRE Inc. dba Lee Ryder Lamination
6187 NW 167th St Unit H-10
Miami, FL 33015
Contact: Lee Ryder President
Tel: 305-893-2762
Email: office@leeryder.com
Website: www.leeryder.com
Computerized photo id systems & supplies: Hid Global, Edisecure, Magicard, Eltron, Fargo, Nisca, Zebra, Evolis, Datacard. retractable id badge reels, laminator, pouch laminator, roll laminator, laminating pouches. (Woman, estab 1980, empl 2, sales $350,000, cert: State, City)

5584   R&D Systems Group, Inc.
19140 SW 24th St
Miramar, FL 33029
Contact: patricia Garcia Acct Exec
Tel: 305-528-9402
Email: pgarcia@rdsgi.com
Website: www.rdsgi.com
Resell IBM software & hardware. (Minority, Woman, estab 2004, empl 6, sales $400,000, cert: NMSDC)

5585   Solares Electrical Services, Inc.
10421 NW 28th St Ste D105
Miami, FL 33172
Contact: A. Solares President
Tel: 305-717-6184
Email: asolares@solareselectrical.com
Website: www.solareselectrical.com
Communication, Lightning Protection, Utilites. Experience in Toll Collection Equipment, wiring and testing. (Hisp, estab 1997, empl 40, sales $3,500,000, cert: State)

5586   Telecom Resources of America, Inc.
205 Goolsby Blvd
Deerfield Beach, FL 33442
Contact: Toni Mastrullo President
Tel: 954-427-1104
Email: toni@telrecusa.com
Website: www.telrecusa.com
Dist data switch & networking products, space parts & peripherals. (Woman, estab 2000, empl 3, sales , cert: WBENC)

5587   Touchpoint Inc.
7200 Lake Ellenor Dr, Ste 101
Orlando, FL 32809
Contact: Jim Soloway Sr Acct Mgr
Tel: 407-977-0507
Email: jsoloway@touchpoint-inc.com
Website: www.touchpoint-inc.com
Dist computer equipment, supplies, PC's, laptops, servers, storage, security, etc. (Woman, estab 1999, empl 18, sales , cert: WBENC)

Georgia

5588   Eastern Data, Inc.
4386 Park Dr
Norcross, GA 30093
Contact: JoAnn Pfeiffer Natl Accounts Mgr
Tel: 770-279-8888
Email: jo.pfeiffer@ediatlanta.com
Website: www.ediatlanta.com
Dist computer systems, components & peripherals. (Minority, Woman, estab 1997, empl 27, sales $20,906,578, cert: NMSDC, WBENC)

5589   Worldwide Audio Visual Services Inc
5040 Bakers Ferry Rd SW
Atlanta, GA 30336
Contact: Bradford McWhorter CEO
Tel: 404-745-9842
Email: brad@atlanta-audiovisual.com
Website: www.atlantaav.com
Audio visual equipment, audio reinforcement, video production, lighting design & corporate set design. (AA, estab 2005, empl 8, sales $374,970, cert: NMSDC)

5590   XentIT, LLC
5425 Peachtree Pkwy
Norcross, GA 30092
Contact: Tariq Alvi President
Tel: 678-906-4046
Email: talvi@xentit.com
Website: www.xentit.com
Value Added Reseller, System Integrator & Cloud Managed Service provider. (As-Ind, estab 2006, empl 7, sales $2,247,000, cert: NMSDC)

Illinois

5591   Flexaco, Inc.
936 W Lake St
Roselle, IL 60172
Contact: Donna Fiedler President
Tel: 630-529-4510
Email: Donnafiedler@flexaco.com
Website: www.flexaco.com
Dist flexographic & rotogravure printers: 10 color printing, 2 color backside printing, surface & reverse printing, laminating, shrink sleeves, lidding material, paper, poly, foil & poly. (Woman, estab 1981, empl 5, sales $1,000,000, cert: WBENC)

5592 Liberty Laser Solutions
375 Commercial St
Marseilles, IL 61341
Contact: President
Tel: 800-570-1987
Email: sales@libertylasersolutions.com
Website: www.libertylasersolutions.com
Mfr & dist laser, ink jet & MICR products. (Woman, estab 1996, empl 42, sales $3,700,000, cert: WBENC)

5593 Mercommbe Inc.
2101 Estes Ave
Elk Grove Village, IL 60007
Contact: Eric Moe Sales
Tel: 847-290-0368
Email: eric@mercommbe.com
Website: www.mercommbe.com
Dist datacom & networking products; fiber optic, structured wiring, low voltage cable & connectors. (Minority, Woman, estab 1989, empl 7, sales $5,686,000, cert: State, City, NMSDC, WBENC)

5594 MNJ Technologies Direct, Inc.
1025 Busch Pkwy
Buffalo Grove, IL 60089
Contact: Holly Hayward
Tel: 312-591-5167
Email: hhayward@mnjtech.com
Website: www.mnjtech.com
Dist computer hardware, software & peripheral products. (Woman, estab 2002, empl 85, sales $25,000,000, cert: WBENC)

5595 RPT Toner LLC
475 Supreme Dr
Bensenville, IL 60106
Contact: Jamie Sr VP Sales/Mktg
Tel: 630-694-0400
Email: jamie@rpttoner.com
Website: www.rpttoner.com
Re-manufacture laser toner cartridges. (As-Ind, estab , empl , sales $10,770,000, cert: NMSDC)

Indiana

5596 ASAP Identification Security, Inc.
212 W 10th St, Ste F-100
Indianapolis, IN 46202
Contact: Sheila Brown President
Tel: 317-488-1030
Email: sbrown@asapident.com
Website: www.asapident.com
Photo ID printers, supplies, service, software and accessories. (Woman, estab 1982, empl 3, sales , cert: State, WBENC)

5597 Convenient Tape & Supplies LLC
545 Industrial Dr
Carmel, IN 46032
Contact: Jennifer Pippen President
Tel: 317-846-0335
Email: jencts1@sbcglobal.net
Website: www.sundsales.com
Distributors of point-of-sale (pos) paper rolls, cash register rolls, printer ribbons, toner cartridges, ink-jet cartridges, printer cleaning supplies, scale labels, industrial bar code labels, pos printers to small computer printer users. (Woman, estab 2002, empl 3, sales $244,000, cert: State)

Kansas

5598 Inland Associates, Inc.
18965 W 158th St
Olathe, KS 66062
Contact: Peggy Meader President
Tel: 913-764-7977
Email: pmeader@inlandassoc.com
Website: www.inlandassoc.com
Dist computer peripherals, data communications equipment. (Woman, estab 1969, empl 7, sales $4,000,000, cert: WBENC)

Louisiana

5599 Dempsey Business Systems of Louisiana
1201 3rd St Ste 210
Alexandria, LA 71301
Contact: Freddie Price, Sr. President
Tel: 318-704-6061
Email: fprice@dempseybus.com
Website: www.dempseybus.com
Dist Computer & Computer Peripheral equipment & software, custom computer programing services, computer systems design services, computer facilities management services, information technology value added reseller. (AA, estab 2004, empl 1, sales $278,789, cert: NMSDC)

5600 The Lazers Edge LLC
2168 Airline Dr, Ste C
Bossier City, LA 71111
Contact: Sandra Nix Owner
Tel: 318-742-6232
Email: nix@lazers-edge.com
Website: www.lazers-edge.com
Remanufactured Toner cartridges, laser printer service & repair. (Woman, estab 1989, empl 7, sales , cert: City)

Massachusetts

5601 Alpha Identification, Inc.
7 Spanish River Rd
Grafton, MA 01519
Contact: Frank Ng Treasurer
Tel: 508-839-6144
Email: alphaidinc@gmail.com
Website: www.alphaidinc.com
Dist photo ID equip & supplies for employee & student ID badges: Polaroid films, cameras, laminators, die-cutters, etc. (Minority, Woman, estab 1987, empl 2, sales $918,810, cert: State, City, CPUC)

5602 Encore Images
21 Lime St
Marblehead, MA 01945
Contact: Laurel Mervis President
Tel: 781-631-4568
Email: laurel.mervis@encoreimages.com
Website: www.encoreimages.com
Remanufacture toner cartridges: monochrome & color laser printers, copiers & facsimile machines. (Woman, estab 1989, empl 14, sales $2,020,000, cert: State)

5603   Pro AV Systems, Inc.
       275 Billerica Road Ste 3
       Chelmsford, MA 01824
       Contact: President
       Tel: 978-692-5111
       Email:
       Website: www.proavsi.com
Dist audiovisual products & installation services. (Woman/
As-Ind, estab 2006, empl 58, sales $16,100,000, cert:
State)

Maryland

5604   Laser Printers Plus
       PO Box 264
       Greenbelt, MD 20768
       Contact: Sales
       Tel: 301-933-9007
       Email: info@laserprintersplus.com
       Website: www.laserprintersplus.com
Dist new & remanufactured laser & toner cartridges, drum
units, fusers, ribbons, developers, parts. (As-Ind, estab
1998, empl 4, sales $500,000, cert: State)

Michigan

5605   AVE Solutions
       1155 Brewery Park Blvd., #350
       Detroit, MI 48207
       Contact: Carol Kirkland Exec VP
       Tel: 313-347-8592
       Email: carol@avesolutions.net
       Website: www.avesolutions.net
Dist office supplies, office furniture, office equipment,
audio visual equipment, computer equipment & supplies,
printer equipment & supplies, paper, janitorial supplies,
first aid supplies. (Woman/AA, estab 1990, empl 6, sales ,
cert: NMSDC, WBENC)

5606   Data Ranger Computer Products
       507 E Main St
       Manchester, MI 48158
       Contact: Andrea Ranger Owner
       Tel: 734-428-8551
       Email: andrea@datarangercomputerproducts.com
       Website: www.datarangercomputerproducts.com
Dist computer, pos, barcoding & imaging supplies, hard-
ware/equipment & peripherals, toner, ink, ribbons, backup media, paper, labels, custom forms, printers, cables,
scanners, networking hardware, monitors, computers, etc.
(Woman, estab 2002, empl 2, sales , cert: WBENC)

5607   JEM Tech Group
       23537 Lakepointe Dr.
       Clinton Township, MI 48036
       Contact: Shelley Deane Sr Technology Consultant
       Tel: 586-783-3400
       Email: s.deane@jemtechgroup.com
       Website: www.jemtechgroup.com
Dist IT products: toners, tape backup media, printers,
cables, monitors, bar code readers, backup libraries,
furniture, switches, hubs, racks, projectors, hardware &
software, etc. (Woman, estab 1979, empl 14, sales
$10,400,000, cert: WBENC)

5608   M.O.R.E. Computer Supplies, LLC
       384 Park
       Troy, MI 48083
       Contact: Jim Williams CEO
       Tel: 248-733-9011
       Email: jw@more-office.biz
       Website: www.more-office.biz
Dist computer supplies. (AA, estab 2001, empl 9, sales
$16,000,000, cert: NMSDC)

5609   Micro Wise, Inc.
       21421 Hilltop Dr, Unit 4
       Southfield, MI 48034
       Contact: Dan Mamman Sales Mgr
       Tel: 248-350-0066
       Email: dan@microwise.net
       Website: www.microwise.net
Resell computers, servers & networking gear, POS,
access-control, PC repairs, upgrades, service, leasing &
disposal. (Minority, Woman, estab 1989, empl 9, sales ,
cert: NMSDC)

5610   Mikan Corporation
       1271 Industrial, Ste 3
       Saline, MI 48176
       Contact: Maggie Stevens President
       Tel: 734-944-9447
       Email: maggie@mikancorp.com
       Website: www.mikancorp.com
Remanufacture laser toner cartridges. (Woman, estab
1990, empl 7, sales $1,726,617, cert: WBENC)

5611   Open Systems Technologies DE, LLC
       605 Seward NW, Ste 101
       Grand Rapids, MI 49504
       Contact: David Gerrity Exec Dir
       Tel: 616-574-3500
       Email: dgerrity@ostusa.com
       Website: www.ostusa.com
Resell computer hardware & software, business process
solutions, data center solutions, application development, managed services. (Nat Ame, estab 1997, empl
110, sales $68,873,026, cert: NMSDC)

5612   PFA Recycling, Inc.
       50150 E Russell Schmidt
       Chesterfield, MI 48051
       Contact: Peter Feamster VP Business Dev
       Tel: 586-949-5788
       Email: pfeamster92@gmail.com
       Website: www.pfa-recycling.com
Recycle plastic consumer goods, ink jet cartridges. (Hisp,
estab 1991, empl 20, sales $3,306,104, cert: NMSDC)

5613   The Computer Group, Inc.
       32985 Hamilton Ct Ste 135
       Farmington Hills, MI 48331
       Contact: Phillip Ingram President
       Tel: 248-888-6900
       Email: phil@compgroup.com
       Website: www.compgroup.com
Computer systems, copy machines, computer peripherals, computer software networking products. (AA, estab
1982, empl 9, sales $525,000, cert: NMSDC)

Minnesota

5614 All Media Supplies, Inc.
4902 NE Tri Oak Circle S
Wyoming, MN 55092
Contact: Rita Morse President
Tel: 763-413-1907
Email: shelly@allmediasuppliesinc.com
Website: www.allmediasuppliesinc.com
Dist magnetic computer products: 4MM,8MM,CD-Rom, labels & racking. (Woman, estab 1997, empl 5, sales $729,000, cert: WBENC)

5615 Best Datacom, Inc.
8405 First Ave NE
Stacy, MN 55079
Contact: Doug Anderson Acct Mgr
Tel: 715-398-0342
Email: doug@best-datacom.com
Website: www.best-datacom.com
Computer & network hardware & peripheral products, copper & fiber cable assemblies, cabinets/racks & computer/network enclosures. (Minority, Woman, estab 2007, empl 3, sales $264,000, cert: NMSDC)

5616 CaDan Technologies
4131 Old Sibley Memorial Hwy Ste 200
Eagan, MN 55122
Contact: Tom Kreiling Sales
Tel: 952-278-0560
Email: sales@cadan.com
Website: www.cadan.com
Computer hardware, software & services, new & refurbished hardware, hardware/software installations, new site setups or site tear downs. (Woman, estab 1992, empl 32, sales $9,300,000, cert: WBENC)

5617 Kelly Computer Supply
2042 Wooddale Dr Ste 250
Woodbury, MN 55125
Contact: Bob Kelly President
Tel: 651-773-1109
Email: bobkelly@kellyrest.com
Website: www.kellyrest.com
Ergonomic equip; mfr "KellyRest" computer products: wrist & foot rests, adjustable copy holders, keyboard drawers & articulating keyboard trays; workstations. (Nat Ame, estab 1983, empl 10, sales , cert: State, NMSDC, CPUC)

5618 Magnetic Products and Services, Inc.
7600 Boone Ave N. Ste 1
Minneapolis, MN 55428
Contact: Michelle Morey VP
Tel: 800-447-1277
Email: mmorey@mpsinc.org
Website: www.mpsinc.org
Dist electrical products & computer supplies: magnetic tapes, cartridges, optical disks, etc. (Woman, estab 1989, empl 14, sales $9,520,000, cert: WBENC)

Missouri

5619 Desktop Color Systems
1675 Larkin Williams Rd
Fenton, MO 63122
Contact: Maryann Gephardt CEO
Tel: 636-343-4600
Email: info@dtcolor.com
Website: www.dtcolor.com
Resell imaging supplies & office equipment hardware, service agreements, break-fix & warranty service. (Woman, estab 1993, empl 5, sales $1,546,000, cert: WBENC)

5620 Huber & Associates, Inc.
1400 Edgewood Dr
Jefferson City, MO 65109
Contact: Elizabeth Huber CEO
Tel: 573-634-5000
Email: ehuber@teamhuber.com
Website: www.teamhuber.com
Dist IBM hardware, software, maintenance & services. (Woman, estab 1986, empl 80, sales , cert: WBENC)

5621 Missouri Office Systems & Supplies, Inc.
941 W 141st Terrace Ste B
Kansas City, MO 64145
Contact: Virgie Dillard President
Tel: 816-761-5152
Email: vld@8asupplier.com
Website: www.8asupplier.com
Dist office supplies, furniture, ethernet, media, printers, software, hardware, ribbons, fax, scanners, computers, typewriters, routers, hubs, toners, servers. (Woman/AA, estab 1993, empl 9, sales $8,775,113, cert: State, City, NMSDC)

North Carolina

5622 Carolina Cartridge Systems, Inc.
516 E Hebron St
Charlotte, NC 28273
Contact: CEO
Tel: 704-347-2447
Email:
Website: www.ccsinside.com
Mfr toner cartridges. (Woman, estab 1991, empl 35, sales $2,200,000, cert: State, WBENC)

5623 Key Services, Inc.
3921 Westpoint Blvd
Winston-Salem, NC 27103
Contact: Lisa Hodges VP & Quality Assurance Mgr
Tel: 336-397-2129
Email: arice@key-services.com
Website: www.key-services.com
Dist & repair computer hardware & software, displays, touchscreens, printers, scanners, barcoding products & networking equipment. (Woman, estab 1976, empl , sales $2,749,120, cert: WBENC)

5624 Stay Online Corp.
3301 Bramer Dr
Raleigh, NC 27604
Contact: Jim Higgins GM
Tel: 919-510-5464
Email: jim@stayonline.com
Website: www.stayonline.com/
Power and data products. (Minority, Woman, estab 1987, empl 13, sales $6,050,000, cert: NMSDC)

New Hampshire

5625 110 Technology LLC
27 Technology Way
Nashua, NH 03060
Contact: Gary Nicoll Sales Mgr
Tel: 603-886-2800
Email: sales@110technology.com
Website: www.110technology.com
Resell information technology products: Hewlett Packard, IBM, Dell, Apple, Microsoft, Cisco, 3Com, APC, Philips, Xerox, NEC, Infocus, Intel, Viewsonic. (Minority, Woman, estab 2004, empl 8, sales $11,000,000, cert: NMSDC, WBENC)

5626 Tape Services, Inc.
15 Londonderry Rd, Unit 11
Londonderry, NH 03053
Contact: Bryan Webb Sales Mgr
Tel: 603-425-2202
Email: bwebb@tapeservices.com
Website: www.tapeservices.com/
Pro Audio; Videotape; Back Up Tape; Data Media;Hard Drives; CD;Computer Media; Digital Media; Pro Tape; Professional Media; Recording Media; Computer Media; Data Migration; DBeta; DVCam; DVCPro; DVD; Glyph; G-Tech. (Woman, estab 1989, empl 8, sales $4,314,589, cert: WBENC)

New Jersey

5627 Baanyan Software Services, Inc.
399 Thornall St Fisrt Fl
Edison, NJ 08837
Contact: VP Sales
Tel: 732-595-9006
Email: nshah@baanyan.com
Website: www.baanyan.com
IT staffing, ERP, BI, Data Warehousing, Cloud and Mobile Computing, and Big Data. (Minority, Woman, estab 2009, empl 100, sales $7,091,695, cert: City, NMSDC)

5628 DATA Inc. USA
72 Summit Ave
Montvale, NJ 07645
Contact: Deepali Schwarz Dir Corporate Affairs
Tel: 201-802-9800
Email: dschwarz@dataincusa.com
Website: www.datainc.biz
IT solutions: staff augmentation & custom application development solutions. (As-Pac, estab 1983, empl 400, sales $49,079,601, cert: State, NMSDC)

5629 First Call Services, Inc.
121 Chestnut St
Roselle Park, NJ 07204
Contact: Fred Bonda President
Tel: 908-620-1240
Email: firstcallsvcs@live.com
Website: www.firstcallservicesinc.com
Repair & service office machines, fax machines, typewriters, scanners, micro-graphics, computers, printers & shredders. dist toners, ribbons, drums, fuser units & additional parts. (Hisp, estab 1995, empl 10, sales , cert: State)

5630 High Point Solutions
5 Gail Ct
Sparta, NJ 07871
Contact: Rich McDonald Acct Mgr
Tel: 973-940-6516
Email: rmcdonald@highpt.com
Website: www.highpoint.com
Resell networking products: Cisco, Juniper, Bay, Fore, IBM, Lucent, Extreme, Nortel, Cables, memory, Digital Link, Paradyne. (Hisp, estab 1997, empl , sales $170,000,000, cert: City)

New York

5631 BXI Consultants, Inc.
33 Peuquet Pkwy
Tonawanda, NY 14150
Contact: Ingrid Charlton President
Tel: 716-693-0343
Email: icharlton@bxiconsultants.com
Website: www.bxiconsultants.com
Xerox copying, printing & scanning. (Minority, Woman, estab 1993, empl 15, sales , cert: State)

5632 Garic Inc.
68 35th St Ste C653
Brooklyn, NY 11232
Contact: Patrick OKeefe Principal
Tel: 646-487-0105
Email: patrick@garicinc.com
Website: www.garicinc.com
Technology leasing & computer remarketing, financial services, computer & telecommunications equipment, computers, telephone systems, switches, networks, peripherals, etc. (AA, Hisp, estab 2000, empl 7, sales $5,000,000, cert: State, City, NMSDC)

5633 Gholkar's, Inc.
7321 State Rt 251
Victor, NY 14564
Contact: Preeya Gholkar President
Tel: 585-924-2050
Email: info@gholkars.com
Website: www.gholkars.com
Dist computer supplies: magnetic media, CAD plotter paper, ribbons, barcode labels, & ribbons. (As-Ind, estab 1988, empl 7, sales $3,400,000, cert: State)

5634 GT Business Supplies LLC
115-13 Linden Blvd
South Ozone park, NY 11420
Contact: Jodhan Basanta Managing Dir
Tel: 718-659-9165
Email: jodhanb@gttoner.com
Website: www.gttoner.com
Dist printers, ink cartridges & toners. (Hisp, estab 2003, empl 4, sales $400,000, cert: City)

5635 Hugo Neu Recycling, LLC
249 E Sandford Blvd
Mount Vernon, NY 10550
Contact: Joseph Claiborne Dir sourcing
Tel: 917-566-8464
Email: info@hugoneu.com
Website: www.hugoneurecycling.com
IT asset disposal & advance electronic e-waste recycler. (Minority, Woman, estab 2009, empl 90, sales , cert: NMSDC, WBENC)

5636 Minoria Tech LLC
326 Broad St
Utica, NY 14476
Contact: Robles President
Tel: 315-628-0021
Email: rose@minoriatech.com
Website: www.minoriatech.com/
We are a computer, hardware, software, and peripherals value added reseller. (Minority, Woman, estab 2017, empl 3, sales $854,026, cert: State, City, WBENC)

5637 New Computech, Inc.
39 Broadway Ste 1630
New York, NY 10006
Contact: Abraham President
Tel: 212-406-1801
Email: mona@newcomputech.com
Website: www.newcomputech.net
Resell computer hardware & software products. (Woman/AA, estab 1996, empl 12, sales $1,500,000, cert: City, WBENC)

5638 Pioneer Business Systems
165 W 29th St
New York, NY 10001
Contact: James Breland Dir Business Devel
Tel: 212-594-2614
Email: jamesb@pioneercopier.com
Website: www.pioneercopier.com
Lease, rentals, purchase copiers, prints, scanners, MFP equipment, wide format printers. Service copiers, printers, fax & MFP equipment. (As-Pac, estab , empl , sales $13,500,000, cert: City, NMSDC)

5639 Sidewinder Holdings, Inc.
245 Mineola Blvd
Mineola, NY 11501
Contact: Stacey Rose President
Tel: 516-742-1700
Email: srose@cartridgeworldusa.com
Website: www.cartridgeworldusa.com/store76
Dist laser, toner & inkjet cartridges for printers, copiers & fax machines. (Woman/AA, estab 2005, empl 5, sales $211,429, cert: City, NMSDC)

Ohio

5640 Integrated Business Supplies Inc.
17381 Old Tannery Trail
Chagrin Falls, OH 44023
Contact: Judy Wardley VP
Tel: 440-498-3888
Email: judyw@misibs.com
Website: www.askibs.com
Dist computers & equipment, office machines, supplies, paper, furniture, vellum. (Woman, estab 1990, empl 5, sales $546,600, cert: State, City)

5641 SpaceBound, Inc.
280 Opportunity Way
LaGrange, OH 44050
Contact: Cindi Duesler Sales Mgr
Tel: 440-355-8008
Email: govtbids@spaceboundsolutions.com
Website: www.spaceboundsolutions.com
Computer hardware, software, peripherals, accessories, electronics, office supplies, office equipment, audio, video, cameras, phones telephone, etc. (Woman, estab 1987, empl 38, sales $34,000,000, cert: WBENC)

5642 Tape Central, Inc.
7020 Huntley Rd, Ste C
Columbus, OH 43229
Contact: Jeff Alan Commercial Sales
Tel: 866-701-0098
Email: southeasternmedia@juno.com
Website: www.tapecentral.com
Dist digital cameras, video cameras & camcorders, lighting, cables, microphones, LCD & Plasma TV-monitors, projectors, duplicators, CD - DVD disk printers, toner and ink, plus pro video & audio tape, CDR, Blu-Ray & DVD media, cases & sleeves. (Woman, estab 2001, empl 10, sales $6,820,168, cert: WBENC)

5643 WMG, LLC
PO Box 3115
Dayton, OH 45401
Contact: William Michael Green CEO
Tel: 937-268-0773
Email: info@wmgreensales.com
Website: www.WMGreensales.com
Office equipment, hardware & doftware multifunctional devices, copiers, scanners, plotters & faxes. (AA, estab 2011, empl 1, sales $1,250,000, cert: State, City, NMSDC)

Pennsylvania

5644 Parmetech, Inc.
137 W Eagle Ave
Havertown, PA 19083
Contact: Ana Fernandez-Parmet President
Tel: 610-446-4000
Email: afparmet@parmetech.com
Website: www.parmetech.com
Dist printers, scanners, multifuction machines & storage devices. (Minority, Woman, estab 1991, empl 23, sales $4,900,000, cert: NMSDC, WBENC)

Rhode Island

5645 NetCablesPlus Inc.
PO Box 7815
Cumberland, RI 02864
Contact: John Rodrigues President
Tel: 401-475-6040
Email: sales@netcablesplus.com
Website: www.netcablesplus.com
Network & PC cables & accessories, ethernet, fiber optic, USB, firewire. (Hisp, estab 2004, empl 3, sales $135,000, cert: State)

Tennessee

5646 Columbia Data Systems, Inc.
2002 Oakland Pkwy
Columbia, TN 38401
Contact: Julie Baker President
Tel: 931-381-4660
Email: julie.baker@edge.net
Website: www.cdsmicro.com
Dist & service computer & peripherals. (Woman, estab 1983, empl 3, sales $308,690, cert: State)

5647 Guy Brown, LLC
      7111 Commerce Way
      Brentwood, TN 37027
      Contact: Lauren Dooros Sales & Marketing Mgr
      Tel: 615-777-1500
      Email: lauren.dooros@guybrown.com
      Website: www.guybrown.com
Mfr recycled laser toner cartridges & office products.
(Minority, Woman, estab 1997, empl 45, sales
$204,877,006, cert: NMSDC, WBENC)

5648 Laser Recharge Inc.
      485 E South St Ste 100
      Collierville, TN 38017
      Contact: John Ferris VP
      Tel: 901-853-0742
      Email: jferris@laser-recharge.com
      Website: www.laser-recharge.com
Laser Printers, Ink Jet Printers, Copiers, Fax, Machines,
Multi Function Machines, Scanners, Digital Senders,
Plotters, Printer & Copier Supplies, Printer Repair Service.
(Woman, estab 1986, empl 11, sales $2,780,000, cert:
State)

5649 RLB Procurement
      1180 Gunter Smith Rd
      Pulaski, TN 38478
      Contact: Cassandara Moore Sales
      Tel: 931-548-1170
      Email: cassandara@rlbprocurement.com
      Website: www.rlbprocurement.com
Systems, switches, servers, software, computers, printers,
toners, inks, security cameras, monitors, displays, storage,
cables, automation, racks & IT related products. (Woman,
estab 2006, empl 3, sales , cert: WBENC)

5650 Unistar-Sparco Computers, Inc.
      7089 Ryburn Dr
      Millington, TN 38053
      Contact: SooTsong Lim CEO
      Tel: 901-872-2272
      Email: lim@sparco.com
      Website: www.sparco.com
IT solutions, hardware, computer systems, desktops,
notebooks, thin clients, tablet PCs, PDAs, workstations,
rack-mount servers, blade servers, monitors, displays,
Plasma TVs, LCD monitors, flat-screen monitors, LCD TVs.
(As-Pac, estab 1992, empl 35, sales $38,700,641, cert:
NMSDC)

Texas

5651 ARDETECH Industries, Inc.
      11526 Pagemill Rd
      Dallas, TX 75243
      Contact: Sales Rep
      Tel: 800-821-5678
      Email:
      Website: www.ardetech.com
Dist IT products, cable assemblies, computer peripherals,
data & telecomm supplies. (Woman, estab 1996, empl 14,
sales $2,415,008, cert: State, WBENC)

5652 CompuPro Global
      15720 Park Row Ste 400
      Houston, TX 77084
      Contact: Randy Pfeiffer VP Business Dev
      Tel: 713-934-9633
      Email: ginnib@compuproglobal.com
      Website: www.compuproglobal.com
Dist computer tape, computer media, computer
accessories, hardware, toner, wide format printer
supplies (Woman, estab 1999, empl 9, sales $5,600,000,
cert: State, WBENC)

5653 Designs That Compute
      1778 N Plano Rd, Ste 211B
      Richardson, TX 75081
      Contact: Gregg Coapman Technical Sales Consult-
      ant
      Tel: 214-276-0124
      Email: sales@visionality.com
      Website: www.visionality.com
Videoconferencing & audio/visual solutions, digital
signage, interactive whiteboards & displays, video walls,
projectors/screens, audio/speakers, recording, streaming video. (Woman, estab 1986, empl 14, sales
$5,400,000, cert: State)

5654 ELP Enterprises, Inc.
      9346 Rosstown Way
      Houston, TX 77080
      Contact: Martha Ceballos CEO
      Tel: 832-969-9947
      Email: mceball@aol.com
      Website: www.elpenterprisesinc.com
Dist computer supplies. (Minority, Woman, estab 1999,
empl 2, sales $813,923, cert: City, NMSDC, WBENC)

5655 JHJ Computer Supplies, Inc.
      3901 Arlington Highlands Blvd. Ste 200
      Arlington, TX 76018
      Contact: Jessie Jones President
      Tel: 817-861-0888
      Email: jhampton@jhjcs.com
      Website: www.jhjcs.com
Dist computer supplies: printers, keyboards, flash drives,
ink & toner cartridges, magnetic media, media storage,
anti-glare screens, mouse pads, optical mouse devices,
wireless devices, computer bags, USB cables. (Woman/
AA, estab 2007, empl 3, sales $116,336, cert: State)

5656 Meridian Office Systems, Inc.
      4113 Lindbergh Dr
      Addison, TX 75001
      Contact: Jeff Emery Mgr
      Tel: 972-690-3661
      Email: jemery@meridianoffice.com
      Website: www.meridianoffice.com
Sell, lease, rent, repair, service & maintenance office
copiers, laser printers & multifunction color copiers.
(Minority, Woman, estab 1994, empl 15, sales
$3,200,000, cert: State)

5657 OAS Computer Supplies
      3333 Earhart Dr, Ste 120
      Carrollton, TX 75006
      Contact: Sales Exec
      Tel: 972-267-8020
      Email: sales @ oas-supplies . com
      Website: www.oas-supplies.com
Resell office supplies & computer supplies. (Woman,
estab 1986, empl 12, sales $150,500,000, cert: State)

5658 Patriot Group, Ltd.
      5000 Terminal St
      Bellaire, TX 77401
      Contact: Lois Livingston Acct Mgr
      Tel: 713-664-1172
      Email: llivingston@patriotgroup.com
      Website: www.patriotgroup.com
Dist business equipment, equipment supplies, service and support. (Woman, estab 1979, empl 22, sales $5,137,000, cert: State)

5659 RLS Interests, Inc.
      10402 Harwin Dr
      Houston, TX 77036
      Contact: Michael Chang
      Tel: 713-933-0934
      Email: directron@globalxlr.com
      Website: www.directron.com
DIY computer components, CPUs, memory, hard drives, optical drives, hardware & software, pre-built systems, notebooks, netbooks, tablets, peripherals & accessories. (As-Pac, estab 1990, empl 157, sales $51,100,000, cert: NMSDC)

5660 Southwest Office Systems, Inc.
      13960 Trinity Blvd
      Fort Worth, TX 76040
      Contact: Debbie Sorrells COO
      Tel: 817-730-8000
      Email: rjasper@sostexas.com
      Website: www.sostexas.com
Copiers, printers, print management, plotters, digital white boards. (Hisp, estab , empl , sales $10,819,775, cert: State, City, NMSDC)

5661 TAPEANDMEDIA.COM, LLC
      450 Colorado Dr
      Cedar Creek, TX 78612
      Contact: Bennie Wallace VP
      Tel: 877-938-0901
      Email: bennie@tapeandmedia.com
      Website: www.tapeandmedia.com
Dist blank media: computer back-up tapes, video tapes, audio tapes, DVD's, CD's, DVD/CD cases. (Woman, estab 2000, empl 6, sales $5,000,000, cert: State)

Virginia

5662 Advanced Business Software Consulting dba NCN
      11890 Sunrise Valley Dr, Ste 515
      Reston, VA 20191
      Contact: Sharon Muniz CEO
      Tel: 703-298-2468
      Email: sharon@ncntechnology.com
      Website: www.ncntechnology.com
Mobile & web application development, SharePoint services. (Minority, Woman, estab 2006, empl 3, sales $520,000, cert: State, WBENC, 8(a), SDB)

5663 Computer Upgrade King, LLC
      1555 Standing Ridge Dr Ste A-1
      Powhatan, VA 23139
      Contact: Robert Robinson VP
      Tel: 800-985-9364
      Email: sales@computerupgradeking.com
      Website: www.computerupgradeking.com
Computers (laptops, desktops), Custom Desktops, Components, Cases, Laser Etching. (Minority, Woman, estab 2008, empl 45, sales $846,956, cert: State)

Washington

5664 EC Corporation Export
      22307 Marine View Dr S
      Des Moines, WA 98198
      Contact: Patricio Mendoza Mgr
      Tel: 206-878-3321
      Email: patricio@eccomputer.com
      Website: www.eccomputer.com
Computers Peripherals, Cartridges, Office Supply, External hard drives, Keyboard, Mouse, Monitors, Software, Licenses, Office Supplies, PC'S. (Hisp, estab 1991, empl 4, sales $250,000, cert: State)

5665 Evergreen Computer Products Inc
      2720 1st Ave S
      Seattle, WA 98134
      Contact: Barbara Anderson VP
      Tel: 206-624-3722
      Email: banderson@evergreencomp.com
      Website: www.evergreencomp.com
Printer repair services. (Woman/AA, estab 1977, empl 10, sales $10,116,295, cert: State, NMSDC)

Wisconsin

5666 Cartridge Savers, Inc.
      2801 Coho St Ste 206
      Madison, WI 53713
      Contact: Thomas Wangard President
      Tel: 608-663-5126
      Email: tom.w@cartridgesavers.com
      Website: www.cartridgesavers.com
Dist remanufactured & new laser printer toner cartridges, laser printers. (Hisp, estab 1994, empl 8, sales $6,843,995, cert: State, NMSDC)

5667 Vanguard Computers, Inc.
      13100 W Lisbon Rd, Ste 100
      Brookfield, WI 53005
      Contact: Owner
      Tel: 262-317-1900
      Email: sales@vanguardinc.com
      Website: www.vanguardinc.com
Dist, svc & rent computer equipment & peripherals; network configuration, installation & maintenance. (Minority, Woman, estab 1982, empl 39, sales , cert: WBENC)

INFORMATION TECHNOLOGY: Systems/Machines

Design, manufacture, lease and/or distribute information processing systems, machines and components. Many of these firms also distribute information processing supplies. (See also INFORMATION TECHNOLOGY: Services and INFORMATION TECHNOLOGY: Supplies). NAICS Code 33

California

5668   CB Technologies, Inc.
       750 The City Dr South Ste 225
       Orange, CA 92868
       Contact: Dwanna Lynch Dir/ Corporate Relations
       Tel: 714-573-7733
       Email: dwanna.lynch@cbtechinc.com
       Website: www.cbtechinc.com
Information technology hardware. (Woman, estab 2001, empl , sales $1,400,000, cert: CPUC, WBENC)

5669   CCIntegration, Inc.
       2060 Corporate Ct
       San Jose, CA 95131
       Contact: Stephanie Stoller Dir Business Dev
       Tel: 408-228-1314
       Email: stephanie.stoller@ccintegration.com
       Website: www.ccintegration.com
Technology, Computer, Server, Storage, Networking, Rack, On-site Service, Integration, Global Logistics, Hardware Engineering Support, Life Cycle Management, Appliance, System Platform, Dell, Lenovo, Supermicro, HPe. (As-Pac, estab 1985, empl 81, sales $108,000,000, cert: WBENC)

5670   DuraTech USA, Inc.
       6765 Westminster Blvd Ste 314
       Westminster, CA 92683
       Contact: Skip Howland Govt Business Dev
       Tel: 831-419-8179
       Email: showland@duratechusa.com
       Website: www.Duratechusa.com
Dist semi rugged & MIL-STD 810F laptops, rugged & submersible tablet pc's. (Minority, Woman, estab 2005, empl 3, sales $2,500,000, cert: State)

5671   Elgin Micro
       14271 Jeffrey Rd Ste 247
       Irvine, CA 92620
       Contact: Daniel Laterneau Sales Dir
       Tel: 949-878-7461
       Email: dan@elginmicro.com
       Website: www.elginmicro.com
Dist HP, IBM, SUN Microsystems (Oracle), Dell, Cisco, Emulex, Qlogic, Juniper, EMC, NetApp, Nortel, Lenovo, Toshiba, Acer, Operating systems, Security, Applications, Design, Accounting, Training & Utilities. (Minority, Woman, estab 2012, empl 8, sales , cert: NMSDC)

5672   JE Components Inc.
       8709 Aviation Blvd
       Inglewood, CA 90301
       Contact: Joni Paulo President
       Tel: 310-645-6021
       Email: joni@jecom.com
       Website: www.jecom.com
Resell PC & network hardware. (Minority, Woman, estab 1995, empl 7, sales , cert: NMSDC, NWBOC)

5673   Performance Designed Products
       14144 Ventura Blvd Ste 200
       Sherman Oaks, CA 91423
       Contact: Theresa Harrell Natl Acct Mgr
       Tel: 479-445-8612
       Email: theresa.harrell@pdp.com
       Website: www.pdp.com
Design & mfr video game peripherals & accessories: PS2, PS3, PSP PS Vita, Xbox, Xbox 360, Wii, Wii U, 3DS, DS Lite. (Woman, estab 1990, empl 200, sales , cert: WBENC)

5674   Premio, Inc.
       918 Radecki Court
       City of Industry, CA 91748
       Contact: Debby Dodd Mktg Mgr
       Tel: 626-839-3128
       Email: debby.dodd@premioinc.com
       Website: www.premioinc.com
Oem Systems, desktop PCs, servers. (Minority, Woman, estab , empl , sales , cert: CPUC)

5675   RICOM
       26062 Merit Circle Bldg. 108
       Laguna Hills, CA 92653
       Contact: Isaac Buchanan Acct Exec
       Tel: 949-788-9939
       Email: isaac@ricom.net
       Website: www.shopricom.com
Computers: Cisco; IBM; Hewlett Packard; Emulex; Sun Microsystems; Dell; EMC; Nimble Storage; F5 Networks; VMware; citrix. (Minority, Woman, estab 1998, empl 9, sales $13,000,000, cert: NMSDC, CPUC, WBENC)

Colorado

5676   CounterTrade Products Inc.
       7585 W 66th Ave
       Arvada, CO 80003
       Contact: Angela Dumm Dir of Contracts & Security
       Tel: 303-424-9710
       Email: adumm@countertrade.com
       Website: www.COUNTERTRADE.COM
Dist computer porducts: IBM, Compaq, Hewlett Packard, Epson, Toshiba, Microsoft, Novell, Apple, Citrix, Viewsonic & 3COM. (Woman, estab 1985, empl 45, sales $275,000,000, cert: WBENC)

5677   SF&B, LLC
       9585 Niwot Rd
       Longmont, CO 80504
       Contact: Mgr
       Tel: 703-297-7447
       Email: support@sfbllc.com
       Website: www.sfbllc.com
Dist top-tier computer hardware. (Woman, estab 2011, empl 4, sales , cert: WBENC)

Connecticut

5678　PCNet, Inc.
100 Technology Dr
Trumbull, CT 06611
Contact: VP Finance/Operations
Tel:　203-452-8559
Email: teric@pcnet-inc.com
Website: www.pcnet-inc.com
Network systems integrator; e-commerce, Internet/
Intranet; resell of personal computer products & svcs.
(Hisp, estab 1993, empl 65, sales $26,000,000, cert:
NMSDC)

Florida

5679　United Data Technologies
8825 NW 21 Terrace
Doral, FL 33172
Contact: Mariana Lugaro Mgr Sales Operations
Tel:　305-882-0435
Email: sales.operations@udtonline.com
Website: www.udtonline.com
Dist, install & repair IT equipment: desktops, laptops,
servers, printers, switches, peripherals, & audio visual
equipment. (Hisp, estab 1995, empl 94, sales , cert: State)

Georgia

5680　American Megatrends Inc.
5555 Oakbrook Pkwy, Ste 200
Norcross, GA 30093
Contact: Srivatsan Ramachandran Dir Business Dev
Tel:　770-246-8600
Email: srivatsanr@ami.com
Website: www.ami.com
Mfr key hardware & software solutions, StorTrends, IP
Storage Area Network (IP-SAN) and Network Attached
Storage (NAS) solutions, Aptio and AMIBIOS system
software and firmware, MegaRAC remote management
software & firmware. (As-Ind, estab 1985, empl 1345, sales
$10,000,000, cert: NMSDC)

5681　Eastern Data, Inc.
4386 Park Dr
Norcross, GA 30093
Contact: JoAnn Pfeiffer Natl Accounts Mgr
Tel:　770-279-8888
Email: jo.pfeiffer@ediatlanta.com
Website: www.ediatlanta.com
Dist computer systems, components & peripherals.
(Minority, Woman, estab 1997, empl 27, sales
$20,906,578, cert: NMSDC, WBENC)

Illinois

5682　Hagerman & Company Inc.
505 Sunset Ct
Mount Zion, IL 62549
Contact: Sandy Hagerman President
Tel:　217-972-7268
Email: sandyhagerman@hagerman.com
Website: www.hagerman.com
Platinum Autodesk Reseller, System Integrator and
Consultant. (Woman, estab 1985, empl 89, sales
$43,800,000, cert: WBENC)

5683　Koi Computers Inc.
200 W North Ave
Lombard, IL 60148
Contact: Ayde Chavez Acct Rep
Tel:　630-627-8811
Email: ayde@koicomputer.com
Website: www.koicomputer.com
Dist computers, servers, printers, copiers, digital imaging
& networking equipments. (Minority, Woman, estab
1995, empl 6, sales $7,500,000, cert: State)

5684　Sayers Technology
825 Corporate Woods Pkwy
Vernon Hills, IL 60061
Contact: Adam Shipp Reg Sales Mgr
Tel:　404-695-2707
Email: ashipp@sayers.com
Website: www.sayers.com
IT Solutions, Servers & Storage, Virtualization, Security &
Mobility, Networking & Professional Services. Storage,
Servers, Cloud, Virtualization, Networking, Data Man-
agement, Archiving & Disaster Recovery Security. (AA,
estab 1984, empl , sales , cert: NMSDC)

Indiana

5685　Professional Information Systems
232 S Linda St
Hobart, IN 46342
Contact: Paulette Hill President
Tel:　219-947-4349
Email: paulette@proinfosys.com
Website: www.proinfosys.com
Hardware & software, build customize computers or
prebuilt computers. (Woman, estab 1992, empl 4, sales
$172,000, cert: State, 8(a))

5686　Qumulus Solutions LLC
101 N Michigan St Ste 300
South Bend, IN 46601
Contact: Russell Ford President
Tel:　574-208-6772
Email: rford@qumulussolutions.com
Website: www.qumulussolutions.com
Resell servers, storage, data backup hardware & soft-
ware. (AA, estab 2010, empl 7, sales $644,000, cert:
State, NMSDC)

Kansas

5687　ProActive Solutions Inc.
5625 Foxridge Dr
Shawnee Mission, KS 66202
Contact: Dean Thiede Exec VP
Tel:　913-948-8000
Email: dthiede@proactivesolutions.com
Website: www.proactivesolutions.com
IBM Hardware Power, System i, AS400, System p,
RS6000, System x, Storage, SAN, Lotus, Domino, Notes,
Websphere, Tivoli, TSM, VMWare, virtualization,
Disaster Recovery, DR, High Availability, HA, Business
Continuity, BC, Linux, (Woman, estab 1996, empl 30,
sales $45,029,277, cert: CPUC, WBENC)

Massachusetts

5688 Concord Information Systems, LLC
165 Middlesex Turnpike Ste 201
Bedford, MA 01730
Contact: Suzanne Hiniker Partner
Tel: 781-863-7200
Email: suzy@concordinfo.com
Website: www.concordinfo.com
Computers, laptops, tablets, servers, monitors, printers, networking hardware, cloud & email services & technical consulting services. (Woman, estab 1994, empl 10, sales $10,000,000, cert: State)

5689 Fenco Global Industries Corp.
1 Federal St
Springfield, MA 01105
Contact: Fenella Sitati President
Tel: 413-308-8800
Email: fenella@winningtek.com
Website: www.winningtek.com
Technology hardware for application security, datacenters & cloud virtualization, F5 Networks, VMware, Palo Alto, Cisco Networks, RedHat, Microsoft, NetApp, EMC, HP, IBM, Dell & ExtraHop. (Woman/AA, estab 2009, empl 5, sales $450,000, cert: NMSDC)

Michigan

5690 Dynamic Computer Corporation
23400 Industrial Park Court
Farmington Hills, MI 48335
Contact: Tami Schultz VP Business Dev
Tel: 248-473-2200
Email: tschultz@dynamictech.solutions
Website: www.dynamictech.solutions
Dist IT equipment: HP/Compaq, Dell, IBM, Microsoft, Symantec & Gateway. (Minority, Woman, estab 1979, empl 24, sales $29,500,000, cert: NMSDC, WBENC)

New Hampshire

5691 Worldcom Exchange Inc.
43 Northwestern Dr
Salem, NH 03079
Contact: Matt Good
Tel: 603-893-0900
Email: matt.good@wei.com
Website: www.wei.com
Dist computer hardware, integration & installation, enterprise storage, servers & PC solutions. (Hisp, estab 1989, empl , sales $265,000,000, cert: NMSDC)

New Jersey

5692 CPI (USA) Inc.
6 Doreen Court
Edison, NJ 08820
Contact: Deepak Advani
Tel: 732-494-0007
Email: dadvani@cpiusainc.com
Website: www.cpiusainc.com
Workstations, Laptops, Servers, Tablets, Multifunction Printers, Held Workstations, CCTV
Phone Systems (Panasonic, Mitel), Enterprise Business, Industry Standard Servers and Options
Routers & Add On, Switches & Add On, UPS & Generators. (Minority, Woman, estab 1997, empl 2, sales $375,000, cert: NMSDC)

New York

5693 Empire Electronics Inc.
103 Fort Salonga Rd
Northport, NY 11768
Contact: Krista Fisher
Tel: 631-544-9111
Email: kfisher@empireusa.com
Website: www.empireusa.com
Dist information technology equip, computer hardware & components. (Woman, estab 1983, empl 6, sales $10,400,000, cert: City, WBENC)

5694 Ergonomic Group, Inc.
200 Robbins Ln
Jericho, NY 11753
Contact: David Ferguson Sr Acct Exec
Tel: 516-746-7777
Email: dave.ferguson@ergogroup.com
Website: www.ergogroup.com
Resell computer equipment, peripherals & computer related services. (Woman, estab 1984, empl , sales , cert: WBENC)

Ohio

5695 Northern Technical Group LLC
14500 Industrial Ave N
Maple Heights, OH 44137
Contact: Mary Fink President
Tel: 216-662-0561
Email: mfink@northerntechnicalgroup.com
Website: www.northerntechnicalgroup.com
IT Asset Management, removal, audit, sanitizing, remarketing & recycling of computer related asset. (Woman, estab 2003, empl 17, sales $921,316, cert: NWBOC)

Texas

5696 Computize Inc.
80 E. McDermott Dr.
Allen, TX 75002
Contact: Bennie Moore Sr Sales Dir
Tel: 972-437-3100
Email: benniem@computize.com
Website: www.computize.com
Resell computers. (Minority, Woman, estab 1982, empl 125, sales $4,000,000, cert: WBENC)

5697 M&A Technology Inc.
2045 Chenault Dr
Carrollton, TX 75006
Contact: Donna Shepard Exec VP
Tel: 469-767-6657
Email: dshepard@macomp.com
Website: www.macomp.com
Custom intergration, servers, workstation, high performance intergrating, data center, on line back up, disater recovery. (AA, estab 1984, empl 55, sales $75,000,000, cert: State)

5698   Via Technology
      906 Fredericksburg Rd
      San Antonio, TX 78201
      Contact: Manuel Rosabal President
      Tel: 210-227-7726
      Email: manuelv@800viatech.com
      Website: www.800viatech.com
Hardware, software, peripherals, storage. (Minority, Woman, estab 1995, empl 10, sales $1,400,000, cert: State)

Virginia

5699   US21, Inc.
      2721 Prosperity Ave, Ste 300
      Fairfax, VA 22031
      Contact: Bassel Shubassi Business Devel Mgr
      Tel: 703-560-0021
      Email: info@us21.com
      Website: www.us21.com
Dist IT hardware: SMB & Enterprise. (Woman, estab 1998, empl 20, sales $10,000,000, cert: State)

INSURANCE COMPANIES
Firms carry life, accident, auto and health insuance policies. Most are licensed in several states. NAICS Code 52

California

5700   Definiti Healthcare Management
       26445 Rancho Pkwy South
       Lake Forest, CA 92630
       Contact: Mike Guerrero CEO
       Tel: 949-716-1890
       Email: mike.guerrero@definiti.net
       Website: www.definiti.net
National Workers Compensation Cost Containment provider. (Woman/Hisp, estab 2002, empl 27, sales $3,300,000, cert: NMSDC, CPUC)

5701   La Canada Ventures Inc.
       448 N San Mateo Dr
       San Mateo, CA 94401
       Contact: Susan Lin CEO
       Tel: 650-340-8688
       Email: drlin@susanlinmd.com
       Website: www.boozaid.com
Insurance services. (Minority, Woman, estab 2006, empl 8, sales $7,500,000, cert: WBENC)

5702   Merriwether & Williams Insurance Services
       550 Montgomery St Ste 550
       San Francisco, CA 94111
       Contact: Donna Hart CEO
       Tel: 415-986-3999
       Email: dhart@imwis.com
       Website: www.imwis.com
Commercial insurance marketing & placements, surety bonding, OCIP, third party administration. (Woman/AA, estab 1997, empl 35, sales $2,292,090, cert: NMSDC, CPUC)

5703   Mudrasys Inc.
       6200 Stoneridge Mall Rd, Ste 300
       Pleasanton, CA 94588
       Contact: Narsi Ayyagari CEO
       Tel: 925-353-3888
       Email: narsi@mudrasys.com
       Website: www.mudrasys.com
AgeAlert is the first thermal age sensor for use in predicting remaining thermal life of propellants as well as other thermally degradable components in ordnance and aircraft and other aerospace platforms. These sensors, weighing less than 1/4 gram, elim (Woman/As-Ind, estab 2009, empl 59, sales $4,200,000, cert: NMSDC, CPUC)

5704   Sovereign Employee Benefits, Inc.
       10630 Town Center Dr, Ste 113
       Rancho Cucamonga, CA 91730
       Contact: Katie King Owner
       Tel: 909-948-7779
       Email: melissadickson@sebins.com
       Website: www.sebins.com
Insurance brokerage services: group medical, customized employee benefit packages, liability, workers' comp & consulting services. (AA, estab 1982, empl 10, sales , cert: CPUC)

Florida

5705   Epiphany Insurance Company LLC
       6073 NW 167 St, Ste C7
       Hialeah, FL 33015
       Contact: Martine Miller Mgr
       Tel: 305-783-1487
       Email: epiphanyinsures@gmail.com
       Website: www.epiphanyinsures.com
Health and Life Insurance, Group Benefits, Supplemental Benefits, Dental & Vision. (Woman/AA, estab 2017, empl 4, sales , cert: State, SDB)

5706   Havens & Company
       586 Bay Villas Lane
       Naples, FL 34108
       Contact: Diane Green COO
       Tel: 978-283-4366
       Email: dgreen@havensandcompany.com
       Website: www.havensandcompany.com
Designing and negotiating benefits programs for life, accident, disability, dental, vision, along with retiree, voluntary, and executive benefits. (Woman, estab 2007, empl 6, sales $2,807,521, cert: WBENC)

5707   Leslie Saunders Insurance Agency, Inc.
       1535 N Dale Mabry Hwy
       Lutz, FL 33548
       Contact: Leslie Saunders President
       Tel: 813-949-8964
       Email: lsaunders@lsimi.com
       Website: www.lesliesaunders.com
Insurance agency: property casualty; employee benefits; life, health, STD, LTD & disablity insurance. (Woman, estab 1988, empl 7, sales , cert: WBENC)

Georgia

5708   Atlanta Life Insurance Company
       191 Peachtree St. Ste 2500
       Atlanta, GA 30303
       Contact: Howard Stephenson President
       Tel: 404-654-8842
       Email: hstephenson@atlantalife.com
       Website: www.atlantalife.com
Financial services, employee benefits, reinsurance, asset mgmt, etc. (AA, estab 2001, empl 68, sales $64,845,989, cert: NMSDC)

5709   Benalytics Consulting Group, LLC
       1850 Pkwy Place SE Ste 730
       Marietta, GA 30067
       Contact: Charles Atkinson Principal
       Tel: 770-420-0525
       Email: catkinson@benalytics.com
       Website: www.benalytics.com
Benefit consulting & insurance brokerage services. (AA, estab 2005, empl 12, sales , cert: NMSDC, 8(a), SDB)

5710   JLM Risk Management Group
       201 17th St Ste 300
       Atlanta, GA 30363
       Contact: Joseph L Moore
       Tel: 404-874-2929
       Email: jmoore@jlmriskmgmt.com
       Website: www.jlmriskmgmt.com
Property, casualty, life & employee benefits insurance brokerage. Risk management, claims management & loss control consultation. (AA, estab 1996, empl 7, sales $600,000, cert: NMSDC)

5711 Premier Benefit Consultants, Inc.
2470 Windy Hill Rd Ste 300
Marietta, GA 30068
Contact: Maureen Jurgelas President
Tel: 678-794-8104
Email: maureen@premierbenefit.com
Website: www.Premierbenefit.com
Insurance agency & consulting: group medical, dental, vision plans, LTD, STD, life insurance, AD&D, etc. (Woman, estab 2000, empl 4, sales $240,000, cert: WBENC)

Illinois

5712 CS Insurance Strategies
542 S Dearborn St
Chicago, IL 60605
Contact: Charles Smith CEO
Tel: 312-566-9700
Email: csmith@csstrategy.com
Website: www.csstrategy.com
Comprehensive risk management, commercial insurance & group employee benefit solutions. (AA, estab 2006, empl 4, sales $500,000, cert: City)

5713 Insurers Review Services, Inc.
225 N Michigan Ave Ste 902
Chicago, IL 60601
Contact: Alvin Robinson President
Tel: 312-938-0900
Email: arobin3172@aol.com
Website: www.insurersreviewservices.com
Insurance coverages, employee benefits, property coverages, special events, travel accident insurance & expatriate benefits. (AA, estab 1983, empl 5, sales $450,000, cert: State, City, NMSDC)

5714 Lambent Risk Management Services, Inc.
33 N. La Salle St Ste 1150
Chicago, IL 60602
Contact: Shirley Evans-Wofford CEO
Tel: 866-419-1415
Email: shirley_evans@lambent-rms.com
Website: www.lambent-rms.com
Insurance brokerage: property & casualty, third party theft, construction builders risk, insurance bonding, travel accident, healthcare & life, 401(k). (Woman/AA, estab 2000, empl 21, sales $2,433,496, cert: State, City)

5715 Prairie States Enterprises, Inc.
101 West Grand Ave., Ste 404
Chicago, IL 60654
Contact: Felicia Wilhelm CEO
Tel: 312-464-1888
Email: fwilhelm@prairieontheweb.com
Website: www.prairieontheweb.com
Health benefit plan administration svcs: medical, dental, vision, health savings account & eeimbursement accounts, short term disability, subrogation, COBRA&HIPAA certifications. (Woman, estab 1989, empl 64, sales $5,000,000, cert: WBENC)

5716 Risk & Insurance Management Services, Inc.
80 Burr Ridge Pkwy, Ste 121
Burr Ridge, IL 60527
Contact: Elizabeth Rodriguez-Spreck President
Tel: 630-655-0800
Email: lspreck@21chc.com
Website: www.21chc.com
Risk mgmt & insurance consulting svcs: employee benefits, group health, property & casualty, workers' comp, liability, product liability, auto, short-term disability, long-term disability, third-party claims admin svcs, healthcare & managed care. (Minority, Woman, estab 1991, empl 23, sales $2,282,406, cert: WBENC)

Louisiana

5717 1st Team Insurance Agency
3745 Choctaw Dr
Baton Rouge, LA 70805
Contact: Harold Williams Owner
Tel: 225-806-6923
Email: hwilliams@1stteaminsurance.com
Website: www.1stteaminsurance.com
Property & casualty insurance, property management, public relations, lobbying. (AA, estab 2005, empl 3, sales $350,000, cert: State)

5718 Hammerman and Gainer, Inc.
2400 Veterans Blvd Ste 510
Kenner, LA 70062
Contact: Kelisha Garrett Business Devel/PMO
Tel: 504-982-5030
Email: kelishag@hgi-global.com
Website: www.hgi.global
Risk management & insurance consulting services. (AA, estab 1929, empl 85, sales $38,000,000, cert: NMSDC)

Michigan

5719 Brownrigg Companies LTD
840 W Long Lake Rd Ste 100
Troy, MI 48098
Contact: Nancy Brownrigg CEO
Tel: 248-373-5580
Email: nbrownrigg@brownrigg.com
Website: www.brownrigg.com
Specialty insurance. (Woman, estab 1990, empl 14, sales $11,000,000, cert: WBENC)

5720 Custom Results Corporate Consulting LLC
101 W Big Beaver Rd Ste 115
Troy, MI 48084
Contact: Diane Christensen President
Tel: 248-572-1160
Email: diane@customresults.com
Website: www.customresults.com
Insurance, design, implementation, service & communication of Employee Benefit Plans & Retiree Medicare Advantage plans. (Woman, estab 2001, empl 6, sales , cert: WBENC)

5721 Employee Solve
725 S Adams Ste L-140
Southfield, MI 48009
Contact: Kenneth Hurtt, RHU, REBC President
Tel: 248-438-0096
Email: info1@employeesolve.com
Website: www.employeesolve.com
Health & welfare plans for employer groups. (AA, estab 1987, empl 6, sales $3,000,000, cert: NMSDC)

5722 Goss LLC
      600 Renaissance Ctr, Ste 1200
      Detroit, MI 48243
      Contact: Vincent Davis Dir of Mktg
      Tel: 313-446-9636
      Email: vdavis@gossllc.com
      Website: www.gossllc.com
Commercial risk & risk consulting svcs: group benefits,
property, casualty, liability, E&O, D&O, workers comp,
business auto, etc. (AA, estab 2001, empl 7, sales
$37,150,000, cert: State, NMSDC)

5723 Laurie Sall & Associates
      201 West Big Beaver Road #300
      Troy, MI 48084
      Contact: Laurie Sall President
      Tel: 248-641-2755
      Email: laurie@lauriesall.com
      Website: www.lauriesall.com
Life, disability & health insurance. (Minority, Woman,
estab 1980, empl 3, sales $8,532,047, cert: NMSDC,
WBENC)

5724 ReviewWorks
      21500 Haggerty Rd Ste 250
      Northville, MI 48167
      Contact: Carolyn Lahousse President
      Tel: 248-848-5067
      Email: carolyn_lahousse@reviewworks.com
      Website: www.reviewworks.com
Medical cost containment solutions & disability services
for workers' compensation, LTD & auto injury related
claims & claimants. (Woman, estab 1989, empl 70, sales
$11,650,921, cert: WBENC)

5725 The Dearborn Agency
      22691 Michigan Ave
      Dearborn, MI 48124
      Contact: Wendy Beaver Sales Mgr
      Tel: 313-562-8373
      Email: wendyb@dearbornagency.com
      Website: www.dearbornagency.com
Insurance. (Woman, estab 1924, empl 10, sales , cert:
WBENC)

5726 Yee & Associates LLC
      20789 Harper
      Harper Woods, MI 48225
      Contact: Matthew Yee Member
      Tel: 313-886-6770
      Email: matthew@bakerhopp.com
      Website: www.bakerhopp.com
Property & casualty life and health insurance agency. (As-
Pac, estab 2002, empl 1, sales , cert: NMSDC)

Minnesota

5727 Integrated Benefits Group, Inc.
      601 Carlson Pkwy Ste 1097
      Hopkins, MN 55305
      Contact: Deborah J. Dybdahl CEO
      Tel: 952-449-5290
      Email: deborah@integratedbenefitsgroup.com
      Website: www.integratedbenefitsgroup.com
Auto/home, legal, long term care, critical illnesss, supplemental disability, retirement planning, PET, etc. (Woman,
estab 1992, empl 16, sales $550,000, cert: WBENC)

Ohio

5728 Pinkney-Perry Insurance Agency, Inc.
      2143 Stokes Blvd
      Cleveland, OH 44106
      Contact: Patricia L. Welcome VP
      Tel: 216-795-1995
      Email: pwelcome@pinkney-perry.com
      Website: www.pinkney-perry.com
Insurance. (AA, estab 0, empl , sales , cert: NMSDC)

Pennsylvania

5729 Benefits Plus Consulting Group
      1807 Pine St 1st Fl
      Philadelphia, PA 19103
      Contact: Norma Romero-Mitchell CEO
      Tel: 215-564-0288
      Email: norma@consultbenefitsplus.com
      Website: www.benefitsplusconsulting.com
Benefits consulting & advisory services, insurance, long
term care. (Minority, Woman, estab 1993, empl 8, sales
$403,180, cert: NMSDC, WBENC)

Tennessee

5730 Diversity Benefits
      230 N 4th Ave, Ste 162
      Nasville, TN 37219
      Contact: David Carter President
      Tel: 615-515-3329
      Email: davidc@diversitybenefits.net
      Website: www.diversitybenefits.net
Health insurance/self-funded health plans, Prescription
drug coverage, Reinsurance ,Dental insurance, Vision
insurance, Life and AD&D insurance, Disability insurance, Voluntary benefits, Retirement plans. (AA, estab
2012, empl 2, sales , cert: NMSDC)

Texas

5731 CPR Insurance Group LLC
      600 E John Carpenter Frwy Ste 365
      Irving, TX 75062
      Contact: Les Titus President
      Tel: 972-887-3660
      Email: ltitus@cprins.com
      Website: www.cprins.com
Insurance claims: property, liability/casualty & auto
claims. (AA, Hisp, estab 2013, empl 19, sales $1,200,000,
cert: State)

LABORATORY/SCIENTIFIC SUPPLIES & SERVICES
Manufacture or distribute products or provide services for scientific laboratories. Products include glassware, disposables, chemicals, safety items. etc.
NAICS Code 33

California

5732 Accurate C&S Services, Inc.
8105 Edgewater Dr Ste 225
Oakland, CA 94621
Contact: Regina Jones President
Tel: 510-387-0324
Email: rjones@accuratemgmt.com
Website: www.accureatecsservices.com
Drug & alcohol testing. (Woman/AA, estab 2006, empl 12, sales $1,500,000, cert: City, NMSDC, WBENC)

5733 BC Laboratories, Inc.
4100 Atlas Court
Bakersfield, CA 93308
Contact: Mark Ellis Business Devel Dir
Tel: 800-878-4911
Email: mark.ellis@bclabs.com
Website: www.bclabs.com
Analytical Services for Groundwater, Drinking Water, Wastewater, Soils & Air, Certified Testing Services, Sampling & Monitoring. (Woman, estab 1949, empl 97, sales $1,000,000,000, cert: CPUC)

5734 BIO PLAS, Inc.
4340 Redwood Hwy Ste A1
San Rafael, CA 94903
Contact: Jeananne McGrath VP
Tel: 415-472-3777
Email: jam@bioplas.com
Website: www.bioplas.com
Mfr disposable laboratory supplies. (Woman, estab 1977, empl 10, sales , cert: State)

5735 Brylen Technologies
275 Orange Ave
Santa Barbara, CA 93117
Contact: Barbara Tzur President
Tel: 805-692-9300
Email: barbara.tzur@brylen.com
Website: www.brylen.com
Calibration & testing laboratory, clean room & clean bench certifications, calibration is electro-magnetic, thermodynamics, dimensional, angle, & mechanical areas, calibrate equipment. (Woman, estab 1985, empl 10, sales $571,850, cert: State)

5736 Comprehensive Drug Testing, Inc. (CDT, Inc.)
PO Box 11869
Santa Ana, CA 92711
Contact: Kim Jasper President
Tel: 800-440-3784
Email: kimj@cdtsolutions.com
Website: www.cdtsolutions.com
Substance abuse program management, drug testing, collections, laboratory, education. (Woman, estab 1985, empl 13, sales $2,400,000, cert: State, CPUC)

5737 Core Diagnostics
3535 Breakwater Ave
Hayward, CA 94545
Contact: Krishnamurthy Balachandran CEO
Tel: 650-532-9500
Email: balachandran@corediagnostics.net
Website: www.corediagnostics.net
Laboratory offering biomarker analysis & translational research support for studies ranging from early discovery to analyses of Phase III clinical trial samples. (As-Ind, estab 2009, empl 12, sales $3,259,000, cert: NMSDC)

5738 CP Lab Safety
14 Commercial Blvd, Ste 113
Novato, CA 94949
Contact: Jessica Kurtz Cstmr Service
Tel: 415-883-2600
Email: info@cplabsafety.com
Website: www.calpaclab.com
Mfr environmentally conscious laboratory safety products & dist leading lab supply brands. (Woman, estab 1996, empl 6, sales $3,069,391, cert: State, 8(a))

5739 Discount Lab Supplies
3201 Verdant Way
San Jose, CA 95117
Contact: Stacey Blanding President
Tel: 408-246-4024
Email: stacey@discountlabs.com
Website: www.discountlabs.com
Dist lab products: cryogenic storage vessels, DI water systems, furnaces, harvey sterilizers, incubators, NANOpure water systems, ovens, rotators & rockers, spectrophotometers, turner fluorometers, ultrasonic cleaners. (Minority, Woman, estab 2004, empl 1, sales , cert: NMSDC)

5740 Fulgent Therapeutics LLC
4978 Santa Anita Ave Ste 205
Temple City, CA 91780
Contact: Joe Roach VP
Tel: 626-350-0537
Email: joeroach@fulgentdiagnostics.com
Website: www.fulgentdiagnostics.com
Hereditary genetic testing. (As-Pac, estab 2013, empl 30, sales $1,000,000, cert: NMSDC)

5741 InterWorking Labs, Inc.
PO Box 66190
Scotts Valley, CA 95067
Contact: Judy Jones Marketing Mgr
Tel: 831-460-7010
Email: info@iwl.com
Website: www.iwl.com
Network Emulation for testing Products. (Woman, estab 1993, empl 10, sales $800,000, cert: WBENC)

5742 Orange Coast Analytical, Inc.
3002 Dow Ave, Ste 532
Tustin, CA 92780
Contact: Cindy Noorani President
Tel: 714-832-0064
Email: cindyn@ocalab.com
Website: www.ocalab.com
Environmental & analytical testing laboratory, organic & inorganic testing-water, waste water, soil, air, industial, chemical & food products. (Woman, estab 1990, empl 15, sales $1,450,178, cert: State, CPUC)

5743 Phamatech, Inc.
10151 Barnes Canyon Rd
San Diego, CA 92121
Contact: Jodee Callaghan Natl Sales Consultant
Tel: 888-635-5840
Email: jodee@phamatech.com
Website: www.phamatech.com
Drug testing laboratory. (As-Pac, estab 1991, empl 185, sales $22,277,000, cert: NMSDC)

5744 Pure Lab Solutions, Inc.
4901 Morena Blvd, Ste 118
San Diego, CA 92117
Contact: Pam Wammes President
Tel: 619-840-5858
Email: pwammes@purelabsolutions.com
Website: www.purelabsolutions.com
Dist Sartorius lab equipment, ultrapure water purification & lab bench scales. (Woman, estab 2012, empl 2, sales , cert: WBENC)

5745 The Andwin Corp.
6636 Variel Ave
Canoga Park, CA 91303
Contact: Arnie Shedlow Sr VP Sales
Tel: 818-999-2828
Email: jpalaganas@andwin.com
Website: www.andwinsci.com
Dist medical & lab supplies & product kits: boxes, labels, bar codes, instruction inserts & kit components. (Woman, estab 1950, empl 98, sales $32,000,000, cert: WBENC)

Connecticut

5746 PRO Scientific Inc.
99 Willenbrock Rd
Oxford, CT 06478
Contact: Holly Archibald Sales Dir
Tel: 203-267-4600
Email: sales@proscientific.com
Website: www.proscientific.com
Mfr PRO Scientific laboratory equipment, PRO homogenizers, mixers, shakers & stirrers. Dist Andreas Hettich Centrifuges. (Woman, estab 1992, empl 15, sales , cert: State)

Florida

5747 Algon Corporation
12000 SW 132 Court
Miami, FL 33186
Contact: Eduardo Suarez-Troconis Dir
Tel: 305-253-6901
Email: edal@algon.com
Website: www.algon.com
Chemical raw materials, laboratory supplies & machine parts. (Minority, Woman, estab 1989, empl 24, sales $20,570,883, cert: NMSDC)

5748 Kramer Laboratories, Inc.
400 University Dr Ste 400
Coral Gables, FL 33134
Contact: Myrna Patterson Sales Mgr
Tel: 800-824-4894
Email: mpatterson@kramerlabs.com
Website: www.kramerlabs.com
Fungi Nail Brand, Safetussin CD Cough Relief/Nasal Decongestant Formula, Safetussin DM Cough Formula. (Minority, Woman, estab 1987, empl 14, sales , cert: NMSDC, WBENC)

5749 VetMeds, Inc.
8950 SW 74th Court Ste 2201
Miami, FL 33156
Contact: President
Tel: 786-220-3634
Email: vetmeds@gmx.com
Website: www.vetmedsinc.com
Dist medical equipment, medical apparel, wound care supplies, medical furniture, exam room supplies, extrication-patient transport equipment, surgical gloves, IV therapy & laboratory supplies. (Woman/AA, estab 2012, empl 5, sales , cert: State)

Massachusetts

5750 Cross-Spectrum Acoustics Inc
PO Box 90842
Springfield, MA 01139
Contact: Herbert Singleton Managing Partner
Tel: 413-315-5770
Email: dbe@csacoustics.com
Website: www.csacoustics.com
Acoustical consulting, noise and vibration control, sound measurements, noise & vibration mitigation. (AA, estab 2003, empl 1, sales , cert: State)

Maryland

5751 Quality Biological, Inc.
7581 Lindbergh Dr
Gaithersburg, MD 20879
Contact: Basile Whitaker VP Operations
Tel: 301-840-9331
Email: whitakerb@qualitybiological.com
Website: www.qualitybiological.com
Mfr tissue culture & molecular biology products, bacteriological plates, dist Corning glass & plastics, Corning lab equipment, Microflex gloves & JT Baker chemicals. (Woman/AA, estab 1983, empl 24, sales , cert: NMSDC)

5752 Trinity Sterile, Inc.
201 Kiley Dr
Salisbury, MD 21801
Contact: Crystal Lutz VP Sales
Tel: 410-860-5123
Email: crystal.lutz@trinitysterile.com
Website: www.trinitysterile.com
Production & sterilization equipment: clinical kits, trays or instruments. (As-Ind, estab , empl , sales , cert: NMSDC)

Michigan

5753 Forensic Fluids Laboratories Inc.
225 Parsons St
Kalamazoo, MI 49007
Contact: Bridget Lemberg CEO
Tel: 269-492-7700
Email: blemberg@forensicfluids.com
Website: www.Forensicfluids.com
Drug testing & screening. (Woman, estab 2005, empl 60, sales $19,861,000, cert: WBENC)

5754   RTI Laboratories, Inc.
      33080 Industrial Rd
      Livonia, MI 48150
      Contact: Kae Trojanowski President
      Tel: 734-422-8000
      Email: ktrojanowski@rtilab.com
      Website: www.rtilab.com
Analytical testing laboratory: environmental, chemical &
metallurgical testing, environmental compliance field
sampling services. (Minority, estab 1986, empl 40, sales
$5,000,000, cert: NMSDC, SDB)

5755   Structural Testing Laboratory
      397 Washington St, Ste B
      Brighton, MI 48116
      Contact: Tracy LaCroix Owner
      Tel: 734-476-9882
      Email: sales@stlbrighton.com
      Website: www.stlbrighton.com
Vibration & shock testing services for automotive, aero-
space & defense, transportation & packaging & military.
(Nat Ame, estab 2005, empl 3, sales , cert: NMSDC)

Minnesota

5756   LKT Laboratories, Inc.
      545 Phalen Blvd
      Saint Paul, MN 55130
      Contact: Luke Lam President
      Tel: 651-644-8424
      Email: llam@lktlabs.com
      Website: www.lktlabs.com/
Mfr biochemicals for life science research, inhibitors,
activators, modulators, and many other high purity small
molecules, phytochemical isolation and analysis. (As-Pac,
estab 1990, empl 11, sales $1,300,000, cert: NMSDC)

Missouri

5757   HERA Laboratory Planners
      411 N. Tenth St, Ste 400
      St. Louis, MO 63101
      Contact: Laurie Sperling President
      Tel: 314-289-9202
      Email: lauries@herainc.com
      Website: www.herainc.com
Laboratory planning, design, programming & equipment
planning. (Woman, estab 1996, empl 22, sales $8,113,716,
cert: State, WBENC)

5758   Taylor Scientific
      950 Hanley Industrial Ct
      St. Louis, MO 63144
      Contact: Jill Taylor President
      Tel: 800-727-0467
      Email: jill@taylorscientific.com
      Website: www.taylorscientific.com
Dist laboratory supplies. (Woman, estab 1972, empl 12,
sales , cert: WBENC)

North Carolina

5759   Clinical Choice LLC
      5574 Garden Village Way Ste D400
      Greensboro, NC 27410
      Contact: Minerva Loran President
      Tel: 336-841-0919
      Email: mloran@clinicalchoice.com
      Website: www.clinicalchoice.com
Lab supplies, cleaning brushes, bite blocks, filters for the
reprocessing scope washing machines, Endo supplies,
SafeCap Endoscope Transport Trays, ScopeVault Endoscope Storage Cabinets, OneTab Powder and Liquid
detergent. (Minority, Woman, estab 2001, empl 7, sales
$3,751,424, cert: NMSDC)

5760   LJP Lab LLC
      495-S Arbor Hill Rd
      Kernersville, NC 27284
      Contact: Thomas Stith President
      Tel: 336-992-3902
      Email: tstith@ljplab.com
      Website: www.ljplab.com
Urine drug screen & confirmation services. (As-Pac,
estab 2017, empl 6, sales $500,000, cert: State)

Nebraska

5761   Midland Scientific Inc.
      10651 Chandler Rd Ste 102
      Lavista, NE 68128
      Contact: Shane Hanzlik
      Tel: 402-346-8352
      Email: shanzlik@midlandsci.com
      Website: www.midlandsci.com
Dist lab supplies & equipment. (Woman, estab , empl ,
sales $48,000,000, cert: WBENC)

New Jersey

5762   AGC Products Inc.
      3740 NW Blvd
      Vineland, NJ 08360
      Contact: Subu Natesan CEO
      Tel: 856-692-4435
      Email: snatesan@andrews-glass.com
      Website: www.andrews-glass.com
Manufacture specialty and precision glass products for
industrial and scientific applications. (As-Ind, estab
1948, empl 40, sales $4,000,000, cert: State, NMSDC)

5763   BioRepository Resources, LLC
      755 Central Ave, Unit 3
      New Providence, NJ 07974
      Contact: Catherine Chin CEO
      Tel: 908-790-8890
      Email: cchin@brr.us.com
      Website: www.brr.us.com
Long term storage of biological & clinical trial samples:
blood, plasma, urine, tissue, biomarkers, retain drug
product, API, pathology slides, blocks. (Minority,
Woman, estab 2008, empl 2, sales , cert: State)

5764 Laboratory Disposable Products
1 Como Court
Towaco, NJ 07082
Contact: Cindy Beatty President
Tel: 973-335-2966
Email: mail@labdisposable.com
Website: www.labdisposable.com
Laboratory Disposable Products. (Woman, estab 1979, empl 10, sales $3,549,720, cert: City, WBENC)

5765 Neta Scientific Inc.
4206 Sylon Blvd
Hainesport, NJ 08036
Contact: Winfred Sanders, PhD President
Tel: 609-265-8210
Email: sales@netascientific.com
Website: www.netascientific.com
Dist laboratory instruments & supplies safety & environmental supplies. (Woman/AA, estab 1999, empl 45, sales , cert: State, NMSDC, WBENC)

5766 Sarchem Laboratories, Inc.
5012 Industrial Rd
Farmingdale, NJ 07727
Contact: Arun Kumar VP
Tel: 732-938-2777
Email: arun.kumar@sarchemlabs.com
Website: www.sarchemlabs.com
Custom Synthesis, Process development from concept to lab scale preparation, Contract Research and Development. Supply small scale diagnostic reagents, chemical reagents and EPA samples in customer required ampules. (Woman/As-Ind, estab 1984, empl 6, sales $1,215,000, cert: NMSDC)

Ohio

5767 DHDC Engineering Consulting Services, Inc.
2390 Advanced Business Center Dr
Columbus, OH 43228
Contact: Savvas Sophocleous President
Tel: 614-527-7656
Email: sophocleous@dhdcinc.com
Website: www.dhdcinc.com
Laboratory testing services, geotechnical (engineering, drilling, and laboratory) & subsurface utility engineering (SUE). (As-Pac, estab 2012, empl 15, sales $500,000, cert: State)

5768 Midtown Scientific, Inc.
4415 Euclid Ave, Ste 343
Cleveland, OH 44103
Contact: Darlene Darby Baldwin CEO
Tel: 216-431-0110
Email: ddarbywatt@aol.com
Website: www.midtownscientific.com
Dist scientific laboratory research supplies & equipment, chemicals. (Woman/AA, estab 2002, empl 4, sales , cert: City)

Pennsylvania

5769 MB Research Laboratories
1765 Wentz Rd
Spinnerstown, PA 18968
Contact: Betty Salyer Accounts Receivable
Tel: 215-536-4110
Email: blandis@mbresearch.com
Website: www.mbresearch.com
Contract Research Toxicology Laboratory. (Hisp, estab 1972, empl 28, sales , cert: WBENC)

Puerto Rico

5770 Instrumed Services Corp.
10th St O 14 Castellana G
Carolina, PR 00983
Contact: Luis Peña President
Tel: 787-257-9249
Email: luis.pena@instrumed.net
Website: www.instrumed.net
Sales, Service, Validation and Calibration of Laboratory Equipments. (Minority, Woman, estab 1999, empl 10, sales , cert: NMSDC)

5771 J.C. Gonzalez, Inc.
2 St KM 178.2 Interior BO. Minillas Alto
San German, PR 00683
Contact: Julio C. Gonzalez Santiago CEO
Tel: 787-892-0047
Email: sales@jcgonzalezinc.com
Website: www.jcgonzalezinc.com
Dist & service scientific & research equipment, laboratory equipment & consumables, microscopes, stereoscopes, freezers, refrigerators. (Hisp, estab 2001, empl 6, sales $865,047, cert: NMSDC, SDB)

5772 MentorTechnical Group, Corp.
PO Box 6857
Caguas, PR 00726
Contact: Luis David Soto President
Tel: 787-743-0897
Email: jose.gonzalez@mentortg.com
Website: www.mentortg.com
Calibration, Instrumentation, and Control Systems Laboratory. (Hisp, estab 2000, empl 450, sales $27,500,000, cert: NMSDC)

Tennessee

5773 Safety Plus, LLC
PO Box 2549
Chattanooga, TN 37409
Contact: Alexa Wardlaw VP/Member
Tel: 423-822-0487
Email: alexa@safetyplusllc.com
Website: www.safetyplusllc.com
Safety solutions: fume hood, biosafety cabinet & clean air bench testing & maintenance, employee training, lab design & equipment recommendations. (Woman, estab 2005, empl 7, sales $284,017, cert: WBENC)

5774 Scientific Sales, Inc.
130 Valley Ct St
Oak Ridge, TN 37830
Contact: Ember Murphy President
Tel: 865-483-9332
Email: emurphy@scisale.com
Website: www.scisale.com
Dist laboratory supplies, equipment, chemicals, safety, industrial & environmental products. (Minority, Woman, estab 1987, empl 30, sales , cert: State, NMSDC)

5775   The Premier Group
      4600 Cromwell Ave, Ste 101
      Memphis, TN 38118
      Contact: JW Gibson CEO
      Tel: 901-346-9002
      Email: jwgibson@gibsoncompanies.com
      Website: www.gibsoncompanies.com
Dist medical supplies, laboratory & scientific equipment & related supplies. (AA, estab 1991, empl 7, sales $8,692,576, cert: NMSDC)

Texas

5776   Affirmative Biosolutions
      PO Box 2274
      Stafford, TX 77497
      Contact: seble woubshet Owner
      Tel: 713-256-8996
      Email: abiosolutions@hotmail.com
      Website: www.abiosolutions.com
Dist laboratories, medical & industrial products (Woman/AA, estab 2010, empl 3, sales , cert: State, City)

5777   Duran Industries Inc.
      504 Business Pkwy
      Richardson, TX 75081
      Contact: Richard Duran President
      Tel: 972-238-7122
      Email: rduran@duranco.com
      Website: www.duranco.com/
Dist industrial, commercial, MRO, safety, scientific & lab products. (Hisp, estab 1995, empl 20, sales $14,050,000, cert: NMSDC)

5778   Fox Scientific, Inc.
      8221 East FM 917
      Alvarado, TX 76009
      Contact: Jetta Lewis Sales
      Tel: 800-369-5524
      Email: paisleyg@foxscientific.com
      Website: www.foxscientific.com
Dist laboratory supplies, equipment & chemicals. (Hisp, estab 1988, empl 21, sales $5,420,000, cert: State, City, NMSDC)

5779   Products Unlimited, Inc.
      PO Box 339
      Justin, TX 76247
      Contact: Raithel Susan Sales Mgr
      Tel: 940-648-3073
      Email: sraithel@products-unlimited.com
      Website: www.products-unlimited.com
Dist medical, lab & safety supplies & equipment. (Woman, estab 1992, empl 7, sales $5,020,000, cert: State)

LEGAL SERVICES

Legal counsel, process services, patent agents, public notaries, paralegal services, court reporting, litigation, mediation, law firms. NAICS Code 54

California

5780 Apogee Law Group, P.C.
      100 Sprectrum Center Dr Ste 900
      Irvine, CA 92618
      Contact: Francisco Rubio President
      Tel: 949-862-8484
      Email: frubio@goapogee.com
      Website: www.apogeelawgroup.com
Specialize in patents, trademarks, and corporate law. (Hisp, estab 2015, empl 6, sales $820,000, cert: NMSDC)

5781 Baer Reed
      8 Sunburst
      Irvine, CA 92603
      Contact: Danielle Buglino SVP
      Tel: 516-658-5003
      Email: dbuglino@baerreed.com
      Website: www.baerreed.com
Virtual Paralegals, Virtual Assistants, Legal Assistants, Global Shared Services, Legal Billing, Management & Review, Ediscovery, Real Estate Law, Contract Analysis, AI Support, Due Diligence, Document Review & Foreign Language Review, Legal Research, Litigation / Internal Investigation, Deposition Summaries, Content Moderation & Social Media Monitoring (Woman, estab 2011, empl 85, sales $1,038,084, cert: NWBOC)

5782 Banker's Hill Law Firm, A.P.C.
      160 Thorn St, Ste 200
      San Diego, CA 92103
      Contact: Carlos Alvarez Tostado Marketing Rep
      Tel: 619-230-0330
      Email: carlosa@bhlflaw.com
      Website: www.bhlflaw.com
Personal injury, immigration law, criminal defense, bankruptcy, and family law. (AA, estab 1991, empl 12, sales $3,154,988, cert: NMSDC)

5783 Behmke Reporting & Video Services
      160 Spear St Ste 300
      San Francisco, CA 94105
      Contact: Paula Behmke Owner
      Tel: 415-597-5600
      Email: paula.behmke@behmke.com
      Website: www.behmke.com
Court reporting, realtime reporting, legal videography, litigation support services with local, state, and nationwide coverage. Cetralized scheduling and billing. (Woman, estab 1989, empl 7, sales $2,168,392, cert: CPUC, WBENC)

5784 Ben Hyatt Corporation
      17835 Ventura Blvd Ste 310
      Encino, CA 91316
      Contact: Mitch Hyatt VP
      Tel: 888-272-0022
      Email: mhyatt@benhyatt.com
      Website: www.benhyatt.com
Court reporting, litigation support services. (Woman, estab 1998, empl 10, sales $3,300,000, cert: WBENC)

5785 California Deposition Reporters
      599 S Barranca
      Covina, CA 91723
      Contact: Jamie Kirk President
      Tel: 800-274-1996
      Email: jamie@caldepo.com
      Website: www.caldepo.com
Court reporting, deposition transcription, videography for depositions, legal depositions, civil trial reporting, video conferencing. (Woman, estab 1979, empl 15, sales $1,687,887, cert: State, CPUC)

5786 Carol Nygard & Associates
      2295 Gateway Oaks Dr, Ste 170
      Sacramento, CA 95833
      Contact: John Nygard VP Business Dev
      Tel: 877-438-7787
      Email: john@walnutcreekcourtreporter.com
      Website: www.nygardreporting.com
Full-service court reporting agency specializing in complex litigation 24/7. (Woman, estab 2000, empl 5, sales $1,257,000, cert: State)

5787 CIR Law Offices International
      2650 Camino Del Rio N, Ste 308
      San Diego, CA 92108
      Contact: Amanda Cinq-Mars Business Devel Mgr
      Tel: 858-496-8909
      Email: acinq-mars@cirlaw.com
      Website: www.cirlaw.com/
Business law, International law, Intellectual Property counseling and Litigation. (Hisp, estab 1997, empl 35, sales $2,608,078, cert: NMSDC)

5788 EcoTeal, Inc.
      18685 Main St, 101-144
      Huntington Beach, CA 92648
      Contact: Maria Tettman President
      Tel: 714-375-5700
      Email: mtettman@ecoteal.com
      Website: www.ecoteal.com
Accident Investigation and Reporting, Acquisitions and Divestitures, Construction Safety, Emergency Preparedness and Response, Energy Efficiency and Conservation. (Woman, estab 2012, empl 1, sales $100,000, cert: City, CPUC)

5789 Kupferstein Manuel LLP
      865 S Figueroa St Ste 3338
      Los Angeles, CA 90017
      Contact: Phyllis Kupferstein Managing Partner
      Tel: 213-988-7531
      Email: pk@kupfersteinmanuel.com
      Website: www.kupfersteinmanuel.com
Trial law firm specializing in employment and general business litigation. (Woman, estab 2014, empl 3, sales $1,406,238, cert: WBENC)

5790 Kusar Court Reporters & Legal Services, Inc.
      111 W Ocean Blvd Ste 1200
      Long Beach, CA 90802
      Contact: Amber Kusar Contract Mgr
      Tel: 800-282-3376
      Email: info@kusar.com
      Website: www.kusar.com
Court reporters specializing in complex litigation & medmal, and they are professional, accurate, on time, accommodating, friendly, andhelpful. (Woman, estab 1983, empl 12, sales $3,600,000, cert: City, CPUC, WBENC)

5791   Lafayette & Kumagai LLP
1300 Clay St Ste 810
Oakland, CA 94612
Contact: Clara Marigmen Office Admin
Tel: 415-357-4600
Email: cmarigmen@lkclaw.com
Website: www.lkclaw.com
Civil litigation law firm, motion practice, jury trials, appeals, mediations, arbitrations, other ADR procedures and hearings. (AA, As-Pac, estab 1994, empl 15, sales $3,285,704, cert: NMSDC, CPUC)

5792   Livingston Law Firm, A Professional Corporation
1600 S Main St, Ste 280
Walnut Creek, CA 94596
Contact: Renee Livingston President
Tel: 925-952-9880
Email: rlivingston@livingstonlawyers.com
Website: www.livingstonlawyers.com
Provide high quality, cost efficient legal services in California. We specialize in product liability litigation. (Woman, estab 2000, empl 11, sales $1,976,196, cert: CPUC, WBENC)

5793   Parker Law Group, Inc.
27815 Barbate
Mission Viejo, CA 92692
Contact: Claudia Parker CEO
Tel: 949-916-9910
Email: cparker@parkerlawgroup.com
Website: www.parkerlawgroup.com
Transactional business legal services to publicly traded, private companies in the manufacturing and technology sectors as well as to non-profit companies covering general business law, technology law. (Woman/As-Pac, Hisp, estab 2008, empl 2, sales $0, cert: NMSDC)

5794   Sideman & Bancroft LLP
1 Embarcadero Center #2200
San Francisco, CA 94111
Contact: Ellen Kahn
Tel: 415-392-1960
Email: ekahn@sideman.com
Website: www.sideman.com
Legal services, civil, business, real estate, professional liability, intellectual property and tax litigation; trademarks, copyrights, domain names, brand protection, technology licensing and transfers; corporate; mergers, acquisitions, joint ventures, strategic alliances; commercial contracts; real estate transactions; tax planning; business crimes defense. (Woman, estab , empl , sales $0, cert: WBENC)

5795   Urrabazo Law, P.C.
2029 Century Park E Ste 400
Los Angeles, CA 90067
Contact: Donald Urrabazo President
Tel: 310-388-9099
Email: durrabazo@ulawpc.com
Website: www.ulawpc.com
Full range of complex litigation matters, contractual and commercial disputes in federal and state courts throughout California. (Hisp, estab 2011, empl 6, sales $1,500,000, cert: NMSDC, CPUC)

5796   Wang & Chang
255 California St Ste 525
San Francisco, CA 94111
Contact: Justin Chang Partner
Tel: 415-599-2828
Email: justin@wangchanglaw.com
Website: www.wangchanglaw.com
Litigation matters, complex commercial cases, class actions, and civil lawsuits. (As-Pac, estab 2011, empl 4, sales $1,300,000, cert: NMSDC)

5797   Wilson Turner Kosmo LLP
550 West C St, Ste 1050
San Diego, CA 92101
Contact: Robin Wofford Partner
Tel: 619-236-9600
Email: rwofford@wilsonturnerkosmo.com
Website: www.wilsonturnerkosmo.com
Legal services: employment law, product liability, contract disputes, real property litigation, health care, warranty, first amendment, trade secret and trust litigation. (Woman/AA, estab 1991, empl 55, sales $11,770,943, cert: CPUC, WBENC)

5798   Yang Professional Law Corporation
80 S. Lake Ave, Ste 820
Pasadena, CA 91101
Contact: Rey Shung President
Tel: 626-921-4300
Email: ryang@yangpc.com
Website: www.yangpc.com
Civil litigation, insurance defense, personal injury, premises liability, product liability, insurance, subrogation, indemnity, employment, automobile, labor, transportation. (As-Pac, estab 2014, empl 3, sales $350,000, cert: NMSDC, CPUC)

5799   Zuber Lawler & Del Duca LLP
350 S Grand Ave, 32nd Floor
Los Angeles, CA 90071
Contact: Tom Zuber Managing Partner
Tel: 213-596-5620
Email: contact@zuberlaw.com
Website: www.zuberlaw.com
IP, environment, class action, and commercial litigation. (As-Pac, estab 2003, empl 54, sales $14,565,000, cert: NMSDC, CPUC)

5800   Zumizi Corp, dba iDepo Reporters
898 N Pacific Coast Hwy, Ste 475
El Segundo, CA 90245
Contact: Tina Mason-Hicks Dir of Operations
Tel: 323-393-3768
Email: tm@ideporeporters.com
Website: www.ideporeporters.com
Full-service court reporting & record retrieval, document retrieval, process service, subpoenas, depositions, court stenographic reporting, transcriptions, legal videography and translation/interpreter services. (As-Pac, estab 2013, empl 10, sales $2,894,115, cert: NMSDC)

Colorado

5801 Campbell Litigation, P.C.
730 17th St, Ste 740
Denver, CO 80202
Contact: Michelle Campbell VP Operations
Tel: 303-536-1833
Email: michelle@campbell-litigation.com
Website: www.campbell-litigation.com/
Employment, labor and commercial litigation defense trial lawyers. (AA, estab 2015, empl 5, sales $1,000,000, cert: NMSDC)

5802 Fair Measures, Inc.
PO Box 22939
Denver, CO 80222
Contact: Jo-Ann Birch President
Tel: 800-458-2778
Email: jbirch@fairmeasures.com
Website: www.fairmeasures.com
Legal services and training on management law for line Mgrs, business owners, Human Resource professionals and lawyers. (Woman, estab , empl , sales $640,000, cert: WBENC)

5803 Gibson Arnold & Associates, Inc.
518 17th St, Ste 1125
Denver, CO 80202
Contact: Elizabeth Dahill Exec VP
Tel: 303-595-3655
Email: denver@gibsonarnold.com
Website: www.gibsonarnold.com
Natl legal recruiting firm with offices in Denver, Houston, and Los Angeles. We have over 29 years experience in placing attorneys, paralegals, and legal support staff. (Woman, estab 1981, empl 16, sales $5,228,089, cert: WBENC)

5804 Wells, Anderson & Race, LLC
1700 Broadway, Ste 1020
Denver, CO 80290
Contact: Jaime Heveron CFO
Tel: 303-830-1212
Email: jheveron@warll.com
Website: www.warllc.com
Litigation and appeals for local, regional and national clients. (Woman, estab 1995, empl 28, sales , cert: WBENC)

Connecticut

5805 Reardon Scanlon LLP
45 S Main St, Ste 305
Hartford, CT 06107
Contact: Katherine Scanlon Managing Partner
Tel: 860-955-9450
Email: katherine.scanlon@reardonscanlon.com
Website: www.reardonscanlon.com
Insurance industry litigation boutique. (Woman, estab 2012, empl 3, sales $899,950, cert: WBENC)

5806 Varunes & Assocaites, P.C.
5 Grand St
Hartford, CT 06106
Contact: Anita Varunes President
Tel: 860-541-1675
Email: avarunes@varuneslaw.com
Website: www.varuneslaw.com
Liability defense litigation and workers' compensation defense litigation. The attorneys in our office handle all aspects of civil lititgation from inception, discovery and trials before a jury or judge. (Woman, estab 2006, empl 9, sales $996,810, cert: WBENC)

District of Columbia

5807 Garrison & Sisson, Inc.
1620 Eye St, NW Ste 501
Washington, DC 20006
Contact: Kathy Charlwood
Tel: 202-429-5630
Email: kcharlwood@g-s.com
Website: www.g-s.com
Attorney Referral and Placement. (Woman, estab 1986, empl 8, sales $1,565,495, cert: WBENC)

5808 Ifrah PLLC
1717 Pennsylvania Ave, NW Ste 650
Washington, DC 20006
Contact: Kyle Ueyama Legal Asst
Tel: 202-524-4140
Email: kyle@ifrahlaw.com
Website: www.ifrahlaw.com
Successful defense strategies, successfully manage, navigate and negotiate federal investigations. (Hisp, estab 2009, empl 7, sales $4,500,000, cert: City)

5809 Livesay IP Law, PLLC
888 16th St, NW, Ste 800
Washington, DC 20006
Contact: Margo Livesay Owner
Tel: 202-684-8685
Email: Margo@Livesay-IP.com
Website: www.Livesay-IP.com
Patent attorney services - patent prosecution, opinion work, due diligence, litigation support, software-related inventions, systems, architectures. (Woman, estab 2009, empl 1, sales $186,590, cert: WBENC)

5810 The O'Riordan Bethel Law Firm, LLP
1314 19th St NW
Washington, DC 20036
Contact: Carol O'Riordan Managing Partner
Tel: 202-822-1720
Email: coriordan@oriordan-law.com
Website: www.oriordan-law.com
Trial, appellate, ADR, counseling and drafting, administrative, civil and criminal law; fiduciary matters, government procurement, Title VII, construction, Sarbanes Oxley. Document review, discovery support, drafting, analysis, contracts, disparity and inclusion, compliance, good governance. (Woman/AA, estab 1997, empl 5, sales $649,874, cert: State, City, WBENC, 8(a))

Florida

5811 Alvin K. Brown, P.A.
1001 3rd Ave West Ste 375
Bradenton, FL 34203
Contact: Alvin Brown President
Tel: 941-953-2825
Email: alvin@akbrownlaw.com
Website: www.brownandbrown.legal/
Security assessments, risk assessments, security training, investigation & litigation svcs. (AA, estab 2002, empl 1, sales $0, cert: State)

5812 DeMahy Labrador & Drake PA (DLD Lawyers)
806 Douglas Rd 12th Fl
Coral Gables, FL 33134
Contact: Greg Victor Partner
Tel: 305-443-4850
Email: gvictor@dldlawyers.com
Website: www.dldlawyers.com
Trial practice for large corporations. Our lawyers have over 1,000 completed jury trials. (Hisp, estab 1984, empl 56, sales $10,000,000, cert: NMSDC)

5813 Hudson & Calleja LLC
355 Alhambra Circle Ste 801
Coral Gables, FL 33134
Contact: Alexis Calleja Attorney Majority Shareholder
Tel: 305-444-6628
Email: acalleja@hudsoncalleja.com
Website: www.hudsoncalleja.com
Legal services. (Woman/Hisp, estab 2011, empl 20, sales $1,700,000, cert: NMSDC, WBENC)

5814 Leon Cosgrove, LLC
255 Alhambra Circle, Ste 800
Coral Gables, FL 33134
Contact: Maricarmen Ortega Firm Admin
Tel: 305-740-1975
Email: mortega@leoncosgrove.com
Website: www.leoncosgrove.com
Complex litigation with offices in Miami, FL, Washington, DC and Dallas, Texas. (Hisp, estab 2013, empl 23, sales , cert: NMSDC)

5815 Levi G. Williams, Jr., P.A.
12 SE 7th St Ste 700
Fort Lauderdale, FL 33301
Contact: Levi Williams President
Tel: 954-463-1626
Email: levi@leviwilliamslaw.com
Website: www.leviwilliamslaw.com
Business Consulting, Litigation, Mediation, Administrative Hearings, Employment, Wage, Civil Rights, Sexual Harassment, Contracts, Negligence, Third Party Litigation, Premises Liability, Negotiations, Bonds, Mergers. (AA, estab 2011, empl 2, sales $300,000, cert: NMSDC)

5816 Losey PLLC
450 S Orange Ave, Ste 550
Orlando, FL 32801
Contact: M. Catherine Losey Managing Partner
Tel: 407-986-0406
Email: closey@losey.law
Website: www.losey.law
Legal services, litigations, arbitrations, and negotiations, manage cybersecurity risks, manage data breach response. (Woman, estab 2016, empl 5, sales $949,437, cert: WBENC)

5817 Marrero & Wydler
2600 Douglas Rd, PH-4
Coral Gables, FL 33113
Contact: Oscar Marrero President
Tel: 305-446-5528
Email: oem@marrerolegal.com
Website: www.marrerolegal.com
Litigation management. (Hisp, estab 2002, empl 6, sales $833,348, cert: State, NMSDC)

5818 Mint Legal Solutions
150 South Pine Island Rd Ste 300
Plantation, FL 33324
Contact: Zully Vergel President
Tel: 954-241-1300
Email: zully@mintlegalsolutions.com
Website: www.mintlegalsolutions.com
Electronic discovery and litigation support. Services include data identification, collection, processing (and culling for review), managed review/document review including but not limited to, physical facilities, review software, contractor staffing. (Woman/Hisp, estab 2017, empl 5, sales , cert: State, WBENC)

5819 Orange Legal Inc.
633 E Colonial Blvd
Orlando, FL 32803
Contact: Kim Henderson Corporate Acct Mgr
Tel: 404-400-6289
Email: kim.henderson@orangelegal.com
Website: www.orangelegal.com
Litigation support and unmatched customer service to the legal community, court reporting, process service, interpreting, videography. (Woman, estab , empl , sales $15,542,932, cert: State, City)

5820 Phipps Reporting, Inc.
1615 Forum Place, Ste 500
West Palm Beach, FL 33401
Contact: Christine Phipps Owner
Tel: 888-811-3408
Email: christine@phippsreporting.com
Website: www.phippsreporting.com
Court reporting. (Woman, estab 2010, empl 10, sales $2,862,699, cert: NWBOC)

5821 Quintairos, Prieto, Wood, and Boyer
255 S Orange Ave Ste 900
Orlando, FL 32801
Contact: Frank Alvarez Attorney/Partner
Tel: 407-872-6011
Email: frank.alvarez@qpwblaw.com
Website: www.QPWBlaw.com
Workers compensation appeals. (Woman/Hisp, estab 1998, empl 125, sales $17,012,551, cert: NMSDC)

5822 Roig Lawyers
1255 S Military Trail Ste 100
Deerfield Beach, FL 33442
Contact: Michael Rosenberg Managing Partner
Tel: 954-462-0330
Email: mrosenberg@roiglawyers.com
Website: www.roiglawyers.com
dDefense law firm: premises liability; workers' compensation; wrongful death (Hisp, estab 2000, empl 300, sales $19,452,441, cert: NMSDC)

5823 Romaguera Law Group, PA
11911 US Hwy 1, Ste 303
North Palm Beach, FL 33408
Contact: Raul Romaguera President
Tel: 561-472-1077
Email: rromaguera@romagueralaw.com
Website: www.romagueralaw.com
Professional liability, Products liability, Specialty risk liability, Breach of contract, Slip and fall, trip and fall and other premises liability, Wrongful death, Automotive liability, Medical malpractice, Construction defects, Dog bites, Property damage, arson and fire damage, Claims counsel oversight. (As-Ind, estab 2013, empl 4, sales $691,239, cert: NMSDC)

5824 Sanchez-Medina, Gonzalez, Quesada, et al.
201 Alhambra Circle Ste 1205
Miami, FL 33134
Contact: Emilia Quesada Partner
Tel: 305-377-1000
Email: equesada@smgqlaw.com
Website: www.smgqlaw.com
Legal services. (Hisp, estab 2007, empl 40, sales $0, cert: NMSDC)

5825 Steven C. Fraser, P.A.
221 W Hallandale Beach Blvd, Ste 201
Hallandale Beach, FL 33009
Contact: Steve Fraser Managing Dir
Tel: 305-809-6781
Email: sfraser@fraserlawfl.com
Website: www.fraserlawfl.com
Civil trial lawyers. We handle all kinds of claims, defense and liability cases throughout Florida in county, state and federal. (AA, estab 2008, empl 2, sales , cert: State)

5826 Torricella Law, PLLC
4551 Ponce de Leon Blvd
Coral Gables, FL 33146
Contact: Roberto A. Torricella, Jr. Managing Member
Tel: 786-693-6644
Email: Robert@TorricellaPastor.com
Website: www.TorricellaLaw.com
Civil and commercial litigation firm that practices in the areas of business, insurance, aviation, real estate, professional liability, employment and general liability litigation. (Hisp, estab 2014, empl 4, sales , cert: NMSDC)

5827 Van Ness Law Firm, PLC
1239 E Newport Center Dr, Ste 110
Deerfield Beach, FL 33442
Contact: John Van President
Tel: 954-571-2031
Email: compliance@vanlawfl.com
Website: www.vanlawfl.com
Law Firm, Commercial and Real Estate Litigation. (AA, estab 2004, empl 75, sales , cert: NMSDC)

Georgia

5828 Benefits Law Group, PK Keesler, PC
945 E Paces Ferry Rd Ste 2515
Atlanta, GA 30326
Contact: Patricia Keesler Owner
Tel: 404-995-9505
Email: pkeesler@benefitslawgroup.com
Website: www.benefitslawgroup.com
Law firm: employee benefits & executive compensation matters. (Woman, estab 1996, empl 8, sales $0, cert: WBENC)

5829 Friese Legal, LLC
1100 Spring St NW, Ste 730
Atlanta, GA 30309
Contact: Stephanie Friese Aron Managing Partner
Tel: 404-876-4880
Email: stephanie@frieselegal.com
Website: www.frieselegal.com
Commercial real estate transactions, including multi-family development, acquisitions, dispositions, and leasing and asset management of commercial properties. (Woman, estab 2001, empl 6, sales $350,000, cert: WBENC)

5830 Lee, Hong, Degerman, Kang & Waimey, APC
133 Main St
LaGrange, GA 30240
Contact: Bernard Ham Partner
Tel: 706-298-0134
Email: bham@lhlaw.com
Website: www.lhlaw.com
intellectual property, business and corporate transactions, commercial litigation, products liability, labor & employment, international arbitration, banking & financial services, and real estate. (As-Pac, estab 1991, empl 70, sales $17,290,000, cert: NMSDC, CPUC)

5831 Moser Law Co LLC
112 Krog St NE, Ste 26
Atlanta, GA 30307
Contact: Theresia Moser Owner
Tel: 404-537-5339
Email: tmoser@moserlawco.com
Website: www.moserlawco.com
Employment Lawyers & Litigators (Woman, estab 2014, empl 5, sales $250,000, cert: WBENC, NWBOC)

5832 Patrick Law Group, LLC
3705 Canyon Ridge Ct, NE
Atlanta, GA 30319
Contact: Founder
Tel: 404-437-6731
Email: info@patricklawgroup.com
Website: www.patricklawgroup.com
Construction Law and Commerical Contracting. We have prepared and negotiated hundreds of design, architect, construction, procurement and other contracts. (Woman, estab 2006, empl 4, sales $1,281,125, cert: WBENC)

5833 Pursley Friese Torgrimson, LLP
1230 Peachtree St., NE Ste 1200
Atlanta, GA 30309
Contact: Maxine Buchman Office Mgr
Tel: 404-665-1226
Email: marketing@pftlegal.com
Website: www.pftlegal.com
Commercial real estate transactions and eminent domain litigation. (Woman, estab 2013, empl 15, sales $1,853,288, cert: WBENC)

5834   Rutherford & Christie LLP
      225 Peachtree St South Tower, Ste 1750
      Atlanta, GA 30303
      Contact: Carrie Christie Managing Partner
      Tel: 404-522-6888
      Email: clc@rclawllp.com
      Website: www.rutherfordchristie.com
Defense litigation in the areas of general liability, employment, construction, contracts, constitutional law, aviation, products liability and workers's compensation. (Woman, estab 1999, empl 12, sales $2,600,000, cert: WBENC)

5835   Shingler Lewis LLC
      1230 Peachtree St Ste 1075
      Atlanta, GA 30309
      Contact: Joyce Gist Lewis Managing Partner
      Tel: 404-907-1999
      Email: jlewis@shinglerlewis.com
      Website: www.shinglerlewis.com
General liability defense, employment discrimination defense, and commercial litigation. (Woman/AA, estab 2012, empl 4, sales $510,000, cert: NMSDC)

Hawaii

5836   Carlsmith Ball LLP
      1001 Bishop St, Ste 2100
      Honolulu, HI 96809
      Contact: Michael Dolan COO
      Tel: 808-523-2500
      Email: mdolan@carlsmith.com
      Website: www.carlsmith.com
Law firm providing legal advise in Hawaii and California. Specialize in real estate and land use, corporate, litigation, energy and environmental. (Woman/As-Pac, estab , empl 180, sales $32,450,000, cert: CPUC)

Iowa

5837   MWH Law Group LLP
      1501 42nd St Ste 465
      West Des Moines, IA 50266
      Contact: Kerrie Murphy Managing Partner
      Tel: 515-453-8509
      Email: kerrie.murphy@mwhlawgroup.com
      Website: www.mwhlawgroup.com
Corporate & Transactional, Real Estate, Contract Support, Employment and Labor Law, Litigation, Intellectual Property. (AA, estab 2016, empl 14, sales $2,563,000, cert: NMSDC)

Illinois

5838   Advitam IP, LLC
      160 N Wacker Dr, 2nd Fl
      Chicago, IL 60606
      Contact: Michele Katz Founding Partner
      Tel: 312-332-7700
      Email: MKatz@AdvitamIP.com
      Website: www.advitamip.com
Legal services in the field of intellectual property, patent and trademark prosecution and litigation, copyright and domain name registration. (Woman, estab 2012, empl 4, sales , cert: WBENC)

5839   Chico & Nunes, P.C.
      333 W. Wacker Dr. Ste 1420
      Chicago, IL 60606
      Contact: Marcus Nunes Partner
      Tel: 312-463-1000
      Email: mnunes@chiconunes.com
      Website: www.chiconunes.com
Legal Services, Government Relations Services. (Hisp, estab 2004, empl 33, sales , cert: NMSDC)

5840   Clayborne, Sabo, and Wagner LLP
      525 W Main St Ste 105
      Belleville, IL 62220
      Contact: John Sabo Partner
      Tel: 618-239-0187
      Email: jsabo@cswlawllp.com
      Website: www.cswlawllp.com
The Firm consists of attorneys independently recognized by the Leading Lawyers Network and Martindale-Hubble as being in the top 5% of lawyers in their state in their fields of practice. (AA, estab 2013, empl 10, sales $1,580,000, cert: State, NMSDC)

5841   Grant Law, LLC
      230 W Monroe St Ste 240
      Chicago, IL 60606
      Contact: Maurice Grant Principal
      Tel: 312-551-0111
      Email: Mgrant@grantlawllc.com
      Website: www.grantlawllc.com
Commercial and Corporate Litigation: Real Estate, Commercial Lending and Corporate Services, Employment Law, Estate Planning. (Woman/AA, estab 2004, empl 6, sales $315,000, cert: NMSDC)

5842   Heavner Beyers & Mihlar LLC
      PO Box 740
      Decatur, IL 62525
      Contact: Faiq Mihlar Managing Member
      Tel: 217-422-1719
      Email: faiqmihlar@hsbattys.com
      Website: www.hsbattys.com
Law firm representing leading financial corporations, as well as middle and small-market clients in the default space. (Woman, estab 1978, empl 143, sales $11,771,967, cert: WBENC)

5843   Johnson Blumberg & Associates
      230 W Monroe Ste 1125
      Chicago, IL 60606
      Contact: Kenneth Johnson Sr Partner
      Tel: 312-541-9713
      Email: ken@johnsonblumberg.com
      Website: www.johnsonblumberg.com
Legal services. (Minority, estab 0, empl , sales $0, cert: NMSDC)

5844   LAW Ventures, Ltd.
      2970 Maria
      Northbrook, IL 60062
      Contact: Lori Ward President
      Tel: 847-791-1396
      Email: lori@lawventuresltd.com
      Website: www.lawventruesltd.com
Services provided leasing, management, acquistions, disposition, cost anaysis, re posistioning, sale lease back, nvestment and auction services. (Woman, estab 2004, empl 2, sales , cert: State)

5845   McClain & Canoy, LLC
       10 S Riverside Plaza Ste 875
       Chicago, IL 60606
       Contact: Salina Canoy Managing Member
       Tel: 312-474-6030
       Email: salina@mcclaincanoy.com
       Website: www.mcclaincanoy.com
Comprehensive legal services to businesses for transactional matters concerning health care, regulatory compliance, information privacy and security, health care information technology, government affairs, public policy. (Woman/AA, estab 2015, empl 5, sales $702,892, cert: State, NMSDC)

5846   McCormack Schreiber Legal Solutions Inc.
       303 W Madison St Ste 1725
       Chicago, IL 60606
       Contact: Amy McCormack Co-President
       Tel: 312-827-6470
       Email: amy@mslegalsolutions.com
       Website: www.thelawrecruiters.com
Contract attorney staffing firm. (Woman, estab 2007, empl 12, sales $458,579, cert: WBENC)

5847   Reyes Kurson, Ltd.
       328 S Jefferson St Ste 909
       Chicago, IL 60661
       Contact: Amy Kurson Managing Partner
       Tel: 312-332-0055
       Email: akurson@rkchicago.com
       Website: www.rkchicago.com
Boutique law firm. (AA, As-Pac, Hisp, estab 2005, empl 14, sales , cert: NMSDC)

5848   Sanchez Daniels & Hoffman, LLP
       333 W Wacker Dr Ste 500
       Chicago, IL 60606
       Contact: Heather D. Erickson Partner
       Tel: 312-641-1555
       Email: herickson@sanchezdh.com
       Website: www.sanchezdh.com
Mid-sized civil defense litigation firm with over 35 attorneys. (Hisp, estab 1987, empl 70, sales $9,480,000, cert: City, NMSDC)

5849   Valentine Austriaco & Bueschel, P.C.
       105 W Adams St 35th Fl
       Chicago, IL 60603
       Contact: Aurora Austriaco Partner
       Tel: 312-288-8285
       Email: aaustriaco@vablawfirm.com
       Website: www.vablawfirm.com
Experience resolving and litigating business disputes and handling real estate related matters, employment law, commercial litigation, contract dispute. (Woman, estab 2016, empl 8, sales $500,000, cert: WBENC)

5850   Victoria Legal + Corporate Services
       2 N. LaSalle St Ste 1615
       Chicago, IL 60602
       Contact: Victoria Rock CEO
       Tel: 312-443-1025
       Email: victoria@victorialcs.com
       Website: www.VictoriaLCS.com
Court reporting, complex litigation, accurate, verbatim transcripts, comprehensive services. (Woman, estab 1981, empl 4, sales $1,034,478, cert: State, WBENC)

Indiana

5851   Delaney & Delaney LLC
       3640 N Washington Blvd
       Indianapolis, IN 46205
       Contact: Kathleen Delaney President
       Tel: 317-920-0400
       Email: kathleen@delaneylaw.net
       Website: www.delaneylaw.net
Law Firm (Woman, estab 0, empl , sales $1,500,000, cert: State)

Kansas

5852   Barbera & Watkins, LLC
       6701 W 64th St., Ste 315
       Overland Park, KS 66202
       Contact: Natalie Stice Office Mgr
       Tel: 913-677-3800
       Email: nstice@bwaerolaw.com
       Website: www.bwaerolaw.com
Legal Services. (Woman, estab 2008, empl 7, sales $0, cert: State, WBENC)

Louisiana

5853   Courington Kiefer & Sommers, LLC
       650 Poydras St Ste 2105
       New Orleans, LA 70130
       Contact: Valerie Matherne Member
       Tel: 504-524-5510
       Email: vmatherne@courington-law.com
       Website: www.courington-law.com
Defending cases in Louisiana, Mississippi, and Texas. (Woman, estab 2011, empl 29, sales $3,854,117, cert: WBENC)

Massachusetts

5854   Fitzhugh & Mariani LLP
       155 Federal St, Ste 1700
       Boston, MA 02110
       Contact: Amy Crowley Partner
       Tel: 617-695-2330
       Email: acrowley@fitzhughlaw.com
       Website: www.fitzhughlaw.com
Environmental law, employment law, products liability, personal injury and general corporate litigation. (Woman/AA, estab 1986, empl 22, sales $1,700,000, cert: NMSDC)

5855   Schwartz Hannum PC
       11 Chestnut St Ste 11
       Andover, MA 01810
       Contact: Sara Goldsmith Schwartz President
       Tel: 978-623-0900
       Email: schwartz@shpclaw.com
       Website: www.shpclaw.com
Labor and Employment law firm representing employers with respect to a full spectrum of labor and employment issues, including Immigration-related matters. (Woman, estab 1995, empl 24, sales $5,639,572, cert: State, WBENC)

5856   The Wagner Law Group
99 Summer St. 13th Fl
Boston, MA 02110
Contact: Marcia Wagner Cheif Marketing Officer
Tel: 617-357-5200
Email:
Website: www.wagnerlawgroup.com
Employee benefits, estate planning, employment, labor and human resources and investment management. (Woman, estab 1996, empl 38, sales $7,709,000, cert: WBENC)

5857   West Hill Technology Counsel, Inc.
900 Cummings Center Ste 206-T
Beverly, MA 01915
Contact: Louise Kennedy President
Tel: 978-338-4082
Email: llkennedy@westhillcounsel.com
Website: www.westhillcounsel.com
Boutique business and technology law firm. (Woman, estab 2008, empl 9, sales $563,930, cert: State, WBENC)

Maryland

5858   A&E Enterprises II
18403 Woodfield Rd, Ste A
Gaithersburg, MD 20879
Contact: Torri Schaffer President
Tel: 301-869-5081
Email: torri@torrilegalservices.com
Website: www.torrilegalservices.com
We serve court papers, do skip tracing and document retrieval in Maryland, DC, Virginia as well as nationwide. We are a Small Women Owned Business, Minority certified. We have been in business for over 20 years. (Woman, estab 1998, empl 6, sales $831,388, cert: State)

5859   For The Record, Inc.
10760 Demarr Rd
White Plains, MD 20695
Contact: Sara Vance CFO
Tel: 800-921-5555
Email: svance@ftrinc.net
Website: www.ftrinc.net
Court reporting, transcription, legal video and litigation support. (Woman, estab 1991, empl 12, sales $2,265,600, cert: State, WBENC)

5860   Rahman LLC
10025 Governor Warfield Pkwy Ste 212
Columbia, MD 21044
Contact: Mohammad Rahman Owner
Tel: 443-283-7000
Email: rahman@rahmanllc.com
Website: www.rahmanllc.com
Intellectual property, patents, trademarks, copyrights, trade secrets, legal, strategy, valuation, IP (As-Ind, estab 2008, empl 3, sales , cert: State, NMSDC)

5861   Taylor & Ryan, LLC
1777 Reisterstown Rd CommereCenter E, Ste 265
Pikesville, MD 21208
Contact: Frances Taylor Member
Tel: 410-486-5800
Email: ftaylor@taylor-ryan.com
Website: www.taylor-ryan.com
Immigration legal services to employers of all sizes. (Woman, estab 2005, empl 6, sales $851,000, cert: State)

Michigan

5862   A.K.Adams, PLC dba A|Squared Legal Group, PLC
615 Griswold Ste 714
Detroit, MI 48226
Contact: Alari Adams Managing Member
Tel: 313-702-2222
Email: aa@asquaredlegal.com
Website: www.asquaredlegal.com
Provide legal counseling to businesses for litigation and transactional matters pertaining to business law, labor/employment law, and human resources management. (Woman/AA, estab 2014, empl 2, sales $100,000, cert: NMSDC, WBENC)

5863   Americlerk, Inc. dba Lumen Legal
1025 N. Campbell Rd
Royal Oak, MI 48067
Contact: Iris Dalfrey VP Southern Region
Tel: 281-853-9295
Email: idalfrey@lumenlegal.com
Website: www.lumenlegal.com
Contract Legal Services, Secondments, Process Assessment, Spend Optimization, Document Review, Six Sigma Project Management, Lumen Review Center, Legal Spend Analysis with Sky Analytics, Document Automation. (Woman, estab 1993, empl 25, sales $8,000,000, cert: WBENC)

5864   Apis LLC
2216 Northlawn Blvd
Birmingham, MI 48009
Contact: Turkia Mullin CEO
Tel: 313-468-4932
Email: tmullin@apisconsultinggroup.com
Website: www.apisconsultinggroup.com
Corporate transactional attorney providing legal, financial and business consulting advice and support, drafting and negotiating all aspects of a deal, including all agreements for such transactions. (Woman, estab 2013, empl 1, sales , cert: WBENC)

5865   Banas and Associates PLLC
330 Hamilton Ste 350
Birmingham, MI 48009
Contact: Leslie Banas Managing Member
Tel: 248-203-5400
Email: leslie.banas@banaslegal.net
Website: www.banaslegal.net
Commercial real estate and corporate legal services; negotiation and documentation of office leases; sales and purchases of manufacturing and warehouse facilities; construction contracts and tenant build. (Woman, estab 2009, empl 4, sales $400,000, cert: WBENC)

5866   Bush Seyferth PLLC
3001 W Big Beaver Rd
Troy, MI 48084
Contact: Cheryl Bush President
Tel: 248-822-7800
Email: bush@bsplaw.com
Website: www.bsplaw.com
Law Firm; legal services (Woman, estab 0, empl , sales $5,344,367, cert: WBENC)

5867   LegalEase Solutions LLC
       2301 Platt Rd, Ste 20
       Ann Arbor, MI 48104
       Contact: Teri Whitehead VP Global Strategy
       Tel: 866-534-6177
       Email: teri.whitehead@lgles.com
       Website: www.legaleasecorporate.com
Customized legal support, including legal research and
drafting service, compliance support, contract lifecycle
management, transactional and litigation support. (Minority, estab 2005, empl 6, sales $80,000,000, cert: NMSDC)

5868   Lewis & Munday
       2490 First Natl Bldg
       Detroit, MI 48226
       Contact: Gerald W. Helms Controller
       Tel: 313-961-2550
       Email: ghelms@lewismunday.com
       Website: www.lewismunday.com
Law firm, legal services. (AA, estab 1972, empl 31, sales $0,
cert: NMSDC)

5869   Rona M. Lum, P.C., dba Law Offices of Rona M. Lum
       691 N Squirrel Rd Ste 185
       Auburn Hills, MI 48326
       Contact: Rona Lum, Esq. President
       Tel: 248-340-1854
       Email: rlum@corpimmigration.us
       Website: www.corpimmigration.us
Immigration Law - corporate and business immigration
related matters. (Woman, estab 0, empl , sales $0, cert:
WBENC)

5870   Skye Suh, PLC.
       32000 Northwestern Hwy, Ste 260
       Farmington Hills, MI 48334
       Contact: Skye Suh Managing Member
       Tel: 248-932-8844
       Email: ssuh@skyesuhplc.com
       Website: www.skyesuhplc.com
Law firm, legal services. (Woman/As-Pac, estab 2002, empl
8, sales $0, cert: NMSDC)

5871   Sowell Law Partners PLLC
       300 River Place Dr Ste 5500
       Detroit, MI 48207
       Contact: Leamon R. Sowell Managing Partner
       Tel: 313-964-7900
       Email: lrsowell@sowellpartners.com
       Website: www.sowellpartners.com
Mergers, acquisitions, joint ventures and strategic alli-
ances. (AA, estab 2000, empl 5, sales $300,000, cert:
NMSDC)

Minnesota

5872   Blackwell Burke P.A.
       431 S 7th St Ste 2500
       Minneapolis, MN 55415
       Contact: Kandy Branch FIRM Admin
       Tel: 612-343-3200
       Email: info@blackwellburke.com
       Website: www.blackwellburke.com
Law Firm (AA, estab 2006, empl 34, sales $6,250,000, cert:
NMSDC)

5873   Depo International
       1330 Jersey Ave South
       Minneapolis, MN 55426
       Contact: CEO
       Tel: 763-591-0535
       Email:
       Website: www.depointernational.com
Court reporting, videography, digital litigation tools,
online repository, trial consulting, videoconferencing on
a national/international level. (Woman, estab 2008,
empl 15, sales $2,420,000, cert: WBENC)

5874   Fondungallah & Kigham, LLC
       2499 Rice St, Ste 145
       Saint Paul, MN 55113
       Contact: Mike Essien Attorney
       Tel: 651-482-0520
       Email: messien@fondlaw.com
       Website: www.fondlaw.com
Legal services: Intellectual property; immigration &
nationality law; business & corporate law; business &
commercial litigation; employment issues; international
law. (AA, estab 2005, empl 3, sales $650,000, cert: State,
NMSDC)

5875   Hollingsworth Davis, LLC
       8500 Normandale Lake Blvd Ste 320
       Minneapolis, MN 55437
       Contact: Tracey Dotter Exec Dir
       Tel: 952-854-2700
       Email: info@hdpatlaw.com
       Website: www.hdpatlaw.com
U.S. and international patent procurement, strategic
patent portfolio Devel and management, legal analysis
and opinion work, pre-litigation and M&A due diligence,
litigation support. (Woman, estab 2005, empl 12, sales
$2,600,000, cert: WBENC)

5876   Hope Law PLLC
       4999 France Ave S, Ste 245
       Minneapolis, MN 55410
       Contact: Rosanne Hope President
       Tel: 612-669-7017
       Email: roseanne@hopelawoffice.com
       Website: www.hopelawoffice.com
Commercial real estate law firm. (Woman, estab 2015,
empl 4, sales $212,880, cert: WBENC)

5877   Igbanugo Partners Int'l Law Firm, PLLC
       250 Marquette Ave Ste 1075
       Minneapolis, MN 55401
       Contact: Herbert Igbanugo CEO
       Tel: 612-746-0360
       Email: higbanugo@igbanugolaw.com
       Website: www.igbanugolaw.com
U.S. Immigration & Nationality Law and International
Trade Law limited to Sub-Saharan Africa. (AA, estab
2006, empl 13, sales $1,011,828, cert: NMSDC)

5878   Integrity Medicolegal Enterprises
       4800 Olson Memorial Hwy Ste 250
       Minneapolis, MN 55422
       Contact: Amy Berg President
       Tel: 763-398-5300
       Email: amy@integrityme.com
       Website: www.integrityme.com
Independent Medical Exams, workers compensation,
liablity and disablity claims, Peer Reviews. (Woman,
estab 2002, empl 50, sales $20,000,000, cert: WBENC)

5879　J. Selmer Law, P.A.
　　　500 Washington Ave S Ste 2010
　　　Minneapolis, MN 55415
　　　Contact: James Selmer Managing Partner
　　　Tel:　612-338-6005
　　　Email: jselmer@jselmerlaw.com
　　　Website: www.jselmerlaw.com
Defense law firm specializing in litigation and appellate practice, civil litigation process, from initial case evaluation through appellate proceedings. (AA, estab 1983, empl 10, sales $747,769, cert: NMSDC)

5880　Kelly & Berens, P.A. dba Berens & Miller, P.A.
　　　80 S Eighth St
　　　Minneapolis, MN 55402
　　　Contact: Barbara Podlucky Berens President
　　　Tel:　612-349-6171
　　　Email:
　　　Website: www.berensmiller.com
Law firm, legal services. (Woman, estab 1989, empl 10, sales $2,280,000, cert: WBENC)

5881　Nightowl Document Management Services, Inc.
　　　724 N First St
　　　Minneapolis, MN 55401
　　　Contact: Andrea Wallack CEO
　　　Tel:　612-337-0448
　　　Email: awal2652@msn.com
　　　Website: www.nightowldiscovery.com
Full service litigation support, single-source solution for both paper and electronic document collections. (Woman, estab 1991, empl 100, sales $3,800,000, cert: WBENC)

5882　Nwaneri Law Firm, PLLC
　　　1885 University Ave W, Ste 222
　　　St. Paul, MN 55104
　　　Contact: Patrick Nwaneri Managing Partner
　　　Tel:　651-917-0633
　　　Email: nwaneri@nwaneri.com
　　　Website: www.nwaneri.com
Professional legal services. (AA, estab 2002, empl 5, sales $153,743, cert: State, City, NMSDC)

Missouri

5883　Boggs, Avellino, Lach & Boggs
　　　9326 Olive Blvd Ste 200
　　　St. Louis, MO 63131
　　　Contact: Beth Boggs Managing Partner
　　　Tel:　314-726-2310
　　　Email: bbblawyers@aol.com
　　　Website: www.balblawyers.com
Legal services in Missouri & southern Illinois. (Woman/AA, estab 1999, empl 45, sales $5,000,000, cert: City, WBENC)

5884　Optitek, Inc.
　　　2001 S Hanley Rd Ste 250
　　　Brentwood, MO 63144
　　　Contact: Ricki McGuire President
　　　Tel:　314-644-2880
　　　Email: ricki@optitek.com
　　　Website: www.optitek.com
Electronic remittance processing, electronic lockbox services, forms processing, legal services & electronic document management systems. (Woman, estab 1992, empl 30, sales $1,796,300, cert: WBENC)

5885　Taylor and Associates, Inc.
　　　711 N 11th St
　　　St. Louis, MO 63101
　　　Contact: Deborah Weaver CEO
　　　Tel:　314-644-2191
　　　Email: dweaver@alaris.us
　　　Website: www.alaris.us/
Court Reporting, Video Depositions, Video Conferencing, digital video services, video-to-text synchronization in multiple formats, photo, document scanning, real time reporting, on-line scheduling, repository for depositions and exhibits. (Woman, estab 1985, empl 63, sales , cert: State, WBENC)

North Carolina

5886　Stanek Lemon Crouse + Meeks, PA
　　　982 Trinity Rd
　　　Raleigh, NC 27607
　　　Contact: Ron Baker Patent Attorney
　　　Tel:　919-944-4006
　　　Email:
　　　Website: www.staneklemon.com
Intellectual property and technology law firm having patent attorneys and patent practitioners with a proven record of success. (Woman, estab 2019, empl 7, sales , cert: WBENC)

New Jersey

5887　Hudson Reporting & Video Inc.
　　　90 Woodbridge Center Dr Ste 240
　　　Woodbridge, NJ 07095
　　　Contact: Geeta Sundrani Communications Specialist
　　　Tel:　732-906-2078
　　　Email: geeta@hudsonreporting.com
　　　Website: www.hudsonreporting.com
Boutique court reporting agency servicing the legal industry. (Woman/As-Ind, estab 1998, empl 6, sales $2,541,000, cert: NMSDC, WBENC)

5888　Johnson & Associates
　　　280 Amboy Ave
　　　Metuchen, NJ 08840
　　　Contact: Al Gil VP Business Dev
　　　Tel:　848-229-2254
　　　Email: agil@johnsonlegalpc.com
　　　Website: www.johnsonlegalpc.com
Law Firm, Corporate & Business Law, Litigation, Immigration, Appeals, Real Estate, Bankruptcy, Municipal Court. (AA, estab 2012, empl 42, sales , cert: NMSDC)

5889　Kim Winston LLP
　　　1307 White Horse Rd, Ste 601
　　　Voorhees, NJ 08043
　　　Contact: Jae Kim Partner
　　　Tel:　856-520-8991
　　　Email: yjaekim@kimwinston.com
　　　Website: www.kimwinston.com
Intellectual property law firm, legal services for patents, patent prosecution, patent procurement, trademarks, trademark prosecution, copyright, intellectual property litigation, patent litigation, trademark litigation, copyright litigation, trademark. (As-Pac, estab 2013, empl 14, sales $850,000, cert: NMSDC)

5890 Love and Long, LLP
      108 Washington St
      Newark, NJ 07102
      Contact: Lisa Love Partner
      Tel: 215-546-8433
      Email: llove@lovandlonglaw.com
      Website: www.loveandlonglaw.com
Law firm specializing in commercial transactions. (Woman/
AA, estab 1992, empl 5, sales $500,000, cert: State,
NMSDC)

5891 Rosenberg & Associates
      425 Eagle Rock Ave, Ste 201
      Roseland, NJ 07068
      Contact: Catherine Kane VP Operations
      Tel: 973-618-2101
      Email: ckane@trantech.net
      Website: www.rosenbergandassociates.com
Court reporting, litigation support, trial presentation,
stenographic transcription services, audiography,
videography, video conferencing, interpreting, database
consulting. (Woman, estab 1973, empl 48, sales , cert:
WBENC)

5892 RVM Enterprises, Inc.
      525 Washington Blvd. 25th Fl
      Jersey City, NJ 07310
      Contact: Cheryl A. Brunetti Exec Chairwoman
      Tel: 212-693-1525
      Email: cbrunetti@rvminc.com
      Website: www.rvminc.com
Litigation, litigation support, ediscovery, e-discovery,
Information Governance, Managed Review, document
review , ESI Processing , ESI Hosting, data hosting, Kcura,
Relativity, clearwell, Predictive Coding, Legal, Litigation
Consulting (Woman, estab 1996, empl 62, sales
$15,000,000, cert: State, City, WBENC)

5893 Wall & Tong, LLP
      25 James Way
      Eatontown, NJ 07724
      Contact: Robert Traina Business Mgr
      Tel: 732-542-2280
      Email: rtraina@walltong.com
      Website: www.walltong.com
Patent, Trademark and related Intellectual Property Legal
Services. (As-Pac, estab 2009, empl 15, sales $3,993,003,
cert: CPUC)

5894 Wong Fleming
      821 Alexander Rd, Ste 200
      Princeton, NJ 08540
      Contact: Linda Wong CEO
      Tel: 609-951-9520
      Email: lwong@wongfleming.com
      Website: www.wongfleming.com
Employment Law, Civil Rights, Commercial Law, Real
Estate, Education Law, Intellectual Property, and Interna-
tional Law. (Woman/As-Pac, estab 1994, empl 65, sales
$2,590,897, cert: NMSDC, WBENC)

New Mexico

5895 Ortiz & Lopez, LLC
      PO Box 4484
      Albuquerque, NM 87196
      Contact: Kermit Lopez Patent Attorney
      Tel: 505-314-1312
      Email: klopez@olpatentlaw.com
      Website: www.olpatentlaw.com
Patent and other intellectual property legal services.
(Hisp, estab 2001, empl 8, sales $1,000,000, cert:
NMSDC)

New York

5896 A. Kershaw, PC//Attorneys & Consultants
      161 Grove St, Ste 200
      Tarrytown, NY 10591
      Contact: Anne Kershaw Owner
      Tel: 914-332-0438
      Email: anne.kershaw@akershaw.com
      Website: www.akershaw.com
Litigation management consulting, providing innovative
and impartial analysis and recommendations for the
management of all aspects of volume litigation.
(Woman, estab 1999, empl 1, sales $0, cert: WBENC)

5897 B&N Legal Interpreting, Inc.
      350 Fifth Ave, 59th Floor
      New York, NY 10118
      Contact: Livingston Buchanan President
      Tel: 866-661-1053
      Email: lbuchanan@bninterpreting.com
      Website: www.bninterpreting.com
Provides interpreting, translation and sign language
services to court reporting agencies, law firms, fortune
100 & 500 companies, individuals for all language needs.
(AA, estab 2004, empl 2, sales , cert: City)

5898 Brune & Richard LLP
      80 Broad St, 30th Fl
      New York, NY 10004
      Contact: Laurie Edelstein Managing Attorney, San
      Francisco Office
      Tel: 212-668-1900
      Email: info@brunelaw.com
      Website: www.bruneandrichard.com
Our commercial cases include securities fraud, breach of
contract, trade secrets, intellectual property, successor
liability, and consumer class actions. Our white-collar
matters include alleged securities fraud, accounting
fraud, insider trading, (Woman, estab 1998, empl 30,
sales $15,000,000, cert: WBENC)

5899 Burgher Gray Jaffe LLP
      535 Fifth Ave 16th Fl
      New York, NY 10017
      Contact: Ron Llewellyn Managing Partner
      Tel: 646-513-3231
      Email: rllewellyn@grayhaile.com
      Website: www.burghergray.com
Boutique corporate law firm, corporate services &
middle market transactions, partnership, stockholders &
operating agreements, corporate governance & securities law advice, angel & venture capital investments,
securities offerings, mergers, acquisitions, divestitures,
joint ventures. (AA, estab 2006, empl 4, sales $360,000,
cert: State, NMSDC)

5900   Complete Discovery Source Inc.
       345 Park Ave Level B
       New York, NY 10154
       Contact: Bibi Bacchus
       Tel: 212-813-7005
       Email: bbacchus@cdslegal.com
       Website: www.cdslegal.com
eDiscovery services, litigation support, and software
supporting planning, early case assessment, information
governance, processing and production, software, data
analytics, review hosting, managed review, and cross-
border. (As-Ind, estab , empl , sales $39,601,399, cert: City,
NMSDC)

5901   David Carrie LLC
       155 E 55th St Ste 4K
       New York, NY 10022
       Contact: Carrie Printz Managing Dir
       Tel: 212-308-6560
       Email:
       Website: www.davidcarrie.com
Full-service legal search firm specializing in career counseling & the placement of talented attorneys in the U.S. &
throughout the world. (Woman, estab 2003, empl 7, sales ,
cert: WBENC)

5902   Drohan Lee LLP
       489 Fifth Ave
       New York, NY 10017
       Contact: Vivian Drohan Partner
       Tel: 212-710-0000
       Email: vdrohan@dlkny.com
       Website: www.dlkny.com
Boutique law firm with capabilities to provide legal
services in corporate, contract transactions and litigation.
(As-Pac, Hisp, estab 2007, empl 5, sales $1,400,000, cert:
State, City)

5903   Frank, Frank, Goldstein & Nager, PC
       330 West 38th St Ste 701
       New York, NY 10018
       Contact: Jocelyn Nager President
       Tel: 212-686-0100
       Email: jnager@ffgnesqs.com
       Website: www.ffgnesqs.com
Law Firm devoted exclusively to the collection of bad debt,
commercial and consumer. (Woman, estab 2000, empl 12,
sales $1,405,280, cert: City)

5904   Green Point Technology Services LLC
       555 Theodore Fremd Ave Ste A102
       Rye, NY 10580
       Contact: Shirley Sharma President
       Tel: 212-913-0500
       Email: shirley@greenpointglobal.com
       Website: www.greenpointglobal.com/
Legal and Compliance, Regulatory Tracking, Publishing &
Editorial services, Software Development, Professional
development. (Woman/As-Ind, estab 2001, empl 350, sales
, cert: State)

5905   JG Advisory Services LLC
       200 E 27th St
       New York, NY 10016
       Contact: Judith Gross Principal
       Tel: 917-375-6852
       Email: judy@jgadvisory.com
       Website: www.jgadvisory.com
Specialty consulting related to hedge funds, particularly
on legal/regulatory/compliance issues. Devel of technology in this area. "Industry intelligence" on hedge funds,
and analysis of market. (Woman, estab 2005, empl 1,
sales $200,000, cert: City)

5906   Johnson Liebman, LLP
       305 Broadway Ste 801
       New York, NY 10007
       Contact: Robert Johnson Partner
       Tel: 212-619-6744
       Email: robert.johnson@johnsonliebman.com
       Website: www.johnsonliebman.com
Insurance defense firm, handle defense and subrogation
cases for various insurers for flat fees. (AA, estab 1999,
empl 6, sales $875,000, cert: City)

5907   Law Office of Marian Polovy
       192 Lexington Ave, Ste 903
       New York, NY 10016
       Contact: Marian Polovy Owner
       Tel: 212-696-0133
       Email: marianpolovy@aol.com
       Website: www.lawofficeofmarianpolovy.com
Law firm-trial attorneys, defense negligence, product
liability, general liability, defense medical malpractice,
employment law and general civil litigation. (Woman,
estab 1983, empl 4, sales $635,382, cert: State, City)

5908   Lee Anav Chung White Kim Ruger & Richter LLP
       156 Fifth Ave Ste 303
       New York, NY 10010
       Contact: Annie Chen Legal Asst
       Tel: 212-271-0664
       Email: anniechen@lacwkrr.com
       Website: www.leeanavchung.com
LEE ANAV CHUNG LLP is a law firm committed to
providing its clients with sophisticated legal advice and
representation on complex legal matters. (As-Pac, estab
2003, empl 30, sales $3,100,000, cert: NMSDC)

5909   Pittleman & Associates
       336 E 43rd St
       New York, NY 10017
       Contact: Linda Pittleman Chairman
       Tel: 212-370-9600
       Email: lindap@pittlemanassociates.com
       Website: www.pittlemanassociates.com
Placement of attorneys. Our candidates span the full
range of legal specialties and levels of expertise. At least
50% of our search activity is for in-house law departments. (Woman/Hisp, estab 1993, empl 7, sales
$1,625,000, cert: NMSDC)

5910 Pride Healthcare, LLC
      222 S 9th St
      New York, NY 10170
      Contact: Jenny Davis Dir of Strategic Accts
      Tel: 612-806-0971
      Email: jennifer.davis@russelltobin.com
      Website: www.pridehealthcare.com
Direct Hire, Temporary, and Temp to Hire staffing services
for Administrative, Allied Health, Healthcare IT, Clinical
Research, Pharmacy, and Travel/Local Nursing. (Hisp, estab
2010, empl 35, sales $40,000,000, cert: NMSDC)

5911 QuisLex
      126 E 56th St
      New York, NY 10022
      Contact: Adam Beschloss Exec Dir Client Solutions
      Tel: 917-512-4447
      Email: adam.beschloss@quislex.com
      Website: www.quislex.com
Premier legal services provider founded by attorneys from
Skadden Arps, Shearman & Sterling and Sidley Austin
QuisLex offers multi-shore capabilities through execution
centers in Chicago and Hyderabad, India. (As-Ind, estab
2004, empl 9, sales $30,500,000, cert: NMSDC)

5912 Quislex, Inc
      Jayabheri Silicon, Towers, Kondapur, Hyderabad,
      Telangana 500084
      Hyderabad, NY 10022
      Contact: Leonard Harmon DEI Mgr & Business
      Dvlpmnt
      Tel: 984-893-6764
      Email: leonard.harmon@quislex.com
      Website: www.quieslex.com
Specialize in complex document review, contract management, compliance, and legal operations projects. (As-Ind,
estab 2005, empl 1000, sales $80,000,000, cert: NMSDC)

5913 Rozario & Associates, P.C.
      55 Broadway 20th Fl
      New York, NY 10006
      Contact: Rovin Rozario Managing Partner
      Tel: 212-301-2770
      Email: rrozario@rozariolaw.com
      Website: www.rozariolaw.com
Rozario & Associates, P.C., is a New York City-based law
firm, certified by NMSDC as a Minority Business Enterprise. We have built our reputation on the quality of our
attorneys and staff members, who provide superior client
service, high-quality legal (AA, estab 2005, empl 9, sales
$821,000, cert: NMSDC)

5914 Schoeman Updike Kaufman & Gerber LLP
      551 Fifth Ave 12th Fl
      New York, NY 10176
      Contact: Beth L. Kaufman Managing Partner
      Tel: 212-661-5030
      Email: bkaufman@schoeman.com
      Website: www.schoeman.com
Law firm specializing in litigation (employment, commer-
cial, personal injury and product liability) and real estate
(commercial transactions and leasing, financing). (Woman/
As-Pac, Hisp, estab 1969, empl 39, sales $5,054,048, cert:
State, City)

5915 Silverman Shin & Byrne PLLC
      88 Pine St, 22nd Fl
      New York, NY 10005
      Contact: Gerard Crowe Partner
      Tel: 212-779-8600
      Email: gcrowe@silverfirm.com
      Website: www.silverfirm.com
Corporate/Commercial realm, we represent small startup companies to multinationals alike in both
tranactional adn litigation. In the Insurance/Tort defense
realsm, we represent a host of insurance carriers,
municipalites, and privately insured (Woman/AA, As-Pac,
Hisp, estab 1986, empl 46, sales $9,188,231, cert:
NMSDC)

5916 Yorkson Legal, Inc.
      800 2nd Ave 804, 8th Fl
      New York, NY 10017
      Contact: Gail Reichwald Managing Dir
      Tel: 212-265-1400
      Email: greichwald@yorkson.com
      Website: www.yorkson.com
Legal staffing and recruiting serves. We deal with
contract attorneys and legal support staff, and both
temporary and permanent paralegals. (Woman, estab
2003, empl 10, sales $6,207,569, cert: WBENC)

5917 Younkins & Schecter LLP
      420 Lexington Ave Ste 2050
      New York, NY 10170
      Contact: Mardi Schecter Partner
      Tel: 212-286-0040
      Email: mschecter@ys-law.com
      Website: www.ys-law.com
Legal Counsel And Prosecution; Legal Services; Property
Management Services; Real Estate Agents (Woman,
estab 1996, empl 12, sales $0, cert: City, WBENC)

Ohio

5918 Curtin & Associates, LLP
      159 S Main St, Ste 920
      Akron, OH 44308
      Contact: Cynthia K. Curtin President
      Tel: 330-376-7245
      Email: dbudny@curtinlawfirm.com
      Website: www.curtinlawfirm.com
Tort Litigation; emphasis on defense. (Woman, estab
2003, empl 9, sales $1,200,000, cert: WBENC)

5919 DCR Denmark Court Reporting Agency, LLC
      810 Sycamore St, 3rd Fl
      Cincinnati, OH 45202
      Contact: Angela Denmark CEO
      Tel: 513-254-8753
      Email: angela@dcragency.com
      Website: www.dcragency.com
Independent, freelance court reporting agency. Are
services are typically requested by legal professionals,
educational, business and government entities.
(Woman/AA, estab 2006, empl 1, sales , cert: State)

5920   Giffen & Kaminski, LLC
1300 E Ninth St Ste 1600
Cleveland, OH 44114
Contact: Karen Giffen Partner
Tel: 216-621-5161
Email: kgiffen@thinkgk.com
Website: www.thinkgk.com
Legal Services; Arbitration; Mediation; Creditor's Rights;
Business Torts; Criminal Defense; White Collar Criminal
Defense; Employment Law; Employment Litigation;
Immigration Law; Product Liability; Real Estate. (Woman,
estab 2004, empl , sales $0, cert: WBENC)

5921   Litigation Management, Inc.
6000 Parkland Blvd
Mayfield Heights, OH 44124
Contact: Megan Pizor Exec Dir
Tel: 440-484-2000
Email: megan.pizor@lmiweb.com
Website: www.lmiweb.com
Comprehensive management and analysis of medical
information for the defense of claims, individual lawsuits,
mass torts or class actions where health, illness or injury .
(Woman, estab 1984, empl 600, sales , cert: WBENC)

5922   Perez & Morris LLC
8000 Ravine's Edge Ct, Ste 300
Columbus, OH 43235
Contact: Juan Jose Perez Partner
Tel: 614-431-1500
Email: jperez@perez-morris.com
Website: www.perez-morris.com
Legal services. (Hisp, estab 1997, empl 29, sales
$2,350,000, cert: NMSDC)

5923   Safety Controls Technology Inc.
6993 Pearl Rd
Middleburg Heights, OH 44130
Contact: Annette Plavny GM
Tel: 440-449-6000
Email: APlavny@sct.us.com
Website: www.sct.us.com
Occupational Health and Safety Services. (Woman, estab
1999, empl 50, sales $500,000,000, cert: City, WBENC)

5924   Thacker Martinsek LPA
2330 One Cleveland Ctr 1375 E 9th St
Cleveland, OH 44114
Contact: John Larger President
Tel: 216-456-3840
Email: jlarger@TMLPA.com
Website: www.thackermartinsek.com
Law firm specializing in business & commercial litigation,
insurance recovery, litigation management, employment
law, intellectual property and civil rights. (Woman, estab
2010, empl 33, sales $6,590,743, cert: WBENC)

5925   Walker & Jocke Co., LPA
231 S Broadway
Medina, OH 44256
Contact: Patricia A. Walker President
Tel: 330-721-0000
Email: paw@walkerandjocke.com
Website: www.walkerandjocke.com
Legal services related to patents, trademarks and
copyrights, infringement analysis, claim mitigation and
infringement defense, IT agreements, software licensing,
outsourcing agreements, electronic funds transfer
agreements, hosting agreements and SaaS arrangements. (Woman, estab 1993, empl 13, sales $3,518,153,
cert: WBENC, NWBOC)

Oregon

5926   Gordon & Polscer LLC
9755 SW Barnes Rd Ste 650
Portland, OR 97225
Contact: Diane Polscer Managing Partner
Tel: 503-242-2922
Email: dpolscer@gordon-polscer.com
Website: www.gordon-polscer.com
Represent insurers, corporate, business clients for:
Insurance Coverage Advice & Litigation; Civil Litigation;
Extra-contractual Claim Advice & Litigation; Class-Action
Defense. (Woman, estab 0, empl , sales $5,253,027, cert:
WBENC)

Pennsylvania

5927   Assigned Counsel Inc.
950 W Valley Rd Ste 2600
Wayne, PA 19087
Contact: Bob Murphy President
Tel: 610-964-8300
Email: nabrams@assignedcounsel.com
Website: www.assignedcounsel.com
Provide attorneys on a temporary, temp-to-perm and
direct hire basis to corporate law departments, non-
profit organizations, federal agencies, and law firms.
(AA, estab , empl , sales $5,084,003, cert: NMSDC)

5928   Ellen Freeman Immigration Law Group
303 Timber Court
Pittsburgh, PA 15238
Contact: Ellen Freeman Managing Partner
Tel: 412-822-6500
Email: efreeman@freemanimmigration.com
Website: www.freemanimmigration.com
A full-service immigration law firm. (Woman, estab
2019, empl 4, sales $750,000, cert: WBENC)

5929   Griesing Law, LLC
1880 John F. Kennedy Boulevard Ste 1800
Philadelphia, PA 19103
Contact: Francine Griesing Managing Member
Tel: 215-618-3720
Email: fgriesing@griesinglaw.com
Website: www.griesinglaw.com
Represent public Fortune 1000 corporations and closely
held companies in complex business transactions and
high stakes litigation, as well as advises its clients on how
to reduce risk and contain litigation costs. (Woman,
estab 2010, empl 15, sales , cert: WBENC)

5930 JURISolutions, Inc.
1500 Joh F Kennedy Blvd Ste 1850
Philadelphia, PA 19102
Contact: Fawn Linn Operations
Tel: 215-383-3517
Email: flinn@jsl-hq.com
Website: www.jurisolutions.com
Legal services and recruitment firm providing innovative, cost-effective legal solutions to corporations, government entities and law firms. (Woman, estab 1997, empl 125, sales $14,085,967, cert: CPUC, WBENC)

5931 Parrish Law Offices
788 Washington Rd
Pittsburgh, PA 15228
Contact: Debra Parrish Partner
Tel: 412-561-6250
Email: debbie@dparrishlaw.com
Website: www.dparrishlaw.com
Legal support for provider and beneficiary appeals of denied claims by payers, including Medicare through the administrative process up to and including Federal court litigation; appeals of post-payment overpayment determinations (Woman, estab 2000, empl 4, sales $833,635, cert: WBENC)

5932 Summit Court Reporting, Inc.
1500 Market St 12th Fl - East Tower
Philadelphia, PA 19102
Contact: Yvette Samuel President
Tel: 215-665-5633
Email: ysamuel@summitreporting.com
Website: www.summitreporting.com
Court Reporting & Legal Video & Videoconference Services for legal proceedings held in depositions, hearings, meetings, video depositions, video playbacks at trial. (Woman, estab 1993, empl 4, sales $958,498, cert: State)

5933 The Axelrod Firm, PC
1125 Walnut St
Philadelphia, PA 19107
Contact: Sheryl Axelrod President
Tel: 215-461-1768
Email: saxelrod@theaxelrodfirm.com
Website: www.theaxelrodfirm.com
Assist individuals, businesses and non-profit organizations with appellate, commercial, real estate, estate planning and bodily injury / product liability lawsuit needs. (Woman, estab 2007, empl 4, sales $386,272, cert: State, WBENC)

5934 Tiagha & Associates, Ltd.
2112 Walnut St
Philadelphia, PA 19103
Contact: Kahiga Tiagha Attorney At Law
Tel: 215-543-7970
Email: info@tiaghalaw.com
Website: www.tiaghalaw.com
Law firm providing tailored solutions in Corporate and Real Estate transactional services. (AA, estab 2009, empl 7, sales $0, cert: NMSDC)

5935 Walker Nell Partners Inc.
1515 Market St, Ste 820
Philadelphia, PA 19102
Contact: Wayne Walker CEO
Tel: 215-569-1660
Email: WalkerNell@walkerNell.com
Website: www.WalkerNell.com
Litigation Support and Insolvency, Restructuring, Valuation and Fiduciary Services; Accounting; Management and Technology Governance, Risk and Compliance; Forensic and Dispute. (AA, estab 2004, empl 7, sales $249,000, cert: City, NMSDC)

Puerto Rico

5936 Del Toro & Santana
Plaza 273, Ste 900
San Juan, PR 00917
Contact: Roberto Santana Sr Partner
Tel: 787-754-8700
Email: rsantana@dtslaw.com
Website: www.dtslaw.com
Litigation and counseling representing a number of industrial and commercial firms, (Hisp, estab 1984, empl 12, sales $1,400,000, cert: NMSDC)

5937 Estrella LLC
PO Box 9023596
San Juan, PR 00902
Contact: Alberto Estrella Managing Member
Tel: 787-977-5050
Email: agestrella@estrellallc.com
Website: www.estrellallc.com
Legal Services. (Hisp, estab 1974, empl 31, sales $4,622,484, cert: NMSDC)

5938 Fiddler Gonzalez & Rodriguez, PSC
PO Box 363507
San Juan, PR 00936
Contact: Kenneth Bury General Admin
Tel: 787-759-3145
Email: kcbury@fgrlaw.com
Website: www.fgrlaw.com
Full-service law firm with well established practice areas encompassing nearly all areas of law. With over 100 lawyers, the firm is one of the largest in the Caribbean and Latin America. (Hisp, estab 1932, empl 209, sales $0, cert: NMSDC)

Texas

5939 Akula & Associates, P.C.
4835 LBJ Freeway Ste 750
Dallas, TX 75244
Contact: Kavitha Akula Marketing Mgr
Tel: 972-241-4698
Email: kavitha.akula@akulalaw.com
Website: www.akulalaw.com
Intellectual Property Business & Transactional Law. (Minority, Woman, estab 2007, empl 9, sales $500,000, cert: State)

5940 Bennett Law Office, PC
132 W Main St
Lewisville, TX 75057
Contact: Tamera H. Bennett President
Tel: 972-436-8141
Email: info@tbennettlaw.com
Website: www.tbennettlaw.com
Intellectual Property Law, Trademark Law, Copyright Law,
Entertainment Law. (Woman, estab 2001, empl 2, sales ,
cert: State)

5941 Brewer & Lormand, PLLC
5910 N Central Expressway, Ste 730
Dallas, TX 75206
Contact: Ruth Brewer Managing Partner
Tel: 214-420-6001
Email: rbrewer@brewerlormand.com
Website: www.brewerlormand.com
Legal Services, Attorneys, Lawyers. (Woman, estab 2008,
empl 11, sales $1,140,687, cert: State, WBENC)

5942 Callier & Garza, L.L.P.
4900 Woodway, Ste 700
Houston, TX 77056
Contact: Bernardo Garza Partner
Tel: 713-439-0248
Email: garza@callierandgarza.com
Website: www.callierandgarza.com
The firm specializes in representing large entities, private
and government, insured and self insured, in State and
Federal co urtsin the following areas: (1) Employment
Litigation (including age, gender, race, ADA and FLA (AA,
Hisp, estab 1985, empl 8, sales $1,650,000, cert: State,
NMSDC)

5943 Carter Scholer Arnett Hamada & Mockler PLLC
8150 N Central Expressway Ste 500
Dallas, TX 75206
Contact: Helen Gilliland Partner
Tel: 214-550-8188
Email: helen@carterscholer.com
Website: www.carterscholer.com
Legal Services (Woman/AA, As-Ind, As-Pac, estab 2012,
empl 14, sales $6,000,000, cert: NMSDC)

5944 Cluso Investigation LLC
4500 Mercantile Plaza Dr Ste 106
Fort Worth, TX 76137
Contact: Sharon Sutila CEO
Tel: 817-422-2289
Email: ssutila@cluso.com
Website: www.cluso.com
Provides comprehensive reports for fraud prevention,
asset recovery, collection, skip tracing, litigation & employ-
ment screening. (Woman, estab 2008, empl 10, sales
$923,433, cert: State, WBENC)

5945 ELS ESQ. LLC
400 N Ervay St No. 131612
Dallas, TX 75201
Contact: E. Lynette Stone Attorney
Tel: 972-383-9499
Email: inquire@elsesq.com
Website: www.elsesq.com
Legal services (commercial litigation). (Woman/AA, estab
2008, empl 1, sales $150,000, cert: WBENC)

5946 Farrow-Gillespie & Heath LLP
1700 Pacific Ave Ste 3700
Dallas, TX 75201
Contact: Liza Farrow-Gillespie Managing Partner
Tel: 214-361-5600
Email: liza@fghlaw.net
Website: www.fghlaw.com
Employment law; employment litigation and arbitration
defense; internal employment investigations; internal
audits; employee handbooks; contract preparation and
review; personal injury defense; advertising (Woman,
estab 2007, empl 22, sales $1,761,000, cert: CPUC,
WBENC)

5947 Henjum Goucher Reporting Services, LP
2777 N Stemmons Fwy, Ste 1025
Dallas, TX 75207
Contact: Kristin Neerhof Dir Business Dev
Tel: 214-521-1188
Email: kneerhof@hglitigation.com
Website: www.hglitigation.com
Deposition provider with over 35 years in the litigation
support industry. (Woman, estab 1979, empl 33, sales ,
cert: WBENC)

5948 Janik Vinnakota LLP
8111 LBJ Freeway, Ste 790
Dallas, TX 75251
Contact: Shelbye Harbour Office Admin
Tel: 214-390-9999
Email: sharbour@jvllp.com
Website: www.jvllp.com
Litigation Services, State and Federal for intellectual
property, business, and contract disputes, Business Legal
Services, Business Formation, Contracts and Legal
Agreements, Business Liability Consulting and Diligence.
(Minority, estab 2016, empl 7, sales $950,000, cert:
State, NMSDC)

5949 Lehtola & Cannatti PLLC
5001 Spring Valley Rd, Ste 400 E
Dallas, TX 75244
Contact: Patricia Lehtola Managing Member
Tel: 972-383-1515
Email: plehtola@lc-lawfirm.com
Website: www.lc-lawfirm.com
Legal services. (Minority, Woman, estab 0, empl , sales
$0, cert: NMSDC)

5950 Lindsay Law
11700 Preston Rd, Ste 660-167
Dallas, TX 75230
Contact: John Lindsay Principal Attorney
Tel: 214-736-4306
Email: supplier@inventiveiplaw.com
Website: www.inventiveiplaw.com
Provides intellectual property law services, namely
patent, copyright, trademark, and technology services.
The firm focuses on the legal aspects of analysis,
protection. (AA, estab 2009, empl 2, sales , cert: CPUC)

5951 Owens Hervey PLLC
901 Main St, Ste 3612
Dallas, TX 75202
Contact: Maurice Owens Jr Member
Tel: 214-741-2288
Email: mowens@owenshervey.com
Website: www.owenshervey.com
Civil litigation and trial experience. (AA, estab 2008,
empl 3, sales $254,446, cert: State)

5952   Reeves & Brightwell LLP
       221 W 6th St
       Austin, TX 78701
       Contact: Beverly Reeves President
       Tel: 512-334-4501
       Email: breeves@reevesbrightwell.com
       Website: www.reevesbrightwell.com
Commercial Litigation firm. (Woman, estab 0, empl , sales
$0, cert: WBENC)

5953   State Tax Group, LLC
       5050 Quorum Dr, Ste 700
       Dallas, TX 75254
       Contact: Richard Fleming
       Tel: 972-492-9841
       Email: rfleming@statetaxgroup.com
       Website: www.statetaxgroup.com
State audit representation, sales tax compliance review,
tax refund reviews, litigation support, dispute resolution,
sampling analysis & evaluation, voluntary disclosures. (AA,
estab 2005, empl 4, sales $518,000, cert: NMSDC)

5954   Stratos Legal Services
       4299 San Felipe, Ste 350
       Houston, TX 77027
       Contact: Bert Farris Exec. VP
       Tel: 713-481-2180
       Email: bfarris@stratoslegal.com
       Website: www.stratoslegal.com
Litigation support: court reporting, videography, interpreters, records retrieval, process serving, and electronic
discovery. (Woman/Hisp, estab 2005, empl 40, sales
$8,100,000, cert: WBENC)

5955   The Law Office of Kathryn N Karam
       2200 Southwest Frwy Ste 400
       Houston, TX 77098
       Contact: Kathryn Karam President
       Tel: 832-582-0620
       Email: katie@immisolver.com
       Website: www.immisolver.com
Law firm: internal I-9 audit, immigration liabilities of a
merger or acquisition by reviewing all employees' immigration documentation. (Woman, estab 2013, empl 4,
sales , cert: WBENC)

5956   The Marker Group, Inc.
       13105 Northwest Frwy
       Houston, TX 77040
       Contact: Hillary Johnson GM
       Tel: 713-460-9070
       Email: supplierdiversity@marker-group.com
       Website: www.marker-group.com
Litigation support services, medical record (MR) collection,
MR retrieval, MR review, record analysis, reprographics,
scanning, subpoenas, litigation management, chronolo-
gies, oral despositions, evidentiary chain of custody, real
time reporting. (Woman, estab 1985, empl 289, sales
$33,542,107, cert: WBENC)

5957   We Muv U, LLC
       3948 Legacy Dr Ste 106
       Plano, TX 75023
       Contact: Jessica Oliver Dir
       Tel: 214-208-1313
       Email: jessica@wmull.com
       Website: www.wmull.com
Manage trial logistics for corporations in a manner that
minimizes cost and maximizes desired productivity. (AA,
estab 2014, empl 5, sales $225,000, cert: NMSDC)

Virginia

5958   Gavin Law Offices, PLC
       2500 Gaskins Rd, Ste B
       Richmond, VA 23238
       Contact: Pamela Gavin Managing Member
       Tel: 804-784-4427
       Email: pgavin@gavinlawoffices.com
       Website: www.gavinlawoffices.com
Legal services, intellectual property (transfers, licensing,
protection, enforcement, commercial transactional
services, entertainment focused legal services, litigation,
trademark preclearance and prosecution, managing
trademark portfolios. (Woman, estab 2004, empl 9, sales
$1,345,216, cert: State, WBENC)

5959   Guidance Law Firm, P.C.
       440 Monticello Ave, Ste 1834
       Norfolk, VA 23510
       Contact: Lamont Maddox President
       Tel: 757-454-2045
       Email: lmaddox@guidancelaw.com
       Website: www.guidancelaw.com
Legal services, contract review, contract drafting,
document review, regulatory compliance, corporate
governance, policy drafting, policy review, corporate
transactions, general business law, negotiations,
settlements, consulting. (AA, estab 2010, empl 1, sales ,
cert: State, NMSDC)

Washington

5960   Focal PLLC
       900 1st Ave S, Ste 201
       Seattle, WA 98134
       Contact: Venkat Balasubramani Owner/Partner
       Tel: 206-718-4250
       Email: info@focallaw.com
       Website: www.focallaw.com
Boutique law firm specializing in internet and technol-
ogy-related issues. (As-Ind, estab 2009, empl 11, sales
$666,153, cert: NMSDC)

5961   Mayner Business Law, P.S.
       19495 SE 57th Pl
       Issaquah, WA 98027
       Contact: Andrea Mayner Owner
       Tel: 425-996-7335
       Email: andrea@maynerlaw.com
       Website: www.maynerlaw.com
Provides exceptional value and personal services.
(Woman, estab 2008, empl 1, sales $287,385, cert:
WBENC)

Wisconsin

5962   Bell & Manning, LLC
       2801 W Beltline Hwy Ste 210
       Madison, WI 53713
       Contact: Callie Bell Shareholder
       Tel: 608-661-3590
       Email: cbell@bellmanning.com
       Website: www.bellmanning.com/
Intellectual property, with an emphasis on U.S. and
international patents. (Woman, estab 2010, empl 6,
sales $1,312,916, cert: WBENC)

5963   JAC Consulting LLC dba The Champagne Group
       2233 N Summit Ave Ste 315
       Milwaukee, WI 53202
       Contact: Jacquie Champagne President
       Tel: 414-704-0602
       Email: jacquie@champagnegrp.com
       Website: www.champagnegrp.com
Executive search, legal services. (Woman, estab 2015,
empl 1, sales , cert: WBENC)

5964   Midwest Legal and eData Services, Inc.
       7625 S Howell Ave
       Oak Creek, WI 53154
       Contact: Shawn Olley Owner
       Tel: 414-764-2772
       Email: solley@mwedata.com
       Website: www.mwedata.com
Provides experienced paralegals on an as-needed basis
charged at an hourly rate. (Woman, estab 1989, empl ,
sales , cert: WBENC)

MATERIAL HANDLING EQUIPMENT
Manufacturers or distributors of handtrucks, hoists, dollies, conveyors, racks, forklifts, etc. (See also HARDWARE & TOOLS, HYDRAULIC & COMPRESSED AIR EQUIPMENT, INDUSTRIAL EQUIPMENT & SUPPLIES and INDUSTRIAL MACHINES. NAICS Code 42

Alabama

5965 Southeastern Conveyor Services, Inc.
870 Minor Pkwy
Birmingham, AL 35224
Contact: Stephanie Weeks President
Tel: 205-785-6884
stephanie.weeks@southeasternconveyorservices.com
Website: www.southeasternconveyorservices.com
Conveyor solutions for all types of conveyor systems, belt sales, belt vulcanizing, change-outs and replacement, mechanical splices, new installations, wiper replacements, roller change-outs. (Woman, estab 2014, empl 15, sales $1,800,000, cert: WBENC)

5966 Springer Equipment Co., Inc.
4263 Underwood Industrial Dr
Birmingham, AL 35210
Contact: Annette Springer CEO
Tel: 205-951-3675
Email: annettes@springerequip.com
Website: www.SpringerEquipment.com
New & used forklift equipment sales, service, parts rentals & leasing. (Woman, estab 1992, empl 52, sales $19,225,692, cert: WBENC)

California

5967 Bench-Tek Solutions, LLC
525 Aldo Ave
Santa Clara, CA 95054
Contact: Maria Castellon CEO
Tel: 408-653-1100
Email: mcastellon@bench-tek.com
Website: www.bench-tek.com
Custom workbenches, materials handling & storage. (Minority, Woman, estab , empl , sales $4,000,000, cert: NMSDC, WBENC)

5968 Can Lines Engineering
9839 Downey-Norwalk Rd
Downey, CA 90241
Contact: Erik Koplien
Tel: 800-233-4597
Email: erik.koplien@canlines.com
Website: www.canlines.com
Engineer, design, fabricate, install & service container & material operational & conveying systems. (Hisp, estab 1960, empl 100, sales , cert: NMSDC)

5969 ELA Enterprises
1813 Lexington Dr
Fullerton, CA 92835
Contact: President
Tel: 714-738-0397
Email: info@elaent.com
Website: www.elaent.com
Design & mfr custom material handling solutions: dollies, service carts, platform trucks, hand trucks, electric tugs, tow vehicles, trailers, food containers, packaging for transportation & storage solutions. (Minority, Woman, estab 2006, empl 2, sales $115,000, cert: CPUC, WBENC)

5970 McMurray-Stern Inc.
15511 Carmenita Rd
Santa Fe Springs, CA 90670
Contact: Edward Stern Design Consultant
Tel: 562-623-3000
Email: pferro@mcstern.com
Website: www.mcmurraystern.com
Design build specialty contractor offering storage, work space and records management solutions, warehouse & industrial racking, storage systems & material handling equipment. (Woman, estab 1984, empl 50, sales $16,000,000, cert: CPUC, WBENC)

5971 Quality Material Handling
900 W Foothill Blvd
Azusa, CA 91702
Contact: Hector Pinto President
Tel: 626-812-9722
Email: info@qmhinc.com
Website: www.qmhinc.com
Material handling equipment distribution & services, pallet racking, boltless shelving, yard ramps, warehouse racks, pallet rack installation, city permits, high pile & fire permits. (Hisp, estab 1991, empl 40, sales , cert: CPUC)

Colorado

5972 Advanced Manufacturing Technology For Bottles
3920 Patton Ave
Loveland, CO 80538
Contact: Jamie Maier Accounting
Tel: 970-612-0315
Email: jmaier@amtcolorado.com
Website: www.amtcolorado.com
Mfr conveyor systems, integrated systems, conveyors, controls & mechanical & electrical installation services, primarily for the packaging industry. (Woman, estab 1996, empl 57, sales , cert: WBENC)

Connecticut

5973 Warner Specialty Products, Inc.
40-B Montowese Ave
North Haven, CT 06473
Contact: Jack Norton VP
Tel: 203-691-9030
Email: amy@warnerspecialty.com
Website: www.warnerspecialty.com
Dist material handling & ergonomic equipment solutions. (Woman, estab 1991, empl 8, sales $4,228,000, cert: WBENC)

Florida

5974 Teknia Networks & Logistics, Inc.
10451 66th St N
Pinellas Park, FL 33782
Contact: Jorge Monsalve President
Tel: 813-918-8417
Email: laura@teknialogistics.com
Website: www.TEKNIANETWORKS.COM
Teknia Networks and Logistics provides rental of machinery, copiers, printers, material handling machines like Toyota foklifts, racking systems, power generators (Hisp, estab 2010, empl 10, sales $5,000,000, cert: NMSDC)

5975 The Bernd Group Inc.
1251 Pinehurst Rd
Dunedin, FL 34698
Contact: Pilar Bernd President
Tel: 727-733-0122
Email: businessdevelopment@berndgroup.com
Website: www.berndgroup.com
Material handling equip, safety products, hand & power tools, pumps & compressors, motors, generators, electrical hardware, batteries, lighting fixtures, lockers, bins, shelving, lab equip. (Minority, Woman, estab 1992, empl 66, sales , cert: NMSDC)

5976 TriFactor Solutions, LLC
2401 Drane Field Rd
Lakeland, FL 33811
Contact: JJ Phelan Managing Member
Tel: 863-646-9671
Email: jjphelan@trifactor.com
Website: www.trifactor.com
Material handling systems, services, parts & integrations: conveyors, racking, palletizers, diverters, storage systems, pallets, work stations. (Woman, estab 2007, empl 25, sales $756,831, cert: State, WBENC)

Georgia

5977 Atlanta Caster & Equipment
1810-E Auger Dr
Tucker, GA 30084
Contact: John Brumbaugh Govt Sales Mgr
Tel: 770-492-0682
Email: atlantacaster@atlantacaster.com
Website: www.atlantacaster.com
Dist casters, wheels & non-powered material handling equipment. (Woman, estab 1986, empl 8, sales $2,010,000, cert: WBENC)

5978 Material Handling Inc.
PO Box 1045
Dalton, GA 30722
Contact: William Gleaton CFO
Tel: 706-278-1104
Email: billgleaton@mhiusa.net
Website: www.mhiusa.net
New & used lift trucks, lift truck parts, service, maintenance, rental & leasing. (As-Ind, estab 1975, empl 93, sales $33,707,229, cert: NMSDC)

Illinois

5979 Kamflex Conveyor Corporation
2312 Oak Leaf St
Joliet, IL 60436
Contact: Grant Branch III President
Tel: 800-323-2440
Email: gbranch@kamflex.com
Website: www.kamflex.org
Mfr sanitary machinery: conveyors (bucket, trough, vertical lift & conveyors), robotic integration (product picking and assembly, case packing vision guided), palletizers, stretch wrappers, case erectors. (AA, estab 1974, empl 72, sales $13,000,000, cert: NMSDC)

5980 Midway Industrial Equipment Inc..
660 Heartland Dr
Sugar Grove, IL 60554
Contact: Dawn Adams President
Tel: 630-466-7700
Email: dawn@midwaylift.com
Website: www.midwaylift.com
Material Handling Services, sales, service, rental & parts for forklifts, scrubbers, aerial. (Minority, Woman, estab 2003, empl 42, sales $11,200,000, cert: State)

5981 Stevenson Crane Service, Inc.
410 Stevenson Dr
Bolingbrook, IL 60440
Contact: John Edmonson President
Tel: 630-972-9199
Email: john@stevensoncrane.com
Website: www.stevensoncrane.com
Material handling equipment: truck cranes, carrydeck cranes, crawler cranes, rough terrain cranes, material & personnel hoists, material handlers, scissor lifts & boom lifts. (Woman, estab 1989, empl 85, sales $17,779,999, cert: WBENC)

Indiana

5982 Courtney Material Handling, Inc.
PO Box 6925
South Bend, IN 46660
Contact: Beth Courtney President
Tel: 574-231-0094
Email: beth@cmhionline.com
Website: www.cmhionline.com
Dist safety items: hard hats, vests, safety glasses, gloves, tools, fire & detection, bins, cabinets, carts, casters, chairs & stools. (Woman, estab 2003, empl 2, sales $213,673, cert: State)

5983 Handling Technologies, Inc.
51024 Portage Rd
South Bend, IN 46628
Contact: Randy Trowbridge Natl Acct Mgr
Tel: 706-495-7683
Email: rtrowbridge@handlingtechnologies.com
Website: www.handlingtechnologies.com
Dist material handling products - shelving, racking systems, decking, conveyor systems, shop equipment (i.e., carts, bins, tables, hoists). (Woman, estab 1982, empl 10, sales $5,000,000, cert: WBENC)

5984 Harriman Material Handling
511 N Range Line Rd
Morristown, IN 46161
Contact: Ashley Larochelle President
Tel: 765-763-8985
Email: ashlar@harrimanmaterialhandling.com
Website: www.HarrimanMaterialHandling.com
Overhead Cranes, Hoists, Jib Cranes, Monorails, Gantry Cranes, Custom Lifting Devices, Slings/Rigging, Fall Protection Equipment, Crane Components & Parts, Dock Equipment, Storage Equipment, Drum Handling Equipment (Woman, estab 2004, empl 5, sales $3,528,300, cert: WBENC)

5985 Meyer Material Handling Products Inc.
PO Box 47366
Indianapolis, IN 46247
Contact: Carolyn F. Meyer Chairman
Tel: 317-786-9214
Email: cfmeyer@meyermat.com
Website: www.meyermat.com
Material handling equipment. (Woman, estab 1974, empl 11, sales , cert: WBENC)

Michigan

5986 Dynamic Conveyor Corp
5980 Grand Haven Rd
Muskegon, MI 49441
Contact: Tracy Powers Business Devel
Tel: 800-640-6850
Email: tpowers@dynamicconveyor.com
Website: www.dynamicconveyor.com
Quality built radius turns, metal detection, clean room, water tanks, cooling fans, box filling, split belt, ergonomic tilt, etc. (Woman, estab 1991, empl 24, sales $5,700,000, cert: WBENC)

5987 ECI Unlimited, Inc.
110 Trealout Dr Ste 102
Fenton, MI 48430
Contact: Lance Stokes President
Tel: 810-354-2775
Email: powertrain@ecienv.com
Website: www.ecipowertrain.webs.com
Install & refurbish material handling & machine loading & unloading equipment: chain conveyors, roller conveyors, pallet conveyors, accumulating conveyors, overhead conveyors, inverted conveyors, skillet conveyors, assembly machines. (AA, estab 1993, empl 4, sales , cert: NMSDC)

5988 Econobuild, LLC
21060 Bridge St
Southfield, MI 48033
Contact: Ramiro Salazar Managing Member
Tel: 248-799-7500
Email: rsalazar@econobuild.com
Website: www.econobuild.com
Material handling equip: flow-thru racks, rack systems, industrial carts, fork-free environment, plant engineering, facility improvements. (As-Pac, estab 1999, empl 15, sales $3,100,000, cert: NMSDC)

5989 Jarvis Handling Equipment Co.
PO Box 140767
Grand Rapids, MI 49514
Contact: Susan Smith President
Tel: 616-363-9847
Email: ssmith@jarvishandling.com
Website: www.jarvishandling.com
Dist material handling equipment: racks, containers, modular offices mezzanines, and all basics and essentials, i.e. pallet trucks, carts, drum dumpers, lockers, work benches, etc. (Woman, estab 1966, empl 1, sales $1,010,000, cert: WBENC)

5990 Kenowa Industries
11405 E Lakewood Blvd
Holland, MI 49424
Contact: Dan Houle Sales Mgr
Tel: 616-392-7080
Email: dan.houle@kenowa.com
Website: www.kenowa.com
Fabricate material handling racks, baskets, workstations, containers, work-in-process carts, dollies, signboards, mezzanines, steel containers, tubs, steel skids, steel pallets, stands, shelf units. (Hisp, estab 1979, empl 26, sales $3,964,542, cert: NMSDC)

5991 Technical Conveyor Group, Inc.
5918 Meridian Blvd, Ste 2
Brighton, MI 48116
Contact: Rob Tarrien President
Tel: 810-229-5811
Email: rtarrien@tcginc.org
Website: www.tcginc.org
Material handling systems: floor conveyors, overhead/ inverted power & free systems, chain-on-edge systems, AGV, electrified monorails, indexing systems, AS/AR systems. (Nat Ame, estab 2000, empl 5, sales $650,956, cert: NMSDC)

5992 Ultimation Industries LLC
27930 Groesbeck Hwy
Roseville, MI 48066
Contact: Jacqueline Canny CEO
Tel: 586-771-1881
Email: jcanny@ultimationinc.com
Website: www.ultimationinc.com
Design, mfr & install assembly line equipment & services, automation devices & conveyor systems, tire & wheel mounting & inflation devices, tire processing lines, TPMS & soaping machines. (Woman, estab 1989, empl 14, sales $4,855,120, cert: WBENC)

5993 Valmec Inc.
1274 S Holly Rd
Fenton, MI 48430
Contact: Krystn Tatus CEO
Tel: 810-629-8750
Email: valmec@comcast.net
Website: www.valmecinc.com
Material handling & packaging, conveyors, returnable packaging, installation, tear-outs & complete system integration. (Woman, estab 1971, empl 5, sales $1,344,664, cert: WBENC)

Minnesota

5994 J & B Equipment Company, Inc.
8200 Grand Ave S
Bloomington, MN 55420
Contact: David Heggem VP/COO
Tel: 952-884-2040
Email: office@jbeq.com
Website: www.jbeq.com
Design & sell engineered overhead crane & monorail systems; hoists; lift tables; specialty carts; and engineered ergonomic material handling systems. (AA, As-Pac, estab 1961, empl 10, sales , cert: NMSDC)

Missouri

5995 C&B Lift Truck Service, Inc.
6250 Knox Industrial Dr
High Ridge, MO 63049
Contact: Melinda Barbaglia Owner
Tel: 314-781-5438
Email: sales@cbforklift.com
Website: www.cbforklift.com
Dist & service forklifts, aerial/scissor lifts, sweepers, scrubbers, golf carts, dollies, dock equipment, warehouse & distribution equipment (Woman, estab 1976, empl 12, sales $1,000,000, cert: State)

5996 Warehouse One Inc.
7800 E 12th St
Kansas City, MO 64126
Contact: Mary L Jacoby President
Tel: 816-255-2250
Email: garys@wh1.com
Website: www.wh1.com
Dist lifts, hoists, conveyors, racks, cabinets, storage, furniture, work benches, lockers, file cabinets, ladders, shelving, bins, casters, industrial compactors, dock boards, ramps, dollies, platform trucks, etc. (Woman, estab , empl , sales $12,000,000, cert: WBENC)

North Carolina

5997 Guna Enterprises, Inc.
1104 Commercial Ave
Charlotte, NC 28205
Contact: Sales
Tel: 704-358-8787
Email: info@gandrcasters.com
Website: www.gandrcasters.com
Mfr industrial, institutional, special & custom made casters, wheels & floor locks. (Woman/As-Ind, estab 1994, empl 60, sales $2,400,000, cert: State)

5998 MYCA Material Handling Solutions, Inc.
223 E. Chatham St, Ste 102
Cary, NC 27511
Contact: Maria Ezell CFO
Tel: 919-378-9409
Email: mezell@mycagroup.com
Website: www.mycamaterialhandling.com
Material handling equipment, lift trucks, safety programs & safety equipment, training, warehouse systems, conveyor systems. (Woman, estab , empl , sales $4,600,000, cert: WBENC)

5999 WARP Services, LLC
1316 Providence Rd
Charlotte, NC 28207
Contact: Dr. Patrick LaRive CEO
Tel: 888-547-9277
Email: patrick@warprobotics.com
Website: www.warprobotics.com
Intall, repair & replace conveyors, motors, compressors, electrical safety equipment, material handling, industrial robotics, laser navigation, anything mechanical or electrical. (Woman/AA, estab 2005, empl 4, sales $298,000, cert: State, NWBOC)

New Jersey

6000 Hu-Lift Equipment
400 Apgar Dr, Unit F
Somerset, NJ 08873
Contact: Ming Gang Guo Mgr
Tel: 908-874-5585
Email: mgguo@hu-liftusa.com
Website: www.hu-liftusa.com
Dist material handling products: lift table, cart, platform trucks, furniture movers, skid lifters, highlifts, scale jacks, hydraulic jacks, skates, pallet trucks, industrial class portable air conditioners, pallet tilters, forklift jacks. (As-Pac, estab 1999, empl 5, sales , cert: State)

Ohio

6001 Caster Connection, Inc.
2380 International St
Columbus, OH 43228
Contact: Joe Lyden Dir of Sales
Tel: 800-544-8978
Email: joe.lyden@casterconnection.com
Website: www.casterconnection.com
Mfr & dist institutional & industrial casters and wheels, hand trucks, pallet jacks, dollies & manual materials handling products. (Minority, Woman, estab 1987, empl 36, sales , cert: WBENC)

6002 Darana Hybrid
345 High St, STE 510
Hamilton, OH 45011
Contact: Darryl Cuttell CEO
Tel: 513-785-7540
Email: development@daranahybrid.com
Website: www.daranahybrid.com
Industrial electrical & mechanical installations of processing, packaging, and conveyor equipment systems and machinery for the food & beverage industry. (Nat Ame, estab 1995, empl 50, sales , cert: NMSDC)

6003 WHM Equipment Co.
11775 Enterprise Ave
Cincinnati, OH 45241
Contact: Joan Morgan President
Tel: 513-771-3200
Email: joan@whmequipment.com
Website: www.whmequipment.com
Design, fabricate & assemble conveyors & material handling systems. (Woman, estab 1968, empl 12, sales $1,920,869, cert: WBENC)

6004 Shingle Belting
420 Drew Court
King of Prussia, PA 19406
Contact: Bob Frasetto
Tel: 610-239-6667
Email: bfrasetto@shinglebelting.com
Website: www.shinglebelting.com
Dist industrial conveyors & power transmission belting. (Woman, estab 1979, empl 31, sales , cert: WBENC)

Tennessee

6005 Kenco Group
2001 Riverside Dr
Chattanooga, TN 37406
Contact: Lindsey Shrader Business Dev Mgr
Tel: 706-766-9554
Email: lindsey.shrader@kencogroup.com
Website: www.kencogroup.com
Fleet management program, material handling fleet, regardless of OEM, we offer battery and charger maintenance. (Woman, estab 1950, empl 5737, sales $947,075,000, cert: WBENC)

Texas

6006 Design Associates International, Inc
11615 Forest Central Dr, Ste 101
Dallas, TX 75243
Contact: Lucia Fredenburgh President
Tel: 214-720-6083
Email: luciaf@daiinc.com
Website: www.daiinc.com
Dist materials handling equipment: casters, wheels, carts, dollies, hand trucks, facilities planning & design. (Minority, Woman, estab 1994, empl 8, sales $1,250,000, cert: State)

6007 Mighty Lift Inc.
PO Box 14998
Houston, TX 77221
Contact: Helen Fu President
Tel: 713-668-0263
Email: helenfu@mightylift.com
Website: www.mightylift.com
Dist pallet jacks, lifting tables, hand trucks, casters and wheels, wire containers, wire partitions, pallet racks & guard rails, electric personnel & burden carriers & scooters. (Minority, Woman, estab 2002, empl 15, sales $4,042,931, cert: State, NMSDC, WBENC)

6008 Permian Machinery Movers Inc.
2200 W Interstate 20
Odessa, TX 79763
Contact: Robert M. Chavez President
Tel: 432-333-1777
Email: robert@permianmachineryinc.com
Website: www.permianmachineryinc.com
Dist, rent & lease forklifts. (Hisp, estab 1981, empl 45, sales $11,100,000, cert: State)

6009 Texas Storage Systems
PO Box 751632
Houston, TX 77075
Contact: Karen Cato Owner
Tel: 713-991-1089
Email: tssinc@ymail.com
Website: www.catoindustries.com
Material handling & warehouse equipment. (Woman/AA, estab 2010, empl 5, sales $100,000, cert: State)

Washington

6010 Washington Liftruck
700 S Chicago
Seattle, WA 98108
Contact: Jeff Darling VP
Tel: 206-762-2040
Email: darling@forkliftsamerica.com
Website: www.washingtonlift.com
Dist forklifts & material handling equipment. (Woman, estab 1973, empl 34, sales $21,260,000, cert: City, WBENC)

MEASURING INSTRUMENTS

Manufacturers and distributors of counters and timers, X-ray spectrometers, voltage and frequency indicators, gas analyzers, thermocouples, thermometers, etc. (See also ELECTRONIC categories and HARDWARE & TOOLS). NAICS Code 42

California

6011 Technical Maintenance, Inc.
117 Jetplex Circle, Ste C4
Madison, AL 35758
Contact: Scott Chamberlain Quality Mgr
Tel: 256-772-4115
Email: scott.chamberlain@tmicalibration.com
Website: www.tmicalibration.com
Calibrate test & measurement equipment (Minority, Woman, estab 1991, empl 162, sales $22,700,000, cert: WBENC)

6012 Alloy Valves and Control
3210 S Susan St
Santa Ana, CA 92704
Contact: Phyllis Abrams Dir Sales/Marketing
Tel: 714-427-0877
Email: pabrams@avcovalve.com
Website: www.avcovalve.com
Design & mfr ball valves & flow measurement products, manual & automated ball valve assemblies. (Woman, estab 2000, empl 15, sales , cert: CPUC)

6013 Brylen Technologies
275 Orange Ave
Santa Barbara, CA 93117
Contact: Barbara Tzur President
Tel: 805-692-9300
Email: barbara.tzur@brylen.com
Website: www.brylen.com
Calibration & testing laboratory, clean room & clean bench certifications, calibration is electro-magnetic, thermodynamics, dimensional, angle, & mechanical areas, calibrate equipment. (Woman, estab 1985, empl 10, sales $571,850, cert: State)

6014 RHF, Inc.
16202 Keats Circle
Westminster, CA 92683
Contact: Robert Friesen President
Tel: 714-848-9367
Email: rhf.radar@earthlink.net
Website: www.radaretc.com
Repair & calibration of speed radar & lidar equipment. (Woman, estab 1983, empl 3, sales $300,000, cert: State)

6015 STB Electrical Test Equipment, Inc.
1666 Auburn Ravine Rd
Auburn, CA 95603
Contact: Patricia Tavare President
Tel: 530-823-5111
Email: pat@stbinc.com
Website: www.stbinc.com
Mfr phasing voltmeters, voltage detectors, voltage sensors, ground detectors, clamp-on ammeters, phase rotation meters, ground cable testers, drain tools. (Woman, estab 1979, empl 6, sales $1,329,220, cert: State, CPUC)

6016 Vanguard Instruments Company, Inc.
1520 S. Hellman Ave
Ontario, CA 91761
Contact: Timm Smith Natl Sales Mgr
Tel: 513-477-2965
Email: timm.s@vanguard-instruments.com
Website: www.vanguard-instruments.com
Mfr measuring & testing electricity & electrical signal instruments. (As-Pac, estab 1993, empl 11, sales , cert: CPUC)

Connecticut

6017 Environics, Inc.
69 Industrial Park Rd E
Tolland, CT 06084
Contact: Cathy Dunn CEO
Tel: 860-872-1111
Email: cdunn@environics.com
Website: www.environics.com
Design, mfr, dist & service computerized gas flow instruments, gas mixing systems, gas on-demand systems, gas calibration systems, gas dilution systems, gas flow management systems. (Woman, estab 1986, empl 20, sales $3,000,000, cert: State)

Florida

6018 Diverse Services USA, Inc.
11111 N 46th St
Tampa, FL 33617
Contact: Michael Schmidt VP
Tel: 813-988-6000
Email: michael.schmidt@diverseservicesusa.com
Website: www.diverseservicesusa.com
Mfr & install all signs: interior, exterior, graphics, LED message centers, millwork (counters, cabinetry), architectural imaging (ACM panel systems, awnings) and lighting (general illumination, specialty/accent, energy savings (Hisp, estab 2009, empl 650, sales $152,000,000, cert: NMSDC)

Georgia

6019 Georgia Time Recorder Co., Inc.
722 Collins Hill Rd Ste H-283
Lawrenceville, GA 30046
Contact: Andrea Drath President
Tel: 770-441-2879
Email: andrea@georgiatime.com
Website: www.gtrbusinesssystems.com
Time & Attendance, Time clocks, Wireless Synchronized clocks & master clocks, Temperature Sensors, temp/humidity sensors, CO2 sensors, emergency lighting, event monitoring. (Woman, estab 1982, empl 6, sales $550,000, cert: WBENC)

Illinois

6020 B&B Instruments, Inc.
145 W Taft Dr
South Holland, IL 60473
Contact: Bob Samoska Owner
Tel: 708-596-1700
Email: bobsamoska@bbinstruments.com
Website: www.bbinstruments.com
Dist pressure, temperature, level, flow, humidity gauges & instrumentation, NiST shop calibrations, testing type calibrators. (As-Pac, estab 1972, empl 8, sales , cert: NMSDC)

Indiana

6021 AFC International Inc
PO Box 894
DeMotte, IN 46310
Contact: Pamela Seneczko President
Tel: 219-987-6825
Email: pjseneczko@afcintl.com
Website: www.afcintl.com
Gas detectors, respiratory protection, detector tubes, self contained breathing apparatus, heat stress monitors, CO detectors, toxic gas detectors. (Woman, estab 1992, empl 6, sales $3,000,000, cert: WBENC)

6022 The CREW Corporation
PO Box 254
Brownsburg, IN 46112
Contact: Kathy Adkins President
Tel: 317-713-7777
Email: kadkins@crewcorp.com
Website: www.crewcorp.com
Validation services: qualification testing & validation, change control, FAT & SAT, IQ/OQ/PQ protocols & execution, instrument calibration, supporting documentation. (Woman, estab 1995, empl 38, sales $2,970,000, cert: WBENC)

Michigan

6023 Hines Industries, Inc.
793 Airport Blvd.
Ann Arbor, MI 48108
Contact: Beverly Monge Sales Admin
Tel: 734-769-2300
Email: ddonall@hinesindustries.com
Website: www.hinesindustries.com
Balancing machines, rebuild balancing equipment & balancing instrumentation services, balancing equipment design innovation & manufacturing process improvement. (Woman, estab 1971, empl 25, sales $8,400,000, cert: WBENC)

6024 M & B Holdings, LLC
5594 E Ten Mile Rd
Warren, MI 48091
Contact: Brian McMillan GM
Tel: 586-427-9971
Email: bmcmillan@gsnscorp.com
Website: www.gsnscorp.com
Gage Commodity Management, Gage Purchasing, Gage Design & Manufacturing. (As-Ind, estab 2005, empl 31, sales $4,420,017, cert: NMSDC)

6025 Omni-Tech Sales, Inc.
31189 Schoolcraft Rd
Livonia, MI 48150
Contact: Deborah Denne CEO
Tel: 734-425-5730
Email: omnitech_sales@ameritech.net
Website: www.omnitech-sales.com
Dist precision measuring equipment, CMM's, Vision Systems, Roundness & Form Measurement, Surface Finish equipment & fixturing, Hardness Testers, Optical Comparators. (Woman, estab 1988, empl 6, sales $3,975,637, cert: WBENC)

6026 River City Metrology LLC
2215 29th St SE, Ste B1
Grand Rapids, MI 49508
Contact: Victor Barker Owner
Tel: 616-530-4899
Email: vbarker@rcmetrology.com
Website: www.rcmetrology.com
Dimensional Inspection, CMM calibration & sales, Dimensional inspection product sales. (As-Pac, estab 2004, empl 5, sales , cert: NMSDC)

6027　Standard Scale & Supply Co.
　　　25421 Glendale
　　　Redford, MI 48239
　　　Contact: John Bowman GM
　　　Tel:　313-255-6700
　　　Email: jbowman@standardscale.com
　　　Website: www.standardscale.com
Dist & service weight-based measuring equipment &
accessories. (Hisp, estab 1946, empl 12, sales , cert:
NMSDC)

6028　Universal Tool Equipment & Controls, Inc.
　　　6525 Center Dr
　　　Sterlng Heights, MI 48312
　　　Contact: Bill Bartolotta VP
　　　Tel:　586-268-4380
　　　Email: bbartolotta@universaltecinc.com
　　　Website: www.universaltecinc.com
Automation & welding systems, robotics, weld guns, vision
systems, sealant systems, drawn arc welders, projection
welders, material handling end effectors & welding
fixtures. (Woman/AA, estab 2009, empl 29, sales
$10,000,000, cert: WBENC)

North Carolina

6029　Cooper Electrical Construction
　　　1706 E Wendover Ave
　　　Greensboro, NC 27405
　　　Contact: Beverly Brown CEO
　　　Tel:　336-275-8439
　　　Email: beverly.brown@coopereic.com
　　　Website: www.coopereic.com
Electrical D/B, BIM, Prefabrication, Instrumentation &
Controls, and Calibration services. (Woman, estab 1954,
empl 120, sales $41,509,090, cert: WBENC)

6030　Measurement Controls, Inc.
　　　PO Box 562775
　　　Charlotte, NC 28256
　　　Contact: Paresh Patel President
　　　Tel:　704-921-1101
　　　Email: sales@measurementcontrols.com
　　　Website: www.measurementcontrols.com
Refurbish, mfr & dist rotary, diaphragms & turbine gas
meters, meter sets with regulators, filters & by-pass, install
index, connections, swivels, nuts, & washers, electro
mechanical correctors, dust caps & blind disc. (As-Ind,
estab 1999, empl 9, sales $400,000, cert: State, City,
NMSDC)

Ohio

6031　AVM Industries
　　　30505 Bainbridge Rd, Ste 100
　　　Solon, OH 44139
　　　Contact: Linda Holt Dir
　　　Tel:　440-349-1849
　　　Email: lholt@hawthornmc.com
　　　Website: www.avminc.com
Mfr & dist climate control actuators & counterbalancing
systems for the automotive, commercial & aftermarket
industries. (As-Pac, estab 2006, empl 376, sales
$34,000,000, cert: NMSDC)

6032　Cooper Atkins
　　　11353 Reed Hartman Hwy Ste 110
　　　Cincinnati, OH 45241
　　　Contact:　Sr VP Sales
　　　Tel:　847-373-2033
　　　Email: gmarcus@cooper-atkins.com
　　　Website: www.cooper-atkins.com
Wireless temperature / environmental monitoring
systems, software, hardware, installation & support.
(Woman, estab , empl , sales , cert: WBENC)

6033　Intek, Inc.
　　　751 Intek Way
　　　Westerville, OH 43082
　　　Contact: Audrey Myers Customer Service Assoc.
　　　Tel:　614-895-0301
　　　Email: amyers@intekflow.com
　　　Website: www.intekflow.com
Mfr & dist thermal low flow meters & switches, mea-
sures liquid flow rates, also mfr RheoVac line of vacuum
monitoring equipment. (As-Pac, estab 1976, empl 17,
sales , cert: City)

6034　Precision Gage & Tool Co.
　　　375 Gargave Rd
　　　Dayton, OH 45449
　　　Contact: Victoria Mack Admin
　　　Tel:　937-866-9666
　　　Email: vmack@pgtgage.com
　　　Website: www.pgtgage.com
Custom grind gauges. (Woman/AA, estab , empl 16, sales
, cert: WBENC)

Oregon

6035　Component Design Northwest, Inc.
　　　PO Box 10947
　　　Portland, OR 97296
　　　Contact: Krissy McKay VP
　　　Tel:　503-225-0900
　　　Email: krissy@cdnw.com
　　　Website: www.cdn-timeandtemp.com
Thermometers & timers. (Woman, estab 1983, empl 7,
sales $4,700,100, cert: WBENC)

Pennsylvania

6036 RNDT, Inc.
      228 Maple Ave
      Johnstown, PA 15901
      Contact: VP Technical Dir
      Tel: 814-535-5448
      Email: info@rndt.net
      Website: www.rndt.net
Nondestructive testing services, radiographic, magnetic
particle, liquid penetrant, ultrasonic and visual testing
services. Also offer Positive Material Identification (PMI),
remote video, certified welding inspector services (CWI).
(Woman, estab 2002, empl 35, sales $5,800,000, cert:
WBENC)

Puerto Rico

6037 American Test & Balance
      PO Box 366584
      San Juan, PR 00936
      Contact: David Rosa President
      Tel: 787-781-7654
      Email: d.rosa@american-test.com
      Website: www.american-test.com
Testing, adjusting and balancing (TAB) services for heating,
ventilating and air conditioning systems. We also provide
Cleanroom Performance Testing (CPT) services. (Hisp,
estab 1994, empl 21, sales , cert: NMSDC)

6038 Instrumentation Corps, Inc.
      PO Box 2116
      Barceloneta, PR 00617
      Contact: Juan Oliveras President
      Tel: 787-970-0746
      Email: jaoliver@instrumentationcorps.com
      Website: www.instrumentationcorps.com
Process instrumentation & weight scales sales, installation,
configuration, calibration & certification svcs, equipment
repair & technical services. (Hisp, estab 1998, empl 40,
sales $4,851,214, cert: NMSDC)

6039 PAS Technologies, Inc.
      9 Pedro Arzuaga W
      Carolina, PR 00984
      Contact: Alfredo Agelviz President
      Tel: 787-775-2237
      Email: alfredo.agelviz@pastechnologies.com
      Website: www.pastechnologies.com
Dist & service instrumentation & control products. (Hisp,
estab 1993, empl 3, sales $1,300,000, cert: NMSDC)

Wisconsin

6040 Precision Metrology, Inc.
      7350 N Teutonia Ave
      Milwaukee, WI 53209
      Contact: Carol Shipley President
      Tel: 414-351-7420
      Email: carol@precisionmetrology.com
      Website: www.precisionmetrology.com
Calibrate & repaire precision measuring instruments.
(Woman, estab , empl , sales , cert: WBENC)

MEDICAL SUPPLIES & SERVICES
Manufacturers and distributors of over the counter drugs, dental supplies, diagnostic equipment and supplies, glass containers, labwear, veterinary products, latex, hospital supplies & apparel, etc. NAICS Code 32

Alabama

6041   NuAngel Inc.
14717 Friend Rd
Athens, AL 35611
Contact: Teresa Carroll President
Tel: 256-729-5000
Email: info@nuangel.com
Website: www.NuAngel.com
Mfr breastfeeding & infant items: washable nursing pads, biodegradable disposable nursing pads, burp cloths, washable baby wipes, receiving blankets, bra extenders. (Woman, estab 1990, empl 10, sales $450,000, cert: WBENC)

6042   VELOX Integration Services, LLC
600 S Court St, Ste 322
Montgomery, AL 36104
Contact: Sherrell Love CEO
Tel: 334-233-3328
Email: sherrell@veloxintegration.com
Website: www.veloxintegration.com
Dist medical supplies & equipment, construction management. (Woman/AA, estab 2014, empl 2, sales , cert: State)

Arizona

6043   Magnum Medical LLC
3265 N Nevada St
Chandler, AZ 85225
Contact: Omar Hameed Mktg Dir
Tel: 800-336-9710
Email: ohameed@magnummed.com
Website: www.magnummed.com
Import & dist surgical instruments, plastic instruments & related items. (As-Ind, estab 1984, empl 9, sales $3,000,000, cert: NMSDC)

6044   Magnum Medical, Inc.
3265 N Nevada St
Chandler, AZ 85225
Contact: Omar Hameed Mktg Dir
Tel: 480-633-2777
Email: magnummed@earthlink.net
Website: www.magnummedical.com
Dist medical equip: handheld surgical dental instruments, hemostats, scissors, needle holders, etc. (As-Ind, estab , empl , sales , cert: NMSDC)

California

6045   Abell Marketing Group, Inc.
15057 Avenida De Las Flores
Chino Hills, CA 91709
Contact: James Lohan Project Mgr
Tel: 909-456-8905
Email: james@abellmarketinggroup.com
Website: www.abellmarketinggroup.com
Protective clothing & medical/industrial nitrile, vinyl & latex gloves. (Woman, estab 1998, empl 2, sales $375,000, cert: WBENC)

6046   Advanced ImmunoChemical, Inc.
111 W Ocean Blvd, 4th Fl
Long Beach, CA 90802
Contact: President
Tel: 562-434-4676
Email: order@advimmuno.com
Website: www.advimmuno.com
Mfr laboratory reagents for In vitro diagnostics & research, Cardiac Disease, Tumor Markers, Metabolic Syndrome, Inflammation, Emerging Infectious Diseases, Biowarfare Threats, Hormones, Autoimmune Disease, Neuroscience. (Woman, estab 1986, empl 2, sales , cert: WBENC)

6047   Alcam Medical Inc.
1760 Chicago Ave, Ste L-21
Riverside, CA 92507
Contact: Cameron Stewart VP
Tel: 866-847-7187
Email: cameron@alcammedical.com
Website: www.alcammedical.com
We provide Orthotic and Prosthetic Services. We evaluate and fit for upper and lower extremity prosthetics, custom orthotics, diabetic shoes, compression garments, cranial helmets, knee braces, back braces, pediatric orthotics, mastectomy bras. (AA, estab 2006, empl 69, sales $8,100,000, cert: CPUC)

6048   Ames Medical Equipment, Inc.
301 N Jackson Ave, Ste 7A
San Jose, CA 95133
Contact: patel Mike Treasurer
Tel: 408-942-9000
Email: mspatel101@hotmail.com
Website: www.Alliancemedsupply.com
Dist durable medical equipment & supplies. (Minority, Woman, estab 2005, empl 2, sales , cert: State)

6049   BioMed Resources Inc.
6646 Doolittle Ave
Riverside, CA 92503
Contact: Lisa Liu CEO
Tel: 310-323-3888
Email: lisal@bmres.com
Website: www.bmres.com
Dist specimen containers, transfer pipettes, conical tubes, irrigation syringes, lab jackets, lab coats, isolation gowns & cover gowns. (Minority, Woman, estab 2002, empl 15, sales $4,300,000, cert: NMSDC)

6050   Broadline Medical, Inc.
2100 Atlas Rd, Ste E
Richmond, CA 94806
Contact: Georgia W. Richardson President
Tel: 510-662-5270
Email: grichardson@broadline.com
Website: www.broadline.com
Dist disposable medical apparel: headwear, footwear, labcoats & lab jackets, OR towels, lap sponges, gowns & non sterile kits. (Woman/AA, estab 1994, empl 10, sales $3,000,000, cert: NMSDC)

6051 Clariti Eyewear, Inc.
      940 Ajax Ave
      City of Industry, CA 91748
      Contact: Dominique Yonemoto President
      Tel: 800-372-6372
      Email: gene@claritieyewear.com
      Website: www.claritieyewear.com
Eyeglasses, Optical frames, Eyeglass frames, Eyewear,
Sunglasses, Eyeglass cases, Cleaning cloths, Cleaning Kit.
(Minority, Woman, estab 1993, empl 14, sales $3,219,627,
cert: State, NMSDC)

6052 Duncan & Duncan Medical, Inc.
      911 Marina Way S Unite E2
      Richmond, CA 94804
      Contact: Luta Duncan President
      Tel: 510-799-0100
      Email: glovesbylu@aol.com
      Website: www.duncanmeds.com
Medical, surgical, laboratory supplies & equipment,
medical books, cleaning supplies, housekeeping supplies,
apparel, gloves, incontinence, textiles, orthopedic ,
nutritional & feeding supplies, personal hygiene, physical
therapy. (Woman/AA, estab 2011, empl 3, sales $429,000,
cert: CPUC)

6053 EMS Safety Services, Inc.
      1046 Calle Recodo Ste K
      San Clemente, CA 92673
      Contact: Marian Lepore CEO
      Tel: 800-215-9555
      Email: bids@emssafety.com
      Website: www.emssafetyservices.com
Training curriculums & products: CPR, AED, First Aid &
Bloodborne Pathogens. (Minority, Woman, estab 1993,
empl 18, sales $2,700,000, cert: NMSDC, CPUC, WBENC)

6054 Flying Medical USA
      18187 Valley
      La Puente, CA 91744
      Contact: Conrad Reveles Sales Exec
      Tel: 855-227-3080
      Email: sales3@flyingmedusa.com
      Website: www.flyingmedusa.com
Mfr medical supplies: band aid, ice packs, finger splints,
etc. (As-Pac, estab 2008, empl 4, sales , cert: State)

6055 Hand and Hand Medical
      822 Wakefield Dr
      Oakdale, CA 95361
      Contact: Sharon Devereaux CEO
      Tel: 209-322-2699
      Email: dwight@handandhand.com
      Website: www.handandhandmed.com
Dist surgical post-op "JP Drain" Management Systems,
unique effective product, US Patent Awarded 2015.
(Woman, estab 2016, empl 3, sales $750,000, cert:
WBENC)

6056 IDEAON
      1855, Gateway Blvd Ste 170
      Concord, CA 94520
      Contact: Shankar Krishna Dir
      Tel: 925-465-2175
      Email: shankar@ideaoninc.com
      Website: www.ideaoninc.com
Custom Programming Services. (As-Ind, estab 2003, empl
5, sales $1,500,000, cert: NMSDC)

6057 J2 Medical Supply
      28790 W Chase
      Valencia, CA 91355
      Contact: Roland Williams Dir Contracts & Compli-
      ance
      Tel: 855-615-8633
      Email: heather.alnimri@j2medicalsupply.com
      Website: www.raelife.co
Mfr & dist high-quality medical solutions. (AA, estab
2020, empl 5, sales $6,728,535, cert: NMSDC)

6058 Kili Summit Corporation
      102 Cross St Ste 220
      San Luis Obispo, CA 93401
      Contact: Cinde Dolphin CEO
      Tel: 916-768-1690
      Email: cinde@medicaldraincarrier.com
      Website: www.medicaldraincarrier.com
Manage JP wound-care drains after mastectomy, cancer,
cardiac and organ transplant surgeries. (Woman, estab
2015, empl 2, sales , cert: WBENC)

6059 Legend Medical Devices Inc.
      16714 E Johnson Dr
      City of Industry, CA 91745
      Contact: Mark Sevilla Dir of Sales
      Tel: 626-350-9733
      Email: msevilla@legendmd.com
      Website: www.legendmd.com
Mfr & dist CPAP, anesthesia, respiratory care & infection
control products. (Minority, Woman, estab 2006, empl 8,
sales $1,500,000, cert: CPUC)

6060 Medi Max Tech
      2805 E Ana St
      East Rancho Dominguez, CA 90221
      Contact: Natl Contracting Mgr
      Tel: 716-868-6108
      Email: Support@MediMaxTech.com
      Website: www.medimaxtech.com
Dist electrosurgical pencils: Telescopic Smoke and
Ergonomic Pencils. (Minority, Woman, estab 2012, empl
10, sales , cert: NMSDC, WBENC)

6061 Medical Receivables Solutions, Inc.
      802 Wilmington
      Fairfield, CA 94533
      Contact: Aleshia Hunter President
      Tel: 415-377-3775
      Email: aleshia@medicalreceivables.net
      Website: www.medicalreceivables.net
Account receivables and medical billing shortage,
Medical Receivables Solutions Inc. (Woman/AA, estab
2002, empl 7, sales $250,000, cert: CPUC)

6062 Plus One Lab Works Inc.
      2872 Walnut Ave, Ste C
      Tustin, CA 92780
      Contact: Jason Vi Mgr
      Tel: 714-558-8009
      Email: jason@plusonelab.com
      Website: www.plusonelab.com
Dist disposable products for use in labs, clean rooms,
hospitals, dental & medical offices. (As-Pac, estab 2010,
empl 5, sales , cert: NMSDC)

6063   ProTrials Research, Inc.
       333 W San Carlos St Ste 800
       San Jose, CA 95110
       Contact: Jodi Andrews CEO
       Tel: 650-864-9180
       Email: jandrews@protrials.com
       Website: www.protrials.com/
Project Management, Clinical Trial Monitoring, Regional
Clinical Trial Monitoring, Clinical Training, SOP Development. (Woman, estab 1996, empl 160, sales $27,000,000,
cert: WBENC)

6064   Shen Wei USA Inc.
       33278 Central Ave, Ste 102
       Union City, CA 94587
       Contact: James Lee President
       Tel: 510-429-8692
       Email: james@shenweiusa.com
       Website: www.shenweiusa.com
Mfr latex & non-latex disposable gloves. (Minority,
Woman, estab 1984, empl 20, sales $45,234,000, cert:
WBENC)

6065   Small Beginnings, Inc.
       17229 Lemon St Ste B2
       Hesperia, CA 92345
       Contact: Kelly Brockelmeyer Exec Admin
       Tel: 760-949-7707
       Email: kelly@small-beginnings.com
       Website: www.small-beginnings.com
Mfr Neonatal Intensive Care Unit disposable products:
diapers, photo-therapy masks, suction devices, pacifiers, &
meconium aspirators. (Woman, estab 2001, empl 8, sales
$1,071,101, cert: WBENC)

6066   Special Respiratory Care, Inc.
       18327 NAPA St
       Northridge, CA 91325
       Contact: Don Reiter President
       Tel: 818-717-8807
       Email: dreiter@src-medical.com
       Website: www.src-medical.com
Dist, rent and service respiratory, anesthesia and critical
care products. Portable ventilators, BiPaps/CPAPs/BiLevels,
airway clearance devices, high flow humidification systems, ventilation monitors, pulse oximeters, intubation
products, patient circuit (Woman, estab 1982, empl 33,
sales $6,000,000, cert: WBENC)

6067   Strive Well-Being, Inc.
       5920 Friars Rd, Ste103
       San Diego, CA 92108
       Contact: Amit Sangani President
       Tel: 619-684-5700
       Email: reg@strive2bfit.com
       Website: www.strive2bfit.com
Onsite Physical Activity Classes, Onsite Stress Management
Classes, Musculoskeletal Strengthening Classes, Fitness
Center Staffing & Management, Fitness & Wellness
Program Management, Fitness Facility Design & Develop-
ment. (As-Ind, estab 2008, empl 40, sales $1,500,000, cert:
City, NMSDC, 8(a))

6068   Teco Diagnostics Inc.
       1268 N Lakeview Ave
       Anaheim, CA 92807
       Contact: Lewis Cabrera Dir of Sales
       Tel: 714-463-1111
       Email: lewis@tecodiagnostics.com
       Website: www.tecodiag.com
Mfr vitro clinical diagnostic tests and instruments. (As-
Pac, estab 1987, empl 50, sales $7,000,000, cert:
NMSDC)

6069   The Andwin Corp.
       6636 Variel Ave
       Canoga Park, CA 91303
       Contact: Arnie Shedlow Sr VP Sales
       Tel: 818-999-2828
       Email: jpalaganas@andwin.com
       Website: www.andwinsci.com
Dist medical & lab supplies & product kits: boxes, labels,
bar codes, instruction inserts & kit components.
(Woman, estab 1950, empl 98, sales $32,000,000, cert:
WBENC)

6070   Total Resources International
       420 S Lemon Ave
       Walnut, CA 91789
       Contact: Andre Dela Victoria Sales Mgr
       Tel: 909-594-1220
       Email: andrev@totalresourcesintl.com
       Website: www.totalresourcesintl.com
Mfr First Aid Kits & Emergency Survival Essentials. (As-
Pac, estab 1990, empl 150, sales $13,000,000, cert:
NMSDC)

6071   Trademark Plastics, Inc.
       807 Palmyrita Ave
       Riverside, CA 92507
       Contact: Gilbert McMoran Sales Mgr
       Tel: 909-941-8810
       Email: gmcmoran@trademarkplastics.com
       Website: www.TrademarkPlastics.com
Mfr plastic, medical components. (Woman, estab 1989,
empl 150, sales $14,000,000, cert: WBENC)

Colorado

6072   in3corp Inc.
       1750 30th St, Ste 216
       Boulder, CO 80301
       Contact: Patricia Gilpin Acct Coord
       Tel: 303-448-1191
       Email: gilpin@in3corp.com
       Website: www.in3corp.com/
Our firm has a variety of capabilities to help audit
supplier invoice payments. Our projects find transaction
errors in order to deliver lost money to clients; but we
also reinforce existing best practices, identify new
optimization strategies (Hisp, estab 2000, empl 79, sales
$2,200,000, cert: NMSDC)

6073   LifeHealth LLC
       5951 S Middlefield Rd, Ste 102
       Littleton, CO 80123
       Contact: Margot Langstaff Managing Partner
       Tel: 303-730-1902
       Email: margot@lifehealthcorp.com
       Website: www.lifehealthcorp.com
Clinical health care services & solutions. (Woman, estab
2004, empl 5, sales $870,000, cert: State, WBENC)

6074 Mountainside Medical Colorado, LLC
6165 Lookout Rd
Boulder, CO 80301
Contact: Susan Neidecker President
Tel: 303-222-1271
Email: sneidecker@mountainsidemed.com
Website: www.mountainsidemed.com
Contract manufacturing for complex, tight-tolerance
medical products, Multi-axis Machining Assembly, Wire
EDMCNC, Swiss type machining centers, Laser welding &
Laser marking, Finishing Metal Forming. (Woman, estab
2006, empl 90, sales $12,731,416, cert: WBENC)

6075 Relius Medical LLC
615 Wooten Rd Ste 150
Colorado Springs, CO 80915
Contact: Lauralee Martin Owner
Tel: 719-725-6444
Email: lmartin@reliusmed.com
Website: www.reliusmed.com
Orthopedic Medical Device Manufacturer: Implants,
External Fixation Devices, Instrumentation. (Woman, estab
2014, empl 125, sales $1,010,907,952, cert: WBENC)

6076 The Medcom Group, Ltd.
541 East Garden Dr, Unit Q
Windsor, CO 80550
Contact: Steven Barnett
Tel: 970-674-3032
Email: novation@medcomgroup.com
Website: www.medcomgroup.com
Dist orthopedic rehabilitative equipment. (Woman, estab ,
empl , sales $2,500,000, cert: WBENC)

Connecticut

6077 PL Medical Co., LLC
117 West Dudley Town Road
Bloomfield, CT 06002
Contact: Rahul Kanwar Owner
Tel: 860-243-2100
Email: r.kanwar@plmedical.com
Website: www.plmedical.com
Dist IV lines (sets), surgical blades, opthalmic products, x-
ray film, x-ray envelopes, safety instruments. (Woman/As-
Ind, estab 1998, empl 8, sales $2,172,116, cert: NMSDC)

Delaware

6078 Med-Tech Equipment, Inc.
2207 Concord Pike Ste 135
Wilmington, DE 19803
Contact: David Gentile VP
Tel: 800-322-2609
Email: info@buymedtech.com
Website: www.buymedtech.com
Dist, service & maintain sport medicine modalities &
training equipment: Electrotherapy Ultrasound, Stim, Laser
and Combo units, Hydrotherapy Whirlpools, Traction/
Decompression Systems, Treatment Tables, Extremity
Testing Systems. (Woman, estab 1989, empl 2, sales
$250,000, cert: State)

6079 QPS, LLC
3 Innovation Way Ste 240
Newark, DE 19711
Contact: Lily Rosa Sr Dir Business Dev
Tel: 302-369-5601
Email: lily.rosa@qps.com
Website: www.qps.com
GLP/GCP compliant CRO supporting discovery, preclinical
and clinical drug development. (As-Pac, estab 1995,
empl 251, sales $19,999,999,998, cert: NMSDC)

6080 SIVAD PPE, LLC
703 Carson Dr
Bear, DE 19701
Contact: Lenzie Davis CEO
Tel: 313-285-9821
Email: Sivad@sivadppe.com
Website: www.sivadppe.com
Provide durable PPE and Janitorial supply chain, special-
izing in trailblazing technology, such as UV-C Disinfec-
tion. (AA, estab 2020, empl 30, sales $47,000,000, cert:
City, NMSDC)

Florida

6081 Advanced Surgical Technologies, Inc.
901 SW Martin Downs Blvd, 200A
Palm City, FL 34990
Contact: Barbara Alfaro President
Tel: 561-801-2314
Email: balfaro@astlaser.com
Website: www.astlaser.com
Medical laser rental and related supplies. (Hisp, estab
2017, empl 10, sales $1,010,000, cert: NMSDC, 8(a))

6082 American Medicals
8900 Corporate Square Court
Jacksonville, FL 32216
Contact: B G Bihani President
Tel: 904-636-9451
Email: bg.bihani@americanmedicals.com
Website: www.americanmedicals.com
Mfr & dist medical, surgical & healthcare products. (As-
Ind, estab 2001, empl 3, sales , cert: State)

6083 American Purchasing Services
10315 USA Today Way
Miramar, FL 33025
Contact: Akhil Agrawal President
Tel: 305-364-0888
Email: akhil.agrawal@american-depot.com
Website: www.american-depot.com
Dist medical supplies. (Minority, estab , empl , sales ,
cert: NMSDC)

6084 Anexa Biomedical, Inc.
40423 Air Time Ave
Zephyrhills, FL 33542
Contact: Lenny Budloo President
Tel: 813-780-7927
Email: lenny@anexabiomedical.com
Website: www.anexabiomedical.com
Mfr USP Sterile Saline and Sterile Water solutions for
moistening of wound dressings, wound debridement,
and device irrigation. (Hisp, estab 2010, empl 8, sales ,
cert: State)

6085   Care-Full Products
3905 Tampa Rd, Ste 432
Oldsmar, FL 34677
Contact: Colleen Meloff President
Tel: 813-602-2824
Email: cmeloff@carefullproducts.com
Website: www.carefullproducts.com
Mfr CareFull Catch disposable specimen cup holder.
(Woman, estab 2015, empl 1, sales , cert: NWBOC)

6086   Customed USA, LLC
10805 Southport Dr
Orlando, FL 32824
Contact: Milexis Torres Dir of Sales
Tel: 407-850-5558
Email: milexis.torres@prhospital.com
Website: www.customedhealing.com
Dist hospital, medical supplies, imaging products, custom
surgical products. (Hisp, estab 2010, empl 240, sales , cert:
NMSDC)

6087   Dazmed, Inc.
508 NW 77th St
Boca Raton, FL 33487
Contact: Amio Das President
Tel: 561-414-3733
Email: amio@dazmed.com
Website: www.dazmed.com
Prescription drug, over-the counter, cosmetics, and
prescription drug re-packager. (As-Ind, estab 2011, empl
11, sales , cert: State)

6088   ECI Holdings, LLC dba Exam Coordinators Network
6111 Broken Sound Pkwy NW Ste 207
Boca Raton, FL 33487
Contact: Barbara Levine CEO
Tel: 561-922-5200
Email: supplierdiversity@ecnime.com
Website: www.ecnime.com
Claim evaluation services, independent medical examina-
tions, functional capacity evaluations, fitness for duty
exams, 2nd opinion exams & medical file, film & bill
reviews. (Woman, estab 1999, empl 75, sales $16,300,000,
cert: WBENC)

6089   EncompasUnlimited, Inc.
2219 Whitfield Park Dr
Sarasota, FL 34243
Contact: Marybeth Flynn VP
Tel: 941-751-3385
Email: marybeth@encompasunlimited.com
Website: www.encompasunlimited.com
Dist endoscopy accessories, specimen caddies, multiple
glove dispenser boxes, endoscopy wedges & headrests.
(Woman, estab 1977, empl 4, sales $2,400,000, cert:
NWBOC)

6090   Global Sourcing, LLC
2415 Albany Ave
Tampa, FL 33607
Contact: Tom Irby VP Strategic Partnerships
Tel: 512-293-8709
Email: tom.irby@globalsourcingppe.com
Website: www.globalsourcingppe.com
Dist PPE items, N95 masks, ASTM level 1,2,3 surgical
masks, face shields, surgical gowns level 1/2/3/4, nitrile
FDA 510k exam gloves, latex gloves, vinyl gloves, show
covers/boots, alcohol EPA list N wipes, hand sanitizers.
(Woman, estab 2020, empl 20, sales $25,500,000, cert:
WBENC)

6091   Healthcare Supply Solutions, Inc.
13949 Alvarez Rd Ste 100
Jacksonville, FL 32218
Contact: Lara Cheek
Tel: 904-638-5520
Email: lcheek@hssone.com
Website: www.hssone.com
Dist healthcare products & services. (Hisp, estab 2008,
empl 14, sales $10,000,000, cert: NMSDC)

6092   HNM Medical USA
20855 Northeast 16th Ave, Ste C15
Miami, FL 11111
Contact: Yoav Anisz President
Tel: 866-291-8498
Email: yanisz@hnmmedical.com
Website: www.hnmmedical.com
Dist medical equipment and supplies. (Hisp, estab , empl
, sales $7,000,000, cert: NMSDC)

6093   Kramer Laboratories, Inc.
400 University Dr Ste 400
Coral Gables, FL 33134
Contact: Myrna Patterson Sales Mgr
Tel: 800-824-4894
Email: mpatterson@kramerlabs.com
Website: www.kramerlabs.com
Fungi Nail Brand, Safetussin CD Cough Relief/Nasal
Decongestant Formula, Safetussin DM Cough Formula.
(Minority, Woman, estab 1987, empl 14, sales , cert:
NMSDC, WBENC)

6094   Lifeline Pharmaceuticals LLC
1301 NW 84th Ave Ste 101
Miami, FL 33126
Contact: Benjamin Rivera Jr SVP
Tel: 877-430-6337
Email: ben@lifelinepharm.com
Website: www.lifelinepharm.com
Dist medical supplies & equipment, medical-surgical
products, specialty pharmaceuticals, anesthesia,
controlled medications, blood & plasma products,
generic & branded chemotherapy products, vaccines,
albumin, IVIG. (AA, estab 2006, empl 37, sales
$29,000,000, cert: State, NMSDC)

6095   Lipotriad LLC
219 Via Emilia
Palm Beach Gardens, FL 33418
Contact: Joan McCabe CEO
Tel: 203-561-0970
Email: joan@lipotriad.com
Website: www.lipotriadvitamins.com
Eye vitamins for eye health (Woman, estab 2009, empl
13, sales $2,000,000, cert: WBENC, NWBOC)

6096   Medgluv Inc
4100 Coral Ridge Dr Ste 100
Coral Springs, FL 33065
Contact: Jerry Leong CEO
Tel: 954-586-5309
Email: jleong@medgluv.com
Website: www.medgluv.com
Mfr & dist examination gloves. (As-Pac, estab 2001, empl
6, sales $8,000,000, cert: State, NMSDC)

6097   Medical Support International, LLC
       2626 Sawyer Terr
       Wellington, FL 33414
       Contact: Edgar Rivera CEO
       Tel: 561-337-4866
       Email: edgar.rivera@medsupportintl.com
       Website: www.medsupportintl.com
Dist medical, dental, veterinary, surgical & hospital
supplies & equipment. (Hisp, estab 2009, empl 2, sales ,
cert: NMSDC)

6098   Med-Lab Supply Co. Inc
       800 Waterford Way Ste 950
       Miami, FL 33126
       Contact: Lucas Diaz VP Sales
       Tel: 800-330-3183
       Email: lucas.diaz@med-lab.com
       Website: www.med-lab.com
Dist & service Siemens medical equipment. (Hisp, estab
1964, empl 79, sales $25,000,000, cert: NMSDC)

6099   Mellow Enterprises LLC
       201 SW 63rd Ave
       Plantation, FL 33317
       Contact: Helen F Litsky President
       Tel: 954-312-7175
       Email: me@mellowllc.com
       Website: www.voacorp.com/mellowenterprises.net
Safety & fire related training, medical supplies. (Woman/
AA, estab 2010, empl 1, sales , cert: City)

6100   Surgimed Corporation
       1303 NW 78th Ave
       Doral, FL 33126
       Contact: Luis Arias VP
       Tel: 305-594-1121
       Email: larias@surgimedcorp.com
       Website: www.surgimedcorp.com/
Dist endotracheal tubes, stylets, guedels, suction catheters, tracheostomy tubes, endobroncheal tubes, foley
catheters, urinary collection bags, leg bags, urine meters,
pediatric urine collectors, foley Catheterization trays,
irrigation syringes & trays. (Hisp, estab 1981, empl 13,
sales $4,000,000, cert: NMSDC)

6101   US Medical International LLC
       6989 NW 82nd Ave
       Miami, FL 33166
       Contact: Ryan Kissane Sales/Operations Mgr
       Tel: 305-468-3248
       Email: ryan@usmedicalintl.com
       Website: www.usmedicalintl.com
Mfr & dist disposable medical supplies. (Hisp, estab 2009,
empl 3, sales , cert: State, NMSDC)

6102   ValorPoint, LLC
       7827 Chase Meadows Dr E
       Jacksonville, FL 32256
       Contact: Markus hardy CEO
       Tel: 904-321-7007
       Email: mark.hardy@valorpointllc.com
       Website: www.valorpointllc.com
Dist Personal Protective Equipment (PPE) for government
and non-government entities. (AA, estab 2016, empl 2,
sales , cert: NMSDC)

6103   VetMeds, Inc.
       8950 SW 74th Court Ste 2201
       Miami, FL 33156
       Contact: President
       Tel: 786-220-3634
       Email: vetmeds@gmx.com
       Website: www.vetmedsinc.com
Dist medical equipment, medical apparel, wound care
supplies, medical furniture, exam room supplies,
extrication-patient transport equipment, surgical gloves,
IV therapy & laboratory supplies. (Woman/AA, estab
2012, empl 5, sales , cert: State)

Georgia

6104   American Clinics for Preventive Medicine
       1343 Terrell Mill Rd Ste 100
       Marietta, GA 30067
       Contact: Juanita Cato Office Assistant
       Tel: 767-836-3477
       Email: americanclinicpm@gmail.com
       Website: www.acpm.net
Provide physical exams, alternative medical treatment
options, nutritional infusion therapy, high dose Vitamin
C infusions, primary prevention exams, alternative
complimentary cancer therapies, detoxification programs. (AA, estab 1985, empl 10, sales , cert: State)

6105   Attain Med, Inc.
       5825 Glenridge Dr NE Bldg 4, Ste 106
       Atlanta, GA 30328
       Contact: Charles Stafford VP Diversity Partner-
       ships
       Tel: 770-288-2466
       Email: charles.stafford@attainmed.com
       Website: www.attainmed.com
Dist pharmaceuticals. (Minority, estab , empl , sales
$8,000,000, cert: NMSDC, 8(a))

6106   Black Knight Medical, LLC
       50 Hurt Plaza SE, Ste 803
       Atlanta, GA 30303
       Contact: Ron Thomas President
       Tel: 877-767-3792
       Email: ron@blackknightmedical.com
       Website: www.blackknightmedical.com
Medical supply distributor servicing healthcare systems
both
domestically and abroad. (AA, estab 2017, empl 4, sales
$5,900,000, cert: City)

6107   Canterbury Pointe LLC
       3350 Riverwood Pkwy, Ste 1900
       Atlanta, GA 30339
       Contact: Diane Dixon Principal
       Tel: 770-633-2570
       Email:
       Website: www.cpointellc.com
Medical Supplies, Pharmacy Benefit Management,
Energy Management & Insurance Services. (Woman/AA,
estab 2015, empl 1, sales , cert: WBENC)

6108 MedX Diagnostic Solutions, LLC
2004 Eastview Pkwy Ste 108
Conyers, GA 30013
Contact: Gerald Patterson COO
Tel: 770-278-0199
Email: gpatterson@medxghs.com
Website: www.medxghs.com
Dist healthcare materials, supplies, furniture, diagnostic kits, biomedical equipment services & repairs. (Woman/AA, estab 2014, empl 3, sales , cert: NMSDC)

6109 U.S. Imaging, Inc.
2234 Bryant Place Court
Marietta, GA 30066
Contact: Sherman Weston President
Tel: 404-934-9054
Email: sweston@bellsouth.net
Website: www.usimagingsite.com
Dist bio-medical, medical supplies & medical imaging equipment. (AA, estab , empl , sales $949,000, cert: NMSDC)

6110 Unyter Enterprises
6065 Pkwy North Dr Ste 200
Cumming, GA 30040
Contact: Rayfus D'Yana President
Tel: 678-500-9568
Email: drayfus@unyter.com
Website: www.unyter.com
Dist pharmaceuticals, medical/surgical supplies & equipment. (AA, estab 2009, empl 10, sales , cert: City)

6111 Vanguard Safety Company LLC
PO Box 608
Savannah, GA 31402
Contact: Howard Genser Jr. Exec VP/COO
Tel: 912-236-1766
Email: howardg@vanguardsafetyco.com
Website: www.vanguardsafetyco.com
Dist occupational health & safety products. (AA, estab 1985, empl 21, sales $8,700,000, cert: NMSDC)

6112 WellSol Medical Inc.
1261 LaVista Rd, Ste D1
Atlanta, GA 30324
Contact: William Moylan CFO/COO
Tel: 855-935-5765
Email: bill@wellsolmed.com
Website: www.wellsolmed.com
Dist medical equipment. (Hisp, estab 2015, empl 4, sales , cert: NMSDC)

Illinois

6113 Ekla Corporation
1707 Quincy Ave, Ste 127
Naperville, IL 11111
Contact: Jeff Prendergast President
Tel: 630-258-6242
Email: jeff@eklacorp.com
Website: www.eklacorp.com
Medcal surgical and equipment supplies and services. (Minority, Woman, estab , empl , sales $7,100,000, cert: City, WBENC)

6114 ESM Products LLC
245 W Roosevelt Rd, Bldg 10, Ste 71
West Chicago, IL 60185
Contact: Roger Sudnick VP Sales
Tel: 630-965-4569
Email: rsudnick@trademanagementpartners.com
Website: www.esmproducts.com
Provides high quality, low cost PPE (personal protective equipment such as nitrile gloves, masks, hairnets, etc.) to the CPG industry in North America. (Woman, estab 2012, empl 6, sales $3,000,000, cert: WBENC)

6115 Goodhealth Medical Products
14818 Drexel Ave
Dolton, IL 60419
Contact: David Wilson President
Tel: 708-841-1700
Email: info@goodhealthmed.com
Website: www.goodhealthmed.com
Dist medical, dental, and surgical supplies. (AA, estab 2001, empl 15, sales $2,000,000, cert: State, NMSDC)

6116 JERO Medical Equipment & Supplies, Inc.
4108 W Division St
Chicago, IL 60651
Contact: President
Tel: 312-829-5376
Email:
Website: www.jeromedical.com
Mfr disposbable wearing apparels, kit assembler, 1st aid, disaster, admission. (AA, estab 1987, empl 24, sales $4,000,000, cert: City)

6117 Medefil, Inc.
405 Windy Point Dr
Glendale Heights, IL 60139
Contact: Praveen Aggarwal Exec VP
Tel: 630-682-4600
Email: manoj@medefilinc.com
Website: www.medefilinc.com
Mfr prefilled syringes filled with saline & hepain for IV flush. (As-Ind, estab , empl , sales , cert: NMSDC)

6118 MEDGYN PRDT INC
PO Box 3126
Oak Brook, IL 60522
Contact: Susan Bendle Finance & HR Mgr
Tel: 630-627-4105
Email: sbendle@medgyn.com
Website: www.medgyn.com
Provides high-quality medical devices: sterile disposable medical devices, stainless steel instruments, equipment, diagnostic test kits & various OB/GYN procedure kits. (As-Ind, estab 1983, empl 50, sales , cert: NMSDC)

6119 Nexus Pharmaceuticals, Inc.
400 Knightsbridge Pkwy
Lincolnshire, IL 60069
Contact: Chris Conroy Dir Natl Accouts
Tel: 847-996-3790
Email: cconroy@nexuspharma.net
Website: www.nexuspharma.net
Mfr sterile generic injectable pharmaceuticals. (Minority, Woman, estab , empl , sales $750,000, cert: NMSDC, WBENC)

6120 Saris and Things Inc.
3836 Mistflower Ln
Naperville, IL 60564
Contact: Shital Daftari CEO
Tel: 630-346-6531
Email: shital@sntbiotech.com
Website: www.sntbiotech.com
Dist PPE and Hand Sanitizers and Covid Tests and testing supplies for labs. NIOSH N95, CDC & EAU KN95, Hand Sanitizers, Covid Tests, Swabs, VTM Kits, Cryovial Tubes, Extraction Tubes, Covid Antigen Tests. (Woman/As-Ind, estab 2011, empl 6, sales $31,250,000, cert: City, WBENC)

Indiana

6121 Bryton Corporation
4001 Methanol Ln
Indianapolis, IN 46268
Contact: James Waldrop Controller
Tel: 317-334-8700
Email: j.waldrop@brytoncorp.com
Website: www.brytoncorp.com
Mfr & dist medical equipment, supplies & accessories. (Woman, estab 1981, empl 40, sales $9,000,000, cert: City)

6122 Hapak Enterprises Inc.
PO Box 21
Crawfordsville, IN 47933
Contact: Shannon Payne Mgr Operations
Tel: 765-364-0490
Email: shannon.payne@currtech.net
Website: www.currtechinc.com
Bio-Check® BioHazard wipes & Benchliners. (Woman, estab 1994, empl 50, sales $15,000,000, cert: WBENC)

Kentucky

6123 Blu Pharmaceuticals
301 Robey St
Franklin, KY 42134
Contact: Bill Luster Contract Mgr
Tel: 270-586-6386
Email: jfurlong@blurx.us
Website: www.blurx.us
mfr & dist generic pharmaceuticals. (Minority, Woman, estab 2006, empl 15, sales $39,613,667, cert: State)

6124 Marian Medical, Inc.
319 Westport Dr
Louisville, KY 40207
Contact: Lisa Stewart Clinical Sales Mgr
Tel: 502-425-6363
Email: lisa@marianmedicalonline.com
Website: www.marianmedicalonline.com
Neonatal products: Enteral System, Urinary Catheters, Urinary Collection Kit, Circumcision Tray, Chest Tube Kit, Exchange Transfusion Tray, Blood Administration Syringe Sets, PICC Procedure Kits. (Woman, estab , empl , sales , cert: City)

Louisiana

6125 AOSS Medical Supply, Inc.
4971 Central Ave
Monroe, LA 71203
Contact: Claudia Sikes President
Tel: 318-325-8290
Email: claudia@aossmedical.com
Website: www.aossmedicalsupply.com
Dist medical supplies. (As-Pac, estab 1979, empl 46, sales $18,000,000, cert: NMSDC)

Massachusetts

6126 Asaman, Inc.
258 Bodwell St
Avon, MA 02322
Contact: Marie Vrakking VP Operations
Tel: 508-588-2008
Email: mvrakking@asaman.com
Website: www.asaman.com
Source Comparator Drugs for Clinical Trials and Analytical testing. (AA, estab 1995, empl 22, sales $17,900,000, cert: State, NMSDC)

6127 Genesis Medical Products, Inc.
40 Farm Hill Rd
Wrentham, MA 02093
Contact: Kevin Kelliher Principal
Tel: 877-933-5437
Email: genesismedical@aol.com
Website: www.iGenesisMedical.com
Dist neonatal, pediatric, labor & delivery soft goods. (Woman, estab 1996, empl 10, sales $300,000, cert: State)

6128 Intelimas Corporation
177 Huntington Ave
Boston, MA 02115
Contact: Charles Mwangi CEO
Tel: 781-388-3300
Email: charles@intelimas.com
Website: www.intelimas.com
Mfr & dist devices, mfr pharmaceutical, generic injectables, pharmaceutical & medical courier, non-emergency medical transportation. (AA, estab 2020, empl 44, sales $22,000,000, cert: NMSDC)

6129 Shinemound Enterprise Inc.
17A Sterling Rd
North Billerica, MA 01862
Contact: Gloria Shiao VP
Tel: 978-436-9980
Email: info@shinemound.com
Website: www.shinemound.com
Mfr latex & non-latex products: disposable PVC, synthetic, vinyl & nitrile, CPE & PE gloves. (As-Pac, estab 1988, empl 6, sales , cert: State)

6130 Westnet Inc.
55 North St
Canton, MA 02021
Contact: Gordon Thompson CEO
Tel: 781-828-7772
Email: gordon@westnetmed.com
Website: www.westnetmed.com
Dist medical/surgical supplies & equipment; life science products & industrial paper. (AA, estab 1994, empl 37, sales , cert: NMSDC)

Maryland

6131 1st Needs Medical LLC
7003 Glenn Dale Rd Ste 151
Glenn Dale, MD 20769
Contact: Vernon White Partner
Tel: 301-928-2557
Email: info@1stneedsmedical.com
Website: www.1stneedsmedical.com
Durable Medical Equipment & daily use medical supplies. (AA, estab 2014, empl 2, sales , cert: State, NMSDC)

6132   Lifeline Medical Services, Inc.
2955 Mercy Lane
Cheverly, MD 20785
Contact: Eze Nwoji President
Tel: 301-386-0000
Email: eze@lifelinemeds.com
Website: www.lifelinemedicalsupplies.com
Dist automatic sanitary shoe dispenser, hand held EKG monitor, ambulatory product, bathroom product, gloves, dental supplies, woundcare supplies, diagnotics equipment, medical apparels hospital beds & accessories. (AA, estab 2003, empl 4, sales $385,000, cert: State)

6133   Universal Medical Associates, Inc.
111 Hamlet Hill Rd Ste 710
Baltimore, MD 21210
Contact: Renee Parks
Tel: 443-765-9366
Email: reneeparks@universalmedicalassociates.com
Website: www.UniversalMedicalAssociates.com
Medical & surgical implants, osteobiologics & regenerative medicine products, Osteobiologics, Sports Medicine Allografts, Synthetic Biologics & Regenerative Tissue products. (AA, estab 2010, empl 3, sales $621,930, cert: NMSDC)

Michigan

6134   Heritage Vision Plans, Inc.
One Woodward Ave Ste 2020
Detroit, MI 48226
Contact: Leonard T. Barnes VP Sales & BD
Tel: 313-863-1633
Email: lbarnes@heritagevisionplans.com
Website: www.heritagevisionplans.com
Optical goods & services: eye exams, frames, lenses & contact lenses. (AA, estab 1975, empl 18, sales $11,154,350, cert: NMSDC)

6135   J and B Medical Supply Company Inc.
50496 W Pontiac Trail
Wixom, MI 48393
Contact: Julian Shaya Exec VP
Tel: 800-737-0045
Email: jshaya@jandbmedical.com
Website: www.jandbmedicalsupply.com
Dist Medical Surgical & Emergency Medical Supplies. (Woman, estab 1996, empl 500, sales , cert: WBENC)

6136   MMS Holdings Inc.
6880 Commerce Blvd
Canton, MI 48187
Contact: Prasad M. Koppolu EVP & COO
Tel: 734-245-0310
Email: pkoppolu@mmsholdings.com
Website: www.mmsholdings.com
Clinical research, regulatory submission support for the pharmaceutical, biotech and medical device industries. (Minority, Woman, estab 2005, empl 362, sales $82,294,495, cert: NMSDC)

6137   OCS Inc.
916 Fremont St
Bay City, MI 48708
Contact: Amy Swackhamer Dir of communications
Tel: 989-714-0719
Email: amy@ocsmgt.com
Website: www.ocsmgt.com
Medical & vocational management, occupational therapy consulting & cost containment services. (Woman, estab 2010, empl 12, sales $1,000,000, cert: WBENC)

6138   TerryWorldWide, LLC
6505 Grandville Ave
Detroit, MI 48228
Contact: Terry Willis CEO
Tel: 313-974-8341
Email: terry@terryworldwide.com
Website: www.terryworldwide.com
Dist CanAm Medical/SiO2 Ultra Thin Liquid Glass Coatings. (AA, estab 2010, empl 1, sales , cert: NMSDC)

6139   The Black Moon Group dba BMG Medical Supply
6026 Kalamazoo Ave, Ste 237
Grand Rapids, MI 49508
Contact: Bill McCurdy CEO
Tel: 616-275-9109
Email: bmccurdy@theblackmoongroup.com
Website: www.BMGmed.com
Dist Medline and McKesson Medical Supply and Equipment. (AA, estab 2015, empl 5, sales , cert: NMSDC)

6140   Veteran Medical Products, Inc.
813 Franklin St SE
Grand Rapids, MI 49507
Contact: Roosevelt Tillman President
Tel: 616-451-8486
Email: rt@veteranmedical.com
Website: www.veteranmedical.com
Disposable medical supplies. (AA, estab 2005, empl 2, sales $100,000, cert: NMSDC)

Minnesota

6141   Global International LLC
P.O.BOX 240385
Apple Valley, MN 55124
Contact: Ambrose Kpoto Dir Strategic Partnership
Tel: 612-404-1051
Email: ambrose@fgmmedical.com
Website: www.fgmmedical.com
Dist medical, dental, and pharmaceuticals. (AA, estab 2014, empl 30, sales $3,000,000, cert: NMSDC)

6142   NavasDRSTi, LLC
1714 Basswood Court
Carver, MN 55315
Contact: Yog Ohneswere CEO
Tel: 888-628-2860
Email: yohnes@navadrsti.com
Website: www.navadrsti.com
Electro-Surgical Units, Cardio-Vascular & Cardiology Equipment & Instruments, Radiology, Ultrasound, Diagnostic Imaging & Testing Equipment, Orthopedic Devices, Implants & Tools, Surgical Equipment, Instruments, Supplies & Disposables. (As-Ind, estab 2016, empl 2, sales , cert: State)

6143   Ulmer Pharmacal
1614 Industry Ave W
Park Rapids, MN 56470
Contact: Brent Swanson CFO
Tel: 218-732-2656
Email: bswanson@lobanaproducts.com
Website: www.ulmerpharmacal.com
Mfr premium cleaning & infection control products, patient lubricating jellies & skin care products.. (Woman, estab 2013, empl 10, sales $520,000, cert: State)

Missouri

6144 Emed Medical Company
11551 Adie Rd
Maryland Heights, MO 63043
Contact: Bailey Eric President
Tel: 314-291-3633
Email: sjones@emedmedical.com
Website: www.emedmedical.com
Dist medical & pharmaceutical products. (AA, estab , empl
, sales $26,000,000, cert: State, NMSDC)

6145 I.V. House, Inc.
418 Seven Gables Ct
Chesterfield, MO 63017
Contact: Angela Cressey
Tel: 314-453-9200
Email: angela@ivhouse.com
Website: www.ivhouse.com
Mfr & dist I.V. House Ultra Dressings & Ultra Domes, IV site
protectors for all ages. (Woman, estab , empl , sales , cert:
State)

6146 RDB Enterprises II LLC
10011 E 67th St
Raytown, MO 64133
Contact: Robert Branscumb President
Tel: 888-626-1577
Email: rmeeks7@aol.com
Website: www.RDBenterprisesllc.com
Dist medical supplies, first-aid, safety, lab equip, food
services & industrial supplies. (AA, estab 1991, empl 35,
sales , cert: City)

6147 SimmCo Distribution
4813 Lee Ave
St. Louis, MO 63115
Contact: Shaun Simms President
Tel: 314-389-3630
Email: info@simmcodistribution.com
Website: www.simmcodistribution.com
Dist Medical Devices, Medical Supplies & Pharmaceuticals.
(AA, estab 2012, empl 5, sales , cert: State, City)

North Carolina

6148 MYCO Medical Supplies, Inc.
2015 Production Dr
Apex, NC 27539
Contact: Sanjiv Kumar President
Tel: 919-460-2535
Email: kkennedy@mycomedical.com
Website: www.mycomedical.com
Dist medical supplies, needles, blunt fill needles, blood
collection sets, sutures, syringes, PPE, blades and scalpels.
(Minority, estab 1993, empl 22, sales , cert: NMSDC)

6149 Playtime Edventures LLC
9905 Running Cedar Ln
Indian Trail, NC 28079
Contact: Kevin Gatlin CEO
Tel: 704-806-5692
Email: playtimebedsheets@gmail.com
Website: www.PlaytimeEdventures.com
Interactive therapy bed sheets for hospitalized children.
(AA, estab 2014, empl 4, sales , cert: NMSDC)

6150 Seniors Medical Supply, Inc.
540 W Elm St
Graham, NC 27253
Contact: Gavin Coble President
Tel: 336-227-0730
Email: seniorsmedical@bellsouth.net
Website: www.seniorsmedicalsupply.net
Dist medical equipment: power & manual wheelchairs,
canes, commodes, walkers, lift chairs, surgical equipment & supplies, hospital beds & sheets, oxygen, wound
care products, compression therapy, ED pumps, diabetic
shoes. (Woman/AA, estab 2004, empl 6, sales $345,789,
cert: WBENC)

New Jersey

6151 Amneal Pharmaceuticals
400 Crossing Blvd 3rd Fl
Bridgewater, NJ 08807
Contact: Brown Massey Dir Sales
Tel: 908-947-3120
Email: bmassey@amneal.com
Website: www.amneal.com
Develop, mfg & dist generic pharmaceutical products.
(As-Ind, estab 2002, empl 4727, sales , cert: NMSDC)

6152 BLOXR Solutions LLC
PO Box 5148
North Branch, NJ 08876
Contact: John Buday Customer Service
Tel: 801-590-9880
Email: order@bloxr.com
Website: www.bloxr.com
Mfr radiation protection cream and apparel. (Minority,
Woman, estab 2015, empl 14, sales , cert: WBENC)

6153 Cenmed Enterprises
121 Jersey Ave
New Brunswick, NJ 08901
Contact: Rizwan Chaudhry Operations
Tel: 732-447-1100
Email: rizwan@cenmed.com
Website: www.cenmed.com
Dist medical supplies, laboratory supplies, hospital
supplies, surgical supplies, emt supplies, safety supplies,
fire supplies. (Woman/As-Ind, estab 1992, empl 25,
sales $8,400,000, cert: State, City, NMSDC, WBENC,
SDB)

6154 Discovery ChemScience LLC
66 Witherspoon St, Ste 1100
Princeton, NJ 08542
Contact: Qun Sun President
Tel: 609-475-5097
Email: qsun@dischemsci.com
Website: www.dischemsci.com
Provide discovery, medicinal chemistry & custom
synthesis CRO services. (As-Pac, estab 2004, empl 2,
sales $2,900,000, cert: NMSDC)

6155 Earth2Earth LLC
      8 Promenade Place
      Voorhees, NJ 08043
      Contact: Sita Rentala Owner
      Tel: 856-843-1441
      Email: earth2earth45@gmail.com
      Website: www.earth2earthonline.com
PPE products to the Health Care Industry, as well as
Biodegradable Toothbrushes to Dentists and Environmen-
talists. Our products are made from renewable resources
that include plant fiber, bamboo, sugar cane, unbleached,
and recycled items. (Woman/As-Ind, estab 2018, empl 5,
sales , cert: City, WBENC)

6156 Eastmed Enterprises, Inc.
      11 Brandywine Dr
      Marlton, NJ 11111
      Contact: Supti Putatunda President
      Tel: 856-797-0131
      Email: mona.p@eastmedent.com
      Website: www.eastmedent.com
Mfr & dist laryngoscope systems, airway management &
intubation products. (Woman/As-Ind, estab 1987, empl 4,
sales , cert: WBENC)

6157 IBS Solutions Corporation
      9 Peach Tree Hill Rd
      Livingston, NJ 07039
      Contact: Matthew ODoherty Strategic Acct Dir
      Tel: 973-994-8000
      Email: matto@pittplastics.com
      Website: www.ibssolutionsgroup.com
Dist can liners and medical waste bags. (As-Pac, estab
2011, empl 10, sales $45,000,000, cert: NMSDC)

6158 NCT Holdings, Inc.
      212 Carnegie Center Blvd Ste 301
      Princeton, NJ 08540
      Contact: Duane Clark Dir Business Devel
      Tel: 609-945-0101
      Email: dclark@wcgclinical.com
      Website: www.wcgclinical.com
Clinical Trials, rater training, certification and data review.
(Woman, estab 2005, empl , sales $15,000,000, cert:
WBENC)

6159 NEXT Medical Products Company, LLC
      45 Columbia Road
      Branchburg, NJ 08876
      Contact: John Buday Dir CS & Sales Support
      Tel: 800-458-4254
      Email: jbuday@nextmedicalproducts.com
      Website: www.nextmedicalproducts.com
Mfr Clear Image & LithoClear Ultrasound Gel brands,
sterile & non-sterile single patient packets. (Minority,
Woman, estab 2012, empl 13, sales $5,000,000, cert:
WBENC)

6160 Precision Medical Devices, Inc.
      121 Jersey Ave
      New Brunswick, NJ 08901
      Contact: Lynn Indyk Business Devel Mgr
      Tel: 732-447-2587
      Email: lindyk@pmdmfg.com
      Website: www.pmdinstruments.com
Mfr medical devices, instrument systems & clinical
products, surgical instruments. (As-Ind, estab 2008, empl
6, sales $275,000, cert: NMSDC)

6161 Siris Pharmaceutical Services
      75 North St Ste 1
      Bloomsbury, NJ 08804
      Contact: Andrew Voigt Business Devel
      Tel: 908-479-1331
      Email: andrewv@sirispharma.com
      Website: www.sirispharma.com
Clinical packaging, distribution, drug storage, and drug
returns/destruction services. (Woman, estab 2001, empl
12, sales $672,000, cert: WBENC)

6162 United Medical Supplies Inc.
      25 Craig Place
      North Plainfield, NJ 07059
      Contact: Raman Alaigh CEO
      Tel: 908-757-0075
      Email: rayalaigh@unitedmedsupplies.com
      Website: www.unitedmedsupplies.com
Dist synthetic, latex & nitrile exam gloves, walkers,
wheelchairs, bathroom accessories, bath benches,
commodes, rollators, crutches, disposable medical
supplies, alternating pressure relief mattress, overlay
mattress. nebulizers, oxygen tubing. (Minority, Woman,
estab 2007, empl 4, sales , cert: State)

New Mexico

6163 R & M Government Services
      650 Montana Ave, Ste A
      Las Cruces, NM 88001
      Contact: Sharon Guerrero VP
      Tel: 575-522-0430
      Email: sharon@rmgovernmentservices.com
      Website: www.rmgovernmentservices.com
Abaxis Veterinary Diagnostics, Vetscan, ACR Mechanical
Construction A-dec Dental Chairs, Handpieces, Delivery
Systems. (Minority, Woman, estab 2011, empl 8, sales ,
cert: WBENC)

Nevada

6164 PPE Catalog LLC
      2300 W Sahara Ave Ste. 800
      Las Vegas, NV 89102
      Contact: Michael Gordon Chairman
      Tel: 702-856-4459
      Email: michaelgordon@ppecatalog.com
      Website: www.ppecatalog.com
Dist PPE equipment and supplies, disinfectant wipes,
and other disinfectant products, sanitizing products,
NIOSH N95 respirators, N95 masks. (Woman, estab
2020, empl 5, sales $3,500,000, cert: WBENC)

New York

6165 Alpha Medical Distributor, Inc.
      60-B Commerce Place Unit B
      Hicksville, NY 11801
      Contact: Jonathan Lee President
      Tel: 516-681-5290
      Email: alphameddis@aol.com
      Website: www.MortuarySuppliesUSA.com
Dist body bags, cadaver bags, transport bags & mortuary
supplies. (Minority, Woman, estab 2000, empl 4, sales
$500,000, cert: State)

6166   BFFL Co., LLC
       20 Kensington Rd
       Scarsdale, NY 10583
       Contact: Elizabeth Thompson CEO
       Tel: 914-713-8550
       Email: drelizabeth@bfflco.com
       Website: www.bfflco.com
Surgical Bras, surgical vests, compression bras, comfort
and recovery garments, compression wear, hospital
gowns, orthopedic dressings. (Woman, estab 2011, empl
5, sales $1,549,736, cert: WBENC)

6167   Danlee Medical Products, Inc.
       6075 E Molloy Rd, Ste 5 Bldg. 5
       Syracuse, NY 13211
       Contact: Joni Walton operations
       Tel: 315-431-0143
       Email: joni@danleemedical.com
       Website: www.danleemedical.com
Mfr custom hook-up kits, boxer shorts & endoscopy
shorts, disposable pouches for holter & event recording,
disposable scrubs & disposable blood pressure cuff liners.
(Woman, estab 1994, empl 13, sales $2,900,000, cert:
State, City, WBENC)

6168   JLGJ Trading, Inc.
       65 East Bethpage Rd Ste 400
       Plainview, NY 11803
       Contact: Edie Berntson VP Sales
       Tel: 888-222-2237
       Email: edie@jlgjtrading.com
       Website: www.ourcaresupplies.com
Dist medical supplies. (Woman, estab 2004, empl 4, sales ,
cert: NWBOC)

6169   Silarx Pharmaceuticals, Inc.
       19 West St
       Spring Valley, NY 10977
       Contact: George Hauss RA/QA coord
       Tel: 845-325-4020
       Email: ghauss@silarx.com
       Website: www.silarx.com
Mfr liquid generic pharmaceutical & nutritional supplements. (As-Ind, estab 1985, empl 40, sales $11,130,742,
cert: NMSDC)

6170   SPS Medical Supply Corp.
       6789 W HENRIETTA RD
       RUSH, NY 14543
       Contact: Mariann Hughes Dir of Sales & Marketing
       Tel: 585-359-0130
       Email: mhughes@spsmedical.com
       Website: www.spsmedical.com
Mfr & dist sterility assurance products: biological &
chemical indicators, integrators, bowie dick tests, autoclave tape, pouches & record keeping products. (Woman,
estab , empl , sales , cert: WBENC)

6171   XGen Pharmaceuticals DJB, Inc.
       300 Daniel Zenker Dr
       Horseheads, NY 14845
       Contact: Liz Carbon Dir Natl Accounts
       Tel: 607-562-2700
       Email: ecarbon@xgenpharmadjb.com
       Website: www.xgenpharmadjb.com
Provide affordable generic equivalents that enhance
patient care, today and tomorrow. (Woman, estab , empl
55, sales $57,250,000, cert: WBENC)

Ohio

6172   889 Global Solutions
       1943 W 5th Ave.
       Columbus, OH 43212
       Contact: Govt Sales Project Mgr
       Tel: 614-235-8889
       Email: info@889globalsolutions.com
       Website: www.889globalsolutions.com
Healthcare Components & Equipment. Consumer Goods
& Promotional Products. Industrial Products. (Minority,
Woman, estab 2000, empl 20, sales , cert: State,
NMSDC)

6173   C&M Medical Supply, Inc.
       8600 S Wilkinson Way, Ste C
       Perrysburg, OH 43551
       Contact: Creston Tarrant President
       Tel: 419-872-0033
       Email: ctarrant@cmmedicalsupply.com
       Website: www.cmmedicalsupply.com
Diagnostic & respiratory equipment & supplies, advanced woundcare, latex, vinyl & nitrile exam gloves,
ultrasound & electro medical products, portable EKG,
spirometry, holter, blood pressure & oximetry. (AA,
estab 2005, empl 8, sales $486,000, cert: State, NMSDC)

6174   Cincinnati Sub-Zero Products, LLC
       12011 Mosteller Rd
       Cincinnati, OH 45241
       Contact: Matt McCurdy Natl Accts Mgr
       Tel: 513-772-8810
       Email: mmccurdy@genthermcsz.com
       Website: www.cszindustrial.com
Hyper-Hypothermia systems for use in hosptials before
during and after surgery. Patient temperature controlled. (Woman, estab 1940, empl 200, sales , cert:
City)

6175   Kadiri Health, LLC
       PO Box 746
       Yellow Springs, OH 45387
       Contact: Christopher Cox Owner, Sr Consultant
       Tel: 310-435-5455
       Email: ccox@kadirihealth.com
       Website: www.kadirihealth.com
Dist medical, laboratory, scientific, diagnostic, &
research equipment, supplies & furniture. (AA, estab ,
empl , sales , cert: NMSDC)

6176   Medical Resources
       8377 Green Meadows Dr N Ste C
       Lewis Center, OH 43035
       Contact: Randy Reichenbach VP
       Tel: 740-201-3300
       Email: Randy@MedicalResources.com
       Website: www.MedicalResources.com
Mfr Stainless Steel Products for Healthcare Facilities:
blanket warming cabinets, instrument cabinets, instru-
ment stands, back tables, and endoscope cabinets.
(Woman, estab 1987, empl 18, sales $8,400,000, cert:
State, NWBOC)

6177   MediGreen Medical Supplies & Services, LLC
340 Echo Valley Dr
Vandalia, OH 45377
Contact: Veronica Green Owner
Tel: 937-776-3113
Email: veronica.green@medigreenmedsupplies.com
Website: www.medigreenmedsupplies.com
Disposable Gowns, Apparel, Patient Care Items, Operating Room/ER Items Gloves. (Woman/AA, estab 2012, empl 1, sales , cert: State, City)

6178   Premium Contractor Solution LLC
2601 W Stroop Rd, Ste 500
Moraine, OH 45439
Contact: Dexiang Bao Sales Dir
Tel: 216-527-4338
Email: dbao@premiumcontractorsolution.com
Website: www.premiumcontractorsolution.com
Provide PPE, N95 mask, KN95 mask, Gowns, Thermometer, surgical mask, cotton face mask, Ventilator, gloves and etc. (Woman, estab 2014, empl 15, sales $4,134,000, cert: WBENC)

6179   Procura Select
30700-E Carter St
Solon, OH 44139
Contact: Patricia Palermo President
Tel: 440-248-1622
Email: ppalermo@procuraselect.com
Website: www.procuraselect.com
Dist medical carts, shelving, storage & organization products. (Woman, estab 2014, empl 3, sales , cert: WBENC)

6180   Reidy Medical Supply, Inc.
PO Box 713079
Cincinnati, OH 45271
Contact: Ted Stitzel President
Tel: 330-686-4485
Email: tstitzel@reidymed.com
Website: www.reidymed.com
Dist disposable medical supplies. (Woman, estab 1992, empl 26, sales $9,000,000, cert: WBENC)

6181   SGM Contracting Inc.
9485 Root Rd
North Ridgeville, OH 44039
Contact: Regina Morris Owner
Tel: 216-337-0742
Email: ginamorris@sgmcontracting.com
Website: www.sgmcontracting.com
Engineered medical support systems: cath, x-ray, surgical & exam light supports, operable walls & specialty support systems. (Woman, estab 2008, empl 3, sales $265,000, cert: City)

6182   Transworld Supply Network, LLC
3850 Winning Stakes Way
Mason, OH 45040
Contact: Christopher Che President
Tel: 513-229-7595
Email: dsmith@transworldsn.com
Website: www.transworldsn.com
Global importer of healthcare disposables. (AA, estab 2018, empl 3, sales $10,000,000, cert: NMSDC)

Oklahoma

6183   Mobile Cardiac Imaging LLC
7018 South Utica Ave
Tulsa, OK 74136
Contact: Kristy Yang Sr Operations Mgr
Tel: 918-744-1001
Email: kyang@mcidiagnostics.com
Website: www.mcidiagnostics.com
Dist medical and laboratory products, services, and equipment. (AA, estab 1998, empl 27, sales $4,900,000, cert: NMSDC)

6184   NeoChild
8213 SW 23rd Place
Oklahoma City, OK 73128
Contact: Chad Kennard VP Operations
Tel: 888-887-6428
Email: chad@neochild.com
Website: www.neochild.com
Neonatal specialty products, (Woman, estab , empl , sales $3,200,000, cert: WBENC)

Oregon

6185   Ascent Group Medical LLC
1631 NE Broadway St, Ste 308
Portland, OR 97211
Contact: Nuradin Kariye CEO
Tel: 888-386-1112
Email: nuradin@ascentgroupmedical.com
Website: www.ascentgroupmedical.com
Dist medical surgical supplies, equipment & medical staffing. (AA, estab 2011, empl 1, sales , cert: State)

6186   Panga Eco-Friendly Dental Supply
2269 SE Lindenbrook Ct
Milwaukie, OR 97222
Contact: Ingrid Adeogun Owner
Tel: 503-523-9442
Email: ingrid@wearepanga.com
Website: www.wearepanga.com
Mfr & dist eco-friendly dental products: Tongue Scraper, Bamboo Toothbrush, eco-friendly floss. (AA, Hisp, estab 2019, empl 1, sales , cert: WBENC)

Pennsylvania

6187   Actuated Medical, Inc.
310 Rolling Ridge Dr
Bellefonte, PA 16823
Contact: Rachael Bernier President
Tel: 814-380-2879
Email: rachael.bernier@actuatedmedical.com
Website: www.actuatedmedical.com/face-shield.html
Provide reusable face shield with a reinforced headband & manufacture a face shield attachment for hard hats. (Woman, estab , empl , sales , cert: WBENC)

6188   Coleman Laboratories
1150 First Ave, Ste 501
King of Prussia, PA 19406
Contact: Le-Jun Yin President
Tel: 267-644-7767
Email: lejun.yin@colemanlabs.com
Website: www.colemanlabs.com
Develop & mfr IV status monitors. The LM series Fluid Level Monitor is a passive sensing device that alarms when the infusion fluid level is low. Provides both visual and audible alarms when preset condition is met. (As-Pac, estab 2010, empl 4, sales $200,000, cert: NMSDC)

6189 Regulatory and Quality Solutions LLC
2790 Mosside Blvd Ste 800
Monroeville, PA 15146
Contact: Maria Fagan CEO
Tel: 877-652-0830
Email: accounting@rqteam.com
Website: www.rqteam.com
Medical device regulatory & quality consulting support organization. (Woman, estab 2008, empl 100, sales $15,200,000, cert: WBENC)

6190 SlateBelt Safety
1694 Southlawn Dr
Lancaster, PA 17603
Contact: Robert D Williams President
Tel: 888-642-0001
Email: robert@slatebeltsafety.com
Website: www.slatebeltsafety.com
Dist occupational safety prescription eyewear. (AA, estab 2006, empl 21, sales $1,000,000, cert: NMSDC)

6191 UMF Medical
1316 Eisenhower Boulevard
Johnstown, PA 15904
Contact: Eileen Melvin Dir Marketing & Cstmr Care
Tel: 814-266-8726
Email: emelvin@umfmedical.com
Website: www.umfmedical.com
Mfr exam tables, podiatry chairs, Procedure Chairs, phlebotomy chairs, power & manual exam tables, treatment & orthopedic tables, pediatric examination tables, clinical casework, modular cabinetry, stools, side chairs, treatment & supply cabinets. (Woman, estab , empl , sales $16,000,000, cert: WBENC)

Puerto Rico

6192 Cesar Castillo, Inc.
361 Calle Angel Buonomo St Tres Monjitas Industrial Pk
Hato Rey, PR 00917
Contact: Luis Vazquez VP
Tel: 787-999-1616
Email: lvazquez@cesarcastillo.com
Website: www.cesarcastillo.com
Dist pharmaceutical products, health & beauty care, consumer goods, Specialty Pharmaceutical Products to Physicians and Specialty Pharmacies. (Hisp, estab 1946, empl 400, sales $177,000,000, cert: NMSDC)

6193 J.C. Gonzalez, Inc.
2 St KM 178.2 Interior BO. Minillas Alto
San German, PR 00683
Contact: Julio C. Gonzalez Santiago CEO
Tel: 787-892-0047
Email: sales@jcgonzalezinc.com
Website: www.jcgonzalezinc.com
Dist & service scientific & research equipment, laboratory equipment & consumables, microscopes, stereoscopes, freezers, refrigerators. (Hisp, estab 2001, empl 6, sales $865,047, cert: NMSDC, SDB)

6194 R & G Clean Room Laboratory, Inc.
Ave Esmeralda #53 PMB 112
Guaynabo, PR 00969
Contact: Ruben Gomez President
Tel: 787-993-1781
Email: rgomez@crlrd.com
Website: www.cleanroomlab.com
R & G Clean Room Laboratory, Inc provides specialty laboratory and clean room products to Biotech, Medical Devices, Animal Research and Pharmaceutical. (Hisp, estab 2007, empl 10, sales $700,000, cert: NMSDC)

6195 Steri-Tech Inc.
Road 701 Km. 0.7, Salinas Ind. Park
Salinas, PR 00751
Contact: Juan Argüelles Managing Dir
Tel: 787-824-4040
Email: jarguelles@steri-tech.com
Website: www.steri-tech.com
Dist cleanroom products & contract sterilization services. (Hisp, estab 1986, empl 30, sales $3,020,000, cert: NMSDC)

South Carolina

6196 Bennett Wholesale Distributors LLC
300 Long Point Ln Ste 220-O
Columbia, SC 29229
Contact: Jameel Bennett Owner
Tel: 800-650-0616
Email: jb@bennettwholesale.com
Website: www.bennettwholesale.com
Dist medical supplies / equipment and laboratory services. (AA, estab 2003, empl 1, sales $250,000, cert: NMSDC)

6197 Cambridge Marketing, Inc.
PO Box 4481
Rock Hill, SC 39732
Contact: Carol Ballard Owner
Tel: 803-328-3167
Email: carolcmi@aol.com
Website: www.cambridgemarketingcorp.com
Dist hospital products: custom sterile kits, suture removal kits & ER kits. (Minority, Woman, estab 1983, empl 2, sales $326,813, cert: State)

6198 Carolina Diagnostic Solutions
100 Old Cherokee Rd Ste F 301
Lexington, SC 29072
Contact: Amanda Clark President
Tel: 803-360-3410
Email: amanda@carolinadxsol.com
Website: www.carolinadiagnosticsolutions.com/
Pulmonary diagnostic related equipment, supplies, consultation & clinical service, body box/ plethysmography, gas measurement (FRC lung volumes, diffusing capacity), Spirometry equipment, handheld spirometer, portable spirometer. (Woman, estab 2014, empl 2, sales , cert: State)

6199   Pediatric Medical Solutions
974 Harbortowne Rd
Charleston, SC 29412
Contact: Heather Able Owner
Tel: 843-762-6769
Email: theableco@aol.com
Website: www.pediatricmedicalsolutions.com
Snuggle Wraps, Pediatric Elbow Immobilizers, are the cool and comfortable solution to keep little hands safely away! Snuggle Wraps are the world's best elbow immobilizers! (Woman, estab 1998, empl 2, sales $155,000, cert: City)

6200   Professional Healthcare Services LLC
1007 Pendleton St
Greenville, SC 29601
Contact: Doris Haley President
Tel: 864-505-6747
Email: dhaley@phsonline.com
Website: www.phsonline.com
Alcohol & drug screening, pre employment physicals & health screening & health fairs, injury management programs & medical case management, On Site nursing care. (Woman/AA, estab 1998, empl 7, sales $259,000, cert: NMSDC)

6201   Rhino Medical Supply
649 Rosewood Dr, Ste B
Columbia, SC 29201
Contact: Elliott Haynie COO
Tel: 404-704-7961
Email: info@rhinomedicalsuppy.com
Website: www.rhinomedicalsupply.com/
Dist Personal Protective Equipment (PPE), medical devices, and disinfectants. (AA, estab 2020, empl 10, sales $8,500,000, cert: NMSDC)

Tennessee

6202   Arch Plastics Packaging, LLC
2010 Polymer Dr
Chattanooga, TN 37421
Contact: Shital Rali Sales/Mktg Exec
Tel: 423-553-7751
Email: srali@archplasticsllc.com
Website: www.archplasticsllc.com
Dist high quality HDPE & PET bottles for the pharmaceutical and personal health care industries. (Woman/As-Ind, estab 2006, empl 94, sales $12,000,000, cert: NMSDC, NWBOC)

6203   Direct Medical Supplies, LLC
7285 Winchester Rd Ste 104
Memphis, TN 38125
Contact: Robert E Williams GM
Tel: 901-461-5379
Email: robert@directmedicalofamerica.com
Website: www.directmedicalsuppliesonline.com
Dist medical equipment & supplies: vinyl gloves, masks, shoes, wheelchairs, hospital beds, motorized wheelchairs, walkers, canes, commodes, rollators, wound dressings, diabetic test supplies, etc. (AA, estab 1999, empl 4, sales $425,000, cert: State)

6204   Global Industrial Components Inc.
705 S College St
Woodbury, TN 37190
Contact: David W. Vance Automtive Product Mgr
Tel: 615-563-5120
Email: dvance@gic-co.com
Website: www.gic-co.com
Dist medical kits, ER kits, roadside emergency kits, dental & medical supplies & equipment, component hardware. (Hisp, estab 1994, empl 47, sales $14,900,000, cert: NMSDC)

6205   GQSI
3777 Winchester Rd Ste 1
Memphis, TN 38118
Contact: Williette Graham President
Tel: 901-365-9566
Email: willgraham@gqsi.net
Website: www.gqsi.net
Engineering & technical services, medical devices, process & special processes equipment & validation, laser marking, CMM inspection services, product inspection, engineering support, supplier support services. (Woman/AA, estab 2005, empl 6, sales , cert: NMSDC)

6206   Innovate Medical, LLC
2210 Buffalo Rd
Johnson City, TN 37604
Contact: Susan Johnston Owner
Tel: 423-461-3558
Email: susanj@innovatemed.com
Website: www.innovatemed.com
Medical rubber products: tourniquets, esmark bandages, exercise bands, dental dams & component parts. (Woman, estab 2001, empl , sales $11,231,046, cert: WBENC)

6207   International Medical & Laboratory Supply, LLC
9093 Valkrie Lane
Lakeland, TN 38002
Contact: Michael Tharps VP
Tel: 901-377-0191
Email: michaeltharps@bellsouth.net
Website: www.internationalmedlab.com
Dist medical, safety, automotive, print management & labopratory supplies. (AA, estab 2004, empl 2, sales , cert: NMSDC)

6208   MRP, LLC   dba Aquabiliti & AmUSA
5209 Linbar Dr Ste 640
Nashville, TN 11111
Contact: Timir Patel CEO
Tel: 615-833-2633
Email: accounts@aquabiliti.com
Website: www.aquabiliti.com
Mfr terminally sterilized pre-filled flush syringes used for maintaining IV (intravenous) catheter patency. (Minority, estab 2005, empl 25, sales $8,016,000, cert: NMSDC)

6209   Princeton Medical Group, Inc.
1601 Championship Blvd Ste 233
Franklin, TN 37064
Contact: Terry Rust VP Marketing & Sales
Tel: 601-594-9495
Email: tcrust50@gmail.com
Website: www.princetonmedical.net
Dist surgical instruments. (Woman, estab 1991, empl 20, sales $1,400,000, cert: WBENC)

6210 The Premier Group
4600 Cromwell Ave, Ste 101
Memphis, TN 38118
Contact: JW   Gibson CEO
Tel: 901-346-9002
Email: jwgibson@gibsoncompanies.com
Website: www.gibsoncompanies.com
Dist medical supplies, laboratory & scientific equipment & related supplies. (AA, estab 1991, empl 7, sales $8,692,576, cert: NMSDC)

Texas

6211 Accel Lifestyle LLC
2014 Bailey St
Houston, TX 77006
Contact: Megan Eddings CEO
Tel: 832-980-0875
Email: megan@accelunite.com
Website: www.accelunite.com
We worked with infection control to design a new style of reusable isolation gowns. (Woman, estab 2020, empl 3, sales , cert: State, WBENC)

6212 Adair Visual, Inc.
3550 W 7th St
Fort Worth, TX 76107
Contact: Alyce Jones President
Tel: 817-377-3500
Email: melanie@adaireyewear.com
Website: www.adaireyewear.com
Protective eyewear & surgical loupes. (AA, estab 1980, empl 6, sales $1,484,023, cert: State, NMSDC)

6213 Affirmative Biosolutions
PO Box 2274
Stafford, TX 77497
Contact: seble woubshet Owner
Tel: 713-256-8996
Email: abiosolutions@hotmail.com
Website: www.abiosolutions.com
Dist laboratories, medical & industrial products (Woman/AA, estab 2010, empl 3, sales , cert: State, City)

6214 Alea Health dba Kersh Health
2600 Technology Dr, Ste 100
Plano, TX 75074
Contact: Bruce Brown VP Advanced Clinical Services
Tel: 469-241-2500
Email: program.coordinator@aleahealth.com
Website: www.kershhealth.com
Population health management, Health Risk Assessment, Diabetes Disease Management, Weight Loss, Stop Smoking, Activity Monitoring, Wellness Programs. (Nat Ame, estab 2015, empl 37, sales , cert: City)

6215 BayLab USA
2230 LBJ Frwy, Ste 100
Dallas, TX 75234
Contact: Joseph Petroni VP Operations
Tel: 214-907-2527
Email: joseph.petroni@baylabusa.com
Website: www.baylabusa.com
Medical device and supplies, designing, manufacturing, sourcing, and marketing a wide range of disposable medical and surgical supplies. (As-Pac, estab 2019, empl 27, sales $15,000,000, cert: WBENC)

6216 Bracane Company, Inc.
1201 W. 15th St. Ste 330
Plano, TX 75075
Contact: Cheryl Barrett Admin
Tel: 888-568-4271
Email: mail@bracaneco.com
Website: www.bracaneco.com
Dist medical supplies: lab equipment, Iv pumps, hospital beds, lab kits and supplies. (Woman/AA, estab 2002, empl 12, sales , cert: NMSDC, WBENC)

6217 Dalton Medical Corp.
4259 McEwen Rd
Farmers Branch, TX 75244
Contact: Jennifer Yu COO
Tel: 469-329-5200
Email: jennifery@daltonmed.net
Website: www.daltonmedical.com
Dist bariatric wheelchairs; walking aids, rollators, forearm rollators, walkers, and U-shape moving walkers with seat; cane stand; knee walker; foot pillow; acrylic medicine organizer; DryAid incontinence supply, protective underwear. (As-Pac, estab 1993, empl 25, sales $4,500,000, cert: State, NMSDC)

6218 GTL Supply Solutions, LLC
101C N Greenville Ave, Ste 423
Allen, TX 75002
Contact: Famira Green Inside Sales Acct Mgr
Tel: 972-359-7300
Email: fgreen@gtlsolutions.com
Website: www.gtlsolutions.com
Dist medical supplies & equipment. (Woman/AA, estab 2007, empl 10, sales $2,300,000, cert: State)

6219 Jackson & Associates, Inc.
8633 Schumacher Ln
Houston, TX 77063
Contact: Saul Szub President
Tel: 713-777-1155
Email: saul@dealmedical.com
Website: www.dealmedical.com
Dist medical, dental, surgical, pharmaceuticals, beauty, health & safety supplies & equipment. (Hisp, estab 1998, empl 6, sales $1,210,000, cert: State, City)

6220 MDD Marketing Inc.
5773 Woodway, Ste 214
Houston, TX 77057
Contact: Jennifer Hess Acct Mgr
Tel: 713-647-8240
Email: jennifer.hess@sterlingtonmedical.com
Website: www.aedtoday.com
AEDs and Manual Defibrillators. (Woman, estab 2000, empl 7, sales $2,000,000, cert: State)

6221 Mpulse Healthcare, LLC
54 Sugar Creek Center Ste 300
Sugarland, TX 77478
Contact: Tyrone Dixon CEO
Tel: 281-277-4410
Email: tdixon@mpulsehealth.com
Website: www.mpulsehealth.com
Dist medical, veterinary, dental, athletic & scientific supplies, products & equipment. (AA, estab 2005, empl 2, sales $100,000, cert: State, NMSDC)

6222   MRC - Medical Research Consultants
10550 Richmond Ave Ste 310
Houston, TX 77042
Contact: Gretchen Watson CEO
Tel: 713-528-6326
Email: gwatson@mrchouston.com
Website: www.mrchouston.com
Medical litigation support services: nurse reviews, mass tort expertise, record retrieval & document management. (Woman, estab 1983, empl 268, sales $9,102,297, cert: WBENC)

6223   Prestige Ameritech LTD
7201 Iron Horse Blvd
North Richland Hills, TX 76180
Contact: Elizabeth Givens
Tel: 817-427-7200
Email: elizabeth@prestigeam.com
Website: www.prestigeameritech.com
Mfr surgcal masks & face shields. (Nat Ame, estab , empl , sales $7,000,000, cert: State)

6224   Products Unlimited, Inc.
PO Box 339
Justin, TX 76247
Contact: Raithel Susan Sales Mgr
Tel: 940-648-3073
Email: sraithel@products-unlimited.com
Website: www.products-unlimited.com
Dist medical, lab & safety supplies & equipment. (Woman, estab 1992, empl 7, sales $5,020,000, cert: State)

6225   VM Cardio Vascular Inc.
4235 Centergate St
San Antonio, TX 78217
Contact: Sara Weyman President
Tel: 800-247-6294
Email: info@vossmedicalproducts.com
Website: www.vossmedicalproducts.com
Manufacture & dist disposable surgical products used in open heart surgeries, bypass graft markers, vein clamps & cannulas. (Woman, estab 2005, empl 4, sales $409,000, cert: WBENC)

6226   Zeitgeist Expressions, Inc.
1222 N Main Ste 740
San Antonio, TX 78212
Contact: Patricia Adams President
Tel: 210-271-7411
Email: padams@zeitgeistexpressions.com
Website: www.zwgroup.net
Employee assistance programs, critical incident debriefing, chaplains, MINT programs, counselors, psychiatrists, psychologists, nurses, social workers & educators. (Woman/AA, estab 2001, empl 47, sales $14,000,000, cert: WBENC)

Utah

6227   Acquire Med LLC
528 N Kays Dr, Ste 1
Kaysville, UT 84037
Contact: Austin Wood Dir of Contracts
Tel: - -
Email: sales@acquiremed.com
Website: www.acquiremed.com
Sales of Urology disposables and surgical equipment rental to Hospital and Surgery center operating rooms. (Woman, estab 2013, empl 4, sales $3,325,000, cert: WBENC)

6228   CAO Group, Inc.
4628 W Skyhawk Dr
West Jordan, UT 84084
Contact: Michael Tippets
Tel: 801-256-9282
Email: pilot@caogroup.com
Website: www.caogroup.com
Mfr & develop veterinary, dental, medical and forensic products and solutions. (As-Pac, estab 2000, empl 50, sales , cert: NMSDC)

Virginia

6229   Evident, Inc.
739 Brooks Mill Rd
Union Hall, VA 24176
Contact: Michael Grimm President
Tel: 800-576-7606
Email: michael@evident.cc
Website: www.ShopEVIDENT.com
Crime scene & forensic identification products: fingerprint products, evidence supplies, DNA collection materials, identification equipment, & crime scene kits for police & law enforcement. (Woman, estab 1992, empl 15, sales , cert: State)

6230   Global PPE Inc.
11490 Commerce Park Dr, Ste 400
Reston, VA 20191
Contact: Andrew Treanor SVP
Tel: 703-488-6912
Email: inquiry@global-ppe.com
Website: www.global-ppe.com
Dist certified diagnostic, testing kits, medical consumables, surgical masks & respirators, gloves, face shields, protective eyewear, surgical gowns, shoe coverings. (As-Ind, estab 2020, empl 30, sales $15,000,000, cert: State)

6231   JKICT, Inc.
11240 Waples Mill Rd Ste 400
Fairfax, VA 22030
Contact: Jay Kim President
Tel: 703-474-4924
Email: jeakuk@gmail.com
Website: www.jkict.net
Digital X-Ray Imaging System, High frequency X-Ray generator, Digital Radiology System, ECG Electrodes, ESU Pencils, ESU Plates, TENS/EMS Units, Cutaneous Electrodes, Robotic Assisted Gait Training System. (As-Pac, estab 2008, empl 2, sales , cert: State)

6232   M.E.Z Distributors LLC
45910 Transamerica Plaza Ste 104
Sterling, VA 20166
Contact: Adeel Shah President
Tel: 703-821-6760
Email: adeel@sterlingsurgical.com
Website: www.sterlingsurgical.com
Dist medical supplies, medical equipment & equipment maintenance/service. (Minority, estab , empl , sales $1,700,000, cert: State)

6233 Reliant Medical Supply
1431 Abingden Road
W. Chesterfield, VA 23236
Contact: stacey worthington Owner
Tel: 804-814-3180
Email:
staceyworthington@reliantmedicalsupply.com
Website: www.reliantmedicalsupply.com
Dist medical supplies. (Woman, estab 2008, empl 2, sales , cert: State)

6234 Triton Light Medical, LLC
8412 MacAndrew Terr
Chesterfield, VA 23838
Contact: Kennon Artis Principal
Tel: 804-543-8137
Email: kennon@tritonlightmedical.com
Website: www.tritonlightmedical.com
Dist our proprietary line of instruments crafted in Tuttlingen, Germany, the global center of first-quality, surgical-grade instruments and operating room (OR) equipment. (AA, estab 2017, empl 1, sales , cert: State, NMSDC)

Washington

6235 Anesthesia Equipment Supply, Inc.
24301 Roberts Dr.
Black Diamond, WA 98010
Contact: Michelle Norrie President
Tel: 253-631-8008
Email: michelle@aesol.com
Website: www.aesol.com
Dist custom medical equipment. (Woman, estab 1967, empl 15, sales , cert: WBENC)

6236 Attunix Corporation
405 114th Ave SE Ste 110
Bellevue, WA 98004
Contact: Matt O'Donnell CEO
Tel: 206-774-3163
Email: matto@attunix.com
Website: www.attunix.com
Custom Development, Portals and Web, Cloud Integration, and Mobile Solutions, Program Management. Technology capabilities include Microsoft .Net, SQL Server, Windows Phone 7, SharePoint (Hisp, estab 2006, empl 12, sales $1,935,000, cert: State, NMSDC)

6237 Summit Imaging
15000 Woodinville Redmond Rd Bldg B, Ste 800
Woodinville, WA 98072
Contact: Jessica Curtiss Customer Outreach Coord
Tel: 866-586-3744
Email: sales@mysummitimaging.com
Website: www.mysummitimaging.com
Ultrasound transducers & parts. (As-Ind, estab 2006, empl 41, sales , cert: NMSDC)

Wisconsin

6238 Alpha Source Inc.
6619 W Calumet Rd
Milwaukee, WI 53223
Contact: Norine Carlson-Weber
Tel: 800-654-9845
Email: norine.carlson-weber@alphasource.com
Website: www.alphasource.com
Mfr medical batteries, dist medical lighting, diagnostic instruments, repair parts for medical equipment. (Woman, estab 1986, empl 40, sales $18,219,000, cert: WBENC)

6239 Fox Converting, Inc.
PO Box 12795
Green Bay, WI 54307
Contact: Accounting Mgr
Tel: 920-434-5272
Email:
Website: www.foxconverting.com
Sterilization Bags/Envelopes, 8" & 16" Swabs - Sterilizable, CSR Sterilizer Wraps, Hospital Bedside Disposal Bags, X-Ray Envelopes. (As-Pac, estab 1960, empl 60, sales $15,150,000, cert: State)

METAL CASTING
Non-ferrous foundries and molds. (Also see six other METAL categories). NAICS Code 33

California

6240   JDH Pacific Inc.
14821 Artesia Blvd.
La Mirada, CA 90638
Contact: David Unger Sales Mgr
Tel: 562-207-1764
Email: dunger@jdhpacific.com
Website: www.jdhpacific.com
Cast & forged components. (As-Pac, estab 1989, empl 35, sales $18,000,000, cert: NMSDC)

6241   KFM International Industries, Inc.
20277 Valley Blvd, Ste L
Walnut, CA 91789
Contact: Dennis Boribor Engineer
Tel: 626-369-9556
Email: dennis@kfmii.com
Website: www.kfmii.com
Casting: Sand Cast, Die Casting, Investment Casting & Permanent Mold Forging: Hot & Cold Formed Sheet Metal Stamping Machining: CNC,Turning & Milling Powder Metal. (Minority, Woman, estab 2000, empl 6, sales $2,500,000, cert: City, CPUC)

Illinois

6242   Calumet Brass Foundry, Inc.
14610 Lakeside Ave
Dolton, IL 60419
Contact: Dawn Stromberg President
Tel: 708-344-7874
Email: dawn@calumetbrassfoundry.com
Website: www.calumetbrassfoundry.com
Mfr bushings, bearings, liners & guides, bronze sand casting, foundry. (Minority, Woman, estab , empl , sales , cert: WBENC)

Michigan

6243   Aerostar Manufacturing
28275 Northline Rd
Romulus, MI 48174
Contact: Robert Johnson VP
Tel: 734-942-8440
Email: rjohnson@aerostarmfg.com
Website: www.aerostarmfg.com
CNC machining assembly, prototyping, machine castings & forgings, sand casting. (As-Pac, estab 1970, empl 200, sales , cert: NMSDC)

6244   Allied Technology Inc.
6830 Metro Plex Dr
Romulus, MI 48174
Contact: Annie Shen President
Tel: 734-728-6688
Email: ati.purchasing@alliedtech-eng.com
Website: www.alliedtech-eng.com
Castings, forgings, cold forming products, stampings and screw machine products. (As-Pac, estab 1999, empl 12, sales $6,000,000, cert: NMSDC)

6245   GK Tech, LLC
3331 W Big Beaver Rd Ste 106
Troy, MI 48084
Contact: Kelly Choi
Tel: 248-494-1960
Email: kellychoi@gktechusa.com
Website: www.gktechllc.com
Marketing specialist, consulting, business development, forging, die-casting, stamping, spring, magnesium pulley, rubber bushing, fasteners, machining, plastic injection molding. (Minority, Woman, estab 2015, empl 3, sales , cert: NMSDC)

6246   Lucerne International
40 Corporate Dr
Auburn Hills, MI 48326
Contact: Karen Ryan Finance Mgr
Tel: 248-674-7210
Email: kryan@lucerneintl.com
Website: www.lucerneintl.com
Advanced metal forming components & assemblies, body structures, chassis systems & powertrain systems. Mfg aluminum & steel forgings, stampings, aluminum & zinc die castings & steel. (Woman, estab 1993, empl 58, sales , cert: WBENC)

6247   New Products Corporation
448 North Shore Dr
Benton Harbor, MI 49022
Contact: Kristy Lovejoy VP
Tel: 269-925-2161
Email: kristy.lovejoy@newproductscorp.com
Website: www.newproductscorp.com
Custom, precision, high-pressure aluminum and zinc die casting. (Woman, estab , empl 50, sales , cert: WBENC)

6248   Precision Components Manufacturing, LLC
35855 Stanley
Sterling Heights, MI 48312
Contact: Tommy Longest CEO
Tel: 586-939-8500
Email: tommy@pcmfettes.com
Website: www.pcmfettes.com
Mfr cast tooling, castings iron/aluminum, steel forging, fully machined castings & assembly, ferrous & non-ferrous products, forging, sand & die casting. (AA, estab 2009, empl 30, sales $7,010,000, cert: NMSDC)

METAL COATING

Includes plating, polishing, spray painting, metal finishing, paint stripping, de-oiling, anodizing, etc. (Also see six other METAL categories). NAICS Code 33

Arizona

6249 Best Finishing, Inc.
7670 E Broadway Blvd Ste 203
Tucson, AZ 85710
Contact: Chris Schlesinger President
Tel: 520-546-7763
Email: chris@bestfinishing.com
Website: www.bestfinishing.com
Metal finishing, polishing & buffing: aluminum castings, exhaust systems, metal moldings, body hardware, stampings, aluminum heads & blocks, magnesium components, closures. (Woman, estab 2000, empl 5, sales $985,981, cert: WBENC)

California

6250 Dean Baldwin Painting, LP
2395 Bulverde Rd Ste 105
Bulverde, CA 78163
Contact: Rick Smith Dir Business Dev
Tel: 830-438-5340
Email: ricks@deanbaldwinpainting.com
Website: www.deanbaldwinpainting.com
High quality aircraft painting: commercial, regioanl, military and VIP corporate aircraft. (Woman/Hisp, estab 1972, empl 560, sales $28,730,962, cert: State, NMSDC, WBENC)

Florida

6251 AmeriCoat Corporation
2935 Barneys Pumps Pl
Lakeland, FL 33812
Contact: Shrikant Desai President
Tel: 863-667-1035
Email: americoatusa@yahoo.com
Website: www.ameri-coat.com
Powder coating, fluoropolymers, metal finishing, coating, blasting, stripping. (As-Ind, estab 1995, empl 5, sales , cert: State)

Illinois

6252 Advance Coating Solutions
748 E Sunnyside Ave
Libertyville, IL 60048
Contact: Joseph Webb CEO
Tel: 847-732-1118
Email: joseph@acsco.us
Website: www.acsco.us
Epoxy coating solutions. (AA, estab 2008, empl 7, sales , cert: State, NMSDC)

Massachusetts

6253 The Falmer Associates, Inc.
96 Swampscott Road Unit 10
Salem, MA 01970
Contact: Stacy Ames President
Tel: 978-745-4000
Email: sames@falmer.com
Website: www.falmer.com
Machining, grinding & thermal spray coating svcs: metal, ceramic & carbide coatings, wear, corrosion, erosion, galling, thermal insulation or conduction, electrical insulation or conduction, anti-skid. (Woman, estab 1961, empl 4, sales $400,000, cert: WBENC)

Michigan

6254 Dhake Industries
15169 Northville Rd
Plymouth, MI 48170
Contact: Arjun Dhake VP
Tel: 734-420-0101
Email: adhake@dhakeindustries.com
Website: www.dhakeindustries.com
Mfr automotive coatings. (As-Ind, estab 1979, empl 25, sales $12,000,000, cert: NMSDC)

6255 Great Lakes Finishing, Inc.
510 W Hackley Ave
Muskegon, MI 49444
Contact: Diana Bench President
Tel: 231-733-9566
Email: dbench@greatlakesfinishinginc.com
Website: www.greatlakesfinishinginc.com
Alkaline and Chloride zinc plating. Barrel plating for small parts. Rack plating for parts up to 12' long. Two automatic lines. RoHS compliant. Chromates: bright, yellow, black and olive drab. (Woman, estab 2002, empl 12, sales $1,000,000, cert: WBENC)

6256 Jackson Tumble Finish
1801 Mitchell St
Jackson, MI 49203
Contact: Denise L. Losey President
Tel: 517-787-0368
Email: denise@jacksontumble.com
Website: www.jacksontumble.com
Zinc phosphate, fine, med, heavy grain; calcium modified fine grain phosphate, manganese phosphate, phos. and lube, black oxide, tumble and vibratory deburr, shot blast, glass bead, acid pickle, wash/degrease, and passivate, sort and packaging. (Woman, estab 1956, empl 45, sales $4,700,000, cert: WBENC)

Minnesota

6257 Coating Solutions, Inc.
      13525 Fenway Blvd N
      Hugo, MN 55038
      Contact: Kimberly Northrop CFO
      Tel: 651-762-5700
      Email: knorthrop@coatingsolutions.com
      Website: www.coatingsolutions.com
DuPont teflon industrial coatings. (Woman, estab 1995, empl 7, sales , cert: WBENC)

New Jersey

6258 Karnak Corporation
      330 Central Ave
      Clark, NJ 07066
      Contact: Sarah Jane Jelin President
      Tel: 800-526-4236
      Email: sjjelin@karnakcorp.com
      Website: www.karnakcorp.com
Protective roof coatings, reflective roof coatings, aluminum coatings, elastomeric coatings, Energy Star & LEED compliant coatings, dampproofing, waterproofing, flashing cements, primers, sealants, membranes, reinforcing fabrics. (Woman, estab 1933, empl 97, sales $60,000,000, cert: WBENC)

Ohio

6259 Cleveland Die & Mfg. Co.
      20303 First Ave
      Middleburg Heights, OH 44130
      Contact: Marty Curry Sales/Engineering
      Tel: 440-243-3404
      Email: mcurry@clevelanddie.com
      Website: www.clevelanddie.com/
Ecoat & powder coat line, automatic & single hit presses, spot & robotic welders, CNC machining. (Hisp, estab 1973, empl 300, sales $24,000,000, cert: NMSDC)

6260 Great Lakes Maintenance, Inc.
      1213 Maple Ave.
      Hamilton, OH 45011
      Contact: Marilyn Barlow President
      Tel: 513-423-0800
      Email: glmbarlow@hotmail.com
      Website: www.greatlakesmtce.com
Tank linings & coatings, abrasive blasting, industrial & maintenance painting, leak repair to live gas, water, sludge, fume exhaust & liquor piping, secondary containment coatings & repairs, fiberglass repairs & fabrications. (Minority, Woman, estab 1997, empl 14, sales $14,000,000, cert: State, NMSDC, WBENC)

6261 Herbert E. Orr Comany, Inc.
      335 W Wall St
      Paudling, OH 45879
      Contact: Greg Johnson President
      Tel: 419-399-4866
      Email: gjohnson@heorr.com
      Website: www.heorr.com
Hot Forged Wheel Wrenches; Jack Tool Kits; Hood Support Rods; E-Coat Painting & powder coating; wire forms (pnuematic and CNC); assembly and kitting. (Woman, estab 1957, empl 51, sales $12,656,024, cert: WBENC)

6262 Steelcote, Inc.
      215 Eastview Dr
      Brooklyn Hts., OH 44131
      Contact: Mohan Kapahi President
      Tel: 216-635-2585
      Email: mohan_kapahi@steelcoteinc.com
      Website: www.steelcoteinc.com
Anti-corrosion coatings on metal stampings & assemblies. (As-Ind, estab 2002, empl 9, sales $1,000,000, cert: NMSDC)

South Carolina

6263 JBE, Inc.
      512 Hartland Dr
      Hartsville, SC 29551
      Contact: John Miller Dir Business Devel
      Tel: 843-332-0589
      Email: johnmiller@jbeinc.net
      Website: www.jbeinc.net
Metal finishing; preplate finishing; abrasive blasting, manual & auto buffing, plating needs, chrome, decorative & hard, brite & electroless, silver & tin. Pre-eng bldgs; structure steel & metal fab. Sub-assembly for auto field. (AA, estab 1982, empl 40, sales $348,000,000, cert: NMSDC)

Tennessee

6264 Y&W Technologies LLC
      2883 Director Cove
      Memphis, TN 38131
      Contact: Willis Yates President
      Tel: 901-396-3380
      Email: wyates@ywtech.com
      Website: www.ywtech.com
Chrome plating, titantium anodizing, metal finishing, electroplating, laser marking, critic & nitric passivation. (AA, estab 2001, empl 20, sales $1,200,000, cert: NMSDC)

Texas

6265 Carrco Painting Contractors, Inc.
       10944 Alder Cir
       Dallas, TX 75238
       Contact: Rudy Cox Business Dev Mgr
       Tel: 214-624-7560
       Email: rcox@carrcopainting.com
       Website: www.carrcopainting.com
We are a provider of painting, pressure cleaning,
wallcovering, drywall repair, epoxy and urethane floor,
specialty coating, wall and ceiling coating, protective
coating, Cool Seal Roof Coating and Industrial Painting
(Hisp, estab 1994, empl 250, sales $8,000,000, cert: State,
City)

6266 Cimcon Finishing, LLC
       2314 Executive Dr
       Garland, TX 75041
       Contact: Mike Gilbert VP Sales
       Tel: 972-840-0934
       Email: mike@cimconfinishing.com
       Website: www.cimconfinishing.com
Electroplate: hard anodize, anodize, chemfilm, electroless
nickel, nickel, tin, zinc, powder coat. (AA, estab 1994, empl
48, sales $3,200,000, cert: NMSDC)

6267 Texas Finishing Company
       PO Box 59445
       Dallas, TX 75229
       Contact: Carolyn Beard President
       Tel: 972-416-2961
       Email: cbeard@texasfinishing.com
       Website: www.texasfinishing.com
Paint application & custom metal fabrication. (Woman,
estab 1982, empl 45, sales , cert: State, WBENC)

Washington

6268 Dunkin & Bush, Inc.
       PO Box 97080
       Kirkland, WA 98083
       Contact: Deidre Dunkin President
       Tel: 425-885-7064
       Email: ddunkin@dunkinandbush.com
       Website: www.dunkinandbush.com
Industrial painting, scaffolding, insulation, rigging, containment, lead abatement, shop coating aplication, concrete
restoration, plural applied tank linings, abrasive blasting,
specialty blasting, water jetting, high heat coating applications. (Woman, estab 2008, empl 300, sales , cert: WBENC)

> **METAL FABRICATION**
> Includes tanks and tank liners, steel containers, aircraft framework parts, electronic chassis, work stands, ornamental ironwork, fences, sheet metal components, etc. (Also see six other METAL categories). NAICS Code 33

Alabama

6269   Majestic Solutions, Inc.
       241 Production Ave
       Madison, AL 35758
       Contact: Grace Lo President
       Tel: 256-772-3232
       Email: grace@majesticsolutionsinc.net
       Website: www.majesticsolutionsinc.net
Mfr institutional metal furniture & security products: lockers, bunk beds, electronic enclosures, dayroom tables, benches, access panel, shelves, storage cabinets, railings, stairs, wire mesh partition/fence, tubings. (Minority, Woman, estab 2004, empl 10, sales $1,000,000, cert: State, City, SDB)

Arizona

6270   K&R Holdings, Inc.
       2322 W Detroit Pl
       Chandler, AZ 85224
       Contact: Wayne Armoogam President
       Tel: 480-236-2682
       Email: warmoogam@lumawaresafety.com
       Website: www.lumawaresafety.com
Supply and install photoluminescent egress systems for facilities. Our technologies for egress requires no electricity, external power source or batteries to provide the illumination required for safe movement of employees (As-Ind, estab 2007, empl 5, sales $100,000, cert: NMSDC)

6271   Vics Welding Company, LLC
       8376 N El Mirage Rd Bldg 3
       El Mirage, AZ 85335
       Contact: Victor Valencia President
       Tel: 623-925-5696
       Email: vic@vicswelding.com
       Website: www.vicswelding.com
Metal fabrication, field welding, structural, piping, ASME pressure vessel repair or manufacturing, aerospace welding. (Minority, Woman, estab 1996, empl 6, sales $970,000, cert: City)

California

6272   A-1 Truck and Equipment, Inc.
       1588 Los Angeles Ave
       Ventura, CA 93004
       Contact: Dan Poole President
       Tel: 805-659-1817
       Email: dan@a1truck.com
       Website: www.a1truck.com
Rotating equipment repair, body repair, truck, trailers & equipment blasting & paint repairs, metal fabrication & welding. (Hisp, estab 2008, empl 30, sales $2,200,000, cert: NMSDC)

6273   Bueno Enterprises
       25589 Seaboard Ln
       Hayward, CA 94545
       Contact: Lydia Bueno Sec/Treas
       Tel: 510-782-2225
       Email: lydia@metalspecialists.com
       Website: www.metalspecialists.com
Precision sheet metal, laser cutting, machining & powder coat painting, fabricate metal parts. (Hisp, estab 1988, empl 10, sales , cert: CPUC)

6274   Columbia Sanitary Products, Inc.
       1622 Browning
       Irvine, CA 92606
       Contact: Paul Escalera
       Tel: 847-559-6132
       Email: p.escalera@columbiasinks.com
       Website: www.columbiasinks.com
Mfr stainless steel products: sinks, wash stations, sink accessories, faucets, heavy-duty forks, shovels, scoops, valves, knife sterilizers & trays. (Woman, estab 1949, empl 8, sales , cert: State)

6275   CX Enterprise Inc.
       14408 Iseli Rd
       Santa Fe Springs, CA 90670
       Contact: Steve Chin Mgr
       Tel: 562-407-1088
       Email: stevechin@cxenterprise.com
       Website: www.cxenterprise.com
Steel strapping. (Minority, Woman, estab 1991, empl 5, sales $1,771,000, cert: CPUC)

6276   Pacific HVAC Depot Corporation
       3029 Teagarden St
       San Leandro, CA 94577
       Contact: Phyllis La Voy CEO
       Tel: 510-346-6500
       Email: pacifichvacdepot@aol.com
       Website: www.pacifichvacdepot.com
Dist hardcast duct sealants, coils & condensers, sheet metal products, fittings & heat ducts. (Minority, Woman, estab 2000, empl 6, sales $2,300,000, cert: WBENC)

6277   Scott Engineering, Inc.
       5051 Edison Ave
       Chino, CA 91710
       Contact: CFO/COO
       Tel: 909-594-9637
       Email: info@scott-eng.com
       Website: www.scott-eng.com
Mfr medium voltage custom fabricated mild steel, stainless steel, & aluminum electrical cabinets & metal fabricated products. (Hisp, estab 1967, empl 75, sales $14,990,887, cert: CPUC)

6278   Tanfel
       1945 Camino Vida Roble, Ste J
       Carlsbad, CA 92008
       Contact: Greg Lange Owner
       Tel: 760-720-9632
       Email: glange@tanfel.com
       Website: www.tanfel.com
Custom metal parts: stamping, extrusion, casting, metal injection molding, machining, turning, prototype to large production with warehousing capabilities. (Hisp, estab 2008, empl 5, sales , cert: NMSDC)

6279 THISAI LLC
1834 Blazewood St
Simi Valley, CA 93063
Contact: Ramalingam Subramaniam Owner
Tel: 747-206-3886
Email: ram@thisaillc.com
Website: www.thisaillc.com
Electrical products, cables, switches, wire, lighting fixtures, metal products, aluminum, sheet metal, laser cut, bent & fabricated. (Minority, estab 2015, empl 2, sales , cert: State)

6280 West Coast Form Grinding
2548 S Fairview St
Santa Ana, CA 92704
Contact: Adrian Calderon President
Tel: 714-540-5621
Email: adrian@precisioncorepins.com
Website: www.precisioncorepins.com
Mfr mold components, core pins, sleeves, ejector pins, luer taper pins. (Hisp, estab 2005, empl 10, sales $1,222,670, cert: NMSDC)

Colorado

6281 Excalibur Machine & Sheet Metal
208 W Buchanan St, Unit C
Colorado Springs, CO 80907
Contact: Douglas McDaniel Plant Mgr
Tel: 719-520-5404
Email: doug@excaliburmfg.com
Website: www.excaliburmfg.com/
Precision machining & sheet metal fabrication, welding, assembly, powder coating. (Hisp, estab 1989, empl 25, sales $2,600,000, cert: NMSDC)

Connecticut

6282 Turbo America Technology, LLC
1400 Old North Colony Rd
Meriden, CT 06450
Contact: Liliane Yebarth
Tel: 860-970-8777
Email: liliane@turboamericatech.com
Website: www.turboamericatech.com
Mfr & repair Industrial Gas Turbine components. (Hisp, estab 2014, empl 5, sales $341,000, cert: NMSDC)

Florida

6283 Blue Water Dynamics LLC dba Dougherty Mfg.
301 S Old County Rd
Edgewater, FL 32132
Contact: Davey Carroll Sales Dir
Tel: 386-316-5939
Email: dcarroll@dougherty-mfg.com
Website: www.doughertymanufacturing.com
Fabricate metals (aluminum, steel & stainless steel) & composites/FRP, engineering, design, tooling, prototyping & manufacturing. (Woman, estab 2010, empl 46, sales $2,500,000, cert: State, WBENC)

6284 Coastal Steel Inc.
870 Cidco Rd
Cocoa, FL 32926
Contact: Dale Coxwell
Tel: 321-632-8228
Email: dcoxwell@coastalsteelmfg.com
Website: www.coastalsteel.com
Complex & Iconic Structures (AISC Fabrication & Erection), Ride & Show (AISC Fabrication & Installation), Machining (Large Capacity 5 Axis Vertical & Horiz), CMM (Zeiss Contra G2 & FERO). (Nat Ame, estab 1976, empl 90, sales $14,000,000, cert: State, NMSDC)

6285 Cool Tactics LLC
910 S 8th St, Ste 302
Fernandina Beach, FL 32034
Contact: Dana Brodsky President
Tel: 904-420-0070
Email: contact@cooltactics.com
Website: www.cooltactics.com
Installs Insulated Metal Panels (IMPs), underfloor insulation systems, and specialty doors for cold storage and food processing facilities, refrigerated warehouses and distribution. (Woman, estab 2019, empl 7, sales , cert: WBENC)

Georgia

6286 Harbor Enterprises, LLC
1207 Sunset Dr
Thomasville, GA 31792
Contact: Brandy Spradlin CEO
Tel: 229-226-0911
Email: sba@harborenterprisesllc.com
Website: www.survive-a-storm.com
Wood & metal fabrication, mfr solid steel above ground safe rooms & underground storm shelters. (Nat Ame, estab 2009, empl 25, sales $5,500,000, cert: NMSDC, 8(a))

Iowa

6287 Air Control, Inc.
80 14th Ave N
Clinton, IA 52732
Contact: Mary Connell President
Tel: 563-243-7228
Email: marypat@acifabricators.com
Website: www.acifabricators.com
HVAC contracting, specialty steel fabrication, tank fabrication. (Woman, estab 1956, empl 45, sales $8,000,000, cert: WBENC, 8(a))

6288 EIP Manufacturing, LLC
2677 - 221st St
Earlville, IA 52041
Contact: Kathy Krapfl VP Sales & Mktg
Tel: 800-942-2226
Email: kkrapfl@eipmfg.com
Website: www.eipmfg.com
Steel fabricated components, structural steel, rebar. (Woman, estab 1975, empl 45, sales $7,700,000, cert: State)

Idaho

6289   Burly Products, Inc.
3999 St. Joe Ave
Post Falls, ID 83854
Contact: Stephani Morris Admin Asst
Tel: 208-262-9531
Email: stephani@burlyproducts.com
Website: www.burlyproducts.com
Design & mfr steel & aluminum products. (Nat Ame, estab 2006, empl 18, sales , cert: State)

Illinois

6290   Ace Metal Craft
484 Thomas Dr
Bensenville, IL 60106
Contact: Kevin Bailey Sales
Tel: 847-455-1010
Email: kevin.bailey@acemetal.com
Website: www.acemetal.com
Structural Metal Fabrication (Woman, estab 1960, empl 150, sales $10,000,000, cert: WBENC)

6291   American Chrome Chicago Company, Inc.
518 W Crossroads Pkwy
Bolingbrook, IL 60440
Contact: Linda Hou President
Tel: 630-685-2200
Email: linda.hou@americanchrome.com
Website: www.americanchrome.com
Dist chrome, stainless steel & PC/ABS chrome products, mirrors, exhaust products, clam shells for catalytic converters, shock absorbers & components, rubber products / bushings, u-joints, grease caps, air tubes, clutch control rods. (Minority, Woman, estab 1983, empl 26, sales $11,695,000, cert: NMSDC, WBENC)

6292   Combined Metals of Chicago LLC
2401 W Grant Ave
Bellwood, IL 60104
Contact: John Dicello Dir Diversity Devel
Tel: 708-547-8800
Email: johnd@combmet.com
Website: www.combmet.com
Stainless steel: flat rolled stainless steel strip, sheet & foil. (As-Pac, estab 1975, empl 279, sales $0, cert: NMSDC)

6293   Great Lakes Metals
8920 S Octavia
Bridgeview, IL 60455
Contact: Donna Herpich President
Tel: 708-430-0500
Email: glmcdonna@aol.com
Website: www.greatlakesmetals.com
Steel & metal svcs. (Woman, estab 1994, empl 6, sales $0, cert: WBENC)

6294   KSO Metalfab, Inc.
250 Roma Jean Pkwy
Streamwood, IL 60107
Contact: Dora Kuzelka President
Tel: 630-372-1200
Email: dkuzelka@kso.com
Website: www.kso.com
Precision sheet metal fabrication: short to large runs. (Woman, estab 1973, empl 33, sales $3,700,000, cert: State)

6295   Patel International
30 N River Rd Ste 102
Des Plaines, IL 60016
Contact: Steve Gordon Sales Rep
Tel: 847-795-3006
Email: sgordon@patelintl.com
Website: www.sejasmi.com
Injection molding, aluminum die casting. (As-Ind, estab 2005, empl 65, sales $8,000,000, cert: NMSDC)

6296   Premier Manufacturing Corporation
3008 Malmo Dr
Arlington Heights, IL 60005
Contact: Susan Fischer President
Tel: 847-640-6644
Email: sfischer@premiermfgcorp.com
Website: www.Premiermfgcorp.com
Sheet metal fabrication: punching, forming, welding, painting, powder coating & assembly. (Woman, estab 1999, empl 9, sales $920,000, cert: WBENC)

6297   Rockford Specialties Company
5601 Industrial Ave
Rockford, IL 61111
Contact: Lisa Stankey President
Tel: 815-877-6000
Email: lisas@rswire.com
Website: www.rockfordspecialties.com
Mfr wire, tube & sheet metal custom displays & components, counter racks, free standing floor displays, wire dividers & aisle extenders, plating & powder painting, laser cutting, forming & welding, MIG, TIG, resistance & robotic welding. (Woman, estab 1979, empl 45, sales $10,780,000, cert: WBENC)

6298   W.E.B. Production & Fabricating, Inc.
448 N Artesian Ave
Chicago, IL 60612
Contact: Maureen Kendziera President
Tel: 312-733-6800
Email: maureenk@webproductionandfabricating.com
Website: www.webproductionandfabricating.com
Welding, shearing, bending, punching, stamping, & drilling, MIG & TIG welding, aluminum, stainless steel, carbon steel, handrails, guardrails & metal stair frames. (Woman, estab 1993, empl 24, sales $3,068,370, cert: State)

6299   Young Technology Inc.
900 W. Fullerton Ave.
Addison, IL 60101
Contact: Young Sohn President
Tel: 630-690-4320
Email: youngsohn@ytinc.com
Website: www.ytinc.com
Mfr molded rubber, plastic & forged steel: shifter knobs, bezels, decorative molding & cable components, leather wrapped & chrome plated. (As-Pac, estab 1985, empl 350, sales $6,000,000, cert: NMSDC)

Indiana

6300 Circle City Rebar, LLC
4002 Industrial Blvd
Indianapolis, IN 46254
Contact: Heidi Russo Controller
Tel: - -
Email: hrusso@circlecityrebar.com
Website: www.circlecityrebar.com
Supplier and Fabricator of concrete reinforcing steel bars (rebar) in all sizes; plain and epoxy coated. (AA, estab 2005, empl 14, sales $7,541,942, cert: NMSDC)

6301 Diversified Quality Services of Indiana, LLC
1315 W 18th St
Anderson, IN 46016
Contact: Sharon Montgomery CEO
Tel: 765-644-7712
Email: sharon.montgomery@dqsicorp.com
Website: www.dqsicorp.com
Design, prototyping, production, modification & repair steel racks, containers & dunnage. (AA, estab 2003, empl 123, sales $5,000,000, cert: NMSDC)

6302 Eagle Magnetic Company Inc.
7417 Crawfordsville Rd
Indianapolis, IN 46214
Contact: Ron Jaggers VP Inside Sales
Tel: 317-297-1030
Email: rjaggers@eaglemagnetic.com
Website: www.eaglemagnetic.com
Magnetic shielding, precision sheet metal fabrication, precision machining. (Woman, estab 1970, empl 39, sales $3,275,000, cert: State)

6303 Electric Metal Fab, Inc.
4889 Helmsburg Rd
Nashville, IN 47448
Contact: Mandy Chittum President
Tel: 812-988-9353
Email: mandy@electricmetalfab.com
Website: www.electricmetalfab.com
Mfr Stainless Steel Equipment & Products for the Pharmaceutical & Food Industries, turn-key conveyor systems for production lines, specialty products, etc. Cabinets, Carts, Tables, Racks, Platforms, Lab Furnishings, etc. (Woman, estab 1993, empl 16, sales $1,177,089, cert: WBENC)

6304 Indiana Bridge
1810 S Macedonia Ave
Muncie, IN 47302
Contact: Sheryl Bronnenberg Mgr
Tel: 765-288-1985
Email: sheryl.bronnenberg@indianabridge.net
Website: www.indianabridge.net
Steel fabrication and erection services. (As-Pac, estab 2001, empl 47, sales $6,348,823, cert: NMSDC)

6305 Indiana Bridge-Midwest Steel, Inc.
1810 S Macedonia Ave
Muncie, IN 47307
Contact: Sheryl Bronnenberg Office Mgr
Tel: 765-288-1985
Email: sheryl@indianabridge.net
Website: www.indianabridge.net/
Fabricate structural steel & rack structures, design build & erection services. (As-Pac, estab , empl 35, sales $26,790,376, cert: NMSDC)

6306 Irons Metal Processing LLC
1605 Adler Cir Ste I
Portage, IN 46368
Contact: Earmon Irons CEO
Tel: 219-764-9999
Email: earmon@ironsmetalprocessing.com
Website: www.ironsmetalprocessing.com
Processed metal products. (AA, estab 2007, empl 3, sales , cert: NMSDC)

6307 Lacay Fabrication and Mfg Inc.
52941 Glenview Dr
Elkhart, IN 46514
Contact: Ann Filley President
Tel: 574-288-4678
Email: ann@lacayfab.com
Website: www.lacayfab.com
Mfr material handling racks, Baskets, Industrial & Production Welding, Machining, Robotic Welding, Stamping, Custom Fabrication, Prototyping. (Woman, estab 1975, empl 70, sales , cert: WBENC)

6308 Refractory Service Corp.
4900 Cline Ave
East Chicago, IN 46312
Contact: Laura Bianchi Eikenmeyer President
Tel: 219-397-7108
Email: laura@refractoryservice.net
Website: www.refractoryservice.net
Mfr high temperature refractories: lances & precast shapes (Woman, estab 1979, empl 85, sales $15,092,895, cert: WBENC)

6309 Royalty Investments, LLC
2476 E US Hwy 50
Seymour, IN 47274
Contact: Marshall Royalty Member
Tel: 812-358-3534
Email: mroyalty@cranehillmachine.com
Website: www.cranehillmachine.com
Machining, fabricating & assembly: steel, aluminum & plastic components. Design, engineering & coating applications. (Woman, estab 1989, empl 30, sales $3,714,618, cert: State, WBENC)

6310 The Phillips Company, Inc.
6330 East 100 South
Columbus, IN 47201
Contact: Valerie Phillips CEO
Tel: 812-378-3797
Email: valeriephillips@thephillipscompany.com
Website: www.thephillipscompany.com
Cast iron & aluminum parts: pulleys, lube pumps, oil coolers, wire harnesses, water pumps, blocks, heads, gear covers. (Woman/AA, estab 1986, empl 47, sales $2,800,000, cert: NMSDC)

Kansas

6311 American Energy Products, Inc.
1105 Industrial St
Lansing, KS 66043
Contact: Gail Watson President
Tel: 913-351-3388
Email: administrator@americanenergyinc.com
Website: www.americanenergyinc.com
Mfr metal products: corrugated seal plate, seal skirting, dip seal plate, drip screen, wire cloth, drip lips, wareplate, scrubber modules, coal piping, pyrite hoppers, ducting work, seal trough, water trough, telescopic coal chutes. (Woman, estab 2000, empl 3, sales $1,200,000, cert: WBENC)

6312 Industrial Metal Fabrication, Inc.
      1401 S Spencer
      Newton, KS 67114
      Contact: Jere Dean Sales Mgr
      Tel: 316-650-4068
      Email: jere@imfinc.com
      Website: www.imfinc.com
Welding, submerged arc, metal plate and sheet rolling, shearing, laser cutting, fabrication, Spouting, Millwright Crew, Transitions, Feed Funnel, Steam Vent, Platform, Pipe Support, Hopper, Silo, Cover Plate, Manhole, ,Weldment, Industrial Bed, Bin. (Woman, estab 2002, empl 41, sales $5,851,062, cert: WBENC)

6313 PTMW, Inc.
      5040 NW US Hwy 24
      Topeka, KS 66618
      Contact: Ashley Bettis President
      Tel: 785-232-7792
      Email: abettis@ptmw.com
      Website: www.ptmw.com
OEM metal fabrication & assembly: metal parts, enclosures & cases, assembly & powdercoating. (Woman, estab 1983, empl 250, sales $55,000,000, cert: CPUC, WBENC)

Louisiana

6314 JRE LLC dba Ascension Roofing and Sheet Metal
      2140 S Philippe Ave
      Gonzales, LA 70737
      Contact: Rebecca Evans President
      Tel: 225-647-3576
      Email: rebevans@ascensionrsm.com
      Website: www.ascensionrsm.com
Metal fabrication: stainless steel, carbon steel, galvanized metal & specialty alloys. (Woman, estab 1954, empl 31, sales $2,260,000, cert: WBENC)

Massachusetts

6315 Heat Exchanger Products Corp.
      55 Industrial Park Rd
      Hingham, MA 02043
      Contact: Tracy Hennigan Bonnyman President
      Tel: 781-749-0220
      Email: hepco@heatexchangerproducts.com
      Website: www.HeatExchangerProducts.com
Mfr tube plugs for condensers, heat exchangers, boilers in sizes 5/8" up to 1 1/4" in materials; Brass, 316 and 314 Stainless Steel, Titanium and Ultem & Non-Metallic High Performance Polymer plug. (Woman, estab 1985, empl 5, sales $0, cert: WBENC)

6316 Wrobel Engineering Co., Inc.
      154 Bodwell St
      Avon, MA 02322
      Contact: Michael Long General/QA Mgr.
      Tel: 508-586-8338
      Email: mlong@wrobeleng.com
      Website: www.wrobeleng.com
Mfr precision sheet metal fabricated parts per customer specs, precision machining, milling & turning, metal stamping, long & short runs, tool & die making, assembly mechanical & electrical, welding all materials. (Woman, estab 1976, empl 86, sales $14,800,000, cert: State, City)

Maryland

6317 Waltons Welding & Fabrication, Inc.
      155 Prospect Dr
      Huntingtown, MD 20639
      Contact: Fay Walton President
      Tel: 301-855-2944
      Email: metalfab@waltonswelding.net
      Website: www.waltonswelding.com
Metal fabrication: elctrode welding, mig welding, tig welding, aluminum welding, stainless steel welding, tourch cutting, saw cutting, plasma cutting, shear cutting, drilling, rolling, bending, sanding, grinding, tapping & punching. (Woman, estab 2000, empl 5, sales $154,007, cert: State)

Michigan

6318 Airodyne Industries, Inc.
      95 E 10 Mile Rd
      Madison Heights, MI 48071
      Contact: Celeste Herpel President
      Tel: 248-548-3336
      Email: caherpel@airodyne.com
      Website: www.airodyne.com
Mfr & dist aerodynamic & fuel-saving devices. (Woman, estab 2004, empl 3, sales $1,265,000, cert: WBENC)

6319 Anderson Express, Inc.
      580 W Sherman Blvd
      Muskegon Heights, MI 49444
      Contact: Angel Ball HR Mgr
      Tel: 231-733-6001
      Email: aball@andersonexpressinc.com
      Website: www.andersonexpressinc.com
Rapid tooling & tooling prototypes for small & medium projects. (Woman, estab 2011, empl 17, sales $0, cert: WBENC)

6320 Clips & Clamps Industries
      15050 Keel St
      Plymouth, MI 48170
      Contact: Jeff Aznavorian President
      Tel: 734-455-0880
      Email: jaznavorian@clipsclamps.com
      Website: www.clipsclamps.com
Metal forming, progressive dies, four slide, CNC wire forming, tool building, MIG & TIG welding, tapping, riveting, automated assemblies, prototyping & production volumes, engineering services, design services, sales support. (Woman, estab 1954, empl 62, sales $0, cert: WBENC)

6321 Dawson Mfg Co. - Benton Harbor Division
      1042 N Crystal Ave
      Benton Harbor, MI 49022
      Contact: Neil Trivedi VP
      Tel: 269-925-0100
      Email: neil.trivedi@vibracoustic.com.com
      Website: www.dawsonmfg.com
Mfr body mounts, engine mounts, strut mounts, link assemblies & bushings, dist anti-vibration components, rubber injection molding. (As-Pac, estab 1988, empl 90, sales $36,000,000, cert: NMSDC)

6322 DGH Enterprises, Inc. dba K-O Products Co.
1225 Milton St
Benton Harbor, MI 49022
Contact: Barbara Herrold CEO
Tel: 269-925-0657
Email: barbaraherrold@koproducts.com
Website: www.koproducts.com
Metal stampings, welded & fabricated assemblies, electrical & mechanical assemblies, metal hardware, metal truck parts & assemblies, metal stamped components for auto, appliances, off-road equipment, metal welding, mig welding, spot welding. (Woman, estab 1938, empl 28, sales $5,700,000, cert: WBENC)

6323 Gill Industries Inc.
5271 Plainfield Ave
Grand Rapids, MI 49525
Contact: Regina Wilk Sales Acct Mgr
Tel: 616-559-2700
Email: rwilk@gill-industries.com
Website: www.gill-industries.com/
Stamped weldments & structural assemblies, seat, chassis, body & powertrain structural assemblies, folding head restraint & seat mechanisms. (Woman, estab 1964, empl 1923, sales $340,000,000, cert: WBENC)

6324 Globe Tech LLC.
101 Industrial Dr
Plymouth, MI 48170
Contact: Amanda Menchinger President
Tel: - -
Email: mmenchinger@globe-tech.biz
Website: www.globe-tech.biz
Machining, fabrication & welding, metal stamping. (Woman, estab 2009, empl 72, sales , cert: WBENC)

6325 Harbin Steel
440 Burroughs St, Ste 133
Detroit, MI 48202
Contact: Anthony Harbin President
Tel: - -
Email: anthony@harbinsteel.com
Website: www.harbinsteel.com
Miscellaneous/structural steel fabrication & installation. (AA, estab 2016, empl 1, sales , cert: NMSDC)

6326 HDN F&A, Inc. dba F&A Fabricating
104 Arbor St
Battle Creek, MI 49015
Contact: Hiep Nguyen President
Tel: 269-965-3268
Email: hiep.nguyen@fa-fabricating.com
Website: www.fa-fabricating.com
Custom sheet metal fabrication, food grade stainless steel, dist sheet metal, tubing. (As-Pac, estab 1956, empl 25, sales $3,000,000, cert: NMSDC)

6327 I F Metalworks
14009 Achyl
Warren, MI 48313
Contact: Karen Arondoski President
Tel: 586-776-8311
Email: karen@ifmetalworks.com
Website: www.ifmetalworks.com
Welding, fabrication, design, weldments, assemblies, prototype, short & long run, decorative, railings, staircases, ballisters, custom furniture, artistic works, architectural, trailers, foodservice production equipment, racks & repair. (Woman, estab 2002, empl 10, sales $425,000, cert: WBENC)

6328 International Specialty Tube
6600 Mt. Elliott
Detroit, MI 48124
Contact: Jason VanDeVen Sales Mgr
Tel: 313-841-6900
Email: quality@istube.com
Website: www.istube.com
Mfr stainless steel tubing for automotive exhaust. (AA, estab 0, empl , sales $29,000,000, cert: NMSDC)

6329 JLC Group LLC
287 Executive Dr
Troy, MI 48083
Contact: William Chen Dir Ph.D.
Tel: 248-792-3281
Email: wchen@jlcgroupllc.com
Website: www.jlcgroupllc.com
Dist casting parts, forging parts & machine finished parts, plastic injected molds & plastic parts. (Minority, Woman, estab 2010, empl 5, sales , cert: WBENC)

6330 Jorgensen Steel Machining & Fabrication
101 Spires Pkwy
Tekonsha, MI 49092
Contact: Matt Jorgensen President
Tel: 517-767-4600
Email: mjorgensen@jorgensen-usa.com
Website: www.jorgensen-usa.com
Design & manufacture contract machinery & contour formed products for the aviation, space & defense industries. (Nat Ame, estab 2001, empl 26, sales $6,334,000, cert: State, NMSDC)

6331 Midbrook Industrial Washers Inc.
2080 Brooklyn Rd
Jackson, MI 49204
Contact: Rodney Sims Govt & diversity Sales
Tel: 517-787-3481
Email: rsims@midbrookindustrial.com
Website: www.midbrookindustrial.com
Custom sheet metal fabrication. (Woman/AA, As-Pac, estab 2012, empl 70, sales $0, cert: WBENC)

6332 Mintech LLC
PO Box 428
Niles, MI 49120
Contact: Minnie Warren President
Tel: 269-683-4551
Email: minnie@mintechllc.com
Website: www.mintechllc.com
Metal fabrication, stamping, light assembly, sort, vibratory deburring, rollforming. (Woman, estab 0, empl , sales $0, cert: WBENC)

6333 MNP Corporation
44225 Utica Rd
Utica, MI 48317
Contact: Donna DeSantis Dir Special Applications
Tel: 586-254-1320
Email: donna.desantis@mnp.com
Website: www.mnp.com
Mfr Specialty Fasteners & Engineered Cold Formed Components. Heat Treatment, Plating Stampings, Powder Metal, Machining. Fastener Design and Testing, Steel processing, Rod and Wire, Flat roll slitting (Woman, estab 1970, empl 540, sales $160,000,000, cert: WBENC)

6334 Rochester Tube Products, Ltd.
      51366 Fischer Park Dr
      Shelby Township, MI 48316
      Contact: Jennie Preston Dir of Mktg
      Tel: 586-726-4816
      Email: jennie@rochestertube.com
      Website: www.rochestertube.com
Fabricate steel parts; specifically tube. (Woman, estab 1973, empl 25, sales $0, cert: WBENC)

6335 Rose-A-Lee Technologies, Inc
      7448 19 Mile Rd
      Sterling Heights, MI 48314
      Contact: Julie Wood Dir Business Dev
      Tel: 586-799-4555
      Email: jwood@rosealeetechnologies.com
      Website: www.rosealeetechnologies.com
CAD design (surface and solid modeling), stamping, assembly/kitting, tube bending, welding (mig, tig, stud arc), etc. (Woman, estab 2013, empl 2, sales , cert: WBENC)

6336 Santanna Tool &Design LLC
      25880 Commerce Dr 48071
      Madison Hgts, MI 48071
      Contact: Jamilce & Newton President
      Tel: 248-541-3500
      Email: jsnewton@santannatool.com
      Website: www.santannatool.com
Design & mfr conveyors, tooling & welding. (Minority, Woman, estab , empl , sales $1,376,927,385, cert: NMSDC, WBENC)

6337 The Ideal Group
      2525 Clark St
      Detroit, MI 48209
      Contact: Linzie Venegas Sales
      Tel: 313-842-7290
      Email: linzie@idealshield.com
      Website: www.weareideal.com
Architectural & engineering svcs; general contracting & construction mgmt, rigging. Mfr, dist, fabricate & erect structural & misc steel. Patent for "Ideal Shield" Protective Guard Rail System. (Hisp, estab 1979, empl 120, sales $0, cert: NMSDC)

6338 Thompson Marketing, LLC
      15890 Sturgeon CT
      Roseville, MI 48066
      Contact: Derek Thompson President
      Tel: 248-761-6802
      Email: derek@tmsglobalservices.com
      Website: www.tmsglobalservices.com
Mfr shipping racks & fixtures. (AA, estab 1999, empl 7, sales $370,000, cert: NMSDC)

6339 Vari-Form, Inc.
      17199 North Laurel Park, Ste #322
      Livonia, MI 48152
      Contact: Derek W. Ochodnicky Acct Specialist
      Tel: 248-641-2816
      Email: dochodnicky@vari-form.com
      Website: www.vari-form.com
Advanced tube hydro-forming technology, laser cut, assembly & various welding applications, instrument panel beams, radiator enclosures, roof rails & front end structures. (As-Ind, estab 1989, empl 402, sales $0, cert: NMSDC)

6340 W.S Molnar Co. dba SlipNOT Metal Safety Flooring
      2545 Beaufait St
      Detroit, MI 48207
      Contact: Christina Molnar Metrose President
      Tel: 313-923-0400
      Email: info@slipnot.com
      Website: www.slipnot.com
Mfr non slip metal products (Woman, estab , empl , sales $20,700,000, cert: WBENC)

Minnesota

6341 Electrical Builders, Inc.
      2720 1 1/2 St S
      St. Cloud, MN 56301
      Contact: Jessica Netter Ducharme President
      Tel: 320-257-9008
      Email: jnetter@electricalbuilders.com
      Website: www.electricalbuilders.com
Turnkey Substation Construction, Iso Phase and Aluminum Bus Welding (Woman, estab 1974, empl 65, sales $12,500,000, cert: WBENC)

6342 JML Fabrication, LLC
      21054 Chippendale Ct
      Farmington, MN 55024
      Contact: Margo Lackore President
      Tel: 612-444-3025
      Email: margo@jmlfabrication.com
      Website: www.jmlfabrication.com
Aluminum welding, Aluminum Fabrication, Stainless steel welding, Stainless steel fabrication, Steel welding, Steel fabrication, Certified Welding, Bending, Shearing. MIG/TIG welding, Flux core welding, large structural steel fabrication. (Minority, Woman, estab 2004, empl 7, sales $2,400,000, cert: WBENC)

6343 Jones Metal Inc.
      3201 3rd Ave
      Mankato, MN 56001
      Contact: John Clifford Natl Business Devel
      Tel: 507-625-4436
      Email: jclifford@jonesmetalinc.com
      Website: www.jonesmetalinc.com
Metal fabrication, laser technology, water jet, saw, punch presses, press brakes, rollers & machining capabilities. (Woman, estab 1942, empl 100, sales $12,000,000, cert: WBENC)

6344 LAI International, Inc.
      4255 Pheasant Ridge Dr NE #405
      Minneapolis, MN 55449
      Contact: Terri Lambert Dir Sales
      Tel: 480-469-4170
      Email: tlambert@laico.com
      Website: www.laico.com
Cutting-Edge Precision Component Manufacturing. (AA, estab 1979, empl 287, sales $73,113,237, cert: NMSDC)

6345 Wyoming Machine, Inc.
      30680 Forest Blvd
      Stacy, MN 55079
      Contact: Lori Tapani President
      Tel: 651-462-4156
      Email: ltapani@wyomingmachine.com
      Website: www.wyomingmachine.com
Precision metal fabrication: aser cutting, CNC punching, forming & welding. (Woman, estab 1974, empl 65, sales $0, cert: WBENC)

Missouri

6346   Sinclair Industries, Inc.
       1317 Kentucky Ave
       St. Louis, MO 63110
       Contact: Jagdish Hinduja President
       Tel: 314-535-6335
       Email: sinclair.inc@sbcglobal.net
       Website: www.snclr.com
Metal fabrication. (As-Ind, estab 1978, empl 9, sales
$1,200,000, cert: City)

North Carolina

6347   QMF Metal & Electronic Solutions, Inc.
       324 Berry Garden Rd
       Kernersville, NC 27284
       Contact: Raymond Polomski Sales Assoc
       Tel: 336-992-6501
       Email: rpolomski@qmf-usa.com
       Website: www.qmf-usa.com
Custom sheet metal fabrication, punching, forming,
welding, robotic welding, machining, hardware installation, wet and powder coat painting, silk screening,
mechanical & electronic assembly. (Woman, estab 1978,
empl 75, sales $7,000,000, cert: WBENC)

6348   Structural Steel of Carolina, LLC
       1720 Vargrave St
       Winston-Salem, NC 27107
       Contact: Mary Brewer President
       Tel: 336-725-0521
       Email: mbrewer@steelofcarolina.com
       Website: www.steelofcarolina.com
Fabrication & erection of structural & miscellaneous steel.
(Woman, estab 2004, empl 85, sales $20,000,000, cert:
State)

New Jersey

6349   Central Metals, Inc.
       1054 S 2nd St
       Camden, NJ 08103
       Contact: Susan Vilotti President
       Tel: 856-963-5844
       Email: vilotti@aol.com
       Website: www.centralmetals.com
Steel fabrication, structural steel, miscellaneous metals,
ornamental metals, railings, stairs & iron. (Woman, estab
1981, empl 57, sales $29,770,000, cert: WBENC, NWBOC)

6350   Holtec International
       1 Holtec Blvd
       Camden, NJ 08104
       Contact: Jordan Landis Sales & Marketing Mgr
       Tel: 856-797-0900
       Email: j.landis@holte.com
       Website: www.holtecinternational.com
Design & mfr storage systems for wet & dry spent nuclear
fuel, takes, vessels, hoists, cranes. (As-Ind, estab , empl ,
sales $99,000,000, cert: NMSDC)

New York

6351   ASP Industries
       9 Evelyn St
       Rochester, NY 14606
       Contact: Robert Uerkvitz Acct Exec
       Tel: 585-254-9130
       Email: robert@aspindustries.com
       Website: www.aspindustries.com
Sheet metal fabrication, laser, welding, machine.
(Woman, estab 1980, empl 25, sales , cert: State)

6352   Bailey Manufacturing Co., LLC
       10987 Bennett State Rd
       Forestville, NY 14062
       Contact: John Hines President
       Tel: 716-965-2731
       Email: bailey03@netsync.net
       Website: www.baileymfgcollc.com
Metal Stamping, Sheet Metal Fabrication, Welding,
Multi-Part Assemblies, Zinc Plating, Rust Proofing,
Quality Inspection, E-Coat Painting. (AA, estab 2002,
empl 100, sales $8,500,000, cert: NMSDC)

6353   Technical Welding Fabricators LLC
       27 Thatcher St
       Albany, NY 12207
       Contact: Carole Boyer Owner
       Tel: 518-463-2229
       Email: caroleboyer@aol.com
       Website: www.technicalweldingfabricators.com
Metals & structural steel, railings, columns, beams,
repairs. (Woman, estab 2006, empl 5, sales $1,600,000,
cert: State)

Ohio

6354   Armor Metal Group
       4600 Mason-Montgomery Rd
       Mason, OH 45040
       Contact: John Ravana Inside Sales
       Tel: 800-543-7417
       Email: jravana@witt.com
       Website: www.witt.com
Fabrication, burn, grind, machining, lathe, blanchard,
surface, roll, laser, form, weld, paint, blast. (Woman,
estab 1950, empl 250, sales $51,000,000, cert: WBENC)

6355   Aster Industries
       275-299 N Arlington St
       Akron, OH 44305
       Contact: Kaitlyn Oplinger Admin Asst
       Tel: 330-762-7965
       Email: kmoplinger@asterind.com
       Website: www.asterind.com
Custom millwork manufacturing, commercial booth
seating, interior design, stainless steel fabrication, and
full construction management. (Woman, estab 1990,
empl 25, sales $6,000,000, cert: WBENC)

6356   Extol of Ohio, Inc.
       208 Republic St
       Norwalk, OH 44857
       Contact: Andrea Buggele Inside Sales
       Tel: 419-668-2072
       Email: andrea@extolohio.com
       Website: www.extolohio.com
Fabricate & dist thermally efficient, non-wicking rigid
pipe insulation products & accessories. (Woman, estab
1985, empl 50, sales $22,919,925, cert: WBENC)

6357   Fabrication Group LLC
3453 W 140th St
Cleveland, OH 44111
Contact: Patricia Setlock President
Tel: 216-251-1125
Email: patty@fabricationgroup.com
Website: www.fabricationgroup.com
Metal fabrications, welded assemblies, guardrails, hand-rails, bollards, stair railings, cutting, shearing, roll forming, punch presses, sheet metal fabrication equipment. (Woman, estab 2008, empl 10, sales $433,345, cert: WBENC)

6358   Ferragon Corporation
11103 Memphis Ave
Cleveland, OH 44144
Contact: Luis J. Gonzalez Mgr
Tel: 216-671-6161
Email: lgonzalez@ferrousmetalprocessing.com
Website: www.ferrousmetalprocessing.com
Hot roll steel toll processing: pickle, slit, level, shear, decamber & warehousing. (Hisp, estab 1983, empl 144, sales $16,200,000, cert: NMSDC)

6359   Forest City Erectors, Inc.
8200 Boyce Pkwy
Twinsburg, OH 44087
Contact: Eric Swinehart Project Mgr
Tel: - -
Email: eswinehart@forestcityerectors.com
Website: www.forestcityerectors.com
Structural Steel & Steel Erection, Precast erection, Tower crane & personnel hoist erection & dismantle, Blast furnace rebuilds/repairs. (Woman, estab 1960, empl 45, sales $27,500,000, cert: City)

6360   GOJO Industries, Inc.
1 Gojo Plz
Akron, OH 44311
Contact: Kerry Bingham Sr Corporate Accounts Dir
Tel: 330-255-6000
Email: binghamk@gojo.com
Website: www.gojo.com
All Other Miscellaneous Fabricated Metal Product Manufacturing. (Woman, estab 1946, empl 3500, sales $0, cert: WBENC)

6361   Journey Steel, Inc.
7655 Production Dr
Cincinnati, OH 45237
Contact: Barbara Smith President
Tel: 513-731-2930
Email: bsmith@journeysteel.com
Website: www.journeysteel.com/
Remodeling & Expanding: retrofit piping, staircases, overhead walkways. Structural & Mechanical Erector: mechanical devices & assorted equipment supported & erected. (Woman/AA, estab 2009, empl 4, sales $3,900,000, cert: State, NMSDC, WBENC)

6362   KeYAH International Trading, LLC
4655 Urbana Rd
Springfield, OH 45502
Contact: Ramon Vasquez VP
Tel: 937-399-3140
Email: rvasquez@keyahint.com
Website: www.keyahint.com
Die cut, RF weld/sonic weld, automotive interior trim components, sub-assemblies. (Minority, Woman, estab 2000, empl 85, sales $2,000,000, cert: WBENC)

6363   Magni-Power Company
5511 Lincoln Way E
Wooster, OH 44691
Contact: Kim Coblentz New Business Dev Mgr
Tel: 330-264-3637
Email: kcoblentz@magnipower.com
Website: www.magnipower.com
Metal fabrication & stamping: process steel, aluminum, stainless steel, CNC punching, forming, laser cutting, robotic welding, in-house powder coating & assembly. (As-Ind, estab 1948, empl 230, sales $27,000,000, cert: NMSDC)

6364   MCM Ind. Co., Inc.
22901 Millcreek Blvd., Ste 250
Highland Hills, OH 44122
Contact: Gloria Reljanovic Owner
Tel: 216-292-4708
Email: greljanovic@mcmindustries.com
Website: www.mcmindustries.com
Mfr, dist & import finished steel & plastic parts: precision & bicycle chains, non-metal chains, steel ball bearings. (Minority, Woman, estab 1986, empl 50, sales $0, cert: NMSDC)

6365   Middletown Tube Works, Inc.
2201 Trine St
Middletown, OH 45044
Contact: Angela Phillips CEO
Tel: 513-727-0080
Email: aphillips@middletowntube.com
Website: www.middletowntube.com
Mfr as-welded steel tubes for Automotive, Appliance, HVAC and Packaging industries. (Woman, estab 0, empl , sales $0, cert: WBENC)

6366   Mid-West Materials, Inc.
3687 Shepard Rd
Perry, OH 44081
Contact: Scott Dennis Sales Rep
Tel: 440-259-5200
Email: scott.dennis@midwestmaterials.com
Website: www.midwestmaterials.com
Flat rolled steel service center, hot rolled, hot rolled, pickled & oiled & coated steel in commercial quality, high strength-low alloy & low through high carbon chemistries. (Woman, estab 1952, empl 50, sales $50,000,000, cert: State)

6367   Morrison Metalweld Process Corporation
3685 Stutz Dr, Ste 102
Canfield, OH 44406
Contact: Robin Eisenbrei CEO
Tel: 330-702-5188
Email: robin@morrisonmetalweld.com
Website: www.morrisonmetalweld.com
Railroad track & crane rail welding services & products. (Woman, estab 1929, empl 9, sales $0, cert: WBENC)

6368   Shelby Welded Tube
5578 State Route 61 North
Shelby, OH 44875
Contact: Kelly Kleman Sales
Tel: 419-347-1720
Email: kkleman@shelbytube.com
Website: www.shelbytube.com
Dist welded steel tubes. (Woman, estab 1967, empl 81, sales $22,000,000, cert: WBENC)

6369   Thieman Quality Metal Fab, Inc.
       05140 Dicke Rd
       New Bremen, OH 45869
       Contact: Ben Wissman Sales Mgr
       Tel: 419-629-2612
       Email: bwissman@thieman.com
       Website: www.thieman.com
Engineering: AutoCAD, 2000i, Solid Edge & Metamation
CAD/CAM Software, Welding: MIG, TIG, Robotic & Spot
welding, Fabrication: Sawing, Machining, Drilling, Hy Def
Plasma, Turret Punch, Lasers, Press Break. (Woman, estab
1951, empl 90, sales $16,200,000, cert: NWBOC)

6370   Tylok International, Inc.
       1061 E 260th St
       Euclid, OH 44132
       Contact: Michael Palinkas VP Sales
       Tel: 216-261-7310
       Email: mpalinkas@tylok.com
       Website: www.tylok.com
Mfr stainless steel, brass & steel tube fittings, pipe & weld
fittings, ball valves, needle valves, manifolds & double
block & bleed valves. (Woman, estab 1955, empl 75, sales
$8,600,000, cert: WBENC)

Oregon

6371   General Sheet Metal Works, Inc.
       PO Box 1490
       Clackamas, OR 97015
       Contact: Carol Duncan President
       Tel: 503-650-0405
       Email: carol@gsmw.com
       Website: www.gsmw.com
Sheet metal fabrication, installation, design & support.
(Woman, estab 1932, empl 40, sales $7,620,093, cert:
WBENC)

Pennsylvania

6372   Cromedy Construction Corporation
       5702 Newtown Ave
       Philadelphia, PA 19120
       Contact: Bill Cromedy President
       Tel: 215-437-7606
       Email: bcromedy@cromedyconstruction.com
       Website: www.cromedyconstruction.com
HVAC, Sheetmetal (AA, estab 2004, empl 15, sales
$14,000,000, cert: State, NMSDC, 8(a))

6373   Flexospan Steel Buildings, Inc.
       PO Box 515
       Sandy Lake, PA 16145
       Contact: Karla Black Exec Asst
       Tel: 724-376-7221
       Email: karla@flexospan.com
       Website: www.flexospan.com
Mfr metal roofing and siding panels, matching trims,
decking, structural components, custom engineered metal
buildings, as well as complete self storage building
packages. (Woman, estab 1969, empl 44, sales
$10,872,000, cert: WBENC)

6374   General Carbide Corporation
       1151 Garden St
       Greensburg, PA 15601
       Contact: Carrie Gartland Admin Exec
       Tel: 800-245-2465
       Email: sales@generalcarbide.com
       Website: www.generalcarbide.com
Mfr tungsten carbide preforms & blanks used in wear
resistant, cutting & metal forming operations. (Woman,
estab 0, empl , sales $0, cert: WBENC)

6375   Specialty Steel Supply Co., Inc.
       225 Lincoln Hwy
       Fairless Hills, PA 19030
       Contact: Green-Campbell President
       Tel: 215-949-8800
       Email: pat@225steel.com
       Website: www.225steel.com
Dist steel beams, angles shapes & plates, fabricate to
specs & prototypes. (Woman, estab 1993, empl 10, sales
$1,600,000, cert: WBENC)

Puerto Rico

6376   Alonso & Carus Iron Works, Inc.
       PO Box 566
       Cataño, PR 00963
       Contact: Jorge L Ramos, Jr. VP
       Tel: 787-788-1065
       Email: jramosjr@alonsocarus.com
       Website: www.alonsocarus.com
Structural Steel odd-shaped buildings, conventional
buildings, steel bridges. Storage tanks for portable
water, firewater, waste water and fuel oil. (Hisp, estab
1961, empl 135, sales $12,000,000, cert: NMSDC)

6377   RAC Enterprises, Inc.
       Road 1, KM 24.8
       Caguas, PR 00726
       Contact: Vivian Carballo President
       Tel: 787-789-9338
       Email: rac@racsteeldrums.com
       Website: www.racsteeldrums.com
Mfr steel drums, dist plastic, steel & stainless containers, sorbent products, secondary containment: spill
pallets, drain seals. Stormwater management products,
PPE & material handling, monitors. (Hisp, estab 1995,
empl 15, sales $2,300,000, cert: NMSDC)

South Carolina

6378   J.I.T. Manufacturing, Inc.
       428 Oglesby Lane
       Cowpens, SC 29330
       Contact: Dan Hunter Production / Sales Mgr.
       Tel: 864-463-0581
       Email: dan@jitmanufacturing.com
       Website: www.jitmfg.net
Laser cutting, welding, forming, CNC punching, CNC
machines, fabrication, sheetmetal, powdercoating,
pressbrakes, modifications, spot welding, control boxes,
mounting plates, brackets, CAD programing, Cad design.
(Woman, estab 1992, empl 22, sales $2,910,792, cert:
City, WBENC)

6379   Lamar's Fabrication, Inc.
       210 Ashley Circle
       North Augusta, SC 29841
       Contact: Michael Lamar CEO
       Tel: 706-513-1992
       Email: michael.lfab@gmail.com
       Website: www.LamarsFabrication.com
Process Pipe, Structural Steel, Carbon steel, Stainless
steel, Chromemoly, Inconel, Hastelloy, GTAW, SMAW,
FCAW, CNC Plasma cutting, C.A.D. Detailing and Design,
3D Modeling. (AA, estab 2008, empl 2, sales , cert:
State, City, NMSDC)

Tennessee

6380 Manufacturers Industrial Group, LLC
      228 Rush St
      Lexington, TN 38351
      Contact: Andre Gist CEO
      Tel: 731-967-6442
      Email: agist@migllc.com
      Website: www.migllc.com
Metal, fabrication, assembly, structural steel, rebar, concrete, reinforcement, welding, racks, metal containers, formed wire and bent tube. (AA, estab 1998, empl 407, sales $0, cert: State, NMSDC)

Texas

6381 A & A Aero Structures Inc.
      800 Schneider Bldg M
      Cibolo, TX 78108
      Contact: Ronald D Atkins Owner
      Tel: 210-566-3660
      Email: ron@aaaerostructures.com
      Website: www.aaaerostructures.com
Fabricate, assemble & mfr aircraft parts & components. (AA, estab 2007, empl 4, sales , cert: State)

6382 Advanced Turbine Solutions LLC
      15653 N Brentwood
      Channelview, TX 77530
      Contact: Tim Donohue InterNatl Sales Mgr
      Tel: 314-494-1900
      Email: donohuet@atshouston.com
      Website: www.ATSHouston.com
Fabrication, piping, structural & skids, welding, carbon steel to exotic metals. (Minority, estab 2010, empl 12, sales $2,850,000, cert: NMSDC)

6383 GABS LLC
      1011 Regal Row
      Dallas, TX 75247
      Contact: Dot Haymann CEO
      Tel: 972-354-6512
      Email: dhaymann@guard-all.com
      Website: www.guard-all.com
Engineer, design & manufacture steel framed, tension fabric buildings for a multitude of applications. (Woman, estab 2011, empl 45, sales $4,990,000, cert: State, WBENC)

6384 GST Manufacturing, Ltd.
      4201 Janada St
      Haltom City, TX 76117
      Contact: Sharrian Lamberth Owner
      Tel: 817-520-2320
      Email: info@gstmanufacturing.com
      Website: www.gstmanufacturing.com
Metal fabrication, in plant maintenance. (Woman, estab 2000, empl 250, sales $50,800,000, cert: State)

6385 Hanstine LLC
      14027 Memorial Dr, Ste 145
      Houston, TX 77079
      Contact: Shawn Gao Sales Mgr
      Tel: 281-712-1588
      Email: shawn.gao@sorogo.com
      Website: www.sorogo.com
Hardware cloth, chainlink fence, barbed wire, welded mesh, hexagonal wire mesh, field fence, horse fence, yard fence, metal wires, window screens (Minority, Woman, estab 2009, empl 2, sales , cert: WBENC)

6386 Harris Composites, Inc.
      600 Holmes Dr
      Granbury, TX 76048
      Contact: Debra Harris CEO
      Tel: 817-279-9546
      Email: hci@itexas.net
      Website: www.harriscomposites.com
Mfr & produce all size composite parts. (Woman, estab 2000, empl 25, sales $3,500,000, cert: State, WBENC)

6387 Llano River Fence Company, LLC
      11418 Lake June Rd
      Balch Springs, TX 75180
      Contact: Ashanti Smith President
      Tel: 972-286-4316
      Email: asmith@llanoriverfence.com
      Website: www.llanoriverfence.com
Custom iron products: gates, iron doors, handrails, & puppy panels, fencing, automatic gates installation & automatic gate operator maintenance. (Woman/AA, estab 2006, empl 13, sales $1,250,000, cert: State)

6388 Magni-Fab Southwest Company
      PO Box 578
      Howe, TX 75459
      Contact: Wayne Swineford Dir Sales/Marketing
      Tel: 903-532-5533
      Email: wswineford@mfsw.net
      Website: www.magnifab.com
Sheet metal fabrication, shearing, CNC punching, laser cutting, stamping, forming, sawing, spot welding, arc welding, robotic welding, powder coating. (As-Pac, estab 1971, empl 105, sales $10,350,000, cert: NMSDC)

6389 MagRabbit-Alamo Iron Works, LLC
      PO Box 2341
      San Antonio, TX 78298
      Contact: Wayne Dennis Diversity Coord
      Tel: 210-704-8520
      Email: wdennis@aiwnet.com
      Website: www.magrabbit-aiw.com
Dist industrial supplies, steel service & fabrication, hand & power tools, equipment repair & installation, logistics, transportation & freight forwarding. (As-Pac, estab 2004, empl 150, sales , cert: NMSDC)

6390 Quality Fabrication & Design
      955 Freeport Pkwy Ste 400
      Coppell, TX 75019
      Contact: Alex Pier President
      Tel: 972-304-3266
      Email: alexpier@quality-fabrication.com
      Website: www.quality-fabrication.com
Mfr custom stainless steel & mild steel equipment: conveyors, drags, belts & bucket, structural steel platforms, waterjet cutting & complete food processing lines. (Hisp, estab 1987, empl 65, sales $6,000,000, cert: State, NMSDC)

6391 Texas Finishing Company
      PO Box 59445
      Dallas, TX 75229
      Contact: Carolyn Beard President
      Tel: 972-416-2961
      Email: cbeard@texasfinishing.com
      Website: www.texasfinishing.com
Paint application & custom metal fabrication. (Woman, estab 1982, empl 45, sales , cert: State, WBENC)

Virginia

6392   Metal Tech Inc.
       2629 Richard Ave NE
       Roanoke, VA 24012
       Contact: Natasha Crowder Project estimator
       Tel: 540-798-4193
       Email: metaltech@cox.net
       Website: www.metaltechincorporated.com
Custom metal fabrication: sandblasting, punching, machine cutting, CNC plasma cutting, water jet cutting, pipe bending, ornamental bender machine, surface preparation & coating. (Woman, estab 1996, empl 2, sales $150,000, cert: State)

6393   Shickel Corporation
       115 Dry River Rd
       Bridgewater, VA 22812
       Contact: Don Crawford Sales Mgr
       Tel: 540-828-2536
       Email: donc@shickel.com
       Website: www.shickel.com
Custom metal fabricating, engineering, design, project management, welding, fabrication, precision machining, finishing & installation services. (Woman, estab 1938, empl 80, sales $11,200,000, cert: State)

6394   Valley Industrial Piping, Inc.
       P O Box 1751
       Waynesboro, VA 22980
       Contact: Michelle Carter President
       Tel: 540-942-4469
       Email: michelle@valleypipes.com
       Website: www.valleypipes.com
Industrial maintenance, fabricate & install process skid systems, pressure vessels, tank installation & repair, structural steel, carbon & stainless steel platforms, mezzanines, ladders & stairways, piping, in-line instrumentation & equipment installation (Woman, estab 2004, empl 10, sales $984,906, cert: State, WBENC)

Vermont

6395   Vermont Precision Tools, Inc.
       10 Precision Ln
       Swanton, VT 05488
       Contact: Monica Greene President
       Tel: 802-868-4246
       Email: mgreene@vermontprecisiontools.com
       Website: www.vermontprecisiontools.com
Mfr high quality precision ground medical burr blanks for the OEM medical industry. (Woman, estab 1968, empl 190, sales $32,527,681, cert: WBENC)

Washington

6396   JIT Manufacturing
       19510 144th Ave NE, Ste E 7
       Woodinville, WA 98072
       Contact: Duane Parrish Sales Mgr
       Tel: 425-487-0672
       Email: duanep@jit-mfg.com
       Website: www.jit-mfg.com
Aerospace Sheet Metal Manufacturing, complete parts, Punching, Laser, Bending, Forming, Hardware & Assembly, Finish, Chem Treat, Paint, Primer. (Woman, estab 1985, empl 60, sales $0, cert: State)

Wisconsin

6397   Church Metal Spinning Company
       5050 N 124th St
       Milwaukee, WI 53225
       Contact: Brenda Birno President
       Tel: 414-461-6460
       Email: markv@churchmetal.com
       Website: www.churchmetal.com
Metal fabrications including metal stampings, metal spun, laser cut, press brake parts. Also, complete assembly and welding of multi-part components. (Woman, estab 1944, empl 30, sales $6,600,000, cert: State)

6398   Creative CNC LLC
       16620 W Rogers Dr
       New Berlin, WI 53151
       Contact: Janet Murphy President
       Tel: 262-347-3939
       Email: jmurphy@creativecnc.net
       Website: www.creativecnc.net/
Mfr metal parts: aerospace, medical, automotive, turbomachinery, etc. (Woman, estab 2010, empl 3, sales , cert: WBENC)

6399   Metal-Era, Inc.
       1600 Airport Rd
       Waukesha, WI 53188
       Contact: Jody Delie Channel Marketing Mgr
       Tel: 800-373-9156
       Email: info@metalera.com
       Website: www.metalera.com
Mfr perimeter edge metal for the low sloped commercial roofing industry. (Hisp, estab 1980, empl 148, sales $36,700,000, cert: State, NMSDC)

6400   Ridgway LLC dba The Price Erecting Co.
       10910 W Lapham St
       Milwaukee, WI 53214
       Contact: Fred Quilling Estimator
       Tel: 414-778-0300
       Email: fquilling@priceerecting.com
       Website: www.priceerecting.com
Equipment installation & removal, steel erection, fabrication & machining. (Minority, estab , empl 40, sales $9,000,000, cert: State)

6401   Safeway Sling USA, Inc.
       6209 Industrial Ct
       Greendale, WI 53129
       Contact: Susan Szymczak President
       Tel: 414-421-7303
       Email: sales@safewaysling.com
       Website: www.safewaysling.com
Mfr nylon & polyester web lifting slings, polyester round slings, alloy chain slings, wire rope slings, metal mesh slings & tie down assemblies. (Woman, estab 1980, empl 36, sales $6,800,000, cert: WBENC)

METAL STAMPING
Services include forming, welding, tapping, tooling, tube fabrication and bending, etc. (Also see six other METAL categories). NAICS Code 33

California

6402   Proformance Manufacturing, Inc.
1922 Elise Circle
Corona, CA 92879
Contact: Tim Borth Technical Sales Mgr
Tel: 951-279-1230
Email: tborth@proformancemfg.com
Website: www.proformancemfg.com
Precision metal stampings, deep draw parts & machined components & parts. Components formed from flat sheet stock are produced in mechanical & hydraulic presses. (Hisp, estab 1987, empl 21, sales $2,200,000, cert: NMSDC)

6403   Tanfel
1945 Camino Vida Roble, Ste J
Carlsbad, CA 92008
Contact: Greg Lange Owner
Tel: 760-720-9632
Email: glange@tanfel.com
Website: www.tanfel.com
Custom metal parts: stamping, extrusion, casting, metal injection molding, machining, turning, prototype to large production with warehousing capabilities. (Hisp, estab 2008, empl 5, sales , cert: NMSDC)

Connecticut

6404   Hylie Products, Inc.
669 Straits Tpke
Watertown, CT 06795
Contact: Bill Thompson CEO
Tel: 860-274-5447
Email: donna@hylie.com
Website: www.hylie.com
Mfr high-volume, customer-specific, high-precision, quality-critical, metal stampings & progressively drawn eyelets, four-slide stamped & formed parts. (Woman, estab 1963, empl 17, sales $2,500,000, cert: WBENC)

6405   WCES, Inc.
225 S Leonard St
Waterbury, CT 06708
Contact:
Tel: 203-573-1325
Email: sales@waterburycontract.com
Website: www.waterburycontract.com
Deep drawn eyelets & metal stampings, die design & manufacture, long run production, assembly, finishing & plating. (Woman, estab , empl , sales , cert: WBENC)

Georgia

6406   Dixien LLC
5286 Circle Dr
Lake City, GA 30260
Contact: Alex Garcia VP Mktg
Tel: 404-366-7427
Email: agarcia@dixien.com
Website: www.dixien.com
Stamping 100 ton to 1000 ton, welded sub-assemblies, tooling, plastic injection molding, blow molding & vaccum forming. (Hisp, estab 1961, empl 400, sales $25,000,000, cert: NMSDC)

Illinois

6407   Altak Inc.
250 Covington Dr
Bloomingdale, IL 60108
Contact: Steve Janas Sales Mgr
Tel: 630-622-0300
Email: rtakayama@arktechno.com
Website: www.altakinc.com
Wire Harness manufacturing, Switch Assembly manufacturing, Spring manufacturing, Stampings - 30 to 800 ton, Wire Forms, IATF 16949 and ISO 9001 certified. (As-Pac, estab 1980, empl 400, sales $37,000,000, cert: NMSDC)

6408   North Star Stamping & Tool, Inc.
1264 Industrial Dr
Lake in the Hills, IL 60156
Contact: Catherine O'Brien
Tel: 847-658-9400
Email: nstar9400@aol.com
Website: www.northstarstampingandtool.com
Metal stamping & assembly: 32 ton press to 200 ton press. (Woman, estab 1993, empl 9, sales , cert: WBENC)

6409   Reliable Machine Company
1327 10th Ave
Rockford, IL 61104
Contact: Gloria Pernacciaro CEO
Tel: 815-968-8803
Email: gloriap@reliablemachine.com
Website: www.reliablemachine.com
Metal Stampings, Part Production Capabilities: Deep draw up to 5 inches, Flat stampings, Stampings with multiple geometric forms, Secondary operations (piercing, staking, trimming and forming). (Woman, estab 1921, empl 40, sales $8,000,000, cert: WBENC)

Indiana

6410   Lacay Fabrication and Mfg Inc.
52941 Glenview Dr
Elkhart, IN 46514
Contact: Ann Filley President
Tel: 574-288-4678
Email: ann@lacayfab.com
Website: www.lacayfab.com
Mfr material handling racks, Baskets, Industrial & Production Welding, Machining, Robotic Welding, Stamping, Custom Fabrication, Prototyping. (Woman, estab 1975, empl 70, sales , cert: WBENC)

Kentucky

6411 Lincoln Manufacturing USA, LLC
102 Industrial Park Dr
Stanford, KY 40484
Contact: Tetsuya Hatta President
Tel: 606-365-3016
Email: blunsford@lincolnmfg.com
Website: www.lincolnmfg.com
Metal stamping services. (As-Pac, estab 1996, empl 150, sales $24,000,000, cert: State)

Massachusetts

6412 Springfield Spring
311 Shaker Rd
Longmeadow, MA 01028
Contact: Norman Rodriques President
Tel: 413-525-6837
Email: pat@springfieldspring.com
Website: www.springfieldspring.com
Mfr precision engineered compression springs, torsion springs, extension springs, wire forms, fourslide-produced stampings, assemblies. (Hisp, estab 1942, empl 39, sales $7,200,000, cert: NMSDC)

Michigan

6413 Allied Technology Inc.
6830 Metro Plex Dr
Romulus, MI 48174
Contact: Annie Shen President
Tel: 734-728-6688
Email: ati.purchasing@alliedtech-eng.com
Website: www.alliedtech-eng.com
Castings, forgings, cold forming products, stampings and screw machine products. (As-Pac, estab 1999, empl 12, sales $6,000,000, cert: NMSDC)

6414 Apex Spring & Stamping
11420 First Ave
Grand Rapids, MI 49544
Contact: Doug Furness Sales/Eng Mgr
Tel: 616-453-5463
Email: djf@apexspring.com
Website: www.apexspring.com
4 slide & vertislide, CNC winders, stamping presse to 110 ton & various assembly equipment, in-house tool room, proto-type capability. (Minority, estab 1977, empl 40, sales $12,000,000, cert: NMSDC)

6415 Atlas Tool Inc.
29880 Groesbeck Hwy
Roseville, MI 48066
Contact: Douglas Flanagan Business Devel Mgr
Tel: 586-778-3570
Email: doug@atlastool.com
Website: www.atlastool.com
Stamping dies, service parts production, prototype parts, machining, engineering, die repair. (Woman, estab 1962, empl 200, sales , cert: WBENC)

6416 Delaco Steel Corporation
8111 Tireman, Ste 1
Dearborn, MI 48126
Contact: Michael Roualet VP Quality
Tel: 313-491-1200
Email: mike.roualet@delacosteel.com
Website: www.delacosteel.com
Dist & process steel & aluminum. Blanking, warehousing, slitting, stampings, etc. (Minority, Woman, estab 1974, empl 650, sales , cert: NMSDC, WBENC)

6417 DGH Enterprises, Inc. dba K-O Products Co.
1225 Milton St
Benton Harbor, MI 49022
Contact: Barbara Herrold CEO
Tel: 269-925-0657
Email: barbaraherrold@koproducts.com
Website: www.koproducts.com
Metal stampings, welded & fabricated assemblies, electrical & mechanical assemblies, metal hardware, metal truck parts & assemblies, metal stamped components for auto, appliances, off-road equipment, metal welding, mig welding, spot welding. (Woman, estab 1938, empl 28, sales $5,700,000, cert: WBENC)

6418 Die Cad Group
3258 Clear Vista Court NE
Grand Rapids, MI 49525
Contact: Bobbie Blanton President
Tel: 616-365-2454
Email: bobbie@diecadgroup.com
Website: www.diecadgroup.com
Product & process simulation, tool & die design, mold design, special purpose machine design, transfer press simulation, die details sourcing, metal stamping die design, metal stamping process development, stamped parts formation. (Woman, estab 1995, empl 41, sales $8,150,746, cert: WBENC)

6419 GK Tech, LLC
3331 W Big Beaver Rd Ste 106
Troy, MI 48084
Contact: Kelly Choi
Tel: 248-494-1960
Email: kellychoi@gktechusa.com
Website: www.gktechllc.com
Marketing specialist, consulting, business development, forging, die-casting, stamping, spring, magnesium pulley, rubber bushing, fasteners, machining, plastic injection molding. (Minority, Woman, estab 2015, empl 3, sales , cert: NMSDC)

6420 Globe Tech LLC.
101 Industrial Dr
Plymouth, MI 48170
Contact: Amanda Menchinger President
Tel: 734-656-2200
Email: mmenchinger@globe-tech.biz
Website: www.globe-tech.biz
Machining, fabrication & welding, metal stamping. (Woman, estab 2009, empl 72, sales , cert: WBENC)

6421 Lapeer Metal Stamping Companies, Inc.
930 S Saginaw St
Lapeer, MI 48446
Contact: Joe Wierbicki VP Sales
Tel: 810-664-8588
Email: jwierbicki@lapeermetal.com
Website: www.lapeermetal.com
Mfr metal stampings & assemblies: seat frame assemblies, dash panels assemblies, heat shields, fuel tank straps, pedals, brake, clutch, latches & hinges, crossmembers, air bag components & structural body components. (Hisp, estab 1960, empl 500, sales $101,781,836, cert: NMSDC)

6422 Lucerne International
40 Corporate Dr
Auburn Hills, MI 48326
Contact: Karen Ryan Finance Mgr
Tel: 248-674-7210
Email: kryan@lucerneintl.com
Website: www.lucerneintl.com
Advanced metal forming components & assemblies, body structures, chassis systems & powertrain systems. Mfg aluminum & steel forgings, stampings, aluminum & zinc die castings & steel. (Woman, estab 1993, empl 58, sales , cert: WBENC)

6423 McKechnie Vehicle Components
27087 Gratiot Ave, 2 Fl
Roseville, MI 48066
Contact: Linda Torakis President
Tel: 586-491-2622
Email: ltorakis@mvcusa.com
Website: www.mvcusa.com
Mfr decorative trim products: nickel chrome plating on plastic and stainless surfaces, plastic injection molding, metal stamping, base and clear coat painting and assembly. (Woman, estab 0, empl , sales , cert: WBENC)

6424 Metalbuilt LLC
50171 E Russell Schmidt
Chesterfield, MI 48051
Contact: Don Wood
Tel: 586-786-9106
Email: dwood@metalbuiltllc.com
Website: www.metalbuiltllc.com
Prototype Stampings, Die development, Laser Cutting, engineering simulation, Short run production. (Woman, estab 2006, empl 35, sales $6,050,000, cert: WBENC)

6425 Mico Industries, Inc.
2929 32nd St SE
Kentwood, MI 49512
Contact: Tracy DeKlein VP Technical Sales
Tel: 616-245-6426
Email: tdeklein@micoind.com
Website: www.micoindustries.com
Mfr metal stampings, welding, assemblies. (Hisp, estab 1983, empl 75, sales $12,000,000, cert: NMSDC)

6426 MNP Corporation
44225 Utica Rd
Utica, MI 48317
Contact: Donna DeSantis Dir Special Applications
Tel: 586-254-1320
Email: donna.desantis@mnp.com
Website: www.mnp.com
Mfr Specialty Fasteners & Engineered Cold Formed Components. Heat Treatment, Plating Stampings, Powder Metal, Machining. Fastener Design and Testing, Steel processing, Rod and Wire, Flat roll slitting (Woman, estab 1970, empl 540, sales $160,000,000, cert: WBENC)

6427 Motor City Stamping
47783 N Gratiot Ave
Chesterfield Twp, MI 48051
Contact: Paul Lachowicz Controller
Tel: 586-949-8420
Email: plachowicz@mcstamp.com
Website: www.mcstamp.com
Medium stampings & multi-welded assemblies. (Minority, Woman, estab 1969, empl 350, sales $48,000,000, cert: WBENC)

6428 Proos Manufacturing, Inc.
1037 Michigan St NE
Grand Rapids, MI 49503
Contact: Amy Engelsman CEO
Tel: 616-454-5622
Email: aengelsman@proos.com
Website: www.proos.com
Metal stampings & assemblies. (Woman, estab , empl , sales , cert: WBENC)

6429 PTM Corporation
6560 Bethuy
Fair Haven, MI 48023
Contact: Nicole Robinson Sales
Tel: 248-670-2650
Email: nrobinson@ptmcorporation.com
Website: www.ptmcorporation.com
Metal stamping, production up to 600 ton, prototype/low volume up to 1000 ton, tool design & build, laser, EDM, CNC, welding & assemblies. (Woman, estab 1972, empl 196, sales $60,000,000, cert: WBENC)

6430 Rose-A-Lee Technologies, Inc
7448 19 Mile Rd
Sterling Heights, MI 48314
Contact: Julie Wood Dir Business Dev
Tel: 586-799-4555
Email: jwood@rosealeetechnologies.com
Website: www.rosealeetechnologies.com
CAD design (surface and solid modeling), stamping, assembly/kitting, tube bending, welding (mig, tig, stud arc), etc. (Woman, estab 2013, empl 2, sales , cert: WBENC)

6431 Roth-Williams Industries Inc. dba Lunar Industries
34335 Groesbeck Hwy
Clinton Township, MI 48035
Contact: Patricia Williams President
Tel: 586-792-0090
Email: pat@lunarind.com
Website: www.lunarind.com
Design & mfr custom tooling, fixtures, gages, stamping dies, prototype parts & stamped metal parts. (Woman, estab 1966, empl 9, sales $670,000, cert: NWBOC)

6432 Sequoia Tool
44831 N Groesbeck Hwy
Clinton Township, MI 48036
Contact: James Coates Acct Mgr
Tel: 586-463-4400
Email: bcoates@sequoiatool.net
Website: www.sequoiatool.net
Mfr prototype sheet metal stampings & assemblies, low volume production and short run svcs. (Nat Ame, estab 1988, empl 65, sales $10,000,000, cert: NMSDC)

Minnesota

6433 Bokers Inc.
3104 Snelling Ave
Minneapolis, MN 55406
Contact: Linda Demma CFO
Tel: 800-448-7492
Email: ldemma@bokers.com
Website: www.bokers.com
Mfr precision metallic & non-metallic stampings & washers. (Woman/AA, estab , empl 110, sales , cert: WBENC)

6434 Top Tool Company
3100 84th Lane Northeast
Blaine, MN 55449
Contact: Duane Kari Sales Mgr
Tel: 763-786-0030
Email: dakari@toptool.com
Website: www.toptool.com
Dies, precision metal stampings & wire EDM, exotic & precious metals, platinum, iridium, titanium, MP35N, copper alloys, phos bronze, gold & silver plating. (Woman, estab 1966, empl 30, sales $4,427,000, cert: State)

Missouri

6435 Thiel Tool & Engineering Co., Inc.
4622 Bulwer Ave
St. Louis, MO 63147
Contact: Gary Shamel Sales Mgr
Tel: 314-241-6121
Email: gshamel@thieltool.com
Website: www.thieltool.com
Automotive stampings & sub-assemblies. (Woman, estab 1945, empl 42, sales $10,000,000, cert: WBENC)

New York

6436 Bailey Manufacturing Co., LLC
10987 Bennett State Rd
Forestville, NY 14062
Contact: John Hines President
Tel: 716-965-2731
Email: bailey03@netsync.net
Website: www.baileymfgcollc.com
Metal Stamping, Sheet Metal Fabrication, Welding, Multi-Part Assemblies, Zinc Plating, Rust Proofing, Quality Inspection, E-Coat Painting. (AA, estab 2002, empl 100, sales $8,500,000, cert: NMSDC)

6437 Cannon Industries, Inc.
525 Lee Rd
Rochester, NY 14606
Contact: Reggie Cannon President
Tel: 585-254-8080
Email: rcannon@cannonind.com
Website: www.cannonind.com
Sheet metal fabrication, welding fabrication, laser & plasma cutting, metal stamping, CNC machining & turning, mechanical assembly, spot welding. (AA, estab 1979, empl 104, sales $16,000,000, cert: NMSDC)

Ohio

6438 Die-Mension Corporation
3020 Nationwide Pkwy
Brunswick, OH 44212
Contact: Karen Thompson President
Tel: 330-273-5872
Email: karen@diemension.com
Website: www.diemension.com
Mfr & design precision progressive die & metal stampings. (Woman, estab 1985, empl 8, sales $1,500,000, cert: WBENC)

6439 GB Manufacturing Company
100 Adams St
Delta, OH 43515
Contact: Teresa Elling Sales
Tel: 419-822-5323
Email: apetree@gbmfg.com
Website: www.gbmfg.com
Stamping, laser blanking, fabrication & assembly, tool making, robotic & hand welding, spot welding, press braking, productin machining, prototyping. (Minority, estab 1975, empl 85, sales $24,500,000, cert: NMSDC)

6440 Green Rock Lighting, LLC
3175 W 33rd St
Cleveland, OH 44109
Contact: Tina Haddad CEO
Tel: 216-651-6446
Email: thaddad@greenrocklighting.com
Website: www.greenrocklighting.com
Laser cutting, wire bending & forming, press brake, spinning, stamping, mig, tig & stick welding, spot welding, machining, destructive & non-destructive testing, packaging & assembly. (Woman, estab 2011, empl 20, sales , cert: State, WBENC)

6441 Hamlin Acquisition, LLC dba Hamlin Steel Products
2741 Wingate Ave
Akron, OH 44314
Contact: Lal Tekchandani President
Tel: 330-753-7791
Email: jkunczt@hnmetalstamping.com
Website: www.hamlinsteel.com
Small to medium size metal stampings, assembly & robotic welding capabilities. (As-Ind, estab 1953, empl 95, sales $15,000,000, cert: NMSDC)

6442 Hamlin Newco, LLC
2741 Wingate Ave
Akron, OH 44314
Contact: Rick Sadd Sales Mgr
Tel: 216-924-5449
Email: ricksadd@gmail.com
Website: www.hnmetalstamping.com/
Metal stampings & welded assemblies with presses up to 800 tons for the automotive industry. (As-Pac, estab 1945, empl 105, sales $16,000,000, cert: NMSDC)

6443   Magni-Power Company
5511 Lincoln Way E
Wooster, OH 44691
Contact: Kim Coblentz New Business Dev Mgr
Tel: 330-264-3637
Email: kcoblentz@magnipower.com
Website: www.magnipower.com
Metal fabrication & stamping: process steel, aluminum, stainless steel, CNC punching, forming, laser cutting, robotic welding, in-house powder coating & assembly. (As-Ind, estab 1948, empl 230, sales $27,000,000, cert: NMSDC)

6444   Mohr Stamping, Inc.
22038 Fairgrounds Rd
Wellington, OH 44090
Contact: Amber Mohrman CEO
Tel: 440-647-4316
Email: sales@mohrstamping.com
Website: www.mohrstamping.com
Metal Stampings, Die design and Build, Assembly. (Woman, estab 1967, empl 25, sales $4,000,000, cert: WBENC)

6445   Select Industries Corp
60 Heid Ave
Dayton, OH 45404
Contact: Timothy Gonyeau Corp Acct Mgr
Tel: 586-337-1006
Email: tgonyeau@select.org
Website: www.select.org
TC clutch & damper assemblies; stamped components; stamped steel synchronizer cores & cone sets, 3-pin synchronizer rings with Gylon friction material for the heavy truck market. (Woman, estab 1970, empl 130, sales $35,400,000, cert: WBENC)

6446   Tech-Matic Industries, Inc.
17941 Englewood Dr
Middleburg Heights, OH 44130
Contact: Kathleen Byrnes President
Tel: 440-826-3191
Email: kbyrnes@tc-tm.com
Website: www.tc-tm.com
Metal stamping for automotive industry. (Woman, estab 1985, empl 9, sales $4,000,000, cert: WBENC)

6447   Wrena, LLC dba Angstrom-USA, LLC
265 Lightner Rd
Tipp City, OH 45371
Contact: Nagesh Palakurthi CEO
Tel: 937-667-4403
Email: pyenger@wrenallc.com
Website: www.angstrom-usa.com
Stampings, tubular products, machining, welding, robotic welding, steel forgings (Warm & Cold), aluminum forgings, assemblies, plastic injection molding, needle bearings, starter assemblies (As-Pac, estab 2011, empl 46, sales , cert: NMSDC)

6448   Zip Tool & Die Inc.
12200 Sprecher Ave
Cleveland, OH 44135
Contact: Victor De Leaon CEO
Tel: 216-267-1117
Email: vdeleon@tritonduro.com
Website: www.ziptool.com
Engineering, Prototyping, Metal Forming, Metal Stamping & Tool & Die solutions. (Hisp, estab 1968, empl 10, sales $650,000, cert: NMSDC)

Pennsylvania

6449   Spalding Automotive, Inc.
1011 Cedar Ave
Croydon, PA 19021
Contact: Vincent Florio Business Devel
Tel: 215-826-4061
Email: vflorio@spaldingautomotive.com
Website: www.spaldingautomotive.com
Metal stampings, roll form components, welding, mechanical assemblies & design & build tooling. (Hisp, estab 1987, empl 75, sales $18,518,000, cert: NMSDC)

6450   Tottser Tool and Manufacturing
1630 Republic Rd
Huntingdon Valley, PA 19006
Contact: Linda Macht President
Tel: 215-357-7600
Email: lmacht@tottser.com
Website: www.tottser.com
Metal stampings, tool & die. (Woman, estab 0, empl , sales , cert: WBENC)

Wisconsin

6451   Church Metal Spinning Company
5050 N 124th St
Milwaukee, WI 53225
Contact: Brenda Birno President
Tel: 414-461-6460
Email: markv@churchmetal.com
Website: www.churchmetal.com
Metal fabrications including metal stampings, metal spun, laser cut, press brake parts. Also, complete assembly and welding of multi-part components. (Woman, estab 1944, empl 30, sales $6,600,000, cert: State)

6452   Universal Die & Stampings
735 15th St
Prairie du Sac, WI 53555
Contact: Karl Andersson Sales Mgr
Tel: 608-643-2477
Email: kanders@unidie.com
Website: www.unidie.com
Precision, high volume metal stamping, full tooling. (Woman, estab 1967, empl 32, sales $6,000,000, cert: City)

METAL, GENERAL MACHINING
Job shops, prototypes, short and long run production work. Tool and dies, jigs and fixtures, electromechanical assemblies, etc. (Also see six other METAL categories). NAICS Code 33

Alabama

6453 Theonics Inc.
12525 Memorial Pkwy SW
Huntsville, AL 35803
Contact: Shelley Coxwell President
Tel: 256-885-3500
Email: shelley.coxwell@theonicsinc.com
Website: www.theonicsinc.com
Precision machining, CMM inspection & assembly of complex hardware. (Woman, estab 2012, empl 31, sales $1,300,000, cert: WBENC)

Arizona

6454 Conway Machine, Inc.
192 Commerce Rd
Conway, AR 72032
Contact: Anthony Davis President
Tel: 501-327-1311
Email: tonyd@conwaymachine.com
Website: www.ConwayMachine.com
Precision milling & turning machining. (Woman, estab 1970, empl 25, sales $2,400,000, cert: WBENC)

6455 Pivot Manufacturing
2602 E Magnolia
Phoenix, AZ 85034
Contact: Steve Macias President
Tel: 602-306-2923
Email: smacias@klmanufacturing.com
Website: www.pivotmfg.com
CNC machining: metals & plastics. (Hisp, estab 2000, empl 17, sales $36,000,010, cert: NMSDC)

6456 State Technology & Manufacturing
2555 E University Dr
Phoenix, AZ 85034
Contact: Ruben Cadena CEO
Tel: 602-275-0990
Email: ruben@azsip.com
Website: www.azsip.com
Machinng, mill, lathe, CNC, welding, fabricating, dist steel, copper, brass, bronze, stainless steel, aluminum. (Hisp, estab 2003, empl 21, sales $3,000,000, cert: State, City, NMSDC)

California

6457 3D Machine Company, Inc.
4790 E Wesley Dr
Anaheim, CA 92807
Contact: Maria Falcusan President
Tel: 714-777-8985
Email: costel@3dmachineco.com
Website: www.3dmachineco.com
CNC machining, 5-axis CNC capability, CAD/CAM software, precision-machined parts & assemblies. (Woman, estab 1996, empl 35, sales , cert: CPUC)

6458 Acutek US
1488 E Valencia Dr
Fullerton, CA 92831
Contact: Charley Yoo Owner
Tel: 714-278-0912
Email: cyoo@acutekus.com
Website: www.acutekus.com
CNC milling, turning: aluminum, steel, titanium, copper, brass. 3 & 4 axis programming tooling fixtures, electronic file transfer. (As-Pac, estab 2003, empl 60, sales $10,700,000, cert: CPUC)

6459 Aranda Tooling, Inc.
15301 Springdale St
Huntington Beach, CA 92649
Contact: Gerrard Connolly GM
Tel: 714-379-6565
Email: gerrard.connolly@arandatooling.com
Website: www.arandatooling.com
Medium to high production metal stamping, assembly, robotic welding, tooling, EDM, prototypes. (Hisp, estab 1975, empl 125, sales , cert: NMSDC)

6460 Azachorok Contract Services LLC
320 Grand Cypress Ave Ste 502
Palmdale, CA 93551
Contact: Gene Souza Mgr
Tel: 661-951-6566
Email: gsouza@azachorok.com
Website: www.azcsllc.com
Precision CNC machining & turnining, aircraft structures, machined housings, castings, aluminum, steel, titanium, copper, brass etc. (Nat Ame, estab 1998, empl 12, sales $550,000, cert: 8(a), SDB)

6461 Bay Tank and Boiler Works
825 W 14th St
Eureka, CA 95501
Contact: Amandy Massey Office Mgr
Tel: 707-443-0934
Email: info@btmetals.com
Website: www.baytankandboilerworks.com
Carbon Steel Products Stainless Steel Products Aluminum Products Rebar Industrial Fasteners (Stock and Custom) We specialize in Made in the USA Certified Welding Drilling, Milling, Plasma Cutting, Oxy Fuel Cutting, laser Forming, Press (Woman, estab 1956, empl 7, sales $500,000, cert: CPUC, WBENC)

6462 Bishop-Wisecarver Corporation
2104 Martin Way
Pittsburg, CA 94565
Contact: Barbara Williams Supplier Diversity Admin
Tel: 888-580-8272
Email: bwilliams@bwc.com
Website: www.bwc.com
Mfr linear & rotary motion components, custom engineering services, bearings, vee guide wheels, linear guides, linear actuator, custom machine shop, XYZ systems, gantry, rotary tables, custom assembly, linear slides, linear bearing, dualvee. (Woman, estab 1950, empl 64, sales $21,000,000, cert: WBENC)

6463   Dinucci Corporation
1057 Shary Cir
Concord, CA 94518
Contact: Gabriela Dinucci COO
Tel: 925-798-3946
Email: gabriela@dinuccicorp.com
Website: www.dinuccicorp.com
Machine shop; computerized mfg & precision prototypes. (Minority, Woman, estab 1978, empl 25, sales $4,227,662, cert: NMSDC)

6464   Fabtronics, Inc.
5026 Calmview Ave
Baldwin Park, CA 91706
Contact: David K. Thompson VP Operations
Tel: 626-962-3293
Email: contact@fabtronics.com
Website: www.fabtronics.com
Precision sheet metal mfg, CNC turret punching, spot welding, enclosures, tubular frame weldments, skins & chassis. (Hisp, estab 1976, empl 14, sales $3,500,000, cert: NMSDC)

6465   Hunter Hawk, Inc.
1842 Taft St
Concord, CA 94521
Contact: Sandy Hunter President
Tel: 925-798-4950
Email: sandy@hunterhawk.com
Website: www.hunterhawk.com
Precision mechanical components, fabrication, reverse engineering, documentation, critical inventory & equipment boxes. (Woman, estab 1994, empl 4, sales $1,886,100, cert: State, CPUC, WBENC)

6466   Infinity Precision Inc.
6919 Eton Ave
Canoga Park, CA 91303
Contact: President
Tel: 818-447-3008
Email: sales@ipinc-usa.com
Website: www.ipinc-usa.com
Hydroforming, Machined parts per print, CAD/CAM/ CNC Machining, 5-Axiss Water Jet Cutting, Honing, Sheet Metal Fabrication (Woman, estab 1996, empl 19, sales $2,338,000, cert: WBENC)

6467   Ingels Engineering Inc.
1828 Evergreen St
Duarte, CA 91010
Contact: Enilde Ingels VP
Tel: 626-256-1967
Email: eeemachineshop@earthlink.net
Website: www.ingelsengineeringservices.com
Machining & engineering consulting services, specialized medical devices, prototype works, short run productions in Stainless Steel, Aluminum, Delrin, Brass, Copper or plastics. (Minority, Woman, estab 1997, empl 7, sales $230,000, cert: State, City)

6468   JB Manufacturing
2814 Aiello Dr Ste D
San Jose, CA 95111
Contact: Jim Ogawa GM
Tel: 408-281-9994
Email: jim@jb-mfg.com
Website: www.jb-mfg.com
CNC milling & turning, 5 CNC vertical mills & 1 CNC lathe. (As-Pac, estab 1985, empl 4, sales $325,000, cert: NMSDC)

6469   KFM International Industries, Inc.
20277 Valley Blvd, Ste L
Walnut, CA 91789
Contact: Dennis Boribor Engineer
Tel: 626-369-9556
Email: dennis@kfmii.com
Website: www.kfmii.com
Casting: Sand Cast, Die Casting, Investment Casting & Permanent Mold Forging: Hot & Cold Formed Sheet Metal Stamping Machining: CNC,Turning & Milling Powder Metal. (Minority, Woman, estab 2000, empl 6, sales $2,500,000, cert: City, CPUC)

6470   LT CNC Machining, Inc.
7945 Silverton Ave, Ste 1103
San Diego, CA 92126
Contact: Liem Phan President
Tel: 858-586-7705
Email: liem@ltmachininginc.com
Website: www.ltmachininginc.com
CNC milling & machining. (Minority, Woman, estab 2006, empl 7, sales $800,000, cert: State)

6471   M&L Precision Machining
18655 Madrone Pkwy
Morgan Hill, CA 95037
Contact: Mike Sullivan Business Specialist
Tel: 408-436-3955
Email: mikes@mlprecision.com
Website: www.mlprecision.com
Precision machining done with over 55 mills and multiple lathes. (Woman, estab 1971, empl 110, sales $18,000,000, cert: WBENC)

6472   QMP Inc.
25070 Ave. Tibbitts
Valencia, CA 91355
Contact: Freddy Vidal CEO
Tel: 661-294-6860
Email: sales@qmpusa.com
Website: www.qmpusa.com
Mfr water filtration systems and components, injection molding and machine shop. (Woman/Hisp, estab 1994, empl 44, sales , cert: NMSDC)

6473   Qualitask, Inc.
2840 E Gretta Lane
Anaheim, CA 92806
Contact: Som Suntharaphat President
Tel: 714-237-0900
Email: soms@qualitask.net
Website: www.qualitask.com
CNC Milling & Turning, Research & Development, Prototype & Production Machining, Jigs & Fixtures, steel, stainless steel, titanium, aluminum, plastics. (As-Pac, estab 1992, empl 30, sales $1,187,381, cert: NMSDC)

6474   Spec-Metal Inc.
PO Box 660536
Arcadia, CA 91066
Contact: Evelyn Chen
Tel: 626-301-7969
Email: evelync@spec-metal.com
Website: www.Spec-Metal.com
Machine metal precision machined parts: aluminum, brass, copper, carbon steel & stainless steel. Engineering design, product development, manufacturing, logistics & customer service. (Minority, Woman, estab 2008, empl 4, sales $2,600,000, cert: NMSDC)

Colorado

6475   Custom Machining Corporation
       2090 W College Ave
       Englewood, CO 80110
       Contact: Terri Yount-Ross
       Tel: 303-762-0333
       Email: terri.ross@cmc1.net
       Website: www.cmc1.net
Can lining machining. (Woman, estab 0, empl , sales , cert: WBENC)

6476   Excalibur Machine & Sheet Metal
       208 W Buchanan St, Unit C
       Colorado Springs, CO 80907
       Contact: Douglas McDaniel Plant Mgr
       Tel: 719-520-5404
       Email: doug@excaliburmfg.com
       Website: www.excaliburmfg.com/
Precision machining & sheet metal fabrication, welding, assembly, powder coating. (Hisp, estab 1989, empl 25, sales $2,600,000, cert: NMSDC)

6477   Mountainside Medical Colorado, LLC
       6165 Lookout Rd
       Boulder, CO 80301
       Contact: Susan Neidecker President
       Tel: 303-222-1271
       Email: sneidecker@mountainsidemed.com
       Website: www.mountainsidemed.com
Contract manufacturing for complex, tight-tolerance medical products, Multi-axis Machining Assembly, Wire EDMCNC, Swiss type machining centers, Laser welding & Laser marking, Finishing Metal Forming. (Woman, estab 2006, empl 90, sales $12,731,416, cert: WBENC)

Connecticut

6478   Precision Metal Products, Inc.
       307 Pepes Farm Rd
       Milford, CT 06460
       Contact: Sean O'Brien VP
       Tel: 203-877-4258
       Email: seanobrien@pmpinc.biz
       Website: www.pmpinc.biz
CNC milling, CNC Swiss, CNC turning, wire EDM, stamping. (Woman, estab 1975, empl 145, sales $19,000,000, cert: WBENC)

Florida

6479   Custom Manufacturing & Engineering, Inc.
       3690 70th Ave North
       Pinellas Park, FL 33781
       Contact: Fred Munro VP
       Tel: 727-547-9799
       Email: fmunro@custom-mfg-eng.com
       Website: www.custom-mfg-eng.com
Subassemblies, turn-key, integrated test systems & process equip. (Woman, estab 1997, empl 40, sales $10,300,000, cert: WBENC)

6480   KN Machine & Tool, Inc.
       3125 Jupiter Park Circle Ste 4
       Jupiter, FL 33458
       Contact: Ron Passino Operations Mgr
       Tel: 561-748-3035
       Email: ron@knmachine.com
       Website: www.knmachine.com
High Speed Machining on Milling machines capable of handling parts up 40"x20"x20".
Turning w/ Live Tooling up to 2-5/8" Bar Capacity and up to 12" O.D. Turning. (As-Pac, estab 2000, empl 10, sales $1,300,000, cert: State)

6481   Tychon, Inc.
       2360 Clark St, Unit J
       Apopka, FL 32703
       Contact: Cindy Wiley President
       Tel: 407-293-7601
       Email: tychon_machining@hotmail.com
       Website: www.tychoninc.com
CNC manufacturing, close tolerance, precision machining, CNC mills & CNC lathes. (Woman, estab 2003, empl 3, sales $339,648, cert: WBENC)

Georgia

6482   Omni Machine Works, Inc.
       30-A Chamisa Rd
       Covington, GA 30016
       Contact: Claudia Engelbracht President
       Tel: 404-861-9035
       Email: claudia@omnimachineworks.com
       Website: www.omnimachineworks.com
Full service machine shope, custom machine manufacturer & engineering/design resource. (Woman, estab 0, empl , sales , cert: WBENC)

Iowa

6483   Indoshell Precision Technologies, LLC
       435 Precision Pkwy
       Story City, IA 50248
       Contact: Ramki Ramakrishan Owner
       Tel: -   -
       Email: paul.diggins@isptglobal.com
       Website: www.isptglobal.com
Precision machine aluminum and steel, CNC Turning Centers and Swiss Turning Centers; Multi axis CNC HMC and VMC Machining Centers with pallet changers; as well as lapping, honing and grinding work centers. (As-Ind, estab 2009, empl 75, sales $12,000,000, cert: NMSDC)

Illinois

6484   ADC LP
       1720 Wolf Rd
       Wheeling, IL 60090
       Contact: Patrick Tang President
       Tel: 847-541-3030
       Email: ptang@adclp.com
       Website: www.adclp.com
High pressure aluminum die casting, CNC machining, automated assembly. (As-Pac, estab 1991, empl 243, sales $35,000,000, cert: NMSDC)

6485　Craftsman Custom Metals, LLC
　　　3838 N River Rd
　　　Schiller Park, IL 60176
　　　Contact: William Johnson Business Devel Mgr
　　　Tel:　847-655-0040
　　　Email: wjohnson@ccm.com
　　　Website: www.ccm.com
Custom chassis & enclosures, cabinets, brackets, structural components, OEM's & EMS's, prototype development, precision milling, metal stamping, testing, weilding, engineering support, mechanical & electro-mechanical assembly. (Hisp, estab 1953, empl 65, sales $10,000,000, cert: NMSDC)

6486　Edmik Inc.
　　　3850 Grove Ave
　　　Gurnee, IL 60031
　　　Contact: Heidi Knill VP
　　　Tel:　847-263-0460
　　　Email: edmik@edmik1.com
　　　Website: www.edmik1.com/
Production, custom tooling, machinery & engineering, CAD/CAM, contract & production assembly, industrial appliances, machining & tooling services. (Minority, Woman, estab 1957, empl 32, sales $3,200,000, cert: NMSDC)

6487　KrisDee & Associates, Inc.
　　　755 Schneider Dr
　　　South Elgin, IL 60177
　　　Contact: Hermann VP
　　　Tel:　847-608-8300
　　　Email: gregg.m@krisdee.com
　　　Website: www.krisdee.com
Precision machining of non ferrous prismatic components. (Nat Ame, estab 1983, empl 65, sales $14,000,000, cert: NMSDC)

6488　Lakeview Precision Machining, Inc.
　　　751 Schneider Dr
　　　South Elgin, IL 60177
　　　Contact: President
　　　Tel:　847-742-7170
　　　Email: sales@lakeviewprecision.com
　　　Website: www.lakeviewprecision.com
CNC precision machining. (Woman, estab 2006, empl 15, sales $1,600,000, cert: WBENC)

6489　Machined Products Co.
　　　2121 Landmeier Rd
　　　Elk Grove Village, IL 60007
　　　Contact: Mohammed Qureshi President
　　　Tel:　847-718-1300
　　　Email: mirna@machinedproducts.com
　　　Website: www.machinedproducts.com
Machine iron, steel & aluminum. (As-Ind, estab 1958, empl 100, sales , cert: NMSDC)

6490　Mennie's Machine Company
　　　10549 Mennie Ln
　　　Mennie, IL 61326
　　　Contact: Mark Stengel Dir Sales
　　　Tel:　815-339-2226
　　　Email: markstengel@mennies.com
　　　Website: www.mennies.com
Supplier of precision machined components and assemblies. (Woman, estab 1970, empl 175, sales $34,100,000, cert: WBENC)

6491　Microtech Machine Company, Inc.
　　　222 Camp McDonald Rd
　　　Wheeling, IL 60090
　　　Contact: Elizabeth A. Iwanicki CEO
　　　Tel:　847-870-0707
　　　Email: microcamp@aol.com
　　　Website: www.microtech-machine.com
Engineering services & precision machined prototype & production components, precision machining, machine design & building, assembly & welding. (Woman, estab 1984, empl 22, sales $4,000,000, cert: NWBOC)

6492　Monnex Precision Inc.
　　　476 Diens Dr
　　　Wheeling, IL 60090
　　　Contact: James E. Wallace Sr. President
　　　Tel:　847-478-1800
　　　Email: jwallace@monnex.net
　　　Website: www.monnex.net
Metals, die casting, stampings & fasteners. (AA, As-Pac, estab 1985, empl 620, sales $5,000,000, cert: NMSDC)

6493　Multitech Industries, Inc.
　　　350 Village Dr
　　　Carol Stream, IL 60188
　　　Contact: Nick S. Anastopoulos Business Acct Mgr
　　　Tel:　630-784-9200
　　　Email: nick@multitechind.com
　　　Website: www.multitechind.com
Wire forms, castings, forgings, stampings, machining, cold-heading. (As-Ind, estab 1993, empl 60, sales $100,000,000, cert: NMSDC)

6494　Pioneer Service Inc. - Addison, IL
　　　542 W Factory Rd
　　　Addison, IL 60101
　　　Contact: Beth Swanson VP Sales & Mktg
　　　Tel:　630-628-0249
　　　Email: bswanson@pioneerserviceinc.com
　　　Website: www.pioneerserviceinc.com/
Contract mfr screw machine products & centerless grinding services: shafts, axles, bolts, bushings, dowels, pins, rods, spacers, valve stems, deburring, drilling, flatting, grinding, knurling, slotting, tapping, threading, heat treating. (Woman, estab 1990, empl 40, sales $5,000,000, cert: CPUC, WBENC)

6495　Precise Products Inc.
　　　3286 Talbot Ave
　　　Warrenville, IL 60555
　　　Contact: Ernest Tucker CEO
　　　Tel:　630-393-9698
　　　Email: sales@preciseproductsinc.com
　　　Website: www.precise-products-inc.com
Automatic screw & CNC machined parts. (AA, estab 1966, empl 30, sales $3,000,000, cert: NMSDC)

6496　Tuson Corporation
　　　475 Bunker Court
　　　Vernon Hills, IL 60061
　　　Contact: Michael Jin Sales Mgr
　　　Tel:　847-816-8800
　　　Email: michael-jin@tuson.com
　　　Website: www.tuson.com
Precision CNC machining, powdered metal, forging, casting, gear, hydraulic relief valve assembly, pump, motor & cylinder components, electric motor. (As-Pac, estab 1987, empl 200, sales $29,000,000, cert: NMSDC)

Indiana

6497 A&A Custom Automation, Inc.
2125 Bergdolt Rd
Evansville, IN 47711
Contact: Bill Frey Sales Rep
Tel: 812-464-3650
Email: bfrey@aacustomautomation.com
Website: www.AAcustomautomation.com
Precision CNC machining, steel fabrication, design, mfg & rebuild automated equipment, mechanical & electrical engineering, (Woman, estab 1989, empl 55, sales , cert: NWBOC)

6498 Accutech Mold & Machine, Inc.
2817 Goshen Rd
Fort Wayne, IN 46808
Contact: Darrin Geiger VP
Tel: 260-471-6102
Email: dgeiger@accutechmoldinc.com
Website: www.accutechmoldinc.com
Plastic injection molding, Insert plastic injection molder of cables/connectors, rapid prototype tooling builder/ injection molding, production machining of brass, aluminum & metals, prototype machining of brass, aluminum & metals. (Woman, estab 1996, empl 70, sales $3,000,000, cert: WBENC)

6499 AMG Engineering & Machining, Inc.
4030 Guion Ln
Indianapolis, IN 46268
Contact: Chris Chadd Business Devel
Tel: 317-329-4000
Email: cchadd@amgindy.com
Website: www.amgindy.com
Mfr & design machined components, fluid controls & connectors, adapters, fittings, plugs, check valves, gas regulators & pressure relief valves. (AA, estab 1989, empl 46, sales , cert: NMSDC)

6500 Brinly-Hardy Company
3230 Industrial Pkwy
Jeffersonville, IN 47130
Contact: Scott Whitehouse Sales Mgr
Tel: 812-218-7219
Email: swhitehouse@brinly.com
Website: www.brinly.com
Bending & forming, welding, powder painting, assembly & packaging. (Woman, estab , empl 150, sales $28,000,001, cert: WBENC)

6501 Exacto, Inc. of South Bend
1137 S Lafayette Blvd
South Bend, IN 46601
Contact: Barbara Jordan CEO
Tel: 574-288-4716
Email: bjordan@exacto-inc.com
Website: www.exacto-inc.com
CNC turning, CNC milling, OD/ID grinding, lapping & honing (Woman, estab 1970, empl 52, sales $4,000,000, cert: WBENC)

6502 Mercer Machine
1421 S Holt Rd
Indianapolis, IN 46241
Contact: Joe Robinson VP Sales
Tel: 317-441-0877
Email: jrobinson@mercermachine.net
Website: www.mercermachine.net
CNN machining. (Woman, estab 1954, empl 20, sales $2,000,000, cert: WBENC)

6503 Precision Cadcam, Inc.
8446 Brookville Rd
Indianapolis, IN 46239
Contact: Darryl Williams President
Tel: 317-353-8058
Email: precisioncadcam@sbcglobal.net
Website: www.pccinc.org
Precision maching and molding, tool & dies. (AA, estab 2004, empl 2, sales $170,000, cert: NMSDC)

6504 Royalty Investments, LLC
2476 E US Hwy 50
Seymour, IN 47274
Contact: Marshall Royalty Member
Tel: 812-358-3534
Email: mroyalty@cranehillmachine.com
Website: www.cranehillmachine.com
Machining, fabricating & assembly: steel, aluminum & plastic components. Design, engineering & coating applications. (Woman, estab 1989, empl 30, sales $3,714,618, cert: State, WBENC)

Louisiana

6505 Vast Industries
108 Venus St Ste 200
Morgan City, LA 70380
Contact: Yvette Archuleta-Tudury Owner
Tel: 985-312-1592
Email: yvette@vast-ind.com
Website: www.Vast-Ind.com
Wire EDM & precision machined parts manufacturing, custom product design, reverse engineering & aluminum & steel fabrication. (Minority, Woman, estab 2007, empl 7, sales $600,000, cert: NMSDC, WBENC, 8(a))

Massachusetts

6506 Boulevard Machine & Gear
326 Lockhouse Road
Westfield, MA 01085
Contact: Susan Kasa President
Tel: 413-788-6466
Email: tanya@boulevardmachine.com
Website: www.boulevardmachine.com/
Mfr aerospace, defense, paper & commercial parts, precision machining, CNC turning, lathe & milling, manual lathes & millers, grinding, splines, rack cutting, turning, honing, stamping & assembly. (Woman, estab 1954, empl 22, sales , cert: WBENC)

6507　Fitz Machine Inc.
4 Railroad Ave
Wakefield, MA 01880
Contact: Kathleen Fitzgerald President
Tel:　781-245-5966
Email: kathleen@fitzmachine.com
Website: www.fitzmachine.com
Precision CNC machined components, multi axis capabilities, prototype & production machining, long & short production runs, in-house tooling design. (Woman, estab 1994, empl 15, sales $1,300,000, cert: WBENC)

6508　M&K Engineering
66 Concord St
North Reading, MA 01864
Contact: Gene Ungvarsky Business Dev Mgr
Tel:　978-276-1973
Email: gene@mkeng.com
Website: www.mkeng.com
Precision machining: CNC & swiss screw CNC. (Woman, estab 1990, empl 28, sales $4,464,492, cert: NMSDC)

6509　PremaTech Advanced Ceramics
2 Coppage Dr
Worcester, MA 01603
Contact: Thomas Shearer Dir Business Dev
Tel:　508-791-9549
Email: info@prematechac.com
Website: www.PremaTechAC.com
Fabricate technical ceramics, sapphire, composite & exotic materials, machining & grinding, ceramic components, refractories, cordierite, kiln furniture, porous metal parts, stainless steel, bronze & titanium filters, zinc, zinc selenide. (Woman, estab 1980, empl 35, sales $3,525,000, cert: WBENC)

6510　Wrobel Engineering Co., Inc.
154 Bodwell St
Avon, MA 02322
Contact: Michael Long General/QA Mgr.
Tel:　508-586-8338
Email: mlong@wrobeleng.com
Website: www.wrobeleng.com
Mfr precision sheet metal fabricated parts per customer specs, precision machining, milling & turning, metal stamping, long & short runs, tool & die making, assembly mechanical & electrical, welding all materials. (Woman, estab 1976, empl 86, sales $14,800,000, cert: State, City)

Maryland

6511　FlexFit Hose LLC
7948 E. Baltimore St.
Baltimore, MD 21224
Contact: Arjun Radhakrishnan Managing Partner
Tel:　410-327-0758
Email: sales@flexfithose.com
Website: www.ffhose.com
CNC Swiss machining, MNT, Female NPT, Female JIC, Tube Adaptors, Tri-Clamps, Mini Tri-Clamps. (AA, estab 2008, empl 4, sales $1,400,000, cert: NMSDC, SDB)

6512　Ray Machine Inc.
12 Lynbrook Rd
Baltimore, MD 21220
Contact: Dan Solomon General Mgr
Tel:　410-686-6955
Email: dsolomon@rayamch.com
Website: www.raymachine.com
CNC & conventional machining; precision sheet metal fab, welding, mechanical & elec assembly, etc. (As-Ind, estab 1950, empl 42, sales $4,711,000, cert: NMSDC)

Michigan

6513　2K Tool LLC
3025 Madison Ave SE
Wyoming, MI 49548
Contact: Kevin Smith Engineering Mgr
Tel:　616-452-4927
Email: kevin@2ktool.com
Website: www.2ktool.com
Moldmaker, machining, tooling, plastic injection molds, compression tooling, composite machining, casting machining part Injection molding. (Woman, estab 2004, empl 19, sales $2,269,151, cert: WBENC)

6514　Accu-Shape Die Cutting, Inc.
4050 Market Place Dr
Flint, MI 48507
Contact: Joe Brooks New Business Dev
Tel:　810-230-2445
Email: joebrooks@accushape.com
Website: www.accushape.com
Large parts a specialty up to 84" x 75" in size with kiss cutting capability from larger roll stock. Lamination of pressure sensitive adhesives up to 54" wide. Slitting and Sheeting of rolled goods up to 85" wide. (AA, estab 1998, empl 36, sales $3,200,000, cert: NMSDC)

6515　Action Tool & Machine Inc.
5976 Ford Ct
Brighton, MI 48116
Contact: Doug Lademan Dir minority bus dev
Tel:　810-229-6300
Email: actiontool@actiontoolmachine.com
Website: www.actiontoolmachine.com
Machining & assembly svcs: build-to-print, part-to-print reverse engineering svcs. (As-Pac, estab 1993, empl 30, sales $3,700,000, cert: NMSDC)

6516　Aerostar Manufacturing
28275 Northline Rd
Romulus, MI 48174
Contact: Robert Johnson VP
Tel:　734-942-8440
Email: rjohnson@aerostarmfg.com
Website: www.aerostarmfg.com
CNC machining assembly, prototyping, machine castings & forgings, sand casting. (As-Pac, estab 1970, empl 200, sales , cert: NMSDC)

6517 ALBAH Manufacturing Technologies Corp.
1985 Ring Rd
Troy, MI 48083
Contact: Kofi Adomako VP
Tel: 519-972-7222
Email: kadomako@albah.com
Website: www.albah.com
Automation & robotics, machine load/unload, material handling, assembly, dispensing, palletizing & material removal. (Woman/AA, estab 1992, empl 27, sales $5,000,000, cert: NMSDC)

6518 Alphi Manufacturing, LLC
576 Beck St
Jonesville, MI 49250
Contact: Ed Carter Dir Diversity Devel
Tel: - -
Email: ecarter@crownegroupllc.com
Website: www.alphimfg.com/
Fabrication (bending, piercing, end forming, miter cutting, welding) of ferrous and non-ferrous tubalur products. Fabricated exhaust components, Fabricated structural components. (Nat Ame, estab 1959, empl 125, sales $19,939,913, cert: NMSDC)

6519 Aluminum Blanking Company, Inc
360 W Sheffield
Pontiac, MI 48340
Contact: Michael Rutkowski VP Finance & Admin
Tel: 248-338-4422
Email: mrutkowski@albl.com
Website: www.albl.com
Leveling, Blanking, lubing, edge-trimming and slitting of Aluminum, Stainless and other surface sensitive materials. (Woman, estab 1979, empl 120, sales $9,864,397, cert: WBENC)

6520 Aztec Manufacturing Corporation
15378 Oakwood Dr
Romulus, MI 48174
Contact: Richard Johnson President
Tel: 734-942-7433
Email: rjohnson@aztecmfgcorp.com
Website: www.aztecmfgcorp.com
Machined aluminum, ductile iron castings & forgings. (Hisp, estab 1983, empl 55, sales $25,000,000, cert: NMSDC)

6521 Casemer Tool
2765 Metamora Rd
Oxford, MI 48371
Contact: Ray Wrubel Sales
Tel: 248-860-3689
Email: Ray@casemer.com
Website: www.casemer.com
CNC machining, large diameter turning 32" x 120 ", bridge Mill 59" x 119" (Woman, estab 1979, empl 85, sales $15,000,000, cert: WBENC)

6522 Chippewa Industries, Inc.dba Thaymar Medical
1223 Greenleaf Dr
Royal Oak, MI 48067
Contact: Jeff St. Louis President
Tel: 248-266-1206
Email: jstlouis@thaymar.com
Website: www.thaymar.com
CNC Machining, vertical and horizontal 3 Axis, 4 Axis and 5 Axis CNC machining capabilities. We provide Billet, Sand Castings, Metal Castings, Aluminum Castings, Investment Castings, Plaster Casting, Die Casting, Prototype, and Short to Medium Production. (Nat Ame, estab 2015, empl 25, sales $6,000,000, cert: NMSDC)

6523 CKS Precision Machining
700 E Soper Rd
Bad Axe, MI 48413
Contact: Frank Gerbig Dir of Sales
Tel: 989-269-9702
Email: fgerbig@geminigroup.net
Website: www.ckstool.com
CNC machining: lathe, mill, grind & heat treating. (Woman, estab 1979, empl 100, sales $15,709,000, cert: WBENC)

6524 Clips & Clamps Industries
15050 Keel St
Plymouth, MI 48170
Contact: Jeff Aznavorian President
Tel: 734-455-0880
Email: jaznavorian@clipsclamps.com
Website: www.clipsclamps.com
Metal forming, progressive dies, four slide, CNC wire forming, tool building, MIG & TIG welding, tapping, riveting, automated assemblies, prototyping & production volumes, engineering services, design services, sales support. (Woman, estab 1954, empl 62, sales , cert: WBENC)

6525 CNC Products Inc.
2126 S 11th St
Niles, MI 49120
Contact: President
Tel: 269-684-5500
Email: orders@cncproductsinc.com
Website: www.cncproductsinc.com/
CNC machining. (Woman, estab 2019, empl 18, sales $2,500,000, cert: WBENC)

6526 Costello Enterprises, LLC
56358 Precision Dr
Chesterfield Township, MI 48051
Contact: Tom Orban VP
Tel: 586-615-6307
Email: torban@costelloenterprises.com
Website: www.costelloenterprises.com
CNC machining & dimensional inspection services. (Hisp, estab 2000, empl 25, sales , cert: NMSDC)

6527 Costello Machine LLC
56358 Precision Dr
Chesterfield, MI 48051
Contact: Frank Keena Operations Mgr
Tel: 586-749-0136
Email: fkeena@costellomachine.com
Website: www.costellomachine.com
Precision machining, boring mill & assemblies. (Hisp, estab 2000, empl 25, sales $3,500,000, cert: NMSDC)

6528 Dalany Metal Products Inc.
4450 13th St
Wyandotte, MI 48192
Contact: Al Yglesias President
Tel: 734-282-6666
Email: al.yglesias@dalany.com
Website: www.dalany.com
Machine formed metal parts: cold heading, rod heading, wire forming, stampers & screw machine, grooves, reamed holes, cross holes, plating. (Hisp, estab 2004, empl 9, sales $525,000, cert: NMSDC)

6529 Dienamic Tool Corporation
4541 Patterson Ave SE
Kentwood, MI 49512
Contact: Rogelio (Roger) Ramirez President
Tel: 616-954-7882
Email: rramirez@dienamictoolcorp.com
Website: www.dienamictoolcorp.com
Die Build, Reverse Engineering, CNC Machining, Fixture Build. (Hisp, estab 1998, empl 16, sales $1,856,444, cert: NMSDC)

6530 Dowding Industries
503 Marilin
Eaton Rapids, MI 48827
Contact: Roger Cope VP Sales
Tel: 517-663-5455
Email: roger@willowhill.net
Website: www.dowdingindustries.com
CNC machining, milling & boring. (Woman, estab 1965, empl 150, sales , cert: WBENC)

6531 GK Tech, LLC
3331 W Big Beaver Rd Ste 106
Troy, MI 48084
Contact: Kelly Choi President
Tel: 248-494-1960
Email: kellychoi@gktechusa.com
Website: www.gktechllc.com
Marketing specialist, consulting, business development, forging, die-casting, stamping, spring, magnesium pulley, rubber bushing, fasteners, machining, plastic injection molding. (Minority, Woman, estab 2015, empl 3, sales , cert: NMSDC)

6532 Jolico/J-B Tool, Inc.
4325 22 Mile Rd
Utica, MI 48317
Contact: Patricia Wieland President
Tel: 586-739-5555
Email: pwieland@jolico.com
Website: www.jolico.com
CNC turning, vertical, multipallet machining, welding, suface, wet & blanchard grinding. (Woman, estab 1963, empl 38, sales , cert: WBENC)

6533 KJL Industries, Inc.
44057 Phoenix Dr
Sterling Heights, MI 48314
Contact: Kristin Wikol President
Tel: 586-803-1818
Email: kwikol@kjlindustries.com
Website: www.kjlindustries.com
Precision machining, tight tolerance, complex parts. (Woman, estab 1984, empl 15, sales $2,000,000, cert: WBENC)

6534 Maya Jig Grinding & Gage Co.
20770 Parker Rd
Farmington Hills, MI 48336
Contact: Jeff Beier VP
Tel: 248-471-0802
Email: jbeier@mayagage.com
Website: www.MayaGage.com
Automatic gages, variable gages, functional gages, hand gages, masters, fixtures & tooling. (Woman, estab 1976, empl 20, sales $3,000,000, cert: WBENC)

6535 PGS Incorporated
2565 Industrial Row Dr
Troy, MI 48084
Contact: Vicki Kafura Exec Admin
Tel: 248-280-1142
Email: vkafura@pgsinc.net
Website: www.pgsinc.net
Prototype, product machining, assembly, steel & plastic component washing & cleaning, sorting, gage/testing, kitting & crisis manufacturing management. (Woman, estab 1983, empl 17, sales $3,844,800, cert: WBENC)

6536 Pioneer Machine & Tech
1167 East 10 Mile Rd
Madison Heights, MI 48071
Contact: Jeffery Harris President
Tel: 248-546-4451
Email: jharris@pioneermachinetech.com
Website: www.pioneermachinetech.com
Machining: custom & precision machining, fabrication, grinding & repair of components & fixtures. (AA, estab 1998, empl 15, sales $1,500,000, cert: NMSDC)

6537 Precision Components Manufacturing, LLC
35855 Stanley
Sterling Heights, MI 48312
Contact: Tommy Longest CEO
Tel: 586-939-8500
Email: tommy@pcmfettes.com
Website: www.pcmfettes.com
Mfr cast tooling, castings iron/aluminum, steel forging, fully machined castings & assembly, ferrous & non-ferrous products, forging, sand & die casting. (AA, estab 2009, empl 30, sales $7,010,000, cert: NMSDC)

6538 Robinson Industries, Inc.
3051 W Curtis Rd
Coleman, MI 48618
Contact: Marvin Ries Sales
Tel: 989-465-6111
Email: mries@robinsonind.com
Website: www.robinsonind.com
Custom design & mfg, vacuum forming, injection molding, extrusion, tool & die shop. (Woman, estab 1950, empl 200, sales $28,348,370, cert: WBENC)

6539 Sequoia Tool
44831 N Groesbeck Hwy
Clinton Township, MI 48036
Contact: James Coates Acct Mgr
Tel: 586-463-4400
Email: bcoates@sequoiatool.net
Website: www.sequoiatool.net
Mfr prototype sheet metal stampings & assemblies, low volume production and short run svcs. (Nat Ame, estab 1988, empl 65, sales $10,000,000, cert: NMSDC)

6540 Set Enterprises, Inc.
38600 Van Dyke Ave Ste 325
Sterling Heights, MI 48093
Contact: Antoinette Turner Mgr Corp Communication
Tel: 586-573-3600
Email: aturner@setenterprises.com
Website: www.setenterprises.com
Metal processing services, blanking, slitting & warehousing of metal products. (AA, estab 0, empl 310, sales , cert: NMSDC)

6541 Steadfast Engineered Products, LLC
775 Woodlawn Ave
Grand Haven, MI 49417
Contact: Jay Cutie Managing Partner
Tel: 616-846-4747
Email: jcutie@steadfastep.com
Website: www.steadfastep.com
Screw machine products, turned parts. (AA, Hisp, estab 1986, empl 12, sales $6,000,000, cert: NMSDC)

6542 Sure Solutions LLC
5385 Perry Dr
Waterford, MI 48329
Contact: Art Huge Sales
Tel: 248-674-7210
Email: info@suresolutionsmbe.com
Website: www.suresolutionsmbe.com/
Stampings, plating, coatings, roll forming, machining, castings, forgings, assembly, packaging, warehousing & distribution, containment. (Minority, Woman, estab 1990, empl 25, sales $8,250,000, cert: WBENC)

6543 Systrand Manufacturing Corporation
19050 Allen Rd
Brownstown, MI 48329
Contact: Jim Meadows Dir of Finance
Tel: 734-479-8100
Email: jim.meadows@systrand.com
Website: www.systrand.com
High volume production machining: cast iron, aluminum, steel & powdered metal components. (Minority, Woman, estab 1982, empl 200, sales $65,000,000, cert: NMSDC, WBENC)

6544 Trutron Corporation
274 Executive Dr
Troy, MI 48083
Contact: Lisa Kingsley President
Tel: 248-583-9166
Email: lkingsley@trutron.com
Website: www.trutron.com
Precision machining, CNC turning, milling, grinding: pressure plates, valve plates, wafer plates, cam rings, rotors, housings, manifolds, radial rings, levers, sleeves, actuator pistons, tooling & gauging. (Woman, estab 1967, empl 26, sales $5,239,911, cert: WBENC)

6545 United Manufacturing Network Inc.
12 Lincoln St
Mt. Clemens, MI 48043
Contact: Cathy DeNardo President
Tel: 586-468-7443
Email: cathydenardo@comcast.net
Website: www.unitedmanufacturingnetwork.com
Design & build fixtures & gages, tool & dies injection molds, molded parts & rapid prototype CNC machining, turning, milling & boring mill OD, ID, surface & centerless grinding, precision jig grinding & wire EDM. (Woman, estab 2004, empl 3, sales $104,202, cert: WBENC)

6546 West Michigan Flocking
78277 County Road 378
Covert, MI 49043
Contact: Garrett Fox VP Sales
Tel: 269-639-1634
Email: gfox@wmflocking.com
Website: www.wmflocking.com
Object flocking, injection molding, in-line attachment assembly, sub assembly & sonic welding. (AA, estab 1978, empl 50, sales $4,500,000, cert: NMSDC)

6547 Witco Inc.
6401 Bricker Rd
Avoca, MI 48006
Contact: Tom Kean Sales Engineer
Tel: 810-387-4231
Email: tomk@witcoinc.com
Website: www.witcoinc.com
CNC precision machine parts: milling, turning, grinding, gear shaping & assembly. (Woman, estab 1977, empl 60, sales $7,000,000, cert: WBENC)

6548 Zoatex
25580 Brest Road
Taylor, MI 48180
Contact: Hamid Servati Partner
Tel: 734-697-5555
Email: hservati@zoatex.com
Website: www.zoatex.com
Manufacturing & machining, powertrain devel, emissions, durability testing, project mgmt, prototyping. (AA, estab 2002, empl 20, sales $12,000,000, cert: NMSDC)

Minnesota

6549 LAI International, Inc.
4255 Pheasant Ridge Dr NE #405
Minneapolis, MN 55449
Contact: Terri Lambert Dir Sales
Tel: 480-469-4170
Email: tlambert@laico.com
Website: www.laico.com
Cutting-Edge Precision Component Manufacturing. (AA, estab 1979, empl 287, sales $73,113,237, cert: NMSDC)

6550 Mack Engineering Corporation
3215 E 26th St
Minneapolis, MN 55406
Contact: Jennifer Salisbury President
Tel: 612-721-2471
Email: info@mackengineering.com
Website: www.mackengineering.com
Mfr precision-machined components utilizing a dock to stock quality system. (Woman, estab 1943, empl 30, sales , cert: WBENC)

6551   Metal Craft Machine & Engineering, Inc.
13760 Businesss Center Dr
Elk River, MN 55330
Contact: Trisha Mowry CEO
Tel: 763-441-1855
Email: trisha@metal-craft.com
Website: www.metal-craft.com
Contract manufacturing & engineering design: CNC milling & turning, multi-tasking machining, 7-axis CNC grinding, wire EDM, swiss gundrilling, laser & GTAW (Tig.), welding blasting, deburring, & finishing. (Woman, estab 1978, empl 185, sales , cert: WBENC)

6552   Miller Machine Company
14105 Commerce Dr
Becker, MN 55308
Contact: Cynthia Wahl President
Tel: 763-263-0091
Email: cyndiw@millermachinecompany.com
Website: www.millermachinecompany.com
CNC mills & lathes, brown & sharpe screw machines, automatice saws, bridgeports, hardinges. (Woman, estab 1944, empl 15, sales $1,764,305, cert: WBENC)

6553   Modern Manufacturing & Engineering, Inc.
9380 Winnetka Ave N
Brooklyn Park, MN 55445
Contact: Nancy Lien Berndt President
Tel: 612-781-3347
Email: nancyl@mmeincmn.com
Website: www.mmeincmn.com
Precision custom machining, milling, turning, grinding, assembly, plating, painting. (As-Pac, estab 1958, empl 156, sales , cert: NMSDC)

6554   Northern U & S, Inc. dba Quali-Mac, Inc.
9208 James Ave S, Ste 11
Bloomington, MN 55431
Contact: Shawn Thai President
Tel: 952-881-6677
Email: shawnt@qualimac-inc.com
Website: www.qualimac-inc.com
Precision, CNC machining, metal/plastic machining, turning, vertical milling, protoype, production machining. (As-Pac, estab 1974, empl 7, sales $400,000, cert: NMSDC)

6555   Permac Industries, Inc.
14401 Ewing Ave S
Burnsville, MN 55306
Contact: Mike Bartizal VP
Tel: 952-746-0289
Email: mbartizal@permacindustries.com
Website: www.permacindustries.com
Precision machining: CNC lathe, swiss & screw machined custom components. (Woman, estab 1966, empl 30, sales $5,000,000, cert: WBENC)

6556   Riverside Manufacturing, Inc.
14280 Sunfish Lake Blvd NW
Ramsey, MN 55303
Contact: Mic Wieshaar President
Tel: 763-274-2193
Email: riversidemnf@earthlink.net
Website: www.riversidemnf.com
CNC machining, complex horizontal machining. (Nat Ame, estab 1997, empl 15, sales $3,450,000, cert: NMSDC)

New Hampshire

6557   Maclean Precision Machine
1928 Village Rd
Madison, NH 03849
Contact: Deborah Folsom President
Tel: 603-367-9011
Email: d.folsom@macleanprecision.com
Website: www.macleanprecision.com
Precision machining, tight tolerance parts, Titanium, Inconel, Stainless Steel, Aluminum, Castings, Bar Stock & Plate. (Woman, estab 1977, empl 33, sales $3,800,000, cert: NWBOC)

New Jersey

6558   Arlington Machine & Tool
90 New Dutch Ln
Fairfield, NJ 07004
Contact: Susan Blanck President
Tel: 973-276-1377
Email: sblanck@arlingtonmachine.com
Website: www.arlingtonmachine.com
CNC machining & turning, manufacturing, assemblies & systems. (Woman, estab 1963, empl 100, sales $16,000,000, cert: State, WBENC)

6559   Computa-Base Machining
411 N Grove St
Berlin, NJ 08009
Contact: Agustin Rosado President
Tel: 856-767-3509
Email: cbmpresident@computabase.com
Website: www.computabase.com
Close tolerance, special metals, nickel, inconell, kamenell, etc. (Hisp, estab 1981, empl 20, sales $1,000,000, cert: NMSDC, SDB)

6560   Kaizen Technologies Inc.
1 Lincoln Hwy, Ste 10
Edison, NJ 08820
Contact: Prakash Bahumanyam VP
Tel: 732-452-9555
Email: prakashb@kaizentek.com
Website: www.kaizentek.com
Precision machining, tooling, jigs & fixtures. (As-Ind, estab 1995, empl 150, sales $11,000,000, cert: State)

6561   Progressive Machinery Inc.
19 E Centre St
Nutley, NJ 07110
Contact: VP Finance
Tel: 833-776-6224
Email: info@pro-machinery.com
Website: www.pro-machinery.com
CNC milling and turning, grinding, welding, die & mold fabrication, multi-slide forming & assembly on Bihler machines & CMM inspections, molding, stamping forming, punching, cutting, welding, tapping, inserting, assembling, and sheet metal fabrication. (Woman, estab 2009, empl 10, sales $1,500,000, cert: State, WBENC)

New Mexico

6562 Las Cruces Machine, Mfg. & Engineering
6000 S Main, Ste B
Mesilla Park, NM 88047
Contact: Rod Mitchell President
Tel: 575-526-1411
Email: rmitchell@lascrucesmachine.com
Website: www.lascrucesmachine.com
CNC precision machining capabilities. (Woman, estab 1975, empl 40, sales $3,907,000, cert: WBENC)

New York

6563 Cannon Industries, Inc.
525 Lee Rd
Rochester, NY 14606
Contact: Reggie Cannon President
Tel: 585-254-8080
Email: rcannon@cannonind.com
Website: www.cannonind.com
Sheet metal fabrication, welding fabrication, laser & plasma cutting, metal stamping, CNC machining & turning, mechanical assembly, spot welding. (AA, estab 1979, empl 104, sales $16,000,000, cert: NMSDC)

6564 Greno Industries Inc.
PO Box 542
Schenectady, NY 12301
Contact: Joe Vainauskas VP Operations
Tel: 518-393-4195
Email: jvainauskas@greno.com
Website: www.greno.com
Contract OEM machining, milling & turning services, CAD/CAM capabilities, modern equipment. (Woman, estab 1961, empl 65, sales $15,500,000, cert: WBENC)

6565 Ingleside Machine Company, Inc.
1120 Hook Rd
Farmington, NY 14425
Contact: Gary Veomett
Tel: 585-924-3046
Email: office@inglesidemachine.com
Website: www.Inglesidemachine.com
CNC milling, turning, sheet metal fabrication, welding, finishing & assembly. (Woman, estab 1974, empl 85, sales , cert: State)

6566 Park Enterprises
226 Jay St
Rochester, NY 14608
Contact: Robert Amo Sales
Tel: 716-393-7106
Email: rob@questsls.com
Website: www.parkent.com
CNC machining, screw machining, prototypes, electrical assemblies. (As-Pac, estab 1991, empl 160, sales $20,000,000, cert: NMSDC)

Ohio

6567 Action Precision Products Inc.
100 E North Ave Box 188
Pioneer, OH 43554
Contact: Linda Heisler President
Tel: 419-737-2348
Email: linda@actionprecision.com
Website: www.actionprecision.com
Machining: low volume, high tolerance blue print items, steel, brass, bronze & plastics, CNC turning, milling & grinding operations. (Woman, estab 1972, empl 10, sales $1,020,000, cert: WBENC)

6568 Cleveland Die & Mfg. Co.
20303 First Ave
Middleburg Heights, OH 44130
Contact: Marty Curry Sales/Engineering
Tel: 440-243-3404
Email: mcurry@clevelanddie.com
Website: www.clevelanddie.com/
Ecoat & powder coat line, automatic & single hit presses, spot & robotic welders, CNC machining. (Hisp, estab 1973, empl 300, sales $24,000,000, cert: NMSDC)

6569 Covert Manufacturing, Inc.
328 S East St
Galion, OH 44833
Contact: Steve Lamontagne VP Sales
Tel: 419-468-1761
Email: stevel@covertmfg.com
Website: www.covertmfg.com
CNC Machine Shop specializing in the machining of castings, Forgings, and Bar. Heavy Truck parts, engine components, suspension components, driveline components, Braking systems. (Woman, estab 1967, empl 140, sales , cert: WBENC)

6570 EnKon, LLC dba Broadway
6344 Webster St
Dayton, OH 45414
Contact: Jodi Walters Member
Tel: 937-890-2221
Email: jodi.walters@enkonllc.com
Website: www.broadwaymold.com
Injection molds, components, mold repairs, Precision Fabrication,
CNC Machining, welding, turning, Electrode manufacturing, EDM'ING, Wire EDM, Polish, Milling, OD, ID, and surface grinding, Design. (Woman, estab 1955, empl 12, sales , cert: WBENC)

6571 GB Manufacturing Company
100 Adams St
Delta, OH 43515
Contact: Teresa Elling Sales
Tel: 419-822-5323
Email: apetree@gbmfg.com
Website: www.gbmfg.com
Stamping, laser blanking, fabrication & assembly, tool making, robotic & hand welding, spot welding, press braking, productin machining, prototyping. (Minority, estab 1975, empl 85, sales $24,500,000, cert: NMSDC)

6572 Green Rock Lighting, LLC
3175 W 33rd St
Cleveland, OH 44109
Contact: Tina Haddad
Tel: 216-651-6446
Email: thaddad@greenrocklighting.com
Website: www.greenrocklighting.com
Laser cutting, wire bending & forming, press brake, spinning, stamping, mig, tig & stick welding, spot welding, machining, destructive & non-destructive testing, packaging & assembly. (Woman, estab 2011, empl 20, sales , cert: State, WBENC)

6573 Kaskell Manufacturing, Inc.
240 Hiawatha Trail
Springboro, OH 45066
Contact: Brian Harris VP
Tel: 937-704-9700
Email: bharris@kaskellmfg.com
Website: www.kaskellmfg.com
CNC machining, milling & turning. (Woman, estab 2000, empl 12, sales $1,250,000, cert: WBENC)

6574 Lewis Unlimited, Inc.
165 Jackson Dr
Cleveland, OH 44022
Contact: Joseph Lewis, Jr. President
Tel: 216-514-8282
Email: jlewis@lewisunlimited.com
Website: www.lewisunlimited.com
CNC precision machined components, multi axis machining centers, single & multi-spindle screw products, CNC Swiss machined components. (AA, estab 1991, empl 10, sales $6,043,537, cert: State, NMSDC)

6575 Magni-Power Company
5511 Lincoln Way E
Wooster, OH 44691
Contact: Kim Coblentz New Business Dev Mgr
Tel: 330-264-3637
Email: kcoblentz@magnipower.com
Website: www.magnipower.com
Metal fabrication & stamping: process steel, aluminum, stainless steel, CNC punching, forming, laser cutting, robotic welding, in-house powder coating & assembly. (As-Ind, estab 1948, empl 230, sales $27,000,000, cert: NMSDC)

6576 Mantych Metalworking, Inc.
3175 Plainfield Rd
Dayton, OH 45432
Contact: Bill Sewell Sales
Tel: 937-258-1373
Email: bill@mantych.net
Website: www.mantych.net
Precision CNC machining & sheet metal fabrication. (Woman, estab 1971, empl 34, sales $8,000,000, cert: WBENC)

6577 Ohio Transitional Machine & Tool Inc.
3940 Castener St
Toledo, OH 43612
Contact: Marten Whalen President
Tel: 419-476-0820
Email: ohiotransitional@hotmail.com
Website: www.ohiotransitional.com
CNC milling & turning, wire EDM, boringmill, general machining, blanchard grinding, 3D machining, jigs & fixtures, prototypes, R&D, welding, painting & assembly. (Nat Ame, estab 1985, empl 10, sales $800,000, cert: NMSDC)

6578 Vantage Agora
23811 Chagrin Blvd Ste 244
Beachwood, OH 44122
Contact: Sudhir Achar President
Tel: 888-246-7211
Email: sudhir@vantageagora.com
Website: www.vantageagora.com
Mfr turned parts, machining, hot & cold forging, printing, precision parts. (As-Ind, estab 2004, empl 19, sales $3,697,558, cert: NMSDC)

6579 Wrena, LLC dba Angstrom-USA, LLC
265 Lightner Rd
Tipp City, OH 45371
Contact: Nagesh Palakurthi CEO
Tel: 937-667-4403
Email: pyenger@wrenallc.com
Website: www.angstrom-usa.com
Stampings, tubular products, machining, welding, robotic welding, steel forgings (Warm & Cold), aluminum forgings, assemblies, plastic injection molding, needle bearings, starter assemblies (As-Pac, estab 2011, empl 46, sales , cert: NMSDC)

Oregon

6580 Browns Machine
90500B Hwy 99N
Eugene, OR 97402
Contact: Kevin Brown President
Tel: 541-344-1466
Email: kevin@brownsmachine.com
Website: www.brownsmachine.com
Custom machining, first article inspections, material certifications. (Nat Ame, estab 2003, empl 31, sales , cert: State)

6581 Hy Speed Machining, Inc.
353 California Ave
Grants Pass, OR 97526
Contact: Rachel Chamberland HR Mgr
Tel: 541-476-0769
Email: rachelc@hyspeedmachining.com
Website: www.hyspeedmachining.com
Machine shop specializing in machined parts; all materials; close tolerance, high volume. (Minority, Woman, estab 1984, empl 19, sales $3,049,034, cert: State)

Pennsylvania

6582 Acutec Precision Aerospace Inc.
13555 Broadway
Meadville, PA 16335
Contact: Rich Shaffer Sr Acct Mgr
Tel: 814-763-3214
Email: rshaffer@acutecprecision.com
Website: www.acutecprecision.com
Milling, turning, grinding, honing, lapping, EDM & light assembly of aluminum, titanium, stainless steel, inconel, hastalloy, hastx, plastics. (Woman, estab 1988, empl 385, sales $100,000,000, cert: WBENC)

6583 Agape Precision Manufacturing, LLC
320 Circle of Progress Dr Ste 108
Pottstown, PA 19464
Contact: Dana Wolfe President
Tel: 484-824-3134
Email: dana.wolfe@agapeprecision.com
Website: www.agapeprecision.com
Machining, fabrication, bending, assemblies, hardware, some special processes, brackets, prototyping, metals, delron, plastics, aerospace manufacturing. (Woman, estab 2006, empl 11, sales $1,100,000, cert: State)

6584 Amity Industries
491 Old Swede Rd
Douglassville, PA 19518
Contact: Monica Lubinsky CEO
Tel: 610-385-6075
Email: mlubins@amityindustries.com
Website: www.amityindustries.com
Custom fabrication, machining & assembly. (Nat Ame, estab 1973, empl 45, sales $10,000,000, cert: NMSDC)

6585 Atlas Machining & Welding, Inc.
777 Smith Lane
Northampton, PA 18067
Contact: Andrew Weiss Project Mgr
Tel: 610-262-1374
Email: info@atlasmw.com
Website: www.atlasmw.com
CNC machine & steel fabrication, vertical & horizontal boring mills, vertical machine centers, lathes & turning. (Woman, estab 1981, empl 65, sales $13,000,000, cert: NWBOC)

6586 C.A. Spalding, Co.
1011 Cedar Ave
Croydon, PA 19021
Contact: Javier Kuehnle CEO
Tel: 215-850-5777
Email: nteubert@spaldingautomotive.com
Website: www.caspalding.com
High-precision forming, laser cutting & bracket machining. (Hisp, estab 1938, empl 30, sales $18,231,344, cert: NMSDC)

6587 D & R Machine Co.
1330 Industrial Hwy
Southampton, PA 18966
Contact: Nelson Redante Mgr Business Dev
Tel: 215-526-2080
Email: nelsonredante@drmachine.com
Website: www.drmachine.com
Mfr precision machine parts to cstmr specs. (Hisp, estab 1971, empl 38, sales , cert: NMSDC)

Puerto Rico

6588 SQS, Inc. (Successful Quality Systems)
Palmas Industrial Park Road 869 KM. 2.0 Street 4
Catano, PR 00962
Contact: WILDA AGUIRRE President
Tel: 787-275-2424
Email: wildaaguirre@sqswarehouse.com
Website: www.sqswarehouse.com
Specialized Storage and Inventory Management Services of materials and products for the pharmaceutical, medical devices, biotech and consumer industries as well as to the safe-guarding of documents (Minority, Woman, estab 2003, empl 8, sales $2,500,000, cert: NMSDC)

Rhode Island

6589 East Bay Manufacturing
400 Franklin St
Bristol, RI 02809
Contact: Randy Medina General Mgr
Tel: 401-254-2960
Email: randy@eastbaymfg.com
Website: www.eastbaymfg.com
CNC machining & fabrication resources. (Hisp, estab 1985, empl 14, sales , cert: State)

South Carolina

6590 Bunty, LLC
444 Fairforest Way
Greenville, SC 29607
Contact: Rajeev Jindal President
Tel: 864-567-0498
Email: rajeev@buntyllc.com
Website: www.buntyllc.com
Precision machined components, assemblies, metal fabrication, jigs & fixtures, forgings, castings, dies, re-engineered OEM parts, CNC milling, CNC turning. (As-Pac, estab 2000, empl 10, sales $1,600,000, cert: NMSDC)

6591 J.I.T. Manufacturing, Inc.
428 Oglesby Lane
Cowpens, SC 29330
Contact: Dan Hunter Production / Sales Mgr.
Tel: 864-463-0581
Email: dan@jitmanufacturing.com
Website: www.jitmfg.net
Laser cutting, welding, forming, CNC punching, CNC machines, fabrication, sheetmetal, powdercoating, pressbrakes, modifications, spot welding, control boxes, mounting plates, brackets, CAD programing, Cad design. (Woman, estab 1992, empl 22, sales $2,910,792, cert: City, WBENC)

6592 Secondary Solutions, Inc.
101 Northeast Dr
Spartanburg, SC 29303
Contact: Mark Mahaffey Sales
Tel: 864-494-5337
Email: markmahaffey@secondarysolutionsinc.net
Website: www.ssiservesyou.net
Machining, fabrication, drilling, tapping, grinding, warehousing, assembly, boring, wire marking, wire harness assembly, 3rd party inspection services, buffing, polishing, packaging. (Woman, estab 1997, empl 10, sales $550,000, cert: WBENC)

Tennessee

6593   Engineered Mechanical Systems
118 Parmenas Lane
Chattanooga, TN 37405
Contact: Brenna Fairchild CEO
Tel: 423-624-3300
Email: brenna@emsfab.com
Website: www.emsfab.com
Design & build custom machines/equipment, multiple lasers & CNC sheet metal machines, certified welders. (Minority, Woman, estab 1990, empl 67, sales $13,000,000, cert: WBENC)

6594   Gonzalez Group LLC/
237 Kraft St
Clarksville, TN 37040
Contact: Felix Gonzalez CEO
Tel: 517-542-2928
Email: fg@gonzalezmfg.com
Website: www.gonzalezmfg.com
Mfr precision turned machined parts. (Hisp, estab 1974, empl 135, sales $14,000,000, cert: NMSDC)

6595   Southern Precision Machining, LLC
220 Calsonic Way
Shelbyville, TN 37160
Contact: President
Tel: 931-685-9057
Email: info@spm-precisionmachining.com
Website: www.spm-precisionmachining.com
3, 4, & 5 axis CNC machining: aluminum, stainless steel & titanium components. (Minority, Woman, estab 2005, empl 30, sales $4,500,000, cert: WBENC)

Texas

6596   365 Machine Inc.
27890 Commercial Park Lane
Tomball, TX 77375
Contact: Billy Helveston VP Sales & Mktg
Tel: 281-378-7811
Email: billy@365-machine.com
Website: www.365-machine.com
Precision CNC machining, 4 CNC lathes, 5 CNC mills, horizontal mill. (Woman, estab 2013, empl 13, sales $1,200,000, cert: State, WBENC)

6597   Best Sheet Metal Solutions
923 KCK Way, Ste A
Cedar Hill, TX 75104
Contact: Jacob Bell Owner
Tel: 214-384-1951
Email: jacob@bestsheetmetalsolutions.com
Website: www.bestsheetmetalsolutions.com
Close Tolerance CNC Machining, CNC Vertical Machining Center & Haas CNC Horitzonal Turning Center (Lathe), Machine Heat Sinks, Buss bar, Surfacing, Profiling, Casting Molds, (AA, estab 2008, empl 3, sales $150,000, cert: NMSDC)

6598   Buks Tool Company, Inc.
6410-X Langfield Rd
Houston, TX 77092
Contact: Danielle Buks President
Tel: 713-974-5187
Email: danielle@bukstool.com
Website: www.bukstool.com
CNC Machining, Conventional machining, coordinate measuring machine, welding, grinding, boring, jig bore, tooling, design, EDM, sawing, hydrostatic pressure testing, high pressure pumps, components & assemblies. (Woman, estab 1978, empl 22, sales , cert: WBENC)

6599   Clay Precision, Ltd.
1102 FM 1417 NE
Sherman, TX 75090
Contact: J. Diann Spencer President
Tel: 903-891-9022
Email: jspencer@clayprecision.com
Website: www.clayprecision.com
Milling, turning, 4th axis capabilities, fixturing, plastic weldment, assemblies, heat treating, grinding, dock-to-stock quality, fabrication of custom metal and plastic machined parts and assemblies, prototypes, exotic metals, exotic plastics. (Woman, estab 1996, empl 11, sales $1,293,930, cert: State, WBENC)

6600   Coastal Machine & Mechanical, LLC
14004 S Hwy 288B
Angleton, TX 77515
Contact: Mike Adams GM
Tel: 979-848-8900
Email: madams@coastalmandm.com
Website: www.coastalmandm.com
Custom machining & fabrication, millwright & welding services, maintenance services & balancing, rebuild pumps, gearboxes, ASME "R" stamp certificate. (Hisp, estab 2010, empl 28, sales , cert: State)

6601   Cutting Source Precision, Inc.
14011 Fm 529 Bldg B
Houston, TX 77065
Contact: Larry Boyd Dir Govt Sale
Tel: 281-859-2900
Email: info@cspmachine.com
Website: www.cspmachine.com
Machining, CNC milling & turning, waterjet saw cutting, carbon, aluminum, stainless, Monel, Inconel, Ferrilum, Titanium, Delrin, & Duplex. (Woman, estab 2000, empl 20, sales $1,900,000, cert: WBENC, NWBOC)

6602   Gretna Machine Shop, Inc.
3450 Lang Rd
Houston, TX 77092
Contact: Aerospace Div. Mgr.
Tel: 713-690-7328
Email:
Website: www.gretnamachine.com
CNC turning machines, CAD/CAM software programming, Sawing, Marking, Deburring services, Real-time order tracking, Worldwide Packaging & Delivery. (Minority, Woman, estab 1980, empl 85, sales , cert: WBENC)

6603 Guzman Manufacturing, Inc.
4206 Industrial St
Rowlett, TX 75088
Contact: Annabell Acuna Office Mgr
Tel: 972-475-3003
Email: info@gzmfg.com
Website: www.gzmfg.com
Machine shop: precision sheet metal, spot welding, CNC, etc. (Hisp, estab 1975, empl 15, sales , cert: State)

6604 Mentco Inc.
15926 University Oak
San Antonio, TX 78249
Contact: Matt Weber Sr Mgr
Tel: 210-494-3100
Email: matt.weber@mentco.com
Website: www.mentcoinc.com
Mfr high precision, tight tolerance machined parts from bar stock, castings or forgings. Stainless Steel, (all grades), Inconel, Monel, Hastelloy, 15-5PH, 17-4PH, Titanium, Aluminum, Copper, Brass, Bronze. (As-Ind, estab 2006, empl 55, sales , cert: State, NMSDC)

6605 QMF Steel, Inc.
3846 IH-30 East
Campbell, TX 75422
Contact: Sherrill Lester President
Tel: 903-455-3618
Email: sherrill@qmfsteel.com
Website: www.qmfsteel.com
CNC plate saw precision cutting, CNC plasma cutting, CNC machining, CNC lathe/turning, bundle cutting, threading, polishing: aluminum, stainless, hot roll, cold roll, alloy, magnesium, brass, copper & other metal products. (Woman, estab 1994, empl 49, sales $15,000,000, cert: State, WBENC)

6606 Spring International
23594 Dogwood Trail Dr Ste A
Hockley, TX 77447
Contact: President
Tel: 281-966-5109
Email: support@springintl.net
Website: www.springintl.net
Machining, turn key, assembly, coat. etc. (Woman/AA, estab 2014, empl 5, sales $500,000, cert: State)

6607 Standard Industrial Products Company
12610 Galveston Rd
Webster, TX 77059
Contact: Walter Gomez Dir Operation & Mktg
Tel: 281-480-8711
Email: wgomez@sipco-mls.com
Website: www.sipco-mls.com
Engineering, Electro - Mechanical Design, Validation & System Integration, CNC Milling, CNC Turning, Sawing, Mechanical System assembly & integration, Gearing - Design, Sourcing, Assembly & System Integration. (Hisp, estab 1984, empl 15, sales $2,099,000, cert: NMSDC)

6608 Systems Integration, Inc.
7316 Business Pl
Arlington, TX 76001
Contact: Rhonda Smith Acct Mgr
Tel: 817-468-1494
Email: rsmith@sitexas.com
Website: www.sitexas.com
Engineering & Design, Reverse Engineering, Fabrication, Installation, Structural & Civil, Manufacturing, Machinery, Mechanical, CNC Machining, Electrical & Controls, Test Structures, Tooling. (Hisp, estab 1992, empl 20, sales $4,000,000, cert: State)

6609 VLJ Inc. dba Smith Tool & Mfg.
116 Regency Dr
Wylie, TX 75098
Contact: Kevin Hefley Sales Mgr
Tel: 972-442-4673
Email: smithtoolsales@airmail.net
Website: www.smithtoolmfg.com
Precision sheet metal mfg, stamping, tool & die, laser cutting, spinning, maching, turning. (Woman, estab 2001, empl 35, sales $570,000, cert: State)

Virginia

6610 High-Tech Machine Mfg, Inc.
11010 Trade Rd
North Chesterfield, VA 23236
Contact: Cheryl P Cacciotti President
Tel: 804-794-8640
Email: sales@hightechmachineinc.com
Website: www.htmachineinc.com
Production machining, swiss screw machine, CNC milling & turning, stock & release program. (Woman, estab 1984, empl 10, sales $1,100,000, cert: State, WBENC)

6611 HUB Corporation
2113 Salem Ave SW
Roanoke, VA 24016
Contact: Hubert Humphrey CEO
Tel: 540-342-3505
Email: hhumphrey@hubcorp.net
Website: www.hubcorp.net
Custom manufacturing CNC specializing in true 5-axis contour programming and machining with the ability to make incredibly complex shapes. (AA, estab 1957, empl 20, sales $5,000,000, cert: NMSDC)

6612 Metal Tech Inc.
2629 Richard Ave NE
Roanoke, VA 24012
Contact: Natasha Crowder Project estimator
Tel: 540-798-4193
Email: metaltech@cox.net
Website: www.metaltechincorporated.com
Custom metal fabrication: sandblasting, punching, machine cutting, CNC plasma cutting, water jet cutting, pipe bending, ornamental bender machine, surface preparation & coating. (Woman, estab 1996, empl 2, sales $150,000, cert: State)

Washington

6613   Premier Manufacturing
1711 N Madison
Liberty Lake, WA 99019
Contact: Britt La Chance Sales Dir
Tel: 509-993-6800
Email: britt@premier-manufacturing.com
Website: www.premier-manufacturing.net
Mfr precision sheet metal products. (Woman, estab 2001, empl 100, sales $8,486,433, cert: WBENC)

Wisconsin

6614   American Metal Technologies LLC
8213 Durand Ave
Sturtevant, WI 53177
Contact: San Santharam President
Tel: 262-633-1756
Email: san@amermetals.com
Website: www.amermetals.com
Precision CNC machining & assembly: ferrous & non-ferrous components, fluid retention components, FEAD brackets & vibration dampening products. (As-Pac, estab 2000, empl 142, sales $25,500,000, cert: NMSDC)

6615   Bothe Associates Inc.
6901-46th St
Kenosha, WI 53144
Contact: Laura Bothe VP
Tel: 262-656-1860
Email: lbothe@bothe.com
Website: www.bothe.com
Machine shop & assembly: prototype, short & long run metal & plastic parts, high tolerance, tooling lathes, mills. (Woman, estab 1950, empl 42, sales $5,876,062, cert: WBENC)

6616   Cardinal Components, Inc.
N59W13500 Manhardt Dr
Menomonee Falls, WI 53051
Contact: Leann Kurey President
Tel: 262-437-1510
Email: nelsonm@cardinalcomponents.com
Website: www.cardinalcomponents.com
Dist Metal Components: Rivet-Nut Fasteners; Precision Machining: CNC Turning and Milling; Metal Fabrication: Brake Press, Laser, Stamping and Welding-Spot; Wire Forming and Springs. (Woman, estab 1983, empl 17, sales $7,000,100, cert: CPUC)

6617   Mantz Automation
1630 Innovation Way
Hartford, WI 53027
Contact: Gary Sonnenburg Sales Rep
Tel: 262-224-7528
Email: tnewman@mantzautomation.com
Website: www.mantzautomation.com
Machining components: alloys, design & build tooling, gages, fitures, CNC machinery, 5 axis machinng centers with large envelope of 60" x 120" x 48". (Minority, Woman, estab 1986, empl 105, sales $22,300,000, cert: State)

6618   R.J. Zeman Tool & Mfg. Co., Inc.
W228 N575 Westmound Dr
Waukesha, WI 53186
Contact: Spencer Schreindl President
Tel: 262-549-4400
Email: sschreindl@zemantool.com
Website: www.zemantool.com
Machining, design, mfr & inspect fixtures, special machines, gages, die cast dies, plastic injection molds, permanent molds, core boxes, patterns for sand casting & short and long-run production parts. (Woman, estab 1966, empl 48, sales $9,600,000, cert: WBENC)

6619   Stanek Tool Corporation
2500 S Calhoun Rd
New Berlin, WI 53151
Contact: Paul Bartkowiak VP Workholding
Tel: 262-786-0120
Email: pbartkowiak@stanektool.com
Website: www.stanektool.com
Design & build machining fixtures, plastic molds, & precision machined parts & assemblies. (Woman, estab 1924, empl 50, sales $10,000,000, cert: WBENC)

METAL RAW STOCK

Includes distributors of metal sheets, plates, rods, pipe, etc. Many can provide cutting and other metal processing services. (Also see six other METAL categories). NAICS Code 33

Arizona

6620 K&R Holdings, Inc.
2322 W Detroit Pl
Chandler, AZ 85224
Contact: Wayne Armoogam President
Tel: 480-236-2682
Email: warmoogam@lumawaresafety.com
Website: www.lumawaresafety.com
Supply and install photoluminescent egress systems for facilities. Our technologies for egress requires no electricity, external power source or batteries to provide the illumination required for safe movement of employees (As-Ind, estab 2007, empl 5, sales $100,000, cert: NMSDC)

California

6621 California Metal & Supply Inc.
10230 Freeman Ave
Santa Fe Springs, CA 90670
Contact: Kenneth Minkyu Lee President
Tel: 800-707-6061
Email: klee@californiametal.com
Website: www.CaliforniaMetal.com
Titanium, Inconel, Aluminum, Stainless, Magnesium Sheet, Plate, Bar, Tube & Tubing, Pipe, Tubing: Stainless, Carbon Steel, Aluminum, Brass, Valves. (As-Pac, estab 1984, empl 12, sales $60,000,000, cert: NMSDC)

6622 Global Steel Alliance Corp.
14241 E Firestone Blvd, Ste 400
La Mirada, CA 90638
Contact: Keith Shiozaki President
Tel: 562-293-4086
Email: keith@steel-alliance.net
Website: www.steel-alliance.net
Dist carbon steel pipe. (As-Pac, estab 2008, empl 1, sales $2,779,880, cert: NMSDC, CPUC)

6623 International Metal Source
17605 Fabrica Way Ste E & F
Cerritos, CA 90703
Contact: Jaymee Del Rosario Founder/CEO
Tel: 714-676-5669
Email: jaymee@imetalsource.com
Website: www.imetalsource.com
Dist Aluminum, Nickel, Titanium, Stainless Steel, High-Temperature & Specialty Steels, Ferrous, Non-Ferrous & Non-Metallic Raw Material in Sheet, Plate, Rod, Bar, Extrusions, Tubes & Formed Shapes. (Minority, Woman, estab 2009, empl 10, sales $889,000, cert: CPUC, SDB)

6624 Southern California Metals, Inc.
9900 Bell Ranch Dr
Santa Fe Springs, CA 90670
Contact: Alisa Thorpe President
Tel: 562-941-1616
Email: alisa@socalmetals.com
Website: www.socalmetals.com
Dist alloys, steels, stainless steels, titanium, nickel based alloys, aluminum & copper alloys in plate, sheet, bar, extrusion, forgings & castings, plastic lexan sheets, aviation rivets, nuts, fasteners, screws & seat tracks. (Woman, estab 1995, empl 15, sales $4,001,000, cert: State, CPUC)

Florida

6625 Aluminum Distributing, Inc. dba ADI Metal
2930 SW Second Ave
Fort Lauderdale, FL 33315
Contact: Betsy McGee President
Tel: 954-523-6474
Email: betsy@adimetal.com
Website: www.adimetal.com
Dist aluminum for the marine and industrial markets. (Woman, estab 1958, empl 16, sales $5,300,000, cert: State, WBENC)

6626 ASM Aerospace Specifications Metals, Inc.
2501 NW 34th Place, B28
Pompano Beach, FL 33069
Contact: Douglas Bridges VP
Tel: 954-977-0666
Email: dbridges@aerospacemetals.com
Website: www.aerospacemetals.com
Dist raw materials: aircraft quality metals, sheet, plate, rod, wire, bar, tubing & extruded shapes. (Minority, Woman, estab 2001, empl 14, sales $7,000,000, cert: NMSDC)

6627 Manzi Metals, Inc.
15293 Flight Path Dr
Brooksville, FL 34604
Contact: Dorsey Peterson Small Bus Specialist
Tel: 352-277-5852
Email: dpeterson@manzimetals.com
Website: www.manzimetals.com
Dist aerospace & commercial metals: aluminum, stainless, alloy steel, copper, brass, titanium, high temps in sheet, plate, bar, rod, hex, tube, etc. forgings, castings, ingots, billets. (Woman/AA, estab 1993, empl 10, sales $3,600,000, cert: State, City, NMSDC, SDB)

Illinois

6628 Elgiloy Specialty Metals
1565 Fleetwood Dr
Elgin, IL 60123
Contact: Margaret Wilson Wire Sales Rep
Tel: 847-695-1900
Email: margaretw@elgiloy.com
Website: www.elgiloy.com
Strip, wire, rod & bar specialty alloys; various gauges/
diameters and widths. Strip: rolling, slitting, annealing.
Wire/bar/rod: drawing, annealing. In-house lab. (As-Pac,
estab 1975, empl 75, sales , cert: NMSDC)

6629 HL Metals, LLC
910 Spruce St
Winnetka, IL 60093
Contact: Hui Lin Lim President
Tel: 312-590-3360
Email: hlim@hlmetalsllc.com
Website: www.hlmetalsllc.com
Dist P1020 aluminum sows/aluminum sheet ingot.
(Minority, Woman, estab 2007, empl 1, sales $55,000,000,
cert: CPUC, NWBOC)

6630 National Material Company, L.L.C.
1965 Pratt Blvd
Elk Grove Village, IL 60007
Contact: Jim Osborne Dir Minority Dev
Tel: 847-806-4742
Email: josborne@nmlp.com
Website: www.nmlp.com
Steel service & processing. (As-Pac, estab 1999, empl 299,
sales $370,000,000, cert: NMSDC)

6631 National Material Trading, LLC
1965 Pratt Blvd
Elk Grove Village, IL 60007
Contact: Jim Osborne Dir of Minority Dev
Tel: 847-806-4742
Email: josborne@nmlp.com
Website: www.nationalmaterialtrading.com
Dist carbon flat rolled steel. (As-Pac, estab 1964, empl 12,
sales $0, cert: NMSDC)

6632 North States Steel Corp.
12255 Hwy 173
Hebron, IL 60034
Contact: Sandra Myers President
Tel: 815-648-1500
Email: smyers@northstatessteel.com
Website: www.northstatessteel.com
Hot rolled, cold rolled, aluminum stainless steel sheets.
(Woman, estab 1971, empl 25, sales $14,000,000, cert:
State, WBENC, SDB)

6633 S & S International,Inc.
457 St. Paul Blvd
Carol Stream, IL 60188
Contact: Rich Isom Sr Acct Exec
Tel: 708-805-5701
Email: icemanandfamily1@msn.com
Website: www.ssistainless.com
Dist stainless steel: sheet, plate, strip, coil, bars, struc-
tural shapes, square & rectangular tubing, pipe &
fittings, aluminum sheet, strip & coil. (Minority, estab
1991, empl 105, sales $30,000,000, cert: NMSDC)

Indiana

6634 Circle City Rebar, LLC
4002 Industrial Blvd
Indianapolis, IN 46254
Contact: Heidi Russo Controller
Tel: 317-917-8566
Email: hrusso@circlecityrebar.com
Website: www.circlecityrebar.com
Supplier and Fabricator of concrete reinforcing steel bars
(rebar) in all sizes; plain and epoxy coated. (AA, estab
2005, empl 14, sales $7,541,942, cert: NMSDC)

6635 Eagle Steel Products, Inc.
5150 Loop Rd
Jeffersonville, IN 47130
Contact: Gary Shumate GM Sales
Tel: 812-282-7090
Email: gshumate@eaglesteelproducts.com
Website: www.eaglesteelproducts.com
Mfr strip steel; flat rolled products, blanking; covered
barge & rail loading & unloading svcs, warehousing, etc.
(Minority, Woman, estab 1982, empl 83, sales
$32,000,000, cert: NMSDC)

Michigan

6636 Delaco Steel Corporation
8111 Tireman, Ste 1
Dearborn, MI 48126
Contact: Michael Roualet VP Quality
Tel: 313-491-1200
Email: mike.roualet@delacosteel.com
Website: www.delacosteel.com
Dist & process steel & aluminum. Blanking, warehous-
ing, slitting, stampings, etc. (Minority, Woman, estab
1974, empl 650, sales $0, cert: NMSDC, WBENC)

6637   Ferrous Processing & Trading
2920 Scotten
Detroit, MI 48210
Contact: Kristy Boismier President
Tel: 313-567-9710
Email: kristy.boismier@fptscrap.com
Website: www.fptscrap.com
Process, distribute & recycle scrap metals. (AA, estab 0, empl , sales $0, cert: NMSDC)

6638   H&H Metal Source
1909 Turner Ave NW
Grand Rapids, MI 49504
Contact: JR Hartman Operations Mgr
Tel: 616-364-0113
Email: jr@hhmetalsource.com
Website: www.hhmetalsource.com
Flat rolled steel in coil or blanks. (Woman, estab 1992, empl 30, sales $38,000,000, cert: WBENC)

6639   Instramed
3071 Commerce Dr. Ste. C
Ft. Gratiot, MI 48059
Contact: Cori Bonkoske Office Mgr
Tel: 800-451-5840
Email: allinfo@instramedinc.com
Website: www.instramedinc.com
Scrap metal & recyclable materials, ferrous & non-ferrous scrap metal. (Woman, estab 1987, empl , sales , cert: NWBOC)

6640   Marwol Metals, Ltd.
PO Box 252464
West Bloomfield, MI 48325
Contact: VP
Tel: 248-356-3444
Email: info@marwolmetals.com
Website: www.marwolmetals.com
Dist & buy ferrous & non-ferrous scrap metals. (Woman, estab 1981, empl 2, sales $950,000, cert: WBENC)

6641   National Material Co.
1505 N Dixie Dr, Ste 2
Monroe, MI 48162
Contact: John Allen Sales Rep
Tel: 734-384-9720
Email: jballen53@msn.com
Website: www.nmcmonroe.com
Steel coil, sheet, blank, painted steel, galvanized, aluminum,stainless HSLA, CS, DS. (As-Pac, estab 0, empl 0, sales $750,000,000, cert: NMSDC)

6642   Scion Steel
21555 Mullin Ave
Warren, MI 48089
Contact: Micky Tschirhart VP
Tel: 800-288-2127
Email: mtschirhart@scionsteel.com
Website: www.scionsteel.com
Full line steel service center - processed & fabricated to order. (Hisp, estab 1984, empl 51, sales $0, cert: NMSDC)

6643   Torch Steel Sales LLC
18501 Krause St
Riverview, MI 48193
Contact: Cristina Simone Owner
Tel: 734-783-2018
Email: csimone@torchsteelsales.com
Website: www.torchsteelsales.com
Steel service center: slitting, blanking, shearing, & slearing of non-ferrous flat rolled steel products, Hot Rolled, Cold Rolled, Hot Dipped Galvanized, Electro Galvanized, Galvanneal, & Aluminized. (Woman, estab 2013, empl 2, sales $700,600, cert: WBENC)

North Carolina

6644   Accro-Met, Inc.
3406 Westwood Industrial Dr
Monroe, NC 28110
Contact: Andrea Doolittle Sales
Tel: 704-283-2111
Email: alm@accromet.com
Website: www.accromet.com
Dist metal: stainless, nickel, aluminum, copper, brass, bronze, sheet, plate, bar, shapes. (Woman, estab 1988, empl 15, sales $6,000,000, cert: WBENC)

New Jersey

6645   L-E-M Plastics& Supply Inc.
255 Highland Cross
Rutherford, NJ 07070
Contact: Ellen Pietrowitz-Phillips President
Tel: 201-933-9150
Email: ellenp@l-e-mplastics.com
Website: www.l-e-mplastics.com
Fabriate & dist raw material plastic & rubber, Sheet, rod, tubing & film cut to size. Machining of all plastic, build to print. Steel rule die punching of thin plastic & rubber. (Woman, estab 1974, empl 12, sales $1,200,000, cert: WBENC)

Ohio

6646   CT Metal Source
9551 St Christine Ct
Sylvania, OH 43560
Contact: Chad Crooks President
Tel: 419-779-6172
Email: ccrooks@ctmetalsource.com
Website: www.ctmetalsource.com
Dist metal castings, rail car parts, vent registers & steel coils. (Hisp, estab 2005, empl 5, sales $7,000,000, cert: NMSDC)

6647   Ferrolux Metals Co. of Ohio, LLC
8055A Highland Pointe Pkwy
Macedonia, OH 44056
Contact: Mark Nester GM
Tel: 330-468-1008
Email: mnester@ferrolux.com
Website: www.ferrolux.com
Dist flat rolled processed steel, Cold rolled, Coated, Slitting & Inspection, Storage, Transportation. (Hisp, estab 2004, empl 22, sales , cert: NMSDC)

6648   Mid-West Materials, Inc.
3687 Shepard Rd
Perry, OH 44081
Contact: Scott Dennis Sales Rep
Tel: 440-259-5200
Email: scott.dennis@midwestmaterials.com
Website: www.midwestmaterials.com
Flat rolled steel service center, hot rolled, hot rolled, pickled & oiled & coated steel in commercial quality, high strength-low alloy & low through high carbon chemistries. (Woman, estab 1952, empl 50, sales $50,000,000, cert: State)

6649   Nu Tek Steel, LLC
6180 American Road
Toledo, OH 43612
Contact: Sarah Bates President
Tel: 419-724-0891
Email: sarah.bates@ntsteel.net
Website: www.ntsteel.net
Steel services: slitting, pickling, blanking, leveling, special bar quality, construction & medical. (Woman/AA, estab 2000, empl 10, sales $4,300,000, cert: State, WBENC)

Texas

6650   Midwest Steel Company, Inc.
9825 Moers Rd
Houston, TX 77075
Contact: Christopher Given VP
Tel: 713-991-7843
Email: chrisgiven@midwest-steel.com
Website: www.midwest-steel.com
Dismantling & demolition contracting. (Woman, estab 1968, empl 89, sales $10,755,892, cert: State, WBENC)

Virginia

6651   United Scrap Metal
2900 Terminal Ave
Richmond, VA 23234
Contact: Owen Tomlinson Recycling Consultant
Tel: 434-430-1039
Email: otomlinson@unitedscrap.com
Website: www.unitedscrap.com
Metal recycling. (Woman, estab 1978, empl 170, sales , cert: WBENC)

METAL, WIRE PRODUCTS
See six other METAL categories. NAICS Code 33

California

6652   Top-Shelf Fixtures
       5263 Schaefer Ave
       Chino, CA 91710
       Contact: Michelle Burguan Controller
       Tel: 909-627-7423
       Email: sprochnow@topshelffixtures.com
       Website: www.topshelffixtures.com
Wire fabrication: sheet metal & structural steel for
gondola shelving. (Hisp, estab 2002, empl 123, sales
$8,500,000, cert: NMSDC)

Georgia

6653   Healthier & Happier, Inc.
       1853 Whitehall Forest Ct.
       Atlanta, GA 30316
       Contact: Jing Carter-Lu President
       Tel: 678-900-6617
       Email: jing.carter-lu@healthier-happier.com
       Website: www.healthier-happier.com
Dist wire rope, steel rope, carbon spring steel wire, bead
wire, hose wire, plastic coated wire rope, PC stranded
wire, bunched wire, galvanized stranded wire & zinc-plated
steel wire. (Minority, Woman, estab 2003, empl 2, sales
$120,000, cert: City)

Illinois

6654   Altak Inc.
       250 Covington Dr
       Bloomingdale, IL 60108
       Contact: Steve Janas Sales Mgr
       Tel: 630-622-0300
       Email: rtakayama@arktechno.com
       Website: www.altakinc.com
Wire Harness manufacturing, Switch Assembly manufacturing, Spring manufacturing, Stampings - 30 to 800 ton,
Wire Forms, IATF 16949 and ISO 9001 certified. (As-Pac,
estab 1980, empl 400, sales $37,000,000, cert: NMSDC)

6655   Solar Spring & Wire Forms
       345 Criss Circle
       Elk Grove Village, IL 60007
       Contact: Aida Carrera Dir of Global Sales
       Tel: 847-437-7838
       Email: acarrera@solarspring.com
       Website: www.solarspring.com
Mfr springs, wire forms & stampings. (Hisp, estab 1979,
empl 110, sales $11,100,000, cert: NMSDC)

Louisiana

6656   Vast Industries
       108 Venus St Ste 200
       Morgan City, LA 70380
       Contact: Yvette Archuleta-Tudury Owner
       Tel: 985-312-1592
       Email: yvette@vast-ind.com
       Website: www.Vast-Ind.com
Wire EDM & precision machined parts manufacturing,
custom product design, reverse engineering & aluminum
& steel fabrication. (Minority, Woman, estab 2007, empl
7, sales $600,000, cert: NMSDC, WBENC, 8(a))

Massachusetts

6657   Springfield Spring
       311 Shaker Rd
       Longmeadow, MA 01028
       Contact: Norman Rodriques President
       Tel: 413-525-6837
       Email: pat@springfieldspring.com
       Website: www.springfieldspring.com
Mfr precision engineered compression springs, torsion
springs, extension springs, wire forms, fourslide-
produced stampings, assemblies. (Hisp, estab 1942,
empl 39, sales $7,200,000, cert: NMSDC)

Ohio

6658   Herbert E. Orr Comany, Inc.
       335 W Wall St
       Paudling, OH 45879
       Contact: Greg Johnson President
       Tel: 419-399-4866
       Email: gjohnson@heorr.com
       Website: www.heorr.com
Hot Forged Wheel Wrenches; Jack Tool Kits; Hood
Support Rods; E-Coat Painting & powder coating; wire
forms (pnuematic and CNC); assembly and kitting.
(Woman, estab 1957, empl 51, sales $12,656,024, cert:
WBENC)

6659   Mid West Fabricating
       313 N Johns St
       Amanda, OH 43102
       Contact: Dave Gallimore Business Devel
       Tel: 740-969-4411
       Email: dgallimore@midwestfab.com
       Website: www.midwestfab.com
Cold formed rod & wire products, fasteners, CNC
wireforming, cold forming. (Woman, estab 1945, empl
200, sales $32,000,000, cert: WBENC)

Oklahoma

6660   Ebsco Spring Company, Inc.
4949 S 83rd Ave E
Tulsa, OK 74145
Contact: Todd Pfeifer Sales
Tel: 918-628-1680
Email: toddp@ebscospring.com
Website: www.ebscospring.com
Mfr & engineer custom, high quality compression, extension & torsion springs. (Woman, estab 1940, empl 75, sales $6,500,000, cert: WBENC)

Pennsylvania

6661   LEM Products, Inc.
147 Keystone Dr
Montgomeryville, PA 18936
Contact: Nicole Adamczyk Sales
Tel: 800-220-2400
Email: nadamczyk@lemproductsinc.com
Website: www.lemproductsinc.com
Mfr wire identification safety products: wire marker cards & books, voltage markers, transformer marking, hand writeable cable markers, laser coded bar codes, lockout tags, roll
dispensers, heat shrinkables, etc. (Woman, estab 1967, empl 38, sales $5,500,000, cert: CPUC, WBENC)

6662   R.A.W. Consulting, LLC
126 Mervis Dr
Beaver Falls, PA 15010
Contact: Robert Washington President
Tel: 724-384-1559
Email: rawconsultantsllc@gmail.com
Website: www.R-A-W-LLC.com
Distribution & warehousing of Stainless & alloy tubing, Cold rolled wire, Metal grating, Deformed wire. (AA, estab 2013, empl 3, sales $309,996, cert: State, NMSDC)

Texas

6663   M3 Associates, Inc.
PO Box 224075
Dallas, TX 75222
Contact: Yvonne Newhouse President
Tel: 214-339-2117
Email: yvonne@m3associatesinc.com
Website: www.m3associatesinc.com
Distributor of wire, cable, tubing, sleeving, solder sleeves, heat shrink molded, shapes, boots (Woman/AA, estab 1988, empl 5, sales $0, cert: State)

Virginia

6664   Jo Kell, Inc.
1716 Lambert Ct
Chesapeake, VA 23320
Contact: Patricia Galiney Sales
Tel: 904-260-8420
Email: customerservice@jokell.com
Website: WWW.JOKELL.COM
Dist electrical apparatus & equipment, wiring supplies & related equipment. (Woman, estab 1977, empl 50, sales $30,383,075, cert: WBENC)

26th Annual
Supplier Diversity Seminar

"Best Practices in Supplier Diversity Strategies and Initiatives"

February 2023 • Location TBD

Join experienced Supplier Diversity Professionals and subject matter experts for a series of presentations and networking events

> "One of the best all-around events that I have attended ... this is an event that I definitely want to have in my yearly budget! "
>
> "Great! I'm glad I attended."
>
> —2019 attendees

AGENDA
Day One
Seminar General Session
8:00 am - 4:00 pm

Networking Reception
5:30 - 7:00 pm

Day Two
Seminar General Session
8:00 am - 12:00 pm

SEMINAR LOCATION
TBD

ACCOMMODATIONS
DIR has reserved a block of rooms at TBD. Reservation information will be sent with registration confirmation.

FEE
$999/person
Fee includes all sessions. seminar materials, continental breakfast, lunch and networking reception

SEMINAR REGISTRATION
www.diversityinforesources.com
or contact DIR directly at:
612-781-6819
info@diversityinforesources.com
NOTE: There is NO on-site registration

SPONSORED BY
Diversity Information Resources
2300 Kennedy Street NE, Suite 230
Minneapolis, MN 55413
www.diversityinforesources.com

TOPICS: Seminar agenda features noted supplier diversity professional and cover topics including (subject to change):

- Raising Social Awareness and Fostering Inclusive Sourcing
- Environmental, Social and Governance (ESG)
- Second Tier Program Design and Development
- Looking Beyond Spend: Supplier Diversity Economic Impact
- How to Identify and Vett Potential Diverse Suppliers: Mitigating and Understanding Risk, Who Qualifies, Capturing and Reporting Diverse Spend, Importance of Certification, etc.
- Managing Government Contracting Requirements and Practical Solutions

WHO ATTENDS?

- Supplier Diversity Professionals
- Purchasing Managers/Buyers
- VP's of Materials and Purchasing Procurement Managers
- Small Business Liaison Officers (SBLO's)
- Lead staff with responsibility for implementing supplier diversity programs
- Graduates of DIR's "Building Strategic Phases of a Supplier Diversity Process" Seminar

Since 1968, DIR has been a leader in providing information resources that support and enhance diversity initiatives.

OFFICE SUPPLIES

Manufacturers and distributors of office supplies and equipment: rubber stamps, writing implements, binders and portfolios, business forms, calculators, envelopes, tape, ink, office machines and furniture, paper and maintenance products, paper recycling, paper conversion, toner cartridges, printers, etc. NAICS Code 42

Alabama

6665   E.S. Robbins Corp.
2802 E Avalon Ave
Muscle Shoals, AL 35661
Contact: Bonnie Donato Channel Marketing Mgr
Tel: 256-248-2494
Email: badonato@esrobbins.com
Website: www.esrchairmats.com
Dist office products & furnishings. Mfr polymer products. (Woman, estab 1967, empl 187, sales , cert: WBENC)

Arkansas

6666   Burris Inc.
113 S Arkansas Ave
Russellville, AR 72801
Contact: President
Tel: 479-968-4888
Email:
Website: www.burrisinc.com
Office supplies & office furniture, panel systems, custom millwork, office layout & design. (Woman, estab 1953, empl 15, sales $3,374,600, cert: WBENC)

Arizona

6667   Goddess Products, Inc.
6142 Getty Dr
North Little Rock, AR 72117
Contact: Andrew Sigeti Acct Mgr
Tel: 501-372-4002
Email: asigeti@ussco.com
Website: www.goddessproductsinc.com
Dist office products, office equipment, office furniture, computer peripherals, janitorial supplies & safety equipment. (Woman/AA, estab 2006, empl 5, sales $375,000, cert: WBENC)

California

6668   American Textile Systems, Inc. DBA American Paper
13151 Midway Place
Cerritos, CA 90703
Contact: Mike Khan VP Corporate Markets
Tel: 562-229-0036
Email: mike@amtexsys.com
Website: www.amtexsys.com
Healthcare & hospitality related textile & paper products. (As-Ind, estab 1993, empl 25, sales $20,000,000, cert: State)

6669   Big Red Print Solutions, LLC
2100 Sawtelle Blvd Ste 201
Los Angeles, CA 90025
Contact: Rudy Wrabel Dir
Tel: 213-985-7201
Email: rudy@bigredink.com
Website: www.bigredink.com
Dist office equipment, supplies & technology products. (Minority, Woman, estab 2010, empl 7, sales $1,100,000, cert: NMSDC, CPUC)

6670   DD Office Products, Inc
5025 Hampton St
Los Angeles, CA 90058
Contact: John Kim GSA Contract Admin
Tel: 323-973-4569
Email: johnk@libertypp.com
Website: www.libertypp.com
Dist office paper. (As-Ind, estab 2001, empl 14, sales $36,617,778, cert: NMSDC)

6671   Garza Industries
1870 N Glassell St
Orange, CA 92865
Contact: James Garza
Tel: 714-769-2777
Email: james@garzaindustries.com
Website: www.garzaindustries.com
Dist office supplies: copy paper, laser toner cartridges, fax & copier supplies, furniture, direct mail svcs, commercial printing, corporate apparel, promotional items. (Minority, Woman, estab 1991, empl 35, sales , cert: CPUC)

6672   Kleenslate Concepts, LP
14997 Camage Ave, Unit B
Sonora, CA 94370
Contact: Julia Rhodes CEO
Tel: 209-588-0375
Email: julia@kleenslate.com
Website: www.kleenslate.com
Dist attachable white board markers erasers, white board products (Minority, Woman, estab 2001, empl 12, sales , cert: WBENC)

6673   Z Venture Capital Frontiers, Inc.
1625 W Vernon Ave
Los Angeles, CA 90062
Contact: Karim Zaman President
Tel: 323-596-4690
Email: karim@thezamangroup.com
Website: www.thezamangroup.com
Dist office supplies, inkjet, laser, toner cartridge, thermal fax ribbon. (AA, estab 1997, empl 2, sales $1,300,000, cert: State, City, CPUC)

Colorado

6674   Eon Office
60 Tejon St
Denver, CO 80223
Contact: Jeniffer Beam VP Sales
Tel: 720-570-5400
Email: jbeam@eonoffice.com
Website: www.eonoffice.com
Office Supplies, Furniture and Design, Printing, Breakroom, Janitorial (Woman, estab 2001, empl 86, sales , cert: WBENC)

6675 Faison Office Products, Inc
      12508 E Briarwood Ave Ste 1A
      Centennial, CO 80012
      Contact: Bonnie Key Exec Coordinator
      Tel: 303-340-3672
      Email: bkey@faisonopc.com
      Website: www.faisonopc.com
Dist office supplies & furniture; word processing & data processing supplies & furniture. (AA, estab 1981, empl 55, sales $45,000,000, cert: NMSDC)

District of Columbia

6676 The Hamilton Group
      4406 Gault Place NE
      Washington, DC 20019
      Contact: Kaari Hamilton President
      Tel: 202-689-4304
      Email: kayhhpbp@verizon.net
      Website: www.thehamiltongroupllc.net
Dist office supplies, advertisement & promotional products, office equipment & clothing wearables. (Woman/AA, estab 2007, empl 1, sales $731,000, cert: City, NMSDC, WBENC)

Florida

6677 Apex Office Products, Inc.
      5209 N Howard Ave
      Tampa, FL 33603
      Contact: Aurelio Llorente, Jr President
      Tel: 800-227-1563
      Email: allorentejr@apexop.com
      Website: www.apexofficeproducts.com
Dist office supplies & furniture, data supplies & furniture, paper products, rubber stamps. (Minority, Woman, estab 1981, empl 55, sales , cert: State, NMSDC)

6678 Konie Cups International, Inc.
      9001 NW 105th Way
      Medley, FL 33178
      Contact: Fiorella Roversi Sales Analyst
      Tel: 786-337-7967
      Email: fiorellaroversi@koniecups.com
      Website: www.koniecups.com
Mfr paper cone cups & funnels. (Hisp, estab 1991, empl 56, sales $9,223,670, cert: NMSDC)

6679 Mammoth Office Products, LLC
      7351 Southampton Terr
      Boynton Beach, FL 33436
      Contact: Lynn Pilato Owner
      Tel: 561-251-8662
      Email: Info@MammothOfficeProducts.com
      Website: www.mammothofficeproducts.com
Office products & supplies. (Woman, estab 2012, empl 1, sales $200,000, cert: WBENC)

6680 MarkMaster, Inc.
      11111 N 46th St
      Tampa, FL 33617
      Contact: Deborah Jordan Sales Rep
      Tel: 813-988-6000
      Email: sales@markmasterinc.com
      Website: www.markmasterinc.com
Mfr rubber stamps, engraved & screened signage & badges; industrial marking equip. (Hisp, estab 1933, empl 65, sales $8,700,993, cert: NMSDC)

Georgia

6681 ABC Laser USA, Inc.
      6000 G Unity Dr
      Norcross, GA 30092
      Contact: Kammie Lee Acct Mgr
      Tel: 770-448-5867
      Email: kmichell@abclaserusa.com
      Website: www.abclaserusa.com
Office Supplies, Ink, Toner, Furniture, Paper, Disc, Printers, Faxes, Pens, Pencils, Maintenance, Service, Janitorial Supplies, Cleaners, Toilet Paper, Paper Towels, Recycle Toner, Hewlett Packard, Lexmark, Dell, Canon. (Minority, Woman, estab 1996, empl 6, sales , cert: City)

6682 Interface Consulting Services, LLC
      4525 Flat Shoals Pkwy Ste 405
      Decatur, GA 30034
      Contact: Anthony Sylvester CEO
      Tel: 404-243-4954
      Email: anthony@interface-cs.com
      Website: www.interface-cs.com
Provide quality consulting advice & paper solutions. (AA, estab 2008, empl 3, sales $20,000,000, cert: NMSDC)

6683 Peachtree Supplies, Inc.
      233 Peachtree St NE, Ste 1265
      Atlanta, GA 30303
      Contact: Al Graham President
      Tel: 404-963-2410
      Email: agraham@peachtreesupplies.com
      Website: www.peachtreesupplies.com
Office supplies, furniture, ink & toner, paper, cleaning supplies, technology. (Woman/AA, estab 2009, empl 10, sales $1,350,000, cert: NMSDC)

6684 South Coast Paper LLC
      2300 Windy Ridge Pkwy, Ste 830
      Atlanta, GA 30339
      Contact: LaJoia Broughton Supplier Diversity
      Tel: 770-933-3411
      Email: supplierdiversity@southcoastpaper.com
      Website: www.southcoastpaper.com
Mfr & convert uncoated, coated, photographic & digital paper grades, cut, wrap, package, palletize & ship product. (AA, estab 2000, empl 49, sales $18,000,000, cert: NMSDC)

Iowa

6685 American Diversity Business Solutions
      9834 Hickory Dr
      Urbandale, IA 50322
      Contact: Joe Riggsbee Sr Acct Exec
      Tel: 515-276-1232
      Email: jriggsbee@americanmin.com
      Website: www.americandiv.com
Dist custom business forms, office supplies, & promotional items. (Woman, estab 1992, empl 15, sales $23,941,250, cert: WBENC)

6686   Bailey Office Equipment, Inc.
       123 E 2nd St
       Ottumwa, IA 52501
       Contact: Linda Gardner President
       Tel: 800-728-0407
       Email: linda@baileyoffice.com
       Website: www.baileyoffice.com
Dist office supplies, business machines, office furniture, cleaning supplies, safety equipment & breakroom essentials. (Woman, estab 1925, empl 10, sales $2,798,000, cert: WBENC)

Illinois

6687   Chicago Green Office Company dba National Office Works, Inc.
       7930 S Madison St
       Burr Ridge, IL 60527
       Contact: Joanna Davidson President
       Tel: 312-455-9343
       Email: joanna.davidson@nationalofficeworks.com
       Website: www.nationalofficeworks.com
Dist office supplies. (Woman, estab , empl , sales $750,000, cert: State, WBENC)

6688   Gorilla Paper Inc.
       1125 Lunt Ave
       Elk Grove Village, IL 60007
       Contact: Su Chang Lim President
       Tel: 773-789-8113
       Email: suchang@gorillapaper.com
       Website: www.gorillapaper.com
POS Thermal Paper rolls, carbonless paper rolls, & related Ink Ribbons. (As-Pac, estab 2009, empl 3, sales $18,598,936, cert: NMSDC)

6689   Logsdon Office Supply
       111 S Fairbank
       Addison, IL 60101
       Contact: Jack Dern VP
       Tel: 847-593-8282
       Email: jdern@logsdonofficesupply.com
       Website: www.logsdonofficesupply.com
Dist office supplies. (AA, estab 1966, empl 25, sales $7,000,000, cert: City, NMSDC)

6690   Norwood Paper
       7001 W 60th St
       Chicago, IL 60674
       Contact: Laura Martin Natl Accts Mgr
       Tel: 773-788-1508
       Email: laura@norwoodpaper.com
       Website: www.norwoodpaper.com
Dist non-box related packaging chipboard, skid liners, dust covers, interleavers, divider sheets, pallet liners, pallet pads. (Woman, estab 1972, empl 1, sales $8,000,000, cert: WBENC)

6691   Pointe International
       234 Oakwood Road
       Lake Zurich, IL 60047
       Contact: Sheila Liao President
       Tel: 847-550-7001
       Email: sheila.liao@pointecompany.com
       Website: www.pointecompany.com
Mfr & dist wooden case pencils, mechanic pencils, desk stapler, office supplies & promotional items. (Minority, Woman, estab 1997, empl 12, sales $1,800,000, cert: NMSDC, WBENC)

6692   Taylor Made Business Solutions LLC
       318 W. Adams St 16th Fl
       Chicago, IL 60606
       Contact: Evonne Taylor CEO
       Tel: 312-803-5635
       Email: etaylor@tmbsllc.com
       Website: www.TMBSLLC.com
Dist general office supplies, office furniture, break room & janitorial supplies. (Woman/AA, estab 2011, empl 3, sales $2,762,000, cert: State, NMSDC)

6693   Working Hands, Inc.
       39W254 Sheldon Ct
       Geneva, IL 60134
       Contact: Maureen Vedder President
       Tel: 630-270-1097
       Email: maureen@workinghandsinc.com
       Website: www.workinghandsinc.com
GBC equipment & supplies, copier tabs, laminating rolls & pouches, clear presentation covers, black composition back covers prepunched, binding coils, 3 ring clear view binders, plain or mylar docucopy copier tabs. (Woman, estab 2003, empl 2, sales $250,000, cert: NWBOC)

Indiana

6694   Kramer & Leonard, Inc.
       312 Roberts Rd
       Chesterton, IN 46304
       Contact: Mary Fox President
       Tel: 219-926-1171
       Email: mfox@kramerleonard.com
       Website: www.kramerleonard.com
Office products, office supplies, computer supplies, office furniture, commercial interior design services, copier sales, copier service. (Woman, estab 0, empl , sales , cert: State, WBENC)

6695   OfficeWorks Services LLC
       12000 Exit Five Pkwy
       Fishers, IN 46037
       Contact: Joyce Posson VP Admin
       Tel: 317-577-3519
       Email: jposson@officeworks.net
       Website: www.officeworks.net
Dist office furniture & material handling equip. (Hisp, estab 1984, empl 60, sales $43,000,000, cert: State, NMSDC)

6696   Rite Quality Office Supplies, Inc.
       710 N Washington St
       Kokomo, IN 46901
       Contact: Douglas Vaughn President
       Tel: 765-459-4788
       Email: riteq@netusa1.net
       Website: www.ritequality.com
Dist office & janitorial supplies & office furniture. (AA, estab 1989, empl 10, sales , cert: State, NMSDC)

Kansas

6697   Supplies Express LLC
       626 S 10th St
       Manhattan, KS 66502
       Contact: Enrique Garibay Managing Partner
       Tel: 785-341-2123
       Email: suppliesexpressllc@gmail.com
       Website: www.suppliesexpress.us
Mfr the world's only water-resistant paper drinking straws, import water-resistant paper grocery bags. (Hisp, estab 2017, empl 4, sales , cert: State)

Maryland

6698 Rudolph's Office & Computer Supply, Inc.
5020 Campbell Blvd Ste C
Baltimore, MD 21014
Contact: Henry Dow VP Sales
Tel: 410-931-4150
Email: henry@rudolphsupply.com
Website: www.rudolphsupply.com
Dist office, computer & janitorial supplies, custom stamps, office furniture, space planning. (Woman, estab 1980, empl 60, sales $1,600,000, cert: State)

6699 Sue-Ann's Office Supply, Inc.
4147 Hayward Ave
Baltimore, MD 21215
Contact: Beverly Williams CEO
Tel: 410-664-6226
Email: bwms@sueannsofficesupply.com
Website: www.sueannsofficesupply.com
Dist office products; office furniture; workstations; computer products. (Woman/AA, estab 1986, empl 5, sales $1,503,484, cert: State, City)

Michigan

6700 AVE Solutions
1155 Brewery Park Blvd., #350
Detroit, MI 48207
Contact: Carol Kirkland Exec VP
Tel: 313-347-8592
Email: carol@avesolutions.net
Website: www.avesolutions.net
Dist office supplies, office furniture, office equipment, audio visual equipment, computer equipment & supplies, printer equipment & supplies, paper, janitorial supplies, first aid supplies. (Woman/AA, estab 1990, empl 6, sales , cert: NMSDC, WBENC)

6701 Caracal Products & Services Inc.
6500 E Warren Ave
Detroit, MI 48207
Contact: Rebecca Miller Dir Sales/Marketing
Tel: 877-898-2847
Email: edis@caracalcorp.com
Website: www.caracalcorp.com
Paper (roll, cut, coated, uncoated), Print Management, office supplies, PPE (to include disposable and cloth 3-ply customizable masks, hand sanitizer, disinfectant spray, wipes, air filters), surgical apparel. (AA, estab 2004, empl 42, sales $81,000,000, cert: NMSDC)

6702 Hercules & Hercules, Inc.
19055 W Davison
Detroit, MI 48223
Contact: Belinda Jefferson President
Tel: 313-933-6669
Email: bjefferson@herculesandherculesinc.com
Website: www.herculesandherculesinc.com
Dist maintenance supplies & equip, office supplies & equip, office furniture. (AA, estab , empl , sales $7,000,000, cert: NMSDC)

6703 Integrated Supply Chain Solutions LLC
21056 Bridge St
Southfield, MI 48033
Contact: Cassaundra Bing President
Tel: 248-354-3445
Email: cbing@iscsupplysolutions.com
Website: www.iscsupplysolutions.com
Office products and print management services. (Woman/AA, estab 2008, empl 30, sales $11,000,000, cert: NMSDC, WBENC)

6704 KamarOE
1280 E Big Beaver Ste A
Troy, MI 48083
Contact: Devin Durrell
Tel: 866-996-8952
Email: devind@kamaroe.com
Website: www.kamaroe.com
Dist office supplies. (AA, estab 2005, empl 15, sales , cert: NMSDC)

6705 Nationwide Envelope Specialists, Inc.
1259 Doris Rd
Auburn Hills, MI 48326
Contact: David Dzuris Sales
Tel: 248-373-0111
Email: sales@nespn.com
Website: www.nespn.com
Printed & plain envelopes: special sizes & windows; commercial, booklet & open-end. (Hisp, estab 1990, empl 16, sales $5,200,000, cert: NMSDC)

6706 Paperworks, Inc.
15477 Woodrow Wilson St
Detroit, MI 48238
Contact: Katrece Business Unit Mgr
Tel: 800-243-1424
Email: customerservice@pwi-inc.com
Website: www.dchem.com
Dist paper & paper related products & office supplies. (AA, estab 1981, empl 23, sales $26,000,000, cert: NMSDC)

6707 Remco Storage Systems, Inc.
2328 Livernois Road Ste 1070
Troy, MI 48083
Contact: Donna Tamburo-Wilson President
Tel: 248-362-0500
Email: donna@remcoequipment.com
Website: www.remcoequipment.com
Storage & retrieval systems: vertical lifts & carousels, electric lateral filing systems, movable shelving, rotary files, cabinets, records mgmt systems, color coded labels, custom filing systems, folders & indexes. (Woman, estab 1976, empl 7, sales $2,000,000, cert: WBENC)

6708 RM International Resource Group. Ltd.
22759 Heslip Dr
Novi, MI 48375
Contact: Reuben Levy President
Tel: 877-637-6468
Email: rlevy@rmintrg.com
Website: www.rmintrg.com
Dist office supplies & furniture. (AA, estab 1998, empl 1, sales $800,000, cert: NMSDC)

6709 Rubber Stamps Unlimited, Inc.
334 S Harvey St
Plymouth, MI 48170
Contact: Maryellen Lewandowski President
Tel: 888-451-7300
Email: mlew@thestampmaker.com
Website: www.thestampmaker.com
Custom rubber stamps, self inking stamps, date stamps, seals, embossers & signs in one day. (Woman, estab 1993, empl 12, sales $3,306,000, cert: WBENC)

6710 Swift Computer Supply, Inc.
37676 Enterprise Court
Farmington Hills, MI 48331
Contact: Henry Swift President
Tel: 248-489-9250
Email: meberle@smartofficedeals.com
Website: www.shopSOSnow.com
Office supplies, furniture, printing, promotional items, janitorial & break room supplies. (AA, estab 1985, empl 1, sales $467,200, cert: NMSDC)

6711 Workplace Integrators
30700 Telegraph, Ste 4800
Bingham Farms, MI 48025
Contact: Joe Eatman President
Tel: 248-430-2345
Email: jeatman@wp-int.com
Website: www.wp-int.com
Dist office supplies: paper, writing instruments, folders, technology products, fastners, etc. (AA, estab 1938, empl 1, sales $50,000,000, cert: NMSDC)

Minnesota

6712 Crown Marking, Inc.
4270 Dahlberg Dr
Golden Valley, MN 55422
Contact: Gregg Prest Treasurer
Tel: 763-543-8243
Email: gprest@crownmarking.com
Website: www.crownmarking.com
Mfr & dist rubber & photopolymer stamps, daters, embossers & related stamping supplies. (Woman, estab 1928, empl 9, sales $5,000,000, cert: WBENC)

6713 ecoThynk
607 Dayton Ave
Saint Paul, MN 55012
Contact: Gale Ward President
Tel: 612-605-4885
Email: gale@ecoenvelopes.com
Website: www.ecothynk.com
Mfr reusable envelopes. (Woman, estab 2002, empl 5, sales $210,000, cert: WBENC)

6714 Innovative Office Solutions, LLC
151 E Cliff Rd
Burnsville, MN 55337
Contact: Kathy Hovde Sr Acct Exec, Sales & Diversity
Tel: 952-808-9900
Email: khovde@innovativeos.com
Website: www.innovativeos.com
Dist office, school, janitorial supplies & furniture. (Woman, estab 2001, empl 213, sales $100,000,000, cert: WBENC)

Missouri

6715 Missouri Office Systems & Supplies, Inc.
941 W 141st Terrace Ste B
Kansas City, MO 64145
Contact: Virgie Dillard President
Tel: 816-761-5152
Email: vld@8asupplier.com
Website: www.8asupplier.com
Dist office supplies, furniture, ethernet, media, printers, software, hardware, ribbons, fax, scanners, computers, typewriters, routers, hubs, toners, servers. (Woman/AA, estab 1993, empl 9, sales $8,775,113, cert: State, City, NMSDC)

6716 Offices Unlimited Inc.
2127 William St
Cape Girardeau, MO 63703
Contact: Celeste "Sally" LeGrand Owner
Tel: 573-332-0202
Email: sally@officesunlimited.com
Website: www.officesunlimited.com
Office supplies, stationary, office furniture, office partitions, panel systems, office equipment, copiers, faxes, toners, medical supplies, break room furniture, break room foods, janitorial products. (Woman, estab 2001, empl 6, sales $2,000,000, cert: State)

North Carolina

6717 American Product Distributors, Inc.
8350 Arrowridge Blvd
Charlotte, NC 28273
Contact: Ray Kennedy CEO
Tel: 704-522-9411
Email: registration@americanproduct.com
Website: www.americanproduct.com
Dist office imaging supplies, remanufactured toner cartridges, cut sheet paper, wide format paper, rolled paper & ribbons, business & manufacturing labels. (AA, estab 1992, empl 50, sales $40,000,000, cert: NMSDC)

6718 Kennedy Office Supply Inc.
4211-A Atlantic Ave
Raleigh, NC 27604
Contact: Linda McCotter Accounting Mgr
Tel: 919-878-5400
Email: lmccotter@kennedyoffice.com
Website: www.kennedyofficesupply.com
Dist office supplies, breakroom products, technology & janitorial supplies. (Woman, estab 1960, empl 50, sales $13,200,000, cert: State)

6719 New Generation Product, Inc.
5736 North Tryon St Ste 223B
Charlotte, NC 28213
Contact: Donald Allen Black President
Tel: 704-596-5327
Email: don.black@newgenproduct.com
Website: www.NewGenProduct.com
Provide biomass papers made from recycled agricultural fibers. (AA, estab 2010, empl 1, sales , cert: State, CPUC)

New Hampshire

6720 Gorham Paper and Tissue LLC
72 Cascade Flats
Gorham, NH 03581
Contact: Greg Kane VP Sales & Mktg
Tel: 603-342-3300
Email: greg.kane@gorhampt.com
Website: www.gorhampt.com
Mfr recycled & virgin fiber towel & tissue products.
(Woman, estab 2012, empl 130, sales $50,000,000, cert: WBENC)

New Jersey

6721 Corporate Diversity Solutions
615 Franklin Turnpike Ste 5
Ridgewood, NJ 07450
Contact: Stacey Scarpa President
Tel: 201-444-1506
Email: stscarpa@corporatediversitysolutions.com
Website: www.corporatediversitysolutions.com
Dist stationery & office supplies. (Woman, estab 2009, empl 7, sales $4,300,000, cert: WBENC)

6722 CSS Building Services Inc.
12 Stults Rd, Ste 132
Dayton, NJ 08810
Contact: Vic Tartara Sales
Tel: 732-246-0554
Email: lcoury@cssbuildingservices.com
Website: www.cssofficesupply.com
Dist office supplies. (Hisp, estab 2004, empl 25, sales , cert: WBENC)

6723 Officemate International Corporation
90 Newfield Ave
Edison, NJ 08837
Contact: Sharon Kiefer Natl Sales Mgr
Tel: 732-225-7422
Email: skiefer@officemate.com
Website: www.officemate.com
Mfr & dist office supply products. (As-Pac, estab 1978, empl 100, sales , cert: NMSDC)

6724 Thayer Distribution, Inc.
333 Swedesboro Ave
Gibbstown, NJ 08027
Contact: Nicholas diRenzo Dir sales/mktg
Tel: 856-687-0000
Email: nick@thayerdist.com
Website: www.thayerdist.com
Confectionery wholesalers, break room products, office coffee, candy, snacks, chips, creamer, sugar, k-cups. (Hisp, estab 1987, empl 100, sales , cert: State, City, NMSDC)

6725 The Fisher Group
PO Box 1653
Dover, NJ 07802
Contact: Irving Fisher Managing Partner
Tel: 973-442-3000
Email: irving@fisherpaper.net
Website: www.fisherpaper.net
Dist paper. (AA, estab 2000, empl 4, sales $3,556,001, cert: NMSDC)

New Mexico

6726 Desert Paper & Envelope Company, Inc.
2700 Girard Blvd NE
Albuquerque, NM 87107
Contact: VP Finance
Tel: 800-228-2298
Email: info@desertpaper.com
Website: www.desertpaper.com
Mfr & print envelopes. (Minority, Woman, estab 1973, empl 40, sales $5,435,600, cert: NMSDC, WBENC)

6727 Midway Office Supply Inc.
5900 Midway Park Blvd NE
Albuquerque, NM 87109
Contact: Mike Sei President
Tel: 505-345-3414
Email: mikesei@midwayos.com
Website: www.midwayos.com
Dist office supplies. (As-Pac, estab 1980, empl 10, sales $9,000,000, cert: NMSDC)

6728 Roses Southwest Paper, Inc.
1701 2nd St SW
Albuquerque, NM 87102
Contact: James Hinkle NSM
Tel: 734-968-8103
Email: jmhinkle@aol.com
Website: www.rosessouthwest.com
Mfr sanitary paper products: hard roll towels, multi fold towels, jumbo roll toilet tissue, standard roll toilet tissue, facial tissue, seat covers, dispenser napkins, dinner napkins, cocktail napkins, kitchen roll towels. (Hisp, estab 1984, empl 215, sales $58,980,000, cert: NMSDC)

6729 Stride Inc.
1021 Carlisle Blvd SE
Albuquerque, NM 87106
Contact: Kerry Bertram President
Tel: 505-232-3201
Email: info@stridewrite.com
Website: www.stridewrite.com
Writing instruments & binders, hinged lid cigar boxes. (Woman, estab , empl , sales $7,000,000, cert: WBENC)

6730 Stride, Inc.
1021 Carlisle Blvd SE
Albuquerque, NM 87106
Contact: Kerry Bertram President
Tel: 505-232-3201
Email: kerry@strideinc.com
Website: www.strideinc.com
Mfr & dist writing instruments, binders & office products: pens & markers for wood finishes, parts marking, black light, crafts, photographic, cosmetics, cleaning devices & voter marking pens. (Woman, estab 1988, empl 11, sales $2,778,019, cert: State, WBENC)

New York

6731 Asian & Hispanic Trading & Consulting Inc.
37 West 39th St Ste 503
New York, NY 10018
Contact: Suzanne Cohon Business Devel
Tel: 212-252-8988
Email: suzanne@asc-to.com
Website: www.aandhtc.com
Dist office supplies, furniture, computer equipment, and promotional products. (Minority, Woman, estab 2016, empl 3, sales $295,000, cert: State, City)

6732   Ebony Office Products, Inc.
10-17 44th Ave
Long Island City, NY 11101
Contact: Michael Ukhueduan Dir Business Dev
Tel: 718-706-8200
Email: info@ebonyproducts.com
Website: www.ebonyofficeusa.com
Dist office supplies, office furniture, computer supplies, printing services. (AA, estab 1982, empl 10, sales $1,500,000, cert: State, City)

6733   FM Office Express dba FM Resources
One Woodbury Blvd
Rochester, NY 14604
Contact: Fabricio Morales President
Tel: 585-238-2895
Email: fmorales@fmop.com
Website: www.fmop.com
Dist office supplies, office furniture, janitorial supplies & computer supplies. (Hisp, estab 1995, empl 83, sales , cert: State)

6734   Impact Enterprises, Inc.
11 Horse Hill Lane
Warwick, NY 10990
Contact: Ralph Salisbury Sr VP
Tel: 845-988-1900
Email: rsalisbury@impactenterprises.com
Website: www.impactenterprises.com
Mfr custom binder covers, award covers, presentation folders, portfolio covers, sales kits & other custom covers. (Woman, estab 1987, empl 8, sales $2,500,000, cert: WBENC)

6735   Mrs. Paper
31 West 34th St, Ste 8044
New York, NY 10001
Contact: Marion Hindenburg President
Tel: 212-532-7777
Email: marion@mrspaper.com
Website: www.mrspaper.com
Dist copy & computer paper, janitorial/sanitary supplies & advertising specialties. (Woman, estab 1982, empl 3, sales $4,082,000, cert: City, WBENC)

6736   Proftech LLC
200 Clearbrook Rd
Elmsford, NY 10523
Contact: JOSE R. MONTIEL President
Tel: 800-937-8354
Email: jmontiel@proftech.com
Website: www.proftech.com
Dist office supplies; computer supplies; packaging supplies; drafting & art supplies; furniture; janitorial supplies; remanufactured toner cartridges. (Hisp, estab 1998, empl 55, sales , cert: State, City, NMSDC)

6737   Royal Automation Supplies
1982 Crotona Pkwy
Bronx, NY 10460
Contact: David Changar VP
Tel: 718-842-5900
Email: royalautomation@aol.com
Website: www.royalautomation.com
Dist paper & office supplies. (As-Ind, estab 1954, empl 5, sales $1,200,000, cert: City, NMSDC)

6738   S & B Computer & Office Products Inc.
17 Wood Road Ste 700
Round Lake, NY 12151
Contact: Brittany Woods-Holmes President
Tel: 518-877-9500
Email: info@royalflashphotobooths.com
Website: www.sbcomputers-office.com
Dist office & computer supplies, office furniture & promotional products. (Minority, Woman, estab 1989, empl 9, sales $5,695,685, cert: State)

6739   Seating, Inc.
PO Box 898
Nunda, NY 14517
Contact: Emily Hart Dir Business Dev
Tel: 585-468-2875
Email: emily@seatinginc.com
Website: www.seatinginc.com
Mfr quality ergonomic office seating for business and government buyers in the form of task, swivel, executive, multi-purpose, stacking, and nesting chairs as well as stools. (Woman, estab 1987, empl 25, sales $4,315,077, cert: City, WBENC)

Ohio

6740   BoLinds Solutions Services, Inc.
850 Euclid Ave, Ste 1314
Cleveland, OH 44114
Contact: Sales Sales
Tel: 216-479-0290
Email: service@bolinds.com
Website: www.bolinds.com
Dist office products, office furniture, remanufactured & compatible toner cartridges, fax machines & office equipment repair. (Woman/AA, estab 1990, empl 6, sales , cert: State, NMSDC)

6741   Office Partners, LLC
826 E Edgerton
Bryan, OH 43506
Contact: Cookie Lehman President
Tel: 419-636-7260
Email: cookie1@bright.net
Website: www.officepartnersonline.com
Office products. (Hisp, estab 2002, empl 3, sales , cert: NMSDC)

6742   Quality Ribbons and Supplies Co.
2769 Commercial Rd
Cleveland, OH 44113
Contact: Jacqueline Litz Owner
Tel: 216-579-6200
Email: jackielitz@qr-s.com
Website: www.qr-s.com
Dist office, computer & janitorial supplies & small equip. (Woman, estab 1982, empl 5, sales , cert: City)

6743   SeaGate Office Products, Inc.
1044 Hamilton Dr
Holland, OH 43528
Contact: Connie Leonardi President
Tel: 419-861-6161
Email: cleonardi@seagateop.com
Website: www.seagteop.com
Dist office supplies: copy & writing paper, pens, post it notes, toner cartridges, ink, stamps, computer supplies, promotional items, mugs, golf balls and, pens, uniforms, desk accessories, binder clips, pencils, staples, tape & dispensers. (Woman, estab 1985, empl 14, sales $5,300,000, cert: WBENC)

6744 The Millcraft Paper Company
6800 Grant Ave
Cleveland, OH 44105
Contact: Lisa Rogala Corporate Business Dev
Tel: 216-441-5500
Email: rogalal@millcraft.com
Website: www.millcraft.com
Paper converting, mfr envelopes, printing, inventory management. (Woman, estab 1920, empl 225, sales $139,988,865, cert: WBENC)

6745 World Pac Paper, LLC
1821 Summit Rd, Ste 317
Cincinnati, OH 45237
Contact: Edgar Smith CEO
Tel: 513-779-9595
Email: elsmith@worldpacpaperllc.com
Website: www.worldpacpaperllc.com
Dist printing & packaging papers. (AA, estab 2004, empl 22, sales $3,563,898, cert: NMSDC)

Pennsylvania

6746 Alpha Office Supplies, Inc.
4950 Parkside Ave Ste 500
Philadelphia, PA 19131
Contact: Chester Riddick CEO
Tel: 215-226-2690
Email: chet.riddick@alphaos.com
Website: www.alphaos.com
Dist office furniture & supplies, paper, computers & accessories; desktop delivery, installation, space planning & project mgmt. (AA, estab 1985, empl 29, sales $26,000,000, cert: NMSDC)

6747 Ardian Group, Inc.
7 Creek Pkwy, Ste 710
Boothwyn, PA 19342
Contact: Jeffrey Shelton COO
Tel: 610-459-4975
Email: jlshelton@ardiangroup.com
Website: www.ardiangroup.com
Dist photo & nonphoto badges: clips, laminates, lanyards, software, laminators, etc. (Minority, Woman, estab 1999, empl 20, sales $2,700,000, cert: WBENC)

6748 Max International
2360 Dairy Rd
Lancaster, PA 17603
Contact: Tiffanie Shaud Mktg Dir
Tel: 800-233-0222
Email: tjs@maxintl.com
Website: www.maxintl.com
Roll paper converting: standard & special sizes, slittering, 4-color printing. (Woman, estab 1992, empl 22, sales $7,500,000, cert: WBENC)

6749 SUPRA Office Solutions, Inc.
5070 PArkside Ave Ste 3200
Philadlephia, PA 19131
Contact: FirstName LastName COO
Tel: 855-777-8772
Email: ken.carter@supraos.com
Website: www.supraos.com
Office supplies, office furniture, janitorial & break-room, paper & paper products, technology items, medical & chemical supplies. (AA, estab 2011, empl 16, sales $19,000,000, cert: State, NMSDC)

6750 Telrose Corporation
3801 Ridge Ave
Philadelphia, PA 19132
Contact: CEO
Tel: 215-229-0500
Email: support@telrosecorp.com
Website: www.telrosecorp.com
Dist office supplies, equipment & furniture. (AA, estab 1995, empl 19, sales $8,000,000, cert: City, NMSDC)

South Carolina

6751 Ebony Holding
1204 Lexington Ave Unit 1, A-2
Irmo, SC 29063
Contact: Pam Heirs Acct Exec
Tel: 803-798-7777
Email: pamh@jmgrace.com
Website: www.jmgrace.com
Office Supplies, Office Furniture, Business Machines, Printing, Promotional Items, Embroidered Apparel, Janitorial Supplies, Breakroom Items, Safety Equipment. (Woman/AA, estab 2013, empl 7, sales $590,692, cert: State)

Tennessee

6752 DevMar Products, LLC
1865 Air Lane Dr
Nashville, TN 37210
Contact: Sharon W. Reynolds CEO
Tel: 615-232-7040
Email: sharaon@devmarproducts.com
Website: www.devmarproducts.com
Janitorial supplies; chemicals; personal paper; MRO; biohazard spill kits/risk management; safety; Clean Up; Safety Sweep; green; sustainable; Ada[t ASB; Oil & Gas; Automotive; Healthcare; Furniture; Chemicals; Forest Products & Paper; Wholesale Dist. (Woman/AA, estab 2007, empl 5, sales $1,000,000, cert: NMSDC, WBENC)

6753 Guy Brown, LLC
7111 Commerce Way
Brentwood, TN 37027
Contact: Lauren Dooros Sales & Marketing Mgr
Tel: 615-777-1500
Email: lauren.dooros@guybrown.com
Website: www.guybrown.com
Mfr recycled laser toner cartridges & office products. (Minority, Woman, estab 1997, empl 45, sales $204,877,006, cert: NMSDC, WBENC)

Texas

6754 Dallas Paper & Packaging
880 Gerault Rd
Flower Mound, TX 75028
Contact: Nemosthenes Baker Owner
Tel: 817-422-3089
Email: nemo@dallaspaperpackaging.com
Website: www.dallaspaperpackaging.com
Dist toner & ink cartridges, trash bags, food gloves, white T-shirts, grey sweat pants, shirts, drinking water carts, janitorial supplies, ribbons, first aid kits, popcorn, hazard & medical supplies. (AA, estab 1984, empl 2, sales $745,963, cert: State, NMSDC)

6755   Derrah Morrison Enterprises, LLC
      1120 Toro Grande Blvd Bldg 2, Ste 208
      Cedar Park, TX 78613
      Contact: Chelsea Derrah CEO
      Tel: 512-879-3088
      Email: cderrah@dme-vet.com
      Website: www.dme-vet.com
resell recycled copy paper, office products, industrial supplies, and medical-surgical products and equipment. (Woman, estab 2009, empl 2, sales $47,611,687, cert: WBENC)

6756   EIS Office Solutions, Inc.
      5803 Sovereign Dr, Ste 214
      Houston, TX 77036
      Contact: Judy Lanum Acct Exec
      Tel: 713-484-7300
      Email: judy.lanum@secor.cc
      Website: www.eisoffice.net
Provide OEM & Compatible printer ink & toner cartridges, office supplies. (As-Pac, estab 2004, empl 11, sales $1,700,000, cert: State)

6757   General Office Plus
      1020 W 8th Ave
      Amarillo, TX 79101
      Contact: Loretta Redmon President
      Tel: 806-373-2877
      Email: lredmon@generalofficeplus.com
      Website: www.general-officesupply.com
Dist office supplies, machines, furniture. (Woman, estab 1948, empl 15, sales $1,803,887, cert: State)

6758   Houdal Corporation dba 2M Business Products
      2630 Nova Dr
      Dallas, TX 75229
      Contact: shabbir mamdani President
      Tel: 972-484-0000
      Email: cs@2mbp.com
      Website: www.2mofficesupplies.com
Dist office supplies, computer supplies, office furniture, new & remanufactured toner cartridges. rubber stamps, printing. (As-Ind, estab 1980, empl 3, sales $980,770, cert: NMSDC)

6759   J R Rodriguez International Corporation
      4541 Leston St
      Dallas, TX 75247
      Contact: Jim Lohr Natl Acct Mgr
      Tel: 214-905-5086
      Email: jim@interconpaper.com
      Website: www.interconpaper.com
Printing paper in rolls & sheets: offset, gloss & matte/dull, board (C1S and C2S), Hi-Brite, groundwood coated, newsprint, digital sizes, cut size xerographic, slitting & rewinding. (Hisp, estab 1998, empl 61, sales $25,100,000, cert: NMSDC)

6760   Lee Office Solutions
      202 Travis ST, Ste 205
      Houston, TX 77002
      Contact: Cathleen Nguyen Exec Asst
      Tel: 713-227-1010
      Email: cathleen@leeofficesolutions.com
      Website: www.leeofficesolutions.com
Dist office supplies & products, electronics, furniture, paper, facilities mgmt & system design. (As-Pac, estab 1970, empl 5, sales $308,647, cert: NMSDC)

6761   Limitless Office Products
      1778 N Plano Rd Ste 114
      Richardson, TX 75081
      Contact: Mita Guha President
      Tel: 214-764-4092
      Email: mg@limitlessofficeproducts.com
      Website: www.LimitlessOfficeProducts.com
Dist office products: printer, copier, fax, ink & laser cartridges, digital cameras, digital storage devices, paper, pens, pencils, file folders etc. (Woman/As-Ind, estab 2005, empl 2, sales , cert: State, NMSDC)

6762   Longhorn Office Products, Inc.
      2210 Denton Dr. Ste. 109
      Austin, TX 78758
      Contact: Marcia Winkler CEO
      Tel: 512-672-4567
      Email: mswinkler@longhornop.com
      Website: www.longhornop.com
Dist office products & furniture. (Woman, estab 1999, empl 13, sales $2,386,005, cert: State, City, WBENC)

6763   P.D. Morrison Enterprises, Inc.
      1120 Toro Grande Blvd Bldg 2, Ste 208
      Cedar Park, TX 78613
      Contact: P.D. Morrison CEO
      Tel: 512-879-3070
      Email: pd@pdme.com
      Website: www.pdme.com
Dist office & computer supplies, office furniture. (AA, estab 1994, empl 10, sales , cert: NMSDC)

6764   Pearle, Inc.
      3660 Richmond Ave Ste 370
      Houston, TX 77046
      Contact: Erskine Black Jr. President
      Tel: 832-304-9571
      Email: eblack@pearle-inc.com
      Website: www.pearle-inc.com
Dist disposable paper goods. (AA, estab 2013, empl 1, sales , cert: State, City, NMSDC)

6765   R.W. Gonzalez Office Products, Inc.
      600 Congress Ave 14th Fl
      Austin, TX 78701
      Contact: Pamela Gonzalez VP
      Tel: 512-717-6623
      Email: diversity@gonzalezop.com
      Website: www.MBEpartners.com
Dist office products. (Hisp, estab 2002, empl 7, sales , cert: State, NMSDC)

6766   Reliant Business Products, Inc
      10641 Haddington Dr, Ste 100
      Houston, TX 77043
      Contact: Steven Woodall VP Sales & IT
      Tel: 713-980-7140
      Email: stevenw@rbp.com
      Website: www.rbp.com
Office Products, Office Supplies, Industrial Supplies, HS&E, MRO, Office Furniture, Coffee Service, Break Room Supplies, Printing. (Nat Ame, estab 1984, empl 17, sales $7,000,000, cert: State, NMSDC)

6767 Summus Industries, Inc.
      245 Commerce Green Blvd Ste 155
      Sugar Land, TX 77478
      Contact: Rodney Craig CEO
      Tel: 281-640-1765
      Email: rcraig@summusindustries.com
      Website: www.summusindustries.com
Dist office supplies. (AA, estab 1997, empl 21, sales
$21,000,000, cert: State, City, NMSDC)

6768 Tejas Office Products, Inc.
      1225 W 20th St
      Houston, TX 77008
      Contact: Stephen M. Fraga President
      Tel: 713-864-6004
      Email: stephenf@tejasoffice.com
      Website: www.tejasoffice.com
Dist office products. (Hisp, estab 1962, empl 50, sales ,
cert: NMSDC)

6769 Today's Business Solutions
      1920 N Memorial Way
      Houston, TX 77007
      Contact: Priscilla Luna President
      Tel: 713-861-8508
      Email: priscilla@tbsconnection.com
      Website: www.tbsknows.com
Dist office supplies. (Hisp, estab 2003, empl 25, sales
$19,000,000, cert: State, NMSDC)

Virginia

6770 Access Office Products
      6 W Cary St
      Richmond, VA 23220
      Contact: AJ Scott President
      Tel: 804-767-7211
      Email: aj@accessofficeproducts.com
      Website: www.AccessOfficeProducts.com
Dist office supplies, technology & furniture. (AA, estab
2009, empl 2, sales $119,231, cert: State, NMSDC)

6771 Ball Office Products, LLC
      2218 Tomlyn St
      Richmond, VA 23230
      Contact: Melissa Ball Managing Member
      Tel: 804-204-1774
      Email: melissa@ballop.com
      Website: www.ballop.com
Dist business furniture & office supplies. (Woman, estab
2000, empl 17, sales $7,050,591, cert: State, WBENC)

6772 Corporate Office Solutions, LLC
      4094 Majestic Ln, Ste 33
      Fairfax, VA 22033
      Contact: Katrina Funkhouser President
      Tel: 703-352-2029
      Email: kf@cosdirect.com
      Website: www.cosdirect.com
Dist computer products, office equipment & supplies,
printer service, computer repair, networking & office
furniture. (Woman/As-Ind, estab 1996, empl 8, sales
$2,386,109, cert: State)

6773 Snap Office Supplies, LLC
      9710 Farrar Court Ste M
      Richmond, VA 23236
      Contact: Andy Todd VP Sales
      Tel: 804-794-9387
      Email: andy@snapsupplies.com
      Website: www.snapsupplies.com
Dist Office & Point-of-Sale supplies. (Woman, estab
1980, empl 7, sales $1,500,000, cert: State)

6774 TSRC, Inc.
      PO Box 1810
      Ashland, VA 23005
      Contact: David Johnson Acct Mgr
      Tel: 804-412-1200
      Email: djohnson@thesupplyroom.com
      Website: www.thesupplyroom.com
Dist office supplies & furniture. (Woman, estab 1986,
empl 187, sales $45,000,000, cert: State)

Washington

6775 American Paper Converting Inc.
      1845 Howard Way
      Woodland, WA 98674
      Contact: Lydia Work President
      Tel: 360-225-0488
      Email: Storneby@americanpaperco.com
      Website: www.americanpaperco.com
Mfr paper towel, bathroom tissue & napkins. (Minority,
Woman, estab 1997, empl 60, sales $32,185,106, cert:
NMSDC)

Wisconsin

6776 H.Derksen & Sons Co., Inc.
      250 Industrial Dr
      Omro, WI 50310
      Contact: Mike Willeford VP
      Tel: 920-685-4000
      Email: mike@hderksen.com
      Website: www.hderksen.com
Pressure sensitive labels, wide format digital printing,
business forms, computer paper, paper & packaging
products, mobility solutions, bar code label printers, bar
coding software. (Nat Ame, estab , empl 11, sales
$8,000,000, cert: NMSDC)

PACKAGING & PACKING SERVICES & SUPPLIES
Contract packaging and crating, shrink or blister packaging and bagging. Manufacturers and distributors of foam packaging, rope and twine, bottles, shrink wrap, corrugated cardboard boxes or bags of various materials such as paper, plastic, etc. NAICS Code 32

Alabama

6777 ARD Logistics, LLC
10098 Brose Dr
Vance, AL 35490
Contact: Courtney Waters Sales & Marketing Rep
Tel: 205-393-5207
Email: cwaters@ardlogistics.com
Website: www.ardlogistics.com
Distribution operations: sequencing, sub-assembly, warehousing, inventory mgmt, shipping & receiving materials handling maintenance, packaging & repackaging, transportation mgmt, transportation svcs. (AA, estab 1998, empl 900, sales $68,717,549, cert: NMSDC)

6778 Containers Plus, Inc.
3068 Alabama Hwy 53
Huntsville, AL 35806
Contact: Ajesh Khanijow Business Devel
Tel: 256-746-8002
Email: akhanijow@containersplususa.com
Website: www.containersplususa.com
Wooden crates, pallets, cardboard boxes, heat shrink, milspec packaging, packaging, RFID, UID, Mil-std-129, mil-std-2073, warehousing, logistics, hazmat packaging. (As-Pac, estab 2014, empl 5, sales $180,000, cert: NMSDC)

6779 Coxco, Inc.
3603 Pine Lane SE
Bessemer, AL 35022
Contact: Renee Cox President
Tel: 205-428-6223
Email: renee@coxcoinc.com
Website: www.coxcoinc.com
Dist wooden & plastic pallets, new & reconditioned, custom packaging. (Woman, estab 1983, empl 4, sales $6,000,000, cert: WBENC)

6780 Prystup Packaging Products
430 North Industrial PArk Dr
Livingston, AL 35470
Contact: Corey Hayden Technical Sales Engineer
Tel: 205-499-9397
Email: chayden@prystup.com
Website: www.prystup.com
Mfr folding paper cartons: food, consumer goods & electronics. (Minority, Woman, estab 1980, empl 160, sales $38,000,000, cert: WBENC)

6781 The Trinity Design Group, LLC
1107 Dowzer Ave
Pell City, AL 35125
Contact: Fernando Valentin CEO
Tel: 205-338-6888
Email: fvalentin@thetrinitydesigngroup.com
Website: www.thetrinitydesigngroup.com
Design, mfr & copack packaging, corrugated, paper, plastics, point of purchase & promotional materials. (AA, Hisp, estab 2004, empl 15, sales $2,028,500, cert: NMSDC)

Arkansas

6782 Alliance Rubber Company, Inc.
210 Carpenter Dam Rd
Hot Springs, AR 71901
Contact: Sheryl Koller Natl Accounts
Tel: 501-262-2700
Email: skoller@alliance-rubber.com
Website: www.rubberband.com/
Mfr & dist mailing, packaging & shipping products. (Woman, estab 1923, empl , sales $35,529,619, cert: WBENC)

6783 Sigma Supply North America
824 Mid America Blvd
Hot Springs, AR 71913
Contact: Brooke Griffin Natl Acct Mgr
Tel: 501-760-1151
Email: supplierdiversity@sigmasupply.com
Website: www.sigmasupply.com
Packaging solutions, turnkey solution for warehouse equipment, bulk storage, individual shipment packaging, labeling & inventory control. (Woman, estab 2003, empl 371, sales $380,900,000, cert: WBENC)

Arizona

6784 All-Pac Distributng LLC
4859 E Gleneagle Dr
Chandler, AZ 85249
Contact: Adam Snow Sales Mgr
Tel: 480-861-0842
Email: asnow@allpaconline.com
Website: www.allpaconline.com
Mfr & dist returnable plastic packaging, injection molding, compression molding. (Woman, estab 2001, empl 3, sales $1,150,000, cert: NWBOC)

6785 La Fiesta Label & Packaging Systems
6162 W Detroit St
Chandler, AZ 85226
Contact: Kirk Valadez VP Operations
Tel: 480-785-3900
Email: kvaladez@lafiestalabel.com
Website: www.lafiestalabel.com
Mfr shrink sleeves, unsupported film pouches & packets, pressure sensitive labels, fold out coupons, cartons, static cling, consecutive number, UV & laminate coating. (Hisp, estab 1985, empl 20, sales $0, cert: NMSDC)

California

6786 ACME Bag Inc Dba The Bulk Bag Company
14730 Northam St, La Mirada, CA,
La Mirada, CA 90638
Contact: John Willoughby Natl Sales Dir
Tel: 866-517-4699
Email: john@thebulkbagcompany.com
Website: www.thebulkbagcompany.com
Soilsaver Rolls, SOD Staples, Construction Fabrics, Landscaping Fabrics & Tarps, Agriculture Packaging, FIBC Bags & Woven Polypropyline Bags, Sand Bags- Burlap & WPP, Treated Burlap Sqares, Silt Fences, Truncated Wire Baskets. (As-Pac, estab 1975, empl 24, sales $20,000,000, cert: NMSDC)

6787 ALOM Technologies Corporation
48105 Warm Springs Blvd
Fremont, CA 94539
Contact: Lisa Dolan VP Supply Chain Strategy
Tel: 510-360-3600
Email: customerservice@alom.com
Website: www.alom.com
Fulfillment, assembly, contract packaging, video & audio tape duplication, CD & DVD duplication (Woman, estab 1997, empl 256, sales $132,400,000, cert: WBENC)

6788 American Supply
PO Box 2322
Chino, CA 91710
Contact: Vonn Castillo Business Devel Mgr
Tel: 949-216-0468
Email: vcastillo@myamericansupply.com
Website: www.myamericansupply.com
Mfr & customize bags & covers, janitorial, housekeeping, promotional & OEM products. Mfr replacement cart bags, laundry bags, caddy bags, laundry truck liners, hair dryer bags, etc. (Minority, Woman, estab 2013, empl 5, sales $300,000, cert: CPUC)

6789 Atlantis Paper & Packaging
13405 Benson Ave
Chino, CA 91710
Contact: James Montano Sales Rep
Tel: 909-591-1809
Email: james@atlantispkg.com
Website: www.atlantispkg.com
Dist packaging products & machinery, corrugated boxes, stretch wrap, poly bags, ice pages, tape, cold storage, pallets, etc. (Hisp, estab 1984, empl 15, sales $15,000,000, cert: NMSDC)

6790 Future Commodities Int'l Inc.
10676 Fulton Ct
Rancho Cucamonga, CA 91730
Contact: Matthew Lim VP Operations
Tel: 909-987-4258
Email: mlim@bestpack.com
Website: www.bestpack.com
Mfr & import carton sealing equipment, carton sealing tape. (As-Pac, estab 1984, empl 14, sales $10,200,000, cert: NMSDC)

6791 Industrial Container Corporation
2015 Acacia Court
Compton, CA 90220
Contact: Josh Rodgers Operations
Tel: 310-763-3550
Email: sales@industrialcontainer.com
Website: www.industrialcontainer.com
Packaging design services & protective packaging, Customer Design/CAD Documentation, Prototyping, Performance Certification, Manufacturing Responsibility, Total Quality control, Supply Chain Management, Maquiladora/JIT & warehousing. (Hisp, estab 1971, empl 35, sales $0, cert: NMSDC)

6792 MikaPak Inc.
PO Box 4276
Walnut Creek, CA 94596
Contact: Helen Ma President
Tel: 800-579-0880
Email: helen@mikapak.com
Website: www.mikapak.com
Sustainable, compostable products from plate wares, utensils, drink cups, food containers to packaging labels using renewable plant base raw materials. (Minority, Woman, estab 1995, empl 1, sales $279,000, cert: NMSDC)

6793 PKG Packaging
311 Hearst Dr
Oxnard, CA 93030
Contact: Carlos Rodriguez Customer Service Mgr
Tel: 805-278-6648
Email: c.rodriguez@pkgpackaging.com
Website: www.pkgpackaging.com
Design, mfr & dist packaging material. (Minority, Woman, estab 1987, empl 10, sales $3,805,000, cert: NMSDC, WBENC)

6794 Premier Packaging/Assembly div of Haringa Inc.
14422 Best Ave
Santa Fe Springs, CA 90670
Contact: Vicki Haringa CEO
Tel: 562-802-2765
Email: vharinga@premierpkg.com
Website: www.premierpkg.com
Packaging services. (Woman, estab 1987, empl 6, sales $13,882,899, cert: WBENC)

6795 Thoro Packaging
1467 Davril Cir
Corona, CA 92880
Contact: Andrea Percy Marketing Liaison
Tel: 951-278-2100
Email: apercy@thoropkg.com
Website: www.thoropkg.com
Mfr & print custom folding cartons. (Woman, estab 1967, empl 184, sales $29,750,000, cert: WBENC)

6796 TransPak
520 N. Marburg Way
San Jose, CA 95133
Contact: Sharon Spina Strategic Accounts Mgr
Tel: 408-590-6543
Email: sharon.spina@transpak.com
Website: www.transpak.com
Mfr wood crates & crating systems, custom packaging solutions, logistics, transportation & rigging services. (Woman, estab 1952, empl 800, sales $120,000,000, cert: WBENC)

6797 Uniq Seal, LLC
5753-G Santa Ana Canyon Rd
Anaheim, CA 92807
Contact: Jacek Zdzienicki VP Sales
Tel: 714-299-5899
Email: jacek@nafm.com
Website: www.nafm.com
Contract sleeving & shrink labeling, multi-pack assemblies, shrink overwrap, tray assembly, re-packing & special assemblies, casing & cartoning, displays assembly, packaging R&D, fulfillment. (Minority, Woman, estab 1993, empl 7, sales $3,500,000, cert: NMSDC)

6798 World Centric
      101 H St, Ste M
      Petaluma, CA 94956
      Contact: Matt Mgr, Natl Accounts
      Tel: -   -
      Email: mattw@worldcentric.org
      Website: www.worldcentric.org
Sustainable, Compostable, Plant-based foodservice
disposables (As-Ind, estab , empl , sales $36,000,000, cert:
NMSDC)

Colorado

6799 Craters and Freighters
      331 Corporate Circle, Ste J
      Golden, CO 80401
      Contact: Chad Brockmeyer Natl Sales Mgr
      Tel: 720-287-7805
      Email: chad@cratersandfreighters.com
      Website: www.cratersandfreighters.com
Custom wood crating, plastic hard cases and freight
services. (Woman, estab 1990, empl 12, sales $55,000,000,
cert: WBENC)

6800 Die Cut Technologies/Denver Gasket
      10943 Leroy Dr
      Northglenn, CO 80233
      Contact: Evelyn Meyers CEO
      Tel: 303-452-4600
      Email: evelyn@diecuttech.com
      Website: www.diecuttech.com
Mfr gaskets, die cut parts & converted non-metallic
materials. Also dist sponge, foam tapes rubber, bridge
bearing pads, expansion joints, impact attenuators &
adhesives, contract assembly & packaging svcs. (Hisp,
estab 1961, empl 20, sales $2,524,000, cert: NMSDC, SDB)

6801 Rocky Mountain Pioneer, LLC
      13802 E 33rd Pl, Unit B
      Aurora, CO 80011
      Contact: Diane Hamilton Acct Mgr
      Tel: 303-371-6070
      Email: diane@pioneerdenver.com
      Website: www.hpcorporategroup.com
Custom & stock packaging materials: corrugated boxes,
folding carton, bubble, foam protective packaging, shrink
& stretch films, banding & tapes, fulfillment services.
(Woman, estab 2004, empl 9, sales $5,000,000, cert:
WBENC)

6802 Summit Container Corporation
      901Synthes Ave
      Monument, CO 80132
      Contact: Adam Walker CEO
      Tel: 719-481-8400
      Email: awalker@summitcontainer.com
      Website: www.summitcontainer.com
Packaging solutions, custom packaging, warehousing,
distribution, assembly & kitting, (AA, estab 1989, empl
200, sales , cert: NMSDC)

6803 Universal Packaging Corp
      11440 E 56th Ave
      Denver, CO 80239
      Contact: Karen Millwater VP
      Tel: 303-373-2523
      Email: kmillwater@upc-solutions.com
      Website: www.upc-solutions.com
Dist industrial packaging supplies: bubble, foam, tape,
stretch, shrink wrap, banding, bags, cable ties, boxes,
styrofoam, rolled corrugated, mailing tubes, etc.
(Woman, estab 1980, empl 13, sales $8,000,000, cert:
City)

Connecticut

6804 Eastern Bag & Paper Company, Inc.
      200 Research Dr
      Milford, CT 06460
      Contact: Meredith Reuben CEO
      Tel: 203-878-1814
      Email: mreuben@ebpsupply.com
      Website: www.ebpsupply.com
Dist paper, packaging & allied products. (Woman, estab ,
empl 270, sales $196,987,948, cert: WBENC)

6805 Flexo Converters USA, Inc.
      1200 Northrop Rd
      Meridan, CT 06450
      Contact: Emily Gerrard Mktg/Sales Mgr
      Tel: 203-639-7070
      Email: egerrard@flexobags.com
      Website: www.flexobags.com
Mfr twisted handle paper shopping & merchandise bags.
(Minority, estab 1994, empl 51, sales $15,000,000, cert:
NMSDC)

6806 New England Packaging Co. LLC
      119 Sherman Ct
      Fairfield, CT 06824
      Contact: Mark Hyman President
      Tel: 203-256-2350
      Email: mark@zero-contact.com
      Website: www.zero-contact.com
Dist corrugated & paper products. (Hisp, estab 1997,
empl 6, sales $200,000, cert: NMSDC)

6807 Penmar Industries, Inc.
      35 Ontario St
      Stratford, CT 06615
      Contact: Ed Rodriguez President
      Tel: 203-853-4868
      Email: eddy@penmar-industries.com
      Website: www.penmar-industries.com
Mfr & convert custom labels & tapes, dist packaging
materials, carton sealing tapes, cartons & shipping room
supplies. (Hisp, estab 1964, empl 15, sales $2,900,000,
cert: NMSDC)

Florida

6808 3 Points Packaging LLC
      3505 NW 123rd St
      Miami, FL 33167
      Contact: Noel Bosh President
      Tel: 305-624-8343
      Email: info@3pointspackaging.com
      Website: www.3PointsPackaging.com
Packaging & janitorial products. (AA, estab 2011, empl 2,
sales $660,000, cert: NMSDC)

6809 All American Containers, Inc
9330 NW 110th Ave
Miami, FL 33178
Contact: Richard Cabrera VP Int'l Division
Tel: 305-913-0624
Email: richardc@americancontainers.com
Website: www.americancontainers.com
Dist packaging supplies. (Minority, Woman, estab 1991, empl 284, sales $0, cert: NMSDC)

6810 Containers Unlimited, Inc.
636 Volterra Blvd
Kissimmee, FL 34759
Contact: C. Eric Jones President
Tel: 678-833-4575
Email: cjones@containersunlimited.net
Website: www.containersunlimited.net
Dist stock & custom boxes & packaging materials. (AA, estab 1999, empl 4, sales $2,729,551, cert: SDB)

6811 Diverse Solution and Supplies
7305 Lismore Ct.
Orlando, FL 32835
Contact: Carolyn Griffin President
Tel: 407-256-2653
Email: carolyn.griffin@div-erse.com
Website: www.div-erse.com
Dist packaging & facility supplies: stretch wrap, corrugated, tapes, cushioning, bundling material, void fill, floor cleaning equipment, mats, bags, etc. (Woman, estab 2013, empl 2, sales $279,000, cert: WBENC)

6812 FlexSol Packaging Corp.
1531 NW 12th Ave
Pompano Beach, FL 33069
Contact: Bonni O'Connell Dir Sales/Marketing
Tel: 800-325-7740
Email: bonnio@flexsolpackaging.com
Website: www.flexsolpackaging.com
Mfr flexible packaging & value-added plastic films, custom bags & film, shrink & hood films, performance & barrier films & can liners. (As-Pac, estab 2009, empl 425, sales , cert: NMSDC)

6813 National Packaging, LLC
6346-65 Lantana Rd, Ste 126
Lake Worth, FL 33463
Contact: Kerry Lowe Mgr
Tel: 561-968-4420
Email: klowe@nationalpack.net
Website: www.nationalpack.net
Flexible packaging, Bag films. (Woman/AA, estab 2006, empl 2, sales , cert: NMSDC)

6814 Soule Medical
4322 Pet Ln
Lutz, FL 33559
Contact: Tim Goode Natl Accounts Mgr
Tel: 800-999-2928
Email: tim.goode@soulemedical.com
Website: www.soulemedical.com
Dist packaging products: crates, corrugated cartons, military type board, hard & soft cases, foams, bubble, tapes, poly bags, ect. (Woman, estab 1957, empl 31, sales $10,000,000, cert: WBENC)

6815 Totalpack, Inc.
2151 NW 72nd Ave
Miami, FL 33122
Contact: Robert Kweller GM
Tel: 305-597-9955
Email: robert@totalpack.com
Website: www.totalpack.com
Mfr & dist boxes, custom printed tapes & labels, double studs, fittings with ring polyfilm, stretchfilm & cargo straps & tapes. (Minority, Woman, estab 1990, empl 24, sales $0, cert: WBENC)

Georgia

6816 Alliance Packaging Group, Inc.
940 Sherwin Pkwy, Ste 100
Buford, GA 30517
Contact: Michelle Calvert CEO
Tel: 770-309-1012
Email: mcalvert@alliancepkggroup.com
Website: www.alliancepkggroup.com
Packaging, janitorial & shipping supplies. (Woman, estab 2007, empl 5, sales $2,733,290, cert: WBENC)

6817 E. Smith Box, Inc.
1875 Rockdale Industrial Blvd
Conyers, GA 30012
Contact: Jaquacer Middlebrooks President
Tel: 770-388-7787
Email: sales@esmithbox.com
Website: www.esmithbox.com
Mfr corrugated boxes. (AA, estab 1987, empl 35, sales $1,300,000, cert: NMSDC)

6818 FilmLOC Inc.
4190 Thurmon Tanner Pkwy
Flowery Branch, GA 30542
Contact: Shirl Handly President
Tel: 404-892-8778
Email: shirl@filmloc.com
Website: www.filmloc.com
Mfr Intelli-Placï¿½ placards for labeling & re-labeling reusable containers, totes & pallets, shelves, equipment, racking, manufactured goods in process, shipping crates. (Woman, estab 2002, empl 5, sales $749,359, cert: WBENC)

6819 Flexstar Packaging, Inc.
1902 Kimberly Park Dr
Dalton, GA 30720
Contact: Alan DaCosta GM
Tel: 706-272-3575
Email: alan@flexstarinc.com
Website: www.flexstarinc.com
Packaging, flexographic. (Woman, estab 2005, empl 21, sales $2,680,000, cert: WBENC)

6820 Meristem Packaging Company LLC
5090 Old Ellis Point
Roswell, GA 30076
Contact: Paige Mesaros Supply Chain Mgr
Tel: 770-998-7120
Email: pmesaros@meristempkg.com
Website: www.meristempkg.com
Packaging, folding cartons/boxes, plastic bags & styrofoam coolers. (AA, Hisp, estab 2009, empl 5, sales $7,444,000, cert: NMSDC)

6821 Palmetto Industries International, Inc.
6001 Horizon West Pkwy
Grovetown, GA 30813
Contact: Purvis King VP
Tel: 706-737-7995
Email: customerservice@palmetto-industries.com
Website: www.palmetto-industries.com
Mfr & dist polymer & paper packaging products. (Minority, estab , empl , sales $20,000,000, cert: NMSDC)

6822 SquarePac LTD
7115 Oak Ridge Pkwy Ste 110
Austell, GA 30168
Contact: Walter Griggs CFO
Tel: 770-617-5688
Email: admin@squarepac.us
Website: www.squarepac.us
Returnable packaging & material handling solutions, eco-friendly containers & packaging, totes, pallets & metal racks. (AA, estab 2013, empl 8, sales $0, cert: NMSDC, SDB)

Illinois

6823 Action Bag Company
1001 Entry Dr.
Bensenville, IL 60640
Contact: Martha Quintero
Tel: 866-349-8853
Email: mquintero@actionbag.com
Website: www.actionhealth.com
Printed bags, bags, retail packaging products, printed promotional products, promotional items, packaging supplies, labels, tissue paper, gift cards, specialty packaging, custom bags, custom printed items, rush orders, in-stock products. (Woman, estab , empl , sales $0, cert: City, WBENC)

6824 Alta Packaging, Inc.
150 Chaddick Dr
Wheeling, IL 60090
Contact: Jill Zienkiewicz
Tel: 847-215-2582
Email: jillz@altapackaging.com
Website: www.altapackaging.com
Dist industrial packaging supplies. (Woman, estab 1995, empl 10, sales $5,276,581, cert: WBENC)

6825 AREM Container & Supply Co.
6153 W Mulford Unit D
Niles, IL 60714
Contact: Brian Shifrin VP
Tel: 847-673-6184
Email: brian@aremcontainer.com
Website: www.aremcontainer.com
Dist shipping, packaging & warehouse supplies: corrugated boxes & sheets, chipboard, poly bags, bubble & foam wrap, tape & spray adhesives, stretch wrap, kraft paper, padded mailers, bubble mailers, poly courier bags, chipboard mailers, etc. (Woman, estab 1961, empl 7, sales $2,182,000, cert: WBENC)

6826 BAF Packaging, LLC
1053 E. 95th St.
Chicago, IL 60619
Contact: Valerie Matthews President
Tel: 888-225-8221
Email: vam@bafpack-rite.com
Website: www.bafpack-rite.com
Contract Packaging, shrink wrap packaging, Light industrial assembly, Fulfillment, Distribution warehouse capabilities. (Woman/AA, estab 2013, empl 3, sales $350,000, cert: NMSDC)

6827 Cano Container Corporation
3920 Enterprise Court
Aurora, IL 60504
Contact: Juventino Cano President
Tel: 630-585-7500
Email: juventino@canocontainer.com
Website: www.canocontainer.com
Mfr corrugated shipping containers. (Hisp, estab 1986, empl 2, sales $20,000,000, cert: NMSDC)

6828 Carter Paper & Packaging, Inc.
3400 SW Washington St
Peoria, IL 61607
Contact: Mike Krost Sales
Tel: 309-637-7711
Email: mike@carterpaper.com
Website: www.erpaper.com
Dist paper & plastic packaging, bags, towels, wipers, tissue, VCI paper, loose fill, foam, tape, adhesives & specialty items. (Woman, estab 1957, empl 18, sales $0, cert: WBENC)

6829 Commercial Bag Company
1 Paper Chase
Normal, IL 61761
Contact: Rachel Bowling
Tel: 309-862-0144
Email: rbowling@commercialpackaging.com
Website: www.commercialpackaging.com
Flexible Packaging, stand up pouches, Bulk Bags/Totes, Woven Poly Bags, Multiwall Bags. (Woman, estab , empl , sales $95,000,000, cert: WBENC)

6830 Cross Packaging Supply, Inc.
968 Dundee Ave Ste B
Elgin, IL 60120
Contact: AJ Loredo President
Tel: 847-780-7225
Email: aloredo@crosspackaging.com
Website: www.crosspackaging.com
Packaging supplies (boxes, paper, tape, stretch film, bubble wrap, poly bags, bubble mailers, mailers, labels, can liners, etc). (Hisp, estab 2013, empl 2, sales $500,000, cert: NMSDC)

6831 Dynamic Packaging
1248 W Jackson Blvd, Ste 2E
Chicago, IL 60607
Contact: Elson Seale President
Tel: 312-374-4445
Email: elson@dynam-pak.com
Website: www.dynam-pak.com
Dist industrial & janitorial supplies: corrugated boxes, tape, stretch-film, shrink-film, poly-bags, bubble wrap. (Woman/AA, estab 2014, empl 5, sales $250,000, cert: NMSDC)

6832 Food Packaging Consultants, Inc.
1601 Pleasant Ct
Libertyville, IL 60048
Contact: Laura Boucher President
Tel: 708-883-7240
Email: laura@pripackaging.com
Website: www.pripackaging.com
Flexible & rigid packaging & food processing materials.
(Woman, estab 2004, empl 1, sales $3,535,219, cert:
WBENC)

6833 H&H Sorting Services
1021 St. Charles St
Elgin, IL 60120
Contact: Jeanne Hintz President
Tel: 847-741-8479
Email: jeanne@hhsort.com
Website: www.hhsort.com
Sorting & inspection, assembly, packaging, labeling of
fasteners & molded plastics & other pre-manufactured
parts. (Woman, estab 1989, empl 48, sales $1,737,436,
cert: WBENC)

6834 Magenta LLC
15160 New Ave
Lockport, IL 60441
Contact: Stephanie Smith Business Dev Exec
Tel: 630-737-9606
Email: ssmith@magentallc.com
Website: www.magentallc.com
Design, development & mfr injection molded components-
primarily packaging— closures and containers. (Woman,
estab 1969, empl 81, sales $14,900,000, cert: WBENC)

6835 Midwest Mailing & Shipping Systems Inc.
3006 Gill St, Ste A
Bloomington, IL 61704
Contact: Dave Rappa VP Sales
Tel: 309-661-1144
Email: dave@midwestmailing.com
Website: www.midwestmailing.com
Dist mailing systems, folder inserters, letter openers,
inbound letter & parcel tracking systems, shipping sys-
tems, addressing systems, CASS/PAVE certified software,
electronic scales, shredders, pressure sealers, bursters,
collators, etc. (Woman, estab 1988, empl 9, sales
$1,650,000, cert: WBENC)

6836 Montenegro Paper, Ltd.
25 E Main St. Ste 205
Roselle, IL 60172
Contact: Ed Enciso President
Tel: 630-894-0350
Email: mbe@montenegro-inc.com
Website: www.montenegro-inc.com
Dist commercial printing paper & packaging supplies.
(Hisp, estab 1996, empl 6, sales $23,173,000, cert: State,
City, NMSDC)

6837 Morris Packaging
211 N Williamsburg Dr, Ste A
Bloomington, IL 61701
Contact: Penny Steinwagner Sales & Marketing
Tel: 309-663-9100
Email: psteinwagner@morrispkg.com
Website: www.morrispkg.com
Flexible packaging manufacturer. (Nat Ame, estab 2004,
empl 263, sales $100,000,000, cert: NMSDC)

6838 Numeridex, Inc.
632 Wheeling Rd
Wheeling, IL 60090
Contact: Alberto Hoyos President
Tel: 847-541-8840
Email: debbie@numeridex.com
Website: www.numeridex.com
Dist labeling & bar code products: thermal transfer
printers, labels, ribbons, scanners, packaging & shipping
supplies, corrugated cartons, stretch film, carton sealing
tape. (Hisp, estab 1967, empl 10, sales $2,370,000, cert:
NMSDC)

6839 Planned Packaging of Illinois Corp.
19558 S Harlem Ave Ste 5
Frankfort, IL 60423
Contact: Jack Callham Exec VP
Tel: 815-277-5270
Email: jack@ppoic.com
Website: www.ppoic.com
Dist industrial packaging supplies: corrugated boxes,
film, foams, pallets, etc. (AA, estab 2001, empl 30, sales ,
cert: NMSDC)

6840 Poly-Pak and Ship, Inc.
2021 Illini Ave
Vandalia, IL 62471
Contact: JoAnn Boggs President
Tel: 618-283-2397
Email: joannboggs@polypakusa.com
Website: www.polypakusa.com
Warehousing, packaging, labeling, addressing, mailing,
distribution printed matter, direct mail svcs.
 (Woman, estab 1985, empl 85, sales $2,658,671, cert:
State, City, WBENC)

6841 Primary Resources Inc.
405 Busse Road
elk Grove Village, IL 60007
Contact: Enza Fragassi President
Tel: 847-808-7684
Email: enza@primarypkg.com
Website: www.primaryresources.net
Corrugated packaging, fibre board slip sheets, folding
cartons, corrugated, chip partitions, flexible films,
barrier bags, pouches, bundling, film products, shrink,
stretch, polyethylene, labels, tamper evident products,
bio-degradable materials. (Minority, Woman, estab
2001, empl 10, sales , cert: NMSDC)

6842 Scout Sourcing, Inc.
2340 South River Road Ste 309
Des Plaines, IL 60018
Contact: Anne Cowherd President
Tel: 917-428-8184
Email: acowherd@scoutsourcinginc.com
Website: www.scoutsourcinginc.com
Dist paper & packaging. (Woman, estab 2006, empl 6,
sales $95,000,000, cert: WBENC)

6843 Service Packaging Design, Inc.
6238 Lincoln Ave
Morton Grove, IL 60053
Contact: Norman Croft President
Tel: 847-966-6556
Email: ncroft@servicepackaging.com
Website: www.servicepackaging.com
Mfr & dist corrugated boxes, wood products, tags &
labels, gum & poly tape, stretch wrap. (AA, estab 1982,
empl 7, sales $1,250,000, cert: NMSDC)

6844   Skyline Container Corporation
9755 W 143rd St
Orland Park, IL 60462
Contact: Dawn Souliotis President
Tel: 708-460-7965
Email: dawn@skyline99.com
Website: www.skyline99.com
Dist corrugated boxes. (Woman, estab 1990, empl 5, sales $1,697,049, cert: City, WBENC)

6845   TransWorld Plastic Films, Inc.
150 N 15th St
Rochelle, IL 61068
Contact: Rodolfo Hernandez Business Devel
Tel: 815-561-7117
Email: rhernandez@transworldplasticfilms.com
Website: www.transworldplasticfilms.com
Polyethylene film for the automotive, tire & rubber industries used in the manufacturing & packaging process. (Minority, Woman, estab 2007, empl 31, sales , cert: NMSDC, WBENC)

6846   Trinity Graphic & Packaging Solutions, LLC
28W031 Greenview Ave
Warrenville, IL 60555
Contact: Hardy Leonard President
Tel: 630-393-7550
Email: len.hardy@trinitygraphic.net
Website: www.trinitygraphic.net
Dist thermal transfer ribbons, thermal transfer printers, thermal transfer print heads, printed labels, warehouse labels, promotional labels. (AA, Nat Ame, estab 2001, empl 1, sales , cert: State)

Indiana

6847   AIM Solutions, Inc.
PO Box 340
McCordsville, IN 46055
Contact: John Laakso Dir
Tel: 239-316-0004
Email: john.laakso@aimsolutionsinc.net
Website: www.aimsolutionsinc.net
Packaging & shipping supplies, pallets, boxes, film, bubble sheet stock, package automation engineering, foam, packaging equipment, plastic trays, labeling products & equipment, tape. (As-Pac, estab 2006, empl 7, sales $1,500,000, cert: State)

6848   Brown Tape Products Company
8909 Sargent Rd
Indianapolis, IN 46256
Contact: Janice Brown President
Tel: 866-276-9682
Email: janbrown@browntapeproducts.com
Website: www.browntapeproducts.com
Adhesive tape, cardboard boxes, mailers, steel banding, plastic banding, banding tools, stretch film, bubble pack, foam packaging, tape dispensers, newsprint, nylon cable ties, rolled corrugated, packing slip envelopes, plastic bags. (Woman, estab 1984, empl 5, sales $1,000,000, cert: City)

6849   Morales Group, Inc.
5628 W 74th St
Indianapolis, IN 46278
Contact: Seth Morales Sales Mgr
Tel: 317-334-0950
Email: smorales@moralesgroup.net
Website: www.moralesgroup.net
Assembly, packaging & warehousing services, Point of Purchase display assembly, Kitting, Literature collation, insertion, Sort/rework. (Hisp, estab 2003, empl 28, sales $14,900,000, cert: NMSDC)

6850   MSW   (Mahomed Sales & Warehousing, LLC)
8258 Zionsville Rd
Indianapolis, IN 46268
Contact: Keith Kanipe Sr VP
Tel: 317-472-5800
Email: kkanipe@whse.com
Website: www.whse.com
Assembly, Sub-assembly Packaging, Kitting, Warehousing, Supply Chain Mgmt & Sorting services. (As-Ind, estab 1996, empl 110, sales $87,000,000, cert: NMSDC)

6851   Premier Business Solutions
3202 N Kenmore
South Bend, IN 46628
Contact: President
Tel: 574-232-8840
Email: PBSAdmin@premierbus.com
Website: www.premierbus.com
Fulfillment & marketing services: product & literature fulfillment, rebate & free offer processing, network programs, lead mgmt programs, pick pack, warehousing & inventory management.
We help our clients execute all facets of their marketing plan. (Woman, estab 2001, empl 15, sales $0, cert: WBENC)

6852   The Servants, Inc.
3145 Lottes Dr
Jasper, IN 47546
Contact: Jerome Balbach Controller
Tel: 812-634-2201
Email: jerome@servants.com
Website: www.servants.com
Corrugated packaging & packaging accessories. (Woman/AA, estab 1973, empl 55, sales $10,000,000, cert: NWBOC)

6853   Vesta Ingredients, Inc.
5767 Thunderbird Rd
Indianapolis, IN 46236
Contact: Richard Pinner Client Relationship Mgr
Tel: 317-397-9004
Email: richard@vestaingredients.com
Website: www.vestaingredients.com
Contract manufacturing & packaging. (As-Pac, estab 1997, empl 20, sales $10,000,010, cert: NMSDC)

Kansas

6854   Pitt Plastics, Inc.   dba IBS Solutions
PO Box 356
Pittsburg, KS 66762
Contact: Randy Orscheln VP Sales, Strategic Accts
Tel: 800-835-0366
Email: randyo@pittplastics.com
Website: www.pittplastics.com
Dist bags: can liners & poly bags, rolls or flat pack. (Nat Ame, estab 1971, empl 450, sales , cert: NMSDC)

Kentucky

6855 CSS Distribution Group, Inc.
3600 Chamberlain Ln Ste 216
Louisville, KY 40241
Contact: Sandy Allemang CEO
Tel: 502-423-1011
Email: sandya@customersourcingsolutions.com
Website: www.customersourcingsolutions.com
Dist packaging tape, edge protector, pallets, packaging & automation equipment, forklift software tracking program. (Woman, estab 2006, empl 12, sales $2,200,000, cert: WBENC)

6856 Kyana Packaging & Industrial Supply, Inc.
2501 Ampere Dr
Louisville, KY 40291
Contact: Kimberly Osborne CEO
Tel: 502-992-3333
Email: kim@kyanaind.com
Website: www.kyanaind.com
Dist packaging & shipping supplies: boxes, tape, stretch wrap, bubble wrap, strapping, adhesives, air pillow machines, stretch wrappers, strapping machines, automatic tape machines, shrink wrap equipment & film, poly bags, plastic films. (Woman, estab 1976, empl 37, sales $9,737,350, cert: WBENC)

6857 P3 Protective Packaging Products
PO Box 3583
Louisville, KY 40201
Contact: Anne Sizemore VP
Tel: 502-357-6872
Email: annes@p3products.com
Website: www.p3products.com
Expendable/Returnable Packaging & design. Retail package supplier/distributor. (Woman, estab 2001, empl 22, sales $7,000,000, cert: WBENC)

Massachusetts

6858 Lancaster Packaging, Inc.
560 Main St, Ste 2
Hudson, MA 01749
Contact: Marianne Lancaster President
Tel: 978-562-0100
Email: mlancaster@lancasterpackaging.com
Website: www.lancasterpackaging.com
Dist bank tamper evident bags, file storage boxes, corrugated materials, stretch wrap, shipping supplies. (Woman/AA, estab 1989, empl 10, sales $10,320,151, cert: WBENC)

Maryland

6859 Vac Pac, Inc.
150 W Ostend St, Ste 160
Baltimore, MD 21230
Contact: Hessa Tary CEO
Tel: 410-685-5181
Email: hessa.tary@vacpacinc.com
Website: www.vacpacinc.com
Print & convert flexible packaging, poly, polyprop, polyester, cellophane, nylon
high temeprature. (Woman, estab 1949, empl 25, sales $4,000,000, cert: WBENC)

Michigan

6860 Aldez Containers, LLC
4260 Van Dyke, Ste 109
Almont, MI 48003
Contact: Diane Pattison VP
Tel: 586-243-0596
Email: dpattison@aldezcontainers.com
Website: www.aldezcontainers.com
Mfr corrugated packaging & dunnage, service parts packaging. (Minority, Woman, estab 1998, empl 78, sales $10,000,000, cert: NMSDC)

6861 Bay Corrugated Container, Inc.
1655 W 7th St
Monroe, MI 48161
Contact: Judy Thoma Exec Admin
Tel: 734-243-5400
Email: jthoma@baycorr.com
Website: www.baycorr.com
Mfr corrugated boxes/folding cartons, corrugated pallets, corrugated interior packaging materials, stretchwrap, chipboard, board coatings, linerboard/fine paper, stickers, labels, etc. (Minority, Woman, estab 1964, empl 250, sales $65,027,000, cert: NMSDC, WBENC)

6862 Contract Source & Assembly Inc.
5230 33rd St SE
Grand Rapids, MI 49512
Contact: Bryce Cooper
Tel: 616-897-2185
Email: bryce@contractmi.com
Website: www.contractmi.com
Light Manufacturing & Contract Assembly, Contract Packaging & Inventory Management, Supply Chain Management, Inspection & Re-work. (As-Pac, estab 2001, empl 13, sales $18,000,000, cert: NMSDC)

6863 Diversity Products
32031 Howard St
Madison Heights, MI 48071
Contact: Darlene Fleser Operations Dir
Tel: 248-585-1200
Email: dfleser@diversityproducts.com
Website: www.diversityproducts.com
Packaging engineering support, cost reduction, vendor consolidation, packaging program mgmt, returnable container repair, cleaning & tracking, inventory management. (Woman/AA, estab 1998, empl 35, sales $9,000,000, cert: NMSDC)

6864 Galaxy Forest Products LLC
1655 W 7th St
Monroe, MI 48161
Contact: Judy Thoma Exec Admin
Tel: 734-243-5400
Email: jthoma@galaxyforestproducts.com
Website: www.galaxyforestproducts.com
Packaging materials, pulp, microflute, consumer boxes, corrugated containers, slip sheets, folding cartons, corner/angle protectors, dunnage packaging. (Minority, Woman, estab 2005, empl 1, sales $2,058,358, cert: State, NMSDC)

6865   Genesee Packaging, Inc (The Genesee Group)
2010 N. Dort Hwy, PO Box 7716
Flint, MI 48506
Contact: Ken Miller Sales Mgr
Tel: 248-514-1883
Email: kmiller@genpackaging.com
Website: www.genpackaging.com
Packaging supplies & services. (Woman, estab 1979, empl 125, sales $190,000,000, cert: WBENC)

6866   Global Strategic Supply Solutions
34450 Industrial Rd
Livonia, MI 48150
Contact: Lisa Williams-Lunsford CEO
Tel: 734-525-9100
Email: lisa@gs3global.com
Website: www.gs3global.com
Warehousing Operations, Consigned Packaging, Order Fulfillment and Distribution, Kit Building, Assembly. (Woman/AA, estab 2010, empl 50, sales $0, cert: WBENC)

6867   Integrated Packaging Company
6400 Harper Ave
Detroit, MI 48211
Contact: Jeffrey Laney Strategic Accounts Mgr
Tel: 612-802-1736
Email: jeff.laney@ipcboxes.com
Website: www.ipcboxes.com
Packaging solutions, packaging & displays, Design, Concept & Development. (AA, estab 1992, empl 30, sales $20,000,000, cert: NMSDC)

6868   James Group International
4335 W Fort St
Detroit, MI 48209
Contact: Lorron James Sales Mgr
Tel: 313-842-4543
Email: lorron.james@jamesgroupintl.com
Website: www.jamesgroupintl.com
Logistics, sequencing, warehousing & distribution, deconsidation, re-packing, sub-assembly, inventory management. (AA, estab 1971, empl 171, sales $30,000,000, cert: NMSDC)

6869   Macomb Wholesale Supply Corp.
17730 E 14 Mile Rd
Fraser, MI 48026
Contact: Catherine David President
Tel: 586-415-7400
Email: online@macombwholesale.com
Website: www.macombwholesale.com
Dist Packaging, Safety, Janitorial & Facility Maintenance Supplies, corrugated, poly bags, tape, paper, chemical, packaging, gloves, safety & facility cleaning supplies. (Woman, estab 1988, empl 10, sales $2,500,000, cert: WBENC)

6870   Packaging Integration, LLC
13235 Avalon Ct
Brighton, MI 48116
Contact: Scott Bradford President
Tel: 248-437-1900
Email: scott.bradford@packagingintegration.com
Website: www.packagingintegration.com
Dist packaging materials. (Hisp, estab 2005, empl 5, sales $5,000,000, cert: NMSDC)

6871   Patriot Packaging Solutions and Consulting
269 Walker St, Ste 522
Detroit, MI 48207
Contact: Jay Jackson VP
Tel: 313-580-1538
Email: jay.jackson@patriotgm1.com
Website:
www.patriotpackagingsolutionsconsuting.com
Packaging services: corrugated box, bulk boxes, displays, single face, bubble wrap, stretch wrap, trays, sheets, tape & labels. (AA, estab 2011, empl 4, sales $500,250, cert: NMSDC)

6872   Peach State Packaging Solutions
8803 Cairn Hwy
Elk Rapids, MI 49629
Contact: Lisa McCririe President
Tel: 819-599-2594
Email:
lmccririe@peachstatepackagingsolutions.com
Website:
www.peachstatepackagingsolutions.com
Dist packaging supplies. (Woman, estab 2006, empl 1, sales $800,000, cert: WBENC)

6873   Pro-Pak Products, Ltd.
17580 Helro Dr
Fraser, MI 48026
Contact: Nancy Stachnik President
Tel: 586-415-1500
Email: propakltd@aol.com
Website: www.propakproductsltd.com
Packaging supplies & services. (Woman, estab 1993, empl 5, sales , cert: NWBOC)

6874   Qualfon Solutions, Inc,
13700 Oakland Ave
Highland Park, MI 48203
Contact: Alisha McNary SVP Cstmr Solutions
Tel: 877-261-0804
Email: alisha.mcnary@qualfon.com
Website: www.qualfon.com
Fulfillment, Literature & Product Fulfillment, Kitting/ Production Support, B2B & B2C fulfillment support, Sampling Packaging & Fulfillment Support, Trade Show, Convention, Event Fulfillment, Promotional Offer/Rebate Support • Inventory Management. (Hisp, estab 2021, empl 16000, sales $379,030,000, cert: NMSDC)

6875   Quixerve Corporation
341 N Helmer Rd
Springfield, MI 49037
Contact: Linda Gillett President
Tel: 269-441-0700
Email: lgillett@quixerve.com
Website: www.quixerve.com
Printing, Labeling, Packaging, Fulfillment, Warehousing, Inventory Control, Distribution. (Woman, estab 2003, empl 3, sales $225,000, cert: WBENC)

6876   Ryan Industries, Inc.
30369 Beck Rd
Wixom, MI 48382
Contact: Brenda Ryan President
Tel: 248-926-5254
Email: bryan@ryanind.net
Website: www.ryanind.net
Warehousing, packaging, light assembly, kitting, distribution, rework. (Woman/AA, estab 1995, empl 10, sales $0, cert: NMSDC, WBENC)

6877   Sibley Laboratories LLC
       8816 Charbane St
       White Lake, MI 48386
       Contact: Kathleen Sibley Managing Partner
       Tel: 248-363-3972
       Email: ksibley@sibleylabs.com
       Website: www.sibleylabs.com
Dist ergonomically safe trash collection receptacles & trash
bags. (Woman, estab 2001, empl 3, sales $0, cert: WBENC)

6878   STEWART Industries, LLC
       150 McQuiston Dr
       Battle Creek, MI 49037
       Contact: Matt Amos Business Dev Mgr
       Tel: 269-998-0608
       Email: mamos@stewartindustriesusa.com
       Website: www.stewartindustriesusa.com
Third party inspection, sorting, rework, light assembly,
packaging. (AA, estab 2000, empl 60, sales $37,615,000,
cert: NMSDC)

6879   Tabb Packaging Solutions
       41605 Ann Arbor Rd Ste 2
       Plymouth, MI 48170
       Contact: Julie Kavulich Business Devel Mgr
       Tel: 734-254-0251
       Email: jkavulich@tabbpackaging.com
       Website: www.tabbpackaging.com
Post Consumer Recycled Materials, HDPE & PET, Primary
Processing Operations, Market Color Concentrates &
Additives, Packaging Materials & Label Substrate (IML),
Virgin & PCR Pre-blend Resins. (Woman, estab 2007, empl
7, sales , cert: WBENC)

6880   Total Packaging Solutions LLC
       900 Wilshire Dr STE 202
       Troy, MI 48084
       Contact: Liz Dzuris Owner
       Tel: 248-505-4419
       Email: servie@totalpkgsolutions.com
       Website: www.totalpackaging.biz
Mfr custom returnable & expendable packaging. (Woman,
estab 2005, empl 3, sales $708,000, cert: WBENC)

6881   Valmec Inc.
       1274 S Holly Rd
       Fenton, MI 48430
       Contact: Krystn Tatus CEO
       Tel: 810-629-8750
       Email: valmec@comcast.net
       Website: www.valmecinc.com
Material handling & packaging, conveyors, returnable
packaging, installation, tear-outs & complete system
integration. (Woman, estab 1971, empl 5, sales
$1,344,664, cert: WBENC)

6882   Venchurs, Inc.
       800 Liberty St
       Adrian, MI 49221
       Contact: Erica Wilt Program Mgr
       Tel: 517-264-4392
       Email: esellers@venchurs.com
       Website: www.venchurs.com
Custom package design & flexible packaging solutions.
Global Sourcing, Supply Chain Management, Inventory
Management, Packaging, Warehousing & Distribution.
(Hisp, estab 1973, empl 86, sales $0, cert: NMSDC)

6883   World Corrugated Container
       PO Box 840
       Albion, MI 49224
       Contact: Tara Saumier Human Resources
       Tel: 517-629-9400
       Email: tsaumier@worldcorrugated.com
       Website: www.worldcorrugated.com
Mfr & dist corrugated containers. (Minority, Woman,
estab 1991, empl 40, sales $7,900,000, cert: WBENC)

Minnesota

6884   Independent Packing Services, Inc.
       7600 32nd Ave N
       Crystal, MN 55427
       Contact: Joseph Wallace President
       Tel: 763-425-7155
       Email: jwallace@ipsipack.com
       Website: www.ipsipack.com
Mfr industrial crating for domestic & export shipments;
electronics & fragile artwork. (AA, estab 1976, empl 60,
sales $0, cert: NMSDC)

6885   Polybest, Inc.
       2962 Cleveland Ave N
       Roseville, MN 55113
       Contact: Zongzhao Li President
       Tel: - -
       Email: johnli@polybestinc.com
       Website: www.polybestinc.com
Mfr packaging materials such as all kinds of plastic and
compostable bags, hazard trash bags, disposal bags,
trash canliners, wrapping film, etc. (As-Pac, estab 2006,
empl 4, sales $2,007,686, cert: NMSDC)

6886   Promotion Management Center, Inc.
       31205 Falcon Ave
       Stacy, MN 55079
       Contact: DeAnn Monson Business Devel
       Tel: 612-801-7921
       Email: dmonson@pmci.com
       Website: www.pmci.com
Fulfillment, direct mail, sweepstakes, packaging.
(Woman, estab 1983, empl 40, sales $3,000,000, cert:
WBENC)

6887   SeaChange Print Innovations
       14505 27th Ave N
       Plymouth, MN 55447
       Contact: Nancy Servais Business Devel
       Tel: 763-586-3700
       Email: nancy.servais@seachangem.com
       Website: www.seachangemn.com
Folding carton & marketing print production, Folding
Carton Packaging, Marketing Printing, Commercial
Printing, Direct Mail Printing, Digital Printing. (Woman,
estab 2014, empl 90, sales $13,100,000, cert: WBENC)

6888   TJ's Packaging Inc
       19950 177th St NW
       Big Lake, MN 55309
       Contact: Kristy Murray COO
       Tel: 763-241-2022
       Email: jfarrington@tjpackaging.com
       Website: www.tjpackaging.com
Packaging supplies & automated packaging equipment.
(Woman, estab 1998, empl 4, sales $1,862,202, cert:
WBENC)

Missouri

6889 Bennett Packaging of Kansas City, Inc.
220 NW Space Center Cir
Lee's Summit, MO 64064
Contact: Traci Strickert Dir of Marketing
Tel: 816-379-5001
Email: traci.strickert@bpkc.com
Website: www.BennettKC.com
Design & mfr corrugated boxes, point-of-purchase displays, co-packing, fulfillment, warehousing & distribution. (Woman, estab 1987, empl 240, sales $65,153,256, cert: WBENC)

6890 Crossroads USA
14004 Century Lane
Grandview, MO 64030
Contact: Jason Begnaud Dir of Sales
Tel: 816-767-8008
Email: service@bestwaylogistics.com
Website: www.bestwaylogistics.com/
Single source packaging & shipping solutions nationwide. (Woman, estab 2000, empl 14, sales $5,050,000, cert: WBENC)

6891 Engineered Packaging Systems, Inc.
16141 Westwoods Business Park
Ellisville, MO 63021
Contact: Debra Debra Runtzel-Young CEO
Tel: 636-227-8600
Email: info@packeps.com
Website: www.packeps.com
Full service packaging machinery and packaging materials or consumables, CAD layout drawings, installation, service, shrink film, stretch film, tapes, adhesives, cartons, custom printed bags, powder filling, liquid filling, labeling machines and labels. (Woman, estab 2004, empl 11, sales $9,000,000, cert: WBENC)

6892 Swan Packaging Inc.
PO Box 1558
St. Louis, MO 63026
Contact: President
Tel: 314-771-9777
Email: info@swanpackaginginc.com
Website: www.swanpackaginginc.com
Dist shrink sleeves, lidding films, printed rollstock & pouches, rotogravure & flexographic printing, multilayer films, extrusion & off-line lamination, films, paper & foil. (Woman, estab 1999, empl 6, sales $3,519,000, cert: WBENC)

Mississippi

6893 Innpack LLC
10511 High Point Rd
Olive Branch, MS 38654
Contact: Jin Ahn CFO
Tel: 901-949-4977
Email: jahn@innpack.com
Website: www.innpack.com
Mfr & dist packaging solutions: burlap, cotton, PP woven, laminated & FBIC bags. (As-Pac, estab 1997, empl 20, sales $9,000,000, cert: NMSDC)

North Carolina

6894 Carolina Industrial Resources, Inc
4303 Oak Level Rd
Rocky Mount, NC 27803
Contact: Margaret Hoyle President
Tel: 800-849-1819
Email: tphoyle@cir-poly.com
Website: www.cir-poly.com
Dist polyethylene plastic packaging products. (Woman, estab 1986, empl 359, sales $155,000,000, cert: WBENC)

6895 Packrite, LLC
PO Box 2438
High Point, NC 33688
Contact: Kevin Spencer Business Devel
Tel: - -
Email: mark@packrite.net
Website: www.packrite.net
Single face-lamination corrugated products. (Woman, estab 2008, empl 90, sales $28,262,000, cert: WBENC)

6896 PolySi Technologies, Inc.
5108 Rex McLeod Dr
Sanford, NC 27330
Contact: LYNN RICHARDSON Operations Mgr
Tel: 919-775-4989
Email: lynn@polysi.com
Website: www.polysi.com
Mfr silicone, synthetic greases & silicone fluids, industrial packaging, retail packaging, contract filling & custom packaging. (Woman, estab 1995, empl 25, sales $7,000,000, cert: WBENC)

6897 SLR Designs, LLC
11220 Elm Lane, Ste 200
Charlotte, NC 28277
Contact: Linda Tilley Managing Member
Tel: 704-546-8448
Email: linda@slrdesignsllc.com
Website: www.slrdesignsllc.com
Design & dist customer packaging, PVC, mPE & phthalate free materials. (Woman, estab 2011, empl 4, sales $3,247,681, cert: WBENC)

6898 Southern Film Extruders, Inc.
2319 English Rd
High Point, NC 27265
Contact: John Barnes VP Finance
Tel: 800-334-6101
Email: sales@southernfilm.com
Website: www.southernfilm.com
Extrudes polyethylene packaging films using LDPE, LLDPE,HDPE and Metallocene resins for various packaging applications, shrink film, film for bags, laminations etc. (Hisp, estab 1965, empl 150, sales $65,000,000, cert: NMSDC)

Nebraska

6899 Frontier Bag Company, Inc
2520 Grant St
Omaha, NE 68111
Contact: Rendell Gines Reg Sales Mgr
Tel: 402-342-0992
Email: jplee@frontierbagco.com
Website: www.frontierbagco.com
Dist plastic bags & packaging, film wrap & shrink wrap. (Woman/AA, estab 1946, empl 15, sales $1,430,000, cert: WBENC)

New Jersey

6900 Accurate Box Company
86 Fifth Ave
Paterson, NJ 07524
Contact: Samara Schlossman Sales & Marketing Mgr
Tel: 973-345-2000
Email: sschlossman@accuratebox.com
Website: www.accuratebox.com
Litholaminated E, B & F flute packaging & displays. (Woman, estab 1944, empl 315, sales $138,000,000, cert: WBENC)

6901 Alpha Industries Inc. dba Sigma Stretch Film
Page and Schuyler
Lyndhurst, NJ 07071
Contact: John Buchan Mgr strategic accts
Tel: 214-799-3975
Email: johnbuchan@sigmaplastics.com
Website: www.sigmaplastics.com
Mfr custom barrier & sealant mono & co-ex blown films for dry,frozen, refrigerated & liquid food applications.. (As-Pac, estab 1997, empl 70, sales $57,500,000, cert: NMSDC)

6902 Creative Packaging Solutions Corporation
5 W First St
Keyport, NJ 07735
Contact: Coni Lefferts President
Tel: 732-335-3700
Email: info@packaging-usa.com
Website: www.packaging-usa.com
Dist packaging containers, parts & components: bottles, jars, flexible tubes, rigid tubes aand canister, caps, sprayers, lotion pumps, folding boxes, rigid gift set up boxes, ribbons, thermoformed blisters and trays. (Woman, estab 2003, empl 2, sales $176,677, cert: State, WBENC)

6903 G&T Trading International
128 Circle Ave
Clifton, NJ 07011
Contact: George Chen President
Tel: 973-340-8003
Email: philipgttic@gmail.com
Website: www.gttic.com
Dist stretch film, wooden pallets, chipboard, stretch film equip, annual equipment audits, shrink film, shrink wrap & bundling equip, carton sealing & bagging equip, supporting films & tapes. (As-Pac, estab 1977, empl 6, sales $23,987,513, cert: State, NMSDC)

6904 Glopak Corporation
132 Case Dr
South Plainfield, NJ 07080
Contact: Elyne Williams Sales Dir
Tel: 908-753-8735
Email: glopakinc@aol.com
Website: www.glopakcorp.com
Dist plastic bags & liners. (Woman/AA, estab 1966, empl 33, sales $0, cert: NMSDC)

6905 Kampack, Inc
100 Frontage Rd
Newark, NJ 07114
Contact: Patrick J Fox Strategic Accounts Mgr
Tel: 804-370-0351
Email: pat.fox@kampackinc.com
Website: www.kampackinc.com
Mfr corrugated packaging. (Woman/Hisp, estab 1959, empl 250, sales $60,000,000, cert: State, NMSDC, WBENC)

6906 Modpak, Inc.
317 Godwin Ave
Midland Park, NJ 07432
Contact: CEO
Tel: 201-493-7677
Email: Modpak@Aol.Com
Website: www.modpakinc.com
Packaging & printing. (Woman, estab 1977, empl 4, sales $0, cert: WBENC)

6907 Pro Pack Inc.
500 W Main St
Wyckoff, NJ 07481
Contact: Peter Quercia CEO
Tel: 201-337-1001
Email: peter@shrinkfilm.com
Website: www.shrinkfilm.com
Packaging materials, form, fill & seal systems, doy-pack systems, metal detectors & check weighers, labeling systems, clip & twist systems, shrink wrappers, carton sealers, stretch wrappers, strapping machines, conveyors, band sealers, filling systems. (Woman, estab 1976, empl 10, sales $4,000,000, cert: WBENC)

6908 Products Distribution, Inc.
7 Santa Fe Way Ste 701
Cranbury, NJ 08512
Contact: Dawn Dunbar President
Tel: 609-655-1341
Email: requests@productsdistribution.com
Website: www.productsdistribution.com
Warehousing, distribution, fulfillment, assembly, kitting, pick pack, container unloading, palletizing, ingredient storage, bulk storage, EDI, custom assembly, display assembly, GWP assembly, rack storage, raw material storage. (Woman, estab 1979, empl 7, sales $1,119,000, cert: WBENC)

6909 Quality Packaging Specialists International, LLC
2030 US 130 N
Florence, NJ 08518
Contact: Jeff Lemke Sales Exec
Tel: 609-239-0503
Email: jlemke@qpsiusa.com
Website: www.qpsiusa.com
Packaging & fulfillment, merchandising displays, contract packaging, logistics & distribution services. (AA, estab 1972, empl 1500, sales $300,000,000, cert: NMSDC)

6910 RKS Plastics Inc.
100 Jersey Ave
New Brunswick, NJ 08903
Contact: Sudhir Shah President
Tel: 800-635-9959
Email: srshah@rksplastics.com
Website: www.rksplastics.com
Dist polyethylene & polyproylene bags, drum/box liners, sheeting & tubing, zipper lock bags, anti-static bags, printed bags, wicket/staple pack, stretch wrap & tapes. In addition, we also offer design services. (AA, As-Pac, estab 1993, empl 7, sales $4,223,000, cert: NMSDC)

6911 SunFlex Packagers Inc.
2 Commerce Dr
Cranford, NJ 07016
Contact: Manny Patel CEO
Tel: 908-709-1500
Email: mannypatel@sunflexpackagers.com
Website: www.sunflexpackagers.com
Convert & dist flexible packaging material: roll form, bags & specialty pouches. (As-Ind, estab 2002, empl 15, sales $5,900,000, cert: NMSDC)

6912 West Pack Industries, LLC.
2225 E Greg St, Ste 107
Sparks, NV 89431
Contact: James Alford General Mgr
Tel: 775-351-3345
Email: james@westpackcopack.com
Website: www.westpackcopack.com/
Flexible packaging, contract packaging, dry product filling, mixing, blending. Stand up pouch filling, Vertical Form Fill Seal filling, volume metric filling, scale filling. Snack Foods, candy, confectionery, powdered beverages. (Nat Ame, estab 2003, empl 44, sales $1,850,000, cert: NMSDC)

New York

6913 Aluf Plastics div. of API Industries, Inc.
2 Glenshaw St
Orangeburg, NY 10962
Contact: Tom Cross VP Retail Sales
Tel: 845-365-2200
Email: tom.c@alufplastics.com
Website: www.alufplastics.com
Mfr plastic bags. (Woman, estab 1977, empl 314, sales , cert: WBENC)

6914 Berry Industrial Group, Inc.
30 Main St
Nyack, NY 10960
Contact: Debra Berry CEO
Tel: 845-353-8338
Email: debra.berry@berryindustrial.com
Website: www.berryindustrial.com
Mfr, recycle & dist industrial shipping pallets. (Woman, estab 1984, empl 7, sales $22,636,656, cert: WBENC)

6915 Bluepack
215 John Glenn Dr
Amherst, NY 14228
Contact: Helen Ma President
Tel: 716-923-0032
Email: hma@bluepackinc.com
Website: www.bluepackinc.com
Mfr printed & unprinted shrink labels, neck bands & safety seals. We have 8 color flexo and rotogravure presses. (Minority, Woman, estab 1999, empl 65, sales $10,000,000, cert: NMSDC)

6916 Diamond Packaging
111 Commerce Dr
Rochester, NY 14623
Contact: Dennis Bacchetta Dir of Marketing
Tel: 585-334-8030
Email: sales@diamondpkg.com
Website: www.diamondpackaging.com
Contract mfg & packaging services: automatic cartoning, bagging bar coding, blister sealing, EAS source tagging, flexible packaging, form, fill & seal, fulfillment, labeling, POP displays, product assembly, RF sealing, shrink wrapping & skin packaging. (Woman, estab , empl 230, sales $59,180,000, cert: WBENC)

6917 Global Packaging Solutions LLC
70 E Sunrise Hwy Ste 611
Valley Stream, NY 11581
Contact: Mitchell Sloane Managing Dir
Tel: 516-256-7416
Email: msloane@glopackllc.com
Website: www.glopackllc.com
Bags, plastic bags, reusable bags, trash liners, shopping bags. (AA, estab 2011, empl 5, sales $3,500,000, cert: State)

6918 Golden Group International, Ltd.
305 Quaker Rd
Patterson, NY 12563
Contact: Transue President
Tel: 845-440-5220
Email: jackiet@goldengroupinternational.com
Website: www.goldengroupinternational.com
Mfr & dist bags, dispensers, receptacles and cabinets. (Woman, estab 2009, empl 8, sales , cert: WBENC)

6919 Howell Packaging
79 Pennsylvania Ave
Elmira, NY 14904
Contact: Katherine Roehlke CEO
Tel: 607-734-6291
Email: khr@howellpkg.com
Website: www.howellpkg.com
Mfr printed folding cartons and thermo-formed plastic components internally. (Woman, estab , empl 240, sales $41,000,000, cert: WBENC)

6920 Ongweoweh Corp
5 Barr Road
Ithaca, NY 14850
Contact: Brett Bucktooth Supplier Diversity Mgr
Tel: 607-266-7070
Email: supplierdiversity@ongweoweh.com
Website: www.ongweoweh.com
Mfr & dist wooden pallets & specialty containers. (Nat Ame, estab 1978, empl 96, sales $252,000,000, cert: NMSDC)

6921 Star Poly Bag Inc.
200 Liberty Ave.
Brooklyn, NY 11207
Contact: Rachel Posen President
Tel: 718-384-3130
Email: rachel@starpoly.com
Website: www.starpoly.com
Mfr poly bags. (Woman, estab 1961, empl 15, sales $3,550,000, cert: State, City, WBENC)

6922 The Standard Group
1010 Northern Blvd Ste 236
Great Neck, NY 11021
Contact: James Gregory Acct Exec
Tel: 718-310-5512
Email: jamesg@thestandardgroup.com
Website: www.thestandardgroup.com
Folding carton, specialty printed packaging & paperboard converter. (Hisp, estab 1932, empl 130, sales $35,000,000, cert: NMSDC)

6923   Universal Packaging Systems
       6080 Jericho Turnpike
       commack, NY 11725
       Contact: David Boone Natl Acct Mgr
       Tel: 404-554-0770
       Email: dboone@paklab.com
       Website: www.paklab.com
Contract manufacturing & flexible film, extended gamut flexographic printing of roll stock & pouches with gussets & fitments. (AA, estab 1987, empl 600, sales $116,400,000, cert: NMSDC)

Ohio

6924   Accel inc.
       9000 Smith's Mill Road
       New Albany, OH 43054
       Contact: Chairwoman
       Tel: 614-656-1100
       Email:
       Website: www.accel-inc.com
Contract packaging & fulfillment svcs: design, sourcing, assembly, shrink-wrapping, warehousing, dist & e-fulfillement svcs. (Woman, estab 1995, empl 375, sales $25,890,000, cert: WBENC)

6925   Allied Shipping and Packaging Supplies
       3681 Vance Road
       Moraine, OH 45439
       Contact: Shelly Heller President
       Tel: 937-222-7422
       Email: sheller@asapi.com
       Website: www.asapi.com
Dist packaging supplies: special size boxes, printed boxes, printed tape, special inserts or cell partitions, printed poly bags or special size poly bags. (Woman, estab 1982, empl 12, sales $4,034,225, cert: WBENC)

6926   Arrowhead Packaging Services
       PO Box 1284
       Perrysburg, OH 43551
       Contact: Brian Deiger VP Sales
       Tel: 419-344-7373
       Email: brian@apackserv.com
       Website: www.apackserv.com
Packaging & packaging services, fulfillment operations, sequencing, storage & logistics. (AA, estab 2010, empl 2, sales $120,000, cert: NMSDC)

6927   Bickley Innovations, LLC
       607 Redna Terr, Ste 700
       Cincinnati, OH 45215
       Contact: Kendra Alexander President
       Tel: 513-655-6074
       Email: information@bickleyllc.com
       Website: www.bickleyllc.com
Dist packaging & industrial supplies. (Woman/AA, estab 2015, empl 1, sales , cert: NMSDC, WBENC)

6928   Custom Paper Tubes
       15900 Industrial Pkwy
       Cleveland, OH 44135
       Contact: Emily Miller Marketing Mgr
       Tel: 216-362-2964
       Email: emiller@custompapertubes.com
       Website: www.custompapertubes.com
Produce sustainable, recyclable & biodegradable packaging for all types of products. (Woman/AA, Hisp, estab 1964, empl 25, sales $5,500,000, cert: WBENC, SDB)

6929   Forest City Companies, Inc.
       3607 W 56th St
       Cleveland, OH 44102
       Contact: Anthony Galang
       Tel: 216-634-9000
       Email: tgalang@forestcityco.com
       Website: www.forestcityco.com
Military packaging service & supplies, laser marking services, wood boxes, export packing & crating, hazmat packaging service & supplies, induatrial sewing, bellows, insulated blankets. (Minority, estab 1993, empl 14, sales $3,600,000, cert: NMSDC)

6930   Fre-Flo Distribution
       3700 Inpark Circle
       Dayton, OH 45414
       Contact: Theodore R. Ross, III President
       Tel: 937-233-1997
       Email: tross@freflo.com
       Website: www.freflo.com
Warehousing, distribution, containment, quality inspection, assembly, sub-assembly, power-washing returnable containers, reworking, components recovery, packaging, labeling, kitting, pick & pack, bulk repacking. (AA, estab 1991, empl 26, sales $1,495,883, cert: State, NMSDC)

6931   Joshen Paper and Packaging
       5800 Grant Ave
       Cuyahoga Heights, OH 44105
       Contact: Anthony Salyers
       Tel: 216-441-5600
       Email: greiser@joshen.com
       Website: www.joshen.com
Dist packaging supplies, bags, office supplies, custom printing, sanitation, chemicals & floor care programs. (Woman, estab 1988, empl 152, sales $180,500,000, cert: NWBOC)

6932   LEFCO Worthington, LLC
       18451 Euclid Ave
       Cleveland, OH 44112
       Contact: Larry Fulton President
       Tel: 216-432-4422
       Email: larry.fulton@lefcoworthington.com
       Website: www.LEFCOWorthington.com
Dist wooden crates, OSB Boxes, custom pallets, sub-assembly & packaging services. (AA, estab 2003, empl 30, sales $3,600,000, cert: State, NMSDC)

6933   TrueChoicePack Corp.
       9565 Cincinnati Columbus Road
       Cincinnati, OH 45069
       Contact: Rakesh Rathore COO
       Tel: 513-759-5540
       Email: info@truechoicepack.com
       Website: www.truechoicepack.com
Mfr environmentally friendly green packaging products, biodegradable & compostable food service packaging & disposable products. (Woman/As-Ind, estab 2008, empl 10, sales $50,560,000, cert: NMSDC, WBENC)

6934 Vista Industrial Packaging, Inc.
      4700 Fisher Rd
      Columbus, OH 43228
      Contact: Michael Houser Business Devel
      Tel: 614-372-9951
      Email: mhouser@vistaindustrialpackaging.com
      Website: www.vistaindustrialpackaging.com
Contract or co-packaging, hand assembly work, shrink
wrapping, build POP displays, HazMat packing, kit or
giftset assembly, auto or manual bagging, ticketing,
sorting, returns processing, pick and pack, QA, warehousing, direct shipments, distribution. (Woman, estab 1983,
empl 70, sales $0, cert: WBENC)

Oregon

6935 Standard Bag Manufacturing Company
      1800 SW Merlo Dr
      Beaverton, OR 97003
      Contact: Rita Fung Controller
      Tel: 503-616-7307
      Email: rfung@standardbag.com
      Website: www.standardbag.com
Mfr bags: sewn open mouth, pinch bottom open mouth &
pinch block bottom bags. (As-Pac, estab 1985, empl 140,
sales $0, cert: NMSDC)

6936 Yoshida Foods International
      8440 NE Alderwood Rd, Ste A
      Portland, OR 97220
      Contact: Junki Yoshida Sales Mgr
      Tel: 503-872-8450
      Email: junki.yoshida@yoshida.com
      Website: www.yoshidafoodsinternational.com
Liquid hot-fill bottling, industrial packaging, portion
packaging. (As-Pac, estab 1982, empl 241, sales $0, cert:
NMSDC)

Pennsylvania

6937 Alpine Packaging Inc.
      4000 Crooked Run Rd
      North Versailles, PA 15137
      Contact: Jan Lehigh President
      Tel: 412-664-4000
      Email: jlehigh@alpinepackaging.com
      Website: www.alpinepackaging.com
Packaging supplies & services. (Woman, estab 1972, empl
38, sales $14,180,198, cert: WBENC)

6938 Carlisle Packaging Company, Inc.
      750 Claremont Rd
      Carlisle, PA 17013
      Contact: Ed Schimmel CEO
      Tel: 717-249-2444
      Email: eschimmel@carlislecontainer.net
      Website: www.carlislecontainer.net
Mfr corrugated packaging & displays. (Woman, estab 1965,
empl 40, sales $7,173,000, cert: State, WBENC)

6939 Evco Industries, Inc.
      126 Talbot Ave
      Holmes, PA 19043
      Contact: Kathleen Evans President
      Tel: 610-586-9842
      Email: kitty@evcoindustries.com
      Website: www.evcoindustries.com
Dist industrial packaging products: adhesives, adhesive
applicating equipment, marking/coding equipment &
drying systems. (Woman, estab 1979, empl 8, sales
$2,230,099, cert: WBENC)

6940 Kalstar Enterprises, LLC
      PO Box 931
      Scranton, PA 18501
      Contact: Adam Zaranski Dir Client Solutions
      Tel: 973-553-5370
      Email: adam.zaranski@kalstar.com
      Website: www.kalstar.com
Packaging, kitting other labor services to manufacturing
companies. (Woman, estab 2004, empl 206, sales
$33,600,000, cert: WBENC)

6941 S&G Corrugated Packaging
      195 Slocum St
      Swoyersville, PA 18704
      Contact: Earl Sampson CEO
      Tel: 570-287-1718
      Email: sgcorrugated@verizon.net
      Website: www.s-gcorrugatedpackaging.com
Mfr corrugated cartons & corrugated sheets: assembled
partitions, corrugated trays, half slotted cartons, one &
five panel folders, scored sheets, coated pads, telescoping cartons, die cutting items, slip sheets, packaging
tapes. (AA, estab 2007, empl 10, sales , cert: NMSDC)

6942 Secure Applications, LLC
      419 West Market St Ste C
      Bethlehem, PA 18018
      Contact: Gina Uzzolino President
      Tel: 732-874-0954
      Email: guzzolino@secureapplications.net
      Website: www.secureapplications.net
Packaging materials for Product Security, Tamper
Evident, Non-Tamper Evident tapes & labels, security
bags, stretch film & Temperature Monitoring Systems for
cold chain applications as well as security containers &
seals. (Woman, estab 2011, empl 2, sales $110,000, cert:
State, CPUC)

6943 Union Packaging, LLC
      6250 Baltimore Ave
      Yeadon, PA 19050
      Contact: Michael K. Pearson President
      Tel: 610-622-7001
      Email: mpearson@unionpkg.com
      Website: www.unionpkg.com
Mfr folding cartons, paperboard printing & converting.
(AA, estab 1999, empl 82, sales $9,287,115, cert:
NMSDC)

6944 Wexler Packaging Products, Inc.
      777-M Schwab Rd
      Hatfield, PA 19440
      Contact: Tara Utain VP Sales
      Tel: 800-878-3878
      Email: tara@wexlerpackaging.com
      Website: www.wexlerpackaging.com
Packaging products. (Woman, estab 1997, empl 20, sales
$0, cert: WBENC)

Puerto Rico

6945 3A Press
PO Box 47
Lajas, PR 00667
Contact: Marie Rosado President
Tel: 787-899-0110
Email: mrosado@3apress.com
Website: www.3apress.com
Mfr & print pharmaceutical, commercial & folding cartons, inserts, stitched & perfect bound booklets/magazines, printed literature. (Hisp, estab 1996, empl 126, sales $11,200,000, cert: NMSDC)

6946 Flexible Packaging Company, Inc.
KM 5 1 BO Guaragua RR 176 Bayamon Gardens Station
Bayamon, PR 00959
Contact: Esteban Serrano Sales Mgr
Tel: 787-622-7225
Email: eserrano@flepak.com
Website: www.flepak.com
Flexible packaging solutions. (Hisp, estab 1976, empl 170, sales , cert: NMSDC)

6947 Inter-Strap Packaging Systems
PO Box 12367
San Juan, PR 00914
Contact: Antonio Fernández GM
Tel: 787-771-5230
Email: afernandez@inter-strap.com
Website: www.inter-strap.com
Dist packaging equipment & materials. (Minority, Woman, estab 1991, empl 18, sales $6,317,564, cert: NMSDC)

6948 Johnny Rullan & Co.,
Road # 1 Km. 20.9 RR-3 Box 3710
San Juan, PR 00926
Contact: Julio Pizarro Accounting Clerk
Tel: 787-789-3050
Email: accountsreceivable@johnnyrullan.com
Website: www.johnnyrullan.com
Packaging equipment sales & service. (Hisp, estab 1970, empl 25, sales , cert: NMSDC)

Rhode Island

6949 Banneker Industries, Inc.
582 Great Rd, Ste 101
North Smithfield, RI 02896
Contact: Joe Cefalo Sales & Marketing Mgr
Tel: 603-819-6966
Email: marketing@banneker.com
Website: www.banneker.com
Supply chain management services: e-business services, assembly & packaging, bar coding, dist packaging materials, third party logistics (3PL), warehousing, material flow & inventory management. (Woman/AA, estab 1991, empl 72, sales $10,072,400, cert: NMSDC, WBENC)

South Carolina

6950 Alpha Pack LLC
PO Box 30266
Charleston, SC 29417
Contact: Carver Wright Jr. Owner
Tel: 843-737-3931
Email: wright.pkg@alphapackllc.com
Website: www.alphapackllc.com
Flexible packaging,polybags, shrink bags, printed bags, tubing, vci bags, sheeting & can liners. (AA, estab 2012, empl 2, sales , cert: NMSDC)

6951 Milagro Packaging LLC
60 Fairview Church Rd
Spartanburg, SC 29306
Contact: Jill McCurry President
Tel: 864-578-0085
Email: jillm@concept-pkg.com
Website: www.milagro-pkg.com
Mfr corrugated & solid fiber boxes, polystyrene foam products & urethane foam products. (Hisp, estab 2001, empl 425, sales $94,873,435, cert: NMSDC)

6952 Progressive Packaging
1224 Old Stage Rd
Greenville, SC 29681
Contact: Mark Hutcherson Sales Exec
Tel: 864-271-8106
Email: hutcherson64@gmail.com
Website: www.progpack.com
Corrugated packaging, boxes, sheet plant, assembly. (Woman, estab 1996, empl , sales $19,000,000, cert: WBENC)

6953 Solution Packaging LLC
2131 Woodruff Rd, Ste 196
Greenville, SC 29607
Contact: Joe Nichol VP Sales
Tel: 864-313-9595
Email: joe@solutionplastics.net
Website: www.solutionplastics.net
Mfr & dist polyethylene based end product & solutions, packaging, poly film, etc. (Minority, Woman, estab 2013, empl 2, sales , cert: WBENC)

6954 WDS, Inc.
1414 Village Harbor Dr
Lake Wylie, SC 29710
Contact: Jennfer Maier CEO
Tel: 803-619-0301
Email: jennifer.maier@womends.com
Website: www.womends.com
Dist industrial supplies: paper products, chipboard, films & plastics. (Woman, estab 2007, empl 180, sales $186,000,000, cert: WBENC)

Tennessee

6955 DSI Warehouse Inc
1315 Farmville Rd
Memphis, TN 38122
Contact: Debbie Martin President
Tel: 901-345-6608
Email: debbiemartin@dsiwarehouse.com
Website: www.dsiwarehouseandstorage.com
Warehousing & Storage, Packing & Crating, Packaging & Labeling, Kitting Pack Services, Storage & Handling Equipment & Supplies, Distribution Fulfillment. (Woman/AA, estab 2013, empl 20, sales $1,455,421, cert: NMSDC, WBENC)

6956 Interstate Packaging
2285 Hwy 47 N
White Bluff, TN 37187
Contact: Marketing Dir
Tel: 615-797-9000
Email: ldoochin@interstatepkg.com
Website: www.interstatepkg.com
Flexible packaging, labels, bags, and pouches. (Woman, estab 1969, empl 210, sales $42,000,000, cert: WBENC)

6957 Johnson Bryce, Inc.
5405 Hickory Hill
Memphis, TN 38141
Contact: Ron Purifoy CEO
Tel: 901-942-6522
Email: rpurifoy@johnsonbryce.com
Website: www.johnsonbryce.com
Mfr flexible packaging. (AA, estab 1991, empl 25, sales $27,500,000, cert: NMSDC)

6958 OTB Container, LLC
1380 Poplar Ave
Memphis, TN 38104
Contact: Daniel Coates President
Tel: 901-270-5407
Email: daniel@otbcontainer.com
Website: www.otbcontainer.com
Supplies corrugated shipping boxes. (AA, estab 2015, empl 5, sales $589,000, cert: NMSDC)

6959 Puffy Stuff
9 Music Square S, Ste 376
Nashville, TN 37203
Contact: Sales
Tel: 877-833-9872
Email: info@puffystufftn.com
Website: www.puffystufftn.com
Mfr 100% biodegradable packing peanuts. (Woman, estab 2000, empl 20, sales , cert: State)

6960 RD Plastics
PO Box 111300
Nashville, TN 37222
Contact: Jeffrey D. Loveless VP Natl Accts
Tel: 615-781-0007
Email: jeffl@rdplastics.com
Website: www.rdplastics.com
Bags: biohazard ziplock, clear ziplock, adhesive closure, specimen transport, open end, security seals, pill crushers, personal belonging. (Woman, estab , empl , sales $16,502,500, cert: WBENC)

6961 Remar Inc
6200 E. Division St
Lebanon, TN 37090
Contact: Lee Whittaker President
Tel: 720-601-4785
Email: lwhittaker@remarinc.com
Website: www.remarinc.com
Dist blister packaging, fin seal wrap, shrink wrap, inventory mgmt, point of purchase displays, media replication, direct mail services, turn key or component projects. (Hisp, estab , empl 150, sales $0, cert: State, NMSDC)

6962 TSS Industrial Packaging, LLC
PO Box 3181
Jackson, TN 38303
Contact: Michelle Boyd CEO
Tel: 888-424-1946
Email: mboyd@tssip.com
Website: www.tssip.com
Dist industrial packaging materials: industrial sewing thread & yarn for closing bags, crepe paper sewing tape, pull tape, twine, slip sheets, pallet covers, stretch film & stretch wrap. (Woman, estab 2006, empl 4, sales $3,803,124, cert: State, WBENC)

6963 Worldwide Label & Packaging LLC
158 Madison Ave Ste 101
Memphis, TN 38103
Contact: Anthony Norris President
Tel: 901-454-9290
Email: anorris@worldwidebg.com
Website: www.worldwidebg.com
Mfr printed packaging: pressure sensitive labels, flexible packaging & continuous roll forms. (AA, estab 2000, empl 26, sales $5,000,000, cert: NMSDC)

Texas

6964 Accredo Packaging, Inc.
12682 Cardinal Meadow Dr
Sugar Land, TX 77478
Contact: Malcolm Cohn Dir of Sustainability
Tel: 713-580-4872
Email: mcohn@accredopkg.com
Website: www.accredopackaging.com
Dist biopolymer resins. (As-Pac, estab 2007, empl 350, sales $305,000,000, cert: State, NMSDC)

6965 Age Industries, Ltd.
3601 County Rd, Ste 316C
Cleburne, TX 76031
Contact: Max Walls GM/VP Packaging Div
Tel: 281-799-0935
Email: max@ageindustries.com
Website: www.ageindustries.com
Mfr & dist packaging products. (Woman, estab 1974, empl 247, sales $72,000,000, cert: WBENC)

6966 Argent Associates, Inc.
2800 E Plano Pkwy Ste 400
Plano, TX 75074
Contact: Betty Manetta VP Supply Chain
Tel: 732-512-9009
Email: bmanetta@argentassociates.com
Website: www.argentassociates.com
Inventory mgmt, warehousing, dist, logistics, packaging, installation & commercial construction. (Minority, Woman, estab 1998, empl 65, sales $181,676,013, cert: NMSDC, CPUC, WBENC)

6967 Austin Foam Plastics, Inc.
2933 AW Grimes Blvd
Pflugerville, TX 78660
Contact: Lisa Carnett Project Leader
Tel: 512-251-6300
Email: lisa.carnett@a-f-p.com
Website: www.a-f-p.com
Packaging Design and testing; logistics; sustainable
solutions; manufacturing - corrugated (boxes; die cut;
pallets; solid fiber folding cartons) wood (custom crates;
pallets; floating pallets) custom cases; custom cushions;
plastic corrugated; sourcing ((Woman, estab 1978, empl
228, sales $0, cert: WBENC)

6968 B.A.G. Corp.
1155 Kas Dr. Ste 170
Richardson, TX 75081
Contact: Sherlene A Wegner Marketing Assistant
Tel: 214-340-7060
Email: sherlene@bagcorp.com
Website: www.bagcorp.com
Bulk handling & supply chain solutions. (Woman, estab
1969, empl 100, sales $70,000,000, cert: WBENC)

6969 Boxes 4 U, Inc.
1405 E Plano Pkwy
Plano, TX 75074
Contact: Nikki Hernandez VP
Tel: 972-516-0002
Email: nikki@boxes4u.com
Website: www.boxes4u.com
Corrugated boxes and packaging materials. Shipping
boxes, heavy duty boxes, cardboard sheets, bubblewrap,
tape, stretch film, packing paper, kraft paper, styrofoam
peanuts, biodegradeable peanuts, biodegradeable bubble,
custom boxes, etc. (Hisp, estab 1991, empl 11, sales $0,
cert: State, 8(a))

6970 Castle Business Solutions, LLC
2777 North Stemmons Frwy Ste 1242
Dallas, TX 75207
Contact: Sharon King CEO
Tel: 214-599-2880
Email: sharon@castlebusinesssolutions.net
Website: www.castlebusinesssolutions.com/
Directory & mailing list publishing, direct mail advertising,
packaging & labeling services, warehousing & storage,
custom computer programming services, data processing,
hosting & related services. (Woman/AA, estab 2010, empl
3, sales $615,880, cert: State, NMSDC)

6971 CCA Distributions
12832 Tierra Karla Dr
El Paso, TX 79938
Contact: Carlos Camarena Owner
Tel: 915-239-1870
Email: carlos@ccadistributions.com
Website: www.ccadistributions.com
Dist Packaging Material: Stretch Film, Kraft Paper, Tape,
Poly Strapping, Metal Strapping, Boxes, Kraft Paper Tubes,
Chipboard. Poly Sheeting, Poly Bags, and more. (Minority,
Woman, estab 2007, empl 2, sales , cert: State, NMSDC)

6972 Diamond Display Group Partners, Inc.
2637 Summit Ave Ste 303
Plano, TX 75074
Contact: Glenn Towery Business Devel Mgr
Tel: 972-636-0781
Email: glenn@ddg-corp.com
Website: www.diamonddisplaygroup.com
Corrugated & permanent displays & packaging, shipper
style corrugated displays & POS signage, styrene,
foamboard, vinyl, acrylic and metal. (Woman, estab
2003, empl 5, sales , cert: State, WBENC)

6973 Formers International, Inc.
3533 Preston Ave
Pasadena, TX 77505
Contact: Corina Carmona Business Dev Mgr
Tel: 281-998-9570
Email: corina@formers.com
Website: www.formers.com
Mfr bag forming assemblies: vertical form, fill & seal
packaging machines. (Hisp, estab 1975, empl 39, sales
$0, cert: City)

6974 Guardian Packaging Industries, LP
3615 Security St
Garland, TX 75042
Contact: President
Tel: 214-349-1500
Email:
Website: www.guardianpackaging.com
Design & manufacture protective packaging, Polyure-
thanes, Polyethylene's, Expanded Polystyrene, Rigid
Urethanes and all Military Spec Foams, corrugated box
shop. (Woman, estab 2005, empl 35, sales $3,900,000,
cert: State, WBENC)

6975 Harris Packaging Corporation
1600 Carson St
Haltom City, TX 76117
Contact: Jana Harris-Bickford CEO
Tel: 817-429-6262
Email: janab@harrispackaging.com
Website: www.harrispackaging.com
Mfr corrugated & folding carton trays & boxes. (Woman,
estab 1976, empl 130, sales $22,000,000, cert: WBENC)

6976 International Print & Packaging, Inc.
951 Hwy 183 N.
Liberty Hill, TX 78642
Contact: Shelly Armstrong Digital Solutions Spec.
Tel: 512-515-6333
Email: shelly@dle-corp.com
Website: www.ipp-corp.com
Mfr flexible packaging: labels, stickers, decals, shrink
film, printed film, lidding materials, POP products,
displays, table tents, shelf strips, hang tags, folding
cartons, self sufficient manufacturing, inhouse graphics
design department. (Woman, estab 1996, empl 90, sales
$0, cert: State)

6977 Komplete Group, Inc.
202 N Great Southwest Pkwy
Grand Prairie, TX 75050
Contact: Tariq Usmani Diversity Coord
Tel: 214-252-8102
Email: tusmani@kpak.com
Website: www.kpak.com
Food copackaging, packaging equipment & supplies,
thermoforming, commercial printing. (As-Pac, estab
1995, empl 150, sales , cert: State, NMSDC)

6978 New Century Packaging Systems, LLC
      401 N Carrol Ave, Ste 124
      Southlake, TX 76092
      Contact: Vanessa Brown General Mgr
      Tel: 972-725-0311
      Email: vbrown@newcenturypkg.net
      Website: www.newcenturypkg.net
Dist packaging materials & packaging equipment. (AA,
estab 1972, empl 4, sales $1,900,000, cert: NMSDC)

6979 Southwest Packaging Solutions, LLC
      2472 Southwell Rd
      Dallas, TX 75229
      Contact: Edgar Sotelo President
      Tel: 903-440-3628
      Email: edgar@southwestpackaging.net
      Website: www.southwestpackaging.net
Contract packaging services, printed registered film
packaging services, warehousing, display building, bundling, reverse logistics, blister pack, skin pack, mfg consulting for improved efficiencies. (Hisp, estab 2009, empl 30,
sales $1,800,000, cert: NMSDC)

6980 Starpak Ltd.
      9690 W Wingfoot Rd
      Houston, TX 77041
      Contact: Catherine Beers Customer Service Dir
      Tel: 713-329-9183
      Email: cbeers@starpakltd.com
      Website: www.starpakltd.com
Converter and printer of flexible films for packaging of
Food and Beverage products (Hisp, estab 2003, empl 350,
sales $106,196,322, cert: NMSDC)

6981 Superbag USA Corp.
      9291 Baythorne Dr
      Houston, TX 77041
      Contact: Woody Hunt VP Sales
      Tel: 713-462-1173
      Email: whunt@superbag.com
      Website: www.superbag.com
Dist high density polyethylene grocery, retail bags &
woven polypropylene bags. (Hisp, estab 1999, empl 250,
sales $149,000,000, cert: NMSDC)

6982 TCP Universal
      3536 Hwy 6 South, Ste 118
      Sugarland, TX 77478
      Contact: Pep Ly President
      Tel: 281-966-8208
      Email: pep.ly@tcpuniversal.com
      Website: www.tcpuniversal.com
Can Liners, Biohazard Bags, Composite Bags, Ice Bags, Poly
Bags, Produce Bags. (Minority, Woman, estab 2015, empl
3, sales , cert: State, City)

Washington

6983 Kalani Packaging, Inc.
      2525 W Casino Rd, Ste 8C
      Everett, WA 98204
      Contact: Shelly Dickson
      Tel: 425-347-0330
      Email: shelly@kalanipkg.com
      Website: www.kalanipkg.com
Dist packaging supplies: tape, stretch wrap, shipping
labels, poly bags & sheeting, boxes, bubble wrap & custom
printed labels. Also dist janitorial supplies, boxes & bags.
(As-Pac, estab 2000, empl 12, sales , cert: NMSDC)

Wisconsin

6984 Chryspac - Quality Custom Solutions
      130 W Edgerton Ave Ste 130
      Milwaukee, WI 53207
      Contact: Warren Scurlock Business Devel Mgr
      Tel: 414-372-0541
      Email: Sales@Chryspac.com
      Website: www.chryspac.com
Packaging & assembly: quality inspection, containment
sorting, assembling, re-work, reclamation, shrink
wrapping & labeling. (AA, estab 2000, empl 50, sales
$816,456, cert: NMSDC)

6985 Pac Basic
      S10744 State Road 93
      Eleva, WI 54738
      Contact: Mindy Pedersen President
      Tel: 715-552-1722
      Email: mpedersen@pacbasic.com
      Website: www.pacbasic.com
Packaging, corrugated, molded pulp & other various
protective materials. (Woman, estab 2007, empl 4, sales
$1,978,000, cert: WBENC)

6986 Packaging Specialties Inc.
      W130 N10751 Washington Dr
      Germantown, WI 53022
      Contact: Hugh Ahn President
      Tel: 262-512-1261
      Email: hahn@packaging-specialties.com
      Website: www.packaging-specialties.com
Dist packaging systems & materials. (As-Pac, estab 1973,
empl 30, sales $0, cert: NMSDC)

6987 TechniSource Services Group
      1025 S Moorland Rd 2057
      Brookfield, WI 53005
      Contact: Elizabeth Tran President
      Tel: 800-864-2317
      Email: james@technisourcegroup.com
      Website: www.technisourcegroup.com
Dist packaging products & services: stretch films, shrink
film, poly films, carton sealers, erectors, stretch wrappers, tapes & adhesives, corrugated & fiber boxes.
(Minority, Woman, estab 1994, empl 50, sales
$25,000,000, cert: NMSDC)

6988 Twin River LLC
      2721 Harvey St
      Hudson, WI 54016
      Contact: Kathy Enerson President
      Tel: 715-381-3067
      Email: kathyb@twinriverllc.com
      Website: www.twinriverllc.com
Packaging, fulfillment, high-speed shrink wrapping,
blister pack, clamshells, poly & paper banding, labeling,
barcoding, kitting, assembly, distribution, warehousing,
POP displays, quality inspections & mailings. (Woman,
estab 2009, empl 8, sales $357,450, cert: WBENC)

VALIDATION
data management
EVALUATE
engage strategy
BEST PRACTICES
reporting
data scrubs
SOURCING
SUPPORT

PHOTOGRAPHY, MOTION & STILL
Commercial photographers. Includes aerial photography, topographic mapping, film processors, photo labs, corporate and professional photography. NAICS Code 54

California

6989   Number 3 Inc.
       108 W 2nd St, Ste 706
       Los Angeles, CA 90012
       Contact: Kal Yee
       Tel: 323-646-8764
       Email: kal@kalyee.com
       Website: www.kalyee.com
Photography & videography. (As-Pac, estab 2000, empl 2, sales $100,000, cert: CPUC)

Florida

6990   APImaging, Inc.
       19 SW 6th St
       Miami, FL 33130
       Contact: Diana Herrera VP Sales
       Tel: 305-373-4774
       Email: dianah@apimaging.com
       Website: www.apimaging.com
Photo imaging & photo finishing services, commercial printing, studio photography, self adhesive signs & graphics, directional signs, posters, point of purchase signs, graphic displays, graphic design, trade shows & exhibits. (Minority, Woman, estab 2013, empl 22, sales , cert: WBENC)

6991   Kerrick Williams Photography LLC
       811 Hickory Glen Dr
       Seffner, FL 33584
       Contact: Kerrick Williams Owner
       Tel: 813-571-3768
       Email: kerrick@kerrickwilliams.com
       Website: www.KerrickWilliams.com
Corporate Photography, Video Production: special event coverage, advertising, marketing archival. Onsite printing, Executive portraits, Head Shots, group functions. (AA, estab 1992, empl 1, sales , cert: State, City, NMSDC)

Illinois

6992   McLaren Photographic LLC
       1482 Armstrong Court
       Elk Grove Village, IL 60007
       Contact: Fiona McLaren Owner
       Tel: 847-668-8615
       Email: fmclaren@mclarenphotographic.com
       Website: www.mclarenphotographic.com
HD video, time-lapse, commercial photography, gigapanography & virtual mobile tours, commercial photographic services with portable studios & editing capabilities. (Woman, estab 2009, empl 1, sales , cert: WBENC)

6993   Powell Photography, Inc.
       531 S Plymouth Court, Ste 101
       Chicago, IL 60605
       Contact: Victor Powell President
       Tel: 312-922-6366
       Email: vpowell@powellphotography.com
       Website: www.powellphotography.com
Photography, photography services, digital imaging & retouching, photo composition, video, multi-media & graphics pre-production. (AA, estab 1976, empl 3, sales $440,000, cert: State, NMSDC)

6994   Yates Enterprises
       213 N Stetson Ave
       Chicago, IL 60601
       Contact: Owen Donnelly VP Operations
       Tel: 419-308-9938
       Email: owen@yatesprotect.com
       Website: www.yatesprotect.com
We believe safety is a right not a privilege and do everything we can to help public entities and companies protect their people. We offer high-quality goods and the best technologies on the market to deliver peace of mind so your hospitals, schools, offi (AA, estab 2013, empl 10, sales $2,000,000, cert: NMSDC)

Massachusetts

6995   Melvin's Photo
       34 Frank st
       Watertown, MA 02472
       Contact: Melvin Guante Owner
       Tel: 617-942-3432
       Email: melvin@melvinsphoto.com
       Website: www.Melvinsphoto.com
Portrait photographic studios, still or video photography, business portrait, commercial, real estate & corporate event. (AA, Hisp, estab 2001, empl 1, sales , cert: State)

Michigan

6996   Stage 3 Productions
       1532 N. Opdyke Rd Ste 700
       Auburn Hills, MI 48326
       Contact: Andre LaRoche President
       Tel: 248-955-1250
       Email: andre@stage3.com
       Website: www.stage3.com
Commercial, advertising photography, digital imaging, illustration, graphic design, stage rental. (AA, estab 1984, empl 8, sales , cert: NMSDC)

Minnesota

6997 Code Creative Services
6001 Code Ave
Edina, MN 55436
Contact: Erin Schwind Owner
Tel: 952-922-8348
Email: erin@codecreativeservices.com
Website: www.codecreativeservices.com
Photography production, Estimating, Crew Sourcing,
Location Scouting, Casting, Talent Negotiations, Budget
Management, Catering, Travel Arrangements, Props,
Permits & Insurance & Billing. (Woman, estab 2012, empl
1, sales $120,262, cert: WBENC)

Nevada

6998 Infinity Enterprises, Inc.
3347 S Highland Dr, Ste 304
Las Vegas, NV 89109
Contact: Audrey Dempsey President
Tel: 702-837-1128
Email: audrey@infinity-photo.com
Website: www.infinity-photo.com
Photography & graphic design: conventions & special
events, food, corporate headshots, products & architec-
ture, private sittings, weddings & retouching, web & print
design, company branding, logo design & marketing, video
editing. (Woman, estab 1993, empl 5, sales $532,467, cert:
WBENC)

6999 Square Shooting
1800 Industrial Rd, Ste 103
Las Vegas, NV 89102
Contact: Jennifer Burkart Managing Partner
Tel: 702-721-9893
Email: jennifer@squareshooting.com
Website: www.squareshooting.com
Commercial photography, professional photographer,
executive portrait photography, architecture, interior
design, editorial, food & cocktail photography, advertising,
fashion, lifestyle, resort, product, photography studio.
Established in 2013, Square (Woman, estab 2013, empl 2,
sales , cert: WBENC)

New York

7000 5th Avenue Digital
231W 29th St, Ste 1006
New York, NY 10001
Contact: Caitlin Elby Corporate Sales Assoc
Tel: 212-741-6427
Email: caitlin@5thavenuedigital.com
Website: www.5thavenuedigital.com
Corporate photography: promotional & marketing events,
meetings & conventions, galas & award ceremonies,
headshots, group photos & product shots. (Woman, estab
2008, empl 5, sales $2,560,552, cert: WBENC)

7001 Adrienne Nicole Productions, LLC
14 Dekalb Ave 3rd Fl
Brooklyn, NY 11201
Contact: Adrienne Nicole Exec Producer
Tel: - -
Email: info@producedbyanp.com
Website: www.producedbyanp.com
Videography, aerial video, drone video photography,
drone photography, progress photos, story develop-
ment, pre-production, post-production, motion graphics
and animation, casting, photography, progress photos.
(Woman/AA, estab 2011, empl 1, sales $986,000, cert:
State, City, NMSDC)

7002 E. Lee White Photography, LLC
116 Duane St, 3rd F
New York, NY 10007
Contact: E. Lee White President
Tel: 917-584-8000
Email: lee@leewhite.com
Website: www.leewhite.com
Advertising photography, executive portraits. (AA, estab
2004, empl 1, sales , cert: NMSDC)

7003 SPA Digital Images, Ltd.
54 W 39th St, 16th fl
New York, NY 10018
Contact: Kelly Murphy President
Tel: 917-420-0940
Email: janine@spadigital.com
Website: www.spadigital.com
Commercial digital photography & digital retouching
services. (Woman, estab 1994, empl 15, sales
$5,165,450, cert: WBENC)

Washington

7004 Mike Nakamura Photography LLC
7414 337th Place SE
Fall CIty, WA 98024
Contact: Mike Nakamura Owner
Tel: 425-260-4033
Email: mike@mikenakamuraphotography.com
Website: www.mikenakamuraphotography.com/
Headshots, event & lifestyle photography, aerial &
commercial photography. (As-Pac, estab 2013, empl 1,
sales $110,000, cert: NMSDC)

PLASTIC PRODUCTS

Manufacturers and distributors of plexiglass, plastic, rubber and fiberglass products. Products range from supplies to aircraft and automobile parts, housewares and apparel accessories. NAICS Code 42

Arizona

7005   4front Tooling LLC dba 4front Manufacturing
3820 E Watkins St
Phoenix, AZ 85034
Contact: Joseph Baiz Owner
Tel: 480-966-1088
Email: joebaiz@4frontmfg.com
Website: www.4frontmfg.com
Plastic injection mold making, molding prototype & production, stampings, assembly & decorating. (Hisp, estab 2008, empl 20, sales $2,595,172, cert: NMSDC)

7006   All-Pac Distributng LLC
4859 E Gleneagle Dr
Chandler, AZ 85249
Contact: Adam Snow Sales Mgr
Tel: 480-861-0842
Email: asnow@allpaconline.com
Website: www.allpaconline.com
Mfr & dist returnable plastic packaging, injection molding, compression molding. (Woman, estab 2001, empl 3, sales $1,150,000, cert: NWBOC)

California

7007   Benchmark Displays LLC
75-145 St. Charles Place Ste 5
Palm Desert, CA 92211
Contact: Bonnie Miller VP Sales
Tel: 760-775-2424
Email: bonnie@benchmarkdisplays.com
Website: www.benchmarkdisplays.com
Mfr soft & hard vinyl store merchandising products, acrylic pos displays & fixtures, stock & custom molded & fabricated plastic literature holders. (Woman, estab 2009, empl 3, sales $349,750, cert: WBENC)

7008   Fairway Injection Molding Systems, Inc.
20109 Paseo Del Prado
Walnut, CA 91789
Contact: David Cockrell VP General Mgr
Tel: 909-595-2201
Email: dcockrell@fairwaymolds.com
Website: www.fairwaymolds.com
Plastic injection molding. (As-Pac, estab 2006, empl 72, sales , cert: NMSDC)

7009   L.W. Reinhold Plastics
8763 Crocker St
Los Angeles, CA 90003
Contact: Everett Woolum Engineering Mgr
Tel: 562-862-2714
Email: brenda@rpiplastics.com
Website: www.rpiplastics.com
Injection molded thermosets & thermoplastics, compression molded thermosets & transfer molded thermoset, prototyping, machining. (Minority, Woman, estab 1943, empl 26, sales $1,800,000, cert: NMSDC)

7010   MJB Plastics, Inc.
6615 E Pacifc Coast Hwy, Ste 270
Long Beach, CA 90803
Contact: Martin Brunn VP
Tel: 562-431-3337
Email: martybrunn@mjbplastics.com
Website: www.mjbplastics.com
Dist plastic materials. (Minority, Woman, estab 1993, empl 6, sales , cert: WBENC)

7011   Plastek Cards, Inc.
24412 S Main St Ste 104
Carson, CA 90745
Contact: Mark Robinson Dir of Marketing
Tel: 888-762-2737
Email: mark.robinson@plastekcards.com
Website: www.plastekcards.com
Blank, white PVC plastic cards with & without a magnetic strip, high coercivity Hi-Co or low coercivity Lo-Co. (As-Pac, estab 2004, empl 51, sales , cert: NMSDC)

7012   Plastikon Industries, Inc.
688 Sandoval Way
Hayward, CA 94544
Contact: Ron Yerrick Sales Specialist
Tel: 989-525-3310
Email: ryerrick@plastikon.com
Website: www.plastikon.com
Custom injection molding of thermal plastic products & packaging. (Nat Ame, estab 1984, empl 100, sales $38,000,000, cert: NMSDC)

7013   Prestige Mold
11040 Tacoma Dr
Rancho Cucamonga, CA 91730
Contact: Curt Corte Tech Sales
Tel: 909-980-6600
Email: curt.corte@prestigemold.com
Website: www.prestigemold.com
Mfr precision plastic injection molds. (Woman, estab 2004, empl 65, sales $11,000,000, cert: WBENC)

7014   Trademark Plastics, Inc.
807 Palmyrita Ave
Riverside, CA 92507
Contact: Gilbert McMoran Sales Mgr
Tel: 909-941-8810
Email: gmcmoran@trademarkplastics.com
Website: www.TrademarkPlastics.com
Mfr plastic, medical components. (Woman, estab 1989, empl 150, sales $14,000,000, cert: WBENC)

7015   Weldon Works, Inc.
1650 Mabury Rd
San Jose, CA 95133
Contact: Jennifer Easom CEO
Tel: 408-251-1161
Email: jenn@weldonworks.com
Website: www.weldonworks.com
Plastic Fabrication & Signage, Interior & Exterior Signs, ADA Signage, Lobby Signs, Window Graphics & Lettering, Menu Boards, Isle Signage, Banner, Stencils, Reflective Road Work/ Parking Signs, Full Color Digital Printing. (Woman, estab 1982, empl 3, sales $100,000, cert: State)

7016 Wright Engineered Plastics, Inc.
      3663 N Laughlin Road Ste 201
      Santa Rosa, CA 95403
      Contact: Mike Nellis VP Mfg
      Tel: 707-575-1218
      Email: mnellis@wepmolding.com
      Website: www.wepmolding.com
Plastic injection molding & contract manufacturing.
(Woman, estab 1970, empl 48, sales $5,040,000, cert:
CPUC)

7017 Yamada Enterprises Inc.
      14070 Montfort Ct
      San Diego, CA 92128
      Contact: Hidehiko Yamada President
      Tel: 858-248-1928
      Email: hyamada@ugoplastics.com
      Website: www.ugoplastics.com
Outsourcing plastic parts manufacturing. Plastic injection
machine sales. Packaging machine sales. SMT surface
mount technology machines sales. Consultation production machines. Capital equipment consultant. Cartner,
Caser, palletizer. Conveyors. (As-Pac, estab 2013, empl 2,
sales $300,000, cert: NMSDC)

Connecticut

7018 Technical Industries, Inc.
      336 Pinewoods Rd
      Torrington, CT 06790
      Contact: Susan O. Parent CEO
      Tel: 860-489-2160
      Email: susan.parent@technicalindustriesinc.com
      Website: www.technicalindustriesinc.com
Mfr plastic injection molded parts. (Woman, estab 1994,
empl 30, sales $4,700,000, cert: WBENC)

Florida

7019 American Tool and Mold LLC
      1700 Sunshine Dr
      Clearwater, FL 33765
      Contact: Phil Gaitan Dir of Sales
      Tel: 727-447-7377
      Email: pgaitan@a-t-m.com
      Website: www.atmmolding.com
Design & construct complex, precision, multi-cavity plastic
injection molding, thin-wall, stack, hot runner, unscrewing
& two-shot molds built with the latest methods & technologies available. (Woman, estab 1992, empl 220, sales ,
cert: WBENC)

7020 Plastec USA Inc.
      7752 NW 74th Ave
      Miami, FL 33166
      Contact: Julio Mejia Dir Reg Sales
      Tel: 513-708-9091
      Email: julio.mejia@mejiatechnologies.com
      Website: www.plastecusa.com
Dist plastics processing machinery, ancillary equipment,
spare parts & MRO services, chemicals & plastic goods.
(Hisp, estab 1985, empl 23, sales $20,000,000, cert:
NMSDC)

7021 Precision Tool and Mold, Inc.
      12050 44th St N
      Clearwater, FL 33762
      Contact: Sherry Mowery President
      Tel: 727-573-4441
      Email: sherry@precisiontoolmoldinc.com
      Website: www.precisiontoolmoldinc.com
Design build & run plastic injection molded parts. Small
to medium sized molds. Assembly work, pad printing,
over molding & insert molding. (Woman, estab 1981,
empl 30, sales $2,665,365, cert: WBENC)

Georgia

7022 Citation Plastics, LLC
      5828 Riverstone Circle
      Atlanta, GA 30339
      Contact: Gregory Collingwood President
      Tel: 248-798-7705
      Email: gregcollingwood@citationplastics.com
      Website: www.citationplastics.com
Dist Plastic Resins: High Density Polyethylene (HDPE)-
Polypropylene (PP)- Talc & Glassed Filled Polypropylene-
Glass Filled Nylon 6 & 66 (AA, estab 1998, empl 7, sales
$189,000, cert: NMSDC)

7023 Dixien LLC
      5286 Circle Dr
      Lake City, GA 30260
      Contact: Alex Garcia VP Mktg
      Tel: 404-366-7427
      Email: agarcia@dixien.com
      Website: www.dixien.com
Stamping 100 ton to 1000 ton, welded sub-assemblies,
tooling, plastic injection molding, blow molding &
vaccum forming. (Hisp, estab 1961, empl 400, sales
$25,000,000, cert: NMSDC)

7024 Joyce Fabrication LLC dba Custom Plastics & More
      2625 Jason Industrial Pkwy Ste 700
      Winston, GA 30187
      Contact: Gail Moore President
      Tel: 770-577-0661
      Email: gailmoore@customplasticsandmore.com
      Website: www.customplasticsandmore.com
Rigid plastic fabrication, hand cut sheet plastic; die
stamped parts, CNC or hand routed plastic. (Woman,
estab 2004, empl 4, sales $318,365, cert: WBENC)

7025 Marglen Industries
      1748 Ward Mountain Rd
      Rome, GA 30161
      Contact: Ben McElrath President
      Tel: 706-295-5621
      Email: bmcelrath@marglen.us
      Website: www.marglen.us
Recycle PET plastic containers, convert recycled PET
water & soda bottles into cleaned washed flake, then
convert the clean washed flake into a FDA approved,
high IV, melt filtered pellet that can be used to make
new bottles. (Woman, estab 1971, empl 150, sales
$62,513,555, cert: WBENC)

7026   Standridge Color Corp.
1196 E Hightower Trail
Social Circle, GA 30025
Contact: Sherry Waters President
Tel: 770-464-3362
Email: swaters@standridgecolor.com
Website: www.standridgecolor.com
Mfr pellitized plastic pellets and color concentrates for the plastics industry. (Woman, estab 0, empl 1, sales , cert: WBENC)

7027   United Seal & Rubber Co. Inc.
7025 C Amwiler Industrial Dr
Atlanta, GA 30360
Contact: Kathy Alonso VP/General Mgr
Tel: 770-729-8880
Email: kalonso@unitedseal.com
Website: www.unitedseal.com
Mfr seals, gaskets, custom molded rubber parts, EMI Shielding products, lathe cut seals, extrusions, rubber to metal bonded parts, spliced & vulcanized parts. (Hisp, estab 1974, empl 28, sales $8,000,000, cert: NMSDC, SDB)

Iowa

7028   Engineered Plastic Components Inc.
1408 Zimmerman Dr S
Grinnell, IA 50112
Contact: Jeremy Barger Sales
Tel: 641-236-3100
Email: jbarger@epcmfg.com
Website: www.epcmfg.com
Mfr wire harness cover caps, injection molding. (As-Ind, estab 1998, empl 500, sales $200,000,000, cert: NMSDC)

Illinois

7029   Amtec Molded Products, Inc.
1355 Holmes Road Unit A
Elgin, IL 60123
Contact: Adithya Jayakar Sales Mgr
Tel: 815-226-0187
Email: adithyaj@amtecmolded.com
Website: www.amtecmolded.com
Plastic injection molding, insert molding, pad printing & sub-assemblies. (As-Ind, estab 1998, empl 35, sales $3,862,500, cert: NMSDC)

7030   Best Foam Fabricators, Inc.
9633 S Cottage Grove
Chicago, IL 60628
Contact: Aqui Hasty Mktg Mgr
Tel: 773-721-1006
Email: aqui@bff.com
Website: www.bff.com
Mfr thermoforming, high speed die cutting, heat sealing, CNC machining & injection molding. (Woman/AA, estab 1981, empl 60, sales $14,750,000, cert: NMSDC)

7031   Cope Plastics Inc.
PO Box 368
Godfrey, IL 62002
Contact: Bryan Cox COO
Tel: 618-467-7357
Email: bcox@copeplastics.com
Website: www.copeplastics.com
Plastic stock shapes (rod, sheet & tube) distribution & fabrication. (Woman, estab 1946, empl 350, sales $86,000,000, cert: NWBOC)

7032   E James & Co.
6000 S Oak Park Ave
Chicago, IL 60638
Contact: Mike Romano
Tel: 773-788-1881
Email: mike.romano@ejames.com
Website: www.ejames.com
Mfr & dist rubber & plastic products: V belts, rubber hose, plastic hose & hose assemblies. (Hisp, estab 1955, empl 14, sales $2,200,000, cert: NMSDC)

7033   Ebco
1330 Holmes Rd
Elgin, IL 60123
Contact: Bill Bernardo Sales
Tel: 847-531-9500
Email: bbernardo@ebcoinc.com
Website: www.ebcoinc.com
Rubber products: molded, extruded, rubber bonded, metal vibration isolators & plastic extrusions. (Hisp, estab 1951, empl 48, sales $20,000,000, cert: NMSDC)

7034   First American Plastics Molding Enterprise
810 Progressive Ln
South Beloit, IL 61080
Contact: Steven McGaw Sales Engineer
Tel: 815-624-8538
Email: info@firstamericanplastic.com
Website: www.firstamericanplastic.com
Custom plastic injection molding. (Nat Ame, estab 1993, empl 130, sales $12,000,000, cert: NMSDC)

7035   HST Materials, Inc.
1631 Brummel Ave
Elk Grove Village, IL 60007
Contact: Kathryn Miller President
Tel: 847-640-1803
Email: kmiller@hstmaterials.com
Website: www.hstmaterials.com
Custom die-cutting & fabrication of non-metallics, including sponge & dense rubber, plastic, films & tapes used as gaskets & sealing devices. (Woman, estab 1987, empl 20, sales $4,428,617, cert: WBENC)

7036   LSL Industries, Inc.
5535 N Wolcott Ave
Chicago, IL 60640
Contact: Jerry Czaja
Tel: 773-878-1100
Email: jerry.czaja@lslhealthcare.com
Website: www.lslhealthcare.com
Mfg plastics & procedural kit assembly & packaging. (As-Ind, estab , empl , sales , cert: NMSDC)

7037   Magenta LLC
15160 New Ave
Lockport, IL 60441
Contact: Stephanie Smith Business Dev Exec
Tel: 630-737-9606
Email: ssmith@magentallc.com
Website: www.magentallc.com
Design, development & mfr injection molded components-primarily packaging— closures and containers. (Woman, estab 1969, empl 81, sales $14,900,000, cert: WBENC)

7038 Matrix IV, Inc.
610 E Judd St
Woodstock, IL 60098
Contact: Patrica Miller President
Tel: 815-338-4500
Email: pmiller@matrix4.com
Website: www.matrix4.com
Mfr injection molded parts, 3D printing, design & engineering. (Woman, estab 1976, empl 25, sales $2,450,000, cert: WBENC)

7039 Midwest Insert Composite Molding & Assembly
Corp.
3940 Industrial Ave
Rolling Meadows, IL 60008
Contact: Chirag Patel President
Tel: 847-818-8444
Email: chirag.pate@micmolding.com
Website: www.micmolding.com
Mfr plastic injection molded products. (Minority, estab 2015, empl 23, sales $2,526,000, cert: NMSDC)

7040 Thermal-Tech Systems, Inc.
750 W Hawthorne Lane
West Chicago, IL 60185
Contact: Joe Majchrowski Sales
Tel: 630-639-5115
Email: jm@thermal-tech.com
Website: www.thermal-tech.com
Dist plastic injection molders, service and repair of manifolds. (Woman, estab 1986, empl 10, sales $2,500,000, cert: WBENC)

7041 TransWorld Plastic Films, Inc.
150 N 15th St
Rochelle, IL 61068
Contact: Rodolfo Hernandez Business Devel
Tel: 815-561-7117
Email: rhernandez@transworldplasticfilms.com
Website: www.transworldplasticfilms.com
Polyethylene film for the automotive, tire & rubber industries used in the manufacturing & packaging process. (Minority, Woman, estab 2007, empl 31, sales , cert: NMSDC, WBENC)

7042 Young Technology Inc.
900 W. Fullerton Ave.
Addison, IL 60101
Contact: Young Sohn President
Tel: 630-690-4320
Email: youngsohn@ytinc.com
Website: www.ytinc.com
Mfr molded rubber, plastic & forged steel: shifter knobs, bezels, decorative molding & cable components, leather wrapped & chrome plated. (As-Pac, estab 1985, empl 350, sales $6,000,000, cert: NMSDC)

Indiana

7043 A. H. Furnico, Inc.
6425 English Ave. Unit 1A
Indianapolis, IN 46278
Contact: Benjamin Liu President
Tel: 317-802-9363
Email: ben.liu@ahfurnico.com
Website: www.ahfurnico.com
Polystyrene extruded mouldings with PVC veneers. (As-Pac, estab 1999, empl 5, sales $3,880,000, cert: NMSDC)

7044 Accutech Mold & Machine, Inc.
2817 Goshen Rd
Fort Wayne, IN 46808
Contact: Darrin Geiger VP
Tel: 260-471-6102
Email: dgeiger@accutechmoldinc.com
Website: www.accutechmoldinc.com
Plastic injection molding, Insert plastic injection molder of cables/connectors, rapid prototype tooling builder/injection molding, production machining of brass, aluminum & metals, prototype machining of brass, aluminum & metals. (Woman, estab 1996, empl 70, sales $3,000,000, cert: WBENC)

7045 Calico Precision Molding, LLC
1211 Progress Rd
Fort Wayne, IN 46808
Contact: Nancy Rivera Sales Rep
Tel: 260-484-4500
Email: nancyr@calicopm.com
Website: www.calicopm.com/
Custom plastic injection molding. (AA, estab 2001, empl 28, sales , cert: NMSDC)

7046 Hi-Tech Foam Products, LLC
One Technology Way
Indianapolis, IN 46268
Contact: John Metaxas VP
Tel: 317-615-1515
Email: jmetaxas@hitechfoam.com
Website: www.hitechfoam.com
Convert, design, package, mold, form, cut & route foam rubber. Laminating foam to foam, foam to corrugated, foam to plastic. Protective, cushioning, acoustical, thermal, polyethylene, polyurethane, crosslink, EVA, EDPM rubber. (AA, estab , empl 35, sales $6,000,000, cert: NMSDC)

7047 Hoosier Molded Products
3603 Progress Dr
South Bend, IN 46628
Contact: Brian Johnson Sales Mgr
Tel: 574-235-7900
Email: johnson@hoosiermp.com
Website: www.hoosiermp.com
Mfr quality injecting molded products. (Hisp, estab 1996, empl 100, sales $14,000,000, cert: NMSDC)

7048 Lorentson Manufacturing Co., Inc.
PO Box 932
Kokomo, IN 46903
Contact: John Routt VP / COO
Tel: 765-452-4425
Email: jroutt@lorentson.com
Website: www.lorentson.com
Design & build plastic injection molds, injection molding machines. (Woman, estab 1949, empl 100, sales $16,000,000, cert: WBENC)

7049 Tomken Plastic Technologies, Inc.
4601 N Superior Dr.
Muncie, IN 47303
Contact: Kevin Undem Sales/Engineering
Tel: 765-284-2472
Email: kevinu@tomkenplastics.com
Website: www.tomkenplastics.com
Precision plastic injection molding, tooling, & injection molding. (Woman, estab 1960, empl 40, sales $6,000,000, cert: WBENC)

7050   Vidal Plastics, LLC
318 Main St Ste 207
Evansville, IN 47708
Contact: Alfonso Vidal President
Tel: 812-431-8075
Email: alfonso@vidalplastics.com
Website: www.vidalplastics.com
Dist resins, prime raw materials to recycled compounds. (Minority, estab 2009, empl 2, sales , cert: NMSDC)

Kentucky

7051   Foam Design Inc.
444 Transport Ct
Lexington, KY 40511
Contact: Chris Harrod Sales Engineer
Tel: 502-682-8562
Email: charrod@foamdesign.com
Website: www.foamdesign.com
Commercial and industrial foam conversion capabilities and design, intricate parts cut to precise tolerances. (Woman, estab 1974, empl 102, sales $18,500,000, cert: WBENC)

Louisiana

7052   Noble Plastics Inc.
318 Burleigh Lane
Grand Coteau, LA 70541
Contact: Sandy Rowell Inside Sales
Tel: 337-662-5374
Email: sandy@nobleplastics.com
Website: www.nobleplastics.com
SPE, MAPP, ASME, Product design, Contract manufacturing, Scientific molding, Inspection, Assembly & fulfillment, Automation systems. (Woman, estab 2000, empl 30, sales $4,900,000, cert: WBENC)

Massachusetts

7053   Polyneer, Inc.
259D Samuel Barnet Blvd
New Bedford, MA 02745
Contact: Nancy DeOliveira Customer Service
Tel: 508-998-5225
Email: ndeoliveira@polyneer.com
Website: www.polyneer.com
Design & mfg polymeric products. (Hisp, estab 2001, empl 39, sales $2,600,000, cert: NMSDC)

7054   TPE Solutions, Inc.
3 Patterson Rd
Shirley, MA 01464
Contact: Jonas Angus President
Tel: 978-425-3033
Email: jonas.angus@tpesinc.com
Website: www.tpesinc.com
Design, mfr & dist Thermoplastic elastomers (TPEs). (AA, estab 2004, empl 5, sales $3,000,000, cert: NMSDC)

Michigan

7055   Accu-Mold, LLC
7622 S Sprinkle Rd
Portage, MI 49002
Contact: Dave Felicijan President
Tel: 269-323-0388
Email: davidf@accu-moldinc.com
Website: www.accum-moldinc.com
Overmold & two shot mold, hybrid metal/plastic parts, high & low pressure plastic injection molds, machined plastic or metal parts, SLA plastic parts, metal-to-plastic conversions. (Nat Ame, estab 1977, empl 15, sales $4,118,893, cert: NMSDC)

7056   Agape Plastics, Inc.
11474 1st Ave NW
Grand Rapids, MI 49534
Contact: Jeff Powers Sales Admin
Tel: 616-735-4091
Email: jpowers@agapeplastics.com
Website: www.agapeplastics.com
Plastic Injection molder serving the automotive and furniture industries. (Woman, estab 1975, empl 150, sales , cert: WBENC)

7057   Ammex Plastics
725 Ternes Dr
Monroe, MI 48162
Contact: David Ayala President
Tel: 734-241-9622
Email:
Website: www.ammexplastics.com
Mfr & design plastic injection molded parts. (Hisp, estab 1999, empl 17, sales $3,300,000, cert: NMSDC)

7058   Argent International
41016 Concept Dr
Plymouth, MI 48170
Contact: Tomas Flores Sales Mgr
Tel: 734-582-9800
Email: tflores@argent-international.com
Website: www.argent-international.com
Die cut foam, felt, fabric adhesive. (Woman, estab 1976, empl 120, sales , cert: WBENC)

7059   Atlantic Precision Products
51234 Filomena Dr
Shelby Township, MI 48315
Contact: Rob Pryomski General Mgr
Tel: 586-532-9420
Email: rpryomski@atlanticpp.com
Website: www.atlanticpp.com
Custom injection molding, functional/decorative plastics, insert molding, welding, sonic, vibration, heatstaking, assembly. Fully certified CMM Lab with color approval capabilities. (Minority, Woman, estab 2004, empl 26, sales $5,200,000, cert: NMSDC)

7060   CG Plastics, Inc.
5349 Rusche Dr NW
Comstock Park, MI 49321
Contact: Shelly Miller CFO
Tel: 616-308-7838
Email: shelly.miller@commercialtool.com
Website: www.cgplastics.com
Tryout, sampling and production plastic injection molding. Capabilities for design and manufacturing of plastic injection molds and custom molding. Gauge & Fixture, Automation, 6-axis robots, Large 5-axis CNC machining. (Woman, estab 0, empl , sales , cert: WBENC)

7061   Colonial Plastics, Inc
51734 Filomena Dr
Shelby Township, MI 48315
Contact: Michele Simo
Tel: 586-991-5150
Email: mms@colgrp.com
Website: www.colgrp.com
Injection molds, compression molds, blow molds, vacuum molds, prototype molds, hybrid molds, bridge molds, production molds, machining, assemblies, tryouts, product developement, product design & sorting. (Woman, estab 1988, empl 110, sales $8,200,000, cert: WBENC)

7062 Concordant Healthcare Solutions, Inc.
200 E. Big Beaver
Troy, MI 48083
Contact: James P Young CEO
Tel: 248-321-3899
Email: jyoung@concordanthealth.com
Website: www.concordanthealth.com
NCQA Certified in Patient Centered Medical Home Recognition for PCPs and Specialists. Staff training in cultural competency and communication skills. Improve hospital HCAHPS total performance scores. (AA, estab 2009, empl 8, sales , cert: NMSDC)

7063 Diversified Engineering & Plastics
1801 Wildwood Ave
Jackson, MI 49202
Contact: Anita Quillen President
Tel: 517-789-8118
Email: aquillen@deplastics.com
Website: www.wwww.deplastics.com
Plastic Injection Molding, Design/Engineering Services, Plastic Part Assembly. (Minority, Woman, estab 2010, empl 130, sales $14,497,480, cert: NMSDC)

7064 DN Plastics
1415 Steele Ave SW
Grand Rapids, MI 49507
Contact: Raj Agrawal President
Tel: 616-942-6060
Email: raj@dnplasticscorp.com
Website: www.dnplasticscorp.com
Polymer compounding for custom & toll manufacturing, Thermoplastic Elastomers (TPE), Thermoplastic Olefins (TPO) & filled Polypropylene compounds. (As-Ind, estab 0, empl 1, sales , cert: NMSDC)

7065 Eagle Fasteners
185 Park Dr
Troy, MI 48083
Contact: Theresa C. Srock President
Tel: 248-373-1441
Email: tsrock@eaglefasteners.com
Website: www.eaglefasteners.com
Custom injection molded plastic parts, design & fabricate tooling. (Woman, estab 1976, empl 9, sales , cert: WBENC)

7066 Elite Mold & Engineering
51548 Filomena Dr
Shelby Township, MI 48315
Contact: Daniel Mandeville Sales Engineer
Tel: 586-314-4000
Email: dj@teameliteonline.com
Website: www.teameliteonline.com
Dist close tolerance plastic parts for the automotive, consumer product, electronic & medical device industries. (Nat Ame, estab 1982, empl 34, sales $3,576,887, cert: NMSDC)

7067 Engineered Plastic Products
699 James L. Hart Pkwy
Ypsilanti, MI 48197
Contact: Aschandria Fisher Business Mgr
Tel: 734-483-2500
Email: afisher@eppmfg.com
Website: www.eppmfg.com
Injection molded plastic assembly & sequencing. (AA, estab 1987, empl 500, sales $50,000,000, cert: NMSDC)

7068 Gemini Plastics, Inc.
4385 Garfield St
Ubly, MI 48475
Contact: Melanie Cappello Mgr Business Devel
Tel: 248-435-7271
Email: melaniecappello@geminigroup.net
Website: www.geminigroup.net
Mfr engineered plastic extrusion products: transportation, medical, lawn & garden, consumer, & appliance. (Woman, estab 1972, empl 110, sales $60,000,000, cert: WBENC)

7069 Intex Technologies LLC
3133 Highland Dr
Hudsonville, MI 49426
Contact: Randi Sniegowski Sales
Tel: 616-662-0276
Email: randi.sniegowski@intextech.net
Website: www.intextech.net
Mfr integral skin flexible foam automotive interior parts: arm rests, center console, console door, sun visor, steering wheel, soft-touch points on door handles, cup holders, seals, jounce bumpers & insulation components. (Hisp, estab 2008, empl 50, sales $14,800,000, cert: NMSDC)

7070 Jenerxx Inc.
307 West Sixth St Ste 209
Royal Oak, MI 48067
Contact: Paul Chaplin Acct Mgr
Tel: 810-225-1600
Email: paul@jenerxx.com
Website: www.jenerxx.com
Dist injection grade resins ranging from engineered plastics to commodities. (Woman, estab 2000, empl 5, sales $760,000, cert: WBENC)

7071 JLC Group LLC
287 Executive Dr
Troy, MI 48083
Contact: William Chen Dir Ph.D.
Tel: 248-792-3281
Email: wchen@jlcgroupllc.com
Website: www.jlcgroupllc.com
Dist casting parts, forging parts & machine finished parts, plastic injected molds & plastic parts. (Minority, Woman, estab 2010, empl 5, sales , cert: WBENC)

7072 Latin American Industries, LLC
1036 Ken-O-Sha Industrial Dr SE
Grand Rapids, MI 49508
Contact: Scott Bigger General Mgr
Tel: 616-301-1878
Email: sbigger@laiinc.net
Website: www.laiinc.net
Plastic injection molding & assembly, molding machines. (Minority, Woman, estab 2000, empl 10, sales $1,000,000, cert: NMSDC)

7073 Molding Concepts, Inc.
6700 Sims St
Sterling Heights, MI 48313
Contact: Norman Fouts President
Tel: - -
Email: slfouts@moldingconcepts.com
Website: www.moldingconcepts.com
Plastic injection molds, plastic injection parts, plastic parts, CNC machining, 3D printing, Additive manufacturing, Prototype, Short run, Production, High heat resin. (Woman, estab 1987, empl 9, sales $800,000, cert: WBENC)

7074　Premier Plastic Resins, Inc.
　　　3079 S Baldwin Rd
　　　Orion, MI 48359
　　　Contact: Michelle Cloutier Sales Engineer
　　　Tel:　877-777-4514
　　　Email: mcloutier@premierplasticresins.com
　　　Website: www.premierplasticresins.com
Dist thermoplastic resins for injection molding. ABS, Nylon, Polycarbonate, PBT, Acetal. Automotive approved grades. Prime branded materials available, such as DuPont, Sabic, Covestro, etc. (Woman, estab 2007, empl 5, sales $1,200,000, cert: WBENC)

7075　Primera Plastics
　　　3424 Production Court
　　　Zeeland, MI 49464
　　　Contact: Noel Cuellar President
　　　Tel:　616-748-6248
　　　Email: noelc@primera-inc.com
　　　Website: www.primera-inc.com
Plastic injection molding & assembly. (Hisp, estab 1994, empl 140, sales , cert: NMSDC)

7076　Quality Assured Plastics, Inc.
　　　1200 Crandall Pkwy
　　　Lawrence, MI 49064
　　　Contact: Annette Crandall President
　　　Tel:　269-674-3888
　　　Email: acrandall@qapinc.com
　　　Website: www.qapinc.com
Custom injection molding, insert/overmolding, & assembly capabilities, molding commodity & engineering resins, Nylon, TPE, ABS, PEEK, Valox, Polystyrene, HDPE, TPO & Polypropylene. (Woman, estab 1986, empl 60, sales $5,200,000, cert: WBENC)

7077　Sejasmi Industries, Inc.
　　　6100 Bethuy
　　　Fair Haven, MI 48023
　　　Contact: Nichole Roemer Production Control
　　　Tel:　586-725-5300
　　　Email: nicholer@us.sejasmi.com
　　　Website: www.us.sejasmi.com
Contract manufacturer of plastic injection molded parts & light assemblies. (As-Ind, estab 2007, empl 50, sales , cert: NMSDC)

7078　Sur-Flo Plastics & Engineering, Inc.
　　　24358 Groesbeck Hwy
　　　Warren, MI 48089
　　　Contact: Jean Douglass IT Security Mgr
　　　Tel:　586-859-6050
　　　Email: jdouglass@sur-flo.com
　　　Website: www.sur-flo.com
Custom injection molded component or assembly: Plastic Injection Molding, Engineering, Program Management, Assembly, Quality. (Woman, estab 1977, empl 207, sales , cert: NMSDC)

7079　Western Diversified Plastics LLC
　　　53150 N Main St
　　　Mattawan, MI 49071
　　　Contact: George Kawwas Dir of Business Dev
　　　Tel:　269-668-3377
　　　Email: george.kawwas@westerndp.com
　　　Website: www.westerndp.com
Mfr close tolerance injection & insert molded electro-mechanical components, engineering grade plastic resin. (AA, estab 2005, empl 75, sales , cert: NMSDC)

7080　Williamston Products, Inc.
　　　845 Progress Ct
　　　Williamston, MI 48895
　　　Contact: Nigam Tripathi President
　　　Tel:　517-655-2131
　　　Email: nigam@wpius.com
　　　Website: www.wpius.com
Blow mold, injection mold, foaming, hand wrapping, cutting, trim, sewing, lamination, prototyping, assembly. (As-Ind, estab 2006, empl 450, sales $42,000,000, cert: NMSDC)

Minnesota

7081　Classic Acrylics Inc.
　　　11040 Industrial Circle NW
　　　Elk River, MN 55330
　　　Contact: Kathy Berg Sales Exec
　　　Tel:　763-241-5221
　　　Email: kberg@classicacrylics.com
　　　Website: www.classicacrylics.com
Plastic fabrication: POP & POS displays, acrylic cereal boxes, literature & brochure holders, advertising & specialty items, sign holders, screened acrylic signs, display cases, food service bins, LED lighting. (Hisp, estab 1998, empl 22, sales $3,754,000, cert: NMSDC)

7082　Lakeview Industries
　　　1225 Lakeview Dr
　　　Chaska, MN 55318
　　　Contact: DeDe Bennett inside Sales
　　　Tel:　952-368-3500
　　　Email: dbennett@lakeviewindustries.com
　　　Website: www.lakeiveiwindustries.com
Dist molded rubber products & fabricate flexible products. (Woman, estab 1974, empl 49, sales $1,000,000, cert: WBENC)

7083　Proto Edge Inc.
　　　8550 Revere Lane N Ste 228
　　　Maple Grove, MN 55369
　　　Contact: Louis Roberts President
　　　Tel:　612-432-4303
　　　Email: lou@protoedge.com
　　　Website: www.protoedge.com
Dist metal & plastic parts for existing and new product development engineered designs, focused on a wide range of processes and materials. (AA, estab 2011, empl 3, sales $125,000, cert: NMSDC)

7084　Thermotech, Inc.
　　　1302 S 5th St
　　　Hopkins, MN 55343
　　　Contact: Andrea Hinrichs
　　　Tel:　734-634-1816
　　　Email: andrea.hinrichs@thermotech.com
　　　Website: www.thermotech.com
Mfr precision plastic parts, thermoplastic molding, thermoset molding, insert molding, two-shot molding, micromolding & assembly. (As-Ind, estab 1949, empl 522, sales $83,000,000, cert: NMSDC)

7085 TMI Coatings, Inc.
3291 Terminal Dr
St. Paul, MN 55121
Contact: Tracy Gliori President
Tel: 651-452-6100
Email: tmi@tmicoatings.com
Website: www.tmicoatings.com
Protective coatings & linings, spray on urethane foam insulation, chemical resistant floor coverings & containment dike linings. (Woman, estab 1985, empl 75, sales $12,162,000, cert: WBENC)

North Carolina

7086 Central Carolina Products
250 W Old Glencoe Rd
Burlington, NC 27217
Contact: Jason Greenhill President
Tel: 336-226-0005
Email: jgreenhill@isotechintl.com
Website: www.centralcarolinaproducts.com
Plastic injection molding: assembly & finishing capabilities. (Hisp, estab 1993, empl 72, sales , cert: NMSDC)

7087 Core Technology Molding Corp.
2911 E. Gate City Blvd
Greensboro, NC 27410
Contact: Brandon Frederick Manufacturing Engineer
Tel: 919-273-3408
Email: brandon.frederick@coretechnologycorp.com
Website: www.coretechnologycorp.com
Product concept & design services, CAD part & mold design, Mold Flow analysis, Prototyping, raw material selection & testing, New all-electric injection molding machines ranging from 200 ton to 400 ton. (AA, estab 2007, empl 25, sales $10,000,000, cert: NMSDC)

7088 Raleigh-Durham Rubber & Gasket Co., Inc.
PO Box 90397
Raleigh, NC 27675
Contact: Judy Hooks President
Tel: 919-781-6817
Email: judyh@raleighdurhamrubber.com
Website: www.raleighdurhamrubber.com
Mfr & dist rubber gaskets. (Woman, estab , empl , sales , cert: WBENC)

7089 RubberMill, Inc.
9897 Old Liberty Rd
Liberty, NC 27298
Contact: Shawn Baldwin Sales Mgr
Tel: 704-458-2653
Email: sbaldwin@rubbermill.com
Website: www.rubbermill.com
OEM custom parts manufactured from solid and sponge rubber, foams, and nonwovens. Gaskets and Seals, Custom Molded Parts, Acoustical Insulation Parts, Urethane Products, Balls, Lab Stoppers, Cleanout Balls. (Woman, estab 1987, empl 56, sales $11,000,000, cert: WBENC)

7090 Sky Leap LLC
PO Box 16368
Chapel Hill, NC 27516
Contact: Lili Engelhardt CEO
Tel: 919-338-2580
Email: office@skyleapllc.com
Website: www.skyleapllc.com
Mfr & design injected molded tool organizers for tools: wrenches, screw drivers, pliers, and sockets. (Minority, Woman, estab 2013, empl 2, sales $425,000, cert: NMSDC)

Nebraska

7091 Lenco, Inc. - PMC
10240 Deer Park Rd
Waverly, NE 68462
Contact: Clarke McGuire VP
Tel: 402-786-2000
Email: cmcguire@pmc-group.com
Website: www.lencopmc.com
Dist defect-free molded & assembled products, injection molding. (As-Ind, estab 1963, empl 160, sales , cert: State, NMSDC)

New Jersey

7092 L-E-M Plastics& Supply Inc.
255 Highland Cross
Rutherford, NJ 07070
Contact: Ellen Pietrowitz-Phillips President
Tel: 201-933-9150
Email: ellenp@l-e-mplastics.com
Website: www.l-e-mplastics.com
Fabriate & dist raw material plastic & rubber, Sheet, rod, tubing & film cut to size. Machining of all plastic, build to print. Steel rule die punching of thin plastic & rubber. (Woman, estab 1974, empl 12, sales $1,200,000, cert: WBENC)

7093 Sigma Extruding Corp. DBA Sigma Stretch Film
808 Page Ave, Bldg 8 Bldg 8
Lyndhurst, NJ 07071
Contact: Maria Samuelson
Tel: 201-507-9100
Email: maria.samuelson@sigmaplastics.com
Website: www.sigmastretchfilm.com
Mfr plastics. (As-Pac, estab 1988, empl 354, sales $396,000,000, cert: NMSDC)

7094 SYSMIND LLC
38 Washington Rd
Princeton Junction, NJ 08550
Contact: Business Devel Specialist
Tel: 609-897-9670
Email: info@sysmind.com
Website: www.sysmind.com
Fabricate plastic components & fasteners for computer, aerospace, electronic, instrumentation, etc. applications. Prototype to production. Also stock molded nylon fasteners. (Woman/As-Ind, estab 1999, empl 456, sales $45,000,000, cert: NMSDC, WBENC)

New York

7095 Extreme Molding LLC
25 Gibson St
Watervliet, NY 12189
Contact: Joanne Moon Managing Partner
Tel: 518-266-6261
Email: joanne@extrememolding.com
Website: www.extrememolding.com
Injection molding: silicone, TPE, floropolymers, teflon, polycarbonate, polypropelene, Ultem, CAD design, material selection assistance, rapid prototyping, overmolding, compression molding, packaging. (Woman, estab 2002, empl 20, sales $1,000,000, cert: State)

7096　Mechanical Rubber Products Company, Inc.
77 Forester Ave, Ste 1
Warwick, NY 10990
Contact: Cedric Glasper President
Tel:　845-986-2271
Email: alisa.sherow@mechanicalrubber.com
Website: www.mechanicalrubber.com
Mfr elastomeric (rubber) products. (AA, estab 1995, empl 21, sales $945,000, cert: NMSDC)

Ohio

7097　Advanced Engineering Solutions Incorporated
250 Advanced Dr
Springboro, OH 45066
Contact: Scott Paulson Business Dev
Tel:　937-743-6900
Email: spaulson@aesi-usa.com
Website: www.advancedinternational.com
Tooling, CNC, punch press, subassembly, automated equipment, injection molded plastics. (Minority, Woman, estab 1995, empl 35, sales $2,250,000, cert: NMSDC)

7098　Axium Plastics LLC
9005 Smiths Mill Rd N
Johnstown, OH 43031
Contact: Tammy Hoffman Business Devel Mgr
Tel:　678-464-2259
Email: thoffman@axiumplastics.com
Website: www.axiumplastics.com
Extrusion Blow Molding, Injection Stretch Blow Molding, Injection Molding, Modeling, Design, Silk Screening, Pressure Sensitive Labeling (As-Ind, estab 2010, empl 250, sales $102,000,000, cert: NMSDC)

7099　Composite Technologies LLC
401 N Keowee St
Dayton, OH 45404
Contact: Karen Pierce Sales & Marketing Mgr
Tel:　937-228-2880
Email: kpierce@ctcplastics.com
Website: www.ctcplastics.com
Mfr plastic pallets made from 100% recycled plastic, compression & injection molding, of plastic parts made from recycled & virgin materials. (As-Pac, estab 1994, empl 150, sales $27,000,000, cert: NMSDC)

7100　Cox Financial Corporation
105 E Fourth St
Cincinnati, OH 45202
Contact: Ethan Cox CEO
Tel:　513-621-1771
Email: ethancox@coxfinco.com
Website: www.coxfinco.com
(AA, estab 1972, empl 12, sales $1,436,689, cert: NMSDC)

7101　EnKon, LLC dba Broadway
6344 Webster St
Dayton, OH 45414
Contact: Jodi Walters Member
Tel:　937-890-2221
Email: jodi.walters@enkonllc.com
Website: www.broadwaymold.com
Injection molds, components, mold repairs, Precision Fabrication, CNC Machining, welding, turning, Electrode manufacturing, EDM'ING, Wire EDM, Polish, Milling, OD, ID, and surface grinding, Design. (Woman, estab 1955, empl 12, sales , cert: WBENC)

7102　Ernie Green Industries
2030 Dividend Dr
Columbus, OH 43228
Contact: Bill Dunlevy VP Sales & Marketing
Tel:　614-949-1714
Email: bdunlevy@egindustries.com
Website: www.egi.net/
Plastic injection molding, paint, pad print, silk screen, hot stamp, graphic emblems, sonic welding, chrome plating, assembly, bar code labeling, shrink wrap & kit/unitized packaging. (AA, estab 1987, empl 450, sales $28,000,000, cert: NMSDC)

7103　HESS Advanced Technology, Inc.
PO Box 17669
Dayton, OH 45417
Contact: Frederick Edmonds CEO
Tel:　937-268-4377
Email: fred.edmonds@gmail.com
Website: www.plastikleen.net
Mfr protective coatings: surveillance cameras, lens/domes, PC's, laptops, PDA's, plasma screens & anti-microbial skin protector. (AA, estab , empl , sales $825,000, cert: NMSDC)

7104　Industry Products Company
500 Statler Rd
Piqua, OH 45356
Contact: Aaron Blakely Sales Specialist
Tel:　937-778-0585
Email: ablakely@industryproductsco.com
Website: www.industryproductsco.com
Mfr precision die-cut & formed products, gasket & sealing products, rubber-coated steel & alloys, compressed fiber, cork, neoprene, phenolic, nylon, Mylar, felts, PE, PP, rubber, etc. (Woman, estab 1966, empl 450, sales $80,000,000, cert: WBENC)

7105　MVP Plastics, Inc.
15005 Enterprise Way
Middlefield, OH 44062
Contact: Darrell McNair President
Tel:　440-834-1790
Email: darrellm@mvpplastics.com
Website: www.mvpplastics.com
Custom injection molding, decorating & assembly of plastics components. (AA, estab 2009, empl 30, sales $20,000,000, cert: NMSDC)

7106　PMC SMART Solutions LLC
9825 Kenwood Rd Ste 302
Cincinnati, OH 45242
Contact: Lisa Jennings CEO
Tel:　513-557-5222
Email: ljennings@pmcsmartsolutions.com
Website: www.pmcsmartsolutions.com
Development engineering, contract manufacturing & injection molding services for medical device, transportation & commercial electronics markets. (Woman, estab 1929, empl 200, sales $33,000,000, cert: WBENC)

7107 Polymer Technologies
      1835 James Pkwy
      Heath, OH 43056
      Contact: Sharad Thakkar President
      Tel: 740-929-5500
      Email: sharad@polymertechnologiesinc.com
      Website: www.polymertechnologiesinc.com
Provide reprocessed & wide spec resins, form, film.
powder, parts & return back in certified pellet form. (As-
Ind, estab 2002, empl 38, sales $7,000,000, cert: NMSDC)

7108 Shirley K's Storage Trays LLC
      PO Box 2519
      Zanesville, OH 43702
      Contact: Devin Hall Sales & Marketing Coord
      Tel: 740-868-8140
      Email: devin.hall@shirleyks.com
      Website: www.shirleyks.com
Mfr storage products, high-impact polystyrene or high-
density polyethylene; labeling tags, casters, locking lids &
imprinting. (Woman, estab 2013, empl 8, sales $1,410,400,
cert: WBENC)

7109 Tom Smith Industries, Inc.
      500 Smith Dr
      Clayton, OH 45315
      Contact: James Pugh Sales Mgr
      Tel: 937-832-1555
      Email: jpugh@tomsmithindustries.com
      Website: www.tomsmithindustries.com
Design & build plastic injection molds. Custom injection
molding of thermoplastics; assemble computer components. (Woman, estab 1980, empl 85, sales $25,367,000,
cert: WBENC)

7110 Triple Diamond Plastics, Inc.
      405 N Pleasantview Dr
      Liberty Center, OH 43532
      Contact: Josh Purdy VP
      Tel: 941-484-7750
      Email: josh.purdy@tdplastics.com
      Website: www.tdplastics.com
Mfr structural foam, multiple plastic pallets & collapsible
bins, large plastic contract products. (Woman, estab 2005,
empl 35, sales $3,500,000, cert: WBENC)

Oklahoma

7111 DA/PRO Rubber Inc.
      601 N Poplar Ave
      Broken Arrow, OK 74012
      Contact: Gretchen Brauninger CEO
      Tel: 918-258-9386
      Email: gbrauninger@daprorubber.com
      Website: www.daprorubber.com
High quality rubber, TPE & plastic custom components,
diaphragms, seals, connectors, custom molded shapes,
rubber-to-metal parts & molded to precision tolerances.
(Woman, estab 1961, empl 320, sales , cert: WBENC)

Oregon

7112 Griffith Rubber Mills
      2625 NW Industrial
      Portland, OR 97296
      Contact: Rick McClain Corporate Quality Mgr
      Tel: 503-226-6971
      Email: rickm@griffithrubber.com
      Website: www.griffithrubber.com
Custom rubber products (Woman, estab , empl 250,
sales , cert: NWBOC)

Pennsylvania

7113 Accudyn Products Inc.
      2400 Yoder Dr
      Erie, PA 16506
      Contact: Leanne Sheldon President
      Tel: 814-833-7615
      Email: lsheldon@accudyn.com
      Website: www.accudyn.com
Various high tolerance plastics parts servicing the
following industries: Appliance, Automotive, Business
Equipment, Electronics, Heating and Cooling, and
Medical. (Woman, estab 0, empl , sales , cert: WBENC)

7114 Pittsburgh Plastics Manufacturing
      140 Kriess Rd
      Butler, PA 16001
      Contact: Emily Crawford Acct Mgr
      Tel: 724-789-9300
      Email: ecrawford@pittsburghplastics.com
      Website: www.pittsburghplastics.com
Polyurethanes, TPEs, Silicones, Hydrogels & Foams.
(Woman, estab 1977, empl 100, sales , cert: WBENC)

7115 PMC-Polymer Products Company, Inc.
      100 Station Ave
      Stockertown, PA 18083
      Contact: Don Barber Business Mgr
      Tel: 610-759-3690
      Email: donbarber@pmc-group.com
      Website: www.polymerproductscompany.com/
      index.htm
Design & develop additive masterbatches & ignition
resistant thermoplastic compounds. (As-Ind, estab 1965,
empl 75, sales $25,500,000, cert: NMSDC)

Puerto Rico

7116 Vassallo International
      1000 St 506
      Cotolaurel, PR 00780
      Contact: Rafael Vassallo CEO
      Tel: 787-848-1515
      Email: faelo@vassalloindustries.com
      Website: www.vassallointernational.com
Lines of PVC & plastics, Water Tanks. (Minority, Woman,
estab 1962, empl 90, sales $15,000,000, cert: NMSDC)

South Carolina

7117   Milagro Packaging LLC
60 Fairview Church Rd
Spartanburg, SC 29306
Contact: Jill McCurry President
Tel: 864-578-0085
Email: jillm@concept-pkg.com
Website: www.milagro-pkg.com
Mfr corrugated & solid fiber boxes, polystyrene foam products & urethane foam products. (Hisp, estab 2001, empl 425, sales $94,873,435, cert: NMSDC)

Tennessee

7118   Innovative Plastics
2900 Old Franklin Rd
Antioch, TN 37013
Contact: Tom Florence Sales
Tel: 404-402-8062
Email: tomf4plastics@aol.com
Website: www.innovative-plastics.com
Custom thermoform & RF contract packaging: PVC, PETG, Styrene, Barex & HDPE. (Woman, estab 1985, empl 350, sales , cert: NWBOC)

7119   Precision Molding Inc.
5500 Roberts Matthews Hwy
Sparta, TN 38583
Contact: Ray Sachs Sales
Tel: 931-738-8376
Email: ray.sachs@precision-molding.com
Website: www.precision-molding.com
High-Pressure injection, inserts & blow molding. (Woman, estab 1987, empl 200, sales $20,000,000, cert: WBENC)

Texas

7120   Austin Foam Plastics, Inc.
2933 AW Grimes Blvd
Pflugerville, TX 78660
Contact: Lisa Carnett Project Leader
Tel: 512-251-6300
Email: lisa.carnett@a-f-p.com
Website: www.a-f-p.com
Packaging Design and testing; logistics; sustainable solutions; manufacturing - corrugated (boxes; die cut; pallets; solid fiber folding cartons) wood (custom crates; pallets; floating pallets) custom cases; custom cushions; plastic corrugated; sourcing ((Woman, estab 1978, empl 228, sales , cert: WBENC)

7121   Belco Manufacturing Company, Inc.
2303 Taylor's Valley Rd
Belton, TX 76513
Contact: Steve Macy President
Tel: 254-933-9000
Email: sales@belco-mfg.com
Website: www.belco-mfg.com
Industrial fiberglass reinforced plastics products. (Woman, estab 0, empl , sales , cert: WBENC)

7122   CamLow, LLC
105 S Friendswood Dr, Ste B
Friendswood, TX 77546
Contact: Karen Wiest President
Tel: 281-474-2613
Email: kawiest@camlow.com
Website: www.camlow.com
Polyurethane spray foam insulation, closed cell spray foam, open cell spray foam, roof spray foam insulation, hurricane protection, hurricane panels, storm panels, storm shutters, roll down shutters, accordian shutters, stainless steel screens. (Woman, estab 2005, empl 4, sales $317,000, cert: State, City)

7123   Chemplast, Inc.
1002 Texas Pkwy, Ste A
Stafford, TX 77477
Contact: Jubin Alexander Business Dev Mgr
Tel: 281-208-2585
Email: jubin@chemplastinc.com
Website: www.chemplastinc.com
Plastic Injection Molding with high performance Engineering Grade Plastics, Compression Molding, Thermoforming, Parts Assembly. (As-Ind, estab 2000, empl 47, sales $15,000,000, cert: NMSDC, CPUC)

7124   Clay Precision, Ltd.
1102 FM 1417 NE
Sherman, TX 75090
Contact: J. Diann Spencer President
Tel: 903-891-9022
Email: jspencer@clayprecision.com
Website: www.clayprecision.com
Milling, turning, 4th axis capabilities, fixturing, plastic weldment, assemblies, heat treating, grinding, dock-to-stock quality, fabrication of custom metal and plastic machined parts and assemblies, prototypes, exotic metals, exotic plastics. (Woman, estab 1996, empl 11, sales $1,293,930, cert: State, WBENC)

7125   Idea Planet, LP
6001 Summerside Dr Ste 204
Dallas, TX 75252
Contact: Michael Flecker President
Tel: 972-380-9867
Email: mflecker@ideaplanetinc.com
Website: www.ideaplanetinc.com
Plastic injected molding, resin, metal & glass manufacturing. (Woman, estab 1999, empl 18, sales $19,000,000, cert: WBENC)

7126   King's Eco Plastics, LLC
4001 W Military Hwy
McAllen, TX 78503
Contact: Owen Stewart President
Tel: 956-631-1115
Email: ostewart@kingsecoplastics.com
Website: www.kingsecoplastics.com
Custom-molded plastics, product assembly & finishing services. (Woman/AA, As- Pac, estab 1986, empl 75, sales $8,109,000, cert: NMSDC, WBENC)

7127 Mexican Technologies Co
8650 Yermoland Dr
El Paso, TX 79907
Contact: Alfredo Baca Sales Mgr
Tel: 915-595-2285
Email: abaca@uniqueproductsinc.com
Website: www.uniqueproductsinc.com
Die cutting, converting, lamination, plastic fabrication, extrusion & coextrusion, slitting, sewing. (Hisp, estab 2002, empl 20, sales , cert: State)

7128 Nicor Inc.
100 Commons Rd, Ste 7-355
Dripping Springs, TX 78620
Contact: Jeff Cook VP Sales & Mktg
Tel: 707-484-0835
Email: jeffacook@nicorinc.net
Website: www.nicorinc.net
Custom injection molding, polymer replacement meter pit lids that are traffic rated. (Woman, estab 1988, empl 5, sales $2,000,000, cert: State)

7129 Precision Mold & Tool Group
315 N Park Dr
San Antonio, TX 78216
Contact: Domingo Auces Dir of Marketing
Tel: 210-525-0094
Email: dhauces@pmtool.com
Website: www.precision-group.com
Injection molding & mold making. (Woman, estab 1985, empl 36, sales $6,505,000, cert: WBENC)

7130 Premier Polymers LLC
16800 Imperial Valley, Ste 200
Houston, TX 77060
Contact: Melwani Kwan Supply Chain Mgr
Tel: 281-902-0909
Email: mkwan@premierpolymers.com
Website: www.premierpolymers.com
Dist Plastic Resin. (As-Pac, estab 2009, empl 22, sales , cert: State, NMSDC)

Utah

7131 Kaddas Enterprises, Inc.
255 N. Apollo Rd. Ste 500
Salt Lake City, UT 84116
Contact: Patrick Scott Dir of Sales
Tel: 801-972-5400
Email: patricks@kaddas.com
Website: www.kaddas.com
Custom Thermoforming, Pressure Forming, Hand Fabrication, 5-Axis CNC Router, Master CAM, Solid Works Modeling, 3-Axis CNC Router, vacuum formed or hand fabricated polymer solutions. (Woman, estab 1966, empl 28, sales $4,296,559, cert: CPUC, WBENC)

Virginia

7132 Dynaric Inc.
5740 Bayside Rd
Virginia Beach, VA 23455
Contact: Kenny Samdahl Cstmr Service
Tel: 757-363-5851
Email: kens@dynaric.com
Website: www.dynaric.com
Mfr plastic strapping & strapping systems. (Hisp, estab 1973, empl 150, sales $122,000,000, cert: NMSDC)

7133 Polyfab Display Company
14892 Persistence Dr
Woodbridge, VA 22191
Contact: Al Parker Owner
Tel: 703-497-4577
Email: al@polyfab-display.com
Website: www.polyfab-display.com
Mfr & dist acrylic fabricated products: point-of-purchase displays (countertop, wall-mount, slatwall and free-standing), fixtures, signage, protective covers & medical device holders. (AA, estab 1987, empl 15, sales $1,189,000, cert: State, NMSDC)

Wisconsin

7134 Custom Service Plastics, Inc.
1101 S Wells St
Lake Geneva, WI 53147
Contact: Minoo Seifoddini President
Tel: 262-248-9557
Email: john@csplastics.com
Website: www.csplastics.com
Plastics injection molding: autotmotive & non automaotive parts & assemblies. (Minority, Woman, estab 0, empl 160, sales $12,000,000, cert: WBENC)

7135 Molded Dimensions, Inc.
701 Sunset Rd
Port Washington, WI 53074
Contact: Sue Bialzik Cstmr Service
Tel: 262-284-9455
Email: sue@moldeddimensions.com
Website: www.moldeddimensions.com
Rubber & polyurethane custom molded components. (Woman, estab 1952, empl 70, sales $12,500,000, cert: WBENC)

7136 Shell Plastics LLC
1010 Valley Rd
Plymouth, WI 53073
Contact: Mary Beth Dellger President
Tel: 920-893-6281
Email: marybeth@shellplastics.com
Website: www.shellplastics.com
Job Shop, Plastic Fabrication, Screen Printing, Vacuum Forming, CNC routing, Heat Bending, Cold Bending, Flame Polishing, Solvent Bonding, Laminating, Spray Painting, Die Cutting, Buffing, Drape Forming, Assembly, Packaging, Fulfillment. (Woman, estab 1953, empl 15, sales $2,924,884, cert: State)

7137 SMC Ltd.
330 SMC Dr
Somerset, WI 54025
Contact: Eugene Puckhaber Corporate Controller
Tel: 978-422-6800
Email: eugene.puckhaber@smcltd.com
Website: www.smcltd.com
Contract manufacturing & molding services, design, engineering, thermoplastic molding including insert & two-shot, micro molding. (As-Ind, estab 1989, empl 700, sales , cert: State, NMSDC)

PRINTING & ENGRAVING
Full service printers with layout, composition, binding and trimming, digital, multi-color, large format, etc. Also included are silkscreen printers, nameplate and trophy engravers, manufacturers or distributors of labels, decals and pressure sensitive materials. NAICS Code 32

Alabama

7138　Advanced Label Worx
1006 Larsen Dr
Oak Ridge, AL 37830
Contact: Lana Sellers President
Tel:　865-966-8711
Email: lsellers@advancedlabelworx.com
Website: www.advancedlabelworx.com
Flexographic pressure-sensitive labels, specialty converting, die-cut components, digital imprinting. (Woman, estab 1968, empl 120, sales , cert: WBENC)

7139　Precision Graphics Inc.
4121 Lewisburg Rd
Birmingham, AL 35207
Contact: Robert Grant President
Tel:　205-841-2072
Email: robertg@precisiongraphicsinc.net
Website: www.precisiongraphicsinc.net
Design, layout, printing, mailing, warehouse, direct mail, packaging, die cut. (Minority, Woman, estab 2002, empl 25, sales $3,529,600, cert: WBENC)

Arizona

7140　Courier Graphics Corporation
2621 S 37th St
Phoenix, AZ 85034
Contact: Renee Teper Acct Exec
Tel:　602-437-9700
Email: renee_teper@couriergraphics.com
Website: www.couriergraphics.com
Commercial printing. (Woman, estab 1975, empl 70, sales $13,789,000, cert: WBENC)

7141　Sapphire Printing Group, Inc.
3800 N. 38th Ave
Phoenix, AZ 85019
Contact: Kenn Gary Dir of Sales
Tel:　714-941-9534
Email: kenng@sapphireprinting.com
Website: www.sapphireprinting.com
Commercial web printing, mailing & fulfillment services. (Woman, estab 2004, empl 115, sales $22,000,000, cert: CPUC)

California

7142　Acme Press Inc., dba California Lithographers
2312 Stanwell Dr
Concord, CA 94520
Contact:　VP
Tel:　925-682-1111
Email:
Website: www.Calitho.com
Commercial printing, digital printing, fulfillment, mailing, packaging. (Woman, estab 1976, empl 75, sales $11,530,090, cert: WBENC)

7143　Advantage Mailing, LLC.
1600 N Kraemer Blvd
Anaheim, CA 92806
Contact: Nicholas Lancione Natl Acct Dir
Tel:　414-379-5210
Email: nlancione@advantageinc.com
Website: www.advantageinc.com
Printing, Mailing, Fulfillment. (As-Pac, estab 1994, empl 450, sales $95,000,000, cert: NMSDC)

7144　Alpha Printing & Graphics, Inc.
12758 schabarum ave
irwindale, CA 91706
Contact: Kelly Ngo VP Sales
Tel:　626-851-9800
Email: kelly.ngo@alphaprinting.com
Website: www.alphaprinting.com
Commercial & digital printing. (Minority, Woman, estab 1995, empl 20, sales $3,000,000, cert: CPUC)

7145　Clear Image Printing, Inc.
12744 San Fernando Road Bldg 2
Sylmar, CA 91342
Contact: Gene Byrne Dir Mktg/Sales
Tel:　818-630-7670
Email: eugene@clearimageprinting.com
Website: www.clearimageprinting.com
Offset sheet fed & digital printing, Brochures, Catalogues, Direct mail campaigns, Special Packaging, Books, Foil stamping, Die-cutting, Posters, Large Format Banners, Graphic Design, Modern-Media. (As-Pac, estab 2008, empl 45, sales $5,005,000, cert: CPUC)

7146　Digital Mania, Inc.
455 Market St Ste 180
San Francisco, CA 94105
Contact: Darius Meykadeh CEO
Tel:　415-896-0500
Email: copymat@copymatsf.com
Website: www.copymat1.com
Indoor & outdoor signs, brochures, booklets, RFPs, oversized prints, desktop publishing & design, mailing services, newsletters, name tents, name badges, conference materials, etc. (As-Ind, estab 1994, empl 20, sales $4,000,000, cert: City)

7147　Digital Services Enterprises
40 Tesla, Ste B
Irvine, CA 92618
Contact:　Sales Mgr
Tel:　949-387-6200
Email: orders@sirspeedyprinter.com
Website: www.sirspeedyprinter.com
Offset printing, digital printing, color copies, photocopying, promotional products, Signs, banners, posters, floor graphics, direct mail, fulfillment, high speedy copies, training manuals, human resource manuals, direct marketing. (Woman, estab 1974, empl 17, sales $2,757,000, cert: CPUC)

7148　Essence Printing
151 Mitchell Ave
South San Francisco, CA 94080
Contact: Bau-Lin Yueh President
Tel:　650-952-5072
Email: baulin@essenceprinting.com
Website: www.essenceprinting.com
Printing: marketing material, brochures, datasheets, newsletters, tradeshow posters, business cards, letterheads, etc. (As-Pac, estab 1976, empl 60, sales , cert: CPUC)

7149 Financial Statement Services, Inc.
3300 S Fairview St
Santa Ana, CA 92704
Contact: Jennifer Dietz CEO
Tel: 714-436-3300
Email:
Website: www.fssi-ca.com
Printing, mailing & electronic invoices, statements, bills & marketing communications. (Woman, estab 1980, empl 187, sales $5,000,000, cert: WBENC)

7150 Fong & Fong Printers and Lithographers
3009 65th St
Sacramento, CA 95820
Contact: Karen Cotton Controller
Tel: 916-739-1313
Email: kcotton@fongprinters.com
Website: www.fongprinters.com
Commercial printing services: sales literature, brochures, folders, packaging, annual reports, data sheets, direct mail & posters. (Minority, Woman, estab 1962, empl 51, sales $12,000,000, cert: CPUC)

7151 Fruitridge Printing and Lithograph
3258 Stockton Blvd
Sacramento, CA 95820
Contact: Karen Young VP
Tel: 916-452-9213
Email: karen@fruitridge.com
Website: www.fruitridge.com
Commercial offset and digital printing, in house bindery & mailing capabilities. (Woman, estab 1970, empl 35, sales $5,100,000, cert: CPUC)

7152 Gibraltar Graphics
5075 Brooks St
Montclair, CA 91763
Contact: Hector Rosado Sales Mgr
Tel: 909-624-6171
Email: hectorr@gprint4u.com
Website: www.gPrint4u.com
Printing, inhouse bindery, heatset web presses, pick up and delivery, brochures, envelopes, laser forms, newsletters, booklets, scratch pads, laser forms, (Hisp, estab 1989, empl 18, sales $410,000, cert: CPUC)

7153 Image Quest Plus, LLC
215 No Marengo Ave. Third Floor
Pasadena, CA 91101
Contact: Margaret Floyd Member
Tel: 626-744-1333
Email: margaret@iqcopy.com
Website: www.iqcopy.com
Photocopy services: document reproduction, scanning & imaging, color copies, wideformat printing, binding, off-site document reproduction. (Woman/AA, estab 1998, empl 5, sales $661,441, cert: NMSDC, CPUC)

7154 Impact Printing
23278 Bernhardt St
Hayward, CA 94545
Contact: Sarah Elder VP Sales
Tel: 510-783-7977
Email: impactprint@impactprint.com
Website: www.impactprint.com
Digital & offset printing, full bindery, graphics. (Minority, Woman, estab 1985, empl 25, sales $2,500,000, cert: CPUC)

7155 Ink Link, Incorporated
351 Oak Place, Ste J
Brea, CA 92821
Contact: Linda Brooking CEO
Tel: 714-256-9700
Email: linda@myinklink.com
Website: www.myinklink.com
Commercial printing: banners, signs, displays, floor graphics. (Woman, estab 2003, empl 4, sales $850,000, cert: State, CPUC, WBENC)

7156 International Diversified Marketing, Inc.
18277 Pasadena St., Ste B102
Lake Elsinore, CA 92530
Contact: Jan Northcutt President
Tel: 714-550-4971
Email: jn@comfortfirst.us
Website: www.ComfortFirstProducts.com
Comfort First Filtered Diffuser™If you want to go GREEN and save energy, improve employee comfort and health, all while improving indoor air quality, this diffuser is the solution you've been looking for. (Woman, estab 2003, empl 3, sales $458,000, cert: WBENC)

7157 Lester Lithograph Inc. (dba Castle Press)
1128 N Gilbert St
Anaheim, CA 92801
Contact: Larry Lester Retired
Tel: - -
Email: amy@castlepress.com
Website: www.castlepress.com
Commercial printing. (Woman, estab 1980, empl 45, sales $5,500,000, cert: CPUC, WBENC)

7158 Marina Graphic Center, Inc.
12903 Cerise Ave
Hawthorne, CA 90250
Contact: Sr Acct Exec
Tel: 310-970-1777
Email:
Website: www.marinagraphics.com
Commercial Printing, Pre-Press, Offset Printing, Digital Printing, Mail fulfillment & Mailing services, Full Bindery, Letterpress, Die Cutting & Embossing. (Woman, estab 1964, empl 125, sales $14,000,000, cert: WBENC)

7159 Metropolitan West, Inc.
130 Pine Ave Ste 400
Long Beach, CA 90802
Contact: Kelly Taylor CEO
Tel: 562-426-7701
Email: nikki@metwest.com
Website: www.metwest.com
Dist film products: solar, safety, anti-graffiti, designer, custom & digital film. (Woman, estab 1992, empl 5, sales $1,200,000, cert: WBENC)

7160 Monarch Litho, Inc.
1501 Date St
Montabella, CA 90640
Contact: Gerry Lewis Acct Exec
Tel: 323-727-0300
Email: gerry.lewis@monarchlitho.com
Website: www.monarchlitho.com
Printing svcs: small & large format sheet fed press; digital pre-press (Hisp, estab 1974, empl 275, sales , cert: NMSDC, CPUC)

7161   PGI Pacific Graphics International
14938 Nelson Ave
City of Industry, CA 91744
Contact: Rick Wasson President
Tel: 626-336-7707
Email: rwasson@pacgraphics.com
Website: www.pacgraphics.com
Printing & graphics, business forms, etc. (Minority, Woman, estab 1989, empl 20, sales $3,600,372, cert: NMSDC, CPUC, SDB)

7162   Photomation
2551 W La Palma Ave
Anaheim, CA 92801
Contact: Francisco Flores Production Mgr/Sales
Tel: 714-236-2121
Email: fflores@photomation.com
Website: www.photomation.com
Digital Graphics, Trade show, Digital Imaging, Photographics prints, Banners, POP displays, Standees, Wallcovering, Large wall Murals, Lobby art, Custom framing, Awards and recognition, office décor. (Woman, estab 1955, empl 21, sales , cert: State, CPUC, WBENC)

7163   Summit Graphics Inc.
11354 Burbank Blvd, Ste A
North Hollywood, CA 91601
Contact: Jorge Ververa VP Diversity
Tel: 818-753-5075
Email: jorge@summit-graphics.net
Website: www.summit-graphics.net
Medium to large runs in offset, digital & large format printing: mailers, inkjet address, brochures, catalogues, booklets, bindery, die-cutting, packaging, coallating, hand fulfillment. (Hisp, estab 2001, empl 4, sales $1,436,504, cert: State, NMSDC)

7164   Transworld Printing Services, Inc.
2857 Transworld Dr
Stockton, CA 95206
Contact: Daphyne Brown CEO
Tel: 209-982-1511
Email: daphyne@tpslabels.com
Website: www.tpslabels.com
Flexographic & digital label manufacturer. (Woman/AA, estab 1996, empl 15, sales $2,065,000, cert: NMSDC, NWBOC)

Colorado

7165   DT Investments Inc. dba Beacon Printing Inc.
2161 S Platte River Dr
Denver, CO 80223
Contact: Terri Witt CEO
Tel: 303-922-4384
Email: beacon.sales@qwestoffice.net
Website: www.beaconprintingdenver.com
Printing services, large format sheetfed, digital, full color, PMS color, pocket folders, post cards, letterhead, envelopes, posters, booklets, annual reports, brochures, forms, rack cards, pamphlets, catalogs, tabs, loose leaf, inserts. (Minority, Woman, estab 1995, empl 10, sales $1,200,000, cert: City)

7166   Mar-Tek Industries, Inc.
3545 S Platte River Dr, Ste G
Englewood, CO 80110
Contact: Irene Smith President
Tel: 303-789-4067
Email: irene@mar-tekind.com
Website: www.mar-tekind.com
Mfr & dist screen printed & digital graphic labels, decals, overlays. (Woman, estab 1987, empl 45, sales $4,500,000, cert: WBENC)

Connecticut

7167   Enhance a Colour Corp.
43b Beaver Brook Road
Danbury, CT 06810
Contact: Lenore Nespoli Sales Mgr
Tel: 203-748-5111
Email: lnespoli@eacgs.com
Website: www.eacgs.com
Large format digitally printed graphics, printing dyesub fabrics & carpets up to 16' wide, UV printing, full color & white ink direct to rigid and flexible substrates, pressure sensitive, regular & mesh substrates. (Woman, estab 1988, empl 32, sales $4,014,058, cert: WBENC)

7168   Kool Ink/Sir Speedy Printing
21 Old Windsor Rd
Bloomfield, CT 06002
Contact: Mark Jacobs Owner
Tel: 860-242-0303
Email: mark@sirspeedy.cc
Website: www.sirspeedy.com
Offset printing, copying, black & white, color, scanning, posters banners & signs. (AA, estab 2001, empl 15, sales $3,500,000, cert: State, NMSDC)

7169   Turnstone Inc. dba Alphagraphics
915 Main St
Hartford, CT 06103
Contact: VP Sales
Tel: 860-247-3766
Email: us667@alphagraphics.com
Website: www.hartford.alphagraphics.com
Brochures, Reports, Training books, Posters, Reports, mailings. Forms, labels, Flyers, Design Services. Fulfillment, Signs & banners, marketing material. (Woman, estab 1989, empl 23, sales $3,100,000, cert: WBENC)

Florida

7170   Alpha Press, Inc.
3804 N John Young Pkwy, Ste 2
Orlando, FL 32804
Contact: GM
Tel: 407-299-2121
Email: sales@apiprint.net
Website: www.apiprint.net
Four color press: brochures, business cards, envelopes, pamplets, magazines & publications. (Minority, Woman, estab 1996, empl 5, sales $870,000, cert: City)

7171 Amazon Services Inc.
7186 SW 47th St
Miami, FL 33155
Contact: Cristina Serralta Founder/CEO
Tel: 305-663-0585
Email: cristina@amazonprinters.com
Website: www.amazonprinters.com
Commercial printers with in-house bindery equipment for booklet making, continuous forms, carbonless, logo, graphics, invoices, checks, brochures, flyers, digital printing, quick printing, envelopes, stationery, cards, and more. (Minority, Woman, estab 1987, empl 12, sales , cert: WBENC)

7172 APImaging, Inc.
19 SW 6th St
Miami, FL 33130
Contact: Diana Herrera VP Sales
Tel: 305-373-4774
Email: dianah@apimaging.com
Website: www.apimaging.com
Photo imaging & photo finishing services, commercial printing, studio photography, self adhesive signs & graphics, directional signs, posters, point of purchase signs, graphic displays, graphic design, trade shows & exhibits. (Minority, Woman, estab 2013, empl 22, sales , cert: WBENC)

7173 Bellak Color
PO Box 227656
Miami, FL 33222
Contact: Manny Fernandez VP
Tel: 305-854-8525
Email: manny@bellak.com
Website: www.bellak.com
Commerical sheet-fed printing - print publications, magazines, brochures, rack brochures, catalogs, stationery packages, POS pieces, postcards, pamplets, invitations, folders. (Hisp, estab 1960, empl 47, sales $6,500,000, cert: NMSDC)

7174 Colonial Press International, Inc.
3690 NW 50th St
Miami, FL 33142
Contact: Jeff Statler EVP Corporate Sales
Tel: 540-347-1402
Email: jstatler@colonialpress.com
Website: www.colonialpressintl.com
Printing svcs: web & sheet fed, 4-6 color, brochures, rack cards, magazines, etc. (Hisp, estab 1952, empl 120, sales $31,000,000, cert: NMSDC)

7175 Innovative Printing & Graphics
310 S Federal Hwy
Boynton Beach, FL 33435
Contact: Amy Bernard Sales Assoc
Tel: 561-742-2977
Email: info@ipgprinting.com
Website: www.ipgprinting.com
Commercial printing: full color, magazines, NCR forms, pocket folders, postcard mailiers, letterhead, invitations, etc. (Woman, estab 2006, empl 9, sales $250,000, cert: City)

7176 Lawton Printers, Inc.
649 Triumph Court
Orlando, FL 32804
Contact: Kimberly Lawton Koon President
Tel: 407-260-0400
Email: kimberly@lawtonprinters.com
Website: www.LawtonPrinters.com
Printing ; offset, digital & wide-format printing equipment. (Woman, estab , empl 27, sales $3,600,000, cert: State, WBENC)

7177 Martin Litho, Inc.
505 N Rome Ave
Tampa, FL 33606
Contact: Martin Saavedra CEO
Tel: 813-254-1553
Email: martin@martinlitho.com
Website: www.mlicorp.com
Commercial sheet-fed, multi-color printing. (Minority, Woman, estab 1970, empl 42, sales $5,116,143, cert: State, NMSDC)

7178 Quadco Printing & Signs
8953 NW 23rd St
Doral, FL 33172
Contact: Jorge Quadreny President
Tel: 305-519-1234
Email: jorge@quadcoonline.com
Website: www.quadcoonline.com
Full color printing services, advertising specialties, promotional items, trade show & retractable banner stands. (Hisp, estab 1982, empl 8, sales $140,000,000, cert: State)

7179 Sol Davis Printing, Inc.
5205 N Lois Ave
Tampa, FL 33614
Contact: Solomon E. Davis President
Tel: 813-353-3609
Email: soldavis.print@verizon.net
Website: www.soldavisprinting.com
Offset printing: 1, 2, 3 & 4 color process, graphic design, typesetting & bindery services. (Woman/AA, estab 1999, empl 9, sales , cert: State, City, NMSDC)

7180 Vista Color Corporation
1401 NW 78th Ave
Miami, FL 33126
Contact: Catherine Finnemore Sr Acct Exec
Tel: 305-635-2000
Email: cfinnemore@vistacolor.com
Website: www.vistacolor.com
Pre-press & printing svcs. (Hisp, estab 1968, empl 120, sales $22,000,000, cert: NMSDC)

Georgia

7181 American Reprographics Corporation
7800 Jett Ferry Rd
Atlanta, GA 30350
Contact: Mindy Godwin President
Tel: 770-394-2465
Email: mindy@arcinatlanta.com
Website: www.arcinatlanta.com
Full service printing: business cards, letterhead, envelopes, check stock, brochures, mailings, graphic design services. (Woman, estab 1978, empl 3, sales , cert: WBENC)

7182   Barcode Warehouse
101 Smoke Hill Lane Ste 130
Woodstock, GA 30188
Contact: Margie Benton VP Sales Operations
Tel: 888-422-9249
Email: mbenton@barcodewarehouse.biz
Website: www.barcodewarehouse.biz
Mfr labels & tags, full color product branding labels, blank labels & tags for variable data printing. (Woman, estab 2004, empl 18, sales $4,225,778, cert: WBENC)

7183   Basiqa, LLC
1555 Oakbrook Dr Ste 135
Norcross, GA 30093
Contact: Winston Dzose VP Digital Marketing
Tel: 678-824-6460
Email: winston@basiqa.com
Website: www.basiqa.com
Direct mail, advertising, material preparation services for mailing or other direct distribution, digital printing. (AA, estab 2009, empl 16, sales $3,000,000, cert: NMSDC)

7184   Dixie Graphics
2074 E Park Dr NE
Conyers, GA 30013
Contact: Denise Hindle COE
Tel: 770-972-2354
Email: dhindle@dixiegraphicsinc.com
Website: www.dixiegraphicsinc.com
Commercial offset printing & large format, graphics design & full mail room capabilities. (Woman, estab 1980, empl 14, sales $2,012,337, cert: WBENC)

7185   Fuentes Enterprises, Inc
2605 Park Central Blvd
Decatur, GA 30035
Contact: Monica Maldonado CEO
Tel: 770-987-7400
Email: monica@weareipcomm.com
Website: www.weareipcomm.com
Commercial printing, graphic design, posters, billboards, marketing collateral materials, annual reports, ads, etc. (Minority, Woman, estab 1984, empl 12, sales $1,649,328, cert: NMSDC)

7186   LittKare, LLC
200 Cobb Pkwy N Ste 130
Marietta, GA 30062
Contact: Littie Brown President
Tel: 770-693-1767
Email: lbrown@speedpro.com
Website: www.speedpromarietta.com
Large format digital printing: banners, posters, signs, trade show displays & banner stands, vehicle wraps, vinyl lettering, wall, window & floor graphics, stickers & decals. (Woman/AA, estab 2010, empl 2, sales $373,880, cert: NMSDC, WBENC)

7187   Matoaka Enterprises, LLC
2455 Bridlewood Dr
Smyrna, GA 30080
Contact: Julie Custalow Owner
Tel: 404-932-6825
Email: julie@matoaka.com
Website: www.matoaka-ent.com
Large format graphics, banners, signs, window clings, vehicle wraps, LEED certified wall paper, custom printed litho & digital printing, custom printed promotional items, apparel. (Minority, Woman, estab 2010, empl 1, sales $181,611, cert: NMSDC)

7188   NorthStar Print, LLC
6050 Peachtree Pkwy Ste 240359
Norcross, GA 30092
Contact: Jacki Suckow President
Tel: 770-490-6251
Email: jacki@northstarprint.net
Website: www.northstarprint.net
Print & promotional products, marketing materials, traditional business forms, POP items, promotional items & just-in-time digital printing, distribution & kitting services. (Woman, estab 1991, empl 8, sales $3,000,000, cert: NWBOC)

7189   PrinTech Label Corporation
2550 Collins Springs Dr
Smyrna, GA 30080
Contact: Kelly Weaver CFO
Tel: 404-792-1133
Email: kelly@printechlabel.com
Website: www.printechlabel.com
Pressure senstive labels, custom printed tags, 4 color process, 6 color capability, hot stamp labels, cold foil labels, UL registered label vendor, IRC's, IRC, redeemable coupons, silver coupon, thermal transfer blanks, direct thermal blanks. (Minority, Woman, estab 1993, empl 14, sales $1,701,002, cert: WBENC)

7190   Printing and Marketing Services, Inc.
1500 Southland Circle, Ste A
Atlanta, GA 30318
Contact: BRIAN MCDANIEL Sr Acct Mgr
Tel: 404-724-9080
Email: bmcdaniel@alphagraphics.com
Website: www.us756.alphagraphics.com
Printing: digital color, digital black & white, offset printing, envelopes, stationery, large format signs & banners. (AA, estab 2015, empl 13, sales $1,695,647, cert: NMSDC)

7191   The Printing People, Inc.
3427 Oakcliff Rd. Ste 112
Doraville, GA 30340
Contact: Misael Millan VP
Tel: 770-452-7561
Email: misa@printingpeople.com
Website: www.printingpeople.com
Commercial offset & digital printing: brochures, post-cards, catalogs, posters, folders, manuals & stationery. (Hisp, estab 1980, empl 13, sales $1,400,000, cert: NMSDC)

Iowa

7192   Promotion Support Services, Inc.
1320 W Kimberly Rd
Davenport, IA 52806
Contact: Terance VanWinkle Dir
Tel: 563-362-6002
Email: tvanwinkle@pss-inc.net
Website: www.pss-inc.net
Offset printing, Digital printing (static & variable), Commercial printing, Transactional print & mail services, Transcription Services, Data capture, Medical Transcription, Outbound call center, warehousing, Fulfillment, Kitting. (Woman, estab 1989, empl 56, sales $5,600,000, cert: WBENC)

Illinois

7193 AmeriPrint Corporation
1401 W Diggins St
Harvard, IL 60098
Contact: Taylor Schulty Marking & Sales Dir
Tel: 800-366-8573
Email: taylors@ameriprint.com
Website: www.ameriprint.com
Continuous forms & checks, snap sets, laser cut-sheets, booked & padded sets, integral card forms & labels, decals, re-positionable labels, key tags, magnets, thermal labels, barcoding, jumbo numbering & rolls. (Woman, estab 1990, empl 63, sales $8,603,265, cert: NWBOC)

7194 Clyde Printing Company
3520 S Morgan
Chicago, IL 60609
Contact: Colleen Woulfe President
Tel: 773-847-5900
Email: clydeprint@sbcglobal.net
Website: www.clydeprinting.com
Sheet fed commercial printing, conventional & digital printing, fullfillment & mailing. (Woman, estab 1942, empl 10, sales $792,852, cert: WBENC)

7195 ComGraphics Inc.
329 W 18th St, 10 Fl
Chicago, IL 60616
Contact: Lydia Erickson CFO
Tel: 312-226-0900
Email: lydiae@cgichicago.com
Website: www.cgichicago.com
Digital printing svcs, folding & inserting operations, internet hosting, statement processing, web statement, laser svcs, invoicing, marketing & fulfillment, data archiving, scanning svcs, direct mail. (Woman, estab 1980, empl 55, sales , cert: WBENC)

7196 Consolidated Printing Company
5942 N Northwest Hwy
Chicago, IL 60631
Contact: Marilyn Jones President
Tel: 773-631-2800
Email: marilyn@consolidatedprinting.net
Website: www.consolidatedprinting.net
Commercial printing includes: design, computer to plate, color digital, offset short & long run: advertising materials, annual reports, banners, brochures, booklets, buttons, business cards, conference materials, digital printing, door hangers. (Woman, estab 1973, empl 15, sales , cert: WBENC)

7197 D&D Business Inc. dba DDI Printing
7830 Quincy St
Willowbrook, IL 60527
Contact: Darmi Parikh CEO
Tel: 630-734-1455
Email: darmi@ddimage.com
Website: www.ddimage.com
Graphic design, Commercial colored printing, digital printing, full bindery & fullfillment. (Minority, Woman, estab 1994, empl 5, sales $560,000, cert: State, City, NMSDC)

7198 Krick Enterprises, Inc.
1548 Ogden Ave
Downers Grove, IL 60515
Contact: President Sales & Marketing
Tel: 630-515-1085
Email: info@signsnowdownersgrove.com
Website: www.signsnowdownersgrove.com
Graphic Design & Layout, commercial & digital printing. Signs & Posters, Brochures, Business Cards, Training Manuals & materials, Promotional items. (Minority, Woman, estab 1991, empl 7, sales $600,000, cert: State, NMSDC)

7199 M & R Graphics
2401 Bond St
University Park, IL 60466
Contact: Keith Reimel VP
Tel: 708-534-6621
Email: kreimel@mrgraphics.biz
Website: www.mrgraphics.biz
Mfr pressure sensitive labels & flexographic printing. (Woman/AA, estab 1989, empl 17, sales , cert: NMSDC)

7200 Master Marketing International
280 Gerzverske Lane
Carol Stream, IL 60188
Contact: Rene Asselmeier Sr Sales Exec
Tel: 630-653-5525
Email: rasselmeier@magnetstreet.com
Website: www.magnetstreet.com
Magnet printing, high-end stationary products, digital printer and mail house. (Woman, estab 1990, empl 66, sales $10,800,000, cert: WBENC)

7201 MOTR GRAFX, LLC
225 Larkin Dr Unit 5
Wheeling, IL 60090
Contact: Lissette Herin VP/Partner
Tel: 847-529-7454
Email: Lherin@motrgx.com
Website: www.motrgrafx.com
Print/media production, design, print, finishing, fulfillment & distribution, digital, sheet fed, large format, web printing, screen printing, direct mail, POP/packaging services. (Minority, Woman, estab 2011, empl 10, sales $2,980,000, cert: City, NMSDC, WBENC)

7202 Orion Offset
236 E Northwest Hwy
Palatine, IL 60067
Contact: President
Tel: 847-776-2300
Email: info@orionoffset.com
Website: www.orionoffset.com
Commercial printers, design, pre-press, digital printing, mailing, fulfillment. (Woman, estab 1993, empl 9, sales , cert: WBENC)

7203 Richards Graphic Communications, Inc.
2700 Van Buren St
Bellwood, IL 60104
Contact: Mary Lawrence President
Tel: 708-731-2103
Email: maryl@rgcnet.com
Website: www.rgcnet.com
Printing & communications, creative concept development, language translations, digital imaging, printing, finishing & mailing. (Woman, estab 1925, empl 23, sales $4,400,000, cert: State, WBENC)

7204 Shree Ganesha, Inc.
      311 S Wacker Dr
      Chicago, IL 60606
      Contact: Tina Kuvadia Production Mgr
      Tel: 312-408-1080
      Email: printxpress@printx-press.com
      Website: www.printx-press.com
Offset printing, copying, binding, large format, digital
printing & graphic designing capabilities. (Minority,
Woman, estab 2008, empl 9, sales , cert: City)

7205 Signcraft Screenprint, Inc.
      100 AJ Harle Dr
      Galena, IL 61036
      Contact: Sandy Redington President
      Tel: 815-777-3030
      Email: sandy@signcraftinc.com
      Website: www.signcraftinc.com
Custom screen printing, mfr pressure sensitive decals,
signs & anti-skid plates. (Woman, estab 1947, empl 133,
sales $11,500,000, cert: NWBOC)

7206 Sunrise Hitek Service, Inc.
      5915 N Northwest Hwy
      Chicago, IL 60631
      Contact: Mark Finch VP
      Tel: 773-792-8880
      Email: mfinch@sunrisedigital.us
      Website: www.sunrisehitek.com
Large format printing; displays, exhibit boards, POP
displays, signs, floor graphics, etc. (As-Pac, estab 1987,
empl 15, sales $3,700,000, cert: State, NMSDC)

7207 THM Creative, Inc. dba Advanced Imaging Inc.
      1944 University Lane
      Lisle, IL 60532
      Contact: Tim Donnell Sales
      Tel: 630-969-1300
      Email: tim@aiprolab.com
      Website: www.aiprolab.com
Digital Color Lab, Photographic Printing & Processing,
Enlargements to 30x40, Inkjet/Giglee Printing, Online
Order Fulfillment. (Minority, Woman, estab 1994, empl 6,
sales , cert: NMSDC)

7208 Wyka LLC d/b/a Edison Graphics
      1515 S Mt. Prospect Rd
      Des Plaines, IL 60018
      Contact: Larae J. Breitenstein CEO
      Tel: 847-298-0740
      Email: larae@edison-graphics.com
      Website: www.edison-graphics.com
Printing svcs: 6 colors & coater sheet fed printing, in-house
finishing, cutters, MBO folders, stitcher, digital printing &
wide format printing. (Woman, estab 1998, empl 14, sales
$3,215,000, cert: WBENC)

Indiana

7209 Fineline Printing Group
      8081 Zionsville Rd
      Indianapolis, IN 46268
      Contact: Richard Miller President
      Tel: 317-802-1964
      Email: richardm@finelineprintinggroup.com
      Website: www.FinelinePrintingGroup.com
Commercial sheetfed printing, inhouse bindery, mailing
svcs, prepress svcs: scanning, design, ctp & high end color
corrections. (Minority, Woman, estab 1981, empl 59, sales
$11,500,000, cert: State, NMSDC)

7210 International Label Mfg.
      1925 S 13th St
      Terre Haute, IN 47802
      Contact: Lisa Gonzales VP
      Tel: 800-525-8469
      Email: lisagonzales@internationallabelmfg.com
      Website: www.internationallabelmfg.com
Custom label mfr & commercial printer. (Woman, estab
1972, empl 18, sales , cert: State, WBENC)

7211 Miles Printing Corporation
      4923 W 78th St
      Indianapolis, IN 46268
      Contact: Exec VP
      Tel: 317-870-6145
      Email: ap@miles2.mystagingwebsite.com
      Website: www.milesprinting.com
Commercial printing, offering digital, multi-color UV
sheet-fed, large format printing, complete bindery,
mailing & fulfillment capabilities. (Woman, estab 2006,
empl 38, sales $13,600,000, cert: State, WBENC)

7212 Nicholson Printing Inc.
      209 Eastern Blvd
      Jeffersonville, IN 47130
      Contact: Chris Nicholson VP
      Tel: 812-283-1200
      Email: chris@nicholsonprinting.com
      Website: www.nicholsonprinting.com
Commercial & quick printing, graphic design, full-color
printing, disk to print, digital color, digital black & white,
copying, letterheads, envelopes, business cards, time
cards, folders, books. (Woman, estab 1979, empl 12,
sales $1,118,000, cert: State)

7213 Offset House Printing, Inc.
      9374 Castlegate Dr
      Indianapolis, IN 46256
      Contact: Jay Williamson Acct Mgr
      Tel: 317-849-5155
      Email: jwilliamson@offsethouse.biz
      Website: www.offsethouseinc.com
Commercial printing, graphic design & direct mail.
(Woman, estab 1964, empl 13, sales , cert: State)

7214 Printing Inc of Louisville Kentucky
      1600 Dutch Lane Ste A
      Jeffersonville, IN 47130
      Contact: Kelly Abney Mgr Business Devel
      Tel: 502-368-6555
      Email: wbe@prettyincredible.com
      Website: www.prettyincredible.com
Print, fulfillment, distribution, marketing consulting,
project management, direct mail with management of
distributions, inventory & fulfillment of literature,
bindery & kit packing. (Woman, estab 1971, empl 19,
sales $3,000,000, cert: State)

7215 Thomas E. Slade, Inc.
      6220 Vogel Road
      Evansville, IN 47715
      Contact: Lisa Slade President
      Tel: 812-437-5233
      Email: tom@sladeprint.com
      Website: www.sladeprint.com
Printing, graphic & website design, wide format posters
& banners, mailing, promotional products, envelopes,
labels, tags, inserts, marketing services, augmented
reality, QR codes for tracking, signs. (Woman, estab
1993, empl 17, sales $2,500,000, cert: State)

7216 Town & Country Printing
1001 E Summit St
Crown Point, IN 46307
Contact: Debera Hinchy President
Tel: 219-924-0441
Email: dhinchy@tandcii.com
Website: www.townandcountryprinting.com
Commercial printing - offset & digital. Traditional, large/
grand format printing. Full color business cards, statio-
nery, notepads, banners, indoor and outdoor signage,
brochures, booklets, wall and floor graphics, decals
(window, wall, floor). (Woman, estab 1970, empl 18, sales
$1,800,000, cert: WBENC)

7217 UN Communications Group, Inc.
1429 Chase Court
Carmel, IN 46032
Contact: Denise Purvis President
Tel: 317-218-8262
Email: dpurvis@uncommgroup.com
Website: www.uncommgroup.com
Commercial, digital & wide format print services, mailing
services, brochures, catalogs & annual reports, banners,
vehicle wraps & tradeshow signage. (Woman, estab 1975,
empl 32, sales $4,500,000, cert: State, City, WBENC)

7218 Valley Screen Process Company, Inc.
58740 Executive Dr
Mishawaka, IN 46544
Contact: Karen Barnett CEO
Tel: 574-256-0901
Email: karenb@valleyscreen.com
Website: www.valleyscreen.com
Commercial screen & digital printing. (Woman, estab 1967,
empl 50, sales $7,445,882, cert: WBENC)

Kansas

7219 Total Print Solutions, Inc.
3220 W 121st Terr
Leawood, KS 66209
Contact: Constance Kingsley President
Tel: 913-481-7393
Email: ckingsley@tpsmidwest.com
Website: www.tpsmidwest.com
Commercial printing, pharma labels, digital print, maga-
zine type publications, business forms, direct mail,
warehousing & distribution. (Minority, Woman, estab
2000, empl 2, sales $800,000, cert: State, NMSDC)

Kentucky

7220 EDJ Inc.
8158 Mall Rd
Florence, KY 41042
Contact: Maureen Schuler President
Tel: 859-525-1199
Email: maureen.schuler@fastsigns.com
Website: www.fastsigns.com/226
Banners, posters, foam boards, decals,
site signs, dimensional logos, coroplast signs, now hiring
signs, production boards,
& tradeshow products and graphics. (Woman, estab 1995,
empl 5, sales $856,000, cert: WBENC)

7221 Multi-Craft Litho, Inc.
131 E Sixth St
Newport, KY 41072
Contact: Debbie Simpson President
Tel: 859-655-8863
Email: dsimpson@multi-craft.com
Website: www.multi-craft.com
Commercial printing: pocket folders, annual reports,
posters, brochures, sell sheets, packaging, etc. (Woman,
estab 1955, empl 50, sales $9,500,000, cert: WBENC)

Louisiana

7222 Advanced Graphic Engraving, LLC
3105 Melancon Rd
Broussard, LA 70518
Contact: Monica Duplantis Mgr
Tel: 337-364-1991
Email: monica@tagsfast.com
Website: www.tagsfast.com
Industrial Engraving: Safety Signage, Architectural
signage, Vinyl signs & decals, Master/Well Control
Panels, Sub Sea Well Control Panels, Flow Schematics,
Data Tags, Operating Instruction Tags, Dual Language
Tags, Angle Indicators, Crane Hand Signals. (Woman,
estab 1997, empl 21, sales $2,000,000, cert: WBENC)

7223 Walle Corporation
600 Elmwood Park Blvd
Harahan, LA 70123
Contact: Dave Taylor Business Devel
Tel: 504-734-8000
Email: dave_taylor@walle.com
Website: www.walle.com
Lithographic & flexographic label printing. (Woman,
estab , empl 175, sales , cert: WBENC)

Massachusetts

7224 Adam Graphic Corporation
16 Mason Ave Unit 4
North Attleboro, MA 02760
Contact: Nancy Ruo President
Tel: 508-699-2089
Email: nancy@adamgraphic.com
Website: www.adamgraphic.com
Printing, print management, forms, envelopes, marketing brochures, folders, binders, ID cards, labels,
commerical print, digital print, signage, mailings,
fulfillment, kitting, warehousing, on-line ordering,
promotional products. (Woman, estab 1985, empl 5,
sales $1,193,045, cert: State, WBENC)

7225 CSW Inc.
45 Tyburski Rd
Ludlow, MA 01056
Contact: Scott Ellison VP Sales
Tel: 800-800-9522
Email: scotte@cswgraphics.com
Website: www.cswgraphics.com
Packaging pre press, design, flexo plates, cutting dies.
(Woman, estab 1936, empl 150, sales $16,160,013, cert:
State, WBENC)

7226 Gangi Printing, Inc.
17 Kensington Ave
Somerville, MA 02145
Contact: Stephen Gangi Sales
Tel: 617-776-6071
Email: steve@gangiprinting.com
Website: www.gangiprinting.com
Promotional printing & book binding services, printed apparel, trade show displays & direct mail pieces. (Woman, estab 1972, empl 9, sales $1,200,000, cert: State)

7227 Print & More Associates
143 North St
Mattapoisett, MA 02739
Contact: Fred Ford Sales Rep
Tel: 617-899-3664
Email: frford@p-massociates.com
Website: www.p-massociates.com
Commercial printing, stationary, brochures, catalogs, window displays, POP, floor mats & banners. (AA, estab 2005, empl 6, sales $1,000,000, cert: NMSDC)

7228 Pyramid Printing and Advertising Inc
58 Mathewson Dr
Weymouth, MA 02189
Contact: Bill Scheufele Sales Rep
Tel: 781-337-7609
Email: bill@pyramidprinting.net
Website: www.pyramidprinting.net
Multicolor offset & digital graphics. (Woman, estab 1978, empl 14, sales $1,400,000, cert: State)

7229 Schmidt Printing, Inc.
237 Chandler St
Worcester, MA 01609
Contact: Ariel Schmidt Dir Sales/Marketing
Tel: 508-752-7600
Email: ariel@schmidtprinting.ink
Website: www.schmidtprinting.ink
Eight Color Offset Printing, HP Indigo Printing, Variable Data Printing, Stochastic Screening, Online Remote Proofing, In-House Mailing Services, Full Service Bindery & Fulfillment. (Hisp, estab 2011, empl 2, sales , cert: NMSDC)

7230 Shafiis' Inc.
PO Box 215
East Longmeadow, MA 01028
Contact: Jennifer Shafii CEO
Tel: 413-224-2100
Email: jennifer@tigerpress.com
Website: www.tigerpress.com
Custom printing, digital prepress, packaging & bindery services. (Woman, estab 1985, empl 70, sales $8,800,000, cert: State)

7231 Spotlight Graphics, Inc.
9-B Whalley Way
Southwick, MA 01077
Contact: DIANE DEMARCO Sales
Tel: 413-998-3232
Email: info@SpotlightGraphicsInc.com
Website: www.SpotlightGraphicsInc.com
Large format printing. (Woman, estab 2013, empl 5, sales $165,000, cert: State, WBENC)

7232 Standard Modern Company, Inc.
186 Duchaine Blvd.
New Bedford, MA 02745
Contact: Bob Crowell Sales
Tel: 508-586-4300
Email: bcrowell@standardmodern.com
Website: www.standardmodern.com
Commercial printing. (Woman, estab 1974, empl 44, sales $7,596,467, cert: WBENC)

7233 Starburst Printing & Graphics
300 Hopping Brook Rd
Holliston, MA 01764
Contact: Jason Grondin VP
Tel: 800-244-8396
Email: jgrondin@starburstprinting.com
Website: www.starburstprinting.com
Printing svcs: prepress, digital & offset & post press services. (Hisp, estab 1988, empl 22, sales $2,600,000, cert: State, NMSDC)

7234 Summit Press Inc.
63 Sixth St
Chelsea, MA 02150
Contact: Lenore DelVecchio President
Tel: 617-889-3991
Email: lsava@summitpress.com
Website: www.summitpress.com
Printing services: 2-6 color sheetfed. (Woman, estab 1961, empl 22, sales $2,910,000, cert: State)

7235 The Matlet Group
30 Industrial Way
Wilmington, MA 01887
Contact: Sheldon Ross Dir of Natl Accounts
Tel: 401-834-3007
Email: sross@thematletgroup.com
Website: www.thematletgroup.com
Printing & graphic services. (As-Pac, estab 2005, empl 408, sales $99,498,000, cert: NMSDC)

Maryland

7236 Alpha Graphics, Inc.
1750 Union Ave, Unit B
Baltimore, MD 21211
Contact: Christine Walsh President
Tel: 410-727-1400
Email: cwalsh@alphagrap.com
Website: www.alpha-graphics.net
Large format printing: banners & signs, posters, mounting, laminating, framing, graphic design, menu boards, point of purchase, adhesive vinyl, cut vinyl, trade show display (Woman, estab 1972, empl 7, sales $853,948, cert: State, City, WBENC)

7237 Art & Negative Graphics, Inc.
4621 Boston Way Ste C
Lanham, MD 20706
Contact: Adrienne Myers Strategic Acct Exec
Tel: 301-459-8911
Email: amyers@artneg.com
Website: www.artneg.com
Prepress, digital & offset printing; full bindery; mailing services; storage and fulfillment. (Woman, estab 1981, empl 42, sales $6,425,530, cert: State, WBENC)

7238 Black Classic Press
3921 Vero Rd Ste F
Halethorpe, MD 21227
Contact: Principal
Tel: 410-242-6954
Email:
Website: www.bcpdigital.com
Printing svcs: ultra short-run book & document printing, digital. (AA, estab 1978, empl 9, sales $1,500,000, cert: State)

7239 Britt's Industries Inc.
40 Hudson St Ste 112
Annapolis, MD 21401
Contact: President
Tel: 410-266-8100
Email: contact@wosbprinting.com
Website: www.wosbprinting.com
Commercial printing, offset, digital, prepress, graphic design, business cards, envelopes, letterhead, brochures, pamphlets. (Woman/As-Pac, estab 1976, empl , sales $784,035, cert: WBENC, 8(a))

7240 Centaur Graphics LLC
12109 Glissans Mill Rd
Union Bridge, MD 21791
Contact: Carl wurzer VP Sales
Tel: 202-297-7575
Email: carl@centaurgraphics.com
Website: www.centaurgraphics.com
Commercial Printing, Direct Mail Printing, Digital Printing, Labels, Envelopes, Fulfillment, Warehousing, Logistics, Mailing , packaging, assembly, print on demand, web to print, saddle stich, perfect bound. (Woman, estab 1994, empl 4, sales $784,000, cert: WBENC)

7241 IVY Services, LLC
PO Box 20092
Baltimore, MD 21284
Contact: Tammy Boccia VP
Tel: 410-235-1489
Email: tboccia@ivy-services.com
Website: www.ivy-services.com
Offset printing: letterhead, envelopes, business cards, brochures, flyers, string & button, metal clasp, latex, peel & seal, tear strip & shrink wrapping. (Woman, estab 2004, empl 2, sales $5,511,950, cert: State, WBENC)

7242 Strouse
1211 Independence Way
Westminster, MD 21157
Contact: Scott Chambers Business Devel Mgr
Tel: 410-848-1611
Email: dchambers@strouse.com
Website: www.strouse.com
Rotary die-cutting, slitting, 6 color printing, laminations. (Woman, estab 1986, empl 70, sales $18,500,000, cert: WBENC)

Michigan

7243 Argent Tape & Label, Inc.
41016 Concept Dr, Ste A
Plymouth, MI 48170
Contact: Lynn Perenic President
Tel: 734-582-9955
Email: lperenic@argent-label.com
Website: www.argent-label.com
Custom tape and label solutions. (Woman, estab 1995, empl 20, sales $14,000,000, cert: WBENC)

7244 Graphic Resource Group
528 Robbins Dr
Troy, MI 48083
Contact: Allen Pyc President
Tel: 248-588-6100
Email: apyc@graphicresource.com
Website: www.graphicresource.com
Large format digital & screen printing, offset printing on plastics, promotional products. (Woman, estab 1990, empl 20, sales , cert: WBENC)

7245 Graywolf Printing
757 S Eton St
Birmingham, MI 48009
Contact: Max Grayvold President
Tel: 248-540-5930
Email: graywolf@ameritech.net
Website: www.graywolfprinting.com/
Printing services. (Nat Ame, estab 0, empl 0, sales $772,368, cert: NMSDC)

7246 Hatteras Printing, Inc.
12801 Prospect St
Dearborn, MI 48126
Contact: Rebecca McFarlane VP
Tel: 313-624-3300
Email: bmcfarlane@4hatteras.com
Website: www.4hatteras.com
Commercial printing. (Woman, estab 1977, empl 70, sales , cert: WBENC)

7247 Imax Company Inc.
22326 Woodward Ave
Ferndale, MI 48220
Contact: Jay Williams President
Tel: 248-629-9680
Email: jay@imaxprinting.com
Website: www.imaxprinting.com
Commercial printing, offset full color printing, multi page booklets, manuals, business cards, brochures, sales sheets, envelopes, posters, postcards, flyers, rack cards, special shapes (die cutting). (AA, estab 2009, empl 5, sales $879,852, cert: NMSDC)

7248 Impact Label Corp.
3434 S Burdick St
Kalamazoo, MI 49001
Contact: Jill Jones Acct Mgr
Tel: 269-381-4280
Email: jillj@impactlabel.com
Website: www.impactlabel.com
Labels, domed labels,tamper evident labels, name-plates, tags, polycarbonate overlays, control panel overlays, warning labels, product identification, serial numbers, security tags, inventory tags, asset labels, ingredient labels. (Woman, estab 1964, empl 50, sales , cert: WBENC)

7249 Kimprint, Inc. dba Progressive Printing
1326 Goldsmith
Plymouth, MI 48170
Contact: Bruce Price vp
Tel: 734-459-2960
Email: sales@progressiveprint.com
Website: www.progressiveprint.com
Full color printing: flyers, brochures, postcards, directmail, stock & color consulting. (Woman, estab 1989, empl 20, sales $2,300,000, cert: WBENC)

7250   New Echelon
280 S Southbound Gratiot Ave
Mt. Clemens, MI 48043
Contact: Michael Arnold President
Tel: 586-307-8001
Email: mcarnold@newechelon.com
Website: www.newechelon.com
Printing, bindery, big color output services. (AA, estab 1996, empl 8, sales , cert: NMSDC)

7251   Stylerite Label Corporation
2140 Avon Industrial Dr
Rochester Hills, MI 48309
Contact: Danielle J. Kay Sales Exec
Tel: 419-367-3772
Email: dkay@styleritelabel.com
Website: www.styleritelabel.com
Mfr Tags & Forms, short to long runs, 4 color process up to 8 colors, rolls, sheets, singles, fan-folded, continuous, printing on adhesive side of labels, lamination, UV varnish. (Woman, estab 1989, empl 25, sales $6,200,000, cert: WBENC)

7252   The MardonGroup LLC
701 Woodward Heights Ste 128
Ferndale, MI 48220
Contact: Shawn Torrence VP Business Dev
Tel: 248-336-3376
Email: s.torrence@mardongroup.com
Website: www.mardongroup.com
Sheet-Fed Printing, Digital Printing, Design, Creative, Layout, Binding, Envelopes, Mail list Processing, List Rental/Purchase, Offline Finishing, Digital/Mobile marketing. (AA, estab 2005, empl 15, sales , cert: NMSDC)

Minnesota

7253   Booth Publications Ink
1217 Seminole Ave
West St Paul, MN 55118
Contact: Jason Booth CEO
Tel: 651-338-8140
Email: jason@boothpublications.com
Website: www.boothpublications.com
Print services: off-set (web & sheet fed), digital, large format & plastic card printing. (Nat Ame, estab 1999, empl 6, sales $3,000,000, cert: NMSDC)

7254   Bromley Printing, Inc.
514 Northdale Blvd
Minneapolis, MN 55448
Contact: Elizabeth Bromley President
Tel: 763-767-0000
Email: elizabeth@bromleyprinting.com
Website: www.bromleyprinting.com
Printing, graphic design & marketing, multi-color printing, digital printing, in-house pre-press, graphic design, bindery & mailing services. (Woman, estab 1986, empl 10, sales , cert: WBENC)

7255   Bywater Business Solutions LLC
800 Washington Ave SE Ste 203
Minneapolis, MN 55414
Contact: Christopher Ferguson CEO
Tel: 763-244-1090
Email: chris@bywater.co
Website: www.bywater.co
Printing: envelopes, labels, letterhead, notecards, folders, business forms, booklets, checks, business cards, direct mail, signs, annual reports, post-it notes. (Hisp, estab 2009, empl 3, sales $185,000, cert: State)

7256   Char-Dell Sign Co.
1017 109th Ave NE
Blaine, MN 55434
Contact: Charlette Grandell VP
Tel: 763-784-8252
Email: ken.grandell@fastsigns.com
Website: www.fastsigns.com/337
Wide Format Digital Printing, Banners, Banner Stands, Trade Show Booths, Trade Show Graphics, ADA & OSHA Compliant, Safety & Identification Materials, Presentation Materials, Posters, Name Tags, Large & Small Vehicle. (Woman, estab 1998, empl 4, sales $400,000, cert: City)

7257   Cimarron Graphics
15400 28th Ave N
Plymouth, MN 55447
Contact: Barbara Schulz CEO
Tel: 952-697-3400
Email: barb@cimgraphics.com
Website: www.cimgraphics.com
Commercial sheet fed & digital printing: brochures, postcards, catalogs, business forms, calendars, tabs, magnets, greeting cards, envelopes, letterhead, labels, annual reports, flyers, header cards, inserts, pocket folders. (Woman, estab 2004, empl 15, sales $1,598,609, cert: State)

7258   Clear Lake Press, Inc.
300 16th Ave SE
Waseca, MN 56093
Contact: Phyllis Beschnett CEO
Tel: 507-835-4430
Email: pbeschnett@clearlakepress.com
Website: www.clearlakepress.com
Marketing & printing solutions, sheet-fed, digital & variable, fulfillment, design services, collateral development & direct marketing, outdoor advertising & customized apparel services. (Woman, estab 1988, empl 34, sales $4,099,574, cert: WBENC)

7259   Dan Dolan Printing
2301 E Hennepin Ave
Minneapolis, MN 55413
Contact: Jeanne Dolan CEO
Tel: 612-379-2311
Email: jeannedolan@dolanprinting.com
Website: www.dolanprinting.com
Printing & marketing services: offset/lithographic printing, digital printing, large format printing, signage, banners, publications, business cards, textile printing, light boxes, trade show displays, pamphlet, letterhead, stationary, printed packaging. (Woman, estab 1985, empl 28, sales $6,434,227, cert: WBENC)

7260   Docunet Corporation
2435 Xenium Ln N
Plymouth, MN 55441
Contact: Wendy Morical President
Tel: 800-936-2863
Email: wnm@docunetworks.com
Website: www.docunetworks.com
Digital printing: black & white, color, database management, direct mail & fulfillment. (Woman, estab 1991, empl 12, sales $1,790,000, cert: WBENC)

7261 Highlight Printing Inc.
3839 Washington Ave N
Minneapolis, MN 55412
Contact: Lisa Bickford President
Tel: 612-522-7600
Email: lisab@highlightprinting.com
Website: www.highlightprinting.com
Offset & digital 1-4 color printing, high-impact high-touch projects, thermography, design, direct mail, warehousing, kitting, niche fulfillment, distribution, work-flow system, saddle stitching, wire-o binding, binding. (Woman, estab , empl , sales $1,205,000, cert: WBENC)

7262 Ideal Printers
645 Olive St
Saint Paul, MN 55130
Contact: Emily Stevenson Acct Rep
Tel: 651-855-1064
Email: emily.stevenson@idealprint.com
Website: www.idealprint.com
Commercial sheetfed printing: 1-6 color & aqueous coating, brochures, newsletters, annual reports, posters, catalogs, packaging, stationary products. (Woman, estab 1979, empl 85, sales $12,625,028, cert: WBENC)

7263 IntegriPrint, Inc.
309 12th Ave S
Buffalo, MN 55313
Contact: Jacqueline Wurm Owner
Tel: 763-682-3750
Email: jackie@integriprint.com
Website: www.integriprint.com
Printing, graphic design & mailing services. (Woman, estab 1994, empl 5, sales $590,338, cert: WBENC)

7264 Lightning Printing dba Wallace Carlson Co.
10825 Greenbrier Rd
Minnetonka, MN 55305
Contact: Ann Turbeville CEO
Tel: 952-277-1210
Email: ann@wc-print.com
Website: www.wc-print.com
Printing svcs: 1-6color offset, sheetfed, aqueous coating, full color & B/W digital printing, mailing & fullfillment services. (Woman, estab 1984, empl 47, sales $9,128,000, cert: WBENC)

7265 Northstar Imaging Services, Inc.
1325 Eagandale Court Ste 130
Eagan, MN 55121
Contact: Martha Smyre CEO
Tel: 651-686-0477
Email: planroom@northstarimaging.com
Website: www.northstarimaging.com
Reprographic services, large & small format copying, plotting, scanning, color imagery & document management. (Woman, estab 1997, empl 5, sales $6,500,000, cert: State, City)

7266 SeaChange Print Innovations
14505 27th Ave N
Plymouth, MN 55447
Contact: Nancy Servais Business Devel
Tel: 763-586-3700
Email: nancy.servais@seachangem.com
Website: www.seachangemn.com
Folding carton & marketing print production, Folding Carton Packaging, Marketing Printing, Commercial Printing, Direct Mail Printing, Digital Printing. (Woman, estab 2014, empl 90, sales $13,100,000, cert: WBENC)

7267 Team One Printing, Inc.
635 Ninth St SE, Ste 180
Minneapolis, MN 55414
Contact: Grace Wong President
Tel: 612-481-5907
Email: grace@teamoneprinting.com
Website: www.teamoneprinting.com
Commercial print & display graphics: brochures, newsletters, manuals, directories, catalogs, labels, direct mail pieces, portable trade show displays, banner stands, wall murals, vehicle graphics, sign & banner graphics, large format posters. (Minority, Woman, estab 2006, empl 3, sales , cert: NMSDC)

Missouri

7268 Complete Solutions LLC
2233 N Village
St. Charles, MO 63303
Contact: Donna Gastreich Owner
Tel: 314-640-6633
Email: dgastreich@complete-solutionsllc.com
Website: www.complete-solutionsllc.com
Printing svcs: letterhead, business cards, envelopes, invoices, BOL, labels, tags, folders, binders, index tabs, brochures, catalogs & checks, direct mail services, promotional products & advertising specialty items. (Woman, estab 2008, empl 1, sales , cert: State, City)

7269 Isringhaus Printing LLC
11012 Lin Valle Dr, Ste D
Affton, MO 63123
Contact: Patricia Isringhaus Owner
Tel: 314-416-9955
Email: patti@isringhausprinting.com
Website: www.isringhausprinting.com
Commercial printing services. (Woman, estab 2002, empl 6, sales $600,000, cert: State, WBENC)

7270 Modern Litho-Print Co.
6009 Stertzer Rd
Jefferson City, MO 65101
Contact: Debra Patterson Cstmr Service
Tel: 573-635-6119
Email: debra@modernlitho.com
Website: www.modernlitho.com
Printing: annual reports, newsletters, books, magazines, promotional materials, labels, etc. (Woman, estab 1937, empl 88, sales $14,500,000, cert: State)

7271 PrintCOR Solutions
826 Heatherhaven Dr
Ballwin, MO 63011
Contact: Kelly Kohn Owner
Tel: 636-891-9900
Email: customerservice@printcorsolutions.com
Website: www.printcorsolutions.com
Labels/tags: blank stock labels, barcode pre-printed product labels, consecutively numbered barcode labels, thermal ribbons, integrated labels, piggy back labels, full color labels, die cut labels & custom labels. (Woman, estab 2006, empl 2, sales $1,500,000, cert: State)

7272   PrintFlex Graphics
        2201 January Ave
        St. Louis, MO 63110
        Contact: Elizabeth Pecha-Poelker CEO
        Tel: 800-406-7093
        Email: eap@print-flex.com
        Website: www.printflexgraphics.com
Promotional printing: instant redeemable coupons, dry
release, folded & placed booklets, USDA & FDA direct food
contact printing. (Woman, estab 1995, empl 35, sales
$6,128,000, cert: State, NWBOC)

Mississippi

7273   Ranger Distributing, Inc dba Ranger Label
        286 Commerce Park Dr
        Ridgeland, MS 39157
        Contact: Bob Anger VP
        Tel: 601-898-1380
        Email: banger@rangerlabel.com
        Website: www.rangerlabel.com
Prime 8 color pressure sensitive labels, blank thermal
labels, complete color process controls. (Woman, estab
1979, empl 14, sales $3,000,000, cert: WBENC)

North Carolina

7274   DocuSource of North Carolina
        2800 Slater Rd
        Morrisville, NC 27560
        Contact: Michael Chorba President
        Tel: 919-459-5909
        Email: mchorba@docusourceofnc.com
        Website: www.docusourceofnc.com
Commercial digital printing, bindery, fulfillment & distribution services. (Woman, estab 2002, empl 46, sales
$8,000,000, cert: State)

7275   Labels, Tags & Inserts, Inc.
        2302 Air Park Dr
        Burlington, NC 27215
        Contact: Rhonda Baker President
        Tel: 336-227-8485
        Email: rhondab@lti-us.com
        Website: www.labelstagsandinserts.com
Flexographic printing services: pressure sensitive labels,
shrink film sleeves, vinyl labels, scratch off labels, tamper-
evident labels, clear labels, hot foil labels, embossed
labels, holographic labels. (Woman, estab 1995, empl 27,
sales $7,000,000, cert: WBENC)

7276   PharmaPress, Inc.
        3360 Old Lexington Rd
        Winston-Salem, NC 27107
        Contact: Terri Roth President
        Tel: 973-376-6625
        Email: pharmapress@gmail.com
        Website: www.pharmapressinc.com
Mfr inserts, outserts, booklets, pamphlets, cards and pads.
(Woman, estab 2004, empl 164, sales $2,400,000, cert:
State)

7277   Progressive Business Solutions, Inc.
        508 New Hope Rd
        Raleigh, NC 27610
        Contact: Tim Catlett President
        Tel: 919-255-6500
        Email: tcatlett@progform.com
        Website: www.progform.com
Commercial printing, business forms, promotional products, copy & computer paper, web ordering capabilities,
office supplies, forms mgmt & warehouse dist. (AA, estab
1988, empl , sales $6,000,000, cert: NMSDC)

7278   Southern Print & Imaging, Inc.
        9311-D Monroe Rd
        Charlotte, NC 28270
        Contact: Barbara Jones President
        Tel: 704-708-5818
        Email: barbara@allegracharlotte.com
        Website: www.allegracharlotte.com
Offset & digital printing, mail services, list sourcing,
direct mail, brochures, flyers, newsletters, postcards,
booklets & promotional products. (Woman, estab 2004,
empl 4, sales $411,000, cert: City)

New Jersey

7279   4 Banner Inc. (DBA Alchemy Printing)
        125 5th Ave
        Paterson, NJ 07524
        Contact: Brett Haikins Production Coordinator
        Tel: 973-341-1311
        Email: jobs@4banner.com
        Website: www.4banner.com
Large format printing: vinyl banners, mesh banners, dye
sublimation fabric banners, trade show displays, banner
stands, flatbed UV printing. Printing up to 10ft seamless.
(As-Pac, estab 2010, empl 6, sales $550,000, cert:
NMSDC)

7280   A+ Letter Service
        200 Syracuse Ct
        Lakewood, NJ 08701
        Contact: Elizabeth Fricke Sales Support Sspecialist
        Tel: 732-905-2010
        Email: aplus@aplusletter.com
        Website: www.aplusletter.com
Print mailing inserts, postcards, brochures, marketing
fulfillment, four-color digital printing, mailing services.
(Woman, estab 1986, empl 75, sales $5,000,000, cert:
State)

7281   AJ Images.com
        259 E First Ave
        Roselle, NJ 07203
        Contact: Lisa Greebel
        Tel: 908-241-6900
        Email: lisa@ajimages.com
        Website: www.ajimages.com
Commercial printing: brochures, newsletters, annual
reports, magazines, technical pieces, posters, postcards,
bill stuffers, direct mail, price lists & catalogs. (Woman,
estab 1967, empl 23, sales $4,500,000, cert: State)

7282   Arna Marketing
        60 Readington Road
        Branchburg, NJ 08876
        Contact: Jakob Hegna Sales Rep
        Tel: 908-231-1100
        Email: jhegna@arnamarketing.com
        Website: www.arnamarketing.com
Digital printing: mailings, brochures, flyers, booklets,
envelopes, letterhead, business cards, newsletters,
coupons, etc. (Woman, estab 2005, empl 80, sales
$40,000,000, cert: WBENC)

7283   Capital Printing Corporation
        420 South Ave
        Middlesex, NJ 08846
        Contact: Brett Russo
        Tel: 732-560-1515
        Email: brettr@capitalprintingcorp.com
        Website: www.capitalprintingcorp.com
Printing services, die cutting & binding, automated in-line gluing & inserting, warehouse & mailing abilities. (Woman, estab 1983, empl 85, sales $15,100,000, cert: WBENC)

7284   CCG Marketing Services
        14 Henderson Dr
        West Caldwell, NJ 07006
        Contact: Steve Stern Sr Acct Exec
        Tel: 973-808-0009
        Email: sstern@corpcomm.com
        Website: www.ccgms.com
Printing, offset, digital with variable data, web 1:1 Marketing with Variable Data, Digital Print Technology, Sales Collateral & Promotional Materials, Sales Force Support, Order Fulfillment. (Woman, estab , empl , sales $20,000,000, cert: WBENC)

7285   CRW Graphics
        9100 Pennsauken Hwy
        Pennsauken, NJ 08110
        Contact: Kathleen Chinnici Acct Dir
        Tel: 800-820-3000
        Email: kchinnici@crwgraphics.com
        Website: www.crwgraphics.com
Digital & critical color prepress services & printing: 1 to 6 colors, bindery, fulfillment & mailing services. (Woman, estab 1993, empl 90, sales $15,500,000, cert: WBENC)

7286   Direct Mail Depot
        200 Circle Dr N
        Piscataway, NJ 08854
        Contact: Terrie Stonack President
        Tel: 305-819-1065
        Email: tstonack@dtsdirectmail.com
        Website: www.directmaildepot.com
Postal services, digital printing, finishing, lettershop services, data processing, mail tracking & handling & fulfillment services (Woman/Hisp, estab 1999, empl 150, sales $14,300,000, cert: State)

7287   Federal Business Products Inc.
        150 Clove Road, 5th Floor 5th Fl
        Little Falls, NJ 07424
        Contact: Angela Stubbs President
        Tel: 973-272-7066
        Email: astubbs@feddirect.com
        Website: www.feddirect.com
Print, direct mail data & fulfillment services: data processing, sheet digital print, continuous form printing to 10 colors, continuous form laser (simplex, duplex, MICR) & inkjet personalization, bindery, fulfillment lettershop mailing services. (Woman, estab , empl , sales $15,663,435, cert: WBENC)

7288   FrontEnd Graphics Inc.
        1951 Old Cuthbert Road, Ste 414
        Cherry Hill, NJ 08034
        Contact: Elizabeth Maul President
        Tel: 856-547-1600
        Email: bettymaul@frontendgraphics.com
        Website: www.frontendgraphics.com
Layout, design, database mgmt, large project mgmt, digital photography, large output, direct to plate & press, finishing, distribution, kitting, mailing. Sheet fed, web, envelopes, label, manual, technical illustration, book publishing. (Woman, estab 1983, empl 13, sales $1,300,000, cert: WBENC)

7289   HighRoad Press, LLC
        220 Anderson Ave
        Moonachie, NJ 07074
        Contact: Hallie Satz CEO
        Tel: 201-708-6900
        Email: hallie@highroadpress.com
        Website: www.highroadpress.com
Printing: web & sheet fed, offset sheet fed printing up to 8/C aqueous coating, offset half web didde press, coldset web & offset full web, packaging & DVD packaging. (Woman, estab 2004, empl 45, sales $10,000,000, cert: State, WBENC)

7290   Industrial Labeling Systems, Inc.
        50 Kulick Rd
        Fairfield, NJ 07004
        Contact: Keith Meyer Reg Sales Mgr
        Tel: 973-882-9688
        Email: kmeyer@e-ilsi.com
        Website: www.e-ilsi.com
Mfr & dist pressure-sensitive labels, prime labels, mailing labels, product ID labels, direct thermal labels, supermarket thermal scale labels, coupons, bar codes, tub labels, retail shelf marketing labels. (As-Pac, estab 1997, empl 23, sales $3,500,000, cert: State)

7291   Mahin Impressions, Inc. DBA Kirkwood Mahin
        600 Meadowlands Pkwy
        Secaucus, NJ 07094
        Contact: Sharon Mahin President
        Tel: 201-870-6300
        Email: smahin@kirkwood-mahin.com
        Website: www.kirkwood-mahin.com/
Offset & digital printing, digital & xerograhpy services, large format, finishing, binding, fullfillment & mailing. (Woman, estab 1983, empl 250, sales $20,000,000, cert: WBENC, SDB)

7292   Mountain Printing Company Inc.
        PO Box 608
        Berlin, NJ 08009
        Contact: Mark DiClementi Dir of Operations
        Tel: 856-767-7600
        Email: mark@mountainprinting.com
        Website: www.mountainprinting.com
Commerical, packaging & digial printing services: bindery, pre-press, press, bindery, coatings, die cutting, foil stamping, embossing, box manufacturing & mailing capabilities. (Woman, estab 1962, empl 25, sales $2,499,116, cert: State)

7293   P/EK Press
7 Essex Rd
Scotch Plains, NJ 07076
Contact: Ann Kahn Owner
Tel: 908-305-1960
Email: annelizabethkahn@gmail.com
Website: www.pekpress.com
Commercial printing & graphic design: NCR forms, Brochures, Stationery, Posters, Direct Mail, Envelopes, Business Cards, Postcards, Presentation Folders, Pads. (Woman, estab 1989, empl 1, sales $126,000, cert: State)

7294   Positive Publications LLC
65 Madison Ave Ste 510
Morristown, NJ 07960
Contact: Susan Poeton COO
Tel: 973-218-0310
Email: spoeton@positivepublications.us
Website: www.positivepublications.us
Publishing, magazines, guides, pamphlets, periodicals, reprints, newsletters & e-newsletters. (Woman, estab 1998, empl 8, sales $827,880, cert: State)

7295   Primary Colors Graphics Inc.
629 Grove St 7th Fl
Jersey City, NJ 07310
Contact: Cecilia Chin Controller
Tel: 201-526-9300
Email: cecilia@primarycolorsgraphics.com
Website: www.primarycolorsgraphics.com
Commercial Offset Printing, Lithographic Printing, business cards, posters, finishing, trimming, die-cut, score, foil stamping, embossing. (As-Pac, estab 2012, empl 12, sales $1,303,673, cert: State)

7296   Riegel Printing Inc.
One Graphics Dr
Ewing, NJ 08628
Contact: Brian Haley President
Tel: 609-771-0555
Email: brian.haley@riegelprintinginc.com
Website: www.riegelprintinginc.com
Commercial printing svcs: pre-press, bindery, one to six color. (Woman, estab 1935, empl 75, sales $28,000,000, cert: WBENC)

7297   RJ Graphics, Inc.
206 Crown Point Rd
West Deptford, NJ 08086
Contact: John Iannelli Dir
Tel: 856-848-1986
Email: jiannelli@rjgraphicsprinting.com
Website: www.rjgraphicsprinting.com
Commercial sheet-fed printing, digital printing, fulfillment, direct mail & web creative services. (Woman, estab 1979, empl 22, sales $3,300,000, cert: WBENC)

7298   Sheroy Printing
220 Entin Rd
Clifton, NJ 07014
Contact: Robert Sternau Dir New Business Dev
Tel: 973-242-4040
Email: roberts@onesourcenj.com
Website: www.onesourcenj.com
Graphic communications, marketing collateral, annual reports, catalogs, presentation kits, packaging, wide format point-of-purchase materials, direct mail & publications. (Woman, estab 1984, empl 65, sales $2,000,000, cert: State)

7299   Wheal-Grace Corporation
300 Ralph St
Belleville, NJ 07109
Contact: Emil Salvini Dir of Marketing
Tel: 973-450-8100
Email: salvini@wheal-grace.com
Website: www.wheal-grace.com
Corporate literature, product info, news magazines, business cards, letterheads, portfolios, posters. (Woman, estab 1946, empl 16, sales $11,301,000, cert: State)

New Mexico

7300   Captiva Group
3838 Bogan Ave NE
Albuquerque, NM 87109
Contact: Jane Fernandez VP Business Dev
Tel: 505-872-2200
Email: jfernandez@thecaptivagroup.com
Website: www.thecaptivagroup.com
Four color offset commercial printing; newsletters, business forms, envelopes, posters, books, etc. (Hisp, estab 1981, empl 100, sales $22,000,000, cert: NMSDC)

7301   R.W. Chavez, Inc.
1361 Flight Way SE
Albuquerque, NM 87106
Contact: Nate Tapia Sales
Tel: 505-264-2453
Email: nate@stixon.com
Website: www.stixon.com
Commercial flexographic printing & mfr labels, pressure sensitive labels. (Minority, Woman, estab 1985, empl 15, sales $2,800,000, cert: NWBOC)

Nevada

7302   Haig's Quality Printing
6360 Sunset Corporate Dr
Las Vegas, NV 89120
Contact: Garo Atamian VP
Tel: 702-966-1000
Email: gatamian@haigsprinting.com
Website: www.haigsprinting.com
Commercial print and mail shop, off-set and digital. (Woman, estab 1996, empl 25, sales $3,500,000, cert: WBENC)

New York

7303   Ampie Enterprises, Inc.
100 College Ave Ste 130
Rochester, NY 14607
Contact: Tina Paradiso President
Tel: 585-482-4400
Email: tinap@imprintablesolutions.com
Website: www.imprintablesolutions.com
Envelopes, forms, carbonless sheets, reports, brochures & informational collateral. (Woman, estab 2013, empl 8, sales $1,500,000, cert: State)

7304   Bell Imaging Inc.
2055 Cruger Ave, Ste 5E
Bronx County, NY 10462
Contact: Megan Blackburn Sales Mgr
Tel: 862-262-6128
Email: mblackburn@bellimagingonline.com
Website: www.bellimagingonline.com
Printing services, 1 to 6 color, commercial & direct mail, bindery, pre-press, fullfilment. (AA, estab 2004, empl 8, sales , cert: NMSDC)

7305 Brigar XPress Solutions Inc, dba Digital XPress
5 Sand Creek Rd
Albany, NY 12205
Contact: Tracy Terry VP Sales
Tel: 518-437-5349
Email: tracy@dxp1.com
Website: www.dxp1.com
Print and mail services, offset, digital, and large format printing. (Woman, estab 1988, empl 72, sales $9,435,127, cert: State)

7306 Classic Labels Inc.
217 River Ave
Patchogue, NY 11772
Contact: Steven Ayala President
Tel: 718-463-0256
Email: sayala@classiclabels.com
Website: www.classiclabels.com
Specialty pressure sensitive labels. (Hisp, estab 1979, empl 100, sales , cert: NMSDC)

7307 Dakota Print and Premiums LLC
150 Barton Road
White Plains, NY 10605
Contact: Stuart Standard President
Tel: 914-831-9101
Email: stuart@fuseprinting.com
Website: www.fuseprinting.com
Promotional products, commercial printing, wide format & transit advertising, vehicle wraps, directories, transit & marketing tools provider, screen printing, banners, posters, postcards, journals, award items, etc. (Woman/AA, estab 2004, empl 3, sales $606,000, cert: State, City, NMSDC)

7308 Duggal Visual Solutions
63 Flushing Ave, Bldg 25
Brooklyn, NY 11205
Contact: George Whalen CFO
Tel: 212-242-7000
Email: cm@duggal.com
Website: www.duggal.com
Digital Sheet Fed Print, Wide Format Print, Photographic Print, 3D Print, Painting, Mounting, Laser cutting, Routering, Finishing, Framing, Digital Display, Lightboxes, SEG Graphics, Digital Animation. (As-Ind, estab 1963, empl 400, sales $92,000,000, cert: State, City, NMSDC)

7309 Fred Weidner & Daughter Printers
15 Maiden Ln, Ste 1601
New York, NY 10038
Contact: Cynthia Weidner President
Tel: 212-964-8676
Email: cynthia@fwdprinters.com
Website: www.fwdprinters.com
Printing services. (Woman, estab , empl 6, sales , cert: State)

7310 Graphic Arts Inc.
11 Bertel Ave
Mount Vernon, NY 10550
Contact: Wayne Purveille
Tel: 914-663-8395
Email: wp@graphicartsinc.net
Website: www.graphicartsinc.net
Design & print brochures, newsletters, pamphlets, pocket folders, annual reports, sheets catalog mailing inserts, etc. (Woman/AA, estab 1994, empl 9, sales , cert: State, City, NMSDC)

7311 Millennium Signs & Display, Inc.
90 W Graham Ave
Hempstead, NY 11550
Contact: Saj Khalfan President
Tel: 516-292-8000
Email: saj@msdny.com
Website: www.msdny.com
Signs and Graphics; Point of Purchase Displays; Large Format Digital Printing; Wayfinding Signage; 3-Dimensional Letters and Logos; Lenticular Graphics; Laser & Waterjet Cutting; Architectural Signage. (Minority, estab 2008, empl 28, sales $5,255,000, cert: City, NMSDC)

7312 Minority Graphics Inc.
4202 Third Ave
Brooklyn, NY 11232
Contact: FirstName LastName President
Tel: 212-255-4355
Email: alec@minoritygraphics.com
Website: www.minoritygraphics.com
Offset & digital printing, fulfillment. (Woman/AA, estab 2004, empl 3, sales $190,000, cert: City, NMSDC)

7313 No Other Impressions, Inc.
27 Tower Dr
Rochester, NY 14623
Contact: Elaine McCarthy CEO
Tel: 585-436-8500
Email: elaine@nootherimpressions.com
Website: www.nootherimpressions.com
Commercial color printing & fullfillment, digital & offset printing process. Complete in house bindery & fullfillment services. (Woman, estab 1990, empl 15, sales $1,800,000, cert: WBENC)

7314 North American D.F., Inc.
280 Watchogue Rd
Staten Island, NY 10314
Contact: Debbie Ayala President
Tel: 718-698-2500
Email: debbie@northamericandf.com
Website: www.northamericandf.com
Commercial printing: 8 color, web & sheet fed, business forms, brochures, booklets, folders, direct mailers, posters labels. (Woman, estab 1992, empl 10, sales $3,000,000, cert: State, City, WBENC)

7315 Panther Graphics Inc.
465 Central Ave
Rochester, NY 14605
Contact: Henry Ehindero Sales Mgr
Tel: 585-546-7163
Email: henry@panthergraphics.net
Website: www.panthergraphics.net
Commercial printing: brochures, coupons, marketing & promotional materials, large format printing, folding cartons, kit packing & distribution.
 (AA, estab 1993, empl 25, sales $1,035,000, cert: City)

Ohio

7316 Associated Visual Communications, Inc.
200 Cherry Ave NE
Canton, OH 44702
Contact: Raymond J Gonzalez President
Tel: 330-452-4449
Email: rgonzalez@avcprint.com
Website: www.avcprint.com
Printing services: screen, digital & offset. (Hisp, estab 1979, empl 32, sales $2,814,501, cert: NMSDC)

7317 Bridge Media, LLC
1457 E 252nd St Ste 100
Euclid, OH 44117
Contact: Craig Brooks, Sr. President
Tel: 216-526-3044
Email: craig@bridge-ohio.com
Website: www.bridge-ohio.com
Printing: professional business cards, brochures & promotional materials, annual reports & glossy publications. (AA, estab 2008, empl 4, sales , cert: State)

7318 Cannell Graphics
5787 Linworth Rd
Worthington, OH 43085
Contact: Phil Ferguson CEO
Tel: 614-330-9110
Email: pferguson@cannellgraphics.biz
Website: www.cannellgraphics.biz
Large & small digital, screen, offset format, mounting & laminating, scanning, document management, litigation support, copier services. (Woman/AA, estab 1964, empl 7, sales , cert: State, NMSDC)

7319 Commodity Management Services CMS
7233 Freedom Ave. NW
North Canton, OH 44720
Contact: Curt Keels Business Dev Exec
Tel: 614-207-2707
Email: ckeels@cmsprintsolutions.com
Website: www.cmsprintsolutions.com
Printing: business forms, print mgmt, print solutions, labels. (AA, estab 1999, empl 525, sales $72,893,797, cert: NMSDC)

7320 Copy King, Inc.
3333 Chester Ave
Cleveland, OH 44114
Contact: Peg Walsh President
Tel: 216-861-3377
Email: peg@copy-king.com
Website: www.copy-king.com
Digital & offset press printing, binding, in house graphic design services, digital color printing, posters & large format printing, business cards. (Woman, estab 1995, empl 21, sales , cert: City)

7321 Corporate Document Solutions, Inc.
11120 Ashburn Rd
Cincinnati, OH 45240
Contact: Mary Percy President
Tel: 513-595-8200
Email: mpercy@cdsprint.com
Website: www.cdsPRINT.com
Design & pre-press services, layout compatibility, graphic file resolution, press imaging sizes & preferred file submission methods, black & white printing. (Woman, estab 1992, empl 18, sales $2,000,000, cert: WBENC)

7322 Dana Graphics, Inc.
PO Box 42219
Cincinnati, OH 45242
Contact: Debbie Coad Mgr, cstmr service
Tel: 513-351-4400
Email: debbie@danalink.com
Website: www.danalink.com
Graphic design, commercial & digital printing. (Woman, estab 1980, empl 8, sales $387,000, cert: WBENC)

7323 Dancor Inc.
2155 Dublin Rd
Columbus, OH 43228
Contact: Michael Michalski Controller
Tel: 614-737-3221
Email: mmichalski@dancorinc.com
Website: www.dancorinc.com
Commercial printing. (Woman, estab 0, empl , sales $8,041,000, cert: WBENC)

7324 DINATCO Inc.
814 Morrison Rd
Gahanna, OH 43230
Contact: Tony Segarra President
Tel: 614-367-1910
Email: tony-segarra@crossbowsystems.net
Website: www.crossbowsystems.net
Design and Installation Services, Technology Infrastructure Engineering, and Media Services. Our core competency is voice and data structural cable infrastructure design and installation. (Hisp, estab 2009, empl 8, sales , cert: State)

7325 Hooven-Dayton Corporation
511 Byers Rd
Miamisburg, OH 45342
Contact: Evan Arrindell VP Sales & Marketing
Tel: 937-233-4473
Email: diversesupplier1@hoovendayton.com
Website: www.hoovendayton.com
print & convert pressure sensitive labels, coupons & custom specific solutions. (AA, estab 1935, empl 101, sales $24,899,000, cert: NMSDC)

7326 IC3D
1697 Westbelt Dr
Columbus, OH 43228
Contact: Michael Cao CEO
Tel: 614-260-5631
Email: michael@ic3dprinters.com
Website: www.ic3dprinters.com/
3D printing services, prototyping & low volume manufacturing. (As-Pac, estab 2012, empl 10, sales $500,000, cert: NMSDC)

7327 Identification Systems, Inc. dba Identity Systems,
1324 Stimmel Road
Columbus, OH 43223
Contact: DeeDee Warden Acct Exec
Tel: 614-448-1741
Email: dwarden@identitysystemsinc.com
Website: www.identitysystemsinc.com
Commercial screen printing: vinyl, styrene, ABS & engraveable stock. Mfr name badges, signage, architectural signage, signage systems inserts, accordion/ spiral signs, engraved signs, nameplates, equipment tags, decals, plaques. (Woman, estab 1986, empl 34, sales $3,626,392, cert: WBENC)

7328 JSCS Group, Inc. dba Market Direct
3478 Hauck Road, Ste C
Cincinnati, OH 45241
Contact: Stephanie Harmon President
Tel: 513-563-4900
Email: stephanie@marketdirectinc.com
Website: www.marketdirectinc.com
Printing: offset & digital on-demand, direct marketing, direct mailing & fulfillment, mailing, target list development & management, graphic design. (AA, estab 2004, empl 5, sales $130,000, cert: NMSDC)

7329 Link to Success dba HARKNESServices
947 E Johnstown Rd, Ste 127
Gahanna, OH 43230
Contact: Tara Harkness President
Tel: 888-959-4203
Email: tharkness@harknessservices.com
Website: www.harknesservices.com
Our service; Kitchen exhaust cleaning with the added services of Install hinges on fans and secure to stack for optimal cleaning access Install grease containment systems to prevent grease from accumulating on the roof Cut access panels in (Woman/AA, estab 2011, empl 8, sales $41,222,200, cert: State, NMSDC)

7330 RPI Color Service, Inc.
1950 Radcliff Dr
Cincinnati, OH 45204
Contact: Karen Rellar EVP Mktg/Communications
Tel: 513-471-4040
Email: karen.rellar@rpigraphic.com
Website: www.rpigraphic.com
Off-set & digital printing, large & small format printing, die cutting, bindery & finishing, on demand printing, signage, packaging, sales samples, prototyping, displays, mailing services, point of sale materials, web-based tools. (Woman, estab 1969, empl 50, sales $8,500,000, cert: WBENC)

7331 Swimmer Printing dba Alphagraphics
1701 E 12th St
Cleveland, OH 44114
Contact: Judith Swimmer President
Tel: 216-623-1005
Email: us320@alphagraphics.com
Website: www.J2MedicalSupply.com
One to four color offset printing, B&W & color copy services, Mailing services, Digital archiving, Poster & banner printing, Prepress & design services, Finishing & bindery services. (Woman, estab 1991, empl 9, sales $1,400,000, cert: City)

7332 Ten 10 Design LLC
119 Main St
Chardon, OH 44024
Contact: Casey Zulandt Owner
Tel: 440-286-4367
Email: casey@ten10design.com
Website: www.ten10design.com
Printing (offset and digital), promotional items, ad specialties, mailing services, labels & decals, graphic design, web design. (Woman/AA, estab 2009, empl 5, sales $3,093,663, cert: State, NMSDC, WBENC)

7333 Three Leaf Productions, Inc.
261 West Johnstown Road Ste 200
Gahanna, OH 43230
Contact: Ron Stokes President
Tel: 614-626-4941
Email: rstokes@three-leaf.com
Website: www.three-leaf.com
Commercial & large digital format printing: retail packaging, point of purchase displays, banners & signs, fulfillment services, pick & pack, kitting, promotional premiums. (AA, estab 1995, empl 15, sales $10,271,000, cert: State, NMSDC)

Oklahoma

7334 OakTree Software, Inc.
1437 S Boulder Ave, Ste 300
Tulsa, OK 74119
Contact: Tony Floyd Business Devel
Tel: 918-584-7900
Email: tony.floyd@oaktreesoftware.com
Website: www.oaktreesoftware.com
IT Consulting, training and services (Woman, estab 1995, empl 100, sales $10,000,000, cert: WBENC)

Oregon

7335 Industrial Safety Solutions Corporation
14791 SE 82nd Dr
Clackamas, OR 97015
Contact: Rhonda Evans President
Tel: 503-303-5958
Email: revans@industrialsafetysolution.com
Website: www.industrialsafetysolution.com
Industrial labeling systems, in-house pipe marking, 5S, Kaizen & general directional labeling. (Minority, Woman, estab 2004, empl 6, sales $854,257, cert: State)

7336 PrintSync, Inc.
6775 SW 111th Ave, Ste 10
Beaverton, OR 97008
Contact: President
Tel: 503-520-2000
Email: customerservice@printsync.com
Website: www.printsync.com
Printing & copying, direct mail & fulfillment. (Woman, estab 1991, empl 10, sales $2,048,000, cert: WBENC)

Pennsylvania

7337 Brenneman Printing, Inc.
1909 Olde Homestead Lane
Lancaster, PA 17601
Contact: Dir Sales/Marketing
Tel: 717-299-2847
Email: ed.nevling@brennemaninc.com
Website: www.brennemaninc.com
Commercial printing: offset printing 1-5 colors, thermography, digital printing, variable data printing, inkjet addressing, mailing services, inserting, database management, online ordering storefronts, mail list acquisition, custom distribution services. (Woman, estab 1969, empl 30, sales , cert: State, WBENC)

7338 Chaucer Press, Inc.
535 Stewart Rd
Hanover Township, PA 18706
Contact: Patricia Frances CEO
Tel: 570-825-2005
Email: pfrances@chaucerpress.com
Website: www.chaucerpress.com
Printed packaging & on-pack promotional materials: pressure-sensitive, cut & extended content labels, folding cartons, inserts, on-serts, blister cards, sleeves, foilstamping, embossing, screen printing, structural design. (Woman, estab 1965, empl 49, sales $15,000,000, cert: WBENC)

7339 Diamond Graphics Inc.
456 Acorn Lane
Downingtown, PA 19335
Contact: Barbara Martin Owner
Tel: 610-269-7010
Email: barb@diamondgraphicsprint.com
Website: www.diamondgraphicsprint.com
Commercial Printing, Direct Mail, Web Offset, Brochures, Pharmaceutical inserts, Flyers, Circulars, Instruction Manuals, Note Pads, Inserts, Reply Cards. (Woman, estab 1999, empl 40, sales $6,500,000, cert: WBENC)

7340 Graphic Arts, Incorporated
2867 East Alleghany Ave
Philadelphia, PA 19134
Contact: Fred Binder Acct Exec
Tel: 215-382-5500
Email: fbinder@galitho.com
Website: www.galitho.com
Full color sheet fed printing: finish, fulfill & mail. (Woman, estab 1928, empl 100, sales $6,135,881, cert: City, WBENC)

7341 Innovation Marketing Communications LLC
232 Conestoga Rd
Wayne, PA 19154
Contact: George Slater Major Accounts Mgr
Tel: 215-802-2885
Email: gslater@phoenixlitho.com
Website: www.innomc.com
Creative, offset & digital printing, wide format, physical & virtual events, warehousing & web-to-print solutions. (As-Pac, estab 1973, empl 92, sales $20,500,000, cert: NMSDC)

7342 Lizzie Bullets LLC dba KDC
2100 Babcock Blvd.
Pittsburgh, PA 15209
Contact: Kristine King CEO
Tel: 412-446-2784
Email: kking@printpgh.com
Website: www.printpgh.com
Print and communication: digital printing, conventional/ commercial offset printing & wide format signage & banners, design, data archiving, direct mail, variable data and web-to-print services. (Woman, estab 2005, empl 22, sales $2,650,000, cert: WBENC)

7343 Migu Press Inc.
260 Ivyland Rd
Warminster, PA 18974
Contact: Ken Bucker New Business Dev
Tel: 215-957-9763
Email: kenb@migu4u.com
Website: www.migu4u.com
Commercial printing. (Woman, estab 1988, empl 28, sales , cert: State, WBENC)

7344 Movad
801 Bristol Pike
Bensalem, PA 19020
Contact: Terri Gasbarra Business Devel
Tel: 215-638-2679
Email: bhanf@gostrata.com
Website: www.movadcorp.com
Digital & offset printing, mailing services, bindery & finishing, fulfillment, variable data printing, database services, graphic design & pre-press, online ordering & proofing. (Woman, estab 1986, empl 11, sales $1,500,000, cert: WBENC)

7345 PAP Technologies, Inc.
1813 Colonial Village Ln
Lancaster, PA 17601
Contact: Michael Robinson President
Tel: 717-399-3333
Email: mrobinson@paptech.net
Website: www.paptech.net
Printing, warehousing, distribution, fulfillment & machine automation, electrical control panels. (AA, estab 1988, empl 54, sales , cert: State, NMSDC)

7346 TMMPROMOS.COM dba The Artifactori
140 Christopher Ln, Ste 101
Harleysville, PA 19438
Contact: Victoria Magagna President
Tel: 215-513-1693
Email: tori@theartifactori.com
Website: www.theartifactori.com
Commercial Printing, Large-Format Printing, Direct mail, Fulfillment, Warehousing, and Custom Distribution, Branded Promotional Products, and Custom Apparel. (Woman, estab 2014, empl 3, sales $617,000, cert: WBENC)

7347 Triangle Press Inc.
6720 Allentown Blvd
Harrisburg, PA 17112
Contact: Tammy Shelley VP
Tel: 717-541-9315
Email: tammy@trianglepress.net
Website: www.trianglepress.net
Graphic design, wide format printing, digital printing, variable data, 5-color offset printing, fulfillment & delivery. (Woman, estab 1970, empl 21, sales $3,175,100, cert: WBENC)

7348 Unity Printing Co., Inc.
5848 State Route 981
Latrobe, PA 15650
Contact: Lori Askins President
Tel: 724-537-5800
Email: lori@unipakcorp.net
Website: www.UnityPrinting.com
Digital Printing, Offset Printing, Direct Mail, services, Variable Data Services, Warehousing. (Woman, estab 1979, empl 40, sales $3,660,000, cert: WBENC)

7349 Universal Printing Company LLC
1205 O'Neill Hwy
Dunmore, PA 18512
Contact: Margaret McGrath CEO
Tel: 570-342-1243
Email: mah@universalprintingcompany.com
Website: www.universalprintingcompany.com
Commercial printing, fulfillment, 4, 8 & 10 color presses with roll-to-sheet capabilities. (Woman, estab 1995, empl 150, sales $32,396,000, cert: WBENC)

Puerto Rico

7350 3A Press
PO Box 47
Lajas, PR 00667
Contact: Marie Rosado President
Tel: 787-899-0110
Email: mrosado@3apress.com
Website: www.3apress.com
Mfr & print pharmaceutical, commercial & folding cartons, inserts, stitched & perfect bound booklets/ magazines, printed literature. (Hisp, estab 1996, empl 126, sales $11,200,000, cert: NMSDC)

South Carolina

7351 National Beverage Screen Printers, Inc
12000 Main St
Williston, SC 29853
Contact: Janet Roberson President
Tel: 803-266-5272
Email: jroberson@nbsinc.net
Website: www.nbsinc.net
Screen printing, digital printing, plastic injection & metal fabrication. (Woman, estab 1984, empl 38, sales $7,000,000, cert: WBENC)

7352 Print Solutions Inc.
1273 Bowater Rd
Rock Hill, SC 29732
Contact: Wyman Wilson Acct Rep
Tel: 803-366-1510
Email: wyman.wilson@printsolutions.org
Website: www.printsolutions.org
Thermal Products, Printheads, Ribbons, Labels & Tags, Continuous Labels & Tags Laser Labels & Tags Custom, Stock Labels & Tags. (Woman, estab 2001, empl 3, sales $325,000, cert: State)

Tennessee

7353 A-1 Printing Services
810 E Brooks Rd
Memphis, TN 38116
Contact: Frazer Windless President
Tel: 901-396-2023
Email: fwindless@a1printingsvc.com
Website: www.a1printingsvc.com
Commercial sheet-fed printing. (AA, estab 1988, empl 12, sales $1,179,800, cert: NMSDC)

7354 Graphic Label Solutions
2407 Pulaski Hwy
Columbia, TN 38401
Contact: Bob Offord VP
Tel: 931-490-0019
Email: bob.offord@abrandcompany.com
Website: www.graphiclabelsolutions.com/
Labels, decals, overlays, nameplates, membrane switches, RFID, EAS. (Woman, estab 2002, empl 5, sales $5,000,000, cert: State, WBENC)

7355 O'Ryan Group
4010 Pilot Dr, Ste 108 Ste 108
Memphis, TN 38118
Contact: Sara O'Ryan Acct Exec
Tel: 901-794-4610
Email: sara@oryangroup.com
Website: www.oryangroup.com
Printing, screen printing, offset printing, web printing, digital printing, hardware, structural, POP, kit packing, installation. (Woman, estab 1997, empl 52, sales $44,000,000, cert: WBENC)

7356 Resource Regeneration LLC dba S3 Asset Mgmt
1309 Elm Hill Pike
Nashville, TN 37210
Contact: Rod McDaniel CEO
Tel: 615-873-4466
Email: rmcdaniel@s3rs.com
Website: www.s3rs.com
(AA, estab 2006, empl 20, sales $500,000, cert: NMSDC)

7357 Tec-Print, LLC
4600 Cromwell Ave, Ste 101
Memphis, TN 38118
Contact: Lynn Higgs Business Devel Mgr
Tel: 865-471-1846
Email: lhiggs@nashua.com
Website: www.tec-print.com
Printing: labels, tickets, cash register receipts, brochures, pamphlets, forms, digital off-set or roll fed web, etc. (AA, estab 2004, empl 23, sales $896,000, cert: NMSDC)

7358 Women in Printing, LLC
2285 Hwy 47 N
White Bluff, TN 37187
Contact: Teri Doochin President
Tel: 615-797-9811
Email: tdoochin@womeninprinting.com
Website: www.womeninprinting.com
Flexographic & offset printing, films & laminated structures, labels, coupons, blister-board, offset and rotary printing, finished pouches & bags. (Woman, estab 2004, empl 15, sales $2,500,000, cert: WBENC)

7359 Worldwide Label & Packaging LLC
158 Madison Ave Ste 101
Memphis, TN 38103
Contact: Anthony Norris President
Tel: 901-454-9290
Email: anorris@worldwidebg.com
Website: www.worldwidebg.com
Mfr printed packaging: pressure sensitive labels, flexible packaging & continuous roll forms. (AA, estab 2000, empl 26, sales $5,000,000, cert: NMSDC)

Texas

7360 AC Printing LLC
3400-1 S Raider Dr
Euless, TX 76040
Contact: Robert Bolt Sales
Tel: 817-267-8990
Email: acpsales@acprinting.com
Website: www.acprinting.com
Commercial printing. (As-Ind, estab 1989, empl 40, sales $7,790,014, cert: State, NMSDC, SDB)

7361 Advanced Business Graphics, Inc.
680 S Royal Lane, Ste 200
Coppell, TX 75019
Contact: Sales Sales
Tel: 972-471-3740
Email: abgi@abgi.com
Website: www.abgi.com
Printed products-business forms, checks, labels, commercial printing, promotional items, packaging, printer supplies, stationery items, presentation materials, office supplies. (Woman, estab 1995, empl 8, sales $5,884,880, cert: State, WBENC)

7362 Alliance of Diversity Printers, LLC
15950 Dallas Pkwy Ste 400
Dallas, TX 75248
Contact: Terri Quinton CEO
Tel: 214-856-8368
Email: terri@adp-llc.com
Website: www.adp-llc.com
Print management solution. (Woman, estab 2008, empl 12, sales $12,700,000, cert: State, NMSDC, WBENC)

7363 Bayside Printing Co, Inc
160 Lockhaven Dr
Houston, TX 77073
Contact: David Solis VP Business Dev
Tel: 281-209-9500
Email: david@baysideprinting.com
Website: www.baysideprinting.com
Commercial multi-color printing: prepress, multiple sheet fed presses, 6 color, coaters, in-house bindery, die cutting & assembly, mailing & fulfillment. (Minority, Woman, estab 1973, empl 30, sales $7,000,000, cert: NMSDC, WBENC)

7364 Best Press Inc.
4201 Airborn Dr
Addison, TX 75001
Contact: Bobby Yocum Marketing/Business Develop
Tel: 972-930-1000
Email: admin@bestpress.com
Website: www.bestpress.com
Commercial printing. (Woman, estab 1993, empl 100, sales $13,200,000, cert: State, WBENC)

7365 Creative Menus & Folders, LLC dba Texas Covers
409 Old Hwy 80
Olden, TX 76466
Contact: Renee Forguson Asst Production Mgr
Tel: 254-653-2775
Email: reneeforguson@texascovers.com
Website: www.texascovers.com
Presentation/Executive Binders, folders, business cards, printing (screen, digital, offset, foil stamp, deboss, specialty color cast printing, plastic ID badge holders, ID badges, name tags, souvenir printing, banners, signage, laminating, caps. (As-Pac, estab 2015, empl 19, sales , cert: NMSDC)

7366 Digi-Color, LP
4414 Hollister
Houston, TX 77040
Contact: Barkla Tully Managing Partner
Tel: 713-934-9800
Email: barkla@digi-color.com
Website: www.digi-color.com
Digital printing; climate-controlled warehousing & fulfillment, mailing, on-line inventory management - ordering & reporting, on-demand 4 color & black/white digital printing, document management services, binding & finishing, packaging, kitting. (Woman, estab 2004, empl 20, sales $4,525,142, cert: State, WBENC)

7367 Dragonfly Group
1015 Amesbury Dr
Murphy, TX 75094
Contact: Laura McClain President
Tel: 972-742-2215
Email: laura@thedragonflygroup.net
Website: www.thedragonflygroup.net
Print production & creative design: litho, UV, web, silkscreen, digital & flexo printing, full bindery, finishing, diecutting, assembly, kitting & fulfillment. (Minority, Woman, estab 2004, empl 1, sales $1,163,510, cert: WBENC)

7368 Dream Big Media Solutions/Alphagraphics 114
7801 Mesquite Bend Dr
Irving, TX 75063
Contact: Sam Reed Owner
Tel: 972-570-0868
Email: us114@alphagraphics.com
Website: www.us114.alphagraphics.com
Printing, graphic design, marketing, and signage, envelopes, brochures, blueprints, business cards, digital printing, letterhead, forms, postcards, stationery, banners, signs, wall graphics. (AA, estab 1984, empl 5, sales $1,047,076, cert: State, NMSDC)

7369 Dynamic Color Graphics
PO Box 161758
Fort Worth, TX 76161
Contact: Kathy Bowers President
Tel: 817-520-6631
Email: kathy@dynamiccolorgraphics.com
Website: www.dynamiccolorgraphics.com
Large format digital printing, banners, posters, trade show graphics, vehicle graphics, floor graphics, murals, fine art reproduction, digital photo lab. (Woman, estab 2000, empl 19, sales $9,403,342, cert: State)

7370 Exalt Printing Solutions
1628 W Crosby Rd Ste 104
Carrollton, TX 75006
Contact: Lisa Marta CEO
Tel: 972-245-3858
Email: lisa@exaltprinting.com
Website: www.exaltprinting.com
Printing, promotional & office products, forms, labels, brochures, checks, direct mail. (Woman, estab , empl , sales $8,150,000, cert: State, WBENC)

7371 FBC Enterprises, Inc.
5110 Rondo Dr
Fort Worth, TX 76106
Contact: Teresa McClain Sales Rep
Tel: 817-740-1951
Email: tmcclain@customgs.com
Website: www.customgs.com
Commercial printing, web & sheetfed, bindery svcs: direct mail, booklets, catalogs, posters, pocket folders, door hangers & brochures, hand assembly, kitting, custom distribution & fulfillment. (Woman, estab 1990, empl 45, sales $4,500,000, cert: WBENC)

7372 Global Bridge Infotech Inc.
5525 N Macarthur Blvd, Ste 670
Irving, TX 75038
Contact: Vishnu Sethuraman Swarna Dir Bus Dev
Tel: 972-550-9400
Email: vishnu@gbitinc.com
Website: www.gbitinc.com
Commercial, full-color web offset printing, sheet-fed, digital design & print. (As-Ind, estab 2006, empl 97, sales $9,000,000, cert: State, NMSDC)

7373 ISSGR, Inc. dba ImageSet
6611 Portwest Dr Ste 190
Houston, TX 77024
Contact: President
Tel: 713-869-7700
Email: sales@imageset.com
Website: www.imageset.com
Digital printing, large format graphics, premedia & graphic design. (Woman, estab 1985, empl 31, sales $4,325,248, cert: WBENC)

7374 Label Systems, Inc.
      4111 Lindberg Dr
      Addison, TX 75001
      Contact: Amy Van Brunt President
      Tel: 972-387-4512
      Email: amy@labelsystemsinc.com
      Website: www.labelsystemsinc.com
Mfr custom labels, flexography, hot stamping &
silkscreening, promotional products & incentive programs
(Woman, estab 1994, empl 10, sales $350,000, cert: State,
WBENC)

7375 Marfield Corporate Stationery
      1225 E Crosby Rd Ste B-1
      Carrollton, TX 75006
      Contact: Andrea Rowe SVP-Sales
      Tel: 877-245-9122
      Email: accounting@marfield.com
      Website: www.marfield.com
Printing, engraving, embossing, foil stamping: business
cards, letterheads & envelopes. (Woman, estab 1968, empl
17, sales $2,100,000, cert: State, WBENC)

7376 Mastercraft Printed Products & Services
      2150 Century Circle
      Irving, TX 75062
      Contact: Eoff Suzanne VP
      Tel: 214-455-4148
      Email: txmx1144@yahoo.com
      Website: www.mbfi.com
Commercial print, direct mail, operational forms, ASI
speciality items, document retention, kitting, fulfillment,
warehousing, logistics. (Woman, estab 1979, empl 45,
sales $15,200,000, cert: WBENC)

7377 Nicholas Earth Printing, LLC
      7021 Portwest Dr. Ste 100
      Houston, TX 77024
      Contact: Marvin (Bob) Nicholas President
      Tel: 713-880-0195
      Email: bnicholas@nicholasearth.com
      Website: www.nicholasearth.com
Sheetfed printing, UV & aqueous coating, web printing &
inline, digital prepress & computer to plate, digital
archiving, bindery, fulfillment, outdoor advertising.
(Woman/AA, estab 2003, empl 18, sales , cert: State)

7378 Nieman Printing
      10615 Newkirk St
      Dallas, TX 75220
      Contact: James Quinonez Acct Rep
      Tel: 214-458-8011
      Email: jq@niemanprinting.com
      Website: www.niemanprinting.com
Digital pritning: short runs press, large press up to 12
colors with UV or AQ on paper or plastic. (Woman, estab
1984, empl 160, sales $22,000,000, cert: State, WBENC)

7379 Parker Business Forms, Inc.
      7395 Frint Dr
      Beaumont, TX 77705
      Contact: Heather Camp VP
      Tel: 409-842-5251
      Email: heather@parkerbf.com
      Website: www.parkerbf.com
Commercial & industrial printing: letterheads, envelopes,
thank you cards, note cards, Christmas Cards, carbonless
forms - invoices, purchase orders, shipping manifest, etc.,
full color(shortand long run). (Woman, estab 0, empl 20,
sales $6,000,000, cert: WBENC)

7380 Peacock Press LLC
      538 Shepherd
      Garland, TX 75042
      Contact: Ru Patel COO
      Tel: 972-272-7764
      Email: ru@peacockpress.net
      Website: www.peacockpress.net
Digital printing, offset printing, complete finishing
capabilities. (As-Ind, estab 2003, empl 15, sales
$2,500,000, cert: State, NMSDC)

7381 Technology Media Group
      1262 Viceroy Dr
      Dallas, TX 75247
      Contact: Amanda Clarke Business Devel
      Tel: 214-267-0535
      Email: amandaclarke@tmguniverse.com
      Website: www.tmguniverse.com
Offset print, digital print, high speed web printing,
signage, wearables, screenprint, embroidery, promotional, warehousing, fulfillment, distribution, graphic
design, envelope mfg, foil stamp, die cut. (Woman, estab
1986, empl 75, sales $9,000,000, cert: State)

Virginia

7382 BBR Print Inc.
      807 Oliver Hill Way
      Richmond, VA 23219
      Contact: Brooke Rhodes Cstmr Service
      Tel: 804-901-2535
      Email: brooke@jamesriverpress.com
      Website: www.bambooink.com
Printing services: in-house art dept, offset press & copy
svcs, bindery. (Woman, estab 1997, empl 15, sales
$1,143,000, cert: State)

7383 Grubb Printing & Stamp Co.
      3303 Airline Blvd, Ste 1G
      Portsmouth, VA 23701
      Contact: Darla Alexander Sales Rep
      Tel: 757-465-7855
      Email: darla@grubbprint.com
      Website: www.grubbprint.com
Commercial printing. (Woman, estab , empl 16, sales
$17,002,000, cert: State)

7384 JoMoCo Studio LLC
      8416 Staples Mill Rd
      Richmond, VA 23228
      Contact: Joe Coleman Mgr
      Tel: 804-262-3555
      Email: engraving@jomocostudio.com
      Website: www.jomocostudio.com
Engraving: stainless steel, brass, aluminum & plastic
signs, nameplates, name badges, labels, legends, tags,
awards & plaques, vinyl signs, braille signs, acrylic
awards & laser engraved metals & glass. (Woman, estab
1985, empl 3, sales $523,155, cert: State)

7385 Premier Reprographics, Inc.
      4701-A Eisenhower Ave
      Alexandria, VA 22304
      Contact: Vickie Banks CEO
      Tel: 703-370-6612
      Email: vickie@premierrepro.com
      Website: www.premierrepro.com
Digital printing, copying, binding, scanning, posters,
manuals, newsletters, booklets, reports, proposals,
marketing collateral, presentations, laminating,
blueprinting, drymounting, large & small format color.
(Woman/AA, estab 1993, empl 10, sales $1,000,000,
cert: State)

Washington

7386 Angel Screen Printing, Inc.
8459 S 208th St, Bldg N
Kent, WA 98031
Contact: Rex Korrell Mktg Mgr
Tel: 206-755-7737
Email: rex@angelscreenprinting.net
Website: www.angelscreenprinting.net
Screen printing and Embroidery services. (Minority, Woman, estab 2004, empl 8, sales $672,896, cert: State, NMSDC)

7387 EE Printing. LLC
8258 S 192nd St
Kent, WA 98032
Contact: Tory Nguyen
Tel: 425-656-1250
Email: tory@eeprinting.com
Website: www.eeprinting.com
From one color to full color, offset to digital, business forms, business cards, stationary, bulk volume envelopes, signs, posters, manuals, books, NCR forms, flyer, brochures. (Minority, Woman, estab 2007, empl 3, sales $190,752, cert: State, NMSDC)

7388 Risque Inc.
1122 N State St
Bellingham, WA 98225
Contact: Nadeem Israr President
Tel: 360-738-1280
Email: nadeem@copysource.com
Website: www.copysource.com
Printing services: digital printing, poster printing, offset printing, copying, publishing, etc. (Minority, Woman, estab 1990, empl 15, sales $1,200,000, cert: State)

Wisconsin

7389 Crossmark Graphics, Inc.
16100 W Overland Dr
New Berlin, WI 53151
Contact: Tammy Rechner President
Tel: 262-821-1343
Email: trechner@crossmarkgraphicsinc.com
Website: www.crossmarkgraphicsinc.com
Print communication, litho, UV printing, lenticular, POS, digital, PURLs, fulfillment/kit packing & web-to-print. (Woman, estab 1987, empl 48, sales $12,703,065, cert: WBENC)

7390 Flex Pre-Press, Inc.
6812 S 112th St
Franklin, WI 53132
Contact: Burt Tabora President
Tel: 414-427-8833
Email: btabora@flexprepress.com
Website: www.flexprepress.com
Photopolymer printing plates, DuPont WaterProofs, color keys, film negatives, analog & digital proofing, high-end color separations, photo retouching, package design, file management & printing, digital plates. (Hisp, estab 1995, empl 15, sales $1,100,000, cert: State, NMSDC)

7391 H.Derksen & Sons Co., Inc.
250 Industrial Dr
Omro, WI 50310
Contact: Mike Willeford VP
Tel: 920-685-4000
Email: mike@hderksen.com
Website: www.hderksen.com
Pressure sensitive labels, wide format digital printing, business forms, computer paper, paper & packaging products, mobility solutions, bar code label printers, bar coding software. (Nat Ame, estab , empl 11, sales $8,000,000, cert: NMSDC)

7392 Industrial Graphics Inc.
304 Industrial Dr
Fredonia, WI 53021
Contact: Teri Swenson Acct Mgr
Tel: 262-692-2424
Email: tswenson@igc-image.com
Website: www.industrialgraphics.com
Digital Printing, Screen Printing, Creative Services, Cad Cut Lettering, Fleet Wrapping, Advertising, Point of Purchase Displays, Priting on Metals, Prototyping, High Volume Sourcing, Architectural Decorating, Wall Paper Printing, Ceiling Tile Printing. (Woman, estab 1969, empl 20, sales $2,750,000, cert: State)

7393 Kubin-Nicholson Corporation
8440 N 87th St
Milwaukee, WI 53224
Contact: Margaret Rees CEO
Tel: 414-586-4300
Email: rees.p@kubin.com
Website: www.kubin.com
Commerical printed products: billboards, banners, transit posters, in store signs, floor graphics, wall scapes, vehicle wraps, building wraps, POP displays. (Woman, estab 1935, empl 63, sales $16,000,000, cert: State)

7394 Promo Print Solutions Inc.
420 S Koeller St, Ste 208
Oshkosh, WI 54902
Contact: Paula Condor President
Tel: 920-233-7900
Email: paula.condor@promoprintsolutions.com
Website: www.promoprintsolutions.com
print collateral: in-store promotions, sales promotions, commerical printing, giveaways & sampling. (Woman, estab 2000, empl 4, sales $2,087,395, cert: WBENC)

7395 Red Oak Label, LLC
2923 S 160th St
New Berlin, WI 53151
Contact: President
Tel: 262-780-9797
Email: CustomerService@RedOakLabel.com
Website: www.redoaklabel.com
Pressure sensitive flexographic labels & tags. (Woman, estab 1997, empl 6, sales $510,900, cert: WBENC)

Alaska

7396 Delta Leasing LLC
      8101 Dimond Hook Dr
      Anchorage, AK 99507
      Contact: Sam Amato VP
      Tel: 907-771-1300
      Email: lmorgan@deltaleasing.com
      Website: www.deltaleasing.com
Commercial leasing services of vehicles, equipment for oil & gas, construction, mining, (Nat Ame, estab 2002, empl 32, sales $13,000,000, cert: NMSDC)

Alabama

7397 Optimum Financial Corporation
      1300 Meridian St Ste 12
      Huntsville, AL 35801
      Contact: Thomas Parker Dir Business Dev
      Tel: 256-539-3994
      Email: tparker@optimumcorp.com
      Website: www.optimumcorp.com
Administrative & financial support services, revenue cycle, management consulting, asset managment, budgeting, const analysis, data entry, debt collection and records management. (AA, estab 1995, empl 20, sales $1,000,000, cert: NMSDC)

California

7398 Advertising Audit Services International, LLC
      32663 Red Maple St Ste 100
      Union City, CA 94587
      Contact: Pankaj Sewal Chief Auditing Officer
      Tel: 415-828-0779
      Email: psewal@adauditservintl.com
      Website: www.adauditservintl.com
Contract compliance audits & analysis: vendor compliance, financial accounting accuracy & advertiser best practices. (Minority, estab 2005, empl 5, sales $3,000,000, cert: NMSDC)

7399 Amerivet Securities, Inc.
      26550 Silverado Court
      Moreno Valley, CA 92555
      Contact: Steven Kay President
      Tel: 888-960-0644
      Email: skay@amerivetsecurities.com
      Website: www.amerivetsecurities.com
Securities business, commodities business & registered investment advisory business. (AA, estab 1993, empl 20, sales $862,000, cert: CPUC)

7400 Blaylock Van, LLC
      350 Frank H Ogawa Plaza 10th Fl
      Oakland, CA 94612
      Contact: Tarrell Gamble VP
      Tel: 510-208-6100
      Email: tgamble@brv-llc.com
      Website: www.brv-llc.com
Investment banking & financial services: corporate debt & equity underwriting, equity research, share repurchase, pension sales & trading & municipal finance. (AA, estab 1991, empl 48, sales , cert: State, NMSDC)

7401 Coast to Coast Financial Solutions Inc.
      101 Hodencamp Rd Ste 120
      Thousand Oaks, CA 91360
      Contact: John Mastro Dir
      Tel: 888-877-4700
      Email: jmastro@c2cfsi.com
      Website: www.c2cfsi.com
Debt collection services. (AA, estab 2002, empl 14, sales $1,412,059, cert: NMSDC)

7402 Consumer Financial Service Corporation
      1500 Park Ave Ste 116
      Emeryville, CA 94608
      Contact: Loy Sheflott President
      Tel: 510-596-4100
      Email: lsheflott@consumerfinancial.com
      Website: www.consumerfinancial.com
Financial services. (Woman, estab 1994, empl 30, sales $1,100,000, cert: WBENC)

7403 Corporate Tax Incentives
      PO Box 2770
      Rancho Cordova, CA 95670
      Contact: Shawn Battle Controller
      Tel: 916-366-0144
      Email: ebarajas@ctillc.com
      Website: www.ctillc.com
State and federal tax incentives, provide complete business incentives consulting services. (AA, As-Pac, estab 2008, empl 44, sales $10,542,392, cert: NMSDC)

7404 Garnier Group and Associates
      10679 Westview Pkwy, 2nd Fl.
      San Diego, CA 92126
      Contact: Winslow Garnier President
      Tel: 858-530-2468
      Email: winslow@garniergroup.com
      Website: www.garniergroup.com
Equipment finance leasing, appraisal services, computer leasing, analytical lab instrumentation leasing. (AA, estab 2003, empl 19, sales $7,023,000, cert: NMSDC, CPUC)

7405 Great Pacific Securities
      151 Kalmus Dr Ste H-8
      Costa Mesa, CA 92626
      Contact: Christopher Vinck-Luna CEO
      Tel: 714-619-3000
      Email: cvinck@greatpac.com
      Website: www.greatpac.com
Financial svcs: equity & fixed income execution, debt underwriting, equity underwriting & corporate buy backs. (Hisp, estab 1990, empl 30, sales $13,926,000, cert: State, City, NMSDC, CPUC)

7406 Jules & Associates, Inc.
      515 S Figeroa St, Ste 1950
      Los Angeles, CA 90071
      Contact: Vincent Alexander Sr acc exec
      Tel: 213-362-5600
      Email: vincea@julesandassociates.com
      Website: www.julesandassociates.com
Equipment finance corporate acquisitions. (Hisp, estab 1989, empl 31, sales $0, cert: CPUC)

7407 Liberty Commercial Finance
      250 El Camino Real, Ste 110
      Tustin, CA 92780
      Contact: Frank Jansen Sr Acct Mgr
      Tel: 949-484-7611
      Email: fjansen@libertycommercial.com
      Website: www.libertycommercial.com
Commercial equipment finance company. (Minority, Woman, estab 2017, empl 10, sales $75,000,000, cert: NMSDC)

7408 LNL Solutions LLC
      423 W Adams Ave
      Alhambra, CA 91801
      Contact: Philip Li Dir of Finance
      Tel: 424-256-5894
      Email: info@lnl-solutions.com
      Website: www.lnl-solutions.com
Middle market & boutique accounting & financial services. (As-Pac, estab 2013, empl 2, sales , cert: State, City, NMSDC)

7409 Pacific Rim Capital, Inc.
      525 Technology Dr Ste 400
      Irvine, CA 92618
      Contact: Tom Budnick VP Sales
      Tel: 949-389-0800
      Email: sales@pacrimcap.com
      Website: www.pacificrimcapital.com
Lease financing: materials handling & IT equip, also dist new & reconditioned IT hardware. (AA, estab 1990, empl 90, sales $42,568,153, cert: NMSDC)

7410 Receivables Solutions, Inc.
      2910 Inland Empire Blvd Ste 100
      Ontario, CA 91764
      Contact: Regina Cameron
      Tel: 909-360-8140
      Email: rcameron@rsinc.us
      Website: www.rsinc.us
National accounts receivable management (ARM), 1st party collections (pre-charge off), 3rd party collections & billing. (Woman/AA, estab 2015, empl 2, sales , cert: CPUC)

7411 Sequoia Financial Services
      28632 Roadside Dr Ste 110
      Agoura Hills, CA 91301
      Contact: Olivia Romero Business Dev Dir
      Tel: 818-409-6000
      Email: secon@sequoiafinancial.com
      Website: www.sequoiafinancial.com
Collection services. (Woman/AA, estab 1991, empl 73, sales $3,000,000, cert: CPUC, WBENC)

7412 Southern California Leasing Inc.
      180 E Main, Ste 204
      Tustin, CA 92780
      Contact: Barbara Griffith President
      Tel: 714-573-9804
      Email: bgriffith@socalleasing.com
      Website: www.socalleasing.com
Equipment leasing & financing. (Woman, estab 1992, empl 7, sales $1,200,000, cert: WBENC)

7413 Strategic Partners Consultants
      8889 W Olympic Blvd, Ste 1000
      Beverly Hills, CA 90211
      Contact: Brenda West CEO
      Tel: 310-870-7055
      brenda.west@strategicpartnersconsultants.com
      Website: www.strategicpartnersconsultants.com
Consulting & outsourcing, Bank Regulatory Compliance issues, Internal Audit functions & Risk Assessment activities. (Woman, estab 2014, empl 3, sales , cert: WBENC)

7414 The Gilson Group, LLC
      2967 Michelson Dr Ste G102
      Irvine, CA 92612
      Contact: Catherine Doll CEO
      Tel: 949-830-3499
      Email: catherine@thegilsongroup.com
      Website: www.TheGilsonGroup.com
Accounting, mergers, financial analysis, due diligence, internal controls, general ledger, forecasting, cash flow, process improvement, Quickbooks, SOX, SEC, cost accounting, financial reporting, internal audit, risk management, GAAP. (Woman, estab 2006, empl 20, sales $502,000, cert: WBENC)

7415 The Zamzow Group, Inc.
      264 S La Cienega Blvd, Ste 1120
      Beverly Hills, CA 90211
      Contact: Brenda Zamzow President
      Tel: 310-551-3000
      Email: wbe@thezamzowgroup.com
      Website: www.thezamzowgroup.com
Accounting services. (Woman, estab 2003, empl 20, sales $1,600,000, cert: State, City)

7416 Venpalia LLC
      1331 N Cuyamaca St, Ste G
      El Cajon, CA 92020
      Contact: Liza Amog Principal
      Tel: 619-788-3781
      Email: liza@venpalia.com
      Website: www.venpalia.com
Finance, risk management. (Minority, Woman, estab 2010, empl 1, sales $150,000, cert: NMSDC, CPUC)

Colorado

7417 Aspen Capital Company, Inc.
      530 North Jefferson Ave Unit A
      Loveland, CO 80537
      Contact: Peggy Tomcheck
      Tel: 303-716-2898
      Email: plapp@aspencapitalcompany.com
      Website: www.aspencapitalcompany.com
Custom asset tracking & invoicing solutions, educational laptop program lease structures, unique iPad refresh programs, consignment solutions, electronic invoicing & billing processes, web based equipment stores. (Woman, estab 2001, empl 8, sales $10,385,908, cert: WBENC)

Connecticut

7418 Airlink Ground Transportation, LLC
      39 Old Ridgebury Rd D1-243
      Danbury, CT 06810
      Contact: Atif Jilani Member
      Tel: 203-297-6060
      Email: atif@airlinklimo.com
      Website: www.airlinklimo.com
Black Car Service to/from CT,NY,NJ airports (As-Ind, estab 2011, empl 3, sales $185,320, cert: NMSDC)

7419 Argus Investors' Counsel, Inc.
      1266 E Main St 4th Fl
      Stamford, CT 06902
      Contact: Sharon Wagoner President
      Tel: 203-316-9000
      Email: clesko@argusinvest.com
      Website: www.argusinvest.com
Manage portfolios: pensions, endowments & foundations. (Woman, estab 1960, empl 6, sales $0, cert: WBENC)

7420 SCG Capital Leasing, LLC
      74 West Park Place
      Stamford, CT 06901
      Contact: Sam Goichman Sr Vice President
      Tel: 917-597-8568
      Email: sgoichman@scgwbe.com
      Website: www.scgwbe.com/
Equipment Leasing, Operating Leases. (Woman, estab 2005, empl 20, sales $30,000,000, cert: WBENC)

7421 Soundview Capital Solutions
      116 Washington Ave
      North Haven, CT 06473
      Contact: John Abella CEO
      Tel: 203-821-7830
      Email: johnabella@soundviewcapitalsolutions.com
      Website: www.soundviewcapitalsolutions.com
Third-party leasing specializing in technology financing. (Hisp, estab 2009, empl 3, sales $100,000, cert: NMSDC)

District of Columbia

7422 McKissack & McKissack of Washington, Inc.
      901 K St, NW 6th Fl
      Washington, DC 20001
      Contact: Pamela Prue Marketing & Proposal Mgr
      Tel: 202-347-1446
      Email: registrations@mckinc.com
      Website: www.mckinc.com
Budget preparation, scheduling, programming, scope preparation, financial consulting. (Woman/AA, estab 1990, empl 130, sales $24,010,225, cert: State, City, NMSDC, WBENC)

Delaware

7423 Faw Casson
      160 Greentree Dr, Ste 203
      Dover, DE 19904
      Contact: Tammy Ordway Dir of ES
      Tel: 302-674-4305
      Email: tjo@fawcasson.com
      Website: www.fawcasson.com
Employee benefit plan audits, business valuations, fraud services, EBP audits, agreed-upon procedures, internal audit staffing & tax services. (Woman, estab 1944, empl 39, sales $6,460,702, cert: WBENC)

Florida

7424 AMI Risk Consultants
      1336 SW 146th Court
      Miami, FL 33184
      Contact: Actuary Analyst/Admin
      Tel: 305-173-1589
      Email: cingo@comcast.net
      Website: www.amirisk.com
Property/casualty actuarial & risk management consulting. (As-Pac, estab 1992, empl 7, sales , cert: NMSDC)

7425 Carter-Health LLC
      4201 Vineland Road Ste I-13-14
      Orlando, FL 32811
      Contact: Rodney Carter President
      Tel: 407-296-6689
      Email: rodney@carterhealth.com
      Website: www.carter-health.com
Carter-Health is a turn-key solutions provider for creating sterile environments for I.V. compounding facilities. Our expertise in this area assists healthcare facilities in meeting the stringent requirements of (AA, estab 2007, empl 5, sales $2,500,000, cert: NMSDC)

7426 Commonwealth Capital Corp
      4532 US Hwy 19 Ste 200
      New Port Richey, FL 34652
      Contact: Kim Springsteen-Abbott Business Devel
      Tel: 800-249-3700
      Email: kspringsteen@ccclease.com
      Website: www.ccclease.com
Equipment leasing: IT, telecom & medical equipment. (Woman, estab 1978, empl 45, sales $10,000,000, cert: WBENC)

7427 Empower Benefits Inc. dba Corestream
      3606 Enterprise Ave, Ste 304
      Naples, FL 34104
      Contact: Neil Vaswani CEO
      Tel: 917-686-5886
      Email: info@corestream.com
      Website: www.corestream.com
Provides consolidated payroll deduction, voluntary benefits portals, employee discount shopping portals, group auto insurance real time comparative quoting, online enrollment and voluntary benefits brokerage. (As-Ind, estab 2006, empl 30, sales , cert: NMSDC)

7428 Enfusion, Inc.
      2429 Grand Teton Circle
      Winter Park, FL 32792
      Contact: Anita White CEO
      Tel: 407-802-0006
      Email: anita@enfusionfinance.com
      Website: www.enfusionfinance.com
Financial intelligence consulting, expense & cost management. (Woman/AA, estab 2007, empl 1, sales , cert: WBENC)

7429 Risk & Re-Insurance Solutions Corporation
      1500 San Remo Ave Ste 247B
      Coral Gables, FL 33146
      Contact: Steven Pacholick VP
      Tel: 770-437-8880
      Email: spacholick@rrisc.com
      Website: www.rrisc.com
Risk management, advisory & risk financing needs to corporate & governmental clients. (Hisp, estab 2001, empl 10, sales $2,550,000, cert: NMSDC)

Georgia

7430 À la Carte Investments, LLC
4480 S. Cobb Dr Ste H-158
Smyrna, GA 30080
Contact: Joseph Harland, II President
Tel: 415-857-4779
Email: jharland@alacarteinvestments.com
Website: www.alacarteinvestments.com
Private equity investment and commercial real estate brokerage advisory firm (AA, estab 2017, empl 1, sales $0, cert: NMSDC)

7431 Accountant In A Minute
1781 Chadds Lake Dr
Marietta, GA 30068
Contact: Alison Nicholson President
Tel: 404-804-5778
Email: alison.nicholson@aimaccountingservices.com
Website: www.aimaccountingservices.com
Accounting Services: Reconciliations Statement reconciliations & Expenses Bank reconciliations, Recording transactions Financial Statement preparation & tutorials Month, Quarter close support, Audit support (Failing Audits) System Migration. (Woman, estab 2017, empl 2, sales $100,000, cert: NWBOC)

7432 Corporate Reports, Inc.
3610 Piedmont Rd NE Ste 200
Atlanta, GA 30305
Contact: Angela King Controller
Tel: 404-233-2230
Email: angela.king@corporatereport.com
Website: www.corporatereport.com
Annual (financial) & sustainability/corporate responsibility/citizenship reporting. (Woman, estab , empl , sales $3,500,000, cert: WBENC)

7433 Harris Group Services, Inc.
PO Box 2244
Alpharetta, GA 30023
Contact: Marine Harris CEO
Tel: 404-243-5600
Email: contact@harrisgs.com
Website: www.harrisgs.com
Project management & support, accounting & finance services, audit support svcs, business analysis & communication, financial compliance & reviews, asset management & valuation. (Woman/AA, estab 2009, empl 3, sales , cert: WBENC)

7434 Infinite Financial Concepts, LLC
PO Box 953
Stone Mountain, GA 30086
Contact: Amin Hassan President
Tel: 678-933-5304
Email: amin@ifc326.com
Website: www.ifc326.com
Accounting & financial reporting. (AA, estab 2011, empl 1, sales , cert: City)

7435 Real Property Tax Advisors
3525 Piedmont Rd, Ste 7-300
Atlanta, GA 30305
Contact: Anne Sheehan CEO
Tel: 404-816-2050
Email: asheehan@realpropertytaxadvisors.com
Website: www.realpropertytaxadvisors.com
Property tax consulting services. (Woman, estab 1972, empl 45, sales , cert: WBENC)

7436 Resurgens Risk Management, Inc.
1201 Peachtree St NE
Atlanta, GA 30361
Contact: Clifton McKnight, Sr. Asst VP
Tel: 678-298-5119
Email: cmcknight@rrmgt.com
Website: www.rrmgt.com
Human resources consulting services, financial products, employee benefits, commercial property & liability insurance & consultative services. (AA, estab 1987, empl 33, sales $3,000,000, cert: NMSDC)

7437 RiverStone Associates, LLC
750 Olde Clubs Dr
Alpharetta, GA 30022
Contact: Monty Brinkley President
Tel: 770-656-7820
Email: mbrinkley@riverstone-us.com
Website: www.riverstone-us.com
Professional svcs: internal audit, accounting, IT security, process improvement & risk management solutions. (AA, estab 2007, empl 2, sales , cert: State)

Illinois

7438 A3B, LLC
100 S Saunders Rd, Ste 150
Lake Forest, IL 60045
Contact: Betsey Robinson President
Tel: 847-574-7227
Email: betsey@a3bllc.com
Website: www.a3bllc.com
Accounting & Finance Consulting Services, business process improvements resulting in cost savings, financial accounting reporting & analysis, financial transformation of shared services centers, management of change. (Woman/AA, estab 2013, empl 3, sales , cert: NMSDC, WBENC)

7439 Adelfia LLC
400 E Randolph Str Ste 705
Chicago, IL 60601
Contact: Stella Marie Santos
Tel: 312-240-9500
Email: sbsantos@adelfiacpas.com
Website: www.adelfiacpas.com
Assurance & advisory services: financial audit, compliance examination, internal audit, agreed-upon procedures, tax services, tax preparation, payroll tax returns, tax notices/audit assistance, tax planning, accounting services. (Minority, Woman, estab 2011, empl 30, sales $541,996, cert: State, City, NMSDC)

7440 Ariel Investments
200 E Randolph St Ste 2900
Chicago, IL 60601
Contact: Gary L. Rozier Sr VP
Tel: 312-726-0140
Email: grozier@arielinvestments.com
Website: www.arielinvestments.com
Financial management services. (AA, estab 1983, empl , sales $54,074,660, cert: NMSDC)

7441 Barbee Tax Consulting, LLC
18700 Wolf Rd Ste 206
Mokena, IL 60448
Contact: Prentice Barbee President
Tel: 708-945-8334
Email: pbarbee@barbeetax.com
Website: www.barbeetax.com
Certified tax, accounting, and affordable care act (ACA) provider to corporate taxpayers. Compliance, contract services, tax preparation, assistance with state audits and notices, research and planning, and much more. (AA, estab 2013, empl 1, sales $145,680, cert: NMSDC, 8(a))

7442 Benford Brown & Associates LLC
8334 S Stony Island Ave
Chicago, IL 60617
Contact: Kim Ellen Partner
Tel: 773-731-1300
Email: kellen@benfordbrown.com
Website: www.benfordbrown.com
Auditing, accounting, tax & small business consulting services. (Woman/AA, estab 1996, empl 7, sales $1,005,155, cert: State, NMSDC, WBENC)

7443 Cabrera Capital Markets, LLC
10 S LaSalle St Ste 1050
Chicago, IL 60603
Contact: William Feeley Managing Dir
Tel: 312-236-8888
Email: mfeeley@cabreracapital.com
Website: www.cabreracapital.com
Investment banking services, domestic & international equity brokerage, taxable fixed income brokerage, mergers & acquisitions. (Hisp, estab 2001, empl 74, sales $25,109,305, cert: State, NMSDC)

7444 Davenport Capital Management
312 N Clark St Ste 500
Chicago, IL 60654
Contact: Thomas Davenport Managing Partner
Tel: 312-445-6406
Email: thomas@davenportcap.com
Website: www.davenportcap.com
Merchant banking, strategic advisory & investments. (AA, estab 2014, empl 4, sales $800,000, cert: NMSDC)

7445 E.C. Ortiz & Co., LLP
333 S Des Plaines St, Ste 2-N
Chicago, IL 60661
Contact: Edilberto C. Ortiz Managing Partner
Tel: 312-876-1900
Email: ecortiz@ecortiz.com
Website: www.ecortiz.com
Auditing, accounting, consulting, taxation, employee benefit plan audits, management services & financial advice. (As-Pac, estab 1974, empl 65, sales $3,968,725, cert: State, City, NMSDC)

7446 Global Capital, Ltd.
205 W. Wacker Dr. Ste 730
Chicago, IL 60606
Contact: Terri McNally President
Tel: 312-846-6918
Email: brian@globelease.com
Website: www.globalcapitalltd.com
Equipment leasing & financing: aircraft, rails, trailers, vehicles, computers, manufacturing & construction equipment. (Woman, estab 1999, empl 7, sales $34,465,113, cert: WBENC)

7447 Holland Capital Management LLC
303 West Madison Ste 700
Chicago, IL 60606
Contact: Valerie King Dir of Marketing
Tel: 312-553-4830
Email: vking@hollandcap.com
Website: www.hollandcap.com
Equity & fixed income institutional management. (Minority, Woman, estab 1991, empl 22, sales $6,966,000, cert: State, NMSDC)

7448 Loop Capital Markets
111 W Jackson Blvd Ste 1901
Chicago, IL 60604
Contact: Sidney Dillard Partner
Tel: 312-356-5008
Email: nancy.ziagos@loopcapital.com
Website: www.loopcapital.com
Corporate debt & issuances, sub notes, floating rate notes, bonds, securities, credit cards, equity, common stock, variable rate debt, etc. (AA, estab 1997, empl 150, sales , cert: NMSDC)

7449 MWM Consulting Group Inc.
55 E Jackson Blvd Ste 1000
Chicago, IL 60604
Contact: Managing Principal
Tel: 312-987-9097
Email: mail@mwmcg.com
Website: www.mwmcg.com
Actuarial analysis, valuations & admin services. (Woman, estab 1993, empl 12, sales $2,350,000, cert: WBENC)

7450 Sierra Forensic Group
30 S Wacker Dr Ste 2200
Chicago, IL 60606
Contact: Adrian Sierra CEO
Tel: 312-674-7100
Email: adrian.sierra@sfg-global.com
Website: www.sfg-global.com
Forensic accounting & investigative services. (Hisp, estab 2005, empl 8, sales $327,688, cert: NMSDC)

Indiana

7451 Engaging Solutions, LLC
3965 N Meridian St Ste 1B
Indianapolis, IN 46208
Contact: Debbie Wilson Managing Principal
Tel: 317-283-8300
Email: debbie@engagingsolutions.net
Website: www.engagingsolutions.net
Fiscal Management & Accountability, Financial Compliance Audits, Program Audits, Financial Reviews, Compilations, Internal Controls Reviews, Tax Preparation, Ta Audit Representation. (Woman/AA, estab 2005, empl 26, sales $2,009,000, cert: State)

7452 Moore Accounting, LLC
9465 Counselors Row, Ste 200
Indianapolis, IN 46240
Contact: April Moore Owner
Tel: 317-504-0296
Email: afreeman@mooreacctg.com
Website: www.mooreacctg.com
Accounting, Tax, Payroll, Tier 2 Audit Services, Davis Bacon & Related Acts, Long-Term Care, Mental Health, Transportation, A133, Echos, Housing Authority, Section 8, Tax Credit Housing, Public Housing. (Woman/AA, estab 2010, empl 3, sales , cert: State, City, WBENC)

7453   Putnam Industries Inc.
4582 NW Plaza W Dr# 100
Zionsville, IN 46077
Contact: Jim Pickens President
Tel: 317-275-3153
Email: jpickens@putnamindustriesinc.com
Website: www.putnamindustriesinc.com
Equipment leasing & finance: computers, software, hardware, copiers, office furniture, fleet vehlices, medical equipment, trucks, buses, lighting, HVAC systems, bulldozers, forklifts, heavy machinery, telephone systems, alarm systems. (AA, estab 2007, empl 5, sales $3,836,816, cert: NMSDC)

7454   Solace Risk Management
9247 N Meridian St Ste 221
Indianapolis, IN 46260
Contact: Charles Moorer President
Tel: 317-423-3947
Email: charles.moorer@srm-cs.com
Website: www.srm-cs.com
Designs comprehensive fully insured & self-insured risk financing & risk management programs. (AA, estab 2011, empl 3, sales , cert: State, NMSDC)

7455   Thomas & Reed, LLC
148 E. Market St Ste 300
Indianapolis, IN 46204
Contact: Stephen A Reed
Tel: 317-955-6933
Email: tclemons@trlllc-cpa.com
Website: www.trlllc-cpa.com
Certified public accounting: auditing, reviews, compilations, controllership, bookkeeping, financial software system installation & training, payroll, staff outsourcing, rate analysis, Davis Bacon Compliance, contract compliance. (Woman/AA, estab 2004, empl 3, sales $267,340, cert: City)

Kansas

7456   Asset LifeCycle, LLC
PO Box 19286
Topeka, KS 66619
Contact: President
Tel: 785-272-8288
Email:
Website: www.assetlc.com
Asset disposition, electronics asset remarketing & recycling solutions. (Woman, estab 2004, empl 10, sales $450,000, cert: WBENC)

Massachusetts

7457   Spafford Leasing Associates, Inc.
1350 Main St Ste 318
Springfield, MA 01103
Contact: Angela Flebotte CEO
Tel: 413-526-0975
Email: angelaf@spafford.com
Website: www.spafford.com
Equipment leasing, computer systems, hospital equipment, copiers, telephone systems, computer software, manufacturing equipment, for lease terms ranging from 3-7 years. (Woman, estab 1989, empl 2, sales $500,000, cert: WBENC)

Maryland

7458   AdNet/AccountNet, Inc.
757 Frederick Rd Ste 102
Catonsville, MD 21228
Contact: Betsy Cerulo CEO
Tel: 410-715-4040
Email: bcerulo@adnetp3.com
Website: www.adnetp3.com
Accounting/Financial, Information Tecnology, Human Resources and Administrative staffing. (Woman, estab 1990, empl 23, sales $2,000,000, cert: State, WBENC)

7459   Beasley Financial Group LLC
4815 Coyle Rd, Ste 103
Owings Mills, MD 21117
Contact: Marcus Beasley CEO
Tel: 877-265-1264
Email: mbeasley@beasleyfinancialgroup.com
Website: www.beasleyfinancialgroup.com
Financial advisory, brokerage & consulting: 401(k) retirement plans, life, health, dental, disability & long term care insurance benefit plans. (Woman/AA, estab 2005, empl 3, sales , cert: State)

7460   Beyond The Bottom Line, Inc.
1300 Mercantile Lane Ste 139
Largo, MD 20774
Contact: Corinda Davis President
Tel: 301-322-4083
Email: bblinc@beyondbottomline.com
Website: www.beyondbottomline.com
Budget formulation, execution & monitoring processes, data mining to compile raw data to help clients recognize significant facts, relationships, trends, patterns, exceptions & anomalies. (Woman/AA, estab 2003, empl 16, sales $1,202,364, cert: State)

7461   EurekaFacts, LLC
51 Monroe St, PE-10
Rockville, MD 20850
Contact: Jorge Restrepo Dir Business Devel
Tel: 240-403-1646
Email: certifications@eurekafacts.com
Website: www.eurekafacts.com
Research design, rigorous data collection, & advanced analytic & statistical services. (Hisp, estab 2003, empl 23, sales $4,281,146, cert: NMSDC)

7462   Gonzalez, Hawkins & Johnson LLC
PO Box 2705
Upper Marlboro, MD 20772
Contact: Alejandro Gonzalez Partner
Tel: 240-865-6052
Email: agonzalez@ghjaccounting.com
Website: www.ghjaccounting.com
Federal Financial Consulting. (Woman/AA, Hisp, estab 2008, empl 3, sales , cert: State, 8(a))

7463   IMB Development Corporation, LLC
7201 Wisconsin Ave., Ste 440
Bethesda, MD 20814
Contact: Tarrus Richardson CEO
Tel: 240-507-1660
Email: trichardson@imbdc.com
Website: www.imbdc.com
Enterprise risk management & insurance solutions, supplier diversity strategy & capacity building, M&A advisory & direct private equity investing. (AA, estab 2010, empl 6, sales $2,012,892, cert: State, NMSDC)

7464 New Century Advisors, LLC
2 Wisconsin Circle, Ste 940
Chevy Chase, MD 20815
Contact: Ellen Safir President
Tel: 240-395-0550
Email: esafir@ncallc.com
Website: www.newcenturyadvisors.com
Investment Management Services. (Woman, estab 2002, empl 14, sales $4,695,000, cert: WBENC)

7465 Premier Group Services, Inc
7404 Executive Pl
Lanham, MD 20706
Contact: Joye Sistrunk Principal
Tel: 301-577-6444
Email: joyes@pgs-cpa.com
Website: www.pgservicesinc.com
Audits, fraud, waste & abuse support, govt contracting consulting & audits, temporary accounting staff, attestation services, business consulting, budgeting, taxes & payroll, financial forecasting & projections. (Woman/AA, estab 2005, empl 5, sales $139,000, cert: State, 8(a))

7466 SB & Company, LLC.
200 International Cir, Ste 5500
Hunt Valley, MD 21030
Contact: Stacy Wenzl Principal of Practice Dev
Tel: 410-584-9302
Email: swenzl@sbandcompany.com
Website: www.sbandcompany.com
Accounting services. (Woman/AA, estab 2005, empl 95, sales $14,050,000, cert: State, NMSDC)

7467 The CTS Group, LLC
13407 Tamarack Rd
Silver Spring, MD 20904
Contact: Calvin L. Scott, Jr. Managing Member
Tel: 301-801-1193
Email: cscott@ctsgroupllc.com
Website: www.ctsgroupllc.com
Comprehensive accounting & advisory business services, account maintenance, financial mgmt, budget devel & analysis, interim outsourcing, transaction analysis, transaction processing, data analysis & summarization. (AA, estab 2007, empl 1, sales $175,000, cert: State, 8(a))

7468 TSC Enterprise
5211 Auth Rd Ste 100
Suitland, MD 20746
Contact: Salome Tinker Managing Partner
Tel: 240-455-7848
Email: sjtinker@tsccpas.com
Website: www.TSCcpas.com
Certified public accounting, FIAR, audit readiness, tax, financial transition, compliance, assurance, management consulting, A133, yellow book, cost recovery, performance reviews, financial system implementation, financial support & staffing. (Woman/AA, estab 2001, empl 6, sales $250,000, cert: WBENC)

Maine

7469 Absolute Credit LLC
175 Exchange St, Ste 225
Bangor, ME 04401
Contact: President
Tel: 800-680-5000
Email: info@absolutecreditllc.com
Website: www.AbsoluteCreditLLC.com
Nationwide collections. (Woman, estab 2006, empl 28, sales $980,000, cert: WBENC)

Michigan

7470 Baron Wealth Management
3150 Livernois Rd, Ste 250
Troy, MI 48083
Contact: Beth Zilka Operations Mgr
Tel: 248-251-0161
Email: bzilka@baron-wealth.com
Website: www.baron-wealth.com
Comprehensive wealth management services, income tax, retirement, cash flow, estate, investment, compensation, benefits & insurance planning. (Woman, estab 2010, empl 6, sales $0, cert: WBENC)

7471 Centennial Securities Advisory Services
515 Ship St, Ste 211
Saint Joseph, MI 49085
Contact: Jim Roberts President
Tel: 269-982-4188
Email: jim@jrcent.com
Website: www.jrcent.com
Registered Investment Advisory firm, wealth management, investments, investing, 401k, IRA, pension, foundation, financial advisor. (Minority, estab 2014, empl 3, sales $300,000, cert: NMSDC)

7472 Chippewa Capital LLC
3190 Tri Park Dr
Grand Blanc, MI 48439
Contact: Thomas Barrett VP
Tel: 810-579-0579
Email: thomas.barrett@macarthurcorp.com
Website: www.chippewacapital.com
Equipment leasing, painting, trucking, warehousing & distribution. (Nat Ame, estab 2000, empl 35, sales $2,000,000, cert: NMSDC)

7473 First Independence Bank
44 Michigan Ave
Detroit, MI 48226
Contact: Rhonda Pugh Branch Admin
Tel: 313-256-8400
Email: rhondapugh@firstindependence.com
Website: www.firstindependence.com
Banking services. (AA, estab 1970, empl 62, sales $13,737,000, cert: NMSDC)

7474 Gonzales Financial Consulting, LLC
4707 Charest
Waterford, MI 48327
Contact: Rogelio Gonzales Managing Member
Tel: 810-706-1687
Email: roy@gonzalesfc.com
Website: www.gonzalesfc.com
Retirement plan consulting services, insurance coverage review, broker management & risk management support services, commercial liability, property, general liability, worker's compensation. (Hisp, estab 2015, empl 4, sales , cert: NMSDC)

7475 KCM Technical Inc.
850 Stephenson Hwy, Ste 603
Troy, MI 48083
Contact: Pamela Williford President
Tel: 877-996-3749
Email: cjohnson@kcmtech.net
Website: www.kcmtech.net
Offers Payroll, Accounting & Help Supply Services. (AA, estab 2005, empl 350, sales , cert: NMSDC)

7476   L J Ross Associates, Inc.
       4 Universal Way
       Jackson, MI 49204
       Contact: Kaylyn Todd Marketing & Business Dev Mgr
       Tel: 517-544-9100
       Email: kaylyn@ljross.com
       Website: www.ljross.com
Debt collection: consumer & commercial debts. (Woman, estab 1992, empl 60, sales $8,012,319, cert: WBENC)

7477   Lakefront Capital, LLC
       28175 Haggerty Rd
       Novi, MI 48377
       Contact: Sandy Fuchs Dir Ops & Client Service
       Tel: 248-994-9001
       Email: sandy.fuchs@lakefrontts.com
       Website: www.lakefrontts.com
Lease financing & portfolio management. (As-Pac, estab 2002, empl 8, sales $10,000,000, cert: NMSDC)

7478   Minority Alliance Capital, LLC
       6960 Orchard Lake Rd Ste 306
       West Bloomfield, MI 48322
       Contact: Tim McCormick VP- Sales
       Tel: 248-236-5182
       Email: mccormick.t@mac-leasing.com
       Website: www.mac-leasing.com
Equipment leasing: computer & software, office furniture & fixtures, production & process control. (AA, estab 1999, empl 14, sales $248,000,000, cert: NMSDC)

7479   Optimal Leasing LLC
       4301 Orchard Lake Rd, Ste 180-173
       West Bloomfield, MI 48323
       Contact: Larry Robinson CEO
       Tel: 248-738-2699
       Email: larry@optimaleasingcompany.com
       Website: www.optimalleasingcompany.com
Third party lease financing of capital equipment. (AA, estab 1996, empl 50, sales , cert: NMSDC)

7480   Renaissance Capital Alliance
       5440 Corporate Dr, Ste 275
       Troy, MI 48098
       Contact: Kyle Bell Natl Acct Mgr
       Tel: 248-821-1811
       Email: kylebell@rcalliance.com
       Website: www.rcalliance.com
Equipment leasing: materials handling, lift trucks, transportation & warehousing equipment; fleet mgmt services. (AA, estab 2001, empl 13, sales $50,000,000, cert: NMSDC, CPUC)

Minnesota

7481   Amare & Associates LLC dba ABA Tax Accounting
       10670 Hawthorn Trail
       St. Paul, MN 55129
       Contact: Amare Berhie CEO
       Tel: 866-936-0430
       Email: amare@abataxaccounting.com
       Website: www.abataxaccounting.com
Finance & accounting outsourcing svcs: transaction processing & staffing services. (AA, estab 1989, empl 2, sales , cert: State, City, NMSDC)

7482   Certes Financial Pros, Inc.
       5775 Wayzata Blvd, Ste 550
       St. Louis Park, MN 55416
       Contact: Sally Mainquist President
       Tel: 952-345-4141
       Email: getalife@certespros.com
       Website: www.certespros.com
Provide high-end financial professionals on an interim & project basis. (Woman, estab 1994, empl 170, sales $12,000,000, cert: State)

7483   Diversified Adjustment Service, Inc.
       600 Coon Rapids Blvd
       Coon Rapids, MN 55433
       Contact: Michelle Wendell Admin Asst
       Tel: 763-783-2334
       Email: diversity@diversifiedadjustment.com
       Website: www.diversifiedadjustment.com
Managed collection svcs: accounts recievable mgmt & credit reporting, debt collection, pre-collect & skip-tracing svcs. (Woman, estab 1981, empl 60, sales $14,400,000, cert: CPUC, WBENC)

Missouri

7484   Stern Brothers & Co.
       8000 Maryland Ave, Ste 800
       Saint Louis, MO 63105
       Contact: Lisa Liebschutz Marketing
       Tel: 314-727-5519
       Email: lliebschutz@sternbrothers.com
       Website: www.sternbrothers.com
Full service investment bank. Lines of business include public and project finance, corporate and equity finance, sales and trading. (Woman, estab 1985, empl 42, sales $20,766,637, cert: WBENC)

North Carolina

7485   Falcon Square Capital, LLC
       4000 Westchase Blvd
       Raleigh, NC 27607
       Contact: Melissa Pendergrass CEO
       Tel: 919-825-1534
       Email: mpendergrass@falconsquarecapital.com
       Website: www.falconsquarecapital.com
Trading, research, portfolio construction, transition management, client commission arrangements & other institutional brokerage services. (Woman, estab 2013, empl 16, sales $1,711,975, cert: WBENC)

7486   Innovation Partners LLC
       5950 Fairview Road, Ste 140
       Charlotte, NC 28210
       Contact: Anthony Lawrence Principal
       Tel: 704-708-5461
       Email: alawrence@innovationpartnersllc.com
       Website: www.innovationpartnersllc.com
Deferred compensation plans, retirement planning, actuarial, pension funds, investment banking, reinsurance, securities portfolio management, risk management, asset portfoilo management, underwriting services. (Woman/AA, estab 2007, empl 20, sales $1,500,000, cert: NMSDC)

7487 Red Bridge Consulting Group
10700 Sikes Place, Ste 305
Charlotte, NC 28277
Contact: Judith Mackesy Owner
Tel: 704-375-2040
Email: jmackesy@redbridgecg.com
Website: www.redbridgecg.com
Recruiting, Consulting and Staffing Services, permanent
placement, project-based consulting, temporary contract,
and contract-to-hire services. (Woman, estab 2009, empl
12, sales $0, cert: WBENC)

7488 Tryon Clear View Group, LLC
816 W Mills St
Columbus, NC 28722
Contact: Mary Thompson Exec VP
Tel: 314-255-6279
Email: mthompson@tryonclearview.com
Website: www.tryonclearviewgroup.com
Detect & recover overpayments to vendors, improved
financial & operational practices & procedures. (Woman,
estab , empl 13, sales $2,200,000, cert: WBENC)

New Jersey

7489 Allen, Maxwell & Silver, Inc.
17-17 Route 208 N Ste 340
Fair Lawn, NJ 07401
Contact: Lisa Freidman CEO
Tel: 201-871-0044
Email: lisa@amscollections.com
Website: www.amscollections.com
Commercial collections. (Woman, estab 1992, empl 38,
sales $2,650,000, cert: WBENC)

7490 Ateeca Inc.
107 B1 Corporate Blvd,
South Plainfield, NJ 07080
Contact: Adam Lee Sr Business Dev
Tel: 908-427-5591
Email: gdavis@ateeca.com
Website: www.ateeca.com/
Payroll services. (Minority, Woman, estab 2005, empl 180,
sales $6,830,000, cert: NMSDC, WBENC)

7491 Broad Street Capital Markets LLC
494 Broad St Ste 206
Newark, NJ 07102
Contact: Andrew Adderly CEO
Tel: 862-367-9930
Email: mdejesus@broadscm.com
Website: www.broadscm.com
Investment Banking & Securities Dealing, Investment
Advice, Administrative Management & General Manage-
ment Consulting. (AA, Hisp, estab 2000, empl 8, sales $0,
cert: State, NMSDC)

7492 Business Processes Redefined, LLC
155 Passaic Ave, Ste 470
Fairfield, NJ 07004
Contact: President
Tel: 800-470-6622
Email: customerservice@bprllc.com
Website: www.bprllc.com
Collection services. (Woman, estab 2007, empl 12, sales
$500,000, cert: WBENC)

7493 Enhanced Due Diligence Advisory, Inc.
910 Garden St
Hoboken, NJ 07030
Contact: Wayne Chau
Tel: 973-727-7248
Email: wchau@eddadvisory.com
Website: www.eddadvisory.com
Risk assessment of domestic/international assets,
compliance, audit & logistics strategy. (As-Pac, estab
2015, empl 3, sales , cert: State, NMSDC)

7494 First Credit Services, Inc.
9 Wills Way
Piscataway, NJ 08854
Contact: Rajesh Chhabria CEO
Tel: 732-305-8301
Email: rchhabria@fcsbpo.com
Website: www.firstcreditonline.com
Collection & business process outsourcing, past-due A/R
for medium & large businesses. (As-Ind, estab 1993,
empl 50, sales $6,934,493, cert: NMSDC)

7495 Runnymede Capital Management, Inc.
10 Wilrich Glen Rd
Morristown, NJ 07960
Contact: Andrew Wang Sr VP
Tel: 973-267-6886
Email: awang@runnymede.com
Website: www.runnymede.com
Manages investment portfolios of institutions (Taft-
Hartley, captive insurance, public pension fund, corpo-
rate, non-profit) & high-net-worth individuals. (As-Pac,
estab 1993, empl 8, sales $1,500,000, cert: NMSDC)

Nevada

7496 ReCredit
1925 Village Center Circle Ste 150-11
Las Vegas, NV 89134
Contact: Katrina Screen Owner
Tel: 650-539-0800
Email: katrina@thepremierconcierge.com
Website: www.recredit.co/bp/
Offers a turn-key solution to personal debt and credit
matters by providing financial literacy education via our
digital content, phone consultations and our credit
services work, which produces maximum credit score
improvement. (Minority, Woman, estab 2016, empl 15,
sales , cert: NMSDC, SDB)

New York

7497 All Occasions Concierge, LLC
1333A North Ave, Ste 149
New Rochelle, NY 10804
Contact: Sterling Jasper CEO
Tel: 914-481-8312
Email: sterling.jasper@alloccasionsconcierge.com
Website: www.alloccasionsconcierge.com
(AA, estab 2006, empl 4, sales , cert: NMSDC)

7498 BCA Watson Rice LLP
5 Penn Plaza, 15th Fl
New York, NY 10001
Contact: Bennie Hadnott Managing Partner
Tel: 212-447-7300
Email: blhadnott@bcawatsonrice.com
Website: www.bcawatsonrice.com
Financial auditing services, retirement plan audits,
forensic accounting services, internal control services &
tax compliance services. (AA, As-Pac, estab 1982, empl
299, sales $4,597,538, cert: State)

7499   C.L. King & Associates, Inc.
410 Park Ave
New York, NY 10022
Contact: Jason Freed Sales
Tel: 212-364-1834
Email: jcf@clking.com
Website: www.clking.com
Investment banking services, stock (equity) underwriting, bond (fixed income/debt) underwriting, mergers & acquisitions advisory, securities sales, trading & distribution, stock buybacks & pension fund asset mgmt. (Woman, estab 1972, empl 125, sales $45,242,635, cert: WBENC)

7500   CastleOak Securities, L.P.
110 E 59th St, 2nd Fl
New York, NY 10022
Contact: Philip Ippolito CFO
Tel: 646-521-6700
Email: ochukwu@castleoaklp.com
Website: www.castleoaklp.com
Primary & secondary sales & trading of fixed income, equity, municipal & money market securities. (AA, estab , empl , sales $23,087,000, cert: NMSDC)

7501   CAVU Securities, LLC.
52 Vanderbilt Ave. Ste 403
New York, NY 10017
Contact: Karin Sheehy Managing Dir
Tel: 212-916-3855
Email: ksheehy@cavusecurities.com
Website: www.cavusecurities.com
Full service brokerage, investment banking & funds distribution. (AA, estab 2013, empl 12, sales $1,500,000, cert: NMSDC, CPUC)

7502   Corporate Leasing Associates, Inc.
21 Morris Ave
Rockville Center, NY 11570
Contact: Mitch Gelnick Diversity Sales
Tel: 212-732-5571
Email: mitch@corplease.com
Website: www.corplease.com
Operating lease structures, lease purchase, sale & lease-back, step down & step up payments, balloon payments, single investor leases, etc. (Woman, estab 1982, empl 6, sales $4,654,218, cert: State, CPUC, WBENC)

7503   DACK Consulting Solutions
2 William St Ste 202
White Plains, NY 10601
Contact: Aleksandra Chancy CEO
Tel: 914-686-7102
Email: ggayle@dackconsulting.com
Website: www.dackconsulting.com
Cost consulting, estimating, scheduling & project management services. (Woman/AA, estab 1997, empl 24, sales $1,000,000, cert: State, City)

7504   Delta Risk Capital Group LLC
860 Fifth Ave (2L)
New York, NY 10065
Contact: Shanker Merchant Principal
Tel: 212-961-6825
Email: shanker.merchant@deltariskcapital.com
Website: www.DeltaRiskCapital.com
Model Validation Services pursuant to FHFA Requirements and Dodd-Frank Financial Regulations, Valuation on Securities, Valuation of Residential and Commercial Mortgages, Mortgage and Asset backed securities, Investment Banking, Capital Raising. (As-Pac, estab , empl , sales , cert: NMSDC)

7505   Divine Capital Markets
39 Broadway, 36 Fl
New York, NY 10006
Contact: Hughes Sales
Tel: 212-344-5867
Email: dani@divinecapital.com
Website: www.divinecapital.com
Investment banking, underwriting & distributions, research, corporate share repurchase programs, proprietary VWAP trading, municipal & corporate bonds, international equities. (Woman, estab 1997, empl 12, sales $13,900,000, cert: WBENC)

7506   EXIGIS LLC
589 8th Ave Fl 8
New York, NY 10018
Contact: Armand Alvarez CEO
Tel: 800-928-1963
Email: sales@exigis.com
Website: www.exigis.com
Risk management services, risk, insurance & business process automation technology. (Hisp, estab 2002, empl 35, sales $1,550,000, cert: NMSDC)

7507   Flash Exterminating, Inc.
164 Maujer St
Brooklyn, NY 11206
Contact: James Swint President
Tel: 347-748-8023
Email: flashexterminating@gmail.com
Website: www.flashexterminating.net
Flash stands for pest elimination. Sealing entry points and having Certified Food Safety handlers on staff to act as consultants to city and state department inspections ensures your facility is in top notch order avoiding the penalties and fines (AA, estab 2009, empl 3, sales $197,000, cert: City, NMSDC)

7508   KBL, LLP Certified Public Accountants & Advisors
110 Wall St, 11th Fl
New York, NY 10005
Contact: Richard Levychin Partner
Tel: 212-785-9700
Email: rlevychin@kbl.com
Website: www.kbl.com
Audit & assurance, agreed-upon procedures, compilation & review procedures, business process outsourcing, risk management & advisory services, cross border international practices business services, tax compliance. (AA, estab 1994, empl 50, sales $5,000,000, cert: NMSDC)

7509   Lebenthal Holdings, LLC
521 Fifth Ave Fl 15
New York, NY 10175
Contact: Steven Willis Sr managing dir
Tel: 877-425-6006
Email: swillis@lebenthal.com
Website: www.lebenthalcapitalmarkets.com
Underwrites securities, equity & corporate debt underwriting. (Woman, estab 2007, empl 38, sales $13,179,068, cert: WBENC)

7510 Masterpiece Accounting Services LLC
2 Hamilton Ave Ste 206
New Rochelle, NY 10801
Contact: Ibanessa Hogan Principal
Tel: 914-661-2798
Email: i.hogan@masterpieceaccounting.com
Website: www.masterpieceaccounting.com
Accounting & bookkeeping services, tax preparation &
QuickBooks consulting. (Minority, Woman, estab 2010,
empl 1, sales , cert: State, WBENC)

7511 Mitchell & Titus LLP
1 Battery Parkm Plaza, Fl 27
New York, NY 10004
Contact: Irene Davis CFO
Tel: 312-325-7422
Email: IDavis@MitchellTitus.com
Website: www.mitchelltitus.com
Certified public accounting & mgmt consulting. (AA, estab
1974, empl 200, sales $17,000,000, cert: State, NMSDC)

7512 Samuel A. Ramirez & Company, Inc.
61 Broadway 29th Fl
NewYork, NY 10006
Contact: Lawrence Goldman Managing Dir
Tel: 212-248-1214
Email: larry.goldman@ramirezco.com
Website: www.ramirezco.com
Investment banking & capital markets, distribution,
brokerage, corporate share repurchase & research services.
(Hisp, estab , empl 150, sales $72,950,961, cert: State, City,
NMSDC)

7513 Sunrise Credit Services, Inc.
260 Airport Plaza
Farmingdale, NY 11735
Contact: BENJAMIN CARROCCIO Sr VP/ General
Counsel
Tel: 800-208-8565
Email: bcarroccio@sunrisecreditservices.com
Website: www.SunriseCreditServices.com
Credit & collection services. (Woman, estab 1974, empl
425, sales $15,500,000, cert: WBENC)

7514 SWS Capital Management, LLC (formerly Williams
Capital Management, LLC
100 Wall St, 18th Floor
New York, NY 10005
Contact: Lorna Maye Administrative Mgr
Tel: 212-461-6500
Email: lmaye@swscapitalmanagement.com
Website: www.swscapitalmanagement.com
Investment svcs: cash management & short-term fixed
income investment strategies. (AA, estab 2002, empl 11,
sales $1,073,590, cert: City, NMSDC)

7515 Tigress Financial Partners LLC
114 W 47th St
New York, NY 10036
Contact: George Orr
Tel: 212-430-8700
Email: gorr@tigressfp.com
Website: www.tigressfp.com
Financial services: rtesearch, trade execution, asset
management, corporate advisory & investment banking.
(Woman, estab 2010, empl 9, sales $100,000, cert: State,
City, WBENC)

7516 Topeka Capital Markets Inc.
40 Wall St, Ste 1702
New York, NY 10005
Contact: Sylvester McClearn COO
Tel: 212-709-5706
Email: sm@topekacapitalmarkets.com
Website: www.topekacapitalmarkets.com
Agency-only trading domestic & international equities,
traders, sales traders & research analysts. (AA, estab
2010, empl 28, sales , cert: City, NMSDC)

7517 Torres Llompart, Sanchez Ruiz LLP
Bowling Green Station
New York, NY 10274
Contact: Frank Sanchez-Ruiz Partner
Tel: 646-214-1064
Email: fsanchez@tlsr.com
Website: www.tlsr.com
Certified public accountants & business consulting:
accounting, auditing, tax & corporate advisory, opera-
tional studies, management advisory, risk management,
marketing consulting, franchising services, international
commerce. (Hisp, estab 1989, empl 35, sales
$2,410,000, cert: City, NMSDC)

7518 VJN Associates. LLC
39-38 Bell Blvd, Ste 202
Bayside, NY 11361
Contact: Victor Chin Operations Mgr
Tel: - -
Email: victorc@vjnassociates.com
Website: www.vjnassociates.com
Assurance, accounting, book keeping, audits both
financial & compliance. (Minority, Woman, estab 2012,
empl 10, sales , cert: City, NMSDC)

Ohio

7519 Chard Snyder
3510 Irwin Simpson Rd
Mason, OH 45040
Contact: Deborah Meek
Tel: 513-754-3121
Email: deborah.meek@chard-snyder.com
Website: www.chard-snyder.com
Flexible Spending Accounts, Health Reimbursement
Accounts, Health Savings Account, Parking and Trans-
portation Accounts, COBRA and Billing Administration.
(Woman, estab 1988, empl , sales $0, cert: WBENC)

7520 Kaiser Consulting, LLC
818 Riverbend Ave
Powell, OH 43065
Contact: Lori Kaiser CEO
Tel: 614-300-1088
Email: lkaiser@kaiserconsulting.com
Website: www.kaiserconsulting.com
Financial & accounting consulting. (Woman, estab 1994,
empl 63, sales $4,440,000, cert: WBENC)

7521 Kanu Asset Managment, LLC
4015 Executive Park Dr Ste 402
Cincinnati, OH 45241
Contact: Enyi Kanu CEO
Tel: 513-769-2700
Email: ktrent@kanuinvestments.com
Website: www.kanuasset.com
Investments, Wealth Management, Financial Planning,
Insurance, Portfolio Management, Institutional Consult-
ing & Advisory Services. (AA, estab 1996, empl 5, sales ,
cert: NMSDC)

7522 McCarthy, Burgess & Wolff
       26000 Cannon Rd
       Cleveland, OH 44146
       Contact: Paul Joseph Dir Business Devel
       Tel: 440-735-5100
       Email: paul.joseph@mbandw.com
       Website: www.mbandw.com
Commercial collections & receivables. (Woman, estab 2000, empl 203, sales $17,200,000, cert: WBENC)

7523 Parms & Company, LLC
       585 S Front St Ste 220
       Columbus, OH 43215
       Contact: John Parms
       Tel: 614-224-3078
       Email: jparms@parms.com
       Website: www.parms.com
Auditing, accounting, agreed-upon procedures, forensic accounting, consulting & tax-related services. (AA, estab 1983, empl 14, sales $1,335,851, cert: State, NMSDC)

7524 Richardson and Associates, LLC
       427 Appaloosa Ct
       Cincinnati, OH 45231
       Contact: Sherri Richardson Owner
       Tel: 513-772-8348
       Email: sherri@richardsonandassociates.com
       Website: www.richardsonandassociates.com
Accounting services, audits, writing policies & procedures. (Woman/AA, estab 2007, empl 12, sales , cert: State, NMSDC, WBENC)

7525 The Pension & Retirement Group LLC
       5900 Roche Dr Ste 435
       Columbus, OH 43229
       Contact: Curtis Clark Managing Partner
       Tel: - -
       cclark@thepensionandretirementgroup.com
       www.thepensionandretirementgroup.com
Financial Wellness, Retirement Planning, Insurance, Investments, 401(k) & 403(b) Plan Management, Retirement Income Planning, Supplement Benefits, Securities, Mutual Funds, IRA's. (AA, estab 2005, empl 3, sales $500,000, cert: NMSDC)

Oklahoma

7526 First Financial Network, Inc.
       9211 Lake Hefner Pkwy, Ste 200
       Oklahoma City, OK 73120
       Contact: John A. Morris President
       Tel: 405-748-4100
       Email: jmorris@ffncorp.com
       Website: www.ffncorp.com/
Provides the financial community with turnkey solutions to loan disposition. (Woman, estab 0, empl , sales $0, cert: WBENC)

Pennsylvania

7527 Caterpillar to Butterfly, LLC
       12575 Chilton Rd
       Philadelphia, PA 19154
       Contact: Davida Godett CEO
       Tel: 215-632-2575
       Email: godett@caterpillartobutterfly.net
       Website: www.caterpillartobutterfly.net
(Woman/AA, estab 2013, empl 1, sales , cert: NMSDC)

7528 Exude, LLC
       325 Chestnut St Ste 1000
       Philadelphia, PA 19106
       Contact: Marcos Lopez CEO
       Tel: 215-875-8730
       Email: mlopez@exudeinc.com
       Website: www.exudeinc.com
Employee Benefits, Human Resources & Risk Management Consulting. (Hisp, estab 2013, empl 2, sales $293,231, cert: State, NMSDC)

7529 Milligan & Company LLC
       105 N 22nd St, 2nd Fl
       Philiadelphia, PA 19103
       Contact: Angela Giunta Dir of Marketing
       Tel: 215-496-9100
       Email: agiunta@milligancpa.com
       Website: www.milligancpa.com
Consulting & certified public accounting. (AA, estab 1985, empl 45, sales $6,400,000, cert: State)

7530 Relevante, Inc
       1235 Westlakes Dr Ste 280
       Berwyn, PA 19312
       Contact: William Brassington CEO
       Tel: 484-403-4100
       Email: wbrassington@relevante.com
       Website: www.relevante.com
Accounting & technology consultants. (As-Ind, estab 2002, empl 130, sales $6,100,000, cert: NMSDC)

Puerto Rico

7531 Alvarado Tax & Business Advisors LLC
       PO Box 195598
       San Juan, PR 00918
       Contact: Miguel Rodriguez Admin
       Tel: 787-620-7744
       Email: mrodriguez@alvatax.com
       Website: www.alvatax.com
Tax & business consulting, outsourcing, business operations, government compliance resolution issues, financial management, business, development, business continuation & succession, business governance. (Hisp, estab 2002, empl 32, sales $5,506,828, cert: NMSDC)

Texas

7532 Akisha Networks, Inc.
       5868 A-1 Westheimer Rd, Ste 224
       Houston, TX 77057
       Contact: Ronald Smith VP
       Tel: 713-840-7424
       Email: info@akisha.net
       Website: www.akisha.net
Akisha Networks Inc (ANI) is a full service Digital Systems Integrator that designs, builds and manages IP convergence solutions for today's intelligent commercial buildings. (AA, estab 2001, empl 8, sales $395,776, cert: NMSDC)

7533 Bley Investment Group
       4200 S Hulen, Ste 519
       Fort Worth, TX 76109
       Contact: Laura Bley President
       Tel: 817-732-2442
       Email: laurab@bleyinvestments.com
       Website: www.bleyinvestments.com
Financial services. (Woman, estab 1990, empl 7, sales $565,000, cert: State, WBENC)

7534 Credit Systems International, Inc.
1277 Country Club Lane
Fort Worth, TX 76112
Contact: Kathy Faith Strategic Devel Dir
Tel: 800-405-7546
Email: kathy@creditsystemsintl.com
Website: www.creditsystemsintl.com
Provides debt collection services. (Woman, estab 1980, empl 70, sales $708,000,000, cert: State, City)

7535 Davis & Davis Professional Services Firm LLC
12300 Ford Rd, Ste 290
Dallas, TX 75234
Contact: Chanel Davis Partner
Tel: 972-488-5000
Email: chanel.davis@davisanddavisllc.com
Website: www.DavisandDavisLLC.com
Sales tax consultants, state tax audit consulting & audit defense. (Woman/AA, estab , empl , sales $1,376,000, cert: NMSDC, WBENC)

7536 DWG CPA PLLC
5100 Westheimer, Ste 200
Houston, TX 77056
Contact: Darrell Groves Managing Dir
Tel: 281-201-8348
Email: info@dwgcpatx.com
Website: www.dwgcpatx.com
Tax, accounting, auditing & financial management. (AA, estab 2005, empl 2, sales , cert: State, NMSDC)

7537 Galosi LLC
16800 Dallas Pkwy, Ste 210
Dallas, TX 75248
Contact: J. Wayne Trimmer EVP
Tel: 972-267-9907
Email: wayne.trimmer@galosi.com
Website: www.galosi.com
Cost of Money, Audit Discounts, Credit Memo Errors, Defective or Spoiled Goods Audit, Duplicate Payments, Errors Involving Returns. (Hisp, estab 2001, empl 27, sales $2,100,000, cert: State, NMSDC)

7538 Goldman, Imani & Goldberg, Inc.
9894 Bissonnet St Ste 900
Houston, TX 77036
Contact: Karl Miller Dir of Marketing & Client Dev
Tel: 713-395-5120
Email: kmiller@giginconline.com
Website: www.giginconline.com
Collection programs, accounts receivable management, third party recovery. (AA, estab 2003, empl 26, sales $2,800,000, cert: NMSDC, 8(a))

7539 Harris & Dickey, LLC.
4127 Wycliff Ave
Dallas, TX 75219
Contact: Kelly Harris Partner
Tel: 972-672-7597
Email: kelly.harris@harris-dickey.com
Website: www.harris-dickey.com
Accounting, finance, tax, internal audit, technology risk & special project assistance. (Woman, estab 2010, empl 12, sales $1,662,658, cert: State, City, WBENC)

7540 JN3 Global Enterprises LLC
3302 Far View Dr
Austin, TX 78730
Contact: James Nowlin CEO
Tel: 512-501-1155
Email: Assistant@egpventures.com
Website: www.excelglobalpartners.com/
Corporate financial strategy & implementation. (AA, estab 2007, empl 20, sales $5,920,000, cert: State, NMSDC, CPUC)

7541 Kipling Jones & Co., Ltd.
1200 Smith St Ste 1600
Houston, TX 77002
Contact: Robbi Jones President
Tel: 713-353-4688
Email: rjones@kiplingjones.com
Website: www.kiplingjones.com
Investment banking, financial advisory, bond underwriting & guidance. (Woman/AA, estab 2008, empl 7, sales $500,000, cert: State, City)

7542 McConnell & Jones LLP
4828 Loop Central Dr, Ste 1000
Houston, TX 77081
Contact: Lori Jamail Marketing Dir
Tel: 713-968-1600
Email: info@mjlm.com
Website: www.mcconnelljones.com
Financial statement audits, benefit plan audits, tax returns, compilations, accounting & bookkeeping services, SEC compliance services & single audits. (AA, estab , empl , sales $14,048,077, cert: NMSDC)

7543 Pharos Financial Services LP
3889 Maple Ave Ste 400
Dallas, TX 75219
Contact: Vince Mullins Program Mgr Pharos/DFS-Del
Tel: 770-330-9105
Email: cswain@pharosfinancial.com
Website: www.pharosfinancial.com
Financial loan & lease products. (AA, estab 2002, empl 20, sales , cert: State, NMSDC)

7544 PMB Precision Medical Billing Inc.
8203 Willow Place Dr S Ste 230
Houston, TX 77070
Contact: Petria McKelvey CEO
Tel: 713-672-7211
Email: petria@precisionmedicalbilling.com
Website: www.precisionmedicalbilling.com
Revenue recovery & collections services. (Woman/AA, estab 1995, empl 13, sales $1,611,635, cert: State, WBENC)

7545 PRO Consulting Services, Inc.
500 Lovett Blvd Ste 250
Houston, TX 77006
Contact: Victor Juarez CEO
Tel: 713-523-1800
Email: vjuarez@proconsrv.com
Website: www.proconsrv.com
Accounts receivables management services, commercial collections. (Hisp, estab 1992, empl 90, sales $4,500,000, cert: NMSDC)

7546   Real Time Resolutions, Inc.
1349 Empire Central Dr Ste 150
Dallas, TX 75247
Contact: Mark Hutto SVP Business Dev
Tel: 214-599-6557
Email: client.services@rtresolutions.com
Website: www.realtimeresolutions.com
Financial services & asset recovery: auto, credit card, mortgages, direct demand accounts, student loans, installment loans & commercial loans. (Woman, estab 2000, empl 320, sales , cert: WBENC)

Utah

7547   Merrimak Capital Company LLC
823 Norfolk Ave
Park City, UT 84060
Contact: Dan Crowl VP Human Resources
Tel: 415-475-4100
Email: rfq@merrimak.com
Website: www.merrimak.com
Financing solutions: operating leases, capital leases, lease lines, sale leasebacks & technology refresh leases. (Woman, estab 1991, empl 42, sales $150,655,616, cert: CPUC, WBENC)

Virginia

7548   BME Ventures LLC
PO Box 2675
Ashburn, VA 20146
Contact: Bianca Ellis Owner
Tel: 571-342-7774
Email: bellis@projacctworkflow.com
Website: www.projacctworkflow.com
Accounting, bookkeeping, and consulting services. (Woman/AA, estab 2019, empl 1, sales , cert: NMSDC, WBENC)

7549   Kodiak Finance LLC
8000 Towers Crescent Dr Ste 1350
Vienna, VA 22182
Contact: Marcy Dilworth President
Tel: 703-266-9199
Email: mdilworth@kodiakfinance.com
Website: www.kodiakfinance.com
Computer leasing & sales, asset management. (Minority, Woman, estab 2004, empl 10, sales $560,357, cert: NMSDC, WBENC)

7550   RER Solutions Inc.
950 Herndon Pkwy, Ste 200
Herndon, VA 20170
Contact: Errin Green CEO
Tel: 703-742-6789
Email: errin.green@rer-solutions.com
Website: www.rer-solutions.com
Comprehensive business, real estate & financial mgmt. services, asset sale support, due diligence, portfolio management systems, technical & admin support personnel, financial modeling, document & records management, risk management. (Woman/AA, estab 1989, empl 27, sales $2,633,597, cert: State, 8(a))

7551   Technology Ventures
7930 Jones Branch Dr Ste 310
McLean, VA 22102
Contact: John Earl Dir Business Dev
Tel: 703-917-1650
Email: jearl@tventures.net
Website: www.tventures.net
IT & Financial Staffing, Government & Consulting Services, Financial Services, Healthcare Communications, Consumer & Retail. (As-Ind, estab 1998, empl 150, sales , cert: State)

Washington

7552   Adekoya Business Consulting LLC
33021 Hoyt Rd SW
Federal Way, WA 98023
Contact: Andre Adekoya CEO
Tel: 206-817-9775
Email: andrew@adekoyabc.com
Website: www.adekoyabc.com
Business solutions, strategic financial planning & analysis, audits, market (digital) competitive analytics & revenue growth opportunities identification, resource planning, process re-engineering & system implementation. (AA, estab 2013, empl 5, sales $425,000, cert: State)

Wisconsin

7553   One Accord, LLC
PO Box 241763
Milwaukee, WI 53224
Contact: Shanna Reid President
Tel: 414-855-6342
Email: smreid@oneaccord.biz
Website: www.oneaccord.biz
Risk management & reinsurance brokerage. (Woman/AA, estab 2002, empl 3, sales , cert: State, City)

PROFESSIONAL SERVICES: Human Resources
Provide training and seminars on a variety of human resources topics: diversity, supplier diversity programs, team building, customer relations, staff development, wellness programs, policy and procedure manuals, coaching, etc. NAICS Code 54

Alabama

7554 C. Edward Lewis & Associates
3415 Buckboard Rd
Montgomery, AL 36116
Contact: Charles Lewis President
Tel: 334-272-3365
Email: charleslewis@celewisohs.com
Website: www.celewisohs.com
EEO & human resources training & consulting. (AA, estab 2004, empl 2, sales , cert: NMSDC)

7555 EAP Lifestyle Management, LLC
805 Daphne Ave Ste B
Daphne, AL 36526
Contact: Patricia Vanderpool Owner
Tel: 800-788-2077
Email: pvanderpool@eaplifestyle.com
Website: www.eaplifestyle.com
Employee assistance program & work/life svcs, substance abuse professional svcs, workplace training & presentation, continuing education, critical incident stress svcs. (Woman, estab 1998, empl 12, sales , cert: WBENC)

Arizona

7556 HR Wise, LLC
8399 E Indian School Rd Ste 101
Scottsdale, AZ 85251
Contact: Gregory O'Keefe CEO
Tel: 480-626-2109
Email: gokeefe@hrwisellc.com
Website: www.hrwisellc.com
Davis Bacon-Act Certified Payroll, Payroll Services, Human Resource Management, Talent Management, Benefits Administration, Time and Attendance, Human Capital Management, HR Business Process Outsourcing (HRBPO). (Hisp, estab 2008, empl 6, sales $290,000, cert: NMSDC, 8(a))

California

7557 ClearPath Management Group, Inc
165 N Maple Ave #1930 Ste 102
Manteca, CA 95336
Contact: ClearPath WM Corporate Services Mgr
Tel: 209-239-8700
Email: wbe@clearpathwm.com
Website: www.clearpathwm.com
Contractor payroll, employer of record service, Contingent workforce management, business process outsourcing, Independent contractor compliance. (Woman, estab 2010, empl 16, sales $49,491,482, cert: WBENC)

7558 E. L. Goldberg & Associates
950 Siskiyou Dr
Menlo Park, CA 94025
Contact: Edie Goldberg CEO
Tel: 650-854-0854
Email: edie@elgoldberg.com
Website: www.elgoldberg.com
Human Resources Mgmt Consulting, Talent Management, Performance Mgmt, Career Mgmt, Succession Planning, Leadership Devel, Competency Modeling, Benchmarking, HR Strategic Planning. (Woman, estab 2001, empl 1, sales $300,000, cert: CPUC)

7559 Employers Choice Online Inc.
9845 Painter Ave. Ste B
Whittier, CA 90605
Contact: Jesus Ariel Lopez Procurement Contracts Mgr
Tel: 562-319-0413
Email: bids@ecoinc.us
Website: www.employerschoicescreening.com
Employment background checks, drug testing, physical exams & Form 1-9 services. (Hisp, estab 2011, empl 20, sales $2,034,818, cert: NMSDC, CPUC, 8(a), SDB)

7560 HR Allen Consulting Services
6065 Sundale Way Ste. 98
Fair Oaks, CA 95628
Contact: Michael Allen President
Tel: 916-370-7849
Email: mallen@hrallenconsulting.com
Website: www.hrallencs.com
Human resource consulting & outsourcing. (AA, Hisp, estab 2005, empl 10, sales , cert: State)

7561 RehabWest, Inc. (RWI)
277 Rancheros Dr Ste 190
San Marcos, CA 92025
Contact: CEO
Tel: 760-759-7500
Email: info@rehabwest.com
Website: www.RehabWest.com
Workers' compensation, risk management & human resources. (Woman, estab 1977, empl 55, sales $6,200,000, cert: WBENC)

7562 Translating Services, Inc.
22141 Ventura Blvd Ste 210
Woodland Hills, CA 91364
Contact: Mel Menendez President
Tel: 310-453-3302
Email: mel@lazar.com
Website: www.lazar.com
Translation, interpreting. (Woman, estab 1999, empl 8, sales $0, cert: WBENC)

Colorado

7563 Champion Business Services
2668 Dexter St
Denver, CO 80207
Contact: Carol Sales
Tel: 303-873-9147
Email: info@championbusiness.com
Website: www.championbusiness.com
Clerical support svcs, help supply svcs, Ccmputer pogramming, data entry processing & preparation, business svcs, clerical skills training, facilities management support svcs. (Woman/AA, estab 1986, empl 3, sales , cert: WBENC)

7564   Employee Development Systems, Inc.
7300 S Alton Way Ste 5J
Centennial, CO 80112
Contact: Sherman Updegraff Managing Dir
Tel: 800-282-3374
Email: sherm@edsiusa.com
Website: www.employeedevelopmentsystems.com
Personal training: self-confidence, understanding behavioral styles, communication skills, listening skills, self-motivation & personal accountability. (Woman, estab , empl , sales $0, cert: NWBOC)

7565   FirstIdea, Inc.
19029 E Plaza Dr, Ste 200
Parker, CO 80134
Contact: Annette Alvarez President
Tel: 303-840-3346
Email: info@firstidea.org
Website: www.firstidea.org
Human Resources consulting and recruitment services. (Woman/Hisp, estab 1989, empl 9, sales $600,000, cert: NMSDC, WBENC)

7566   PayTech, Inc.
7979 E Tufts Ave Ste 1000
Denver, CO 80237
Contact: Julie Knabenshue
Tel: 303-617-0030
Email: jknabenshue@paytech.com
Website: www.paytech.com
Global Payroll & HRIS consulting. (Woman, estab 1999, empl , sales $20,000,000, cert: WBENC)

Florida

7567   DDM Professional Leasing Services
2100 Ponce de Leon Ave Ste 1260
Coral Gables, FL 33134
Contact: Magda Vargas Dir Region North America
Tel: 305-495-6889
Email: mvargas@bmapr.com
Website: www.bmagroupglobal.com
HR Consulting: BPO, Headhunting, Culture-Fit Staffing, Temporary/Contract Employees, Outplacement, Training and Development, Engagement Survey, Employee Values Survey, Behavioral assessments. (Woman/Hisp, estab 2000, empl 20, sales $11,178,587, cert: WBENC)

7568   HRSS Consulting Group
125 E Merritt Island Cswy Ste 107 246
Merritt Island, FL 32952
Contact: Karen Gregory President
Tel: 321-576-1314
Email: kgregory@hrssconsultinggroup.com
Website: www.hrssconsultinggroup.com
Organizational development and talent management. (Woman, estab 2012, empl 6, sales $230,000, cert: State, WBENC)

7569   Midwest Background Inc.
200 Central Ave, Ste 820
St. Petersburg, FL 33701
Contact: Syan Kazi Dir of Business Dev
Tel: 727-592-8275
Email: media@mbiworldwide.com
Website: www.mbiworldwide.com
Background screening & hiring solutions. (Woman, estab 1998, empl 27, sales $2,700,000, cert: NWBOC)

7570   Moten Tate, Inc.
301 E. Pine St Ste 250
Orlando, FL 32801
Contact: Kenneth Moten CEO
Tel: 407-843-3277
Email: kmoten@motentate.com
Website: www.motentate.com
Human resource management: staffing, HR project mgmt, reward strategies, employee development & HR outsourcing. (AA, estab 1997, empl 100, sales $3,400,000, cert: State, NMSDC)

7571   Resource Management 1, LLC
520 N Semoran Blvd
Orlando, FL 32807
Contact: Leyla Eagle Dir strategic alliance
Tel: 800-508-0048
Email: leagle@rmi-solutions.com
Website: www.helpmewithhr.com
Payroll, workers compensation, regulatory compliance, risk management & benefits admin. (Hisp, estab 1995, empl 45, sales $114,000,000, cert: State, NMSDC)

7572   Sobriety On the Sea / Danette Arthur MD PA
4302 Hollywood Blvd 125
Hollywood, FL 33021
Contact: Danette Arthur MD President
Tel: 954-923-7333
Email: sos@doctorsos.org
Website: www.DrArthur.org
Pre-employment & drug testing services. (Woman/AA, estab 2001, empl 4, sales $140,000, cert: State)

7573   Suncoast Compliance Services, LLC
16765 Fishhawk Dr, Ste 325
Lithia, FL 33547
Contact: Vincent McGrew President
Tel: 813-653-4559
Email: vroy.mcgrew@usamdt.com
Website: www.usamdt.com/westcentralflorida
Pre-employment background screening, drug-free workplace policy devel & implementation, on-site drug & alcohol testing, Employer Assistance Program referral, supervisor training for DOT & non-DOT employees. (AA, estab 2012, empl 1, sales , cert: State, NMSDC)

7574   The Management Edge, Inc.
12360 66th St, Ste S
Largo, FL 33773
Contact: Patty Dunn Dir ops/finance
Tel: 727-588-9481
Email: patty.dunn@mgtedge.com
Website: www.themanagementedge.com
Organization dev, team building & partnering, executive & staff dev, training & coaching, conflict resolution, consensus building. (Woman, estab 1986, empl 18, sales $908,000, cert: State, WBENC)

Georgia

7575   Assessment Plus, Inc.
2180 Satellite Blvd Ste 400
Duluth, GA 30097
Contact: Brielle Fetrow Project Coord
Tel: 770-925-3990
Email: brielle.fetrow@assessmentplus.com
Website: www.assessmentplus.com
Employee opinion surveys, customers satisfaction surveys, leadership dev, 360-degree feedback assessments, executive & leadership coaching, exit interviews & team assessments. (Woman, estab 1984, empl 14, sales $650,000, cert: WBENC)

7576 Career Connection, Inc.
1170 Peachtree St Ste 1200
Atlanta, GA 30309
Contact: Cody Stowers
Tel: 404-814-5282
Email: cstowers@ccicareers.com
Website: www.ccicareers.com
Staff augmentation, workforce solutions, permanent placement, recruitment, personnel management, HR services, administrative management, call center, customer support, IT support, Information technology, facilities management. (Woman, estab 1986, empl 1000, sales $40,000,000, cert: WBENC)

7577 CyQuest Business Solutions, Inc.
3645 Market Place Blvd Ste 130
East Point, GA 30344
Contact: DeVan Brown CEO
Tel: 404-761-6699
Email: devan@cyquesthr.com
Website: www.cyquesthr.com
HR outsourcing solutions: compensation, employee benefits, retirement plans, HRIS systems, payroll processing, employee recruitment & retention. (AA, estab 2004, empl 8, sales , cert: State, NMSDC)

7578 eVerifile.com Inc.
900 Circle 75 Pkwy Ste 1550
Atlanta, GA 30339
Contact: Jennifer Brown VP Business Dev
Tel: 404-585-4487
Email: jennifer.brown@everifile.com
Website: www.everifile.com
Criminal background investigations, action notification and/or information analytics & grading, US Government watch searches, certificate & license verification, motor vehicle reports, employment & reference verification. (AA, estab , empl , sales $12,000,000, cert: NMSDC)

7579 JNX Partners, LLC
2935 Haynes Club Cir
Grayson, GA 30017
Contact: Judy Swanier President
Tel: 770-982-0043
Email: judy.swanier@jnxpartners.com
Website: www.jnxpartners.com
Executive staffing, HR & career transition: sourcing, screening, testing, hiring & retention
practices, coaching & support. (Woman/AA, estab 2005, empl 3, sales , cert: WBENC)

7580 McPherson, Berry & Associates, Inc.
4158 S River Ln Ste 110
Ellenwood, GA 30294
Contact: LaSonya Berry CEO
Tel: 800-325-5269
Email: lasonya@mcphersonberryassoc.com
Website: www.mcphersonberry.com
Human Rrsource training, consulting & team building event planning. (Woman/AA, estab 2000, empl 3, sales $250,000, cert: NMSDC, WBENC)

7581 Springboard Benefits, LLC
695 Pylant St NE Ste 232
Atlanta, GA 30306
Contact: Amy Parkman CEO
Tel: 205-790-1060
Email: aparkman@springboardbenefits.com
Website: www.springboardbenefits.com
Project management & consulting, employee on-boarding & off-boarding, hire to retire, new hires, open enrollment, ACA, variable hour tracking, medicare exchange & early termination exchanges. (Woman, estab 2014, empl 6, sales $250,000, cert: WBENC)

7582 Steelbridge Solutions, Inc
2451 Cumberland Pkwy Ste 3228
Atlanta, GA 30339
Contact: Susan Richards President
Tel: 404-259-0865
Email: susan.richards@steelbridgesolutions.com
Website: www.SteelBridgeSolutions.com
Human Capital Consulting, Human Resource Consulting, Business Transformation Consulting, Change Management Consulting, Human resource Information System Consulting, HR Transformation, HR Strategy, HR Technology. (Woman, estab 2013, empl 1, sales $900,000, cert: WBENC)

Illinois

7583 Clark Consulting Group, Inc.
1220 South Blvd
Evanston, IL 60202
Contact: Dr. Marilyn A. Clark CEO
Tel: 847-332-1778
Email: contact@ccg-solutions.com
Website: www.ccg-solutions.com
Human resource development consulting: organizational development, learning & development & career development. (Woman/AA, estab 2002, empl 2, sales $150,000, cert: WBENC)

7584 Executive Coaching Connections
1000 Skokie Blvd, Ste 340
Wilmette, IL 60091
Contact: Kathy Green President
Tel: 847-920-0190
Email: info@executivecoachingconnections.com
www.executivecoachingconnections.com
Organizational development, executive coaching, leadership acceleration, introspection guide, development planning template. (Woman, estab 1995, empl 30, sales $0, cert: WBENC)

7585 JRA Consulting Services, Inc.
10225 W Higgins Rd
Rosemont, IL 60018
Contact: Ross Wolfson Talent Acquisition Mgr
Tel: 847-430-3682
Email: rwolfson@hrcontracting.com
Website: www.hrcontracting.com
Human resources staffing, permanent & contract positions. (Woman, estab 1997, empl 4, sales $2,000,000, cert: NWBOC)

7586   Quantum Associates Inc.
459 Lambert Tree Ave
Highland Park, IL 60035
Contact: Willie L. Carter President
Tel: 847-919-6127
Email: wcarter@quantumassocinc.com
Website: www.quantumassocinc.com
Operations management, process redesign, team building & team problem solving. (AA, estab 1999, empl 4, sales $215,000, cert: NMSDC)

7587   Ossanna Corporation
48 Hawthorne Lane
Barrington Hills, IL 60010
Contact: Mariaelena Estrada Office/Contracts Mgr
Tel: 847-255-2800
Email: mestrada@ossanna.com
Website: www.ossanna.com
Human resource professionals: consulting, option-to-hire & permanent basis. (Woman, estab 1988, empl 16, sales $3,313,000, cert: State, WBENC)

Indiana

7588   HR Alternative Consulting, Inc.
10641 Medinah Dr
Indianapolis, IN 46234
Contact: Ann Fisher President
Tel: 317-852-3590
Email: afisher@hralternativeconsulting.com
Website: www.hralternativeconsulting.com
Customized human resources services. (Woman, estab 2003, empl 2, sales , cert: State, City)

7589   Work-Comp Management Services
760 Park East Blvd #5
Lafayette, IN 47905
Contact: Julie Ott, Owner/Nurse Mgr
Tel: 765-447-7473
Email: jott@workcompms.com
Website: www.workcompms.net
On-site occupational health services, work comp case management, pre-employment random drug screening, certified collections. (Woman, estab 1996, empl 55, sales $3,600,000, cert: WBENC)

Louisiana

7590   Debra Gould & Associates, Inc.
PO Box 871211
New Orleans, LA 70187
Contact: Debra Gould President
Tel: 504-244-6576
Email: djgould@gouldassoc.com
Website: www.gouldassoc.com
Diversity, change management, team building, leadership, project management, Six Sigma & communication. (Woman/AA, estab 1996, empl 2, sales , cert: WBENC)

Maryland

7591   Full Disclosure
2 Industrial Park Dr Ste B
Waldorf, MD 20602
Contact: Felicia Denman President
Tel: 877-214-4717
Email: fdenman@full-disclosure.org
Website: www.full-disclosure.org
Preemployment screening, background checks, criminal records, employment verification, education verification, terrorist watch list, reference check, civil records, professional license verification. (Woman/AA, estab 2006, empl 1, sales , cert: State)

7592   HR Anew, Inc.
6350 Stevens Forest Rd Ste 250
Columbia, MD 21046
Contact: Melanie Freeman President
Tel: 410-381-5220
Email: mfreeman@hranew.com
Website: www.hranew.com
HR management & consulting, training & professional development, mgmt & employee coaching, recruitment & hiring, executive search, staff augmentation, event & conference planning , employee relations. (Woman/AA, estab 1999, empl 17, sales $2,200,000, cert: State)

7593   Managed Care Advisors
2 Wisconsin Cir, Ste 800
Chevy Chase, MD 20815
Contact: Lisa Firestone President
Tel: 301-951-4344
Email:
Website: www.managedcareadvisors.com
Consulting svcs: employee health benefits, workers compensation, disability, case, claims management. (Woman, estab 1997, empl 5, sales $0, cert: WBENC)

7594   Rickinson Marketing Inc.
302 Treemont Way
Rockville, MD 20850
Contact: Janette Rickinson President
Tel: 240-683-6550
Email: janette@therickinsongroup.com
Website: www.therickinsongroup.com
Market research consulting, qualitative & quantative research. (Woman, estab 1998, empl 2, sales $450,000, cert: WBENC)

7595   The HR Source
8181 Professional Place Ste 120
Landover, MD 20785
Contact: Patricia Hall Jaynes CEO
Tel: 301-459-3133
Email: pathj@thehrsource.com
Website: www.thehrsource.com
HR staffing & consulting services, interim/temporary & permanent staffing services, outplacement & payroll services, administrative interim/temporary & permanent staffing services. (Woman/AA, estab 1994, empl 5, sales $2,894,265, cert: State, NMSDC, WBENC)

Michigan

7596   Aha! Leadership LLC
49425 Deer Run
Northville, MI 48167
Contact: Robyn Marcotte President
Tel: 248-882-2354
Email: robyn.marcotte@ahaleadership.com
Website: www.ahaleadership.com
Leadership Training & Dev, Human Resources Consulting Services; Customer Service Training & Development. (Woman, estab 0, empl , sales $0, cert: WBENC)

7597   Ashlor Management Corporation
3710 Davison Rd
Flint, MI 48506
Contact: Charles Kuta President
Tel: 810-275-0690
Email: charles@ashlorstaffing.com
Website: www.ashlorstaffing.com
Human resources, staffing, payroll & complete benefit administration. (Hisp, estab 2015, empl 5, sales , cert: NMSDC)

7598 The Orsus Group, Inc.
      3155 W Big Beaver Rd Ste 216
      Troy, MI 48084
      Contact: Brandon Meagher Business Devel Mgr
      Tel: 248-530-3685
      Email: bmeagher@theorsusgroup.com
      Website: www.theorsusgroup.com
Employment screening: criminal checks, sex offender
registry, employment & education verification, motor
vehicle records, credit checks, sanctions checks, drug
screening, prohibited parties. (AA, estab 2007, empl 22,
sales $900,000, cert: NMSDC)

Minnesota

7599 Inclusion, Inc.
      126 N 3rd St Ste 412
      Minneapolis, MN 55401
      Contact: Shirley Engelmeier CEO
      Tel: 612-339-2202
      Email: shirley@inclusion-inc.com
      Website: www.inclusion-inc.com
Diversity & inclusion strategies: web based survey, diversity & inclusion assesment, customized skills based
training, changing business behaviors, micro-inequities &
on-the-job application. (Woman, estab 2001, empl 21,
sales , cert: WBENC)

Missouri

7600 Hicks-Carter-Hicks, LLC
      12747 Olive Blvd, Ste 300
      St. Louis, MO 63141
      Contact: Gloria Carter-Hicks CEO
      Tel: 314-260-7587
      Email: info@h-c-h.com
      Website: www.h-c-h.com
Performance improvement consulting: mgmt & human
resources, performance coaching, training & dev, facilitation, keynote presentations. (Woman/AA, estab 1999,
empl 5, sales $0, cert: NMSDC, WBENC)

North Carolina

7601 Benefit Advocates, Inc.
      514 S Stratford Rd
      Winston-Salem, NC 27103
      Contact: Mary Kesel President
      Tel: 336-721-2029
      Email: mkesel@benefitadvocates.net
      Website: www.benefitadvocates.net
Health Advocacy and billing claim assistance. Work with
HR in managing employees health benefits and medicare.
(Woman, estab 2001, empl 10, sales $500,000, cert:
WBENC, 8(a))

7602 CareerUnlocked, Inc.
      626 N Graham St, Ste 203
      Charlotte, NC 28202
      Contact: Andrew Lee President
      Tel: 919-264-1288
      Email: andrew@careerunlocked.com
      Website: www.Careerunlocked.com
Human resources consulting, business process improvements, executive search, professional and management
development training & talent management. (AA, estab
2015, empl 1, sales , cert: State)

New Jersey

7603 Diversified Consulting Consortium, LLC
      5 Tenalfy Rd, Ste 404
      Englewood, NJ 07631
      Contact: Antonette Alonso
      Tel: 908-669-4633
      talonso@diversifiedconsultingconsortium.com
      www.diversifiedconsultingconsortium.com
Human resources management consulting, training,
investigations, diversity management, affirmative action,
employee coaching & counseling, labor relations.
(Woman/AA, Hisp, estab 2012, empl 6, sales , cert:
NMSDC)

7604 Fintech Consulting LLC DBA ApTask
      120 Wood Ave South, Ste 300
      Iselin, NJ 08830
      Contact: Taj Haslani Founder
      Tel: 212-256-9131
      Email: joshua@aptask.com
      Website: www.aptask.com
Staffing, workforce solutions, strategic outsourcing. (As-
Ind, estab 2010, empl 367, sales $32,000,000, cert:
NMSDC)

7605 SHIFT Employment Law Training, LLC
      26 Main St, Ste 301
      Chatham, NJ 07928
      Contact: Regina Feeney Dir of Operations
      Tel: 800-790-5030
      Email: regina@shiftelt.com
      Website: www.shiftelt.com
Online HR Compliance Training courses. (Woman, estab
2015, empl 14, sales $1,788,000, cert: WBENC)

New York

7606 Can-Am Consultants Inc.
      208 Mill St
      Rochester, NY 14614
      Contact: Cathryn Bell CEO
      Tel: 585-777-4040
      Email: carrie.bell@can-amconsultants.com
      Website: www.can-amconsultants.com
Recruitment & Payroll, Recruitment, Staffing & Payroll
of Engineering, Technical & IT Personnel. (Woman, estab
2003, empl 150, sales $19,494,834, cert: State)

7607 Corporate Screening Consulting, LLC
      4201 N Buffalo Rd Ste 10
      Orchard Park, NY 14127
      Contact: Maria DiPirro President
      Tel: 716-583-4629
      Email: mdipirro@corpscreen.com
      Website: www.corpscreen.com
Risk management advisory services, Risk Avoidance
consulting, litigation support, corporate compliance, due
diligence, fraud analysis, background investigations &
loss prevention program design. (Woman, estab 2007,
empl 3, sales $250,000, cert: State)

Ohio

7608 Global to Local Language Solutions, LLC
1776 Mentor Ave Ste 319
Cincinnati, OH 42512
Contact: Grace Bosworth President
Tel: 513-526-5011
Email: grace@g2local.com
Website: www.g2local.com
Interpreting/translation services, interpreter training &
language training. (Woman, estab 2009, empl 3, sales ,
cert: State, WBENC)

7609 Strategic Performance Systems, LLC
2206 Highland Ave
Cincinnati, OH 45219
Contact: Deborah Heater CEO
Tel: 513-602-6200
debheater@strategicperformancesystems.com
Website: www.strategicperformancesystems.com
Employee Development: management, leadership,
compliance & risk reduction strategies, Human Resources
Best Practices: effective human resources functions,
Diversity Climate Assessments. (Woman/AA, estab 2013,
empl 1, sales $130,000, cert: State)

7610 Stryker Green, LLC
1240 Sharonbrook Dr
Twinsburg, OH 44087
Contact: Sandy Moore CEO
Tel: 330-963-9985
Email: sjohnson@strykergreen.com
Website: www.strykergreen.com
Human Resource Solutions consulting & managed ser-
vices. (Woman/AA, estab 2012, empl 2, sales , cert:
NMSDC)

7611 TriCor Employment Screening
110 Blaze Industrial Pkwy
Berea, OH 44017
Contact: Gary Becher Co-Owner
Tel: 800-818-5116
Email: gbecher@tricorinfo.com
Website: www.tricorinfo.com
Employment screening, background checks, personal &
business credit reports, social security number verifica-
tions, driving records, criminal & civil record searches,
verifications of educational degrees, terrorist checks &
drug screening. (Woman, estab 1998, empl 18, sales
$3,252,000, cert: WBENC)

Pennsylvania

7612 Advance Sourcing Concepts, LLC
3000 McKnight East Dr Ste 201
Pittsburgh, PA 15237
Contact: Judith Bernhard President
Tel: 412-415-5081
Email: jbernhard@ascpeople.com
Website: www.ascpeople.com
Human Resources contract & sourcing. (Woman, estab
2005, empl 4, sales $1,200,000, cert: State, WBENC)

7613 American Personnel Managers & Consultants, Inc.
3607 Rosemont Ave, Ste 101
Camp Hill, PA 17011
Contact: Pat Gingrich CEO
Tel: 717-465-5637
Email: patg@apmci.com
Website: www.amerijob.com
Staffing, Human Resource Management, Consulting,
Testing & Training, Procurement, Information Technol-
ogy Staffing, Project Management. (Woman, estab 1998,
empl 45, sales $3,000,000, cert: State)

7614 BRODY Professional Development
115 West Ave Ste 114
Jenkintown, PA 19046
Contact: Laura Gabor Accounting Department
Tel: 215-886-1688
Email: laura@BrodyPro.com
Website: www.BrodyPro.com
Training & coaching. (Woman, estab 1983, empl 15,
sales $2,520,316, cert: WBENC)

7615 Career Concepts, Inc.
Arborcrest 2, 721 Arbor Way
Blue Bell, PA 19422
Contact: Sharon Imperiale CEO
Tel: 610-941-4455
Email: simperiale@cciconsulting.com
Website: www.cciconsulting.com
Management consulting, HR, outplacement/career
transition, recruiting, managerial & executive coaching,
leadership development, training. (Woman, estab 1988,
empl 40, sales $7,000,000, cert: State, WBENC)

7616 FCF Schmidt Public Relations
600 W Germantown Pike, Ste 380
Plymouth Meeting, PA 19462
Contact: Maribeth Schmidt President
Tel: 610-941-0395
Email: mschmidt@fcfschmidtpr.com
Website: www.fcfschmidtpr.com
Strategic, integrated business-to-business & consumer
public relations programs: technical writing, media
relations, special events management, public service.
(Woman, estab 1989, empl 43, sales $8,700,000, cert:
WBENC)

7617 Strategic Benefit Solutions
204 Rivercrest Dr
Phoenixville, PA 19460
Contact: Le Phan CEO
Tel: 609-957-5309
Email: lphan@sbscompanies.com
Website: www.sbscompanies.com
Strategic Benefit Solutions is a full service consulting
firm for voluntary worksite benefit solutions with a
proven track record of delivering successful benefit
solutions that deliver the results you and your employees require. (Minority, Woman, estab 2011, empl 6,
sales $500,000, cert: NMSDC)

7618 The Bradley Partnerships, Inc.
207 Malbec Lane Ste 100
Wexford, PA 15090
Contact: Lois Bradley President
Tel: 724-779-8170
Email: lois@bradleypartnerships.com
Website: www.bradleypartnerships.com
Organizational & human resource consulting services.
(Woman, estab 2002, empl 6, sales $325,000, cert:
State, City, WBENC, 8(a))

7619 The JPI Group LLC
1700 Market St, Ste 1005
Philadelphia, PA 19103
Contact: Paul Douglas Exec
Tel: 267-688-9606
Email: paul@thejpigroup.com
Website: www.thejpigroup.com
HR Consulting Services for Technology & Software Development. (Woman/AA, estab 2012, empl 6, sales $16,925,273, cert: NMSDC, WBENC)

Puerto Rico

7620 Smart Option Search
PO Box 194088
San Juan, PR 00917
Contact: Melissa Concepcion Esterrich President
Tel: 787-767-2373
Email: mconcepcion@smartoptionsearch.com
Website: www.smartoptionsearch.com
Recruiting and HR Consulting. (Minority, Woman, estab 2000, empl 10, sales $398,000, cert: NMSDC)

South Carolina

7621 RL Enterprise & Associates, LLC
319 Garlington Rd Ste D-3
Greenville, SC 29615
Contact: Rick Harris CEO
Tel: 864-234-8788
Email: rharris@rlenterprisellc.com
Website: www.rlenterprisellc.com
Human resource lifecycle from candidate placement through career development, and even outplacement, in unfortunate circumstances. (AA, estab 2006, empl 21, sales $11,800,000, cert: NMSDC)

7622 Sunkiko
280 Hindman Rd
Travelers Rest, SC 29690
Contact: Sonja Milisic President
Tel: 864-660-6958
Email: sonja@sunkiko.com
Website: www.sunkiko.com
Outsourced solutions for payroll, benefits, HR, workers' comp, tax reporting and more. (Woman, estab 2009, empl 3, sales $356,408, cert: WBENC)

Texas

7623 24/7 Background Checks LLC
11520 N Central Expressway Ste 230
Dallas, TX 75243
Contact: Jones Ajatuaewo President
Tel: 214-206-3565
Email: jones@criminal411.com
Website: www.criminal411.com
Pre employment screening services: driving records, education & employment verification. (Woman/AA, estab 2004, empl 25, sales $600,000, cert: State, NMSDC)

7624 AGResearch International, LLC
PO Box 460
McKinney, TX 75070
Contact: Patti T. Mayer President
Tel: 214-842-4540
Email: patti.mayer@agresearch.info
Website: www.agresearch.info
Human capital services, benchmarking studies. (Woman, estab 2002, empl 15, sales $1,450,278, cert: State, WBENC)

7625 Aspire HR, Inc.
5151 Belt Line Rd Ste 1125
Dallas, TX 75254
Contact: Kevin Vonderschmidt Managing Partner
Tel: 972-372-2815
Email: kvonder@aspirehr.com
Website: www.aspirehr.com
HR services for SAP ERP HCM solutions, implementations, upgrades & support, payroll, HR renewal, data conversions & migrations. (Woman, estab 1998, empl , sales , cert: WBENC)

7626 Bashen Corporation
2603 Augusta Dr, Ste 200
Houston, TX 77057
Contact: Janet Bashen CEO
Tel: 800-994-1554
Email: sales@bashencorp.com
Website: www.bashencorp.com
HR consulting services: EEO compliance administration, EEO investigations/ position statements & investigative reports, workplace training, affirmative action planning, diversity strategies, risk mgmt. (Woman/AA, estab 2013, empl 20, sales $1,578,181, cert: NMSDC, WBENC)

7627 Brook Consultants Inc.
2500 N Dallas Pkwy Ste 180
Plano, TX 75093
Contact: Matt Jones VP Sales
Tel: 972-473-8918
Email: sales@brookvms.com
Website: www.brookvms.com
Human Resource Management services, Contractor onboarding, competence evaluation, E-Verify & background checks. (Woman, estab 2006, empl 125, sales $60,000,000, cert: WBENC)

7628 Cruvel Data Analytics
6315 Liberty ct
Frisco, TX 75035
Contact: Jose Owner
Tel: 214-250-8937
Email: jvel2572@gmail.com
Website: www.cruvel.com
Translation & interpretation services. (Hisp, estab 2018, empl 6, sales , cert: City)

7629 DIVERSA LLC
7003 Viscount Blvd Ste 103
El Paso, TX 79925
Contact: Eleanor Euler VP Business Devel
Tel: 915-781-2665
Email: eleanor.euler@ihcus.com
Website: www.diversaus.com
HR Solutions with focus on MSP services. (Woman/Hisp, estab 2009, empl 1, sales $16,158,922, cert: NMSDC, WBENC)

7630 Excellian Inc.
2301 Ohio Dr, Ste 285
Plano, TX 75093
Contact: Linda Labrada HR Services & Business Dev
Tel: 972-499-0525
Email: llabrada@excellian.com
Website: www.excellian.com
Human Resources | Payroll | Training | Coaching | Management Consulting | Diversity & Inclusion. (Woman/AA, estab 2014, empl 20, sales , cert: NMSDC, WBENC)

7631 G&A Partners
4801 Woodway Ste 210
Houston, TX 77056
Contact: David Vasquez VP
Tel: 713-784-1181
Email: dvasquez@gnapartners.com
Website: www.gnapartners.com
Professional Employer Organization (PEO) & Human Resources Outsourcing & Consulting. (Hisp, estab 1995, empl 175, sales $131,230,000, cert: State)

7632 Human Capital International, LLC dba Integrated Human Capital
7300 Viscount Blvd Ste 103
El Paso, TX 79925
Contact: Rosa Santana CEO
Tel: 915-781-2665
Email: rosa.santana@ihcus.com
Website: www.ihcus.com
HR consulting, temporary staffing, professional & executive placement, payroll svcs, skill testing, vendor mgmt, on-site staff mgmt. (Minority, Woman, estab 2002, empl 34, sales $16,171,166, cert: State, NMSDC, WBENC)

7633 InGenesis, Inc.
10231 Kotzebue St
San Antonio, TX 78217
Contact: Dr. Veronica Edwards CEO
Tel: 210-366-0033
Email: commercial@ingenesis.com
Website: www.ingenesis.com
Workforce solutions: direct placement, direct hire, executive search, temporary staffing, contingent staffing, managed vendor, recruitment process outsourcing, managed services programs & locum tenens. (Minority, Woman, estab , empl , sales $174,785,000, cert: NMSDC, WBENC)

7634 KAS Consulting Group
3625 North Hall Ste 610
Dallas, TX 75219
Contact: Keith Scott CEO
Tel: 214-528-3326
Email: keith@kasconsulting.com
Website: www.kasconsulting.com
Human resources consulting, direct staffing & placement svcs, outplacement svcs, performance mgmt & appraisals, leadership & performance coaching. (AA, estab 2002, empl 3, sales $1,000,000, cert: State)

7635 Pursuit of Excellence Inc.
10440 N Central Expwy Ste 1250
Dallas, TX 75231
Contact: Glenda Scott Finance Admin
Tel: 214-452-7881
Email: gscott@pursuitofexcellenceinc.com
Website: www.pursuitofexcellenceinc.com
Outsourcing for Human Resources/Payroll. (Minority, Woman, estab 1995, empl 6, sales , cert: State)

Virginia

7636 Helios HR LLC
1925 Isaac Newton Sq E Ste 200
Reston, VA 20190
Contact: VP Finance
Tel: 703-860-3882
Email: ekrause@helioshr.com
Website: www.helioshr.com
HR Effectiveness & Compliance Analysis, Employee Assimilation & Onboarding, Employee Regulation Requirements, Policy Maintenance, Employee Relations & Retention, Maintain & Implement Employee Performance Management. (Woman, estab 2001, empl 20, sales $3,670,154, cert: State, WBENC)

7637 Human Capital Consultants, LLC
4201 Wilson Blvd Ste 320
Arlington, VA 22203
Contact: Milton Hall President
Tel: 202-601-1080
Email: SupplierDiversity@humancapitalllc.com
Website: www.humancapitalllc.com
Employee benefit consulting & workplace diversity training. (AA, estab 2004, empl 14, sales $2,497,097, cert:)

7638 RKL Resources
6933 Commons Plaza Ste 245
Chesterfield, VA 23831
Contact: Tawanda Johnson Owner
Tel: 804-638-5991
Email: tjohnson@rklresources.com
Website: www.rklresources.com
Human resources solutions: recruitment, training, organizational development, employee relations & audits. (Woman/AA, estab 2013, empl 2, sales $552,167, cert: State)

West Virginia

7639 Edwards Management Consultants, Inc.
110 S. George St Ste 1
Charles Town, WV 25414
Contact: Christine Edwards President
Tel: 703-349-1412
Email: christinec@edwardsemc.com
Website: www.edwardsemc.com
HR Advisor/Consulting Services, HR Support Services, Recruitment - Short/Long Term Entry Level/Mid to Senior Level Candidates Managenment and Performance Management. (Woman/AA, estab 2005, empl 5, sales , cert: NMSDC)

PROFESSIONAL SERVICES: Management Consulting

Provide general management consulting services: survey research, economic forecasting, transportation studies, facilities and program management, strategic planning, training and development. NAICS Code 54

Alaska

7640 Teya Technologies, LLC
101 E 9th Ave, Ste 9B
Anchorage, AK 99501
Contact: Ronald Perry CEO
Tel: 907-339-4901
Email: ron.perry@teyatech.com
Website: www.teyatech.com
Construction, demolition, project management, custodial and janitorial services, administrative services, product manufacturing, housing maintenance, and conference and event planning/management. (Nat Ame, estab 2005, empl 46, sales $14,422,189, cert: NMSDC)

Alabama

7641 Paragon Management Group
PO Box 687
Cotondale, AL 35453
Contact: Ty Jones President
Tel: 205-409-2948
Email: tjones@paragon-mgmt.com
Website: www.paragon-mgt.com
Management consulting, supply chain mgmt strategy, operations, technology & organization solutions. (Woman/AA, estab 2006, empl 5, sales $180,000, cert: NMSDC)

7642 Terrell & Associates, LLC
2210 S Tallassee Dr
Tallassee, AL 36078
Contact: Shandra Terrell President
Tel: 334-283-5156
Email: sterrell@terrellassociates.net
Website: www.terrellassociates.net
Training: diversity, difficult people, teamwork, customer service, speaking engagements, research & evaluation, etc. (Woman/AA, estab 2001, empl 1, sales , cert: NWBOC)

Arizona

7643 Banda Group International, LLC
1799 E Queen Creek Rd Ste 1
Chandler, AZ 85286
Contact: Elisonia Valle Marketing & Communications
Tel: 480-636-8734
Email: elisoniav@bandagroupintl.com
Website: www.bandagroupintl.com
Safety management, risk management, project management, training & associated engineering disciplines. (Hisp, estab 2003, empl 88, sales $9,049,000, cert: NMSDC, SDB)

7644 BLeadersEdge LLC
721 N 106th St
Mesa, AZ 85207
Contact: Michael Nadeau President
Tel: 480-269-7438
Email: mike@bleadersedge.com
Website: www.bleadersedge.com
Personal, team & organizational leadership devel, leadership development. (Nat Ame, estab 2019, empl 1, sales , cert: NMSDC)

7645 Tax Roof, LLC dba JT Project Management Office
1 E Washington St Ste 500
Phoenix, AZ 85004
Contact: Dionne Joseph Thomas President
Tel: 623-374-6455
Email: admin@taxroof.com
Website: www.jtprojectmanagementoffice.com
Program/Project Management & Implementation, Initiation; Planning; Execution; Monitoring & Control; Closing. (Woman/AA, estab 2011, empl 2, sales , cert: State, City, WBENC)

California

7646 Agile Sourcing Partners, Inc.
2385 Railroad St
Corona, CA 92880
Contact: Gabriela Lozano CEO
Tel: 951-279-4154
Email: glozano@agilesp.com
Website: www.agilesp.com/
Procurement, warehousing, assembly, logistics, managing suppliers, and professional staff augmentation. (Woman/Hisp, estab 2006, empl 200, sales $222,512,779, cert: State, NMSDC, WBENC)

7647 Alorica Inc.
5 Park Plaza Ste 1100
Irvine, CA 92614
Contact: Kyle Baker VP Sales
Tel: 949-527-4600
Email: kyle.baker@alorica.com
Website: www.alorica.com
Business process outsourcing, customer management solutions. (As-Pac, estab , empl 22000, sales $570,000,000, cert: State, NMSDC, CPUC)

7648 Being Present Inc
8601 Sunland Blvd, Ste 53
Sun Valley, CA 91352
Contact: Sonya Shelton CEO
Tel: 818-473-5323
Email: sonya@executiveleader.com
Website: www.ExecutiveLeader.com
Management consulting & executive coaching services. (Minority, Woman, estab 2006, empl 4, sales $970,003, cert: NMSDC, WBENC)

7649 causeIMPACTS
5301 W 119th Pl
Inglewood, CA 90304
Contact: Jessica Daugherty Principal
Tel: 714-390-6301
Email: jessica@causeimpacts.com
Website: www.causeimpacts.com
Social impact strategy consulting. (Woman, estab 2015, empl 2, sales $500,000, cert: WBENC)

7650 Celerity Consulting Group, Inc.
2 Gough St, Ste 300
San Francisco, CA 94103
Contact: Yinna Wong CEO
Tel: 415-986-8850
Email: ywong@consultcelerity.com
Website: www.consultcelerity.com
Litigation & business consulting: strategic planning, quality control processes. (Woman, estab 2001, empl 98, sales $16,604,529, cert: CPUC)

7651 Dilan Consulting Group
550 15th St Ste M-13
San Francisco, CA 94103
Contact: Eugene Dilan CEO
Tel: 415-937-0621
Email: office@dilanconsulting.com
Website: www.dilanconsulting.com
Organizational Development & Change. (Hisp, estab , empl , sales $1,004,136, cert: NMSDC)

7652 Elia Erickson, LLC
11620 Wilshire Blvd. 9th Fl
Los Angeles, CA 90025
Contact: Lisa Elia CEO
Tel: 310-479-0217
Email: team@expertmediatraining.com
Website: www.expertmediatraining.com
Media training, presentation training, public speaking training, communication consulting, business coaching, publicity training. (Woman, estab 1999, empl 1, sales $128,741, cert: State, City, CPUC)

7653 Emerson Human Capital Consulting, Inc.
2199 Harbor Bay Pkwy
Alameda, CA 94502
Contact: Tricia Emerson CEO
Tel: 510-545-4435
Email: temerson@emersonhc.com
Website: www.emersonhc.com
Training, diversity training & workshops, change management, organizational design, communications, intercultural svcs, process design, IT implementation, user acceptance. (Woman, estab 2001, empl 35, sales $7,459,817, cert: WBENC)

7654 Extron-Knurr USA
496 S Abbott Ave
Milpitas, CA 95035
Contact: Cobey Cross Business Devel Mgr
Tel: 510-353-0177
Email: diversity@extroninc.com
Website: www.knurrUSA.com
Product Assembly, Warehousing, Order Fulfillment, Returns Management, and Repairs. (As-Ind, estab 1999, empl 65, sales $0, cert: CPUC)

7655 ICE Safety Solutions Inc.
47703 Fremont Blvd
Fremont, CA 94538
Contact: Pamela ISom CEO
Tel: 877-743-8423
Email: accounting@getice.com
Website: www.getice.com
Safety training: CPR, first aid, ERT, AED, forklift, Fire safety, fire extinguisher training, safety consulting & curriculum dev. (Woman/AA, Hisp, estab , empl , sales $1,800,000, cert: NMSDC, CPUC, WBENC)

7656 Imani Lee, Inc.
11297 Senda Luna Llena Bldg. B
San Diego, CA 92130
Contact: Lee Martin CEO
Tel: 858-523-9733
Email: translations@imanilee.com
Website: www.imanilee.com
Translation & Localization, Transcription, Transcreation, Interpreting, International Social Media Management, Consulting Services, Language & Culture training, Subtitling & Voiceover, Educational Curriculum Development. (AA, estab 2002, empl 10, sales $1,526,000, cert: NMSDC, CPUC)

7657 Julianna Hynes & Associates
1638 Freed Circle
Pittsburg, CA 94565
Contact: Julianna Hynes Principal
Tel: 925-207-1578
Email: julianna@juliannahynes.com
Website: www.juliannahynes.com
Executive coaching & leadership development services. (Woman/AA, estab 2003, empl 1, sales $139,599, cert: WBENC)

7658 K'ontinuous Technologies, Inc.
1304 W 2nd St, Ste 346
Los Angeles, CA 90026
Contact: Steve Buchanan President
Tel: 213-334-3951
Email: sbuchanan@kontinuoustech.com
Website: www.kontinuoustech.com
Program Management Oversight, Program/Project Definition & Direction, Program/Project Tracking & Documentation, Technical Resource Allocation, Client/Vendor Relations, Change Management, Risk Management. (AA, Hisp, estab 2015, empl 1, sales , cert: State)

7659 LKG-CMC, Inc.
707 Wilshire Blvd, Ste 3600
Los Angeles, CA 90017
Contact: Kathy Simons vp
Tel: 213-892-0789
Email: ksimons@lkgcmc.com
Website: www.lkgcmc.com
Project controls & configuration mgmt consulting: document control, cost control & estimating, scheduling & business continuity planning. (Woman, estab 1987, empl 70, sales $0, cert: CPUC)

7660 LUZ, Inc.
555 Montgomery St Ste 720
San Francisco, CA 94111
Contact: Katie Levenstein Marketing Communications Specialist
Tel: 415-981-5890
Email: register@luz.com
Website: www.luz.com
Translation & localization solutions. (Woman, estab , empl , sales $29,000,000, cert: WBENC)

7661 Nesso Strategies
4142 Adams Ave Ste 103-256
San Diego, CA 92116
Contact: Judy Hissong President
Tel: 619-546-7885
Email: judy@nessostrategies.com
Website: www.NessoStrategies.com
Speaking, training, consulting & facilitation, communication & conflict management, leadership development, accountability, diversity & inclusion. (Woman, estab 2009, empl 3, sales $240,000, cert: City, CPUC)

7662 OneSource Supply Solutions (OSS)
3951 Oceanic Dr
Oceanside, CA 92506
Contact: John Maybeery Exec VP
Tel: - -
Email: jmayberry@1sourcesupplysolutions.com
Website: www.1sourcesupplysolutions.com
Supply chain solutions to industry leading utilities, contractors and manufacturers. (Hisp, estab 2010, empl 60, sales $295,000,000, cert: NMSDC)

7663 Osceola Consulting llc
One Blackfield Dr, Ste 410
Tiburon, CA 94920
Contact: Neda Najibi VP Business Operations
Tel: 800-986-1960
Email: nnajibi@osceolac.com
Website: www.osceolac.com
Management consulting, business process consulting, information technology procurement, & computer & data processing services. (Nat Ame, estab 2006, empl 27, sales $6,103,929, cert: NMSDC, CPUC)

7664 ROI Communication Inc.
5274 Scotts Valley Dr Ste 207
Scotts Valley, CA 95066
Contact: Tricia Deeter VP Finance
Tel: 831-430-0170
Email: accounting@roico.com
Website: www.roico.com/index.html
Strategy & planning, leader & manager communication, measurement, benchmarking & analysis, employee experience, change communication, creative & visual design, sales communication, communication architecture. (Woman, estab 2001, empl 73, sales $0, cert: WBENC)

7665 Ruiz Strategies
1900 Ave of the Stars Ste 1800
Los Angeles, CA 90067
Contact: Michele Ruiz CEO
Tel: 310-853-3605
Email: inquiries@ruizstrategies.com
Website: www.ruizstrategies.com
Strategic communications, change management, reputational management, internal communications, and unconscious bias training and assessments. (Woman/Hisp, estab 2011, empl 10, sales $1,200,000, cert: NMSDC, CPUC, WBENC)

7666 SCMSP (dba) of Spotswood Consulting
92 Corporate Park Ste 812
Irvine, CA 92606
Contact: Derek Spotswood President
Tel: 800-716-2360
Email: derek@scmsp.com
Website: www.scmsp.com
Management consulting, business & technology solutions. (AA, estab 2006, empl 20, sales $2,200,000, cert: NMSDC, 8(a))

7667 Wentworth Consulting Group, LLC
4616 Dolores Ave
Oakland, CA 94602
Contact: Audrey Waidelich Business Mgr
Tel: 510-482-6278
Email: info@wentworthconsulting.com
Website: www.wentworthconsulting.com
Training, leadership development, organization develop-ment, executive coaching, instructional design, workplace mediation & meeting facilitation. (Woman, estab 2011, empl 1, sales $890,200, cert: CPUC, WBENC)

Colorado

7668 LFL International Inc.
4 W Dry Creek Circle Ste 100
Littleton, CO 80120
Contact: Loretta Lovell CEO
Tel: 303-791-8405
Email: lflinc@aol.com
Website: www.LFLINC.com
Professional, administrative & anagement support services: program/, project & construction management services. (Woman/AA, estab 1990, empl 1300, sales $3,150,000, cert: City, NMSDC)

7669 Sanchez, Tennis & Associates, LLC
470 Fountaintree Ln
Boulder, CO 80304
Contact: Anita Sanchez Dir
Tel: 303-449-5921
Email: anita@sancheztennis.com
Website: www.SanchezTennis.com
Organizational development consulting. (Minority, Woman, estab 1976, empl 2, sales $230,000, cert: NMSDC)

Connecticut

7670 Daniel Penn Associates, LLC
151 New Park Ave, Ste 106
Hartford, CT 06106
Contact: Tony Rodriguez President
Tel: 860-232-8577
Email: info@danielpenn.com
Website: www.danielpenn.com
Mgmt consutling firm, consulting svcs, productivity improvement, supply chain optimization, lean mfg, maintenance mgmt, supplier diversity, mfr systems improvement. (Hisp, estab 1978, empl 11, sales $0, cert: State, NMSDC)

7671 Framework LLC
1 Atlantic St, Ste 405
Stamford, CT 06901
Contact: Cecile Girard COO
Tel: 203-563-0644
Email: cgirard@framework-llc.com
Website: www.framework-llc.com
Develop & integrate sustainable business strategy & practices & communicate performance to stakeholders. (Woman, estab 2003, empl 6, sales , cert: WBENC)

7672 HOPET Engineering Services LLC
151 New Park Ave
Hartford, CT 06106
Contact: Rosa Valenzuela President
Tel: 860-251-9587
Email: rosa@hopetengineeringservices.com
Website: www.hopetengineeringservices.com
Project management & engineering, government & commercial contracts project management, supply chain, value stream mapping, sourcing strategies, risk mitigation plans & root cause analysis. (Minority, Woman, estab 2013, empl 1, sales , cert: State)

7673 N-Touch Strategies, LLC
263 Tresser Blvd, 9 Fl
Stamford, CT 06901
Contact: Natasha Williams Managing Partner
Tel: 855-686-8247
Email: nwilliams@ntouchstrategies.com
Website: www.ntouchstrategies.com
Strategic management, Initiate & Accelerate growth, Improve organizational efficiency, Leadership Development. (Woman/AA, estab 2010, empl 17, sales $2,250,000, cert: NMSDC, WBENC, 8(a))

District of Columbia

7674 H Rizvi Consulting Inc.
1345 S Capitol St SW 807
Washington, DC 20003
Contact: Hamid Rizvi President
Tel: 832-640-7374
Email: hamid.rizvi@hrizviconsulting.com
Website: www.hrizviconsulting.com
Consulting, Administrative, and Training Services. (Minority, estab 2017, empl 0, sales $0, cert: NMSDC)

7675 Nexlevel Consulting Services, LLC
611 Pennsylvania Ave SE Ste 197
Washington, DC 20003
Contact: Tammy Davis CEO
Tel: 202-417-7495
Email: tldavis@nexlevelconsultingllc.com
Website: www.nexlevelconsultingllc.com/
Training, Organizational Change Management, Communications (Woman/AA, estab 2006, empl 3, sales $500,000, cert: NMSDC, 8(a))

Delaware

7676 DecisivEdge LLC
131 Continental Dr Ste 409
Newark, DE 19713
Contact: Michele Frayler
Tel: 302-299-1570
Email: michele.frayler@decisivedge.com
Website: www.decisivedge.com
Business consulting & technology services, business architecture & performance, business analytics, data warehouse strategy, design, development & governance, marketing analytics development. (As-Ind, estab 2007, empl 41, sales $4,739,862, cert: NMSDC)

7677 Jackson LMS and Associates Inc.
1328 W 4th St
Wilmington, DE 19805
Contact: Samuel Jackson Dir
Tel: 678-477-8355
Email: sam@jacksonlms.com
Website: www.jacksonlms.com
Change Management, Communications and Training, Program and Project Management, Customer Relationship Management, IT Project Portfolio Management, Vendor Evaluation and Selection, Certified Technologists/Staffing, Regulatory Support. (AA, estab 2012, empl 2, sales $500,000, cert: CPUC)

Florida

7678 Advaion LLC
1560 Sawgrass Corporate Pkwy 4th Fl
Sunrise, FL 33323
Contact: Pavan Satyaketu Operations Mgr
Tel: 954-331-7969
Email: bhuvan@advaion.com
Website: www.advaion.com
Transaction & risk solutions, acquisition integration svcs, risk assessment, Sarbanes-Oxley section svcs, process & control documentation, entity level controls review, corporate governance. (Minority, Woman, estab 2003, empl 10, sales $1,900,000, cert: NMSDC)

7679 Aikerson Consulting Group
51 SW 11th St 634
Miami, FL 33130
Contact: LaShanya Aikerson President
Tel: 678-522-1545
Email: lashanya@aikersonconsulting.com
Website: www.AikersonConsulting.com
Training, speaking, coaching, talent development, and meeting facilitation services. (Woman/AA, estab 2004, empl 1, sales $165,709, cert: NMSDC, WBENC)

7680 American Sign Language Services Corporation
3700 Commerce Blvd Ste. 216
Kissimmee, FL 34741
Contact: Julian Ignatowski CFO
Tel: 407-518-7900
Email: gabrielle@aslservices.com
Website: www.aslservices.com
Interpretation services, sign language, onsite interpreting, Video Relay Services (VRS) & Video Remote Interpreting (VRI). (Minority, Woman, estab 1997, empl 125, sales $8,750,000, cert: State, NMSDC)

7681 Argos Global Partner Services, LLC
240 Crandon Blvd. Ste 201
Key Biscayne, FL 33149
Contact: Luciana Ciuchini CEO
Tel: 305-365-1096
Email: lciuchini@argosus.com
Website: www.argosgps.com
Supply chain solutions, sourcing, consolidation, import, export, purchasing, quality control, logistics and warehousing. (Minority, Woman, estab 2005, empl 15, sales $20,120,630, cert: NMSDC, WBENC)

7682 Blue Isis LLC
525 Caribbean Dr E
Summerland Key, FL 33042
Contact: Dawn Mahan CEO
Tel: 717-412-1900
Email: dmahan@blueisisllc.com
Website: www.blueisisllc.com
Project management consulting & talent development services, management consulting services, program management, portfolio management, governance, budgeting, forecasting, strategic planning, resource management. (Minority, Woman, estab 2009, empl 10, sales $1,000,000, cert: State)

7683   Caraballo Consulting & Associates, LLC
11312 NW 65 St
Doral, FL 33178
Contact: Lourdes Cordeiro Dir New Business Dev
Tel: 305-204-2493
Email: lourdes@caraballoconsulting.com
Website: www.caraballoconsulting.com
Regulatory Compliance & Submissions, Clinical, Quality Assurance, Manufacturing, Project Management, Black Belt, Lean Manufacturing, Engineering & Specialized Engineering. (Minority, Woman, estab 2015, empl 10, sales , cert: NMSDC)

7684   CMA Enterprise Incorporated
207 Laurel Oak Lane Ste B
Davie, FL 33325
Contact: Gail Birks Williams President
Tel: 954-476-3525
Email: cma@cma-ent.com
Website: www.cma-ent.com
Management consulting, business process re-engineering, supplier/corporate diversity initiatives, employee relations, training. (Woman/AA, estab 1990, empl 2, sales $0, cert: State, WBENC)

7685   Corporate Fitness Works, Inc.
1200 16TH ST N
Saint Petersburg, FL 33705
Contact: Ken Viglio Sr Dir of Business Dev
Tel: 727-522-2900
Email: kviglio@teamcfw.com
Website: www.corporatefitnessworks.com/
Manage customized fitness centers & wellness programs, feasibility studies, facility layout & design, equipment recommendations. (Minority, Woman, estab 1988, empl 370, sales $9,587,182, cert: NMSDC, CPUC, WBENC)

7686   Enhance Performance Consulting, Inc.
1724 Bella Lago Dr
Clermont, FL 34711
Contact: Donnie Cochran CEO
Tel: 404-277-1950
Email: dcec1@outlook.com
Website: www.donniecochran.com/
Leadership Development Keynote • Motivational Teaching • Team Building & Development Strategies • Personal Excellence Strategies • Leadership Mentorship Support • Law Enforcement Motivational Wellness Support • Mental Toughness Strategies (AA, estab 2000, empl 2, sales , cert: State)

7687   Global Gateway Solutions Inc.
8201 Peters Rd Ste 1000
Plantation, FL 33324
Contact: Jacqueline Sutherland CEO
Tel: 877-447-4627
Email: asutherland@callggs.com
Website: www.callggs.com
Outsourced contact center solutions, customer service, sales, and collections. (Woman/AA, estab 2007, empl 450, sales $14,113,423, cert: NMSDC, WBENC)

7688   Government Business Solutions
12905 SW 132nd St, Ste 4
Miami, FL 33186
Contact: Lourdes Martin-Rosa President
Tel: 786-293-1601
Email: lourdes@govbizsolutions.com
Website: www.govbizsolutions.com
Educate small businesses on procuring federal, state & local government contracts. (Minority, Woman, estab 2002, empl 6, sales , cert: State, WBENC, 8(a))

7689   GreenPath Energy Solutions
3218 E Colonial Dr Ste G
Orlando, FL 32803
Contact: Samuel Graham CEO
Tel: 321-948-3623
Email: sgraham@greenpathes.com
Website: www.greenpathenergysolutions.com
Energy monitoring, energy auditing, retro-commissioning, web-based energy dashboard management software. (AA, estab 2006, empl 3, sales $175,000, cert: State, City, NMSDC)

7690   Impresiv Health
145 Bellagio Way
Sanford, FL 32771
Contact: Marcus Fontaine President
Tel: 305-407-0218
Email: mfontaine@impresivhealth.com
Website: www.impresivhealth.com
Accreditation Readiness, Care Management, Program Development, Regulatory Compliance Readiness, Clinical & Non-Clinical Managed, Care Training, System Redesign, Process & Workflow Improvement. (AA, estab 2015, empl 17, sales $2,500,000, cert: State)

7691   Maria R Pearson Inc dba Own Your World
101 Del Sol Circle
Tequesta, FL 33469
Contact: Maria Pearson President
Tel: 772-287-5833
Email: mariapearson@ownyourworld.net
Website: www.OwnYourWorld.net
Training & management consulting: communication, presentation skills, leadership effectiveness, time mgmt, process & system improvement. (Minority, Woman, estab 1993, empl 1, sales , cert: State)

7692   Premier Remodeling Services, Inc.
5703 Red Bug Lake Rd, Ste 328
Winter Springs, FL 32708
Contact: Geoff Gilpin
Tel: 407-489-8510
Email: ggilpin@premiergroupadvisors.com
Website: www.premiergroupadvisors.com
Policy, Planning & Program Support, Information Management, Human Capital Optimization, Education & Training, Infrastructure Management, Sustainability Planning, Engineering & Technical Assistance, Supplier Management. (AA, estab 2006, empl 8, sales $1,500,000, cert: NMSDC, 8(a))

7693   Program Evaluation Services Inc.
5521 Oak Hollow Dr
Titusville, FL 32780
Contact: Gina Beckles CEO
Tel: 321-243-4809
Email: ginabeckles@cfl.rr.com
Website: www.programevaluationservices.com
Program evaluation & performance measurement, analytical & administrative services. (Woman/AA, estab 2006, empl 2, sales , cert: NMSDC)

7694 Trustee Capital LLC
100 S Ashley Dr, Ste 600
Apollo Beach, FL 33572
Contact: Andre Fair CEO
Tel: 813-397-3648
Email: info@trusteecap.com
Website: www.trusteecap.com
Business valuations and custom analytics solutions. (AA, estab 2017, empl 2, sales , cert: NMSDC)

7695 Wightman & Associates LLC
720 W Montrose St
Clermont, FL 34711
Contact: Louis Dommer III CFO
Tel: 757-574-4386
Email: ldommer@wightman-associates.com
Website: www.Wightman-Associates.com
Training & organizational development products & services. (Woman, estab 2011, empl 12, sales $836,000, cert: State)

Georgia

7696 Asil White Enterprises, Inc.
642 Concord Lake Circle Se
Smyrna, GA 30082
Contact: Lisa L White President
Tel: 404-786-8931
Email: lw@thinkaweinc.com
Website: www.thinkaweinc.com
Instructional design, training materials, professional & mgmt dev training, coaching, time mgmt , organizational dev, performance improvement, project mgmt. (Woman/AA, estab 2004, empl 1, sales , cert: State)

7697 BDM2
235 Peachtree St, Ste 400
Atlanta, GA 30303
Contact: Missy Pitcher CEO
Tel: 404-301-5879
Email: missy.pitcher@bdmsquared.com
Website: www.bdmsquared.com
BDM Squared is a premier professional services consultancy providing our clients with Project Delivery; PMO Creation and Management; and Project Planning for Rapid Ignition Project Startup and Launching. (AA, estab 2016, empl 8, sales $284,000, cert: NMSDC)

7698 Full Circle Events
6070 Black Water Trail
Atlanta, GA 30328
Contact: Sally Silverman Owner
Tel: 404-236-0440
Email: sally.fullcircle@comcast.net
Website: www.fullcircleeventsinc.com
Event, meeting & conference planning. (Woman, estab 2002, empl 5, sales $416,897, cert: WBENC)

7699 Horizon Leadership, Inc.
3295 River Exchange Dr Ste 560
Norcross, GA 30092
Contact: Cindy Larkin President
Tel: 770-552-5511
Email: clarkin@horizonleadership.com
Website: www.horizonleadership.com
Facilitation, presentation & influencing skills, teambuilding, change management, coaching skills, etc. (Woman, estab 2002, empl 4, sales $2,300,000, cert: WBENC)

7700 LBJR Consulting LLC
2942 Darlington Run
Duluth, GA 30097
Contact: Lavoska Barton President
Tel: 678-662-9159
Email: lbarton@lbjrconsulting.com
Website: www.lbjrconsulting.com
Project Management & Planning, Cost management & Control, Budget prioritization & Management, Vendor Management & Control, Financial / Variance Analysis of projects, Process Management, Six Sigma Black Belt. (AA, estab 2005, empl 4, sales , cert: State)

7701 LEAP Leadership
1011 Carriage Lane SE
Smyrna, GA 30082
Contact: Kim Radford Partner
Tel: 404-414-8624
Email: kr@leaplead.com
Website: www.leaplead.com
Leadership education, executive coaching & organizational development services. (Woman/AA, estab 2009, empl 3, sales $590,405, cert: NMSDC)

7702 Peerless Performance, LLC
9040 Roswell Road Ste 460
Atlanta, GA 30350
Contact: LeeAnne Canecchio Acct Dir
Tel: 404-551-5181
Email: leeannecanecchio@peerlessperformance.net
Website: www.peerlessperformance.net
Performance Improvement, Culture Engineering Agency. (Woman, estab 2017, empl 8, sales $550,000, cert: WBENC)

7703 The Cadence Group, Inc.
1095 Zonolite Rd Ste 105
Atlanta, GA 30306
Contact: Tina Teree Baker President
Tel: 404-874-0544
Email:
Website: www.cadence-group.com
Information management: acquire, organize & disseminate information. (Woman, estab 1988, empl 46, sales $2,890,048, cert: WBENC)

7704 The Intuition Consulting Firm, LLC.
2870 Peachtree Rd NW Ste 404
Atlanta, GA 30305
Contact: Roy Broderick Jr President
Tel: 404-861-2661
Email: team@authentiqueagency.com
Website: www.authentiqueagency.com
Multicultural integration and programming. (AA, estab 2016, empl 25, sales $1,500,000, cert: NMSDC)

7705 Translation Station, Inc.
3460 Chamblee Dunwoody Way
Chamblee, GA 30341
Contact: Lindsey Cambardella CEO
Tel: 770-234-9387
Email: lindsey@translationstation.com
Website: www.translationstation.com
Foreign language translation: technical, legal,medical documents, benefits, software localization, website translation, interpretation for meetings, conferences, courts, depositions, conflict resolution, etc. (Woman, estab 1998, empl 10, sales $703,000, cert: WBENC)

7706 Tricia Browning Design Group
      102 Westside Dr
      LaGrange, GA 30240
      Contact: Tim Donahue
      Tel: 706-883-7741
      Email: tdonahue@nimlok-westgeorgia.com
      Website: www.nimlok-westgeorgia.com
Trade Show booths, Exhibits, Graphic Design, Display
Advertising, Commercial Photography, Advertising Ser-
vices, Design Services (Woman, estab 1996, empl 8, sales
$2,180,000, cert: WBENC)

7707 VetWorks LLC
      5865 N Point Pkwy, Ste 320 Ste 320
      Alpharetta, GA 30022
      Contact: Avilala Thanuja HR Mgr
      Tel: 770-561-3929
      Email: Thanuja@vetworksus.com
      Website: www.vetworksus.com/
Design & implement customized recruiting solutions that
deliver proven, dependable Leaders and Technicians
transitioning from the military. (Woman/AA, estab 2008,
empl 100, sales $1,062,323, cert: NMSDC, WBENC)

7708 VYD and Associates, LLC
      3306 Blanton Dr
      Scottdale, GA 30079
      Contact: Vonetta Daniels CEO
      Tel: 404-966-8411
      Email: vonetta.daniels@gmail.com
      Website: www.vydandassociates.com
Management consulting: business strategy, business
process engineering, supply chain management, revenue
cycle & cost optimization; program performance measurement & evaluation, strategic planning, budget & performance. (Woman/AA, estab 2010, empl 1, sales , cert:
NMSDC, WBENC, 8(a))

Hawaii

7709 Native Hawaiin Veterans LLC
      3375 Koapaka St, Ste F238-20
      Honolulu, HI 96819
      Contact: Rebecca McKee Sr Program Mgr
      Tel: 808-792-7528
      Email: rebecca.mckee@nativehawaiianveterans.com
      Website: www.nativehawaiianveterans.com
Homeland Security, Emergency Management, Information
Technology, Communication Equipment, Professional Staff
Augmentation, Munitions and Explosives of Concern (MEC)
Remediation, and Strategic Communications/Creative
Services. (Minority, estab 2004, empl 190, sales $0, cert:
NMSDC)

Illinois

7710 Administrative Resource Options Inc.
      200 W Adams St Ste 2000
      Chicago, IL 60606
      Contact: Alecia McClung CEO
      Tel: 312-634-0300
      Email: ammcclung@aroptions.com
      Website: www.aroptions.com
Managed & on-site services outsourcing, customized
workplace & workspace solutions, print & document
management, mail center, front of office, conference room
services. (Woman, estab 1990, empl 394, sales
$22,827,215, cert: WBENC)

7711 B2B Strategic Solutions, Inc.
      150 N Michigan Ave Ste 2800
      Chicago, IL 60601
      Contact: Donna Bryant President
      Tel: 312-368-1700
      Email: info@b2bssi.com
      Website: www.b2bssi.com
Management consulting, information technology,
technical training, strategic planning, professional
development, leadership, customer service, training,
business writing. (Woman/AA, estab 2003, empl 20,
sales $1,254,000, cert: State, NMSDC)

7712 CGN & Associates, Inc.
      415 SW Washingotn
      Peoria, IL 61602
      Contact: Patrick Dierker Associate Partner
      Tel: 309-495-2100
      Email: patrick.dierker@cgnglobal.com
      Website: www.cgnglobal.com
Business consulting: operations, execution & technology
mgmt, analysis, design & implementation complex
operational transformations, strategy dev, solution
design, implementation & optimization techniquies. (As-
Pac, estab 1995, empl 125, sales $0, cert: State, NMSDC)

7713 EMS Consulting
      477 W Happfield Dr
      Arl, IL 60004
      Contact: Liz Kistner President
      Tel: 224-465-1115
      lkistner@enrollmentmarketingsolutions.com
      Website: www.emsconsultgroup.com
Project & program management consulting. (Woman,
estab 2006, empl 1, sales $0, cert: WBENC)

7714 Executive Consultants United, LLC
      180 N Stetson Ave, Ste 3500
      Chicago, IL 60601
      Contact: Wheeler Coleman CEO
      Tel: 312-268-5829
      Email: wcoleman@ec-united.com
      Website: www.ec-united.com
Data Strategy, Roadmap, Advanced Analytics, Reporting,
Dashboards & Scorecards, Data Strategies, Data Lakes,
Data Platforms & Data Mgmt, Data Scientists & DBAs
Specialists, Analytics (Consumer, Provider, etc.) (AA,
estab 2016, empl 10, sales $1,020,000, cert: NMSDC)

7715 Hendon Group, Inc.
      165 Robincrest Ln
      Lindenhurst, IL 60046
      Contact: Ira M. Hendon President
      Tel: 847-245-8722
      Email: imh@hendon-group.com
      Website: www.hendon-group.com
Program and Project Leadership Professional Services
and Consulting. (AA, estab 2006, empl 1, sales , cert:
State, NMSDC)

7716 Kairos Consulting Worldwide
      935 West Chestnut Ste 455
      Chicago, IL 60642
      Contact: Managing Principal
      Tel: 312-757-5197
      Email: info@kairosworldwide.com
      Website: www.kairosworldwide.com
Technology consulting: change management & process
reengineering, process management, strategic planning
& project management. (Woman/AA, estab 2004, empl
1, sales , cert: State, WBENC)

7717 MarketZing Inc.
      875 N Michigan Ave Ste 3100
      Chicago, IL 60611
      Contact: Aleen Bayard Principal
      Tel: 312-794-7880
      Email: aleen@aleenbayard.com
      Website: www.marketzing.org
Change management project design & execution, culture
& values alignment work, strategic planning facilitation &
implementation support, employee engagement and team
effectiveness, organizational & leadership development.
(Woman, estab 1999, empl 1, sales $350,000, cert:
WBENC)

7718 Mary O'Connor & Company
      220 W River Dr
      St. Charles, IL 60174
      Contact: Mary O'Connor President
      Tel: 630-443-4300
      Email: moconnor@mocandco.com
      Website: www.mocandco.com
Meeting & event mgmt, online event registration, program
dev, employee training & dev, speaker svcs, hotel mgmt,
transportation, food & beverage mgmt. (Woman, estab
1995, empl 17, sales $3,400,000, cert: WBENC)

7719 MJ Learning Inc.
      605 S Maple Ave
      Oak Park, IL 60304
      Contact: Sarah Gee CEO
      Tel: 708-613-5401
      Email: sarah@mjlearning.com
      Website: www.mjlearning.com
Professional & management development training.
(Woman, estab 2010, empl 5, sales $500,000, cert:
WBENC)

7720 Multilingual Connections, LLC
      847 Chicago Ave, Ste 250
      Evanston, IL 60202
      Contact: Jill Bishop CEO
      Tel: 773-292-5500
      Email: jill@mlconnections.com
      Website: www.multilingualconnections.com
Translation/interpretation services, workplace language
training (Spanish and ESL - English as a Second Language),
diversity training and workplace harassment prevention
training and leadership development. (Woman, estab
2005, empl 25, sales $3,122,086, cert: WBENC)

7721 Nancy Conner Consulting, LLC
      1235 Berry Lane
      Flossmoor, IL 60422
      Contact: Nancy Conner CEO
      Tel: 847-456-5601
      Email: nancy@nancyconner.com
      Website: www.nancyconner.com
Supply chain, supplier development business partnerships,
negotiation, community outreach & advocacy. (Woman,
estab 2016, empl 1, sales , cert: WBENC)

7722 PTS Consulting Services LLC
      1700 Park St, Ste 212
      Naperville, IL 60563
      Contact: Reshma Multani Client Servicing Mgr
      Tel: 630-635-8328
      Email: reshma.multani@ptscservices.com
      Website: www.ptscservices.com
IT consulting and Business Consulting Services. (As-Pac,
estab 2012, empl 50, sales $7,000,000, cert: NMSDC)

7723 RGMA
      980 N Michigan Ave Ste 1230
      Chicago, IL 60611
      Contact: Ralph Moore President
      Tel: 312-419-7250
      Email: ralphmoore@rgma.com
      Website: www.rgma.com
Provides supplier diversity services to drive shareholder
value in an increasingly diverse, global economy. (AA,
estab 1979, empl 6, sales , cert: City, NMSDC)

7724 Sandstorm Design
      4422 N Ravenswood Ave Ste 50
      Chicago, IL 60640
      Contact: Amanda Heberg VP Business Dev
      Tel: 773-348-4200
      Email: aheberg@sandstormdesign.com
      Website: www.sandstormdesign.com
Internal Communications, Annual Reports. (Woman,
estab 1998, empl 14, sales $0, cert: WBENC)

7725 SB Services, Inc.
      888 E Belvidere Rd, Ste 309
      Grayslake, IL 60030
      Contact: Sharon Castillo Principal
      Tel: 847-223-5712
      Email: scastillo@sbservicesinc.com
      Website: www.sbservicesinc.com
Supplier diversity program development & process
improvement. (Woman, estab 2003, empl 5, sales
$150,000, cert: WBENC)

7726 TrainSmart, Inc.
      1600 Golf Rd, Ste 1200
      Rolling Meadows, IL 60008
      Contact: President
      Tel: 847-991-8181
      Email: inquiries@trainsmartinc.com
      Website: www.trainsmartinc.com
Computer training, performance solutions, team
building, customer service, leadership skills, manufacturing quality training, needs analysis, instructural design,
assessments, programming. (Woman, estab 1994, empl
6, sales $1,500,000, cert: WBENC)

7727 Trilogy Consulting Group, Inc.
      2021 Midwest Rd, Ste 200
      Oak Brook, IL 60523
      Contact: Kathy Martin-Smith VP
      Tel: 630-953-6278
      Email: kmartin-smith@trilogy-consulting.com
      Website: www.trilogy-consulting.com
Health plan administration reviews & audits. (Woman,
estab 1995, empl 3, sales $679,217, cert: State, WBENC)

7728 Trinal, Inc.
      329 W 18th St, Ste 401
      Chicago, IL 60616
      Contact: Gladys Rodriguez GM
      Tel: 312-738-0500
      Email: info@trinalinc.com
      Website: www.trinalinc.com
Strategic business management consulting, procurement policy development & economic development
program monitoring. (Woman/AA, Hisp, estab 1997,
empl 14, sales , cert: State)

7729   Tristana R Harvey Career Planning & Consulting Series LLC
5135 S Kenwood Ave, Box 504
Chicago, IL 60615
Contact: Tristana Harvey Owner
Tel: 312-351-0272
Email: tristana_harvey@harveycareerplanning.com
Website: www.harveycareerplanning.com
Counseling, coaching & consulting, training programs that create awareness, increase education & produce behavior change. (Woman/AA, estab 2010, empl 2, sales $125,000, cert: State, City, 8(a))

7730   Universal. Innovative. Intelligent, Inc.
PO Box 1711
Bolingbrook, IL 60440
Contact: Kimberly Johnson President
Tel: 630-981-1931
Email: kjohnson@universal3i.com
Website: www.myfavoritethings-u3i.com
Management & marketing consulting. (Woman/AA, estab 2003, empl 1, sales , cert: State)

7731   ZOI Incorporated
2114 Rugen Rd, Unit A
Glenview, IL 60026
Contact: Susanna Alvarado CEO
Tel: 847-834-4787
Email: info@zoiinc.com
Website: www.zoiinc.com
Project, Product and Logistics Management, Change Management, and Training Development, e-Commerce, Cloud, Cognitive & Data Analysis. (Woman/Hisp, estab 2011, empl 5, sales $115,000, cert: NMSDC, WBENC)

Indiana

7732   Advanced Systems
508 Sunshine Dr
Valparaiso, IN 46385
Contact: Christy Poturkovic Reg Sales Mgr
Tel: 317-845-5017
Email: christyp@successstrategiesllc.com
Website: www.processspecialist.com
Business consulting services, education & training: process improvement, strategic planning, leadership development, management & supervision training, sales training, customer service training, quality improvement. (Woman, estab 1997, empl 1, sales , cert: City)

7733   Bulldog Consulting Services
PO Box 65
Leo, IN 46765
Contact: Sharon Miller President
Tel: 517-455-7016
Email: smiller@bulldogmeansbusiness.com
Website: www.BulldogMeansBusiness.com
Process Assessment & improvements, Program/Project Management, Process Documentation, and Training. (Woman, estab 2007, empl 3, sales $200,000, cert: State)

7734   Growing Kids Pediatrics, LLC
3707 Charlestown Rd, Ste C1
New Albany, IN 47150
Contact: Rosie Nolot Office Mgr
Tel: 812-944-4575
Email: contact@growingkidspediatrics.com
Website: www.growingkidspediatrics.com/
Pediatric Office-we see children from 0 - 21 years of age. (Woman, estab 2010, empl 4, sales , cert: State)

7735   Intrinz Inc.
12175 Visionary Way
Fishers, IN 46038
Contact: Patricia Musariri Gurnell President
Tel: 317-288-2267
Email: patricia.musariri@intrinzincorp.com
Website: www.intrinzincorp.com
Project Management, Corporate Treasury, Corporate Tax, International Business, Global Sourcing, Language Translation, Business Strategy & Business Consulting Services. (Woman/AA, estab 2011, empl 5, sales $1,250,000, cert: NMSDC)

7736   Prairie Quest Consulting
4211 Hobson Court Ste A
Fort Wayne, IN 46815
Contact: Martha Martin Program Mgr
Tel: 260-420-7374
Email: mmartin@pqcworks.com
Website: www.pqcworks.com
Project mgmt: application development, business case analysis, conceptual & functional process design, project plans, budgets, tracking assessment & metrics. (Woman, estab 2004, empl 150, sales $12,340,945, cert: WBENC)

7737   Raymond Young & Associates, LLC
10705 Club Chase
Fishers, IN 46037
Contact: Raymond Young President
Tel: 317-459-0797
Email: rayyoungjr@msn.com
Website: www.raymondyoungassociates.com
Business consulting, planning, business preformance, competitive analysis, service quality & retention, project management & six sigma principals. (AA, estab 2007, empl 1, sales , cert: State)

Kentucky

7738   Catalyst Learning Co.
310 W Liberty St, Ste 403
Louisville, KY 40202
Contact: Elizabeth LaRue Accountant
Tel: 502-584-7737
Email: elarue@catalystlearning.com
Website: www.catalystlearning.com
Provides proven learning & development tools. (Woman, estab 1994, empl 14, sales , cert: NWBOC)

Louisiana

7739   Henry Consulting LLC
1010 Common St Ste 2500
New Orleans, LA 70112
Contact: Allen Square Dir
Tel: 504-529-9890
Email: allen.square@henryconsulting.net
Website: www.henryconsulting.net
Management consulting services. (AA, estab 2001, empl 15, sales $1,941,921, cert: NMSDC)

Massachusetts

7740   3D Leadership Group LLC
396 Washington St, Ste 207
Wellesley, MA 02481
Contact: Sue Williamson Co-Founder
Tel: 781-453-9800
Email: sue.williamson@3dleadershipgroup.com
Website: www.3dleadershipgroup.com
Executive Coaching, Team Coaching, Transition Coaching, Leadership Workshops, Assessments. (Woman, estab 2008, empl 2, sales $1,528,044, cert: WBENC)

7741　Chrysalis Coaching & Consulting
　　　　595 E Fourth St Ste 1
　　　　Boston, MA 02127
　　　　Contact: Karen Carmody President
　　　　Tel:　617-283-8705
　　　　Email: kcarmody@chrysaliscoachingconsulting.com
　　　　Website: www.chrysaliscoachingconsulting.com/
Corporate coaching, organizational effectiveness, &
corporate wellness services. (Woman, estab 2012, empl 1,
sales , cert: WBENC)

7742　Communication Management, Inc.
　　　　5 Perkins Glen
　　　　Eastham, MA 02642
　　　　Contact: Joseph Perkins President
　　　　Tel:　508-255-3789
　　　　Email: jperkins@cmiglobal.com
　　　　Website: www.cmiglobal.com
Communications skills, training, onsite & online business
writing & presentation skills training programs. (AA, estab
1991, empl 1, sales , cert: State, NMSDC)

7743　Culture Coach International
　　　　259 Walnut St, Ste 17
　　　　Newton, MA 02460
　　　　Contact: Kari Heistad CEO
　　　　Tel:　617-795-1688
　　　　Email: admin@culturecoach.biz
　　　　Website: www.CultureCoach.biz
Consulting, strategic planning & training. (Woman, estab
1998, empl 10, sales , cert: WBENC)

7744　EnVision Performance Solutions
　　　　9 Pond View Cir
　　　　Sharon, MA 02067
　　　　Contact: Irene Stern Frielich President
　　　　Tel:　617-877-2719
　　　　Email: irene.frielich@envision-performance.com
　　　　Website: www.envision-performance.com/
Custom instructional design & training development
services; needs assessment, curriculum development,
instructor-led classes, virtual classes, elearning, on-the-job
training, performance support. (Woman, estab 1998, empl
1, sales $448,000, cert: State, WBENC)

7745　Incite, Inc.
　　　　14 St. Charles St
　　　　Boston, MA 02116
　　　　Contact: Beth Rogers President
　　　　Tel:　617-521-9050
　　　　Email: brogers@pointtaken.net
　　　　Website: www.pointtaken.net
Custom communication skills training workshops; Presen-
tation Skills, Facilitation Skills, Negotiation Skills. (Woman,
estab 1997, empl 4, sales $1,800,000, cert: WBENC)

7746　The Asaba Group
　　　　220 N Main St, Ste 102
　　　　Natick, MA 01760
　　　　Contact: Katrice Rivers Business Mgr
　　　　Tel:　508-655-8100
　　　　Email: krivers@asabagroup.com
　　　　Website: www.asabagroup.com
Strategic assessments, strategic support services, organiza-
tional improvement. (AA, estab 1999, empl 10, sales
$1,000,000, cert: NMSDC)

Maryland

7747　Andean Consulting Solutions International, LLC
　　　　11140 Rockville Pike Ste 100-155
　　　　Rockville, MD 20852
　　　　Contact: Andres Echeverri President
　　　　Tel:　202-618-1455
　　　　Email: andres@acsitranslations.com
　　　　Website: www.acsitranslations.com
Language translation & interpretation services in over
60 languages. (Hisp, estab 2011, empl 2, sales $585,000,
cert: State, 8(a))

7748　Applied Development LLC
　　　　7 S Front St Ste 200
　　　　Baltimore, MD 21202
　　　　Contact: Kimberly Citizen
　　　　Tel:　410-571-4016
　　　　Email: kcitizen@applied-dev.com
　　　　Website: www.applied-dev.com
Process improvement, automation, analytics & cyber
security, project management, business process improvement, strategic communications, cybersecurity &
administrative support. (Woman/AA, estab 2011, empl
12, sales $687,000, cert: State, City, NMSDC, WBENC,
8(a))

7749　BETAH Associates, Inc.
　　　　199 E. Montgomery Ave. Ste 100
　　　　Rockville, MD 20815
　　　　Contact: Meisha Robinson Mktg & Proposals
　　　　Coord
　　　　Tel:　301-657-4254
　　　　Email: mrobinson@betah.com
　　　　Website: www.betah.com
Professional, technical & communications consulting:
social marketing & outreach, management consulting,
technical assistance, research & evaluation, communica-
tions & media relations, event planning. (Woman/AA,
estab 1988, empl 105, sales $0, cert: WBENC)

7750　Cheseldine Management Consulting, LLC
　　　　PO Box 1307
　　　　Leonardtown, MD 20650
　　　　Contact: Margaret Cheseldine CEO
　　　　Tel:　301-475-2272
　　　　Email: margiec@md.metrocast.net
　　　　Website: www.cheseldine.org
Management consulting, asset, property & construction
management. (Woman, estab 2008, empl 11, sales
$512,000, cert: State)

7751　Destiny Management Services, LLC
　　　　8737 Colesville Rd Ste 710
　　　　Silver Spring, MD 20910
　　　　Contact: Donna Mitchell President
　　　　Tel:　301-650-0047
　　　　Email: donnam@destinymgmtsvcs.com
　　　　Website: www.destinymgmtsvcs.com
Management Consulting, Business Solutions, Informa-
tion Technology, Staff Augmentation, Compliance
Reviews, Contacts Management, Human Capitol
Development. (Woman/AA, estab 1996, empl 10, sales
$1,300,000, cert: State, WBENC)

7752 DPN Group, LLC
516 N Charles St Ste 303
Baltimore, MD 21201
Contact: Andrea Jackson Principal
Tel: 410-905-4036
Email: ajackson@dpngroup.net
Website: www.dpngroup.net
Management consulting: public outreach, supplier diversity & inclusion consulting, strategic planning, workforce development, performance evaluation, policy development, & compliance monitoring. (Woman/AA, estab 2008, empl 4, sales $204,000, cert: State)

7753 Ivy Planning Group, LLC
15204 Omega Dr, Ste 110
Rockville, MD 20850
Contact: Cynthia Featherson President
Tel: 301-963-1669
Email: cfeatherson@ivygroupllc.com
Website: www.ivygroupllc.com
Diversity consulting & training, strategic planning, change mgmt, customer service, executive coaching, assessments & surveys, knowledge mgmt, performance measurement & mgmt, training & development. (Woman/AA, estab 1990, empl 30, sales $0, cert: WBENC)

7754 Lord and Tucker Management Consultants, LLC
4140 Holbrook Ln
Huntingtown, MD 20639
Contact: Dawn Tucker President
Tel: 866-517-0477
Email: info@ltmctraining.com
Website: www.ltmctraining.com
Staff development & training: life skills, career development & entrepreneurship, customer service, time mgmt, organizational dev, financial mgmt, budgeting, resume writing & interview skills. (Woman/AA, estab 2004, empl 1, sales , cert: State)

7755 Muse GME Enterprises LLC
2 Wisconsin Circle, Ste 700
Chevy Chase, MD 20815
Contact: Gwen Muse-Evans CEO
Tel: 301-244-4947
Email: g.museevans@gmeenterprises.net
Website: www.gmeenterprises.net
Organizational governance, program review and development, professional and management development, quality management, strategic planning, committee establishment, regulatory compliance, risk governance. (Woman/AA, estab 2014, empl 3, sales $154,300, cert: State, WBENC, SDB)

7756 Performance Development Corporation
17308 Twin Ridge Court
Silver Spring, MD 20905
Contact: Sharon Fountain President
Tel: 301-421-0118
Email: sharon@sharonfountain.com
Website: www.SharonFountain.com
Training: interpersonal competence, communication, feedback, assertiveness, conflict management, self-esteem/self confidence, leadership/management/supervisory skills, team building, organizational skills, time management/managing multiple priorities. (Woman, estab 1980, empl 1, sales , cert: NWBOC)

7757 Pivotal Practices Consulting
6301 Ivy Lane, Ste 800
Greenbelt, MD 20770
Contact: Patrina Clark Business Devel
Tel: 301-220-3179
Email: info@pivotalpractices.com
Website: www.pivotalpractices.com
Organizational climate assessments & engagements: surveys & diagnostic tools, improve individual, team & organizational performance. (Woman/AA, estab 2011, empl 10, sales $2,307,552, cert: NMSDC, WBENC, 8(a))

7758 Sheila Lee & Associates, LLC
1518 W Pratt St
Baltimore, MD 21223
Contact: Sheila S. Lee CEO
Tel: 410-233-6922
Email: sheilalee@learningeverywhere.com
Website: www.learningeverywhere.com
Organizational development, curriculum design & training. (Woman/AA, estab 2005, empl 8, sales $0, cert: State, NMSDC, WBENC)

7759 Starr and Associates LLC
10707 Heather Glen Way
Bowie, MD 20720
Contact: Jamal Starr CEO
Tel: 888-727-3017
Email: jamalstarr@starrconsultant.com
Website: www.starrconsultant.com
Management consulting practices and technologies to improve productivity and reduce costs. (AA, estab 2004, empl 30, sales $0, cert: NMSDC)

7760 The Fehlig Group, LLC
1 Arch Pl, Ste 421
Gaithersburg, MD 20878
Contact: Mary Fehlig President
Tel: 240-912-9422
Email: maryfehlig@fehliggroup.com
Website: www.fehliggroup.com
Corporate Social Responsibility, Corporate Social Responsibility Development, Sustainability Action Plans, Award Applications, Local, National, Global: Great Place To Work Strategy & Recognition, Green Business Strategy & Recognition, Capacity Building. (Woman, estab 1993, empl 1, sales $435,227, cert: WBENC)

7761 The Stroud Group
9130 Red Branch Rd, Ste S
Columbia, MD 21045
Contact: Theo Bell VP Business Dev
Tel: 410-964-2222
Email: theo@stroudgroup.com
Website: www.stroudgroup.com
Procurement & project management services. (Woman, estab 1987, empl 22, sales $22,000,000, cert: WBENC)

Michigan

7762 ASG Renaissance
27655 Middlebelt Rd Ste 140
Farmington Hills, MI 48334
Contact: Maureen Michaels Acct Mgr
Tel: 248-477-5432
Email: mmichaels@asgren.com
Website: www.asgren.com
Consulting svcs: information technology, public relations, engineering, mktg, minority technical assistance programs, etc. (Minority, Woman, estab 1987, empl 200, sales $206,586,000, cert: NMSDC, WBENC)

7763   Bigelow Family Holdings LLC
       3223 15 Mile Rd
       Sterling Heights, MI 48310
       Contact: President
       Tel: 586-306-8962
       Email: info@mettleops.com
       Website: www.mettleops.com
Program management, engineering, and business development. (Woman, estab 2013, empl 10, sales , cert: WBENC, 8(a))

7764   BTS Consulting & Training LLC
       211 N. First St Ste 200
       Brighton, MI 48116
       Contact: Mary Temple Managing Partner
       Tel: 586-322-3065
       Email: mary.temple@btsmichigan.com
       Website: www.btsmichigan.com/
Designs, develops & delivers customized training solutions, instructional design, course development, training delivery, project and curriculum management, conference and event coordination, travel administration. (Woman, estab 1991, empl 10, sales $2,600,000, cert: WBENC)

7765   Coach for Higher
       2015 Geddes Ave
       Ann Arbor, MI 48104
       Contact: Nan Owner
       Tel: 734-255-7833
       Email: nan@coachforhigher.com
       Website: www.CoachForHigher.com
Executive & Leadership Coaching Services for Individuals, Teams & Organizations. (Woman, estab 2010, empl 1, sales , cert: WBENC)

7766   Contract Source & Assembly Inc.
       5230 33rd St SE
       Grand Rapids, MI 49512
       Contact: Bryce Cooper
       Tel: 616-897-2185
       Email: bryce@contractmi.com
       Website: www.contractmi.com
Light Manufacturing & Contract Assembly, Contract Packaging & Inventory Management, Supply Chain Management, Inspection & Re-work. (As-Pac, estab 2001, empl 13, sales $18,000,000, cert: NMSDC)

7767   DSSI LLC
       40 Oak Hollow St Ste 225
       Southfield, MI 48033
       Contact: Kathy Young
       Tel: 248-208-8340
       Email: kyoung@directsourcing.com
       Website: www.directsourcing.com
Purchasing services. (As-Ind, estab 2000, empl 100, sales $110,000,000, cert: NMSDC)

7768   Focused Coaching LLC
       2022 Liberty HTS
       Ann Arbor, MI 48103
       Contact: Lisa Pasbjerg CEO
       Tel: 734-663-0420
       Email: lpasbjerg@focusedcoaching.net
       Website: www.focusedcoaching.net
Leadership development, executive coaching, assessment & facilitation services. (Woman, estab 2006, empl 1, sales $104,000, cert: WBENC)

7769   Global LT, Inc.
       1871 Woodslee Dr
       Troy, MI 48083
       Contact: Chris Brotherson VP Sales
       Tel: 248-786-0999
       Email: CBrotherson@global-lt.com
       Website: www.Global-LT.com
English, foreign language, cross-cultural, diversity training; relocation translation, interpreting svcs; video/film narration. (AA, estab 1979, empl , sales $25,000,000, cert: NMSDC)

7770   GSHA Quality Services
       PO Box 1452
       Ann Arbor, MI 48103
       Contact: CEO
       Tel: 734-263-7399
       Email:
       Website: www.gshasolutions.org
Quality management services, stabilize processes, reduce cost, reduce waste, improve effectiveness, and efficiency to achieve sustainable, transformational performance improvements. (Woman/AA, estab 2009, empl 8, sales $400,000, cert: NMSDC, WBENC)

7771   Innovative Learning Group, Inc.
       1130 Coolidge Hwy
       Troy, MI 48084
       Contact: Gayle Holsworth Performance Consultant
       Tel: 248-544-1568
       Email: gayle.holsworth@innovativelg.com
       Website: www.innovativeLG.com
Human performance consulting, needs assessment, training design & development, evaluation. (Woman, estab 2004, empl 17, sales $5,000,000, cert: WBENC)

7772   Jim Roberts Enterprises LLC
       515 Ship St Ste 211
       Saint Joseph, MI 49085
       Contact: Jim Roberts President
       Tel: 269-982-4188
       Email: jim@jimrobertsenterprises.com
       Website: www.jimrobertsenterprises.com
Management consulting, financial, facility management, real estate & project mgmt consulting services. (Minority, estab 2004, empl 1, sales $163,000, cert: NMSDC)

7773   Learning Designs, Inc.
       6001 North Adams, Ste 100
       Bloomfield Hills, MI 48304
       Contact: Julie Gieraltowski Operations Mgr
       Tel: 248-269-0808
       Email: jgieral@learningdesigns.com
       Website: www.learningdesigns.com
Training & consulting: performance consulting, instructional design, training delivery, technology solutions & evaluation. (Woman, estab 1984, empl 18, sales $2,029,000, cert: WBENC)

7774   LWH Enterprises
       1515 W. Wackerly St.
       Midland, MI 48640
       Contact: Anne Herron VP
       Tel: 989-835-5811
       Email: aherron@allisinfo.com
       Website: www.allisinfo.com
Business research, market research, business intelligence, marketing services, IT support. (Minority, Woman, estab 1979, empl 17, sales $1,884,979, cert: WBENC)

7775 OMNEX
    315 E Eisenhower Pkwy Ste 110
    Ann Arbor, MI 48108
    Contact: Jason Hicks Pulishing Coord
    Tel: 734-761-4940
    Email: jhicks@omnex.com
    Website: www.omnex.com
Consulting & training services in Quality, Environmental, Health & Safety standards-based management systems, ISO 9001:2000, ISO 14000, ISO/TS 16949:2002 & QOS. (As-Ind, estab 1985, empl 200, sales $2,000,001, cert: NMSDC)

7776 Pyramid Quality Solutions & Innovations, Inc.
    2075 West Big Beaver Ste 415
    Troy, MI 48084
    Contact: Ossie Nunn CEO
    Tel: 248-577-1356
    Email: onunn@pqsiinc.com
    Website: www.pqsiinc.com
Quality & industrial engineering consulting: sequencing (JIT), rework & repair svcs, manuals & procedures, kitting & assembly, supplier representation, logistics, quality standards implementation, error & mistake proofing, etc. (AA, estab 2002, empl 150, sales $3,450,000, cert: NMSDC)

7777 Richalin Digue, LLC
    46036 Michigan Ave Ste 201
    Canton, MI 48188
    Contact: Richalin Digue Mgr
    Tel: 313-213-3103
    Email: rich.digue@rnd-engineering.com
    Website: www.rnd-engineering.com
Marketing & project management. (AA, estab 2004, empl 2, sales $800,000, cert: NMSDC)

7778 Syncreon.US Inc.
    2851 High Meadow Circle Ste 250
    Auburn Hills, MI 48326
    Contact: Oswald Reid CEO
    Tel: 248-377-4700
    Email: oswald.reid@syncreon.com
    Website: www.syncreon-us.com
Supply chain management, material follow-up & transportation management and cross-dock. Complex material handling and material integration. (AA, estab 2000, empl 1100, sales $671,200,000, cert: NMSDC)

7779 Utility Reduction Analysts, Inc.
    12935 S West Bay Shore Dr Ste 240
    Traverse City, MI 49684
    Contact: Jennifer Wynn Stoll President
    Tel: 888-586-2121
    Email: jwstoll@utilityreduction.com
    Website: www.utilityreduction.com
Full service utility cost reduction company. Our thorough analysis provides information on rates/tariffs, promotions, refund processing, market opportunities, consumption patterns, & available deregulation options. (Woman, estab 1991, empl 5, sales $410,000, cert: WBENC)

7780 Vani Quality Quest, Inc.
    41000 Woodward Ave Ste 350
    Bloomfield Hills, MI 48304
    Contact: Jagdish Vani President
    Tel: 248-733-0000
    Email: jvani@vqqinc.com
    Website: www.vqqinc.com
Containment inspection, rework svcs, SQI consulting & training, problem solving, customer liaison, QC employee staffing services. (As-Pac, estab 1992, empl 60, sales $0, cert: NMSDC)

7781 VAS Consulting Services
    33228 W 12 Mile Rd
    Farmington Hills, MI 48334
    Contact: Glenn Stafford President
    Tel: 248-553-6603
    Email: gstafford@vas4.com
    Website: www.vas4.com
Consulting services: develop minority supplier programs, strategic alliances & joint ventures. (AA, estab 2001, empl 1, sales $250,000, cert: NMSDC)

Minnesota

7782 Alliant Consulting, Inc.
    555 7th St W, Ste 101
    Saint Paul, MN 55102
    Contact: CFO
    Tel: 651-291-0607
    Email: solutions@alliantconsulting.com
    Website: www.alliantconsulting.com
Management consulting: operational assessment, redesign & implementation to improve service, quality & productivity (Woman, estab 1997, empl 4, sales $505,200, cert: WBENC)

7783 Beehive Strategic Communication GBC
    PO BOX 11373
    Saint Paul, MN 55111
    Contact: Rebecca Martin SVP Culture & Talent
    Tel: 651-789-2236
    Email: rmartin@beehivepr.biz
    Website: www.beehivepr.biz
Strategic planning, competitive intelligence, brand positioning, crisis management, media coaching, communications. (Woman, estab 1998, empl 14, sales $3,000,000, cert: WBENC)

7784 CultureBrokers, LLC
    1610 5th St NE
    Minneapolis, MN 55413
    Contact: Lisa Tabor President
    Tel: 651-321-2167
    Email: lisa@culturebrokers.com
    Website: www.culturebrokers.com
Diversity & inclusion services, diversity recruitment, cultural competence training, strategic planning, inclusion initiatives, employee engagement and retention, community relations, community engagement, equity initiatives. (Woman/AA, estab 2005, empl 1, sales , cert: City)

7785 ECM Instructional Systems
    5816 11th Ave S
    Minneapolis, MN 55417
    Contact: Michael Mazyck President
    Tel: 888-685-0877
    Email: mazyck@ecminstructionalsystems.com
    Website: www.ecminstructionalsystems.com
Instructional design, training, professional development & evaluation services, Learning & Development. (AA, estab 2004, empl 4, sales , cert: State, City)

7786 Hollstadt & Associates, Inc.
      1333 Northland Dr, Ste 220
      Mendota Heights, MN 55120
      Contact: Molly Jungbauer CEO
      Tel: 952-898-6813
      Email: mjungbauer@hollstadt.com
      Website: www.hollstadt.com/
Management & technology consulting: portfolio, program
& project management, business analysis, training programs. (Woman, estab 1990, empl 200, sales $26,053,034,
cert: WBENC)

7787 JIT Energy Services
      23505 Smithtown Rd Ste 280
      Excelsior, MN 55331
      Contact: Jamie Aragon CEO
      Tel: 952-474-3410
      Email: jamie.a@jitservicesinc.com
      Website: www.jitservicesinc.com
Energy efficiency consulting & energy mgmt services.
(Minority, Woman, estab 1991, empl 12, sales
$173,840,860, cert: NMSDC, WBENC)

7788 MDA Leadership Consulting
      150 S 5th St, Ste 3300
      Minneapolis, MN 55402
      Contact: Linda Barrett Dir Business Svcs
      Tel: 612-332-8182
      Email: info@mdaleadership.com
      Website: www.mdaleadership.com
Talent management, leadership development, organizational performance (Woman, estab 1981, empl 31, sales
$4,422,000, cert: State)

7789 Nelson Consulting LLC
      1330 Lagoon Ave 4th Fl
      Minneapolis, MN 55408
      Contact: Owner
      Tel: 612-460-5250
      Email: info@pivotstrategies.com
      Website: www.pivotstrategies.com
Communications strategy, organizational change management, reputation management, sustainability, corporate
social responsibility, (Woman, estab 2015, empl 12, sales
$1,500,000, cert: WBENC)

7790 ON Point Next Level Leadership
      5775 Wayzata Blvd, Ste 700
      Minneapolis, MN 55416
      Contact: Pam Borton CEO
      Tel: 612-418-7776
      Email: pam@onpointnextlevel.com
      Website: www.onpointnextlevel.com
Leadership development, strategic succession planning
and innovative training. (Woman, estab 2015, empl 3,
sales , cert: WBENC)

7791 Risk Management Consulting Services, LLC.
      35 Pineview Lane N
      Plymouth, MN 55441
      Contact: Gwen McFadden Managing Partner
      Tel: 952-544-0354
      Email: gwen@rmcsllc.com
      Website: www.riskconsultingservices.net
Insurance placement, insurance & risk management
consulting services, RFP/RFQ consulting, insurance
placement, risk management consulting, due diligence
projects, claims consulting & management. (Woman/AA,
estab 1997, empl 2, sales $150,000, cert: NMSDC, 8(a))

7792 Talencio, LLC
      708 N 1st St Ste 341
      Minneapolis, MN 55401
      Contact: Paula Norbom President
      Tel: 612-703-4236
      Email: pnorbom@talencio.com
      Website: www.talencio.com
Accounting & Finance, Clinical Research, Data Analysis &
Statistics, Engineering, Health Care Policy & Reform,
Human Resource Management, Informatics, Information
Technology, Interim Leadership, Lean & Six Sigma,
Marketing, Operations. (Woman, estab 2008, empl 6,
sales $1,037,000, cert: WBENC)

7793 The Improve Group
      700 Raymond Ave Ste 140
      St. Paul, MN 55114
      Contact: Leah Goldstein Moses Founder & CEO
      Tel: 651-315-8919
      Email: leah@theimprovegroup.com
      Website: www.theimprovegroup.com
Professional services: evaluation, strategic planning,
management consulting & facilitation. (Woman, estab
2000, empl 11, sales $973,523, cert: WBENC)

7794 Vuelta Management Group, LLC
      1507 Chelmsford St
      Saint Paul, MN 55108
      Contact: Scott Hamilton President
      Tel: 651-329-8609
      Email: shamilton@vueltamanagement.com
      Website: www.vueltamanagement.com
Project Management; Process Improvement; Lean Six
Sigma; Supply Chain Management; Inventory Management; Purchasing; Production Management. (Hisp, estab
2009, empl 1, sales $162,117, cert: State, NMSDC)

Missouri

7795 Kwame Building Group, Inc.
      1204 Washington Ave, Ste 200
      Saint Louis, MO 63103
      Contact: Joshua Randall VP
      Tel: 314-862-5344
      Email: jrandall@kwamebuildinggroup.com
      Website: www.kwamebuildinggroup.com
Program & construction mgmt services: project scheduling, estimating, cost controls, document controls, value
engineering, quality assurance & project inspection. (AA,
Hisp, estab 1991, empl 75, sales $6,100,000, cert: City)

7796 Mustardseed Cultural & Environmental Services,
      LLC
      222 W Gregory Blvd, Ste 211
      Kansas City, MO 64114
      Contact: Timberlyn Smith, CHMM President
      Tel: 816-333-2424
      Email: tsmith@m-c-e-services.net
      Website: www.m-c-e-services.net
Environmental, safety & cultural resource management
consulting. (Woman/AA, estab 2003, empl 5, sales
$227,305, cert: State, City)

7797 P/Strada, LLC
      406 W 34th st.
      Kansas City, MO 64111
      Contact: Patrice Manuel CEO
      Tel: 816-256-4577
      Email: pat@pstrada.com
      Website: www.pstrada.com
Organizational development & homeland security consulting. (Woman/AA, estab 2001, empl 42, sales $3,370,000, cert: State, City, NMSDC)

7798 Project Controls Group, Inc.
      2 Campbell Plaza, Bldg C
      St. Louis, MO 63139
      Contact: Viola Pancratz Principal
      Tel: 314-647-0707
      Email: vpancratz@projectcontrolsgroup.com
      Website: www.projectcontrolsgroup.com
Cost engineering & estimating, CPM scheduling, claims analysis, document control, claims analysis, construction management, program management. (AA, estab 2003, empl 22, sales $1,430,353, cert: State, NMSDC)

7799 PryCor Technologies, LLC
      20 S Sarah St
      St. Louis, MO 63108
      Contact: Seqwana Pryor CEO
      Tel: 302-528-0965
      Email: ceo.prycortechnologies@gmail.com
      Website: www.prycortechnologies.com
Management consulting & training: Lean Six Sigma & operational excellence. (Woman/AA, estab 2016, empl 1, sales , cert: WBENC)

7800 Standing Partnership
      1610 Des Peres Rd Ste 200
      St. Louis, MO 63131
      Contact: Melissa Lackey CEO
      Tel: 314-469-3500
      Email: mlackey@standingpartnership.com
      Website: www.standingpartnership.com
Strategy, corporate social responsibility (CSR), public affairs, internal communications and issues and crisis management. (Woman, estab 1991, empl 26, sales $3,824,984, cert: WBENC)

Mississippi

7801 AGF Enterprise LLC
      1060 E Countyline Rd Ste 3A-104
      Ridgeland, MS 39157
      Contact: Anthony Fairley Managing Partner
      Tel: 601-500-2325
      Email: anthonygf@agfenterprise.com
      Website: www.agfenterprise.com
Learning Management System (LMS), Tracking & Reporting Easily track goal progress, knowledge gains, ROI, Regulatory Compliance Train, assess, and report for compliance purposes. (AA, estab 2013, empl 1, sales $376,000, cert: NMSDC)

North Carolina

7802 Aseptic Haven LLC
      3330 Black Jack Simpson Rd
      Greenville, NC 27858
      Contact: Felicia Richardson Owner
      Tel: 252-258-5935
      Email: feliciarichardson@aseptichaven.com
      Website: www.aseptichaven.com
Consulting & training services, Life Sciences, Workforce Development, Inclusion & Diversity. (Woman/AA, estab 2014, empl 1, sales , cert: State)

7803 Flynn Heath Holt Leadership, LLC
      309 E Morehead St, Ste 230
      Charlotte, NC 28202
      Contact: Maggie Norris COO
      Tel: 704-632-6712
      Email: mnorris@flynnheath.com
      Website: www.flynnheath.com/
Development programs and workshops, executive coaching and speaking. (Woman, estab , empl , sales $4,415,000, cert: WBENC)

7804 LMK Clinical Research Consulting, LLC
      9815 J Sam Furr Rd
      Huntersville, NC 28078
      Contact: Isaiah Howard Dir of Marketing
      Tel: 704-464-3291
      Email: isaiah.howard@lmkclinicalresearch.com
      Website: www.lmkclinicalresearch.com
Strategic development, project management & quality control of documents & content that support clinical development. (Woman/AA, estab 2013, empl 10, sales , cert: WBENC)

7805 Proficient Learning LLC
      1508 Military Cutoff Rd Ste 304
      Wilmington, NC 28403
      Contact: Pamela Marinko CEO
      Tel: 910-795-1376
      Email: pam.marinko@proficientlearning.com
      Website: www.proficientlearning.com
Instructor-led, virtual, eLearning & mobile learning solutions. (Woman, estab 2005, empl 23, sales $3,200,000, cert: WBENC)

7806 Tactegra
      18 Cabarrus Ave W
      Concord, NC 20825
      Contact: Leanne Kinsella Dir Business Devel
      Tel: 704-793-0800
      Email: info@tactegra.com
      Website: www.tactegra.com
Management consulting, program/project management, IT project support services, staff augmentation & process management. (AA, Hisp, estab 2007, empl 50, sales $3,700,000, cert: NMSDC)

7807 The Future Procurement Group, LLC
      3513 McPherson St
      Waxhaw, NC 28173
      Contact: Silas Carter
      Tel: 203-913-9598
      Email: scarter@thefutureprocurementgroup.com
      Website: www.thefutureprocurementgroup.com
Consulting Services, Strategic Sourcing, Procurement Management, Supplier Diversity, Program Devel, Training, Vendor Mgmt, Supplier Evaluation, Process Review & Analysis, Cost Management, Mgmt Consulting. (AA, estab 2011, empl 1, sales , cert: NMSDC)

7808 The Thrower Group, LLC.
11204 Waightstill Way
Charlotte, NC 28277
Contact: Baron Thrower CEO
Tel: 704-215-4946
Email: baron.thrower@thethrowergroupllc.com
Website: www.thethrowergroupllc.com
Management consulting firm. (AA, estab 2010, empl 35, sales , cert: NMSDC)

New Jersey

7809 Bardess Group Ltd.
15 Morey Ln, Ste 100
Randolph, NJ 07869
Contact: Barbara Pound President
Tel: 973-584-9100
Email: bspound@bardess.com
Website: www.bardess.com
Management consulting; data management, business performance management, IT, business planning & process improvement, reveune & asset management. (Woman, estab 1997, empl 25, sales $0, cert: State, WBENC)

7810 Candid Services
80 Pine St
Bridgewater, NJ 08807
Contact: Meghana Patel CEO
Tel: 732-874-1345
Email: contact@candidcorp.com
Website: www.candidcorp.com
Pharmaceutical & medical device consulting services, computer system validation, non compartmental analysis (NCA), Clinical data analysis & handling, SAS programming & Regulatory Affairs consulting. (Minority, Woman, estab 2015, empl 2, sales , cert: WBENC)

7811 Davis & Company, Inc.
11 Harristown Rd
Glen Rock, NJ 07452
Contact: David Pitre VP Sonsulting Svcs
Tel: 201-445-5100
Email: david.pitre@davisandco.com
Website: www.davisandco.com
Communication consulting & implementation, strategic planning & research, writing & design. (Woman, estab 1984, empl 17, sales $3,350,000, cert: State, WBENC)

7812 Microexcel Inc.
One Harmon Plaza, 10th Fl
Secaucus, NJ 07094
Contact: Ayub Qhadri President
Tel: 201-787-4562
Email: ayub.qhadri@microexcel.com
Website: www.microexcel.com
Global management consulting, technology services & outsourcing. (As-Ind, estab 2001, empl 75, sales $28,000,000, cert: State)

7813 QualComp Consulting Services LLC
675 US Hwy One Ste B203
North Brunswick, NJ 08902
Contact: Victor Arriaran Principal
Tel: 800-511-8758
Email: victor.arriaran@qualcomp.com
Website: www.qualcomp.com
Quality systems design & implementation, audit & inspection readiness, complaint remediation, process control & process improvement, risk management , design control, root cause analysis, Corrective & Preventive Action. (Hisp, estab 2010, empl 4, sales $1,521,586, cert: NMSDC)

7814 The Forefront Group
26 Sunflower Circle
Lumberton, NJ 08048
Contact: Bonnie Keith Owner
Tel: 609-265-1825
Email: bkeith@theforefrontgroup.com
Website: www.theforefrontgroup.com
Admin management consulting, education support svcs, professional & management development training. (Woman, estab 2002, empl 10, sales , cert: WBENC)

7815 Trascent Management Consulting LLC
460 US Hwy 22 West
Whitehouse Station, NJ 08889
Contact: Neha Patel Dir Finance
Tel: 973-641-8806
Email: npatel@trascent.com
Website: www.trascent.com
Corporate Real Estate & Facilities management consulting. (As-Ind, estab 2014, empl 45, sales , cert: NMSDC)

7816 Vitiello Communications Group
825 Georges Rd Ste 6
North Brunswick, NJ 08902
Contact: Nadine Green COO
Tel: 732-238-6622
Email: nadine.green@vtlo.com
Website: www.vtlo.com
Communications, employee engagement, strategic change & leadership communications. (Woman, estab 1990, empl 20, sales $3,600,000, cert: WBENC)

7817 Wet Cement, Inc.
18 Yardley Manor Dr
Matawan, NJ 07747
Contact: Jennifer Willey CEO
Tel: 917-334-3653
Email: info@wet-cement.com
Website: www.wet-cement.com/
Coach and train on powerful presenting, public speaking and pitching skills to drive sales and develop talent. (Woman, estab 2017, empl 3, sales $120,000, cert: WBENC)

Nevada

7818 American Project Management LLC
11700 W Charleston Blvd, Ste 170-315
Las Vegas, NV 89135
Contact: Jane Lee Managing Partner
Tel: 702-220-4562
Email: jlee@apmlasvegas.com
Website: www.apmlasvegas.com
Project Scheduling & Cost Control, Earned Value Management System (EVMS) Implementation, Computer Programming & Embedded Software Development Services & Staff Augmentation. (Minority, Woman, estab 2003, empl 2, sales , cert: NMSDC, NWBOC)

7819 Operations Service Systems
9716 Terrace Green Ave
Las Vegas, NV 89117
Contact: Susan Beyer President
Tel: 800-878-6906
Email: sue@suebeyer.com
Website: www.suebeyer.com
Training & development: operations, dev, customer service & results oriented training systems. (Woman, estab 2000, empl 2, sales $255,000, cert: WBENC)

7820 Purpose & Action, LLC
3225 McLeod Dr, Ste 100
Las Vegas, NV 89121
Contact: Miguel de Jesus President
Tel: 760-438-9907
Email: miguel@coachmiguel.com
Website: www.coachmiguel.com
Business management, global sales/marketing. (Hisp, estab 2011, empl 1, sales , cert: NMSDC)

New York

7821 AIOPX Management Consulting
1007 La Quinta Dr
Webster, NY 14580
Contact: David Powe Partner & Lead Consultant
Tel: 585-627-1716
Email: dpowe@aiopx.com
Website: www.aiopx.com
Operation Excellence (OpEx): lean, six sigma, total quality, practical process improvement & the Toyota production system. (AA, estab 2012, empl 1, sales $125,000, cert: NMSDC)

7822 Axiom Consulting LLC
126 W Main St
Endicott, NY 13760
Contact: Wayne McCray CEO
Tel: 800-563-2758
Email: info@4axiomcorp.com
Website: www.4axiomcorp.com
MRO sales, business process outsourcing, staffing, training. (AA, estab 2001, empl 150, sales $6,000,000, cert: NMSDC)

7823 Carlin Solutions, LLC
237 Flatbush Ave Ste 128
Brooklyn, NY 11217
Contact: Carla Franklin Managing Dir
Tel: 917-463-3592
Email: carla@carlinsolutions.com
Website: www.carlinsolutions.com
Requirements analysis, staff augmentation, program management, project management, operational improvement, management consulting, Strategic Planning, Business Development, Strategic Market Analysis. (Woman/AA, estab 2003, empl 3, sales $414,000, cert: City, NMSDC, WBENC)

7824 Chapman Lean Enterprise
81 Rock Hill Rd
Rochester, NY 14618
Contact: Christopher Chapman President
Tel: 585-406-7804
Email: cdchapman1@chapmanlean.com
Website: www.chapmanlean.com
Lean process improvement training & consultation services. (AA, estab 2010, empl 1, sales , cert: NMSDC)

7825 Gillespie Associates, Ltd.
1501 East Ave Ste 200
Rochester, NY 14610
Contact: Karen Barrow President
Tel: 585-287-8191
Email: kbarrow@gillespieassociates.com
Website: www.gillespieassociates.com
Performance consulting, customized training & development, sales performance institute, e-learning solutions, web-based learning, technical documentation, business process documentation. (Woman, estab 1989, empl 9, sales $1,292,286, cert: State, WBENC)

7826 Green Silk Associates, LLC
10440 Queens Blvd., Ste 5J
Forest Hills, NY 11375
Contact: Deb Seidman President
Tel: 917-445-2443
Email: dseidman@greensilkassociates.com
Website: www.greensilkassociates.com
Organizational effectiveness & leadership development, innovation, planning, problem-solving meeting/offsite facilitation; team development; organization design; executive coaching; & talent management consulting. (Woman, estab 2009, empl 1, sales , cert: State, City)

7827 Hyun & Associates, Inc.
222 Riverside Dr, #3B
New York, NY 10025
Contact: Jane Hyun President
Tel: 917-327-0992
Email: jhyun@hyunassociates.com
Website: www.hyunassociates.com
Leadership, diversity training & coaching services. (Minority, Woman, estab 1997, empl 3, sales $275,000, cert: NMSDC)

7828 Impact Consulting, LLC
1177 Ave of the Americas
New York, NY 10036
Contact: Lucy Sorrentini Founder & CEO
Tel: 973-727-1574
Email: team@impactconsultingus.com
Website: www.impactconsultingus.com
Leadership & organizational development, consulting, coaching & training services. (Minority, Woman, estab 2015, empl 6, sales $1,038,000, cert: State, City, NMSDC, WBENC)

7829 International Institute for Learning, Inc. (IIL)
110 E 59th St, 31st Fl
New York, NY 10022
Contact: Amy Gershen
Tel: 212-758-0177
Email: amy.gershen@iil.com
Website: www.iil.com
Project management, six sigma & MSP training & consulting services. (Woman, estab 1991, empl 87, sales $1,300,000,000, cert: WBENC)

7830 JDR Consulting, LLC
4305 Broadway Ste 41
New York, NY 10033
Contact: John Rivers CEO
Tel: 917-324-2443
Email: jrivers@jdrconsulting.net
Website: www.jdrconsulting.net
Management consulting, program & project management, systems & and accounting services. (AA, estab 2004, empl 9, sales $6,000,000, cert: State, NMSDC)

7831 Jennifer Brown LLC
20 E 9th St, Ste 4U
New York, NY 10003
Contact: Jennifer Brown CEO
Tel: 917-769-1599
Email: info@jenniferbrownconsulting.com
Website: www.jenniferbrownconsulting.com
Leadership consulting, HR training, coaching, speaker, communications, diversity, global, teams, facilitator, facilitation, career planning, leaders, inclusive, inclusion, innovative, innovation, empowered, empowerment. (Woman, estab 2004, empl 15, sales $1,400,000, cert: City, WBENC)

7832   JR Language Translation Services, Inc.
       2112 Empire Blvd, Ste 1C
       Rochester, NY 14580
       Contact: d'Empaire Language Solutions Specialist
       Tel: 877-771-0145
       Email: info@jrlanguage.com
       Website: www.jrlanguage.com
Document Translation - Web site and software localization
- Scripts - Manuals - Brochures - Contracts. (Minority,
Woman, estab 2006, empl 8, sales $1,680,371, cert: State,
WBENC)

7833   KGM Consulting Inc.
       30 Wall St
       New York, NY 10005
       Contact: Martell Admin
       Tel: 212-791-1555
       Email: mmcgovern@kgmcon.com
       Website: www.kgmit.com
Technology management solutions: echnology project
mgmt, circuit provisioning mgmt & voice systems admin,
carrier & telecom expense mgmt svcs, staff augmentation.
(Woman, estab 1996, empl 30, sales $3,952,677, cert: City,
WBENC)

7834   KnowledgeSources Consulting Inc.
       23 W 73rd St Ste 1103
       New York, NY 10023
       Contact: Peggy Decker Principal
       Tel: 212-362-1606
       Email: peggy@knowledgesources.com
       Website: www.knowledgesources.com
Employee/Financial Advisor Learning & Development;
Customer Events.
Specifically: employee engagement, organizational
development, professional development, training, coach-
ing, facilitating. (Woman, estab 2009, empl 1, sales
$400,000, cert: WBENC)

7835   Shaheen & Associates, Inc.
       37 Maple Ave
       Armonk, NY 10504
       Contact: William Shaheen COO
       Tel: 914-273-9000
       Email: w.shaheen@shaheeninc.com
       Website: www.shaheeninc.com
Telecom auditing & cost-containment services. (Woman,
estab 1988, empl 8, sales $2,400,000, cert: WBENC)

7836   The Caswood Group, Inc.
       811 Ayrault Rd, Ste 2
       Fairport, NY 14450
       Contact: Isabel Casamayor President
       Tel: 585-425-0332
       Email: icasamayor@caswood.com
       Website: www.caswood.com
Specialty sales teams, analytics, data collection & management, sample management. (Woman, estab 1996, empl
38, sales $5,054,073, cert: WBENC)

7837   The Madison Consulting Group, Inc.
       41 Madison Ave 31st Fl
       New York, NY 10010
       Contact: Fisher Consultant & Marketing Mgr
       Tel: 212-532-0703
       Email: n.carrington@tmcginc.com
       Website: www.tmcginc.com
Training & consulting: executive coaching, organizational
consulting & strategic resourcing. (Woman, estab 1993,
empl 11, sales $1,103,130, cert: City, WBENC)

7838   The Real Advice Plus LLC
       108 5th Ave, Ste 20-B
       New York, NY 10011
       Contact: Tony Brown President
       Tel: 718-812-8856
       Email: tbrown@t-rap.com
       Website: www.t-rap.com
Management consulting, executive search consulting,
diversity consulting & career development coaching
services. (AA, estab 2006, empl 1, sales , cert: State, City)

7839   Tribal Capital Markets, LLC
       405 Lexington Ave 54th Fl
       New York, NY 10174
       Contact: Sean Harte CEO
       Tel: 212-850-2295
       Email: sharte@tribalcap.com
       Website: www.tribalcap.com
With a strong capital structure, TCM offers client
focused services in both Fixed Income trading and
origination as well as Equity trading. Our Equity staff
provides proficient execution capabilities (Nat Ame,
estab 1995, empl 14, sales $4,000,000, cert: NMSDC)

Ohio

7840   Alegre, Inc.
       3101 W Tech Rd
       Miamisburg, OH 45342
       Contact: Don Phillips Business Dev Mgr
       Tel: 937-885-6786
       Email: dphillips@alegreinc.com
       Website: www.alegreinc.com
Supply chain mgmt, program mgmt, customer engineering & quality interface, warehousing & distribution
processes, sorting & containment, rework processes,
light assembly processes. (Minority, Woman, estab 1992,
empl 30, sales $20,000,000, cert: NMSDC)

7841   APB & Associates, Inc.
       55 Erieview Plaza Ste 328
       Cleveland, OH 44114
       Contact: Andre Bryan President
       Tel: 216-541-2900
       Email: abryan@apbandassociates.com
       Website: www.apbandassociates.com
Document management services, office technology,
organizational design, business process improvement,
telecommunications & office automation consulting.
(AA, estab 2004, empl 12, sales $2,200,000, cert: State,
NMSDC, SDB)

7842   Arnold Solutions, LLC
       4228 E 178th St
       Cleveland, OH 44128
       Contact: Reginald E. Arnold CEO
       Tel: 216-533-2837
       Email: arnoldsolutionsllc@gmail.com
       Website: www.arnoldsolutionsllc.com
Consulting, administrative & innovative leadership,
Federal Law, HR, PMP, Fleet Management, IT, BPM,
Supply Chain Management, Strategic Analysis, Construc-
tion Management, Contract Procurement. (Woman/AA,
estab 2014, empl 2, sales , cert: State, City)

7843   ATS Training and Consulting Co
       1991 Crocker Rd Ste 340
       Westlake, OH 44145
       Contact: P. Rani Maddali President
       Tel: 440-249-0095
       Email: pm@ats-tc.com
       Website: www.ats-tc.com
Training & consulting services: lean, Six Sigma, supply
chain, organizational devel, change mgmt, team building
& executive coaching. (Woman/As-Ind, estab 2001, empl
20, sales $1,060,000, cert: NMSDC, WBENC, 8(a))

7844   Berkshire Group Inc.
       2711 W Market St, Ste 5310
       Akron, OH 44334
       Contact: Janet Kendall White CEO
       Tel: 800-556-5549
       Email: janet@berkshire-leadership.com
       Website: www.berkshire-leadership.com
Consulting & leadership development, strategic planning, process & profit improvement; training & development; executive coaching & facilitation. (Woman, estab
1993, empl 4, sales $309,000, cert: WBENC)

7845   C H Smith & Associates dba Scale Strategic
       Solution
       1329 E Kemper Rd, Ste 4218E
       Cincinnati, OH 45246
       Contact: Calista Smith President
       Tel: 513-252-8129
       Email: chs@scalestrategicsolutions.com
       Website: www.scalestrategicsolutions.com
Management consulting and evaluation services for the
public and non-profit sectors. (Woman/AA, estab 2011,
empl 3, sales $290,354, cert: WBENC)

7846   Compass Consulting Services, LLC
       PO Box 221347
       Beachwood, OH 44122
       Contact: Tameka Taylor President
       Tel: 216-299-7335
       Email: tameka@compassconsultingservices.com
       Website: www.compassconsultingservices.com
Organizational development, diversity & inclusion
management, conflict mgmt, communication, leadership
development, team building. (Woman/AA, estab 2008,
empl 2, sales $170,000, cert: State, NMSDC, WBENC)

7847   Diverse Supply Chain Partner, LLC
       4132 E Village Dr
       Mason, OH 45040
       Contact: Cheryl El-Alfi President
       Tel: 513-274-8035
       Email: cheryl@diversepartner.com
       Website: www.diversepartner.com
Strategic business development consulting services to
help diverse business enter & grow within the corporate
supply chain. (Woman, estab 2014, empl 1, sales , cert:
WBENC)

7848   Equilibrium Perceptum LLC
       11839 Pearl Rd, Ste 101
       Strongsville, OH 44136
       Contact: Ramana Gaddamanugu
       Tel: 216-278-1866
       Email: ramana@epfocus.com
       Website: www.epfocus.com
Systems & process reviews, strategy documentation, risk
management / risk assessments / risk analysis assistance, data analysis, data review, data preparation. (As-
Pac, estab 2014, empl 1, sales , cert: State, City)

7849   GPI Enterprises Inc.
       3637 Medina Rd, Ste 60
       Medina, OH 44256
       Contact: Christopher Murillo President
       Tel: 330-321-2461
       Email: chris.murillo@e-gpi.com
       Website: www.e-gpi.com
Management consulting services, process analysis/
development, data analysis, project management & IT
support. (Hisp, estab 2001, empl 16, sales $1,050,000,
cert: State, 8(a))

7850   Howse Solutions LLC
       17325 Euclid Ste 2030
       Cleveland, OH 44112
       Contact: Christopher Howse President
       Tel: 440-318-4720
       Email: chowse@howsesolutions.com
       Website: www.howsesolutions.com
Experience leading analysts, developers, and project
teams; and defining, creating, and delivering business
solutions. (AA, estab , empl 1, sales $255,000, cert:
State, City, SDB)

7851   Improve Consulting & Training Group LLC
       4600 Euclid Ave Ste 320
       Cleveland, OH 44103
       Contact: Ellen Burts-Cooper Sr Managing Partner
       Tel: 216-539-8737
       Email: ellen@improveconsulting.biz
       Website: www.improveconsulting.biz
Leadership development & continuous improvement.
(Woman/AA, estab 2005, empl 10, sales $700,000, cert:
State)

7852   Integrity Development
       8050 Beckett Center Dr Ste 317
       West Chester, OH 45069
       Contact: Eric Ellis CEO
       Tel: 513-874-6836
       Email: ericellis@integritydev.com
       Website: www.integritydev.com
Diversity training, leadership development, conflict
mgmt, strategic planning, cultural assessment, executive
coaching & team building. (AA, estab 1991, empl 6, sales
, cert: NMSDC)

7853   Monterey Consultants, Inc.
       5335 Far Hills Ave, Ste 311
       Dayton, OH 45429
       Contact: Gary Munoz President
       Tel: 937-436-4536
       Email: gary.munoz@mcix.com
       Website: www.mcix.com
Management consulting, organizational development &
business process improvement, strategic planning,
change management, process improvement, outreach &
marketing & customer service. (Hisp, estab , empl , sales
$2,704,856, cert: NMSDC)

7854   Pep Promotions
       151 W Fourth St Ste 700
       Cincinnati, OH 45202
       Contact: Dave Kroeger President
       Tel: 513-826-3871
       Email: kroegerd@peppromotions.com
       Website: www.peppromotions.com
Project management, promotional programs. (AA, estab
2004, empl 125, sales $11,000,000, cert: NMSDC)

7855 SimpleQuE, Inc.
249 S Garber Dr
Tipp City, OH 45371
Contact: Jim Lee President
Tel: 740-305-0868
Email: jlee@simpleque.com
Website: www.simpleque.com
Management consulting services. (As-Pac, estab 2005, empl 26, sales $2,100,000, cert: NMSDC)

7856 Sritech Global Inc.
341 S 3rd St, Ste 100
Columbus, OH 43215
Contact: Sheela Kunduru President
Tel: 614-477-2944
Email: ksheela@sritechglobal.com
Website: www.sritechglobal.com
Business process consulting, Business process improvement, Enterprise process & product quality assurance, Independent verification & validation. (Minority, Woman, estab 2013, empl 1, sales $339,640, cert: State, WBENC)

7857 SRM & Associates, LLC
1123 Firth Ave
Worthington, OH 43085
Contact: Victoria Schneider President
Tel: 614-505-1209
Email: vschneider@srm-consulting.net
Website: www.srm-consulting.net
Risk Management Consulting services, Safety & Environmental Consulting, Process Safety Management, Risk Management Planning, Safety & Environmental Program Development, Auditing & Training. (Woman, estab 2011, empl 4, sales $370,000, cert: WBENC)

7858 The CADD Department, Inc.
13916 Euclid Ave Ste 5
East Cleveland, OH 44112
Contact: Wayne Grant CEO
Tel: 216-269-5901
Email: wgrant@thecaddept.net
Website: www.thecaddept.net
Progressive civil / structural engineering, construction supervision & surveying, design, surveying & construction phase services. (AA, estab 2007, empl 4, sales , cert: State, City)

Oklahoma

7859 CDR Assessment Group, Inc.
1644 S Denver Ave
Tulsa, OK 74119
Contact: President
Tel: 918-488-0722
Email: cdrinfo@cdrassessmentgroup.com
Website: www.cdrassessmentgroup.com
Mfr CDR 3-Dimensional Assessment Suite® accurately revealing a leader's Character, Risk Factors for Derailment, and Drivers & Reward Needs. (Woman, estab 1998, empl 5, sales $0, cert: WBENC)

7860 Gina Sofola & Associates, Inc.
5801 Broadway Extension Ste 310
Oklahoma City, OK 73118
Contact: Gina Sofola President
Tel: 203-613-9471
Email: gsofola@sofolaassociates.com
Website: www.sofolaassociates.com
Project mgmt: facility mgmt, transportation, strategic planning, engineering & feasibility studies, cost control, scheduling, building assessment, document mgmt, contract admin, interior design, transportation analysis, environmental assessment. (Woman/AA, estab 1999, empl 20, sales $0, cert: State)

Pennsylvania

7861 Clarity Concepts Inc.
240 Dechert Dr
Gulph Mills, PA 19406
Contact: Jane Downey President
Tel: 610-825-3705
Email: janedowney@clarityconceptsinc.com
Website: www.clarityconceptsinc.com
Customized training programs. Leadership training. Personal branding. Team development. Risk mgmt services. (Woman, estab 1996, empl 2, sales $220,000, cert: WBENC)

7862 Evolve Advisors I, LLC
85 Overhill Rd
Bala Cynwyd, PA 19004
Contact: Peri Higgins President
Tel: 610-420-5535
Email: phiggins@evolveadvisors.com
Website: www.evolveadvisors.com
Management consulting, assess, baseline, restructure & redesign business processes. (Woman/AA, estab 2012, empl 3, sales $108,000, cert: NMSDC, WBENC)

7863 Innovative Business Products & Services, LLC
514 Firethorne Dr
Monroeville, PA 15146
Contact: Harvey Smith, Sr. CEO
Tel: 412-894-3132
Email: ibpshssr@outlook.com
Website: www.artistecard.com/ibps
Diversity, inclusion & sensitivity training, recruiting diversity talent services; diversity website review; diversity mission/vision statement development; & re-entry of ex-offenders into job market services. (Woman/AA, estab 2015, empl 7, sales , cert: NMSDC)

7864 KnowledgeStart, Inc.
300 King St
Pottstown, PA 19464
Contact: Bryan Yingst Internet Dir
Tel: 610-650-0448
Email: byingst@knowledgestart.com
Website: www.knowledgestart.com
Diversity & Inclusion training. (Minority, estab 2001, empl 12, sales $850,000, cert: NMSDC)

7865 Lapine Group, Inc.
8200 Greensboro Dr Ste 900
McLean, PA 22102
Contact: Judy Honig Managing Partner
Tel: 703-940-6005
Email: lapineinfor@lapinegroup.com
Website: www.lapinegroup.com
Management consulting. (Woman, estab 2006, empl 10, sales $3,770,000, cert: WBENC)

7866 Lima Consulting Group, LLC
40 Lloyd Ave Ste 108B
Malvern, PA 19335
Contact: Paul Lima Managing Partner
Tel: 212-671-0309
Email: plima@limaconsulting.com
Website: www.LimaConsulting.com
Administrative Management & General Management
Consulting, Marketing Consulting, Process, Physical
Distribution & Logistics Consulting. (Hisp, estab 2004, empl
26, sales $739,087, cert: NMSDC)

7867 Quacoapit LLC
7121 Lynford St
Philadelphia, PA 19149
Contact: Chea Kunwon CEO
Tel: 267-315-5147
Email: ckunwon@quacoapit.com
Website: www.quacoapit.com
Quality & Compliance Consulting Services. (AA, estab
2017, empl 3, sales , cert: NMSDC)

7868 Quality Solutions Now, Inc.
3251 Olympic Dr
Emmaus, PA 18049
Contact: Brette Travaglio President
Tel: 610-462-4090
Email: brette@qualitysolutionsnow.com
Website: www.qualitysolutionsnow.com
Strategic, on-demand support & tactical project manage-
ment svcs, product launch, regulatory compliance, large-
scale change, process improvement. (Woman, estab 2004,
empl 1, sales $2,064,000, cert: NWBOC)

7869 Sustainable Solutions Corporation
155 Railroad Plaza Ste 203
Royersford, PA 19468
Contact: Tara Radzinski CEO
Tel: 610-569-1047
tara@sustainablesolutionscorporation.com
www.sustainablesolutionscorporation.com
Sustainable Buildings & Operations, Corporate
Sustainability, Training & Education, Seminars. (Woman,
estab 2001, empl 16, sales $882,045, cert: WBENC)

7870 Talson Solutions, LLC
41 N. 3rd St
Philadelphia, PA 19106
Contact: Robert S. Bright President
Tel: 215-592-9634
Email: rbright@talsonsolutions.com
Website: www.talsonsolutions.com
Independent contract audits & compliance reviews,
project risk analysis, due diligence services & project
reporting. (AA, estab 2001, empl 4, sales $330,000, cert:
NMSDC)

7871 TayganPoint Consulting Group
1118 General Washington Memorial Blvd. Ste 210
Washington Crossing, PA 08977
Contact: R CEO
Tel: 215-302-2500
Email: info@tayganpoint.com
Website: www.tayganpoint.com
Consulting services: business process improvement,
strategy development & execution, change management &
communications, program management. (Woman, estab
2009, empl 69, sales $18,700,000, cert: WBENC)

7872 The Claiborne Consulting Group, Inc.
1800 JFK Blvd, Ste 300
Philadelphia, PA 19103
Contact: Julian Gray VP HR, Staffing GM
Tel: 914-388-4165
Email: julian.gray@claibornecg.com
Website: www.claibornecg.com
Management Consulting Services: Business Process Re-
engineering, Business Case Development, Software
Selection, Organization Change Management, Technical
Content Writing, Startup Consultation, Digital Brand
Management. (AA, As-Pac, estab 2015, empl 10, sales ,
cert: NMSDC)

7873 Veris Associates, Inc. dba VerisVisalign
PO Box 245
West Point, PA 19486
Contact: Trisha Daly Office Mgr
Tel: 267-649-5007
Email: trishadaly@verisvisalign.com
Website: www.verisvisalign.com
Consulting & training: process engineering, compliance
consulting & corporate learning. (Woman, estab 2003,
empl 38, sales $3,500,000, cert: State, WBENC)

7874 XCELLAS, LLC
275 Dilworth Ln
Langhorne, PA 19047
Contact: Maria T. Alvarez CEO
Tel: 215-287-9488
Email: maria.alvarez@xcellas.com
Website: www.xcellas.com
Consulting assessment & requirements, project man-
agement solution strategies, implementation & optimi-
zation. (Minority, Woman, estab 2013, empl 10, sales
$1,308,715, cert: State, NMSDC, WBENC)

Puerto Rico

7875 Development Management & Consulting Group,
Inc.
PO Box 142343
Arecibo, PR 00614
Contact: Eduardo Hernandez Principal Engineer
Tel: 787-897-0830
Email: eduardo.hernandez@dmcginc.com
Website: www.dmcginc.com
Validation Master Planning/Management, Commission-
ing & Qualification (C&Q), Decommissioning & Records
Management, GMP Documentation Review / Genera-
tion, Cleaning & Process/Packaging Validation. (Hisp,
estab 2000, empl 44, sales $4,089,547, cert: NMSDC)

7876 Impactivo LLC
PMB 140 1357 Ashford Ave
San Juan, PR 00907
Contact: Maria Fernanda Levis-Peralta CEO
Tel: 787-993-1508
Email: maria.levis@gmail.com
Website: www.impactivo.com
Systems Research, Policy Analysis, Strategic Planning &
Financial Sustainability, Community Health Needs
Assessment, Strategic Planning, Data Driven Decision
Making, Project Planning, Technical Assistance, Perfor-
mance Improvement. (Minority, Woman, estab 2010,
empl 5, sales $0, cert: NMSDC)

7877 Integrated Management & Controls, Inc.
PO Box 229
Manati, PR 00674
Contact: Ismael Jaime President
Tel: 787-462-4739
Email: ismael.jaime@imanagementcontrols.com
Website: www.imanagementcontrols.com
Program Management, Portfolio Management, Project Management, Construction Management, Project Controls, Cost Control, Planning, Scheduling, Document & Contract Management, Engineering, Design, Qualification Schedule, Design Schedules. (Hisp, estab 2014, empl 3, sales $390,000, cert: NMSDC)

7878 Process Excellence & Engineering Consultants Inc
Zona Industrial Las Palmas Calle 4, Edificio, Ste 8
Catano, PR 00962
Contact: Michael Garcia Business Devel Dir
Tel: 787-565-9970
Email: info@peec-inc.com
Website: www.peec-inc.com
Six Sigma, Process Excellence, Lean Manufacturing, Validation, IQ, OQ, PQ, CAPA, Installation Qualification, Operational Qualification, Process Qualification, Commissioning, Computer Systems (Hisp, estab 2006, empl 25, sales $400,000, cert: NMSDC)

Rhode Island

7879 Granger Warburton Consulting, LLC
79 West St
East Greenwich, RI 02818
Contact: Bethany Warburton Principal Consultant
Tel: 401-965-1288
Email: bethany@grangerwarburton.com
Website: www.grangerwarburton.com
Learning management system design & deployment, elearning creation, software application development, project management, business analysis, change management, documentation & process design. (Woman, estab 2013, empl 2, sales $127,000, cert: State)

South Carolina

7880 DESA, Inc
400 Percival Rd
Columbia, SC 29206
Contact: Diane Sumpter CEO
Tel: 803-256-3212
Email: dianes@desainc.com
Website: www.desainc.com
Conference management, construction management, facilities management, business services. (Woman/AA, estab 1986, empl 75, sales $1,811,901, cert: State)

7881 Elevate USA Inc
509 Colony Dr
Ridgeland, SC 29936
Contact: Delvon Survine President
Tel: 843-441-6478
Email: delvon@elevate4success.com
Website: www.elevate4success.com
Workforce management, training, and consulting, customized solutions, interactive training, executive coaching, account management, and online learning solution delivery. (Woman, estab 2008, empl 12, sales $600,000, cert: State, WBENC)

7882 Sharp Business Consulting Services LLC
1320 Main St Ste 300
Columbia, SC 29210
Contact: Mitchell Wyatt CEO
Tel: 803-600-7941
Email: mitchell.wyatt@gmail.com
Website: www.sharpbusinessconsulting.com
Growth & market penetration, profitability, repeat clients, customer service & strong community presence. (AA, estab 2006, empl 23, sales $1,642,774, cert: State, 8(a))

Tennessee

7883 PEOPLE3, Inc.
91 Antioch Pike, Ste 603
Nashville, TN 37211
Contact: Candace Warner CEO
Tel: 615-340-6896
Email: candace@people3.co
Website: www.people3.co
Provides diversity and inclusion training, workshops, and inclusion-centered consulting. (Woman, estab 2016, empl 5, sales , cert: WBENC)

7884 Performance Consulting Group, Inc.
100 Saddle Springs Blvd Ste 100
Thompsons Station, TN 37179
Contact: Marcy Willerton VP
Tel: 303-709-3889
Email: mwillerton@eperformax.com
Website: www.eperformax.com
providing the highest levels of customer service and BPO to a select group of Fortune 500 and other global companies to support their English-speaking customers from the U.S., Canada and Australia. (Woman, estab 2000, empl 6000, sales $65,900,000, cert: WBENC)

7885 Remnant Management Group Inc.
2550 Meridian Blvd Ste 200
Franklin, TN 37067
Contact: Stephanie Beard CEO
Tel: 615-403-1567
Email: info@remnantgroup.com
Website: www.theremnantgroup.com
Employee development training & construction management services, leadership training & development, workforce development, curriculum selection & customization, construction management workforce development. (Woman/AA, estab 2006, empl 5, sales , cert: State)

Texas

7886 Access Sciences Corporation
1900 West Loop South Ste 1450
Houston, TX 77027
Contact: Todd Brown
Tel: 713-664-4357
Email: tbrown@accesssciences.com
Website: www.accesssciences.com
Information & records mgmt, enterprise content mgmt & regulatory compliance, information management consulting & outsourcing. (Woman, estab 1985, empl 62, sales $0, cert: State, WBENC)

7887 AHRMDCO International LLC
      14405 Walters Road Ste 1002
      Houston, TX 77014
      Contact: Roderick Lemon President
      Tel: 713-589-3688
      Email: rlemon@ahrmdcoint.com
      Website: www.ahrmdcoint.com
Organizational development: customer service, time
mgmt, partenering & team building, supervisor, executive
coaching, project mgmt, web & graphic design, employee
assessment surveys & interviewing techniques. (AA, estab
2002, empl 20, sales , cert: State, NMSDC)

7888 Austin Texas Mediators LLC
      4500 Williams Dr. Ste 212-111
      Georgetown, TX 78633
      Contact: Barbara Allen Owner
      Tel: 512-966-9222
      Email: info@motexas.com
      Website: www.mediatorsoftexas.com
Train the trainer; sensitivity training; sexual harassment in
the workplace training; non-confrontational communication skills training; conflict resolution in the work place.
(Woman, estab 2014, empl 15, sales , cert: State, WBENC)

7889 Beacon Training Services Inc.
      1229 Mohawk Trail
      Richardson, TX 75080
      Contact: Diana Stein Managing Principal
      Tel: 972-404-0069
      Email: diana@beacontraining.com
      Website: www.beacontraining.com
Computer/technical, management/supervisory, profes-
sional development & project management training.
(Woman, estab 1987, empl 4, sales $1,000,000, cert: State,
WBENC)

7890 Brittain-Kalish Group, LLC
      PO Box 8577
      Fort Worth, TX 76124
      Contact: Heather Randolph Consultant
      Tel: 817-991-0705
      Email: bkg@theupconsultants.com
      Website: www.brittainkalishgroup.com
Management consulting firm comprised of trusted
advisors, valued resources and trainers who strategically
collaborate to create optimal results in a timely manner.
(Woman, estab 2010, empl 3, sales , cert: WBENC)

7891 CAET Project Management Consultants
      1139 Keller Pkwy Ste B
      Keller, TX 76248
      Contact: President
      Tel: 817-741-6546
      Email: info@caetpmc.com
      Website: www.caetpmc.com
Owner Representation & Financial Consulting, Development of project budget, cost estimation, Assist & develop
contract strategies, Conduct requests for proposals (RFPs)
& manage process for receipt & review. (Woman, estab
2016, empl 5, sales $150,000, cert: State, WBENC)

7892 Caldwell Everson PLLC
      2777 Allen Pkwy, Ste 950
      Houston, TX 77019
      Contact: Faye Caldwell Managing Partner
      Tel: 713-654-3000
      Email: fcaldwell@caldwelleverson.com
      Website: www.caldwelleverson.com
Management employment, drug-testing, commercial,
product liability & general civil litigation. (Woman, estab
1997, empl 6, sales $940,180, cert: State, WBENC)

7893 Career Management International, Inc.
      4801 Woodway Dr Ste 300 East
      Houston, TX 77056
      Contact: Jim Tye CEO
      Tel: 713-623-8780
      Email: jimt@careermanagement.com
      Website: www.careermanagement.com
Career transition & outplacement; training; team
building & organizational development. (Woman, estab
1975, empl 18, sales $3,000,000, cert: City, WBENC)

7894 Deirdre Sanborn & Associates
      4321 Bretton Bay Lane
      Dallas, TX 75287
      Contact: Deirdre Sanborn Owner
      Tel: 214-308-1408
      Email: deirdre@deirdresanborn.com
      Website: www.deirdresanborn.com
Executive Coaching, Leadership Coaching, Team Integra-
tion, Team Management & Strategic consulting.
(Woman, estab 2014, empl 3, sales , cert: WBENC)

7895 DiversityInPromotions, Inc.
      5057 Keller Springs Rd Ste 300
      Addison, TX 75001
      Contact: Rodney Woods
      Tel: 469-718-5589
      Email: rwoods@diversityinpromotions.com
      Website: www.diversityinpromotions.com
Program Assessment, Strategic Planning, Policy Develop-
ment, Metrics Development, Communication Plan
(Internal & External), Mentor/Protege Development,
Government Reporting (Subcontract Plan). (AA, estab
1998, empl 18, sales $1,200,000, cert: State, NMSDC)

7896 D'Onofrio Consulting Partners
      1700 Post Oak Blvd
      Houston, TX 77056
      Contact: Margaret D'Onofrio Principal
      Tel: 713-963-3673
      Email: margaret@donofrioconsultingpartners.com
      Website: www.donofrioconsultingpartners.com
Coaching for individuals, teams & organizations.
(Woman, estab 2007, empl 1, sales $1,168,885, cert:
WBENC, NWBOC)

7897 Dramatic Conclusions, LLC
      3900 Vitruvian Way Ste 231
      Addison, TX 75001
      Contact: Pam Boyd Owner
      Tel: 469-855-0543
      Email: pam@dramaticconclusions.com
      Website: www.dramaticconclusions.com
Management & employee training & consulting.
(Woman, estab 1999, empl 1, sales , cert: State, WBENC)

7898 FFG Strategic Consulting LLC
      363 N. Houston Pkwy E Ste 1100
      Houston, TX 77060
      Contact: Colette Lewis
      Tel: 832-412-2524
      Email: colette.lewis@ffgsconsulting.com
      Website: www.ffgsconsulting.com
Program/project mgmt, engineering consulting, technical resources, project planning, construction mgmt, project scheduling, system engineering, six sigma methodology analysis, mechanical engineering. (Woman/AA, estab 2011, empl 5, sales , cert: State, NMSDC, WBENC)

7899 Hybrid Teams, Inc.
      3023 Cape Buffalo Trail
      Frisco, TX 75034
      Contact: Mac Choi President
      Tel: 847-530-9034
      Email: info@hybridteams.com
      Website: www.hybridteams.com
Enterprise content management professional services, document management, consulting services. (As-Pac, estab 2006, empl 3, sales $306,000, cert: NMSDC)

7900 JFE International Consultants, Inc.
      18705 Stoneridge Dr
      Dallas, TX 75252
      Contact: J. Francisco Escobar President
      Tel: 214-728-6903
      Email: francisco@jfeintl.com
      Website: www.jfeintl.com
Management consulting, contract diagnostics, compensation principles, negotiations, performance evaluations & measurements, internal/external process audits. (Hisp, estab 2003, empl 1, sales $214,595, cert: NMSDC)

7901 Jill Hickman Companies
      1721 Palomino Ln
      Kingwood, TX 77339
      Contact: Jill Hickman President
      Tel: 281-358-8580
      Email: jill@jillhickman.com
      Website: www.jillhickman.com
Training & development services: leadership, supervision, consultative sales, customer service & team building, pre-employment assessment, executive advisement, strategic planning. (Minority, Woman, estab 1998, empl 1, sales $141,956, cert: WBENC)

7902 Languages Houston
      1001 S Dairy Ashford Ste 100
      Houston, TX 77077
      Contact: Elena Tsilina CEO
      Tel: 832-359-4226
      Email: info@languageshouston.com
      Website: www.languageshouston.com
Foreign language classes & translation services. (Woman, estab 2015, empl 20, sales , cert: State, WBENC)

7903 Lone Star Interpreters LLC
      2800 Post Oak Blvd, Ste 1400 Ste 4100
      Houston, TX 77056
      Contact: Marie Mills CEO
      Tel: 832-399-2100
      Email: marie.mills@lonestarinterpreters.com
      Website: www.lonestarinterpreters.com
Language services in over 200 languages: Translation & Localization, Transcription, Interpretation: On Site, Telephonic & Video, Voice Prompt Translating, Voice Prompt Recording. (Woman/AA, estab 2007, empl 40, sales $2,480,000, cert: State)

7904 Michael Resource Group LLC
      1325 Daja Lane Ste 604
      Grand Prairie, TX 75050
      Contact: Brandon Russell Sales
      Tel: 888-313-8688
      Email: brussell@mrgroupllc.com
      Website: www.mrgroupllc.com
Management Consulting. (AA, estab 2014, empl 4, sales $100,000, cert: State, NMSDC)

7905 Mind The Gap, LLC
      901 Parkwood Ct
      McKinney, TX 75070
      Contact: Beth Anagnos Principal
      Tel: 314-378-6426
      Email: betha@mindthegapcoaching.com
      Website: www.mindthegapcoaching.com
Leadership coaching, customized coaching programs for all levels of leadership. (Woman, estab 2007, empl 5, sales , cert: WBENC)

7906 Mohr Partners, Inc.
      14643 Dallas Pkwy Ste 1000
      Dallas, TX 75254
      Contact: Robert Shibuya CEO
      Tel: 214-907-8094
      Email: robert.shibuya@mohrpartners.com
      Website: www.mohrpartners.com
Portfolio management, lease administration, horizon business intelligence, research and site selection, incentive practices, and project management. (As-Pac, estab 1986, empl 120, sales $29,056,140, cert: NMSDC)

7907 Niche Assurance LLC
      9894 Bissonnet St
      Houston, TX 77036
      Contact: Peter Kiilu
      Tel: 281-636-2749
      Email: peter.kiilu@nicheconsult.net
      Website: www.nicheconsult.net
Financial & IT risk management, business performance improvement, Internal control design & implementation, Sarbanes-Oxley Act compliance, FCPA compliance, internal audits, I.T. audits, cyber security, SAP security. (AA, estab 2007, empl 4, sales $150,000, cert: State, NMSDC)

7908 Obsidian Technical Communications, Ltd.
      3522 White Oak Dr
      Houston, TX 77007
      Contact: Erik Pettine Dir of Sales
      Tel: 281-732-5940
      Email: erikp@obsidianlearning.com
      Website: www.obsidianlearning.com
Consulting: job performance, end-user performance support, custom training strategy & development, documentation, e-learning, knowledge mgmt & change mgmt. (Woman, estab 1998, empl 26, sales $3,700,000, cert: WBENC)

7909 PABULUM Consulting, LLC
      1002 Gemini St Ste 225D
      Houston, TX 77058
      Contact: Ferrel Bonner CEO
      Tel: 713-538-4719
      Email: ferrelbonner@pabulumconsulting.com
      Website: www.pabulumconsulting.com
Military Intelligence, Security & Emergency Management, Special Operations & Tactical Communications. (AA, estab 2007, empl 4, sales $150,000, cert: State, City, 8(a))

7910   Peck Training Group LLC
907 Glen Rose Dr
Allen, TX 75013
Contact: Holly St John Peck President
Tel: 214-495-9499
Email: holly@pecktraining.com
Website: www.pecktraining.com
Professional development training & coaching. (Woman, estab 1985, empl 2, sales $325,000, cert: WBENC)

7911   Phoenix Translations
2110 White Horse Trail
Austin, TX 78757
Contact: Deborah Wright CEO
Tel: 512-343-8389
Email: service@phoenixtranslations.com
Website: www.phoenixtranslations.com
Technical translation services. (Woman/AA, Hisp, estab 2000, empl , sales $2,500,000, cert: State, WBENC)

7912   Phronetik
5851 Legacy Circle 6th Fl
Plano, TX 75024
Contact: Tania Martin-Mercado President
Tel: 877-844-3575
Email: taniame@phronetik.com
Website: www.phronetik.com
Research & Development, Technical Support, Interoperability, Patient Portal Development, Privacy & Security, Clinical Documentation, Mobile Health, Decision Support Systems, Telemedicine, Custom Development. (Minority, Woman, estab 2013, empl 11, sales , cert: WBENC)

7913   Possible Missions, Inc.
150 W Parker Rd., Ste 602
Houston, TX 77076
Contact: Paula Mendoza CEO
Tel: 713-271-3746
Email: paula@possiblemissions.com
Website: www.possiblemissions.com
Project management solutions, plan, execute & complete projects within budget and on schedule. (Minority, Woman, estab 2001, empl 33, sales $2,100,000, cert: State, City, NMSDC, WBENC, 8(a))

7914   Proje Inc.
6942 FM 1960 E, Ste 362
Humble, TX 77346
Contact: Violet Stephens President
Tel: 832-293-5633
Email: info@projeinc.com
Website: www.projeinc.com
Project Management Leadership & analytical thinking, Crisis Management, Integration & Consolidation,   Risk Analysis & Adjustment, Medicare Advantage. (Woman, estab 2004, empl 38, sales $8,800,119, cert: WBENC)

7915   Risk Mitigation Worldwide
9800 Northwest Frwy Ste 600
Houston, TX 77092
Contact: Michele Ward VP Business Dev
Tel: 713-864-9997
Email: michele@legalwatch.com
Website: www.legalwatch.com
Training & consulting services: communications to minimize & avoid potential lawsuits, claims & internal disputes. (Woman/AA, estab 1997, empl 6, sales $0, cert: State, NMSDC, WBENC)

7916   RWG Consulting, Inc.
2560 King Arthur Blvd. Ste 124-34
Dallas, TX 75056
Contact: Anton Gates Managing Partner
Tel: 972-386-7601
Email: agates@rwgconsulting.com
Website: www.rwgconsulting.com
Training, Instructional Design, Project Management, Organizational Change Management, SAP Training Development,
Staff Augmentation, Business Process Optimization, Contract to Hire. (AA, estab 2013, empl 15, sales $900,000, cert: State, NMSDC)

7917   Sales Trac Coaching & Mgmt Development
10012 SIlvertree Dr
Dallas, TX 75243
Contact: David Tyson CEO
Tel: 214-215-1108
Email: davidt@salestrac.net
Website: www.salestrac.net
Leadership Development & Performance Management, Management training, Sales Management training, sales training, service focused training, customer service training
Generational training. (AA, estab 2007, empl 1, sales , cert: State, NMSDC)

7918   Seilevel Partners, LP
3410 Far West Blvd Ste 265
Austin, TX 78731
Contact: Christine Wollmuth
Tel: 512-527-9952
Email: cwollmuth@seilevel.com
Website: www.seilevel.com
Business analysis consulting, business analyst staffing, assessment, mentoring & training. (As-Ind, estab 2000, empl 30, sales , cert: State, NMSDC)

7919   Shea Writing and Training Solutions, Inc.
5807 Benning Dr
Houston, TX 77096
Contact: Evalyn Shea President
Tel: 713-723-9142
Email: info@sheaws.com
Website: www.sheaws.com
Technical writing & editing, risk assessment & meeting scribing, web content, training materials, proposals, presentations, reports, technical manuals, etc. (Woman, estab 1997, empl 12, sales $861,472, cert: WBENC)

7920   Sirius Solutions, LLLP
1233 West Loop South Ste 1800
Houston, TX 77027
Contact: Kathy Pattillo Dir Business Devel
Tel: 713-888-0488
Email: kpattillo@sirsol.com
Website: www.sirsol.com
Management consulting: finance, internal audit, information technology, accounting, risk, operations, process improvement, strategy & tax. (Woman, estab 1998, empl 230, sales , cert: WBENC, NWBOC)

7921 The Conxsis Group, Inc.
1910 McCartney Court
Arlington, TX 76012
Contact: Abdul Shakir President
Tel: 817-348-0060
Email: ashakir@conxsis.com
Website: www.conxsis.com
Environmental consulting, financial, economic, business consulting, large & small business teaming, M/WBE Programs, marketing & business development. (AA, estab 2002, empl 16, sales , cert: State)

7922 The I4 Group Consulting, LLC
1206 Rio Grande Ct
Allen, TX 75013
Contact: Charles Maddox Sr. Business Dir
Tel: 612-207-2751
Email: charles.sr@thei4group.com
Website: www.thei4group.com
Training & coaching for Scaled Agile, Agile, and IT business process improvement, Lean Six Sigma, project management training & certification. (AA, estab 2013, empl 42, sales $8,250,120, cert: NMSDC, 8(a))

7923 The Tagos Group, LLC
8 E Greenway Plaza Ste 1340
Houston, TX 77046
Contact: Maria Traver Office Mgr
Tel: 713-850-7031
Email: mtraver@tagosgroup.com
Website: www.tagosgroup.com
Business consulting, services & products: supply chain mgmt, transportation & logistics mgmt, speciality maintenance & call center operations. (AA, estab 2007, empl 9, sales $500,000, cert: NMSDC)

7924 Tray-Tec, Inc.
2598 Wilson Rd
Humble, TX 77396
Contact: Darell Fowler VP
Tel: 281-441-7314
Email: traytec@traytec.com
Website: www.traytec.com
Installers of process equipment such as trays, packings, distributors in towers, reactors, and drums. We perform installation and repairs of nozzles, and we perform vessel shell repairs. (Hisp, estab 2005, empl 20, sales $10,000,000, cert: State)

7925 Tre Weekly Magazine
3202 N Shiloh Rd
Garland, TX 75044
Contact: Shayne Hohman Marketing Coord
Tel: 972-675-4383
Email: marketing@trenews.com
Website: www.baotreonline.com/
Tre magazine circulates nearly 125,000 publications nationwide on a weekly basis: with a readership census of 112,000 people in Dallas alone. (As-Pac, estab 1997, empl 25, sales $1,600,000, cert: NMSDC)

Virignia

7926 3DIF LLC
47 E Queens Way Ste 204-C
Hampton, VA 23669
Contact: Indy Freeman CEO
Tel: 757-905-0631
Email: indy.freeman@3dif.co
Website: www.3dif.co
Professional & Management Consulting Services, Staff Augmentation and Job Placement Services, i3DReadiness Training & Custom Facilitation Solutions and Events Management & Custom Branded Products to individuals, businesses, organizations and local, state (Minority, Woman, estab 2011, empl 3, sales , cert: State)

7927 A. Reddix & Associates Inc.
1215 N Military Hwy, Ste 754
Norfolk, VA 23502
Contact: Contracts Dir
Tel: 757-410-7704
Email: info@ardx.net
Website: www.ardx.net
Workforce training & technical assistance, innovative information technology & security solutions & support, collaborative conferencing & events management, quality, compliance & revenue audits, policy documentation & management. (Minority, Woman, estab 2006, empl 105, sales , cert: State)

7928 Aerobodies Fitness Company, Inc.
950 N Washington St Ste 311
Alexandria, VA 22314
Contact: CEO
Tel: 703-402-8477
Email: contact@aerobodies.com
Website: www.aerobodies.com
Program management services, acquisition support, organizational development, and occupational health services to federal and private sector agencies. (AA, estab 1997, empl 25, sales $750,000, cert: WBENC, 8(a))

7929 Assura, Inc.
7814 Carousel Ln, Ste 202
Richmnod, VA 23294
Contact: Karen Cole CEO
Tel: 804-672-8714
Email: karen.cole@assuraconsulting.com
Website: www.assurainc.com
Consulting: Governance, Risk & Compliance (GRC), Enterprise Risk Management (ERM), cyber-security, business continuity planning & Information Technology (IT) audit. (Woman, estab , empl , sales , cert: State, WBENC)

7930 Burton-Fuller Managment
4905 Radford Ave Ste 105
Richmond, VA 23230
Contact: Vicki Funk Office Mgr
Tel: 804-217-6380
Email: support@burtonfuller.com
Website: www.burtonfuller.com
Management consulting. (Woman, estab 1989, empl 5, sales $0, cert: State)

7931   C.W. Hines and Associates, Inc.
344 Churchill Cir, Sanctuary Bay
White Stone, VA 22578
Contact: Cheryl Hudson President
Tel: 804-435-8844
Email: turtlecwh@aol.com
Website: www.cwhinesassociates.org
Management training & consulting: performance excellence coaching, diversity, teambuilding, leadership development, communications, customer service, strategic thinking, strategic planning, supervisory effectiveness, executive coaching, mediation. (Woman/AA, estab , empl , sales $850,000, cert: State, City)

7932   Capitol Management Consulting Services, Inc.
1600 Chain Bridge Rd
McLean, VA 22101
Contact: Akshat Prasad President
Tel: 571-318-6404
Email: akshat@capitolmcs.com
Website: www.capitolmcs.com
Management consulting, organizational governance, performance optimization, strategy, technology, and training services. (Minority, estab 2011, empl 7, sales , cert: NMSDC, 8(a))

7933   DP Distribution & Consulting, LLC
12240 Hunting Horn Lane
Rockville, VA 23146
Contact: Darren Reeves President
Tel: 804-307-7706
Email: dreeves@dpdconline.com
Website: www.dpdconline.com/
Quality Assurance & Regulatory for Manufacturing, Auditing, 510K, FDA regulation. (Woman, estab 2000, empl 1, sales $300,000, cert: State)

7934   EMY Consulting LLC
13406 Poplar Woods
Chantillly, VA 20151
Contact: Elena Yearly President
Tel: 703-943-8129
Email: eyearly@emyconsulting.biz
Website: www.emyconsulting.biz
Management consulting solutions. (Woman, estab 2013, empl 1, sales $201,000, cert: State, WBENC)

7935   Evans Inc.
2750 Properity Ave, Ste 425
Fairfax, VA 22031
Contact: Sue Evans Founder
Tel: 703-663-2480
Email: info@evansconsulting.com
Website: www.evansincorporated.com
Business process consulting, change mgmt & reengineering, enterprise IT investment analysis & integration, ethical leadership training, process & data modeling, performance mgmt, competency framework changes & development, user interface. (Woman, estab 1993, empl 10, sales $1,500,000, cert: WBENC)

7936   FM Solutions, PLLC
901 E Byrd St Ste 1210
Richmond, VA 23219
Contact: Wendy Henley Principal
Tel: 804-288-3173
Email: wendyh@fmsolutions-us.com
Website: www.fmsolutions-us.com
Project & program mgmt, facilities mgmt, consulting & supplemental staffing, space allocation analyses & programming, strategic space & facilities planning, relocation mgmt. (Woman, estab 2003, empl 4, sales $394,143, cert: State)

7937   Intelligent Decision Systems, Inc.
5870 Trinity Pkwy
Centreville, VA 20120
Contact: Joe Collins VP Business Devel
Tel: 703-766-9631
Email: bd@idsi.com
Website: www.idsi.com
Human Performance Management, Research, analysis & assessment studies. (Woman, estab 1995, empl 133, sales $15,000,000, cert: WBENC)

7938   KAPAX Solutions LLC
44308 Navajo Dr
Ashburn, VA 20147
Contact: Katrecia Nolen President
Tel: 571-239-0653
Email: katrecia.nolen@kapaxsolutions.com
Website: www.kapaxsolutions.com
Professional services & management consulting, strategic planning, system integration & project management support services. (Woman/AA, estab 2011, empl 1, sales , cert: State)

7939   KickStart Specialists, LLC
11809 Crown Prince Circle
Henrico, VA 23238
Contact: Robert Riley Principal
Tel: 855-454-2578
Email: rriley@kickstartspecialists.com
Website: www.kickstartspecialists.com
Leadership development & training; roles & responsibilities, business objectives, business case evaluation, teambuilding; project & program management consulting; project board training; health checks. (Woman, estab 2011, empl 2, sales , cert: State)

7940   Mindseeker, Inc.
20130 Lakeview Center Plaza, Ste 320
Ashburn, VA 20147
Contact: Cassie Kelly VP Client Services & Operations
Tel: 304-549-9281
Email: ckelly@mindseeker.com
Website: www.mindseeker.com
Information Technology, Financial, Clerical and Enterprise Performance Management services and solutions. (Woman, estab , empl 234, sales $2,000,000, cert: State, WBENC)

7941   OmniTek Consulting, Inc.
       8260 Greensboro Dr Ste 120
       McLean, VA 22102
       Contact: Matthew Donahue GM
       Tel: 240-344-7914
       Email: support@omnitekconsulting.com
       Website: www.omnitekconsulting.com/
Consulting, Contingent, and Professional Service Engage-
ments: Program & Project Management, Business Process
Management (BPM), Change Management & Training,
Systems Implementation & Integration, Business Analytics
& Data Management. (As-Pac, estab 2005, empl 41, sales
$3,736,515, cert: NMSDC)

7942   Project Management and Consulting LLC
       512 Lafayette Boulevard, Ste 2
       Fredericksburg, VA 22401
       Contact: Bryan Rock CEO
       Tel: 800-971-3194
       Email: brock@pmcllcva.com
       Website: www.pmcva.com
Business management & consulting business consulting,
minority-owned business consulting. (AA, estab 2007,
empl 1, sales $195,000, cert: State)

7943   Savi Solutions, Inc.
       8200 Greensboro Dr, Ste 900
       McLean, VA 22102
       Contact: Smita Iyer CEO
       Tel: 571-258-7602
       Email: siyer@savisolutions.biz
       Website: www.savisolutions.biz
Strategic Planning, Program/Project Management, Merger
& Acquisition Support, Systems Implementation (ERP/
CRM/SCM), Cloud Based Implementation Solutions,
Business Requirement Analysis, System Design and
Development. (Minority, estab 2010, empl 3, sales
$552,551, cert: WBENC)

7944   The Perspectives Group
       7620 Little River Turnpike Ste 205
       Annandale, VA 22003
       Contact: Dir Business Dev
       Tel: 703-837-1197
       Email: info@theperspectivesgroup.com
       Website: www.theperspectivesgroup.com
Public participation & outreach, advisory boards &
governance, collaboration, facilitation, graphic design,
mediation & dispute resolution, message development,
policy development, process design, strategic planning,
training & education. (Woman, estab 1991, empl 6, sales
$990,000, cert: State)

7945   TMS Consulting LLC
       2776 S Arlington Mill Dr Ste 114
       Arlington, VA 22206
       Contact: Tafadzwa Matinenga President
       Tel: 703-864-9965
       Email: info@tmsconsultingservices.us
       Website: www.tmsconsultingservices.us
Global management consulting. (Woman/AA, estab 2015,
empl 3, sales , cert: State)

7946   Visions2000 Inc.
       312 Tides Run
       Yorktown, VA 23692
       Contact: Che Henderson VP
       Tel: 757-898-5010
       Email: che@visions2000inc.com
       Website: www.visions2000inc.com
Consulting & training solutions: diversity, leadership,
teambuilding, change management, life work planning &
job search assistance. (Woman/AA, estab 1990, empl 2,
sales , cert: NMSDC)

Washington

7947   Blueprint Consulting Services, LLC
       350 106th Ave NE, 2nd Fl
       Bellevue, WA 98004
       Contact: Ryan Neal President
       Tel: - -
       Email: ryanh@bpcs.com
       Website: www.bpcs.com
Business management and technology solutions. (Nat
Ame, estab 2013, empl 650, sales , cert: NMSDC)

7948   Brightwork Consulting, Inc.
       200 W Mercer St, Ste 108
       Seattle, WA 98119
       Contact: Shannan Epps CEO
       Tel: 206-659-0643
       Email: info@brightworkhealthit.com
       Website: www.brightworkhealthit.com
Risk management, solution deployment, smart decisions, and change management. (Woman, estab 2017,
empl 15, sales $4,000,000, cert: WBENC)

7949   Cascade Management and Consulting
       26211 178th St SE
       Monroe, WA 98272
       Contact: Amy Hoyt Owner
       Tel: 206-778-4322
       Email: info@cascademgtconsulting.com
       Website: www.cascademgtconsulting.com
Project & program management, IT & global rollouts,
business continuity/disaster recovery, brand integrity,
change management & collaborative communications.
(Woman, estab 2015, empl 1, sales , cert: State)

7950   Eagle Hill Consulting
       10400 NE 4th St
       Bellevue, WA 98004
       Contact: Jordan Henry Dir Seattle Office
       Tel: 301-980-2910
       Email: jhenry@eaglehillconsulting.com
       Website: www.eaglehillconsulting.com/seattle
Management consulting services, change management,
organizational design, human capital management,
strategy, and business process improvement. (Woman,
estab 2003, empl 185, sales $30,000,000, cert: WBENC,
NWBOC)

7951 Groundwork Tech, LLC
      PO Box 489
      Bellevue, WA 98004
      Contact: Jeff Foster Principal
      Tel: 425-209-0588
      Email: jeff@groundworktech.com
      Website: www.groundworktech.com
Professional Management Services, consulting services &
resources to enhance, re-engineer & develop customer
business. (AA, estab 2014, empl 3, sales $180,000, cert:
State)

7952 Humbition Consulting, LLC
      4123 NE 9th Pl
      Renton, WA 98059
      Contact: Steven Sun Managing Partner
      Tel: 206-618-2080
      Email: ssun@humbitionconsulting.com
      Website: www.humbitionconsulting.com
Program Leadership, Innovation & Planning, Technology
Operations, Financial & Insights. (Woman/As-Pac, estab
2019, empl 5, sales $1,491,154, cert: NMSDC, WBENC)

7953 Rafael A Colon Voices Internacional
      5145 Illahee Ln NE
      Olympia, WA 98516
      Contact: Rafael Colon President
      Tel: 360-459-7228
      Email: rafael@voicesinternacional.com
      Website: www.voicesinternacional.com
Consulting, training, organizational operations & administration, leadership & management development, program
development & management, communication effectiveness & meeting facilitation, peak performance & team
unity practices. (Hisp, estab 1994, empl 1, sales $217,500,
cert: State, NMSDC)

7954 Rivet Consulting LLC
      2212 Queen Anne Ave N, Ste 127
      Seattle, WA 98109
      Contact: Courtney Klein Managing Partner
      Tel: 888-201-1422
      Email: courtney@rivetconsulting.com
      Website: www.rivetconsulting.com
Project Managers, Program Managers, Marketing Managers, Marketing Coordinators, Financial Analysts, Business
Analysts, Social Media Experts, Search Marketing Experts,
Data Analysts,   Market Researchers, Marketing Communications Managers. (Woman, estab 2013, empl 30, sales ,
cert: WBENC)

Wisconsin

7955 Advantage Research, Inc.
      W162N11840 Fond Du Lac Ave
      Germantown, WI 53022
      Contact: Adam Hale Dir Research & Business Dev
      Tel: 262-502-7001
      Email: ahale@advantageresearchinc.com
      Website: www.advantageresearchinc.com
Awareness, attitude and usage studies; Customer satisfaction, retention and loyalty studies. (Woman, estab 1992,
empl 7, sales $0, cert: WBENC)

7956 Cross Management Services, Inc.
      1815 N 4th St
      Milwaukee, WI 53212
      Contact: Demeke Meri President
      Tel: 414-449-4920
      Email:
      Website: www.cross-management.com
Supplier & workforce diversity consulting, real estate
development management. (Woman/AA, estab 1999,
empl , sales $436,000, cert: NMSDC)

7957 Urban Strategies US LLC DBA SMCG
      759 N Milwaukee St Ste 414
      Milwaukee, WI 53202
      Contact: Jim Milner CEO
      Tel: 414-221-9500
      Email: jmilner@sectormanagement.biz
      Website: www.sectormcg.com
Leadership development, assessing/shaping organizational culture, stretching leadership capacity & acceler-
ating the development of those who follow through
effective coaching. (AA, estab 2002, empl 3, sales , cert:
State, NMSDC)

PROFESSIONAL SERVICES: Public Relations/Marketing

Provide services including business research and marketing plans, data collection and analysis, meeting planning, needs assessments, corporate imaging enhancement, focus groups, fundraising, technical writing, media relations, etc. NAICS Code 54

Alabama

7958 Marketry Inc.
1630 29th Ct S
Birmingham, AL 35209
Contact: Gillian Waybright Business Mgr
Tel: 205-802-7252
Email: gwaybright@marketryinc.com
Website: www.marketryinc.com
Qualitative marketing research: focus groups, ethnography, online discussions, online video focus groups, interviews, dyads, triads, observational research, ideation, shop-a-longs, online bulletin boards, video diaries. (Woman, estab 1995, empl 5, sales , cert: WBENC)

7959 PM Group, Inc.
4324 Midmost Dr
Mobile, AL 36685
Contact: Juan Peasant
Tel: 251-445-7804
Email: juan@pmgroupnow.com
Website: www.TheCultureExperts.com
Branding & Marketing, Social Media Marketing, creative & design development, print, web development & video production. (AA, estab 2004, empl 3, sales $226,910, cert: NMSDC)

Arizona

7960 Denise Meridith Consultants Inc.
1201 E Palo Verde Dr
Phoenix, AZ 85014
Contact: Denise Meridith CEO
Tel: 602-763-9900
Email: denisemeridithconsultants@cox.net
Website: www.denisemeridithconsultants.com
Public relations, marketing, lobbying, human resources management, training, organizational development. (Woman/AA, estab 2001, empl 1, sales , cert: City)

7961 EventPro Strategies, Inc.
7373 N. Scottsdale Road, Ste B-120
Scottsdale, AZ 85283
Contact: Kelly Springs-Kelley Dir of Marketing
Tel: 480-449-4100
Email: kkelley@eventprostrategies.com
Website: www.eventprostrategies.com
Marketing, PR & promotional events. (Woman, estab 1999, empl 32, sales $6,700,000, cert: WBENC)

7962 JVJ Can 22 Corp
3260 N Hayden, Ste 210
Scottsdale, AZ 85251
Contact: Michelle Candelaria CEO
Tel: 480-626-7919
Email: mc@cts10.com
Website: www.CTS10.com
SEO Search Engine Optimization, Social Media Mgmt Reputation monitoring. (Minority, Woman, estab 2016, empl 7, sales , cert: NMSDC)

7963 Katherine Christensen & Associates, Inc.
107 S Southgate Dr
Chandler, AZ 85226
Contact: Katherine Christensen, President
Tel: 480-893-6110
Email: kc@kc-a.com
Website: www.kc-a.com
Meeting management, trade association management & public relations. (Woman, estab 1992, empl 12, sales $731,957, cert: WBENC)

7964 Morrissey & Associates, LLC
PO Box 25967
Scottsdale, AZ 85255
Contact: Neysa Morrissey CEO
Tel: 480-515-2688
Email: admin@morrisseytravel.com
Website: www.MorrisseyTravel.com
Meeting, Event & Travel, Site Research & Selection, Analysis & Cost Containment Solutions, Contract Negotiations & Risk Mitigation, Strategic Meetings Management (SMM); Program Itinerary & Agenda Development, Housing & Registration, Trade Show Management. (Minority, Woman, estab 2007, empl 1, sales $151,168, cert: State, WBENC, 8(a))

7965 Scarritt Group
7620 N Hartman Ln, Ste 100
Tucson, AZ 85743
Contact: Adrienne Williams CEO
Tel: 520-529-0000
Email: Edson.Ribeiro@scarrittgroup.com
Website: www.scarrittgroup.com
Meeting planning: contract negotiations, budgeting, registration, invitations, online registration, confirmation & welcome packets, name badges, etc. (Woman, estab 2000, empl 23, sales $4,100,000, cert: WBENC)

7966 The Event Concierge
3218 E Bell Rd, Ste 142
Phoenix, AZ 85032
Contact: Julie Wong President
Tel: 602-569-5333
Email: julie@eventconcierge.com
Website: www.eventconcierge.com
Event Planning and Meeting Management. (Minority, Woman, estab 2005, empl 2, sales $330,029, cert: State, City, WBENC)

7967 The Translation Team
4960 S Gilbert Rd, Ste 1-115
Chandler, AZ 85249
Contact: Micaela Novas Owner
Tel: 720-394-0109
Email: micaela.novas@thetranslationteam.com
Website: www.thetranslationteam.com
Spanish translations for the U.S Hispanic market. We support the multicultural communication efforts. (Woman/Hisp, estab 2014, empl 1, sales $936,000, cert: CPUC, WBENC)

California

7968 Acento Advertising, Inc.
11400 West Olympic Blvd 12th Fl
Los Angeles, CA 90064
Contact: Donnie Broxson CEO
Tel: 310-843-8300
Email: dbroxson@acento.com
Website: www.acento.com
Integrated marketing programs for the U.S. Hispanic & total market segments. (Hisp, estab 1983, empl 30, sales $32,067,933, cert: NMSDC, CPUC)

7969 Acme Arts Inc.
19709 Horseshoe Dr
Topanga, CA 90290
Contact: Scott Ferguson Partner
Tel: 310-455-1413
Email: scott@sferguson.com
Website: www.sferguson.com
Marketing communications services, copywriting, creative direction, strategic brand consulting, original music, complete production for educational & promotional corporate videos. (Minority, Woman, estab 1990, empl 2, sales $234,000, cert: CPUC, WBENC)

7970 Afaf Translations, LLC
15655 Liberty St
San Leandro, CA 94578
Contact: Afaf Steiert President
Tel: 510-684-4586
Email: afaf@afaftranslations.com
Website: www.afaftranslations.com
Translation, interpreting, voice-over, desktop publishing, transcription, localization, language proficiency evaluations & cultural consultation. (Woman/AA, estab 2004, empl 2, sales , cert: WBENC)

7971 AfterViolet Inc.
1100 Glendon Ave Ste 1715
Los Angeles, CA 90024
Contact: Christopher Bodmer Innovation Consultant
Tel: 917-331-5637
Email: cab@afterviolet.com
Website: www.afterviolet.com
Innovation & branding, Product, service & experience design, Marketing & innovation strategy, Graphic design services, Consumer research. (Hisp, estab 2013, empl 6, sales $243,857, cert: NMSDC)

7972 Alter Agents
617 S Olive St, Ste 1010
Los Angeles, CA 90014
Contact: Angela Woo Co-Founder
Tel: 213-612-0356
Email: angela@alteragents.com
Website: www.alteragents.com
Market research & brand strategy, brand building, targeting, marketing strategy/development, product development, shopper insights & in-market performance. (Woman, estab 2010, empl 10, sales , cert: NWBOC)

7973 AP42
2303 Camino Ramon, Ste 280
San Ramon, CA 94583
Contact: CEO
Tel: 925-901-1100
Email: info@ap42.com
Website: www.ap42.com
Create ads, direct marketing programs, website content, logo design, email blasts, collateral materials. (Minority, Woman, estab 2001, empl 7, sales $720,000, cert: WBENC)

7974 Artisan Creative Inc.
1830 Stoner Ave Ste 6
Los Angeles, CA 90025
Contact: Katty Douraghy President
Tel: 310-312-2062
Email: kattyd@artisancreative.com
Website: www.artisancreative.com
Design & development solutions: marketing, advertising, communications & production teams in the digital, broadcast, mobile & print space. (Woman, estab 1996, empl 15, sales $3,000,000, cert: WBENC)

7975 Bleu Marketing Solutions
101 Lucas Valley Road Ste 300
San Rafael, CA 94903
Contact: Jennifer Giordano Acct Dir
Tel: 415-345-3317
Email: jgiordano@bleusf.com
Website: www.bleumarketing.com
Direct marketing, strategy & consulting, media planning & procurement, design & creative implementation, marketing program systems & IT support. (Woman, estab 2001, empl 25, sales $2,500,000, cert: WBENC)

7976 BrandGov
125 Humphrey Lane
Vallejo, CA 94591
Contact: K Patrice Williams President
Tel: 800-215-0280
Email: supplier@brandgov.com
Website: www.brandgov.com
Brand Strategy & Lobbying, Integrated Branding & Marketing Solutions, Supplier Diversity Outreach, Website & Mobile Application Dev, Logo Dev, Brochures, Graphic Designs, Technical Procurement. (Woman/AA, estab 2007, empl 4, sales , cert: NMSDC, CPUC)

7977 Briabe Media, Inc.
634A Venice Blvd
Venice, CA 90291
Contact: James Briggs CEO
Tel: 310-694-3283
Email: james.briggs@briabemedia.com
Website: www.briabemedia.com
Multicultural mobile marketing solutions, SMS & MMS campaigns, mobile advertising & mobile website development. (AA, Hisp, estab 2006, empl 15, sales $3,000,000, cert: NMSDC)

7978 Captura Group
408 Nutmeg St
San Diego, CA 92103
Contact: Walter Boza GM
Tel: 619-681-1856
Email: diversity@capturagroup.com
Website: www.capturagroup.com/
Strategic, data-driven consulting with digital first in-language and in-culture marketing services. (Hisp, estab 2001, empl 16, sales $4,800,000, cert: WBENC)

7979 CCS/PR, Inc.
2888 Loker Ave East Ste 316
Carlsbad, CA 92010
Contact: Gayle Mestel President
Tel: 760-929-7514
Email: gaylem@ccspr.com
Website: www.ccspr.com/
Marketing communications/consulting products & services: case studies, magazine articles, press releases/kits, video scripts, website content, blogs, PPTs, newsletters, marketing collateral, testimonial quotes, brochures, pitches. (Woman, estab 1966, empl 6, sales $1,405,334, cert: WBENC)

7980 Chica Intelligente LLC
5757 Wilshire Blvd
Los Angeles, CA 90036
Contact: Katrina Jefferson Owner
Tel: 323-360-4191
Email: katrina@chicaintelligente.com
Website: www.chicaintelligente.com
Digital marketing, enhance or develop digital marketing programs through integrated experiential Marketing, online branding & increase target audience. (Woman/AA, Hisp, estab 2013, empl 2, sales , cert: CPUC)

7981 CLC Publicidad dba Sherpa Marketing Solutions
4528 Stern Ave
Sherman Oaks, CA 91423
Contact: Carlos Cordoba President
Tel: 818-635-7318
Email: ccordoba@sherpa-marketing.com
Website: www.sherpa-marketing.com/
Consumer research & insights into the Hispanic population, qualitative & quantitative research services. (Hisp, estab 1996, empl 5, sales $1,500,000, cert: State, CPUC)

7982 Coast to Coast Conferences & Events
100 W Broadway Ste 250
Long Beach, CA 90802
Contact: Michelle Manire President
Tel: 562-980-7566
Email: michelle@ctcconferences.com
Website: www.ctcconferences.com
Meeting & event management: site selection, contract negotiations, housing, on line registration, transportation, on site services, on site registration, exhibit management, event planning & destination management. (Woman, estab 1994, empl 4, sales $700,000, cert: State, WBENC)

7983 Cook & Schmid, LLC
740 13th St, Ste 502
San Diego, CA 92101
Contact: Jon Schmid President
Tel: 619-814-2370
Email: jschmid@cookandschmid.com
Website: www.cookandschmid.com
Public relations, advertising and marketing agency. (Minority, estab 2006, empl 10, sales $1,006,305, cert: NMSDC, CPUC)

7984 Corporate Translations, Inc.
222 N. Pacific Coast Hwy., Ste 2000
El Segundo, CA 90245
Contact: Toni Andrews President
Tel: 310-376-1400
Email: projects@corporatetranslations.com
Website: www.CorporateTranslations.com
Provides native-speaking, technical language translation, multilingual document publishing, audio/video production & certified interpreting. (Woman, estab 1995, empl 10, sales $1,205,000, cert: State, CPUC)

7985 Culturati Research & Consulting, Inc.
12625 High Bluff Dr, Ste 218
San Diego, CA 92130
Contact: Lisa Raggio Acct Exec
Tel: 858-750-2600
Email: lisa.raggio@culturatiresearch.com
Website: www.CulturatiResearch.com
Market research, custom research solutions. (Minority, Woman, estab 2004, empl 18, sales $1,000,000,000, cert: CPUC)

7986 DM Connect LLC
4223 Glencoe Ave, Ste A-130
Marina Del Rey, CA 90292
Contact: Dawn Perdew Managing Partner
Tel: 800-778-2990
Email: accounting@dumontproject.com
Website: www.thedumontproject.com
Marketing Consulting Services. (Woman, estab 2008, empl 23, sales $1,700,000, cert: WBENC)

7987 DoubleShot Creative, LLC
499 Seaport Court Ste 205
Redwood City, CA 94063
Contact: Kathy Hutton VP Strategy
Tel: 415-992-7468
Email: kathy@doubleshotcreative.com
Website: www.doubleshotcreative.com
Creative & strategic marketing services, executive communications, marketing strategy and implementation, presentations, videos, messaging, campaign strategy, event creative concepts, social media, blogs, professional bios. (Woman, estab 2007, empl 2, sales $1,000,000, cert: WBENC)

7988 Duarte Communications, Inc.
3200 Coronado Dr
Santa Clara, CA 95054
Contact: Nancy Duarte CEO
Tel: 650-625-8200
Email: nancy@duarte.com
Website: www.duarte.com/
Presentation Development, Speaker Coaching, Communication Strategy and Presentation Coaching, graphic design, management consulting, and marketing research (Woman, estab 1994, empl 117, sales $20,000,000, cert: WBENC)

7989 Elevate Planning
13575 Zivi Ave
Chino, CA 91710
Contact: Viviana Salvia Owner
Tel: 951-217-1028
Email: viviana@elevateplanning.com
Website: www.elevateplanning.com
Experiential marketing & event planning. (Woman, estab 2003, empl 1, sales , cert: WBENC)

7990 Everfield Consulting, LLC
2075 W 235th Pl
Torrance, CA 90501
Contact: Delbara Dorsey Partner
Tel: 310-251-7165
Email: deldorsey@everfieldconsulting.com
Website: www.everfieldconsulting.com
Marketing Consulting, Administrative & Management, Display Advertising, Advertising, Public Relations, Media Buying, Direct Mail Advertising, Advertising Material Distribution Services. (Woman/AA, As- Pac, estab 2011, empl 2, sales , cert: State, City, CPUC)

7991 ExpoMarketing Group LLC
2741 Dow Ave
Tustin, CA 92780
Contact: Laurie Pennacchi CEO
Tel: 949-777-1051
Email: laurie@expomarketing.com
Website: www.expomarketing.com
Trade show exhibits: custom rental & custom-built exhibits, portable exhibits & peripherals, large format graphics, program management & logistics, & in-house design & creative services. (Woman, estab 1991, empl 13, sales $2,596,339, cert: CPUC, WBENC)

7992 Freddie Georges Production Group
15362 Graham St
Huntington Beach, CA 92649
Contact: Melanie Chomchavalit CFO
Tel: 714-367-9260
Email: mchomchavalit@fgpg.com
Website: www.freddiegeorges.com
Trade show & special events: design, fabrication, project management, rental solutions & logistical support. (Woman, estab 2001, empl 24, sales $7,079,500, cert: WBENC)

7993 HispaniSpace LLC
2100 W Magnolia Blvd Ste A/B
Burbank, CA 91506
Contact: Mario X. Carrasco Partner
Tel: 818-843-0220
Email: mario@thinknowresearch.com
Website: www.thinknowresearch.com
Online market research solutions for the U.S. Hispanic consumer. (Hisp, estab 2010, empl 8, sales $1,583,661, cert: NMSDC, CPUC)

7994 Hunter-Blyden, Katherine
PO Box 94893
Pasadena, CA 91104
Contact: Katherine Hunter-Blyden Managing Dir
Tel: 626-344-8730
Email: khb@katherinehunterblyden.com
Website: www.khbmarketinggroup.com
Develop marketing strategies, evaluate marketing channels & tactics & define programs that align with growth profitable goals. (Woman/AA, estab 2012, empl 1, sales , cert: CPUC)

7995 Ilana Ashley Events
24226 Park Granada
Calabasas, CA 91302
Contact: Ilana Rosenberg CEO
Tel: 818-963-8670
Email: ilana@ilanaashleyevents.com
Website: www.IlanaAshleyEvents.com
Full-service event production, plan and design corporate events, gala affairs, holiday parties, soirées, weddings, and other social events. (Woman, estab 2013, empl 2, sales $108,476, cert: WBENC)

7996 Innovate Marketing Group
300 S Raymond Ave
Pasadena, CA 91105
Contact: Amanda Ma CEO
Tel: 626-817-9588
Email: amanda@innovatemkg.com
Website: www.innovatemkg.com
Experiential event & production agency, product launch, conferences, meetings, sponsorship activations, award & galas. (Minority, Woman, estab 2014, empl 3, sales , cert: NMSDC, CPUC, WBENC)

7997 JR Resources
1130 Camino Del Mar Ste H
Del Mar, CA 92014
Contact: Waren Katz Acct Exec
Tel: 858-481-1074
Email: warren@jrresources.com
Website: www.jrresources.com
Promotional products & marketing services. (Woman, estab 1991, empl 10, sales $4,151,500, cert: CPUC, WBENC)

7998 Language Select, LLC.
7590 N Glenoaks Blvd, Ste 100
Los Angeles, CA 91504
Contact: Paolo Santa
Tel: 818-394-3407
Email: psantamaria@languageselect.com
Website: www.languageselect.com
Simultaneous & consecutive interpreting services. (Hisp, estab , empl , sales $11,700,000, cert: NMSDC)

7999 Latin Nation Live LLC
3245 N San Fernando Rd
Los Angeles, CA 90065
Contact: Ricardo Gieseken President
Tel: 213-924-5683
Email: ricardo@lnlagency.com
Website: www.lnlagency.com
Experiential Marketing, Diversity Marketing, Taste-maker/influencer marketing, Event production, Government affairs/tradeshows, Asset design & procurement, Brand Strategy, Brand Development, Shopper Marketing. (Hisp, estab 2008, empl 10, sales $1,000,000, cert: NMSDC)

8000 Liehr Marketing & Communications, Inc.
1899 Western Way Ste 400A
Torrance, CA 90501
Contact: Elisa Liehr President
Tel: 310-781-3727
Email: eliehr@lmconline.net
Website: www.lmconline.net
Marketing & research, copywriting, design, interactive, video, web development, design & programing. (Woman, estab 1987, empl 6, sales $780,000, cert: WBENC)

8001 Lightbox Libraries
320 Hedge Rd
Menlo Park, CA 94025
Contact: Cindy Lee Founder
Tel: 650-298-4759
Email: cindy.lee@lightboxlibraries.com
Website: www.lightboxlibraries.com
Lightbox Libraries is a custom photography and video production company. We specialize in producing On-Brand image libraries for all your Marcom materials, shooting both domestic and internationally. (Minority, Woman, estab 2011, empl 2, sales $1,954,051, cert: NMSDC)

8002 Luth Research
1365 4th Ave
San Diego, CA 92101
Contact: Candice Hinds Assoc Business Dev Mgr
Tel: 619-234-5884
Email: chinds@luthresearch.com
Website: www.luthresearch.com
Market research, enhanced data & data collection solutions, qualitative & quantitative research methodologies. (Woman, estab 1977, empl 90, sales , cert: WBENC)

8003 Marketing Maven Public Relations, Inc.
2390 C Las Posas Rd, Ste 479
Camarillo, CA 93010
Contact: John Carnett Dir Business Dev
Tel: 310-994-7380
Email: john@marketingmavenpr.com
Website: www.marketingmavenpr.com
Public Relations, Hispanic Marketing, Social Media Management, Digital Advertising, Deep Dive Research, Brand Analysis, Graphic Design, Media Traning, Clip Tracking, Event Execution. (Minority, Woman, estab 2009, empl 13, sales $1,259,534, cert: State, CPUC, WBENC, 8(a), SDB)

8004 Meeting Planners Plus
3069 Taylor Way
Costa Mesa, CA 92626
Contact: Rosa McArthur President
Tel: 714-668-1126
Email: rlmcarthur@meetingplannersplus.com
Website: www.meetingplannersplus.com
Meeting & special event management; tradeshow production, seminars, conferences, retreats, board meetings. (Woman/AA, estab 1993, empl 1, sales , cert: CPUC)

8005 Meijun LLC
9888 Carroll Centre Rd Ste#210
San Diego, CA 92126
Contact: Huy Ly
Tel: 619-333-8698
Email: hly@meijun.cc
Website: www.meijun.cc
Web development & marketing, custom software solutions, web & mobile development, design & strategy, digital marketing services, SEO, content marketing & marketing automation integration. (As-Pac, estab 2011, empl 5, sales , cert: NMSDC, CPUC)

8006 Multi-Cultural Convention Services Network
(MCCSN)
212 Sweetwood St
San Diego, CA 92114
Contact: Clara Carter CEO
Tel: 619-265-2561
Email: info@mccsn.com
Website: www.mccsn.com
Meeting & event management, hotel sourcing & contract negotiations & business consulting services. (Woman/AA, estab 2004, empl 1, sales , cert: CPUC)

8007 Netpace Inc.
5000 Executive Pkwy, Ste 530
San Ramon, CA 94583
Contact: Omar Khan President
Tel: 925-543-7760
Email: rfp@netpace.com
Website: www.netpace.com
Lead generation and brand awareness, web development and design practices. (As-Ind, estab 1996, empl 120, sales $22,771,314, cert: NMSDC)

8008 Nostrum, Inc.
401 E Ocean Blvd Ste M101
Long Beach, CA 90802
Contact: Alice Kijak VP
Tel: 562-437-2200
Email: alicekijak@verizon.net
Website: www.nostruminc.com
Strategic marketing communications: advertising, direct marketing, brand optimization, concept development, creative & print production services. (Woman, estab 1981, empl 9, sales $2,452,000, cert: WBENC)

8009 Outward Media, Inc.
9229 Sunset Blvd, Ste 410
Los Angeles, CA 90069
Contact: Paula Chiocchi President
Tel: 310-274-5312
Email: paula@outwardmedia.com
Website: www.outwardmedia.com
Email marketing; creative design, deployment, statistical reporting & campaign management. (Woman, estab 1998, empl 8, sales $5,000,000, cert: WBENC)

8010 Parle Enterprises, Inc.
800 Airport Blvd, Ste 21
Burlingame, CA 94010
Contact: Mary Shulenberger CEO
Tel: 415-467-3100
Email: mary@parle.com
Website: www.parle.com
Media, marketing sponsorships, advertising, oppportunity programs, promotional marketing. (Minority, Woman, estab 1997, empl 8, sales $1,400,000, cert: NMSDC, CPUC)

8011 ProExhibits
48571 Milmont Dr
Fremont, CA 94538
Contact: Acct Exec
Tel: 916-364-9013
Email: msanzone@proexhibits.com
Website: www.proexhibits.com
Trade show exhibit & events. (Woman, estab 1987, empl 40, sales $1,040,000, cert: CPUC)

8012 Purpose Generation LLC
535 Mission St 14th Fl
San Francisco, CA 94105
Contact: Nellie Morris Co-Founder
Tel: 917-243-4777
Email: nellie@purposegeneration.com
Website: www.purposegeneration.com/
Millennial marketing, market research, millennials, gen Y, project mgmt, consulting, strategy, consumer insights, quantitative research, product sampling, product co-creation, quantitative research, influencer strategy. (Woman, estab 2013, empl 4, sales $758,280, cert: WBENC, NWBOC)

8013 RED Company
10323 Los Alamitos Blvd
Long Beach, CA 90720
Contact: President
Tel: 562-498-1270
Email: hello@redcompany.com
Website: www.redcompany.com
Meeting & event planning: site review, contract negotiation, vendor relations, sponsorship cultivation to onsite management, ground transportation, registration services, staffing, hotel block/rooming lists, hospitality, activities. (Woman, estab 2007, empl 22, sales $11,600,000, cert: WBENC)

8014 Red Kite Business Advisors LLC
3525 Del Mar Heights Rd, Ste 202
San Diego, CA 92130
Contact: Principal
Tel: 858-232-4555
Email: info@redkitecorp.com
Website: www.redkitesite.com
Marketing, advertising, public speaking, seminars, workshops, strategic planning, brand assessment & dev, integrated campaign strategies, media plan development, online & traditional marketing. (Minority, Woman, estab 2007, empl 1, sales , cert: CPUC, WBENC)

8015   RevOne Design, Inc.
         1649B Adrian Rd
         Burlingame, CA 94010
         Contact: Sean Carlin Dir Business Dev
         Tel: 650-468-2996
         Email: sean@revonedesign.com
         Website: www.revonedesign.com
Graphic & Production Design, Photography & Photo
Retouching, Digital/Web & Print Communications, Creative
Concepting & Campaign Design & Copywriting. (Minority,
Woman, estab 2011, empl 7, sales $300,000, cert: NMSDC,
WBENC)

8016   RMD Group Inc.
         2311 E South St
         Long Beach, CA 90805
         Contact: Laura Milanes COO
         Tel: 562-866-9288
         Email: laura@rmdgroupinc.com
         Website: www.rmdgroupinc.com
Experiential Marketing, Digital & Social Media, Large
Format Graphic Printing, Vehicle Fabrication, Trade Show
Design, Trade Show Booth Builder, Millwork, Data Collec-
tion. (Hisp, estab 1993, empl 25, sales $6,000,000, cert:
NMSDC)

8017   Samantha Smith Productions LLC
         2325 Third St Ste 407
         San Francisco, CA 94107
         Contact: Samantha Smith Owner
         Tel: 415-626-7925
         Email: samantha@samanthasmithproductions.com
         Website: www.samanthasmithproductions.com
Meeting & event planning. (Woman, estab 2003, empl 5,
sales $1,500,000, cert: WBENC)

8018   Sax Productions Inc.
         1055 W 7th St 33rd Fl PH
         Los Angeles, CA 90017
         Contact: Tamara Keller COO
         Tel: 213-232-1682
         Email: tamara@saxproductions.com
         Website: www.saxproductions.com
Brand marketing & storytelling, digital strategy, innovation
& public relation. (Woman/AA, estab 2012, empl 6, sales ,
cert: NMSDC, WBENC)

8019   Shiloh Event Management
         PO Box 2772
         Santa Clara, CA 95050
         Contact: Huong Burrow Dir of Events
         Tel: 408-899-5464
         Email: huong@shiloh-events.com
         Website: www.shiloh-events.com
Event strategies, event production, event marketing
solutions & event management services. (As-Pac, estab
2013, empl 3, sales , cert: NMSDC)

8020   Specialized Marketing Services, Inc.
         3421 W Segerstrom Ave
         Santa Ana, CA 92704
         Contact: John Snook Exec VP
         Tel: 714-955-5450
         Email: jsnook@teamsms.com
         Website: www.teamsms.com
Strategic marketing devel, copywriting, print mgmt,
database mgmt/processing, mailing svcs, warehousing,
fulfillment/hand assembly, internet application,
telemarketing. (Minority, Woman, estab 1988, empl 23,
sales $8,161,000, cert: WBENC)

8021   Stage 4 Solutions, Inc.
         4701 Patrick Henry Dr, #19
         Santa Clara, CA 95054
         Contact: Niti Agrawal CEO
         Tel: 408-868-9739
         Email: niti@stage4solutions.com
         Website: www.stage4solutions.com
Marketing & strategy consulting services: strategic
business & product plan dev, focused sales tools,
competitive analyses, new product introduction mgmt &
interim marketing staffing solutions. (Woman/As-Ind,
estab , empl , sales , cert: NMSDC, WBENC)

8022   Strategic Business Communications
         12175 Dearborn Pl
         Poway, CA 92064
         Contact: Jim Hernandez President
         Tel: 858-679-1805
         Email: jhernandez@sbcinc.com
         Website: www.sbcinc.info
Sales & Marketing Training & Consulting, Meeting &
Event Planning. (As-Pac, estab 1987, empl 10, sales
$2,400,000, cert: NMSDC)

8023   Sundial Marketing Research, Inc.
         30 Center St
         San Rafael, CA 94901
         Contact: Nancy Kelber President
         Tel: 415-200-1461
         Email: nancy@sundialresearch.com
         Website: www.sundialresearch.com
Market research to the medical device, pharmaceutical
& biotechnology industries. (Woman, estab 2010, empl
6, sales $2,500,000, cert: WBENC)

8024   The Mark USA, Inc.
         4482 Barranca Pkwy, Ste 220
         Newport Beach, CA 92663
         Contact: Traci Shirachi CEO
         Tel: 949-396-6053
         Email: tshirachi@themarkusa.com
         Website: www.themarkusa.com
Research and evaluation through innovative data
collection, analytics, and visualization in order to help
clients achieve better outcomes and demonstrate the
impact of an organization. (Woman/As-Pac, estab 2007,
empl 15, sales $1,250,000, cert: NMSDC, WBENC)

8025   Undisclosed Location, Inc
         5761 Sonoma Mountain Rd
         Santa Rosa, CA 95404
         Contact: Barbara Gorder President
         Tel: 415-295-4920
         Email: barbara.gorder@unlo.com
         Website: www.unlo.com
Marketing, advertising & communications solutions,
strategic brand advertising, mobile marketing consulting
& content dev, website development, packaging design,
presentation consulting & event promotions. (Woman,
estab 2003, empl 10, sales $1,000,000, cert: WBENC)

8026   Valencia, Perez & Echeveste
         1605 Hope St, Ste 250
         South Pasadena, CA 91030
         Contact: Patricia Perez President
         Tel: 626-403-3200
         Email: patricia@vpepr.com
         Website: www.vpepr.com
Public relations & marketing communications. (Hisp,
estab 1987, empl 25, sales , cert: NMSDC)

8027 Vic Salazar Enterprises, LLC
2514 Jamacha Rd, Ste 502-21
El Cajon, CA 92019
Contact: Vic Salazar President
Tel: 619-517-4744
Email: vicsalazar@cox.net
Website: www.vicsalazar.com
Public Relations, Hispanic Marketing, Video Production, Media Training, Advertising, Crisis Communications, Hard Drive Storage, Printing, Labeling, Promotional Items, Event Production. (Hisp, estab 2008, empl 1, sales , cert: CPUC)

Colorado

8028 Egg Strategy, Inc.
1360 Walnut St Ste 102
Boulder, CO 80302
Contact: Matthew Sommers Dir of Operations
Tel: 303-546-9311
Email: boulderinfo@eggstrategy.com
Website: www.eggstrategy.com
Marketing consulting, innovation, brand strategy, market research, consumer insight. (Woman, estab 2005, empl 50, sales $10,000,000, cert: WBENC)

8029 MorSports & Events, Inc.
3333 S Bannock St Ste 790
Englewood, CO 80110
Contact: Betsy Mordecai President
Tel: 720-381-5000
Email: betsy@morevents.com
Website: www.morevents.com
Event planning, meeting coordination & hospitality mgmt. (Woman, estab 1996, empl 13, sales $6,000,000, cert: WBENC)

8030 Translation Excellence
2620 S Parker Rd Ste 210
Aurora, CO 80014
Contact: Nisar Nikzad President
Tel: 720-325-0459
Email: info@translationexcellence.com
Website: www.translationexcellence.com
Translation, interpretation, interpretation equipment & language classes. (As-Ind, estab 2010, empl 5, sales $422,000, cert: City, 8(a))

8031 Vladimir Jones
PO Box 387
Colorado Springs, CO 80901
Contact: Trudy Rowe CFO
Tel: 719-473-0704
Email: trowe@vladimirjones.com
Website: www.vladimirjones.com
Marketing services: strategic planning, research, advertising & public relations, creative development & production, television, print, radio, out of home, digital & on-line communications, media planning & buying, account planning. (Woman, estab 1970, empl 71, sales $21,863,320, cert: NWBOC)

Connecticut

8032 Axiom Actuarial Consulting, LLC
462 Firetown Rd
Simsbury, CT 06070
Contact: Carlos Sanchez-Fuentes Partner
Tel: 860-651-7573
Email: carlos-fuentes@axiom-actuarial.com
Website: www.axiom-actuarial.com
Market research, Strategic studies, Decision analysis, Development of business strategies. (Hisp, estab 2008, empl 2, sales , cert: NMSDC)

8033 BCM Media
30 Old Kings Hwy S
Darien, CT 06820
Contact: S. McKenna Managing Dir
Tel: 203-326-1477
Email: smckenna@bcmmedia.biz
Website: www.bcmmedia.biz/
Advertising, Media Consulting, Media Planning, Negotiations, B2B Advertising, B2C Advertising, Trade Advertising, Multimedia Planning and Buying, Global Media Planning, National Media Planning, Local Media Planning, Public Relations. (Woman, estab 2013, empl 9, sales $855,047, cert: WBENC)

8034 CYMA Systems Inc.
360 Tolland Turnpike Ste 2D
Manchester, CT 06042
Contact: Nisha Sunil HR Mgr
Tel: 860-791-6356
Email: hr@cymasys.com
Website: www.cymasys.com
CYMA Systems Inc. is a professional staffing and solutions firm headquartered in the Greater Hartford Area, CT. We provide customers with leading edge technology solutions and augment their IT staff needs. (As-Ind, estab 2006, empl 179, sales $16,800,000, cert: NMSDC)

8035 Domo Domo IMG
28 Castle Meadow Road
Newtown, CT 06470
Contact: Deb Adams Founder & CCO
Tel: 203-270-3515
Email: judy@domomarketing.com
Website: www.domomarketing.com
Brand strategy & optimization, strategic positioning, new product launches, line extensions, NPD innovation, trend & market analyses. (Woman, estab 1997, empl 10, sales $845,000, cert: WBENC)

8036 Peralta Illustration & Design LLC
431 Howe Ave
Shelton, CT 06484
Contact: Ramon Peralta
Tel: 203-513-2222
Email: ramon@peraltadesign.com
Website: www.peraltadesign.com
Digital interactive design: web development, web applications, corporate identity & marketing, branding. (Hisp, estab 2003, empl 6, sales , cert: NMSDC)

8037   Touchpoint Integrated Communications, LLC
       16 Thorndal Circle
       Darien, CT 06820
       Contact: Karen Kluger CEO
       Tel: 203-665-7705
       Email: kkluger@tpointmedia.com
       Website: www.tpointmedia.com
Communication: broadcast, print, digital, social, mobile, email, direct mail, out of home & alternative. (Woman, estab 2005, empl 40, sales $9,591,292, cert: WBENC)

8038   TruEvents LLC
       PO Box 893
       Madison, CT 06443
       Contact: CEO
       Tel: 203-980-3495
       Email: Info@BE-TRU.com
       Website: www.be-tru.com
Marketing, Graphic Design, Creative Design, Web, Retail Packaging, Retail Strategy, Digital, Digital Store Displays, Retail POS, Merchandising, Tradeshows, Meeting Production, Event Production, Ideation, Strategy. (Woman, estab 2000, empl 4, sales $2,082,729, cert: WBENC)

District of Columbia

8039   JPA Health Communications
       1101 Connecticut Ave NW Ste 600
       Washington, DC 20036
       Contact: Carrie Jones Principal
       Tel: 202-591-4000
       Email: carrie@jpa.com
       Website: www.jpa.com
Public Relations, Health Communications, Influencer Relations (Media relations, advocacy engagement, social & digital media, policy & issues advocacy, stakeholder engagement). (Woman, estab 2007, empl 21, sales $7,700,000, cert: NWBOC)

8040   Premier Consultants International, Inc.
       1020 16th St NW Ste 201
       Washington, DC 20036
       Contact: Renard H. Marable
       Tel: 202-319-1211
       Email: rmarable@premiercon.com
       Website: www.premiercon.com
Marketing & business development services. (AA, estab 2000, empl 1, sales , cert: State, City)

8041   Scott Circle Communications, Inc.
       1307 New York Ave NW Ste 702
       Washington, DC 20005
       Contact: Laura Gross President
       Tel: 202-695-8225
       Email: lgross@scottcircle.com
       Website: www.scottcircle.com
Public relations & event-planning. (Woman, estab 2006, empl 11, sales $1,614,156, cert: WBENC)

8042   SEW, Inc.
       717 D St NW Ste 300
       Washington, DC 20004
       Contact: Thedis Miller CEO
       Tel: 202-403-4739
       Email: tmiller@4sew.com
       Website: www.4sew.com
Human capital mgmt svcs, customer relationship mgmt (CRM), large team operations support, business planning, executive coaching, administrative support. (Woman/AA, estab 2004, empl 1, sales $104,000, cert: NMSDC)

8043   Washingtonian Custom Media
       1828 L St NW, Ste 200
       Washington, DC 20036
       Contact: James Byles President
       Tel: 202-862-3500
       Email: jbyles@washingtonian.com
       Website: www.washingtoniancustommedia.com
Communications strategy, print & digital publications, magazines, brochures, white papers, annual reports, content development, content strategy, audience development, writing, editing, website design, graphic design, website development. (Woman, estab 1965, empl 80, sales $10,000,000, cert: WBENC)

Delaware

8044   Barron Marketing Communications
       833 Washington St
       Wilmington, DE 19801
       Contact: Patricia D. Barron President
       Tel: 302-658-1627
       Email: pbarron@barronmarketing.com
       Website: www.barronmarketing.com
Mktg print communications: direct mail, catalogs, displays, premiums, POS, broadcast, packaging, media, outdoor. (Woman, estab 1976, empl 9, sales $1,000,000, cert: State)

Florida

8045   A-Plus Meetings and Incentives
       901 Ponce de Leon Blvd. Ste 600
       Coral Gables, FL 33134
       Contact: Jay Klein COO
       Tel: 786-888-3203
       Email: jklein@aplusmeetings.com
       Website: www.aplusmeetings.com
Meeting planning, online registration, venue selection, audio-visual management, production development, airline travel, ground transportation & hospitality desk staffing. (Woman, estab 1993, empl 21, sales $10,382,504, cert: CPUC, WBENC)

8046   Avenue Event Group LLC
       501 N Orlando Ave Ste 313-312 Orlando, FL 32789
       Orlando, FL 32801
       Contact: Sean Hughes Marketing
       Tel: 650-784-0175
       Email: sean@avenueeventgroup.com
       Website: www.avenueeventgroup.com
National event planning & logistics services: Venue Selection, Meeting Logistics, Hotel Coordination, Group Transportation, Vendor Procurement, Unique Entertainment. (Woman, estab 2013, empl 5, sales $1,300,000, cert: WBENC)

8047   Chasm Communications, Inc.
       13045 W Linebaugh Ave Ste 101
       Tampa, FL 33626
       Contact: Jennifer Williams President
       Tel: 813-283-0908
       Email: jwilliams@chasmcommunications.com
       Website: www.chasmcommunications.com
Marketing & web design, app design, digital marketing & traditional print marketing. (Woman, estab 2006, empl 7, sales $845,317, cert: WBENC)

8048 Cordova Marketing Group
2702 Wright Ave
Winter Park, FL 32789
Contact: Tom Cordova President
Tel: 321-972-8181
Email: tom@covacova.com
Website: www.covacova.com
Multi-culutral Marketing, Sponsorship, Broadcasting, Naming Rights, Events, Ticket Sales, Community Outreach, Executive Recruitment. (Hisp, estab 1998, empl 2, sales $375,000, cert: NMSDC)

8049 Creative Zing Promotion Group
189 S Orange Ave Ste 1130a
Orlando, FL 32801
Contact: Pamela D Aniello President
Tel: 407-514-0044
Email: pamela@creativezing.com
Website: www.creativezing.com
Integrated marketing & promotions, complex contest & sweepstakes administration. (Woman, estab 2007, empl 9, sales $1,300,000, cert: WBENC)

8050 CRG Global, Inc.
3 Signal Ave, Ste B
Ormong Beach, FL 32174
Contact: Anastasia Mentavlos VP Sensory
Tel: 386-677-5644
Email: am@cssdatatelligence.com
Website: www.crgglobalinc.com
Custom market research services. (Woman, estab 1989, empl 530, sales $28,446,000, cert: WBENC)

8051 Detail Planners, LLC
1452 Distant Oaks Dr
Wesley Chapel, FL 33543
Contact: Anita Jentzen CEO
Tel: 813-991-1348
Email:
Website: www.detailplanners.com
Plan & manage corporate meetings & events. (Woman, estab 2004, empl 5, sales $1,900,000, cert: WBENC)

8052 Diper Designers LLC
7306 Exchange Dr
Orlando, FL 32809
Contact: Ricardo Contreras Business Devel Mgr
Tel: 407-208-2226
Email: rcontreras@diper.com
Website: www.diper.com
Designing & build customized exhibit displays; booths, pavilions, corporate events, retail stores, kiosks, among others. (Hisp, estab 1999, empl 19, sales $516,352, cert: City)

8053 EuroAmerican IP, LLC
2511 NW 16th Lane Bay 2
Pompano Beach, FL 33064
Contact: Tami Dana Mgr of Operations
Tel: 866-972-6467
Email: tami@euroamericanproducts.com
Website: www.EuroAmericanProducts.com
Manufacturers Reps/Distribution based business that provides various industries and government facilities with our unique line of products within the medical, outdoor and health & beauty arenas. (Woman, estab 2007, empl 15, sales $500,000, cert: State)

8054 Executive Meeting Management, Inc.
6996 Piazza Grande Ave Ste 314
Orlando, FL 32835
Contact: Heather Wilson President
Tel: 407-399-7681
Email: hwilson@execmm.com
Website: www.execmm.com
Meeting management. (Woman, estab 2004, empl 1, sales $1,026,779, cert: WBENC)

8055 Fortes Laboratories
1005 W Busch Blvd Ste 101
Tampa, FL 33612
Contact: Steven Seigel CFO
Tel: 813-390-6536
Email: info@forteslabs.com
Website: www.forteslabs.com
Drug testing, national forensic, toxicology laboratory, drug & alcohol testing. (Woman, estab 1994, empl 15, sales , cert: State)

8056 Fusion Communications, Inc.
8725 NW 18 Terrace, Ste 103
Miami, FL 33172
Contact: Annabel Beyra Partner
Tel: 786-574-2330
Email: annabel@fusioncomminc.com
Website: www.fusioncomminc.com
Public relations agency. (Minority, Woman, estab 2006, empl 5, sales $1,279,242, cert: NMSDC)

8057 Gossett Marketing
3701 Poinciana Ave
Coconut Grove, FL 33133
Contact: President
Tel: 305-443-1332
Email: danette@gossettmktg.com
Website: www.gossettmktg.com
Promotional products, awards, corporate apparel, banners, trade show booths, POP, creative design, direct mail, advertising. (Woman, estab 1992, empl 4, sales , cert: WBENC)

8058 HAS Art Solutions LLC
3139 Philips Hwy, Ste 100
Jacksonville, FL 32207
Contact: Heather Sams President
Tel: 904-503-9800
Email: hasams@hasartsolutions.com
Website: www.HASartsolutions.com
We are an art consulting, art design, and procurement firm with over 25 years of experience in providing clients with solutions to their aesthetic needs. We provide artwork and artwork programs to all types of businesses, from interior design (Woman, estab 2010, empl 7, sales $355,000, cert: State)

8059 HMB Enterprises LLC
5401 S Kirkman Rd, Ste 310
Orlando, FL 32819
Contact: Harry Bailey President
Tel: 678-887-7670
Email: hbailey@hmbenterprises.net
Website: www.hmbenterprises.net
Healthcare Risk Management System (HRMS) Airborne Pathogen Elimination system (KIlls MRCR, Staph and many other airborne pathogens under 3 microns) Purlalizer(KIlls MRCR, Staph (AA, estab 2005, empl 5, sales $425,000, cert: State, NMSDC)

8060   Imagine Enterprises International
8600 Commodity Circle, Ste 109
Orlando, FL 32819
Contact: Heidi Brumbach CEO
Tel: 407-409-7310
Email: heidi@technischcreative.com
Website: www.technischcreative.com
Event Planning & Production, Venue Research & Selection, Venue Negotiation & Contracting, Room Block Management, Speaker Selection, Event Marketing, Food & Beverage Management, Event Registration, Audio Visual. (Woman, estab 1999, empl 4, sales , cert: WBENC)

8061   Ingenium Research Boutique, Inc.
8057 Solitaire Ct
Orlando, FL 32836
Contact: Maria Parra President
Tel: 407-309-2742
Email: mlparra@ingeniumresearch.com
Website: www.ingeniumresearch.com
Qualitative marketing research, focus groups, ethnographic interviews, in-depth interviews, shop-alongs, qualitative techniques. (Minority, Woman, estab 2011, empl 2, sales $500,000, cert: WBENC)

8062   Inktel Direct
13975 NW 58th Ct
Miami Lakes, FL 33014
Contact: Jason Schlenker VP Business Dev
Tel: 305-523-1129
Email: jason.schlenker@inktel.com
Website: www.inktel.com
Direct marketing: call center, fulfillment, direct mail, database marketing. (Hisp, estab 1997, empl 580, sales , cert: NMSDC)

8063   ITC Translations USA Inc.
900 E Indiantown Rd, Ste 302
Jupiter, FL 33477
Contact: Allison Paxton Business Dev Mgr
Tel: 561-746-6242
Email: a.paxton@itcglobaltranslations.com
Website: www.itcglobaltranslations.com
Technical, scientific & communication translation services in over 25 languages. (Woman, estab 1999, empl 68, sales $8,600,000, cert: WBENC)

8064   JCQ Services, Inc
7200 Lake Ellenor Dr, Ste 130
Orlando, FL 32809
Contact: Eliana Fuguet Project Coord
Tel: 407-889-4944
Email: eliana@jcqservices.com
Website: www.jcqservices.com
We are a complete renovation subcontractor, from flooring to ceiling and moving, storage and transportation and selective demolition (Hisp, estab 2000, empl 25, sales $1,550,000, cert: State)

8065   Key Lime Interactive
8750 NW 36th St, Ste 475
Doral, FL 33178
Contact: Ania Rodriguez
Tel: 305-809-0555
Email: accounting@keylimeinteractive.com
Website: www.keylimeinteractive.com
Qualitative & quantitative research, usability testing, mobile research, card sorting, remote intercept testing, expert reviews, ethnography, competitive benchmarking, eye tracking, shop along. (Minority, Woman, estab 2009, empl 17, sales $3,686,319, cert: NMSDC, WBENC)

8066   Lingua Franca Translations, LLC
1111 Brickell Ave Ste 1140
Miami, FL 33156
Contact: Marcela Arbelaez CEO
Tel: 305-913-7193
Email: marcela.arbelaez@lftranslations.com
Website: www.lftranslations.com
Translations, interpretations & transcriptions into and from over 240 languages. (Minority, Woman, estab 2011, empl 3, sales $138,000, cert: NMSDC)

8067   M. Gill & Associates, Inc.
4770 Biscayne Blvd, Ste 1050
Miami, FL 33137
Contact: Marie Gill President
Tel: 305-576-7888
Email: info@mgillonline.com
Website: www.mgillonline.com
Management & public relations consulting. (Woman/AA, estab 1990, empl 10, sales , cert: State)

8068   Media Global Group, LLC
2000 Ponce de Leon Blvd
Coral Gables, FL 33134
Contact: Maria Gonzalez-Pacheco CEO
Tel: 786-431-4555
Email: mgonzalez@mggmedia.com
Website: www.mggmedia.com
Digital Media Outlets & Out-of-Home (OOH), TV, Radio & Print Media. (Minority, Woman, estab 2008, empl 10, sales $3,600,000, cert: NMSDC)

8069   Nobles Research, Inc.
8321 Golden Prairie Dr
Tampa, FL 33647
Contact: Kevin Nobles President
Tel: 813-977-7700
Email: kevin@noblesresearch.com
Website: www.noblesresearch.com
Qualitative research. (AA, estab 2001, empl 1, sales $270,000, cert: NMSDC)

8070   Orlando Conference Management Group, Inc.
13124 Sunkiss Loop
Windermere, FL 34786
Contact: Lori Lombardi Ryan President
Tel: 407-948-5706
Email: llr@ocmg.net
Website: www.ocmg.net
Meeting management, logistics & events planning. (Woman, estab 1993, empl 2, sales , cert: State, WBENC)

8071   Paragon Events, Inc.
352 NE 3rd Ave
Delray Beach, FL 33444
Contact: Renee Radabaugh CEO
Tel: 561-243-3073
Email: info@paragon-events.com
Website: www.paragon-events.com
Meeting & special events. (Woman, estab 1989, empl 12, sales $5,514,280, cert: WBENC)

8072   Pierson Grant Public Relations
6301 NW 5th Way, Ste 2600
Fort Lauderdale, FL 33309
Contact: President
Tel: 954-776-1999
Email: info@piersongrant.com
Website: www.piersongrant.com
Public relations planning; media relations; publicity; crisis communications; creating & managing community relations programs; writing newsletters, brochures, speeches; graphic design. (Woman, estab 1995, empl 15, sales $1,840,898, cert: WBENC)

8073   Prestige Auto Specialists
4250 St. Charles Way
Boca Raton, FL 33434
Contact: Marcello Serrato President
Tel: 954-428-6689
Email: mserrato@prestigeautous.com
Website: www.prestigeautous.com
Event production, media fleet management, marketing &
communication. (Hisp, estab 1985, empl 30, sales
$52,000,000, cert: NMSDC)

8074   Quest Corporation of America
17220 Camelot Court
Land O'Lakes, FL 34638
Contact: Sharlene Francois President
Tel: 813-926-2942
Email: corporate@usa.com.com
Website: www.QCAusa.com
Public relations, partnering, marketing, creative services,
media, publications, printing, aerial photography, advertis-
ing, technology support, web design & data storage,
transportation support svcs. (Woman, estab 1995, empl
14, sales $3,075,300, cert: State)

8075   RBB Public Relations LLC
355 Alhambra Cir Ste 800
Coral Gables, FL 33134
Contact: Marsha Rhymer Controller
Tel: 305-448-7450
Email: marsha.rhymer@rbbpr.com
Website: www.rbbpr.com
Marketing, Public Relations. (Woman, estab 2001, empl
81, sales $6,401,984, cert: WBENC)

8076   Republica, LLC
2153 Coral Way 5th Fl
Miami, FL 33145
Contact: Jorge A. Plasencia CEO
Tel: 786-347-4700
Email: jp@republica.net
Website: www.republica.net
Branding, advertising, promotions, digital and communica-
tions company. (Hisp, estab 2006, empl 100, sales
$14,500,000, cert: State, NMSDC)

8077   ROUGE 24, Inc.
5279 Grande Palm Cir
Delray Beach, FL 33484
Contact: Todd Victor Dir of Accounts
Tel: 561-213-0260
Email: todd.victor@rouge24.com
Website: www.rouge24.com
Brand Strategy, Identity Design, Packaging, Style Guides,
Adaptation, Process Management, Marketing Materials,
In-Store Signage. (Woman, estab 2009, empl 1, sales
$2,500,000, cert: WBENC)

8078   SFM Services, Inc.
9700 NW 79th Ave
Hialeah Gardens, FL 33016
Contact: Christian Infante VP
Tel: 305-818-2424
Email: cinfante@sfmservices.com
Website: www.sfmservices.com
Complete janitorial services, landscape services, and
security guard services. (Hisp, estab 1987, empl 480, sales
$12,000,000, cert: NMSDC)

8079   T. Mak's International, Inc.
2100 Corporate Sq Blvd, Ste 100
Jacksonville, FL 32216
Contact: Shannon Stoddard GBD
Tel: 904-855-4188
Email: shannon@2100tmaks.com
Website: www.2100tmaks.com
Mfr, international sourcing, advertising & marketing,
custom promotional products, advertising signage.
(Minority, Woman, estab 1985, empl 11, sales
$2,200,000, cert: WBENC)

8080   Trickey Jennus, Inc.
5300 W Cypress St Ste 285
Tampa, FL 33607
Contact: Kathie Craft Comella COO
Tel: 813-831-2325
Email: kathie@trickeyjennus.com
Website: www.trickeyjennus.com
Strategy review & rational, collaborative account
planning, strategic media planning, specialized direct
marketing, campaign development, web services, social
media strategy, creative services. (Woman, estab 2005,
empl 7, sales $1,015,266, cert: State)

8081   Vistra Communications, LLC
18315 N US Hwy 41
Lutz, FL 33549
Contact: Brian A. Butler President
Tel: 813-961-4700
Email: brian@consultvistra.com
Website: www.ConsultVistra.com
Public relations, strategic communications, homeland
security, information technology, management consult-
ing, training & curriculum development. (AA, estab
2007, empl 112, sales $22,716,235, cert: City, NMSDC,
8(a))

8082   Wragg & Casas Public Relations, Inc.
3191 Coral Way 607
Miami, FL 33145
Contact: Ramon Casas President
Tel: 305-372-1234
Email: rcasas@wraggcasas.com
Website: www.wraggcasas.com
Strategic counseling, media relations, reputation & crisis
management, brand visibility & public affairs. (Hisp,
estab 1991, empl 8, sales $1,200,000, cert: NMSDC)

Georgia

8083   Benchmarc360, Inc.
6340 Sugarloaf Pkwy Ste 200
Atlanta, GA 30097
Contact: CEO
Tel: 678-291-0011
Email:
Website: www.benchmarc360.com
Strategic solutions, strategic event marketing, confer-
ence, meeting & event mgmt, destination mgmt, trade
shows, incentive programs, site selection & contract
negotiations. (Woman, estab , empl , sales $32,800,000,
cert: NWBOC)

8084　BLH Consulting, Inc.
　　　502 Pryor St Ste 301
　　　Atlanta, GA 30312
　　　Contact: Betsy Helgager Hughes
　　　Tel:　404-688-0415
　　　Email: betsy@blhconsulting.net
　　　Website: www.blhconsulting.net
Multicultural public relations & marketing services.
(Woman/AA, estab 2002, empl 2, sales $350,000, cert:
WBENC)

8085　CMT Agency
　　　1417 Dutch Valley Place Ste A
　　　Atlanta, GA 30324
　　　Contact: Shelly Justice CEO
　　　Tel:　404-233-4644
　　　Email: sjustice@cmtagency.com
　　　Website: www.cmtagency.com
Spokesmodels, event staffing, brand ambassadors, product
demonstrators, celebrity look-a-likes & corporate present-
ers. (Woman, estab 2001, empl 11, sales $2,119,677, cert:
WBENC)

8086　Colour One O One, Inc.
　　　4995 Avalon Ridge Pkwy Ste 100
　　　Norcross, GA 30071
　　　Contact: Taylor Lepera Sales Assoc
　　　Tel:　404-350-1700
　　　Email: tlepera@studio101.com
　　　Website: www.colour101.com
Strategic marketing programs for the retail, food, bever-
age, sports & entertainment industries. (Woman, estab
1983, empl 9, sales $697,000, cert: WBENC)

8087　Creative Juice LLC
　　　75 Marietta St, Ste 503
　　　Atlanta, GA 30303
　　　Contact: Octavia Gilmore Owner
　　　Tel:　404-947-8599
　　　Email: octavia@itscreativejuice.com
　　　Website: www.itscreativejuice.com
Graphic design & web design services, logo, branding,
print design, infographics, brochures, tradeshow graphics,
marketing, web design & development, Wordpress, email
marketing, copy writing, blogging, local SEO & motion
graphics. (Woman/AA, Hisp, estab 2013, empl 4, sales
$315,000, cert: City)

8088　CyberAnalysis, LLC
　　　427 Rhodes House Dr
　　　Suwanee, GA 30024
　　　Contact: Jeanne Eidex President
　　　Tel:　770-614-6334
　　　Email: jeidex@eidexgroup.com
　　　Website: www.cyberanalysisllc.com
Market research: questionnaire design, data collection,
data analysis, reports, presentations, recommendations.
(Woman, estab 1999, empl 5, sales , cert: WBENC)

8089　EventEssentials, LLC
　　　1227 Rockbridge Rd Ste 208-238
　　　Stone Mountain, GA 30087
　　　Contact: Qualena Odom-Royes President
　　　Tel:　404-642-6064
　　　Email: qualena@eventsessential.com
　　　Website: www.eventsessential.com
Marketing, branding & messaging, special events, meet-
ings, corporate sponsorships, event promotion & produc-
tion, best practices, public relations. (Woman/AA, estab
2002, empl 2, sales $125,055, cert: NMSDC)

8090　Folio, Inc. Design & Illustration
　　　1145 Zonolite Rd NE, Ste 2
　　　Atlanta, GA 30306
　　　Contact: Margaret Lisi
　　　Tel:　404-888-6599
　　　Email: margaret@stir-marketing.com
　　　Website: www.stir-marketing.com
Marketing & communications services, create content &
media, employee engagement/change management &
event marketing. (Woman, estab 1993, empl 10, sales
$1,200,000, cert: WBENC)

8091　Global Organization and Planning Services, LLC
　　　2727 Skyview Dr. Unit 76
　　　Lithia Springs, GA 30122
　　　Contact: Vanessa Whitehead Managing Dir
　　　Tel:　770-574-4415
　　　Email: vanessa@globalorganizationplanning.com
　　　Website: www.globalorganizationplanning.com
Event planning & management services: business
meetings, conferences, tours, trips, receptions, cruises,
accommodations & travel, program & agenda develop-
ment, logistics management, etc. (Woman, estab 2002,
empl 20, sales , cert: State, City)

8092　Grow Now, LLC
　　　1320 Ellsworth Industrial Blvd NW
　　　Atlanta, GA 30318
　　　Contact: Bob McNeil CEO
　　　Tel:　404-254-3281
　　　Email: b.mcneil@grownowllc.com
　　　Website: www.grownowllc.com
Marketing communications, advertising, promotional
marketing, public relations & activations. (AA, estab
2013, empl 24, sales $8,600,000, cert: State, NMSDC)

8093　Insights Marketing
　　　3131 Piedmont Rd. Ste 205
　　　Atlanta, GA 30305
　　　Contact: Keshia Walker President
　　　Tel:　404-872-9899
　　　Email: kw@insights-mpc.com
　　　Website: www.insights-mpc.com
Multi-cultural research development & analysis, market-
ing, promotion, special event program development &
execution. (Woman/AA, estab 1998, empl 10, sales
$390,000, cert: NMSDC, WBENC)

8094　IROK Solutions, Inc.
　　　4002 Hwy 78, Ste 530-192
　　　Snellville, GA 30039
　　　Contact: Kunmi Oluleye President
　　　Tel:　770-982-1000
　　　Email: kunmi@shebafoods.com
　　　Website: www.shebafoods.com
Marketing consulting. (Woman/AA, estab 2000, empl 4,
sales , cert: WBENC)

8095　Juice Studios
　　　1123 Zonolite Rd, Ste 7B
　　　Atlanta, GA 30306
　　　Contact:　Co-Owner
　　　Tel:　404-817-9369
　　　Email: Atlanta@TheJuiceStudios.com
　　　Website: www.thejuicestudios.com
Meeting planning & special events. (Woman, estab
2004, empl 1, sales $2,560,189, cert: WBENC)

8096   LightPath OM LLC dba strut AGENCY
1235 Oriole Dr, SW
Atlanta, GA 30311
Contact: Tashion Macon, PhD, MBA President
Tel: 404-855-4568
Email: tashion@strutagency.com
Website: www.strutagency.online
Creative design, cross-cultural communications, and consumer marketing strategy. (Woman/AA, estab 2008, empl 15, sales , cert: NMSDC, WBENC)

8097   Maveryck Marketing Group, LLC
3726 Upton Ct
Ellenwood, GA 30294
Contact: Keith Philpot Managing Member
Tel: 770-681-0731
Email: kphilpot@maveryckmarketing.com
Website: www.maveryckmarketing.com
Strategic market planning & implementation. (AA, estab 2005, empl 1, sales , cert: NMSDC)

8098   McDowell Information Group Public Relations LLC.
233 Mitchell St, Ste 500
Atlanta, GA 30303
Contact: Anita Carlyle Sr Managing Partner
Tel: 844-462-3693
Email: acarlyle@mccevents.ca
Website: www.mcdowellpr.com
Public relations, Web Development, Voice Overs, Military/ Corporate engagement, Minority Community Relations, Stage Productions, lighting & Event Planning. (AA, estab 2014, empl 10, sales , cert: NMSDC)

8099   Modo Modo Agency LLC
3175 Northside Pkwy NW Bldg 300, Ste 700
Atlanta, GA 30327
Contact: Moira Vetter CEO
Tel: 770-436-3100
Email: moira@modomodoagency.com
Website: www.modomodoagency.com
Marketing, brand development, thought leadership, lead generation, internal communications, publications, web sites, integrated marketing campaigns, direct response. (Woman, estab 2007, empl 15, sales $1,535,000, cert: WBENC)

8100   National Business Advisory Group, Inc.
540 Powder Springs St, Ste C16
Marietta, GA 30064
Contact: Silah Williams CEO
Tel: 770-974-8100
Email: swilliams@mynbag.com
Website: www.mynbag.com
Market research & strategy consulting services. (AA, estab 2011, empl 5, sales $150,000, cert: NMSDC)

8101   Outsource Events, Inc.
1647 Emory Place Dr, NE
Atlanta, GA 30329
Contact: President
Tel: 404-982-1640
Email: info@blackironbystro.com
Website: www.outsourceevents.com
Event & meeting planning. (Woman, estab 2003, empl 2, sales $156,620, cert: WBENC)

8102   Phase 3 Marketing and Communications
280 Interstate North Circle SE, Ste 300
Atlanta, GA 30339
Contact: Jim Cannata EVP Strategic Growth
Tel: 404-367-9898
Email: jim.cannata@phase3mc.com
Website: www.phase3mc.com
Integrated marketing services from ideation to execution, including creative, digital, public relations- and large- format printing and warehousing and distribution. (As-Pac, estab 2001, empl 167, sales $28,000,000, cert: NMSDC)

8103   Printing Systems, LLC
2759 Delk Rd, Ste 2300
Marietta, GA 30067
Contact: Sherrica Davis New Business Specialist
Tel: 404-855-3021
Email: sdavis@printingsys.com
Website: www.printingsys.com
At Printing Systems we utilize innovation to maximize target marketing success, increase return on investments and impact CRM through increasing consumer databases and identifying consumer purchasing habits. (AA, estab 2002, empl 7, sales $2,300,000, cert: NMSDC)

8104   Q&A Entertainment Inc.
1514 E Cleveland Ave Ste 116
East Point, GA 30344
Contact: Sheila Merritt Dir New Business Dev
Tel: 404-762-5665
Email: smerritt@qandaentertainment.com
Website: www.QandAEntertainment.com
Event production & marketing services: production & management, marketing & promotion, ideation & creation & sponsorships. (Woman, estab 1999, empl 3, sales $830,788, cert: WBENC)

8105   Sojo, Inc.
4400 N Point Pkwy Ste 153
Alpharetta, GA 30022
Contact: Sophie Gibson President
Tel: 770-360-6330
Email: sophie.gibson@sojoinc.com
Website: www.sojoinc.com
Technology marketing, marketing communications. (Woman/AA, estab 2001, empl 11, sales $2,300,000, cert: NMSDC)

8106   Southeast Exhibits and Events
1000 Marietta St Ste 124
Atlanta, GA 30318
Contact: Jamal Lewis President
Tel: 470-865-2007
Email: info@southeastexhibit.com
Website: www.Southeastexhibit.com
Trade show exhibits & design. (Woman/AA, estab 2014, empl 5, sales , cert: NMSDC)

8107   SPAR Solutions, LLC
360 Interstate North Pkwy SE Ste 220
Atlanta, GA 30339
Contact: Swami Ganapathy Solutions Consulting
Tel: 855-772-7765
Email: sganapathy@sparsolutions.com
Website: www.sparsolutions.com
CRM Solutions for Sales, Marketing, Customer Service, Field Service, Contract Management, telephony, Email, Chat, Social Media. (As-Ind, estab 2003, empl 60, sales $3,670,000, cert: NMSDC)

8108   TDEFERIAMEDIA, Inc.
9795 Talisman Dr
Johns Creek, GA 30022
Contact: Antenor Tony President
Tel: 404-630-0639
Email: contact@tdeferiamedia.com
Website: www.tdeferiamedia.com
Marketing, branding consulting & creative production, ethnic market study & plans, media buying, translation & interpretation in Spanish, digital & social media expertise. (Hisp, estab 2007, empl 1, sales $140,000, cert: NMSDC)

8109   The Capre Group
115 Perimeter Center Place Ste 1120
Atlanta, GA 30346
Contact: Kim Gavlak Controller
Tel: 678-443-2280
Email: kgavlak@capregroup.com
Website: www.capregroup.com
Strategic marketing consulting. (Woman, estab 2001, empl 14, sales $4,750,000, cert: WBENC)

8110   The Crafton Group, Inc.
1107 Lanier Blvd Atlanta
Georgia, GA 30306
Contact: Crafton Langley President
Tel: 404-873-3019
Email: crafton.langley@thecraftongroup.com
Website: www.thecraftongroup.com
Marketing & communications: research, strategy, branding, design, advertising, promotion, product development, media. (Woman, estab 1996, empl 15, sales , cert: City, WBENC)

8111   V & L Research and Consulting, Inc.
3340 Peachtree Rd Ste 1800
Atlanta, GA 30326
Contact: Dydra Virgil Principal
Tel: 770-908-0003
Email: vlresearch@mindspring.com
Website: www.vlresearch.com
Market research: focus groups; in-depth interviews; Ethnographies, telephone & intercept surveys. (Woman/AA, estab 1991, empl 2, sales $492,052, cert: WBENC)

8112   VonCreations, Inc.
2886 Branchwood Dr
East Point, GA 30344
Contact: Yvonne J. Wiltz CEO
Tel: 404-347-1054
Email: vonco3@bellsouth.net
Website: www.voncreations.com
Meeting planning & management, conferences, special events & marketing campaigns. (Woman/AA, estab 1989, empl 2, sales $145,279, cert: NMSDC, WBENC, 8(a))

Idaho

8113   Milligan Events
1116 S Vista Ave #189
Boise, ID 83705
Contact: Milligan Events Owner
Tel: 208-387-0770
Email: diversitymatters@milliganevents.com
Website: www.milliganevents.com
Event & meeting planning & logistics. (Woman, estab 1994, empl 8, sales $756,972, cert: WBENC)

Illinois

8114   Bamboo Worldwide Inc.
30 N Racine Ave, Ste 300
Chicago, IL 60607
Contact: Tracy Thirion President
Tel: 773-227-4848
Email: tracyt@bambooinc.com
Website: www.bambooworldwide.com
Consulting services specializing in branding, innovation & market research. (Woman, estab , empl , sales $1,700,545, cert: WBENC)

8115   Beaman Public Relations, Inc.
401 N Michigan Ave, Ste 1300
Chicago, IL 60611
Contact: Robin Beaman President
Tel: 312-751-9689
Email: rbeaman@beamaninc.com
Website: www.beamaninc.com
Public relations, marketing & advertising services. (Woman/AA, estab 1996, empl 7, sales $1,084,431, cert: State, City, NMSDC, WBENC)

8116   Belle Communications
1390 Jaycox Rd
Chicago, IL 60673
Contact: Kate Finley CEO
Tel: 614-304-1463
Email: kate@bellecommunication.com
Website: www.bellecommunication.com/
Digital public relations and social media. (Woman, estab 2013, empl 16, sales $1,112,921, cert: WBENC)

8117   Classical Marketing LLC
2300 Cabot Dr Ste 390
Lisle, IL 60532
Contact: Susan Mazanek Managing Partner
Tel: 847-969-9006
Email: smazanek@classicalmarketing.com
Website: www.classicalmarketing.com
Marketing programs in Business to Business and Business to Consumer categories for clients in retail, financial services, automotive, health care. (Woman, estab 1999, empl 8, sales $1,700,687, cert: WBENC)

8118   Creative & Response Research Services, Inc.
500 N Michigan Ave, 12th Fl
Chicago, IL 60611
Contact: Robbin Jaklin CFO
Tel: 312-828-9200
Email: robbinj@crresearch.com
Website: www.crresearch.com
Custom market research, internet surveys, phone surveys, focus groups, qualitative & quantitative research. (Woman, estab 1960, empl 120, sales $23,268,888, cert: State, WBENC)

8119   Customer Lifecycle, LLC
1112 W Boughton Rd, Ste 365
Bolingbrook, IL 60440
Contact: Principal
Tel: 630-412-8989
Email: info@customerlifecycle.us
Website: www.customerlifecycle.us
Full-service qualitative and quantitative market research, plan, support and deploy customer satisfaction and loyalty research and align the stages of the customer lifecycle to improve customer loyalty. (Woman, estab 2008, empl 16, sales , cert: WBENC)

8120 Data Research Inc.
2525 Cabot Dr Ste 107
Lisle, IL 60532
Contact: Leslie Gunner Losh President
Tel: 630-281-8307
Email: lgunnerlosh@mindseyeresearch.com
Website: www.mindseyeresearch.com
Market research services. (Woman, estab 1982, empl 46, sales $3,600,000, cert: WBENC)

8121 DCC Marketing, LLC
2130 N 22nd St
Decatur, IL 62526
Contact: Kara Demirjian Huss President
Tel: 217-421-7580
Email: ksd@dccmarketing.com
Website: www.dccmarketing.com
Integrated marketing, communications and digital services. (Woman, estab 2000, empl 10, sales $1,200,000, cert: State, WBENC)

8122 Elemento L2, LLC
401 S LaSalle St, Ste 1501
Chicago, IL 60605
Contact: Ivan Lopez Managing Dir
Tel: 312-465-2355
Email: chemistry@elementol2.com
Website: www.elementol2.com
Multicultural marketing, experiential, PR, shopper & digital marketing. (Hisp, estab 2011, empl 15, sales $1,048,333, cert: NMSDC)

8123 Eved Services, Inc.
4811 Oakton St, Ste 250
Skokie, IL 60077
Contact: Alexis Feczko Dir of Sales Operations
Tel: 773-764-7000
Email: sales@eved.com
Website: www.eved.com/
Event services, destination management, technology services. (Woman, estab 2004, empl 25, sales $8,100,000, cert: WBENC)

8124 Fridkin Valo, Inc. dba TPG Live Events
210 N Cass Ave, Ste A
Westmont, IL 60559
Contact: Christina Piedlow CEO
Tel: 630-353-1308
Email: cpiedlow@tpgliveevents.com
Website: www.tpgliveevents.com
Event management and marketing expertise, creativity. (Woman, estab 1994, empl 9, sales $3,835,057, cert: WBENC)

8125 Frontline Public Strategies, Inc.
100 E. Washington St
Springfield, IL 62701
Contact: Kim Robinson President
Tel: 217-528-3434
Email: kimrobinson@frontline-online.net
Website: www.frontline-online.net
Public relations, marketing, event planning & public affairs. (Woman, estab 2001, empl 12, sales $1,200,000, cert: State, WBENC)

8126 Gerard Design, Inc.
28371 Davis Pkwy
Warrenville, IL 60555
Contact: Carolyn Gerard President
Tel: 630-355-0775
Email: carolyn@gerarddesign.com
Website: www.gerarddesign.com
Strategic Branding and Design, Communications, Graphic Design. (Woman, estab 0, empl , sales , cert: WBENC)

8127 Group O, Inc.
4905 77th Ave
Milan, IL 61264
Contact: Mike De La Cruz Sr VP Bus Dev & Div
Tel: 210-213-2258
Email: supplierdiversity@groupo.com
Website: www.groupo.com
Single source integrated marketing solutions, customer loyalty, rebate administration & fulfillment, gift cards, inbound & outbound call center services, 4-color printing, print personalization, direct mail & fulfillment. (Hisp, estab 1974, empl 1200, sales $900,424,000, cert: NMSDC)

8128 Ivan Carlson & Associates
2224 W Fulton
Chicago, IL 60612
Contact: Tina Carlson President
Tel: 312-829-4616
Email: tina@ivancarlson.com
Website: www.ivancarlson.com
Event production & management, logistics, staging, sound & lighting. (Woman, estab 1974, empl 25, sales $3,370,000, cert: WBENC)

8129 JAK Graphic Design, LLC
4949 Forest Ave
Downers Grove, IL 60515
Contact: Jill Kerrigan Founder & CEO
Tel: 630-512-0500
Email: jill@jakcd.com
Website: www.jakcd.com
Creative concepting, design and final art production in both print and digital channels including, direct mail, internal corporate employee communications, POP, emails, landing pages, animated and static banner ads, wireframes and web. (Woman, estab 1995, empl 6, sales $1,500,000, cert: WBENC)

8130 JRS Consulting, Inc.
1316 Gregory Ave
Wilmette, IL 60091
Contact: Jenny Schade President
Tel: 847-920-1701
Email: jenny.schade@JRSConsulting.net
Website: www.JRSconsulting.net
Market research, management consulting, marketing & internal & external communications initiatives. (Woman, estab 2002, empl 1, sales , cert: WBENC)

8131 JumpGarden Consulting, LLC
1534 Washington Ave
Wilmette, IL 60091
Contact: Sheila Cahnman President
Tel: 312-286-0119
Email: sheila@jumpgardenllc.com
Website: www.jumpgardenllc.com
Healthcare design, planning & marketing solutions. (Woman, estab 2014, empl 1, sales , cert: State, City, WBENC)

8132   K.O. Strategies
       2903 N Wolcott Ave, Ste B
       Chicago, IL 60657
       Contact: Kate O'Malley CEO
       Tel: 312-307-4206
       Email:
       Website: www.kostrategies.com
Strategic communications, public affairs, stakeholder
relations, crisis leadership & strategic planning/presenta-
tions. (Woman, estab 2006, empl 1, sales , cert: WBENC)

8133   Kathy Schaeffer and Associates, Inc.
       17 N State St, Ste 1690
       Chicago, IL 60602
       Contact: Kathy Schaeffer President
       Tel: 312-251-5100
       Email: kschaeffer@ksapr.com
       Website: www.ksapr.com
Public relations. (Woman, estab 1994, empl 5, sales , cert:
City)

8134   L3 Agency
       1452 E 53rd
       Chicago, IL 60615
       Contact: Larvetta Loftin CEO
       Tel: 312-268-5207
       Email: larvetta.loftin@l3eventeurs.com
       Website: www.thel3agency.com
Marketing and communications, digital content creation,
PR, advertising, brand experiences, corporate sponsorship,
community outreach, and social philanthropy. (Woman/
AA, estab 2000, empl 4, sales , cert: NMSDC)

8135   Liberty Lithographers, Inc.
       18625 W Creek Dr
       Tinley Park, IL 60477
       Contact: Angela Hipelius CEO
       Tel: 708-633-7450
       Email: ahipelius@libertycreativesolutions.com
       Website: www.libertycreativesolutions.com
Marketing services: graphic design, direct mail campaigns,
research, promotions & loyalty campaigns, marketing
collateral, advertising, web design, brand development,
corporate identity. (Woman, estab 1964, empl 65, sales
$12,000,001, cert: WBENC)

8136   Live Marketing
       1201 N Clark St
       Chicago, IL 60610
       Contact: Alyssa Lavik Relationship Mgr
       Tel: 312-787-4800
       Email: alavik@livemarketing.com
       Website: www.livemarketing.com
Trade show engagement strategies. (Woman, estab 1978,
empl 175, sales $7,100,000, cert: WBENC)

8137   Magnolia Insights
       350 N Orleans St, Ste 9000N
       Chicago, IL 60654
       Contact: Tania Haigh CEO
       Tel: 646-768-4279
       Email:
       Website: www.magnoliainsights.com
Integrated marketing communications agency. (Hisp, estab
2014, empl 5, sales , cert: NMSDC)

8138   Marketing Innovators International Inc.
       9701 W Higgins Rd Ste 400
       Rosemont, IL 60018
       Contact: Merrie Marinovich Acct Exec
       Tel: 847-696-1111
       Email: mmarinovich@marketinginnovators.com
       Website: www.marketinginnovators.com
Employee recognition award programs. (Woman, estab
1978, empl 70, sales , cert: WBENC)

8139   Matrex Exhibits
       301 S Church St
       Addison, IL 60101
       Contact: VP Business Dev
       Tel: 630-628-2233
       Email:
       Website: www.matrexhibits.com
Tradeshow exhibits, design, construction & mgmt,
graphic design & production, tradeshow svcs. (Woman,
estab 1987, empl 66, sales $27,000,000, cert: WBENC)

8140   Mekky Media Relations
       913 S. I-Oka Ave
       Mount Prospect, IL 60056
       Contact: Bill Rossi COO
       Tel: 312-315-0181
       Email: supplierdiversity@mekkymedia.com
       Website: www.mekkymedia.com
Public relations firm. (Woman, estab 2016, empl 5, sales
$1,125,901, cert: WBENC)

8141   Metaphrasis Language and Cultural Solutions, LLC
       1147 W Ohio, Ste 306
       Chicago, IL 60714
       Contact: Elizabeth Colon President
       Tel: 815-464-1423
       Email: ecolon@metaphrasislcs.com
       Website: www.metaphrasislcs.com
Language services, interpretation, translation & corporate trainings. (Minority, Woman, estab 2007, empl 6,
sales , cert: State, WBENC)

8142   MHJohnson & Associates, Inc.
       1918 S Michigan Ave Ste 302
       Chicago, IL 60616
       Contact: Marilyn Johnson Principal
       Tel: 312-949-9164
       Email: marilyn@mhjohnson.com
       Website: www.mhjohnson.com
Marketing management, program, product development
& mgmt, organizational development. (Woman/AA, estab
2001, empl 2, sales $225,000, cert: WBENC)

8143   ModelPeople Inc
       301 W Grand Ave Ste 139
       Chicago, IL 60654
       Contact: Claire Brooks President
       Tel: 858-755-7150
       Email: cbrooks@modelpeopleinc.com
       Website: www.modelpeopleinc.com
Qualitative research, ethnographic research, consumer
research, deep insights research, consumer video
production, consumer brand consulting. (Woman, estab
2000, empl 3, sales $1,400,000, cert: WBENC)

8144 Neiger Design, Inc.
1515 Sherman Ave
Evanston, IL 60201
Contact: President
Tel: 847-328-1328
Email: info@neigerdesign.com
Website: www.neigerdesign.com
Graphic design, marketing & communications: website design, annual reports, logos & corporate identity, brochures, employee communications, packaging, magazine &book design. (Woman, estab 1989, empl 6, sales , cert: WBENC)

8145 PACO Communications, Inc. d/b/a PACO Collective
400 S. Green St Unit H
Chicago, IL 60607
Contact: Ozzie Godinez CEO
Tel: 312-281-2040
Email: marketing@pacocollective.com
Website: www.pacocollective.com
Hispanic marketing, advertising, public relations & community outreach, web design & development. (Hisp, estab 2006, empl 40, sales $19,900,000, cert: NMSDC)

8146 PCH Communications
600 W Fluton Fl 4
Chicago, IL 60661
Contact: Alice Pollard SVP Operations
Tel: 312-384-1906
Email: alice@discovercg.com
Website: www.commongroundmgs.com
Advertising/Marketing, Strategic Planning/Dev, Creative, PR, Event Marketing, Multicultural Marketing, Digital Marketing , Shopper/Retail Marketing, Content Development, Research Promotions/Sponsorship's. (AA, Hisp, estab 2014, empl 256, sales $35,276,000, cert: NMSDC)

8147 Production Partners Company LLC
911 Rock Spring Rd
Naperville, IL 60565
Contact: Haves McNeal CEO
Tel: 312-735-1486
Email: haves@pp-co.biz
Website: www.pp-co.biz
Marketing Communications. (AA, estab 2017, empl 5, sales , cert: NMSDC)

8148 Public Communications Inc.
1 E Wacker Dr Ste 2450
Chicago, IL 60601
Contact: Pamela Oettel CFO/COO
Tel: 312-558-1770
Email: poettel@pcipr.com
Website: www.pcipr.com
Develop integrated communications strategies: Advocacy Programs, Board Counsel, Branding & Positioning, Competitive Analysis, Consumer Mktg, Conservation & Wildlife Issues, Crisis/Issues Mgmt & Monitoring. (Woman, estab 1962, empl 50, sales $6,111,500, cert: State, WBENC)

8149 Quicksilver Associates, Inc.
18 W Ontario St
Chicago, IL 60654
Contact: Diane MacWilliams President
Tel: 312-943-7622
Email: dianem@quicksilvernow.com
Website: www.quicksilvernow.com
Print, video, meeting planning, production, web & interactive media. (Woman, estab 1976, empl 22, sales $4,600,000, cert: WBENC)

8150 Reilly Connect
625 N Michigan Ave Ste 1705
Chicago, IL 60611
Contact: Kim Smith President
Tel: 312-600-6780
Email: ksmith@tcgad.com
Website: www.tcgad.com
Social media marketing, brand activation & events, video production, public relations. (Woman, estab 1996, empl 5, sales , cert: WBENC)

8151 Research Explorers, Inc
1111 New Trier Ct
Wilmette, IL 60091
Contact: Lisa Gaines McDonald President
Tel: 847-853-0237
Email: lisa@researchexplorers.com
Website: www.reserachexplorers.com
Market research & consulting services: qualitative research, focus groups, in-depth interviews, ethnographies, brain storming & idea generation sessions. (Woman/AA, estab 1994, empl 1, sales $305,087, cert: City, NMSDC)

8152 Revel Global Events
1402 N Western Ave
Chicago, IL 60622
Contact: Dir of Sales
Tel: 773-292-9100
Email: hello@therevelgroup.com
Website: www.revelglobalevents.com
Event planning & production, experiential events. (Woman, estab 2007, empl 15, sales $3,000,000, cert: WBENC)

8153 Signature Media Group Talk
1327 W Washington Blvd
Chicago, IL 60607
Contact: Pam Redwood President
Tel: 312-226-5552
Email: pam@smgspeakers.com
Website: www.smgspeakers.com
Public communications, speakers bureau, brand creation awareness, client advertising, ad management, creative services, custom publishing, event planning, media planning, media relations, corporate communications. (Woman/AA, estab 2009, empl 2, sales $400,000, cert: State, City)

8154 Simple Truth Communication Partners Inc
314 W Superior St Ste 300
Chicago, IL 60654
Contact: Rhonda Kokot Managing Partner
Tel: 312-376-0360
Email: m.person@yoursimpletruth.com
Website: www.yoursimpletruth.com
Brand strategy & positioning, B2B, sales force & corporate/internal communications. (Woman, estab 1988, empl 20, sales $9,803,864, cert: WBENC)

8155 Strategic Marketing, Inc.
350 S Northwest Hwy Ste 304
Park Ridge, IL 60068
Contact: Leslie Reinhardt Controller
Tel: 847-720-7500
Email: lreinhardt@smialcott.com
Website: www.smialcott.com
Marketing research services. (Woman, estab 1980, empl 23, sales $7,636,812, cert: WBENC)

8156   The Wynning Experience
      2325 South Michigan Ave
      Chicago, IL 60616
      Contact: Lead Event Planner
      Tel: 312-800-3605
      Email: hello@thewynningexperience.com
      Website: www.thewynningexperience.com
Event & meeting mgmt. (Woman/AA, estab 1996, empl 5, sales $400,000, cert: NMSDC, WBENC)

8157   Total Event Resources
      1920 N Thoreau Dr Ste 105
      Schaumburg, IL 60173
      Contact: Lynnea Walsh Dir of Operations
      Tel: 847-397-2200
      Email: lwalsh@total-event.com
      Website: www.total-event.com
Corporate communications, event production, entertainment [roduction, meeting management, experiential learning & destination management. (Woman, estab 1995, empl 15, sales $3,320,000, cert: WBENC)

8158   Wedgeworth Business Communications
      2215 Enterprise Dr, Ste 1506
      Westchester, IL 60154
      Contact: Pamela G. Wedgeworth President
      Tel: 708-223-0019
      Email: pamela@wedgeworthbiz.com
      Website: www.wedgeworthbiz.com
Visual communications: video production, multimedia creation, print & electronic collateral, event coordination. (Woman/AA, estab 1999, empl 2, sales $320,000, cert: City, WBENC)

Indiana

8159   Avant Healthcare
      630 W Carmel Dr
      Carmel, IN 46032
      Contact: Jeff Sears Exec Dir
      Tel: 317-208-3600
      Email: info@avanthc.com
      Website: www.AvantHC.com
Peer-to-peer marketing for pharmaceutical and biotechnology companies, creating comprehensive communication strategies & plans. (Woman, estab 1994, empl 200, sales $22,000,000, cert: WBENC)

8160   Coles Marketing Communications
      3950 Priority Way Ste 106
      Indianapolis, IN 46240
      Contact: Barbara Coles President
      Tel: 317-571-0051
      Email: bcoles@colesmarketing.com
      Website: www.colesmarketing.com
Marketing communications services: graphic design, web design, e-communications, public relations, media relations, word of mouth marketing, videography, photography. (Woman, estab 1985, empl 10, sales $1,250,000, cert: State, City)

8161   TalentCode Management Group
      1801 S Liberty Dr, Ste 300
      Bloomington, IN 47403
      Contact: Melanie Hoffman Business Devel
      Tel: 888-381-7248
      Email: melanie.hoffman@employbridge.com
      Website: www.employbridge.com
Staffing services. (Minority, estab 1997, empl 3000, sales $3,000,000,000, cert: NMSDC)

Kansas

8162   A.S.K. Associates, Inc.
      1505 Kasold Dr
      Lawrence, KS 66047
      Contact: Kenneth Martinez President
      Tel: 800-315-4333
      Email: kenm@askusa.com
      Website: www.askusa.com
Conference, convention, trade show, meeting, seminar support services. (Minority, Woman, estab 1979, empl 15, sales $6,600,000, cert: WBENC)

8163   Exhibit Arts, LLC
      326 N Athenian
      Wichita, KS 67203
      Contact: Beth Harshfield Managing Member
      Tel: 316-264-2915
      Email: beth@exhibitarts.net
      Website: www.exhibitarts.net
Exhibit design, fabrication & management, project management, conference support services, warehousing & fulfillment center services. (Minority, Woman, estab 2000, empl 160, sales $18,843,000, cert: NMSDC, NWBOC)

8164   Meeting Excellence, Inc.
      7300 West 110th St Ste 700
      Overland Park, KS 66210
      Contact: Kory Oplinger Dir of Sales
      Tel: 913-693-4675
      Email: koplinger@meeting-excellence.com
      Website: www.meeting-excellence.com
Corporate meetings, events & incentive travel services. (AA, estab 2003, empl 4, sales $1,113,929, cert: NMSDC)

8165   Sassafras Marketing, Inc.
      13600 Santa Fe Trail Dr
      Lenexa, KS 66215
      Contact: Jenny Holton CEO
      Tel: 913-888-7400
      Email: creativejobs@sassafrasmarketing.co
      Website: www.sassafrasmarketing.com
Marketing, customer/consumer promotions & B2B communication. (Woman, estab 2000, empl 8, sales $1,342,000, cert: WBENC)

8166   The Lexinet Corporation
      701 N Union
      Council Grove, KS 66846
      Contact: Lindsey Boyer President
      Tel: 620-767-7000
      Email: indseyb@lexinetcorporation.com
      Website: www.lexinetcorporation.com
Marketing campaigns & programs, custom personalized variable data printed direct mail, fully-integrated marketing centers, multi-channel solutions. (Woman, estab 1991, empl 18, sales $3,100,000, cert: WBENC)

Kentucky

8167   ConvenePro
      1792 Alysheba Way Ste 160
      Lexington, KY 40509
      Contact: Delphine Hepp Acct Dir
      Tel: 859-276-0065
      Email: dhepp@convenepro.com
      Website: www.convenepro.com
Event management, marketing & communications, live speaker programs, conferences & trade shows, promotional presentations, satellite broadcasts/webcasts, live & virtual training workshops, product training. (Woman, estab 1995, empl 50, sales , cert: NWBOC)

8168   Corporate World Public Relations
4017 Whiteblossom Estates Ct
Louisville, KY 40241
Contact: Ray Callender, Jr. VP
Tel: 678-592-8516
Email: ray.callender@corpworldpr.com
Website: www.corpworldpr.com
Exhibits design & management services. (AA, estab , empl , sales $262,000, cert: NMSDC)

8169   Digital Business Solutions, Inc.
517 S Fourth St
Louisville, KY 40202
Contact: Cynthia Masters CEO
Tel: 502-562-7895
Email: rfp@dbswebsite.com
Website: www.dbswebsite.com
Web & digital development, design, strategy & marketing, websites, apps, mobile, hosting, interactive infographics, SEO, digital business strategy, lead generation online marketing. (Woman, estab 2000, empl 20, sales $1,700,000, cert: WBENC)

8170   Intrinzic Marketing & Design
One Levee Way, Ste 3121
Newport, KY 41071
Contact: Tami Beattie Office Mgr
Tel: 859-292-5061
Email: tami@intrinzicinc.com
Website: www.intrinzicinc.com
Marketing & design: marketing, design & interactive svcs, creative concepting, campaign dev, graphic design, copywriting, public relations, website design, email marketing & media planning. (Woman, estab 1989, empl 12, sales , cert: WBENC)

8171   Mackey Group LLC
2250 Mackey Pike
Nicholasville, KY 40356
Contact: Nancy Wiser President
Tel: 859-887-0866
Email: nancy@wiserstrategies.com
Website: www.wiserstrategies.com
Public relations, marketing, market research, corporate relations, crisis planning & response, media relations, branding creative services, writing, graphic design, photography, video production & editing, print production management. (Woman, estab 2011, empl 1, sales $300,000, cert: WBENC)

8172   New West LLC
9630 Ormsby Station Rd
Louisville, KY 40223
Contact: Melvin Graham Managing Dir
Tel: 888-867-7811
Email: mgraham@newwestagency.com
Website: www.newwestagency.com
Advertising, Public Relations, Brand Strategy, Website & Mobile App Development, Social Media, Multicultural Marketing, SEO/SEM/PPC, Event Planning & Video Production. (AA, estab 2002, empl 28, sales $5,500,000, cert: NMSDC)

Massachusetts

8173   Causemedia, Inc.
50 Hunt St Ste 140
Watertown, MA 02472
Contact: Donna Latson Gittens Principal
Tel: 617-558-6850
Email: info@causemedia.com
Website: www.moreadvertising.com
Communications, advertising & marketing agency. (Woman/AA, estab 1997, empl 8, sales $4,636,330, cert: State, NMSDC, WBENC)

8174   Color Media Group, LLC
4 Copley Pl, Ste 120
Boston, MA 02116
Contact: Josefina Bonilla President
Tel: 617-266-6961
Email: josefina@colorboston.com
Website: www.colormagazineusa.com
Web advertising, signature events, event management, strategic marketing initiatives, new markets, media buying services, public relations. (Minority, Woman, estab 2007, empl 3, sales $289,000, cert: State)

8175   Conover + Gould Strategic Communications, Inc.
69 Milk St Ste 101
Westborough, MA 01581
Contact: Heather Conover CEO
Tel: 508-789-9273
Email: hconover@conovergould.com
Website: www.conovergould.com
Public relations & marketing communications, environmental communications & event management. (Woman, estab 1984, empl 9, sales $1,528,016, cert: State)

8176   Consolidated Marketing Services, Inc.
841 Woburn St
Wilmington, MA 01887
Contact: Andrew Bausman key acct Mgr
Tel: 800-474-5756
Email: abausman@cmsassociates.com
Website: www.cmsassociates.com
Marketing svcs: fulfillment, printing, mailing, promotional products, graphics & catalogs. (Woman, estab , empl , sales $4,000,000, cert: WBENC)

8177   Early Bird Power LLC
1 Adams St
Milton, MA 02186
Contact: Shaun Pandit CEO
Tel: 888-763-2759
Email: shaunpandit@earlybirdpower.com
Website: www.earlybirdpower.com
Facilitator of procurement services for electricity, natural gas, and renewable energy credits. Energy Consulting and risk management. (As-Ind, estab 2009, empl 1, sales $500,000, cert: State)

8178   EMI Strategic Marketing Inc.
15 Broad St
Boston, MA 02109
Contact: Paul OBrien VP Finance
Tel: 617-224-1101
Email: pobrien@emiboston.com
Website: www.emiboston.com
Marketing services. (Woman, estab 1989, empl 45, sales $7,000,000, cert: State, WBENC)

8179 Global Link Language Services, Inc.
71 Commercial St Ste 218
Boston, MA 02109
Contact: Carol Ann Managing Dir
Tel: 617-451-6655
Email: cmichel@gleneagleadv.com
Website: www.languagetranslate.com
Intl communication svcs: translation, interpretation,
localization, multilingual typesetting & desktop publishing.
(Woman, estab 1996, empl 4, sales $650,000, cert: State)

8180 Grand Design, Inc.
42 Chestnut St Ste 2
Salem, MA 01970
Contact: Debra Glabeau Principal
Tel: 978-741-0112
Email: dglabeau@greatisland.com
Website: www.greatisland.com
Graphic design & marketing communications solutions,
brand development, logos & corporate identity systems,
naming & taglines, collateral & brochures, websites, email
& direct mail programs, print advertising, sales kits.
(Woman, estab 1982, empl 4, sales $223,742, cert: State)

8181 Inspired Marketing
20 Maple St 4th Fl, Ste 1
Springfield, MA 01103
Contact: Lauren Mendoza Office Mgr
Tel: 413-303-0101
Email: lauren@inspiredmarketing.biz
Website: www.inspiredmarketing.biz
Marketing, Event Planning, Social Media, Media Buying,
Advertising, Graphic Design (Woman, estab 2009, empl 6,
sales $632,920, cert: WBENC)

8182 Kelley Chunn & Associates
184 Dudley St, Ste 106
Boston, MA 02119
Contact: Kelley Chunn Principal
Tel: 617-427-0997
Email: kc4info@aol.com
Website: www.kelleychunn.com
Multicultural marketing & public relations services.
(Woman/AA, estab 1991, empl 1, sales $160,000, cert:
State)

8183 NXTevent, Inc.
60K St, 4th Fl
Boston, MA 02127
Contact: Joanne O'Connell General Mgr
Tel: 617-904-9053
Email: connect@nxtevent.com
Website: www.nxtevent.com
Event & destination management. (Woman, estab 2001,
empl 8, sales $2,447,766, cert: State, WBENC)

8184 The Castle Group, Inc.
38 Third Ave Ste 200
Charlestown, MA 02129
Contact: Wendy Spivak Treasurer
Tel: 617-337-9535
Email: wspivak@thecastlegrp.com
Website: www.thecastlegrp.com/
Public relations & events management. (Woman, estab
1996, empl 23, sales $5,300,000, cert: WBENC)

8185 Twirling Tiger Press Inc.
7 Jeffrey Road
Franklin, MA 02038
Contact: Maureen Joyce President
Tel: 508-520-3258
Email: mjoyce@twirlingtigermedia.com
Website: www.twirlingtigermedia.com
Writing & graphic design, creation of design & imagery,
development, scheduling & trafficking, & content
generation, advertising, printing, promotions, publications, RFPs & proposals, social media, websites, white
papers. (Woman, estab 2013, empl 2, sales $270,000,
cert: WBENC)

Maryland

8186 Bates Creative Group, LLC
1119 East West Hwy
Silver Spring, MD 20910
Contact: Debra Bates Schrott President
Tel: 301-495-8844
Email: debbie@batescreative.com
Website: www.batescreative.com
Branding & Identity, Magazine Design & Redesign, Event
Marketing, Marketing Collateral, Web Design & Develop-
ment, iPad UI Design, Annual Reports, Media Kits.
(Woman, estab 2003, empl 11, sales , cert: WBENC)

8187 BrightKey, Inc.
60 West St Ste 300
Annapolis, MD 21401
Contact: Krystal Dyer Business Solutions
Tel: 301-604-3305
Email: businessdevelopment@brightkey.net
Website: www.brightkey.net/
Marketing research, strategy & creative services.
(Woman, estab 1988, empl 600, sales $34,212,531, cert:
WBENC)

8188 Hargrove Inc.
One Hargrove Dr
Lanham, MD 20706
Contact: Meghan Muniz Natl Sales Exec
Tel: 301-306-3000
Email: meghanmuniz@hargroveinc.com
Website: www.hargroveinc.com
Events, exhibits & trade shows: venue selection, staffing,
design, menu development, security, building of stages,
set design, AV & lighting services. (Woman, estab 1946,
empl 225, sales $73,000,000, cert: WBENC)

8189 Humdinger Enterprises LLC
PO Box 4542
Crofton, MD 21114
Contact: Alexis Jenkins Managing Member
Tel: 410-279-0205
Email: alexis@humdingerenterprise.com
Website: www.humdingerenterprises.com
Event planning: festivals, concerts, meetings, award
shows & broadcast events. (Woman, estab 2008, empl 5,
sales $230,681, cert: State)

8190 JDC Events, LLC
8720 Georgia Ave Ste 801
Silver Spring, MD 20910
Contact: Jennifer Collins President
Tel: 240-512-4219
Email: jennifer@jdc-events.com
Website: www.jdc-events.com
Meeting & event management: custom-designed
logistical solutions, guidance & communications,
meetings, conferences & special events. (Woman/AA,
estab 1997, empl 4, sales $2,040,000, cert: NMSDC,
WBENC, 8(a))

8191 McMillon Communications, Inc.
      12902 Argyle Circle
      Fort Washington, MD 20744
      Contact: Doris McMillon CEO
      Tel: 301-292-9141
      Email: Doris@McMillonCommunications.com
      Website: www.mcmilloncommunications.com
Marketing support solutions, public relations & strategic
partnership development. (Woman/AA, estab 1986, empl
1, sales $4,528,979, cert: State, WBENC)

8192 Mjach Designs
      5100 Buckeystown Pike Ste 250
      Frederick, MD 21704
      Contact: FirstName LastName Admin
      Tel: 410-366-0505
      Email: rose@mjachdesigns.com
      Website: www.mjachdesigns.com
Graphic design, marketing & communications, web design
& implementation, print production, marketing & advertising, public relations, media planning & buying, research &
copywriting. (Woman, estab 2003, empl 5, sales $336,640,
cert: State, City)

8193 MultiLingual Solutions, Inc.
      11 N Washington St Ste 300
      Rockville, MD 20850
      Contact: Paul Keys VP Business Dev
      Tel: 301-424-7444
      Email: pkeys@mlsolutions.com
      Website: www.mlsolutions.com
Document Translation, On-site and Remote Interpretation,
Website & Software Localization, Multicultural Marketing
& Advertising, Language, Cultural and Executive Training &
Curriculum Development, Desktop Publishing. (Minority,
Woman, estab 2002, empl 162, sales $9,729,040, cert:
NMSDC, WBENC)

8194 Pensari, LLC
      107 Theodora Court
      Forest Hill, MD 21050
      Contact: Hans Plate
      Tel: 410-588-5465
      Email: hans.plate@pensari.com
      Website: www.pensari.com
Market research specializing in healthcare research,
qualitative & quantitative research. (Hisp, estab 2013,
empl 1, sales , cert: NMSDC)

8195 Slice, Inc dba SliceWorks
      20301 Highland Hall Dr
      Montgomery Village, MD 20886
      Contact: Kathleen Rabil CEO
      Tel: 301-519-8101
      Email: kathi@slice-works.com
      Website: www.slice-works.com
Graphic design, marketing strategy consulting, marketing
communications & campaign development, social media
strategy consulting & execution, website design & development, brand consulting, publication layout & design.
(Woman, estab 1997, empl 4, sales $445,690, cert:
WBENC)

8196 Sutter Design, Inc. dba The Sutter Group
      4640 Forbes Blvd. Ste 160A
      Lanham, MD 20706
      Contact: Karen Sutter President
      Tel: 301-459-5445
      Email: karen@sutter-group.com
      Website: www.sutter-group.com
Marketing, advertising & public relations: brand,
creating logos, corporate collateral, websites, direct mail
& e-marketing campaigns, advertising & public relations.
(Woman, estab 1987, empl 8, sales $1,000,000, cert:
State)

8197 The Hannon Group, LLC
      10002 Edgewater Terr, Ste 100
      Fort Washington, MD 20744
      Contact: Sandra Wills Hannon President
      Tel: 301-839-2744
      Email: info@thehannongroup.com
      Website: www.thehannongroup.com
Public relations, strategic planning, market research,
materials development, communications training &
consulting services. (Woman/AA, estab 1991, empl 2,
sales $2,404,262, cert: WBENC)

8198 TMNcorp
      8720 Georgia Ave, Ste 206
      Silver Spring, MD 20910
      Contact: Nhora Barrera Murphy President
      Tel: 301-565-0770
      Email: nbarrera@tmncorp.com
      Website: www.tmncorp.com
Communication & social marketing, advertising, media
relations, research & evaluation & cultural adaptation
services. (Minority, Woman, estab 1999, empl 20, sales
$4,850,000, cert: State)

8199 Transient Identiti, Inc.
      11 Webster Hill Ct
      Clarksburg, MD 20871
      Contact: Albert Thompson Dir Brand Strategy
      Tel: 301-792-8535
      Email: albert@transientidentiti.com
      Website: www.transientidentiti.com
Digital Marketing: mobile, social, display, search, apps,
email, advanced targeting. (AA, estab 2002, empl 7,
sales $424,000, cert: NMSDC)

8200 What Works Studio LLC
      8 Market Pl, Ste 300
      Baltimore, MD 21202
      Contact: Brooke Allen CEO
      Tel: 410-800-0788
      Email: hello@whatworksstudio.com
      Website: www.whatworksstudio.com
Full service creative marketing agency, digital, social
media, and content marketing. (Woman, estab 2009,
empl 2, sales $560,557, cert: City, WBENC)

Michigan

8201 Airfoil Public Relations, Inc.
      336 N Main St
      Royal Oak, MI 48067
      Contact: Sharon Neumann SVP Finance & Admin
      Tel: 248-304-1400
      Email: neumann@airfoilgroup.com
      Website: www.airfoilgroup.com
Marketing communications. (Woman, estab 2000, empl
37, sales $7,200,000, cert: WBENC)

8202 Archer Corporate Services
6703 Haggerty Ste B
Belleville, MI 48111
Contact: Dennis Archer Dir of Operations
Tel: 734-713-3100
Email: diversity@theacsadvantage.com
Website: www.theacsadvantage.com
Marketing support svcs: B2B fulfillment, rebates, direct
response, sweepstakes, customer service, merchandising.
(AA, estab 2004, empl 25, sales $15,400,000, cert: NMSDC)

8203 BPI Communications, LLC
13700 Oakland Ave
Highland Park, MI 48203
Contact: Jim Suddendorf EVP Sales/mlktg
Tel: 313-957-5459
Email: j.suddendorf@bpicommunications.com
Website: www.bpicommunications.com
Fulfillment & direct marketing solutions. (AA, estab 2005,
empl 10, sales $107,000,000, cert: NMSDC)

8204 Bromberg & Associates, LLC
3141 Caniff St.
Hamtramck, MI 48212
Contact: Carly Priehs Business Devel Specialist
Tel: 313-871-0080
Email: carly@brombergtranslations.com
Website: www.brombergtranslations.com
Translations & interpretations: over 60 languages.
(Woman, estab 1999, empl 20, sales , cert: WBENC)

8205 Collaborative Advantage Marketing
2987 Franklin St
Detroit, MI 48207
Contact: Sales Rep
Tel: 248-723-0793
Email: accounting@camtrade.com
Website: www.camtrade.com
Category Management Quality Assurance Programs Total
Product Design Business Analysis Brand Management Full
Service Marketing Headquarter Selling. (Woman, estab
1999, empl 18, sales , cert: WBENC)

8206 Harris Marketing Group, Inc.
102 Pierce St
Birmingham, MI 48009
Contact: Wendy Vadnais Finance Dir
Tel: 248-723-6300
Email: wvadnais@harris-hmg.com
Website: www.harris-hmg.com/
Integrated marketing campaigns, loyalty programs, brand
advertising, targeted direct mail, fulfillment, media, public
relations, training materials, website development, event
marketing & viral marketing. (Woman, estab 1976, empl
10, sales $4,425,995, cert: WBENC)

8207 Maestro LLC
7107 Elm Valley Dr
Kalamazoo, MI 49009
Contact: Tagg Petersen Dir Business Dev
Tel: 800-319-2122
Email: tagg@meetmaestro.com
Website: www.meetmaestro.com
Training, brand consulting, management consulting
services, solution based contractors. (Woman, estab 2007,
empl 31, sales $7,612,178, cert: WBENC)

8208 RSVP Premier Group, LLC
900 Wilshire Dr Ste 202
Troy, MI 48084
Contact: Tamika Brown CEO
Tel: 248-663-4107
Email: tbrown@rsvppremier.com
Website: www.rsvppremier.com
Event planning & management, meeting planning,
conference planning, incentive trips, trade shows/expos,
event design & décor, event production, celebrity
entertainment, talent & speaker booking. (Woman/AA,
estab 2002, empl 4, sales $109,450, cert: WBENC)

8209 Skyline Exhibits West Michigan
4768 Danvers Dr. SE
Kentwood, MI 49512
Contact: Eloy Cantu President
Tel: 616-301-8708
Email: cantul@skylinewm.com
Website: www.skyline.com
Trade show marketing, seminars, workshops. (Hisp,
estab 2004, empl 5, sales $900,000, cert: NMSDC)

8210 Smith-Dahmer Associates, LLC
116 State St
Saint Joseph, MI 49085
Contact: Lori Stanwood Dir Key Accounts
Tel: 269-983-4748
Email: loristanwood@smithdahmer.com
Website: www.smithdahmer.com
Marketing research & consulting, custom qualitative &
quantitative methodologies, innovation & design
research processes. (Woman, estab 1995, empl 30, sales
$9,000,000, cert: WBENC)

8211 Special D Events, Inc.
535 Woodward Heights
Ferndale, MI 48220
Contact: Carol Galle CEO
Tel: 248-336-8600
Email: administrator@specialdevents.com
Website: www.specialdevents.com
Corporate event planning. (Woman, estab 1992, empl
17, sales $2,200,000, cert: WBENC)

8212 Strategic Market Research Group, Inc.
37129 Saint Martins St
Livonia, MI 48152
Contact: Ami Nienus President
Tel: 734-452-9104
Email: ami@smrginc.com
Website: www.smrginc.com
Market research. (Woman/As-Ind, estab 2007, empl 1,
sales , cert: WBENC)

8213 Vista Latinos LLC
6582 Horncliffe
Clarkston, MI 48346
Contact: Terry Beltran-Miller President
Tel: 248-978-7491
Email: tbm@vistalatinos.com
Website: www.VistaLatinos.com
Marketing consulting services. (Minority, Woman, estab
2005, empl 1, sales $150,000, cert: WBENC)

8214   Wilson-Taylor Associates, Inc.
242 Lighthouse Circle
Manistee, MI 49660
Contact: Joanne Cleaver President
Tel: 231-291-1275
Email: jycleaver@wilson-taylorassoc.com
Website: www.wilson-taylorassoc.com
Content strategy & execution, writing, editing, research, website content, digital publishing, strategic communication consulting, communication training, career training, media training, communication coaching. (Woman, estab 1998, empl 2, sales $110,000, cert: WBENC)

Minnesota

8215   AllOut Marketing, Inc.
5775 Wayzata Blvd Ste 700
St. Louis Park, MN 55416
Contact: Ruth Lane CEO
Tel: 952-404-0800
Email: ruthlane@alloutsuccess.com
Website: www.alloutsuccess.com
Medical marketing consulting, market research, web development, graphic design, event management & public relations. (Minority, Woman, estab 1995, empl 8, sales $722,000, cert: State)

8216   Azul 7, Inc.
800 Hennepin Ave Ste 700
Minneapolis, MN 55403
Contact: Sara O'Brien Business Devel Lead
Tel: 612-767-4335
Email: hello@azul7.com
Website: www.azul7.com
Build better brands, products & services, strategy & innovation consulting, research, digital product & service design along with innovation process training. (Woman, estab 2007, empl 16, sales $1,868,437, cert: WBENC)

8217   Char Mason & Associates, LLC, dba Mason Creative
695 Mount Curve Blvd
Saint Paul, MN 55116
Contact: Owner
Tel: 651-698-2678
Email: char@masoncreative.biz
Website: www.masoncreative.biz
Event planning agency. (Woman, estab 2000, empl 1, sales $117,469, cert: State)

8218   Creative Connections
4049 Blackhawk Rd
Eagan, MN 55122
Contact: Marianne Badar Ohman Owner
Tel: 651-261-7886
Email: marianne@creativeconnections.net
Website: www.creativeconnections.net
Communications consulting, marketing communications project management, conference, meeting, tradeshow & event planning & production, team leadership, teambuilding training & services. (Woman, estab 1998, empl 1, sales , cert: City)

8219   D.Trio Marketing Group
401 N Third St, Ste 480
Minneapolis, MN 55401
Contact: Fred Driver Business Dev Dir
Tel: 612-436-0401
Email: fdriver@dtrio.com
Website: www.dtrio.com
Direct marketing, strategy, creative, list, DP, print and lettershop production, fulfillment & graphic design services. (Woman, estab 2000, empl 12, sales $3,500,000, cert: WBENC)

8220   deZinnia, Inc.
1032 W 7th St
St. Paul, MN 55102
Contact: Michele Boone CEO
Tel: 651-695-1041
Email: sbboone@dezinnia.com
Website: www.dezinnia.com
Program management, graphic design, marketing, marketing communications, digital architecture. (Woman, estab 1993, empl 14, sales $1,322,045, cert: State, City, WBENC)

8221   Five Star Productions
7400 Metro Blvd
Minneapolis, MN 55439
Contact: Cindy Black President
Tel: 952-831-7309
Email: cjblack@fivestarproductions.net
Website: www.fivestarproductions.net
Full-service production & event mgmt, natl sales meetings & conventions; recognition, incentive, & awards programs; entertainment and keynote speakers; product launches; philanthropic & special events. (Woman, estab 1989, empl 3, sales $1,300,000, cert: WBENC)

8222   Futura Marketing, Inc.
9531 W 78th St Ste 250
Eden Prairie, MN 55344
Contact: Kelly Wold Smith President
Tel: 952-843-5400
Email: kelly@futuramarketing.com
Website: www.futuramarketing.com
Marketing svcs: strategic planning, project management & creative design. (Woman, estab 1999, empl 13, sales $1,146,520, cert: WBENC)

8223   Group Ventures Inc.
1770 James Ave S, Ste 2
Minneapolis, MN 55403
Contact: Ann Wellmuth President
Tel: 612-821-0511
Email: ann@groupventuresinc.com
Website: www.groupventuresinc.com
Event & meeting planning, coordination & execution of incentive trips, sales & organizational meetings, board of directors meetings, conventions & tradeshows. (Woman, estab 1997, empl , sales $14,000,000, cert: WBENC)

8224   KDG InterActive, Inc.
8010 Demontreville Trail
Lake Elmo, MN 55042
Contact: Lynette Kramer President
Tel: 651-748-8480
Email: lynette@kdg.com
Website: www.kdg.com
Design & develop interactive marketing, education & training solutions. (Woman, estab 1991, empl 11, sales $1,200,000, cert: WBENC)

8225   LEE Branding
       945 Broadway St NE Ste 280
       Minneapolis, MN 55413
       Contact: Terri Lee CEO
       Tel: 612-843-8477
       Email: terri@leebranding.com
       Website: www.leebranding.com
Consumer-minded, strategic brand development. (Woman, estab 2011, empl 15, sales $4,100,000, cert: WBENC)

8226   Neka Creative LLC
       PO Box 211481
       Saint Paul, MN 55121
       Contact: Rosemary Ugboajah President
       Tel: 651-207-9656
       Email: rosemaryu@nekacreative.com
       Website: www.nekacreative.com
Brand development, Competitive Analysis, Brand Audits, Qualitative Research, Quantitative Research, Strategic Positioning, Brand Development, Culture Plans, Brand Workshops
Brand Blueprints, Marketing/Communication. (Woman/AA, estab 2009, empl 1, sales , cert: NMSDC)

8227   Nina Hale Inc.
       100 S 5th St, Ste 2000
       Minneapolis, MN 55402
       Contact: Sarah Petit Sales & Marketing Mgr
       Tel: 612-392-2427
       Email: businessinquiry@ninahale.com
       Website: www.ninahale.com
Digital direct marketing; search engine optimization (SEO), paid placement, social media consulting, analytics & reporting, local search. (Minority, Woman, estab , empl , sales $14,000,000, cert: WBENC)

8228   One 2 One Marketing Inc.
       12101 12th Ave South
       Burnsville, MN 55337
       Contact: Elaine Grundhauser CEO
       Tel: 952-567-2730
       Email: elaine.g@one2onemktg.com
       Website: www.one2onemktg.com
Strategic promotional programs. (Woman, estab 1995, empl 9, sales $1,606,966, cert: WBENC)

8229   Perkins & Associates, LLC
       400 Grovaland Ave, Ste 2309
       Minneapolis, MN 55403
       Contact: Frank Perkins Owner
       Tel: 612-810-8361
       Email: frank@perkinsbridge.com
       Website: www.perkinsbridge.com
Marketing & business development. (AA, estab 2000, empl 1, sales $125,000, cert: City, NMSDC)

8230   Showcraft, Inc.
       1357 Larc Industrial Blvd
       Burnsville, MN 55337
       Contact: Jeryl Beaulieu President
       Tel: 952-890-4200
       Email: jeryl@showcraft.com
       Website: www.showcraft.com
Trade show exhibits, events & environments. (Minority, Woman, estab 1996, empl 14, sales $500,000, cert: WBENC)

8231   SmartBase Solutions LLC
       411 Washington Ave N
       Minneapolis, MN 55401
       Contact: Kris Lynch CEO
       Tel: 612-767-9940
       Email: klynch@smartbasesolutions.com
       Website: www.smartbasesolutions.com
Database marketing solutions, measure, analyze, & improve marketing & sales activities. (Woman, estab 2005, empl 20, sales , cert: WBENC)

8232   The Research Edge LLC
       1821 University Ave W, Ste N177
       St. Paul, MN 55104
       Contact: Cheryl Powers President
       Tel: 651-644-6006
       Email: cheryl@theresearchedge.com
       Website: www.theresearchedge.com
Marketing research services, focus groups, in-depth interviews, qualitative research, quantitative research, phone surveys, online surveys, online focus groups, customized market research services full-service market research services. (Woman, estab 1995, empl 5, sales $303,360, cert: WBENC)

8233   The Social Lights, LLC
       610 SE 9th St, Ste 101
       Minneapolis, MN 55414
       Contact: Emily Pritchard CEO
       Tel: 612-803-8833
       Email: emily@thesocial-lights.com
       Website: www.thesociallights.com
Strategy development, creative production, influencer management, media buying, and social media management. (Woman, estab 2011, empl 40, sales $4,632,928, cert: WBENC)

8234   Touch Of Magic Inc.
       PO Box 9311
       St. Paul, MN 55109
       Contact: Lori Hurley Chief Entertainment Officer
       Tel: - -
       Email: lori@atouchofmagicentertainment.com
       Website: www.atouchofmagicentertainment.com
Event planning, Company Picnics, Corporate Events, Holiday Parties, Banquets, Trade Shows, Sales Meetings, Festivals, Fairs, Mitzvahs, Birthday Parties, Team Building, Schools, Churches, etc. (Woman, estab 1986, empl 2, sales $250,000, cert: WBENC)

8235   Tunheim
       8009 34th Ave South
       Minneapolis, MN 55425
       Contact: Ginny Melvie Sr Exec Assistant/Consultant
       Tel: 952-851-1600
       Email: gmelvie@tunheim.com
       Website: www.tunheim.com
Public Relations, Public Affairs, Strategic Communications, Crisis Communications, Branding - Marketing, Research & Opinion Polling. (Woman, estab 1990, empl 25, sales $5,000,000, cert: WBENC)

8236 Type A Events, LLC
10701 Red Circle Dr
Minnetonka, MN 55343
Contact: CEO
Tel: 763-682-4846
Email: events@typeaevents.com
Website: www.typeaevents.com
Strategic event management. (Woman, estab 2009, empl 40, sales $9,000,000, cert: WBENC)

8237 Visions, Inc.
8801 Wyoming Ave N
Brooklyn Park, MN 55445
Contact: Jon Otto President
Tel: 763-425-4251
Email: jon.otto@visionsfirst.com
Website: www.visionsfirst.com
Web design, print design, advertising & promotion, corporate identification, logo branding, packaging, interactive media, flash animation, video & special effects, 3D animation, web-based applications. (Nat Ame, estab 1985, empl 109, sales $14,207,330, cert: NMSDC)

Missouri

8238 Brighton Agency, Inc.
7711 Bonhomme Ave Ste 100
Saint Louis, MO 63105
Contact: Tina VonderHaar CEO
Tel: 314-726-0700
Email: accounting@brightonagency.com
Website: www.brightonagency.com
Strategic planning, brand development, digital marketing & production, marketing consulting, public relations, advertising, promotions, media planning, audio & video production, event marketing, online, mobile & app development. (Woman, estab 1989, empl 71, sales $9,030,143, cert: State, WBENC)

8239 Credit Financial Group Inc.
141 Chesterfield Business Pkwy
Chesterfield, MO 63005
Contact: Vincent Andaloro President
Tel: 636-536-5344
Email: vince@latinpak.com
Website: www.latinpak.com
Direct marketing services. (Hisp, estab 1996, empl 11, sales $1,600,000, cert: State, NMSDC)

8240 Decision Insight Inc.
2940 Main St
Kansas City, MO 64108
Contact: Tami Kaegi Office Mgr
Tel: 816-221-0445
Email: info@decisioninsight.com
Website: www.decisioninsight.com
Market research services. (Woman, estab 1983, empl 22, sales $3,440,000, cert: WBENC)

8241 Moxi Events, LLC
1904 Grassy Ridge Rd
Saint Louis, MO 63122
Contact: Jaime Ratino Acct Mgr
Tel: 615-454-2008
Email: jratino@moxievents.com
Website: www.moxievents.com
Corporate event planning, meetings, conferences, incentive programs & special events. (Woman, estab 2008, empl 7, sales $267,125, cert: WBENC)

8242 Mozaic Management, Inc.
5257 Shaw Ave Ste 204
St. Louis, MO 63110
Contact: Mary Ann Gibson CEO
Tel: 314-446-6400
Email: mgibson@mozaicltd.com
Website: www.mozaicltd.com
Marketing communications: strategic brand consulting, concept & design, creative execution, digital photography, illustration, photo retouching, interactive web services, art production, prepress, large format digital printing, sales promotion, etc. (Woman, estab 2003, empl 130, sales $30,000,000, cert: WBENC)

8243 MT & Associates, LLC
222 S Meramec Ave, Ste 202
St. Louis, MO 63105
Contact: Mishely Tisius President
Tel: 314-896-0275
Email: mt@mtapractice.com
Website: www.mtapractice.com
Sign language interpreting services. (Woman, estab 2013, empl 5, sales , cert: State, City, WBENC)

8244 Pixie Stuff LLC
18 Brighton Way
Clayton, MO 63105
Contact: Jennifer Hein Chief Business Officer
Tel: 314-368-4730
Email: jennifer@hiredink.com
Website: www.hiredink.com
Develop outreach programs that engage, educate and empower your target audience. (Woman, estab 2003, empl 10, sales $800,000, cert: State, WBENC)

8245 Stakeholder Insights, LLC
319 N 4th St Ste 820
St. Louis, MO 63102
Contact: Lisa Richter Managing Principal
Tel: 314-454-1923
Email: lisa@stakeholderinsights.com
Website: www.stakeholderinsights.com
Market & employee research services, supports branding, change management, competitive intelligence, customer experience, employee engagement and retention, message testing, public opinion & website usability. (Woman, estab 2006, empl 3, sales $408,312, cert: WBENC)

8246 The Vandiver Group, Inc.
16052 Swingley Ridge Road Ste 210
St. Louis, MO 63017
Contact: Donna Vandiver CEO
Tel: 314-991-4641
Email: tvg@vandivergroup.com
Website: www.vandivergroup.com
Strategic communications & public relations, corporate image & reputation management, branding, market research & training. (Woman, estab 1993, empl 10, sales $1,432,900, cert: State, WBENC)

North Carolina

8247 3 Birds Marketing, LLC
505-B W Franklin St
Chapel Hill, NC 27516
Contact: Layton Judd President
Tel: 919-913-2750
Email: layton@3birdsmarketing.com
Website: www.3birdsmarketing.com
Technology, software, integrated marketing platform, marketing, digital marketing, multichannel marketing, email marketing, email newsletters, digital newsletters, social media mgmt, social media mktg. (Woman, estab 2009, empl 60, sales $3,769,500, cert: WBENC, NWBOC)

8248 ABZ Creative Partner
1300 S Mint St, Ste 100
Charlotte, NC 28203
Contact: President
Tel: 704-374-1072
Email: worksmart@abzcreative.com
Website: www.abzcreativepartners.com
Marketing communications & graphic design. (Woman, estab 1982, empl 11, sales , cert: State)

8249 Avantgarde Translations
5960 Fairview Rd Ste 400
Charlotte, NC 28210
Contact: Jael Williams Administrative Asst
Tel: 704-496-2735
Email: submissions@avantgardetranslations.com
Website: www.avantgardetranslations.com
Translating written material, interpretation services, revising, editing, proofreading & laying out translated documents, cultural consulting. (Woman/AA, estab 2004, empl 3, sales $200,789, cert: NMSDC, WBENC)

8250 Bellomy Research, Inc.
175 Sunnynoll Ct
Winston-Salem, NC 27106
Contact: Glen Kelley Sr Dir of Admin
Tel: 336-721-1140
Email: glen.kelley@bellomy.com
Website: www.bellomyresearch.com
Marketing research services: design, data collection, analysis, interpretation, reporting & delivering point-of-view. (Woman, estab 1977, empl 100, sales $14,600,000, cert: State)

8251 Confero, Inc.
535 Keisler Dr Ste 204
Cary, NC 27518
Contact: Elaine Buxton President
Tel: 919-469-5200
Email: ebuxton@conferoinc.com
Website: www.conferoinc.com
Mystery shopping & customer satisfaction studies, training, brand management. (Woman, estab 1987, empl 23, sales $2,670,000, cert: WBENC)

8252 Content Spectrum
1832 Folly Gate Ct
Charlotte, NC 28262
Contact: David Springston Owner
Tel: 980-309-1465
Email: contentspectrum@gmail.com
Website: www.contentspectrum.net
Copywriting, Editing, Graphic design (banners, fliers, magazines, newsletters, posters, etc.), Translation services, Website development & maintenance. (Woman/AA, estab 2015, empl 1, sales , cert: NMSDC)

8253 It's My Affair, LLC
8711 Walden Ridge Dr
Charlotte, NC 28216
Contact: Kenneth Fields President
Tel: 704-394-4928
Email: kffields@it-henhouse.com
Website: www.itsmyaffair.com
Special events & meeting management: meetings, conferences, tradeshow management, grand openings, corporate recognition, launch parties, incentives. (Woman/AA, estab 2002, empl 2, sales , cert: WBENC, 8(a))

8254 Lockman-Brooks Marketing Services, LLC
6135 Park Dr S Ste 510
Charlotte, NC 28210
Contact: Linda Lockman-Brooks President
Tel: 704-293-5666
Email: linda@lockmanbrooks.com
Website: www.lockmanbrooks.com
Strategic marketing consulting: commununity relations & outreach, leadership consulting, communications planning & project management. (Woman/AA, estab 1998, empl 1, sales , cert: NMSDC)

8255 Lyerly Agency
4819 Park Rd
Charlotte, NC 28209
Contact: Elaine Lyerly CEO
Tel: 704-525-3937
Email:
Website: www.lyerly.com
Advertising, marketing, public relations & interactive svcs. (Woman, estab 1977, empl 4, sales $976,184, cert: State, City)

8256 TCG Events
2923 S. Tryon St Ste 230
Charlotte, NC 28203
Contact: Travis Holmes President
Tel: 704-376-1943
Email: info@tbsfreightmanagement.com
Website: www.tcgevents.com
Event planning & production, video production, graphic design and art direction, conference mgmt, entertainment production, incentive programs, corporate awards programs, destination management. (Woman, estab 1985, empl 5, sales $2,400,000, cert: WBENC)

8257 The Media Pro
4613 Hunters Creek Lane
Raleigh, NC 27606
Contact: Jill Hammergren Owner
Tel: 919-805-1061
Email: jill@themediapro.biz
Website: www.themediapro.biz
Media, marketing & communications, visual storytelling, creative writing, videos, animations & graphic, live TV, network programming, PSAs, video, film, e-learning, government, training & & multimedia purposes. (Woman, estab 1987, empl 0, sales , cert: WBENC)

8258 The Special Event Company
6112 Saint Giles St
Raleigh, NC 27612
Contact: Ly Nguyen Dir Business Devel
Tel: 919-459-8785
Email: bp@recredit.co
Website: www.specialeventco.com/
Event & meeting management. (Woman, estab 2001, empl 15, sales $5,000,000, cert: WBENC)

Nebraska

8259 Bozell and Jacobs LLC
1022 Leavenworth St
Omaha, NE 68102
Contact: Robin Donovan President
Tel: 402-965-4300
Email: rdonovan@bozell.com
Website: www.bozell.com
Marketing Communications, Branding, Digital Marketing, Interactive Design & Development, Social Media, Media, Public Relations, Market Research, Data Analytics. (Woman, estab 1921, empl 38, sales $3,200,000, cert: WBENC)

New Jersey

8260 AG Marketing & Consulting Group
554 W Broad St 1st Fl Rear
Westfield, NJ 07090
Contact: April Gregory President
Tel: 908-456-5700
Email: april@aprilgregoryinc.com
Website: www.agmarketingconsulting.com
Brand development, event marketing & marketing planning, social media & web implementation services. (Woman/AA, estab 2000, empl 3, sales $250,000, cert: State)

8261 Baldwin & Obenauf, Inc.
50 Division St Ste 401
Somerville, NJ 08876
Contact: Joanne Obenauf Founder
Tel: 908-685-1510
Email: jmobenauf@baldwinandobenauf.com
Website: www.bnoinc.com
Marketing & communications, strategic, creative & production, brand strategy, identity packages, advertising, print & digital collateral, web & mobile sites, corporate intranets, mobile apps, social media campaigns, videos. (Woman, estab 1981, empl 46, sales $7,824,663, cert: State, WBENC)

8262 Breakthrough Marketing Technology
110 E. Shearwater Court Ste 11
Jersey City, NJ 07305
Contact: Elaine Harris President
Tel: 201-604-3600
Email: elaine@breakthroughgroup.com
Website: www.breakthroughgroup.com
Marketing, strategic planning, market research, learning, coaching, implementation planning. (Woman/AA, estab 2002, empl 13, sales $432,000, cert: State, WBENC)

8263 BUZZRegistration
3525 Quakerbridge Rd Ste 908
Hamilton, NJ 08619
Contact: Michael Rayner CEO
Tel: 888-202-2262
Email: michaelr@buysmart-gsa.com
Website: www.buzzregistration.com
Registration management services for meeting planners. Focus on the core planning of your events and leave attendee management to our registration team. (Woman, estab 2011, empl 25, sales $4,647,794, cert: WBENC)

8264 Cajam Marketing, Inc.
8 Haviland Dr
Millstone Twp, NJ 08535
Contact: Kathy Gould President
Tel: 609-371-1325
Email: kgould@cajammarketing.com
Website: www.cajammarketing.com
Offline & online marketing initiatives through analytics. (Woman, estab 2001, empl 5, sales $400,000, cert: State)

8265 Classic Conferences Inc.
1 University Plaza, Ste 310
Hackensack, NJ 07601
Contact: Andrea Strauss President
Tel: 201-343-1999
Email: astrauss@classicconferences.com
Website: www.classicconferences.com
Corporate meeting & event planning. (Woman, estab 1990, empl 7, sales $20,000,000, cert: WBENC)

8266 Command Marketing Innovations
70 Outwater Lane
Garfield, NJ 07026
Contact: Michele Murphy Acct Exec
Tel: 201-835-4588
Email: mmurphy@commandmi.com
Website: www.commandmarketinginnovations.com
Best in-class, data-driven, print & multi-channel based marketing solutions. (Woman, estab 2016, empl 25, sales $14,000,000, cert: WBENC)

8267 Digital Brand Expressions
100 Overlook Center 2nd Fl
Princeton, NJ 08540
Contact: Veronica Fielding President
Tel: 609-688-8558
Email: vfielding@digitalbrandexpressions.com
Website: www.digitalbrandexpressions.com
Search engine marketing consultancy & services firm. Focus: search engine marketing/optimization/advertising and/or search engine image protection. (Woman, estab 2002, empl 10, sales $860,000, cert: WBENC)

8268 Distinctive Marketing, Inc.
516 Bloomfield Ave
Montclair, NJ 07042
Contact: Diane Spencer
Tel: 973-746-9114
Email: dmiassociates@verizon.net
Website: www.distinctivemktg.com
Marketing research, focus groups, telephone surveys, event planning & mgmt, consulting, etc. (Woman/AA, estab 1990, empl 12, sales , cert: State)

8269 Diversity Marketing and Communications
28 Washington St, Ste 103 Ste 103
East Orange, NJ 07017
Contact: Susan Cohen Managing Partner
Tel: 973-377-0300
Email: susan.cohen@diversitymc.com
Website: www.diversitymc.com
Marketing & advertising, public relations, special events management, crisis communications & partnership alliance development. (Woman, estab 2004, empl 5, sales $286,787, cert: State, WBENC)

8270   Executive Meetings & Incentives, Inc.
       685 US Hwy 202/206 N 2nd Fl
       Bridgewater, NJ 08876
       Contact: Larry Hambro Business Devel
       Tel: 908-864-5800
       Email: rgiaimo@eminj.com
       Website: www.eminj.com
Meeting planning, global, full service meeting, event &
incentive planning, logistic services. (Woman, estab 1982,
empl 18, sales $2,746,000, cert: State)

8271   FirstEye Media Works
       59 Lincoln Park Ste 375
       Newark, NJ 07102
       Contact: Kimberlee Williams CEO
       Tel: 973-494-9705
       Email: kwilliams@femworksllc.com
       Website: www.femworksllc.com
Integrated campaigns, events & custom campaign photography. (Woman/AA, estab 2004, empl 5, sales $503,611,
cert: NMSDC, WBENC)

8272   Focus USA, Inc
       95 North State Route 17 Ste 109
       Paramus, NJ 07652
       Contact: Meg Ugenti Corporate Dir of Sales &
       Marketing
       Tel: 201-489-2525
       Email: megu@focus-usa.com
       Website: www.focus-usa.com
Direct & data marketing services, consumer & business
database aggregator, buyer behavior profiling, data &
email appending, email marketing, digital solutions,
mobile marketing, social media marketing. (Woman, estab
1994, empl 14, sales $3,840,000, cert: WBENC)

8273   Global Planners, Inc.
       3525 Quakerbridge Rd Ste 909
       Hamilton, NJ 08619
       Contact: Megan Buzzetta CEO
       Tel: 609-689-0001
       Email: wbereg@globalplanners.com
       Website: www.globalplanners.com
Meeting & event coordination, contract negotiation, on
line attendee registration, on site staff support, site
selection, travel agency. (Woman, estab 2000, empl 14,
sales $3,368,000, cert: WBENC)

8274   HAP Marketing Services, Inc.
       1511 Wayside Rd
       Tinton Falls, NJ 07724
       Contact: Lorenzo Fernandez Managing Partner
       Tel: 732-982-8222
       Email: lorenzo.fernandez@hapmarketing.com
       Website: www.hapmarketing.com
Advertising, public relations, promotional items, graphics
design. (Hisp, estab 1984, empl 24, sales $5,063,096, cert:
State)

8275   InGroup, Inc.
       PO Box 206
       Midland Park, NJ 07432
       Contact: Marlene Bauer President
       Tel: 201-612-1230
       Email: mbaur@ingroupinc.com
       Website: www.ingroupinc.com
Strategy & customized support services for marketing
programs, outreach communications & public relations.
(Woman, estab 1995, empl 5, sales $461,884, cert: State,
City, SDB)

8276   Iris Communications LLC
       11 Belaire Dr
       Roseland, NJ 07068
       Contact: Barbara Bochese Managing Dir
       Tel: 973-902-7027
       Email: bbochese@iriscommunications.org
       Website: www.iriscommunications.org
Marketing services, corporate communications &
branding, presentations, brand deliverables, educa-
tional/training, video production & animation, website
design & dev, media planning & buying. (Woman, estab
2011, empl 12, sales , cert: State, NWBOC)

8277   Magee Enterprises, LLC dba Event1Source
       68 Abbond Court
       Plainfield, NJ 07063
       Contact: Dion Magee Co-Owner
       Tel: 888-299-2250
       Email: dion@event1source.com
       Website: www.event1source.com
Event management & meeting sourcing. (Woman/AA,
estab 1994, empl 2, sales $195,000, cert: State)

8278   Marketsmith Inc.
       2 Wing Dr
       Cedar Knolls, NJ 07927
       Contact: Smith President
       Tel: 973-889-0006
       Email: nmichael@marketsmithinc.com
       Website: www.marketsmithinc.com
Media: strategic consulting; media planning, buying &
optimization; traditional; programmatic display; mobile;
paid social; social CRM. (Woman, estab 1999, empl 72,
sales $9,417,082, cert: WBENC)

8279   MarketView Research Group, Inc.
       115 River Rd, Ste 105
       Edgewater, NJ 07020
       Contact: Gail Apkarian President
       Tel: 201-840-5300
       Email: sales@mvrg.com
       Website: www.mvrg.com
Quantitative marketing research. (Woman, estab 1989,
empl 35, sales $8,021,000, cert: State, WBENC)

8280   Meadowlands Consumer Center Global Marketing
       Resea
       301 Rt. 17N Ste 503
       Rutherford, NJ 07070
       Contact: Andrea C. Schrager CEO
       Tel: 201-865-4900
       Email: info@consumercenters.com
       Website: www.consumercenters.com
Qualitative market research & strategic consulting: study
design, strategy development, branding & new product
R & D. (Woman, estab 1984, empl 50, sales $5,200,000,
cert: State, WBENC)

8281   Meeting Logistics, LLC
       890 Mountain Ave
       New Providence, NJ 07974
       Contact: President
       Tel: 908-771-0804
       Email:
       Website: www.mtglogistics.com
Meeting, event, convention management, trade show
support, incentive programs, special events, advisory
boards, awards, educational programs, training programs. (Woman, estab 2000, empl 5, sales $1,933,790,
cert: WBENC)

8282 MMI Inc.
350 W Passaic St
Rochelle Park, NJ 07662
Contact: Michele McKenna President
Tel: 201-556-1188
Email: info@MarketAnalytics.com
Website: www.marketanalytics.com
International research: customer, competitive & market intelligence solutions, qualitative & quantitative solutions. (Woman, estab 2002, empl 10, sales $1,200,000, cert: State, WBENC)

8283 Mona Terrell & Associates LLC
1610 Division Ave
Piscataway, NJ 08854
Contact: Mona Terrell President
Tel: 732-752-4690
Email: mona@monaterrell.com
Website: www.monaterrell.com
Corporate communications, public relations, public affairs, social responsibility & sustainability programs. (Woman/AA, estab 2009, empl 1, sales $150,000, cert: State, WBENC)

8284 Paragon Productions Inc.
1900 Shadow Brook Dr
Wall Township, NJ 07719
Contact: Susanne Ardolino President
Tel: 732-282-9088
Email: susanne@paragonproductionsinc.com
Website: www.paragonproductionsinc.com
Marketing & communications, Design, Scheduling, Staging, Audio Visual, Guest Speaker & Entertainment requirements. (Woman, estab 1995, empl 4, sales $895,000, cert: State)

8285 Raare Solutions LLC
4 Lorettacong Dr
Lake Hopatcong, NJ 07849
Contact: Business Dev Dir
Tel: 800-693-2994
Email: sales@raaresolutions.com
Website: www.raaresolutions.com
CRM & customer data analysis, marketing campaign design & management services, focusing on luxury brands. (Woman, estab 2004, empl 17, sales $2,100,000, cert: WBENC)

8286 Smith Design Associates Inc.
8 Budd St
Morristown, NJ 07960
Contact: Jenna Smith President
Tel: 973-429-2177
Email: jenna@smithdesign.com
Website: www.smithdesign.com
Brand Identity & Package Design, Seamless Account + Project Management, Visual Strategy + Positioning, Verbal Expression + Brand Package Design, Design Production + Realization.
Visual (Woman, estab 1978, empl 25, sales $7,200,000, cert: State, WBENC)

8287 Snap Creative Marketing
425 Sand Shore Rd
Hackettstown, NJ 07840
Contact: Roberta Rivinius Managing Partner
Tel: 908-441-6220
Email: roberta@snapcreativemarketing.com
Website: www.snapcreativemarketing.com
Campaign Dev & Strategy, Brand Mgmt, Direct Mail & Fulfillment, Lettershop/Mailhouse, Print Production, Multicultural Marketing, Graphic Design, Web Dev & Interactive Design, Social Media & TV & Radio Production, Promotions. (Woman, estab 2013, empl 21, sales $13,800,000, cert: WBENC)

8288 Stokes Creative Group, Inc.
1666 Route 206
Vincentown, NJ 08088
Contact: Diane Konopka President
Tel: 609-859-8400
Email: diane@stokescg.com
Website: www.stokescg.com
Marketing agency, public outreach, videography, marketing, advertising, and photography. (Woman, estab 1989, empl 32, sales $2,970,811, cert: WBENC)

8289 Strategic Research I
101 Morgan Lane
Plainsboro, NJ 08536
Contact: Venky Jagannathan Principal
Tel: 609-751-5231
Email: venky.jagan@srinsights.com
Website: www.srinsights.com
Pharmaceutical Marketing Research, Marketing Consulting, Big Data Analysis. (As-Ind, estab 2006, empl 20, sales , cert: State)

8290 Taurus Market Research
1810 Englishtown Rd
Old Bridge, NJ 08857
Contact: Beth Kamenitz Dir Client Dev
Tel: 732-251-7772
Email: beth@taurusresearch.com
Website: www.taurusresearch.com
Qualitative & quantitative market research: concept, product, packaging & advertising testing, one-on-one in-depth interviewing, intercept/exit interviewing, ethnographies & consumer panels, in-house recruiting. (Woman, estab 1992, empl 53, sales $1,000,000, cert: City)

8291 The Lane Group LLC
14-25 Plaza Rd North Ste 3N
Fair Lawn, NJ 07410
Contact: Tracey Lane President
Tel: 201-398-9230
Email: tlane@tlgmeetings.com
Website: www.tlgmeetings.com
Event & meeting planning, production & management (Woman, estab 2000, empl 15, sales $2,226,800, cert: State, WBENC)

8292 TMW Enterprises, Inc.
76 Park Ave
Flemington, NJ 08822
Contact: President, Exec Producer
Tel: 908-638-6070
Email: tmwinfo@tmwenterprises.com
Website: www.tmwenterprises.com
Audio visual equipment & staging services: sales meetings, product launches & award ceremonies. (Woman, estab 1992, empl 6, sales $2,650,000, cert: WBENC)

8293 Trimensions Inc.
      One Engle St
      Englewood, NJ 07631
      Contact: Maria Maceri President
      Tel: 201-816-8820
      Email: mmaceri@trimensionsinc.com
      Website: www.trimensionsinc.com
Printed material for sales & promotional purposes, design
& manufacturing of displays, direct mail, packaging, detail
aids & interactive pieces. (Woman, estab 1975, empl 6,
sales $4,500,000, cert: WBENC)

8294 Vanadams Sports Group LLC
      623 Eagle Rock Ave Ste 317
      West Orange, NJ 07052
      Contact: Van Adams Principal
      Tel: 888-435-8006
      Email: vadams@vanadamssports.com
      Website: www.VanAdamsSports.com
Marketing Athletes & Events, Consulting, Event Development, national events and promotions, contract negotiations, budget creation. (Woman/AA, estab 2004, empl 1,
sales $225,000, cert: State)

8295 VS Research LLC
      411 Hackensack Ave, 10 Fl
      Hackensack, NJ 07601
      Contact: Steven Segal CFO
      Tel: 201-498-9333
      Email: steven@vsresearch.com
      Website: www.vsresearch.com
Qualitative & quantitative market research. (Woman, estab
1997, empl 9, sales , cert: WBENC)

8296 Websignia
      60 Park Place Ste 404
      Newark, NJ 07102
      Contact: Steve Jones CEO
      Tel: 973-732-4750
      Email: diversity@websignia.net
      Website: www.websignia.net
Digital marketing, visual design for web & print, digital
marketing & custom web & mobile applications. (AA, estab
2003, empl 13, sales $670,000, cert: NMSDC)

New Mexico

8297 Slow Life Games, LLC
      9 Piedras Negras
      Santa Fe, NM 87505
      Contact: Jason Zeaman President
      Tel: 505-603-8930
      Email: jason@handcraftedlearning.com
      Website: www.HandcraftedLearning.com
We design and develop custom training for our clients in
multiple formats: virtual webinars, in-person classroom,
and stand alone eLearning. We specialize in highly interactive training that simulates what people do on the job and
allows them to practice (Minority, Woman, estab 2011,
empl 2, sales $716,617, cert: NMSDC, WBENC)

Nevada

8298 Ad Hoc Communication Resources, LLC
      6 Benevolo Dr
      Henderson, NV 89011
      Contact: Shelli Ryan President
      Tel: 702-567-1115
      Email: shelli@adhoccr.com
      Website: www.adhocCR.com
Business & corporate management consulting svcs:
editing, technical writing, public realtions, news &
publicity, product launches, media outreach, industry
analyst outreach, whitepapers, press releases. (Woman,
estab 1996, empl 2, sales $304,129, cert: WBENC)

8299 Fresh Wata, LLC
      3905 W Diablo Dr, Ste 100
      Las Vegas, NV 89118
      Contact: Tricia Costello President
      Tel: 913-269-3849
      Email: tricia@freshwata.com
      Website: www.freshwata.com
Create extraordinarily meaningful brand moments that
drive connection, engagement and dialogue. (Woman/
AA, estab , empl , sales $10,400,000, cert: WBENC)

8300 INTU Corporation
      7065 W Ann Rd, Ste 130-332
      Las Vegas, NV 89130
      Contact: Joanna Lai Project Coord
      Tel: 702-656-4503
      Email: events@intucorporation.com
      Website: www.intucorporation.com
Chair massage therapy, corporate wellness, spa oasis,
casino gaming, luxury poolside services, sporting sky
boxes, golf tournaments, themed parks, special events.
(Woman, estab 2005, empl 150, sales , cert: WBENC)

8301 MYS LLC
      1000 N Green Valley Pkwy, Ste 440-592
      Henderson, NV 89074
      Contact: Laura Silva Project Dir
      Tel: 800-933-9720
      Email: info@mysfirm.com
      Website: www.mysfirm.com
Project management & brand management services,
strategic marketing services, print & digital media.
(Woman/AA, Hisp, estab 2014, empl 2, sales $122,600,
cert: NMSDC, WBENC)

New York

8302 Adrea Rubin Marketing Inc.
      19 W 44th St Ste 1415
      New York, NY 10036
      Contact: Jennifer Vilkelis CFO
      Tel: 212-983-0020
      Email: jenniferv@adrearubin.com
      Website: www.adrearubin.com
Provides a unique perspective in direct marketing,
identifying new consumer populations, and the marketing strategies to engage these consumers, we have the
ability to grow businesses. (Woman, estab 1990, empl
14, sales , cert: WBENC)

8303 aLanguageBank
159 W 25th St, 6th Fl
New York, NY 10001
Contact: Maxwell Davidson Mgr of New Business
Tel: 212-213-3336
Email: maxwelld@alanguagebank.com
Website: www.alanguagebank.com
Translation & localization services. (As-Pac, estab 1999, empl 10, sales $950,000, cert: NMSDC)

8304 Beardwood&Co. LLC
40 Wooster St, 4th Fl
New York, NY 10013
Contact: Partner
Tel: 212-334-5689
Email: hello@beardwood.com
Website: www.beardwood.com
Branding & design, qualitative research, naming & voice, logos, packaging structures, packaging graphics, point-of-purchase displays, point-of-purchase advertising, brand books, brand guidelines. (Woman, estab 2004, empl 12, sales $2,294,723, cert: WBENC)

8305 BuzzBack Market Research dba Buzzback LLC
989 Sixth Ave
New York, NY 10036
Contact: Andrea Levene SVP Finance & Admin
Tel: 646-315-7575
Email: info@buzzback.com
Website: www.buzzback.com
Full service market research. (Woman, estab 2000, empl 37, sales , cert: WBENC)

8306 Buzzword PR Corp.
34 N 6th St
Brooklyn, NY 11249
Contact: Eva Dilmanian Owner
Tel: 718-599-2591
Email: eva@buzzwordpr.com
Website: www.buzzwordpr.com
Media relations. (Minority, Woman, estab 2003, empl 1, sales , cert: WBENC)

8307 CBA Research Corp.
59 Clubhouse Ln
Scarsdale, NY 10583
Contact: Judy Bernstein VP Qualitative Insights
Tel: 914-478-9355
Email: judy_bernstein@cba-link.com
Website: www.cba-link.com
Qualitative marketing research, focus groups, insights, moderating, analysis, ethnographies, depth interviews, shop-alongs, brand imagery, new product development, concept/messaging. (Woman, estab 1967, empl 3, sales $1,063,279, cert: WBENC)

8308 Company 20, Inc.
555 Eighth Ave Ste 2201
New York, NY 10018
Contact: Michele Lasky VP
Tel: 212-784-6453
Email: michelelasky@company20.com
Website: www.company20.com
Event marketing; planning; management; consulting; production; charity fundraisers; celebrity; athlete foundations; cause-related; sports; special events; corporate meetings; consumer promotions; incentives; hospitality. (Woman, estab 2005, empl 5, sales $2,085,000, cert: WBENC)

8309 Complemar Partners
500 Lee Rd Ste 200
Rochester, NY 14606
Contact: President
Tel: 585-647-5890
Email: info@complemar.com
Website: www.complemar.com
Marketing & sales communication programs. (Woman, estab 2004, empl 65, sales $5,195,389, cert: WBENC)

8310 Converge Marketing Services, LLC
33 E 33rd St 3rd Fl
New York, NY 10016
Contact: Maarten Terry President
Tel: 203-536-9414
Email: maartent@convergedirect.com
Website: www.convergemarketingservices.com
Media buying, planning & strategy, print production services & paper procurement. (AA, estab 2017, empl 17, sales , cert: NMSDC)

8311 D Exposito & Partners, LLC
875 6th Ave, 25th Fl
New York, NY 10001
Contact: Louis Maldonado Managing Dir
Tel: 646-747-8814
Email: lmaldonado@dex-p.com
Website: www.newamericanagency.com
Hispanic Marketing Solutions, Spanish language, In-Culture and English language communications programs to reach America's Hispanics no matter where they live, work or play. (Minority, Woman, estab 2005, empl 28, sales $5,077,000, cert: State, NMSDC, WBENC)

8312 Design & Source Productions, Inc.
143 W 29th St 3rd Fl
New York, NY 10001
Contact: Laura Tufariello President
Tel: 212-265-8632
Email: laura@dsnyc.com
Website: www.design-and-source.com
Design & develop branded & private label products, custom creative packaging solutions. (Woman, estab 1996, empl 7, sales $8,400,000, cert: City, WBENC)

8313 DEVLINHAIR Production Inc.
120 Wooster Dr 3rd Fl
New York, NY 10012
Contact: Dorothy Devlin Co-Founder
Tel: 212-941-9009
Email: supplier-diversity@devlinhair.com
Website: www.devlinhair.com
Corporate event planning: meetings, conferences, internal sales/mktg campaigns, film, video training programs, interactive media. (Woman, estab 1991, empl 13, sales $14,938,324, cert: WBENC)

8314 Drury Design Dynamics, Inc.
275 7th Ave Ste 2001
New York, NY 10001
Contact: Liza Handman VP Creative Devel Group
Tel: 212-576-1314
Email: l.handman@drurydesign.com
Website: www.drurydesign.com
Planning & production of meetings, learning & performance (training) programs, corporate. (Woman, estab 1981, empl 35, sales $20,000,000, cert: WBENC)

8315   Ebony Marketing Systems, Inc.
79 Alexander Ave, Ste 31-A
Bronx, NY 10454
Contact: FirstName LastName Operations Dir
Tel: 718-742-0006
Email: kfuentes@ebonysystems.com
Website: www.ebonysystems.com
Market research studies & services. (Woman/AA, estab 2011, empl 1, sales $650,000, cert: City, NMSDC)

8316   Eclipse Direct Marketing LLC
173 Mineola Blvd Ste 402
Mineola, NY 11501
Contact: Kris Thelen CEO
Tel: 212-931-8344
Email: kthelen@eclipsedm.com
Website: www.eclipsedm.com
Tracking & analytics, strategy planning with marketing departments. (Woman, estab 2003, empl 7, sales $1,600,000, cert: WBENC)

8317   Egami Group, Inc.
212 W. 35th St 10th Fl
New York, NY 10001
Contact: Teneshia Jackson CEO
Tel: 917-720-5580
Email: teneshia@egamigroup.com
Website: www.egamigroup.com
Maketing consulting, branding, events, custom community programs, campaigns & new products. (Woman/AA, estab 2004, empl 12, sales $401,000, cert: NMSDC, WBENC)

8318   Extrovertic Communications, LLC
30 W 21st St 3rd Fl
New York, NY 10010
Contact: Dorothy Wetzel CEO
Tel: 646-312-6001
Email: dorothy@extrovertic.com
Website: www.extrovertic.com
Creative (print, video and digital), relationship marketing, patient education, social media, & marketing consulting. (Woman, estab 2009, empl 27, sales $7,933,003, cert: WBENC)

8319   Foglamp Research Corp.
100 Greenwich Rd
Bedford, NY 10506
Contact: Kate Horn CEO
Tel: 914-682-4127
Email: kate.horn@foglampresearch.com
Website: www.foglampresearch.com
Due diligence, reputational risk inquiries, surveys, interviews & local market intelligence research in emerging & frontier markets. (Woman, estab 2013, empl 3, sales $237,811, cert: WBENC)

8320   Gammon & Associates
152 Madison Ave, Ste 400
New York, NY 10016
Contact: Fred Gammon President
Tel: 212-725-6710
Email: admin@thegroagency.com
Website: www.thegroagency.com
Branding and Package Design Agency. (AA, estab 1988, empl 13, sales $1,771,414, cert: NMSDC)

8321   Greater Than One Inc.
395 Hudson St
New York, NY 10014
Contact: Elizabeth Izard Apelles CEO
Tel: 917-549-4202
Email: eapelles@gthegtogroup.com
Website: www.thegtogroup.com
marketing services: strategies, assessments, metrics analytics, consumer research, behavior analytics, communications planning, engagement. (Woman, estab 2000, empl 120, sales $28,000,000, cert: WBENC)

8322   Human Touch Translations Ltd.
1010 Northern Boulevard Ste 208
Great Neck, NY 11021
Contact: FirstName LastName President
Tel: 646-358-4972
Email: enagy@humantouchtranslations.com
Website: www.humantouchtranslations.com
Translation servivces, 120 languages, interpreting documents, technical documents, legal documents, scientific papers, journal and magazine articles, educational materials, medical documents, market research surveys. (Woman, estab 2010, empl 5, sales , cert: State, WBENC)

8323   Imagine 360 Marketing
340 E 64th St Ste 17N
New York, NY 10065
Contact: President
Tel: 212-313-9616
Email: info@i360m.com
Website: www.i360m.com
Strategic marketing and innovative design to increase brand awareness, acquire new business and retain existing customers. (Woman, estab 2005, empl 7, sales , cert: WBENC)

8324   Intstrux LLC
15 W 39th St, 13th Fl
New York, NY 10018
Contact: Sanjiv Mody CEO
Tel: 646-688-2782
Email: sanjiv.mody@pixacore.com
Website: www.pixacore.com
Digital communication, strategy & implementation services, marketing, training, corporate communication, live events initiatives. (As-Ind, estab 2007, empl 30, sales $7,577,436, cert: NMSDC)

8325   Ivy Cohen Corporate Communications, Inc.
2098 Frederick Douglass Blvd. Ste 10M
New York, NY 10026
Contact: Ivy Cohen CEO
Tel: 212-399-0026
Email: ivy@ivycohen.com
Website: www.ivycohen.com
Branding, promotions, corporate communications & organizational issues. (Woman, estab 2001, empl 1, sales $326,063, cert: City, WBENC)

8326   Jeannette McClennan LLC
109 W 118th St
New York, NY 10026
Contact: Jeannette McClennan President
Tel: 917-842-0364
Email: jeannette@mcclennangroup.com
Website: www.mcclennangroup.com
Digital products and marketing programs for its corporate clients quickly and cost-effectively. (AA, estab 2004, empl 50, sales , cert: WBENC)

8327 Keeper of the Brand
894 Otsego Rd
West Hempstead, NY 11552
Contact: Donyshia Boston-Hill CEO
Tel: 917-697-1699
Email: db@keeperofthebrand.com
Website: www.keeperofthebrand.com/
Marketing Plans & Strategies, Media Buying, TV, Radio,
Print & Digital Solutions, Broadcast Media Distribution,
Brand Development, Consumer Insight, Copyright, Trans-
actional Engagement, Programming & Campaign Mgmt,
Graphic Design, Creative Services. (Woman/AA, estab
2013, empl 6, sales , cert: State, NMSDC, WBENC)

8328 Kipany Productions, Ltd.
32 E 39 St
New York, NY 10016
Contact: Salman Ali President
Tel: 212-883-8300
Email: rfp@kipany.com
Website: www.kipany.com
Marketing communication svcs: direct response TV sales &
outbound telemarketing; video, print, Internet direct
mktg/web design & placement. (Woman, estab 1979, empl
30, sales , cert: WBENC)

8329 Kupcha Marketing Services
2 Hayes Rd
Amity Harbor, NY 11701
Contact: Elizabeth Kupcha President
Tel: 917-432-9481
Email: liz@kupchamkt.com
Website: www.kupchamkt.com
Marketing consulting: proposal management, presentation
preparation/coaching, publicity & event planning.
(Woman/AA, estab 2010, empl 1, sales , cert: State, City)

8330 Lightbeam Communications Corp
1787 Madison Ave, Ste 710
New York, NY 10035
Contact: Roben Allong CEO
Tel: 917-498-1738
Email: robena@lightbeamnyc.com
Website: www.lightbeamnyc.com
Qualitative research. (Woman/AA, estab 2009, empl 1,
sales $284,000, cert: City)

8331 LilyGild Ltd.
199 Carlton Ave
Brooklyn, NY 11205
Contact: Ann Chitwood Co-President
Tel: 718-797-4656
Email: ilygild@lilygild.com
Website: www.lilygild.com
Communications svcs: event, meeting & media production.
(Woman, estab 1991, empl 3, sales $890,323, cert:
WBENC)

8332 MedEdNow, LLC
29 W 35th St Ste 10A
New York, NY 10001
Contact: Alexis Pone VP Strategy & Business Dev
Tel: 646-674-9549
Email: apone@medednow.com
Website: www.medednow.com
Marketing; medical education; medical communication;
content development & medical writing; brand strategy;
brand planning; sales training; global; conferences and
society meetings; symposia and product theaters.
(Woman, estab 2001, empl 35, sales $12,952,301, cert:
WBENC)

8333 Meeting Management Associates, Inc.
16 W State St
Sherburne, NY 13460
Contact: Lisa Denton Dir Sales
Tel: 607-674-2666
Email: lisa@mma-inc.com
Website: www.mma-inc.com
Manage conventions, tradeshows, meetings, special
events & develop promotional, specialty items. Housing, electronic registrations, registrations via phone,
travel arrangements, sales correspondence, exhibit
routing, labor management. (Woman, estab 1994, empl
17, sales $1,355,199, cert: WBENC)

8334 Mico Promotions, Inc.
1350 6th Ave, 4th Fl
New York, NY 10019
Contact: Maia Michaelson President
Tel: 212-255-5785
Email: maia@micopromotions.com
Website: www.micopromotions.com
Creative and art studio services. (Woman, estab 1992,
empl 5, sales $1,295,287, cert: WBENC)

8335 Mirror Show Management
855 Hard Rd
Webster, NY 14580
Contact: Devon Donatello Marketing & Sales
Enablement Specialist
Tel: 585-232-4020
Email: supplierdiversity@msmxp.com
Website: www.msmxp.com
Exhibit design & management firm. (Woman, estab
1993, empl 50, sales $20,000,000, cert: WBENC)

8336 Novatek Communications, Inc.
500 Helendale Road Ste 280
Rochester, NY 14609
Contact: Amy Castronova CEO
Tel: 585-482-4070
Email: patty.setchell@novatekcom.com
Website: www.novatekcom.com
User & service writing, computer-based training, e-
learning & multimedia. (Woman, estab 1989, empl 29,
sales $1,504,910, cert: State, WBENC)

8337 Percepture
104 W 40th St.
New York, NY 10018
Contact: Thor Harris CEO
Tel: 800-707-9190
Email: supplierdiversity@percepture.com
Website: www.percepture.com
Public relations & marketing. (AA, estab 2004, empl 4,
sales $3,389,825, cert: State)

8338 Sage Advertising LLC
71 Atkinson Rd
Rockville Centre, NY 11570
Contact: Jodi O'Sullivan Owner
Tel: 516-320-9225
Email: jodi@sage-agency.com
Website: www.sage-agency.com
Marketing strategies & materials, print, collateral,
digital, trade show & video production. (Woman, estab
2008, empl 5, sales $454,000, cert: WBENC)

8339 Site Solutions Worldwide
      1023 Route 146
      Clifton Park, NY 12065
      Contact: Nathalie Whitton President
      Tel: 518-399-7181
      Email: nathalie@sswmeetings.com
      Website: www.sitesolutionsworldwide.com
Meeting svcs: site selection, meeting management,
contract negotiations, online registration, speaker coordination, exhibitor coordination & on-site meeting management. (Woman, estab 2001, empl 14, sales $8,764,783,
cert: State, WBENC)

8340 Spiral Design Studio, LLC
      135 Mohawk St
      Cohoes, NY 12047
      Contact: Lauren Payne Managing Partner
      Tel: 518-326-1135
      Email: lauren@spiraldesign.com
      Website: www.spiraldesign.com
Graphic design, advertising, marketing, website design, web
page design, responsive design, mobile website design,
internet marketing, digital marketing, email marketing,
branding, logo design, corporate identity, print design, print
marketing. (Woman, estab 1989, empl 10, sales $948,500,
cert: State, WBENC)

8341 Strategic Marketing & Promotions, Inc.
      10 N Main St
      Pearl River, NY 10965
      Contact: Greg Caglione President
      Tel: 845-623-7777
      Email: gcaglione@smpglobal.com
      Website: www.smpglobal.com
Mfr, design & produce point of purchase display fixtures,
signage, retail consumer packaging. Assembly, fulfillment,
inventory management, distribution center. (Woman, estab
2001, empl 85, sales $5,000,000, cert: State)

8342 StudioLabs LLC.
      247 W 30th St Ste 12A
      New York, NY 10001
      Contact: Liz Young CEO
      Tel: 646-880-6892
      Email: liz@studiolabs.com
      Website: www.studiolabs.com
Websites, online software, mobile applications, digital ads,
online tools & digital marketing products. (Woman, estab
2003, empl 27, sales $3,999,300, cert: WBENC)

8343 The CementBloc
      32 Old Slip 15th Fl
      New York, NY 10005
      Contact: Art Chavez Partner
      Tel: 646-829-2002
      Email: achavez@thebloc.com
      Website: www.thebloc.com
Global branding, full-service professional promotion,
medical strategy, patient education, payer strategy, digital
strategy & communications planning/execution. (Woman,
estab 2000, empl 175, sales $41,900,000, cert: WBENC)

8344 The Mixx
      350 7th Ave Ste 1403
      New York, NY 10001
      Contact: Olympia Lambert Client Services Dir
      Tel: 212-695-6663
      Email: hi@themixxnyc.com
      Website: www.themixxnyc.com
Strategic branding, messaging & marketing firm:
corporate identity & brand platforms, brand collateral,
annual reports & Bbochures, advertising campaigns,
direct mail campaigns, web design & development,
multi-media marketing plans. (Woman, estab 1996,
empl 18, sales $16,968,000, cert: WBENC)

8345 The Mundial Group, Inc.
      28 E 28th St
      New York, NY 10016
      Contact: Felix Sencion
      Tel: 212-213-1400
      Email: billing@mundialgroup.net
      Website: www.mundialsportsnetwork.com
Marketing; Print Sport Publication; Print Advertising;
Digital Advertidsing: display, flash, mobile, pre-roll,
branded content production (Hisp, estab 1999, empl 11,
sales , cert: NMSDC)

8346 The Thomas Collective LLC
      37 w 28th st 12th floor
      New York, NY 10001
      Contact: Erin Donley Special Projects Coordinator
      Tel: 212-229-2294
      Email: edonley@thethomascollective.com
      Website: www.thethomascollective.com
Marketing communications, Brand Development, Public
Relations & Digital/Social Media. (Woman, estab 2004,
empl 20, sales $700,000, cert: WBENC)

8347 TITANIUM Worldwide LLC
      350 7th Ave Ste 1403
      New York, NY 10001
      Contact: Streisand Chief Financial Operations
      Officer
      Tel: 646-952-8440
      Email: accounting@titaniumww.com
      Website: www.titaniumww.com
Media, marketing, communications & consulting:
Branding/Creative/Strategy, Content/Messaging, Digital/
Social/Mobile, Film/Video Production, Event Marketing,
Business Intelligence, Data Warehousing, Development/
Deployment. (Woman, estab 2014, empl 4, sales , cert:
WBENC)

8348 UX Design Collective LLC
      672 Carroll St, Unit 3
      Brooklyn, NY 11215
      Contact: Ariel Rey Head of Product & Projects
      Tel: 929-352-4489
      Email: services@uxdesigncollective.com
      Website: www.uxdesigncollective.com
Design websites, mobile apps, strategize, design, and
build thoughtful, transformative digital products. (As-
Pac, estab 2017, empl 4, sales , cert: State, City, WBENC)

8349   View Finders Market Research
       11 Sandra Ln
       Pearl River, NY 10965
       Contact: Janet Gaines Owner
       Tel: 845-735-7022
       Email: jgaines@view-finders.com
       Website: www.view-finders.com
Focus group management, consumer & business research,
advertising testing, product definition, concept development, attitudinal research, usage testing, customer
satisfaction & new product development. (Woman, estab
1983, empl 25, sales $700,000, cert: WBENC)

8350   Weinman Schnee Morais, Inc.
       250 W 57th St Ste 2212
       New York, NY 10107
       Contact: Cynthia Weinman Principal
       Tel: 212-906-1900
       Email: cweinman@wsm-inc.com
       Website: www.wsm-inc.com
Marketing research, 50% qualitative & 50% quantitative.
(Woman, estab 1993, empl 12, sales , cert: WBENC)

8351   Yorkville Marketing Consulting LLC
       425 E 79 St Ste 11M
       New York, NY 10075
       Contact: Dina Shapiro CEO
       Tel: 646-284-2481
       Email: dina.shapiro@yorkvilleconsulting.com
       Website: www.YorkvilleConsulting.com
Corporate Brand Strategy, Marketing, Organization
Planning, Marketing Capabilities, Training. (Woman, estab
2013, empl 1, sales , cert: WBENC)

8352   Zebra Strategies
       421 7th Ave Ste 1100
       New York, NY 10001
       Contact: Denene Jonielle Rodney CEO
       Tel: 212-244-3960
       Email: denene@zstrategies.net
       Website: www.zebrastrategies.com
Qualitative market research services. (Woman/AA, estab
2001, empl 10, sales $1,541,000, cert: NMSDC, WBENC)

Ohio

8353   Abercrumbie Group
       10301 Giverny Blvd
       Cincinnati, OH 45241
       Contact: Claudia Abercrumbie President
       Tel: 513-733-1555
       Email: claudia@theabercrumbiegroup.com
       Website: www.theabercrumbiegroup.com
Event management. (Woman/AA, estab 2005, empl 1,
sales $350,000, cert: WBENC)

8354   Acadia Lead Management Services Inc.
       4738 Gateway Circle Ste A100
       Kettering, OH 45440
       Contact: Tami Randall Mgr
       Tel: 888-605-3194
       Email: tlr@acadialms.com
       Website: www.acadialms.com
Customized industry data, marketing information & sales
leads, lead qualification, lead nurturing, marketing
dashboard & lead management. (Woman, estab 1999,
empl 21, sales $958,835, cert: WBENC)

8355   Affordable Language Services
       8944 Blue Ash Road
       Cincinnati, OH 45242
       Contact: Kristi Reynek CEO
       Tel: 513-745-0888
       Email: kreynek@affordablelanguages.com
       Website: www.affordablelanguages.com
Translation & interpreting services, voice-over &
transcription. (Woman, estab 2000, empl 14, sales
$2,209,000, cert: WBENC)

8356   Baker Creative Ltd.
       386 Main St
       Groveport, OH 43125
       Contact: Michele Cuthbert Principal
       Tel: 614-836-3845
       Email: mbaker@baker-creative.com
       Website: www.baker-creative.com
Graphic Design, Marketing Consulting, Advertising,
Public Relations, Display Advertising. (Minority, Woman,
estab 2003, empl 10, sales , cert: State, WBENC, SDB)

8357   Bascom & Adams Business Solutions, LLC
       1209 Hill St North Ste 227
       Pickerington, OH 43147
       Contact: Christine Adams President
       Tel: 614-252-7880
       Email: chrisadams@bascomadams.com
       Website: www.bascomadams.com
Marketing communications, public relations, special
events, outreach & engagement. (Woman/AA, estab
2002, empl 1, sales , cert: State, City)

8358   Charm Consulting
       2957 Cranbrook Dr
       Cincinnati, OH 45251
       Contact: Toyia Montgomery CEO
       Tel: 513-290-6357
       Email: charmconsulting3@gmail.com
       Website: www.charmconsulting3.com
Branding, public relations & event services. (Woman/AA,
estab 2014, empl 3, sales , cert: State)

8359   EVOLUTION Creative Solutions
       7107 Shona Dr Ste 110
       Cincinnati, OH 45237
       Contact: Robert Miller Sales Rep
       Tel: 513-864-3761
       Email: bob.miller@evo-creative.com
       Website: www.evo-creative.com
Marketing plans, graphic design & production, website
creation & maintenance, and social media. (Woman,
estab 2011, empl 6, sales , cert: WBENC)

8360   Exhibit Concepts Inc.
       700 Crossroads Ct
       Vandalia, OH 45377
       Contact: Ellen Kaminski VP Sales and Marketing
       Tel: 937-535-0224
       Email: ekaminski@exhibitconcepts.com
       Website: www.exhibitconcepts.com
Strategic design, graphic design and production, engineering and fabrication, program management, custom,
rental, hybrid, modular exhibits, interior nvironments,
events, museum design, fabrication. (Woman, estab
1978, empl 106, sales $280,000,000, cert: WBENC)

8361 Gong Gong Communications
746 Green Crest Dr
Westerville, OH 43081
Contact: Amanda Sage CEO
Tel: 614-388-8918
Email: amanda@gonggongcommunications.com
Website: www.gonggongcommunications.com
Corporate, non-profit event planning & marketing, Offline
& online experiential marketing campaigns, Target social
media & e-mail marketing campaigns, Podcast production
& promotion. (Woman, estab 2009, empl 3, sales , cert:
WBENC)

8362 Illumination Research, Inc.
5947 Deerfield Blvd Ste 203
Mason, OH 45040
Contact: Karri Bass President
Tel: 513-774-9588
Email: kbass@illumination-research.com
Website: www.illumination-research.com
Qualitative market research. (Woman, estab 0, empl 29,
sales $6,593,000, cert: WBENC)

8363 Incite Visual Communications
PO Box 1017
Milford, OH 45150
Contact: Michael Perry Business Dev Dir
Tel: 513-575-5100
Email: mike@incitevisual.com
Website: www.incitevisual.com
Branding/marketing design, Branding, Package Design, Print
& Digital Sales/Marketing Assets, Point of Sale materials,
Product Sell Sheets, FSI, Event Promotional assets. (Woman,
estab 2001, empl 2, sales $186,000, cert: WBENC)

8364 Market Inquiry, Inc.
5825 Creek Rd
Cincinnati, OH 45242
Contact: Cathy Noyes Owner
Tel: 513-794-1088
Email: cathy@marketinquiry.com
Website: www.marketinquiry.com
Qualitative & quantitative research. (Woman, estab 1995,
empl 20, sales $1,164,000, cert: WBENC)

8365 MMP LLC
7588 Central Parke Blvd, Ste 321
Mason, OH 45040
Contact: Linda Dektas Owner
Tel: 513-234-0560
Email: linda@creativestorm.com
Website: www.creativestorm.com
Websites, ads-print & broadcast, brochures, logo design,
digital marketing, direct mail, social media, promotions,
displays, promotional items & apparel. (Woman, estab
1999, empl 5, sales $1,000,000, cert: WBENC)

8366 Modern Technique, LLC
1050 Lear Industrial Pkwy
Avon, OH 44011
Contact: Kristi Blosser President
Tel: 440-497-8547
Email: kristi@whatsyourtechnique.com
Website: www.whatsyourtechnique.com
Advertising, digital & mobile media development, website
design, SEO & email marketing, broadcast & social media
planning & devel, mobile app devel & mobile marketing.
(Woman, estab 2012, empl 4, sales $250,000, cert: WBENC)

8367 Partners In Planning One Inc.
7061 Larkspur Lane
Liberty Township, OH 45044
Contact: Nancy Caine President
Tel: 513-755-1091
Email: ncainepip@aol.com
Website: www.partnersinplanning.org
Meeting planning & event svcs: food & beverage
negotiation, budget control, meeting set up & contract
negotiations. (Woman, estab 1997, empl 1, sales , cert:
WBENC)

8368 Power Presentations, Inc.
8225 Brecksville Rd, Ste 100
Brecksville, OH 44141
Contact: Cate Huff Finance/Admin Mgr
Tel: 440-526-4400
Email: ch@power-presentations.com
Website: www.power-presentations.com
Communication and presentations skills training for all
types of communication, standing, seated and virtual.
(Woman, estab 1993, empl 7, sales , cert: WBENC)

8369 Quez Media Marketing
1138 Prospect Ave E
Cleveland, OH 44115
Contact: Jose Vasquez CEO
Tel: 216-910-0202
Email: info@quezmedia.com
Website: www.quezmedia.com
Marketing communications, online storefronts, data
services, creative services, print. (Hisp, estab 2009, empl
17, sales $1,646,098, cert: State, City, NMSDC)

8370 R/P Marketing Public Relations
1500 Timberwolf Dr
Holland, OH 43528
Contact: Robin Walters VP Business Dev
Tel: 614-428-6056
Email: rwalters@r-p.com
Website: www.r-p.com
Marketing, advertising & public relations services.
(Woman, estab 1993, empl 25, sales $5,559,217, cert:
WBENC)

8371 Rhonda Crowder & Associates LLC
1465 E 112th St
Cleveland, OH 44106
Contact: Wayne Dailey Creative Dir
Tel: 216-352-3330
Email: wayne@rhondacrowderllc.com
Website: www.rhondacrowderllc.com
Communications, content creation, graphic design,
fundraising & media relations services. (Woman/AA,
estab 2011, empl 5, sales , cert: State)

8372 SCANVenger Hunt LLC
1275 Kinnear Rd
Columbus, OH 43212
Contact: Sean Fields Dir Business Dev
Tel: 800-975-5161
Email: sean@scanvengerhunt.biz
Website: www.scanvengerhunt.biz
Event services, event applications, registration badges
for attendees. (AA, estab 2012, empl 3, sales $155,000,
cert: NMSDC)

8373 Various Views Research, Inc.
      11353 Reed Hartman Hwy, Ste 200
      Cincinnati, OH 45241
      Contact: Doug van der Zee Dir Business Dev
      Tel: 513-387-2208
      Email: dvanderzee@variousviews.com
      Website: www.variousviews.com
Market research, qualitative research methodologies,
focus groups, in-depth interviews & product tests.
(Woman, estab 2007, empl 75, sales $3,500,000, cert:
WBENC)

8374 Visibility Marketing, Inc.
      24700 Chagrin Blvd Ste 306
      Beachwood, OH 44122
      Contact: Montrie Rucker Adams Chief Visibility
      Officer
      Tel: 440-684-9920
      Email: mra@visibilitymarketing.com
      Website: www.visibilitymarketing.com
Marketing communications & public relations, public &
media relations services & strategic marketing campaigns.
(Woman/AA, estab 2000, empl 2, sales , cert: State, City,
WBENC, 8(a))

Oklahoma

8375 Bullseye Database Marketing, LLC
      5546 S 104th East Ave
      Tulsa, OK 74146
      Contact: Deborah Kobe Norris CEO
      Tel: 918-587-1731
      Email: dnorris@bullseyedm.com
      Website: www.bullseyedm.com
Direct marketing, direct mail, email, mobile & social
media, strategic campaign direction, creative services, on-
time, on-budget, error-free production, response tracking
& analysis. (Woman, estab 1988, empl 8, sales $1,638,390,
cert: WBENC)

Oregon

8376 Paulette Carter Design, Inc. (PCD Group)
      5257 NE MLK Jr Blvd, Ste 301
      Portland, OR 97211
      Contact: Danielle Bastron Controller
      Tel: 503-525-2989
      Email: danielle@pcdgroup.com
      Website: www.pcdgroup.com
Marketing svcs: custom websites, intranets & online
applications, content mgmt, customer relationship mgmt
tools, custom work flow & productivity applications, e-
commerce, systems & data integration. (Woman, estab
1996, empl 12, sales , cert: WBENC)

8377 Stewart Marketing Group, LLC
      905 N Harbour Dr, Unit 3
      Portland, OR 97217
      Contact: Michael Stewart President
      Tel: 503-270-7857
      Email: michael@stewartmarketinggroup.com
      Website: www.stewartmarketinggroup.com
Conference & event planning, training & seminar materials, travel & hospitality, point of purchase displays, media
& CD/DVD disc storage, office supplies. (AA, estab 2006,
empl 1, sales $130,000, cert: State)

8378 The Kingfisher Group, LLC
      10260 SW Greenburg Rd Ste. 400
      Portland, OR 97223
      Contact: Mary Lou Kayser CEO
      Tel: 503-567-8730
      Email: mlk@maryloukayser.com
      Website: www.maryloukayser.com
Content Marketing Strategies, Visual Strategic Planning,
Creativity & Innovation, Training & Development,
Presentation Skills Development. (Woman, estab 2012,
empl 1, sales , cert: State)

Pennsylvania

8379 2nd Spark Consulting LLC
      31 E Butler Ave 1st Fl
      Ambler, PA 19002
      Contact: Stefanie Freeling Finance Mgr
      Tel: 215-948-3055
      Email: sfreeling@2ndspark.com
      Website: www.2ndspark.com
Marketing consulting & creative advertising, customer
insights, situation analysis, war games, portfolio architecture strategy, buying process, positioning, messaging,
branding, campaign development, media planning,
tactical planning. (Minority, Woman, estab 2009, empl
20, sales $1,726,022, cert: WBENC)

8380 aiaTranslations LLC
      4387 W. Swamp Rd
      Doylestown, PA 18902
      Contact: Molly Naughton President
      Tel: 908-955-5201
      Email: molly.naughton@aiatranslations.com
      Website: www.aiaTranslations.com
aiaTranslations is the only full-service US-based agency
specializing in healthcare and life science translation.
(Woman, estab 2010, empl 4, sales $1,500,000, cert:
WBENC)

8381 Albrecht Events LLC
      209 Providence Ln
      Lansdale, PA 19446
      Contact: Ashley Albrecht Managing Dir
      Tel: 215-699-3784
      Email: aalbrecht@albrechtevents.com
      Website: www.albrechtevents.com
Corporate meeting, event planning & destination
management services. (Woman, estab 2005, empl 1,
sales $171,228, cert: WBENC)

8382 Apex Impact Marketing LLC
      1720 Kendarloren Dr Ste. 714
      Jamison, PA 18929
      Contact: Howard Wilensky Partner
      Tel: 215-489-5460
      Email: howard@focusmx.com
      Website: www.focusmx.com
Marketing Strategy, Digital Strategy & Planning
Websites, Microsites, Landing Pages, Creative & Design
(Wordpress,Kentico, Sitecore, .NET), eCRM Programs,
Social Media Campaigns, Mobile & Tablet Applications,
Online Advertising. (Woman, estab 2009, empl 14, sales
, cert: WBENC)

8383   Bosha Design Inc.
       921 Childs Ave
       Drexel Hill, PA 19026
       Contact: Barbara Bosha President
       Tel: 610-622-4422
       Email: BarbBosha@boshadesign.com
       Website: www.boshadesign.com
Print & web graphic design: corporate communications,
business collateral, annual reports, web design & dev,
identity systems, brochures, newsletters, advertising,
exhibits & signage. (Woman, estab 1986, empl 5, sales
$85,019,107, cert: WBENC)

8384   Brandwidth Solutions, LLC
       108 Samantha Lane
       Lansdale, PA 19446
       Contact: Debra Harrsch CEO
       Tel: 215-997-8575
       Email: dharrsch@brandwidthsolutions.com
       Website: www.brandwidthsolutions.com
Marketing communications, digital, 3D interactive, video &
social media. (Woman, estab 2005, empl 7, sales $718,392,
cert: WBENC)

8385   Chelsea Partners Inc.
       108 Arch St Ste 1202
       Philadelphia, PA 19106
       Contact: Tempa Berish President
       Tel: 215-603-7300
       Email: tempa@chelseapartners.com
       Website: www.chelseapartners.com
Graphic design, printing (digital, flat sheet and web),
presort mailing services & fulfillment. (Woman, estab 1998,
empl 13, sales $2,120,795, cert: State, City, WBENC)

8386   Community Marketing Concepts, Inc.
       7300 City Ave Ste 330
       Philadelphia, PA 19151
       Contact: Daud Hadi Public Relations
       Tel: 215-871-0900
       Email: johnpaul@communitymarketingconcepts.com
       Website: www.communitymarketingconcepts.com
Public relations & marketing, research, strategic development, social & issue management programs, brand messaging, publicity & media placement, event planning, corporate & community relations, sponsorships, graphic & web
design. (Woman/AA, estab 1998, empl 10, sales
$2,400,000, cert: State, City, NMSDC)

8387   DaBrian Marketing Group
       500 Penn St, Ste 201
       Reading, PA 19602
       Contact: Daniel Laws, Jr. President
       Tel: 610-743-5602
       Email:
       Website: www.dabrianmarketing.com
Digital marketing agency, original and strategic digital
marketing solutions. (AA, estab 2008, empl 9, sales
$949,000, cert: State, NMSDC)

8388   Direct Marketing Alliance Inc.
       104 Park Dr
       Montgomeryville, PA 18936
       Contact: Ted Gramiak VP
       Tel: 215-619-8800
       Email: tgramiak@directma.com
       Website: www.directma.com
Direct marketing fulfillment services, direct mail package
production. (Woman, estab 2003, empl 45, sales
$6,000,000, cert: WBENC)

8389   Eitzen Creative LLC
       202 Dudley Ave
       Narberth, PA 19072
       Contact: Pamela Eitzen President
       Tel: 610-660-0220
       Email: pam@eobcreative.com
       Website: www.eobcreative.com
Graphic design, strategic communications, branding,
advertising, video, animation, corp & employee communications, corp identity, investor relations materials,
websites, exhibit design & meeting support. (Woman,
estab 2012, empl 3, sales $268,944, cert: WBENC)

8390   Fox Specialties, Inc. dba Encompass Elements
       2750 Morris Rd Ste C
       Lansdale, PA 19446
       Contact: Nadine Hodges New Business Dev
       Tel: 267-209-4133
       Email: nhodges@encompasselements.com
       Website: www.encompasselements.com
Marketing communications. (Woman, estab 1995, empl
65, sales $34,000,000, cert: WBENC)

8391   Lead Dog, Inc.
       305 S Chester Rd
       Swarthmore, PA 19081
       Contact: Mary Susan Milbourne, CMM CEO
       Tel: 610-690-5184
       Email: marysusan@leaddogonline.com
       Website: www.leaddogonline.com
Plan & manage meetings, conferences & special events:
budget dev, site selection, attendee registration,
multimedia presentations. (Woman, estab 1997, empl 3,
sales $275,232, cert: WBENC)

8392   Linguis-Techs, Inc.
       408 Executive Dr
       Langhorne, PA 19047
       Contact: Lisa O'Rourke Dir of Finance
       Tel: 215-860-8152
       Email: lisa@sommerconsulting.com
       Website: www.sommerconsulting.com
Qualitative marketing research, strategy & motivational
profile of target audiences on conscious, unconscious &
emotional levels. (Minority, Woman, estab 1991, empl
11, sales $3,855,315, cert: NMSDC, WBENC)

8393   Markitects, Inc.
       107 W Lancaster Ave, Ste 203
       Wayne, PA 19087
       Contact: Francine Carb CEO
       Tel: 610-687-2200
       Email: fcarb@markitects.com
       Website: www.markitects.com
Strategic marketing, branding, public relations &
communications. (Woman, estab 1994, empl 12, sales
$2,000,000, cert: WBENC)

8394   Maven Communications, LLC
       123 S Broad St Ste 1645
       Philadelphia, PA 19109
       Contact: Jessica Sharp Principal
       Tel: 215-434-7190
       Email: jsharp@mavenagency.com
       Website: www.mavenagency.com
Public relations: strategic planning, community affairs,
issues management, crisis communications & planning,
internal communications, product & corporate launches,
spokesperson & media training. (Woman, estab 2006,
empl 4, sales $315,839, cert: WBENC)

8395 MFR Consultants, Inc.
       128 Chestnut St
       Philadelphia, PA 19106
       Contact: Maria Roberts CEO
       Tel: 215-238-9270
       Email: mfrizelle@mfrconsultants.com
       Website: www.mfrconsultants.com
Strategic marketing, multimedia, graphic design, web &
application development, management consulting.
(Woman/AA, estab 1989, empl 15, sales $4,114,966, cert:
State, WBENC)

8396 MOD Worldwide
       1429 Walnut St Fl 2
       Philadelphia, PA 19102
       Contact: Nina Stanley President
       Tel: 215-732-7666
       Email: nina@modworldwide.com
       Website: www.modworldwide.com
Brand, marketing, digital, 3D visualization, graphic design,
digital media, internet marketing, film, website develop-
ment, production, visual effects, and print production.
(Woman, estab 2002, empl 20, sales $3,000,000, cert: City,
WBENC)

8397 Modern Graphics
       118 Dickerson Rd Ste B
       North Wales, PA 19454
       Contact: Diane Connor President
       Tel: 215-619-4700
       Email: dconnor@modernsbc.com
       Website: www.modernsbc.com
Branding, web design, collateral & digital literature, logo
design, graphic design, internal & external corporate
communications. (Woman, estab 1999, empl 8, sales
$2,100,000, cert: WBENC)

8398 Rector Communications, Inc.
       2300 Chestnut St, Ste. 360
       Philadelphia, PA 19103
       Contact: Marion Rector President
       Tel: 215-963-9661
       Email: marion@rector.com
       Website: www.rector.com
Corporate Communications, Employee Communications,
Branding, Business Development, Marketing Services,
Management Consulting, Graphic Design & Annual
Reports. (Woman, estab 1983, empl 5, sales $654,514,
cert: City, WBENC)

8399 Slice Communications, LLC
       234 Market St, Fl 4
       Philadelphia, PA 19106
       Contact: Brian McDonnell Business Devel
       Tel: 215-600-0050
       Email: bmcdonnell@slicecommunications.com
       Website: www.slicecommunications.com/
Public relations & social media, stories, editorials, re-
search, data, trends, case studies, events & digital assets.
(Woman, estab 2008, empl 15, sales , cert: City, WBENC)

8400 SPRYTE Communications
       200 S Broad St, Ste 1160
       Philadelphia, PA 19102
       Contact: Lisa Simon CEO
       Tel: 215-545-4715
       Email: lsimon@sprytecom.com
       Website: www.sprytecom.com
Public relations & marketing consulting. (Woman, estab
1990, empl 6, sales $1,527,267, cert: State, WBENC)

8401 The Melior Group, Inc.
       1528 Walnut St, Ste 1414
       Philadelphia, PA 19102
       Contact: Linda McAleer President
       Tel: 215-545-0054
       Email: lmcaleer@meliorgroup.com
       Website: www.meliorgroup.com
Marketing research & consulting, analysis, implications
& recommendations. (Woman, estab 1982, empl 10,
sales $1,500,000, cert: State)

Puerto Rico

8402 DC Engineering Group, PSC
       FIrst Federal Savings Bldg, Ste 820 Ponce de Leon
       Ave 1519
       San Juan, PR 00693
       Contact: Daianyk Cordova CEO
       Tel: 787-477-1789
       Email: dcordova@dc-eng.com
       Website: www.dc-eng.com
DC Engineering is a Professional Services Corporation
that offer Project Management and Inspection Services
During Construction. We also provide permit procure-
ment services and environmental services. (Minority,
Woman, estab 2011, empl 8, sales , cert: NMSDC)

8403 Desde Mi Huerto, Inc.
       PO Box 61
       Patillas, PR 00723
       Contact: Raul Rosado Admin
       Tel: 787-202-0392
       Email: desdemihuerto@gmail.com
       Website: www.caribbeanecoseeds.com
We can deliver and merchandize in the island of Puerto
Rico and ship to the southern USA (Minority, Woman,
estab 2012, empl 6, sales , cert: NMSDC)

8404 Maremar Design, Inc.
       Urb Casa Linda Court 20 B St
       Bayamon, PR 00959
       Contact: Marina Rivon President
       Tel: 787-731-8795
       Email: marina@maremar.com
       Website: www.maremar.com
Graphic design, corporate identity, logos, stationary,
graphic standards manual, design consultancy, sales
literature, collateral, point of purchase, annual peports,
corporate profiles, brochures, newsletters. (Minority,
Woman, estab 1997, empl 2, sales , cert: NMSDC)

Rhode Island

8405 Advertising Ventures, Inc. dba (add)ventures
       20 Risho Ave
       East Providence, RI 02914
       Contact: Joseph R Miech COO
       Tel: 401-453-4748
       Email: jmiech@addventures.com
       Website: www.addventures.com
Marketing, branding, public relations, advertising,
graphic & interactive design. (Hisp, estab 1989, empl 42,
sales $9,891,991, cert: State)

8406   FAVOR Design + Communications
       582 Great Rd Ste 201
       North Smithfield, RI 02896
       Contact: Rene Payne Principal
       Tel: 508-272-0522
       Email: rene@favordesignco.com
       Website: www.favordesignco.com
Graphic & web design services, branding, creative direction,
brand identity, content creation, copywriting, positioning,
book design, packaging, interactive design, product design,
typography, editorial, environmental retail. (Woman/AA,
estab 2004, empl 1, sales $335,817, cert: WBENC)

8407   Katie Schibler & Associates LLC
       5875 Post Rd, Unit 1
       East Greenwich, RI 02818
       Contact: Katie Schibler Founder
       Tel: 401-398-0830
       Email: partnerships@schiblerandassociates.com
       Website: www.katieschibler.com
Project Management, Event Planning, Marketing Consult-
ing, Social Media Planning, Social Media Strategy,
Copywriting, Sales Strategy, Strategic Planning, Partnership
Consulting, PR/Media Relations. (Woman, estab 2011, empl
4, sales , cert: WBENC)

8408   North Star Marketing, Inc.
       1130 Ten Rod Rd Ste D-208
       North Kingstown, RI 02852
       Contact: April Williams President
       Tel: 401-294-0133
       Email: april@fortheloveofmarketing.com
       Website: www.fortheloveofmarketing.com
Marketing & PR: direct mail, advertising, strategy, email
marketing & public relations. (Woman, estab 1997, empl
10, sales $708,613, cert: State, WBENC)

Tennessee

8409   Behind the Scenes
       7850 Stage Hills Blvd Ste 103
       Bartlett, TN 38133
       Contact: Dusky Project Mgr
       Tel: 901-937-3926
       Email: dusky@btsmemphis.com
       Website: www.btsmemphis.com
Procurement, warehousing, mail merge & related activities,
event & production management. (Woman, estab 2000,
empl 17, sales $2,000,000, cert: WBENC)

8410   Bytes of Knowledge, Inc.
       1212 6th Ave N
       Nashville, TN 37208
       Contact: Nancy Bass Lead Visual Artist, eLearning
       Tel: 615-383-9005
       Email: sales@bytesofknowledge.com
       Website: www.bytesofknowledge.com
Website design, mobile & software development, brand
support, social marketing, digital elearning, business
strategy, network design & maintenance & entrepreneur
consulting. (Woman, estab 1995, empl 22, sales
$2,964,288, cert: WBENC)

8411   Miller Tanner Associates, LLC
       2070 Lebanon Rd
       Lebanon, TN 37087
       Contact: Dawn Barnes Dir Global Sales
       Tel: 615-466-2600
       Email: dawn@millertanner.com
       Website: www.millertanner.com
Global meeting & event planning. (Woman, estab 1997,
empl 50, sales $26,000,000, cert: WBENC)

8412   Shelton Communications Group, Inc.
       111 E Jackson Ave, Ste 201
       Knoxville, TN 37915
       Contact: Gwen Meadows Accounting Asst
       Tel: 865-524-8385
       Email: gmeadows@sheltongrp.com
       Website: www.sheltongrp.com
Green advertising; green marketing; consumer research;
enviironmental research. (Woman, estab 0, empl , sales ,
cert: WBENC)

Texas

8413   70kft, LLC
       325 N. St. Paul St Ste 3000
       Dallas, TX 75201
       Contact: Tiffany Bryant
       Tel: 214-653-1600
       Email: tiffany@70kft.com
       Website: www.70kft.com
Design, public relations & digital marketing disciplines.
(AA, estab 2003, empl 25, sales $3,251,230, cert: State,
NMSDC)

8414   All About Events
       7810 Chinon Circle
       Houston, TX 77071
       Contact: Elmer Rogers Owner
       Tel: 713-723-1618
       Email: elmer@allaevents.com
       Website: www.allaevents.com
Event planning, ceremonies, conferences, conventions,
exhibitions, fundraisers, meetings, receptions, seminars
& trade shows. (Woman/AA, estab 2005, empl 2, sales ,
cert: State, City, NMSDC)

8415   Boone DeLeon Communications, Inc.
       3100 S Gessner, Ste 110
       Houston, TX 77063
       Contact: Leo De Leon Jr President
       Tel: 713-952-9600
       Email: leo@boonedeleon.com
       Website: www.boonedeleon.com
Marketing, advertising, public relations, promotions,
retail overlays, couponing & sampling, Spanish translations. (Hisp, estab 1979, empl 7, sales $1,656,911, cert:
State, City)

8416   BrandEra, Inc.
       219 S Main St Ste 301
       Fort Worth, TX 76104
       Contact: Elizabeth Owens Principal
       Tel: 817-927-7750
       Email: bo@branderamarketing.com
       Website: www.branderamarketing.com
Strategic planning, sales/promotional initiatives,
advertising, press materials, designing/maintaining
websites, marketing materials, planning special events.
(Woman, estab 2004, empl 4, sales $935,118, cert:
State, WBENC)

8417   Consumer and Market Insights, LLC (CMI)
       3010 Lyndon B Johnson Fwy Ste 1200
       Dallas, TX 75234
       Contact: Royalyn Reid CEO
       Tel: 972-939-9500
       Email: madisen@thecmiteam.com
       Website: www.thecmiteam.com
Market research, training & strategic event planning.
(Woman/AA, estab 1998, empl 16, sales , cert: State,
NMSDC, WBENC, SDB)

8418 CS Creative
      9108 Chancellor Row
      Dallas, TX 75247
      Contact: Cindy Slayton President
      Tel: 214-905-8008
      Email: cindy@cs-creative.com
      Website: www.cs-creative.com
Graphic design svcs: corporate communications, identity
devel & mgmt. (Woman, estab 1989, empl 17, sales
$1,886,000, cert: WBENC)

8419 Cybersoft Technologies Inc.
      4422 FM 1960 W, Ste 300
      Houston, TX 77068
      Contact: Milind Sethi
      Tel: 281-453-8504
      Email: milind.sethi@cybersoft.net
      Website: www.cybersoft.net
Cybersoft Technologies was founded in Houston, Texas in
1996, providing "superior" IT Business solutions an
services to clients nation-wide.
Solutions include ERP, WEB Technologies, EAI, Microsoft
Technologies, Data Management, (As-Ind, estab 1996,
empl 50, sales $7,000,000, cert: State, NMSDC)

8420 Dallas Fan Fares, Inc.
      14900 Landmark Blvd. Ste 300
      Dallas, TX 75254
      Contact: Christine Spradling
      Tel: 972-239-9969
      Email: cspradling@fanfares.com
      Website: www.fanfares.com
Corporate meeting, incentive trips & sporting event
planning. (Woman, estab 1980, empl 35, sales
$14,412,000, cert: WBENC)

8421 DirecToHispanic, LLC
      4909 N McColl Rd
      McAllen, TX 78504
      Contact: Lauren Boyle
      Tel: 562-624-4680
      Email: lauren.boyle@directohispanic.com
      Website: www.directohispanic.com
Marketing promotions agency. (Hisp, estab 2004, empl 12,
sales $2,700,000, cert: NMSDC)

8422 Elias Events, LLC
      6214 Beverly Hill, Ste 24
      Houston, TX 77057
      Contact: Deborah Elias President
      Tel: 713-334-1800
      Email: deborah@eliasevents.com
      Website: www.eliasevents.com
Meeting planning, production schedules, resource & staff
management, marketing & communications strategy &
delivery, graphic design, public relations, marketing/press
collateral, website development & social media support.
(Woman, estab 1998, empl 2, sales $10,111,567, cert: City)

8423 ETC Group, Inc.
      1112 Copeland Rd Ste 400
      Arlington, TX 76011
      Contact: Bill Nichols vp
      Tel: 817-462-0103
      Email: bnichols@etconline.net
      Website: www.etconline.net
Corporate travel management, groups, meeting & incentive, promotional marketing. (Woman, estab 1989, empl
25, sales $40,000,000, cert: State, WBENC)

8424 Event Source Professionals, inc.
      4109 Gateway Court 300
      Colleyville, TX 76034
      Contact: Dara Hall EVP
      Tel: 817-267-6698
      Email: dara@espinc-usa.com
      Website: www.espinc-usa.com
Executive meeting, corporate conference & event
planning services, travel, site selection, trade shows,
exhibits, security, destination management, online and/
or onsite registration. (Woman, estab 1988, empl 4,
sales $2,489,000, cert: WBENC)

8425 EventLink International, Inc.
      5910 N Central Expressway Ste 1665
      Dallas, TX 75206
      Contact: Teri Abram Sales
      Tel: 214-750-9229
      Email: tabram@eventlinkintl.com
      Website: www.eventlinkintl.com
Global corporate event management: conferences,
incentive trips, sales kick-offs, conventions, trade shows,
business meetings, user conferences, retreats, leadership forums, etc. (Woman, estab 1998, empl 4, sales
$330,000, cert: WBENC)

8426 Focus Latino
      720 Barton Creek Blvd
      Austin, TX 78746
      Contact: Guy Antonioli President
      Tel: 512-306-7393
      Email: gcafocuslatino@austin.rr.com
      Website: www.focuslatino.com
Qualitative Research & Strategic Planning, Focus Groups,
Triads, Dyads, IDIs, Ethnographies (In-Homes & Shop-
Alongs) & Quanti-Qualis. (Minority, Woman, estab 1996,
empl 5, sales $814,366, cert: State)

8427 Garcia Baldwin Inc.
      8647 Wurzbach Rd Ste J100
      San Antonio, TX 78240
      Contact: Yvonne Garcia CEO
      Tel: 210-222-1933
      Email: ygarcia@mvculture.com
      Website: www.mvculture.com
Market & advertising, promotions/merchandising, event
marketing, market research creative services, media
strategies. (Minority, Woman, estab 1998, empl 42, sales
$12,791,077, cert: State, NMSDC, WBENC, NWBOC)

8428 Global Exhibit Management
      PO Box 331641
      Fort Worth, TX 76163
      Contact: President
      Tel: 817-370-1400
      Email: info@globalexhibitmanagement.com
      Website: www.globalexhibitmanagement.com
Exhibit & event svcs: rental or purchase options, design
& project management. (Woman, estab 2002, empl 10,
sales $737,681, cert: State, WBENC)

8429 Impact Strategies Consultants
      PO Box 266232
      Houston, TX 77207
      Contact: Debny Greenlee President
      Tel: 713-446-4600
      Email: debny@impact06.com
      Website: www.impact06.com
Business development, diversity marketing, meeting &
special events planning. (Woman/AA, estab 2006, empl
12, sales , cert: WBENC)

8430　Integrated Focus
6523 Embers Rd
Dallas, TX 75248
Contact: Valerie Pelan President
Tel:　214-454-5376
Email: vpelan@integratedfocus.com
Website: www.integratedfocus.com
Leadership management, sales training, branding, sales marketing integration. (Woman, estab 2004, empl 1, sales , cert: WBENC)

8431　Integrity International, Inc.
11767 Katy Frwy, Ste 750
Houston, TX 77079
Contact: Susan Lake Project Mgr
Tel:　877-955-0707
Email: info@tarrenpoint.com
Website: www.tarrenpoint.com
Documentation consulting services, project management, content development (technical documentation), graphic design, technical illustration, desktop publishing, editing & quality assurance, indexing, localization & translation. (Woman, estab 1994, empl 63, sales $6,000,000, cert: State, WBENC)

8432　Ivie & Associates, Inc.
601 Silveron Blvd
Flower Mound, TX 75028
Contact: Jodi Marsh SVP Communications & Bus Dev
Tel:　972-899-4723
Email: jodi.marsh@ivieinc.com
Website: www.ivieinc.com
Advertising & marketing support services: print procurement, print management, media, creative, digital, development, communication/PR services, shopper marketing, kitting & fulfillment, staffing, publishing, CRM. (Woman, estab 1993, empl 650, sales $1,065,000,000, cert: WBENC)

8433　J.O. Agency
440 S Main St
Fort Worth, TX 76104
Contact:　Business Dev Mgr
Tel:　817-335-0100
Email:
Website: www.joagency.com
Full service marketing, public relations and advertising: branding, public relations, graphic design, market research, marketing campaigns, digital marketing, etc. (Woman, estab 1998, empl 10, sales $950,825, cert: WBENC)

8434　K. Fernandez and Associates LLC
10601 RR 2222 Ste R13
Austin, TX 78730
Contact: Karla Fernandez Parker CEO
Tel:　210-614-1052
Email: karla@kfernandez.com
Website: www.kfernandez.com
Marketing services. (Minority, Woman, estab 1996, empl 11, sales $2,640,615, cert: State)

8435　Listo Translating Services & More LLC
830 S Mason Rd, Ste B2-A
Katy, TX 77450
Contact: Roxana Heredia CEO
Tel:　832-592-9264
Email: roxana@listotranslating.com
Website: www.houston-translation.com/
Translation & interpretation services. (Minority, Woman, estab 2012, empl 2, sales $150,000, cert: State, City, NMSDC)

8436　LNT 3 Group
545 E John Carpenter Frwy Ste 300
Irving, TX 75062
Contact: Marqueax Price President
Tel:　214-650-9966
Email: marqueax.price@lnt3group.com
Website: www.lnt3group.com
Marketing, e-communications, business development & new media services & support. (Woman/AA, estab 2010, empl 1, sales , cert: State)

8437　Magic Moments Parties and Events
4760 Preston Rd Ste 244-257
Frisco, TX 75034
Contact: Courtney Rai VP Sales & Mktg
Tel:　214-688-9900
Email: courtney@magicmomentsevents.com
Website: www.magicmomentsevents.com
Event planning, custom design & décor, floral design, event lighing, drapery, theme decor, props, interactive LED dance floor, custom artwork. (Woman, estab 2004, empl 12, sales $550,000, cert: WBENC)

8438　Malkoff Promotions
4904 Stony Ford Dr
Dallas, TX 75287
Contact: Lynne Malkoff President
Tel:　972-248-4354
Email: lynne@lmpspecialties.com
Website: www.lmpspecialties.com
Marketing & promotional solutions. (Woman, estab 1989, empl 5, sales , cert: State, WBENC)

8439　Mobius Partners Enterprise Solutions
1711 Citadel Plaza
San Antonio, TX 78209
Contact: Arlene Watson Principal
Tel:　216-621-9653
Email: arlene@mobiusgrey.com
Website: www.mobiusgrey.com
Design & visual communications, marketing development & branding. (Woman/AA, Hisp, estab 2002, empl 4, sales $33,600,000, cert: State, NMSDC)

8440　MSR Group, Inc.
3060 Communications Pkwy, Ste 200
Plano, TX 75093
Contact: Lauren Dunnaway Dir Sales & Marketing
Tel:　214-291-2920
Email: lauren.dunnaway@infinxglobal.com
Website: www.infinixglobal.com
Meeting management, Site selection, negotiation & venue contracting. (Woman, estab 1994, empl 25, sales $14,787,000, cert: State, WBENC)

8441　n8 Solutions
18650 Martinique
Houston, TX 77058
Contact: Dawn Magnan Owner
Tel:　281-333-3428
Email: dawn@n8s.cc
Website: www.n8s.cc
Marketing communications, marketing plans, packaging, advertising, sales materials & public relations, design brochures, trade show displays, point-of-purchase, billboards, direct mail, ads, corporate identity logos and standards, catalogs. (Woman, estab 1996, empl 3, sales $700,000, cert: WBENC)

8442 OMS Strategic Advisors, LLC
2591 Dallas Pkwy, Ste 300
Frisco, TX 75034
Contact: Lawrence Gardner President
Tel: 214-207-7720
Email: lawrence.gardner@omsstrategicadvisors.com
Website: www.omsstrategicadvisors.com
commercial real estate services firm specializing in tenant representation, project leasing, strategic marketing and related consulting. We are a network of senior professionals with extensive relationships in the industry. (Woman/AA, estab 2009, empl 2, sales $560,000, cert: State, NMSDC)

8443 Onyx Power and Gas LLC
13155 Noel Rd Ste 900
Dallas, TX 75240
Contact: Loraine Sutton Mgr
Tel: 214-871-5574
Email: vinnies@onyxpg.com
Website: www.onyxpg.com
Energy management and procurement; power sales; consultation concerning strategies to control and reduce energy costs; consultation concerning market and bid analysis and contract evaluation. (AA, estab 2009, empl 14, sales , cert: State, NMSDC)

8444 Open Channels Group, LLC
1320 S. University Dr Ste 220
Fort Worth, TX 76107
Contact: Tonya Veasey CEO
Tel: 817-332-0404
Email: info@ocgpr.com
Website: www.ocgpr.com
Public Relations, Multicultural Strategy Development, Integrated Communications, Digital Strategies, Public Involvement, Advertising & Marketing. (Woman/AA, estab 2005, empl 20, sales $1,794,160, cert: NMSDC)

8445 Outreach Strategists LLC
2727 Allen Pkwy., Ste 1300
Houston, TX 77019
Contact: Mustafa Tameez Managing Dir
Tel: 713-247-9600
Email: marketing@outreachstrategists.com
Website: www.outreachstrategists.com
Corporate & strategic communications, messaging, government affairs, public relations & marketing, ethnic & media relations, advocacy, constituent engagement, community outreach, graphic design, crisis management. (As-Ind, estab 2003, empl 5, sales $500,000, cert: State)

8446 Planning Professionals, Ltd.
1210 W McDermott Ste 111
Allen, TX 75013
Contact: Mollie Wallace CEO
Tel: 469-854-6991
Email: mwallace@planningprofessionals.com
Website: www.planningprofessionals.com
Web dev, logistical support, hotel site selection, electronic mktg, on-site staffing, food & beverage selection, contract negotiation, transportation, airfare, event marketing, signs, graphics, premiums & giveaways, mail fulfillment. (Woman, estab 1994, empl 12, sales $6,265,000, cert: WBENC)

8447 Production & Event Services, Inc.
9425 Sandy Ln
Manvel, TX 77578
Contact: Cindy Kutch President
Tel: 281-585-0569
Email: cindy@eventsplanning.com
Website: www.EventsPlanning.com
Special event services: sound, lighting, staging, theme decor, drapery, entertainment, catering, event planning, production & show management. (Woman, estab 2003, empl 10, sales , cert: WBENC)

8448 Regali Inc.
518 N Interurban St
Richardson, TX 75081
Contact: Renee Dutia President
Tel: 972-726-8830
Email: renee@regaliinc.com
Website: www.regaliinc.com
Diversified global marketing & technology services, integrating promotional programs, creative development & technology. (Woman/As-Ind, estab 1989, empl 7, sales , cert: State, NMSDC)

8449 Rutherford Enterprises, Inc.
17304 Preston Rd Ste 1020
Dallas, TX 75252
Contact: Al Rutherford President
Tel: 214-438-1185
Email: alrutherford@teamrutherford.net
Website: www.teamrutherford.net
Convention, meeting & event planning, event mgmt, communications, sourcing & site selection, housing management, attrition mitigation, exhibit & logistics mgmt, senior executive travel support. (AA, estab 1998, empl 10, sales $1,032,594, cert: NMSDC)

8450 Sanders Wingo Advertising, Inc.
303 N Oregon Auite 1200
El Paso,, TX 79901
Contact: Leslie Wingo President
Tel: 915-533-9583
Email: lwingo@sanderswingo.com
Website: www.sanderswingo.com
Strategic planning, account planning, public relations, research, brand creation, account services, media planning, buying & creative services. (AA, Hisp, estab 1958, empl 76, sales $27,800,000, cert: NMSDC)

8451 Steel Digital Studios, Inc.
6414 Bee Cave Rd, Ste B
Austin, TX 78746
Contact: Andrea Wallace Business Dev Dir
Tel: 800-681-8809
Email: andrea.wallace@steelbranding.com
Website: www.steelbranding.com
Family targeted marketing. (Woman, estab 2000, empl 25, sales $4,321,750, cert: State, WBENC)

8452 Strategar LLC
3100 Independence Pkwy, Ste 311-204
Plano, TX 75075
Contact: Yareli Esteban CEO
Tel: 972-948-3781
Email: yareli@strategar.com
Website: www.strategar.com
Marketing services: marketing, advertising, translations, web development, creative services, SEM, traditional media, content production & support of promotional events. (Minority, Woman, estab 2013, empl 3, sales , cert: State)

8453 Studio B Dallas, LLC
2719 Randal Lake lane
Spring, TX 77388
Contact: MJ Moreau President
Tel: 281-528-7000
Email: mj@studiobdallas.com
Website: www.studiobdallas.com
Strategic design, brand identity, packaging, retail store design & restaurant store design & merchandising. (Woman, estab 2009, empl 1, sales $165,000, cert: City)

8454 Studio J Designworks LLC
7750 N. Macarthur Blvd Ste 120-356
Irving, TX 75063
Contact: Gina Jacobson Owner
Tel: 972-556-0511
Email: gina.jacobson@studiojdesignworks.com
Website: www.studiojdesignworks.com
Visual communication solutions, branding, tag line development, trade show & event marketing, copywriting & copy editing, flash animation & development. (Woman, estab 2008, empl 2, sales , cert: State, WBENC)

8455 T3
1801 N Lamar Blvd
Austin, TX 78701
Contact: Gay Gaddis Founder & CEO
Tel: 512-499-8811
Email: austin.hegarty@t-3.com
Website: www.t-3.com
Integrated marketing solutions. (Woman, estab 1989, empl 150, sales , cert: WBENC)

8456 Tandem Axle Inc. dba Mixed Media Creations
2300 Rockbrook Dr Ste D
Lewisville, TX 75067
Contact: Whitney Stockstill Business Operations Mgr
Tel: 972-221-1600
Email: whitney@mailmmc.com
Website: www.mixedmediacreations.com
Graphic Design, Large-Scale Design, Web Development, Digital Media, Photography / Videography, Printing Services, Creative Consultation, Copywriting / Editing, Marketing Campaigns, Branded Merchandise. (Woman, estab 2007, empl 27, sales $2,800,000, cert: State, WBENC)

8457 Teneo Linguistics Company, LLC
4700 Bryant Irvin Ct. Ste 301
Fort Worth, TX 76107
Contact: Hana Laurenzo CEO
Tel: 817-441-9974
Email: hana@tlctranslation.com
Website: www.tlctranslation.com
Foreign language translation & interpreting services. (Woman, estab , empl , sales $1,400,000, cert: State, WBENC)

8458 The Backshop, Inc. DBA Mercury Mambo
1107 S 8th St
Austin, TX 78704
Contact: Liz Arreaga Partner
Tel: 512-447-4440
Email: liz@mercurymambo.com
Website: www.mercurymambo.com
Research & strategic planning, sales promotions, shopper marketing, retail merchandising, online/social media, field management, brand advertising experiential marketing, bilingual local market staffing. (Minority, Woman, estab 1999, empl 3, sales $1,062,732, cert: NMSDC, WBENC)

8459 The ID Development Group
8811 Teel Pkwy, Ste 100 - 5233
Frisco, TX 75035
Contact: Julian Dorise President
Tel: 214-295-5414
Email: jdorise@iddevelop.com
Website: www.iddevelop.com
Project designs, creative interior environments, tradeshow events & marketing campaigns. (AA, estab 2010, empl 5, sales , cert: NMSDC)

8460 The Maxcel Company
6600 LBJ Freeway Ste 109
Dallas, TX 75240
Contact: Gwenna Brush President
Tel: 972-644-0880
Email: gwenna.brush@maxcel.net
Website: www.maxcel.net
Plan & manage meetings, conventions & incentive travel programs. (Woman, estab 1995, empl 6, sales , cert: State, WBENC)

8461 Trilogy LLC
5601 Democracy Dr Ste 105
Plano, TX 75024
Contact: Jeff Hoedebeck VP Business Dev
Tel: 972-473-8911
Email: jeffh@trilogymktg.com
Website: www.trilogymktg.com
Experiential marketing: product sampling, product demonstrations, product merchandising & sponsorship activations. (AA, Hisp, estab 2002, empl 10, sales $3,500,000, cert: State, NMSDC)

8462 Ultimate Ventures
4400 Beltway Dr
Addison, TX 75001
Contact: Val Lenington VP
Tel: 972-732-8433
Email: val@ultimateventures.com
Website: www.ultimateventures.com
Special events, transportation, conference & convention services, corporate meeting & team building, inbound incentive programs & customized sightseeing tours. (Woman, estab 1993, empl 12, sales , cert: WBENC)

8463 Ward Creative Communications, Inc.
PO Box 701219
Houston, TX 77270
Contact: Deborah Buks President
Tel: 713-869-0707
Email: dbuks@wardcc.com
Website: www.wardcc.com
Media, community & employee relations; public affairs; marketing communications, graphic design; special events; crisis management. (Woman, estab 1990, empl 1, sales $1,200,000,000, cert: State)

8464 Winkler Public Relations
PO Box 73404
Houston, TX 77273
Contact: Kathleen Winkler CEO
Tel: 713-259-0189
Email: kathy@winklerpr.com
Website: www.winklerpr.com
Public relations services, crisis mgmt, media training. (Woman, estab 2003, empl 2, sales , cert: WBENC)

Utah

8465 Andavo Meetings & Incentives
5588 S Green St Ste 300
Salt Lake City, UT 84123
Contact: Jessica Perez
Tel: 720-398-5504
Email: jessica.perez@andavomeetings.com
Website: www.andavomeetings.com
Meetings, incentives & event planning & management. (Woman, estab 1982, empl 162, sales $36,989,079, cert: WBENC)

8466 Andinas dba/ Inlingua Utah
602 E 300 S
Salt Lake City, UT 84102
Contact: Don Durham Business Devel
Tel: 801-355-3775
Email: don@inlinguautah.com
Website: www.inlinguautah.com
Language classes, interpretation & translation services, translate websites, technical & legal documents. (Minority, Woman, estab 1996, empl 15, sales $1,013,000, cert: NMSDC)

8467 Craig Enterprises, Inc.
7069 S Highland Dr Ste 201
Salt Lake City, UT 84121
Contact: Lelani Craig President
Tel: 801-944-4049
Email: lelani@commgap.com
Website: www.commgap.com
Communications, interpretation, document translation, voice-over, website development, language training, cultural consulting & localization. (Minority, Woman, estab 2000, empl 4, sales $350,000, cert: WBENC)

Virginia

8468 360 Virtual Assistance, LLC
905 22nd St
Newport News, VA 23607
Contact: Natalie Robertson CEO
Tel: - -
Email: sales@360virtualassistance.com
Website: www.360virtualassistance.com
Integrated document preparation, multimedia creation, content design, layout, printing, optical scanning, research, technical writing. (AA, estab 2013, empl 1, sales , cert: State, NMSDC)

8469 All About Presentation, LLC
707 E Main St Ste 1615
Richmond, VA 23219
Contact: Andrea M. Lyons CEO
Tel: 804-381-4002
Email: andrea@allaboutpresentation.com
Website: www.allaboutpresentation.com
Event management: plan, design, manage and produce corporate events. (Woman/AA, estab 2007, empl 5, sales , cert: State, NMSDC)

8470 Bare International Inc.
3702 Pender Dr, Ste 305
Fairfax, VA 22030
Contact: Lynne Brighton Sr VP
Tel: 703-995-3132
Email: lbrighton@bareinternational.com
Website: www.bareinternational.com
Mystery shopping, employee surveys, video mystery shopping. (Woman, estab 1987, empl 300, sales $16,000,000, cert: WBENC)

8471 Candice Bennett & Associates, Inc.
9621 Masey McQuire Ct
Lorton, VA 22079
Contact: Candice Bennett President
Tel: 703-919-6231
Email: clb@candicebennett.com
Website: www.candicebennett.com
Market research, communications, organizational assessment & development. (Woman, estab 2003, empl 7, sales $619,866, cert: State, WBENC)

8472 Customer Relationship Metrics
100 Glenn Dr, Ste A-11
Sterling, VA 20164
Contact: Dr. Jodie Monger President
Tel: 410-643-1136
Email: jmonger@metrics.net
Website: www.metrics.net
Automated, email & website customer surveys, metrics designs, customer satisfaction & loyalty programs, data collection, analysis, reporting & consulting. (Woman, estab 1993, empl 14, sales $3,500,000, cert: WBENC)

8473 DGS Create, Inc.
6400 Arligton Blvd
Falls Church, VA 22042
Contact: Christine Francis Owner
Tel: 703-776-1919
Email: christine@printdgs.com
Website: www.dgscreate.com
Graphic design, digital printing, mailing & e-mailing
services & online communication channels. (Woman, estab
2012, empl 21, sales $1,854,501, cert: NMSDC)

8474 Elizabeth Coffey Design
1616 Claremont Ave
Richmond, VA 23227
Contact: Elizabeth Coffey Principal
Tel: 804-266-2193
Email: ecoffey@elizabethcoffeydesign.com
Website: www.estrategicdesign.com
Graphic design solutions, brochures, publications, catalogs,
advertisements, direct mail, websites, displays and
banners, invitations, logos & identity packages. (Woman,
estab 2000, empl 1, sales , cert: State)

8475 Exhibit Edge Inc.
4315-A Walney Road
Chantilly, VA 20151
Contact: Bev Gray President
Tel: 703-230-0000
Email: bev.gray@exhibitedge.com
Website: www.exhibitedge.com
Trade show exhibit services: design & fabricate custom
exhibits, rent trade show displays & exhibits, large format
graphics & banners. (Woman, estab 1992, empl 20, sales
$3,450,000, cert: WBENC)

8476 Frontline Marketing LLC
2248 Dabney Rd, Ste J
Richmond, VA 23230
Contact: Henry Howells President
Tel: 804-359-2422
Email: h.howells@frontline-exhibits.com
Website: www.frontline-exhibits.com
Mfr, design & dist trade show & outdoor event exhibits &
office environments. (Woman, estab 1992, empl 5, sales
$635,000, cert: State)

8477 Johnson, Inc.
201 W Broad St Ste 600
Richmond, VA 23220
Contact: Andre Dean Corp VP
Tel: 804-644-8515
Email: adean@johnsonmarketing.com
Website: www.johnsonmarketing.com
Marketing & communications. (AA, estab 1993, empl 15,
sales $2,750,000, cert: State)

8478 KTL Communications LLC
5055 Seminary Rd, 1220 Unit
Alexandria, VA 22311
Contact: Amir Khan Owner
Tel: 703-662-0465
Email: amir@ktl-communications.com
Website: www.ktl-communications.com
Language Service Provider (LSP), translation, in person
interpretation, DTP, localization, language tutoring &
language authentication services. (Minority, Woman, estab
2013, empl 2, sales , cert: State)

8479 LeapFrog Solutions, Inc.
3201 Jermantown Rd Ste 350
Fairfax, VA 22030
Contact: Kathleen Jerabek Contracts & Pricing
Mgr
Tel: 703-273-7900
Email: kjerabek@leapfrogit.com
Website: www.leapfrogit.com
Strategic marketing communications: web site design,
graphic design, branding/marketing campaigns, multi-
media, corporate collateral materials. (Woman, estab
1996, empl 11, sales $893,494, cert: State, WBENC)

8480 Montage Marketing Group, LLC
8000 Westpark Dr Ste 480
McLean, VA 22102
Contact: Mercedita Roxas-Murray CEO
Email:
mroxasmurray@montagemarketinggroup.com
Website: www.montagemarketinggroup.com
Full cycle integrated experiential marketing: Audience
intelligence/data & market analysis, Strategy development, campaign conceptualization, creative development, experiential design. (Minority, Woman, estab
2015, empl 3, sales $1,900,000, cert: State, NMSDC,
WBENC, 8(a))

8481 National Events LLC
4003 Westfax Dr, Ste L
Chantilly, VA 20151
Contact: Ruth Crout CEO
Tel: 703-961-1105
Email: RCrout@nationaleventsllc.com
Website: www.nationaleventsllc.com
Strategic event planning, comprehensive event manage-
ment, and all-inclusive event production services for
private, corporate, government, and not-for-profit
organizations. (Woman, estab 2003, empl 8, sales
$2,154,730, cert: WBENC)

8482 Nexus Direct, LLC
101 W Main St Ste 400
Norfolk, VA 23510
Contact: Suzanne Nowers CEO
Tel: 757-340-5960
Email: suzanne@nexusdirect.com
Website: www.nexusdirect.com
Direct marketing, marketing spend, strategy, creative,
messaging, production, media buying, data analytics,
processing, modeling & overall analysis & attribution of
the direct marketing program results. (Woman, estab
2004, empl 30, sales $6,243,833, cert: WBENC)

8483 Omega World Travel
3102 Omega Office Park
Fairfax, VA 22031
Contact: Jackie Olt Marketing & PR Specialist
Tel: 703-359-0200
Email: jolt@owt.net
Website: www.OmegaTravel.com
Full service travel agency. Meeting Planning & Strategic
Meetings Management Services. (Minority, Woman,
estab 1972, empl 475, sales $1,400,000,000, cert:
WBENC)

8484   ORI
171 Elden St Ste 160
Herndon, VA 20170
Contact: Kathleen Benson CEO
Tel: 571-257-3205
Email: kathyb@oriresults.com
Website: www.ORIresults.com
Strategic research planning, sample & questionnaire
design, qualitative & quantitative research, data collection,
technology-based online research, data coding & entry,
database mgmt & integration, statistical analysis &
interpretation. (Woman, estab 1988, empl 75, sales
$22,971,050, cert: WBENC)

8485   Rhudy & Co. Communications and Marketing, Inc.
14342 Lander Rd
Midlothian, VA 23113
Contact: Michele Rhudy President
Tel: 804-897-0762
Email: michele@rhudy.biz
Website: www.rhudy.biz
Public relations, communications & marketing consulting:
strategic communications planning, media relations,
writing services. (Woman, estab 2003, empl 16, sales
$2,200,000, cert: State, WBENC)

8486   The Dominion Group Marketing Research & Consult-
ing
1800 Alexander Bell Dr Ste 515
Reston, VA 20191
Contact: Susan Wyant President
Tel: 703-234-2360
Email: swyant@thedominiongrp.com
Website: www.thedominiongrp.com
Marketing research, competitive intelligence, & consulting,
qualitiative methodologies. (Woman, estab 1993, empl 7,
sales $2,934,757, cert: WBENC)

8487   The InnovateHers
713 Huntsman Rd
Sandston, VA 23150
Contact: Tasha Chambers Principal
Tel: 804-263-0491
Email: info@theinnovatehers.com
Website: www.theinnovatehers.com
PR Communications Plans News Releases Crisis Communi-
cations Executive Speeches Media Monitoring Community
Engagement Events Theme Conceptualization Venue
Selection Celebrity/Talent Contract Negotiation Event
Styling Volunteer Management Guest Management.
(Woman/AA, estab 2017, empl 1, sales , cert: State)

Washington

8488   Blue Crest Creative, LLC
5108 S Myrtle St
Seattle, WA 98118
Contact: Troy Shelby Creative Dir
Tel: 800-476-0128
Email: shelbyt@bluecrestcreative.com
Website: www.bluecrestcreative.com
Corporate Identity Design, Branding, Logo, Letterhead,
Business Cards, Print Design, Brochures, Invitations, Direct
Mail, Newsletters, Internet Design, Architecture planning,
Web Design, eNewsletters, Maintenance, SharePoint. (AA,
estab 2011, empl 1, sales $105,600, cert: City, NMSDC)

8489   Dynamic Events Inc
6715 NE 63rd St
Vancouver, WA 98661
Contact: Tim Fish Dir Sales/Marketing
Tel: 503-686-1498
Email: tfish@dynamicevents.com
Website: www.dynamicevents.com
Professional event management company committed to
strategic management and execution of our global
client's requirements, extraordinary service and cutting
edge planning.
Area (Woman, estab 1998, empl 40, sales $5,000,000,
cert: WBENC)

8490   Elite Meetings & Events of Washington
2606 81st Court NW
Gig Harbor, WA 98332
Contact: Eileen Higgins President
Tel: 866-734-9990
Email: ehiggins@emeworldwide.com
Website: www.emeworldwide.com
Meetings, trade shows & incentives, event planning.
(Woman, estab 1998, empl 3, sales $25,000,000, cert:
WBENC)

8491   Green Cat Dzine, Inc.
5412 101st St SW
Mukilteo, WA 98275
Contact: Elisabeth Rumpelsberger President
Tel: 206-406-8329
Email: liz@greencatdzine.com
Website: www.greencatdzine.com
Graphic design: print, online (web), environmental
graphics, strategic branding, promotions, online devel-
opment, logo work, posters, brochures, invitations,
tradeshow exhibit designs. (Woman, estab 2001, empl 1,
sales $148,000, cert: State)

8492   PRR, Inc.
1501 4th Ave, Ste 550
Seattle, WA 98101
Contact: Rachel Novotny Business Devel
Tel: 206-623-0735
Email: bd@prrbiz.com
Website: www.prrbiz.com
Public relations, marketing, market research, social &
digital media, graphic design, facilitation, public involve-
ment & advertising services. (Minority, Woman, estab
1981, empl 86, sales , cert: State)

Wisconsin

8493   Market Probe, Inc.
2655 N Mayfair Rd
Milwaukee, WI 53226
Contact: Bonnie Lockwood Sr VP
Tel: 414-778-6000
Email: info@marketprobe.com
Website: www.marketprobe.com
Market research & cstmr satisfaction research svcs. (As-
Ind, estab 1976, empl 125, sales $40,000,000, cert:
State, NMSDC)

8494 Mazur/Zachow, Inc.
      1025 S Moorland Rd Ste 300
      Brookfield, WI 53005
      Contact: Michele Conway President
      Tel: 262-938-9244
      Email: michelec@mazurzachow.com
      Website: www.mazurzachow.com
data collection services, marketing research studies, focus
groups, IDI's, ethnographic studies, in-home product
placements & music tests. (Woman, estab 1983, empl 16,
sales , cert: WBENC)

8495 Meetings & Incentives Worldwide, Inc.
      10520 7 Mile Road
      Caledonia, WI 53108
      Contact: Dan Tarpey VP Sales & Marketing
      Tel: 773-851-0908
      Email: dtarpey@meetings-incentives.com
      Website: www.meetings-incentives.com
Global strategic meeting & event management, strategic
meeting management implementation, global strategic
sourcing & contracting, attendee management. (Woman,
estab 1967, empl 350, sales $90,000,000, cert: WBENC)

8496 Revelation, LLC
      222 N Midvale Blvd Ste 18
      Madison, WI 53705
      Contact: Brian Lee President
      Tel: 608-622-7767
      Email: brian@experiencerevelation.com
      Website: www.experiencerevelation.com
Public relations, media buying, ad buying, advertising,
social media consulting, internet marketing, web marketing & speaking engagements. (As-Pac, estab 2010, empl 3,
sales $170,000, cert: NMSDC)

8497 Rivera & Associates, Inc.
      1543 S 14th St
      Milwaukee, WI 53204
      Contact: Michael Rivera CEO
      Tel: 414-736-1255
      Email: michael.rivera@riveraprfirm.com
      Website: www.riveraprfirm.com
Public Relations, Marketing, Strategic Communication,
Multicultural Marketing, Public Information & Outreach,
Media Relations, Language Translations, Management
Consulting, Brand Awareness, Environmental Marketing.
(Hisp, estab , empl , sales , cert: State)

8498 The Dieringer Research Group, Inc.
      200 Bishops Way
      Brookfield, WI 53005
      Contact: Shelley Ahrens Chief Customer Officer
      Tel: 262-432-5231
      Email: shelley.ahrens@thedrg.com
      Website: www.thedrg.com
Customer Experience, Brand Awareness, Product Development, and Market Opportunity. (Woman, estab 1974, empl
74, sales $6,720,000, cert: WBENC)

West Virginia

8499 CRA Communications LLC
      601 Morris St Ste 301
      Charleston, WV 25301
      Contact: Susan Lavenski CEO
      Tel: 304-342-0161
      Email: slavenski@charlesryan.com
      Website: www.charlesryan.com
Account Management, Planning, Advertising, Branding,
Communications, Crisis Communications, Graphic
Design, Media Buying, Media Relations, Media Training,
Message Development, Public Relations, Social Media,
Strategy. (Woman, estab 2015, empl 25, sales
$6,402,960, cert: WBENC)

PROFESSIONAL SERVICES: Staffing Services
Firms provide temporary and permanent personnel placement, contract and direct hire, personnel consulting, training and employment services. NAICS Code 54

Alabama

8500 CD Covenant Distributors International LLC
1400 Commerce Blvd Ste 12
Anniston, AL 36207
Contact: Rod Lemon CEO
Tel: 256-832-4385
Email: rlemon@cdcovenant.com
Website: www.cdcovenant.com
CD Covenant Distributors International (CD) is a Minority Owned/ Disadvantage, Service Disable Veteran Owned Small Business Business (MBE, SBE, DBE). CD was incorporated in 2001 in the State of Alabama. We are a reputable provider of MRO Products a (AA, estab 2001, empl 6, sales $254,000, cert: City, NMSDC, 8(a))

8501 EALI Logistics Solutions LLC
123 N 7th St
Gadsden, AL 35901
Contact: JT Johnson President
Tel: 785-213-5493
Email: jt@ealilogistics.com
Website: www.EaliLogistics.com
EcoChemPro product is 100% biodegradable cleaner/ degreaser, contains no VOC's, no acids, no alkalis, no butyl, and has a neutral pH, and it is safe for people to use and it is environmental friendly. This product can replace multiple (AA, estab 2014, empl 6, sales , cert: NMSDC)

8502 Providence Staffing LLC
15 Windsweep Ct, Ste 114
Phenix City, AL 36870
Contact: Albert Williams President
Tel: 706-358-8926
Email: albertwilliams@get2worknow.com
Website: www.get2worknow.com
Broad-based staffing and recruiting solutions, temporary, temp-to-hire, and permanent employees. (AA, estab 2018, empl 1, sales , cert: State)

8503 RecruitSource, Inc.
3532 Seventh Ct S
Birmingham, AL 35222
Contact: Jane Smith CEO
Tel: 205-322-6822
Email: jsmith@recruitsource.org
Website: www.rsi-services.com
Contract management services: staff augmentation, advertising & marketing. (Minority, Woman, estab 2001, empl 4, sales , cert: WBENC)

8504 SK Services, LLC
45281 US Hwy 78
Lincoln, AL 35096
Contact: Sonya Jacks President
Tel: 205-763-1818
Email: job4u@skstaffing.com
Website: www.skstaffing.com
Staffing, temp to hire & contingent staffing. (Woman, estab 2010, empl 9, sales , cert: WBENC)

8505 Tech Providers, Inc.
2117 Magnolia Ave S
Birmingham, AL 35205
Contact: Eleanor Estes CEO
Tel: 205-930-9664
Email: eleanorestes@techproviders.com
Website: www.techproviders.com
Permanent IT staffing needs, IT software developers, IT systems or database administrators, financial staffing & engineering staffing. (Woman, estab 1998, empl 135, sales $10,701,387, cert: WBENC)

Arkansas

8506 Temporaries Plus, Inc.
601 E Eighth Ave
Pine Bluff, AR 71601
Contact: Kayla Cheatwood Sales
Tel: 870-535-5507
Email: kcheatwood@ateamtemp.com
Website: www.ateamtemp.com
Temporary staffing services. (Woman/AA, estab 1995, empl 7, sales $5,300,000, cert: WBENC)

Arizona

8507 All About People, Inc.
4422 East Indian School Road
Phoenix, AZ 85018
Contact: Charles Mitchell CEO
Tel: 602-955-1212
Email: charles@allaboutpeople.net
Website: www.allaboutpeople.net/
Temporary & executive level staffing. (AA, estab 2002, empl 87, sales , cert: NMSDC)

8508 Axis Employment Services
7000 N 16th St, Ste 120-501
Phoenix, AZ 85020
Contact: Tran Tran CEO
Tel: 602-301-8115
Email: tran@axisemployment.com
Website: www.axisemployment.com
Temporaries, temp-to-hire & direct hire searches, drug testing, Criminal/County searches, software testing, education & employment verification. (Minority, Woman, estab 2002, empl 6, sales $2,130,000, cert: State, City)

8509 AZ Construction Resources, Inc., dba AZCR Staffing
2601 W Dunlap Ave Ste #4
Phoenix, AZ 85021
Contact: Kim Jones Dir of Sourcing
Tel: 602-870-3515
Email: kjones@azcrstaffing.com
Website: www.azcrstaffing.com
Temporary and Temp to Perm Employees to the Industrial, Oil & Construction Industries (Minority, Woman, estab 2006, empl 100, sales $11,093,000, cert: NMSDC, WBENC)

8510   Bridgeport Resources, LLC
930 W Watson Dr
Tempe, AZ 85283
Contact: Diana Lemos-Marquez
Tel: 480-456-6031
Email: diana@bridgeportresources.com
Website: www.bridgeportresources.com
Direct placement staffing service, Finance, Accounting, Administration, Customer Service, Education, Engineering, IT, Healthcare, Management, Manufacturing, Sales/Marketing, Human Resources. (Minority, Woman, estab 2013, empl 2, sales , cert: NMSDC)

8511   Creative Human Resources Concepts LLC
4710 E Falcon Dr, Ste 125
Mesa, AZ 85215
Contact: Rosa Roy President
Tel: 480-654-4606
Email: rosa@chrc4work.com
Website: www.chrc4work.com
Staffing: contract, full-time, part-time, temporary, long & short-term. (Minority, Woman, estab 1997, empl 205, sales $1,723,389, cert: NMSDC, CPUC, WBENC)

8512   DuffyGroup, Inc.
4727 E Union Hills Dr, Ste 200
Phoenix, AZ 85050
Contact: Kathleen Duffy Ybarra President
Tel: 602-942-7112
Email: kduffy@duffygroupinc.com
Website: www.duffygroupinc.com
Executive search, sourcing, HR contracting & direct hire, short-term, extended assignments. (Woman, estab 1991, empl 25, sales $2,600,000, cert: WBENC)

8513   Egnite LLC
4747 E Elliot Rd Bldg 29, Ste 600
Phoenix, AZ 85044
Contact: Alex Luevano VP
Tel: 602-931-5000
Email: alex.luevano@egniteinc.com
Website: www.egniteinc.com
Direct placement, contract, contract to hire & project solutions. (Minority, Woman, estab 2007, empl 5, sales $325,000, cert: State)

8514   Elsner Human Resources
7409 E Chaparral Rd Ste A110
Scottsdale, AZ 85250
Contact: Krisanne Elsner CEO
Tel: 480-657-8638
Email: ke@southwestrecruiting.com
Website: www.elsnerhr.com
Recruiting, talent acquisition, executive search. (Woman, estab 2003, empl 1, sales $115,000, cert: WBENC)

8515   JBN & Associates, LLC.
4040 E Camelback Rd Ste 280
Phoenix, AZ 85018
Contact: Dainiz Alvarez Exec Search Mgr
Tel: 480-344-2822
Email: info@jbnassociates.com
Website: www.jbnassociates.com
Recruiting firm, direct/perm placements, executive search & C-level positions. (Woman, estab 1999, empl 12, sales , cert: WBENC)

8516   Safe T Professionals LLC
241 S Washington St
Chandler, AZ 85249
Contact: Anna Martinez CEO
Tel: 800-502-9481
Email: info@safetpros.com
Website: www.safetpros.com
Safety staff augmentation and consulting services. (Woman/Hisp, estab 2011, empl 57, sales $8,700,000, cert: NMSDC)

8517   Scott Business Group, LLC
668 N 44th St Ste 300
Phoenix, AZ 85008
Contact: Milagros Gonzalez-Scott
Tel: 480-694-2619
Email: millie@scottbiz.net
Website: www.scottbiz.net
Contract & temporary staffing. (AA, estab 2003, empl 105, sales $3,451,356, cert: State, City, NMSDC)

8518   Source Group Professionals
4729 E Sunrise Dr Ste 244
Tucson, AZ 85718
Contact: GM
Tel: 520-870-5114
Email: info@sourcegrouppros.com
Website: www.sourcegrouppros.com
Staffing services. (Woman, estab 2003, empl 35, sales $1,273,000, cert: WBENC)

California

8519   24-Hour Medical Staffing Services, LLC
21700 East Copley Dr Ste 270
Diamond Bar, CA 09765
Contact: Linda Stone VP Sales & Client Delivery
Tel: 909-895-8960
Email: linda@24-hrmed.com
Website: www.24-hrmed.com
Temporary healthcare staffing services to clients on permanent, per diem, travel, and local contract assignment. (Minority, Woman, estab 2000, empl 150, sales $8,678,030, cert: NMSDC)

8520   3 Bridge Networks LLC
601 Montgomery St Ste 715
San Francisco, CA 94111
Contact: Caleb Hill Managing Partner
Tel: 415-692-6944
Email: caleb.hill@3bridgenetworks.com
Website: www.3bridgenetworks.com
Recruiting services, direct hire & temporary consults ranging from staff to VP levels within Accounting & Finance. (As-Pac, estab 2011, empl 7, sales , cert: NMSDC, CPUC)

8521   A.P.R., Inc. (Alpha Professional Resources)
100 E Thousand Oaks Blvd Ste 240
Thousand Oaks, CA 91360
Contact: Rick C. Ramirez VP Operations
Tel: 805-371-5644
Email: rick@alphaprotemps.com
Website: www.alphaprotemps.com
Technical IT personnel on contract or contract to hire or permanent. (AA, Hisp, estab 1993, empl 155, sales $15,605,246, cert: NMSDC, CPUC)

8522 Absolute Employment Solutions, Inc.
PO Box 2446
Culver City, CA 90231
Contact: Penelope Sherman- Hunt President
Tel: 323-931-6262
Email: phunt@absoluteemploymentsolutions.com
Website: www.absoluteemploymentsolutions.com
Staffing services: direct-hire, temporary-to-hire & temporary. (Woman/AA, estab 2001, empl 3, sales $350,000, cert: State, CPUC, SDB)

8523 Accelon Inc.
2410 Camino Ramon, Ste 194
San Mateo, CA 94583
Contact: Kelda Williams Acct Mgr
Tel: 925-216-5735
Email: kelda@acceloninc.com
Website: www.AccelonInc.com
Staffing, managed services, project management and application development. (As-Pac, estab 2014, empl 65, sales $52,300,000, cert: NMSDC, CPUC)

8524 Agile1
1999 W 190th St
Torrance, CA 90504
Contact: Bobbi Babcock Regional Vice President
Tel: 480-209-0374
Email: bbabcock@agile1.com
Website: www.agile-1.com
Workforce management, human capital management, talent acquisition and contingent staffing services, payrolling, and 1099 independent contractor compliance. (Woman/AA, estab 1978, empl , sales $971,113,334, cert: NMSDC, CPUC, WBENC)

8525 AgileTalent, Inc.
1900 S Norfolk Ave.
San Mateo, CA 94403
Contact: Jay Singh
Tel: 650-931-2572
Email: jay.singh@agiletalentinc.com
Website: www.agiletalentinc.com
IT contract staffing & recruiting. (As-Ind, estab 2011, empl 48, sales $4,600,000, cert: NMSDC, CPUC)

8526 Allstem Connections, Inc.
327 W Broadway
Glendale, CA 91204
Contact: Penni Rich VP
Tel: - -
Email: prich@ain1.com
Website: www.allstemconnections.com
Specialty recruiting and staffing firm for the temporary, temp-to-permanent and direct hire placement of talent in STEM (Science, Technology, Engineering and Mathematics) positions. Unique talent development programs include apprenticeships, internships, (Woman/AA, estab 2018, empl 2800, sales $965,741,349, cert: NMSDC, WBENC)

8527 AppleOne Employment Services
327 W Broadway
Glendale, CA 91204
Contact: Lea Murga Sr Dir Business Devel
Tel: 714-404-6068
Email: lmurga@ain1.com
Website: www.appleone.com
Contingent Workforce Services and Technologies. (Woman/AA, estab 1963, empl 1535, sales $1,038,404,566, cert: NMSDC, WBENC)

8528 APR Consulting, Inc.
1370 Valley Vista Dr Ste 280
Diamond Bar, CA 91765
Contact: Daniel Benninghoff VP
Tel: 909-396-5375
Email: dbenninghoff@aprconsulting.com
Website: www.aprconsulting.com
Supporting Managed Staffing (MSP)/Vendor Management, System (VMS) Programs, Direct Hire Search, Contract Labor, Administrative & Clerical, Accounting & Finance, Human Resources, Call Center & Customer Care, Information Technology. (Minority, Woman, estab 1980, empl 1382, sales $75,000,000, cert: NMSDC, CPUC, WBENC)

8529 ATR International, Inc.
1230 Oakmead Pkwy Ste 110
Sunnyvale, CA 94085
Contact: Angelique Alvarez Chief Diversity Relations Officer
Tel: 408-328-8085
Email: angeliques@atr1.com
Website: www.atrinternational.com
Temporary employment svcs. (Minority, Woman, estab 1988, empl 100, sales $96,000,000, cert: NMSDC)

8530 Bench International Search Inc.
120 S Doheny Dr
Beverly Hills, CA 90211
Contact: Mary Kelley CFO
Tel: 310-854-9900
Email: mkelley@benchinternational.com
Website: www.benchinternational.com
Executive search services. (Woman, estab 1974, empl 23, sales $8,865,478, cert: WBENC)

8531 Berkhemer Clayton
241 S Figueroa St Ste 300
Los Angeles, CA 90012
Contact: Exec Admin
Tel: 213-621-2300
Email: Info@berkhemerclayton.com
Website: www.berkhemerclayton.com
Executive search firm. (Woman, estab 1994, empl 8, sales , cert: CPUC, WBENC)

8532 Bratton & Co., Inc. DBA Hyperdrive Agile
1547 Palos Verdes Mall, Ste 198
Walnut Creek, CA 94597
Contact: Mary Louie Owner
Tel: 925-330-6970
Email: mary@brattoninc.com
Website: www.hyperdriveagile.com
Temporary staffing: administration, project management, technology, marketing & public relations. (Minority, Woman, estab 2009, empl 2, sales $3,000,000, cert: WBENC)

8533 Canon Recruiting Group LLC
26531 Summit Circle
Santa Clarita, CA 91351
Contact: Recruiting Mgr
Tel: 661-252-7400
Email: Careers@canonrecruiting.com
Website: www.canonrecruiting.com
Identification, evaluation & recruit Executives, Professionals, IT Technical, Accounting, Environmental & Industrial staffing. (Woman, estab 1980, empl 300, sales $15,000,000, cert: WBENC)

8534 Coneybeare Inc.
      2003 N Broadway
      Santa Ana, CA 92706
      Contact: Victoria Betancourt President
      Tel: 714-547-8546
      Email: vicky@coneybeare.com
      Website: www.coneybeare.com
Staffing services: technical, skilled industrial, administrative, clerical & professional. (Woman, estab 1986, empl 5, sales , cert: WBENC)

8535 Crowdstaffing, a Zenith Talent Company
      6030 Hellyer Ave Ste 100
      San Jose, CA 95138
      Contact: Bret Bass Dir Content Strategy
      Tel: 844-467-2300
      Email: bret@crowdstaffing.com
      Website: www.crowdstaffing.com
Staffing & recruiting: software and OS, hardware, QA & automation, IT, mobile applications & platforms & professional. (As-Ind, estab 2000, empl 25, sales $14,000,000, cert: NMSDC)

8536 Dawson & Dawson Staffing Inc.
      26522 La Alameda Ste 110
      Mission Viejo, CA 92691
      Contact: Kathy Dawson President
      Tel: 949-421-3966
      Email: kathy.dawson@dawsondawsoninc.com
      Website: www.dawsondawsoninc.com
National search & staffing employment services. (Woman, estab 2008, empl 14, sales $3,544,239, cert: WBENC)

8537 Delta Computer Consulting, Inc.
      25550 Hawthorne Blvd Ste 106-108
      Torrance, CA 90505
      Contact: Alisa Spiegel VP Sales
      Tel: 310-541-9440
      Email: A.Spiegel@deltacci.com
      Website: www.deltacci.com
Human Capital Recruiting & Deployment, IT Staff Recruiting & Augmentation. (Woman, estab 1987, empl 165, sales $28,000,000, cert: WBENC, NWBOC)

8538 Domar Companies, LLC
      14742 Beach Blvd, Ste 256
      La MIrada, CA 90638
      Contact: Don Martinez CEO
      Tel: 714-674-0391
      Email: martinezd@domarcompanies.com
      Website: www.domarcompanies.com
Executive search recruiting Hispanic & Multicultural Diversity Executives & Professionals. (Minority, Woman, estab 2011, empl 8, sales $27,500,000, cert: CPUC)

8539 Enterprise Resource Services, Inc.
      400 Continental Blvd Ste 6170
      El Segundo, CA 90245
      Contact: Ladie Ella Daya Natl Acct Mgr
      Tel: 424-888-3771
      Email: ella@ersstaffing.com
      Website: www.ersstaffing.com
Staffing, payroll & IT consulting services: temp, temp-to-hire & direct hire. (As-Pac, estab 2001, empl 25, sales $3,851,150, cert: CPUC)

8540 Genesis Professional Staffing, Inc.
      2600 West Olive Ave 5th Fl
      Burbank, CA 91505
      Contact: Marcus T. Moore CEO
      Tel: 818-333-5153
      Email: marcus.moore@gpstaffing.com
      Website: www.gpstaffing.com
Staffing: permanent hires, temp-to-hire, temporary placement, payrolling & consulting. (AA, estab 2003, empl 25, sales , cert: NMSDC)

8541 Government Staffing Associates
      101 Howard St, Ste 490
      San Francisco, CA 94105
      Contact: Steven Strawser Owner
      Tel: 415-692-6905
      Email: sf@govstaff.org
      Website: www.govstaff.org
Temporary, contract & permanent staffing solutions. (As-Pac, estab 2009, empl 11, sales $833,429, cert: City, NMSDC, CPUC)

8542 Grove Technical Resources
      9035 Rosewood Ave
      West Hollywood, CA 90048
      Contact: Debra Polister President
      Tel: 786-390-7119
      Email: dpolister@grovetr.com
      Website: www.grovetr.com
Technical staffing & consulting services. (Woman, estab 2005, empl 2, sales , cert: CPUC, WBENC)

8543 Hart Employment Services
      220 S Kenwood St Ste 320
      Glendale, CA 91205
      Contact: Rhonda Minarcin President
      Tel: 626-405-0778
      Email: gsa@hartjobs.com
      Website: www.hartjobs.com
Staffing services. (Woman, estab 1988, empl 6, sales $1,833,485, cert: WBENC)

8544 Harvest Technical Services
      1839 Ygnacio Valley Rd, Ste 390
      Walnut Creek, CA 94598
      Contact: Renee Bush Sales
      Tel: 925-937-4874
      Email: renee@harvtech.com
      Website: www.harvtech.com
Temporary technical staffing personnel. (Woman, estab 1997, empl 85, sales $12,018,213, cert: WBENC)

8545 HBL Search
      118 Prospect Ave Ste 4
      Long Beach, CA 90803
      Contact: Halvern Logan President
      Tel: 562-754-6925
      Email: halvern@hblsearch.com
      Website: www.hblsearch.com
Staffing: accountants, finance, banking, IT, engineering, sales & HR. (AA, estab 2013, empl 1, sales , cert: NMSDC)

8546 Human Potential Consultants, LLC
454 E Carson Plaza Dr, Ste 102
Carson, CA 90746
Contact: Garnett Newcombe CEO
Tel: 310-756-1560
Email: drnewcombe@aol.com
Website: www.hpcemployment.org
Staffing services: administrative, janitorial, warehouse & production service workers. (Woman/AA, estab 1997, empl 7, sales $580,000, cert: City, NMSDC, WBENC)

8547 Inconen Corporation
6133 Bristol Pkwy Ste 232
Culver City, CA 90230
Contact: Gordon Ross CEO
Tel: 310-410-1931
Email: register@inconen.com
Website: www.inconen.com
Temporary employees & pay-rolled employees. (As-Ind, estab 1978, empl 120, sales $13,351,317, cert: NMSDC, CPUC)

8548 Inconen Temporary Services, Inc.
6133 Bristol Pkwy Ste 225
Culver City, CA 90230
Contact: Gordon Ross CEO
Tel: 310-216-6715
Email: gordon@e-its.com
Website: www.e-its.com
Staffing svcs: temporary, payroll svcs, engineers & IT professionals. (As-Ind, estab 1996, empl 25, sales $1,592,435, cert: NMSDC, CPUC)

8549 Integrated Talent Solutions, Inc. dba Vivo
7901 Stoneridge Dr Ste 440
Pleasanton, CA 94588
Contact: Marilyn Weinstein CEO
Tel: 925-271-6800
Email: info@vivoinc.com
Website: www.vivoinc.com
Staffing services: contract, contract-to-hire & full-time/direct positions. (Woman, estab 2006, empl 15, sales $5,100,000, cert: WBENC)

8550 Integritas Resources, Inc.
12304 Santa Monica Blvd. Ste 300
Los Angeles, CA 90025
Contact: Lindy Huang Werges CEO
Tel: 310-584-7295
Email: lhwerges@integritasresources.com
Website: www.integritasresources.com
Executive search, recruitment & staffing, direct hire, contract, contract-to-hire, temporary, or project basis. (Minority, Woman, estab 2014, empl 3, sales $646,557, cert: City, NMSDC, CPUC, WBENC)

8551 Invero Group
8560 Vineyard Ave Ste 504
Rancho Cucamonga, CA 91730
Contact: Daniel Phillips President
Tel: 909-373-8120
Email: daniel@inverogroup.com
Website: www.inverogroup.com
Staffing & recruiting: temporary, direct hire & contingent staffing solutions. (Woman, estab 2001, empl 75, sales $1,988,644, cert: WBENC)

8552 Josephine's Professional Staffing, Inc.
2158 Ringwood Ave
San Jose, CA 95131
Contact: Josephine Hughes CEO
Tel: 408-943-0111
Email: josephine@jps-inc.com
Website: www.jps-inc.com
Staffing svcs: temp, contract, yemporary-to-hire, full-time placement, payroll svcs, vendor-on-site. (Minority, Woman, estab 1988, empl 10, sales $3,248,000, cert: State, NMSDC, WBENC)

8553 Kavaliro
5401 Old Redwood Hwy Ste 104
Petaluma, CA 94954
Contact: Timothy M. Harrington Managing Dir
Tel: 704-525-3457
Email: tharrington@kavaliro.com
Website: www.kavaliro.com
Staffing services: Information Technology (IT); Engineering; Finance & Accounting; Administrative & Professional; & Project Solutions & Delivery. (Minority, Woman, estab 2003, empl 200, sales $41,700,000, cert: NMSDC, CPUC)

8554 Lighthouse Management Group Inc.
1650 The Alameda
San Jose, CA 95126
Contact: Nirav Shah Managing Dir
Tel: 408-579-6200
Email: nirav.shah@lighthousemg.com
Website: www.lighthousemg.com
Staffing, temporary & temp-to-hire, senior-level consulting & management professionals. (As-Ind, estab 2006, empl 20, sales $8,500,000, cert: NMSDC)

8555 Loan Administration Network Inc.
18952 MacArthur Blvd Ste 315
Irvine, CA 92612
Contact: Charlene Nichols President
Tel: 949-752-5246
Email: charlene_nichols@lani.com
Website: www.lani.com
Temporary, Temp-to-Hire, Direct Hire staffing services: Accounting, Finance, Healthcare, Banking, Credit Unions, Title, Escrow, Mortgage industries. Clerical, mid-level, Management, Executive positions. (Woman, estab 1992, empl 12, sales $5,600,000, cert: CPUC)

8556 Marquee Workforce Solutions, Inc.
338 Via Vera Cruz, Ste 140
San Marcos, CA 92078
Contact: Emily Salanio CEO
Tel: 949-271-0502
Email: workforcesolutions@marqueewfs.com
Website: www.marqueewfs.com
Workforce solutions. (Minority, Woman, estab 2013, empl 43, sales $12,000,000, cert: NMSDC)

8557 MIDCOM
1275 N Manassero St
Anaheim, CA 92807
Contact: Anastacia Warunek VP
Tel: 714-507-3723
Email: stacy@midcom.com
Website: www.midcom.com
Recruit & place technical & professional personnel. (Woman, estab 1979, empl 635, sales $120,000,000, cert: CPUC, WBENC)

8558   Mynela Staffing LLC
       17777 Center Court Dr N Ste 600
       Cerritos, CA 90703
       Contact: CEO
       Tel: 562-246-5317
       Email:
       Website: www.mynela.com
Healthcare staffing services, per diem, temp & direct hire services of physicians, nurses, clinical, allied & administrative staff. (Minority, estab 2015, empl 75, sales $2,000,000, cert: NMSDC)

8559   netPolarity, Inc.
       900 E Campbell Ave
       Campbell, CA 95008
       Contact: Jeremy Schiff Sr Acct Mgr
       Tel: 408-200-3230
       Email: jeremys@netpolarity.com
       Website: www.netpolarity.com
Temporary staffing, staff augmentation, contingent workforce staffing for information technology, project management, application development, professional services, marketing, finance and accounting. (Minority, Woman, estab 2000, empl 500, sales $55,000,000, cert: NMSDC, CPUC)

8560   NetSource, Inc.
       PO Box 590665
       San Francisco, CA 94159
       Contact: VP Sales
       Tel: 415-831-3681
       Email: resumes@netsourceweb.com
       Website: www.netsourceweb.com
pPacement, contracting & consulting services. (Woman, estab 1997, empl 50, sales $800,000, cert: State, CPUC, WBENC)

8561   Occasions Staffing Solutions, LLC
       2191 S El Camino Real, Ste 206
       Oceanside, CA 92821
       Contact: Derek Rippy President
       Tel: 760-439-7500
       Email: derek@occasionsstaffing.com
       Website: www.occasionsstaffing.com
Temporary staffing requirements for Warehouse, Customer Service, Data Entry, Convention Services. (AA, estab 2017, empl 12, sales , cert: NMSDC)

8562   Partners In Diversity, Inc.
       690 E Green St Ste 101
       Pasadena, CA 91101
       Contact: Arlene Apodaca President
       Tel: 626-793-0020
       Email: arlene.apodaca@p-i-d.biz
       Website: www.partnersindiversity.com
Staffing support: clerical & non-clerical. (Minority, Woman, estab 2002, empl 10, sales $14,130,878, cert: State, CPUC, WBENC)

8563   Patricia J. Mayer & Associates, LLC
       2395 Lake Meadow Cir
       Martinez, CA 94553
       Contact: Patricia Mayer CEO
       Tel: 925-689-1440
       Email: pattmayer@earthlink.net
       Website: www.pjmstaffing.com
Staffing services: temporary & permanent employees. (Woman, estab 2003, empl 1, sales $1,000,000, cert: WBENC)

8564   Peoples Choice Staffing, Inc.
       1269 W Pomona Rd, Ste 107
       Corona, CA 92882
       Contact: Denise Peoples CEO
       Tel: 951-735-0550
       Email: dapeoples@peopleschoicestaffing.com
       Website: www.peopleschoicestaffing.com
Staffing: temporary, temporary-Hire or full-time placement services. (Woman/AA, estab 2003, empl 200, sales $19,037,280, cert: NMSDC, CPUC)

8565   PFITECH
       17011 Beach Blvd, Ste 9
       Huntington Beach, CA 92647
       Contact: Sean Scully Reg Sales Mgr
       Tel: 310-824-1800
       Email: sean.scully@PFITECH.COM
       Website: www.PFITECH.com
Staffing and desktop solutions. (Hisp, estab 2001, empl 200, sales $16,318,677, cert: NMSDC, CPUC)

8566   Pivotal Search Partners
       2531 Greenwich St
       San Francisco, CA 94123
       Contact: President
       Tel: 415-323-6339
       Email:
       Website: www.pivotalsearchpartners.com
Staffing Solutions: IT, Engineering & Accounting & Finance, Direct Hire, Contract & Contract to Hire & VSP / MSP Contingent Workforce staffing solutions. (As-Ind, estab 2012, empl 6, sales $538,000, cert: NMSDC, CPUC)

8567   PM Business Holdings LLC
       733 Hindry Ave, Ste C205
       Inglewood, CA 90301
       Contact: Derrick Ferguson CEO
       Tel: 310-242-3171
       Email: pmbh14@gmail.com
       Website: www.brilliantmindssolutions.com
Computer Systems Design Services, employment placement & executive search services (AA, estab 2012, empl 1, sales , cert: NMSDC)

8568   POGO Inc.
       6265 Greenwich Dr Ste 103
       San Diego, CA 92122
       Contact: Reg Dir
       Tel: 858-587-4970
       Email:
       Website: www.getpogo.com
Temporary staffing services. (Woman, estab 2011, empl 7, sales $2,500,000, cert: CPUC, WBENC)

8569   Premier Staffing, Inc
       3595 Mt Diablo Blvd Ste 340
       Lafayette, CA 94549
       Contact: Andrew Melgar Acct Mgr
       Tel: 415-362-2211
       Email: andrewm@premiertalentpartners.com
       Website: www.premiertalentpartners.com/
Direct-hire & temporary/contract staffing. (Woman, estab , empl , sales $6,778,631, cert: WBENC)

8570 Proven Solutions Inc
9444 Waples St Ste 440
San Diego, CA 92121
Contact: Louis Song Sr Partner
Tel: 858-412-1122
Email: lsong@provenrecruiting.com
Website: www.provenrecruiting.com
Consulting, staffing & solutions. (As-Pac, estab 2007, empl 49, sales $16,800,000, cert: NMSDC, CPUC)

8571 PTS Advance Life Sciences
2860 Michelle Dr, Ste 150
Irvine, CA 92606
Contact: Jayne Gill Managing Dir
Tel: 949-268-4021
Email: jayne.gill@ptsadvance.com
Website: www.ptsadvance.com
Engineering & professional staffing: petrochemical, power, transportation & infrastructure. (Woman, estab 1995, empl 200, sales $28,000,000, cert: WBENC)

8572 Quality Driver Solutions, Inc.
320 S Milliken Ave, Ste A
Ontario, CA 91761
Contact: Angelica Dazhan Reg Mgr
Tel: 510-453-4655
Email: angelica@qualitydriversolutions.com
Website: www.qualitydriversolutions.com
Offices located in Northern California and Pacific Northwest. In addition, we have offices in Southern California, Houston and Dallas, TX, with plans for Full service staff: temps, temp to hire, long term dedicated & direct hire placements. (Hisp, estab 2004, empl 23, sales , cert: NMSDC)

8573 RennickBarrett Recruiting, Inc.
82-408 Brewster Dr
Indio, CA 92203
Contact: Vinette Morris President
Tel: 760-863-0076
Email: vinette@rennickbarrett.com
Website: www.rennickbarrett.com
Direct & temporary/contract labor, high level, hard to fill positions at the senior and executive management levels. (Woman/AA, estab 2008, empl 4, sales $1,246,000, cert: City)

8574 SearchPros
6363 Auburn Blvd
Citrus Heights, CA 95621
Contact: Myla Ramos CEO
Tel: 916-721-6000
Email: myla@spstaffing.com
Website: www.spstaffing.com
Human capital staffing & solutions: temporary staffing, contract to hire, long-term contract, project staffing, direct hire, payrolling services, retained searches, outplacement services. (Woman/AA, As- Pac, estab 2005, empl 100, sales $20,000,000, cert: NMSDC)

8575 SuperbTech, Inc.
5800 Hannm Ave Ste 150
Culver City, CA 90230
Contact: Jan Davis President
Tel: 310-645-1199
Email: jdavis@superbtechinc.com
Website: www.superbtechinc.com
Staffing:contract, temporary & permanent placement. (Woman/AA, estab 1998, empl 7, sales , cert: CPUC, WBENC)

8576 TEKtalent Inc.
26250 Industrial Blvd, Ste 110
Hayward, CA 94545
Contact: Kishore Pallapothu CEO
Tel: 510-256-7311
Email: joeparker@tektalentinc.com
Website: www.tektalentinc.com
End-to-end recruitment and service solutions. (Woman/As-Ind, estab 2015, empl 25, sales , cert: NMSDC, WBENC)

8577 The ACT 1 Group, Inc.
1999 W 190th St
Torrance, CA 90504
Contact: Gary Randazzo Dir of Natl communications
Tel: 800-383-1965
Email: hrcg-rfxmanager@act-1.com
Website: www.act1group.com
Staffing, payrolling & workforce mgmt svcs: financial, energy, healthcare & high technology industries. (Woman/AA, estab 1978, empl 1535, sales $476,000,000, cert: NMSDC, CPUC)

8578 The Mice Groups, Inc.
1730 S Amphlett Blvd Ste 100
San Mateo, CA 94402
Contact: Sofia Gomez VP Recruiting & Strategy
Tel: 650-655-7655
Email: sofia@micegroups.com
Website: www.micegroups.com
IT contract, contract-to-hire & full-time employment positions. (Hisp, estab 2000, empl 100, sales $100,000,000, cert: NMSDC, CPUC)

8579 TheraEx Rehab Services, Inc.
1191 Central Blvd Ste E
Brentwood, CA 94513
Contact: Rey Rivera President
Tel: 707-342-5200
Email: info@theraexstaffing.com
Website: www.theraexstaffing.com
Healthcare staffing: Registered Nurses (RN), Licensed Vocational Nurses (LVN), Certified Nurse Assistants (CNA), Physical therapist (PT), Occupational Therapist (OT). (As-Pac, estab 2009, empl 64, sales $3,545,324, cert: NMSDC)

8580 Tiffany Stuart Solutions, Inc.
390 Diablo Rd. Ste 220
Danville, CA 94526
Contact: President
Tel: 925-855-3600
Email: AR@Go2Dynamic.com
Website: www.go2dynamic.com
Temporary contractors, temp to hire & direct hire. (Woman, estab 1997, empl 100, sales $5,200,000, cert: CPUC, WBENC)

8581 Two Roads Professional Resources, Inc.
5122 Bolsa Ave, Ste 112
Huntington Beach, CA 92649
Contact: Tammy Gottschalk President
Tel: 714-901-3804
Email: tgotts@2roads.com
Website: www.2roads.com
Provide temporary staffing in the technical, engineering, and information technology services. (Woman, estab 1996, empl 125, sales $12,168,000, cert: CPUC)

8582 Vertisystem Inc.
      39300 Civic Center Dr, Ste 230
      Fremont, CA 94538
      Contact: Shaloo Jeswani Sr BDM
      Tel: 702-241-5131
      Email: shaloo@vertisystem.com
      Website: www.vertisystem.com
Staff Augmentation, Full-Time Placements, contract to Hire,
IT Projects & Consulting. (Minority, Woman, estab 2008,
empl 120, sales $20,000,000, cert: City, CPUC)

8583 Vidhwan Inc dba E-Solutions, Inc.
      2 N Market St Ste 400
      San Jose, CA 95113
      Contact: Eric Kumar Acct Mgr
      Tel: 408-239-4647
      Email: eric.kumar@e-solutionsinc.com
      Website: www.e-solutionsinc.com
IT & ITES staffing, recruitment & deployment: permanent,
contract, contract to hire & project based staffing.
(Woman/As-Ind, estab 2003, empl 450, sales $22,800,000,
cert: NMSDC, CPUC)

8584 Vitesse Recruiting & Staffing, Inc.
      1432 Edinger Ave, Ste 100
      Tustin, CA 92780
      Contact: Kim N. Zastrow President
      Tel: 714-210-5959
      Email: knzastrow@vitesserecruiting.com
      Website: www.VitesseRecruiting.com
Temporary or permanent human resources employment
services. (Minority, Woman, estab 2000, empl 3, sales ,
cert: State, CPUC)

8585 Voigt & Associates, Inc.
      22981 Sonriente Trail
      Coto de Caza, CA 92679
      Contact: Barbara Voigt President
      Tel: 949-766-1100
      Email: bvoigt@voigtinc.com
      Website: www.voigtinc.com
Executive search services. (Woman, estab 2005, empl 1,
sales $1,200,000, cert: CPUC)

8586 Whitham Group Executive Search
      8130 Luisa Way
      Windsor, CA 95492
      Contact: President
      Tel: 888-238-1273
      Email: Info@WhithamGroup.com
      Website: www.WhithamGroup.com
Executive search & recruiting specializing in Utilities,
Renewable Energy & Environmental Services. (Woman,
estab 2010, empl 2, sales $1,174,000, cert: CPUC, WBENC)

8587 Workforce Solutions Group
      26090 Towne Centre Dr
      Foothill Ranch, CA 92679
      Contact: Colleen Jones COO
      Tel: 949-588-5812
      Email: cjones@wsgcorp.com
      Website: www.workforcesolutionsgroup.com
Staffing & direct hire: contract, temporary & direct hire
placement. (Minority, Woman, estab 2002, empl 11, sales ,
cert: City, NWBOC)

8588 WorkSquare West
      4401 Crenshaw Blvd, Ste 220
      Los Angeles, CA 90043
      Contact: Natasha White President
      Tel: 323-294-9675
      Email: natasha@worksquare.com
      Website: www.worksquare.com
Recruiting,Temporary to Permanente Staffing Firm
(Woman/AA, estab 2008, empl 4, sales , cert: NMSDC)

8589 Xtra Pair of Hands
      4307 San Joaquin Plz
      Newport Beach, CA 92660
      Contact: Kym Smith Managing Partner
      Tel: 404-825-4398
      Email: info@xtrapairofhands.com
      Website: www.xtrapairofhands.com
Staffing & recruiting: temp, temp-to-hire & direct hire
placements. (Woman/AA, estab 2007, empl 4, sales
$250,000, cert: State, CPUC)

8590 Zempleo, Inc.
      4000 Executive Pkwy Ste 240, Bishop Ranch 8
      San Ramon, CA 94583
      Contact: SABRINA CHISHOLM VP
      Tel: 925-284-0377
      Email: schisholm@zempleo.com
      Website: www.zempleo.com
Temporary staffing, payrolling & direct hire services.
(Hisp, estab 2005, empl 1000, sales $62,860,000, cert:
NMSDC, CPUC)

8591 Action Staffing Solutions
      1409 W 29th St
      Loveland, CO 80538
      Contact: Robin Fischer CEO
      Tel: 970-667-4202
      Email: robin@myactionstaffing.com
      Website: www.myactionstaffing.com
Temporary to permanent employee placement, contract
personnel, long-term, executive placement, direct hire,
on-site management. (Woman/AA, estab 2008, empl 7,
sales $1,500,000, cert: State, City, 8(a))

Colorado

8592 EGS, Inc.
      333 W Hampden Ave, Ste 530
      Englewood, CO 80111
      Contact: Susan Fenske President
      Tel: 303-477-6800
      Email: susan@egs-partners.com
      Website: www.egs-partners.com
Provide staffing & consulting assistance to public and
private sector organizations. (Woman, estab 2002, empl
120, sales $12,000,000, cert: WBENC)

8593 Equity Staffing Group, Inc.
      8310 S. Valley Hwy Ste 135
      Englewood, CO 80112
      Contact: Stacey L Moore Operations Mgr
      Tel: 720-897-8714
      Email: stacey.moore@equitystaffing.com
      Website: www.equitystaffing.com
Staffing, consulting, contingent, or direct-hire workforce
solutions. (Nat Ame, estab 2009, empl 60, sales
$85,617,000, cert: NMSDC)

8594 IntelliSource
1899 Wynkoop St Ste 900
Denver, CO 80202
Contact: Matt Pollard SVP
Tel: 303-692-1100
Email: mpollard@intellisource.com
Website: www.intellisource.com
Staffing solutions, temporary, temp to perm, project management, outsourcing, contract & direct hire. (Woman, estab 1999, empl 300, sales , cert: WBENC)

8595 Job Store, Inc.
7100 E Hampden Ave Ste A
Denver, CO 80224
Contact: Julie DeGolier President
Tel: 303-757-7686
Email: julie@jobstorestaffing.com
Website: www.jobstorestaffing.com
Tempoary office, clerical admin support, accounting & technical & light industrial personnel. (Woman, estab 1974, empl 14, sales $8,400,419, cert: WBENC)

8596 Lakeshore Talent, LLC
5251 DTC Pkwy, Ste 400
Denver, CO 80111
Contact: Mary Clark President
Tel: 303-483-1100
Email: mclark@lakeshoretalent.com
Website: www.lakeshoretalent.com
Staffing and recruiting, contract, contract to hire, direct hire and payroll services. (Woman, estab 2017, empl 15, sales $10,529,849, cert: WBENC)

8597 MHa Technical Staffing, Inc.
7475 Dakin St, Ste 350
Denver, CO 80221
Contact: Thomas R. Leyba VP Operations
Tel: 303-428-1728
Email: t.leyba@martinez-hromada.com
Website: www.mhatech.com/
Temporary eng support personnel: civil, electrical, structural, mechanical, HVAC, programmers, subcontract, construction mgmt, designers & drafters. (Hisp, estab 1992, empl 65, sales , cert: City, NMSDC)

8598 Nexus Staffing Solutions Corp.
4701 Marion St, Ste 307
Denver, CO 80216
Contact: Barbara Butler Business Devel Mgr
Tel: 303-736-2008
Email: bonnie@nexusstaffingllc.com
Website: www.nexusstaffingllc.com/
Staffing: Engineering, Construction & Call Centers. (Woman, estab 2010, empl 12, sales , cert: WBENC)

8599 Prestige Staffing, Inc.
1873 S Bellaire St, Ste 320
Denver, CO 80222
Contact: President
Tel: 303-691-0111
Email: contactus@prestigecareer.com
Website: www.prestigecareer.com
Permanent, contract & temp positions. (Woman, estab 2003, empl 2, sales $350,000, cert: WBENC)

8600 Primesource Staffing
400 S. Colorado Blvd, Ste 400
Denver, CO 80246
Contact: Dennis Hatcher Controller
Tel: 303-869-2990
Email: dhatcher@primesourcestaffing.com
Website: www.primesourcestaffing.com
Staffing services. (Woman, estab 1996, empl 27, sales $20,600,000, cert: WBENC)

8601 The Maris Group
2696 S Colorado Blvd, Ste 595
Denver, CO 80222
Contact: Kathryn Ake Principal
Tel: 303-778-1962
Email: info@marisgroup.com
Website: www.marisgroup.com
Staffing: contract, marketing & communications. (Woman, estab 1999, empl 2, sales $2,500,000, cert: WBENC)

Connecticut

8602 JOBPRO Temporary Services, Inc.
36 Main St
East Hartford, CT 06118
Contact: Catherine Beck President
Tel: 800-404-7795
Email: cbeck@job-pro.com
Website: www.jobproworks.com
Staffing: temporary, temp-to-hire & direct placements: office, accounting, light industrial & technical niches. (Woman, estab 1981, empl 10, sales , cert: State)

8603 Key Alliance Staffing, LLC
406 Farmington Ave
Farmington, CT 06032
Contact: Sandra Hathaway
Tel: 860-676-7733
Email: shathaway@keyalliancestaff.com
Website: www.kas-consulting.com
Staffing: contract, contract to hire, or direct hire personnel. (Woman, estab 2008, empl 32, sales $2,586,000, cert: State)

8604 MY HR Supplier
1266 E Main St Ste 700R
Stamford, CT 06902
Contact: Omer Mutaqi COO
Tel: 203-274-8595
Email: omutaqi@myhrsupplier.cm
Website: www.myhrsupplier.com
Human capital talent: IT, administrative & office support, clerical & accounting. (Woman/As-Ind, estab 2011, empl 53, sales , cert: State, NMSDC)

8605 Skylightsys, LLC
175 Capital Blvd Ste 402
Rocky Hill, CT 06067
Contact: Shalu Arora President
Tel: 860-289-9096
Email: arora@skylightsys.com
Website: www.skylightsys.com
Staffing services. (Woman/As-Ind, estab 2005, empl 9, sales , cert: State)

8606 Stratoserve LLC
18 Colonial Ct
Cheshire, CT 06410
Contact: Subroto Roy President
Tel: 203-768-5690
Email: subroto.roy@stratoserve.com
Website: www.stratoserve.com
consulting, research and training for the following NAICS codes:541720,541613,611430 and is committed to provide quick and measurable value to its clients. (As-Pac, estab 2005, empl 1, sales , cert: NMSDC)

8607 Talus Partners, LLC
321 Main St
Farmington, CT 06032
Contact: Steve Massucci Mgr
Tel: 860-678-4410
Email: accounting@taluspartners.com
Website: www.taluspartners.com
IT, Engineering & Accounting contract & direct hire staffing. Certified Project Managers, Web Developers, Analysts. (Woman, estab 2011, empl 35, sales $5,500,000, cert: NWBOC)

8608 The Good Search, LLC
4 Valley Rd
Westport, CT 06880
Contact: CEO
Tel: 203-227-8615
Email: info@tgsus.com
Website: www.tgsus.com
Retained search & recruitment research, strategic recruitment initiatives of internal search teams. (Woman, estab 1999, empl 1, sales $662,398, cert: State, WBENC)

8609 Walt Medina & Associates, LLC
1224 Mill St Bldg D, Ste 200
East Berlin, CT 06023
Contact: Walt Medina CEO
Tel: 860-357-5002
Email: wm@waltmedina.com
Website: www.waltmedina.com
Healthcare recruiting, recruit military personnel (veterans). (Hisp, estab 2003, empl 2, sales $400,000, cert: NMSDC)

District of Columbia

8610 Adept Professional Staffing Inc.
1629 K St, NW Ste 300
Washington, DC 20006
Contact: Elizabeth Joseph CEO
Tel: 301-883-4308
Email: tavares@adeptprostaffing.com
Website: www.adeptprostaffing.com
Recruitment service for Accounting, Legal & Administrative Assistants, Permanent & Temporary placements. (Woman/AA, estab 2010, empl 1, sales $795,000, cert: State, WBENC, 8(a))

8611 JustinBradley, Inc.
1725 I St, NW Ste 300
Washington, DC 20006
Contact: Andrew Chase EVP
Tel: 202-457-8400
Email: asc@justinbradley.com
Website: www.JustinBradley.com
Recruiting & staff augmentation. (Woman, estab 2002, empl 65, sales $5,566,000, cert: WBENC)

8612 Midtown Personnel, Inc.
1130 Connecticut Ave. NW Ste 1101
Washington, DC 20036
Contact: Proposal Mgr
Tel: 202-887-4747
Email: Accounting@themidtowngroup.com
Website: www.themidtowngroup.com
Staffing services: direct hire, temp to hire, temporary, executive search. (Woman, estab 1989, empl 35, sales $15,400,000, cert: WBENC)

8613 National Associates, Inc.
1130 Connecticut Ave, NW Ste 530
Washington, DC 20036
Contact: Oscar Hannaway President
Tel: 202-223-7606
Email: ohannaway@naipersonnel.com
Website: www.naipersonnel.com
Permanent & temporary staffing: administrative, clerical, professional, technical & light industrial. (AA, estab 1987, empl 18, sales $9,600,000, cert: NMSDC)

8614 Pat Taylor and Associates, Inc.
1101 17th St, NW Ste 707
Washington, DC 20036
Contact: Pat Taylor President
Tel: 202-466-5622
Email: pat@pattaylor.com
Website: www.pattaylor.com
Temporary, temp to perm & permanent employment of attorneys, law clerks, paralegals, legal technology & court reporting services. (Woman, estab 1992, empl 6, sales $1,400,000, cert: WBENC)

Florida

8615 Airetel Staffing, Inc.
PO Box 915864
Longwood, FL 32791
Contact: Mike Tomaso Natl Aquisitions Mgr
Tel: 407-788-2015
Email: mt@airetel.com
Website: www.airetel.com
Full-time, contract & contract-to-hire staffing solutions. (Woman, estab 2000, empl 10, sales $3,570,000, cert: WBENC)

8616 Albion Healthcare Staffing
10162 W Sample Rd
Coral Springs, FL 33065
Contact: Francisco Arteaga Division Dir
Tel: 954-796-3336
Email: francisco@albionbiomed.com
Website: www.albionstaffing.com
Staffing services for Pharmaceutical & Medical Device companies. (Woman, estab 2005, empl 5, sales , cert: State)

8617 Alpha1 Staffing/Search Firm, LLC.
3350 SW 148th Ave, Ste 220
Miramar, FL 33027
Contact: Garrie Harris President
Tel: 954-734-2744
Email: gharris@alpha1staffing.com
Website: www.alpha1staffing.com
Staffing solutions, recruitment, assessment, training, development, and career management, to outsourcing and workforce consulting. (Woman/AA, estab 2007, empl 500, sales $13,000,000, cert: NMSDC)

8618 Ascendo Resources, LLC
    500 West Cypress Creek Road Ste 230
    Fort Lauderdale, FL 33309
    Contact: Melissa Mitchell Partner
    Tel: 321-251-3762
    Email: mmitchell@ascendo.com
    Website: www.ascendo.com
Executive recruiting & temporary staffing, temporary & project opportunities. (Hisp, estab 2009, empl 100, sales $39,000,000, cert: NMSDC)

8619 Bear Staffing Services Corporation
    10501 Six Mile Cypress Pkwy, Ste 104
    Fort Myers, FL 33966
    Contact: Gary Johnson CEO
    Tel: 856-848-0082
    Email: gjohnson@bearstaff.com
    Website: www.bearstaff.com
Temporary, temp to hire & direct hire staffing services. (Woman, estab , empl 475, sales , cert: WBENC)

8620 BioStaff Solutions Inc.
    4007 Blushing Rose Court
    Oviedo, FL 32766
    Contact: Jim Owens
    Tel: 407-542-6006
    Email: jowens@biostaffsolutions.com
    Website: www.biostaffsolutions.com
Provide clinical staffing services: contract, contract to hire & direct placements in SAS Programming, Clinical Programming, Biostatistics, Clinical Data Management, Pharmacovigilance, Clinical Monitoring. (Minority, Woman, estab 2014, empl 3, sales , cert: NMSDC)

8621 Career Center, Inc.
    1236 NW 18th Ave
    Gainesville, FL 32609
    Contact: Carolynn Buchanan Owner
    Tel: 352-378-2300
    Email: cbuchanan@tempforce.net
    Website: www.tempforcegainesville.com
Staffing: temporary, temp to perm & direct hire. (Woman, estab , empl , sales $934,261, cert: State, City)

8622 Career Solutions International Inc.
    400 Lexington Green Lane
    Sanford, FL 32771
    Contact: Suzette DiMascio CEO
    Tel: 866-484-4752
    Email: suzette@csigroup.net
    Website: www.csigroup.net
Executive search & recruiting services. (Woman, estab 2002, empl 8, sales $3,400,000, cert: WBENC)

8623 CareersUSA, Inc.
    6501 Congress Ave Ste 200
    Boca Raton, FL 33487
    Contact: Jennifer Johnson Exec VP & General Counsel
    Tel: 561-995-7000
    Email: jjohnson@careersusa.com
    Website: www.careersusa.com
Temporary, temp-to-hire, direct hire placements & payrolling services. (Woman, estab 1981, empl 10000, sales $32,000,000, cert: State, WBENC)

8624 Future Force Personnel
    15800 NW 57th Ave
    Miami Lakes, FL 33014
    Contact: Adela Gonzalez CEO
    Tel: 407-851-0039
    Email: adela@futureforcepersonnel.com
    Website: www.futureforcepersonnel.com
Temporary, temp to hire & direct hire placements. (Minority, Woman, estab 1992, empl 15, sales $17,500,000, cert: NMSDC)

8625 Garcia & Ortiz Staffing, LLC
    888 Executive Center Dr W, Ste 101
    St. Petersburg, FL 33702
    Contact: Jeremy Lavin Operations Mgr
    Tel: 727-342-1007
    Email: jlavin@garciaortiz.com
    Website: www.garciaortiz.com
Staffing: accounting, finance & banking professionals on a temporary, project & permanent basis. (Hisp, estab 2005, empl 5, sales $900,000, cert: State)

8626 GDKN Corporation
    9700 Stirling Road Ste 110
    Cooper City, FL 33024
    Contact: Gary Dhir VP
    Tel: 954-985-6650
    Email: gdhir@gdkn.com
    Website: www.gdkn.com
Staffing: information technology, engineering, professional, administrative & clerical, IT consulting, custom application development. (As-Ind, estab 1993, empl 400, sales $18,000,000, cert: NMSDC)

8627 Genesis Global Recruiting
    3000 SW 148 Ave, Ste 116
    Miramar, FL 33027
    Contact: Jim Cochran Dir of Recruiting
    Tel: 800-780-2232
    Email: jcochran@genesis-global.com
    Website: www.genesis-global.com
Staffing & workforce solutions: direct hire, temporary workforce & contract consulting. (Minority, Woman, estab 1999, empl 167, sales $16,500,000, cert: WBENC)

8628 Genoa Employment Solutions, Inc
    1560 Sawgrass Corporate Pkwy
    Sunrise, FL 33323
    Contact: Walter Ruf CEO
    Tel: 954-604-6056
    Email: wruf@genoausa.com
    Website: www.genoausa.com
Staffing services: engineering, IT, office support, human resources & purchasing. (Hisp, estab 2009, empl 162, sales $15,000,000, cert: NMSDC)

8629 GlobalVise Inc.
    10335 Cross Creek Blvd Ste 8
    Tampa, FL 33647
    Contact: Sanjay Mehta President
    Tel: 813-333-0400
    Email: sanjay@globalvise.com
    Website: www.globalvise.com
Permanent, temporary & contract staffing solutions. (As-Ind, estab 2008, empl 8, sales $2,758,764, cert: State, NMSDC, 8(a))

8630   Hamilton-Malone Corp
31958 US 19 N
Palm Harbor, FL 34684
Contact: Eileen McQuown President
Tel: 727-781-7747
Email: eileen@accordstaff.com
Website: www.accordstaff.com
Temporary & temp to hire staffing, executive search.
(Woman, estab 1993, empl 4, sales $80,000,000, cert:
State)

8631   Hanker Systems, Inc.
5401 W Kennedy Blvd, Ste 100
Tampa, FL 33609
Contact: Shravan Bommireddy Business Dev Mgr
Tel: 813-710-1444
Email: ranjithk@hankersystems.com
Website: www.HankersystemsInc.com
Permanent and Temporary staffing. (As-Ind, estab 2013,
empl 62, sales $4,000,000, cert: State)

8632   Innovative Systems Group of Florida, Inc. dba ISGF
100 E Pine St Ste 605
Orlando, FL 32801
Contact: Thomas Bryan Managing Partner
Tel: 407-481-9580
Email: tbryan@isgf.com
Website: www.isgf.com
Temporary, contract, contract to hire, direct hire staffing &
recruitment in information technology, accounting &
finance, sales & marketing. (As-Pac, estab 1996, empl 30,
sales $3,210,000, cert: State, City, NMSDC, CPUC)

8633   I-Tech Personnel Services, Inc.
5627 Atlantic Blvd, Ste 1
Jacksonville, FL 32207
Contact: Marco Tran President
Tel: 904-381-1911
Email: mtran@itechpersonnel.com
Website: www.itechpersonnel.net
Staffing svcs: clerical, technical professionals & light
industrial, temporary to permanent, direct hire placement
& on-site management. (As-Pac, estab 1998, empl 125,
sales $3,580,000, cert: State, NMSDC)

8634   Key Technical Resources, Inc.
5763 N Andrews Way
Fort Lauderdale, FL 33309
Contact: President
Tel: 954-771-1554
Email:
Website: www.keytechnical.com
Full time, contract & temporary placement: information
technology, accounting & finance. (Woman, estab 1999,
empl 15, sales $1,828,000, cert: WBENC)

8635   KeyStaff, Inc.
3540 Forest Hill Blvd Ste 203
West Palm Beach, FL 33406
Contact: Jessica Irons Business Devel
Tel: 561-688-9184
Email: jirons@mykeystaff.com
Website: www.mykeystaff.com/
IT/technical staffing solutions. (Woman, estab 1990, empl
60, sales $50,000,000, cert: State, WBENC)

8636   Nurses And Medical Staffing Agency LLC
37 N Orange Ave, Ste 328
Orlando, FL 32801
Contact: Triffina Brown Admin
Tel: 954-608-7971
Email: admin@wholecaremedicalstaffing.com
Website: www.wholecaremedicalstaffing.com/
Medical Staffing provides healthcare facilities (hospitals,
rehabilitation center, nursing care centers, Assisted
living facilities) in Florida with local nursing staff. (AA,
estab 2021, empl 14, sales , cert: State)

8637   Premier Advisors Staffing and Sales, LLC
7138 Spikerush Ct
Lakewood Ranch, FL 34202
Contact: Richard Burns President
Tel: 313-869-8868
Email: rburns@premierhealthcareadvisors.com
Website: www.premierhealthcareadvisors.com
Staffing and Recruiting. (AA, estab 2015, empl 1, sales
$1,000,000, cert: State, NMSDC)

8638   Pro-Staffing Agency
981 W Commercial Blvd
Fort Lauderdale, FL 33309
Contact: Marie Morency Owner
Tel: 954-530-2894
Email: marie@pro-staffinggroup.com
Website: www.pro-staffinggroup.com
Recruiting, staffing & business management. (Woman/
AA, estab 2016, empl 2, sales , cert: NMSDC)

8639   Qualese, LLC
3035 Honeysuckle Rd
Largo, FL 33770
Contact: Roberto Filippelli President
Tel: 727-488-6373
Email: roberto.filippelli@qualese.com
Website: www.qualese.com
Recruiting & staffing agency. (Hisp, estab 2015, empl 1,
sales , cert: NMSDC)

8640   Rapid Staffing, Inc.
PO Box 602
Valrico, FL 33595
Contact: Lani Harless President
Tel: 813-651-1242
Email: lani@rapidstaffing.com
Website: www.rapidstaffing.com
Staffing services: temporary & temporary to permanent
employees. (Minority, Woman, estab 2002, empl 5, sales
$2,227,174, cert: State, NMSDC)

8641   Resource Employment Solutions
5900 Lake Ellenor Dr, Ste 100
Orlando, FL 32809
Contact: Eddy Dominguez VP Business Dev
Tel: 321-234-9363
Email: eddy_d@resourceemployment.com
Website: www.resourceemployment.com
Employment agency, staffing services & recruitment
company. (Hisp, estab 1995, empl 35000, sales
$111,000,000, cert: NMSDC)

8642 Search Wizards, Inc.
15 Paradise Plaza Ste 261
Sarasota, FL 34239
Contact: Miranda Hinshaw CEO
Tel: 941-932-4108
Email: miranda@searchwizards.com
Website: www.searchwizards.com
Staffing: IT, finance & human resources, contract, contract-to-hire & full time. (Woman, estab 2000, empl 71, sales $35,000,000, cert: WBENC)

8643 Spherion Corporation
8130 Baymeadows Way W Ste 103
Jacksonville, FL 32256
Contact: Shelley Sherman Sr Mgr Qualification
Tel: 904-448-9102
Email: info@spherion.com
Website: www.spherion.com
National staffing: temp, temp to perm & direct placement staffing. (Woman, estab 1946, empl 1500, sales $14,089,000, cert: WBENC)

8644 Staffing By Choice LLC
7975 NW 154th St, Ste 380
Miami Lakes, FL 33016
Contact: Matthew Marsh VP Business Acquisition
Tel: 954-417-5627
Email: mmarsh@cpabychoice.com
Website: www.staffingbychoice.com
Staffing, recruiting & executive search services: accounting, finance, sales & operations professionals, permanent, temp to perm & contract roles. (As-Pac, estab 2002, empl 7, sales $360,000, cert: NMSDC)

8645 Techno-Transfers of Florida, Inc.
4609 NW 26th Ave
Boca Raton, FL 33434
Contact: Virginia Mendiola Dir
Tel: 561-212-2383
Email: vmendiola@techno-transfers.com
Website: www.techno-transfers.com
IT personnel for temporary contract, temp-to-perm roles & full-time positions. (Minority, Woman, estab 1992, empl 6, sales $350,000, cert: State)

8646 The CALER Group, Inc.
23337 Lago Mar Cir
Boca Raton, FL 33433
Contact: Colleen Perrone President
Tel: 561-394-8045
Email: cperrone@calergroup.com
Website: www.calergroup.com
Executive recruiting. (Woman, estab 1995, empl 6, sales $1,200,000, cert: WBENC)

8647 The Fountain Group, LLC
4505 Woodland Corporate Blvd Ste 200
Tampa, FL 33614
Contact: Rachel Slowey VP
Tel: 813-439-8393
Email: rachel.slowey@thefountaingroup.com
Website: www.thefountaingroup.com
Match top contingent talent with Fortune 100 to Fortune 500 companies. Life Sciences, Clinical, Engineering, IT. (Woman, estab 2001, empl 1000, sales $91,000,000, cert: WBENC)

8648 TransHire
3601 W Commercial Blvd Ste 12
Fort Lauderdale, FL 33309
Contact: Yvonne Rasbach President
Tel: 954-484-5401
Email: yvonne@transhiregroup.com
Website: www.TransHiregroup.com
Staffing svcs: office, clerical, admin support, word processing, light industrial, on-site mgmt programs & payrolling svcs, temp, contract & permanent placement. (Minority, Woman, estab 1984, empl 9, sales $21,575,122, cert: State, NMSDC)

8649 Victoria & Associates Career Services, Inc.
8181 NW 36 St, Ste 22
Miami, FL 33166
Contact: Victoria Villalba President
Tel: 305-477-2233
Email: victoria@victoriaassociates.com
Website: www.victoriaassociates.com
Staffing svcs: temp, temp to hire, direct hire, vendor on premise, payrolling, background checks, etc. (Minority, Woman, estab 1992, empl 6, sales , cert: WBENC)

8650 Vinali LLC
2860 Delaney Ave
Orlando, FL 32806
Contact: Acct Mgr
Tel: 407-574-2000
Email:
Website: www.vinalistaffing.com/
Permanent and temporary staffing services across technology, accounting, logistics and healthcare. (Minority, Woman, estab 2016, empl 15, sales $5,000,000, cert: State, WBENC)

Georgia

8651 Apollos Partners LLC
PO Box 49755
Atlanta, GA 30359
Contact: Bryan Payne Managing Partner
Tel: 404-437-7500
Email: bryan@apollospartners.com
Website: www.apollospartners.com
Direct-hire placements, accounting & finance positions. (AA, estab 2009, empl 1, sales $225,000, cert: NMSDC)

8652 ARK Temporary Staffing, LLC
221 Scenic Hwy
Lawrenceville, GA 30046
Contact: Alvin Keitt Business Devel Mgr
Tel: 770-962-5099
Email: akeitt@arktempstaffing.com
Website: www.arktempstaffing.com
Staffing services providing reliable, quality Temporary and Permanent personnel for business and government agencies. (Woman/AA, estab 2004, empl 100, sales $4,324,547, cert: NMSDC)

8653 Ashton Staffing, Inc
3590 Cherokee St Ste
Kennesaw, GA 30144
Contact: Jennifer Coon-Leeper Major Accts Mgr
Tel: 770-419-1776
Email: jleeper@ashtonstaffing.com
Website: www.ashtonstaffing.com
Direct hire & contract recruiting: technology, financial, management. (Woman, estab 1995, empl 35, sales $16,100,000, cert: WBENC)

8654   ASK Staffing, Inc.
6495 Shiloh Road Ste 300
Alpharetta, GA 30005
Contact: Manish Karani President
Tel: 770-813-8947
Email: mkarani@askstaffing.com
Website: www.askconsulting.com/
Permanent placement & information technology staff augmentation. (Minority, Woman, estab 1995, empl , sales $22,000,000, cert: NMSDC, WBENC)

8655   Bison Data Systems, Inc.
5425 Peachtree Pkwy
Peachtree Corners, GA 30092
Contact: Wesley Owens CEO
Tel: 888-242-5737
Email: sscott@bisonstaffing.com
Website: www.bisonstaffing.com
Staffing, Technology, Light, Industrial & Health Care industries. (AA, estab 2014, empl 37, sales $12,000,000, cert: NMSDC)

8656   Blue Ocean Ventures LLC
2814 Spring Rd Ste 116
Atlanta, GA 30339
Contact: Robert Jordan
Tel: 404-279-2777
Email: robert.jordan@blue-oceanventures.com
Website: www.blue-oceanventures.com
Recruiting, permanent hire & staffing. (AA, estab 2012, empl 10, sales , cert: NMSDC)

8657   Boomers Consulting, LLC
PO Box 246
Lithonia, GA 30058
Contact: Pamela Garr Managing Dir
Tel: 678-476-8243
Email: info@boomersconsultingllc.com
Website: www.boomersconsultingllc.com
Talent acquisition & consulting, staffing/recruiting. (Woman/AA, estab 2011, empl 1, sales , cert: State, City)

8658   COMFORCE
2400 Meadowbrook Pkwy
Duluth, GA 30096
Contact: Shivani Sardana Recruiter
Tel: 678-648-7422
Email: shivani.sardana@comforce.com
Website: www.comforce.com
Contingent staffing, information technology consulting & human resource outsourcing solutions. (As-Ind, estab 1962, empl 500, sales $438,000,000, cert: NMSDC)

8659   Corporate Temps, Inc.
5950 Live Oak Pkwy Ste 230
Norcross, GA 30093
Contact: Shawn Menefee President
Tel: 770-934-1710
Email: shawn@corporatetemps.com
Website: www.corporatetemps.com
Temporary & permanent staffing. (AA, estab 1991, empl 250, sales $11,670,618, cert: State, City, NMSDC)

8660   CorTech
710 Morgan Falls Road
Atlanta, GA 30350
Contact: JP Rogers Sr VP Sales
Tel: 770-628-0268
Email: jrogers@cor-tech.net
Website: www.cor-tech.net
Recruiting svcs: technical, professional services, vendor mgmt (VMS). (Hisp, estab 1999, empl 7500, sales $260,543,521, cert: NMSDC)

8661   DoverStaffing
2451 Cumberland Pkwy Ste 3418
Atlanta, GA 30339
Contact: Sanquinetta Dover CEO
Tel: 770-434-3040
Email: sdover@doverstaffing.com
Website: www.doverstaffing.com
Staffing, training, call center svcs. (Woman/AA, estab 1996, empl 200, sales , cert: NMSDC)

8662   EC London & Associates
101 Marietta St NW, Ste 3310
Atlanta, GA 30303
Contact: Edward C. London CEO
Tel: 404-688-6607
Email: elondon@bellsouth.net
Website: www.eclondon.com
Facilities support & staffing services. (AA, estab 1981, empl 50, sales $1,821,984, cert: City)

8663   Ellsworth Healthcare Staffing LLC
160 Clairemont Ave, Ste 200
Decatur, GA 30030
Contact: Terri Lawson-Adams CEO
Tel: 404-806-8164
Email: tadams@ehstaffing.com
Website: www.ehstaffing.com
Healthcare staffing, highly qualified professional and medical staff. (Woman/AA, estab 2016, empl 10, sales $920,000, cert: NMSDC, WBENC)

8664   Enterprise Project Solutions Group Corporation
204 Kobuk Court
Canton, GA 30114
Contact: Dir of Sales
Tel: 678-592-2256
Email: sales@epsgcorp.com
Website: www.epsgcorp.com
Staff Augmentation (Woman, estab 2005, empl 5, sales $1,500,000, cert: WBENC)

8665   Excel Staffing Inc.
1174 Grimes Bridge Rd Ste 100
Roswell, GA 30075
Contact: Khushnood Elahi Sales/ Marketing Mgr
Tel: 678-461-8701
Email: k.elahi@4esi.com
Website: www.4esi.com
Staffing svcs: sales & marketing, executive, accounting & finance, engineering & manufacturing, industrial, office professionals, IT managed svcs & e-business svcs. (As-Ind, estab 2001, empl 10, sales $9,000,000, cert: NMSDC)

8666   FirstPro Inc.
PO Box 420559
Atlanta, GA 30342
Contact: Michelle Kennedy Dir of Mktg
Tel: 404-250-7179
Email: m.kennedy@firstproinc.com
Website: www.firstproinc.com
Executive search, professional placement & staffing: accounting, administrative, call center, clerical, collections, finance, healthcare, human resources, information technology, legal, light industrial, life sciences, management consulting. (Woman, estab 1986, empl 125, sales $31,900,000, cert: WBENC)

8667 Futurewave Systems Inc.
5 Concourse Pkwy Ste 3000
Roswell, GA 30075
Contact: Raj Prabhu CEO
Tel: 678-640-1167
Email: raj.prabhu@futurewavesystems.com
Website: www.futurewavesystems.com
Staffing services. (As-Ind, estab 2006, empl 267, sales
$3,292,000, cert: NMSDC)

8668 Global Personnel Solutions, Inc.
1143 Laney Walker Blvd
Augusta, GA 30901
Contact: Giselle Brown Acct Mgr
Tel: 706-722-4222
Email: gbrown@gapersonnel.com
Website: www.globalpersonnelsol.com
Full service staffing services. (Woman/AA, estab 1987,
empl 10, sales $4,475,681, cert: NMSDC)

8669 Heagney Logan Group, LLC
2002 Summit Blvd Ste 300
Atlanta, GA 30319
Contact: Jeannette Weigelt Principal
Tel: 404-267-1351
Email: info@heagneylogan.com
Website: www.heagneylogangroup.com
Management Consulting, IT Consultant Staffing, Project
Management, ERP Consulting, Remote Development,
Contract Technical Staffing. (AA, estab 2009, empl 3, sales
$924,954, cert: State, NMSDC)

8670 Healthcare Resources Staffing Agency
2107 N Decatur Rd, Ste 256
Decatur, GA 30033
Contact: Terrilyn Ferguson Dir
Tel: 770-820-7874
Email: terri@hrsagency.com
Website: www.hrsagency.com
Healthcare Resources Staffing (HRS) Agency is a medical
staffing company providing Nurses, Therapists, Nursing
Assistants and other Healthcare medical and non-medical
professionals.
We provide medical staffing services and related products
to Medical (AA, estab 2016, empl , sales $1,100,000, cert:
NMSDC)

8671 Homrich, Klein & Associates
3500 Lenox Rd
Atlanta, GA 30326
Contact: Amy Dresser Principal
Tel: 404-541-9010
Email: adresser@hkasearch.com
Website: www.hkasearch.com
Accounting & financial recruiting. (Woman, estab 2003,
empl 5, sales $1,000,400, cert: WBENC)

8672 Infinite Resouce Solutions
2400 Herodian Way SE Ste 205
Smyrna, GA 30080
Contact: Leigh Sicina COO
Tel: 404-645-7065
Email: lsicina@infiniters.com
Website: www.infiniters.com
Resource management & professional staffing. (Woman,
estab 2013, empl 50, sales $2,464,410, cert: WBENC)

8673 JNX Partners, LLC
2935 Haynes Club Cir
Grayson, GA 30017
Contact: Judy Swanier President
Tel: 770-982-0043
Email: judy.swanier@jnxpartners.com
Website: www.jnxpartners.com
Executive staffing, HR & career transition: sourcing,
screening, testing, hiring & retention
practices, coaching & support. (Woman/AA, estab 2005,
empl 3, sales , cert: WBENC)

8674 Lorentine Green & Associates, Inc.
12104 Jefferson Creek Dr
Alpharetta, GA 30005
Contact: Lorentine F. Green President
Tel: 770-616-6326
Email: lorentine@lorentinegreen.com
Website: www.lorentinegreen.com
Recruiting & project management, Permanent Place-
ment, Contract & Contract to Permanent. (AA, estab
2013, empl 7, sales $300,000, cert: NMSDC)

8675 Management, Analysis & Utilization, Inc. d.b.a 3Ci
501 Greene St
Augusta, GA 30901
Contact: Harlee Bush Marketing Asst
Tel: 706-823-2337
Email: mausupplier@mau.com
Website: www.mau.com
Strategic temporary staffing, professional recruiting,
outsourcing, outplacement and managed services. (Nat
Ame, estab 1973, empl 10729, sales $433,592,830, cert:
NMSDC)

8676 MarketPro Inc.
53 Perimeter Center E Ste 200
Atlanta, GA 30346
Contact: Cindy Underwood VP
Tel: 404-978-1005
Email: cindy@marketproinc.com
Website: www.marketproinc.com
Contract, contract to hire or direct hire: marketing,
advertising & communications. (Woman, estab 1996,
empl 20, sales $15,650,000, cert: WBENC)

8677 Olivine LLC
970 Peachtree Industrial Blvd. Ste 100
Suwanee, GA 30024
Contact: Rajeev Maddur Sr Acct Mgr
Tel: 770-596-5155
Email: rajeevm@olivinellc.com
Website: www.olivinellc.com
IT Consulting Services, Contract, Contract to Hire and
Direct hire placements. (As-Ind, estab 2006, empl 20,
sales , cert: NMSDC)

8678 Pareto Solutions Group, Inc.
8 Piedmont Center Ste 210
Atlanta, GA 30305
Contact: Shaun Harvill CEO
Tel: 770-804-8020
Email: sharvill@paretosg.com
Website: www.paretosg.com
Staffing: temporary, temp-to-hire & direct hire place-
ment of accounting, finance & IT professionals. (Minor-
ity, Woman, estab 2006, empl 55, sales , cert: WBENC)

8679 Perimeter Entertainment, Inc.
PO Box 464003
Lawrenceville, GA 30042
Contact: CEO
Tel: 678-866-4066
Email: info@perimeterent.com
Website: www.perimeterent.com
Content Creation & Professional Recruiting Services for Entertainment, Media, Government and Big Brand Companies. (Woman/AA, estab 2010, empl 4, sales , cert: NMSDC, WBENC)

8680 Peritia LLC
4751 Best Rd Ste 179
College Park, GA 30337
Contact: Panseh Tsewole President
Tel: 404-224-9692
Email: ptsewole@peritiafederal.com
Website: www.peritiafederal.com
Program Management, IT Services, Administrative Support Services & Staff Augmentation. (AA, estab 2016, empl 2, sales $123,240, cert: NMSDC)

8681 PharmaCare Solutions, Inc.
5555 Glenridge Connector Ste 200
Atlanta, GA 30342
Contact: Cassandra Tancil CEO
Tel: 404-459-2847
Email: ctancil@pharmacaresolutions.com
Website: www.pharmacaresolutions.com
Contract & temporary health professional staffing, analytical data reporting, health management initiatives & clinical support services. (Woman/AA, estab 2003, empl 1, sales , cert: NMSDC)

8682 Preferred Personnel Solutions, Inc.
425 Barrett Pkwy Ste 4045
Kennesaw, GA 30144
Contact: Business Devel Specialist
Tel: 678-662-6471
Email: cartersville@preferredpersonnel.com
Website: www.preferredpersonnel.com
Staffing svcs: light industrial, manufacturing, logistics & distribution, office & admin, call center, accounting & finance, executive search. (Woman, estab 2002, empl 500, sales $11,900,000, cert: WBENC)

8683 ProKatchers LLC
1766 Baxley Pine Trce
Suwanee, GA 30024
Contact: Samay Shah CEO
Tel: 706-254-7008
Email: samay@prokatchers.com
Website: www.prokatchers.com/
Traditional staffing & recruiting, direct placement & payroll services, workforce solution programs. (As-Pac, estab 2015, empl , sales $12,000,000, cert: NMSDC, CPUC)

8684 Quality Staffing of America, Inc.
3525 Piedmont Rd NE
Atlanta, GA 30305
Contact: Ken Richards President
Tel: 404-477-0020
Email: ken@qualitystaffingamerica.com
Website: www.QualityStaffingAmerica.com
Temporary/contingent staffing services. (Woman, estab 2013, empl 200, sales $7,400,000, cert: WBENC)

8685 R. Beverly Consulting, LLC dba Silver Fox Staffing
1140 Newpark View Place
Mableton, GA 30126
Contact: Jeannine Lewis Managing Dir
Tel: 404-512-6441
Email: info@silverfoxstaffs.com
Website: www.silverfoxstaffs.com
Staffing, temporary, part-time and seasonal employees for sporting and special events, conferences, corporate and organizational meetings, trade shows. (AA, estab 2011, empl 1, sales $167,000, cert: NMSDC)

8686 Southern Crescent Personnel, Inc.
7179 Jonesboro Rd Ste 101
Morrow, GA 30260
Contact: Krystal Pate President
Tel: 770-968-4602
Email:
Website: www.scp-jobs.com
Temporary, temp-to-hire & perm placement: administrative, medical & dental positions. (Woman, estab 1993, empl 4, sales , cert: WBENC)

8687 The Experts Bench, Inc.
1325 Satellite Blvd 615
Suwanee, GA 30024
Contact: Ramsey A'Ve Market Practice Lead
Tel: 770-757-5831
Email: ramseya@tebww.com
Website: www.tebww.com/
Professional services. staff marketing & accounting contractors. (Woman, estab 2002, empl 20, sales $1,819,000, cert: WBENC)

8688 The Mom Corps, Inc.
1205 Johnson Ferry Rd Ste 136-507
Marietta, GA 30068
Contact: Allison OKelly CEO
Tel: 888-438-8122
Email: allison@momcorps.com
Website: www.momcorps.com
Temporary staffing. (Woman, estab 2005, empl 15, sales $11,240,405, cert: WBENC)

8689 The Royster Group, Inc.
934 Glenwood Ave SE Ste 280
Atlanta, GA 30316
Contact: Taunton Ken President
Tel: 770-507-3353
Email: krtaunton@roystergroup.com
Website: www.roystergroup.com
Diversity search: healthcare, financial services, consumer products & industrial. (AA, estab 2001, empl 80, sales $18,000,000, cert: NMSDC)

Iowa

8690 CareerPros, LLC dba Sedona Staffing Services
2065 Holliday Dr
Dubuque, IA 52002
Contact: Nikki Kiefer President
Tel: 563-556-3040
Email: nikki@careerpros.com
Website: www.careerpros.com
Staffing services: temporary, temp-to-hire, smart-hire, contract & staff leasing. (Woman, estab 1993, empl 18, sales $11,700,000, cert: WBENC)

8691 Chenhall's Staffing, Inc
2119 E 12th St
Davenport, IA 52803
Contact: Bob Hickman President
Tel: 563-386-3800
Email: bhickman@chenhallstaffing.com
Website: www.chenhallstaffing.com
Staffing augmentation, recruiting & HR, contingent staffing augmentation; temp to perm & transitional probationary staffing recruitment, screening, testing & placement; corporate recruitment, career counseling & outplacement. (Nat Ame, estab 1955, empl 7, sales , cert: NMSDC, 8(a))

8692 SelectOne Staffing Services LLC
222 Third Ave SE Ste 240-B
Cedar Rapids, IA 52401
Contact: Vincent Clayton President
Tel: 319-373-2325
Email: vclayton@genatek.net
Website: www.genatek.net
Recruiting & staffing: engineering, IT development, telecommunications, technical support. (AA, estab 2003, empl 10, sales , cert: NMSDC)

Illinois

8693 AltaStaff LLC
19 S La Salle Ste 800
Chicago, IL 60603
Contact: Taz Wilson President
Tel: 312-269-9990
Email: kkossack@altastaff.com
Website: www.altastaff.com
Staffing services: temporary, temp-to-hire & direct-hire placements for administrative, creative, financial & sales support. (Woman, estab 2007, empl 5, sales , cert: State)

8694 Amazing Edibles Gourmet Catering, Inc.
2419 W 14th St Unit C
Chicago, IL 60608
Contact: Andrea Herrera President
Tel: 312-563-1600
Email: amazingedibles@aol.com
Website: www.amazingediblescatering.com
(Minority, Woman, estab 1994, empl 10, sales $963,488, cert: State)

8695 Anchor Staffing Inc.
9901 S Western Ave, Ste 206
Chicago, IL 60643
Contact: Joyce Johnson CEO
Tel: 773-881-0530
Email: jjohnson@anchorstaffing.com
Website: www.anchorstaffing.com
Temporary & direct hire staffing & employment services. (Minority, estab 2002, empl 350, sales $2,600,000,000, cert: State, City, NMSDC)

8696 Apidel Technologies LLC
13550 U.S. 30, Unit 204 F
Plainfield, IL 60544
Contact: Chris Raut Business Devel Exec
Tel: 847-483-8565
Email: chris@apideltech.com
Website: www.apideltech.com
Temporary Placement, Permanent Placement, Temp to Direct Placement & Payroll, SOW & Call Center. (Woman/As-Ind, estab 2012, empl 770, sales $26,000,000, cert: NMSDC, WBENC)

8697 A-PRO EXECS, LLC
208 S Lasalle St Ste 1450
Chicago, IL 60604
Contact: Gladys Jossell Owner
Tel: 312-855-1515
Email: gjossell@aol.com
Website: www.aprotemps.com
Temporary & permanent placement services:administrative/legal office support, accounting, customer service & information technology. (Woman/AA, estab 2004, empl 4, sales $2,700,000, cert: WBENC)

8698 Arlington Resources, Inc.
4902 Tollview Dr
Rolling Meadows, IL 60008
Contact: Patricia Casey President
Tel: 224-232-5900
Email: pcasey@arlingtonresources.com
Website: www.arlingtonresources.com
Temporary staffing services, temp to hire & direct hire placement of Human Resources Professionals. (Woman, estab 1997, empl 25, sales $6,000,000, cert: City)

8699 Arrow Strategies
233 N. Michigan Ave Ste 1960
Chicago, IL 60601
Contact: Mike Colles Division Dir
Tel: 312-561-9202
Email: mikec@arrowstrategies.com
Website: www.arrowstrategies.com
Recruiting: source, profile & present high-end talent. (Nat Ame, estab 2002, empl 300, sales $48,000,000, cert: NMSDC)

8700 Aspen Technical Staffing, Inc.
10123 Mandel Rd
Plainfield, IL 60544
Contact: Amy Negrete VP
Tel: 630-904-8566
Email: amy@atstaffing.net
Website: www.atstaffing.net
Temporary staffing. (Woman, estab 2001, empl 6, sales $2,400,000,000, cert: WBENC)

8701 Assured Healthcare Staffing LLC - Gurnee, IL
495 N Riverside Dr Ste 203
Gurnee, IL 60031
Contact: Leslie Kischer President
Tel: 847-775-7445
Email: leslie.kischer@assuredhealthcare.com
Website: www.assuredhealthcare.com
Healthcare staffing: Registered Nurses, Licensed Practical Nurses, Certified Nurses Aids, Pharmacists, Pharmacy Techs, Medical Assistants, Medical Billers. (Woman, estab 2007, empl 70, sales $2,751,000, cert: WBENC)

8702 Carrington & Carrington
230 W Monroe St Ste 2250
Chicago, IL 60606
Contact: Marian H Carrington Principal
Tel: 312-606-0503
mcarrington@carringtonandcarrington.com
Website: www.carringtonandcarrington.com
Executive search, recruitment & placement of diverse professionals for senior management & executive level positions. (Woman/AA, estab 1979, empl 6, sales , cert: City, WBENC)

8703 Crystal Equation Corporation
1111 Plaza Dr. Ste 480
Schaumburg, IL 60173
Contact: Julie Selders Dir Marketing & Sales
Tel: 847-715-0453
Email: jselders@crystalequation.com
Website: www.crystalequation.com
Information Technology (IT), contract/consulting, direct placement, Software engineers, System Engineers, Testers, Project Management, Database, Administrators, Developers, Network Engineers. (Woman, estab 2006, empl 350, sales $51,000,000, cert: CPUC, WBENC, NWBOC)

8704 Cube Hub Inc.
600 N Commons Dr Ste 109
Aurora, IL 60504
Contact: Sunil Bakhshi Business Devel Mgr
Tel: 630-746-1239
Email: sunil@cube-hub.com
Website: www.cube-hub.com
Technology, Training, Staffing & Professional Services, Staffing/Recruiting services, Software Development, IT, Engineering, Professional, Marketing, Healthcare, Clinical, Scientific, Finance/Audit, Telecommunication, etc. (Minority, Woman, estab 2014, empl 28, sales $3,580,640, cert: NMSDC)

8705 DC McIssac Corp. dba FPC Arlington, Inc.
1400 Renaissance Dr Ste 100
Park Ridge, IL 60068
Contact: Cathy McIsaac President
Tel: 847-228-7205
Email: cathy@fpcarlington.com
Website: www.fpcarlington.com
Executive search & recruiting services. (Woman, estab 1959, empl 7, sales $800,000, cert: WBENC, NWBOC)

8706 Deegit, Inc.
1900 E Golf Rd. Ste 925
Schaumburg, IL 60173
Contact: Jim Dimitriou CEO
Tel: 847-330-1985
Email: jdimitriou@deegit.com
Website: www.deegit.com
Temp and Perm, project-based services(SOW) & Recruitment process outsourcing(RPO). (As-Ind, estab 1993, empl 150, sales $30,000,000, cert: State, NMSDC)

8707 DMD Consulting, LLC
230 S Clark St Ste 113
Chicago, IL 60604
Contact: Darlene Drab CEO
Tel: 312-809-6987
Email: darlene@dmdconsulting.net
Website: www.dmdconsulting.net
Permanent placement, interim resourcing, and co-sourcing, Audit & Compliance, Accounting and Finance, Tax and Information Technology. (Woman/AA, estab 2008, empl 20, sales $408,865, cert: State, City, WBENC)

8708 Elsko, Inc.
3601 Algonquin Rd, Ste 130
Rolling Meadows, IL 60008
Contact: Christina LaSalvia President
Tel: 847-691-2869
Email: clasalvia@elskoinc.com
Website: www.elskoinc.com/home
Executive staffing. (Minority, Woman, estab 1976, empl 8, sales $550,000, cert: WBENC)

8709 Furst Services
2580 Charles St
Rockford, IL 61125
Contact: Darlene Furst President
Tel: 815-997-1426
Email: darlene.furst@furststaff.com
Website: www.furststaff.com
Recruiting services. (Woman, estab 1971, empl 55, sales $25,000,000, cert: WBENC)

8710 Global Staffing Services, Inc.
925 S Main St
Rockford, IL 61101
Contact: Michele Caldwell CEO
Tel: 815-968-5797
Email: mec611@earthlink.net
Website: www.global-staffing.com
Staffing: flexible, contract & permanent placement, employment & background assessment. (Woman/AA, estab 2000, empl 4, sales , cert: NMSDC)

8711 Granthium Corporation
1111 Plaza Dr
Schaumburg, IL 60173
Contact: Salim Mehdi VP Finance & HR
Tel: 224-353-6427
Email: salimmehdi@granthium.com
Website: www.granthium.com
Staffing resources: Information Technology, Project Management, Legacy Modernization, Cloud Migration, Digital Transformation, Telecom, IOT, Retail & Pharmaceutical, Banking & Finance.
We build on a clear (As-Ind, estab 2019, empl 3, sales $310,000, cert: NMSDC)

8712 Ignition Network dba Fieldday
400 W Erie
Chicago, IL 60654
Contact: Josh Miller Partner
Tel: 708-223-1191
Email: diversesupplier@fieldaymarketing.com
Website: www.fieldaymarketing.com
Recruit human resources professionals. (Woman, estab , empl 5, sales $753,000, cert: WBENC)

8713 IlinkResources Staffing
24402 W Lockport Rd Ste 226
Plainfield, IL 60544
Contact: VP Sales
Tel: 815-230-5256
Email: info@ilinkresources.com
Website: www.ilinkresources.com
Recruiting & staffing. (Woman, estab 2011, empl 6, sales , cert: WBENC)

8714 Instant Technology LLC
200 W Adams, Ste 1440
Chicago, IL 60606
Contact: Monica Lee Corporate Communications Mgr
Tel: 312-582-2600
Email: mlee@instanttechnology.com
Website: www.instanttechnology.com
Technical professionals, contract, contract-to-hire and permanent placement. (Woman, estab 2001, empl 150, sales $19,787,595, cert: State, City)

8715 JRA Consulting Services, Inc.
      10225 W Higgins Rd
      Rosemont, IL 60018
      Contact: Ross Wolfson Talent Acquisition Mgr
      Tel: 847-430-3682
      Email: rwolfson@hrcontracting.com
      Website: www.hrcontracting.com
Human resources staffing, permanent & contract positions. (Woman, estab 1997, empl 4, sales $2,000,000, cert: NWBOC)

8716 LBF Recruitment Strategies, LLC
      330 N Clinton St Ste 606
      Chicago, IL 60661
      Contact: Lisa Frank CEO
      Tel: 312-725-8544
      Email: lisa@lbfstrategies.com
      Website: www.LBFStrategies.com
Executive Search & Career Coaching. (Woman, estab 2012, empl 1, sales $112,000, cert: WBENC)

8717 Loftus & O'Meara Staffing Inc.
      211 E Ontario Ste 1050
      Chicago, IL 60611
      Contact: Cindy Loftus Co-Owner
      Tel: 312-944-2102
      Email: cloftus@loftusomeara.com
      Website: www.loftusomeara.com
Staffing: temporary, temp-to-hire & direct hire. (Woman, estab 1978, empl 7, sales $1,804,597, cert: WBENC)

8718 Mutual Target Associates, Inc.
      7002 Hamilton Dr
      Gurnee, IL 60031
      Contact: Chandra Govind CEO
      Tel: 847-855-0059
      Email: cgovind@mtaincorporated.com
      Website: www.mtaincorporated.com
Permanent placements, contract & contract to hire services. (As-Pac, estab 2005, empl 6, sales $750,000, cert: NMSDC)

8719 My Future Consulting, Inc.
      15255 S 94th Ave Ste 500
      Orland Park, IL 60462
      Contact: Anthony Fletcher CEO
      Tel: 708-428-6462
      Email: anthony.fletcher@myfutureconsulting.com
      Website: www.myfutureconsulting.com
Executive search & recruitment. (AA, estab 2012, empl 17, sales $420,000, cert: NMSDC)

8720 Myriad Technical Services
      40 Shuman Blvd Ste 210
      Naperville, IL 60563
      Contact: Mihir Dash President
      Tel: 630-369-6369
      Email: jobs@myriadcorp.com
      Website: www.myriadcorp.com
Staffing recruiting. (As-Pac, estab 1997, empl 40, sales $4,000,000, cert: State)

8721 Premier Systems, Inc
      14489 John Humphrey Ste 202 Ste 202
      Orland Park, IL 60462
      Contact: Tariq Khan Acct Mgr
      Tel: 708-349-9200
      Email: tkhan@premiersystemsinc.com
      Website: www.premiersystemsinc.com
IT consulting & staffing, project mgmt, systems programming & admin. (As-Pac, estab 1993, empl 30, sales $2,713,000, cert: City, NMSDC)

8722 PSI Resources, LLC
      2001 Butterfield Rd, Ste 1040
      Downers Grove, IL 60515
      Contact: Scott Fleckenstein SVP Strategic Partnerships
      Tel: 602-696-5727
      Email: sfleckenstein@psiresources.com
      Website: www.psiresources.com
Staffing & recruiting services. (Woman, estab 1993, empl 45, sales $1,411,062, cert: State, City, WBENC)

8723 Remedy Intelligent Staffing
      211 53rd St
      Moline, IL 61265
      Contact: Dir of Sales
      Tel: 309-762-7716
      Email: kathys@remedystaff.com
      Website: www.remedystaff.com
Staffing services: administrative, finance, accounting, customer service, IT, logistics & light industrial. (Woman, estab 1963, empl 8, sales $6,000,000,000, cert: State)

8724 Resource Technology Associates, LLC
      10225 W Higgins Rd
      Rosemont, IL 60018
      Contact: Andrew Konik VP
      Tel: 847-430-3667
      Email: akonik@rta-inc.com
      Website: www.rta-inc.com
Staffing support, outbound recruitment. (Woman, estab 1984, empl 22, sales $2,000,000, cert: NWBOC)

8725 RJSL Group
      1956 W Erie St Unit 1E
      Chicago, IL 60622
      Contact: Richard Lee CEO
      Tel: 312-282-4654
      Email: richard@rjslgroup.com
      Website: www.rjslgroup.com
Staffing and recruiting agency, IT & business resources. (As-Pac, estab 2006, empl 10, sales , cert: State, City, NMSDC)

8726 Shar Enterprises Inc dba HKA Staffing Services
      800 Waukegan Rd Ste 200
      Glenview, IL 60025
      Contact: Kristin Haffner President
      Tel: 847-998-9300
      Email: khaffner@hkastaffing.com
      Website: www.hkastaffing.com
Staffing services. (Woman, estab 1989, empl 45, sales $1,200,000, cert: WBENC)

8727 Smartdept. Inc.
      39W581 Bealer Cir
      Geneva, IL 60134
      Contact: Michelle Pairitz Owner
      Tel: 847-579-8202
      Email: michelle@thesmartdept.com
      Website: www.thesmartdept.com
Creative staffing resources: art directors, graphic designers, presentation specialists, copywriters, project managers, technical writers, etc. (Woman, estab 2001, empl 9, sales $250,000, cert: WBENC)

8728   Special Project Staffing by Salem, Inc.
Two Trans Am Plaza Dr
Oakbrook Terrace, IL 60181
Contact: Don Kraus Managing Dir
Tel: 630-932-7000
Email: dkraus@saleminc.com
Website: www.saleminc.com
Temporary staffing agency for both short term assignments and long term projects. (Woman, estab 1980, empl , sales , cert: WBENC)

8729   Sterling Engineering, Inc.
Two Westbrook Corporate Center Ste 300
Westchester, IL 60154
Contact: Rama Kavaliauskas President
Tel: 630-993-3433
Email: rama@sterling-engineering.com
Website: www.sterling-engineering.com
Engineering & technical staff augmentation solutions. (Woman, estab 1969, empl 75, sales $2,691,294, cert: WBENC)

8730   Superior Staffing
PO Box 1551
Melrose Park, IL 60161
Contact: Heriberto Vale CEO
Tel: 630-516-3505
Email: hvale@superior-staffing.com
Website: www.superior-staffing.com
Staffing: temp light industrial & clerical. (Hisp, estab 2001, empl 600, sales $15,000,000, cert: NMSDC)

8731   Synergy Global Systems Inc
1580 S Milwaukee Ave, Ste # 425 Ste 425
Libertyville, IL 60048
Contact: Renu Suri Dir
Tel: 630-768-2975
Email: renusuri@synergygbl.com
Website: www.synergygbl.com/
Staffing solutions & services, temporary staffing, permanent placement, career transition, talent development, outsourcing. (Woman/As-Ind, estab 2006, empl 1113, sales $434,765,600, cert: NMSDC, WBENC)

8732   The Wellington Group, Inc.
317 S Third St
Geneva, IL 60134
Contact: Ann Anastasio President
Tel: 630-262-2000
Email: ann@wellingtongroupinc.com
Website: www.wellingtongroupinc.com
Staffing services: contract, contract to hire. (Woman, estab 2002, empl 8, sales $10,791,915, cert: WBENC)

8733   Theophany Staffing, Inc.
1601 Bond St Ste 106
Naperville, IL 60563
Contact: Tracy McLean President
Tel: 630-983-5200
Email: tracy@theophanystaffing.com
Website: www.theophanystaffing.com
Staffing services. (Woman, estab 2001, empl 5, sales $1,000,000, cert: WBENC)

8734   US Surgitech Inc.
551 Kimberly Dr
Carol Sream, IL 60188
Contact: Alyssa Cantore
Tel: 630-456-4114
Email: alyssa@ussurgitech.com
Website: www.ussurgitech.com
Temporary & permanent staffing solutions. (As-Ind, estab 2003, empl 7, sales $1,206,246, cert: NMSDC)

Indiana

8735   Alpha Rae Personnel, Inc.
347 W Berry St, Ste 700
Fort Wayne, IN 46802
Contact: Rae Pearson President
Tel: 260-426-8227
Email: businessoffice@alpha-rae.com
Website: www.alpha-rae.com
Contract & temporary staffing, executive search, HR management & HR department outsourcing, employee training, electronics & embedded software contract engineering & manufacturing development. (Woman/AA, estab 1980, empl 400, sales , cert: State, WBENC)

8736   CFA Inc.
2461 E. Main St.
Plainfield, IN 46248
Contact: Teresa Wade President
Tel: 317-354-1102
Email: twade@cfastaffing.com
Website: www.cfastaffing.com
Temporary personnel & mgmt recruiting svcs. (Woman/AA, estab 1999, empl 5179, sales $131,000,000, cert: WBENC)

8737   DaMar Staffing Solutions
8900 Keystone Crossing, Ste 1060
Indianapolis, IN 46240
Contact: Tiffany Thompson President
Tel: 317-566-8320
Email: tthompson@damarstaff.com
Website: www.damarstaffing.com
Staffing: direct hire, temp-to-hire, temporary. (Woman/AA, estab 2003, empl 7, sales $622,423, cert: State, City, 8(a))

8738   Diverse Staffing Services
6325 Digital Way, Ste #100
Indianapolis, IN 46278
Contact: Amber Slaughter Business Devel Mgr
Tel: 317-813-8000
Email: aslaughter@diversestaffing.com
Website: www.diversestaffing.com
Recruiting & staffing solutions: information technology, engineering, life sciences, sales & business operations. (AA, estab 1999, empl 3000, sales , cert: State, NMSDC)

8739   First Call Temporary Services Inc.
6960 Hillsdale Ct
Indianapolis, IN 46250
Contact: John Kulish Sales Mgr
Tel: 317-596-3280
Email: jkulish@fcqs.com
Website: www.firstcallinc.com
Staffing services: temp and temp-hire. (Woman, estab 1991, empl 31, sales $18,000,000, cert: WBENC)

8740   MS Inspection & Logistics, Inc.
710 E 64th St
Indianapolis, IN 46220
Contact: Nicky Benefiel CEO
Tel: 855-447-3968
Email: nicky.benefiel@ms-il.com
Website: www.ms-il.com
Warehousing, contingent labor, staffing, temporary staffing, temporary to full time. (Woman/Hisp, estab 2001, empl 76, sales $45,000,000, cert: NMSDC)

8741   Smart IT Staffing, Inc.
6500 Technology Center Dr Ste 300
Indianapolis, IN 46278
Contact: Bill Ryle Dir of Sales
Tel: 513-530-0600
Email: bryle@getsmarterit.com
Website: www.getsmarterit.com
Information Technology Workforce Solutions. (Woman/AA, estab 2005, empl 480, sales $47,900,000, cert: NMSDC, WBENC)

8742   Specialized Staffing Solutions, LLC
1001 E Jefferson
South Bend, IN 46617
Contact: Jacqueline Barton President
Tel: 574-234-9944
Email: jbarton@specializedstaffing.biz
Website: www.specializedstaffing.biz
Temporary, permanant, technical & professional staffing, employment services, human resource mgmt, managed services. (Minority, Woman, estab 2002, empl 27, sales $17,000,000, cert: State, WBENC)

Kansas

8743   Choson Resource LLC
1999 N Amidon, Ste 100B
Wichita, KS 67203
Contact: Kim Silcott President
Tel: 316-729-0312
Email: kim@chosonresource.com
Website: www.Chosonresource.com
Aerospace engineering & staffing services for the air, defense & space industries. (Minority, Woman, estab 2010, empl 4, sales $4,254,100, cert: NMSDC)

8744   Staffing Kansas City Inc.
9930 College Blvd
Overland Park, KS 66210
Contact: Michelle Hays Sales Exec
Tel: 913-663-5627
Email: michelle@staffingkc.com
Website: www.staffingkc.com
Temporary & permanent employment placement. (Woman, estab 1998, empl 5, sales $2,283,865, cert: State)

Kentucky

8745   Astute Sourcing, LLC
10200 Forest Green Blvd Ste 112
Louisville, KY 40223
Contact: Dorothy Abernathy Exec Asst
Tel: 502-499-9440
Email: info@tktandassociates.com
Website: www.astutesourcing.com
Staffing services: telecommunications, healthcare, government, financial services, utilities, manufacturing and supply/chain logistics, contingent staffing, direct hire, permanent staffing, rapid deployment. (Woman/AA, estab 2012, empl 7, sales $1,683,311, cert: NMSDC, WBENC)

8746   J.Y. Legner Associates, Inc.
800 W Market St, Ste 102
Louisville, KY 40202
Contact: Josephine Legner CEO
Tel: 502-585-9000
Email: jlegner@jyla.com
Website: www.jyla.com
Staffing & HR mgmt, temporary staffing, long-term employee leasing. (Woman/AA, estab 1999, empl 70, sales $1,000,000, cert: NMSDC)

8747   QP1, Inc. dba Luttrell Staffing Group
1435 Campbell Ln
Bowling Green, KY 42104
Contact: Monica Shuffett VP
Tel: 270-250-3446
Email: mshuffett@lstaff.com
Website: www.lstaff.com
Manufacturing and industrial employment agency, exceptional administrative, call center, technical and professional placement services. (Woman, estab 1977, empl 185, sales $152,475,221, cert: WBENC)

Louisiana

8748   Delta Personnel, Inc.
2709 L & A Rd
Metairie, LA 70001
Contact: Ingrid Delahoussaye Owner
Tel: 504-833-5200
Email: tlawrence@deltapersonnel.com
Website: www.deltapersonnel.com/
Staffing & payroll payroll services. (Minority, Woman, estab 1968, empl 6, sales $3,000,000, cert: State, NMSDC, WBENC)

8749   Frazee Recruiting Consultants, Inc.
2351 Energy Dr, Ste 1100
Baton Rouge, LA 70808
Contact: Chris Bien Business Dev
Tel: 225-231-7880
Email: sales@frazeerecruit.com
Website: www.frazeerecruit.com
Professional staffing, direct hire search, contract/ temporary. (Woman, estab 1998, empl 150, sales $6,000,000, cert: WBENC)

8750   Jean Simpson Personnel Services, Inc.
1318 Shreveport-Barksdale Hwy
Shreveport, LA 71105
Contact: Angel Scott Admin Asst
Tel: 318-869-3494
Email: ascott@jeansimpson.com
Website: www.jeansimpson.com
Temporary & full-time staffing: clerical, industrial & professional. (Woman, estab 1974, empl 33, sales , cert: WBENC)

8751   Preferred Standards, LLC
654 Lobdell Ave
Baton Rouge, LA 70806
Contact: Derrick Toussaint CEO
Tel: 225-924-9552
Email: dtoussaint@pstandards.net
Website: www.pstandards.org
Professional staffing, recruiting & payroll services. (AA, estab 2013, empl 5, sales $1,312,529, cert: NMSDC)

8752 SureTemps LLC
1631 Elysian Fields Ave
New Orleans, LA 70117
Contact: Maxine A. President
Tel: 504-947-3353
Email: sunsoundconcerts@yahoo.com
Website: www.suretemps.biz
Personnel staffing: labors, data entry clerks, custodial services, full food services & supervisors/managers for long or short term basis. (AA, estab 2011, empl 500, sales , cert: City)

8753 Topp Knotch Personnel, Inc.
401 Whitney Ave Ste 312
Gretna, LA 70056
Contact: Diedria Joseph CEO
Tel: 866-744-2974
Email: diedria@tkpsi.com
Website: www.tkpsi.com
Staffing svcs: admin, clerical, customer service, accounting, marketing, computer technology. (Woman/AA, estab , empl , sales $4,055,182, cert: City, WBENC)

8754 Universal Personnel, LLC
1100 Poydras St Ste 1300
New Orleans, LA 70163
Contact: Michele Vignes President
Tel: 504-561-5627
Email: michelev@universal-personnel.com
Website: www.universal-personnel.com
Technical staffing, career & contract job placement: engineering, drafting, architecture & information technology, professional, administrative & clerical. (Woman, estab 1980, empl 650, sales $57,118,011, cert: WBENC)

Massachusetts

8755 Aries Group, Inc.
500 Cummings Center Ste 1750
Beverly, MA 01915
Contact: Frances Dichner President
Tel: 877-806-7977
Email: fran@ariesgroupinc.com
Website: www.ariesgroupinc.com
Contract & permanent placement staffing services. (Woman, estab 2000, empl 10, sales $7,732,415, cert: WBENC)

8756 East Coast Staffing Solutions
651 Orchard St Ste 307
New Bedford, MA 02744
Contact: Randy Silva Business Devel
Tel: 508-990-7670
Email: randy@eastcoaststaffingsolutions.com
Website: www.eastcoaststaffingsolutions.com
Staffing, direct hires, temporary placements & contractual assignments. (AA, estab 2009, empl 5, sales $105,650,836, cert: State)

8757 Griffin Staffing Network, LLC
1145 Main St Ste 508
Springfield, MA 01103
Contact: Michelle O'Meara
Tel: 413-788-0751
Email: momeara@griffinstaffingnetwork.com
Website: www.griffinstaffingnetwork.com
Staffing services. (Woman/AA, estab 2013, empl 2, sales , cert: State)

8758 Hollister Staffing, Inc.
75 State St, 9th Fl
Boston, MA 02109
Contact: Kip Hollister Founder & CEO
Tel: 617-654-0200
Email: kip@hollisterstaff.com
Website: www.hollisterstaff.com
Recruiting services: direct hire, contract & contract-to-hire. (Woman, estab 1988, empl 70, sales $31,100,000, cert: WBENC)

8759 Integration Technology, Inc.
167 Washington St Ste 32
Norwell, MA 02061
Contact: Sean Stewart Acct mgr
Tel: 781-569-4949
Email: sean.stewart@it-inc.us
Website: www.integration-technology.com
IT, SAP staffing and consulting services (Woman, estab 1998, empl 4, sales $1,300,000, cert: State)

8760 John Leonard Employment Services, Inc.
75 Federal St, Ste 1120
Boston, MA 02110
Contact: Linda Poldoian CEO
Tel: 617-348-2607
Email: Info@johnleonard.com
Website: www.johnleonard.com
Temporary employment: office support personnel. (Woman, estab 1969, empl 18, sales $7,009,497, cert: State, City, WBENC)

8761 KNF&T Staffing Resources
3 Post Office Square
Boston, MA 02109
Contact: Joanna DiTrapano Dir of Marketing
Tel: 617-574-8200
Email: jditrapano@knft.com
Website: www.knft.com
Staffing services: administrative, accounting, finance & healthcare personnel. (Woman, estab 1983, empl , sales $14,000,000, cert: State, WBENC)

8762 S & S Staffing, LLC
50 Lake Ave
Worcester, MA 01604
Contact: Karen DeMichele President
Tel: 508-799-7171
Email: karen@savvystaffing.com
Website: www.savvystaffing.com
Staffing solutions: long or short term, temporary & permanent. (Woman, estab 2006, empl 15, sales $12,000,000, cert: State)

8763 Scout Exchange LLC
501 Boylston St, Ste 3101
Boston, MA 02116
Contact: Farla Russo Dir of Admin
Tel: 617-535-4561
Email: frusso@goscoutgo.com
Website: www.goscoutgo.com
Hosted software to find specialty recruiters to fill their positions. integrated with Applicant Tracking System (ATS). (As-Pac, estab 2013, empl 58, sales , cert: NMSDC)

8764 Snelling Staffing Services
3 Courthouse Lane Ste 2
Chelmsford, MA 01824
Contact: Bernice Kaiser Owner/General Mgr
Tel: 978-970-3434
Email: bernice@snelling-ma.com
Website: www.snelling.com/chelmsford
Staffing: engineering, administrative, finance & accounting, sales & marketing, manufacturing direct hire/temp-to-hire/contract labor. (Woman, estab 1988, empl 6, sales $2,000,000, cert: WBENC)

8765 Staffing Solutions, Inc.
225 Friend St
Boston, MA 02114
Contact: Earl Tate CEO
Tel: 617-248-0048
Email: earl@staffingww.com
Website: www.staffingsolutionsworldwide.com
Temporary & permanent staffing service. (Woman/AA, estab 1996, empl 1, sales $4,650,000, cert: WBENC)

8766 The Resource Connection, Inc.
161 S Main St Ste 300
Middleton, MA 01949
Contact: President
Tel: 978-777-9333
Email: staff@resource-connection.com
Website: www.resource-connection.com
Staffing services: temporary, temp-to-hire, & direct placement of administrative, clerical & light industrial personnel. (Woman, estab 1987, empl 9, sales $8,300,000, cert: State, City, WBENC)

8767 The Vesume Group, LLC
21 High St Ste 210A
North Andover, MA 01845
Contact: Jori Blumsack COO
Tel: 978-687-6000
Email: jori@thevesumegroup.com
Website: www.thevesumegroup.com
Staffing, contract, contract-to-hire & permanent placement of IT, Engineering, Manufacturing, Accounting/Finance & Call Center professionals. (Woman, estab 2009, empl 9, sales $3,663,666, cert: WBENC)

8768 Total Technical Services, Inc.
225 Wyman St
Waltham, MA 02451
Contact: Tim Hovey VP
Tel: 800-776-0562
Email: thovey@total-tech.com
Website: www.total-tech.com
Temporary, contract & permanent staffing svcs, on-site managed vendor program & payroll svcs. (AA, Hisp, estab 1992, empl 300, sales , cert: NMSDC)

8769 United Personnel Services
289 Bridge St
Springfield, MA 01103
Contact: Jennifer Brown VP Business Dev
Tel: 413-314-6073
Email: jbrown@unitedpersonnel.com
Website: www.unitedpersonnel.com
Staffing: temporary, temp-to-hire & full-time placements. (Woman, estab 1984, empl 39, sales $27,000,000, cert: State, WBENC)

Maryland

8770 All-Pro Placement Service, Inc.
116 Old Padonia Rd, Ste D
Cockeysville, MD 21030
Contact: Jennifer Quinn VP
Tel: 410-308-9050
Email: jennifer@allproplacement.com
Website: www.allproplacement.com
Staffing: temp, temp-to-perm & direct hire permanent placements, clerical, executive level, warehousing. (Woman, estab 2002, empl 8, sales $4,364,791, cert: State, City)

8771 Beacon Staffing Alternatives
16-2 S Philadelphia Blvd
Aberdeen, MD 21001
Contact: Sheryl Kohl President
Tel: 410-297-6600
Email: sheryl@beaconstaffing.com
Website: www.Beaconstaffing.com
Staffing services. (Woman, estab 1999, empl 300, sales $4,441,779, cert: State, WBENC)

8772 BizyBee Professional Staffing & Biz'Ness Solutions
8181 Professional Place ste 205
Hyattsville, MD 20785
Contact: Danae Hubbard President
Tel: 301-459-1233
Email: bzbpro@yahoo.com
Website: www.bzbpro.com
Temporary staffing, employment, recruitment, staff augmentation & HR that services. (Woman/AA, estab 2011, empl 5, sales $500,000, cert: State, 8(a))

8773 Contemporaries, Inc.
1010 Wayne Ave, Ste 400
Silver Spring, MD 20910
Contact: Erin Allen President
Tel: 301-775-4392
Email:
Website: www.contemps.com
Administrative temporary & permanent placement services. (Woman, estab 1991, empl 6, sales $1,021,514, cert: WBENC)

8774 Crews Control Inc
11820 West Market Place Ste L
Fulton, MD 20759
Contact: Laura A. Monaco VP Operations
Tel: 301-604-1200
Email: Laura@crewscontrol.com
Website: www.crewscontrol.com
Recruitment, staffing & payroll services. (Woman, estab 1988, empl 12, sales , cert: WBENC)

8775 Crosby Corporation
14405 Laurel Place, Ste 201
Laurel, MD 20707
Contact: Howard Petty President
Tel: 301-585-3105
Email: hpetty@crosbycorp.com
Website: www.crosbycorp.com
Human capital solutions: technical staff augmentation, direct placement services, outsourced projects, educational services & comprehensive workforce management solutions. (AA, estab 2001, empl 100, sales $4,000,000, cert: City, 8(a))

8776 Federal Staffing Resources LLC
      2200 Somerville Rd Ste 300
      Annapolis, MD 21401
      Contact: Tracy Balazs CEO
      Tel: 410-990-0795
      Email: tbalazs@fsrpeople.com
      Website: www.fsrpeople.com
Workforce solutions & integrative business solutions,
recruitment & staffing. (Minority, Woman, estab 2004,
empl 266, sales $31,325,000, cert: State, NMSDC, WBENC)

8777 Infojini Inc.
      10015 Old Columbia Rd Ste B 215
      Columbia, MD 21046
      Contact: Sandeep Harjani Dir
      Tel: 443-257-0086
      Email: commercialrfi@infojiniconsulting.com
      Website: www.infojiniconsulting.com/
Recruitment, training, assessment, outsourcing & consulting services, temporary & permanent positions. (As-Pac,
estab 2006, empl 700, sales $54,000,000, cert: NMSDC)

8778 Innova Project Services LLC
      1150 Ripley St, Ste 1616
      Silver Spring, MD 20910
      Contact: Molly Donaldson CEO
      Tel: 301-275-7262
      Email: mdonaldson@innovaprojectservices.com
      Website: www.innovaprojectservices.com/
Project controls services and staffing. (Woman, estab
2021, empl 5, sales , cert: WBENC)

8779 nTech Solutions, Inc.
      9256 Bendix Road Ste 208
      Columbia, MD 21045
      Contact: Sridhar Kunadi CEO
      Tel: 877-689-8448
      Email: sridhar@ntechsol.com
      Website: www.ntechsol.com
IT staffing/consulting services. (As-Pac, estab 2012, empl
45, sales , cert: State, NMSDC)

8780 PMC Group Inc dba Piper Staffing
      8117 Harford Rd, Ste D
      Baltimore, MD 21234
      Contact: Kimberley West President
      Tel: 410-286-1874
      Email: kimberley@pmcgrpinc.com
      Website: www.piperstaffing.com
Multiple & diverse staffing solutions. (Woman/AA, estab
2010, empl 104, sales $1,669,345, cert: State)

8781 The BOSS Group
      4350 East West Hwy, Ste 307
      Bethesda, MD 20814
      Contact: Truelove, Charisse Owner
      Tel: 301-802-3672
      Email: linda@thebossgroup.com
      Website: www.thebossgroup.com
Human capital solutions, source, evaluate & place exclusive creative, marketing, communications & interactive
talent. (Woman, estab 0, empl , sales , cert: WBENC)

8782 The HR Source
      8181 Professional Place Ste 120
      Landover, MD 20785
      Contact: Patricia Hall Jaynes CEO
      Tel: 301-459-3133
      Email: pathj@thehrsource.com
      Website: www.thehrsource.com
Human resources staffing & consulting services, interim/
temporary & permanent staffing services, outplacement
& payroll services, administrative interim/temporary &
permanent staffing services. (Woman/AA, estab 1994,
empl 5, sales $2,894,265, cert: State, NMSDC, WBENC)

Michigan

8783 Abacus Service Corporation
      25925 Telegraph Rd Ste 206
      Southfield, MI 48033
      Contact: April Szlaga VP
      Tel: 248-522-8005
      Email: april@abacusservice.com
      Website: www.abacusservice.com
Staff augmentation, contract, temporary & permanent
placement services. (Minority, Woman, estab 2004,
empl 325, sales $22,200,000, cert: NMSDC, WBENC)

8784 Accura Services, LLC
      51470 Oro Dr
      Shelby Township, MI 48315
      Contact: Jenifer Cugliari Member
      Tel: 586-884-4417
      Email: jen@accuraservicesllc.com
      Website: www.accuraservicesllc.com
Direct & contract staffing services specializing in Engineering, Technical & Professional areas. (Woman, estab
2015, empl 3, sales , cert: WBENC)

8785 Aegis Group Search Consultants, LLC
      1358 Village Dr
      Detroit, MI 48207
      Contact: John Green President
      Tel: 248-344-1450
      Email: jgreen@aegis-group.com
      Website: www.aegis-group.com
Executive search services. (AA, estab 1991, empl 4, sales
$700,000, cert: NMSDC)

8786 Arps International LLC
      3003 Silver Spring Dr
      Ann Arbor, MI 48103
      Contact: Arun Nikore VP
      Tel: 734-945-3000
      Email: sales@arpsint.com
      Website: www.arpsint.com
Executive recruiting services: engineering, information
technology, manufacturing & operations, supply chain.
(Woman/As-Ind, estab 2002, empl 2, sales $106,127,
cert: NMSDC)

8787 Blake Group LLC
      30986 Stoneridge Dr Ste 14205
      Wixom, MI 48393
      Contact: Jim Blake Sr Exec VP
      Tel: 248-238-5776
      Email: james@blakegroupllc.com
      Website: www.blakegrouptechnicalstaffing.com
Information Technology professional executive staffing.
(Woman/AA, estab 2010, empl 7, sales , cert: NMSDC)

8788 Boston Contemporaries, Inc.
55 Court St Ste 330
Boston, MI 02108
Contact: Ron Porter Sr Acct Mgr
Tel: 617-723-9797
Email: ron@bostoncontemporaries.com
Website: www.bostoncontemporaries.com
Staffing temporary and temp to hire Administrative Support, Accounting & Finance, and IT Support professionals. (Woman, estab 1998, empl 20, sales $1,150,000, cert: State)

8789 CIMA Consulting Group
901 Tower Dr, Ste 420
Troy, MI 48098
Contact: Scott Foreman CFO
Tel: 586-226-2000
Email: sforeman@cimacg.com
Website: www.cimacg.com
Talent Management Solutions. (Woman/Hisp, estab 2016, empl 6, sales $260,000, cert: NMSDC, WBENC)

8790 Community Based Staffing
4369 Seebaldt
Detroit, MI 48204
Contact: David Cross President
Tel: 313-744-5771
Email: david.cross@cb-staffing.com
Website: www.cb-staffing.com
Direct hire & staffing: machine operators, production associates, welders, quality inspectors, press operators. (AA, estab 2016, empl 50, sales , cert: NMSDC)

8791 CrossFire Group LLC
691 N Squirrel Rd Ste 118
Auburn Hills, MI 48326
Contact: Deborah Schneider CEO
Tel: 866-839-2600
Email: dschneider@xfiregroup.com
Website: www.xfiregroup.com
Recruiting, Staffing, Business Process Outsourcnig, professional temporary & contract staffing, permanent placement, vendor management &payroll services to large and medium size firms. (Woman, estab 2002, empl 1500, sales $10,000,000, cert: WBENC)

8792 Crystal Employment Services, LLC
32355 Howard St
Madison Heights, MI 48071
Contact: Michael Stanley Partner
Tel: 248-588-9540
Email: mstanley@crystaleng.com
Website: www.crystaleng.com
Staffing services. (Hisp, estab 2004, empl 300, sales , cert: NMSDC)

8793 Entech Staffing Solutions
1800 Crooks Road
Troy, MI 48084
Contact: Colleen Myers Dir of Sales & Recruiting
Tel: 248-528-1444
Email: cmyers@teamentech.com
Website: www.teamentech.com
Temporary staffing: administrative, technical, medical & light industrial positions, short term, long term & permanent employment. (Woman, estab , empl , sales $11,500,000, cert: WBENC)

8794 Galaxy Software Solutions, Inc.
5820 N Lilley Rd, Ste 8
Canton, MI 48187
Contact: Dileep Tiwari VP
Tel: 734-717-7969
Email: dileep@galaxy-soft.com
Website: www.galaxy-soft.com
Staffing highly skilled candidates/consultants on contract and on a full-time basis. (Minority, Woman, estab 2004, empl 251, sales $24,000,000, cert: WBENC)

8795 Gonzalez Production Systems
1670 Highwood East
Pontiac, MI 48340
Contact: Bill Kelly New Business Dev
Tel: 248-884-0315
Email: bkelly@gonzales-group.com
Website: www.gonzalez-group.com
Contract Placement, Contract to Direct, Direct Placement, Managed Services. (Hisp, estab 1975, empl 800, sales $50,000,000, cert: NMSDC)

8796 G-TECH Services, Inc.
17101 Michigan Ave
Dearborn, MI 48126
Contact: Shelby Medina Dir of Business Dev
Tel: 313-425-3666
Email: smedina@gogtech.com
Website: www.gogtech.com
Contract & direct hire staffing solutions, engineering/technical support; information technology; finance/accounting; scientific; administration/clerical; co-employment training & payroll services. (Woman, estab 1986, empl 650, sales $56,000,000, cert: WBENC)

8797 Harvard Resource Group
210 W Big Beaver Rd Ste 310
Troy, MI 48084
Contact: Mark Hicks VP
Tel: 248-528-1110
Email: mhicks@hrgus.com
Website: www.harvardresourcegroup.com
Staffing: permanent, contract, temp to perm, professional & organizational dev, mgmt & leadership dev, wireless dev & deployment svcs. (Nat Ame, estab 2001, empl 6, sales $3,000,000, cert: NMSDC)

8798 Hattrick Professional Staffing
3228 Norton Lawn
Rochester Hills, MI 48307
Contact: Julie Campbell Owner
Tel: 248-289-6241
Email: julie.campbell@hattrick-staffing.com
Website: www.hattrick-staffing.com
Staffing, Direct Hire, Contract or Temp to hire placements within areas of Engineering, Design, Finance/Accounting, IT, Professional, Technical placements & Executive positions. (Woman, estab 2015, empl 1, sales , cert: WBENC)

8799 Human Capital Staffing LLC
6001 N Adams Rd, Ste 208
Bloomfield Hills, MI 48304
Contact: Mary Adams President
Tel: 248-593-1950
Email: madams@hcsteam.com
Website: www.hcsteam.com
Staffing services. (Minority, Woman, estab 0, empl 10, sales , cert: NMSDC, WBENC)

8800   Industry Specific Solutions LLC
       24901 Northwestern Hwy Ste 400
       Southfield, MI 48075
       Contact: Earl Newman President
       Tel: 248-356-3400
       Email: enewman@isscompanies.com
       Website: www.isscompanies.com
Full-service staffing in logistics, manufacturing, accounting
& finance, education, technology & office administration.
(AA, estab 2006, empl 150, sales $122,000, cert: NMSDC)

8801   Inteligente Solutions, Inc.
       17199 N Laurel Park Dr Ste 321
       Livonia, MI 48152
       Contact: Kathy DeCaires VP
       Tel: 734-338-8970
       Email: kdecaires@igsstaff.com
       Website: www.igsstaff.com
Staffing svcs; general labor & light industrial; long term to
permanent, clerical & admin support staffing. (Hisp, estab
1993, empl 500, sales , cert: NMSDC)

8802   K&A Staffing, LLC
       38700 Van Dyke Rd. Ste 150
       Sterling Heights, MI 48312
       Contact: Justin Tappero COO
       Tel: 586-806-6614
       Email: jtappero@knaresourcegroup.com
       Website: www.knaresourcegroup.com
Staffing services. (As-Ind, estab 2011, empl 16, sales , cert:
NMSDC)

8803   Linked, LLC
       6633 18 Mile Rd
       Sterling Heights, MI 48314
       Contact: Marie Khoury President
       Tel: 586-231-1234
       Email: marie.khoury@linkedps.com
       Website: www.linkedps.com
Staffing, candidate search, recruitment, contract & direct
placement services. (Woman, estab 2012, empl 4, sales ,
cert: WBENC)

8804   MCM Staffing, LLC
       415 W 11 Mile Rd
       Madison Heights, MI 48076
       Contact: Courtney Morales Hofmann President
       Tel: 248-436-2616
       Email: courtney@mcmstaffing.com
       Website: www.mcmstaffing.com
Staffing services. (Minority, Woman, estab 2011, empl 950,
sales $19,500,000, cert: NMSDC, WBENC)

8805   Michigan Staffing
       29400 Van Dyke Ste 308
       Warren, MI 48093
       Contact: Frances Lucido VP
       Tel: 586-506-7524
       Email: francy@michiganstaffing.com
       Website: www.michiganstaffing.com
Temporary, contract & direct staffing services: administrative, customer service, light industrial, technical, professional & skilled trades. (Woman, estab 2002, empl 75,
sales , cert: WBENC)

8806   Moreno Services LLC
       5140 State St #103
       Saginaw, MI 48603
       Contact: Yvette Serrato CEO
       Tel: 989-401-3996
       Email: yvette@morenoservices.com
       Website: www.morenoservices.com
Professional recruiting, on site services, and indirect and
direct placements, temporary staffing. (Hisp, estab 2010,
empl 4, sales $12,564,679, cert: NMSDC)

8807   National Career Group
       1745 Hamilton Rd
       Okemos, MI 48864
       Contact: Nadia Sellers CEO
       Tel: 517-706-0111
       Email: nadia@nationalcareergroup.com
       Website: www.nationalcareergroup.com
Permanent staffing & Human Relations Training.
(Woman/AA, estab 1997, empl 10, sales $700,000, cert:
WBENC)

8808   NexTech Professional Services
       25200 Telegraph Rd. Ste 110
       Southfield, MI 48033
       Contact: Rosanne Davis President
       Tel: 248-416-1718
       Email: rosanne.davis@nextechps.com
       Website: www.nextechps.com
Contract & permanent placement: engineering, technology, finance & executive recruiting. (As-Pac, estab
1994, empl 10, sales $2,600,000, cert: NMSDC)

8809   OpTech, LLC
       5440 Corporate Dr
       Troy, MI 48098
       Contact: Ronia Kruse CEO
       Tel: 313-962-9000
       Email: info@optechus.com
       Website: www.optechus.com
Talent, Business consulting, business strategy, Informa-
tion Technology, Engineering, Healthcare, Financial,
Assessments, Marketing, Training, Technical Services,
Business Support, Staffing. (Woman, estab 1999, empl
250, sales $49,032,035, cert: WBENC)

8810   PDS Services, LLC
       37633 Pembroke
       Livonia, MI 48152
       Contact: Derek Dyer President
       Tel: 734-953-3300
       Email: derek@pdsstaffing.com
       Website: www.pdsstaffing.com
Staffing services: contract, contract to hire & permanent
placements. (AA, estab 2005, empl 260, sales
$9,000,000, cert: NMSDC)

8811   Personnel Unlimited Inc.
       29400 Van Dyke Ave
       Warren, MI 48093
       Contact: Frances Lucido President
       Tel: 586-751-5608
       Email: fllucido@personnel-unlimited.com
       Website: www.personnel-unlimited.com
Temporary & Contract Staffing for Admin, Clerical, Tech/
Professional. (Woman, estab 2008, empl 7, sales
$2,462,679, cert: WBENC)

8812 Populus Group, LLC
3001 W Big Beaver Rd Ste 400
Troy, MI 48084
Contact: Danielle Hein Sr Proposal Mgr
Tel: 248-712-7900
Email: dhein@populusgroup.com
Website: www.PopulusGroup.com
Temporary staffing services. Professional Payrolling
Services, Independent Contractor Engagement Services/
1099 Compliance, Immigration Employment Solutions,
Managed Services, Strategic Partnerships, Diverse Talent
Management Solutions. (Hisp, estab 2002, empl 270, sales
$577,322,374, cert: NMSDC)

8813 Premier Automation Contractors
9015 Davison Rd
Davison, MI 48423
Contact: Lisa VanWyk Engineering Accts Dir
Tel: 248-421-7360
Email: lisa@premierac.com
Website: www.premierac.com
Direct & contract hire staffing for skilled trades. (Woman,
estab 2008, empl 200, sales $12,000,000, cert: WBENC)

8814 Premier Staff Services
16250 Northland Dr Ste 224
Southfield, MI 48075
Contact: Michael Garcia Acct Mgr
Tel: 248-809-9675
Email: michael.garcia.rep@gmail.com
Website: www.premierstaffservices.net
Contract staffing, temporary help & direct placement of
clerical, administrative, financial, janitorial, maintenance,
engineering & IT human resources. (AA, estab 2011, empl
24, sales $11,000,000, cert: NMSDC, 8(a))

8815 Reliance One, Inc.
1700 Harmon Rd Ste One
Auburn Hills, MI 48326
Contact: Chad Toms VP Sales
Tel: 248-922-4500
Email: ctoms@reliance-one.com
Website: www.reliance-one.com
Staffing, direct & contract, employment, payroll. (Hisp,
estab 1998, empl 700, sales , cert: NMSDC)

8816 Scope Services, Inc.
2095 Niles Rd
St. Joseph, MI 49085
Contact: TRISH MELCHER President
Tel: 269-982-2888
Email: tmmelcher@scope-services.com
Website: www.scope-services.com
Human capital management, contract &project staffing &
managed staffing/consulting, executive search, contin-
gency direct hire placement, career consulting &
outplacement services. (Woman, estab 1965, empl 569,
sales $58,000,000, cert: WBENC)

8817 Smart Folks, Inc.
29445 Beck Rd, Ste 202N
Wixom, MI 48393
Contact: Lalitha Nandyala President
Tel: 313-671-5767
Email: lalitha@smartfolksinc.com
Website: www.smartfolksinc.com
Provide flexible and permanent staffing solutions.
(Woman/As-Ind, estab 2011, empl 50, sales $483,035,949,
cert: NMSDC, CPUC, WBENC)

8818 Staffing Source Personnel dba DriverSource
15340 Michigan Ave
Dearborn, MI 48126
Contact: David J. Olshansky Co-Founder
Tel: 313-624-9500
Email: dolshansky@driversource.net
Website: www.driversource.net
Commercial driver leasing & recruiting services.
(Woman, estab 1998, empl 350, sales , cert: WBENC)

8819 The Targa Group
33228 W 12 Mile Rd Ste 108
Farmington Hills, MI 48334
Contact: Rob Ganesan President
Tel: 248-514-2295
Email: rganesan@thetargagroup.com
Website: www.thetargagroup.clom
Staffing, Process Improvement & Information Technol-
ogy. (As-Pac, estab 2009, empl 6, sales $250,000, cert:
NMSDC)

8820 Therapy Staff, LLC
801 W Ann Arbor Trail, Ste 200
Pylmouth, MI 48170
Contact: William Klabo RVP
Tel: 877-366-2580
Email: wklabo@therapystaff.com
Website: www.Therapystaff.com
Therapist recruiting and staffing. (As-Ind, estab 2000,
empl 53, sales $15,400,000, cert: NMSDC)

8821 Trialon Corporation
1477 Walli Strasse Blvd
Burton, MI 48509
Contact: Robert Feys Sales Engineer
Tel: 810-742-8500
Email: rfeys@trialon.com
Website: www.trialon.com
Technical Staffing and Engineering & Test Services to the
Automotive, Aerospace, Military, Consumer Electronics,
Medical, and Telecommunications Industries. (Woman,
estab 1982, empl 750, sales $25,050,000, cert: WBENC)

8822 Trusted Link Staffing Services LLC
12966 Brixham Dr
Warren, MI 48088
Contact: Tochukwu (Tochi) Anyadibe Dir
Tel: 248-403-0689
Email: admin@trustedlinkstaffingservices.com
Website: www.tl-staffing.com
Hospital staffing services, Care facility staffing services,
Registered Nurse, Licensed Practical Nurse LPN / LVN
Travel contracts, Certified Nurse Assistant CNA Travel
contracts. (AA, estab 2022, empl 42, sales , cert: WBENC)

8823 Venator Staffing
888 W Big Beaver Rd, Ste 450
Troy, MI 48084
Contact: Michael Teats Sales Mgr
Tel: 248-269-0000
Email: michael@venatornet.com
Website: www.venatornet.com
Accounting, finance & administrative staffing: temp &
permanent placement. (As-Pac, estab 2001, empl 25,
sales $2,500,000, cert: NMSDC)

8824 VETBUILT Services, Inc.
1927 Rosa Parks Blvd Ste 125
Detroit, MI 48216
Contact: Hector Malacara CEO
Tel: 989-493-1240
Email: hmalacara@vetbuilt.com
Website: www.vetbuiltservices.com
Staffing services. (Hisp, estab 2013, empl 300, sales $6,853,851, cert: NMSDC)

Minnesota

8825 Advent Creative Group
7101 York Ave S, Ste 240
Edina, MN 55435
Contact: Mary Younggren Owner
Tel: 952-746-5668
Email: maryy@adventcreativegroup.com
Website: www.adventcreativegroup.com
Advertising, communications, creative, marketing & interactive hiring resources, contract & full-time basis. (Woman, estab 2007, empl 4, sales $606,822, cert: WBENC)

8826 Avenue Staffing Inc.
7000-57th Ave N Ste 120
Minneapolis, MN 55428
Contact: Chuck Okitikpi President
Tel: 763-537-6104
Email: chuck@avenuestaffing.com
Website: www.Avenuestaffing.com
Temporary & permanent employment. (AA, estab 2006, empl 48, sales $1,200,000, cert: NMSDC)

8827 Billinda Group LLC
4651 Nicols Rd, Ste 106-108
Eagan, MN 55122
Contact: Bill Fitch CEO
Tel: 651-379-5082
Email: bill@techpoweres.com
Website: www.Techpoweres.com
Contract, contract to permanent & direct placement. (Woman, estab 2005, empl 28, sales $3,700,000, cert: WBENC)

8828 Celarity
8120 Penn Ave Ste 220
Minneapolis, MN 55431
Contact: Marlene Phipps President
Tel: 952-941-0022
Email: marlene@celarity.com
Website: www.celarity.com
Contract, temporary recruiting, staffing, full-time direct hires. (Woman, estab 1992, empl 110, sales $7,092,546, cert: WBENC)

8829 Dahl Consulting, Inc.
418 County Rd D East
St. Paul, MN 55117
Contact: Corey Johnson CEO
Tel: 651-772-9225
Email: corey@dahlconsulting.com
Website: www.dahlconsulting.com
Vendor management services, staff augmentation, permanent search. (Woman, estab 1993, empl 808, sales $87,902,216, cert: WBENC)

8830 Doherty Staffing Solutions, Inc.
7645 Metro Blvd
Edina, MN 55439
Contact: David Tuenge Program Mgr
Tel: 952-818-3251
Email: dtuenge@dohertystaffing.com
Website: www.dohertystaffing.com
Contract & temporary staffing. (Woman, estab 1980, empl 151, sales $400,337,900, cert: WBENC)

8831 Finnesse Partners LLC
5000 W 36th St Ste 220
St. Louis Park, MN 55416
Contact: Janie Finn President
Tel: 952-232-6170
Email: janie@finnessepartners.com
Website: www.finnessepartners.com
Recruit for the medical device industry. (Woman, estab 2012, empl 5, sales $804,442, cert: WBENC)

8832 HighCloud Solutions Inc
445 Minnesota St Ste 1552
Saint Paul, MN 55101
Contact: Raghu Chejarla President
Tel: 612-479-3333
Email: raghu@highcloudsolutions.com
Website: www.highcloudsolutions.com/
Staffing, contracting/temp job positions. (Woman/As-Ind, estab 2015, empl 9, sales $774,113, cert: State, City, NMSDC, 8(a))

8833 IG, Inc. dba Indrotec
17 Washington Ave N
Minneapolis, MN 55401
Contact: Kathleen Dolphin CEO
Tel: 612-371-7402
Email: kathydolphin@mydolphingroup.com
Website: www.myindrotec.com
We supply companies with light industrial and assembly staff. (Woman, estab 1968, empl 16, sales $20,000,100, cert: WBENC)

8834 Just In Case, Inc.
6900 Shady Oak Rd, Ste 250
Eden Praire, MN 55344
Contact: Diane Blomberg CEO
Tel: 952-925-3789
Email: diane.blomberg@justincasestaffing.com
Website: www.casestaffingsolutions.com/
Staffing, consulting & integration: packaging, shipping & receiving, taping & assembly, clerical positions, administrative jobs, inbound call center positions, customer support. (Woman, estab 1981, empl 9, sales $5,900,000, cert: WBENC)

8835 Latitude Technology Group, Inc.
6800 France Ave South Ste 500
Edina, MN 55435
Contact: Dorreen Schmidt CEO
Tel: 952-767-6802
Email: dschmidt@latitude-group.com
Website: www.latitude-group.com
Staffing svcs: contract, contract to hire & permanent placement services. (Woman, estab 2002, empl 45, sales $6,000,000, cert: WBENC)

8836   Nexpro Personnel Services, Inc.
       5353 Gamble Dr, Ste 112
       Minneapolis, MN 55416
       Contact: Julia Zimmer Owner
       Tel: 952-224-9855
       Email: jzimmer@nexprojobs.com
       Website: www.nexprojobs.com
Staffing services: administrative, clerical, temporary,
contract, word processors, data entry, customer service
reps, accounting & payroll, light industrial, receptionist,
executive assistants (Woman, estab 2000, empl 40, sales
$5,000,000, cert: WBENC)

8837   Pelican Staffing Solutions
       2323 N 2nd St
       Minneapolis, MN 55411
       Contact: Ebi Itie President
       Tel: 612-545-5330
       Email: ebi@pelicanstaffing.com
       Website: www.pelicanstaffing.com
Contract & temporary staffing, staff & vendor management. (Woman/AA, estab 2011, empl 11, sales , cert: City)

8838   Select Source International
       13911 Ridgedale Dr, Ste 230
       Minnetonka, MN 55305
       Contact: Mandeep Sodhi CEO
       Tel: 952-546-3300
       Email: sales@selectsourceintl.com
       Website: www.SelectSourceIntl.com
Temporary Staffing, Information Technology Staffing,
Information Technology Services, Engineering Services,
Financial Services, Government Services, Retail Services,
Energy & Utility Services, Application Development,
Mobile Development. (Nat Ame, estab 2000, empl 771,
sales , cert: NMSDC)

8839   Serenity Staffing LLC
       6180 W 143rd St
       Savage, MN 55378
       Contact: Jennifer Sabby President
       Tel: 612-834-6444
       Email: jsabby@serenity-staffing.com
       Website: www.serenity-staffing.com
Place Human Resource professionals. (Woman, estab 2005,
empl 5, sales $281,316, cert: WBENC)

8840   Synico Staffing
       3033 Excelsior Blvd Ste 495
       Minneapolis, MN 55416
       Contact: Jerry Marsh VP
       Tel: 612-926-6000
       Email: jmarsh@synico.com
       Website: www.synico.com
Staffing services. (AA, estab 1996, empl 450, sales
$13,000,000, cert: NMSDC)

8841   TCG, Inc.
       17 Washington Ave N Ste 500
       Minneapolis, MN 55401
       Contact: Kathleen Dolphin President
       Tel: 612-338-7581
       Email: kathydolphin@mydolphingroup.com
       Website: www.mydolphingroup.com
Workforce management solutions. (Woman, estab 1969,
empl 70, sales $52,000,000, cert: WBENC)

8842   The Advent Group
       7101 York Ave S, Ste 240
       Edina, MN 55435
       Contact: Mary Younggren Owner
       Tel: 952-920-9119
       Email: mary@adventgroupco.com
       Website: www.adventgroupofcompanies.com
Staffing office support positions, administrative &
accounting support, call center/customer service,
human resources, mortgage/financial areas, manufacturing & logistics. (Woman, estab 2002, empl 12, sales ,
cert: WBENC)

8843   The Mazzitelli Placement Group
       500 Lake St, Ste 212
       Excelsior, MN 55331
       Contact: Teresa Mazzitelli President
       Tel: 952-476-5449
       Email: tm@mazzsearch.com
       Website: www.mazzsearch.com
Executive search, recruitment & placement services.
(Woman, estab 1988, empl 1, sales $110,000, cert:
WBENC)

Missouri

8844   Above All Personnel dba S.M. Huber Ent., Inc.
       2228 S Big Bend Blvd
       Saint Louis, MO 63117
       Contact: Susan Huber President
       Tel: 314-781-6008
       Email: team@aboveallpersonnel.com
       Website: www.aboveallpersonnel.com
Temporary, temp-to-hire, direct hire employment svcs:
clerical, accounting, customer service, data processing.
(Woman, estab 1995, empl 450, sales , cert: State)

8845   American Staffing LLC
       11424A Dorsett Rd
       Maryland Heights, MO 63043
       Contact: Diane Fennel President
       Tel: 314-872-7070
       Email: dfennel@americanstaffingstl.com
       Website: www.americanstaffingstl.com
Staffing: temp, temp to hire & permanent. (Woman,
estab 2002, empl 12000, sales $6,777,000, cert: State)

8846   Applications Engineering Group
       12300 Old Tesson Rd, Ste 100-G
       St. Louis, MO 63128
       Contact: Chris Rakel VP Operations
       Tel: 314-842-9110
       Email: chris.rakel@aeg-inc.com
       Website: www.aeg-inc.com
Provide contract, contract to hire & direct hire IT
employment services. (Hisp, estab 1992, empl 35, sales ,
cert: State)

8847   C & S Business Services, Inc.
       1731 Southridge Dr
       Jefferson City, MO 65109
       Contact: Paula Benne President
       Tel: 573-635-9295
       Email: paula@cs-business.com
       Website: www.cs-business.com
Staffing, temporary, direct hire, contract, employment
verification, criminal background checks. (Woman, estab
1977, empl 12, sales $4,000,000, cert: State)

8848   Chief of Staff LLC
601 E 63rd St
Kansas City, MO 64110
Contact: Marny Burke Govt Accounts Mgr
Tel: 816-581-2776
Email: government@chiefofstaffkc.com
Website: www.chiefofstaffkc.com
Temporary administrative staffing services, office management, receptionist, accounting & finance, HR, customer service/call room & data entry/records management positions. (Woman, estab 2011, empl 8, sales $1,190,023, cert: State)

8849   Creatives On Call Inc.
101 S Hanley Road Ste 710
St. Louis, MO 63105
Contact: Corey Zinser Acct Exec
Tel: 513-218-5596
Email: corey.zinser@creativesoncall.com
Website: www.creativesoncall.com
Placement agency, recruit professionals with creative, marketing, communications and/or interactive expertise for permanent, contract & freelance positions. (Woman, estab 1995, empl 12, sales $4,500,000, cert: State, WBENC)

8850   Critique Personnel Service, Inc.
1100 S Jefferson Ave
St. Louis, MO 63104
Contact: Monique Jeans Dir Client Services
Tel: 314-772-5445
Email: mjeans@critiquepersonnel.com
Website: www.critiquepersonnel.com
Temporary & permanent staffing services. (AA, estab 1997, empl 50, sales , cert: State)

8851   EH, Inc. dba HireLevel
415 S 18th St. Ste 205
St. Louis, MO 63103
Contact: Nicole Kline Sr Natl Business Dev
Tel: 314-550-8626
Email: nkline@hirelevel.com
Website: www.hirelevel.com
Staffing services, temporary employment, temporary-to-hire & direct hire. (Woman, estab 1995, empl 60, sales $37,813,000, cert: WBENC)

8852   NextGen Information Services Inc.
906 Olive St Ste 600
Saint Louis, MO 63101
Contact: Christy Herschbach Admin Asst
Tel: 314-588-1212
Email: supplierdiversity@nextgen-is.com
Website: www.nextgen-is.com
IT consulting services: project mgmt, custom application dev, legacy transition svcs & staff augmentation, staff augmentaion. (Minority, Woman, estab 1997, empl 300, sales , cert: State, City, WBENC)

8853   Pangaea, Inc.
1403 Hwy F
Defiance, MO 63341
Contact: Heather Everett President
Tel: 314-925-1783
Email: heverett@pangaea-inc.com
Website: www.Pangaea-inc.com
Supplemental staffing services, contract, direct placement, and contract to hire resources. (Woman, estab 2008, empl 10, sales $750,000, cert: State)

8854   Shelgin Partners
9211 Phoenix Village Pkwy
O'Fallon, MO 63368
Contact: Gerri Lynn Zschetzsche Partner
Tel: 636-625-2333
Email: glz@shelgin.com
Website: www.shelgin.com
Recruiting agency: direct recruitment, advertising, job boards, candidate referrals & partner referrals. (Woman, estab 2005, empl 5, sales $553,000, cert: State)

8855   Supplemental Medical Services, Inc.
10916 Schuetz Road
St. Louis, MO 63146
Contact: Gretchen Curry President
Tel: 314-997-8833
Email: gcurry@stafflinkusa.com
Website: www.stafflinkusa.com
Temporary, contract, travel & direct hire healthcare personnel. (Woman/AA, estab 1987, empl 125, sales $2,643,128, cert: State, NMSDC)

8856   The Herring IMPACT Group
12977 N Outer 40 Dr Ste 300
St. Louis, MO 63141
Contact: Kristy King Exec Asst
Tel: 314-453-9002
Email: diversity1@impactgrouphr.com
Website: www.impactgrouphr.com
Career transitions, relocation support, talent development, and outplacement services. (Woman, estab 1988, empl 121, sales $15,000,000, cert: State, WBENC)

Mississippi

8857   TempStaff Inc.
2282 Lakeland Dr
Flowood, MS 39232
Contact: Jamie Higdon VP Operations
Tel: 601-353-4200
Email: jamie@tempstaff.net
Website: www.tempstaff.net
Temporary & permanent employment. (Woman, estab 1979, empl 24, sales , cert: WBENC)

Montana

8858   Brady Co., Inc
50 West 14th St Ste 300
Helena, MT 59601
Contact: Anna Kazmierowski CEO
Tel: 406-443-7664
Email: anna@a2zmontana.com
Website: www.a2zmontana.com
Workforce solutions, temp staffing, temp to permanent placement & direct hire services, employee payroll, scientific & technical staffing, technical & professional recruitment & construction labor. (Woman, estab 2003, empl 7, sales $4,517,215, cert: State, WBENC, SDB)

North Carolina

8859   AccruePartners, Inc.
1000 W Morehead St Ste 200
Charlotte, NC 28208
Contact: Amy Pack Principal Partner
Tel: 704-632-9955
Email: amy@accruepartners.com
Website: www.accruepartners.com
Contract to contract-to-hire, direct hire and executive search, project solutions. (Woman, estab 2002, empl 50, sales $28,000,000, cert: WBENC)

8860 Associate Staffing, LLC
      303C Atkinson St
      Laurinburg, NC 28352
      Contact: Dir
      Tel: 980-224-8754
      Email: info@astaff.us
      Website: www.associatestaffingllc.com
Recruiting & staffing, contract, contract to permanent &
direct placement basis. (Woman, estab 2008, empl 450,
sales $13,400,000, cert: WBENC)

8861 Aten Solutions, Inc.
      5404 Hillsborough St Ste A
      Raleigh, NC 27606
      Contact: COO
      Tel: 919-949-3503
      Email: info@a10clinical com
      Website: www.a10clinical.com
Staffing solutions: clinical research, clinical data management, statistical programming & biostatistics space, clinical
trial svcs & staffing support. (Woman/AA, estab 2004,
empl 64, sales $1,800,000, cert: NMSDC, WBENC)

8862 Best National Services Inc. dba Latin Labor Staffi
      4917 South Blvd
      Charlotte, NC 28217
      Contact: Frank Colunga Sr Acct Mgr
      Tel: 704-877-8241
      Email: fcolunga@latinlabor.net
      Website: www.latinlabor.net
Light Industrial staffing services: General Labor, Logistics,
manufacturing, cleaning, events, etc. (Hisp, estab 2005,
empl 600, sales $13,000,000, cert: NMSDC)

8863 BPN Concepts
      8305 University Executive Park Dr Ste 330
      Charlotte, NC 28262
      Contact: Brenda Harris Owner
      Tel: 980-335-0656
      Email: info@bpnconcepts.com
      Website: www.bpnconcepts.com
Executive search & staffing services. (Woman/AA, estab
2011, empl 6, sales , cert: State, City)

8864 CEO Inc.
      412 Louise Ave
      Charlotte, NC 28204
      Contact: Deborah Millhouse President
      Tel: 704-372-4701
      Email: debby@ceohr.com
      Website: www.ceohr.com
Temporary staffing, payrolling, HR consulting, executive
search & placement. (Woman, estab 1994, empl 15, sales
$2,995,605, cert: State)

8865 Concierge Staffing LLC
      160 S Main St
      Graham, NC 27253
      Contact: Denise Brown Owner
      Tel: 336-270-3035
      Email: denise.brown@concierge-staffing.com
      Website: www.concierge-staffing.com
Staffing services and solutions. (Woman/AA, estab 2014,
empl 50, sales , cert: State)

8866 CrossComm, Inc.
      PO Box 673
      Durham, NC 27702
      Contact: Beverly Williams Business Operations
      Mgr
      Tel: 919-667-9432
      Email: beverlywilliams@crosscomm.com
      Website: www.crosscomm.com
Mobile and web application development studio that
builds custom iOS, Android, Web and Augmented
Reality/Virtual Reality apps. (As-Pac, estab 2000, empl 8,
sales $975,000, cert: NMSDC)

8867 Cyber Shield Consulting Inc.
      8300 Boone Blvd, Ste 500
      Vienna, NC 22182
      Contact: Doug Marland Business Devel Mgr
      Tel: 571-358-5602
      Email: operations@cybershieldincorporated.com
      Website: www.cybershieldincorporated.com
Human capital services, temporary & permanent on a
nationwide. (AA, estab 2013, empl 25, sales , cert:
NMSDC)

8868 Debbie's Staffing Services, Inc.
      4431 N Cherry St
      Winston-Salem, NC 27105
      Contact: Joanne Altieri Business Devel Mgr
      Tel: 704-682-0036
      Email: mwoodson@debbiesstaffing.com
      Website: www.debbiesstaffing.com
Temporary staffing, distribution, warehouse, data-entry,
IT, cashiers. (Woman, estab 1986, empl 105, sales
$94,000,000, cert: WBENC)

8869 Elite Touch Cleaning Services, Inc.
      4105-A Stuart Andrew Blvd
      Charlotte, NC 28217
      Contact: Mario Mendigana President
      Tel: 704-266-0623
      Email: mario@elitetouchcleaning.com
      Website: www.elitetouchcleaning.com
Janitorial Services, Floor Maintenance, Carpet care,
Construction clean up (Hisp, estab 2007, empl 5, sales
$1,668,000, cert: NMSDC)

8870 ER Select
      6100 Fairview Road Ste 545
      Charlotte, NC 28210
      Contact: Jeremy Holland Dir Strategic Accounts
      Tel: 407-221-1000
      Email: jholland@talentbridge.com
      Website: www.talentbridge.com
Recruiting and staffing, short-term, permanent and
contract solutions. (Woman, estab 2011, empl 100, sales
$83,000,000, cert: WBENC)

8871 Global Pros Staffing Solutions
      9635 Southern Pine Blvd Ste 102
      Charlotte, NC 28273
      Contact: TaWanda Duncan CEO
      Tel: 704-648-7355
      Email: globalprosstaffingsolutions@gmail.com
      Website: www.globalprosstaffingsolutions.com
Staffing: Administrative, Call Center, Healthcare, Human
Resources, Warehouse, Forklift, Landscaping
Janitorial. (AA, estab 2015, empl 50, sales , cert: City)

8872　Golden Tech Systems Inc.
2704 Twinberry Ln
Waxhaw, NC 28173
Contact: Pushpinder Garcha President
Tel:　704-236-2939
Email: pushpinder@golden-tech-systems.com
Website: www.golden-tech-systems.com
Staffing, Enterprise Application Development, n-tier Web Development, Systems Integration, SCRUM Development. (As-Ind, estab 2007, empl 5, sales $753,550, cert: State, City, NMSDC, 8(a))

8873　Greer Group
3109 Charles B. Root Wynd
Raleigh, NC 27612
Contact: Mark Blume Client Devel Mgr
Tel:　919-571-0051
Email: sales@thegreergroup.com
Website: www.thegreergroup.com
Staffing services: temporary staffing, temporary to direct hire staffing, direct hire recruitment, payrolling services & onsite staffing management. (Woman, estab 1986, empl 16, sales $15,802,034, cert: WBENC)

8874　GREGORY ART SERVICES INC
10806 Reames Rd, Ste A
Charlotte, NC 28269
Contact: Eugene Gregory President
Tel:　980-949-7355
Email: info@gregoryartservices.com
Website: www.gregoryartservices.com
We provide artwork and custom picture framing, security mount installations, repairs, refurbish pick-up and delivery, art consulting, art placement, large art installations on time service and all work is guaranteed with competitive pricing. (AA, estab 2001, empl 4, sales $275,558, cert: NMSDC)

8875　Greytree Partners
121 Greenwich Rd Ste 211
Charlotte, NC 28211
Contact: Clarence Fisher Chief Solutions Architect
Tel:　704-899-4082
Email: clarence.fisher@greytreepartners.com
Website: www.GreytreePartners.com
Identification, recruitment & placement of information technology and engineering services professionals on a contract or permanent basis. (AA, estab 2004, empl 30, sales $2,400,000, cert: State, NMSDC)

8876　In-Flight Crew Connections
338 S Sharon Amity Rd, Ste 311
Charlotte, NC 28211
Contact: Jennifer Guthrie Owner
Tel:　704-236-3647
Email: jennifer.guthrie@inflightcrewconnections.com
Website: www.inflightcrewconnections.com
Temporary Flight Attendants, Pilots & Technicians. (Woman, estab 2002, empl 55, sales $16,000,000, cert: WBENC)

8877　Jennifer Temps, Inc.
1973 JN Pease Pl Ste 201
Charlotte, NC 28262
Contact: Jennifer Singleton President
Tel:　212-964-8367
Email: jsingleton@jennifertemps.com
Website: www.jennifertemps.com
Temporary staffing. (Woman/AA, estab 1992, empl 8, sales $4,500,000, cert: NMSDC)

8878　Omni Source Solutions
13016 Eastfield Rd
Huntersville, NC 28078
Contact: Charisma Smith Managing Member
Tel:　704-412-3031
Email: charisma@omnisourcesolutions.net
Website: www.omnisourcesolutions.net
Offer skilled quality self-performing contractors throughout the Southeast. We provide flexible, reliable and safety-minded tradesmen for a wide range of commercial construction jobs. We understand the importance of having the right (Woman/AA, estab 2012, empl 2, sales , cert: City, NMSDC)

8879　Quality Staffing Solutions, Inc.
120 Towerview Ct
Cary, NC 27513
Contact: Phyllis Eller-Moffett CEO
Tel:　919-481-4114
Email: pmoffett@quality-staffing.com
Website: www.quality-staffing.com
Staffing solutions. (Woman, estab 1995, empl 400, sales $6,526,751, cert: WBENC)

8880　Right Choice Solutions, Inc.
316 W Millbrook Rd Ste. 213
Raleigh, NC 27609
Contact: Layce Adams Operations Mgr
Tel:　919-324-3557
Email: layce@thercsolutions.com
Website: www.thercsolutions.com
Staffing: temporary staffing, temp to hire & direct hire quality candidates. (Woman/AA, estab 2005, empl 7, sales , cert: NMSDC)

8881　Talented Fish, Inc.
111 W Lewis St Ste 120
Greensboro, NC 27406
Contact: Tracey Wallace COO
Tel:　336-279-7665
Email: tracey@talentedfish.com
Website: www.talentedfish.com
Executive Search & Placement. (AA, estab 2017, empl 3, sales , cert: NMSDC)

8882　Two Hawk Employment Services, Inc.
3021 N Roberts Ave
Lumberton, NC 28360
Contact: Harvey Godwin, Jr. Owner
Tel:　910-738-3014
Email: harvey.godwin@twohawk.net
Website: www.twohawk.net
Temporary & permanent employment services: general labor, supervisory & administration positions. (Nat Ame, estab 1999, empl 50, sales $24,000,000, cert: NMSDC)

8883　Xcentri, Inc.
412 Louise Ave
Charlotte, NC 28204
Contact: Debby Millhouse President
Tel:　704-369-3211
Email: deborah.millhouse@xcentri.com
Website: www.xcentri.com
Staffing & recruiting (temp, contract to hire and direct hire); HR Consulting; Background Checks; Drug Screening (Woman, estab 2014, empl 200, sales $9,586,491, cert: WBENC)

New Hampshire

8884 CCSI Inc.
62 Portsmouth Ave
Stratham, NH 03885
Contact: Sarah Latiolais Acct Mgr
Tel: 800-598-0255
Email: sarah@ccsiinc.com
Website: www.ccsiinc.com
Temporary & permanent staffing: IT, accounting, finance, HR, sales, administration, marketing & clinical staff. (Woman, estab 1998, empl 256, sales $16,000,000, cert: WBENC)

8885 The Spencer Thomas Group LLC
One Falkland Place
Portsmouth, NH 03801
Contact: Lori Perkins Acct Mgr
Tel: 603-835-3707
Email: lori.perkins@spencer-thomas.com
Website: www.spencer-thomas.com
Recruiting, staffing, consulting, PeopleSoft, SAP, Oracle, web deveoplers, project management, program managers, outsourced payroll services, employee leasing. (Woman, estab 1998, empl , sales $20,000,000, cert: WBENC)

New Jersey

8886 Accountants For You Inc.
1175 Marlkress Road, Ste 1040
Cherry Hill, NJ 08034
Contact: Marcia Libes President
Tel: 215-988-7200
Email: marcia.libes@accountantsforyou.com
Website: www.accountantsforyou.com
Staffing & recruiting: temporary, temporary to permanent & permanent placement of accounting, finance, human resource & office professionals. (Woman, estab 2006, empl 10, sales $1,376,195, cert: WBENC)

8887 ACCU Staffing Services
911 Kings Hwy N
Cherry Hill, NJ 08034
Contact: Debra Fordyce Operations Mgr
Tel: 856-482-2222
Email: cherryhill@accustaffing.com
Website: www.accustaffing.com
Staffing svcs: human resources, planned staffing, direct placement, corporate outplacement svcs & on-site consulting/mgmt funcations. (Woman, estab 1979, empl 100, sales , cert: WBENC)

8888 APN Consulting Inc.
1100 Cornwall Rd
Monmouth Junction, NJ 08852
Contact: Francis Moser Business Devel Mgr
Tel: 609-924-3400
Email: francis@apnconsultinginc.com
Website: www.apnconsultinginc.com
Contract, contract-to-hire & full time staffing services. (As-Ind, estab 2002, empl 250, sales $20,300,000, cert: NMSDC)

8889 ATRIA Consulting, LLC
1 Aaa Dr Ste 206
Robbinsville, NJ 08691
Contact: Melissa Bordman Managing Member
Tel: 646-722-8702
Email: mbordman@atriaconsutling.com
Website: www.atriaconsulting.com
Staffing & Solutions: Information Technology, Accounting/Finance, Administrative/Clerical, Human Resources, Customer Service, and Online Media Permanent and Contract Placement services. (Woman, estab 2006, empl 30, sales $1,640,850, cert: WBENC)

8890 CNC Consulting
50 E Palisades Ave Ste 422
Englewood, NJ 07631
Contact: Fred Seltzer Business Devel Mgr
Tel: 201-541-9122
Email: fseltzer@cncconsult.com
Website: www.cncconsulting.com
IT professionals for consulting contracts. (AA, estab 1996, empl 25, sales $3,000,000, cert: State)

8891 Datanomics, Inc.
991 US Hwy 22 West Ste 201
Bridgewater, NJ 08807
Contact: Lori Vail CEO
Tel: 908-707-8200
Email: vail@datanomics.com
Website: www.datanomics.com
IT staffing, helpdesk, desktop support, administration, technical writers, validation specialists, business/systems
analysts, programmers, mainframe, client/server, & web. (Woman, estab 1982, empl 100, sales , cert: State)

8892 Elite Personnel Group, LLC
220 Davidson Ave. Ste 102
Somerset, NJ 08873
Contact: Junior Recruiter
Tel: 908-722-1111
Email: apply@cosmostaff.com
Website: www.eliteitpersonnel.com
National recruiting and talent acquisition. (As-Pac, estab 2007, empl 40, sales $45,000,000, cert: State)

8893 Fabergent, Inc.
63 Ramapo Valley Rd, Ste 214
Mahwah, NJ 07430
Contact: Ratna Silpa Gorantla President
Tel: 201-378-0036
Email: ratna@fabergent.com
Website: www.fabergent.com
Contract & full-time positions IT staffing in Java, .Net, SharePoint, SAP, Oracle, BI, Analytics, networking & IT security. (Minority, Woman, estab 2005, empl 125, sales , cert: State)

8894 Frink-Hamlett Legal Solutions
PO Box 2022
Teaneck, NJ 07666
Contact: Katherine Frink-Hamlett President
Tel: 201-357-8975
Email: katherine@frinkhamlett.com
Website: www.frinkhamlett.com
Provide legal professionals: attorneys, compliance & paralegals on a temporary and permanent basis. (Woman/AA, estab 2004, empl 3, sales $1,383,371, cert: State, City, NMSDC, WBENC)

8895 Glenmont Group Inc.
39 S Fullerton Ave Ste 9
Montclair, NJ 07042
Contact: President
Tel: 973-746-0600
Email: info@glenmontgroup.com
Website: www.glenmontgroup.com
Recruiting & staffing. (Woman, estab 2001, empl 22, sales $2,404,882, cert: State, WBENC)

8896 Harita Infotech
601 Crest Stone Circle
Princeton, NJ 08540
Contact: Kaushal Sampat President
Tel: 609-216-1844
Email: kaushalsampat@haritainfotechinc.com
Website: www.haritainfotechinc.com
Consulting & Permanent resources in the Business, IT & general fields. (As-Pac, estab 2014, empl 10, sales , cert: State)

8897 Industrial Staffing Services inc.
25 Kennedy Blvd Ste 200
East Brunswick, NJ 08816
Contact: Steve Dern VP
Tel: 303-323-5179
Email: SDern@evaluentsolutions.com
Website: www.industrial-staffing.com
Place contract & permanent workers for all types of staffing needs: staff augmentation, payroll-servicing, &project staffing with qualified & certified pre-screened personnel in all industrial, technical and administrative positions. (Woman, estab 2003, empl 25, sales , cert: State, City, WBENC)

8898 Integrated Resources, Inc.
4 Ethel Rd, Ste 403B
Edison, NJ 08817
Contact: Chris Byram VP
Tel: 732-549-2030
Email: chris@irionline.com
Website: www.irionline.com
Staffing services, Direct Hire, Temporary/Contract and Contract-to-Hire. (Minority, estab 1996, empl 750, sales $53,000,000, cert: State, NMSDC)

8899 IT Staffing, Inc.
5 Bliss Court Ste 200
Woodcliff Lake, NJ 07677
Contact: Jerry G. Myers Dir Business Dev
Tel: 201-505-0493
Email: jerry.myers@itstaffinc.com
Website: www.itstaffinc.com
Strategic contract sourcing, consulting, staff augmentation, managed teams & outsourcing. (Minority, Woman, estab 1998, empl 78, sales $11,500,000, cert: State)

8900 JBK Associates International, Inc.
607 E Palisade Ave
Englewood Cliffs, NJ 07632
Contact: Shari Caloz Exec Admin
Tel: 201-567-9070
Email: scaloz@jbkassociates.net
Website: www.jbkassociates.net
Executive recruitment. (Woman, estab 2003, empl 17, sales $4,642,327, cert: WBENC)

8901 Jersey Staffing Solutions, LLC
400 Valley Rd Ste 106
Mt. Arlington, NJ 07856
Contact: Kristi Telschow CEO
Tel: 973-810-4495
Email: ktelschow@jerseystaffing.com
Website: www.jerseystaffing.com
Staffing, temporary, temp-to-perm & permanent staffing. (Woman, estab 2010, empl 35, sales $2,160,000, cert: WBENC)

8902 Jomsom Staffing Services
4390 US Hwy One, Ste 203
Princeton, NJ 08540
Contact: Ross Lazio Business Dev Exec
Tel: 973-446-5627
Email: rlazio@jomsomjobs.com
Website: www.jomsomstaffing.com
Staffing solutions, full-time & part-time resources, temporary, temporary to permanent & permanent placement basis. (Woman/As-Ind, estab 2008, empl 55, sales $3,500,000, cert: NMSDC)

8903 Knoodae Staffing, LLC
525 Rt 73N, Ste 104
Marlton, NJ 08053
Contact: Anitra Green Owner
Tel: 856-804-0321
Email: anitra@knoodaestaffing.com
Website: www.knoodaestaffing.com
Professional recruiting and staffing. (AA, estab 2021, empl 70, sales , cert: State)

8904 MetaSense Inc.
100 Technology Way, Ste 320
Mt. Laurel, NJ 08054
Contact: Jatin V Mehta CEO
Tel: 856-873-9950
Email: jmehta@metasenseusa.com
Website: www.metasenseusa.com
Information system staffing, software development, web design, outsourcing, business process outsourcing, knowledge pocess outsourcing. (Minority, Woman, estab 1999, empl 5, sales $767,000, cert: State)

8905 Net2Source Inc
270 Davidson Ave, Ste 704 Ste 704
Somerset, NJ 08873
Contact: Ashish Garg Founder & CEO
Tel: 201-340-8700
Email: supplier_registrations@net2source.com
Website: www.net2source.com
Staffing & recruitment services. (Minority, estab 2007, empl 5000, sales $172,000,000, cert: NMSDC)

8906 Next Step Staffing
725 River Road
Edgewater, NJ 07020
Contact: Pratcher CEO
Tel: 646-829-1800
Email: joy@nsstaff.com
Website: www.nsstaff.com
IT solutions, full-time, permanent placement or temporary contract basis. (Woman/AA, Hisp, estab 2012, empl 5, sales $1,804,633, cert: NMSDC, WBENC)

8907 Perry Temps, Inc.
      525 Route 73, South Ste 201
      Marlton, NJ 08053
      Contact: Wendy Brooks Dir Business Dev
      Tel: 856-596-9400
      Email: wbrooks@perryresources.com
      Website: www.perryresources.com
Temporary staffing: administrative, accounting, clerical,
customer service call center personnel. (Woman, estab
1986, empl 8, sales $2,174,927, cert: WBENC)

8908 Pride Veteran Staffing
      15 Union Ave
      Rutherford, NJ 07070
      Contact: Beth Firgau CEO
      Tel: 732-318-5985
      Email: Beth@prideveteran.com
      Website: www.prideveteran.com/
Staffing agency. (Woman, estab 2019, empl 21, sales
$500,000, cert: WBENC)

8909 Professional Resource Partners
      14 Rickland Dr
      Randolph, NJ 07869
      Contact: Stefanie Wichansky CEO
      Tel: 201-259-4739
      Email: swichansky@prp-us.com
      Website: www.professionalresourcepartners.com
Life Science Consulting & Staffing: contract, contract-to-
perm, permanent basis across functional areas. (Woman,
estab 2012, empl 20, sales $454,478, cert: WBENC)

8910 Protocall NJ, Inc.
      One Mall Dr
      Cherry Hill, NJ 08002
      Contact: Janis LeBude President
      Tel: 856-667-7500
      Email: lebude@protocallstaffing.com
      Website: www.protocallstaffing.com
General laborers, assemblers, maintenance staff, import/
export clerks, bi-Lingual supervisors, warehouse manag-
ers/supervisors, quality control inspectors, shipping/
receiving clerks, packers, event staff & mail room staff.
(Woman, estab 1965, empl 70, sales $23,059,418, cert:
WBENC)

8911 RHO, Inc.
      507 Omni Dr
      Hillsborough, NJ 08844
      Contact: Deborah Johnson President
      Tel: 908-359-0808
      Email: deborah.johnson@rho-inc.com
      Website: www.rho-inc.com
Staffing, consulting & training services. (Minority, Woman,
estab 1981, empl 120, sales , cert: WBENC)

8912 Sage Group Technologies Inc
      3400 Hwy 35 S Ste 9A
      Hazlet, NJ 07730
      Contact: Shruthi Reddy Exec VP
      Tel: 732-994-6792
      Email: sreddy@sagegroupinc.com
      Website: www.sagegroupinc.com
Contingent Workforce Services • Contract Staffing,
Contract to Hire Staffing • IT & Non-IT Staffing • Clinical &
Scientific Staffing • Permanent Staffing • Professional
Staffing • Payroll Services. (Minority, estab 2004, empl
120, sales $63,200,000, cert: State, NMSDC)

8913 Software Folks, Inc. dba Saviance Technologies
      16 Bridge St
      Metuchen, NJ 08840
      Contact: Anuj Sakhuja Client Relationship Mgr
      Tel: 732-593-8015
      Email: anuj.sakhuja@saviance.com
      Website: www.saviance.com
Information technology staffing: contract, contract-to-
hire & permanent. (As-Pac, estab 1999, empl 60, sales
$7,725,180, cert: NMSDC)

8914 Software Galaxy Systems, LLC
      4390 US Route 1 N, Ste 210A
      Princeton, NJ 08540
      Contact: Srini Vengad Sr VP
      Tel: 609-919-1133
      Email: srini.vengad@sgsconsulting.com
      Website: www.sgsconsulting.com
Contingent Workforce Services, integrated suite of
services through our global delivery platform. (As-Pac,
estab 1997, empl 220, sales $18,000,000, cert: NMSDC)

8915 Synasha LLC
      100 Matawan Rd Ste 130
      Matawan, NJ 07747
      Contact: Geoffrey Crawley VP
      Tel: 732-705-3553
      Email: geoffrey.crawley@synasha.com
      Website: www.synasha.com
Direct Mail, Direct Ship, Retail Display Assembly & Pack
Out Drop Ship, Kitting, Multi Branded Displays, Primary
Packaging, Promotional Packaging, Rework Repackaging
VMI & Sequenced Material Replenishment. (AA, estab
2015, empl 7500, sales $40,000,000, cert: NMSDC)

8916 TNT Staffing
      70 Kinderkamack Rd, Ste 202
      Emerson, NJ 07630
      Contact: Jacqueline Tarnowski Dir of Recruiting
      Tel: 201-497-6305
      Email: jackie@tntstaffing.com
      Website: www.tntstaffing.com
Staff Augmentation & Direct Full Time Placement
Services. (Woman/AA, estab 2005, empl 25, sales
$4,328,500, cert: State, WBENC)

8917 TSK Products, Inc.
      12 Windsor Dr
      Eatontown, NJ 07724
      Contact: Eric Klein VP
      Tel: 732-982-1090
      Email: esklein@tskproducts.com
      Website: www.tskproducts.com
(Minority, Woman, estab 2000, empl 3, sales $989,849,
cert: State, City)

8918 UserEdge Technical Personnel
      1812 Front St.
      Scotch Plains, NJ 07076
      Contact: Jay Madlangbayan President
      Tel: 908-387-7601
      Email: jay@useredge.com
      Website: www.useredge.com
Direct hire recruitment, short & long-term contract
assignments, outsourced staffing. (As-Pac, estab 1995,
empl 30, sales $1,750,000, cert: State, NMSDC)

Nevada

8919 ActOne Government Solutions, Inc.
8330 W Sahara Ave, Ste 290
Las Vegas, NV 89117
Contact: Millton Perkins SVP
Tel: 866-493-8343
Email: GovNotices@A1GovernmentSolutions.com
Website: www.A1GovernmentSolutions.com
General HR consulting/solutions related to the lifecycle of
an employee, Diversity/Equity & Inclusion, commodities
(PPE, durable/non-durable med/surg products, office
supplies) (Woman/AA, estab 2015, empl , sales , cert:
NMSDC, WBENC)

8920 My Next Career Path Staffing, LLC
400 S. Fourth St, Ste 500
Las Vegas, NV 89101
Contact: Renee Boyce President
Tel: 844-579-6627
Email: rboyce@mncpstaffing.com
Website: www.mncpstaffing.com
Consulting & staffing: analysts, system/network administra-
tors, project managers, developers, bookkeepers, design-
ers, customer service experts & marketing specialists. (AA,
estab 2014, empl 40, sales $1,000,000, cert: State, NMSDC,
CPUC, 8(a))

New York

8921 24 Seven Inc.
120 Wooster St, 4th Floor
New York, NY 10012
Contact: Meghan Dewey President
Tel: 212-966-4426
Email: mdewey@24seveninc.com
Website: www.24seveninc.com
Staffing svcs: freelance, freelance to fulltime, fulltime &
executive search services. (Woman, estab 2000, empl 93,
sales $125,326,911, cert: WBENC)

8922 Admiral Staffing Inc.
18 W 30th St
New York, NY 10001
Contact: Ray Rafeek
Tel: 212-714-3543
Email: irshaad@admiralstaffinginc.com
Website: www.admiralstaffinginc.com
Temporary to permanent staffing services. (As-Pac, estab
2010, empl 25, sales $492,000, cert: City, NMSDC)

8923 Amtex System, Inc
28 Liberty St, 6th Fl
New York, NY 10005
Contact: Rob Collins Sr BDM
Tel: 646-200-7115
Email: rob@amtexsystems.com
Website: www.amtexsystems.com
IT Placement firm. (As-Pac, estab 1997, empl 260, sales
$30,000,000, cert: City)

8924 ANR Staffing Solutions, LLC
21702 Jamaica Ave, Ste 2
Queens Village, NY 11428
Contact: Alecia C. Grant CEO
Tel: - -
Email: agrant@anrstaffingsolutions.com
Website: www.anrstaffingsolutions.com
ANR Staffing Solutions, LLC provides supplemental staffing
of clinical and non-clinical personnel to hospitals, homecare
agencies, government agencies and individuals. (AA, estab
2013, empl 40, sales , cert: City)

8925 Associate Resource Management, Inc.
2527 Merrick Rd
Bellmore, NY 11710
Contact: Kim Robertson Exec Dir
Tel: 516-785-6211
Email: kim@armi.bz
Website: www.armi.bz
Staffing solutions: Front Desk Staff, Receptionist,
Centralized Scheduling, Clerical Staff, Human Resources,
Customer Service, Office Support Staff, Office Manager,
Data Entry Clerks, Accounting, Bookkeepers, Administra-
tive. (Woman, estab 2006, empl 6, sales $1,700,000,
cert: WBENC)

8926 ATRIUM STAFFING LLC
387 Park Ave S 3rd Fl
New York, NY 10016
Contact: Kelly Couto VP
Tel: 732-902-5917
Email: supplierdiversity@atriumstaff.com
Website: www.atriumworks.com
Temporary & direct-hire staffing: administration,
finance, professional services & science. (Woman, estab
1995, empl 240, sales $293,646,368, cert: WBENC)

8927 Axelon Services Corporation
44 Wall St Fl 18
New York, NY 10005
Contact: Cynthia Lah COO
Tel: 212-306-0104
Email: cynthia@axelon.com
Website: www.axelon.com
Powerful staffing cloud technologies and processes
deliver precise talent matches. (Woman, estab 1977,
empl 961, sales $89,000,000, cert: City, WBENC,
NWBOC)

8928 Broadleaf Results, Inc.
250 International Dr
Williamsville, NY 14221
Contact: Michelle Prue Client Liaison
Tel: 800-574-5021
Email: pruem@broadleafresults.com
Website: www.broadleafresults.com
Staffing svcs: temp, direct hire, payrolling svcs, on-site
staffing & web-based vendor mgmt programs. (Woman,
estab 1965, empl 500, sales $352,440,788, cert: WBENC)

8929 CompliStaff, Inc.
381 Lewis St
West Hempstead, NY 11552
Contact: April Bernstein VP
Tel: 646-595-0040
Email: april.bernstein@complistaff.com
Website: www.complistaff.com
Staffing & recruitment solutions in legal, compliance,
accounting, audit & risk management. (Woman, estab
2010, empl 8, sales $1,270,000, cert: City, WBENC)

8930 Custom Staffing, Inc.
420 Lexington Ave Ste 550
New York, NY 10017
Contact: Managing Dir
Tel: 212-818-0300
Email: mrodriguez@customstaffing.com
Website: www.customgroupofcompanies.com
Staffing, temporary and permanent positions, contract
and permanent attorneys and paralegals. (Woman/AA,
estab , empl , sales $17,240,885, cert: State)

8931 Dale Workforce Solutions, LLC
      1751 2nd Ave, Ste 103
      New York, NY 10128
      Contact: Lois Dale Holtzman President
      Tel: 212-860-2000
      Email: ldale@daleworkforce.com
      Website: www.daleworkforce.com/
Staff Augmentation, Independent Contractor Compliance,
Payroll Services. (Woman, estab 2012, empl 10, sales
$1,200,000, cert: WBENC)

8932 Distinctive Personnel
      424 W 33rd St
      New York, NY 10001
      Contact: Gonzalo Vergara Founder/Chairman
      Tel: 917-952-2766
      Email: gus@distinctivepersonnel.com
      Website: www.distinctivepersonnel.com
Staffing services: temporary, permanent, executive search,
managed service providers, vendor managed services/,
payroll outsourcing. (Hisp, estab , empl , sales
$710,000,000, cert: City)

8933 Elmark Group, Inc.
      499 7th Ave 22 N Tower
      New York, NY 10018
      Contact: President
      Tel: 212-856-9888
      Email: info@marcusjobs.com
      Website: www.marcusjobs.com
Contingency & retained accounting & finance search
services in the areas of financial reporting, general
accounting, accounting policy, internal audit, SOX compliance, risk management, financial & strategic analysis.
(Woman, estab 1991, empl 5, sales $1,243,000, cert:
WBENC)

8934 Gainor Temporaries, Inc.
      489 Fifth Ave
      New York, NY 10017
      Contact: Sr Acct Exec
      Tel: 212-697-4145
      Email:
      Website: www.gainor.net
Temporary & permanent administrative personnel placement. (Woman, estab 1984, empl 20, sales $9,064,000,
cert: WBENC)

8935 Geneva Consulting Group, Inc.
      14 Vanderventer Ave Ste 250
      Port Washington, NY 11050
      Contact: Gina Santorio Dir Business Dev
      Tel: 516-767-6695
      Email: gsantorio@genevaconsulting.com
      Website: www.genevaconsulting.com
IT consulting & full-time placement services, payrolling
services. (Woman, estab 1997, empl 50, sales $8,021,175,
cert: WBENC)

8936 HireTalent
      135 W 26th St, Ste 7B
      New York, NY 10001
      Contact: Ashish Kaushal President
      Tel: 646-495-1558
      Email: vms@hiretalent.com
      Website: www.hiretalent.com
Staffing services. (As-Ind, estab 1996, empl 250, sales
$29,105,000, cert: NMSDC)

8937 iT Resource Solutions.net, Inc.
      10 Technology Dr, Ste 1
      East Setauket, NY 11733
      Contact: Andrea Dunkle Dir of Diversity Manage-
      ment
      Tel: 631-941-2622
      Email: adunkle@it-rs.net
      Website: www.it-rs.net
Staffing: information technology consultants. (Woman,
estab 1995, empl 45, sales , cert: City, WBENC)

8938 Journee Technology Staffing Inc..
      2117Buffalo Rd Ste 275
      Rochester, NY 14624
      Contact: Dixon President
      Tel: 585-210-5314
      Email: orville@journeetechnologystaffing.com
      Website: www.journeetechnologystaffing.com
Staffing solutions. (Woman/AA, estab 2007, empl 2,
sales $310,000, cert: State)

8939 NetPro Resources, Inc.
      444 E 75th St, Ste 16e
      New York, NY 10021
      Contact: Pam Lindheim VP Client Relations
      Tel: 212-650-1665
      Email: pam@netproresources.com
      Website: www.netproresources.com
Accounting, finance, Human Resources, Administrative,
Legal and Treasury recruitment and placement of
temporary, permanent and consultative professionals
(Woman, estab 1999, empl 1, sales $175,000, cert:
WBENC)

8940 Noor Associates, Inc.
      622 Third Ave, 7th Floor
      New York, NY 10017
      Contact: Jake Eletto Chief of Staff
      Tel: 212-812-3390
      Email: jake@noorinc.com
      Website: www.noorinc.com
Professional services: staffing, consulting & project
based solutions. (As-Ind, estab 2005, empl 100, sales
$10,000,000, cert: City, NMSDC)

8941 Noor Staffing Group, LLC
      295 Madison Ave 14th Fl
      New York, NY 10017
      Contact: Frank Cumbo Sr VP
      Tel: 212-878-2000
      Email: contracts@noorgov.us
      Website: www.promptpersonnel.com
Staffing, skills evaluation, reference, background checks
& market intelligence. (As-Ind, estab 2005, empl 200,
sales $55,000,000, cert: City, NMSDC)

8942 Nueva Solutions Inc
      1410 Broadway Ste 1904
      New York, NY 10018
      Contact: Punit Shetty Business Devel
      Tel: 212-937-0056
      Email: punit@nuevainc.com
      Website: www.nuevainc.com
IT Staffing - contingent & permanent. (Woman/As-Ind,
estab 2008, empl 17, sales $3,200,000, cert: State)

8943 Penda Aiken, Inc.
330 Livingston St, 2 Fl
Brooklyn, NY 11217
Contact: Susie Fryer Business Devel Mgr
Tel: 718-643-4880
Email: sfryer@pendaaiken.com
Website: www.pendaaiken.com
Staffing & HR solutions: testing & evaluating, recruiting & retention, quality control, insurance protection, prompt service & guarantee. (Woman/AA, estab 1990, empl 225, sales $6,815,855, cert: State, City, NMSDC)

8944 Pride Technologies LLC
420 Lexington Ave Ste 2220
New York, NY 10170
Contact: David Hellard Major Accounts Mgr
Tel: 614-991-5895
Email: joshua.kaplan@pridetech.com
Website: www.pridetech.com
Project management & staffing services. (Hisp, estab 1983, empl 800, sales $97,000,000, cert: NMSDC)

8945 Procare USA, LLC
845 3rd Ave, Fl 6
New York, NY 10022
Contact: Dominic Sequeira President
Tel: 631-880-6917
Email: dominic@procareus.com
Website: www.procareus.com
Short-term and long-term healthcare staffing solutions. (As-Ind, estab 2011, empl 80, sales $6,200,000, cert: City)

8946 QED National
350 Seventh Ave, 10 Fl
New York, NY 10001
Contact: Colleen Molter President
Tel: 212-481-6868
Email: cmolter@qednational.com
Website: www.qednational.com
IT temporary & permanent staffing. (Woman, estab 1993, empl 40, sales $14,281,567, cert: State)

8947 Russell Tobin & Associates, LLC
420 Lexington Ave, 29th Floor
New York, NY 10170
Contact: Jenny Davis Sr Dir
Tel: 212-235-5300
Email: jennifer.davis@russelltobin.com
Website: www.russelltobin.com
Recruitment and staffing, labor staffing, direct hire recruitment and payroll services. (Hisp, estab , empl 500, sales $80,000,000, cert: NMSDC)

8948 Synergy Staffing & Solutions Inc.
200 Park Ave S Ste 1411
New York, NY 10003
Contact: Ryan Watson President
Tel: 646-553-4458
Email: ryan@sinyc.com
Website: www.sinyc.com
Full-Time Staffing & Freelance Consulting Recruitment. (Minority, estab 2008, empl 50, sales $10,961,383, cert: NMSDC)

8949 Temporary Staffing by Suzanne, Ltd.
370 Lexington Ave, Ste 902
New York, NY 10017
Contact: Suzanne G. Davis President
Tel: 212-856-9500
Email: sdavis@suzannenyc.com
Website: www.suzannenyc.com
Temporary staffing: administrative, secretarial, computer, reception, research, clerical, editorial, project coordinator, events registration & data entry positions. (Woman, estab 1999, empl 6, sales $3,085,963, cert: State, City)

8950 The Burgess Group - Corporate Recruiters Intl
10 Barclay St Ste 16-C
New York, NY 10007
Contact: William H. Burgess, III CEO
Tel: 212-406-2400
Email: billburgess@theburgessgroup.com
Website: www.theburgessgroup.com
Mid to senior level executive search, diversity recruiting, training & management development consulting. (AA, estab 1997, empl 5, sales , cert: NMSDC)

8951 The May Consulting Group Inc.
174 County Hwy 67
Amsterdam, NY 12010
Contact: Sheila Greco CEO
Tel: 518-843-4611
Email: sgreco@sgatalent.com
Website: www.sgatalent.com
Recruitment research & strategic recruiting solutions. (Woman, estab 1989, empl 20, sales , cert: WBENC)

8952 Tower Legal Solutions
65 Broadway 17th Fl.
New York, NY 10006
Contact: Firtell Founder & CEO
Tel: 212-430-6300
Email: rchristenlall@towerls.com;ar@towerls.com
Website: www.towerls.com
Staffing: temporary attorneys, paralegals & project space. (Woman, estab 2007, empl 74, sales $51,956,340, cert: WBENC)

Ohio

8953 Acloche Staffing
1800 Watermark Dr Ste 430
Columbus, OH 43215
Contact: Kimberly Shoemaker CEO
Tel: 614-824-3700
Email: kshoemaker@acloche.com
Website: www.acloche.com
Human capital strategies & workforce resources, recruiting, customized search program. (Woman, estab 1968, empl 100, sales $36,494,135, cert: WBENC, NWBOC)

8954 Career Connections Staffing Services Inc.
26260 Center Ridge Road
Westlake, OH 44145
Contact: Brian DeChant President
Tel: 866-424-1233
Email: bdechant@go2itgroup.com
Website: www.go2itgroup.com
Temporary & permanent information technology & medical support staffing. (Woman, estab 1996, empl 45, sales $3,776,350, cert: WBENC)

8955 Crown Services, Inc.
2800 Corporate Exchange Dr Ste 120
Columbus, OH 43231
Contact: Stacey Diana VP Business Dev
Tel: 614-844-5429
Email: sdiana@crownservices.com
Website: www.crownservices.com
Staffing services. (Woman, estab 1968, empl 245, sales $123,000,000, cert: WBENC)

8956 Eastern Personnel Services, Inc.
619 Central Ave.
Cincinnati, OH 45202
Contact: Angelita Jones VP Smployment Svcs
Tel: 513-421-4666
Email: ajones@easternpersonnelservices.com
Website: www.easternpersonnelservices.com
Staffing: professional, contract, temporary, temp to hire, contract management & on-site supervision. (Woman/AA, estab 1987, empl 7, sales $3,625,356, cert: State, NMSDC, WBENC)

8957 Great Work Employment Services, Inc.
2034 E Market St
Akron, OH 44312
Contact: Bob Frankish Dir Business Dev
Tel: 330-535-3800
Email: bfrankish@greatwork.jobs
Website: www.greatwork.cc
Temporary staffing services. (Woman, estab 1992, empl 16, sales $7,600,000, cert: WBENC)

8958 Howard & O
29525 Chagrin Blvd Ste 100
Cleveland, OH 44122
Contact: Lee Ann Howard
Tel: 216-514-8980
Email: lah@howardobrien.com
Website: www.howardobrien.com
Executive search consulting services. (Woman, estab 2001, empl 4, sales $1,900,000, cert: WBENC)

8959 Hunter International, Inc.
38100 Colorado Ave
Avon, OH 44011
Contact: Gabrielle Christman President
Tel: 440-389-0023
Email: gchristman@hirecruiting.com
Website: www.hirecruiting.com
Project based staffing solutions, contract or temporary, contract to permanent. (Woman, estab 2006, empl 100, sales $15,700,000, cert: WBENC)

8960 JLS Staffing & Management dba Total Staffing Solutions
11562 Chester Rd
Cincinnati, OH 45246
Contact: Amy Mullett Owner
Tel: 513-771-9675
Email: tmullett@totalstaffsolutions.com
Website: www.totalstaffsolutions.com
Staffing Solutions: temporary positions, temp to hire, as well as direct hire placements. (Woman, estab 2012, empl 10, sales $10,200,000, cert: WBENC)

8961 KNK Recruiting, LLC
6562 Pleasant Valley Court
Loveland, OH 45140
Contact: Matt Baker CEO
Tel: 513-265-5741
Email: mbaker@knkrecruiting.com
Website: www.knkrecruiting.com
Recruitment Process Outsourcing (RPO), recruiting & placement solutions. (AA, estab 2009, empl 1, sales $230,871, cert: State)

8962 Maverick Direct, Inc.
PO Box 1247
Bath, OH 44210
Contact: Cindy Janos President
Tel: 330-668-1800
Email: cjanos@callmaverick.com
Website: www.callmaverick.com
Staffing & search firm capabilities in the IT and IS arena. (Woman, estab 1999, empl 43, sales $5,200,000, cert: NWBOC)

8963 Minority Executive Search
3060 Monticello Blvd.
Cleveland, OH 44118
Contact: Eral Burks CEO
Tel: 216-932-2022
Email: eral@minorityexecsearch.com
Website: www.minorityexecsearch.com
Women & Minority job placements. (AA, estab 1985, empl 10, sales , cert: NMSDC)

8964 Multitec, Inc./Next Step Resources
2731 Sawbury Blvd
Columbus, OH 43235
Contact: Tim Weber
Tel: 614-798-0671
Email: info@nextsr.com
Website: www.nextsr.com
Ppermanent placement, contract staffing, and consulting services (As-Pac, estab 1995, empl 40, sales , cert: NMSDC)

8965 OneSource Services
6700 Beta Dr Ste 110
Mayfield Village, OH 44143
Contact: Tom Puletti Operations
Tel: 440-565-4434
Email: tpuletti@1-sourceservices.com
Website: www.1-sourceservices.com
Temporary, temporary to hire, direct hire & payroll services for technical, professional, and light industrial skill sets. (Woman, estab 2014, empl 25, sales $500,000, cert: NWBOC)

8966 Pearl Interactive Network
1105 Schrock Rd Ste 107
Columbus, OH 43229
Contact: Merry Korn Owner
Tel: 614-258-2943
Email: mkcontracts@pinsourcing.com
Website: www.pinsourcing.com
Provides contact center, and business and staffing services. (Woman, estab 2004, empl 214, sales $11,984,822, cert: WBENC)

8967 Portfolio Creative, LLC
      777 Goodale Blvd Ste 300
      Columbus, OH 43212
      Contact: Shelli Welch Dir Operations
      Tel: 614-839-4897
      Email: shelli@portfoliocreative.com
      Website: www.portfoliocreative.com/
Staffing services: marketing, advertising, design, project management. (Woman, estab 2005, empl 60, sales $6,500,000, cert: WBENC)

8968 Proteam Solutions, Inc.
      2750 Airport, Ste 120
      Columbus, OH 43219
      Contact: Tracy Stearns Dir Client Relations
      Tel: 614-454-6488
      Email: tstearns@psi92.com
      Website: www.psi92.com
Supplemental staffing, direct hire, temp-to-hire, light industrial, administrative & career placement. (AA, estab 1992, empl 16, sales $10,482,357, cert: NMSDC)

8969 Quick Employment LLC
      2800 Euclid Ave, Ste 310
      Cleveland, OH 44101
      Contact: Sherall Hardy President
      Tel: 216-361-3030
      Email: quickemp@cs.com
      Website: www.quickemp.com
Employment services: office services, data entry, receptionist, accounting clerks, file clerks, office administrative, IT, General Labor, shipping & receiving, porters, maintenance, drivers, CDL A, CDL B, dental assistants & medical assistants. (Woman/AA, estab 2001, empl 30, sales , cert: State, City)

8970 Reesential Inc.
      15804 Terrace Dr
      Cleveland, OH 44112
      Contact: Charee Fountain President
      Tel: 216-451-1820
      Email: cfountain@reesential.com
      Website: www.reesential.com
Information Technology Staffing: contract, contract to hire & direct hire placement services. (Woman/AA, estab 2014, empl 2, sales , cert: WBENC)

8971 Spherion of Lima Inc.
      216 N Elizabeth St
      Lima, OH 45801
      Contact: Judith Cowan VP
      Tel: 419-224-8367
      Email: judithc@spherion-schulte.com
      Website: www.spherion.com/nwohio
Recruiting and staffing. (Woman, estab 1982, empl 38, sales $26,000,000, cert: WBENC)

8972 Staffing Solutions Enterprises
      5915 Landerbrook Dr Ste 100
      Cleveland, OH 44124
      Contact: Amy Elder Sales Team Mgr
      Tel: 440-684-7218
      Email: aelder@staffsol.com
      Website: www.staffsol.com
Staffing & workforce management: temporary, temp-to-hire, direct placement, recruiting, managed staffing services, payrolling. (Woman, estab 1974, empl 20, sales $10,434,625, cert: City, WBENC)

8973 Supplemental Staffing
      5333 Southwyck Blvd.
      Toledo, OH 43614
      Contact: Mary Stoneking President
      Tel: 419-866-8367
      Email: mstoneking@supplemental.com
      Website: www.supplemental.com
Employment services. (Woman, estab 1978, empl 3000, sales , cert: WBENC)

Oregon

8974 BeginRight Employment Services
      3708 NE 122nd Ave.
      Portland, OR 97220
      Contact: Cindy Wilkerson VP Sales & Service
      Tel: 503-254-5959
      Email: cwilkerson@beginright.com
      Website: www.beginright.com/
Temporary, seasonal, contract to hire & direct hire staffing services: clerical, administrative, accounting, technical, engineering & professional placements, payrolling services. (Woman, estab 1985, empl 15, sales $7,200,000, cert: State)

8975 Boly-Welch, Inc.
      920 SW 6th Ave, Ste 100
      Portland, OR 97204
      Contact: Kathleen Everett Dir Client Relations
      Tel: 503-242-1300
      Email: k.everett@bolywelch.com
      Website: www.bolywelch.com
Recruiting/Staffing/Consulting agency. (Woman, estab 1986, empl 46, sales $16,000,000, cert: State, WBENC)

8976 Collaborative Vision LLC
      7883 SW Barnard Dr
      Beaverton, OR 97007
      Contact: Lisa Matar Founder
      Tel: 503-941-9444
      Email: lisa@cvhires.com
      Website: www.cvhires.com
Staffing, Direct Hire, Permanent, Contract, Temp, Contingent Staffing Support. (Woman/As-Ind, estab 2008, empl 19, sales $579,845, cert: State)

8977 OLSA Resources, Inc
      3485 NE John Olsen Ave
      Hillsboro, OR 97124
      Contact: Olsa Martini President
      Tel: 503-608-7895
      Email: olsamartini@olsaresources.com
      Website: www.olsaresources.com
Staffing & recruiting svcs: IT & engineering. (Woman, estab 1996, empl 75, sales $12,000,000, cert: WBENC, SDB)

8978 S. Brooks and Associates Inc.
      1130 NE Alberta St
      Portland, OR 97211
      Contact: Lynn Sanders
      Tel: 503-284-7930
      Email: lsanders@sbrooks.com
      Website: www.sbrooks.com
Staffing: permanent & temporary. (Woman/AA, estab 1981, empl 5, sales $3,000,000, cert: State)

Pennsylvania

8979 Abel Personnel, Inc.
3356 Paxton St
Harrisburg, PA 17111
Contact: Deborah Abel
Tel: 717-561-2222
Email: dabel@abelpersonnel.com
Website: www.abelpersonnel.com
Temp & contract employees, perm placement, business &
professional employers. (Woman, estab 1969, empl 12,
sales , cert: WBENC)

8980 Advantage Resource Group
1600 Valley View Blvd
Altoona, PA 16602
Contact: Bonnie Williams VP Admin
Tel: 814-944-3571
Email: bonnie.williams@theadvantages.com
Website: www.theadvantages.com
Temporary to hire/contract staffing, Direct Hire, Executive
Placement, HR audits, Employee handbooks & Job Descrip-
tions, HR Consulting & training, Resume writing & exit
interviews. (Woman, estab 1953, empl 12, sales
$3,000,000, cert: State)

8981 American Personnel Managers and Consultants, Inc.
3607 Rosemont Ave, Ste 101
Camp Hill, PA 17011
Contact: Pat Gingrich CEO
Tel: 717-465-5637
Email: patg@apmci.com
Website: www.amerijob.com
Staffing, Human Resource Management, Consulting,
Testing & Training, Procurement, Information Technology
Staffing, Project Management. (Woman, estab 1998, empl
45, sales $3,000,000, cert: State)

8982 Assurance Staffing, Inc.
4660 Trindle Rd Ste 100
Camp Hill, PA 17011
Contact: Cinde Holste Mgr
Tel: 717-920-9190
Email: jobs@assurancestaf.com
Website: www.assurancestaf.com
Professional Staffing Services, Temporary, Temp to Hire &
Direct Hire placements. (Woman, estab 2003, empl 35,
sales $879,179, cert: State, WBENC)

8983 Becker Technical Staffing, Inc.
312 Old Lancaster Rd
Merion Station, PA 19066
Contact: Renee Becker CEO
Tel: 610-667-9155
Email: renee@beckertek.com
Website: www.beckertek.com
Staffing: technical, pharmaceutical/healthcare, marketing
sciences & financial/accounting talent acquisition.
(Woman, estab 2008, empl 30, sales $2,000,000, cert:
State, WBENC)

8984 Blue Plate Minds, Inc.
PO Box 1428
Paoli, PA 19301
Contact: Owner
Tel: 610-240-9001
Email: info@blueplateminds.com
Website: www.blueplateminds.com
Full time & freelance staffing: advertising & marketing,
graphic & web designers/directors, editors, writers &
proofreaders. (Woman, estab 1999, empl 25, sales
$1,893,000, cert: WBENC)

8985 Bradley Temporaries, Inc. dba Bradley Staffing Gro
1400 Liberty Ridge Dr Ste 103
Wayne, PA 19087
Contact: Brad Burns VP
Tel: 610-254-9999
Email: brad@bradleystaffinggroup.com
Website: www.BradleyStaffingGroup.com
Temporary & direct hire placement services. (Woman,
estab 1984, empl 6, sales $2,030,000, cert: WBENC)

8986 Choice Counsel, Inc.
535 Smithfield St, Ste 614 Oliver Bldg
Pittsburgh, PA 15222
Contact: Cynthia Scott President
Tel: 412-355-0900
Email: cynthiascott@choicecounsel.com
Website: www.choicecounsel.com
Legal staffing, attorneys & paralegals in temporary and
temporary-to-hire positions. (Woman, estab 1998, empl
50, sales $2,400,000, cert: WBENC)

8987 Choice One Staffing Group, Inc.
2009 MacKenzie Way Ste 250
Cranberry Township, PA 16066
Contact: Julie Sacriponte President
Tel: 724-452-5800
Email: julie@choice1staffing.com
Website: www.choice1staffing.com
Temporary, temp to hire & direct hire capacities, custom
employee testing, background screens, drug screens,
payroll services & skill marketing. (Woman, estab 2003,
empl 525, sales $3,300,000, cert: WBENC)

8988 Clutch Group LLC DBA-Clutch
417 N 8th St Ste 500
Philadelphia, PA 19123
Contact: Jewel Schmitz Business Devel
Tel: 215-240-6672
Email: jewel@clutchnow.com
Website: www.clutchnow.com
Flexible staffing solutions: Advertising, Digital, Creative,
and Marketing, Freelance/Contract, Temp to Hire, Direct
Hire, and Retained Search. (Woman, estab 2018, empl
15, sales $3,500,000, cert: WBENC)

8989 HTSS, Inc.
860 Broad St Ste 111
Emmaus, PA 18049
Contact: Pat Howells President
Tel: 610-432-4161
Email: phowells@htss-inc.com
Website: www.htss-inc.com
Staffing & recruiting services. (Woman, estab 1993, empl
7, sales $4,900,000, cert: State, WBENC)

8990 JH Technical Services, Inc.
3935 Washington Road Unit 1405
Canonsburg, PA 15317
Contact: Cynthia Harrison Henry President
Tel: 412-788-1174
Email: charrison@jhtechnical.com
Website: www.jhtechnical.com
Staffing services. (Woman, estab 1996, empl 20, sales
$3,443,126, cert: State, WBENC)

8991 Krown Employment Services, LLC
801 Vinial St, Ste 102
Pittsburgh, PA 15212
Contact: President
Tel: 412-567-7136
Email: jobs@krownempsvc.com
Website: www.krownempsvc.com
Staffing: Administrative, Accounts Payable/Receivable Call
Center, Clerical, General Labor, Hospitality, Light Industrial,
Janitorial, Maintenance & Warehouse. (Woman, estab
2013, empl 250, sales , cert: WBENC)

8992 McCallion Temps, Inc.
601A Bethlehem Pike
Montgomeryville, PA 18936
Contact: Lisa McCallion President
Tel: 215-855-8000
Email: lmccallion@mccalliongroup.com
Website: www.mccallionstaffing.com
Staffing, temporary, temp to hire & direct hire personnel.
(Woman, estab 1979, empl 12, sales $7,001,821, cert:
NWBOC)

8993 Partner's Consulting, Inc.
2004 Sproul Road, Ste 206
Broomall, PA 19008
Contact: Delivery & Engagement Mgr
Tel: 215-939-6294
Email: info@partners-consulting.com
Website: www.partners-consulting.com
Information technology recruiting for full-time, temp-to-
perm & contract positions. (Woman, estab 2006, empl 40,
sales $6,000,000, cert: State, WBENC)

8994 RomAnalytics
1117 Bridge Road, #34 34
Creamery, PA 19430
Contact: Kathy Roman President
Tel: 484-961-8213
Email: kathy.roman@romanalytics.com
Website: www.romanalytics.com/
Recruiting & staffing, contract staffing or permanent staff
recruiting. (Woman, estab 2013, empl 15, sales $1,900,000,
cert: State, WBENC)

8995 Solomon International, LLC
635 Coles Ct
Harleysville, PA 19438
Contact: Paul Solomon President
Tel: 609-510-9705
Email: paul.solomon@solomonsint.com
Website: www.solomonsint.com
Employment services, temporary & direct hire employment
& IT consulting services. (Minority, Woman, estab 2004,
empl 20, sales $1,018,354, cert: State)

8996 Staffing Pharm, LLC
PO Box 23
Cresco, PA 18326
Contact: Dora Pereda President
Tel: 610-272-4993
Email: dora.pereda@staffingpharm.com
Website: www.staffingpharm.com/
Professional staffing services: pharmaceutical, healthcare,
biotechnology & research industries. (Minority, Woman,
estab 2012, empl 1, sales , cert: NMSDC)

8997 STAFFusion
210 W. Pike St Ste 3
Canonsburg, PA 15317
Contact: Paula Davey President
Tel: 724-916-4772
Email: paula@staffusion.us
Website: www.staffusion.com
Staffing, recruiting professionals, personnel, office,
administrative, (Woman, estab 2003, empl 5, sales
$2,800,000, cert: WBENC)

8998 StarsHR, Inc.
1700 N Highland Rd Ste 200
Pittsburgh, PA 15241
Contact: Dir Placement Svcs
Tel: 412-927-0369
Email: sales@StarsHR.com
Website: www.StarsHR.com
Executive placement services. (As-Ind, estab 2007, empl
5, sales $2,700,000, cert: State)

8999 The Carney Group
1777 Sentry Pkwy West VEVA 14, Ste 301
Blue Bell, PA 19422
Contact: Jacquelyn Fowler Client Relationship Mgr
Tel: 215-646-6200
Email: jfowler@carneyjobs.com
Website: www.carneyjobs.com
Staff augmentation or permanent hire. (Woman, estab
1992, empl 20, sales $10,000,000, cert: State, WBENC)

9000 The Drexel Group, Inc
1832 Market St
Camp Hill, PA 17011
Contact: Romayne Johnson President
Tel: 717-730-9841
Email: romayne@thedrexelgroup.com
Website: www.thedrexelgroup.com
Staffing: temporary, permanent, temp to hire, direct hire
& contingency. (Woman, estab 1994, empl 200, sales
$3,430,086, cert: State, WBENC)

Puerto Rico

9001 Careers Inc.
208 Ave Ponce De Leon, Ste 1100 Banco Popular
Ctr
San Juan, PR 00918
Contact: Blankie Hernandez Curt VP Admin
Tel: 787-764-2298
Email: blankieh@careersincpr.com
Website: www.careersincpr.com
Executive Search & Management Recruiting. (Minority,
Woman, estab 1970, empl 21, sales $2,179,173, cert:
NMSDC)

9002 Caribbean Temprorary Services, LLC
PO Box 11873
San Juan, PR 00910
Contact: Xiomara Villamil VP Corporate Affairs
Tel: 787-620-5500
Email: xiomara.villamil@ctspr.com
Website: www.ctspr.com
Staffing services. (Minority, Woman, estab 1983, empl
5000, sales , cert: NMSDC)

9003 Job Hunters LLC
PO Box 56012
Bayamon, PR 00960
Contact: JOHN BRUNO
Tel: 787-998-7210
Email: bruno@jobhunters-pr.com
Website: www.clasificadosonline.com/
PartnersListingJ
Temporary & permanent staffing. (Minority, Woman, estab 2013, empl 50, sales $1,200,000, cert: NMSDC)

9004 PSS Pathfinders Inc.
90 carr 165 Ste 310
Guaynabo, PR 00958
Contact: Georyanne Rios Alvarez President
Tel: 787-622-6868
Email: grios@psspathfinders.com
Website: www.psspathfinders.com
Staffing solutions: temporary, temporary to hire & executive search. (Minority, Woman, estab 1985, empl 425, sales $8,448,618, cert: WBENC, SDB)

9005 The Cervantes Group
PO Box 16409
San Juan, PR 00908
Contact: Joanna Bauza President
Tel: 787-729-7597
Email: joanna@thecervantesgroup.com
Website: www.thecervantesgroup.com
Staffing solutions, short or long-term requirements. (Minority, Woman, estab 2004, empl 22, sales $2,800,000, cert: WBENC)

9006 Weil Group, Inc.
Urb. Villa Blanca Calle Aquamarina #78 Ste 1
Caguas, PR 00725
Contact: Milagros del R Gonzalez GM
Tel: 787-633-0025
Email: clopez@weilgroup.com
Website: www.weilgroup.com
Temporary employment agency, outsourcing IT & automation services: management and/or admin, help desk, servers, WAN, email system, desktop, maintenance, backup & restore. (Hisp, estab 1994, empl 215, sales $12,000,000, cert: NMSDC)

9007 Wisdom Resources, Inc.
350 Chardon Ave. Ste 119
San Juan, PR 00918
Contact: Aissa Betancourt President
Tel: 787-963-1048
Email: aissa@snellingpr.com
Website: www.snellingpr.com
Staffing services: executive, career, temporary, temp-to-hire & contractors, background check & drug testing services. (Minority, Woman, estab 2008, empl 137, sales $5,200,000, cert: NMSDC, WBENC)

Rhode Island

9008 Silverman McGovern Staffing
284 W Exchange St
Providence, RI 02903
Contact: Faye Silverman Managing Partner
Tel: 401-632-0580
Email: Faye@silvermanmcgovern.com
Website: www.silvermanmcgovern.com
Staffing: Legal, Marketing/Creative, Accounting/Finance, Administrative, Technical. (Woman, estab 2003, empl 7, sales , cert: WBENC)

South Carolina

9009 Augusta Temporaries, Inc. dba Manpower
101 Broadus Ave
Greenville, SC 29601
Contact: Pamelia Davis COO
Tel: 864-233-4162
Email: pamelia.davis@manpowersc.com
Website: www.manpowersc.com
Temporary staffing & customer service. (Woman, estab 1978, empl 300, sales $16,711,520, cert: WBENC)

9010 Benchmark Contracting, Inc.
215 E Bay St
Charleston, SC 29401
Contact: Jennifer Courville Dir of Business Dev
Tel: 843-628-5999
Email: courvillej@benchmarkcontracting.org
Website: www.BenchmarkContractingSC.com
General Contracting staffing. (AA, estab 1998, empl 20, sales $10,267,000, cert: State, City)

9011 Eastern Design Services
25 Woods Lake Rd, Ste 301
Greenville, SC 29607
Contact: John Crain Office Mgr
Tel: 864-271-1228
Email: jcrain@easterndesign.com
Website: www.easterndesign.com
Technical & professonal staffing: engineers, designers, drafters, office professionals, information technology & administrative personnel. (Woman, estab 1979, empl 5, sales $2,714,000, cert: State)

9012 Express Employment Professionals
9557 Two Notch Rd Ste N
Columbia, SC 29223
Contact: Northan Golden CEO
Tel: 803-788-8721
Email: northan.golden@expresspros.com
Website: www.expresspros.com
Temporary & permanent staffing. (AA, estab 2007, empl 4, sales $450,000, cert: NMSDC)

9013 Godshall and Godshall Personnel Consultants, Inc.
310 University Ridge
Greenville, SC 29601
Contact: Julie Brown President
Tel: 864-242-3491
Email: julie.brown@godshallstaffing.com
Website: www.SCcareerSearch.com
Staffing and recruiting, temporary, contract, temp to direct hire, and direct hire positions. (Woman, estab 1968, empl 18, sales $12,000,005, cert: WBENC)

9014 Marketplace Staffing Services Inc.
200 Adley Way
Greenville, SC 29606
Contact: Jason Mitchell Dir of Sales
Tel: 864-286-3900
Email: jmitchell@marketplacestaffing.com
Website: www.marketplacestaffing.com
Comprehensive staffing & onsite managed contract labor services: manufacturing, warehouse & light industrial staffing solutions. (AA, estab 1996, empl 25, sales $9,000,000, cert: NMSDC)

9015   Onin Staffing
950 Sunset Blvd.
Columbia, SC 29169
Contact: Cierra Belser Dir of Natl Partnersh
Tel: 334-313-6477
Email: cbelser@excelsiorstaffing.com
Website: www.excelsiorstaffing.com
Staffing services: temporary, temporary to permanent,
direct placement & VNP. (AA, estab 2008, empl 1000, sales
$9,542,011, cert: NMSDC)

9016   Perceptive Recruiting, LLC
221 Meadow Rose Dr
Travelers Rest, SC 29690
Contact: Jill Rose President
Tel: - -
Email: info@perceptiverecruiting.com
Website: www.perceptiverecruiting.com
Recruiting and staffing services. (Woman, estab 2014, empl
5, sales $3,311,462, cert: WBENC)

Tennessee

9017   A-One, LLC
3639 New Getwell Rd., Ste 1 & 2
Memphis, TN 38118
Contact: Sterlyn Howell Owner
Tel: 901-367-5757
Email: astaffing2@yahoo.com
Website: www.aonestaffing.com
Temp, temp-to-perm & permanent placement. (Woman/
AA, estab 2001, empl 32, sales $2,200,000, cert: City,
WBENC)

9018   Atlas Management Corporation
750 Old Hickory Blvd Bldg Two, Ste 265
Brentwood, TN 37027
Contact: Warren Sawyers President
Tel: 615-620-0977
Email: wsawyers@atlasmanagement.us
Website: www.atlasmanagement.us
Recruiting, staffing, call center services, business unit
outsourcing. (AA, estab 2003, empl 10, sales $2,600,000,
cert: State, SDB)

9019   Gem Quality
2033 Castaic Lane
Knoxville, TN 37932
Contact: Jason Campbell President
Tel: 865-560-9891
Email: jcampbell@gem-quality.com
Website: www.gemcareinc.com
HR services, temporary to hire, direct placement, commer-
cial & professional staffing. (Woman/AA, estab 2005, empl
200, sales $6,428,737, cert: NMSDC, WBENC)

9020   MasterStaff, Inc.
611 Potomac Pl, Ste 103
Smyrna, TN 37167
Contact: Jennifer Sheets CEO
Tel: 615-223-5627
Email: jennifer@masterstaffemployment.com
Website: www.masterstaffemployment.com
Professional recruitment & placement, temporary & temp
to hire employees, human resource consulting & contract
staffing. (Woman, estab 1999, empl 450, sales
$12,789,203, cert: WBENC)

9021   neMarc Professional Services, Inc.
2500 Mt. Moriah Rd, Ste H231
Memphis, TN 38115
Contact: Carmen Bassett President
Tel: 901-360-1804
Email: carmenbassett@bellsouth.net
Website: www.nemarcstaffing.com
Temp, permanent placement, temp-to-perm staffing
svcs: clerical, administrative, distribution, warehouse, IT,
accounting & professional placement. (Woman/AA,
estab 2002, empl 5, sales $742,000, cert: State, NMSDC)

9022   Omni Staffing Plus, Inc.
80 N Tillman, Ste 201
Memphis, TN 38111
Contact: Dinah Terry
Tel: 901-843-8433
Email: dterry@omnistaffingplus.com
Website: www.omnistaffingplus.com
Temporary/permanent staffing. (Woman/AA, estab
1999, empl 6, sales $1,874,214, cert: NMSDC)

9023   Provide Staffing Services LLC
6765 E Shelby Dr
Memphis, TN 38141
Contact: Pat Morris Mgr
Tel: 901-505-0005
Email: pat@provide-staffing.com
Website: www.pscstaffing.net
Temporary Employees, Clerical positions. (Woman, estab
2013, empl 170, sales , cert: City)

9024   Reliable Building Solutions, Inc.
6232 Airpark Dr
Chattanooga, TN 37421
Contact: Kathy Sok President
Tel: 423-954-9834
Email: ksok6322@aol.com
Website: www.rbsi-online.com
We provide Complete facility management service to
include: Janitorial, Floor maintenance, Emergency
services, and provide wholesale of Janitorial supplies,
equipment and chemicals. (Minority, Woman, estab
1992, empl 45, sales $2,800,000, cert: State)

Texas

9025   ADASTAFF, Inc.
702 Hunters Row Court
Mansfield, TX 76063
Contact: Aaron Flaherty Call Ctr Solutions Expert
Tel: 817-469-6234
Email: aflaherty@adastaff.com
Website: www.adastaff.com
Temporary, Temporary-to-Hire Staffing, Payroll Adminis-
tration, Executive Placement, Safety Consulting and
Training, Direct Hire and Special Project Outsourcing.
Our specialty is in Administrative, Clerical. (Woman,
estab 1993, empl 225, sales $7,187,978, cert: WBENC)

9026   Adventus Technologies, Inc.
6001 Savoy Ste 511
Houston, TX 77036
Contact: Vicki Semander
Tel: 713-995-4446
Email: vsemander@adventus-tech.com
Website: www.adventus-tech.com
Professional, para professional & admin personnel:
Project Mgt, Finance & Accounting Support, General
Consulting Svcs, Acquisition & Procurement Mgt,
Publication, & Logistic Support Svcs. (Woman/AA, estab
2005, empl 8, sales $376,000, cert: State, City, NMSDC,
8(a))

9027 All Temps 1 Personnel
2606 MLK Jr. Blvd
Dallas, TX 75215
Contact: Stacie McGill Sales & Mktg Mgr
Tel: 214-426-2700
Email: jjeffrey@alltemps1.com
Website: www.alltemps1.com
Staffing services. (AA, estab 1994, empl 15, sales
$11,800,000, cert: NMSDC)

9028 Alleare Consulting, LLC
3625 N. Hall St Ste 685
Dallas, TX 75219
Contact: Lana Arnold CFO
Tel: 214-559-9878
Email: larnold@alleareconsulting.com
Website: www.alleareconsulting.com
Recruiting, staffing & consulting services: permanent
placement, contract & contract-to-hire. (Woman, estab ,
empl , sales $816,030, cert: State, WBENC)

9029 All-N-One Services, LLC
12115 English Brook Cir
Humble, TX 77346
Contact: Ann Guliex CEO
Tel: 281-812-3553
Email: annguliex@all-n1.com
Website: www.all-n1.com
Temp to hire, direct-hire, contract & temporary staffing
svcs. (Woman/AA, estab 2002, empl 3, sales $583,000,
cert: WBENC)

9030 AllTex Staffing & Consulting LLC dba Abba Staffing
2350 Airport Fwy Ste 130
Bedford, TX 76022
Contact: Darla Beggs CEO
Tel: 817-354-2800
Email: darla@abbastaffing.com
Website: www.abbastaffing.com
Direct Placement, Contingent-to-hire-Personnel, Contract
personnel, Temporary personnel. (Woman, estab 2001,
empl 5, sales $390,000,000, cert: State, WBENC)

9031 AMP Personnel Services, LLC
3700 N 10th St, Ste 302
McAllen, TX 78501
Contact: Marisa Sonnier Admin
Tel: 956-627-0477
Email: amppersonnelservices@gmail.com
Website: www.amppersonnel.com
Staffing services: professional, administrative & commer-
cial job placement. (Minority, Woman, estab 2012, empl 2,
sales $100,000, cert: State, 8(a))

9032 ANSERTEAM, LLC
4835 LBJ Freeway Ste 1000
Dallas, TX 75244
Contact: Ann Kramer Dir Strategic Partnerships
Tel: 888-932-6737
Email: akramer@anserteam.com
Website: www.anserteam.com
Specialize in clerical, administrative, customer service,
accounting and technical staffing. (Woman, estab 2004,
empl 8, sales $47,095,422, cert: WBENC)

9033 Applicantz, Inc.
10235 W Little York Road, Ste 235
Houston, TX 77040
Contact: Nikhil Jain Dir
Tel: 713-834-4909
Email: nikhilj@applicantz.com
Website: www.applicantz.com
IT Contingent Staffing: Contract, Contract-to-hire, and
Permanent and Remote Technology Staffing. (Minority,
Woman, estab 2001, empl 125, sales $14,800,000, cert:
NMSDC)

9034 ASAP Personnel Inc.
17311 Dallas Pkwy
Dallas, TX 75248
Contact: Evelyn Touchette President
Tel: 972-432-6667
Email: evelyn@asapdo.com
Website: www.asapdo.net
Staffing & Personnel Services. (Woman, estab 2010,
empl 22, sales $500,000, cert: State, City)

9035 AXIS Staffing
1111 W Mockingbird Ln
Dallas, TX 75247
Contact: Jacob Joseph President
Tel: 214-638-4000
Email: jacob_joseph@axisstaff.com
Website: www.axisstaff.com
Staffing services. (As-Pac, estab 1993, empl 10, sales
$4,500,000, cert: State)

9036 Barbara J. Charles dba Perfection Staffing
16502 Brightling Ln
Houston, TX 77090
Contact: Barbara Charles Owner
Tel: 281-781-7587
Email: bcharles@perfectionstaffing.agency
Website: www.perfectionstaffing.agency
Staffing and Recruitment Agency, Direct Hire, Contract/
Contract-to-Hire, and Temporary talent for Exempt and
Non-Exempt positions.
Our staffing efforts are (AA, estab 2018, empl 2, sales ,
cert: City, NMSDC)

9037 BBM Staffing
4242 Medical Dr, Bldg 2200
San Antonio, TX 78229
Contact: Liz Moreno Operations Mgr
Tel: 210-822-0717
Email: lmoreno@bbmstaffing.com
Website: www.bbmstaffing.com
Recruiting, temporary, temp to hire & direct hire
solutions. (Minority, Woman, estab 2009, empl 300,
sales $11,000,000, cert: State, NMSDC)

9038 Bestica, Inc.
3463 Magic Dr Ste 303
San Antonio, TX 78229
Contact: Harvinder Singh CEO
Tel: 210-614-4198
Email: harvinder@bestica.com
Website: www.bestica.com
IT consulting & staffing firm. (As-Ind, estab 2005, empl
198, sales $7,500,000, cert: NMSDC, 8(a))

9039 Brooke Staffing Companies, Inc.
3900 Essex, Ste 555
Houston, TX 77027
Contact: Joe Stephens Treasurer
Tel: 713-337-2222
Email: joes@brookecompanies.com
Website: www.brookecompanies.com
Temporary & full-time placement services. (Woman, estab 1989, empl 213, sales $8,718,523, cert: City, WBENC)

9040 Burnett Specialists
9800 Richmond Ave Ste 800
Houston, TX 77042
Contact: Rick Burnett VP Reg Mgr
Tel: 713-358-1437
Email: rick@burnettspecialists.com
Website: www.burnettspecialists.com
Temporary, contract & direct-hire placement: clerical & administrative, accounting & financial, legal, human resources, information technology, sales, medical, customer service, light industrial & electronics personnel. (Woman, estab 1974, empl 115, sales $66,200,000, cert: WBENC)

9041 Burns Search LLC
1415 Legacy Dr, Ste 310
Frisco, TX 75034
Contact: CEO
Tel: 214-213-4053
Email:
Website: www.burnssearch.com
Staffing, recruiting, consulting: technical, accounting, finance, executive search. (Woman, estab 1999, empl 8, sales $1,394,555, cert: WBENC)

9042 Business Control Systems LP
16415 Addison Rd Ste 150
Addison, TX 75001
Contact: Chevalier Francis Business Devel Mgr
Tel: 972-241-8392
Email: chevalier.francis@bcsmis.com
Website: www.bcsmis.com
Project resources planning, enterprise business architecture, mediation, and outplacement services. (Woman/AA, estab 1981, empl 150, sales $19,127,630, cert: State, WBENC)

9043 C&T Information Technology Consulting, Inc.
201 S Lakeline Ste 803
Cedar Park, TX 78613
Contact: Jennifer Conway Dir Sales/Marketing
Tel: 512-610-0040
Email: sales@candttech.com
Website: www.candttech.com
Entry level, High End & Mid-Level Technical Staffing & Consulting. Project Management, Enterprise Architecture & Technical Solutions Provider Perm Placement, Technical Recruiting. (Woman, estab 2003, empl 34, sales $5,115,202, cert: State)

9044 Cambay Consulting LLC
1838 Snake River Road, Ste A
Katy, TX 77449
Contact: ashwani sharma Business Devel Mgr
Tel: 469-393-9501
Email: ashwani.sharma@cambaycs.com
Website: www.cambaycs.com
Temporary & permanent staffing solutions. (Minority, estab 2012, empl 137, sales $19,200,000, cert: NMSDC)

9045 Choice Hire Staffing LLC
3106 Hwy 377 S
Brownwood, TX 76801
Contact: Melissa Mauricio Owner
Tel: 325-643-1416
Email: melissa@choicehirestaffing.com
Website: www.choicehirestaffing.com
Temporary, seasonal, temp to hire & direct placement. (Woman, estab 2013, empl 3, sales , cert: State)

9046 Employee Risk Management Co. Inc.
4639 Corona, Ste 99
Corpus Christi, TX 78411
Contact: Laura Escobar President
Tel: 361-808-8367
Email: laura@atrecruiters.com
Website: www.atpersonnelservices.com
Recruiting, direct hire & temporary placement, Background checks, Drug screens, Safety Assured. (Minority, Woman, estab 1994, empl 10, sales $6,000,000, cert: State)

9047 Evins Personnel Consltants
6430 Richmond Ave Ste 415
Houston, TX 77057
Contact: Helen Royston Acct Rep
Tel: 713-977-8555
Email: staffing@hrnetconnection.com
Website: www.HRnetConnection.com
Temporary staffing, direct hire, temp to hire staffing. (Woman, estab 1967, empl 5000, sales $15,000,000, cert: State)

9048 Execusane Inc
2306 Stillwater Dr
Mesquite, TX 75181
Contact: Shiree Alexander President
Tel: 972-277-1176
Email: shayes@execusane.com
Website: www.execusane.com
Direct Placement, Executive Recruiting, HR Consulting, Staffing/Contract Recruiting. (Woman/AA, estab 2012, empl 1, sales , cert: State)

9049 Foremost Staffing, Inc.
3991 West Vickery
Fort Worth, TX 76107
Contact: Vicki Jordan President
Tel: 817-346-4738
Email: vjordan@foremoststaffing.com
Website: www.foremoststaffing.com
Staffing: temporary, temp to hire, direct placements & payroll services. (Woman, estab 2007, empl 100, sales $2,261,595, cert: State, WBENC)

9050 Fulgent Solutions Inc.
5700 Granite Pkwy Ste 200
Plano, TX 75024
Contact: Shan Adaikalam President
Tel: 972-506-7335
Email: shan.adaikalam@fulgentsol.com
Website: www.fulgentsol.com
Enterprise business consulting & staffing, technology, temporary, temporary-to-hire & permanent placement services. (As-Ind, estab 2013, empl 15, sales $1,500,000, cert: State)

9051 Getcorp Payroll Accounting & Tax dba Get Hire
Staffing
8104 Southwest Fwy, Ste C
Houston, TX 77074
Contact: Gloria Towolawi CEO
Tel: 832-680-5225
Email: info@gethirestaffing.com
Website: www.gethirestaffing.com
Employment placement agency that provides pre-screened
and qualified candidates- eliminating time and money
wasting unproductive job boards. (AA, estab 2019, empl 3,
sales , cert: State, City, WBENC)

9052 GS Infovision LLC dba Global Systems LLC
1200 Walnut Hill Lane, Ste 2220
Irving, TX 75038
Contact: Shekhar Gupta VP
Tel: 214-717-4344
Email: account@globalsyst.com
Website: www.globalsyst.com
IT Consulting, Staffing, BPO, IT Consulting, temporary,
contract, temp to perm & permanent staffing solutions.
(Minority, Woman, estab 2005, empl 110, sales
$11,000,000, cert: NMSDC)

9053 Hawkins, Associates, Inc.
909 NE Loop 410, Ste 104
San Antonio, TX 78209
Contact: Elizabeth Hawkins VP
Tel: 210-349-9911
Email: liz@hawkinspersonnel.com
Website: www.hawkinspersonnel.com
Temporary, temp-to-hire, direct hire professional services,
payrolling services & on-site management services.
(Woman, estab 1977, empl 35, sales $18,000,000, cert:
State, City)

9054 HirePower Personnel, Inc.
14100 Southwest Freeway Ste 320
Sugar Land, TX 77478
Contact: Travis Hamblet Global Operations Mgr
Tel: 281-455-6802
Email: travis.hamblet@hppstaffing.com
Website: www.hppstaffing.com
Temp, Temp to Hire & Direct Hire Placements. (Woman,
estab 0, empl , sales $4,000,000, cert: State, WBENC)

9055 ICON Information Consultants, LP
100 Waugh Dr Ste 300
Houston, TX 77007
Contact: Pamela O'Rourke Founder & CEO
Tel: 713-438-0919
Email: porourke@iconconsultants.com
Website: www.iconconsultants.com
Recruit information technology, accounting & finance
professionals. (Woman, estab 1998, empl 6000, sales
$589,013,900, cert: WBENC)

9056 Imprimis Group
4835 LBJ Frwy, Ste 1000
Dallas, TX 75244
Contact: Valerie Freeman CEO
Tel: 972-419-1635
Email: vfreeman@imprimis.com
Website: www.imprimis.com
Staffing; temp, temp to hire, direct hire: admin/office,
accounting, bilingual, cstnmr svc, legal, mktg, medical,
mortgage, etc. (Woman, estab 1982, empl 60, sales
$21,000,000, cert: State, WBENC)

9057 InGenesis, Inc.
10231 Kotzebue St
San Antonio, TX 78217
Contact: Dr. Veronica Edwards CEO
Tel: 210-366-0033
Email: commercial@ingenesis.com
Website: www.ingenesis.com
Workforce solutions: direct placement, direct hire,
executive search, temporary staffing, contingent
staffing, managed vendor, recruitment process
outsourcing, managed services programs & locum
tenens. (Minority, Woman, estab , empl , sales
$174,785,000, cert: NMSDC, WBENC)

9058 International Genesis Professional Solutions, Inc.
PO Box 692205
San Antonio, TX 78269
Contact: Shelah Simmons CEO
Tel: 210-867-4182
Email: simmons@genesisprofsol.com
Website: www.genesisprofsol.com
Human Capital, Business Process Optimization & Project
Management, Strategic Executive Recruitment, Human
Resources Staffing (Temporary Help Service). (Woman/
AA, estab 2006, empl 5, sales $149,100, cert: State)

9059 JK Flenory & Company, LLC
PO Box 5069
Frisco, TX 75035
Contact: Marcellas Flenory Sr. CEO
Tel: 972-480-2667
Email: recruiter@jkfcompany.com
Website: www.JKFCompany.com
Staffing, recruiting, retention & outplacement services.
(AA, estab 2012, empl 1, sales , cert: City)

9060 KeyStaff Inc.
2909 Hillcroft St, Ste 620 Ste 620
Houston, TX 77057
Contact: Tammie Jeffers Branch Mgr
Tel: 713-422-2710
Email: tammie.jeffers@keystaffinc.com
Website: www.keystaffinc.com
Staffing: temporary, temp-to-perm & direct-hire place-
ments. (Woman, estab 2004, empl 20, sales
$18,989,644, cert: State, City)

9061 King Finders, LLC
6575 West Loop South, Ste 500
Bellaire, TX 77401
Contact: Manny Coronado President
Tel: 713-936-2695
Email: mcoronado@kingfinders.com
Website: www.kingfinders.com
Temp-to-Hire, Contingent & Direct Hire placements:
Business & Administrative Professionals, Oil & Gas,
Energy, Finance & Accounting, Information Technology
and Mfg. (Hisp, estab 2018, empl 25, sales , cert: State)

9062 Labor On Demand Inc., Dba, LOD Resource Group
851 Culebra Road
San Antonio, TX 78201
Contact: Richard Tovar Business Devel
Tel: 210-865-0445
Email: rtovar@lodresourcegroup.com
Website: www.lodresourcegroup.com/
Temporary & permanent employment services. (Minor-
ity, Woman, estab 2003, empl 31, sales $13,475,568,
cert: State, 8(a), SDB)

9063 LaneStaffing Inc.
2211 Norfolk, Ste 150
Houston, TX 77098
Contact: Elaine Jackson Sr Recruiter
Tel: 713-522-0000
Email: ejackson@lanestaff.com
Website: www.lanestaff.com
Staffing: light industrial, construction, information technology, administrative/clerical, security, call center, finance, accounting, and engineering/technical support specialists. (Woman/AA, estab 2007, empl 525, sales $20,000,000, cert: City)

9064 LiveWell Insurance Products, Inc.
2425 Holly Hall, Ste H 106
Houston, TX 77054
Contact: Glen Reaux President
Tel: 281-827-7909
Email: g.reaux@thenewfaceofhealthcare.com
Website: www.thenewfaceofhealthcare.com
Marketing & advertising services. (AA, estab 2013, empl 4, sales , cert: State, NMSDC)

9065 LK Jordan & Associates
7550 IH 10 West Ste 105
San Antonio, TX 78229
Contact: Stefanie Chavez Business Devel
Tel: 210-488-9360
Email: stefanie.chavez@lkjordan.com
Website: www.lkjordan.com
Staffing services: temporary, temporary to hire & direct hire employees. (Woman, estab 1990, empl 52, sales $25,000,000, cert: State)

9066 Lotus Staffing Group, LLC
1925 E Beltline Rd Ste 419
Carrollton, TX 75006
Contact: Tyra Roberts Managing Dir
Tel: 972-410-3685
Email: tyra@lotusstaffingagency.com
Website: www.lotusstaffingagency.com
Contingent staffing solutions. (Woman/AA, Hisp, estab 2008, empl 23, sales $3,450,000, cert: State, City)

9067 Magnum Staffing Services, Inc.
2900 Smith St, Ste 250
Houston, TX 77006
Contact: Caroline Brown President
Tel: 713-658-0068
Email: caroline.brown@magnumstaffing.com
Website: www.magnumstaffing.com
Background, drug-screening, SS verification, temporary placement, temp-to-hire, direct hire, industrial, clerical & managerial arenas. (Woman, estab 1996, empl 43, sales $38,000,000, cert: WBENC)

9068 MIT Professionals, Inc.
22611 Duncan Brush Trace
Richmond, TX 77469
Contact: Rebecca Morgan President
Tel: 713-934-9700
Email: rebecca@mitprof.com
Website: www.mitprof.com
Staffing services: information technology, supply chain resources, engineering & professional services. (Woman, estab 1995, empl 50, sales , cert: State)

9069 Mobile Temporary Services
9110 Jones Rd Ste 131
Houston, TX 77065
Contact: Allison Holmes President
Tel: 713-344-4148
Email: allison@mobiletempstaff.com
Website: www.mobiletempstaff.com
Temporary employees, direct hire, temp-to-perm & contract employees, on-site applications, backgrounds checks, drug-screen & on-boarding. (Woman/AA, estab 2016, empl 4, sales , cert: WBENC, SDB)

9070 Nelson Search Group
3001 Lake Oak Dr
Arlington, TX 76017
Contact: D. Gayle Barton Principal
Tel: 817-466-7117
Email: gayle@nelsonsearchgroup.com
Website: www.nelsonsearchgroup.com
Ethical, consultative, confidential, quality-driven direct recruiting & on-boarding (full life-cycle). (Woman, estab 2009, empl 1, sales $150,000, cert: State, WBENC)

9071 Peyton Resource Group, LP
100 Decker Ct, Ste 140
Irving, TX 75062
Contact: Bryan Mayhew
Tel: 972-717-7701
Email: bmayhew@prg-usa.com
Website: www.prg-usa.com
Staffing services, temp, temp to perm: IT, telecom, engineering, finance, accounting, clerical, admin & customer support. (Hisp, estab 2001, empl 15, sales , cert: State, NMSDC)

9072 Primary Services LP
520 Post Oak Blvd Ste 550
Houston, TX 77027
Contact: MaryKay Foy-Hinton Strategic Accounts Mgr
Tel: 713-850-7010
Email: marykay@primaryservices.com
Website: www.primaryservices.com
Staffing solutions, contract, contract-to-hire & direct hire placement. (Woman, estab 1988, empl 39, sales $44,928,501, cert: WBENC)

9073 QSTAFF Incorporated
PO Box 580622
Houston, TX 77258
Contact: Richard Green
Tel: 281-218-6574
Email: r.green@qualified-staff.com
Website: www.qualified-staff.com
Staffing svcs: accounting, admin, clerical, chemical plant operators, data entry, engineering, IT, light industrial. (Minority, Woman, estab 1999, empl 75, sales $3,000,000, cert: State, WBENC)

9074 RD Data Solutions
2340 E Trinity Mills Ste 349
Carrollton, TX 75006
Contact: Reuben D'Souza CEO
Tel: 972-899-2334
Email: reuben.dsouza@rddatasolutions.com
Website: www.rddatasolutions.com
Technology staffing: SAP & ERP. (Minority, Woman, estab 2002, empl 26, sales $25,000,000, cert: State, NMSDC)

9075 Recruiting Force, LLC
1464 E. Whitestone Blvd. Ste 1903
Cedar Park, TX 78613
Contact: Rudy Uribe President
Tel: 512-996-0999
Email: rudy.uribe@recruitveterans.com
Website: www.recruitveterans.com
Direct hire professional executive search, permanent placement, information technology, engineering, project management, logisitics, finance, accounting. (Hisp, estab 2003, empl 60, sales $4,437,363, cert: NMSDC, 8(a))

9076 Recruiting Source International
21414 Julie Marie Ln, Ste 2301
Katy, TX 77449
Contact: Bianca Jackson COO
Tel: 281-277-1411
Email: bjackson@recruiting-source.com
Website: www.recruiting-source.com
Executive Search, Staffing & 1099 Management Services. (Woman/AA, estab , empl , sales $1,410,000, cert: State, City, NMSDC, WBENC, SDB)

9077 Resource Personnel Consultants, LLC
14070 Proton Rd
Farmers Branch, TX 75244
Contact: Acct Mgr
Tel: 972-371-2934
Email: hmckinley@rpccompany.com
Website: www.rpccompany.com
Staffing: clerical, administrative & customer service employees, temporary, temporary to permanent or direct hire. (Minority, Woman, estab 2001, empl 8, sales $1,827,499, cert: State)

9078 RG Talent Solutions, LLC
726 Dalworth St Ste 1000
Grand Prairie, TX 75050
Contact: Reginald W Calhoun, Sr. CEO
Tel: 817-405-2838
Email: rcalhoun@rgtalentsolutions.com
Website: www.rgtalentsolutions.com
Business process outsourcing (BPO), talent management, talent acquisition, agency and marketing firm. (AA, estab 2009, empl 14, sales $4,000,000, cert: State, NMSDC)

9079 RightStaff, Inc
6060 N Central Expy Ste 222
Dallas, TX 75206
Contact: Shelley Amason CEO
Tel: 214-615-6015
Email: samason@rightstaffinc.com
Website: www.rightstaffinc.com
Staffing services: permanent, temporary, project staff augmentation, computer software & hardware, computer programing, systems design, technology infrastructure. (Woman, estab 1998, empl 20, sales $2,862,677, cert: State, WBENC)

9080 Riverway Business Services
5213 Spruce St Ste 100
Bellaire, TX 77401
Contact: Margo Costello President
Tel: 713-664-5900
Email: margo.costello@riverway.jobs
Website: www.riverway.jobs
Staffing services: administrative/clerical, accounting, human resource, professional & information technology. (Woman, estab 1990, empl 22, sales $2,000,000, cert: WBENC)

9081 RMPersonnel, Inc.
4707 Montana Ave
El Paso, TX 79903
Contact: Debra Underwood Branch Mgr
Tel: 915-565-7674
Email: debras@rmpersonnel.com
Website: www.rmpersonnel.com
Staffing services: employee leasing, temporaries, temp to hire, executive recruiting & HR consulting services. (Minority, Woman, estab 1990, empl 33, sales $34,000,000, cert: WBENC)

9082 Saba Quaility System
1456 FM 1960 W
Houston, TX 77090
Contact: Patricia Carter Mgr/HR Business Devel
Tel: 281-537-7676
Email: qualitysystem.qs@gmail.com
Website: www.qualitysystemssite.com
IT staffing, sourcing, prescreening, interviewing & placement. (Minority, Woman, estab 2010, empl 14, sales $1,700,000, cert: State)

9083 Search Plus International
5900 Balcones Dr Ste 242
Austin, TX 78731
Contact: Bruce Bagwell Managing Dir
Tel: 512-459-8200
Email: bbagwell@searchplustexas.com
Website: www.searchplustexas.com
Executive mid-management & highly-technical searches. (Woman, estab 1988, empl 9, sales $500,000, cert: WBENC)

9084 Smith & Dean, Inc.
11511 Katy Freeway Ste 430
Houston, TX 77079
Contact: Jennifer Dean President
Tel: 713-785-7483
Email: jdean@dpsinc-texas.com
Website: www.deansprofessionalservices.com
Staffing solutions, recruiting, workshops & seminars, IT consulting. (Woman/AA, estab 1993, empl 2180, sales $10,681,149, cert: State, City, NMSDC, WBENC)

9085 Snelling Employment, LLC
4055 Valley View Lane Ste 700
Dallas, TX 75244
Contact: Bryan Lee
Tel: 972-776-1309
Email: bryan.lee@snelling.com
Website: www.snelling.com
Temporary, temp-to-hire, contract, contract-to-direct hire, direct hire, executive search, and payrolling services. (Woman, estab 1951, empl 2300, sales $144,376,000, cert: WBENC)

9086 SNS Global Corporation
1000 Heritage Center Circle
Round Rock, TX 78664
Contact: Misty Carr HR
Tel: 512-250-2959
Email: m.carr@snsglobalstaffing.com
Website: www.snsglobalstaffing.com
Staffing services. (As-Ind, estab 2003, empl 20, sales , cert: State, NMSDC)

9087 Softel Techsource LLC
2100 Alamo Rd., Ste T,
Richardson, TX 75080
Contact: Mohammed Al-Baki Managing Partner
Tel: 469-475-2297
Email: malbaki@softeltechsource.com
Website: www.softeltechsource.com
Recruiting practices & continuous training. (Woman/As-Ind, estab 2010, empl 10, sales , cert: State)

9088 SOLRAC Corporation
6 Founders Blvd Ste A
El Paso, TX 79906
Contact: Masazumi Aso Exec VP & COO
Tel: 915-772-3073
Email: maso@solraccorp.com
Website: www.solraccorp.com
Assembly, sorting & rework operation, staffing services, warehouse & logistic operation. (Hisp, estab 1989, empl 300, sales , cert: State, NMSDC)

9089 Solution Tech Staffing Inc.
2825 Wilcrest, Ste 678
Houston, TX 77042
Contact: Emon Carroll President
Tel: 713-988-5325
Email: emon@ststaff.com
Website: www.ststaff.com
Staffing: short term temporary, long term temporary, temp-to-hire & direct hire. (Woman/AA, estab 2001, empl 7, sales , cert: State, City)

9090 Southwest Staffing
12025 Rojas, Ste L
El Paso, TX 79936
Contact: James Tidwell Dir
Tel: 915-857-9719
Email: info@southweststaffing.com
Website: www.southweststaffing.com
Temporary employee placement & management, staffing & recruiting solutions in technical & professional placement. (Minority, Woman, estab 1994, empl 23, sales $15,298,011, cert: State)

9091 SV Meditrans, Inc.
100 S 8th St
Richmond, TX 77469
Contact: Rohini Dinesh CEO
Tel: 832-520-8742
Email: rohinid@svmtinc.com
Website: www.svmtinc.com
Staffing services, interviews, screening & training. (Minority, Woman, estab 2002, empl 20, sales $1,650,000, cert: WBENC)

9092 Tek Leaders, Inc
4975 Preston Park Blvd, Ste 500, Plano 75093
Plano, TX 75093
Contact: 774001 VP Enterprise Accounts
Tel: 214-244-3753
Email: hr@tekleaders.com
Website: www.tekleaders.com
IT Services, IT Staffing, Data Analytics and Business Intelligence. (As-Pac, estab 2008, empl 150, sales $20,000,000, cert: NMSDC)

9093 The Burchell Group
11200 W Broadway, Ste 2348
Pearland, TX 77584
Contact: Jamie Burchell President
Tel: 281-607-5990
Email: jamie@theburchellgroup.com
Website: www.theburchellgroup.com
Staffing solutions: engineering, information technology & GIS. (Hisp, estab 2001, empl 45, sales , cert: NMSDC)

9094 The HR Source, Inc.
2307 Oak Ln, Ste 2B-213
Grand Prairie, TX 75051
Contact: Brett Farley Acct Exec
Tel: 972-264-9800
Email: contactus@thehrsource.net
Website: www.thehrsource.net
Temporary, temp to hire & permanent placement: IT, administrative, engineering, clerical & general labor. (Woman/AA, estab 2003, empl 101, sales , cert: WBENC)

9095 The Omega Staff, LLC
14756 Dallas Pkwy, Ste 805
Dallas, TX 75254
Contact: Michelle Deriggs Owner
Tel: 972-948-7754
Email: mderiggs@omegastaff.com
Website: www.omegastaff.com
Professional recruiting & staffing services to automotive, engineering, defense, and manufacturing companies. (Woman/AA, estab 2007, empl 6, sales $130,000, cert: State, City)

9096 The Unbeatable Connection LLC
111 Brand Lane, Ste 3
Stafford, TX 77477
Contact: La Teasha Smith Owner
Tel: 832-363-2566
Email: tuctruckingsales@gmail.com
Website: www.tuctrucking.com/
Staffing services: temp, temp to perm & direct hire positions. (Woman/AA, estab 2010, empl 5, sales $308,826, cert: City)

9097 TMC Workforce Solutions
2313 W Sam Houston Pkwy N Ste 155
Houston, TX 77043
Contact: James Morris President
Tel: 832-473-3993
Email: james.morris@tmcworkforce.com
Website: www.tmcworkforce.com
Staffing, Recruiting and Procurement Services. (AA, estab 2016, empl 342, sales $12,000,000, cert: NMSDC)

9098 TriQuest Business Services, LLC
13526 George Rd, Ste 201
San Antonio, TX 78230
Contact: Stephanie Balditt President
Tel: 210-598-1539
Email: stephanie@triquestbusiness.com
Website: www.triquestbusiness.com
Temporary & permanent placement services: IT, Accounting, Finance, Administrative & Human Resource placement. (Minority, Woman, estab 2010, empl 6, sales $931,239, cert: State)

9099 Walker Elliott, LP
11200 Westheimer
Houston, TX 77042
Contact: Victor M. Taveras Contract Mgr
Tel: 713-482-3750
Email: belliott@walker-elliott.com
Website: www.walker-elliott.com
Information technology & healthcare direct hire, contract & contract to hire placement firm. (Woman, estab 2006, empl 17, sales , cert: WBENC)

Utah

9100 Premier Employee Solutions LLC
3596 Mountain Vista Pkwy, #2
Provo, UT 84606
Contact: Dan Riley Dir of Natl Sales
Tel: 800-385-0855
Email: driley@thepremierpride.com
Website: www.thepremierpride.com
Staffing & payroll services. (Woman, estab 2005, empl 500, sales $391,331,571, cert: WBENC)

Virginia

9101 22nd Century Solutions Inc
8251 Greensboro Dr Ste 900
McLean, VA 22102
Contact: Avinash Singh President
Tel: 866-537-9191
Email: ravis@22csi.com
Website: www.22csi.com
Staffing services, IT staffing & workforce management services, contract or permanent positions. (Woman/As-Ind, estab 1997, empl 6500, sales $350,000,000, cert: WBENC)

9102 Action Technology, Inc.
3121 E Boundary Ct
Midlothian, VA 23112
Contact: Thomas Hammerstone Reg Mgr
Tel: 804-464-1271
Email: thammerstone@action-tech.com
Website: www.action-tech.com
Staff augmentation: direct hire, contract & temporary. (Woman, estab 1982, empl 200, sales $8,000,000, cert: State, CPUC, WBENC)

9103 Alcove Resources
1900 Campus Commons Dr, Ste 100
Reston, VA 20191
Contact: Quan Woodard CEO
Tel: 703-652-4732
Email: info@alcoveresources.com
Website: www.alcoveresources.com
Recruiting & executive search services, information management consulting. (Woman/AA, estab 2005, empl 5, sales $100,000, cert: State)

9104 ARK Solutions Inc.
1939 Roland Clarke Pll Ste 300
Reston, VA 20191
Contact: Anuj Khurana Managing Dir
Tel: 703-502-6999
Email: anuj@arksolutionsinc.com
Website: www.arksolutionsinc.com
Staffing & consulting, staffing support, Enterprise IT Solutions, Information Assurance Solutions, Business Process Management & Integration Competency. (Minority, Woman, estab 2003, empl 43, sales , cert: State, NMSDC)

9105 Arthur Grand Technologies Inc.
44355 Premier Plaza, Ste 110
Ashburn, VA 20147
Contact: Jeff Prater Sr VP
Tel: 571-251-9509
Email: contracts@arthurgrand.com
Website: www.arthurgrand.com
Staffing and technology consulting services. (Minority, estab 2012, empl 25, sales $1,750,000, cert: NMSDC)

9106 BEST Employment SoluTions, LLC
110 Coliseum Crossing
Hampton, VA 23666
Contact: Kipland Albright Owner
Tel: 757-589-2675
Email: kalbright@thebestllc.com
Website: www.thebestllc.com
Staffing: Light Industrial, Warehousing, Manufacturing, Admin Clerical, Customer Support, & Transportation positions. (AA, estab 2016, empl 20, sales , cert: State, NMSDC)

9107 Cammas & Associates
5870 Trinity Pkwy Ste 170
Centreville, VA 20120
Contact: Diane Cammas Owner/Mgr
Tel: 703-579-1100
Email: diane.cammas@snelling.com
Website: www.Snelling.com/NoVa
Staffing & recruiting services: Administrative & Support, Information Technology, Accounting & Finance, Human Resources, Engineering, Manufacturing & Production, Construction, Pharmaceutical, Sales & Marketing. (Woman, estab 2008, empl 3, sales , cert: WBENC)

9108 Checks and Balances, Inc.
10550 Linden Lake Plaza Ste 200
Manassas, VA 20109
Contact: Lovey Hammel Owner
Tel: 703-361-2220
Email: aharkins@eeihr.com
Website: www.checksbalancesinc.com
Workforce solutions, Employer of Record, Independent Contractor/1099, Corp-to-Corp (SOW). (Woman, estab 1989, empl 46, sales $13,000,000, cert: State, WBENC)

9109 Cynet Systems Inc.
21000 Atlantic Blvd #700
Sterling, VA 20166
Contact: Arpit Paul VP Strategy & Partnerships
Tel: 571-442-1007
Email: arpitp@cynetsystems.com
Website: www.cynetsystems.com
IT & engineering staffing consulting, direct/full time hiring, contract (temp hiring) or contract to hire services. (Minority, estab 2010, empl 1200, sales $65,000,000, cert: NMSDC)

9110 Gillman Services, Inc.
3300 Tyre Neck Rd Ste E
Portsmouth, VA 23703
Contact: Jeremy Andrews Exec Acct Mgr
Tel: 757-439-0800
Email: jandrews@gillmannservices.com
Website: www.gillmannservices.com
Staffing services. (Woman, estab 2008, empl 300, sales $8,850,000, cert: State)

9111 Hire 1 Staffing
PO Box 34337
Richmond, VA 23234
Contact: Sandra Smith Owner
Tel: 804-223-2110
Email: ssmith@hire1staffing.net
Website: www.hire1staffing.net
Temporary staffing: administrative, clerical, call center/ customer service representatives & light industrial positions. (Woman/AA, estab 2005, empl 1, sales , cert: State)

9112 Key Personnel, Inc.
5540 Falmouth St, Ste 100
Richmond, VA 23230
Contact: Thomas Bowles President
Tel: 804-716-9450
Email: thomasbowles@keypersonnel.net
Website: www.keypersonnel.net
Staffing: temporary, temporary to hire & direct hire employment services. (AA, estab 1998, empl 40, sales $2,000,000, cert: State)

9113 Leading Edge Systems Richmond
3711-A Westerre Pkwy
Richmond, VA 23233
Contact: Adish Jain Mgr
Tel: 804-673-5100
Email: adishj@leadingedgesys.com
Website: www.leadingedgesys.com
Staffing svcs; information tech, clerical support & professional svcs. (Minority, estab 1997, empl 42, sales $4,500,000, cert: State)

9114 McKinley Marketing Partners, Inc.
201 N. Union St Ste 110
Alexandria, VA 22314
Contact: Susie President
Tel: 703-836-4445
Email: clientservices@mckinleyinc.com
Website: www.mckinleymarketingpartners.com/
Staffing: short-term marketing mgrs. (Woman, estab 1995, empl 15, sales $9,395,256, cert: WBENC)

9115 MillenniumSoft, Inc
8301 Arlington Blvd, Ste 504,
Fairfax, VA 22031
Contact: Swathi Billa
Tel: 703-698-9232
Email: time@millenniumsoft.com
Website: www.millenniumsoft.com
Permanent, long term or short term staffing. (Minority, Woman, estab 2000, empl 45, sales $293,466,000, cert: State, NMSDC)

9116 Outcomes Inc.
4215 Lafayette center Dr Ste 6
Chantilly, VA 20151
Contact: Sonali Kakatkar CEO
Tel: 703-996-8833
Email: sonali@out-comes.com
Website: www.out-comes.com
Staffing, recruiting, payroll services & vendor managed services. (Minority, Woman, estab 2002, empl 8, sales $3,000,000, cert: State, WBENC, SDB)

9117 Preferred Staffing Group/Preferred Temporary Services, Inc.
2001 Jefferson Davis Hwy Ste 303
Arlington, VA 22202
Contact: Barbara Posner President
Tel: 703-415-0182
Email: ejackson@ourpsg.com
Website: www.ourpsg.com
Staffing svcs: administrative, telecommunications fiber optic, IT, legal, light construction, housekeeping. (Woman, estab 1987, empl 150, sales , cert: WBENC)

9118 ProTask Inc.
542 Springvale Road
Great Falls, VA 22066
Contact: Jessie Covington Sr Acct Mgr
Tel: 703-231-4275
Email: jcovington@protaskinc.com
Website: www.protaskinc.com/
Staffing solutions, IT contractors, IT consultants, IT Staff Augmentation, Traditional direct hire talent search (full life cycle), Executive recruitment. (Woman, estab 2010, empl 22, sales $3,300,000, cert: State, WBENC)

9119 Pyramind LLC
1069 W Broad St, Ste 781
Falls Church, VA 22046
Contact: Hope Johnson CEO
Tel: 703-241-2996
Email: hope@pyramindsearch.com
Website: www.pyramindsearch.com
Executive search. (Woman, estab 2001, empl 5, sales $400,000, cert: WBENC)

9120 Skill Path Talent, Inc.
8300 Boone Blvd, Ste 500
Vienna, VA 22182
Contact: Sharon Campbell Business Devel Mgr
Tel: 571-358-5602
Email: operatons@skillstalent.com
Website: www.skillstalent.com
Human capital services, temporary & permanent placement. (AA, estab 2013, empl 25, sales , cert: NMSDC)

9121 TeamPeople LLC
180 S Washington St Ste 200
Falls Church, VA 22046
Contact: Kathy Roma Dev Consultant
Tel: 917-751-6088
Email: kroma@teampeople.tv
Website: www.teampeople.tv
Media Staffing & Support Services. (Woman, estab 2004, empl 600, sales $51,714,354, cert: WBENC)

9122 Temporary Solutions, Inc.
      10550 Linden Lake Plaza, Ste 200
      Manassas, VA 20109
      Contact: Lovey Hammel VP Mktg & Contract Svcs
      Tel: 703-361-2220
      Email: lhammel@eeihr.com
      Website: www.eeihr.com
Staffing services: temporary staffing, temp-to-hire staffing,
direct placement, on-site services & single source mgmt
solutions. (Woman, estab 1980, empl 921, sales
$7,245,894, cert: State, WBENC)

Washington

9123 2rbConsulting, Inc.
      19515 North Creek Pkwy Ste 310
      Bothell, WA 98011
      Contact: Betta Beasley CEO
      Tel: 425-406-7644
      Email: betta@2rbconsulting.com
      Website: www.2rbconsulting.com
Provide contract consultants, permanent staff & managed
services at all levels of expertise. (Woman, estab 2007,
empl 25, sales $3,200,000, cert: WBENC)

9124 Aditi Staffing LLC
      2002 156th Ave NE Ste 200
      Bellevue, WA 98004
      Contact: Malcolm Cooper Strategic Relations
      Tel: 425-305-5091
      Email: malcolm@aditistaffing.com
      Website: www.aditistaffing.com
Staff Aug/Contingent Labor/SOW. (As-Ind, estab 2007,
empl 516, sales $38,691,000, cert: NMSDC)

9125 All StarZ Staffing & Consulting, Inc.
      24437 Russell Rd, Ste 200
      Kent, WA 98032
      Contact: Tyler Crass COO
      Tel: 253-277-4000
      Email: inquiries@allstarzstaffing.com
      Website: www.allstarzstaffing.com
Staffing consulting services. (Woman, estab 2011, empl 10,
sales $4,000,000, cert: WBENC)

9126 Allegiance Staffing
      400 Industry Dr, Ste 180
      Tukwila, WA 98188
      Contact: Luis Perez Acct Mgr
      Tel: 253-854-7000
      Email: lperez@allegiancestaffing.com
      Website: www.allegiancestaffing.com
Staffing solutions: temporary, contract employees,
executive search & permanent placement. (Minority, estab
1994, empl 10, sales $6,500,000, cert: State)

9127 Allovus Design, Inc.
      15822 Peacock Hill Ave NW
      Gig Harbor, WA 98332
      Contact: Hayley Nichols Client Services Dir
      Tel: 253-222-0274
      Email: hayley@allovus.com
      Website: www.allovus.com
Staffing services, direct hire, staff augmentation & studios
project teams. (Woman, estab 2009, empl 75, sales
$9,000,000, cert: WBENC)

9128 Archer & Associates I, Inc.
      16625 Redmond Way, Ste M8
      Redmond, WA 98052
      Contact: Ann-Marie Archer CEO
      Tel: 425-869-6350
      Email: aarcher@archer-associates.com
      Website: www.archer-associates.com
Executive search & consulting. (Woman, estab 2000,
empl 2, sales $852,500, cert: State)

9129 Ci2i Services, Inc.
      410 Bellevue Way SE Ste 205
      Bellevue, WA 98004
      Contact: Raul Ramos CEO
      Tel: 425-279-7992
      Email: raul@ci2iservices.com
      Website: www.Ci2iServices.com
IT Consulting & Staffing services: Program & Project
Management, Software development, Business strategy
& Marketing resource needs. (As-Ind, estab 1998, empl
40, sales $3,600,000, cert: State, NMSDC)

9130 MB Diversity
      6523 California Ave SW, Ste B-255
      Seattle, WA 98136
      Contact: Anthony Burnett Owner
      Tel: 206-941-2834
      Email: anthony@mbdiversity.com
      Website: www.MBDiversity.com
Staffing recruiting & managed resources. (AA, estab
2014, empl 10, sales $573,315, cert: State, City, NMSDC)

9131 VanderHouwen & Associates, Inc.
      2018 156th Ave NE Ste 220
      Bellevue, WA 98007
      Contact: Jennifer Boyle Client Specialist
      Tel: 425-453-7300
      Email: jennifer@vanderhouwen.com
      Website: www.vanderhouwen.com
Professional Staffing Services: IT, Engineering, Accounting, and Administrative talent. (Woman, estab 1987,
empl 410, sales , cert: WBENC)

Wisconsin

9132 Division 10 Personnel Services of Milwaukee, Inc.
      4425 N Port Washington Rd, Ste 401
      Milwaukee, WI 53212
      Contact: Wendy Koppel, CPC President
      Tel: 414-963-8700
      Email: wendy@division10personnel.com
      Website: www.division10personnel.com
Recruiting & staffing: Administrative & Professional level
candidates. (Woman, estab 1980, empl 30, sales
$1,563,690, cert: State, WBENC)

9133 Hatch Staffing Services
      700 W Virginia St, Ste 400
      Milwaukee, WI 53204
      Contact: Lucas Harvey Branch Mgr
      Tel: 414-272-4544
      Email: lucas@hatch.com
      Website: www.hatch.com
Staffing services: temp, temp to hire & direct hire
candidates. (Woman, estab 1983, empl 23, sales
$12,269,000, cert: WBENC)

9134   ON-SITE Inc.
      4635 South 108th St
      Milwaukee, WI 53228
      Contact: Crystal Kent President
      Tel: 414-349-8546
      Email: ckent@onsitestaffing.com
      Website: www.onsitestaffing.com
Employee leasing, payrolling, on site mgmt, permanent placement, contract engineering, temporary help. (Minority, Woman, estab 1998, empl 5, sales $531,825, cert: WBENC)

9135   SEEK Careers/Staffing, Inc.
      PO Box 148
      Grafton, WI 53024
      Contact: Debbie Fedel VP Business Dev
      Tel: 262-377-8888
      Email: dfedel@seekcareers.com
      Website: www.seekcareers.com
Staffing services, office/accounting, light industrial & skilled manufacturing positions. (Woman, estab 1971, empl 96, sales $53,824,639, cert: WBENC)

9136   TotalMed Staffing, Inc.
      5517 Waterford Ln
      Appleton, WI 54913
      Contact: Nick Palleria Dir Sales
      Tel: 920-750-7157
      Email: npalleria@totalmed.com
      Website: www.totalmedstaffing.com
Clinical Staffing, Registered Nurses & Allied Health, temporary staffing shortages. (As-Ind, estab , empl , sales $22,000,000, cert: NMSDC)

9137   Victory Personnel Services, Inc.
      735 N Water St Ste 1411
      Milwaukee, WI 53202
      Contact: Mike Farrell VP
      Tel: 414-271-0749
      Email: mfarrell@victoryprofessional.com
      Website: www.victorypersonnel.com
Staffing: temporary, permanent & payroll services. (AA, estab 1991, empl 400, sales $18,510,506, cert: NMSDC)

PROFESSIONAL SERVICES: Technical
Provide consulting services on a variety of technically oriented topics: technical writing and editing, information systems, record management, educational research, scientific research, program evaluation, nuclear energy consulting, technical manuals. NAICS Code 54

Connecticut

9138 Access Consulting
31 Island Heights Circle
Stamford, CT 06902
Contact: Arun Sinha President
Tel: 203-975-2950
Email: contact@accessc.com
Website: www.accessc.com/
Corporate communications, marketing communications & technical writing services. (As-Ind, estab 2003, empl 2, sales , cert: NMSDC)

Florida

9139 The Med Writers LLC
9314 Forest Hill Blvd, Ste 6
Wellington, FL 33411
Contact: Karen Vieira President
Tel: 561-247-2190
Email: karen@themedwriters.com
Website: www.themedwriters.com
Medical & scientific writing, offsite writing services. (Woman/AA, estab 2007, empl 8, sales , cert: CPUC)

9140 The Solers Reseach Group
1445 Dolgner Place #10
Sanford, FL 32771
Contact: Thomas Wilson Sr Strategy Mgr
Tel: 407-873-1456
Email: twilson@solersrg.com
Website: www.solersrg.com
Cyber awareness interventions, mobile & game-based learning; digital propensity, learning & literacy; examine learning & evidence-based practice in gifted, special education & assistive technology. (Woman, estab 2008, empl 15, sales $1,500,000, cert: 8(a))

Georgia

9141 A-Z Sophisticated Solutions
12850 Hwy 9 N, Ste 600-205
Alpharetta, GA 30004
Contact: Ana Maria Marin Managing Dir
Tel: 404-996-1358
Email: ap@a-zssolutions.com
Website: www.a-zssolutions.com
Engineering, Technical Writing, Technical Instruction & written Translation services. Technical Writing: brochures, user manuals, creation, proofread & editorial. Technical Instruction: plastics seminars & CAE plastics. (Minority, Woman, estab 2010, empl 1, sales , cert: WBENC)

9142 Continental Technical Services
260 Peachtree St, Ste 2200
Atlanta, GA 30303
Contact: Willie Dunlap CEO
Tel: 404-527-6297
Email: henri@ctsnationally.com
Website: www.ctsnationally.com
Staff augmentation, temporary personnel, technical publications, integrated logistics support, validations & verifications, ECPs, technical writing, quality assurance & control, quality inspection. (AA, estab 1992, empl 54, sales $7,400,000, cert: NMSDC)

9143 Eubio, LLC
PO Box 16555
Atlanta, GA 30321
Contact: Alita Anderson Principal
Tel: 404-632-2435
Email: alita@eubiomed.com
Website: www.eubiomed.com
Medical communications, medical writing. (Woman/AA, estab 2012, empl 2, sales $885,503, cert: City, NMSDC, WBENC)

Indiana

9144 Techcom, Inc.
PO Box 39206
Indianapolis, IN 46239
Contact: Ilene Adams President
Tel: 317-865-2530
Email: inadams@techcom.com
Website: www.techcom.com
Technical publications producer including: engineering, research, writing, data management, photography, illustration, CAD drawing, video production, animation, interactive multimedia creation. (Woman, estab 1976, empl 38, sales , cert: WBENC)

Michigan

9145 Good Fortune Trading Co. dba GFT Services
3959 Nash Dr
Troy, MI 48083
Contact: Janice Girling President
Tel: 248-884-4635
Email: janice.girling@gftservices.com
Website: www.gftservices.com
Procurement services, project planning, technical writing. (Woman, estab 2016, empl 1, sales , cert: WBENC)

Minnesota

9146 Shepherd Data Services, Inc.
527 Marquette Ave 400 Rand Tower
Minneapolis, MN 55402
Contact: Dennis Waldrop VP
Tel: 612-659-1234
Email: cchalstrom@shepherddata.com
Website: www.shepherddata.com
Data collection for litigation. (Woman, estab 2002, empl 12, sales $2,283,392, cert: WBENC)

North Carolina

9147 Hurley Write Inc
      21835 Advocates Ct
      Cornelius, NC 28031
      Contact: pamela hurley President
      Tel: 910-233-7670
      Email: info@hurleywrite.com
      Website: www.hurleywrite.com
Develop and teach customized onsite technical, business,
and scientific writing courses, online writing courses,
webinars and series. (Woman, estab 2000, empl 1, sales
$388,000, cert: WBENC)

9148 Whitsell Innovations Inc.
      18 Kendall Dr
      Chapel Hill, NC 27517
      Contact: Robin Whitsell President
      Tel: 919-321-9017
      Email: robin.whitsell@whitsellinnovations.com
      Website: www.whitsellinnovations.com
Medical, scientific & technical writing, GCP, GMP & GLP,
clinical regulatory writing, clinical study reports, protocols,
investigator brochures, narratives & full submissions of
investigational new drug, applications & new drug applications. (Woman, estab 2006, empl 32, sales $5,262,000,
cert: WBENC)

Pennsylvania

9149 FMD K&L Inc.
      1300 Virginia Dr Ste 408
      Fort Washington, PA 19034
      Contact: Xin Ke President
      Tel: 215-283-6035
      Email: xin.ke@klserv.com
      Website: www.klserv.com
Data Management, Biostatistics, Statistical Programming,
Medical Writing. (As-Pac, estab 1995, empl 200, sales
$27,000,000, cert: NMSDC)

9150 KB COMM LLC
      985 State Rd
      West Grove, PA 19390
      Contact: Kathy Breuninger Owner
      Tel: 610-357-8625
      Email: kathy@kbcommllc.com
      Website: www.kbcommllc.com
Scientific & technical writing services, business & marketing communications; instructions & procedures; installation, operation & maintenance manuals; computer
documentation; training materials & document templates.
(Woman, estab 2006, empl 8, sales $610,154, cert:
WBENC)

9151 Provider Resources Inc.
      153 E 13th St Ste 1400
      Erie, PA 16503
      Contact: Nadine Manzi Program Mgr
      Tel: 814-480-8732
      Email: nmanzi@provider-resources.com
      Website: www.provider-resources.com
Policy and Regulatory, Healthcare Quality & Disparities,
Program Integrity, and Education. (Woman, estab 2003,
empl 130, sales $13,400,000, cert: NWBOC)

Texas

9152 A. Miller Consulting Services, Inc.
      4425 Plano Pkwy, Ste 803
      Carrollton, TX 75010
      Contact: Carie Joyce Team Lead
      Tel: 972-580-0812
      Email: cjoyce@mcs.biz
      Website: www.mcs.biz
Technical documentation: technical writing, project
mgmt, technical illustration & graphics creation, web
design, web-based training dev, manual dev & consolidation, proposal writing & consulting, process dev &
documentation, engineering guides. (Woman, estab
2000, empl 13, sales $2,449,127, cert: WBENC)

9153 Integrity International, Inc.
      11767 Katy Frwy, Ste 750
      Houston, TX 77079
      Contact: Susan Lake Project Mgr
      Tel: 877-955-0707
      Email: info@tarrenpoint.com
      Website: www.tarrenpoint.com
Documentation consulting services, project management, content development (technical documentation),
graphic design, technical illustration, desktop publishing,
editing & quality assurance, indexing, localization &
translation. (Woman, estab 1994, empl 63, sales
$6,000,000, cert: State, WBENC)

9154 QA Consulting Inc.
      7500 Rialto Blvd Bldg 1, Ste 225
      Austin, TX 78735
      Contact: Amber Hilfiger Dir of Operations
      Tel: 512-328-9404
      Email: info@qaconsultinginc.com
      Website: www.qaconsultinginc.com
Quality, Microbiology, Regulatory & Auditing consulting
services, QMS development, design, risk management,
biocompatibility, verification and validation. (Woman,
estab 2000, empl 6, sales $1,294,768, cert: State,
WBENC)

9155 TECHNIKOS Information Development, LLC
      PO Box 2693
      Stafford, TX 77497
      Contact: Ora Gibson CEO
      Tel: 281-568-7955
      Email: ora@technicallyclear.com
      Website: www.technicallyclear.com
Technical writing, editing, formatting, reviewing,
proofreading, documentation, manuals, guides, web
content, user guides, operations manuals, procedure
manuals, processes, procedures, training guides.
(Woman/AA, estab 2007, empl 2, sales , cert: State,
NMSDC)

Virginia

9156 AccuWrit Inc.
      118 Primrose Dr
      Blacksburg, VA 24060
      Contact: Eileen Y. Ivasauskas President
      Tel: 540-961-1611
      Email: eileen@accuwrit.com
      Website: www.accuwrit.com
Editorial consulting — Editorial specialist in medical,
scientific, and technical information and communication
materials. Custom writing services and editorial support
for the preparation of manuscripts, monographs,
abstracts, critiques. (Woman, estab 1984, empl 1, sales ,
cert: State)

RECORDING & VIDEO PRODUCTION
Produce videos (in studio or remote), TV shows, records, sound recordings, pre and post production services, talent arrangers, video distribution. NAICS Code 51

Arizona

9157   Blade Inc
3033 N Central Ave Ste 440
Phoenix, AZ 85012
Contact: Louise Parker President
Tel: 602-307-5577
Email: louise@bladeinc.com
Website: www.bladeinc.com
Production, Editing, Video Production, Video Editing, Post Production, 3D Animation, Animation, Motion Graphics, VFX, Visual Effects, Visual Design, Motion Design, Illustration. TV Commercials, Web, Training, Corporate. (Woman, estab 2002, empl 65, sales , cert: WBENC)

California

9158   Aahs Entertainment, Inc.
10707 Camarillo St, Ste 312
Toluca Lake, CA 91602
Contact: Gwenn Smith President
Tel: 818-279-2416
Email: gwenn@aahsentertainment.com
Website: www.aahsentertainment.com
Video Production Services, Media Production, Media Services, Advertising, Marketing, Content Creation, Branded Content, Brand Marketing, DVD Extras, DVD Special Features, Marketing, Advertising, EPKs. (Woman/ AA, estab 2011, empl 1, sales , cert: WBENC)

9159   Agnew Multilingual
2625 Townsgate Road Ste 330
Westlake Village, CA 91361
Contact: Irene Agnew President
Tel: 805-494-3999
Email: i.agnew@agnew.com
Website: www.agnew.com
Translation, interpretation & audiovisual production. (Woman, estab 1986, empl 9, sales $800,000, cert: CPUC, WBENC, SDB)

9160   Backhand Productions, Inc.
12400 Wilshire Blvd, Ste 1275
Los Angeles, CA 90025
Contact: Jeff Atlas President
Tel: 626-351-4390
Email: BackhandProductionsInc@cmcregistrations.com
Website: www.backhandproductions.com
Full service production company with an experienced staff of industry pros. Our team has executed dozens of successful TV shows and special projects and have overcome almost every type of production challenge imaginable. (AA, estab 2000, empl 1, sales $335,109, cert: NMSDC)

9161   CF Entertainment, Inc.
1925 Century Park E Ste 1000
Los Angeles, CA 90067
Contact: Darren Galatt
Tel: 310-277-3500
Email: darren@es.tv
Website: www.es.tv
Media & advertising, produce, distribute & sell commercials in 25+ first-run programs for TV stations & high definition cable networks. (AA, estab 1993, empl 75, sales $44,987,627, cert: NMSDC)

9162   Fire Starter Studios, LLC
28348 Constellation Rd Ste 820
Santa Clarita, CA 91355
Contact: Rachel Klein CEO
Tel: 747-201-7400
Email: bids@firestarterstudios.com
Website: www.firestarterstudios.com
Media, animation, live-action and VR/AR. (Woman, estab 2012, empl 5, sales , cert: WBENC)

9163   Hybrid Edit, LLC
5782 W. Jefferson blvd.
Los Angeles, CA 90016
Contact: Susan Munro President
Tel: 310-586-9799
Email: diversity@hybridcollective.tv
Website: www.hybridcollective.tv
Commercial, television & motion picture post production & production services: creative editorial offline, online/compositing, color correction, graphic design, motion graphic design, sound design & mixing. (Woman, estab 2009, empl 8, sales $1,400,000, cert: WBENC)

9164   International Communication Network
901 Lane Ave, Ste 200
Chula Vista, CA 91914
Contact: Michelle Diaz COO
Tel: 619-421-0426
Email: mdiaz@inctv50.com
Website: www.Inctv50.com
Television broadcasting, video production, marketing, Hispanic market. (AA, estab 1997, empl 5, sales , cert: NMSDC)

9165   Kaboom Productions
2169 Folsom St Ste 201M
San Francisco, CA 94110
Contact: Denise Militzer Exec Producer
Tel: 415-434-2666
Email: denise@jzuntosmedia.com
Website: www.kaboomproductions.com
TV commercials, corporate videos, branded content, TV shows, feature films. (Woman, estab 1997, empl 3, sales $3,051,256, cert: WBENC)

9166   Showreel International Inc.
639 S. Glenwood Place, Ste. 200
Burbank, CA 90038
Contact: Jessica Ristic CEO
Tel: 323-464-5111
Email: jessica@weareshotglass.com
Website: www.weareshotglass.com
Film & video production. (Woman, estab 1985, empl 7, sales , cert: State)

9167   The Traveling Picture Show Company
1531 N. Cahuenga Blvd
Los Angeles, CA 90028
Contact: Partner
Tel: 323-769-1115
Email: info@thetpsc.com
Website: www.thetpsc.com
Commercial video production services, television commercials, online branded content &visual media. (Woman, estab 2011, empl 9, sales $5,500,000, cert: WBENC)

9168   Total Media Group
432 N Canal St
South San Francisco, CA 94080
Contact: Megan McKenna Acct Exec
Tel: 650-583-8236
Email: megan@totalmediagroup.com
Website: www.totalmediagroup.com
Video production, motion graphics, 3D animation, editorial, event production, web design & mobile apps. (Woman, estab 1971, empl 10, sales $4,900,000, cert: WBENC)

Colorado

9169   PayReel, Inc.
211 Violet St Unit 100
Golden, CO 80401
Contact: Heidi McLean President
Tel: 303-526-4900
Email: heidi@payreel.com
Website: www.payreel.com
Provides outsourcing services for corporate video and media production departments. (Woman, estab 1995, empl 7, sales $15,914,000, cert: WBENC)

Connecticut

9170   Anderson Productions Inc.
71 Dolphin Rd
Bristol, CT 06010
Contact: Tom Stanwicks Sales/Mktg
Tel: 503-287-3004
Email: tstanwicks@anderson3.com
Website: www.andersonprod.com
Video production, post production, graphics, animations, sound design, audio editing, product models, digital signage. (Woman, estab 1994, empl 24, sales $4,500,000, cert: WBENC)

9171   Creative Video Corporation
9 Mott Ave, Ste 108
Norwalk, CT 06850
Contact: Francisca Bogdan Production Specialist
Tel: 203-866-8700
Email: francisca.bogdan@creativevideocorp.com
Website: www.creativevideocorp.com
Corporate communication videos & multi-media products, internal communications, sales & markeitng, event opening video, promotional video, event coverage. (Minority, Woman, estab 1997, empl 4, sales $380,000, cert: NMSDC)

Delaware

9172   DelVideo Productions
583 Barley Court
Smyrna, DE 19977
Contact: Milton Melendez VP
Tel: 302-223-4049
Email: info@delvideo.com
Website: www.delvideo.com
Bilingual video production, Pre-Production, Pre-Planning & vision writing, Location & set assessment, Research, Script writing, Talent arrangement, Recording Services, Video recording, Audio capture & recording, Project management, Directing. (Woman/AA, Hisp, estab 2013, empl 2, sales , cert: State, 8(a))

Florida

9173   Campbell Advertising and Design, LLC
103 NE 4th St
Delray Beach, FL 33444
Contact: Lucia Alvarez Principal
Tel: 561-562-6119
Email: info@campbellcreative.com
Website: www.campbellcreative.com
Photography, art direction, web videos, social content, broadcast commercials, testimonial videos, training videos, animated videos. (Woman/Hisp, estab 2010, empl 6, sales $1,600,000, cert: WBENC)

9174   Coda Sound Inc.
4819 N Hale Ave
Tampa, FL 33614
Contact: Maritza Astorquiza Owner
Tel: 813-353-8151
Email: maritza@codasoundusa.com
Website: www.codasoundusa.com
Event production: sound, lights, stages & audio visual. (Minority, Woman, estab 1998, empl 2, sales $471,000, cert: State, City, NMSDC)

9175   Graphix 360, LLC
7777 N Wickham Rd Ste 12710
Melbourne, FL 32940
Contact: Bobbi Gerardot CEO
Tel: 321-693-9293
Email: bobbi@graphix360.com
Website: www.Graphix360.com
Multimedia design, photo, video, graphic/web design & printing services, multimedia equipment. (Woman, estab 2013, empl 4, sales , cert: City)

9176   Kreative Kontent Co.
3019 Ravenswood Road Ste 110
Fort Lauderdale, FL 33312
Contact: Debbie Margolis-Horwitz Exec Producer
Tel: 954-312-3660
Email: debbie@kreativekontent.com
Website: www.kreativekontent.com
Production specializing in content creation, broadcast, web based, theatrical & marketing fulfillment programs, broadcast commercials, corporate video communications, product placement, branded content, promotional products. (Woman, estab 2010, empl 4, sales $2,000,000, cert: State, WBENC)

Georgia

9177 A-1 Audio Visual, LLC
863 Flat Shoals Rd SE Ste C359
Conyers, GA 30094
Contact: Keith McNeil CEO
Tel: 800-805-7210
Email: kmcneil@a1audiovisual.com
Website: www.a1audiovisual.com
Audio visual, video & lighting. (AA, estab 2003, empl 6, sales $190,000, cert: State, NMSDC)

9178 One Production Place
1945 Colland Dr, NW
Atlanta, GA 30318
Contact: Elisa Gambino President
Tel: 404-452-3500
Email: elisa@oneproductionplace.com
Website: www.oneproductionplace.com
Multi media video production & communications: shooting, lighting, editing, color grading, writing & scoring music. (Woman, estab 2002, empl 2, sales $300,000, cert: WBENC)

9179 Onyx Media Services, Inc.
57 Forsyth St NW Ste 250-G
Atlanta, GA 30303
Contact: Jennifer Rocke VP Finance
Tel: 404-420-0030
Email: info@onyxmsgroup.com
Website: www.onyxmsgroup.com
Production services: audio visual, facility, technical production design, presentation video, graphic design, sound reinforcement, theatrical lighting. (AA, estab 2006, empl 15, sales , cert: NMSDC)

9180 Popoff Enterprises Inc.
3035 Wallace Circle SE
Atlanta, GA 30339
Contact: Dana Popoff President
Tel: 404-307-1979
Email: popoffdana@gmail.com
Website: www.popoffenterprises.com
Video production & still photography services, commercial distribution, web sites, point of purchase, social media, internal corporate communications - training, company meetings & conferences, President's address, legacy knowledge, etc. (Woman, estab 1997, empl 1, sales $138,750, cert: WBENC)

9181 Works of Bawbee Films
704 Brambling Way
Stockbridge, GA 30281
Contact: Brian Ezeike Video Producer
Tel: 478-390-7375
Email: info@wobfilms.com
Website: www.wobfilms.com
Video production/digital content creation, write, shoot & edit a wide variety of video content. (AA, estab 2010, empl 1, sales , cert: NMSDC)

Illinois

9182 Hootenanny LLC
230 E Ohio St Ste 700
Chicago, IL 60611
Contact: Elizabeth Tate President
Tel: 312-266-0777
Email: liz@hootenanny.tv
Website: www.hootenanny.tv
Post-production, creative editorial, finishing, graphic design & visual effects, television, print, web, corporate video & interactive media. (Woman, estab 2008, empl 11, sales $2,100,000, cert: State, WBENC)

Indiana

9183 Multitek Corporate Communications
6531 Greencove Ave
Evansville, IN 47715
Contact: Earl Milligan President
Tel: 812-760-7488
Email: earl.milligan@gmail.com
Website: www.multitekcorporate.com
Corporate safety & training video production services, construction archival videos, 3 d survey mapping, drone aerial photography & videography. (AA, estab 1984, empl 1, sales , cert: State)

Massachusetts

9184 Real Cool Productions, Inc. dba RCP Learning
800 S Main St, Ste 203
Mansfield, MA 02048
Contact: President
Tel: 508-878-8907
Email: info@rcplearning.com
Website: www.rcplearning.com
Integrated communications, technology & production services, internal & external facing content (mixed media, animations and videos), corporate overviews, business documentaries, executive interviews & announcements, testimonials, product videos, training (Woman, estab 2010, empl 10, sales $1,100,000, cert: WBENC)

Michigan

9185 Freshwater Film, Inc.
3061 Myddleton Court
Troy, MI 48084
Contact: Sue Witham CEO
Tel: 248-840-5400
Email: sue@mediumfilm.com
Website: www.mediumfilm.com
Film & digital production, influential storytelling, relevant creative content & serious production expertise. (Woman, estab 1991, empl 1, sales $656,756, cert: WBENC)

9186 Seventy 7 Productions
620 Cherry Ave
Royal Oak, MI 48073
Contact: Nora Urbanski Producer
Tel: 313-610-0109
Email: nora@seventy7productions.com
Website: www.seventy7productions.com
Full service video production, post production & creative services for broadcast commercials, social media videos, 360 and VR videos, etc. (Hisp, estab 2011, empl 5, sales , cert: NMSDC)

9187   ShawneTV Inc
29558 English Way
Novi, MI 48377
Contact: CEO
Tel: 248-444-7573
Email: info@shawnetv.com
Website: www.shawnetv.com
Promotional & sponsorships, media & networking training, TV production. (Woman, estab 1999, empl 2, sales $150,000, cert: WBENC)

9188   VideoWorks Production Services, Inc.
4851 Fernlee Ste 100
Royal Oak, MI 48073
Contact: Ruben Rodriguez President
Tel: 248-563-0371
Email: ruben@videoworksonline.com
Website: www.videoworksonline.com
Video production: instructional & training videos, corporate, communications, news-style event coverage, multi-camera events & live media tours. (Hisp, estab 1995, empl 2, sales $150,000, cert: NMSDC)

Minnesota

9189   Orange Filmworks Inc.
3912 Harriet Ave
Minneapolis, MN 55409
Contact: Marco Baca Owner
Tel: 612-868-7875
Email: marco@orangefilmworks.com
Website: www.orangefilmworks.com
Broadcast television commercials, videos or commercials for web, long format instructional video, internal & in-store content. (Hisp, estab 2005, empl 1, sales $674,623, cert: NMSDC).

9190   Peterson Productions LLC
1501 Spring Valley Rd
Golden Valley, MN 55422
Contact: Janie Peterson President
Tel: 763-521-4746
Email: janie@petersonproductionslive.com
Website: www.PetersonProductionsLive.com
Video production house for corporate communications. (Woman, estab 2007, empl 2, sales $195,000, cert: State)

9191   Slang Productions, LLC
3207 E 51st St
Minneapolis, MN 55417
Contact: Sue Lang Principal
Tel: 612-310-4622
Email: sue@slangproductions.net
Website: www.slangproductions.net
Production: live events, video, audio & interactive media. (Woman, estab 2003, empl 2, sales $200,560, cert: WBENC)

Missouri

9192   CAC REPS, LLC
5965 Jamison Ave
St. Louis, MO 63109
Contact: Charlene Colombini Owner
Tel: 314-752-0994
Email: charlenecolo@hotmail.com
Website: www.cacreps.com
Design, illustration, photography, computer imaging, computer 3D Rendering, video production & post, videography & on set styling. (Woman, estab 2008, empl 1, sales , cert: State, CPUC)

9193   Haller Concepts, Inc.
4501 Mattis Rd
St. Louis, MO 63128
Contact: Mike Haller President
Tel: 314-913-5626
Email: mikeh@hallerconcepts.com
Website: www.hallerconcepts.com
Corporate, event, training, web & TV video production filming. (Woman, estab 1982, empl 2, sales $174,400, cert: State)

New Jersey

9194   Harlan Media LLC
494 Broad St, Ste 104
Newark, NJ 07102
Contact: Harlan Brandon CEO
Tel: 973-623-6200
Email: hb@harlanmedia.com
Website: www.harlanmedia.com
Film & Video Production, Marketing, Advertising, Public Relations, Graphic Design, Independent Artist and Writers, Direct Mail Advertising, Commercial Photography (AA, estab 2008, empl 8, sales , cert: NMSDC)

9195   KVibe Productions, LLC
591 Summit Ave Ste 101
Jersey City, NJ 07306
Contact: Khoa Le CEO
Tel: 201-936-8033
Email: khoa.le@kvibe.com
Website: www.kvibe.com
Video production, product video, corporate video, commercial production, feature films. (As-Pac, estab 2005, empl 2, sales , cert: State)

9196   Modat Productions
29 Windermere Rd
Montclair, NJ 07043
Contact: Shana Scott Founder & Content Creator
Tel: 201-763-6666
Email: shana@mOdatVideo.com
Website: www.mOdatVideo.com
Full service video production, digital and broadcast content for television, businesses, social media and the government with end to end production. (Woman, estab 2010, empl 2, sales $150,000, cert: State, WBENC)

New York

9197   Adrienne Nicole Productions, LLC
14 Dekalb Ave 3rd Fl
Brooklyn, NY 11201
Contact: Adrienne Nicole Exec Producer
Tel: - -
Email: info@producedbyanp.com
Website: www.producedbyanp.com
Videography, aerial video, drone video photography, drone photography, progress photos, story development, pre-production, post-production, motion graphics and animation, casting, photography, progress photos. (Woman/AA, estab 2011, empl 1, sales $986,000, cert: State, City, NMSDC)

9198 Amber Heavenly USA, Ltd.
      250 Lafayette St 4th Fl
      New York, NY 10012
      Contact: Michelle Curran President
      Tel: 212-352-1888
      Email: michelle@ambermusic.com
      Website: www.ambermusic.com
Commercial music production, composition, music
licensing & publishing. (Woman, estab 1997, empl 7, sales
$1,400,000, cert: State, WBENC)

9199 Bardin Palomo Ltd.
      432 W 19th St Ste 3
      New York, NY 10011
      Contact: Robert Palomo President
      Tel: 212-989-6113
      Email: rrpalomo@bardinpalomo.com
      Website: www.bardinpalomo.com
Special Events design and production company specializing
in floral design, lighting design, stage design, prop and
furniture rental. We sdesign and supply all visuals for any
type of event. (Hisp, estab 1992, empl 5, sales $3,200,000,
cert: NMSDC)

9200 Be Real Company
      114 W 26th St, Fl 8
      New York, NY 10001
      Contact: CEO
      Tel: 551-574-7006
      Email: ola@berealcompany.com
      Website: www.berealcompany.com
Integrated creative & production services: Live Action
Shoots: commercials, documentaries, social videos,
branded content Post-Production: editing, CGI, color
correction, animation, music composing and mix,
websites. (Woman, estab 2017, empl 5, sales $100,000,
cert: WBENC)

9201 Cutter Productions
      236 W 27th St Ste 1001
      New York, NY 10001
      Contact: Hillary Cutter Exec Producer
      Tel: 646-588-1133
      Email: hillary@cutterproductions.com
      Website: www.cutterproductions.com
Full-service production. (Woman, estab 2005, empl 4, sales
, cert: WBENC)

9202 Loftin Productions
      104 Belmont Pkwy
      Hempstead, NY 11550
      Contact: Dushka Petkovich Co-Owner
      Tel: 917-825-5412
      Email: vze26rdi@verizon.net
      Website: www.loftinpro.com/
Produce product demonstration & employee training
videos. (Woman/AA, estab 1991, empl 2, sales , cert:
State)

9203 Media2, Inc. dba M2
      72 Madison Ave, Fl 2
      New York, NY 10016
      Contact: Cathy Humphrey Producer
      Tel: 212-213-4004
      Email: cathy@m2nyc.tv
      Website: www.m2nyc.tv
Creative offline editorial, 2D/3D design & animation,
television & live event production, install digital & high
definition production studios, monitors, cameras &
lighting. (AA, Hisp, estab 1997, empl 10, sales
$25,000,000, cert: NMSDC)

9204 Resilient Media
      10 E 39th St, 4th Fl
      New York, NY 10016
      Contact: Emilio Mahomar CEO
      Tel: 646-580-9391
      Email: emilio@resilient.tv
      Website: www.resilient.tv
Production, post production, duplication & language
localization (translation, closed captions, subtitles,
language dubbing). (Hisp, estab 2010, empl 2, sales
$200,000, cert: NMSDC)

9205 The Studio
      80- 8th Ave Ste 307
      New York, NY 10011
      Contact: Mary Nittolo Founder / CCO
      Tel: 212-661-1363
      Email: mary@studionyc.com
      Website: www.studionyc.com
Art & animation studio, 3d/2d animation, motion
capture, animatics, pre-vis, storyboards, presentation
art, digital art, comps & character design. (Woman,
estab 1988, empl 30, sales $3,500,000, cert: WBENC)

9206 TimeLine Video
      One Bridge St
      Irvington, NY 10533
      Contact: Timothy Englert VP Dev
      Tel: 914-591-7360
      Email: tim@timelinevideo.com
      Website: www.timelinevideo.com
Video, production & post-production, graphic design.
(Woman, estab 1994, empl 7, sales $1,700,000, cert:
WBENC)

9207 Transcendent Enterprise
      37 W 26th St, Ste 408
      New York, NY 10010
      Contact: Chris Alvarez Founder & CEO
      Tel: 718-304-6384
      Email: chris@t-enter.com
      Website: www.transcendententerprise.com
Video production, live stream services, post production,
editing & filming, photography. (Hisp, estab 2004, empl
4, sales $230,000, cert: City, NMSDC)

9208   United Sources of America, Inc.
253 West 35th St 2nd Fl
New York, NY 10001
Contact: Kenny Khan CEO
Tel: 212-398-6400
Email: kkhan@usastudios.tv
Website: www.usastudios.tv
Post-production facilities, motion picture or video, TV commercial spot distribution to station services, edit, direct response prep, closed caption, legalize, encode for broadcast verification, format spot for each station and network specs, final qualit (As-Ind, estab 1988, empl 27, sales $2,528,241, cert: NMSDC)

9209   VMIX, LLC.
163 William St, 3 Fl
New York, NY 10038
Contact: Wening Cintron relationship Mgr
Tel: 800-436-8618
Email: wening@vmix.tv
Website: www.vmix.tv
Digital media, audio/visual (A/V) content, music, television & urban entertainment. (AA, estab 2004, empl 2, sales , cert: State)

9210   Wild Child Editorial, Inc.
44 West 28th St
New York, NY 10001
Contact: Scott Spanjich Managing Dir
Tel: 212-725-5333
Email: scott@wildchildpost.com
Website: www.wildchildpost.com
TV commercials, music videos, feature films & emerging media. (Minority, Woman, estab , empl , sales $4,500,000, cert: WBENC)

Ohio

9211   MMG Corporate Communication, Inc.
515 W Loveland Ave
Loveland, OH 45140
Contact: President
Tel: 513-677-8787
Email: info@mmgonline.com
Website: www.mmgonline.com
Multi-media production: in-studio & field video production, multiple non-linear digital post production, CD & DVD-ROM programming, 2D & 3D animation, web site dev, duplication svcs, public relations, marketing & broadcast. (Woman, estab 1993, empl 7, sales $804,000, cert: WBENC)

9212   New Vision Media Inc.
6804 Caine Rd
Columbus, OH 43235
Contact: Jerrud Smith Co-Owner
Tel: - -
Email: jsmith@newvisionmediainc.com
Website: www.newvisionmediainc.com
Video production services including aerial drone cinematography. (AA, estab 2000, empl 3, sales $350,000, cert: NMSDC)

Pennsylvania

9213   Crossover Ent. LLC
728 Copeland St
Pittsburgh, PA 15232
Contact: Freya Saxon Producer
Tel: 651-347-3831
Email: fs@deepcea.com
Website: www.deepcea.com
Script to screen production, Corporate Videos, Training Videos, Commercials, Film & Documentaries. (AA, estab 2014, empl 14, sales , cert: State)

9214   Karasch & Associates
1646 W Chester Pike Ste 4
West Chester, PA 19382
Contact: Edward Sarkissian Sales Mgr
Tel: 800-621-5689
Email: esarkissian@karasch.com
Website: www.karasch.com
Video production, duplications & captioning services. (Woman, estab 1980, empl 25, sales $4,000,000, cert: State, WBENC)

9215   Panta Rhei Media, Inc.
565 Beulah Rd
Turtle Creek, PA 15145
Contact: Martha O'Grady President
Tel: 412-824-8858
Email: info@panta-rhei.com
Website: www.panta-rhei.com
Video production with a specialty in health care, product demonstration and promotion, web testimonials, employee communications and streaming live events, consultation, concepts, script writing, location and studio video. (Woman, estab 1984, empl , sales , cert: WBENC)

South Carolina

9216   Mad Monkey, Inc.
1631 Main St
Columbia, SC 29201
Contact: Lorie Gardner CEO
Tel: 803-252-2211
Email: lorie@gomadmonkey.com
Website: www.gomadmonkey.com
Creates video stories for television, laptops, mobile devices & social platforms. (Woman, estab 2000, empl 15, sales $1,650,351, cert: State, WBENC)

Texas

9217   1820 Productions, LLC
6301 N Riverside Dr Bldg One, Ste 2C
Irving, TX 75039
Contact: Sara Madsen Miller COO
Tel: 972-869-7777
Email: sara@1820productions.com
Website: www.1820productions.com
Television & film production, creative concept development, producing, directing, editing, graphics and animation, marketing, script writing, industrial or marketing videos from script to screen. (AA, estab 2001, empl 5, sales $1,012,000, cert: State, NMSDC)

9218 Abernethy Media Professionals, Inc.
10763 Sanden Dr
Dallas, TX 75355
Contact: Sandy Mason Abernethy President
Tel: 214-632-4518
Email: mason@ampcreative.com
Website: www.ampcreative.com
Video production services. (Woman, estab 2002, empl 25, sales $4,021,000, cert: State, WBENC)

9219 Cactex Media
2231 Valdina St, Unit 100
Dallas, TX 75207
Contact: Claire Brooks Head of Business Devel
Tel: 214-346-3456
Email: claire@cactexmedia.com
Website: www.cactexmedia.com
Video & Interactive production, video production, B2B videos, Web video, Webcast/live stream, Sales tools, Explainer videos, Training videos, Executive interviews, Customer testimonials, Case studies. (Woman, estab 2006, empl 14, sales $4,000,000, cert: State, WBENC)

9220 CM Productions, Inc.
4228 North Central Expressway Ste 340
Dallas, TX 75206
Contact: Carrie Martinez President
Tel: 214-528-2700
Email: carrie@cmproductions.tv
Website: www.cmproductions.tv
Video production, employee & marketing communications, documentaries, commercials, scriptwriting, stunning photography & sharp editing, still photography. (Woman, estab , empl , sales $194,628, cert: WBENC)

9221 Julye Newlin Productions, Inc.
129 E 13th St
Houston, TX 77008
Contact: Julye Newlin Owner
Tel: 713-869-3609
Email: julye@julyenewlin.com
Website: www.julyenewlin.com
Video, film & photography services: digital video, digital editing, web, broadcast, print advertising, CD business cards, DVD presentations, etc. (Woman, estab 1993, empl 3, sales , cert: City, WBENC)

9222 Small Pond Video Productions, Inc.
2217 Clarebrooke Dr.
Grand Prairie, TX 75050
Contact: Silvana Rosero President
Tel: 214-686-1092
Email: silvana@lagunamg.com
Website: www.lagunamg.com
Video production & meeting support, marketing, motivational, product introductions, testimonials, training videos & broadcast commercials. (Minority, Woman, estab , empl , sales $178,412, cert: State, NMSDC, WBENC)

9223 Sue Abrams Productions, LLC
2709 Prestonwood Dr
Plano, TX 75093
Contact: Sue Abrams Owner
Tel: 972-418-2034
Email: sue@saproductions.net
Website: www.saproductions.net
Video production: sales pieces, public education videos, corporate overviews, recruiting videos, commercials, training pieces, product launches, event videos & video news releases. (Woman, estab 1999, empl 1, sales $152,620, cert: WBENC)

9224 ZapBoomBang Studios, LLC
3336 Richmond Ave
Houston, TX 77098
Contact: Catherine Lopez Negrete
Tel: 713-877-8777
Email: cathy@zapboombang.com
Website: www.zapboombang.com
Audio, Video Post Production Services (Woman, estab 0, empl , sales , cert: WBENC)

Washington

9225 Native Ways LLC - Apachewolf Productions
15313 NE 13th Place
Bellevue, WA 98008
Contact: Freddie Begay CEO
Tel: 360-930-9615
Email: chipbegay@gmail.com
Website: www.apachewolf.com
Video productions, video shooting & editing services, develop & create television & radio commercials, video streaming, DVD & CD duplication, Radio/TV broadcast development & marketing. (Minority, estab 2015, empl 1, sales , cert: State, SDB)

TELECOMMUNICATIONS
Manufacture and distribute telecommunications systems and products: CATV, telephones, intercoms, test and control equipment, etc. Includes firms which provide cellular and internet services, phone line installation, service and consulting. NAICS Code 51

Alabama

9226 Palco Telecom Service Inc.
      2914 Green Cove Rd
      Huntsville, AL 35803
      Contact: Phil Terry Vice President
      Tel: 256-426-5272
      Email: pterry@gotopalco.com
      Website: www.gotopalco.com
Telecommunications: logistics, forward & reverse, technical product repair upgrade & remanufacture, warranty fulfillment. (Woman, estab 1986, empl 250, sales $17,193,208, cert: WBENC)

Arizona

9227 Denali Telecom Solutions, Inc.
      6524 S McAllister Ave
      Tempe, AZ 85283
      Contact: Karen Tynan CEO
      Tel: 855-239-7776
      Email: karen.tynan@denalicorp.com
      Website: www.denalicorp.com
Mfr telecommunications products & service solutions for Broadband & Network Projects. (Minority, Woman, estab 2013, empl 4, sales $1,000,000, cert: WBENC)

9228 Native Technology Solutions Inc.
      7065 W Allison Rd
      Chandler, AZ 85226
      Contact: Mabel Tsosie
      Tel: 480-639-1234
      Email: mtsosie@gilarivertel.com
      Website: www.native-tech.net
Cabling & computing services, structured cabling, phone, security systems, video conferencing, & technology solutions. (Nat Ame, estab 2007, empl 14, sales $4,000,000, cert: State)

9229 Tower Safety and Instruction
      3620 S 40th St
      Phoenix, AZ 85040
      Contact: Kathy Brand CEO
      Tel: 480-313-0678
      Email: kathy@towersafety.com
      Website: www.towersafety.com
Safety School for the Wireless/Crane Industry, Wireless & Microwave, Construction & Telecommunications-Fiber Optics/Copper Installation & Testing, Project Management, Installation, Telecommunications Maintenance & Testing. (Woman, estab 2013, empl 8, sales , cert: WBENC)

California

9230 Aponi Products and Services
      3805 Florin Rd Ste 1228
      Sacramento, CA 95823
      Contact: Lisa M Davis lacy Owner
      Tel: 916-392-6571
      Email: lisad@aponitelecommunication.com
      Website: www.aponitelecom.com
Telecommunication Equip, Installation, Voice, Data, Cabling, Maintenance, Repair, Security System, DVR, Security Cameras. (Minority, Woman, estab 2007, empl 7, sales $360,000, cert: State, 8(a))

9231 Business Communications Solutions
      9910 Irvine Center Dr
      Irvine, CA 92618
      Contact: Afsaneh Rajab CEO
      Tel: 949-333-1000
      Email: srajab@bcsconsultants.com
      Website: www.bcsconsultants.com
Telecommunication & networking: phone systems, internet & telephone services, cabling, networking, & server room design & installation. (Woman, estab 2001, empl 15, sales $3,700,000, cert: State)

9232 Cico Electrical Contractors Inc.
      365 Whipporwill Dr
      Riverside, CA 92507
      Contact: Ron Veloz Office Mgr
      Tel: 951-213-2229
      Email: ron.veloz@cicoele.com
      Website: www.cicoele.com
Electrical, Electrical Subcontractor, New Construction, Remodeling, Renovations, Improvements-Relocations, Maintenance, Switchgear Change out, Critical Power-UPS, Generators, Predictive Maintenance (circuit (Hisp, estab 2004, empl 25, sales $4,464,384, cert: NMSDC)

9233 Clean Sweep Group Inc
      8306 Wilshire Blvd Ste 7009
      Beverly Hills, CA 90211
      Contact: Leo Williams, II CEO
      Tel: 310-985-0504
      Email: leo.williams@csgiusa.com
      Website: www.csgiusa.com
We are a veteran minority business enterprise. We provide an ultraviolet light disinfection and education service which greatly reduces the threat of hospital acquired infections and their increased costs and safety risks. (AA, estab 2011, empl 16, sales , cert: NMSDC)

9234 Coast to Coast Communications
      34145 Pacific Coast Hwy 635
      Dana Point, CA 92629
      Contact: Nikki Clark Natl Acct Exec
      Tel: 949-481-6550
      Email: nikki@c2ccomm.com
      Website: www.c2ccomm.com
Voice, data cabling & phone systems. (Woman, estab 2000, empl 10, sales $5,040,175, cert: WBENC)

9235 Dataoptek Corp
      573 E. Fairview Blvd. #43
      Inglewood, CA 90302
      Contact: Roderick Byrd CEO
      Tel: 310-367-2826
      Email: rbyrd@dataoptek.com
      Website: www.dataoptek.com
Structured cabling, LAN, WAN, VoIP, wireline, wireless network infrastructure installations & maintenance. (AA, estab 1999, empl 10, sales , cert: NMSDC)

9236 E-3 Systems
1220 Whipple Rd
Union City, CA 94587
Contact: Kofi Tawiah President
Tel: 510-487-7393
Email: kofi@e3systems.com
Website: www.e3systems.com
Low voltage voice & data structured cabling, electronic security systems & telecom. (AA, estab 1989, empl 58, sales $3,900,000, cert: NMSDC, CPUC)

9237 JM Fiber Optics, Inc.
13941 Ramona Ave Ste A
Chino, CA 91710
Contact: Marlene Vidana Business Devel Mgr
Tel: 909-628-3445
Email: mvidana@jmfiberoptics.com
Website: www.jmfiberoptics.com
Fiber optic & copper voice, video & data communication systems, transit system passenger information systems & intrusion dectection systems. (Hisp, estab 1992, empl 8, sales $5,701,490, cert: State, City, NMSDC, CPUC, SDB)

9238 Pinnacle Telecommunications, Inc. (PTI Solutions)
4242 Forcum Ave, Ste 200
McClellan, CA 95652
Contact: Accounts Payable Marketing Program Mgr
Tel: 916-426-1046
Email: ap@pti-s.com
Website: www.pti-s.com
Install communications cabling & equipment, cell tower upgrades, structured wire, WiFi & laser communications. (Woman, estab 1984, empl 140, sales $17,000,000, cert: CPUC, WBENC)

9239 Rincon Technology
810 East Montecito St
Santa Barbara, CA 93103
Contact: Mike Bartling Founder EVP Sales
Tel: 805-319-7830
Email: mbartling@rincontechnology.com
Website: www.rincontechnology.com
Wireless transmission gear T1 to 3DS3 capacity, native Ethernet/IP backhaul, up to 800mbps transmission, wireless SONET backhaul. (Hisp, estab 2003, empl 45, sales $55,000,000, cert: State, NMSDC)

9240 Serene Innovations
14731 Carmenita Rd
Norwalk, CA 90650
Contact: James McGehee Sales Coord
Tel: 562-407-5400
Email: j.mcgehee@sereneinnovations.com
Website: www.sereneinnovations.com/
Amplified Phones, TV Listening Devices, Ringer/Flasher, Alerting Notification System, Telephone Amplifier. (As-Pac, estab 2004, empl 15, sales $3,000,000, cert: NMSDC)

9241 Solutionz Videoconferencing Inc. (Solutionz Conferencing, Inc.)
901 Bringham Ave
Los Angeles, CA 90049
Contact: Paul Mitnick Sales Acct Exec
Tel: 234-303-2300
Email: pmitnick@solutionzinc.com
Website: www.solutionzinc.com
Audio, video, Videoconferencing, Telecommunications retailer. (Hisp, estab 2001, empl 295, sales $140,000,000, cert: NMSDC, CPUC)

9242 Tempest Telecom Solutions, LLC
136 W Canon Perdido Ste 100
Santa Barbara, CA 93101
Contact: Elda Rudd VP Mktg
Tel: 805-879-4800
Email: tempestsupplier@tempesttelecom.com
Website: www.tempesttelecom.com
New & refurbished networking equipment. (Woman, estab 2005, empl 160, sales $0, cert: CPUC, WBENC)

9243 Towne Communications, Inc.
4640 Duckhorn Dr
Sacramento, CA 95834
Contact: Jeanette Towne CEO
Tel: 916-993-2100
Email: jmtowne@synectic.us
Website: www.synectic.us
Voice, data, VOIP, telecommunication services. (Woman, estab 1995, empl 35, sales $4,200,000, cert: WBENC)

9244 Unified TelData Inc.
425 2nd St
San Francisco, CA 94107
Contact: Eric Clauss GSS
Tel: 415-977-7031
Email: eclauss@utdi.com
Website: www.utdi.com
Communications solutionsL Avaya, Cisco & Nortel hardware & services. (Woman, estab 1981, empl 50, sales $10,000,000, cert: CPUC, 8(a))

9245 Universal Network Development Corp.
2555 Third St Ste 112
Sacramento, CA 95818
Contact: Cinthia Larkin Kazee President
Tel: 916-475-1200
Email: undc@undc.com
Website: www.undc.com
Telecommunication eng, fiber optic & copper splicing, installation & repair, project mgmt, CAD drafting. (Minority, Woman, estab 1980, empl 75, sales $4,234,625, cert: CPUC, WBENC)

9246 WP Electric & Communications, Inc.
14198 Albers Way
Chino, CA 91710
Contact: LAURA NESBITT President
Tel: 909-606-3510
Email: ROSEANN@WPELECTRIC.COM
Website: www.wpelectric.com
Electrical & network cabling services. (Woman, estab 1975, empl 45, sales $7,800,000, cert: CPUC, WBENC)

Colorado

9247 M.R. Research
8003 S Corona Way
Centennial, CO 80122
Contact: Madeline K. Reilly President
Tel: 303-795-4353
Email: rkreilly@aol.com
Website: www.m-r-research.com
Applied research, electronic design & telecommunications components for satellites, base stations & mobile wireless systems. (Minority, Woman, estab 2010, empl 4, sales $334,900, cert: NMSDC)

9248　Sage Telecommunications Corp.
6700 Race St
Denver, CO 80229
Contact: President
Tel: 303-227-0986
Email:
Website: www.sagecom.net
Engineers, build & maintain fiber optic, cable & other networks. (Woman, estab 1992, empl 90, sales $10,000,000, cert: State)

9249　Tripwireless, Inc.
4941 Allison St Ste 7 & 8
Arvada, CO 80022
Contact: Kimberly Koch Founder
Tel: 720-361-4998
Email: kym@tripwireless.com
Website: www.tripwireless.com
Network infrastructure equipment & services, cell sites, microwave, outside power plant, transmission, routers, data centers, de-commissioning, trenching, fiber, installation & preventative maintenance. (Woman, estab 2005, empl 6, sales $0, cert: WBENC)

Connecticut

9250　IQ Telcom, LLC dba IQ Telecom
78 Beaver Road
Wethersfield, CT 06109
Contact: Carol Guerra Dir Business Devel
Tel: 860-882-0500
Email: carol.guerra@iqt360.com
Website: www.iqt360.com
Telecommunications expense: voice, data & wireless, audit, optimization, spend base lining, invoice processing, monthly reporting for cost allocation, vendor/carrier mgmt; contract negotiation, network design & optimization. (Woman, estab 2001, empl 35, sales $3,000,000, cert: State, WBENC)

9251　VisionPoint LLC
152 Rockwell Rd
Newington, CT 06111
Contact: Louise Mastroianni Acct Mgr
Tel: 860-436-9673
Email: visionpointct@gmail.com
Website: www.visionpointllc.com
Technology acquisition, integration, design, installation, technical meeting support & service. (Woman, estab 2003, empl 24, sales $7,002,015, cert: WBENC)

District of Columbia

9252　MJS Communications LLC
1343 First St NW
Washington, DC 20001
Contact: Marlon Boykin President
Tel: 888-829-1658
Email: mboykin@mjscommunications.biz
Website: www.mjscommunications.biz
Information technology, telecommunications services, structure cabling system, voice/data cabling, CCTV cabling, POS & wireless, CCTV, digital video recorders, Interior/exterior cameras, monitors, perimeter security. (AA, estab 2009, empl 2, sales $110,000, cert: State, City)

9253　National Fiber and Copper, Inc.
1701 Pennsylvania Ave NW Ste 300
Washington, DC 20006
Contact: Kimberly Valentine President
Tel: 202-729-6339
Email: kimvalentine@nationalfiberandcopper.com
Website: www.nationalfiberandcopper.com
Low-voltage communication installation & services, structured cabling, fiber optics, network installation & mgmt, VOIP, phone systems, security solutions, on-site & support services. (Woman, estab 1999, empl 10, sales $1,350,000, cert: City, WBENC, SDB)

9254　Tecknomic LLC
2322 First St NW
Washington, DC 20001
Contact: Dexter Spencer President
Tel: 202-829-2953
Email: dspencer@tecknomic.com
Website: www.tecknomic.com
Emergency management & services training, information technology, wireless/wireline communications. (AA, estab 2003, empl 12, sales $391,000, cert: State, 8(a))

Florida

9255　Advanced IT Concepts, Inc.
1351 Sundial Point
Winter Springs, FL 32708
Contact: Gabriel Ruiz President
Tel: 407-914-2484
Email: eve.maldonado@aitcinc.com
Website: www.aitcinc.com
Telecommunications & Information Technology services. (Hisp, estab 2006, empl 51, sales $24,860,693, cert: City, 8(a))

9256　Cell Antenna
12453 NW 44th St
Coral Springs, FL 33065
Contact: Barbara Melamed Owner
Tel: 954-340-7053
Email: barbara@cellantenna.com
Website: www.cellantenna.com
Signal enhancement using Distributed Antenna Systems for cell phone carriers (AT&T, Verizon, T-Mobile and Sprint) (Woman, estab 2002, empl 21, sales $8,000,000, cert: State)

9257　ClearTone Communications Inc.
840 Edgewood Ave S, Ste 209
Jacksonville, FL 32205
Contact: Jerry Irizarry President
Tel: 904-240-0490
Email: jerry@cleartonejax.com
Website: www.cleartonejax.com
Telecommunications, voice, data & structured cabling. (Hisp, estab 2007, empl 1, sales , cert: State)

9258　Satya Acquisition Management, Inc. dba SAM, Inc.
3300 South OBT Ste 106
Orlando, FL 32839
Contact: Bob Chopra President
Tel: 267-973-4228
Email: bchopra@sam-inc.com
Website: www.sam-inc.com
Telecommunications, new site builds, antenna modifications, generator installations, microwave installations, temporary cell site installations cells & Distributed Antenna Systems. (As-Pac, estab 2006, empl 2, sales $350,000, cert: NMSDC)

9259 SENCOMMUNICATIONS, INC.
9208 FLORIDA PALM Dr
Tampa, FL 33619
Contact: STACIE MILLER CEO
Tel: 813-626-4404
Email: rgeneral@sencomm.com
Website: www.sencomm.com
Provides telephone headsets, desksets, teleconferencing units, and other products. (Woman, estab 1989, empl 16, sales $14,528,491, cert: WBENC)

9260 Smith Corona/Comfort Telecommunications
1407 SE 47th Terr
Cape Coral, FL 33904
Contact: Louise Bergen Sales
Tel: 800-399-3224
Email: louise@comfortel.com
Website: www.comfortel.com
Mfr & dist telephone headsets & accessories. (Woman, estab 1985, empl 15, sales $11,000,000, cert: State)

9261 TSG Enterprises, LLC dba RadiusPoint
1211 State Road 436, Ste 295
Casselberry, FL 32707
Contact: CEO
Tel: 407-661-6840
Email: sales@radiuspoint.com
Website: www.radiuspoint.com
Telecommunications & utility invoices auditing, expense management & bill processing. (Woman, estab 1992, empl 42, sales , cert: WBENC)

Georgia

9262 Agile Perspective
27 Edwin Pl
Atlanta, GA 30318
Contact: Rae-Anne Alves
Tel: 917-648-7544
Email: rae-anne.alves@anagileperspective.com
Website: www.anagileperspective.com
Telecommunication sourcing, cost reduction initiatives, strategic management, best practice benchmarking, technology integration. (Woman/AA, Hisp, estab 2012, empl 1, sales , cert: NMSDC, WBENC)

9263 Atlanta Communications Co.
1510 Huber St
Atlanta, GA 30318
Contact: Carrie Davis Exec Asst
Tel: 404-875-9316
Email: cdavis@atlantacomm.com
Website: www.atlantacomm.com
Dist, service, install, rent, site preparation & project management of two-way communications equipment. (Woman/AA, estab 1947, empl 43, sales , cert: WBENC)

9264 Concise, Inc.
191 Peachtree St, Ste 3300
Alanta, GA 30303
Contact: David Johnson CEO
Tel: 404-736-3669
Email: info@conciseinc.com
Website: www.conciseinc.com
Telecommunications svcs: network & telephone cabling, wireless networks, surveillance & security systems. (AA, estab 2003, empl 2, sales $560,000, cert: NMSDC, 8(a))

9265 Digicomm Systems, Inc.
3221 Hill St, Ste 103-B
Duluth, GA 30096
Contact: Undra Patrick VP Operations
Tel: 770-497-8080
Email: management@digicommsystems.com
Website: www.digicommsystems.com
Telecommunication services: data center design & consulting, data network design & consulting, systems integration & installation, internal communications, low-voltage cabling, equipment relocation. (Woman/AA, estab 1988, empl 7, sales $0, cert: City, NMSDC)

9266 FamTeck, LLC
4484 Covington Hwy, Ste 105
Decatur, GA 30038
Contact: Conrad Meertins CEO
Tel: 404-822-1117
Email: cmeertins@famteck.com
Website: www.famteck.com
FamTeck leverages new technologies and mobility to provide next generation applications to meet today's challenges. We develop solutions that provide optimal performance allowing you to do more with less.Core Competencies•Streamline IT Operations with Pre (AA, estab 2006, empl 7, sales $0, cert: NMSDC)

9267 HYPEFAN
3560 Morning Ivy Way
Suwanee, GA 30024
Contact: Derrick Brown CEO
Tel: 404-217-7933
Email: ds@hypefan.com
Website: www.hypefan.com
No Cheerstix! No Thunderstix! No foam hands! Bring the HYPE with HypeSticks . There is nothing quite like the HypeStick, with 6 distinct areas of real estate for cross-marketing opportunities, two faces on the main, two on the handle, a lanyard can be at (AA, estab 2004, empl 3, sales , cert: NMSDC)

9268 Litra Manufacturing Inc.
6733-A Jones Mill Ct
Norcross, GA 30092
Contact: Skip York Sales Mgr
Tel: 800-445-4617
Email: skipyork@litramfg.com
Website: www.litramfg.com
Mfr copper & pre-terminated fiber optic cable assemblies: coax, multipair copper cable assemblies, high strand fiber assemblies, single-mode, multi-mode, fiber jumpers, components & accessories. (Woman, estab 1986, empl 25, sales $0, cert: CPUC)

9269 North Georgia Telecom, Inc.
4200 Steve Reynolds Blvd., Ste 12
Norcross, GA 30093
Contact: Brittany Gold President
Tel: 678-482-0015
Email: b.gold@ngtinc.com
Website: www.ngtinc.com
Install, deinstall, switching sales, asset mgmt. (Woman, estab 1994, empl 20, sales $0, cert: WBENC)

9270   ProComm Telecommunications, Inc.
        1377 Business Center Dr
        Conyers, GA 30094
        Contact: Josh Franklin Sales
        Tel: 770-760-8660
        Email: jfranklin@ptinc.org
        Website: www.ptinc.org
Installation, engineering & design telecommunications
networks: wireless, fiber optics, digital cross connects,
switch, multiplexer & channel bank, calibrate & repair test
equipment. (Minority, Woman, estab 1989, empl 55, sales
$7,000,000, cert: WBENC)

9271   VanRan Communications Services, Inc.
        2939 Pacific Dr
        Norcross, GA 30071
        Contact: Dir Govt & Enterprise Solutions
        Tel: 540-728-1941
        Email: sales@vanran.com
        Website: www.vanran.com
Telecommunications systems: traditional, converged, voice
over internet protocol, voice mail & unified messaging,
contact ctr solutions, networking services. (Woman, estab
1986, empl 35, sales $9,650,000, cert: WBENC)

9272   Washington Communications Group LLC
        6465 Hwy 85
        Riverdale, GA 30274
        Contact: Stacy Washington President
        Tel: 770-991-3000
        Email: washingtoncommunication@yahoo.com
        Website: www.washingtoncommunication.com
Structured Network Cabling, Fiber Optic Installation, Single
mode, Multimode, Fiber Optic Testing & Terminations,
Voice/Data Network Installation, Business & VoIP Phone
Systems, Patch panel installation & termination. (AA, estab
2013, empl 10, sales , cert: State)

Illinois

9273   Chicago Communications, LLC
        200 W Spangler Ave
        Elmhurst, IL 60126
        Contact: Lisa MacGillivray Mktg Dir
        Tel: 630-832-3311
        Email: sales@chicomm.com
        Website: www.chicomm.com
Dist, install & maintain communication equipment.
(Woman, estab 2004, empl 68, sales $10,000,000, cert:
State, WBENC)

9274   ClearSounds Communication
        1743 Quincy Ave, Ste 155
        Naperville, IL 60540
        Contact: Michelle Maher Dir of Sales/ops
        Tel: 866-657-2855
        Email: michelle.maher@clearsounds.com
        Website: www.clearsounds.com
Amplified phones, Bluetooth headsets, amplified
neckloops, mobile accessories & listening systems for
people with hearing loss and those looking for a remark-
able listening experience. (Woman, estab 2004, empl 15,
sales , cert: WBENC)

9275   Cymbal Communications Corporation
        4N419 Mountain Ash Dr
        Wayne, IL 60184
        Contact: Antoinette Calarco Dir Sales/service
        Tel: 877-296-2666
        Email: antoinette@cymbalcomm.com
        Website: www.cymbalcomm.com
Dist telecommunication products: VXi, GN Netcom,
Plantronics, Polycom,ClearOne, Avaya & Nortel Phones.
(Minority, Woman, estab 2005, empl 5, sales $930,000,
cert: WBENC)

9276   Integrated Installations, inc.
        514 Pratt Ave N
        Schaumburg, IL 60193
        Contact: Kate Novelle Contracts/Sales Dir
        Tel: 847-985-1170
        Email: kate@i3install.com
        Website: www.i3install.com
Telecom installation services, Wireless & Wireline
Industries. (Woman, estab 2000, empl 25, sales
$2,330,161, cert: State, City, WBENC, NWBOC)

9277   Level-(1) Global Solutions, LLC
        233 S. Wacker Dr 84th Fl
        Chicago, IL 60606
        Contact: CEO
        Tel: 312-202-3300
        Email:
        Website: www.level-1.com
Infrastructure solutions: office technology & data ctr
facilities, IDF/telecom infrastructure, UPS power protection, emergency generator power, HVAC environmental
systems, fire protection, security & access control, CATV
& LAN/WAN video surveillance. (AA, estab 2001, empl
25, sales $1,800,000, cert: City)

9278   Phoenix Business Solutions LLC
        12543 S Laramie Ave
        Alsip, IL 60803
        Contact: Peggy Hrindak CEO
        Tel: 708-388-1330
        Email: phrindak@getpbsnow.com
        Website: www.getpbsnow.com
Design, install & maintain telecom & data systems.
(Woman, estab 2000, empl 35, sales $5,853,538, cert:
WBENC)

9279   Pilot Services, Inc.
        317 Mustang Dr
        Oswego, IL 60543
        Contact: Kimberly Warren President
        Tel: 630-554-7413
        Email: kwarren@pilotservicesinc.com
        Website: www.pilotservicesinc.com
Telecommunications, voice & data, cabling, wiring,
installation & maintenance for telecommunications
equipment. (Woman, estab 1996, empl 10, sales
$817,915, cert: WBENC)

9280   Raptor Industries, Inc.
        1602 N Park Dr
        Mount Prospect, IL 60056
        Contact: Anthony Kalama
        Tel: 708-417-9190
        Email: gkalama@raptorindustriesinc.com
        Website: www.raptorindustriesinc.com
Voice, Data, Fiber Optic & CATV Cable Installation and
Certification, Copper and Fiber Optic Splicing, Audio/
Visual, CCTV, Riser Management, Intercom. (As-Pac,
estab 2013, empl 5, sales $162,554, cert: State, City,
NMSDC)

9281 SI Tech Inc.
1101 N Raddant Rd
Batavia, IL 60510
Contact: Ramesh Sheth (ramesh@sitech-bitdriver.com) President
Tel: 630-761-3640
Email: admin@sitech-bitdriver.com
Website: www.sitech-bitdriver.com
Mfr & develop fiber optic communications products. (As-Ind, estab 1984, empl 20, sales $0, cert: NMSDC)

9282 TelePlus, Inc.
724 Racquet Club Dr
Addison, IL 60101
Contact: Mike Warda Sales Mgr
Tel: 630-543-3066
Email: mwarda@telepluscom.com
Website: www.telepluscom.com
Voice/data low voltage cabling systems, electrical, paging systems, CCTV, Nortel BCM and Norstar telephone systems. (Woman, estab 1986, empl 56, sales $6,250,000, cert: City, WBENC)

9283 The Northridge Group, Inc.
9700 W Higgins Rd Ste 600
Rosemont, IL 60018
Contact: Sue Antkowiak Dir of Program Mgmt & Compliance
Tel: 847-692-7002
Email: registrations@northridgegroup.com
Website: www.northridgegroup.com
Telecommunications. (Woman/AA, Hisp, estab 1999, empl 82, sales $10,000,000, cert: City, WBENC)

9284 Viadata1 Communications Inc.
3118 Elder Ln
Franklin Park, IL 60131
Contact: Eddie Villariny President
Tel: 773-593-1346
Email: edvilla@viadata1.net
Website: www.viadata1.net
Low Voltage Cabling, Fiber Optic, CCTV, Card Access, Wireless Access Points, Network Data Center design & Installation, Data & Voice Cabling. Computer equipment installation. (Hisp, estab 2008, empl 4, sales $800,000, cert: NMSDC)

Indiana

9285 C-CAT, Inc.
1726 W. 15th St
Indianapolis, IN 46202
Contact: Kristi Johnson President
Tel: 317-568-2899
Email: kjohnson@c-cat.com
Website: www.c-cat.com
Infrastructure & low-voltage cabling services: video, voice & data, security/safety cabling & Cat 5E, Cat-6 & fiber-optic wiring systems. (Woman, estab 2001, empl 30, sales $5,200,000, cert: WBENC)

9286 Dixon Phone Place, Inc.
5335 N Tacoma Ave, Ste 3
Indianapolis, IN 46220
Contact: Juli Fritsch
Tel: 317-251-3504
Email: dixonphoneplace1@att.net
Website: www.dixonphone.com
Telephone equipment, plantronics telephone & computer headsets, cell phone corded & bluetooth headsets, corded & wireless headsets, telephone parts, line & handset cords, polycom conference equipment, cordless phones, business phones. (Woman, estab 1983, empl 2, sales $0, cert: State, City)

9287 Summitline Industries, Inc.
7822 Opportunity Dr
Fort Wayne, IN 46825
Contact: Stan Richard President
Tel: 260-490-2213
Email: stan.richard@summitline.com
Website: www.Summitline.com
Telecommunications, supply chain solutions, material mgmt, warehousing & kit fulfillment. (AA, estab 1983, empl 20, sales $15,000,000, cert: NMSDC, CPUC)

9288 Telamon Corporation
1000 E 116th St
Carmel, IN 46032
Contact: John L. Weeks Dir of Sales
Tel: 317-818-6757
Email: john.weeks@telamon.com
Website: www.telamon.com
Mfr & dist voice & data communications products: cables & connectors to cstmrs specs, modular voice & data accessories; engineering & install telecommunication equip. (As-Pac, estab 1984, empl 1100, sales $0, cert: NMSDC)

Kentucky

9289 Strategic Communications, LLC
310 Evergreen Rd, Ste 100
Louisville, KY 40243
Contact: Kathy Mills CEO
Tel: 502-493-7234
Email: info@yourstrategic.com
Website: www.stratcomllc.com
Voice, data & communications solutions: structured cabling, telecommunications systems, carrier services, security/alarm, data communications products & services. (Minority, Woman, estab 1993, empl 40, sales $4,200,000, cert: NMSDC, WBENC)

Louisiana

9290 TCN
1016 Harimaw Court E
Metairie, LA 70001
Contact: Victor Hess Sales Mgr
Tel: 504-838-9600
Email: vhess@executonesystems.com
Website: www.executonesystems.com
Furnish & install wiring, digital & Voice over IP telephone systems, Overhead Paging, Music, Sound, Masking, School Intercom & Mass Notification Systems. (Woman, estab 1947, empl 28, sales $357,531,124, cert: WBENC)

Massachusetts

9291 C.E. Communication Services, Inc.
25 Grove St
Franklin, MA 02038
Contact: Bruce Baltz
Tel: 866-966-1555
Email: bruceb@cecommunication.com
Website: www.cecommunication.com/
Dist telecommuncations & networking products. (Woman, estab 1998, empl 10, sales $0, cert: State)

9292 C4Cable, LLC
257 Scadding St
Taunton, MA 02780
Contact: Carole Derringer Principal
Tel: 508-944-5573
Email: caroled@c4cable.com
Website: www.c4cable.com
Dist Telecommunications & Data Networking Products: Bulk Copper & Fiber Optic Cables, Patch Panels, Enclosures, Copper & Fiber Patch Cords, Pre-Terminated MTP/MPO Backplane Fiber Cables & Cassettes, Free Standing Racks. (Woman, estab 2014, empl 2, sales , cert: State, WBENC)

9293 Coastal Telecommunications Inc.
35 Main St Ste 116C
Topsfield, MA 01983
Contact: Angela Gill President
Tel: 978-744-4900
Email: angela@gocti.us
Website: www.gocti.us
Low Voltage Cabling, Voice & Data Structured Cabling, Communication System Design, Installation & Maintenance, Voice & Network Equipment & Service Solutions. (Woman/AA, estab 1990, empl 5, sales $250,000, cert: State, WBENC)

9294 Mallory Headsets
679 N Main St
West Bridgewater, MA 02379
Contact: Kelly Mallory President
Tel: 508-586-0117
Email: donna@malloryheadsets.com
Website: www.malloryheadsets.com
Telecommunications products, audio conferencing products. (Woman/AA, estab 1997, empl 10, sales $0, cert: State)

Maryland

9295 Crest Telecom, Inc.
PO Box 410
Bel Air, MD 21014
Contact: Tammy Halley Principal
Tel: 410-420-1044
Email: tammy.halley@cresttelecom.com
Website: www.cresttelecom.com
Wireless & wireline telecommunication products: routers, microwave radios, central service units, cross connect panels, fuse alarm panels, racks, fiber management systems, filters, duplexers, cable, channel element cards, etc. (Woman, estab 2007, empl 10, sales , cert: WBENC)

9296 KSC Consultant Services LLC
18216 Darnell Dr
Olney, MD 20832
Contact: Kimberlie Manns Owner
Tel: 240-389-1882
Email: kmanns@kscconsultants.net
Website: www.kscconsultants.net
Telecommunication consulting & infrastructure wiring, designing & installing voice & data infrastructure/cabling, troubleshoot, repair, testing & installing voice & data lines, rewiring, installing & replacing jacks. (Woman/AA, estab 2004, empl 2, sales , cert: State, SDB)

9297 SRL TotalSource LLC
83 High St Ste B
Waldorf, MD 20602
Contact: John Johnson COO
Tel: 301-885-0097
Email: jjohnson@srltotalsource.com
Website: www.srltotalsource.com/
Wireless Telecommunications Carriers, Data Processing, Hosting, and Related Services. (AA, estab 2011, empl 6, sales $589,253, cert: State, 8(a))

Michigan

9298 Advanced Communication Cabling, Inc.
PO Box 308
Spring Arbor, MI 49283
Contact: Ruth Fritz President
Tel: 517-524-2224
Email: ruthacci@direcway.com
Website: www.acci-mi.com
Voice, data, video, sound reinforcement, networking, copper & fiber optics, feed cable installation, cable repair & removal, testing & inspection, emergency repair, project mgmt, engineering, consulting & surveys. (Woman, estab 1992, empl 22, sales $0, cert: WBENC)

9299 Cellular Solutions Signal Enhancing Specialists
2737 N Meridian Rd
Sanford, MI 48657
Contact: Devin O'Neil Acct Exec
Tel: 989-687-4023
Email: aimeek@cellularsolutions.com
Website: www.cellularsolutions.com
Cellular signal enhancement throughout homes, vehicles commercial buildings & large facilities. (Woman, estab 2004, empl 13, sales $8,000,000, cert: WBENC)

9300 Communication Brokers, Inc.
437 44th St SW
Grand Rapid, MI 49548
Contact: Mimi Micu CEO
Tel: 616-301-3733
Email: mmicu@cbitelecom.com
Website: www.cbitelecom.com
Telecommunications consulting services, data, local & wireless communications analysis. (Woman, estab 1991, empl 30, sales $5,000,000, cert: WBENC)

9301 Federated Service Solutions, Inc.
41100 Plymouth Rd Ste 165
Plymouth, MI 48170
Contact: Susan Troyer Sales Admin
Tel: 248-539-9000
Email: stroyer@federatedservice.com
Website: www.federatedservice.com
POS, server, kiosks/self-service, low voltage cabling (voice/data/video/audio), security/LP, network devices, and wireless (Woman, estab 2004, empl 70, sales $21,500,000, cert: WBENC)

9302 Prima Communications, Inc.
PO Box 338
Schoolcraft, MI 49087
Contact: Charlotte Hubbard Owner
Tel: 269-679-3800
Email: primaadmin@voyager.net
Website: www.primacommunications.com
Technical communications. (Woman, estab 1991, empl 25, sales $0, cert: WBENC)

Minnesota

9303 Building Systems Solutions, Inc.
1250 E Moore Lake Dr Ste 230
Fridley, MN 55432
Contact: Megan Beaver CEO
Tel: 763-502-1515
Email: meganb@bssmn.com
Website: www.buildingsystemssolutions.com
Design commercial audio & communications systems: paging, sound masking, music & emergency notification systems. (Woman, estab 2003, empl 2, sales $200,145, cert: State)

9304 Seacom, LLC
160 Birchwood Ave
Saint Paul, MN 55110
Contact: Sandee Ebbott President
Tel: 612-207-7423
Email: sandee@seacomllc.com
Website: www.seacomllc.com
Telecommunication solutions: legacy equipment, VoIP, video conferencing, voice & data cabling, electrical cabling, data networking & security systems. (Woman, estab 2010, empl 10, sales $1,500,000, cert: WBENC)

9305 Technology Management Corporation
4790 Lakeway Terr
Shorewood, MN 55331
Contact: Brendon O'Brien Dir Business Devel
Tel: 952-470-0217
Email: bobrien@tmc-1.com
Website: www.tmc-1.com
Telecommunications consulting: cable design; phone system design; phone, data, & internet network design, data/server room design. telecommunications audit & contract negotiation. (Woman, estab 1988, empl 12, sales $788,715, cert: State, City, WBENC, NWBOC)

9306 TRiCOM Communications
1301 Corporate Center Dr, Ste 160
Eagan, MN 55121
Contact: Diane Evans President
Tel: 651-686-9000
Email: diane.evans@tricom1.com
Website: www.tricom1.com
Design & install structured cabling: copper & fiber optics, Data Centers, Telecom Rooms, Equipment Rooms, Outside Plant Construction, Security Cameras, Card Access Systems, In-Building Wireless Distributed Antenna Systems (DAS). (Woman, estab 1989, empl 20, sales $2,250,000, cert: State, City, WBENC)

Missouri

9307 American Cable Products LLC
4 Forest Park Circle Dr
Lake St. Louis, MO 63367
Contact: Richard Politte Managing Partner
Tel: 636-265-6602
Email: rmpolitte@amercp.net
Website: www.americancableproducts.com
Install voice & data cable, routers, switches, modems, racks, wireless equipment, fiber optic cable & hardware, PA & video systems, arial cable & single mode fiber & buried drop service, trenching, boring, etc. (As-Pac, estab 2002, empl 25, sales $12,000,000, cert: State, City, CPUC, SDB)

9308 eTech Solutons, LLC
1813 Zumbehl Rd
Saint Charles, MO 63303
Contact: Sara Hagemeyer Owner
Tel: 314-282-8318
Email: brad@etechstl.com
Website: www.etechstl.com
Cellphone supplier, Cellphone repair, Tablet repair, Tablet supplier electronic repair - ie micro soldering, laptop repair, Cellphone & tablet data recovery, Chipoff data recovery, jtag data recovery, cellphone forensics. (Woman, estab 2012, empl 2, sales $530,000, cert: WBENC)

9309 TSI Global Companies LLC
700 Fountain Lakes Blvd
Saint Charles, MO 63301
Contact: Christine Robinson Accounting Dept
Tel: 636-949-8889
Email: crobinson@tsi-global.com
Website: www.tsi-global.com
Electrical & Low-voltage systems integrator providing convergent audio and video, networked communications & security system solutions. (Nat Ame, estab 1980, empl 100, sales $43,110,684, cert: State, City, NMSDC)

Montana

9310 Alamon Telco, Inc.
315 W. Idaho St
Kalispell, MT 59901
Contact: Margaret Gebhardt President
Tel: 800-252-8838
Email: peg@alamon.com
Website: www.alamon.com
Communication svcs: outside plant engineering, splicing & inspection; cable installations; CO transmission, engineering, installation, testing, maintenance & support. (Woman, estab 1975, empl 150, sales $14,053,000, cert: WBENC)

North Carolina

9311 Atlantic Communication Products, Inc.
4324 Barringer Dr Ste. 112
Charlotte, NC 28217
Contact: Winn Pray President
Tel: 704-676-5880
Email: w.pray@goacp.com
Website: www.goacp.com
Resell voice & data products, installation & maintenance services of wire & cabling. (Hisp, estab 1997, empl 10, sales $900,000, cert: NMSDC)

9312 Lexair Electronics Sales Corp.
      4807-B Koger Blvd
      Greensboro, NC 27407
      Contact: Paula Edwards Contract Mgr
      Tel: 336-294-5300
      Email: alisawatts@lexairsales.com
      Website: www.lexair.com
Dist communications equipment: headsets, telephones, audio conferencing equipment & peripherals. (Woman, estab 1998, empl 15, sales $6,550,000, cert: WBENC)

9313 Team Telecom, LLC
      220 N. Main St
      Lexington, NC 27292
      Contact: Jennifer Sturgell
      Tel: 888-305-4772
      Email: jsturgell@teamtelecom.net
      Website: www.teamtelecom.net
Dist new, surplus & refurbished telecommunications equipment. (Woman/AA, estab 2005, empl 8, sales $3,050,000, cert: State, NMSDC, WBENC)

9314 TelExpress
      406 Interstate Dr
      Archdale, NC 27263
      Contact: Tabitha Brock Sr Acct Mgr
      Tel: 434-990-2644
      Email: tabitha@telexpressinc.com
      Website: www.telexpressinc.com
Mfr central office, wireless,cable, fiber & DC power equipment. (Woman, estab 1992, empl 35, sales $5,785,800, cert: WBENC)

9315 Walker and Associates, Inc.
      7129 Old Hwy 52
      Welcome, NC 27374
      Contact: Jane Brightwell VP Business Dev
      Tel: 336-731-5236
      Email: governcon@walkerfirst.com
      Website: www.walkerfirst.com
Dist data & telecommunication equip, material mgmt & installation. (Woman, estab 1970, empl 120, sales $0, cert: CPUC)

New Jersey

9316 D.M. Radio Service Corp.
      45 Perry St
      Chester, NJ 07930
      Contact: Sandy Drysdale President
      Tel: 908-879-2525
      Email: sdrysdale@csiradio.com
      Website: www.csiradio.com
Dist two-way radio communications equipment, design/build service, supply & support for radio systems, Emergency Call Boxes, BDA & DAS systems. (Woman, estab 1968, empl 6, sales $700,000, cert: State, WBENC)

9317 e.comm Technologies
      11 Melanie Ln
      East Hanover, NJ 07936
      Contact: Chuck Tarantino global acct Mgr
      Tel: 973-503-5814
      Email: ctarantino@ecommt.com
      Website: www.ecommtechnologies.com
Avaya's Radvision video conferencing, contact center, call recording, speech access, predictive dialers, wireless solutions, video conferencing both room to room & desktop to desktop. (Woman, estab 1999, empl 20, sales $6,622,113, cert: State)

9318 Office Solutions Inc.
      217 Mount Horeb Rd
      Warren, NJ 07059
      Contact: Michael Scannelli Div Mgr
      Tel: 732-356-0200
      Email: mscannelli@osidirect.com
      Website: www.osidirect.com
Designs & implement converged voice & data solutions: VoIP, IP telephony telecommunications equipment, telephone maintenance contracts, headsets, media servers & gateways, voice messaging, call centers, contact centers, video conferencing. (Woman, estab 1982, empl 30, sales $6,200,000, cert: WBENC)

9319 Spectrotel
      3535 Route 66, Building 7
      Neptune, NJ 07753
      Contact: Jack Dayan President
      Tel: 732-345-7936
      Email: sales@spectrotel.com
      Website: www.spectrotel.com
Dedicated Voice Services, Business Calling Services (POTs), VoIP Services, Conferencing Services, Managed Services, Network Monitoring, Managed Security, Cyber Security, SD-WAN, Dedicated Network Services, Dedicated Internet Access, Virtual Network Svcs. (Hisp, estab 1997, empl 130, sales $78,000,000, cert: NMSDC)

9320 The Seideman Company
      4 Canterbury Ct
      Marlton, NJ 08053
      Contact: Patricia Seideman Owner
      Tel: 856-988-0117
      Email: pseideman@aol.com
      Website: www.seidemancompany.com
Telecommunications & data networking services. (Woman, estab 1991, empl 2, sales $156,382, cert: WBENC)

9321 TRAK Communications, Inc.
      710 Tennant Rd Ste 101
      Manalapan, NJ 07726
      Contact: President
      Tel: 732-786-1355
      Email: rsmaldone@trakcommunications.com
      Website: www.trakcommunications.com
Telecommunications Billing Audit & Consulting Services, Contract Negotiations, contract compliance audits, wireless audits & optimizations, Bid Management Services, Vendor Management, Telecom Expense Management. (Woman, estab 1999, empl 2, sales $338,371, cert: WBENC)

New York

9322 Annese & Associates, Inc.
      4781 Route 5 W
      Herkimer, NY 13350
      Contact: Yvonne Annese LoRe VP Corp Projects
      Tel: 315-849-9194
      Email: yannese@annese.com
      Website: www.annese.com
Design, install & maintain IP telephony, wireless, voice & data networks, remote monitoring, 24 x 7 maintenance, security. (Woman, estab 1970, empl 94, sales $53,000,010, cert: State)

9323 Coranet Corp
277 Fairfield Road Ste 320A
Fairfield, NY 07004
Contact: Kevin O'Brien Acct Exec
Tel: 212-635-2770
Email: kobrien@coranet.com
Website: www.coranet.com
VoIP convergence solutions, data networking, project mgmt, video networking, structured cabling systems, mobility & wireless solutions, installation & maintenance, IP audits, call center applications, billing audits, e-collaboration. (Woman, estab 1987, empl 85, sales $63,000,000, cert: State, WBENC)

9324 HAVE, Inc.
309 Power Ave
Hudson, NY 12534
Contact: Lowell Stringer Sales
Tel: 518-828-2000
Email: lstringer@haveinc.com
Website: www.haveinc.com
Custom audio/video/data cable assemblies, dist bulk cable, connectors, tools & accessories. (Woman, estab 1977, empl 18, sales $3,120,541, cert: City)

9325 Information Transport Solutions Inc.
3204 Route 22
Patterson, NY 12563
Contact: President
Tel: 855-472-7701
Email: Info@4yourITS.com
Website: www.4yourITS.com
Wireless & structured cabling: wifi, DAS, AV, Access Control & Sound Masking. (Woman, estab 2001, empl 5, sales $2,000,000, cert: WBENC)

9326 Pivotel LLC
6066 State Hwy 12
Norwich, NY 13815
Contact: Ronald Martin Jr Tech Sales Eng
Tel: 607-334-7400
Email: ron.martin@pivotelonline.com
Website: www.pivotelonline.com
Communications & network wiring: AC/DC & fiber optic cabling & terminations. (Woman, estab 2001, empl 30, sales , cert: WBENC)

9327 Reliance Communications, LLC
555 Wireless Blvd
Hauppauge, NY 11788
Contact: Jeanne Healey VP Marketing
Tel: 631-952-4800
Email: jeanne.healey@reliance.us
Website: www.reliance.us
Dist wireless communications handsets & accessories. (As-Ind, estab 2005, empl 290, sales $715,079,538, cert: NMSDC)

9328 Saia Communications, Inc.
100 Stradtman St
Buffalo, NY 14206
Contact: Cheryl Kirchmeyer Sales
Tel: 716-892-2900
Email: cheryl.kirchmeyer@saiacomm.com
Website: www.saiacomm.com
Motorola two-way radio products. (Woman, estab 1980, empl 25, sales $5,000,000, cert: State)

9329 Sintel Satellite Services
373 Nesconset Hwy Ste 133
Hauppauge, NY 11788
Contact: Sanjay Singhal COO
Tel: 212-202-0678
Email: sanjay@sintelsat.com
Website: www.sintelsat.com
Satellite communication & terrestrial telecom solutions, infrastructure rebuilding, IP connectivity, fiber, microwave & satellite, Vsat, broadcasting & IT solutions. (Minority, Woman, estab 1997, empl 30, sales $1,132,000, cert: State, City)

Ohio

9330 Ameridial, Inc.
4877 Higbee Ave NW, 2nd Fl
Canton, OH 44718
Contact: Ganesh Marve SVP
Tel: 234-401-8104
Email: ganesh.marve@fusionbposervices.com
Website: www.ameridial.com
Customer service,Tele-sales,Telephone Answering Services, Debt recovery,Technical support services, Order Taking, Online Order Processing, Collection Services. (As-Pac, estab 1987, empl 663, sales $42,391,472, cert: CPUC)

9331 Cincinnati Cable Technology
1177 W 8th St, Ste A
Cincinnati, OH 45203
Contact: Sheryl Yeager President
Tel: 513-579-1888
Email: sherylyeager@ccablet.com
Website: www.ccablet.com
Structured cabling, fiber optics, coax network infrastructure, wireless networks, security solutions, IP based door entrance, IP security cameras, audio/visual system design. (Woman, estab 2010, empl 7, sales $1,500,000, cert: WBENC)

9332 ClarkTel Communications Corp.
1661 Copley Rd
Akron, OH 44320
Contact: Terence N Clark President
Tel: 330-869-8657
Email: tclark@clarktel.net
Website: www.clarktel.net
Design, installation, warranty & service business telephone systems: NEC, Nortel, Mitel, Toshiba, Panasonic, Comdial, Vodavi Sprint, voice/data cable. (AA, estab 1996, empl 10, sales , cert: NMSDC)

9333 Fine Line Communications Inc.
PO Box 91
Aurora, OH 44202
Contact: Barbara Hoover President
Tel: 330-562-0731
Email: bhoover@finelinecomm.com
Website: www.finelinecomm.com
Design, intall & maintain voice & data network systems. (Woman, estab 1981, empl 25, sales $2,480,000, cert: State, WBENC)

9334 Ohio Cables, LLC
5288 Dietrich Ave
Orient, OH 43146
Contact: MINDY DIMEL Owner
Tel: 614-991-0404
Email: mindy@ohiocables.com
Website: www.ohiocables.com
Mfr & dist cables. (Woman, estab 2008, empl 2, sales $950,000, cert: City)

9335   One Source Mobile
        1066 Reading Rd
        Mason, OH 45040
        Contact: Amy Baumhower President
        Tel: 513-870-9300
        Email: abaumhower@onesourcemobile.com
        Website: www.onesourcemobile.com
Telecommunication services: wireless cell phone accessories, bluetooth items, car chargers & holsters etc. (Woman, estab 2005, empl 10, sales $925,000, cert: WBENC)

9336   SpeakSpace, LLC
        600 Superior Ave, Ste 1300
        Cleveland, OH 44114
        Contact: Behan Rebecca Managing Partner
        Tel: 440-263-1919
        Email: beckybehan@speakspace.com
        Website: www.speakspace.com
Teleconferencing services/conference calling, audio, web & video conferencing services. (Woman, estab 1999, empl 5, sales $800,000, cert: WBENC)

9337   The Fishel Company
        1366 Dublin Road
        Columbus, OH 43215
        Contact: Erick Piscopo Dir Marketing & BD
        Tel: 614-274-8100
        Email: ejpiscopo@teamfishel.com
        Website: www.teamfishel.com
Underground & aerial utility construction; inside & outside installation of fiber optic, copper, coaxial cabling; right of way services; structured cabling; network electronic installation; conduit construction & maintenance (Woman, estab 1936, empl 2575, sales $438,251,280, cert: WBENC)

9338   US Communications and Electric
        4933 Neo Pkwy
        Garfield Heights, OH 44128
        Contact: Jim Connole COO
        Tel: 216-478-0810
        Email: jconnole@uscande.com
        Website: www.uscande.com
Technology-based communications cabling systems, design & install outdoor copper systems, horizontal copper cabling solutions. (Woman, estab , empl , sales $17,000,000, cert: State, City, WBENC)

Oklahoma

9339   Ford Audio-Video Systems, LLC
        4800 West Interstate 40
        Oklahoma City, OK 73128
        Contact: Sales Center Mgr
        Tel: 405-946-9966
        Email: johnj@fordav.com
        Website: www.fordav.com
Design, mfr & install audio video communication equip: conference & board rooms, network operation ctrs, war rooms, command & control rooms, emergency response ctrs, video conferencing, media streaming, educational & training facilities. (Woman, estab 1973, empl , sales $200,000,000, cert: WBENC)

Pennsylvania

9340   Clark Resources, Inc.
        321 N Front St
        Harrisburg, PA 17101
        Contact: Christa Anderson
        Tel: 717-230-8861
        Email: christaanderson@fclarkresources.com
        Website: www.fclarkresources.com
Inbound and outbound telephone services. Call Center/Customer Support Center. (AA, estab 2002, empl 180, sales $6,000,000, cert: State, NMSDC)

9341   Enterprise Cable Group, Inc.
        805 W Fifth St
        Lansdale, PA 19446
        Contact: WBE Dir
        Tel: 215-361-4114
        Email: Sales@EnterpriseCableGroup.com
        Website: www.enterprisecablegroup.com
Communication & computer cable systems design & installation. (Woman, estab 2001, empl 20, sales $2,420,839, cert: WBENC)

9342   Fiber Business Solutions Inc.
        PO Box 103
        Fairview Village, PA 19409
        Contact: Cindy Gallo President
        Tel: 484-576-0876
        Email: cgallo@fbsginc.com
        Website: www.fbsginc.com
Fiber Optic Cable Placement & Splicing, Copper Cable Placement & Splicing, Right of Way & Permit Acquisition Services, Engineering & Design Services, CAD & As-Built Services, Project Management Services. (Woman, estab 2004, empl 8, sales $1,300,000, cert: WBENC, 8(a))

9343   MobileStrat, Inc.
        642 Cowpath Rd, Ste 390
        Lansdale, PA 19446
        Contact: Larry Blackshear CEO
        Tel: 215-237-3874
        Email: lb@mobilestrat.com
        Website: www.mobilestrat.com
Wireless, cellular, voice & data, gap analysis, billing management, WiFi site surveys
wire line, WAN design, WiFi security. (AA, estab 2004, empl 18, sales $0, cert: NMSDC)

9344   Pagoda Electrical
        2003 Friedensburg Rd
        Reading, PA 19606
        Contact: Bernette Wrobel President
        Tel: 610-779-3216
        Email: bernie@pagoda-electrical.com
        Website: www.pagoda-electrical.com
Electrical Contractor, Tele/Data. (Woman, estab 1994, empl 70, sales $24,248,481, cert: WBENC)

9345   Telecom Electric Supply Inc.
        320 Constance Dr, Bldg 5
        Warminster, PA 18974
        Contact: Theresa Flaherty CEO
        Tel: 267-960-2601
        Email: theresa@tessupply.com
        Website: www.tessupply.com
Dist central office installation supplies, telecommunication & electrical equipment. (Woman, estab 1995, empl 6, sales $1,295,272, cert: WBENC)

Puerto Rico

9346   B&B Communications Group
       220 Plaza Western Auto PMB-370 Ste 101
       Trujillo Alto, PR 00976
       Contact: Benjamin Bravo Sales
       Tel: 787-760-2698
       Email: bbravo@bbcorp.net
       Website: www.bbcorp.net
Communications, Fiber Optics, UPS, Cabling, Network, Cat-5e, cat-6, cat-6a, telecomm, telecommunications, voice, data, IP phones, power supply, design, site survey, training, service (Minority, Woman, estab 2014, empl 5, sales , cert: State, NMSDC)

South Carolina

9347   Globenet Telecommunications, LLC
       210 Titus Ln
       Pineville, SC 29468
       Contact: Cavid Middleton President
       Tel: 828-320-3291
       Email: dlmiddleton@charter.net
       Website: www.globenetusa.net
Low voltage system integration, install security devices & fiber optic cable. (AA, estab 2007, empl 32, sales $14,500,000, cert: CPUC)

Tennessee

9348   1 Point Procurement Solutions, LLC
       406 N Irish St, Ste 206
       Greeneville, TN 37745
       Contact: Steve Meriweather President
       Tel: 423-702-4700
       Email: steve.meriweather@1pointps.com
       Website: www.1pointps.com
Value-added reseller of wireless products from base station infrastructure, broadband connectivity, critical communications, indoor/outdoor network architecture, remote monitoring and control, and mobile devices. (AA, estab 2012, empl 1, sales $1,063,916, cert: State)

9349   Ashaun
       5100 Poplar Ave Ste 726
       Memphis, TN 38137
       Contact: Anthony Tate CEO
       Tel: 901-312-7025
       Email: atate@ashaun.com
       Website: www.ashaun.com
Call center services. (AA, estab 2000, empl 35, sales , cert: State, NMSDC)

9350   Power & Telephone Supply Co,
       2673 Yale Ave
       Memphis, TN 38112
       Contact: Annmarie Templeton Natl Acct Mgr
       Tel: 800-238-7514
       Email: annmarie.templeton@ptsupply.com
       Website: www.ptsupply.com
Communications products. (Woman, estab 1963, empl 350, sales , cert: State, City, CPUC, WBENC)

9351   Televergence Solutions, Inc.
       424 Church St, Ste 2000
       Nashville, TN 37219
       Contact: Ira Globerson VP Enterprise & Govt Sales
       Tel: 213-943-2023
       Email: igloberson@televergence.com
       Website: www.televergence.com
Toll Free, Long Distance and Cloud Phone System services, high call volume and/or in-house or outsourced Contact Centers. (Woman, estab 1988, empl 19, sales $2,982,863, cert: WBENC)

9352   Tel-XL
       5462 McGill
       Memphis, TN 38120
       Contact: Linda Hawkins President
       Tel: 866-848-3595
       Email: lhawkins@tel-xl.com
       Website: www.tel-xl.com
Dist new & refurb telecom equip, systems, accessories. (Woman, estab , empl , sales $0, cert: WBENC)

9353   Walker Warren Communications
       155 S Mendenhall Rd
       Memphis, TN 38117
       Contact: Sharlene H. Warren Principal
       Tel: 901-337-6326
       Email: Sharlene@ww911.net
       Website: www.ww911.net
Radio Systems /Infrastructure, 2-way radios, mobile (vehicles), Telephone Systems, GPS, Logger Recorders, Computer Aided Dispatch Systems, Redundancy analysis for critical applications. (Woman/AA, estab 2016, empl 2, sales , cert: City, WBENC)

Texas

9354   Austin Tele-Services Partners, LP dba Genesis ATS
       4209 S Industrial Dr Ste 300
       Austin, TX 78744
       Contact: Patrick Manning VP Business Dev
       Tel: 512-437-3041
       Email: pmanning@genesis-ats.com
       Website: www.genesis-ats.com
IT, Networking, Telecommunications & Computer related equipment & services. (Hisp, estab 2003, empl 45, sales $25,000,000, cert: State, NMSDC)

9355   Can-Am Wireless LLC dba Can-Am IT Solutions
       1333 Corporate Dr, Ste 110
       Irving, TX 75038
       Contact: Johan Rahardjo Dir of Engineering
       Tel: 866-976-4177
       Email: johan.rahardjo@canamitsolutions.com
       Website: www.canamitsolutions.com
Telecommunications and Information Technology Hardware & Software. (As-Pac, estab 2001, empl 7, sales $1,020,000, cert: NMSDC)

9356   Clayborn Inc.
       PO Box 703212
       Dallas, TX 75370
       Contact: Jacquelyn Clayborn CEO
       Tel: - -
       Email: onc@oncnational.com
       Website: www.oncnational.com
Installation (Cat5 Cat6) Voice, Data, Fiber Optic, Coax (tv), Wireless access point installation, splicing of building entrance and riser cable, cable abatement, abandoned cable removal, sound masking systems, extensions services. (Woman/AA, estab 2016, empl 5, sales $569,399, cert: NMSDC, WBENC)

9357   Clearvue Networks, LLC
       100 E Main St Ste 201
       Round Rock, TX 78664
       Contact: Shanna Schmidt Admin Asst
       Tel: 512-861-5319
       Email: shanna.schmidt@clearvuenetworks.com
       Website: www.clearvuenetworks.com
Business networking solutions, work station installs/configs, server installs/configs, network assessments, wireless installs, telecom services, voice/data/fiber cabling, alarm/surveillance systems, card access security systems. (Hisp, estab 2011, empl 9, sales , cert: State)

9358　Continental Wireless
10455 VISTA PARK RD
Dallas, TX 75238
Contact: RITA WEBER President
Tel:　972-926-7443
Email: RITA.WEBER@CNTLWIRE.COM
Website: www.cntlwire.com
Wireless communication, dist & rent two way radios.
(Woman, estab 2000, empl 25, sales $15,263,348, cert:
WBENC)

9359　Crystal Application Software Services, LLC
3201 Cherry Ridge Dr Ste B-218
San Antonio, TX 78230
Contact: Veronica Vela Acct Mgr
Tel:　210-698-2410
Email: veronica.vela@cnetcable.com
Website: www.cnetcable.com
Design-build telecommunications, low voltage cabling,
wireless & access points, voice & data networks, security
cameras, audio & visual, fiber optics, phone systems &
microwave. (Hisp, estab 2014, empl 10, sales , cert: State)

9360　Diamond P Enterprises, Inc.
PO Box 483
Brownwood, TX 76804
Contact: Erin Toft Operations Mgr
Tel:　325-643-5629
Email: admin.assist@diamondpenterprises.com
Website: www.diamondpenterprises.com
Cable Placing Materials, Closures/Splicing Materials,
Copper Cable, Cutting & Distribution, Corrugated Products,
Fiber Optic Cable, Cutting & Distribution. (Hisp, estab ,
empl , sales $60,309,360, cert: NMSDC, CPUC)

9361　DMI Technologies, Inc.
14900 Grand River Rd, Ste 100
Fort Worth, TX 76155
Contact: L Samentha Tiller President
Tel:　817-355-5385
Email: stiller@dmitechinc.com
Website: www.dmitechinc.com
Voice, data, audio, video, CCTV, CATV cabling contractor.
(Woman, estab , empl , sales $27,000,000, cert: WBENC)

9362　Dynamic Voice Data
4403 Greenbriar Dr
Stafford, TX 77477
Contact: Tina Greenfield Business Devel Mgr
Tel:　800-838-5070
Email: tgreenfield@dvd-inc.com
Website: www.dvd-inc.com
Mfr custom OEM products using injection mould technol-
ogy, interconnect products & telephone parts, harnesses &
power supplies. (Minority, Woman, estab 1993, empl 15,
sales $11,300,000, cert: State, NMSDC)

9363　KMM Telecommunications
4051 N Hwy 121 Ste 400
Grapevine, TX 76051
Contact: Sarah McNab Dir HR & Marketing
Tel:　844-566-8488
Email: s.mcnab@kmmcorp.net
Website: www.kmmcorp.net
Sourcing products & services; contract management;
inventory planning & procurement; material management
& deployment; material warehousing; material fulfillment,
3PL services; last-mile staging services; reverse logistics.
(Woman, estab 1991, empl 130, sales $892,823,959, cert:
CPUC, WBENC)

9364　Micro-Design, Inc.
10210 Monroe Dr
Dallas, TX 75229
Contact: Douglas Ramsey VP Operations
Tel:　972-488-8725
Email: dramsey@levelcon.com
Website: www.micro-design.com
Remote telemetry solutions: wireless, WiFi, cellular &
satellite, engineering & solutions for CNG pump stations
& infrastructure. (Woman, estab 1984, empl 15, sales
$2,000,000, cert: State)

9365　Operational Technologies Corporation
4100 NW Loop 410, Ste 23
San Antonio, TX 78229
Contact: Louisa Alaniz Sr Mgr. Client Services
Tel:　210-731-0000
Email: louisa.alaniz@otcorp.com
Website: www.otcorp.com
Fulfillment center kitting, warehousing & distribution,
telecommunications & communications engineering &
installation, environmental svcs. (Hisp, estab 1986, empl
70, sales $15,192,216, cert: State, NMSDC)

9366　Premier Paging, Inc.
12220 Murphy Rd Ste F
Stafford, TX 77477
Contact: Lea Bogle President
Tel:　281-575-8500
Email: lea.bogle@premierwirelesstx.com
Website: www.premierwirelesstx.com
Wireless equipment, accessories & service, GPS tracking
for fleets & assets, electronic forms. (Woman, estab
1993, empl 17, sales $2,500,000, cert: State, WBENC)

9367　Ransor, Inc.
7055 Pipestone
Schertz, TX 78154
Contact: Randy Sorrell VP
Tel:　210-651-6451
Email: randy@ransor.com
Website: www.ransor.com
Install communication equipment & maintains mono-
poles, guyed & self supporting towers, tower construc-
tion, tower modifications & tower maintenance.
(Woman, estab 1987, empl 7, sales $984,000, cert:
State)

9368　Sky Communications, Inc.
6101 Long Prairie Rd, Ste 744-162
Flower Mound, TX 75028
Contact:　Exec VP
Tel:　214-789-5090
Email: contact@skycomglobal.com
Website: www.skycomglobal.com
Telecommunications services, engineering, design,
implementation & managed services, unified communi-
cations, VOIP, call center & project management. (AA,
estab 1995, empl 13, sales $1,735,567, cert: State,
NMSDC)

9369 Telecom Electric Supply Company
1304 Capital Ave
Plano, TX 75074
Contact: Christy Moses Sales Exec
Tel: 972-422-0012
Email: cmoses@tes85.com
Website: www.tes85.com
Dist electric, utility, construction & telecommunication supplies. (AA, estab , empl , sales $33,858,031, cert: State, NMSDC)

9370 Teltech Communications LLC
3211 Internet Blvd Ste 300
Frisco, TX 75034
Contact: Lisa Hanlon CEO
Tel: 469-713-3801
Email: lhanlon@teltech.com
Website: www.teltech.com
Network infrastructure equipment, wireless, wireline, asset & inventory management services. (Minority, Woman, estab 1999, empl 106, sales $34,827,298, cert: NMSDC, CPUC, WBENC)

9371 The Wilkins Group, Inc.
1710 Firman Dr, Ste 200
Richardson, TX 75081
Contact: ConTrenia McKinzie Cameron VP Admin
Tel: 972-479-1090
Email: trenia@wilkins.com
Website: www.wilkins.com
Telecommunications services, equipment installation, voice, video & data systems. (Woman/AA, estab 1986, empl 30, sales $7,400,000, cert: State, NMSDC)

Utah

9372 Discountcell Inc.
350 West 500 South
Provo, UT 84601
Contact: Janiel Jones Mgr
Tel: 801-235-9809
Email: corp@discountcell.com
Website: www.discountcell.com
Dist cell phone accessories: antennas, boosters, cases, chargers, holsters, screen protectors, batteries, headsets, Bluetooth, data kits, data cables, covers, stylus, neoprene, canvas, heavy duty, leather. (Woman, estab 1998, empl 10, sales $700,000, cert: WBENC)

Virginia

9373 Opterna-AM Inc.
44901 Falcon Pl Ste 116
Sterling, VA 20166
Contact: Matt Onojafe Dir Govt Contracting
Tel: 571-294-7652
Email: matt.onojafe@opterna.com
Website: www.opterna.com
Fiber optic products & solutions, fiber optic communication solutions. (As-Ind, estab 1994, empl 17, sales $10,000,000, cert: NMSDC)

9374 Secured Network Solutions, Inc.
929 Ventures Way Ste 113
Chesapeake, VA 23320
Contact: Alphonzo Barney President
Tel: 757-819-7647
Email: abarney@teamsns.com
Website: www.teamsns.com
Telecommunications & information technology: cabling, design, install, fiber optics single/multi-strand, fiber fusion & splicing, LAN/WAN/wireless network engineering, drafting & information systems security. (AA, estab 2006, empl 11, sales , cert: State)

9375 Shore Communications, Inc.
600 N Witchduck Rd, Ste 106
Virginia Beach, VA 23462
Contact: Laura Castner President
Tel: 757-468-0855
Email: lcastner@shorecomusa.com
Website: www.shorecomusa.com
Engineering, design, installation & testing structured cabling systems, telephone & paging systems, including adds, moves or changes to existing systems. (Woman, estab 1995, empl 28, sales , cert: State)

9376 TEKCONNX
608 Westwood Office Park
Fredericksburg, VA 22401
Contact: Kevin Wlliams CEO
Tel: 703-635-4439
Email: kevinw@tekconnx.com
Website: www.tekconnx.com
Interactive Audio Visual (IAVT) Solutions & Integration, A/V Telepresence Conferencing (HW & SW), Design/ Build Interactive Audio Visual Solutions, Command & Control Centers, Wireless Video/Audio Solutions. (AA, estab 2013, empl 3, sales $850,000, cert: State, NMSDC)

9377 Roadswest Construction Inc.
307 N Olympic Ave, Ste 209
Arlington, WA 98223
Contact: Kirby Lundberg VP
Tel: 360-403-8782
Email: roadswestinc@verizon.net
Website: www.RoadsWestInc.com
Dist, service & install voice & data wiring & audio/vidio systems. (Nat Ame, estab 1987, empl 30, sales $873,949, cert: State)

Wisconsin

9378 1Prospect Technologies, LLC
PO Box 1045
Rhinelander, WI 54501
Contact: Brad Kowieski Dir of Business Dev
Tel: 715-369-1119
Email: info@1prospect.com
Website: www.oneprospect.com
Design & build flexible cabling infrastructure supporting multiple voice, data, video & multimedia systems. (Nat Ame, estab 2000, empl 33, sales $10,400,000, cert: State)

> ### TEXTILES
> Includes thread, trimmings, woven and nonwoven material manfucaturers. NAICS Code 31

California

9379 A & R Tarpaulins Inc.
16246 Valley Blvd
Fontana, CA 92335
Contact: Didi Truong Aerospace Project Mgr
Tel: 909-829-4444
Email: didi@artech2000.com
Website: www.artech2000.com
We specialize in MLI (Multilayer insulation), Acoustic blankets, payload fairing, sound barriers, high temperture insulation & protection, thermal radiational heat control, EMI & RFI shielding, antistatic & security enclosures. (Minority, Woman, estab 1976, empl 49, sales $4,500,000, cert: CPUC)

9380 H & A Enterprise
530 N Baldwin Park Blvd
City of Industry, CA 91746
Contact: Huma Latif Owner
Tel: 909-714-3960
Email: ahuma@hotmail.com
Website: www.hnaenterprise.com
Dist textile goods, socks, towels, bar mops . (Woman/As-Ind, estab 2012, empl 1, sales , cert: NMSDC)

9381 International Textile and Apparel, Inc.
1875 Century Park E Ste 1040
Los Angeles, CA 90067
Contact: Shoaib Kothawala CEO
Tel: 310-556-8088
Email: nbaresabidia@intlinen.com
Website: www.donothaveone.com
Mfr towels, bar mop towels & shop towels, weaving dye & finish, cut & sew. (As-Pac, estab 1983, empl 15, sales , cert: NMSDC)

9382 Venus Group, Inc.
25861 Wright St
Foothill Ranch, CA 92610
Contact: Ryen Masters Sales Mgr
Tel: 800-421-4595
Email: rmasters@venusgroup.com
Website: www.venusgroup.com
Mfr, cut and sew textiles, towels, sheets and napery. (As-Ind, estab 1972, empl 130, sales $75,000,000, cert: NMSDC)

Georgia

9383 PBR Inc.
335 Athena Dr
Athens, GA 30601
Contact: Palak Patel Exec Business Devel
Tel: 706-354-3700
Email: palak@skaps.com
Website: www.skaps.com
Fabricate Geosynthetic & nonwoven drainage products, produce polypropylene & polyester needle-punched nonwoven geotextiles from 2 to 32 ounces per square yard. (As-Pac, estab 1995, empl 250, sales $390,000,000, cert: NMSDC)

9384 Unitex International Inc.
2222 Northmont Pkwy Ste 100
Duluth, GA 30096
Contact: Anwer Anwer Shakoor Dir
Tel: 770-232-0060
Email: a.shakoor@unitexonline.com
Website: www.unitexonline.com
Textile & fabric finishing. (Minority, estab 1990, empl 29, sales $83,000,000, cert: NMSDC)

Illinois

9385 R&R Textile Mills Inc.
1101 N Lombard Rd
Lombard, IL 60148
Contact: Rajan Barad COO
Tel: 630-424-8000
Email: rbarad@rrtextilemills.com
Website: www.rrtextilemills.com
Mfr & dist textile products. (Minority, estab 1988, empl 40, sales $9,800,000, cert: NMSDC)

9386 Revere Mills International Group, Inc.
2860 S River Rd Ste 250
Des Plaines, IL 60018
Contact: Jeff Gregg President
Tel: 847-759-6800
Email: jgregg@reveremills.com
Website: www.reveremills.com
Mfr, import & dist textile products: beach towels, bath towels, kitchen towels, golf & rally towels. (Woman, estab , empl 22, sales $24,000,000, cert: WBENC)

Massachusetts

9387 Spectro Coating Corp.
101 Scott Dr
Leominster, MA 01453
Contact: Wayne Turcotte VP Sales
Tel: 978-534-1800
Email: ssnyer@spectrocoating.com
Website: www.spectrocoating.com
Mfr fibers: silk, cotton, rayon, Kevlar, Tencel, bamboo, nylon, acrylic, polyester, etc. (As-Pac, estab 1988, empl 70, sales $12,000,000, cert: NMSDC)

Maine

9388 Auburn Manufacturing, Inc.
PO Box 220
Mechanic Falls, ME 04256
Contact: Kathie M Leonard CEO
Tel: 207-345-8771
Email: kleonard@auburnmfg.com
Website: www.auburnmfg.com
Design & mfr heat-resistant textiles for MRO applications. (Minority, Woman, estab 1979, empl 49, sales $10,300,000, cert: WBENC)

Michigan

9389 National Manufacturing, Inc.
25426 Ryan Rd
Warren, MI 48091
Contact: Paul Cano Sales
Tel: 586-755-8983
Email: paul.cano@nationalmanufacturinginc.com
Website: www.nationalmanufacturinginc.com
Leather & vinyl wrapping of steering wheels, pull handles, shift knobs, arm rests, bolsters, sewn by hand or machine, emergency kits, jack bags, utility bags, tools bags for the automotive industry. (Woman/Hisp, estab 1964, empl 32, sales , cert: NMSDC, WBENC)

9390 Plastikon Michigan
      2300 Pine Lake Rd
      West Bloomfield, MI 48324
      Contact: Martin Fisher Dir
      Tel: 248-798-8292
      Email: mfisher@trimsllc.com
      Website: www.trimsllc.com
Contract mfr sew leather, vinyl, cloth for automotive interiors, boat seats, office chairs, top of bed for hotel industry. (As-Ind, estab 1980, empl 16, sales , cert: NMSDC)

9391 Star Textile, Inc.
      2333 John B
      Warren, MI 48091
      Contact: Marketing
      Tel: 586-758-2700
      Email: info@startextile.com
      Website: www.startextile.com
Provides bedding & draperies in the hospitality industry. (Woman, estab 1999, empl 60, sales $2,500,000, cert: WBENC)

Missouri

9392 Phoenix Textile Corporation
      21 Commerce Dr
      OFallon, MO 63366
      Contact: Laura Mahnken Sales Admin
      Tel: 314-291-2151
      Email: lmahnken@phoenixtextile.com
      Website: www.phoenixtextile.com
Reusable institutional textiles & interior products. (Woman, estab , empl , sales , cert: WBENC)

North Carolina

9393 Kilop USA, Inc.
      4100 Mendenhall Oaks Pkwy
      High Point, NC 27265
      Contact: Christine Chen President
      Tel: 336-402-5979
      Email: cchen@kilopusa.com
      Website: www.kilopusa.com
Global nonwoven and textile raw material supply chain services. (Minority, Woman, estab 0, empl , sales $0, cert: NMSDC, WBENC)

New Jersey

9394 Centryco Inc.
      300 W Broad St
      Burlington, NJ 08016
      Contact: Mary Gordon President
      Tel: 609-386-6448
      Email: mtg@centryco.com
      Website: www.centryco.com
Mfr point of operation barriers for machinery & equipment: bellows, way covers, telescoping covers, flat bellows & screens, spring guards/covers. (Woman, estab 1949, empl 35, sales $3,910,958, cert: WBENC)

9395 Offray Specialty Narrow Fabrics, Inc.
      4 Essex Ave Ste 403
      Bernardsville, NJ 07924
      Contact: Denise A. Offray CEO
      Tel: 908-879-3636
      Email: doffray@osnf.com
      Website: www.osnf.com
Engineer & mfr quality, high performance, innovative narrow fabric textiles, weave specialty branded yarns. (Woman, estab 1921, empl 45, sales $8,674,420, cert: State)

New York

9396 Sigmatex, Inc
      551 Fifth Ave, Ste 1110
      New York, NY 10176
      Contact: Marcia Rodriguez General Mgr
      Tel: 212-593-0934
      Email: mrodriguez@sigmatexlanier.com
      Website: www.sigmatexlanier.com
Mfr institutional textile products: terry towels, sheets & pillowcases, table linens. (Minority, Woman, estab 1976, empl 25, sales $18,155,425, cert: State)

Ohio

9397 Casco Manufacturing Solutions, Inc.
      3107 Spring Grove Ave
      Cincinnati, OH 45225
      Contact: Melissa Mangold President
      Tel: 800-843-1339
      Email: mmangold@cascosolutions.com
      Website: www.cascosolutions.com
Design & mfr fabric or textiles products. (Woman, estab , empl , sales $5,300,000, cert: WBENC)

South Carolina

9398 Calitex International
      106 Thousand Oaks Ct
      Summerville, SC 29485
      Contact: John Sylvester President
      Tel: 864-278-2621
      Email: john@calitexintl.com
      Website: www.calitex.us
Dist Industrial Fabrics, Cotton Canvas, Single fill duck, Numbered Ducks, Army Duck, Twill, Treated fabric for Tarps, Tents, Tipis, Boat covers. (Minority, Woman, estab 2005, empl 2, sales $1,500,000, cert: NMSDC)

9399 MVP Textiles and Apparel, Inc.
      1031 Le Grand Blvd
      Charleston, SC 29492
      Contact: Mary Propes CEO
      Tel: 843-216-8380
      Email: marypropes@mvpgroupint.com
      Website: www.mvptextiles.com
Mfr textiles. (Woman, estab 2005, empl 15, sales $16,800,000, cert: WBENC)

Texas

9400 Orr Textile Co., Inc.
      4777 Blalock
      Houston, TX 77041
      Contact: Hilary Orr VP Sales
      Tel: 713-939-7788
      Email: hilary@orrtextile.com
      Website: www.orrtextile.com
Dist sheets, towels, blankets, pillows, bath mats, robes, slippers, bar mops, table linen, napkins, janitorial supplies, mops, buckets & wringers, mattress pads, pillow slips, pool towels, spa linen, chef wear, etc. (Woman, estab 1967, empl 11, sales , cert: WBENC)

Washington

9401 Lancs Industries Holdings, LLC
      12704 NE 124th St, Bldg 36
      Kirkland, WA 98034
      Contact: Raymond Suarez
      Tel: 425-823-6634
      Email: rsuarez@lancsindustries.com
      Website: www.lancsindustries.com
Mfr custom lead wool blankets, glovebags, tents, protective clothing, related shielding & containment products for nuclear naval shipyards; nuclear remediation, decontamination. (AA, estab 2010, empl 65, sales $6,000,000, cert: State)

TRANSPORTATION SERVICES
Transport office and household furniture and equipment. Commercial freight and general commodities and have ICC rights for other states. Storage, wharehousing and packaging services. Charter bus, limousine service and air couriers. Custom house clearance, export documentation, export packing and crating. NAICS Code 48

Alabama

9402 ARD Logistics, LLC
10098 Brose Dr
Vance, AL 35490
Contact: Courtney Waters Sales & Marketing Rep
Tel: 205-393-5207
Email: cwaters@ardlogistics.com
Website: www.ardlogistics.com
Distribution operations: sequencing, sub-assembly, warehousing, inventory mgmt, shipping & receiving materials handling maintenance, packaging & repackaging, transportation mgmt, transportation svcs. (AA, estab 1998, empl 900, sales $68,717,549, cert: NMSDC)

9403 ARI Logistics LLC
204 20th St North Ste 200
Birmingham, AL 35203
Contact: Brennan Waters Sales
Tel: 205-271-4434
Email: brennan.waters@actn.com
Website: www.actn.com
Hazardous waste transport, in-plant, remediation, & logistics services. (AA, estab 2008, empl 55, sales $202,000,000, cert: NMSDC)

9404 Universal Logistics Services, Inc.
5330 Stadium Trace Pkwy, Ste 200
Birmingham, AL 35244
Contact: Alan Washburn Operations Mgr
Tel: 205-682-8505
Email: awashburn@ufsystems.com
Website: www.universallogisticsservices.com
Transportation services. (AA, estab 1999, empl 100, sales $3,500,000, cert: NMSDC)

Arkansas

9405 Heartland Supply Company
1248 Pump Station Rd
Fayetteville, AR 72702
Contact: Timothy J McNicholas Key Acct Mgr
Tel: 773-617-6214
Email: tmcnicholas@heartlandsupply.com
Website: www.heartlandsupply.com
Logistic, distribution, supply chain optimization & warehousing services. (Nat Ame, estab 1987, empl 15, sales $100,000,000, cert: NMSDC)

9406 WMJ Enterprises, LLC.
PO Box 979
Lowell, AR 72745
Contact: Justin Winberry VP
Tel: 888-782-5828
Email: jwinberry@leon-cannon.com
Website: www.leon-cannon.com
Asset based transportation & logsitics. (Hisp, estab 1994, empl 38, sales $27,200,000, cert: State)

Arizona

9407 Aerocean Freight Solutions, Inc.
9414 E. San Salvador Dr Ste 242
Scottsdale, AZ 85258
Contact: Yeon-Hee (Jennifer) Hwang President
Tel: 480-515-1912
Email: jennifer@aeroceanfreight.com
Website: www.aeroceanfreight.com
Third party logistical services, road transportation, rail, ocean freight transportation. (Minority, Woman, estab 2006, empl 4, sales $5,314,734, cert: WBENC)

9408 BC Logistics LLC
4405 E Baseline Rd Ste 114
Phoenix, AZ 85042
Contact: Vicki Boisjolie President
Tel: 480-966-5000
Email: phx@bclogisticsllc.com
Website: www.bclogisticsllc.com
Air afreight, ground transportation, domestic & international, next flight out, same day, conventions, blank wrap, pad van, flat beds, double flat beds. (Woman, estab , empl , sales $3,061,531, cert: WBENC)

9409 GIT Global Services
2049 W Hwy Dr
Tucson, AZ 85705
Contact: D'Angelo Brenda Dir of Operations
Tel: 520-269-6372
Email: info@gitgs.com
Website: www.gitgs.com
Freight forwarding company offering worldwide logistics services. (Hisp, estab 2011, empl 10, sales $3,000,000, cert: City, NMSDC)

9410 Mach 1 Global Services, Inc.
1530 W Broadway Rd
Tempe, AZ 85282
Contact: Jamie Fletcher CEO
Tel: 480-921-3900
Email: jfletcher@mach1global.com
Website: www.mach1global.com
Transportation & logistics, domestic heavy weight expedited freight forwarding, international freight forwarding, ocean & air import & export, distribution, warehousing & supply chain management. (Minority, Woman, estab 1988, empl 290, sales $165,000,000, cert: WBENC)

9411 Patriot Movers, LLC
3060 N Ridgecrest, Unit 128
Mesa, AZ 85207
Contact: Christopher Palos COO
Tel: 877-793-7775
Email: patriotmovers57@yahoo.com
Website: www.Patriotmover.us
Moving & Transportation, Local a& nd Long Distance Moving, (intrastate and interstate), Packing, Unpacking, Crating, Specialized Freight,   Residential, Commercial, Office, Relocation services. (Minority, Woman, estab 2012, empl 5, sales , cert: City)

9412   QBP Logistics, Inc.
       6006 N 83rd Ave Ste 201
       Glendale, AZ 85303
       Contact: Marlin Banks Operations Mgr
       Tel: 602-314-5099
       Email: marlin@landstarmail.com
       Website: www.qbpfreight.com
Transportation. Truckload transportation, Rail Intermodal service, Heavy Haul Specialized transport, Ocean freight forwarding, Expedited ground transport & Air freight forwarding. (AA, estab 2007, empl 6, sales $560,000, cert: CPUC)

9413   Reflex Logistics, LLC
       7114 E Stetson Dr Ste 400
       Scottsdale, AZ 85251
       Contact: Cory Clapper VP Sales
       Tel: 602-859-5969
       Email: coryclapper@reflexlogistics.com
       Website: www.reflexlogistics.com
Domestic full truckload van, refrigerated & flatbed transportation services. (Woman, estab 2013, empl 8, sales $750,000, cert: WBENC)

9414   The ILS Company
       8350 E Old Vail Rd
       Tucson, AZ 85747
       Contact: Roy Austin Business Dev Dir
       Tel: 520-618-4309
       Email: roy.austin@ilscompany.com
       Website: www.ilscompany.com
International Freight Forwarding & Logistics Services, Door to Door Transportation Management (Air, Ground, Ocean and Rail), Project Cargo Management, Vendor Managed Inventory, Hot Shot, Remote & White Glove. (Hisp, estab 2002, empl 54, sales $24,320,000, cert: NMSDC)

California

9415   Aeronet Logistics Inc.
       42 Corporate Park
       Irvine, CA 92606
       Contact: Andres Aceves President
       Tel: 949-474-9292
       Email: diversity@aeronet.com
       Website: www.aeronet.com
Global integrated logistics svcs: freight & cargo transportation, distribution & supply chain mgmt, air freight, expedited ground freight & urgent shipments, ocean cargo, import & export. (Hisp, estab 1982, empl 125, sales $70,858,000, cert: NMSDC, CPUC)

9416   ASI Computer Technologies, Inc.
       48289 Fremont Blvd
       Fremont, CA 94538
       Contact: Louis Kim Business Devel Mgr
       Tel: 510-445-4112
       Email: louis.kim@asipartner.com
       Website: www.asipartner.com
Freight dispatch capabilities, containers by Sea, air or Ground Trucking, Supply Chain Programs. (Minority, Woman, estab 1987, empl , sales $23,000,000, cert: NMSDC, WBENC)

9417   Bulk or Liquid Transport, LLC
       576 Camino Mercado
       Arroyo Grande, CA 93420
       Contact: Tracy Thomas CEO
       Tel: 800-975-2658
       Email: tthomas@bolt-transport.com
       Website: www.BOLT-Transport.com
Interstate transportation: liquid food-grade products. (Woman, estab 2006, empl 10, sales $2,253,148, cert: WBENC)

9418   Cargo Solutions Express
       14587 Valley Blvd
       Fontana, CA 92335
       Contact: Harsimran Singh Operations Mgr
       Tel: 909-350-1644
       Email: karan@cargosolutionexpress.com
       Website: www.cargosolutionexpress.com/
Transportation: fleet of 1500+ tractors and 2700+ trailers. (As-Pac, estab 2001, empl 550, sales $106,521,000, cert: NMSDC)

9419   Casas International Brokerage, Inc.
       9355 Airway Rd, Ste 4 Otay Mesa
       San Diego, CA 92154
       Contact: Syliva Casas President
       Tel: 619-710-4619
       Email: s.casas@casasinternational.com
       Website: www.casasinternational.com
US Customs broker & freight forwarder, warehouse & distribution. (Minority, Woman, estab 1984, empl 85, sales $6,055,615, cert: NMSDC)

9420   Contractors Cargo Companies
       500 S Alameda St
       Compton, CA 90221
       Contact: Steve Cummins Natl Sales Mgr
       Tel: 310-609-1957
       Email: scummins@contractorscargo.com
       Website: www.contractorscargo.com
Heavy haul transportation company, oversized, overweight or overdimensional cargo, rail logistics, heavy haul transport & shipping, nationally & internationally. (Woman, estab 1929, empl 85, sales $24,000,000, cert: CPUC)

9421   Crown Xpress Transport Inc.
       9931 Via de la amistad
       San Diego, CA 92154
       Contact: Lorena Guillen Business Devel
       Tel: 619-671-9611
       Email: assistant@crownxt.com
       Website: www.crownxt.com
FTL freight services. (Minority, Woman, estab 2003, empl 39, sales $12,434,665, cert: NMSDC, WBENC)

9422   CurDor Group Inc.
       2321 Del Amo Blvd
       Rancho Dominguez, CA 90220
       Contact: Curlee Dorn President
       Tel: 310-885-5200
       Email: curlee.dorn@360globaltransportation.com
       Website: www.360globaltransportation.com
Intermodal, Import / Export, Haz-mat, Over-Weight Containers, Warehousing, Less Than truck Load, Transloading, Dedicated Services, Flatbed, Reefer, Rail Services, Cross-Drocking, Truckload (TL), Outsourcing, Dryvan. (AA, estab 2012, empl 7, sales $400,000, cert: NMSDC)

9423 D.W. Morgan Company, Inc.
4185 Blackhawk Plaza Circle Ste 260
Danville, CA 94506
Contact: Dawn Kim Dir of Business Dev
Tel: 310-938-9091
Email: dawn.kim@dwmorgan.com
Website: www.dwmorgan.com
Supply chain consulting, transportation management, and thrid-party logistics. (As-Pac, estab 1990, empl 750, sales $98,310,000, cert: NMSDC)

9424 EXCEL Moving Services
30047 Ahern Ave
Union City, CA 94587
Contact: Bruce Owashi President
Tel: 800-392-3596
Email: bruce@excelmoving.com
Website: www.excelmoving.com
Moving & storage, employee relocations, storage & distribution, air-ride inside PU/Del transportation, intl shipping/receiving, household goods specialist. (AA, As-Pac, estab 1994, empl 55, sales $4,000,000, cert: State, NMSDC, CPUC)

9425 FNS, Inc.
18301 S Broadwick St
Rancho Dominguez, CA 90220
Contact: Josh Taxon Sales/Mktg Mgr
Tel: 310-747-8530
Email: joshua.taxon@pantos.com
Website: www.fnsusa.com
Global third party logistics: ocean transport, air transport, trucking, warehousing & custom house brokerage. (As-Pac, estab 1995, empl 250, sales $12,881,358, cert: NMSDC)

9426 Freight Express Shipping Corp (FESCO)
15330 Fairfield Ranch Rd., Unit G
Chino Hills, CA 91709
Contact: Michael Yu General Mgr
Tel: 909-586-3000
Email: service@fescous.com
Website: www.fescous.com
Import & export freight forwarding services. (Minority, Woman, estab 2012, empl 6, sales $900,000, cert: State)

9427 Global Freight Experts, Inc.
1950 E Miner Ave
Stockton, CA 95205
Contact: Rajinder Singh President
Tel: 209-547-9210
Email: raj@gfbontime.com
Website: www.gfbontime.com
Asset based trucking. (As-Pac, estab 2010, empl 25, sales $3,100,000, cert: NMSDC)

9428 Golden Gate Air Freight Inc.
1809 Sabre St
Hayward, CA 94545
Contact: John Cardenas President
Tel: 510-785-5720
Email: jcardenas@ggaf.com
Website: www.ggaf.com
Domestic & international freight forwarding. (Hisp, estab 1982, empl 22, sales $8,055,928, cert: NMSDC)

9429 Intrade Industries, Inc.
2559 S East Ave
Fresno, CA 93706
Contact: Tracy Farrell logistics/Mktg Mgr
Tel: 559-256-3291
Email: tracy.intradeindustries@gmail.com
Website: www.intradeindustries.com
Transportation services for refrigerated cargo & freight from coast to coast. (Minority, Woman, estab 1997, empl 14, sales $23,000,000, cert: NMSDC)

9430 KLS Air Express, Inc. dba Freight Solution Provide
2870 Gold Tailings Ct.
Rancho Cordova, CA 95670
Contact: Chrissie Cruz Natl Exec Accounts Mgr
Tel: 513-532-1297
Email: chrissie_cruz@shipfsp.com
Website: www.shipfsp.com/about/index.html
Customized frieght transportation, logistics, warehousing & supply chain management solutions. (Minority, Woman, estab 1989, empl 110, sales $42,000,000, cert: NMSDC, WBENC)

9431 KW International, Inc.
18655 Bishop Ave
Carson, CA 90746
Contact: Steve Cho Sr Mgr
Tel: 310-354-6944
Email: steve@kwinternational.com
Website: www.kwinternational.com/default.aspx
Total logistics, transportation, freight forwarding, in-house customs brokerage, warehousing & distribution, reverse logistics, customer call center, field service, drayage, information & technology. (As-Pac, estab 1996, empl 1000, sales , cert: NMSDC)

9432 Mayor Logistics Inc.
17214 S Figueroa St
Gardena, CA 90248
Contact: Henry Mayor
Tel: 424-221-5225
Email: hruiz@mayorusa.com
Website: www.mayorusa.com
Domestic drayage, import/export, truckload, local & over the road, regional carrier. (Hisp, estab 2004, empl 10, sales $5,636,670, cert: NMSDC)

9433 Mosaic Global Transportation
743 S Winchester Blvd Ste 210
San Jose, CA 95128
Contact: Maurice Brewster CEO
Tel: 800-398-7881
Email: info@mosaicglobaltransportation.com
Website: www.mosaicglobaltransportation.com
Transportation & corporate charters. (AA, estab 2001, empl 101, sales $11,100,000, cert: NMSDC)

9434 Music Express Limousine Service
2601 Empire Ave
Burbank, CA 91504
Contact: Gary Dye General Counsel
Tel: 818-260-6630
Email: gdye@musiclimo.com
Website: www.musiclimo.com
National & international limousine svcs. (Woman, estab , empl , sales $0, cert: WBENC)

9435 National Freight Logistics Inc.
3150 N Weber Ave
Fresno, CA 93722
Contact: Ethan Lee
Tel: 559-827-4092
Email: ethan@nflfreight.com
Website: www.NFLfreight.com
Freight transportation & logistics. (Minority, Woman, estab 2006, empl 4, sales $1,534,690, cert: NMSDC)

9436 Northwest Freightway Inc.
3421 Industrial Dr
Yuba City, CA 95991
Contact: Nicholas Schlaff Dir of Sales
Tel: 539-788-2742
Email: nick@nwfreightway.com
Website: www.nwfreightway.com
Freight transportation services. (AA, estab 2007, empl 26, sales $28,000,000, cert: NMSDC)

9437 Oakley Relocation LLC
13026 Stowe Dr
Poway, CA 92064
Contact: Dir of Business Dev
Tel: 858-602-1010
Email:
Website: www.oakleyrelocation.com
Full-service moving & storage company. (Woman, estab 2008, empl 15, sales $4,250,000, cert: WBENC)

9438 Public Special
3147 Progress Circle
Mira Loma, CA 91752
Contact: Anna Aguiar President
Tel: 951-360-4466
Email: aaguiar@publicspecial.net
Website: www.publicspecial.net
Transportation, US and Canada. (Minority, Woman, estab 1980, empl 4, sales $22,048,000, cert: NMSDC)

9439 Red Rose Transportation, Inc
5705 N West Ave
Fresno, CA 93711
Contact: Mark Rose Operations Mgr
Tel: 559-277-1060
Email: mark@redrosetrans.net
Website: www.redrosetransportation.com
Logistic services, dedicated truckloads, Heavy haul, 53' dry van & reefers, flatbeds & LTL. (Minority, Woman, estab 2007, empl 7, sales $8,300,000, cert: CPUC, WBENC)

9440 Roland International Freight Services, Inc.
5710 W Manchester Ave Ste 104
Los Angeles, CA 90045
Contact: Roland Furtado President
Tel: 310-337-1775
Email: roland@rolandfreight.com
Website: www.rolandfreight.com
International freight forwarder handling shipments by air & ocean. (As-Ind, estab 1991, empl 4, sales $1,310,617, cert: State, CPUC, 8(a))

9441 Say Cargo Express, Inc.
700 E Debra Lane
Anaheim, CA 92805
Contact: Doug Childers President
Tel: 714-772-7735
Email: dchilders@saycargo.com
Website: www.saycargo.com
Freight; Shipping; Expedited; Cargo; Oversized; Tradeshows; Logistics; LTL; Air Freight; Truckload, domestic freight forwarder that specializes in expedited freight. (Minority, Woman, estab 2000, empl 13, sales $2,700,000, cert: CPUC, WBENC)

9442 Tina Miller, Inc
30025 Alicia Pkwy, Box 172
Laguna Niguel, CA 92677
Contact: Faith Kennedy Acct exec
Tel: 877-211-7767
Email: info@tmisalesinc.com
Website: www.tmisalesinc.com
Customized traffic & freight management. (Woman, estab 2004, empl 14, sales $14,337,571, cert: WBENC)

9443 Trans Global Shipping Alliance, LLC
25255 Cabot Rd, Ste 212
Laguna Hills, CA 92653
Contact: William Cordova President
Tel: 949-699-1491
Email: bill@trustglobal.com
Website: www.trustglobal.com
Global shipping, trucking, ocean, air & special air couriers - standard & charter, full truckloads, flatbeds to LTL. (Woman, estab 2000, empl 5, sales $338,896, cert: State, CPUC)

9444 Transit Air Cargo Inc.
2204 East 4th St
Santa Ana, CA 92705
Contact: Gulnawaz Khodayar President
Tel: 714-915-0657
Email: gkhodayar@transitair.com
Website: www.transitair.com
Global tradeshow logistics: air, ocean & ground. Product freight services international & domestic. (Woman/As-Ind, estab 1989, empl 55, sales $23,933,988, cert: NMSDC, WBENC)

9445 Tricor America, Inc.
PO Box 8100 - SFIA
San Francisco, CA 94128
Contact: Scott Tanaka Major Acct Exec
Tel: 650-877-3650
Email: scott.tanaka@mail.tricor.com
Website: www.tricor.com
National & intl courier services. (As-Pac, estab 1957, empl 500, sales , cert: NMSDC)

Colorado

9446 Corporate GT Denver, Inc.
505 Nucla Way, Unit D
Aurora, CO 80011
Contact: Mary Norby VP
Tel: 303-243-3900
Email: mary@gtdenver.com
Website: www.corporategtdenver.com
Luxury Ground Transportation. Sedan, Vans, SUVs, Limousines. (Woman, estab 1985, empl 31, sales $2,000,000, cert: WBENC)

9447　Craters and Freighters
　　　331 Corporate Circle, Ste J
　　　Golden, CO 80401
　　　Contact: Chad Brockmeyer Natl Sales Mgr
　　　Tel:　720-287-7805
　　　Email: chad@cratersandfreighters.com
　　　Website: www.cratersandfreighters.com
Custom wood crating, plastic hard cases and freight services. (Woman, estab 1990, empl 12, sales $55,000,000, cert: WBENC)

9448　FAK, Inc.
　　　10885 E 51st Ave
　　　Denver, CO 80239
　　　Contact: Ron Harms GM
　　　Tel:　303-289-5433
　　　Email: rharms@fakinc.com
　　　Website: www.fakinc.com
Transportation: refrigerated, dry van, flatbed, specialized & intermodal. US & Canada. (Woman, estab 1983, empl 62, sales $69,359,561, cert: WBENC)

9449　Logistics Innovators Inc. dba Adcom Worldwide
　　　16600 E 33rd Dr, Unit 26
　　　Aurora, CO 80011
　　　Contact: Toni Brock President
　　　Tel:　303-329-0702
　　　Email: tbrock@adcomworldwide.com
　　　Website: www.adcomworldwide.com
Worldwide logistics, customs brokerage, ocean, air ground, warehouse. (Woman, estab 1997, empl 10, sales $2,167,000, cert: WBENC)

Delaware

9450　Bayshore Transportation System, Inc.
　　　901 Dawson Dr
　　　Newark, DE 19713
　　　Contact: M FOLZ
　　　Tel:　651-430-2929
　　　Email: mfolz@bayshoreteam.com
　　　Website: www.bayshoreallied.com
Transportation svcs, moving & storage, relocation. (Woman, estab 1973, empl , sales $24,000,000, cert: WBENC)

Florida

9451　Air Marine Forwarding Company
　　　3409-B NW 72 Ave
　　　Miami, FL 33122
　　　Contact: Roger Madan President
　　　Tel:　305-477-3496
　　　Email: r.madan@airmarine.com
　　　Website: www.airmarine.com
Global logistics, intl air & ocean freight forwarding, customs brokerage, NVOCC, warehousing & distribution, bonded facilities & trucks, packing & crating. (Hisp, estab 1968, empl 28, sales $3,108,366, cert: NMSDC)

9452　Avanti Limousine Service, LLC.
　　　5425 N Dixie Hwy
　　　Boca Raton, FL 33487
　　　Contact: Serena Leverrier Affiliate Relations Dir
　　　Tel:　561-241-9955
　　　Email: res@avanticar.com
　　　Website: www.avanticar.com
Global ground transportation to and from anywhere in the world. (Woman, estab 1985, empl 12, sales $1,000,000, cert: WBENC)

9453　Clover Systems Inc.
　　　1910 NW 97th Ave
　　　Miami, FL 33172
　　　Contact:　Dir Business Dev
　　　Tel:　305-499-7056
　　　Email: houston@clovergroup.com
　　　Website: www.clovergroup.com
Integrated logistics, air & ocean shipping, domestic & intl distribution svcs, warehouse, export packing & trucking. (Hisp, estab 1985, empl 70, sales $0, cert: NMSDC)

9454　CW Carriers USA Inc.
　　　509 S Falkenburg Rd
　　　Tampa, FL 33619
　　　Contact: Zach Valjarevic Sr Sales Mgr
　　　Tel:　813-771-0391
　　　Email: zach@cwcarriersinc.com
　　　Website: www.cwcarriersinc.com
Asset-based trucking company with a brokerage arm. (Woman, estab 2009, empl 151, sales $96,000,000, cert: WBENC)

9455　Edward Estevez CHB, Inc.
　　　6910 Main St, Ste 150
　　　Miami Lakes, FL 33014
　　　Contact: Edward Estevez President
　　　Tel:　786-247-1961
　　　Email: admin@eechb.com
　　　Website: www.eechb.com
U.S. Customs brokerage & logistics services. (Hisp, estab 2004, empl 1, sales , cert: State)

9456　Faith Transport & Logistics, Inc.
　　　190 SE 3rd Ave
　　　Deerfield Beach, FL 33441
　　　Contact: Aldo Goncalves Jr. President
　　　Tel:　954-274-0357
　　　Email: transportwithfaith@faithtlinc.com
　　　Website: www.transportwithfaith.com
Transportation & logistics, United States & Canada as an Interstate Motor Carrier. (Hisp, estab 2012, empl 3, sales $244,948, cert: NMSDC)

9457　Florida Freight Lines Inc.
　　　451 Harbor Dr N
　　　Indian Rocks Beach, FL 33785
　　　Contact: Marie Mazzara President
　　　Tel:　727-800-9870
　　　Email: mmazzara@floridafreightlines.com
　　　Website: www.FloridaFreightLines.com
LTL (Less Than Truckload), Full Truckload, Dry, Fresh, Frozen. (Woman, estab 2013, empl 2, sales $245,570, cert: WBENC)

9458　Giovanni Transport, LLC
　　　3066 Shady Dr
　　　Jacksonville, FL 32257
　　　Contact: Shatise Johnson President
　　　Tel:　904-612-5988
　　　Email: smjohnson@giovannitrans.com
　　　Website: www.giovannitrans.com
Transportation solutions, ship truckload freight, dedicated dry van transportation. (Woman/AA, estab 2006, empl 4, sales $230,000, cert: State)

9459   GuyDlogistics Corp.
        10200 W State Road 84 Ste. 205
        Davie, FL 33324
        Contact: Tatiana Guydouk President
        Tel: 954-414-0561
        Email: tatiana@globaltransservicecorp.com
        Website: www.globaltransservicecorp.com/
Dry Van, Reefer, Flat Bed, Tracking Shipment, Logistics.
(Woman, estab 2014, empl , sales $5,105,052, cert:
WBENC)

9460   Harbor Transport, Inc.
        7320 NW 70th St
        Miami, FL 33166
        Contact: Roberto Victorero President
        Tel: 305-592-5357
        Email: roberto@harbor.com
        Website: www.harbor.com
Transportation services. (Minority, Woman, estab 1987,
empl 7, sales $0, cert: NMSDC)

9461   Hermes Global Logistic Services, LLC
        5323 Millenia Lakes Blvd Ste 300
        Orlando, FL 32839
        Contact: Dena Kirschbaum
        Tel: 407-734-4046
        Email: dena.kirschbaum@hglservices.com
        Website: www.hglservices.com
3PL supply chain management solutions, integrating
operations, warehousing & transportation services.
(Woman/AA, estab 2015, empl 4, sales $500,000, cert:
NMSDC)

9462   Interstate Transport, Inc.
        324 1st Ave North
        St. Petersburg, FL 33701
        Contact: Zach Aufmann COO
        Tel: 727-822-9999
        Email: WBENC@interstatetransport.com
        Website: www.InterstateTransport.com
TL (truckload) & LTL (less than truckload) freight in US &
Canada. Specialized freight capabilities (live goods, plants,
perishables, lumber) dry, flatbed & refrigerated (reefer/
refer) trailers, utilizing single or team drivers. (Woman,
estab 2002, empl 40, sales $43,524,625, cert: WBENC)

9463   Magno International LP
        11014 NW 33 St, Ste 100
        Doral, FL 33172
        Contact: Jesus Lovo Exec VP
        Tel: 305-392-4726
        Email: jesus.lovo@magnointl.com
        Website: www.magnointl.com
Multi modal domestic & international transportation,
warehouse & distribution, customs. (Hisp, estab 2005,
empl 18, sales , cert: NMSDC)

9464   Newco Services, Inc.
        1831 16th St
        Boynton Beach, FL 33435
        Contact: Sales
        Tel: 561-375-9930
        Email: info@newcoservices.com
        Website: www.newcoservices.com
Transportation, warehousing, repair, refurbishment,
prevenative maintenance, data reporting & consolidated
billing svcs. (Woman, estab 1994, empl 20, sales
$4,200,000, cert: WBENC)

9465   North American Transport Services LLC
        160 Ali baba Ave
        Opa-Locka, FL 33054
        Contact: Kasey Cano Business Devel Rep
        Tel: 305-455-1150
        Email: kcano@nalogistics.com
        Website: www.nalogistics.com
Assist customers with inbound & outbound freight,
manage pick-up & delivery schedules. (Hisp, estab 2004,
empl 45, sales $45,000,000, cert: NMSDC)

9466   One Horn Transportation Inc.
        8374 Market St #470
        Lakewood Ranch, FL 34202
        Contact: Mary Morra Operations Mgr
        Tel: 973-595-7700
        Email: help@onehorn.com
        Website: www.OneHorn.com
Freight brokerage, flatbed & dry van tractor-trailer
services, 48 contiguous states & Canada. (Woman/AA,
estab 2005, empl 40, sales $20,000,000, cert: NMSDC,
WBENC)

9467   Prime Air Cargo Inc.
        1316 NW 78th Ave
        Doral, FL 33126
        Contact: Omar Zambrano GM
        Tel: 305-592-2044
        Email: ozambrano@primeaircargo.com
        Website: www.primeaircargo.com
Air, land & ocean transport services. (Hisp, estab 2004,
empl 15, sales , cert: NMSDC)

9468   Raven Transport Company, Inc.
        6800 Broadway Ave
        Jacksonville, FL 32254
        Contact: Andrew Rhodes VP Sales & Marketing
        Tel: 904-425-5230
        Email: andrew.rhodes@raventrans.com
        Website: www.raventrans.com
Truckload carrier, 48 states authority. (AA, estab 1985,
empl 579, sales $85,297,000, cert: NMSDC)

9469   Time Definite Services Transportation, LLC
        1935 CR525E
        Sumterville, FL 33521
        Contact: Michael Suarez President
        Tel: 800-466-8040
        Email: sales@timedefinite.com
        Website: www.timedefinite.com
Freigth transportation: truckload LTL air freight, hot
shots, warehousing, domestic & international. (Hisp,
estab 1990, empl 60, sales $45,700,000, cert: NMSDC)

Georgia

9470   AFCLS Logistics Services LLC
        975 Cobb Place Blvd Ste 101
        Kennesaw, GA 30144
        Contact: Brenda Collins Brown VP
        Tel: 770-514-1456
        Email: brenda.collinsbrown@afcls.com
        Website: www.afcls.com
Global freight logistics svcs: motor freight forwarding,
freight brokerage, ocean transportation intermediary &
non-vessel operating common carrier services & indirect
air carriage. (AA, estab 2008, empl 10, sales $1,300,000,
cert: NMSDC)

9471   Atlanta Peach Movers, Inc.
2911 Northeast Pkwy
Doraville, GA 30360
Contact: Orlando Lynch Office Mgr
Tel: 770-447-5121
Email: olynch@atlpeachmovers.com
Website: www.atlantapeachmovers.com
Moving & storage, furnishings & equipment. (AA, estab , empl , sales $0, cert: NMSDC)

9472   Axiom Logistics LLC
5000 Austell-Powder Springs Rd Ste 189
Austell, GA 30106
Contact: Morgan Perry Founder & CEO
Tel: 770-694-6248
Email: morgan@axiomtrans.com
Website: www.axiomtrans.com
Logistics, Dry, frozen & refrigerated truckload, Flatbed, drop deck & double drop, Over-Dimensional, heavy haul & expedited, Power Only, Team & expedited truckload and (LTL) less than truckload services. (Woman/AA, estab 2012, empl 6, sales $1,099,963, cert: NMSDC, WBENC)

9473   Bennett International Group LLC
1001 Industrial Pkwy
McDonough, GA 30253
Contact: Marcia Taylor CEO
Tel: 770-957-1866
Email:
Website: www.bennettig.com
Transportation: NVOCC, customs brokerage, freight forwarding air & ocean, project cargo, domestic trucking, oversized & over weight cargo, warehousing, third party logistics. (Woman, estab 1973, empl 650, sales $0, cert: WBENC)

9474   CorTrans Logistics, LLC
6465 E Johns Crossing Ste 300
Johns Creek, GA 30097
Contact: Gloria Cortez CEO
Tel: 678-969-9529
Email: gcortez@cortrans.com
Website: www.cortrans.com
Transportation svcs: air freight, charters, next day, second day, and deferred delivery, logistics svcs & supply chain mgmt. (Hisp, estab 1999, empl 20, sales $35,290,000, cert: WBENC)

9475   Eagle Transportation Services, Inc.
731 Queen City Pkwy Ste 101
Gainesville, GA 30501
Contact: Lynn Mull President
Tel: 770-965-1242
Email: lynn@eagletransportation.com
Website: www.eagletransportation.com
Third party logistics. (Woman, estab 1988, empl 6, sales , cert: WBENC)

9476   Efficient Courier & Logistics Services LLC
5475 Tulane Dr
Atlanta, GA 30336
Contact: Patrick Chukwudolue Exec Dir
Tel: 800-590-2155
Email: partners@ecourierlogistics.com
Website: www.ecourierlogistics.com
Integrated end to logistics & freight services, customized supply chain, warehousing, logistics & delivery. (AA, estab 2013, empl 5, sales , cert: NMSDC)

9477   Expedited Transportation Services, Inc
505 Plantation Park Dr
Atlanta, GA 30052
Contact: Traci Taylor President
Tel: 770-413-1700
Email: expedited@ets-atlanta.com
Website: www.ets-atlanta.com
Mail & cargo transport, air cargo, local area trucking, marine cargo, rail cargo, regional or natl trucking, vehicle carrier services, air charter transport. (Woman, estab 1982, empl 11, sales $0, cert: WBENC)

9478   KCH Trucking, LLC
6695 Peachtree Industrial Blvd Ste 250
Atlanta, GA 30360
Contact: Alan Whitten VP Sales
Tel: 770-962-6829
Email: awhitten@kchtrans.com
Website: www.kchtrans.com
National truckload transportation services. (Woman, estab 2006, empl 5, sales $8,000,001, cert: WBENC)

9479   Premier Expediters, Inc.
598 Red Oak Rd
Stockbridge, GA 30281
Contact: Jay Patterson Exec Dir
Tel: 888-744-7911
Email: jpatterson@shippei.com
Website: www.shippei.com
Transportation, Carrier Authority, Freight Forwarding Authority & Brokerage, FTL, LTL, Expedited, Specialized, Air & Ocean Freight services. (Woman, estab 1992, empl 32, sales $13,000,000, cert: WBENC)

9480   R2 Trucking Solutions
1882 Princeton Ave, Ste 1
College Park, GA 30337
Contact: Amari Ruff CEO
Tel: 770-892-3699
Email: aruff@r2truckingsolutions.com
Website: www.r2truckingsolutions.com
Global logistics, air, ocean & ground carriers. (AA, estab 2014, empl 22, sales $1,867,989, cert: NMSDC)

9481   S-2international LLC
395 McDonough Pkwy
McDonough, GA 30253
Contact: Jennifer Mead CEO
Tel: 678-432-9502
Email: jennifer.mead@s-2international.com
Website: www.s-2international.com
Transportation services, expedited/JIT movement, LTL, Airfreight, Charter & Ocean shipments. (Woman, estab 2005, empl 37, sales $17,200,000, cert: WBENC)

9482   Scott Logistics Corp.
375 Technology Pkwy
Rome, GA 30165
Contact: Jayme Gauthreaux Dir of Natl Sales
Tel: 470-419-6209
Email: jayme.gauthreaux@scottlogistics.com
Website: www.scottlogistics.com
Transportation brokerage. (Woman, estab 1995, empl 165, sales $155,000,000, cert: WBENC)

9483 Southeastern Transfer & Storage Co., Inc.
2561 Plant Atkinson Rd
Smyrna, GA 30080
Contact: Debra Wallace Co-Owner
Tel: 404-794-2401
Email: dwallace@setransfer.com
Website: www.setransfer.com
Transportation services: heavy-haul trucking & storage, 48 states authority. (Woman, estab 1929, empl 30, sales $3,000,000, cert: WBENC)

9484 The FSL Group
200 Corporate Center Dr
Stockbridge, GA 30253
Contact: Cheryl Gaita Admin Asst
Tel: 770-506-9100
Email: kcrowley@fslgroup.com
Website: www.fslgroup.com
Consulting & management services, logistics operations, Transportation, Shipment Auditing. (Woman, estab 1996, empl 21, sales $45,241,000, cert: CPUC, WBENC)

9485 Transgroup World Wide Logistics
650 Atlanta S Pkwy, Ste 109
Atlanta, GA 30349
Contact: Tamara Barnes President
Tel: 404-725-3660
Email: tamib.atl@transgroup.com
Website: www.transgroup.cam
Domestic Air: Next flight out, Next Day AM, Second day, 3-5 day service, Air Charters, Express LTL & Full Truckload, Flatbed/Oversize loads, Trade Show Services, Canada/Mexico TransBoarder. (Woman, estab 1986, empl 37, sales $291,000,000, cert: NWBOC)

9486 Tribe Express
2251 Jesse Jewell Pkwy NE
Gaineville, GA 30507
Contact: Fred Schloth Dir New Business Dev
Tel: 904-222-0445
Email: fschloth@tribetrans.com
Website: www.tribeexpress.com
Asset based transportation, Expedited Services, Power Only, Dedicated Services, Logistics Services for Temp Controlled, Deep Frozen & all Dry modes. (Minority, Woman, estab 2005, empl 118, sales $39,000,000, cert: NMSDC)

9487 Vector Global Logistics LLC
887 W Marietta St NW, Ste M201
Atlanta, GA 30318
Contact: Enrique Alvarez Managing Dir
Tel: 404-554-1150
Email: enrique.alvarez@vectorgl.com
Website: www.VectorGL.com
Sea freight, air freight, truck, rail & general logistics. (Hisp, estab 2012, empl 19, sales $9,100,000, cert: NMSDC)

Hawaii

9488 Hawaii Transfer Company, Ltd.
94-1420 Moaniani St
Waipahu, HI 96797
Contact: Financial Analyst
Tel: 770-496-9500
Email: rshumake@lanier.com
Website: www.hawaiitransfer.com
Transportation, warehousing and other services. (As-Pac, estab 1931, empl 180, sales $20,000,000, cert: NMSDC)

Iowa

9489 JMS Transportation Inc.
5650 6th St SW
Cedar Rapids, IA 52404
Contact: Riley Larson GM
Tel: 800-877-1529
Email: rileylarson@jmstransport.com
Website: www.jmstransport.com
Trucking & logistics, asset-based transportation, Midwest regional LTL & FTL dry van freight hauling. (Woman, estab 1990, empl 39, sales $19,048,850, cert: NWBOC)

9490 Johnsrud Transport, Inc.
200 SE 34th St
Des Moines, IA 50317
Contact: Jackie Johnsrud CEO
Tel: 800-237-9795
Email: jjohnsrud@johnsrudtransport.com
Website: www.johnsrudtransport.com
Transport bulk foodgrade liquids. (Woman, estab 1963, empl 170, sales $21,000,000, cert: WBENC)

9491 Legacy Logistics Freight, Inc.
500 College Dr, Ste 127B
Mason City, IA 50401
Contact: President
Tel: 641-423-5187
Email: legacylogisticsandfreight@gmail.com
Website: www.legacylogisticsfreight.com
Freight brokerage, 48 states in the lower continental US. (Woman, estab 2006, empl 8, sales , cert: WBENC)

9492 Weinrich Truck Line, Inc.
27932 C 60
Hinton, IA 51024
Contact: Ranae Allen Operations Mgr
Tel: 800-831-0814
Email: ranaewtl@hotmail.com
Website: www.weinrichtruckline.com
Liquid bulk food grade transportation. (Woman, estab 1960, empl 75, sales $9,284,328, cert: WBENC)

Illinois

9493 AGT Global Logistics
800 Roosevelt Rd, Building C, Ste 300
Glen Ellyn, IL 60137
Contact: Jeff Mock MR
Tel: 630-953-4366
Email: jeffm@agt3pl.com
Website: www.agt3pl.com
Certified 3rd Party Logistics, air freight carrier, asset based. (Woman, estab 2005, empl 21, sales $1,141,103,297, cert: WBENC, NWBOC)

9494 All Girl Transportation & Logistics, Inc
216 S Prater
Northlake, IL 60164
Contact: Angela Mock President
Tel: 877-816-5477
Email: amock@allgirlstrucking.com
Website: www.allgirlstrucking.com
Transportation: ground & ground expedited, air & airfreight package, auditing, transportation management services. (Woman, estab 2005, empl 30, sales $12,000,000, cert: WBENC)

9495 Box Truck Logistics, LLC
      1517 Golfview Court
      Glendale Heights, IL 60139
      Contact: Hayden Lynch President
      Tel: 312-602-2639
      Email: hlynch@boxtrucklogistics.com
      Website: www.boxtrucklogistics.com
Freight brokerage - FTL, LTL shipments, project freight &
out of gauge shipments. (AA, estab 2014, empl 2, sales ,
cert: NMSDC)

9496 Chela Logistics Inc.
      1521 Brummel Ave
      Elk Grove Village, IL 60007
      Contact: President
      Tel: 847-290-9040
      Email: marcela@chelalogistics.com
      Website: www.chelalogistics.com
Local & nationwide transportation. (Woman, estab 2001,
empl 11, sales $2,500,000, cert: WBENC)

9497 CTL Global, Inc.
      11697 W Grand Ave
      Northlake, IL 60164
      Contact: Sharon Dalenberg President
      Tel: 708-223-1196
      Email:
      Website: www.ctlglobalsolutions.com
Fulfillment & logistics, transportation & technology
services. (Woman, estab 1978, empl 250, sales
$53,723,000, cert: WBENC)

9498 DSC Logistics, Inc.
      1750 S Wolf Rd
      Des Plaines, IL 60018
      Contact: Tracy Drake Dir Diversity
      Tel: 847-390-6800
      Email: tracy.drake@dsc-logistics.com
      Website: www.dsclogistics.com
Supply chain mgmt, strategic solutions-based consulting,
business process integration, process improvement &
management, logistics operations, warehousing, transportation, packaging & fulfillment. (Woman, estab 1960, empl
2200, sales $330,000,000, cert: WBENC)

9499 GTS Express, Inc.
      13851 S Janas Pkwy
      Homer Glen, IL 60491
      Contact: Olivia Metelanski President
      Tel: 844-487-9777
      Email: olivia@gtsexpressinc.com
      Website: www.gtsexpressinc.com
Asset based transportation logistics & 3PL. (Woman, estab
2013, empl 12, sales $550,000, cert: NWBOC)

9500 Hassett Express
      17W775 Butterfield Rd. Ste 109
      Oakbrook Terrace, IL 60181
      Contact: Tim Cunningham Business Devel Mgr
      Tel: 630-730-7346
      Email: tim.cunningham@teamhassett.com
      Website: www.hassettlogistics.com
Transportation, Domestic Air Freight, Domestic Ground
Freight, White Glove, Logistics Services, International Air,
International Moving. (Woman, estab 1980, empl 133,
sales $52,000,000, cert: WBENC)

9501 Mid-West Moving & Storage, Inc.
      1255 Tonne Rd
      Elk Grove Village, IL 60007
      Contact: Luis Toledo President
      Tel: 847-593-7201
      Email: diversity@midwestmoving.com
      Website: www.midwestmoving.com
Office & residential moving, record storage & destruction, ware housing, dist & local hauling. (Hisp, estab
1983, empl 100, sales $7,306,878, cert: NMSDC, 8(a))

9502 Milano Railcar Services
      PO Box 1357
      Mount Vernon, IL 62864
      Contact: Mary Burgan President
      Tel: 618-242-4004
      Email: mary@milanorail.com
      Website: www.milanorail.com
Logistics, Storage, Pipe Laydown Yard, Trucking, Logistics, Inventory Control, Warehousing, Materials Handling, Transloading, Consulting. (Woman, estab 2009,
empl 3, sales $264,085, cert: WBENC)

9503 New Age Transportation, Distribution & Ware-
      housing
      1881 Rose Rd
      Lake Zurich, IL 60047
      Contact: Pam Troy VP Admin
      Tel: 847-545-9200
      Email: pamt@newagetransportation.com
      Website: www.newagetransportation.com
National & international transportation & logistics: dist,
warehousing, fulfillment & e-commerce, expedition &
rail shipments, freight bill auditing. (Woman, estab
1989, empl 45, sales $28,000,000, cert: WBENC)

9504 Pactrans Air & Sea, Inc.
      951-961 W Thorndale Ave
      Bensenville, IL 60106
      Contact: Kitty Pon President
      Tel: 847-766-9988
      Email: kittyp@pactrans.com
      Website: www.pactrans.com
International freight forwarding: air & sea freight
consolidation logistics, world wide charter, warehousing,
distribution, trucking & Customs brokerage services.
(Minority, Woman, estab 1991, empl 50, sales
$30,000,000, cert: City, NMSDC)

9505 Par Logistics, Inc.
      1251 N Plum Grove Rd, Ste 120
      Schaumburg, IL 60173
      Contact: Jim Vasquez President
      Tel: 847-519-1990
      Email: jvasquez@parlogistics.net
      Website: www.parlogsitics.net
Transportation svcs: truckload, domestic air freight,
ground expedite, air charter services, int'l air & ocean.
(Hisp, estab 2006, empl 8, sales $35,000,000, cert:
NMSDC)

9506 Passion Transportation Inc.
      145 Sayton Road Ste C
      Fox Lake, IL 60020
      Contact: Suzanne Thompson WBE Liasion
      Tel: 847-587-2700
      Email: quotes@passiontrans.com
      Website: www.passiontrans.com
Truckload, less than truckload & partial truckloads, air,
ocean, expidited, temperature controlled & flatbed
freight. (Woman, estab 2007, empl 6, sales $4,134,507,
cert: WBENC)

9507 Pelican Logistics Inc.
      101 Frontier way
      Bensenville, IL 60106
      Contact: Keith Kim Sales Mgr
      Tel: 847-337-5255
      Email: keith.kim@pelicanloginc.com
      Website: www.pelicanti.com
Air freight transportation. (As-Pac, estab 1995, empl 8,
sales $10,000,000, cert: WBENC)

9508 Precision Transportation, Inc.
      1010 Dixie Hwy Ste 309
      Chicago Heights, IL 60411
      Contact: Division VP
      Tel: 630-352-3311
      Email: service@precisiontransportation.net
      Website: www.precision-nal.com
Logistics, transportation, warehousing, project management & inventory control. (Woman, estab 1992, empl 10,
sales , cert: State, WBENC)

9509 Reilly International Ltd.
      1555 N Michael Dr
      Wood Dale, IL 60191
      Contact: Vickie Reilly President
      Tel: 630-238-4900
      Email: vickie@reillyinternational.com
      Website: www.reillyinternational.com
International freight forwarding, consolidation & broker-
age. (Woman, estab 1984, empl 20, sales $8,417,000, cert:
WBENC)

9510 Riverbend Logistics Solutions, Inc.
      65 E Ferguson Ave
      Wood River, IL 62095
      Contact: Murdock Moss
      Tel: 618-254-2687
      Email: mmoss@rls-global.com
      Website: www.rls-global.com
Third-party logistics, freight mgmt & shipping. (Woman,
estab 1992, empl 8, sales $2,680,000, cert: State, NWBOC)

9511 Select Logistics Network Inc.
      PO Box 496
      Clinton, IL 61727
      Contact: Lisa Edwards President
      Tel: 800-353-9113
      Email: lisa@selectlogistics.net
      Website: www.selectlogistics.net
Freight logistics: rail, intermodal, over the road, in North
America. (Woman, estab 1997, empl 6, sales $2,599,924,
cert: WBENC)

9512 Servex, Inc.
      1567 Frontenac Rd
      Naperville, IL 60563
      Contact: John Rizek Dir Mktg
      Tel: 630-369-9500
      Email: j.rizek@servex.com
      Website: www.servex.com
Third party warehousing & warehousing services (Woman,
estab 1981, empl 35, sales $0, cert: CPUC)

9513 Williams NationaLease, Ltd.
      404 W Northtown Road Ste B
      Normal, IL 61761
      Contact: Sandy Hotlen President
      Tel: 800-779-8785
      Email: shotlen@wnlgroup.com
      Website: www.wnlgroup.com
Truck leasing & rental: 130 power units & 180 trailers.
(Woman, estab 1984, empl 210, sales $36,000,000, cert:
State, WBENC)

9514 Worldwide Freight Solutions Inc.
      6518 Marble Lane
      Carpentersville, IL 60110
      Contact: Bob Grady CEO
      Tel: 847-915-1025
      Email: bob@wwfsolutions.com
      Website: www.wwfsolutions.com
Transportation Brokerage Organization. (AA, estab 2019,
empl 1, sales , cert: NMSDC)

Indiana

9515 Butler Tillman Express Trucking, Inc.
      PO Box 1017
      Belverly Shores, IN 46301
      Contact: Sue Lundberg Office Mgr
      Tel: 219-764-2100
      Email: info@btexpresstrucking.com
      Website: www.btexpresstrucking.com
Tanker trucking, bulk liquid and dry materials. (Woman/
AA, estab 2003, empl 6, sales $388,518, cert: NMSDC)

9516 Chaser, LLC
      415 E 31st St
      Anderson, IN 46016
      Contact: Nammy Eskar CEO
      Tel: 765-640-8620
      Email: neskar@chaserllc.com
      Website: www.chaserllc.com
Transportation & logistics, hauling truckload shipments
of general commodities in both interstate & intrastate
commerce. (Minority, estab 2011, empl 50, sales , cert:
NMSDC)

9517 HeLP Logistics, Inc.
      2130 S Oakwood Dr
      New Palestine, IN 46163
      Contact: Lorri Lord President
      Tel: 866-504-9620
      Email: lorri.lord@helplogistics.com
      Website: www.helplogistics.com
Transportation & logistics. (Woman, estab 2007, empl
12, sales $3,768,517, cert: WBENC)

9518 Langham Logistics Inc.
      5335 W 74th St
      Indianapolis, IN 46268
      Contact: Cathy Langham President
      Tel: 317-471-5120
      Email: cathylangham@elangham.com
      Website: www.elangham.com
Global freight management: FF, expedite, warehousing,
distribution, fulfillment. (Woman, estab 1988, empl 150,
sales $0, cert: State, WBENC)

9519 Mid-American Specialized Transport, Inc.
      2827 W State Rd 66
      Rockport, IN 47635
      Contact: Paula Joyner President
      Tel: 812-649-2599
      Email: paula.joyner@mastusa.com
      Website: www.mastusa.com
General freight & hazardous materials, transportation
logistics, brokerage, third party logistics & transportation consutling services. (Woman, estab 2008, empl 19,
sales $8,000,000, cert: WBENC)

9520 MyWay Logistics LLC
1300 E 86th St, Ste 14 # 128
Indianapolis, IN 46240
Contact: Owner
Tel: 888-557-4213
Email: admin@myway-logistics.com
Website: www.myway-logistics.com
Non-asset based logistics. Licensed & bonded to service all 48 states & Canada. (Woman, estab 2014, empl 3, sales $913,754, cert: WBENC)

9521 Pinnacle Industries LLC
717 Ley RD
Fort Wayne, IN 46825
Contact: Stan Richards President
Tel: 260-267-9199
Email: stan.richard@pinnacleindustriesllc.com
Website: www.pinnacleindustriesllc.com
Material management services, Supply Chain Management, logistical fulfillment operations and warehousing services. (AA, estab 2014, empl 10, sales $15,000,000, cert: NMSDC)

9522 TOC Logistics International, LLC
2601 Fortune Circle East Ste 201B
Indianapolis, IN 46241
Contact: Gary Cardenas CEO
Tel: 317-759-2132
Email: gcardenas@toclogistics.com
Website: www.toclogistics.com
Logistics management organization. (Hisp, estab 2010, empl 20, sales $15,000,000, cert: NMSDC)

Kansas

9523 Butler Transport, Inc
347 N James St
Kansas City, KS 66118
Contact: Bill Taylor Controller
Tel: 913-321-0047
Email: billtaylor@butlertransport.com
Website: www.butlertransport.com
Transportation (Woman, estab 1991, empl 350, sales $67,000,000, cert: WBENC, NWBOC)

9524 Gold Star Transportation, Inc.
9424 Reeds Rd
Overland Park, KS 66207
Contact: Anthony Janiak
Tel: 913-433-4133
Email: tonyj@goldstartrans.com
Website: www.goldstartransportation.com
Third party transportation logistics. (Woman, estab 1982, empl 29, sales $24,781,811, cert: NWBOC)

9525 Nationwide Transportation & Logistics Services Inc.
PO Box 3190
Shawnee, KS 66203
Contact: Kim Isenhower President
Tel: 913-888-1685
Email: kim@nationwidetransportation.com
Website: www.nationwidetransportation.com
Transportation freight brokerage services. (Woman, estab 1998, empl 18, sales $20,000,000, cert: WBENC)

Kentucky

9526 A. Blair Enterprises Inc.
3801 Springhurst Blvd Ste 106
Louisville, KY 40241
Contact: Steve Orlowski General Mgr
Tel: 502-326-0500
Email: sorlowski@goablair.com
Website: www.goablair.com
Ground Expedite Freight Carrier with a fleet of over 1000 trucks of all sizes, from a cargo van to a tractor trailer at our disposal. (Woman, estab 1984, empl 5, sales $30,000,000, cert: WBENC)

9527 HJI -Vascor Logistics LLC
13200 Complete Court
Louisville, KY 40223
Contact: Brian Palmer Sr Mgr inbound logistics
Tel: 502-638-8021
Email: bpalmer@vascorltd.com
Website: www.vascorlogistics.com
Transportation services. (Woman/AA, estab 2012, empl 500, sales $20,000,000, cert: WBENC)

9528 Liberty Transportation, Inc. dba Team Worldwide
1348 Jamike Dr
Erlanger, KY 41018
Contact: Bobbie Mattis President
Tel: 859-282-0505
Email: bobbie.mattis@teamww.com
Website: www.teamww.com
Freight forwarding & logistics services. (Woman, estab 1989, empl 15, sales $6,000,000, cert: WBENC)

9529 Missouri Sea & Air Services, Inc.
500 Meijer Dr Ste 107
Florence, KY 41042
Contact: Katie Adler GM
Tel: 859-283-1919
Email: katie.adler@msatrans.com
Website: www.msatrans.com
Transportation, Truckload, LTL, Air, Intermodal, counter to counter and ocean. (Woman, estab 1982, empl 17, sales $27,000,000, cert: WBENC)

9530 Stett Transportation Inc.
224 Grandview Dr
Ft. Mitchell, KY 41017
Contact: Chris Jolevski Sales Team Lead
Tel: 859-384-2400
Email: chris@stett.net
Website: www.stett.net
Non-asset based 3PL transporting liquid bulk, both Hazmat & non hazardous products. (Woman, estab 1995, empl 24, sales $11,500,000, cert: WBENC)

Massachusetts

9531 Advantage Global Logistics
41 Highland Ave
Randolph, MA 02368
Contact: Maureen Powers VP Sales
Tel: 781-986-3832
Email: maureen.powers@landstarmail.com
Website: www.landstar.com
Domestic & international, white glove inside delivery, debris removal & scheduled appointment deliveries, exporting & importing, air or ocean, door to door or door to airport/port, clear customs. (Woman, estab 1960, empl 5000, sales , cert: State)

9532 Normandin Transportation Services Inc.
10 Tandem Way, Ste B
Hopedale, MA 01747
Contact: Stephen Normandin VP Strategy
Tel: 508-278-6579
Email: steve@normandintrans.com
Website: www.normandintrans.com
Transportation & logistics, LTL & truckload service.
(Woman, estab 2008, empl 56, sales $0, cert: WBENC)

9533 Performance Trans. Inc.
70 Benson St
Fitchburg, MA 01420
Contact: Julie Taylor President
Tel: 978-345-5300
Email: julie@performancetransinc.com
Website: www.performancetransinc.com
Transportation: haul petroleum products (gas,diesel,
heating oil, bio diesel, etc), building materials. (Woman,
estab 1985, empl 45, sales $8,000,000, cert: State)

Maryland

9534 C J International Inc.
519 S Ellwood Ave
Baltimore, MD 21224
Contact: Samya Murray Compliance Officer
Tel: 410-563-6020
Email: sdmurray@cjinternational.com
Website: www.cjinternational.com
Global Logistics: air/ocean/ground freight transportation,
warehousing & Customs brokerage services. (Woman,
estab 1987, empl 50, sales $3,600,000, cert: WBENC)

9535 Patriot Air Freight, Inc.
806 Cromwell Park Dr
Glen Burnie, MD 21061
Contact: Heidi Gordon Acct Exec
Tel: 410-766-2422
Email: hgordon@aitworldwide.com
Website: www.aitworldwide.com
Domestic Air Freight, Ground Transportation, International
Air & Ocean, Custom House Brokerage, Transborder
Services. (Woman, estab 1980, empl 16, sales $4,790,000,
cert: WBENC)

9536 Samuel Shapiro & Company, Inc.
1215 E Fort Ave Ste 201
Baltimore, MD 21230
Contact: Olga Lyakhovetskaya Mktg & Bus Dev
Tel: 410-539-0540
Email: web@shapiro.com
Website: www.shapiro.com
Transport management/freight forwarding, ocean, air,
surface, documentation & letters of credit, Automated
Export System (AES), classification & binding rulings,
export compliance & consulting, public & private export
seminars. (Woman, estab , empl 120, sales $12,284,800,
cert: WBENC)

9537 Velocity Global Logistics, Inc.
6805 Douglas Legum Dr Ste 201
Elkridge, MD 21075
Contact: Joseph Armstead President
Tel: 888-845-9855
Email: joe.armstead@velocitygloballogistics.com
Website: www.velocitygloballogistics.com
Global transportation. (Woman/AA, estab 2005, empl 2,
sales $158,000, cert: NMSDC)

Michigan

9538 Acme Global Logistics, Inc.
31500 W 13 Mile Rd, Ste 219
Farmington Hills, MI 48334
Contact: Corey Dickerson Freight Broker
Tel: 844-260-0463
Email: cdickerson@aglogistics.us
Website: www.aglogistics.us
Freight Brokerage, Logistics Consulting, Specialized Pick-
Up & Delivery, Intermodal. (AA, estab 2015, empl 6,
sales , cert: NMSDC)

9539 ADED Logistics a Division of Hearn Industrial
Services NA, Inc
13500 Huron St
Taylor, MI 48180
Contact: Johanna Leon Dir Business Devel
Tel: 519-990-1207
Email: johanna.leon@hearnindustrial.com
Website: www.hearnindustrial.com
Transportation, Supply Chain and Quality Services to the
automotive industry. (AA, estab 2016, empl 75, sales ,
cert: NMSDC)

9540 BLT Logistics LLC
34450 Goddard Rd
Romulus, MI 48174
Contact: Joe Goryl VP Supply Chain
Tel: 586-467-1437
Email: jgoryl@bltship.com
Website: www.bltship.com
Transportation & logistics services in the U.S., Canada,
and Mexico, domestic intermodal, drayage, air & ocean
forwarding services. (Woman, estab 2014, empl 22, sales
$1,500,000, cert: WBENC)

9541 BNM Transportation Services
91 N Saginaw, Ste 100
Pontiac, MI 48342
Contact: Marsha Rutherford Owner
Tel: 888-621-5592
Email: m.rutherford@bnmtrans.com
Website: www.bnmtransportation.com
Third party logistics, warehousing basics, public storage
& order fulfillment for manufacturers. (Woman/AA,
estab 2008, empl 45, sales $12,000,000, cert: NMSDC,
WBENC)

9542 Camryn Logistics LLC
36500 Ford Rd
Westland, MI 48185
Contact: JIMMIE COMER Business Dev Mgr
Tel: 866-670-8680
Email: jcomer@camrynlogistics.com
Website: www.camrynlogistics.com
Freight management, warehousing, sequencing, parts
assembly, custom packing & transportation. (AA, estab
2008, empl 15, sales $600,000, cert: NMSDC)

9543 Chat of Michigan Inc.
35790 Northline Rd
Romulus, MI 48174
Contact: Greg Katcher President
Tel: 734-941-5004
Email: chatgk@aol.com
Website: www.chatofmichigan.com
Transportation, crating, rigging, plant relocation, freight
forwarding. (AA, estab 1995, empl 40, sales $5,758,000,
cert: NMSDC)

9544 D & D Logistics, LLC
      3130 Glade St, Ste A
      Muskegon Heights, MI 49444
      Contact: Denise Kanaar CEO
      Tel: 231-737-0100
      Email: denise.kanaar@d-dlogistics.com
      Website: www.d-dlogistics.com
Logistics services. (Woman, estab 2005, empl 12, sales
$16,000,000, cert: WBENC)

9545 E.L. Hollingsworth & Co.
      3039 Airpark Dr N
      Flint, MI 48507
      Contact: Steven Barr President
      Tel: 810-233-7331
      Email: sbarr@hollingsworthgroup.com
      Website: www.elhc.net
Transportation services: truckload & expedite delivery,
warehouse & packaging svcs. (Nat Ame, estab 1927, empl
501, sales $45,000,000, cert: NMSDC)

9546 El Camino Transport Logistics & Management, LLC
      PO Box 28
      Union Lake, MI 48387
      Contact: Mary Kilgore President
      Tel: 248-242-0047
      Email: mkilgore@elcaminotransport.com
      Website: www.elcaminotransport.com
Warehousing specializing in pick & pack, kitting, sequencing & building batches. (Minority, Woman, estab 2007,
empl 4, sales , cert: NMSDC)

9547 EPJ Logistics Inc.
      50270 E Russell Schmidt
      Chesterfield Township, MI 48051
      Contact: Pamela Flynn CEO
      Tel: 586-421-1375
      Email: pflynn@epjlogistics.com
      Website: www.epjlogistics.com
Domestic & international transportation svcs, warehouse
storage, fulfillment, inventory control, design & layout.
(Woman, estab 1998, empl 9, sales $2,200,000, cert:
WBENC)

9548 Expedite Express Transportation Inc.
      20411 W 12 Mile Rd Ste 200
      Southfield, MI 48076
      Contact: William Hamblin VP
      Tel: 248-443-1970
      Email: dispatch@expeditexp.com
      Website: www.expeditexp.com
Local & long distance TL & FTL, dedicated, same day &
next day services to small & large businesses within the
auto industry. (Woman/AA, estab 2005, empl 7, sales
$622,635, cert: WBENC)

9549 February 14 Inc.
      4525 - 50th St SE
      Grand Rapids, MI 49512
      Contact: Bridget Carey President
      Tel: 616-656-0267
      Email: bridgetcarey@ffitransportation.com
      Website: www.FFItransportation.com
Transportation logistics. (Woman, estab 1984, empl 75,
sales $18,875,000, cert: WBENC)

9550 First Choice of Elkhart
      10888 US Hwy 12
      White Pigeon, MI 49099
      Contact: Misty Campagna President
      Tel: 269-483-2010
      Email: mfirstchoice@gmail.com
      Website: www.firstchoiceautotransport.com
Automotive transportation & logistics. (Woman, estab
1992, empl 2, sales $3,407,867, cert: WBENC)

9551 Foreway Management Services Inc.
      1413 W Randall St
      Coopersville, MI 49404
      Contact: Pam Hassevoort President
      Tel: 616-997-9771
      Email: pamh@foreway.com
      Website: www.foreway.com
Qualcomm equipped 53' dry van units, 48 state cover-
age specializing in time sensitive and job site deliveries.
(Woman, estab 1977, empl 60, sales $33,000,000, cert:
WBENC)

9552 Global TEAM Associates, LLC
      11301 Metro Airport Center Dr Ste 170
      Romulus, MI 48174
      Contact: Petra Clark CEO
      Tel: 734-992-3208
      Email: petra.clark@globalteamusa.com
      Website: www.globalteamusa.com
Freight Forwarding & Customs House Brokerage ser-
vices. (Woman, estab 2013, empl 21, sales , cert:
WBENC)

9553 Go-To Transport
      1320 Washington Ave
      Bay City, MI 48708
      Contact: Allison Short President
      Tel: 989-891-2521
      Email: ashort@gototransport.com
      Website: www.gototransport.com
Truckload carrier: 48 contiguous states & Canada.
(Woman, estab 2003, empl 160, sales $38,900,000, cert:
WBENC)

9554 Grupo Logico, LLC
      42400 Grand River Ave, Ste 103
      Novi, MI 48375
      Contact: Darin Dittenber Dir Sales/Marketing
      Tel: 248-613-1699
      Email: ddittenber@grupologico.com
      Website: www.grupologico.com
Full service logistics solutions. (Hisp, estab 2004, empl
25, sales $0, cert: NMSDC)

9555 Gumro and Associates
      69 N Squirrel Ct
      Auburn Hills, MI 48326
      Contact: Ryan Gumro CEO
      Tel: 248-652-6200
      Email: rgumro@gumroandassociates.com
      Website: www.gumroandassociates.com
3PL trucking logistics, heavy haul, curtain sides, double
drop, Lift-gate Straight truck & Vans. (Woman, estab
1974, empl 15, sales $20,000,000, cert: WBENC)

9556 HNT Logistics LLC
PO Box 603
New Boston, MI 48164
Contact: Mark Bowers VP Operations
Tel: 866-984-8840
Email: sales@hntlogistics.net
Website: www.hntlogistics.com
3PL logistics, truck freight, bulk freight, ocean freight, air freight, expedited freight & rail freight. (Woman, estab 2005, empl 34, sales $23,000,000, cert: WBENC)

9557 Hollingsworth Logistics Group, L.L.C.
14225 W Warren Ave
Dearborn, MI 48126
Contact: Greg Martinez Jr Dir of Govt Sales
Tel: 313-768-1306
Email: gmartinez@hlgllc.com
Website: www.hlgllc.com
Warehousing, container management, packaging services, kit packaing, fullfillment services, direct ship,d istribution, transportation OTR/LTL. (Nat Ame, estab 1991, empl 1900, sales , cert: NMSDC)

9558 KC Transportation Inc.
862 Will Carleton Rd
Carleton, MI 48117
Contact: Chad A. Lechy Corporate Controller
Tel: 734-654-4644
Email: lechyc@kcintegrated.com
Website: www.kcintegrated.com
Logistics management, freight brokerage & management, parts sequencing, parts sub assembly, quality containment & rework
warehousing. (Minority, estab 1986, empl 250, sales $70,000,000, cert: NMSDC)

9559 LB Transportation Group & Omni Warehouse
966 Bridgeview S
Saginaw, MI 48604
Contact: Tony Lander CEO
Tel: 989-759-5544
Email: tlander@lb-omni.com
Website: www.lb-omni.com
Transportation: expediting & dedicated svcs, warehousing, inspection, kitting, assembly, repacking. (Hisp, estab 1976, empl 70, sales $9,859,567, cert: NMSDC)

9560 Mexus Transport, Inc.
18600 Northville Rd, Ste 900
Northville, MI 48167
Contact: Alba R. McConell President
Tel: 248-344-8060
Email: alba@mexustransport.com
Website: www.mexustransport.com
Transportation: general freight, machinery & heavy haul, Canada, United States & Mexico. (Minority, Woman, estab 2003, empl 5, sales $300,000, cert: State)

9561 New Dimension Logistics, LLC
12256 Universal Dr
Taylor, MI 48180
Contact: Kurmmell Knox CEO
Tel: 734-865-9960
Email: kwknox@ndlx.us
Website: www.ndlx.us
Integrated supply chain solutions delivering safe, specialized transportation, warehousing and logistics services. (AA, estab 2007, empl 14, sales $3,588,000, cert: NMSDC)

9562 Northfield Trucking Company, Inc.
28800 Nothline Rd
Romulus, MI 48174
Contact: Leigh Ann Frederick President
Tel: 313-624-4900
Email: leighannl@northfieldtruck.com
Website: www.northfieldtruck.com
Transportation, regional, long haul & dry freight long distances operation. (Woman, estab 2002, empl 100, sales $12,000,000, cert: WBENC)

9563 O & I Transport Inc.
PO Box 807
Dearborn, MI 48121
Contact: Mike Schofiled Sales Mgr
Tel: 800-270-0020
Email: mschofield@oitransport.com
Website: www.oitransport.com
Flatbed trucking. (AA, estab 1981, empl 21, sales $25,000,000, cert: NMSDC)

9564 Oneida Solutions Group
10049 Harrison, Ste 500A
Romulus, MI 48174
Contact: Fred Rogers Exec Dir
Tel: 248-252-2260
Email: frogers@oneidasolutions.com
Website: www.oneidasolutions.com
Transportation svcs: intl household & office moving, project mgmt. (Nat Ame, estab 2001, empl 200, sales , cert: WBENC)

9565 Palmer Logistic Services
24660 Dequindre Rd
Warren, MI 48091
Contact: Terri Palmer Burton President
Tel: 313-220-5433
Email: terripb@palmerlogisticsservices.com
Website: www.palmerls.com
Global household relocation, commercial relocation, regional distribution, trade show transportation & store fixture distribution. (Woman, estab 2007, empl 9, sales $42,000,000, cert: WBENC)

9566 Prime Time Delivery
9354 Harrison Rd
Romulus, MI 48174
Contact: Paul Davis CEO
Tel: 800-336-3678
Email: pdavis@ptlogistics.com
Website: www.ptlogistics.com
Nationwide airfreight & ground transportation. (AA, estab 1997, empl 11, sales $3,000,000, cert: NMSDC)

9567 Promesa Logistics, LLC
3068 Highland Dr
Hudsonville, MI 49426
Contact: Lon Agular President
Tel: 800-646-1016
Email:
Website: www.promesalogistics.com
Dedicated route transportation, Local Transportation, Brokerage, Warehouse, Distribution, Consolidation, Expediting, Cargo Van, Straight Truck, Semis. (Hisp, estab 1997, empl 10, sales $2,400,000, cert: NMSDC)

9568 Promesa Transportation
3068 Highland Dr
Hudsonville, MI 49426
Contact: Lon Aguilar President
Tel: 616-748-2340
Email: lonagu@chartermi.net
Website: www.chartermi.net
Transportation services. (Hisp, estab 0, empl , sales $0, cert: NMSDC)

9569 Rich Davis Enterprises, Inc.
4831 Wyoming Ave
Dearborn, MI 48126
Contact: Melissa Matsos Acct Exec
Tel: 313-584-3334
Email: melmatsos@richdavistrucking.com
Website: www.richdavistrucking.com
Transport auto parts, steel, machinery & general commodity freight. (Woman, estab 1987, empl 17, sales $1,995,074, cert: WBENC)

9570 Rodriguez Expedited Freight Systems, Inc.
9400 Pelham
Taylor, MI 48180
Contact: Dennis Schmidt VP Operations
Tel: 800-718-0066
Email: dschmidt@rodexp.com
Website: www.rodexp.com
Ground & air expedition: cargo van, cube truck, straight truck & semi, 48 state authority, plus Canada. (Minority, Woman, estab 1992, empl 20, sales $5,600,000, cert: NMSDC)

9571 Rose-Allied International
41775 Ecorse Rd Ste 190
Belleville, MI 48111
Contact: Brad Koch Global Business
Tel: 734-957-8000
Email: bkoch@rosemoving.com
Website: www.rosemoving.com
Global Relocation services. (Woman, estab 1964, empl 200, sales $30,020,000, cert: WBENC)

9572 RSP Express Inc.
28169 Van Born Road
Romulus, MI 48174
Contact: Maria Pop President
Tel: 734-578-0799
Email: rspexpress1@yahoo.com
Website: www.rspexpress.com
Brokerage and Transportation Services. (Woman, estab 2006, empl 140, sales $19,896,325, cert: WBENC)

9573 Rush Trucking Corporation
35160 E Michigan Ave
Wayne, MI 48184
Contact: Rob Allgary Dir of Sales
Tel: 800-526-7874
Email: rallgary@rushtrucking.com
Website: www.rushtrucking.com
Truckload transportation, expedited transportation. (Minority, Woman, estab 1984, empl 950, sales $125,000,000, cert: NMSDC, WBENC)

9574 Sterling Services Ltd.
1530 Commor
Hamtramck, MI 48212
Contact: Jason Eddleston VP
Tel: 248-298-2973
Email: jason@sterlingoilchem.com
Website: www.sterlingoilchem.com
Provides high-quality bulk liquid storage, custom blending, warehousing & bulk liquid transport services. (Woman, estab 1985, empl 9, sales $2,036,474, cert: WBENC)

9575 T & M Incorporated
930 Interchange Dr
Holland, MI 49423
Contact: Helen Zeerip President
Tel: 269-751-8050
Email: helen@teddystransport.com
Website: www.teddystransport.com
Transportation svcs, expediting to all 48 states & Ontario/Quebec, Canada, dedicated fleet services, full-truck load services. (Woman, estab 1982, empl 75, sales $7,276,168, cert: WBENC)

9576 Technology Ventures, Inc.
25200 Malvina Ave
Warren, MI 48089
Contact: Constance E. Blair President
Tel: 586-573-6000
Email: cblair@tvihq.com
Website: www.tvihq.com
Logistics, warehousing, light assembly, fulfillment, kitting, distribution & foreign trade zone. (Minority, Woman, estab 1992, empl 30, sales $0, cert: NMSDC, NWBOC)

9577 The Outbound Group
9900 Harrison
Romulus, MI 48174
Contact: Karl Randolph President
Tel: 734-947-1333
Email: karlr@outboundgroup.com
Website: www.outboundgroup.com
Interstate & intrastate motor truck transportation service, fright brokerage, air freight forwarding services & warehouseing. (Woman/AA, estab 1982, empl 100, sales $7,200,000, cert: NMSDC)

9578 Three Star Trucking Co.
36860 Van Born Rd
Wayne, MI 48184
Contact: Tedd Rowe Logistics Mgr
Tel: 734-728-5500
Email: operations@threestartrucking.com
Website: www.threestartrucking.com
Transportation svcs; automotive. (Minority, Woman, estab 1979, empl 60, sales , cert: NMSDC, WBENC)

9579 Top Worldwide, LLC
3039 Air Park Dr N
Flint, MI 48507
Contact: B. Hall VP Sales
Tel: - -
Email: bhall@elhc.net
Website: www.topworldwide.com/
Third Party Logistics. (Nat Ame, estab 2007, empl 15, sales $15,000,000, cert: NMSDC)

9580 Trans Overseas Corporation
28000 Goddard Road
Romulus, MI 48174
Contact: Brett Ouellette VP- Sales & Logistics
Tel: 734-946-8750
Email: bouellette@trans-overseas.com
Website: www.trans-overseas.com
US Customs Broker, International Air/Ocean Freight
Forwarder, Bonded Warehouse, Foreign Trade Zone,
Container Freight Station, Barcode Labeling, Inspections,
Repackaging & Distribution. (Woman, estab 1978, empl 65,
sales $6,200,000, cert: WBENC)

9581 Transphere Inc.
5800 Commerce Dr
Westland, MI 48185
Contact: Smita Koradia CEO
Tel: 734-727-1307
Email: skoradia@transphereinc.net
Website: www.transphereinc.com
International logistics/transportation, warehousing, cargo
by sea, air & land. (Woman/As-Ind, estab 1987, empl 3,
sales $980,000, cert: NMSDC)

9582 University Moving & Storage
23305 Commerce Dr
Farmington Hills, MI 48335
Contact: Ben Cross VP
Tel: 248-949-5755
Email: bcross@universitymoving.com
Website: www.universitymoving.com
Transportation, moving & storage. (Woman, estab 1969,
empl 150, sales $14,490,725, cert: WBENC)

9583 Warehouse Properties, Inc.
16000 W. Nine Mile Rd. Ste 302
Southfield, MI 48075
Contact: Kathleen Eberle President
Tel: 248-569-6106
Email: keberle@npotransportation.com
Website: www.npotransportation.com
Truckload transportation services: seating companies,
kitting & JIT components. (Woman, estab 1984, empl 4,
sales $1,641,592, cert: WBENC)

Minnesota

9584 Assure Shipping, LLC
9462 Stevens Ave S
Bloomington, MN 55420
Contact: Jane Mahowald CEO
Tel: 612-270-6889
Email: jane@assureshipping.com
Website: www.assureshipping.com
Logistics: air, truck & rail, import/export. (Minority,
Woman, estab 2008, empl 2, sales , cert: NMSDC)

9585 Jade Logistics, Inc.
1333 Northland Dr Ste 210
Mendota Heights, MN 55120
Contact: Ni Suphavong Owner
Tel: 651-405-3141
Email: ni@shipjade.com
Website: www.shipjade.com
Domestic & international freight transportation services.
(Minority, Woman, estab 2007, empl 20, sales
$13,000,000, cert: State, NMSDC, WBENC)

9586 Malark Logistics
PO Box 438
Maple Grove, MN 55369
Contact: Sr Sales Exec
Tel: 763-428-3564
Email: info@malark.com
Website: www.malark.com
Logistics, transportation, warehousing, trucking,
airfreight, expedited, freight auditing, crating, claims
filing, distribution, pick and pack, LTL, tradeshow
services, 3PL & 4PL. (Woman, estab 1994, empl 60, sales
$35,000,000, cert: WBENC)

Missouri

9587 All America Transportation, Inc.
910 S Kirkwood Rd Ste 120
St. Louis, MO 63122
Contact: Lianne Reizer President
Tel: 314-835-9499
Email: lianne@allamericatrans.com
Website: www.allamericatrans.com
Licensed freight broker, truckload shipments throughout
US & Canada. (Woman, estab 1996, empl 7, sales
$2,579,000, cert: State, CPUC, WBENC)

9588 Crossland Carriers Inc.
421 Cedar Hills Rd
Ozark, MO 65721
Contact: Patricia Schmig President
Tel: 800-217-0898
Email: tschmig@crosslandcarriers.us
Website: www.crosslandcarriers.com
Trucking long haul, short haul, partial truckload, logis-
tics, mobile home, mobile office moves, heavy haul,
specialized logistics. (Woman, estab 1999, empl 3, sales
$1,750,000, cert: State)

9589 Kings Warehouse Logistics LLC
6008 N Lindbergh Blvd Ste B
Hazelwood, MO 63042
Contact: Eric Wright Dir Sales Operations
Tel: 314-716-3499
Email: ericwright@kingswarehouselogistics.com
Website: www.kingswarehouselogistics.com
Cross Docking, FTL and LTL Trucking, General 3PL,
General Warehousing & Dist, Labeling, Light Assembly
Outsourcing Services, Logistic Transportation of General
Merchandise. (AA, estab 2014, empl , sales , cert: State)

9590 LHP Transportation Services, Inc.
2032 E Kearney St Ste 213
Springfield, MO 65803
Contact: Greg Gloeckner
Tel: 972-812-7370
Email: gloeg@lhptransport.com
Website: www.lhptransport.com
Multimodal transportation: truck, rail, LTL, steamship &
air, 48 states, Canada, Mexico & abroad. (Minority,
Woman, estab 1993, empl 9, sales $30,000,001, cert:
NMSDC)

9591 Marleon International, LLC
5630 NE Lake Dr
Kansas City, MO 64118
Contact: Marquez Cesar CEO
Tel: 816-249-2319
Email: camarquez@mar-leon.com
Website: www.marleoninternational.com
Freight transportation: less than container load, less
than truckload, full truckload, flatbed freight, air
transportation services, distribution & warehousing.
(Hisp, estab 2005, empl 4, sales $560,000, cert: State,
NMSDC)

9592   The Thomas Family Business, Inc.
8194 Lackland Rd
Saint Louis, MO 63114
Contact: Rolondo Thomas CEO
Tel: 314-423-6111
Email: rolondo.thomas@ttfbcompanies.com
Website: www.ttfbcompanies.com
Transportation services, local & regional, warehousing, supply chain management & logistics. (AA, estab 2009, empl 7, sales $750,000, cert: City)

9593   ValDivia Enterprises, Inc.
#5C The Pines Court
St. Louis, MO 63141
Contact: steve ellis VP Sales
Tel: 314-275-7941
Email: steve@valdiviaenterprises.net
Website: www.valdiviaenterprises.net
Transportation services serving North America & Mexico. (Minority, Woman, estab 2006, empl 1450, sales , cert: State)

Montana

9594   Bridger Trnasportation LLC
186 Garden Dr, Ste 103
Bozeman, MT 59718
Contact: Kyle Pena broker
Tel: 888-586-0648
Email: orders@bridgertrans.com
Website: www.bridgertrans.com
Full service logistics, supply chain management, OTR, LTL, FTL & rail in the U.S. & Canada. (Woman, estab 2007, empl 11, sales $10,000,000, cert: WBENC)

9595   Meadow Lark Companies
935 Lake Elmo Dr
Billings, MT 59105
Contact: Chris Verlanic Dir of Freight Management
Tel: 406-657-8645
Email: cverlanic@meadowlarkco.com
Website: www.meadowlarkco.com
Transportation, Freight Management & Logistics: TL, LTL, Vans/Reefers, Flatbed & Heavy Haul. (Woman, estab 1983, empl 160, sales $65,000,000, cert: WBENC)

North Carolina

9596   All-State Express, Inc.
121-I Shields Park Dr
Kernersville, NC 27284
Contact: Sherri Squier President
Tel: 336-992-6880
Email: sherri@all-stateexpress.com
Website: www.all-stateexpress.com
Transportation Services, Expedited Trucking, Air Charter, TruckLoad, Expedite Trucking, Truck Load (TL), Milk Runs, Dedicated Truck Load, Air Freight, Air Charter, Hazmat Carrier 48 States, Canada and Mexico. (Woman, estab 1996, empl 28, sales $23,755,580, cert: WBENC)

9597   Graebel Vanlines Holdings, LLC
2901 Stewart Creek Blvd
Charlotte, NC 28216
Contact: Colin Holden VP Corporate Sales
Tel: 704-281-7129
Email: colin.holden@graebelmoving.com
Website: www.graebelmoving.com
Facility management services, commercial moving services, warehousing services. (Woman, estab 1960, empl 1360, sales $266,000,000, cert: WBENC)

9598   Logical Logistics Solutions
7508 E Independence Blvd Ste 112
Charlotte, NC 28227
Contact: Noel Sanchez President
Tel: 704-566-4770
Email: nsanchez@llsolutions.com
Website: www.llsolutions.com
Logistics services: freight cost reduction & administration, warehousing, consolidation & distribution & inventory management. (AA, estab 1996, empl 5, sales $3,128,798, cert: City)

9599   PWJ Enterprises   dba as Team Worldwide
3400 Yorkmont Rd Ste 700
Charlotte, NC 28208
Contact: Mark Patrick Dir of Business Dev
Tel: 704-357-9857
Email: mark.patrick@teamww.com
Website: www.teamww.com
Freight forwarding: air, ocean, logistics, charter, warehousing, distribution, order fulfillment. (AA, estab 2006, empl 7, sales $6,500,000, cert: NMSDC)

9600   Southeastern Fleet Management, LLC
215 W Plaza Dr, Ste 200
Mooresville, NC 28117
Contact: Patty Bretz Procurement Mgr
Tel: 704-658-1613
Email: patty@sefmgt.com
Website: www.southeasternfleet.com
Transportation solutions, Vehicle Acquisitions Leasing Maintenance Licensing & Registration Remarketing Funding Solutions Personal Fleet Advisor. (Woman, estab 2012, empl 2, sales $2,400,156, cert: State)

9601   Synchrogistics, LLC
900 Ridgefield Dr Ste 350
Raleigh, NC 27609
Contact: Mary MacIsaac Mgr Admin
Tel: 877-879-0668
Email: mary@synchrogistics.com
Website: www.synchrogistics.com
National transportation, domestic truckload and LTL transportation, intermodal, international shipping, warehousing. (Woman, estab 2010, empl 24, sales $18,803,598, cert: WBENC)

North Dakota

9602   S & S Transport, Inc
PO Box 12579
Grand Forks, ND 58208
Contact: Brian Seng Operations Mgr
Tel: 701-746-8484
Email: brian_seng@sstransport.com
Website: www.sstransport.com
Trucking Transportation Services (Woman, estab 1981, empl 120, sales $18,500,000, cert: State)

Nebraska

9603   Kirsch Transportation Services Inc.
1102 Douglas St
Omaha, NE 68102
Contact: Lucas Bird Govt Operations
Tel: 531-213-2153
Email: lucasb@kirschtrans.com
Website: www.kirschtrans.com
Dry Van, Open Deck and Temp Control Over-Dimensional and Heavy Haul Intermodal - Domestic and Cross Border Freight Management. (Woman, estab 2001, empl 60, sales $128,033,344, cert: NWBOC)

9604 Nationwide Auto Transport, Inc.
730 Pier 3
Lincoln, NE 68528
Contact: Julie Delp President
Tel: 402-742-4000
Email: nwat90@tahoo.com
Website: www.nwat.com
Automobile transport services. (Woman, estab 2001, empl 35, sales $3,900,000, cert: WBENC, SDB)

New Jersey

9605 Andrew Vazquez Inc.
24 Tuttle Ave
Bedminster, NJ 07921
Contact: Andrew Vazquez President
Tel: 908-719-2444
Email: avaquez@dlgroup.com
Website: www.aviquality.com
Vehicle Logistics Services (Hisp, estab 1979, empl 30, sales $4,500,000, cert: NMSDC)

9606 Bett-A-Way Traffic Systems Inc.
110 Sylvania Pl
South Painfield, NJ 07080
Contact: Betty Vaccaro VP
Tel: 908-222-2500
Email: laura.vaccaro@bettaway.com
Website: www.bett-a-way.com
Logistics management, freight nationwide, truck load & LTL, dry & refrigerated. (Woman, estab 1982, empl 107, sales $0, cert: WBENC)

9607 Blisset Transportation
50 Triangle Blvd.
Carlstadt, NJ 07072
Contact: Roseanne Magliato President
Tel: 201-549-0672
Email: rmagliato@blissetllc.com
Website: www.blissetllc.com
Transportation & logistics services, warehousing, fulfillment & technology solutions. (Minority, Woman, estab 1991, empl 35, sales $10,000,001, cert: NMSDC, WBENC)

9608 Bohren's Moving & Storage/United Van Lines
3 Applegate Dr
Robbinsville, NJ 08691
Contact: Charlene Heath Sales/Mktg Mgr
Tel: 800-326-4736
Email: cheath@bohrensmoving.com
Website: www.bohrensmoving.com
Transportation & storage svcs; brokerage & international divisions. (Woman, estab 1924, empl 90, sales $28,798,613, cert: WBENC)

9609 Business Relocation Services, Inc.
20 Aquarium Dr
Secaucus, NJ 07094
Contact: Jesus Linares President
Tel: 718-399-8000
Email: jesus.linares@brsrelocations.com
Website: www.brsmove.com
Commercial Relocation services, Warehousing, Trucking, Project Management, Furniture Installation & Storage. (Hisp, estab 1987, empl 45, sales $14,133,451, cert: City, NMSDC)

9610 Gem Limousine Service, Inc.
70 Amboy Ave
Woodbridge, NJ 07095
Contact: Ed Walch VP Client Relations
Tel: 732-596-0900
Email: ewalch@gemlimo.com
Website: www.gemlimo.com
Provider of worldwide ground transportation for individual and group needs. (Woman, estab 1976, empl 140, sales $14,485,851, cert: WBENC)

9611 Global Transit Solutions
110 Chestnut Ridge Rd, Ste 188
Montvale, NJ 07645
Contact: Fernando Mateo Co-Owner
Tel: 201-949-8755
Email: FM@gowithgts.com
Website: www.gowithgts.com
Third Party Logistics throughout the nation, transportation services, trucks, and intermodal, full truck loads (FTL), and less than a trailer. (Hisp, estab 2018, empl 2, sales , cert: State)

9612 Ltd Logistics, Inc.
222 Outwater Lane Ste 3
Garfield, NJ 07026
Contact: Tracy Flood Transportation Sales Rep
Tel: 973-340-4428
Email: tracy.flood@ltdnj.com
Website: www.ltdnj.com
Ground & air freight transportation, full truckload & LTL/ partials via over the road, intermodal & air freight. (Woman, estab 1995, empl 10, sales $4,922,477, cert: State, City)

9613 ProFreight Inc.
35A Brunswick Ave
Edison, NJ 08817
Contact: Ben Leuenberger President
Tel: 732-429-1600
Email: ben@profreight.us
Website: www.profreight.us
Licensed US customs brokerage, int'l freight forwarding, 3PL supply chain management. (Woman, estab 1989, empl 37, sales $15,000,000, cert: State)

9614 Royal Coachman Worldwide
88 Ford Rd, Unit 26
Denville, NJ 07834
Contact: Amy Birnbaum CEO
Tel: 973-400-3200
Email: amy.birnbaum@royalcoachman.com
Website: www.royalcoachman.com
Corporate limousine & transportation svcs: luxury sedans, stretch limousines, 14 passenger motor coaches. (Woman, estab 1969, empl 150, sales $13,034,000, cert: WBENC)

New Mexico

9615 Loadstone Transportation, LLC
1811 Copper Loop, Ste K
Las Cruces, NM 88007
Contact: Bridgette Snow Marketing Coord
Tel: 575-523-7000
Email: bridgette@loadstonetransportation.com
Website: www.loadstonetransportation.com
Transportation services, multitude of local, state, & federal government contracts. (Woman, estab 2011, empl 6, sales $5,823,500, cert: State, WBENC)

Nevada

9616 Full Tilt Logistics LLC
150 Isidor Court
Sparks, NV 89441
Contact: Customer Management Team
Tel: 702-852-2228
Email: remit@fulltiltlogistics.com
Website: www.fulltiltlogistics.com
LTL, Partial loads, Full truck load, Rail, Heavy haul. (Woman, estab 2014, empl 11, sales $16,403,958, cert: WBENC)

9617 Railroad Industries Inc.
1575 Delucchi Ln, Ste 210
Reno, NV 89502
Contact: Anastacia Sullivan Dir of Operations
Tel: 775-329-4855
Email: reg@railroadindustries.com
Website: www.railroadindustries.com
Transportation consulting. (Woman/AA, As- Pac, estab 1983, empl 9, sales $775,382, cert: State)

New York

9618 A & Z Trucking, Inc.
115 Corporate Dr
New Windsor, NY 12550
Contact: Maria Zakar Broker
Tel: 845-569-7299
Email: az.trucking01@gmail.com
Website: www.AandZtrucking.com
Transportation solutions, temperature-controlled reefer trucks, dry vans, flatbeds, full truckload (TL), less-than-truckload (LTL), refrigerated freight. (Minority, Woman, estab 2003, empl 15, sales , cert: NMSDC)

9619 AWLI Group, Inc.
147-60 175 St
Jamaica, NY 11434
Contact: Keith Milliner VP
Tel: 718-244-8923
Email: keith@amberworldwide.com
Website: www.amberworldwide.com
International freight forwarding. (Woman, estab 1990, empl 20, sales $12,594,223, cert: State)

9620 Continental Trading & Services, Inc.
167-43 148th Ave
Jamaica, NY 11434
Contact: Gabriel Gorre
Tel: 718-995-9560
Email: ggorre@ctslogi.com
Website: www.ctslogi.com
Domestic & international transportation. (Hisp, estab 1994, empl 10, sales $3,329,233, cert: State, NMSDC)

9621 Deluxe Delivery Systems, Inc.
729 7th Ave 2nd Fl
New York, NY 10019
Contact: Yoindra Ramnarayan President
Tel: 212-376-4500
Email: ryan@deluxedelivery.com
Website: www.deluxedelivery.com
Distribution services, regional & local trucking, moving (internal and external), overnight mail and messenger service. (As-Ind, estab 1985, empl 500, sales $18,000,000, cert: NMSDC)

9622 Eagle Transfer Corporation
23-02 49 Ave
Long Island City, NY 11101
Contact: Marisol Morales Dir Mktg
Tel: 718-663-0400
Email: mmorales@eagletransfer.com
Website: www.eagletransfer.com
Office moving & storage, installation, dissasemble modular furniture & shelving, project mgmt, records storage. (AA, Hisp, estab 1971, empl 74, sales $0, cert: NMSDC)

9623 Native Trax Logistics LLC
767 Warren Rd
Ithaca, NY 14850
Contact: Ryan Van Alstine GM
Tel: 607-319-5122
Email: ryan@nativetraxlogistics.com
Website: www.nativetraxlogistics.com
Transportation Mgmt, Asset tracking & reporting, Driver safety screenings, Driver credential checks, Timely proof of delivery, On call 24 hours. (Nat Ame, estab 2014, empl 5, sales $3,500,000, cert: NMSDC)

9624 Spearhead Transportation Services, Inc.
PO Box 1984
Blasdell, NY 14219
Contact: Joe Dotterweich CFO
Tel: 716-823-4942
Email: joed@spearheadlogistics.com
Website: www.spearheadlogistics.com
Transportation & logistics services. (Nat Ame, estab 0, empl , sales $14,000,000, cert: NMSDC)

9625 V G Francis Logistics Inc.
800 Et 180th St
Bronx, NY 10460
Contact: Victor Francis President
Tel: 866-970-8866
Email: vgfrancislogistics@gmail.com
Website: www.vgfrancislogistics.com
Transportation, logistics & related information services: air, rail & sea transportation. (AA, estab 2006, empl 1, sales , cert: City, NMSDC)

9626 Walker SCM, LLC
70 E Sunrise Hwy Ste 611
Valley Stream, NY 11581
Contact: Emmett F. Walker CEO
Tel: 516-568-2080
Email: sales@walkerscm.com
Website: www.walkerscm.com
International transportation, logistics, sub- assembly, sequencing, kitting, warehousing, distribution & customs brokarage. (AA, estab 1989, empl 700, sales $163,000,000, cert: NMSDC, SDB)

Ohio

9627 ASW Global, LLC
3375 Gilchrist Rd
Mogadore, OH 44260
Contact: Pam Harris Dir Mktg & Supplier Diversity
Tel: 330-733-8176
Email: pharris@aswglobal.com
Website: www.aswglobal.com
Third-party logistics, warehousing, order fulfillment, pick pack & ship, pkging/re-packaging, contract logistics retail supply chain support, real estate devel proj mgmt, bulk resin transloading, records retention, file storage, & retrieval services. (AA, estab 1983, empl 120, sales $27,000,000, cert: NMSDC)

9628   BD Transportation, Inc.
        9590 Looney Rd
        Piqua, OH 45356
        Contact: Tom Stirnaman Sales
        Tel: 309-531-1370
        Email: toms@ptc-inc.net
        Website: www.ptc-inc.net
Dry van freight, 62 tractors & 125 dry van trailers.
(Woman, estab 2000, empl 95, sales $14,600,000, cert:
WBENC)

9629   Black Star Logistics Inc.
        2350 Greenvale Rd
        Cleveland, OH 44121
        Contact: Malike Moore President
        Tel: 216-307-0767
        Email: mmoore@blackstarlogisticsincorporated.org
        Website: www.blackstarlogisticsincorporated.org
Shipping commercial freight and all other courier services.
(AA, estab 2017, empl 4, sales , cert: State)

9630   Cam Logistics, LLC
        7800 Robinett Way
        Canal Winchester, OH 43110
        Contact: Patrick Shea VP
        Tel: 614-409-1776
        Email: patrick@camlogisticsllc.com
        Website: www.camlogisticsllc.com
Third party logistics, transportation, truckload &
intermodal arrangements. (Woman, estab 2006, empl 9,
sales $5,400,000, cert: WBENC)

9631   Cimarron Express Inc.
        21611 State Rt 51
        Genoa, OH 43430
        Contact: Jim Shepperd/Gloria Snow VP /Admin Asst
        Tel: 419-855-7713
        Email: jshepperd@cimarronexpress.com
        Website: www.cimarronexpress.com
Motor carrier svcs, truckload. (AA, estab 1984, empl 325,
sales $0, cert: NMSDC)

9632   Cordell Transporation Company LLC
        2942 Boulder Ave
        Dayton, OH 45414
        Contact: Lori Van Opstal President
        Tel: 937-277-7271
        Email: lvanopstal@cordelltransportation.com
        Website: www.cordelltransportation.com
Provides dedicated Truckload Transportation services
throughout the US and Canada. (Minority, Woman, estab
1999, empl 225, sales $20,947,709, cert: NMSDC, WBENC)

9633   Debo Enterprises Incorporated
        16021 Dunbury Dr Ste 103
        Maple Heights, OH 44137
        Contact: Tommie Rodgers Operations Dir/Co-Owner
        Tel: 404-333-5008
        Email: deboenterprise@gmail.com
        Website: www.deboenterprises.com
Logistics & transportation services, Short term & long term
line haul services, railroad/shipyards, Hauling services for
construction worksites. (AA, estab 2001, empl 3, sales
$137,000, cert: State)

9634   Grand Aire, Inc.
        11777 W. Airport Service Road
        Swanton, OH 43558
        Contact: Katrina Cheema Business Advisor
        Tel: 419-861-6700
        Email: diversity@grandaire.com
        Website: www.grandaire.com
Air charter transportation: passengers & cargo. (As-Ind,
estab 1997, empl , sales $18,894,688, cert: NMSDC, SDB)

9635   H & W Trucking
        15 W Locust St
        Newark, OH 43055
        Contact: Barcy Vidt President
        Tel: 800-572-2120
        Email: barcy@handwtrucking.com
        Website: www.handwtrucking.com
Third party logistics & freight, LTL & rail, US & Canada.
(Woman, estab 1979, empl 3, sales $5,300,000, cert:
WBENC)

9636   InterChez Global Services, Inc.
        600 Alpha Pkwy
        Stow, OH 44224
        Contact: Ivette Tam Exec VP
        Tel: 330-923-5080
        Email: itam@interchez.com
        Website: www.interchezglobal.com
Logistics engineering, network modeling, logistics
execution, freight bill payment, premium freight
management, logistics consulting, translation, interpretation. (Minority, Woman, estab 2001, empl 12, sales
$18,000,000, cert: State, NMSDC, WBENC)

9637   J Rayl Trasnport Inc.
        1016 Triplett Blvd
        Akron, OH 44306
        Contact: Tara Vance President
        Tel: 800-753-5050
        Email: tara.rayl@jrayl.com
        Website: www.jrayl.com
Asset based transportation firm. (Woman, estab 1987,
empl 20, sales $68,000,000, cert: WBENC)

9638   Kingsgate Transportation Services LLC
        9100 West Chester Towne Centre
        West Chester, OH 45069
        Contact: AMY BARNETT Managing Partner
        Tel: 513-874-7447
        Email: abarnett@kingsgatetrans.com
        Website: www.kingsgatetrans.com
Freight services: truck, rail, air or ocean. (Woman, estab
1986, empl 21, sales $19,500,000, cert: WBENC)

9639   KLN Logistics dba AIT Worldwide Logistics
        6749 Eastland Rd, Ste C
        Middleburg Heights, OH 44130
        Contact: Kimberly Martinez-Giering Owner
        Tel: 440-816-1505
        Email: info@klnlogistics.com
        Website: www.klnlogistics.com
Air freight, expedited trucking, import, export, logistics.
(Minority, Woman, estab 2005, empl 28, sales
$427,000,000, cert: State, NMSDC, WBENC)

9640   Marine Services International, Inc.
       14508 S Industrial Ave
       Cleveland, OH 44137
       Contact: Kenton Woodhead President
       Tel: 216-587-3500
       Email: kenton@marineservicesintl.com
       Website: www.marineservicesintl.com
Air, Sea, Land International Freight Transportation (freight
forwarder), warehousing, labeling, repackaging, packaging
& re-palletizing capabilities. (Minority, Woman, estab
2006, empl 18, sales $5,000,000, cert: State)

9641   Rush Expediting, Inc.
       PO Box 2810
       Dayton, OH 45401
       Contact: Steve Parker President
       Tel: 800-989-7874
       Email: parkersl@rush-delivery.com
       Website: www.rush-delivery.com
Freight transportation services. (Woman, estab 2004, empl
200, sales $36,361,000, cert: WBENC)

9642   T.V. Minority Company, Inc.
       30 Lau Pkwy
       Clayton, OH 45315
       Contact: Sales Mgr
       Tel: 313-299-2177
       Email: info@tvmtrucking.com
       Website: www.tvmtrucking.com
Freight distribution and transportation. (AA, estab 1990,
empl 2, sales , cert: NMSDC)

9643   Trio Trucking, Inc.
       7750 Reinhold Dr
       Cincinnati, OH 45237
       Contact: Carvel Simmons President
       Tel: 513-679-7100
       Email: simmons.ce@onecalldoesall.com
       Website: www.trioenterprises.com
Transportation svcs: intermodal & full truckload transpor-
tation. (AA, estab 1982, empl 75, sales $18,300,000, cert:
State, NMSDC)

9644   Western Reserve Technology
       34194 Aurora Rd, Ste 200
       Solon, OH 44139
       Contact: Kim Cahuas Owner
       Tel: 440-498-9500
       Email: kim@gowrt.com
       Website: www.gowrt.com
(Minority, Woman, estab 2005, empl 1, sales $1,100,000,
cert: State, NMSDC)

Oklahoma

9645   STI Trucking LLC
       PO Box 700
       Kiefer, OK 74041
       Contact: Sam Mookerjee Accountant
       Tel: 918-446-6181
       Email: twyla.johnson@stonetrucking.com
       Website: www.stonetrucking.com
Premier legal flatbed, oversize & heavy haul carrier
servicing the US, Canada & Mexico. Hot shot trucks,
tankers, pole trucks, slick backs, RGN's. (AA, estab 1945,
empl 200, sales , cert: NMSDC)

Oregon

9646   Alliance Trucking Inc.
       1209 Stowe Ave
       Medford, OR 97501
       Contact: Jordan Kell Acct Exec
       Tel: 541-734-4844
       Email: jkell@alliancetrucking.com
       Website: www.alliancetrucking.com
Asset-based trucking, haul truckload & LTL shipments via
vans, flatbeds, step decks & multi-axle heavy haul
trailers, 48 states, Canada & Mexico. (Woman, estab
1996, empl 20, sales $9,726,975, cert: State)

9647   Lile International Companies
       8060 SW Pfaffle St, Ste 200
       Tigard, OR 97223
       Contact: Diane DeAutremont President
       Tel: 503-726-4800
       Email: diane.deautremont@lile.com
       Website: www.lile.com
National & international transportation svcs, warehousing, distribution & logistics. (Woman, estab 1959, empl
275, sales $0, cert: WBENC)

9648   Mulino Trading, LLC
       16570 SE McLoughlin Blvd
       Oak Grove, OR 97267
       Contact: Mike Theis Agent
       Tel: 503-786-8000
       Email: info@mulinotrading.com
       Website: www.mulinotrading.com
Freight truck transportation, broker forwarding. (Hisp,
estab 2012, empl 6, sales , cert: State)

Pennsylvania

9649   Advanced Shipping Technologies
       526 W Ogle St
       Ebensburg, PA 15931
       Contact: Emily Steberger Business Dev Dir
       Tel: 877-692-0570
       Email: diversity@astship.com
       Website: www.astship.com
Third party logistics: on-line transportation management
system. (Woman, estab 2002, empl 18, sales $0, cert:
WBENC)

9650   Allegheny Valley Transfer Co., Inc.
       1512 Lebanon Church Rd
       Pittsburgh, PA 15236
       Contact: Mary Jessup Owner
       Tel: 412-653-1200
       Email: alleghenyallied@aol.com
       Website: www.pghmover.com
Moving, storage & packing of household & office goods.
(Woman, estab 1925, empl 45, sales $1,561,882, cert:
State, WBENC)

9651   C.B. Transportation Inc
       2452 Horseshoe Trail
       Chester Springs, PA 19425
       Contact: Carole Borden CEO
       Tel: 610-416-4058
       Email: clborden@cbtransportation.com
       Website: www.cbtransportation.com
Provides truckload, distribution and logistics services.
(Woman, estab 1995, empl 11, sales $11,200,000, cert:
WBENC)

9652 Horwith Trucks, Inc.
      1449 Nor-Bath Blvd.
      Northampton, PA 18067
      Contact: Regina Grim President
      Tel: 610-261-2220
      Email: info@horwithfreightliner.com
      Website: www.horwithfreightliner.com
Transportation of hazardous and non hazardous waste, deicing salt, wall panels, general freight. (Woman, estab 1968, empl 84, sales , cert: WBENC)

9653 Knichel Logistics
      5347 William Flynn Hwy
      Gibsonia, PA 15044
      Contact: Ashley Caloia Marketing Coord
      Tel: 724-449-3300
      Email: acaloia@knichellogistics.com
      Website: www.knichellogistics.com
Intermodal, drayage & truckload services. (Woman, estab 2003, empl 42, sales $73,000,000, cert: WBENC)

9654 Maroadi Transfer & Storage
      1801 Lincoln Hwy
      North Versailles, PA 15137
      Contact: Mary V. Maroadi President
      Tel: 412-824-4420
      Email: mary@maroadi.com
      Website: www.maroadi.com
Local, interstate & international moving services, office & electronics moving, household goods moving, displays & exhibits. (Woman, estab 1967, empl 45, sales $3,800,000, cert: WBENC)

9655 Parks Moving Systems
      1234 Wrights Ln
      West Chester, PA 19380
      Contact: Relocation Consultant
      Tel: 610-429-4125
      Email:
      Website: www.parksmoving.com
Transportation: local, long distance, storage, record storage, trade show moves, etc. (Woman, estab 1992, empl 20, sales $1,300,000, cert: WBENC)

9656 Shepherd Transport, LLC
      296 Cumberland Rd
      Bedford, PA 15522
      Contact: Sandy Jones CEO
      Tel: 814-623-9346
      Email: sandy@shepherdtransport.com
      Website: www.shepherdtransport.com
Third party Logistics (3PL), non-asset based platform to serve a variety of transportation requirements. (Woman, estab 2008, empl 12, sales $7,682,700, cert: WBENC)

9657 Yourway Transport Inc.
      6681 Snowdrift Rd
      Allentown, PA 18106
      Contact: Frank DiStefano Sr VP Global Sales
      Tel: 442-222-4665
      Email: frank.distefano@yourwaytransport.com
      Website: www.yourway.com
Clinical supply chain management, 24x7 door to door transport, cold chain packaging, distribution, bio sample management, IRT, and a proprietary inventory management system. (As-Ind, estab 1997, empl 75, sales $55,000,000, cert: NMSDC)

Puerto Rico

9658 Allied Logistics Corp.
      PO Box 101
      Guaynabo, PR 00970
      Contact: Alberto Cruz VP
      Tel: 787-622-9393
      Email: alberto@alliedpr.com
      Website: www.alliedpr.com
Logistic services (Hisp, estab 2001, empl 14, sales , cert: NMSDC)

9659 Nestor Reyes, Inc.
      PO Box 9023474
      San Juan, PR 00902
      Contact: Edmundo Rodriguez President
      Tel: 787-289-6465
      Email: e.rodriguez@nreyes.com
      Website: www.nreyes.com
Foreign freight forwarding. (Hisp, estab 1973, empl 35, sales $7,753,580, cert: NMSDC)

9660 PR Global Logistics JP Corporation
      200 Rafael Cordero Ave, Ste 140
      Caguas, PR 00726
      Contact: Ivelisse Baba-Portalatin VP
      Tel: 787-653-5070
      Email: ivelisse@prgloballogistics.com
      Website: www.prgloballogistics.com
Logistics & distribution operations, packaging, quality control, supply chain technology, and organizational excellence. (Minority, Woman, estab 2007, empl 2, sales , cert: NMSDC)

Rhode Island

9661 Trans-Link LLC
      1249 Oaklawn Ave
      Cranston, RI 02920
      Contact: President
      Tel: 401-463-3862
      Email: Info@Translinkllc.com
      Website: www.translinkllc.com
Transportation & trucking: LTL, truckload, rail & flatbeds, refrigerated & dry freight, 48 states & Canada. (Woman, estab 2000, empl 5, sales $5,600,000, cert: State)

South Carolina

9662 Alpha Logistics Solutions, LLC
      8201 Arrowridge Blvd ste 123
      Charlotte, SC 28273
      Contact: Arthur Cottingham COO
      Tel: 877-356-6102
      Email: arthur@alphals-biz.com
      Website: www.alphals-biz.com/
Less Than Truckload (LTL), Truckload (TL), Domestic Air & Ground Expedited Shipping, International, Intermodal. (Woman/AA, estab 2014, empl 5, sales $350,000, cert: NMSDC)

9663 Atlantic-Pacific Express, Inc.
      1350 Browning Rd, Ste B
      Columbia, SC 29210
      Contact: Irene Brotherton President
      Tel: 877-739-1116
      Email: irene@apexpedite.com
      Website: www.apexpedite.com
Asset & non-asset based ground & air freight. (Woman, estab , empl 13, sales $28,000,000, cert: WBENC)

9664   Key Logistics Solutions, LLC
    4279A Cross Point Dr.
    Ladson, SC 29456
    Contact: Sylvester Hester President
    Tel: 404-597-1652
    Email: shester@keylogistics.com
    Website: www.keylogistics.com
3rd Party Logistics, Sorting, Kitting, Warehousing, Inventory mgmt,Transportation, Sequencing, Light assembly. (AA, estab 2003, empl 410, sales $218,796,533, cert: NMSDC)

9665   Kontane Inc.
    1000 Charleston Regional Pkwy
    Charleston, SC 29492
    Contact: Rusty Byrd President
    Tel: 843-352-0011
    Email: rusty@kontanelogistics.com
    Website: www.kontanelogistics.com
Logistics, warehousing & distribution, cross-docking, freight consolidation, import material receipt, line sequencing, parts distribution, development of logistics information systems, sub-assembly & foreign trade zones services. (Woman, estab 1975, empl 100, sales $40,000,000, cert: WBENC)

9666   Logisticus Projects Group
    20 W North St
    Greenville, SC 29601
    Contact: Vikash Patel President
    Tel: - -
    Email: commercial@logisticusgroup.com
    Website: www.logisticusgroup.com
Turnkey Transportation, Barge, Rail, Heavy Haul Truck, Crane & Rigging, Port, Distribution Centers, Warehousing, Field Support, Owners Representatives, GPS Tracking. (As-Pac, estab 2012, empl 25, sales $14,000,000, cert: NMSDC)

9667   Premier Logistics Solutions Warehousing, LLC
    904 Commerce Circle
    Hanahan, SC 29410
    Contact: Stewart Bauknight Dir Sales
    Tel: 843-554-7529
    Email: bauknights@premier3pl.com
    Website: www.premier3pl.com
Provide transportation, transportation brokerage, fulfillment, packaging, just in time deliveries, trans loading of bulk products, rail service with CSX, a container freight station, foreign trade zone. (Woman, estab 2003, empl 100, sales $15,000,000, cert: WBENC)

9668   TPS Logistics
    PO Box 9493
    Columbia, SC 29229
    Contact: Al Stokes VP Sales & Mktg
    Tel: 803-622-2970
    Email: alstokes@tpslogisticsinc.com
    Website: www.tpslogisticsinc.com
Transportation services. (Woman, estab 2004, empl 3, sales $20,000,000, cert: NWBOC)

9669   Warehouse Services, Inc.
    58 S Burty Rd
    Piedmont, SC 29673
    Contact: Michelle Dender Mktg Coord
    Tel: 864-422-6079
    Email: michelledender@wsi-ismi.com
    Website: www.wsionline.com
Warehousing, transportation svcs: distribution, client system integration, domestic & international supply chain (SC) enhancement. (Woman, estab 1985, empl 2000, sales $220,000,000, cert: WBENC)

South Dakota

9670   K & J Trucking, Inc.
    1800 East 50th St North
    Sioux Falls, SD 57104
    Contact: John Kemp Marketing Mgr
    Tel: 605-332-5531
    Email: jkemp@kandjtrucking.com
    Website: www.kandjtrucking.com
Long haul & regional refrigerated transportation services. (Woman, estab 1979, empl 45, sales $21,235,776, cert: WBENC)

Tennessee

9671   Ewing Moving Services
    4006 Air Park St
    Memphis, TN 38118
    Contact: Ashleigh Hayes Natl Acct Coordinator
    Tel: 901-774-2197
    Email: admin@ewingmovingservice.com
    Website: www.ewingmovingservice.com
Moving & storage services. (AA, estab 1980, empl 57, sales $3,047,104, cert: NMSDC)

9672   Infinity Logistics Group, LLC
    2115 Chapman Rd
    Chattanooga, TN 37421
    Contact: Dallas Holder Sales Mgr
    Tel: 423-373-2600
    Email: Dholder@infinitylogisticsgroup.com
    Website: www.infinitylogisticsgroup.com
Transportation, warehousing, storage, logistic services. (As-Ind, estab 2019, empl 18, sales $3,131,559, cert: NMSDC)

9673   Lanigan Worldwide Moving & Warehousing, Inc.
    1870 Airways Blvd
    Memphis, TN 38114
    Contact: Lynn L. Lanigan CEO
    Tel: 901-744-7070
    Email: llanigan@alliedagent.com
    Website: www.laniganmoving.com
Transportation svcs: local, intrastate, interstate & international relocations. (Woman, estab 1955, empl 38, sales $3,600,000, cert: WBENC)

9674   Time Logistics, Inc
    1406 Nashville Hwy
    Columbia, TN 38401
    Contact: Laura Shorette Business Devel Exec
    Tel: 866-293-8463
    Email: lshorette@timelogisticsinc.com
    Website: www.timelogisticsinc.com
Transporation provider that specializes in the managment of pre-printed inserts and direct mail promotions. (Woman, estab 2001, empl 50, sales $12,010,000, cert: WBENC)

9675   Total Control Logistics
    1519 Union Ave, Ste 177
    Memphis, TN 38104
    Contact: Terica Lamb President
    Tel: 901-830-1864
    Email: tlamb@tclogistix.com
    Website: www.tclogistix.com
Third party logistics provider (3PL), Warehousing & Distribution. (Woman/AA, estab 2009, empl 1, sales , cert: NMSDC)

9676   Western Express Inc.
       7135 Centennial Place
       Nashville, TN 37209
       Contact: Hannah Sweeney
       Tel: 615-369-8208
       Email: hyoung@westernexp.com
       Website: www.westernexp.com
Full truck load carrier operates 3800 power units 48 states,
Canada & Mexico border cities. (Woman, estab 1991, empl
3600, sales $430,250,000, cert: WBENC)

Texas

9677   A-1 Freeman Relocation
       4727 Macro
       San Antonio, TX 78218
       Contact: Jonathan Hightower Corporate Relocation
       & Logistics Consultant
       Tel: 210-661-1404
       Email: jhightower@a-1freeman.com
       Website: www.a-1freemanrelo.com
Domestic & international household goods moving &
transportation services. (Woman, estab 1994, empl 450,
sales $10,000,000, cert: WBENC)

9678   Action Transportation Services, Inc.
       PO Box 15711
       Houston, TX 77220
       Contact: Lucy Bowerman Sales
       Tel: 713-673-4817
       Email: actiontransport@sbcglobal.net
       Website: www.actionfrtservices.com
Transportation services: flatbeds, van, stepdecks, hotshots,
power only, local & specialized equipment for partial & full
loads, US & Canada, 24 hrs a day 7 days a week. (Woman,
estab 1998, empl 3, sales $245,878, cert: State, WBENC)

9679   Americorp Xpress Carriers
       5201 N Veterans Blvd
       Pharr, TX 78577
       Contact: Frank Flores President
       Tel: 956-283-0052
       Email: fflores@axcarriers.com
       Website: www.axcarriers.com
Transportation services. (Hisp, estab 2010, empl 250, sales
, cert: NMSDC)

9680   A-Rocket Moving & Storage, Inc.
       3401 Corder St
       Houston, TX 77021
       Contact: Lewis Grisby TQM
       Tel: 713-748-6024
       Email: arocket@arocket.com
       Website: www.arocket.com
Relocation services: material handling & warehousing,
local, long-distance & international. (AA, estab 1959, empl
120, sales $3,700,000, cert: State, City, NMSDC)

9681   Best Logistics and Freight LLC
       3516 Chatham Green Ln
       Arlington, TX 76014
       Contact: Domonique Chantal Donegan Freight
       Broker
       Tel: 682-208-1193
       Email: broker@blnfreight.com
       Website: www.blnfreight.com
Freight transportation services. (AA, estab 2020, empl 3,
sales , cert: State)

9682   Candor Expedite
       1404 Gables Court, Ste 202
       Plano, TX 75075
       Contact: John Kennedy Sr Business Dev
       Tel: 469-661-3360
       Email: jkennedy@candorexp.com
       Website: www.candorexp.com
Expedite transportation and nationwide hotshot
services. (Woman, estab 2017, empl 21, sales
$6,000,000, cert: WBENC)

9683   Cargo One Logistics, LLC
       5802 Val Verde, Ste 165
       Houston, TX 77057
       Contact: Diego Alexander President
       Tel: 713-290-9922
       Email: dalexander@cargo1logistics.com
       Website: www.cargo1logistics.com
Transportation services, over the road, full truck load,
Mexico, US & Canada. (Hisp, estab 2000, empl 7, sales
$4,000,000, cert: NMSDC)

9684   DFW LinQ Transport
       2300 Valley View Ste 100
       Irving, TX 75062
       Contact: Sylvia Dayer Dir Brokerage Div
       Tel: 972-522-1500
       Email: sdayer@linqtransport.com
       Website: www.linqtransport.com
Transportation & logistic services. (Hisp, estab 2005,
empl 52, sales $39,400,000, cert: NMSDC)

9685   EP Logistics LLC
       9601 Pan American Dr
       El Paso, TX 79927
       Contact: Ingrid Hurtado Marketing Business Dev
       Mgr
       Tel: 915-881-9100
       Email: ingridh@eplogistics.com
       Website: www.eplogistics.com
Warehousing, customs brokerage, sorting/rework
services, transportation. (Hisp, estab 2005, empl 50,
sales $1,200,000, cert: State, NMSDC)

9686   Epsilon Brokerage Corporation
       12110 Sara Rd
       Laredo, TX 78045
       Contact: Rick Laurel President
       Tel: 956-728-8713
       Email: rick.laurel@epsilonbrokerage.com
       Website: www.epsilonbrokerage.com
Logistics, customs broker, freight forwarding, warehous-
ing. (Hisp, estab 2011, empl 50, sales $4,000,000, cert:
State, NMSDC)

9687   Expedited Specialized Logistics LLC
       801 Pellegrino Court
       Laredo, TX 78045
       Contact: Armando Correa Commercial Dir
       Tel: 956-712-8350
       Email: acorrea@es-logistics.net
       Website: www.es-logistics.net
USA and International Truck Load Transportation
Services. Dryvan Trailers Flatbeds Stepdecks double drop
open or curtain trailers. RGN Lowboys. (Hisp, estab
2011, empl 30, sales $7,661,250, cert: NMSDC)

9688   Group of Global Suppliers, LLC
      279 Shadow Mountain, Ste 200
      El Paso, TX 79912
      Contact: Roberto Gonzalez President
      Tel: 915-727-2811
      Email: sales@ggscorporation.com
      Website: www.ggscorporation.com
Logistics, warehousing, inspection, sorting, etc. (Minority, estab 2013, empl 5, sales $1,620,000, cert: State, NMSDC)

9689   Hazel's Hot Shot, Inc.
      2009 McKenzie Dr Ste 110
      Carrollton, TX 75006
      Contact: Dustin Marshall CEO
      Tel: 972-620-8812
      Email: dustin@hazels.com
      Website: www.hazels.com
Expedited freight, 48 contiguous states. (Woman, estab , empl , sales $6,000,000, cert: State, WBENC)

9690   InstiCo Freight Management, Inc.
      3011 Gateway Dr. Ste 340
      Irving, TX 75063
      Contact: Cory Allen Business Dev Exec
      Tel: 469-293-9549
      Email: callen@insticologistics.com
      Website: www.insticologistics.com
International Services- Ocean cargo, Air cargo, and Non-Vessel Operating Common Carrier. (Hisp, estab 2011, empl 25, sales , cert: NMSDC)

9691   Intercon Carriers
      19810 FM 1472
      Laredo, TX 78045
      Contact: Enrique Serna Managing Partner
      Tel: 956-725-7275
      Email: enrique.serna@intercomlogistics.com
      Website: www.interconcarriers.com
Transportation & logistics services in the United States, Canada & Mexico. (Hisp, estab 1996, empl 175, sales , cert: State, NMSDC)

9692   Kaliber Choice, LLC
      12705 S Kirkwood Rd, Ste 213
      Stafford, TX 77477
      Contact: Valesco Raymond President
      Tel: 512-774-5838
      Email: vraymond@nxglogistics.com
      Website: www.nxglogistics.com
Freight brokerage: LTL (Less-Than-Truckload), Full Truck-load (FTL), Airfreight, Ocean Container (20/40ft) Drayage package ecommerce shipping (Fedex, UPS, DHL). (AA, estab 2016, empl 9, sales $997,898, cert: NMSDC)

9693   Logisti-K USA, LLC
      13151 S Unitec
      Laredo, TX 78045
      Contact: Cesar Roberto Flores Dir Inland Forwarding
      Tel: 956-723-7606
      Email: cflores@logisti-k.com.mx
      Website: www.logisti-k.com.mx
Truckload, Flatbed, Refrigerated & Intermodal services. (Hisp, estab 2005, empl 30, sales $1,225,062, cert: State, NMSDC)

9694   MagRabbit, Inc.,
      1464 E. Whitestone Blvd Ste 1001
      Cedar Park, TX 78613
      Contact: Tommy Hodinh President
      Tel: 512-993-5730
      Email: tommy.hodinh@magrabbit.com
      Website: www.magrabbit.com
Global supply chain solutions, air, surface & ocean tranportation. (As-Pac, estab 1990, empl 1001, sales , cert: State, NMSDC)

9695   MagRabbit-Alamo Iron Works, LLC
      PO Box 2341
      San Antonio, TX 78298
      Contact: Wayne Dennis Diversity Coord
      Tel: 210-704-8520
      Email: wdennis@aiwnet.com
      Website: www.magrabbit-aiw.com
Dist industrial supplies, steel service & fabrication, hand & power tools, equipment repair & installation, logistics, transportation & freight forwarding. (As-Pac, estab 2004, empl 150, sales , cert: NMSDC)

9696   Moore Transport of Tulsa LLC
      661 N Plano Rd Ste 319
      Richardson, TX 75081
      Contact: Gary Moore Owner
      Tel: 972-578-0606
      Email: danchase@mooretransport.com
      Website: www.mooretransport.com
Freight transportation. (AA, estab 2005, empl 300, sales $63,000,000, cert: NMSDC)

9697   Multi-Trans, Inc.
      606 Grand Central Blvd.
      Laredo, TX 78045
      Contact: Emilio Villarreal New Projects
      Tel: 210-418-4889
      Email: evillarreal@multitransinc.com
      Website: www.multitransinc.com
Air, Sea & Land Transportation service, LTL, TL & Sea Containers, Flat Beds, Lowboys, Drop Decks & Heavy Equipment Hauling, Air Charters. (Minority, Woman, estab 2000, empl 8, sales $10,000,000, cert: State)

9698   Munoz Trucking, Inc.
      12460 Weaver Rd
      El Paso, TX 79928
      Contact: Marvin Arellano Dir of Sales
      Tel: 915-852-7722
      Email: marvin@munoztruckinginc.com
      Website: www.munoztrucking1@verizon.net
Over the Road Transportation Services, 300 plus dry vans , 5 reefers, 150+ Units, drop trailer, long haul, 48 states. (Hisp, estab 1994, empl 175, sales $25,000,000, cert: NMSDC)

9699   Mustang Express Ltd.
      11436 Rojas Dr, Ste B-10
      El Paso, TX 79936
      Contact: Josh Hernandez Dir Operations
      Tel: 915-598-2600
      Email: jhernandez@mustangexpress.net
      Website: www.mustangexpress.net
Freight transportation. (Minority, estab 2001, empl 15, sales , cert: NMSDC)

9700   MW Logistics, LLC
       12770 Coit Road, Ste 1040
       Dallas, TX 75251
       Contact: Brian Thompson Sr Dir
       Tel: 214-393-8211
       Email: bthompson@mwlogistics.com
       Website: www.mwlogistics.com
Transportation & logistics: over the road, intermodal & bulk. (AA, estab 2001, empl 17, sales $16,800,000, cert: NMSDC)

9701   Navigator Express
       14587 Kelmscot Dr
       Frisco, TX 75035
       Contact: Furqan Khan VP Operations
       Tel: 972-330-2340
       Email: ops@navex.us
       Website: www.navex.us
Authorized motor carrier, interstate transportation of commodities to all 48 contiguous states. (As-Ind, estab 2009, empl 15, sales , cert: State)

9702   Nobis Logistics LLC
       1100 E Campbell Rd Ste 247
       Richardson, TX 75081
       Contact: Bonnie MacEslin Owner
       Tel: 214-446-2400
       Email: bonnie.maceslin@gonobis.com
       Website: www.gonobis.com
Transportation management, manufacturing, distribution, supply chain, executive management & logistics. (Woman, estab , empl , sales $3,000,000, cert: WBENC)

9703   Pan American Express, Inc.
       4848 Riverside Dr
       Laredo, TX 78041
       Contact: Ric Guardado CEO
       Tel: 214-762-9912
       Email: ric@panamex-zero.com
       Website: www.panamex-zero.com
International transportation svcs; 48 states, Mexico & Canada. (Hisp, estab 1988, empl 185, sales $43,000,000, cert: NMSDC)

9704   Perimeter Global Logistics (PGL)
       2800 Story Rd W Ste 100
       Irving, TX 75038
       Contact: Tammy Williams Global Sales Exec
       Tel: 214-914-2654
       Email: tammy.williams@shippgl.com
       Website: www.shippgl.com
Freight forwarding, contract logistics, transportation and distribution management. (Woman, estab 2007, empl 140, sales $120,000,000, cert: WBENC)

9705   Pronto Delivery, Courier, and Logistics, LLC
       7420 S Cooper St
       Arlington, TX 76001
       Contact: Matthew Hince Mgr
       Tel: 817-261-0035
       Email: matt.hince@pronto-delivery.com
       Website: www.pronto-delivery.com
Hot Shot delivery, Route delivery, Scheduled delivery, pick-up truck, cargo van, pipe rack truck, box truck, flatbed, tractor trailer. (Woman, estab 1984, empl 85, sales $13,000,000, cert: WBENC)

9706   Purpose Transportation, LLC
       701 Hanover Dr
       Grand Prairie, TX 75053
       Contact: Greg Crawford VP Sales
       Tel: 972-746-4585
       Email: chuck@purposetransportation.com
       Website: www.purposetransportation.com
Domestic transportation, freight & logistics services. (Woman, estab 2011, empl 10, sales $4,874,185, cert: State, WBENC)

9707   Royal Freight, LP
       407 W Sioux Rd
       Pharr, TX 78577
       Contact: Mike Kelley Sales Mgr
       Tel: 956-283-2200
       Email: mikek@royalfreight.net
       Website: www.royalfreight.net
Direct, Truckload, Asset Based Carrier, serving U.S.(48), Canada, and Mexico, Satelitte equipped (tractors and trailers). (Woman, estab 2001, empl 350, sales , cert: State)

9708   Russell Transport Inc.
       12365 Pine Springs
       El Paso, TX 79928
       Contact: Rosa Marin President
       Tel: 915-542-1495
       Email: rmarin@russelltransport.com
       Website: www.russelltransport.com
Full TL & logistics. (Minority, Woman, estab 1992, empl 300, sales $27,000,000, cert: State, NMSDC)

9709   Shire Express Transportation
       6651 Watauga Rd, Ste 48803
       Fort Worth, TX 76148
       Contact: Brenda Jackson Logistics Coord
       Tel: 214-243-5872
       Email: brenda.jackson@landstarmail.com
       Website: www.shireexpressgov.com/
Transportation & logistic services across the United States and Canada. (AA, estab 2015, empl 7, sales , cert: State)

9710   Siam Logistics
       2320 Dean Way Ste 160
       Southlake, TX 76092
       Contact: Sarah Baldwin Acct Mgr
       Tel: 734-619-8576
       Email: sarah.baldwin@siam-logistics.com
       Website: www.siam-logistics.com
Transportation, oversized loads, specialized equipment & special weight requirements, US, Mexico & Canada. (Minority, Woman, estab 2009, empl 13, sales $1,920,000, cert: NMSDC, WBENC)

9711   Southwest Freight Lines
       PO Box 371736
       El Paso, TX 79936
       Contact: Jesus Lares Operations Mgr
       Tel: 915-860-8592
       Email: jesus.lares@swflines.com
       Website: www.swflines.com
Truckload services, 48 states & Mexico. (Hisp, estab 1988, empl 300, sales $50,000,000, cert: State)

9712 Spirit Truck Lines
      200 W Nolana
      San Juan, TX 78589
      Contact: Steve Garza VP Ops & Sales
      Tel: 956-781-7715
      Email: sgarza@spirittrucklines.com
      Website: www.spirittrucklines.com
Dedicated carrier service, bonded shipmment, expedited
loads, cargo tracking. (Hisp, estab 1990, empl 300, sales
$30,000,000, cert: NMSDC)

9713 Sun City Group Inc
      1009 Myrtle Ave Ste 100 A
      El Paso, TX 79901
      Contact: Patrick Warrington Dir of Sales
      Tel: 915-593-5900
      Email: pwarrington@suncitygroup.com
      Website: www.suncitygroup.com
Multimodal transportation services, over the road,
intermodal, sea & air. (Hisp, estab 2006, empl 21, sales
$15,000,000, cert: NMSDC)

9714 Sunrise Delivery Inc.
      2020 Lawrence St
      Houston, TX 77008
      Contact: Lanette Martinez President
      Tel: 713-864-2020
      Email: lm@sditex.com
      Website: www.sunrisedeliveryinc.com
LTL freight, warehousing & logistics. (Minority, Woman,
estab 1981, empl 15, sales $799,616, cert: City, NMSDC,
CPUC, WBENC)

9715 Swift Logistics, Inc.
      1809 Stoney Brook Dr Ste 204
      Houston, TX 77063
      Contact: Rosemarie Patterson Logistics Consultant
      Tel: 713-425-4175
      Email: rpatterson@swiftlogisticsinc.com
      Website: www.swiftlogisticsinc.com
Freight brokerage. (Woman, estab 2014, empl 4, sales ,
cert: WBENC)

9716 TBM Carriers
      4241 E. Piedras, Ste. 200
      San Antonio, TX 78228
      Contact: Gerardo Villarreal Natl Accts mgr
      Tel: 830-775-8283
      Email: gerardo@tbmcarriers.com
      Website: www.tbmcarriers.com
Logistics solution. (Hisp, estab 1999, empl 250, sales
$45,000,001, cert: State, NMSDC)

9717 Texas Freight
      1207 NE Big Bend Trail, Ste L
      Glen Rose, TX 76043
      Contact: Preston Shuffield Broker
      Tel: 254-898-1117
      Email: preston@texasfreight.net
      Website: www.texasfreight.net
Commercial motor carrier, brokerage authority serving 48
states, flatbeds, drop decks, RGN's, lowboys, and dry vans.
(Woman, estab 2002, empl 8, sales , cert: NWBOC)

9718 Trans-Expedite Inc
      7 Founders Blvd Ste 100
      El Paso, TX 79906
      Contact: Claudia Fuentes CEO
      Tel: 915-205-5500
      Email: diversity@trans-expedite.com
      Website: www.trans-expedite.com
Transportation & logistics: air charters, warehousing,
customs brokerage. (Minority, Woman, estab 2001, empl
11, sales $30,000,000, cert: NMSDC, WBENC)

9719 Transmaquila, Inc.
      1385 Cheers Blvd
      Brownsville, TX 78521
      Contact: Alejandra Torres HR Asst
      Tel: 956-831-0128
      Email: alejandra.torres@transmaquila.com
      Website: www.transmaquila.com
Cargo transportation throughout Mexico, the United
States and Canada. (Hisp, estab 2002, empl 32, sales ,
cert: NMSDC)

9720 Tri Star Freight System Inc.
      5407 Mesa Dr
      Houston, TX 77028
      Contact: Shana Whittington Administrative Asst
      Tel: 713-631-1095
      Email: shanaw@tristarfreightsys.com
      Website: www.tristarfreightsys.com
Linehaul, FTL & LTL, airport pick up & delivery, drayage,
local & OTR container drayage, warehousing. (Woman,
estab 1987, empl 89, sales $32,634,980, cert: NWBOC)

9721 Twenty-Two Global Transport, LP
      PO Box 62588
      Houston, TX 77205
      Contact: Kevin Smoot Reg Mgr
      Tel: 901-362-3707
      Email: ksmoot@22global.com
      Website: www.xxiiglobal.com
International ocean freight forwarding, customs brokerage, hot shot/expedited services, logistics services,
global information services. (AA, estab 2007, empl 4,
sales $200,000, cert: NMSDC)

9722 Verde Logistics, LLC
      9525 Escobar Dr
      El Paso, TX 79907
      Contact: Holly Webb Business Devel
      Tel: 915-791-4034
      Email: holly.jones@verdelogistics.com
      Website: www.verdelogisticsllc.com/home
Third party transportation, full truck load van, reefer, flat
bed & heavy haul. (Minority, Woman, estab 2010, empl
6, sales $20,000,000, cert: NMSDC, WBENC)

Virginia

9723 Accurate Courier Express
      1711 Ellen Rd
      Richmond, VA 23230
      Contact: Dwight Hicks CEO
      Tel: 804-354-8880
      Email: dhicks@accuratecourierexpress.com
      Website: www.accuratecourierexpress.com
Transportation and delivery services. (AA, estab 1990,
empl 80, sales $15,000,000, cert: State)

9724 High Plains Logistics Consulting, LLC
      PO Box 8
      Highland Springs, VA 23057
      Contact: Burt Epps VP
      Tel: 804-437-0066
      Email: HGPSlogistics@gmail.com
      Website: www.highplainslogistics.com
Transprotation brokerage & third party logistics. (Nat
Ame, estab 2002, empl 3, sales $8,200,000, cert:
NMSDC)

9725 LAS Logistical Services LLC
3031 N Lakebridge Dr
Norfolk, VA 23324
Contact: Sam Kearson CEO
Tel: 855-232-5866
Email: samkearson@laslogistical.com
Website: www.laslogistical.com
Logistic services: land, air & sea. (AA, estab 2012, empl 10, sales , cert: State)

9726 TH Logistics,LLC
2150 Magnolia St
Richmond, VA 23223
Contact: Devon Henry President
Tel: 888-929-7323
Email: dhenry@thlogistics.net
Website: www.thlogistics.net
Third party logistics & supply chain services, value added warehousing distribution, contract packaging, product acquisition, transload & transportation. (AA, estab 2016, empl 200, sales $50,000,000, cert: NMSDC)

Washington

9727 Radiant Logistics Partners, LLC
405 114th Ave SE, 3rd Fl
Bellevue, WA 98004
Contact: Bohn Crain Managing Member
Tel: 425-462-1094
Email: mbe@radiantdelivers.com
Website: www.radiantdelivers.com
Domestic and international transportation and logistics services. (Nat Ame, estab 2006, empl 20, sales $102,000,000, cert: NMSDC)

9728 Red Arrow Logistics
150 120th Ave NE, Ste F110
Bellevue, WA 98005
Contact: Liz Lasater CEO
Tel: 425-747-7914
Email: ashley.moise@redarrowlogistics.com
Website: www.redarrowlogistics.com
Warehousing & distribution services, vendor compliance programs, ground, sea & air transportation. (Woman, estab 2003, empl 8, sales $6,747,398, cert: WBENC)

9729 VETRANS LLC
1420 Meridian E Ste 2
Milton, WA 98354
Contact: Vincent W. Santiago Owner
Tel: 253-833-4688
Email: vince@go-vetrans.com
Website: www.go-VETrans.com
Transportation, railroad transloading, other transporation brokerage services. (Minority, Woman, estab 2006, empl 3, sales $3,967,124, cert: NMSDC)

Wisconsin

9730 Black River Truck Brokers, LLC
N613 Colonial Ave
Pittsville, WI 54466
Contact: Heather Jacobson Owner
Tel: 800-241-2785
Email: heather.brtb@yahoo.com
Website: www.blackrivertruckbroker.com
Transportation & Logistics Services. (Woman, estab 2007, empl 2, sales $4,800,000, cert: State, WBENC)

9731 KM Logistics LLC
4375 S Kansas Ave
Saint Francis, WI 53235
Contact: Muny Chen Sales
Tel: 414-856-0020
Email: mchen@SHIPKML.com
Website: www.shipkml.com
Nationwide direct/exclusive transporation services. (Minority, Woman, estab 2008, empl 15, sales $2,500,000, cert: State)

9732 Merchants Delivery Moving & Storage Co.
1215 State St
Racine, WI 53404
Contact: Jennifer Eastman President
Tel: 262-631-5680
Email: jeastman@merchants-moving.com
Website: www.merchants-moving.com
Moving services. (Woman, estab 1921, empl 84, sales $0, cert: WBENC)

9733 Trans International, LLC
N93 W16288 Megal Dr
Menomonee Falls, WI 53051
Contact: Denise Lawien CSMO
Tel: 262-253-3500
Email: sales@ticominc.com
Website: www.ticominc.com
Transportation consulting & logistics services: freight pre-audit & payment, post audit, transportation reporting software & tools, freight rating & routing, carrier contract negotiations & general logistics consulting. (Woman, estab 1975, empl 115, sales $5,790,000, cert: State, WBENC)

9734 Veriha Trucking, Inc.
2830 Cleveland Ave
Marinette, WI 54143
Contact: Kyle Cheney Sales Mgr
Tel: 715-330-5921
Email: kcheney@veriha.com
Website: www.veriha.com
Transportation services. (Woman, estab 1978, empl 300, sales $45,000,000, cert: WBENC)

9735 Wisconsin International Services Inc.
5600 S Westridge Dr
New Berlin, WI 53151
Contact: Michael Pflugheoft Dir of Sales
Tel: 262-501-0098
Email: mpflughoeft@wislogistics.com
Website: www.wislogistics.com
Full service logistics solutions. (As-Pac, estab 1996, empl 9, sales $10,000,000, cert: NMSDC)

TRAVEL ARRANGEMENTS
Full service travel agencies with domestic and international capabilities. NAICS Code 48

Arizona

9736   El Sol Travel, Inc.
4500 S. Lakeshore Dr Ste 450
Tempe, AZ 85282
Contact: Christine Davidson VP Business Travel
Solutions Strategist
Tel: 480-693-0218
Email: cdavidson@elsoltravel.net
Website: www.elsoltravel.net
Full service travel agency. (Woman, estab 1986, empl 27, sales $213,395,700, cert: WBENC)

California

9737   Incentive Travel Inc.
311 Fourth Ave, Ste 617
San Diego, CA 92101
Contact: Penny Wing President
Tel: 619-515-0880
Email: penny@incentiveinc.com
Website: www.incentiveinc.com
Incentive & meeting planning, consulting, creating, promoting. (Woman, estab 1988, empl 14, sales $5,000,000, cert: WBENC)

9738   Pinnacle Travel Services, LLC
390 N Sepulveda Blvd Ste 3100
El Segundo, CA 90245
Contact: Bob Singh President
Tel: 310-343-4284
Email: ptsbsingh@earthlink.net
Website: www.pinnaclecallsolutions.com
Full service travel agency. (Hisp, estab 1999, empl 150, sales $10,600,000, cert: NMSDC)

Florida

9739   Cruise.Com
255 E Dania Beach Blvd
Dania Beach, FL 33004
Contact: Jessica Speirs Reg Sales Dir
Tel: 954-805-7810
Email: jspeirs@cruise.com
Website: www.cruise.com
Leisure products: cruise, affinity revenue share program. (Woman, estab 2002, empl 200, sales , cert: WBENC)

9740   Landry & Kling, Inc.
1390 S Dixie Hwy
Coral Gables, FL 33146
Contact: Cyndi Murphy VP Corporate Planning
Tel: 305-661-1880
Email: cmurphy@landrykling.com
Website: www.landrykling.com
Full service travel agency. (Woman, estab 1982, empl 24, sales $11,739,216, cert: WBENC)

Georgia

9741   Four Seasons Travel
4060 Johns Creek Pkwy Bldg. D
Suwanee, GA 30024
Contact: Michael Morrison Business Devel
Tel: 770-441-2170
Email: mmorrison@travelleaders.com
Website: www.fscorporatetravel.com
Travel Fulfillment, Consulting & Analytics, and Meetings Management. (Woman, estab 1979, empl 30, sales $35,000,000, cert: WBENC)

9742   Georgia International Travel, Inc.
6285 Barfield Rd Ste 150
Atlanta, GA 30328
Contact: Vela McClam Mitchell CEO
Tel: 404-851-9166
Email: corporatetravel@dt.com
Website: www.gitravel.com
Corporate travel management. (Woman/AA, estab 1984, empl 24, sales $21,000,000, cert: NMSDC)

9743   Teplis Travel Service
244 Perimeter Center Pkwy, Ste 280
Atlanta, GA 30346
Contact: Van Henderson VP Business Dev
Tel: 404-843-7460
Email: van@teplis.com
Website: www.teplis.com
Full service travel agency. (Woman, estab 1972, empl 45, sales $50,000,000, cert: WBENC)

Illinois

9744   Travelex International, Inc.
2500 W. Higgins Road
Hoffman Estates, IL 60169
Contact: Ursula Pearson President
Tel: 847-882-0400
Email: ursulap@travelexonline.com
Website: www.travelexonline.com
Full service travel agency, travel management. (Woman, estab 1992, empl 12, sales $725,435, cert: State, WBENC)

Kansas

9745   WingGate Travel, Inc.
8645 College Blvd, Ste 100
Overland Park, KS 66210
Contact: Young Sexton CEO
Tel: 913-451-9200
Email: young.sexton@winggatetravel.com
Website: www.winggatetravel.com
Full service travel management, online fulfillment, VIP executive travel & leisure travel services. (Minority, Woman, estab 1991, empl 38, sales $4,000,000, cert: NMSDC)

Massachusetts

9746 Atlas Travel & Technology Group, Inc.
One Maple St
Milford, MA 01757
Contact: Kerin McKinnon SVP Global
Tel: 508-488-1160
Email: kerin.mckinnon@atlastravel.com
Website: www.atlastravel.com
Full service travel agency. (Woman, estab 1986, empl 138, sales $179,000,000, cert: WBENC)

Michigan

9747 American Center Travel
2451 W Stadium Blvd
Ann Arbor, MI 48103
Contact: Sue Konarska Owner
Tel: 734-827-1030
Email: sue.act@travelleaders.com
Website: www.travelleaders.com
Full service travel agency. (Woman/As-Ind, estab 1986, empl 4, sales $0, cert: NMSDC)

9748 Boersma Travel Services
3368 Washtenaw Ave
Ann Arbor, MI 48104
Contact: James Kimble President
Tel: 734-971-3148
Email: jkimble@boersmatravel.com
Website: www.boersmatravel.com
Full svc travel agency. (AA, estab 1945, empl 23, sales $24,000,000, cert: NMSDC)

9749 Departure Travel Management
344 N Old Woodward, Ste 100
Birmingham, MI 48011
Contact: Maria Garcia Reg acct exec
Tel: 210-913-8016
Email: maria@dtmdeparture.com
Website: www.dtmdeparture.com
Full service travel agency. (Woman/AA, estab 1999, empl 21, sales $29,000,000, cert: NMSDC, WBENC)

9750 Global Business Travel, LLC
2100 Coe Court Ste A
Auburn Hills, MI 48326
Contact: Nick Ladney Sales Mgr
Tel: 877-227-8770
Email: globaltravel@myway.com
Website: www.gbtah.com
Full service travel agency. (AA, estab 0, empl 1, sales $4,600,000, cert: NMSDC)

9751 Motor City Travel
29566 Northwestern Hwy Ste 400
Southfield, MI 48034
Contact: Tracey Campbell VP Business Dev
Tel: 248-799-0752
Email: tcampbell@motorcitytravel.com
Website: www.motorcitytravel.com
Full service travel agency. (Woman/AA, estab 0, empl , sales $12,095,618, cert: NMSDC)

9752 Sky Bird Travel & Tours Inc.
26500 Northwestern Hwy Ste 260
Southfield, MI 48076
Contact: Arvin Shah President
Tel: 248-727-1697
Email: info@skybirdtravel.com
Website: www.skybirdtravel.com
Full svc travel agency. (As-Ind, estab 1976, empl 52, sales $0, cert: NMSDC)

9753 The Travel Exchange
755 W Big Beaver Ste 100
Troy, MI 48084
Contact: Pamela Edwartoski President
Tel: 248-269-9721
Email: pam@travelexchangemi.com
Website: www.travelexchangemi.com
Full service travel agency. (Woman, estab 1976, empl 15, sales $0, cert: WBENC)

Minnesota

9754 Metro Travel
9298 Central Ave NE, Ste 222
Minneapolis, MN 55434
Contact: Diane Cyrus CEO
Tel: 763-784-0560
Email: dianecyrus@metrotravel.biz
Website: www.metrotravel.biz
Full service travel management. (As-Ind, estab 1982, empl 14, sales $890,000, cert: NMSDC)

North Carolina

9755 Aquila Travel & Events
2 Mill Creek Ct
Greensboro, NC 27407
Contact: Yolande Wainwright President
Tel: 336-580-9796
Email: aquila@triad.rr.com
Website: www.eventsbyaquila.com
Corporate event & travel services. (Woman/AA, estab 2008, empl 1, sales , cert: State)

New York

9756 Global Network Tours, Inc.
1 West 34 St Ste 1203
New York, NY 10001
Contact: Farida Garda President
Tel: 212-695-1647
Email: fgarda@air-supply.com
Website: www.air-supply.com/
Corporate travel agency. (Woman/As-Ind, estab 1993, empl 4, sales $2,750,000, cert: WBENC)

9757   Van Zile Travel
3540 Winton Place
Rochester, NY 14623
Contact: Rebecca Mineo VP
Tel: 585-244-1100
Email: katie@vanzile.com
Website: www.vanzile.com
Full service travel agency. (Woman, estab , empl 45, sales $35,000,000, cert: WBENC)

Ohio

9758   ATG
7775 Walton Pkwy Ste 100
New Albany, OH 43054
Contact: Paula Aquizap Sr Proposal Admin
Tel: 614-901-4100
Email: paquizap@atg.travel
Website: www.atgtravel.com
Full service travel agency. (Woman, estab 1995, empl 3000, sales $593,580,200, cert: WBENC)

9759   Uniglobe Travel Designers
480 S Third St
Columbus, OH 43215
Contact: Elizabeth Blount McCormick President
Tel: 614-237-4488
Email: elizabethb@uniglobetd.com
Website: www.uniglobetraveldesigners.com
Full service travel agency. (Woman/AA, estab , empl , sales $22,500,000, cert: NMSDC, WBENC)

Tennessee

9760   World Ventures Tours and Travel Inc.
6601 Kingston Pike
Knoxville, TN 37919
Contact: Constantine Christodoulou President
Tel: 865-588-7426
Email: cdc@wvtt.com
Website: www.wvtt.com
Travel and meeting management, airline reservarions, car rental reservations, hotel reservations, travel insurance, domestic travel, international travel. (Woman, estab 1977, empl 20, sales $8,000,000, cert: WBENC)

Texas

9761   The Alamo Travel Group LP
8930 Wurzbach Rd Ste 100
San Antonio, TX 78240
Contact: Patricia Pliego Stout President
Tel: 210-593-0084
Email: pstout@alamotravel.com
Website: www.alamotravel.com
Full service travel agency. (Minority, Woman, estab 1990, empl 11, sales $111,000,000, cert: State, NMSDC, WBENC)

9762   The Travel Group LLC
5930 Royal Lane Ste E277
Dallas, TX 75230
Contact: Greg Corley COO/CFO
Tel: 800-514-9132
Email: info@thetravelgroup.travel
Website: www.thetravelgroup.travel
Full service travel agency. (Minority, Woman, estab 1986, empl 55, sales $15,000,000, cert: WBENC)

9763   Travel Acquisition Group, Ltd.
5700 W Plano Pkwy Ste 1400
Plano, TX 75093
Contact: Exec VP
Tel: 972-422-4000
Email: info@artatravel.com
Website: www.artatravel.com
Corporate travel, management & consulting. (Woman, estab 1980, empl 21, sales $30,500,000, cert: State, WBENC)

Virginia

9764   Omega World Travel
3102 Omega Office Park
Fairfax, VA 22031
Contact: Jackie Olt Marketing & PR Specialist
Tel: 703-359-0200
Email: jolt@owt.net
Website: www.OmegaTravel.com
Full service travel agency. Meeting Planning & Strategic Meetings Management Services. (Minority, Woman, estab 1972, empl 475, sales $1,400,000,000, cert: WBENC)

Wisconsin

9765   JCCOB Smith Gardner Smith/Keystone AMEX Tvl Svs
16735 W Greenfield Ave
New Berlin, WI 53151
Contact: Art Smith President
Tel: 262-782-8750
Email: artkeystone@yahoo.com
Website: www.travelbykeystone.com
Full service travel agency. (AA, estab 1990, empl 12, sales $705,000, cert: NMSDC)

> **WOOD PRODUCTS**
> Produce videos (in studio or remote), TV shows, records, sound recordings, pre and post production services, talent arrangers, video distribution. NAICS Code 51

Alabama

9766 Containers Plus, Inc.
3068 Alabama Hwy 53
Huntsville, AL 35806
Contact: Ajesh Khanijow Business Devel
Tel: 256-746-8002
Email: akhanijow@containersplususa.com
Website: www.containersplususa.com
Wooden crates, pallets, cardboard boxes, heat shrink, milspec packaging, packaging, RFID, UID, Mil-std-129, mil-std-2073, warehousing, logistics, hazmat packaging. (As-Pac, estab 2014, empl 5, sales $180,000, cert: NMSDC)

California

9767 Commercial Lumber & Pallet Company, Inc.
135 Long Ln
City of Industry, CA 91746
Contact: Kathleen Dietrich VP
Tel: 626-968-0631
Email: kathy@clcpallets.com
Website: www.clcpallets.com
Mfr & dist wooden pallets, skids & boxes. (Hisp, estab 1941, empl 100, sales $35,000,000, cert: CPUC)

9768 Cutter Lumber Products
10 Rickenbacker Cir
Livermore, CA 94550
Contact: Todd Samuels General Mgr
Tel: 925-443-5959
Email: todd@cutterlumber.com
Website: www.cutterlumber.com/
Mfr wooden pallets, wooden boxes. (As-Pac, estab 1965, empl 85, sales , cert: NMSDC, CPUC)

9769 Pallet Recovery Service Inc.
PO Box 35
Westley, CA 95387
Contact: Lisa Kilcoyne President
Tel: 209-839-1224
Email: lisa@palletrecoveryservice.com
Website: www.palletrecoveryservice.com
Mfr new pallets, dist repairable pallets, remove unwanted scrap pallets. (Woman, estab 2007, empl 14, sales $596,456, cert: WBENC)

9770 TransPak
520 N. Marburg Way
San Jose, CA 95133
Contact: Sharon Spina Strategic Accounts Mgr
Tel: 408-590-6543
Email: sharon.spina@transpak.com
Website: www.transpak.com
Mfr wood crates & crating systems, custom packaging solutions, logistics, transportation & rigging services. (Woman, estab 1952, empl 800, sales $120,000,000, cert: WBENC)

9771 Winship Stake and Lath
PO Box 909
Riverside, CA 92502
Contact: Lisa Winship Hankin President
Tel: 951-682-8761
Email: lisa@winshipstakeandlath.com
Website: www.winshipstakeandlath.com
Mfr & dist wood stakes & lath used in building, surveying & landscaping. (Woman, estab 1972, empl 8, sales $400,000, cert: CPUC)

Colorado

9772 Pro Pallet, Inc.
920 E Collins
Eaton, CO 80615
Contact: Jean Kyne President
Tel: 970-353-5311
Email: propallet@qwestoffice.net
Website: www.propallet.net
New, recycled & new/recycled pallets, crates & boxes. (Woman, estab 1988, empl 45, sales $8,258,291, cert: WBENC)

Florida

9773 Pallet Consultants Corporation
951 SW 12th Ave
Pompano Beach, FL 33069
Contact: Brian Groene President
Tel: 954-946-2212
Email: brian.groene@palletconsultants.com
Website: www.palletconsultants.com
Recycle wood pallets, mfr new & used pallets. (Hisp, estab 1996, empl 178, sales $45,000,000, cert: NMSDC)

Georgia

9774 A & B Pallets, Inc.
6323 Riverview Rd
Mableton, GA 30126
Contact: Alberto Dominguez President
Tel: 404-691-0567
Email: aandbpalletsinc@yahoo.com
Website: www.aandbpalletsinc.com
Recycled, new & remanufactured pallets. (Hisp, estab 1997, empl 15, sales , cert: NMSDC)

9775　Pallet Central Enterprises, Inc.
2B Lenox Pointe
Atlanta, GA 30324
Contact: Jameson Humber Assistant Sales Mgr
Tel:　404-671-3494
Email: jhumber@palletcentralent.com
Website: www.palletcentralent.com
Pallets. (Minority, Woman, estab 2005, empl 25, sales $26,000,000, cert: WBENC)

Illinois

9776　Harvey Pallets Inc.
2200 W 139th St
Blue Island, IL 60406
Contact: Manuel Tavarez President
Tel:　708-293-1831
Email: manuel@harveypallets.com
Website: www.harveypallet.com
Mfr wood pallets, skids, crates & lumber. (Hisp, estab 1997, empl 50, sales $24,000,000, cert: NMSDC)

9777　Perma Treat of Illinois
PO Box 99
Marion, IL 62959
Contact: Sara Bond CEO
Tel:　618-694-2898
Email: sara@permatreatlumber.com
Website: www.permatreatlumber.com
Wood Treated products: Utility Poles, Railroad Ties, Pallets, Wood Quality Control Inspection, Rail Spur on site can ship via rail or truck. (Woman, estab 1982, empl 7, sales $330,866, cert: State, WBENC)

9778　Phoenix Woodworking Corporation
PO Box 459
Woodstock, IL 60098
Contact: Sandra Pierce President
Tel:　815-338-9338
Email: spierce@phoenixwoodworking.com
Website: www.phoenixwoodworking.com
Custom & commercial cabinetry & casework, reception centers, filing cabinets, wooden lockers & millwork, custom desks & wooden store fixtures. (Woman, estab 1996, empl 10, sales , cert: State, WBENC)

Massachusetts

9779　Native Lumber LLC dba Paper City Bat Company
653 Northampton St
Holyoke, MA 01040
Contact: Kipngetich Rutto Owner
Tel:　413-265-0920
Email: Kip@nativelumberllc.com
Website: www.papercitybatco.com
Farm-to-Table Manufacturer of Custom Baseball Bats. Log-to-Bat, we process the Highest Quality Lumber Species: Ash, Birch and Hard Maple- The Best, tested and approved Wood. (AA, estab 2016, empl 2, sales , cert: State)

Maryland

9780　Timber Industries, LLC
PO Box 6879
Towson, MD 21285
Contact: Danielle Sutphen Sales & Mktg Coord
Tel:　410-823-8300
Email: danielle.sutphen@timberindustries.com
Website: www.timberindustries.com
Custom & standard pallets, skids & crates. (Woman, estab 2013, empl 6, sales $2,500,000, cert: State, WBENC)

Michigan

9781　J&G Pallets and Trucking, Inc.
2971 Bellevue
Detroit, MI 48207
Contact: Les Lance Business Mgr
Tel:　313-921-0222
Email: llance@jgpalletsandtrucking.com
Website: www.jgpalletsandtrucking.com
Wood pallets, design custom pallets, recycle/reuse wood pallets & wood pallet materials. (Woman/AA, estab 1992, empl 22, sales $1,625,000, cert: NMSDC)

Minnesota

9782　R and L Woodcraft, Inc
823 Industrial Park Dr SE
Lonsdale, MN 55046
Contact: Randall Rivers Business Devel
Tel:　507-744-2318
Email: randall@randlwoodcraft.com
Website: www.randlwoodcraft.com
Mfr commercial millwork & casework: cabinets, countertops, workstations, service counters, point of service counters, tables, booths, upholstered seating, running trim, trash recepticles, lockers & toilet partitions. (Woman, estab 1986, empl 22, sales $3,600,000, cert: WBENC)

North Carolina

9783　The Pallet Alliance
200 N Greensboro St Ste D-8
Carrboro, NC 27510
Contact: Joe Movic Program Specialist
Tel:　919-442-1400
Email: joe@tpai.com
Website: www.tpai.com
Design & implement national pallet management programs. (Woman, estab 1995, empl 16, sales $50,000,000, cert: WBENC)

New Jersey

9784   Bett-A-Way Pallet Systems
       110 Sylvania Pl
       South Plainfield, NJ 07080
       Contact: Laura Vaccaro VP Business Dev
       Tel: 800-795-7255
       Email: laura.vaccaro@bettaway.com
       Website: www.bettaway.com
Pallet management: sales, repairs, retrievals & inventory management. (Woman, estab 1996, empl 15, sales $20,986,000, cert: WBENC)

New York

9785   Ongweoweh Corp
       5 Barr Road
       Ithaca, NY 14850
       Contact: Brett Bucktooth Supplier Diversity Mgr
       Tel: 607-266-7070
       Email: supplierdiversity@ongweoweh.com
       Website: www.ongweoweh.com
Mfr & dist wooden pallets & specialty containers. (Nat Ame, estab 1978, empl 96, sales $252,000,000, cert: NMSDC)

Ohio

9786   LEFCO Worthington, LLC
       18451 Euclid Ave
       Cleveland, OH 44112
       Contact: Larry Fulton President
       Tel: 216-432-4422
       Email: larry.fulton@lefcoworthington.com
       Website: www.LEFCOWorthington.com
Dist wooden crates, OSB Boxes, custom pallets, sub-assembly & packaging services. (AA, estab 2003, empl 30, sales $3,600,000, cert: State, NMSDC)

9787   Prime WoodCraft
       5755 Granger Rd Ste 900
       Independence, OH 44131
       Contact: Michelle Morere Admin
       Tel: 216-588-9053
       Email: michelle@primewoodcraft.com
       Website: www.primewoodcraft.com
Warehousing, pallets, third party logistics. (As-Ind, estab 1997, empl 300, sales , cert: NMSDC)

9788   The Lima Pallet Company, Inc.
       1470 Neubrecht Rd
       Lima, OH 45801
       Contact: Brian Cunningham VP
       Tel: 419-229-5736
       Email: bcunningham@limapallet.com
       Website: www.limapallet.com
Mfr wood pallets & crates. ISP certified. (Woman, estab 1977, empl 49, sales $3,000,000, cert: WBENC)

9789   Wood Concepts
       2401 Train Ave
       Cleveland, OH 44113
       Contact: Jacquline Even President
       Tel: 216-579-0500
       Email: jackieeven@att.net
       Website: www.woodconceptsinc.com
Mfr & fabricate casework, millwork & cabinetry. (Woman, estab 1983, empl 8, sales $1,025,215, cert: City)

Texas

9790   Apache Products Inc.
       PO Box 187
       Silsbee, TX 77656
       Contact: Brenda Killingsworth President
       Tel: 409-385-7021
       Email: acmeskid@aol.com
       Website: www.pallet-mall.com/apache/
Mfr & dist wooden pallets, skids & crates for shipping & storage. (Woman, estab 1952, empl 90, sales $11,000,000, cert: WBENC)

9791   Austin Lumber Company, Inc.
       630 S Washington St
       La Grange, TX 78945
       Contact: Laura Culin President
       Tel: 512-476-5534
       Email: info@austinlumbercompany.com
       Website: www.austinlumbercompany.com
Construction mill. (Woman, estab 1929, empl 5, sales , cert: State, City)